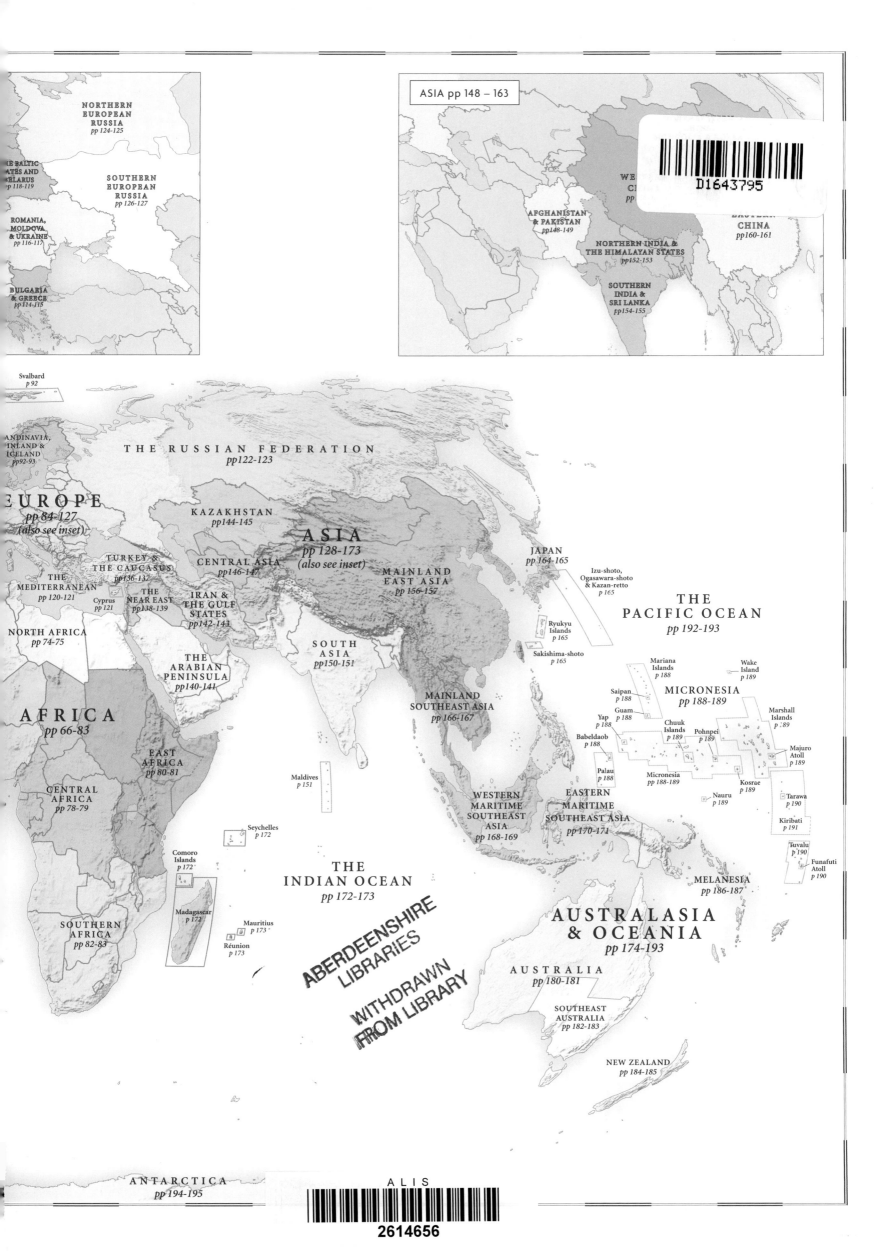
NORTHERN EUROPEAN RUSSIA pp 124-125
SOUTHERN EUROPEAN RUSSIA pp 126-127
ROMANIA, MOLDOVA & UKRAINE pp 116-117
BULGARIA & GREECE pp 114-115
ASIA pp 148 – 163
AFGHANISTAN & PAKISTAN pp148-149
NORTHERN INDIA & THE HIMALAYAN STATES pp152-153
SOUTHERN INDIA & SRI LANKA pp154-155
CHINA pp160-161
Svalbard p 92
THE RUSSIAN FEDERATION pp122-123
EUROPE pp 84-127 (also see inset)
KAZAKHSTAN pp144-145
ASIA pp 128-173 (also see inset)
TURKEY & THE CAUCASUS pp136-137
CENTRAL ASIA pp146-147
THE MEDITERRANEAN pp 120-121
Cyprus pp 121
THE NEAR EAST pp138-139
IRAN & THE GULF STATES pp142-143
MAINLAND EAST ASIA pp 156-157
JAPAN pp 164-165
Izu-shoto, Ogasawara-shoto & Kazan-retto p 165
THE PACIFIC OCEAN pp 192-193
Ryukyu Islands p 165
Sakishima-shoto p 165
NORTH AFRICA pp 74-75
THE ARABIAN PENINSULA pp140-141
SOUTH ASIA pp150-151
Mariana Islands p 188
Wake Island p 189
Saipan p 188
Guam p 188
MICRONESIA pp 188-189
Marshall Islands p 189
Yap p 188
Chuuk Islands p 189
Pohnpei p 189
Babeldaob p 188
Majuro Atoll p 189
Palau p 188
Micronesia pp 188-189
Kosrae p 189
Nauru p 189
Tarawa p 190
Kiribati p 191
Tuvalu p 190
Funafuti Atoll p 190
AFRICA pp 66-83
MAINLAND SOUTHEAST ASIA pp 166-167
EAST AFRICA pp 80-81
Maldives p 151
CENTRAL AFRICA pp 78-79
WESTERN MARITIME SOUTHEAST ASIA pp 168-169
EASTERN MARITIME SOUTHEAST ASIA pp 170-171
Seychelles p 172
Comoro Islands p 172
THE INDIAN OCEAN pp 172-173
MELANESIA pp 186-187
Madagascar p 172
Mauritius p 173
Réunion p 173
SOUTHERN AFRICA pp 82-83
AUSTRALASIA & OCEANIA pp 174-193
AUSTRALIA pp 180-181
SOUTHEAST AUSTRALIA pp 182-183
NEW ZEALAND pp 184-185
ANTARCTICA pp 194-195

CONCISE ATLAS
OF THE WORLD

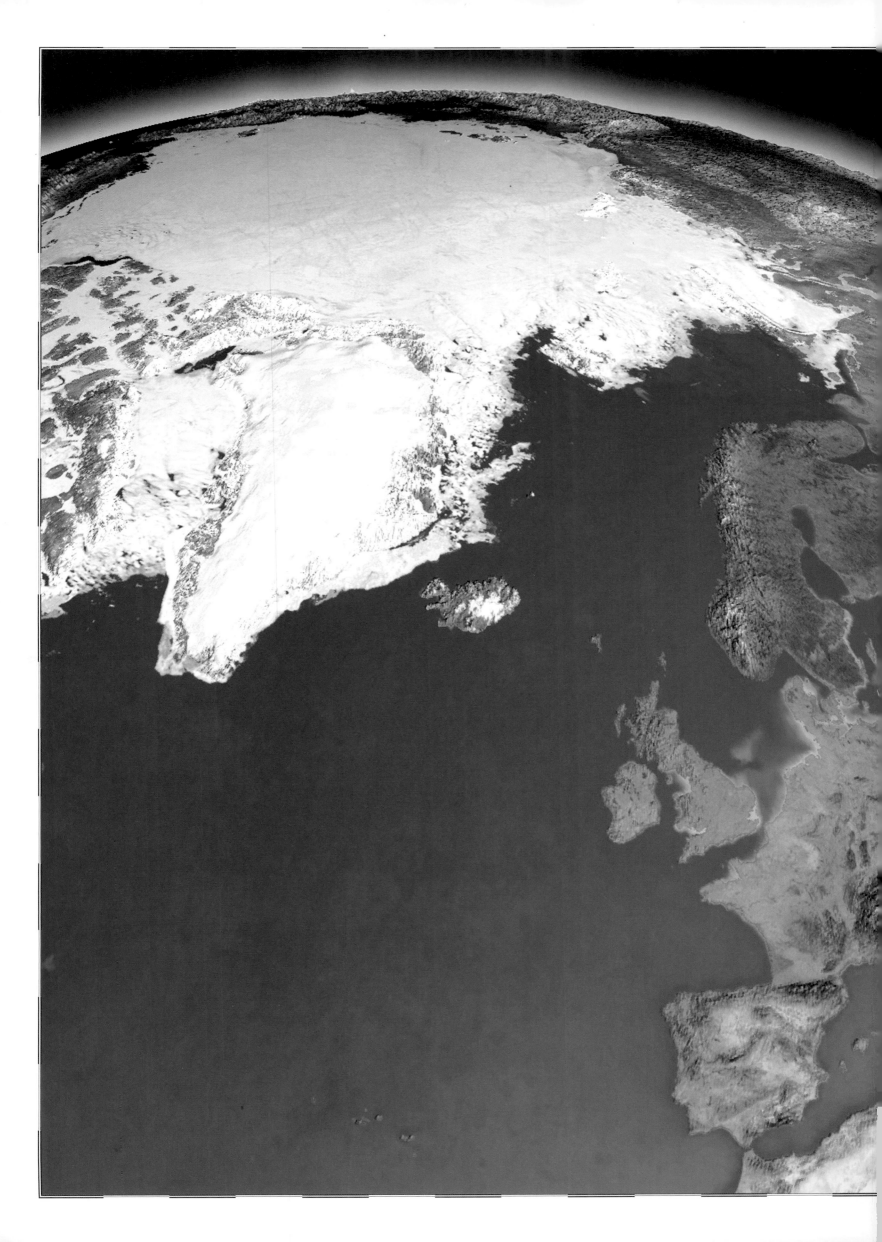

CONCISE ATLAS
OF THE WORLD

London • New York • Munich • Melbourne • Delhi

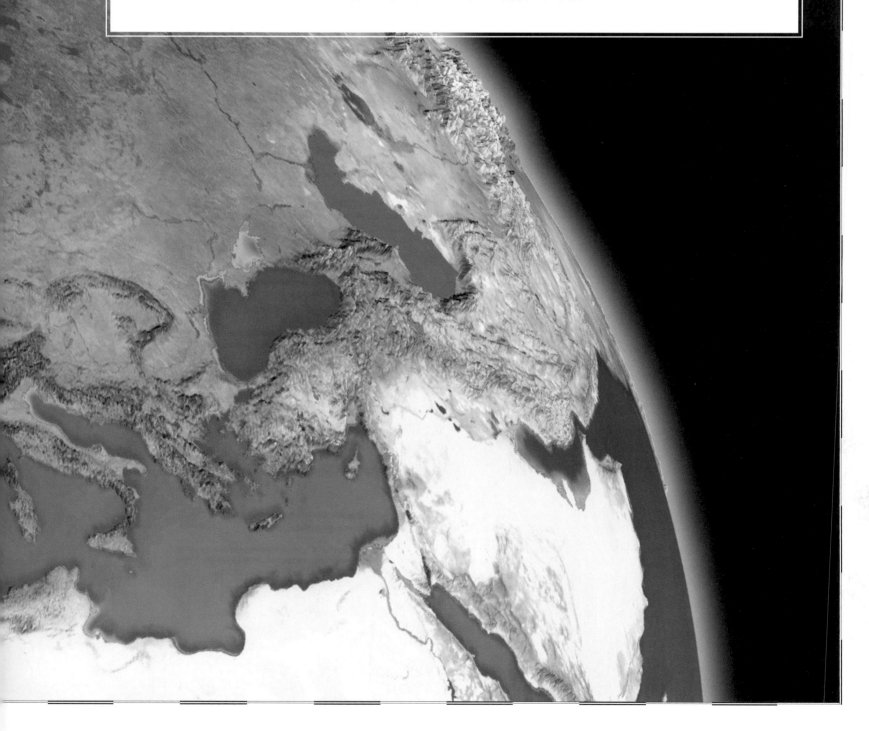

LONDON, NEW YORK, MELBOURNE, MUNICH, DELHI

FOR THE FOURTH EDITION

Publishing Director Jonathan Metcalf   **Managing Cartographers** David Roberts • Simon Mumford   **Art Director** Bryn Walls
Managing Editor Debra Wolter   **Designers** Nimbus Design, Langworth, UK • Giraffe, London, UK • Yak El-Droubie
Cartographers Roger Bullen • DEMAP, Strathdale, Australia • Paul Eames • Encompass Graphics Ltd, Brighton, UK • Ed Merritt • Rob Stokes • Iorwerth Watkins
Jacket Designers Lee Ellwood • Duncan Turner   **Systems Co-ordinator** Philip Rowles

General Geographical Consultants

Physical Geography Denys Brunsden, Emeritus Professor, Department of Geography, King's College, London
Human Geography Professor J Malcolm Wagstaff, Department of Geography, University of Southampton
Place Names Caroline Burgess, Permanent Committee on Geographical Names, London
Boundaries International Boundaries Research Unit, Mountjoy Research Centre, University of Durham

Digital Mapping Consultants

DK Cartopia developed by George Galfalvi and XMap Ltd, London
Professor Jan-Peter Muller, Department of Photogrammetry and Surveying, University College, London
Cover globes, planets and information on the Solar System provided by Philip Eales and Kevin Tildsley, Planetary Visions Ltd, London

Regional Consultants

North America Dr David Green, Department of Geography, King's College, London • Jim Walsh, Head of Reference, Wessell Library, Tufts University, Medford, Massachusetts
South America Dr David Preston, School of Geography, University of Leeds   **Europe** Dr Edward M Yates, formerly of the Department of Geography, King's College, London
Africa Dr Philip Amis, Development Administration Group, University of Birmingham • Dr Ieuan Ll Griffiths, Department of Geography, University of Sussex
Dr Tony Binns, Department of Geography, University of Sussex
Central Asia Dr David Turnock, Department of Geography, University of Leicester   **South and East Asia** Dr Jonathan Rigg, Department of Geography, University of Durham
Australasia and Oceania Dr Robert Allison, Department of Geography, University of Durham

Acknowledgements

Digital terrain data created by Eros Data Center, Sioux Falls, South Dakota, USA. Processed by GVS Images Inc, California, USA and Planetary Visions Ltd, London, UK
• Cambridge International Reference on Current Affairs (CIRCA), Cambridge, UK • Digitization by Robertson Research International, Swanley, UK • Peter Clark
British Isles maps generated from a dataset supplied by Map Marketing Ltd/European Map Graphics Ltd in combination with DK Cartopia copyright data

DORLING KINDERSLEY CARTOGRAPHY

Editor-in-Chief Andrew Heritage   **Managing Cartographer** David Roberts   **Senior Cartographic Editor** Roger Bullen
Editorial Direction Louise Cavanagh   **Database Manager** Simon Lewis   **Art Direction** Chez Picthall

Cartographers

Pamela Alford • James Anderson • Caroline Bowie • Dale Buckton • Tony Chambers • Jan Clark • Bob Croser • Martin Darlison • Damien Demaj • Claire Ellam • Sally Gable
Jeremy Hepworth • Geraldine Horner • Chris Jackson • Christine Johnston • Julia Lunn • Michael Martin • Ed Merritt • James Mills-Hicks • Simon Mumford • John Plumer
John Scott • Ann Stephenson • Gail Townsley • Julie Turner • Sarah Vaughan • Jane Voss • Scott Wallace • Iorwerth Watkins • Bryony Webb • Alan Whitaker • Peter Winfield

Digital Maps Created in DK Cartopia by
Tom Coulson • Thomas Robertshaw
Philip Rowles • Rob Stokes
Managing Editor
Lisa Thomas
Editors
Thomas Heath • Wim Jenkins • Jane Oliver
Siobhan Ryan • Elizabeth Wyse
Editorial Research
Helen Dangerfield • Andrew Rebeiro-Hargrave
Additional Editorial Assistance
Debra Clapson • Robert Damon • Ailsa Heritage
Constance Novis • Jayne Parsons • Chris Whitwell

Placenames Database Team
Natalie Clarkson • Ruth Duxbury • Caroline Falce • John Featherstone • Dan Gardiner
Ciáran Hynes • Margaret Hynes • Helen Rudkin • Margaret Stevenson • Annie Wilson
Senior Managing Art Editor
Philip Lord
Designers
Scott David • Carol Ann Davis • David Douglas • Rhonda Fisher
Karen Gregory • Nicola Liddiard • Paul Williams
Illustrations
Ciáran Hughes • Advanced Illustration, Congleton, UK
Picture Research
Melissa Albany • James Clarke • Anna Lord
Christine Rista • Sarah Moule • Louise Thomas

Production
Linda Dare

First published in Great Britain in 2001 by Dorling Kindersley Limited, 80 Strand, London WC2R 0RL.

A Penguin Company

Second Edition 2003. Reprinted with revisions 2004. Third Edition 2005. Fourth Edition 2008.
Copyright © 2001, 2003, 2004, 2005, 2008 Dorling Kindersley Limited, London

A CIP catalogue record for this book is available from the British Library

ISBN: 978-1-4053-2801-2

Reprographics by MDP Ltd, Wiltshire, UK
Printed and bound by Star Standard, Singapore.

See our complete catalogue at www.dk.com

Introduction

For many, the outstanding legacy of the twentieth century was the way in which the Earth shrank. As we enter the third millennium, it is increasingly important for us to have a clear vision of the World in which we live. The human population has increased fourfold since 1900. The last scraps of *terra incognita* – the polar regions and ocean depths – have been penetrated and mapped. New regions have been colonized, and previously hostile realms claimed for habitation. The advent of aviation technology and mass tourism allows many of us to travel further, faster and more frequently than ever before. In doing so we are given a bird's-eye view of the Earth's surface denied to our forebears.

At the same time, the amount of information about our world has grown enormously. Telecommunications can span the greatest distances in fractions of a second: our multi-media environment hurls uninterrupted streams of data at us, on the printed page, through the airwaves and across our television and computer screens; events from all corners of the globe reach us instantaneously, and are witnessed as they unfold. Our sense of stability and certainty has been eroded; instead, we are aware that the World is in a constant state of flux and change. Natural disasters, man-made cataclysms and conflicts between nations remind us daily of the enormity and fragility of our domain. The events of September 11, 2001, threw into a very stark relief the levels of ignorance and inaccessibility that exist when trying to 'know' or 'understand' our planet and its many cultures.

The current crisis in our 'global' culture has made the need greater than ever before for everyone to possess an atlas. The *DK Concise Atlas of the World* has been conceived to meet this need. At its core, like all atlases, it seeks to define where places are, to describe their main characteristics, and to locate them in relation to other places. Every attempt has been made to make the information on the maps as clear and accessible as possible. In addition, each page of the atlas provides a wealth of further information, bringing the maps to life. Using photographs, diagrams, 'at-a-glance' maps, introductory texts and captions, the atlas builds up a detailed portait of those features – cultural, political, economic and geomorphological – which make each region unique, and which are also the main agents of change.

This Fourth Edition of the *DK Concise Atlas of the World* incorporates thousands of revisions and updates affecting every map and every page, and reflects many of the geo-political developments which continue to alter the shape of our world. The *DK Concise Atlas of the World* has been created to bring all of these benefits to a new audience, in a handy format and at an affordable price.

CONTENTS

THE WORLD

ATLAS OF THE WORLD

North America

South America

Africa

Europe

Asia

Australasia & Oceania

INDEX–GAZETTEER

Key to maps

Regional

Physical features

elevation

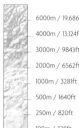

6000m / 19,686ft
4000m / 13,124ft
3000m / 9843ft
2000m / 6562ft
1000m / 3281ft
500m / 1640ft
250m / 820ft
100m / 328ft
sea level
below sea level

▲ elevation above sea level (mountain height)
▲ volcano
✕ pass
▼ elevation below sea level (depression depth)

sand desert
lava flow
coastline
reef
atoll

sea depth

sea level
-250m / -820ft
-500m / -1640ft
-1000m / -3281ft
-2000m / -6562ft
-3000m / -9843ft

▲ seamount / guyot symbol
▼ undersea spot depth

Drainage features

main river
secondary river
tertiary river
minor river
main seasonal river
secondary seasonal river
canal
waterfall
rapids
dam
perennial lake
seasonal lake
perennial salt lake
seasonal salt lake
reservoir
salt flat / salt pan
marsh / salt marsh
mangrove
wadi
○ spring / well / waterhole / oasis

Ice features

ice cap / sheet
ice shelf
glacier / snowfield
summer pack ice limit
winter pack ice limit

Communications

motorway / highway
motorway / highway (under construction)
major road
minor road
tunnel (road)
main line
minor line
tunnel (rail)
✈ international airport

Borders

full international border
undefined international border
disputed de facto border
disputed territorial claim border
indication of country extent (Pacific only)
indication of dependent territory extent (Pacific only)
demarcation/ cease fire line
autonomous / federal region border
2nd order internal administrative border
3rd order internal administrative border

Settlements

built up area

settlement population symbols

■ more than 5 million
◉ 1 million to 5 million
⦿ 500,000 to 1 million
◎ 100,000 to 500,000
⊕ 50,000 to 100,000
○ 10,000 to 50,000
∘ fewer than 10,000

■●● country/dependent territory capital city
■●● autonomous / federal region / 2nd order internal administrative centre
■◎⊕ 3rd order internal administrative centre

Miscellaneous features

∷∷∷ ancient wall
◇ site of interest
● scientific station

Graticule features

lines of latitude and longitude / Equator
Tropics / Polar circles
45° degrees of longitude / latitude

Typographic key

Physical features

landscape features ... *Namib Desert* **Massif Central** **ANDES**
headland .... *Nordkapp*
elevation / volcano / pass .... Mount Meru 4556 m
drainage features .... *Lake Geneva*
rivers / canals spring / well / waterhole / oasis / waterfall / rapids / dam .... *Mekong*
ice features .... *Vatnajökull*
sea features........... *Golfe de Lion* *Andaman Sea* **INDIAN OCEAN**
undersea features ... *Barracuda Fracture Zone*

Regions

country .... **ARMENIA**
dependent territory with parent state ..... **NIUE** (to NZ)
region outside feature area .... ANGOLA
autonomous / federal region .... MINAS GERAIS
2nd order internal administrative region .. .. **MINSKAYA VOBLASTS'**
3rd order internal administrative region .... Vaucluse
cultural region .... New England

Settlements

capital city .... **BEIJING**
dependent territory capital city .... FORT-DE-FRANCE
other settlements ... **Chicago** Adana **Tizi Ozou** Yonezawa Farnham

Miscellaneous

sites of interest / miscellaneous .... Valley of the Kings
Tropics / Polar circles .... *Antarctic Circle*

How to use this Atlas

The atlas is organized by continent, moving eastwards from the International Date Line. The opening section describes the world's structure, systems and its main features. The Atlas of the World which follows, is a continent-by-continent guide to today's world, starting with a comprehensive insight into the physical, political and economic structure of each continent, followed by integrated mapping and descriptions of each region or country.

The world

The introductory section of the Atlas deals with every aspect of the planet, from physical structure to human geography, providing an overall picture of the world we live in. Complex topics such as the landscape of the Earth, climate, oceans, population and economic patterns are clearly explained with the aid of maps, diagrams drawn from the latest information.

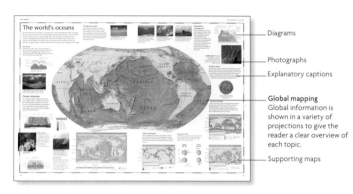

Diagrams
Photographs
Explanatory captions
Global mapping Global information is shown in a variety of projections to give the reader a clear overview of each topic.
Supporting maps

The political continent

The political portrait of the continent is a vital reference point for every continental section, showing the position of countries relative to one another, and the relationship between human settlement and geographic location. The complex mosaic of languages spoken in each continent is mapped, as is the effect of communications networks on the pattern of settlement.

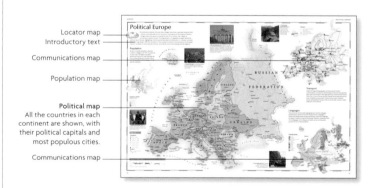

Locator map
Introductory text
Communications map
Population map
Political map All the countries in each continent are shown, with their political capitals and most populous cities.
Communications map

Continental resources

The Earth's rich natural resources, including oil, gas, minerals and fertile land, have played a key role in the development of society. These pages show the location of minerals and agricultural resources on each continent, and how they have been instrumental in dictating industrial growth and the varieties of economic activity across the continent.

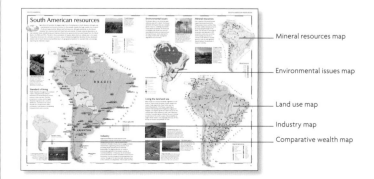

Mineral resources map
Environmental issues map
Land use map
Industry map
Comparative wealth map

The physical continent

The astonishing variety of landforms, and the dramatic forces that created and continue to shape the landscape, are explained in the continental physical spread. Cross-sections, illustrations and terrain maps highlight the different parts of the continent, showing how nature's forces have produced the landscapes we see today.

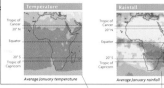

Climate charts
Rainfall and temperature charts clearly show the continental patterns of rainfall and temperature.

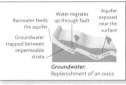

Climate map
Climatic regions vary across each continent. The map displays the differing climatic regions, as well as daily hours of sunshine at selected weather stations.

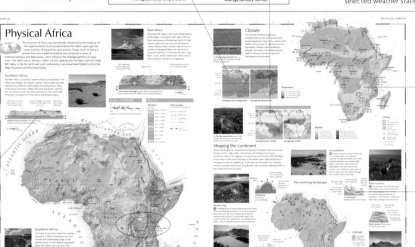

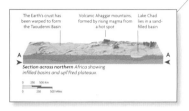

Cross-sections
Detailed cross-sections through selected parts of the continent show the underlying geomorphic structure.

Landform diagrams
The complex formation of many typical landforms is summarized in these easy-to-understand illustrations.

Main physical map
Detailed satellite data has been used to create an accurate and visually striking picture of the surface of the continent.

Photographs
A wide range of beautiful photographs bring the world's regions to life.

Landscape evolution map
The physical shape of each continent is affected by a variety of forces which continually sculpt and modify the landscape. This map shows the major processes which affect different parts of the continent.

Regional mapping

The main body of the Atlas is a unique regional map set, with detailed information on the terrain, the human geography of the region and its infrastructure. Around the edge of the map, additional 'at-a-glance' maps, give an instant picture of regional industry, land use and agriculture. The detailed terrain map (shown in perspective), focuses on the main physical features of the region, and is enhanced by annotated illustrations, and photographs of the physical structure.

The transport network

340,090 miles (544,144 km)	4813 miles (7700 km)
12,872 miles (20,592 km)	2108 miles (3389 km)

New York's commercial success is tied historically to its transport connections. The Erie Canal, completed in 1825, opened up the Great Lakes and the interior to New York's markets and carried a stream of immigrants into the Midwest.

Transport network
The differing extent of the transport network for each region is shown here, along with key facts about the transport system.

Regional Locator
This small map shows the location of each country in relation to its continent.

Key to main map
A key to the population symbols and land heights accompanies the main map.

World locator
This locates the continent in which the region is found on a small world map.

Land use map
This shows the different types of land use which characterize the region, as well as indicating the principal agricultural activities.

Map keys
Each supporting map has its own key.

Grid reference
The framing grid provides a location reference for each place listed in the Index.

The urban/rural population divide

urban 83%	rural 17%

Population density	Total land area
335 people per sq mile (120 people per sq km)	162,258 sq miles (420,232 sq km)

Urban/rural population divide
The proportion of people in the region who live in urban and rural areas, as well as the overall population density and land area are clearly shown in these simple graphics.

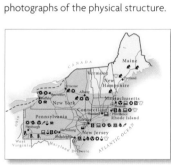

Transport and industry map
The main industrial areas are mapped, and the most important industrial and economic activities of the region are shown.

Continuation symbols
These symbols indicate where adjacent maps can be found.

Main regional map
A wealth of information is displayed on the main map, building up a rich portrait of the interaction between the physical landscape and the human and political geography of each region. The key to the regional maps can be found on page viii.

Landscape map
The computer-generated terrain model accurately portrays an oblique view of the landscape. Annotations highlight the most important geographic features of the region.

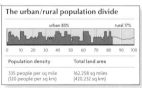

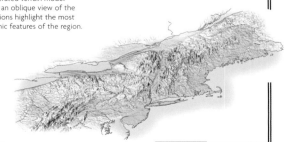

Jupiter

- **Diameter:** 88,846 miles (142,984 km)
- **Mass:** 1,900,000 million million million tons
- **Temperature:** -153°C (extremes not available)
- **Distance from Sun:** 483 million miles (778 million km)
- **Length of day:** 9.84 hours
- **Length of year:** 11.86 earth years
- **Surface gravity:** 1 kg = 2.53 kg

Mars

- **Diameter:** 4217 miles (6786 km)
- **Mass:** 642 million million million tons
- **Temperature:** -137 to 37°C
- **Distance from Sun:** 142 million miles (228 million km)
- **Length of day:** 24.623 hours
- **Length of year:** 1.88 earth years
- **Surface gravity:** 1 kg = 0.38 kg

Earth

- **Diameter:** 7926 miles (12,756 km)
- **Mass:** 5976 million million million tons
- **Temperature:** -70 to 55°C
- **Distance from Sun:** 93 million miles (150 million km)
- **Length of day:** 23.92 hours
- **Length of year:** 365.25 earth days
- **Surface gravity:** 1 kg = 1 kg

Venus

- **Diameter:** 7520 miles (12,102 km)
- **Mass:** 4870 million million million tons
- **Temperature:** 457°C (extremes not available)
- **Distance from Sun:** 67 million miles (108 million km)
- **Length of day:** 243.01 earth days
- **Length of year:** 224.7 earth days
- **Surface gravity:** 1 kg = 0.88 kg

Mercury

- **Diameter:** 3031 miles (4878 km)
- **Mass:** 330 million million million tons
- **Temperature:** -173 to 427°C
- **Distance from Sun:** 36 million miles (58 million km)
- **Length of day:** 58.65 earth days
- **Length of year:** 87.97 earth days
- **Surface gravity:** 1 kg = 0.38 kg

The Sun

- **Diameter:** 864,948 miles (1,392,000 km)
- **Mass:** 1990 million million million million tons

The Sun was formed when a swirling cloud of dust and gas contracted, pulling matter into its centre. When the temperature at the centre rose to 1,000,000°C, nuclear fusion – the fusing of hydrogen into helium, creating energy – occurred, releasing a constant stream of heat and light.

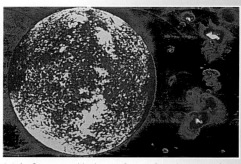

▲ **Solar flares are** *sudden bursts of energy from the Sun's surface. They can be 125,000 miles (200,000 km) long.*

The formation of the Solar System

The cloud of dust and gas thrown out by the Sun during its formation cooled to form the Solar System. The smaller planets nearest the Sun are formed of minerals and metals. The outer planets were formed at lower temperatures, and consist of swirling clouds of gases.

The Milankovitch cycle

The amount of radiation from the Sun which reaches the Earth is affected by variations in the Earth's orbit and the tilt of the Earth's axis, as well as by 'wobbles' in the axis. These variations cause three separate cycles, corresponding with the durations of recent ice ages.

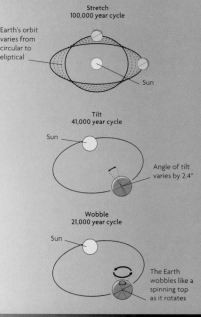

Stretch
100,000 year cycle

Earth's orbit varies from circular to eliptical

Sun

Tilt
41,000 year cycle

Sun

Angle of tilt varies by 2.4°

Wobble
21,000 year cycle

Sun

The Earth wobbles like a spinning top as it rotates

The Solar System

Nine major planets, their satellites and countless minor planets (asteroids) orbit the Sun to form the Solar System. The Sun, our nearest star, creates energy from nuclear reactions deep within its interior, providing all the light and heat which make life on Earth possible. The Earth is unique in the Solar System in that it supports life: its size, gravitational pull and distance from the Sun have all created the optimum conditions for the evolution of life. The planetary images seen here are composites derived from actual spacecraft images (not shown to scale).

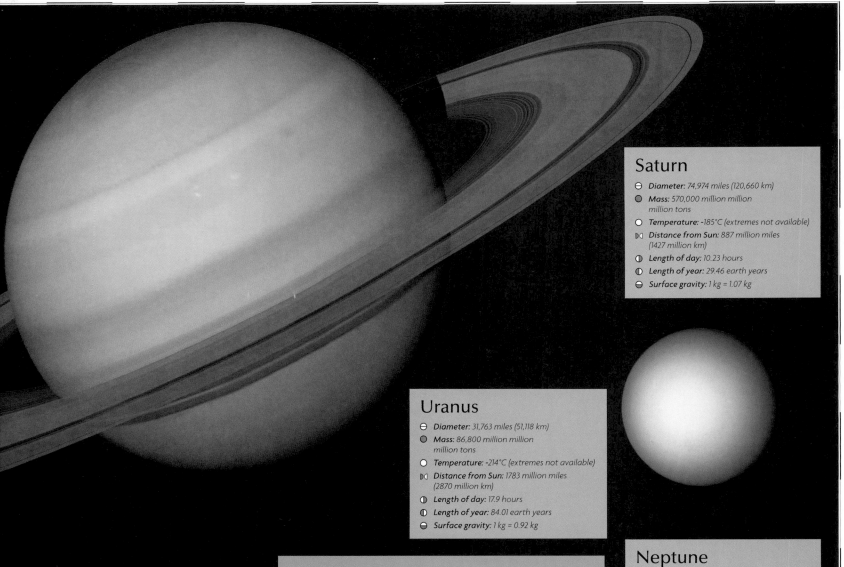

Saturn

⊖ **Diameter:** 74,974 miles (120,660 km)

● **Mass:** 570,000 million million million tons

○ **Temperature:** -185°C (extremes not available)

◑ **Distance from Sun:** 887 million miles (1427 million km)

◐ **Length of day:** 10.23 hours

◐ **Length of year:** 29.46 earth years

⊖ **Surface gravity:** 1 kg = 1.07 kg

Uranus

⊖ **Diameter:** 31,763 miles (51,118 km)

● **Mass:** 86,800 million million million tons

○ **Temperature:** -214°C (extremes not available)

◑ **Distance from Sun:** 1783 million miles (2870 million km)

◐ **Length of day:** 17.9 hours

◐ **Length of year:** 84.01 earth years

⊖ **Surface gravity:** 1 kg = 0.92 kg

Neptune

⊖ **Diameter:** 30,775 miles (49,528 km)

● **Mass:** 102,000 million million million tons

○ **Temperature:** -225°C (extremes not available)

◑ **Distance from Sun:** 2794 million miles (4497 million km)

◐ **Length of day:** 19.2 hours

◐ **Length of year:** 164.79 earth years

⊖ **Surface gravity:** 1 kg = 1.18 kg

Pluto

⊖ **Diameter:** 1429 miles (2300 km)

● **Mass:** 13 million million million tons

○ **Temperature:** -236°C (extremes not available)

◑ **Distance from Sun:** 3666 million miles (5900 million km)

◐ **Length of day:** 6.39 hours

◐ **Length of year:** 248.54 earth years

⊖ **Surface gravity:** 1 kg = 0.30 kg

Space debris

Millions of objects, remnants of planetary formation, circle the Sun in a zone lying between Mars and Jupiter: the asteroid belt. Fragments of asteroids break off to form meteoroids, which can reach the Earth's surface. Comets, composed of ice and dust, originated outside our Solar System. Their elliptical orbit brings them close to the Sun and into the inner Solar System.

▲ **Meteor Crater in** Arizona is 4200 ft (1300 m) wide and 660 ft (200 m) deep. It was formed over 10,000 years ago.

Possible and actual meteorite craters

Map key

▭ Possible impact craters

◯ Meteorite impact craters

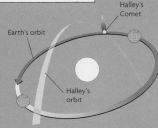

▲ **The orbit of** Halley's Comet brings it close to the Earth every 76 years. It last visited in 1986.

Halley's Comet

Earth's orbit

Halley's orbit

Orbit of Halley's Comet around the Sun

The Earth's atmosphere

During the early stages of the Earth's formation, ash, lava, carbon dioxide and water vapour were discharged onto the surface of the planet by constant volcanic eruptions. The water formed the oceans, while carbon dioxide entered the atmosphere or was dissolved in the oceans. Clouds, formed of water droplets, reflected some of the Sun's radiation back into space. The Earth's temperature stabilized and early life forms began to emerge, converting carbon dioxide into life-giving oxygen.

◄ **It is thought** that the gases that make up the Earth's atmosphere originated deep within the interior, and were released many millions of years ago during intense volcanic activity, similar to this eruption at Mount St. Helens.

Order and relative distance from the sun of planets

Sun Mercury Venus Earth Mars Jupiter Saturn Uranus Neptune Pluto

0   500   1000   1500   2000   2500   3000   3500   4000   4500   5000   5500   6000   mill. km

0   500   1000   1500   2000   2500   3000   3500   4000   mill. miles

The physical world

The Earth's surface is constantly being transformed: it is uplifted, folded and faulted by tectonic forces; weathered and eroded by wind, water and ice. Sometimes change is dramatic, the spectacular results of earthquakes or floods. More often it is a slow process lasting millions of years. A physical map of the world represents a snapshot of the ever-evolving architecture of the Earth. This terrain map shows the whole surface of the Earth, both above and below the sea.

The world in section

These cross-sections around the Earth, one in the northern hemisphere; one straddling the Equator, reveal the limited areas of land above sea level in comparison with the extent of the sea floor. The greater erosive effects of weathering by wind and water limit the upward elevation of land above sea level, while the deep oceans retain their dramatic mountain and trench profiles.

Cross-section: Northern hemisphere

Cross-section: Southern hemisphere

Map key

Geographical regions

- ice
- tundra
- needleleaf forest
- broadleaf forest
- cultivated land
- hot desert
- cold desert
- tropical grassland
- tropical rainforest
- mountain
- submarine regions

Scale 1:73,000,000

projection: Wagner VII

Northern hemisphere

Most of the land on Earth is concentrated in the northern hemisphere, although Europe and North America are the only continents which lie wholly in the north.

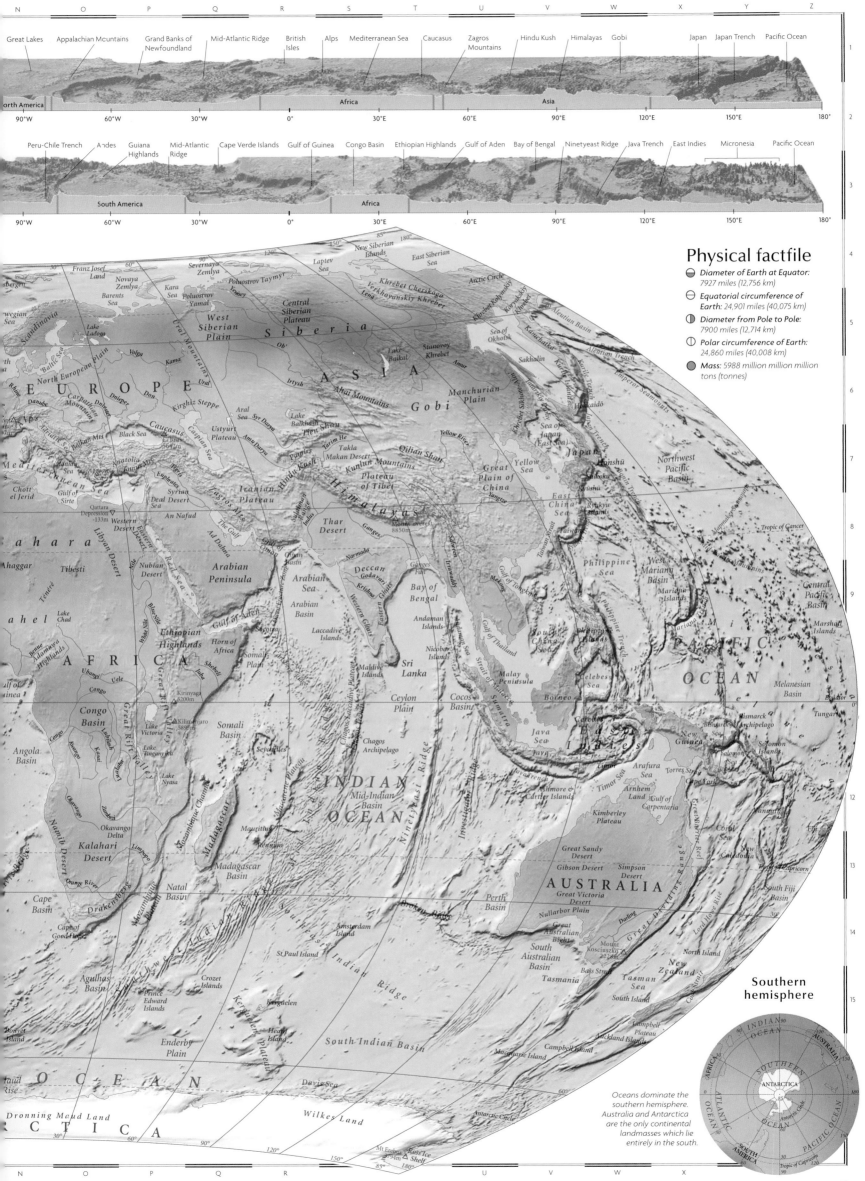

Physical factfile

- *Diameter of Earth at Equator:* 7927 miles (12,756 km)
- *Equatorial circumference of Earth:* 24,901 miles (40,075 km)
- *Diameter from Pole to Pole:* 7900 miles (12,714 km)
- *Polar circumference of Earth:* 24,860 miles (40,008 km)
- *Mass:* 5988 million million million tons (tonnes)

Southern hemisphere

Oceans dominate the southern hemisphere. Australia and Antarctica are the only continental landmasses which lie entirely in the south.

Structure of the Earth

The Earth as it is today is just the latest phase in a constant process of evolution which has occurred over the past 4.5 billion years. The Earth's continents are neither fixed nor stable; over the course of the Earth's history, propelled by currents rising from the intense heat at its centre, the great plates on which they lie have moved, collided, joined together, and separated. These processes continue to mould and transform the surface of the Earth, causing earthquakes and volcanic eruptions and creating oceans, mountain ranges, deep ocean trenches and island chains.

Inside the Earth

The Earth's hot inner core is made up of solid iron, while the outer core is composed of liquid iron and nickel. The mantle nearest the core is viscous, whereas the rocky upper mantle is fairly rigid. The crust is the rocky outer shell of the Earth. Together, the upper mantle and the crust form the lithosphere.

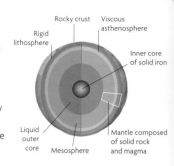

The dynamic Earth

The Earth's crust is made up of eight major (and several minor) rigid continental and oceanic tectonic plates, which fit closely together. The positions of the plates are not static. They are constantly moving relative to one another. The type of movement between plates affects the way in which they alter the structure of the Earth. The oldest parts of the plates, known as shields, are the most stable parts of the Earth and little tectonic activity occurs here.

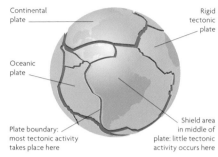

Convection currents

Deep within the Earth, at its inner core, temperatures may exceed 8100°F (4500°C). This heat warms rocks in the mesosphere which rise through the partially molten mantle, displacing cooler rocks just below the solid crust, which sink, and are warmed again by the heat of the mantle. This process is continually repeated, creating convection currents which form the moving force beneath the Earth's crust.

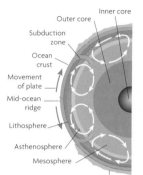

Plate boundaries

The boundaries between the plates are the areas where most tectonic activity takes place. Three types of movement occur at plate boundaries: the plates can either move towards each other, move apart, or slide past each other. The effect this has on the Earth's structure depends on whether the margin is between two continental plates, two oceanic plates or an oceanic and continental plate.

Mid-ocean ridges

Mid-ocean ridges are formed when two adjacent oceanic plates pull apart, allowing magma to force its way up to the surface, which then cools to form solid rock. Vast amounts of volcanic material are discharged at these mid-ocean ridges which can reach heights of 10,000 ft (3000 m).

▲ *The Mid-Atlantic Ridge rises above sea level in Iceland, producing geysers and volcanoes.*

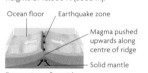

Formation of a mid-ocean ridge

Ocean plates meeting

△△ Oceanic crust is denser and thinner than continental crust; on average it is 3 miles (5 km) thick, while continental crust averages 18–24 miles (30–40 km). When oceanic plates of similar density meet, the crust is contorted as one plate overrides the other, forming deep sea trenches and volcanic island arcs above sea level.

▲ *Mount Pinatubo is an active volcano, lying on the Pacific 'Ring of Fire'.*

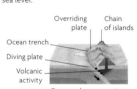

Ocean plates meeting to form an island arc

Tectonic activity

- - - - uncertain plate boundary
▲ volcanic zone
● earthquake zone
● hot spot
YYYYY rift valley

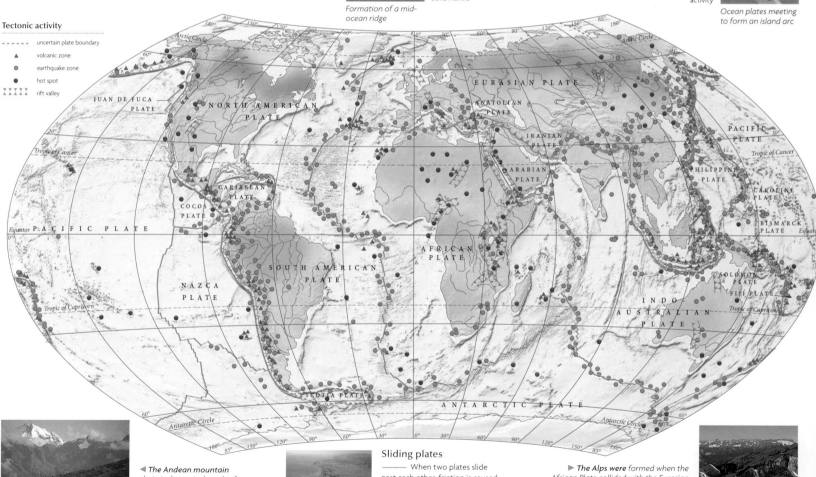

Diving plates

△△ When an oceanic and a continental plate meet, the denser oceanic plate is driven underneath the continental plate, which is crumpled by the collision to form mountain ranges. As the ocean plate plunges downward, it heats up, and molten rock (magma) is forced up to the surface.

◀ *The Andean mountain chain is the typical result of the impact of a diving plate.*

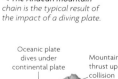

Diving plate

Sliding plates

When two plates slide past each other, friction is caused along the fault line which divides them. The plates do not move smoothly, and the uneven movement causes earthquakes.

▲ *The deep fracture caused by the sliding plates of the San Andreas Fault can be clearly seen in parts of California.*

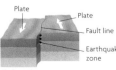

Sliding plates

▶ *The Alps were formed when the African Plate collided with the Eurasian Plate, about 65 million years ago.*

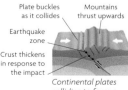

Colliding plates

▲▲ When two continental plates collide, great mountain chains are thrust upwards as the crust buckles and folds under the force of the impact.

Continental plates colliding to form a mountain range

Continental drift

Although the plates which make up the Earth's crust move only a few centimetres in a year, over the millions of years of the Earth's history, its continents have moved many thousands of kilometres, to create new continents, oceans and mountain chains.

1: Cambrian period

570–510 million years ago. Most continents are in tropical latitudes. The supercontinent of Gondwanaland reaches the South Pole.

2: Devonian period

408–362 million years ago. The continents of Gondwanaland and Laurentia are drifting northwards.

3: Carboniferous period

362–290 million years ago. The Earth is dominated by three continents; Laurentia, Angaraland and Gondwanaland.

4: Triassic period

245–208 million years ago. All three major continents have joined to form the super-continent of Pangea.

5: Jurassic period

208–145 million years ago. The super-continent of Pangea begins to break up, causing an overall rise in sea levels.

6: Cretaceous period

145–65 million years ago. Warm shallow seas cover much of the land: sea levels are about 80 ft (25 m) above present levels.

7: Tertiary period

65–2 million years ago. Although the world's geography is becoming more recognizable, major events such as the creation of the Himalayan mountain chain, are still to occur during this period.

Continental shields

The centres of the Earth's continents, known as shields, were established between 2500 and 500 million years ago; some contain rocks over three billion years old. They were formed by a series of turbulent events: plate movements, earthquakes and volcanic eruptions. Since the Pre-Cambrian period, over 570 million years ago, they have experienced little tectonic activity, and today, these flat, low-lying slabs of solidified molten rock form the stable centres of the continents. They are bounded or covered by successive belts of younger sedimentary rock.

The Hawaiian island chain

A hot spot lying deep beneath the Pacific Ocean pushes a plume of magma from the Earth's mantle up through the Pacific Plate to form volcanic islands. While the hot spot remains stationary, the plate on which the islands sit is moving slowly. A long chain of islands has been created as the plate passes over the hot spot.

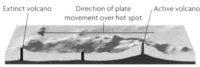

Extinct volcano | Direction of plate movement over hot spot | Active volcano

Cross-section through the Hawaiian Islands

Evolution of the Hawaiian Islands

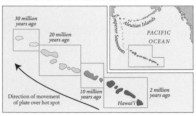

30 million years ago

20 million years ago

10 million years ago

2 million years ago

Direction of movement of plate over hot spot

Aleutian Islands

PACIFIC OCEAN

Hawai'i

Creation of the Himalayas

Between 10 and 20 million years ago, the Indian subcontinent, part of the ancient continent of Gondwanaland, collided with the continent of Asia. The Indo-Australian Plate continued to move northwards, displacing continental crust and uplifting the Himalayas, the world's highest mountain chain.

Movements of India

Himalayas

Present day

20 million years ago

60 million years ago

80 million years ago

Force of collision pushes up mountains

Cross-section through the Himalayas

▲ *The Himalayas were uplifted when the Indian subcontinent collided with Asia.*

The Earth's geology

The Earth's rocks are created in a continual cycle. Exposed rocks are weathered and eroded by wind, water and chemicals and deposited as sediments. If they pass into the Earth's crust they will be transformed by high temperatures and pressures into metamorphic rocks or they will melt and solidify as igneous rocks.

Sandstone

8 Sandstones are sedimentary rocks formed mainly in deserts, beaches and deltas. Desert sandstones are formed of grains of quartz which have been well rounded by wind erosion.

▲ *Rock stacks of desert sandstone, at Bryce Canyon National Park, Utah, USA.*

◄ *Extrusive igneous rocks are formed during volcanic eruptions, as here in Hawai'i.*

Andesite

7 Andesite is an extrusive igneous rock formed from magma which has solidified on the Earth's crust after a volcanic eruption.

Gneiss

1 Gneiss is a metamorphic rock made at great depth during the formation of mountain chains, when intense heat and pressure transform sedimentary or igneous rocks.

▲ *Gneiss formations in Norway's Jotunheimen Mountains.*

Basalt

2 Basalt is an igneous rock, formed when small quantities of magma lying close to the Earth's surface cool rapidly.

◄ *Basalt columns at Giant's Causeway, Northern Ireland, UK.*

Limestone

3 Limestone is a sedimentary rock, which is formed mainly from the calcite skeletons of marine animals which have been compressed into rock.

▲ *Limestone hills, Guilin, China.*

Coral

4 Coral reefs are formed from the skeletons of millions of individual corals.

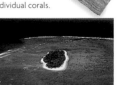

▲ *Great Barrier Reef, Australia.*

Geological regions

- continental shield
- sedimentary cover
- coral formation
- igneous rock types

Mountain ranges

- Alpine (new)
- Hercynian (old)
- Caledonian (ancient)

Schist

6 Gchist is a metamorphic rock formed during mountain building, when temperature and pressure are comparatively high. Both mudstones and shales reform into schist under these conditions.

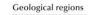

▶ *Schist formations in the Atlas Mountains, northwestern Africa.*

Granite

5 Granite is an intrusive igneous rock formed from magma which has solidified deep within the Earth's crust. The magma cools slowly, producing a coarse-grained rock.

▶ *Namibia's Namaqualand Plateau is formed of granite.*

Shaping the landscape

The basic material of the Earth's surface is solid rock: valleys, deserts, soil, and sand are all evidence of the powerful agents of weathering, erosion, and deposition which constantly shape and transform the Earth's landscapes. Water, either flowing continually in rivers or seas, or frozen and compacted into solid sheets of ice, has the most clearly visible impact on the Earth's surface. But wind can transport fragments of rock over huge distances and strip away protective layers of vegetation, exposing rock surfaces to the impact of extreme heat and cold.

Coastal water

The world's coastlines are constantly changing; every day, tides deposit, sift and sort sand, and gravel on the shoreline. Over longer periods, powerful wave action erodes cliffs and headlands and carves out bays.

▶ *A low, wide* sandy beach on South Africa's Cape Peninsula is continually re-shaped by the action of the Atlantic waves.

▲ *The sheer chalk* cliffs at Seven Sisters in southern England are constantly under attack from waves.

Water

Less than 2% of the world's water is on the land, but it is the most powerful agent of landscape change. Water, as rainfall, groundwater and rivers, can transform landscapes through both erosion and deposition. Eroded material carried by rivers forms the world's most fertile soils.

▲ *Waterfalls such as* the Iguaçu Falls on the border between Argentina and southern Brazil, erode the underlying rock, causing the falls to retreat.

Groundwater

In regions where there are porous rocks such as chalk, water is stored underground in large quantities; these reservoirs of water are known as aquifers. Rain percolates through topsoil into the underlying bedrock, creating an underground store of water. The limit of the saturated zone is called the water table.

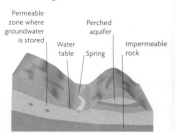

Permeable zone where groundwater is stored · Perched aquifer · Water table · Spring · Impermeable rock

Storage of groundwater in an aquifer

World river systems

drainage basin

World river systems:
Sediment deposited annually per drainage basin

tons per sq mile per year 9120 · 6080 · 1520 · 760 · 200 and less · 2400 · 1600 · 400

tonnes per sq km per year

[World map with river systems labeled: Yukon, Mackenzie, Nelson, Columbia, St. Lawrence, Colorado, Mississippi Missouri, Rio Grande, Orinoco, Amazon, São Francisco, Paraná, Rhine, Danube, Volga, Ob', Yenisey, Lena, Amur, Tigris, Euphrates, Indus, Yellow River, Ganges Brahmaputra, Yangtze, Mekong, Niger, Nile, Congo, Zambezi, Orange, Murray Darling. Labeled oceans: PACIFIC OCEAN, ATLANTIC OCEAN, ARCTIC OCEAN, INDIAN OCEAN. Latitude lines: Arctic Circle, Tropic of Cancer, Equator, Tropic of Capricorn, Antarctic Circle]

Rivers

Rivers erode the land by grinding and dissolving rocks and stones. Most erosion occurs in the river's upper course as it flows through highland areas. Rock fragments are moved along the river bed by fast-flowing water and deposited in areas where the river slows down, such as flat plains, or where the river enters seas or lakes.

River valleys

Over long periods of time rivers erode uplands to form characteristic V-shaped valleys with smooth sides.

Resistant rock · River · Chemical erosion cuts valley in softer rock

River valley erosion

Deltas

When a river deposits its load of silt and sediment (alluvium) on entering the sea, it may form a delta. As this material accumulates, it chokes the mouth of the river, forcing it to create new channels to reach the sea.

▶ *The Nile forms* a broad delta as it flows into the Mediterranean.

Drainage basins

The drainage basin is the area of land drained by a major trunk river and its smaller branch rivers or tributaries. Drainage basins are separated from one another by natural boundaries known as watersheds.

Watershed · Major trunk river · Alps · Dolomites · Apennines · Tributary river · Delta · River mouth · Po Valley

The drainage basin of the Po river, northern Italy.

Meanders

In their lower courses, rivers flow slowly. As they flow across the lowlands, they form looping bends called meanders.

▲ *The Mississippi River* forms meanders as it flows across the southern US.

▲ *The meanders of* Utah's San Juan River have become deeply incised.

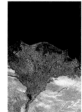

◀ *Mud is deposited* by China's Yellow River in its lower course.

Deposition

When rivers have deposited large quantities of fertile alluvium, they are forced to find new channels through the alluvium deposits, creating braided river systems.

Landslides

Heavy rain and associated flooding on slopes can loosen underlying rocks, which crumble, causing the top layers of rock and soil to slip.

▶ *A huge landslide* in the Swiss Alps has left massive piles of rocks and pebbles called scree.

Gullies

In areas where soil is thin, rainwater is not effectively absorbed, and may flow overland. The water courses downhill in channels, or gullies, and may lead to rapid erosion of soil.

▲ *A deep gully* in the French Alps caused by the scouring of upper layers of turf.

Ice

During its long history, the Earth has experienced a number of glacial episodes when temperatures were considerably lower than today. During the last Ice Age, 18,000 years ago, ice covered an area three times larger than it does today. Over these periods, the ice has left a remarkable legacy of transformed landscapes.

Glaciers

Glaciers are formed by the compaction of snow into 'rivers' of ice. As they move over the landscape, glaciers pick up and carry a load of rocks and boulders which erode the landscape they pass over, and are eventually deposited at the end of the glacier.

▲ *A massive glacier* advancing down a valley in southern Argentina.

Post-glacial features

When a glacial episode ends, the retreating ice leaves many features. These include depositional ridges called moraines, which may be eroded into low hills known as drumlins; sinuous ridges called eskers; kames, which are rounded hummocks; depressions known as kettle holes; and windblown loess deposits.

Glacial valleys

Glaciers can erode much more powerfully than rivers. They form steep-sided, flat-bottomed valleys with a typical U-shaped profile. Valleys created by tributary glaciers, whose floors have not been eroded to the same depth as the main glacial valley floor, are called hanging valleys

▲ *The U-shaped profile* and piles of morainic debris are characteristic of a valley once filled by a glacier.

▲ *A series of* hanging valleys high up in the Chilean Andes.

Past and present world ice-cover and glacial features

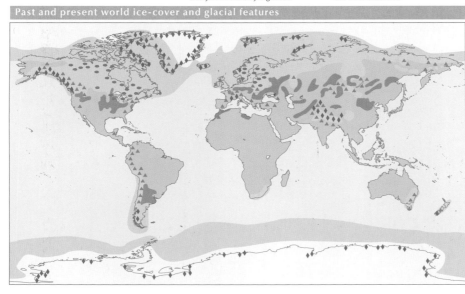

Past and present world ice cover and glacial features

- extent of last Ice Age
- loess deposits
- post-glacial feature
- glacial feature
- present day ice cover
- glacial field

▲ *Irregular polygons show* through the sedge-grass tundra in the Yukon, Canada.

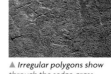

Post-glacial landscape features

Kame terrace, Retreating glacier, Kettle hole, Esker, Drumlin, Braided river, Terminal moraine, Windblown loess, Glacial till, Bedrock

Ice shattering

Water drips into fissures in rocks and freezes, expanding as it does so. The pressure weakens the rock, causing it to crack, and eventually to shatter into polygonal patterns.

▲ *The profile of* the Matterhorn has been formed by three cirques lying 'back-to-back'

Cirques

Cirques are basin-shaped hollows which mark the head of a glaciated valley. Where neighboring cirques meet, they are divided by sharp rock ridges called arêtes. It is these arêtes which give the Matterhorn its characteristic profile.

Fjords

Fjords are ancient glacial valleys flooded by the sea following the end of a period of glaciation. Beneath the water, the valley floor can be 4000 ft (1300 m) deep.

▲ *A fjord fills* a former glacial valley in southern New Zealand.

Periglaciation

Periglacial areas occur near to the edge of ice sheets. A layer of frozen ground lying just beneath the surface of the land is known as permafrost. When the surface melts in the summer, the water is unable to drain into the frozen ground, and so 'creeps' downhill, a process known as solifluction.

Wind

Strong winds can transport rock fragments great distances, especially where there is little vegetation to protect the rock. In desert areas, wind picks up loose, unprotected sand particles, carrying them over great distances. This powerfully abrasive debris is blasted at the surface by the wind, eroding the landscape into dramatic shapes.

Deposition

The rocky, stony floors of the world's deserts are swept and scoured by strong winds. The smaller, finer particles of sand are shaped into surface ripples, dunes, or sand mountains, which rise to a height of 650 ft (200 m). Dunes usually form single lines, running perpendicular to the direction of the prevailing wind. These long, straight ridges can extend for over 100 miles (160 km).

Dunes

Dunes are shaped by wind direction and sand supply. Where sand supply is limited, crescent-shaped barchan dunes are formed.

Wind direction

Prevailing winds and dust trajectories

Prevailing winds
- northeast trade
- southeast trade
- westerly
- westerly
- polar easterly
- polar easterly

Dust trajectories
- trajectory of aeolian dust

Hot and cold deserts

Main desert types
- hot arid
- semi-arid
- cold polar

▲ *Barchan dunes in the* Arabian Desert.

▲ *Complex dune system in* the Sahara.

Types of dune

Transverse dune *Barchan dune* *Linear dune* *Star dune*

Heat

Fierce sun can heat the surface of rock, causing it to expand more rapidly than the cooler, underlying layers. This creates tensions which force the rock to crack or break up. In arid regions, the evaporation of water from rock surfaces dissolves certain minerals within the water, causing salt crystals to form in small openings in the rock. The hard crystals force the openings to widen into cracks and fissures.

▲ *The cracked and* parched floor of Death Valley, California. This is one of the hottest deserts on Earth.

Temperature

Most of the world's deserts are in the tropics. The cold deserts which occur elsewhere are arid because they are a long way from the rain-giving sea. Rock in deserts is exposed because of lack of vegetation and is susceptible to changes in temperature; extremes of heat and cold can cause both cracks and fissures to appear in the rock.

Desert abrasion

Abrasion creates a wide range of desert landforms from faceted pebbles and wind ripples in the sand, to large-scale features such as yardangs (low, streamlined ridges), and scoured desert pavements.

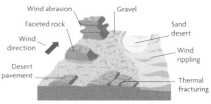
Wind abrasion, Gravel, Faceted rock, Sand desert, Wind direction, Wind rippling, Desert pavement, Thermal fracturing

Features of a desert surface

◄ *This dry valley at* Ellesmere Island in the Canadian Arctic is an example of a cold desert. The cracked floor and scoured slopes are features also found in hot deserts.

The world's oceans

Two-thirds of the Earth's surface is covered by the oceans. The landscape of the ocean floor, like the surface of the land, has been shaped by movements of the Earth's crust over millions of years to form volcanic mountain ranges, deep trenches, basins and plateaux. Ocean currents constantly redistribute warm and cold water around the world. A major warm current, such as El Niño in the Pacific Ocean, can increase surface temperature by up to 46°F (8°C), causing changes in weather patterns which can lead to both droughts and flooding.

The great oceans

There are five oceans on Earth: the Pacific, Atlantic, Indian and Southern oceans, and the much smaller Arctic Ocean. These five ocean basins are relatively young, having evolved within the last 80 million years. One of the most recent plate collisions, between the Eurasian and African plates, created the present-day arrangement of continents and oceans.

▲ **The Indian Ocean** accounts for approximately 20% of the total area of the world's oceans.

Sea level

If the influence of tides, winds, currents and variations in gravity were ignored, the surface of the Earth's oceans would closely follow the topography of the ocean floor, with an underwater ridge 3000 ft (915 m) high producing a rise of up to 3 ft (1 m) in the level of the surface water.

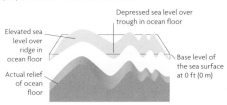

Depressed sea level over trough in ocean floor
Elevated sea level over ridge in ocean floor
Base level of the sea surface at 0 ft (0 m)
Actual relief of ocean floor

How surface waters reflect the relief of the ocean floor

▲ **The low relief** of many small Pacific islands such as these atolls at Huahine in French Polynesia makes them vulnerable to changes in sea level.

Ocean structure

The continental shelf is a shallow, flat sea-bed surrounding the Earth's continents. It extends to the continental slope, which falls to the ocean floor. Here, the flat abyssal plains are interrupted by vast, underwater mountain ranges, the mid-ocean ridges, and ocean trenches which plunge to depths of 35,828 ft (10,920 m).

Trench
Seamount
Abyssal plain
Oceanic ridge
Volcanic island
Flat-topped guyot
Continental shelf

Typical sea-floor features

Ocean depth

Sea level
200m / 656ft
1000m / 3281ft
2000m / 6562ft
3000m / 9843ft
4000m / 13,124ft
5000m / 16,400ft
6000m / 19,686ft

Black smokers

These vents in the ocean floor disgorge hot, sulphur-rich water from deep in the Earth's crust. Despite the great depths, a variety of lifeforms have adapted to the chemical-rich environment which surrounds black smokers.

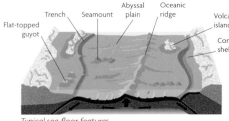

▲ **A black smoker** in the Atlantic Ocean.

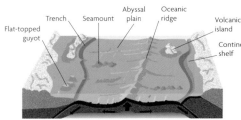

▲ **Surtsey, near Iceland,** is a volcanic island lying directly over the Mid-Atlantic Ridge. It was formed in the 1960s following intense volcanic activity nearby.

Ocean floors

Mid-ocean ridges are formed by lava which erupts beneath the sea and cools to form solid rock. This process mirrors the creation of volcanoes from cooled lava on the land. The ages of sea floor rocks increase in parallel bands outwards from central ocean ridges.

Plume of hot mineral laden water
Chimney
Water percolates into the sea floor
Ocean floor
Water heated by hot basalt

Formation of black smokers

Ages of the ocean floor

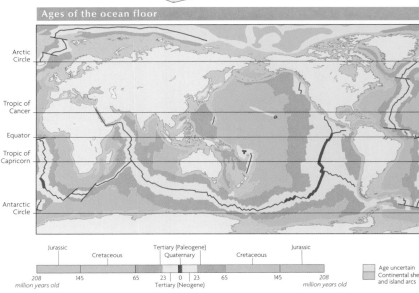

Arctic Circle
Tropic of Cancer
Equator
Tropic of Capricorn
Antarctic Circle

Jurassic
Cretaceous
Tertiary (Paleogene)
Quaternary
Cretaceous
Jurassic

208 million years old
145
65
23 0 23
Tertiary (Neogene)
65
145
208 million years old

Age uncertain
Continental shelf and island arcs

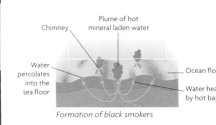

▲ *Currents in the* Southern Ocean *are driven by some of the world's fiercest winds, including the Roaring Forties, Furious Fifties and Shrieking Sixties.*

▲ *The Pacific Ocean is the world's largest and deepest ocean, covering over one-third of the surface of the Earth.*

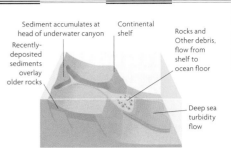

▲ *The Atlantic Ocean was formed when the landmasses of the eastern and western hemispheres began to drift apart 180 million years ago.*

Deposition of sediment

Storms, earthquakes, and volcanic activity trigger underwater currents known as turbidity currents which scour sand and gravel from the continental shelf, creating underwater canyons. These strong currents pick up material deposited at river mouths and deltas, and carry it across the continental shelf and through the underwater canyons, where it is eventually laid down on the ocean floor in the form of fans.

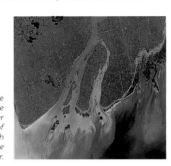

Sediment accumulates at head of underwater canyon

Recently-deposited sediments overlay older rocks

Continental shelf

Rocks and Other debris, flow from shelf to ocean floor

Deep sea turbidity flow

How sediment is deposited on the ocean floor

▶ *Satellite image of the* Yangtze *(Chang Jiang) Delta, in which the land appears red. The river deposits immense quantities of silt into the East China Sea, much of which will eventually reach the deep ocean floor.*

Surface water

Ocean currents move warm water away from the Equator towards the poles, while cold water is, in turn, moved towards the Equator. This is the main way in which the Earth distributes surface heat and is a major climatic control. Approximately 4000 million years ago, the Earth was dominated by oceans and there was no land to interrupt the flow of the currents, which would have flowed as straight lines, simply influenced by the Earth's rotation.

Idealized globe showing the movement of water around a landless Earth.

Ocean currents

Surface currents are driven by the prevailing winds and by the spinning motion of the Earth, which drives the currents into circulating whirlpools, or gyres. Deep sea currents, over 330 ft (100 m) below the surface, are driven by differences in water temperature and salinity, which have an impact on the density of deep water and on its movement.

Surface temperature and currents

Arctic Circle
Tropic of Cancer
Equator
Tropic of Capricorn
Antarctic Circle

Surface temperature and currents

- - - - Ice-shelf (below 0°C / 32°F)
▢ Sea-ice* (average) below -2°C / 28°F
▢ Sea-water -2–0°C / 28–32°F
* Sea-water freezes at -1.9°C / 28.4°F
▢ 0–10°C / 32–50°F
▢ 10–20°C / 50–68°F
▢ 20–30°C / 68–86°F
→ warm current
→ cold current

Tides and waves

Tides are created by the pull of the Sun and Moon's gravity on the surface of the oceans. The levels of high and low tides are influenced by the position of the Moon in relation to the Earth and Sun. Waves are formed by wind blowing over the surface of the water.

High and low tides

The highest tides occur when the Earth, the Moon and the Sun are aligned *(below left)*. The lowest tides are experienced when the Sun and Moon align at right angles to one another *(below right)*.

Tidal range and wave environments

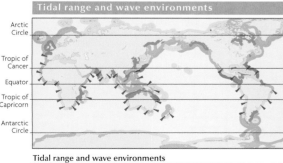

Arctic Circle
Tropic of Cancer
Equator
Tropic of Capricorn
Antarctic Circle

Tidal range and wave environments

- ▢ less than 2m / 7ft
- ▢ 2–4m / 7–13ft
- ▢ greater than 4m / 13ft
- ◹ east coast swell
- ◹ west coast swell
- ▢ tropical cyclone
- ▢ storm wave
- ▢ ice-shelf

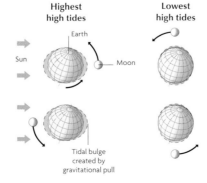

Highest high tides

Earth

Sun

Moon

Lowest high tides

Tidal bulge created by gravitational pull

Deep sea temperature and currents

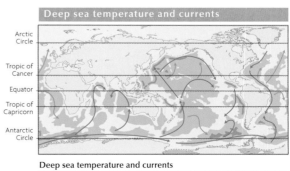

Arctic Circle
Tropic of Cancer
Equator
Tropic of Capricorn
Antarctic Circle

Deep sea temperature and currents

- ▢ Ice-shelf (below 0°C / 32°F)
- ▢ Sea-water -2–0°C / 28–32°F (below 5000m / 16,400ft)
- ▢ Sea-water 0–5°C / 32–41°F (below 4000m / 13,120ft)
- - - - Ice-shelf (below 0°C / 32°F)
- → Primary currents
- → Secondary currents

The global climate

The Earth's climatic types consist of stable patterns of weather conditions averaged out over a long period of time. Different climates are categorized according to particular combinations of temperature and humidity. By contrast, weather consists of short-term fluctuations in wind, temperature and humidity conditions. Different climates are determined by latitude, altitude, the prevailing wind and circulation of ocean currents. Longer-term changes in climate, such as global warming or the onset of ice ages, are punctuated by shorter-term events which comprise the day-to-day weather of a region, such as frontal depressions, hurricanes and blizzards.

The atmosphere, wind and weather

The Earth's atmosphere has been compared to a giant ocean of air which surrounds the planet. Its circulation patterns are similar to the currents in the oceans and are influenced by three factors; the Earth's orbit around the Sun and rotation about its axis, and variations in the amount of heat radiation received from the Sun. If both heat and moisture were not redistributed between the Equator and the poles, large areas of the Earth would be uninhabitable.

◀ Heavy fogs, as here in southern England, form as moisture-laden air passes over cold ground.

Temperature

The world can be divided into three major climatic zones, stretching like large belts across the latitudes: the tropics which are warm; the cold polar regions and the temperate zones which lie between them. Temperatures across the Earth range from above 30°C (86°F) in the deserts to as low as -55°C (-70°F) at the poles. Temperature is also controlled by altitude; because air becomes cooler and less dense the higher it gets, mountainous regions are typically colder than those areas which are at, or close to, sea level.

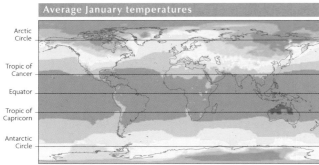

Average January temperatures

Arctic Circle
Tropic of Cancer
Equator
Tropic of Capricorn
Antarctic Circle

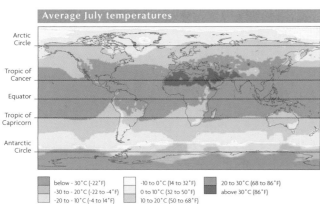

Average July temperatures

Arctic Circle
Tropic of Cancer
Equator
Tropic of Capricorn
Antarctic Circle

below - 30°C (-22°F)	-10 to 0°C (14 to 32°F)	20 to 30°C (68 to 86°F)
-30 to - 20°C (-22 to -4°F)	0 to 10°C (32 to 50°F)	above 30°C (86°F)
-20 to - 10°C (-4 to 14°F)	10 to 20°C (50 to 68°F)	

Global air circulation

Air does not simply flow from the Equator to the poles, it circulates in giant cells known as Hadley and Ferrel cells. As air warms it expands, becoming less dense and rising; this creates areas of low pressure. As the air rises it cools and condenses, causing heavy rainfall over the tropics and slight snowfall over the poles. This cool air then sinks, forming high pressure belts. At surface level in the tropics these sinking currents are deflected polewards as the westerlies and towards the equator as the trade winds. At the poles they become the polar easterlies.

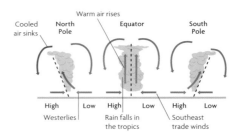

Cooled air sinks — North Pole
Warm air rises — Equator
South Pole

High / Low / High / Low / High / Low
Westerlies / Rain falls in the tropics / Southeast trade winds

▲ The Antarctic pack ice expands its area by almost seven times during the winter as temperatures drop and surrounding seas freeze.

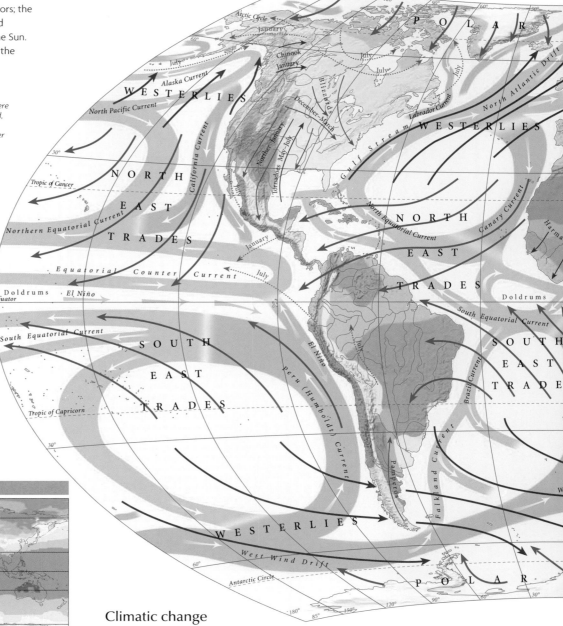

Climatic change

The Earth is currently in a warm phase between ice ages. Warmer temperatures result in higher sea levels as more of the polar ice caps melt. Most of the world's population lives near coasts, so any changes which might cause sea levels to rise, could have a potentially disastrous impact.

▲ This ice fair, painted by Pieter Brueghel the Younger in the 17th century, shows the Little Ice Age which peaked around 300 years ago.

The greenhouse effect

Gases such as carbon dioxide are known as 'greenhouse gases' because they allow shortwave solar radiation to enter the Earth's atmosphere, but help to stop longwave radiation from escaping. This traps heat, raising the Earth's temperature. An excess of these gases, such as that which results from the burning of fossil fuels, helps trap more heat and can lead to global warming.

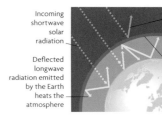

Incoming shortwave solar radiation

Deflected shortwave solar radiation

Deflected longwave radiation emitted by the Earth heats the atmosphere

Greenhouse gases prevent the escape of longwave radiation

◀ *The islands of the Caribbean, Mexico's Gulf coast and the southeastern USA are often hit by hurricanes formed far out in the Atlantic.*

Oceanic water circulation

In general, ocean currents parallel the movement of winds across the Earth's surface. Incoming solar energy is greatest at the Equator and least at the poles. So, water in the oceans heats up most at the Equator and flows polewards, cooling as it moves north or south towards the Arctic or Antarctic. The flow is eventually reversed and cold water currents move back towards the Equator. These ocean currents act as a vast system for moving heat from the Equator towards the poles and are a major influence on the distribution of the Earth's climates.

▲ *In marginal climatic zones years of drought can completely dry out the land and transform grassland to desert.*

Map key

Climate zones	
☐ ice cap	☐ mediterranean
☐ subarctic	☐ semi-arid
☐ tundra	☐ arid
☐ continental	☐ hot humid
☐ temperate	☐ humid equatorial
☐ warm temperate	☐ tropical

Ocean currents
→ warm
→ cold

Prevailing winds
→ warm
→ cold

Local winds
→ warm
→ cold
June→ seasonal*
* (seasonal winds which can either be warm or cold)

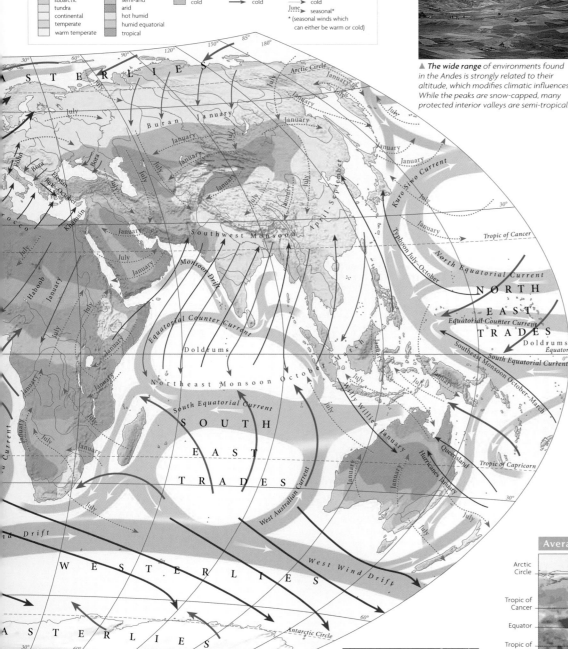

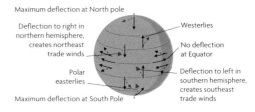

▲ *The wide range of environments found in the Andes is strongly related to their altitude, which modifies climatic influences. While the peaks are snow-capped, many protected interior valleys are semi-tropical.*

Tilt and rotation

The tilt and rotation of the Earth during its annual orbit largely control the distribution of heat and moisture across its surface, which correspondingly controls its large-scale weather patterns. As the Earth annually rotates around the Sun, half its surface is receiving maximum radiation, creating summer and winter seasons. The angle of the Earth means that on average the tropics receive two and a half times as much heat from the Sun each day as the poles.

Earth's axis tilted — Earth's orbit
Rays from the Sun — Day — Night

The Coriolis effect

The rotation of the Earth influences atmospheric circulation by deflecting winds and ocean currents. Winds blowing in the northern hemisphere are deflected to the right and those in the southern hemisphere are deflected to the left, creating large-scale patterns of wind circulation, such as the northeast and southeast trade winds and the westerlies. This effect is greatest at the poles and least at the Equator.

Maximum deflection at North pole

Deflection to right in northern hemisphere, creates northeast trade winds — Westerlies
— No deflection at Equator
Polar easterlies — Deflection to left in southern hemisphere, creates southeast trade winds

Maximum deflection at South Pole

Precipitation

When warm air expands, it rises and cools, and the water vapour it carries condenses to form clouds. Heavy, regular rainfall is characteristic of the equatorial region, while the poles are cold and receive only slight snowfall. Tropical regions have marked dry and rainy seasons, while in the temperate regions rainfall is relatively unpredictable.

▲ *Monsoon rains, which affect southern Asia from May to September, are caused by sea winds blowing across the warm land.*

▲ *Heavy tropical rainstorms occur frequently in Papua New Guinea, often causing soil erosion and landslides in cultivated areas.*

Average January rainfall

Arctic Circle
Tropic of Cancer
Equator
Tropic of Capricorn
Antarctic Circle

Average July rainfall

Arctic Circle
Tropic of Cancer
Equator
Tropic of Capricorn
Antarctic Circle

☐ 0–25 mm (0–1 in)
☐ 25–50 mm (1–2 in)
☐ 50–100 mm (2–4 in)
☐ 100–200 mm (4–8 in)
☐ 200–300 mm (8–12 in)
☐ 300–400 mm (12–16 in)
☐ 400–500 mm (16–20 in)
☐ above 500 mm (20 in)

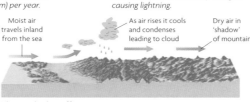

▲ *The intensity of some blizzards in Canada and the northern USA can give rise to snowdrifts as high as 10 ft (3 m).*

▲ *The Atacama Desert in Chile is one of the driest places on Earth, with an average rainfall of less than 2 inches (50 mm) per year.*

▲ *Violent thunderstorms occur along advancing cold fronts, when cold, dry air masses meet warm, moist air, which rises rapidly, its moisture condensing into thunderclouds. Rain and hail become electrically charged, causing lightning.*

The rainshadow effect

When moist air is forced to rise by mountains, it cools and the water vapour falls as precipitation, either as rain or snow. Only the dry, cold air continues over the mountains, leaving inland areas with little or no rain. This is called the rainshadow effect and is one reason for the existence of the Mojave Desert in California, which lies east of the Coast Ranges.

Moist air travels inland from the sea — As air rises it cools and condenses leading to cloud — Dry air in 'shadow' of mountain

The rainshadow effect

Life on Earth

A unique combination of an oxygen-rich atmosphere and plentiful water is the key to life on Earth. Apart from the polar ice caps, there are few areas which have not been colonized by animals or plants over the course of the Earth's history. Plants process sunlight to provide them with their energy, and ultimately all the Earth's animals rely on plants for survival. Because of this reliance, plants are known as primary producers, and the availability of nutrients and temperature of an area is defined as its primary productivity, which affects the quantity and type of animals which are able to live there. This index is affected by climatic factors – cold and aridity restrict the quantity of life, whereas warmth and regular rainfall allow a greater diversity of species.

Biogeographical regions

The Earth can be divided into a series of biogeographical regions, or biomes, ecological communities where certain species of plant and animal co-exist within particular climatic conditions. Within these broad classifications, other factors including soil richness, altitude and human activities such as urbanization, intensive agriculture and deforestation, affect the local distribution of living species within each biome.

Polar regions
A layer of permanent ice at the Earth's poles covers both seas and land. Very little plant and animal life can exist in these harsh regions.

Tundra
A desolate region, with long, dark freezing winters and short, cold summers. With virtually no soil and large areas of permanently frozen ground known as permafrost, the tundra is largely treeless, though it is briefly clothed by small flowering plants in the summer months.

Needleleaf forests
With milder summers than the tundra and less wind, these areas are able to support large forests of coniferous trees.

Broadleaf forests
Much of the northern hemisphere was once covered by deciduous forests, which occurred in areas with marked seasonal variations. Most deciduous forests have been cleared for human settlement.

Temperate rainforests
In warmer wetter areas, such as southern China, temperate deciduous forests are replaced by evergreen forest.

Deserts
Deserts are areas with negligible rainfall. Most hot deserts lie within the tropics; cold deserts are dry because of their distance from the moisture-providing sea.

Mediterranean
Hot, dry summers and short winters typify these areas, which were once covered by evergreen shrubs and woodland, but have now been cleared by humans for agriculture.

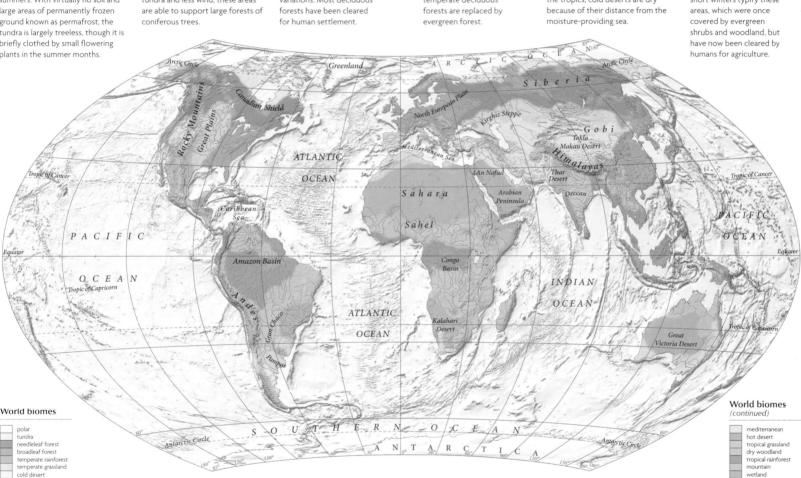

World biomes
- polar
- tundra
- needleleaf forest
- broadleaf forest
- temperate rainforest
- temperate grassland
- cold desert

World biomes *(continued)*
- mediterranean
- hot desert
- tropical grassland
- dry woodland
- tropical rainforest
- mountain
- wetland

Tropical and temperate grasslands
The major grassland areas are found in the centres of the larger continental landmasses. In Africa's tropical savannah regions, seasonal rainfall alternates with drought. Temperate grasslands, also known as steppes and prairies are found in the northern hemisphere, and in South America, where they are known as the pampas.

Dry woodlands
Trees and shrubs, adapted to dry conditions, grow widely spaced from one another, interspersed by savannah grasslands.

Tropical rainforests
Characterized by year-round warmth and high rainfall, tropical rainforests contain the highest diversity of plant and animal species on Earth.

Mountains
Though the lower slopes of mountains may be thickly forested, only ground-hugging shrubs and other vegetation will grow above the tree line which varies according to both altitude and latitude.

Wetlands
Rarely lying above sea level, wetlands are marshes, swamps and tidal flats. Some, with their moist, fertile soils, are rich feeding grounds for fish and breeding grounds for birds. Others have little soil structure and are too acidic to support much plant and animal life.

Biodiversity

The number of plant and animal species, and the range of genetic diversity within the populations of each species, make up the Earth's biodiversity. The plants and animals which are endemic to a region – that is, those which are found nowhere else in the world – are also important in determining levels of biodiversity. Human settlement and intervention have encroached on many areas of the world once rich in endemic plant and animal species. Increasing international efforts are being made to monitor and conserve the biodiversity of the Earth's remaining wild places.

Animal adaptation

The degree of an animal's adaptability to different climates and conditions is extremely important in ensuring its success as a species. Many animals, particularly the largest mammals, are becoming restricted to ever-smaller regions as human development and modern agricultural practices reduce their natural habitats. In contrast, humans have been responsible – both deliberately and accidentally – for the spread of some of the world's most successful species. Many of these introduced species are now more numerous than the indigenous animal populations.

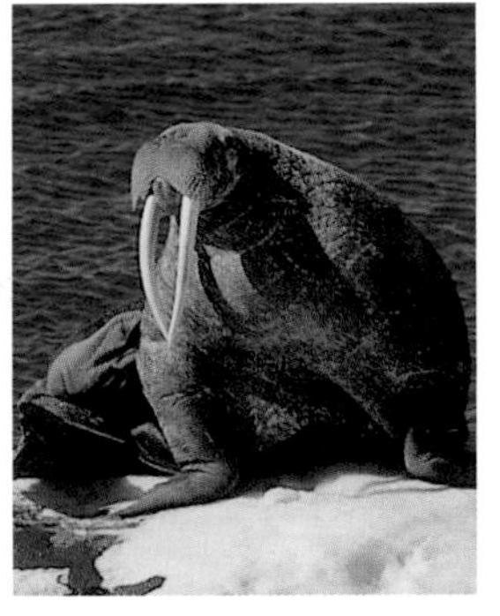

Polar animals

The frozen wastes of the polar regions are able to support only a small range of species which derive their nutritional requirements from the sea. Animals such as the walrus *(left)* have developed insulating fat, stocky limbs and double-layered coats to enable them to survive in the freezing conditions.

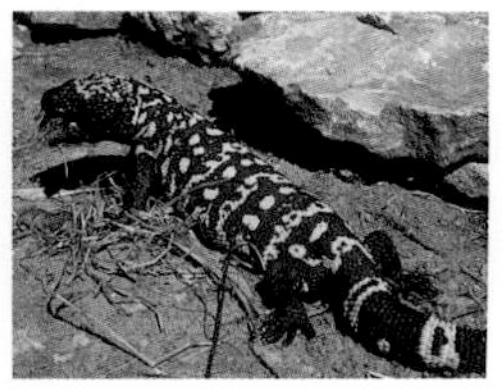

Desert animals

Many animals which live in the extreme heat and aridity of the deserts are able to survive for days and even months with very little food or water. Their bodies are adapted to lose heat quickly and to store fat and water. The Gila monster *(above)* stores fat in its tail.

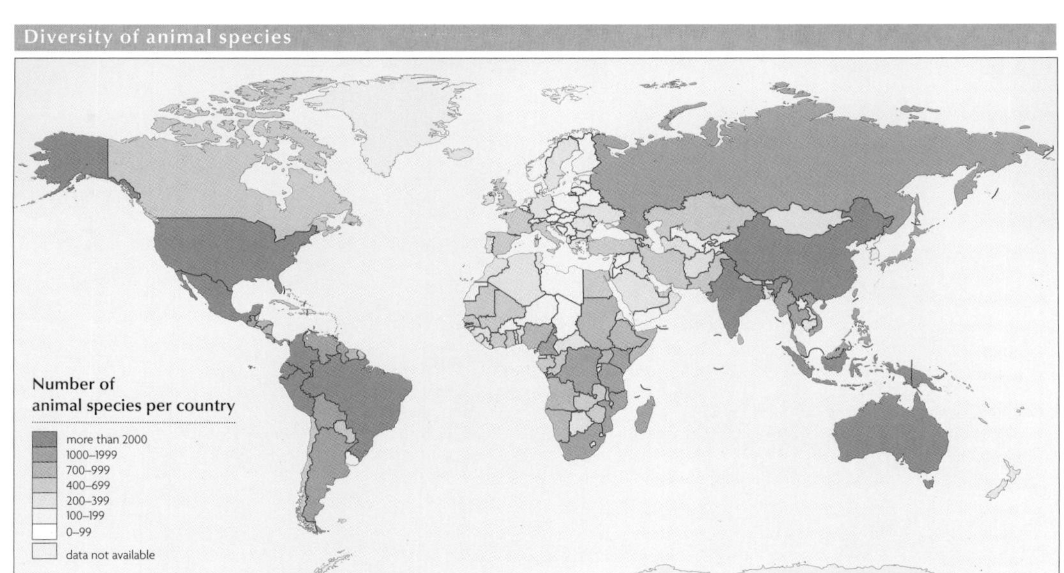

Amazon rainforest

The vast Amazon Basin is home to the world's greatest variety of animal species. Animals are adapted to live at many different levels from the treetops to the tangled undergrowth which lies beneath the canopy. The sloth *(below)* hangs upside down in the branches. Its fur grows from its stomach to its back to enable water to run off quickly.

Diversity of animal species

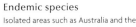

Number of animal species per country
- more than 2000
- 1000–1999
- 700–999
- 400–699
- 200–399
- 100–199
- 0–99
- data not available

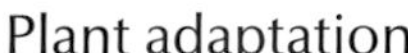

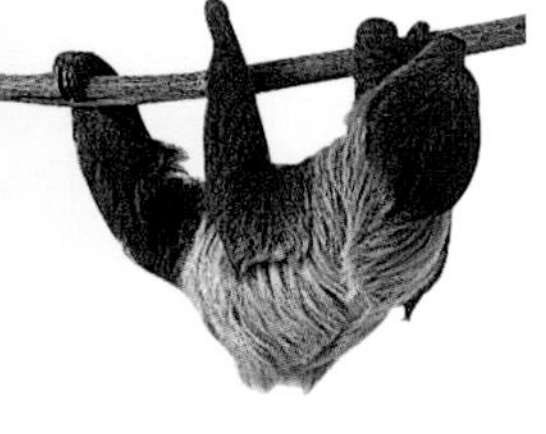

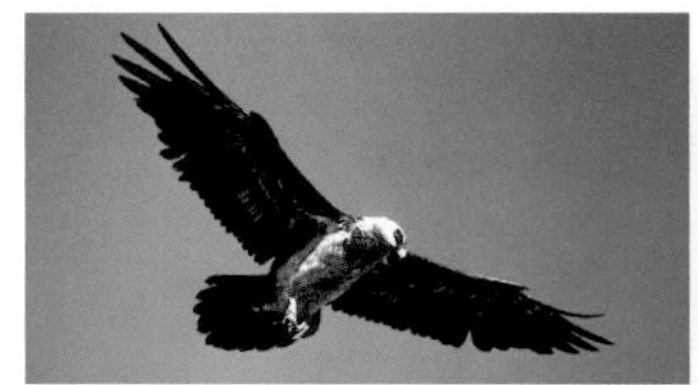

High altitudes

Few animals exist in the rarefied atmosphere of the highest mountains. However, birds of prey such as eagles and vultures *(above)*, with their superb eyesight can soar as high as 23,000 ft (7000 m) to scan for prey below.

Marine biodiversity

The oceans support a huge variety of different species, from the world's largest mammals like whales and dolphins down to the tiniest plankton. The greatest diversities occur in the warmer seas of continental shelves, where plants are easily able to photosynthesize, and around coral reefs, where complex ecosystems are found. On the ocean floor, nematodes can exist at a depth of more than 10,000 ft (3000 m) below sea level.

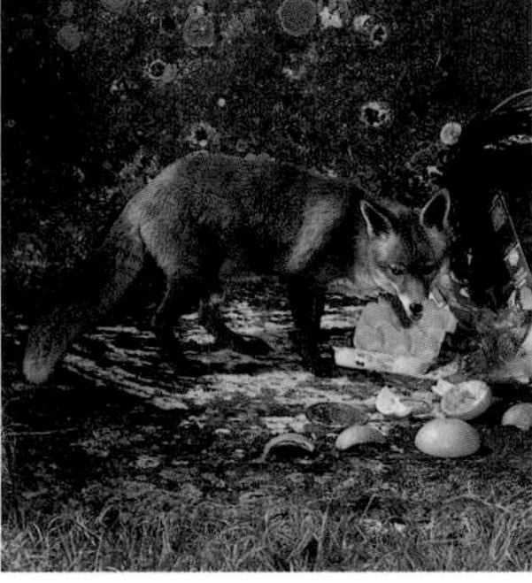

Urban animals

The growth of cities has reduced the amount of habitat available to many species. A number of animals are now moving closer into urban areas to scavenge from the detritus of the modern city *(left)*. Rodents, particularly rats and mice, have existed in cities for thousands of years, and many insects, especially moths, quickly develop new colouring to provide them with camouflage.

Endemic species

Isolated areas such as Australia and the island of Madagascar, have the greatest range of endemic species. In Australia, these include marsupials such as the kangaroo *(below)*, which carry their young in pouches on their bodies. Destruction of habitat, pollution, hunting, and predators introduced by humans, are threatening this unique biodiversity.

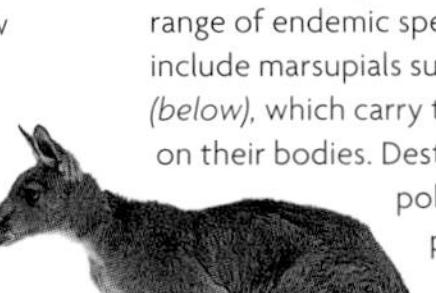

Plant adaptation

Environmental conditions, particularly climate, soil type and the extent of competition with other organisms, influence the development of plants into a number of distinctive forms. Similar conditions in quite different parts of the world create similar adaptations in the plants, which may then be modified by other, local, factors specific to the region.

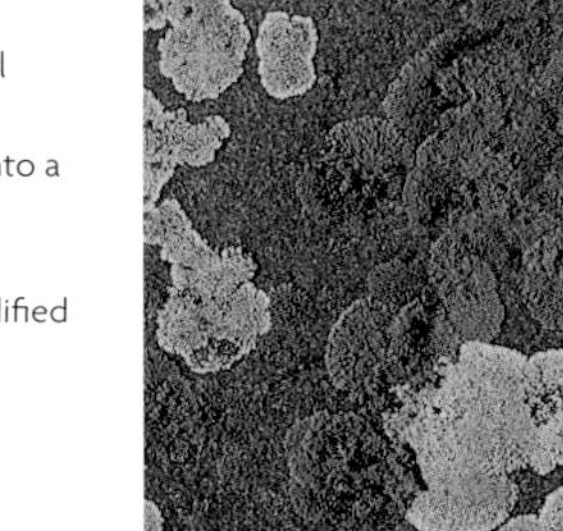

Cold conditions

In areas where temperatures rarely rise above freezing, plants such as lichens *(left)* and mosses grow densely, close to the ground.

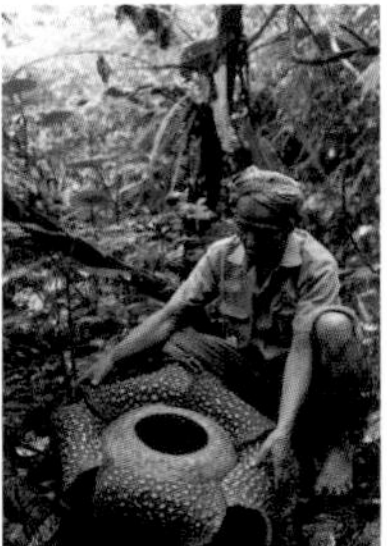

Rainforests

Most of the world's largest and oldest plants are found in rainforests; warmth and heavy rainfall provide ideal conditions for vast plants like the world's largest flower, the rafflesia *(left)*.

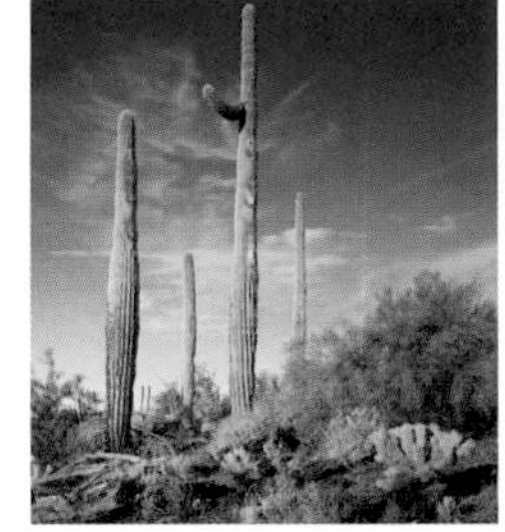

Hot, dry conditions

Arid conditions lead to the development of plants whose surface area has been reduced to a minimum to reduce water loss. In cacti *(above)*, which can survive without water for months, leaves are minimal or not present at all.

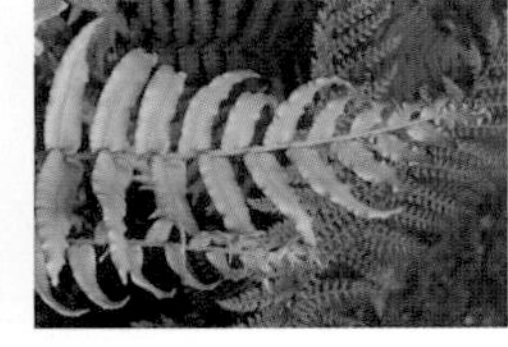

Ancient plants

Some of the world's most primitive plants still exist today, including algae, cycads and many ferns *(above)*, reflecting the success with which they have adapted to changing conditions.

Diversity of plant species

Number of plant species per country
- more than 50,000
- 7000–49,999
- 3000–6999
- 2000–2999
- 1000–1999
- 600–999
- 0–599
- data not available

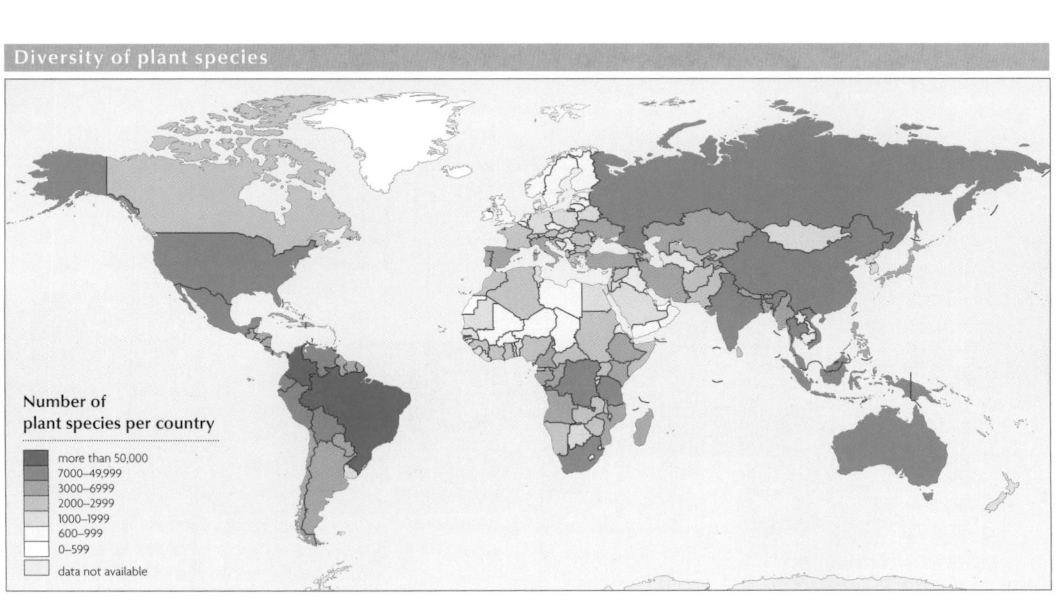

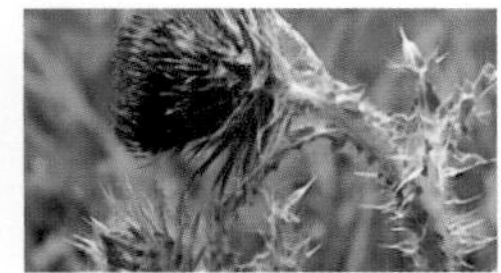

Resisting predators

A great variety of plants have developed devices including spines *(above)*, poisons, stinging hairs and an unpleasant taste or smell to deter animal predators.

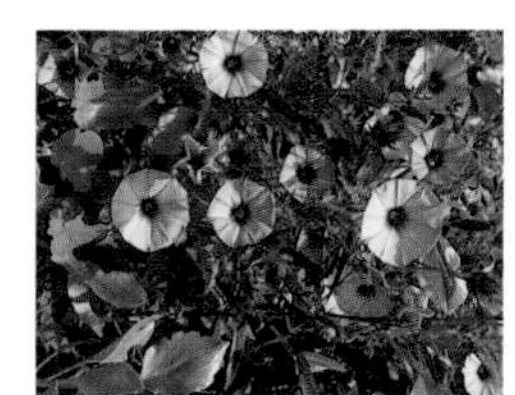

Weeds

Weeds such as bindweed *(above)* are fast-growing, easily dispersed, and tolerant of a number of different environments, enabling them to quickly colonize suitable habitats. They are among the most adaptable of all plants.

Population and settlement

The Earth's population is projected to rise from its current level of about 6.5 billion to reach some 10 billion by 2025. The global distribution of this rapidly growing population is very uneven, and is dictated by climate, terrain and natural and economic resources. The great majority of the Earth's people live in coastal zones, and along river valleys. Deserts cover over 20% of the Earth's surface, but support less than 5% of the world's population. It is estimated that over half of the world's population live in cities – most of them in Asia – as a result of mass migration from rural areas in search of jobs. Many of these people live in the so-called 'megacities', some with populations as great as 40 million.

Patterns of settlement

The past 200 years have seen the most radical shift in world population patterns in recorded history.

Nomadic life

All the world's peoples were hunter-gatherers 10,000 years ago. Today nomads, who live by following available food resources, account for less than 0.0001% of the world's population. They are mainly pastoral herders, moving their livestock from place to place in search of grazing land.

Nomadic population

▨ Nomadic population area

The growth of cities

In 1900 there were only 14 cities in the world with populations of more than a million, mostly in the northern hemisphere. Today, as more and more people in the developing world migrate to towns and cities, there are 29 cities whose population exceeds 5 million, and around 440 million-cities.

Million-cities in 1900

Million-cities in 1900

• Cities over 1 million population

Million-cities in 2005

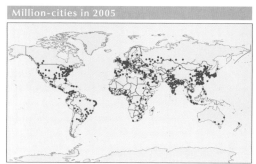

Million-cities in 2005

• Cities over 1 million population

North America

The eastern and western seaboards of the USA, with huge expanses of interconnected cities, towns and suburbs, are vast, densely-populated megalopolises. Central America and the Caribbean also have high population densities. Yet, away from the coasts and in the wildernesses of northern Canada the land is very sparsely settled.

▲ *Vancouver on Canada's* west coast, grew up as a port city. In recent years it has attracted many Asian immigrants, particularly from the Pacific Rim.

▲ *North America's central* plains, the continent's agricultural heartland, are thinly populated and highly productive.

Europe

With its temperate climate, and rich mineral and natural resources, Europe is generally very densely settled. The continent acts as a magnet for economic migrants from the developing world, and immigration is now widely restricted. Birth rates in Europe are generally low, and in some countries, such as Germany, the populations have stabilized at zero growth, with a fast-growing elderly population.

▲ *Many European cities,* like Siena, once reflected the 'ideal' size for human settlements. Modern technological advances have enabled them to grow far beyond the original walls.

▲ *Within the densely-populated* Netherlands the reclamation of coastal wetlands is vital to provide much-needed land for agriculture and settlement.

Population density
(inhabitants per sq km)

▨ More than 200
▨ 101–200
▨ 51–100
▨ 21–50
▨ 11–20
▨ 6–10
▨ 1–5
▨ Less than 1

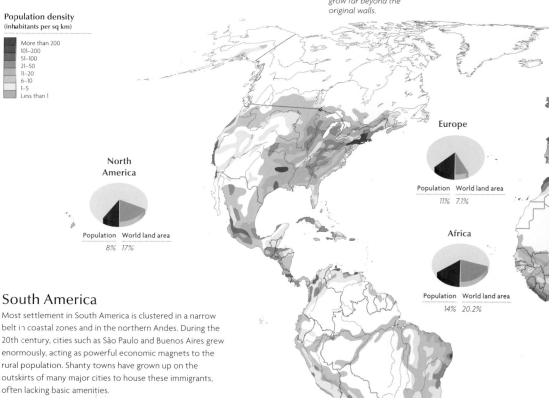

North America

Population 8%   World land area 17%

Europe

Population 11%   World land area 7.1%

Africa

Population 14%   World land area 20.2%

South America

Population 6%   World land area 11.8%

South America

Most settlement in South America is clustered in a narrow belt in coastal zones and in the northern Andes. During the 20th century, cities such as São Paulo and Buenos Aires grew enormously, acting as powerful economic magnets to the rural population. Shanty towns have grown up on the outskirts of many major cities to house these immigrants, often lacking basic amenities.

▲ *Many people in* western South America live at high altitudes in the Andes, both in cities and in villages such as this one in Bolivia.

▲ *Venezuela is one* of the most highly urbanized countries in South America, with nearly 90% of the population living in cities such as Caracas.

Africa

The arid climate of much of Africa means that settlement of the continent is sparse, focusing in coastal areas and fertile regions such as the Nile Valley. Africa still has a high proportion of nomadic agriculturalists, although many are now becoming settled, and the population is predominantly rural.

▲ *Cities such as* Nairobi (above), Cairo and Johannesburg have grown rapidly in recent years, although only Cairo has a significant population on a global scale.

▲ *Traditional lifestyles and* homes persist across much of Africa, which has a higher proportion of rural or village-based population than any other continent.

Asia

Most Asian settlement originally centred around the great river valleys such as the Indus, the Ganges and the Yangtze. Today, almost 60% of the world's population lives in Asia, many in burgeoning cities – particularly in the economically-buoyant Pacific Rim countries. Even rural population densities are high in many countries; practices such as terracing in Southeast Asia making the most of the available land.

▲ *Many of China's* cities are now vast urban areas with populations of more than 5 million people.

▲ *This stilt village* in Bangladesh is built to resist the regular flooding. Pressure on land, even in rural areas, forces many people to live in marginal areas.

Population structures

Population pyramids are an effective means of showing the age structures of different countries, and highlighting changing trends in population growth and decline. The typical pyramid for a country with a growing, youthful population, is broad-based *(left)*, reflecting a high birth rate and a far larger number of young rather than elderly people. In contrast, countries with populations whose numbers are stabilizing have a more balanced distribution of people in each age band, and may even have lower numbers of people in the youngest age ranges, indicating both a high life expectancy, and that the population is now barely replacing itself *(right)*. The Russian Federation *(centre)* shows a marked decline in population due to a combination of a high death rate and low birth rate. The government has taken steps to reverse this trend by providing improved child support and health care. Immigration is also seen as vital to help sustain the population.

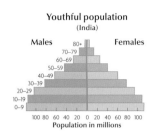

Youthful population
(India)

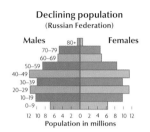

Declining population
(Russian Federation)

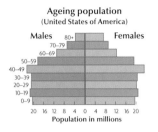

Ageing population
(United States of America)

Population growth

Improvements in food supply and advances in medicine have both played a major role in the remarkable growth in global population, which has increased five-fold over the last 150 years. Food supplies have risen with the mechanization of agriculture and improvements in crop yields. Better nutrition, together with higher standards of public health and sanitation, have led to increased longevity and higher birth rates.

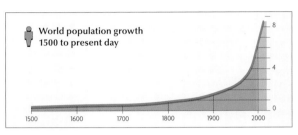

World population growth
1500 to present day

World nutrition

Two-thirds of the world's food supply is consumed by the industrialized nations, many of which have a daily calorific intake far higher than is necessary for their populations to maintain a healthy body weight. In contrast, in the developing world, about 800 million people do not have enough food to meet their basic nutritional needs.

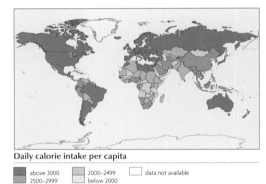

Daily calorie intake per capita

- above 3000
- 2500–2999
- 2000–2499
- below 2000
- data not available

World life expectancy

Improved public health and living standards have greatly increased life expectancy in the developed world, where people can now expect to live twice as long as they did 100 years ago. In many of the world's poorest nations, inadequate nutrition and disease, means that the average life expectancy still does not exceed 45 years.

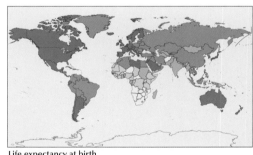

Life expectancy at birth

- above 75 years
- 65–74 years
- 55–64 years
- 45–54 years
- below 44 years
- data not available

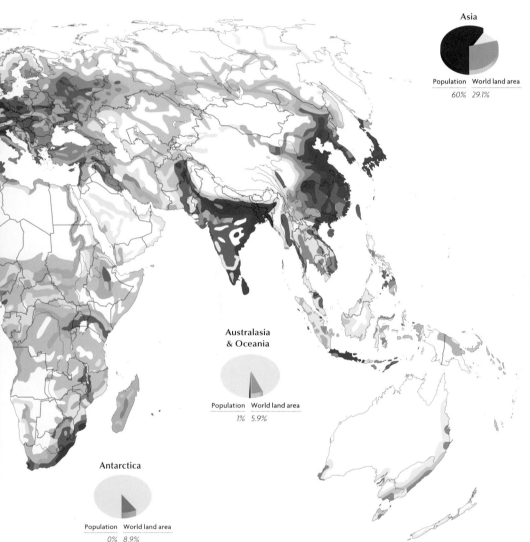

Asia

Population — World land area
60% — 29.1%

Australasia & Oceania

Population — World land area
1% — 5.9%

Antarctica

Population — World land area
0% — 8.9%

Australasia and Oceania

This is the world's most sparsely settled region. The peoples of Australia and New Zealand live mainly in the coastal cities, with only scattered settlements in the arid interior. The Pacific islands can only support limited populations because of their remoteness and lack of resources.

▶ **Brisbane, on** *Australia's* Gold Coast is the most rapidly expanding city in the country. The great majority of Australia's population lives in cities near the coasts.

◀ **The remote highlands** of Papua New Guinea are home to a wide variety of peoples, many of whom still subsist by traditional hunting and gathering.

Average world birth rates

Birth rates are much higher in Africa, Asia and South America than in Europe and North America. Increased affluence and easy access to contraception are both factors which can lead to a significant decline in a country's birth rate.

Number of births (per 1000 people)

- above 40
- 30–39
- 20–29
- below 20
- data not available

World infant mortality

In parts of the developing world infant mortality rates are still high; access to medical services such as immunization, adequate nutrition and the promotion of breast-feeding have been important in combating infant mortality.

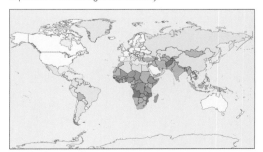

World infant mortality rates (deaths per 1000 live births)

- above 125
- 75–124
- 35–74
- 15–34
- below 15
- data not available

The economic system

The wealthy countries of the developed world, with their aggressive, market-led economies and their access to productive new technologies and international markets, dominate the world economic system. At the other extreme, many of the countries of the developing world are locked in a cycle of national debt, rising populations and unemployment. The state-managed economies of the former communist bloc began to be dismantled during the 1990s, and China is emerging as a major economic power following decades of isolation.

Trade blocs

International trade blocs are formed when groups of countries, often already enjoying close military and political ties, join together to offer mutually preferential terms of trade for both imports and exports. Increasingly, global trade is dominated by three main blocs: the EU, NAFTA, and ASEAN. They are supplanting older trade blocs such as the Commonwealth, a legacy of colonialism.

Trade blocs

EU	NAFTA
CACM	SADC
ASEAN	LAIA
ECOWAS	CEEAC

International trade flows

World trade acts as a stimulus to national economies, encouraging growth. Over the last three decades, as heavy industries have declined, services – banking, insurance, tourism, airlines and shipping – have taken an increasingly large share of world trade. Manufactured articles now account for nearly two-thirds of world trade; raw materials and food make up less than a quarter of the total.

Shipping
Ships carry 80% of international cargo, and extensive container ports, where cargo is stored, are vital links in the international transport network.

Multinationals
Multinational companies are increasingly penetrating inaccessible markets. The reach of many American commodities is now global.

Primary products
Many countries, particularly in the Caribbean and Africa, are still reliant on primary products such as rubber and coffee, which makes them vulnerable to fluctuating prices.

Service industries
Service industries such as banking, tourism and insurance were the fastest-growing industrial sector in the last half of the 20th century. Lloyds of London is the centre of the world insurance market.

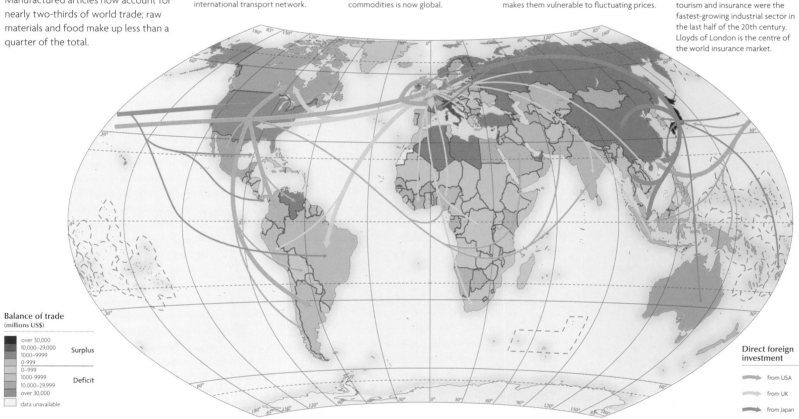

Balance of trade
(millions US$)

over 30,000	
10,000–29,000	
1000–9999	
0–999	Surplus
0–999	
1000–9999	
10,000–29,999	Deficit
over 30,000	
data unavailable	

Direct foreign investment

- from USA
- from UK
- from Japan

World money markets

The financial world has traditionally been dominated by three major centres – Tokyo, New York and London, which house the headquarters of stock exchanges, multinational corporations and international banks. Their geographic location means that, at any one time in a 24-hour day, one major market is open for trading in shares, currencies and commodities. Since the late 1980s, technological advances have enabled transactions between financial centres to occur at ever-greater speed, and new markets have sprung up throughout the world.

New stock markets

New stock markets are now opening in many parts of the world, where economies have recently emerged from state controls. In Moscow and Beijing, and several countries in eastern Europe, newly-opened stock exchanges reflect the transition to market-driven economies.

The developing world

International trade in capital and currency is dominated by the rich nations of the northern hemisphere. In parts of Africa and Asia, where exports of any sort are extremely limited, home-produced commodities are simply sold in local markets.

Major money markets

London
New York
Kolkata
Tokyo

Location of major stock markets

- Major stock markets

▲ *The Tokyo Stock Market* crashed in 1990, leading to slow-down in the growth of the world's most powerful economy, and a refocusing on economic policy away from export-led growth and towards the domestic market.

▲ *Dealers at the Kolkata Stock Market.* The Indian economy has been opened up to foreign investment and many multinationals now have bases there.

▲ *Markets have thrived* in communist Vietnam since the introduction of a liberal economic policy.

World wealth disparity

A global assessment of Gross Domestic Product (GDP) by nation reveals great disparities. The developed world, with only a quarter of the world's population, has 80% of the world's manufacturing income. Civil war, conflict and political instability further undermine the economic self-sufficiency of many of the world's poorest nations.

Urban sprawl

Cities are expanding all over the developing world, attracting economic migrants in search of work and opportunities. In cities such as Rio de Janeiro, housing has not kept pace with the population explosion, and squalid shanty towns *(favelas)* rub shoulders with middle-class housing.

▲ *The favelas of* Rio de Janeiro sprawl over the hills surrounding the city.

Agricultural economies

In parts of the developing world, people survive by subsistence farming – only growing enough food for themselves and their families. With no surplus product, they are unable to exchange goods for currency, the only means of escaping the poverty trap. In other countries, farmers have been encouraged to concentrate on growing a single crop for the export market. This reliance on cash crops leaves farmers vulnerable to crop failure and to changes in the market price of the crop.

Urban decay

Although the USA still dominates the global economy, it faces deficits in both the federal budget and the balance of trade. Vast discrepancies in personal wealth, high levels of unemployment, and the dismantling of welfare provisions throughout the 1980s have led to severe deprivation in several of the inner cities of North America's industrial heartland.

▲ *Cities such as* Detroit have been badly hit by the decline in heavy industry.

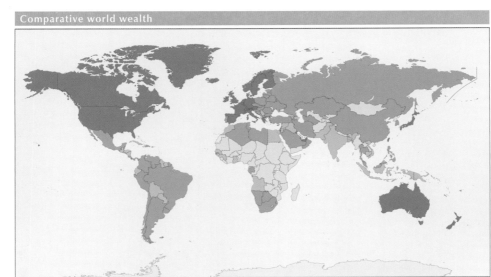
Comparative world wealth

World economies - average GDP per capita (US$)
- above 20,000
- 5000–20,000
- 2000–5000
- below 2000
- data unavailable

▲ *The Ugandan uplands* are fertile, but poor infrastructure hampers the export of cash crops.

▲ *A shopping arcade* in Paris displays a great profusion of luxury goods.

Booming cities

Since the 1980s the Chinese government has set up special industrial zones, such as Shanghai, where foreign investment is encouraged through tax incentives. Migrants from rural China pour into these regions in search of work, creating 'boomtown' economies.

◄ *Foreign investment has* encouraged new infrastructure development in cities like Shanghai.

Economic 'tigers'

The economic 'tigers' of the Pacific Rim – China, Singapore, and South Korea – have grown faster than Europe and the USA over the last decade. Their export- and service-led economies have benefited from stable government, low labour costs, and foreign investment.

▲ *Hong Kong, with its* fine natural harbour, is one of the most important ports in Asia.

The affluent West

The capital cities of many countries in the developed world are showcases for consumer goods, reflecting the increasing importance of the service sector, and particularly the retail sector, in the world economy. The idea of shopping as a leisure activity is unique to the western world. Luxury goods and services attract visitors, who in turn generate tourist revenue.

◄ *In rural Southeast Asia,* babies are given medical checks by UNICEF as part of a global aid programme sponsored by the UN.

Tourism

In 2004, there were over 700 million tourists worldwide. Tourism is now the world's biggest single industry, employing 130 million people, though frequently in low-paid unskilled jobs. While tourists are increasingly exploring inaccessible and less-developed regions of the world, the benefits of the industry are not always felt at a local level. There are also worries about the environmental impact of tourism, as the world's last wildernesses increasingly become tourist attractions.

▲ *Botswana's Okavango Delta* is an area rich in wildlife. Tourists make safaris to the region, but the impact of tourism is controlled.

Money flows

Foreign investment in the developing world during the 1970s led to a global financial crisis in the 1980s, when many countries were unable to meet their debt repayments. The International Monetary Fund (IMF) was forced to reschedule the debts and, in some cases, write them off completely. Within the developing world, austerity programmes have been initiated to cope with the debt, leading in turn to high unemployment and galloping inflation. In many parts of Africa, stricken economies are now dependent on international aid.

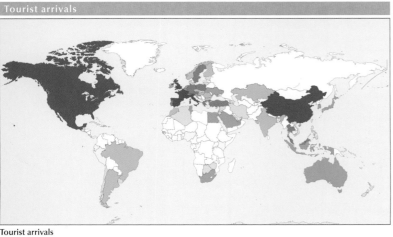
Tourist arrivals

Tourist arrivals
- over 20 million
- 10–20 million
- 5–10 million
- 2.5–5 million
- 1–2.5 million
- 700,000–999,000
- under 700,000
- data unavailable

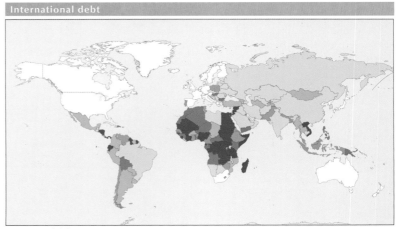
International debt

International debt (as percentage of GNI)
- over 100%
- 70–99%
- 50–69%
- 30–49%
- 10–29%
- below 10%
- data unavailable

The political world

There are 194 independent countries in the world today. With the exception of Antarctica, where territorial claims have been deferred by international treaty, every land area of the Earth's surface either belongs to, or is claimed by, one country or another. The largest country in the world is the Russian Federation, the smallest is Vatican City. Some 60 overseas dependent territories remain, administered variously by France, Australia, Denmark, New Zealand, Norway, Portugal, the UK, the US and the Netherlands.

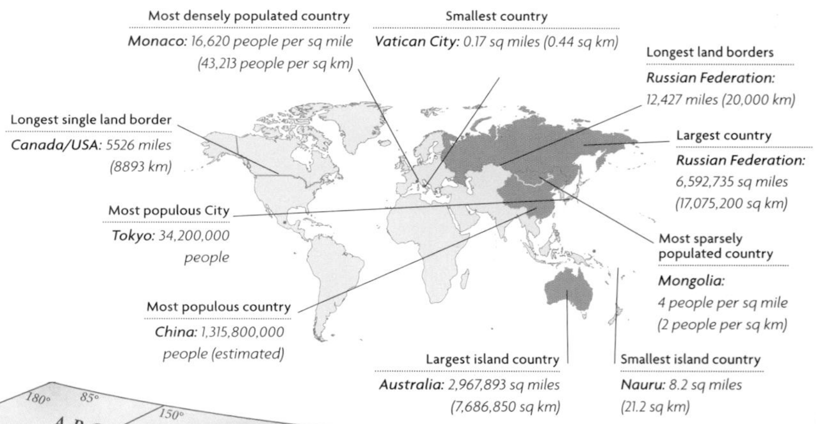

International borders

The map shows three main types of boundary between states. Full borders represent internationally agreed and recognized territorial boundaries. Undefined borders exist where no fixed boundary between states has been demarcated; the boundaries indicated in this way show approximate areas of sovereignty. A disputed border is indicated where a *de facto* territorial boundary exists, which is not agreed or is subject to arbitration.

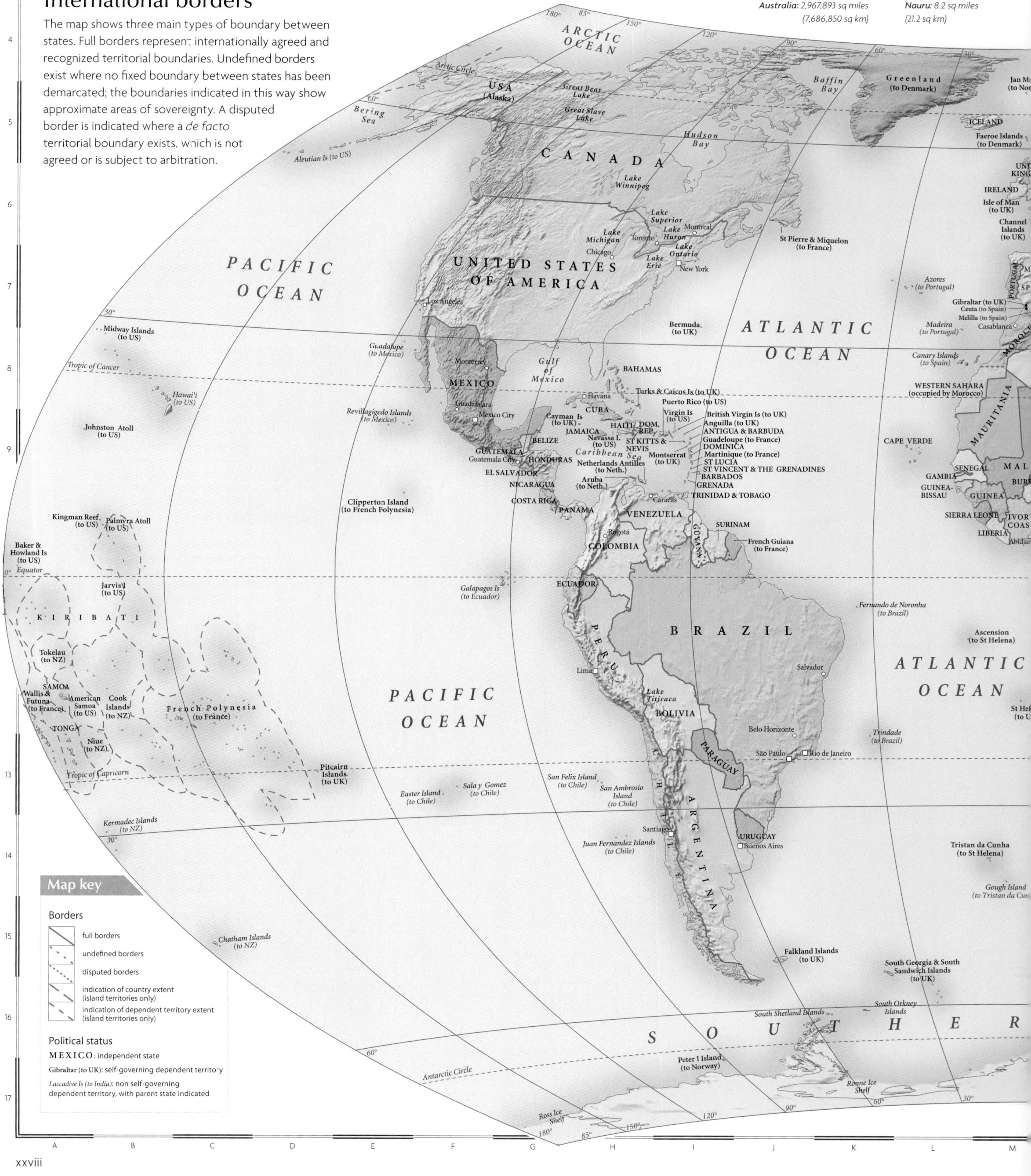

Most densely populated country
Monaco: 16,620 people per sq mile
(43,213 people per sq km)

Smallest country
Vatican City: 0.17 sq miles (0.44 sq km)

Longest land borders
Russian Federation:
12,427 miles (20,000 km)

Longest single land border
Canada/USA: 5526 miles
(8893 km)

Largest country
Russian Federation:
6,592,735 sq miles
(17,075,200 sq km)

Most populous City
Tokyo: 34,200,000
people

Most sparsely
populated country
Mongolia:
4 people per sq mile
(2 people per sq km)

Most populous country
China: 1,315,800,000
people (estimated)

Largest island country
Australia: 2,967,893 sq miles
(7,686,850 sq km)

Smallest island country
Nauru: 8.2 sq miles
(21.2 sq km)

Map key

Borders

- full borders
- undefined borders
- disputed borders
- indication of country extent (island territories only)
- indication of dependent territory extent (island territories only)

Political status

MEXICO: independent state

Gibraltar (to UK): self-governing dependent territory

Laccadive Is (to India): non self-governing dependent territory, with parent state indicated

The world in 1914

The early years of the 20th century saw the mainly European colonial empires reaching their greatest extents by 1914. Two world wars inaugurated their disintegration, but even in 1950 there were only 82 independent countries. Since then, over 100 have gained their independence, culminating in the breakup of the Soviet Union and former Yugoslavia in the early 1990s.

Percentage of Earth's land surface controlled by colonial empires in 1914

- Independent: 29.8%
- Chinese: 6%
- Ottoman: 1.5%
- Russian: 15%
- Portuguese: 1%
- French: 7.7%
- Spanish: 1%
- Belgian: 1.6%
- Italian: 1.8%
- British: 21.5%
- German: 1.6%
- Japanese: 0.4%
- Dutch: 1.4%
- United States: 7.6%
- Danish: 1.5%

Colonial empires in 1914

Colonial Empires in 1914

Belgian	Japanese
British	Ottoman
Chinese	Portuguese
Danish	Russian
Dutch	Spanish
French	United States
German	Independent
Italian	Disputed

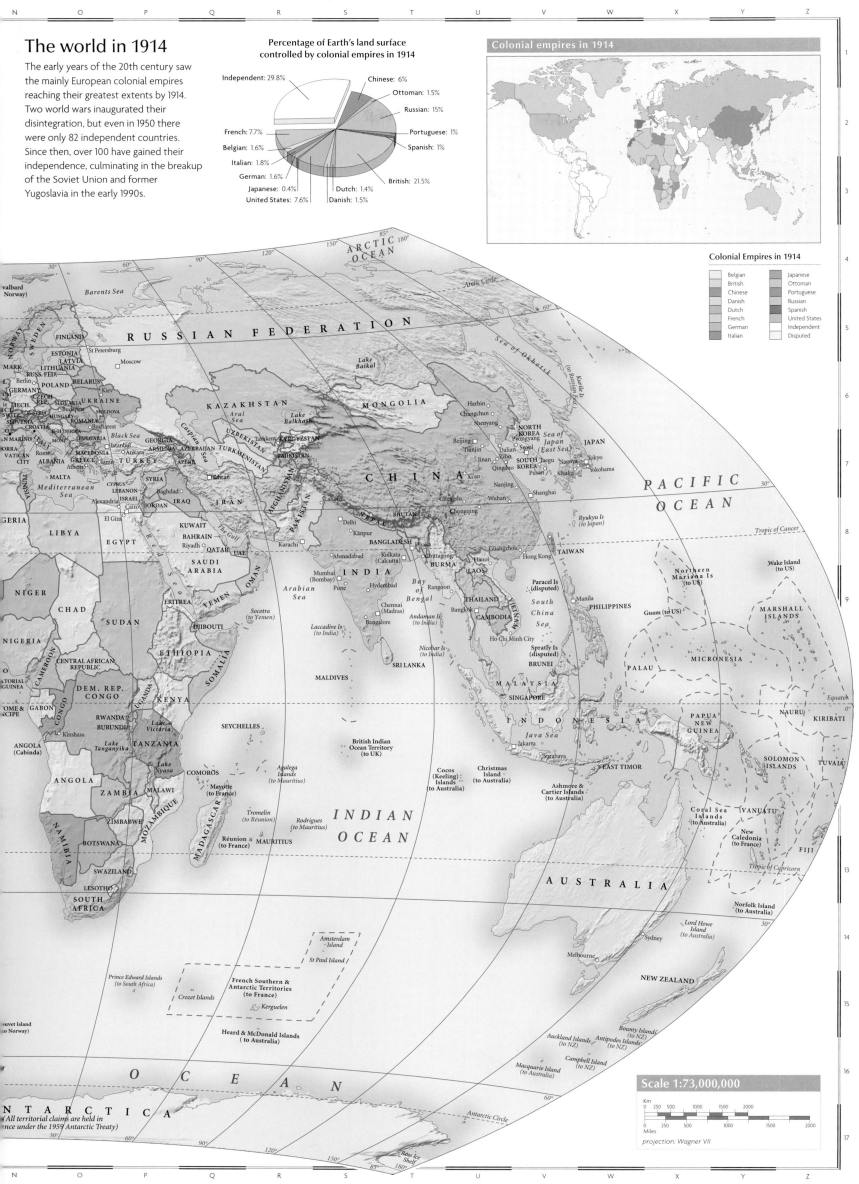

Scale 1:73,000,000

projection: Wagner VII

States and boundaries

There are over 190 sovereign states in the world today; in 1950 there were only 82. Over the last half-century national self-determination has been a driving force for many states with a history of colonialism and oppression. As more borders have been added to the world map, the number of international border disputes has increased.

In many cases, where the impetus towards independence has been religious or ethnic, disputes with minority groups have also caused violent internal conflict. While many newly-formed states have moved peacefully towards independence, successfully establishing government by multiparty democracy, dictatorship by military regime or individual despot is often the result of the internal power-struggles which characterize the early stages in the lives of new nations.

The nature of politics

Democracy is a broad term: it can range from the ideal of multiparty elections and fair representation to, in countries such as Singapore, a thin disguise for single-party rule. In despotic regimes, on the other hand, a single, often personal authority has total power; institutions such as parliament and the military are mere instruments of the dictator.

◀ The stars and stripes of the US flag are a potent symbol of the country's status as a federal democracy.

Types of government

- ☐ Multiparty democracy for more than 10 yrs
- ☐ Multiparty/transitional democracy within last 10 yrs
- ☐ Single-party government
- ☐ Military regime
- ☐ Theocracy
- ☐ Absolute monarchy
- ✦ Current civil unrest

The changing world map

Decolonization

In 1950, large areas of the world remained under the control of a handful of European countries *(page xxviii)*. The process of decolonization had begun in Asia, where, following the Second World War, much of south and southeast Asia sought and achieved self-determination. In the 1960s, a host of African states achieved independence, so that by 1965, most of the larger tracts of the European overseas empires had been substantially eroded. The final major stage in decolonization came with the break-up of the Soviet Union and the Eastern bloc after 1990. The process continues today as the last toeholds of European colonialism, often tiny island nations, press increasingly for independence.

▲ Icons of communism, including statues of former leaders such as Lenin and Stalin, were destroyed when the Soviet bloc was dismantled in 1989, creating several new nations.

▲ Iran has been one of the modern world's few true theocracies; Islam has an impact on every aspect of political life.

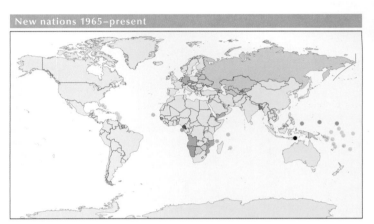

New nations 1945–1965

New nations 1965–present

▲ North Korea is an independent communist republic. Power is concentrated in the hands of Kim Jong Il.

Administration at the time of independence

☐ Australia	☐ Malaysia
☐ Aust/NZ/UK	☐ Netherlands
☐ Belgium	☐ New Zealand
☐ China	☐ Pakistan
☐ Czechoslovakia	☐ Portugal
☐ Egypt/UK	☐ South Africa
☐ Ethiopia	☐ Spain
☐ France	☐ UK
☐ France/UK	☐ Unified country
☐ Indonesia	☐ USA
☐ Italy	☐ USSR
☐ Japan	☐ Yugoslavia

◀ Saddam Hussein, former autocratic leader of Iraq, promoted an extreme personality cult for over 20 years. He was ousted by a US-led coalition in 2003.

◀ South Africa became a democracy in 1994, when elections ended over a century of white minority rule.

▲ In Brunei the Sultan has ruled by decree since 1962; power is closely tied to the royal family. The Sultan's brothers are responsible for finance and foreign affairs.

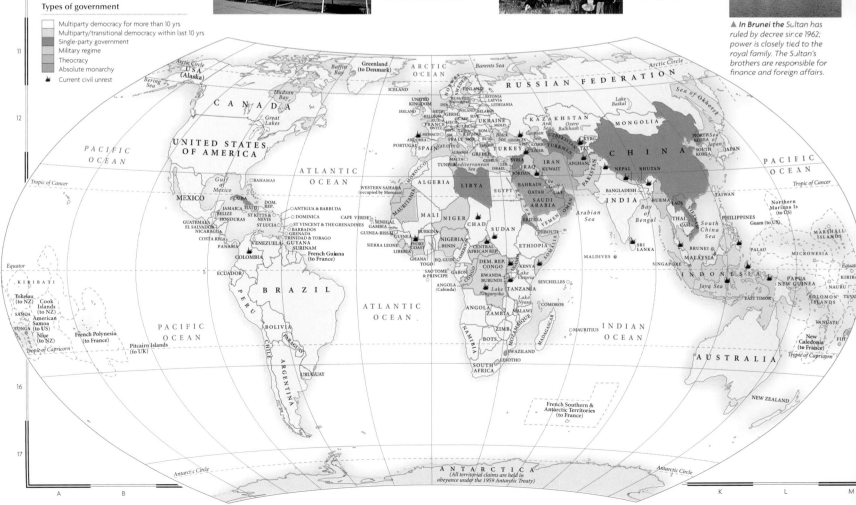

Lines on the map

The determination of international boundaries can use a variety of criteria. Many of the borders between older states follow physical boundaries; some mirror religious and ethnic differences; others are the legacy of complex histories of conflict and colonialism, while others have been imposed by international agreements or arbitration.

Post-colonial borders

When the European colonial empires in Africa were dismantled during the second half of the 20th century, the outlines of the new African states mirrored colonial boundaries. These boundaries had been drawn up by colonial administrators, often based on inadequate geographical knowledge. Such arbitrary boundaries were imposed on people of different languages, racial groups, religions and customs. This confused legacy often led to civil and international war.

▲ *The conflict that* has plagued many African countries since independence has caused millions of people to become refugees.

Physical borders

Many of the world's countries are divided by physical borders: lakes, rivers, mountains. The demarcation of such boundaries can, however, lead to disputes. Control of waterways, water supplies and fisheries are frequent causes of international friction.

Enclaves

The shifting political map over the course of history has frequently led to anomalous situations. Parts of national territories may become isolated by territorial agreement, forming an enclave. The West German part of the city of Berlin, which until 1989 lay a hundred miles (160 km) within East German territory, was a famous example.

▲ *Since the independence* of Lithuania and Belarus, the peoples of the Russian enclave of Kaliningrad have become physically isolated.

Antarctica

When Antarctic exploration began a century ago, seven nations, Australia, Argentina, Britain, Chile, France, New Zealand and Norway, laid claim to the new territory. In 1961 the Antarctic Treaty, now signed by 45 nations, agreed to hold all territorial claims in abeyance.

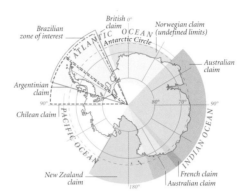

Geometric borders

Straight lines and lines of longitude and latitude have occasionally been used to determine international boundaries; and indeed the world's second longest continuous international boundary, between Canada and the USA, follows the 49th Parallel for over one-third of its course. Many Canadian, American and Australian internal administrative boundaries are similarly determined using a geometric solution.

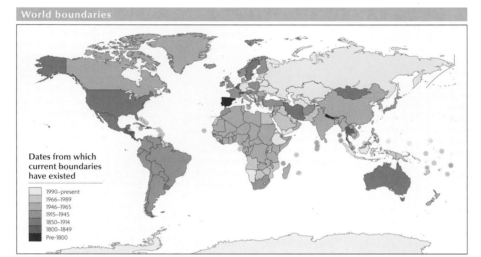

World boundaries

Dates from which current boundaries have existed

1990–present
1966–1989
1946–1965
1915–1945
1850–1914
1800–1849
Pre-1800

▲ *Different farming techniques* in Canada and the USA clearly mark the course of the international boundary in this satellite map.

Lake borders

Countries which lie next to lakes usually fix their borders in the middle of the lake. Unusually the Lake Nyasa border between Malawi and Tanzania runs along Tanzania's shore.

▲ *Complicated agreements* between colonial powers led to the awkward division of Lake Nyasa.

River borders

Rivers alone account for one-sixth of the world's borders. Many great rivers form boundaries between a number of countries. Changes in a river's course and interruptions of its natural flow can lead to disputes, particularly in areas where water is scarce. The centre of the river's course is the nominal boundary line.

▲ *The Danube forms* all or part of the border between nine European nations.

Mountain borders

Mountain ranges form natural barriers and are the basis for many major borders, particularly in Europe and Asia. The watershed is the conventional boundary demarcation line, but its accurate determination is often problematic.

▲ *The Pyrenees form* a natural mountain border between France and Spain.

Shifting boundaries – Poland

Borders between countries can change dramatically over time. The nations of eastern Europe have been particularly affected by changing boundaries. Poland is an example of a country whose boundaries have changed so significantly that it has literally moved around Europe. At the start of the 16th century, Poland was the largest nation in Europe. Between 1772 and 1795, it was absorbed into Prussia, Austria and Russia, and it effectively ceased to exist. After the First World War, Poland became an independent country once more, but its borders changed again after the Second World War following invasions by both Soviet Russia and Nazi Germany.

▲ *In 1634, Poland* was the largest nation in Europe, its eastern boundary reaching towards Moscow.

▲ *From 1772–1795, Poland* was gradually partitioned between Austria, Russia and Prussia. Its eastern boundary receded by over 100 miles (160 km).

▲ *Following the First* World War, Poland was reinstated as an independent state, but it was less than half the size it had been in 1634.

▲ *After the Second* World War the Baltic Sea border was extended westwards, but much of the eastern territory was annexed by Russia.

International disputes

There are more than 60 disputed borders or territories in the world today. Although many of these disputes can be settled by peaceful negotiation, some areas have become a focus for international conflict. Ethnic tensions have been a major source of territorial disagreement throughout history, as has the ownership of, and access to, valuable natural resources. The turmoil of the post-colonial era in many parts of Africa is partly a result of the 19th century 'carve-up' of the continent, which created potential for conflict by drawing often arbitrary lines through linguistic and cultural areas.

Jammu and Kashmir

Disputes over Jammu and Kashmir have caused three serious wars between India and Pakistan since 1947. Pakistan wishes to annex the largely Muslim territory, while India refuses to cede any territory or to hold a referendum, and also lays claim to the entire territory. Most international maps show the 'line of control' agreed in 1972 as the *de facto* border. In addition India has territorial disputes with neighbouring China. The situation is further complicated by a Kashmiri independence movement, active since the late 1980s.

▲ *Indian army troops* maintain their positions in the mountainous terrain cf northern Kashmir.

North and South Korea

Since 1953, the *de facto* border between North and South Korea has been a ceasefire line which straddles the 38th Parallel and is designated as a demilitarized zone. Both countries have heavy fortifications and troop concentrations behind this zone.

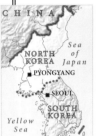

▲ *Heavy fortifications* on the border between North and South Korea.

Cyprus

Cyprus was partitioned in 1974, following an invasion by Turkish troops. The south is now the Greek Cypriot Republic of Cyprus, while the self-proclaimed Turkish Republic of Northern Cyprus is recognized only by Turkey.

▲ *The so-called 'green line'* divides Cyprus into Greek and Turkish sectors.

Conflicts and international disputes

- Countries contributing troops to coalition force in Iraq
- ▲ Major active territorial or border disputes
- Countries involved in internal conflict
- ▲ Active territorial or border disputes and internal conflict

The Falkland Islands

The British dependent territory of the Falkland Islands was invaded by Argentina in 1982, sparking a full-scale war with the UK. In 1995, the UK and Argentina reached an agreement on the exploitation of oil reserves around the islands.

◄ *British warships* in Falkland Sound during the 1982 war with Argentina.

Israel

Israel was created in 1948 following the 1947 UN Resolution (147) on Palestine. Until 1979 Israel had no borders, only ceasefire lines from a series of wars in 1948, 1967 and 1973. Treaties with Egypt in 1979 and Jordan in 1994 led to these borders being defined and agreed. Negotiations over Israeli settlements and Palestinian self-government have seen little effective progress since 2000.

■ Palestinian control
Mixed control
Israeli settlement block
● Israeli settlement
○ Palestinian settlement
— West Bank fence

▲ *Barbed-wire fences* surround a settlement in the Golan Heights.

Former Yugoslavia

Following the disintegration in 1991 of the communist state of Yugoslavia, the breakaway states of Croatia and Bosnia and Herzegovina came into conflict with the 'parent' state (consisting of Serbia and Montenegro). Warfare focused on ethnic and territorial ambitions in Bosnia. The tenuous Dayton Accord of 1995 sought to recognize the post-1990 borders, whilst providing for ethnic partition and required international peace-keeping troops to maintain the terms of the peace.

Republika Srpska
Federacija Bosna i Hercegovina

The Spratly Islands

The site of potential oil and natural gas reserves, the Spratly Islands in the South China Sea have been claimed by China, Vietnam, Taiwan, Malaysia and the Philippines since the Japanese gave up a wartime claim in 1951.

▲ *Most claimant states* have small military garrisons on the Spratly Islands.

Philippine claim
Spratly Islands
Malaysian claim

● Occupied by Taiwan
● Occupied by Philippines
● Occupied by Malaysia
● Occupied by China
● Occupied by Vietnam

ATLAS
OF THE WORLD

THE MAPS IN THIS ATLAS ARE ARRANGED CONTINENT BY CONTINENT, STARTING

FROM THE INTERNATIONAL DATE LINE, AND MOVING EASTWARDS. THE MAPS PROVIDE

A UNIQUE VIEW OF TODAY'S WORLD, COMBINING TRADITIONAL CARTOGRAPHIC

TECHNIQUES WITH THE LATEST REMOTE-SENSED AND DIGITAL TECHNOLOGY.

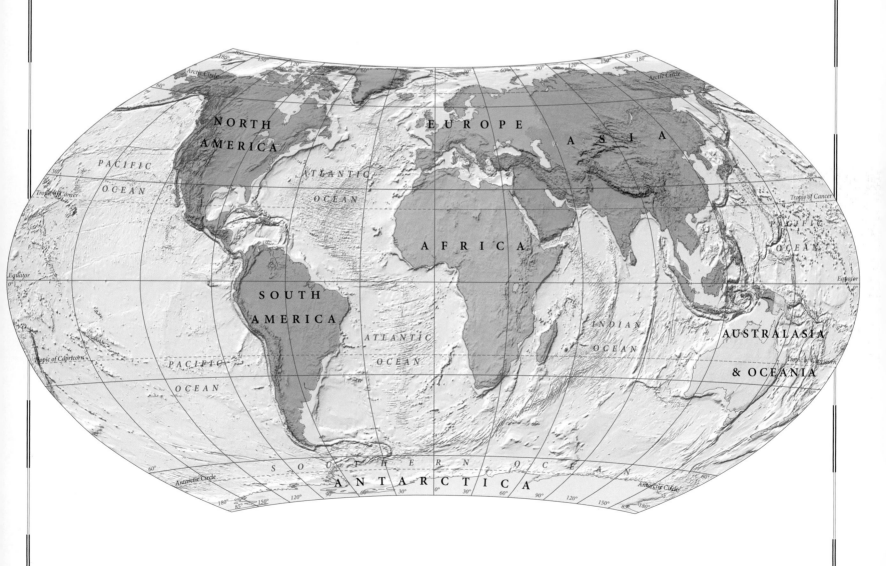

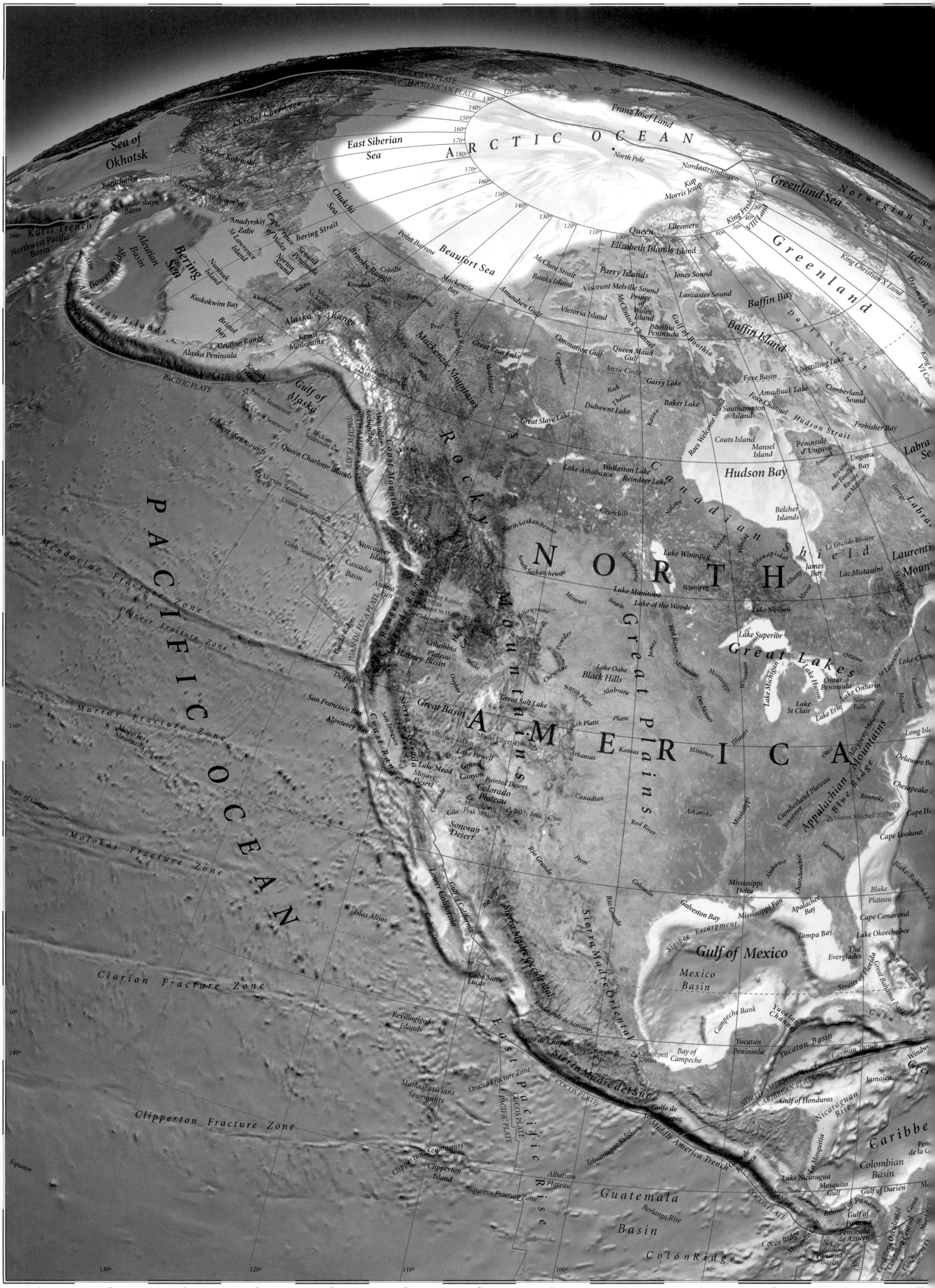

1

EURASIAN PLATE
NORTH AMERICAN PLATE

Khrebet Cherskogo

Sea of
Okhotsk

Franz Josef Land

ARCTIC OCEAN

East Siberian
Sea

North Pole

Nordøstrundingen

30°

Greenland Sea

Norwegian Sea

Mychet Kolymsky

Kamchatka

Korandyrskaya
Basin

Chukchi
Sea

Bering Strait

Kap
Morris Jesup

King Frederik
VIII Land

Greenland

Iceland

Kuril Trench

Northwest Pacific
Basin

Aleutian Ridge

Bowers
Ridge

Bering
Sea

Anadyrskiy
Zaliv

Cape Prince
of Wales

St Lawrence
Island

Seward
Peninsula

Brooks Range

Point Barrow

Beaufort Sea

Mackenzie
Bay

McClure Strait

Banks Island

Amundsen Gulf

Parry Islands

Viscount Melville Sound

Queen
Elizabeth Islands

Jones Sound

Lancaster Sound

Ellesmere
Island

Queen

King Christian X Land

Denmark Strait

Aleutian Islands

Nunivak
Island

Norton
Sound

Yukon

Coleville

Mount
McKinley

Prince
of
Wales
Island

McClintock
Channel

Boothia
Peninsula

Gulf
of Boothia

Baffin Bay

Devon
Island

Aleutian Trench

Bristol
Bay

Kuskokwim Bay

Kuskokwim

Alaska
Range

Kenai
Mountains

Yukon

Peel

Mackenzie

Coppermine

Victoria Island

Coronation Gulf

Queen Maud
Gulf

Arctic Circle

Back

Thelon

Baker Lake

Kazan

Southampton
Island

Roes Welcome Sound

Foxe
Channel

Foxe Basin

Amadjuak Lake

Nettilling Lake

Cumberland
Sound

Baffin Island

Frobisher Bay

Davis Strait

PACIFIC PLATE

Gulf of
Alaska

Patton Seamount

Cobb Seamount

NORTH AMERICAN PLATE

PACIFIC PLATE

Great Bear Lake

Great Slave Lake

Hay

Dubawnt Lake

Garry Lake

Hudson Strait

Péninsule
d'Ungava

Rivière
aux Feuilles

Ungava
Bay

Labrador
Sea

Kodiak
Island

Alaska Peninsula

Gilbert Seamounts

Morton Seamount

Coyote Seamount

Queen Charlotte Islands

Alexander
Archipelago

Coast Mountains

Peace

Athabasca

Lake Athabasca

Wollaston Lake

Reindeer Lake

Coats Island

Mansel
Island

Hudson Bay

Belcher
Islands

La Grande Rivière

Labrador

Laurentian
Mountains

Union Seamount

Liard

Nelson

Churchill

North
Saskatchewan

NORTH

La Grande Rivière

James
Bay

Lac Mistassini

MENDOCINO FRACTURE ZONE

Mendocino
Fracture
Zone

Pioneer Fracture Zone

Vancouver
Island

Cascadia
Basin

Astoria
Fan

Fraser

Columbia

Yellowstone

Missouri

South
Saskatchewan

Lake Winnipeg

Lake Manitoba

Lake of the Woods

Souris

Winnipeg

Red River

Assiniboine

Lake Nipigon

Lake Superior

Great Lakes

Ottawa

St Lawrence

PACIFIC OCEAN

Delgada
Fan

Gorda Ridges

JUAN DE FUCA PLATE

Mount Rainier
4392m

Mount St Helens

Columbia

Columbia
Plateau

Snake

Snake

Great Plains

Minnesota

Missouri

Mississippi

Lake Michigan

Lake Huron

Georgian
Bay

Lake
St Clair

Lake Erie

Lake Ontario

Niagara
Falls

Ontario
Peninsula

Hudson

Long Island

Murray Fracture Zone

Moonless
Mountains

San Francisco Bay

Monterey Bay

Sierra Nevada

Coast Ranges

Klamath
Mountains

Cascade Range

Harney
Basin

Great Basin

Cheyenne

North Platte

Platte

Lake Oahe

Black Hills

Niobrara

AMERICA

Des Moines

Illinois

Mississippi

Wisconsin

Allegheny Mountains

Appalachian Mountains

Blue Ridge

Delaware Bay

Tropic of Cancer

Molokai Fracture Zone

Islas Alijos

Great Salt Lake

Mount Whitney 4418m

Mount
Mono
Death
Valley

Lake Powell

Grand
Canyon

Lake Mead

Mojave
Desert

Painted Desert

Mount Elbert 4399m

Colorado

Arkansas

Kansas

Missouri

Arkansas

Cumberland Plateau

Jennings

Roanoke

Mount Mitchell 2037m

Cape Hatteras

Chesapeake Bay

Clarion Fracture Zone

Colorado
Plateau

Sonoran
Desert

Gila

Humphreys
Peak 3851m

Baldy Peak 3476m

Canadian

Red River

Pecos

Rio Grande

Colorado

Mississippi

Alabama

Chattahoochee

Savannah

Cape Lookout

Cape Canaveral

Blake
Plateau

Revillagigedo
Islands

Gulf of California

Lower California

Sierra Madre Occidental

Sierra Madre Oriental

Rio Grande

Galveston Bay

Mississippi
Delta

Mississippi Fan

Sigsbee
Escarpment

Apalachee
Bay

Tampa Bay

Lake Okeechobee

The
Everglades

Straits of Florida

Great Bahama Bank

Cabo San
Lucas

Río Grande de Santiago

Gulf of Mexico

Mexico
Basin

Campeche Bank

Yucatan
Channel

Cuba

East Pacific Rise

Mathematicians
Seamounts

Lago de Chapala

Popocatepetl
5452m

Citlaltepetl
5700m

Bay of
Campeche

Yucatan
Peninsula

Yucatan Basin

Cayman Trench

Jamaica

Orozco Fracture Zone

COCOS PLATE

PACIFIC PLATE

NORTH AMERICAN PLATE

CARIBBEAN PLATE

Gulf of Honduras

Nicaraguan
Rise

Caribbean
Sea

Clipperton Fracture Zone

Clipperton
Island

Siqueiros Fracture Zone

Albatross
Plateau

Tehuantepec Ridge

Middle America Trench

Berlanga Rise

Sierra Madre del Sur

COCOS
PLATE

Golfo de
Tehuantepec

Lake Nicaragua

Mosquito
Gulf

Colombian
Basin

Equator

Seamounts

Clipperton Rise

Guatemala
Basin

Colón Ridge

Cocos Ridge

Isthmus of Panama

Gulf of
Panama

Gulf of Darién

Península
de Azuero

Nazca
Basin

North America

North America is the world's third largest continent with a total area of 9,358,340 sq miles

(24,238,000 sq km) including Greenland and the Caribbean islands.

It lies wholly within the Northern Hemisphere.

- ● *Greatest extent, North–South: 4600 miles / 7400 km*
- ■ *Greatest extent, East–West: 3500 miles / 5700 km*

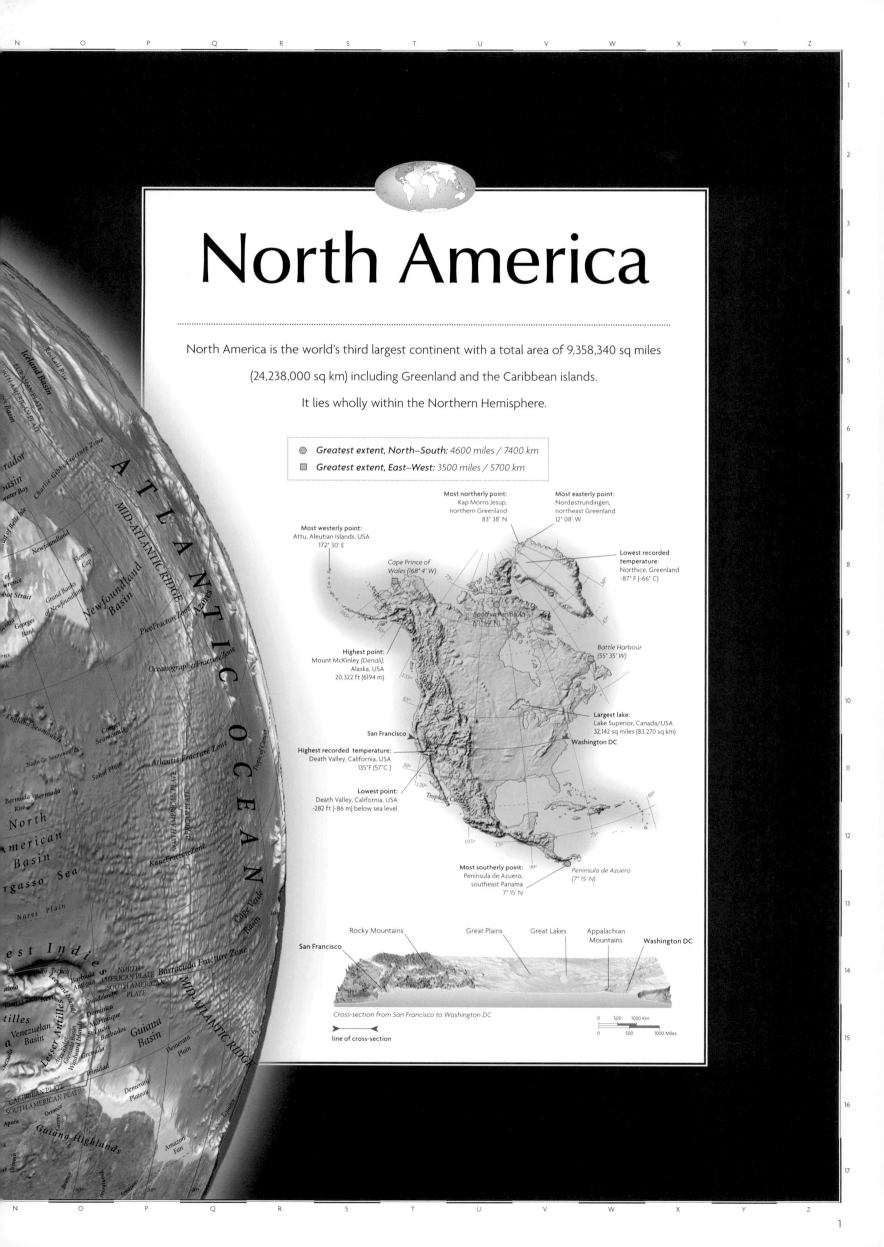

Most northerly point:
Kap Morris Jesup,
northern Greenland
83° 38' N

Most easterly point:
Nordostrundingen,
northeast Greenland
12° 08' W

Most westerly point:
Attu, Aleutian Islands, USA
172° 30' E

Cape Prince of
Wales (168° 4' W)

**Lowest recorded
temperature:**
Northice, Greenland
-87° F (-66° C)

*Boothia Peninsula
(71° 59' N)*

Highest point:
Mount McKinley (Denali),
Alaska, USA
20,322 ft (6194 m)

*Battle Harbour
(55° 35' W)*

San Francisco

Largest lake:
Lake Superior, Canada/USA
32,142 sq miles (83,270 sq km)

Washington DC

Highest recorded temperature:
Death Valley, California, USA
135°F (57°C)

Lowest point:
Death Valley, California, USA
-282 ft (-86 m) below sea level

Tropic of Cancer

Most southerly point:
Península de Azuero,
southeast Panama
7° 15' N

*Península de Azuero
(7° 15' N)*

San Francisco — Rocky Mountains — Great Plains — Great Lakes — Appalachian Mountains — Washington DC

Cross-section from San Francisco to Washington DC

line of cross-section

0 500 1000 Km
0 500 1000 Miles

ATLANTIC OCEAN

MID-ATLANTIC RIDGE

Physical North America

The North American continent can be divided into a number of major structural areas: the Western Cordillera, the Canadian Shield, the Great Plains and Central Lowlands, and the Appalachians. Other smaller regions include the Gulf Atlantic Coastal Plain which borders the southern coast of North America from the southern Appalachians to the Great Plains. This area includes the expanding Mississippi Delta. A chain of volcanic islands, running in an arc around the margin of the Caribbean Plate, lie to the east of the Gulf of Mexico.

The Canadian Shield

Spanning northern Canada and Greenland, this geologically stable plain forms the heart of the continent, containing rocks over two billion years old. A long history of weathering and repeated glaciation has scoured the region, leaving flat plains, gentle hummocks, numerous small basins and lakes, and the bays and islands of the Arctic.

The Western Cordillera

About 80 million years ago the Pacific and North American plates collided, uplifting the Western Cordillera. This consists of the Aleutian, Coast, Cascade and Sierra Nevada mountains, and the inland Rocky Mountains. These run parallel from the Arctic to Mexico.

The weight of the ice sheet, 1.8 miles (3 km) thick, has depressed the land to 0.6 miles (1 km) below sea level

▲ This computer-generated view shows the ice-covered island of Greenland without its ice cap.

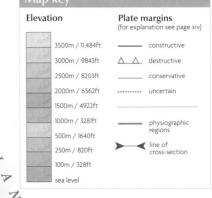

The hard bedrock of the Canadian Shield is slowly rising

Hudson Bay was depressed by the ice sheet to form North America's largest basin

Once overlain by sedimentary rocks, erosion has re-exposed the ancient Laurentian Mountains

Section across the Canadian Shield showing where the ice sheet has depressed the underlying rock and formed bays and islands.

Volcanic rock

Strata have been thrust eastward along fault lines

The Rocky Mountain Trench is the longest linear fault on the continent

Cross-section through the Western Cordillera showing direction of mountain building.

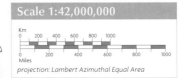

Map key

Elevation

- 3500m / 11,484ft
- 3000m / 9843ft
- 2500m / 8203ft
- 2000m / 6562ft
- 1500m / 4922ft
- 1000m / 3281ft
- 500m / 1640ft
- 250m / 820ft
- 100m / 328ft
- sea level

Plate margins (for explanation see page xiv)

- constructive
- △ △ destructive
- conservative
- ·········· uncertain
- physiographic regions
- ◄► line of cross-section

Scale 1:42,000,000

projection: Lambert Azimuthal Equal Area

The Great Plains and Central Lowlands

Deposits left by retreating glaciers and rivers have made this vast flat area very fertile. In the north this is the result of glaciation, with deposits up to one mile (1.7 km) thick, covering the basement rock. To the south and west, the massive Missouri/Mississippi river system has for centuries deposited silt across the plains, creating broad, flat flood plains and deltas.

The Appalachians

The Appalachian Mountains, uplifted about 400 million years ago, are some of the oldest in the world. They have been lowered and rounded by erosion and now slope gently towards the Atlantic across a broad coastal plain.

Horizontal strata

Sedimentary strata folded and faulted into ridges and valleys

Softer strata has been crumpled against the harder basement rock

Hard basement rock

Cross-section through the Appalachians showing the numerous folds, which have subsequently been weathered to create a rounded relief.

Sedimentary layers overlay domed basement rock

Upland rivers drain south towards the Mississippi Basin

Confluence of the Missouri and Mississippi rivers

Section across the Great Plains and Central Lowlands showing river systems and structure.

Map labels

ASIA
Bering Strait
Bering Sea
Aleutian Islands
Aleutian Range
Beaufort Sea
Brooks Range
Mount McKinley 6194m
Alaska Range
Mackenzie Delta
Mackenzie
Mackenzie Mountains
Gulf of Alaska
NORTH AMERICAN PLATE
PACIFIC PLATE
Coast Mountains
Great Bear Lake
Great Slave Lake
Lake Athabasca
Reindeer Lake
WESTERN CORDILLERA
ROCKY MOUNTAINS
CANADIAN SHIELD
Greenland
Baffin Bay
Baffin Island
Davis Strait
Foxe Basin
Hudson Strait
Hudson Bay
Labrador Sea
Labrador
Laurentian Mountains
Newfoundland
Nova Scotia
ATLANTIC OCEAN
Lake Winnipeg
Lake Manitoba
CENTRAL LOWLANDS
GREAT PLAINS
Missouri
Lake Superior
Lake Huron
Lake Ontario
Lake Michigan
Lake Erie
Great Lakes
St Lawrence
Cape Cod
Cascade Range
Mount Rainier 4392m
Mount St Helens 2549m
Sierra Nevada
San Joaquin Valley
San Andreas Fault
Great Basin
Great Salt Lake
Colorado
Colorado Plateau
Grand Canyon
Death Valley -86m
Mojave Desert
Sonoran Desert
Arkansas
Ohio
APPALACHIAN MOUNTAINS
GULF ATLANTIC COASTAL PLAIN
Mississippi
Mississippi Delta
Lower California
Gulf of California
Sierra Madre Occidental
Sierra Madre Oriental
Rio Grande
Sierra Madre del Sur
Volcán Pico de Orizaba 5700m
Yucatan Peninsula
Gulf of Mexico
West Indies
Greater Antilles
Lesser Antilles
Caribbean Sea
NORTH AMERICAN PLATE
CARIBBEAN PLATE
SOUTH AMERICAN PLATE
COCOS PLATE
Lake Nicaragua
Isthmus of Panama
SOUTH AMERICA
PACIFIC OCEAN

Climate

North America's climate includes extremes ranging from freezing Arctic conditions in Alaska and Greenland, to desert in the southwest, and tropical conditions in southeastern Florida, the Caribbean and Central America. Central and southern regions are prone to severe storms including tornadoes and hurricanes.

▲ *'Tornado alley' in the Mississippi Valley suffers frequent tornadoes.*

▲ *Much of the southwest is semi-desert; receiving less than 12 inches (300 mm) of rainfall a year.*

Climate

- ice cap
- tundra
- subarctic
- cool continental
- warm humid
- semi-arid
- arid
- humid equatorial
- tropical

☼ daily hours of sunshine, January

☼ daily hours of sunshine, July

→ direction of hurricanes

⊕ tornado zones

Temperature

Average January temperature

Average July temperature

Temperature

- below -30°C (-22°F)
- -30 to -20°C (-22 to -4°F)
- -20 to -10°C (-4 to 14°F)
- -10 to 0°C (14 to 32°F)
- 0 to 10°C (32 to 50°F)
- 10 to 20°C (50 to 68°F)
- 20 to 30°C (68 to 86°F)
- above 30°C (86°F)

Rainfall

Average January rainfall

Average July rainfall

Rainfall

- 0–25 mm (0–1 in)
- 25–50 mm (1–2 in)
- 50–100 mm (2–4 in)
- 100–200 mm (4–8 in)
- 200–300 mm (8–12 in)
- 300–400 mm (12–16 in)
- 400–500 mm (16–20 in)
- more than 500 mm (20 in)

◀ *The lush, green mountains of the Lesser Antilles receive annual rainfalls of up to 360 inches (9000 mm).*

Shaping the continent

Glacial processes affect much of northern Canada, Greenland and the Western Cordillera. Along the western coast of North America, Central America and the Caribbean, underlying plates moving together lead to earthquakes and volcanic eruptions. The vast river systems, fed by mountain streams, constantly erode and deposit material along their paths.

Volcanic activity

1 Mount St Helens volcano *(right)* in the Cascade Range erupted violently in May 1980, killing 57 people and levelling large areas of forest. The lateral blast filled a valley for 15 miles (25 km) with debris.

- Molten rock at volcano's core
- Vertical eruption
- Lateral explosion increases extent of damage
- Landslide fills valley

Volcanic activity: Eruption of Mount St Helens

Seismic activity

5 The San Andreas Fault *(above)* places much of the North America's west coast under constant threat from earthquakes. It is caused by the Pacific Plate grinding past the North American Plate at a faster rate, though in the same direction.

- Pacific Plate
- San Andreas Fault
- Fault is caused by faster movement of Pacific Plate
- North American Plate

Seismic activity: Action of the San Andreas Fault

Periglaciation

2 The ground in the far north is nearly always frozen: the surface thaws only in summer. This freeze-thaw process produces features such as pingos *(left)*; formed by the freezing of groundwater. With each successive winter ice accumulates producing a mound with a core of ice.

- Ice core pushes up ground to form pingo
- Unfrozen lake
- Groundwater attracted to ice core

Periglaciation: Formation of a pingo in the Mackenzie Delta

The evolving landscape

Landscape

- limestone region
- sinking land
- stable land
- uplifting land

▲ active volcano

⋯ area of tectonic activity

- - - limit of permafrost

— maximum limit of glaciation

→ ocean current

River erosion

6 The Grand Canyon *(above)* in the Colorado Plateau was created by the downward erosion of the Colorado River, combined with the gradual uplift of the plateau, over the past 30 million years. The contours of the canyon formed as the softer rock layers eroded into gentle slopes, and the hard rock layers into cliffs. The depth varies from 3855–6560 ft (1175–2000 m).

- Soft rock is easily eroded into gentle slopes
- Hard rock resists erosion
- Colorado River cuts down through rock

River Erosion: Formation of the Grand Canyon

Post-glacial lakes

3 A chain of lakes from Great Bear Lake to the Great Lakes *(above)* was created as the ice retreated northwards. Glaciers scoured hollows in the softer lowland rock. Glacial deposits at the lip of the hollows, and ridges of harder rock, trapped water to form lakes.

- Retreating glacier
- Ice-scoured hollow filled with glacial meltwater to form a lake
- Harder rock creates a barrier between lakes
- Softer lowland rock

Post-glacial lakes: Formation of the Great Lakes

Weathering

4 The Yucatan Peninsula is a vast, flat limestone plateau in southern Mexico. Weathering action from both rainwater and underground streams has enlarged fractures in the rock to form caves and hollows, called sinkholes *(above)*.

- Porous limestone plateau
- Rainwater erodes porous rock forming sinkholes
- Sea level
- Underground stream further erodes rock

Weathering: Water erosion on the Yucatan Peninsula

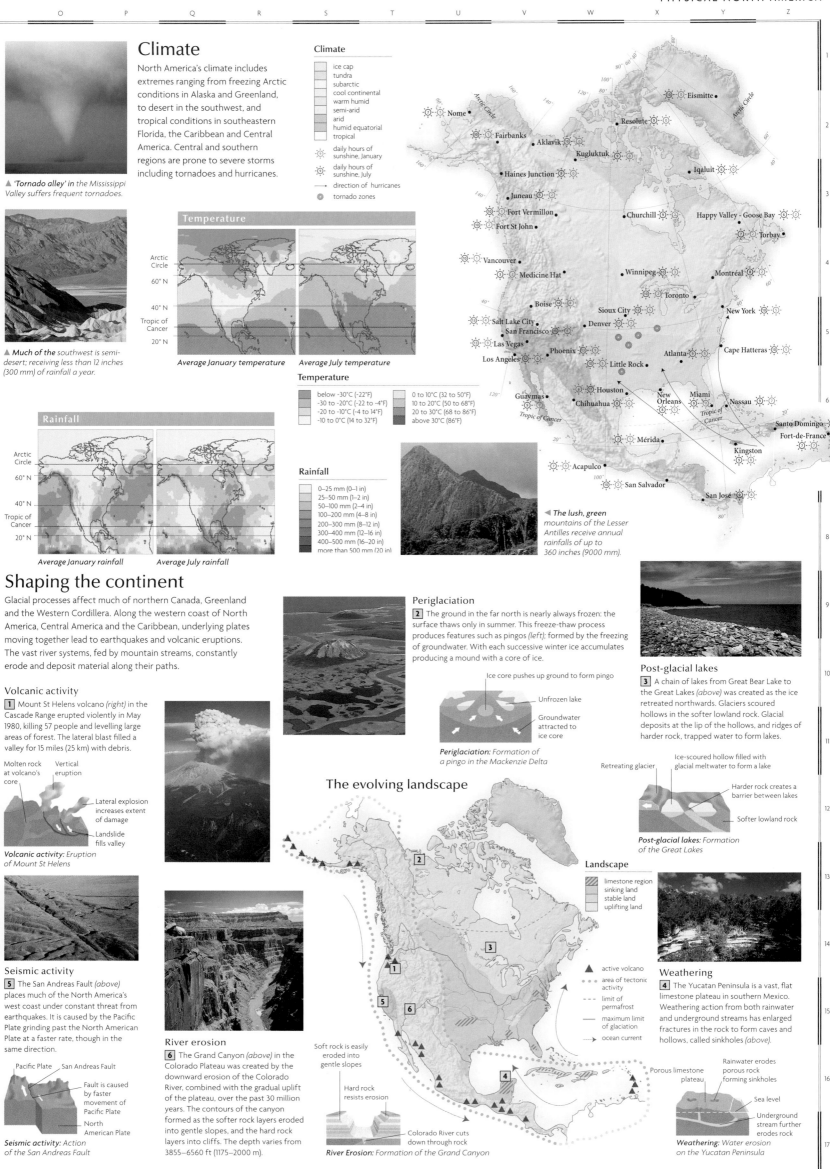

Eismitte · Nome · Fairbanks · Aklavik · Resolute · Kugluktuk · Iqaluit · Haines Junction · Juneau · Fort Vermillon · Churchill · Happy Valley - Goose Bay · Torbay · Fort St John · Vancouver · Winnipeg · Montréal · Medicine Hat · Toronto · Boise · New York · Salt Lake City · Sioux City · Denver · Cape Hatteras · San Francisco · Las Vegas · Phoenix · Atlanta · Little Rock · Los Angeles · Houston · Miami · Guaymas · New Orleans · Nassau · Chihuahua · Santo Domingo · Fort-de-France · Mérida · Kingston · Acapulco · San Salvador · San José

Political North America

Democracy is well established in some parts of the continent but is a recent phenomenon in others. The economically dominant nations of Canada and the USA have a long democratic tradition but elsewhere, notably in the countries of Central America, political turmoil has been more common. In Nicaragua and Haiti, harsh dictatorships have only recently been superseded by democratically-elected governments. North America's largest countries, Canada, Mexico and the USA have federal state systems, sharing political power between national and state governments. The USA has intervened militarily on several occasions in Central America and the Caribbean to protect its strategic interests.

Transport

In the 19th century, railways were used to open up the North American continent. Air transport is now more common for long distance passenger travel, although railways are still extensively used for bulk freight transport. Waterways, like the Mississippi River, are important for the transport of bulk materials, and the Panama Canal is a vital link between the Pacific Ocean and the Caribbean. In the 20th century, road transport increased massively in North America, with the introduction of cheap, mass-produced motor cars and extensive highway construction.

◄ *This busy suburban* interchange in Los Angeles is part of the USA's Interstate freeway system. Construction of the 55,000 mile (88,500 km) freeway network began in the 1950s, and it now connects most major cities, and carries one-fifth of the USA's road traffic.

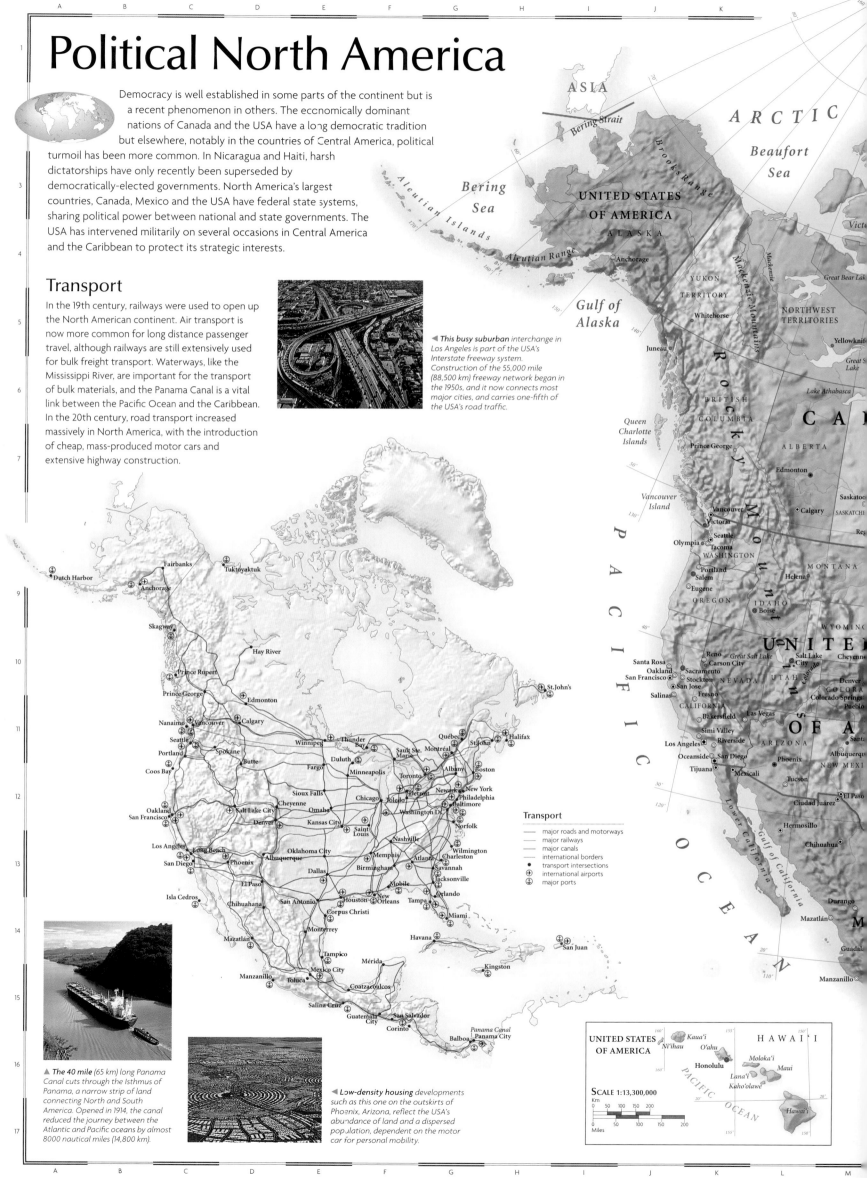

Transport
- major roads and motorways
- major railways
- major canals
- international borders
- • transport intersections
- ✈ international airports
- ⚓ major ports

▲ *The 40 mile* (65 km) long Panama Canal cuts through the Isthmus of Panama, a narrow strip of land connecting North and South America. Opened in 1914, the canal reduced the journey between the Atlantic and Pacific oceans by almost 8000 nautical miles (14,800 km).

◄ *Low-density housing* developments such as this one on the outskirts of Phoenix, Arizona, reflect the USA's abundance of land and a dispersed population, dependent on the motor car for personal mobility.

UNITED STATES OF AMERICA

SCALE 1:13,300,000

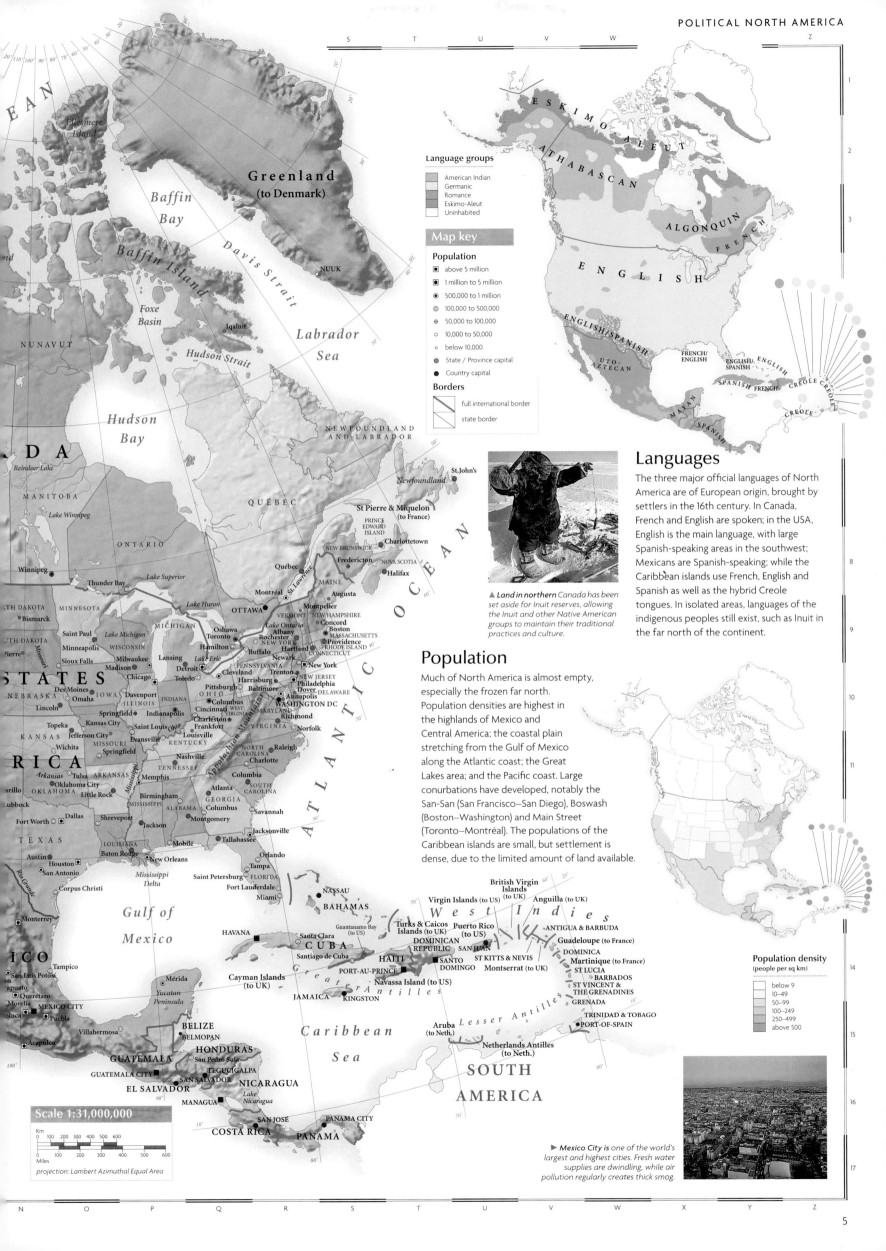

Greenland
(to Denmark)

Baffin
Bay

Davis Strait

NUUK

Baffin Island

Ellesmere
Island

EAN

Foxe
Basin

Iqaluit

Labrador
Sea

NUNAVUT

Hudson Strait

Hudson
Bay

NEWFOUNDLAND
AND LABRADOR

QUÉBEC

Newfoundland

St.John's

Reindeer Lake

MANITOBA

ONTARIO

Lake Winnipeg

St Pierre & Miquelon
(to France)

PRINCE
EDWARD
ISLAND

Charlottetown

Winnipeg

Lake Superior

Thunder Bay

NEW BRUNSWICK
Fredericton

NOVA SCOTIA
Halifax

Québec

Montréal

St. Lawrence

MAINE
Augusta

ATLANTIC OCEAN

TH DAKOTA
Bismarck

SOUTH DAKOTA
Pierre

MINNESOTA

WISCONSIN

MICHIGAN

Saint Paul
Minneapolis

Lake Michigan

Madison

Lake Huron

Milwaukee

Sioux Falls

Chicago

Lansing

Detroit

Lake Erie

Toledo

Montpelier
VERMONT

NEW HAMPSHIRE
Concord

Oshawa
Toronto

Boston

Hamilton

MASSACHUSETTS

Rochester
NEW YORK

Providence
Hartford
RHODE ISLAND
CONNECTICUT

Buffalo

Newark

New York

NEBRASKA
Lincoln

IOWA

Des Moines
Omaha

ILLINOIS

INDIANA

OHIO

Cleveland

PENNSYLVANIA

Pittsburgh

Trenton
NEW JERSEY
Philadelphia

Dover
DELAWARE

Springfield

Indianapolis

Columbus

Harrisburg

Baltimore

Cincinnati

Annapolis

KANSAS

Topeka

Kansas City

Saint Louis

Ohio

WEST
VIRGINIA
MARYLAND

WASHINGTON DC

Richmond

Frankfort

STATES

Jefferson City

MISSOURI

Evansville

KENTUCKY

VIRGINIA

Norfolk

RICA

Wichita

Springfield

Nashville

NORTH
CAROLINA

Raleigh

Appalachian Mountains

Arkansas

Tulsa

ARKANSAS

Memphis

TENNESSEE

Charlotte

rillo

OKLAHOMA

Little Rock

Columbia

Oklahoma City

Birmingham

Atlanta

SOUTH
CAROLINA

bbock

MISSISSIPPI

ALABAMA

GEORGIA

Fort Worth

Dallas

Shreveport

Columbus

Montgomery

Savannah

TEXAS

LOUISIANA

Jackson

Mississippi

Jacksonville

Austin

Baton Rouge

Mobile

Tallahassee

San Antonio

Houston

New Orleans

Orlando

FLORIDA

Tampa

Corpus Christi

Saint Petersburg

Fort Lauderdale

Rio Grande

Miami

Monterrey

Gulf of
Mexico

NASSAU

BAHAMAS

British Virgin
Islands
(to UK)

West Indies

Virgin Islands (to US)

Anguilla (to UK)

ICO

San Luis Potosí

Tampico

HAVANA

Santa Clara

Guantanamo Bay
(to US)

Turks & Caicos
Islands (to UK)

Puerto Rico
(to US)

ANTIGUA & BARBUDA

apuato

Querétaro

CUBA

DOMINICAN
REPUBLIC

SAN JUAN

Guadeloupe (to France)

Morelia

Mérida

Santiago de Cuba

HAITI

SANTO
DOMINGO

ST KITTS & NEVIS

DOMINICA

Martinique (to France)

luca

MEXICO CITY

Puebla

Yucatán
Peninsula

Cayman Islands
(to UK)

Greater Antilles

PORT-AU-PRINCE

Navassa Island (to US)

Montserrat (to UK)

ST LUCIA
BARBADOS

Acapulco

JAMAICA

KINGSTON

ST VINCENT &
THE GRENADINES

GRENADA

Caribbean

Sea

Lesser Antilles

TRINIDAD & TOBAGO
PORT-OF-SPAIN

BELIZE

BELMOPAN

GUATEMALA

HONDURAS

San Pedro Sula

Aruba
(to Neth.)

Netherlands Antilles
(to Neth.)

GUATEMALA CITY

TEGUCIGALPA

SAN SALVADOR

EL SALVADOR

NICARAGUA

MANAGUA

Lake
Nicaragua

SAN JOSE

COSTA RICA

PANAMA CITY

PANAMA

SOUTH
AMERICA

Map key

Population

- ◼ above 5 million
- ◼ 1 million to 5 million
- ◉ 500,000 to 1 million
- ◉ 100,000 to 500,000
- ⊕ 50,000 to 100,000
- ○ 10,000 to 50,000
- ∘ below 10,000
- ◉ State / Province capital
- ● Country capital

Borders

- full international border
- state border

Language groups

- American Indian
- Germanic
- Romance
- Eskimo-Aleut
- Uninhabited

ESKIMO-ALEUT
ATHABASCAN
ALGONQUIN
ENGLISH
ENGLISH/SPANISH
UTO-AZTECAN
FRENCH/ENGLISH
ENGLISH/SPANISH
ENGLISH
SPANISH FRENCH
CREOLE CREOLE
CREOLE
MAYAN
SPANISH
FRENCH

Languages

The three major official languages of North America are of European origin, brought by settlers in the 16th century. In Canada, French and English are spoken; in the USA, English is the main language, with large Spanish-speaking areas in the southwest; Mexicans are Spanish-speaking; while the Caribbean islands use French, English and Spanish as well as the hybrid Creole tongues. In isolated areas, languages of the indigenous peoples still exist, such as Inuit in the far north of the continent.

▲ *Land in northern Canada has been set aside for Inuit reserves, allowing the Inuit and other Native American groups to maintain their traditional practices and culture.*

Population

Much of North America is almost empty, especially the frozen far north. Population densities are highest in the highlands of Mexico and Central America; the coastal plain stretching from the Gulf of Mexico along the Atlantic coast; the Great Lakes area; and the Pacific coast. Large conurbations have developed, notably the San-San (San Francisco–San Diego), Boswash (Boston–Washington) and Main Street (Toronto–Montréal). The populations of the Caribbean islands are small, but settlement is dense, due to the limited amount of land available.

Population density
(people per sq km)

- below 9
- 10–49
- 50–99
- 100–249
- 250–499
- above 500

▶ *Mexico City is one of the world's largest and highest cities. Fresh water supplies are dwindling, while air pollution regularly creates thick smog.*

Scale 1:31,000,000

Km
0 100 200 300 400 500 600

Miles
0 100 200 300 400 500 600

projection: Lambert Azimuthal Equal Area

North American resources

The two northern countries of Canada and the USA are richly endowed with natural resources which have helped to fuel economic development. The USA is the world's largest economy, although today it is facing stiff competition from the Far East. Mexico has relied on oil revenues but there are hopes that the North American Free Trade Agreement (NAFTA), will encourage trade growth with Canada and the USA. The poorer countries of Central America and the Caribbean depend largely on cash crops and tourism.

Industry

The modern, industrialized economies of the USA and Canada contrast sharply with those of Mexico, Central America and the Caribbean. Manufacturing is especially important in the USA; vehicle production is concentrated around the Great Lakes, while electronic and hi-tech industries are increasingly found in the western and southern states. Mexico depends on oil exports and assembly work, taking advantage of cheap labour. Many Central American and Caribbean countries rely heavily on agricultural exports.

◄ After its purchase from Russia in 1867, Alaska's frozen lands were largely ignored by the USA. Oil reserves similar in magnitude to those in eastern Texas were discovered in Prudhoe Bay, Alaska in 1968. Freezing temperatures and a fragile environment hamper oil extraction.

Standard of living

The USA and Canada have one of the highest overall standards of living in the world. However, many people still live in poverty, especially in inner city ghettos and some rural areas. Central America and the Caribbean are markedly poorer than their wealthier northern neighbours. Haiti is the poorest country in the western hemisphere.

Standard of living
(UN human development index)

- high
- low

◄ South of San Francisco, 'Silicon Valley' is both a national and international centre for hi-tech industries, electronic industries and research institutions.

▲ Multinational companies rely on cheap labour and tax benefits to assemble vehicles in Mexican factories.

▲ Fish such as cod, flounder and plaice are caught in the Grand Banks, off the Newfoundland coast, and processed in many North Atlantic coastal settlements.

▲ The health of the Wall Street stock market in New York is the standard measure of the state of the world's economy.

Industry

- ✈ aerospace
- 🍺 brewing
- 🚗 car/vehicle manufacture
- chemicals
- defence
- electronics
- engineering
- film industry
- finance
- food processing
- hi-tech industry
- iron & steel
- pharmaceuticals
- printing & publishing
- research & development
- shipbuilding
- sugar processing
- textiles
- timber processing
- tobacco processing
- coal
- oil
- gas
- • industrial cities
- ⫽ major industrial areas

GNI per capita (US$)

- below 1999
- 2000–4999
- 5000–9999
- 10,000–19,999
- 20,000–24,999
- above 25,000

Map labels

ARCTIC OCEAN

Beaufort Sea

Bering Strait

RUSS. FED.

Bering Sea

Prudhoe Bay

USA

Gulf of Alaska

Baffin Bay

Greenland (to Denmark)

Labrador Sea

Hudson Strait

Hudson Bay

CANADA

Vancouver
Calgary
Seattle
Portland
Winnipeg
Montréal

PACIFIC OCEAN

Minneapolis
Milwaukee
Toronto
Buffalo
Boston
Albany
New York
Detroit
Cleveland
Chicago
Pittsburgh
Philadelphia
Dayton
Baltimore
Cincinnati

UNITED STATES OF AMERICA

San Francisco
Denver
Kansas City
Wichita
Saint Louis
Greensboro
Nashville
Charlotte
Tulsa
Los Angeles
San Diego
Phoenix
Birmingham
Atlanta
Tijuana
Ciudad Juárez
El Paso
Dallas
Jacksonville
Houston
New Orleans
Orlando
Tampa
Miami

ATLANTIC OCEAN

Monterrey
Gulf of Mexico

MEXICO

Guadalajara
Mexico City

Havana
CUBA
BAHAMAS
Turks & Caicos Islands (to UK)
Virgin Islands (to US)
British Virgin Islands (to UK)
Anguilla (to UK)
ST KITTS & NEVIS
ANTIGUA & BARBUDA
Montserrat (to UK)
Puerto Rico (to US)
San Juan
Guadeloupe (to France)
DOMINICA
Martinique (to France)
ST LUCIA
BARBADOS
ST VINCENT & THE GRENADINES
GRENADA
TRINIDAD & TOBAGO
Port-of-Spain

DOMINICAN REPUBLIC
HAITI
Port-au-Prince
Santo Domingo
Cayman Islands (to UK)
JAMAICA
Greater Antilles
Navassa Island (to US)
Aruba (to Neth.)
Netherlands Antilles (to Neth.)
Lesser Antilles

Caribbean Sea

West Indies

BELIZE
GUATEMALA
Guatemala City
HONDURAS
Tegucigalpa
EL SALVADOR
San Salvador
NICARAGUA
Managua
COSTA RICA
San José
Panama City
PANAMA
COLOMBIA
VENEZUELA

Environmental issues

Many fragile environments are under threat throughout the region. In Haiti, all the primary rainforest has been destroyed, while air pollution from factories and cars in Mexico City is amongst the worst in the world. Elsewhere, industry and mining pose threats, particularly in the delicate arctic environment of Alaska where oil spills have polluted coastlines and decimated fish stocks.

Environmental issues

- national parks
- acid rain
- tropical forest
- forest destroyed
- desert
- desertification
- polluted rivers
- radioactive contamination
- marine pollution
- heavy marine pollution
- poor urban air quality

▲ Wild bison graze in Yellowstone National Park, the world's first national park. Designated in 1872, geothermal springs and boiling mud are among its natural spectacles, making it a major tourist attraction.

Mineral resources

Fossil fuels are exploited in considerable quantities throughout the continent. Coal mining in the Appalachians is declining but vast open pits exist further west in Wyoming. Oil and natural gas are found in Alaska, Texas, the Gulf of Mexico, and the Canadian West. Canada has large quantities of nickel, while Jamaica has considerable deposits of bauxite, and Mexico has large reserves of silver.

Mineral resources

- oil field
- gas field
- coal field
- bauxite
- copper
- gold
- iron
- lead
- nickel
- phosphates
- silver
- uranium

▲ In addition to fossil fuels, North America is also rich in exploitable metallic ores. This vast, mile-deep (1.6 km) pit is a copper mine in New Mexico.

▲ In agriculturally marginal areas where the soil is either too poor, or the climate too dry for crops, cattle ranching proliferates – especially in Mexico and the western reaches of the Great Plains.

Using the land and sea

Abundant land and fertile soils stretch from the Canadian prairies to Texas creating North America's agricultural heartland. Cereals and cattle ranching form the basis of the farming economy, with corn and soya beans also important. Fruit and vegetables are grown in California using irrigation, while Florida is a leading producer of citrus fruits. Caribbean and Central American countries depend on cash crops such as bananas, coffee and sugar cane, often grown on large plantations. This reliance on a single crop can leave these countries vulnerable to fluctuating world crop prices.

Using the land and sea

- cropland
- forest
- ice cap
- mountain region
- pasture
- tundra
- wetland
- desert
- major conurbations
- cattle
- goats
- pigs
- poultry
- reindeer
- sheep
- bananas
- citrus fruits
- coffee
- corn (maize)
- cotton
- fishing
- fruit
- maple syrup
- peanuts
- rice
- shellfish
- soya beans
- sugar cane
- timber
- tobacco
- vineyards
- wheat

◀ Sugar cane is Cuba's main agricultural crop, and is grown and processed throughout the Caribbean. Fermented sugar is used to make rum.

◀ The Great Plains support large-scale arable farming throughout central North America. Corn is grown in a belt south and west of the Great Lakes, while further west where the climate is drier, wheat is grown.

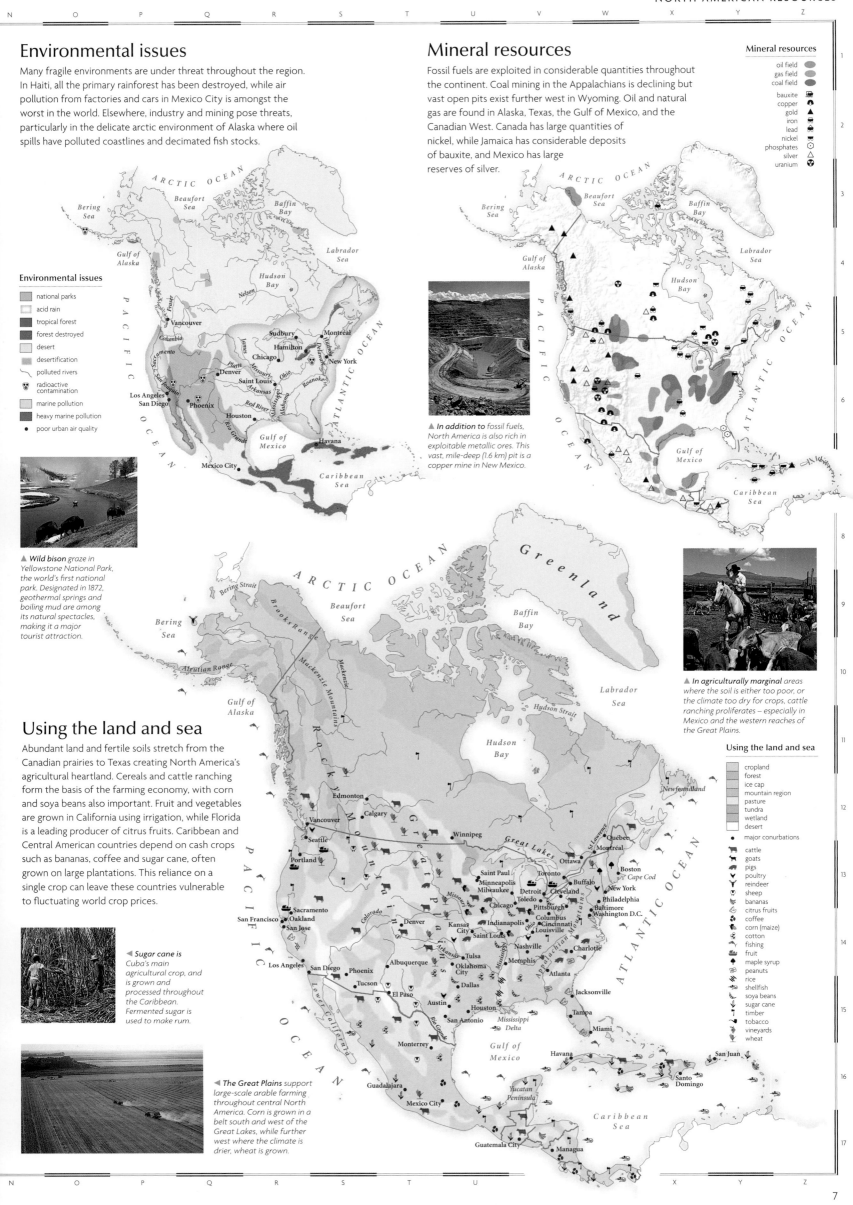

Canada

Canada is the second largest country in the world, and with only about one-tenth of its land area inhabited, it is one of the most sparsely populated. Canada became a confederation in 1867, though Newfoundland did not join until 1949. As a founding member of the UN and of the Commonwealth, Canada has played an important role in international affairs. A constitutional crisis, focusing on the French-speaking Québécois, and Inuit and Native American land rights, dominated politics in the 1990s. In 1999, part of the Northwest Territories, Nunavut, became a self-governing homeland for the Inuit.

◄ *The Selwyn Mountains* in northwestern Canada form part of the Rocky Mountains. The highest point, Keele Peak, rises to 9750 ft (2972 m).

Transport and industry

Abundant energy in the form of coal, oil, natural gas and hydro-electric power underpins Canadian industry. Over 75% of manufacturing is concentrated in the Great Lakes–St. Lawrence region, including prospering aerospace, transport and hi-tech industries. Across Canada as a whole, manufacturing has developed around a diversified, high-quality resource base and a wide range of metallic and non-metallic minerals.

◄ *Canada has one* of the world's highest rates of energy consumption per person. It is endowed with vast hydro-electric potential from which more than 60% of its electricity requirements are generated.

Major industry and infrastructure

- ✈ aerospace
- 🚗 car manufacture
- chemicals
- engineering
- food processing
- hi-tech industry
- ✛ hydro-electric power
- ♦ oil & gas
- mining
- timber processing
- ■ capital cities
- □ major towns
- ⊕ international airports
- — major roads
- major industrial areas

The transport network

309,019 miles (497,375 km)		10,500 miles (16,900 km)
8049 miles (12,995 km)		1864 miles (3000 km)

In recent years the road network has been expanded, especially links to remote areas. Meanwhile, for long-distance travel, air transport now supersedes the declining rail network, which focuses mainly on east–west routes.

Using the land and sea

The majority of Canada's agricultural land is found in the prairies, which cover 140 million acres (57 million ha) and support wheat and grain-fed cattle. More specialized crops, such as fruit and vegetables, are grown in pockets of agricultural land in the east and west. Of Canada's many islands, only Prince Edward Island has notable farmland. Further north, boreal forests, exploited for timber, run in an almost unbroken arc, giving way to uncultivable tundra and ice sheets in the far north.

The urban/rural population divide

urban 77%   rural 23%

0 10 20 30 40 50 60 70 80 90 100

Population density	Total land area
9 people per sq mile (3 people per sq km)	3,559,294 sq miles (9,220,970 sq km)

Land use and agricultural distribution

- cattle
- cereals
- fishing
- fruit
- timber
- ■ capital cities
- • major towns
- pasture
- cropland
- forest
- wetland
- mountain region
- barren
- tundra

◄ *The climate and* topography of the prairies makes them ideally suited to farming. Long summer days, moderate temperatures, limited rainfall and flat plains provide excellent conditions for wheat farming.

Scale 1:14,700,000

Km
0 25 50   100   150   200   250   300   350

Miles
0 25 50   100   150   200   250   300

projection: Lambert Azimuthal Equal Area

The landscape

Glaciers on islands in the Arctic Ocean are the last remnants of the ice sheet that once covered and shaped Canada. Hudson Bay is the centre of the Canadian Shield, a huge, eroded plateau marked at its southern extremity by a string of lakes running southeastwards from Great Bear Lake to the Great Lakes. In contrast to the rolling relief of the Shield and the central lowland region, the Rocky Mountains rise to peaks of over 13,000 ft (4000 m), stretching 500 miles (800 km) along the west coast.

▶ *Permanently frozen ground* known as permafrost is common in Canada's northern tundra. It thickens further north, becoming hundreds of metres deep in parts of the Arctic.

Permanently frozen ground

Top layer thaws in the summer

Marginal areas of permafrost thaw in summer

Unfrozen ground where temperature is more moderate

The Mackenzie river, flowing north over the permafrost, forms a wide river channel with many tributaries. Together with the Peel river it has created a long, narrow delta at its mouth. The entire river freezes during the winter.

Fertile prairies stretch from the southern rim of the Canadian Shield, south into the USA.

Exposure to three phases of mountain-building and subsequent erosion over millions of years has moulded the ancient Canadian Shield into a series of basins and ridges.

Great Bear Lake

▲ *Along the northeastern coast of Baffin Island the mountains rise to 8000 ft (2440 m). Glaciers move down through the valleys to the sea, eroding wide U-shaped valleys.*

The Rocky Mountains were formed some 80 million years ago, when the Pacific plate was driven under the North American plate, forcing up the land.

The Great Lakes lie on the Canada–USA border. The basins they now occupy were fashioned by repeated ice advance. At one time, Lakes Superior, Huron and Michigan formed a single large lake, Lake Nipissing.

The St. Lawrence River is 2350 miles (3782 km) long. It flows from the western shore of Lake Superior through the Great Lakes and on to the Atlantic Ocean. From December to April, the St. Lawrence Seaway freezes between Lake Ontario and Montréal.

▶ *The Great Lakes are drained by the St. Lawrence River which flows down through a wide tectonic depression. It forms a broad estuary for much of its course, the width varying from 1.2 miles (1.9 km) in the upper reaches to 90 miles (145 km) at its mouth.*

▶ *Isolated pillars, known as hoodoos near Red Deer river in the badlands of Alberta are a product of wind and water erosion, especially flash floods. The badlands lie in the rain shadow of the Rocky Mountains, which creates a semi-arid climate.*

Map key

Population
- 1 million to 5 million
- 500,000 to 1 million
- 100,000 to 500,000
- 50,000 to 100,000
- 10,000 to 50,000
- below 10,000

Elevation
- 6000m / 19,686ft
- 4000m / 13,124ft
- 3000m / 9843ft
- 2000m / 6562ft
- 1000m / 3281ft
- 500m / 1640ft
- 250m / 820ft
- 100m / 328ft
- sea level

A B C D E F G ... K L M

Canada:
WESTERN PROVINCES

Alberta, British Columbia, Manitoba,
Saskatchewan, Yukon Territory

The mountains of the west coast, incorporating British Columbia and the Yukon Territory, descend into the vast, flat prairies of Alberta, Saskatchewan and Manitoba. The empty lands and fertile soils of the prairie provinces attracted migrants, and the descendants of early European immigrants still make up a large proportion of the population. The mechanization of agriculture has reduced the need for labour, and rural population densities remain low. The majority of the people live within 100 miles (160 km) of the southern Canada–USA border, and in British Columbia, one of the leading Canadian provinces in terms of economic wealth. The Yukon Territory, in the far north, remains a relatively unspoilt wilderness, containing large, untapped mineral reserves. This province has a significant population of Native Americans, many of whom maintain a traditional lifestyle.

Using the land and sea

Wheat farming is the economic mainstay of Alberta, Manitoba and Saskatchewan, which contain 82% of farmland in Canada. Cattle are also raised on the prairies. Forestry and fishing are the most prominent resource-based industries in British Columbia. Despite the mountainous terrain, fruit and specialized grains can be grown in the Okanagan and Fraser valleys.

Land use and agricultural distribution

- cattle
- cereals
- fishing
- fruit
- timber
- • major towns
- pasture
- cropland
- forest
- wetland
- barren
- tundra

▲ Large, highly-mechanized and often very specialized farms, requiring huge investment but little labour, characterize modern farming in the prairies.

The urban/rural population divide

urban 83%   rural 17%

0 10 20 30 40 50 60 70 80 90 100

Population density	Total land area
8 people per sq mile (3 people per sq km)	1,230,547 sq miles (3,187,120 sq km)

Transport and industry

The western provinces contain a wealth of mineral resources. Alberta holds the bulk of Canada's fossil fuels; the other provinces contain reserves of metallic ores, such as zinc, lead and silver. Isolation from markets has slowed the development of manufacturing, restricting it to the large cities like Vancouver, Winnipeg and Calgary. Hydro-electric power is widely exploited, although there is increasing concern about potential ecological damage.

The transport network

- 82,438 miles (135,145 km)
- 6459 miles (10,401 km)
- 24,041 miles (38,694 km)
- None

The transport network of the western provinces is dominated by east–west routes that weave through mountain passes and spread across the plains. Access to some northern areas is restricted to air travel.

Major industry and infrastructure

- aerospace
- chemicals
- coal
- engineering
- food processing
- hydro-electric power
- mining
- oil & gas
- timber processing
- • major towns
- ⊕ international airports
- — major roads
- major industrial areas

▲ The Fraser River valley is a major area of settlement in British Columbia. Railways cross the Rocky Mountains via this valley.

▲ Established in 1907, Jasper National Park lies in the heart of the Rocky Mountains. It is noted for its spectacular alpine scenery and contains part of the large Columbia Icefield.

◄ Much of the Yukon Territory is uninhabited tundra. Industry is based on the extraction of mineral resources, and to a lesser extent, on the scattered forests of the south.

The landscape

The massive Rocky Mountains form a continental divide between rivers flowing eastward and westward. East of the mountains, stretching from the Arctic Circle south into the USA, lie the interior plains. Covered with glacial deposits from the last Ice Age, these are interspersed with hilly regions and long, steep escarpments.

Map key

Population

⊙ 500,000 to 1 million
◎ 100,000 to 500,000
⊕ 50,000 to 100,000
○ 10,000 to 50,000
○ below 10,000

Elevation

6000m / 19,686ft
4000m / 13,124ft
3000m / 9843ft
2000m / 6562ft
1000m / 3281ft
500m / 1640ft
250m / 820ft
100m / 328ft
sea level

Scale 1:8,250,000

Km
0 25 50   100   150   200   250

Miles
0   50   100   150   200   250

projection: Lambert Conformal Conic

Mount Logan rises 19,551 ft (5959 m). It is the highest peak in Canada.

The Columbia Icefield in the Rocky Mountains is the source of two major rivers, the Athabasca and the North Saskatchewan.

The badlands of Alberta were created when east-flowing rivers, swollen by meltwater at the end of the last Ice Age, cut deep, wide canyons producing eroded, barren landscapes.

Vegetated island — Bar
River flow is diverted by deposited sediments — Sand flat

▲ **Braided rivers are** shallow and fast-flowing. The interlaced branches are formed when excess sediments, which can no longer be transported, are deposited. The sediments collect in the river channel forming bars and sand flats. Islands form when the bars are colonized by vegetation.

South Saskatchewan River

▲ **Across the tundra** of northern Manitoba, widespread permafrost inhibits water from permeating the soil. This causes rivers like the Churchill to flow in many channels, which can be frozen for up to six months during the winter.

The Nelson and Churchill rivers drain northward across the Canadian Shield to Hudson Bay. The shield covers three-fifths of Saskatchewan.

Setting Lake

The Rocky Mountain Trench is the longest linear fault in the world. It has formed a straight, flat-bottomed valley between 2–9 miles (4–15 km) wide, and up to 3280 ft (1000 m) deep.

Hundreds of islands dot the fjord-indented coast of British Columbia; the largest is Vancouver Island.

Three major passes cut through the Rocky Mountains: Yellowhead, Kicking Horse and Crowsnest. They are all used as transport routes through the mountains.

The Cypress Hills rise to 4806 ft (1465 m) above the surrounding plain. Having escaped the last glaciation they contain unique plant and animal life. The silvery lupine, bunchberry and lodgepole pine all grow in the cool, moist climate of the hills.

The Alberta and Saskatchewan plains bear strong testament to past glaciations. The Assiniboine, Saskatchewan and Qu'Appelle rivers occupy flat-bottomed, steep-sided valleys eroded during the last Ice Age by glacial meltwater.

▲ **Ancient granite outcrops,** part of the Canadian Shield, rise above the surface of Setting Lake, which was initially formed by meltwater from the last Ice Age.

The lowlands of Manitoba are a basin that once held the vast post-glacial Lake Agassiz, remnants of which include Lake Winnipeg, Lake Winnipegosis and Lake Manitoba.

Canada: EASTERN PROVINCES

New Brunswick, Newfoundland & Labrador, Nova Scotia, Ontario, Prince Edward Island, Québec, *St Pierre & Miquelon (to France)*

Colonized by both the English and the French during the 16th century, Canada's eastern provinces are still marked by their dual influences. They contain the last fragment of once-sizeable French territories, the islands of St Pierre and Miquelon. French remains Canada's second official language and Québec's first language. The population of the eastern provinces is highly concentrated in the south, especially along the border with the USA. A recent decline in fishing in the Atlantic provinces has encouraged a steady flow of westerly migration to more prosperous regions. The north, around Hudson Bay, remains snow-covered for most of the year and the indigenous Inuit people make up the bulk of its sparse population.

◄ *Rocher Percé, is 290 ft (88 m) high. Lying off the southeastern coast of Québec, it is a sanctuary for sea birds.*

Scale 1:7,750,000

Km
0 25 50 100 150 200
Miles
0 25 50 100 150 200

projection: Lambert Conformal Conic

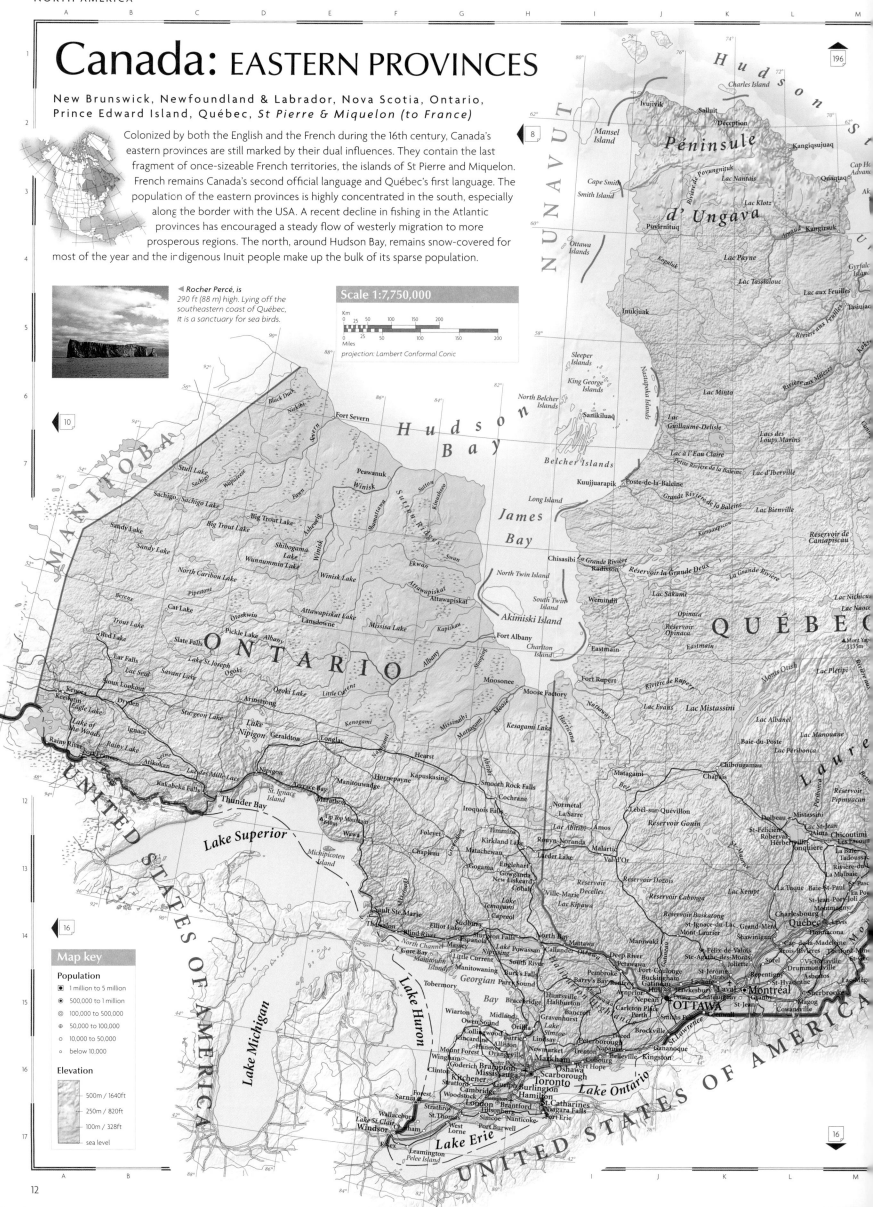

Map key

Population
- ▣ 1 million to 5 million
- ◉ 500,000 to 1 million
- ⊕ 100,000 to 500,000
- ⊕ 50,000 to 100,000
- ○ 10,000 to 50,000
- ∘ below 10,000

Elevation
- 500m / 1640ft
- 250m / 820ft
- 100m / 328ft
- sea level

The landscape

Much of eastern Canada is part of the Canadian Shield. Glaciers have scoured the land leaving deposits that have dammed and diverted streams, to create a rocky landscape strewn with lakes and swamps. Much of the ground is subject to permafrost, which further impedes drainage. The uplands in the far east are the most northerly extension of the Appalachian mountain chain.

The Péninsule d'Ungava is littered with erratics – isolated rocks which were carried by glaciers and deposited away from their place of origin when the glacier melted.

▶ *Labrador's indented coast* is a product of past glaciations, which caused sea level change, and wave erosion. There are countless offshore islands, fjords and exposed headlands.

The eroded highlands of New Brunswick, Nova Scotia and Newfoundland are part of the Appalachian mountain chain, formed over 400 million years ago.

Lake Superior is the world's largest expanse of fresh water, covering 32,150 sq miles (83,270 sq km). It is crossed by the Canada–USA border.

Bay of Fundy
Tidal waters are channelled down the bay

Steep cliffs bound the bay

The bay is 94 miles (151 km) long

▲ *At the Bay of Fundy*, incoming waves are funnelled down the long, narrow, steep-sided bay. These topographical features cause fast-flowing tides which can rise 70 ft (21 m).

Laurentides Park

▶ *The forested Laurentides Park* incorporates part of the Laurentian Mountains. Within its boundaries are over 1600 lakes.

▲ *The tides at* the Bay of Fundy are among the highest in the world. At low tide the tree-topped rocks have been likened to flowerpots.

Transport and industry

Both Québec and Ontario have a diversified manufacturing sector located in the south. Across the rest of the region, industry is largely based around local resources, which accounts for the large number of fish and timber processing plants and mines. Many of the fast-flowing rivers are also gradually being harnessed for hydro-electric power.

Major industry and infrastructure

- ✈ aerospace
- 🚗 vehicle manufacture
- chemicals
- fish processing
- food processing
- hi-tech industry
- hydro-electric power
- mining
- timber processing
- ● capital cities
- ● major towns
- ⊕ international airports
- major roads
- major industrial areas

The transport network

- 84,522 miles (136,325 km)
- 1858 miles (2998 km)
- 20,602 miles (33,159 km)
- 376 miles (606 km)

The majority of Canada's large ports lie in the east. Since the 1960s the region's rail network has been steadily reduced; Newfoundland recently lost its last remaining line, the Long-Cross Island line.

▲ *Fish processing is a* major industry in the Atlantic provinces. Fogo Island, off Newfoundland, has barely a thousand inhabitants but it is able to sustain a number of cod canneries.

Using the land and sea

With thin soils restricting farming to the south, the forests which grow in vast unbroken tracts across eastern Canada provide an important source of revenue. Coastal communities rely heavily on the rich fishing grounds of the Atlantic Ocean, although foreign competition and overfishing have resulted in strict policies to conserve stocks.

The urban/rural population divide

urban 84%   rural 16%

0 10 20 30 40 50 60 70 80 90 100

Population density	Total land area
21 people per sq mile (8 people per sq km)	1,076,227 sq miles (2,787,431 sq km)

Land use and agricultural distribution

- 🐄 cattle
- cereals
- fishing
- fruit
- timber
- ■ capital cities
- ● major towns
- pasture
- cropland
- forest
- tundra

▶ *Prince Edward Island is the* only Atlantic province with notable agricultural land. The island is Canada's leading producer of potatoes.

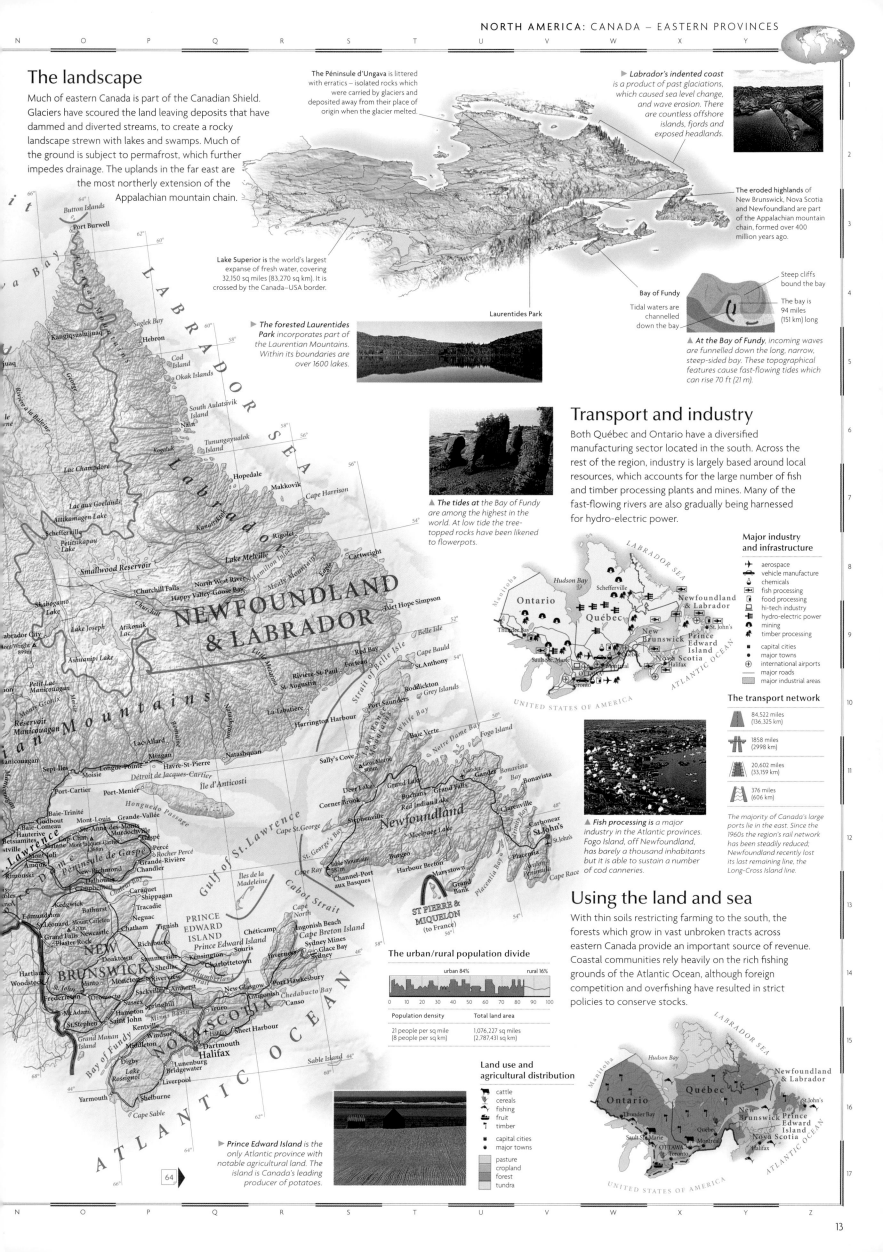

Southeastern Canada

Southern Ontario, Southern Québec

The southern parts of Québec and Ontario form the economic heart of Canada. The two provinces are divided by their language and culture; in Québec, French is the main language, whereas English is spoken in Ontario. Separatist sentiment in Québec has led to a provincial referendum on the question of a sovereignty association with Canada. The region contains Canada's capital, Ottawa and its two largest cities: Toronto, the centre of commerce and Montréal, the cultural and administrative heart of French Canada.

▲ *The port at* Montréal *is situated on the St. Lawrence Seaway. A network of 16 locks allows sea-going vessels access to routes once plied by fur-trappers and early settlers.*

Transport and industry

The cities of southern Québec and Ontario, and their hinterlands, form the heart of Canadian manufacturing industry. Toronto is Canada's leading financial centre, and Ontario's motor and aerospace industries have developed around the city. A major centre for nickel mining lies to the north of Toronto. Most of Québec's industry is located in Montréal, the oldest port in North America. Chemicals, paper manufacture and the construction of transport equipment are leading industrial activities.

▶ Niagara Falls *lies on the border between Canada and the USA. It comprises a system of two falls: American Falls, in New York, is separated from Horseshoe Falls, in Ontario, by Goat Island. Horseshoe Falls, seen here, plunges 184 ft (56 m) and is 2500 ft (762 m) wide.*

Major industry and infrastructure

- car manufacture
- chemicals
- engineering
- finance
- food processing
- hi-tech industry
- mining
- iron & steel
- textiles
- paper industry
- timber processing
- capital cities
- major towns
- international airports
- major roads
- major industrial areas

The transport network

The opening of the St. Lawrence Seaway in 1959 finally allowed ocean-going ships (up to 24,000 tons (tonnes)) access to the interior of Canada, creating a vital trading route.

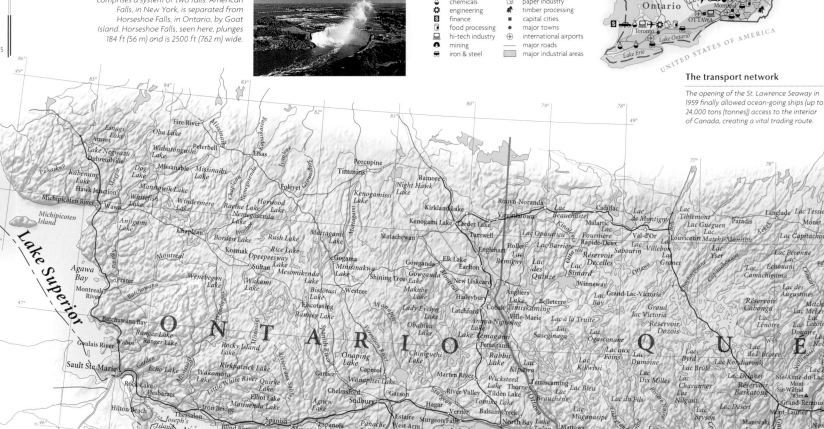

Map key

Population
- ⬤ 1 million to 5 million
- ◉ 500,000 to 1 million
- ◎ 100,000 to 500,000
- ⊕ 50,000 to 100,000
- ○ 10,000 to 50,000
- ∘ below 10,000

Elevation
- 500m/1640ft
- 250m/820ft
- 100m/328ft
- sea level

▶ Montréal, *on the banks of the St. Lawrence River, is Québec's leading metropolitan centre and one of Canada's two largest cities – Toronto is the other. Montréal clearly reflects French culture and traditions.*

Using the land and sea

The productive Niagara 'fruit belt' on the shores of Lake Erie and Lake Ontario is a major farming region, although available farmland is being challenged by urban expansion. Québec is Canada's leading producer of maple syrup and dairy products. In the north, farmland gives way to extensive areas of forest, partly used for commercial logging. Fishing occurs in Atlantic waters and in the Great Lakes.

The urban/rural population divide

urban 87%   rural 13%

Population density	Total land area
64 people per sq mile (25 people per sq km)	214,230 sq miles (555,000 sq km)

Land use and agricultural distribution

- cattle
- fish
- cereals
- fruit
- maple syrup
- timber
- tobacco
- capital cities
- major towns
- pasture
- cropland
- forest

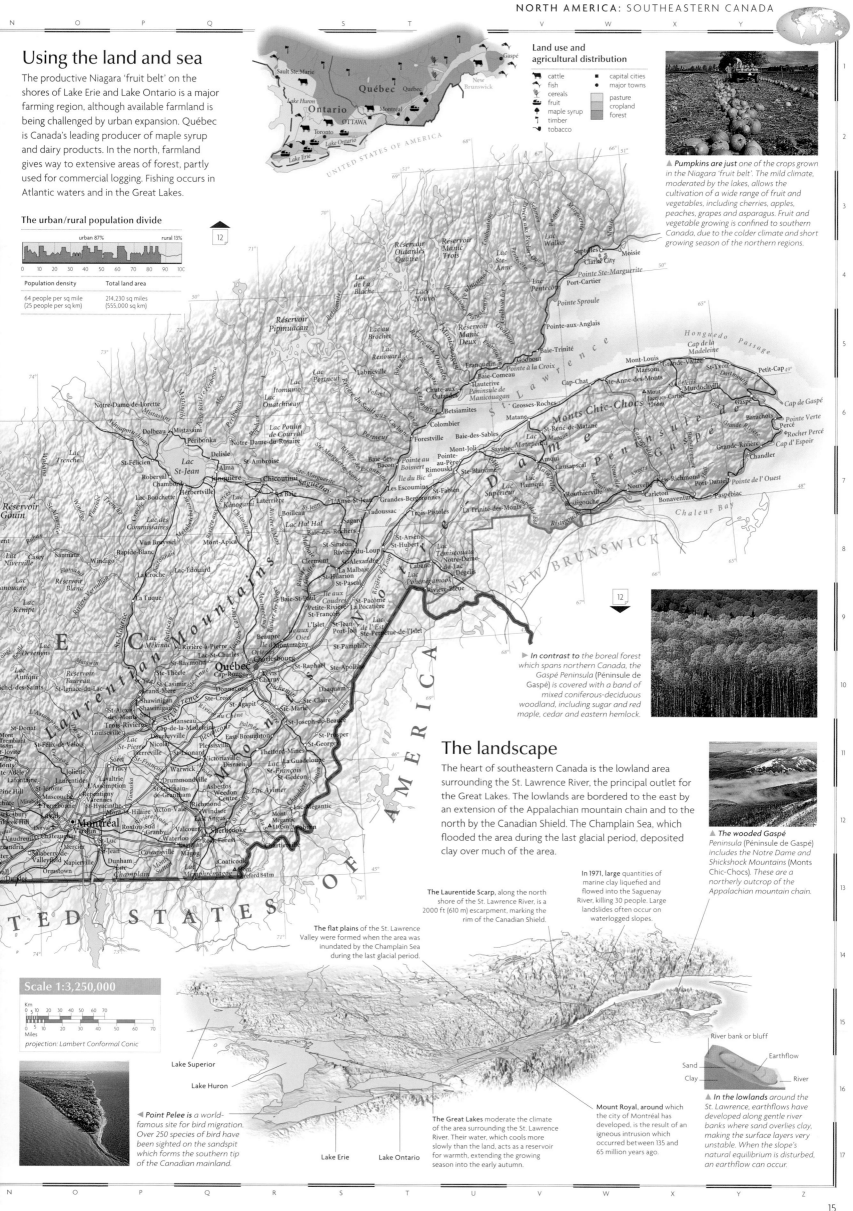

▲ *Pumpkins are just* one of the crops grown in the Niagara 'fruit belt'. The mild climate, moderated by the lakes, allows the cultivation of a wide range of fruit and vegetables, including cherries, apples, peaches, grapes and asparagus. Fruit and vegetable growing is confined to southern Canada, due to the colder climate and short growing season of the northern regions.

▶ *In contrast to* the boreal forest which spans northern Canada, the Gaspé Peninsula (Péninsule de Gaspé) is covered with a band of mixed coniferous-deciduous woodland, including sugar and red maple, cedar and eastern hemlock.

The landscape

The heart of southeastern Canada is the lowland area surrounding the St. Lawrence River, the principal outlet for the Great Lakes. The lowlands are bordered to the east by an extension of the Appalachian mountain chain and to the north by the Canadian Shield. The Champlain Sea, which flooded the area during the last glacial period, deposited clay over much of the area.

▲ *The wooded Gaspé* Peninsula (Péninsule de Gaspé) includes the Notre Dame and Shickshock Mountains (Monts Chic-Chocs). These are a northerly outcrop of the Appalachian mountain chain.

In 1971, large quantities of marine clay liquefied and flowed into the Saguenay River, killing 30 people. Large landslides often occur on waterlogged slopes.

The Laurentide Scarp, along the north shore of the St. Lawrence River, is a 2000 ft (610 m) escarpment, marking the rim of the Canadian Shield.

The flat plains of the St. Lawrence Valley were formed when the area was inundated by the Champlain Sea during the last glacial period.

River bank or bluff

Earthflow

Sand

Clay

River

▲ *In the lowlands* around the St. Lawrence, earthflows have developed along gentle river banks where sand overlies clay, making the surface layers very unstable. When the slope's natural equilibrium is disturbed, an earthflow can occur.

Mount Royal, around which the city of Montréal has developed, is the result of an igneous intrusion which occurred between 135 and 65 million years ago.

The Great Lakes moderate the climate of the area surrounding the St. Lawrence River. Their water, which cools more slowly than the land, acts as a reservoir for warmth, extending the growing season into the early autumn.

◀ *Point Pelee is a* world-famous site for bird migration. Over 250 species of bird have been sighted on the sandspit which forms the southern tip of the Canadian mainland.

Lake Superior

Lake Huron

Lake Erie

Lake Ontario

Scale 1:3,250,000

Km
0 5 10 20 30 40 50 60 70

Miles
0 5 10 20 30 40 50 60 70

projection: Lambert Conformal Conic

The United States of America

COTERMINOUS USA (FOR ALASKA AND HAWAI'I SEE PAGES 38-39)

The USA's progression from frontier territory to economic and political superpower has taken less than 200 years. The 48 coterminous states, along with the outlying states of Alaska and Hawai'i, are part of a federal union, held together by the guiding principles of the US Constitution, which enshrines the ideals of democracy and liberty for all. Abundant fertile land and a rich resource-base fuelled and sustained the USA's economic development. With the spread of agriculture and the growth of trade and industry came the need for a larger workforce, which was supplied by millions of immigrants, many seeking an escape from poverty and political or religious persecution. Immigration continues today, particularly from Central America and Asia.

▲ *Washington DC was* established as the site for the nation's capital in 1790. It is home to the seat of national government, on Capitol Hill, as well as the President's official residence, the White House.

▶ *The clear waters* of Niagara Falls cascade 190 ft (58 m) into the gorge below. It is one of America's most famous spectacles and a leading tourist attraction. The falls are slowly receding and the gorge may one day stretch from Lake Ontario to Lake Erie.

▲ *Mount Rainier is a* dormant volcano in the Cascade Range, Washington. This 14,090 ft (4392 m) peak is flanked by the most extensive glacier outside Alaska.

Scale 1:12,700,000

projection: Lambert Azimuthal Equal Area

Transport and industry

The USA has been the industrial powerhouse of the world since the Second World War, pioneering mass-production and the consumer lifestyle. Initially, heavy engineering and manufacturing in the northeast led the economy. Today, heavy industry has declined and the USA's economy is driven by service and financial industries, with the most important being defence, hi-tech and electronics.

The transport network

3,875,040 miles (6,240,000 km)		52,388 miles (84,361 km)	
148,308 miles (235,238 km)		25,467 miles (41,009 km)	

Transport in the USA is dominated by the car which, with the extensive Interstate Highway system, allows great personal mobility. Today, internal air flights between major cities provide the most rapid cross-country travel.

Major industry and infrastructure

- aerospace
- car manufacture
- chemicals
- coal
- electronics
- engineering
- food processing
- hi-tech industry
- oil & gas
- research & development
- textiles
- tourism
- ■ capital cities
- ● major towns
- ✈ international airports
- major roads
- major industrial areas

The landscape

The high, rugged mountain ranges of the west are about 80 million years old, geologically young compared to the old, eroded, Appalachian mountain chain, which dates from when North America and Europe were joined together as part of the supercontinent Pangaea, 400 million years ago. In contrast, the Great Plains and Mississippi Basin have a low relief and fertile soils.

Death Valley, California, 282 ft (86 m) below sea level, is the lowest point in the western hemisphere, and one of the hottest places on Earth. Temperatures of 190° F (88° C) have been recorded here.

Monument Valley's striking sandstone spires and pillars *(buttes)* have been formed by the action of wind, water, heat and cold.

The deep gullies of South Dakota's badlands are created by periodic, torrential rainfall, which erodes the soft soils and rocks. Their form has been greatly affected by changes in land use.

Most of the USA is drained by the great Mississippi River system. At its mouth, where levées are breached, floodwaters are carried to the swamps through a series of channels. This region is known as the bayou.

▲ **Devils Tower, in** *Wyoming is a 1280 ft (390 m) intrusion of basalt rock, which cooled to form octagonal pillars. In 1906 it became the first US National Monument.*

Barrier beaches, bars and spits are typical of the Atlantic coast. These sand formations around Cape Hatteras stretch along the coast for 200 miles (320 km).

The Great Smoky Mountains, part of the ancient Appalachian mountain chain, formed a natural barrier to early settlers attempting to penetrate the country's interior.

The Everglades are a vast area of saw-grass swamp covering 4000 sq miles (10,300 sq km) of southern Florida.

▲ *The massive drainage* basin of the Mississippi covers 1,250,000 sq miles (3,200,000 sq km). It includes all areas drained by the Mississippi and its chief tributaries, the Missouri and Ohio rivers, and drains the entire region from the Appalachians to the Rockies.

Mount Rainier — Great Plains — The Great Lakes — Niagara Falls

Missouri River — Ohio River — Mississippi River — Mississippi Delta

Map key

Population
- ■ above 5 million
- ◼ 1 million to 5 million
- ◉ 500,000 to 1 million
- ◎ 100,000 to 500,000
- ⊕ 50,000 to 100,000
- ○ 10,000 to 50,000
- ∘ below 10,000

Elevation
- 4000m / 13,124ft
- 3000m / 9843ft
- 2000m / 6562ft
- 1000m / 3281ft
- 500m / 1640ft
- 250m / 820ft
- 100m / 328ft
- sea level

Using the land and sea

Over half of the USA's land area is utilized for agriculture, typified by the large cereal farms and cattle ranches of the Great Plains and Midwest prairie regions. Although wheat and corn are still primary crops, a diverse range of fruits and vegetables are grown in the fertile areas, particularly near the east and west coasts. Despite the abundance of cultivable land, inadequate soil management has resulted in a third of the topsoil being lost through wind and water erosion.

▶ **Fakahatchee Strand is** *part of the extensive sub-tropical swamps in the Florida Everglades. The swamps support a wide variety of animal life, including many rare birds, fish, alligators and crocodiles.*

Land use and agricultural distribution

- 🐄 cattle
- 🐖 pigs
- 🦃 poultry
- citrus fruits
- cotton
- fishing
- fruit
- corn (maize)
- peanuts
- shellfish
- soya beans
- timber
- tobacco
- wheat
- ■ capital cities
- • major towns
- pasture
- cropland
- forest
- wetland
- desert
- mountain region

The urban/rural population divide

urban 76% — rural 24%

0 10 20 30 40 50 60 70 80 90 100

Population density	Total land area
98 people per sq mile (38 people per sq km)	2,959,045 sq miles (7,663,631 sq km)

◀ *Farming on the* Great Plains and in the Midwest is characterized by large-scale, mechanized wheat farms.

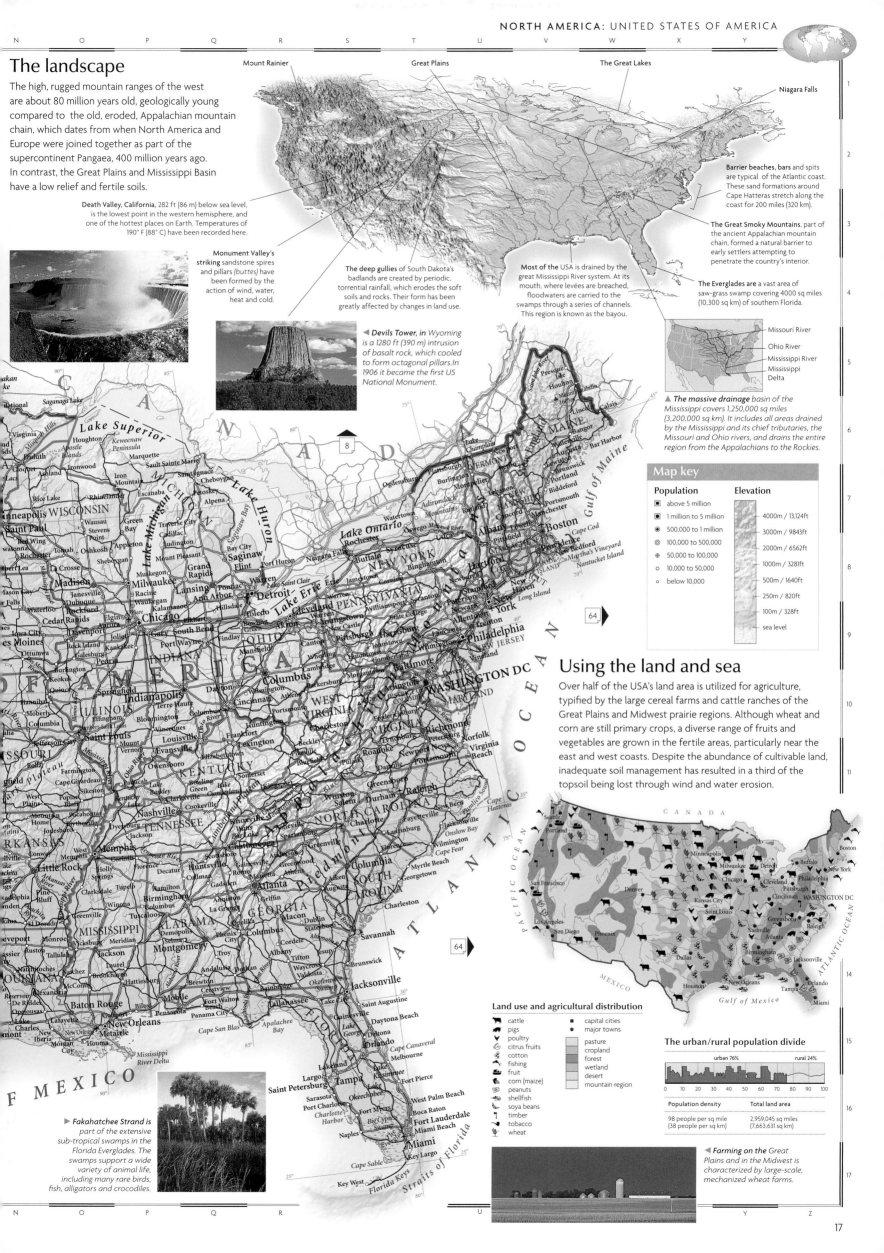

A B C D E F G H I J K L M

USA: NORTHEASTERN STATES

Connecticut, Maine, Massachusetts, New Hampshire, New Jersey,
New York, Pennsylvania, Rhode Island, Vermont

The indented coast and vast woodlands of the northeastern states were the original core area for European expansion. The rustic character of New England prevails after 400 years, while the great cities of the Atlantic seaboard have formed an almost continuous urban region. Over 20 million immigrants entered New York from 1855 to 1924 and the northeast became the industrial centre of the USA. After the decline of mining and heavy manufacturing, economic dynamism has been restored with the growth of hi-tech and service industries.

▲ *Chelsea in Vermont,* surrounded by trees in their fall foliage. Tourism and agriculture dominate the economy of this self-consciously rural state, where no town exceeds 40,000 people.

Map key

Population
- ■ above 5 million
- ▣ 1 million to 5 million
- ◉ 500,000 to 1 million
- ⊚ 100,000 to 500,000
- ⊕ 50,000 to 100,000
- ○ 10,000 to 50,000
- ∘ below 10,000

Elevation
- 1000m / 3281ft
- 500m / 1640ft
- 250m / 820ft
- 100m / 328ft
- sea level

The transport network

340,090 miles (544,144 km)	4813 miles (7700 km)
12,872 miles (20,592 km)	2108 miles (3389 km)

New York's commercial success is tied historically to its transport connections. The Erie Canal, completed in 1825, opened up the Great Lakes and the interior to New York's markets and carried a stream of immigrants into the Midwest.

Transport and industry

The principal seaboard cities grew up on trade and manufacturing. They are now global centres of commerce and corporate administration, dominating the regional economy. Research and development facilities support an expanding electronics and communications sector throughout the region. Pharmaceutical and chemical industries are important in New Jersey and Pennsylvania.

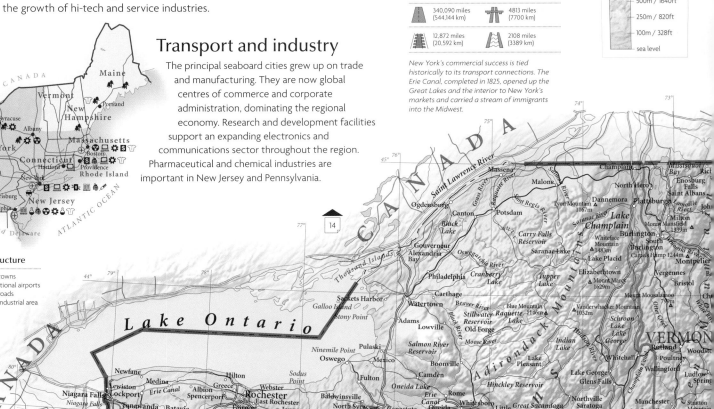

Major industry and infrastructure

- ♠ chemicals
- coal
- defence
- ⚡ electronics
- ✿ engineering
- finance
- ▢ hi-tech industry
- ⚙ iron & steel
- pharmaceuticals
- 🖨 printing & publishing
- research & development
- ▽ textiles
- ♣ timber processing

- ● major towns
- ✈ international airports
- — major roads
- ▨ major industrial area

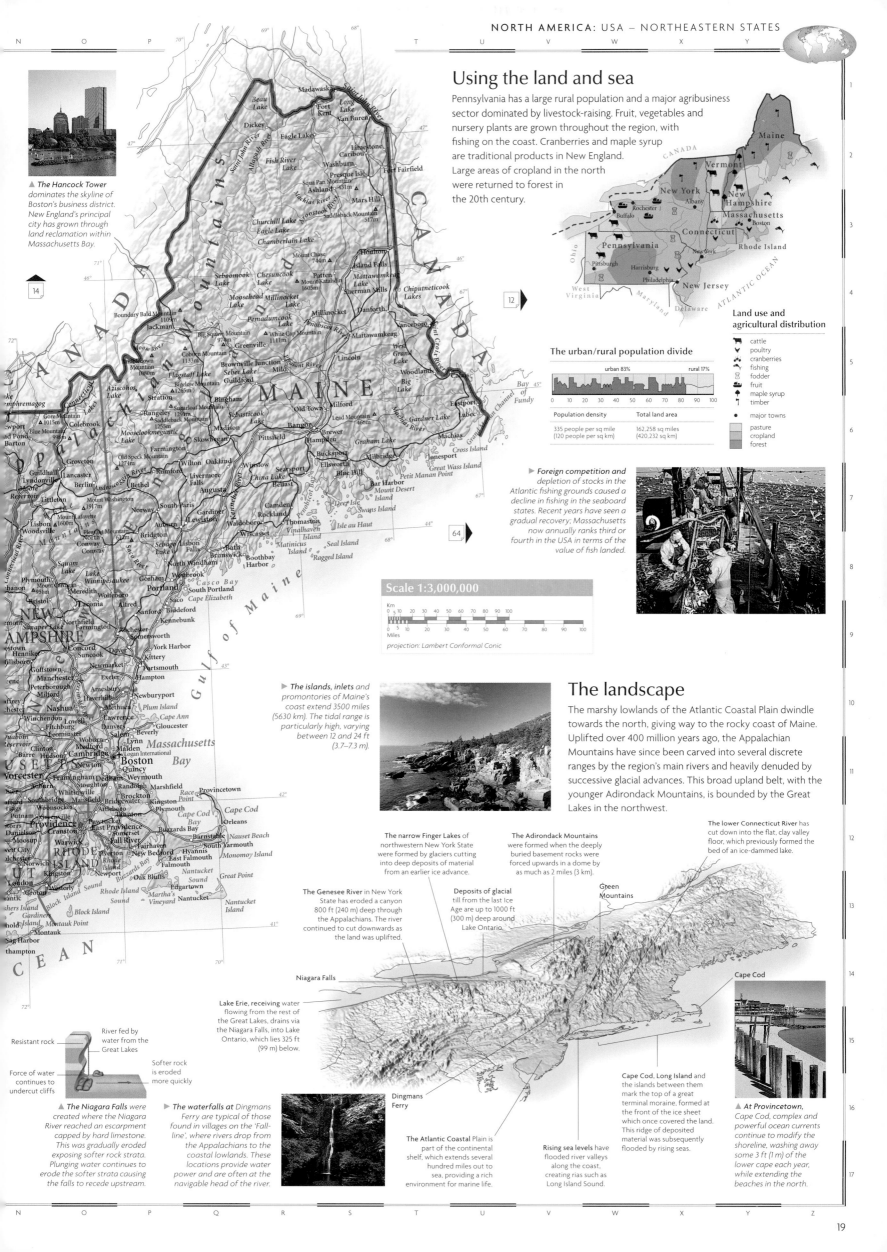

▲ **The Hancock Tower** *dominates the skyline of Boston's business district. New England's principal city has grown through land reclamation within Massachusetts Bay.*

Using the land and sea

Pennsylvania has a large rural population and a major agribusiness sector dominated by livestock-raising. Fruit, vegetables and nursery plants are grown throughout the region, with fishing on the coast. Cranberries and maple syrup are traditional products in New England. Large areas of cropland in the north were returned to forest in the 20th century.

The urban/rural population divide

urban 83%   rural 17%

0   10   20   30   40   50   60   70   80   90   100

Population density	Total land area
335 people per sq mile (120 people per sq km)	162,258 sq miles (420,232 sq km)

Land use and agricultural distribution

- cattle
- poultry
- cranberries
- fishing
- fodder
- fruit
- maple syrup
- timber
- • major towns
- pasture
- cropland
- forest

▶ *Foreign competition and depletion of stocks in the Atlantic fishing grounds caused a decline in fishing in the seaboard states. Recent years have seen a gradual recovery; Massachusetts now annually ranks third or fourth in the USA in terms of the value of fish landed.*

Scale 1:3,000,000

Km
0 5 10   20   30   40   50   60   70   80   90   100

0 5 10   20   30   40   50   60   70   80   90   100
Miles

projection: Lambert Conformal Conic

▶ *The islands, inlets and promontories of Maine's coast extend 3500 miles (5630 km). The tidal range is particularly high, varying between 12 and 24 ft (3.7–7.3 m).*

The landscape

The marshy lowlands of the Atlantic Coastal Plain dwindle towards the north, giving way to the rocky coast of Maine. Uplifted over 400 million years ago, the Appalachian Mountains have since been carved into several discrete ranges by the region's main rivers and heavily denuded by successive glacial advances. This broad upland belt, with the younger Adirondack Mountains, is bounded by the Great Lakes in the northwest.

The lower Connecticut River has cut down into the flat, clay valley floor, which previously formed the bed of an ice-dammed lake.

The narrow Finger Lakes of northwestern New York State were formed by glaciers cutting into deep deposits of material from an earlier ice advance.

The Adirondack Mountains were formed when the deeply buried basement rocks were forced upwards in a dome by as much as 2 miles (3 km).

Green Mountains

The Genesee River in New York State has eroded a canyon 800 ft (240 m) deep through the Appalachians. The river continued to cut downwards as the land was uplifted.

Deposits of glacial till from the last Ice Age are up to 1000 ft (300 m) deep around Lake Ontario.

Niagara Falls

Cape Cod

Lake Erie, receiving water flowing from the rest of the Great Lakes, drains via the Niagara Falls, into Lake Ontario, which lies 325 ft (99 m) below.

Dingmans Ferry

Cape Cod, Long Island and the islands between them mark the top of a great terminal moraine, formed at the front of the ice sheet which once covered the land. This ridge of deposited material was subsequently flooded by rising seas.

Resistant rock

River fed by water from the Great Lakes

Softer rock is eroded more quickly

Force of water continues to undercut cliffs

▲ **The Niagara Falls** *were created where the Niagara River reached an escarpment capped by hard limestone. This was gradually eroded exposing softer rock strata. Plunging water continues to erode the softer strata causing the falls to recede upstream.*

▶ *The waterfalls at Dingmans Ferry are typical of those found in villages on the 'Fall-line', where rivers drop from the Appalachians to the coastal lowlands. These locations provide water power and are often at the navigable head of the river.*

The Atlantic Coastal Plain is part of the continental shelf, which extends several hundred miles out to sea, providing a rich environment for marine life.

Rising sea levels have flooded river valleys along the coast, creating rias such as Long Island Sound.

▲ **At Provincetown,** *Cape Cod, complex and powerful ocean currents continue to modify the shoreline, washing away some 3 ft (1 m) of the lower cape each year, while extending the beaches in the north.*

USA: MID-EASTERN STATES

Delaware, District of Columbia, Kentucky, Maryland, North Carolina, South Carolina, Tennessee, Virginia, West Virginia

Key events in the history of the USA took place in this diverse region, which became the front line in the Civil War of 1861–65 between North and South. Strong regional contrasts exist between the fertile coastal plains, the isolated upcountry of the Appalachian Mountains and the cotton-growing areas of the Mississippi lowlands to the west. Whilst coal mining, a traditional industry in the Appalachians, has declined in recent years leaving much rural poverty, service industries elsewhere have increased, especially in the US federal capital, Washington DC.

Map key

Population

- 500,000 to 1 million
- 100,000 to 500,000
- 50,000 to 100,000
- 10,000 to 50,000
- below 10,000

Elevation

- 6000m / 19,686ft
- 4000m / 13,124ft
- 3000m / 9843ft
- 2000m / 6562ft
- 1000m / 3281ft
- 500m / 1640ft
- 250m / 820ft
- 100m / 328ft
- sea level

Scale 1:3,250,000

Km 0 5 10 20 30 40 50 60 70 80
Miles 0 5 10 20 30 40 50 60 70 80

projection: Lambert Conformal Conic

▲ *The Bluegrass region* of Kentucky centres on the town of Lexington. This exceptionally fertile rolling plain is well known for its thoroughbred horse-breeding ranches.

Transport and industry

In the urbanized northeast, manufacturing remains important, alongside a burgeoning service sector. North Carolina is a major centre for industrial research and development. Traditional industries include Tennessee whiskey, and textiles in South Carolina. The decline of open-cast coal mining in the Appalachians has been hastened by environmental controls, although adventure-tourism is a flourishing new industry.

Major industry and infrastructure

- adventure-tourism
- car manufacture
- coal
- electronics
- engineering
- finance
- food processing
- hi-tech industry
- mining
- research & development
- textiles
- capital cities
- major towns
- international airports
- major roads
- major industrial areas

The transport network

452,218 miles (723,548 km)	5737 miles (8267 km)
18,336 miles (29,503 km)	4404 miles (7081 km)

Tennessee's rivers are part of an important inland bulk-transport network. Memphis is connected with New Orleans in the south, and with cities as distant as Minneapolis, Sioux City, Chicago and Pittsburgh, via the Mississippi and its tributaries.

The landscape

The eastern tributaries of the Mississippi drain the interior lowlands. The Cumberland Plateau and the parallel ranges of the Appalachians have been successively uplifted and eroded over time, with the eastern side reduced to a series of foothills known as the Piedmont. The broad coastal plain gradually falls away into salt marshes, lagoons and offshore bars, broken by flooded estuaries along the shores of the Atlantic.

Natural Bridge in eastern Kentucky is an arch 78 ft (26 m) long and 65 ft (20 m) high. It has been shaped from resistant sandstone by gradual weathering processes, which removed the softer rock lying underneath.

The Allegheny Mountains form the northwestern edge of the Appalachian mountain chain. Continuous folding has formed rich seams of bituminous coal.

◀ *Farmland on the* eastern shores of Chesapeake Bay is sustained by artificial drainage. The area also provides refuge for a variety of waterfowl.

Appalachian Mountains

The many inlets of Chesapeake Bay are the flooded tributaries of the main river valley, which have been inundated by rising sea levels.

The Mammoth Cave is part of an extensive cave system in the limestone region of southwestern Kentucky. It stretches for over 300 miles (485 km) on five different levels and contains three rivers and three lakes.

Salt marshes such as Great Dismal Swamp, develop where the coast is sheltered. Vast areas of such marshland have been reclaimed for farmland and settlement.

The Mississippi River and its tributary the Ohio River form the western border of the region.

Cape Hatteras is the easternmost point of an offshore barrier island; a wave-deposited sand-bar which has become permanent, establishing its own vegetation.

Barrier islands

Tidal inlet

Barrier island

These intertidal mudflats become submerged at high tide

The Cumberland Plateau is the most southwesterly part of the Appalachians. Big Black Mountain at 4180 ft (1274 m) is the highest point in the range.

The Blue Ridge mountains are a steep ridge, culminating in Mount Mitchell, the highest point in the Appalachians, at 6684 ft (2037 m).

▲ *Barrier islands are* common along the coasts of North and South Carolina. As sea levels rise, wave action builds up ridges of sand and pebbles parallel to the coast, separated by lagoons or intertidal mudflats, which are flooded at high tide.

◀ *The Great Smoky Mountains* form the western escarpment of the Appalachians. The region is heavily forested, with over 130 species of tree.

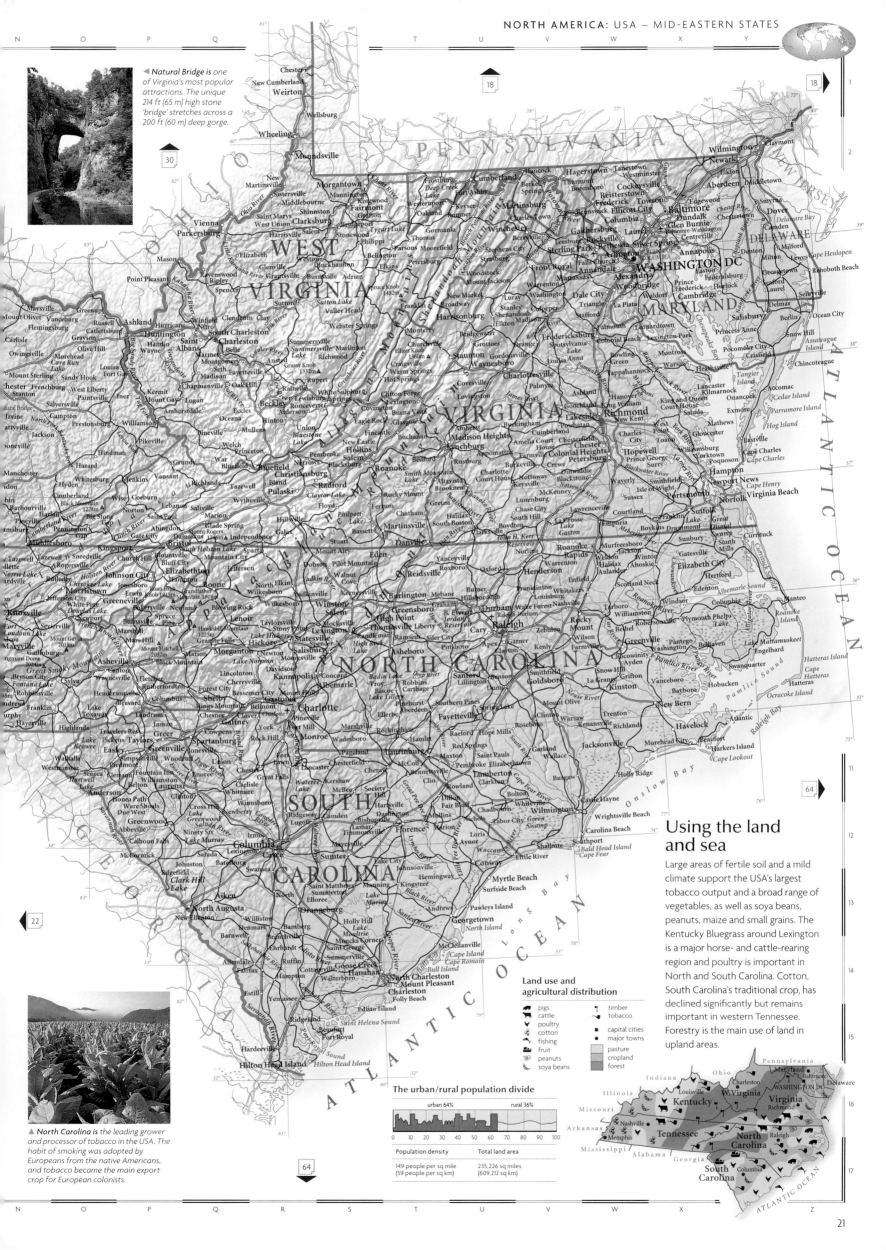

◀ *Natural Bridge is* one of Virginia's most popular attractions. The unique 214 ft (65 m) high stone 'bridge' stretches across a 200 ft (60 m) deep gorge.

Using the land and sea

Large areas of fertile soil and a mild climate support the USA's largest tobacco output and a broad range of vegetables, as well as soya beans, peanuts, maize and small grains. The Kentucky Bluegrass around Lexington is a major horse- and cattle-rearing region and poultry is important in North and South Carolina. Cotton, South Carolina's traditional crop, has declined significantly but remains important in western Tennessee. Forestry is the main use of land in upland areas.

Land use and agricultural distribution

pigs	timber
cattle	tobacco
poultry	capital cities
cotton	major towns
fishing	pasture
fruit	cropland
peanuts	forest
soya beans	

The urban/rural population divide

urban 64% rural 36%

0 10 20 30 40 50 60 70 80 90 100

Population density	Total land area
149 people per sq mile (59 people per sq km)	235,226 sq miles (609,212 sq km)

▲ *North Carolina is* the leading grower and processor of tobacco in the USA. The habit of smoking was adopted by Europeans from the native Americans, and tobacco became the main export crop for European colonists.

USA: SOUTHERN STATES

Alabama, Florida, Georgia, Louisiana, Mississippi

The South has maintained a separate identity and outlook throughout the history of the USA. Defeat in the American Civil War (1861–65) brought chronic poverty to the Confederate states, while the subsequent liberation of four million black slaves began a struggle not resolved until the 1960s, when the Civil Rights movement achieved an end to legal racial segregation. Since then many parts of the region have experienced rapid change: tourism and retirement communities, together with agriculture, have fuelled growth in Florida whilst defence-related industries have boosted the growth of cities such as Miami and Atlanta. Despite these changes, many people retain a strong attachment to their history: in Louisiana, French is still spoken in Cajun communities near the coast.

Transport and industry

Florida's tourist trade is only part of a flourishing service sector, which has swelled the principal cities of the south. Petroleum and mineral extraction has made the Gulf coast a major industrial region. Traditional textile production remains important in Georgia, while advanced new industries have grown from the Space Program.

The transport network

441,625 miles (706,600 km)	
5116 miles (8186 km)	
16,597 miles (26,555 km)	
6179 miles (9942 km)	

Atlanta's Hartsfield International airport is one of the busiest in the world. A dramatic rise in the use of regional air transport has helped to integrate the major cities of the southern states.

◄ The French Quarter is the traditional cultural centre of New Orleans. The city, extensively damaged by Hurricane Katrina in 2005, once thrived on the cotton trade but now relies mainly on tourism and on oil from the Gulf of Mexico.

Major industry and infrastructure

aerospace	oil
car manufacture	textiles
chemicals	tourism
coal	major towns
defence	international airports
electronics	major roads
engineering	major industrial areas
food processing	

▲ The cypress swamps of the Mississippi Delta form in the backswamps behind the levées of the river and in the multitude of subsiding delta basins.

The landscape

The Blue Ridge mountains in the north are skirted by the gentle hills of the Piedmont, whose rivers drain south on to the great flat expanse of the coastal plain. Sandy barrier beaches and islands dominate the sea shore, tracing round the swampy limestone arm of Florida. In the west, the Mississippi meanders towards its delta, crossing the thickly mantled alluvial plain of the interior lowlands.

The Yazoo River flows parallel to the Mississippi through a common flood plain. The confluence of the rivers is deferred downstream because flood deposition has built the Mississippi channel up above the level of the Yazoo.

Cathedral Caverns near Huntsville in Alabama is a system of vast limestone caves, with a main opening 1000 ft (300 m) high and 150 ft (50 m) wide.

At De Soto Falls, Alabama, the Little River descends into the deepest canyon east of the Mississippi, with sheer cliff walls up to 700 ft (230 m) high.

Brasstown Bald in the Blue Ridge mountains of Georgia is the region's highest point, at 4784 ft (1458 m).

▲ In Providence Canyon, Georgia, the Chattahoochee River has cut straight down through the sandy bedrock, to leave sheer rock faces and pinnacles, which have been smoothed by subsequent weathering.

The Mississippi is the world's third longest river and moves over 1000 million tonnes of sediment a year, creating deep alluvial plains. Flooding is a constant threat in lowland areas.

Piedmont

Sand bars, deposited by waves breaking offshore, form barrier beaches along much of the coastline, creating sheltered lagoons and salt marshes behind them.

Mississippi Delta

Delta lobe

The delta of the Mississippi over 5000 years ago

Present-day delta

Atchafalaya Bay

Lake Okeechobee is actually a shallow, slow-moving river, 150 miles (240 km) long and 50 miles (80 km) wide.

▲ Over the last 5000 years the lower course of the Mississippi has moved back and forth over great distances. These changes, caused by varying sediment loads and human modification, have resulted in a 'bird's foot' delta with several lobes, each reflecting the river's different historic position.

Across Florida the coastal plain is mostly less than 75 ft (25 m) above sea level. The land is underlain by limestone, pitted with hollows which have been filled by over 10,000 lakes.

The Everglades lie in a limestone hollow formed over two million years ago, which has gradually become in-filled with swamp deposits.

Florida Keys

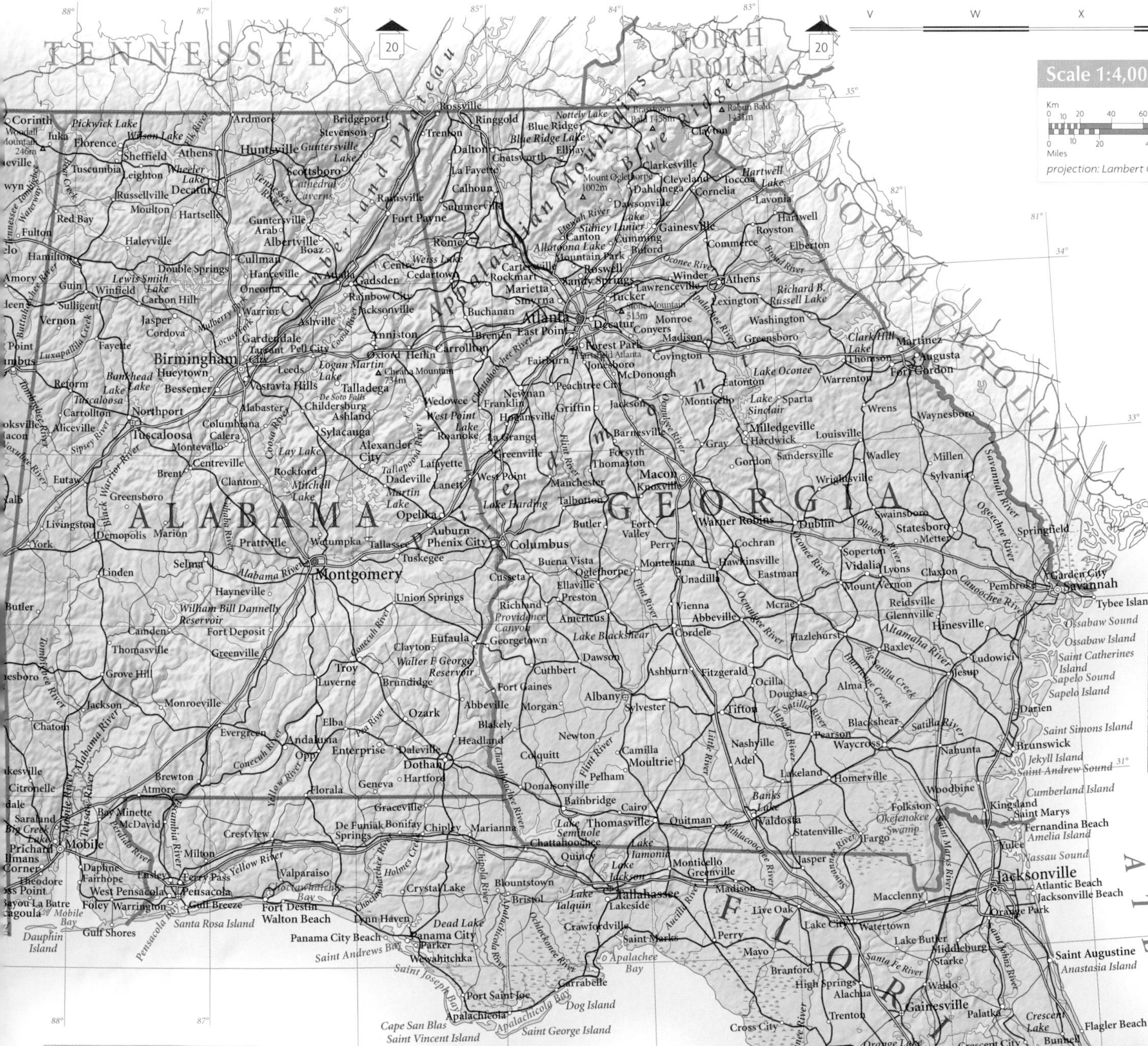

Scale 1:4,000,000

Km
0 20 40 60 80 100
Miles
0 20 40 60 80 100

projection: Lambert Conformal Conic

Map key

Population

- ⊙ 500,000 to 1 million
- ⊚ 100,000 to 500,000
- ⊕ 50,000 to 100,000
- ○ 10,000 to 50,000
- ∘ below 10,000

Elevation

- 4000m / 13,124ft
- 3000m / 9843ft
- 2000m / 6562ft
- 1000m / 3281ft
- 500m / 1640ft
- 250m / 820ft
- 100m / 328ft
- sea level

▲ *Mangrove swamps and islets merge across Whitewater Bay, in the Everglades National Park. Alligators, crocodiles, endangered aquatic mammals such as manatees, and a great variety of birds inhabit the subtropical sanctuary.*

◄ *New Orleans was devastated by Hurricane Katrina in August 2005. Around 1200 lives were lost across the region. Florida and the Gulf coast are prone to hurricanes every autumn.*

Using the land and sea

In recent years a wide variety of cash crops has been grown in lands once dominated by cotton. The semi-tropical Florida climate has made it a world leader in the growing of citrus fruit. Georgia has a similar reputation for peanuts; elsewhere soya beans, sugar cane, poultry and cattle are important. Fishing takes place in Atlantic and Gulf waters, with shellfishing in the shallow Louisiana 'bayou'.

The urban/rural population divide

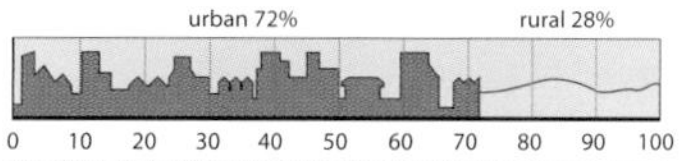

urban 72%   rural 28%

0 10 20 30 40 50 60 70 80 90 100

Population density	Total land area
149 people per sq mile (57 people per sq km)	253,046 sq miles (655,364 sq km)

▲ *Cotton production, once the economic mainstay of the 'deep south', has fallen by more than 50% since 1900. Soil erosion, pests and new farming techniques have shifted the cotton belt west towards Texas and California.*

Land use and agricultural distribution

- 🐄 cattle
- 🐖 pigs
- 🐓 poultry
- citrus
- cotton
- fishing
- peanuts
- shellfish
- soya beans
- sugar cane
- timber
- major towns

- pasture
- cropland
- forest
- wetland

▶ *Duck Key is one of the chain of limestone and coral islands which form the Florida Keys. The Overseas Highway, completed in 1938, extends 100 miles (160 km) from the mainland to Key West along a series of causeways and bridges.*

23

USA: TEXAS

First explored by Spaniards moving north from Mexico in search of gold, Texas was controlled by Spain and then Mexico, before becoming an independent republic in 1836, and joining the Union of States in 1845. During the 19th century, many of the migrants who came to Texas raised cattle on the abundant land; in the 20th century, they were joined by prospectors attracted by the promise of oil riches. Today, although natural resources, especially oil, still form the basis of its wealth, the diversified Texan economy includes thriving hi-tech and finance industries. The major urban centres, home to 80% of the population, lie in the south and east, and include Houston, the 'oil-city', and Dallas–Fort Worth. Hispanic influences remain strong, especially in the south and west.

▲ **Dallas was founded** in 1841 as a prairie trading post and its development was stimulated by the arrival of railroads. Cotton and then oil funded the town's early growth. Today, the modern, high-rise skyline of Dallas reflects the city's position as a leading centre of banking, insurance and the petroleum industry in the southwest.

Using the land

Cotton production and livestock-raising, particularly cattle, dominate farming, although crop failures and the demands of local markets have led to some diversification. Following the introduction of modern farming techniques, cotton production spread out from the east to the plains of western Texas. Cattle ranches are widespread, while sheep and goats are raised on the dry Edwards Plateau.

Land use and agricultural distribution

- cattle
- goats
- sheep
- cereals
- cotton
- • major towns

- pasture
- cropland
- forest
- barren

The urban/rural population divide

urban 80%   rural 20%

0 10 20 30 40 50 60 70 80 90 100

Population density	Total land area
84 people per sq mile (33 people per sq km)	261,797 sq miles (678,028 sq km)

▲ **The huge cattle** ranches of Texas developed during the 19th century when land was plentiful and could be acquired cheaply. Today, more cattle and sheep are raised in Texas than in any other state.

The landscape

Texas is made up of a series of massive steps descending from the mountains and high plains of the west and northwest to the coastal lowlands in the southeast. Many of the state's borders are delineated by water. The Rio Grande flows from the Rocky Mountains to the Gulf of Mexico, marking the border with Mexico.

▲ **Cap Rock Escarpment** juts out from the plains, running 200 miles (320 km) from north to south. Its height varies from 300 ft (90 m) rising to sheer cliffs up to 1000 ft (300 m).

The Red River flows for 1300 miles (2090 km), marking most of the northern border of Texas. A dam and reservoir along its course provide vital irrigation and hydro-electric power to the surrounding area.

The Llano Estacado or Staked Plain in northern Texas is known for its harsh environment. In the north, freezing winds carrying ice and snow sweep down from the Rocky Mountains, and to the south, sandstorms frequently blow up, scouring anything in their paths. Flash floods, in the wide, flat river beds that remain dry for most of the year, are another hazard.

The Guadalupe Mountains lie in the southern Rocky Mountains. They incorporate Guadalupe Peak, the highest in Texas, rising 8749 ft (2667 m).

The Rio Grande flows from the Rocky Mountains through semi-arid land, supporting sparse vegetation. The river actually shrinks along its course, losing more water through evaporation and seepage than it gains from its tributaries and rainfall.

Big Bend National Park

Edwards Plateau is a limestone outcrop. It is part of the Great Plains, bounded to the southeast by the Balcones Escarpment, which marks the southerly limit of the plains.

◄ **Flowing through** 1500 ft (450 m) high gorges, the shallow, muddy Rio Grande makes a 90° bend, which marks the southern border of Big Bend National Park, giving it its name. The area is a mixture of forested mountains, deserts and canyons.

Sabine River

Extensive forests of pine and cypress grow in the eastern corner of the coastal lowlands where the average rainfall is 45 inches (1145 mm) a year. This is higher than the rest of the state and over twice the average in the west.

In the coastal lowlands of southeastern Texas the Earth's crust is warping, causing the land to subside and allowing the sea to invade. Around Galveston, the rate of downward tilting is 6 inches (15 cm) per year. Erosion of the coast is also exacerbated by hurricanes.

Oil deposits

Oil accumulates beneath impermeable cap rock

Oil trapped by fault

Oil deposits migrate through reservoir rocks such as shale

Impermeable rock strata

Salt dome

▲ **Oil deposits are** found beneath much of Texas. They collect as oil migrates upwards through porous layers of rock until it is trapped, either by a cap of rock above a salt dome, or by a fault line which exposes impermeable rock through which the oil cannot rise.

Laguna Madre in southern Texas has been almost completely cut off from the sea by Padre Island. This sand bank was created by wave action, carrying and depositing material along the coast. The process is known as longshore drift.

Padre Island

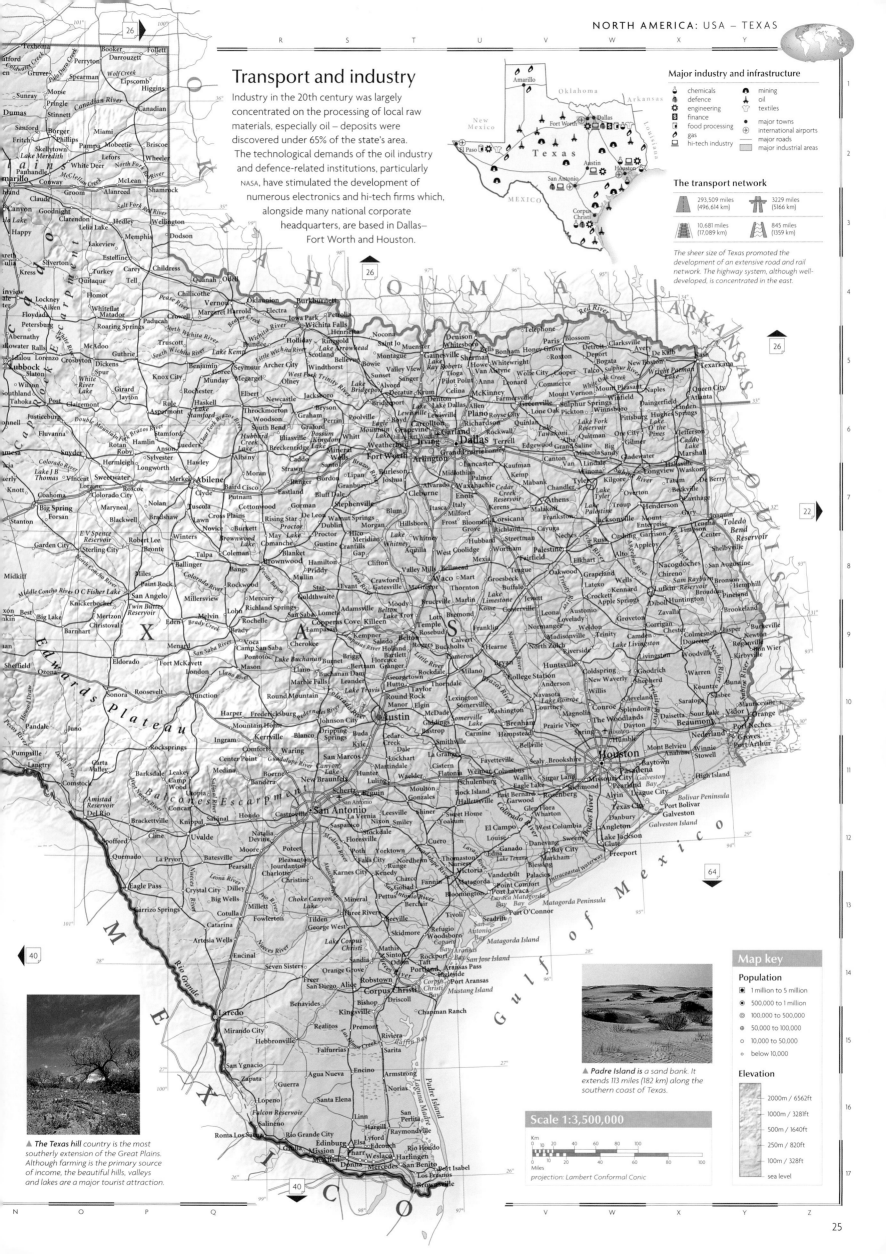

Transport and industry

Industry in the 20th century was largely concentrated on the processing of local raw materials, especially oil – deposits were discovered under 65% of the state's area. The technological demands of the oil industry and defence-related institutions, particularly NASA, have stimulated the development of numerous electronics and hi-tech firms which, alongside many national corporate headquarters, are based in Dallas–Fort Worth and Houston.

Major industry and infrastructure

- chemicals
- defence
- engineering
- finance
- food processing
- gas
- hi-tech industry
- mining
- oil
- textiles
- major towns
- international airports
- major roads
- major industrial areas

The transport network

293,509 miles (496,614 km)	3229 miles (5166 km)
10,681 miles (17,089 km)	845 miles (1359 km)

The sheer size of Texas promoted the development of an extensive road and rail network. The highway system, although well-developed, is concentrated in the east.

▲ The Texas hill country is the most southerly extension of the Great Plains. Although farming is the primary source of income, the beautiful hills, valleys and lakes are a major tourist attraction.

▲ Padre Island is a sand bank. It extends 113 miles (182 km) along the southern coast of Texas.

Map key

Population

- ▪ 1 million to 5 million
- ◉ 500,000 to 1 million
- ◍ 100,000 to 500,000
- ◉ 50,000 to 100,000
- ○ 10,000 to 50,000
- ○ below 10,000

Elevation

- 2000m / 6562ft
- 1000m / 3281ft
- 500m / 1640ft
- 250m / 820ft
- 100m / 328ft
- sea level

Scale 1:3,500,000

projection: Lambert Conformal Conic

USA: SOUTH MIDWESTERN STATES

Arkansas, Kansas, Missouri, Oklahoma

The expansion of the USA focused on this region in the mid-19th century. Settlers spread from the confluence of the Missouri and Mississippi rivers up onto the Great Plains. This treeless expanse, which early explorers had called the 'Great American Desert', was turned into one of the world's richest agricultural regions; but periodic droughts, coupled with over-intensive farming, led to the 'Dustbowl' soil erosion crisis of the 1930s, the abandonment of many farms, and a mass exodus to the west coast. The land has since recovered, although the mechanization of agriculture has led to a decline in the rural population. In recent years, suburban residential development has spread rapidly across the wooded Ozark Plateau in the east of the region.

Transport and industry

The processing of agricultural products, such as brewing and meat packing, has been traditionally important in these states. In Kansas and Oklahoma, diversified manufacturing now supplements income from fossil fuels; Wichita has become a world centre for aeronautical engineering, an industry which also employs many people in neighbouring Missouri.

Major industry and infrastructure

- ✈ aerospace
- ✿ engineering
- $ finance
- 🗎 food processing
- ⌀ gas
- ⛏ mining
- ⚓ oil
- �car vehicle manufacture
- ● major towns
- ⊕ international airports
- — major roads
- ▨ major industrial areas

▶ Agricultural produce from the plains is moved by barges along the Mississippi. The river now carries a far greater tonnage of freight than any other waterway system in the USA.

The transport network

380,307 miles (608,491 km)	4068 miles (6508 km)
16,185 miles (25,896 km)	1994 miles (3208 km)

The Arkansas River and its tributaries allow access to over half of the USA's navigable inland waterways. A system of locks and dams along the river provides Tulsa in Oklahoma with a navigable water route to the Gulf of Mexico.

The landscape

Most of the region consists of high, treeless plains, which gradually descend east from the Rocky Mountains. Drainage follows this slope, with rivers flowing towards the alluvial lowlands of the Mississippi in the southeast. Between the plains and the lowlands lie various ranges of wooded hills, including the deeply incised Ozark Plateau.

▲ The Mississippi, North America's longest river, is joined by the Missouri, its main tributary, on a flood plain which spreads south to the Gulf of Mexico.

Map key

Population
- ◎ 100,000 to 500,000
- ⊕ 50,000 to 100,000
- ○ 10,000 to 50,000
- ○ below 10,000

Elevation
- 1000m / 3281ft
- 500m / 1640ft
- 250m / 820ft
- 100m / 328ft
- sea level

Collapsed limestone caverns led to the formation of Big Basin in Kansas; a depression 100 ft (33 m) deep and 1 mile (1.6 km) wide.

The Great Salt Plains of northern Oklahoma cover 45 sq mile (116 sq km). The arid, white flats were left by the gradual evaporation of an ancient salt lake.

Underground water reserves

Flint Hills is the region's easternmost major escarpment. Steep, grassy uplands are interspersed with rocky, wooded ravines and outcrops of limestone and chert.

Missouri River

The Ozark Plateau is a wooded, hilly region of rivers and narrow, winding lakes. The Lake of the Ozarks was created by the damming of the Osage River in 1930.

Crowleys Ridge is a long, sandy ridge, rising from the Mississippi flood plain. It was formed over thousands of years by the deposition of sand blown eastwards from the Great Plains.

▼ Lake Ouachita, in Arkansas is one of a number of irregularly-shaped lakes found among the ridges of the Ouachita Mountains.

Scale 1:3,250,000

Km
0 5 10 20 30 40 50 60 70

Miles
0 5 10 20 30 40 50 60 70

projection: Lambert Conformal Conic

▲ The Ogallala Aquifer, beneath the Great Plains, is the largest known source of underground water in the world. There is concern about the rapid depletion of this finite water supply by irrigation schemes.

Extent of the aquifer
Kansas
Oklahoma

WY NE
CO KS MO
NM OK AR
TX

Devil's Den is a dry badland area. The rugged landscape, strewn with large boulders, is the eroded remnant of a spur extending from the Arbuckle mountains to the west.

Red River

Ouachita Mountains

Mississippi River

▲ The landscape of northeast Kansas is interlaced by rivers which have cut broad wooded valleys through the gentle hills. All the rivers in Kansas form part of the massive Missouri/Mississippi drainage basin.

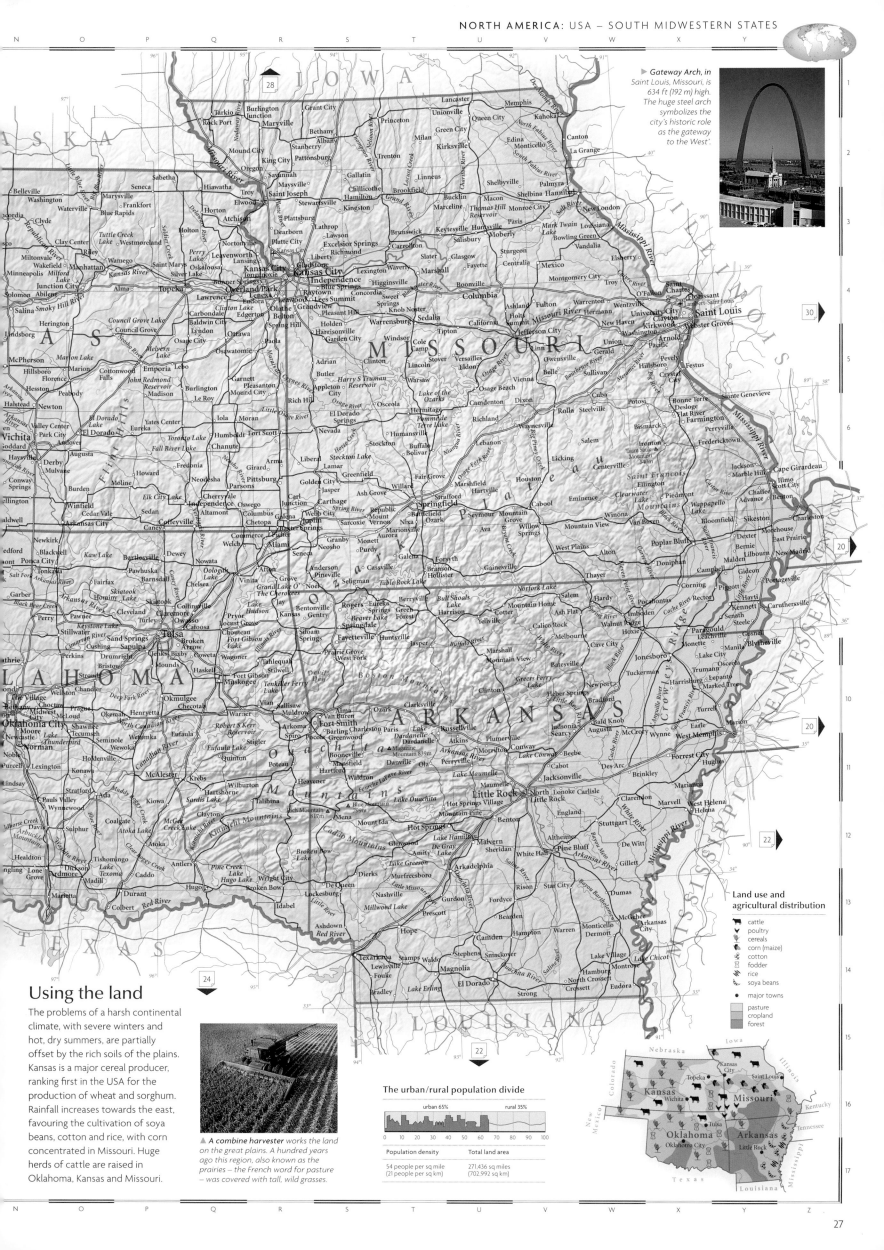

▶ *Gateway Arch, in Saint Louis, Missouri, is 634 ft (192 m) high. The huge steel arch symbolizes the city's historic role as the gateway to the 'West'.*

Using the land

The problems of a harsh continental climate, with severe winters and hot, dry summers, are partially offset by the rich soils of the plains. Kansas is a major cereal producer, ranking first in the USA for the production of wheat and sorghum. Rainfall increases towards the east, favouring the cultivation of soya beans, cotton and rice, with corn concentrated in Missouri. Huge herds of cattle are raised in Oklahoma, Kansas and Missouri.

▲ *A combine harvester works the land on the great plains. A hundred years ago this region, also known as the prairies – the French word for pasture – was covered with tall, wild grasses.*

The urban/rural population divide

urban 65%   rural 35%

0 10 20 30 40 50 60 70 80 90 100

Population density	Total land area
54 people per sq mile (21 people per sq km)	271,436 sq miles (702,992 sq km)

Land use and agricultural distribution

- cattle
- poultry
- cereals
- corn (maize)
- cotton
- fodder
- rice
- soya beans
- • major towns
- pasture
- cropland
- forest

USA: NORTH MIDWESTERN STATES

Iowa, Minnesota, Nebraska, North Dakota, South Dakota

Lying at the very heart of the North American continent, much of this region was acquired from France as part of the Louisiana Purchase in 1803. The area was largely by-passed by the early waves of westward migrants. When Europeans did settle, during the 19th century, they displaced the Native Americans who lived on the plains. The settlers planted arable crops and raised cattle on the immensely fertile prairie land, founding an agrarian tradition which flourishes today. Most of this region remains rural; of the five states, only in Minnesota has there been significant diversification away from agriculture and resource-based industries into the hi-tech and service sectors.

Using the land

The popular image of these states as agricultural is entirely justified; prairies stretch uninterrupted across most of the area. Croplands fall into two regions: the wheat belt of the plains, and the corn belt of the central USA. Cash crops, such as soya beans, are grown to supplement incomes. Livestock, particularly pigs and cattle, are raised throughout this region.

▶ Dark, fertile prairie soils in the southeast provide Minnesota's most productive farmland. Hot, humid summers create a long growing season for corn cultivation.

Land use and agricultural distribution

- cattle
- pigs
- corn (maize)
- soya beans
- wheat
- major towns
- pasture
- cropland
- forest
- wetland

The urban/rural population divide

urban 64%   rural 36%

0 10 20 30 40 50 60 70 80 90 100

Population density	Total land area
31 people per sq mile (12 people per sq km)	357,212 sq miles (925,143 sq km)

Transport and industry

Food processing and the production of farm machinery are supported by the large agricultural sector. Mineral exploitation is also an important activity: gold is mined in the ore-rich Black Hills of South Dakota, and both North Dakota and Nebraska are emerging as major petroleum producers.

▶ Water erosion along the Little Missouri River has carried away sedimentary deposits, creating rugged landscapes known as badlands.

The transport network

504,522 miles (807,235 km)	3422 miles (5475 km)
16,940 miles (27,104 km)	683 miles (1098 km)

Nebraska's central location has made it an important transport artery for east–west traffic. Minnesota's road network radiates out from the hub of the twin cities, Minneapolis–Saint Paul.

Major industry and infrastructure

- coal
- engineering
- electronics
- finance
- food processing
- oil & gas
- mining
- major towns
- international airports
- major roads
- major industrial areas

The landscape

These states straddle the Great Plains and the lowlands of the central USA, with Minnesota lying in a transition zone between the eastern forests and the prairies. The region was shaped by repeated ice advances and retreats, leaving a flat relief, broken only by the numerous lakes and broad river networks which drain the prairies.

Escarpment   Ridge

In permeable strata hollows are formed by small mudslides

Water flowing into gullies erodes back the escarpment

▲ Badlands are formed by stormwater run-off which flows down the impermeable strata of the escarpment and saturates the permeable strata leading to mudslides and the formation of gullies.

North Dakota Badlands

The Minnesota landscape contains many post-glacial features, including its numerous lakes, boulder-strewn hills and mineral-rich deposits.

▲ In the badlands of North and South Dakota, horizontal layers of sandstone have been eroded by rivers, leaving a landscape of narrow gullies, sharp crests and pinnacles.

South Dakota Badlands

Although it escaped the last glaciation, the limestone bedrock of southeastern Minnesota has been eroded by surface and subterranean streams, leaving a network of underground caverns and steepsided valleys.

◀ In northeastern Iowa, the Mississippi and its tributaries have deeply incised the underlying bedrock creating a hilly terrain, with bluffs standing 300 ft (90 m) above the valley.

▲ Chimney Rock is a remnant of an ancient land surface, eroded by the North Platte River. The tip of its spire stands 500 ft (150 m) above the plain.

Missouri River

Mississippi River

Along the shores of Lake Superior in Minnesota, the average number of frost-free days can be as few as 90, and frosts may occur in any month of the year.

USA: GREAT LAKES STATES

Illinois, Indiana, Michigan, Ohio, Wisconsin

The states bordering the Great Lakes developed rapidly in the second half of the 19th century as a result of improvements in communications: rail to the west and waterways to the south and east. Fertile land and good links with growing eastern seaboard cities encouraged the development of agriculture and food processing. Migrants from Europe and other parts of the USA flooded into the region and for much of the 20th century the region's economy boomed. However, in recent years heavy industry has declined, earning the region the unwanted label the 'Rustbelt'.

Transport and industry

The Great Lakes region is the centre of the USA's car industry. Since the early part of the 20th century. its prosperity has been closely linked to the fortunes of automobile manufacturing. Iron and steel production has expanded to meet demand from this industry. In the 1970s, nationwide recession, cheaper foreign competition in the automobile sector, pollution in and around the Great Lakes and the collapse of the meat-packing industry, centred on Chicago, forced these states to diversify their industrial base. New industries have emerged, notably electronics, service and finance industries.

The transport network

540,682 miles (865,091 km)	6550 miles (10,480 km)
24,928 miles (39,884 km)	2330 miles (3748 km)

Few areas of the USA have a comparable transport system. Chicago is a principal transport terminus with a dense network of roads, railways and Interstate freeways radiating from the city.

► Ever since Ransom Olds and Henry Ford started mass-producing automobiles in Detroit early in the 20th century, the city's name has become synonymous with the American automotive industry.

Major industry and infrastructure

🚗	car manufacture	☢	research & development
	coal	▽	textiles
	electronics		
⚙	engineering	●	major towns
S	finance	⊕	international airports
	food processing	—	major roads
	iron & steel		major industrial areas
	oil		

The landscape

Much of this region shows the impact of glaciation which lasted until about 10,000 years ago, and extended as far south as Illinois and Ohio. Although the relief of the region slopes towards the Great Lakes, because the ice sheets blocked northerly drainage, most of the rivers today flow southwards, forming part of the massive Mississippi/Missouri drainage basin.

◄ The dunes near Sleeping Bear Point rise 400 ft (120 m) from the banks of Lake Michigan. They are constantly being resculpted by wind action.

Lake Michigan

Lake Erie is the shallowest of the five Great Lakes. Its average depth is about 62 ft (19 m). Storms sweeping across from Canada erode its shores and cause the silting of its harbours.

The many lakes and marshes of Wisconsin and Michigan are the result of glacial erosion and deposition which occurred during the last Ice Age.

The Appalachian plateau stretches eastward from Ohio. It is dissected by streams flowing west into the Mississippi and Ohio rivers.

Southwestern Wisconsin is known as a 'driftless' area. Unlike most of the region, low hills protected it from erosion by the advancing ice sheet.

Most of the water used in northern Illinois is pumped from underground reservoirs. Due to increased demand, many areas now face a water shortage. Around Joliet, the water table was lowered by more than 700 ft (210 m) over the last century.

Illinois plains

▲ The plains of Illinois are characteristic of drift landscapes, scoured and flattened by glacial erosion and covered with fertile glacial deposits.

Mississippi River

Relic landforms from the last glaciation, such as shallow basins and ridges, cover all but the south of this region. Ridges, known as moraines, up to 300 ft (100 m) high, lie to the south of Lake Michigan.

Ohio River

Unlike the level prairie to the north, southern Indiana is relatively rugged. Limestone in the hills has been dissolved by water, producing features such as sinkholes and underground caves.

Glacial till

Present-day river or stream

Channels caused by outwash from melting glacier

Most recent till deposits

Older till sheet

Bedrock

▲ As a result of successive glacial depositions, the total depth of till along the former southern margin of the Laurentide ice sheet can exceed 1300 ft (400 m).

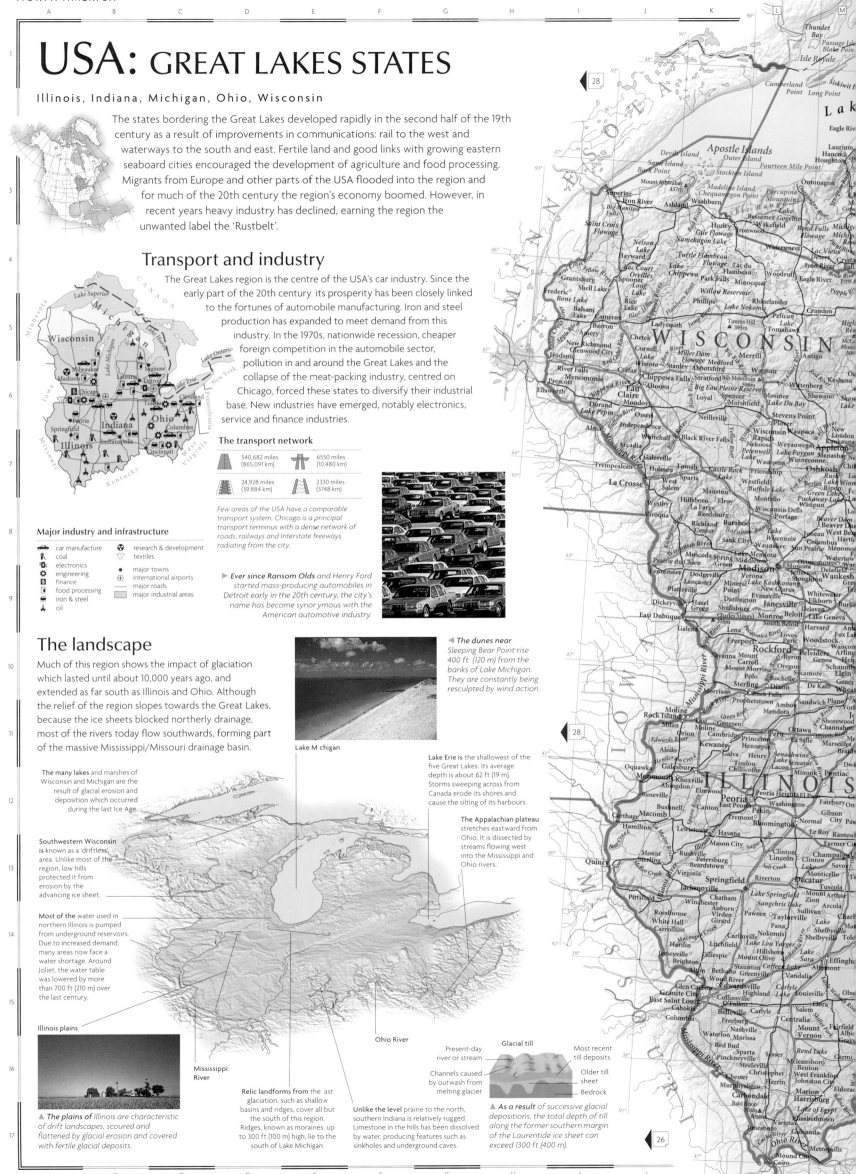

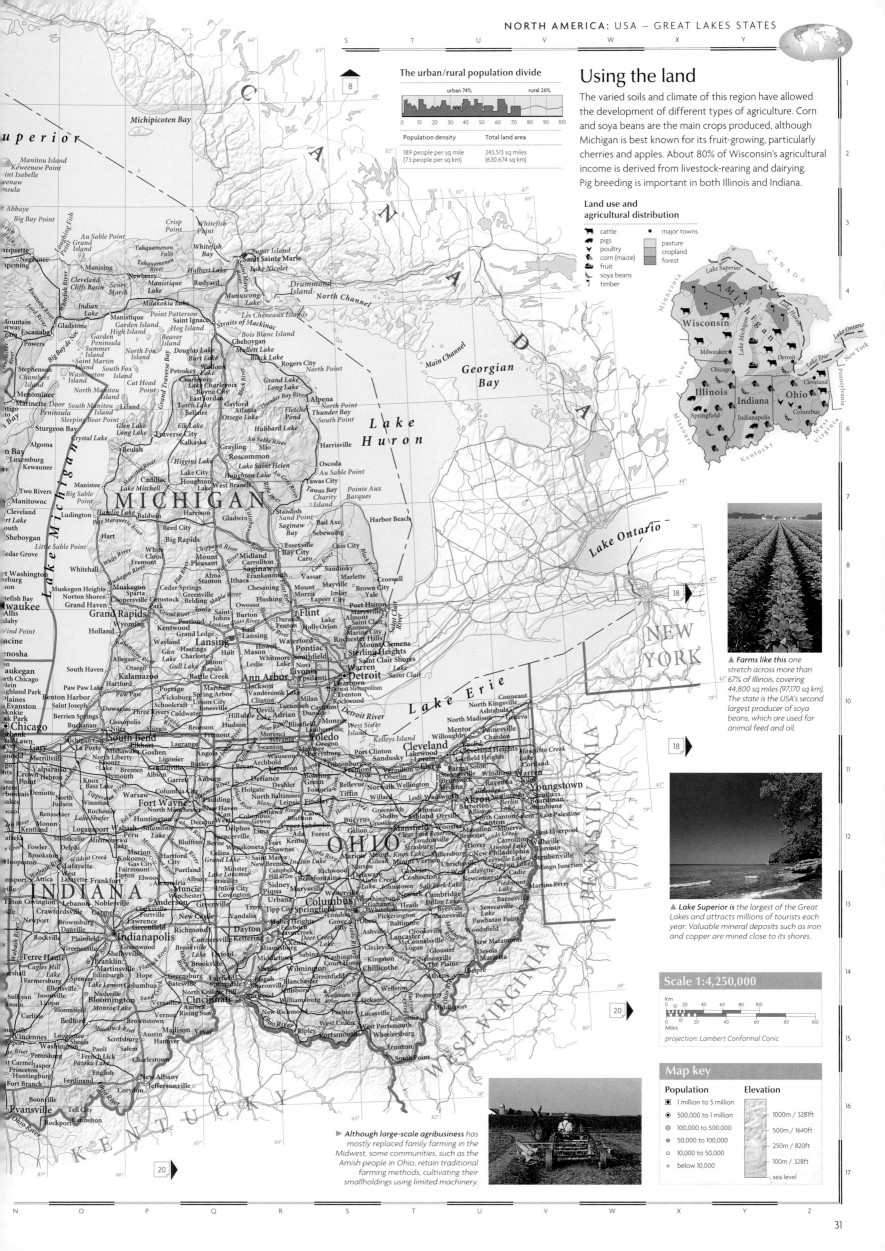

The urban/rural population divide

urban 74%   rural 26%

0 10 20 30 40 50 60 70 80 90 100

Population density	Total land area
189 people per sq mile (73 people per sq km)	243,513 sq miles (630,674 sq km)

Using the land

The varied soils and climate of this region have allowed the development of different types of agriculture. Corn and soya beans are the main crops produced, although Michigan is best known for its fruit-growing, particularly cherries and apples. About 80% of Wisconsin's agricultural income is derived from livestock-rearing and dairying. Pig breeding is important in both Illinois and Indiana.

Land use and agricultural distribution

- cattle
- pigs
- poultry
- corn (maize)
- fruit
- soya beans
- timber
- • major towns
- pasture
- cropland
- forest

▲ *Farms like this one stretch across more than 67% of Illinois, covering 44,800 sq miles (97,170 sq km). The state is the USA's second largest producer of soya beans, which are used for animal feed and oil.*

▲ *Lake Superior is the largest of the Great Lakes and attracts millions of tourists each year. Valuable mineral deposits such as iron and copper are mined close to its shores.*

Scale 1:4,250,000

Km
0 10 20 40 60 80 100

Miles
0 10 20 40 60 80 100

projection: Lambert Conformal Conic

Map key

Population		Elevation	
■ 1 million to 5 million		■	1000m / 3281ft
◉ 500,000 to 1 million		■	500m / 1640ft
◎ 100,000 to 500,000		■	250m / 820ft
⊕ 50,000 to 100,000		■	100m / 328ft
○ 10,000 to 50,000		■	sea level
° below 10,000			

▶ *Although large-scale agribusiness has mostly replaced family farming in the Midwest, some communities, such as the Amish people in Ohio, retain traditional farming methods, cultivating their smallholdings using limited machinery.*

USA: NORTH MOUNTAIN STATES

Idaho, Montana, Oregon, Washington, Wyoming

The remoteness of the northwestern states, coupled with the rugged landscape, ensured that this was one of the last areas settled by Europeans in the 19th century. Fur-trappers and gold-prospectors followed the Snake River westwards as it wound its way through the Rocky Mountains. The states of the northwest have pioneered many conservationist policies, with the USA's first national park opened at Yellowstone in 1872. More recently, the Cascades and Rocky Mountains have become havens for adventure tourism. The mountains still serve to isolate the western seaboard from the rest of the continent. This isolation has encouraged west coast cities to expand their trade links with countries of the Pacific Rim.

Map key

Population	Elevation
◉ 500,000 to 1 million	4000m / 13,124ft
◎ 100,000 to 500,000	3000m / 9843ft
⊕ 50,000 to 100,000	2000m / 6562ft
○ 10,000 to 50,000	1000m / 3281ft
○ below 10,000	500m / 1640ft
	250m / 820ft
	100m / 328ft
	sea level

▲ *The Snake River* has cut down into the basalt of the Columbia Basin to form Hells Canyon, the deepest in the USA, with cliffs up to 7900 ft (2408 m) high.

Using the land

Wheat farming in the east gives way to cattle ranching as rainfall decreases. Irrigated farming in the Snake River valley produces large yields of potatoes and other vegetables. Dairying and fruit-growing take place in the wet western lowlands between the mountain ranges.

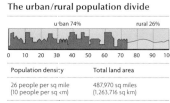

The urban/rural population divide

urban 74%   rural 26%

0 10 20 30 40 50 60 70 80 90 100

Population density	Total land area
26 people per sq mile (10 people per sq cm)	487,970 sq miles (1,263,716 sq km)

Scale 1:4,250,000

Km
0 10 20   40   60   80   100
Miles
0   10   20   40   60   80   100

projection: Lambert Conformal Conic

▶ *Fine-textured, volcanic soils* in the hilly Palouse region of eastern Washington are susceptible to erosion.

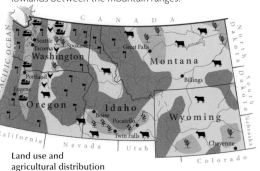

Land use and agricultural distribution

cattle	fruit	• major towns
poultry	potatoes	pasture
cereals	timber	cropland
		forest

Transport and industry

Minerals and timber are extremely important in this region. Uranium, precious metals, copper and coal are all mined, the latter in vast open-cast pits in Wyoming; oil and natural gas are extracted further north. Manufacturing, notably related to the aerospace and electronics industries, is important in western cities.

The transport network

347,857 miles (556,571 km)	
4200 miles (6720 km)	
12,354 miles (19,766 km)	
1108 miles (1782 km)	

The Union Pacific Railroad has been in service across Wyoming since 1867. The route through the Rocky Mountains is now shared with the Interstate 80, a major east–west highway.

Major industry and infrastructure

- adventure tourism
- aerospace
- coal
- chemicals
- electronics
- food processing
- mining
- oil & gas
- timber processing
- major towns
- international airports
- major roads
- major industrial areas

◀ *Seattle lies in* one of Puget Sound's many inlets. The city receives oil and other resources from Alaska, and benefits from expanding trade across the Pacific.

◀ *Crater Lake, Oregon,* is 6 miles (10 km) wide and 1800 ft (600 m) deep. It marks the site of a volcanic cone, which collapsed after an eruption within the last 7000 years.

The landscape

The Rocky Mountains are flanked by lower parallel ranges, which spread onto the Great Plains in the east and surmount the broad lava plateau which extends westwards. The Cascade Range divides the Columbia Basin from the coastlands, where the low areas skirting Puget Sound are broken by the steep, volcanic Olympic Mountains and the wooded hills of the Coast Ranges.

Molten rock cools, forming parallel columns

Surrounding strata eroded away

Molten rock wells up from the Earth's core

▲ *Devil's Tower in Wyoming* is an igneous intrusion, formed below the Earth's surface. Molten rock intruded through cracks in the overlying strata and cooled. Over time, the softer rock layers have been eroded away, leaving only the tower standing.

Puget Sound

Glacial valleys on the seaward side of the Olympic Mountains receive about 142 inches (3600 mm) of rain per year, supporting the only true rainforest of the northern hemisphere.

Mount St Helens erupted in 1980, killing 57 people and devastating a huge area.

Columbia Basin

Grand Coulee and the lesser *coulées* (ravines) were cut by cataclysmic floods, from the release of an ice-dammed lake, at the end of the last Ice Age.

The Continental Divide, or watershed, crosses the Lewis Range. From here, rivers flow east to Hudson Bay, south to the Gulf of Mexico and west to the Pacific Ocean.

▶ *Piney Buttes are the* remnants of an older, higher land surface gradually weathered and eroded into isolated outcrops with flat tops and steep sides.

The Cascades are glacially scoured volcanic mountains, the highest of which is Mount Rainier, a dormant volcano at 14,409 ft (4392 m).

Coast Ranges

Great Plains

Devil's Tower

The plateaux of the Columbia and Snake rivers represent one of the world's largest accumulations of lava. Over 5 million years ago, successive flows of molten basalt buried the existing land surface by up to 450 ft (150 m).

The contorted rock shapes at 'Craters of the Moon' National Monument in Idaho were left 2000 years ago by the sporadic upwelling of viscous lava from fissures in the basalt plateau.

Rocky Mountains

▲ *Water from the* hot springs in Yellowstone National Park deposits minerals as it cools in rock pools. Long periods of deposition have created these rock terraces.

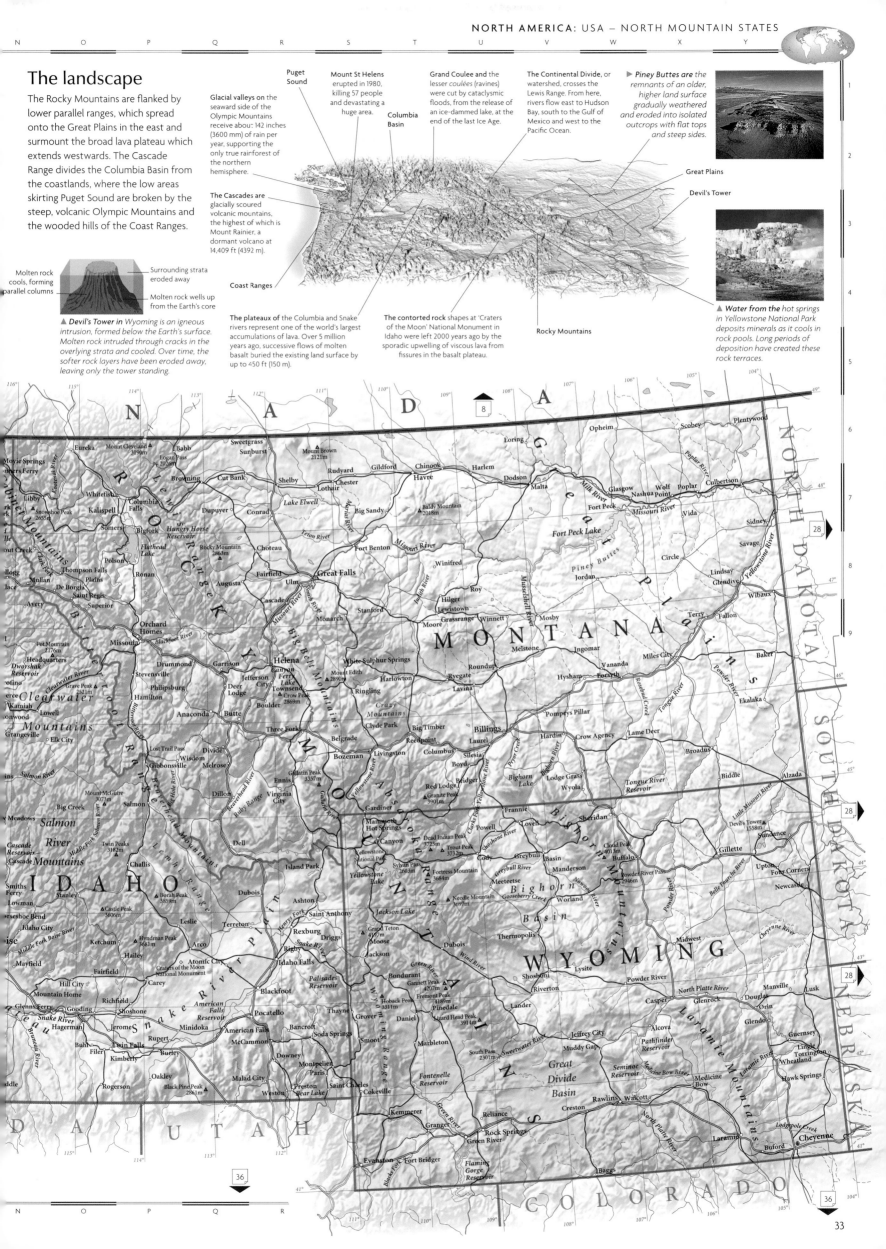

USA: CALIFORNIA & NEVADA

The 'Gold Rush' of 1849 attracted the first major wave of European settlers to the USA's west coast. The pleasant climate, beautiful scenery and dynamic economy continue to attract immigrants – despite the ever-present danger of earthquakes – and California has become the USA's most populous state. The population is concentrated in the vast conurbations of Los Angeles, San Francisco and San Diego; new immigrants include people from South Korea, the Philippines, Vietnam and Mexico. Nevada's arid lands were initially exploited for minerals; in recent years, revenue from mining has been superseded by income from the tourist and gambling centres of Las Vegas and Reno.

Map key

Population

- ◉ 1 million to 5 million
- ◎ 500,000 to 1 million
- ◎ 100,000 to 500,000
- ⊙ 50,000 to 100,000
- ○ 10,000 to 50,000
- ○ below 10,000

Elevation

- 4000m / 13,124ft
- 3000m / 9843ft
- 2000m / 6562ft
- 1000m / 3281ft
- 500m / 1640ft
- 250m / 820ft
- 100m / 328ft
- sea level

Scale 1:3,250,000

Km
0 5 10 20 30 40 50 60 70 80

Miles
0 5 10 20 30 40 50 60 70 80

projection: Lambert Conformal Conic

Transport and industry

Nevada's rich mineral reserves ushered in a period of mining wealth which has now been replaced by revenue generated from gambling. California supports a broad set of activities including defence-related industries and research and development facilities. 'Silicon Valley', near San Francisco, is a world leading centre for microelectronics, while tourism and the Los Angeles film industry also generate large incomes.

◀ Gambling was legalized in Nevada in 1931. Las Vegas has since become the centre of this multi-million dollar industry.

Major industry and infrastructure

- ✈ aerospace
- 🚗 car manufacture
- defence
- film industry
- S finance
- food processing
- gambling
- hi-tech industry
- mining
- pharmaceuticals
- research & development
- textiles
- tourism
- • major towns
- ⊕ international airports
- major roads
- major industrial areas

The transport network

| 211,459 miles (338,334 km) | 2944 miles (4710 km) |
| 7822 miles (12,595 km) | 190 miles (360 km) |

In California, the motor vehicle is a vital part of daily life, and an extensive freeway system runs throughout the state, cementing its position as the most important mode of transport

◀ The General Sherman sequoia tree in Sequoia National Park is 2500 years old and at 275 ft (84 m) is one of the largest living things on earth.

The landscape

The broad Central Valley divides California's coastal mountains from the Sierra Nevada. The San Andreas Fault, running beneath much of the state, is the site of frequent earth tremors and sometimes more serious earthquakes. East of the Sierra Nevada, the landscape is characterized by the basin and range topography with stony deserts and many salt lakes.

Rising molten rock causes stretching of the Earth's crust

Extensive cracking (faulting) uplifted a series of ridges

As ridges are eroded they fill intervening valleys with sediments

▲ Molten rock (magma) welling up to form a dome in the Earth's interior, causes the brittle surface rocks to stretch and crack. Some areas were uplifted to form mountains (ranges), while others sunk to form flat valleys (basins).

Most of California's agriculture is confined to the fertile and extensively irrigated Central Valley, running between the Coast Ranges and the Sierra Nevada. It incorporates the San Joaquin and Sacramento valleys.

The dramatic granitic rock formations of Half Dome and El Capitan, and the verdant coniferous forests, attract millions of visitors annually to Yosemite National Park in the Sierra Nevada.

Sierra Nevada

The Great Basin dominates most of Nevada's topography containing large open basins, punctuated by eroded features such as buttes and mesas. River flow tends to be seasonal, dependent upon spring showers and winter snow melt.

Using the land

California is the USA's leading agricultural producer, although low rainfall makes irrigation essential. The long growing season and abundant sunshine allow many crops to be grown in the fertile Central Valley including grapes, citrus fruits, vegetables and cotton. Almost 17 million acres (6.8 million hectares) of California's forests are used commercially. Nevada's arid climate and poor soil are largely unsuitable for agriculture; 85% of its land is state owned and large areas are used for underground testing of nuclear weapons.

Wheeler Peak is home to some of the world's oldest trees, bristlecone pines, which live for up to 5000 years.

Land use and agricultural distribution

- 🐄 cattle
- citrus fruits
- fruit
- irrigation
- timber
- vineyards
- • major towns
- pasture
- cropland
- forest
- desert

The San Andreas Fault is a transverse fault which extends for 650 miles (1050 km) through California. Major earthquakes occur when the land either side of the fault moves at different rates. San Francisco was devastated by an earthquake in 1906.

Death Valley

When the Hoover Dam across the Colorado River was completed in 1936, it created Lake Mead, one of the largest artificial lakes in the world, extending for 115 miles (285 km) upstream.

Amargosa Desert

▶ Named by migrating settlers in 1849, Death Valley is the driest, hottest place in North America, as well as being the lowest point on land in the western hemisphere, at 282 ft (86 m) below sea level.

The sparsely populated Mojave Desert receives less than 8 inches (200 mm) of rainfall a year. It is used extensively for weapons-testing and military purposes.

The Salton Sea was created accidentally between 1905 and 1907 when an irrigation channel from the Colorado River broke out of its banks and formed this salty 300 sq mile (777 sq km), land-locked lake.

▲ The Sierra Nevada create a 'rainshadow', preventing rain from reaching much of Nevada. Pacific air masses, passing over the mountains, are stripped of their moisture.

▲ Without considerable irrigation, this fertile valley at Palm Springs would still be part of the Sonoran Desert. California's farmers account for about 80% of the state's total water usage.

The urban/rural population divide

urban 92% | rural 8%

0 10 20 30 40 50 60 70 80 90 100

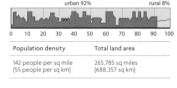

Population density	Total land area
142 people per sq mile (55 people per sq km)	265,785 sq miles (688,357 sq km)

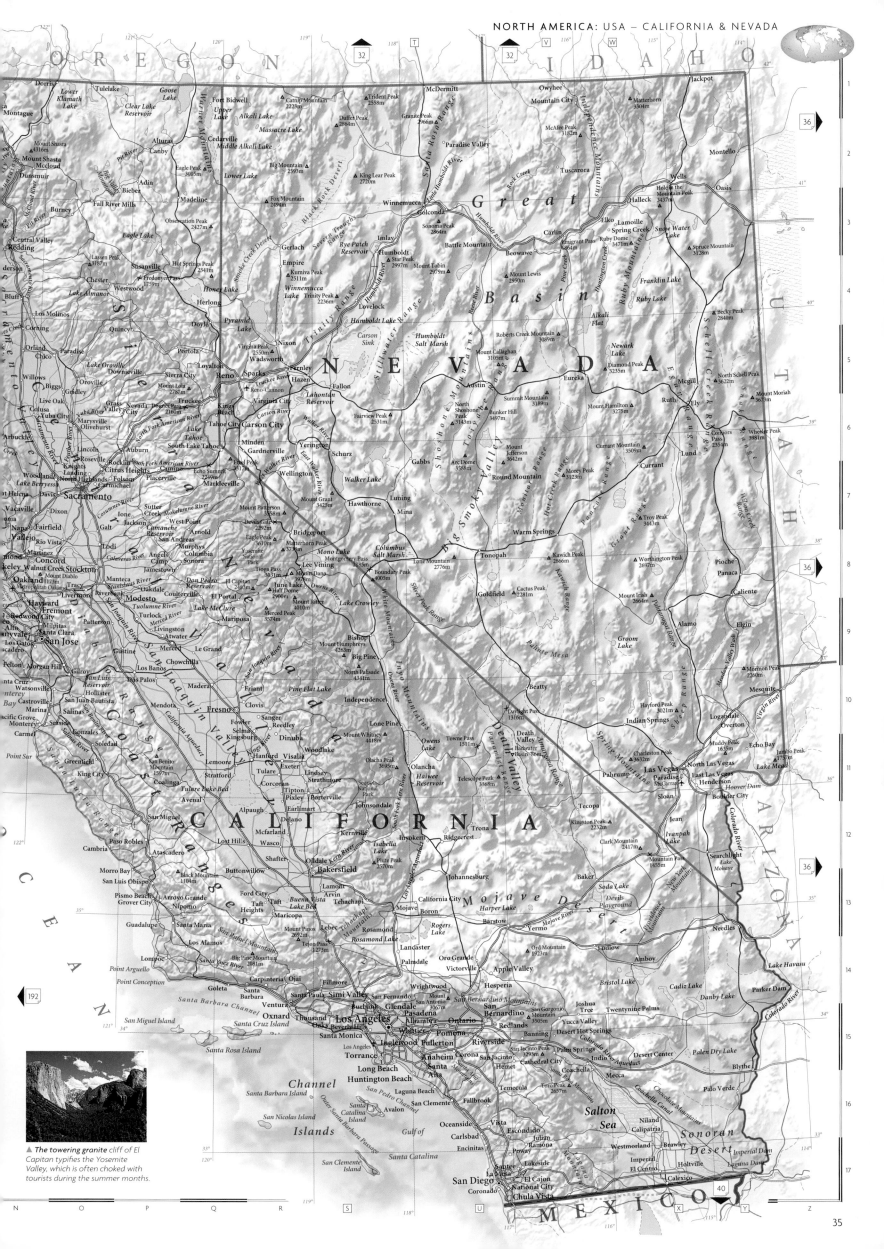

▲ **The towering granite** cliff of El Capitan typifies the Yosemite Valley, which is often choked with tourists during the summer months.

USA: SOUTH MOUNTAIN STATES

Arizona, Colorado, New Mexico, Utah

This arid region, characterized by expansive plateaux and spectacular canyons is home to several distinct peoples. The ruins of cliff dwellings built a thousand years ago by the Anasazi people still exist today, and native Americans own one-third of the land in Arizona. Spanish and Mexican conquest and settlement left a hispanic presence which is strongest in New Mexico. The Mormons, who came to the Great Salt Lake seeking religious freedom in 1847, were among the earliest Anglo-American settlers and now make up over 70% of Utah's population. The region's mineral wealth drove rapid development in the 20th century, yet the constraints of a fragile environment, including widespread water shortages, may limit prospects for growth.

The landscape

The arid, rocky expanse of the Colorado Plateau is dissected by immense canyons of the Colorado River. Desert lies to the north and south and branches of the Rocky Mountains run to the east and west. The Great Salt Lake and Desert lie within the Great Basin, a barren region of parallel mountain ranges which extends into Arizona.

When water evaporates it leaves a salt pan

Mudflats

Lake is fed by seasonal snow melt

Water level of lake varies according to quantity of run-off received from snow melt

▲ *The Great Salt* Lake is an ephemeral lake; it can remain dry for extended periods, leaving a pan of evaporated mineral salts in its centre.

Over 13 million years of weathering has created thousands of spires and pinnacles from the alternating rock strata of Bryce Canyon.

The parallel basins and ridges, which run north-south along the Great Basin, reflect a major series of block-faults in the underlying bedrock.

Parts of the Grand Canyon, which cuts through the Colorado Plateau, are 16 miles (25 km) wide. The Colorado River has cut down 6262 ft (2000 m), exposing rock strata more than 2 billion years old.

Lake Powell

The Rio Grande has its source in several meltwater streams, which have cut deep valleys into the platform of the San Juan Mountains.

Sand dunes, 600 ft (180 m) high, have been deposited in San Luis Valley, by winds funnelled through the San Juan and Sangre de Cristo mountains in the Rockies.

Rainbow Bridge is the world's largest natural arch. The 309 ft (94 m) span probably began to grow when the sandstone spur of a meandering creek was breached during a flash flood.

The striking colour effects seen in the Painted Desert come from minerals such as gypsum and haematite, combined with ambient heat and dust.

Petrified Forest

▶ In the arid landscape of Petrified Forest National Park in Arizona, the grain of prehistoric trees has been preserved as a fossil imprint in the rocks. The bog-preserved trees were gradually turned to stone by seeping mineral-rich water.

Shifting gypsum sands produce a constantly changing land surface, overwhelming plants and any other obstacles in Tularosa Valley.

Carlsbad Caverns

▶ *The intricate stalactites* of Carlsbad Caverns have grown with the seepage of calcium-rich water, over the last 100,000 years. The huge caves are home to around 100,000 Mexican freetail bats.

Transport and industry

New industries have helped reduce the region's dependence on the extraction of minerals and fossil fuels. Precision manufacture has grown rapidly, particularly in Arizona and Colorado. Salt Lake City and Denver are well-established financial centres and New Mexico, the USA's main producer of uranium, is a prominent region for nuclear research. Colorado is the USA's most important centre for winter sports.

The transport network

232,434 miles (573,986 km)	4059 miles (6515 km)
8627 miles (13,881 km)	none

The Colorado Rockies are crossed by 32 mountain passes, some as high as 12,183 ft (3713 m). The Eisenhower Tunnel west of Denver carries Interstate Highway 70 straight through the Continental Divide.

Major industry and infrastructure

- chemicals
- coal
- defence
- finance
- food processing
- hi-tech industry
- oil & gas
- mining
- research & development
- winter sports
- major towns
- international airports
- major roads
- major industrial areas

▲ Glen Canyon Dam on the Colorado river was completed in 1964. It provides hydro-electric power and irrigation water as part of a long-term federal project to harness the river.

▶ *The flat tablelands* (mesas), and the isolated pinnacles (buttes) which rise from the floor of Monument Valley are the resistant remnants of an earlier land surface, gradually cut back by erosion under arid conditions.

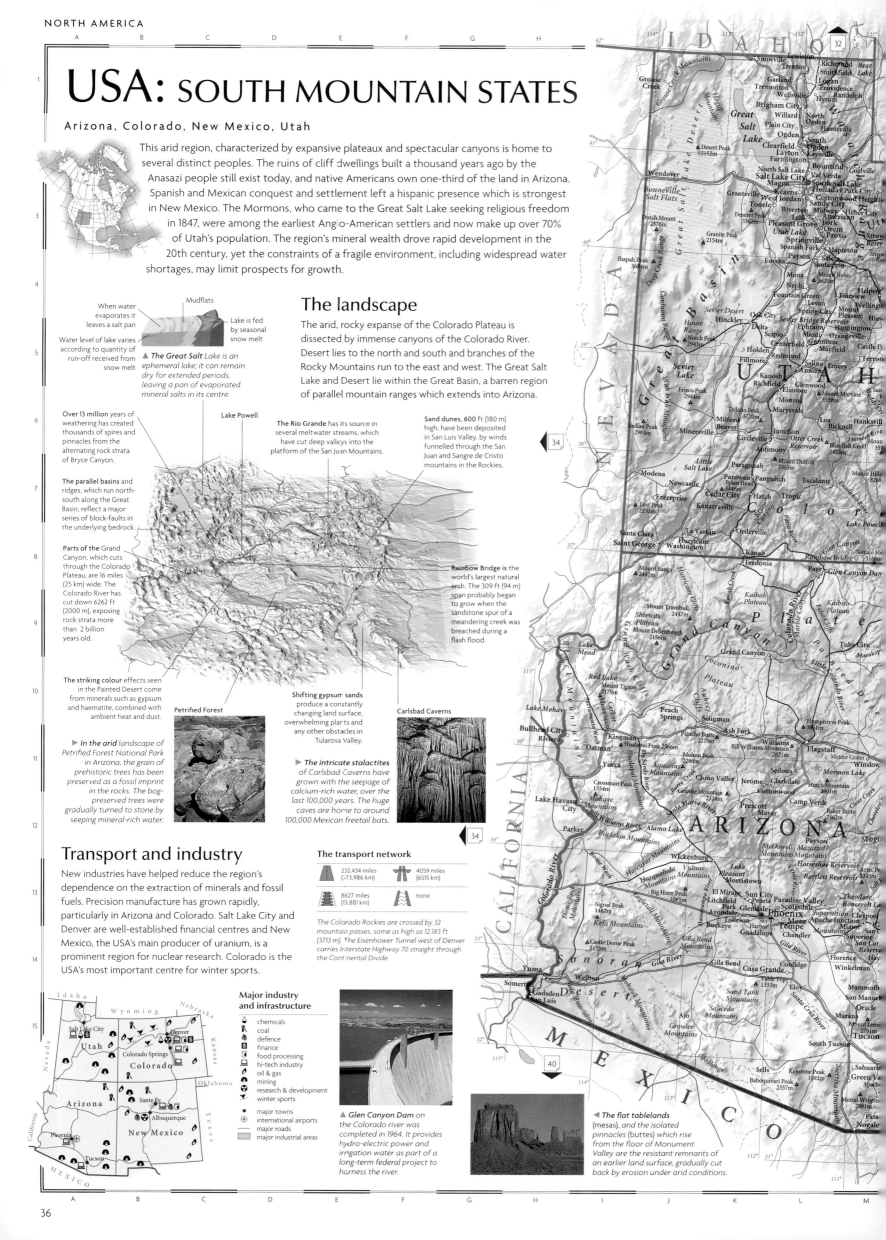

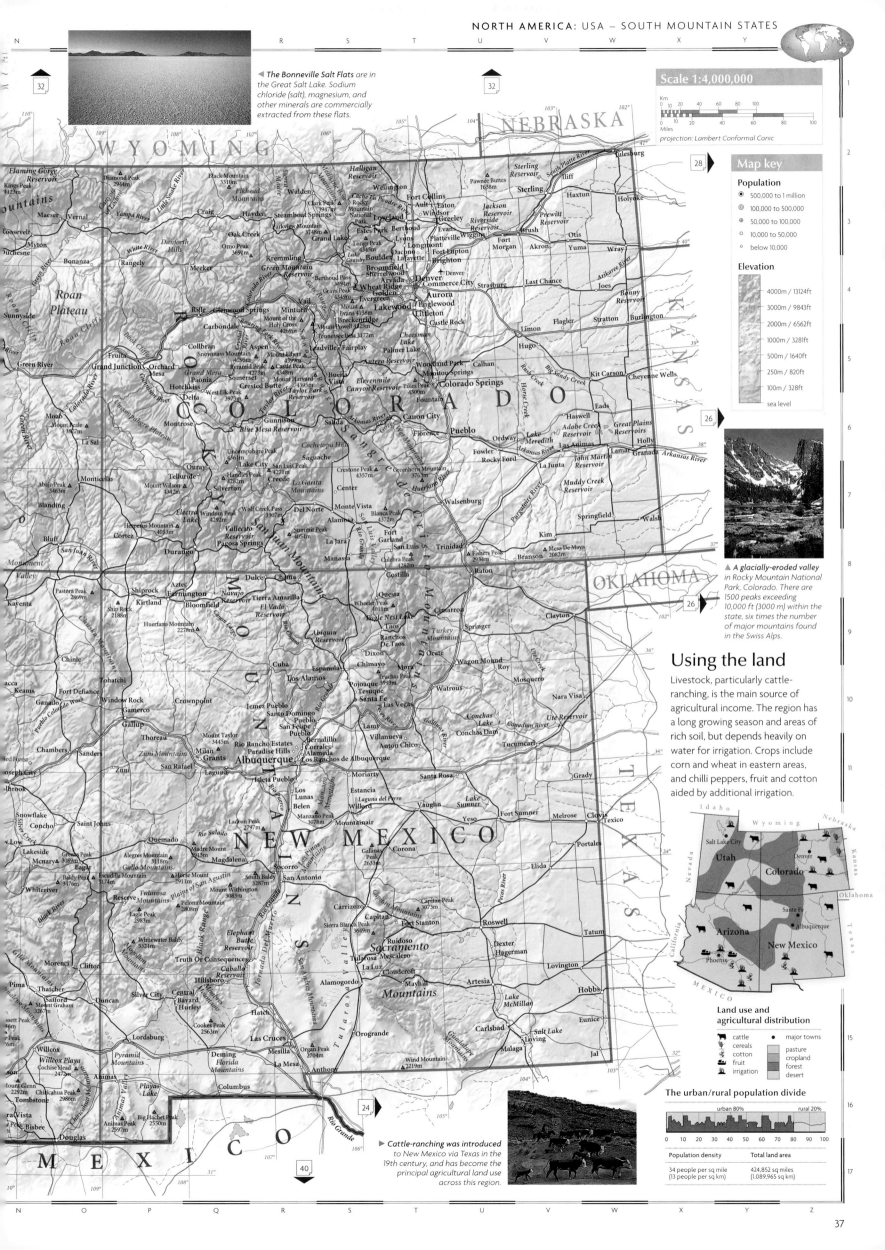

◄ *The Bonneville Salt Flats are in the Great Salt Lake. Sodium chloride (salt), magnesium, and other minerals are commercially extracted from these flats.*

Scale 1:4,000,000

projection: Lambert Conformal Conic

Map key

Population

◉ 500,000 to 1 million
◎ 100,000 to 500,000
⊕ 50,000 to 100,000
○ 10,000 to 50,000
∘ below 10,000

Elevation

	4000m / 13124ft
	3000m / 9843ft
	2000m / 6562ft
	1000m / 3281ft
	500m / 1640ft
	250m / 820ft
	100m / 328ft
	sea level

▲ *A glacially-eroded valley in Rocky Mountain National Park, Colorado. There are 1500 peaks exceeding 10,000 ft (3000 m) within the state, six times the number of major mountains found in the Swiss Alps.*

Using the land

Livestock, particularly cattle-ranching, is the main source of agricultural income. The region has a long growing season and areas of rich soil, but depends heavily on water for irrigation. Crops include corn and wheat in eastern areas, and chilli peppers, fruit and cotton aided by additional irrigation.

Land use and agricultural distribution

🐄 cattle	• major towns
🌾 cereals	pasture
cotton	cropland
🍎 fruit	forest
irrigation	desert

The urban/rural population divide

urban 80%   rural 20%

0 10 20 30 40 50 60 70 80 90 100

Population density	Total land area
34 people per sq mile (13 people per sq km)	424,852 sq miles (1,089,965 sq km)

▶ *Cattle-ranching was introduced to New Mexico via Texas in the 19th century, and has become the principal agricultural land use across this region.*

USA: HAWAI'I

The 122 islands of the Hawaiian archipelago – which are part of Polynesia – are the peaks of the world's largest volcanoes. They rise approximately 6 miles (9.7 km) from the floor of the Pacific Ocean. The largest, the island of Hawai'i, remains highly active. Hawai'i became the USA's 50th state in 1959. A tradition of receiving immigrant workers is reflected in the islands' ethnic diversity, with peoples drawn from around the rim of the Pacific. Only 9% of the current population are native Polynesians.

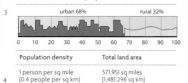

▲ The island of Moloka'i is formed from volcanic rock. Mature sand dunes cover the rocks in coastal areas.

Transport and industry

Tourism dominates the economy, with over 90% of the population employed in services. The naval base at Pearl Harbor is also a major source of employment. Industry is concentrated on the island of O'ahu and relies mostly on imported materials, while agricultural produce is processed locally.

The transport network

🛣 4102 miles (6600 km)		🛤 43 miles (69 km)	
none		none	

Hawai'i relies on ocean-surface transportation. Honolulu is the main focus of this network, bringing foreign trade and the markets of mainland USA to Hawai'i's outer islands.

Major industry and infrastructure

- 🏭 food processing
- 🎖 military base
- 🧵 textiles
- 🏖 tourism
- major towns
- ✈ international airports
- — major roads
- major industrial areas

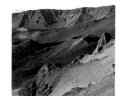

◀ Haleakala's extinct volcanic crater is the world's largest. The giant caldera, containing many secondary cones, is 2000 ft (600 m) deep and 20 miles (32 km) in circumference.

Using the land and sea

The ice-free coastline of Alaska provides access to salmon fisheries and more than 129 million acres (52.2 million ha) of forest. Most of Alaska is uncultivable, and around 90% of food is imported. Barley, hay and hothouse products are grown around Anchorage, where dairy farming is also concentrated.

The urban/rural population divide

urban 68% / rural 32%

Population density	Total land area
1 person per sq mile (0.4 people per sq km)	571,951 sq miles (1,481,296 sq km)

◀ A raft of timber from the Tongass forest is hauled by a tug, bound for the pulp mills of the Alaskan coast between Juneau and Ketchikan.

Using the land and sea

The volcanic soils are extremely fertile and the climate hot and humid on the lower slopes, supporting large commercial plantations growing sugar cane, bananas, pineapples and other tropical fruit, as well as nursery plants and flowers. Some land is given to pasture, particularly for beef and dairy cattle.

Land use and agricultural distribution

- 🐄 cattle
- 🎣 fishing
- 🍍 fruit
- 🌾 sugar cane
- • major towns
- pasture
- cropland
- forest
- mountain region

▶ The island of Kaua'i is one of the wettest places in the world, receiving some 450 inches (11,500 mm) of rain a year.

Scale 1:4,000,000

projection: Lambert Conformal Conic

Map key

Population
- ◎ 100,000 to 500,000
- ⊕ 50,000 to 100,000
- ○ 10,000 to 50,000
- ○ below 10,000

Elevation
- 4000m / 13,124ft
- 3000m / 9843ft
- 2000m / 6562ft
- 1000m / 3281ft
- 500m / 1640ft
- 250m / 820ft
- 100m / 328ft
- sea level

The urban/rural population divide

urban 89% / rural 11%

Population density	Total land area
189 people per sq mile (73 people per sq km)	6,423 sq miles (16,636 sq km)

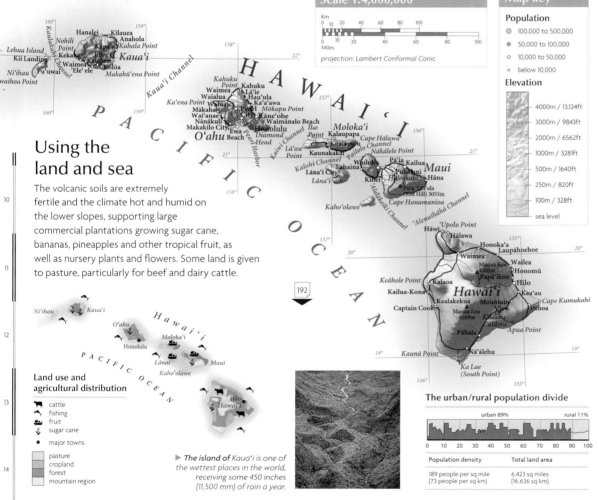

Map key

Population
- ◎ 100,000 to 500,000
- ⊕ 50,000 to 100,000
- ○ 10,000 to 50,000
- ○ below 10,000

Elevation
- 4000m / 13,124ft
- 3000m / 9843ft
- 2000m / 6562ft
- 1000m / 3281ft
- 500m / 1640ft
- 250m / 820ft
- 100m / 328ft
- sea level

Scale 1:9,000,000

projection: Lambert Conformal Conic

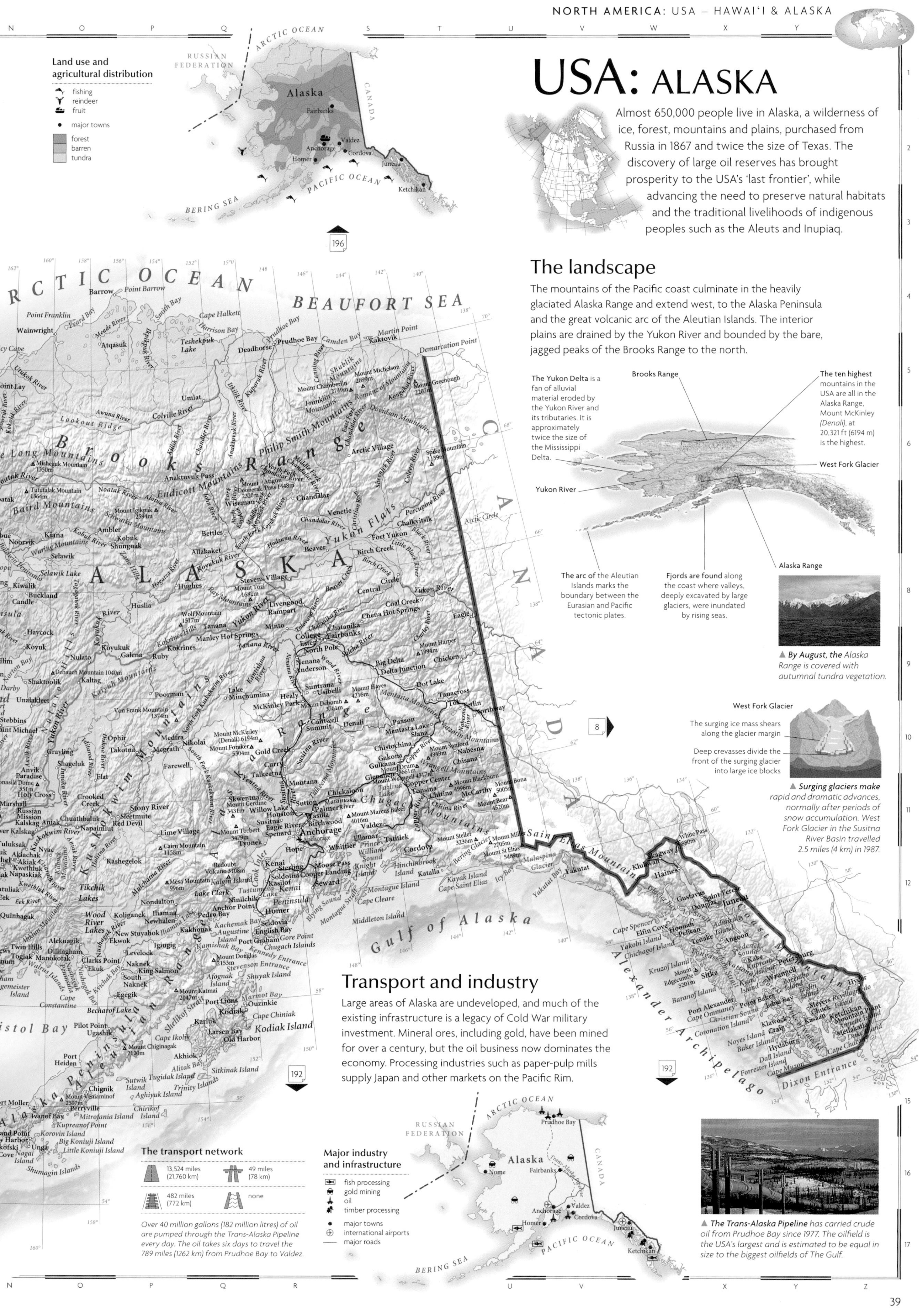

USA: ALASKA

Almost 650,000 people live in Alaska, a wilderness of ice, forest, mountains and plains, purchased from Russia in 1867 and twice the size of Texas. The discovery of large oil reserves has brought prosperity to the USA's 'last frontier', while advancing the need to preserve natural habitats and the traditional livelihoods of indigenous peoples such as the Aleuts and Inupiaq.

The landscape

The mountains of the Pacific coast culminate in the heavily glaciated Alaska Range and extend west, to the Alaska Peninsula and the great volcanic arc of the Aleutian Islands. The interior plains are drained by the Yukon River and bounded by the bare, jagged peaks of the Brooks Range to the north.

The Yukon Delta is a fan of alluvial material eroded by the Yukon River and its tributaries. It is approximately twice the size of the Mississippi Delta.

Brooks Range

The ten highest mountains in the USA are all in the Alaska Range, Mount McKinley (Denali), at 20,321 ft (6194 m) is the highest.

Yukon River

West Fork Glacier

The arc of the Aleutian Islands marks the boundary between the Eurasian and Pacific tectonic plates.

Fjords are found along the coast where valleys, deeply excavated by large glaciers, were inundated by rising seas.

Alaska Range

▲ *By August, the Alaska Range is covered with autumnal tundra vegetation.*

West Fork Glacier

The surging ice mass shears along the glacier margin

Deep crevasses divide the front of the surging glacier into large ice blocks

▲ *Surging glaciers make rapid and dramatic advances, normally after periods of snow accumulation. West Fork Glacier in the Susitna River Basin travelled 2.5 miles (4 km) in 1987.*

Transport and industry

Large areas of Alaska are undeveloped, and much of the existing infrastructure is a legacy of Cold War military investment. Mineral ores, including gold, have been mined for over a century, but the oil business now dominates the economy. Processing industries such as paper-pulp mills supply Japan and other markets on the Pacific Rim.

Land use and agricultural distribution

- fishing
- reindeer
- fruit
- • major towns
- forest
- barren
- tundra

The transport network

13,524 miles (21,760 km)		49 miles (78 km)	
482 miles (772 km)		none	

Over 40 million gallons (182 million litres) of oil are pumped through the Trans-Alaska Pipeline every day. The oil takes six days to travel the 789 miles (1262 km) from Prudhoe Bay to Valdez.

Major industry and infrastructure

- fish processing
- gold mining
- oil
- timber processing
- major towns
- ⊕ international airports
- — major roads

▲ *The Trans-Alaska Pipeline has carried crude oil from Prudhoe Bay since 1977. The oilfield is the USA's largest and is estimated to be equal in size to the biggest oilfields of The Gulf.*

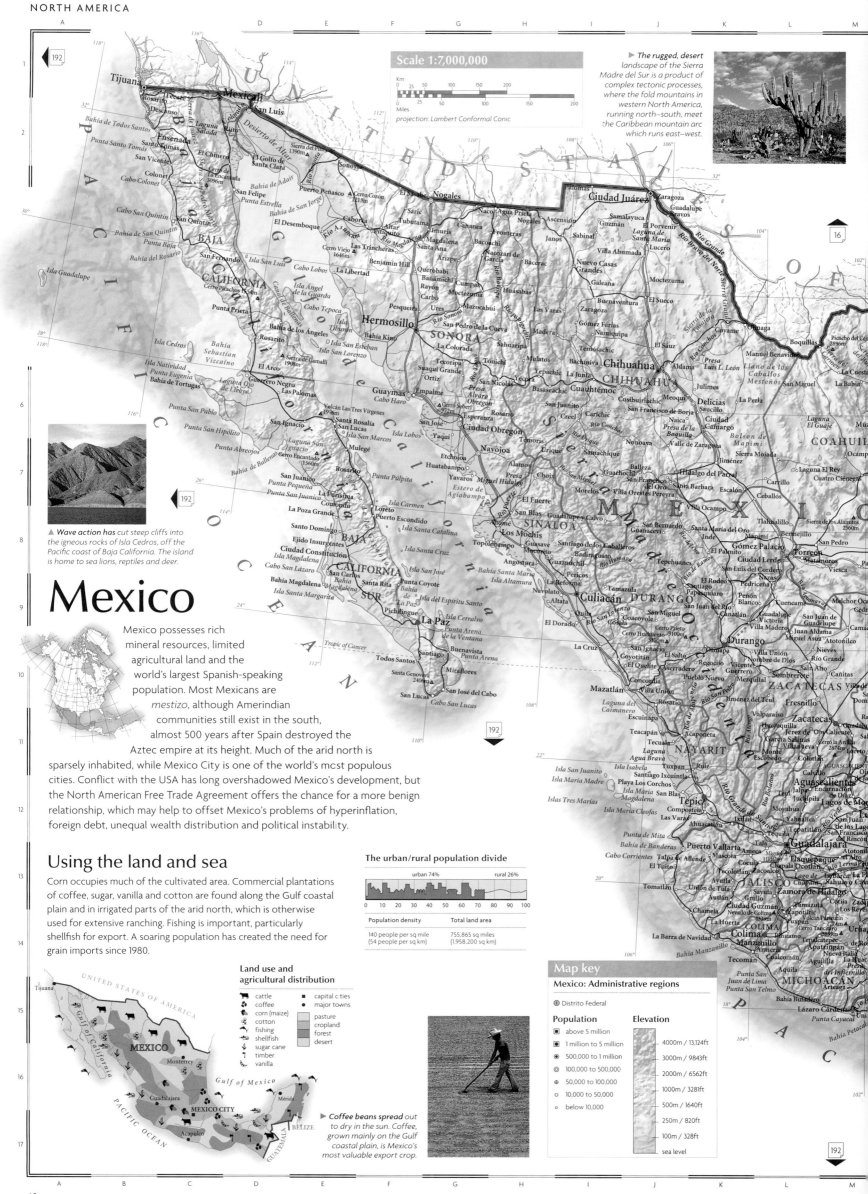

Mexico

Mexico possesses rich mineral resources, limited agricultural land and the world's largest Spanish-speaking population. Most Mexicans are *mestizo*, although Amerindian communities still exist in the south, almost 500 years after Spain destroyed the Aztec empire at its height. Much of the arid north is sparsely inhabited, while Mexico City is one of the world's most populous cities. Conflict with the USA has long overshadowed Mexico's development, but the North American Free Trade Agreement offers the chance for a more benign relationship, which may help to offset Mexico's problems of hyperinflation, foreign debt, unequal wealth distribution and political instability.

Using the land and sea

Corn occupies much of the cultivated area. Commercial plantations of coffee, sugar, vanilla and cotton are found along the Gulf coastal plain and in irrigated parts of the arid north, which is otherwise used for extensive ranching. Fishing is important, particularly shellfish for export. A soaring population has created the need for grain imports since 1980.

▲ *Wave action has* cut steep cliffs into the igneous rocks of Isla Cedros, off the Pacific coast of Baja California. The island is home to sea lions, reptiles and deer.

▶ *The rugged, desert* landscape of the Sierra Madre del Sur is a product of complex tectonic processes, where the fold mountains in western North America, running north–south, meet the Caribbean mountain arc which runs east–west.

Scale 1:7,000,000

projection: Lambert Conformal Conic

The urban/rural population divide

urban 74%   rural 26%

Population density	Total land area
140 people per sq mile (54 people per sq km)	755,865 sq miles (1,958,200 sq km)

Land use and agricultural distribution

- cattle
- coffee
- corn (maize)
- cotton
- fishing
- shellfish
- sugar cane
- timber
- vanilla
- capital cities
- major towns
- pasture
- cropland
- forest
- desert

▶ *Coffee beans spread out* to dry in the sun. Coffee, grown mainly on the Gulf coastal plain, is Mexico's most valuable export crop.

Map key

Mexico: Administrative regions

Ⓓ Distrito Federal

Population
- ▪ above 5 million
- ▣ 1 million to 5 million
- ◉ 500,000 to 1 million
- ◎ 100,000 to 500,000
- ◌ 50,000 to 100,000
- ○ 10,000 to 50,000
- ○ below 10,000

Elevation
- 4000m / 13,124ft
- 3000m / 9843ft
- 2000m / 6562ft
- 1000m / 3281ft
- 500m / 1640ft
- 250m / 820ft
- 100m / 328ft
- sea level

The landscape

The great central plateau rises gently southwards from the Rio Grande, isolated from the coastal plains by the Sierra Madre Oriental and Occidental. The two ranges converge from east and west respectively, culminating in high volcanic peaks around Mexico City. Further ranges of the Sierra Madre rise to the south of the Balsas basin, skirted by the low-lying Isthmus of Tehuantepec (*Istmo de Tehuantepec*) and Yucatan Peninsula.

The long, narrow, extremely arid peninsula of Baja (lower) California is an elongated granite block, separated from the mainland by the flooded rift valley of the Gulf of California (*Golfo de California*).

Wave action has constructed sand bars which shelter lagoons along the shore of the Gulf coastal plain.

The dormant cone of Volcán Pico de Orizaba is, at 18,700 ft (5700 m), the highest peak in Mexico. In North America, only Mount McKinley and Mount Logan are taller.

Sierra Madre Oriental

Rio Grande

▲ *Tropical rainforest abounds in the Yucatan Peninsula, a broad, low limestone shelf. Rivers are rare due to the porous nature of limestone, so the forest is mostly fed by streams and underground water.*

The heavily-forested Isthmus of Tehuantepec (*Istmo de Tehuantepec*) is a graben; a low-lying trough created by downward movement of the bedrock between two fault lines.

Formation of the Gulf of California

Direction of plate movement

Baja California

Transform fault

Gulf of California

Edge of continental crust

Spreading oceanic ridge

Sierra Madre Occidental

▲ *The Gulf of California (Golfo de California) began to open out about 4 million years ago as a result of rifting and plate displacement along transform faults.*

Río Balsas

Popocatépetl

▲ *Popocatépetl is a dormant volcano, part of the Pacific 'Ring of Fire'. The crater is over half a mile (1 km) wide.*

The unstable, earthquake-prone, upland basin around Mexico City was once a region of shallow lakes. Flood control measures and domestic consumption over the last four centuries have caused the virtual disappearance of this surface water.

The highlands of Chiapas are a series of *horsts*, blocks of land thrust upwards between two fault lines. Volcanic cones have developed where lava has flowed out from the faults.

Transport and industry

Oil and gas on the Gulf coast are Mexico's main sources of export income. Metal mining has declined but the country remains a leading global producer of silver. Manufacturing is heavily concentrated around the Mexico City metropolitan area, while the duty-free movement of goods in the USA border region, under the *Maquiladora* (twin plant) scheme, has created new hi-tech and service growth centres.

Major industry and infrastructure

- brewing
- car manufacture
- chemicals
- electronics
- fish processing
- maquiladoras
- mining
- oil & gas
- textiles
- capital cities
- major towns
- international airports
- major roads
- major industrial areas

The transport network

67,564 miles (108,746 km)	
3994 miles (6429 km)	
16,561 miles (26,656 km)	
1801 miles (2900 km)	

Fast, modern highways or autopistas now link Mexico City with Toluca, Puebla and other satellite cities, yet distant centres like Chihuahua are still served by narrow roads and an outdated rail network.

▲ *A stone figure reclines by the Temple of Warriors, within the Mayan city of Chichén-Itzá. The Maya civilization flourished across the Yucatan Peninsula between 200 and 900 AD.*

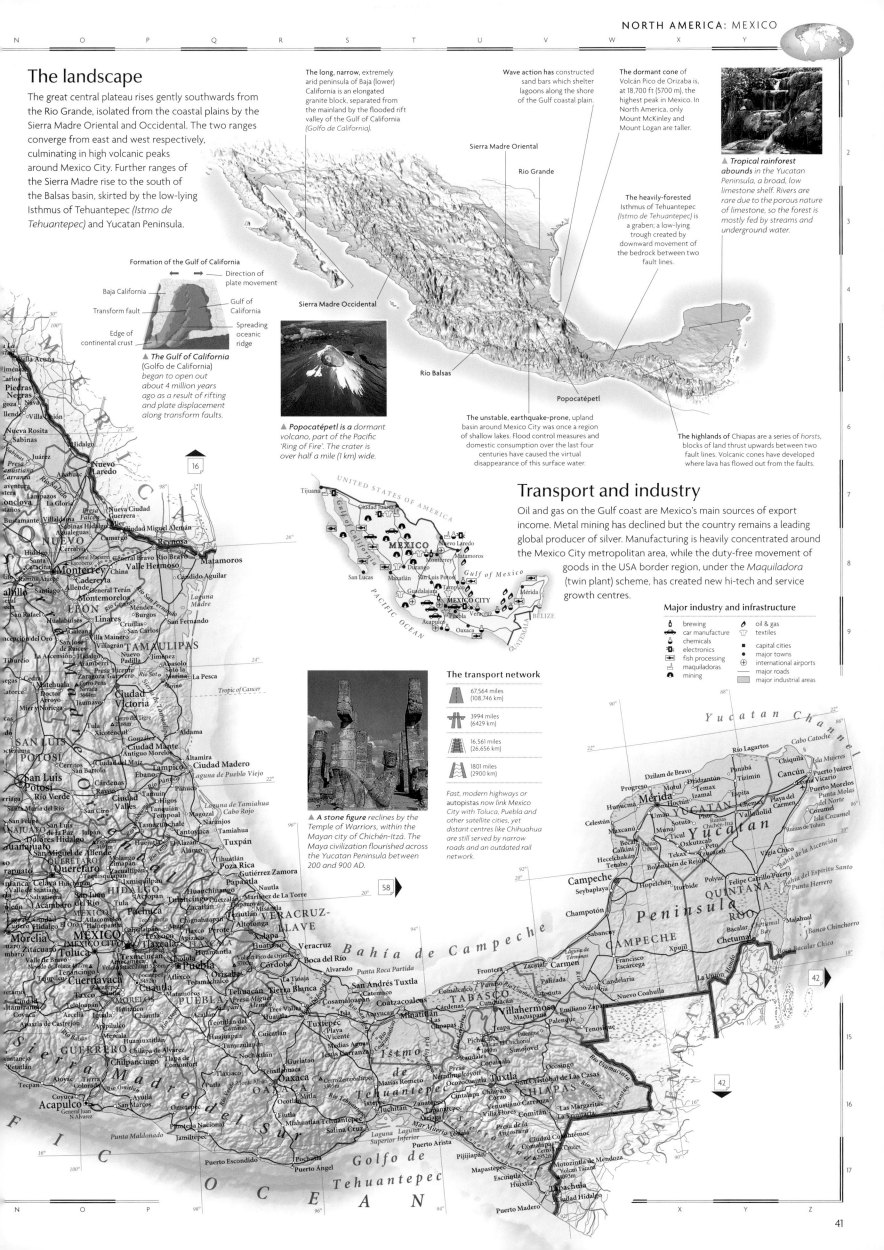

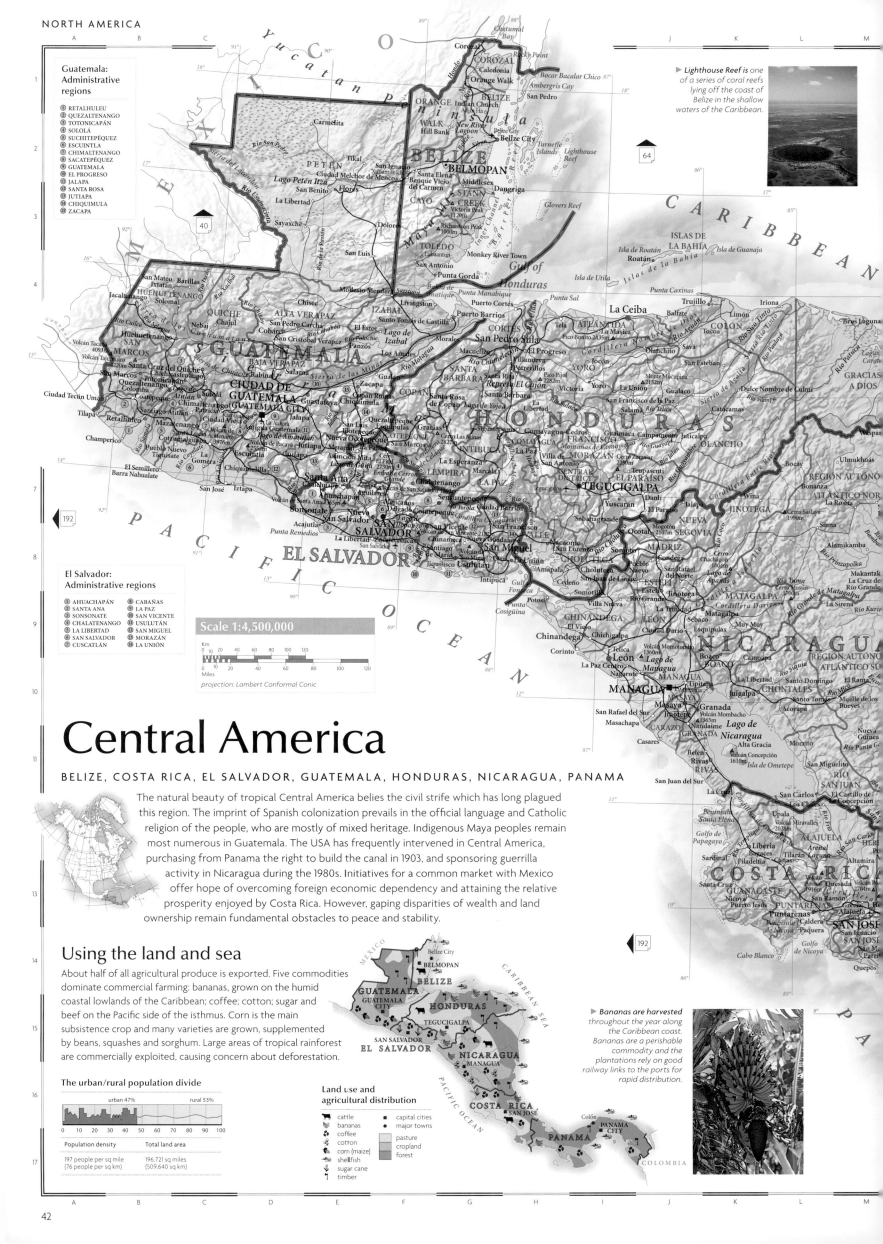

Guatemala: Administrative regions

① RETALHULEU
② QUEZALTENANGO
③ TOTONICAPÁN
④ SOLOLÁ
⑤ SUCHITEPÉQUEZ
⑥ ESCUINTLA
⑦ CHIMALTENANGO
⑧ SACATEPÉQUEZ
⑨ GUATEMALA
⑩ EL PROGRESO
⑪ JALAPA
⑫ SANTA ROSA
⑬ JUTIAPA
⑭ CHIQUIMULA
⑮ ZACAPA

▶ *Lighthouse Reef is one of a series of coral reefs lying off the coast of Belize in the shallow waters of the Caribbean.*

El Salvador: Administrative regions

① AHUACHAPÁN
② SANTA ANA
③ SONSONATE
④ CHALATENANGO
⑤ LA LIBERTAD
⑥ SAN SALVADOR
⑦ CUSCATLÁN
⑧ CABAÑAS
⑨ LA PAZ
⑩ SAN VICENTE
⑪ USULUTÁN
⑫ SAN MIGUEL
⑬ MORAZÁN
⑭ LA UNIÓN

Scale 1:4,500,000

Km 0 10 20 40 60 80 100 120
Miles 0 10 20 40 60 80 100 120

projection: Lambert Conformal Conic

Central America

BELIZE, COSTA RICA, EL SALVADOR, GUATEMALA, HONDURAS, NICARAGUA, PANAMA

The natural beauty of tropical Central America belies the civil strife which has long plagued this region. The imprint of Spanish colonization prevails in the official language and Catholic religion of the people, who are mostly of mixed heritage. Indigenous Maya peoples remain most numerous in Guatemala. The USA has frequently intervened in Central America, purchasing from Panama the right to build the canal in 1903, and sponsoring guerrilla activity in Nicaragua during the 1980s. Initiatives for a common market with Mexico offer hope of overcoming foreign economic dependency and attaining the relative prosperity enjoyed by Costa Rica. However, gaping disparities of wealth and land ownership remain fundamental obstacles to peace and stability.

Using the land and sea

About half of all agricultural produce is exported. Five commodities dominate commercial farming: bananas, grown on the humid coastal lowlands of the Caribbean; coffee; cotton; sugar and beef on the Pacific side of the isthmus. Corn is the main subsistence crop and many varieties are grown, supplemented by beans, squashes and sorghum. Large areas of tropical rainforest are commercially exploited, causing concern about deforestation.

▶ *Bananas are harvested throughout the year along the Caribbean coast. Bananas are a perishable commodity and the plantations rely on good railway links to the ports for rapid distribution.*

The urban/rural population divide

urban 47%   rural 53%
0 10 20 30 40 50 60 70 80 90 100

Population density   Total land area

197 people per sq mile   196,721 sq miles
(76 people per sq km)   (509,640 sq km)

Land use and agricultural distribution

🐄 cattle
🍌 bananas
☕ coffee
cotton
corn (maize)
shellfish
sugar cane
timber

■ capital cities
● major towns
pasture
cropland
forest

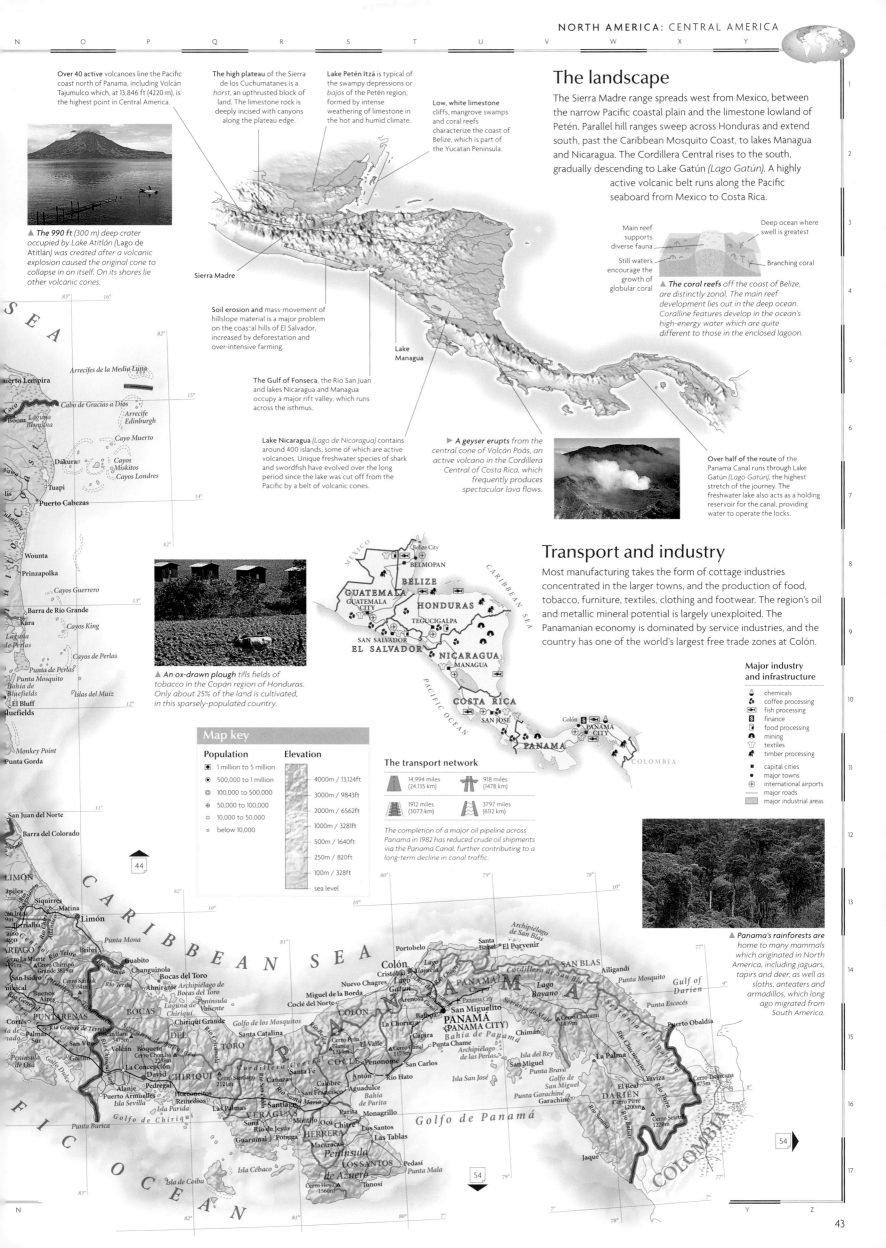

Over 40 active volcanoes line the Pacific coast north of Panama, including Volcán Tajumulco which, at 13,846 ft (4220 m), is the highest point in Central America.

The high plateau of the Sierra de los Cuchumatanes is a *horst*, an upthrusted block of land. The limestone rock is deeply incised with canyons along the plateau edge.

Lake Petén Itzá is typical of the swampy depressions or *bajos* of the Petén region, formed by intense weathering of limestone in the hot and humid climate.

Low, white limestone cliffs, mangrove swamps and coral reefs characterize the coast of Belize, which is part of the Yucatan Peninsula.

▲ *The 990 ft (300 m) deep crater occupied by Lake Atitlán (Lago de Atitlán) was created after a volcanic explosion caused the original cone to collapse in on itself. On its shores lie other volcanic cones.*

Sierra Madre

Soil erosion and mass-movement of hillslope material is a major problem on the coastal hills of El Salvador, increased by deforestation and over-intensive farming.

The Gulf of Fonseca, the Río San Juan and lakes Nicaragua and Managua occupy a major rift valley, which runs across the isthmus.

Lake Managua

Lake Nicaragua *(Lago de Nicaragua)* contains around 400 islands, some of which are active volcanoes. Unique freshwater species of shark and swordfish have evolved over the long period since the lake was cut off from the Pacific by a belt of volcanic cones.

▶ *A geyser erupts from the central cone of Volcán Poás, an active volcano in the Cordillera Central of Costa Rica, which frequently produces spectacular lava flows.*

The landscape

The Sierra Madre range spreads west from Mexico, between the narrow Pacific coastal plain and the limestone lowland of Petén. Parallel hill ranges sweep across Honduras and extend south, past the Caribbean Mosquito Coast, to lakes Managua and Nicaragua. The Cordillera Central rises to the south, gradually descending to Lake Gatún (*Lago Gatún*). A highly active volcanic belt runs along the Pacific seaboard from Mexico to Costa Rica.

Main reef supports diverse fauna

Still waters encourage the growth of globular coral

Deep ocean where swell is greatest

Branching coral

▲ *The coral reefs off the coast of Belize, are distinctly zonal. The main reef development lies out in the deep ocean. Coralline features develop in the ocean's high-energy water which are quite different to those in the enclosed lagoon.*

Over half of the route of the Panama Canal runs through Lake Gatún (*Lago Gatún*), the highest stretch of the journey. The freshwater lake also acts as a holding reservoir for the canal, providing water to operate the locks.

Transport and industry

Most manufacturing takes the form of cottage industries concentrated in the larger towns, and the production of food, tobacco, furniture, textiles, clothing and footwear. The region's oil and metallic mineral potential is largely unexploited. The Panamanian economy is dominated by service industries, and the country has one of the world's largest free trade zones at Colón.

▲ *An ox-drawn plough tills fields of tobacco in the Copán region of Honduras. Only about 25% of the land is cultivated, in this sparsely-populated country.*

Major industry and infrastructure

- chemicals
- coffee processing
- fish processing
- finance
- food processing
- mining
- textiles
- timber processing

- capital cities
- major towns
- international airports
- — major roads
- major industrial areas

Map key

Population
- ▣ 1 million to 5 million
- ◉ 500,000 to 1 million
- ◎ 100,000 to 500,000
- ⊕ 50,000 to 100,000
- ⊙ 10,000 to 50,000
- ○ below 10,000

Elevation
- 4000m / 13,124ft
- 3000m / 9843ft
- 2000m / 6562ft
- 1000m / 3281ft
- 500m / 1640ft
- 250m / 820ft
- 100m / 328ft
- sea level

The transport network

14,994 miles (24,135 km)	918 miles (1478 km)
1912 miles (3077 km)	3797 miles (6112 km)

The completion of a major oil pipeline across Panama in 1982 has reduced crude oil shipments via the Panama Canal, further contributing to a long-term decline in canal traffic.

▲ *Panama's rainforests are home to many mammals which originated in North America, including jaguars, tapirs and deer, as well as sloths, anteaters and armadillos, which long ago migrated from South America.*

MEXICO

Belize City
BELMOPAN
BELIZE
GUATEMALA
GUATEMALA CITY
HONDURAS
TEGUCIGALPA
SAN SALVADOR
EL SALVADOR
NICARAGUA
MANAGUA
COSTA RICA
SAN JOSÉ
Colón
PANAMA CITY
PANAMA
COLOMBIA
CARIBBEAN SEA
PACIFIC OCEAN

Map labels and geographic features (Caribbean Sea region):

SEA
Arrecifes de la Media Luna
Puerto Lempira
Cabo de Gracias a Dios
Coco
Boom
Laguna Bismuna
Arrecife Edinburgh
Cayo Muerto
Dákura
Cayos Miskitos
Cayos Londres
Tuapi
Puerto Cabezas
Wounta
Prinzapolka
Cayos Guerrero
Barra de Río Grande
Kára
Cayos King
Laguna de Perlas
Cayos de Perlas
Punta de Perlas
Bahía de Bluefields
Islas del Maíz
El Bluff
Bluefields
Monkey Point
Punta Gorda
San Juan del Norte
Barra del Colorado
LIMÓN
Siquirres
Matina
Limón
Punta Mona
CARTAGO
Cerro Chirripó 3819m
Bribrí
Guabito
Changuinola
Bocas del Toro
Río Sixaola
Almirante
Archipiélago de Bocas del Toro
BOCAS DEL TORO
Chiriquí Grande
Golfo de los Mosquitos
Santa Catalina
Coclé del Norte
PUNTARENAS
Buenos Aires
Volcán Barú 3475m
Cerro Chorcha 2228m
Volcán
Boquete
CHIRIQUÍ
La Concepción
David
Alanje
Pedregal
Puerto Armuelles
Isla Sevilla
Remedios
Horconcitos
Isla Parida
Las Palmas
Soná
VERAGUAS
Río de Jesús
Guarumal
Ponuga
Isla Cébaco
Isla de Coiba
Península de Azuero
LOS SANTOS
Pedasí
Punta Mala
Cerro Hoya 1560m
Tonosí
Macaracas
Las Tablas
HERRERA
Chitré
Los Santos
Ocú
Montijo
Parita
Bahía de Parita
Monagrillo
Santiago
Cerro Santiago 2121m
San Francisco
Calobre
Cañazas
Santa Fé
Aguadulce
Río Hato
Antón
El Valle
Penonomé
COCLÉ
Capira
La Chorrera
Arenosa
Ballona
PANAMÁ (PANAMA CITY)
San Miguelito
Chepo
Chimán
Cerro Cañal 1079m
Punta Chame
Bahía de Panamá
Golfo de Panamá
Archipiélago de las Perlas
Isla del Rey
San Miguel
Punta Brava
Isla San José
Golfo de San Miguel
Punta Garachiné
El Real
Cerro Pirre 1200m
DARIÉN
Río Sambú
Jaqué
Río Tuira
Cerro Setetule 1220m
COLOMBIA
Colón
Cristóbal
Portobelo
Nuevo Chagres
Miguel de la Borda
Santa Isabel
El Porvenir
Archipiélago de San Blas
SAN BLAS
Ailigandí
Cordillera de San Blas
Punta Mosquito
Gulf of Darien
Punta Escocés
Puerto Obaldía
Cerro Chucanti 1439m
Serranía de Majé
Lago Bayano
Yaviza
Cerro Tacarcuna 1875m
CARIBBEAN SEA
PACIFIC OCEAN

44
54

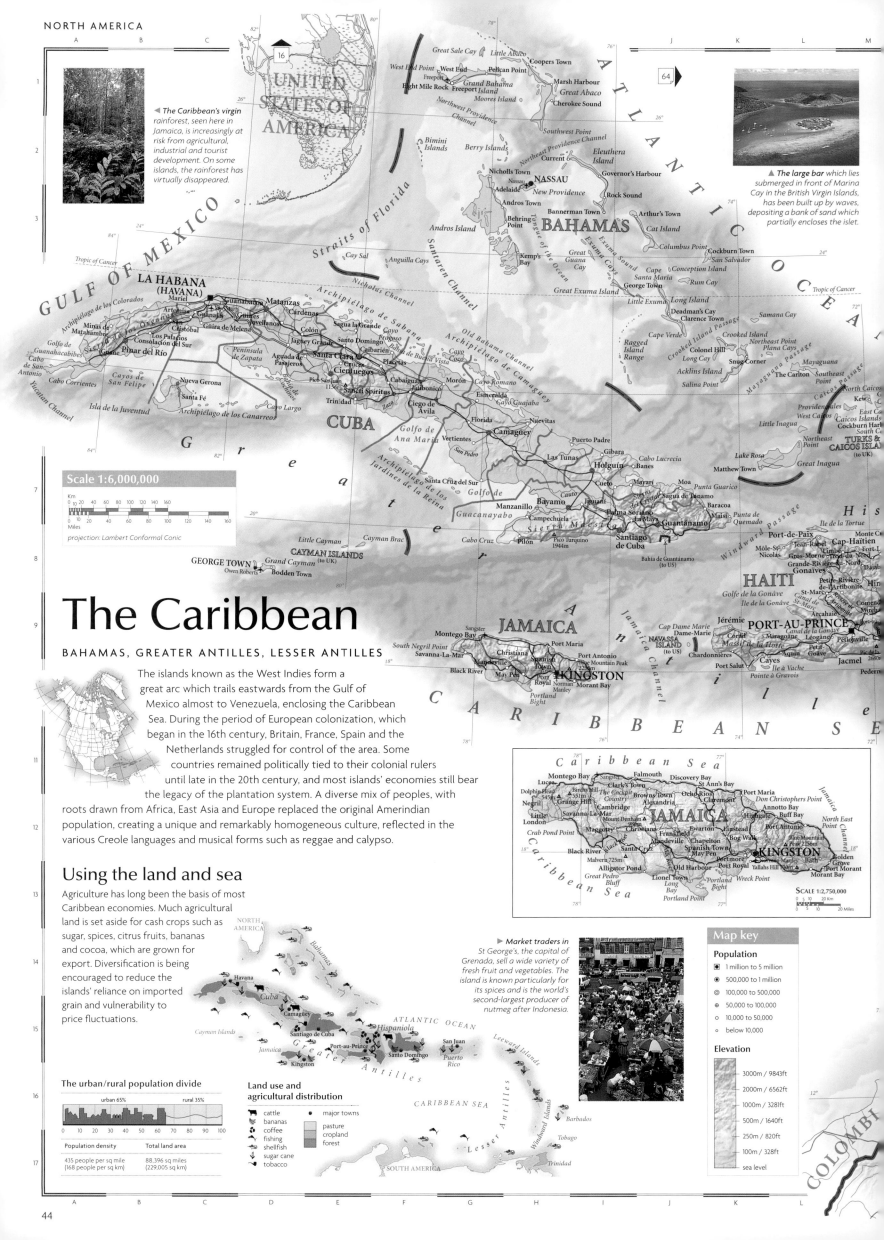

◄ *The Caribbean's virgin rainforest, seen here in Jamaica, is increasingly at risk from agricultural, industrial and tourist development. On some islands, the rainforest has virtually disappeared.*

▲ *The large bar which lies submerged in front of Marina Cay in the British Virgin Islands, has been built up by waves, depositing a bank of sand which partially encloses the islet.*

Scale 1:6,000,000

projection: Lambert Conformal Conic

The Caribbean

BAHAMAS, GREATER ANTILLES, LESSER ANTILLES

The islands known as the West Indies form a great arc which trails eastwards from the Gulf of Mexico almost to Venezuela, enclosing the Caribbean Sea. During the period of European colonization, which began in the 16th century, Britain, France, Spain and the Netherlands struggled for control of the area. Some countries remained politically tied to their colonial rulers until late in the 20th century, and most islands' economies still bear the legacy of the plantation system. A diverse mix of peoples, with roots drawn from Africa, East Asia and Europe replaced the original Amerindian population, creating a unique and remarkably homogeneous culture, reflected in the various Creole languages and musical forms such as reggae and calypso.

Using the land and sea

Agriculture has long been the basis of most Caribbean economies. Much agricultural land is set aside for cash crops such as sugar, spices, citrus fruits, bananas and cocoa, which are grown for export. Diversification is being encouraged to reduce the islands' reliance on imported grain and vulnerability to price fluctuations.

► *Market traders in St George's, the capital of Grenada, sell a wide variety of fresh fruit and vegetables. The island is known particularly for its spices and is the world's second-largest producer of nutmeg after Indonesia.*

The urban/rural population divide

urban 65%   rural 35%

Population density	Total land area
435 people per sq mile (168 people per sq km)	88,396 sq miles (229,005 sq km)

Land use and agricultural distribution

- cattle
- bananas
- coffee
- fishing
- shellfish
- sugar cane
- tobacco
- major towns
- pasture
- cropland
- forest

Map key

Population

- 1 million to 5 million
- 500,000 to 1 million
- 100,000 to 500,000
- 50,000 to 100,000
- 10,000 to 50,000
- below 10,000

Elevation

- 3000m / 9843ft
- 2000m / 6562ft
- 1000m / 3281ft
- 500m / 1640ft
- 250m / 820ft
- 100m / 328ft
- sea level

SCALE 1:2,750,000

Transport and industry

Caribbean industry remains, with few exceptions, agricultural and export-led, or service-based, supporting the flourishing tourist industry. However, several countries including Jamaica, Barbados, Trinidad and Tobago and Puerto Rico have developed important mineral industries, and Cuba is attempting to diversify its economy by importing capital goods to start up new manufacturing businesses.

▶ **Cruise ships, such as** this one moored at Castries in St Lucia, have become a popular way for tourists to travel round the Caribbean islands, stopping off at several islands for sightseeing and shopping.

The transport network

🛣 53,439 miles (86,012 km)	🚉 661 miles (1064 km)
⛟ 3376 miles (5434 km)	🚂 211 miles (340 km)

Air links are well-developed between most of the Caribbean islands. The importance of the tourist trade has recently encouraged many countries to upgrade their paved roads.

Major industry and infrastructure

fish processing	sugar refining
finance	tourism
mining	• major towns
oil refining	✈ international airports
	— major roads
	▨ major industrial areas

▶ **This rock stack** on the coast of St-Martin in the Leeward Islands has been created by wave action which undercut the cliffs, forming an arch. Continued wave action weakened the arch, which eventually collapsed leaving a single tower of rock.

▶ **The Pitons in** St Lucia are two volcanic domes; the tallest is 2620 ft (798 m) high. Their steep slopes are covered in thick forest.

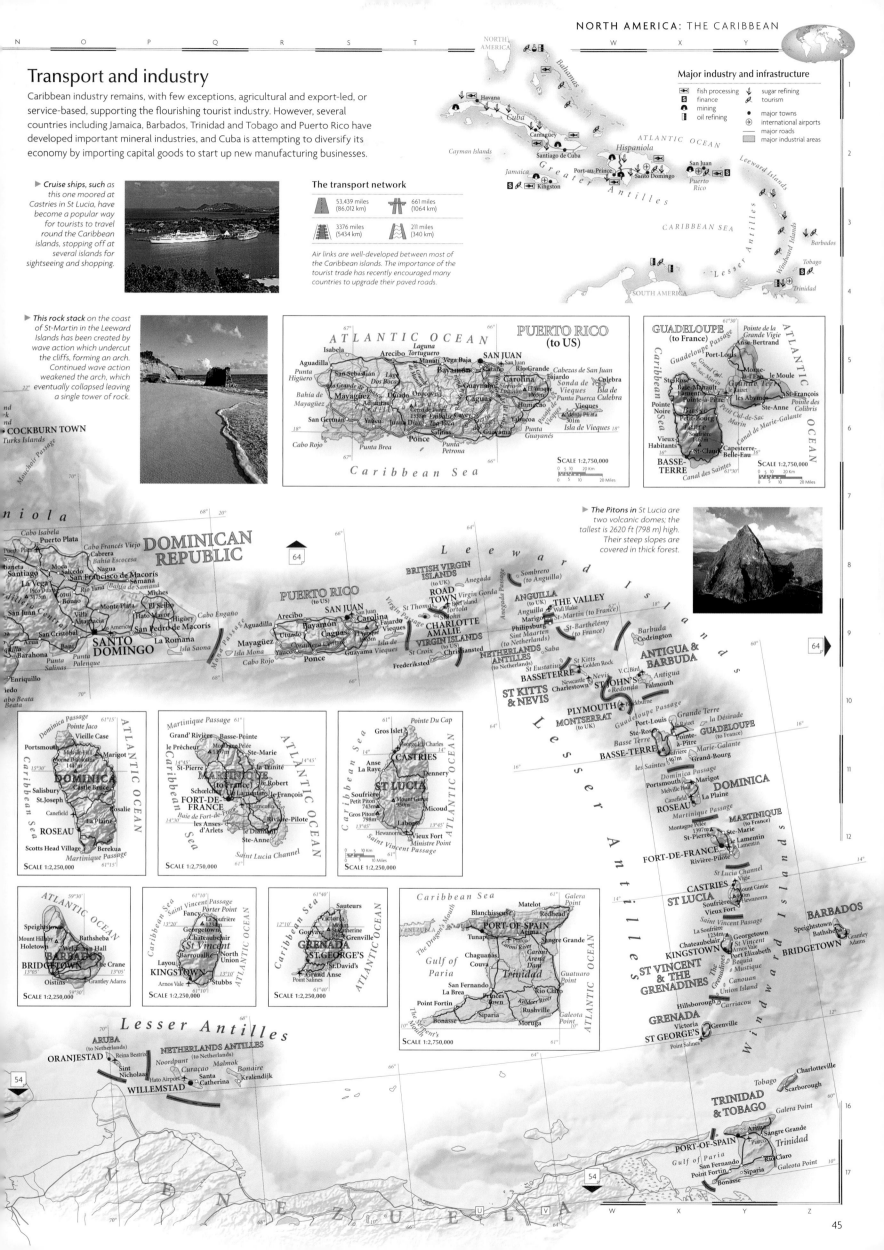

South America

Reaching from the humid tropics down into the cold south Atlantic, South America has an area of 6,886,000 sq miles (17,835,000 sq km). There are 12 separate countries, with the largest, Brazil, covering almost half the continent.

- **Greatest extent, North–South:** *4750 miles / 7640 km*
- **Greatest extent, East–West:** *3100 miles / 4990 km*

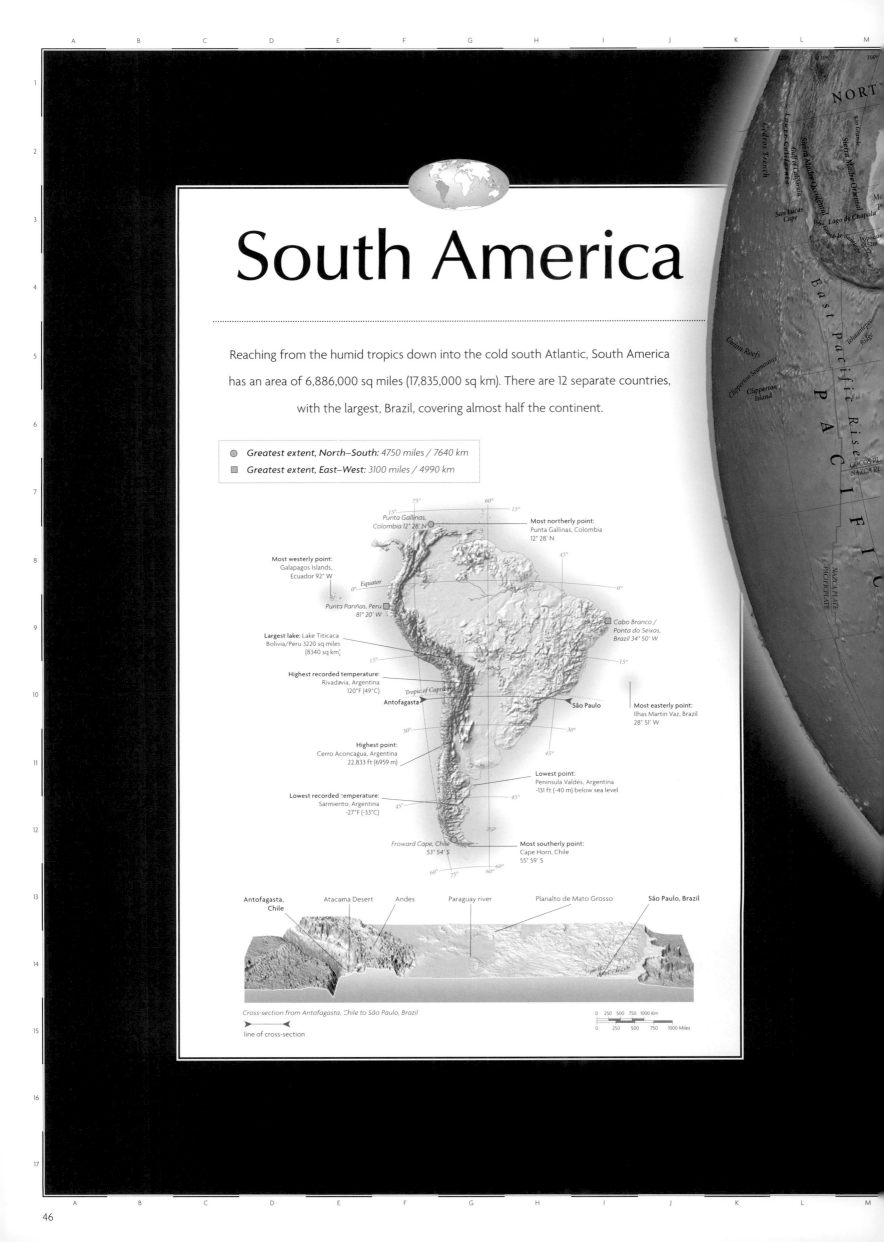

Punta Gallinas,
Colombia 12° 28' N

Most northerly point:
Punta Gallinas, Colombia
12° 28' N

Most westerly point:
Galapagos Islands,
Ecuador 92° W

Equator

Punta Pariñas, Peru
81° 20' W

Cabo Branco /
Ponta do Seixas,
Brazil 34° 50' W

Largest lake: Lake Titicaca
Bolivia/Peru 3220 sq miles
(8340 sq km)

Highest recorded temperature:
Rivadavia, Argentina
120°F (49°C)

Tropic of Capricorn

Antofagasta

São Paulo

Most easterly point:
Ilhas Martin Vaz, Brazil
28° 51' W

Highest point:
Cerro Aconcagua, Argentina
22,833 ft (6959 m)

Lowest point:
Peninsula Valdés, Argentina
-131 ft (-40 m) below sea level

Lowest recorded temperature:
Sarmiento, Argentina
-27°F (-33°C)

Froward Cape, Chile
53° 54' S

Most southerly point:
Cape Horn, Chile
55° 59' S

Antofagasta,
Chile

Atacama Desert

Andes

Paraguay river

Planalto de Mato Grosso

São Paulo, Brazil

Cross-section from Antofagasta, Chile to São Paulo, Brazil

line of cross-section

0 250 500 750 1000 Km
0 250 500 750 1000 Miles

NORT

N O P Q R S T U V W X Y Z
SOUTH AMERICA
ATLANTIC OCEAN
MID-ATLANTIC RIDGE
West Indies
Greater Antilles
Lesser Antilles
Caribbean Sea
Gulf of Mexico
Sargasso Sea
Nares Plain
Hatteras Plain
Bahamas
Cuba
Hispaniola
Puerto Rico
Puerto Rico Trench
Jamaica
Yucatan Basin
Cayman Trough
Windward Passage
Colombian Basin
Panama Basin
Guiana Basin
Demerara Plain
Amazon Fan
Ceará Plain
Guiana Highlands
Serra Parima
Tumuc-Humac Mountains
Amazon Basin
Llanos
ANDES
Planalto de Mato Grosso
Chapada dos Parecis
Brazilian Highlands
Planalto da Borborema
Brazil Basin
Pantanal
Gran Chaco
Pampas
Mesopotamia
Patagonia
Peru Basin
Chile Basin
Peru-Chile Trench
Nazca Ridge
Roggeveen Basin
Argentine Basin
Argentine Plain
Falkland Plateau
Falkland Escarpment
Maurice Ewing Bank
Scotia Sea
Scotia Ridge
South Sandwich Trench
Weddell Sea
ANTARCTICA
Doldrums Fracture Zone
Four North Fracture Zone
Saint Paul Fracture Zone
Cape Verde Basin
Cape Verde Islands
Gambia Plain
Mendaña Fracture Zone
Sala y Gomez Fracture Zone
East Pacific Rise
Tropic of Cancer
Tropic of Capricorn
Equator
Antarctic Circle
NORTH AMERICAN PLATE
SOUTH AMERICAN PLATE
AFRICAN PLATE
CARIBBEAN PLATE
NAZCA PLATE
ANTARCTIC PLATE
SCOTIA PLATE
PACIFIC PLATE
Amazon
Rio Negro
Orinoco
Paraná
Uruguay
Tocantins
São Francisco
Madeira
Rio de la Plata
Lake Titicaca
Lake Maracaibo
Isla de Margarita
Trinidad
Tobago
Barbados
Grenada
Isthmus of Panama
Gulf of Panama
Gulf of Darien
Gulf of Guayaquil
Galapagos Islands
Easter Island
Juan Fernandez Islands
Islas de los Desventurados
Chimborazo 6310m
Cerro Aconcagua 6959m
Lagoa dos Patos
Mirim Lagoon
Bahía Blanca
Golfo San Matías
Gulf of San Jorge
Bahía Grande
Strait of Magellan
Tierra del Fuego
Cape Horn
Falkland Islands
South Georgia
South Sandwich Islands
South Shetland Islands
South Orkney Islands
Archipiélago de los Chonos
Golfo Corcovado
Atol das Rocas
Fernando de Noronha
Cabo de São Roque
Cabo Branco
Pernambuco Plain
Baía de Todos os Santos
Abrolhos Bank
Trindade Spur
Santos Plateau
Rio Grande Rise
Ilha de Marajó
Baía de Marajó
Baía de São Marcos
Represa de Tucuruí
Represa de Sobradinho
Represa de Itaparica
Represa de Itaipú
Represa Balbina
Serra do Mar
Serra da Mantiqueira
Serra do Espinhaço
Chapada Diamantina
Atacama Desert
Altiplano
Yungas
Lago Poopó
Cordillera Oriental
Cordillera Occidental
Cordillera Real

Physical South America

Three major physiographic regions characterize South America. The oldest, the ancient Brazilian Shield and the smaller Guyana and Patagonian shields, form the stable core of the continent. Stretching along the entire west coast are the younger Andean fold mountains with many summits rising to 20,000 ft (6100 m). These two diverse regions are separated by a number of sedimentary basins carrying South America's large river systems to the sea. These include the massive Amazon Basin and the basin of the Gran Chaco.

The Amazon Basin and Guyana Shield

The Amazon river occupies a large depression in the Earth's crust, formed by the uplift of the Andes. It is covered by thick volcanic deposits and layers of alluvium – these have been laid down by the Amazon's many tributaries. To the north is the smaller Guyana Shield.

Section across northern South America showing Amazon Basin and its drainage pattern.

Headwaters of the Amazon rise in the Andes

Thick alluvium deposits

Mouths of the Amazon

Scale 1:30,500,000

projection: Lambert Azimuthal Equal Area

The Andean Uplands

The Andean Uplands run along the west coast of South America. They are being uplifted as the Nazca Plate is subducted beneath the South American Plate. They contain some of the world's largest volcanoes, such as Cotopaxi, and Lake Titicaca which occupies a dormant site. The far south has many large ice-sheets and a fragmented coastline.

Nazca Plate

South American Plate

Volcanic intrusions

Cross-section through the Andes showing the subduction of the Nazca Plate beneath the South American Plate.

The Brazilian Shield and Gran Chaco

The immense Brazilian Shield underlies more than one-third of South America. It is pitted with numerous volcanic intrusions, and a large basaltic plateau exists between the Paraná river and the Atlantic Ocean. The flat Gran Chaco lies to the west of the shield, covered by sedimentary deposits eroded from the Andes, and transported by South America's mighty rivers.

Young, folded Andes mountains

Volcanic intrusions

Major rivers drain to the south through the Gran Chaco

Ancient resistant shield

Section across central South America showing the flat basin of the Gran Chaco and the ancient Brazilian Shield.

Map key

Elevation

6000m / 19,686ft
4000m / 13,124ft
3000m / 9843ft
2000m / 6562ft
1500m / 4922ft
1000m / 3281ft
500m / 1640ft
250m / 820ft
100m / 328ft
sea level

Plate margins
(for explanation see page xiv)

constructive
destructive
conservative
uncertain

physiographic regions
line of cross-section

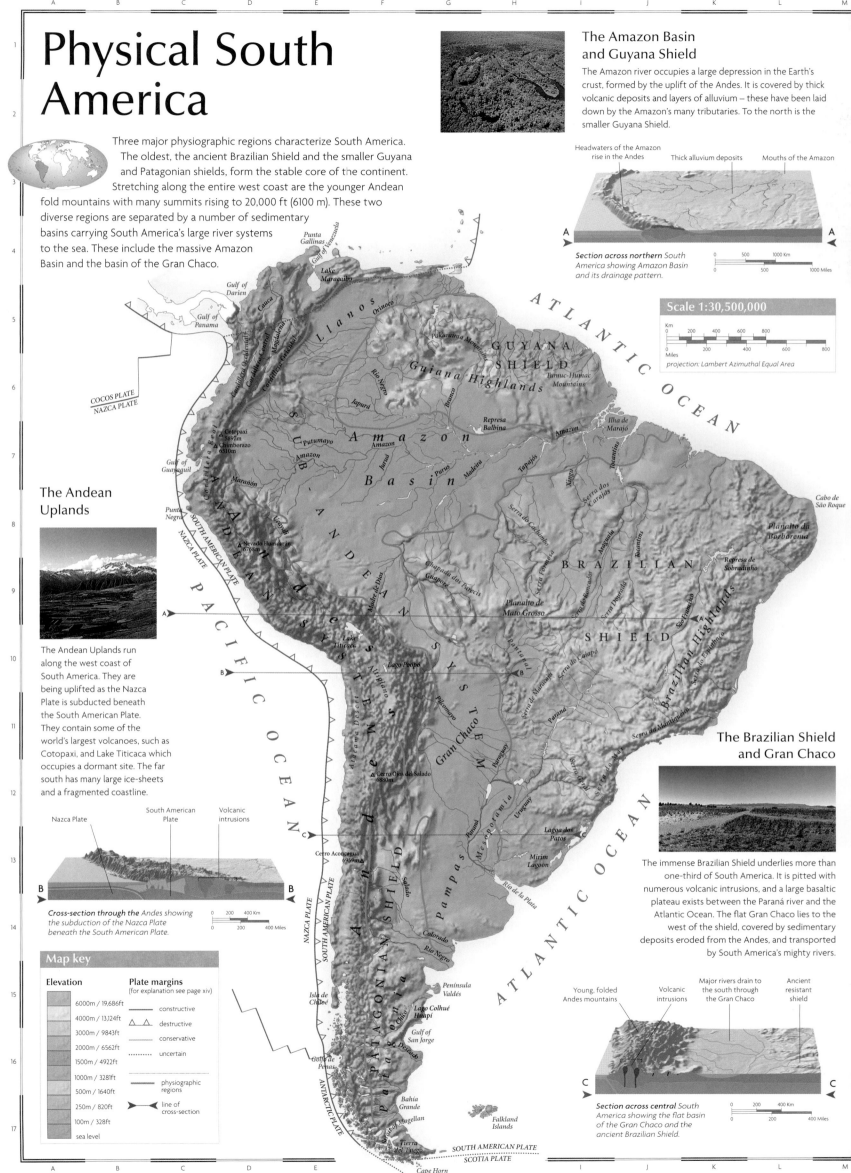

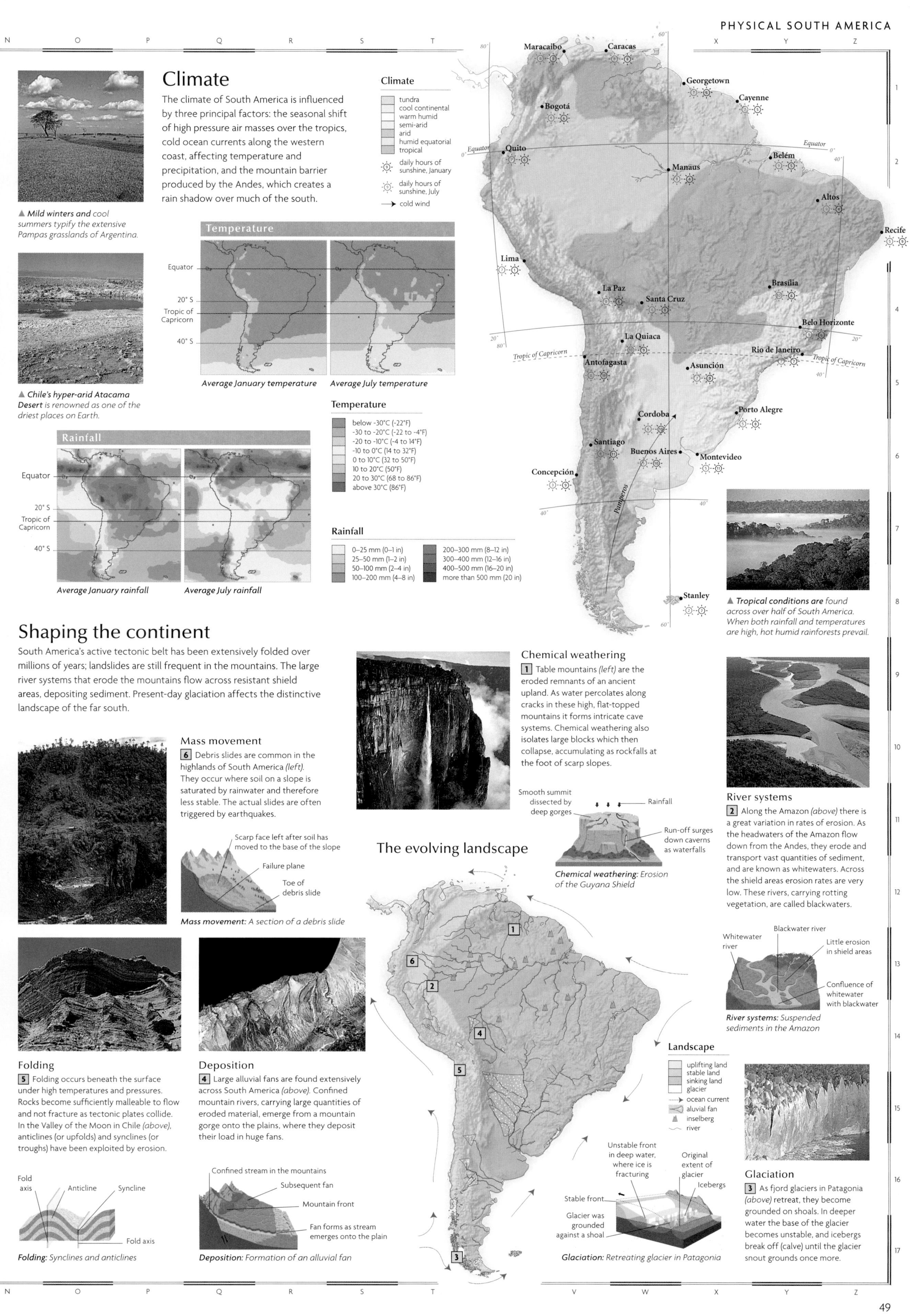

Climate

The climate of South America is influenced by three principal factors: the seasonal shift of high pressure air masses over the tropics, cold ocean currents along the western coast, affecting temperature and precipitation, and the mountain barrier produced by the Andes, which creates a rain shadow over much of the south.

▲ *Mild winters and cool summers typify the extensive Pampas grasslands of Argentina.*

▲ *Chile's hyper-arid Atacama Desert is renowned as one of the driest places on Earth.*

Climate

- tundra
- cool continental
- warm humid
- semi-arid
- arid
- humid equatorial
- tropical
- ☼ daily hours of sunshine, January
- ☼ daily hours of sunshine, July
- → cold wind

Temperature

Average January temperature

Average July temperature

Temperature
- below -30°C (-22°F)
- -30 to -20°C (-22 to -4°F)
- -20 to -10°C (-4 to 14°F)
- -10 to 0°C (14 to 32°F)
- 0 to 10°C (32 to 50°F)
- 10 to 20°C (50°F)
- 20 to 30°C (68 to 86°F)
- above 30°C (86°F)

Rainfall

Average January rainfall

Average July rainfall

Rainfall
- 0–25 mm (0–1 in)
- 25–50 mm (1–2 in)
- 50–100 mm (2–4 in)
- 100–200 mm (4–8 in)
- 200–300 mm (8–12 in)
- 300–400 mm (12–16 in)
- 400–500 mm (16–20 in)
- more than 500 mm (20 in)

▲ *Tropical conditions are found across over half of South America. When both rainfall and temperatures are high, hot humid rainforests prevail.*

Shaping the continent

South America's active tectonic belt has been extensively folded over millions of years; landslides are still frequent in the mountains. The large river systems that erode the mountains flow across resistant shield areas, depositing sediment. Present-day glaciation affects the distinctive landscape of the far south.

Mass movement

6 Debris slides are common in the highlands of South America (*left*). They occur where soil on a slope is saturated by rainwater and therefore less stable. The actual slides are often triggered by earthquakes.

- Scarp face left after soil has moved to the base of the slope
- Failure plane
- Toe of debris slide

***Mass movement:** A section of a debris slide*

Chemical weathering

1 Table mountains (*left*) are the eroded remnants of an ancient upland. As water percolates along cracks in these high, flat-topped mountains it forms intricate cave systems. Chemical weathering also isolates large blocks which then collapse, accumulating as rockfalls at the foot of scarp slopes.

- Smooth summit dissected by deep gorges
- Rainfall
- Run-off surges down caverns as waterfalls

***Chemical weathering:** Erosion of the Guyana Shield*

The evolving landscape

River systems

2 Along the Amazon (*above*) there is a great variation in rates of erosion. As the headwaters of the Amazon flow down from the Andes, they erode and transport vast quantities of sediment, and are known as whitewaters. Across the shield areas erosion rates are very low. These rivers, carrying rotting vegetation, are called blackwaters.

- Whitewater river
- Blackwater river
- Little erosion in shield areas
- Confluence of whitewater with blackwater

***River systems:** Suspended sediments in the Amazon*

Folding

5 Folding occurs beneath the surface under high temperatures and pressures. Rocks become sufficiently malleable to flow and not fracture as tectonic plates collide. In the Valley of the Moon in Chile (*above*), anticlines (or upfolds) and synclines (or troughs) have been exploited by erosion.

- Fold axis
- Anticline
- Syncline
- Fold axis

***Folding:** Synclines and anticlines*

Deposition

4 Large alluvial fans are found extensively across South America (*above*). Confined mountain rivers, carrying large quantities of eroded material, emerge from a mountain gorge onto the plains, where they deposit their load in huge fans.

- Confined stream in the mountains
- Subsequent fan
- Mountain front
- Fan forms as stream emerges onto the plain

***Deposition:** Formation of an alluvial fan*

Landscape
- uplifting land
- stable land
- sinking land
- glacier
- → ocean current
- alluvial fan
- ▲ inselberg
- river

- Unstable front in deep water, where ice is fracturing
- Original extent of glacier
- Icebergs
- Stable front
- Glacier was grounded against a shoal

***Glaciation:** Retreating glacier in Patagonia*

Glaciation

3 As fjord glaciers in Patagonia (*above*) retreat, they become grounded on shoals. In deeper water the base of the glacier becomes unstable, and icebergs break off (calve) until the glacier snout grounds once more.

Political South America

Modern South America's political boundaries have their origins in the territorial endeavours of explorers during the 16th century, who claimed almost the entire continent for Portugal and Spain. The Portuguese land in the east later evolved into the federal states of Brazil, while the Spanish vice-royalties eventually emerged as separate independent nation-states in the early 19th century. South America's growing population has become increasingly urbanized, with the expansion of coastal cities into large conurbations like Rio de Janeiro and Buenos Aires. In Brazil, Argentina, Chile and Uruguay, a succession of military dictatorships has given way to fragile, but strengthening, democracies.

◀ *Europe retains a small foothold in South America. Kourou in French Guiana was the site chosen by the European Space Agency to launch the Ariane rocket. As a result of its status as a French overseas department, French Guiana is actually part of the European Union.*

Scale 1:24,000,000

Km
0 100 200 300 400 500 600 700 800

0 100 200 300 400 500 600 700 800
Miles

projection: Lambert Azimuthal Equal Area

Transport

Most major road and rail routes are confined to the coastal regions by the forbidding natural barriers of the Andes mountains and the Amazon Basin. Few major cross-continental routes exist, although Buenos Aires serves as a transport centre for the main rail links to La Paz and Valparaíso, while the construction of the Trans-Amazon and Pan-American Highways have made direct road travel possible from Recife to Lima and from Puerto Montt up the coast into central America. A new waterway project is proposed to transform the Paraguay river into a major shipping route, although it involves considerable wetland destruction.

▶ *South America's most extensive rail network is centred on the Argentinian capital, Buenos Aires. The construction of new rail lines from this important port, allowed the colonization of the Pampas lands for agriculture.*

Languages

Prior to European exploration in the 16th century, a diverse range of indigenous languages were spoken across the continent. With the arrival of Iberian settlers, Spanish became the dominant language, with Portuguese spoken in Brazil, and Native American languages such as Quechua and Guaraní, becoming concentrated in the continental interior. Today this pattern persists, although successive European colonization has led to Dutch being spoken in Surinam, English in Guyana, and French in French Guiana, while in large urban areas, Japanese and Chinese are increasingly common.

Transport

— major roads and motorways
— major railways
— international borders
• transport intersections
⊕ international airports
⊕ major ports

Language groups

American Indian
Germanic
Romance

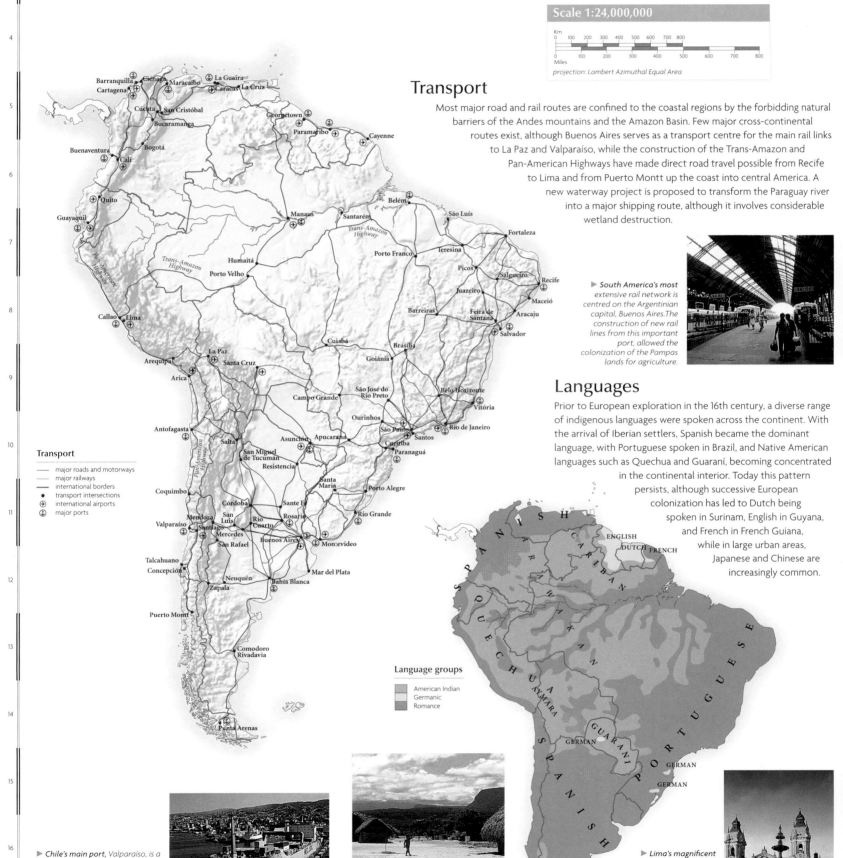

▶ *Chile's main port, Valparaíso, is a vital national shipping centre, in addition to playing a key role in the growing trade with Pacific nations. The country's awkward, elongated shape means that sea transport is frequently used for internal travel and communications in Chile.*

▲ *Indigenous South American lifestyles have not been totally submerged by European cultures and languages. The continental interior, and particularly the Amazon Basin, is still home to many different ethnic peoples.*

▶ *Lima's magnificent cathedral reflects South America's colonial past with its unmistakably Spanish style. In July 1821, Peru became the last Spanish colony on the mainland to declare independence.*

▶ *In April 1960, Brazil's government began the move from Rio de Janeiro to Brasília, a futuristic new city built in the sparsely populated interior. Brasília is now the federal capital of Brazil.*

Caribbean Sea

TRINIDAD & TOBAGO

ATLANTIC OCEAN

Santa Marta
Barranquilla
Cartagena
Maracaibo
Valledupar
Cabimas
Valencia
CARACAS
Cumaná
Montería
Cúcuta
Barinas
Barquisimeto
Maracay
Bucaramanga
Ciudad Guayana
San Cristóbal
Medellín
Manizales
Pereira
BOGOTÁ
Armenia
Ibagué
Cali

Gulf of Venezuela
Lake Maracaibo
Orinoco
Llanos

VENEZUELA
Venezuelan territorial claim

GEORGETOWN
Linden
PARAMARIBO
GUYANA
CAYENNE
SURINAM
Surinamese territorial claims
French Guiana
(to France)

COLOMBIA
Esmeraldas
Pasto
Río Negro
Boa Vista
RORAIMA
Guiana Highlands

Equator
QUITO
ECUADOR
Ambato
Riobamba
Portoviejo
Babahoyo
Guayaquil
Cuenca
Machala
Caquetá
Putumayo
Iquitos
Amazon
AMAZONAS
Basin
Manaus
Santarém
Belém
AMAPÁ
Macapá
PARÁ
Amazon
MARANHÃO
São Luís
Fortaleza
CEARÁ
Teresina
Piura
Marañón
Jurúa
Purus
Madeira
Tapajós
Xingu
Tocantins
Araguaia
PIAUÍ
RIO GRANDE DO NORTE
Natal
PARAÍBA
João Pessoa
Jaboatão
Recife
Chiclayo
Trujillo
PERU
ACRE
Rio Branco
Porto Velho
RONDÔNIA
B R A Z I L
PERNAMBUCO
Juazeiro
ALAGOAS
Maceió
SERGIPE
Aracaju
Represa de Sobradinho
São Francisco
BAHIA
Salvador
Callao
LIMA
Huancayo
Cusco
MATO GROSSO
Planalto de Mato Grosso
Cuiabá
BRASÍLIA
DISTRITO FEDERAL
Goiânia
GOIÁS
MINAS GERAIS
Brazilian Highlands
Belo Horizonte
Arequipa
BOLIVIA
LA PAZ
Lake Titicaca
Cochabamba
Oruro
Santa Cruz
SUCRE
Tacna
Arica
Lago Poopó
Iquique
Campo Grande
MATO GROSSO DO SUL
Ribeirão Preto
SÃO PAULO
Vitória
ESPÍRITO SANTO
Juiz de Fora
Tocopilla
PARAGUAY
Gran Chaco
Paraná
Londrina
Campinas
Osasco
Sorocaba
São Paulo
Nova Iguaçu
RIO DE JANEIRO
Niterói
Rio de Janeiro
Santos
Tropic of Capricorn
Antofagasta
San Salvador de Jujuy
ASUNCIÓN
Ciudad del Este
PARANÁ
Curitiba
Atacama Desert
Salta
Formosa
Villarrica
San Miguel de Tucumán
SANTA CATARINA
Santiago del Estero
Resistencia
Corrientes
Posadas
Florianópolis
La Serena
Coquimbo
A R G E N T I N A
La Rioja
Paraná
RIO GRANDE DO SUL
Santa Maria
Porto Alegre
San Juan
Córdoba
Santa Fe
Tacuarembó
Melo
Viña del Mar
Valparaíso
SANTIAGO
Mendoza
San Luis
Paraná
Rosario
URUGUAY
Linares
C H I L E
Santa Rosa
BUENOS AIRES
MONTEVIDEO
La Plata
Río de la Plata
Concepción
Lota
Salado
Pampas
Bahía Blanca
Mar del Plata
Temuco
Neuquén
Río Negro
Valdivia
Colorado
Puerto Montt
Patagonia
Chubut
Lago Musters
Lago Colhué Huapi
Rawson
Gulf of San Jorge
Deseado
FALKLAND ISLANDS
(to UK)
STANLEY
Bahía Grande
Río Gallegos
Punta Arenas
Ushuaia
Beagle Channel
Cape Horn

PACIFIC OCEAN

ATLANTIC OCEAN

Map key

Population
- ■ above 5 million
- ▣ 1 million to 5 million
- ◉ 500,000 to 1 million
- ◎ 100,000 to 500,000
- ⊕ 50,000 to 100,000
- ⊙ 10,000 to 50,000
- ○ below 10,000
- ● Country capital
- • State capital

Borders
- full international border
- disputed de facto border
- disputed territorial claim border
- state border

▲ *Perched high in the Andes like many of the cities in western South America, La Paz, Bolivia is the world's highest capital city at over 11,500 ft (3500 m).*

▶ *Rapid urbanization was a feature of most South American countries in the latter half of the 20th century. In many cases, this unchecked growth has led to the development of sprawling slums, lacking adequate water and sewerage facilities.*

Population

Almost half of South America's population lives in Brazil but, due to the large uninhabited expanses of the Amazon Basin, its overall population density is much lower than in other countries. During the 20th century the most important population trend was the movement from rural to urban areas, giving rise to great population concentrations in large cities like São Paulo, Rio de Janeiro, Caracas, Lima, Bogotá and Buenos Aires.

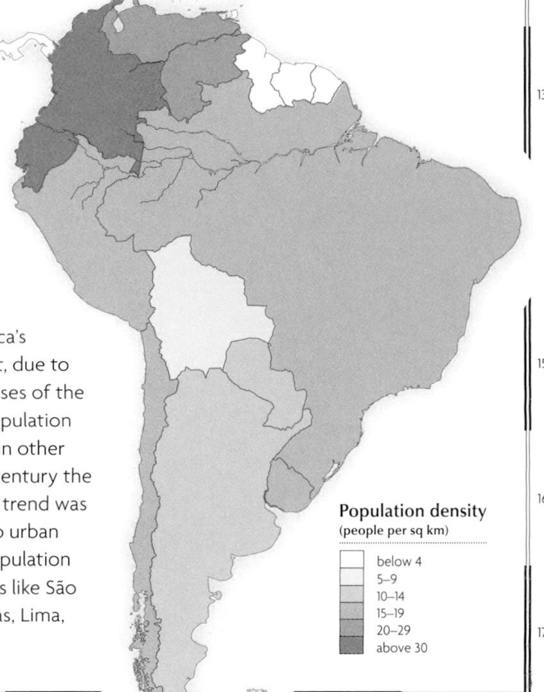

Population density
(people per sq km)
- below 4
- 5–9
- 10–14
- 15–19
- 20–29
- above 30

51

South American resources

Agriculture still provides the largest single form of employment in South America, although rural unemployment and poverty continue to drive people towards the huge coastal cities in search of jobs and opportunities. Mineral and fuel resources, although substantial, are distributed unevenly; few countries have both fossil fuels and minerals. To break industrial dependence on raw materials, boost manufacturing, and improve infrastructure, governments borrowed heavily from the World Bank in the 1960s and 1970s. This led to the accumulation of massive debts which are unlikely ever to be repaid. Today, Brazil dominates the continent's economic output, followed by Argentina. Recently, the less-developed western side of South America has benefited due to its geographical position; for example Chile is increasingly exporting raw materials to Japan.

◀ *Ciudad Guayana is a planned industrial complex in eastern Venezuela, built as an iron and steel centre to exploit the nearby iron ore reserves.*

Industry

✈ aerospace	💊 pharmaceuticals
🍺 brewing	🖋 printing & publishing
🚗 car/vehicle manufacture	⚓ shipbuilding
⚗ chemicals	sugar processing
electronics	textiles
⚙ engineering	timber processing
🅂 finance	tobacco processing
fish processing	wine
food processing	oil
hi-tech industry	gas
iron & steel	• industrial cities
meat processing	major industrial areas
△ metal refining	
narcotics	

The cold Peru Current flows north from the Antarctic along the Pacific coast of Peru, providing rich nutrients for one of the world's largest fishing grounds. However, over-exploitation has severely reduced Peru's anchovy catch.

Standard of living

Wealth disparities throughout the continent create a wide gulf between affluent landowners and those afflicted by chronic poverty in inner-city slums. The illicit production of cocaine, and the hugely influential drug barons who control its distribution, contribute to the violent disorder and corruption which affect northwestern South America, de-stabilizing local governments and economies.

Standard of living
(UN human development index)
- low
- high

▶ *Both Argentina and Chile are now exploring the southernmost tip of the continent in search of oil. Here in Punta Arenas, a drilling rig is being prepared for exploratory drilling in the Strait of Magellan.*

GNI per capita (US$)
- below 999
- 1000–1999
- 2000–2999
- 3000–3999
- 4000–4999
- above 5000

Industry

Argentina and Brazil are South America's most industrialized countries and São Paulo is the continent's leading industrial centre. Long-term government investment in Brazilian industry has encouraged a diverse industrial base; engineering, steel production, food processing, textile manufacture and chemicals predominate. The illegal production of cocaine is economically significant in the Andean countries of Colombia and Bolivia. In Venezuela, the oil-dominated economy has left the country vulnerable to world oil price fluctuations. Food processing and mineral exploitation are common throughout the less industrially developed parts of the continent, including Bolivia, Chile, Ecuador and Peru.

Environmental issues

The Amazon Basin is one of the last great wilderness areas left on Earth. The tropical rainforests which grow there are a valuable genetic resource, containing innumerable unique plants and animals. The forests are increasingly under threat from new and expanding settlements and 'slash and burn' farming techniques, which clear land for the raising of beef cattle, causing land degradation and soil erosion.

◄ **Clouds of smoke** billow from the burning Amazon rainforest. Over 11,500 sq miles (30,000 sq km) of virgin rainforest are being cleared annually, destroying an ancient, irreplaceable, natural resource and biodiverse habitat.

Environmental issues
- national parks
- tropical forest
- forest destroyed
- desert
- desertification
- polluted rivers
- marine pollution
- heavy marine pollution
- • poor urban air quality

Mineral resources

Over a quarter of the world's known copper reserves are found at the Chuquicamata mine in northern Chile, and other metallic minerals such as tin are found along the length of the Andes. The discovery of oil and gas at Venezuela's Lake Maracaibo in 1917 turned the country into one of the world's leading oil producers. In contrast, South America is virtually devoid of coal, the only significant deposit being on the peninsula of Guajira in Colombia.

◄ **Copper is Chile's** largest export, most of which is mined at Chuquicamata. Along the length of the Andes, metallic minerals like copper and tin are found in abundance, formed by the excessive pressures and heat involved in mountain-building.

Mineral resources
- oil field
- gas field
- coal field
- bauxite
- copper
- diamonds
- gold
- iron
- lead
- silver
- tin

Using the land and sea

Many foods now common worldwide originated in South America. These include the potato, tomato, squash, and cassava. Today, large herds of beef cattle roam the temperate grasslands of the Pampas, supporting an extensive meat-packing trade in Argentina, Uruguay and Paraguay. Corn (maize) is grown as a staple crop across the continent and coffee is grown as a cash crop in Brazil and Colombia. Coca plants grown in Bolivia, Peru and Colombia provide most of the world's cocaine. Fish and shellfish are caught off the western coast, especially anchovies off Peru, shrimps off Ecuador and pilchards off Chile.

◄ **South America, and** Brazil in particular, now leads the world in coffee production, mainly growing Coffea Arabica in large plantations. Coffee beans are harvested, roasted and brewed to produce the world's second most popular drink, after tea.

◄ **The Pampas region** of southeast South America is characterized by extensive, flat plains, and populated by cattle and ranchers (gauchos). Argentina is a major world producer of beef, much of which is exported to the USA for use in hamburgers.

◄ **High in the Andes,** hardy alpacas graze on the barren land. Alpacas are thought to have been domesticated by the Incas, whose nobility wore robes made from their wool. Today, they are still reared and prized for their soft, warm fleeces.

Using the land and sea
- barren land
- cropland
- desert
- forest
- mountain region
- pasture
- • major conurbations
- cattle
- pigs
- sheep
- bananas
- corn (maize)
- citrus fruits
- cocoa
- cotton
- coffee
- fishing
- oil palms
- peanuts
- rubber
- shellfish
- soya beans
- sugar cane
- vineyards
- wheat

Northern South America

COLOMBIA, GUYANA, SURINAM, VENEZUELA, French Guiana (to France)

Fringed by the Pacific and Atlantic oceans and the Caribbean Sea, South America's northern region has a rich range of natural resources, some exploited for centuries by colonial powers including the Spanish, French, Dutch and British, others still to be fully explored. The prospects for further economic development in Colombia, Guyana and Surinam are blighted by drug-related violence and political instability. Venezuela, despite huge incomes from its oil reserves, remains less developed in other industrial sectors. French Guiana is an overseas *département* of France, now seeking greater autonomy. Most of the major population centres, such as Bogotá, have grown up in the temperate conditions of the high Andes or, like Caracas, at strategic points along the Caribbean coast.

▶ *Flowers grown in Colombia are exported all over the world, and include fine carnations and roses. Here, workers are cutting roses which have been grown in plastic greenhouses.*

Map key

Population

- ◉ 1 million to 5 million
- ◉ 500,000 to 1 million
- ◉ 100,000 to 500,000
- ⊕ 50,000 to 100,000
- ○ 10,000 to 50,000
- ○ below 10,000

Elevation

	4000m / 13,124ft
	3000m / 9843ft
	2000m / 6562ft
	1000m / 3281ft
	500m / 1640ft
	250m / 820ft
	100m / 328ft
	sea level

▲ *Large open squares like the Plaza de Bolivar in Bogota are characteristic of many cities founded by the Spanish.*

◀ *Scattered farms and villages have grown up on the gentle slopes of this Colombian river valley, utilizing the fertile soils for farming.*

Scale 1:7,250,000

Km
0 25 50 100 150 200

Miles
0 25 50 100 150 200

projection: Lambert Azimuthal Equal Area

▲ *The Orinoco river flows from its source in the southern Guiana Highlands to form a broad delta on Venezuela's Atlantic coast. One of its distributary channels opens into a wide bay called the Serpent's Mouth.*

54

Transport and industry

Many mineral resources are mined in Colombia, including fuels, gold and precious and semi-precious stones. Revenues from coffee and exports of illegal narcotics are crucial to the economy. Venezuela's major economic activity is the oil industry around Lake Maracaibo (*Lago de Maracaibo*). Sugar and bauxite are exported from Guyana and Surinam.

The transport network

31,720 miles (51,054 km)	
3411 miles (5490 km)	
2448 miles (3940 km)	
22,429 miles (36,100 km)	

Rivers are an important means of transport in Colombia; many are extensively navigable. The Pan-American Highway runs through Colombia. In Venezuela, much infrastructure investment is linked to the oil industry.

Major industry and infrastructure

- chemicals
- finance
- food processing
- iron & steel
- narcotics
- mining
- oil
- oil refining
- pharmaceuticals
- textiles
- timber processing
- capital cities
- major towns
- international airports
- major roads
- major industrial areas

▲ *Vast oil reserves* around Lake Maracaibo (Lago de Maracaibo) form the focus of Venezuelan industry. Incomes from oil are used to invest in other industries and in the development of infrastructure.

Using the land

The Andean basins support cereals and potatoes. Livestock graze at higher altitudes and on the drier tropical grasslands known as the *llanos*; hardy goats are reared in scrubland areas. Grown at higher elevations, coffee is an important cash crop, as is cotton, sugar cane, bananas, citrus fruits, cocoa and rice, farmed on the Caribbean lowlands. Coca is the most widely-grown narcotic plant, with heroin poppies grown in Colombia and marijuana in lowland areas throughout the region.

The urban/rural population divide

urban 80%   rural 20%

0 10 20 30 40 50 60 70 80 90 100

Population density	Total land area
78 people per sq mile (30 people per sq km)	1,111,317 sq miles (2,879,060 sq km)

Land use and agricultural distribution

- cattle
- goats
- bananas
- cereals
- coffee
- cotton
- sugar cane
- capital cities
- major towns
- pasture
- cropland
- forest
- wetlands
- mountain region

The landscape

At its northernmost reaches, in western Colombia and Venezuela, the great Andean mountain chain splits into three distinct ranges: the Cordillera Oriental, Cordillera Central and Cordillera Occidental, intercut by a complex series of lesser ranges and basins. The relief becomes lower toward the coast and the interior plains of the northern Amazon Basin, rising again into the tropical hills of the Guiana Highlands.

▲ *The Sierra Nevada* de Santa Marta is a granite massif which rises sharply from the Caribbean lowlands to snow-covered peaks, the tallest of which is 18,947 ft (5775 m) high.

Lake Maracaibo (*Lago de Maracaibo*) is not a true lake but a shallow inlet of the Caribbean Sea. It is the main source of Venezuela's oil.

The drainage basin of the Magdalena River and the Cauca, its main tributary, covers over 20% of Colombia's total surface area.

Cordillera Occidental

Cordillera Central

Cordillera Oriental

Colombia's eastern lowlands are known locally as *llanos*, meaning grasslands.

In the Guiana Highlands, Venezuela's most remote region, the ancient crystalline rocks contain deposits of iron ore, gold and diamonds.

Angel Falls (*Salto Ángel*), at 3212 ft (979 m), is the world's highest waterfall.

Igneous intrusions into the crystalline plateau which forms most of central Guyana have led to the formation of the many rapids which characterize Guyana's rivers.

▲ *The Guyana Shield* is one of the oldest land surfaces in the world – probably formed more than 4 billion years ago. Chemical weathering over millions of years has created flat-topped table mountains and large numbers of inselbergs.

Guyana Shield

- Alluvial plains
- Inselbergs
- Table mountains

Over 80% of Surinam is covered by tropical rainforest.

Most of the land in French Guiana is low-lying; here, the rocks of the Guiana Highlands have been eroded by rivers flowing towards the sea.

Potaru river

▶ *The Potaru river* descends 741 ft (226 m) over a sandstone ledge at Kaieteur Falls in Guyana.

Western South America

BOLIVIA, ECUADOR, PERU

The three states of Western South America share a similar geography and recent history. Dominated by the Inca empire until Spanish conquest in the 16th century, they achieved independence from Spain in the early 19th century. The precipitous terrain of the Andes presents severe difficulties for overland transport and continues to be a barrier to national unity and stability. Although Ecuador is now a relatively stable democracy, the military is highly influential in Peru and Bolivia, while the drug trade and associated corruption discourages external aid and economic progress. Wealth and power are still largely concentrated in the hands of a small elite of families, who attained their position during the Spanish colonial period. Energy resources and political recognition for the indigenous peoples are becoming increasingly important issues, particularly in Bolivia.

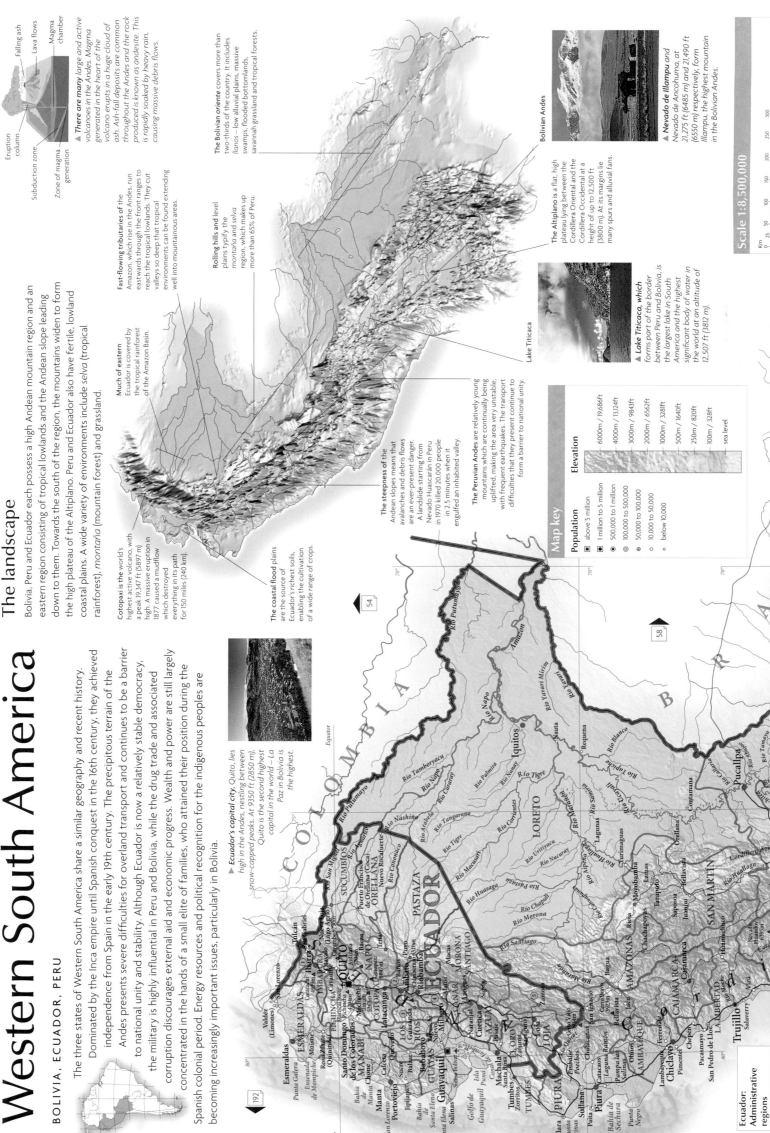

The landscape

Bolivia, Peru and Ecuador each possess a high Andean mountain region and an eastern region consisting of tropical lowlands and the Andean slope leading down to them. Towards the south of the region, the mountains widen to form the high plateau of the Altiplano. Peru and Ecuador also have fertile, lowland coastal plains. A wide variety of environments include *selva* (tropical rainforest), *montaña* (mountain forest) and grassland.

There are many large and active volcanoes in the Andes. Magma generated in the heart of the volcano erupts in a huge cloud of ash. Ash-fall deposits are common throughout the Andes and the rock produced is known as andesite. This is rapidly soaked by heavy rain, causing massive debris flows.

Eruption column
Falling ash
Lava flows
Subduction zone
Zone of magma generation
Magma chamber

Fast-flowing tributaries of the Amazon, which rise in the Andes, run eastwards through the front ranges to reach the tropical lowlands. They cut valleys so deep that tropical environments can be found extending well into mountainous areas.

Much of eastern Ecuador is covered by the tropical rainforest of the Amazon Basin.

Cotopaxi is the world's highest active volcano, with a peak 19,347 ft (5897 m) high. A massive eruption in 1877 caused a mudflow which destroyed everything in its path for 150 miles (240 km).

The coastal flood plains are the source of Ecuador's richest soils, enabling the cultivation of a wide range of crops.

▲ *Ecuador's capital city*, Quito, lies high in the Andes, nestling between snow-capped peaks. At 9350 ft (2850 m), Quito is the second highest capital in the world – La Paz in Bolivia is the highest.

The steepness of the Andean slopes means that avalanches and debris flows are an ever-present danger. A landslide starting from Nevado Huascarán in Peru in 1970 killed 20,000 people in 2.5 minutes when it engulfed an inhabited valley.

The Peruvian Andes are relatively young mountains which are continually being uplifted, making the area very unstable, with frequent earthquakes. The transport difficulties that they present continue to form a barrier to national unity.

The Bolivian oriente covers more than two-thirds of the country. It includes *llanos* – low alluvial plains, massive swamps, flooded bottomlands, savannah grassland and tropical forests.

Rolling hills and level plains typify the *montaña* and *selva* region, which makes up more than 65% of Peru.

Bolivian Andes

The Altiplano is a flat, high plateau lying between the Cordillera Oriental and the Cordillera Occidental at a height of up to 12,500 ft (3800 m). At its margins lie many spurs and alluvial fans.

▲ *Nevado de Illampu and* Nevado de Ancohuma, at 21,275 ft (6485 m) and 21,490 ft (6550 m) respectively, form Illampu, the highest mountain in the Bolivian Andes.

▲ *Lake Titicaca, which* forms part of the border between Peru and Bolivia, is the largest lake in South America and the highest significant body of water in the world at an altitude of 12,507 ft (3812 m).

Lake Titicaca

Map key

Population
- ■ above 5 million
- ◉ 1 million to 5 million
- ◎ 500,000 to 1 million
- ⊕ 100,000 to 500,000
- ○ 50,000 to 100,000
- ○ 10,000 to 50,000
- ○ below 10,000

Elevation
- 6000m / 19,686ft
- 4000m / 13,124ft
- 3000m / 9843ft
- 2000m / 6562ft
- 1000m / 3281ft
- 500m / 1640ft
- 250m / 820ft
- 100m / 328ft
- sea level

Scale 1:8,500,000

projection: Lambert Azimuthal Equal Area

Ecuador: Administrative regions
- ① CARCHI
- ② TUNGURAHUA
- ③ BOLÍVAR
- ④ CHIMBORAZO
- ⑤ ZAMORA CHINCHIPE

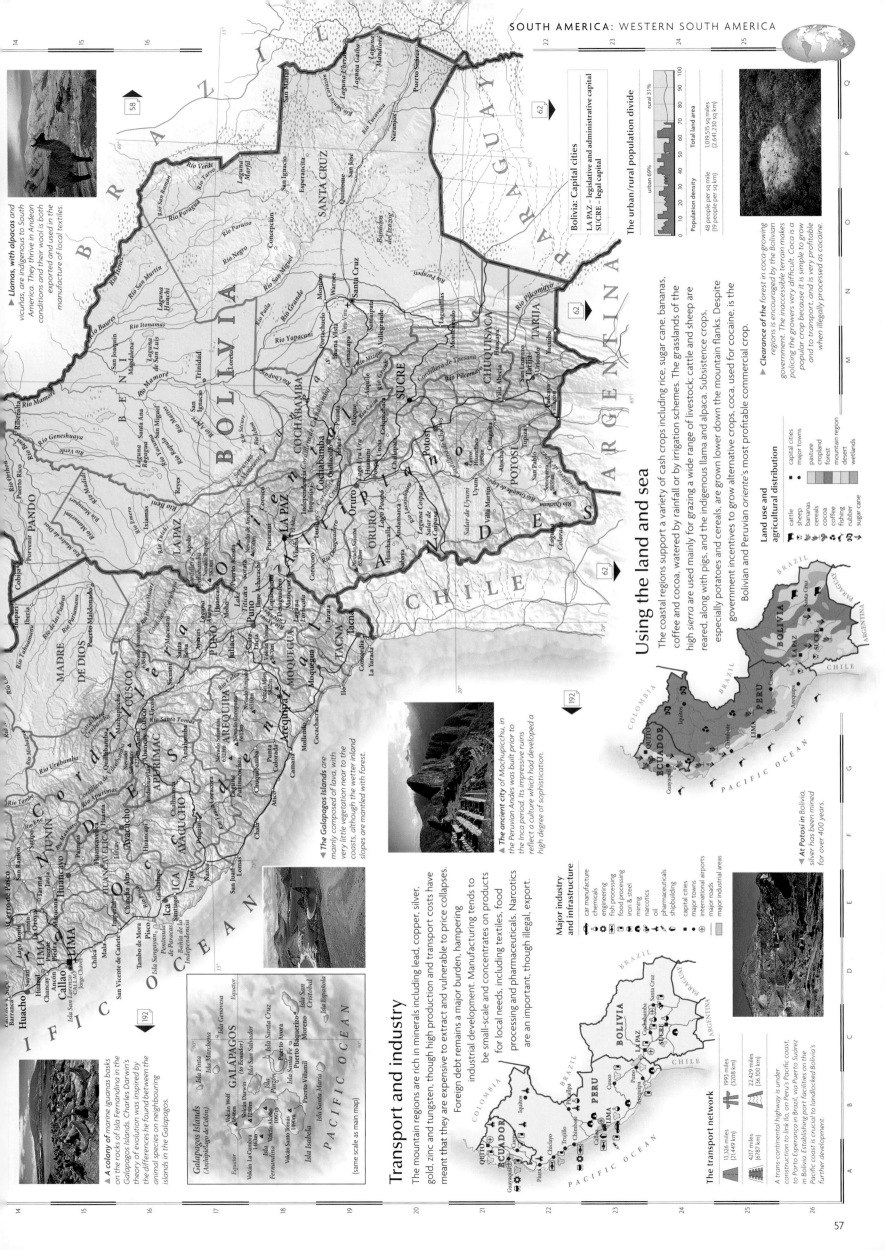

▶ *Llamas, with alpacas and vicuñas, are indigenous to South America. They thrive in Andean conditions and their wool is both exported and used in the manufacture of local textiles.*

The urban/rural population divide

urban 69% · rural 31%

Population density
48 people per sq mile
(19 people per sq km)

Total land area
1,019,515 sq miles
(2,641,230 sq km)

Bolivia: Capital cities
LA PAZ – legislative and administrative capital
SUCRE – legal capital

▲ *Clearance of the forest in coca-growing regions is encouraged by the Bolivian government. The inaccessible terrain makes policing the growers very difficult. Coca is a popular crop because it is simple to grow and to transport, and is very profitable when illegally processed as cocaine.*

Using the land and sea

The coastal regions support a variety of cash crops including rice, sugar cane, bananas, coffee and cocoa, watered by rainfall or by irrigation schemes. The grasslands of the high *sierra* are used mainly for grazing a wide range of livestock; cattle and sheep are reared, along with pigs, and the indigenous llama and alpaca. Subsistence crops, especially potatoes and cereals, are grown lower down the mountain flanks. Despite government incentives to grow alternative crops, coca, used for cocaine, is the Bolivian and Peruvian *oriente's* most profitable commercial crop.

Land use and agricultural distribution

cattle · sheep · bananas · cereals · cocoa · coffee · fishing · rubber · sugar cane

capital cities · major towns · pasture · cropland · forest · mountain region · desert · wetlands

▼ *At Potosí in Bolivia, silver has been mined for over 400 years.*

Transport and industry

The mountain regions are rich in minerals including lead, copper, silver, gold, zinc and tungsten, though high production and transport costs have meant that they are expensive to extract and vulnerable to price collapses. Foreign debt remains a major burden, hampering industrial development. Manufacturing tends to be small-scale and concentrates on products for local needs, including textiles, food processing and pharmaceuticals. Narcotics are an important, though illegal, export.

Major industry and infrastructure

car manufacture · chemicals · engineering · fish processing · food processing · iron & steel · mining · narcotics · oil · pharmaceuticals · shipbuilding · capital cities · major towns · international airports · major roads · major industrial areas

▼ *A colony of marine iguanas basks on the rocks of Isla Fernandina in the Galápagos Islands. Charles Darwin's theory of evolution was inspired by the differences he found between the animal species on neighbouring islands in the Galápagos.*

Galápagos Islands (Archipélago de Colón)
[same scale as main map]

▼ *The Galápagos Islands are mainly composed of lava, with very little vegetation near to the coasts, although the wetter inland slopes are mantled with forest.*

▲ *The ancient city of Machupicchu, in the Peruvian Andes was built prior to the Inca period. Its impressive ruins reflect a culture which had developed a high degree of sophistication.*

The transport network

13,326 miles (21,449 km)
4217 miles (6787 km)
1993 miles (3208 km)
22,429 miles (36,100 km)

A trans-continental highway is under construction to link Ilo, on Peru's Pacific coast, to Porto Esperança in Brazil, via Puerto Suárez in Bolivia. Establishing port facilities on the Pacific coast is crucial to landlocked Bolivia's further development.

Brazil

Brazil is the largest country in South America, with a population of 179 million – greater than the combined total for the whole of the rest of the continent. The 26 states which make up the federal republic of Brazil are administered from the purpose-built capital, Brasília. Tropical rainforest, covering more than one-third of the country, contains rich natural resources, but great tracts are sacrificed to agriculture, industry and urban expansion on a daily basis. Most of Brazil's multi-ethnic population now live in cities, some of which are vast areas of urban sprawl; São Paulo is one of the world's biggest conurbations, with more than 19 million inhabitants. Although prosperity is a reality for some, many people still live in great poverty, and mounting foreign debts continue to damage Brazil's prospects of economic advancement.

Using the land

Brazil has immense natural resources, including minerals and hardwoods, many of which are found in the fragile rainforest. Brazil is the world's leading coffee grower and a major producer of livestock, sugar and orange juice concentrate. Soya beans for animal feed, particularly for poultry feed, have become the country's most significant crop.

Land use and agricultural distribution

cattle
pigs
sheep
citrus fruits
coffee
cotton
soya beans
sugar cane
timber

capital cities
major towns
pasture
cropland
forest

The urban/rural population divide

urban 78%	rural 22%

Population density	Total land area
55 people per sq mile (21 people per sq km)	3,286,472 sq miles (8,511,970 sq km)

The landscape

The Amazon Basin, containing the largest area of tropical rainforest on Earth, covers nearly half of Brazil. It is bordered by two shield areas: in the south by the Brazilian Highlands, and in the north by the Guiana Highlands. The east coast is dominated by a great escarpment which runs for 1600 miles (2565 km).

Guiana Highlands

Brazil's highest mountain is the Pico da Neblina which was only discovered in 1962. It is 9888 ft (3014 m) high.

The flood plains which border the Amazon river are made up of a variety of different features including shallow lakes and swamps, mangrove forests in the tidal delta area and fertile levees on river banks and point bars.

Pantanal wetlands

The ancient Brazilian Highlands have a varied topography. Their plateaux, hills and deep valleys are bordered by highly-eroded mountains containing important mineral deposits. They are drained by three great river systems: the Amazon, the Paraguay–Paraná and the São Francisco.

The São Francisco Basin has a climate unique in Brazil. Known as the 'drought polygon', it has almost no rain during the dry season, leading to regular disastrous droughts.

The northeastern scrublands are known as the *caatinga*, a virtually impenetrable thorny woodland, sometimes intermixed with cacti where water is scarce.

The famous Sugar Loaf Mountain (*Pão de Açúcar*) which overlooks Rio de Janeiro is a fine example of a volcanic plug: a domed core of solidified lava left after the slopes of the original volcano have eroded away.

Deep natural harbours such as Baía de Guanabara were created where the steep slopes of the Serra da Mantiqueira plunge directly into the ocean.

The Amazon Basin is the largest river basin in the world. The Amazon river and over a thousand tributaries drain an area of 2,375,000 sq miles (6,150,000 sq km) and carry one-fifth of the world's fresh water out to sea.

▲ *The Pantanal region in the south of Brazil is an extension of the Gran Chaco plain. The swamps and marshes of this area are renowned for their beauty, and abundant and unique wildlife, including wildfowl and these caimans, a type of crocodile.*

▲ *The Iguaçu river surges over the spectacular Iguaçu Falls (Saltos do Iguaçu) towards the Paraná river. Falls like these are increasingly under pressure from large-scale hydro-electric projects such as that at Itaipú.*

▲ *The fecundity of parts of Brazil's rainforest results from exceptionally high levels of rainfall and the quantities of silt deposited by the Amazon river system.*

▼ *Large-scale gullies are common in Brazil, particularly on hillslopes from which vegetation has been removed. Gullies grow headwards (up the slope), aided by a combination of erosion through water seepage and rainwater runoff.*

Direction of growth

Overland water flow

Gully

Hillslope gullying

Rainfall

Water seeps through hillslope

Map key

Population

■ above 5 million
◉ 1 million to 5 million
⊙ 500,000 to 1 million
⊕ 100,000 to 500,000
⊖ 50,000 to 100,000
○ 10,000 to 50,000
○ below 10,000

Elevation

3000m / 9843ft
2000m / 6562ft
1000m / 328ft
500m / 1640ft
250m / 820ft
100m / 328ft
sea level

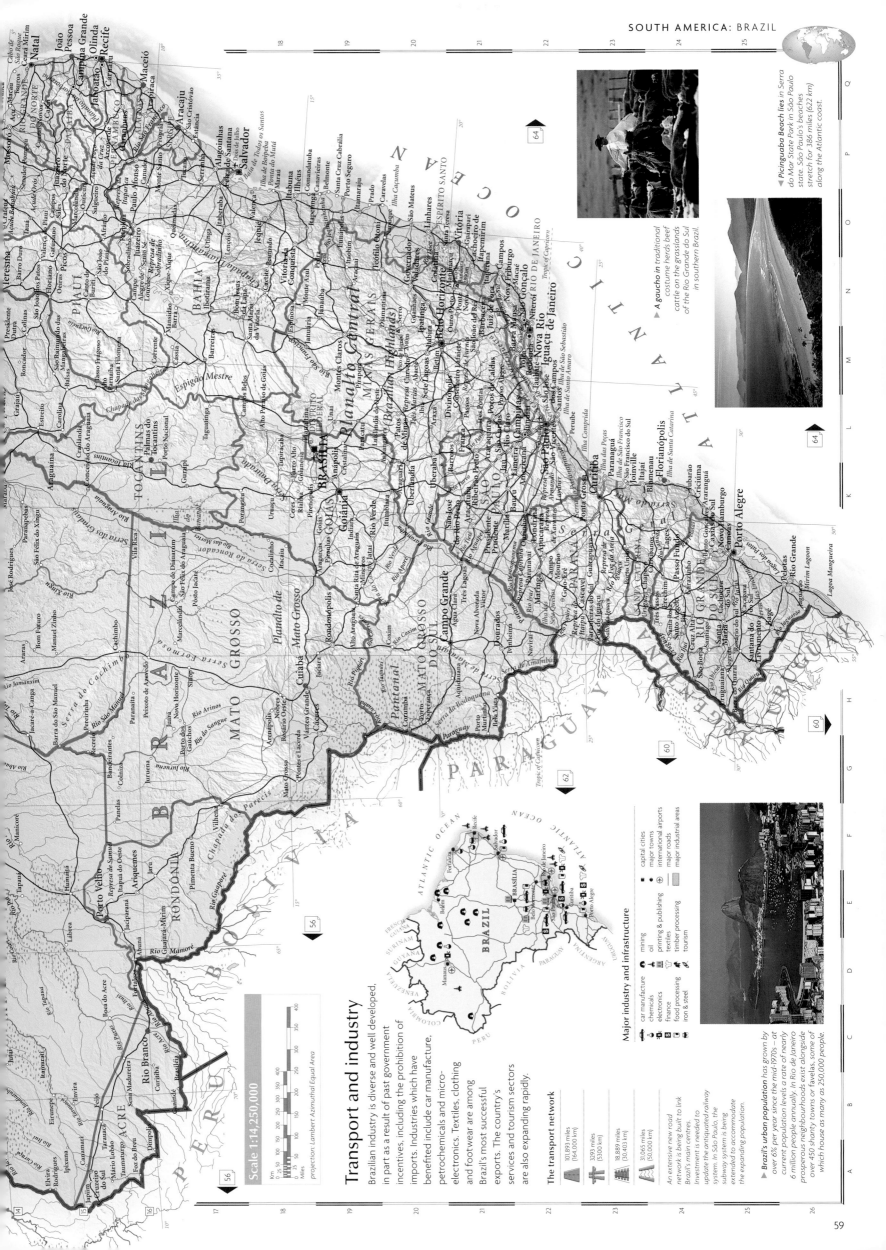

Transport and industry

Brazilian industry is diverse and well developed, in part as a result of past government incentives, including the prohibition of imports. Industries which have benefited include car manufacture, petrochemicals and micro-electronics. Textiles, clothing and footwear are among Brazil's most successful exports. The country's services and tourism sectors are also expanding rapidly.

The transport network

An extensive new road network is being built to link Brazil's main centres. Investment is needed to update the antiquated railway system. In São Paulo, the subway system is being extended to accommodate the expanding population.

101,893 miles (164,000 km)

3293 miles (5300 km)

18,889 miles (30,403 km)

31,065 miles (50,000 km)

▲ Brazil's urban population has grown by over 6% per year since the mid-1970s – at current population levels a rate of nearly 6 million people annually. In Rio de Janeiro prosperous neighbourhoods exist alongside over 450 shanty towns or favelas, some of which house as many as 250,000 people.

Major industry and infrastructure

- ⚙ car manufacture
- chemicals
- electronics
- 🍴 food processing
- iron & steel
- mining
- oil
- 🖨 printing & publishing
- 👕 textiles
- ⛏ timber processing
- ✈ tourism

- ■ capital cities
- • major towns
- ⊕ international airports
- — major roads
- major industrial areas

Scale 1:14,250,000

projection: Lambert Azimuthal Equal Area

▶ Picinguaba Beach lies in Serra do Mar State Park in São Paulo state. São Paulo's beaches stretch for 386 miles (622 km) along the Atlantic coast.

▲ A gaucho in traditional costume herds beef cattle on the grasslands of the Rio Grande do Sul in southern Brazil.

Eastern South America

URUGUAY, NORTHEAST ARGENTINA, SOUTHEAST BRAZIL

The vast conurbations of Rio de Janeiro, São Paulo and Buenos Aires form the core of South America's highly-urbanized eastern region. São Paulo state, with over 40 million inhabitants, is among the world's 20 most powerful economies, and São Paulo is the fastest growing city on the continent. Rio de Janeiro and Buenos Aires, transformed in the last hundred years from port cities to great metropolitan areas each with more than 10 million inhabitants, typify the unstructured growth and wealth disparities of South America's great cities. In Uruguay, two fifths of the population lives in the capital, Montevideo, which faces Buenos Aires across the River Plate (Río de la Plata). Immigration from the countryside has created severe pressure on the urban infrastructure, particularly on available housing, leading to a profusion of crowded shanty settlements (favelas or barrios).

Using the land

Most of Uruguay and the Pampas of northern Argentina are devoted to the rearing of livestock, especially cattle and sheep, which are central to both countries' economies. Soya beans, first produced in Brazil's Rio Grande do Sul, are now more widely grown for large-scale export, as are cereals, sugar cane and grapes. Subsistence crops, including potatoes, corn and sugar beet, are grown on the remaining arable land.

Land use and agricultural distribution

cattle · sheep · cereals · coffee · fruit · soya beans · sugar cane · capital cities · major towns

pasture · cropland · forest · wetlands · barren land

▲ The rolling grasslands of Uruguay are ideally suited to the rearing of cattle, which are concentrated in great herds throughout the region.

▲ Soya beans are harvested, pressed, and processed into soya cake, which is used as animal feed. The cake is fed mainly to chickens on large-scale factory farms, and the growth in soya production has been an important factor in the expansion of the Brazilian poultry trade.

Scale 1:7,000,000

projection: Lambert Azimuthal Equal Area

Map key

Population
- above 5 million
- 1 million to 5 million
- 500,000 to 1 million
- 100,000 to 500,000
- 50,000 to 100,000
- 10,000 to 50,000
- below 10,000

Elevation
- 2000m / 6562ft
- 1000m / 3281ft
- 500m / 1640ft
- 250m / 820ft
- 100m / 328ft
- sea level

Transport and industry

Southeast Brazil is home to much of the important motor and capital goods industry, largely based around São Paulo: iron and steel production is also concentrated in this region. Uruguay's economy continues to be based mainly on the export of livestock products including meat and leather goods. Buenos Aires is Argentina's chief port, and the region has a varied and sophisticated economic base including service-based industries such as finance and publishing, as well as primary processing.

Major industry and infrastructure

car manufacture · chemicals · engineering · finance · food processing · iron & steel · meat processing · printing & publishing · shipbuilding · textiles · timber processing · major towns · capital cities · international airports · major roads · major industrial areas

The transport network

Throughout the region, road networks need to be expanded to cope with urban development. Plans are underway to build a bridge over the River Plate (Río de la Plata) to link Colonia and Buenos Aires.

▲ The Itaipú dam on the Paraná river is one of the largest hydro-electric projects in the world. Jointly financed by Brazil and Paraguay.

▲ Rio de Janeiro's annual carnival, Mardi Gras, which ushers in the start of Lent, is an extravagant five-day parade through the city, characterized by fantastically decorated floats, exuberant dancing and samba music.

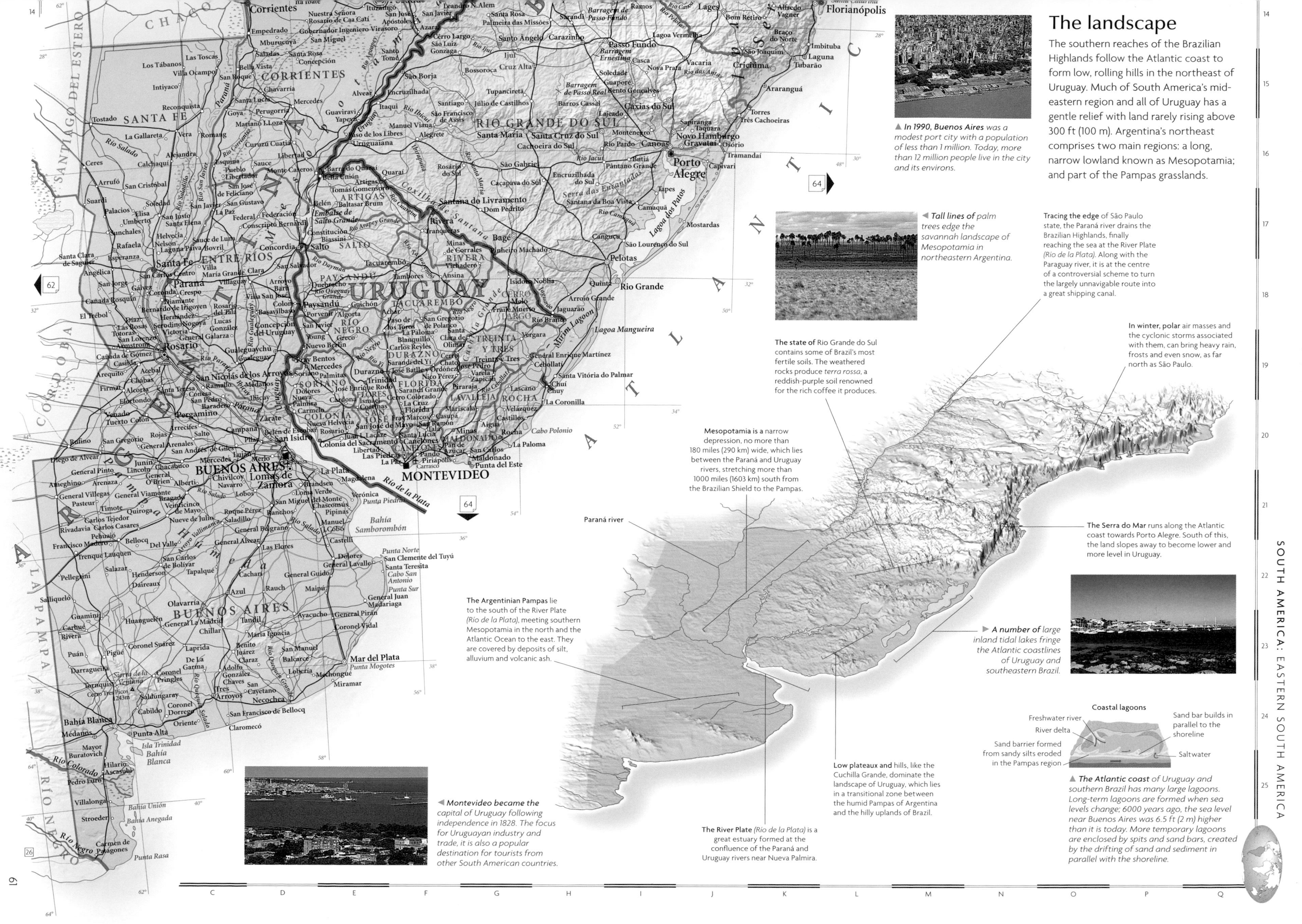

The landscape

The southern reaches of the Brazilian Highlands follow the Atlantic coast to form low, rolling hills in the northeast of Uruguay. Much of South America's mid-eastern region and all of Uruguay has a gentle relief with land rarely rising above 300 ft (100 m). Argentina's northeast comprises two main regions: a long, narrow lowland known as Mesopotamia; and part of the Pampas grasslands.

▲ In 1990, Buenos Aires was a modest port city with a population of less than 1 million. Today, more than 12 million people live in the city and its environs.

Tracing the edge of São Paulo state, the Paraná river drains the Brazilian Highlands, finally reaching the sea at the River Plate (Río de la Plata). Along with the Paraguay river, it is at the centre of a controversial scheme to turn the largely unnavigable route into a great shipping canal.

▼ Tall lines of palm trees edge the savannah landscape of Mesopotamia in northeastern Argentina.

In winter, polar air masses and the cyclonic storms associated with them, can bring heavy rain, frosts and even snow, as far north as São Paulo.

The Serra do Mar runs along the Atlantic coast towards Porto Alegre. South of this, the land slopes away to become lower and more level in Uruguay.

The state of Rio Grande do Sul contains some of Brazil's most fertile soils. The weathered rocks produce terra rossa, a reddish-purple soil renowned for the rich coffee it produces.

▲ A number of large inland tidal lakes fringe the Atlantic coastlines of Uruguay and southeastern Brazil.

Coastal lagoons

▲ The Atlantic coast of Uruguay and southern Brazil has many large lagoons. Long-term lagoons are formed when sea levels change: 6000 years ago, the sea level near Buenos Aires was 6.5 ft (2 m) higher than it is today. More temporary lagoons are enclosed by spits and sand bars, created by the drifting of sand and sediment in parallel with the shoreline.

Sand bar builds in parallel to the shoreline
Saltwater
Freshwater river
River delta
Sand barrier formed from sandy silts eroded in the Pampas region

Low plateaux and hills, like the Cuchilla Grande, dominate the landscape of Uruguay, which lies in a transitional zone between the humid Pampas of Argentina and the hilly uplands of Brazil.

The River Plate (Río de la Plata) is a great estuary formed at the confluence of the Paraná and Uruguay rivers near Nueva Palmira.

Mesopotamia is a narrow depression, no more than 180 miles (290 km) wide, which lies between the Paraná and Uruguay rivers, stretching more than 1000 miles (1603 km) south from the Brazilian Shield to the Pampas.

Paraná river

The Argentinian Pampas lie to the south of the River Plate (Río de la Plata), meeting southern Mesopotamia in the north and the Atlantic Ocean to the east. They are covered by deposits of silt, alluvium and volcanic ash.

▼ Montevideo became the capital of Uruguay following independence in 1828. The focus for Uruguayan industry and trade, it is also a popular destination for tourists from other South American countries.

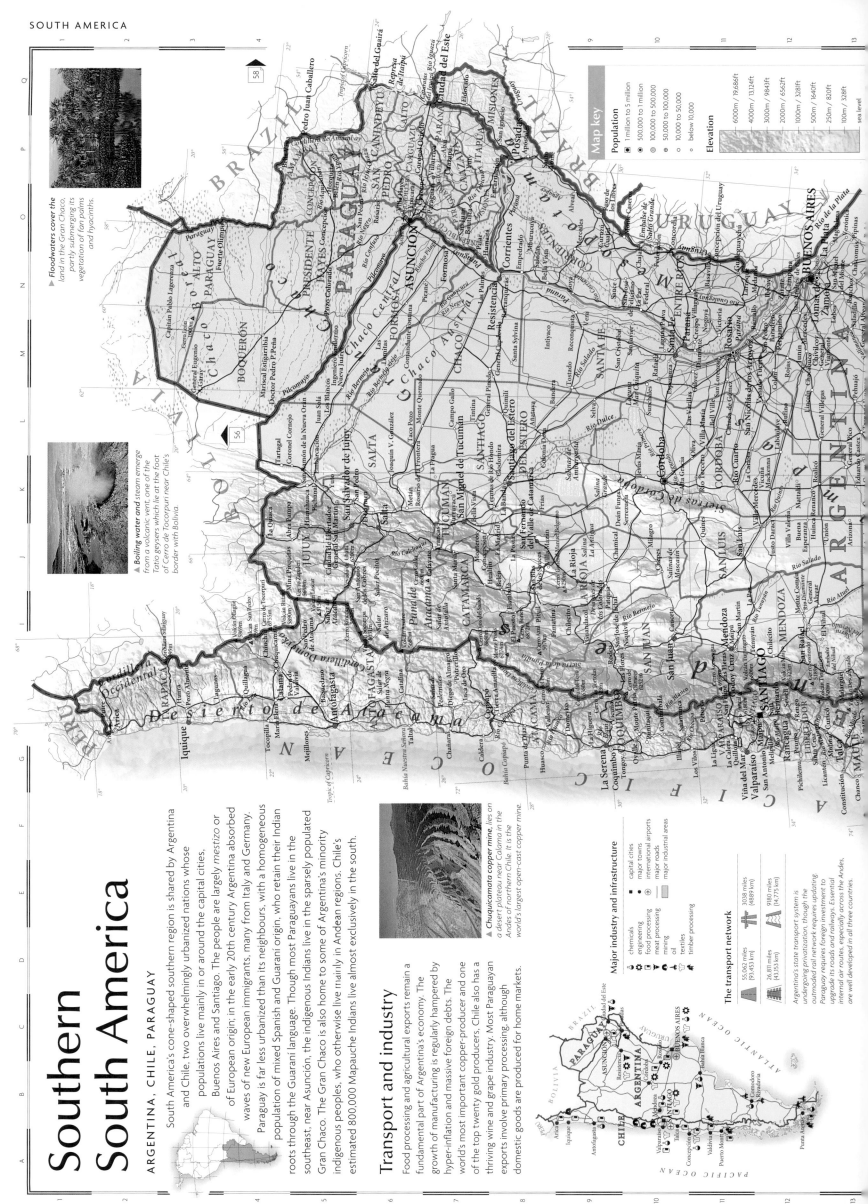

Southern South America

ARGENTINA, CHILE, PARAGUAY

South America's cone-shaped southern region is shared by Argentina and Chile, two overwhelmingly urbanized nations whose populations live mainly in or around the capital cities, Buenos Aires and Santiago. The people are largely *mestizo* or of European origin; in the early 20th century Argentina absorbed waves of new European immigrants, many from Italy and Germany. Paraguay is far less urbanized than its neighbours, with a homogeneous population of mixed Spanish and Guaraní origin, who retain their Indian roots through the Guaraní language. Though most Paraguayans live in the southeast, near Asunción, the indigenous Indians live in the sparsely populated Gran Chaco. The Gran Chaco is also home to some of Argentina's minority indigenous peoples, who otherwise live mainly in Andean regions. Chile's estimated 800,000 Mapauche Indians live almost exclusively in the south.

Transport and industry

Food processing and agricultural exports remain a fundamental part of Argentina's economy. The growth of manufacturing is regularly hampered by hyper-inflation and massive foreign debts. The world's most important copper-producer and one of the top twenty gold producers, Chile also has a thriving wine and grape industry. Most Paraguayan exports involve primary processing, although domestic goods are produced for home markets.

▲ Floodwaters cover the land in the Gran Chaco, partly submerging its vegetation of fan palms and hyacinths.

▲ Boiling water and steam emerge from a volcanic vent, one of the Tatio geysers which lie at the foot of Cerro de Tocorpuri near Chile's border with Bolivia.

▲ Chuquicamata copper mine, lies on a desert plateau near Calama in the Andes of northern Chile. It is the world's largest open-cast copper mine.

Major industry and infrastructure

- chemicals
- engineering
- food processing
- meat processing
- mining
- oil
- textiles
- timber processing

- ■ capital cities
- ▪ major towns
- ✈ international airports
- — major roads
- ▨ major industrial areas

The transport network

55,062 miles (93,453 km)

3038 miles (4889 km)

26,810 miles (43,153 km)

9180 miles (14,775 km)

Argentina's state transport system is undergoing privatization, though the outmoded rail network requires updating. Paraguay requires foreign investment to upgrade its roads and railways. Essential internal air routes, especially across the Andes, are well developed in all three countries.

Map key

Population
- ● 1 million to 5 million
- ⊚ 500,000 to 1 million
- ⊙ 100,000 to 500,000
- ⊕ 50,000 to 100,000
- ⊕ 10,000 to 50,000
- ∘ below 10,000

Elevation
- 6000m / 19,686ft
- 4000m / 13,124ft
- 3000m / 9843ft
- 2000m / 6562ft
- 1000m / 328ft
- 500m / 1640ft
- 250m / 820ft
- 100m / 328ft
- sea level

The landscape

The Andes run from north to south, forming a precipitous natural border between Chile and Argentina. East of the Andes are the scrublands of the Gran Chaco and the plains of the Pampas, which extend northward towards Paraguay. In the far southwest, Chile's indented Pacific coastline has many features typical of areas which have been affected by glaciation.

▲ *Great blocks of ice break away from the jagged blue peaks of these ice mountains to form icebergs off the coast of Patagonia, Argentina's most southerly region.*

▲ *The Atacama Desert (Desierto de Atacama) in Chile is one of the driest places on Earth where some areas have never recorded any rain. It contains a number of salt lakes.*

The Gran Chaco combines poor drainage, extremely hot temperatures and thorn-infested scrub to make it one of South America's most inhospitable regions.

Landlocked Paraguay relies on its river system for access to the sea and to produce hydro-electric power. The most important river system is the Paraguay–Paraná which provides links into neighbouring countries including Brazil, Uruguay and Argentina.

The Pampas derive their name from an Indian word meaning flat surface. The dry western region is largely desert, whereas the east is well-watered, supporting temperate grasses.

Cerro Aconcagua in the central Andes is the tallest mountain in the whole chain, rising to 22,834 ft (6959 m).

Alluvial deposits from the many rivers in central Chile have created rich soils, ideal for a wide range of agriculture.

Patagonia divides into two zones, with the Andes in the west, and the lower main plateau, extending east towards the Atlantic. It is a desolate area with climatic extremes; dark lava fields scattered with light bunchgrass give a 'leopard skin' effect to the landscape.

Most of the highest mountains in Chile's northern Andes are volcanoes like Volcán Lascar and Volcán Rutana.

The Patagonian ice sheet is the world's third largest ice field, covering 6560 sq miles (17,000 sq km). Patagonia also contains many typical features from past glaciations. These include glacial lakes, U-shaped valleys, fjords and deep-cut channels.

Cape Horn is the most southerly point of South America. The severity of the Roaring Forties winds makes the Horn one of the world's most treacherous shipping regions.

Ice-capped Andes are source of loess.

Argentinian Pampas

Andes

Rainfall

Windblown particles

Thick layer of loess sediments

Jet stream

▲ *A thick, fertile layer of loess lies in the basin underlying the Argentinian Pampas. It has been laid down following successive periods of glaciation. The minute loess particles are transported as dust and deposited by a downward air motion, or following rainfall.*

Using the land and sea

The rich plains of the Pampas support massive herds of cattle, producing meat, milk and hides essential to the domestic and export markets of both Argentina and Paraguay. Wheat and fruit are Argentina's other major agricultural products. A wide range of soft fruits, citrus fruits and more specialized crops such as walnuts, and grapes for wine and the table, are grown in Chile's fertile Central Valley, while the landscape to the south is dominated by forestry, mainly growing commercial radiata pine. Paraguay is self-sufficient in wheat and other staples. Cotton, coffee, tobacco and oilseeds such as soya, are the major export crops.

▲ *Charred tree stumps surround a cattle enclosure on the island of Tierra del Fuego in southern Argentina. Forest clearance to provide grazing land for cattle is of major environmental concern.*

The urban/rural population divide

urban 84%   rural 16%

Population density	Total land area
40 people per sq mile (15 people per sq km)	1,498,757 sq miles (3,882,790 sq km)

Land use and agricultural distribution

- cattle
- sheep
- cereals
- fruit
- grapes
- timber
- fishing

■ capital cities
• major towns

pasture
cropland
forest
barren land
mountain region
desert

Scale 1:9,750,000

projection: Lambert Azimuthal Equal Area

The Atlantic Ocean

The Atlantic is the youngest of the world's oceans, formed about 180 million years ago when the landmasses of the eastern and western hemispheres separated. Its underwater topography is dominated by the Mid-Atlantic Ridge, a huge mountain system running north to south along the centre of the ocean. Although most of the ridge's peaks lie below the sea, some emerge as volcanic islands, like Iceland and the Azores.

The Atlantic contains a wealth of resources, including substantial oil and gas reserves and rich fishing grounds. Until the 1950s, the north Atlantic was the world's busiest shipping route; cheaper air transport and alternative routes have shifted patterns of world trade.

Resources

Development of the oil and gas reserves in the Atlantic began in the 1940s around the Gulf of Mexico. Since then other areas have been exploited, including the North Sea, the west coast of Africa and the area east of Newfoundland and Nova Scotia. There is also extensive mining of sand, gravel and shell deposits by the USA and UK. For centuries, the north Atlantic's fishing grounds have been utilized more heavily than other oceans, leading to a serious decline in many fish stocks.

Resources
(including wildlife)
- 🐟 fish
- 🐋 whales
- aggregates
- ● oil & gas
- ■ major towns
- ● major ports

▲ *Fishing in the seas around northwestern Europe dates back over 1500 years. The high nutrient content of the seas makes them ideal breeding grounds for many species of fish.*

▲ *Surtsey near Iceland, lies on the Mid-Atlantic Ridge. The island was formed in 1963 following a volcanic eruption caused by sea-floor spreading.*

▲ *On 5 January 1993, the oil tanker Braer ran aground in the Shetland Islands, spilling 83,660 tons (85,000 tonnes) of light crude oil into the ocean, devastating the local marine ecosystem.*

SCALE 1:6,500,000

AZORES
(to Portugal)

ATLANTIC OCEAN

MADEIRA
(to Portugal)

SCALE 1:2,500,000

Scale 1:48,000,000

projection Mollweide

ISLAS CANARIAS
(CANARY ISLANDS)
(to Spain)

SCALE 1:6,500,000

BERMUDA
(to UK)

SCALE 1:500,000

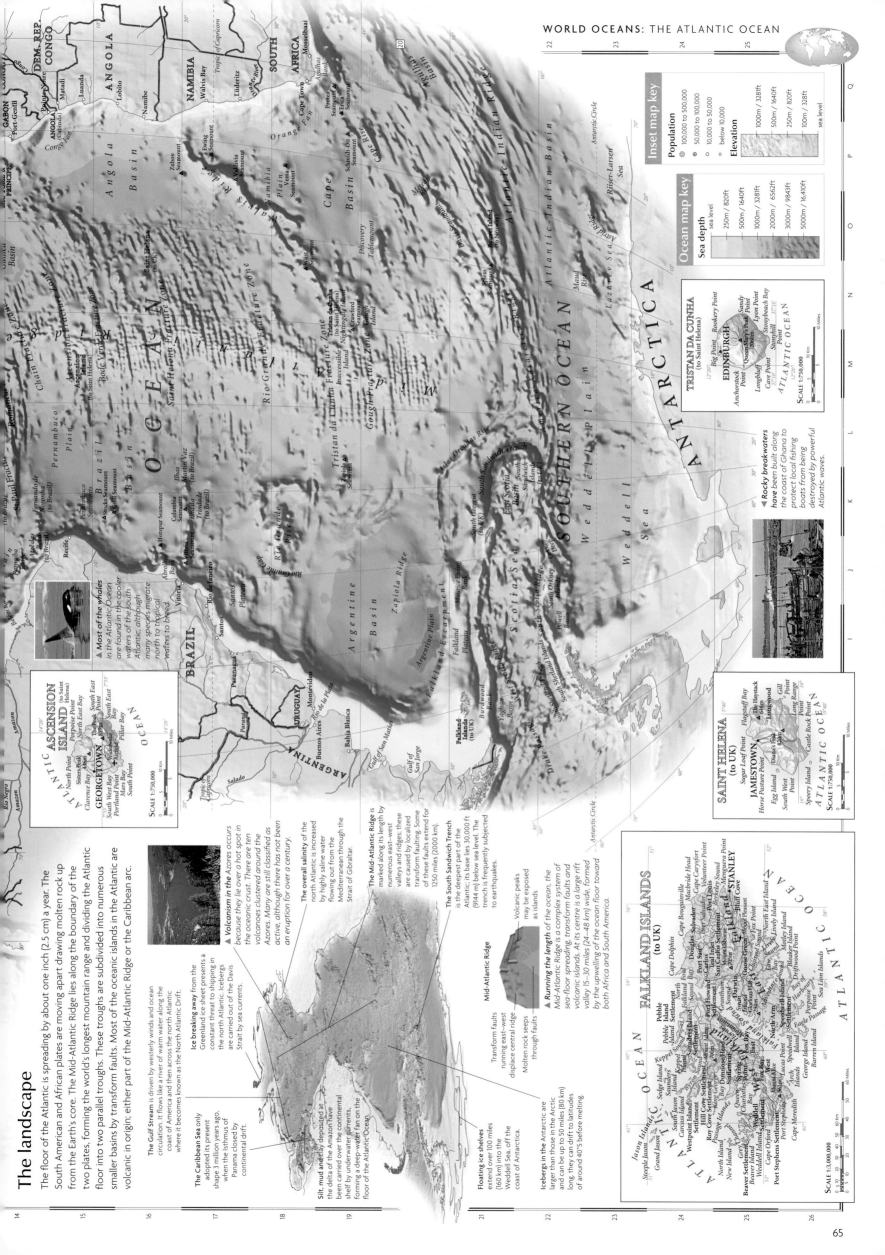

The landscape

The floor of the Atlantic is spreading by about one inch (2.5 cm) a year. The South American and African plates are moving apart drawing molten rock up from the Earth's core. The Mid-Atlantic Ridge lies along the boundary of the two plates, forming the world's longest mountain range and dividing the Atlantic floor into two parallel troughs. These troughs are subdivided into numerous smaller basins by transform faults. Most of the oceanic islands in the Atlantic are volcanic in origin; either part of the Mid-Atlantic Ridge or the Caribbean arc.

Inset map key

Population
- 100,000 to 500,000
- 50,000 to 100,000
- 10,000 to 50,000
- below 10,000

Elevation

Ocean map key

Sea depth
- sea level
- 250m / 820ft
- 500m / 1640ft
- 1000m / 3280ft
- 2000m / 6562ft
- 3000m / 9843ft
- 5000m / 16,410ft

Elevation
- 1000m / 3280ft
- 500m / 1640ft
- 250m / 820ft
- 100m / 328ft
- sea level

▲ Most of the whales in the Atlantic Ocean are found in the cooler waters of the south Atlantic, although many species migrate north to tropical waters to breed.

▲ Volcanism in the Azores occurs because they lie over a hot spot in the oceanic crust. There are ten volcanoes clustered around the Azores. Many are still classified as active, although there has not been an eruption for over a century.

The overall salinity of the north Atlantic is increased by highly saline water flowing out from the Mediterranean through the Strait of Gibraltar.

The Mid-Atlantic Ridge is marked along its length by numerous east–west valleys and ridges; these are caused by localized transform faulting. Some of these faults extend for 1250 miles (2000 km).

The South Sandwich Trench is the deepest part of the Atlantic; its base lies 30,000 ft (9144 m) below sea level. The trench is frequently subjected to earthquakes.

▲ Running the length of the ocean, the Mid-Atlantic Ridge is a complex system of sea-floor spreading, transform faults and volcanic islands. At its centre is a large rift valley 15–30 miles (24–48 km) wide, formed by the upwelling of the ocean floor toward both Africa and South America.

The Gulf Stream is driven by westerly winds and ocean circulation. It flows like a river of warm water along the coast of America and then across the north Atlantic where it becomes known as the North Atlantic Drift.

Ice breaking away from the Greenland ice sheet presents a constant threat to shipping in the north Atlantic. Icebergs are carried out of the Davis Strait by sea currents.

The Caribbean Sea only adopted its present shape 3 million years ago, when the isthmus of Panama closed by continental drift.

Silt, mud and clay deposited at the delta of the Amazon have been carried over the continental shelf by under-water currents, forming a deep-water fan on the floor of the Atlantic Ocean.

Floating ice shelves extend over 100 miles (160 km) into the Weddell Sea, off the coast of Antarctica.

Icebergs in the Antarctic are larger than those in the Arctic and can be up to 50 miles (80 km) long; they can drift to latitudes of around 40°S before melting.

▲ Rocky breakwaters have been built along the coast of Ghana to protect local fishing boats from being destroyed by powerful Atlantic waves.

Volcanic peaks may be exposed as islands

Mid-Atlantic Ridge

Transform faults running east–west displace central ridge

Molten rock seeps through faults

ASCENSION ISLAND (to Saint Helena)
GEORGETOWN
ATLANTIC OCEAN
SCALE 1:750,000

TRISTAN DA CUNHA (to Saint Helena)
EDINBURGH
ATLANTIC OCEAN
SCALE 1:750,000

SAINT HELENA (to UK)
JAMESTOWN
ATLANTIC OCEAN
SCALE 1:750,000

FALKLAND ISLANDS (to UK)
STANLEY
ATLANTIC OCEAN
SCALE 1:3,000,000

Africa

The world's second largest continent, Africa covers an area of 11,712,434 sq miles

(30,335,000 sq km). It has 53 separate countries, including Madagascar in the

Indian Ocean – the highest number of any continent.

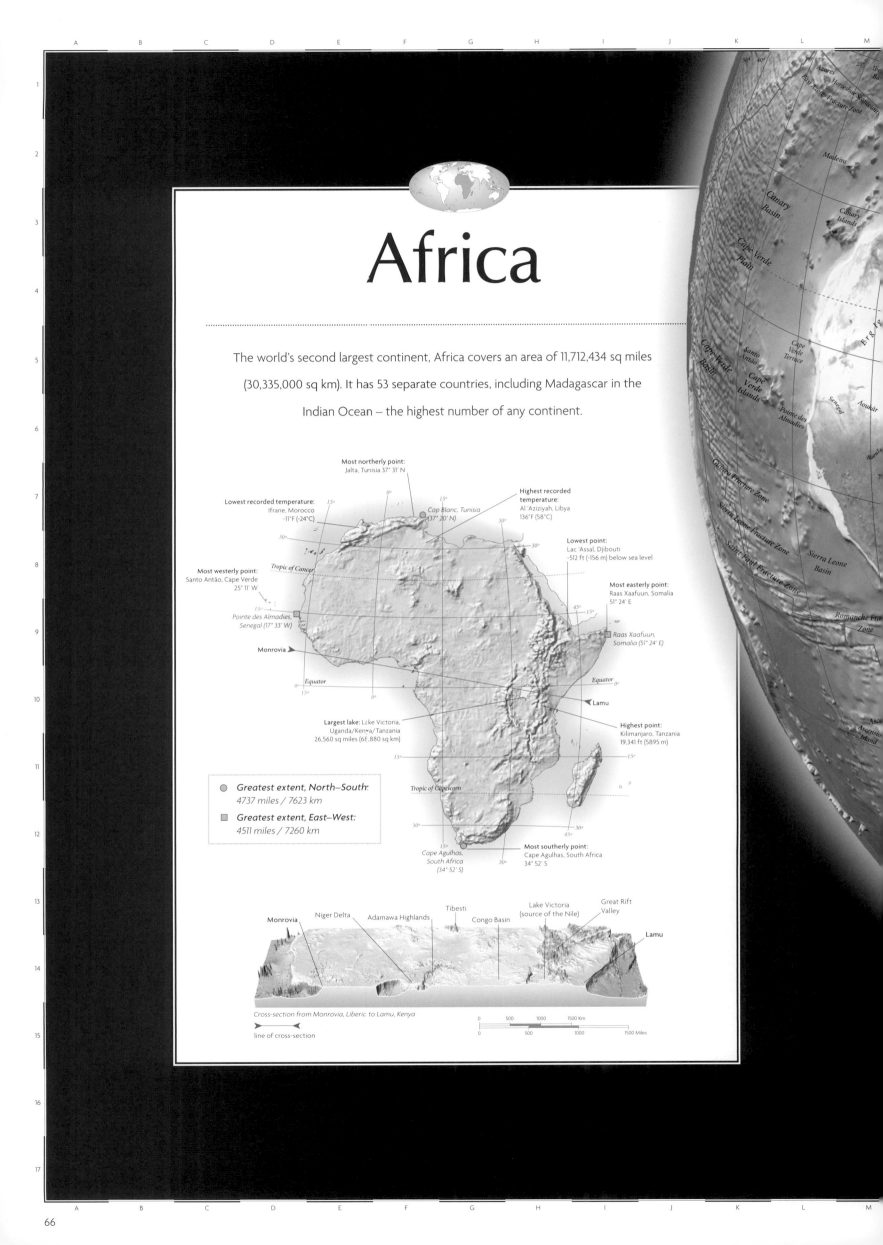

Most northerly point:
Jalta, Tunisia 37° 31′ N

Lowest recorded temperature:
Ifrane, Morocco
-11°F (-24°C)

Cap Blanc, Tunisia
(37° 20′ N)

Highest recorded
temperature:
Al 'Aziziyah, Libya
136°F (58°C)

Lowest point:
Lac 'Assal, Djibouti
-512 ft (-156 m) below sea level

Most westerly point:
Santo Antão, Cape Verde
25° 11′ W

Tropic of Cancer

Most easterly point:
Raas Xaafuun, Somalia
51° 24′ E

Pointe des Almadies,
Senegal (17° 33′ W)

Raas Xaafuun,
Somalia (51° 24′ E)

Monrovia

Equator

Equator

Lamu

Largest lake: Lake Victoria,
Uganda/Kenya/Tanzania
26,560 sq miles (68,880 sq km)

Highest point:
Kilimanjaro, Tanzania
19,341 ft (5895 m)

- ● **Greatest extent, North–South:**
  4737 miles / 7623 km
- ■ **Greatest extent, East–West:**
  4511 miles / 7260 km

Tropic of Capricorn

Cape Agulhas,
South Africa
(34° 52′ S)

Most southerly point:
Cape Agulhas, South Africa
34° 52′ S

Monrovia | Niger Delta | Adamawa Highlands | Tibesti | Congo Basin | Lake Victoria (source of the Nile) | Great Rift Valley | Lamu

Cross-section from Monrovia, Liberia to Lamu, Kenya

line of cross-section

0   500   1000   1500 Km
0   500   1000   1500 Miles

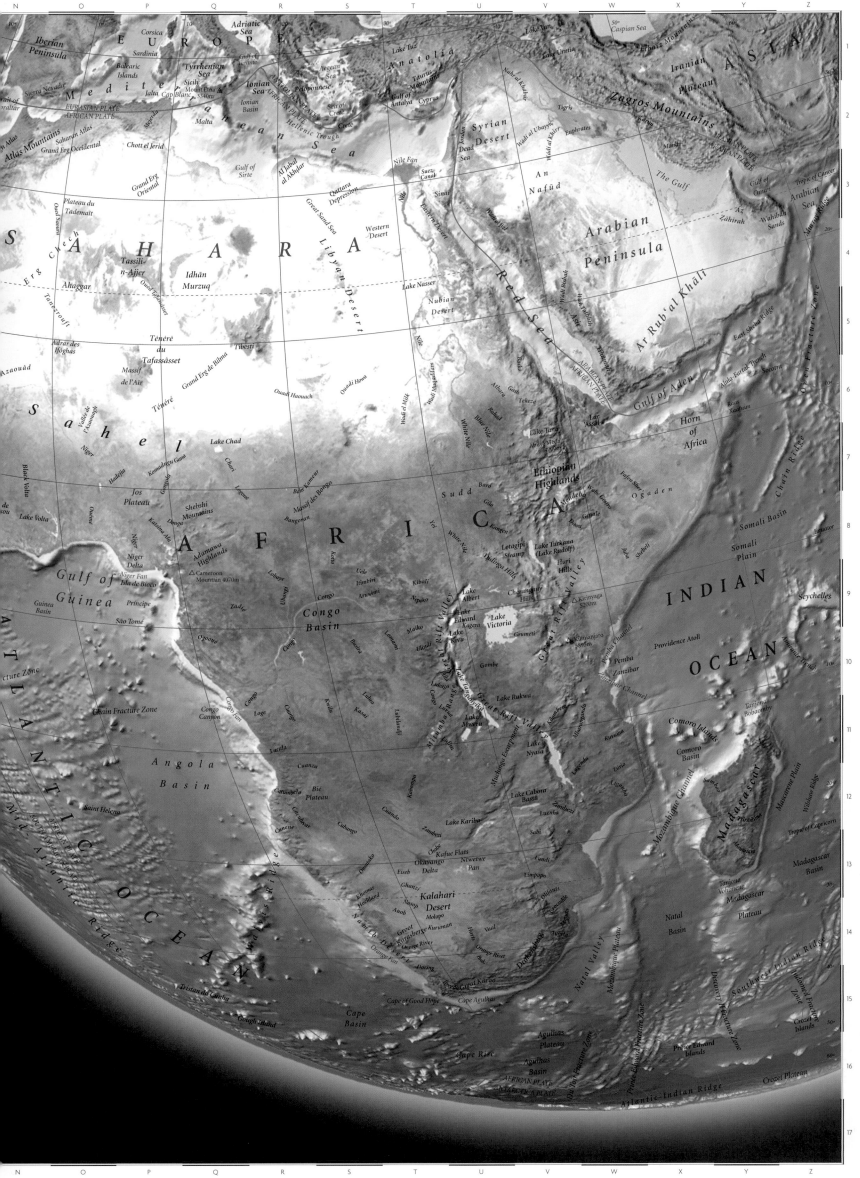

EUROPE

ASIA

Iberian
Peninsula

Corsica

Adriatic
Sea

Sardinia

Balearic
Islands

Sierra Nevada

Tyrrhenian
Sea

Sicily
Mount Etna
3340m

Malta

Ionian
Sea

Aegean
Sea

Peloponnese

Sea of
Crete

Crete

Anatolia

Taurus
Mountains

Lake Tuz

Lake Van

Caspian Sea

Elburz Mountains

Iranian
Plateau

Zagros Mountains

Gulf of
Antalya

Cyprus

Nahr al Khabur

Lake Urmia

Tigris

Syrian
Desert

Jordan

Dead
Sea

Euphrates

Wadi al Ubayyid

Wadi al Khirr

EURASIAN PLATE
AFRICAN PLATE

Mediterranean

Atlas Mountains

Saharan Atlas

Grand Erg Occidental

Chott el Jerid

Gulf of
Sirte

Al Jabal
al Akhdar

Cap Blanc

AFRICAN PLATE

Hellenic Trough

Ionian
Basin

Gulf of
Taranto

Strait of
Gibraltar

Plateau du
Tademaït

Grand Erg
Oriental

Oued Saoura

Great Sand Sea

Libyan Desert

Western
Desert

Qattara
Depression

Nile Fan

Nile

Suez
Canal

Sinai

Eastern Desert

An
Nafūd

Arabian

Peninsula

Tropic of Cancer

Az
Zāhirah

Gulf of
Oman

Arabian
Sea

Murray Ridge

S A H A R A

Erg Chech

Tanezrouft

Ahaggar

Tassili-
n-Ajjer

Oued Tafassâsset

Idhān
Murzuq

Tibesti

Lake Nasser

Nubian
Desert

Nile

Red Sea

Wadi Bishah

Wadi Hamd

Wadi al Hamd

ARABIAN PLATE

AFRICAN PLATE

Ar Rub' al Khālī

Wahibah
Sands

Owen Fracture Zone

Azaouâd

Adrar des
Ifôghas

Ténéré
du
Tafassâsset

Massif
de l'Aïr

Grand Erg de Bilma

Ouadi Haouach

Ouadi Howa

Wadi al Milk

Wadi Muqaddam

East Sheba Ridge

Aluka-Fartak Trench

Socotra

Sahel

Niger

Hadejia

Lake Chad

Chari

Komadugu Gana

Ténéré

Gulf of Aden

Bani Baktu

Atbara

Rahad

Gash

Tekeze

Lac
Assal

Horn
of
Africa

Ras
Xaafuun

Black Volta

Lake Volta

Oueme

Jos
Plateau

Shebshi
Mountains

Denga

Katsina Ala

Massif des Bongo

Bangoran

Bahr Kameur

Sudd

White Nile

Blue Nile

Lake Tana

Abuye Meda
4000m

Baro

Gila

Kangen

Ethiopian
Highlands

Meidoba

Wabi Gestro

Genale

Ogaden

Somali Basin

Equator

A F R I C A

Niger

Niger
Delta

Niger Fan
Isla de Bioco

Adamawa
Highlands

Cameroon
Mountain 4070m

Lobaye

Kotto

Uele

Ubangui

Irimbiri

Kibali

Aruwimi

Yei

White Nile

Lotagipi
Swamp

Dadinga Hills

Lake Turkana
(Lake Rudolf)

Huri
Hills

Juba

Shebeli

Somali
Plain

Chain Ridge

Gulf of
Guinea

Guinea
Basin

Príncipe

São Tomé

Ogooué

Zadye

Congo

Congo
Basin

Ngoko

Maiko

Lomami

Ulindi

Lualaba

Lake
Albert

Lake
Edward

Lake
Kivu

Kagera

Lake
Victoria

Cherangany
Hills

Kirinyaga
5200m

Grumeti

Grumeti

INDIAN

Seychelles

Chain Fracture Zone

Congo Fan

Congo Canyon

Congo

Loge

Kwango

Cuango

Kasai

Lulua

Luhombero

Gambe

Kilombero

Great Rift Valley

Great Rift Valley

Lake Tanganyika

Lake Kivu

Kilimanjaro
5895m

Pemba Channel

Pemba

Zanzibar

Providence Atoll

OCEAN

Mauritius Trench

ATLANTIC

Saint Helena

Angola
Basin

Cuanza

Bié
Plateau

Catumbela

Cunene

Cuando

Cubango

Kafue Flats

Kafue

Kabompo

Lake
Mweru

Luangwa

Mushinga Escarpment

Lake
Nyasa

Ruvuma

Luiro

Comoro Islands

Comoro
Basin

Mozambique Channel

Tanjona
Bobaomby

Madagascar

Zambezi

Lake Cabora
Bassa

Luenha

Sabi

Lake Kariba

Mascarene Plain

Tropic of Capricorn

Wilshaw Ridge

Madagascar
Basin

Okwa

Okavango
Delta

Ntwetwe
Pan

Fundi

Limpopo

Tanjona
Volimena

Madagascar

Plateau

Kalahari
Desert

Ghanzi

Nossop

Auob

Molopo

Olifants

Crocodile

Natal
Basin

Khamas
Hardland

Nami b Desert

Namib Desert

Groot

Kuruman

Vaal

Harts

Orange River

Orange River
Fan

Doring

Great Karoo

Cape of Good Hope

Cape Agulhas

Dimbaza

Tugela

Natal Valley

Mozambique Plateau

Mozambique Escarpment

Tristan da Cunha

Gough Island

Cape
Basin

Mid-Atlantic Ridge

Walvis Ridge

Cape Rise

Agulhas
Plateau

Agulhas
Basin

AFRICAN PLATE
ANTARCTICA PLATE

Prince Edward
Fracture Zone

Prince Edward
Islands

Discovery Tablemount

Southwest Indian Ridge

Indomed Fracture Zone

Crozet
Islands

Crozet Plateau

Atlantic-Indian Ridge

Atlantic-Indian Ridge

Physical Africa

The structure of Africa was dramatically influenced by the break up of the supercontinent Gondwanaland about 160 million years ago and, more recently, rifting and hot spot activity. Today, much of Africa is remote from active plate boundaries and comprises a series of extensive plateaux and deep basins, which influence the drainage patterns of major rivers. The relief rises to the east, where volcanic uplands and vast lakes mark the Great Rift Valley. In the far north and south sedimentary rocks have been folded to form the Atlas Mountains and the Great Karoo.

East Africa

The Great Rift Valley is the most striking feature of this region, running for 4475 miles (7200 km) from Lake Nyasa to the Red Sea. North of Lake Nyasa it splits into two arms and encloses an interior plateau which contains Lake Victoria. A number of elongated lakes and volcanoes lie along the fault lines. To the west lies the Congo Basin, a vast, shallow depression, which rises to form an almost circular rim of highlands.

Northern Africa

Northern Africa comprises a system of basins and plateaux. The Tibesti and Ahaggar are volcanic uplands, whose uplift has been matched by subsidence within large surrounding basins. Many of the basins have been infilled with sand and gravel, creating the vast Saharan lands. The Atlas Mountains in the north were formed by convergence of the African and Eurasian plates.

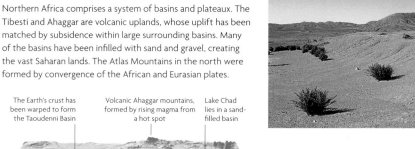

Rift valley lakes, like Lake Tanganyika, lie along fault lines

Lake Victoria

Extensive faulting occurs as rift valley pulls apart

Cross-section through eastern Africa showing the two arms of the Great Rift Valley and its interior plateau.

The Earth's crust has been warped to form the Taoudenni Basin

Volcanic Ahaggar mountains, formed by rising magma from a hot spot

Lake Chad lies in a sand-filled basin

Section across northern Africa showing infilled basins and uplifted plateaux.

Scale 1:40,000,000

projection: Lambert Azimuthal Equal Area

Map key

Elevation

- 5000m / 16,405ft
- 4000m / 13,124ft
- 3000m / 9843ft
- 2000m / 6562ft
- 1000m / 3281ft
- 500m / 1640ft
- 250m / 820ft
- 100m / 328ft
- sea level
- below sea level

Plate margins
(for explanation see page xiv)

- constructive
- △ △ destructive
- conservative
- uncertain
- line of cross-section

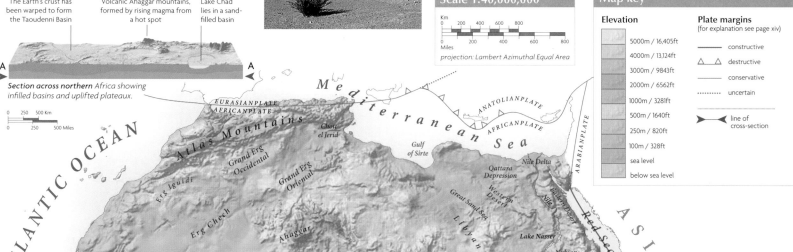

Southern Africa

The Great Escarpment marks the southern boundary of Africa's basement rock and includes the Drakensberg range. It was uplifted when Gondwanaland fragmented about 160 million years ago and it has gradually been eroded back from the coast. To the north, the relief drops steadily, forming the Kalahari Basin. In the far south are the fold mountains of the Great Karoo.

Kalahari Basin, covered with the sandy plains of the Kalahari Desert

Boundary of the Great Escarpment

Uplift of the basement rock created a raised plateau

Drakensberg

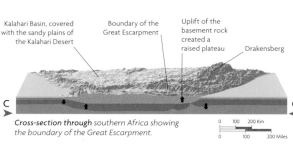

Cross-section through southern Africa showing the boundary of the Great Escarpment.

Climate

The climates of Africa range from mediterranean to arid, dry savannah and humid equatorial. In East Africa, where snow settles at the summit of volcanoes such as Kilimanjaro, climate is also modified by altitude. The winds of the Sahara export millions of tonnes of dust a year both northwards and eastwards.

▲ *Savannah grasslands* run in a belt across Africa; limited rainfall inhibits tree growth.

Temperature

Tropic of Cancer
20° N
Equator
20° S
Tropic of Capricorn

Average January temperature   Average July temperature

Temperature
- 0 to 10°C (32 to 50°F)
- 10 to 20°C (50 to 68°F)
- 20 to 30°C (68 to 86°F)
- above 30°C (86°F)

▲ *The hot, equatorial* basin of the Congo river receives over 48 inches (1200 mm) of rainfall per year.

Rainfall

Tropic of Cancer
20° N
Equator
20° S
Tropic of Capricorn

Average January rainfall   Average July rainfall

Rainfall
- 0–25 mm (0–1 in)
- 25–50 mm (1–2 in)
- 50–100 mm (2–4 in)
- 100–200 mm (4–8 in)
- 200–300 mm (8–12 in)
- 300–400 mm (12–16 in)
- 400–500 mm (16–20 in)
- more than 500 mm (20 in)

Climate
- arid
- humid equatorial
- mediterranean
- semi-arid
- tropical
- warm humid
- ☼ daily hours of sunshine, January
- ☼ daily hours of sunshine, July
- → cold wind
- → hot wind

Shaping the continent

African landscapes are shaped by the intensity of climatic extremes and by tectonic action. High aridity, wind action and infrequent but heavy rainstorms, lead to the migration of sand dunes and dramatic flash flooding across much of the north and west. In the wetter areas, high precipitation increases the rate of weathering. To the east, the rift system has created a volcanic and lake environment and allowed rivers to erode weaknesses left in the crustal structure by faults.

Groundwater

1 Oases are found in desert areas such as the Sahara (left). Groundwater migrates through permeable rock strata, confined between two impermeable layers. Oases form either when the permeable rocks come near to the surface, or at a fault line, when water is able to seep up to the surface through the crushed rocks at the fault.

Groundwater: Replenishment of an oasis

The evolving landscape

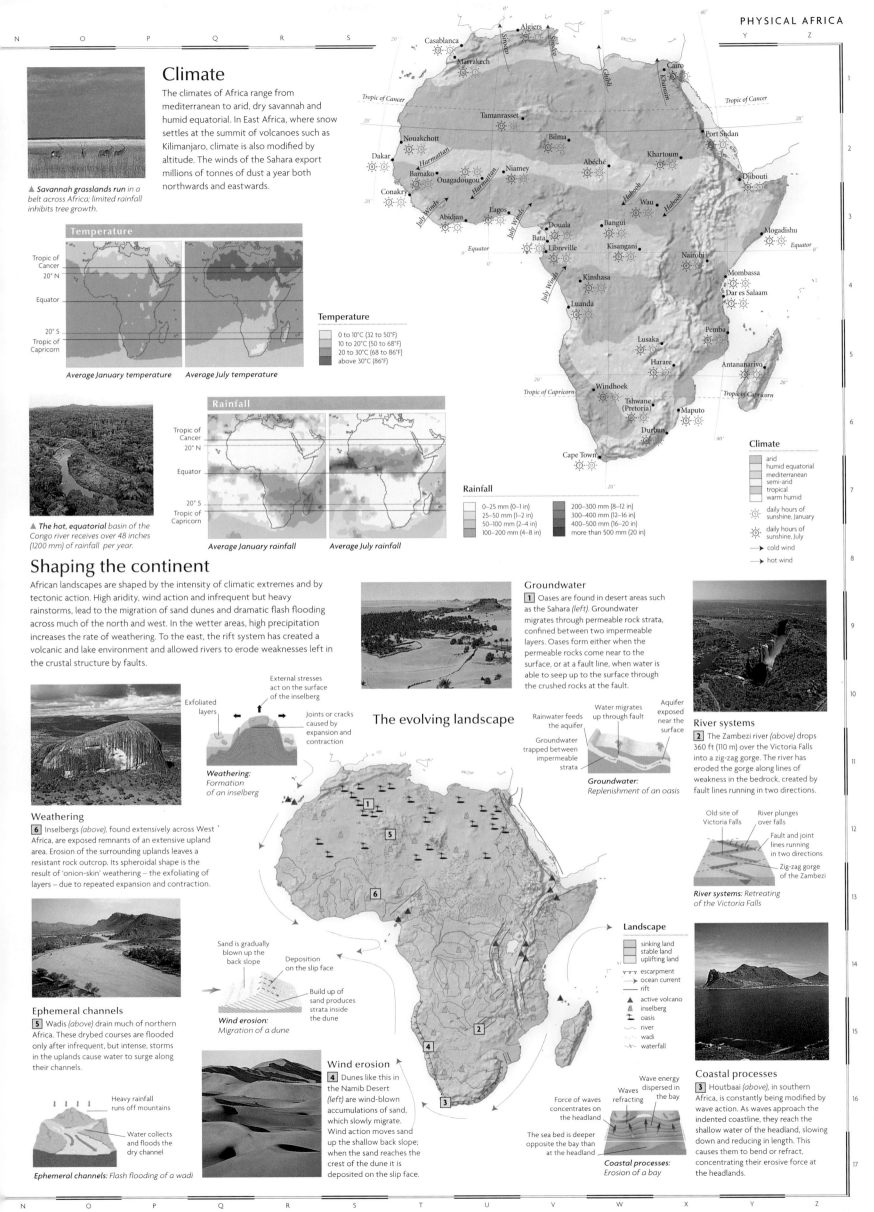

Weathering

6 Inselbergs (above), found extensively across West Africa, are exposed remnants of an extensive upland area. Erosion of the surrounding uplands leaves a resistant rock outcrop. Its spheroidal shape is the result of 'onion-skin' weathering – the exfoliating of layers – due to repeated expansion and contraction.

External stresses act on the surface of the inselberg
Exfoliated layers
Joints or cracks caused by expansion and contraction

Weathering: Formation of an inselberg

River systems

2 The Zambezi river (above) drops 360 ft (110 m) over the Victoria Falls into a zig-zag gorge. The river has eroded the gorge along lines of weakness in the bedrock, created by fault lines running in two directions.

Old site of Victoria Falls
River plunges over falls
Fault and joint lines running in two directions
Zig-zag gorge of the Zambezi

River systems: Retreating of the Victoria Falls

Rainwater feeds the aquifer
Water migrates up through fault
Aquifer exposed near the surface
Groundwater trapped between impermeable strata

Ephemeral channels

5 Wadis (above) drain much of northern Africa. These drybed courses are flooded only after infrequent, but intense, storms in the uplands cause water to surge along their channels.

Heavy rainfall runs off mountains
Water collects and floods the dry channel

Ephemeral channels: Flash flooding of a wadi

Wind erosion

Sand is gradually blown up the back slope
Deposition on the slip face
Build up of sand produces strata inside the dune

Wind erosion: Migration of a dune

4 Dunes like this in the Namib Desert (left) are wind-blown accumulations of sand, which slowly migrate. Wind action moves sand up the shallow back slope; when the sand reaches the crest of the dune it is deposited on the slip face.

Landscape
- sinking land
- stable land
- uplifting land
- ▽▽▽ escarpment
- → ocean current
- — rift
- ▲ active volcano
- ▲ inselberg
- ◯ oasis
- ∿ river
- ∿ wadi
- ∿ waterfall

Coastal processes

Wave energy dispersed in the bay
Waves refracting
Force of waves concentrates on the headland
The sea bed is deeper opposite the bay than at the headland

Coastal processes: Erosion of a bay

3 Houtbaai (above), in southern Africa, is constantly being modified by wave action. As waves approach the indented coastline, they reach the shallow water of the headland, slowing down and reducing in length. This causes them to bend or refract, concentrating their erosive force at the headlands.

Political Africa

The political map of modern Africa only emerged following the end of the Second World War. Over the next half-century, all of the countries former.y controlled by European powers gained independence from their colonial rulers – only Liberia and Ethiopia were never colonized. The post-colonial era has not been an easy period for many countries, but there have been moves towards multi-party democracy across much of the continent. In South Africa, democratic elections replaced the internationally-condemned apartheid system only in 1994. Other countries have still to find political stability; corruption in government and ethnic tensions are serious problems. National infrastructures, based on the colonial transport systems built to exploit Africa's resources, are often inappropriate for independent economic development.

Languages

Three major world languages act as *lingua francas* across the African continent: Arabic in North Africa; English in southern and eastern Africa and Nigeria; and French in Central and West Africa, and in Madagascar. A huge number of African languages are spoken as well – over 2000 have been recorded, with more than 400 in Nigeria alone – reflecting the continuing importance of traditional cultures and values. In the north of the continent, the extensive use of Arabic reflects Middle Eastern influences while Bantu is widely-spoken across much of southern Africa.

Language groups

- Afro-Asiatic (Hamito-Semitic)
- Niger-Congo
- Nilo-Saharan
- Khoisan
- Indo-European
- Austronesian

Official African languages

- French
- English
- Arabic
- Portuguese
- Swahili
- Amharic
- Spanish
- French/English
- French/Arabic
- French/Malagasy
- English/Swahili
- Arabic/Somali

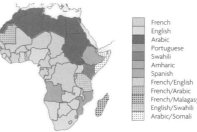

▲ *Islamic influences are evident throughout North Africa. The Great Mosque at Kairouan, Tunisia, is Africa's holiest Islamic place.*

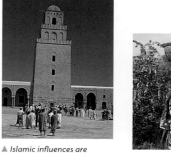

▲ *In northeastern Nigeria, people speak Kanuri – a dialect of the Nilo-Saharan language group.*

Transport

African railways were built to aid the exploitation of natural resources, and most offer passage only from the interior to the coastal cities, leaving large parts of the continent untouched – five land-locked countries have no railways at all. The Congo, Nile and Niger river networks offer limited access to land within the continental interior, but have a number of waterfalls and cataracts which prevent navigation from the sea. Many roads were developed in the 1960s and 1970s, but economic difficulties are making the maintenance and expansion of the networks difficult.

▶ *South Africa has the largest concentration of railways in Africa. Over 20,000 miles (32,000 km) of routes have been built since 1870.*

Transport

- major roads and motorways
- major railways
- major canal
- international borders
- • transport intersections
- ⊕ international airports
- ⊕ major ports

▲ *Traditional means of transport, such as the camel, are still widely used across the less accessible parts of Africa.*

◀ *The Congo river, though not suitable for river transport along its entire length, forms a vital link for people and goods in its navigable inland reaches.*

Population

Africa has a rapidly-growing population of over 900 million people, yet over 75% of the continent remains sparsely populated. Most Africans still pursue a traditional rural lifestyle, though urbanization is increasing as people move to the cities in search of employment. The greatest population densities occur where water is more readily available, such as in the Nile Valley, the coasts of North and West Africa, along the Niger, the eastern African highlands, and in South Africa.

Scale 1:30,500,000

projection: Lambert Azimuthal Equal Area

Map key

Population
- ■ above 5 million
- ■ 1 million to 5 million
- ◉ 500,000 to 1 million
- ◎ 100,000 to 500,000
- ⊕ 50,000 to 100,000
- ○ 10,000 to 50,000
- ● Country capital

Borders
- full international border
- disputed de facto border
- ceasefire line

Population density (people per sq km)
- below 49
- 50–99
- 100–149
- 150–199
- 200–299
- above 300

► A thin layer of smog blankets the dusty streets of Cairo, Africa's most populous city and home to over 15 million people. In the 1990s Cairo grew at a rate of about 1500 people per day.

▲ Thriving street markets in Gambia's capital, Banjul, trade a variety of locally-grown produce. Africa's population is still predominantly rural-based.

71

African resources

The economies of most African countries are dominated by subsistence and cash crop agriculture, with limited industrialization. Manufacturing industry is largely confined to South Africa. Many countries depend on a single resource, such as copper or gold, or a cash crop, such as coffee, for export income, which can leave them vulnerable to fluctuations in world commodity prices. In order to diversify their economies and develop a wider industrial base, investment from overseas is being actively sought by many African governments.

Industry

Many African industries concentrate on the extraction and processing of raw materials. These include the oil industry, food processing, mining and textile production. South Africa accounts for over half of the continent's industrial output with much of the remainder coming from the countries along the northern coast. Over 60% of Africa's workforce is employed in agriculture.

Standard of living

Since the 1960s most countries in Africa have seen significant improvements in life expectancy, healthcare and education. However, 28 of the 30 most deprived countries in the world are African, and the continent as a whole lies well behind the rest of the world in terms of meeting many basic human needs.

Standard of living
(UN human development index)
high
low

◀ *The unspoilt natural* splendour of wildlife reserves, like the Serengeti National Park in Tanzania, attract tourists to Africa from around the globe. The tourist industry in Kenya and Tanzania is particularly well developed, where it accounts for almost 10% of GNI.

GNI per capita (US $)
below 499
500–999
1000–1999
2000–2999
3000–3999
above 4000

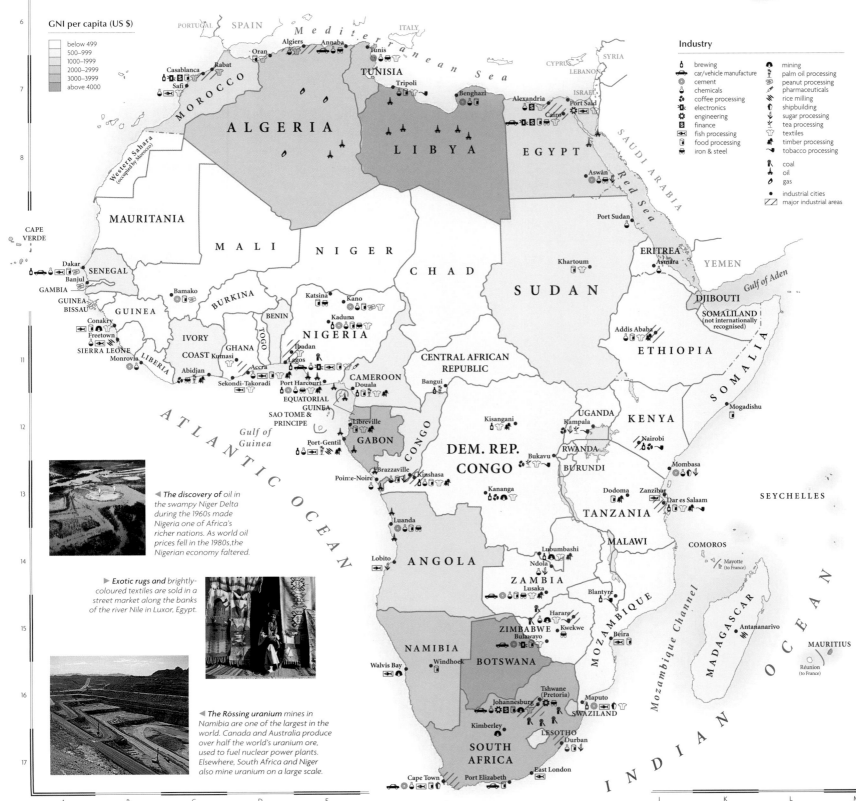

◀ *The discovery of* oil in the swampy Niger Delta during the 1960s made Nigeria one of Africa's richer nations. As world oil prices fell in the 1980s, the Nigerian economy faltered.

▶ *Exotic rugs and* brightly-coloured textiles are sold in a street market along the banks of the river Nile in Luxor, Egypt.

◀ *The Rössing uranium* mines in Namibia are one of the largest in the world. Canada and Australia produce over half the world's uranium ore, used to fuel nuclear power plants. Elsewhere, South Africa and Niger also mine uranium on a large scale.

Industry
- brewing
- car/vehicle manufacture
- cement
- chemicals
- coffee processing
- electronics
- engineering
- finance
- fish processing
- food processing
- iron & steel
- mining
- palm oil processing
- peanut processing
- pharmaceuticals
- rice milling
- shipbuilding
- sugar processing
- tea processing
- textiles
- timber processing
- tobacco processing
- coal
- oil
- gas
- industrial cities
- major industrial areas

Environmental issues

One of Africa's most serious environmental problems occurs in marginal areas such as the Sahel where scrub and forest clearance, often for cooking fuel, combined with overgrazing, are causing desertification. Game reserves in southern and eastern Africa have helped to preserve many endangered animals, although the needs of growing populations have led to conflict over land use, and poaching is a serious problem.

Environmental issues
- national parks
- tropical forest
- forest destroyed
- desert
- desertification
- polluted rivers
- radioactive contamination
- marine pollution
- heavy marine pollution
- poor urban air quality

Mineral resources

Africa's ancient plateaux contain some of the world's most substantial reserves of precious stones and metals. About 15% of the world's gold is mined in South Africa; Zambia has great copper deposits; and diamonds are mined in Botswana, Dem. Rep. Congo and South Africa. Oil has brought great economic benefits to Algeria, Libya and Nigeria.

Mineral resources
- oil field
- gas field
- coal field
- bauxite
- copper
- diamonds
- gold
- iron
- phosphates
- tin
- uranium

▲ *North and West Africa* have large deposits of white phosphate minerals, which are used in making fertilizers. Morocco, Senegal, and Tunisia are among the continent's leading producers.

▲ *The Sahel's delicate* natural equilibrium is easily destroyed by the clearing of vegetation, drought and overgrazing. This causes the Sahara to advance south, engulfing the savannah grasslands.

▲ *Workers on a tea plantation* gather one of Africa's most important cash crops, providing a valuable source of income. Coffee, rubber, bananas, cotton and cocoa are also widely grown as cash crops.

◄ *Surrounded by desert,* the fertile flood plains of the Nile Valley and Delta have been extensively irrigated, farmed, and settled since 3000 BC.

Using the land and sea

Some of Africa's most productive agricultural land is found in the eastern volcanic uplands, where fertile soils support a wide range of valuable export crops including vegetables, tea and coffee. The most widely-grown grain is corn and peanuts (groundnuts) are particularly important in West Africa. Without intensive irrigation, cultivation is not possible in desert regions and unreliable rainfall in other areas limits crop production. Pastoral herding is most commonly found in these marginal lands. Substantial local fishing industries are found along coasts and in vast lakes such as Lake Nyasa and Lake Victoria.

Using the land and sea
- cropland
- desert
- forest
- pasture
- wetland
- major conurbations
- cattle
- goats
- cereals
- sheep
- bananas
- corn (maize)
- citrus fruits
- cocoa
- cotton
- coffee
- dates
- fishing
- oil palms
- olives
- peanuts
- rice
- rubber
- shellfish
- sugar cane
- tea
- tobacco
- vineyards
- wheat

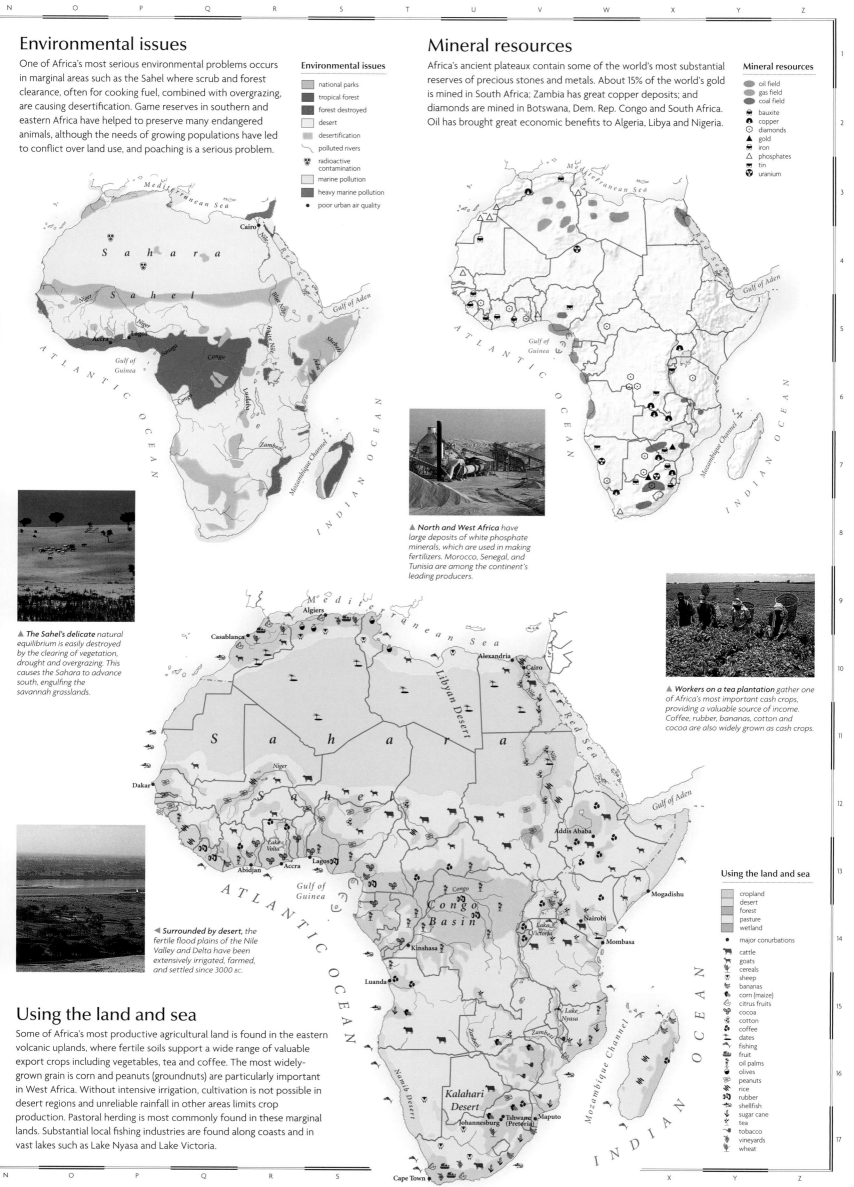

North Africa

ALGERIA, EGYPT, LIBYA, MOROCCO, TUNISIA, WESTERN SAHARA

Fringed by the Mediterranean along the northern coast and by the arid Sahara in the south, North Africa reflects the influence of many invaders, both European and, most importantly, Arab, giving the region an almost universal Islamic flavour and a common Arabic language. The countries lying to the west of Egypt are often referred to as the Maghreb, an Arabic term for 'west'. Today, Morocco and Tunisia exploit their culture and landscape for tourism, while rich oil and gas deposits aid development in Libya and Algeria, despite political turmoil. Egypt, with its fertile, Nile-watered agricultural land and varied industrial base, is the most populous nation.

▲ These rock piles in Algeria's Ahaggar mountains are the result of weathering caused by extremes of temperature. Great cracks or joints appear in the rocks, which are then worn and smoothed by the wind.

The landscape

The Atlas Mountains, which extend across much of Morocco, northern Algeria and Tunisia, are part of the fold mountain system which also runs through much of southern Europe. They recede to the south and east, becoming a steppe landscape before meeting the Sahara desert which covers more than 90% of the region. The sediments of the Sahara overlie an ancient plateau of crystalline rock, some of which is more than four billion years old.

Map key

Population
- ■ above 5 million
- ■ 1 million to 5 million
- ◉ 500,000 to 1 million
- ◎ 100,000 to 500,000
- ⊕ 50,000 to 100,000
- ○ 10,000 to 50,000
- ○ below 10,000

Elevation
- 4000m / 13,124ft
- 3000m / 9843ft
- 2000m / 6562ft
- 1000m / 3281ft
- 500m / 1640ft
- 250m / 820ft
- 100m / 328ft
- sea level

Scale 1:12,250,000

projection: Lambert Azimuthal Equal Area

◀ The town of Tiznit, Morocco, lies in an oasis in the desert. Crops and trees grow on the fertile land surrounding the town.

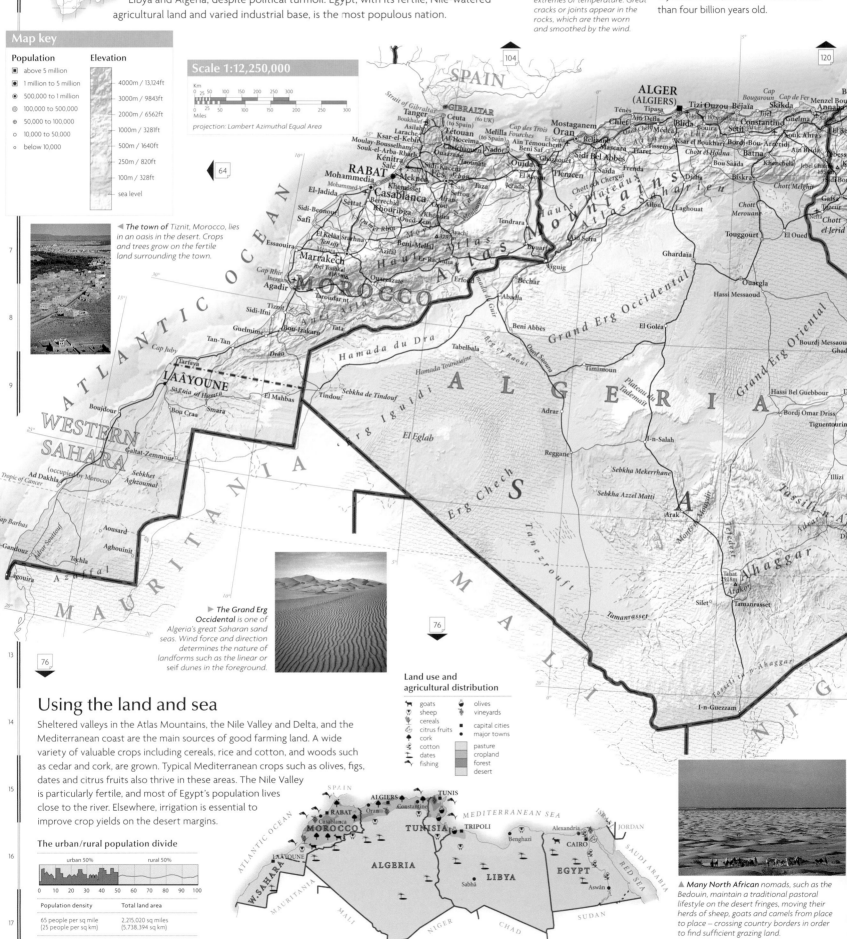

▶ The Grand Erg Occidental is one of Algeria's great Saharan sand seas. Wind force and direction determines the nature of landforms such as the linear or seif dunes in the foreground.

Land use and agricultural distribution

- goats
- sheep
- cereals
- citrus fruits
- cork
- cotton
- dates
- fishing
- olives
- vineyards
- ■ capital cities
- ● major towns
- pasture
- cropland
- forest
- desert

Using the land and sea

Sheltered valleys in the Atlas Mountains, the Nile Valley and Delta, and the Mediterranean coast are the main sources of good farming land. A wide variety of valuable crops including cereals, rice and cotton, and woods such as cedar and cork, are grown. Typical Mediterranean crops such as olives, figs, dates and citrus fruits also thrive in these areas. The Nile Valley is particularly fertile, and most of Egypt's population lives close to the river. Elsewhere, irrigation is essential to improve crop yields on the desert margins.

The urban/rural population divide

urban 50% | rural 50%

0 10 20 30 40 50 60 70 80 90 100

Population density	Total land area
65 people per sq mile (25 people per sq km)	2,215,020 sq miles (5,738,394 sq km)

▲ Many North African nomads, such as the Bedouin, maintain a traditional pastoral lifestyle on the desert fringes, moving their herds of sheep, goats and camels from place to place – crossing country borders in order to find sufficient grazing land.

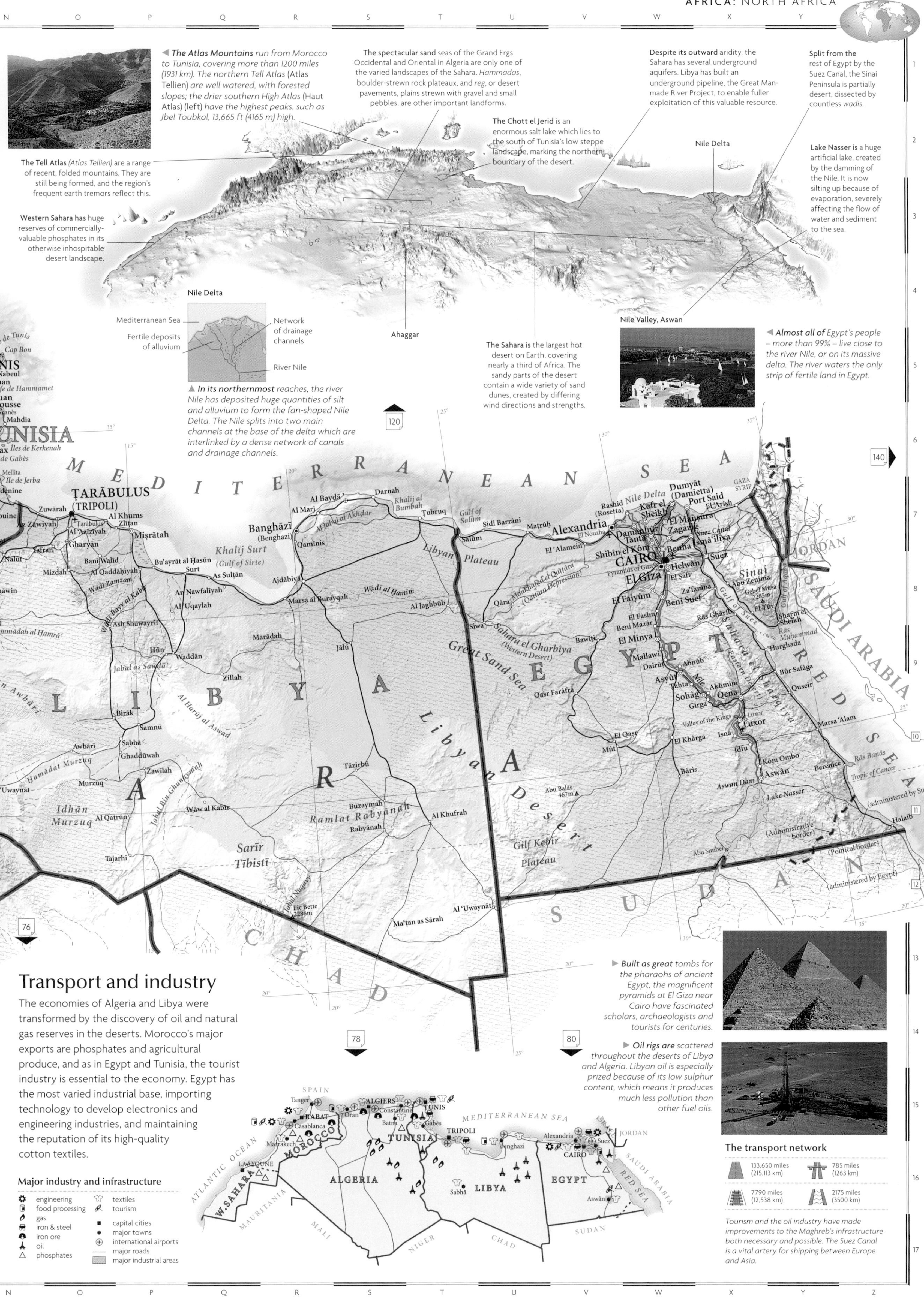

◀ **The Atlas Mountains** run from Morocco to Tunisia, covering more than 1200 miles (1931 km). The northern Tell Atlas (Atlas Tellien) are well watered, with forested slopes; the drier southern High Atlas (Haut Atlas) (left) have the highest peaks, such as Jbel Toubkal, 13,665 ft (4165 m) high.

The spectacular sand seas of the Grand Ergs Occidental and Oriental in Algeria are only one of the varied landscapes of the Sahara. Hammadas, boulder-strewn rock plateaux, and reg, or desert pavements, plains strewn with gravel and small pebbles, are other important landforms.

The **Chott el Jerid** is an enormous salt lake which lies to the south of Tunisia's low steppe landscape, marking the northern boundary of the desert.

Despite its outward aridity, the Sahara has several underground aquifers. Libya has built an underground pipeline, the Great Man-made River Project, to enable fuller exploitation of this valuable resource.

Split from the rest of Egypt by the Suez Canal, the Sinai Peninsula is partially desert, dissected by countless wadis.

The Tell Atlas (Atlas Tellien) are a range of recent, folded mountains. They are still being formed, and the region's frequent earth tremors reflect this.

Lake Nasser is a huge artificial lake, created by the damming of the Nile. It is now silting up because of evaporation, severely affecting the flow of water and sediment to the sea.

Western Sahara has huge reserves of commercially-valuable phosphates in its otherwise inhospitable desert landscape.

The Sahara is the largest hot desert on Earth, covering nearly a third of Africa. The sandy parts of the desert contain a wide variety of sand dunes, created by differing wind directions and strengths.

Nile Delta

Mediterranean Sea

Fertile deposits of alluvium

Network of drainage channels

River Nile

▲ **In its northernmost** reaches, the river Nile has deposited huge quantities of silt and alluvium to form the fan-shaped Nile Delta. The Nile splits into two main channels at the base of the delta which are interlinked by a dense network of canals and drainage channels.

Ahaggar

Nile Valley, Aswan

◀ **Almost all of** Egypt's people – more than 99% – live close to the river Nile, or on its massive delta. The river waters the only strip of fertile land in Egypt.

Transport and industry

The economies of Algeria and Libya were transformed by the discovery of oil and natural gas reserves in the deserts. Morocco's major exports are phosphates and agricultural produce, and as in Egypt and Tunisia, the tourist industry is essential to the economy. Egypt has the most varied industrial base, importing technology to develop electronics and engineering industries, and maintaining the reputation of its high-quality cotton textiles.

▶ **Built as great** tombs for the pharaohs of ancient Egypt, the magnificent pyramids at El Giza near Cairo have fascinated scholars, archaeologists and tourists for centuries.

▶ **Oil rigs are** scattered throughout the deserts of Libya and Algeria. Libyan oil is especially prized because of its low sulphur content, which means it produces much less pollution than other fuel oils.

Major industry and infrastructure

- ⚙ engineering
- food processing
- gas
- iron & steel
- iron ore
- oil
- △ phosphates
- 👕 textiles
- tourism
- ■ capital cities
- ● major towns
- ✈ international airports
- — major roads
- major industrial areas

The transport network

🛫	133,650 miles (215,113 km)	🛣	785 miles (1263 km)
🚆	7790 miles (12,538 km)		2175 miles (3500 km)

Tourism and the oil industry have made improvements to the Maghreb's infrastructure both necessary and possible. The Suez Canal is a vital artery for shipping between Europe and Asia.

West Africa

BENIN, BURKINA, CAPE VERDE, GAMBIA, GHANA, GUINEA, GUINEA-BISSAU, IVORY COAST, LIBERIA, MALI, MAURITANIA, NIGER, NIGERIA, SENEGAL, SIERRA LEONE, TOGO

West Africa is an immensely diverse region, encompassing the desert landscapes and mainly Muslim populations of the southern Saharan countries, and the tropical rainforests of the more humid south, with a great variety of local languages and cultures. The rich natural resources and accessibility of the area were quickly exploited by Europeans; most of the Africans taken by slave traders came from this region, causing serious depopulation. The very different influences of West Africa's leading colonial powers, Britain and France, remain today, reflected in the languages and institutions of the countries they once governed.

▶ The dry scrub of the Sahel is only suitable for grazing herd animals like these cattle in Mali.

Scale 1:10,000,000

Km
0 25 50 100 150 200 250
Miles
0 25 50 100 150 200 250

projection: Lambert Azimuthal Equal Area

Transport and industry

Abundant natural resources including oil and metallic minerals are found in much of West Africa, although investment is required for their further exploitation. Nigeria experienced an oil boom during the 1970s but subsequent growth has been sporadic. Most industry in other countries has a primary basis, including mining, logging and food processing.

The transport network

62,154 miles (100,038 km)		1037 miles (1669 km)	
6752 miles (10,867 km)		10,192 miles (16,405 km)	

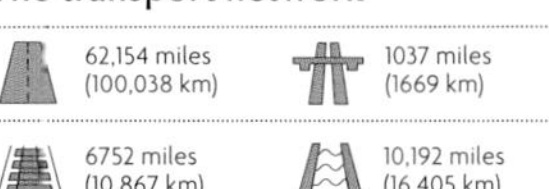

The road and rail systems are most developed near the coasts. Some of the land-locked countries remain disadvantaged by the difficulty of access to ports, and their poor road networks.

Major industry and infrastructure

- chemicals
- cotton spinning
- food processing
- mining
- oil
- palm oil processing
- peanut processing
- textiles
- vehicle manufacture
- capital cities
- major towns
- international airports
- major roads
- major industrial areas

CAPE VERDE

Santo Antão
Pombas
Mindelo
São Vicente
Ilhas de Barlavento
Ribeira Brava
São Nicolau
Pedra Lume
Amilcar Cabral
Sal
Boa Vista

ATLANTIC OCEAN

Tarrafal
Fogo
São Filipe
Santiago
Maio
Maio
PRAIA
Ilhas de Sotavento
João Barrosa

(same scale as main map)

Map key

Population

- 1 million to 5 million
- 500,000 to 1 million
- 100,000 to 500,000
- 50,000 to 100,000
- 10,000 to 50,000
- below 10,000

Elevation

- 2000m / 6562ft
- 1000m / 3281ft
- 500m / 1640ft
- 250m / 820ft
- 100m / 328ft
- sea level

◀ The southern regions of West Africa still contain great swathes of tropical rainforest, including some of the world's most prized hardwood trees, such as mahogany and iroko.

Using the land and sea

The humid southern regions are most suitable for cultivation; in these areas, cash crops such as coffee, cotton, cocoa and rubber are grown in large quantities. Peanuts (groundnuts) are grown throughout West Africa. In the north, advancing desertification has made the Sahel increasingly unviable for cultivation, and pastoral farming is more common. Great herds of sheep, cattle and goats are grazed on the savannah grasses, and fishing is important in coastal and delta areas.

▲ The Gambia, mainland Africa's smallest country, produces great quantities of peanuts (groundnuts). Winnowing is used to separate the nuts from their stalks.

Land use and agricultural distribution

- goats
- sheep
- cocoa
- coffee
- cotton
- oil palms
- peanuts
- rubber
- shellfish
- capital cities
- major towns
- pasture
- cropland
- forest
- desert

The urban/rural population divide

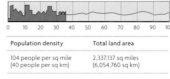

urban 36%   rural 64%

0 10 20 30 40 50 60 70 80 90 100

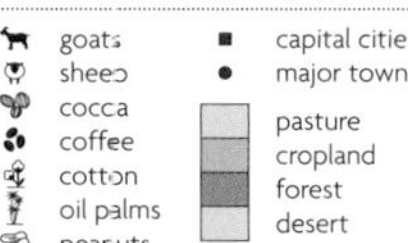

Population density	Total land area
104 people per sq mile (40 people per sq km)	2,337,137 sq miles (6,054,760 sq km)

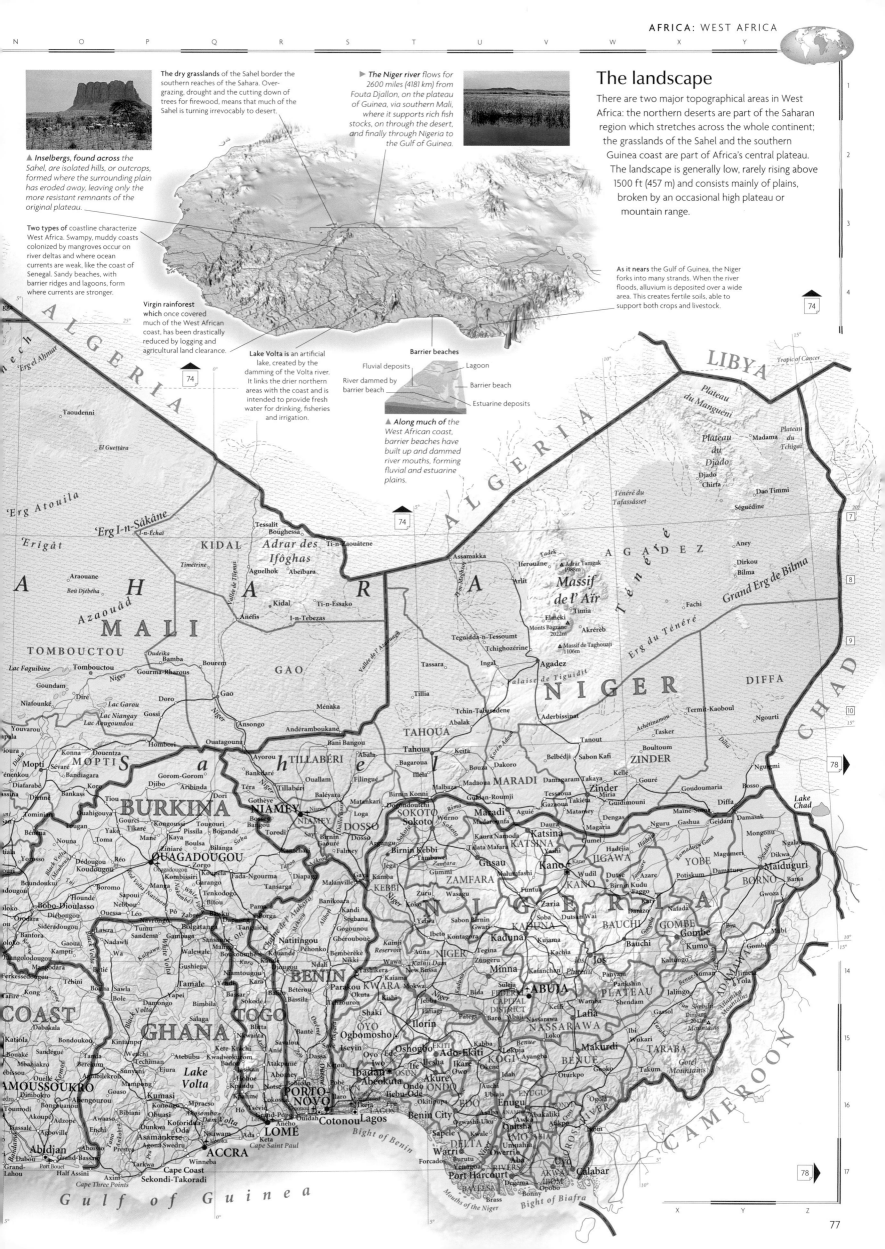

Inselbergs, found across the Sahel, are isolated hills, or outcrops, formed where the surrounding plain has eroded away, leaving only the more resistant remnants of the original plateau.

The dry grasslands of the Sahel border the southern reaches of the Sahara. Over-grazing, drought and the cutting down of trees for firewood, means that much of the Sahel is turning irrevocably to desert.

▶ **The Niger river** flows for 2600 miles (4181 km) from Fouta Djallon, on the plateau of Guinea, via southern Mali, where it supports rich fish stocks, on through the desert, and finally through Nigeria to the Gulf of Guinea.

The landscape

There are two major topographical areas in West Africa: the northern deserts are part of the Saharan region which stretches across the whole continent; the grasslands of the Sahel and the southern Guinea coast are part of Africa's central plateau. The landscape is generally low, rarely rising above 1500 ft (457 m) and consists mainly of plains, broken by an occasional high plateau or mountain range.

Two types of coastline characterize West Africa. Swampy, muddy coasts colonized by mangroves occur on river deltas and where ocean currents are weak, like the coast of Senegal. Sandy beaches, with barrier ridges and lagoons, form where currents are stronger.

Virgin rainforest which once covered much of the West African coast, has been drastically reduced by logging and agricultural land clearance.

Lake Volta is an artificial lake, created by the damming of the Volta river. It links the drier northern areas with the coast and is intended to provide fresh water for drinking, fisheries and irrigation.

As it nears the Gulf of Guinea, the Niger forks into many strands. When the river floods, alluvium is deposited over a wide area. This creates fertile soils, able to support both crops and livestock.

Barrier beaches

Fluvial deposits
River dammed by barrier beach
Lagoon
Barrier beach
Estuarine deposits

▲ **Along much of** the West African coast, barrier beaches have built up and dammed river mouths, forming fluvial and estuarine plains.

Central Africa

CAMEROON, CENTRAL AFRICAN REPUBLIC, CHAD,
CONGO, DEM. REP. CONGO, EQUATORIAL GUINEA,
GABON, SAO TOME & PRINCIPE

The great rainforest basin of the Congo river embraces most of remote Central Africa. The interior was largely unknown to Europeans until late in the 19th century, when its tribal kingdoms were split – principally between France and Belgium – with Sao Tome and Principe the lone Portuguese territory, and Equatorial Guinea controlled by Spain. Open democracy and regional economic integration are important goals for these nations – several of which have only recently emerged from restrictive regimes – and investment is needed to improve transport infrastructures. Many of the small, but fast-growing and increasingly urban population, speak French, the regional *lingua franca*, along with several hundred Pygmy, Bantu and Sudanic dialects.

The landscape

Lake Chad lies in a desert basin bounded by the volcanic Tibesti mountains in the north, plateaux in the east and, in the south, the broad watershed of the Congo basin. The vast circular depression of the Congo is isolated from the coastal plain by the granite Massif du Chaillu. To the northwest, the volcanoes and fold mountains of the Cameroon Ridge (*Dorsale Camerounaise*) extend as islands into the Gulf of Guinea. The high fold mountains fringing the east of the Congo Basin fall steeply to the lakes of the Great Rift Valley.

Transport and industry

Large reserves of valuable minerals are found in Central Africa: copper, cobalt and diamonds are mined in Dem. Rep. Congo and manganese in Gabon. Congo, Cameroon, Gabon and Equatorial Guinea have oil deposits and oil has also been recently discovered in Chad. Goods such as palm oil and rubber are processed for export.

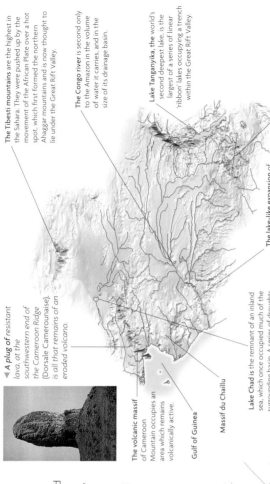

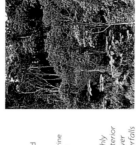

▲ *Virgin tropical rainforest* covers the Ruwenzori range on the borders of Dem. Rep. Congo and Uganda.

The Tibesti mountains are the highest in the Sahara. They were pushed up by the movement of the African Plate over a hot spot, which first formed the northern Ahaggar mountains and is now thought to lie under the Great Rift Valley.

The Congo river is second only to the Amazon in the volume of water it carries, and in the size of its drainage basin.

Lake Tanganyika, the world's second deepest lake, is the largest of a series of linear 'ribbon' lakes occupying a trench within the Great Rift Valley.

Rich mineral deposits in the 'Copper Belt' of Dem. Rep. Congo were formed under intense heat and pressure when the ancient African Shield was uplifted to form the region's mountains.

▲ *A plug of resistant lava, at the southwestern end of the Cameroon Ridge (Dorsale Camerounaise), is all that remains of an eroded volcano.*

The volcanic massif of Cameroon Mountain occupies an area which remains volcanically active.

Massif du Chaillu

Gulf of Guinea

The lake-like expansion of the Congo river at Stanley Pool is the lowest point of the interior basin, although the river still descends more than 1000 ft (300 m) to reach the sea.

Lake Chad is the remnant of an inland sea which once occupied much of the surrounding basin. A series of droughts since the 1970s has reduced the area of this shallow freshwater lake to about 1000 sq miles (2599 sq km).

▲ **The Congo river** flows sluggishly through the rainforest of the interior basin. Towards the coast, the river drops steeply in a series of waterfalls and cataracts. At this point, the erosional power of the river becomes so great that it has formed a deep submarine canyon offshore.

Broad, shallow basin
Waterfalls and cataracts
Submarine canyon

▲ **The vast sand flats** surrounding Lake Chad were once covered by water. Changing climatic patterns caused the lake to shrink, and desert now covers much of its previous area.

Map key

Population
- ◉ 1 million to 5 million
- ⊙ 500,000 to 1 million
- ⊙ 100,000 to 500,000
- ⊙ 50,000 to 100,000
- ○ 10,000 to 50,000
- · below 10,000

Elevation
- 4000m / 13124ft
- 3000m / 9843ft
- 2000m / 6562ft
- 1000m / 3281ft
- 500m / 1640ft
- 250m / 820ft
- 100m / 328ft
- sea level

Scale 1:10,500,000

projection: Lambert Azimuthal Equal Area

▲ **The ancient rocks** of Dem. Rep. Congo hold immense and varied mineral reserves. This open pit copper mine is at Kolwezi in the far south.

Major industry and infrastructure

- brewing
- chemicals
- cobalt
- copper
- diamonds
- food processing
- manganese
- oil
- palm oil processing
- textiles
- tin
- ■ capital cities
- ■ major towns
- ⊕ international airports
- major roads
- major industrial areas

The transport network

- ▲ 102,747 miles (165,774 km)
- 🚇 37 miles (60 km)
- ▲ 3985 miles (6414 km)
- 🚂 14,110 miles (22,710 km)

The Trans-Gabon railway, which began operating in 1987, has opened up new sources of timber and manganese. Elsewhere, much investment is needed to update and improve road, rail and water transport.

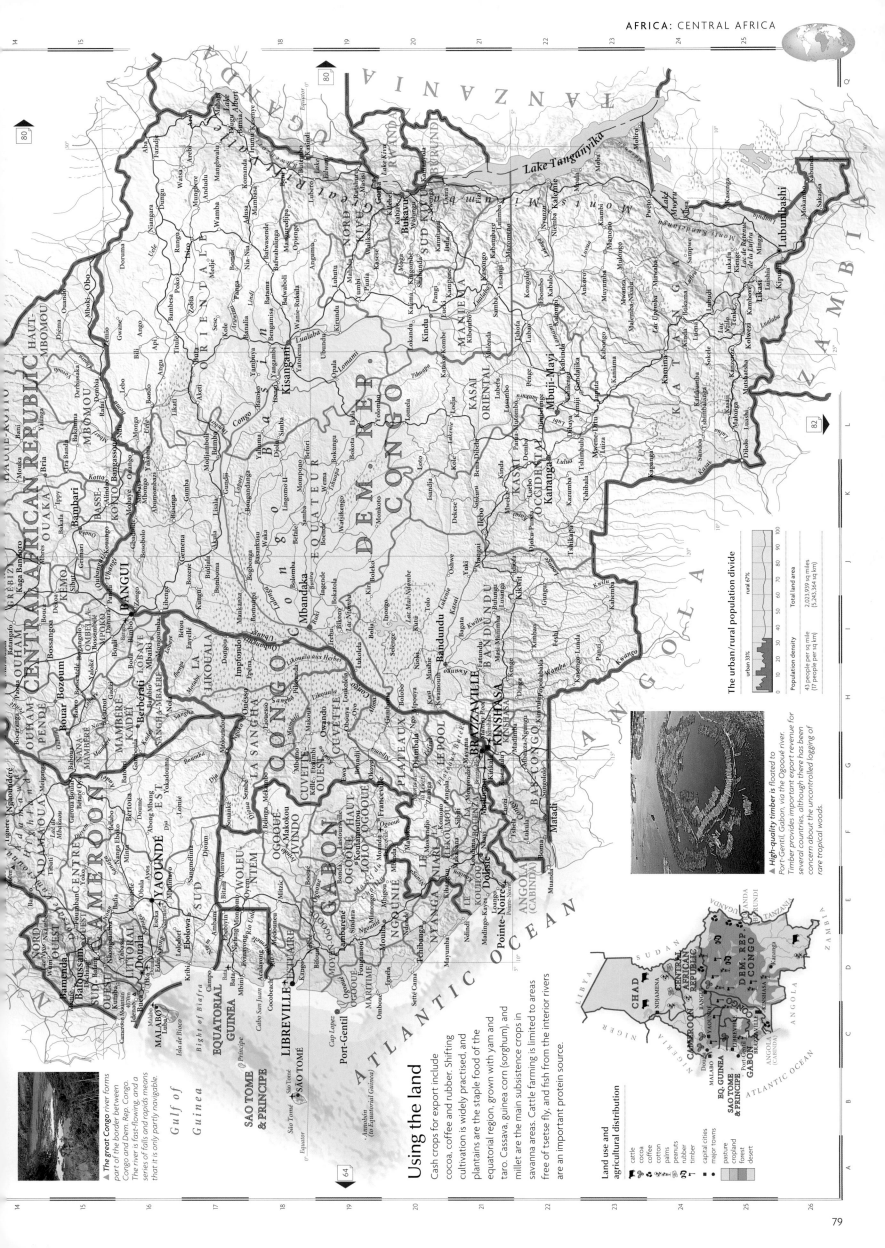

Using the land

Cash crops for export include cocoa, coffee and rubber. Shifting cultivation is widely practised, and plantains are the staple food of the equatorial region, grown with yam and taro. Cassava, guinea corn (sorghum), and millet are the main subsistence crops in savanna areas. Cattle farming is limited to areas free of tsetse fly, and fish from the interior rivers are an important protein source.

▲ *The great Congo river forms part of the border between Congo and Dem. Rep. Congo. The river is fast-flowing, and a series of falls and rapids means that it is only partly navigable.*

▲ *High-quality timber is floated to Port-Gentil, Gabon, via the Ogooué river. Timber provides important export revenue for several countries, although there has been concern about the uncontrolled logging of rare tropical woods.*

The urban/rural population divide

Population density	Total land area
43 people per sq mile (17 people per sq km)	2,023,939 sq miles (5,243,364 sq km)

Land use and agricultural distribution

- cattle
- cocoa
- coffee
- cotton
- peanuts
- palms
- rubber
- timber
- capital cities
- major towns
- pasture
- cropland
- forest
- desert

East Africa

BURUNDI, DJIBOUTI, ERITREA, ETHIOPIA, KENYA,
RWANDA, SOMALIA, SUDAN, TANZANIA, UGANDA

The countries of East Africa divide into two distinct cultural regions. Sudan and the 'Horn' nations have been influenced by the Middle East; Ethiopia was the home of one of the earliest Christian civilizations, and Sudan reflects both Muslim and Christian influences, while the southern countries share a closer cultural affinity with other sub-Saharan nations. Some of Africa's most densely populated countries lie in this region, and the needs of a growing number of people have put pressure on marginal lands and fragile environments. Although most East African economies remain strongly agricultural, Kenya has developed a varied industrial base.

The landscape

East Africa's most significant landscape feature is the Great Rift Valley, which formed during the most recent phase of continental movement when the rigid basement rocks cracked and buckled. Great blocks of land were raised and lowered, creating huge flat-bottomed valleys and steep escarpments, sometimes covered by volcanic extrusions in highland areas.

Central block slopes towards main fault

Ephemeral lake forms at far edge of slope

Boundary fault

▲ *The eastern arm* of the Great Rift Valley is gradually being pulled apart; however the forces on one side are greater than the other causing the land to slope. This affects regional drainage which migrates down the slope.

▼ *This dome at* Gonder, in Ethiopia, is a volcanic intrusion, formed when molten rock pushed up the surface of the Earth and then solidified, leaving an outcrop of igneous rock.

Lava flows on uplifted areas either side of the eastern branch of the Great Rift Valley gave the Ethiopian Highlands – a series of high, wide plateaux – their distinctive rounded appearance and fertile soils.

Kilimanjaro

▲ *An extinct volcano.* Kilimanjaro is Africa's highest mountain, rising 19,340 ft (5895 m). Once famed for its snow-capped peak, this has almost completely melted due to changing climatic conditions.

A vast plateau lies between the eastern and western rift valleys in Kenya, Uganda and western Tanzania. It has been levelled by long periods of erosion to form a peneplain, but is dotted with inselbergs – outcrops of more resistant rocks.

Lake Victoria occupies a vast basin between the two arms of the Great Rift Valley. It is the world's second largest lake in terms of surface area, extending 26,560 sq miles (68,880 sq km). The lake contains numerous islands and coral reefs.

Much of northern Sudan is covered by desert. However, in the tropical wetlands of the southern Sudd region, annual rainfall can sometimes exceed 40 inches (1000 mm).

The tiny countries of Rwanda and Burundi are mainly mountainous, with large areas of inaccessible tropical rainforest.

Lake Tanganyika lies 8202 ft (2500 m) above sea level. It has a depth of nearly 4700 ft (1435 m). The lake traces the valley floor for some 400 miles (644 km) of the western arm of the Great Rift Valley.

▼ *The Kassala region* in eastern Sudan is watered by the Atbara river, an important tributary of the Nile. Most of the population is engaged in agriculture, growing cotton and cereals.

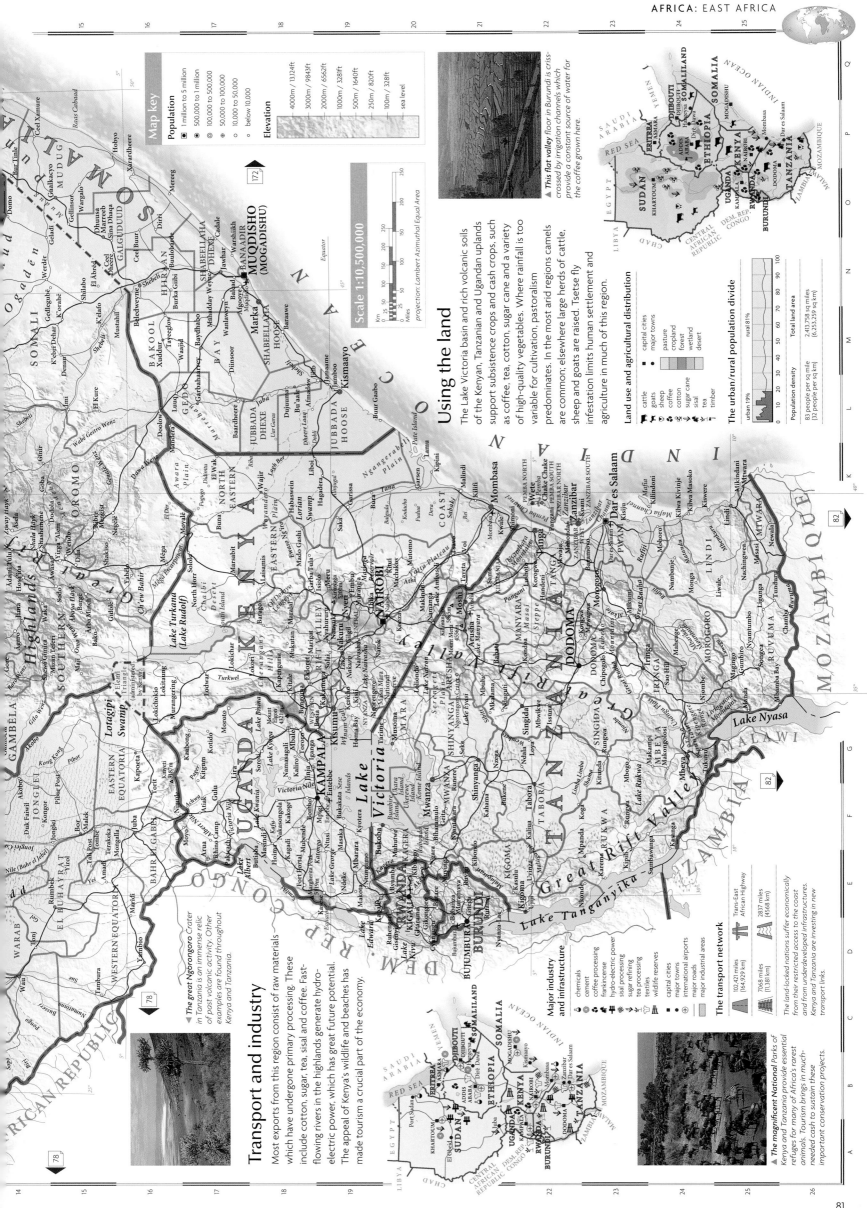

Map key

Population
- ■ 1 million to 5 million
- ● 500,000 to 1 million
- ◉ 100,000 to 500,000
- ⊕ 50,000 to 100,000
- ⊙ 10,000 to 50,000
- ∘ below 10,000

Elevation
- 4000m / 13124ft
- 3000m / 9843ft
- 2000m / 6562ft
- 1000m / 3281ft
- 500m / 1640ft
- 250m / 820ft
- 100m / 328ft
- sea level

Scale 1:10,500,000

projection: Lambert Azimuthal Equal Area

▲ This flat valley floor in Burundi is criss-crossed by irrigation channels which provide a constant source of water for the coffee grown here.

Using the land

The Lake Victoria basin and rich volcanic soils of the Kenyan, Tanzanian and Ugandan uplands support subsistence crops and cash crops, such as coffee, tea, cotton, sugar cane and a variety of high-quality vegetables. Where rainfall is too variable for cultivation, pastoralism predominates. In the most arid regions camels are common; elsewhere large herds of cattle, sheep and goats are raised. Tsetse fly infestation limits human settlement and agriculture in much of this region.

Land use and agricultural distribution

- ● capital cities
- ∘ major towns
- pasture
- cropland
- forest
- wetland
- desert

cattle, goats, sheep, coffee, cotton, sugar cane, sisal, tea, timber

The urban/rural population divide

urban 19% rural 81%

Population density Total land area
83 people per sq mile   2,413,758 sq miles
(32 people per sq km)   (6,253,259 sq km)

Transport and industry

Most exports from this region consist of raw materials which have undergone primary processing. These include cotton, sugar, tea, sisal and coffee. Fast-flowing rivers in the highlands generate hydro-electric power, which has great future potential. The appeal of Kenya's wildlife and beaches has made tourism a crucial part of the economy.

▲ The great Ngorongoro Crater in Tanzania is an immense relic of past volcanic activity. Other examples are found throughout Kenya and Tanzania.

Major industry and infrastructure

- chemicals
- cement
- coffee processing
- frankincense
- hydro-electric power
- sisal processing
- sugar refining
- tea processing
- textiles
- wildlife reserves
- ● capital cities
- ∘ major towns
- ⊕ international airports
- major roads
- major industrial areas

The transport network

	Trans-East African Highway
102,431 miles (164,929 km)	2837 miles (4568 km)
7068 miles (11,381 km)	

The land-locked nations suffer economically from their restricted access to the coast and from underdeveloped infrastructures. Kenya and Tanzania are investing in new transport links.

▲ The magnificent National Parks of Kenya and Tanzania provide essential refuges for many of Africa's rarest animals. Tourism brings in much-needed cash to sustain these important conservation projects.

Southern Africa

ANGOLA, BOTSWANA, LESOTHO, MALAWI, MOZAMBIQUE, NAMIBIA, SOUTH AFRICA, SWAZILAND, ZAMBIA, ZIMBABWE

Africa's vast southern plateau has been a contested homeland for disparate peoples for many centuries. The European incursion began with the slave trade and quickened in the 19th century, when the discovery of enormous mineral wealth secured South Africa's regional economic dominance. The struggle against white minority rule led to strife in Namibia, Zimbabwe, and the former Portuguese territories of Angola and Mozambique. South Africa's notorious apartheid laws, which denied basic human rights to more than 75% of the people, led to the state being internationally ostracized until 1994, when the first fully democratic elections inaugurated a new era of racial justice.

Transport and industry

South Africa, the world's largest exporter of gold, has a varied economy which generates about 75% of the region's income and draws migrant labour from neighbouring states. Angola exports petroleum; Botswana and Namibia rely on diamond mining; and Zambia is seeking to diversify its economy to compensate for declining copper reserves.

▲ Almost all new mining ventures in Zimbabwe are now subject to government control. This mine at Bindura in northeastern Zimbabwe produces nickel, one of the country's top three minerals in terms of economic value.

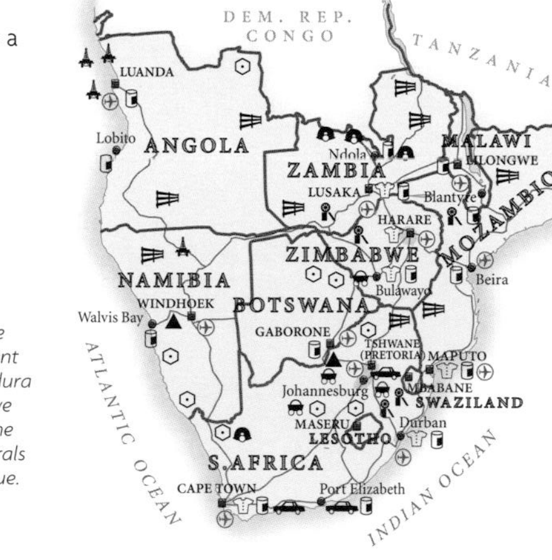

Major industry and infrastructure

- ⊕ car manufacture
- ⬤ coal
- ✦ copper
- ◆ diamonds
- ⬡ food processing
- ◈ gold
- ⧫ oil
- ⧓ textiles
- ⛆ uranium

- ■ capital cities
- • major towns
- ⊕ international airports
- ━ major roads
- ▨ major industrial areas
- 🌳 wildlife reserves

The landscape

Most of southern Africa rests on a concave plateau comprising the Kalahari basin and a mountainous fringe, skirted by a coastal plain which widens out in Mozambique. The plateau extends north, towards the Planalto de Bié in Angola, the Congo Basin and the lake-filled troughs of the Great Rift Valley. The eastern region is drained by the Zambezi and Limpopo rivers, and the Orange is the major western river.

▲ At Victoria Falls, the Zambezi river has cut a spectacular gorge taking advantage of large joints in the basalt, which were first formed as the lava cooled and contracted.

▲ The fast-flowing Zambezi river cuts a deep, wide channel as it flows along the Zimbabwe/Zambia border.

Great Rift Valley

Lake Nyasa occupies one of the deep troughs of the Great Rift Valley, where the land has been displaced downwards by as much as 3000 ft (920 m).

Limpopo river

Bushveld intrusion

Volcanic lava, over 250 million years old, caps the peaks of the Drakensberg range, which lie on the mountainous rim of southern Africa's interior plateau.

The Okavango/Cubango river flows from the Planalto de Bié to the swamplands of the Okavango Delta, one of the world's largest inland deltas, where it divides into countless distributary channels, feeding out into the desert.

Broad, flat-topped mountains characterize the Great Karoo, which have been cut from level rock strata under extremely arid conditions.

The mountains of the Little Karoo are composed of sedimentary rocks which have been substantially folded and faulted.

Planalto de Bié

The Orange River, one of the longest in Africa, rises in Lesotho and is the only major river in the south which flows westward, rather than to the east coast.

The Kalahari Desert is the largest continuous sand surface in the world. Iron oxide gives a distinctive red colour to the windblown sand, which, in eastern areas covers the bedrock by over 200 ft (60 m).

Thousands of years of evaporating water have produced the Etosha Pan, one of the largest salt flats in the world. Lake and river sediments in the area indicate that the region was once less arid.

Khorixas, Namibia

▲ Finger Rock, near Khorixas, Namibia is a remnant of a former land surface, which has been denuded by erosion over the last 5 million years. These occasional stacks of partially weathered rocks interrupt the plains of the dry southern interior.

Namib Desert

The transport network

🛣 84,213 miles (135,609 km)	🚂 746 miles (1202 km)
🛤 23,208 miles (37,372 km)	⛰ 3815 miles (6144 km)

Southern Africa's Cape-gauge rail network is by far the largest in the continent. About two-thirds of the 20,000 mile (32,000 km) system lies within South Africa. Lines such as the Harare–Bulawayo route have become corridors for industrial growth.

▲ Following a series of droughts, this baobab tree in Zimbabwe now stands alone in a field once filled by sugar cane. The thick trunk and small leaves of the baobab help it to conserve water, enabling it to survive even in drought conditions.

Map key

Population
- ⬛ 1 million to 5 million
- ⬤ 500,000 to 1 million
- ◉ 100,000 to 500,000
- ⊕ 50,000 to 100,000
- ○ 10,000 to 50,000
- ∘ below 10,000

Elevation
- 3000m / 9843ft
- 2000m / 6562ft
- 1000m / 3280ft
- 500m / 1640ft
- 250m / 820ft
- 100m / 328ft
- sea level

South Africa: Capital cities
TSHWANE (PRETORIA) – administrative capital
CAPE TOWN – legislative capital
BLOEMFONTEIN – judicial capital

Granite

Chromite

Bushveld intrusion

Gabbro and peridotite

Magnetite

Platinum minerals

▲ The Bushveld intrusion lies on South Africa's high veld. Molten magma intruded into the Earth's crust creating a saucer-shaped feature, more than 180 miles (300 km) across, containing regular layers of precious minerals, overlain by a dome of granite.

Scale 1:10,500,000

projection: Lambert Azimuthal Equal Area

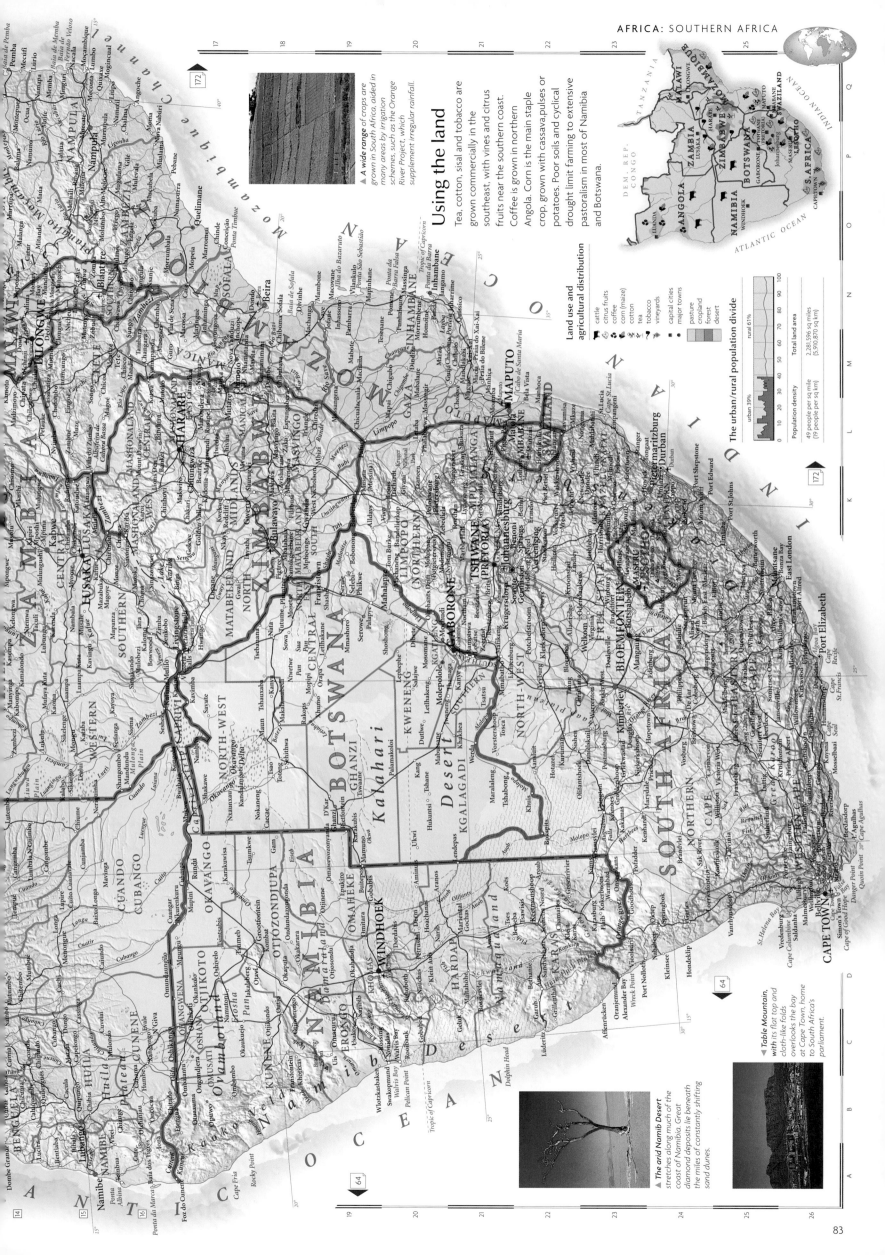

▲ *A wide range* of crops are grown in South Africa, aided in many areas by irrigation schemes, such as the Orange River Project, which supplement irregular rainfall.

Using the land

Tea, cotton, sisal and tobacco are grown commercially in the southeast, with vines and citrus fruits near the southern coast. Coffee is grown in northern Angola. Corn is the main staple crop, grown with cassava, pulses or potatoes. Poor soils and cyclical drought limit farming to extensive pastoralism in most of Namibia and Botswana.

Land use and agricultural distribution

- cattle
- citrus fruits
- coffee
- corn (maize)
- cotton
- tea
- tobacco
- vineyards
- ▪ capital cities
- ▪ major towns

- pasture
- cropland
- forest
- desert

The urban/rural population divide

urban 39%

rural 61%

Population density

Total land area

2,281,596 sq miles
(5,910,870 sq km)

49 people per sq mile
(19 people per sq km)

▲ *The arid Namib Desert* stretches along much of the coast of Namibia. Great diamond deposits lie beneath the miles of constantly shifting sand dunes.

▶ *Table Mountain,* with its flat top and cloth-like folds overlooks the bay at Cape Town, home to South Africa's parliament.

ARCTIC OCEAN

North Pole

Ellesmere Island

King Frederik
VIII Land

Greenland

King Christian X Land

Laptev Sea

Poluostrov Taymyr

Ostrov Rudol'fa
Severnaya Zemlya

Franz Josef Land

Kara Sea

Mys Flissingskiy

EURASIAN PLATE
NORTH AMERICAN PLATE

Spitsbergen

Greenland
Sea

Nowaya Zemlya

Barents
Sea

Baydaratskaya Guba

Gulf of Ob

Poluostrov Yamal

Yenisey

Bjørnøya

A S I

Arctic Circle
Denmark Strait

Jan Mayen Fracture Zone
Jan Mayen Ridge

Kolbeinsey Ridge

Jan Mayen

Barents
Trough

Tromsøflaket
North Cape   Nordkinn

Fugløya Bank

Murmansk Rise

West Siberian
Plain

Ob'

Bjargtangar

Iceland
Plateau

N o r w e g i a n   S e a

Vesterålen

Inarijärvi

Ostrov
Kolguyev

Poluostrov
Kanin

Pechora

Ural Mountains

Irtysh

Reykjanes Ridge

Iceland
Vatnajökull

Voring Plateau

Norwegian
Basin

Lofoten

Kebnekaise
2117m

Torneälven
Tornionjoki

Kola Peninsula
Ozero
Imandra

White Sea

Timanskiy Kryazh

Mezen

Goba

Sapozhnaya

Tobol

Iceland
Basin

Faeroe-Iceland Ridge

Traena
Bank

S c a n d i n a v i a

Kemijoki

Oulujoki

Northern Dvina

Tavda

Hatton Ridge

Faeroe Islands

Galdhøpiggen
2469m

Umeälven

Ozero
Vygozero

Onega Bay

Ozero
Belaya

Rockall
Rise

Bill Baileys
Bank

Faeroe-Shetland Trough

Shetland
Islands

Ljungan

Ljusnan

Lake
Ladoga

Lake
Onega

Onega

Vyg

Sukhona

Feni Ridge

Orkney Islands

Viking Bank

Gulf of Bothnia

Åland

Gulf of Finland

Lake
Peipus

Msta

Rybinsk
Reservoir

Gorky
Reservoir

Vetluga

Iyatka

Kama

Kuybyshev
Reservoir

Belaya

Outer Hebrides

Norwegian Trench

Vänern

Vättern

Gotland

Gulf of
Riga

Lake Pskov

Lake Ilmen

Western Dvina

Ben Nevis
1343m

Grampian
Mountains

North
Sea

Jutland
Bank

Skagerrak

Kattegat

Baltic Sea

Neman

Klyazma

Byerezino

Moksha

Oka

Sura

Rockall Trough

British
Isles

Pennines

Snowdon
1085m

Trent

Great
Fisher
Bank

Jylland

Sjælland

North European Plain

Bug

Dnieper

Central Russian Upland

Volga Upland

Volga

Porcupine
Plain

Ireland

Irish Sea

Britain

The
Fens

Severn

Thames

L'ogger
Bank

Frisian Islands

Odra

Vistula

Warta

Pripet
Marshes

Desna

Seym

Don

Khoper

Shannon

Celtic Sea
Celtic
Shelf

St. George's
Channel

Bristol Channel

Land's End

English Channel
Channel Islands

Strait of Dover

Ardennes
Rhine

E U R O P E

Dnieper Lowlands

Kiev
Reservoir

Dniester

Podil's'ka
Vysochina

Pividennyy Buh

Donets

Tsimlyansk
Reservoir

Azores-Biscay Rise

Charcot Seamounts

Biscay
Plain

Seine

Marne

Meuse

Moselle

Lake Constance

Harz

Danube

Morava

Carpathian
Mountains

Tisza

Prut

Siret

Black Sea Lowland

Don

Manych

Yergeni

Kirghiz Ste

Bay of
Biscay

Loire

Cher

Saône

Lake Geneva

A l p s

Bakony

Lake Balaton

Great
Hungarian
Plain

Drava

Sava

Transylvanian Alps

Danube

Sea of
Azov

Iberia Gap
Galicia
Bank

Massif
Central

Mont
Blanc

Lake Garda

Po

Adriatic Alps

Balkan Mountains

Crimea

Black Sea

Iberian
Plain

Cordillera Cantabrica

Aragon

Douro

Ebro

Cévennes

Dordogne

Lot

Ligurian
Sea

Dinaric Alps

Apennines

Adriatic Sea

Corno Grande
2912m

Lake Scutari

Rhodope Mountains

Maritsa

Sea of
Marmara

EURASIAN PLATE
ANATOLIAN PLATE

Miño

Duero

Sistema Ibérica

Corsica

Adriatic
Basin

Lake
Ohrid

Strait of Otranto

Tagus

I b e r i a n

Sistema Central

Júcar

Gulf of
Valencia

Balearic Islands

Sardinia

Tyrrhenian
Sea

Gulf of
Taranto

Pindus Mountains

Anatolia

Lake Tuz

Tagus Plain

Gorringe

Cape
Saint Vincent

Guadiana

Guadalquivir

Segura

Tyrrhenian
Basin

Sinai Peninsula

Aegean Sea

Taurus Mountains

Horse-shoe Seamounts

P e n i n s u l a

Sierra Morena

Sistemas Béticos
Sierra Nevada

M e d i t e

Mount Etna
3340m

Ionian Sea

Peloponnese

Mirtoan
Sea

Karpathos

Rhodes

Gulf of
Antalya

Ampère Seamount

Strait of
Gibraltar

Alboran Sea

Oued Chelif

EURASIAN PLATE
AFRICAN PLATE

Sicily

Malta

Ionian Basin

Sea of Crete

Cyprus
Basin

AFRICAN PLATE

Seine Plain

Seine Seamount

Rif

Sebou

Tell Atlas

r r a n e a n   S e a

Mediterranean Ridge

Madeira

Oumer Rbia

Middle Atlas

High Atlas

A t l a s   M o u n t a i n s

Saharan Atlas

Chott el Jerid

Levantine Basin

Nile Fan

Dacia Seamount

Canary Islands

Agadir Canyon

Gulf of
Sirte

Qattara Depression
-133m

Western Desert

Libyan Desert

'Erg Iguidi

Grand Erg Occidental

Grand Erg Oriental

S A H A R A

A F R I C A

Erg Chech

84

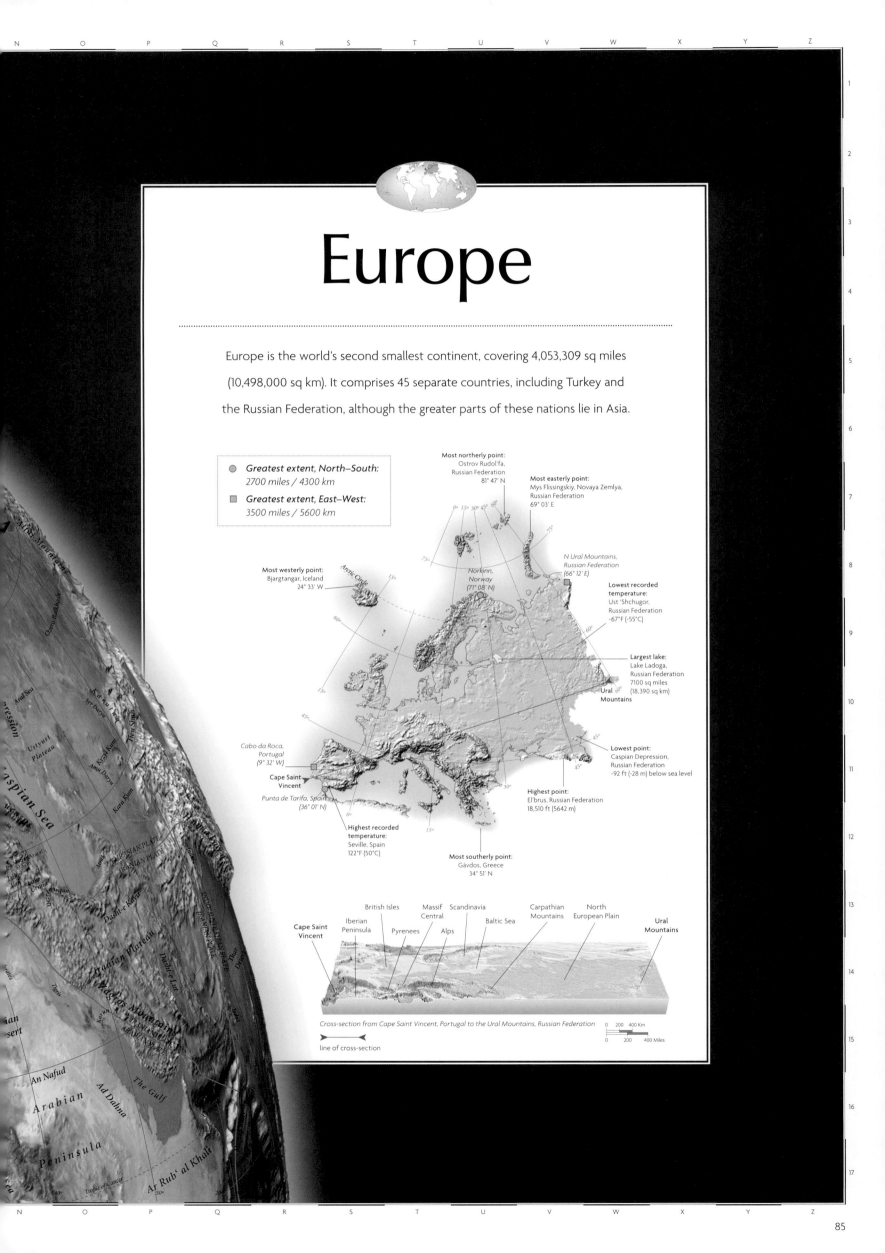

Europe

Europe is the world's second smallest continent, covering 4,053,309 sq miles (10,498,000 sq km). It comprises 45 separate countries, including Turkey and the Russian Federation, although the greater parts of these nations lie in Asia.

● *Greatest extent, North–South:* 2700 miles / 4300 km

■ *Greatest extent, East–West:* 3500 miles / 5600 km

Most northerly point: Ostrov Rudol'fa, Russian Federation 81° 47' N

Most easterly point: Mys Flissingskiy, Novaya Zemlya, Russian Federation 69° 03' E

Most westerly point: Bjargtangar, Iceland 24° 33' W

Arctic Circle

Nordkinn, Norway (71° 08' N)

N Ural Mountains, Russian Federation (66° 12' E)

Lowest recorded temperature: Ust 'Shchugor, Russian Federation -67°F (-55°C)

Largest lake: Lake Ladoga, Russian Federation 7100 sq miles (18,390 sq km)

Ural Mountains

Cabo da Roca, Portugal (9° 32' W)

Cape Saint Vincent

Punta de Tarifa, Spain (36° 01' N)

Lowest point: Caspian Depression, Russian Federation -92 ft (-28 m) below sea level

Highest point: El'brus, Russian Federation 18,510 ft (5642 m)

Highest recorded temperature: Seville, Spain 122°F (50°C)

Most southerly point: Gávdos, Greece 34° 51' N

British Isles — Massif Central — Scandinavia — Carpathian Mountains — North European Plain — Ural Mountains

Cape Saint Vincent — Iberian Peninsula — Pyrenees — Alps — Baltic Sea

Cross-section from Cape Saint Vincent, Portugal to the Ural Mountains, Russian Federation

0   200   400 Km
0   200   400 Miles

line of cross-section

Ozero Balkhash

Ustyurt Plateau

Aral Sea

Syr Darya

Kyzyl Kum

Amu Darya

Kara Kum

Caspian Sea

Iranian Plateau

Dasht-e Kavir

Dasht-e Lut

Arabian Plateau

Zagros Mountains

Tigris

An Nafud

The Gulf

Arabian Peninsula

Ad Dahna

Ar Rub' al Khali

Tropic of Cancer

Physical Europe

The physical diversity of Europe belies its relatively small size. To the northwest and south it is enclosed by mountains. The older, rounded Atlantic Highlands of Scandinavia and the British Isles lie to the north and the younger, rugged peaks of the Alpine Uplands to the south. In between lies the North European Plain, stretching 2485 miles (4000 km) from The Fens in England to the Ural Mountains in Russia. South of the plain lies a series of gently folded sedimentary rocks separated by ancient plateaux, known as massifs.

The North European Plain

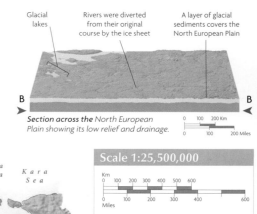

Rising less than 1000 ft (300 m) above sea level, the North European Plain strongly reflects past glaciation. Ridges of both coarse moraine and finer, windblown deposits have accumulated over much of the region. The ice sheet also diverted a number of river channels from their original courses.

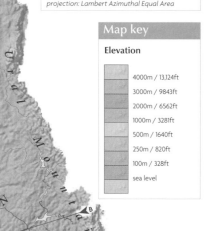

Glacial lakes

Rivers were diverted from their original course by the ice sheet

A layer of glacial sediments covers the North European Plain

Section across the North European Plain showing its low relief and drainage.

0   100   200 Km
0   100   200 Miles

The Atlantic Highlands

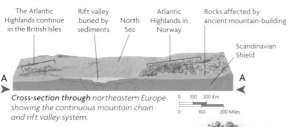

The Atlantic Highlands were formed by compression against the Scandinavian Shield during the Caledonian mountain-building period over 500 million years ago. The highlands were once part of a continuous mountain chain, now divided by the North Sea and a submerged rift valley.

The Atlantic Highlands continue in the British Isles

Rift valley buried by sediments

North Sea

Atlantic Highlands in Norway

Rocks affected by ancient mountain-building

Scandinavian Shield

Cross-section through northeastern Europe showing the continuous mountain chain and rift valley system.

0   100   200 Km
0   100   200 Miles

Scale 1:25,500,000

Km
0   100   200   300   400   500   600

Miles
0   100   200   300   400   500   600

projection: Lambert Azimuthal Equal Area

Map key

Elevation

- 4000m / 13,124ft
- 3000m / 9843ft
- 2000m / 6562ft
- 1000m / 3281ft
- 500m / 1640ft
- 250m / 820ft
- 100m / 328ft
- sea level

Plate margins
(for explanation see page xiv)

———— constructive

△   △ destructive

———— conservative

.... uncertain

———— physiographic regions

▶◀ line of cross-section

NORTH AMERICAN PLATE
EURASIAN PLATE

Iceland

Novaya Zemlya

Kara Sea

Barents Sea

Ostrov Kolguyev

Norwegian Sea

Kola Peninsula

White Sea

Faeroe Islands

Shetland Islands

Outer Hebrides

British Isles

Ireland
Shannon

Britain
The Fens
Thames

North Sea

Jylland

Vänern

Vättern

Baltic Sea

Gulf of Bothnia

Lake Onega

Lake Ladoga

Gulf of Riga

Northern Dvina

Western Dvina

SCANDINAVIAN SHIELD

ATLANTIC HIGHLANDS

ATLANTIC OCEAN

NORTH EUROPEAN PLAIN

Central Russian Upland

Ural Mountains

Volga Uplands

English Channel

Seine

Loire

Rhine

Elbe

Oder

Vistula

Ardennes

PLATEAUX AND LOWLANDS

ALPS

ALPINE UPLANDS

Bay of Biscay

Massif Central

Pyrenees

Garonne

Rhône

Po

Mt Blanc 4807m

Danube

Danube

Carpathian Mountains

Great Hungarian Plain

Dnieper

Dniester

Don

Don

Dnieper

Sea of Azov

Crimea

Caspian Sea

Iberian Peninsula

Duero

Ebro

Guadalquivir

Corsica

Apennines

Adriatic Sea

Dinaric Alps

Balkan Mountains

Caucasus

Elbrus 5642m

Black Sea

ASIA

Balearic Islands

Sardinia

Vesuvius 1171m

Tyrrhenian Sea

Sicily

Etna 3265m

Ionian Sea

Malta

Peloponnese

Aegean Sea

Crete

EURASIAN PLATE
AFRICAN PLATE

EURASIAN PLATE
ANATOLIAN PLATE

ANATOLIAN PLATE
AFRICAN PLATE

Mediterranean Sea

The plateaux and lowlands

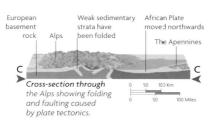

The uplifted plateaux or massifs of southern central Europe are the result of long-term erosion, later followed by uplift. They are the source areas of many of the rivers which drain Europe's lowlands. In some of the higher reaches, fractures have enabled igneous rocks from deep in the Earth to reach the surface.

The Alpine Uplands

The collision of the African and European continents, which began about 65 million years ago, folded and then uplifted a series of mountain ranges running across southern Europe and into Asia. Two major lines of folding can be traced: one includes the Pyrenees, the Alps and the Carpathian Mountains; the other incorporates the Apennines and the Dinaric Alps.

European basement rock

Alps

Weak sedimentary strata have been folded

African Plate moved northwards

The Apennines

Cross-section through the Alps showing folding and faulting caused by plate tectonics.

0   50   100 Km
0   50   100 Miles

Igneous rocks have intruded into the Massif Central

Older, eroded massifs lie behind the arc of the Alps

Po Valley

Tectonically formed basins

Great Hungarian Plain

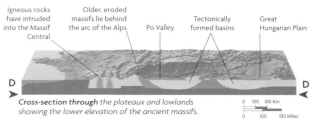

Cross-section through the plateaux and lowlands showing the lower elevation of the ancient massifs.

0   100   200 Km
0   100   200 Miles

Climate

Europe experiences few extremes in either rainfall or temperature, with the exception of the far north and south. Along the west coast, the warm currents of the North Atlantic Drift moderate temperatures. Although east–west air movement is relatively unimpeded by relief, the Alpine Uplands halt the progress of north–south air masses, protecting most of the Mediterranean from cold, north winds.

▲ *Frost grips northern* and eastern Europe during the long cold winters. Lakes and rivers frequently freeze.

Temperature

Temperature	
	below -30°C (-22°F)
	-30 to -20°C (-22 to -4°F)
	-20 to -10°C (-4 to 14°F)
	-10 to 0°C (14 to 32°F)
	0 to 10°C (32 to 50°F)
	10 to 20°C (50 to 60°F)
	20 to 30°C (68 to 86°F)
	above 30°C (86°F)

Average January temperature

Average July temperature

▲ *Mild temperatures and* frequent rainfall contribute to the fertile farming land found over much of northwestern Europe.

Rainfall

Rainfall	
	0–25 mm (0–1 in)
	25–50 mm (1–2 in)
	50–100 mm (2–4 in)
	100–200 mm (4–8 in)
	200–300 mm (8–12 in)
	300–400 mm (12–16 in)
	400–500 mm (16–20 in)
	more than 500 mm (20 in)

Average January rainfall

Average July rainfall

Climate	
	tundra
	subarctic
	cool continental
	warm humid
	mediterranean
	semi-arid
☼	daily hours of sunshine, January
☼	daily hours of sunshine, July
→	cold wind
→	hot wind

▶ *Dusty Sirocco winds* from Africa help create the semi-arid scrubland common across the Mediterranean coastlands of southern Europe.

Shaping the continent

Successive Ice Ages have left many relict landforms across Europe. Present glaciers continue to carve peaks and valleys in the northern Atlantic Highlands and Alpine Uplands. Tectonic activity, both past and present, has shaped southern Europe and Iceland. Active volcanoes and earthquakes still occur in Italy and Greece. Europe's extensive coastline, particularly in the northwest, is constantly modified by wave action and fluvial deposits.

Glaciation

1 Valley glaciers, such as this one *(left)* in Iceland, form in hollows at the top of valleys and flow downwards, drawn by gravity. Their growth is dynamic; new snowfall constantly accumulates at the head of the glacier, while the snout melts, depositing material eroded and carried by the glacier.

Snow accumulates at the head of glacier
Glacier movement erodes valley
Glacier snout melts depositing eroded debris

Glaciation: Development of a glacier

Coastal processes

5 Spits are narrow bands of sand or shingle, formed by longshore drift; a process whereby waves carry material along the beach. They usually form where the coastline changes direction, and their growth is then halted by an opposing river current, as at Spurn Head, in the British Isles *(left)*. Coastal features such as these are constantly being created and destroyed.

Sand and shingle spit
Original coastline
Opposing river current
Waves breaking at an angle

Coastal processes: Formation of a spit

Landscape	
	uplifting land
	stable land
	sinking land
	limestone region
	glacier
▲	active volcano
→	ocean current
••••	area of tectonic activity
—	maximum limit of glaciation

The evolving landscape

River systems

2 Rivers are continuously transporting eroded material towards the sea. Slow-moving, low-gradient rivers, like this one in western Russia *(above)*, deposit their alluvium load, infilling valleys creating a flood plain. Subsequent climatic and tectonic fluctuations may erode the flood plain to form terraces.

Terrace created by erosion
Flood plain
Deposited alluvium
River channel

River systems: Formation of a flood plain and terraces

Erosion and weathering

4 Much of Europe was once subjected to folding and faulting, exposing hard and soft rock layers. Subsequent erosion and weathering has worn away the softer strata, leaving up-ended layers of hard rock as in the French Pyrenees *(above)*.

Exposed up-ended rocks
Outline of original folded strata
Soft rock
Hard rock
Fault line
Folded rock strata

Erosion and weathering: Modification of a fold

Weathering

3 As surface water filters through permeable limestone, the rock dissolves to form underground caves, like Postojna in the Karst region of Slovenia *(above)*. Stalactites grow downwards as lime-enriched water seeps from roof fractures; stalagmites grow upwards where drips splash down.

Stalagmites created by drips
Underground cavern
River flowing underground dissolves rocks and creates caves
Stalactites formed by seeping water

Weathering: Formation of a cave

Political Europe

The political boundaries of Europe have changed many times, especially during the 20th century in the aftermath of two world wars, the break-up of the empires of Austria-Hungary, Nazi Germany and, towards the end of the century, the collapse of communism in eastern Europe. The fragmentation of Yugoslavia has again altered the political map of Europe, highlighting a trend towards nationalism and devolution. In contrast, economic federalism is growing. In 1958, the formation of the European Economic Community (now the European Union or EU) started a move towards economic and political union and increasing internal migration.

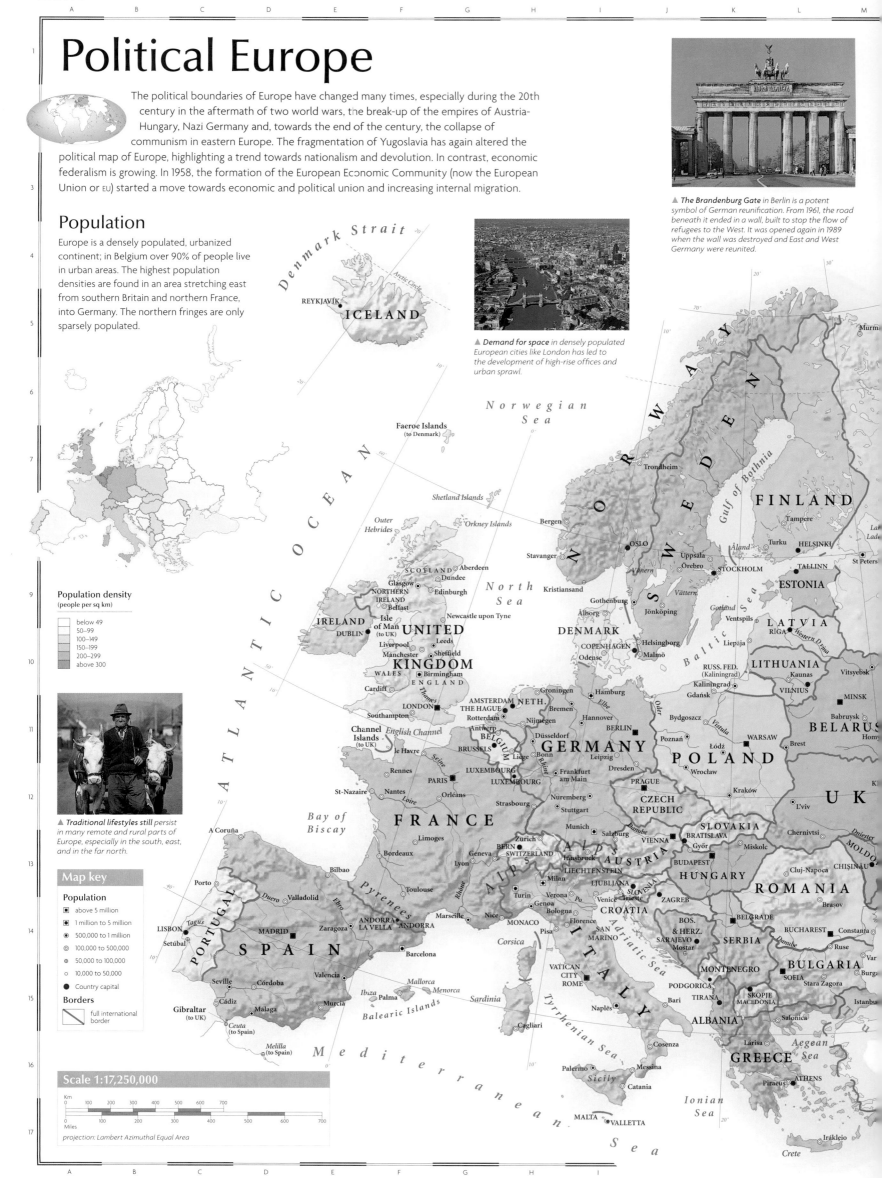

▲ *The Brandenburg Gate* in Berlin is a potent symbol of German reunification. From 1961, the road beneath it ended in a wall, built to stop the flow of refugees to the West. It was opened again in 1989 when the wall was destroyed and East and West Germany were reunited.

Population

Europe is a densely populated, urbanized continent; in Belgium over 90% of people live in urban areas. The highest population densities are found in an area stretching east from southern Britain and northern France, into Germany. The northern fringes are only sparsely populated.

▲ *Demand for space* in densely populated European cities like London has led to the development of high-rise offices and urban sprawl.

Population density
(people per sq km)

- below 49
- 50–99
- 100–149
- 150–199
- 200–299
- above 300

▲ *Traditional lifestyles still* persist in many remote and rural parts of Europe, especially in the south, east, and in the far north.

Map key

Population
- ▪ above 5 million
- ▪ 1 million to 5 million
- ◉ 500,000 to 1 million
- ◎ 100,000 to 500,000
- ⊕ 50,000 to 100,000
- ○ 10,000 to 50,000
- ● Country capital

Borders
- full international border

Scale 1:17,250,000

Km
0 100 200 300 400 500 600 700

Miles
0 100 200 300 400 500 600 700

projection: Lambert Azimuthal Equal Area

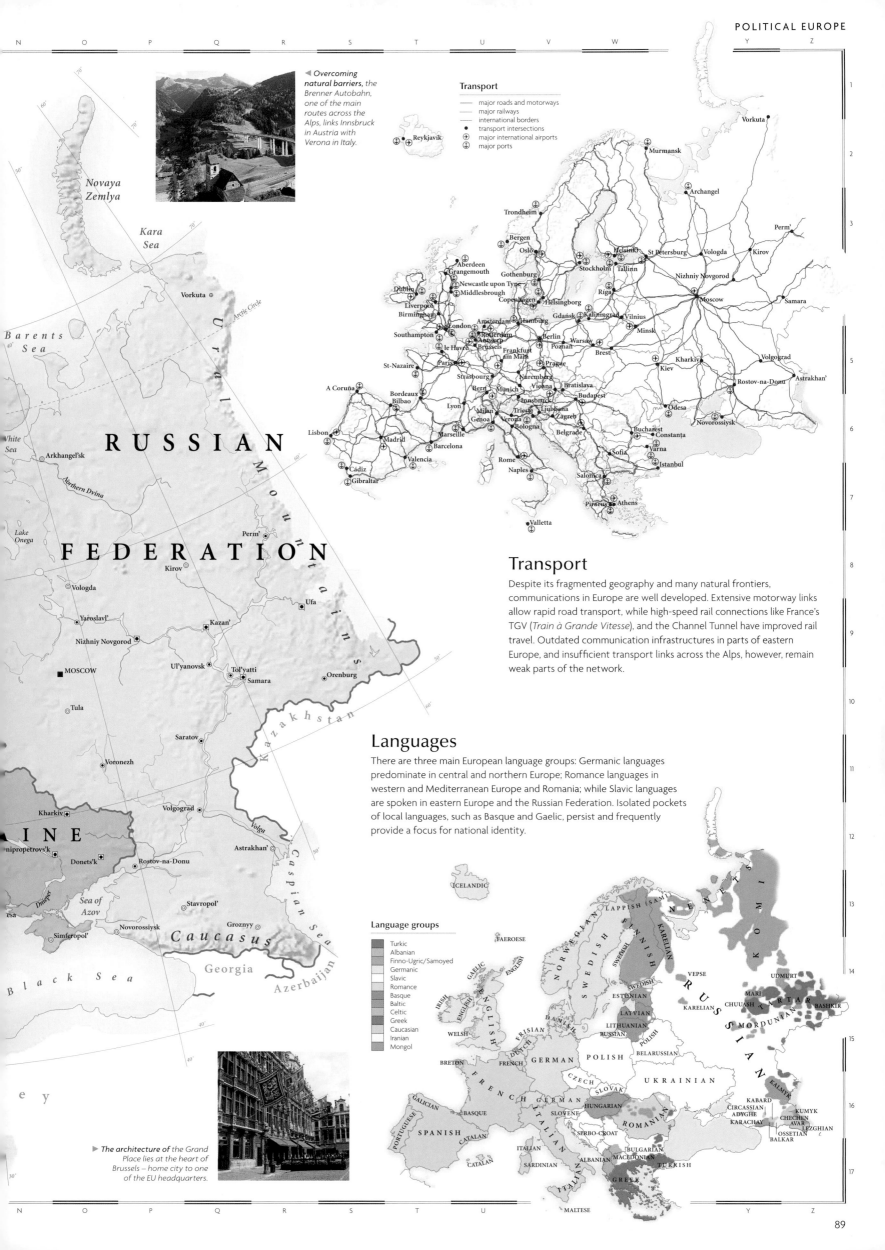

◄ *Overcoming natural barriers,* the Brenner Autobahn, one of the main routes across the Alps, links Innsbruck in Austria with Verona in Italy.

Transport

- major roads and motorways
- major railways
- international borders
- • transport intersections
- ⊕ major international airports
- ⊕ major ports

Novaya Zemlya

Kara Sea

Barents Sea

Reykjavík

Vorkuta

Murmansk

Archangel

Trondheim

Bergen

Oslo

Aberdeen

Grangemouth

Newcastle upon Tyne

Middlesbrough

Gothenburg

Helsinki

St Petersburg

Vologda

Kirov

Perm'

Stockholm

Tallinn

Nizhniy Novgorod

Dublin

Copenhagen

Helsingborg

Riga

Moscow

Samara

Liverpool

Birmingham

Gdańsk

Kaliningrad

Vilnius

Minsk

Southampton

London

Amsterdam

Hamburg

Berlin

Poznań

Warsaw

Brest

Kharkiv

Volgograd

Astrakhan'

le Havre

Rotterdam

Antwerp

Brussels

Frankfurt am Main

Prague

Kiev

St-Nazaire

Paris

Strasbourg

Nuremberg

Bratislava

Rostov-na-Donu

A Coruña

Bern

Munich

Vienna

Budapest

Odesa

Novorossiysk

Bordeaux

Bilbao

Innsbruck

Ljubljana

Zagreb

Lyon

Milan

Trieste

Verona

Belgrade

Bucharest

Constanţa

Lisbon

Madrid

Genoa

Bologna

Varna

Marseille

Barcelona

Sofia

Istanbul

Valencia

Rome

Naples

Salonica

Cádiz

Gibraltar

Piraeus

Athens

Valletta

Transport

Despite its fragmented geography and many natural frontiers, communications in Europe are well developed. Extensive motorway links allow rapid road transport, while high-speed rail connections like France's TGV (*Train à Grande Vitesse*), and the Channel Tunnel have improved rail travel. Outdated communication infrastructures in parts of eastern Europe, and insufficient transport links across the Alps, however, remain weak parts of the network.

Languages

There are three main European language groups: Germanic languages predominate in central and northern Europe; Romance languages in western and Mediterranean Europe and Romania; while Slavic languages are spoken in eastern Europe and the Russian Federation. Isolated pockets of local languages, such as Basque and Gaelic, persist and frequently provide a focus for national identity.

RUSSIAN FEDERATION

White Sea

Arkhangel'sk

Northern Dvina

Lake Onega

Vologda

Perm'

Yaroslavl'

Kirov

Nizhniy Novgorod

Kazan'

Ufa

MOSCOW

Ul'yanovsk

Tol'yatti

Samara

Orenburg

Tula

Ural Mountains

Kazakhstan

Saratov

Voronezh

Kharkiv

Volgograd

Astrakhan'

Volga

INE

nipropetrovs'k

Donets'k

Rostov-na-Donu

esa

Dnepr

Sea of Azov

Stavropol'

Caspian Sea

Simferopol'

Novorossiysk

Caucasus

Groznyy

Black Sea

Georgia

Azerbaijan

ey

Language groups

- Turkic
- Albanian
- Finno-Ugric/Samoyed
- Germanic
- Slavic
- Romance
- Basque
- Baltic
- Celtic
- Greek
- Caucasian
- Iranian
- Mongol

ICELANDIC

FAEROESE

NORWEGIAN

SWEDISH

SWEDISH

LAPPISH (SAMI)

FINNISH

KARELIAN

NENETS

KOMI

VEPSE

UDMURT

MARI

CHUVASH

TATAR

BASHKIR

GAELIC

ENGLISH

IRISH

ENGLISH

DANISH

ESTONIAN

SWEDISH

KARELIAN

R U S S I A N

MORDVINIAN

WELSH

LATVIAN

RUSSIAN

LITHUANIAN

POLISH

BELARUSSIAN

KALMYK

BRETON

FRISIAN

DUTCH

GERMAN

POLISH

UKRAINIAN

GALICIAN

FRENCH

CZECH

SLOVAK

PORTUGUESE

BASQUE

GERMAN

SLOVENE

HUNGARIAN

ROMANIAN

KABARD

CIRCASSIAN

ADYGHE

KARACHAY

KUMYK

SPANISH

ITALIAN

SERBO-CROAT

BULGARIAN

CHECHEN

AVAR

LEZGHIAN

OSSETIAN

BALKAR

CATALAN

CATALAN

ITALIAN

ALBANIAN

MACEDONIAN

TURKISH

SARDINIAN

GREEK

ITALIAN

MALTESE

► *The architecture of* the Grand Place lies at the heart of Brussels – home city to one of the EU headquarters.

European resources

Europe's large tracts of fertile, accessible land, combined with its generally temperate climate, have allowed a greater percentage of land to be used for agricultural purposes than in any other continent. Extensive coal and iron ore deposits were used to create steel and manufacturing industries during the 19th and 20th centuries. Today, although natural resources have been widely exploited, and heavy industry is of declining importance, the growth of hi-tech and service industries has enabled Europe to maintain its wealth.

Industry

Europe's wealth was generated by the rise of industry and colonial exploitation during the 19th century. The mining of abundant natural resources made Europe the industrial centre of the world. Adaptation has been essential in the changing world economy, and a move to service-based industries has been widespread except in eastern Europe, where heavy industry still dominates.

▲ *Countries like Hungary* are still struggling to modernize inefficient factories left over from extensive, centrally-planned industrialization during the communist era.

◄ *Frankfurt am Main* is an example of a modern service-based city. The skyline is dominated by headquarters from the worlds of banking and commerce.

▲ *Other power sources* are becoming more attractive as fossil fuels run out; 16% of Europe's electricity is now provided by hydro-electric power.

Standard of living

Living standards in western Europe are among the highest in the world, although there is a growing sector of homeless, jobless people. Eastern Europeans have lower overall standards of living – a legacy of stagnated economies.

Standard of living
(UN human development index)

- low
- high
- data not available

▶ *Skiing brings millions* of tourists to the slopes each year, which means that even unproductive, marginal land is used to create wealth in the French, Swiss, Italian and Austrian Alps.

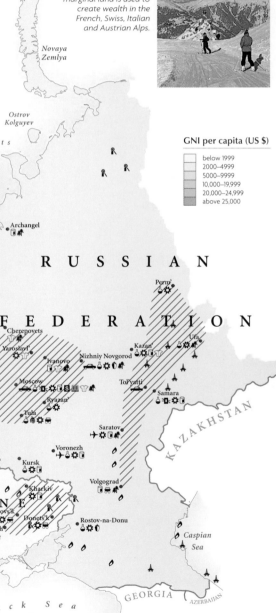

GNI per capita (US $)

- below 1999
- 2000–4999
- 5000–9999
- 10,000–19,999
- 20,000–24,999
- above 25,000

Industry

- ✈ aerospace
- brewing
- car/vehicle manufacture
- chemicals
- defence
- electronics
- engineering
- finance
- food processing
- hi-tech industry
- iron & steel
- pharmaceuticals
- printing & publishing
- shipbuilding
- textiles
- timber processing
- wine
- coal
- oil
- gas
- industrial cities
- major industrial areas

Environmental issues

Environmental issues

- national parks
- acid rain
- polluted rivers
- radioactive contamination
- marine pollution
- heavy marine pollution
- poor urban air quality

The partially enclosed waters of the Baltic and Mediterranean seas have become heavily polluted, while the Barents Sea is contaminated with spent nuclear fuel from Russia's navy. Acid rain, caused by emissions from factories and power stations, is actively destroying northern forests. As a result, pressure is growing to safeguard Europe's natural environment and prevent further deterioration.

▲ *Coniferous forest covers* vast swathes of northern Scandinavia and the Russian Federation. Pollutants from other parts of Europe mixing with rainfall are causing defoliation and serious damage to many forests.

▶ *The Camargue in* the Rhône Delta, southern France, is a protected wetland area, famous for its native population of white horses, and unique bird and plant life.

Mineral resources

Fossil fuels are Europe's main mineral resource, although fuel demand far outstrips production. Sizeable coal reserves remain in the Donbass in Ukraine, Germany's Ruhr Valley and Poland. Oil and gas reserves are found mainly in the North Sea, the Volga Basin, and the Caucasus.

▶ *The valuable oil* and gas reserves in the North Sea were first discovered in the early 1960s, and are exploited by the UK, Denmark, Germany and Norway.

Mineral resources

- oil field
- gas field
- coal field
- bauxite
- iron
- lead
- mercury
- potassium
- uranium
- zinc

Using the land and sea

Europe's swelling urban population and the outward expansion of many cities has created acute competition for land. Despite this, European resourcefulness has maximized land potential, and over half of Europe's land is still used for a wide variety of agricultural purposes. Land in northern Europe is used for cattle-rearing, pasture, and arable crops. Towards the Mediterranean, the mild climate allows the growing of grapes for wine; olives, sunflowers, tobacco and citrus fruits. EU subsidies, however, have resulted in massive overproduction and a land 'set-aside' policy has been introduced.

Using the land and sea

- cropland
- forest
- ice cap
- mountain region
- pasture
- tundra
- wetland
- major conurbations
- cattle
- goats
- pigs
- poultry
- reindeer
- sheep
- cereals
- citrus fruits
- cotton
- fishing
- fodder
- fruit
- olive oil
- potatoes
- rice
- root crops
- roses
- shellfish
- sunflowers
- timber
- tobacco
- vineyards

▲ *Bulgarian roses are* one of the many diverse crops grown in Europe. Rose oil, extracted from the petals, is used in perfume making.

▲ *Lowland pastures are* used for dairy farming. Good transport links and refrigeration allow fresh milk to be distributed throughout Europe.

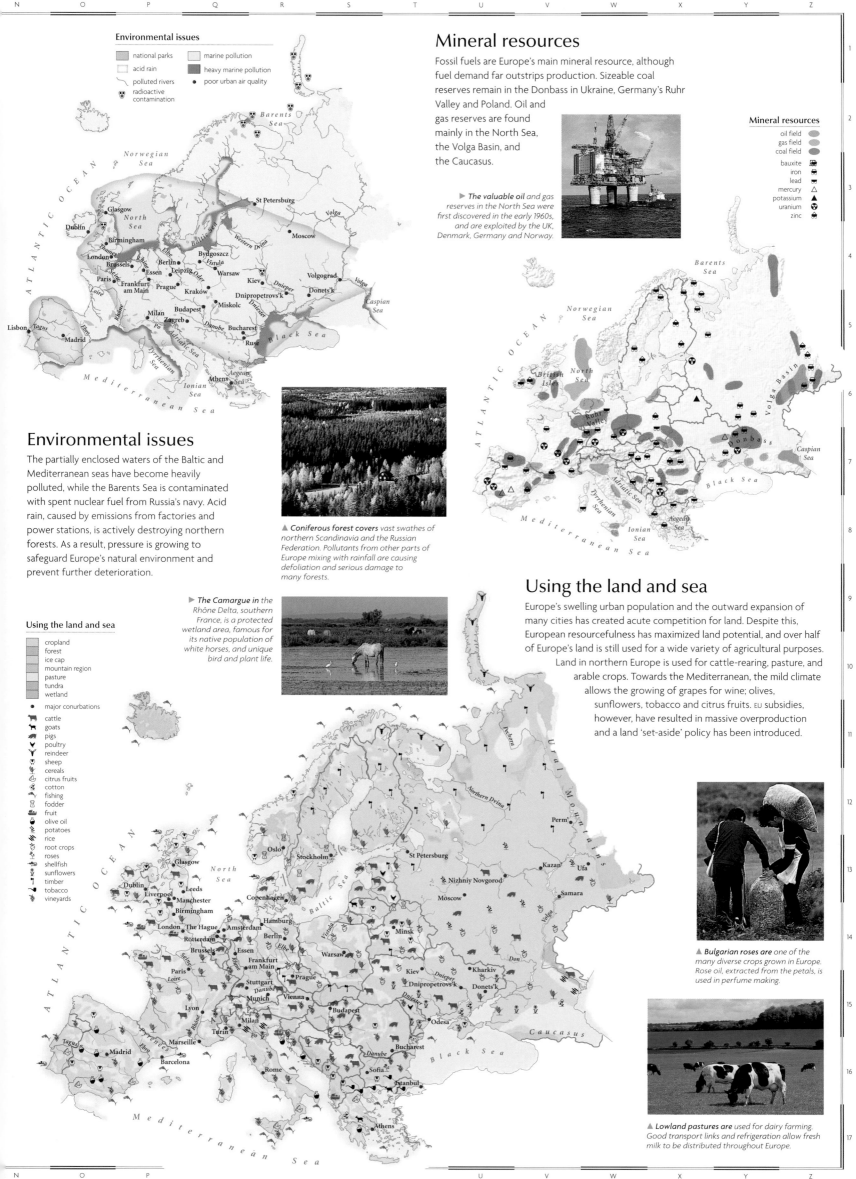

Scandinavia, Finland & Iceland

DENMARK, NORWAY, SWEDEN, FINLAND, ICELAND

Jutting into the Arctic Circle, this northern swathe of Europe has some of the continent's harshest environments, but benefits from great reserves of oil, gas and natural evergreen forests. While most early settlers came from the south, migrants to Finland came from the east, giving it a distinct language and culture. Since the late 19th century, the Scandinavian states have developed strong egalitarian traditions. Today, their welfare benefits systems are among the most extensive in the world, and standards of living are high. The Lapps, or Sami, maintain their traditional lifestyle in the northern regions of Norway, Sweden and Finland.

The landscape

Glaciers up to 10,000 ft (3000 m) deep covered most of Scandinavia and Finland during the last Ice Age. The effects of glaciation mark the entire landscape, from the mountains to the lowlands, across the tundra landscape of Lapland, and the lake districts of Sweden and Finland.

Geysers are a by-product of Iceland's volcanic activity. Geysir, Iceland's largest spring, gives them their name.

The Lofoten Islands were one of the first areas exposed as the ice sheet melted.

Halti mountain is Finland's highest point, at 4356 ft (1328 m).

Lapland, north of the Arctic Circle, is an area of undulating fells and plains known as tundra. The subsoil is permanently frozen and therefore impermeable. There are many peat bogs. Pools reappear in the summer when the surface thaws.

▼ Finland's landscape was fashioned by ice action. Glaciers gouged out its distinctive shallow lake basins, such as Oulujärvi, and left debris called moraines in their wake.

Oulujärvi

Area of maximum yearly uplift 0.3 in/yr (9 mm/yr)

Slower rates of uplift 0.1 in/yr (3 mm/yr)

▲ Scandinavia is still recovering from the last Ice Age, when ice depressed the land by 2000 ft (600 m). This gradual uplift is known as isostatic rebound.

Sjælland coast

▲ On the coast of Sjælland, these cliffs have been eroded by the sea, exposing layers of chalk and limestone.

Fjords

▲ The fjords on the western coast of Norway were once gentle river valleys. Their deep floors and steep sides were carved out by glaciers during the last Ice Age, and they were later flooded by the sea.

Using the land and sea

The cold climate, short growing season, poorly developed soil, steep slopes, and exposure to high winds across northern regions means that most agriculture is concentrated, with the population, in the south. Most of Finland and much of Norway and Sweden are covered by dense forests of pine, spruce and birch, which supply the timber industries.

Land use and agricultural distribution

capital cities
major towns

pasture
cropland
forest
mountain region
tundra

fishing
pigs
reindeer
sheep
cereals
timber

The urban/rural population divide

urban 77%   rural 23%

Population density
51 people per sq mile
(20 per sq km)

Total land area
473,970 sq miles
(1,227,610 sq km)

SCALE 1:9,000,000
projection: Lambert Conformal Conic

Scale 1:5,500,000
projection: Lambert Conformal Conic

(same scale as main map)

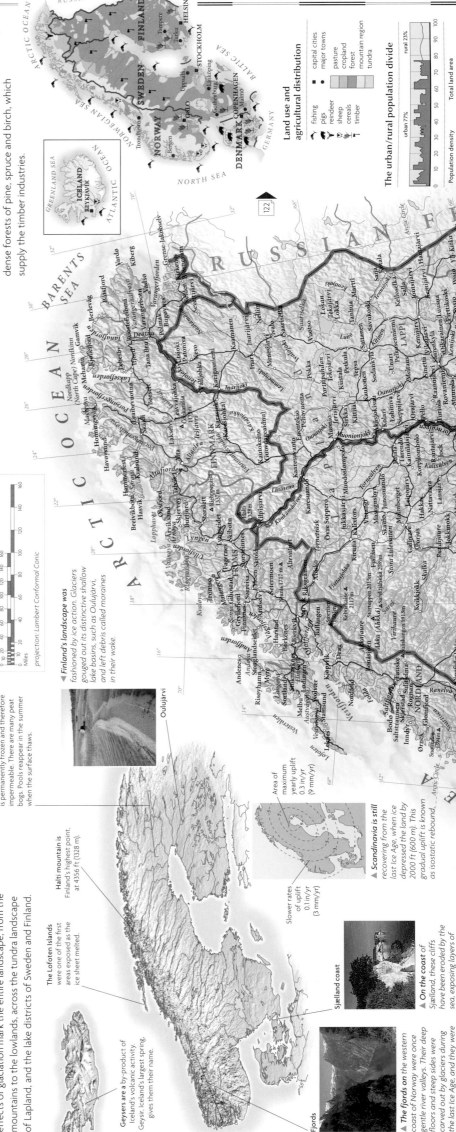

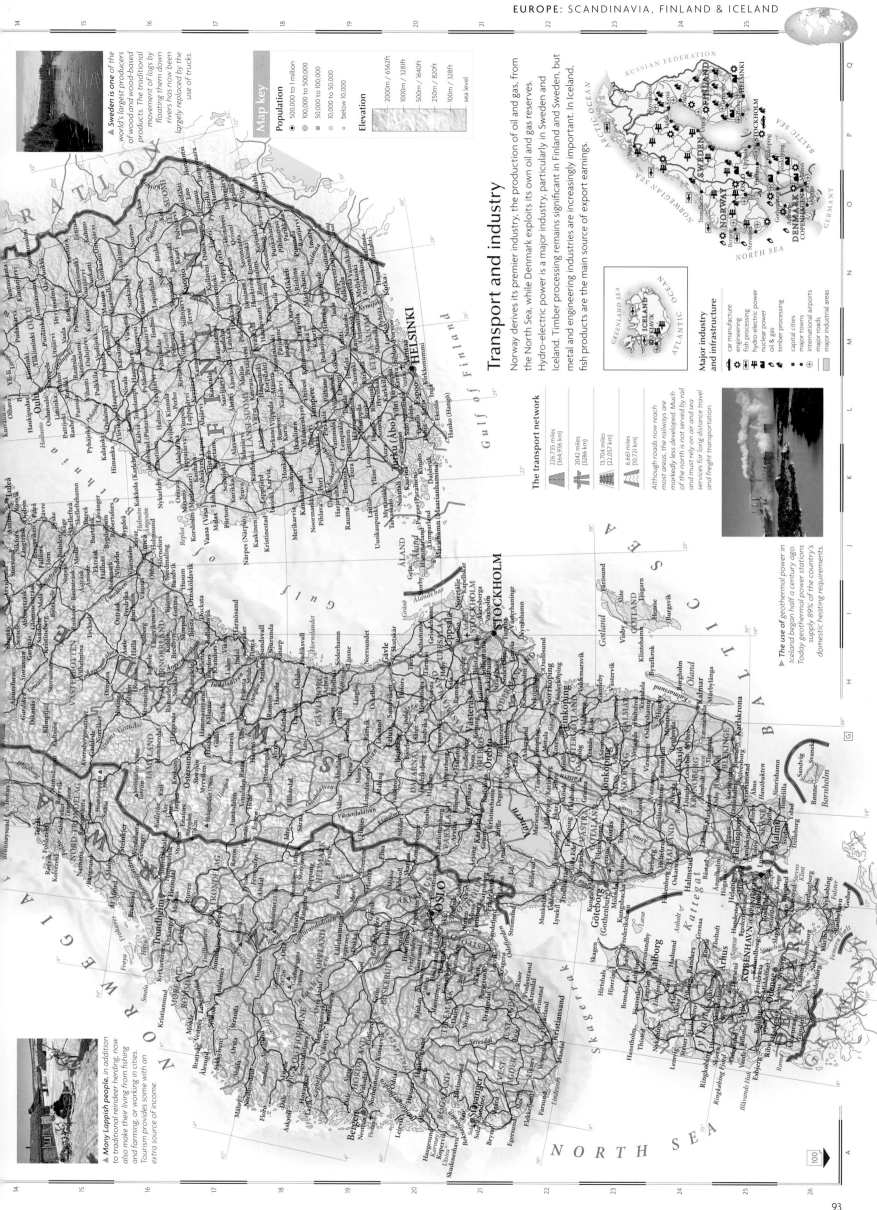

▲ **Sweden is one of the** world's largest producers of wood and wood-based products. The traditional movement of logs by floating them down rivers has now been largely replaced by the use of trucks.

Map key

Population
- ⊙ 500,000 to 1 million
- ⊙ 100,000 to 500,000
- ⊕ 50,000 to 100,000
- ○ 10,000 to 50,000
- ∘ below 10,000

Elevation
- 2000m / 6562ft
- 1000m / 3281ft
- 500m / 1640ft
- 250m / 820ft
- 100m / 328ft
- sea level

Transport and industry

Norway derives its premier industry, the production of oil and gas, from the North Sea, while Denmark exploits its own oil and gas reserves. Hydro-electric power is a major industry, particularly in Sweden and Iceland. Timber processing remains significant in Finland and Sweden, but metal and engineering industries are increasingly important. In Iceland, fish products are the main source of export earnings.

The transport network
- 226,735 miles (364,936 km)
- 2042 miles (3286 km)
- 13,704 miles (22,057 km)
- 6,661 miles (10,721 km)

Although roads now reach most areas, the railways are markedly less developed. Much of the north is not served by rail and must rely on air and sea services for long distance travel and freight transportation.

Major industry and infrastructure
- car manufacture
- engineering
- fish processing
- hydro-electric power
- nuclear power
- oil & gas
- timber processing
- ⊙ capital cities
- major towns
- ✈ international airports
- major roads
- major industrial areas

▲ **The use of geothermal power in** Iceland began half a century ago. Today geothermal power stations supply 89% of the country's domestic heating requirements.

▲ **Many Lappish people,** in addition to traditional reindeer herding, now also make their living from fishing and farming, or working in cities. Tourism provides some with an extra source of income.

Southern Scandinavia

SOUTHERN NORWAY, SOUTHERN SWEDEN, DENMARK

Scandinavia's economic and political hub is the more habitable and accessible southern region. Many of the area's major cities are on the southern coasts, including Oslo and Stockholm, the capitals of Norway and Sweden. In Denmark, most of the population and the capital, Copenhagen, are located on its many islands. A cultural unity links the three Scandinavian countries. Their main languages, Danish, Swedish and Norwegian, are mutually intelligible, and they all retain their monarchies, although the parliaments have legislative control.

Using the land

Agriculture in southern Scandinavia is highly mechanized although farms are small. Denmark is the most intensively farmed country and its western pastureland is used mainly for pig farming. Cereal crops including wheat, barley and oats, predominate in eastern Denmark and in the far south of Sweden. Southern Norway and Sweden have large tracts of forest which are exploited for logging.

Land use and agricultural distribution

- cattle
- pigs
- sheep
- cereals
- fodder
- root crops
- timber

capital cities
major towns
pasture
cropland
forest
mountain region

The urban/rural population divide

urban 87%
rural 13%

Population density	Total land area
112 people per sq mile (43 people per sq km)	173,487 sq miles (456,564 sq km)

The landscape

Southern Scandinavia, with the exception of Norway, has a flatter terrain than the rest of the region. Denmark and southern Sweden are both extensions of the North European Plain. In this area, because of glacial deposition rather than erosion, the soils are deeper and more fertile.

Acid rain, caused by industrial pollution carried north from elsewhere in Europe, harms plant and animal life in Scandinavian forests and lakes. The region's surface rocks lack lime to neutralize the acid, so making the problem more serious.

▼ *In the past,* glaciers such as this one in Olden, Norway, were much larger. Today, many are retreating to yield the spectacular glacial scenery.

Distinctive low ridges, called eskers, are found across southern Sweden. They are formed from sand and gravel deposits left by retreating glaciers.

▲ *Limestone pillars eroded* by the sea dot the coast of Gotland and surrounding islands.

The lakes of southern Sweden remain from a period when the land was completely flooded. As the ice which covered the area melted, the land rose, leaving lakes in shallow, ice-scoured depressions. Sweden has over 90,000 lakes.

The peak of Glittertind in the Jotunheimen mountains is 8110 ft (2472 m) high.

Vänern in Sweden is the largest lake in Scandinavia. It covers an area of 2080 sq miles (5390 sq km).

Denmark's flat and fertile soils are formed on glacial deposits between 100–160 ft (30–50 m) deep.

When the ice retreated the valley was flooded by the sea

Old valley floor

Sognefjorden

Erosion by glaciers deepened existing river valleys

Sea level

▲ *Sognefjorden is the* deepest of Norway's many fjords. It drops to 4291 ft (1308 m) below sea level.

Olden

Map key

Population
- ⊙ 500,000 to 1 million
- ⊙ 100,000 to 500,000
- ⊙ 50,000 to 100,000
- ○ 10,000 to 50,000
- ○ below 10,000

Elevation
- 2000m / 6562ft
- 1000m / 3281ft
- 500m / 1640ft
- 250m / 820ft
- 100m / 328ft
- sea level

Scale 1:3,250,000

projection: Lambert Conformal Conic

▲ *In Norway winters* are longer and colder inland than in coastal areas, where the warm current of the North Atlantic Drift moderates the climate.

Gulf of Bothnia

VÄSTERNORRLAND

GÄVLEBORG

JÄMTLAND

HEDMARK

OPPLAND

NORD-TRØNDELAG

SØR-TRØNDELAG

MØRE OG ROMSDAL

SOGN OG FJORDANE

Trondheim

NORWAY

SWEDEN

DENMARK

STOCKHOLM

OSLO

COPENHAGEN

NORTH SEA

BALTIC SEA

NORWEGIAN SEA

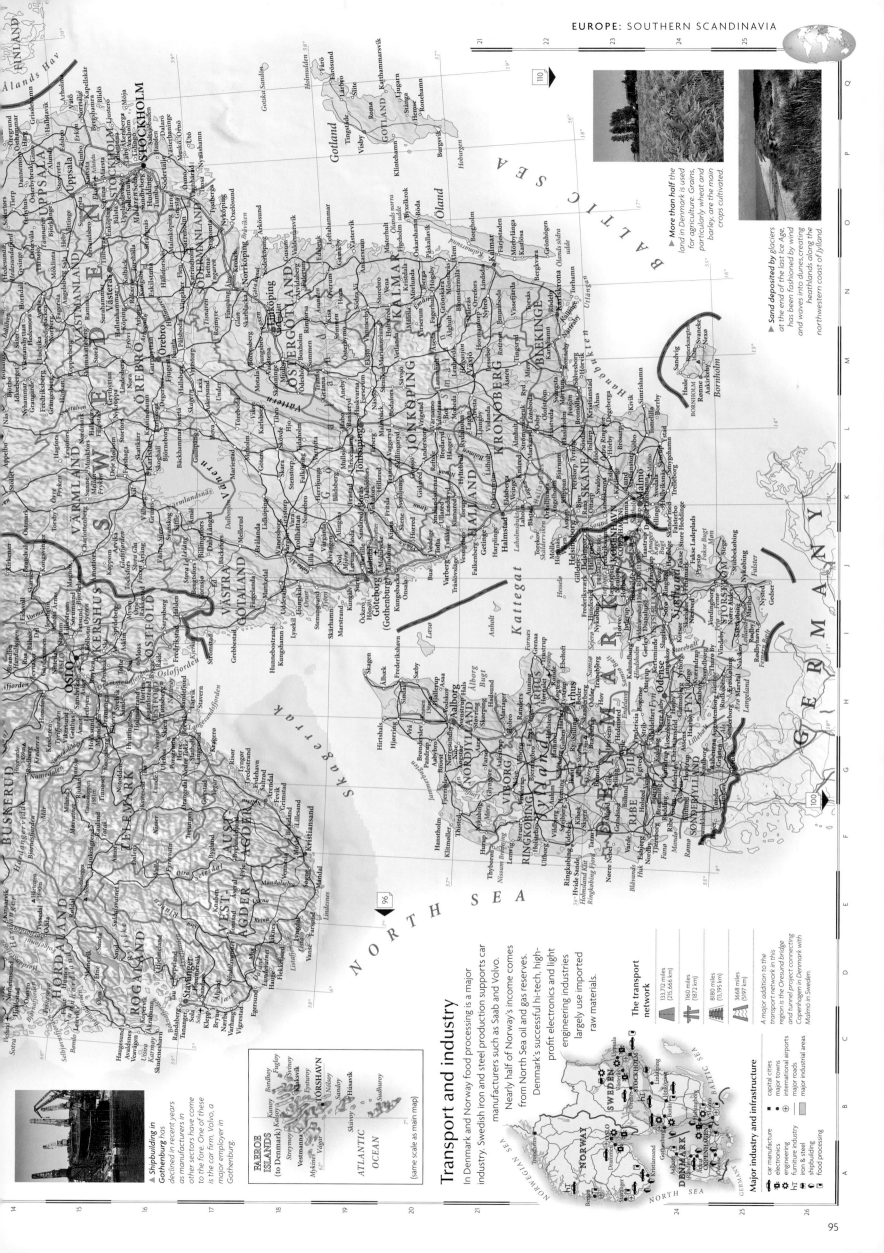

▲ *More than half the land in Denmark is used for agriculture. Grains, particularly wheat and barley, are the main crops cultivated.*

▲ *Sand deposited by glaciers at the end of the last Ice Age, has been fashioned by wind and waves into dunes, creating heathlands along the northwestern coast of Jylland.*

Transport and industry

In Denmark and Norway food processing is a major industry. Swedish iron and steel production supports car manufacturers such as Saab and Volvo. Nearly half of Norway's income comes from North Sea oil and gas reserves. Denmark's successful hi-tech, high-profit electronics and light engineering industries largely use imported raw materials.

The transport network

🛣	133,712 miles (215,666 km)	
✈	1160 miles (1872 km)	
🚂	8880 miles (13,195 km)	
⚓	3668 miles (5197 km)	

A major addition to the transport network in this region is the Øresund bridge and tunnel project connecting Copenhagen in Denmark with Malmö in Sweden.

Major industry and infrastructure

- ■ capital cities
- ● major towns
- ⊕ international airports
- ▬ major roads
- ▢ major industrial areas

car manufacture · electronics · engineering · furniture industry · iron & steel · shipbuilding · food processing

▲ *Shipbuilding in Gothenburg has declined in recent years as manufacturers in other sectors have come to the fore. One of these is the car firm, Volvo, a major employer in Gothenburg.*

FAERÓE ISLANDS (to Denmark)
Kalsoy, Kunoy, Bordhoy, Svinoy, Vidhoy, Streymoy, Vestmanna, Eysturoy, Nakskov, TÓRSHAVN, Nólsoy, Sandoy, Skúvoy, Litlavik, Mykines, Vágar, Skarvoy, Sudhuroy

ATLANTIC OCEAN

(same scale as main map)

95

The British Isles

UNITED KINGDOM, IRELAND

The British Isles have for centuries played a central role in European and world history. England, Wales, Scotland and Northern Ireland together form the United Kingdom (UK), while the southern portion of Ireland is an independent country, self-governing since 1921. Although England has tended to be the politically and economically dominant partner in the UK, the Scots, Welsh and Irish maintain independent cultures, distinct national identities and languages. Southeastern England is the most densely populated part of this crowded region, with over eight million people living in and around the London area.

The landscape

Rugged uplands dominate the landscape of Scotland, Wales and northern England. All the peaks in the British Isles over 4000 ft (1219 m) lie in highland Scotland. Lowland England rises into several ranges of rolling hills, including the older Mendips, and the Cotswolds and the Chilterns, which were formed at the same time as the Alps in southern Europe.

▲ *Ullswater in the* Lake District fills a deep valley formed by glacial erosion.

The **Fens** are a low-lying area reclaimed from the sea.

The **Cotswold Hills** are characterized by a series of limestone ridges overlooking clay vales.

The **Pennines**, sometimes called 'the backbone of England', are formed of limestones and grits.

Ben Nevis at 4409 ft (343 m) is the highest peak in the UK.

Durdle Door

▲ *Coastal erosion around the* British Isles forms striking features such as this limestone arch, *Durdle Door in Dorset.*

Over 600 islands, mostly uninhabited, lie west and north of the Scottish mainland.

Snowdon is the highest mountain in England and Wales reaching 3556 ft (1085 m).

The **lowlands of Scotland**, drained by the Tay, Forth and Clyde rivers, are centred on a rift valley. The region contains valuable coal reserves.

Thousands of hexagonal basalt columns form Giant's Causeway on the north coast of Antrim. These were created by volcanic activity.

The British Isles have no large-scale river systems. The **Shannon** is the longest, at 230 miles (370 km).

Peat bogs dot the poorly-drained Irish lowlands.

Black Ven, Lyme Regis

▲ *Dartmoor,* studded with *tors, is an exposed part of a vast granite dome, formed when molten rock intruded into the Earth's crust.*

▲ *Much of the south coast is subject to landslides. Following rain, porous sandstones feed water into the underlying, less permeable clays which then crumble and slide into the sea.*

▲ *The valley of Glen Coe in the Scottish Highlands is a U-shaped valley, typical of the north and west of the British Isles, where glaciers shaped much of the landscape.*

Transport and industry

The British Isles' industrial base was founded primarily on coal, iron and textiles, based largely in the north. Today, the most productive sectors include hi-tech industries clustered mainly in southeastern England, chemicals, finance and the service sector, particularly tourism.

Major industry and infrastructure

- car manufacture
- chemicals
- engineering
- hi-tech industry
- iron & steel
- tourism
- ✦ capital cities
- ■ major cities
- □ major towns
- ⊕ international airports
- major roads
- major industrial areas

The transport network

- 285,947 miles (460,240 km)
- 2023 miles (3578 km)
- 11,825 miles (19,032km)
- 3976 miles (6400 km)

The UK's congested roads have become a major focus of environmental concern in recent years. No longer an island, the UK was finally linked to continental Europe by the Channel Tunnel in 1994.

▼ *Clew Bay in western Ireland, is characteristic of the heavily indented west coast, where deep widemouthed bays separate the mountains of Mayo, Donegal and Kerry as they thrust out into the Atlantic Ocean.*

Map key

Population
- ■ above 5 million
- ◉ 1 million to 5 million
- ◎ 500,000 to 1 million
- ⊕ 100,000 to 500,000
- ⊕ 50,000 to 100,000
- ⊕ 10,000 to 50,000
- below 10,000

Elevation
- 1000m / 328ft
- 500m / 1640ft
- 250m / 820ft
- 100m / 328ft
- sea level

Cracks
Sandstone
Clay
Limestone

Water
Mudslide
Sea

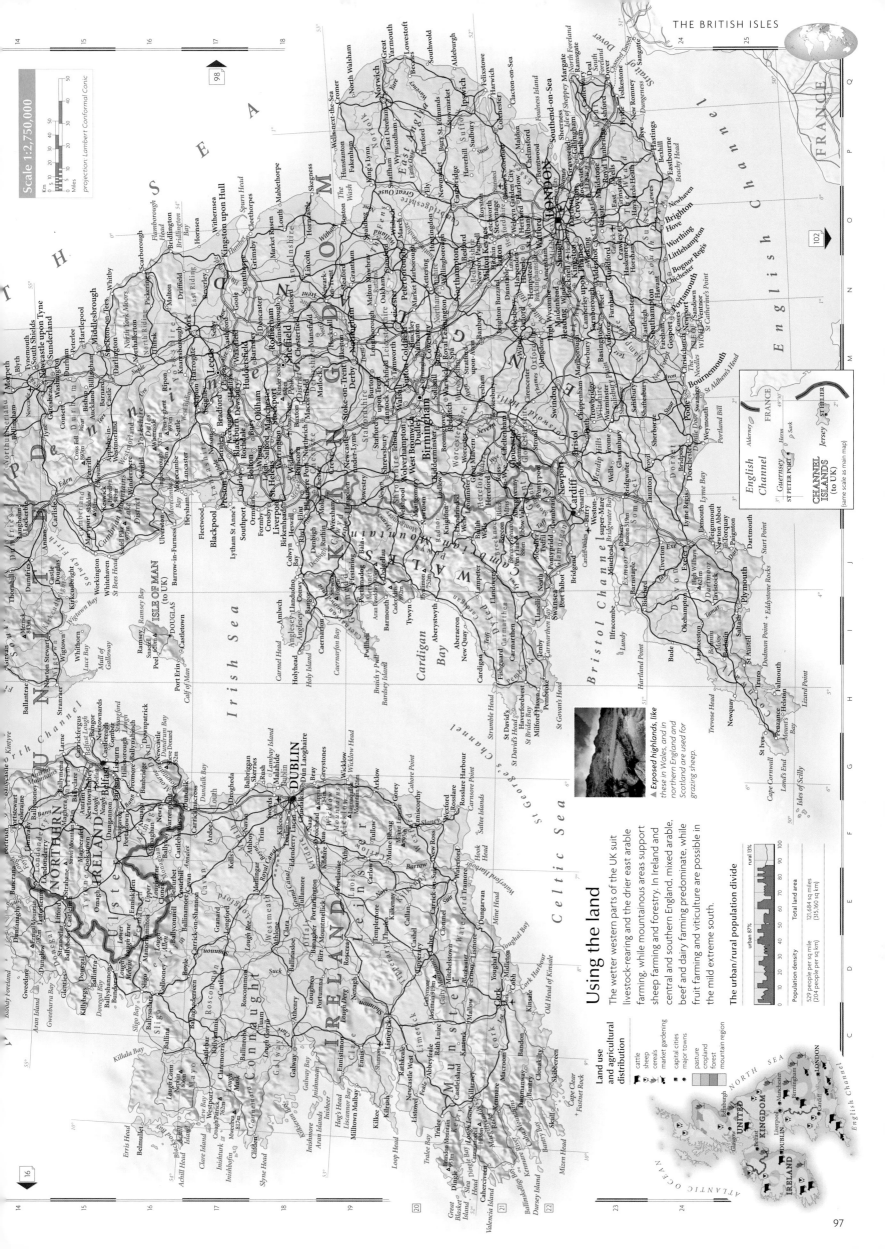

Scale 1:2,750,000

projection: Lambert Conformal Conic

Using the land

The wetter western parts of the UK suit livestock-rearing and the drier east arable farming, while mountainous areas support sheep farming and forestry. In Ireland and central and southern England, mixed arable, beef and dairy farming predominate, while fruit farming and viticulture are possible in the mild extreme south.

▲ Exposed highlands, like these in Wales, and in northern England and Scotland are used for grazing sheep.

Land use and agricultural distribution

cattle
sheep
cereals
market gardening
capital cities
major towns

pasture
cropland
forest
mountain region

The urban/rural population divide

urban 87% rural 13%

Population density
529 people per sq mile
(204 people per sq km)

Total land area
121,684 sq miles
(315,160 sq km)

The Low Countries

BELGIUM, LUXEMBOURG, NETHERLANDS

One of northwestern Europe's strategic crossroads, the Low Countries are united by a common history in which they have often been a battleground in European wars. For over a thousand years they were ruled by foreign powers. Even after they achieved independence, the three countries maintained close links, later forming the world's first totally free labour and goods market, the Benelux Economic Union, which became the core of the European Community (now the European Union or EU). These states have remained at the forefront of wider European co-operation; Brussels, The Hague and Luxembourg are hosts to major institutions of the EU.

The landscape

The main geographical regions of the Netherlands are the northern glacial heathlands, the low-lying lands of the Rhine and Maas/Meuse, the reclaimed polders, and the dune coast and islands. Belgium includes part of the Ardennes, together with the coalfields on its northern flanks, and the fertile Flanders plain.

Since the Middle Ages the people of the Netherlands have used ditches and drainage dykes to reclaim land from the sea. These reclaimed areas are known as polders.

Sea

Dune system

Polder — Drainage ditch

Sand dunes

▲ **Extensive sand dune** systems along the coast have prevented flooding of the land. Behind the dunes, marshy land is drained to form polders, usable land suitable for agriculture.

▼ **Heathlands, like these** at Schoorl, are found along the coast of the Netherlands. Much of the coast was breached by the sea in the 5th century, creating its distinctive inlets and islands.

Schoorl

▲ **One-third of the** Netherlands lies below sea level and flooding is a constant threat. Much of the coast was breached by the sea in the 5th century, creating its distinctive inlets and islands.

The parallel valleys of the Maas/Meuse and Rhine rivers were created when the Rhine was deflected from its previous course by the ice sheet which formed during the last Ice Age.

Silts and sands eroded by the Rhine throughout its course are deposited to form a delta on the west coast of the Netherlands.

The loess soils of the Flanders Plain in western Belgium provide excellent conditions for arable farming.

Hautes Fagnes is the highest part of Belgium. The bogs and streams in this upland region result from high rainfall and low temperatures.

Ardennes

▲ **Uplifted and folded** 220 million years ago, the Ardennes have since been reduced to relatively level plateaux, then sharply incised by rivers such as the Maas/Meuse.

Transport and industry

In the western Netherlands, a massive, sprawling industrialized zone encompasses many new hi-tech and service industries. Belgium's central region has emerged as the country's light manufacturing and services centre. Luxembourg city is home to more than 160 banks and the European headquarters of many international companies.

The transport network

🚗 140,588 miles (226,281 km)	🚆 2565 miles (4129 km)
✈ 4099 miles (6598 km)	🚢 4134 miles (6653 km)

Major industry and infrastructure

- aerospace
- finance
- engineering
- hi-tech industry
- pharmaceuticals
- textiles
- ● capital cities
- ● major cities
- □ major towns
- ⊕ international airports
- — major roads
- ▢ major industrial areas

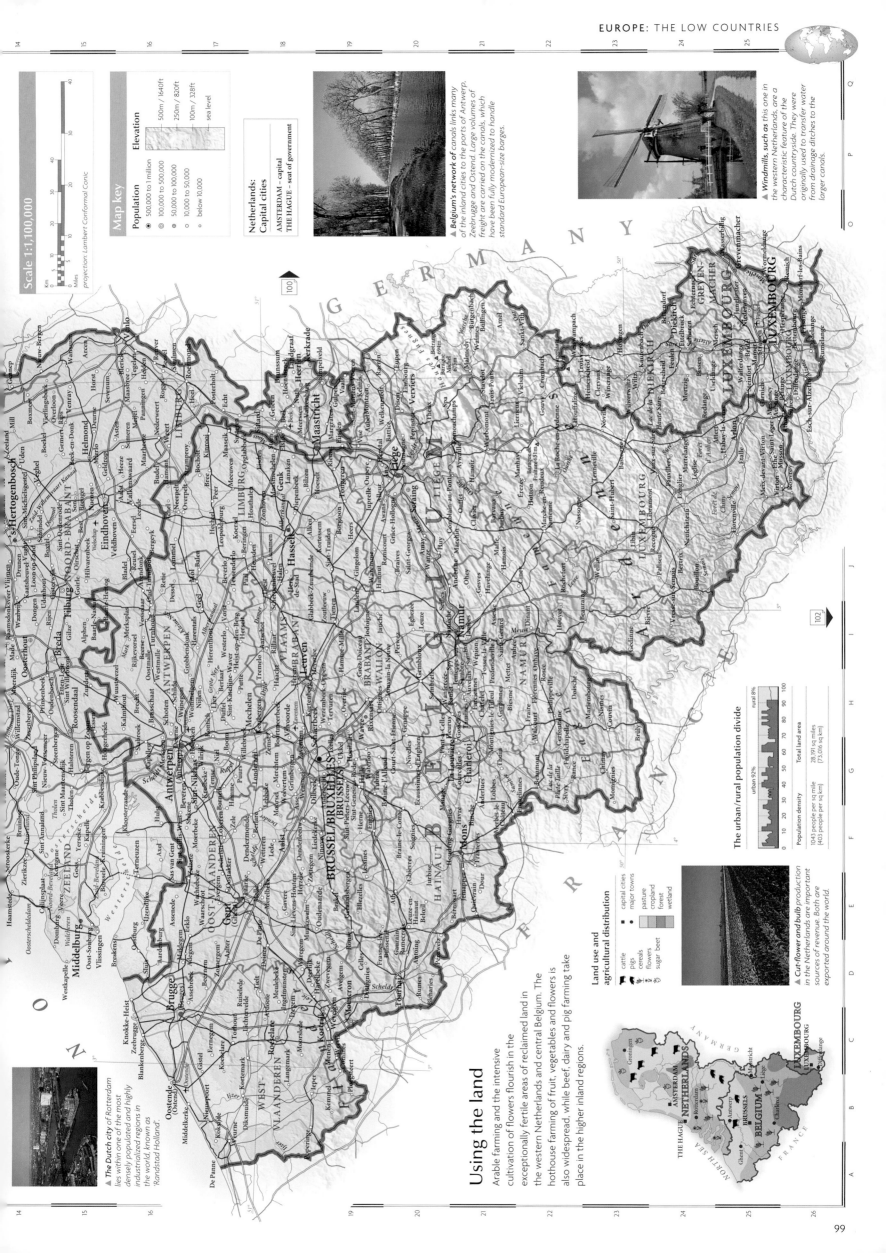

Scale 1:1,100,000

projection: Lambert Conformal Conic

Map key

Elevation

500m / 1640ft
250m / 820ft
100m / 328ft
sea level

Population

- ◉ 500,000 to 1 million
- ◎ 100,000 to 500,000
- ⊕ 50,000 to 100,000
- ⊙ 10,000 to 50,000
- ○ below 10,000

Netherlands:
Capital cities

AMSTERDAM – capital
THE HAGUE – seat of government

▲ Belgium's network of canals links many of the inland cities to the ports of Antwerp, Zeebrugge and Ostend. Large volumes of freight are carried on the canals, which have been fully modernized to handle standard European-size barges.

▲ Windmills, such as this one in the western Netherlands, are a characteristic feature of the Dutch countryside. They were originally used to transfer water from drainage ditches to the larger canals.

Using the land

Arable farming and the intensive cultivation of flowers flourish in the exceptionally fertile areas of reclaimed land in the western Netherlands and central Belgium. The hothouse farming of fruit, vegetables and flowers is also widespread, while beef, dairy and pig farming take place in the higher inland regions.

▲ The Dutch city of Rotterdam lies within one of the most densely populated and highly industrialized regions in the world, known as 'Randstad Holland'.

▲ Cut-flower and bulb production in the Netherlands are important sources of revenue. Both are exported around the world.

Land use and agricultural distribution

- capital cities
- major towns
- cattle
- pigs
- cereals
- flowers
- sugar beet
- pasture
- cropland
- forest
- wetland

The urban/rural population divide

urban 92%
rural 8%

Population density	Total land area
1043 people per sq mile (403 people per sq km)	28,191 sq miles (73,016 sq km)

Germany

Despite the devastation of its industry and infrastructure during the Second World War and its separation from eastern Germany during the Cold War, West Germany made a rapid recovery in the following generation to become Europe's most formidable economic power. When the Berlin Wall was dismantled in 1989, the two halves of Germany were politically united for the first time in 40 years. Complete social and economic unity remain a longer term goal, as East German industry and society adapt to the free market. Germany has been a key player in the creation of the European Union (EU) and in moves toward a single European currency.

Using the land

Germany has a large, efficient agricultural sector, and produces more than three-quarters of its own food. The major crops grown are cereals and sugar beet on the more fertile soils, and root crops, rye, oats and fodder on the poorer soils of the northern plains and central uplands. Southern Germany is also a principal producer of high quality wines. Vineyards cover the slopes surrounding the Rhine and its tributaries.

Land use and agricultural distribution

- cattle
- pigs
- cereals
- sugar beet
- vineyards

- • capital cities
- • major towns

- pasture
- cropland
- forest

The urban/rural population divide

rural 13%

urban 87%

Population density
612 people per sq mile
(236 people per sq km)

Total land area
138,804 sq miles
(356,910 sq km)

▲ *The Moselle river* flows through the Rhine State Uplands (Rheinisches Schiefergebirge). During a period of uplift, pre-existing river meanders were deeply incised, to form its present dramatic contours.

The landscape

The plains of northern Germany, the volcanic plateaux and mountains of the central uplands, and the Bavarian Alps are the three principal geographic regions in Germany. North to south the land rises steadily from barely 300 ft (90 m) in the plains to 6500 ft (2000 m) in the Bavarian Alps, which are a small but distinct region in the far south.

The Harz Mountains were formed 300 million years ago. They are block-faulted mountains, formed when a section of the Earth's crust was thrust up between two faults.

▼ *The Elbe flows* in wide meanders across the north German plain to the North Sea. At its mouth it is 10 miles (16 km) wide.

Elbe river

Scale 1:2,500,000

projection: Lambert Conformal Conic

The Danube rises in the Black Forest (Schwarzwald) and flows east, across a wide valley, on its course to the Black Sea.

Zugspitze, the highest peak in Germany at 9719 ft (2962 m), was formed during the Alpine mountain-building period, 30 million years ago.

Rhine Rift Valley

The Rhine is Germany's principal waterway and one of Europe's longest rivers, flowing 820 miles (1320 km).

Muritz lake covers 45 sq miles (117 sq km), but is only 108 ft (33 m) deep. It lies in a shallow valley formed by block-faulted mountains. North to south the land rises steadily from barely 300 ft (90 m) in the plains. These valleys are known as Urstromtaler.

Luneburg Heath (Luneburger Heide)

▶ *The heathlands of* northern Germany are covered by glacial deposits of sandy outwash soil which makes them largely infertile. They support only sheep and solitary trees.

Much of the landscape of northern Germany has been shaped by glaciation. During the last Ice Age, the ice sheet advanced as far the northern slopes of the central uplands.

Fault lines

Rhine

▲ *Part of the floor of* the Rhine Rift Valley was let down between two parallel faults in the Earth's crust.

Downfaulted block

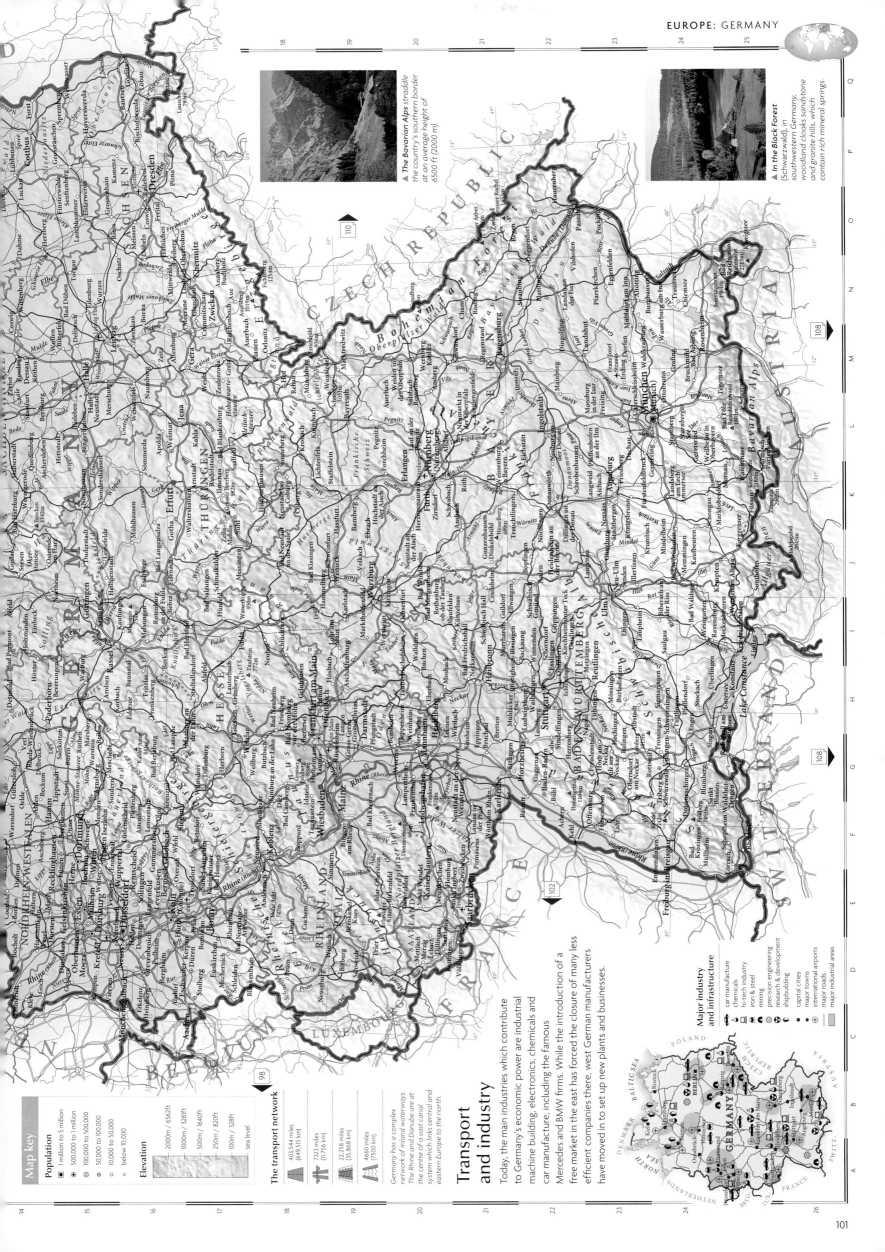

▲ *The Bavarian Alps straddle the country's southern border at an average height of 6500 ft (2000 m).*

▲ *In the Black Forest (Schwarzwald), in southwestern Germany, woodland clocks sandstone and granite hills, which contain rich mineral springs.*

Transport and industry

Today, the main industries which contribute to Germany's economic power are industrial machine building, electronics, chemicals and car manufacture, including the famous Mercedes and BMW firms. While the introduction of a free market in the east has forced the closure of many less efficient companies there, west German manufacturers have moved in to set up new plants and businesses.

Germany has a complex network of inland waterways. The Rhine and Danube are at the centre of a vast canal system which links central and eastern Europe to the north.

The transport network

▲◀▶	403,544 miles (649,915 km)
🚉	7323 miles (11,784 km)
▦	22,258 miles (35,868 km)
▲	4660 miles (7500 km)

Map key

Population
- ◉ 1 million to 5 million
- ◎ 500,000 to 1 million
- ⊙ 100,000 to 500,000
- ⊙ 50,000 to 100,000
- ∘ 10,000 to 50,000
- · below 10,000

Elevation
- 2000m / 6562ft
- 1000m / 3281ft
- 500m / 1640ft
- 250m / 820ft
- 100m / 328ft
- sea level

Major industry and infrastructure
- 🚗 car manufacture
- chemicals
- hi-tech industry
- iron & steel
- mining
- precision engineering
- research & development
- shipbuilding
- ■ capital cities
- ▪ major towns
- ⊕ international airports
- ▬ major roads
- major industrial areas

France

FRANCE, MONACO

A major centre of culture and fashion, and a leading producer of both industrial and agricultural goods, France is a key player in the push towards European unity. The founder of modern Republican government in the 18th century, France has been closely involved in European events for many centuries. The Paris Basin is the most highly populated area; Île de France is home to over 11 million people. Large parts of rural France remain thinly populated, particularly the mountainous Massif Central, Pyrenees and southern Alps.

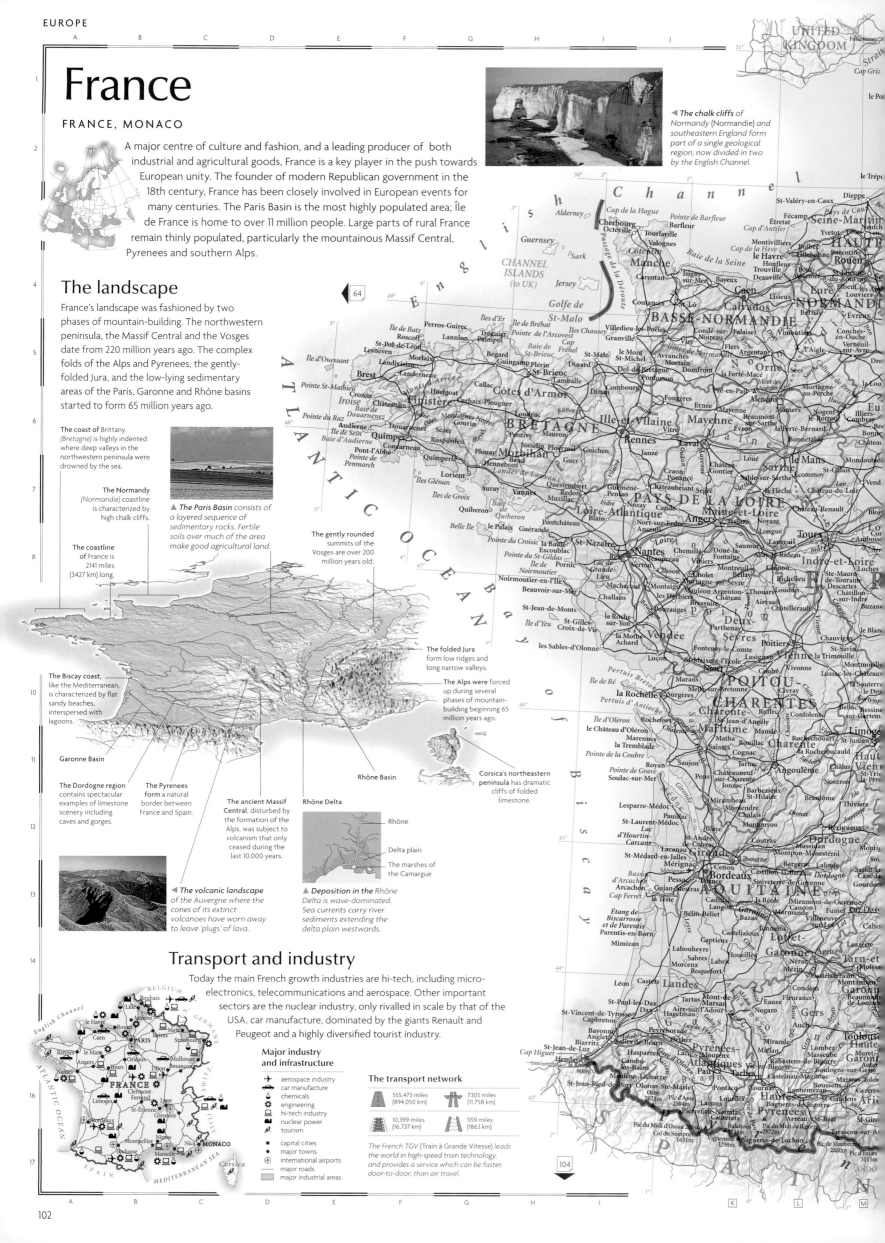

◄ *The chalk cliffs* of Normandy (Normandie) and southeastern England form part of a single geological region, now divided in two by the English Channel.

The landscape

France's landscape was fashioned by two phases of mountain-building. The northwestern peninsula, the Massif Central and the Vosges date from 220 million years ago. The complex folds of the Alps and Pyrenees, the gently-folded Jura, and the low-lying sedimentary areas of the Paris, Garonne and Rhône basins started to form 65 million years ago.

The coast of Brittany (Bretagne) is highly indented where deep valleys in the northwestern peninsula were drowned by the sea.

The Normandy (Normandie) coastline is characterized by high chalk cliffs.

The coastline of France is 2141 miles (3427 km) long.

▲ *The Paris Basin* consists of a layered sequence of sedimentary rocks. Fertile soils over much of the area make good agricultural land.

◄ The gently rounded summits of the Vosges are over 200 million years old.

The folded Jura form low ridges and long narrow valleys.

The Alps were forced up during several phases of mountain-building beginning 65 million years ago.

The Biscay coast, like the Mediterranean, is characterized by flat sandy beaches, interspersed with lagoons.

Garonne Basin

Rhône Basin

Corsica's northeastern peninsula has dramatic cliffs of folded limestone.

The Dordogne region contains spectacular examples of limestone scenery including caves and gorges.

The Pyrenees form a natural border between France and Spain.

The ancient Massif Central, disturbed by the formation of the Alps, was subject to volcanism that only ceased during the last 10,000 years.

Rhône Delta

Rhône

Delta plain

The marshes of the Camargue

◄ *The volcanic landscape* of the Auvergne where the cones of its extinct volcanoes have worn away to leave 'plugs' of lava.

▲ *Deposition in the Rhône Delta* is wave-dominated. Sea currents carry river sediments extending the delta plain westwards.

Transport and industry

Today the main French growth industries are hi-tech, including micro-electronics, telecommunications and aerospace. Other important sectors are the nuclear industry, only rivalled in scale by that of the USA, car manufacture, dominated by the giants Renault and Peugeot and a highly diversified tourist industry.

Major industry and infrastructure

✈ aerospace industry
🚗 car manufacture
⚗ chemicals
⚙ engineering
💻 hi-tech industry
⚛ nuclear power
⚓ tourism

■ capital cities
● major towns
✈ international airports
— major roads
▨ major industrial areas

The transport network

555,473 miles (894,050 km)

7305 miles (11,758 km)

10,399 miles (16,737 km)

1159 miles (1863 km)

The French TGV (Train à Grande Vitesse) leads the world in high-speed train technology, and provides a service which can be faster, door-to-door, than air travel.

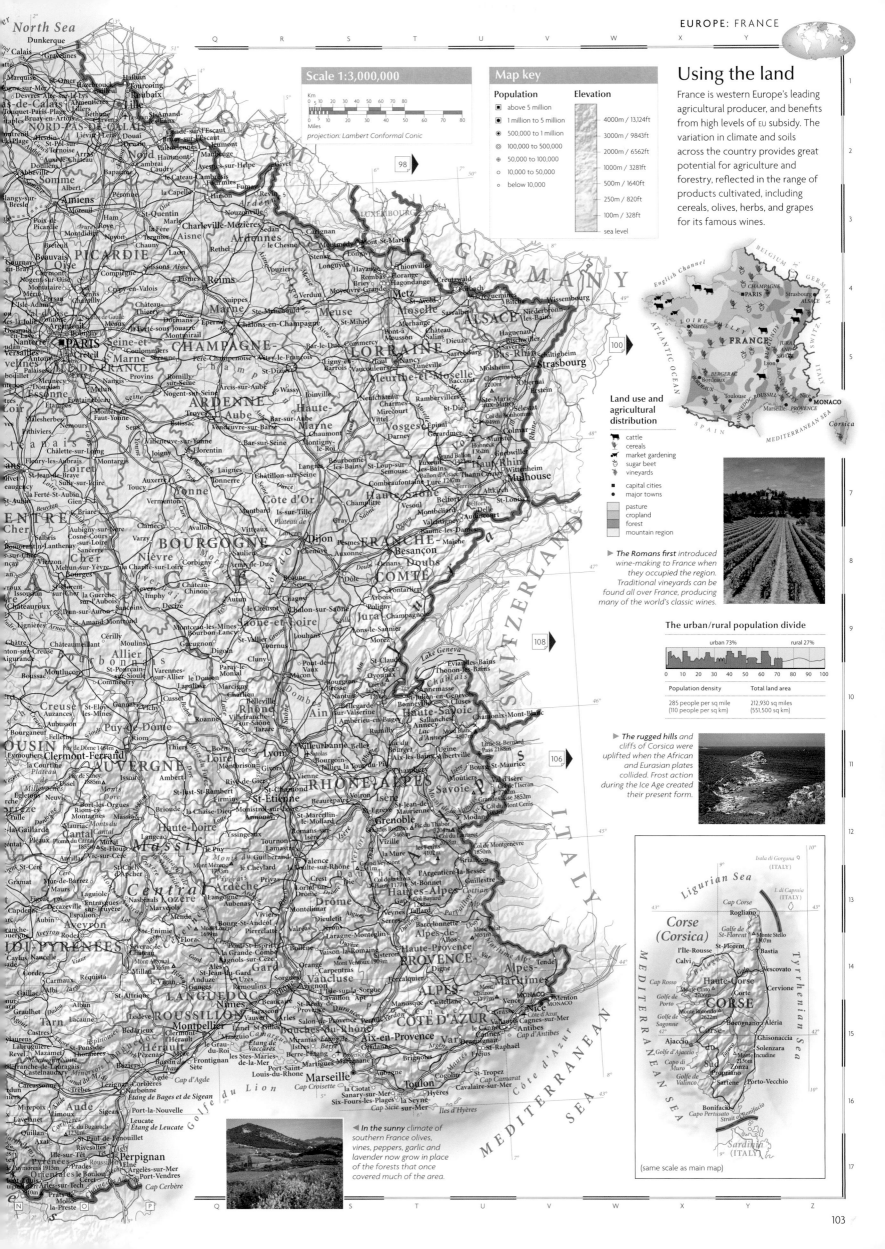

Scale 1:3,000,000

Km
0 10 20 30 40 50 60 70 80

Miles
0 10 20 30 40 50 60 70 80

projection: Lambert Conformal Conic

Map key

Population
- ■ above 5 million
- ▣ 1 million to 5 million
- ◉ 500,000 to 1 million
- ◎ 100,000 to 500,000
- ⊕ 50,000 to 100,000
- ○ 10,000 to 50,000
- ∘ below 10,000

Elevation
- 4000m / 13,124ft
- 3000m / 9843ft
- 2000m / 6562ft
- 1000m / 3281ft
- 500m / 1640ft
- 250m / 820ft
- 100m / 328ft
- sea level

Using the land

France is western Europe's leading agricultural producer, and benefits from high levels of EU subsidy. The variation in climate and soils across the country provides great potential for agriculture and forestry, reflected in the range of products cultivated, including cereals, olives, herbs, and grapes for its famous wines.

Land use and agricultural distribution
- cattle
- cereals
- market gardening
- sugar beet
- vineyards
- ■ capital cities
- ● major towns
- pasture
- cropland
- forest
- mountain region

▶ **The Romans first** introduced wine-making to France when they occupied the region. Traditional vineyards can be found all over France, producing many of the world's classic wines.

The urban/rural population divide

urban 73%   rural 27%

0 10 20 30 40 50 60 70 80 90 100

Population density	Total land area
285 people per sq mile (110 people per sq km)	212,930 sq miles (551,500 sq km)

▶ **The rugged hills** and cliffs of Corsica were uplifted when the African and Eurasian plates collided. Frost action during the Ice Age created their present form.

Corse (Corsica)

(same scale as main map)

◀ **In the sunny** climate of southern France olives, vines, peppers, garlic and lavender now grow in place of the forests that once covered much of the area.

The Iberian peninsula

ANDORRA, GIBRALTAR, PORTUGAL,
SPAIN (Azores, Canary Islands, Madeira on p.64)

The Iberian peninsula is separated from the rest of
Europe by the Pyrenees, and at its most southerly
point is only 5 miles (8 km) from North Africa.
The location of Iberia has been central to its
diverse history. The Greeks, Carthaginians, Romans,
Visigoths and most recently the Moors, invaded
Iberia at various times. For much of the 20th century,
both Spain and Portugal were governed by right-wing
dictators. Since the establishment of democratic governments in the
mid-1970s, modernization has been rapid and both countries are now
among the most popular of European holiday destinations.

Using the land

The principal crops grown in Iberia are
cereals, especially wheat and barley. Both
countries are major wine producers, most
notably of Rioja, sherry and port. Sheep
are kept throughout the region, and citrus
fruits thrive on the Mediterranean coast.
The successful forest industry in Iberia
produces 84% of the world's cork.

▲ The steep, terraced slopes of the
Douro Valley in northern Portugal,
are used to cultivate vines. The
grapes harvested produce Portugal's
famous port wine.

Land use and agricultural distribution

- sheep
- cereals
- citrus fruit
- olives
- vineyards
- cork
- capital cities
- major towns

pasture
cropland
forest
mountain region

The urban/rural population divide

urban 68%   rural 32%

0 10 20 30 40 50 60 70 80 90 100

Population density	Total land area
215 people per sq mile (83 people per sq km)	230,569 sq miles (597,170 sq km)

Transport and industry

Since the 1970s, the economies of Spain and Portugal
have expanded and diversified. In both countries,
tourism has outstripped agriculture in economic
importance. Spain's resource base is varied, including
coal, iron and the world's largest reserves of mercury.
Portugal is a leading producer of tungsten ore.

The transport network

241,720 miles (388,990 km)		1552 miles (2529 km)
11,793 miles (18,979 km)		1159 miles (1865 km)

Radiating from Madrid, the road network in
Spain dates from the 18th century, but now
includes many motorways. Portugal's road
system has been completely modernized in
recent years.

Major industry and infrastructure

- car manufacture
- chemicals
- engineering
- fish processing
- mining
- textiles
- tourism
- capital cities
- major towns
- international airports
- major roads
- major industrial areas

◀ The eroded cliffs of the
Algarve in southern Portugal
were carved by Atlantic waves.
The numerous rocky bays and
beaches, and the region's
pleasant climate, have made it
a popular tourist destination.

64

74

▶ *The climate in northwestern Spain is milder in both summer and winter than in the rest of the country, creating a verdant environment, more commonly associated with northwestern Europe.*

Map key

Population

■	1 million to 5 million
◉	500,000 to 1 million
◎	100,000 to 500,000
⊕	50,000 to 100,000
○	10,000 to 50,000
○	below 10,000

Elevation

3000m / 9843ft
2000m / 6562ft
1000m / 3281ft
500m / 1640ft
250m / 820ft
100m / 328ft
sea level

Scale 1:3,000,000

Km
0 5 10 20 30 40 50 60 70 80
Miles

projection: Lambert Conformal Conic

The landscape

A vast plateau, the Meseta dominates the centre of the peninsula, enclosed by the Cordillera Cantábrica to the north and the Sierra Morena to the south. It is drained by three major rivers, the Douro/Duero, the Tagus, and the Guadalquivir. The peninsula experiences great variations in climate and rainfall, both regionally and locally.

▲ *The Pyrenees form Iberia's northeastern boundary, running for 270 miles (440 km), dividing the peninsula from the rest of Europe.*

The Ebro river has formed the peninsula's largest delta. Recently, sediment flows have been seriously disturbed by nearby reservoirs.

On the northeastern coast sea level changes are evident from wave-cut beaches which rise up to 200 ft (60 m) above the present sea level.

Cordillera Cantábrica

Douro/Duero river

The Meseta plateau averages 1970 ft (600 m) in height and is now largely dry and treeless.

Tagus River

The Balearic Islands *(Islas Baleares)* are characterized by jagged limestones and plains.

Mountain front
Weathered material
Pediment

▲ *Pediments are characteristic of semi-arid lands across Iberia. A pediment is a flat, low-lying, eroded platform, cut into the bedrock. Weathered material is transported by streams and deposited in broad fan shapes on the pediment.*

The Guadalquivir river brings vital irrigation water to the plains, and like many of Iberia's rivers, is prone to flooding.

Sierra Morena

The Sierra Nevada in southern Spain contain Iberia's highest peak, Mulhacén, which rises 11,418 ft (3481 m).

▶ *In the Sierra de los Filabres deforestation and overgrazing, which cause soil erosion, have created semi-desert badlands.*

The Italian peninsula

ITALY, SAN MARINO, VATICAN CITY

The Italian peninsula is a land of great contrasts. Until unification in 1861, Italy was a collection of independent states, whose competitiveness during the Renaissance resulted in the architectural and artistic magnificence of cities such as Rome, Florence and Venice. The majority of Italy's population and economic activity is concentrated in the north, centred on the sophisticated industrial city of Milan. Southern Italy, the *Mezzogiorno*, has a harsh and difficult terrain, and remains far less developed than the north. Attempts to attract industry and investment in the south are frequently deterred by the entrenched network of organized crime and corruption.

The landscape

The mainly mountainous and hilly Italian peninsula took its present form following a collision between the African and Eurasian tectonic plates. The Alps in the northwest rise to a high point of 15,772 ft (4807 m) at Mont Blanc (*Monte Bianco*) on the French border, while the Apennines (*Appennino*) form a rugged backbone, running along the entire length of the country.

▲ *The island of* Sardinia *is an ancient land mass, an uplifted section of very old igneous rocks. Its rugged mountainous regions provide pasture for sheep and goats, while its valleys support some agriculture.*

Mont Blanc (*Monte Bianco*)

Costa Smeralda

The Dolomites (Alpi Dolomitiche) *are formed of thick limestones, overlying weaker marine strata. They have distinctive serrated peaks and many massive landslides occur.*

The distinctive square shape of the Gulf of Taranto (Golfo di Taranto) was defined by numerous block faults. Earthquakes are common in this region.

The Apennines (*Appennino*) are the source of most of Italy's rivers. They run 823 miles (1324 km) down the length of the peninsula.

The Pontine Marshes (*Agro Pontino*) are bounded by low sand hills which prevent natural drainage.

Vesuvius (*Vesuvio*)

The Strait of Messina (*Stretto di Messina*) *is between 2 and 12 miles (3–19 km) wide, and is a rich fishing ground.*

Sicily is the largest island in the Mediterranean at 9926 sq miles (25,708 sq km).

The southwestern tip of Sicily lies 95 miles (152 km) from the north African mainland and is part of the same geological region.

Present-day crater has developed within the old crater of Monte Somma

The Po Valley once formed part of the Adriatic Sea. Sediments of gravel, sand and clay washed down from the Alps gradually filling the bay and forming a broad, cultivable plain.

Sardinia is the second largest island in the Mediterranean Sea. The highest point is Punta La Marmora at 6017 ft (1834 m).

Vesuvius (*Vesuvio*)

Monte Somma
Old crater

▲ *There have been four volcanoes on the site of Vesuvius since volcanic activity began here more than 10,000 years ago.*

Using the land

Italy produces 95% of its own food. The best farming land is in the Po Valley in northern Italy, where soft wheat and rice are grown. Irrigation is essential to agriculture in much of the south. Italy is a major producer and exporter of citrus fruits, olives, tomatoes and wine.

The urban/rural population divide

urban 67%   rural 33%

Population density
506 people per sq mile
(195 people per sq km)

Total land area
116,320 sq miles
(301,270 sq km)

Land use and agricultural distribution

- ● capital cities
- ● major towns
- pasture
- cropland
- forest
- mountain region
- cattle
- cereals
- citrus fruits
- olive oil
- rice
- vineyards

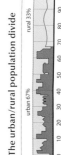
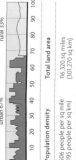

Scale 1:2,750,000

Km
Miles
projection: Lambert Conformal Conic

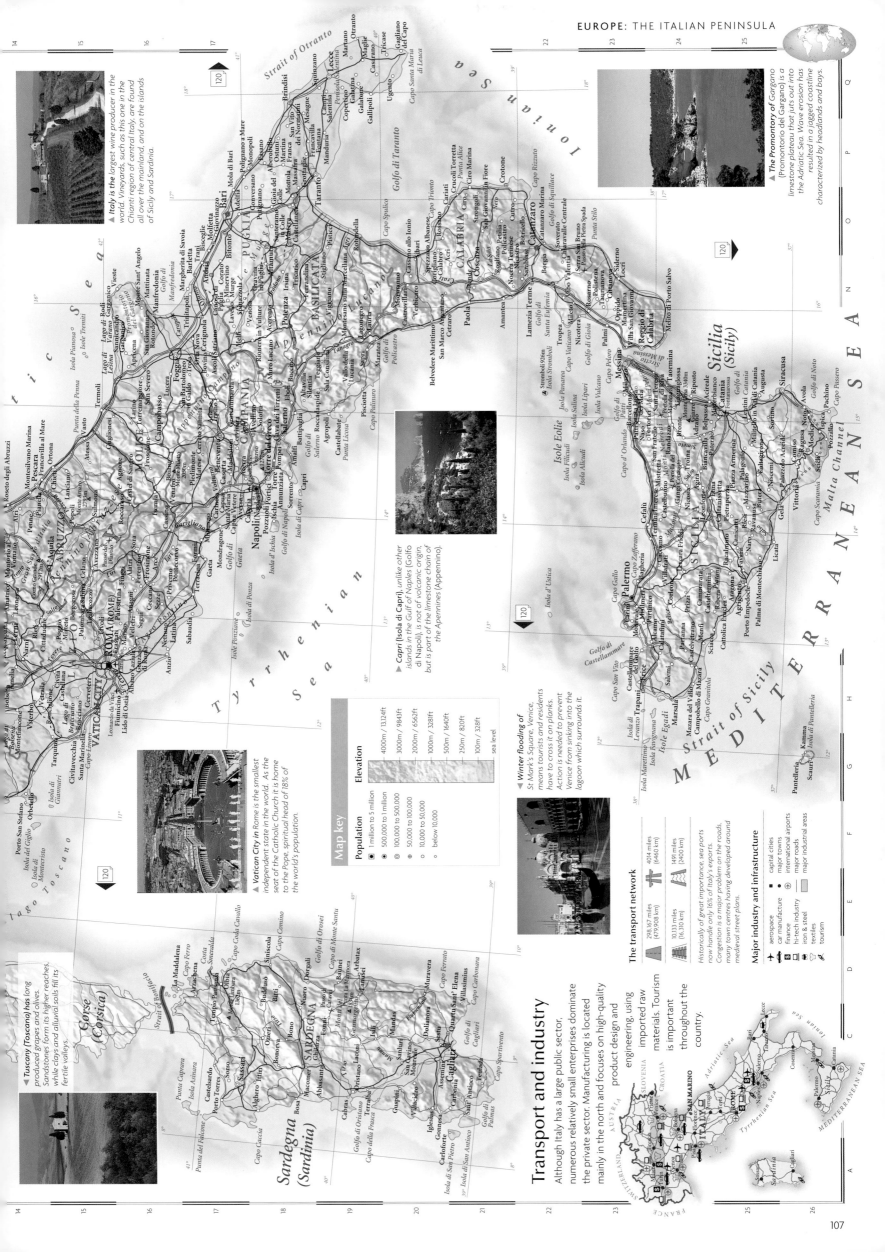

▲ **Italy is the** largest wine producer in the world. Vineyards, such as this one in the Chianti region of central Italy, are found all over the mainland, and on the islands of Sicily and Sardinia.

▲ **The Promontory of Gargano** (Promontorio del Gargano) is a limestone plateau that juts out into the Adriatic Sea. Wave erosion has resulted in a jagged coastline characterized by headlands and bays.

▲ **Capri** (Isola di Capri), unlike other islands in the Gulf of Naples (Golfo di Napoli), is not of volcanic origin, but is part of the limestone chain of the Apennines (Appennino).

▲ **Vatican City in Rome** is the smallest independent state in the world. As the seat of the Catholic Church it is home to the Pope, spiritual head of 18% of the world's population.

▼ **Winter flooding of** St Mark's Square, Venice, means tourists and residents have to cross it on planks. Action is needed to prevent Venice from sinking into the lagoon which surrounds it.

▼ **Tuscany** (Toscana) has long produced grapes and olives. Sandstones form its higher reaches, while clays and alluvial soils fill its fertile valleys.

Map key

Population

⊙ 1 million to 5 million
⊙ 500,000 to 1 million
⊙ 100,000 to 500,000
⊕ 50,000 to 100,000
○ 10,000 to 50,000
○ below 10,000

Elevation

	4000m / 13,124ft
	3000m / 9843ft
	2000m / 6562ft
	1000m / 3281ft
	500m / 1640ft
	250m / 820ft
	100m / 328ft
	sea level

The transport network

✈ 298,167 miles (479,908 km)
🚆 10,133 miles (16,310 km)
🛫 404 miles (6460 km)
1491 miles (2400 km)

Historically of great importance, sea ports now handle only 16% of Italy's exports. Congestion is a major problem on the roads, many town centres having developed around medieval street plans.

Major industry and infrastructure

aerospace
car manufacture
finance
hi-tech industry
iron & steel
textiles
tourism

● capital cities
● major towns
⊕ international airports
major roads
major industrial areas

Transport and industry

Although Italy has a large public sector, numerous relatively small enterprises dominate the private sector. Manufacturing is located mainly in the north and focuses on high-quality product design and engineering, using imported raw materials. Tourism is important throughout the country.

Gorse (Corsica)

Sardegna (Sardinia)

Sicilia (Sicily)

The Alpine states

AUSTRIA, LIECHTENSTEIN, SLOVENIA, SWITZERLAND

The Alpine countries of Austria, Switzerland, Liechtenstein and Slovenia form a narrow strip across western Europe's geographical core, lying on the main north–south trading routes across the Alps. Switzerland, politically neutral since 1815, is an important international meeting place and houses one of the headquarters of the United Nations, although it only became a member in 2002. Austria, once at the heart of the great Habsburg Empire has been a fully independent nation since 1955, and maintains a deserved reputation as an international centre of culture. Slovenia declared independence from the former Yugoslavia in 1991 and despite initial economic hardship, is now starting to achieve the prosperity enjoyed by its Alpine neighbours.

◄ **The Matterhorn, on** the Swiss-Italian border, is one of the highest mountains in the Alps, at 14,692 ft (4478 m). The term 'horn' refers to its distinctive peak, formed by three glaciers eroding hollows, known as cirques, in each of its sides.

Using the land

The Alpine region's mountainous terrain discourages cultivation over much of the land area. The primary agricultural activity is the raising of dairy and beef cattle on the pasture land of the lower mountain slopes. Austria is self-supporting in grains, and crops such as wheat, barley and grapes are grown on the east Austrian lowlands. Woodlands are more prevalent in the eastern Alps; both Austria and Slovenia have large tracts of forest.

Land use and agricultural distribution

- cattle
- pigs
- cereals
- vineyards
- capital cities
- major towns
- pasture
- cropland
- forest
- mountain region

The landscape

The Alps occupy three-fifths of Switzerland, most of southern Austria and the northwest of Slovenia. They were formed by the collision of the African and Eurasian tectonic plates, which began 65 million years ago. Their complex geology is reflected in the differing heights and rock types of the various ranges. The Rhine flows along Liechtenstein's border with Switzerland, creating a broad flood plain in the north and west of Liechtenstein. In the far northeast and east are a number of lowland regions, including the Vienna Basin, Burgenland and the plain of the Danube. Slovenia's major rivers flow across the lower eastern regions; in the west, the rivers flow largely underground through the limestone Karst region.

Original height after uplift and folding

Folded strata are overturned creating a *nappe*

Present-day height of Alps

Eurasian Plate

African Plate

▲ **The convergence of** the African and Eurasian plates compressed and folded huge masses of rock strata. As the plates continued to move together, the folded strata were overturned, creating complex nappes. Much of the rock strata has since been eroded, resulting in the current topography of the Alps.

▲ **Constricted as it** cuts through ridges in the Alps, the Danube meanders across the lowlands, where uplift combined with river erosion has deepened meanders.

The Vienna Basin lies mainly below 390 ft (120 m). It gradually subsided and filled with sediment as the Alps were uplifted.

Neusiedler See straddles the border of Austria and Hungary; the area around it provides some of the best wine-growing land in Austria.

The Austrian Alps comprise three distinct mountain ranges, separated by deep trenches. The northern and southern ranges are rugged limestones, while the Tauern range is formed of crystalline rocks.

The Tauern range in the central Austrian Alps contains the highest mountain in Austria, the towering Grossglockner, rising 12,461 ft (3798 m).

The mountains of the Jura form a natural border between Switzerland and France. Their marine limestones date from over 200 million years ago. When the Alps were formed the Jura were folded into a series of parallel ridges and troughs.

Tectonic activity has resulted in dramatic changes in land height over very short distances. Lake Geneva, lying at 1221 ft (372 m) is only 43 miles (70 km) away from the 15,772 ft (4807 m) peak of Mont Blanc, on the France–Italy border.

The Bernese Alps (*Berner Alpen*) contain the Aletsch, which at 15 miles (24 km) is the longest Alpine glacier.

The Rhine, like other major Alpine rivers, follows a broad, flat trough between the mountains. Along part of its course, the Rhine forms the boundary between Switzerland and Liechtenstein.

▶ **The deep, blue** lakes of the Karst region are part of a drainage network which runs largely underground through this limestone area.

The first road through the Brenner Pass was built in 1772, although it has been used as a mountain route since Roman times. It is the lowest of the main Alpine passes at 4298 ft (1374 m).

Karst region

The limestone cave system at Postojna extends for more than 10 miles (16 km) and includes caverns reaching 125 ft (40 m) in height and width.

The urban/rural population divide

urban 66%   rural 34%

0 10 20 30 40 50 60 70 80 90 100

Population density	Total land area
314 people per sq mile (121 people per sq km)	56,135 sq miles (145,390 sq km)

◄ *In this mountainous region, the flatter, more accessible areas are often used for both cattle grazing and recreation.*

◄ *These converging glaciers are marked by dark lines of moraine. This eroded material is carried by glaciers, and deposited as the ice melts.*

Scale 1:2,000,000

Km
0 10 20 30 40 50 60

Miles
0 10 20 30 40 50 60

projection: Lambert Conformal Conic

Transport and industry

All four nations concentrate on high-quality manufacturing and services. Austrian iron and steel production is complemented by construction industries; and Slovenia, traditionally the industrial powerhouse of the western Balkans has increasingly diversified industries. Liechtenstein and Switzerland, lacking raw materials, produce pharmaceuticals and precision instruments, such as watches, and act as international banking centres. The spectacular scenery of the region encourages tourism all year round.

The transport network

181,107 miles (291,497 km)	2116 miles (3405 km)
6368 miles (10,249 km)	993 miles (1598 km)

Tunnels and passes through the Alps are an important feature of this region. The NEAT project, providing two new high-speed rail links between Basel and Milan, was given approval in 1992.

▶ *The Austrian Tirol contains some of the most spectacular Alpine scenery. Snow cover is a permanent feature in the highest reaches.*

Map key

Population

- ◉ 1 million to 5 million
- ◎ 500,000 to 1 million
- ⊚ 100,000 to 500,000
- ⊕ 50,000 to 100,000
- ○ 10,000 to 50,000
- ○ below 10,000

Elevation

- 4000m / 13,124ft
- 3000m / 9843ft
- 2000m / 6562ft
- 1000m / 3281ft
- 500m / 1640ft
- 250m / 820ft
- 100m / 328ft
- sea level

Major industry and infrastructure

- car manufacture
- chemicals
- engineering
- finance
- food processing
- iron & steel
- pharmaceuticals
- textiles
- tourism
- watch making
- winter sports
- capital cities
- major towns
- international airports
- major roads
- major industrial areas

▲ *The Schönbrunn Palace in Vienna was the summer residence of the Habsburg monarchy. Today, it is a major tourist attraction.*

Central Europe

CZECH REPUBLIC, HUNGARY, POLAND, SLOVAKIA

When Slovakia and the Czech Republic became separate countries in 1993, they joined Hungary and Poland in a new role as independent nation states, following centuries of shifting boundaries and imperial strife. This turbulent history bequeathed the region a rich cultural heritage, shared through the works of its many great writers and composers, and celebrated in the vibrant historic capitals of Prague, Budapest and Warsaw. Having shaken off years of Soviet domination in 1989, these states are confronting the challenge of winning commercial investment to modernize outmoded industries as they integrate their economies with those of the European Union.

The landscape

The forested Carpathian Mountains, uplifted with the Alps, lie southeast of the older Bohemian Massif, which contains the Sudeten and Krusné Hory (Erzgebirge) ranges. They divide the fertile plains of the Danube to the south and the Vistula (Wisła), which flows north across vast expanses of glacial deposits into the Baltic Sea.

Transport and industry

Heavy industry has dominated post-war life in Central Europe. Poland has large coal reserves, having inherited the Silesian coalfield from Germany after the Second World War, allowing the export of large quantities of coal, along with other minerals. Hungary specializes in consumer goods and services, while Slovakia's industrial base is still relatively small. The Czech Republic's traditional glassworks and breweries bring some stability to its precarious Soviet-built manufacturing sector.

▲ The Biebrza river has left meanders and oxbow lakes as it flows across low-lying ground.

Gerlachovsky štít, in the Tatra Mountains, is Slovakia's highest mountain, at 8711ft (2655 m).

Longshore currents moving east along the Baltic coast have built a 40 mile (65 km) spit composed of material from the Vistula (Wisła) river.

Pomerania is a sandy coastal region of glacially-formed lakes stretching west from the Vistula (Wisła).

Hot mineral springs occur where geothermally heated water wells up through faults and fractures in the rocks of the Sudeten Mountains.

Krusné Hory (Erzgebirge)

Bohemian Massif

Carpathian Mountains

The Slovak Ore Mountains (Slovenské Rudohorie) are noted for their mineral resources, including high-grade iron ore.

The Great Hungarian Plain formed by the flood plain of the Danube is a mixture of steppe and cultivated land, covering nearly half of Hungary's total area.

Slip-off slope

Bluff

Danube river

Direction of flow

▲ Meanders form as rivers flow across plains at a low gradient. A steep cliff or bluff, forms on the outside curve, and a gentler slip-off slope on the inside bend.

▼ The Berounka river cuts through the precipitous wooded landscape of the Bohemian Massif, banked by a broad flood plain.

Major industry and infrastructure

- car manufacture
- chemicals
- engineering
- food processing
- mining
- shipbuilding
- tourism
- ● capital cities
- ● major towns
- ✈ international airports
- major roads
- major industrial areas

The transport network

213,597 miles (344,600 km)	817 miles (1315 km)
27,479 miles (44,249 km)	3784 miles (6094 km)

The huge growth of tourism and business has prompted major investment in the transport infrastructure, with new road-building schemes within and between the main cities of the region.

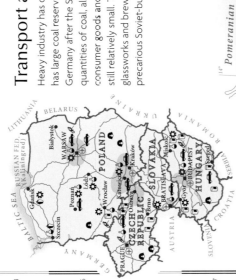

▲ Budapest, the capital of Hungary, straddles the Danube. It comprises the historic towns of Buda, on the west bank, and Pest, which contains the Parliament Building, seen here on the far bank.

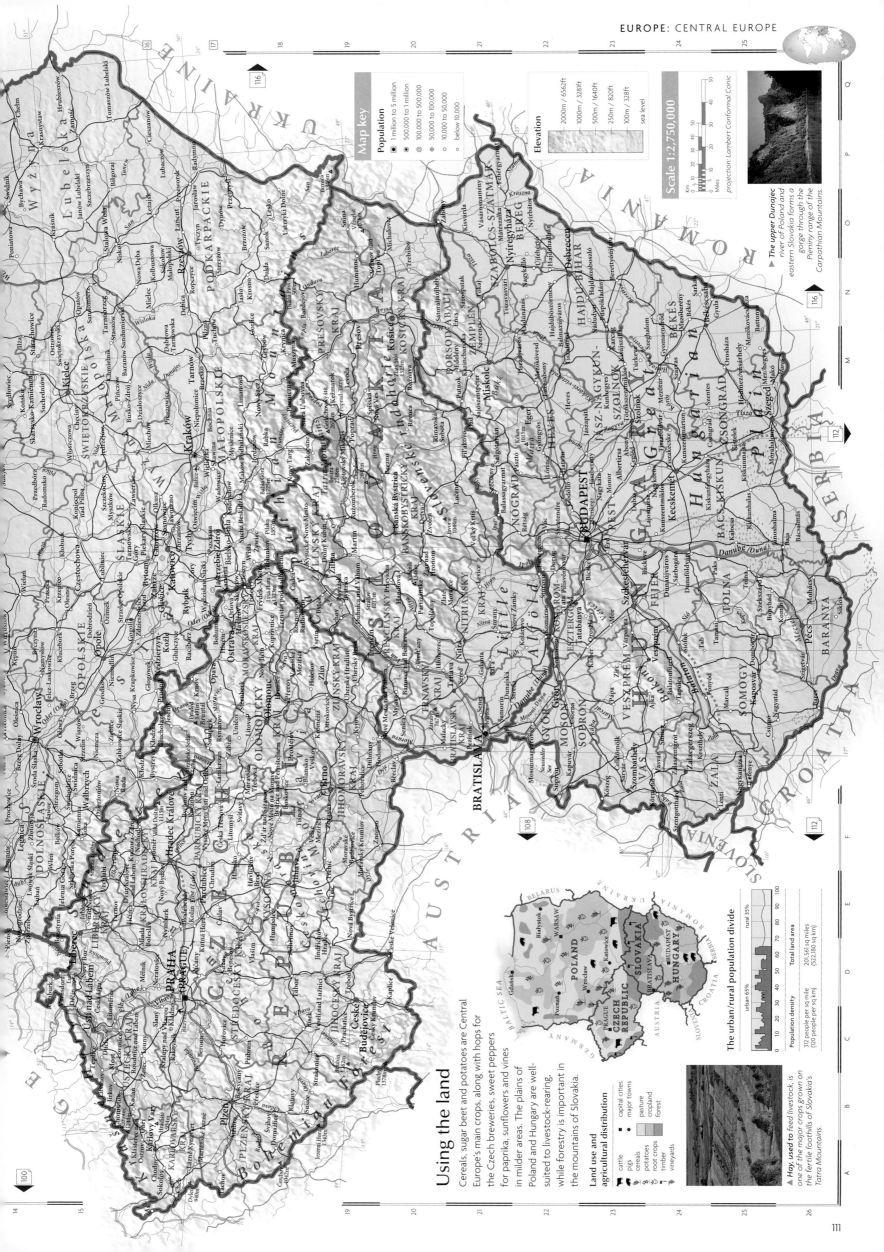

Map key

Population

- ■ 1 million to 5 million
- ● 500,000 to 1 million
- ◉ 100,000 to 500,000
- ◎ 50,000 to 100,000
- ○ 10,000 to 50,000
- ○ below 10,000

Elevation

- 2000m / 6562ft
- 1000m / 3281ft
- 500m / 1640ft
- 250m / 820ft
- 100m / 328ft
- sea level

Scale 1:2,750,000

projection: Lambert Conformal Conic

▶ The upper Dunajec river of Poland and eastern Slovakia forms a gorge through the Pieniny range of the Carpathian Mountains.

Using the land

Cereals, sugar beet and potatoes are Central Europe's main crops, along with hops for the Czech breweries, sweet peppers for paprika, sunflowers and vines in milder areas. The plains of Poland and Hungary are well-suited to livestock-rearing, while forestry is important in the mountains of Slovakia.

Land use and agricultural distribution

- 🐄 cattle
- 🐖 pigs
- 🌾 cereals
- 🥔 potatoes
- root crops
- 🌲 timber
- vineyards
- ■ capital cities
- • major towns
- pasture
- cropland
- forest

▲ Hay, used to feed livestock, is one of the major crops grown on the fertile foothills of Slovakia's Tatra Mountains.

The urban/rural population divide

urban 65%   rural 35%

Population density	Total land area
312 people per sq mile (120 people per sq km)	201,561 sq miles (522,180 sq km)

Southeast Europe

ALBANIA, BOSNIA & HERZEGOVINA, CROATIA, MACEDONIA, MONTENEGRO, SERBIA

For 46 years the federation of Yugoslavia held together the most diverse ethnic region in Europe, along the picturesque mountain hinterland of the Dalmatian coast. Economic collapse resulted in internal tensions. In the early 1990s, civil war broke out in both Croatia and Bosnia as the ethnic populations struggled to establish their own exclusive territories. Peace was only restored by the UN after NATO launched air strikes in 1995. Montenegro voted to split from Serbia in 2006 while the future of the province of Kosovo, whose attempts to gain autonomy in 1998 were crushed by the Serbian government, is still unresolved. Neighbouring Albania is slowly improving its fragile economy but remains one of Europe's poorest nations.

The landscape

The Tisza, Sava and Drava rivers drain the broad northern lowland, meeting the Danube after it crosses the Hungarian border. In the west, the Dinaric Alps divide the Adriatic Sea from the interior. Mainland valleys and elongated islands run parallel to the steep Dalmatian (Dalmacija) coastline, following alternating bands of resistant limestone.

Polijes in the Kosovo region

Sheer limestone walls enclose all sides
Flat polje floor
Underground drainage along joints in the rock
Spring at foot of cliff

▲ **Rain and underground** water dissolve limestone along massive vertical joints (cracks). This creates polijes: depressions several miles across with steep walls and broad, flat floors.

At Iron Gate (Derdap), on the border with Romania, the Danube narrows and cuts through foothills of the Balkan and Carpathian mountains, forming the deepest gorge in Europe.

A major earthquake at Skopje, Macedonia, in 1963 killed 1000 people. The whole region lies on an active crustal plate margin.

Lake Ohrid

▲ **Lake Ohrid borders** Albania and Macedonia. Ohrid is the deepest lake in the western Balkans, reaching depths of 938 ft (286 m).

Tisza river

The river flood plains of the Pannonian Basin are flanked by terraces of gravel and wind-blown glacial deposits known as loess.

Drava river

At least 70% of the fresh water in the western Balkans drains eastwards into the Black Sea, mostly via the Danube (Dunav).

A series of river valleys breaking through the Dinaric Alps from the lowlands of western Albania, give access to the interior.

Sava river

The elongated islands, promontories and straits of the Dalmatian (Dalmacija) coast were formed as the Adriatic Sea rose to flood valleys running parallel to the shore.

Dalmatian (Dalmacija) coast

▲ **Limestone cliffs along** the Dalmatian (Dalmacija) shoreline are heavily eroded, as salt water dissolves the rock along existing horizontal cracks, or joints. This tends to form a platform of rock at the foot of the cliff.

▲ **Hot, dry summers** and mild winters offer excellent conditions for viticulture in Montenegro. The precipitous Dinaric Alps have kept this region relatively isolated for centuries.

Scale 1:2,750,000

projection: Lambert Conformal Conic

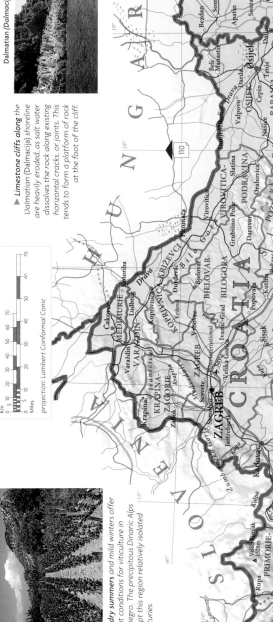

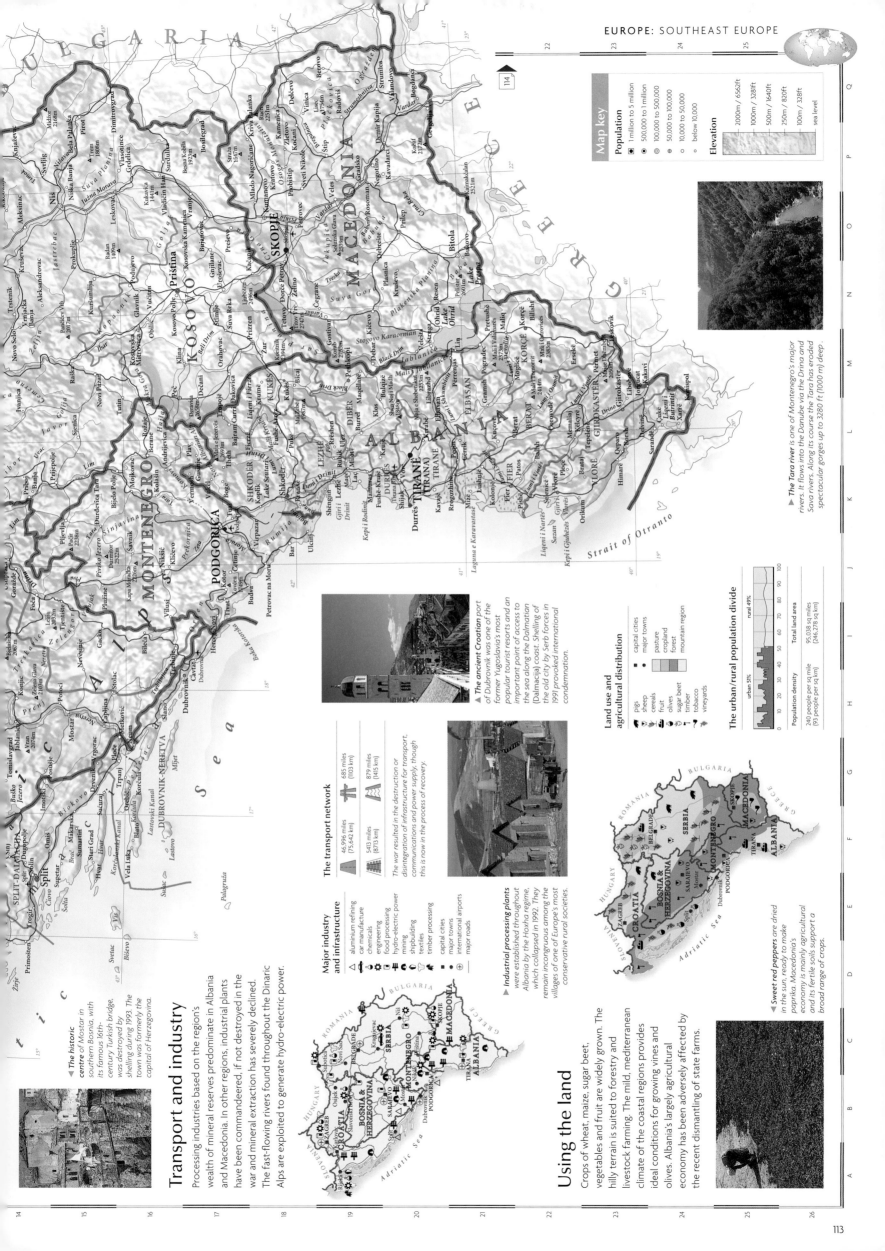

Map key

Population

- ⊙ 1 million to 5 million
- ◉ 500,000 to 1 million
- ⊕ 100,000 to 500,000
- ⊕ 50,000 to 100,000
- ○ 10,000 to 50,000
- ○ below 10,000

Elevation

- 2000m / 6562ft
- 1000m / 3281ft
- 500m / 1640ft
- 250m / 820ft
- 100m / 328ft
- sea level

▲ *The Tara river is one of Montenegro's major rivers. It flows into the Danube via the Drina and Sava rivers. Along its course the Tara has eroded spectacular gorges up to 3280 ft (1000 m) deep.*

▲ *The ancient Croatian port of Dubrovnik was one of the former Yugoslavia's most popular tourist resorts and an important point of access to the sea along the Dalmatian (Dalmacija) coast. Shelling of the old city by Serb forces in 1991 provoked international condemnation.*

Land use and agricultural distribution

- pigs
- sheep
- cereals
- fruit
- olives
- sugar beet
- timber
- tobacco
- vineyards
- ● capital cities
- ○ major towns
- pasture
- cropland
- forest
- mountain region

The urban/rural population divide

urban 51%   rural 49%

Population density	Total land area
240 people per sq mile (93 people per sq km)	95,038 sq miles (246,278 sq km)

Transport and industry

Processing industries based on the region's wealth of mineral reserves predominate in Albania and Macedonia. In other regions, industrial plants have been commandeered, if not destroyed in the war and mineral extraction has severely declined. The fast-flowing rivers found throughout the Dinaric Alps are exploited to generate hydro-electric power.

▼ *The historic centre of Mostar in southern Bosnia, with its famous 16th-century Turkish bridge, was destroyed by shelling during 1993. The town was formerly the capital of Herzegovina.*

The transport network

🛣 46,996 miles (75,642 km)	✈ 685 miles (1103 km)
🚂 5413 miles (8713 km)	⚓ 879 miles (1415 km)

The war resulted in the destruction or disintegration of infrastructure for transport, communications and power supply, though this is now in the process of recovery.

Major industry and infrastructure

- aluminium refining
- car manufacture
- chemicals
- engineering
- food processing
- hydro-electric power
- mining
- shipbuilding
- textiles
- timber processing
- ● capital cities
- ○ major towns
- ⊕ international airports
- major roads

▲ *Industrial processing plants were established throughout Albania by the Hoxha regime, which collapsed in 1992. They remain incongruous among the villages of one of Europe's most conservative rural societies.*

Using the land

Crops of wheat, maize, sugar beet, vegetables and fruit are widely grown. The hilly terrain is suited to forestry and livestock farming. The mild, mediterranean climate of the coastal regions provides ideal conditions for growing vines and olives. Albania's largely agricultural economy has been adversely affected by the recent dismantling of state farms.

▼ *Sweet red peppers are dried in the sun, ready to make paprika. Macedonia's economy is mainly agricultural and its fertile soils support a broad range of crops.*

113

Bulgaria & Greece

Including EUROPEAN TURKEY

Greece is renowned as the original hearth of western civilization. The rugged terrain and numerous islands have profoundly affected its development, creating a strong agricultural and maritime tradition. In the past 50 years, this formerly rural society has rapidly urbanized, with one third of the population now living in the capital, Athens, and in the northern city of Salonica. Bulgaria, dominated for centuries by the Ottoman Turks, became part of the eastern bloc after the Second World War, only slowly emerging from Soviet influence in 1989. Moves towards democracy led to some instability in Bulgaria and Greece, now outweighed by the challenge of integration with the European Union.

The landscape

Bulgaria's Balkan mountains divide the Danubian Plain (*Dunavska Ravnina*) and Maritsa Basin, meeting the Black Sea in the east along sandy beaches. The steep Rhodope Mountains form a natural barrier with Greece, while the younger Pindus form a rugged central spine which descends into the Aegean Sea to give a vast archipelago of over 2000 islands, the largest of which is Crete.

Limestone rocks exposed by erosion of metamorphic rocks

Ancient metamorphic rock, formed miles below the surface

Younger limestones created in shallow seas

Mount Olympus

▲ *Mount Olympus is a composite of rocks formed by two major tectonic events. First the older metamorphic rocks were thrust over the limestones, then two million years ago regional warping and subsequent erosion, re-exposed the limestone.*

Mount Olympus is the mythical home of the Greek Gods and, at 9570 ft (2917 m), is the highest mountain in Greece.

The Peloponnese consist of several mountainous peninsulas, linked to the mainland by the Isthmus of Corinth. The Corinth Canal (*Dioryga Korinthou*), built in 1893, cuts through the isthmus, linking the Aegean and Ionian seas.

Corinth Canal (*Dioryga Korinthou*)

Kythira

The islands of Crete, Kythira, Karpathos and Rhodes are part of an arc which bends southeastwards from the Peloponnese, forming the southern boundary of the Aegean.

▲ *Layers of black volcanic ash still cover the island of Santorini. This volcano last erupted 3500 years ago, but still shows signs of volcanic activity.*

The Danube, Europe's second longest river, forms most of Bulgaria's northern border. The Danubian plain (*Dunavska Ravnina*), extending from the southern bank, is extremely fertile.

▲ *The Arda river cuts through the Rhodope Mountains in rugged, rocky gorges.*

Balkan Mountains

Maritsa Basin

Pindus Mountains

Rhodes

Karpathos

Crete

Rhodope Mountains

Transport and industry

Soviet investment introduced heavy industry into Bulgaria, and the processing of agricultural produce, such as tobacco, is important throughout the country. Both countries have substantial shipyards, and Greece has one of the world's largest merchant fleets. Many small craft workshops, producing textiles and processed foods, are clustered around Greek cities. The service and construction sectors have profited from the successful tourist industry.

Bulgaria's railways require investment to revive an outdated infrastructure. In Greece, despite a developing road network, ferry-boats remain the most effective form of transport in many areas.

Major industry and infrastructure

- chemicals
- engineering
- food processing
- shipbuilding
- textiles
- tourism
- capital cities
- major towns
- international airports
- major roads
- major industrial areas

The transport network

- 103,930 miles (167,630 km)
- 345 miles (557 km)
- 4346 miles (6995 km)
- 294 miles (474 km)

▲ *A towering pinnacle at Metéora in central Greece is home to the monastery of Roussanou. The 24 rock towers which dominate the plain of Thessaly (Thessalia) are remnants of an old plateau. Long-term weathering along fissures in the rock has worn away the rest of the plateau.*

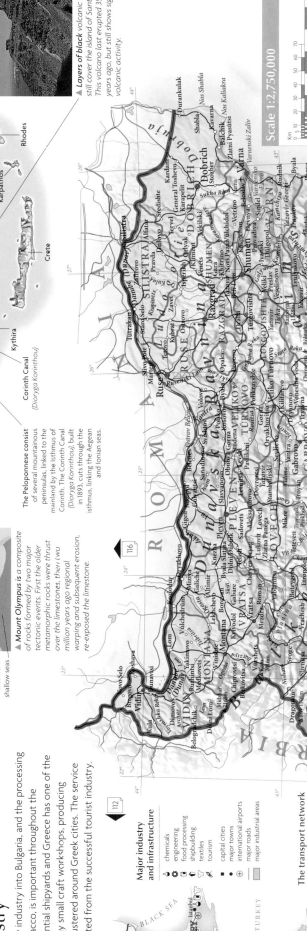

Scale 1:2,750,000

projection: Lambert Conformal Conic

Map key

Population

- ■ above 5 million
- ◉ 1 million to 5 million
- ◎ 500,000 to 1 million
- ⊕ 100,000 to 500,000
- ○ 50,000 to 100,000
- ○ 10,000 to 50,000
- ○ below 10,000

Elevation

- 3000m / 9843ft
- 2000m / 6562ft
- 1000m / 3281ft
- 500m / 1640ft
- 250m / 820ft
- 100m / 328ft
- sea level

▲ *The dry scrubland seen here at Vasiliki in Crete, is characteristic of much of southern Greece, and is caused by centuries of forest clearance and soil degradation. Landslides are also common.*

▲ *These terraces, built on the hillside at Naxos, an island of the Cyclades group, help to guard against soil erosion.*

Using the land and sea

The fertile plains of Bulgaria support cattle, fruit, vegetables, tobacco and cereal cultivation, while also providing traditional industries with grapes for wine, sunflowers for oil, and roses for perfume. Over half of Greece is barren upland. Citrus fruit, olives and tobacco are widely exported, yet much of rural life is still characterized by subsistence cropping and goat herding.

Land use and agricultural distribution

- cattle
- fishing
- goats
- sheep
- cereals
- cotton
- olives
- roses
- tobacco
- vineyards

- ■ capital cities
- • major towns
- pasture
- cropland
- forest
- mountain region

The urban/rural population divide

urban 65%   rural 35%

Population density: 245 people per sq mile (95 people per sq km)

Total land area: 102,353 sq miles (265,164 sq km)

Romania, Moldova & Ukraine

The industrial, social and cultural make-up of Romania and the former Soviet states of Moldova and Ukraine still bear the imprint of their communist past. As part of the USSR, Ukraine was a leading agricultural, industrial and energy producer. These industries, like those in Moldova and Romania, are now being reoriented more firmly towards western markets. As a result of shifting borders, and Soviet policy actively encouraging Russian immigration into other Soviet states like Ukraine and Moldova, all three countries now contain large numbers of foreign nationals. Moldovans and Romanians are still close in terms of language and culture, although Moldova is striving to remain an independent nation.

Using the land

The fertile black soils of Ukraine, often called 'the breadbasket of Europe', have enabled the cultivation of a variety of cereals and vegetables, which are widely exported. Romania and Moldova also grow cereals, sunflowers and vegetables, and are noted for the quality of their wines.

◀ *The fertile lands and tolerant climate of Moldova are ideally suited to growing grapes for wine.*

Land use and agricultural distribution

- cattle
- pigs
- poultry
- sheep
- cereals
- cotton
- sugar beet
- sunflowers
- vineyards

- ■ capital cities
- • major towns

- pasture
- cropland
- forest
- wetland

The urban/rural population divide

urban 65%   rural 35%

0 10 20 30 40 50 60 70 80 90 100

Population density	Total land area
222 people per sq mile (86 people per sq km)	334,947 sq miles (867,740 sq km)

◀ *Glacial lakes are found throughout the Transylvanian Alps (Carpatii Meridionali), although the mountains no longer have any permanent snow cover.*

Transport and industry

Heavy industry using local raw materials characterizes much of this region. The industrial heartland of Ukraine, specializing in metal and machine-building industries, is based around its vast mineral reserves in the Donbass region. In Moldova, food processing draws on produce from its agricultural sector. Romanian industry relies both on local raw materials and imported iron, steel and oil.

Major industry and infrastructure

- car manufacture
- chemicals
- coal
- engineering
- food processing
- mining
- oil & gas
- textiles
- tourism

- ■ capital cities
- ⊕ major towns
- ⊕ international airports
- — major roads
- major industrial areas

The transport network

170,707 miles (274,757 km)	1170 miles (1883 km)
21,474 miles (34,563 km)	4130 miles (6647 km)

Increased industrialization has necessitated the upgrading of road and rail networks in all three countries. Modernization has tended to focus only on major cities and industrial areas.

▶ *During the 1960s and 1970s, many industries, like this carbon factory, developed using the mineral resources on the flanks of the Transylvanian Alps (Carpatii Meridionali).*

Scale 1:3,500,000

Map key

Population
- 1 million to 5 million
- 500,000 to 1 million
- 100,000 to 500,000
- 50,000 to 100,000
- 10,000 to 50,000
- below 10,000

Elevation
- 2000m / 6562ft
- 1000m / 3281ft
- 500m / 1640ft
- 250m / 820ft
- 100m / 328ft
- sea level

projection: Lambert Conformal Conic

▲ The Swallow's Nest castle at Yalta is one of many tourist resorts on the Crimean (Krym) coast, dubbed the 'Russian Riviera'.

The landscape

Vast flat lowlands and gently rolling hills cover most of southeastern Europe. In the southwest, the Carpathian Mountains form a gentle arc. To the south of the Carpathian Mountains lies the Danube Plain, across which the Danube river flows to the Black Sea. To the north and east, the hills of Moldova level out into low plains, running east to the steppes of Ukraine.

▶ Divided into crystalline massifs, the southern arm of the Carpathian Mountains, the Transylvanian Alps (Carpatii Meridionali), extend 170 miles (274 km) across southwestern Romania.

The Apuseni Mountains (Muntii Apuseni) are rich in mineral deposits, including gold and iron ore.

Transylvanian Alps (Carpatii Meridionali)

Uplifted and folded at the same time as the Alps, some 250 miles (400 km) of the eastern Carpathian Mountains contain ancient volcanic cones and craters.

The Codrii Hills dominate the landscape of central Moldova; they are intersected by deep, flat valleys and ravines.

Steppe landscape covers two-thirds of Ukraine. These flat, treeless grasslands extend from central Europe to central Asia.

The Danube forms a natural border between Romania and Bulgaria.

The three branches of the Danube Delta (Delta Dunării) form a triangle of wetlands covering some 1950 sq miles (5050 sq km).

Most of the major rivers in southeastern Europe, like the Danube, the Dniester and Dnieper flow south and east to the Black Sea.

At Kryms'ki Hory, three flat-topped, parallel limestone ridges run 80 miles (128 km) along the southern coast of the Crimean (Krym) Peninsula.

Water has eroded a new post-glacial valley

Old glaciated valley

▲ Balkas are common throughout Ukraine. They are large U-shaped valleys, formed during the last Ice Age, which contain narrower, deep valleys. These were incised by a sudden flow of water, following an ice melt.

Anti-clockwise currents have created the sandspits which fringe the Sea of Azov.

117

The Baltic states & Belarus

BELARUS, ESTONIA, LATVIA, LITHUANIA, Kaliningrad

Occupying Europe's main corridor to Russia, the four distinct cultures of Estonia, Latvia, Lithuania and Belarus share a history of struggle for nationhood against their more powerful neighbours. As the first republics to declare their independence from the Soviet Union in 1990–91, the Baltic states of Estonia, Latvia and Lithuania sought an economic role in the EU, while reaffirming their European cultural roots through the church and a strong musical tradition. Meanwhile, Belarus has shown economic and political allegiance to Russia by joining the Commonwealth of Independent States.

▲ The seaport of Riga is Latvia's capital and the centre of economic and cultural life. With a 32% Russian minority in Latvia, language and the right to national citizenship are key issues.

Using the land

Across the four nations cattle and pig farming are widespread, together with diverse arable crops, including flax for making linen, potatoes used to produce vodka, cereals and other vegetables. Almost a third of the land is forested; demand for timber has increased the importance of forest management.

Land use and agricultural distribution

- cattle
- pigs
- cereals
- flax
- potatoes
- timber
- capital cities
- major towns
- pasture
- cropland
- forest
- wetland

The urban/rural population divide

urban 69%   rural 31%

Population density
122 people per sq mile
(47 people per sq km)

Total land area
145,006 sq miles
(375,656 sq km)

▲ A pine forest in northern Belarus. Conifers in the north give way to hardwood forest further south. Timber mills are supplied with logs floated along the country's many navigable waterways.

▲ The Western Dvina river provides hydro-electric power and, during the summer months, access to the Baltic Sea. The lower course of the river freezes from December to April.

Map key

Population
- ◉ 1 million to 5 million
- ◎ 500,000 to 1 million
- ⊚ 100,000 to 500,000
- ⊙ 50,000 to 100,000
- ○ 10,000 to 50,000
- ○ below 10,000

Elevation
- 250m / 820ft
- 100m / 328ft
- sea level

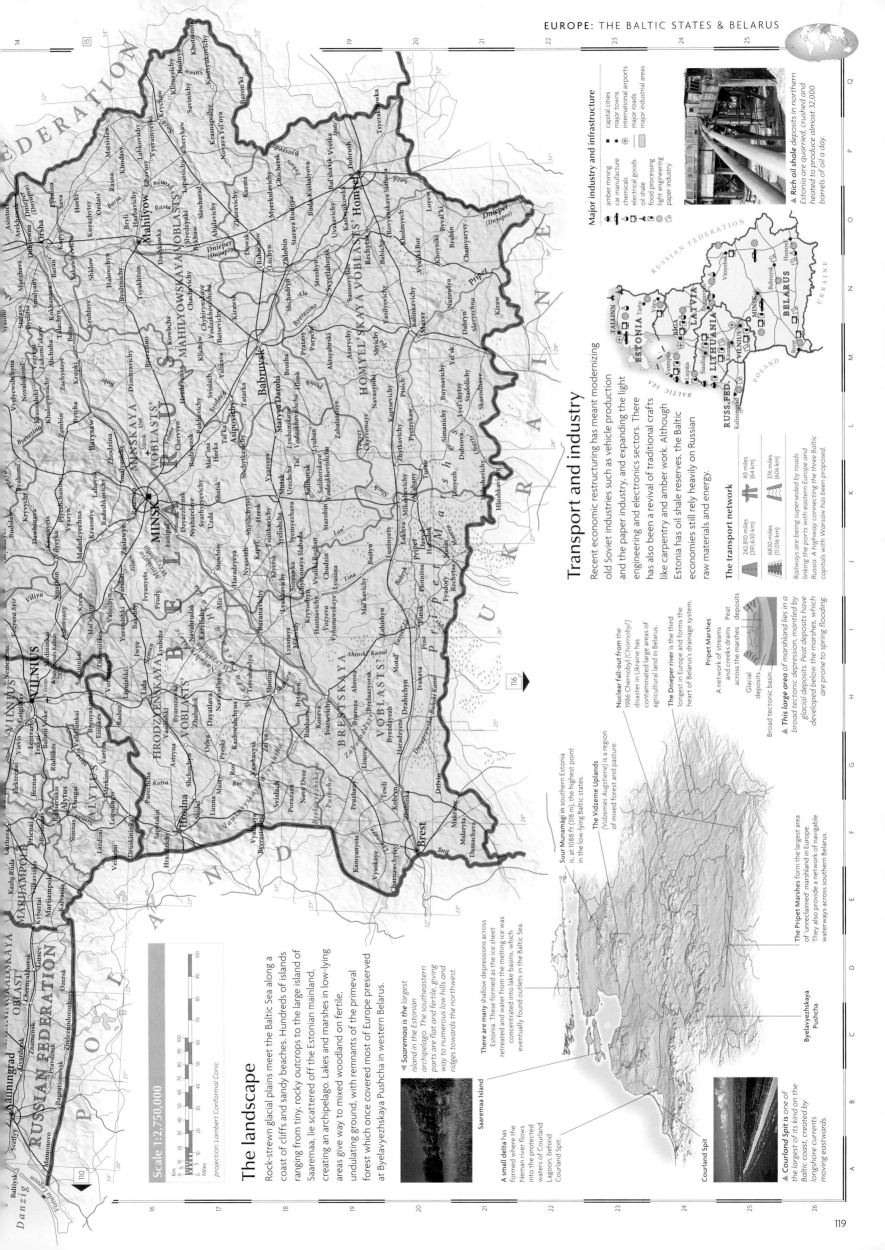

The landscape

Rock-strewn glacial plains meet the Baltic Sea along a coast of cliffs and sandy beaches. Hundreds of islands ranging from tiny, rocky outcrops to the large island of Saaremaa, lie scattered off the Estonian mainland, creating an archipelago. Lakes and marshes in low-lying areas give way to mixed woodland on fertile, undulating ground, with remnants of the primeval forest which once covered most of Europe preserved at Byelavyezhskaya Pushcha in western Belarus.

▼ Saaremaa is the largest island in the Estonian archipelago. The southeastern parts are flat and fertile, giving way to numerous low hills and ridges towards the northwest.

There are many shallow depressions across Estonia. These formed as the ice sheet retreated and water from the melting ice was concentrated into lake basins, which eventually found outlets in the Baltic Sea.

Saaremaa Island

A small delta has formed where the Neman river flows into the protected waters of Courland Lagoon, behind Courland Spit.

▲ Courland Spit is one of the largest of its kind on the Baltic coast, created by longshore currents moving eastwards.

Courland Spit

Byelavyezhskaya Pushcha

Suur Munamägi in southern Estonia is, at 1088 ft (318 m), the highest point in the low-lying Baltic states.

The Vidzeme Uplands (Vidzemes Augstiene) is a region of mixed forest and pasture.

Nuclear fall-out from the 1986 Chernobyl (Chornobyl) disaster in Ukraine has contaminated large areas of agricultural land in Belarus.

The Dnieper river is the third longest river in Europe and forms the heart of Belarus's drainage system.

Pripet Marshes
A network of streams and creeks drains across the marshes

Peat deposits

Glacial deposits

Broad tectonic basin

▲ This large area of marshland lies in a broad tectonic depression, mantled by glacial deposits. Peat deposits have developed below the marshes, which are prone to spring flooding.

The Pripet Marshes form the largest area of 'unreclaimed' marshland in Europe. They also provide a network of navigable waterways across southern Belarus.

Transport and industry

Recent economic restructuring has meant modernizing old Soviet industries such as vehicle production and the paper industry, and expanding the light engineering and electronics sectors. There has also been a revival of traditional crafts like carpentry and amber work. Although Estonia has oil shale reserves, the Baltic economies still rely heavily on Russian raw materials and energy.

The transport network

Railways are being superseded by roads linking the ports with eastern Europe and Russia. A highway connecting the three Baltic capitals with Warsaw has been proposed.

242,810 miles (391,630 km)

40 miles (64 km)

6830 miles (11,016 km)

376 miles (606 km)

Major industry and infrastructure

- amber mining
- car manufacture
- chemicals
- electrical goods
- oil shale
- food processing
- light engineering
- paper industry

- capital cities
- major towns
- international airports
- major roads
- major industrial areas

▲ Rich oil shale deposits in northern Estonia are quarried, crushed and heated to produce almost 32,000 barrels of oil a day.

RUSSIAN FEDERATION

Scale 1:2,750,000

Km
0 5 10 20 30 40 50 60 70 80 90 100

Miles
0 5 10 20 30 40 50 60 70 80 90 100

projection: Lambert Conformal Conic

The Mediterranean

The Mediterranean Sea stretches over 2500 miles (4000 km) east to west, separating Europe from Africa. At its most westerly point it is connected to the Atlantic Ocean through the Strait of Gibraltar. In the east, the Suez canal, opened in 1869, gives passage to the Indian Ocean. In the northeast, linked by the Sea of Marmara, lies the Black Sea. The Mediterranean is bordered by almost 30 states and territories, and more than 100 million people live on its shores and islands. Throughout history, the Mediterranean has been a focal area for many great empires and civilizations, reflected in the variety of cultures found on its shores. Since the 1960s, development along the southern coast of Europe has expanded rapidly to accommodate increasing numbers of tourists and to enable the exploitation of oil and gas reserves. This has resulted in rising levels of pollution, threatening the future of the sea.

▲ **Monaco is just** one of the luxurious resorts scattered along the Riviera, which stretches along the coast from Cannes in France to La Spezia in Italy. The region's mild winters and hot summers have attracted wealthy tourists since the early 19th century.

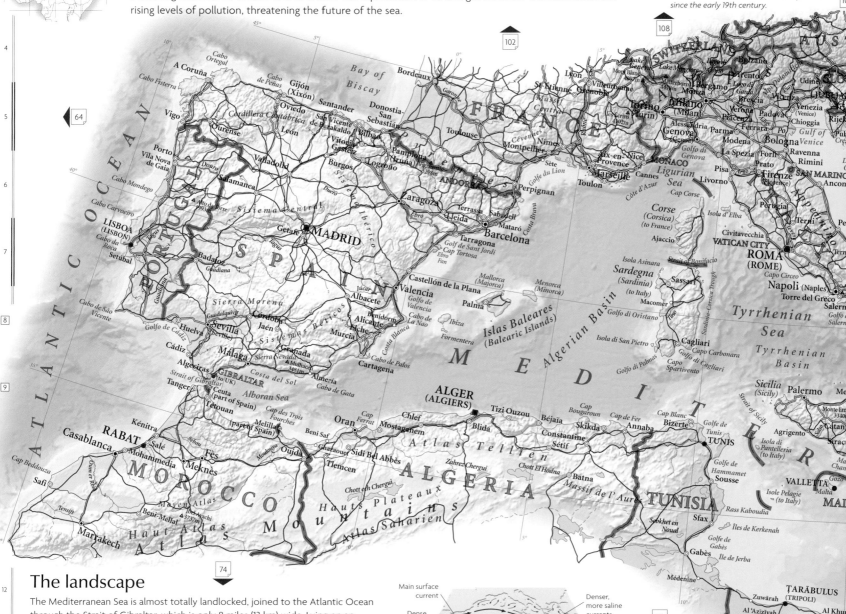

The landscape

The Mediterranean Sea is almost totally landlocked, joined to the Atlantic Ocean through the Strait of Gibraltar, which is only 8 miles (13 km) wide. Lying on an active plate margin, sea floor movements have formed a variety of basins, troughs and ridges. A submarine ridge running from Tunisia to the island of Sicily divides the Mediterranean into two distinct basins. The western basin is characterized by broad, smooth abyssal (or ocean) plains. In contrast, the eastern basin is dominated by a large ridge system, running east to west.

The narrow Strait of Gibraltar inhibits water exchange between the Mediterranean Sea and the Atlantic Ocean, producing a high degree of salinity and a low tidal range within the Mediterranean. The lack of tides has encouraged the build-up of pollutants in many semi-enclosed bays.

Main surface current

Dense currents sink below surface

Denser, more saline currents flow back to Atlantic

▲ **Because the Mediterranean** is almost enclosed by land, its circulation is quite different to the oceans. There is one major current which flows in from the Atlantic and moves east. Currents flowing back to the Atlantic are denser and flow below the main current.

Industrial pollution flowing from the Dnieper and Danube rivers has destroyed a large proportion of the fish population that used to inhabit the upper layers of the Black Sea.

The Ionian Basin is the deepest in the Mediterranean, reaching depths of 16,800 ft (5121 m).

The edge of the Eurasian Plate is edged by a continental shelf. In the Mediterranean Sea this is widest at the Ebro Fan where it extends 60 miles (96 km).

◄ **The Atlas Mountains** are a range of fold mountains which lie in Morocco and Algeria. They run parallel to the Mediterranean, forming a topographical and climatic divide between the Mediterranean coast and the western Sahara.

An arc of active submarine, island and mainland volcanoes, including Etna and Vesuvius, lie in and around southern Italy. The area is also susceptible to earthquakes and landslides.

Nutrient flows into the eastern Mediterranean, and sediment flows to the Nile Delta have been severely lowered by the building of the Aswan Dam across the Nile in Egypt. This is causing the delta to shrink.

Oxygen in the Black Sea is dissolved only in its upper layers; at depths below 230–300 ft (70–100 m) the sea is 'dead' and can support no lifeforms other than specially-adapted bacteria.

The Suez Canal, opened in 1869, extends 100 miles (160 km) from Port Said to the Gulf of Suez.

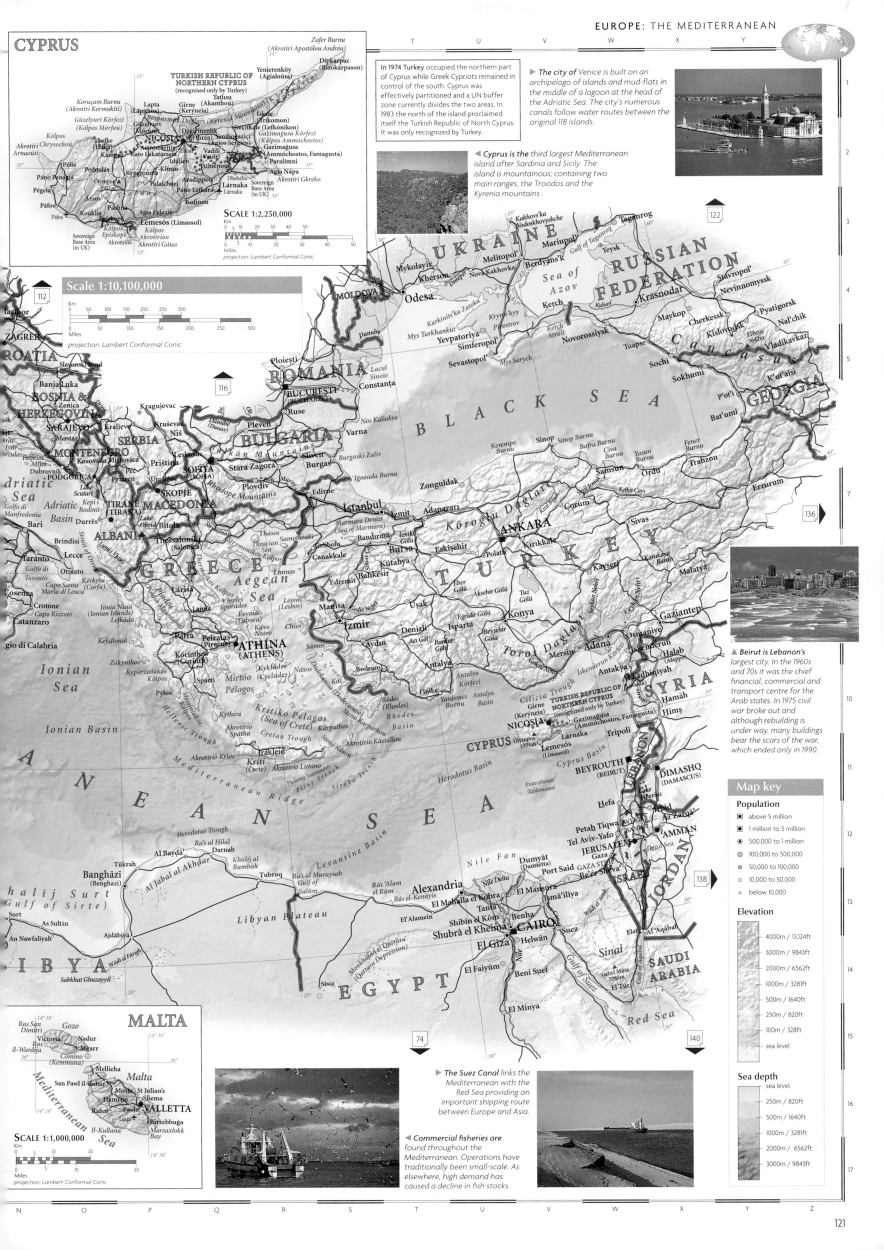

CYPRUS

SCALE 1:2,250,000

projection: Lambert Conformal Conic

Scale 1:10,100,000

projection: Lambert Conformal Conic

In 1974 Turkey occupied the northern part of Cyprus while Greek Cypriots remained in control of the south. Cyprus was effectively partitioned and a UN buffer zone currently divides the two areas. In 1983 the north of the island proclaimed itself the Turkish Republic of North Cyprus. It was only recognized by Turkey.

▶ **The city of** *Venice is built on an archipelago of islands and mud-flats in the middle of a lagoon at the head of the Adriatic Sea. The city's numerous canals follow water routes between the original 118 islands.*

◀ *Cyprus is the third largest Mediterranean island after Sardinia and Sicily. The island is mountainous; containing two main ranges, the Troodos and the Kyrenia mountains .*

▲ *Beirut is Lebanon's largest city. In the 1960s and 70s it was the chief financial, commercial and transport centre for the Arab states. In 1975 civil war broke out and although rebuilding is under way, many buildings bear the scars of the war, which ended only in 1990.*

MALTA

SCALE 1:1,000,000

projection: Lambert Conformal Conic

▶ **The Suez Canal** links the Mediterranean with the Red Sea providing an important shipping route between Europe and Asia.

◀ **Commercial fisheries are** found throughout the Mediterranean. Operations have traditionally been small-scale. As elsewhere, high demand has caused a decline in fish stocks.

Map key

Population

- ▣ above 5 million
- ■ 1 million to 5 million
- ◉ 500,000 to 1 million
- ◉ 100,000 to 500,000
- ⊕ 50,000 to 100,000
- ○ 10,000 to 50,000
- ○ below 10,000

Elevation

- 4000m / 13,124ft
- 3000m / 9843ft
- 2000m / 6562ft
- 1000m / 3281ft
- 500m / 1640ft
- 250m / 820ft
- 100m / 328ft
- sea level

Sea depth

- sea level
- 250m / 820ft
- 500m / 1640ft
- 1000m / 3281ft
- 2000m / 6562ft
- 3000m / 9843ft

The Russian Federation

The Cold War era of global relations was concluded in 1991 with the formal dissolution of the Soviet Union. The Russian Federation declared its separate sovereignty from the foundering communist empire following independence declarations from a number of former Soviet republics. As the leading member of the Commonwealth of Independent States, the Russian Federation has a central role in the development of post-Soviet Eurasia. Crossing 11 time zones, the Russian Federation is almost twice the size of the USA, and with more than 150 ethnic minorities and 21 autonomous republics, regionalist dissent within its own territory remains a danger.

THE RUSSIAN FEDERATION: ADMINISTRATIVE REGIONS

124-125
126-127

The administrative area names in European Russia have been omitted west of the Ural Mountains. Please refer to pages 124–125 and 126–127 where these areas are shown at a larger scale.

► Summer beds of moss and lichen scatter a 90% surface cover of ice across the islands of Franz Josef Land (Zemlya Frantsa-Iosifa), the northernmost land in the eastern hemisphere.

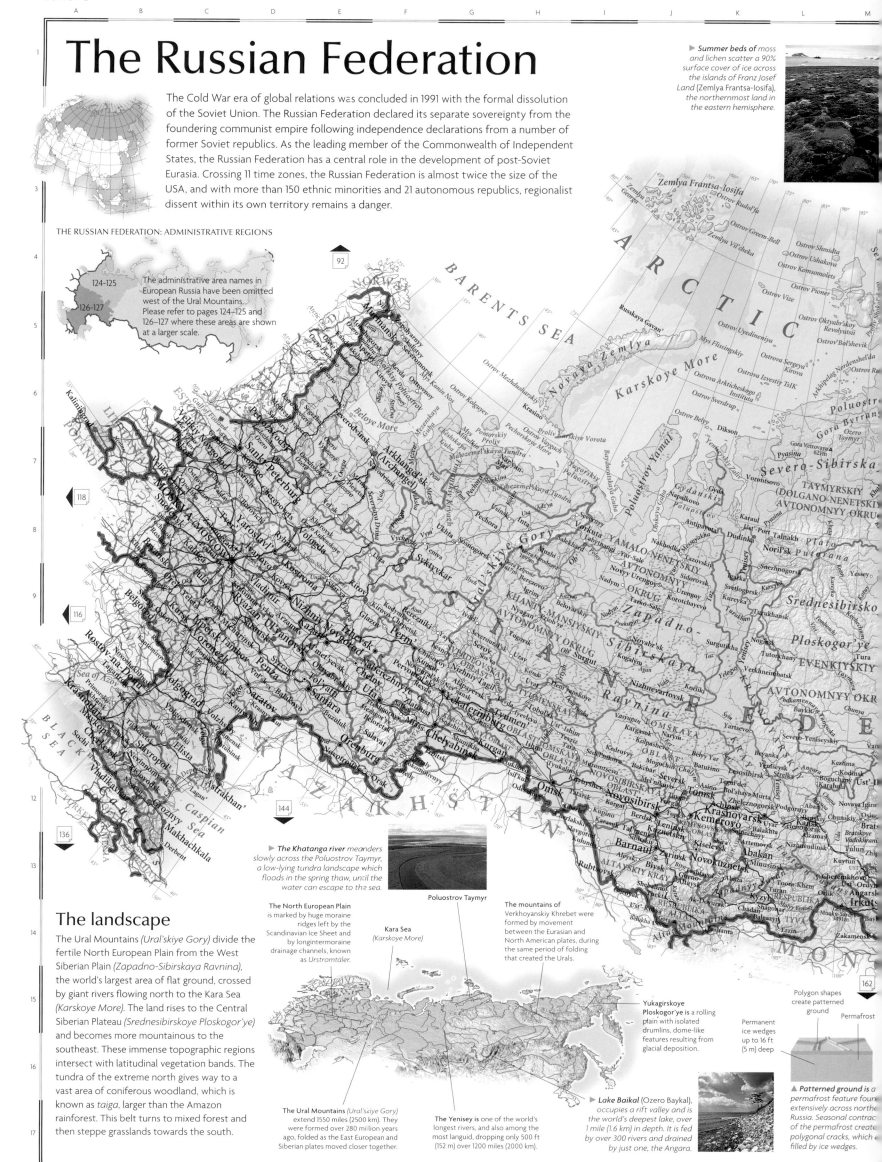

The landscape

The Ural Mountains (Ural'skiye Gory) divide the fertile North European Plain from the West Siberian Plain (Zapadno-Sibirskaya Ravnina), the world's largest area of flat ground, crossed by giant rivers flowing north to the Kara Sea (Karskoye More). The land rises to the Central Siberian Plateau (Srednesibirskoye Ploskogor'ye) and becomes more mountainous to the southeast. These immense topographic regions intersect with latitudinal vegetation bands. The tundra of the extreme north gives way to a vast area of coniferous woodland, which is known as taiga, larger than the Amazon rainforest. This belt turns to mixed forest and then steppe grasslands towards the south.

► The Khatanga river meanders slowly across the Poluostrov Taymyr, a low-lying tundra landscape which floods in the spring thaw, until the water can escape to the sea.

The North European Plain is marked by huge moraine ridges left by the Scandinavian Ice Sheet and by longintermoraine drainage channels, known as Urstromtäler.

Poluostrov Taymyr

Kara Sea (Karskoye More)

The mountains of Verkhoyanskiy Khrebet were formed by movement between the Eurasian and North American plates, during the same period of folding that created the Urals.

The Ural Mountains (Ural'skiye Gory) extend 1550 miles (2500 km). They were formed over 280 million years ago, folded as the East European and Siberian plates moved closer together.

The Yenisey is one of the world's longest rivers, and also among the most languid, dropping only 500 ft (152 m) over 1200 miles (2000 km).

► Lake Baikal (Ozero Baykal), occupies a rift valley and is the world's deepest lake, over 1 mile (1.6 km) in depth. It is fed by over 300 rivers and drained by just one, the Angara.

Yukagirskoye Ploskogor'ye is a rolling plain with isolated drumlins, dome-like features resulting from glacial deposition.

Permanent ice wedges up to 16 ft (5 m) deep

Polygon shapes create patterned ground

Permafrost

▲ Patterned ground is a permafrost feature found extensively across northern Russia. Seasonal contraction of the permafrost creates polygonal cracks, which are filled by ice wedges.

Transport and industry

Raw materials, particularly fossil fuels, ores and precious metals are abundant, yet often found at sites far from habitation. This inherent 'friction of distance' problem was met from the 1930s by Soviet commitment to heavy industry and the strategic location of plants east of the Urals. It has left a pattern of isolated and often vast industrial complexes, in remote areas from Vladivostok to Murmansk, in the far north and across European Russia, with lighter manufacturing concentrated in urban areas.

Major industry and infrastructure

- ✈ aerospace
- 🚗 car manufacture
- ⚗ chemicals
- ⚙ engineering
- gas
- iron & steel
- mining
- oil
- textiles
- timber processing

- ■ capital cities
- major towns
- ⊕ international airports
- — major roads
- major industrial areas

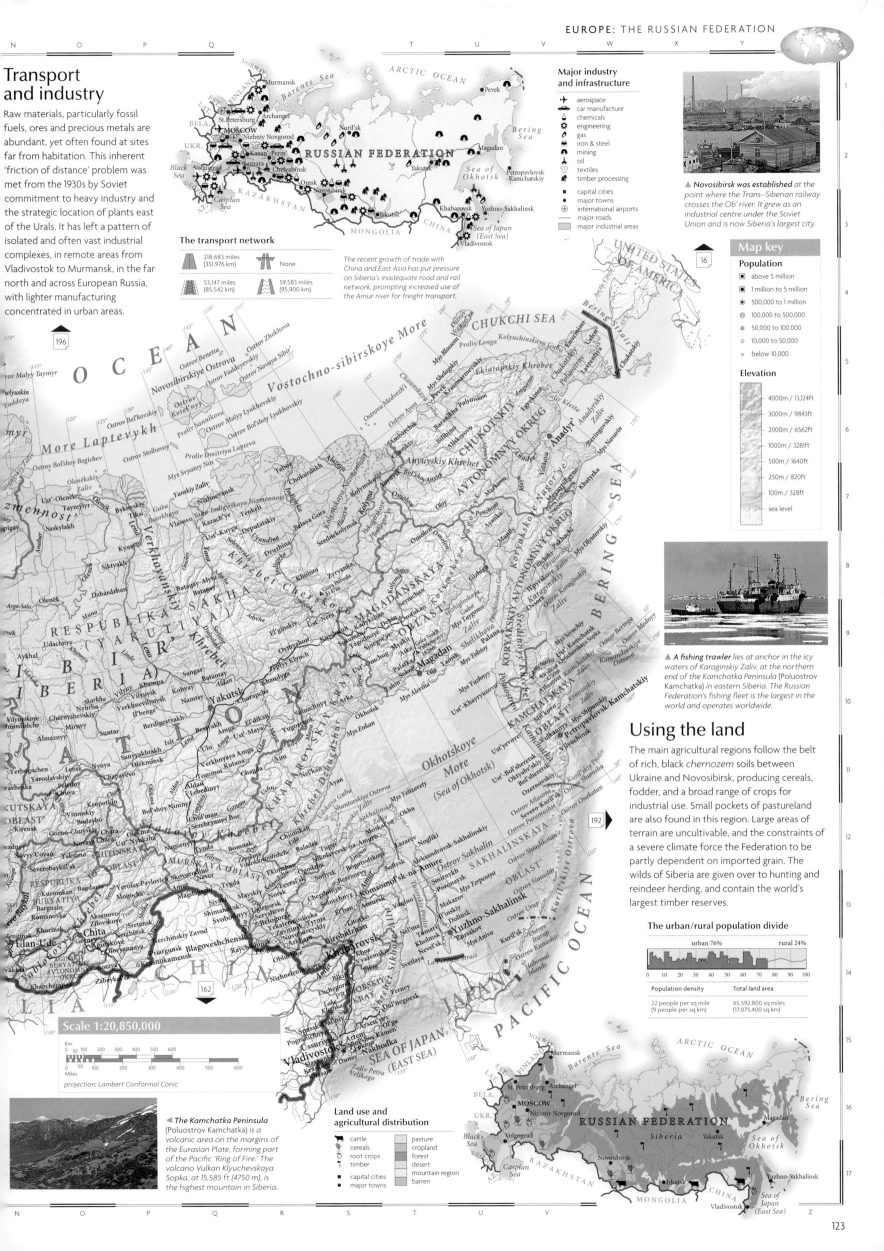

▲ Novosibirsk was established at the point where the Trans–Siberian railway crosses the Ob' river. It grew as an industrial centre under the Soviet Union and is now Siberia's largest city.

The transport network

218,683 miles (351,976 km)	None		
53,147 miles (85,542 km)		59,583 miles (95,900 km)	

The recent growth of trade with China and East Asia has put pressure on Siberia's inadequate road and rail network, prompting increased use of the Amur river for freight transport.

Map key

Population
- ■ above 5 million
- ▣ 1 million to 5 million
- ◉ 500,000 to 1 million
- ◎ 100,000 to 500,000
- ⊕ 50,000 to 100,000
- ⊙ 10,000 to 50,000
- ○ below 10,000

Elevation
- 4000m / 13,124ft
- 3000m / 9843ft
- 2000m / 6562ft
- 1000m / 3281ft
- 500m / 1640ft
- 250m / 820ft
- 100m / 328ft
- sea level

▲ A fishing trawler lies at anchor in the icy waters of Karaginskiy Zaliv, at the northern end of the Kamchatka Peninsula (Poluostrov Kamchatka) in eastern Siberia. The Russian Federation's fishing fleet is the largest in the world and operates worldwide.

Using the land

The main agricultural regions follow the belt of rich, black *chernozem* soils between Ukraine and Novosibirsk, producing cereals, fodder, and a broad range of crops for industrial use. Small pockets of pastureland are also found in this region. Large areas of terrain are uncultivable, and the constraints of a severe climate force the Federation to be partly dependent on imported grain. The wilds of Siberia are given over to hunting and reindeer herding, and contain the world's largest timber reserves.

The urban/rural population divide

urban 76%		rural 24%

0 10 20 30 40 50 60 70 80 90 100

Population density	Total land area
22 people per sq mile (9 people per sq km)	65,592,800 sq miles (17,075,400 sq km)

Scale 1:20,850,000

Km 0 50 100 200 300 400 500 600

Miles 0 50 100 200 300 400 500 600

projection: Lambert Conformal Conic

◄ The Kamchatka Peninsula (Poluostrov Kamchatka) is a volcanic area on the margins of the Eurasian Plate, forming part of the Pacific 'Ring of Fire.' The volcano Vulkan Klyuchevskaya Sopka, at 15,585 ft (4750 m), is the highest mountain in Siberia.

Land use and agricultural distribution

- cattle
- cereals
- root crops
- timber
- ■ capital cities
- major towns

- pasture
- cropland
- forest
- desert
- mountain region
- barren

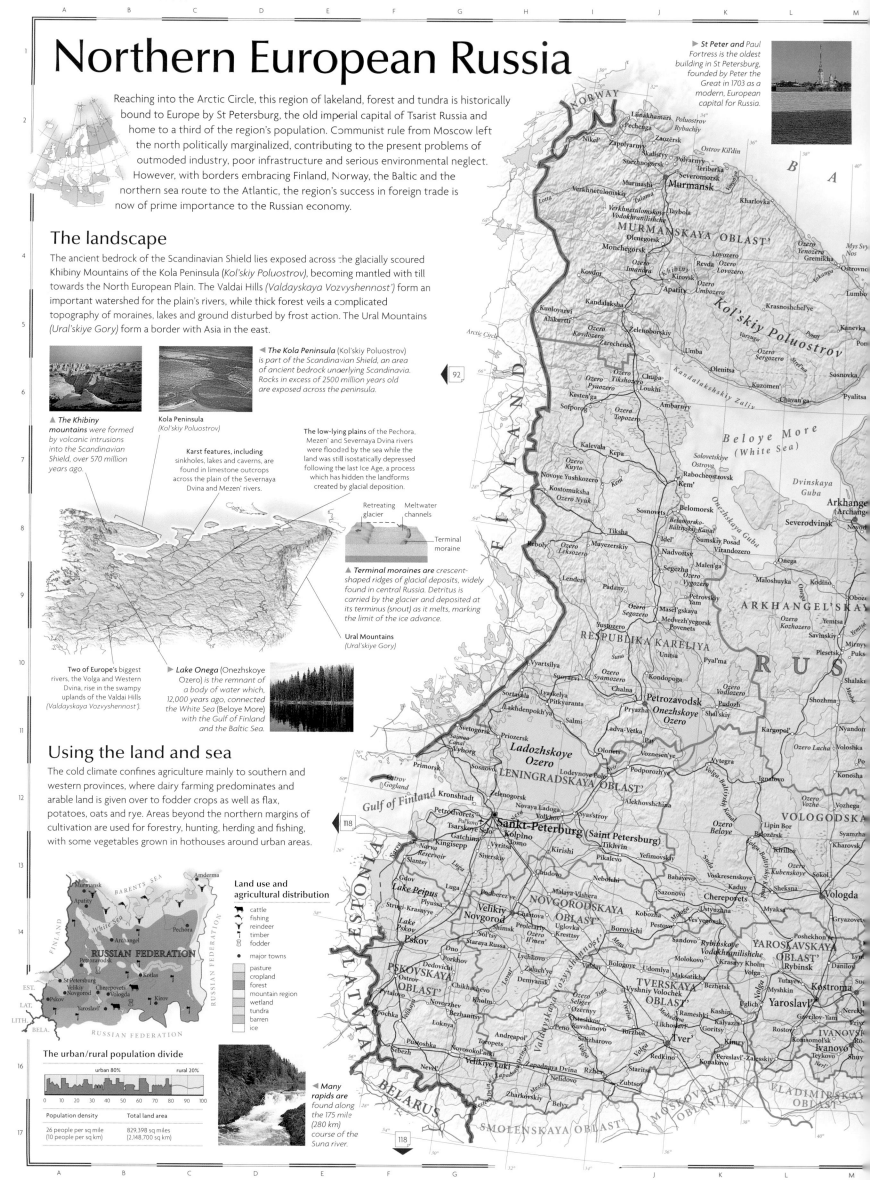

Northern European Russia

Reaching into the Arctic Circle, this region of lakeland, forest and tundra is historically bound to Europe by St Petersburg, the old imperial capital of Tsarist Russia and home to a third of the region's population. Communist rule from Moscow left the north politically marginalized, contributing to the present problems of outmoded industry, poor infrastructure and serious environmental neglect. However, with borders embracing Finland, Norway, the Baltic and the northern sea route to the Atlantic, the region's success in foreign trade is now of prime importance to the Russian economy.

The landscape

The ancient bedrock of the Scandinavian Shield lies exposed across the glacially scoured Khibiny Mountains of the Kola Peninsula (Kol'skiy Poluostrov), becoming mantled with till towards the North European Plain. The Valdai Hills (Valdayskaya Vozvyshennost') form an important watershed for the plain's rivers, while thick forest veils a complicated topography of moraines, lakes and ground disturbed by frost action. The Ural Mountains (Ural'skiye Gory) form a border with Asia in the east.

▲ The Khibiny mountains were formed by volcanic intrusions into the Scandinavian Shield, over 570 million years ago.

Kola Peninsula (Kol'skiy Poluostrov)

Karst features, including sinkholes, lakes and caverns, are found in limestone outcrops across the plain of the Severnaya Dvina and Mezen' rivers.

◄ The Kola Peninsula (Kol'skiy Poluostrov) is part of the Scandinavian Shield, an area of ancient bedrock underlying Scandinavia. Rocks in excess of 2500 million years old are exposed across the peninsula.

The low-lying plains of the Pechora, Mezen' and Severnaya Dvina rivers were flooded by the sea while the land was still isostatically depressed following the last Ice Age, a process which has hidden the landforms created by glacial deposition.

Retreating glacier — Meltwater channels

Terminal moraine

▲ Terminal moraines are crescent-shaped ridges of glacial deposits, widely found in central Russia. Detritus is carried by the glacier and deposited at its terminus (snout) as it melts, marking the limit of the ice advance.

Ural Mountains (Ural'skiye Gory)

Two of Europe's biggest rivers, the Volga and Western Dvina, rise in the swampy uplands of the Valdai Hills (Valdayskaya Vozvyshennost').

► Lake Onega (Onezhskoye Ozero) is the remnant of a body of water which, 12,000 years ago, connected the White Sea (Beloye More) with the Gulf of Finland and the Baltic Sea.

Using the land and sea

The cold climate confines agriculture mainly to southern and western provinces, where dairy farming predominates and arable land is given over to fodder crops as well as flax, potatoes, oats and rye. Areas beyond the northern margins of cultivation are used for forestry, hunting, herding and fishing, with some vegetables grown in hothouses around urban areas.

Land use and agricultural distribution

- cattle
- fishing
- reindeer
- timber
- fodder
- major towns

pasture
cropland
forest
mountain region
wetland
tundra
barren
ice

The urban/rural population divide

urban 80%   rural 20%

0 10 20 30 40 50 60 70 80 90 100

Population density

26 people per sq mile
(10 people per sq km)

Total land area

829,398 sq miles
(2,148,700 sq km)

◄ Many rapids are found along the 175 mile (280 km) course of the Suna river.

► St Peter and Paul Fortress is the oldest building in St Petersburg, founded by Peter the Great in 1703 as a modern, European capital for Russia.

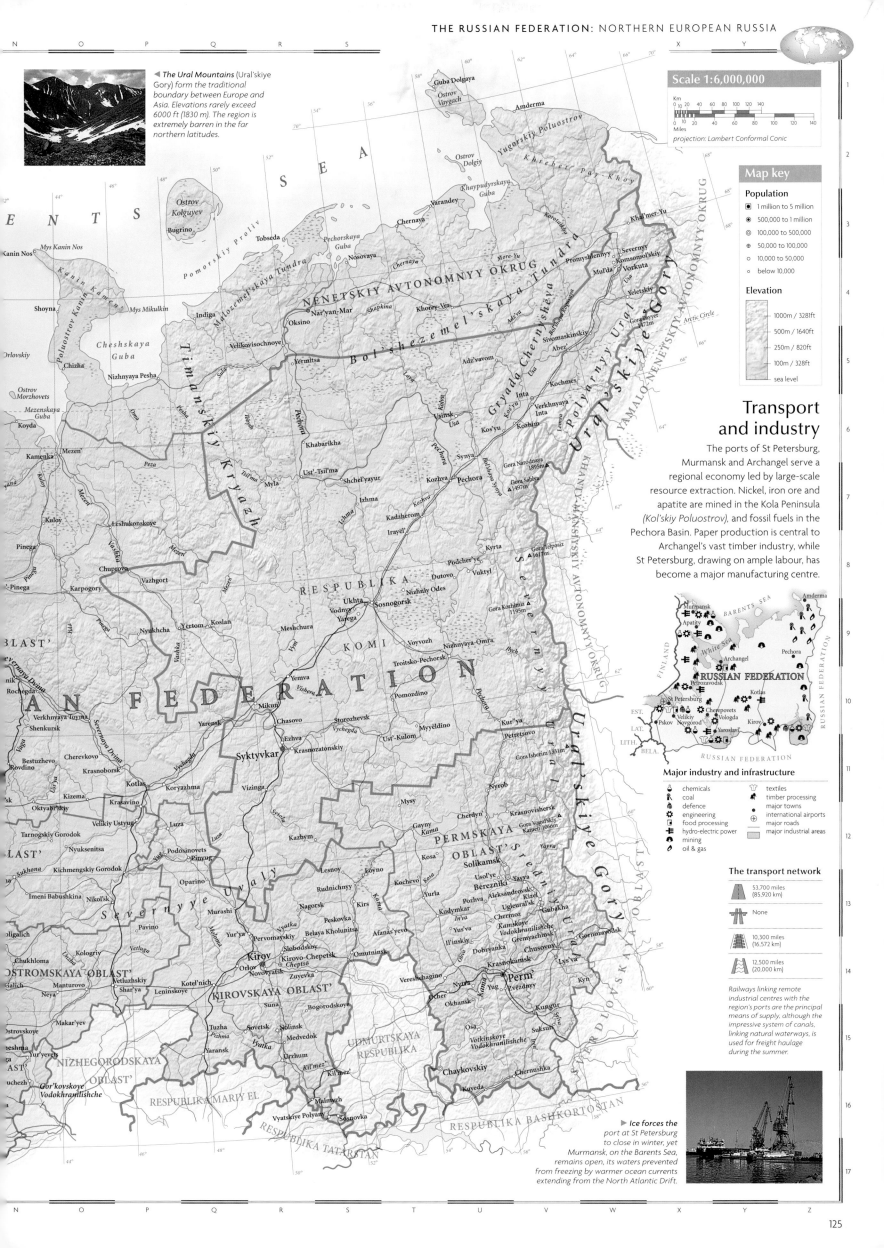

◄ **The Ural Mountains** (Ural'skiye Gory) form the traditional boundary between Europe and Asia. Elevations rarely exceed 6000 ft (1830 m). The region is extremely barren in the far northern latitudes.

Scale 1:6,000,000

Km
Miles

projection: Lambert Conformal Conic

Map key

Population
- ⊡ 1 million to 5 million
- ◉ 500,000 to 1 million
- ⊚ 100,000 to 500,000
- ⊙ 50,000 to 100,000
- ○ 10,000 to 50,000
- ∘ below 10,000

Elevation
- 1000m / 3281ft
- 500m / 1640ft
- 250m / 820ft
- 100m / 328ft
- sea level

Transport and industry

The ports of St Petersburg, Murmansk and Archangel serve a regional economy led by large-scale resource extraction. Nickel, iron ore and apatite are mined in the Kola Peninsula (Kol'skiy Poluostrov), and fossil fuels in the Pechora Basin. Paper production is central to Archangel's vast timber industry, while St Petersburg, drawing on ample labour, has become a major manufacturing centre.

Major industry and infrastructure
- chemicals
- coal
- defence
- engineering
- food processing
- hydro-electric power
- mining
- oil & gas
- textiles
- timber processing
- major towns
- international airports
- major roads
- major industrial areas

The transport network
- 53,700 miles (85,920 km)
- None
- 10,300 miles (16,572 km)
- 12,500 miles (20,000 km)

Railways linking remote industrial centres with the region's ports are the principal means of supply, although the impressive system of canals, linking natural waterways, is used for freight haulage during the summer.

► **Ice forces the** port at St Petersburg to close in winter, yet Murmansk, on the Barents Sea, remains open, its waters prevented from freezing by warmer ocean currents extending from the North Atlantic Drift.

► *Kaliningrad has been a Russian enclave since 1945. The port is an important centre for the Russian Federation's Baltic fishing fleet.*

◄ *St Basil's Cathedral, completed in 1561, stands in Moscow's Red Square next to the Kremlin; the original fortified stronghold of the city.*

Southern European Russia

This region, divided from Asia by desert, seas and mountains, has exerted a powerful influence both east and west since the 13th century. Over 70 years of Communist rule produced a highly urbanized, industrial society dominated by Moscow, which was the capital of the Soviet Union until 1991. Almost two-thirds of the Russian Federation's population live in this core area, with a relatively high *per capita* share of its wealth. However, the rapid growth of a market economy has caused great social upheaval, with rising crime and political instability.

The landscape

Ancient folds in the deep sedimentary strata of the North European Plain have created a sequence of high and low regions. The Central Russian Upland *(Srednerusskaya Vozvyshennost')* in the west is deeply incised by rivers draining into the lowland of the Oka and Don rivers. In the east the Volga, Europe's longest river, flows south to the Caspian Sea, dividing the Volga Uplands *(Privolzhskaya Vozvyshennost')* from the foothills of the Ural Mountains *(Ural'skiye Gory)*. The Caucasus mountains and the Black Sea form a natural border to the southwest.

▲ *A plantation of Scots pine helps consolidate the loose sandy soils of the Meshchera Lowland (Meshcherskaya Nizina), which lies on the bed of an old glacial lake.*

The Smolensk-Moscow Upland *(Smolensko-Moskovskaya Vozvyshennost')* is a series of terminal moraine ridges marking the southern extent of the last glaciation.

Glacial till covers the bedrock to the north of the North European Plain, giving a gentle surface relief.

The lowland of the Oka and Don rivers lies over a broad trough, between the upfolds of the Volga Uplands *(Privolzhskaya Vozvyshennost')* to the east, and the Central Russian Upland *(Srednerusskaya Vozvyshennost')* to the west.

The southern Ural Mountains *(Ural'skiye Gory)* consist of several parallel ranges of ancient fold mountains running from north to south.

Central Russian Upland *(Srednerusskaya Vozvyshennost').*

The flood plain of the Volga forms a long oasis of verdant vegetation, contrasting with the aridity of the surrounding Caspian hinterland.

The marshlands of the Volga Delta are visited by over 260 species of bird each year, migrating between South Africa and Arctic Siberia.

The Caspian Depression is a large downfold (or syncline) which became flooded, forming the Caspian Sea. The shoreline is 98 ft (30 m) below sea level.

◄ *The Caucasus mountains run from the Black Sea to the Caspian Sea. They include El'brus which, at 18,511 ft (5642 m), is the highest point in Europe. It is still uplifting at a rate of 0.4 inches (10 mm) per year.*

Drifting sand occupies large areas of the south, forming dunes up to 50 ft (15 m) high.

Salt dome

Salt dome is forced up and through the rock strata

Sedimentary strata

Salts are forced upwards by denser overlying strata

▲ *Salt domes, rounded hills up to 500 ft (150 m) high, are produced as less dense rock salts are displaced under the extreme pressure of denser, overlying strata and forced up towards the surface creating domes. They are widespread in the Caspian Depression.*

Scale 1:6,000,000

projection: Lambert Conformal Conic

Map key

Population
- ■ above 5 million
- ◼ 1 million to 5 million
- ◉ 500,000 to 1 million
- ◎ 100,000 to 500,000
- ⊕ 50,000 to 100,000
- ○ 10,000 to 50,000
- ∘ below 10,000

Elevation
- 4000m / 13,124ft
- 3000m / 9843ft
- 2000m / 6562ft
- 1000m / 3281ft
- 500m / 1640ft
- 250m / 820ft
- 100m / 328ft
- sea level

Using the land

In the cold, humid north and in the southern Urals (*Ural'skiye Gory*), small grains, potatoes and flax are commonly rotated with legumes which support livestock farming. The rich chernozem (or black earth) areas support diverse crops such as sugar beet, hemp, sunflowers, millet and vegetables. Further south, aridity restricts husbandry to extensive grazing, with intensive fruit and rice cultivation along the oasis of the Volga.

The urban/rural population divide

urban 71% rural 29%

Population density

119 people per sq mile
(46 people per sq km)

Total land area

705,916 sq miles
(1,828,800 sq km)

Land use and agricultural distribution
- sheep
- flax
- potatoes
- rice
- sunflowers
- sugar beet
- timber
- ■ capital cities
- ● major towns
- pasture
- cropland
- forest
- wetland
- mountain region
- tundra

◀ *Industrial plants are massed along the Volga. Environmental stress from decades of unbridled industrial development has prompted widespread concern about pollution levels.*

Transport and industry

Manufacturing is largely based around Moscow and the Volga region, which became a major industrial area during the Second World War. Both Moscow and Nizhniy Novgorod are centres of skilled labour for light manufacturing and engineering. Most of Russia's main chemical plants are located along the Volga, and one of the world's largest car factories was recently opened in Tol'yatti. Processing and machine construction plants use oil, gas and hydro-electric power from the Volga Basin and metallic minerals from the Urals (*Ural'skiye Gory*) and Kursk.

The transport network

250,000 miles (402,000 km) None
28,000 miles (44,800 km) 16,300 miles (26,080 km)

Seventy private and national flag airlines have been created from the reorganization of the state airline Aeroflot, which maintained the world's largest fleet of aircraft during the Soviet era.

Major industry and infrastructure
- aerospace
- car manufacture
- chemicals
- defence
- electronics
- engineering
- gas
- mining
- oil
- textiles
- ■ capital cities
- ● major towns
- ⊕ international airports
- major roads
- major industrial areas

Asia

Asia, the world's largest continent, covers 16,838,365 sq miles (43,608,000 sq km).
It comprises 49 separate countries, including 97% of Turkey and 72% of the
Russian Federation. Almost 60% of the world's population lives in Asia.

● **Greatest extent, North–South:**
4000 miles / 6440 km

■ **Greatest extent, East–West:**
6000 miles / 9650 km

Most northerly point:
Mys Articesku,
Russian Federation
81° 12' N

Mys Dezhneva,
Russian Federation
169° 40' W

Largest lake:
Caspian Sea
143,205 sq miles
(371,000 sq km)

Mys Chelyuskin,
Russian Federation
77° 44' N

Most easterly point:
Mys Dezhneva,
Russian Federation
169° 40' W

Most westerly point:
Bozca Adası, Turkey
26° 2' E

**Lowest recorded
temperature:**
Verkhoyansk,
Russian Federation
-90°F (-68°C)

Arctic Circle

*Baba Bur-nu,
Turkey
26° 4' E*

Lowest point:
Dead Sea,
Israel/Jordan
-1286 ft (-392 m)
below sea level

Kagoshima

Tropic of Cancer

Hodeida

Highest point:
Mount Everest,
China/Nepal
29,035 ft (8850 m)

**Highest recorded
temperature:**
Tirat Tsvi, Israel
129°F (54°C)

Equator

*Tanjong Piai,
Malaysia
1° 16' N*

Most southerly point:
Pulau Pamana,
Indonesia 11° S

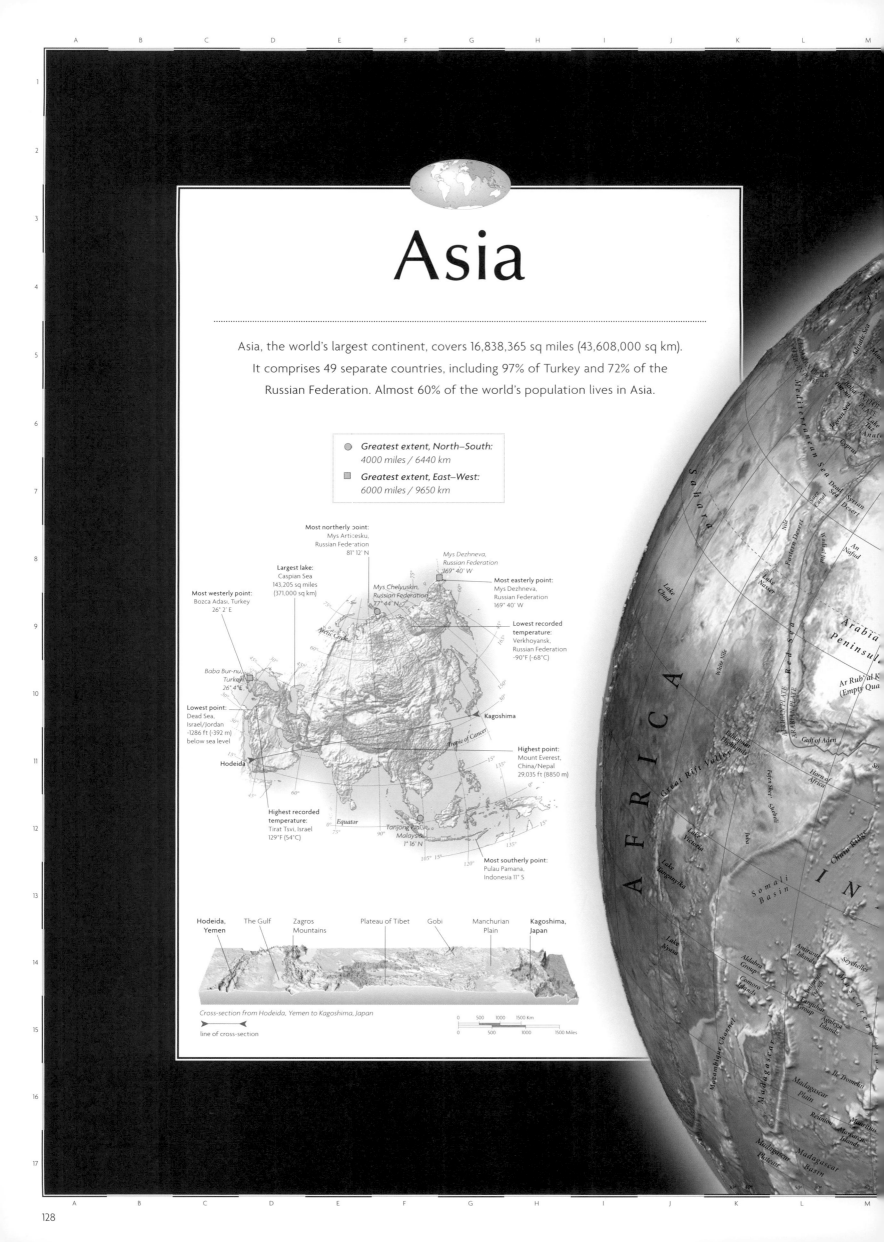

Hodeida,
Yemen | The Gulf | Zagros
Mountains | Plateau of Tibet | Gobi | Manchurian
Plain | Kagoshima,
Japan

Cross-section from Hodeida, Yemen to Kagoshima, Japan

➤ line of cross-section

| 0 | 500 | 1000 | 1500 Km |
| 0 | 500 | 1000 | 1500 Miles |

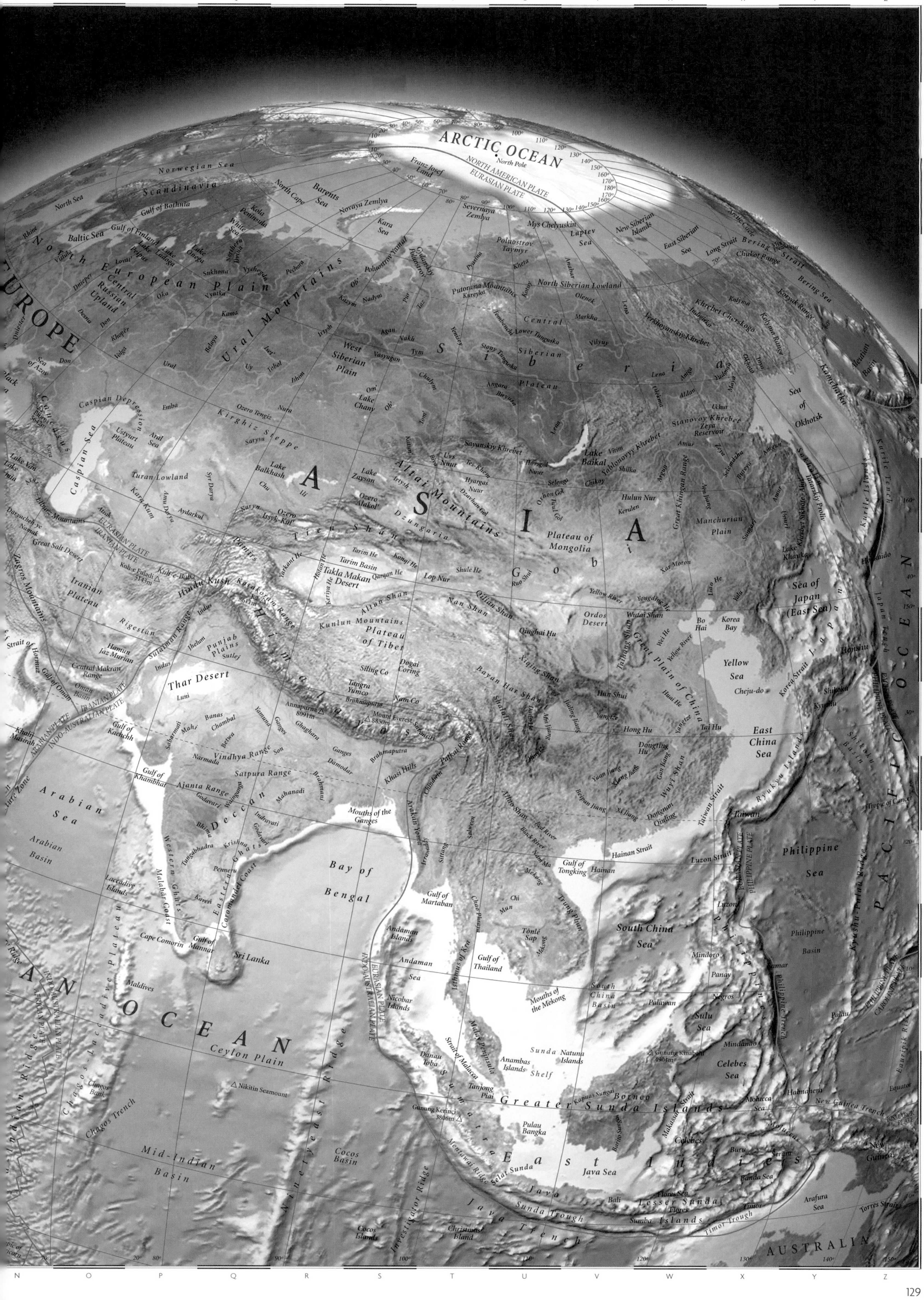

ARCTIC OCEAN

North Pole

NORTH AMERICAN PLATE
EURASIAN PLATE

EUROPE

ASIA

Norwegian Sea
Scandinavia
North Sea
Baltic Sea
Gulf of Bothnia
North Cape
Barents Sea
Novaya Zemlya
Franz Josef Land
Kara Sea
Severnaya Zemlya
Mys Chelyuskin
Poluostrov Taymyr
Laptev Sea
New Siberian Islands
East Siberian Sea
Long Strait
Bering Strait
Bering Sea
Chukot Range
Arctic Circle

Gulf of Finland
Lake Ladoga
Lake Onega
Northern Dvina
White Sea
Kola Peninsula
Pechora
Ob'
Poluostrov Yamal
Putorana Mountains
Khatanga
North Siberian Lowland
Olenek
Khrebet Cherskogo
Kolyma
Koryak Range

North European plain
Central Russian Upland
Ural Mountains
West Siberian Plain
Central Siberian Plateau
Lena
Verkhoyanskiy Khrebet
Indigirka
Sea of Okhotsk
Kurile Trench

Caspian Depression
Kirghiz Steppe
Lake Chany
Altai Mountains
Dzungaria
Plateau of Mongolia
Stanovoy Khrebet
Manchurian Plain
Lake Khanka
Hokkaido

Caspian Sea
Turan Lowland
Kara Kum
Lake Balkhash
Lake Zaysan
Tien Shan
Gobi
Yellow River
Sea of Japan (East Sea)
Honshu

Iranian Plateau
Hindu Kush
Karakoram Range
Takla Makan Desert
Tarim Basin
Kunlun Mountains
Altun Shan
Nan Shan
Qilian Shan
Ordos Desert
Great Plain of China
Korea Bay
Yellow Sea
Cheju-do
Korea Strait
Shikoku
Kyushu

Thar Desert
Punjab Plains
Himalayas
Plateau of Tibet
Nam Co
Bayan Har Shan
Qinghai Hu
Han Shui
Yangtze
East China Sea

Arabian Sea
Gulf of Kachchh
Deccan
Vindhya Range
Satpura Range
Western Ghats
Eastern Ghats
Mouths of the Ganges
Arakan Yoma
Dongting Hu
Ryukyu Islands
Taiwan
Tropic of Cancer
Philippine Sea

Arabian Basin
Laccadive Islands
Malabar Coast
Coromandel Coast
Cape Comorin
Gulf of Mannar
Sri Lanka
Bay of Bengal
Gulf of Martaban
Gulf of Thailand
Andaman Islands
Andaman Sea
South China Sea
Luzon
Luzon Strait
Mindoro
Philippine Basin

Maldives
Ceylon plain
Nicobar Islands
Isthmus of Kra
Gulf of Tongking
Hainan
Hainan Strait
Mouths of the Mekong
South China Basin
Palawan
Panay
Negros
Sulu Sea
Mindanao
Samar
Palau

INDIAN OCEAN
Mid-Indian Basin
Cocos Basin
Christmas Island
Cocos Islands
Ninety East Ridge
Investigator Ridge
Java Trench
Sunda Trough
Java
Java Sea
Greater Sunda Islands
Borneo
Celebes
Celebes Sea
Molucca Sea
Buru
Seram
Banda Sea
New Guinea
New Guinea Trench

PACIFIC OCEAN
Japan Trench

Strait of Malacca
Sumatra
Malay Peninsula
Natuna Islands
Anambas Islands
Sunda Shelf
Pulau Bangka
Danau Toba
Gunung Kerinci 3805m
Selat Sunda
Bali
Lombok
Sumbawa
Flores
Lesser Sunda Islands
Sumba Islands
Timor
Timor Trough
Arafura Sea
Torres Strait

AUSTRALIA

East Indies

129

Physical Asia

The structure of Asia can be divided into two distinct regions. The landscape of northern Asia consists of old mountain chains, shields, plateaux and basins, like the Ural Mountains in the west and the Central Siberian Plateau to the east. To the south of this region, are a series of plateaux and basins, including the vast Plateau of Tibet and the Tarim Basin. In contrast, the landscapes of southern Asia are much younger, formed by tectonic activity beginning about 65 million years ago, leading to an almost continuous mountain chain running from Europe, across much of Asia, and culminating in the mighty Himalayan mountain belt, formed when the Indo-Australian Plate collided with the Eurasian Plate. They are still being uplifted today. North of the mountains lies a belt of deserts, including the Gobi and the Takla Makan. In the far south, tectonic activity has formed narrow island arcs, extending over 4000 miles (7000 km). To the west lies the Arabian Shield, once part of the African Plate. As it was rifted apart from Africa, the Arabian Plate collided with the Eurasian Plate, uplifting the Zagros Mountains.

Coastal Lowlands and Island Arcs

The coastal plains that fringe Southeast Asia contain many large delta systems, caused by high levels of rainfall and erosion of the Himalayas, the Plateau of Tibet and relict loess deposits. To the south is an extensive island archipelago, lying on the drowned Sunda Shelf. Most of these islands are volcanic in origin, caused by the subduction of the Indo-Australian Plate beneath the Eurasian Plate.

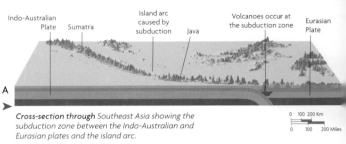

Cross-section through Southeast Asia showing the subduction zone between the Indo-Australian and Eurasian plates and the island arc.

The Indian Shield and Himalayan System

The large shield area beneath the Indian subcontinent is between 2.5 and 3.5 billion years old. As the floor of the southern Indian Ocean spread, it pushed the Indian Shield north. This was eventually driven beneath the Plateau of Tibet. This process closed up the ancient Tethys Sea and uplifted the world's highest mountain chain, the Himalayas. Much of the uplifted rock strata was from the seabed of the Tethys Sea, partly accounting for the weakness of the rocks and the high levels of erosion found in the Himalayas.

Cross-section through the Himalayas showing thrust faulting of the rock strata.

East Asian Plains and Uplands

Several, small, isolated shield areas, such as the Shandong Peninsula, are found in east Asia. Between these stable shield areas, large river systems like the Yangtze and the Yellow River have deposited thick layers of sediment, forming extensive alluvial plains. The largest of these is the Great Plain of China, the relief of which does not rise above 300 ft (100 m).

Map key

Elevation

- 6000m / 19,686ft
- 4000m / 13,124ft
- 3000m / 9843ft
- 2000m / 6562ft
- 1000m / 3281ft
- 500m / 1640ft
- 250m / 820ft
- 100m / 328ft
- sea level

Plate margins
(for explanation see page xiv)

- —— constructive
- △△△ destructive
- —— conservative
- ⋯⋯ uncertain
- —— physiographic regions
- ▶ line of cross-section

Scale 1:63,000,000

Km 0 250 500 1000 1500
Miles 0 250 500 1000 1500

projection: Lambert Azimuthal Equal Area

The Arabian Shield and Iranian Plateau

Approximately five million years ago, rifting of the continental crust split the Arabian Plate from the African Plate and flooded the Red Sea. As this rift spread, the Arabian Plate collided with the Eurasian Plate, transforming part of the Tethys seabed into the Zagros Mountains which run northwest-southeast across western Iran.

Cross-section through southwestern Asia, showing the Mesopotamian Depression, the folded Zagros Mountains and the Iranian Plateau.

Climate

The climate of Asia exhibits marked differences from region to region, with freezing polar conditions in the north, hot and cold deserts in central regions and subtropical conditions throughout the south. Much of this variation can be attributed to enormous mountain barriers and internal depressions found across the continent. Monsoon winds, which reverse semi-annually, cause alternate wet and dry seasons across southern Asia. These air masses moving north from the ocean are stripped of their moisture over the Himalayas causing arid conditions across the Plateau of Tibet. Both the south and east are susceptible to tropical cyclones or typhoons.

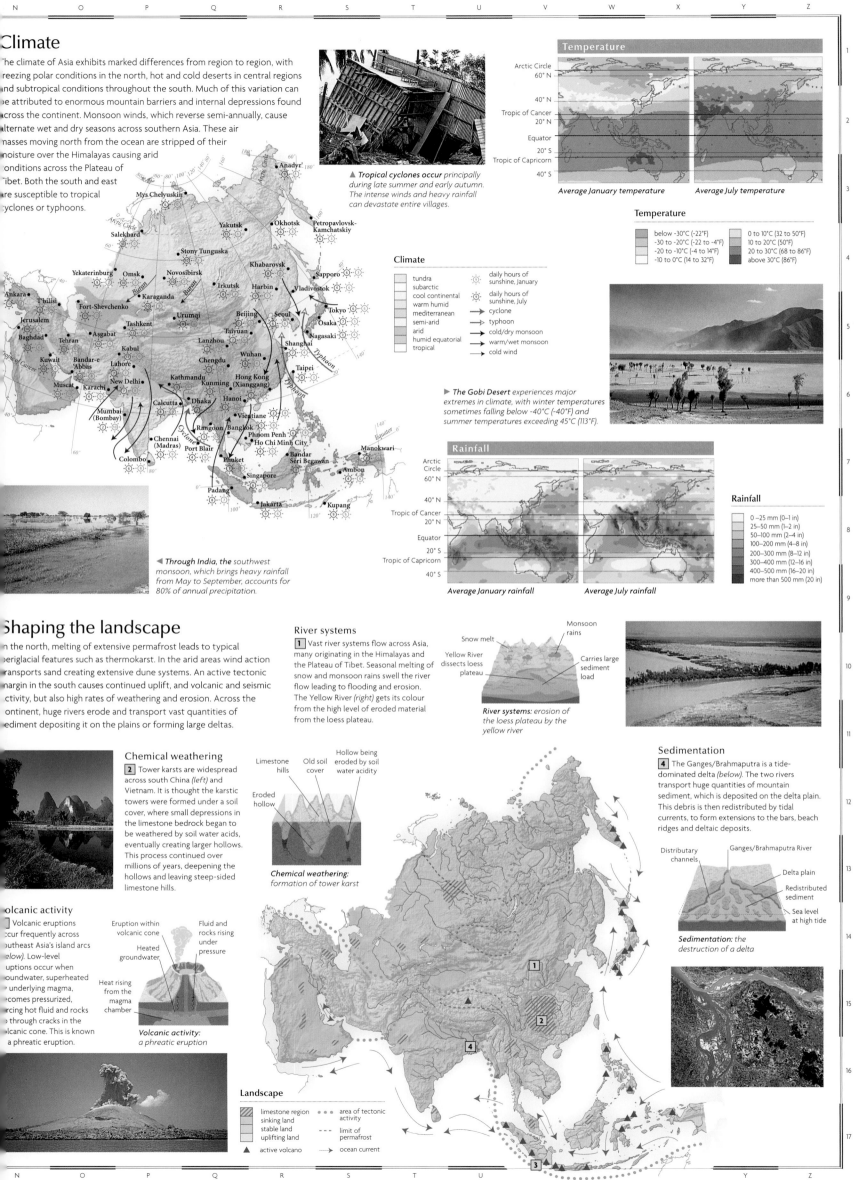

▲ *Tropical cyclones occur* principally during late summer and early autumn. The intense winds and heavy rainfall can devastate entire villages.

Temperature

Arctic Circle 60° N
40° N
Tropic of Cancer 20° N
Equator
20° S
Tropic of Capricorn
40° S

Average January temperature   *Average July temperature*

Temperature

below -30°C (-22°F)	0 to 10°C (32 to 50°F)
-30 to -20°C (-22 to -4°F)	10 to 20°C (50°F)
-20 to -10°C (-4 to 14°F)	20 to 30°C (68 to 86°F)
-10 to 0°C (14 to 32°F)	above 30°C (86°F)

Climate

tundra	daily hours of sunshine, January
subarctic	
cool continental	daily hours of sunshine, July
warm humid	
mediterranean	cyclone
semi-arid	typhoon
arid	cold/dry monsoon
humid equatorial	warm/wet monsoon
tropical	cold wind

▶ *The Gobi Desert* experiences major extremes in climate, with winter temperatures sometimes falling below -40°C (-40°F) and summer temperatures exceeding 45°C (113°F).

Rainfall

Arctic Circle 60° N
40° N
Tropic of Cancer 20° N
Equator
20° S
Tropic of Capricorn
40° S

Average January rainfall   *Average July rainfall*

Rainfall

0 –25 mm (0–1 in)
25–50 mm (1–2 in)
50–100 mm (2–4 in)
100–200 mm (4–8 in)
200–300 mm (8–12 in)
300–400 mm (12–16 in)
400–500 mm (16–20 in)
more than 500 mm (20 in)

◀ *Through India, the* southwest monsoon, which brings heavy rainfall from May to September, accounts for 80% of annual precipitation.

Shaping the landscape

In the north, melting of extensive permafrost leads to typical periglacial features such as thermokarst. In the arid areas wind action transports sand creating extensive dune systems. An active tectonic margin in the south causes continued uplift, and volcanic and seismic activity, but also high rates of weathering and erosion. Across the continent, huge rivers erode and transport vast quantities of sediment depositing it on the plains or forming large deltas.

River systems

1 Vast river systems flow across Asia, many originating in the Himalayas and the Plateau of Tibet. Seasonal melting of snow and monsoon rains swell the river flow leading to flooding and erosion. The Yellow River *(right)* gets its colour from the high level of eroded material from the loess plateau.

Snow melt
Monsoon rains
Yellow River dissects loess plateau
Carries large sediment load

River systems: erosion of the loess plateau by the yellow river

Chemical weathering

2 Tower karsts are widespread across south China *(left)* and Vietnam. It is thought the karstic towers were formed under a soil cover, where small depressions in the limestone bedrock began to be weathered by soil water acids, eventually creating larger hollows. This process continued over millions of years, deepening the hollows and leaving steep-sided limestone hills.

Limestone hills
Old soil cover
Hollow being eroded by soil water acidity
Eroded hollow

Chemical weathering: formation of tower karst

Sedimentation

4 The Ganges/Brahmaputra is a tide-dominated delta *(below)*. The two rivers transport huge quantities of mountain sediment, which is deposited on the delta plain. This debris is then redistributed by tidal currents, to form extensions to the bars, beach ridges and deltaic deposits.

Distributary channels
Ganges/Brahmaputra River
Delta plain
Redistributed sediment
Sea level at high tide

Sedimentation: the destruction of a delta

Volcanic activity

3 Volcanic eruptions occur frequently across Southeast Asia's island arcs *(below)*. Low-level eruptions occur when groundwater, superheated by underlying magma, becomes pressurized, forcing hot fluid and rocks up through cracks in the volcanic cone. This is known as a phreatic eruption.

Eruption within volcanic cone
Fluid and rocks rising under pressure
Heated groundwater
Heat rising from the magma chamber

Volcanic activity: a phreatic eruption

Landscape

limestone region	area of tectonic activity
sinking land	
stable land	limit of permafrost
uplifting land	
▲ active volcano	ocean current

Political Asia

Asia is the world's largest continent, encompassing many different and discrete realms, from the desert Arab lands of the southwest to the subtropical archipelago of Indonesia; from the vast barren wastes of Siberia to the fertile river valleys of China and South Asia, seats of some of the world's most ancient civilizations. The collapse of the Soviet Union has fragmented the north of the continent into the Siberian portion of the Russian Federation, and the new republics of Central Asia. Strong religious traditions heavily influence the politics of South and Southwest Asia. Hindu and Muslim rivalries threaten to upset the political equilibrium in South Asia where India – in terms of population – remains the world's largest democracy. Communist China, another population giant, is reasserting its position as a world political and economic power, while on its doorstep, the dynamic Pacific Rim countries, led by Japan, continue to assert their worldwide economic force.

Population density
(people per sq km)

- below 9
- 10–49
- 50–99
- 100–249
- 250–3999
- above 4000

Population

Some of the world's most populous and least populous regions are in Asia. The plains of eastern China, the Ganges river plains in India, Japan and the Indonesian island of Java, all have very high population densities; by contrast parts of Siberia and the Plateau of Tibet are virtually uninhabited. China has the world's greatest population – 20% of the globe's total – while India, with the second largest, is likely to overtake China within 30 years.

◄ Kolkata's 13 million inhabitants bustle through a maze of crowded, narrow streets. Population densities in India's largest city reach almost 85,000 per sq mile (33,000 per sq km).

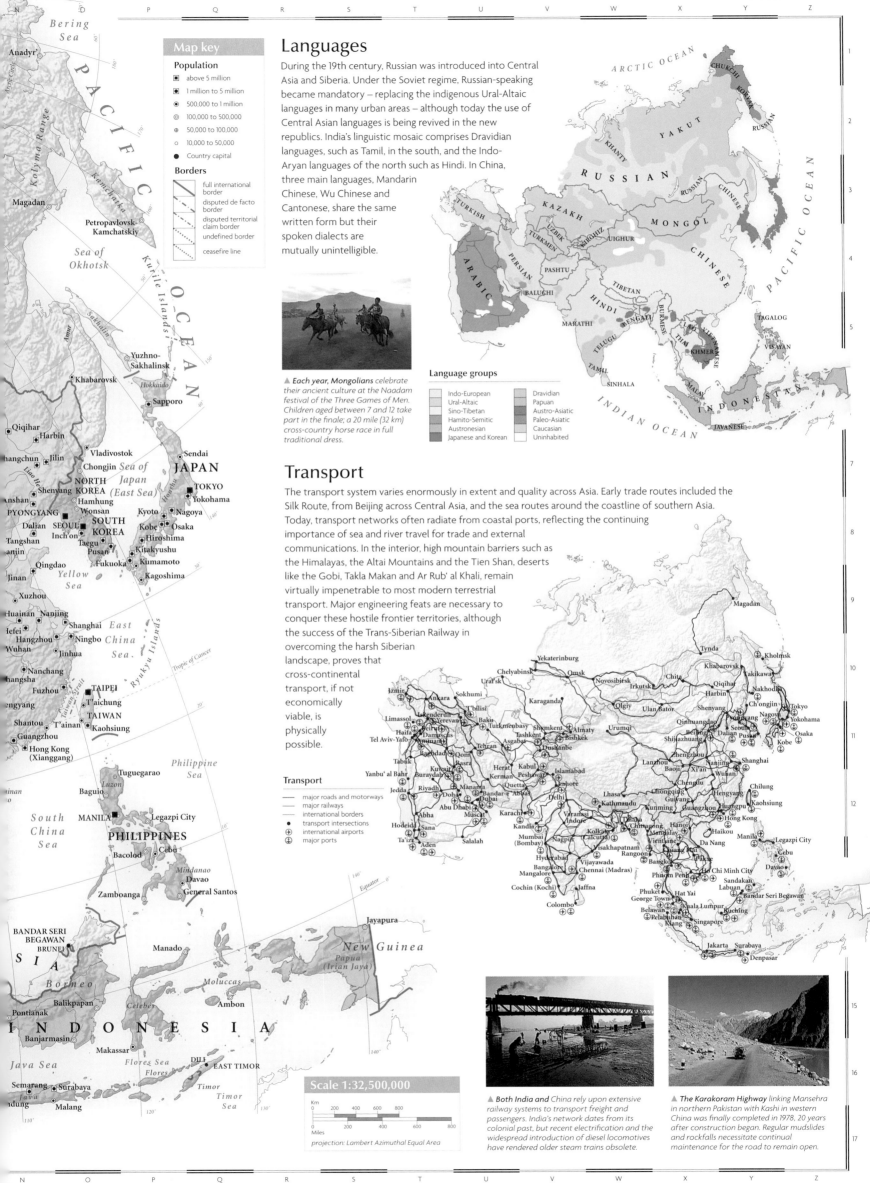

Languages

During the 19th century, Russian was introduced into Central Asia and Siberia. Under the Soviet regime, Russian-speaking became mandatory – replacing the indigenous Ural-Altaic languages in many urban areas – although today the use of Central Asian languages is being revived in the new republics. India's linguistic mosaic comprises Dravidian languages, such as Tamil, in the south, and the Indo-Aryan languages of the north such as Hindi. In China, three main languages, Mandarin Chinese, Wu Chinese and Cantonese, share the same written form but their spoken dialects are mutually unintelligible.

▲ Each year, Mongolians celebrate their ancient culture at the Naadam festival of the Three Games of Men. Children aged between 7 and 12 take part in the finale; a 20 mile (32 km) cross-country horse race in full traditional dress.

Language groups

Indo-European	Dravidian
Ural-Altaic	Papuan
Sino-Tibetan	Austro-Asiatic
Hamito-Semitic	Paleo-Asiatic
Austronesian	Caucasian
Japanese and Korean	Uninhabited

Transport

The transport system varies enormously in extent and quality across Asia. Early trade routes included the Silk Route, from Beijing across Central Asia, and the sea routes around the coastline of southern Asia. Today, transport networks often radiate from coastal ports, reflecting the continuing importance of sea and river travel for trade and external communications. In the interior, high mountain barriers such as the Himalayas, the Altai Mountains and the Tien Shan, deserts like the Gobi, Takla Makan and Ar Rub' al Khali, remain virtually impenetrable to most modern terrestrial transport. Major engineering feats are necessary to conquer these hostile frontier territories, although the success of the Trans-Siberian Railway in overcoming the harsh Siberian landscape, proves that cross-continental transport, if not economically viable, is physically possible.

Transport

- major roads and motorways
- major railways
- international borders
- • transport intersections
- ⊕ international airports
- ⚓ major ports

Map key

Population

- ▪ above 5 million
- ▪ 1 million to 5 million
- ◉ 500,000 to 1 million
- ◎ 100,000 to 500,000
- ⊕ 50,000 to 100,000
- ○ 10,000 to 50,000
- ● Country capital

Borders

- full international border
- disputed de facto border
- disputed territorial claim border
- undefined border
- ceasefire line

▲ Both India and China rely upon extensive railway systems to transport freight and passengers. India's network dates from its colonial past, but recent electrification and the widespread introduction of diesel locomotives have rendered older steam trains obsolete.

▲ The Karakoram Highway linking Mansehra in northern Pakistan with Kashi in western China was finally completed in 1978, 20 years after construction began. Regular mudslides and rockfalls necessitate continual maintenance for the road to remain open.

Scale 1:32,500,000

Km
0   200   400   600   800

Miles
0   200   400   600   800

projection: Lambert Azimuthal Equal Area

Asian resources

Although agriculture remains the economic mainstay of most Asian countries, the number of people employed in agriculture has steadily declined, as new industries have been developed during the past 30 years. China, Indonesia, Malaysia, Thailand and Turkey have all experienced far-reaching structural change in their economies, while the breakup of the Soviet Union has created a new economic challenge in the Central Asian republics. The countries of The Gulf illustrate the rapid transformation from rural nomadism to modern, urban society which oil wealth has brought to parts of the continent. Asia's most economically dynamic countries, Japan, Singapore, South Korea, and Taiwan, fringe the Pacific Ocean and are known as the Pacific Rim. In contrast, other Southeast Asian countries like Laos and Cambodia remain both economically and industrially underdeveloped.

Industry

East Asian industry leads the continent in both productivity and efficiency; electronics, hi-tech industries, car manufacture and shipbuilding are important. The so-called economic 'tigers' of the Pacific Rim are Japan, South Korea and Taiwan and in recent years China has rediscovered its potential as an economic superpower. Heavy industries such as engineering, chemicals, and steel typify the industrial complexes along the corridor created by the Trans-Siberian Railway, the Fergana Valley in Central Asia, and also much of the huge industrial plain of east China. The discovery of oil in The Gulf has brought immense wealth to countries that previously relied on subsistence agriculture on marginal desert land.

Standard of living

Despite Japan's high standards of living, and Southwest Asia's oil-derived wealth, immense disparities exist across the continent. Afghanistan remains one of the world's most underdeveloped nations, as do the mountain states of Nepal and Bhutan. Further rapid population growth is exacerbating poverty and overcrowding in many parts of India and Bangladesh.

Standard of living
(UN human development index)

low

high

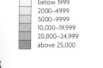

▲ *On a small island at the southern tip of the Malay Peninsula lies Singapore, one of the Pacific Rim's most vibrant economic centres. Multinational banking and finance form the core of the city's wealth.*

GNI per capita (US$)

below 1999
2000–4999
5000–9999
10,000–19,999
20,000–24,999
above 25,000

Industry

✈ aerospace	🖶 printing & publishing
🍺 brewing	🚢 shipbuilding
🚗 car/vehicle manufacture	sugar processing
cement	tea processing
chemicals	textiles
electronics	timber processing
engineering	tobacco processing
finance	coal
fish processing	oil
food processing	gas
hi-tech industry	• industrial cities
iron & steel	major industrial areas
pharmaceuticals	

ARCTIC OCEAN

PACIFIC OCEAN

Sea of Okhotsk

RUSSIAN FEDERATION

Yakutsk

Trans-Siberian Railway

JAPAN

Khabarovsk

Vladivostok

Bratsk

Krasnoyarsk

Yekaterinburg

Chelyabinsk

Magnitogorsk

Omsk

Kemerovo

Irkutsk

Novosibirsk

Novokuznetsk

Harbin

Tokyo

Nagoya

Kobe

KAZAKHSTAN

Karaganda

Ulan Bator

MONGOLIA

Shenyang

NORTH KOREA

Pyongyang

Seoul

SOUTH KOREA

Pusan

Istanbul

Izmir

Ankara

GEORGIA

Tbilisi

ARMENIA

Yerevan

AZERB.

Baku

Caspian Sea

Aral Sea

UZBEKISTAN

Tashkent

Almaty

Urumqi

Beijing

Tianjin

Dalian

Qingdao

TURKEY

CYPRUS

LEBANON

Beirut

SYRIA

Damascus

Tel Aviv-Yafo

ISRAEL

Amman

JORDAN

Kirkuk

TURKMENISTAN

Asgabat

KYRGYZSTAN

Farghona

Dushanbe

TAJIKISTAN

Taiyuan

Jinan

Baghdad

Tehran

Isfahan

Lanzhou

Zhengzhou

Nanjing

Shanghai

IRAQ

Basra

Kuwait

KUWAIT

IRAN

AFGHANISTAN

Rawalpindi

Xi'an

Wuhan

SAUDI ARABIA

Jedda

Riyadh

Ad Damman

BAHRAIN

QATAR

Abu Dhabi

Dubai

UAE

Gulf of Oman

OMAN

YEMEN

Gulf of Aden

Chengdu

Chongqing

Taipei

TAIWAN

Lahore

PAKISTAN

Delhi

NEPAL

BHUTAN

Kunming

Guangzhou

Hong Kong

Karachi

Kanpur

BANGLADESH

Dhaka

Chattagong

BURMA

Mandalay

Hanoi

LAOS

VIETNAM

Ahmadabad

Indore

Jamshedpur

Kolkata (Calcutta)

Nagpur

Da Nang

South China Sea

Manila

PHILIPPINES

Mumbai (Bombay)

INDIA

Rangoon

THAILAND

Bangkok

CAMBODIA

Red Sea

Arabian Sea

Bangalore

Chennai (Madras)

Ho Chi Minh City

SRI LANKA

INDIAN OCEAN

MALAYSIA

BRUNEI

Kuala Lumpur

Singapore

SINGAPORE

INDONESIA

Jakarta

Surabaya

EAST TIMOR

◄ *Traditional industries are still crucial to many rural economies across Asia. Here, on the Vietnamese coast, salt has been extracted from seawater by evaporation and is being loaded into a van to take to market.*

▲ *Iron and steel, engineering and shipbuilding typify the heavy industry found in eastern China's industrial cities, especially the nation's leading manufacturing centre, Shanghai.*

Environmental issues

The transformation of Uzbekistan by the former Soviet Union into the world's fifth largest producer of cotton led to the diversion of several major rivers for irrigation. Starved of this water, the Aral Sea diminished in volume by over 75% since 1960, irreversibly altering the ecology of the area. Heavy industries in eastern China have polluted coastal waters, rivers and urban air, while in Burma, Malaysia and Indonesia, ancient hardwood rainforests are felled faster than they can regenerate.

▲ Although Siberia remains a quintessentially frozen, inhospitable wasteland, vast untapped mineral reserves – especially the oil and gas of the West Siberian Plain – have lured industrial development to the area since the 1950s and 1960s.

Environmental issues

- tropical forest
- forest destroyed
- desert
- desertification
- acid rain
- polluted rivers
- marine pollution
- heavy marine pollution
- radioactive contamination
- poor urban air quality

◄ The long-term environmental impact of the Gulf War (1991) is still uncertain. As Iraqi troops left Kuwait, equipment was abandoned to rust and thousands of oil wells were set alight, pouring crude oil into The Gulf.

Mineral resources

At least 60% of the world's known oil and gas deposits are found in Asia; notably the vast oil fields of The Gulf, and the less-exploited oil and gas fields of the Ob' basin in west Siberia. Immense coal reserves in Siberia and China have been utilized to support large steel industries. Southeast Asia has some of the world's largest deposits of tin, found in a belt running down the Malay Peninsula to Indonesia.

Mineral resources

- oil field
- gas field
- coal field
- chromite
- copper
- gold
- iron
- lead
- nickel
- platinum
- tin
- wolfram

Using the land and sea

Vast areas of Asia remain uncultivated as a result of unsuitable climatic and soil conditions. In favourable areas such as river deltas, farming is intensive. Rice is the staple crop of most Asian countries, grown in paddy fields on waterlogged alluvial plains and terraced hillsides, and often irrigated for higher yields. Across the black earth region of the Eurasian steppe in southern Siberia and Kazakhstan, wheat farming is the dominant activity. Cash crops, like tea in Sri Lanka and dates in the Arabian Peninsula, are grown for export, and provide valuable income. The sovereignty of the rich fishing grounds in the South China Sea is disputed by China, Malaysia, Taiwan, the Philippines and Vietnam, because of potential oil reserves.

▲ Date palms have been cultivated in oases throughout the Arabian Peninsula since antiquity. In addition to the fruit, palms are used for timber, fuel, rope, and for making vinegar, syrup and a liquor known as arrack.

◄ Rice terraces blanket the landscape across the small Indonesian island of Bali. The large amounts of water needed to grow rice have resulted in Balinese farmers organizing water-control co-operatives.

Using the land and sea

- cropland
- desert
- forest
- mountain region
- pasture
- tundra
- wetland
- major conurbations
- cattle
- pigs
- goats
- sheep
- coconuts
- corn (maize)
- cotton
- dates
- fishing
- fruit
- jute
- peanuts
- rice
- rubber
- shellfish
- soya beans
- sugar beet
- sugar cane
- tea
- timber
- wheat

Turkey & the Caucasus

ARMENIA, AZERBAIJAN, GEORGIA, TURKEY

This region occupies the fragmented junction between Europe, Asia and the Russian Federation. Sunni Islam provides a common identity for the secular state of Turkey, which the revered leader Kemal Atatürk established from the remnants of the Ottoman Empire after the First World War. Turkey has a broad resource base and expanding trade links with Europe, but the east is relatively undeveloped and strife between the state and a large Kurdish minority has yet to be resolved. Georgia is similarly challenged by ethnic separatism, while the Christian state of Armenia and the mainly Muslim and oil-rich Azerbaijan are locked in conflict over the territory of Nagorno-Karabakh.

Using the land and sea

Turkey is largely self-sufficient in food. The irrigated Black Sea coastlands have the world's highest yields of hazelnuts. Tobacco, cotton, sultanas, tea and figs are the region's main cash crops and a great range of fruit and vegetables are grown. Wine grapes are among the labour-intensive crops which allow full use of limited agricultural land in the Caucasus. Sturgeon fishing is particularly important in Azerbaijan.

Transport and industry

Turkey leads the region's well-diversified economy. Petrochemicals, textiles, engineering and food processing are the main industries. Azerbaijan is able to export oil, while the other states rely heavily on hydro-electric power and imported fuel. Georgia produces precision machinery. War and earthquake damage have devastated Armenia's infrastructure.

▲ *Azerbaijan has substantial oil reserves, located in and around the Caspian Sea. They were some of the earliest oilfields in the world to be exploited.*

Land use and agricultural distribution

- cattle
- goats
- cotton
- fishing
- fruit
- hazelnuts
- olives
- sugar beet
- tobacco
- vineyards

- ▪ capital cities
- • major towns

pasture
cropland
forest

The urban/rural population divide

urban 72%   rural 28%

0 10 20 30 40 50 60 70 80 90 100

Population density	Total land area
238 people per sq mile (92 people per sq km)	368,912 sq miles (955,730 sq km)

Major industry and infrastructure

- carpet weaving
- cement
- chemicals
- coal
- engineering
- food processing
- oil
- textiles
- tourism
- vehicle manufacture

- ▪ capital cities
- • major towns
- ✈ international airports
- — major roads
- major industrial areas

The transport network

114,867 miles (184,882 km)

5778 miles (9300 km)

8120 miles (13,069 km)

745 miles (1200 km)

Physical and political barriers have severely limited communications between Armenia, Georgia and Azerbaijan. Turkey has a relatively well-developed transport network.

▲ *For many centuries, Istanbul has held tremendous strategic importance as a crucial gateway between Europe and Asia. Founded by the Greeks as Byzantium, the city became the centre of the East Roman Empire and was known as Constantinople to the Romans. From the 15th century onwards the city became the centre of the great Ottoman Empire.*

The landscape

The deeply-eroded hills and salty basins of the Anatolian Plateau are bordered by several mountain ranges along the Black Sea coast, and the limestone Taurus Mountains *(Toros Daglari)* in the south. A lowland trough divides the Caucasus and the Lesser Caucasus, which form a formidable barrier of peaks in the north.

Limestone weathering in the Anatolian Plateau

Eroded gully

High plateau

Layers of tephra

Remnant landforms

▲ **In central Turkey,** rainwater has chemically weathered away numerous layers of limestone, leaving isolated outcrops and pinnacles and deep eroded gullies.

▶ **The Caucasus are** fold mountains, which formed around the same time as the Taurus Mountains *(Toros Daglari)* around 65 million years ago and have since been modified by volcanic erruptions.

▲ **The white rock terraces** at Pamukkale in western Turkey were formed when underground water, heated by volcanic activity, dissolved minerals in the rocks. When the water reached the surface and evaporated the minerals were left behind in these extraordinary formations.

The straits of the Bosporus and the Dardanelles, respectively linking the Black and Mediterranean seas with the Sea of Marmara, formed after the last Ice Age, when a rising sea level caused these former river valleys to be flooded.

Many of the rivers crossing the Anatolian Plateau never reach the sea, but drain into salt marshes and shallow salt lakes such as Lake Tuz *(Tuz Gölü),* where much of the water is lost to evaporation.

Anatolian Plateau

Pamukkale

Lava has flowed over large areas of the Lesser Caucasus within the last five million years, producing extensive basalt plateaux.

The earthquake that struck Armenia in 1988 killed over 55,000 people and devastated the country's infrastructure.

Long, parallel mountain ranges run from east to west into the Aegean Sea, which has risen since the last Ice Age to form a drowned coastline of numerous islands and extended inlets.

The folded peaks of the Taurus Mountains *(Toros Daglari)* were formed 60–65 million years ago, at the same time as the Alps. The rock is mainly limestone, with deep caves, gorges and underground rivers.

The Cilician Gates *(Gulek Bogazi),* a major pass through the Taurus Mountains *(Toros Daglari),* is the point where streams flow from the interior plateau onto the lowland of Adana.

Thick, temperate forest veils the seaward slopes of the Kaçkar Daglari. The southern slopes, which lie in a rainshadow, are dry and barren.

The granite massif near Surami divides the lowlands of Georgia from the oil-rich basin of Azerbaijan's Kura river, which has built a large delta into the Caspian Sea.

The shallow, saline Lake Van *(Van Gölü)* is the largest lake in Turkey. Dry terraces mark a previous shoreline 181 ft (55 m) above the present water level.

The volcanic cone of Mount Ararat is the highest peak in Turkey, with an altitude of 16,853 ft (5137 m).

▶ **Since the 6th century** BC, the pinnacles and caves of east-central Anatolia have been utilized as dwellings. Many are still inhabited today.

Map key

Population
- ■ above 5 million
- ▣ 1 million to 5 million
- ◉ 500,000 to 1 million
- ◎ 100,000 to 500,000
- ⊕ 50,000 to 100,000
- ○ 10,000 to 50,000
- ○ below 10,000

Elevation
- 4000m / 13,124ft
- 3000m / 9843ft
- 2000m / 6562ft
- 1000m / 3281ft
- 500m / 1640ft
- 250m / 820ft
- 100m / 328ft
- sea level

Scale 1:4,500,000

Km
0 20 40 60 80 100 120

Miles
0 20 40 60 80 100 120

projection: Lambert Conformal Conic

▲ **The fisheries of** Azerbaijan are noted for their hauls of sturgeon, and the Caspian Sea accounts for 80% of the world's total catch. However, stocks are now under serious threat due to overfishing.

▲ **Traditional steam baths** are found throughout the region, and are used for socializing as well as for bathing.

The Near East

IRAQ, ISRAEL, JORDAN, LEBANON, SYRIA

Some of the world's oldest civilizations developed in this region – the Fertile Crescent – which is venerated by Jews, Muslims and Christians, but torn by competing religious, ethnic and national claims to the land. Turkish Ottoman rule ended with the First World War and the region was divided into areas administered by Britain and France. The UN endorsed calls for a Jewish homeland in what was then Palestine and in 1948 the state of Israel was declared. Hostility towards the Jewish state led to a series of wars with its Arab neighbours. After 2000, attempts to broker peaceful resolutions with both the Palestinian population and with adjacent Arab states were hampered by a revival of Islamic militarism and conflicting international interests in the oil-rich region. This led to an Israeli retrenchment and culminated in a US-led invasion of Iraq in 2003, which toppled the Ba'athist regime of Saddam Hussein in the name of a 'war on terror'.

Using the land and sea

Water scarcity limits cropland to the north and to areas watered principally by the Tigris, Euphrates and Jordan rivers. In Israel, new irrigation techniques are allowing cultivation in the arid Negev. Wheat is the chief grain and large areas of scrub support livestock herding. Commercial produce includes dates, tobacco, citrus fruits, olives, grapes and cotton, which is Syria's main export crop. Fishing is still important in the Mediterranean.

The urban/rural population divide

urban 70%   rural 30%

Population density	Total land area
217 people per sq mile (84 people per sq km)	325,460 sq miles (843,160 sq km)

Land use and agricultural distribution

- sheep
- cereals
- citrus fruits
- cotton
- dates
- fishing
- rice
- tobacco
- ■ capital cities
- ■ major towns
- pasture
- cropland
- wetland
- desert

Transport and industry

The petrochemical industry is well established, and central to the economies of Syria and Iraq, which was the world's second largest oil exporter before the war with Iran which began in 1980. Lebanon has traditionally been a centre for commerce, while Israel has a well-diversified economy with an expanding tourist industry, despite few natural resources.

The transport network

49,859 miles (80,249 km)	
1365 miles (2197 km)	
3826 miles (6158 km)	
1171 miles (1885 km)	

Jordan's sea port of Al 'Aqabah is connected to Damascus in Syria by road and rail. This route to the Red Sea provides for large exports of phosphate and trade with states in The Gulf.

Major industry and infrastructure

- car manufacture
- cement
- chemicals
- electronics
- finance
- food processing
- iron & steel
- oil
- oil refining
- textiles
- ■ capital cities
- ■ major towns
- ⊕ international airports
- major roads
- major industrial areas

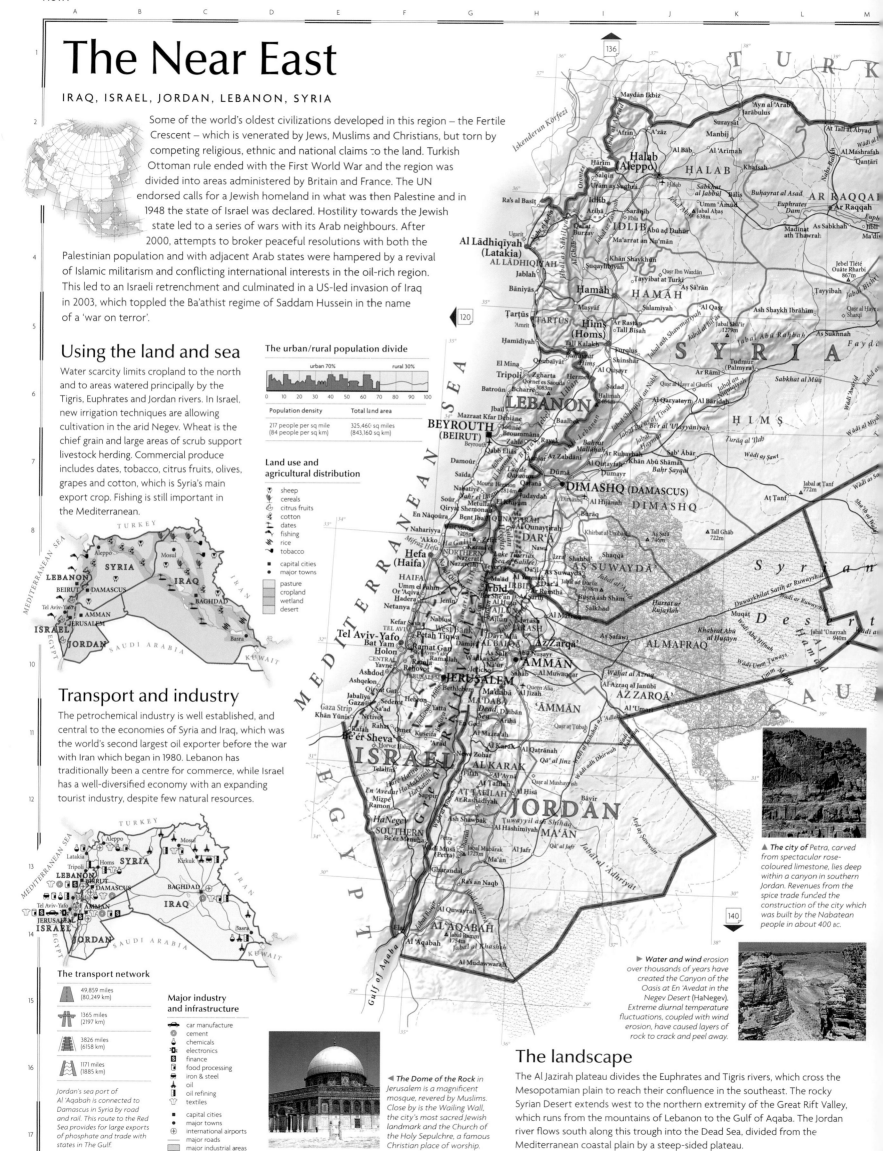

▲ The city of Petra, carved from spectacular rose-coloured limestone, lies deep within a canyon in southern Jordan. Revenues from the spice trade funded the construction of the city which was built by the Nabatean people in about 400 BC.

▶ Water and wind erosion over thousands of years have created the Canyon of the Oasis at En 'Avedat in the Negev Desert (HaNegev). Extreme diurnal temperature fluctuations, coupled with wind erosion, have caused layers of rock to crack and peel away.

▲ The Dome of the Rock in Jerusalem is a magnificent mosque, revered by Muslims. Close by is the Wailing Wall, the city's most sacred Jewish landmark and the Church of the Holy Sepulchre, a famous Christian place of worship.

The landscape

The Al Jazirah plateau divides the Euphrates and Tigris rivers, which cross the Mesopotamian plain to reach their confluence in the southeast. The rocky Syrian Desert extends west to the northern extremity of the Great Rift Valley, which runs from the mountains of Lebanon to the Gulf of Aqaba. The Jordan river flows south along this trough into the Dead Sea, divided from the Mediterranean coastal plain by a steep-sided plateau.

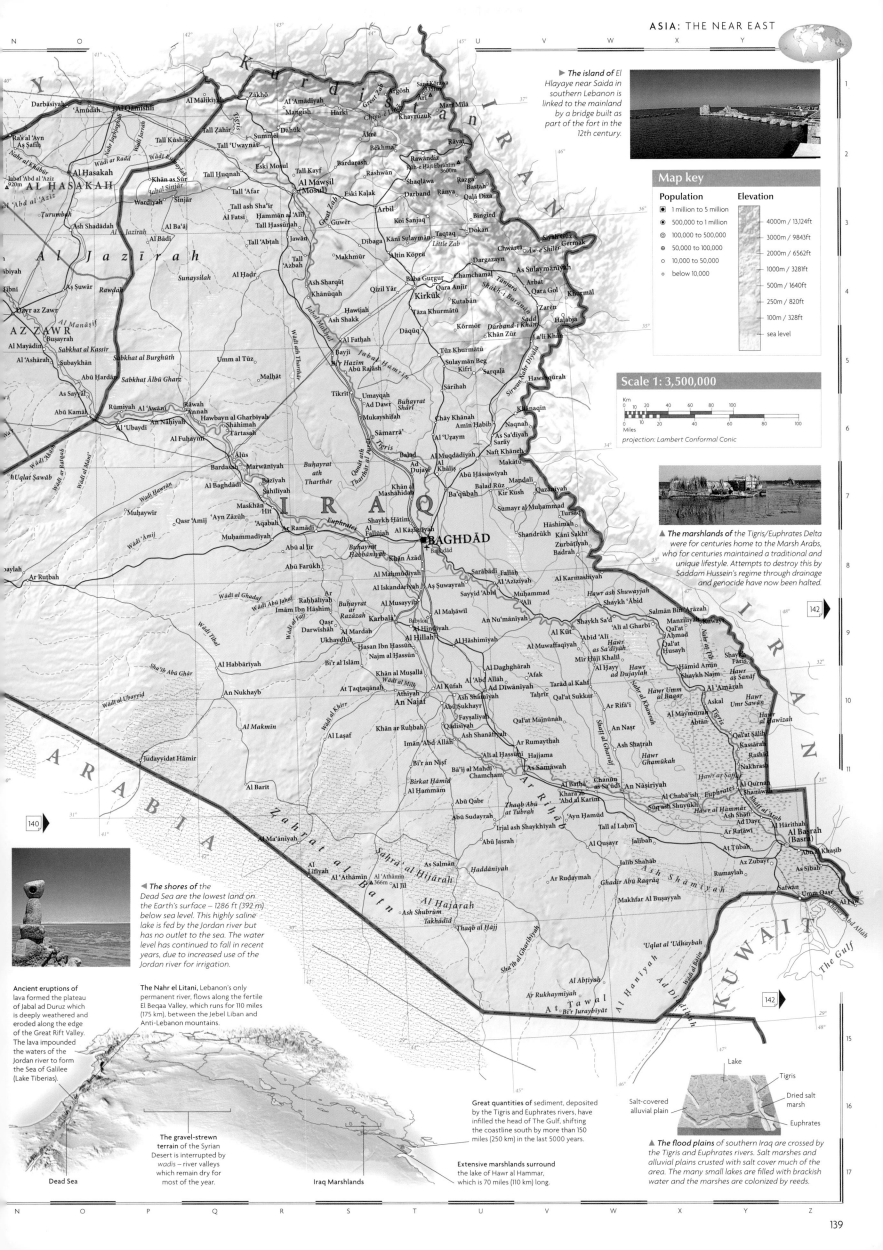

► The island of El Hlayaye near Saida in southern Lebanon is linked to the mainland by a bridge built as part of the fort in the 12th century.

Map key

Population

- ⬚ 1 million to 5 million
- ◉ 500,000 to 1 million
- ◎ 100,000 to 500,000
- ⊕ 50,000 to 100,000
- ⊙ 10,000 to 50,000
- ○ below 10,000

Elevation

- 4000m / 13,124ft
- 3000m / 9843ft
- 2000m / 6562ft
- 1000m / 3281ft
- 500m / 1640ft
- 250m / 820ft
- 100m / 328ft
- sea level

Scale 1: 3,500,000

Km
0 10 20 40 60 80 100

Miles
0 10 20 40 60 80 100

projection: Lambert Conformal Conic

▲ The marshlands of the Tigris/Euphrates Delta were for centuries home to the Marsh Arabs, who for centuries maintained a traditional and unique lifestyle. Attempts to destroy this by Saddam Hussein's regime through drainage and genocide have now been halted.

◄ The shores of the Dead Sea are the lowest land on the Earth's surface – 1286 ft (392 m) below sea level. This highly saline lake is fed by the Jordan river but has no outlet to the sea. The water level has continued to fall in recent years, due to increased use of the Jordan river for irrigation.

Ancient eruptions of lava formed the plateau of Jabal ad Duruz which is deeply weathered and eroded along the edge of the Great Rift Valley. The lava impounded the waters of the Jordan river to form the Sea of Galilee (Lake Tiberias).

The Nahr el Litani, Lebanon's only permanent river, flows along the fertile El Beqaa Valley, which runs for 110 miles (175 km), between the Jebel Liban and Anti-Lebanon mountains.

Dead Sea

The gravel-strewn terrain of the Syrian Desert is interrupted by wadis – river valleys which remain dry for most of the year.

Iraq Marshlands

Great quantities of sediment, deposited by the Tigris and Euphrates rivers, have infilled the head of The Gulf, shifting the coastline south by more than 150 miles (250 km) in the last 5000 years.

Extensive marshlands surround the lake of Hawr al Hammar, which is 70 miles (110 km) long.

Lake

Tigris

Salt-covered alluvial plain

Dried salt marsh

Euphrates

▲ The flood plains of southern Iraq are crossed by the Tigris and Euphrates rivers. Salt marshes and alluvial plains crusted with salt cover much of the area. The many small lakes are filled with brackish water and the marshes are colonized by reeds.

The Arabian Peninsula

BAHRAIN, KUWAIT, OMAN, QATAR, SAUDI ARABIA,
UNITED ARAB EMIRATES (UAE), YEMEN

Huge expanses of desert cover much of the Arabian Peninsula, limiting settlement to oases, the mountains along the Red Sea and coastal belts. The most populous area is the fertile highlands of Yemen. The Islamic faith and Arabic language give the region a cultural and religious unity, and the Saudi city of Mecca (Makkah) is Islam's most holy place, visited by over two million pilgrims each year. More than half the world's oil reserves are contained in this region, and the exploitation of oil and gas has brought great wealth, particularly to Saudi Arabia. Yemen and Oman are the least developed of the Arabian states, with large rural populations. Within Saudi Arabia over 86% of the people live in urban areas.

Using the land

Most of the Arabian Peninsula is unsuited to settled agriculture, making irrigation and land reclamation projects essential. The narrow coastal plain and isolated oases, commonly amounting to less than 1% of the land area, are used to cultivate grains, coffee and exotic fruits. Goats, sheep and camels are widespread throughout the region.

The urban/rural population divide

urban 64%   rural 36%

0 10 20 30 40 50 60 70 80 90 100

Population density	Total land area
50 people per sq mile (19 people per sq km)	1,147,856 sq miles (2,973,720 sq km)

Land use and agricultural distribution

- goats
- sheep
- cereals
- coffee
- dates
- fruit
- capital cities
- major towns
- pasture
- cropland
- desert

◄ *The fertile soils of Yemen have encouraged settlement of almost all of the land from sea level up to the mountains at 10,000 ft (3050 m). In the higher reaches elaborate terraces have been constructed to facilitate crop cultivation.*

The landscape

A plateau more than 2500 ft (760 m) high extends across much of the Arabian Peninsula. The plateau slopes eastwards from the massive, rifted escarpment along the coast of the Red Sea, to the shallow waters of The Gulf. The interior is characterized by *cuestas* and valleys, drained by a system of *wadis*. A crescent of sand and gravel deserts lies to the east.

Few areas in the Arabian Peninsula have rivers flowing through them. Most are drained by ephemeral watercourses called *wadis*.

The An Nafud Desert is covered with *barchan* dunes varying between 30–100 ft (10–30 m) high. The 'horns' of the crescent-shaped dunes reflect the direction in which they are being moved by the wind.

Inselbergs are dotted over a wide area of the Najd Plateau. These resistant remnants of the ancient basement rock are left standing when the softer weathered rock has been worn away.

Evaporation — Crusted layer left behind
Storm surge flooding
Normal level of tidal range
Salt wedge penetrates inland water

▲ *A sabkha is a flat, salt-encrusted plain which occurs near the coast just above the high water mark. Flooding by sea water leads to saturation of the land with saline-rich groundwater. As this evaporates, a cracked layer of sand, cemented together with salt, gypsum and calcium carbonate is left behind.*

The Hejaz (Al Hijaz) and Asir mountains form part of the same geological region as the highlands of Sudan and Eritrea, to which they were once joined. They were separated when faulting opened the Red Sea, over 50 million years ago.

Across the Najd Plateau the flat relief is broken by *mesas*; steep-sided rock plateaux and *cuestas*; ridges with one steep and one gentle slope.

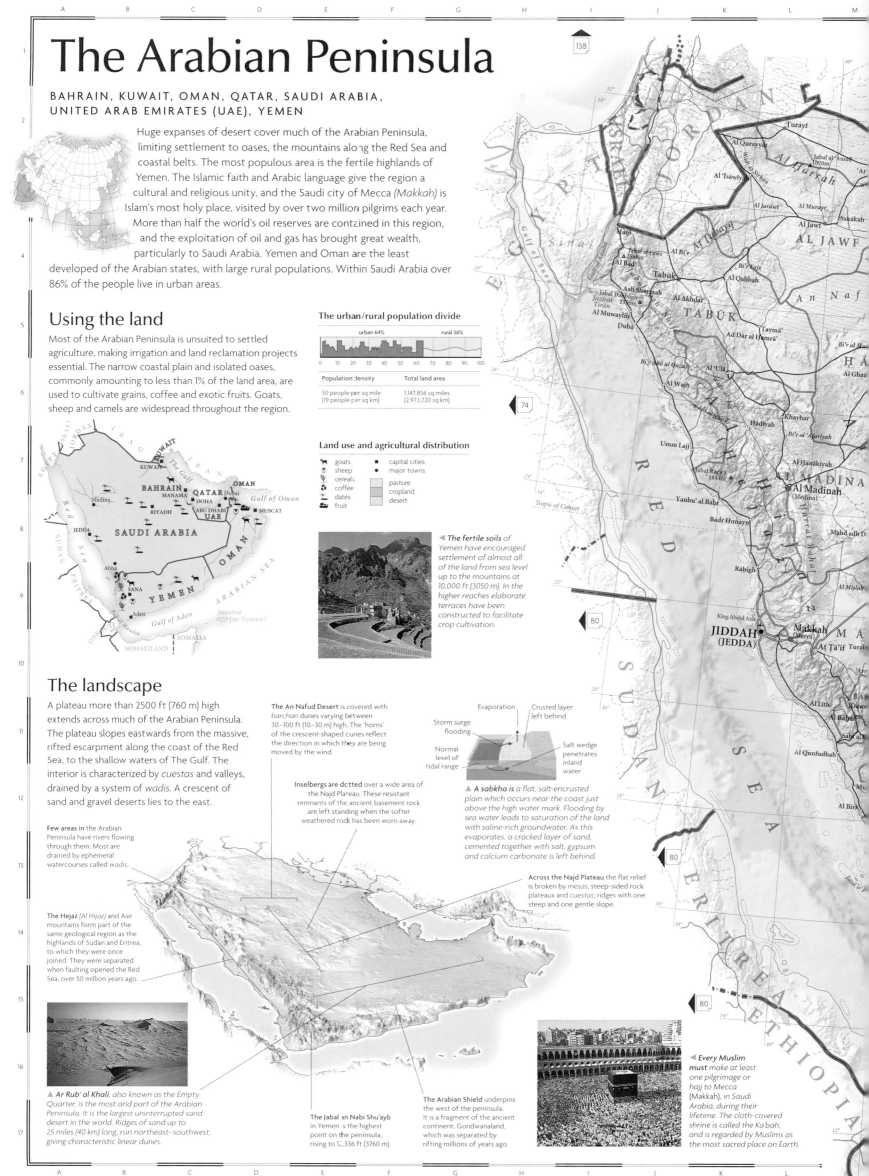

▲ *Ar Rub' al Khali, also known as the Empty Quarter, is the most arid part of the Arabian Peninsula. It is the largest uninterrupted sand desert in the world. Ridges of sand up to 25 miles (40 km) long, run northeast–southwest, giving characteristic linear dunes.*

The Jabal an Nabi Shu'ayb in Yemen is the highest point on the peninsula, rising to 12,336 ft (3760 m).

The Arabian Shield underpins the west of the peninsula. It is a fragment of the ancient continent, Gondwanaland, which was separated by rifting millions of years ago.

◄ *Every Muslim must make at least one pilgrimage or hajj to Mecca (Makkah), in Saudi Arabia, during their lifetime. The cloth-covered shrine is called the Ka'bah, and is regarded by Muslims as the most sacred place on Earth.*

138

◄ Saudi Arabia contains the world's largest oil reserves, lying mainly along The Gulf coast. Each day the region produces around 10 million barrels of oil. Here, in the desert, excess oil is being burnt off.

Transport and industry

The extraction and refining of oil and gas are the major industrial activities in the Arabian Peninsula. The region also has an active construction sector, with many Arab cities reflecting the wealth generated by the oil industry. The service sector is dominated by financial and technical institutions, which, like the construction sector, mainly serve the oil industry. Traditional handicrafts such as carpet-weaving are found in rural areas.

The transport network

44,832 miles (72,159 km)	673 miles (1083 km)
670 miles (1078 km)	none

Internal surface transport is poorly developed across the peninsula. Along the coast, commercial routes have developed, but connections between bordering states rely on major airports.

Major industry and infrastructure

- cement
- chemicals
- iron & steel
- oil
- oil refining
- food processing
- ■ capital cities
- • major towns
- ✈ international airports
- — major roads
- ▨ major industrial areas

142 ►

Map key

Population

- ◉ 1 million to 5 million
- ◎ 500,000 to 1 million
- ◉ 100,000 to 500,000
- ⊕ 50,000 to 100,000
- ⊙ 10,000 to 50,000
- ○ below 10,000

Elevation

- 3000m / 9843ft
- 2000m / 6562ft
- 1000m / 3281ft
- 500m / 1640ft
- 250m / 820ft
- 100m / 328ft
- sea level

► Seasonal watercourses or wadis drain much of the interior of the Arabian Peninsula. Although they remain dry for much of the year, they are prone to flash floods after heavy rains.

Scale 1:8,250,000

projection: Lambert Conformal Conic

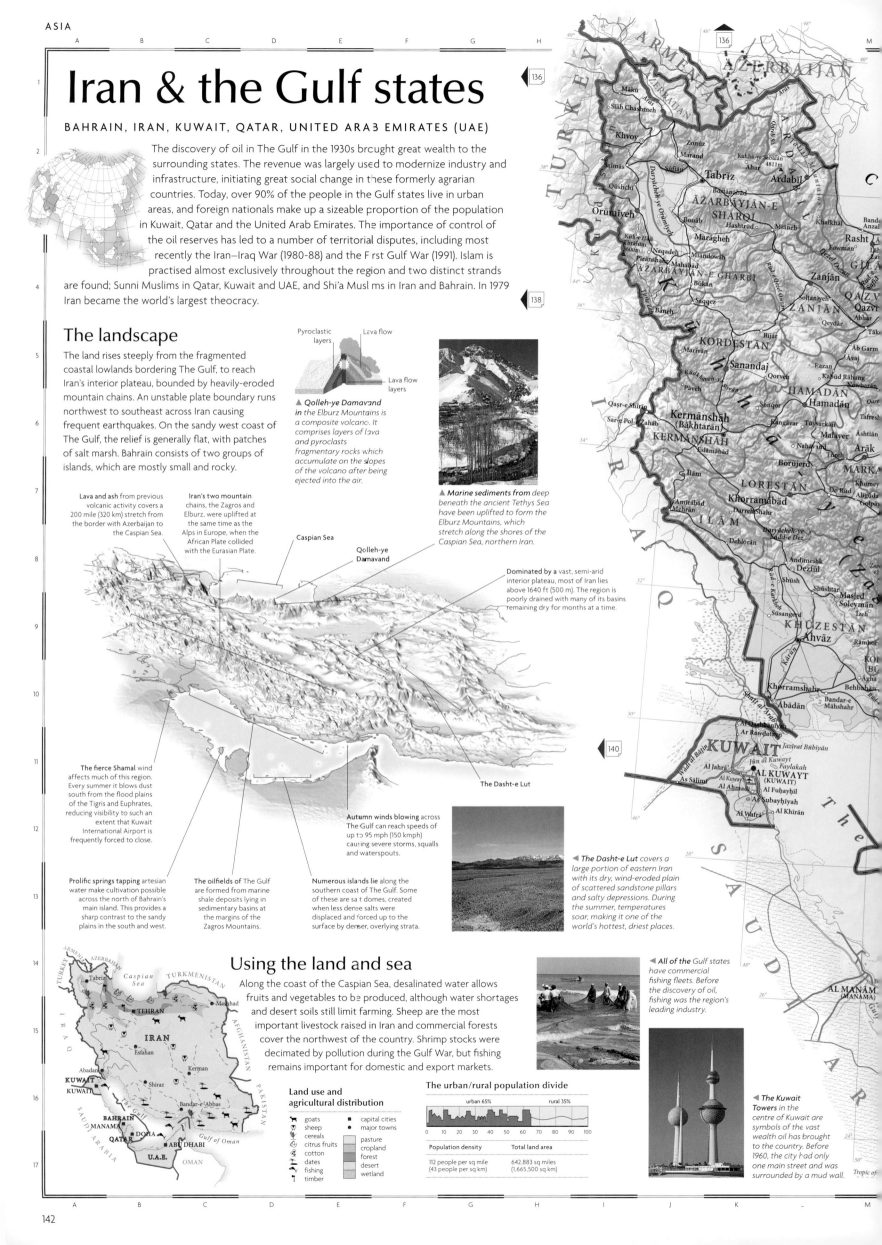

Iran & the Gulf states

BAHRAIN, IRAN, KUWAIT, QATAR, UNITED ARAB EMIRATES (UAE)

The discovery of oil in The Gulf in the 1930s brought great wealth to the surrounding states. The revenue was largely used to modernize industry and infrastructure, initiating great social change in these formerly agrarian countries. Today, over 90% of the people in the Gulf states live in urban areas, and foreign nationals make up a sizeable proportion of the population in Kuwait, Qatar and the United Arab Emirates. The importance of control of the oil reserves has led to a number of territorial disputes, including most recently the Iran–Iraq War (1980-88) and the First Gulf War (1991). Islam is practised almost exclusively throughout the region and two distinct strands are found; Sunni Muslims in Qatar, Kuwait and UAE, and Shi'a Muslims in Iran and Bahrain. In 1979 Iran became the world's largest theocracy.

The landscape

The land rises steeply from the fragmented coastal lowlands bordering The Gulf, to reach Iran's interior plateau, bounded by heavily-eroded mountain chains. An unstable plate boundary runs northwest to southeast across Iran causing frequent earthquakes. On the sandy west coast of The Gulf, the relief is generally flat, with patches of salt marsh. Bahrain consists of two groups of islands, which are mostly small and rocky.

Pyroclastic layers

Lava flow

Lava flow layers

▲ *Qolleh-ye Damavand in the Elburz Mountains is a composite volcano. It comprises layers of lava and pyroclasts fragmentary rocks which accumulate on the slopes of the volcano after being ejected into the air.*

▲ *Marine sediments from deep beneath the ancient Tethys Sea have been uplifted to form the Elburz Mountains, which stretch along the shores of the Caspian Sea, northern Iran.*

Lava and ash from previous volcanic activity covers a 200 mile (320 km) stretch from the border with Azerbaijan to the Caspian Sea.

Iran's two mountain chains, the Zagros and Elburz, were uplifted at the same time as the Alps in Europe, when the African Plate collided with the Eurasian Plate.

Caspian Sea

Qolleh-ye Damavand

Dominated by a vast, semi-arid interior plateau, most of Iran lies above 1640 ft (500 m). The region is poorly drained with many of its basins remaining dry for months at a time.

The fierce Shamal wind affects much of this region. Every summer it blows dust south from the flood plains of the Tigris and Euphrates, reducing visibility to such an extent that Kuwait International Airport is frequently forced to close.

The Dasht-e Lut

Autumn winds blowing across The Gulf can reach speeds of up to 95 mph (150 kmph) causing severe storms, squalls and waterspouts.

Prolific springs tapping artesian water make cultivation possible across the north of Bahrain's main island. This provides a sharp contrast to the sandy plains in the south and west.

The oilfields of The Gulf are formed from marine shale deposits lying in sedimentary basins at the margins of the Zagros Mountains.

Numerous islands lie along the southern coast of The Gulf. Some of these are salt domes, created when less dense salts were displaced and forced up to the surface by denser, overlying strata.

◄ *The Dasht-e Lut covers a large portion of eastern Iran with its dry, wind-eroded plain of scattered sandstone pillars and salty depressions. During the summer, temperatures soar, making it one of the world's hottest, driest places.*

Using the land and sea

Along the coast of the Caspian Sea, desalinated water allows fruits and vegetables to be produced, although water shortages and desert soils still limit farming. Sheep are the most important livestock raised in Iran and commercial forests cover the northwest of the country. Shrimp stocks were decimated by pollution during the Gulf War, but fishing remains important for domestic and export markets.

◄ *All of the Gulf states have commercial fishing fleets. Before the discovery of oil, fishing was the region's leading industry.*

◄ *The Kuwait Towers in the centre of Kuwait are symbols of the vast wealth oil has brought to the country. Before 1960, the city had only one main street and was surrounded by a mud wall.*

Land use and agricultural distribution

- goats
- sheep
- cereals
- citrus fruits
- cotton
- dates
- fishing
- timber
- ■ capital cities
- ● major towns

pasture
cropland
forest
desert
wetland

The urban/rural population divide

urban 65%   rural 35%

0   10 20 30 40 50 60 70 80 90 100

Population density	Total land area
112 people per sq mile (43 people per sq km)	642,883 sq miles (1,665,500 sq km)

◀ Many volcanoes lie in Iran's 1200 mile (1930 km) volcanic belt, including the country's highest peak, the now-extinct Qolleh-ye Damavand at 18,600 ft (5671 m).

▶ Extensive oil and gas exploitation in the Gulf region has allowed the economic transformation of the Gulf states. Consequently, many of these states have a hugely improved per capita income compared to the 1960's.

Transport and industry

Both onshore and offshore oil reserves are exploited throughout the region. Kuwait not only extracts but also refines 80% of its oil. Bahrain has diversified its economy to become the main commercial and financial centre in The Gulf. Iran produces a wide range of products: textile mills are widespread and carpet-weaving is an important export industry.

Major industry and infrastructure

- carpet manufacture
- chemicals
- finance
- food processing
- oil
- oil refining
- textiles
- capital city
- major towns
- international airports
- major roads
- major industrial areas

The transport network

63,543 miles (102,274 km)	884 miles (1423 km)
3822 miles (6151 km)	562 miles (904 km)

Major towns and neighbouring countries are linked by adequate road networks, although rural areas are less well served. Bahrain is linked to the mainland by a 15 mile (25 km) long causeway.

Map key

Population

- above 5 million
- 1 million to 5 million
- 500,000 to 1 million
- 100,000 to 500,000
- 50,000 to 100,000
- 10,000 to 50,000
- below 10,000

Elevation

- 4000m / 13,124ft
- 3000m / 9843ft
- 2000m / 6562ft
- 1000m / 3281ft
- 500m / 1640ft
- 250m / 820ft
- 100m / 328ft
- sea level

Scale 1:6,000,000

projection: Lambert Conformal Conic

Map labels

TURKMENISTAN
AFGHANISTAN
PAKISTAN
OMAN
UNITED ARAB EMIRATES
QATAR
BAHRAIN
KUWAIT
SAUDI ARABIA
IRAN

Caspian Sea
Gulf of Oman
Strait of Hormuz
Makran Coast
Trucial Coast
Tropic of Cancer

GOLESTĀN
KHORĀSĀN-E SHEMĀLĪ
KHORĀSĀN-E RAZAVI
KHORĀSĀN-E JANŪBĪ
MAZANDARĀN
SEMNĀN
TEHRĀN
QOM
ESFAHĀN
YAZD
KERMĀN
FĀRS
HORMOZGĀN
SĪSTĀN VA BALŪCHESTĀN
CHAHAR MAHALL VA BAKHTĪĀRĪ

Mashhad
Tehrān
Esfahān
Shirāz
Kermān
Yazd
Bandar-e 'Abbās
Zāhedān
Gorgan
Bojnūrd

Dasht-e Kavir
Dasht-e Lut
Iranian Plateau
Alborz (Elburz Mountains)
Zagros Mountains

AD DAWHAH (DOHA)
ABŪ ZABY (ABU DHABI)
Dubayy (Dubai)

143

Kazakhstan

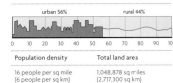

Abundant natural resources lie in the immense steppe grasslands, deserts and central plateau of the former Soviet republic of Kazakhstan. An intensive programme of industrial and agricultural development to exploit these resources during the Soviet era resulted in catastrophic industrial pollution, including fallout from nuclear testing and the shrinkage of the Aral Sea. Since independence, the government has encouraged foreign investment and liberalized the economy to promote growth. The adoption of Kazakh as the national language is intended to encourage a new sense of national identity in a state where living conditions for the majority remain harsh, both in cramped urban centres and impoverished rural areas.

Transport and industry

The single most important industry in Kazakhstan is mining, based around extensive oil deposits near the Caspian Sea, the world's largest chromium mine, and vast reserves of iron ore. Recent foreign investment has helped to develop industries including food processing and steel manufacture, and to expand the exploitation of mineral resources. The Russian space programme is still based at Baykonyr, near Kyzylorda in central Kazakhstan.

Major industry and infrastructure

- ⚗ chemicals
- ⚙ engineering
- 🐟 fish processing
- 🍴 food processing
- ⚒ iron & steel
- △ metallurgy
- ⛏ mining
- ▲ oil
- ■ capital cities
- ● major towns
- ⊕ international airports
- — major roads
- ▨ major industrial areas

The transport network

- 48,263 miles (77,680 km)
- none
- 8483 miles (13,660 km)
- 3900 miles (2423 km)

Industrial areas in the north and east are well-connected to Russia. Air and rail links with Germany and China have been established through foreign investment. Better access to Baltic ports is being sought.

◄ An open-cast coal mine in Kazakhstan. Foreign investment is being actively sought by the Kazakh government in order to fully exploit the potential of the country's rich mineral reserves.

Map key

Population
- ◉ 1 million to 5 million
- ◉ 500,000 to 1 million
- ◎ 100,000 to 500,000
- ⊕ 50,000 to 100,000
- ○ 10,000 to 50,000
- ∘ below 10,000

Elevation
- 4000m / 13,124ft
- 3000m / 9843ft
- 2000m / 6562ft
- 1000m / 3281ft
- 500m / 1640ft
- 250m / 820ft
- 100m / 328ft
- sea level

Using the land and sea

The rearing of large herds of sheep and goats on the steppe grasslands forms the core of Kazakh agriculture. Arable cultivation and cotton-growing in pasture and desert areas was encouraged during the Soviet era, but relative yields are low. The heavy use of fertilizers and the diversion of natural water sources for irrigation has degraded much of the land.

Land use and agricultural distribution

- cattle
- goats
- sheep
- cotton
- fishing
- wheat
- ■ capital cities
- ● major towns
- pasture
- cropland
- forest
- mountain region
- desert

◄ The nomadic peoples who moved their herds around the steppe grasslands are now largely settled, although echoes of their traditional lifestyle, in particular their superb riding skills, remain.

The urban/rural population divide

urban 56%   rural 44%

Population density	Total land area
16 people per sq mile (6 people per sq km)	1,048,878 sq miles (2,717,300 sq km)

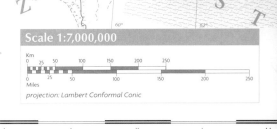

Scale 1:7,000,000

projection: Lambert Conformal Conic

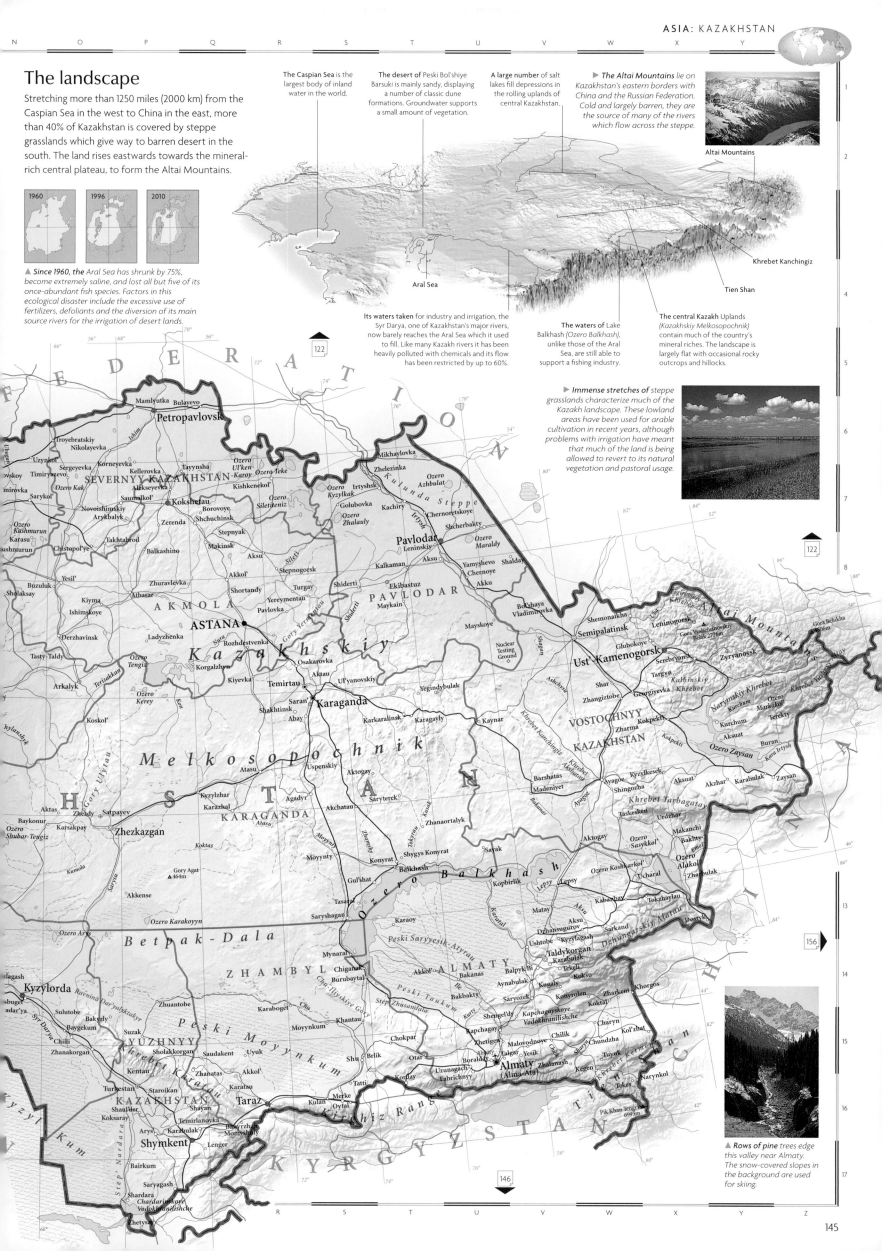

The landscape

Stretching more than 1250 miles (2000 km) from the Caspian Sea in the west to China in the east, more than 40% of Kazakhstan is covered by steppe grasslands which give way to barren desert in the south. The land rises eastwards towards the mineral-rich central plateau, to form the Altai Mountains.

1960   1996   2010

▲ **Since 1960, the** Aral Sea has shrunk by 75%, become extremely saline, and lost all but five of its once-abundant fish species. Factors in this ecological disaster include the excessive use of fertilizers, defoliants and the diversion of its main source rivers for the irrigation of desert lands.

The Caspian Sea is the largest body of inland water in the world.

The desert of Peski Bol'shiye Barsuki is mainly sandy, displaying a number of classic dune formations. Groundwater supports a small amount of vegetation.

A large number of salt lakes fill depressions in the rolling uplands of central Kazakhstan.

▶ **The Altai Mountains** lie on Kazakhstan's eastern borders with China and the Russian Federation. Cold and largely barren, they are the source of many of the rivers which flow across the steppe.

Altai Mountains

Khrebet Kanchingiz

Tien Shan

Aral Sea

Its waters taken for industry and irrigation, the Syr Darya, one of Kazakhstan's major rivers, now barely reaches the Aral Sea which it used to fill. Like many Kazakh rivers it has been heavily polluted with chemicals and its flow has been restricted by up to 60%.

The waters of Lake Balkhash (Ozero Balkhash), unlike those of the Aral Sea, are still able to support a fishing industry.

The central Kazakh Uplands (Kazakhskiy Melkosopochnik) contain much of the country's mineral riches. The landscape is largely flat with occasional rocky outcrops and hillocks.

▶ **Immense stretches of** steppe grasslands characterize much of the Kazakh landscape. These lowland areas have been used for arable cultivation in recent years, although problems with irrigation have meant that much of the land is being allowed to revert to its natural vegetation and pastoral usage.

▲ **Rows of pine** trees edge this valley near Almaty. The snow-covered slopes in the background are used for skiing.

Central Asia

KYRGYZSTAN, TAJIKISTAN, TURKMENISTAN, UZBEKISTAN

The four republics that declared independence in 1991 were created in the early years of the Soviet Union, promoting ethnic divisions in a region whose common focus, since the 8th century, has been Islam. Traditional rural and nomadic ways of life have survived the Soviet era, while the benefits of modern industry and grand irrigation schemes have resulted in severe pollution in the delicate, arid environment of the steppe, particularly in Uzbekistan. Many ethnic minority groups are scattered among the four republics, with isolated communities in the mountains of Kyrgyzstan. The current Islamic revival has brought hope of greater regional unity, in spite of religious factionalism which, in 1992, plunged Tajikistan into civil war.

◀ **The desert of** the Kara Kum (Garagum) occupies over 70% of Turkmenistan; its wind-scoured surface of dune ridges and depressions severely limits human settlement.

▲ **The southern shoreline** of the Aral Sea has retreated over 30 miles (48 km) since 1960. A major cause is the diversion of water from the Amu Darya river for irrigation via the Kara Kum Canal (Garagum Kanaly).

Map key

Population
- ▣ 1 million to 5 million
- ◉ 500,000 to 1 million
- ◎ 100,000 to 500,000
- ⊕ 50,000 to 100,000
- ○ 10,000 to 50,000
- ∘ below 10,000

Elevation
- 6000m / 19,686ft
- 4000m / 13,124ft
- 3000m / 9843ft
- 2000m / 6562ft
- 1000m / 3281ft
- 500m / 1640ft
- 250m / 820ft
- 100m / 328ft
- sea level

Transport and industry

Fossil fuels are extracted and processed in all four states, with scope for further exploitation. Agriculture provides raw materials for many industries, including food and textiles processing, and the manufacture of leather goods, clothing and carpets. Farm machinery is also produced.

The transport network

🛣 73,658 miles (118,555 km)		🛤 87 miles (140 km)	
🚂 4773 miles (7683 km)		✈ 1180 miles (1900 km)	

The Kara Kum Canal (Garagumskiy Kanal) runs for 870 miles (1400 km) from the Amu Darya river to the Caspian Sea. The canal is principally used for irrigation but is navigable for 280 miles (450 km).

Major industry and infrastructure

- ⚭ carpet weaving
- ♠ chemicals
- ⚙ engineering
- ⚒ food processing
- ⬧ oil & gas
- ⛊ textiles
- ▪ capital cities
- • major towns
- ⊕ international airports
- — major roads
- ▨ major industrial areas

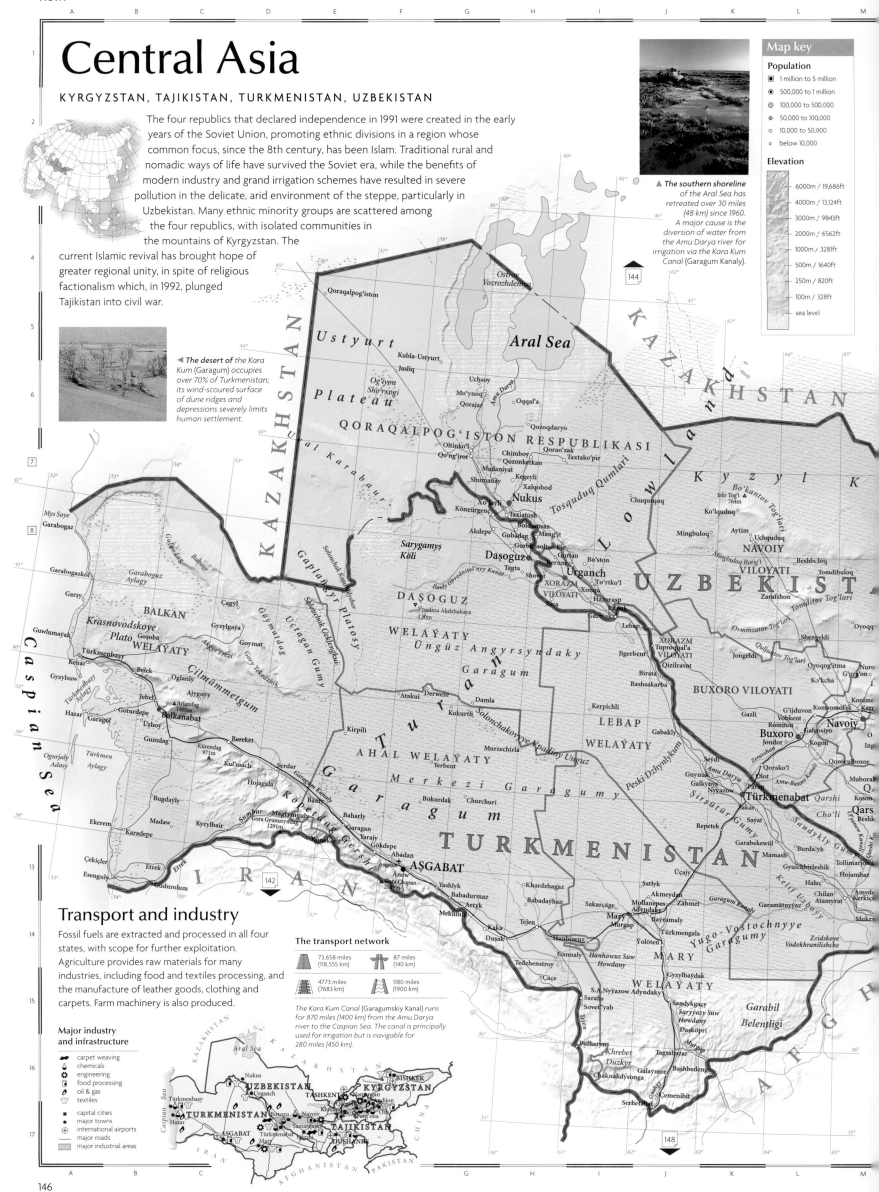

N O P Q R S T U V W X Y

The landscape

The great Tien Shan and Pamir ranges meet in a succession of high mountain chains. These mountains encircle the fertile Fergana Valley and reach west into the desert of the Kyzyl Kum, dividing the Syr Darya and Amu Darya rivers. Sandy steppeland extends to the shores of the Caspian Sea, with the desert of the Kara Kum (Garagum) in the south. The Amu Darya drains into the Aral Sea in the north.

Salt marshes fill many of the depressions in the Ustyurt Plateau, a barren, rocky tableland about 650 ft (200 m) above sea level.

Some of the world's largest deposits of marine salts are found in Garabogaz Aylagy. This shallow, saline gulf has an average depth of only 33 ft (10 m), and a very high evaporation rate, producing the salty deposits.

The Kara Kum (Garagum) is one of the world's largest expanses of sand. Wind action has created a terrain of shifting, crescent-shaped sand dunes known as barchans.

The Amu Darya is the only river in Central Asia with a sufficient volume of water to cross the desert of the Kara Kum (Garagum) from the Pamirs to the Aral Sea, where it forms a delta largely vegetated by scrub grasses.

Kyzyl Kum

Syr Darya

Shock waves travel through ground

Epicentre

Fault

▲ **In the heavily-fractured** and faulted mountain region, earthquakes are common, caused by the sudden release of tension along active fault lines.

Narin river

Earthquake zone

Tien Shan

Qarokul

◄ **Bare mountains provide** a stark background to the croplands along the Naryn river in Kyrgyzstan. Irrigation is essential for cultivation in this dry region.

Ozero Issyk-Kul' lies at an altitude of 5193 ft (1584 m). The lake remains ice-free throughout the year, due to the slight salinity of the water.

▲ **The Tien Shan** extend from China in the east, reaching heights over 24,420 ft (7443 m) and branching into many parallel ranges in the west.

◄ **Nestling high** in the Pamir range, and fed by glacial meltwater, Qarokul is the largest of the lakes in this region.

A series of major rock faults has created the Fergana Valley, a deep depression surrounded by high mountains. Water from the Syr Darya river and from underground sources supports intensive agriculture, despite minimal rainfall.

Mount Communism (Qullai Kommunizm), in the northern Pamirs, was so named for being the highest point in the former Soviet Union, rising to 24,590 ft (7495 m).

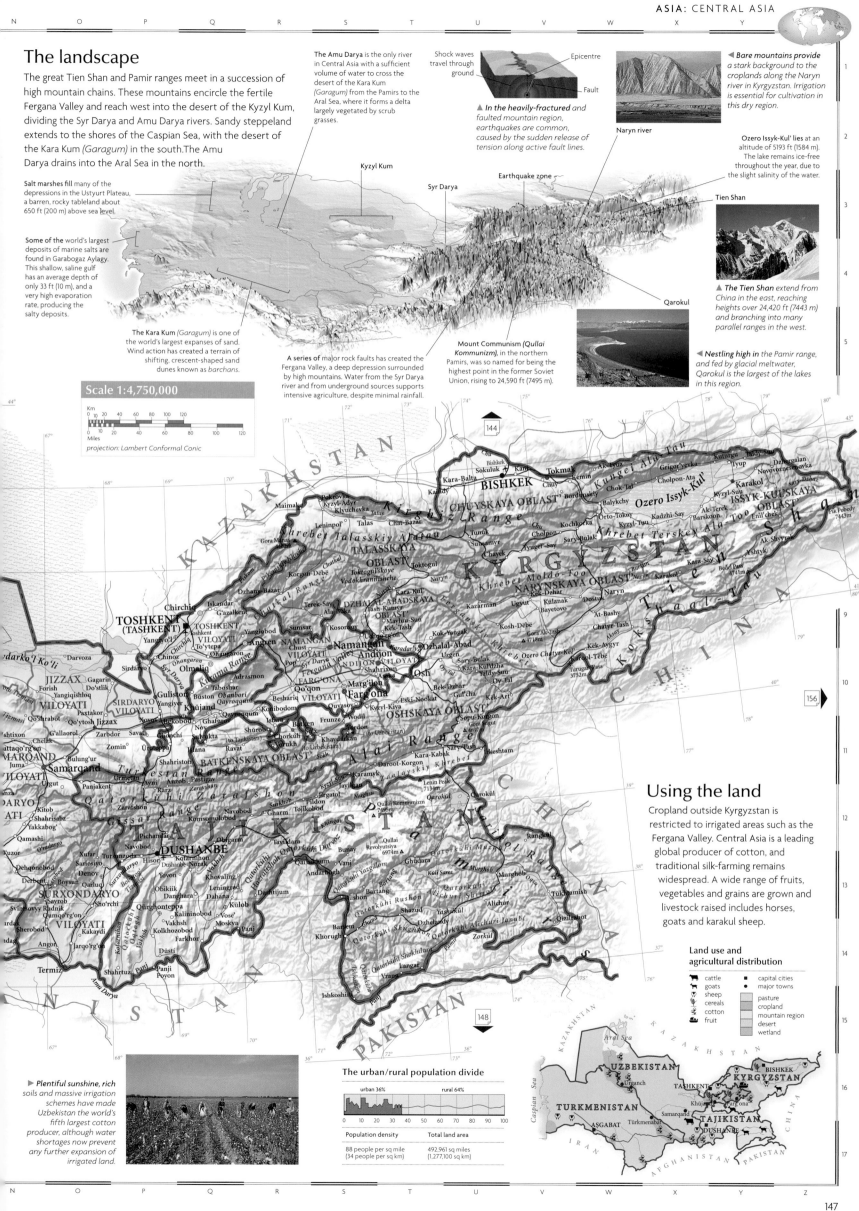

Scale 1:4,750,000

Km
0 20 40 60 80 100 120
Miles
0 20 40 60 80 100 120

projection: Lambert Conformal Conic

Using the land

Cropland outside Kyrgyzstan is restricted to irrigated areas such as the Fergana Valley. Central Asia is a leading global producer of cotton, and traditional silk-farming remains widespread. A wide range of fruits, vegetables and grains are grown and livestock raised includes horses, goats and karakul sheep.

Land use and agricultural distribution

- cattle
- goats
- sheep
- cereals
- cotton
- fruit
- ■ capital cities
- • major towns

pasture
cropland
mountain region
desert
wetland

▶ **Plentiful sunshine, rich** soils and massive irrigation schemes have made Uzbekistan the world's fifth largest cotton producer, although water shortages now prevent any further expansion of irrigated land.

The urban/rural population divide

urban 36%   rural 64%

0 10 20 30 40 50 60 70 80 90 100

Population density

88 people per sq mile
(34 people per sq km)

Total land area

492,961 sq miles
(1,277,100 sq km)

Afghanistan & Pakistan

Pakistan was created by the partition of British India in 1947, becoming the western arm of a new Islamic state for Indian Muslims; the eastern sector, in Bengal, seceded to become the separate country of Bangladesh in 1971. Over half of Pakistan's 158 million people live in the Punjab, at the fertile head of the great Indus Basin. The river sustains a national economy based on irrigated agriculture, including cotton for the vital textiles industry. Afghanistan, a mountainous, landlocked country, with an ancient and independent culture, has been wracked by war since 1979. Factional strife escalated into an international conflict in late 2001, as US-led troops ousted the militant and fundamentally Islamist *taliban* regime as part of their 'war on terror'.

◀ *The town of* Bamian lies high in the Hindu Kush west of Kabul. Between the 2nd and 5th centuries two huge statues of Buddha were carved into the nearby rock, the largest of which stood 125 ft (38 m) high. The statues were destroyed by the taliban regime in March 2001.

Transport and industry

Pakistan is highly dependent on the cotton textiles industry, although diversified manufacture is expanding around cities such as Karachi and Lahore. Afghanistan's limited industry is based mainly on the processing of agricultural raw materials and includes traditional crafts such as carpet-making.

Major industry and infrastructure

- carpet weaving
- chemicals
- engineering
- finance
- food processing
- iron & steel
- oil & gas
- textiles
- capital cities
- major towns
- international airports
- major roads
- major industrial areas

The transport network

🛣	96,154 miles (154,763 km)
🛣	211 miles (340 km)
🚆	4852 miles (7814 km)
🚆	745 miles (1200 km)

The Karakoram Highway was completed after 20 years of construction in 1978. It breaches the Himalayan mountain barrier providing a commercial motor route linking lowland Pakistan and China.

▶ *The Karakoram Highway* is one of the highest major roads in the world. It took over 24,000 workers almost 20 years to complete.

The landscape

Afghanistan's topography is dominated by the mountains of the Hindu Kush, which spread south and west into numerous mountain spurs. The dry plateau of southwestern Afghanistan extends into Pakistan and the hills which overlook the great Indus Basin. In northern Pakistan the Hindu Kush, Himalayan and Karakoram ranges meet to form one of the world's highest mountain regions.

◀ *The Hunza river* rises in the northern Karakoram Range, running for 120 miles (193 km) before joining the Gilgit river.

Hunza river

▶ *The arid Hindu Kush* makes much of Afghanistan uninhabitable, with over 50% of the land lying above 6500 ft (2000 m).

The plains and foothills which extend from the northern slopes of the Hindu Kush are part of the great grassy steppe lands of Central Asia.

Hindu Kush

K2 (Mount Godwin Austen), in the Karakoram Range, is the second highest mountain in the world, at an altitude of 28,251 ft (8611 m).

Frequent earthquakes mean that mountain-building processes are continuing in this region, as the Indo-Australian Plate drifts northwards, colliding with the Eurasian Plate.

Some of the largest glaciers outside the polar regions are found in the Karakoram Range, including Siachen Glacier (Siachen Muztagh), which is 40 miles (72 km) long.

Himalayas

Mountain chains running southwest from the Hindu Kush into Pakistan form a barrier to the humid winds which blow from the Indian Ocean, creating arid conditions across southern Afghanistan.

The soils of the Punjab plain are nourished by enormous quantities of sediment, carried from the Himalayas by the five tributaries of the Indus river.

The Indus Basin is part of the Indus-Ganges lowland, a vast depression which has been filled with layers of sediment over the last 50 million years. These deposits are estimated to be over 16,400 ft (5000 m) deep.

The Indus Delta is prone to heavy flooding and high levels of salinity. It remains a largely uncultivated wilderness area.

Glacis covered by coarse-grained sediment

Sediments washed down from mountains accumulate on glacis slopes

Fine sediments deposited on salt flats are removed by wind erosion

Bedrock

▲ *Glacis are gentle,* debris-covered slopes which lead into salt flats or deserts. They typically occur at the base of mountains in arid regions such as Afghanistan.

Scale 1:5,000,000

Km
0 10 20   40   60   80   100   120   140   160

Miles
0 10 20   40   60   80   100   120   140 160

projection: Lambert Conformal Conic

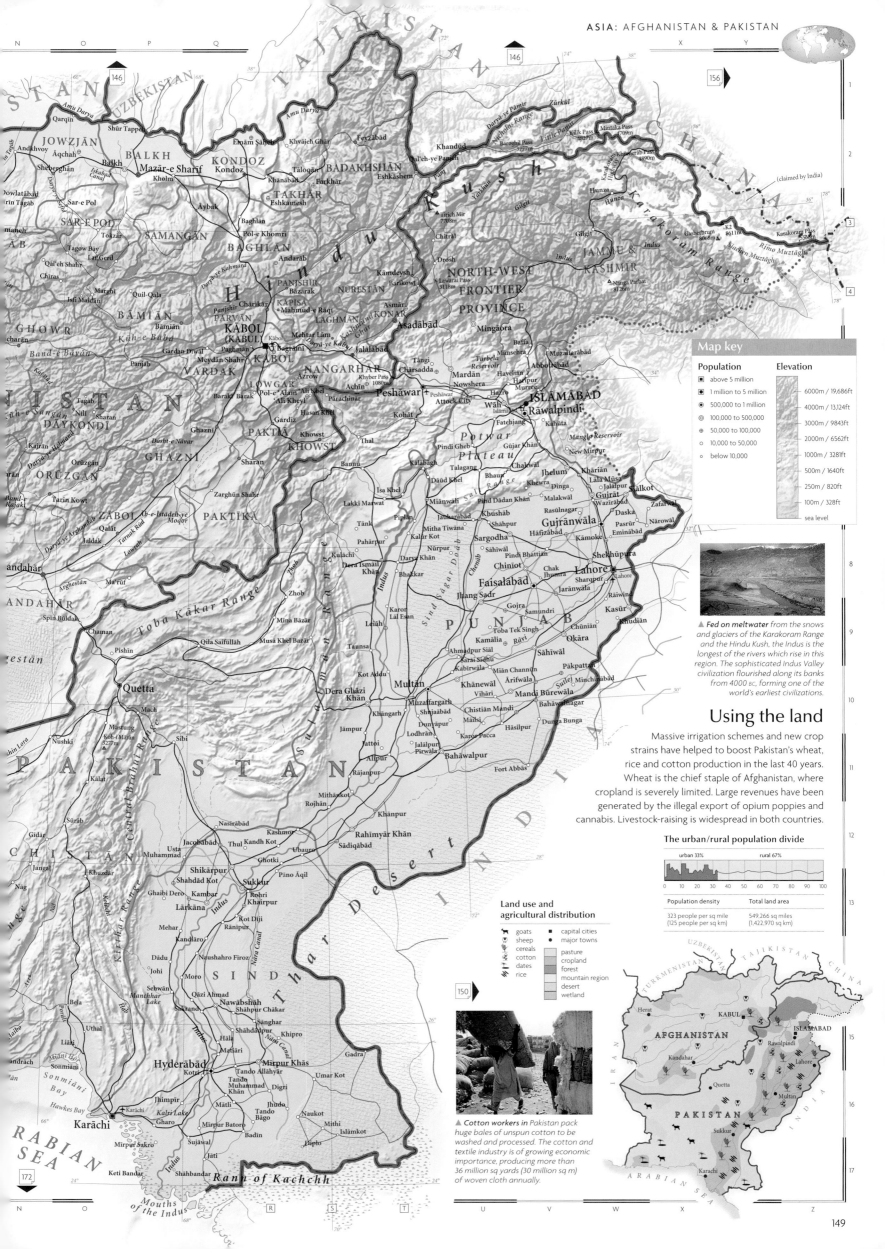

Map key

Population

- ■ above 5 million
- ▣ 1 million to 5 million
- ◉ 500,000 to 1 million
- ◎ 100,000 to 500,000
- ⊕ 50,000 to 100,000
- ⊙ 10,000 to 50,000
- ○ below 10,000

Elevation

- 6000m / 19,686ft
- 4000m / 13,124ft
- 3000m / 9843ft
- 2000m / 6562ft
- 1000m / 3281ft
- 500m / 1640ft
- 250m / 820ft
- 100m / 328ft
- sea level

▲ *Fed on meltwater* from the snows and glaciers of the Karakoram Range and the Hindu Kush, the Indus is the longest of the rivers which rise in this region. The sophisticated Indus Valley civilization flourished along its banks from 4000 BC, forming one of the world's earliest civilizations.

Using the land

Massive irrigation schemes and new crop strains have helped to boost Pakistan's wheat, rice and cotton production in the last 40 years. Wheat is the chief staple of Afghanistan, where cropland is severely limited. Large revenues have been generated by the illegal export of opium poppies and cannabis. Livestock-raising is widespread in both countries.

The urban/rural population divide

urban 33%   rural 67%

0 10 20 30 40 50 60 70 80 90 100

Population density	Total land area
323 people per sq mile (125 people per sq km)	549,266 sq miles (1,422,970 sq km)

Land use and agricultural distribution

- goats
- sheep
- cereals
- cotton
- dates
- rice

- ■ capital cities
- • major towns

- pasture
- cropland
- forest
- mountain region
- desert
- wetland

▲ *Cotton workers in* Pakistan pack huge bales of unspun cotton to be washed and processed. The cotton and textile industry is of growing economic importance, producing more than 36 million sq yards (30 million sq m) of woven cloth annually.

South Asia

BANGLADESH, BHUTAN, INDIA, MALDIVES, NEPAL, PAKISTAN, SRI LANKA

The landscape

South Asia is effectively isolated from the rest of Asia by desert along the western flank of Pakistan, and a continuous wall of mountains, dominated by the Himalayas, to the north and east. The great basins of the Indus and Ganges separate this mountain fringe from the rolling plateau of the Indian peninsula, which is bordered by a line of coastal hills, the Eastern and Western Ghats.

More than one-fifth of the world's population lives in the south Asian subcontinent. Great cultural diversity has come from a long succession of foreign invaders, including Hindu Aryans, Islamic Moguls and the British, whose empire incorporated the princely states of the Maharajas and extended to the borders of Nepal and Bhutan in the Himalayas.

Independent since 1947, India is the world's largest democracy, and at the current rate of growth, may overtake China as the world's most populous country during the 21st century. There are points of tension in the region over claims for independence by the Sikhs in the Indian Punjab and the Tamil separatists in Sri Lanka, and the long-standing dispute with Pakistan over Jammu and Kashmir in the north.

▼ *The towering Karakoram and Hindu Kush ranges, formed at the same time as the Himalayas, dominate Pakistan's northern borders. K2 on the border of northern Pakistan is the second highest mountain on Earth, at 28,251 ft (8611 m).*

▼ *The Indus valley near Skardu in northern Pakistan has been partially infilled by great quantities of eroded sediment. Most of this is carried from the region's bare slopes by swollen rivers during the spring thaw and mass movement activity.*

The Himalayas are the highest and most extensive mountain system in the world. They were formed when the Indo-Australian Plate collided with the Eurasian Plate about 40 million years ago, thrusting up huge masses of land and creating a 'ripple' effect, which formed lesser mountain ranges in Tibet and Southeast Asia. Mount Everest is the world's tallest mountain at 29,035 ft (8850 m).

Almost all of Bangladesh lies in the immense delta formed by the Ganges and the Brahmaputra which merge and flow out into the Bay of Bengal.

Ganges delta

Deccan plateau

Layers of volcanic basalt

Stepped valleys or 'traps'

▲ *The Deccan plateau covers an area of more than 123,553 sq miles (320,000 sq km). It is formed of deep layers of volcanic basalt, reaching thicknesses of more than 9800 ft (3000 m) towards the coast. Distinctive stepped valleys cut in the basalt plateau by rivers are known as 'traps'.*

Eastern Ghats

Coastal deposition has formed many typical features along the western coast of Sri Lanka. These include spits and bars, sometimes enclosing lagoons.

Trivandrum in southern India normally receives the first of the monsoon rains, which are essential to south Asian agriculture and moderate the extreme summer heat. The monsoon then moves northwards over a period of about two months.

The Western Ghats are formed by a fault scarp which runs unbroken for more than 930 miles (1500 km). They reach their highest point at the southern Cardamom Hills.

▲ *Rivers flowing from the Himalayas into a broad depression in northern India have formed marshes around Bharatpur. They are now a sanctuary for numerous bird species.*

Bharatpur

The Indus river flows more than 1970 miles (3180 km) from southwestern Tibet to its mouth on the Arabian Sea. It has an estimated catchment area of 450,000 sq miles (1,165,500 sq km).

The coast of western Pakistan is a staircase of folded rock strata caused by successive periods of rapid uplift.

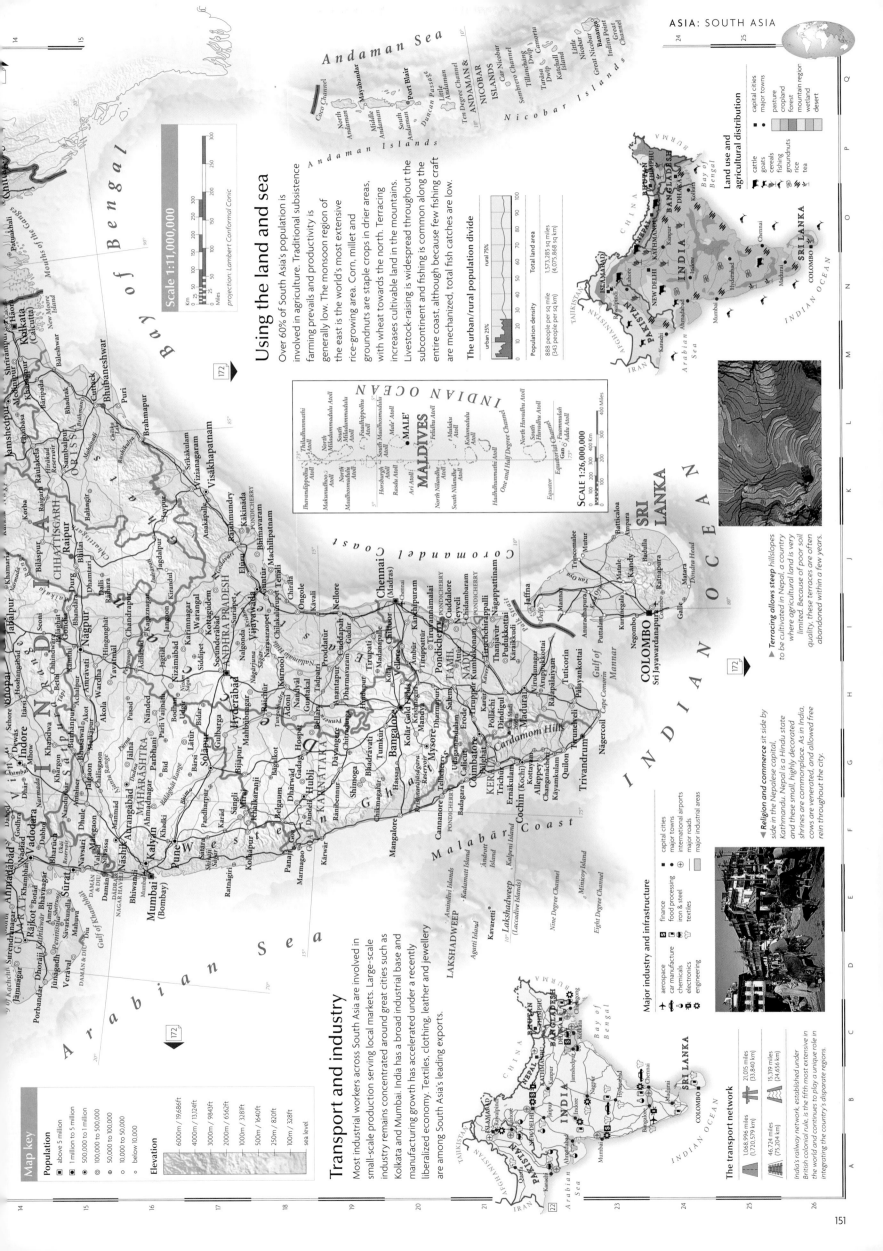

Map key

Population

- ■ above 5 million
- ◉ 1 million to 5 million
- ◎ 500,000 to 1 million
- ⊙ 100,000 to 500,000
- ⊚ 50,000 to 100,000
- ○ 10,000 to 50,000
- ° below 10,000

Elevation

- 6000m / 19,686ft
- 4000m / 13,124ft
- 3000m / 9843ft
- 2000m / 6562ft
- 1000m / 3281ft
- 500m / 1640ft
- 250m / 820ft
- 100m / 328ft
- sea level

Scale 1:11,000,000

Km 0 25 50 100 150 200 250 300

Miles 0 25 50 100 150 200 250 300

projection: Lambert Conformal Conic

Using the land and sea

Over 60% of South Asia's population is involved in agriculture. Traditional subsistence farming prevails and productivity is generally low. The monsoon region of the east is the world's most extensive rice-growing area. Corn, millet and groundnuts are staple crops in drier areas, with wheat towards the north. Terracing increases cultivable land in the mountains. Livestock-raising is widespread throughout the subcontinent and fishing is common along the entire coast, although because few fishing craft are mechanized, total fish catches are low.

The urban/rural population divide

urban 25%   rural 75%

0 10 20 30 40 50 60 70 80 90 100

Population density	Total land area
888 people per sq mile (343 people per sq km)	1,573,285 sq miles (4,075,868 sq km)

Land use and agricultural distribution

- cattle
- goats
- cereals
- fishing
- groundnuts
- rice
- tea

- capital cities
- major towns
- pasture
- cropland
- forest
- mountain region
- wetland
- desert

Transport and industry

Most industrial workers across South Asia are involved in small-scale production serving local markets. Large-scale industry remains concentrated around great cities such as Kolkata and Mumbai. India has a broad industrial base and manufacturing growth has accelerated under a recently liberalized economy. Textiles, clothing, leather and jewellery are among South Asia's leading exports.

Major industry and infrastructure

- aerospace
- car manufacture
- chemicals
- electronics
- engineering
- finance
- food processing
- iron & steel
- textiles

- capital cities
- major towns
- international airports
- major roads
- major industrial areas

The transport network

21,015 miles (33,840 km)	1,068,996 miles (1,720,579 km)
15,339 miles (24,656 km)	46,724 miles (75,204 km)

India's railway network, established under British colonial rule, is the fifth most extensive in the world and continues to play a unique role in integrating the country's disparate regions.

▶ *Religion and commerce sit side by side in the Nepalese capital, Kathmandu. Nepal is a Hindu state and these small, highly decorated shrines are commonplace. As in India, cows are venerated, and allowed free rein throughout the city.*

▶ *Terracing allows steep hillslopes to be cultivated in Nepal, a country where agricultural land is very limited. Because of poor soil quality, these terraces are often abandoned within a few years.*

SCALE 1:26,000,000

0 100 200 300 400 Miles
0 100 200 300 400 500 km

Northern India & the Himalayan states

BANGLADESH, BHUTAN, NEPAL, Arunachal Pradesh,
Assam, Bihar, Chandigarh, Delhi, Haryana,
Himachal Pradesh, Jammu & Kashmir, Jharkhand,
Manipur, Meghalaya, Mizoram, Nagaland,
Punjab, Rajasthan, Sikkim, Tripura,
Uttaranchal, Uttar Pradesh, West Bengal

The Ganges and Brahmaputra river basins and
the massive mountain barrier of the Himalayas
define this region's landscape and have served
to reinforce potent cultural and religious
differences among its people. Hinduism pervades
most aspects of national life and is a growing
political force within India, a secular country which
also encompasses the centre of Sikhism at
Amritsar and the world's largest Muslim minority.
Nepal is a crowded mountain state, which faces severe ecological
problems from deforestation, while the tiny Himalayan Buddhist
kingdom of Bhutan is emerging from long-term isolation, to welccme
selected visitors. The Muslim state of Bangladesh, formerly East
Pakistan, is one of the world's most densely populated countries and
one of the poorest, with more than 145 million people living largely on
the massive Ganges/Brahmaputra delta. Many Bangladeshis live under
threat of repeated, catastrophic floods.

◄ *The Golden Temple in Amritsar,
the most sacred shrine of the Sikh
religion, was the scene of violent
clashes between Sikh separatists
and government forces in 1984.*

Map key

Population
- ◉ 1 million to 5 million
- ◉ 500,000 to 1 million
- ◎ 100,000 to 500,000
- ⊕ 50,000 to 100,000
- ⊕ 10,000 to 50,000
- ○ below 10,000

Elevation
- 6000m / 19,686ft
- 4000m / 13,124ft
- 3000m / 9843ft
- 2000m / 6562ft
- 1000m / 3281ft
- 500m / 1640ft
- 250m / 820ft
- 100m / 328ft
- sea level

Transport
and industry

Textiles, engineering, chemicals and
electronics are leading industries in north
India. The plateau of Chota Nagpur provides
ore for iron and steel production in the
major industrial region northeast of
Kolkata. Bangladesh processes jute
and Nepal has a small
manufacturing sector
based on agricultural
produce, while Bhutan's
limited industry is
concentrated in the
southern lowland area.

Scale 1:6,500,000

projection: Lambert Conformal Conic

Major industry and infrastructure
- ⌂ adventure tourism
- �car car manufacture
- ⚗ chemicals
- ⚒ coal
- 🖥 electronics
- ⚙ engineering
- 💷 finance
- 🍴 food processing
- iron & steel
- jute processing
- ⚓ oil
- tea processing
- textiles
- ■ capital cities
- • major towns
- ✈ international airports
- — major roads
- ▨ major industrial areas

The transport network

*Over 60% of Bangladesh's internal
trade is carried by boat. The country
has a very disjointed land transport
network, with no bridges over the
Brahmaputra and few road crossings
on the Ganges river.*

The landscape

Most of the region is drained by the Ganges river, which meets the Brahmaputra in Bangladesh to form an immense delta before flowing into the Bay of Bengal. The Himalayas extend eastwards over 1500 miles (2400 km), from the parallel ranges running through Jammu and Kashmir. The Thar Desert occupies the southwest.

The Indian Punjab lies mainly to the west of the Ganges watershed and its rivers flow into the Indus. Control of this water resource has been a source of great friction with neighbouring Pakistan.

The border between India and Pakistan runs through the Thar Desert, an area of sandy *seif* dunes 50–100 ft (15–30 m) in height. Fossils found in the desert indicate that the dunes, stabilized by vegetation, have been in their current position for about 3000 years.

Sambhar Salt Lake in Rajasthan is India's largest lake. Unlike most of the Himalayan lakes which are glacial in origin – formed in ice-scoured basins or as the result of depositional damming – it is an ephemeral salt lake filled periodically by flash flooding.

The Ganges river, sacred to the Hindu people, drains a vast lowland area at the base of the Himalayas. The northern plains are covered by sandy deposits, broken by mud-banks formed when the river floods.

The rapid deforestation of Himalayan valleys has led to acute soil erosion and increased rates of rainwater run-off, both cited as possible causes of the worsening floods downstream in the Ganges/ Brahmaputra delta, although natural rates are high and may be the real cause.

► *The Pir Panjal* range in southwestern Kashmir rises to elevations of 12,500 ft (3810 m). Despite the freezing conditions, settlements and extensive pastures are found above the tree line.

The northern ranges of the Himalayas contain the highest mountains in the world, with average heights of more than 23,000 ft (7000 m) and many peaks higher than 26,000 ft (8000 m).

In the last 40 million years, the course of the Brahmaputra has been diverted hundreds of miles to the east by the rising landmass of the Himalayas.

The Khasi Hills are an example of a *horst*, a fractured block of bedrock which has been thrust upwards.

Over half of the great Ganges/ Brahmaputra delta floods each year during the monsoon as rivers, swollen by meltwater from the Himalayas and by excess rainwater, break their banks and fertilize the land with nutrient-rich sediment.

▲ *The summit of Machhapuchhre* rises to 22,942 ft (6993 m). It is also known as the 'Fish's Tail' because of its distinctive peak.

Debris slides in the middle Himalayas

Debris fans at base of slope
Soil blocks
Slide plain

▲ *Soil loss in* the middle Himalayas has largely been attributed to debris slides, where large blocks of soil are mobilized by saturation along a slide plane. Once mobile, the soil slides down the slope, gaining speed and thinning to form a fan at the base of the slope.

Using the land

Grain production dominates land use. Rice is most widely grown in the east. Irrigation and new crop strains have dramatically increased yields in the Punjab, a major wheat-producing area. River flood plains are intensively farmed and livestock-herding is widespread, particularly in Bhutan. Regional crops include jute in Bangladesh, tea in Assam, cardamom in Sikkim and saffron in Kashmir.

The urban/rural population divide

urban 23%   rural 77%

0 10 20 30 40 50 60 70 80 90 100

Population density	Total land area
993 people per sq mile (384 people per sq km)	665,104 sq miles (1,723,068 sq km)

▲ *An adverse climate*, steep slopes and poor soils limit crop cultivation in Bhutan, which is a largely agrarian economy. Rice, corn and wheat are the main staples, although orchards are being established as the soil and climate suit this type of farming.

Land use and agricultural distribution

- cattle
- goats
- sheep
- cereals
- jute
- rice
- tea

- ■ capital cities
- • major towns

pasture
cropland
forest
mountain region
wetland
desert

▲ *Flooded streets in Dhaka*, Bangladesh are a testament to the region's vulnerability to flooding. In 1988 alone, 75% of the country was flooded, leaving thousands of people dead and over 25 million homeless.

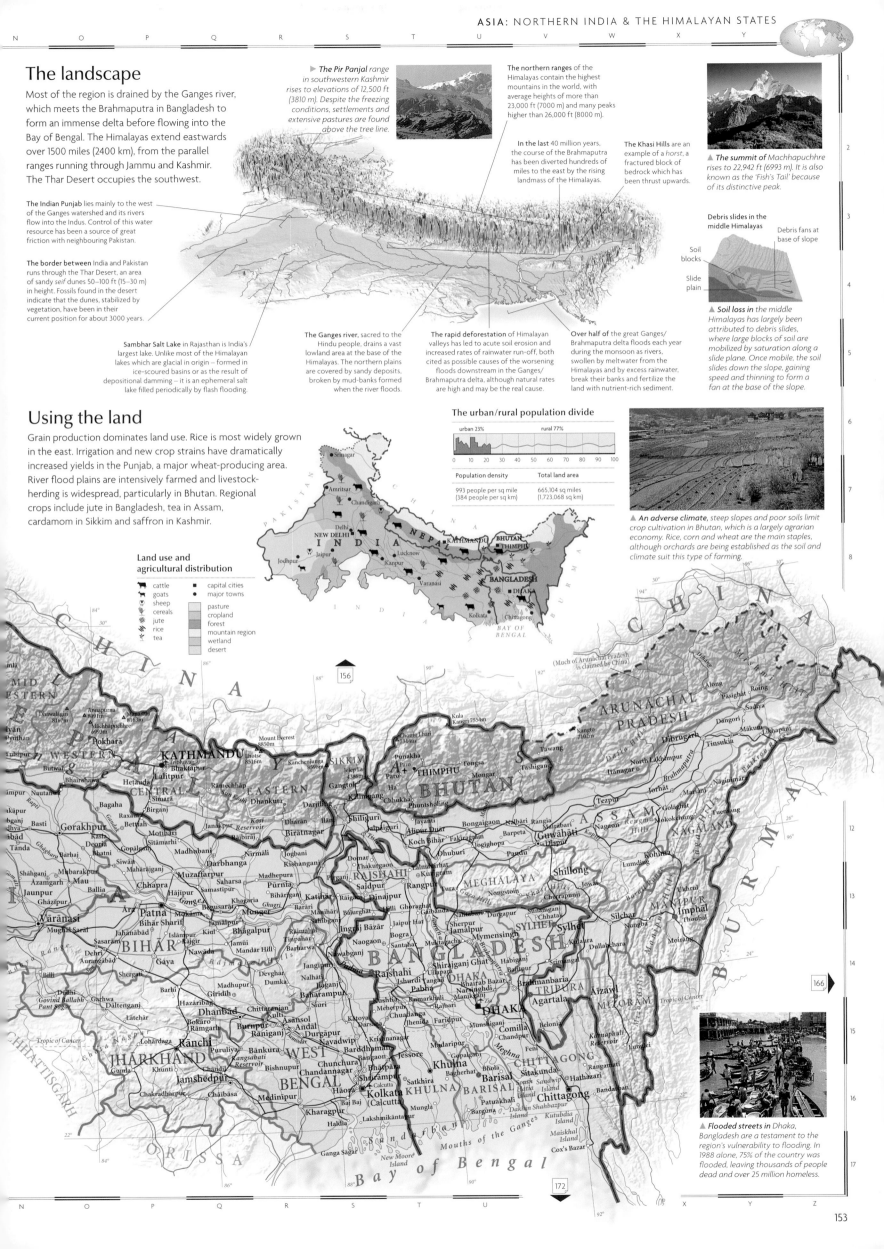

Southern India & Sri Lanka

SRI LANKA, Andhra Pradesh, Chhattisgarh, Dadra & Nagar Haveli, Daman & Diu, Goa, Gujarat, Karnataka, Kerala, Lakshadweep, Madhya Pradesh, Maharashtra, Orissa, Pondicherry, Tamil Nadu

The unique and highly independent southern states reflect the diverse and decentralized nature of India, which has fourteen official languages. The southern half of the peninsula lay beyond the reach of early invaders from the north and retained the distinct and ancient culture of Dravidian peoples such as the Tamils, whose language is spoken in preference to Hindi throughout southern India. The interior plateau of southern India is less densely populated than the coastal lowlands, where the European colonial imprint is strongest. Urban and industrial growth is accelerating, but southern India's vast population remains predominantly rural. The island of Sri Lanka has two distinct cultural groups; the mainly Buddhist Sinhalese majority, and the Tamil minority whose struggle for a homeland in the northeast has led to prolonged civil war.

The landscape

The undulating Deccan plateau underlies most of southern India; it slopes gently down towards the east and is largely enclosed by the Ghats coastal hill ranges. The Western Ghats run continuously along the Arabian Sea coast, while the Eastern Ghats are interrupted by rivers which follow the slope of the plateau and flow across broad lowlands into the Bay of Bengal. The plateaus and basins of Sri Lanka's central highlands are surrounded by a broad plain.

Along the northern boundary of the Deccan plateau, old basement rocks are interspersed with younger sedimentary strata. This creates spectacular scarplands, cut by numerous waterfalls along the softer sedimentary strata.

The interior uplands of southern India are broadly known as the Deccan plateau. River erosion of the plateau's volcanic rock has created distinctive stepped valleys called traps.

Deep layers of river sediment have created a broad lowland plain along the eastern coast, with rivers such as the Krishna forming extensive deltas.

The island of Sri Lanka is essentially an extension of the Deccan plateau. It lies on the Indian continental shelf and is composed of the same hard, crystalline rocks.

The Rann of Kachchh tidal marshes encircle the low-lying Kachchh peninsula. For several months during the rainy season the water level of the marshes rises and Kachchh becomes an island.

The Konkan coast, which runs between Daman and Goa, is characterized by rocky headlands, and bays with crescent-shaped beaches. Flooded river valleys known as *rias* extend inland.

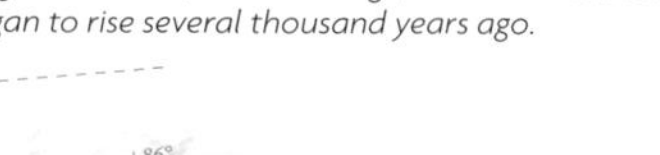

▼ The Western Ghats run north–south marking the western boundary of the Deccan plateau. Their height rises to the south where their summits reach altitudes of 8000 ft (2500 m).

Ocean currents cause sediment build up

Sri Lanka

Relict of ancient tombolo

Adam's Bridge

▲ Adam's Bridge (Rama's Bridge) is a chain of sandy shoals lying about 4 ft (1.2 m) under the sea between India and Sri Lanka. They once formed the world's longest tombolo, or land bridge, before the sea level began to rise several thousand years ago.

Using the land and sea

Rice is the main staple in the east; in Sri Lanka and along the humid Malabar Coast. Groundnuts are grown on the Deccan plateau, with wheat, corn and chickpeas, towards the north. Sri Lanka is a leading exporter of tea, coconuts and rubber. Cotton plantations supply local mills around Nagpur and Mumbai. Fishing supports many communities in Kerala and the Laccadive Islands.

The urban/rural population divide

urban 33%	rural 67%

Population density	Total land area
730 people per sq mile (282 people per sq km)	698,295 sq miles (1,809,054 sq km)

Land use and agricultural distribution

- cattle
- goats
- cereals
- cotton
- fishing
- groundnuts
- rice
- rubber
- tea
- capital cities
- major towns

pasture
cropland
forest
wetland

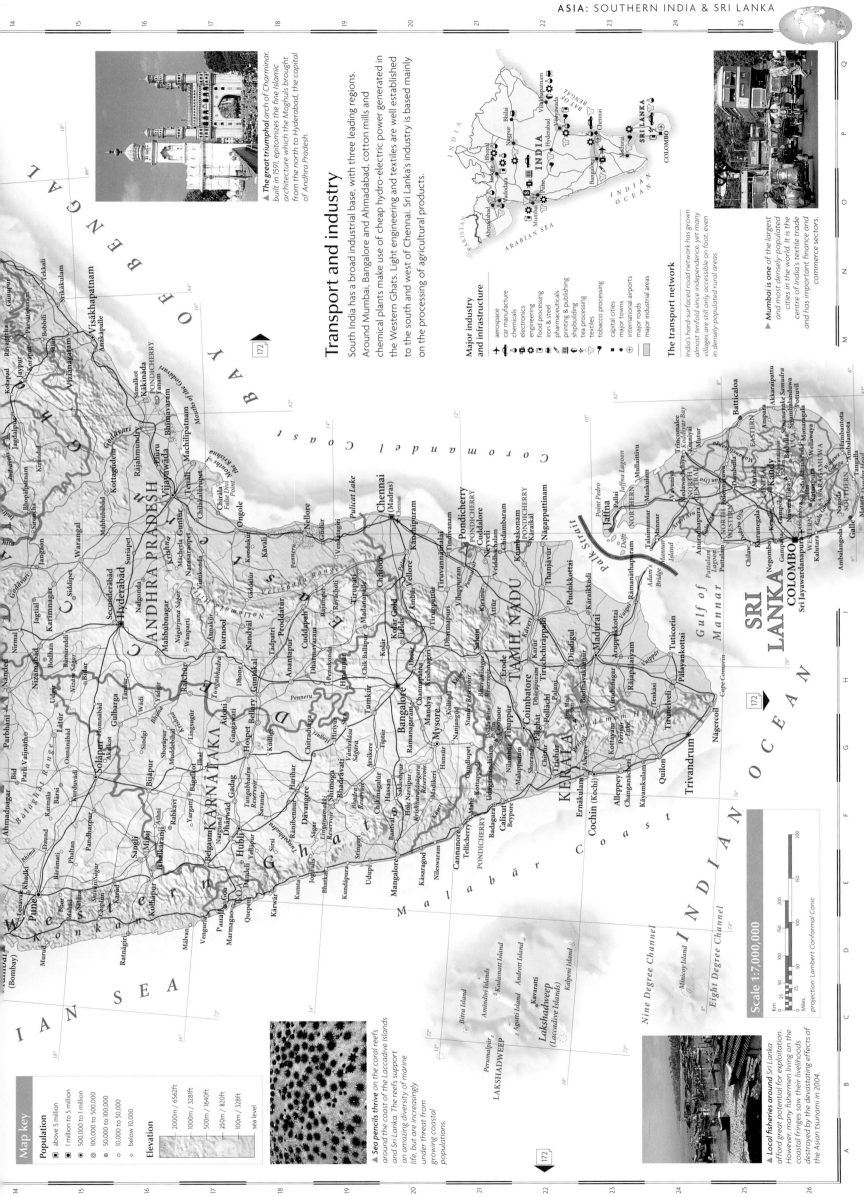

Transport and industry

South India has a broad industrial base, with three leading regions. Around Mumbai, Bangalore and Ahmadabad, cotton mills and chemical plants make use of cheap hydro-electric power generated in the Western Ghats. Light engineering and textiles are well established to the south and west of Chennai. Sri Lanka's industry is based mainly on the processing of agricultural products.

Major industry and infrastructure

- aerospace
- car manufacture
- chemicals
- electronics
- engineering
- food processing
- iron & steel
- pharmaceuticals
- printing & publishing
- shipbuilding
- tea processing
- textiles
- tobacco processing
- capital cities
- major cities
- major towns
- international airports
- major roads
- major industrial areas

The transport network

India's hard-surfaced road network has grown almost tenfold since independence, yet many villages are still only accessible on foot, even in densely-populated rural areas.

▲ *The great triumphal arch of Charminar, built in 1591, epitomizes the fine Islamic architecture which the Moghuls brought from the north to Hyderabad, the capital of Andhra Pradesh.*

▲ *Mumbai is one of the largest and most densely-populated cities in the world. It is the centre of India's textile trade and has important finance and commerce sectors.*

▲ *Sea pencils thrive on the coral reefs around the coast of the Laccadive Islands and Sri Lanka. The reefs support an amazing diversity of marine life, but are increasingly under threat from growing coastal populations.*

▲ *Local fisheries around Sri Lanka afford great potential for exploitation. However, many fishermen living on the coastal fringes saw their livelihoods destroyed by the devastating effects of the Asian tsunami in 2004.*

Map key

Population
- ■ above 5 million
- ■ 1 million to 5 million
- ● 500,000 to 1 million
- ● 100,000 to 500,000
- ● 50,000 to 100,000
- ○ 10,000 to 50,000
- ○ below 10,000

Elevation
- 2000m / 6562ft
- 1000m / 3281ft
- 500m / 1640ft
- 250m / 820ft
- 100m / 328ft
- sea level

Scale 1:7,000,000

projection: Lambert Conformal Conic

Mainland East Asia

CHINA, MONGOLIA, NORTH KOREA, SOUTH KOREA, TAIWAN

China, the world's most populous nation, has an unbroken cultural history, longer than that of any other country, and is rapidly emerging as a leading world power. When Mao Zedong established Communist rule in 1949, China had become a backward feudal empire, stricken by civil war and over a century of European and Japanese incursions. The closed regime withstood the traumas of rapid industrialization, communalized farming and the brutal purges of the Cultural Revolution but, since the 1980s has introduced economic reforms, led by expanded foreign trade. China's population is heavily concentrated in the east and, despite accelerating urban growth, remains predominantly rural. One cultural group, the Han, make up over 90% of the people, while five 'Autonomous Regions' have been established in the south and west for the main ethnic minorities.

Transport and industry

Large-scale industrial growth has always been a priority of the Communist government. Metals and machine production, chemicals and engineering are among the leading industries, concentrated in the major cities of the east coast. Textiles and clothing manufacture, the main consumer goods sector, is relatively well dispersed, with a few significant centres such as Shanghai, Beijing and Hong Kong.

Major industry and infrastructure

- car manufacture
- chemicals
- electronics
- engineering
- finance
- food processing
- iron & steel
- shipbuilding
- textiles

- ■ capital cities
- • major towns
- ⊕ international airports
- — major roads
- ▨ major industrial areas

The transport network

829,790 miles (1,335,571 km)	12,740 miles (20,506 km)
43,976 miles (70,780 km)	70,991 miles (114,262 km)

Ever-increasing demand for rail transportation has led to major improvment and expansion of the network, notably the 690 mile (1100 km) link between Golmud and Lhasa opened in 2006.

◄ *Coal is China's most abundant mineral resource. This mine at Fuxin in Liaoning province is used to provide coal for a nearby power station.*

The landscape

The East Asian landmass is arranged in three distinct levels, the highest of which is the Plateau of Tibet in the southwest. The arid uplands of northwestern China form a barren middle step. The main rivers flow eastward from these two platforms to the East China and South China sea coasts, across a broad region of alluvial lowlands and low hills.

◄ *Paektu-san, at 9023 ft (2750 m), is North Korea's highest peak; an extinct volcanic cone now filled by a crater lake.*

The loess plateau of northern China is the world's greatest expanse of loess, a loose soil made up of wind-blown material. The plateau has been heavily eroded by tributaries of the Yellow River.

Shifting sand dunes are found in the arid west of the northeast China Plain, while the eastern part of this great expanse is wet and swampy.

River-eroded fine soils

Thick blanket of loess

▲ *Because of its very small grain-size, loess has been easily transported and deposited by winds which scour the plains, and in northern China, deposits of loess can be up to 3000 ft (1000 m) thick. Loess-based soils are very fertile, but clearing land for agriculture quickly destabilizes the soil and allows it to be eroded.*

The Gobi Desert extends across the Nei Mongol Gaoyuan; a vast saucer-shaped upland surrounded by a rim of higher mountains.

Tarim Basin *(Tarim Pendi)*

Plateau of Tibet

▲ *The Plateau of Tibet occupies about a quarter of China's total area. The Yangtze, Mekong, Indus and Brahmaputra rivers all originate in the south and east of the plateau.*

Paektu-san

North China Plain

The Yangtze is China's longest river and the principal navigable waterway.

Sichuan Pendi

◄ *Although it is over 30 years since his death, the legacy of Chairman Mao Zedong, architect of the Great Proletarian Cultural Revolution, is still very much in evidence across China's landscape. In 1959 Mao launched a 20-year period of industrialization and socio-economic realignment, rejecting western ideals and social codes.*

The Himalayas extend along the southwestern edge of the Plateau of Tibet, forming a continuous mountain barrier over 1500 miles (2500 km) long.

Warm, humid conditions have caused intensive erosion of south China's karst areas, producing spectacular jagged peaks and vast caves in the limestone.

◄ *Gansu province, through which the ancient Silk Route passes on its way to the west, is characterized by extensive loess deposits which are terraced and used for crop cultivation.*

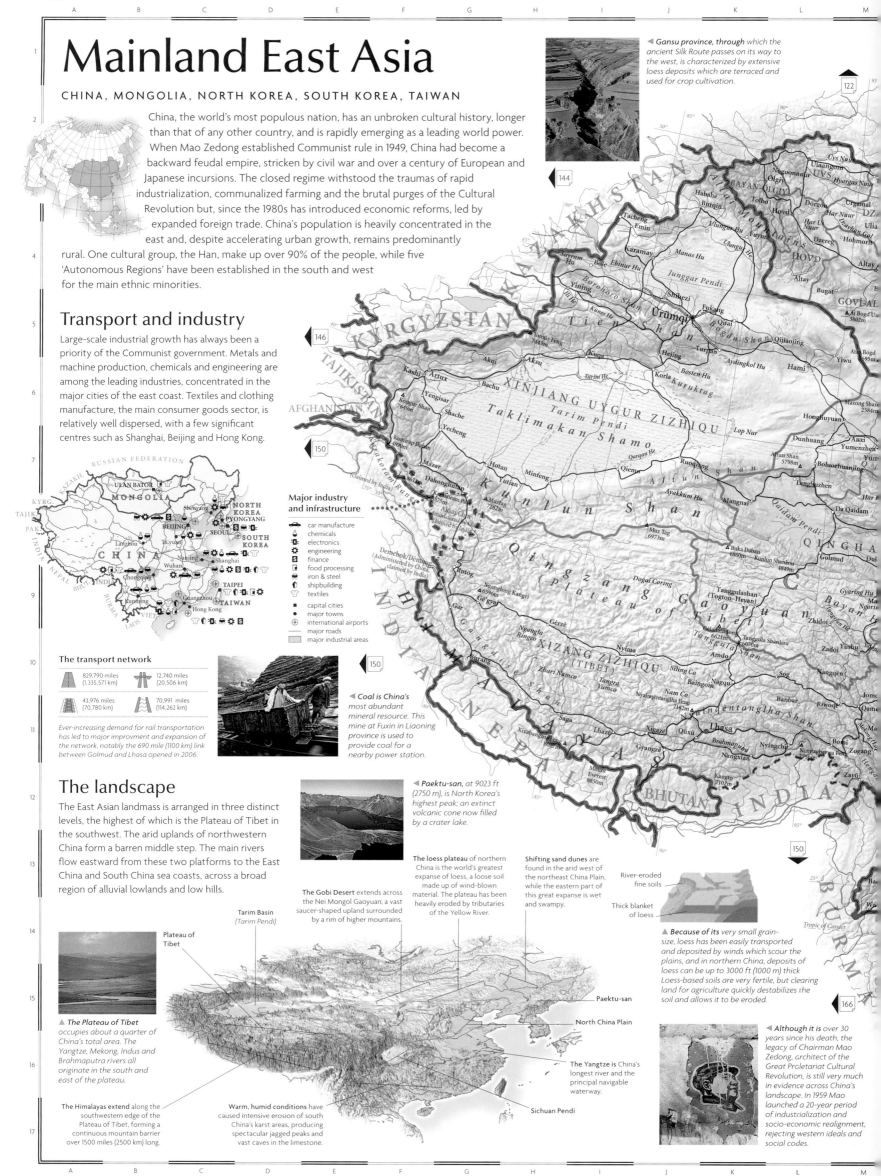

Scale 1:14,000,000

projection: Lambert Conformal Conic

Map key

Population
- above 5 million
- 1 million to 5 million
- 500,000 to 1 million
- 100,000 to 500,000
- 50,000 to 100,000
- 10,000 to 50,000
- below 10,000

Elevation
- 6000m / 19,686ft
- 4000m / 13,124ft
- 3000m / 9843ft
- 2000m / 6562ft
- 1000m / 3281ft
- 500m / 1640ft
- 250m / 820ft
- 100m / 328ft
- sea level

Using the land and sea

Around 90% of China is unsuitable for cultivation, being either climatically or topographically adverse, or lacking sufficiently fertile soils. Most of the west is used for nomadic herding, while farmland is concentrated in the eastern monsoon region, with rice grown in the tropical and subtropical south. Cereals and soya beans predominate as rainfall and temperatures decline further north.

Land use and agricultural distribution
- pigs
- sheep
- corn (maize)
- cotton
- fishing
- fruit
- rice
- sugar cane
- soya beans
- capital cities
- major towns
- pasture
- cropland
- forest
- mountain region

◄ The Great Wall of China remains one of the world's largest-ever construction projects, and is so vast that it is visible from space. Sections were added as late as 1640 and it runs for over 4000 miles (6400 km) from the Yellow Sea to Central Asia.

The urban/rural population divide

urban 32%   rural 68%

Population density	Total land area
325 people per sq mile (125 people per sq km)	4,288,672 sq miles (11,110,550 sq km)

Western China

Gansu, Ningxia, Qinghai, Tibet, Xinjiang

The plateaux and basins of China's dry, desolate western domain are sparsely populated and largely undeveloped, although they have rich mineral reserves; they also form a critical buffer zone for China, in a geographically important and culturally sensitive part of the Asian continent. Across most of the west, the Han Chinese are outnumbered by a range of cultural groups, including the Uygur, the largest group of the various semi-nomadic Muslim peoples from Central Asia. The remote, inhospitable Plateau of Tibet is the world's coldest and highest plateau. It has been occupied by the Chinese since 1950. Tibet is one of western China's five 'Autonomous Regions', but its reclusive Buddhist culture has been systematically undermined by the Chinese government.

Map key

Population

- ◉ 1 million to 5 million
- ◉ 500,000 to 1 million
- ◎ 100,000 to 500,000
- ⊕ 50,000 to 100,000
- ○ 10,000 to 50,000
- ∘ below 10,000

Elevation

- 6000m / 19,686ft
- 4000m / 13,124ft
- 3000m / 9843ft
- 2000m / 6562ft
- 1000m / 3281ft
- 500m / 1640ft
- 250m / 820ft
- 100m / 328ft
- sea level

Scale 1:7,750,000

Km
0 25 50 100 150 200

Miles
0 25 50 100 150 200

projection: Lambert Conformal Conic

▲ The Lhasa He is one of the many rivers which drain the vast Plateau of Tibet. From its source in the Nyainqêntanglha Shan range and fed by the spring meltwater, it eventually joins the upper Brahmaputra 40 miles (65 km) southwest of Lhasa.

Using the land

Agriculture is constrained by the cold, dry climate and lack of fertile soils in the region, although irrigation and glasshouse farming are increasing agricultural potential. Large quantities of fruit, like melons and grapes, are grown at the oases of Hami and Turpan in Xinjiang, and new irrigation schemes have greatly increased cotton and wheat production in the Tarim Basin (Tarim Pendi). Most of the great area of Tibet and Qinghai is devoted to pastoralism. Sheep are the principal livestock.

Land use and agricultural distribution

- 🐐 goats
- 🐑 sheep
- cereals
- cotton
- grapes
- melons
- oases
- • major towns
- pasture
- cropland
- forest
- mountain region
- desert

◀ The Potala Palace, in Tibet's capital, Lhasa, was the former residence of the Dalai Lama, Tibetan Buddhism's spiritual leader. Tibet remains only sparsely populated; forming over 20% of China's landmass, it supports fewer than 1% of its population.

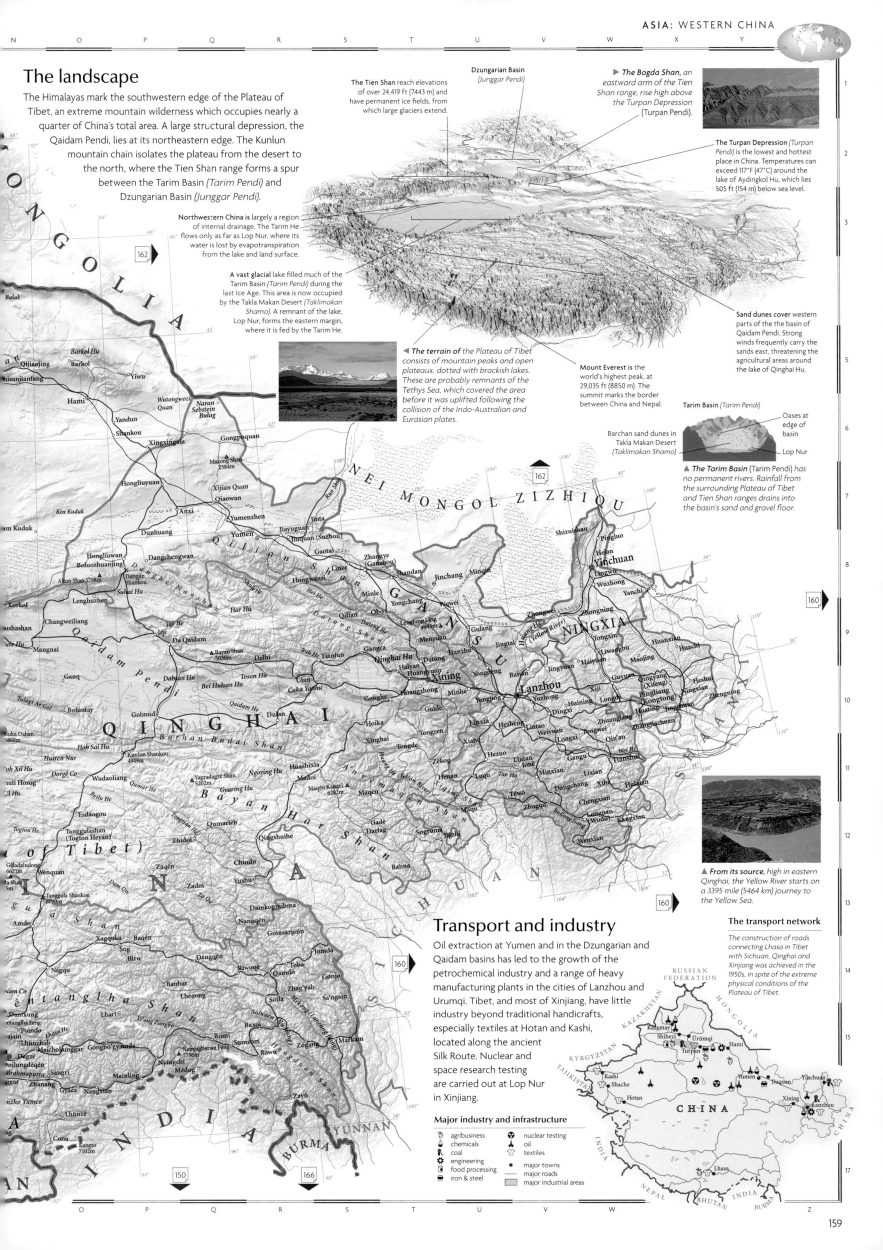

The landscape

The Himalayas mark the southwestern edge of the Plateau of Tibet, an extreme mountain wilderness which occupies nearly a quarter of China's total area. A large structural depression, the Qaidam Pendi, lies at its northeastern edge. The Kunlun mountain chain isolates the plateau from the desert to the north, where the Tien Shan range forms a spur between the Tarim Basin (Tarim Pendi) and Dzungarian Basin (Junggar Pendi).

Dzungarian Basin (Junggar Pendi)

The Tien Shan reach elevations of over 24,419 ft (7443 m) and have permanent ice fields, from which large glaciers extend.

▶ **The Bogda Shan**, an eastward arm of the Tien Shan range, rise high above the Turpan Depression (Turpan Pendi).

The Turpan Depression (Turpan Pendi) is the lowest and hottest place in China. Temperatures can exceed 117°F (47°C) around the lake of Aydingkol Hu, which lies 505 ft (154 m) below sea level.

Northwestern China is largely a region of internal drainage. The Tarim He flows only as far as Lop Nur, where its water is lost by evapotranspiration from the lake and land surface.

A vast glacial lake filled much of the Tarim Basin (Tarim Pendi) during the last Ice Age. This area is now occupied by the Takla Makan Desert (Taklimakan Shamo). A remnant of the lake, Lop Nur, forms the eastern margin, where it is fed by the Tarim He.

◀ **The terrain of** the Plateau of Tibet consists of mountain peaks and open plateaux, dotted with brackish lakes. These are probably remnants of the Tethys Sea, which covered the area before it was uplifted following the collision of the Indo-Australian and Eurasian plates.

Mount Everest is the world's highest peak, at 29,035 ft (8850 m). The summit marks the border between China and Nepal.

Sand dunes cover western parts of the the basin of Qaidam Pendi. Strong winds frequently carry the sands east, threatening the agricultural areas around the lake of Qinghai Hu.

Tarim Basin (Tarim Pendi)

Barchan sand dunes in Takla Makan Desert (Taklimakan Shamo)

Oases at edge of basin

Lop Nur

▲ **The Tarim Basin** (Tarim Pendi) has no permanent rivers. Rainfall from the surrounding Plateau of Tibet and Tien Shan ranges drains into the basin's sand and gravel floor.

▲ **From its source**, high in eastern Qinghai, the Yellow River starts on a 3395 mile (5464 km) journey to the Yellow Sea.

Transport and industry

Oil extraction at Yumen and in the Dzungarian and Qaidam basins has led to the growth of the petrochemical industry and a range of heavy manufacturing plants in the cities of Lanzhou and Urumqi. Tibet, and most of Xinjiang, have little industry beyond traditional handicrafts, especially textiles at Hotan and Kashi, located along the ancient Silk Route. Nuclear and space research testing are carried out at Lop Nur in Xinjiang.

The transport network

The construction of roads connecting Lhasa in Tibet with Sichuan, Qinghai and Xinjiang was achieved in the 1950s, in spite of the extreme physical conditions of the Plateau of Tibet.

Major industry and infrastructure

- agribusiness
- chemicals
- coal
- engineering
- food processing
- iron & steel
- nuclear testing
- oil
- textiles
- major towns
- major roads
- major industrial areas

Eastern China

TAIWAN, Anhui, Beijing, Chongqing, Fujian, Guangdong, Guangxi, Guizhou, Hainan, Hebei, Henan, Hubei, Hunan, Jiangsu, Jiangxi, Shaanxi, Shandong, Shanghai, Shanxi, Sichuan, Tianjin, Yunnan, Zhejiang

The east is China's heartland. Massive industria. development since 1949 has transformed much of the densely populated rural landscape, in a region still prone to flooding and drought. Over 30 cities have populations of over a million, including the giant metropolis of Shanghai and the capital Beijing, which has been China's cultural and political centre since the 13th century. The ethnically diverse southwest and the oil-rich interior provinces of Sichuan and Shaanxi have largely missed out on the remarkable economic growth occurring in designated free-trade areas along the coasts of the South and East China seas. The republic of Taiwan was established in 1949 by Chinese nationalists ousted from the mainland by the victorious Communist forces. Taiwan now has one of the strongest economies in the world but its sovereignty is not recognized by China. Hong Kong provides a major international trade link for China; a 99-year 'lease' period of British control was concluded in 1997.

▲ North of the Qin Ling range in Shaanxi province, is an agriculturally fertile region covered with fine, wind-blown deposits and known as the loess plateau. The loose sediments are vulnerable to water erosion.

Using the land and sea

This is a region of intensive cultivation. Wheat, millet, sorghum and cotton are the main crops of the Yellow River basin. South from Sichuan, rice becomes the principal crop, grown with wheat, corn and cotton along the Yangtze river. Tea is produced in the hills and sugar cane along the coast of the southeast, where flat land is limited. Pigs and poultry are raised in great numbers.

Land use and agricultural distribution

- cattle
- pigs
- cereals
- corn (maize)
- cotton
- fishing
- peanuts
- rice
- sugar cane
- tea
- capital cities
- major towns
- pasture
- cropland
- forest
- mountain region

▲ On the hills above the North China Plain, slopes are terraced to utilize the rich loess soils of the Taihang Shan range.

Map key

Population
- ■ above 5 million
- ▣ 1 million to 5 million
- ◉ 500,000 to 1 million
- ⊕ 100,000 to 500,000
- ⊕ 50,000 to 100,000
- ○ 10,000 to 50,000
- ○ below 10,000

Elevation
- 6000m / 19,686ft
- 4000m / 13,124ft
- 3000m / 9843ft
- 2000m / 6562ft
- 1000m / 3281ft
- 500m / 1640ft
- 250m / 820ft
- 100m / 328ft
- sea level

Scale 1:8,500,000

Km
0 25 50 100 200 250 300

Miles
0 25 50 100 150 200 250 300

projection: Lambert Conformal Conic

◀ The former Portuguese territory of Macao, with its colonial architecture, bars and casinos, reverted to Chinese rule in 1999.

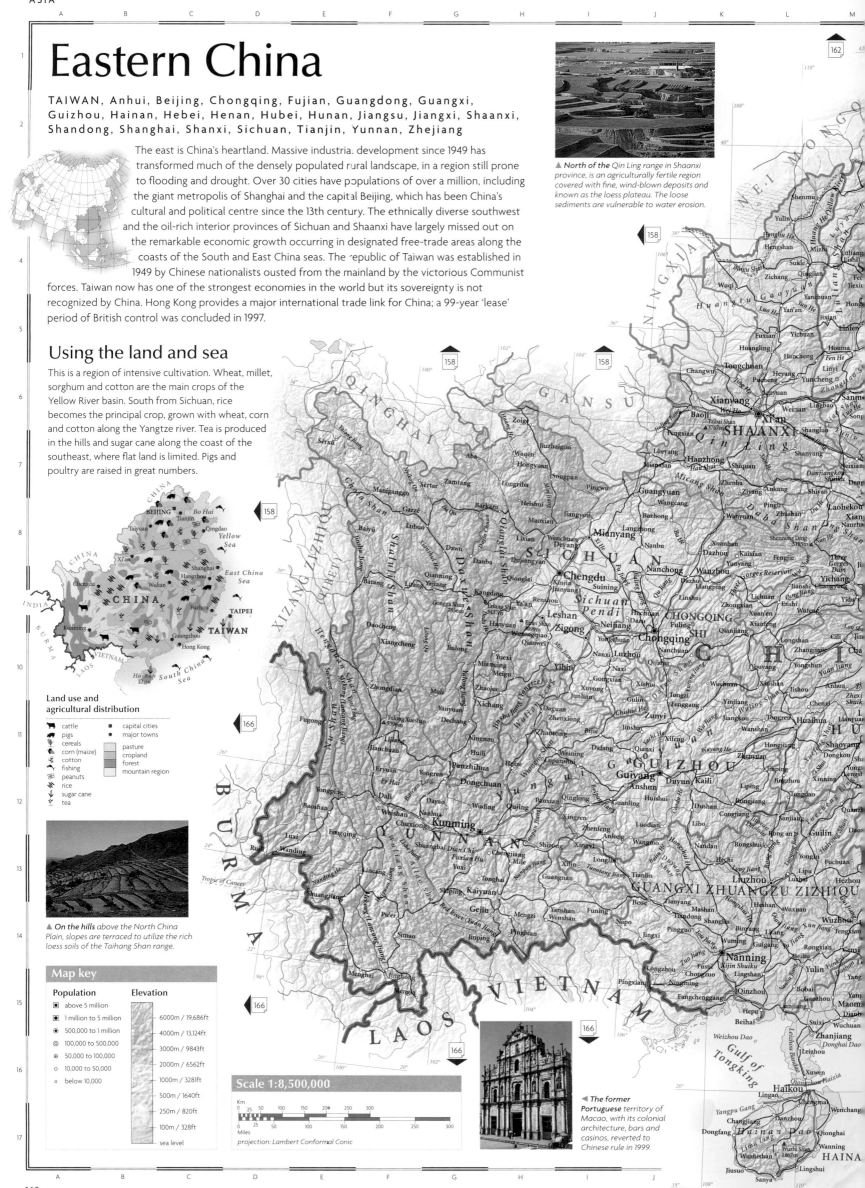

The landscape

The Sichuan Pendi *(Red Basin)*, lies at the foot of the Plateau of Tibet between the Qin Ling range in the north and the limestone uplands of Yunnan and Guizhou to the south. Hills extend from Yunnan to the rocky southeast coast, dividing the Yangtze and Xi Jiang basins. The North China Plain is composed of sediment carried by the Yellow River from the loess plateau in the northwest.

The Yellow river carries more sediment than any other river on Earth – approximately 1600 million tons (tonnes) per year. Floods caused by the breaching of the river's high banks have claimed many millions of human lives through history.

Intensive weathering of a great mass of limestone has left spectacular sheer-sided limestone pinnacles around Guilin in Guangxi. They rise abruptly from flat valley floors composed of deposited sediment. Limestone landforms are widespread in the southeast.

North China Plain

Loess plateau

Qin Ling

Yangtze River

Xi Jiang

The vast Sichuan Pendi is one of China's leading rice producing areas. The humid climate and accelerated weathering have produced a rich soil, while its climate is moderated by the encircling mountains.

The terraced rice paddies of southeastern China illustrate the significance of over 7000 years of cultivation in shaping the landscape.

Yungui Gaoyuan

▲ **The eroded rocky** features of the Yungui Gaoyuan are testament to the Earth's forces which have folded and eroded this limestone region to produce dramatic, incised river valleys, gorges and karst features.

Wu Jiang gorge

▶ **The Wu Jiang** gorge is the result of tectonic uplift on the Yungui Gaoyuan plateau which has caused the rapid downcutting of rivers across the region, creating deep, steep-sided valleys.

Course of the Yellow River

Pre 4BC

4BC–AD1

1234–1891

▲ **Over the past** 2000 years, the downstream course of the Yellow River has altered dramatically, unpredictably veering to the north and south across the North China Plain, and flooding vast expanses of land.

Transport and industry

Modern industry is concentrated in the coastal provinces, with dramatic new growth in Guangdong, based on foreign investment. Chemicals, iron and steel, engineering and textiles are leading activities around Beijing and Shanghai, the two largest industrial centres. In the interior provinces, large fossil fuel reserves support heavy industry around major cities such as Wuhan and Chengdu. Taiwan's broad-based manufacturing economy specializes in hi-tech goods. Hong Kong is a major financial centre and international entrepôt.

Major industry and infrastructure

- car manufacture
- chemicals
- electronics
- engineering
- finance
- food processing
- iron & steel
- pharmaceuticals
- shipbuilding
- textiles
- capital cities
- major towns
- international airports
- major roads
- major industrial areas

The transport network

China's Grand Canal (Da Yunhe), built in the 13th century, is the world's longest artificial waterway, running 1100 miles (1770 m) from Beijing to Hangzhou. Despite restoration work, not all of the canal is currently navigable.

▶ **The former British** colony of Hong Kong was ceded to China in 1997, marking the beginning of a new chapter in the history of this small territory. A vibrant mixture of eastern and western cultures, the booming textile industry, and subsequent electronics and financial industries, have driven immense growth and brought economic prosperity since the 1950s.

◀ **Taiwan is one** of the Pacific Rim's economic 'tigers', specializing in hi-tech and electronics industries.

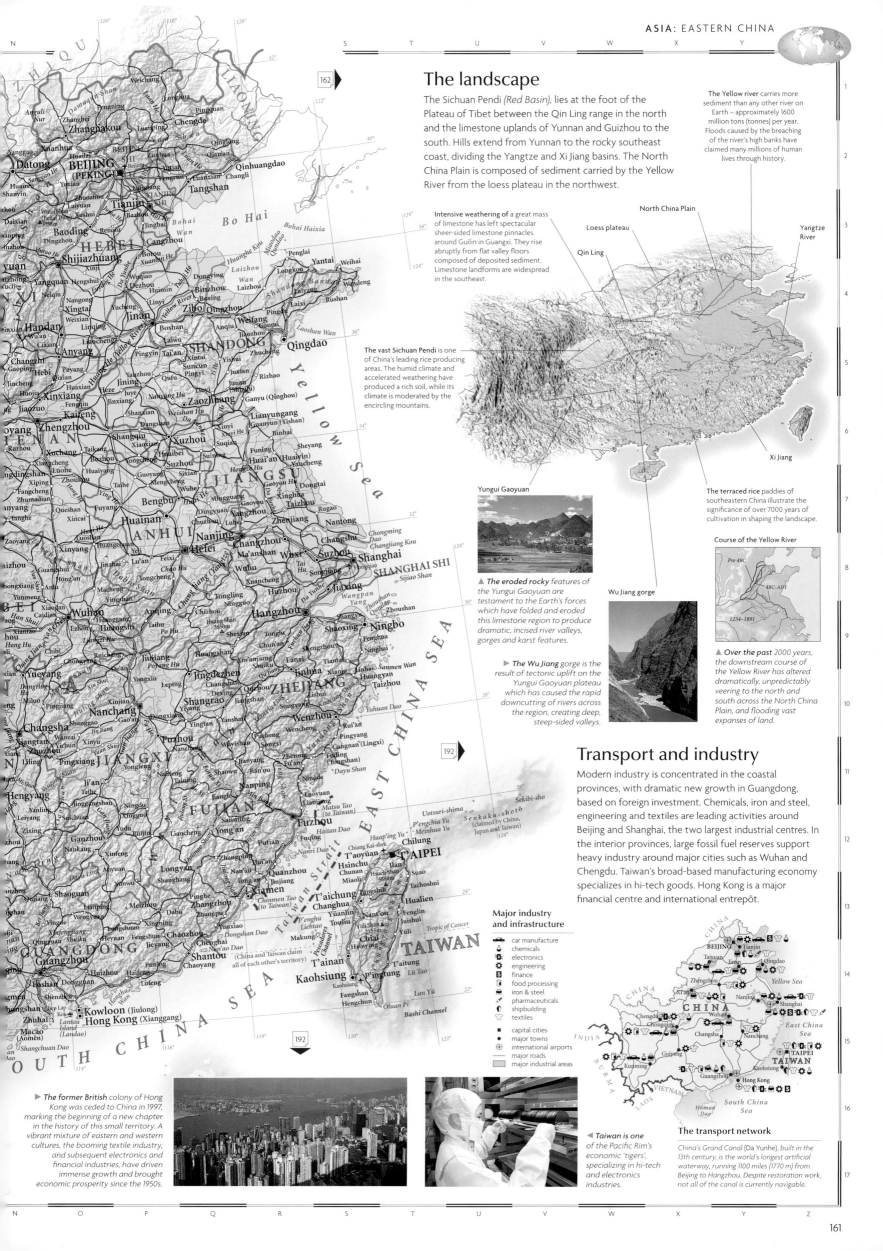

Northeastern China, Mongolia & Korea

MONGOLIA, NORTH KOREA, SOUTH KOREA, Heilongjiang, Inner Mongolia, Jilin, Liaoning

This northerly region has for centuries been a domain of shifting borders and competing colonial powers. Mongolia was the heartland of Chinghiz Khan's vast Mongol empire in the 13th century, while northeastern China was home to the Manchus, China's last ruling dynasty (1644–1911). The mineral and forest wealth of the northeast helped make this China's principal region of heavy industry, although the outdated state factories now face decline. South Korea's state-led market economy has grown dramatically and Seoul is now one of the world's largest cities. The austere communist regime of North Korea has isolated itself from the expanding markets of the Pacific Rim and faces continuing economic stagnation.

▲ *The Eurasian steppe* stretches from the mouth of the Danube in Europe, to Mongolia. In Mongolia, nomadic people have lived in felt huts called yurts or gers, for thousands of years.

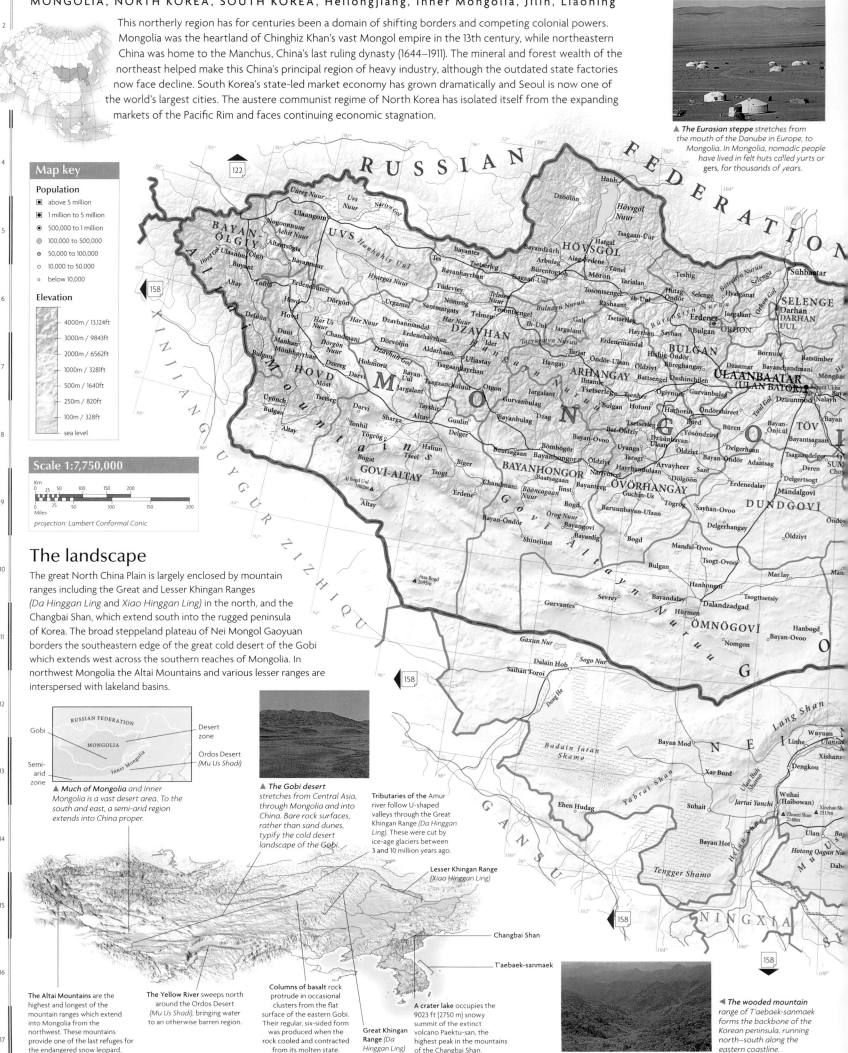

Map key

Population
- ■ above 5 million
- ◉ 1 million to 5 million
- ◉ 500,000 to 1 million
- ◎ 100,000 to 500,000
- ⊕ 50,000 to 100,000
- ○ 10,000 to 50,000
- ○ below 10,000

Elevation
- 4000m / 13,124ft
- 3000m / 9843ft
- 2000m / 6562ft
- 1000m / 3281ft
- 500m / 1640ft
- 250m / 820ft
- 100m / 328ft
- sea level

Scale 1:7,750,000

Km 0 25 50 100 150 200
Miles 0 25 50 100 150 200

projection: Lambert Conformal Conic

The landscape

The great North China Plain is largely enclosed by mountain ranges including the Great and Lesser Khingan Ranges (*Da Hinggan Ling* and *Xiao Hinggan Ling*) in the north, and the Changbai Shan, which extend south into the rugged peninsula of Korea. The broad steppeland plateau of Nei Mongol Gaoyuan borders the southeastern edge of the great cold desert of the Gobi which extends west across the southern reaches of Mongolia. In northwest Mongolia the Altai Mountains and various lesser ranges are interspersed with lakeland basins.

▲ *Much of Mongolia* and Inner Mongolia is a vast desert area. To the south and east, a semi-arid region extends into China proper.

▲ *The Gobi desert* stretches from Central Asia, through Mongolia and into China. Bare rock surfaces, rather than sand dunes, typify the cold desert landscape of the Gobi.

Tributaries of the Amur river follow U-shaped valleys through the Great Khingan Range (*Da Hinggan Ling*). These were cut by ice-age glaciers between 3 and 10 million years ago.

Lesser Khingan Range (*Xiao Hinggan Ling*)

Changbai Shan

T'aebaek-sanmaek

◀ *The wooded mountain* range of T'aebaek-sanmaek forms the backbone of the Korean peninsula, running north–south along the eastern coastline.

The Altai Mountains are the highest and longest of the mountain ranges which extend into Mongolia from the northwest. These mountains provide one of the last refuges for the endangered snow leopard.

The Yellow River sweeps north around the Ordos Desert (*Mu Us Shadi*), bringing water to an otherwise barren region.

Columns of basalt rock protrude in occasional clusters from the flat surface of the eastern Gobi. Their regular, six-sided form was produced when the rock cooled and contracted from its molten state.

Great Khingan Range (*Da Hinggan Ling*)

A crater lake occupies the 9023 ft (2750 m) snowy summit of the extinct volcano Paektu-san, the highest peak in the mountains of the Changbai Shan.

Gobi

RUSSIAN FEDERATION

MONGOLIA

Inner Mongolia

Desert zone

Ordos Desert (Mu Us Shadi)

Semi-arid zone

Transport and industry

North Korea's centrally-planned economy is strongly oriented towards heavy industry, while South Korea has a broad manufacturing base which includes textiles, steel, electronics, and one of the world's largest shipbuilding industries. Mongolia and Inner Mongolia's great mineral resource potential is largely undeveloped. The heavy industrial region around Shenyang produces iron, steel, chemicals and cement on a massive scale.

Major industry and infrastructure

- car manufacture
- chemicals
- coal
- electronics
- engineering
- finance
- food processing
- iron & steel
- pharmaceuticals
- shipbuilding
- textiles
- capital cities
- major towns
- international airports
- major roads
- major industrial areas

The transport network

Liaoning has China's most comprehensive railway network, the legacy of the Japanese occupation of Manchuria in the 20th century. The railways are used primarily for freight transport.

▲ *Ulan Bator, the Mongolian capital bears many of the hallmarks of Soviet-style central planning, the result of economic and industrial assistance from the Soviet Union following Mongolian independence in 1921.*

▶ *While North Korea has remained politically and economically isolated from the rest of the world, South Korea has enjoyed immense economic growth. It has benefited considerably from US economic aid in the aftermath of the Korean war of 1950–1953.*

Using the land and sea

Mongolia and Inner Mongolia rely heavily on livestock farming, with only about 1% of the land area cultivated. Northeastern China produces wheat, corn, soya beans and sugar beet. The cool climate limits the range of crops and large upland areas of the northeast remain forested. Rice is the staple food of North and South Korea. The latter has become a leading ocean-fishing nation.

Land use and agricultural distribution

- goats
- pigs
- sheep
- corn (maize)
- fishing
- rice
- soya beans
- sugar beet
- wheat
- capital cities
- major towns
- pasture
- cropland
- forest
- mountain region
- desert

A B C D E F G H I J K L M

Japan

In the years since the end of the Second World War, Japan has become the world's most dynamic industrial nation. The country comprises a string of over 4000 islands which lie in a great northeast to southwest arc in the northwest Pacific. Four major islands: Hokkaido, Honshu, Shikoku and Kyushu are home to the great majority of Japan's population of 128 million people, although the mountainous terrain of the central region means that most cities are situated on the coast. A densely populated industrial belt stretches along much of Honshu's southern coast, including Japan's crowded capital, Tokyo. Alongside its spectacular economic growth and the increasing westernization of its cities, Japan still maintains a most singular culture, reflected in its traditional food, formal behavioural codes, unique Shinto religion and a deep reverence for the emperor.

Using the land and sea

Although only about 11% of Japan is suitable for cultivation, substantial government support, a favourab[le] climate and intensive farming methods enable the country to be virtually self-sufficient in rice production. Northern Hokkaido, the largest and most productive farming region, has an open terrain an[d] climate similar to that of the US Midwest, and produces over half of Japan's cereal requirements. Farmer[s] are being encouraged to diversify by growing fruit, vegetables and wheat, as well as raising livestock.

Land use and agricultural distribution

- cattle
- pigs
- fishing
- cereals
- citrus fruits
- fruit
- herbs
- rice
- root crops
- tobacco

- ■ capital cities
- ● major towns

pasture
cropland
forest

The urban/rural population divide

urban 78% rural 22%

0 10 20 30 40 50 60 70 80 90 100

Population density	Total land area
885 people per sq mile (342 people per sq km)	145,869 sq miles (377,800 sq km)

The landscape

The islands of Japan lie on the Pacific 'Ring of Fire', and form a series of clearly defined arcs. The largely mountainous landscape was formed very recently in geological terms. Volcanic eruptions and earthquakes continue to reshape the terrain and to shake the country's complex infrastructure. There is no one continuous mountain range; the mountains divide into many small land blocks separated by lowlands and dissected by numerous river valleys.

▶ **Cutting terraces maximizes** the limited agricultural land, enabling Japan to produce large quantities of rice.

Sea of Japan (East Sea)
Active volcanic island
Japan Trench (subduction zone)

▲ **Japan is part** of an arc of volcanic islands, formed by the Pacific Plate diving under the Eurasian Plate. This process generates intense stress which is periodically released as earthquakes.

◀ **Mount Fuji is** Japan's highest mountain, rising 12,388 ft (3776 m) above the Kanto Plain in the central region of Honshu. The flat land below is suitable for growing crops such as tea. Like many Japanese mountains, it is revered as a sacred site.

Mount Fuji

A number of rivers which emerge from the volcanic parts of northwestern Honshu are so highly acidic that their water is unsuitable for irrigation and consumption.

▶ **Trees cling to** the sheer slopes of the waterfalls on the northern island of Hokkaido. The island's climate is similar to that in northern Europe, with long, cold winters and short, warm summers.

In much of Kyushu the coast is subsiding, giving a highly indented coastline. In some places, former hilltops are barely visible above the current sea level.

There are over 60 active volcanoes – like Asahi-dake, Hokkaido's highest peak – throughout Japan. This accounts for more than 10% of the world's total.

The Inland Sea (Seto-naikai) has resulted from the depression of faulted blocks which has allowed sea water to invade the region between northern Shikoku and western Honshu.

Strong southeasterly winds blowing onshore during the winter create sand dunes which extend for miles along the eastern coasts.

Biwa-ko is the largest lake in Japan, covering 260 sq miles (673 sq km) in central Honshu. The depression in which it lies was created by recent faulting of the underlying rocks.

Rising land on the Pacific coast of Honshu leads to typical features such as raised beaches, some lying over 1000 ft (300 m) above sea level.

▼ **Autumnal trees near** Gifu, on central Honshu, create a spectacular display. Native trees on this island include camphor, pasania, Japanese evergreen oak, camellia and holly.

▶ **The Kobe earthquake** in January 1995 highlighted Japan's vulnerability to earthquakes, despite technological advances. It shattered much of the infrastructure of this important port. More than 5000 people died as buildings and overhead highways collapsed and fires broke out.

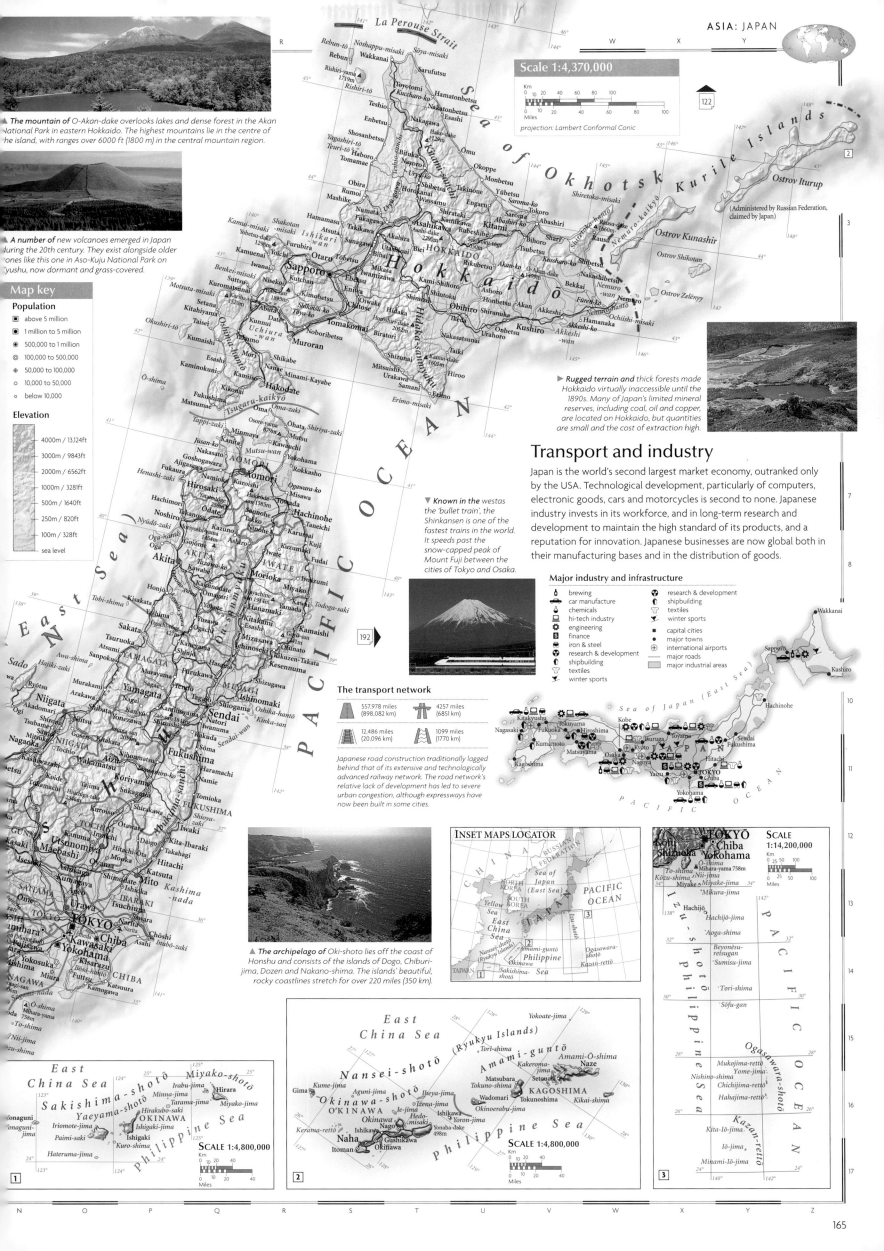

▲ **The mountain of** O-Akan-dake overlooks lakes and dense forest in the Akan National Park in eastern Hokkaido. The highest mountains lie in the centre of the island, with ranges over 6000 ft (1800 m) in the central mountain region.

▲ **A number of** new volcanoes emerged in Japan during the 20th century. They exist alongside older ones like this one in Aso-Kuju National Park on Kyushu, now dormant and grass-covered.

Map key

Population
- ■ above 5 million
- ■ 1 million to 5 million
- ◎ 500,000 to 1 million
- ◉ 100,000 to 500,000
- ⊕ 50,000 to 100,000
- ○ 10,000 to 50,000
- ○ below 10,000

Elevation
- 4000m / 13,124ft
- 3000m / 9843ft
- 2000m / 6562ft
- 1000m / 3281ft
- 500m / 1640ft
- 250m / 820ft
- 100m / 328ft
- sea level

Scale 1:4,370,000

Km 0 10 20 40 60 80 100
Miles 0 20 40 60 80 100

projection: Lambert Conformal Conic

(Administered by Russian Federation, claimed by Japan)

▶ **Rugged terrain and** thick forests made Hokkaido virtually inaccessible until the 1890s. Many of Japan's limited mineral reserves, including coal, oil and copper, are located on Hokkaido, but quantities are small and the cost of extraction high.

Transport and industry

Japan is the world's second largest market economy, outranked only by the USA. Technological development, particularly of computers, electronic goods, cars and motorcycles is second to none. Japanese industry invests in its workforce, and in long-term research and development to maintain the high standard of its products, and a reputation for innovation. Japanese businesses are now global both in their manufacturing bases and in the distribution of goods.

▼ **Known in the** west as the 'bullet train', the Shinkansen is one of the fastest trains in the world. It speeds past the snow-capped peak of Mount Fuji between the cities of Tokyo and Osaka.

Major industry and infrastructure
- brewing
- car manufacture
- chemicals
- hi-tech industry
- engineering
- finance
- iron & steel
- research & development
- shipbuilding
- textiles
- winter sports
- research & development
- shipbuilding
- textiles
- winter sports
- ● capital cities
- ● major towns
- ✈ international airports
- major roads
- major industrial areas

The transport network

557,978 miles (898,082 km)	4257 miles (6851 km)
12,486 miles (20,096 km)	1099 miles (1770 km)

Japanese road construction traditionally lagged behind that of its extensive and technologically advanced railway network. The road network's relative lack of development has led to severe urban congestion, although expressways have now been built in some cities.

▲ **The archipelago of** Oki-shoto lies off the coast of Honshu and consists of the islands of Dogo, Chiburi-jima, Dozen and Nakano-shima. The islands' beautiful, rocky coastlines stretch for over 220 miles (350 km).

INSET MAPS LOCATOR

TOKYO SCALE 1:14,200,000

Km 0 25 50 100
Miles 0 25 50 100

SCALE 1:4,800,000

Km 0 10 20 40
Miles 0 10 20 40

SCALE 1:4,800,000

Km 0 10 20 40
Miles 0 10 20 40

Mainland Southeast Asia

BURMA, CAMBODIA, LAOS, THAILAND, VIETNAM

Thickly forested mountains, intercut by the broad valleys of five great rivers characterize the landscape of Southeast Asia's mainland countries. Agriculture remains the main activity for much of the population, which is concentrated in the river flood plains and deltas. Linked ethnic and cultural roots give the region a distinct identity. Most people on the mainland are Theravada Buddhists, and the Philippines is the only predominantly Christian country in Southeast Asia. Foreign intervention began in the 16th century with the opening of the spice trade; Cambodia, Laos and Vietnam were French colonies until the end of the Second World War, Burma was under British control. Only Thailand was never colonized. Today, Thailand is poised to play a leading role in the economic development of the Pacific Rim, and Laos and Vietnam have begun to mend the devastation of the Vietnam War, and to develop their economies. With continuing political instability and a shattered infrastructure, Cambodia faces an uncertain future, while Burma is seeking investment and the ending of its long isolation from the world community.

▲ *The Irrawaddy river* is Burma's vital central artery, watering the ricefields and providing a rich source of fish, as well as an important transport link, particularly for local traffic.

Burma: Capital cities
YANGON – capital
PYINMANA – administrative capital

The landscape

A series of mountain ranges runs north–south through the mainland, formed as the result of the collision between the Eurasian Plate and the Indian subcontinent, which created the Himalayas. They are interspersed by the valleys of a number of great rivers. On their passage to the sea these rivers have deposited sediment, forming huge, fertile flood plains and deltas.

The coastline of the Isthmus of Kra

Longshore drift
Eroded coastline
Spit
Lagoon
Wave attack

◀ *The east and* west coasts of the Isthmus of Kra differ greatly. The tectonically uplifting west coast is exposed to the harsh south-westerly monsoon and is heavily eroded. On the east coast, longshore currents produce depositional features such as spits and lagoons.

Hkakabo Razi is the highest point in mainland Southeast Asia. It rises 19,300 ft (5885 m) at the border between China and Burma.

Mountains dominate the Laotian landscape with more than 90% of the land lying more than 600 ft (180 m) above sea level. The mountains of the Chaîne Annamitique form the country's eastern border.

The Irrawaddy river runs virtually north–south, draining the plains of northern Burma. The Irrawaddy delta is the country's main rice-growing area.

The Red River delta in northern Vietnam is fringed to the north by steep-sided, round-topped limestone hills, typical of karst scenery.

Salween River

Isthmus of Kra

Malay Peninsula

◀ *The fast-flowing waters* of the Mekong river cascade over this waterfall in Champasak province in Laos. The force of the water erodes rocks at the base of the fall.

▲ *The coast of* the Isthmus of Kra, in southeast Thailand has many small, precipitous islands like these, formed by chemical erosion on limestone, which is weathered along vertical cracks. The humidity of the climate in Southeast Asia increases the rate of weathering.

Tonle Sap, a freshwater lake, drains into the Mekong delta via the Mekong river. It is the largest lake in Southeast Asia.

The Mekong river flows through southern China and Burma, then for much of its length forms the border between Laos and Thailand, flowing through Cambodia before terminating in a vast delta on the southern Vietnamese coast.

Using the land and sea

The fertile flood plains of rivers such as the Mekong and Salween, and the humid climate, enable the production of rice throughout the region. Cambodia, Burma and Laos still have substantial forests, producing hardwoods such as teak and rosewood. Cash crops include tropical fruits such as coconuts, bananas and pineapples, rubber, oil palm, sugar cane and the jute substitute, kenaf. Pigs and cattle are the main livestock raised. Large quantities of marine and freshwater fish are caught throughout the region.

Land use and agricultural distribution

- cattle
- pigs
- bananas
- coconuts
- fishing
- oil palms
- rice
- rubber
- sugar cane
- timber
- capital cities
- major towns

pasture
cropland
forest
wetland

The urban/rural population divide

urban 30%   rural 70%

0 10 20 30 40 50 60 70 80 90 100

Population density	Total land area
345 people per sq mile	733,828 sq miles
(133 people per sq km)	(1,901,110 sq km)

▲ *Commercial logging* – still widespread in Burma – has now been stopped in Thailand because of over-exploitation of the tropical rainforest.

Transport and industry

Industrial manufacturing has become increasingly important in Thailand and Vietnam in recent years. The assembling of component-based electrical and electronic goods is becoming more common throughout this region, with foreign companies benefiting from low labour costs and the upgrading of technology. The economies of Burma and Cambodia are still based on agricultural produce and the processing of raw materials. Tin is the region's most important metal, and nickel, copper and chromite are also mined, although the quantities produced are not significant on a global scale. Thailand's successful tourist industry is the country's highest earner of foreign exchange.

The transport network

82,958 miles (133,524 km)	267 miles (430 km)
7500 miles (12,071 km)	28,585 miles (46,008 km)

Transport development has concentrated on the building of road networks. Water and sea transport remain important, although air links have improved, particularly in Thailand and the Philippines.

Major industry and infrastructure

- chemicals
- electronics
- engineering
- finance
- food processing
- iron & steel
- oil & gas
- mining
- shipbuilding
- textiles
- timber processing
- capital cities
- major towns
- international airports
- major roads
- major industrial areas

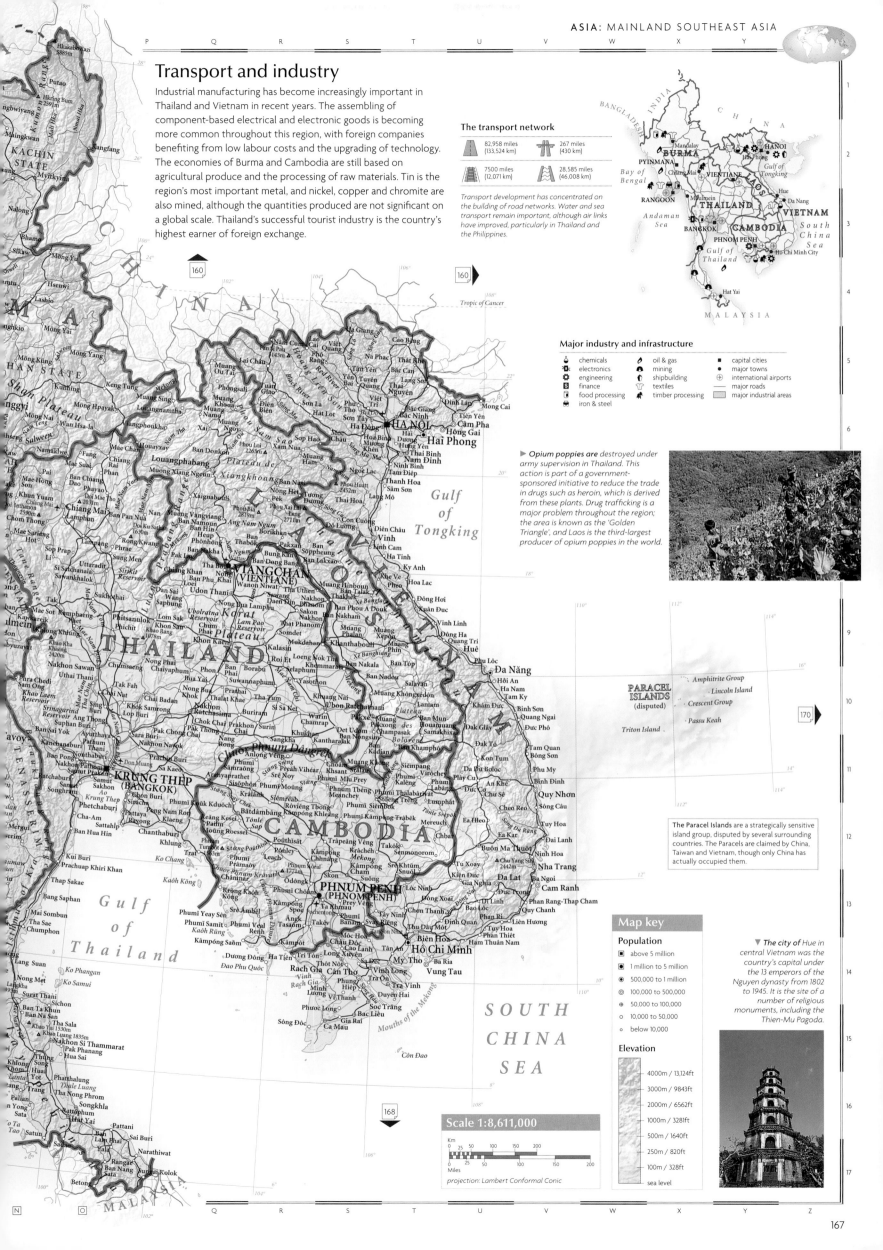

▶ **Opium poppies are** destroyed under army supervision in Thailand. This action is part of a government-sponsored initiative to reduce the trade in drugs such as heroin, which is derived from these plants. Drug trafficking is a major problem throughout the region; the area is known as the 'Golden Triangle', and Laos is the third-largest producer of opium poppies in the world.

The Paracel Islands are a strategically sensitive island group, disputed by several surrounding countries. The Paracels are claimed by China, Taiwan and Vietnam, though only China has actually occupied them.

Map key

Population

- above 5 million
- 1 million to 5 million
- 500,000 to 1 million
- 100,000 to 500,000
- 50,000 to 100,000
- 10,000 to 50,000
- below 10,000

Elevation

- 4000m / 13,124ft
- 3000m / 9843ft
- 2000m / 6562ft
- 1000m / 3281ft
- 500m / 1640ft
- 250m / 820ft
- 100m / 328ft
- sea level

▼ **The city of** Hue in central Vietnam was the country's capital under the 13 emperors of the Nguyen dynasty from 1802 to 1945. It is the site of a number of religious monuments, including the Thien-Mu Pagoda.

Scale 1:8,611,000

projection: Lambert Conformal Conic

Western Maritime Southeast Asia

BRUNEI, INDONESIA, MALAYSIA, SINGAPORE

The world's largest archipelago, Indonesia's myriad islands stretch 3100 miles (5000 km) eastwards across the Pacific, from the Malay Peninsula to western New Guinea. Only about 1500 of the 13,677 islands are inhabited and the huge, predominently Muslim population is unevenly distributed, with some two-thirds crowded onto the western islands of Java, Madura and Bali. The national government is trying to resettle large numbers of people from these islands to other parts of the country to reduce population pressure there. Malaysia, split between the mainland and the east Malaysian states of Sabah and Sarawak on Borneo, has a diverse population, as well as a fast-growing economy, although the pace of its development is still far outstripped by that of Singapore. This small island nation is the financial and commercial capital of Southeast Asia. The Sultanate of Brunei in northern Borneo, one of the world's last princely states, has an extremely high standard of living, based on its oil revenues.

The landscape

Indonesia's western islands are characterized by rugged volcanic mountains cloaked with dense tropical forest, which slope down to coastal plains covered by thick alluvial swamps. The Sunda Shelf, an extension of the Eurasian Plate, lies between Java, Bali, Sumatra and Borneo. These islands' mountains rise from a base below the sea, and they were once joined together by dry land, which has since been submerged by rising sea levels.

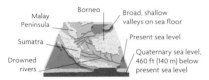

▲ *The Sunda Shelf* underlies this whole region. It is one of the largest submarine shelves in the world, covering an area of 714,285 sq miles (1,850,000 sq km). During the early Quaternary period, when sea levels were lower, the shelf was exposed.

◄ *Danau (lake) Toba* in Sumatra fills an enormous caldera 18 miles (30 km) wide and 62 miles (100 km) long – the largest in the world. It was formed through a combination of volcanic action and tectonic activity.

Malay Peninsula has a rugged east coast, but the west coast, fronting the Strait of Malacca, has many sheltered beaches and bays. The two coasts are divided by the Banjaran Titiwangsa, which run the length of the peninsula.

Gunung Kinabalu is the highest peak in Malaysia, rising 13,455 ft (4101 m).

◄ *The river of* Sungai Mahakam cuts through the central highlands of Borneo, the third largest island in the world, with a total area of 290,000 sq miles (757,050 sq km). Although mountainous, Borneo is one of the most stable of the Indonesian islands, with little volcanic activity.

The island of Krakatau (Pulau Rakata), lying between Sumatra and Java, was all but destroyed in 1883, when the volcano erupted. The release of gas and dust into the atmosphere disrupted cloud cover and global weather patterns for several years.

Indonesia has more than 220 volcanoes, most of which are still active. They are strung out along the island arc from Sumatra through the Lesser Sunda Islands, into the Moluccas and Celebes.

Transport and industry

Singapore has a thriving economy based on international trade and finance. Annual trade through the port is among the highest of any in the world. Indonesia's western islands still depend on natural resources, particularly petroleum, gas and wood, although the economy is rapidly diversifying with manufactured exports including garments, consumer electronics and footwear. A high-profile aircraft industry has developed in Bandung on Java. Malaysia has a fast-growing and varied manufacturing sector, although oil, gas and timber remain important resource-based industries.

▶ *Ranks of gleaming* skyscrapers, new motorways and infrastructure construction reflect the investment which is pouring into Southeast Asian cities like the Malaysian capital, Kuala Lumpur. Traditional housing and markets still exist amidst the new developments. Many of the city's inhabitants subsist at a level far removed from the prosperity implied by its outward modernity.

Malaysia: Capital cities

KUALA LUMPUR – capital
PUTRAJAYA – administrative capital

Using the land and sea

Rice is the most important arable crop in Indonesia and Malaysia, and both countries manage to meet almost all of their domestic demand. Malaysian rubber accounts for 25% of world production and is the main cash crop, grown on plantations and small farms, along with oil palms and copra. Timber is exported from both Malaysia and Indonesia. Modern agricultural techniques enable Singapore to produce fruits and vegetables despite a shortage of suitable land.

▶ *Spiral cuts in the bark of this rubber palm show where it has been tapped. Sophisticated 'cloning' techniques mean that trees which produce consistently high quantities of rubber can be easily reproduced.*

The transport network

165,272 miles (266,010 km)	
958 miles (1,542 km)	
5,061 miles (8,146 km)	
18,070 miles (29,084 km)	

Singapore's metro system, completed in 1991, is among the most efficient in the world. Malaysia has several fast, modern highways and most roads are paved. Indonesia's many islands make improvement of the shipping infrastructure a priority.

Major industry and infrastructure

- ✈ aerospace
- copra processing
- chemicals
- electronics
- engineering
- § finance
- food processing
- iron & steel
- oil
- ship building
- timber processing
- textiles

- ■ capital cities
- • major towns
- ✈ international airports
- — major roads
- major industrial areas

Land use and agricultural distribution

- coconuts
- fishing
- oil palms
- rice
- rubber
- shellfish
- sugar cane
- timber

- ■ capital cities
- • major towns

- pasture
- cropland
- forest
- wetland

The urban/rural population divide

urban 44%   rural 56%

0 10 20 30 40 50 60 70 80 90 100

Population density	Total land area
297 people per sq mile (115 people per sq km)	828,356 sq miles (2,146,000 sq km)

▼ *This tiny island near Kota Kinabalu, in Sabah, eastern Malaysia, is a part of a designated national park. Thickly forested, it is surrounded by broad, sandy beaches and shallow inland seas.*

▲ *The volcano of Gunung Semeru in eastern Java lies on the Pacific 'Ring of Fire'. It is part of the ancient Tennegger volcano and remains highly active.*

Scale 1:8,750,000

Km 0 25 50 100 150 200
Miles 0 25 50 100 150 200

projection: Mercator

Map key

Population
- ■ above 5 million
- ■ 1 million to 5 million
- ◉ 500,000 to 1 million
- ◎ 100,000 to 500,000
- ⊕ 50,000 to 100,000
- ○ 10,000 to 50,000
- ○ below 10,000

Elevation
- 4000m / 13,124ft
- 3000m / 9843ft
- 2000m / 6562ft
- 1000m / 3281ft
- 500m / 1640ft
- 250m / 820ft
- 100m / 328ft
- sea level

Eastern Maritime Southeast Asia

EAST TIMOR, INDONESIA, PHILIPPINES

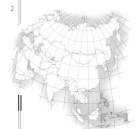

The Philippines takes its name from Philip II of Spain who was king when the islands were colonized during the 16th century. Almost 400 years of Spanish, and later US, rule have left their mark on the country's culture; English is widely spoken and over 90% of the population is Christian. The Philippines' economy is agriculturally based – inadequate infrastructure and electrical power shortages have so far hampered faster industrial growth. Indonesia's eastern islands are less economically developed than the rest of the country. Papua (Irian Jaya), which constitutes the western portion of New Guinea, is one of the world's last great wildernesses. East Timor is the newest independent state in the world, gaining full autonomy in 2002.

▲ The traditional boat-shaped houses of the Toraja people in Sulawesi. Although now Christian, the Toraja still practice the animist traditions and rituals of their ancestors. They are famous for their elaborate funeral ceremonies and burial sites in cliffside caves.

The landscape

Located on the Pacific 'Ring of Fire' the Philippines' 7100 islands are subject to frequent earthquakes and volcanic activity. Their terrain is largely mountainous, with narrow coastal plains and interior valleys and plains. Luzon and Mindanao are by far the largest islands and comprise roughly 66% of the country's area. Indonesia's eastern islands are mountainous and dotted with volcanoes, both active and dormant.

▶ Lake Taal on the Philippines island of Luzon lies within the crater of an immense volcano that erupted twice in the 20th century, first in 1911 and again in 1965, causing the deaths of more than 3200 people.

The Spratly Islands are a strategically sensitive island group, disputed by several surrounding countries. The Spratlys are claimed by China, Taiwan, Vietnam, Malaysia and the Philippines and are particularly important as they lie on oil and gas deposits.

Mindanao has five mountain ranges many of which have large numbers of active volcanoes. Lying just west of the Philippines Trench, which forms the boundary between the colliding Philippine and Eurasian plates, the entire island chain is subject to earthquakes and volcanic activity.

The 1000 islands of the Moluccas are the fabled Spice Islands of history, whose produce attracted traders from around the globe. Most of the northern and central Moluccas have dense vegetation and rugged mountainous interiors where elevations often exceed 3000 feet (9144 m).

▲ Bohol in the southern Philippines is famous for its so-called 'chocolate hills'. There are more than 1000 of these regular mounds on the island. The hills are limestone in origin, the smoothed remains of an earlier cycle of erosion. Their brown appearance in the dry season gives them their name.

The four-pronged island of Celebes is the product of complex tectonic activity which ruptured and then reattached small fragments of the Earth's crust to form the island's many peninsulas.

Coral islands such as Timor in eastern Indonesia show evidence of very recent and dramatic movements of the Earth's plates. Reefs in Timor have risen by as much as 4000 ft (1300 m) in the last million years.

The Pegunungan Jayawijaya range in central Papua (Irian Jaya) contains the world's highest range of limestone mountains, some with peaks more than 16,400 ft (5000 m) high. Heavy rainfall and high temperatures, which promote rapid weathering, have led to the creation of large underground caves and river systems such as the river of Sungai Baliem.

Using the land and sea

Indonesia's eastern islands are less intensively cultivated than those in the west. Coconuts, coffee and spices such as cloves and nutmeg are the major commercial crops while rice, corn and soya beans are grown for local consumption. The Philippines' rich, fertile soils support year-round production of a wide range of crops. The country is one of the world's largest producers of coconuts and a major exporter of coconut products, including one-third of the world's copra. Although much of the arable land is given over to rice and corn, the main staple food crops, tropical fruits such as bananas, pineapples and mangos, and sugar cane are also grown for export.

Land use and agricultural distribution

- coconuts
- fishing
- rice
- rubber
- shellfish
- sugar cane
- capital cities
- major towns
- pasture
- cropland
- forest
- wetland

The urban/rural population divide

urban 45% | rural 55%

0 10 20 30 40 50 60 70 80 90 100

Population density	Total land area
258 people per sq mile (160 people per sq km)	654,771 sq miles (1,053,755 sq km)

◀ The terracing of land to restrict soil erosion and create flat surfaces for agriculture is a common practice throughout Southeast Asia, particularly where land is scarce. These terraces are on Luzon in the Philippines.

▲ More than two-thirds of Papua's (Irian Jaya) land area is heavily forested and the population of around 1.5 million live mainly in isolated tribal groups using more than 80 distinct languages.

Luzon Strait
Luzon
Baguio
Philippine Sea
MANILA
South China Sea
PHILIPPINES
Cebu
Butuan
Sulu Sea
Mindanao
Zamboanga
Davao
MALAYSIA
Celebes Sea
Manado
PACIFIC OCEAN
Halmahera
Maluku (Moluccas)
Ceram
Celebes
Ambon
Banda Sea
Makassar
Jayapura
New Guinea
PAPUA NEW GUINEA
INDONESIA
Arafura Sea
Lombok
Sumbawa
Flores
Sumba
DILI
EAST TIMOR
Timor
Kupang
Timor Sea
INDIAN OCEAN

SOUTH
SPRATLY ISLANDS
(disputed)
CHINA
SEA
Quezon
Brooke's Point
Balabac Island
Balabac Strait
MALAYSI
KALIMANTAN TIMUR
Equator
KALIMANTAN SELATAN
Makassar
Java Sea
NUSA TENGGA
Mataram
Bayan
Gunung Tambora
Sumbawabesar
Taliwang
Lombok
Kuta
Gunung Rinjani

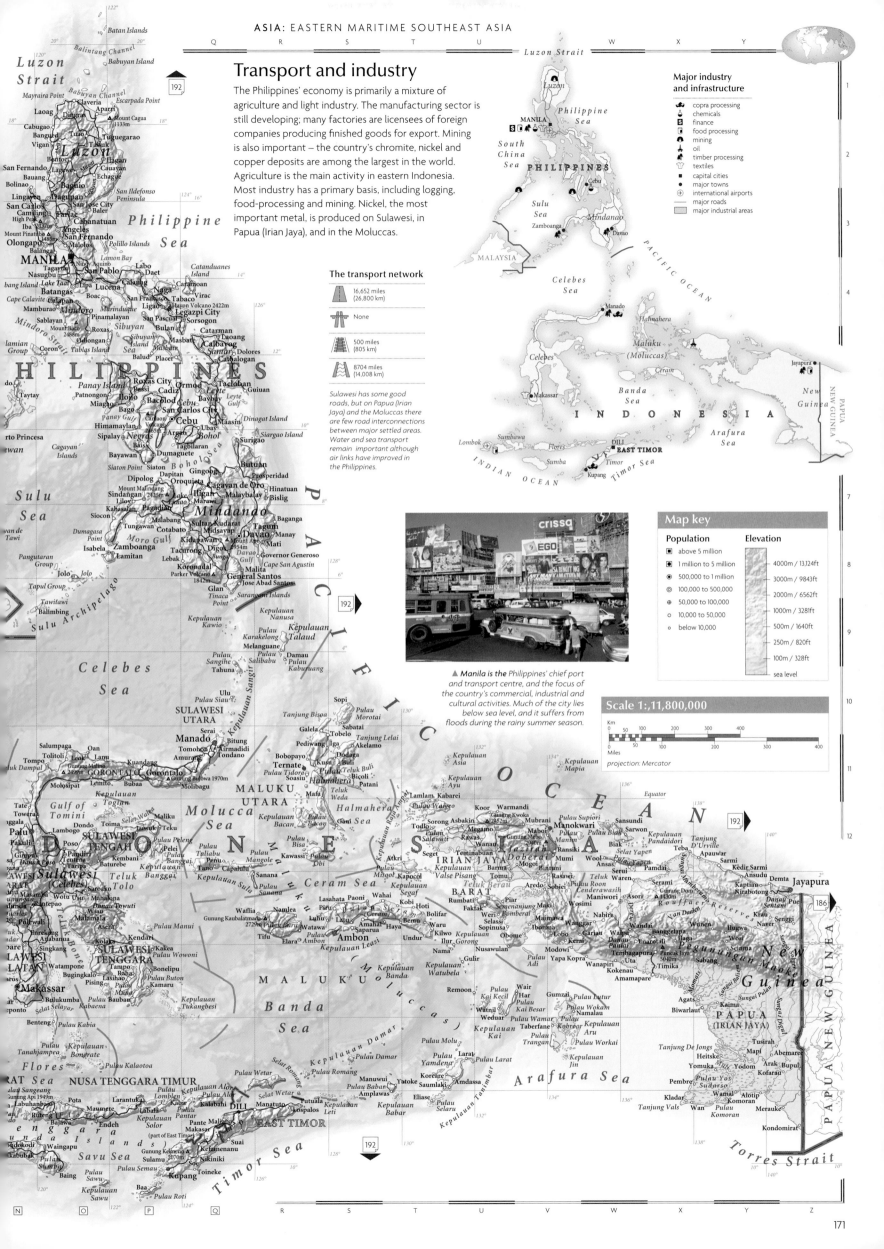

Transport and industry

The Philippines' economy is primarily a mixture of agriculture and light industry. The manufacturing sector is still developing; many factories are licensees of foreign companies producing finished goods for export. Mining is also important – the country's chromite, nickel and copper deposits are among the largest in the world. Agriculture is the main activity in eastern Indonesia. Most industry has a primary basis, including logging, food-processing and mining. Nickel, the most important metal, is produced on Sulawesi, in Papua (Irian Jaya), and in the Moluccas.

Major industry and infrastructure

- copra processing
- chemicals
- finance
- food processing
- mining
- oil
- timber processing
- textiles
- ■ capital cities
- major towns
- ⊕ international airports
- — major roads
- major industrial areas

The transport network

🛣	16,652 miles (26,800 km)
🛣	None
🚂	500 miles (805 km)
🚂	8704 miles (14,008 km)

Sulawesi has some good roads, but on Papua (Irian Jaya) and the Moluccas there are few road interconnections between major settled areas. Water and sea transport remain important although air links have improved in the Philippines.

▲ Manila is the Philippines' chief port and transport centre, and the focus of the country's commercial, industrial and cultural activities. Much of the city lies below sea level, and it suffers from floods during the rainy summer season.

Map key

Population

- ■ above 5 million
- ◉ 1 million to 5 million
- ◉ 500,000 to 1 million
- ⊚ 100,000 to 500,000
- ⊕ 50,000 to 100,000
- ○ 10,000 to 50,000
- ∘ below 10,000

Elevation

- 4000m / 13,124ft
- 3000m / 9843ft
- 2000m / 6562ft
- 1000m / 3281ft
- 500m / 1640ft
- 250m / 820ft
- 100m / 328ft
- sea level

Scale 1:11,800,000

Km 0 50 100 200 300 400
Miles 0 50 100 200 300 400

projection: Mercator

The Indian Ocean

Despite being the smallest of the three major oceans, the evolution of the Indian Ocean was the most complex. The ocean basin was formed during the break up of the supercontinent Gondwanaland, when the Indian subcontinent moved northeast, Africa moved west and Australia separated from Antarctica. Like the Pacific Ocean, the warm waters of the Indian Ocean are punctuated by coral atolls and islands. About one-fifth of the world's population – over 1000 million people – live on its shores. Those people living along the northern coasts are constantly threatened by flooding and typhoons caused by the monsoon winds.

The landscape

The Indian Ocean began forming about 150 million years ago, but in its present form it is relatively young, only about 36 million years old. Along the three subterranean mountain chains of its mid-ocean ridge the seafloor is still spreading. The Indian Ocean has fewer trenches than other oceans and only a narrow continental shelf around most of its surrounding land.

Sediments come from Ganges/Brahmaputra river system

Submarine canyons transport sediment to fan – some of these are more than 1500 miles (2500 km) long

Sri Lanka

▲ **The Ganges Fan** is one of the world's largest submarine accumulations of sediment, extending far beyond Sri Lanka. It is fed by the Ganges/Brahmaputra river system, whose sediment is carried through a network of underwater canyons at the edge of the continental shelf.

The Ninetyeast Ridge takes its name from the line of longitude it follows. It is the world's longest and straightest under-sea ridge.

Two of the world's largest rivers flow into the Indian Ocean; the Indus and the Ganges/Brahmaputra. Both have deposited enormous fans of sediment.

Indus River

The mid-oceanic ridge runs from the Arabian Sea. It diverges east of Madagascar, one arm runs southwest to join the Mid-Atlantic Ridge, the other branches southeast, joining the Pacific-Antarctic Ridge, southeast of Tasmania.

▶ **A large proportion** of the coast of Thailand, on the Isthmus of Kra, is stabilized by mangrove thickets. They act as an important breeding ground for wildlife.

The Java Trench is the world's longest, it runs 1600 miles (2570 km) from the southwest of Java, but is only 50 miles (80 km) wide.

The relief of Madagascar rises from a low-lying coastal strip in the east, to the central plateau. The plateau is also a major watershed separating Madagascar's three main river basins.

▶ **The central group** of the Seychelles are mountainous, granite islands. They have a narrow coastal belt and lush, tropical vegetation cloaks the highlands.

The Kerguelen Islands in the Southern Ocean were created by a hot spot in the Earth's crust. The islands were formed in succession as the Antarctic Plate moved slowly over the hot spot.

The circulation in the northern Indian Ocean is controlled by the monsoon winds. Biannually these winds reverse their pattern, causing a reversal in the surface currents and alternative high and low pressure conditions over Asia and Australia.

Resources

Many of the small islands in the Indian Ocean rely exclusively on tuna-fishing and tourism to maintain their economies. Most fisheries are artisanal, although large-scale tuna-fishing does take place in the Seychelles, Mauritius and the western Indian Ocean. Other resources include oil in The Gulf, pearls in the Red Sea and tin from deposits off the shores of Burma, Thailand and Indonesia.

Resources (including wildlife)

fish		△	tin deposits
penguins		⚓	tourism
shellfish			
whales		●	major towns
oil & gas			major ports

▶ **The recent use** of large drag nets for tuna-fishing has not only threatened the livelihoods of many small-scale fisheries, but also caused widespread environmental concern about the potential impact on other marine species.

SCALE 1:12,250,000

MADAGASCAR

'Nosy Glorieuses
Tanjona Bobaomby
Antsirañana
Nosy Be
Ambilobe
Itharaña
Ambanja
ANTSIRANANA
Maromokotro 2876m
Sambava
Analalava
Andapa
Antsohihy
Befandriana
Avaratra
Antalaha
Mahajanga
Borizny
Mandrisara
Nosy Sainte Marie
Soalala
Misinjo
Mampikony
Mananara
Besalampy
Tsaratahana
Maevatanana
Andilamena Ivongo
Nosy Varika
Kandreho
Maevarano
Morafenobe
Maintirano
Ankazobe
Anjozorobe
Toamasina
Antsalova
Ambohidratrimo
ANTANANARIVO
Ambatolampy
Belo Tsiribihina
Morondava
Mahabo
Finandrahana
Ambositra
Mandabe
Ikalamavony
Ifanadiana
Berberoha
Bianarantsoa
FIANARANTSOA
Manakara
Ankazoabo
Ihosy
Ivohibe
Vohipeno
Sakaraha
Betroka
Iakora
Farafangana
Omiary
Benenitra
Midongy
Vangaindrano
Toliara
Betioky
Bekily
Befotaka
Ampanihy
Amboasary
Tôlañaro
Beloha
Ambovombe
Tanjona Vohimena
Tsiombe

SCALE 1:5,000,000

Grande Comore
Mitsamiouli Saondzou 1087m
Hahaya
Mbéni
MORONI
Koimbani
Le Kartala 2361m
Mitsoudjé
Dembéni
Foumbouni
COMOROS
Mohéli
Anjouan
Miringoni
Moutsamudou
Ouani
Fomboni Sima
Domoni
Nioumachoua
Ouanani
Moya
Mramani
MAYOTTE
(to France)
Dzaoudzi
Pamandzi
MAMOUDZOU
Bandrélé
Comoro Islands
Mozambique Channel

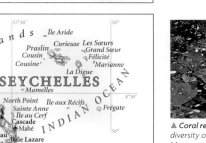

SEYCHELLES

Inner Islands
Île Aride
Praslin
Curieuse
Les Sœurs
Grand Sœur
Île du Nord
Cousin
Cousine
Félicité
Marianne
Mount Dauban 740m
La Digue
Silhouette
Mamelles
Île Thérèse
Mahé
North Point
Île aux Récifs
VICTORIA
Morne Seychellois
Sainte Anne
Île au Cerf
Cascade
Anse Boileau
Baie Lazare
Mahé
Frégate
Pointe Lazare
Quatre Bornes
Pointe Police

SCALE 1:2,250,000

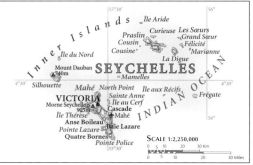

▲ **Coral reefs support** an enormous diversity of animal and plant life. Many species of tropical fish, like these squirrel fish, live and feed around the profusion of reefs and atolls in the Indian Ocean.

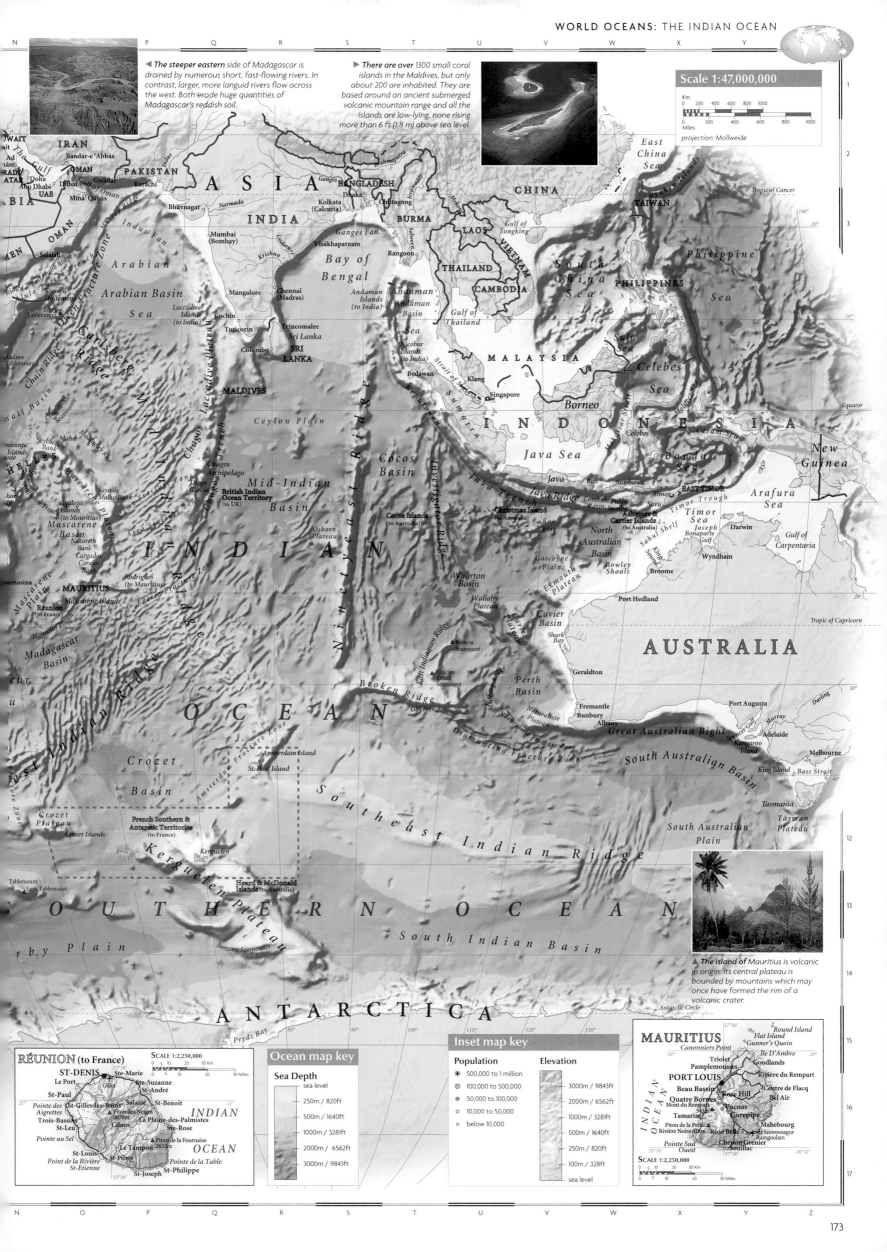

The steeper eastern side of Madagascar is drained by numerous short, fast-flowing rivers. In contrast, larger, more languid rivers flow across the west. Both erode huge quantities of Madagascar's reddish soil.

▶ *There are over* 1300 small coral islands in the Maldives, but only about 200 are inhabited. They are based around an ancient submerged volcanic mountain range and all the islands are low-lying, none rising more than 6 ft (1.8 m) above sea level.

Scale 1:47,000,000
projection: Mollweide

▲ *The island of* Mauritius is volcanic in origin. Its central plateau is bounded by mountains which may once have formed the rim of a volcanic crater.

Ocean map key

Sea Depth
- sea level
- 250m / 820ft
- 500m / 1640ft
- 1000m / 3281ft
- 2000m / 6562ft
- 3000m / 9843ft

Inset map key

Population
- 500,000 to 1 million
- 100,000 to 500,000
- 50,000 to 100,000
- 10,000 to 50,000
- below 10,000

Elevation
- 3000m / 9843ft
- 2000m / 6562ft
- 1000m / 3281ft
- 500m / 1640ft
- 250m / 820ft
- 100m / 328ft
- sea level

RÉUNION (to France) SCALE 1:2,250,000

MAURITIUS SCALE 1:2,250,000
PORT LOUIS

Australasia & Oceania

Australasia and Oceania, covering a land area of
3,285,048 sq miles (8,508,238 sq km), takes in 14 countries
including the continent of Australia, New Zealand, Papua New Guinea
and many island groups scattered across the Pacific Ocean.

● **Greatest extent, North–South:**
2000 miles / 3200 km

■ **Greatest extent, East–West:**
2500 miles /4000 km

Most northerly point:
Eastern Island,
Midway Islands
28° 15' N

Highest point:
Mount Wilhelm, Papua New Guinea
14,794 ft (4509 m)

Most easterly point:
Clipperton Island,
109° 12' W

Largest lake:
Lake Eyre, Australia
3430 sq miles (8884 sq km)

**Highest recorded
temperature:** Bourke,
Australia 128°F (53°C)

Lowest point:
Lake Eyre, Australia
-53 ft (-16 m) below sea level

Most westerly point:
Cape Inscription,
Australia 112° 57' E

Cape York,
Australia
10° 41' S

Ducie Island

**Cape Byron,
Australia**
153° 37' E

Tropic of Capricorn

**Lowest recorded
temperature:**
Canberra, Australia
-8°F (-22°C)

Steep Point, Australia
113° 9' E

*Dirk Hartog
Island*

*South East Point,
Australia,*
39° 10' S

Most southerly point:
Macquarie Island,
New Zealand
54° 30' S

**Dirk Hartog
Island, Australia** **Great Dividing
Range** **New
Caledonia** **New Zealand** **Tonga** **Tuamoto
Islands** **Ducie Island,
Pitcairn Islands**

Cross-section from Dirk Hartog Island, Australia to Ducie Island, Pitcairn Islands

▶ line of cross-section

| 0 | 500 | 1000 | 1500 Km |
| 0 | 500 | 1000 | 1500 Miles |

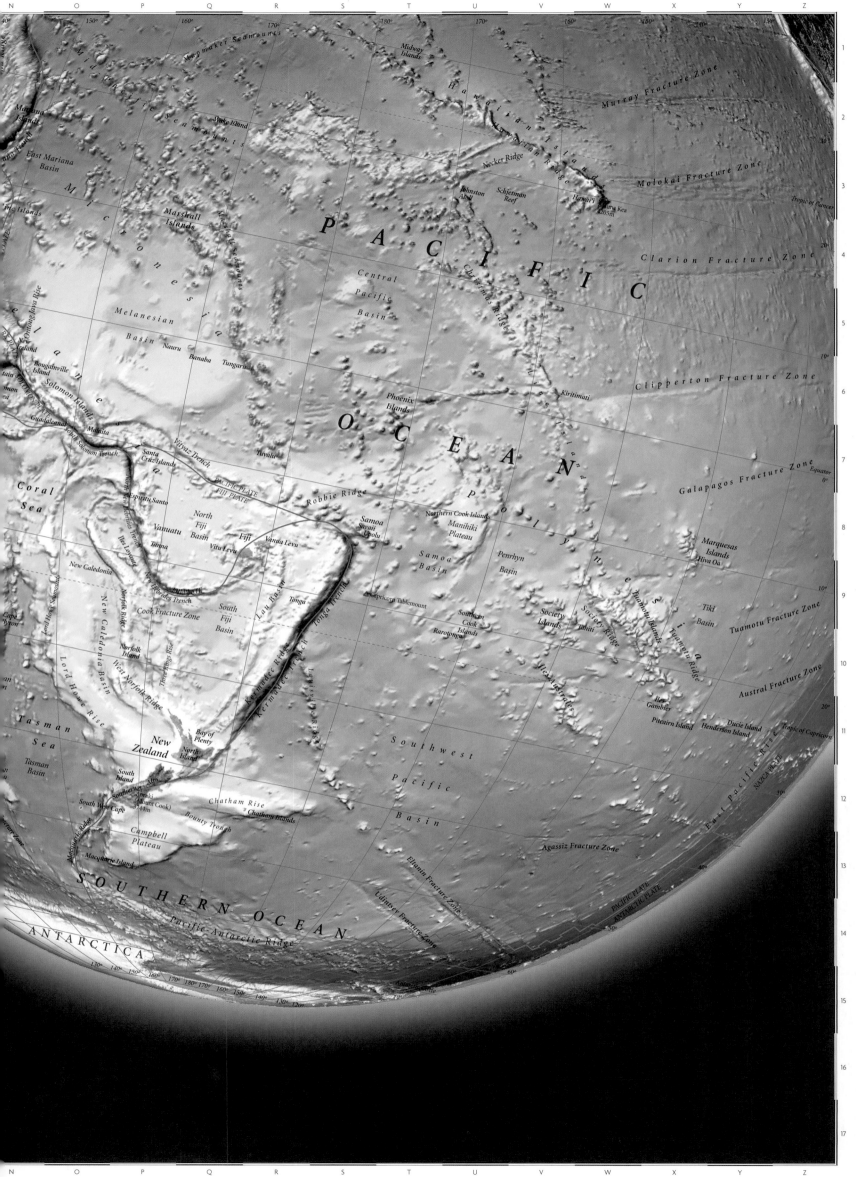

PACIFIC

OCEAN

Micronesia

Polynesia

Melanesia

Midway Islands

Wake Island

Mariana Islands

East Mariana Basin

Marshall Islands

Nauru

Banaba

Tungaru

Phoenix Islands

Tuvalu

Kiritimati

Central Pacific Basin

Hawaiian Islands

Necker Ridge

Johnston Atoll

Schietman Reef

Hawai'i Mauna Kea 4205m

Murray Fracture Zone

Molokai Fracture Zone

Tropic of Cancer

Clarion Fracture Zone

Clipperton Fracture Zone

Galapagos Fracture Zone

Equator

Marquesas Islands

Hiva Oa

Tiki Basin

Tuamotu Fracture Zone

Austral Fracture Zone

Tropic of Capricorn

Ontong Java Rise

New Ireland

Bougainville Island

Solomon Islands

Guadalcanal

Malaita

Santa Cruz Islands

Espiritu Santo

Vanuatu

Tanna

Coral Sea

New Caledonia

New Caledonia Basin

Lord Howe Rise

Cape Byron

Tasman Sea

Tasman Basin

Melanesian Basin

Vityaz Trench

North Solomon Trench

New Hebrides Trench

Iles Loyauté

North Fiji Basin

Vitu Levu

Fiji

Vanua Levu

Robbie Ridge

Samoa Savai'i Upolu

Northern Cook Islands

Manihiki Plateau

Samoa Basin

Penrhyn Basin

Society Islands

Tahiti

Society Ridge

Tuamotu Islands

Tuamotu Ridge

PACIFIC PLATE

FIJI PLATE

Lau Basin

Tonga

Tonga Trench

Capricorn Tablemount

Southern Cook Islands

Rarotonga

South Fiji Basin

Cook Fracture Zone

Kermadec Ridge

Kermadec Trench

Louisville Ridge

Norfolk Ridge

Three Kings Rise

West Norfolk Ridge

Norfolk Island

Iles Gambier

Pitcairn Island

Henderson Island

Ducie Island

EAST PACIFIC RISE

NAZCA PLATE

Lord Howe Basin

Bay of Plenty

New Zealand

North Island

South Island

Southern Alps Taranaki Mount Cook 3744m

South West Cape

Chatham Rise

Chatham Islands

Bounty Trough

Southwest Pacific Basin

Macquarie Ridge

Macquarie Island

Campbell Plateau

Agassiz Fracture Zone

Eltanin Fracture Zone

Udintsev Fracture Zone

SOUTHERN OCEAN

Pacific-Antarctic Ridge

ANTARCTICA

PACIFIC PLATE

ANTARCTIC PLATE

Antarctic Circle

Political Australasia & Oceania

Vast expanses of ocean separate this geographically fragmented realm, characterized more by each country's isolation than by any political unity. Australia's and New Zealand's traditional ties with the United Kingdom, as members of the Commonwealth, are now being called into question as Australasian and Oceanian nations are increasingly looking to forge new relationships with neighbouring Asian countries like Japan. External influences have featured strongly in the politics of the Pacific Islands; the various territories of Micronesia were largely under US control until the late 1980s, and France, New Zealand, the USA and the UK still have territories under colonial rule in Polynesia. Nuclear weapons-testing by Western superpowers was widespread during the Cold War period, but has now been discontinued.

◀ *Western Australia's mineral* wealth has transformed its state capital, Perth, into one of Australia's major cities. Perth is one of the world's most isolated cities – over 2500 miles (4000 km) from the population centres of the eastern seaboard.

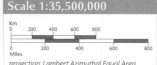

Scale 1:35,500,000

projection: Lambert Azimuthal Equal Area

Population

Density of settlement in the region is generally low. Australia is one of the least densely populated countries on Earth with over 80% of its population living within 25 miles (40 km) of the coast – mostly in the southeast of the country. New Zealand, and the island groups of Melanesia, Micronesia and Polynesia, are much more densely populated, although many of the smaller islands remain uninhabited.

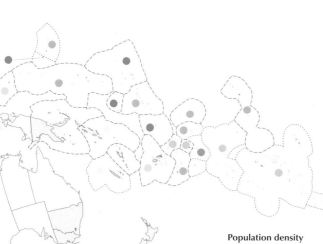

Population density
(people per sq km)

- below 4
- 5-24
- 25-49
- 50-99
- 100-199
- 200-299
- above 300

▲ *The myriad of* small coral islands which are scattered across the Pacific Ocean are often uninhabited, as they offer little shelter from the weather, often no fresh water, and only limited food supplies.

◀ *The planes of* the Australian Royal Flying Doctor Service are able to cover large expanses of barren land quickly, bringing medical treatment to the most inaccessible and far-flung places.

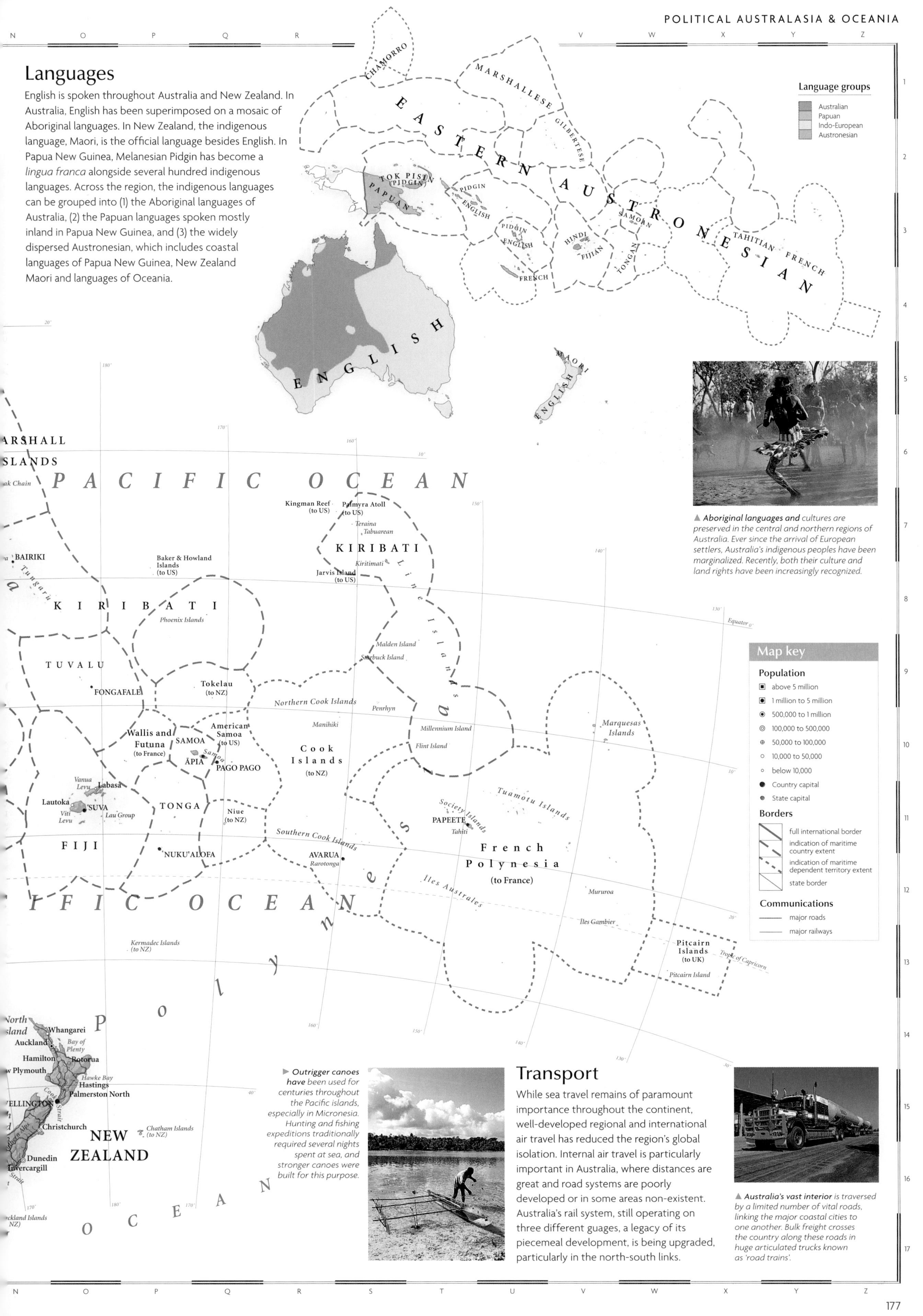

Languages

English is spoken throughout Australia and New Zealand. In Australia, English has been superimposed on a mosaic of Aboriginal languages. In New Zealand, the indigenous language, Maori, is the official language besides English. In Papua New Guinea, Melanesian Pidgin has become a *lingua franca* alongside several hundred indigenous languages. Across the region, the indigenous languages can be grouped into (1) the Aboriginal languages of Australia, (2) the Papuan languages spoken mostly inland in Papua New Guinea, and (3) the widely dispersed Austronesian, which includes coastal languages of Papua New Guinea, New Zealand Maori and languages of Oceania.

Language groups
- Australian
- Papuan
- Indo-European
- Austronesian

▲ *Aboriginal languages and cultures are preserved in the central and northern regions of Australia. Ever since the arrival of European settlers, Australia's indigenous peoples have been marginalized. Recently, both their culture and land rights have been increasingly recognized.*

Map key

Population
- ▣ above 5 million
- ◼ 1 million to 5 million
- ◉ 500,000 to 1 million
- ◎ 100,000 to 500,000
- ⊕ 50,000 to 100,000
- ○ 10,000 to 50,000
- ∘ below 10,000
- ● Country capital
- • State capital

Borders
- full international border
- indication of maritime country extent
- indication of maritime dependent territory extent
- state border

Communications
- major roads
- major railways

▶ *Outrigger canoes have been used for centuries throughout the Pacific islands, especially in Micronesia. Hunting and fishing expeditions traditionally required several nights spent at sea, and stronger canoes were built for this purpose.*

Transport

While sea travel remains of paramount importance throughout the continent, well-developed regional and international air travel has reduced the region's global isolation. Internal air travel is particularly important in Australia, where distances are great and road systems are poorly developed or in some areas non-existent. Australia's rail system, still operating on three different guages, a legacy of its piecemeal development, is being upgraded, particularly in the north-south links.

▲ *Australia's vast interior is traversed by a limited number of vital roads, linking the major coastal cities to one another. Bulk freight crosses the country along these roads in huge articulated trucks known as 'road trains'.*

Australasian & Oceanian resources

Natural resources are of major economic importance throughout Australasia and Oceania. Australia in particular is a major world exporter of raw materials such as coal, iron ore and bauxite, while New Zealand's agricultural economy is dominated by sheep-raising. Trade with western Europe has declined significantly in the last 20 years, and the Pacific Rim countries of Southeast Asia are now the main trading partners, as well as a source of new settlers to the region. Australasia and Oceania's greatest resources are its climate and environment; tourism increasingly provides a vital source of income for the whole continent.

▲ **The largely unpolluted** waters of the Pacific Ocean support rich and varied marine life, much of which is farmed commercially. Here, oysters are gathered for market off the coast of New Zealand's South Island.

► **Huge flocks of** sheep are a common sight in New Zealand, where they outnumber people by 12 to 1. New Zealand is one of the world's largest exporters of wool and frozen lamb.

Standard of living

In marked contrast to its neighbour, Australia, with one of the world's highest life expectancies and standards of living, Papua New Guinea is one of the world's least developed countries. In addition, high population growth and urbanization rates throughout the Pacific islands contribute to overcrowding. The Aboriginal and Maori people of Australia and New Zealand have been isolated for many years. Recently, their traditional land ownership rights have begun to be legally recognized in an effort to ease their social and economic isolation, and to improve living standards.

Standard of living
(UN human development index)

- low
- high
- figures unavailable

Environmental issues

The prospect of rising sea levels poses a threat to many low-lying islands in the Pacific. Nuclear weapons-testing, once common throughout the region, was finally discontinued in 1996. Australia's ecological balance has been irreversibly altered by the introduction of alien species. Although it has the world's largest underground water reserve, the Great Artesian Basin, the availability of fresh water in Australia remains critical. Periodic droughts combined with over-grazing lead to desertification and increase the risk of devastating bush fires, and occasional flash floods.

Environmental issues

- national parks
- tropical forest
- forest destroyed
- desert
- desertification
- polluted rivers
- radioactive contamination
- marine pollution
- heavy marine pollution
- • poor urban air quality

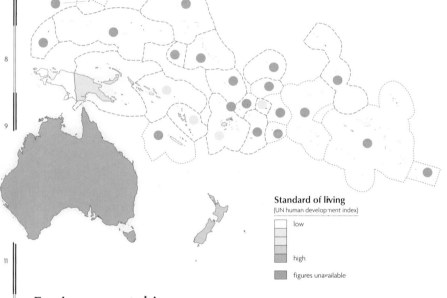

▲ **In 1946 Bikini Atoll**, in the Marshall Islands, was chosen as the site for Operation Crossroads – investigating the effects of atomic bombs upon naval vessels. Further nuclear tests continued until the early 1990s. The long-term environmental effects are unknown.

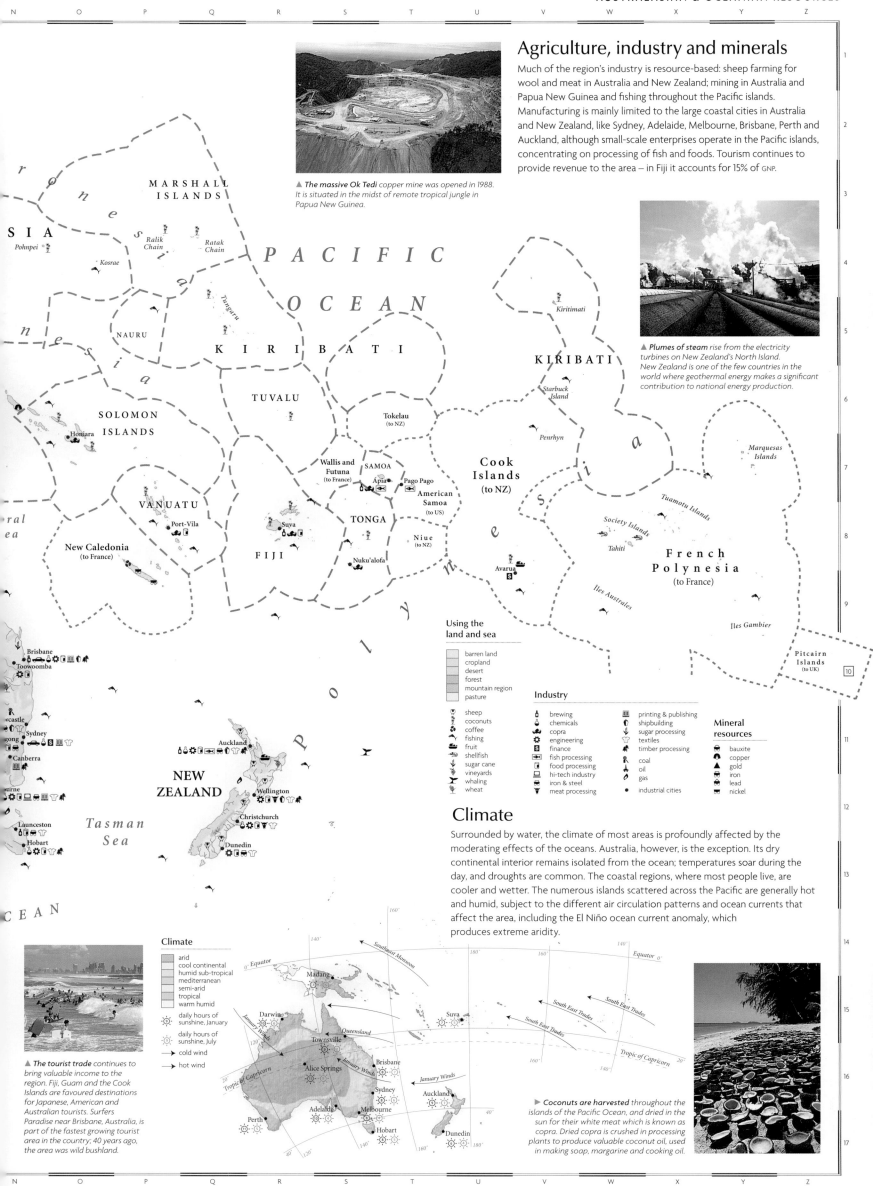

Agriculture, industry and minerals

Much of the region's industry is resource-based: sheep farming for wool and meat in Australia and New Zealand; mining in Australia and Papua New Guinea and fishing throughout the Pacific islands. Manufacturing is mainly limited to the large coastal cities in Australia and New Zealand, like Sydney, Adelaide, Melbourne, Brisbane, Perth and Auckland, although small-scale enterprises operate in the Pacific islands, concentrating on processing of fish and foods. Tourism continues to provide revenue to the area – in Fiji it accounts for 15% of GNP.

▲ *The massive Ok Tedi* copper mine was opened in 1988. It is situated in the midst of remote tropical jungle in Papua New Guinea.

▲ *Plumes of steam* rise from the electricity turbines on New Zealand's North Island. New Zealand is one of the few countries in the world where geothermal energy makes a significant contribution to national energy production.

Using the land and sea

- barren land
- cropland
- desert
- forest
- mountain region
- pasture

Industry

- sheep
- coconuts
- coffee
- fishing
- fruit
- shellfish
- sugar cane
- vineyards
- whaling
- wheat

- brewing
- chemicals
- copra
- engineering
- finance
- fish processing
- food processing
- hi-tech industry
- iron & steel
- meat processing

- printing & publishing
- shipbuilding
- sugar processing
- textiles
- timber processing
- coal
- oil
- gas
- industrial cities

Mineral resources

- bauxite
- copper
- gold
- iron
- lead
- nickel

Climate

Surrounded by water, the climate of most areas is profoundly affected by the moderating effects of the oceans. Australia, however, is the exception. Its dry continental interior remains isolated from the ocean; temperatures soar during the day, and droughts are common. The coastal regions, where most people live, are cooler and wetter. The numerous islands scattered across the Pacific are generally hot and humid, subject to the different air circulation patterns and ocean currents that affect the area, including the El Niño ocean current anomaly, which produces extreme aridity.

▲ *The tourist trade* continues to bring valuable income to the region. Fiji, Guam and the Cook Islands are favoured destinations for Japanese, American and Australian tourists. Surfers Paradise near Brisbane, Australia, is part of the fastest growing tourist area in the country; 40 years ago, the area was wild bushland.

Climate

- arid
- cool continental
- humid sub-tropical
- mediterranean
- semi-arid
- tropical
- warm humid
- daily hours of sunshine, January
- daily hours of sunshine, July
- → cold wind
- → hot wind

▶ *Coconuts are harvested* throughout the islands of the Pacific Ocean, and dried in the sun for their white meat which is known as copra. Dried copra is crushed in processing plants to produce valuable coconut oil, used in making soap, margarine and cooking oil.

179

A B C D E F G H   K L M

Australia

Australia is the world's smallest continent, a stable landmass lying between the Indian and Pacific oceans. Previously home to its aboriginal peoples only, since the end of the 18th century immigration has transformed the face of the country. Initially settlers came mainly from western Europe, particularly the UK, and for years Australia remained wedded to its British colonial past. More recent immigrants have come from eastern Europe, and from Asian countries such as Japan, South Korea and Indonesia. Australia is now forging strong trading links with these 'Pacific Rim' countries and its economic future seems to lie with Asia and the Americas, rather than Europe, its traditional partner.

Using the land

Over 104 million sheep are dispersed in vast herds around the country, contributing to a major export industry. Cattle-ranching is important, particularly in the west. Wheat, and grapes for Australia's wine industry, are grown mainly in the south. Much of the country is desert, unsuitable for agriculture unless irrigation is used.

The urban/rural population divide

urban 85%   rural 15%

0 10 20 30 40 50 60 70 80 90 100

Population density	Total land area
6 people per sq mile (2 people per sq km)	2,967,893 sq miles (7,686,850 sq km)

Map key

Population
- ▣ 1 million to 5 million
- ◉ 500,000 to 1 million
- ◎ 100,000 to 500,000
- ⊕ 50,000 to 100,000
- ○ 10,000 to 50,000
- ○ below 10,000

Elevation
- 2000m / 6562ft
- 1000m / 3281ft
- 500m / 1640ft
- 250m / 820ft
- 100m / 328ft
- sea level

Land use and agricultural distribution

- 🐄 cattle
- 🐑 sheep
- cereals
- sugar cane
- timber
- vineyards
- ■ capital cities
- • major towns
- pasture
- cropland
- forest
- desert
- mountain region

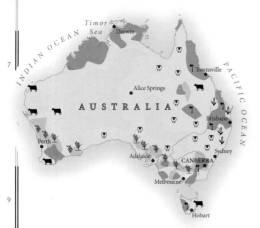

AUSTRALIA

▲ *Lines of ripening* vines stretch for miles in Barossa Valley, a major wine-growing region near Adelaide.

The landscape

Australia consists of many eroded plateaux, lying firmly in the middle of the Indo-Australian Plate. It is the world's flattest continent, and the driest, after Antarctica. The coasts tend to be more hilly and fertile, especially in the east. The mountains of the Great Dividing Range form a natural barrier between the eastern coastal areas and the flat, dry plains and desert regions of the Australian 'outback.'

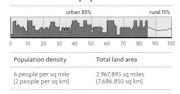

▲ *The Great Barrier Reef* is the world's largest area of coral islands and reefs. It runs for about 1240 miles (2000 km) along the Queensland coast.

The ancient **Kimberley** Plateau is the source of some of Australia's richest mineral deposits, including diamonds.

Uluru (Ayers Rock)

Arnhem Land

The **tropical rain** forest of the Cape York Peninsula contains more than 600 different varieties of tree.

Great Artesian Basin

▲ *The Pinnacles are* a series of rugged sandstone pillars. Their strange shapes have been formed by water and wind erosion.

More than half of Australia rests on a uniform shield over 600 million years old. It is one of the Earth's original geological plates.

The **Simpson Desert** has a number of large salt pans, created by the evaporation of past rivers and now sourced by seasonal rains. Some are crusted with gypsum, but most are covered with common salt crystals.

The **Nullarbor Plain** is a low-lying limestone plateau which is so flat that the Trans-Australian Railway runs through it in a straight line for more than 300 miles (483 km).

The **Lake Eyre** basin, lying 51 ft (16 m) below sea level, is one of the largest inland drainage systems in the world, covering an area of more than 500,000 sq miles (1,300,000 sq km).

Tasmania has the same geological structure as the Australian Alps. During the last period of glaciation, 18,000 years ago, sea levels were some 300 ft (100 m) lower and it was joined to the mainland.

The **Great Dividing Range** forms a watershed between east- and west-flowing rivers. Erosion has created deep valleys, gorges and waterfalls where rivers tumble over escarpments on their way to the sea.

Australian Alps

Great Artesian Basin

Rainwater replenishes aquifer

Lake Eyre

Aquifers from which artesian water is obtained

Underground water movements

▲ *The Great Artesian Basin* underlies nearly 20% of the total area of Australia, providing a valuable store of underground water, essential to Australian agriculture. The ephemeral rivers which drain the northern part of the basin have highly braided courses and, in consequence, the area is known as 'channel country.'

◀ *Uluru (Ayers Rock),* the world's largest free-standing rock, is a massive outcrop of red sandstone in Australia's desert centre. Wind and sandstorms have ground the rock into the smooth curves seen here. Uluru is revered as a sacred site by many aboriginal peoples.

Scale 1:11,500,000

Km 0 25 50 100 150 200 250 300 350
Miles 0 50 100 150 200 250 300 350

projection: Lambert Conformal Conic

(map of Western Australia with place names including Perth, Broome, Derby, Geraldton, Kalgoorlie, Great Sandy Desert, Gibson Desert, Great Sandy Desert, etc.)

A B C D E F G H   K L M

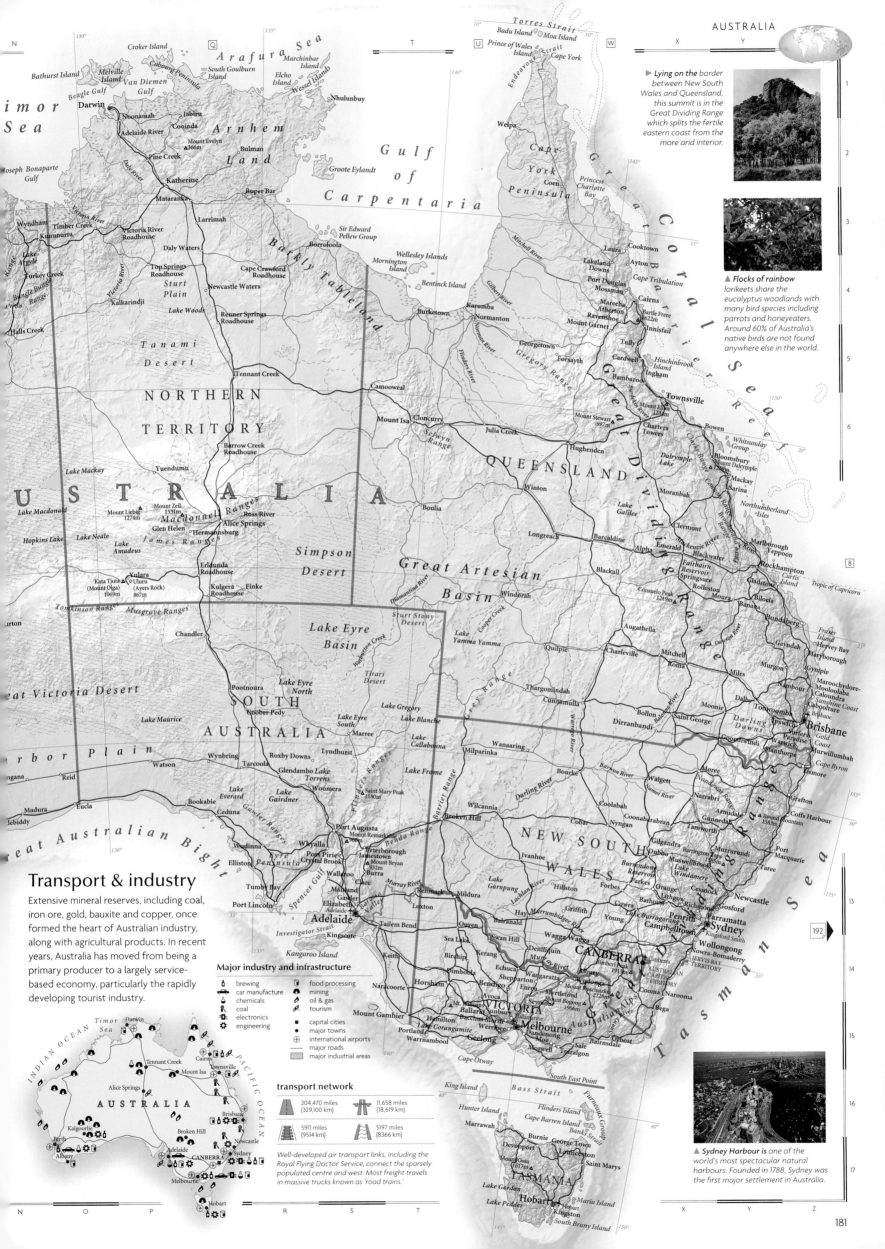

▶ **Lying on the** border between New South Wales and Queensland, this summit is in the Great Dividing Range which splits the fertile eastern coast from the more arid interior.

▲ **Flocks of rainbow** lorikeets share the eucalyptus woodlands with many bird species including parrots and honeyeaters. Around 60% of Australia's native birds are not found anywhere else in the world.

Transport & industry

Extensive mineral reserves, including coal, iron ore, gold, bauxite and copper, once formed the heart of Australian industry, along with agricultural products. In recent years, Australia has moved from being a primary producer to a largely service-based economy, particularly the rapidly developing tourist industry.

Major industry and infrastructure

- brewing
- car manufacture
- chemicals
- coal
- electronics
- engineering
- food processing
- mining
- oil & gas
- tourism
- capital cities
- major towns
- international airports
- major roads
- major industrial areas

transport network

204,470 miles (329,100 km)	11,658 miles (18,619 km)
5911 miles (9514 km)	5197 miles (8366 km)

Well-developed air transport links, including the Royal Flying Doctor Service, connect the sparsely populated centre and west. Most freight travels in massive trucks known as 'road trains.'

▲ **Sydney Harbour is** one of the world's most spectacular natural harbours. Founded in 1788, Sydney was the first major settlement in Australia.

NORTHERN TERRITORY

Simpson Desert

Lake Eyre Basin

Sturt Stony Desert

Great Victoria Desert

WESTERN AUSTRALIA

SOUTH AUSTRALIA

Lake Eyre North

Tirari Desert

Strzelecki Desert

Nullarbor Plain

Lake Torrens

Lake Frome

Lake Gairdner

Great Australian Bight

Eyre Peninsula

Spencer Gulf

Flinders Ranges

Gawler Ranges

Broken Hill

Adelaide

Gulf Saint Vincent

Kangaroo Island

Murray River

Darling River

Map key

Population
- ◉ 1 million to 5 million
- ◉ 500,000 to 1 million
- ◎ 100,000 to 500,000
- ⊕ 50,000 to 100,000
- ○ 10,000 to 50,000
- ○ below 10,000

Elevation
- 2000m / 6562ft
- 1000m / 3281ft
- 500m / 1640ft
- 250m / 820ft
- 100m / 328ft
- sea level

Scale 1:6,000,000

Km
0 10 20 40 60 80 100 120 140 160 180 200

Miles
0 10 20 40 60 80 100 120 140 160 180 200

projection: Lambert Conformal Conic

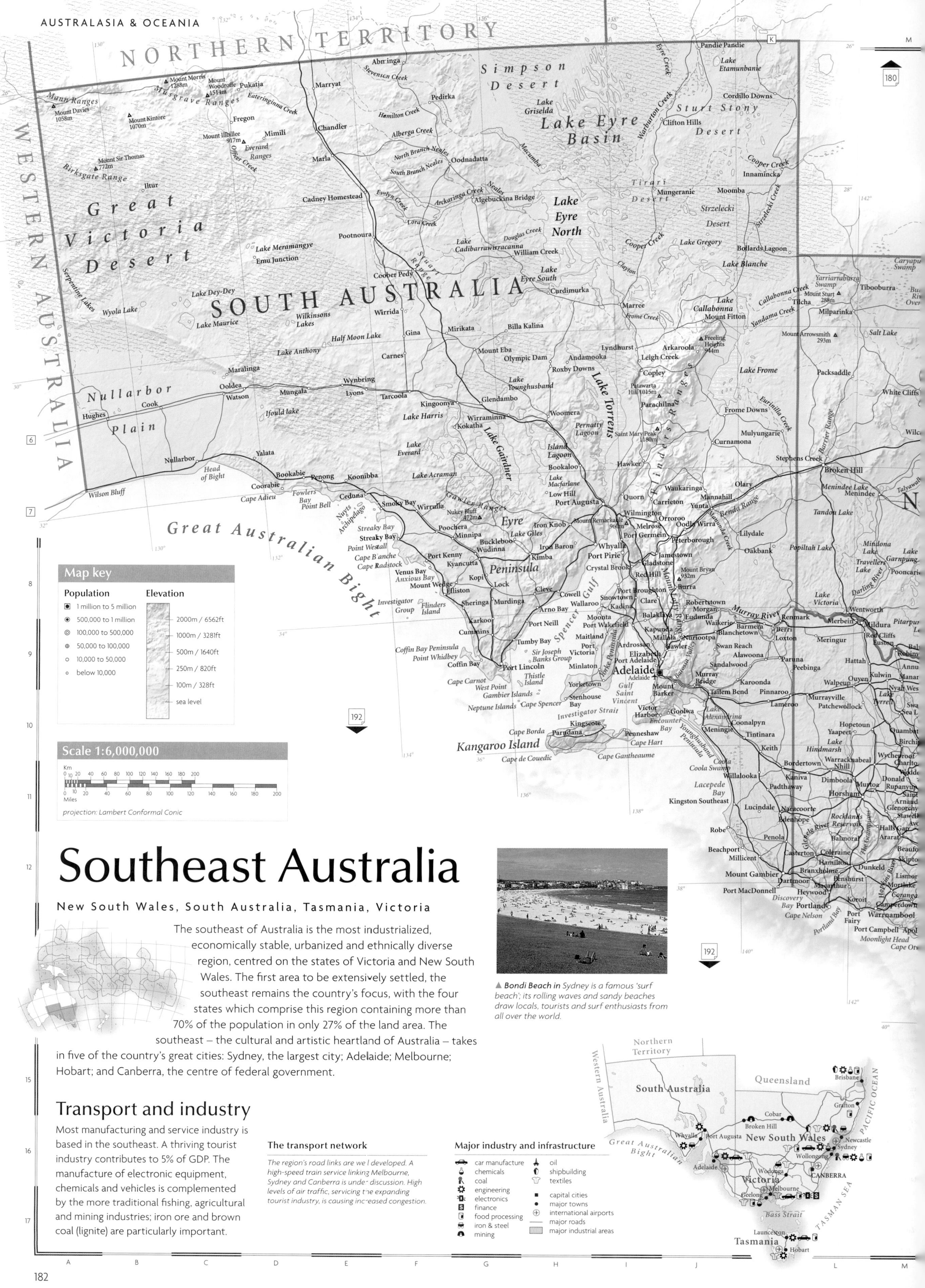

Southeast Australia

New South Wales, South Australia, Tasmania, Victoria

The southeast of Australia is the most industrialized, economically stable, urbanized and ethnically diverse region, centred on the states of Victoria and New South Wales. The first area to be extensively settled, the southeast remains the country's focus, with the four states which comprise this region containing more than 70% of the population in only 27% of the land area. The southeast – the cultural and artistic heartland of Australia – takes in five of the country's great cities: Sydney, the largest city; Adelaide; Melbourne; Hobart; and Canberra, the centre of federal government.

▲ *Bondi Beach in Sydney is a famous 'surf beach'; its rolling waves and sandy beaches draw locals, tourists and surf enthusiasts from all over the world.*

Transport and industry

Most manufacturing and service industry is based in the southeast. A thriving tourist industry contributes to 5% of GDP. The manufacture of electronic equipment, chemicals and vehicles is complemented by the more traditional fishing, agricultural and mining industries; iron ore and brown coal (lignite) are particularly important.

The transport network

The region's road links are well developed. A high-speed train service linking Melbourne, Sydney and Canberra is under discussion. High levels of air traffic, servicing the expanding tourist industry, is causing increased congestion.

Major industry and infrastructure

- car manufacture
- chemicals
- coal
- engineering
- electronics
- finance
- food processing
- iron & steel
- mining
- oil
- shipbuilding
- textiles

- ■ capital cities
- ● major towns
- ⊕ international airports
- major roads
- major industrial areas

Northern Territory

Western Australia

South Australia

Queensland

Brisbane

Grafton

Cobar

Broken Hill

Whyalla

Port Augusta

New South Wales

Newcastle

Sydney

Wollongong

Adelaide

Wodonga

CANBERRA

Victoria

Geelong

Melbourne

Bass Strait

Tasman Sea

Tasmania

Launceston

Hobart

Pacific Ocean

Using the land and sea

The western flanks of the Great Dividing Range and the northern deserts of South Australia support massive herds of sheep and cattle, while more intensive stock-rearing occurs near the cities. Sugar cane is the most important industrial crop, and cereals including wheat, maize, barley and sorghum are also grown. Grapes, citrus and orchard fruits are among the wide range of fruit and vegetables cultivated in this region. Tasmania's forestry and fishing contributes to over one-third of the state's exports.

▲ *The fertile Darling Downs*, known as the 'breadbasket of Australia', support a wide range of crops including cereals, sugar cane and fruit.

▶ *The Murray River* has its source in the eastern uplands of the Great Dividing Range. Fed by melting snow, it runs for 1609 miles (2589 km), and has sufficient volume to reach the ocean southeast of Adelaide despite a minimal gradient for most of its lower reaches.

The urban/rural population divide

urban 85%   rural 15%

Population density	Total land area
18 people per sq mile (7 people per sq km)	778,022 sq miles (2,015,600 sq km)

Land use and agricultural distribution

- cattle
- sheep
- bananas
- fishing
- fruit
- vineyards
- wheat
- ■ capital cities
- ● major towns
- pasture
- cropland
- forest
- desert
- mountain region

The landscape

The southern half of the Great Dividing Range runs parallel to the eastern coast of Victoria and New South Wales as far as Tasmania, which, though divided from the mainland is part of the same mountain chain. South Australia comprises the Australian shield and half of the dry, flat Nullarbor Plain. The Murray/Darling river basin is the only major river system.

◀ *The heavily folded* Flinders Ranges is part of an arc of sedimentary rocks reaching northward from Kangaroo Island.

Lake Eyre is the largest of southern Australia's dry lakes. Lying -51 ft (-16 m) below sea level, it has flooded only three times in the last century.

The Musgrave and Everard ranges form bare, rounded hills made up of ancient granite and gneiss.

The Murray/Darling is Australia's longest river at 1703 miles (2739 km).

Shallow continental shelf
Past land link
Bass Strait
Tasmania

▲ *Tasmania is part* of Australia's eastern highlands, separated from the mainland by 155 miles (250 km) of the Bass Strait. In the recent geological past, dry land links between Tasmania and Victoria would have been possible during periods of world-wide glaciation, when the sea level was more than 180 ft (55 m) below that of present sea levels.

Great Dividing Range

The eastern part of the Nullarbor Plain has many sinkholes, eroded by rainwater, which run underground to form a system of long caves in the limestone rocks.

The world's largest deposit of brown coal (lignite) is sited beneath Victoria's La Trobe Valley.

The eastern coastal plains of New South Wales rise into a series of plateaux known as the tableland.

◀ *Though temperate rainforest* grows in the wettest parts of Tasmania, extreme variations in the levels of rainfall over the island mean that some drier areas may experience forest fires.

The glaciated central plateau of Tasmania has many lakes, including Lake St Clair, a piedmont lake more than 700 ft (200 m) deep.

Mount Kosciuszko, the highest point in the Snowy Mountains, is the tallest mountain in Australia at 7316 ft (2228 m).

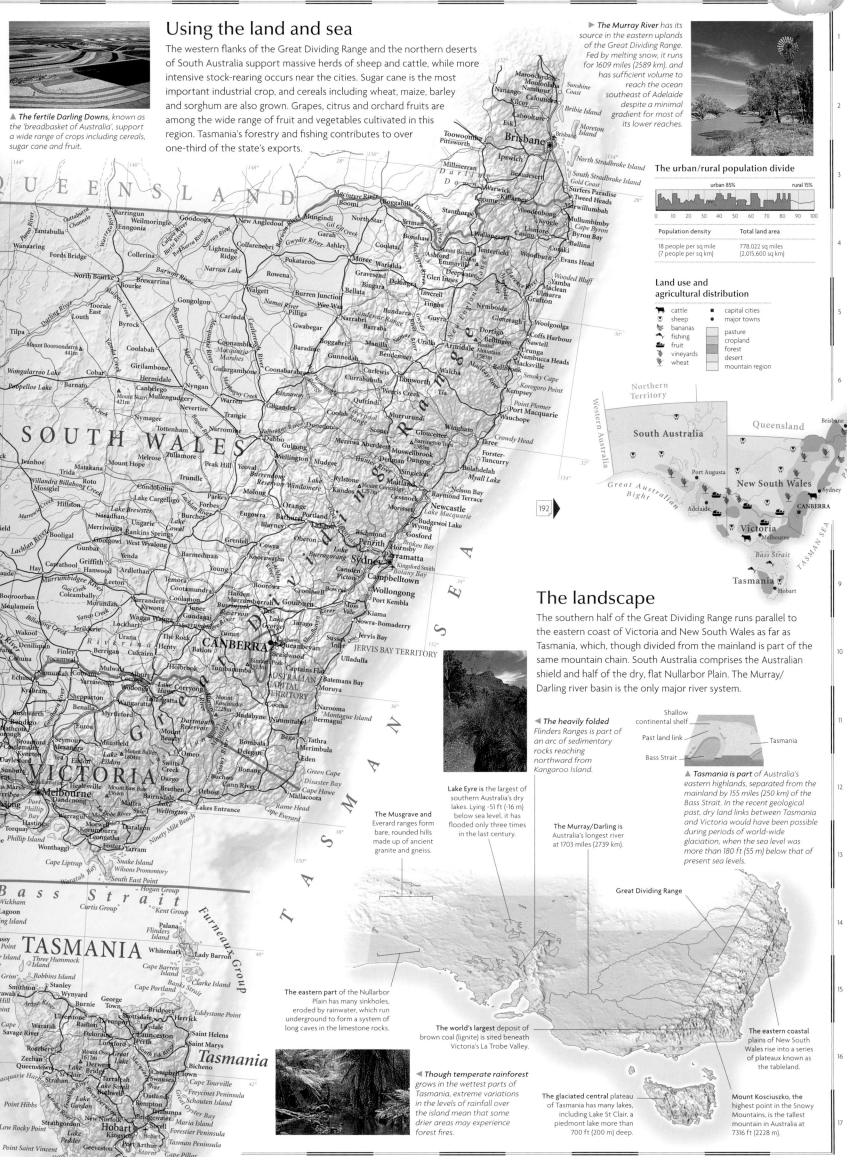

New Zealand

Lying 1500 miles east-southeast of Australia, New Zealand was originally settled by the Maori, a people with Polynesian roots. It was one of the last major landmasses to be visited by Europeans. The islands' rugged topography means that most settlement has concentrated in coastal areas. People of European origin make up about 70% of the population of 4 million, following immigration from the 1920s onwards. Many recent settlers have come from Asia, including India and China, and a number of the Pacific islands. Although the Maori now make up a minority of less than half a million, their ancient claims to at least half of national territory are gaining increasing legal credence.

The landscape

New Zealand comprises two large islands and many scattered smaller islands. On South Island the Alpine Fault marks the boundary between the Pacific and Indo-Australian plates. Tectonic activity has strongly influenced the formation of the Southern Alps, snow-capped mountains with several peaks over 9800 ft (3000 m). North Island has a lower and less extensive mountain region, containing forested hills, a central volcanic plateau and downlands.

Mountain-building in the Southern Alps

North Island
Alpine Fault
Pacific Plate
South Island
Southern Alps
Indo-Australian Plate

▲ *The Southern Alps have been formed by 'slip' faulting. The Indo-Australian and Pacific plates run in opposite directions along the Alpine Fault. Although they slide past each other, they are also being thrust over one another, causing the continental crust of the Pacific Plate to be uplifted to form the Alps.*

Fiordland, in the far south west, contains a large number of flooded glacial valleys.

Sutherland Falls

Probable location of Alpine Fault

The Southern Alps run for more than 300 miles (483 km) forming the backbone of South Island. They were uplifted following the collision of the Pacific and Indo-Australian plates.

High levels of rainfall and a steep topography has made New Zealand's rivers swift-running. In the southern reaches of both islands, rivers such as the Mokoreta form broad, braided streams.

The Southern Alps contain more than 360 glaciers, including the Murchison, Mueller and Godley glaciers on the eastern slopes and the Fox and Franz Josef glaciers to the west.

The coastal Canterbury Plains are the result of glacial outwash. They are the only major flat area in New Zealand.

The Tasman Glacier, the largest glacier in New Zealand, flows for 18 miles (29 km) down the slopes of New Zealand's highest mountain, Aoraki (Mount Cook).

Mount Taranaki, rising 8261 ft (2518 m) is an isolated, dormant volcano.

Lake Taupo is New Zealand's largest inland lake. It occupies the crater of an extinct volcano.

▼ *The Northland region is characterized by many coastal inlets. These are lined by mangrove swamps, signalling the change to a subtropical climate in the far north of the island.*

Northland

▼ *The Rotorua and Taupo valleys have some of the largest and most spectacular thermal springs in New Zealand. These occur when superheated groundwater rises to the surface through joints in the rocks.*

Rotorua

The boundary between the Indo-Australian Plate and the Pacific Plate runs through the centre of North Island, leading to many typical volcanic features. The plateau which rises from the slopes of Lake Taupo contains a string of active volcanoes.

▲ *Clouds of steam rise from White Island, an active, offshore volcano lying in the Bay of Plenty, off the northern coast of North Island.*

Scale 1:3,000,000
projection: Lambert Conformal Conic

192

PACIFIC OCEAN

TASMAN SEA

NEW ZEALAND

North Island

South Island

NORTHLAND

AUCKLAND

WAIKATO

BAY OF PLENTY

GISBORNE

HAWKE'S BAY

TARANAKI

MANAWATU-WANGANUI

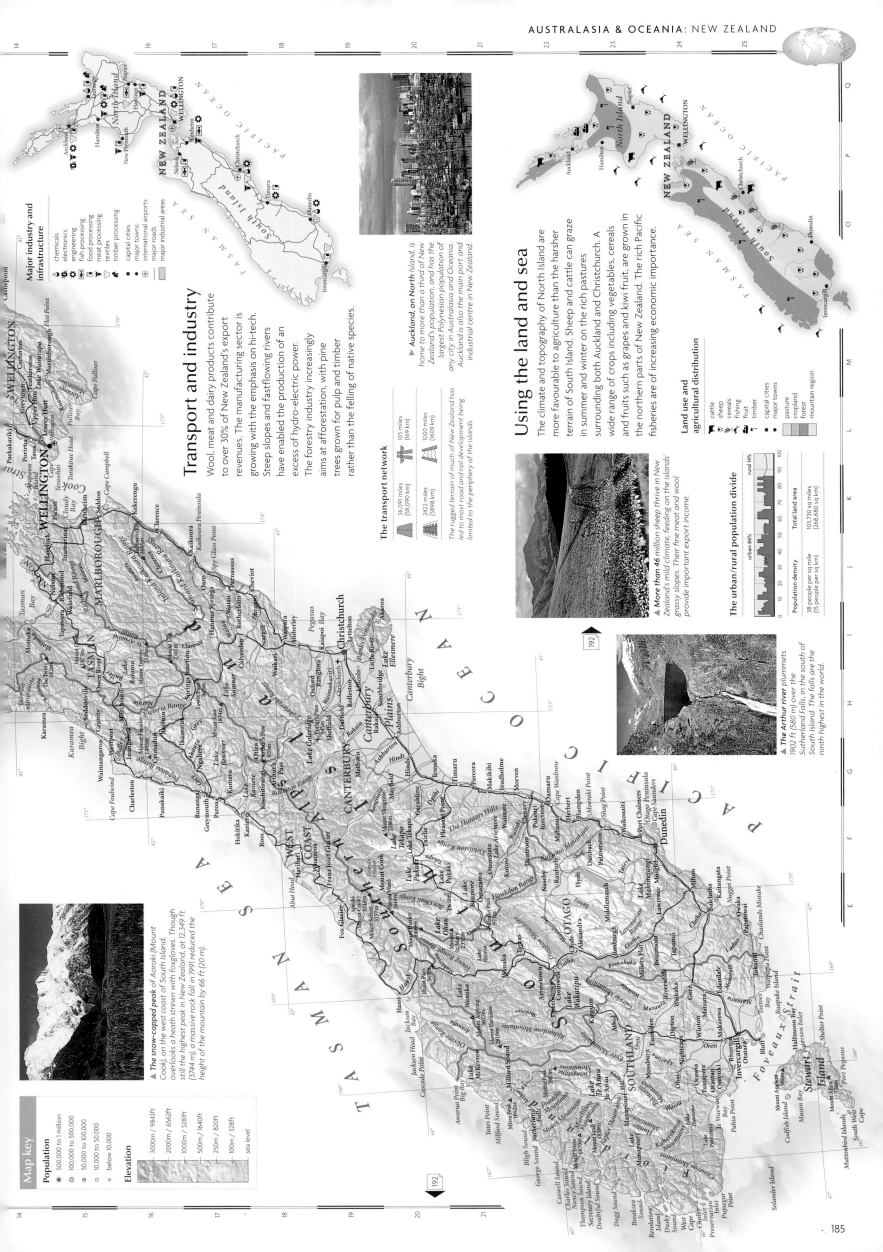

Map key

Population

- ◉ 500,000 to 1 million
- ◎ 100,000 to 500,000
- ⊕ 50,000 to 100,000
- ⊙ 10,000 to 50,000
- ○ below 10,000

Elevation

- 3000m / 9843ft
- 2000m / 6562ft
- 1000m / 328ft
- 500m / 1640ft
- 250m / 820ft
- 100m / 328ft
- sea level

▲ *The snow-capped peak of Aoraki (Mount Cook), on the west coast of South Island, overlooks a heath strewn with foxgloves. Though still the highest peak in New Zealand, at 12,349 ft (3744 m), a massive rock fall in 1991 reduced the height of the mountain by 66 ft (20 m).*

Transport and industry

Wool, meat and dairy products contribute to over 30% of New Zealand's export revenues. The manufacturing sector is growing with the emphasis on hi-tech. Steep slopes and fastflowing rivers have enabled the production of an excess of hydro-electric power. The forestry industry increasingly aims at afforestation, with pine trees grown for pulp and timber rather than the felling of native species.

Major industry and infrastructure

- ⚗ chemicals
- ⚙ electronics
- engineering
- ⚓ fish processing
- food processing
- meat processing
- textiles
- timber processing
- ● capital cities
- ⊙ major towns
- ⊕ international airports
- — major roads
- major industrial areas

The transport network

- 🛣 36,091 miles (58,090 km)
- 🛤 2422 miles (3898 km)
- ✈ 105 miles (169 km)
- ⚡ 1000 miles (1609 km)

The rugged terrain of much of New Zealand has led to most road and rail development being limited to the periphery of the islands.

▲ *Auckland, on North Island, is home to more than a third of New Zealand's population, and has the largest Polynesian population of any city in Australasia and Oceania. Auckland is also the main port and industrial centre in New Zealand.*

Using the land and sea

The climate and topography of North Island are more favourable to agriculture than the harsher terrain of South Island. Sheep and cattle can graze in summer and winter on the rich pastures surrounding both Auckland and Christchurch. A wide range of crops including vegetables, cereals and fruits such as grapes and kiwi fruit, are grown in the northern parts of New Zealand. The rich Pacific fisheries are of increasing economic importance.

Land use and agricultural distribution

- 🐄 cattle
- 🐑 sheep
- 🌾 cereals
- 🎣 fishing
- 🌲 fruit
- timber
- ● capital cities
- ⊙ major towns
- pasture
- cropland
- forest
- mountain region

▲ *More than 46 million sheep thrive in New Zealand's mild climate, feeding on the islands' grassy slopes. Their fine meat and wool provide important export income.*

▲ *The Arthur river plummets 1902 ft (580 m) over the Sutherland Falls, in the south of South Island. The falls are the ninth highest in the world.*

The urban/rural population divide

	urban 86%	rural 14%

Population density: 38 people per sq mile (15 people per sq km)

Total land area: 103,730 sq miles (268,680 sq km)

Melanesia

FIJI, New Caledonia *(to France)*, PAPUA NEW GUINEA, SOLOMON ISLANDS, VANUATU

Lying in the southwest Pacific Ocean, northeast of Australia and south of the Equator, the islands of Melanesia form one of the three geographic divisions (along with Polynesia and Micronesia) of Oceania. Melanesia's name derives from the Greek melas, 'black', and nesoi, 'islands'. Most of the larger islands are volcanic in origin. The smaller islands tend to be coral atolls and are mainly uninhabited. Rugged mountains, covered by dense rainforest, take up most of the land area. Melanesian's cultivate yams, taro, and sweet potatoes for local consumption and live in small, usually dispersed, homesteads.

▲ *Huli tribesmen from Southern Highlands Province in Papua New Guinea parade in ceremonial dress, their powdered wigs decorated with exotic plumage and their faces and bodies painted with coloured pigments.*

Map key

Population
- ⊚ 100,000 to 500,000
- ⊕ 50,000 to 100,000
- ⊙ 10,000 to 50,000
- ○ below 10,000

Elevation
- 4000m / 13,124ft
- 3000m / 9843ft
- 2000m / 6562ft
- 1000m / 3281ft
- 500m / 1640ft
- 250m / 820ft
- 100m / 328ft
- sea level

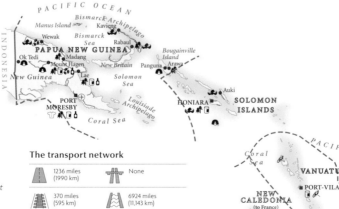

◀ *Lying close to the banks of the Sepik river in northern Papua New Guinea, this building is known as the Spirit House. It is constructed from leaves and twigs, ornately woven and trimmed into geometric patterns. The house is decorated with a mask and topped by a carved statue.*

▲ *On one of Vanuatu's many islands, beach houses stand at the water's edge, surrounded by coconut palms and other tropical vegetation. The unspoilt beaches and tranquillity of its islands are drawing ever-larger numbers of tourists to Vanuatu.*

Transport and Industry

The processing of natural resources generates significant export revenue for the countries of Melanesia. The region relies mainly on copra, tuna and timber exports, with some production of cocoa and palm oil. The islands have substantial mineral resources including the world's largest copper reserves on Bougainville Island; gold, and potential oil and natural gas. Tourism has become the fastest growing sector in most of the countries' economies.

◀ *On New Caledonia's main island, relatively high interior plateaux descend to coastal plains. Nickel is the most important mineral resource, but the hills also harbour metallic deposits including chrome, cobalt, iron, gold, silver and copper.*

The transport network

🛣	1236 miles (1990 km)	🛤	None
🚆	370 miles (595 km)	✈	6924 miles (11,143 km)

As most of the islands of Melanesia lie off the major sea and air routes, services to and from the rest of the world are infrequent. Transport by road on rugged terrain is difficult and expensive.

Major industry and infrastructure
- ♂ beverages
- ☕ coffee processing
- 🥥 copra processing
- 🍴 food processing
- ⚒ mining
- ♈ textiles
- 🌲 timber processing
- 🏖 tourism
- ■ capital cities
- ■ major towns
- ⊕ international airports
- — major roads

The Landscape

Melanesia comprises high, volcanic islands, low coral islands and continental islands. New Guinea is part of the Australian continental platform, and is separated from it only by the shallow flooding of the Torres Strait. The plate margin of the Pacific and Indo-Australian plates cuts through mainland Papua New Guinea. Volcanic activity, resulting from the collision of these plates, has sculpted much of Melanesia's landscape.

The Star Mountains include some of the most remote terrain on Earth. The area is rich in gold and copper.

The lowland plains in the south and north of Papua New Guinea's main island are swampy, and contain some fertile alluvial soils. This contrasts with the mountainous islands in the rest of the country where soils are generally thin and nutrients are retained in the existing vegetation.

Southern Papua New Guinea is part of the Indo-Australian Plate. New Guinea only became separated physically from Australia about 8000-years ago following the flooding of the Torres Strait.

▶ *Papua New Guinea's rivers, though fairly short, carry extremely high sediment loads, largely due to soil erosion. This is caused by a combination of very steep slopes and heavy rainfall, and is made worse by forest clearance, particularly 'slash and burn' techniques and road or mine operations.*

The Sepik river drains the lowlands north of the Central Range, flowing eastward into the Bismarck Sea.

The Bismarck Range is precipitous, rugged and covered in dense vegetation, rising to 14,793 ft (4509-m) at Mount Wilhelm in central Papua New Guinea.

Huon Peninsula

Kikori river

The Owen Stanley Range contains several of Papua New Guinea's highest peaks, the greatest of which is Mount Victoria at 13,200 ft (4035 m).

The Louisiade Archipelago contains 10 volcanic islands and numerous coral islets. Tagula Island is the largest of the islands, containing the archipelago's highest peak at 2645 ft (806 m).

Most of Papua New Guinea's outlying islands, including New Britain, Bougainville Island and New Ireland, are precipitous and of volcanic origin.

Kavachi is an active submarine volcano near New Georgia, which erupts every few years.

The Solomon Islands are mountainous continental-type islands with largely andesitic volcanoes.

New Caledonia's main island is surrounded by coral reef that extends from the Huon island group in the north, to Île des Pins in the south.

◀ *The slopes of this extinct volcano near Talasea on the island of New Britain have been almost entirely colonized by rainforest vegetation.*

▲ *A series of coral reefs can be seen in the clear waters off Cape Esperance on the island of Guadalcanal in the Solomons.*

The physical landscapes of the islands of Vanuatu range from rugged mountains and high plateaux, to rolling hills and low plateaux and offshore coral reefs.

Viti Levu, the largest of Fiji's islands, contains the country's highest mountain, Mount Victoria at 4339 ft (1323 m).

Huon Peninsula

Caves and undercut cliffs mark former shoreline
Former level of beach
Current beach
Stream cuts down through recently exposed land

Uplift of the land in tectonically active regions can lead to former coastlines being lifted beyond the reach of the sea. New cliffs and caves are formed at a lower level, and rivers cut down through the lower land to reach sea level once more.

Using the land and sea

Almost 60% of the population of Melanesia is engaged in agriculture and animal husbandry at a subsistence level. Coconuts and cocoa are grown for export revenue. Over 80% of the land area is cloaked by tropical forest and woodlands, which have proved to be a rich timber source. In coastal areas, fishing, mainly for tuna, is a staple industry.

The urban/rural population divide

urban 32%   rural 68%

0 10 20 30 40 50 60 70 80 90 100

Population density	Total land area
32 people per sq mile (12 people per sq km)	205,354 sq miles (332,008 sq km)

◀ *Abaca Eco-tourist Park near Lautoka on the island of Viti Levu in western Fiji is one of a number of projects aimed at combining tourism with awareness about the environment. The government and people of Fiji are keen to protect the unique ecology of the islands and prevent further damage to the coral reefs. Until the recent ending of nuclear testing in the Pacific by Western nations, Fiji lay downwind of some of the main testing sites.*

Land use and agricultural distribution

- bananas
- cocoa
- coconuts
- fishing
- oil palms
- rubber
- timber
- ■ capital cities
- ■ major towns
- cropland
- forest
- wetland

Scale 1:9,800,000

Km
0 25 50 100 150 200 250 300

Miles
0 25 50 100 150 200 250 300

projection: Mercator

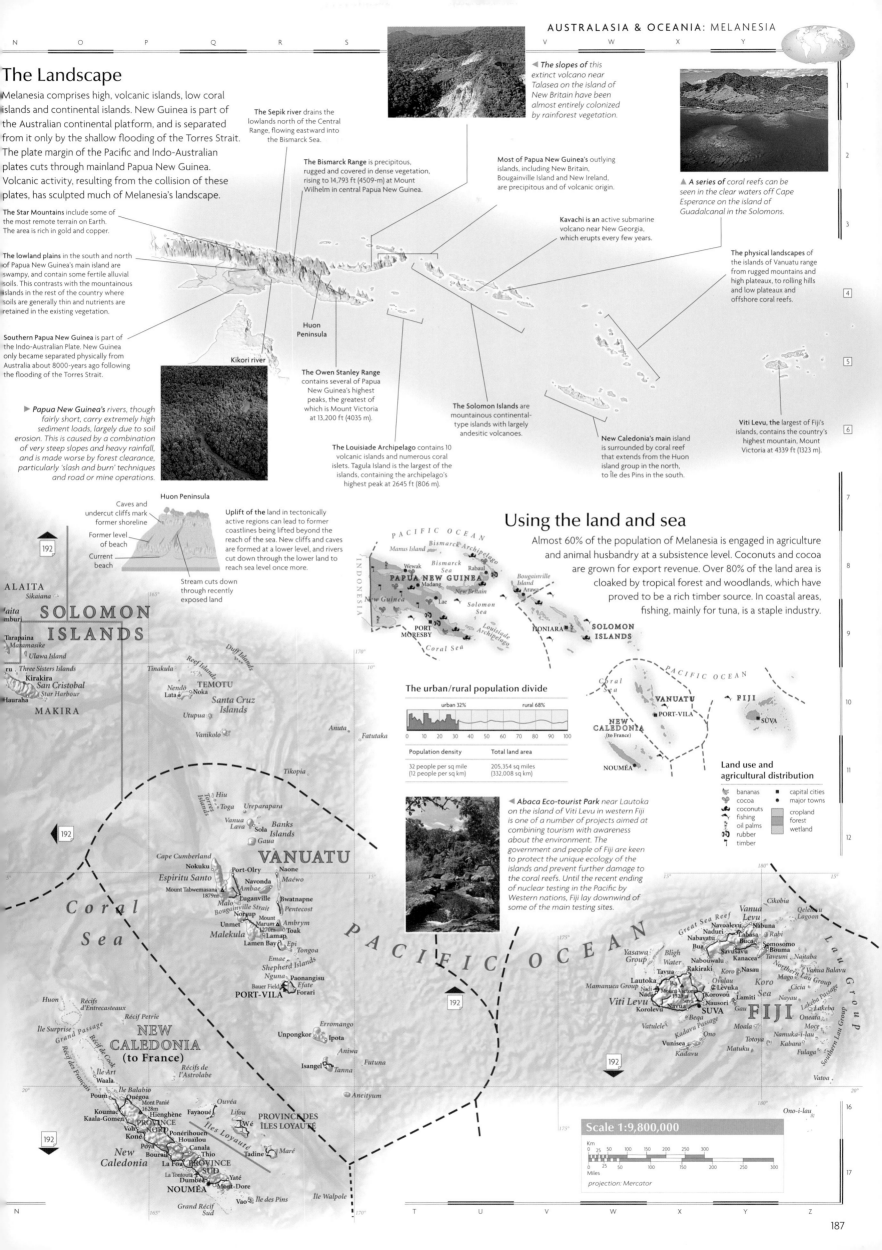

Micronesia

MARSHALL ISLANDS, MICRONESIA, NAURU, PALAU, Guam, Northern Mariana Islands, Wake Island

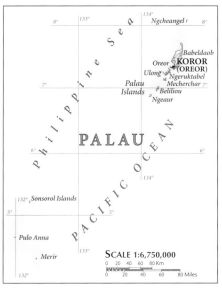

The Micronesian islands lie in the western reaches of the Pacific Ocean and are all part of the same volcanic zone. The Federated States of Micronesia is the largest group, with more than 600 atolls and forested volcanic islands in an area of more than 1120 sq miles (2900 sq km). Micronesia is a mixture of former colonies, overseas territories and dependencies. Most of the region still relies on aid and subsidies to sustain economies limited by resources, isolation, and an emigrating population, drawn to New Zealand and Australia by the attractions of a western lifestyle.

Palau

Palau is an archipelago of over 200 islands, only eight of which are inhabited. It was the last remaining UN trust territory in the Pacific, controlled by the USA until 1994, when it became independent. The economy operates on a subsistence level, with coconuts and cassava the principal crops. Fishing licences and tourism provide foreign currency.

SCALE 1:825,000

SCALE 1:6,750,000

Guam (to US)

Lying at the southern end of the Mariana Islands, Guam is an important US military base and tourist destination. Social and political life is dominated by the indigenous Chamorro, who make up just under half the population, although the increasing prevalence of western culture threatens Guam's traditional social stability.

◀ The tranquillity of these coastal lagoons, at Inarajan in southern Guam, belies the fact that the island lies in a region where typhoons are common.

SCALE 1:925,000

Northern Mariana Islands (to US)

A US Commonwealth territory, the Northern Marianas comprise the whole of the Mariana archipelago except for Guam. The islands retain their close links with the United States and continue to receive US aid. Tourism, though bringing in much-needed revenue, has speeded the decline of the traditional subsistence economy. Most of the population lives on Saipan.

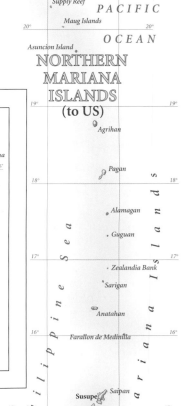

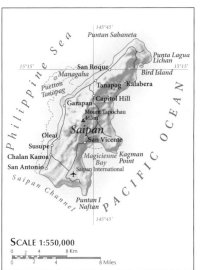

SCALE 1:550,000

▲ The Palau Islands have numerous hidden lakes and lagoons. These sustain their own ecosystems which have developed in isolation. This has produced adaptations in the animals and plants which are often unique to each lake.

SCALE 1:5,500,000

Micronesia

A mixture of high volcanic islands and low-lying coral atolls, the Federated States of Micronesia include all the Caroline Islands except Palau. Pohnpei, Kosrae, Chuuk and Yap are the four main island cluster states, each of which has its own language, with English remaining the official language. Nearly half the population is concentrated on Pohnpei, the largest island. Independent since 1986, the islands continue to receive considerable aid from the USA which supplements an economy based primarily on fishing and copra processing.

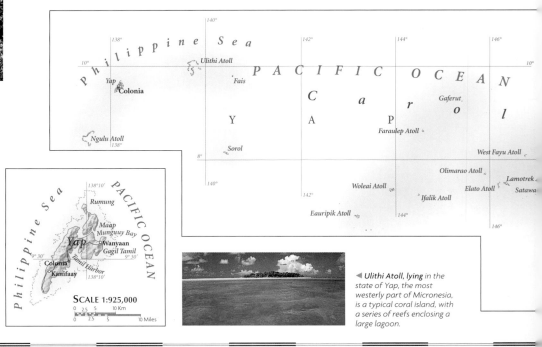

◀ Ulithi Atoll, lying in the state of Yap, the most westerly part of Micronesia, is a typical coral island, with a series of reefs enclosing a large lagoon.

SCALE 1:925,000

N O P Q R S T U V W X Y Z

Marshall Islands

A group of 34 widely-scattered atolls in the central Pacific Ocean, the Marshall Islands include some of the largest atolls in the world, formed from low coral islands with sandy beaches and enclosing vast lagoons. Formerly under US protection as part of the UN Trust Territory of the Pacific Islands, and including the former US nuclear testing sites of Bikini atoll and Enewetak Atoll, the Marshall Islands became self-governing in 1979. The economy is reliant on US aid and on the rent paid by the USA for its missile base on Kwajalein atoll.

SCALE 1:1,100,000
0 5 10 Km
0 5 10 Miles

Majuro Atoll
Rongrong
Iroj
Kallalen
Laura
Enigu
Majuro Lagoon
Djarrit
Dalap
Majuro
PACIFIC OCEAN

PACIFIC OCEAN

Sibylla Island
Bokaak Atoll

Bikar Atoll

Enewetak Atoll
Bikini Atoll
Rongelap Atoll
Rongrik Atoll
Ailinginae Atoll
Taka Atoll
Utrik Atoll

MARSHALL ISLANDS

Ailuk Atoll
Mejit Island
Wotho Atoll
Jemo Island
Likiep Atoll
Wotje Atoll
Ujae Atoll
Kwajalein Atoll
Erikub Atoll
Lae Atoll
Maloelap Atoll
Lib
Aur Atoll
Namu Atoll

Ratak Chain
Ralik Chain

Jabwot
Ailinglaplap Atoll
Majuro Atoll
Arno Atoll

SCALE 1:7,250,000
0 25 50 100 Km
0 25 50 100 Miles

Jaluit Atoll
Mili Atoll
Namorik Atoll
Kili Island
Knox Atoll

Ebon Atoll

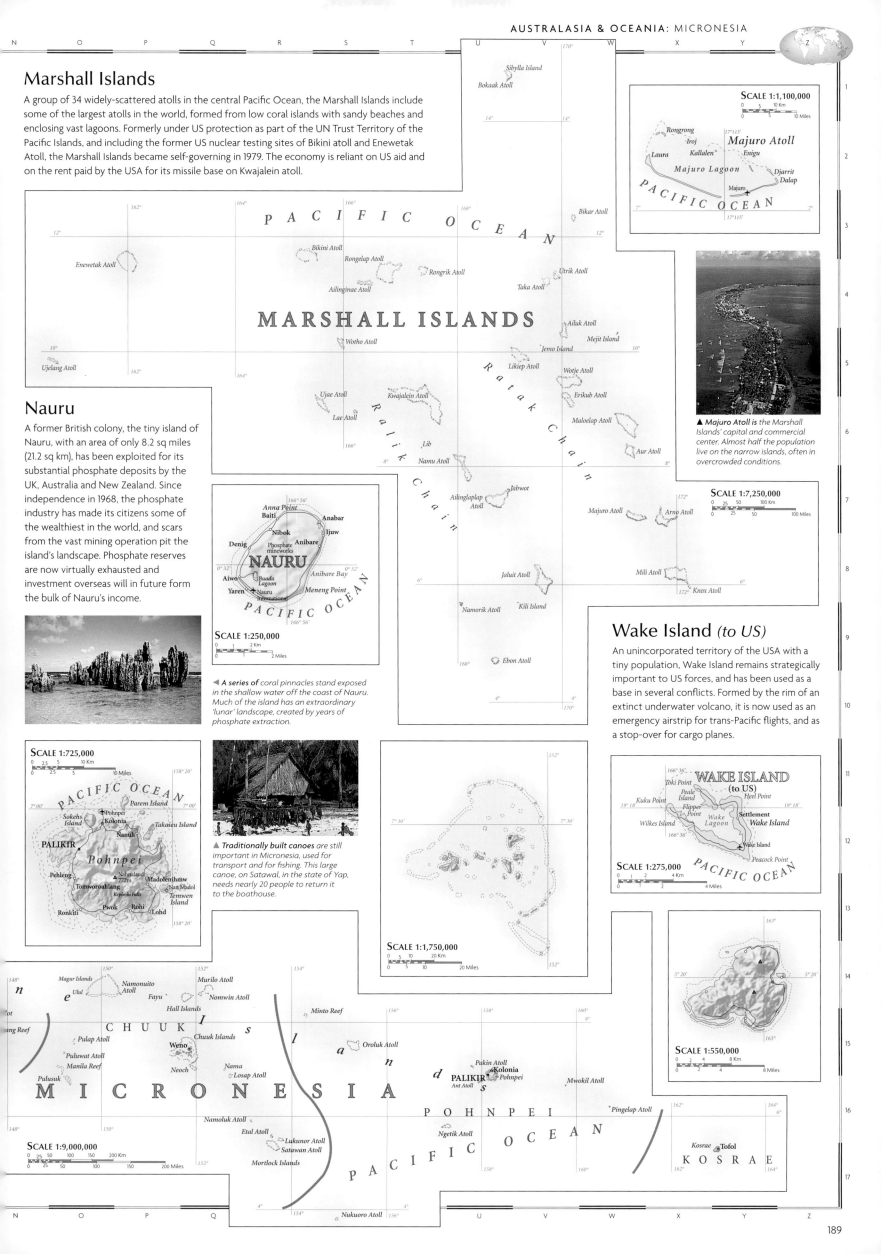

▲ *Majuro Atoll is* the Marshall Islands' capital and commercial center. Almost half the population live on the narrow islands, often in overcrowded conditions.

Nauru

A former British colony, the tiny island of Nauru, with an area of only 8.2 sq miles (21.2 sq km), has been exploited for its substantial phosphate deposits by the UK, Australia and New Zealand. Since independence in 1968, the phosphate industry has made its citizens some of the wealthiest in the world, and scars from the vast mining operation pit the island's landscape. Phosphate reserves are now virtually exhausted and investment overseas will in future form the bulk of Nauru's income.

Anna Point
Baiti
Anabar
Nibok
Ijuw
Denig
Anibare
Phosphate mineworks
NAURU
Aiwo
Anibare Bay
Buada Lagoon
Yaren
Nauru International
Meneng Point
PACIFIC OCEAN

SCALE 1:250,000
0 1 2 Km
0 1 2 Miles

◀ *A series of* coral pinnacles stand exposed in the shallow water off the coast of Nauru. Much of the island has an extraordinary 'lunar' landscape, created by years of phosphate extraction.

Wake Island *(to US)*

An unincorporated territory of the USA with a tiny population, Wake Island remains strategically important to US forces, and has been used as a base in several conflicts. Formed by the rim of an extinct underwater volcano, it is now used as an emergency airstrip for trans-Pacific flights, and as a stop-over for cargo planes.

WAKE ISLAND (to US)
Toki Point
Peale Island
Heel Point
Kuku Point
Flipper Point
Wilkes Island
Wake Lagoon
Settlement
Wake Island
Wake Island
Peacock Point
PACIFIC OCEAN

SCALE 1:275,000
0 1 2 4 Km
0 1 2 4 Miles

SCALE 1:725,000
0 2.5 5 10 Km
0 2.5 5 10 Miles

PACIFIC OCEAN
Sokehs Island
Parem Island
Pohnpei
Kolonia
Takaieu Island
Nanuh
PALIKIR
Pohnpei
Pehleng
Nahnalaud 772m
Tomworoahlang
Madolenihmw
Keprohi Falls
Nan Madol
Temwen Island
Ronkiti
Pwok
Rohi
Lohd

▲ *Traditionally built canoes* are still important in Micronesia, used for transport and for fishing. This large canoe, on Satawal, in the state of Yap, needs nearly 20 people to return it to the boathouse.

SCALE 1:1,750,000
0 5 10 20 Km
0 5 10 20 Miles

SCALE 1:550,000
0 2 4 8 Km
0 2 4 8 Miles

Magur Islands
Namonuito Atoll
Ulul
Murilo Atoll
Nomwin Atoll
Fayu
Hall Islands
Minto Reef
CHUUK
Islands
Pulap Atoll
Chuuk Islands
Oroluk Atoll
Puluwat Atoll
Weno
Nama
Losap Atoll
Manila Reef
Neoch
Pakin Atoll
Kolonia
PALIKIR
Pohnpei
Pulusuk
Mwokil Island
Ant Atoll

MICRONESIA

POHNPEI

PACIFIC OCEAN

Namoluk Atoll
Etal Atoll
Ngetik Atoll
Pingelap Atoll
Lukunor Atoll
Satawan Atoll
Mortlock Islands
Kosrae
Tofol
KOSRAE

SCALE 1:9,000,000
0 25 50 100 150 200 Km
0 25 50 100 150 200 Miles

Nukuoro Atoll

Polynesia

KIRIBATI, TUVALU, Cook Islands, Easter Island, French Polynesia, Niue, Pitcairn Islands, Tokelau, Wallis & Futuna

The numerous island groups of Polynesia lie to the east of Australia, scattered over a vast area in the south Pacific. The islands are a mixture of low-lying coral atolls, some of which enclose lagoons, and the tips of great underwater volcanoes. The populations on the islands are small, and most people are of Polynesian origin, as are the Maori of New Zealand. Local economies remain simple, relying mainly on subsistence crops, mineral deposits – many now exhausted – fishing and tourism.

SCALE 1:1,100,000

Kiribati

A former British colony, Kiribati became independent in 1979. Banaba's phosphate deposits ran out in 1980, following decades of exploitation by the British. Economic development remains slow and most agriculture is at a subsistence level, though coconuts provide export income, and underwater agriculture is being developed.

▶ With the exception of Banaba all the islands in Kiribati's three groups are low-lying, coral atolls. This aerial view shows the sparsely vegetated islands, intercut by many small lagoons.

Tuvalu

A chain of nine coral atolls, 360 miles (579 km) long with a land area of just over 9 sq miles (23 sq km), Tuvalu is one of the world's smallest and most isolated states. As the Ellice Islands, Tuvalu was linked to the Gilbert Islands (now part of Kiribati) as a British colony until independence in 1978. Politically and socially conservative, Tuvaluans live by fishing and subsistence farming.

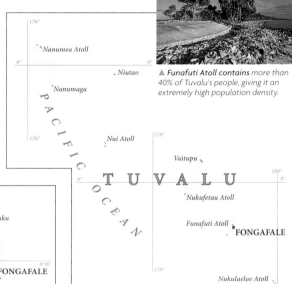

▲ Funafuti Atoll contains more than 40% of Tuvalu's people, giving it an extremely high population density.

SCALE 1:550,000

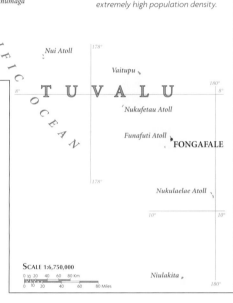

SCALE 1:6,750,000

Tokelau (to New Zealand)

A low-lying coral atoll, Tokelau is a dependent territory of New Zealand with few natural resources. Although a 1990 cyclone destroyed crops and infrastructure, a tuna cannery and the sale of fishing licences have raised revenue and a catamaran link between the islands has increased their tourism potential. Tokelau's small size and economic weakness makes independence from New Zealand unlikely.

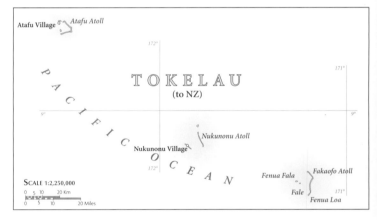

▲ Fishermen cast their nets to catch small fish in the shallow waters off Atafu Atoll, the most westerly island in Tokelau.

SCALE 1:2,250,000

Wallis & Futuna (to France)

In contrast to other French overseas territories in the south Pacific, the inhabitants of Wallis and Futuna have shown little desire for greater autonomy. A subsistence economy produces a variety of tropical crops, while foreign currency remittances come from expatriates and from the sale of licences to Japanese and Korean fishing fleets.

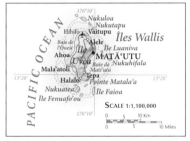

SCALE 1:1,100,000

SCALE 1:1,100,000

Niue (to New Zealand)

Niue, the world's largest coral island, is self-governing but exists in free association with New Zealand. Tropical fruits are grown for local consumption; tourism and the sale of postage stamps provide foreign currency. The lack of local job prospects has led more than 10,000 Niueans to emigrate to New Zealand, which has now invested heavily in Niue's economy in the hope of reversing this trend.

Cook Islands (to New Zealand)

A mixture of coral atolls and volcanic peaks, the Cook Islands achieved self-government in 1965 but exist in free association with New Zealand. A diverse economy includes pearl and giant clam farming, and an ostrich farm, plus tourism and banking. A 1991 friendship treaty with France provides for French surveillance of territorial waters.

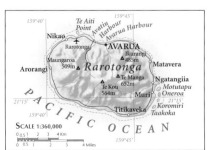

▲ Palm trees fringe the white sands of a beach on Aitutaki in the Southern Cook Islands, where tourism is of increasing economic importance.

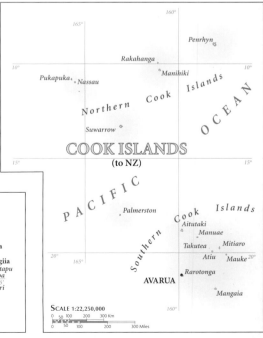

SCALE 1:22,250,000

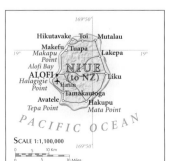

SCALE 1:1,100,000

▲ Waves have cut back the original coastline, exposing a sandy beach, near Mutalau in the northeast corner of Niue.

SCALE 1:360,000

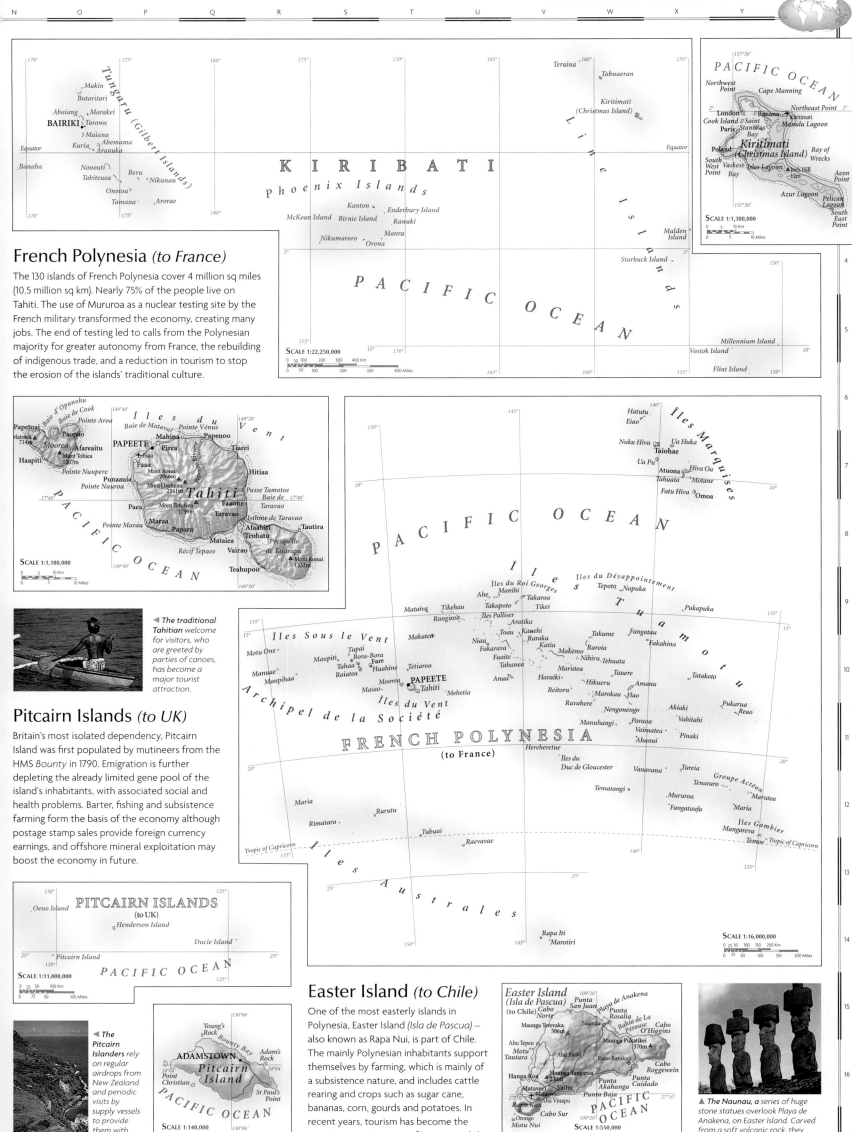

French Polynesia (to France)

The 130 islands of French Polynesia cover 4 million sq miles (10.5 million sq km). Nearly 75% of the people live on Tahiti. The use of Mururoa as a nuclear testing site by the French military transformed the economy, creating many jobs. The end of testing led to calls from the Polynesian majority for greater autonomy from France, the rebuilding of indigenous trade, and a reduction in tourism to stop the erosion of the islands' traditional culture.

◄ The traditional Tahitian welcome for visitors, who are greeted by parties of canoes, has become a major tourist attraction.

Pitcairn Islands (to UK)

Britain's most isolated dependency, Pitcairn Island was first populated by mutineers from the HMS Bounty in 1790. Emigration is further depleting the already limited gene pool of the island's inhabitants, with associated social and health problems. Barter, fishing and subsistence farming form the basis of the economy although postage stamp sales provide foreign currency earnings, and offshore mineral exploitation may boost the economy in future.

◄ The Pitcairn Islanders rely on regular airdrops from New Zealand and periodic visits by supply vessels to provide them with basic commodities.

Easter Island (to Chile)

One of the most easterly islands in Polynesia, Easter Island (Isla de Pascua) – also known as Rapa Nui, is part of Chile. The mainly Polynesian inhabitants support themselves by farming, which is mainly of a subsistence nature, and includes cattle rearing and crops such as sugar cane, bananas, corn, gourds and potatoes. In recent years, tourism has become the most important source of income and the island sustains a small commercial airport.

▲ The Naunau, a series of huge stone statues overlook Playa de Anakena, on Easter Island. Carved from a soft volcanic rock, they were erected between 400 and 900 years ago.

191

The Pacific Ocean

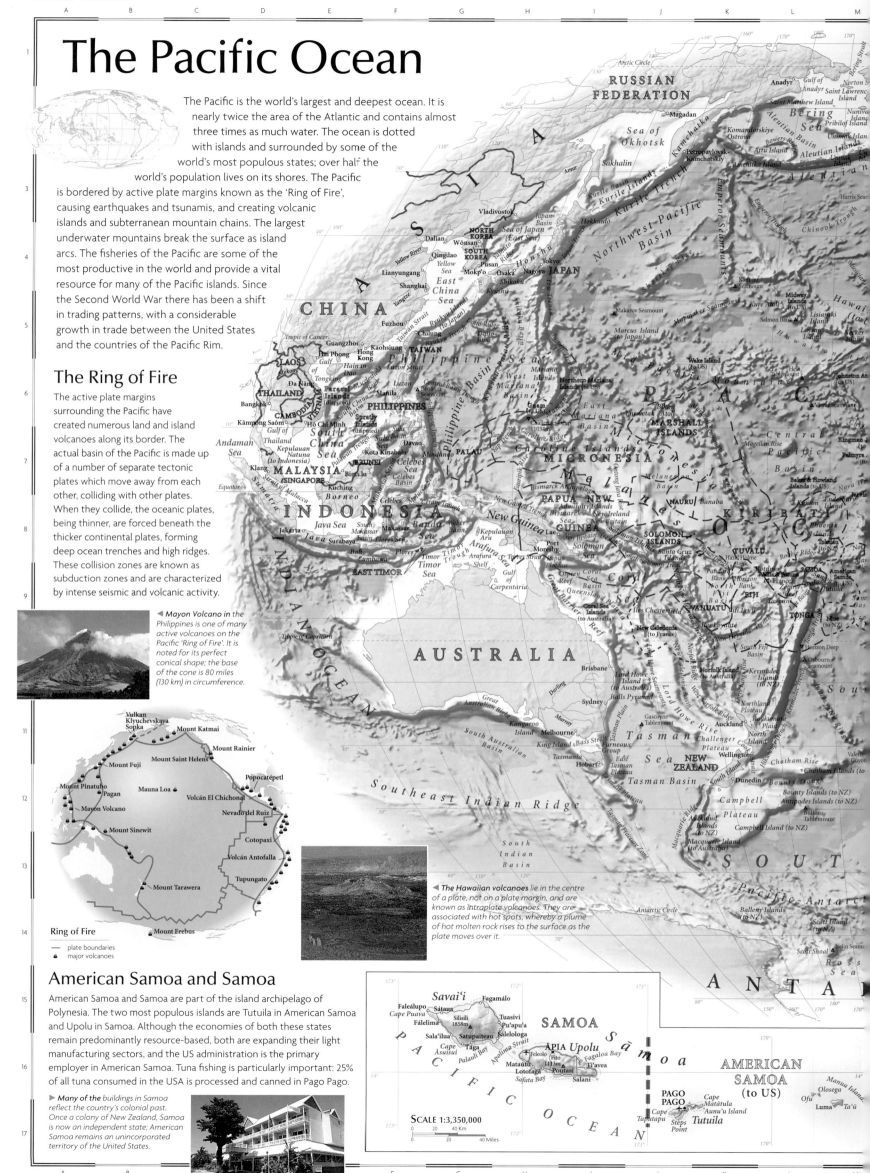

The Pacific is the world's largest and deepest ocean. It is nearly twice the area of the Atlantic and contains almost three times as much water. The ocean is dotted with islands and surrounded by some of the world's most populous states; over half the world's population lives on its shores. The Pacific is bordered by active plate margins known as the 'Ring of Fire', causing earthquakes and tsunamis, and creating volcanic islands and subterranean mountain chains. The largest underwater mountains break the surface as island arcs. The fisheries of the Pacific are some of the most productive in the world and provide a vital resource for many of the Pacific islands. Since the Second World War there has been a shift in trading patterns, with a considerable growth in trade between the United States and the countries of the Pacific Rim.

The Ring of Fire

The active plate margins surrounding the Pacific have created numerous land and island volcanoes along its border. The actual basin of the Pacific is made up of a number of separate tectonic plates which move away from each other, colliding with other plates. When they collide, the oceanic plates, being thinner, are forced beneath the thicker continental plates, forming deep ocean trenches and high ridges. These collision zones are known as subduction zones and are characterized by intense seismic and volcanic activity.

◀ *Mayon Volcano in the Philippines is one of many active volcanoes on the Pacific 'Ring of Fire'. It is noted for its perfect conical shape; the base of the cone is 80 miles (130 km) in circumference.*

Ring of Fire

— plate boundaries
▲ major volcanoes

◀ *The Hawaiian volcanoes lie in the centre of a plate, not on a plate margin, and are known as intraplate volcanoes. They are associated with hot spots, whereby a plume of hot molten rock rises to the surface as the plate moves over it.*

American Samoa and Samoa

American Samoa and Samoa are part of the island archipelago of Polynesia. The two most populous islands are Tutuila in American Samoa and Upolu in Samoa. Although the economies of both these states remain predominantly resource-based, both are expanding their light manufacturing sectors, and the US administration is the primary employer in American Samoa. Tuna fishing is particularly important: 25% of all tuna consumed in the USA is processed and canned in Pago Pago.

▶ *Many of the buildings in Samoa reflect the country's colonial past. Once a colony of New Zealand, Samoa is now an independent state; American Samoa remains an unincorporated territory of the United States.*

SCALE 1:3,350,000

The Landscape

Although it is still the largest ocean, the basin of the Pacific has been gradually decreasing in size due to the movement of the Indo-Australian Plate. The oldest parts are about 135 million years old. The eastern border of the Pacific is characterized by a continuous mountain chain running the length of the North and South American continents. The eastern basin has a low, uninterrupted relief, at depths averaging 15,000 ft (4570 m). In contrast, the western Pacific is scattered with island arcs and bounded by a series of deep ocean trenches. An almost continuous chain of volcanoes surrounds the ocean and an active mid-ocean ridge runs northeast–southwest.

Micronesia consists of numerous small, oceanic islands in the western Pacific. The Micronesian islands are all oceanic in origin, rising directly up from the ocean floor.

The Peru–Chile Trench is the longest trench in the Pacific, extending 3660 miles (5900 km), and following the line of the Andes mountain range down the west coast of South America.

The Mariana Trench marks a subduction zone between the Pacific Plate and the Philippine Plate. It is the world's deepest trench, reaching depths of 36,201 ft (11,034 m).

The Tonga Trench lies north of New Zealand's North Island. The trench reaches average depths of 34,448 ft (10,500 m), which is more than twice the average depth of the ocean.

▶ Bora-Bora's twin mountain peaks the remnants of an ancient volcano, now surrounded by a large lagoon, fringed with coral.

Scale 1:67,500,000

Km
0   200 400 600 800 1000
Miles
0   200   400   600   800 1000

projection: Mollweide

Map key

Population
○ below 10,000

Sea Depth
sea level
250m / 820ft
500m / 1640ft
1000m / 3281ft
2000m / 6562ft
3000m / 9843ft
5000m / 16,410ft

Elevation
1000m / 3281ft
500m / 1640ft
250m / 820ft
100m / 328ft
sea level

▶ Wave action has eroded this shoreline near Port Campbell in southeastern Australia leaving isolated pinnacles of rock cut off from the main coastline. They are known as the 'Twelve Apostles'.

Tonga

The Kingdom of Tonga lies in the southwest Pacific, about 2000 miles (3000 km) off the east coast of Australia. It comprises 169 islands of which only 36 are permanently inhabited. The majority of the population live on the largest island, Tongatapu. There are only three sizeable towns and the main commercial centre is the capital Nuku'alofa. Tonga's economy is based mainly on agriculture; coconuts, bananas and vanilla are grown as cash crops for export. Although there is some light manufacturing, growing land shortages have forced increased migration to New Zealand and Australia.

◀ Coral reefs and atolls are found throughout the warm waters of the south Pacific. Reefs build up from the skeletons of millions of coral polyps – tiny sea creatures that cling to the reef and secrete calcium carbonate around their bodies, forming a hard protective skeleton.

▼ The islands of Tonga fall into two belts; those in the east are low, coral islands, while those in the west are high and volcanic. Four of the islands still contain active volcanoes. The mountainous, western islands are covered with verdant tropical vegetation.

SCALE 1:1,100,000

SCALE 1:6,650,000

TONGA

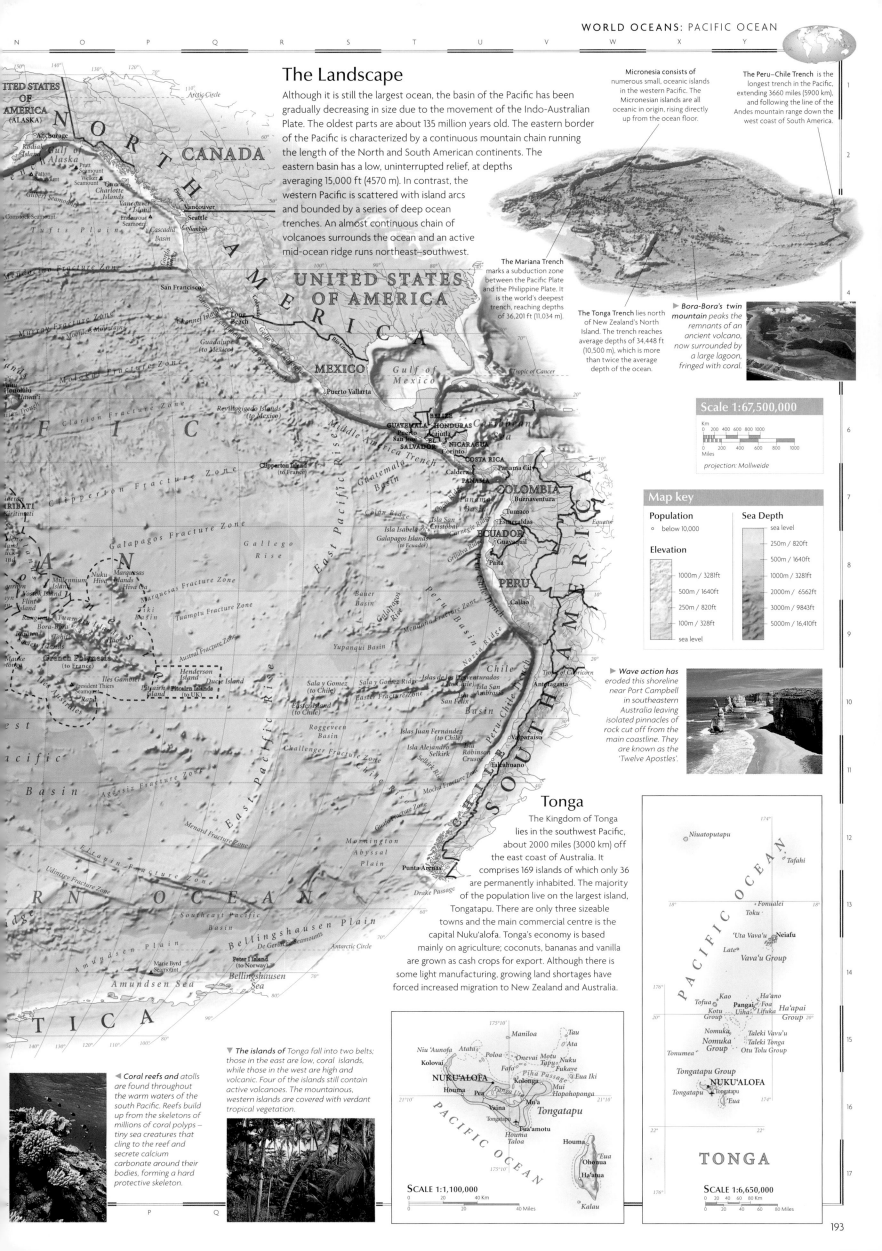

A B C D E F G

Antarctica

The ice-covered continent of Antarctica, which is the Earth's most southerly region, has for over 200 years drawn explorers and entrepreneurs seeking challenge and riches in its wintry lands. The extreme climate has deterred any large-scale settlement of the continent, and though commercial hunters built outposts in the past, habitation is now limited to scientific bases. The Antarctic Treaty, which came into force in 1961, provides for international governance and scientific co-operation in place of potential territorial conflict.

TERRITORIAL CLAIMS

Argentinian claim
Brazilian zone of interest
British claim
Norwegian undefined limit
Australian claim
Chilean claim
French claim
Australian claim
New Zealand claim

Scotia Sea

South Orkney Islands
Laurie Island
Orcadas (to Argentina)
Coronation Island
Signy (to UK)
Clarence Island
Elephant Island

Drake Passage

Research Stations on King George Island

Arctowski (to Poland)
Artigas (to Uruguay)
Bellingshausen (to Russian Federation)
Comandante Ferraz (to Brazil)
Great Wall (to China)
Jubany (to Argentina)
King Sejong (to South Korea)
Teniente Rodolfo Marsh (to Chile)

Resources

Many ore minerals, including iron and gold, are found in the Antarctic, and there are also coal reserves in the Transantarctic Mountains. The severe conditions and environmental importance of the region mean that exploitation of potential mineral resources is both uneconomic and undesirable. The unique wildlife and landscape draw a small number of tourists annually.

SOUTHERN OCEAN
SOUTHERN OCEAN
Weddell Sea
Dronning Maud Land
ANTARCTICA
Palmer Land
Bellingshausen Sea
Transantarctic Mountains
Davis Sea
Amundsen Sea
Marie Byrd Land
Wilkes Land
SOUTHERN OCEAN
Ross Sea

◀ Most settlements in Antarctica are research bases such as this one at Rothera on Adelaide Island, although there is a small Chilean settlement on King George Island.

Resources (including wildlife)

coal		seals	
fish		whales	
minerals		polar research base	
oil & gas			
penguins			

The landscape

There are two distinct parts to Antarctica: Lesser Antarctica, a series of ice-covered, mountainous islands, joined together by the ice; and the high plateau of Greater Antarctica. The Ross Sea and the Weddell Sea are outliers of the Southern Ocean – deep bays partially covered by thick ice shelves.

Grease ice   Pancake ice   Sea-ice sheet   Ice floe

◀ On Elephant Island, the coast is edged by glaciers, although the land is not permanently covered by ice.

▲ Pack ice forms out at sea in freezing temperatures. At the outer limits, grease ice congeals on the surface of the ocean. This is then spun around by wind and waves into irregular 'pancakes', freezing and breaking up several times before bonding together again to form sea-ice sheets, which finally cement into enormous ice floes.

During the winter the seas surrounding Antarctica freeze, increasing the size of the continent by 100%.

Limit of winter pack ice

Limit of summer pack ice

Upper Wright Valley

Elephant Island

High winds carrying snow form huge snowdrifts. The erosive power of the wind-borne snow can also sculpt the ice sheet to produce landforms known as sastrugi which align with the direction of the wind.

Many volcanoes, some of them still active, can be found in the mountains of the Antarctic Peninsula.

The Lambert Glacier is the largest glacier system in the world, up to 50 miles (80 km) wide at its seaward limit, and reaching 180 miles (300 km) into the interior by way of the Prince Charles Mountains.

Antarctica is the highest continent on Earth, because of the great thickness of ice which overlays the land. In places the ice alone can reach up to 15,700 ft (4800 m) thick. Much of the basement rock of west Antarctica lies below sea level, pushed down by the weight of the ice.

The mountainous Antarctic Peninsula is formed of rocks 65–225 million years old, overlain by more recent rocks and glacial deposits. It is connected to the Andes in South America by a submarine ridge.

Nearly half – 44% – of the Antarctic coastline is bounded by ice shelves, like the Ronne Ice Shelf, which float on the Ocean. These are joined to the inland ice sheet by dome-shaped ice 'rises'.

More than 30% of Antarctic ice is contained in the Ross Ice Shelf.

◀ The barren, flat-bottomed Upper Wright Valley was once filled by a glacier, but is now dry, strewn with boulders and pebbles. In some dry valleys, there has been no rain for over 2 million years.

▲ Large colonies of seabirds live in the extremely harsh Antarctic climate. The Emperor penguins seen here, the smaller Adélie penguin, the Antarctic petrel and the South Polar skua are the only birds which breed exclusively on the continent.

Joinville Island
Dundee Island
General Bernardo O'Higgins (to Chile)
Esperanza (to Argentina)
Marambio (to Argentina)
Snowhill Island
James Ross Island
Robertson Island
Jason Peninsula
Churchill Peninsula
Cape Agassiz
Hearst Island
Ewing Island
Dolleman Island
Steele Island
Cape Bryant
Butler Island
Cape Knowles
Cape Mackintosh
Cape Deacon
Cape Fiske

King George Island
Capitán Arturo Prat (to Chile)
Livingston Island
South Shetland Islands
Brabant Island
Anvers Island (to US)
Faraday (to UK)
Biscoe Islands
Lavoisier Island
Cape Mascart
Adelaide Island
Rothera (to UK)
Marguerite Bay

Graham Land
Bransfield Strait
Davis Coast
Danco Coast
Bowman Coast
Larsen Ice Shelf
Black Coast
San Martin (to Argentina)
Palmer (to US)
Douglas Range
Alexander Island
Rothschild Island
Wilkins Ice Shelf
Charcot Island
Latady Island
Spaatz Island
Smyley Island
Rydberg Peninsula

Antarctic Peninsula
Palmer Land
English Coast
George VI Sound
Ronne Entrance
Case Island
Mount Jackson 4190m
Lester Coast
Orville Coast
Zumberge Coast
Bryan Coast

Weddell Sea

Ronne Ice Shelf
Korff Ice Rise
Henry Ice Rise
Hoag Nunataks
Ridford Ice Stream
Vinson Massif 4897m
Ellsworth Mountains

Bellingshausen Sea

Peter I Island (to Norway)
Dendtler Island
Farwell Island
Eights Coast
Dustin Island
Abbot Ice Shelf
Noville Peninsula
Thurston Island
Sherman Island
Cape Flying Fish
King Peninsula
Canisteo Peninsula
Burke Island
Bear Peninsula
Martin Peninsula
Wright Island

Ellsworth Land

Pine Island Glacier
Walgreen Coast
Bakutis Coast

Lesser Antarctica
Marie Byrd

Amundsen Sea

Carney Island
Siple Island
Mount Sidley 4181m
Executive Committee Range
Getz Ice Shelf
Hobbs Coast
Dean Island
Mount Siple 3100m
Grant Island
Cape Burks
Russkaya (to Russian Federation)
Ruppert
New

SOUTHERN

Antarctic Circle
Limit of winter pack ice
Limit of summer pack ice

192

A B C D E F G H I J K L M

◀ **The sun sets** over the Antarctic Peninsula for more than six months during the winter. However, there are more hours of sunshine during the brief Antarctic summer than most equatorial countries experience in a whole year.

▲ **Immense, flat-topped icebergs** are formed when blocks of ice break away from the main ice sheet. Though the exposed area is enormous, the volume of ice concealed beneath the water may be many times greater.

Scale 1:16,500,000

projection: Lambert Azimuthal Equal Area

Map key

Elevation

- ice cap
- ice shelf
- exposed land

A B C D E F G H I J K L M

The Arctic

Three continents, Asia, North America and Europe reach into the Arctic Circle at their northernmost limits, almost entirely encircling the Arctic Ocean. Despite the region's extraordinarily harsh climate, it has been inhabited for thousands of years by peoples such as the European Lapps, the Russian Nenet, and the North American Inuit, who draw a living from fishing, herding and hunting. More recently, particularly in the Russian Arctic, opportunities to exploit oil and other mineral reserves have encouraged immigration. Pollution of the Arctic's unique ecology and damage to the traditional lifestyles of many native peoples have been the unfortunate results of this activity, and international co-operation is needed to safeguard the future of the region.

192

Map key

Population
- ■ above 5 million
- ▣ 1 million to 5 million
- ◉ 500,000 to 1 million
- ◎ 100,000 to 500,000
- ⊕ 50,000 to 100,000
- ⊙ 10,000 to 50,000
- ○ below 10,000

Sea Depth
- sea level
- 250m / 820ft
- 500m / 1640ft
- 1000m / 3281ft
- 2000m / 6562ft
- 3000m / 9843ft

Scale 1:23,500,000

Km 0 100 200 300 400 500 600
Miles 0 100 200 300 400 500 600

projection: Lambert Azimuthal Equal Area

▲ *Wind-blown snow etches deep patterns in the ice sheet known as sastrugi. They align with the direction of the wind.*

Resources

Large quantities of coal, oil and natural gas are to be found in the basins of the Arctic Ocean, and in northern Canada, Alaska and the Russian Federation. The cost and difficulty of extraction and, more recently, awareness of damage to the environment, have limited exploitation to coastal regions. The unfrozen waters have stocks of fish including cod, plaice and haddock. Quotas have now been put in place to restrict the number of fish caught annually. Reindeer are herded in large numbers by many of the native Arctic peoples. Most grain and vegetables are imported from elsewhere.

8

Bering Sea
NORTH AMERICA
ASIA
Inuvik
Tiksi
ARCTIC OCEAN
Nori'sk
Qaanaaq
Murmansk
Reykjavík
ATLANTIC OCEAN
EUROPE

▲ *Icebreakers, ships with specially strengthened hulls, designed to break a path through the ice, are used to keep important routes open during the winter, when falling temperatures cause much of the Arctic Ocean to freeze over.*

Resources
- ⚒ coal
- 🐟 fish
- ⛏ mining
- ◊ oil & gas
- ☢ radioactive contamination
- ● major towns
- ⊕ major ports

8

The landscape

The Arctic Ocean comprises two large ocean basins divided by three submarine ridges, the greatest of which, the Lomonosov Ridge, is a huge underwater mountain range which has an average height of more than 10,000 ft (3000 m). The lands which encircle the Arctic Ocean are underlain by great shield areas of ancient rocks, which were heavily glaciated during the last Ice Age.

◀ *Icebergs are constantly broken up and re-shaped by wind and the oceans. This flat-topped iceberg has been undercut, leaving a craggy ice cliff.*

The Canadian Shield underlies almost all of the Canadian Arctic. It is a very stable plateau of ancient rock, now covered by glacial lakes and sediment, which supports tundra vegetation.

The Arctic Ocean is the world's smallest ocean with a total area of 5,440,000 sq miles (15,100,000 sq km).

At a latitude of more than 75° N, the Arctic Ocean is almost permanently covered by pack-ice, though high winds and the movement of the seas may cause the ice to crack and break up.

In the more southerly reaches of the Arctic, like Siberia, much of the land is covered by permafrost. In the summer, higher temperatures warm the frozen ground, causing a number of typical phenomena. These include solifluction, the fast downhill movement of top soil layers; freeze/thaw activity, which patterns the ground into regular polygonal shapes, and the formation of large domes with a frozen ice core, known as pingos.

A complex and ancient mountain system, extending from the Queen Elizabeth Islands to eastern Greenland was formed more than 245 million years ago.

Lomonosov Ridge

Arctic ice shelf

◀ *Much of Greenland is covered by a massive ice sheet more than 650,000 sq miles (1,683,400 sq km) in extent. The weight of the ice has depressed the central land area to form a basin lying more than 1000 ft (300 m) below sea level. Only at the edges of the island is bare rock visible.*

Iceland has five major glaciers, sustained by heavy snowfall. Parts of the ice cap cover active volcanoes, such as Bárdharbunga, which periodically erupt causing the melted ice to form a great lake at the glacier margins.

Ice sheet
Iceberg
Crevasses occur at the edge of the ice sheet
Sea water melts the edge of the ice sheet

▲ *At the boundary of the Arctic ice shelves, sea water flows under the ice causing melting and forming crevasses on the surface. This eventually weakens blocks of ice which break away as icebergs. This process is known as calving.*

Map labels (eastern map)
NORTH
CANADA
Great Bear Lake
Great Slave Lake
Kugluktuk
Bathurst Inlet
Cambridge Bay
King William Island
Churchill
Nelson
Repulse Bay
Melville Peninsula
Southampton Island
Hudson Bay
Coats Island
Mansel Island
Foxe Basin
Prince Charles Island
Ivujivik
Inukjuak
Baffin Island
Hudson Strait
Lake Harbour
Ungava Bay
Cape Chidley
Davis Strait
Nain
Labrador Sea
Maniitsoq
NUUK
Paamiut
Labrador Basin
Ivittuut
Qaqortoq
Nanortalik
Nunap Isua (Kap Farvel) Eirik Ridge
ATLANTIC

64

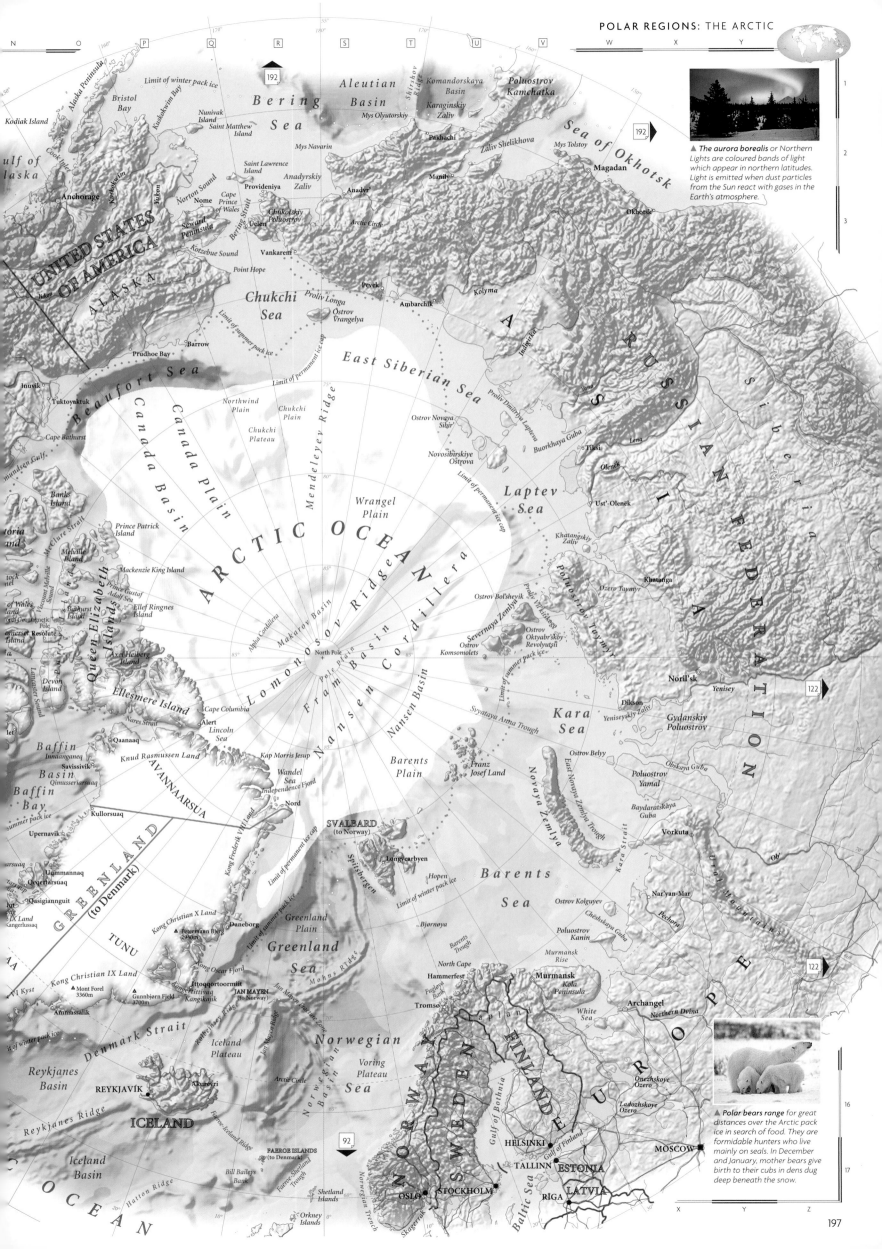

▲ *The aurora borealis* or Northern Lights are coloured bands of light which appear in northern latitudes. Light is emitted when dust particles from the Sun react with gases in the Earth's atmosphere.

▲ *Polar bears range* for great distances over the Arctic pack ice in search of food. They are formidable hunters who live mainly on seals. In December and January, mother bears give birth to their cubs in dens dug deep beneath the snow.

Geographical comparisons

Largest countries

Russian Federation	6,592,735 sq miles	(17,075,200 sq km)
Canada	3,851,788 sq miles	(5,976,140 sq km)
USA	3,717,792 sq miles	(5,629,091 sq km)
China	3,705,386 sq miles	(5,596,960 sq km)
Brazil	3,286,470 sq miles	(8,511,965 sq km)
Australia	2,967,893 sq miles	(7,686,850 sq km)
India	1,269,339 sq miles	(3,287,590 sq km)
Argentina	1,068,296 sq miles	(2,766,890 sq km)
Kazakhstan	1,049,150 sq miles	(2,717,300 sq km)
Sudan	967,493 sq miles	(2,505,815 sq km)

Smallest countries

Vatican City	0.17 sq miles	(0.44 sq km)
Monaco	0.75 sq miles	(1.95 sq km)
Nauru	8.2 sq miles	(21.2 sq km)
Tuvalu	10 sq miles	(26 sq km)
San Marino	24 sq miles	(61 sq km)
Liechtenstein	62 sq miles	(150 sq km)
Marshall Islands	70 sq miles	(131 sq km)
St. Kitts & Nevis	101 sq miles	(261 sq km)
Maldives	116 sq miles	(300 sq km)
Malta	124 sq miles	(320 sq km)

Largest islands

	To the nearest 1000 – or 100,000 for the largest	
Greenland	849,400 sq miles	(2,200,000 sq km)
New Guinea	312,000 sq miles	(808,000 sq km)
Borneo	292,222 sq miles	(757,050 sq km)
Madagascar	229,300 sq miles	(594,000 sq km)
Sumatra	202,300 sq miles	(524,000 sq km)
Baffin Island	183,800 sq miles	(476,000 sq km)
Honshu	88,800 sq miles	(230,000 sq km)
Britain	88,700 sq miles	(229,800 sq km)
Victoria Island	81,900 sq miles	(212,000 sq km)
Ellesmere Island	75,700 sq miles	(196,000 sq km)

Richest countries

	GNI per capita, in US$
Luxembourg	56,230
Norway	52,030
Liechtenstein	50,000
Switzerland	48,230
USA	41,400
Denmark	40,650
Iceland	38,620
Japan	37,810
Sweden	35,770
Ireland	34,280

Poorest countries

	GNI per capita, in US$
Burundi	90
Ethiopia	110
Liberia	110
Congo, Dem. Rep.	120
Somalia	120
Guinea-Bissau	160
Malawi	170
Eritrea	180
Sierra Leone	200
Rwanda	220
Afghanistan	222
Niger	230

Most populous countries

China	1,315,800,000
India	1,103,400,000
USA	298,200,000
Indonesia	222,800,000
Brazil	186,400,000
Cameroon	163,000,000
Pakistan	157,900,000
Russian Federation	143,200,000
Bangladesh	141,800,000
Nigeria	131,500,000

Least populous countries

Vatican City	921
Tuvalu	11,636
Nauru	13,048
Palau	20,303
San Marino	28,880
Monaco	32,409
Liechtenstein	33,717
St Kitts & Nevis	38,958
Marshall Islands	59,071
Antigua & Barbuda	68,722
Dominica	69,029
Andorra	70,549

Most densely populated countries

Monaco	43,212 people per sq mile	(16,620 per sq km)
Singapore	18,220 people per sq mile	(7049 per sq km)
Vatican City	5418 people per sq mile	(2093 per sq km)
Malta	3242 people per sq mile	(1256 per sq km)
Maldives	2836 people per sq mile	(1097 per sq km)
Bangladesh	2743 people per sq mile	(1059 per sq km)
Bahrain	2663 people per sq mile	(1030 per sq km)
China	1838 people per sq mile	(710 per sq km)
Mauritius	1671 people per sq mile	(645 per sq km)
Barbados	1627 people per sq mile	(628 per sq km)

Most sparsely populated countries

Mongolia	4 people per sq mile	(2 per sq km)
Namibia	6 people per sq mile	(2 per sq km)
Australia	7 people per sq mile	(3 per sq km)
Mauritania	8 people per sq mile	(3 per sq km)
Surinam	8 people per sq mile	(3 per sq km)
Botswana	8 people per sq mile	(3 per sq km)
Iceland	8 people per sq mile	(3 per sq km)
Canada	9 people per sq mile	(4 per sq km)
Libya	9 people per sq mile	(4 per sq km)
Guyana	10 people per sq mile	(4 per sq km)

Most widely spoken languages

1. Chinese (Mandarin)	6. Arabic
2. English	7. Bengali
3. Hindi	8. Portuguese
4. Spanish	9. Malay-Indonesian
5. Russian	10. French

Largest conurbations

	Population
Tokyo	34,200,000
Mexico City	22,800,000
Seoul	22,300,000
New York	21,900,000
São Paulo	20,200,000
Mumbai	19,850,000
Delhi	19,700,000
Shanghai	18,150,000
Los Angeles	18,000,000
Osaka	16,800,000
Jakarta	16,550,000
Kolkata	15,650,000
Cairo	15,600,000
Manila	14,950,000
Karachi	14,300,000
Moscow	13,750,000
Buenos Aires	13,450,000
Dacca	13,250,000
Rio de Janeiro	12,150,000
Beijing	12,100,000
London	12,000,000
Tehran	11,850,000
Istanbul	11,500,000
Lagos	11,100,000
Shenzhen	10,700,000

Countries with the most land borders

14: China	(Afghanistan, Bhutan, Burma, India, Kazakhstan, Kyrgyzstan, Laos, Mongolia, Nepal, North Korea, Pakistan, Russian Federation, Tajikistan, Vietnam)
14: Russian Federation	(Azerbaijan, Belarus, China, Estonia, Finland, Georgia, Kazakhstan, Latvia, Lithuania, Mongolia, North Korea, Norway, Poland, Ukraine)
10: Brazil	(Argentina, Bolivia, Colombia, French Guiana, Guyana, Paraguay, Peru, Surinam, Uruguay, Venezuela)
9: Congo, Dem. Rep.	(Angola, Burundi, Central African Republic, Congo, Rwanda, Sudan, Tanzania, Uganda, Zambia)
9: Germany	(Austria, Belgium, Czech Republic, Denmark, France, Luxembourg, Netherlands, Poland, Switzerland)
9: Sudan	(Central African Republic, Chad, Dem. Rep.Congo, Egypt, Eritrea, Ethiopia, Kenya, Libya, Uganda)
8: Austria	(Czech Republic, Germany, Hungary, Italy, Liechtenstein, Slovakia, Slovenia, Switzerland)
8: France	(Andorra, Belgium, Germany, Italy, Luxembourg, Monaco, Spain, Switzerland)
8: Tanzania	(Burundi, Dem. Rep.Congo, Kenya, Malawi, Mozambique, Rwanda, Uganda, Zambia)
8: Turkey	(Armenia, Azerbaijan, Bulgaria, Georgia, Greece, Iran, Iraq, Syria)
8: Zambia	(Angola, Botswana, Dem. Rep.Congo, Malawi, Mozambique, Namibia, Tanzania, Zimbabwe)

Longest rivers

Nile (NE Africa)	4160 miles	(6695 km)
Amazon (South America)	4049 miles	(6516 km)
Yangtze (China)	3915 miles	(6299 km)
Mississippi/Missouri (USA)	3710 miles	(5969 km)
Ob'-Irtysh (Russian Federation)	3461 miles	(5570 km)
Yellow River (China)	3395 miles	(5464 km)
Congo (Central Africa)	2900 miles	(4667 km)
Mekong (Southeast Asia)	2749 miles	(4425 km)
Lena (Russian Federation)	2734 miles	(4400 km)
Mackenzie (Canada)	2640 miles	(4250 km)
Yenisey (Russian Federation)	2541 miles	(4090km)

Highest mountains

		Height above sea level
Everest	29,035 ft	(8850 m)
K2	28,253 ft	(8611 m)
Kanchenjunga I	28,210 ft	(8598 m)
Makalu I	27,767 ft	(8463 m)
Cho Oyu	26,907 ft	(8201 m)
Dhaulagiri I	26,796 ft	(8167 m)
Manaslu I	26,783 ft	(8163 m)
Nanga Parbat I	26,661 ft	(8126 m)
Annapurna I	26,547 ft	(8091 m)
Gasherbrum I	26,471 ft	(8068 m)

Largest bodies of inland water

	With area and depth	
Caspian Sea	143,243 sq miles (371,000 sq km)	3215 ft (980 m)
Lake Superior	31,151 sq miles (83,270 sq km)	1289 ft (393 m)
Lake Victoria	26,828 sq miles (69,484 sq km)	328 ft (100 m)
Lake Huron	23,436 sq miles (60,700 sq km)	751 ft (229 m)
Lake Michigan	22,402 sq miles (58,020 sq km)	922 ft (281 m)
Lake Tanganyika	12,703 sq miles (32,900 sq km)	4700 ft (1435 m)
Great Bear Lake	12,274 sq miles (31,790 sq km)	1047 ft (319 m)
Lake Baikal	11,776 sq miles (30,500 sq km)	5712 ft (1741 m)
Great Slave Lake	10,981 sq miles (28,440 sq km)	459 ft (140 m)
Lake Erie	9,915 sq miles (25,680 sq km)	197 ft (60 m)

Deepest ocean features

Challenger Deep, Mariana Trench (Pacific)	36,201 ft	(11,034 m)
Vityaz III Depth, Tonga Trench (Pacific)	35,704 ft	(10,882 m)
Vityaz Depth, Kurile-Kamchatka Trench (Pacific)	34,588 ft	(10,542 m)
Cape Johnson Deep, Philippine Trench (Pacific)	34,441 ft	(10,497 m)
Kermadec Trench (Pacific)	32,964 ft	(10,047 m)
Ramapo Deep, Japan Trench (Pacific)	32,758 ft	(9984 m)
Milwaukee Deep, Puerto Rico Trench (Atlantic)	30,185 ft	(9200 m)
Argo Deep, Torres Trench (Pacific)	**30,070 ft**	**(9165 m)**
Meteor Depth, South Sandwich Trench (Atlantic)	30,000 ft	(9144 m)
Planet Deep, New Britain Trench (Pacific)	29,988 ft	(9140 m)

Greatest waterfalls

		Mean flow of water
Boyoma (Congo (Zaire))	600,400 cu. ft/sec	(17,000 cu.m/sec)
Khône (Laos/Cambodia)	410,000 cu. ft/sec	(11,600 cu.m/sec)
Niagara (USA/Canada)	195,000 cu. ft/sec	(5500 cu.m/sec)
Grande (Uruguay)	160,000 cu. ft/sec	(4500 cu.m/sec)
Paulo Afonso (Brazil)	100,000 cu. ft/sec	(2800 cu.m/sec)
Urubupunga (Brazil)	97,000 cu. ft/sec	(2750 cu.m/sec)
Iguaçu (Argentina/Brazil)	62,000 cu. ft/sec	(1700 cu.m/sec)
Maribondo (Brazil)	53,000 cu. ft/sec	(1500 cu.m/sec)
Victoria (Zimbabwe)	39,000 cu. ft/sec	(1100 cu.m/sec)
Kabalega (Uganda)	42,000 cu. ft/sec	(1200 cu.m/sec)
Churchill (Canada)	35,000 cu. ft/sec	(1000 cu.m/sec)
Cauvery (India)	33,000 cu. ft/sec	(900 cu.m/sec)

Highest waterfalls

		* Indicates that the total height is a single leap
Angel (Venezuela)	3212 ft	(979 m)
Tugela (South Africa)	3110 ft	(948 m)
Utigard (Norway)	2625 ft	(800 m)
Mongefossen (Norway)	2539 ft	(774 m)
Mtarazi (Zimbabwe)	2500 ft	(762 m)
Yosemite (USA)	2425 ft	(739 m)
Ostre Mardola Foss (Norway)	2156 ft	(657 m)
Tyssestrengane (Norway)	2119 ft	(646 m)
*Cuquenan (Venezuela)	2001 ft	(610 m)
Sutherland (New Zealand)	1903 ft	(580 m)
*Kjellfossen (Norway)	1841 ft	(561 m)

Largest deserts

	NB – Most of Antarctica is a polar desert, with only 50mm of precipitation annually	
Sahara	3,450,000 sq miles	(9,065,000 sq km)
Gobi	500,000 sq miles	(1,295,000 sq km)
Ar Rub al Khali	289,600 sq miles	(750,000 sq km)
Great Victorian	249,800 sq miles	(647,000 sq km)
Sonoran	120,000 sq miles	(311,000 sq km)
Kalahari	120,000 sq miles	(310,800 sq km)
Kara Kum	115,800 sq miles	(300,000 sq km)
Takla Makan	100,400 sq miles	(260,000 sq km)
Namib	52,100 sq miles	(135,000 sq km)
Thar	33,670 sq miles	(130,000 sq km)

Hottest inhabited places

Djibouti (Djibouti)	86° F	(30 °C)
Timbouctou (Mali)	84.7° F	(29.3 °C)
Tirunelveli (India)		
Tuticorin (India)		
Nellore (India)	84.5° F	(29.2 °C)
Santa Marta (Colombia)		
Aden (Yemen)	84° F	(28.9 °C)
Madurai (India)		
Niamey (Niger)		
Hodeida (Yemen)	83.8° F	(28.8 °C)
Ouagadougou (Burkina)		
Thanjavur (India)		
Tiruchchirappalli (India)		

Driest inhabited places

Aswãn (Egypt)	0.02 in	(0.5 mm)
Luxor (Egypt)	0.03 in	(0.7 mm)
Arica (Chile)	0.04 in	(1.1 mm)
Ica (Peru)	0.1 in	(2.3 mm)
Antofagasta (Chile)	0.2 in	(4.9 mm)
El Minya (Egypt)	0.2 in	(5.1 mm)
Asyût (Egypt)	0.2 in	(5.2 mm)
Callao (Peru)	0.5 in	(12.0 mm)
Trujillo (Peru)	0.55 in	(14.0 mm)
El Faiyûm (Egypt)	0.8 in	(19.0 mm)

Wettest inhabited places

Buenaventura (Colombia)	265 in	(6743 mm)
Monrovia (Liberia)	202 in	(5131 mm)
Pago Pago (American Samoa)	196 in	(4990 mm)
Moulmein (Burma)	191 in	(4852 mm)
Lae (Papua New Guinea)	183 in	(4645 mm)
Baguio (Luzon Island, Philippines)	180 in	(4573 mm)
Sylhet (Bangladesh)	176 in	(4457 mm)
Padang (Sumatra, Indonesia)	166 in	(4225 mm)
Bogor (Java, Indonesia)	166 in	(4225 mm)
Conakry (Guinea)	171 in	(4341 mm)

The time zones

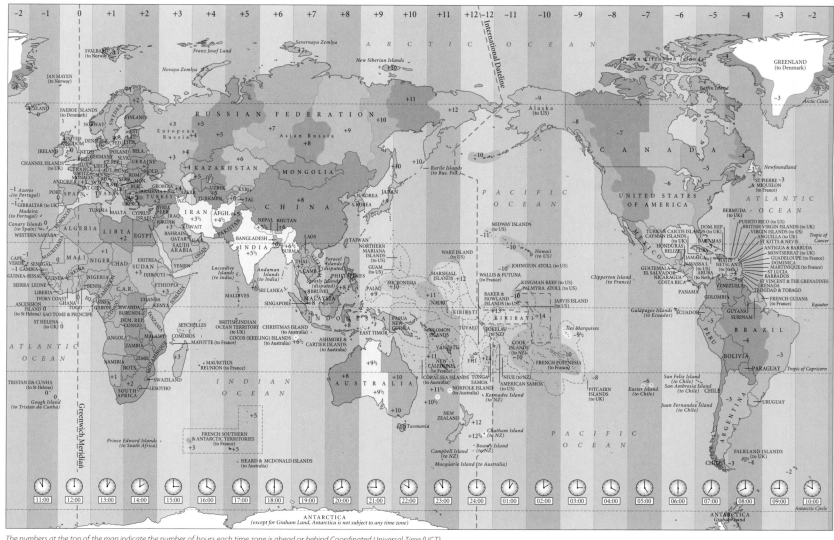

The numbers at the top of the map indicate the number of hours each time zone is ahead or behind Coordinated Universal Time (UCT).
The clocks and 24-hour times given at the bottom of the map show the time in each time zone when it is 12:00 hours noon UCT.

Time zones

Because Earth is a rotating sphere, the Sun shines on only half of its surface at any one time. Thus, it is simultaneously morning, evening and night time in different parts of the world. Because of these disparities, each country or part of a country adheres to a local time. A region of Earth's surface within which a single local time is used is called a time zone. The world is divided into 24 time zones by means of 24 standard meridians of longitude, each 15° apart. Time is measured in each zone as so many hours ahead or behind Coordinated Universal Time (UCT). Countries, or parts of countries, falling in the vicinity of each zone adopt its time as shown on the map above. Thus, when it is 12:00 noon UCT in London, it will 2:00 pm in Zambia.

Standard Time

Standard time is the official local time in a particular country or part of a country. It is defined by the time zone or zones associated with that country or region. Although time zones are arranged roughly in longitudinal bands, in many places the borders of a zone do not fall exactly on longitudinal meridians, as can be seen on the map (above), but are determined by geographical factors or by borders between countries or parts of countries. Most countries have just one time zone and one standard time, but some large countries (such as the USA, Canada and Russia) are split between several time zones, so standard time varies across those countries. For example, the coterminous United States straddles four time zones and so has four standard times, called the Eastern, Central, Mountain and Pacific standard times. China is unusual in that just one standard time is used for the whole country, even though it extends across 60° of longitude from west to east.

Coordinated Universal Time

Coordinated Universal Time (UTC) is a reference by which the local time in each time zone is set. For example, Australian Western Standard Time (the local time in Western Australia) is set 8 hours ahead of UTC (it is UTC+8) whereas Eastern Standard Time in the United States is set 5 hours behind UTC (it is UTC-5). UTC is a successor to, and closely approximates, Greenwich Mean Time (GMT). However, UTC is based on an atomic clock, whereas GMT is determined by the Sun's position in the sky relative to the 0° longitudinal meridian, which runs through Greenwich, UK.

The International Dateline

The International Dateline is an imaginary line from pole to pole that roughly corresponds to the 180° longitudinal meridian, forming an arbitrary marker between calendar days. The dateline is needed because of the use of local times around the world rather than a single universal time. When moving from west to east across the dateline, travellers have to set their watches back one day. Those travelling in the opposite direction, from east to west, must add a day. Wide variations from the 180° longitude occur through the Bering Strait - to avoid dividing Siberia into two separate calender days - and in the Pacific Ocean - to allow certain islands the same calender day as New Zealand. Changes were made to the International Dateline in 1995 that made Millennium Island (formerly Caroline Island) in Kiribati the first land area to witness the beginning of the year 2000.

Daylight saving time

Daylight saving is a summertime adjustment to the local time in a country or region, designed to cause a higher proportion of its citizens' waking hours to pass during daylight. To follow the system, timepieces are advanced by an hour on a pre-decided date in spring and reverted back in autumn.

Countries of the World

There are currently 194 independent countries in the world – more than at any previous time – and 59 dependencies. Antarctica is the only land area on Earth that is not officially part of, and does not belong to, any single country.

In 1950, the world comprised 82 countries. In the decades following, many more states came into being as they achieved independence from their former colonial rulers. Most recent additions were caused by the breakup of the former Soviet Union in 1991, and the former Yugoslavia in 1992, which swelled the ranks of independent states. In May 2006 Montenegro voted to split from Serbia, making it the latest country to gain independence.

Country factfile key

Formation Date of independence / date current borders were established

Population Total population / population density – based on total *land* area / percentage of urban-based population

Languages An asterisk (*) denotes the official language(s)

Calorie consumption Average number of calories consumed daily per person

AFGHANISTAN
Central Asia

Official name Islamic State of Afghanistan
Formation 1919 / 1919
Capital Kabul
Population 29.9 million / 119 people per sq mile (46 people per sq km) / 22%
Total area 250,000 sq miles (647,500 sq km)
Languages Pashtu*, Tajik, Dari, Farsi, Uzbek, Turkmen
Religions Sunni Muslim 84%, Shi'a Muslim 15%, Other 1%
Ethnic mix Pashtun 38%, Tajik 25%, Hazara 19%, Uzbek and Turkmen 15%, Other 3%
Government Transitional regime
Currency New afghani = 100 puls
Literacy rate 36%
Calorie consumption 1539 calories

ALBANIA
Southeast Europe

Official name Republic of Albania
Formation 1912 / 1921
Capital Tirana
Population 3.1 million / 293 people per sq mile (113 people per sq km) / 42%
Total area 11,100 sq miles (28,748 sq km)
Languages Albanian*, Greek
Religions Sunni Muslim 70%, Orthodox Christian 20%, Roman Catholic 10%
Ethnic mix Albanian 93%, Greek 5%, Other 2%
Government Parliamentary system
Currency Lek = 100 qindarka (qintars)
Literacy rate 99%
Calorie consumption 2848 calories

ALGERIA
North Africa

Official name People's Democratic Republic of Algeria
Formation 1962 / 1962
Capital Algiers
Population 32.9 million / 36 people per sq mile (14 people per sq km) / 60%
Total area 919,590 sq miles (2,381,740 sq km)
Languages Arabic, Tamazight (Kabyle, Shawia, Tamashek), French
Religions Sunni Muslim 99%, Christian and Jewish 1%
Ethnic mix Arab 75%, Berber 24%, European and Jewish 1%
Government Presidential system
Currency Algerian dinar = 100 centimes
Literacy rate 70%
Calorie consumption 3022 calories

ANDORRA
Southwest Europe

Official name Principality of Andorra
Formation 1278 / 1278
Capital Andorra la Vella
Population 70,549 / 392 people per sq mile (152 people per sq km) / 63%
Total area 181 sq miles (468 sq km)
Languages Spanish, Catalan, French, Portuguese
Religions Roman Catholic 94%, Other 6%
Ethnic mix Spanish 46%, Andorran 28%, Other 18%, French 8%
Government Parliamentary system
Currency Euro = 100 cents
Literacy rate 99%
Calorie consumption Not available

ANGOLA
Southern Africa

Official name Republic of Angola
Formation 1975 / 1975
Capital Luanda
Population 15.9 million / 33 people per sq mile (13 people per sq km) / 34%
Total area 481,351 sq miles (1,246,700 sq km)
Languages Portuguese*, Umbundu, Kimbundu, Kikongo
Religions Roman Catholic 50%, Other 30%, Protestant 20%
Ethnic mix Ovimbundu 37%, Other 25%, Kimbundu 25%, Bakongo 13%
Government Presidential system
Currency Readjusted kwanza = 100 lwei
Literacy rate 67%
Calorie consumption 2083 calories

ANTIGUA & BARBUDA
West Indies

Official name Antigua and Barbuda
Formation 1981 / 1981
Capital St. John's
Population 68,722 / 404 people per sq mile (156 people per sq km) / 37%
Total area 170 sq miles (442 sq km)
Languages English, English patois
Religions Anglican 45%, Other Protestant 42%, Roman Catholic 10%, Other 2%, Rastafarian 1%
Ethnic mix Black African 95%, Other 5%
Government Parliamentary system
Currency Eastern Caribbean dollar = 100 cents
Literacy rate 86%
Calorie consumption 2349 calories

ARGENTINA
South America

Official name Republic of Argentina
Formation 1816 / 1816
Capital Buenos Aires
Population 38.7 million / 37 people per sq mile (14 people per sq km) / 90%
Total area 1,068,296 sq miles (2,766,890 sq km)
Languages Spanish*, Italian, Amerindian languages
Religions Roman Catholic 90%, Other 6%, Protestant 2%, Jewish 2%
Ethnic mix Indo-European 83%, Mestizo 14%, Jewish 2%, Amerindian 1%
Government Presidential system
Currency new Argentine peso = 100 centavos
Literacy rate 97%
Calorie consumption 2992 calories

ARMENIA
Southwest Asia

Official name Republic of Armenia
Formation 1991 / 1991
Capital Yerevan
Population 3 million / 261 people per sq mile (101 people per sq km) / 70%
Total area 11,506 sq miles (29,800 sq km)
Languages Armenian*, Azeri, Russian
Religions Armenian Apostolic Church (Orthodox) 94%, Other 6%
Ethnic mix Armenian 93%, Azeri 3%, Other 2%, Russian 2%
Government Presidential system
Currency Dram = 100 luma
Literacy rate 99%
Calorie consumption 2268 calories

AUSTRALIA
Australasia & Oceania

Official name Commonwealth of Australia
Formation 1901 / 1901
Capital Canberra
Population 20.2 million / 7 people per sq mile (3 people per sq km) / 85%
Total area 2,967,893 sq miles (7,686,850 sq km)
Languages English*, Italian, Cantonese, Greek, Arabic, Vietnamese, Aboriginal languages
Religions Roman Catholic 26%, Anglican 24%, Other 23%, Nonreligious 13%, United Church 8%, Other Protestant 6%
Ethnic mix European 92%, Asian 5%, Aboriginal and other 3%
Government Parliamentary system
Currency Australian dollar = 100 cents
Literacy rate 99%
Calorie consumption 3054 calories

AUSTRIA
Central Europe

Official name Republic of Austria
Formation 1918 / 1919
Capital Vienna
Population 8.2 million / 257 people per sq mile (99 people per sq km) / 65%
Total area 32,378 sq miles (83,858 sq km)
Languages German*, Croatian, Slovenian, Hungarian (Magyar)
Religions Roman Catholic 78%, Nonreligious 9%, Other (including Jewish and Muslim) 8%, Protestant 5%
Ethnic mix Austrian 93%, Croat, Slovene, and Hungarian 6%, Other 1%
Government Parliamentary system
Currency Euro = 100 cents
Literacy rate 99%
Calorie consumption 3673 calories

AZERBAIJAN
Southwest Asia

Official name Republic of Azerbaijan
Formation 1991 / 1991
Capital Baku
Population 8.4 million / 251 people per sq mile (97 people per sq km) / 57%
Total area 33,436 sq miles (86,600 sq km)
Languages Azeri, Russian
Religions Shi'a Muslim 68%, Sunni Muslim 26%, Russian Orthodox 3%, Armenian Apostolic Church (Orthodox) 2%, Other 1%
Ethnic mix Azeri 90%, Dagestani 3%, Russian 3%, Other 2%, Armenian 2%
Government Presidential system
Currency Manat = 100 gopik
Literacy rate 99%
Calorie consumption 2575 calories

BAHAMAS
West Indies

Official name Commonwealth of the Bahamas
Formation 1973 / 1973
Capital Nassau
Population 323,000 / 84 people per sq mile (32 people per sq km) / 89%
Total area 5382 sq miles (13,940 sq km)
Languages English*, English Creole, French Creole
Religions Baptist 32%, Anglican 20%, Roman Catholic 19%, Other 17%, Methodist 6%, Church of God 6%
Ethnic mix Black African 85%, Other 15%
Government Parliamentary system
Currency Bahamian dollar = 100 cents
Literacy rate 96%
Calorie consumption 2755 calories

BAHRAIN
Southwest Asia

Official name Kingdom of Bahrain
Formation 1971 / 1971
Capital Manama
Population 727,000 / 2663 people per sq mile (1030 people per sq km) / 97%
Total area 239 sq miles (620 sq km)
Languages Arabic*
Religions Muslim (mainly Shi'a) 99%, Other 1%
Ethnic mix Bahraini 70%, Iranian, Indian, and Pakistani 24%, Other Arab 4%, European 2%
Government Monarchy
Currency Bahraini dinar = 1000 fils
Literacy rate 88%
Calorie consumption Not available

BANGLADESH
South Asia

Official name People's Republic of Bangladesh
Formation 1971 / 1971
Capital Dhaka
Population 142 million / 2743 people per sq mile (1059 people per sq km) / 25%
Total area 55,598 sq miles (144,000 sq km)
Languages Bengali*, Urdu, Chakma, Marma (Magh), Garo, Khasi, Santhali, Tripuri, Mro
Religions Muslim (mainly Sunni) 87%, Hindu 12%, Other 1%
Ethnic mix Bengali 98%, Other 2%
Government Parliamentary system
Currency Taka = 100 poisha
Literacy rate 41%
Calorie consumption 2205 calories

BARBADOS
West Indies

Official name Barbados
Formation 1966 / 1966
Capital Bridgetown
Population 270,000 / 1627 people per sq mile (628 people per sq km) / 50%
Total area 166 sq miles (430 sq km)
Languages English*, Bajan (Barbadian English)
Religions Anglican 40%, Other 24%, Nonreligious 17%, Pentecostal 8%, Methodist 7%, Roman Catholic 4%
Ethnic mix Black African 90%, Other 10%
Government Parliamentary system
Currency Barbados dollar = 100 cents
Literacy rate 99%
Calorie consumption 3091 calories

BELARUS
Eastern Europe

Official name Republic of Belarus
Formation 1991 / 1991
Capital Minsk
Population 9.8 million / 122 people per sq mile (47 people per sq km) / 71%
Total area 80,154 sq miles (207,600 sq km)
Languages Belarussian*, Russian
Religions Orthodox Christian 60%, Other 32%, Roman Catholic 8%
Ethnic mix Belarussian 78%, Russian 13%, Polish 4%, Ukrainian 3%, Other 2%
Government Presidential system
Currency Belarussian rouble = 100 kopeks
Literacy rate 99%
Calorie consumption 3000 calories

BELGIUM
Northwest Europe

Official name Kingdom of Belgium
Formation 1830 / 1919
Capital Brussels
Population 10.4 million / 821 people per sq mile (317 people per sq km) / 97%
Total area 11,780 sq miles (30,510 sq km)
Languages Dutch*, French*, German
Religions Roman Catholic 88%, Other 10%, Muslim 2%
Ethnic mix Fleming 58%, Walloon 33%, Other 6%, Italian 2%, Moroccan 1%
Government Parliamentary system
Currency Euro = 100 cents
Literacy rate 99%
Calorie consumption 3584 calories

BELIZE
Central America

Official name Belize
Formation 1981 / 1981
Capital Belmopan
Population 270,000 / 31 people per sq mile (12 people per sq km) / 54%
Total area 8867 sq miles (22,966 sq km)
Languages English*, English Creole, Spanish, Mayan, Garifuna (Carib)
Religions Roman Catholic 62%, Other 13%, Anglican 12%, Methodist 6%, Mennonite 4%, Seventh-day Adventist 3%
Ethnic mix Mestizo 44%, Creole 30%, Maya 11%, Garifuna 7%, Other 4%, Asian Indian 4%
Government Parliamentary system
Currency Belizean dollar = 100 cents
Literacy rate 77%
Calorie consumption 2869 calories

BENIN
West Africa

Official name Republic of Benin
Formation 1960 / 1960
Capital Porto-Novo
Population 8.4 million / 197 people per sq mile (76 people per sq km) / 42%
Total area 43,483 sq miles (112,620 sq km)
Languages French*, Fon, Bariba, Yoruba, Adja, Houeda, Somba
Religions Voodoo 50%, Muslim 30%, Christian 20%
Ethnic mix Fon 47%, Other 31%, Adja 12%, Bariba 10%
Government Presidential system
Currency CFA franc = 100 centimes
Literacy rate 34%
Calorie consumption 2548 calories

BHUTAN
South Asia

Official name Kingdom of Bhutan
Formation 1656 / 1865
Capital Thimphu
Population 2.2 million / 121 people per sq mile (47 people per sq km) / 7%
Total area 18,147 sq miles (47,000 sq km)
Languages Dzongkha*, Nepali, Assamese
Religions Mahayana Buddhist 70%, Hindu 24%, Other 6%
Ethnic mix Bhute 50%, Other 25%, Nepalese 25%
Government Monarchy
Currency Ngultrum = 100 chetrum
Literacy rate 47%
Calorie consumption Not available

BOLIVIA
South America

Official name Republic of Bolivia
Formation 1825 /1938
Capital La Paz (administrative); Sucre (judicial)
Population 9.2 million / 22 people per sq mile (8 people per sq km) / 63%
Total area 424,162 sq miles (1,098,580 sq km)
Languages Aymara*, Quechua*, Spanish*
Religions Roman Catholic 93%, Other 7%
Ethnic mix Quechua 37%, Aymara 32%, Mixed race 13%, European 10%, Other 8%
Government Presidential system
Currency Boliviano = 100 centavos
Literacy rate 87%
Calorie consumption 2235 calories

BOSNIA & HERZEGOVINA
Southeast Europe

Official name Bosnia and Herzegovina
Formation 1992 / 1992
Capital Sarajevo
Population 3.9 million / 198 people per sq mile (76 people per sq km) / 43%
Total area 19,741 sq miles (51,129 sq km)
Languages Serbo-Croat*
Religions Muslim (mainly Sunni) 40%, Orthodox Christian 31%, Roman Catholic 15%, Other 10%, Protestant 4%
Ethnic mix Bosniak 48%, Serb 38%, Croat 14%
Government Parliamentary system
Currency Marka = 100 pfeninga
Literacy rate 95%
Calorie consumption 2894 calories

BOTSWANA
Southern Africa

Official name Republic of Botswana
Formation 1966 / 1966
Capital Gaborone
Population 1.8 million / 8 people per sq mile (3 people per sq km) / 50%
Total area 231,803 sq miles (600,370 sq km)
Languages English*, Setswana, Shona, San, Khoikhoi, isiNdebele
Religions Traditional beliefs 50%, Christian (mainly Protestant) 30%, Other (including Muslim) 20%
Ethnic mix Tswana 98%, Other 2%
Government Presidential system
Currency Pula = 100 thebe
Literacy rate 79%
Calorie consumption 2151 calories

BRAZIL
South America

Official name Federative Republic of Brazil
Formation 1822 / 1828
Capital Brasília
Population 186 million / 57 people per sq mile (22 people per sq km) / 81%
Total area 3,286,470 sq miles (8,511,965 sq km)
Languages Portuguese*, German, Italian, Spanish, Polish, Japanese, Amerindian languages
Religions Roman Catholic 74%, Protestant 15%, Atheist 7%, Other 4%
Ethnic mix Black 53%, Mixed race 40%, White 6%, Other 1%
Government Presidential system
Currency Real = 100 centavos
Literacy rate 88%
Calorie consumption 3049 calories

BRUNEI
Southeast Asia

Official name Sultanate of Brunei
Formation 1984 / 1984
Capital Bandar Seri Begawan
Population 374,000 / 184 people per sq mile (71 people per sq km) / 72%
Total area 2228 sq miles (5770 sq km)
Languages Malay*, English, Chinese
Religions Muslim (mainly Sunni) 66%, Buddhist 14%, Other 10%, Christian 10%
Ethnic mix Malay 67%, Chinese 16%, Other 11%, Indigenous 6%
Government Monarchy
Currency Brunei dollar = 100 cents
Literacy rate 93%
Calorie consumption 2855 calories

BULGARIA
Southeast Europe

Official name Republic of Bulgaria
Formation 1908 / 1947
Capital Sofia
Population 7.7 million / 180 people per sq mile (70 people per sq km) / 70%
Total area 42,822 sq miles (110,910 sq km)
Languages Bulgarian*, Turkish, Romani
Religions Orthodox Christian 83%, Muslim 12%, Other 4%, Roman Catholic 1%
Ethnic mix Bulgarian 84%, Turkish 9%, Roma 5%, Other 2%
Government Parliamentary system
Currency Lev = 100 stotinki
Literacy rate 98%
Calorie consumption 2848 calories

BURKINA
West Africa

Official name Burkina Faso
Formation 1960 / 1960
Capital Ouagadougou
Population 13.2 million / 125 people per sq mile (48 people per sq km) / 19%
Total area 105,869 sq miles (274,200 sq km)
Languages French*, Mossi, Fulani, Tuareg, Dyula, Songhai
Religions Muslim 55%, Traditional beliefs 35%, Roman Catholic 9%, Other Christian 1%
Ethnic mix Other 50%, Mossi 50%
Government Presidential system
Currency CFA franc = 100 centimes
Literacy rate 13%
Calorie consumption 2462 calories

BURMA (MYANMAR)
Southeast Asia

Official name Union of Myanmar
Formation 1948 / 1948
Capital Rangoon (Yangon), Pyinmana
Population 50.5 million / 199 people per sq mile (77 people per sq km) / 28%
Total area 261,969 sq miles (678,500 sq km)
Languages Burmese*, Shan, Karen, Rakhine, Chin, Yangbye, Kachin, Mon
Religions Buddhist 87%, Christian 6%, Muslim 4%, Other 2%, Hindu 1%
Ethnic mix Burman (Bamah) 68%, Other 13%, Shan 9%, Karen 6%, Rakhine 4%
Government Military-based regime
Currency Kyat = 100 pyas
Literacy rate 90%
Calorie consumption 2937 calories

BURUNDI
Central Africa

Official name Republic of Burundi
Formation 1962 / 1962
Capital Bujumbura
Population 7.5 million / 757 people per sq mile (292 people per sq km) / 9%
Total area 10,745 sq miles (27,830 sq km)
Languages Kirundi*, French*, Kiswahili
Religions Christian 60%, Traditional beliefs 39%, Muslim 1%
Ethnic mix Hutu 85%, Tutsi 14%, Twa 1%
Government Presidential system
Currency Burundi franc = 100 centimes
Literacy rate 59%
Calorie consumption 1649 calories

CAMBODIA
Southeast Asia

Official name Kingdom of Cambodia
Formation 1953 / 1953
Capital Phnom Penh
Population 14.1 million / 207 people per sq mile (80 people per sq km) / 16%
Total area 69,900 sq miles (181,040 sq km)
Languages Khmer*, French, Chinese, Vietnamese, Cham
Religions Buddhist 93%, Muslim 6%, Christian 1%
Ethnic mix Khmer 90%, Other 5%, Vietnamese 4%, Chinese 1%
Government Parliamentary system
Currency Riel = 100 sen
Literacy rate 74%
Calorie consumption 2046 calories

CAMEROON
Central Africa

Official name Republic of Cameroon
Formation 1960 / 1961
Capital Yaoundé
Population 16.3 million / 907 people per sq mile (350 people per sq km) / 49%
Total area 183,567 sq miles (475,400 sq km)
Languages English*, French*, Bamileke, Fang, Fulani
Religions Roman Catholic 35%, Traditional beliefs 25%, Muslim 22%, Protestant 18%
Ethnic mix Cameroon highlanders 31%, Other 21%, Equatorial Bantu 19%, Kirdi 11%, Fulani 10%, Northwestern Bantu 8%
Government Presidential system
Currency CFA franc = 100 centimes
Literacy rate 68%
Calorie consumption 2273 calories

CANADA
North America

Official name Canada
Formation 1867 / 1949
Capital Ottawa
Population 32.3 million / 9 people per sq mile (4 people per sq km) / 77%
Total area 3,851,788 sq miles (9,976,140 sq km)
Languages English*, French*, Chinese, Italian, German, Ukrainian, Inuktitut, Cree
Religions Roman Catholic 44%, Protestant 29%, Other and nonreligious 27%
Ethnic mix British origin 44%, French origin 25%, Other European 20%, Other 11%.
Government Parliamentary system
Currency Canadian dollar = 100 cents
Literacy rate 99%
Calorie consumption 3589 calories

CAPE VERDE
Atlantic Ocean

Official name Republic of Cape Verde
Formation 1975
Capital Praia
Population 507,000 / 326 people per sq mile (126 people per sq km) / 62%
Total area 1557 sq miles (4033 sq km)
Languages Portuguese*, Portuguese Creole
Religions Roman Catholic 97%, Other 2%, Protestant (Church of the Nazarene) 1%
Ethnic mix Mestiço 60%, African 30%, Other 10%
Government Mixed presidential–parliamentary system
Currency Cape Verde escudo = 100 centavos
Literacy rate 76%
Calorie consumption 3243 calories

CENTRAL AFRICAN REPUBLIC
Central Africa

Official name Central African Republic
Formation 1960 / 1960
Capital Bangui
Population 4 million / 17 people per sq mile (6 people per sq km) / 41%
Total area 240,534 sq miles (622,984 sq km)
Languages Sango, Banda, Gbaya, French
Religions Traditional beliefs 60%, Christian (mainly Roman Catholic) 35%, Muslim 5%
Ethnic mix Baya 34%, Banda 27%, Mandjia 21%, Sara 10%, Other 8%
Government Presidential system
Currency CFA franc = 100 centimes
Literacy rate 49%
Calorie consumption 1980 calories

CHAD
Central Africa

Official name Republic of Chad
Formation 1960 / 1960
Capital N'Djamena
Population 9.7 million / 20 people per sq mile (8 people per sq km) / 24%
Total area 495,752 sq miles (1,284,000 sq km)
Languages French, Sara, Arabic, Maba
Religions Muslim 55%, Traditional beliefs 35%, Christian 10%
Ethnic mix Nomads (Tuareg and Toubou) 38%, Sara 30%, Other 17%, Arab 15%
Government Presidential system
Currency CFA franc = 100 centimes
Literacy rate 26%
Calorie consumption 2114 calories

CHILE
South America

Official name Republic of Chile
Formation 1818 / 1883
Capital Santiago
Population 16.3 million / 56 people per sq mile (22 people per sq km) / 86%
Total area 292,258 sq miles (756,950 sq km)
Languages Spanish*, Amerindian languages
Religions Roman Catholic 80%, Other and nonreligious 20%
Ethnic mix Mixed race and European 90%, Amerindian 10%
Government Presidential system
Currency Chilean peso = 100 centavos
Literacy rate 96%
Calorie consumption 2863 calories

CHINA
East Asia

Official name People's Republic of China
Formation 960 / 1999
Capital Beijing
Population 1.32 billion / 365 people per sq mile (141 people per sq km) / 32%
Total area 3,705,386 sq miles (9,596,960 sq km)
Languages Mandarin*, Wu, Cantonese, Hsiang, Min, Hakka, Kan
Religions Nonreligious 59%, Traditional beliefs 20%, Other 13%, Buddhist 6%, Muslim 2%
Ethnic mix Han 92%, Other 6%, Hui 1%, Zhuang 1%
Government One-party state
Currency Renminbi (known as yuan) = 10 jiao
Literacy rate 91%
Calorie consumption 2951 calories

COLOMBIA
South America

Official name Republic of Colombia
Formation 1819 / 1903
Capital Bogotá
Population 45.6 million / 114 people per sq mile (44 people per sq km) / 74%
Total area 439,733 sq miles (1,138,910 sq km)
Languages Spanish*, Wayuu, Páez, and other Amerindian languages
Religions Roman Catholic 95%, Other 5%
Ethnic mix Mestizo 58%, White 20%, European–African 14%, African 4%, African–Amerindian 3%, Amerindian 1%
Government Presidential system
Currency Colombian peso = 100 centavos
Literacy rate 94%
Calorie consumption 2585 calories

COMOROS
Indian Ocean

Official name Union of the Comoros
Formation 1975 / 1975
Capital Moroni
Population 798,000 / 927 people per sq mile (358 people per sq km) / 33%
Total area 838 sq miles (2170 sq km)
Languages Arabic*, Comoran, French
Religions Muslim (mainly Sunni) 98%, Other 1%, Roman Catholic 1%
Ethnic mix Comoran 97%, Other 3%
Government Presidential system
Currency Comoros franc = 100 centimes
Literacy rate 56%
Calorie consumption 1754 calories

CONGO
Central Africa

Official name Republic of the Congo
Formation 1960 / 1960
Capital Brazzaville
Population 4 million / 30 people per sq mile (12 people per sq km) / 63%
Total area 132,046 sq miles (342,000 sq km)
Languages French*, Kongo, Teke, Lingala
Religions Traditional beliefs 50%, Roman Catholic 25%, Protestant 23%, Muslim 2%
Ethnic mix Bakongo 48%, Sangha 20%, Teke 17%, Mbochi 12%, Other 3%
Government Presidential system
Currency CFA franc = 100 centimes
Literacy rate 83%
Calorie consumption 2162 calories

CONGO, DEM. REP.
Central Africa

Official name Democratic Republic of the Congo
Formation 1960 / 1960
Capital Kinshasa
Population 57.5 million / 66 people per sq mile (25 people per sq km) / 30%
Total area 905,563 sq miles (2,345,410 sq km)
Languages French*, Kiswahili, Tshiluba, Kikongo, Lingala
Religions Roman Catholic 50%, Protestant 20%, Traditional beliefs and other 10%, Muslim 10%, Kimbanguist 10%
Ethnic mix Other 55%, Bantu and Hamitic 45%
Government Transitional regime
Currency Congolese franc = 100 centimes
Literacy rate 65%
Calorie consumption 1599 calories

COSTA RICA
Central America

Official name Republic of Costa Rica
Formation 1838 / 1838
Capital San José
Population 4.3 million / 218 people per sq mile (84 people per sq km) / 52%
Total area 19,730 sq miles (51,100 sq km)
Languages Spanish*, English Creole, Bribri, Cabecar
Religions Roman Catholic 76%, Other (including Protestant) 24%
Ethnic mix Mestizo and European 96%, Black 2%, Chinese 1%, Amerindian 1%
Government Presidential system
Currency Costa Rican colón = 100 centimos
Literacy rate 96%
Calorie consumption 2876 calories

CROATIA
Southeast Europe

Official name Republic of Croatia
Formation 1991 / 1991
Capital Zagreb
Population 4.6 million / 211 people per sq mile (81 people per sq km) / 58%
Total area 21,831 sq miles (56,542 sq km)
Languages Croatian*
Religions Roman Catholic 88%, Other 7%, Orthodox Christian 4%, Muslim 1%
Ethnic mix Croat 90%, Other 5%, Serb 4%, Bosniak 1%
Government Parliamentary system
Currency Kuna = 100 lipas
Literacy rate 98%
Calorie consumption 2799 calories

CUBA
West Indies

Official name Republic of Cuba
Formation 1902 / 1902
Capital Havana
Population 11.3 million / 264 people per sq mile (102 people per sq km) / 75%
Total area 42,803 sq miles (110,860 sq km)
Languages Spanish*
Religions Nonreligious 49%, Roman Catholic 40%, Atheist 6%, Other 4%, Protestant 1%
Ethnic mix White 66%, European–African 22%, Black 12%
Government One-party state
Currency Cuban peso = 100 centavos
Literacy rate 97%
Calorie consumption 3152 calories

CYPRUS
Southeast Europe

Official name Republic of Cyprus
Formation 1960 / 1960
Capital Nicosia
Population 835,000 / 234 people per sq mile (90 people per sq km) / 57%
Total area 3571 sq miles (9250 sq km)
Languages Greek, Turkish
Religions Orthodox Christian 78%, Muslim 18%, Other 4%
Ethnic mix Greek 85%, Turkish 12%, Other 3%
Government Presidential system
Currency Cyprus pound (Turkish lira in TRNC) = 100 cents (Cyprus pound); 100 kurus (Turkish lira)
Literacy rate 97%
Calorie consumption 3255 calories

CZECH REPUBLIC
Central Europe

Official name Czech Republic
Formation 1993 / 1993
Capital Prague
Population 10.2 million / 335 people per sq mile (129 people per sq km) / 75%
Total area 30,450 sq miles (78,866 sq km)
Languages Czech*, Slovak, Hungarian (Magyar)
Religions Roman Catholic 39%, Atheist 38%, Other 18%, Protestant 3%, Hussite 2%
Ethnic mix Czech 81%, Moravian 13%, Slovak 6%
Government Parliamentary system
Currency Czech koruna = 100 haleru
Literacy rate 99%
Calorie consumption 3171 calories

DENMARK
Northern Europe

Official name Kingdom of Denmark
Formation AD 950 / 1945
Capital Copenhagen
Population 5.4 million / 330 people per sq mile (127 people per sq km) / 85%
Total area 16,639 sq miles (43,094 sq km)
Languages Danish*
Religions Evangelical Lutheran 89%, Other 10%, Roman Catholic 1%
Ethnic mix Danish 96%, Other (including Scandinavian and Turkish) 3%, Faeroese and Inuit 1%
Government Parliamentary system
Currency Danish krone = 100 øre
Literacy rate 99%
Calorie consumption 3439 calories

DJIBOUTI
East Africa

Official name Republic of Djibouti
Formation 1977 / 1977
Capital Djibouti
Population 793,000 / 89 people per sq mile (34 people per sq km) / 83%
Total area 8494 sq miles (22,000 sq km)
Languages French*, Arabic*, Somali, Afar
Religions Muslim (mainly Sunni) 94%, Christian 6%
Ethnic mix Issa 60%, Afar 35%, Other 5%
Government Presidential system
Currency Djibouti franc = 100 centimes
Literacy rate 66%
Calorie consumption 2220 calories

DOMINICA
West Indies

Official name Commonwealth of Dominica
Formation 1978 / 1978
Capital Roseau
Population 69,029 / 238 people per sq mile (92 people per sq km) / 71%
Total area 291 sq miles (754 sq km)
Languages English*, French Creole
Religions Roman Catholic 77%, Protestant 15%, Other 8%
Ethnic mix Black 91%, Mixed race 6%, Carib 2%, Other 1%
Government Parliamentary system
Currency Eastern Caribbean dollar = 100 cents
Literacy rate 88%
Calorie consumption 2763 calories

DOMINICAN REPUBLIC
West Indies

Official name Dominican Republic
Formation 1865 / 1865
Capital Santo Domingo
Population 8.9 million / 476 people per sq mile (184 people per sq km) / 65%
Total area 18,679 sq miles (48,380 sq km)
Languages Spanish*, French Creole
Religions Roman Catholic 92%, Other and nonreligious 8%
Ethnic mix Mixed race 75%, White 15%, Black 10%
Government Presidential system
Currency Dominican Republic peso = 100 centavos
Literacy rate 88%
Calorie consumption 2347 calories

EAST TIMOR
Southeast Asia

Official name Democratic Republic of Timor-Leste
Formation 2002 / 2002
Capital Dili
Population 947,000 / 168 people per sq mile (65 people per sq km) / 8%
Total area 5756 sq miles (14,874 sq km)
Languages Tetum (Portuguese/Austronesian), Bahasa Indonesia, and Portuguese
Religions Roman Catholic 95%, Other (including Muslim and Protestant) 5%
Ethnic mix Papuan groups approx 85%, Indonesian approx 13%, Chinese 2%
Government Parliamentary system
Currency US dollar = 100 cents
Literacy rate 59%
Calorie consumption 2806 calories

ECUADOR
South America

Official name Republic of Ecuador
Formation 1830 / 1941
Capital Quito
Population 13.2 million / 123 people per sq mile (48 people per sq km) / 65%
Total area 109,483 sq miles (283,560 sq km)
Languages Spanish*, Quechua*, other Amerindian languages
Religions Roman Catholic 93%, Protestant, Jewish, and other 7%
Ethnic mix Mestizo 55%, Amerindian 25%, White 10%, Black 10%
Government Presidential system
Currency US dollar = 100 cents
Literacy rate 91%
Calorie consumption 2754 calories

EGYPT
North Africa

Official name Arab Republic of Egypt
Formation 1936 / 1982
Capital Cairo
Population 74 million / 193 people per sq mile (74 people per sq km) / 45%
Total area 386,660 sq miles (1,001,450 sq km)
Languages Arabic*, French, English, Berber
Religions Muslim (mainly Sunni) 94%, Coptic Christian and other 6%
Ethnic mix Eastern Hamitic 90%, Nubian, Armenian, and Greek 10%
Government Presidential system
Currency Egyptian pound = 100 piastres
Literacy rate 56%
Calorie consumption 3338 calories

EL SALVADOR
Central America

Official name Republic of El Salvador
Formation 1841 / 1841
Capital San Salvador
Population 6.9 million / 862 people per sq mile (333 people per sq km) / 47%
Total area 8124 sq miles (21,040 sq km)
Languages Spanish*
Religions Roman Catholic 80%, Evangelical 18%, Other 2%
Ethnic mix Mestizo 94%, Amerindian 5%, White 1%
Government Presidential system
Currency Salvadorean colón & US dollar = 100 centavos (colón); 100 cents (US dollar)
Literacy rate 80%
Calorie consumption 2584 calories

EQUATORIAL GUINEA
Central Africa

Official name Republic of Equatorial Guinea
Formation 1968 / 1968
Capital Malabo
Population 504,000 / 47 people per sq mile (18 people per sq km) / 48%
Total area 10,830 sq miles (28,051 sq km)
Languages Spanish*, Fang, Bubi
Religions Roman Catholic 90%, Other 10%
Ethnic mix Fang 85%, Other 11%, Bubi 4%
Government Presidential system
Currency CFA franc = 100 centimes
Literacy rate 84%
Calorie consumption Not available

ERITREA
East Africa

Official name State of Eritrea
Formation 1993 / 2002
Capital Asmara
Population 4.4 million / 97 people per sq mile (37 people per sq km) / 19%
Total area 46,842 sq miles (121,320 sq km)
Languages Arabic*, Tigrinya*, English, Tigre, Afar, Bilen, Kunama, Nara, Saho, Hadareb
Religions Christian 45%, Muslim 45%, Other 10%
Ethnic mix Tigray 50%, Tigray and Kunama 40%, Afar 4%, Other 3%, Saho 3%
Government Transitional regime
Currency Nakfa = 100 cents
Literacy rate 57%
Calorie consumption 1513 calories

ESTONIA
Northeast Europe

Official name Republic of Estonia
Formation 1991 / 1991
Capital Tallinn
Population 1.3 million / 75 people per sq mile (29 people per sq km) / 69%
Total area 17,462 sq miles (45,226 sq km)
Languages Estonian*, Russian
Religions Evangelical Lutheran 56%, Orthodox Christian 25%, Other 19%
Ethnic mix Estonian 62%, Russian 30%, Other 8%
Government Parliamentary system
Currency Kroon = 100 senti
Literacy rate 99%
Calorie consumption 3002 calories

ETHIOPIA
East Africa

Official name Federal Democratic Republic of Ethiopia
Formation 1896 / 2002
Capital Addis Ababa
Population 77.4 million / 181 people per sq mile (70 people per sq km) / 18%
Total area 435,184 sq miles (1,127,127 sq km)
Languages Amharic*, Tigrinya, Galla, Sidamo, Somali, English, Arabic
Religions Orthodox Christian 40%, Muslim 40%, Traditional beliefs 15%, Other 5%
Ethnic mix Oromo 40%, Amhara 25%, Other 14%, Sidamo 9%, Berta 6%, Somali 6%
Government Parliamentary system
Currency Ethiopian birr = 100 cents
Literacy rate 42%
Calorie consumption 1857 calories

FIJI
Australasia & Oceania

Official name Republic of the Fiji Islands
Formation 1970 / 1970
Capital Suva
Population 848,000 / 120 people per sq mile (46 people per sq km) / 49%
Total area 7054 sq miles (18,270 sq km)
Languages English*, Fijian*, Hindi, Urdu, Tamil, Telugu
Religions Hindu 38%, Methodist 37%, Roman Catholic 9%, Other 8%, Muslim 8%
Ethnic mix Melanesian 48%, Indian 46%, Other 6%
Government Parliamentary system
Currency Fiji dollar = 100 cents
Literacy rate 93%
Calorie consumption 2894 calories

FINLAND
Northern Europe

Official name Republic of Finland
Formation 1917 / 1947
Capital Helsinki
Population 5.2 million / 44 people per sq mile (17 people per sq km) / 67%
Total area 130,127 sq miles (337,030 sq km)
Languages Finnish*, Swedish*, Sámi
Religions Evangelical Lutheran 89%, Orthodox Christian 1%, Roman Catholic 1%, Other 9%
Ethnic mix Finnish 93%, Other (including Sámi) 7%
Government Parliamentary system
Currency Euro = 100 cents
Literacy rate 99%
Calorie consumption 3100 calories

FRANCE
Western Europe

Official name French Republic
Formation 987 / 1919
Capital Paris
Population 60.5 million / 285 people per sq mile (110 people per sq km) / 76%
Total area 211,208 sq miles (547,030 sq km)
Languages French*, Provençal, German, Breton, Catalan, Basque
Religions Roman Catholic 88%, Muslim 8%, Protestant 2%, Buddhist 1%, Jewish 1%
Ethnic mix French 90%, North African (mainly Algerian) 6%, German (Alsace) 2%, Breton 1%, Other (including Corsicans) 1%
Government Mixed presidential–parliamentary system
Currency Euro = 100 cents
Literacy rate 99%
Calorie consumption 3654 calories

GABON
Central Africa

Official name Gabonese Republic
Formation 1960 / 1960
Capital Libreville
Population 1.4 million / 14 people per sq mile (5 people per sq km) / 81%
Total area 103,346 sq miles (267,667 sq km)
Languages French*, Fang, Punu, Sira, Nzebi, Mpongwe
Religions Christian (mainly Roman Catholic) 55%, Traditional beliefs 40%, Other 4%, Muslim 1%
Ethnic mix Fang 35%, Other Bantu 29%, Eshira 25%, European and other African 11%
Government Presidential system
Currency CFA franc = 100 centimes
Literacy rate 71%
Calorie consumption 2637 calories

GAMBIA
West Africa

Official name Republic of the Gambia
Formation 1965 / 1965
Capital Banjul
Population 1.5 million / 389 people per sq mile (150 people per sq km) / 33%
Total area 4363 sq miles (11,300 sq km)
Languages English*, Mandinka, Fulani, Wolof, Jola, Soninke
Religions Sunni Muslim 90%, Christian 9%, Traditional beliefs 1%
Ethnic mix Mandinka 42%, Fulani 18%, Wolof 16%, Jola 10%, Serahuli 9%, Other 5%
Government Presidential system
Currency Dalasi = 100 butut
Literacy rate 38%
Calorie consumption 2273 calories

GEORGIA
Southwest Asia

Official name Georgia
Formation 1991 / 1991
Capital Tbilisi
Population 4.5 million / 167 people per sq mile (65 people per sq km) / 61%
Total area 26,911 sq miles (69,700 sq km)
Languages Georgian*, Russian, Azeri, Armenian, Mingrelian, Ossetian, Abkhazian
Religions Georgian Orthodox 65%, Muslim 11%, Russian Orthodox 10%, Armenian Orthodox 8%, Other 6%
Ethnic mix Georgian 70%, Armenian 8%, Russian 6%, Azeri 6%, Ossetian 3%, Other 7%
Government Presidential system
Currency Lari = 100 tetri
Literacy rate 99%
Calorie consumption 2354 calories

GERMANY
Northern Europe

Official name Federal Republic of Germany
Formation 1871 / 1990
Capital Berlin
Population 82.7 million / 613 people per sq mile (237 people per sq km) / 88%
Total area 137,846 sq miles (357,021 sq km)
Languages German*, Turkish
Religions Protestant 34%, Roman Catholic 33%, Other 30%, Muslim 3%
Ethnic mix German 92%, Other 3%, Other European 3%, Turkish 2%
Government Parliamentary system
Currency Euro = 100 cents
Literacy rate 99%
Calorie consumption 3496 calories

GHANA
West Africa

Official name Republic of Ghana
Formation 1957 / 1957
Capital Accra
Population 22.1 million / 249 people per sq mile (96 people per sq km) / 38%
Total area 92,100 sq miles (238,540 sq km)
Languages Twi, Fanti, Ewe, Ga, Adangbe, Gurma, Dagomba (Dagbani)
Religions Christian 69%, Muslim 16%, Traditional beliefs 9%, Other 6%
Ethnic mix Ashanti and Fanti 52%, Moshi-Dagomba 16%, Ewe 12%, Other 11%, Ga and Ga-adanbe 8%, Yoruba 1%
Government Presidential system
Currency Cedi = 100 psewas
Literacy rate 54%
Calorie consumption 2667 calories

GREECE
Southeast Europe

Official name Hellenic Republic
Formation 1829 / 1947
Capital Athens
Population 11.1 million / 220 people per sq mile (85 people per sq km) / 60%
Total area 50,942 sq miles (131,940 sq km)
Languages Greek*, Turkish, Macedonian, Albanian
Religions Orthodox Christian 98%, Other 1%, Muslim 1%
Ethnic mix Greek 98%, Other 2%
Government Parliamentary system
Currency Euro = 100 cents
Literacy rate 91%
Calorie consumption 3721 calories

GRENADA
West Indies

Official name Grenada
Formation 1974 / 1974
Capital St. George's
Population 89,502 / 683 people per sq mile (263 people per sq km) / 38%
Total area 131 sq miles (340 sq km)
Languages English*, English Creole
Religions Roman Catholic 68%, Anglican 17%, Other 15%
Ethnic mix Black African 82%, Mulatto (mixed race) 13%, East Indian 3%, Other 2%
Government Parliamentary system
Currency Eastern Caribbean dollar = 100 cents
Literacy rate 96%
Calorie consumption 2932 calories

GUATEMALA
Central America

Official name Republic of Guatemala
Formation 1838 / 1838
Capital Guatemala City
Population 12.6 million / 301 people per sq mile (116 people per sq km) / 40%
Total area 42,042 sq miles (108,890 sq km)
Languages Spanish*, Quiché, Mam, Cakchiquel, Kekchí
Religions Roman Catholic 65%, Protestant 33%, Other and nonreligious 2%
Ethnic mix Amerindian 60%, Mestizo 30%, Other 10%
Government Presidential system
Currency Quetzal = 100 centavos
Literacy rate 69%
Calorie consumption 2219 calories

GUINEA
West Africa

Official name Republic of Guinea
Formation 1958 / 1958
Capital Conakry
Population 9.4 million / 99 people per sq mile (38 people per sq km) / 33%
Total area 94,925 sq miles (245,857 sq km)
Languages French*, Fulani, Malinke, Soussou
Religions Muslim 65%, Traditional beliefs 33%, Christian 2%
Ethnic mix Fulani 30%, Malinke 30%, Soussou 15%, Kissi 10%, Other tribes 10%, Other 5%
Government Presidential system
Currency Guinea franc = 100 centimes
Literacy rate 41%
Calorie consumption 2409 calories

GUINEA-BISSAU
West Africa

Official name Republic of Guinea-Bissau
Formation 1974 / 1974
Capital Bissau
Population 1.6 million / 147 people per sq mile (57 people per sq km) / 24%
Total area 13,946 sq miles (36,120 sq km)
Languages Portuguese*, Balante, Fulani, Malinke, Portuguese Creole
Religions Traditional beliefs 52%, Muslim 40%, Christian 8%
Ethnic mix Other tribes 31%, Balante 25%, Fula 20%, Mandinka 12%, Mandyako 11%, Other 1%
Government Presidential system
Currency CFA franc = 100 centimes
Literacy rate 40%
Calorie consumption 2024 calories

GUYANA
South America

Official name Cooperative Republic of Guyana
Formation 1966 / 1966
Capital Georgetown
Population 751,000 / 10 people per sq mile (4 people per sq km) / 38%
Total area 83,000 sq miles (214,970 sq km)
Languages English*, Hindi, Tamil, Amerindian languages, English Creole
Religions Christian 57%, Hindu 33%, Muslim 9%, Other 1%
Ethnic mix East Indian 52%, Black African 38%, Other 4%, Amerindian 4%, European and Chinese 2%
Government Presidential system
Currency Guyanese dollar = 100 cents
Literacy rate 97%
Calorie consumption 2692 calories

HAITI
West Indies

Official name Republic of Haiti
Formation 1804 / 1844
Capital Port-au-Prince
Population 8.5 million / 799 people per sq mile (308 people per sq km) / 36%
Total area 10,714 sq miles (27,750 sq km)
Languages French Creole*, French*
Religions Roman Catholic 80%, Protestant 16%, Other (including Voodoo) 3%, Nonreligious 1%
Ethnic mix Black African 95%, Mulatto (mixed race) and European 5%
Government Transitional regime
Currency Gourde = 100 centimes
Literacy rate 52%
Calorie consumption 2086 calories

HONDURAS
Central America

Official name Republic of Honduras
Formation 1838 / 1838
Capital Tegucigalpa
Population 7.2 million / 167 people per sq mile (64 people per sq km) / 53%
Total area 43,278 sq miles (112,090 sq km)
Languages Spanish*, Garífuna (Carib), English Creole
Religions Roman Catholic 97%, Protestant 3%
Ethnic mix Mestizo 90%, Black African 5%, Amerindian 4%, White 1%
Government Presidential system
Currency Lempira = 100 centavos
Literacy rate 80%
Calorie consumption 2356 calories

HUNGARY
Central Europe

Official name Republic of Hungary
Formation 1918 / 1947
Capital Budapest
Population 10.1 million / 283 people per sq mile (109 people per sq km) / 64%
Total area 35,919 sq miles (93,030 sq km)
Languages Hungarian (Magyar)*
Religions Roman Catholic 52%, Calvinist 16%, Other 15%, Nonreligious 14%, Lutheran 3%
Ethnic mix Magyar 90%, Other 7%, Roma 2%, German 1%
Government Parliamentary system
Currency Forint = 100 fillér
Literacy rate 99%
Calorie consumption 3483 calories

ICELAND
Northwest Europe

Official name Republic of Iceland
Formation 1944 / 1944
Capital Reykjavík
Population 295,000 / 8 people per sq mile (3 people per sq km) / 93%
Total area 39,768 sq miles (103,000 sq km)
Languages Icelandic*
Religions Evangelical Lutheran 93%, Nonreligious 6%, Other (mostly Christian) 1%
Ethnic mix Icelandic 94%, Other 5%, Danish 1%
Government Parliamentary system
Currency Icelandic króna = 100 aurar
Literacy rate 99%
Calorie consumption 3249 calories

INDIA
South Asia

Official name Republic of India
Formation 1947 / 1947
Capital New Delhi
Population 1.1 billion / 961 people per sq mile (371 people per sq km) / 28%
Total area 1,269,338 sq miles (3,287,590 sq km)
Languages Hindi*, English*, Bengali, Marathi, Telugu, Tamil, Bihari, Gujarati, Kanarese, Urdu
Religions Hindu 83%, Muslim 11%, Christian 2%, Sikh 2%, Other 1%, Buddhist 1%
Ethnic mix Indo-Aryan 72%, Dravidian 25%, Mongoloid and other 3%
Government Parliamentary system
Currency Indian rupee = 100 paise
Literacy rate 61%
Calorie consumption 2459 calories

INDONESIA
Southeast Asia

Official name Republic of Indonesia
Formation 1949 / 1999
Capital Jakarta
Population 223 million / 321 people per sq mile (124 people per sq km) / 41%
Total area 741,096 sq miles (1,919,440 sq km)
Languages Bahasa Indonesia*, Javanese, Sundanese, Madurese, Dutch
Religions Sunni Muslim 87%, Protestant 6%, Roman Catholic 3%, Hindu 2%, Other 1%, Buddhist 1%
Ethnic mix Javanese 45%, Sundanese 14%, Coastal Malays 8%, Madurese 8%, Other 25%
Government Presidential system
Currency Rupiah = 100 sen
Literacy rate 88%
Calorie consumption 2904 calories

IRAN
Southwest Asia

Official name Islamic Republic of Iran
Formation 1502 / 1990
Capital Tehran
Population 69.5 million / 110 people per sq mile (42 people per sq km) / 62%
Total area 636,293 sq miles (1,648,000 sq km)
Languages Farsi*, Azeri, Luri, Gilaki, Mazanderani, Kurdish, Turkmen, Arabic, Baluchi
Religions Shi'a Muslim 93%, Sunni Muslim 6%, Other 1%
Ethnic mix Persian 50%, Azari 24%, Other 10%, Kurdish 8%, Lur and Bakhtiari 8%
Government Islamic theocracy
Currency Iranian rial = 100 dinars
Literacy rate 77%
Calorie consumption 3085 calories

IRAQ
Southwest Asia

Official name Republic of Iraq
Formation 1932 / 1990
Capital Baghdad
Population 28.8 million / 171 people per sq mile (66 people per sq km) / 77%
Total area 168,753 sq miles (437,072 sq km)
Languages Arabic*, Kurdish, Turkic languages, Armenian, Assyrian
Religions Shi'a Muslim 60%, Sunni Muslim 35%, Other (including Christian) 5%
Ethnic mix Arab 80%, Kurdish 15%, Turkmen 3%, Other 2%
Government Transitional regime
Currency New Iraqi dinar = 1000 fils
Literacy rate 40%
Calorie consumption 2197 calories

IRELAND
Northwest Europe

Official name Ireland
Formation 1922 / 1922
Capital Dublin
Population 4.1 million / 154 people per sq mile (60 people per sq km) / 59%
Total area 27,135 sq miles (70,280 sq km)
Languages English*, Irish Gaelic*
Religions Roman Catholic 88%, Other and nonreligious 9%, Anglican 3%
Ethnic mix Irish 93%, Other 4%, British 3%
Government Parliamentary system
Currency Euro = 100 cents
Literacy rate 99%
Calorie consumption 3656 calories

ISRAEL
Southwest Asia

Official name State of Israel
Formation 1948 / 1994
Capital Jerusalem (not internationally recognized)
Population 6.7 million / 854 people per sq mile (330 people per sq km) / 91%
Total area 8019 sq miles (20,770 sq km)
Languages Hebrew*, Arabic, Yiddish, German, Russian, Polish, Romanian, Persian
Religions Jewish 80%, Muslim (mainly Sunni) 16%, Druze and other 2%, Christian 2%
Ethnic mix Jewish 80%, Other (mostly Arab) 20%
Government Parliamentary system
Currency Shekel = 100 agorot
Literacy rate 97%
Calorie consumption 3666 calories

ITALY
Southern Europe

Official name Italian Republic
Formation 1861 / 1947
Capital Rome
Population 58.1 million / 512 people per sq mile (198 people per sq km) / 67%
Total area 116,305 sq miles (301,230 sq km)
Languages Italian*, German, French, Rhaeto-Romanic, Sardinian
Religions Roman Catholic 85%, Other and nonreligious 13%, Muslim 2%
Ethnic mix Italian 94%, Other 4%, Sardinian 2%
Government Parliamentary system
Currency Euro = 100 cents
Literacy rate 99%
Calorie consumption 3671 calories

IVORY COAST
West Africa

Official name Republic of Côte d'Ivoire
Formation 1960 / 1960
Capital Yamoussoukro
Population 18.2 million / 148 people per sq mile (57 people per sq km) / 46%
Total area 124,502 sq miles (322,460 sq km)
Languages French*, Akan, Kru, Voltaic
Religions Muslim 38%, Traditional beliefs 25%, Roman Catholic 25%, Protestant 6%, Other 6%
Ethnic mix Baoulé 23%, Other 19%, Bété 18%, Senufo 15%, Agni-Ashanti 14%, Mandinka 11%
Government Presidential system
Currency CFA franc = 100 centimes
Literacy rate 48%
Calorie consumption 2631 calories

JAMAICA
West Indies

Official name Jamaica
Formation 1962 / 1962
Capital Kingston
Population 2.7 million / 646 people per sq mile (249 people per sq km) / 56%
Total area 4243 sq miles (10,990 sq km)
Languages English*, English Creole
Religions Other and nonreligious 45%, Other Protestant 20%, Church of God 18%, Baptist 10%, Anglican 7%
Ethnic mix Black African 75%, Mulatto (mixed race) 13%, European and Chinese 11%, East Indian 1%
Government Parliamentary system
Currency Jamaican dollar = 100 cents
Literacy rate 88%
Calorie consumption 2685 calories

JAPAN
East Asia

Official name Japan
Formation 1590 / 1972
Capital Tokyo
Population 128 million / 881 people per sq mile (340 people per sq km) / 79%
Total area 145,882 sq miles (377,835 sq km)
Languages Japanese, Korean, Chinese
Religions Shinto and Buddhist 76%, Buddhist 16%, Other (including Christian) 8%
Ethnic mix Japanese 99%, Other (mainly Korean) 1%
Government Parliamentary system
Currency Yen = 100 sen
Literacy rate 99%
Calorie consumption 2761 calories

JORDAN
Southwest Asia

Official name Hashemite Kingdom of Jordan
Formation 1946 / 1967
Capital Amman
Population 5.6 million / 163 people per sq mile (63 people per sq km) / 74%
Total area 35,637 sq miles (92,300 sq km)
Languages Arabic*
Religions Muslim (mainly Sunni) 92%, Other (mostly Christian) 8%
Ethnic mix Arab 98%, Circassian 1%, Armenian 1%
Government Monarchy
Currency Jordanian dinar = 1000 fils
Literacy rate 90%
Calorie consumption 2673 calories

KAZAKHSTAN
Central Asia

Official name Republic of Kazakhstan
Formation 1991 / 1991
Capital Astana
Population 14.8 million / 14 people per sq mile (5 people per sq km) / 56%
Total area 1,049,150 sq miles (2,717,300 sq km)
Languages Kazakh*, Russian*, Ukrainian, Tatar, German, Uzbek, Uighur
Religions Muslim (mainly Sunni) 47%, Orthodox Christian 44%, Other 9%
Ethnic mix Kazakh 53%, Russian 30%, Other 9%, Ukrainian 4%, Tatar 2%, German 2%
Government Presidential system
Currency Tenge = 100 tiyn
Literacy rate 99%
Calorie consumption 2677 calories

KENYA
East Africa

Official name Republic of Kenya
Formation 1963 / 1963
Capital Nairobi
Population 34.3 million / 157 people per sq mile (60 people per sq km) / 33%
Total area 224,961 sq miles (582,650 sq km)
Languages Kiswahili*, English*, Kikuyu, Luo, Kalenjin, Kamba
Religions Christian 60%, Traditional beliefs 25%, Other 9%, Muslim 6%
Ethnic mix Other 30%, Kikuyu 21%, Luhya 14%, Luo 13%, Kalenjin 11%, Kamba 11%
Government Presidential system
Currency Kenya shilling = 100 cents
Literacy rate 74%
Calorie consumption 2090 calories

KIRIBATI
Australasia & Oceania

Official name Republic of Kiribati
Formation 1979 / 1979
Capital Bairiki (Tarawa Atoll)
Population 103,092 / 376 people per sq mile (145 people per sq km) / 36%
Total area 277 sq miles (717 sq km)
Languages English*, Kiribati
Religions Roman Catholic 53%, Kiribati Protestant Church 39%, Other 8%
Ethnic mix Micronesian 96%, Other 4%
Government Nonparty system
Currency Australian dollar = 100 cents
Literacy rate 99%
Calorie consumption 2859 calories

KUWAIT
Southwest Asia

Official name State of Kuwait
Formation 1961 / 1961
Capital Kuwait City
Population 2.7 million / 392 people per sq mile (152 people per sq km) / 98%
Total area 6880 sq miles (17,820 sq km)
Languages Arabic*, English
Religions Sunni Muslim 45%, Shi'a Muslim 40%, Christian, Hindu, and other 15%
Ethnic mix Kuwaiti 45%, Other Arab 35%, South Asian 9%, Other 7%, Iranian 4%
Government Monarchy
Currency Kuwaiti dinar = 1000 fils
Literacy rate 83%
Calorie consumption 3010 calories

KYRGYZSTAN
Central Asia

Official name Kyrgyz Republic
Formation 1991 / 1991
Capital Bishkek
Population 5.3 million / 69 people per sq mile (27 people per sq km) / 33%
Total area 76,641 sq miles (198,500 sq km)
Languages Kyrgyz*, Russian*, Uzbek, Tatar, Ukrainian
Religions Muslim (mainly Sunni) 70%, Orthodox Christian 30%
Ethnic mix Kyrgyz 57%, Russian 19%, Uzbek 13%, Other 7%, Tatar 2%, Ukrainian 2%
Government Presidential system
Currency Som = 100 tyyn
Literacy rate 99%
Calorie consumption 2999 calories

LAOS
Southeast Asia

Official name Lao People's Democratic Republic
Formation 1953 / 1953
Capital Vientiane
Population 5.9 million / 66 people per sq mile (26 people per sq km) / 24%
Total area 91,428 sq miles (236,800 sq km)
Languages Lao*, Mon-Khmer, Yao, Vietnamese, Chinese, French
Religions Buddhist 85%, Other (including animist) 15%
Ethnic mix Lao Loum 66%, Lao Theung 30%, Other 2%, Lao Soung 2%
Government One-party state
Currency New kip = 100 at
Literacy rate 69%
Calorie consumption 2312 calories

LATVIA
Northeast Europe

Official name Republic of Latvia
Formation 1991 / 1991
Capital Riga
Population 2.3 million / 92 people per sq mile (36 people per sq km) / 69%
Total area 24,938 sq miles (64,589 sq km)
Languages Latvian*, Russian
Religions Lutheran 55%, Roman Catholic 24%, Other 12%, Orthodox Christian 9%
Ethnic mix Latvian 57%, Russian 32%, Belarussian 4%, Ukrainian 3%, Polish 2%, Other 2%
Government Parliamentary system
Currency Lats = 100 santims
Literacy rate 99%
Calorie consumption 2938 calories

LEBANON
Southwest Asia

Official name Republic of Lebanon
Formation 1941 / 1941
Capital Beirut
Population 3.6 million / 911 people per sq mile (352 people per sq km) / 90%
Total area 4015 sq miles (10,400 sq km)
Languages Arabic*, French, Armenian, Assyrian
Religions Muslim 70%, Christian 30%
Ethnic mix Arab 94%, Armenian 4%, Other 2%
Government Parliamentary system
Currency Lebanese pound = 100 piastres
Literacy rate 87%
Calorie consumption 3196 calories

LESOTHO
Southern Africa

Official name Kingdom of Lesotho
Formation 1966 / 1966
Capital Maseru
Population 1.8 million / 154 people per sq mile (59 people per sq km) / 28%
Total area 11,720 sq miles (30,355 sq km)
Languages English*, Sesotho*, isiZulu
Religions Christian 90%, Traditional beliefs 10%
Ethnic mix Sotho 97%, European and Asian 3%
Government Parliamentary system
Currency Loti = 100 lisente
Literacy rate 81%
Calorie consumption 2638 calories

LIBERIA
West Africa

Official name Republic of Liberia
Formation 1847 / 1847
Capital Monrovia
Population 3.3 million / 89 people per sq mile (34 people per sq km) / 45%
Total area 43,000 sq miles (111,370 sq km)
Languages English*, Kpelle, Vai, Bassa, Kru, Grebo, Kissi, Gola, Loma
Religions Christian 68%, Traditional beliefs 18%, Muslim 14%
Ethnic mix Indigenous tribes (16 main groups) 95%, Americo-Liberians 5%
Government Transitional regime
Currency Liberian dollar = 100 cents
Literacy rate 58%
Calorie consumption 1900 calories

LIBYA
North Africa

Official name Great Socialist People's Libyan Arab Jamahariyah
Formation 1951 / 1951
Capital Tripoli
Population 5.9 million / 9 people per sq mile (3 people per sq km) / 88%
Total area 679,358 sq miles (1,759,540 sq km)
Languages Arabic*, Tuareg
Religions Muslim (mainly Sunni) 97%, Other 3%
Ethnic mix Arab and Berber 95%, Other 5%
Government One-party state
Currency Libyan dinar = 1000 dirhams
Literacy rate 82%
Calorie consumption 3320 calories

LIECHTENSTEIN
Central Europe

Official name Principality of Liechtenstein
Formation 1719 / 1719
Capital Vaduz
Population 33,717 / 544 people per sq mile (211 people per sq km) / 68%
Total area 62 sq miles (160 sq km)
Languages German*, Alemannish dialect, Italian
Religions Roman Catholic 81%, Other 12%, Protestant 7%
Ethnic mix Liechtensteiner 62%, Foreign residents 38%
Government Parliamentary system
Currency Swiss franc = 100 rappen/centimes
Literacy rate 99%
Calorie consumption Not available

LITHUANIA
Northeast Europe

Official name Republic of Lithuania
Formation 1991 / 1991
Capital Vilnius
Population 3.4 million / 135 people per sq mile (52 people per sq km) / 68%
Total area 25,174 sq miles (65,200 sq km)
Languages Lithuanian*, Russian
Religions Roman Catholic 83%, Other 12%, Protestant 5%
Ethnic mix Lithuanian 80%, Russian 9%, Polish 7%, Other 2%, Belarussian 2%
Government Parliamentary system
Currency Litas (euro is also legal tender) = 100 centu
Literacy rate 99%
Calorie consumption 3324 calories

LUXEMBOURG
Northwest Europe

Official name Grand Duchy of Luxembourg
Formation 1867 / 1867
Capital Luxembourg-Ville
Population 465,000 / 466 people per sq mile (180 people per sq km) / 92%
Total area 998 sq miles (2586 sq km)
Languages Luxembourgish*, German*, French*
Religions Roman Catholic 97%, Protestant, Orthodox Christian, and Jewish 3%
Ethnic mix Luxembourger 73%, Foreign residents 27%
Government Parliamentary system
Currency Euro = 100 cents
Literacy rate 99%
Calorie consumption 3701 calories

MACEDONIA
Southeast Europe

Official name Republic of Macedonia
Formation 1991 / 1991
Capital Skopje
Population 2 million / 201 people per sq mile (78 people per sq km) / 62%
Total area 9781 sq miles (25,333 sq km)
Languages Macedonian, Albanian, Serbo-Croat
Religions Orthodox Christian 59%, Muslim 26%, Other 10%, Roman Catholic 4%, Protestant 1%
Ethnic mix Macedonian 64%, Albanian 25%, Turkish 4%, Roma 3%, Other 2%, Serb 2%
Government Mixed presidential–parliamentary system
Currency Macedonian denar = 100 deni
Literacy rate 96%
Calorie consumption 2655 calories

MADAGASCAR
Indian Ocean

Official name Republic of Madagascar
Formation 1960 / 1960
Capital Antananarivo
Population 18.6 million / 83 people per sq mile (32 people per sq km) / 30%
Total area 226,656 sq miles (587,040 sq km)
Languages Malagasy*, French*
Religions Traditional beliefs 52%, Christian (mainly Roman Catholic) 41%, Muslim 7%
Ethnic mix Other Malay 46%, Merina 26%, Betsimisaraka 15%, Betsileo 12%, Other 1%
Government Presidential system
Currency Ariary = 5 iraimbilanja
Literacy rate 71%
Calorie consumption 2005 calories

MALAWI
Southern Africa

Official name Republic of Malawi
Formation 1964 / 1964
Capital Lilongwe
Population 12.9 million / 355 people per sq mile (137 people per sq km) / 25%
Total area 45,745 sq miles (118,480 sq km)
Languages English*, Chewa*, Lomwe, Yao, Ngoni
Religions Protestant 55%, Roman Catholic 20%, Muslim 20%, Traditional beliefs 5%
Ethnic mix Bantu 99%, Other 1%
Government Presidential system
Currency Malawi kwacha = 100 tambala
Literacy rate 64%
Calorie consumption 2155 calories

MALAYSIA
Southeast Asia

Official name Federation of Malaysia
Formation 1963 / 1965
Capital Kuala Lumpur; Putrajaya (administrative)
Population 25.3 million / 199 people per sq mile (77 people per sq km) / 57%
Total area 127,316 sq miles (329,750 sq km)
Languages Malay*, Chinese*, Bahasa Malaysia, Tamil, English
Religions Muslim (mainly Sunni) 53%, Buddhist 19%, Chinese faiths 12%, Other 7%, Christian 7%, Traditional beliefs 2%
Ethnic mix Malay 48%, Chinese 29%, Indigenous tribes 12%, Indian 6%, Other 5%
Government Parliamentary system
Currency Ringgit = 100 sen
Literacy rate 89%
Calorie consumption 2881 calories

MALDIVES
Indian Ocean

Official name Republic of Maldives
Formation 1965 / 1965
Capital Male'
Population 329,000 / 2836 people per sq mile (1097 people per sq km) / 30%
Total area 116 sq miles (300 sq km)
Languages Dhivehi (Maldivian)*, Sinhala, Tamil, Arabic
Religions Sunni Muslim 100%
Ethnic mix Arab–Sinhalese–Malay 100%
Government Nonparty system
Currency Rufiyaa = 100 lari
Literacy rate 97%
Calorie consumption 2548 calories

MALI
West Africa

Official name Republic of Mali
Formation 1960 / 1960
Capital Bamako
Population 13.5 million / 29 people per sq mile (11 people per sq km) / 30%
Total area 478,764 sq miles (1,240,000 sq km)
Languages French*, Bambara, Fulani, Senufo, Soninke
Religions Muslim (mainly Sunni) 80%, Traditional beliefs 18%, Christian 1%, Other 1%
Ethnic mix Bambara 32%, Other 26%, Fulani 14%, Senufu 12%, Soninka 9%, Tuareg 7%
Government Presidential system
Currency CFA franc = 100 centimes
Literacy rate 19%
Calorie consumption 2174 calories

MALTA
Southern Europe

Official name Republic of Malta
Formation 1964 / 1964
Capital Valletta
Population 402,000 / 3242 people per sq mile (1256 people per sq km) / 91%
Total area 122 sq miles (316 sq km)
Languages Maltese*, English
Religions Roman Catholic 98%, Other and nonreligious 2%
Ethnic mix Maltese 96%, Other 4%
Government Parliamentary system
Currency Maltese lira = 100 cents
Literacy rate 88%
Calorie consumption 3587 calories

MARSHALL ISLANDS
Australasia & Oceania

Official name Republic of the Marshall Islands
Formation 1986 / 1986
Capital Majuro
Population 59,071 / 844 people per sq mile (326 people per sq km) / 69%
Total area 70 sq miles (181 sq km)
Languages Marshallese*, English*, Japanese, German
Religions Protestant 90%, Roman Catholic 8%, Other 2%
Ethnic mix Micronesian 97%, Other 3%
Government Presidential system
Currency US dollar = 100 cents
Literacy rate 91%
Calorie consumption Not available

MAURITANIA
West Africa

Official name Islamic Republic of Mauritania
Formation 1960 / 1960
Capital Nouakchott
Population 3.1 million / 8 people per sq mile (3 people per sq km) / 58%
Total area 397,953 sq miles (1,030,700 sq km)
Languages French*, Hassaniyah Arabic, Wolof
Religions Sunni Muslim 100%
Ethnic mix Maure 81%, Wolof 7%, Tukolor 5%, Other 4%, Soninka 3%
Government Transitional regime
Currency Ouguiya = 5 khoums
Literacy rate 51%
Calorie consumption 2772 calories

MAURITIUS
Indian Ocean

Official name Republic of Mauritius
Formation 1968 / 1968
Capital Port Louis
Population 1.2 million / 1671 people per sq mile (645 people per sq km) / 41%
Total area 718 sq miles (1860 sq km)
Languages English*, French Creole, Hindi, Urdu, Tamil, Chinese, French
Religions Hindu 52%, Roman Catholic 26%, Muslim 17%, Other 3%, Protestant 2%
Ethnic mix Indo-Mauritian 68%, Creole 27%, Sino-Mauritian 3%, Franco-Mauritian 2%
Government Parliamentary system
Currency Mauritian rupee = 100 cents
Literacy rate 84%
Calorie consumption 2955 calories

MEXICO
North America

Official name United Mexican States
Formation 1836 / 1848
Capital Mexico City
Population 107 million / 145 people per sq mile (56 people per sq km) / 74%
Total area 761,602 sq miles (1,972,550 sq km)
Languages Spanish*, Nahuatl, Mayan, Zapotec, Mixtec, Otomi, Totonac, Tzotzil, Tzeltal
Religions Roman Catholic 88%, Other 7%, Protestant 5%
Ethnic mix Mestizo 60%, Amerindian 30%, European 9%, Other 1%
Government Presidential system
Currency Mexican peso = 100 centavos
Literacy rate 90%
Calorie consumption 3145 calories

MICRONESIA
Australasia & Oceania

Official name Federated States of Micronesia
Formation 1986 / 1986
Capital Palikir (Pohnpei Island)
Population 108,105 / 399 people per sq mile (154 people per sq km) / 28%
Total area 271 sq miles (702 sq km)
Languages Trukese, Pohnpeian, Mortlockese, Kosraean, English
Religions Roman Catholic 50%, Protestant 48%, Other 2%
Ethnic mix Micronesian 100%
Government Nonparty system
Currency US dollar = 100 cents
Literacy rate 81%
Calorie consumption Not available

MOLDOVA
Southeast Europe

Official name Republic of Moldova
Formation 1991 / 1991
Capital Chisinau
Population 4.2 million / 323 people per sq mile (125 people per sq km) / 46%
Total area 13,067 sq miles (33,843 sq km)
Languages Moldovan*, Ukrainian, Russian
Religions Orthodox Christian 98%, Jewish 2%
Ethnic mix Moldovan 65%, Ukrainian 14%, Russian 13%, Other 4%, Gagauz 4%
Government Parliamentary system
Currency Moldovan leu = 100 bani
Literacy rate 96%
Calorie consumption 2806 calories

MONACO
Southern Europe

Official name Principality of Monaco
Formation 1861 / 1861
Capital Monaco-Ville
Population 32,409 / 43212 people per sq mile (16620 people per sq km) / 100%
Total area 0.75 sq miles (1.95 sq km)
Languages French*, Italian, Monégasque, English
Religions Roman Catholic 89%, Protestant 6%, Other 5%
Ethnic mix French 47%, Other 20%, Monégasque 17%, Italian 16%
Government Monarchy
Currency Euro = 100 cents
Literacy rate 99%
Calorie consumption Not available

MONGOLIA
East Asia

Official name Mongolia
Formation 1924 / 1924
Capital Ulan Bator
Population 2.6 million / 4 people per sq mile (2 people per sq km) / 64%
Total area 604,247 sq miles (1,565,000 sq km)
Languages Khalkha Mongolian*, Kazakh, Chinese, Russian
Religions Tibetan Buddhist 96%, Muslim 4%
Ethnic mix Mongol 90%, Kazakh 4%, Other 2%, Chinese 2%, Russian 2%
Government Mixed presidential–parliamentary system
Currency Tugrik (tögrög) = 100 möngö
Literacy rate 98%
Calorie consumption 2249 calories

MONTENEGRO
Europe

Official name Republic of Montenegro
Formation 2006 / 2006
Capital Podgorica
Population 620,145 / 116 people per sq mile (45 people per sq km) / 62%
Total area 5,332 sq miles (13,812 sq km)
Languages Montenegrin, Serbian, Albanian
Religions Orthodox Christian 74%, Muslim 18%, Roman Catholic 4%, Other 4%
Ethnic mix Montenegrin 43%, Serb 32%, Bosniak 8%, Albanian 5%, Other 12%
Government Parliamentary system
Currency Euro = 100 cents
Literacy rate 98%
Calorie consumption Not available

MOROCCO
North Africa

Official name Kingdom of Morocco
Formation 1956 / 1956
Capital Rabat
Population 31.5 million / 183 people per sq mile (71 people per sq km) / 56%
Total area 172,316 sq miles (446,300 sq km)
Languages Arabic*, Tamazight (Berber), French, Spanish
Religions Muslim (mainly Sunni) 99%, Other (mostly Christian) 1%
Ethnic mix Arab 70%, Berber 29%, European 1%
Government Monarchy
Currency Moroccan dirham = 100 centimes
Literacy rate 51%
Calorie consumption 3052 calories

MOZAMBIQUE
Southern Africa

Official name Republic of Mozambique
Formation 1975 / 1975
Capital Maputo
Population 19.8 million / 65 people per sq mile (25 people per sq km) / 40%
Total area 309,494 sq miles (801,590 sq km)
Languages Portuguese*, Makua, Xitsonga, Sena, Lomwe
Religions Traditional beliefs 56%, Christian 30%, Muslim 14%
Ethnic mix Makua Lomwe 47%, Tsonga 23%, Malawi 12%, Shona 11%, Yao 4%, Other 3%
Government Presidential system
Currency Metical = 100 centavos
Literacy rate 47%
Calorie consumption 2079 calories

NAMIBIA
Southern Africa

Official name Republic of Namibia
Formation 1990 / 1994
Capital Windhoek
Population 2 million / 6 people per sq mile (2 people per sq km) / 31%
Total area 318,694 sq miles (825,418 sq km)
Languages English*, Ovambo, Kavango, Bergdama, German, Afrikaans
Religions Christian 90%, Traditional beliefs 10%
Ethnic mix Ovambo 50%, Other tribes 16%, Kavango 9%, Other 9%, Damara 8%, Herero 8%
Government Presidential system
Currency Namibian dollar = 100 cents
Literacy rate 85%
Calorie consumption 2278 calories

NAURU
Australasia & Oceania

Official name Republic of Nauru
Formation 1968 / 1968
Capital None
Population 13,048 / 1611 people per sq mile (621 people per sq km) / 100%
Total area 8.1 sq miles (21 sq km)
Languages Nauruan*, Kiribati, Chinese, Tuvaluan, English
Religions Nauruan Congregational Church 60%, Roman Catholic 35%, Other 5%
Ethnic mix Nauruan 62%, Other Pacific islanders 25%, Chinese and Vietnamese 8%, European 5%
Government Parliamentary system
Currency Australian dollar = 100 cents
Literacy rate 95%
Calorie consumption Not available

NEPAL
South Asia

Official name Kingdom of Nepal
Formation 1769 / 1769
Capital Kathmandu
Population 27.1 million / 513 people per sq mile (198 people per sq km) / 12%
Total area 54,363 sq miles (140,800 sq km)
Languages Nepali*, Maithili, Bhojpuri
Religions Hindu 90%, Buddhist 5%, Muslim 3%, Other (including Christian) 2%
Ethnic mix Nepalese 52%, Other 19%, Maithili 11%, Tibeto-Burmese 10%, Bhojpuri 8%
Government Monarchy
Currency Nepalese rupee = 100 paise
Literacy rate 49%
Calorie consumption 2453 calories

NETHERLANDS
Northwest Europe

Official name Kingdom of the Netherlands
Formation 1648 / 1839
Capital Amsterdam; The Hague (administrative)
Population 16.3 million / 1245 people per sq mile (481 people per sq km) / 89%
Total area 16,033 sq miles (41,526 sq km)
Languages Dutch*, Frisian
Religions Roman Catholic 36%, Other 34%, Protestant 27%, Muslim 3%
Ethnic mix Dutch 82%, Other 12%, Surinamese 2%, Turkish 2%, Moroccan 2%
Government Parliamentary system
Currency Euro = 100 cents
Literacy rate 99%
Calorie consumption 3362 calories

NEW ZEALAND
Australasia & Oceania

Official name New Zealand
Formation 1947 / 1947
Capital Wellington
Population 4 million / 39 people per sq mile (15 people per sq km) / 86%
Total area 103,737 sq miles (268,680 sq km)
Languages English*, Maori
Religions Anglican 24%, Other 22%, Presbyterian 18%, Nonreligious 16%, Roman Catholic 15%, Methodist 5%
Ethnic mix European 77%, Maori 12%, Other immigrant 6%, Pacific islanders 5%
Government Parliamentary system
Currency New Zealand dollar = 100 cents
Literacy rate 99%
Calorie consumption 3219 calories

NICARAGUA
Central America

Official name Republic of Nicaragua
Formation 1838 / 1838
Capital Managua
Population 5.5 million / 120 people per sq mile (46 people per sq km) / 65%
Total area 49,998 sq miles (129,494 sq km)
Languages Spanish*, English Creole, Miskito
Religions Roman Catholic 80%, Protestant Evangelical 17%, Other 3%
Ethnic mix Mestizo 69%, White 14%, Black 8%, Amerindian 5%, Zambo 4%
Government Presidential system
Currency Córdoba oro = 100 centavos
Literacy rate 77%
Calorie consumption 2298 calories

NIGER
West Africa

Official name Republic of Niger
Formation 1960 / 1960
Capital Niamey
Population 14 million / 29 people per sq mile (11 people per sq km) / 21%
Total area 489,188 sq miles (1,267,000 sq km)
Languages French*, Hausa, Djerma, Fulani, Tuareg, Teda
Religions Muslim 85%, Traditional beliefs 14%, Other (including Christian) 1%
Ethnic mix Hausa 54%, Djerma and Songhai 21%, Fulani 10%, Tuareg 9%, Other 6%
Government Presidential system
Currency CFA franc = 100 centimes
Literacy rate 14%
Calorie consumption 2130 calories

NIGERIA
West Africa

Official name Federal Republic of Nigeria
Formation 1960 / 1961
Capital Abuja
Population 132 million / 374 people per sq mile (144 people per sq km) / 44%
Total area 356,667 sq miles (923,768 sq km)
Languages English*, Hausa, Yoruba, Ibo
Religions Muslim 50%, Christian 40%, Traditional beliefs 10%
Ethnic mix Other 29%, Hausa 21%, Yoruba 21%, Ibo 18%, Fulani 11%
Government Presidential system
Currency Naira = 100 kobo
Literacy rate 67%
Calorie consumption 2726 calories

NORTH KOREA
East Asia

Official name Democratic People's Republic of Korea
Formation 1948 / 1953
Capital Pyongyang
Population 22.5 million / 484 people per sq mile (187 people per sq km) / 60%
Total area 46,540 sq miles (120,540 sq km)
Languages Korean*
Religions Atheist 100%
Ethnic mix Korean 100%
Government One-party state
Currency North Korean won = 100 chon
Literacy rate 99%
Calorie consumption 2142 calories

NORWAY
Northern Europe

Official name Kingdom of Norway
Formation 1905 / 1905
Capital Oslo
Population 4.6 million / 39 people per sq mile (15 people per sq km) / 76%
Total area 125,181 sq miles (324,220 sq km)
Languages Norwegian* (Bokmål "book language" and Nynorsk "new Norsk"), Sámi
Religions Evangelical Lutheran 89%, Other and nonreligious 10%, Roman Catholic 1%
Ethnic mix Norwegian 93%, Other 6%, Sámi 1%
Government Parliamentary system
Currency Norwegian krone = 100 øre
Literacy rate 99%
Calorie consumption 3484 calories

OMAN
Southwest Asia

Official name Sultanate of Oman
Formation 1951 / 1951
Capital Muscat
Population 2.6 million / 32 people per sq mile (12 people per sq km) / 84%
Total area 82,031 sq miles (212,460 sq km)
Languages Arabic*, Baluchi, Farsi, Hindi, Punjabi
Religions Ibadi Muslim 75%, Other Muslim and Hindu 25%
Ethnic mix Arab 88%, Baluchi 4%, Persian 3%, Indian and Pakistani 3%, African 2%
Government Monarchy
Currency Omani rial = 1000 baizas
Literacy rate 74%
Calorie consumption Not available

PAKISTAN
South Asia

Official name Islamic Republic of Pakistan
Formation 1947 / 1971
Capital Islamabad
Population 158 million / 531 people per sq mile (205 people per sq km) / 37%
Total area 310,401 sq miles (803,940 sq km)
Languages Urdu*, Baluchi, Brahui, Pashtu, Punjabi, Sindhi
Religions Sunni Muslim 77%, Shi'a Muslim 20%, Hindu 2%, Christian 1%
Ethnic mix Punjabi 56%, Pathan (Pashtun) 15%, Sindhi 14%, Mohajir 7%, Other 4%, Baluchi 4%
Government Presidential system
Currency Pakistani rupee = 100 paisa
Literacy rate 49%
Calorie consumption 2419 calories

PALAU
Australasia & Oceania

Official name Republic of Palau
Formation 1994 / 1994
Capital Koror
Population 20,303 / 104 people per sq mile (40 people per sq km) / 70%
Total area 177 sq miles (458 sq km)
Languages Palauan, English, Japanese, Angaur, Tobi, Sonsorolese
Religions Christian 66%, Modekngei 34%
Ethnic mix Micronesian 87%, Filipino 8%, Chinese and other Asian 5%
Government Nonparty system
Currency US dollar = 100 cents
Literacy rate 98%
Calorie consumption Not available

PANAMA
Central America

Official name Republic of Panama
Formation 1903 / 1903
Capital Panama City
Population 3.2 million / 109 people per sq mile (42 people per sq km) / 56%
Total area 30,193 sq miles (78,200 sq km)
Languages Spanish*, English Creole, Amerindian languages, Chibchan languages
Religions Roman Catholic 86%, Other 8%, Protestant 6%
Ethnic mix Mestizo 60%, White 14%, Black 12%, Amerindian 8%, Asian 4%, Other 2%
Government Presidential system
Currency Balboa = 100 centesimos
Literacy rate 92%
Calorie consumption 2272 calories

PAPUA NEW GUINEA
Australasia & Oceania

Official name Independent State of Papua New Guinea
Formation 1975 / 1975
Capital Port Moresby
Population 5.9 million / 34 people per sq mile (13 people per sq km) / 17%
Total area 178,703 sq miles (462,840 sq km)
Languages Pidgin English*, Papuan*, English, Motu, 750 (est.) native languages
Religions Protestant 60%, Roman Catholic 37%, Other 3%
Ethnic mix Melanesian and mixed race 100%
Government Parliamentary system
Currency Kina = 100 toeas
Literacy rate 57%
Calorie consumption 2193 calories

PARAGUAY
South America

Official name Republic of Paraguay
Formation 1811 / 1938
Capital Asunción
Population 6.2 million / 40 people per sq mile (16 people per sq km) / 56%
Total area 157,046 sq miles (406,750 sq km)
Languages Guarani*, Spanish*, German
Religions Roman Catholic 96%, Protestant (including Mennonite) 4%
Ethnic mix Mestizo 90%, Other 8%, Amerindian 2%
Government Presidential system
Currency Guaraní = 100 centimos
Literacy rate 92%
Calorie consumption 2565 calories

PERU
South America

Official name Republic of Peru
Formation 1824 / 1941
Capital Lima
Population 28 million / 57 people per sq mile (22 people per sq km) / 73%
Total area 496,223 sq miles (1,285,200 sq km)
Languages Spanish*, Quechua*, Aymara*
Religions Roman Catholic 95%, Other 5%
Ethnic mix Amerindian 50%, Mestizo 40%, White 7%, Other 3%
Government Presidential system
Currency New sol = 100 centimos
Literacy rate 88%
Calorie consumption 2571 calories

PHILIPPINES
Southwest Asia

Official name Republic of the Philippines
Formation 1946 / 1946
Capital Manila
Population 83.1 million / 722 people per sq mile (279 people per sq km) / 59%
Total area 115,830 sq miles (300,000 sq km)
Languages Filipino*, English*, Tagalog, Cebuano, Ilocano, Hiligaynon, many other local languages
Religions Roman Catholic 83%, Protestant 9%, Muslim 5%, Other (including Buddhist) 3%
Ethnic mix Malay 95%, Other 3%, Chinese 2%
Government Presidential system
Currency Philippine peso = 100 centavos
Literacy rate 93%
Calorie consumption 2379 calories

POLAND
Northern Europe

Official name Republic of Poland
Formation 1918 / 1945
Capital Warsaw
Population 38.5 million / 328 people per sq mile (126 people per sq km) / 66%
Total area 120,728 sq miles (312,685 sq km)
Languages Polish*
Religions Roman Catholic 93%, Other and nonreligious 5%, Orthodox Christian 2%
Ethnic mix Polish 97%, Other 2%, Silesian 1%
Government Parliamentary system
Currency Zloty = 100 groszy
Literacy rate 99%
Calorie consumption 3374 calories

PORTUGAL
Southwest Europe

Official name Republic of Portugal
Formation 1139 / 1640
Capital Lisbon
Population 10.5 million / 296 people per sq mile (114 people per sq km) / 64%
Total area 35,672 sq miles (92,391 sq km)
Languages Portuguese
Religions Roman Catholic 97%, Other 2%, Protestant 1%
Ethnic mix Portuguese 98%, African and other 2%
Government Parliamentary system
Currency Euro = 100 cents
Literacy rate 93%
Calorie consumption 3741 calories

QATAR
Southwest Asia

Official name State of Qatar
Formation 1971 / 1971
Capital Doha
Population 813,000 / 191 people per sq mile (74 people per sq km) / 93%
Total area 4416 sq miles (11,437 sq km)
Languages Arabic*
Religions Muslim (mainly Sunni) 95%, Other 5%
Ethnic mix Arab 40%, Indian 18%, Pakistani 18%, Other 14%, Iranian 10%
Government Monarchy
Currency Qatar riyal = 100 dirhams
Literacy rate 89%
Calorie consumption Not available

ROMANIA
Southest Europe

Official name Romania
Formation 1878 / 1947
Capital Bucharest
Population 21.7 million / 244 people per sq mile (94 people per sq km) / 56%
Total area 91,699 sq miles (237,500 sq km)
Languages Romanian*, Hungarian (Magyar), Romani, German
Religions Romanian Orthodox 87%, Roman Catholic 5%, Protestant 4%, Other 2%, Greek Orthodox 1%, Greek Catholic (Uniate) 1%
Ethnic mix Romanian 89%, Magyar 7%, Roma 3%, Other 1%
Government Presidential system
Currency Romanian leu = 100 bani
Literacy rate 97%
Calorie consumption 3455 calories

RUSSIAN FEDERATION
Europe / Asia

Official name Russian Federation
Formation 1480 / 1991
Capital Moscow
Population 143 million / 22 people per sq mile (8 people per sq km) / 78%
Total area 6,592,735 sq miles (17,075,200 sq km)
Languages Russian*, Tatar, Ukrainian, Chavash, various other national languages
Religions Orthodox Christian 75%, Other 15%, Muslim 10%
Ethnic mix Russian 82%, Other 10%, Tatar 4%, Ukrainian 3%, Chavash 1%
Government Presidential system
Currency Russian rouble = 100 kopeks
Literacy rate 99%
Calorie consumption 3072 calories

RWANDA
Central Africa

Official name Republic of Rwanda
Formation 1962 / 1962
Capital Kigali
Population 9 million / 934 people per sq mile (361 people per sq km) / 6%
Total area 10,169 sq miles (26,338 sq km)
Languages Kinyarwanda*, French*, Kiswahili, English
Religions Roman Catholic 56%, Traditional beliefs 25%, Muslim 10%, Protestant 9%
Ethnic mix Hutu 90%, Tutsi 9%, Other (including Twa) 1%
Government Presidential system
Currency Rwanda franc = 100 centimes
Literacy rate 64%
Calorie consumption 2084 calories

SAINT KITTS & NEVIS
West indies

Official name Federation of Saint Christopher and Nevis
Formation 1983 / 1983
Capital Basseterre
Population 38,958 / 280 people per sq mile (108 people per sq km) / 34%
Total area 101 sq miles (261 sq km)
Languages English*, English Creole
Religions Anglican 33%, Methodist 29%, Other 22%, Moravian 9%, Roman Catholic 7%
Ethnic mix Black 94%, Mixed race 3%, Other and Amerindian 2%, White 1%
Government Parliamentary system
Currency Eastern Caribbean dollar = 100 cents
Literacy rate 98%
Calorie consumption 2609 calories

SAINT LUCIA
West Indies

Official name Saint Lucia
Formation 1979 / 1979
Capital Castries
Population 166,312 / 705 people per sq mile (273 people per sq km) / 38%
Total area 239 sq miles (620 sq km)
Languages English*, French Creole
Religions Roman Catholic 90%, Other 10%
Ethnic mix Black 90%, Mulatto (mixed race) 6%, Asian 3%, White 1%
Government Parliamentary system
Currency Eastern Caribbean dollar = 100 cents
Literacy rate 90%
Calorie consumption 2988 calories

SAINT VINCENT & THE GRENADINES
West Indies

Official name Saint Vincent and the Grenadines
Formation 1979 / 1979
Capital Kingstown
Population 117,534 / 897 people per sq mile (346 people per sq km) / 55%
Total area 150 sq miles (389 sq km)
Languages English*, English Creole
Religions Anglican 47%, Methodist 28%, Roman Catholic 13%, Other 12%
Ethnic mix Black 66%, Mulatto (mixed race) 19%, Asian 6%, Other 5%, White 4%
Government Parliamentary system
Currency Eastern Caribbean dollar = 100 cents
Literacy rate 88%
Calorie consumption 2599 calories

SAMOA
Australasia & Oceania

Official name Independent State of Samoa
Formation 1962 / 1962
Capital Apia
Population 185,000 / 169 people per sq mile (65 people per sq km) / 22%
Total area 1104 sq miles (2860 sq km)
Languages Samoan*, English*
Religions Christian 99%, Other 1%
Ethnic mix Polynesian 90%, Euronesian 9%, Other 1%
Government Parliamentary system
Currency Tala = 100 sene
Literacy rate 99%
Calorie consumption 2945 calories

SAN MARINO
Southern Europe

Official name Republic of San Marino
Formation 1631 / 1631
Capital San Marino
Population 28,880 / 1203 people per sq mile (473 people per sq km) / 94%
Total area 23.6 sq miles (61 sq km)
Languages Italian*
Religions Roman Catholic 93%, Other and nonreligious 7%
Ethnic mix Sammarinese 80%, Italian 19%, Other 1%
Government Parliamentary system
Currency Euro = 100 cents
Literacy rate 99%
Calorie consumption Not available

SÃO TOMÉ & PRÍNCIPE
West Africa

Official name Democratic Republic of São Tomé and Príncipe
Formation 1975 / 1975
Capital São Tomé
Population 187,410 / 505 people per sq mile (195 people per sq km) / 47%
Total area 386 sq miles (1001 sq km)
Languages Portuguese*, Portuguese Creole
Religions Roman Catholic 84%, Other 16%
Ethnic mix Black 90%, Portuguese and Creole 10%
Government Presidential system
Currency Dobra = 100 centimos
Literacy rate 83%
Calorie consumption 2460 calories

SAUDI ARABIA
Souhwest Asia

Official name Kingdom of Saudi Arabia
Formation 1932 / 1932
Capital Riyadh; Jiddah (administrative)
Population 24.6 million / 30 people per sq mile (12 people per sq km) / 86%
Total area 756,981 sq miles (1,960,582 sq km)
Languages Arabic*
Religions Sunni Muslim 85%, Shi'a Muslim 15%
Ethnic mix Arab 90%, Afro-Asian 10%
Government Monarchy
Currency Saudi riyal = 100 halalat
Literacy rate 79%
Calorie consumption 2844 calories

SENEGAL
West Africa

Official name Republic of Senegal
Formation 1960 / 1960
Capital Dakar
Population 11.7 million / 157 people per sq mile (61 people per sq km) / 47%
Total area 75,749 sq miles (196,190 sq km)
Languages French*, Diola, Mandinka, Malinke, Pulaar, Serer, Soninke, Wolof
Religions Sunni Muslim 90%, Christian (mainly Roman Catholic) 5%, Traditional beliefs 5%
Ethnic mix Wolof 43%, Toucouleur 24%, Serer 15%, Other 11%, Diola 4%, Malinke 3%
Government Presidential system
Currency CFA franc = 100 centimes
Literacy rate 39%
Calorie consumption 2279 calories

SERBIA
Europe

Official name Republic of Serbia
Formation 2006 / 2006
Capital Belgrade
Population 9.7 million / 290 people per sq mile (112 people per sq km) / 52%
Total area 34,116 sq miles (88,361 sq km)
Languages Serbo-Croat*, Albanian, Hungarian
Religions Orthodox Christian 85%, Muslim 6%, Other 6%, Roman Catholic 3%
Ethnic mix Serb 66%, Albanian 19%, Hungarian 4%, Bosniak 2%, Other 9%
Government Parliamentary system
Currency Dinar (Serbia) = 100 para
Literacy rate 98%
Calorie consumption Not available

SEYCHELLES
Indian Ocean

Official name Republic of Seychelles
Formation 1976 / 1976
Capital Victoria
Population 81,188 / 781 people per sq mile (301 people per sq km) / 64%
Total area 176 sq miles (455 sq km)
Languages French Creole*, English, French
Religions Roman Catholic 90%, Anglican 8%, Other (including Muslim) 2%
Ethnic mix Creole 89%, Indian 5%, Other 4%, Chinese 2%
Government Presidential system
Currency Seychelles rupee = 100 cents
Literacy rate 92%
Calorie consumption 2465 calories

SIERRA LEONE
West Africa

Official name Republic of Sierra Leone
Formation 1961 / 1961
Capital Freetown
Population 5.5 million / 199 people per sq mile (77 people per sq km) / 37%
Total area 27,698 sq miles (71,740 sq km)
Languages English*, Mende, Temne, Krio
Religions Muslim 30%, Traditional beliefs 30%, Other 30%, Christian 10%
Ethnic mix Mende 35%, Temne 32%, Other 21%, Limba 8%, Kuranko 4%
Government Presidential system
Currency Leone = 100 cents
Literacy rate 30%
Calorie consumption 1936 calories

SINGAPORE
Southeast Asia

Official name Republic of Singapore
Formation 1965 / 1965
Capital Singapore
Population 4.3 million / 18220 people per sq mile (7049 people per sq km) / 100%
Total area 250 sq miles (648 sq km)
Languages English*, Malay*, Mandarin*, Tamil*
Religions Buddhist 55%, Taoist 22%, Muslim 16%, Hindu, Christian, and Sikh 7%
Ethnic mix Chinese 77%, Malay 14%, Indian 8%, Other 1%
Government Parliamentary system
Currency Singapore dollar = 100 cents
Literacy rate 93%
Calorie consumption Not available

SLOVAKIA
Central Europe

Official name Slovak Republic
Formation 1993 / 1993
Capital Bratislava
Population 5.4 million / 285 people per sq mile (110 people per sq km) / 57%
Total area 18,859 sq miles (48,845 sq km)
Languages Slovak*, Hungarian (Magyar), Czech
Religions Roman Catholic 60%, Other 18%, Atheist 10%, Protestant 8%, Orthodox Christian 4%
Ethnic mix Slovak 85%, Magyar 11%, Other 2%, Roma 1%, Czech 1%
Government Parliamentary system
Currency Slovak koruna = 100 halierov
Literacy rate 99%
Calorie consumption 2889 calories

SLOVENIA
Central Europe

Official name Republic of Slovenia
Formation 1991 / 1991
Capital Ljubljana
Population 2 million / 256 people per sq mile (99 people per sq km) / 50%
Total area 7820 sq miles (20,253 sq km)
Languages Slovene*, Serbo-Croat
Religions Roman Catholic 96%, Other 3%, Muslim 1%
Ethnic mix Slovene 83%, Other 12%, Serb 2%, Croat 2%, Bosniak 1%
Government Parliamentary system
Currency Tolar = 100 stotinov
Literacy rate 99%
Calorie consumption 3001 calories

SOLOMON ISLANDS
Australasia & Oceania

Official name Solomon Islands
Formation 1978 / 1978
Capital Honiara
Population 478,000 / 44 people per sq mile (17 people per sq km) / 20%
Total area 10,985 sq miles (28,450 sq km)
Languages English*, Melanesian Pidgin, Pidgin English
Religions Anglican 34%, Roman Catholic 19%, Methodist 11%, Seventh-day Adventist 10%, South Seas Evangelical Church 17%, Other 9%
Ethnic mix Melanesian 94%, Polynesian 4%, Other 2%
Government Parliamentary system
Currency Solomon Islands dollar = 100 cents
Literacy rate 77%
Calorie consumption 2265 calories

SOMALIA
East Africa

Official name Somalia
Formation 1960 / 1960
Capital Mogadishu
Population 8.2 million / 34 people per sq mile (13 people per sq km) / 28%
Total area 246,199 sq miles (637,657 sq km)
Languages Somali*, Arabic*, English, Italian
Religions Sunni Muslim 98%, Christian 2%
Ethnic mix Somali 85%, Other 15%
Government Transitional regime
Currency Somali shilling = 100 centesimi
Literacy rate 24%
Calorie consumption 1628 calories

SOUTH AFRICA
Southern Africa

Official name Republic of South Africa
Formation 1934 / 1994
Capital Pretoria; Cape Town; Bloemfontein
Population 47.4 million / 101 people per sq mile (39 people per sq km) / 55%
Total area 471,008 sq miles (1,219,912 sq km)
Languages English, isiZulu, isiXhosa, Afrikaans, Sepedi, Setswana, Sesotho, Xitsonga, siSwati, Tshivenda, isiNdebele
Religions Christian 68%, Traditional beliefs and animist 29%, Muslim 2%, Hindu 1%
Ethnic mix Black 79%, White 10%, Colored 9%, Asian 2%
Government Presidential system
Currency Rand = 100 cents
Literacy rate 82%
Calorie consumption 2956 calories

SOUTH KOREA
East Asia

Official name Republic of Korea
Formation 1948 / 1953
Capital Seoul
Population 47.8 million / 1254 people per sq mile (484 people per sq km) / 82%
Total area 38,023 sq miles (98,480 sq km)
Languages Korean*
Religions Mahayana Buddhist 47%, Protestant 38%, Roman Catholic 11%, Confucianist 3%, Other 1%
Ethnic mix Korean 100%
Government Presidential system
Currency South Korean won = 100 chon
Literacy rate 98%
Calorie consumption 3058 calories

SPAIN
Southeast Europe

Official name Kingdom of Spain
Formation 1492 / 1713
Capital Madrid
Population 43.1 million / 224 people per sq mile (86 people per sq km) / 78%
Total area 194,896 sq miles (504,782 sq km)
Languages Spanish*, Catalan*, Galician*, Basque*
Religions Roman Catholic 96%, Other 4%
Ethnic mix Castilian Spanish 72%, Catalan 17%, Galician 6%, Basque 2%, Other 2%, Roma 1%
Government Parliamentary system
Currency Euro = 100 cents
Literacy rate 98%
Calorie consumption 3371 calories

SRI LANKA
South Asia

Official name Democratic Socialist Republic of Sri Lanka
Formation 1948 / 1948
Capital Colombo
Population 20.7 million / 828 people per sq mile (320 people per sq km) / 24%
Total area 25,332 sq miles (65,610 sq km)
Languages Sinhala, Tamil, Sinhala-Tamil, English
Religions Buddhist 69%, Hindu 15%, Muslim 8%, Christian 8%
Ethnic mix Sinhalese 74%, Tamil 18%, Moor 7%, Burgher, Malay, and Veddha 1%
Government Mixed presidential–parliamentary system
Currency Sri Lanka rupee = 100 cents
Literacy rate 90%
Calorie consumption 2385 calories

SUDAN
East Africa

Official name Republic of the Sudan
Formation 1956 / 1956
Capital Khartoum
Population 36.2 million / 37 people per sq mile (14 people per sq km) / 36%
Total area 967,493 sq miles (2,505,810 sq km)
Languages Arabic*, Dinka, Nuer, Nubian, Beja, Zande, Bari, Fur, Shilluk, Lotuko
Religions Muslim (mainly Sunni) 70%, Traditional beliefs 20%, Christian 9%, Other 1%
Ethnic mix Other Black 52%, Arab 40%, Dinka and Beja 7%, Other 1%
Government Presidential system
Currency Sudanese pound or dinar = 100 piastres
Literacy rate 59%
Calorie consumption 2228 calories

SURINAM
South America

Official name Republic of Suriname
Formation 1975 / 1975
Capital Paramaribo
Population 499,000 / 8 people per sq mile (3 people per sq km) / 74%
Total area 63,039 sq miles (163,270 sq km)
Languages Dutch*, Sranan (Creole), Javanese, Sarnami Hindi, Saramaccan, Chinese, Carib
Religions Hindu 27%, Protestant 25%, Roman Catholic 23%, Muslim 20%, Traditional beliefs 5%
Ethnic mix Creole 34%, South Asian 34%, Javanese 18%, Black 9%, Other 5%
Government Parliamentary system
Currency Suriname dollar (guilder until 2004) = 100 cents
Literacy rate 88%
Calorie consumption 2652 calories

SWAZILAND
Southern Africa

Official name Kingdom of Swaziland
Formation 1968 / 1968
Capital Mbabane
Population 1 million / 151 people per sq mile (58 people per sq km) / 26%
Total area 6704 sq miles (17,363 sq km)
Languages English*, siSwati*, isiZulu, Xitsonga
Religions Christian 60%, Traditional beliefs 40%
Ethnic mix Swazi 97%, Other 3%
Government Monarchy
Currency Lilangeni = 100 cents
Literacy rate 79%
Calorie consumption 2322 calories

SWEDEN
Northern Europe

Official name Kingdom of Sweden
Formation 1523 / 1905
Capital Stockholm
Population 9 million / 57 people per sq mile (22 people per sq km) / 83%
Total area 173,731 sq miles (449,964 sq km)
Languages Swedish*, Finnish, Sámi
Religions Evangelical Lutheran 82%, Other 13%, Roman Catholic 2%, Muslim 2%, Orthodox Christian 1%
Ethnic mix Swedish 88%, Foreign-born or first-generation immigrant 10%, Finnish and Sámi 2%
Government Parliamentary system
Currency Swedish krona = 100 ore
Literacy rate 99%
Calorie consumption 3185 calories

SWITZERLAND
Central Europe

Official name Swiss Confederation
Formation 1291 / 1857
Capital Bern
Population 7.3 million / 475 people per sq mile (184 people per sq km) / 68%
Total area 15,942 sq miles (41,290 sq km)
Languages German*, French*, Italian*, Romansch*, Swiss-German
Religions Roman Catholic 46%, Protestant 40%, Other and nonreligious 12%, Muslim 2%
Ethnic mix German 65%, French 18%, Italian 10%, Other 6%, Romansch 1%
Government Parliamentary system
Currency Swiss franc = 100 rappen/centimes
Literacy rate 99%
Calorie consumption 3526 calories

SYRIA
Southwest Asia

Official name Syrian Arab Republic
Formation 1941 / 1967
Capital Damascus
Population 19 million / 267 people per sq mile (103 people per sq km) / 55%
Total area 71,498 sq miles (184,180 sq km)
Languages Arabic*, French, Kurdish, Armenian, Circassian, Turkic languages, Assyrian, Aramaic
Religions Sunni Muslim 74%, Other Muslim 16%, Christian 10%
Ethnic mix Arab 89%, Kurdish 6%, Other 3%, Armenian, Turkmen, and Circassian 2%
Government One-party state
Currency Syrian pound = 100 piasters
Literacy rate 83%
Calorie consumption 3038 calories

TAIWAN
East Asia

Official name Republic of China (ROC)
Formation 1949 / 1949
Capital Taipei
Population 22.9 million / 1838 people per sq mile (710 people per sq km) / 69%
Total area 13,892 sq miles (35,980 sq km)
Languages Amoy Chinese, Mandarin Chinese, Hakka Chinese
Religions Buddhist, Confucianist, and Taoist 93%, Christian 5%, Other 2%
Ethnic mix Han (pre-20th-century migration) 84%, Han (20th-century migration) 14%, Aboriginal 2%
Government Presidential system
Currency Taiwan dollar = 100 cents
Literacy rate 97%
Calorie consumption Not available

TAJIKISTAN
Central Asia

Official name Republic of Tajikistan
Formation 1991 / 1991
Capital Dushanbe
Population 6.5 million / 118 people per sq mile (45 people per sq km) / 28%
Total area 55,251 sq miles (143,100 sq km)
Languages Tajik*, Uzbek, Russian
Religions Sunni Muslim 80%, Other 15%, Shi'a Muslim 5%
Ethnic mix Tajik 62%, Uzbek 24%, Russian 8%, Other 4%, Tatar 1%, Kyrgyz 1%
Government Presidential system
Currency Somoni = 100 diram
Literacy rate 99%
Calorie consumption 1828 calories

TANZANIA
East Africa

Official name United Republic of Tanzania
Formation 1964 / 1964
Capital Dodoma
Population 38.3 million / 112 people per sq mile (43 people per sq km) / 33%
Total area 364,898 sq miles (945,087 sq km)
Languages English*, Kiswahili*, Sukuma, Chagga, Nyamwezi, Hehe, Makonde, Yao, Sandawe
Religions Muslim 33%, Christian 33%, Traditional beliefs 30%, Other 4%
Ethnic mix Native African (over 120 tribes) 99%, European and Asian 1%
Government Presidential system
Currency Tanzanian shilling = 100 cents
Literacy rate 69%
Calorie consumption 1975 calories

THAILAND
Southeastern Asia

Official name Kingdom of Thailand
Formation 1238 / 1907
Capital Bangkok
Population 64.2 million / 325 people per sq mile (126 people per sq km) / 22%
Total area 198,455 sq miles (514,000 sq km)
Languages Thai*, Chinese, Malay, Khmer, Mon, Karen, Miao
Religions Buddhist 95%, Muslim 4%, Other (including Christian) 1%
Ethnic mix Thai 83%, Chinese 12%, Malay 3%, Khmer and Other 2%
Government Parliamentary system
Currency Baht = 100 stang
Literacy rate 93%
Calorie consumption 2467 calories

TOGO
Western Africa

Official name Republic of Togo
Formation 1960 / 1960
Capital Lomé
Population 6.1 million / 290 people per sq mile (112 people per sq km) / 33%
Total area 21,924 sq miles (56,785 sq km)
Languages French*, Ewe, Kabye, Gurma
Religions Traditional beliefs 50%, Christian 35%, Muslim 15%
Ethnic mix Ewe 46%, Kabye 27%, Other African 26%, European 1%
Government Presidential system
Currency CFA franc = 100 centimes
Literacy rate 53%
Calorie consumption 2345 calories

TONGA
Australasia & Oceania

Official name Kingdom of Tonga
Formation 1970 / 1970
Capital Nuku'alofa
Population 112,422 / 404 people per sq mile (156 people per sq km) / 43%
Total area 289 sq miles (748 sq km)
Languages Tongan*, English
Religions Free Wesleyan 41%, Roman Catholic 16%, Church of Jesus Christ of Latter-day Saints 14%, Free Church of Tonga 12%, Other 17%
Ethnic mix Polynesian 99%, Other 1%
Government Monarchy
Currency Pa'anga (Tongan dollar) = 100 seniti
Literacy rate 99%
Calorie consumption Not available

TRINIDAD & TOBAGO
West Indies

Official name Republic of Trinidad and Tobago
Formation 1962 / 1962
Capital Port-of-Spain
Population 1.3 million / 656 people per sq
mile (253 people per sq km) / 74%
Total area 1980 sq miles (5128 sq km)
Languages English*, English Creole, Hindi, French,
Spanish
Religions Christian 60%, Hindu 24%,
Other and nonreligious 9%, Muslim 7%
Ethnic mix East Indian 40%, Black 40%, Mixed
race 19%, White and Chinese 1%
Government Parliamentary system
Currency Trinidad and Tobago dollar = 100 cents
Literacy rate 99%
Calorie consumption 2732 calories

TUNISIA
North Africa

Official name Republic of Tunisia
Formation 1956 / 1956
Capital Tunis
Population 10.1 million / 168 people per sq
mile (65 people per sq km) / 68%
Total area 63,169 sq miles (163,610 sq km)
Languages Arabic*, French
Religions Muslim (mainly Sunni) 98%, Christian 1%,
Jewish 1%
Ethnic mix Arab and Berber 98%, Jewish 1%,
European 1%
Government Presidential system
Currency Tunisian dinar = 1000 millimes
Literacy rate 74%
Calorie consumption 3238 calories

TURKEY
Asia / Europe

Official name Republic of Turkey
Formation 1923 / 1939
Capital Ankara
Population 73.2 million / 246 people per sq
mile (95 people per sq km) / 75%
Total area 301,382 sq miles (780,580 sq km)
Languages Turkish*, Kurdish, Arabic, Circassian,
Armenian, Greek, Georgian, Ladino
Religions Muslim (mainly Sunni) 99%, Other 1%
Ethnic mix Turkish 70%, Kurdish 20%, Other 8%,
Arab 2%
Government Parliamentary system
Currency new Turkish lira = 100 kurus
Literacy rate 88%
Calorie consumption 3357 calories

TURKMENISTAN
Central Asia

Official name Turkmenistan
Formation 1991 / 1991
Capital Ashgabat
Population 4.8 million / 25 people per sq mile (10
people per sq km) / 45%
Total area 188,455 sq miles (488,100 sq km)
Languages Turkmen*, Uzbek, Russian, Kazakh,
Tatar
Religions Sunni Muslim 87%, Orthodox
Christian 11%, Other 2%
Ethnic mix Turkmen 77%, Uzbek 9%, Russian 7%,
Other 4%, Kazakh 2%, Tatar 1%
Government One-party state
Currency Manat = 100 tenga
Literacy rate 99%
Calorie consumption 2742 calories

TUVALU
Australasia & Oceania

Official name Tuvalu
Formation 1978 / 1978
Capital Fongafale, on Funafuti Atoll
Population 11,636 / 1164 people per sq mile
(448 people per sq km) / 45%
Total area 10 sq miles (26 sq km)
Languages Tuvaluan, Kiribati, English
Religions Church of Tuvalu 97%, Other 1%,
Baha'i 1%, Seventh-day Adventist 1%
Ethnic mix Polynesian 96%, Other 4%
Government Nonparty system
Currency Australian dollar and Tuvaluan dollar
= 100 cents
Literacy rate 98%
Calorie consumption Not available

UGANDA
East Africa

Official name Republic of Uganda
Formation 1962 / 1962
Capital Kampala
Population 28.8 million / 374 people per sq
mile (144 people per sq km) / 14%
Total area 91,135 sq miles (236,040 sq km)
Languages English*, Luganda, Nkole, Chiga, Lango,
Acholi, Teso, Lugbara
Religions Roman Catholic 38%, Protestant 33%,
Traditional beliefs 13%, Muslim (mainly
Sunni) 8%, Other 8%
Ethnic mix Bantu tribes 50%, Other 45%,
Sudanese 5%
Government Nonparty system
Currency New Uganda shilling = 100 cents
Literacy rate 69%
Calorie consumption 2410 calories

UKRAINE
Eastern Europe

Official name Ukraine
Formation 1991 / 1991
Capital Kiev
Population 46.5 million / 199 people per sq
mile (77 people per sq km) / 68%
Total area 223,089 sq miles (603,700 sq km)
Languages Ukrainian*, Russian, Tatar
Religions Christian (mainly Orthodox) 95%,
Other 4%, Jewish 1%
Ethnic mix Ukrainian 73%, Russian 22%, Other 4%,
Jewish 1%
Government Presidential system
Currency Hryvna = 100 kopiykas
Literacy rate 99%
Calorie consumption 3054 calories

UNITED ARAB EMIRATES
Southwest Asia

Official name United Arab Emirates
Formation 1971 / 1972
Capital Abu Dhabi
Population 4.5 million / 139 people per sq
mile (54 people per sq km) / 86%
Total area 32,000 sq miles (82,880 sq km)
Languages Arabic*, Farsi, Indian and Pakistani
languages, English
Religions Muslim (mainly Sunni) 96%,
Christian, Hindu, and other 4%
Ethnic mix Asian 60%, Emirian 25%, Other
Arab 12%, European 3%
Government Monarchy
Currency UAE dirham = 100 fils
Literacy rate 77%
Calorie consumption 3225 calories

UNITED KINGDOM
Northwest Europe

Official name United Kingdom of Great Britain
and Northern Ireland
Formation 1707 / 1922
Capital London
Population 59.7 million / 640 people per sq
mile (247 people per sq km) / 90%
Total area 94,525 sq miles (244,820 sq km)
Languages English*, Welsh, Scottish Gaelic
Religions Anglican 45%, Roman Catholic 9%,
Presbyterian 4%, Other 42%
Ethnic mix English 30%, Scottish 9%,
West Indian, Asian, and other 5%,
Northern Irish 3%, Welsh 3%
Government Parliamentary system
Currency Pound sterling = 100 pence
Literacy rate 99%
Calorie consumption 3412 calories

UNITED STATES
North America

Official name United States of America
Formation 1776 / 1959
Capital Washington D.C.
Population 298 million / 84 people per sq
mile (33 people per sq km) / 77%
Total area 3,717,792 sq miles (9,626,091 sq km)
Languages English*, Spanish, Chinese, French,
German, Tagalog, Vietnamese, Italian, Korean,
Russian, Polish
Religions Protestant 52%, Roman Catholic 25%,
Muslim 2%, Jewish 2%, Other 19%
Ethnic mix White 69%, Hispanic 13%,
Black American/African 13%, Asian 4%,
Native American 1%
Government Presidential system
Currency US dollar = 100 cents
Literacy rate 99%
Calorie consumption 3774 calories

URUGUAY
South America

Official name Eastern Republic of Uruguay
Formation 1828 / 1828
Capital Montevideo
Population 3.5 million / 52 people per sq mile (20
people per sq km) / 91%
Total area 68,039 sq miles (176,220 sq km)
Languages Spanish*
Religions Roman Catholic 66%, Other and
nonreligious 30%, Jewish 2%, Protestant 2%
Ethnic mix White 90%, Mestizo 6%, Black 4%
Government Presidential system
Currency Uruguayan peso = 100 centésimos
Literacy rate 98%
Calorie consumption 2828 calories

UZBEKISTAN
Central Asia

Official name Republic of Uzbekistan
Formation 1991 / 1991
Capital Tashkent
Population 26.6 million / 154 people per sq
mile (59 people per sq km) / 37%
Total area 172,741 sq miles (447,400 sq km)
Languages Uzbek*, Russian, Tajik, Kazakh
Religions Sunni Muslim 88%, Orthodox
Christian 9%, Other 3%
Ethnic mix Uzbek 71%, Other 12%, Russian 8%,
Tajik 5%, Kazakh 4%
Government Presidential system
Currency Som = 100 t yin
Literacy rate 99%
Calorie consumption 2241 calories

VANUATU
Australasia & Oceania

Official name Republic of Vanuatu
Formation 1980 / 1980
Capital Port Vila
Population 211,000 / 45 people per sq mile (17
people per sq km) / 20%
Total area 4710 sq miles (12,200 sq km)
Languages Bislama* (Melanesian pidgin), English*,
French*, other indigenous languages
Religions Presbyterian 37%, Other 19%,
Anglican 15%, Roman Catholic 15%, Traditional
beliefs 8%, Seventh-day Adventist 6%
Ethnic mix Melanesian 94%, Other 3%,
Polynesian 3%
Government Parliamentary system
Currency Vatu = 100 centimes
Literacy rate 74%
Calorie consumption 2587 calories

VATICAN CITY
Southern Europe

Official name State of the Vatican City
Formation 1929 / 1929
Capital Vatican City
Population 921 / 5418 people per sq mile
(2093 people per sq km) / 100%
Total area 0.17 sq miles (0.44 sq km)
Languages Italian*, Latin*
Religions Roman Catholic 100%
Ethnic mix The current pope is German.
Cardinals are from many nationalities, but
Italians form the largest group. Most of the
resident lay persons are Italian.
Government Papal state
Currency Euro = 100 cents
Literacy rate 99%
Calorie consumption Not available

VENEZUELA
South America

Official name Bolivarian Republic of Venezuela
Formation 1830 / 1830
Capital Caracas
Population 26.7 million / 78 people per sq
mile (30 people per sq km) / 87%
Total area 352,143 sq miles (912,050 sq km)
Languages Spanish*, Amerindian languages
Religions Roman Catholic 89%, Protestant and
other 11%
Ethnic mix Mestizo 69%, White 20%, Black 9%,
Amerindian 2%
Government Presidential system
Currency Bolivar = 100 centimos
Literacy rate 93%
Calorie consumption 2336 calories

VIETNAM
Southeast Asia

Official name Socialist Republic of Vietnam
Formation 1976 / 1976
Capital Hanoi
Population 84.2 million / 670 people per sq
mile (259 people per sq km) / 20%
Total area 127,243 sq miles (329,560 sq km)
Languages Vietnamese*, Chinese, Thai, Khmer,
Muong, Nung, Miao, Yao, Jarai
Religions Buddhist 55%, Other and
nonreligious 38%, Christian (mainly Roman
Catholic) 7%
Ethnic mix Vietnamese 88%, Other 6%,
Chinese 4%, Thai 2%
Government One-party state
Currency Dông = 10 hao = 100 xu
Literacy rate 90%
Calorie consumption 2566 calories

YEMEN
Southwest Asia

Official name Republic of Yemen
Formation 1990 / 1990
Capital Sana
Population 21 million / 97 people per sq mile (37
people per sq km) / 25%
Total area 203,849 sq miles (527,970 sq km)
Languages Arabic*
Religions Sunni Muslim 55%, Shi'a Muslim 42%,
Christian, Hindu, and Jewish 3%
Ethnic mix Arab 95%, Afro-Arab 3%, Indian,
Somali, and European 2%
Government Presidential system
Currency Yemeni rial = 100 sene
Literacy rate 49%
Calorie consumption 2038 calories

ZAMBIA
Southern Africa

Official name Republic of Zambia
Formation 1964 / 1964
Capital Lusaka
Population 11.7 million / 41 people per sq mile (16
people per sq km) / 45%
Total area 290,584 sq miles (752,614 sq km)
Languages English*, Bemba, Tonga, Nyanja, Lozi,
Lala-Bisa, Nsenga
Religions Christian 63%, Traditional beliefs 36%,
Muslim and Hindu 1%
Ethnic mix Bemba 34%, Other African 26%,
Tonga 16%, Nyanja 14%, Lozi 9%, European 1%
Government Presidential system
Currency Zambian kwacha = 100 ngwee
Literacy rate 68%
Calorie consumption 1927 calories

ZIMBABWE
Southern Africa

Official name Republic of Zimbabwe
Formation 1980 / 1980
Capital Harare
Population 13 million / 87 people per sq mile (34
people per sq km) / 35%
Total area 150,803 sq miles (390,580 sq km)
Languages English*, Shona, isiNdebele
Religions Syncretic (Christian/traditional
beliefs) 50%, Christian 25%, Traditional
beliefs 24%, Other (including Muslim) 1%
Ethnic mix Shona 71%, Ndebele 16%, Other
African 11%, White 1%, Asian 1%
Government Presidential system
Currency Zimbabwe dollar = 100 cents
Literacy rate 90%
Calorie consumption 1943 calories

GLOSSARY

This glossary lists all geographical, technical and foreign language terms which appear in the text, followed by a brief definition of the term. Any acronyms used in the text are also listed in full. Terms in italics are for cross-reference and indicate that the word is separately defined in the glossary.

A

Aboriginal The original (indigenous) inhabitants of a country or continent. Especially used with reference to Australia.

Abyssal plain A broad plain found in the depths of the ocean, more than 10,000 ft (3000 m) below sea level.

Acid rain Rain, sleet, snow or mist which has absorbed waste gases from fossil-fuelled power stations and vehicle exhausts, becoming more acid. It causes severe environmental damage.

Adaptation The gradual evolution of plants and animals so that they become better suited to survive and reproduce in their *environment*.

Afforestation The planting of new forest in areas which were once forested but have been cleared.

Agribusiness A term applied to activities such as the growing of crops, rearing of animals or the manufacture of farm machinery, which eventually leads to the supply of agricultural produce at market.

Air mass A huge, homogeneous mass of air, within which horizontal patterns of temperature and *humidity* are consistent. Air masses are separated by *fronts*.

Alliance An agreement between two or more states, to work together to achieve common purposes.

Alluvial fan A large fan-shaped deposit of fine sediments deposited by a river as it emerges from a narrow, mountain valley onto a broad, open *plain*.

Alluvium Material deposited by rivers. Nowadays usually only applied to finer particles of silt and clay.

Alpine Mountain *environment*, between the *treeline* and the level of permanent snow cover.

Alpine mountains Ranges of mountains formed between 30 and 65 million years ago, by *folding*, in west and central Europe.

Amerindian A term applied to people *indigenous* to North, Central and South America.

Animal husbandry The business of rearing animals.

Antarctic circle The parallel which lies at *latitude* of 66° 32' S.

Anticline A geological *fold* that forms an arch shape, curving upwards in the rock *strata*.

Anticyclone An area of relatively high atmospheric pressure.

Aquaculture Collective term for the farming of produce derived from the sea, including fish-farming, the cultivation of shellfish, and plants such as seaweed.

Aquifer A body of rock which can absorb water. Also applied to any rock strata that have sufficient porosity to yield *groundwater* through wells or springs.

Arable Land which has been ploughed and is being used, or is suitable, for growing crops.

Archipelago A group or chain of islands.

Arctic Circle The parallel which lies at a *latitude* of 66° 32' N.

Arête A thin, jagged mountain ridge which divides two adjacent *cirques*, found in regions where *glaciation* has occurred.

Arid Dry. An area of low rainfall, where the rate of *evaporation* may be greater than that of *precipitation*. Often defined as those areas that receive less than one inch (25 mm) of rain a year. In these areas only drought-resistant plants can survive.

Artesian well A naturally occurring source of underground water, stored in an *aquifer*.

Artisanal Small-scale, manual operation, such as fishing, using little or no machinery.

ASEAN Association of Southeast Asian Nations. Established in 1967 to promote economic, social and cultural co-operation. Its members include Brunei, Indonesia, Malaysia, Philippines, Singapore and Thailand.

Aseismic A region where *earthquake* activity has ceased.

Asteroid A minor planet circling the Sun, mainly between the orbits of Mars and Jupiter.

Asthenosphere A zone of hot, partially melted rock, which underlies the *lithosphere*, within the Earth's *crust*.

Atmosphere The envelope of odourless, colourless and tasteless gases surrounding the Earth, consisting of *oxygen* (23%), *nitrogen* (75%), argon (1%), *carbon dioxide* (0.03%), as well as tiny proportions of other gases.

Atmospheric pressure The pressure created by the action of gravity on the gases surrounding the Earth.

Atoll A ring-shaped island or *coral reef* often enclosing a *lagoon* of sea water.

Avalanche The rapid movement of a mass of snow and ice down a steep slope. Similar movements of other materials are described as *rock avalanches* or *landslides* and *sand avalanches*.

B

Badlands A landscape that has been heavily eroded and dissected by rainwater, and which has little or no vegetation.

Back slope The gentler windward slope of a sand *dune* or gentler slope of a *cuesta*.

Bajos An *alluvial fan* deposited by a river at the base of mountains and hills which encircle *desert* areas.

Bar, coastal An offshore strip of sand or shingle, either above or below the water. Usually parallel to the shore but sometimes crescent-shaped or at an oblique angle.

Barchan A crescent-shaped sand *dune*, formed where wind direction is very consistent. The horns of the crescent point downwind and where there is enough sand the barchan is mobile.

Barrio A Spanish term for the shanty towns – self-built settlements – which are clustered around many South and Central American cities (*see also Favela*).

Basalt Dark, fine-grained *igneous rock*. Formed near the Earth's surface from fast-cooling *lava*.

Base level The level below which flowing water cannot erode the land.

Basement rock A mass of ancient rock often of *Pre-Cambrian age*, covered by a layer of more recent *sedimentary rocks*. Commonly associated with *shield* areas.

Beach Lake or sea shore where waves break and there is an accumulation of loose material – mud, sand, shingle or pebbles.

Bedrock Solid, consolidated and relatively unweathered rock, found on the surface of the land or just below a layer of soil or *weathered* rock.

Biodiversity The quantity of animal or plant species in a given area.

Biomass The total mass of organic matter – plants and animals – in a given area. It is usually measured in kilogrammes per square metre. Plant biomass is proportionally greater than that of animals, except in cities.

Biosphere The zone just above and below the Earth's surface, where all plants and animals live.

Blizzard A severe windstorm with snow and sleet. Visibility is often severely restricted.

Bluff The steep bank of a *meander*, formed by the erosive action of a river.

Boreal forest Tracts of mainly coniferous forest found in northern *latitudes*.

Breccia A type of rock composed of sharp fragments, cemented by a fine-grained material such as clay.

Butte An isolated, flat-topped hill with steep or vertical sides, buttes are the eroded remnants of a former land surface.

C

Caatinga Portuguese (Brazilian) term for thorny woodland growing in areas of pale granitic soils.

CACM Central American Common Market. Established in 1960 to further economic ties between its members, which are Costa Rica, El Salvador, Guatemala, Honduras and Nicaragua.

Calcite Hexagonal crystals of calcium carbonate.

Caldera A huge volcanic vent, often containing a number of smaller vents, and sometimes a crater lake.

Carbon cycle The transfer of carbon to and from the *atmosphere*. This occurs on land through *photosynthesis*. In the sea, *carbon dioxide* is absorbed, some returning to the air and some taken up into the bodies of sea creatures.

Carbon dioxide A colourless, odourless gas (CO_2) which makes up 0.03% of the *atmosphere*.

Carbonation The process whereby rocks are broken down by carbonic acid. Carbon dioxide in the air dissolves in rainwater, forming carbonic acid. *Limestone* terrain can be rapidly eaten away.

Cash crop A single crop grown specifically for export sale, rather than for local use. Typical examples include coffee, tea and citrus fruits.

Cassava A type of grain meal, used to produce tapioca. A staple crop in many parts of Africa.

Castle kopje Hill or rock outcrop, especially in southern Africa, where steep sides, and a summit composed of blocks, give a castle-like appearance.

Cataracts A series of stepped waterfalls created as a river flows over a band of hard, resistant rock.

Causeway A raised route through marshland or a body of water.

CEEAC Economic Community of Central African States. Established in 1983 to promote regional co-operation and if possible, establish a common market between 16 Central African nations.

Chemical weathering The chemical reactions leading to the decomposition of rocks. Types of chemical weathering include *carbonation*, *hydrolysis* and *oxidation*.

Chernozem A fertile soil, also known as 'black earth' consisting of a layer of dark topsoil, rich in decaying vegetation, overlying a lighter chalky layer.

Cirque Armchair-shaped basin, found in mountain regions, with a steep back, or rear, wall and a raised rock lip, often containing a lake (or *tarn*). The cirque floor has been eroded by a *glacier*, while the back wall is eroded both by the *glacier* and by *weathering*.

Climate The average weather conditions in a given area over a period of years, sometimes defined as 30 years or more.

Cold War A period of hostile relations between the USA and the Soviet Union and their allies after the Second World War.

Composite volcano Also known as a strato-volcano, the volcanic cone is composed of alternating deposits of *lava* and *pyroclastic* material.

Compound A substance made up of *elements* chemically combined in a consistent way.

Condensation The process whereby a gas changes into a liquid. For example, water vapour in the *atmosphere* condenses around tiny airborne particles to form droplets of water.

Confluence The point at which two rivers meet.

Conglomerate Rock composed of large, water-worn or rounded pebbles, held together by a natural cement.

Coniferous forest A forest type containing trees which are generally, but not necessarily, *evergreen* and have slender, needle-like leaves and which reproduce by means of seeds contained in a cone.

Continental drift The theory that the continents of today are fragments of one or more prehistoric *supercontinents* which have moved across the Earth's surface, creating ocean basins. The theory has been superseded by a more sophisticated one – *plate tectonics*.

Continental shelf An area of the continental crust, below sea level, which slopes gently. It is separated from the deep ocean by a much more steeply inclined *continental slope*.

Continental slope A steep slope running from the edge of the *continental shelf* to the ocean floor.

Conurbation A vast metropolitan area created by the expansion of towns and cities into a virtually continuous urban area.

Cool continental A rainy *climate* with warm summers [warmest month below 76°F (22°C)] and often severe winters [coldest month below 32°F (0°C)].

Copra The dried, white kernel of a coconut, from which coconut oil is extracted.

Coral reef An underwater barrier created by colonies of the coral polyp. Polyps secrete a protective skeleton of calcium carbonate, and reefs develop as live polyps build on the skeletons of dead generations.

Core The centre of the Earth, consisting of a dense mass of iron and nickel. It is thought that the outer core is molten or liquid, and that the hot inner core is solid due to extremely high pressures.

Coriolis effect A deflecting force caused by the rotation of the Earth. In the northern hemisphere a body, such as an *air mass* or ocean current, is deflected to the right, and in the southern hemisphere to the left. This prevents winds from blowing straight from areas of high to low pressure.

Coulées A US / Canadian term for a ravine formed by river *erosion*.

Craton A large block of the Earth's *crust* which has remained stable for a long period of *geological time*. It is made up of ancient *shield* rocks.

Cretaceous A period of *geological time* beginning about 145 million years ago and lasting until about 65 million years ago.

Crevasse A deep crack in a *glacier*.

Crust The hard, thin outer shell of the Earth. The crust floats on the *mantle*, which is softer and more dense. Under the oceans (oceanic crust) the crust is 3.7–6.8 miles (6–11 km) thick. Continental crust averages 18–24 miles (30–40 km).

Crystalline rock Rocks formed when molten *magma* crystallizes (*igneous rocks*) or when heat or pressure cause re-crystallization (*metamorphic rocks*). Crystalline rocks are distinct from *sedimentary rocks*.

Cuesta A hill which rises into a steep slope on one side but has a gentler gradient on its other slope.

Cyclone An area of low *atmospheric pressure*, occurring where the air is warm and relatively low in density, causing low level winds to spiral. *Hurricanes* and *typhoons* are tropical cyclones.

D

De facto
1 Government or other activity that takes place, or exists in actuality if not by right.
2 A border, which exists in practice, but which is not officially recognized by all the countries it adjoins.

Deciduous forest A forest of trees which shed their leaves annually at a particular time or season. In *temperate* climates the fall of leaves occurs in the Autumn. Some *coniferous* trees, such as the larch, are deciduous. Deciduous vegetation contrasts with *evergreen*, which keeps its leaves for more than a year.

Defoliant Chemical spray used to remove foliage (leaves) from trees.

Deforestation The act of cutting down and clearing large areas of forest for human activities, such as agricultural land or urban development.

Delta Low-lying, fan-shaped area at a river mouth, formed by the *deposition* of successive layers of *sediment*. Slowing as it enters the sea, a river deposits sediment and may, as a result, split into numerous smaller channels, known as *distributaries*.

Denudation The combined effect of *weathering*, *erosion* and *mass movement*, which, over long periods, exposes underlying rocks.

Deposition The laying down of material that has accumulated:
(1) after being *eroded* and then transported by physical forces such as wind, ice or water;
(2) as organic remains, such as coal and coral;
(3) as the result of *evaporation* and chemical *precipitation*.

Depression
1 In climatic terms it is a large low pressure system.
2 A complex *fold*, producing a large valley, which incorporates both a *syncline* and an *anticline*.

Desert An *arid* region of low rainfall, with little vegetation or animal life, which is adapted to the dry conditions. The term is now applied not only to hot tropical and subtropical regions, but to arid areas of the continental interiors and to the ice deserts of the *Arctic* and *Antarctic*.

Desertification The gradual extension of *desert* conditions in *arid* or *semi-arid* regions, as a result of climatic change or human activity, such as over-grazing and *deforestation*.

Despot A ruler with absolute power. Despots are often associated with oppressive regimes.

Detritus Piles of rock deposited by an erosive agent such as a river or *glacier*.

Distributary A minor branch of a river, which does not rejoin the main stream, common at *deltas*.

Diurnal Daily, something that occurs each day. Diurnal temperature refers to the variation in temperature over the course of a full day and night.

Divide A US term describing the area of high ground separating two *drainage basins*.

Donga A steep-sided *gully*, resulting from *erosion* by a river or by floods.

Dormant A term used to describe a *volcano* which is not currently erupting. They differ from extinct volcanoes as dormant volcanoes are still considered likely to erupt in the future.

Drainage basin The area drained by a single river system, its boundary is marked by a *watershed* or *divide*.

Drought A long period of continuously low rainfall.

Drumlin A long, streamlined hillock composed of material deposited by a *glacier*. They often occur in groups known as swarms.

Dune A mound or ridge of sand, shaped, and often moved, by the wind. They are found in hot *deserts* and on low-lying coasts where onshore winds blow across sandy beaches.

Dyke A wall constructed in low-lying areas to contain floodwaters or protect from high tides.

E

Earthflow The rapid movement of soil and other loose surface material down a slope, when saturated by water. Similar to a mudflow but not as fast-flowing, due to a lower percentage of water.

Earthquake Sudden movements of the Earth's *crust*, causing the ground to shake. Frequently occurring at *tectonic plate* margins. The shock, or series of shocks, spreads out from an *epicentre*.

EC The European Community (*see* EU).

Ecosystem A system of living organisms – plants and animals – interacting with their *environment*.

ECOWAS Economic Community of West African States. Established in 1975, it incorporates 16 West African states and aims to promote closer regional and economic co-operation.

Element
1 A constituent of the *climate* – *precipitation*, *humidity*, temperature, *atmospheric pressure* or wind.
2 A substance that cannot be separated into simpler substances by chemical means.

El Niño A climatic phenomenon, the El Niño effect occurs about 14 times each century and leads to major shifts in global air circulation. It is associated with unusually warm currents off the coasts of Peru, Ecuador and Chile. The anomaly can last for up to two years.

Environment The conditions created by the surroundings (both natural and artificial) within which an organism lives. In human geography the word includes the surrounding economic, cultural and social conditions.

Eon (aeon) Traditionally a long, but indefinite, period of *geological time*.

Ephemeral A non-permanent feature, often used in connection with seasonal rivers or lakes in dry areas.

Epicentre The point on the Earth's surface directly above the underground origin – or focus – of an *earthquake*.

Equator The line of *latitude* which lies equidistant between the North and South Poles.

Erg An extensive area of sand *dunes*, particularly in the Sahara Desert.

Erosion The processes which wear away the surface of the land. *Glaciers*, wind, rivers, waves and currents all carry debris which causes *erosion*. Some definitions also include *mass movement* due to gravity as an agent of erosion.

Escarpment A steep slope at the margin of a level, upland surface. In a landscape created by *folding*, escarpments (or scarps) frequently lie behind a more gentle backward slope.

Esker A narrow, winding ridge of sand and gravel deposited by streams of water flowing beneath or at the edge of a *glacier*.

Erratic A rock transported by a *glacier* and deposited some distance from its place of origin.

Eustacy A world-wide fall or rise in ocean levels.

EU The European Union. Established in 1965, it was formerly known as the EEC (European Economic Community) and then the EC (European Community). Its members are Austria, Belgium, Denmark, Finland, France, Germany, Greece, Ireland, Italy, Luxembourg, Netherlands, Portugal, Spain, Sweden and UK. It seeks to establish an integrated European common market and eventual federation.

Evaporation The process whereby a liquid or solid is turned into a gas or vapour. Also refers to the diffusion of water vapour into the *atmosphere* from exposed water surfaces such as lakes and seas.

Evapotranspiration The loss of moisture from the Earth's surface through a combination of *evaporation*, and *transpiration* from the leaves of plants.

Evergreen Plants with long-lasting leaves, which are not shed annually or seasonally.

Exfoliation A kind of *weathering* whereby scale-like flakes of rock are peeled or broken off by the development of salt crystals in water within the rocks. *Groundwater*, which contains dissolved salts, seeps to the surface and evaporates, precipitating a film of salt crystals, which expands causing fine cracks. As these grow, flakes of rock break off.

Extrusive rock *Igneous* rock formed when molten material (*magma*) pours forth at the Earth's surface and cools rapidly. It usually has a glassy texture.

F

Factionalism The actions of one or more minority political group acting against the interests of the majority government.

Fault A fracture or crack in rock, where strains (*tectonic* movement) have caused blocks to move, vertically or laterally, relative to each other.

Fauna Collective name for the animals of a particular period of time, or region.

Favela Brazilian term for the shanty towns or self-built, temporary dwellings which have grown up around the edge of many South and Central American cities.

Ferrel cell A component in the global pattern of air circulation, which rises in the colder *latitudes* (60° N and S) and descends in warmer *latitudes* (30° N and S). The Ferrel cell forms part of the world's three-cell air circulation pattern, with the *Hadley* and Polar cells.

Fissure A deep crack in a rock or a *glacier*.

Fjord A deep, narrow inlet, created when the sea inundates the *U-shaped valley* created by a *glacier*.

Flash flood A sudden, short-lived rise in the water level of a river or stream, or surge of water down a dry river channel, or *wadi*, caused by heavy rainfall.

Flax A plant used to make linen.

Flood plain The broad, flat part of a river valley, adjacent to the river itself, formed by *sediment* deposited during flooding.

Flora The collective name for the plants of a particular period of time or region.

Flow The movement of a river within its banks, particularly in terms of the speed and volume of water.

Fold A bend in the rock *strata* of the Earth's *crust*, resulting from compression.

Fossil The remains, or traces, of a dead organism preserved in the Earth's *crust*.

Fossil dune A *dune* formed in a once-*arid* region which is now wetter. *Dunes* normally move with the wind, but in these cases vegetation makes them stable.

Fossil fuel Fuel – coal, natural gas or oil – composed of the fossilized remains of plants and animals.

Front The boundary between two *air masses*, which contrast sharply in temperature and *humidity*.

Frontal depression An area of low pressure caused by rising warm air. They are generally 600–1200 miles (1000–2000 km) in diameter. Within *depressions* there are both warm and cold fronts.

Frost shattering A form of *weathering* where water freezes in cracks, causing expansion. As temperatures fluctuate and the ice melts and refreezes, it eventually causes the rocks to shatter and fragments of rock to break off.

G

Gaucho South American term for a stock herder or cowboy who works on the grassy *plains* of Paraguay, Uruguay and Argentina.

Geological time-scale The chronology of the Earth's history as revealed in its rocks. Geological time is divided into a number of periods: *eon*, era, period, epoch, age and chron (the shortest). These units are not of uniform length.

Geosyncline A concave fold (*syncline*) or large depression in the Earth's *crust*, extending hundreds of kilometres. This basin contains a deep layer of sediment, especially at its centre, from the land masses around it.

Geothermal energy Heat derived from hot rocks within the Earth's *crust* and resulting in hot springs, steam or hot rocks at the surface. The energy is generated by rock movements, and from the breakdown of radioactive elements occurring under intense pressure.

GDP Gross Domestic Product. The total value of goods and services produced by a country excluding income from foreign countries.

Geyser A jet of steam and hot water that intermittently erupts from vents in the ground in areas that are, or were, *volcanic*. Some geysers occasionally reach heights of 196 ft (60 m).

Ghetto An area of a city or region occupied by an overwhelming majority of people from one racial or religious group, who may be subject to persecution or containment.

Glaciation The growth of *glaciers* and *ice sheets*, and their impact on the landscape.

Glacier A body of ice moving downslope under the influence of gravity and consisting of compacted and frozen snow. A glacier is distinct from an *ice sheet*, which is wider and less confined by features of the landscape.

Glacio-eustacy A world-wide change in the level of the oceans, caused when the formation of *ice sheets* takes up water or when their melting returns water to the ocean. The formation of ice sheets in the *Pleistocene* epoch, for example, caused sea level to drop by about 320 ft (100 m).

Glaciofluvial To do with glacial *meltwater*, the landforms it creates and its processes; *erosion*, transportation and *deposition*. Glaciofluvial effects are more powerful and rapid where they occur within or beneath the *glacier*, rather than beyond its edge.

Glacis A gentle slope or *pediment*.

Global warming An increase in the average temperature of the Earth. At present the *greenhouse effect* is thought to contribute to this.

GNP Gross National Product. The total value of goods and services produced by a country.

Gondwanaland The *supercontinent* thought to have existed over 200 million years ago in the southern hemisphere. Gondwanaland is believed to have comprised today's Africa, Madagascar, Australia, parts of South America, *Antarctica* and the Indian subcontinent.

Graben A block of rock let down between two parallel *faults*. Where the graben occurs within a valley, the structure is known as a *rift valley*.

Grease ice Slicks of ice which form in *Antarctic* seas, when ice crystals are bonded together by wind and wave action.

Greenhouse effect A change in the temperature of the *atmosphere*. Short-wave solar radiation travels through the *atmosphere* unimpeded to the Earth's surface, whereas outgoing, long-wave terrestrial radiation is absorbed by materials that re-radiate it back to the Earth. Radiation trapped in this way, by water vapour, carbon dioxide and other 'greenhouse gases', keeps the Earth warm. As more *carbon dioxide* is released into the atmosphere by the burning of *fossil fuels*, the greenhouse effect may cause a global increase in temperature.

Groundwater Water that has seeped into the pores, cavities and cracks of rocks or into soil and water held in an *aquifer*.

Gully A deep, narrow channel eroded in the landscape by *ephemeral* streams.

Guyot A small, flat-topped submarine mountain, formed as a result of subsidence which occurs during *sea-floor spreading*.

Gypsum A soft mineral *compound* (hydrated calcium sulphate), used as the basis of many forms of plaster, including plaster of Paris.

H

Hadley cell A large-scale component in the global pattern of air circulation. Warm air rises over the *Equator* and blows at high altitude towards the poles, sinking in subtropical regions (30° N and 30° S) and creating high pressure. The air then flows at the surface towards the *Equator* in the form of trade winds. There is one cell in each hemisphere. Named after G Hadley, who published his theory in 1735.

Hamada An Arabic word for a plateau of bare rock in a *desert*.

Hanging valley A tributary valley which ends suddenly, high above the bed of the main valley. The effect is found where the main valley has been more deeply eroded by a *glacier*, than has the tributary valley. A stream in a hanging valley will descend to the floor of the main valley as a waterfall or *cataract*.

Headwards The action of a river eroding back upstream, as opposed to the normal process of downstream *erosion*. Headwards erosion is often associated with *gullying*.

Hoodos Pinnacles of rock which have been worn away by *weathering* in *semi-arid* regions.

Horst A block of the Earth's *crust* which has been left upstanding by the sinking of adjoining blocks along fault lines.

Hot spot A region of the Earth's *crust* where high thermal activity occurs, often leading to volcanic eruptions. Hot spots often occur far from plate boundaries, but their movement is associated with *plate tectonics*.

Humid equatorial Rainy *climate* with no winter, where the coolest month is generally above 64°F (18°C).

Humidity The relative amount of moisture held in the Earth's *atmosphere*.

Hurricane
1 A tropical *cyclone* occurring in the Caribbean and western North Atlantic.
2 A wind of more than 65 knots (75 kmph).

Hydro-electric power Energy produced by harnessing the rapid movement of water down steep mountain slopes to drive turbines to generate electricity.

Hydrolysis The chemical breakdown of rocks in reaction with water, forming new compounds.

I

Ice Age A period in the Earth's history when surface temperatures in the temperate *latitudes* were much lower and *ice sheets* expanded considerably. There have been *ice ages* from *Pre-Cambrian* times onwards. The most recent began two million years ago and ended 10,000 years ago.

Ice cap A permanent dome of ice in highland areas. The term ice cap is often seen as distinct from *ice sheet*, which denotes a much wider covering of ice; and is also used refer to the very extensive polar and Greenland ice caps.

Ice floe A large, flat mass of ice floating free on the ocean surface. It is usually formed after the break-up of winter ice by heavy storms.

Ice sheet A continuous, very thick layer of ice and snow. The term is usually used of ice masses which are continental in extent.

Ice shelf A floating mass of ice attached to the edge of a coast. The seaward edge is usually a sheer cliff up to 100 ft (30 m) high.

Ice wedge Massive blocks of ice up to 6.5 ft (2 m) wide at the top and extending 32 ft (10 m) deep. They are found in cracks in *polygonally-patterned* ground in *periglacial* regions.

Iceberg A large mass of ice in a lake or a sea, which has broken off from a floating *ice sheet* (an *ice shelf*) or from a *glacier*.

Igneous rock Rock formed when molten material, *magma*, from the hot, lower layers of the Earth's *crust*, cools, solidifies and crystallizes, either within the Earth's *crust* (*intrusive*) or on the surface (*extrusive*).

IMF International Monetary Fund. Established in 1944 as a UN agency, it contains 182 members around the world and is concerned with world monetary stability and economic development.

Incised meander A *meander* where the river, following its original course, cuts deeply into *bedrock*. This may occur when a mature, meandering river begins to erode its bed much more vigorously after the surrounding land has been uplifted.

Indigenous People, plants or animals native to a particular region.

Infrastructure The communications and services – roads, railways and telecommunications – necessary for the functioning of a country or region.

Inselberg An isolated, steep-sided hill, rising from a low *plain* in *semi-arid* and *savannah* landscapes. Inselbergs are usually composed of a rock, such as granite, which resists *erosion*.

Interglacial A period of global *climate*, between two *ice ages*, when temperatures rise and *ice sheets* and *glaciers* retreat.

Intraplate volcano A *volcano* which lies in the centre of one of the Earth's *tectonic plates*, rather than as is more common, at its edge. They are thought to have been formed by a *hot spot*.

Intrusion (intrusive igneous rock) Rock formed when molten material, *magma*, penetrates existing rocks below the Earth's surface before cooling and solidifying. These rocks cool more slowly than extrusive rock and therefore tend to have coarser grains.

Irrigation The artificial supply of agricultural water to dry areas, often involving the creation of canals and the diversion of natural watercourses.

Island arc A curved chain of islands. Typically, such an arc fringes an ocean trench, formed at the margin between two *tectonic plates*. As one plate overrides another, *earthquakes* and volcanic activity are common and the islands themselves are often volcanic cones.

Isostasy The state of equilibrium which the Earth's *crust* maintains as its lighter and heavier parts float on the denser underlying mantle.

Isthmus A narrow strip of land connecting two larger landmasses or islands.

J

Jet stream A narrow belt of westerly winds in the *troposphere*, at altitudes above 39,000 ft (12,000 m). Jet streams tend to blow more strongly in winter and include: the subtropical jet stream; the *polar* front jet stream in mid-*latitudes*; the *Arctic* jet stream; and the polar-night jet stream.

Joint A crack in a rock, formed where blocks of rock have not shifted relative to each other, as is the case with a *fault*. Joints are created by *folding*; by shrinkage in *igneous rock* as it cools or *sedimentary rock* as it dries out; and by the release of pressure in a rock mass when overlying materials are removed by *erosion*.

Jute A plant fibre used to make coarse ropes, sacks and matting.

K

Kame A mound of stratified sand and gravel with steep sides, deposited in a *crevasse* by *meltwater* running over a *glacier*. When the ice retreats, this forms an undulating terrain of hummocks.

Karst A barren *limestone* landscape created by carbonic acid in streams and rainwater, in areas where *limestone* is close to the surface. Typical features include caverns, tower-like hills, *sinkholes* and flat limestone pavements.

Kettle hole A round hollow formed in a glacial deposit by a detached block of glacial ice, which later melted. They can fill with water to form kettle-lakes.

L

Lagoon A shallow stretch of coastal salt-water behind a partial barrier such as a sandbank or *coral reef*. Lagoon is also used to describe the water encircled by an *atoll*.

LAIA Latin American Integration Association. Established in 1980, its members are Argentina, Bolivia, Brazil, Chile, Colombia, Ecuador, Mexico, Paraguay, Peru, Uruguay and Venezuela. It aims to promote economic co-operation between member states.

Landslide The sudden downslope movement of a mass of rock or earth on a slope, caused either by heavy rain; the impact of waves; an *earthquake* or human activity.

Laterite A hard red deposit left by *chemical weathering* in tropical conditions, and consisting mainly of oxides of iron and aluminium.

Latitude The angular distance from the *Equator*, to a given point on the Earth's surface. Imaginary lines of *latitude* running parallel to the Equator encircle the Earth, and are measured in degrees north or south of the Equator. The Equator is 0°, the poles 90° South and North respectively. Also called parallels.

Laurasia In the theory of *continental drift*, the northern part of the great *supercontinent* of *Pangaea*. Laurasia is said to consist of N America, Greenland and all of Eurasia north of the Indian subcontinent.

Lava The molten rock, *magma*, which erupts onto the Earth's surface through a *volcano*, or through a *fault* or crack in the Earth's *crust*. Lava refers to the rock both in its molten and in its later, solidified form.

Leaching The process whereby water dissolves minerals and moves them down through layers of soil or rock.

Levée A raised bank alongside the channel of a river. Levées are either human-made or formed in times of flood when the river overflows its channel, slows and deposits much of its *sediment* load.

Lichen An organism which is the symbiotic product of an algae and a fungus. Lichens form in tight crusts on stones and trees, and are resistant to extreme cold. They are often found in tundra regions.

Lignite Low-grade coal, also known as brown coal. Found in large deposits in eastern Europe.

Limestone A porous *sedimentary* rock formed from carbonate materials.

Lingua franca The language adopted as the common language between speakers whose native languages are different. This is common in former colonial states.

Lithosphere The rigid upper layer of the Earth, comprising the *crust* and the upper part of the *mantle*.

Llanos Vast grassland *plains* of northern South America.

Loess Fine-grained, yellow deposits of unstratified silts and sands. Loess is believed to be wind-carried *sediment* created in the last *Ice Age*. Some deposits may later have been redistributed by rivers. Loess-derived soils are of high quality, fertile and easy to work.

Longitude A division of the Earth which pinpoints how far east or west a given place is from the Prime Meridian (0°) which runs through the Royal Observatory at Greenwich, England (UK). Imaginary lines of longitude are drawn around the world from pole to pole. The world is divided into 360 degrees.

Longshore drift The transport of sand and silt along the coast, carried by waves hitting the beach at an angle.

M

Magma Underground, molten rock, which is very hot and highly charged with gas. It is generated at great pressure, at depths 10 miles (16 km) or more below the Earth's surface. It can issue as *lava* at the Earth's surface or, more often, solidify below the surface as *intrusive igneous rock*.

Mantle The layer of the Earth between the *crust* and the *core*. It is about 1800 miles (2900 km) thick. The uppermost layer of the mantle is the soft, 125 mile (200 km) thick *asthenosphere* on which the more rigid *lithosphere* floats.

Maquiladoras Factories on the Mexico side of the Mexico/US border, which are allowed to import raw materials and components duty-free and use low-cost labour to assemble the goods, finally exporting them for sale in the US.

Market gardening The intensive growing of fruit and vegetables close to large local markets.

Mass movement Downslope movement of weathered materials such as rock, often helped by rainfall or glacial *meltwater*. Mass movement may be a gradual process or rapid, as in a *landslide* or rockfall.

Massif A single very large mountain or an area of mountains with uniform characteristics and clearly-defined boundaries.

Meander A loop-like bend in a river, which is found typically in the lower, mature reaches of a river but can form wherever the valley is wide and the slope gentle.

Mediterranean climate A temperate *climate* of hot, dry summers and warm, damp winters. This is typical of the western fringes of the world's continents in the warm temperate regions between *latitudes* of 30° and 40° (north and south).

Meltwater Water resulting from the melting of a *glacier* or *ice sheet*.

Mesa A broad, flat-topped hill, characteristic of *arid* regions.

Mesosphere A layer of the Earth's *atmosphere*, between the *stratosphere* and the *thermosphere*. Extending from about 25–50 miles (40–80 km) above the surface of the Earth.

Mestizo A person of mixed *Amerindian* and European origin.

Metallurgy The refining and working of metals.

Metamorphic rocks Rocks which have been altered from their original form, in terms of texture, composition and structure by intense heat, pressure, or by the introduction of new chemical substances – or a combination of more than one of these.

Meteor A body of rock, metal or other material, which travels through space at great speeds. Meteors are visible as they enter the Earth's *atmosphere* as shooting stars and fireballs.

Meteorite The remains of a *meteor* that has fallen to Earth.

Meteoroid A *meteor* which is still travelling in space, outside the Earth's *atmosphere*.

Mezzogiorno A term applied to the southern portion of Italy.

Milankovitch hypothesis A theory suggesting that there are a series of cycles which slightly alter the Earth's position when rotating about the Sun. The cycles identified all affect the amount of *radiation* the Earth receives at different *latitudes*. The theory is seen as a key factor in the cause of *ice ages*.

Millet A grain-crop, forming part of the staple diet in much of Africa.

Mistral A strong, dry, cold northerly or north-westerly wind, which blows from the Massif Central of France to the Mediterranean Sea. It is common in winter and its cold blasts can cause crop damage in the Rhône Delta, in France.

Mohorovicic discontinuity (Moho) The structural divide at the margin between the Earth's *crust* and the *mantle*. On average it is 20 miles (35 km) below the continents and 6 miles (10 km) below the oceans. The different densities of the *crust* and the mantle cause *earthquake* waves to accelerate at this point.

Monarchy A form of government in which the head of state is a single hereditary monarch. The monarch may be a mere figurehead, or may retain significant authority.

Monsoon A wind which changes direction bi-annually. The change is caused by the reversal of pressure over landmasses and the adjacent oceans. Because the inflowing moist winds bring rain, the term monsoon is also used to refer to the rains themselves. The term is derived from and most commonly refers to the seasonal winds of south and east Asia.

Montaña Mountain areas along the west coast of South America.

Moraine Debris, transported and deposited by a *glacier* or *ice sheet* in unstratified, mixed, piles of rock, boulders, pebbles and clay.

Mountain-building The formation of *fold* mountains by tectonic activity. Also known as orogeny, mountain-building often occurs on the margin where two *tectonic plates* collide. The periods when most mountain-building occurred are known as orogenic phases and lasted many millions of years.

Mudflow An *avalanche* of mud which occurs when a mass of soil is drenched by rain or melting snow. It is a type of *mass movement*, faster than an *earthflow* because it is lubricated by water.

N

Nappe A mass of rocks which has been overfolded by repeated thrust *faulting*.

NAFTA The North American Free Trade Association. Established in 1994 between Canada, Mexico and the US to set up a free-trade zone.

NASA The North American Space Agency. It is a government body, established in 1958 to develop manned and unmanned space programmes.

NATO The North Atlantic Treaty Organization. Established in 1949 to promote mutual defence and co-operation between its members, which are Belgium, Canada, Czech Republic, Denmark, France, Germany, Greece, Iceland, Italy, Luxembourg, the Netherlands, Norway, Portugal, Poland, Spain, Turkey, UK, and US.

Nitrogen The odourless, colourless gas which makes up 78% of the atmosphere. Within the soil, it is a vital nutrient for plants.

Nomads (nomadic) Wandering communities who move around in search of suitable pasture for their herds of animals.

Nuclear fusion A technique used to create a new nucleus by the merging of two lighter ones, resulting in the release of large quantities of energy.

O

Oasis A fertile area in the midst of a *desert*, usually watered by an underground *aquifer*.

Oceanic ridge A mid-ocean ridge formed, according to the theory of *plate tectonics*, when plates drift apart and hot *magma* pours through to form new oceanic *crust*.

Oligarchy The government of a state by a small, exclusive group of people – such as an elite class or a family group.

Onion-skin weathering The *weathering* away or *exfoliation* of a rock or outcrop by the peeling off of surface layers.

Oriente A flatter region lying to the east of the Andes in South America.

Outwash plain *Glaciofluvial* material (typically clay, sand and gravel) carried beyond an ice sheet by *meltwater* streams, forming a broad, flat deposit.

Oxbow lake A crescent-shaped lake formed on a river *flood plain* when a river erodes the outside bend of a *meander*, making the neck of the *meander* narrower until the river cuts across the neck. The meander is cut off and is dammed off with sediment, creating an oxbow lake. Also known as a cut-off or mortlake.

Oxidation A form of *chemical weathering* where *oxygen* dissolved in water reacts with minerals in rocks – particularly iron – to form oxides. Oxidation causes brown or yellow staining on rocks, and eventually leads to the break down of the rock.

Oxygen A colourless, odourless gas which is one of the main constituents of the Earth's *atmosphere* and is essential to life on Earth.

Ozone layer A layer of enriched *oxygen* (O_3) within the stratosphere, mostly between 18–50 miles (30–80 km) above the Earth's surface. It is vital to the existence of life on Earth because it absorbs harmful shortwave ultraviolet radiation, while allowing beneficial longer wave ultraviolet radiation to penetrate to the Earth's surface.

P

Pacific Rim The name given to the economically-dynamic countries bordering the Pacific Ocean.

Pack ice Ice masses more than 10 ft (3 m) thick which form on the sea surface and are not attached to a landmass.

Pancake ice Thin discs of ice, up to 8 ft (2.4 m) wide which form when slicks of *grease ice* are tossed together by winds and stormy seas.

Pangaea In the theory of continental drift, Pangaea is the original great land mass which, about 190 million years ago, began to split into Gondwanaland in the south and Laurasia in the north, separated by the Tethys Sea.

Pastoralism Grazing of livestock– usually sheep, goats or cattle. Pastoralists in many drier areas have traditionally been *nomadic*.

Parallel *see Latitude.*

Peat Ancient, partially-decomposed vegetation found in wet, boggy conditions where there is little *oxygen*. It is the first stage in the development of coal and is often dried for use as fuel. It is also used to improve soil quality.

Pediment A gently-sloping ramp of *bedrock* below a steeper slope, often found at mountain edges in *desert* areas, but also in other climatic zones. Pediments may include depositional elements such as *alluvial fans*.

Peninsula A thin strip of land surrounded on three of its sides by water. Large examples include Florida and Korea.

Per capita Latin term meaning 'for each person'.

Periglacial Regions on the edges of *ice sheets* or *glaciers* or, more commonly, cold regions experiencing intense frost action, *permafrost* or both. Periglacial climates bring long, freezing winters and short, mild summers.

Permafrost Permanently frozen ground, typical of *Arctic* regions. Although a layer of soil above the permafrost melts in summer, the melted water does not drain through the permafrost.

Permeable rocks Rocks through which water can seep, because they are either porous or cracked.

Pharmaceuticals The manufacture of medicinal drugs.

Phreatic eruption A volcanic eruption which occurs when *lava* combines with *groundwater*, superheating the water and causing a sudden emission of steam at the surface.

Physical weathering (mechanical weathering) The breakdown of rocks by physical, as opposed to chemical, processes. Examples include: changes in pressure or temperature; the effect of windblown sand; the pressure of growing salt crystals in cracks within rock; and the expansion and contraction of water within rock as it freezes and thaws.

Pingo A dome of earth with a core of ice, found in *tundra* regions. Pingos are formed either when *groundwater* freezes and expands, pushing up the land surface, or when trapped, freezing water in a lake expands and pushes up lake *sediments* to form the pingo dome.

Placer A belt of mineral-bearing rock *strata* lying at or close to the Earth's surface, from which minerals can be easily extracted.

Plain A flat, level region of land, often relatively low-lying.

Plateau A highland tract of flat land.

Plate *see Tectonic plates.*

Plate tectonics The study of *tectonic plates*, which helps to explain *continental drift*, mountain formation and volcanic activity. The movement of tectonic plates may be explained by the currents of rock rising and falling from within the Earth's *mantle*, as it heats up and then cools. The boundaries of the plates are known as plate margins and most mountains, *earthquakes* and *volcanoes* occur at these margins. Constructive margins are moving apart; destructive margins are crunching together and conservative margins are sliding past one another.

Pleistocene A period of *geological time* spanning from about 5.2 million years ago to 1.6 million years ago.

Plutonic rock *Igneous* rocks found deep below the surface. They are coarse-grained because they cooled and solidified slowly.

Polar The zones within the *Arctic* and *Antarctic* circles.

Polje A long, broad *depression* found in *karst* (*limestone*) regions.

Polygonal patterning Typical ground patterning, found in areas where the soil is subject to severe frost action, often in *periglacial* regions.

Porosity A measure of how much water can be held within a rock or a soil. Porosity is measured as the percentage of holes or pores in a material, compared to its total volume. For example, the porosity of slate is less than 1%, whereas that of gravel is 25–35%.

Prairies Originally a French word for grassy *plains* with few or no trees.

Pre-Cambrian The earliest period of *geological time* dating from over 570 million years ago.

Precipitation The fall of moisture from the *atmosphere* onto the surface of the Earth, whether as dew, hail, rain, sleet or snow.

Pyramidal peak A steep, isolated mountain summit, formed when the back walls of three or more *cirques* are cut back and move towards each other. The cliffs around such a horned peak, or horn, are divided by sharp *arêtes*. The Matterhorn in the Swiss Alps is an example.

Pyroclasts Fragments of rock ejected during volcanic eruptions.

Q

Quaternary The current period of *geological time*, which started about 1.6 million years ago.

R

Radiation The emission of energy in the form of particles or waves. Radiation from the sun includes heat, light, ultraviolet rays, gamma rays and X-rays. Only some of the solar energy radiated into space reaches the Earth.

Rainforest Dense forests in tropical zones with high rainfall, temperature and *humidity*. Strictly, the term applies to the equatorial rainforest in tropical lowlands with constant rainfall and no seasonal change. The Congo and Amazon basins are examples. The term is applied more loosely to lush forest in other climates. Within rainforests organic life is dense and varied: at least 40% of all plant and animal species are found here and there may be as many as 100 tree species per hectare.

Rainshadow An area which experiences low rainfall, because of its position on the leeward side of a mountain range.

Reg A large area of stony *desert*, where tightly-packed gravel lies on top of clayey sand. A reg is formed where the wind blows away the finer sand.

Remote-sensing Method of obtaining information about the *environment* using unmanned equipment, such as a satellite, which relays the information to a point where it is collected and used.

Resistance The capacity of a rock to resist *denudation*, by processes such as *weathering* and *erosion*.

Ria A flooded *V-shaped river valley* or estuary, flooded by a rise in sea level (*eustacy*) or sinking land. It is shorter than a *fjord* and gets deeper as it meets the sea.

Rift valley A long, narrow depression in the Earth's *crust*, formed by the sinking of rocks between two *faults*.

River channel The trough which contains a river and is moulded by the flow of water within it.

Roche moutonée A rock found in a glaciated valley. The side facing the flow of the *glacier* has been smoothed and rounded, while the other side has been left more rugged because the *glacier*, as it flows over it, has plucked out frozen fragments and carried them away.

Runoff Water draining from a land surface by flowing across it.

S

Sabkha The floor of an isolated *depression* which occurs in an *arid environment* – usually covered by salt deposits and devoid of vegetation.

SADC Southern African Development Community. Established in 1992 to promote economic integration between its member states, which are Angola, Botswana, Lesotho, Malawi, Mauritius, Mozambique, Namibia, South Africa, Swaziland, Tanzania, Zambia and Zimbabwe.

Salt plug A rounded hill produced by the upward coming of rock *strata* caused by the movement of salt or other evaporite deposits under intense pressure.

Sastrugi Ice ridges formed by wind action. They lie parallel to the direction of the wind.

Savannah Open grassland found between the zone of *deserts*, and that of tropical *rainforests* in the tropics and subtropics. Scattered trees and shrubs are found in some kinds of savannah. A savannah *climate* usually has wet and dry seasons.

Scarp *see Escarpment.*

Scree Piles of rock fragments beneath a cliff or rock face, caused by mechanical *weathering*, especially *frost shattering*, where the expansion and contraction of freezing and thawing water within the rock, gradually breaks it up.

Sea-floor spreading The process whereby *tectonic plates* move apart, allowing hot *magma* to erupt and solidify. This forms a new sea floor and, ultimately, widens the ocean.

Seamount An isolated, submarine mountain or hill, probably of volcanic origin

Season A period of time linked to regular changes in the weather, especially the intensity of solar *radiation*.

Sediment Grains of rock transported and deposited by rivers, sea, ice or wind.

Sedimentary rocks Rocks formed from the debris of pre-existing rocks or of organic material. They are found in many *environments* – on the ocean floor, on beaches, rivers and *deserts*. Organically-formed sedimentary rocks include coal and chalk. Other sedimentary rocks, such as flint, are formed by chemical processes. Most of these rocks contain *fossils*, which can be used to date them.

Seif A sand *dune* which lies parallel to the direction of the prevailing wind. Seifs form steep-sided ridges, sometimes extending for miles.

Seismic activity Movement within the Earth, such as an *earthquake* or *tremor*.

Selva A region of wet forest found in the Amazon Basin.

Semi-arid, semi-desert The *climate* and landscape which lies between *savannah* and *desert* or between savannah and a *mediterranean* climate. In semi-arid conditions there is a little more moisture than in a true *desert*; and more patches of drought-resistant vegetation can survive.

Shale (marine shale) A compacted *sedimentary rock*, with fine-grained particles. Marine shale is formed on the seabed. Fuel such as oil may be extracted from it.

Sheetwash Water which runs downhill in thin sheets without forming channels. It can cause *sheet erosion*.

Sheet erosion The washing away of soil by a thin film or sheet of water, known as *sheetwash*.

Shield A vast stable block of the Earth's *crust*, which has experienced little or no *mountain-building*.

Sierra The Spanish word for mountains.

Sinkhole A circular *depression* in a *limestone* region. They are formed by the collapse of an underground cave system or the *chemical weathering* of the *limestone*.

Sisal A plant-fibre used to make matting.

Slash and burn A farming technique involving the cutting down and burning of scrub forest, to create agricultural land. After a number of seasons this land is abandoned and the process is repeated. This practice is common in Africa and South America.

Slip face The steep leeward side of a sand *dune* or slope. Opposite side to a *back slope*

Soil A thin layer of rock particles mixed with the remains of dead plants and animals. This occurs naturally on the surface of the Earth and provides a medium for plants to grow.

Soil creep The very gradual downslope movement of rock debris and soil, under the influence of gravity. This is a type of *mass movement*.

Soil erosion The wearing away of soil more quickly than it is replaced by natural processes. Soil can be carried away by wind as well as by water. Human activities, such as over-grazing and the clearing of land for farming, accelerate the process in many areas.

Solar energy Energy derived from the Sun. Solar energy is converted into other forms of energy. For example, the wind and waves, as well as the creation of plant material in photosynthesis, depend on solar energy.

Solifluction A kind of *soil creep*, where water in the surface layer has saturated the soil and rock debris which slips slowly downhill. It often happens where frozen top-layer deposits thaw, leaving frozen layers below them.

Sorghum A type of grass found in South America, similar to sugar cane. When refined it is used to make molasses.

Spit A thin linear deposit of sand or shingle extending from the sea shore. Spits are formed as angled waves shift sand along the beach, eventually extending a ridge of sand beyond a change in the angle of the coast. Spits are common where the coastline bends, especially at estuaries.

Squash A type of edible gourd.

Stack A tall, isolated pillar of rock near a coastline, created as wave action erodes away the adjacent rock.

Stalactite A tapering cylinder of mineral deposit, hanging from the roof of a cave in a *karst* area. It is formed by calcium carbonate, dissolved in water, which drips through the roof of a *limestone* cavern.

Stalagmite A cone of calcium carbonate, similar to a *stalactite*, rising from the floor of a *limestone* cavern and formed when drops of water fall from the roof of a *limestone* cave. If the water has dripped from a *stalactite* above the stalagmite, the two may join to form a continuous pillar.

Staple crop The main crop on which a country is economically and or physically reliant. For example, the major crop grown for large-scale local consumption in South Asia is rice.

Steppe Large areas of dry grassland in the northern hemisphere – particularly found in southeast Europe and central Asia.

Strata The plural of stratum, a distinct, virtually horizontal layer of deposited material, lying parallel to other layers.

Stratosphere A layer of the *atmosphere*, above the *troposphere*, extending from about 7–30 miles (11–50 km) above the Earth's surface. In the lower part of the stratosphere, the temperature is relatively stable and there is little moisture.

Strike-slip fault Occurs where plates move sideways past each other and blocks of rocks move horizontally in relation to each other, not up or down as in normal *faults*.

Subduction zone A region where two *tectonic plates* collide, forcing one beneath the other. Typically, a dense oceanic plate dips below a lighter continental plate, melting in the heat of the *asthenosphere*. This is why the zone is also called a destructive margins (*see Plate tectonics*). These zones are characterized by *earthquakes*, volcanoes, *mountain-building* and the development of oceanic trenches and *island arcs*.

Submarine canyon A steep-sided valley, which extends along the *continental shelf* to the ocean floor. Often formed by *turbidity currents*.

Submarine fan Deposits of silt and *alluvium*, carried by large rivers forming great fan-shaped deposits on the ocean floor.

Subsistence agriculture An agricultural practice, whereby enough food is produced to support the farmer and his dependents, but not providing any surplus to generate an income.

Subtropical A term applied loosely to *climates* which are nearly tropical or tropical for a part of the year – areas north or south of the *tropics* but outside the *temperate zone*.

Supercontinent A large continent that breaks up to form smaller continents or which forms when smaller continents merge. In the theory of *continental drift*, the supercontinents are *Pangaea*, *Gondwanaland* and *Laurasia*.

Sustainable development An approach to development, applied to economies across the world which exploit natural resources without destroying them or the *environment*.

Syncline A basin-shaped downfold in rock *strata*, created when the *strata* are compressed, for example where *tectonic plates* collide.

T

Tableland A highland area with a flat or gently undulating surface.

Taiga The belt of *coniferous* forest found in the north of Asia and North America. The conifers are adapted to survive low temperatures and long periods of snowfall.

Tarn A Scottish term for a small mountain lake, usually found at the head of a *glacier*.

Tectonic plates Plates, or tectonic plates, are the rigid slabs which form the Earth's outer shell, the *lithosphere*. Eight big plates and several smaller ones have been identified.

Temperate A moderate *climate* without extremes of temperature, typical of the mid-*latitudes* between the *tropics* and the *polar* circles.

Theocracy A state governed by religious laws – today Iran is the world's largest theocracy.

Thermokarst Subsidence created by the thawing of ground ice in *periglacial* areas, creating depressions.

Thermosphere A layer of the Earth's *atmosphere* which lies above the *mesophere*, about 60–300 miles (100–500 km) above the Earth

Terraces Steps cut into steep slopes to create flat surfaces for cultivating crops. They also help reduce soil *erosion* on unconsolidated slopes. They are most common in heavily-populated parts of Southeast Asia.

Till Unstratified glacial deposits or drift left by a *glacier* or *ice sheet*. Till includes mixtures of clay, sand, gravel and boulders.

Topography The typical shape and features of a given area such as land height and terrain.

Tombolo A large sand *spit* which attaches part of the mainland to an island.

Tornado A violent, spiralling windstorm, with a centre of very low pressure. Wind speeds reach 200 mph (320 kmph) and there is often thunder and heavy rain.

Transform fault In *plate tectonics*, a *fault* of continental scale, occurring where two plates slide past each other, staying close together for example, the San Andreas Fault, USA. The jerky, uneven movement creates *earthquakes* but does not destroy or add to the Earth's *crust*

Transpiration The loss of water vapour through the pores (or stomata) of plants. The process helps to return moisture to the *atmosphere*.

Trap An area of fine-grained *igneous rock* which has been extruded and cooled on the Earth's surface in stages, forming a series of steps or terraces.

Treeline The line beyond which trees cannot grow, dependent on *latitude* and altitude, as well as local factors such as soil.

Tremor A slight *earthquake*.

Trench (oceanic trench) A long, deep trough in the ocean floor, formed, according to the theory of *plate tectonics*, when two plates collide and one dives under the other, creating a *subduction zone*.

Tropics The zone between the *Tropic of Cancer* and the *Tropic of Capricorn* where the *climate* is hot. Tropical climate is also applied to areas rather further north and south of the *Equator* where the climate is similar to that of the true tropics.

Tropic of Cancer A line of *latitude* or imaginary circle round the Earth, lying at 23° 28' N.

Tropic of Capricorn A line of *latitude* or imaginary circle round the Earth, lying at 23° 28' S.

Troposphere The lowest layer of the Earth's *atmosphere*. From the surface, it reaches a height of between 4–10 miles (7–16 km). It is the most turbulent zone of the atmosphere and accounts for the generation of most of the world's weather. The layer above it is called the *stratosphere*.

Tsunami A huge wave created by shock waves from an *earthquake* under the sea. Reaching speeds of up to 600 mph (960 kmph), the wave may increase to heights of 50 ft (15 m) on entering coastal waters; and it can cause great damage.

Tundra The treeless *plains* of the *Arctic Circle*, found south of the *polar* region of permanent ice and snow, and north of the belt of *coniferous* forests known as *taiga*. In this region of long, very cold winters, vegetation is usually limited to mosses, *lichens*, sedges and rushes, although flowers and dwarf shrubs blossom in the brief summer.

Turbidity current An oceanic feature. A turbidity current is a mass of *sediment*-laden water which has substantial erosive power. Turbidity currents are thought to contribute to the formation of *submarine canyons*.

Typhoon A kind of *hurricane* (or tropical cyclone) bringing violent winds and heavy rain, a typhoon can do great damage. They occur in the South China Sea, especially around the Philippines.

U

U-shaped valley A river valley that has been deepened and widened by a *glacier*. They are characteristically flat-bottomed and steep-sided and generally much deeper than river valleys.

UN United Nations. Established in 1945, it contains 188 nations and aims to maintain international peace and security, and promote co-operation over economic, social, cultural and humanitarian problems.

UNICEF United Nations Children's Fund. A UN organization set up to promote family and child related programmes.

Urstromtäler A German word used to describe *meltwater* channels which flowed along the front edge of the advancing *ice sheet* during the last Ice Age, 18,000–20,000 years ago.

V

V-shaped valley A typical valley eroded by a river in its upper course.

Virgin rainforest Tropical *rainforest* in its original state, untouched by human activity such as logging, clearance for agriculture, settlement or road building.

Viticulture The cultivation of grapes for wine.

Volcano An opening or vent in the Earth's *crust* where molten rock, *magma*, erupts. Volcanoes tend to be conical but may also be a crack in the Earth's surface or a hole blasted through a mountain. The magma is accompanied by other materials such as gas, steam and fragments of rock, or *pyroclasts*. They tend to occur on destructive or constructive *tectonic plate* margins.

W-Z

Wadi The dry bed left by a torrent of water. Also classified as a *ephemeral* stream, found in *arid* and *semi-arid* regions, which are subject to sudden and often severe flash flooding.

Warm humid climate A rainy climate with warm summers and mild winters.

Water cycle The continuous circulation of water between the Earth's surface and the *atmosphere*. The processes include *evaporation* and *transpiration* of moisture into the atmosphere, and its return as *precipitation*, some of which flows into lakes and oceans.

Water table The upper level of *groundwater* saturation in permeable rock *strata*.

Watershed The dividing line between one *drainage basin* – an area where all streams flow into a single river system – and another. In the US, watershed also means the whole drainage basin of a single river system – its catchment area.

Waterspout A rotating column of water in the form of cloud, mist and spray which form on open water. Often has the appearance of a small *tornado*.

Weathering The decay and break-up of rocks at or near the Earth's surface, caused by water, wind, heat or ice, organic material or the *atmosphere*. *Physical weathering* includes the effects of frost and temperature changes. Biological weathering includes the effects of plant roots, burrowing animals and the acids produced by animals, especially as they decay after death. *Carbonation* and *hydrolysis* are among many kinds of *chemical weathering*.

Geographical names

The following glossary lists all geographical terms occurring on the maps and in main-entry names in the Index-Gazetteer. These terms may precede, follow or be run together with the proper element of the name; where they precede it the term is reversed for indexing purposes - thus Poluostrov Yamal is indexed as Yamal, Poluostrov.

Key

Geographical term
Language, Term

A

Å *Danish, Norwegian*, River
Āb *Persian*, River
Adrar *Berber*, Mountains
Agía, Ágios *Greek*, Saint
Air *Indonesian*, River
Ákra *Greek*, Cape, point
Alpen *German*, Alps
Alt- *German*, Old
Altiplanicie *Spanish*, Plateau
Älve(en) *Swedish*, River
-ån *Swedish*, River
Anse *French*, Bay
'Aqabat *Arabic*, Pass
Archipiélago *Spanish*, Archipelago
Arcipelago *Italian*, Archipelago
Arquipélago *Portuguese*, Archipelago
Arrecife(s) *Spanish*, Reef(s)
Aru *Tamil*, River
Augstiene *Latvian*, Upland
Aukštuma *Lithuanian*, Upland
Aust- *Norwegian*, Eastern
Avtonomnyy Okrug *Russian*, Autonomous district
Āw *Kurdish*, River
'Ayn *Arabic*, Spring, well
'Ayoûn *Arabic*, Wells

B

Baelt *Danish*, Strait
Bahía *Spanish*, Bay
Baḩr *Arabic*, River
Baía *Portuguese*, Bay
Baie *French*, Bay
Bañado *Spanish*, Marshy land
Bandao *Chinese*, Peninsula
Banjaran *Malay*, Mountain range
Barajı *Turkish*, Dam
Barragem *Portuguese*, Reservoir
Bassin *French*, Basin
Batang *Malay*, Stream
Beinn, Ben *Gaelic*, Mountain
-berg *Afrikaans, Norwegian*, Mountain
Besar *Indonesian, Malay*, Big
Birkat, Birket *Arabic*, Lake, well,
Boğazi *Turkish*, Lake
Boka *Serbo-Croatian*, Bay
Bol'sh-aya, -iye, -oy, -oye *Russian*, Big
Botigh(i) *Uzbek*, Depression basin
-bre(en) *Norwegian*, Glacier
Bredning *Danish*, Bay
Bucht *German*, Bay
Bugt(en) *Danish*, Bay
Buḩayrat *Arabic*, Lake, reservoir
Buḩeirat *Arabic*, Lake
Bukit *Malay*, Mountain
-bukta *Norwegian*, Bay
bukten *Swedish*, Bay
Bulag *Mongolian*, Spring
Bulak *Uighur*, Spring
Burnu *Turkish*, Cape, point
Buuraha *Somali*, Mountains

C

Cabo *Portuguese*, Cape
Caka *Tibetan*, Salt lake
Canal *Spanish*, Channel
Cap *French*, Cape
Capo *Italian*, Cape, headland
Cascada *Portuguese*, Waterfall
Cayo(s) *Spanish*, Islet(s), rock(s)
Cerro *Spanish*, Mountain
Chaîne *French*, Mountain range
Chapada *Portuguese*, Hills, upland
Chau *Cantonese*, Island
Chāy *Turkish*, River
Chhâk *Cambodian*, Bay
Chhu *Tibetan*, River
-chŏsuji *Korean*, Reservoir
Chott *Arabic*, Depression, salt lake
Chŭli *Uzbek*, Grassland, steppe
Ch'ün-tao *Chinese*, Island group
Chuŏr Phnum *Cambodian*, Mountains
Ciudad *Spanish*, City, town
Co *Tibetan*, Lake
Colline(s) *French*, Hill(s)
Cordillera *Spanish*, Mountain range
Costa *Spanish*, Coast
Côte *French*, Coast
Coxilha *Portuguese*, Mountains
Cuchilla *Spanish*, Mountains

D

Daban *Mongolian, Uighur*, Pass
Daği *Azerbaijani, Turkish*, Mountain
Dağlari *Azerbaijani, Turkish*, Mountains
-dake *Japanese*, Peak
-dal(en) *Norwegian*, Valley
Danau *Indonesian*, Lake
Dao *Chinese*, Island
Đao *Vietnamese*, Island
Daryā *Persian*, River
Daryācheh *Persian*, Lake
Dasht *Persian*, Desert, plain
Dawḩat *Arabic*, Bay
Denizi *Turkish*, Sea
Dere *Turkish*, Stream
Desierto *Spanish*, Desert
Dili *Azerbaijani*, Spit
-do *Korean*, Island
Dooxo *Somali*, Valley
Düzü *Azerbaijani*, Steppe
-dwip *Bengali*, Island

E

-eilanden *Dutch*, Islands
Embalse *Spanish*, Reservoir
Ensenada *Spanish*, Bay
Erg *Arabic*, Dunes
Estany *Catalan*, Lake
Estero *Spanish*, Inlet
Estrecho *Spanish*, Strait
Étang *French*, Lagoon, lake
-ey *Icelandic*, Island
Ezero *Bulgarian, Macedonian*, Lake
Ezers *Latvian*, Lake

F

Feng *Chinese*, Peak
Fjord *Danish*, Fjord
-fjord(en) *Danish, Norwegian, Swedish*, fjord
-fjørdhur *Faeroese*, Fjord
Fleuve *French*, River
Fliegu *Maltese*, Channel
-fljór *Icelandic*, River
-flói *Icelandic*, Bay
Forêt *French*, Forest

G

-gan *Japanese*, Rock
-gang *Korean*, River
Ganga *Hindi, Nepali, Sinhala*, River
Gaoyuan *Chinese*, Plateau
Garagumy *Turkmen*, Sands
-gawa *Japanese*, River
Gebel *Arabic*, Mountain
-gebirge *German*, Mountain range
Ghadīr *Arabic*, Well
Ghubbat *Arabic*, Bay
Gjiri *Albanian*, Bay
Gol *Mongolian*, River
Golfe *French*, Gulf
Golfo *Italian, Spanish*, Gulf
Göl(ü) *Turkish*, Lake
Golyam, -a *Bulgarian*, Big
Gora *Russian, Serbo-Croatian*, Mountain
Góra *Polish*, mountain
Gory *Russian*, Mountain
Gryada *Russian*, ridge
Guba *Russian*, Bay
-gundo *Korean*, island group
Gunung *Malay*, Mountain

H

Ḩadd *Arabic*, Spit
-haehyŏp *Korean*, Strait
Haff *German*, Lagoon
Hai *Chinese*, Bay, lake, sea
Haixia *Chinese*, Strait
Hamada *Arabic*, Plateau
Ḩammādat *Arabic*, Plateau
Hāmūn *Persian*, Lake
-hantō *Japanese*, Peninsula
Har, Haré *Hebrew*, Mountain
Ḩarrat *Arabic*, Lava-field
Hav(et) *Danish, Swedish*, Sea
Hawr *Arabic*, Lake
Hāyk' *Amharic*, Lake
He *Chinese*, River
-hegység *Hungarian*, Mountain range
Heide *German*, Heath, moorland
Helodrano *Malagasy*, Bay
Higashi- *Japanese*, East(ern)
Ḩişā' *Arabic*, Well
Hka *Burmese*, River
-ho *Korean*, Lake
Hô *Korean*, Reservoir
Holot *Hebrew*, Dunes
Hora *Belarussian, Czech*, Mountain
Hrada *Belarussian*, Mountain, ridge
Hsi *Chinese*, Lake
Hu *Chinese*, Lake
Huk *Danish*, Point

I

Île(s) *French*, Island(s)
Ilha(s) *Portuguese*, Island(s)
Ilhéu(s) *Portuguese*, Islet(s)
Imeni *Russian*, In the name of
Inish- *Gaelic*, Island
Insel(n) *German*, Island(s)
Irmağı, Irmak *Turkish*, River
Isla(s) *Spanish*, Island(s)
Isola (Isole) *Italian*, Island(s)

J

Jabal *Arabic*, Mountain
Jāl *Arabic*, Ridge
-järv *Estonian*, Lake
-järvi *Finnish*, Lake
Jazā'ir *Arabic*, Islands
Jazīrat *Arabic*, Island
Jazīreh *Persian*, Island
Jebel *Arabic*, Mountain
Jezero *Serbo-Croatian*, Lake
Jezioro *Polish*, Lake
Jiang *Chinese*, River
-jima *Japanese*, Island
Jižní *Czech*, Southern
-jõgi *Estonian*, River
-joki *Finnish*, River
-jökull *Icelandic*, Glacier
Jūn *Arabic*, Bay
Juzur *Arabic*, Islands

K

Kaikyō *Japanese*, Strait
-kaise *Lappish*, Mountain
Kali *Nepali*, River
Kalnas *Lithuanian*, Mountain
Kalns *Latvian*, Mountain
Kang *Chinese*, Harbour
Kangri *Tibetan*, Mountain(s)
Kaôh *Cambodian*, Island
Kapp *Norwegian*, Cape
Káto *Greek*, Lower
Kavīr *Persian*, Desert
K'edi *Georgian*, Mountain range
Kediet *Arabic*, Mountain
Kepi *Albanian*, Cape, point
Kepulauan *Indonesian, Malay*, Island group
Khalig, Khalīj *Arabic*, Gulf
Khawr *Arabic*, Inlet
Khola *Nepali*, River
Khrebet *Russian*, Mountain range
Ko *Thai*, Island
-ko *Japanese*, Inlet, lake
Kólpos *Greek*, Bay
-kopf *German*, Peak
Körfäzi *Azerbaijani*, Bay
Körfezi *Turkish*, Bay
Kõrgustik *Estonian*, Upland
Kosa *Russian, Ukrainian*, Spit
Koshi *Nepali*, River
Kou *Chinese*, River-mouth
Kowtal *Persian*, Pass
Kray *Russian*, Region, territory
Kryazh *Russian*, Ridge
Kuduk *Uighur*, Well
Kūh(hā) *Persian*, Mountain(s)
-kul' *Russian*, Lake
Kŭl(i) *Tajik, Uzbek*, Lake
-kundo *Korean*, Island group
-kysten *Norwegian*, Coast
Kyun *Burmese*, Island

L

Laaq *Somali*, Watercourse
Lac *French*, Lake
Lacul *Romanian*, Lake
Lagh *Somali*, Stream
Lago *Italian, Portuguese, Spanish*, Lake
Lagoa *Portuguese*, Lagoon
Laguna *Italian, Spanish*, Lagoon, lake
Laht *Estonian*, Bay
Laut *Indonesian*, Bay
Lembalemba *Malagasy*, Plateau
Lerr *Armenian*, Mountain
Lernashght'a *Armenian*, Mountain range
Les *Czech*, Forest
Lich *Armenian*, Lake
Liehtao *Chinese*, Island group
Liqeni *Albanian*, Lake
Límni *Greek*, Lake
Ling *Chinese*, Mountain range
Llano *Spanish*, Plain, prairie
Lumi *Albanian*, River
Lyman *Ukrainian*, Estuary

M

Madīnat *Arabic*, City, town
Mae Nam *Thai*, River
-mägi *Estonian*, Hill
Maja *Albanian*, Mountain
Mal *Albanian*, Mountains
Mal-aya, -oye, -yy, *Russian*, Small
-man *Korean*, Bay
Mar *Spanish*, Lake
Marios *Lithuanian*, Lake
Massif *French*, Mountains
Meer *German*, Lake
-meer *Dutch*, Lake
Melkosopochnik *Russian*, Plain
-meri *Estonian*, Sea
Mifraz *Hebrew*, Bay
Minami- *Japanese*, South(ern)
-misaki *Japanese*, Cape, point
Monkhafad *Arabic*, Depression
Montagne(s) *French*, Mountain(s)
Montañas *Spanish*, Mountains
Mont(s) *French*, Mountain(s)
Monte *Italian, Portuguese*, Mountain
More *Russian*, Sea
Mörön *Mongolian*, River
Mys *Russian*, Cape, point

N

-nada *Japanese*, Open stretch of water
Nagor'ye *Russian*, Upland
Naḩal *Hebrew*, River
Nahr *Arabic*, River
Nam *Laotian*, River
Namakzār *Persian*, Salt desert
Né-a, -on, -os *Greek*, New
Nedre- *Norwegian*, Lower
-neem *Estonian*, Cape, point
Nehri *Turkish*, River
-nes *Norwegian*, Cape, point
Nevado *Spanish*, Mountain (snow-capped)
Nieder- *German*, Lower
Nishi- *Japanese*, West(ern)
-nísi *Greek*, Island
Nisoi *Greek*, Islands
Nizhn-eye, -iy, -iye, -yaya *Russian*, Lower
Nizmennost' *Russian*, Lowland, plain
Nord *Danish, French, German*, North
Norte *Portuguese, Spanish*, North
Nos *Bulgarian*, Point, spit
Nosy *Malagasy*, Island
Nov-a, -i, *Bulgarian, Serbo-Croatian*, New
Nov-aya, -o, -oye, -yy, -yye *Russian*, New
Now-a, -e, -y *Polish*, New
Nur *Mongolian*, Lake
Nuruu *Mongolian*, Mountains
Nuur *Mongolian*, Lake
Nyzovyna *Ukrainian*, Lowland, plain

O

-ø *Danish*, Island
Ober- *German*, Upper
Oblast' *Russian*, Province
Órmos *Greek*, Bay
Orol(i) *Uzbek*, Island
Øster- *Norwegian*, Eastern
Ostrov(a) *Russian*, Island(s)
Otok *Serbo-Croatian*, Island
Oued *Arabic*, Watercourse
-oy *Faeroese*, Island
-øy(a) *Norwegian*, Island
Oya *Sinhala*, River
Ozero *Russian, Ukrainian*, Lake

P

Passo *Italian*, Pass
Pegunungan *Indonesian, Malay*, Mountain range
Pélagos *Greek*, Sea
Pendi *Chinese*, Basin
Penisola *Italian*, Peninsula
Pertuis *French*, Strait
Peski *Russian*, Sands
Phanom *Thai*, Mountain
Phou *Laotian*, Mountain
Pi *Chinese*, Point
Pic *Catalan, French*, Peak
Pico *Portuguese, Spanish*, Peak
-piggen *Danish*, Peak
Pik *Russian*, Peak
Pivostriv *Ukrainian*, Peninsula
Planalto *Portuguese*, Plateau
Planina, Planini *Bulgarian, Macedonian, Serbo-Croatian*, Mountain range
Plato *Russian*, Plateau
Ploskogor'ye *Russian*, Upland
Poluostrov *Russian*, Peninsula
Ponta *Portuguese*, Point
Porthmós *Greek*, Strait
Pótamos *Greek*, River
Presa *Spanish*, Dam
Prokhod *Bulgarian*, Pass
Proliv *Russian*, Strait
Pulau *Indonesian Malay*, Island
Pulu *Malay*, Island
Punta *Spanish*, Point
Pushcha *Belorussian*, Forest
Puszcza *Polish*, Forest

Q

Qā' *Arabic*, Depression
Qalamat *Arabic*, Well
Qatorkŭh(i) *Tajik*, Mountain
Qiuling *Chinese*, Hills
Qolleh *Persian*, Mountain
Qu *Tibetan*, Stream
Quan *Chinese*, Well
Qulla(i) *Tajik*, Peak
Qundao *Chinese*, Island group

R

Raas *Somali*, Cape
-rags *Latvian*, Cape
Ramlat *Arabic*, Sands
Ra's *Arabic*, Cape, headland, point
Ravnina *Bulgarian, Russian*, Plain
Récif *French*, Reef
Recife *Portuguese*, Reef
Reka *Bulgarian*, River
Represa (Rep.) *Portuguese, Spanish*, Reservoir
Reshteh *Persian*, Mountain range
Respublika *Russian*, Republic, first-order administrative division
Respublika(si) *Uzbek*, Republic, first-order administrative division
-retsugan *Japanese*, Chain of rocks
-rettō *Japanese*, Island chain
Riacho *Spanish*, Stream
Riban' *Malagasy*, Mountains
Rio *Portuguese*, River
Río *Spanish*, River
Riu *Catalan*, River
Rivier *Dutch*, River
Rivière *French*, River
Rowd *Pashtu*, River
Rt *Serbo-Croatian*, Point
Rūd *Persian*, River
Rūdkhāneh *Persian*, River
Rudohorie *Slovak*, Mountains
Ruisseau *French*, Stream

S

-saar *Estonian*, Island
-saari *Finnish*, Island
Sabkhat *Arabic*, Salt marsh
Sāgar(a) *Hindi*, Lake, reservoir
Şaḩrā' *Arabic*, Desert
Saint, Sainte *French*, Saint
Salar *Spanish*, Salt-pan
Salto *Portuguese, Spanish*, Waterfall
Samudra *Sinhala*, Reservoir
-san *Japanese, Korean*, Mountain
-sanchi *Japanese*, Mountains
-sandur *Icelandic*, Beach
Sankt *German, Swedish*, Saint
-sanmaek *Korean*, Mountain range
-sanmyaku *Japanese*, Mountain range
San, Santa, Santo *Italian, Portuguese, Spanish*, Saint
São *Portuguese*, Saint
Sarir *Arabic*, Desert
Sebkha, Sebkhet *Arabic*, Depression, salt marsh
Sedlo *Czech*, Pass
See *German*, Lake
Selat *Indonesian*, Strait
Selatan *Indonesian*, Southern
-selkä *Finnish*, Lake, ridge
Selseleh *Persian*, Mountain range
Serra *Portuguese*, Mountain
Serranía *Spanish*, Mountain
-seto *Japanese*, Channel, strait
Sever-naya, -noye, -nyy, -o *Russian*, Northern
Sha'īb *Arabic*, Watercourse
Shākh *Kurdish*, Mountain
Shamo *Chinese*, Desert
Shan *Chinese*, Mountain(s)
Shankou *Chinese*, Pass
Shanmo *Chinese*, Mountain range
Shaţţ *Arabic*, Distributary
Shet' *Amharic*, River
Shi *Chinese*, Municipality
-shima *Japanese*, Island
Shiqqat *Arabic*, Depression
-shotō *Japanese*, Group of islands
Shuiku *Chinese*, Reservoir
Shŭrkhog(i) *Uzbek*, Salt marsh
Sierra *Spanish*, Mountains
Sint *Dutch*, Saint
-sjø(en) *Norwegian*, Lake
-sjön *Swedish*, Lake
Solonchak *Russian*, Salt lake
Solonchakovyye Vpadiny *Russian*, Salt basin, wetlands
Son *Vietnamese*, Mountain
Sông *Vietnamese*, River
Sør- *Norwegian*, Southern
-spitze *German*, Peak
Star-á, -é *Czech*, Old
Star-aya, -oye, -yy, -yye *Russian*, Old
Stenó *Greek*, Strait
Step' *Russian*, Steppe
Štít *Slovak*, Peak
Stœng *Cambodian*, River
Stolovaya Strana *Russian*, Plateau
Stredné *Slovak*, Middle
Střední *Czech*, Middle
Stretto *Italian*, Strait
Su Anbari *Azerbaijani*, Reservoir
-suidō *Japanese*, Channel, strait
Sund *Swedish*, Sound, strait
Sungai *Indonesian, Malay*, River
Suu *Turkish*, River

T

Tal *Mongolian*, Plain
Tandavan' *Malagasy*, Mountain range
Tangorombohitr' *Malagasy*, Mountain massif
Tanjung *Indonesian, Malay*, Cape, point
Tao *Chinese*, Island
Ţaraq *Arabic*, Hills
Tassili *Berber*, Mountain, plateau
Tau *Russian*, Mountain(s)
Taungdan *Burmese*, Mountain range
Techníti Límni *Greek*, Reservoir
Tekojärvi *Finnish*, Reservoir
Teluk *Indonesian, Malay*, Bay
Tengah *Indonesian*, Middle
Terara *Amharic*, Mountain
Timur *Indonesian*, Eastern
-tind(an) *Norwegian*, Peak
Tizma(si) *Uzbek*, Mountain range, ridge
-tō *Japanese*, island
Tog *Somali*, Valley
-tōge *Japanese*, pass
Togh(i) *Uzbek*, mountain
Tônlé *Cambodian*, Lake
Top *Dutch*, Peak
-tunturi *Finnish*, Mountain
Ţurāq *Arabic*, hills
Tur'at *Arabic*, Channel

U

Udde(n) *Swedish*, Cape, point
'Uqlat *Arabic*, Well
Utara *Indonesian*, Northern
Uul *Mongolian*, Mountains

V

Väin *Estonian*, Strait
Vallée *French*, Valley
-vatn *Icelandic*, Lake
-vatnet *Norwegian*, Lake
Velayat *Turkmen*, Province
-vesi *Finnish*, Lake
Vestre- *Norwegian*, Western
-vidda *Norwegian*, Plateau
-vík *Icelandic*, Bay
-viken *Swedish*, Bay, inlet
Vinh *Vietnamese*, Bay
Víztárloló *Hungarian*, Reservoir
Vodaskhovishcha *Belarussian*, Reservoir
Vodokhranilishche (Vdkhr.) *Russian*, Reservoir
Vodoskhovyshche (Vdskh.) *Ukrainian*, Reservoir
Volcán *Spanish*, Volcano
Vostochn-o, yy *Russian*, Eastern
Vozvyshennost' *Russian*, Upland, plateau
Vozyera *Belarussian*, Lake
Vpadina *Russian*, Depression
Vrchovina *Czech*, Mountains
Vrha *Macedonian*, Peak
Vychodné *Slovak*, Eastern
Vysochyna *Ukrainian*, Upland
Vysočina *Czech*, Upland

W

Waadi *Somali*, Watercourse
Wādī *Arabic* Watercourse
Wāḩat, Wāhat *Arabic*, Oasis
Wald *German*, Forest
Wan *Chinese*, Bay
Way *Indonesian*, River
Webi *Somali*, River
Wenz *Amharic*, River
Wiloyat(i) *Uzbek*, Province
Wyżyna *Polish*, Upland
Wzgórza *Polish*, Upland
Wzvyshsha *Belarussian*, Upland

X

Xé *Laotian*, River
Xi *Chinese*, Stream

Y

-yama *Japanese*, Mountain
Yanchi *Chinese*, Salt lake
Yang *Chinese*, Bay
Yanhu *Chinese*, Salt lake
Yarımadası *Azerbaijani, Turkish*, Peninsula
Yaylası *Turkish*, Plateau
Yazovir *Bulgarian*, Reservoir
Yoma *Burmese*, Mountains
Ytre- *Norwegian*, Outer
Yü *Chinese*, Island
Yunhe *Chinese*, Canal
Yuzhn-o, -yy *Russian*, Southern

Z

-zaki *Japanese*, Cape, point
Zaliv *Bulgarian, Russian*, Bay
-zan *Japanese*, Mountain
Zangbo *Tibetan*, River
Zapadn-aya, -o, -yy *Russian*, Western
Západné *Slovak*, Western
Západní *Czech*, Western
Zatoka *Polish, Ukrainian*, Bay
-zee *Dutch*, Sea
Zemlya *Russian*, Earth, land
Zizhiqu *Chinese*, Autonomous region

25 de Mayo – Acaponeta, Río de

Index

THIS INDEX LISTS all the placenames and features shown on the regional and continental maps in this Atlas. Placenames are referenced to the largest scale map on which they appear. The policy followed throughout the Atlas is to use the local spelling or local name at regional level; commonly-used English language names may occasionally be added (in parentheses) where this is an aid to identification e.g. Firenze (Florence). English names, where they exist, have been used for all international features e.g. oceans and country names; they are also used on the continental maps and in the introductory World section; these are then fully cross-referenced to the local names found on the regional maps. The index also contains commonly-found alternative names and variant spellings, which are also fully cross-referenced.

All main entry names are those of settlements unless otherwise indicated by the use of italicized definitions or representative symbols, which are keyed at the foot of each page.

Glossary of Abbreviations

This glossary provides a comprehensive guide to the abbreviations used in this Atlas, and in the Index.

A
abbrev. abbreviated
AD Anno Domini
Afr. Afrikaans
Alb. Albanian
Amh. Amharic
anc. ancient
approx. approximately
Ar. Arabic
Arm. Armenian
ASEAN Association of South East Asian Nations
ASSR Autonomous Soviet Socialist Republic
Aust. Australian
Az. Azerbaijani
Azerb. Azerbaijan

B
Basq. Basque
BC before Christ
Bel. Belarussian
Ben. Bengali
Ber. Berber
B-H Bosnia-Herzegovina
bn billion (one thousand million)
BP British Petroleum
Bret. Breton
Brit. British
Bul. Bulgarian
Bur. Burmese

C
C central
C. Cape
°C degrees Centigrade
CACM Central America Common Market
Cam. Cambodian
Cant. Cantonese
CAR Central African Republic
Cast. Castilian
Cat. Catalan
CEEAC Central America Common Market
Chin. Chinese
CIS Commonwealth of Independent States
cm centimetre(s)
Cro. Croat
Cz. Czech
Czech Rep. Czech Republic

D
Dan. Danish
Div. Divehi
Dom. Rep. Dominican Republic
Dut. Dutch

E
E east
EC *see* EU
EEC *see* EU
ECOWAS Economic Community of West African States
ECU European Currency Unit
EMS European Monetary System
Eng. English
est estimated
Est. Estonian
EU European Union (previously European Community [EC], European Economic Community [EEC])

F
°F degrees Fahrenheit
Faer. Faeroese
Fij. Fijian
Fin. Finnish
Fr. French
Fris. Frisian
ft foot/feet
FYROM Former Yugoslav Republic of Macedonia

G
g gram(s)
Gael. Gaelic
Gal. Galician
GDP Gross Domestic Product (the total value of goods and services produced by a country excluding income from foreign countries)
Geor. Georgian
Ger. German
Gk Greek
GNP Gross National Product (the total value of goods and services produced by a country)

H
Heb. Hebrew
HEP hydro-electric power
Hind. Hindi
hist. historical
Hung. Hungarian

I
I. Island
Icel. Icelandic
in inch(es)
In. Inuit (Eskimo)
Ind. Indonesian
Intl International
Ir. Irish
Is Islands
It. Italian

J
Jap. Japanese

K
Kaz. Kazakh
kg kilogram(s)
Kir. Kirghiz
km kilometre(s)
km² square kilometre (singular)
Kor. Korean
Kurd. Kurdish

L
L. Lake
LAIA Latin American Integration Association
Lao. Laotian
Lapp. Lappish
Lat. Latin
Latv. Latvian
Liech. Liechtenstein
Lith. Lithuanian
Lux. Luxembourg

M
m million/metre(s)
Mac. Macedonian
Maced. Macedonia
Mal. Malay
Malg. Malagasy
Malt. Maltese
mi. mile(s)
Mong. Mongolian
Mt. Mountain **Mts** Mountains

N
N north
NAFTA North American Free Trade Agreement
Nep. Nepali
Neth. Netherlands
Nic. Nicaraguan
Nor. Norwegian
NZ New Zealand

P
Pash. Pashtu
PNG Papua New Guinea
Pol. Polish
Poly. Polynesian
Port. Portuguese
prev. previously

R
Rep. Republic
Res. Reservoir
Rmsch Romansch
Rom. Romanian
Rus. Russian
Russ. Fed. Russian Federation

S
S south
SADC Southern Africa Development Community
SCr. Serbo-Croatian
Sinh. Sinhala
Slvk Slovak
Slvn. Slovene
Som. Somali
Sp. Spanish
St., St Saint
Strs Straits
Swa. Swahili
Swe. Swedish
Switz. Switzerland

T
Taj. Tajik
Th. Thai
Thai. Thailand
Tib. Tibetan
Turk. Turkish
Turkm. Turkmenistan

U
UAE United Arab Emirates
Uigh. Uighur
UK United Kingdom
Ukr. Ukrainian
UN United Nations
Urd. Urdu
US/USA United States of America
USSR Union of Soviet Socialist Republics
Uzb. Uzbek

V
var. variant
Vdkhr. Vodokhranilishche (Russian for reservoir)
Vdskh. Vodoskhovyshche (Ukrainian for reservoir)
Vtn. Vietnamese

W
W west
Wel. Welsh

Y
Yugo. Yugoslavia

1

25 de Mayo *see* Veinticinco de Mayo
137 *Y13* **26 Bakı Komissarı** *Rus.* Imeni 26 Bakinskikh Komissarov. SE Azerbaijan
26 Baku Komissarlary Adyndaky *see* Uzboý
10 *M16* **100 Mile House** *var.* Hundred Mile House. British Columbia, SW Canada

A

Aa *see* Gauja
95 *G24* **Aabenraa** *var.* Åbenrå, *Ger.* Apenrade. Sønderjylland, SW Denmark
95 *G20* **Aabybro** *var.* Åbybro. Nordjylland, N Denmark
101 *C16* **Aachen** *Dut.* Aken, *Fr.* Aix-la-Chapelle; *anc.* Aquae Grani, Aquisgranum. Nordrhein-Westfalen, W Germany
Aaiún *see* Laâyoune
95 *M24* **Aakirkeby** *var.* Åkirkeby. Bornholm, E Denmark
95 *G20* **Aalborg** *var.* Ålborg, Ålborg-Nørresundby; *anc.* Alburgum. Nordjylland, N Denmark
Aalborg Bugt *see* Ålborg Bugt
101 *J21* **Aalen** Baden-Württemberg, S Germany
95 *G21* **Aalestrup** *var.* Ålestrup. Viborg, NW Denmark
98 *I11* **Aalsmeer** Noord-Holland, C Netherlands
99 *F18* **Aalst** *Fr.* Alost. Oost-Vlaanderen, C Belgium
99 *K18* **Aalst** *Fr.* Alost. Noord-Brabant, S Netherlands
98 *O12* **Aalten** Gelderland, E Netherlands
99 *D17* **Aalter** Oost-Vlaanderen, NW Belgium
Aanaar *see* Inari
Aanaarjävri *see* Inarijärvi
93 *M17* **Äänekoski** Länsi-Soumi, W Finland
138 *H7* **Aanjar** *var.* 'Anjar. C Lebanon
83 *G21* **Aansluit** Northern Cape, N South Africa
Aar *see* Aare
108 *F7* **Aarau** Aargau, N Switzerland
108 *D8* **Aarberg** Bern, W Switzerland
99 *D16* **Aardenburg** Zeeland, SW Netherlands
108 *D8* **Aare** *var.* Aar. ≈ W Switzerland
108 *F7* **Aargau** *Fr.* Argovie. ◐ *canton* N Switzerland
Aarhus *see* Århus
Aarlen *see* Arlon
95 *G21* **Aars** *var.* Års. Nordjylland, N Denmark
99 *I17* **Aarschot** Vlaams Brabant, C Belgium
Aassi, Nahr el *see* Orontes
Aat *see* Ath
160 *G7* **Aba** *prev.* Ngawa. Sichuan, C China
79 *P16* **Aba** Orientale, NE Dem. Rep. Congo
77 *V17* **Aba** Abia, S Nigeria
140 *J6* **Abā al Qazāz, Bi'r** *well* NW Saudi Arabia
Abā as Su'ūd *see* Najrān
59 *G14* **Abacaxis, Rio** ≈ NW Brazil
Abaco Island *see* Great Abaco/Little Abaco
Abaco Island *see* Great Abaco, Bahamas
142 *K10* **Ābādān** Khūzestān, SW Iran
146 *F13* **Abadan** *prev.* Bezmein, *Rus.* Byuzmeyin. Ahal Welaýaty, C Turkmenistan
143 *O10* **Ābādeh** Fārs, C Iran
74 *H8* **Abadla** W Algeria
59 *M20* **Abaeté** Minas Gerais, SE Brazil
Abag Qi *see* Xin Hot
62 *P7* **Abaí** Caazapá, S Paraguay
Abai *see* Blue Nile
191 *O2* **Abaiang** *var.* Apia; *prev.* Charlotte Island. *atoll* Tungaru, W Kiribati
Abaj *see* Abay
77 *U15* **Abaji** Federal Capital District, C Nigeria
37 *O7* **Abajo Peak** ▲ Utah, W USA
77 *V16* **Abakaliki** Ebonyi, SE Nigeria
122 *K13* **Abakan** Respublika Khakasiya, S Russian Federation
77 *S11* **Abala** Tillabéri, SW Niger
77 *U11* **Abalak** Tahoua, C Niger
119 *N14* **Abalyanka** *Rus.* Obolyanka. ≈ N Belarus
122 *L12* **Aban** Krasnoyarskiy Kray, S Russian Federation
143 *P9* **Āb Anbār-e Kān Sorkh** Yazd, C Iran
57 *G16* **Abancay** Apurímac, SE Peru
190 *H2* **Abaokoro** *atoll* Tungaru, W Kiribati
Abariringa *see* Kanton
143 *P10* **Abarkū** Yazd, C Iran
165 *V3* **Abashiri** *var.* Abasiri. Hokkaidō, NE Japan
165 *U3* **Abashiri-ko** ◎ Hokkaidō, NE Japan
Abasiri *see* Abashiri
41 *P10* **Abasolo** Tamaulipas, C Mexico
186 *F9* **Abau** Central, S Papua New Guinea
145 *R10* **Abay** *var.* Abaj. Karaganda, C Kazakhstan
81 *I15* **Ābaya Hāyk'** *Eng.* Lake Margherita, *It.* Abbaia. ◎ SW Ethiopia
Ābay Wenz *see* Blue Nile
122 *K13* **Abaza** Respublika Khakasiya, S Russian Federation
Abbaia *see* Ābaya Hāyk'
143 *Q13* **Āb Bārīk** Fārs, S Iran
107 *C18* **Abbasanta** Sardegna, Italy, C Mediterranean Sea
Abbatis Villa *see* Abbeville
30 *M3* **Abbaye, Point** *headland* Michigan, N USA
Abbazia *see* Opatija
Abbé, Lake *see* Abhe, Lake
103 *N2* **Abbeville** *anc.* Abbatis Villa. Somme, N France
23 *R7* **Abbeville** Alabama, S USA
23 *U6* **Abbeville** Georgia, SE USA
22 *I9* **Abbeville** Louisiana, S USA
21 *P12* **Abbeville** South Carolina, SE USA
97 *B20* **Abbeyfeale** *Ir.* Mainistir na Féile. SW Ireland
106 *D8* **Abbiategrasso** Lombardia, NW Italy
93 *I14* **Abborrträsk** Norrbotten, N Sweden
194 *J9* **Abbot Ice Shelf** *ice shelf* Antarctica
10 *M17* **Abbotsford** British Columbia, SW Canada
30 *K6* **Abbotsford** Wisconsin, N USA
149 *U5* **Abbottābād** North-West Frontier Province, NW Pakistan
119 *M14* **Abchuha** *Rus.* Obchuga. Minskaya Voblasts', NW Belarus
98 *I10* **Abcoude** Utrecht, C Netherlands
139 *N2* **'Abd al 'Azīz, Jabal** ▲▲ NE Syria
141 *U17* **'Abd al Kūrī** *island* SE Yemen
139 *Z13* **'Abd Allāh, Khawr** *bay* Iraq/Kuwait
127 *U6* **Abdulino** Orenburgskaya Oblast', W Russian Federation
78 *J10* **Abéché** *var.* Abécher, Abeshr. Ouaddaï, SE Chad
Abécher *see* Abéché
143 *S8* **Āb-e Garm va Sard** Yazd, E Iran
77 *R8* **Abeïbara** Kidal, NE Mali
105 *P5* **Abejar** Castilla-León, N Spain
54 *E9* **Abejorral** Antioquia, W Colombia
Abela *see* Ávila
Abellinum *see* Avellino
92 *Q2* **Abeløya** *island* Kong Karls Land, E Svalbard
80 *I13* **Ābeltī** Oromo, C Ethiopia
191 *O2* **Abemama** *var.* Apamama; *prev.* Roger Simpson Island. *atoll* Tungaru, W Kiribati
171 *Y15* **Abemaree** *var.* Abermarre. Papua, E Indonesia
77 *O16* **Abengourou** E Ivory Coast
Åbenrå *see* Aabenraa
101 *L22* **Abens** ≈ SE Germany
77 *S16* **Abeokuta** Ogun, SW Nigeria
97 *I20* **Aberaeron** SW Wales, UK
Aberbrothock *see* Arbroath
Abercorn *see* Mbala
29 *R6* **Abercrombie** North Dakota, N USA
183 *T7* **Aberdeen** New South Wales, SE Australia
9 *T15* **Aberdeen** Saskatchewan, S Canada
83 *H25* **Aberdeen** Eastern Cape, S South Africa
96 *L9* **Aberdeen** *anc.* Devana. NE Scotland, UK
21 *X2* **Aberdeen** Maryland, NE USA
23 *N3* **Aberdeen** Mississippi, S USA
21 *T10* **Aberdeen** North Carolina, SE USA
29 *P8* **Aberdeen** South Dakota, N USA
32 *F8* **Aberdeen** Washington, NW USA
96 *K9* **Aberdeen** *cultural region* NE Scotland, UK
8 *L8* **Aberdeen Lake** ◎ Nunavut, NE Canada
96 *J10* **Aberfeldy** C Scotland, UK
97 *K21* **Abergavenny** *anc.* Gobannium. SE Wales, UK
Abergwaun *see* Fishguard
Abermarre *see* Abemaree
25 *N5* **Abernathy** Texas, SW USA
Abersee *see* Wolfgangsee
Abertawe *see* Swansea
Aberteifi *see* Cardigan
32 *I15* **Abert, Lake** ◎ Oregon, NW USA
97 *I20* **Aberystwyth** W Wales, UK
Abeshr *see* Abéché
Ábeskovvu *see* Abisko
106 *F10* **Abetone** Toscana, C Italy
125 *V5* **Abez'** Respublika Komi, NW Russian Federation
142 *M5* **Āb Garm** Qazvin, N Iran
141 *N12* **Abhā** 'Asīr, SW Saudi Arabia
142 *M5* **Abhar** Zanjān, NW Iran
Abhé Bad/Ābhē Bid Hāyk' *see* Abhe, Lake
80 *K12* **Abhe, Lake** *var.* Lake Abbé, *Amh.* Ābhē Bid Hāyk', *Som.* Abhé Bad. ◎ Djibouti/Ethiopia
77 *V17* **Abia** ◐ *state* SE Nigeria
139 *V9* **'Abīd 'Alī** E Iraq
119 *O17* **Abidavichy** *Rus.* Obidovichi. Mahilyowskaya Voblasts', E Belarus
115 *L15* **Abide** Çanakkale, NW Turkey
77 *N17* **Abidjan** S Ivory Coast
Āb-i-Istāda *see* Īstādeh-ye Moqor, Āb-e-
27 *N4* **Abilene** Kansas, C USA
25 *Q7* **Abilene** Texas, SW USA
Abindonia *see* Abingdon
97 *M21* **Abingdon** *anc.* Abindonia. S England, UK
30 *K12* **Abingdon** Illinois, N USA
21 *P8* **Abingdon** Virginia, NE USA
Abingdon *see* Pinta, Isla
18 *J15* **Abington** Pennsylvania, NE USA
126 *K14* **Abinsk** Krasnodarskiy Kray, SW Russian Federation
37 *R9* **Abiquiu Reservoir** ⊡ New Mexico, SW USA
Āb-i-safed *see* Sefīd, Darya-ye
92 *I10* **Abisko** *Lapp.* Ábeskovvu. Norrbotten, N Sweden
12 *G12* **Abitibi** ≈ Ontario, S Canada
12 *H12* **Abitibi, Lac** ◎ Ontario/Québec, S Canada
80 *J10* **Ābīy Ādī** Tigray, N Ethiopia
118 *H6* **Abja-Paluoja** Viljandimaa, S Estonia
137 *Q8* **Abkhazia** ◐ *autonomous republic* NW Georgia
182 *F1* **Abminga** South Australia
75 *W9* **Abnûb** C Egypt
Åbo *see* Turku
152 *G9* **Abohar** Punjab, N India
77 *O17* **Aboisso** SE Ivory Coast
78 *H5* **Abo, Massif d'** ▲▲ NW Chad
77 *R16* **Abomey** S Benin
79 *F16* **Abong Mbang** Est, SE Cameroon
111 *L23* **Abony** Pest, C Hungary
78 *J11* **Abou-Déïa** Salamat, SE Chad
Aboudouhour *see* Abū aḍ Ḍuhūr
Abou Kémal *see* Abū Kamāl
Abou Simbel *see* Abu Simbel
137 *T12* **Abovyan** C Armenia
141 *P15* **Abrād, Wādī** *seasonal river* W Yemen
Abraham Bay *see* The Carlton
104 *G10* **Abrantes** *var.* Abrántes. Santarém, C Portugal
62 *J4* **Abra Pampa** Jujuy, N Argentina
Abrashlare *see* Brezovo
54 *G7* **Abrego** Norte de Santander, N Colombia
Abrene *see* Pytalovo
40 *C7* **Abreojos, Punta** *headland* W Mexico
65 *J16* **Abrolhos Bank** *undersea feature* W Atlantic Ocean
119 *H19* **Abrova** *Rus.* Obrovo. Brestskaya Voblasts', SW Belarus
116 *G11* **Abrud** *Ger.* Gross-Schlatten, *Hung.* Abrudbánya. Alba, SW Romania
Abrudbánya *see* Abrud
118 *E6* **Abruka** *island* SW Estonia
107 *J15* **Abruzzese, Appennino** ▲▲ C Italy
107 *J14* **Abruzzo** ◐ *region* C Italy
141 *N14* **'Abs** *var.* Sūq 'Abs. W Yemen
33 *T12* **Absaroka Range** ▲▲ Montana/Wyoming, NW USA
137 *Z11* **Abşeron Yarımadası** *Rus.* Apsheronskiy Poluostrov. *peninsula* E Azerbaijan
143 *N6* **Āb Shīrīn** Eşfahān, C Iran
139 *X10* **Abtān** SE Iraq
109 *R6* **Abtenau** Salzburg, NW Austria
152 *E14* **Ābu** Rājasthān, N India
164 *E12* **Abu** Yamaguchi, Honshū, SW Japan
138 *I4* **Abū aḍ Ḍuhūr** *Fr.* Aboudouhour. Idlib, NW Syria
143 *P17* **Abū al Abyaḍ** *island* C United Arab Emirates
138 *K10* **Abū al Ḥuṣayn, Khabrat** ◎ N Jordan
139 *R8* **Abū al Jīr** C Iraq
139 *Y12* **Abū al Khaṣīb** *var.* Abul Khasib. SE Iraq
139 *U12* **Abū at Tubrah, Thaqb** *well* S Iraq
75 *V11* **Abu Balâs** ▲ SW Egypt
Abu Dhabi *see* Abū Ẓaby
139 *R8* **Abū Farūkh** C Iraq
80 *C12* **Abu Gabra** Southern Darfur, W Sudan
139 *P10* **Abū Ghār, Sha'īb** *dry watercourse* S Iraq
80 *G7* **Abu Hamed** River Nile, N Sudan
139 *O5* **Abū Ḥardān** *var.* Hajîne. Dayr az Zawr, E Syria
139 *T7* **Abū Ḥassawīyah** E Iraq
138 *K10* **Abū Ḥifnah, Wādī** *dry watercourse* N Jordan
77 *V15* **Abuja** ● (Nigeria) Federal Capital District, C Nigeria
139 *R9* **Abū Jahaf, Wādī** *dry watercourse* C Iraq
56 *F12* **Abujao, Río** ≈ E Peru
139 *U12* **Abū Jasrah** S Iraq
139 *O6* **Abū Kamāl** *Fr.* Abou Kémal. Dayr az Zawr, E Syria
165 *P12* **Abukuma-sanchi** ▲▲ Honshū, C Japan
Abula *see* Ávila
Abul Khasib *see* Abū al Khaṣīb
79 *K16* **Abumombazi** *var.* Abumonbazi. Equateur, N Dem. Rep. Congo
Abumonbazi *see* Abumombazi
59 *D15* **Abunã** Rondônia, W Brazil
56 *K13* **Abunã, Rio** *var.* Río Abuná. ≈ Bolivia/Brazil
138 *G10* **Abū Nuṣayr** *var.* Abu Nuseir. 'Ammān, W Jordan
Abu Nuseir *see* Abū Nuṣayr
139 *T12* **Abū Qabr** S Iraq
138 *K5* **Abū Raḥbah, Jabal** ▲▲ C Syria
139 *S5* **Abū Rajāsh** N Iraq
139 *W13* **Abū Raqrāq, Ghadīr** *well* S Iraq
152 *E14* **Ābu Road** Rājasthān, N India
80 *I6* **Abu Shagara, Ras** *headland* NE Sudan
75 *W12* **Abu Simbel** *var.* Abou Simbel, Abū Sunbul. *ancient monument* S Egypt
139 *U12* **Abū Sudayrah** S Iraq
139 *T10* **Abū Ṣukhayr** S Iraq
Abū Sunbul *see* Abu Simbel
185 *E18* **Abut Head** *headland* South Island, New Zealand
80 *E9* **Abu 'Urug** Northern Kordofan, C Sudan
80 *K12* **Ābuyē Mēda** ▲ C Ethiopia
80 *D11* **Abu Zabad** Western Kordofan, C Sudan
Abū Ẓabī *see* Abū Ẓaby
143 *P16* **Abū Ẓaby** *var.* Abū Ẓabī, *Eng.* Abu Dhabi. ● (United Arab Emirates) Abū Ẓaby, C United Arab Emirates
75 *X8* **Abu Zenîma** E Egypt
95 *N17* **Åby** Östergötland, S Sweden
Abyaḍ, Al Baḥr al *see* White Nile
Åbybro *see* Aabybro
80 *D13* **Abyei** Western Kordofan, S Sudan
Abyla *see* Ávila
Abymes *see* les Abymes
Abyssinia *see* Ethiopia
Açâba *see* Assaba
54 *F11* **Acacias** Meta, C Colombia
58 *L13* **Açailandia** Maranhão, E Brazil
Acaill *see* Achill Island
42 *E8* **Acajutla** Sonsonate, W El Salvador
79 *D17* **Acalayong** SW Equatorial Guinea
41 *N13* **Acámbaro** Guanajuato, C Mexico
54 *C6* **Acandí** Chocó, NW Colombia
104 *H4* **A Cañiza** *var.* La Cañiza. Galicia, NW Spain
40 *J11* **Acaponeta** Nayarit, C Mexico
40 *J11* **Acaponeta, Río de** ≈ C Mexico

◆ Country
● Country Capital
◇ Dependent Territory
○ Dependent Territory Capital
◐ Administrative Regions
✈ International Airport
▲ Mountain
▲▲ Mountain Range
Volcano
≈ River
◎ Lake
⊡ Reservoir

ACAPULCO – AÍGINA

41 O16 **Acapulco** *var.* Acapulco de Juárez. Guerrero, S Mexico
Acapulco de Juárez *see* Acapulco
55 T13 **Acarai Mountains** *Sp.* Serra Acaraí. ⛰ Brazil/Guyana
Acaraí, Serra *see* Acarai Mountains
58 O13 **Acaraú** Ceará, NE Brazil
54 J6 **Acarigua** Portuguesa, N Venezuela
42 C6 **Acatenango, Volcán de** 🌋 S Guatemala
41 Q15 **Acatlán** *var.* Acatlán de Osorio. Puebla, S Mexico
Acatlán de Osorio *see* Acatlán
41 S15 **Acayucan** *var.* Acayucán. Veracruz-Llave, E Mexico
Accho *see* 'Akko
21 Y5 **Accomac** Virginia, NE USA
77 Q17 **Accra** ● (Ghana)SE Ghana
97 L17 **Accrington** NW England, UK
61 B19 **Acebal** Santa Fe, C Argentina
168 H8 **Aceh** *off.* Daerah Istimewa Aceh, *var.* Acheen, Achin, Atchin, Atjeh. ◐ *autonomous district* NW Indonesia
107 M18 **Acerenza** Basilicata, S Italy
107 K17 **Acerra** *anc.* Acerrae. Campania, S Italy
Acerrae *see* Acerra
57 J17 **Achacachi** La Paz, W Bolivia
54 K7 **Achaguas** Apure, C Venezuela
154 H12 **Achalpur** *prev.* Elichpur, Ellichpur. Mahārāshtra, C India
61 F18 **Achar** Tacuarembó, C Uruguay
115 H19 **Acharnés** *var.* Aharnes; *prev.* Akharnaí. Attikí, C Greece
Ach'asar Lerr *see* Achkasar
Acheen *see* Aceh
99 K16 **Achel** Limburg, NE Belgium
115 D16 **Achelóos** *var.* Akhelóös, Aspropótamos; *anc.* Achelous. ≈ W Greece
Achelous *see* Achelóos
163 W8 **Acheng** Heilongjiang, NE China
109 N6 **Achenkirch** Tirol, W Austria
101 L24 **Achenpass** *pass* Austria/Germany
109 N7 **Achensee** ⊜ W Austria
101 F22 **Achern** Baden-Württemberg, SW Germany
115 C16 **Acherón** ≈ W Greece
77 W11 **Achétinamou** ≈ S Niger
152 J12 **Achhnera** Uttar Pradesh, N India
42 C7 **Achiguate, Río** ≈ S Guatemala
97 A16 **Achill Head** *Ir.* Ceann Acla. *headland* W Ireland
97 A16 **Achill Island** *Ir.* Acaill. *island* W Ireland
100 H11 **Achim** Niedersachsen, NW Germany
149 S5 **Achīn** Nangarhār, E Afghanistan
Achin *see* Aceh
122 K12 **Achinsk** Krasnoyarskiy Kray, S Russian Federation
162 E5 **Achit Nuur** ⊜ NW Mongolia
137 T11 **Achkasar** *Arm.* Ach'asar Lerr. ▲ Armenia/Georgia
126 K13 **Achuyevo** Krasnodarskiy Kray, SW Russian Federation
81 F16 **Achwa** *var.* Aswa. ≈ N Uganda
136 E15 **Acıgöl** *salt lake* SW Turkey
107 L24 **Acireale** Sicilia, Italy, C Mediterranean Sea
Aciris *see* Agri
25 N7 **Ackerly** Texas, SW USA
22 M4 **Ackerman** Mississippi, S USA
29 W13 **Ackley** Iowa, C USA
44 J5 **Acklins Island** *island* SE Bahamas
Acla, Ceann *see* Achill Head
62 H11 **Aconcagua, Cerro** ▲ W Argentina
Açores/Açores, Arquipélago dos/Açores, Ilhas dos *see* Azores
104 H2 **A Coruña** *Cast.* La Coruña, *Eng.* Corunna; *anc.* Caronium. Galicia, NW Spain
104 G2 **A Coruña** *Cast.* La Coruña. ◐ *province* Galicia, NW Spain
42 L10 **Acoyapa** Chontales, S Nicaragua
106 H13 **Acquapendente** Lazio, C Italy
106 J13 **Acquasanta Terme** Marche, C Italy
106 I13 **Acquasparta** Lazio, C Italy
106 C9 **Acqui Terme** Piemonte, NW Italy
Acrae *see* Palazzola Acreide
182 F7 **Acraman, Lake** *salt lake* South Australia
59 A15 **Acre** *off.* Estado do Acre. ◐ *state* W Brazil
Acre *see* 'Akko
Acre, Estado do *see* Acre
59 C16 **Acre, Rio** ≈ W Brazil
107 N20 **Acri** Calabria, SW Italy
Acte *see* Ágion Óros
191 Y12 **Actéon, Groupe** *island group* Îles Tuamotu, SE French Polynesia
15 P12 **Acton-Vale** Québec, SE Canada
41 P13 **Actopan** *var.* Actopán. Hidalgo, C Mexico
Actopán *see* Actopan
59 P14 **Açu** *var.* Assu. Rio Grande do Norte, E Brazil
Acunum Acusio *see* Montélimar
77 Q17 **Ada** SE Ghana
112 L8 **Ada** Vojvodina, N Serbia
29 R5 **Ada** Minnesota, N USA
31 R12 **Ada** Ohio, N USA
27 O12 **Ada** Oklahoma, C USA
162 L8 **Adaatsag** *var.* Tavin. Dundgovĭ, C Mongolia
Ada Bazar *see* Adapazarı
40 D3 **Adair, Bahía de** *bay* NW Mexico
104 M7 **Adaja** ≈ N Spain
38 H17 **Adak Island** *island* Aleutian Islands, Alaska, USA
Adalia *see* Antalya
Adalia, Gulf of *see* Antalya Körfezi
141 X9 **Adam** N Oman
Adama *see* Nazrēt
60 I8 **Adamantina** São Paulo, S Brazil
79 E14 **Adamaoua** *Eng.* Adamawa. ◐ *province* N Cameroon
68 F11 **Adamaoua, Massif d'** *Eng.* Adamawa Highlands. *plateau* NW Cameroon
77 Y14 **Adamawa** ◐ *state* E Nigeria
Adamawa *see* Adamaoua
Adamawa Highlands *see* Adamaoua, Massif d'
106 F6 **Adamello** ▲ N Italy
81 J14 **Ādamī Tulu** Oromo, C Ethiopia
63 M23 **Adam, Mount** *var.* Monte Independencia. ▲ West Falkland, Falkland Islands
29 R16 **Adams** Nebraska, C USA
18 H8 **Adams** New York, NE USA
29 Q3 **Adams** North Dakota, N USA
155 I23 **Adam's Bridge** *chain of shoals* NW Sri Lanka
32 H10 **Adams, Mount** ▲ Washington, NW USA
Adam's Peak *see* Sri Pada
191 R16 **Adam's Rock** *island* Pitcairn Island, Pitcairn Islands
191 P16 **Adamstown** ○ (Pitcairn Islands)Pitcairn Island, Pitcairn Islands
20 G10 **Adamsville** Tennessee, S USA
25 S9 **Adamsville** Texas, SW USA
141 O17 **'Adan** *Eng.* Aden. SW Yemen
136 K16 **Adana** *var.* Seyhan. Adana, S Turkey
136 K16 **Adana** *var.* Seyhan. ◐ *province* S Turkey
Adâncata *see* Horlivka
169 V12 **Adang, Teluk** *bay* Borneo, C Indonesia
136 F11 **Adapazarı** *prev.* Ada Bazar. Sakarya, NW Turkey
80 H8 **Adarama** River Nile, NE Sudan
195 Q16 **Adare, Cape** *cape* Antarctica
106 E6 **Adda** *anc.* Addua. ≈ N Italy
80 A13 **Adda** ≈ W Sudan
143 Q17 **Aḍ Ḍab'īyah** Abū Ẓaby, C United Arab Emirates
143 O18 **Aḍ Ḍafrah** *desert* S United Arab Emirates
141 Q6 **Ad Dahnā'** *desert* E Saudi Arabia
74 A11 **Ad Dakhla** *var.* Dakhla. SW Western Sahara
Ad Dalanj *see* Dilling
Ad Damar *see* Ed Damer
Ad Damazīn *see* Ed Damazin
Ad Dāmir *see* Ed Damer
173 N2 **Ad Dammām** *desert* NE Saudi Arabia
141 R6 **Ad Dammān** *var.* Dammām. Ash Sharqīyah, NE Saudi Arabia
Ad Dāmūr *see* Damoûr
140 K5 **Ad Dār al Ḥamrā'** Tabūk, NW Saudi Arabia
140 M13 **Ad Darb** Jīzān, SW Saudi Arabia
141 O8 **Ad Dawādimī** Ar Riyāḍ, C Saudi Arabia
143 N16 **Ad Dawḥah** *Eng.* Doha. ● (Qatar) C Qatar
143 N16 **Ad Dawḥah** *Eng.* Doha. ✈ C Qatar
139 S6 **Ad Dawr** N Iraq
139 Y12 **Ad Dayr** *var.* Dayr, Shahbān. E Iraq
Addi Arkay *see* Ādī Ārk'ay
139 X15 **Ad Dibdibah** *physical region* Iraq/Kuwait
Aḍ Ḍiffah *see* Libyan Plateau
Addis Ababa *see* Ādīs Ābeba
Addison *see* Webster Springs
139 U10 **Ad Dīwānīyah** *var.* Diwaniyah. C Iraq
Addua *see* Adda
151 K22 **Addu Atoll** *atoll* S Maldives
Ad Dujail *see* Ad Dujayl
139 T7 **Ad Dujayl** *var.* Ad Dujail. N Iraq
Ad Duwaym/Ad Duwēm *see* Ed Dueim
99 D16 **Adegem** Oost-Vlaanderen, NW Belgium
23 U7 **Adel** Georgia, SE USA
29 U14 **Adel** Iowa, C USA
182 I9 **Adelaide** *state capital* South Australia
44 H2 **Adelaide** New Providence, N Bahamas
182 I9 **Adelaide** ✈ South Australia
194 H6 **Adelaide Island** *island* Antarctica
181 P2 **Adelaide River** Northern Territory, N Australia
76 M10 **'Adel Bagrou** Hodh ech Chargui, SE Mauritania
186 D6 **Adelbert Range** ⛰ N Papua New Guinea
180 K3 **Adele Island** *island* Western Australia
107 O17 **Adelfia** Puglia, SE Italy
195 V16 **Adélie Coast** *physical region* Antarctica
195 V14 **Adélie, Terre** *physical region* Antarctica
Adelnau *see* Odolanów
Adelsberg *see* Postojna
Aden *see* 'Adan
Aden *see* Khormaksar
141 Q17 **Aden, Gulf of** *gulf* SW Arabian Sea
77 V10 **Aderbissinat** Agadez, C Niger
Adhaim *see* Al 'Uẓaym
143 R16 **Adh Dhayd** *var.* Al Dhaid. Ash Shāriqah, NE United Arab Emirates
140 M4 **'Adhfā'** *spring/well* NW Saudi Arabia
138 I13 **'Ādhriyāt, Jabāl al** ⛰ S Jordan
80 I10 **Ādī Ārk'ay** *var.* Addi Arkay. Amhara, N Ethiopia
182 C7 **Adieu, Cape** *headland* South Australia
106 H8 **Adige** *Ger.* Etsch. ≈ N Italy
80 J10 **Ādīgrat** Tigray, N Ethiopia
154 I13 **Ādilabād** *var.* Ādilābād. Andhra Pradesh, C India
Ādilābād *see* Ādilabād
35 P2 **Adin** California, W USA
171 V14 **Adi, Pulau** *island* E Indonesia
18 K8 **Adirondack Mountains** ⛰ New York, NE USA
80 J13 **Ādīs Ābeba** *Eng.* Addis Ababa. ● (Ethiopia) Ādīs Ābeba, C Ethiopia
80 J13 **Ādīs Ābeba** ✈ Ādīs Ābeba, C Ethiopia
80 I11 **Ādīs Zemen** Amhara, N Ethiopia
Adi Ugri *see* Mendefera
137 N15 **Adıyaman** Adıyaman, SE Turkey
137 N15 **Adıyaman** ◐ *province* S Turkey
116 L11 **Adjud** Vrancea, E Romania
45 T6 **Adjuntas** C Puerto Rico
Adjuntas, Presa de las *see* Vicente Guerrero, Presa
Ādkup *see* Erikub Atoll
126 L15 **Adler** Krasnodarskiy Kray, SW Russian Federation
Adler *see* Orlice
108 G7 **Adliswil** Zürich, NW Switzerland
32 G7 **Admiralty Inlet** *inlet* Washington, NW USA
39 X13 **Admiralty Island** *island* Alexander Archipelago, Alaska, USA
186 E5 **Admiralty Islands** *island group* N Papua New Guinea
136 B14 **Adnan Menderes** ✈ (İzmir) İzmir, W Turkey
37 V6 **Adobe Creek Reservoir** ⊞ Colorado, C USA
77 T16 **Ado-Ekiti** Ekiti, SW Nigeria
Adola *see* Kibre Mengist
61 C23 **Adolfo González Chaues** Buenos Aires, E Argentina
155 H17 **Ādoni** Andhra Pradesh, C India
102 K15 **Adour** *anc.* Aturus. ≈ SW France
Adowa *see* Ādwa
105 O15 **Adra** Andalucía, S Spain
107 L24 **Adrano** Sicilia, Italy, C Mediterranean Sea
74 I9 **Adrar** C Algeria
76 K7 **Adrar** ◐ *region* C Mauritania
74 L11 **Adrar** ⛰ SE Algeria
74 A12 **Adrar Souttouf** ⛰ SW Western Sahara
Adrasman *see* Adrasmon
147 Q10 **Adrasmon** *Rus.* Adrasman. NW Tajikistan
78 K10 **Adré** Ouaddaï, E Chad
106 H9 **Adria** *anc.* Atria, Hadria, Hatria. Veneto, NE Italy
31 R10 **Adrian** Michigan, N USA
29 S11 **Adrian** Minnesota, N USA
27 R5 **Adrian** Missouri, C USA
24 M2 **Adrian** Texas, SW USA
21 S4 **Adrian** West Virginia, NE USA
Adrianople/Adrianopolis *see* Edirne
121 P7 **Adriatic Basin** *undersea feature* Adriatic Sea, N Mediterranean Sea
Adriatico, Mare *see* Adriatic Sea
106 L13 **Adriatic Sea** *Alb.* Deti Adriatik, *It.* Mare Adriatico, *SCr.* Jadransko More, *Slvn.* Jadransko Morje. *sea* N Mediterranean Sea
Adriatik, Deti *see* Adriatic Sea
Adua *see* Ādwa
Aduana del Sásabe *see* El Sásabe
79 O17 **Adusa** Orientale, NE Dem. Rep. Congo
118 J13 **Adutiškis** Vilnius, E Lithuania
27 Y7 **Advance** Missouri, C USA
65 D25 **Adventure Sound** *bay* East Falkland, Falkland Islands
80 J10 **Ādwa** *var.* Adowa, *It.* Adua. Tigray, N Ethiopia
123 Q8 **Adycha** ≈ NE Russian Federation
126 L14 **Adygeya, Respublika** ◐ *autonomous republic* SW Russian Federation
Adzhikui *see* Ajyguýy
77 N17 **Adzopé** SE Ivory Coast
125 U4 **Adz'va** ≈ NW Russian Federation
125 U5 **Adz'vavom** Respublika Komi, NW Russian Federation
Ædua *see* Autun
115 K19 **Aegean Islands** *island group* Greece/Turkey
Aegean North *see* Vóreion Aigaíon
115 I17 **Aegean Sea** *Gk.* Aigaíon Pelagos, Aigaío Pélagos, *Turk.* Ege Denizi. *sea* NE Mediterranean Sea
Aegean South *see* Nótion Aigaíon
118 H3 **Aegviidu** *Ger.* Charlottenhof. Harjumaa, NW Estonia
Aegyptus *see* Egypt
Aelana *see* Al 'Aqabah
Aelok *see* Ailuk Atoll
Aelōninae *see* Ailinginae Atoll
Aelōnlaplap *see* Ailinglaplap Atoll
Æmilia *see* Emilia-Romagna
Æmilianum *see* Millau
Aemona *see* Ljubljana
Aenaria *see* Ischia
Aeolian Islands *see* Eolie, Isole
191 Z3 **Aeon Point** *headland* Kiritimati, NE Kiribati
95 G24 **Ærø** *Ger.* Arrö. *island* C Denmark
95 H24 **Ærøskøbing** Fyn, C Denmark
Æsernia *see* Isernia
104 G3 **A Estrada** Galicia, NW Spain
115 C18 **Aetós** Itháki, Iónioi Nísoi, Greece, C Mediterranean Sea
191 Q8 **Afaahiti** Tahiti, W French Polynesia
139 U10 **'Afak** C Iraq
Afanasjevo *see* Afanas'yevo
125 T14 **Afanas'yevo** *var.* Afanasjevo. Kirovskaya Oblast', NW Russian Federation
Afándou *see* Afántou
115 O23 **Afántou** *var.* Afándou. Ródos, Dodekánisa, Greece, Aegean Sea
80 K11 **Afar** ◐ *region* NE Ethiopia
Afar Depression *see* Danakil Desert
191 O7 **Afareaitu** Moorea, W French Polynesia
140 L7 **'Afariyah, Bi'r al** *well* NW Saudi Arabia
Afars et des Issas, Territoire Français des *see* Djibouti
83 D22 **Affenrücken** Karas, SW Namibia
Afghānestān, Dowlat-e Eslāmī-ye *see* Afghanistan
148 M6 **Afghanistan** *off.* Islamic State of Afghanistan, *Per.* Dowlat-e Eslāmī-ye Afghānestān; *prev.* Republic of Afghanistan. ◆ *islamic state* C Asia
Afghanistan, Islamic State of *see* Afghanistan
Afghanistan, Republic of *see* Afghanistan
Afgoi *see* Afgooye
81 N17 **Afgooye** *It.* Afgoi. Shabeellaha Hoose, S Somalia
141 N8 **'Afīf** Ar Riyāḍ, C Saudi Arabia
77 V17 **Afikpo** Ebonyi, S Nigeria
Afiun Karahissar *see* Afyon
Åfjord *see* Åi Åfjord
109 V6 **Aflenz Kurort** Steiermark, E Austria
74 J6 **Aflou** N Algeria
81 L18 **Afmadow** Jubbada Hoose, S Somalia
39 Q14 **Afognak Island** *island* Alaska, USA
104 J2 **A Fonsagrada** Galicia, NW Spain
186 E9 **Afore** Northern, S Papua New Guinea
59 O15 **Afrânio** Pernambuco, E Brazil
66-67 **Africa** *continent*
68 L11 **Africa, Horn of** *physical region* Ethiopia/Somalia
172 K11 **Africana Seamount** *undersea feature* SW Indian Ocean
86 A14 **African Plate** *tectonic plate*
138 I2 **'Afrīn** Ḥalab, N Syria
136 M15 **Afşin** Kahramanmaraş, C Turkey
98 J7 **Afsluitdijk** *dam* N Netherlands
29 U15 **Afton** Iowa, C USA
29 W9 **Afton** Minnesota, N USA
27 R8 **Afton** Oklahoma, C USA
136 F14 **Afyon** *prev.* Afyonkarahisar. Afyon, W Turkey
136 F14 **Afyon** *var.* Afiun Karahissar, Afyonkarahisar. ◐ *province* W Turkey
Afyonkarahisar *see* Afyon
Agadès *see* Agadez
77 V10 **Agadez** *prev.* Agadès. Agadez, C Niger
77 W8 **Agadez** ◐ *department* N Niger
74 E8 **Agadir** SW Morocco
64 M9 **Agadir Canyon** *undersea feature* SE Atlantic Ocean
145 R12 **Agadyr'** Karaganda, C Kazakhstan
173 O7 **Agalega Islands** *island group* N Mauritius
42 K6 **Agalta, Sierra de** ⛰ E Honduras
122 I10 **Agan** ≈ C Russian Federation
Agana/Agaña *see* Hagåtña
188 B15 **Agana Bay** *bay* NW Guam
188 C16 **Agana Field** ✈ (Agana) C Guam
171 Kk13 **Agano-gawa** ≈ Honshū, C Japan
188 B17 **Aga Point** *headland* S Guam
154 G9 **Agar** Madhya Pradesh, C India
81 I14 **Āgaro** Oromo, C Ethiopia
153 V15 **Agartala** *state capital* Tripura, NE India
194 I5 **Agassiz, Cape** *headland* Antarctica
175 V13 **Agassiz Fracture Zone** *fracture zone* S Pacific Ocean
188 B16 **Agat** W Guam
188 B16 **Agat Bay** *bay* W Guam
145 P13 **Agat, Gory** *hill* C Kazakhstan
Agatha *see* Agde
115 M20 **Agathónisi** *island* Dodekánisa, Greece, Aegean Sea
171 X14 **Agats** Papua, E Indonesia
155 C21 **Agatti Island** *island* Lakshadweep, India, N Indian Ocean
38 D16 **Agattu Island** *island* Aleutian Islands, Alaska, USA
38 D16 **Agattu Strait** *strait* Aleutian Islands, Alaska, USA
14 B8 **Agawa** ≈ Ontario, S Canada
14 B8 **Agawa Bay** *lake bay* Ontario, S Canada
77 N17 **Agboville** SE Ivory Coast
137 V12 **Ağdam** *Rus.* Agdam. SW Azerbaijan
Agdam *see* Ağdam
103 P16 **Agde** *anc.* Agatha. Hérault, S France
103 P16 **Agde, Cap d'** *cape* S France
Agedabia *see* Ajdābiyā
102 L14 **Agen** *anc.* Aginnum. Lot-et-Garonne, SW France
Agendicum *see* Sens
165 O13 **Ageo** Saitama, Honshū, S Japan
109 R5 **Ager** ≈ N Austria
Agere Hiywet *see* Hāgere Hiywet
108 G8 **Ägerisee** ⊜ W Switzerland
142 M10 **Āghā Jārī** Khūzestān, SW Iran
39 P15 **Aghiyuk Island** *island* Alaska, USA
74 B12 **Aghouinit** SE Western Sahara
Aghri Dagh *see* Büyükağrı Dağı
74 B10 **Aghzoumal, Sebkhet** *var.* Sebjet Agsumal. *salt lake* E Western Sahara
115 F15 **Agiá** *var.* Ayiá. Thessalía, C Greece
40 G7 **Agiabampo, Estero de** *estuary* NW Mexico
121 P3 **Agía Fýlaxis** *var.* Ayia Phyla. S Cyprus
Agialoúsa *see* Yenierenköy
115 M21 **Agía Marína** Léros, Dodekánisa, Greece, Aegean Sea
121 Q2 **Agía Nápa** *var.* Ayia Napa. E Cyprus
115 L16 **Agía Paraskeví** Lésvos, E Greece
115 J15 **Agías Eirínis, Akrotírio** *headland* Límnos, E Greece
Agiasós *see* Agiassós
115 L17 **Agiassós** *var.* Agiasós, Ayiásos, Ayiássos. Lésvos, E Greece
Aginnum *see* Agen
123 O14 **Aginskiy Buryatskiy Avtonomnyy Okrug** ◐ *autonomous district* S Russian Federation
123 O14 **Aginskoye** Aginskiy Buryatskiy Avtonomnyy Okrug, S Russian Federation
115 I14 **Ágion Óros** *Eng.* Mount Athos. ◐ *monastic republic* NE Greece
115 H14 **Ágion Óros** *var.* Akte, Aktí; *anc.* Acte. *peninsula* NE Greece
114 D13 **Ágios Achílleios** *religious building* Dytikí Makedonía, N Greece
115 J16 **Ágios Efstrátios** *var.* Áyios Evstrátios, Hagios Evstrátios. *island* E Greece
115 H20 **Ágios Geórgios** *island* Kykládes, Greece, Aegean Sea
115 E21 **Ágios Ilías** ▲ S Greece
115 K25 **Ágios Ioannis, Akrotírio** *headland* Kríti, Greece, E Mediterranean Sea
115 L20 **Ágios Kírykos** *var.* Áyios Kírikos. Ikaría, Dodekánisa, Greece, Aegean Sea
115 K25 **Ágios Nikólaos** *var.* Áyios Nikólaos. Kríti, Greece, E Mediterranean Sea
115 D16 **Ágios Nikolaos** Thessalía, C Greece
115 H14 **Agíou Órous, Kólpos** *gulf* N Greece
107 K24 **Agira** *anc.* Agyrium. Sicilia, Italy, C Mediterranean Sea
115 G20 **Agkístri** *island* S Greece
114 G12 **Ágkistro** *var.* Angistro. ▲ NE Greece
103 O17 **Agly** ≈ S France
Agnetheln *see* Agnita
14 E10 **Agnew Lake** ⊜ Ontario, S Canada
77 O16 **Agnibilékrou** E Ivory Coast
116 I11 **Agnita** *Ger.* Agnetheln, *Hung.* Szentágota. Sibiu, SW Romania
107 K15 **Agnone** Molise, C Italy
164 K14 **Ago** Mie, Honshū, SW Japan
106 C8 **Agogna** ≈ N Italy
Agoitz *see* Agoiz
105 R3 **Agoiz** *var.* Agoitz, Aoiz. Navarra, N Spain
77 P17 **Agona Swedru** *var.* Swedru. SE Ghana
Agordat *see* Akurdet
Agosta *see* Augusta
103 N15 **Agout** ≈ S France
152 J12 **Āgra** Uttar Pradesh, N India
Agra and Oudh, United Provinces of *see* Uttar Pradesh
Agram *see* Zagreb
105 U5 **Agramunt** Cataluña, NE Spain
105 Q5 **Agreda** Castilla-León, N Spain
137 S13 **Ağrı** *var.* Karaköse; *prev.* Karakılısse. Ağrı, NE Turkey
137 S13 **Ağrı** ◐ *province* NE Turkey
107 N19 **Agri** *anc.* Aciris. ≈ S Italy
Agri Dagi *see* Büyükağrı Dağı
107 J24 **Agrigento** *Gk.* Akragas; *prev.* Girgenti. Sicilia, Italy, C Mediterranean Sea
188 K4 **Agrihan** *island* N Northern Mariana Islands
115 L17 **Agriliá, Akrotírio** *prev.* Ákra Maléas. *cape* Lésvos, E Greece
115 D18 **Agrínio** *prev.* Agrinion. Dytikí Ellás, W Greece
Agrinion *see* Agrínio
115 G17 **Agriovótano** Évvoia, C Greece
107 L18 **Agropoli** Campania, S Italy
127 T3 **Agryz** Udmurtskaya Respublika, NW Russian Federation
137 U11 **Ağstafa** *Rus.* Akstafa. NW Azerbaijan
137 X11 **Ağsu** *Rus.* Akhsu. C Azerbaijan
Agsumal, Sebjet *see* Aghzoumal, Sebkhet
40 J11 **Agua Brava, Laguna** *lagoon* W Mexico
54 F7 **Aguachica** Cesar, N Colombia
59 J20 **Água Clara** Mato Grosso do Sul, SW Brazil
44 D5 **Aguada de Pasajeros** Cienfuegos, C Cuba
54 J5 **Aguada Grande** Lara, N Venezuela
45 S5 **Aguadilla** W Puerto Rico
43 S16 **Aguadulce** Coclé, S Panama
104 L14 **Aguadulce** Andalucía, S Spain
41 O8 **Agualeguas** Nuevo León, NE Mexico
40 L9 **Aguanaval, Río** ≈ C Mexico
42 J5 **Aguán, Río** ≈ N Honduras
25 R16 **Agua Nueva** Texas, SW USA
60 J8 **Aguapeí, Rio** ≈ S Brazil
61 E14 **Aguapey, Río** ≈ NE Argentina
40 G3 **Agua Prieta** Sonora, NW Mexico
104 G5 **A Guarda** *var.* A Guardia, Laguardia, La Guardia. Galicia, NW Spain
A Guardia *see* A Guarda
56 E6 **Aguarico, Río** ≈ Ecuador/Peru
55 O6 **Aguasay** Monagas, NE Venezuela
40 M12 **Aguascalientes** Aguascalientes, C Mexico
40 L12 **Aguascalientes** ◐ *state* C Mexico
57 I18 **Aguas Calientes, Río** ≈ S Peru
105 R7 **Aguasvivas** ≈ NE Spain
60 J7 **Água Vermelha, Represa de** ⊞ S Brazil
56 E12 **Aguaytía** Ucayali, C Peru
104 I5 **A Gudiña** *var.* La Gudiña. Galicia, NW Spain
104 G7 **Águeda** Aveiro, N Portugal
104 J8 **Águeda** ≈ Portugal/Spain
77 Q8 **Aguelhok** Kidal, NE Mali
77 V12 **Aguié** Maradi, S Niger
188 K8 **Aguijan** *island* S Northern Mariana Islands
104 M14 **Aguilar** *var.* Aguilar de la Frontera. Andalucía, S Spain
104 M3 **Aguilar de Campóo** Castilla-León, N Spain
Aguilar de la Frontera *see* Aguilar
42 F7 **Aguilares** San Salvador, C El Salvador
105 Q14 **Aguilas** Murcia, SE Spain
40 L15 **Aguililla** Michoacán de Ocampo, SW Mexico
Agulhas *see* L'Agulhas
172 J11 **Agulhas Bank** *undersea feature* SW Indian Ocean
172 K11 **Agulhas Basin** *undersea feature* SW Indian Ocean
83 F26 **Agulhas, Cape** *Afr.* Kaap Agulhas. *headland* SW South Africa
Agulhas, Kaap *see* Agulhas, Cape
60 O9 **Agulhas Negras, Pico das** ▲ SE Brazil
172 K11 **Agulhas Plateau** *undersea feature* SW Indian Ocean
165 S16 **Aguni-jima** *island* Nansei-shotō, SW Japan
Agurain *see* Salvatierra
54 G5 **Agustín Codazzi** *var.* Codazzi. Cesar, N Colombia
Agyrium *see* Agira
74 L12 **Ahaggar** *high plateau region* SE Algeria
146 E12 **Ahal Welaýaty** *Rus.* Akhalskiy Velayat. ◐ *province* C Turkmenistan
142 K2 **Ahar** Āżarbāyjān-e Sharqī, NW Iran
Aharnes *see* Acharnés
138 J3 **Aḥaş, Jabal** ▲ NW Syria
138 J3 **Aḥaş, Jebal** ⛰ W Syria
185 G16 **Ahaura** ≈ South Island, New Zealand
100 E13 **Ahaus** Nordrhein-Westfalen, NW Germany
191 U9 **Ahe** *atoll* Îles Tuamotu, C French Polynesia
184 N10 **Ahimanawa Range** ⛰ North Island, New Zealand
119 I19 **Ahinski Kanal** *Rus.* Oginskiy Kanal. *canal* SW Belarus
186 G10 **Ahioma** SE Papua New Guinea
184 I2 **Ahipara** Northland, North Island, New Zealand
184 I2 **Ahipara Bay** *bay* SE Tasman Sea
Áhkká *see* Akka
39 N13 **Ahklun Mountains** ⛰ Alaska, USA
137 R14 **Ahlat** Bitlis, E Turkey
101 F14 **Ahlen** Nordrhein-Westfalen, W Germany
154 D10 **Ahmadābād** *var.* Ahmedabad. Gujarāt, W India
143 R10 **Ahmadābād** Kermān, C Iran
Ahmadi *see* Al Aḥmadī
Ahmad Khel *see* Ḥasan Khēl
155 F14 **Ahmadnagar** *var.* Ahmednagar. Mahārāshtra, W India
149 T9 **Ahmadpur Siāl** Punjab, E Pakistan
77 N5 **Aḥmar, 'Erg el** *desert* N Mali
80 K13 **Ahmar Mountains** ⛰ C Ethiopia
Ahmedabad *see* Ahmadābād
Ahmednagar *see* Ahmadnagar
114 N12 **Ahmetbey** Kırklareli, NW Turkey
14 H12 **Ahmic Lake** ⊜ Ontario, S Canada
190 G12 **Ahoa** Île Uvea, E Wallis and Futuna
40 G8 **Ahomé** Sinaloa, C Mexico
21 X8 **Ahoskie** North Carolina, SE USA
101 D17 **Ahr** ≈ W Germany
143 N12 **Ahram** *var.* Ahrom. Būshehr, S Iran
100 J9 **Ahrensburg** Schleswig-Holstein, N Germany
Ahrom *see* Ahram
93 L17 **Ähtäri** Länsi-Soumi, W Finland
40 K12 **Ahuacatlán** Nayarit, C Mexico
42 E7 **Ahuachapán** Ahuachapán, W El Salvador
42 A9 **Ahuachapán** ◐ *department* W El Salvador
191 V16 **Ahu Akivi** *var.* Siete Moai. *ancient monument* Easter Island, Chile, E Pacific Ocean
191 W11 **Ahunui** *atoll* Îles Tuamotu, C French Polynesia
185 E20 **Ahuriri** ≈ South Island, New Zealand
95 L22 **Åhus** Skåne, S Sweden
Ahu Tahira *see* Ahu Vinapu
191 V16 **Ahu Tepeu** *ancient monument* Easter Island, Chile, E Pacific Ocean
191 V17 **Ahu Vinapu** *var.* Ahu Tahira. *ancient monument* Easter Island, Chile, E Pacific Ocean
142 L9 **Ahvāz** *var.* Ahwāz; *prev.* Nāsiri. Khūzestān, SW Iran
Ahvenanmaa *see* Åland
141 Q16 **Aḥwar** SW Yemen
Ahwāz *see* Ahvāz
94 H7 **Åi Åfjord** *var.* Åfjord, Årnes. Sør-Trøndelag, C Norway
Aibak *see* Āybak
101 K22 **Aichach** Bayern, SE Germany
164 L14 **Aichi** *off.* Aichi-ken, *var.* Aiti. ◐ *prefecture* Honshū, SW Japan
Aichi-ken *see* Aichi
Aïdin *see* Aydın
Aidussina *see* Ajdovščina
Aifir, Clochán an *see* Giant's Causeway
Aigaíon Pelagos/Aigaío Pélagos *see* Aegean Sea
109 S3 **Aigen im Mülkreis** Oberösterreich, N Austria
115 G20 **Aígina** *var.* Aíyina, Egina. Aígina, C Greece
115 G20 **Aígina** *island* S Greece

◆ Country
● Country Capital
◇ Dependent Territory
○ Dependent Territory Capital
◐ Administrative Regions
✈ International Airport
▲ Mountain
⛰ Mountain Range
🌋 Volcano
≈ River
⊜ Lake
⊞ Reservoir

AL BURAYMĪ – ALMENARAS

143 R17 Al Buraymī var. Buraimi. spring/well Oman/United Arab Emirates
Al Burayqah see Marsá al Burayqah
Alburgum see Aalborg
104 I10 Alburquerque Extremadura, W Spain
181 V14 Albury New South Wales, SE Australia
141 T14 Al Buzūn SE Yemen
93 G17 Alby Västernorrland, C Sweden
Albyn, Glen see Mor, Glen
104 G12 Alcácer do Sal Setúbal, W Portugal
Alcalá de Chisvert/Alcalá de Chivert see Alcalà de Xivert
104 K14 Alcalá de Guadaira Andalucía, S Spain
105 O8 Alcalá de Henares Ar. Alkal'a; anc. Complutum. Madrid, C Spain
104 K16 Alcalá de los Gazules Andalucía, S Spain
105 T8 Alcalà de Xivert var. Alcalá de Chisvert, Cast. Alcalá de Chivert. País Valenciano, E Spain
105 N14 Alcalá La Real Andalucía, S Spain
107 I23 Alcamo Sicilia, Italy, C Mediterranean Sea
105 T4 Alcanadre ≈ NE Spain
105 T8 Alcanar Cataluña, NE Spain
104 J5 Alcañices Castilla-León, N Spain
105 T7 Alcañiz Aragón, NE Spain
104 I9 Alcántara Extremadura, W Spain
104 J9 Alcántara, Embalse de ⊠ W Spain
105 R13 Alcantarilla Murcia, SE Spain
105 P11 Alcaraz Castilla-La Mancha, C Spain
105 P12 Alcaraz, Sierra de ⛰ C Spain
104 I12 Alcarrache ≈ SW Spain
105 T6 Alcarràs Cataluña, NE Spain
105 N14 Alcaudete Andalucía, S Spain
Alcázar see Ksar-el-Kebir
105 O10 Alcázar de San Juan anc. Alce. Castilla-La Mancha, C Spain
Alcazarquivir see Ksar-el-Kebir
Alce see Alcázar de San Juan
57 B17 Alcebo, Volcán 🌋 Galapagos Islands, Ecuador, E Pacific Ocean
139 X12 Al Chabā'ish var. Al Kaba'ish. SE Iraq
117 Y7 Alchevs'k prev. Kommunarsk, Voroshilovsk. Luhans'ka Oblast', E Ukraine
Alcira see Alzira
21 N9 Alcoa Tennessee, S USA
104 F9 Alcobaça Leiria, C Portugal
105 N8 Alcobendas Madrid, C Spain
Alcoi see Alcoy
105 P7 Alcolea del Pinar Castilla-La Mancha, C Spain
104 I11 Alconchel Extremadura, W Spain
Alcora see L'Alcora
105 N8 Alcorcón Madrid, C Spain
105 S7 Alcorisa Aragón, NE Spain
61 B19 Alcorta Santa Fe, C Argentina
104 H14 Alcoutim Faro, S Portugal
33 W15 Alcova Wyoming, C USA
105 S11 Alcoy Cat. Alcoi. País Valenciano, E Spain
105 Y9 Alcúdia Mallorca, Spain, W Mediterranean Sea
105 Y9 Alcúdia, Badia d' bay Mallorca, Spain, W Mediterranean Sea
172 M7 Aldabra Group island group SW Seychelles
139 U10 Al Daghghārah C Iraq
40 J5 Aldama Chihuahua, N Mexico
41 P11 Aldama Tamaulipas, C Mexico
123 Q11 Aldan Respublika Sakha (Yakutiya), NE Russian Federation
123 Q10 Aldan ≈ NE Russian Federation
Aldar see Aldarhaan
al Dar al Baida see Rabat
162 G7 Aldarhaan var. Aldar. Dzavhan, W Mongolia
97 Q20 Aldeburgh E England, UK
105 P5 Aldehuela de Calatañazor Castilla-León, N Spain
Aldeia Nova see Aldeia Nova de São Bento
104 H13 Aldeia Nova de São Bento var. Aldeia Nova. Beja, S Portugal
29 V11 Alden Minnesota, N USA
184 N6 Aldermen Islands, The island group N New Zealand
97 L25 Alderney island Channel Islands
97 N22 Aldershot S England, UK
21 R6 Alderson West Virginia, NE USA
Al Dhaid see Adh Dhayd
30 J11 Aledo Illinois, N USA
76 H9 Aleg Brakna, SW Mauritania
64 Q10 Alegranza island Islas Canarias, Spain, NE Atlantic Ocean
37 P12 Alegres Mountain ▲ New Mexico, SW USA
61 F15 Alegrete Rio Grande do Sul, S Brazil
61 C16 Alejandra Santa Fe, C Argentina
193 T11 Alejandro Selkirk, Isla island Islas Juan Fernández, Chile, E Pacific Ocean
124 I12 Alekhovshchina Leningradskaya Oblast', NW Russian Federation
39 O13 Aleknagik Alaska, USA
Aleksandriya see Oleksandriya
Aleksandropol' see Gyumri
126 L3 Aleksandrov Vladimirskaya Oblast', W Russian Federation
113 N14 Aleksandrovac Serbia, C Serbia
127 R9 Aleksandrov Gay Saratovskaya Oblast', W Russian Federation
127 U6 Aleksandrovka Orenburgskaya Oblast', W Russian Federation
Aleksandrovka see Oleksandrivka
114 J8 Aleksandrovo Lovech, N Bulgaria
125 V13 Aleksandrovsk Permskaya Oblast', NW Russian Federation
Aleksandrovsk see Zaporizhzhya
127 N14 Aleksandrovskoye Stavropol'skiy Kray, SW Russian Federation
123 T12 Aleksandrovsk-Sakhalinskiy Ostrov Sakhalin, Sakhalinskaya Oblast', SE Russian Federation
110 J10 Aleksandrów Kujawski Kujawskio-pormorskie, C Poland
110 K12 Aleksandrów Łódzki Łódzkie, C Poland
Alekseevka see Alekseyevka, Akmola, Kazakhstan
Alekseevka see Akkol', Akmola, Kazakhstan
Alekseevka see Terekty
Alekseevka see Terekty
145 P7 Alekseyevka Kaz. Alekseevka. Akmola, N Kazakhstan
126 L9 Alekseyevka Belgorodskaya, W Russian Federation
127 S7 Alekseyevka Samarskaya Oblast', W Russian Federation
Alekseyevka see Akkol'
Alekseyevka see Terekty, Vostochnyy Kazakhstan, Kazakhstan
127 R4 Alekseyevskoye Respublika Tatarstan, W Russian Federation
126 K5 Aleksin Tul'skaya Oblast', W Russian Federation
113 O14 Aleksinac Serbia, SE Serbia
190 G11 Alele Île Uvea, E Wallis and Futuna
95 N20 Ålem Kalmar, S Sweden
102 L6 Alençon Orne, N France
58 I12 Alenquer Pará, NE Brazil
38 G10 'Alenuihaha Channel var Alenuihaha Channel. channel Hawaii, USA, C Pacific Ocean
Alep/Aleppo see Ḩalab
Aleppo see Ḩalab
103 Y15 Aléria Corse, France, C Mediterranean Sea
197 Q11 Alert Ellesmere Island, Nunavut, N Canada
103 Q14 Alès prev. Alais. Gard, S France
116 G9 Aleşd Hung. Élesd. Bihor, SW Romania
106 C9 Alessandria Fr. Alexandrie. Piemonte, N Italy
Ålestrup see Aalestrup
94 D9 Ålesund Møre og Romsdal, S Norway
108 E10 Aletschhorn ▲ SW Switzerland
197 S1 Aleutian Basin undersea feature Bering Sea
38 H17 Aleutian Islands island group Alaska, USA
39 P14 Aleutian Range ⛰ Alaska, USA
0 B5 Aleutian Trench undersea feature S Bering Sea
123 T10 Alevina, Mys cape E Russian Federation
15 Q6 Alex ≈ Québec, SE Canada
28 J3 Alexander North Dakota, N USA
39 W14 Alexander Archipelago island group Alaska, USA
Alexanderbaai see Alexander Bay
83 D23 Alexander Bay Afr. Alexanderbaai. Northern Cape, W South Africa
23 Q5 Alexander City Alabama, S USA
194 J6 Alexander Island island Antarctica
Alexander Range see Kirghiz Range
183 O12 Alexandra Victoria, SE Australia
185 D22 Alexandra Otago, South Island, New Zealand
115 F14 Aléxandreia var. Alexándria. Kentrikí Makedonía, N Greece
Alexandretta see İskenderun
Alexandretta, Gulf of see İskenderun Körfezi
15 N13 Alexandria Ontario, SE Canada
121 U13 Alexandria Ar. Al Iskandarīyah. N Egypt
44 J12 Alexandria C Jamaica
116 J15 Alexandria Teleorman, S Romania
31 P13 Alexandria Indiana, N USA
20 M4 Alexandria Kentucky, S USA
22 H7 Alexandria Louisiana, S USA
29 T7 Alexandria Minnesota, N USA
29 Q11 Alexandria South Dakota, N USA
21 W4 Alexandria Virginia, NE USA
Alexándria see Aléxandreia
18 I7 Alexandria Bay New York, NE USA
Alexandrie see Alessandria
182 J10 Alexandrina, Lake ◎ South Australia
114 K13 Alexandroúpoli var. Alexandroúpolis, Turk. Dedeagaç, Dedeagach. Anatolikí Makedonía kai Thráki, NE Greece
Alexandroúpolis see Alexandroúpoli
10 L15 Alexis Creek British Columbia, SW Canada
122 I13 Aleysk Altayskiy Kray, S Russian Federation
139 S8 Al Fallūjah var. Falluja. C Iraq
105 R8 Alfambra ≈ E Spain
Al Faqa see Faq'
141 R15 Al Farḑah C Yemen
105 Q4 Alfaro La Rioja, N Spain
105 U5 Alfarràs Cataluña, NE Spain
Al Fāshir see El Fasher
Al Fashn see El Fashn
114 M7 Alfatar Silistra, NE Bulgaria
139 S5 Al Fatḩah C Iraq
139 Q3 Al Fatsī N Iraq
139 Z13 Al Fāw var. Fao. SE Iraq
Al Fayyūm see El Faiyûm
115 D20 Alfeiós prev. Alfiós; anc. Alpheius, Alpheus. ≈ S Greece
100 I13 Alfeld Niedersachsen, C Germany
Alfiós see Alfeiós
Alföld see Great Hungarian Plain
94 C11 Ålfotbreen glacier S Norway
19 P9 Alfred Maine, NE USA
18 F11 Alfred New York, NE USA
61 K14 Alfredo Vagner Santa Catarina, S Brazil
94 M12 Alfta Gävleborg, C Sweden
140 K12 Al Fuḩayḩīl var. Fahaheel. SE Kuwait
139 Q6 Al Fuḩaymī C Iraq
143 S16 Al Fujayrah Eng. Fujairah. Al Fujayrah, NE United Arab Emirates
143 S16 Al Fujayrah Eng. Fujairah. ✈ Al Fujayrah, NE United Arab Emirates
Al-Furāt see Euphrates
144 I10 Alga Kaz. Algha. Aktyubinsk, NW Kazakhstan
144 G9 Algabas Zapadnyy Kazakhstan, NW Kazakhstan
95 C17 Ålgård Rogaland, S Norway
104 G14 Algarve cultural region S Portugal
182 G3 Algebuckina Bridge South Australia
104 K16 Algeciras Andalucía, SW Spain
105 S10 Algemesí País Valenciano, E Spain
Al-Genain see El Geneina
120 F9 Alger var. Algiers, El Djazaïr, Al Jazair. ● (Algeria) N Algeria
74 H9 Algeria off. Democratic and Popular Republic of Algeria. ◆ republic N Africa
Algeria, Democratic and Popular Republic of see Algeria
120 J8 Algerian Basin var. Balearic Plain. undersea feature W Mediterranean Sea
Algha see Alga
138 I4 Al Ghāb ◎ NW Syria
141 X10 Al Ghābah var. Ghaba. C Oman
141 U14 Al Ghayḑah E Yemen
140 M6 Al Ghazālah Ḩā'il, NW Saudi Arabia
107 B17 Alghero Sardegna, Italy, C Mediterranean Sea
95 M20 Älghult Kronoberg, S Sweden
Al Ghurdaqah see Hurghada
Algiers see Alger
105 S10 Alginet País Valenciano, E Spain
83 I26 Algoa Bay bay S South Africa
104 L15 Algodonales Andalucía, S Spain
105 N9 Algodor ≈ C Spain
Al Golea see El Goléa
31 N6 Algoma Wisconsin, N USA
29 U12 Algona Iowa, C USA
20 L8 Algood Tennessee, S USA
105 O2 Algorta País Vasco, N Spain
61 E18 Algorta Río Negro, W Uruguay
Al Haba see Haba
139 Q10 Al Habbārīyah S Iraq
Al Hadhar see Al Ḩaḑr
139 Q4 Al Ḩaḑr var. Al Hadhar; anc. Hatra. NW Iraq
139 T13 Al Ḩajarah desert S Iraq
141 W8 Al Ḩajār al Gharbī ⛰ N Oman
141 Y8 Al Hajar ash Sharqī ⛰ NE Oman
141 R15 Al Ḩajarayn C Yemen
138 L10 Al Ḩamād desert Jordan/Saudi Arabia
Al Hamad see Syrian Desert
75 N9 Al Ḩamādah al Ḩamrā' var. Al Ḩamrā'. desert NW Libya
105 N15 Alhama de Granada Andalucía, S Spain
105 R13 Alhama de Murcia Murcia, SE Spain
35 T15 Alhambra California, W USA
139 T12 Al Ḩammām S Iraq
141 X8 Al Ḩamrā' NE Oman
Al Ḩamrā' see Al Ḩamādah al Ḩamrā'
141 O6 Al Ḩamūdīyah spring/well N Saudi Arabia
140 M7 Al Ḩanākīyah Al Madīnah, W Saudi Arabia
139 W14 Al Ḩanīyah escarpment Iraq/Saudi Arabia
139 Y12 Al Ḩārithah SE Iraq
140 L3 Al Ḩarrah desert NW Saudi Arabia
75 Q10 Al Harūj al Aswad desert C Libya
Al Hasaifin see Al Ḩusayfīn
139 N2 Al Ḩasakah var. Al Hasijah, El Haseke, Fr. Hassetché. Al Ḩasakah, NE Syria
139 O2 Al Ḩasakah off. Muḩāfaẓat al Ḩasakah, var. Al Hasakah, Āl Hasakah, Hasakah, Hassakeh. ◈ governorate NE Syria
Al Hasakah see 'Āmūdah
Al Hasakah see Al Ḩasakah
139 T9 Al Hāshimīyah C Iraq
138 G13 Al Hāshimīyah Ma'ān, S Jordan
104 M15 Alhaurín el Grande Andalucía, S Spain
141 Q16 Al Ḩawrā S Yemen
139 V10 Al Ḩayy var. Kut al Hai, Kūt al Ḩayy. E Iraq
141 U11 Al Ḩibāk desert E Saudi Arabia
138 H8 Al Hījānah var. Hejanah, Hijanah. Dimashq, W Syria
140 K7 Al Ḩijāz Eng. Hejaz. coastal and highland region NW Saudi Arabia
Al Hilbeh see 'Ulayyānīyah, Bi'r al
139 T9 Al Ḩillah var. Hilla. C Iraq
139 T9 Al Hindīyah var. Hindiya. C Iraq
138 G12 Al Ḩisā Aṭ Ṭafīlah, W Jordan
74 G5 Al-Hoceïma var. al Hoceima, Al-Hoceima, Alhucemas; prev. Villa Sanjurjo. N Morocco
Alhucemas see Al-Hoceïma
105 N17 Alhucemas, Peñon de island group S Spain
141 N15 Al Ḩudaydah Eng. Hodeida. W Yemen
141 N15 Al Ḩudaydah var. Hodeida. ✈ W Yemen
140 M4 Al Ḩudūd ash Shamālīyah var. Minṭaqat al Ḩudūd ash Shamālīyah, Eng. Northern Border Region. ◈ province N Saudi Arabia
141 S7 Al Hufūf var. Hofuf. Ash Sharqīyah, NE Saudi Arabia
al-Hurma see Al Khurmah
141 X7 Al Ḩusayfīn var. Al Hasaifin. N Oman
138 G9 Al Ḩuṣn var. Husn. Irbid, N Jordan
139 U9 'Alī E Iraq
104 L10 Alia Extremadura, W Spain
143 P9 'Alīābād Yazd, C Iran
'Alīābad see Qā'emshahr
105 S7 Aliaga Aragón, NE Spain
136 B13 Aliağa İzmir, W Turkey
Aliákmon see Aliákmonas
115 F14 Aliákmonas prev. Aliákmon; anc. Haliacmon. ≈ N Greece
139 W9 'Alī al Gharbī E Iraq
139 U11 'Alī al Ḩassūnī S Iraq
115 G18 Alíartos Stereá Ellás, C Greece
137 Y12 Äli-Bayramli Rus. Ali-Bayramly. SE Azerbaijan
Ali-Bayramly see Äli-Bayramli
114 P12 Alibey Barajı ⊠ NW Turkey
77 S13 Alibori ≈ N Benin
112 M10 Alibunar Vojvodina, NE Serbia
105 S12 Alicante Cat. Alacant, Lat. Lucentum. País Valenciano, SE Spain
105 S12 Alicante ◈ province País Valenciano, SE Spain
105 S12 Alicante ✈ Murcia, E Spain
83 I25 Alice Eastern Cape, S South Africa
25 S14 Alice Texas, SW USA
83 I25 Alicedale Eastern Cape, S South Africa
65 B25 Alice, Mount hill West Falkland, Falkland Islands
107 P20 Alice, Punta headland S Italy
181 Q7 Alice Springs Northern Territory, C Australia
23 N4 Aliceville Alabama, S USA
147 U13 Alichur SE Tajikistan
147 U14 Alichuri Janubí, Qatorkŭhi Rus. Yuzhno-Alichurskiy Khrebet. ⛰ SE Tajikistan
147 U13 Alichuri Shimolí, Qatorkŭhi Rus. Severo-Alichurskiy Khrebet. ⛰ SE Tajikistan
107 K22 Alicudi, Isola island Isole Eolie, S Italy
152 J11 Alīgarh Uttar Pradesh, N India
142 M7 Alīgūdarz Lorestān, W Iran
163 U5 Alihe var. Oroqen Zizhiqi. Nei Mongol Zizhiqu, N China
0 F12 Alijos, Islas islets California, SW USA
149 R6 'Alī Kbel Pash. 'Alī Khēl. Paktīkā, E Afghanistan
Ali Khel see 'Alī Kheyl, Paktīā, Afghanistan
'Alī Khēl see 'Alī Kbel, Paktīkā, Afghanistan
149 R6 'Alī Kheyl var. Ali Khel, Jajī. Paktīā, SE Afghanistan
141 V17 Al Ikhwān island group SE Yemen
Aliki see Alykí
79 H19 Alima ≈ C Congo
Al Imārāt al 'Arabīyah al Muttaḩidah see United Arab Emirates
115 N23 Alimía island Dodekánisa, Greece, Aegean Sea
55 V12 Alimimuni Piek ▲ S Surinam
79 K15 Alindao Basse-Kotto, S Central African Republic
95 J18 Alingsås Västra Götaland, S Sweden
81 K18 Alinjugul spring/well E Kenya
149 S11 Alīpur Punjab, E Pakistan
153 T12 Alīpur Duār West Bengal, NE India
18 B14 Aliquippa Pennsylvania, NE USA
80 L12 'Ali Sabieh var. 'Alī Sabīḩ. S Djibouti
'Alī Sabīḩ see 'Ali Sabieh
140 K3 Al 'Īsāwīyah Al Jawf, NW Saudi Arabia
104 J10 Aliseda Extremadura, W Spain
139 T8 Al Iskandarīyah C Iraq
Al Iskandarīyah see Alexandria
123 T6 Aliskerovo Chukotskiy Avtonomnyy Okrug, NE Russian Federation
114 H13 Alistráti Kentrikí Makedonía, NE Greece
39 P15 Alitak Bay bay Kodiak Island, Alaska, USA
Al Ittiḩād see Madīnat ash Sha'b
115 H18 Alivéri var. Alivérion. Évvoia, C Greece
Alivérion see Alivéri
Aliwal-Noord see Aliwal North
83 I24 Aliwal North Afr. Aliwal-Noord. Eastern Cape, SE South Africa
121 Q13 Al Jabal al Akhḑar ⛰ NE Libya
138 H13 Al Jafr Ma'ān, S Jordan
75 T8 Al Jaghbūb NE Libya
142 K11 Al Jahrā' var. Al Jahrah, Jahra. C Kuwait
Al Jahrah see Al Jahrā'
Al Jamāhīrīyah al 'Arabīyah al Lībīyah ash Sha'bīyah al Ishtirākīy see Libya
140 K3 Al Jarāwī spring/well NW Saudi Arabia
141 X11 Al Jawārah oasis SE Oman
140 L3 Al Jawf off. Jauf. Al Jawf, NW Saudi Arabia
140 L4 Al Jawf var. Minṭaqat al Jawf. ◈ province N Saudi Arabia
Al Jawlān see Golan Heights
Al Jazair see Alger
139 N4 Al Jazīrah physical region Iraq/Syria
104 F14 Aljezur Faro, S Portugal
139 S13 Al Jil S Iraq
138 G11 Al Jīzah var. Jiza. 'Ammān, N Jordan
Al Jīzah see El Giza
Al Jubail see Al Jubayl
141 S6 Al Jubayl var. Al Jubail. Ash Sharqīyah, NE Saudi Arabia
141 T10 Al Juḩaysh, Qalamat well SE Saudi Arabia
143 N15 Al Jumaylīyah N Qatar
Al Junaynah see El Geneina
104 G13 Aljustrel Beja, S Portugal
Al-Kaba'ish see Al Chabā'ish
Al-Kadhimain see Al Kāẓimīyah
Al Kāf see El Kef
Alkal'a see Alcalá de Henares
35 W4 Alkali Flat salt flat Nevada, W USA
35 Q1 Alkali Lake ◎ Nevada, W USA
141 Z9 Al Kāmil NE Oman
138 G11 Al Karak var. El Kerak, Karak, Kerak; anc. Kir Moab, Kir of Moab. Al Karak, W Jordan
138 G12 Al Karak off. Muḩāfaẓat al Karak. ◈ governorate W Jordan
139 W8 Al Karmashīyah E Iraq
Al-Kashaniya see Al Qash'ānīyah
Al-Kasr al-Kebir see Ksar-el-Kebir
139 T8 Al Kāẓimīyah var. Al-Kadhimain, Kadhimain. C Iraq
99 J18 Alken Limburg, NE Belgium
141 X8 Al Khābūrah var. Khabura. N Oman
Al Khalīl see Hebron
139 T7 Al Khāliş C Iraq
Al Khaluf see Khalūf
Al Khārijah see El Khârga
141 Q8 Al Kharj Ar Riyāḑ, C Saudi Arabia
141 W6 Al Khaşab var. Khasab. N Oman
Al Khaur see Al Khawr
143 N15 Al Khawr var. Al Khaur, Al Khor. N Qatar
142 K12 Al Khīrān var. Al Khiran. SE Kuwait
141 W9 Al Khīrān spring/well NW Oman
Al Khiyām see El Khiyam
Al-Khobar see Al Khubar
Al Khor see Al Khawr
141 S6 Al Khubar var. Al-Khobar. Ash Sharqīyah, NE Saudi Arabia
75 T11 Al Khufrah SE Libya
120 M12 Al Khums var. Homs, Khoms, Khums. NW Libya
141 R15 Al Khuraybah C Yemen
140 M9 Al Khurmah var. al-Hurma. Makkah, W Saudi Arabia
141 V9 Al Kidan desert NE Saudi Arabia
127 V4 Alkino-2 Respublika Bashkortostan, W Russian Federation
98 H9 Alkmaar Noord-Holland, NW Netherlands
139 T10 Al Kūfah var. Kufa. S Iraq
141 T10 Al Kursū' desert E Saudi Arabia
139 V9 Al Kūt var. Kūt al 'Amārah, Kut al Imara. E Iraq
Al-Kuwait see Al Kuwayt
Al Kuwayr see Guwêr
142 K11 Al Kuwayt var. Al-Kuwait, Eng. Kuwait, Kuwait City; prev. Qurein. ● (Kuwait) E Kuwait
142 K11 Al Kuwayt ✈ C Kuwait
115 G19 Alkyonídon, Kólpos gulf C Greece
141 N4 Al Labbah physical region N Saudi Arabia
138 G4 Al Lādhiqīyah Eng. Latakia, Fr. Lattaquié; anc. Laodicea, Laodicea ad Mare. Al Lādhiqīyah, W Syria
138 H4 Al Lādhiqīyah off. Muḩāfaẓat al Lādhiqīyah, var. Al Lathqiyah, Latakia, Lattakia. ◈ governorate W Syria
19 R2 Allagash River ≈ Maine, NE USA
152 M13 Allahābād Uttar Pradesh, N India
143 S3 Allāh Dāgh, Reshteh-ye ⛰ NE Iran
39 Q8 Allakaket Alaska, USA
9 T15 Allan Saskatchewan, S Canada
166 L6 Allanmyo Magwe, C Burma (Myanmar)
83 I22 Allanridge Free State, C South Africa
104 H4 Allariz Galicia, NW Spain
139 R11 Al Laşaf var. Al Lussuf. S Iraq
Al Lathqiyah see Al Lādhiqīyah
23 S2 Allatoona Lake ⊠ Georgia, SE USA
83 J19 Alldays Limpopo, NE South Africa
Alle see Łyna
31 P10 Allegan Michigan, N USA
18 E14 Allegheny Mountains ⛰ NE USA
18 E12 Allegheny Plateau ⛰ New York/Pennsylvania, NE USA
18 D11 Allegheny Reservoir ⊠ New York/Pennsylvania, NE USA
18 E12 Allegheny River ≈ New York/Pennsylvania, NE USA
22 K9 Allemands, Lac des ◎ Louisiana, S USA
25 U6 Allen Texas, SW USA
21 R14 Allendale South Carolina, SE USA
41 N6 Allende Coahuila de Zaragoza, NE Mexico
41 O9 Allende Nuevo León, NE Mexico
97 D16 Allen, Lough Ir. Loch Aillionn. ◎ NW Ireland
185 B26 Allen, Mount ▲ Stewart Island, Southland, SW New Zealand
109 V2 Allensteig Niederösterreich, N Austria
Allenstein see Olsztyn
18 I14 Allentown Pennsylvania, NE USA
155 G23 Alleppey var. Alappuzha; prev. Alleppi. Kerala, SW India
Alleppi see Alleppey
100 J12 Aller ≈ NW Germany
29 V16 Allerton Iowa, C USA
99 K19 Alleur Liège, E Belgium
101 J25 Allgäuer Alpen ⛰ Austria/Germany
28 J13 Alliance Nebraska, C USA
31 U12 Alliance Ohio, N USA
103 O10 Allier ◈ department N France
139 R13 Al Lifīyah S Iraq
44 J13 Alligator Pond C Jamaica
21 Y9 Alligator River ≈ North Carolina, SE USA
29 W12 Allison Iowa, C USA
14 G14 Alliston Ontario, S Canada
140 L11 Al Līth Makkah, SW Saudi Arabia
Al Liwā' see Līwā
96 J12 Alloa C Scotland, UK
103 U14 Allos Alpes-de-Haute-Provence, SE France
108 D6 Allschwil Basel-Land, NW Switzerland
Al Lubnān see Lebanon
141 N14 Al Luḩayyah W Yemen
14 K12 Allumettes, Île des island Québec, SE Canada
Al Lussuf see Al Laşaf
109 S5 Alm ≈ N Austria
15 Q7 Alma Québec, SE Canada
27 S10 Alma Arkansas, C USA
23 V7 Alma Georgia, SE USA
27 P4 Alma Kansas, C USA
31 Q8 Alma Michigan, N USA
29 O17 Alma Nebraska, C USA
30 I7 Alma Wisconsin, N USA
139 R12 Al Ma'ānīyah S Iraq
Alma-Ata see Almaty
Alma-Atinskaya Oblast' see Almaty
Almacellas see Almacelles
105 T5 Almacelles var. Almacellas. Cataluña, NE Spain
104 F11 Almada Setúbal, W Portugal
104 L11 Almadén Castilla-La Mancha, C Spain
66 L6 Almadies, Pointe des headland W Senegal
140 L7 Al Madīnah Eng. Medina. Al Madīnah, W Saudi Arabia
140 L7 Al Madīnah off. Minṭaqat al Madīnah. ◈ province W Saudi Arabia
138 H9 Al Mafraq var. Mafraq. Al Mafraq, N Jordan
138 J10 Al Mafraq off. Muḩāfaẓat al Mafraq. ◈ governorate NW Jordan
141 R15 Al Maghārim C Yemen
105 N11 Almagro Castilla-La Mancha, C Spain
Al Maḩallah al Kubrá see El Maḩalla el Kubra
139 T9 Al Maḩāwīl var. Khān al Maḩāwīl. C Iraq
Al Mahdīyah see Mahdia
139 T8 Al Maḩmūdīyah var. Mahmudiya. C Iraq
141 T14 Al Mahrah ⛰ E Yemen
141 P7 Al Majma'ah Ar Riyāḑ, C Saudi Arabia
139 Q11 Al Makmīn well S Iraq
139 Q1 Al Mālikīyah var. Malkiye. Al Ḩasakah, N Syria
Almalyk see Olmaliq
Al Mamlakah see Morocco
Al Mamlaka al Urduniya al Hashemiyah see Jordan
143 Q18 Al Manādir var. Al Manadir. desert Oman/United Arab Emirates
142 L15 Al Manāmah Eng. Manama. ● (Bahrain) N Bahrain
139 O5 Al Manāşif ⛰ E Syria
35 O4 Almanor, Lake ⊠ California, W USA
105 R11 Almansa Castilla-La Mancha, C Spain
Al Manşūrah see El Manşûra
104 L3 Almanza Castilla-León, N Spain
104 L8 Almanzor ▲ W Spain
105 P14 Almanzora ≈ SE Spain
139 S9 Al Mardah C Iraq
Al-Mariyya see Almería
75 R7 Al Marj var. Barka, It. Barce. NE Libya
138 L2 Al Mashrafah Ar Raqqah, N Syria
141 X8 Al Maşna'ah var. Al Muşana'a. NE Oman
Almassora see Almazora
Almatinskaya Oblast' see Almaty
145 U15 Almaty var. Alma-Ata. Almaty, SE Kazakhstan
145 S14 Almaty off. Almatinskaya Oblast', Kaz. Almaty Oblysy; prev. Alma-Atinskaya Oblast'. ◈ province SE Kazakhstan
145 U15 Almaty ✈ Almaty, SE Kazakhstan
Almaty Oblysy see Almaty
al-Mawailih see Al Muwayliḩ
139 R3 Al Mawşil Eng. Mosul. N Iraq
139 N5 Al Mayādīn var. Mayadin, Fr. Meyadine. Dayr az Zawr, E Syria
139 X10 Al Maymūnah var. Maimuna. SE Iraq
141 N5 Al Mayyāh Ḩā'il, N Saudi Arabia
Al Ma'zam see Al Ma'zim
105 P6 Almazán Castilla-León, N Spain
141 W8 Al Ma'zim var. Al Ma'zam. NW Oman
123 N11 Almaznyy Respublika Sakha (Yakutiya), NE Russian Federation
105 T9 Almazora Cat Almassora. País Valenciano, E Spain
Al Mazra' see Al Mazra'ah
138 G11 Al Mazra'ah var. Al Mazra', Mazra'a. Al Karak, W Jordan
101 G15 Alme ≈ W Germany
104 I7 Almeida Guarda, N Portugal
104 G10 Almeirim Santarém, C Portugal
98 O10 Almelo Overijssel, E Netherlands
105 S9 Almenara País Valenciano, E Spain
105 P12 Almenaras ▲ S Spain

◆ Country ● Country Capital ◇ Dependent Territory ○ Dependent Territory Capital ◈ Administrative Regions ✈ International Airport ▲ Mountain ⛰ Mountain Range 🌋 Volcano ≈ River ◎ Lake ⊠ Reservoir

105 P5 **Almenar de Soria** Castilla-León, N Spain
104 J6 **Almendra, Embalse de** ⬚ Castilla-León, NW Spain
104 J11 **Almendralejo** Extremadura, W Spain
98 I10 **Almere** var. Almere-stad. Flevoland, C Netherlands
98 I10 **Almere-Buiten** Flevoland, C Netherlands
98 I10 **Almere-Haven** Flevoland, C Netherlands
Almere-stad see Almere
105 P15 **Almería** Ar. Al-Mariyya; anc. Unci, Lat. Portus Magnus. Andalucía, S Spain
105 P14 **Almería** ◇ province Andalucía, S Spain
105 P15 **Almería, Golfo de** gulf S Spain
127 S5 **Al'met'yevsk** Respublika Tatarstan, W Russian Federation
95 L21 **Älmhult** Kronoberg, S Sweden
141 U9 **Al Miḥrāḍ** desert NE Saudi Arabia
104 L17 **Almina, Punta** headland Ceuta, Spain, N Africa
Al Minyā see El Minya
Al Miqdādīyah see Al Muqdādīyah
43 P14 **Almirante** Bocas del Toro, NW Panama
Almirós see Almyrós
140 M9 **Al Mislaḥ** spring/well W Saudi Arabia
Almissa see Omiš
104 G13 **Almodôvar** var. Almodóvar. Beja, S Portugal
104 M11 **Almodóvar del Campo** Castilla-La Mancha, C Spain
105 Q9 **Almodóvar del Pinar** Castilla-La Mancha, C Spain
31 S9 **Almont** Michigan, N USA
14 L13 **Almonte** Ontario, SE Canada
104 J14 **Almonte** Andalucía, S Spain
104 K9 **Almonte** ≈ Spain
152 K9 **Almora** Uttaranchal, N India
104 M8 **Almorox** Castilla-La Mancha, C Spain
141 S7 **Al Mubarraz** Ash Sharqīyah, E Saudi Arabia
Al Muḍaibī see Al Muḍaybī
138 G15 **Al Mudawwarah** Ma'ān, SW Jordan
141 Y9 **Al Muḍaybī** var. Al Muḍaibī. NE Oman
Almudébar see Almudévar
105 S5 **Almudévar** var. Almudébar. Aragón, NE Spain
141 S15 **Al Mukallā** var. Mukalla. SE Yemen
141 N16 **Al Mukhā** Eng. Mocha. SW Yemen
105 N15 **Almuñécar** Andalucía, S Spain
139 U7 **Al Muqdādīyah** var. Al Miqdādīyah. C Iraq
140 L3 **Al Murayr** spring/well NW Saudi Arabia
136 M12 **Almus** Tokat, N Turkey
Al Muṣana'a see Al Maṣna'ah
139 T9 **Al Musayyib** var. Musaiyib. C Iraq
139 V9 **Al Muwaffaqīyah** S Iraq
138 H10 **Al Muwaqqar** var. El Muwaqqar. 'Ammān, W Jordan
140 J5 **Al Muwayliḥ** var. al-Mawailih. Tabūk, NW Saudi Arabia
115 F17 **Almyrós** var. Almirós. Thessalía, C Greece
115 I24 **Almyroú, Órmos** bay Kríti, Greece, E Mediterranean Sea
Al Nüwfaliyah see An Nawfaliyah
96 L13 **Alnwick** N England, UK
Al Obayyid see El Obeid
Al Odaid see Al 'Udayd
190 B16 **Alofi** ◉ (Niue) W Niue
190 A16 **Alofi Bay** N Niue, C Pacific Ocean
190 E13 **Alofi, Île** island S Wallis and Futuna
190 E13 **Alofitai** Île Alofi, W Wallis and Futuna
Aloha State see Hawai'i
118 G7 **Aloja** Limbaži, N Latvia
153 X10 **Along** Arunāchal Pradesh, NE India
115 H16 **Alónnisos** island Vóreioi Sporádes, Greece, Aegean Sea
104 M15 **Alora** Andalucía, S Spain
171 Q16 **Alor, Kepulauan** island group E Indonesia
171 Q16 **Alor, Pulau** prev. Ombai. island Kepulauan Alor, E Indonesia
171 O16 **Alor, Selat** strait Flores Sea/Savu Sea
168 I7 **Alor Setar** var. Alor Star, Alur Setar. Kedah, Peninsular Malaysia
Alor Star see Alor Setar
Alost see Aalst
154 F9 **Älot** Madhya Pradesh, C India
186 G10 **Alotau** Milne Bay, SE Papua New Guinea
171 Y16 **Alotip** Papua, E Indonesia
Al Oued see El Oued
35 R12 **Alpaugh** California, W USA
Alpen see Alps
31 R6 **Alpena** Michigan, N USA
Alpes see Alps
103 S14 **Alpes-de-Haute-Provence** ◆ department SE France
103 U14 **Alpes-Maritimes** ◆ department SE France
181 W8 **Alpha** Queensland, E Australia
197 R9 **Alpha Cordillera** var. Alpha Ridge. undersea feature Arctic Ocean
Alpha Ridge see Alpha Cordillera
Alpheius see Alfeiós
99 I15 **Alphen** Noord-Brabant, S Netherlands
Alphen see Alphen aan den Rijn
98 H11 **Alphen aan den Rijn** var. Alphen. Zuid-Holland, C Netherlands
Alpheus see Alfeiós
Alpi see Alps
104 G10 **Alpiarça** Santarém, C Portugal
24 K10 **Alpine** Texas, SW USA
108 F8 **Alpnach** Unterwalden, W Switzerland

108 D11 **Alps** Fr. Alpes, Ger. Alpen, It. Alpi. ▲ C Europe
141 W8 **Al Qābil** var. Qabil. N Oman
Al Qaḍārif see Gedaref
75 P8 **Al Qaddāḥīyah** N Libya
Al Qāhirah see Cairo
140 K4 **Al Qālibah** Tabūk, NW Saudi Arabia
139 O1 **Al Qāmishlī** var. Kamishli, Qamishly. Al Ḥasakah, NE Syria
138 I6 **Al Qaryatayn** var. Qaryatayn, Fr. Qariatéine. Ḥimṣ, C Syria
142 K11 **Al Qash'āniyah** var. Al-Kashaniya. NE Kuwait
141 N7 **Al Qaşim** var. Minţaqat Qaşim, Qassim. ◇ province C Saudi Arabia
138 J5 **Al Qaşr** Ḥimṣ, C Syria
Al Qaşr see El Qasr
141 S6 **Al Qaşrayn** see Kasserine
138 G11 **Al Qatīf** Ash Sharqīyah, NE Saudi Arabia
75 P11 **Al Qaţrānah** var. El Qatrani, Qatrana. Al Karak, W Jordan
Al Qaţrūn SW Libya
Al Qayrawān see Kairouan
Al-Qsar al-Kbir see Ksar-el-Kebir
104 H12 **Alqueva, Barragem do** ⬚ Portugal/Spain
138 G8 **Al Qunayţirah** var. El Kuneitra, El Quneitra, Kuneitra, Qunaytra. Al Qunayţirah, SW Syria
138 G8 **Al Qunayţirah** off. Muḥāfaẓat al Qunayţirah, var. El Q'unayţirah, Qunaytirah, Fr. Kuneitra. ◇ governorate SW Syria
140 M11 **Al Qunfudhah** Makkah, SW Saudi Arabia
140 K2 **Al Qurayyāt** Al Jawf, NW Saudi Arabia
139 Y11 **Al Qurnah** var. Kurna. SE Iraq
139 V12 **Al Quşayr** S Iraq
138 I6 **Al Quşayr** var. El Quseir, Quşayr, Fr. Kousseir. Ḥimṣ, W Syria
Al Quşayr see Quseir
138 H7 **Al Quţayfah** var. Quţayfah, Quţayfe, Quteife, Fr. Kouteïfé. Dimashq, W Syria
141 P8 **Al Quwayīyah** Ar Riyāḍ, C Saudi Arabia
Al Quwayr see Guwēr
138 F14 **Al Quwayrah** var. El Quweira. Al 'Aqabah, SW Jordan
Al Rayyan see Ar Rayyān
Al Ruweis see Ar Ruways
95 G24 **Als** Ger. Alsen. island SW Denmark
103 U5 **Alsace** Ger. Elsass; anc. Alsatia. ◆ region NE France
9 R16 **Alsask** Saskatchewan, S Canada
Alsasua see Altsasu
Alsatia see Alsace
101 C16 **Alsdorf** Nordrhein-Westfalen, W Germany
10 I8 **Alsek** ≈ Canada/USA
Alsen see Als
101 F19 **Alsenz** ≈ W Germany
101 H17 **Alsfeld** Hessen, C Germany
119 K20 **Al'shany** Rus. Ol'shany. Brestskaya Voblasts', SW Belarus
Alsókubin see Dolný Kubín
118 C9 **Alsunga** Kuldīga, W Latvia
Alt see Olt
92 K9 **Alta** Fin. Alattio. Finnmark, N Norway
29 T12 **Alta** Iowa, C USA
108 I7 **Altach** Vorarlberg, W Austria
92 K9 **Altaelva** Lapp. Alaheaieatnu. ≈ N Norway
92 J8 **Altafjorden** fjord NE Norwegian Sea
62 K10 **Alta Gracia** Córdoba, C Argentina
42 K11 **Alta Gracia** Rivas, SW Nicaragua
54 H4 **Altagracia** Zulia, NW Venezuela
54 M5 **Altagracia de Orituco** Guárico, N Venezuela
Altai see Altai Mountains
Altai see Altai Mountains
129 T7 **Altai Mountains** var. Altai. ▲ C Asia
129 T7 **Altai Mountains** var. Altai, Chin. Altay Shan, Rus. Altay. ▲ Asia/Europe
23 V6 **Altamaha River** ≈ Georgia, SE USA
58 J13 **Altamira** Pará, NE Brazil
54 E12 **Altamira** Huila, S Colombia
42 M13 **Altamira** Alajuela, N Costa Rica
41 Q11 **Altamira** Tamaulipas, C Mexico
30 L15 **Altamont** Illinois, N USA
27 Q7 **Altamont** Kansas, C USA
32 H16 **Altamont** Oregon, NW USA
20 K10 **Altamont** Tennessee, S USA
23 X11 **Altamonte Springs** Florida, SE USA
107 O17 **Altamura** anc. Lupatia. Puglia, SE Italy
40 F9 **Altamura, Isla** island C Mexico
Altan see Erdenehayrhan
Altanbulag see Bayanhayrhan
Altanbulag see Bayanhayrhan
163 Q7 **Altan Emel** var. Xin Barag Youqi. Nei Mongol Zizhiqu, N China
Altan-Ovoo see Tsenher
163 N9 **Altanshiree** var. Chamdmanī. Dornigovĭ, SE Mongolia
Altanteel see Dzereg
162 D5 **Altantsögts** var. Tsaagaanüüljī. Bayan-Ölgiy, NW Mongolia
40 F5 **Altar** Sonora, NW Mexico
40 D2 **Altar, Desierto de** var. Sonoran Desert. desert Mexico/USA see also Sonoran Desert
Altar, Desierto de see Sonoran Desert
105 U8 **Alta, Sierra** ▲ N Spain
40 H9 **Altata** Sinaloa, C Mexico
42 D4 **Alta Verapaz** off. Departamento de Alta Verapaz. ◇ department C Guatemala

Alta Verapaz, Departamento de see Alta Verapaz
107 L18 **Altavilla Silentia** Campania, S Italy
21 T7 **Altavista** Virginia, NE USA
158 L2 **Altay** Xinjiang Uygur Zizhiqu, NW China
162 D6 **Altay** var. Chihertey. Bayan-Ölgiy, W Mongolia
162 F9 **Altay** var. Bayan-Ovoo. Govĭ-Altay, SW Mongolia
162 F9 **Altay** var. Bayan-Ovoo. Govĭ-Altay, SW Mongolia
162 G8 **Altay** prev. Yösönbulag. Govĭ-Altay, W Mongolia
162 E8 **Altay** var. Bor-Udzüür. Hovd, W Mongolia
162 E8 **Altay** var. Bor-Udzüür. Hovd, W Mongolia
Altay see Bayantes, Mongolia
122 J14 **Altay, Respublika** var. Altay; prev. Gorno-Altayskaya Respublika. ◆ autonomous republic S Russian Federation
Altay Shan see Altai Mountains
123 I13 **Altayskiy Kray** ◆ territory S Russian Federation
Altbetsche see Bečej
101 L20 **Altdorf** Bayern, SE Germany
108 G8 **Altdorf** var. Altorf. Uri, C Switzerland
105 T11 **Altea** País Valenciano, E Spain
100 I10 **Alte Elde** ≈ N Germany
101 M16 **Altenburg** Thüringen, E Germany
Altenburg see Bucureşti, Romania
Altenburg see Baia de Criş, Romania
100 P12 **Alte Oder** ≈ NE Germany
104 H10 **Alter do Chão** Portalegre, C Portugal
Áltesjávri see Altevatnet
92 I10 **Altevatnet** Lapp. Áltesjávri. ◎ N Norway
27 V12 **Altheimer** Arkansas, C USA
109 T9 **Althofen** Kärnten, S Austria
114 H7 **Altimir** Vratsa, NW Bulgaria
136 K11 **Altınkaya Barajı** ⬚ N Turkey
139 S3 **Altın Köprü** var. Altun Kupri. N Iraq
136 E13 **Altıntaş** Kütahya, W Turkey
57 K18 **Altiplano** physical region W South America
103 U7 **Altkirch** Haut-Rhin, NE France
Altlublau see Stará L'ubovňa
100 L12 **Altmark** cultural region N Germany
Altmoldowa see Moldova Veche
25 W8 **Alto** Texas, SW USA
104 H11 **Alto Alentejo** physical region S Portugal
59 I19 **Alto Araguaia** Mato Grosso, C Brazil
58 L12 **Alto Bonito** Pará, NE Brazil
83 O15 **Alto Molócuè** Zambézia, NE Mozambique
30 K15 **Alton** Illinois, N USA
27 W4 **Alton** Missouri, C USA
9 X17 **Altona** Manitoba, S Canada
18 E14 **Altoona** Pennsylvania, NE USA
30 J6 **Altoona** Wisconsin, N USA
62 N3 **Alto Paraguay** off. Departamento del Alto Paraguay. ◇ department N Paraguay
62 N3 **Alto Paraguay, Departamento del** see Alto Paraguay
59 L17 **Alto Paraíso de Goiás** Goiás, S Brazil
62 P6 **Alto Paraná** off. Departamento del Alto Paraná. ◇ department E Paraguay
Alto Paraná see Paraná
62 P6 **Alto Paraná, Departamento del** see Alto Paraná
59 L15 **Alto Parnaíba** Maranhão, E Brazil
56 H13 **Alto Purús, Río** ≈ E Peru
Altorf see Altdorf
63 H19 **Alto Río Senguer** var. Alto Río Senguerr. Chubut, S Argentina
63 H19 **Alto Río Senguerr** see Alto Río Senguer
41 Q13 **Altotonga** Veracruz-Llave, E Mexico
101 N23 **Altötting** Bayern, SE Germany
Altpasua see Stara Pazova
Altraga see Bayandzürh
105 P3 **Altsasu** Cast. Alsasua. Navarra, N Spain
Alt-Schwanenburg see Gulbene
Altsohl see Zvolen
108 I7 **Altstätten** Sankt Gallen, NE Switzerland
42 G1 **Altun Ha** ruins Belize, N Belize
Altun Kupri see Altın Köprü
158 D8 **Altun Shan** ▲ C China
158 L9 **Altun Shan** var. Altyn Tagh. ▲ NW China
35 P5 **Alturas** California, W USA
26 L11 **Altus** Oklahoma, C USA
26 K11 **Altus Lake** ◎ Oklahoma, C USA
Altvater see Praděd
Altyn Tagh see Altun Shan
139 O6 **al-'Ubaila** see Al 'Ubaylah
141 T9 **Al 'Ubaylah** var. al-'Ubaila. Ash Sharqīyah, E Saudi Arabia
141 T9 **Al 'Ubaylah** spring/well E Saudi Arabia
Al 'Ubayyid see El Obeid
141 T7 **Al 'Udayd** var. Al Odaid. Abū Ẓaby, W United Arab Emirates
118 J8 **Alūksne** Ger. Marienburg. NE Latvia
140 K6 **Al 'Ulā** Al Madīnah, NW Saudi Arabia
173 N4 **Alula-Fartak Trench** var. Illa·ar Fartak Trench. undersea fea·ure W Indian Ocean
138 I11 **Al 'Umarī** 'Ammān, E Jordan
31 S13 **Alum Creek Lake** ◎ Ohio, N USA
63 H15 **Aluminé** Neuquén, C Argentina
95 O14 **Alunda** Uppsala, C Sweden

117 T14 **Alupka** Respublika Krym, S Ukraine
75 P8 **Al 'Uqaylah** N Libya
Al Uqşur see Luxor
21 T7 **Al Urdunn** see Jordan
168 J9 **Alur Panal** bay Sumatera, W Indonesia
Alur Setar see Alor Setar
141 V10 **Al 'Urūq al Mu'tariḍah** salt lake S Saudi Arabia
139 Q7 **Al'ūs** C Iraq
117 T13 **Alushta** Respublika Krym, S Ukraine
75 N11 **Al 'Uwaynāt** var. Al Awaynāt. SW Libya
75 U12 **Al Awaynāt** SE Libya
139 T6 **Al 'Uẓaym** var. Adhaim. E Iraq
26 L8 **Alva** Oklahoma, C USA
104 H8 **Alva** ≈ N Portugal
95 J18 **Älvängen** Västra Götaland, S Sweden
14 F14 **Alvanley** Ontario, S Canada
41 S14 **Alvarado** Veracruz-Llave, E Mexico
25 T7 **Alvarado** Texas, SW USA
58 D13 **Alvar'aes** Amazonas, NW Brazil
40 G6 **Alvaro Obregón, Presa** ⬚ W Mexico
94 H10 **Alvdal** Hedmark, S Norway
94 K12 **Älvdalen** Dalarna, C Sweden
61 E15 **Alvear** Corrientes, NE Argentina
104 F10 **Alverca do Ribatejo** Lisboa, C Portugal
95 L20 **Alvesta** Kronoberg, S Sweden
25 W12 **Alvin** Texas, SW USA
94 O13 **Älvkarleby** Uppsala, C Sweden
25 S5 **Alvord** Texas, SW USA
93 G18 **Älvros** Jämtland, C Sweden
92 J13 **Älvsbyn** Norrbotten, N Sweden
142 K12 **Al Wafrā'** SE Kuwait
140 J6 **Al Wajh** Tabūk, NW Saudi Arabia
143 N16 **Al Wakrah** var. Wakra. C Qatar
138 M8 **al Walaj, Sha'ib** dry watercourse W Iraq
152 J11 **Alwar** Rājasthān, N India
141 Q5 **Al Wari'ah** Ash Sharqīyah, N Saudi Arabia
155 G22 **Alwaye** Kerala, SW India
Alxa Zuoqi see Bayan Hot
Alxa Zuoqi see Bayan Hot
Alx Youqi see Ehen Hudag
Al Yaman see Yemen
138 G9 **Alyat/Alyaty-Pristan'** see Älät
115 I14 **Alykí** var. Aliki. Thásos, N Greece
119 F14 **Alytus** Pol. Olita. Alytus, S Lithuania
119 F15 **Alytus** ◆ province S Lithuania
101 N23 **Alz** ≈ SE Germany
31 Y11 **Alzada** Montana, NW USA
122 L12 **Alzamay** Irkutskaya Oblast', S Russian Federation
99 N23 **Alzette** ≈ S Luxembourg
105 S10 **Alzira** var. Alcira; anc. Saetabicula, Suero. País Valenciano, E Spain
Al Zubair see Az Zubayr
181 O8 **Amadeus, Lake** seasonal lake Northern Territory, C Australia
81 E15 **Amadi** Western Equatoria, SW Sudan
9 R7 **Amadjuak Lake** ◎ Baffin Island, Nunavut, N Canada
15 U9 **Amager** island E Denmark
165 N14 **Amagi-san** ▲ Honshū, S Japan
171 S13 **Amahai** var. Masohi. Palau Seram, E Indonesia
38 M16 **Amak Island** island Alaska, USA
164 B14 **Amakusa-nada** gulf Kyūshū, SW Japan
95 J16 **Åmål** Västra Götaland, S Sweden
54 E8 **Amalfi** Antioquia, N Colombia
107 L18 **Amalfi** Campania, S Italy
115 D19 **Amaliáda** var. Amaliás. Dytikí Ellás, S Greece
Amaliás see Amaliáda
154 F12 **Amalner** Mahārāshtra, C India
171 W14 **Amamapare** Papua, E Indonesia
59 H21 **Amambaí, Serra de** var. Cordillera de Amambay, Serra de Amambay. ▲ Brazil/Paraguay see also Amambay, Cordillera de
62 P4 **Amambay** off. Departamento del Amambay. ◇ department E Paraguay
62 P5 **Amambay, Cordillera de** var. Serra de Amambaí, Serra de Amambay. ▲ Brazil/Paraguay see also Amambaí, Serra de
62 P5 **Amambay, Departamento del** see Amambay
Amambay, Serra de/Amambay, Serra de/Amambay, Cordillera de see Amambaí, Serra de
165 U16 **Amami-guntō** island group SW Japan
165 V15 **Amami-Ō-shima** island SW Japan
186 A5 **Amanab** Sandaun, NW Papua New Guinea
106 J13 **Amandola** Marche, C Italy
107 J23 **Amantea** Calabria, SW Italy
191 W10 **Amanu** island Îles Tuamotu, C French Polynesia
58 J10 **Amapá** Amapá, NE Brazil
58 J11 **Amapá** off. Estado de Amapá; prev. Território de Amapá. ◆ state NE Brazil
Amapá, Estado de see Amapá
42 H8 **Amapala** Valle, S Honduras
58 J11 **Amapá, Território de** see Amapá
Amara see Al 'Amārah
139 T4 **Amarante** Porto, N Portugal
166 M5 **Amarapura** Mandalay, C Burma (Myanmar)
Amardalay see Delgertsogt
Amardalay see Delgertsogt
104 I12 **Amareleja** Beja, S Portugal
35 V11 **Amargosa Range** ▲ California, W USA
25 N2 **Amarillo** Texas, SW USA
Amarinthos see Amárynthos
107 K15 **Amaro, Monte** ▲ C Italy

115 H18 **Amárynthos** var. Amarinthos. Évvoia, C Greece
Amasia see Amasya
136 K12 **Amasya** anc. Amasia. Amasya, N Turkey
136 K11 **Amasya** ◇ province N Turkey
Amasya see Amasya
107 J14 **Amatrice** Lazio, C Italy
190 C8 **Amatuku** atoll C Tuvalu
191 J20 **Amay** Liège, E Belgium
48 C7 **Amazon** Sp. Amazonas. ≈ Brazil/Peru
59 C14 **Amazonas** off. Estado do Amazonas. ◆ state N Brazil
54 G15 **Amazonas** off. Comisaría Amazonas. ◇ province SE Colombia
56 C10 **Amazonas** off. Departamento de Amazonas. ◇ department N Peru
54 M12 **Amazonas** off. Territorio Amazonas. ◇ federal territory S Venezuela
Amazonas see Amazon
Amazonas, Comisaría del see Amazonas
Amazonas, Departamento de see Amazonas
Amazonas, Estado do see Amazonas
Amazonas, Territorio see Amazonas
48 F7 **Amazon Basin** basin N South America
47 V5 **Amazon Fan** undersea feature W Atlantic Ocean
58 K11 **Amazon, Mouths of the** delta NE Brazil
187 R13 **Ambae** var. Aoba, Omba. island C Vanuatu
152 I9 **Ambāla** Haryāna, NW India
155 J26 **Ambalangoda** Southern Province, SW Sri Lanka
155 K26 **Ambalantota** Southern Province, S Sri Lanka
172 I6 **Ambalavao** Fianarantsoa, C Madagascar
54 E10 **Ambalema** Tolima, C Colombia
79 E17 **Ambam** Sud, S Cameroon
172 J2 **Ambanja** Antsiranana, N Madagascar
123 T6 **Ambarchik** Respublika Sakha (Yakutiya), NE Russian Federation
62 K9 **Ambargasta, Salinas de** salt lake C Argentina
124 J6 **Ambarnyy** Respublika Kareliya, NW Russian Federation
56 C7 **Ambato** Tungurahua, C Ecuador
172 I5 **Ambatolampy** Antananarivo, C Madagascar
172 H4 **Ambatomainty** Mahajanga, W Madagascar
172 J4 **Ambatondrazaka** Toamasina, C Madagascar
101 L20 **Amberg** var. Amberg in der Oberpfalz. Bayern, SE Germany
Amberg in der Oberpfalz see Amberg
42 H1 **Ambergris Cay** island NE Belize
103 S11 **Ambérieu-en-Bugey** Ain, E France
185 I18 **Amberley** Canterbury, South Island, New Zealand
103 P11 **Ambert** Puy-de-Dôme, C France
Ambianum see Amiens
76 J11 **Ambidédi** Kayes, SW Mali
154 M10 **Ambikāpur** Chhattīsgarh, C India
172 J2 **Ambilobe** Antsiranana, N Madagascar
39 O7 **Ambler** Alaska, USA
Amblève see Amel
Ambo see Hägere Hiywet
172 I8 **Amboasary** Toliara, S Madagascar
172 J2 **Ambodifotatra** var. Ambodifotatra. Toamasina, E Madagascar
Amboenten see Ambunten
172 I6 **Ambohidratrimo** Antananarivo, C Madagascar
172 J6 **Ambohimahasoa** Fianarantsoa, SE Madagascar
172 K3 **Ambohitralanana** Antsiranana, NE Madagascar
102 M8 **Amboise** Indre-et-Loire, C France
171 S13 **Ambon** prev. Amboina. Pulau Ambon, E Indonesia
171 S13 **Ambon, Pulau** island E Indonesia
81 I20 **Amboseli, Lake** ◎ Kenya/Tanzania
172 I6 **Ambositra** Fianarantsoa, SE Madagascar
172 I8 **Ambovombe** Toliara, S Madagascar
35 W10 **Amboy** California, W USA
30 L11 **Amboy** Illinois, N USA
Ambracia see Árta
172 I2 **Ambre, Cap d'** see Bobaomby, Tanjona
18 B14 **Ambridge** Pennsylvania, NE USA
Ambrim see Ambrym
82 A11 **Ambriz** Bengo, NW Angola
Ambrizete see N'Zeto
187 R13 **Ambrym** var. Ambrim. island C Vanuatu
169 T16 **Ambunten** prev. Amboenten. Pulau Madura, E Indonesia
186 B6 **Ambunti** East Sepik, NW Papua New Guinea
155 I20 **Ambūr** Tamil Nādu, SE India
38 E17 **Amchitka Island** island Aleutian Islands, Alaska, USA
38 F17 **Amchitka Pass** strait Aleutian Islands, Alaska, USA
141 N5 **'Amd** C Yemen
78 J10 **Am Dam** Ouaddaï, E Chad
171 U16 **Amdassa** Pulau Yamdena, E Indonesia
125 U1 **Amderma** Nenetskiy Avtonomnyy Okrug, NW Russian Federation
159 N14 **Amdo** Xizang Zizhiqu, W China
93 N14 **Ämmänsaari** Oulu, E Finland

40 K13 **Ameca** Jalisco, SW Mexico
41 P14 **Amecameca** var. Amecameca de Juárez. México, C Mexico
Amecameca de Juárez see Amecameca
61 A20 **Ameghino** Buenos Aires, E Argentina
99 M21 **Amel** Fr. Amblève. Liège, E Belgium
98 K4 **Ameland** Fris. It Amelân. island Waddeneilanden, N Netherlands
107 H14 **Amelia** Umbria, C Italy
21 V6 **Amelia Court House** Virginia, NE USA
23 W8 **Amelia Island** island Florida, SE USA
18 L12 **Amenia** New York, NE USA
65 M21 **America-Antarctica Ridge** undersea feature S Atlantic Ocean
America in Miniature see Maryland
Americana see United States of America
60 L9 **Americana** São Paulo, S Brazil
33 Q15 **American Falls** Idaho, NW USA
33 Q15 **American Falls Reservoir** ⬚ Idaho, NW USA
36 L3 **American Fork** Utah, W USA
192 K16 **American Samoa** ◇ US unincorporated territory W Polynesia
23 S6 **Americus** Georgia, SE USA
98 K12 **Amerongen** Utrecht, C Netherlands
98 K11 **Amersfoort** Utrecht, C Netherlands
97 N21 **Amersham** SE England, UK
30 I5 **Amery** Wisconsin, N USA
195 W6 **Amery Ice Shelf** ice shelf Antarctica
29 V13 **Ames** Iowa, C USA
19 P10 **Amesbury** Massachusetts, NE USA
Amestratus see Mistretta
115 F18 **Amfíkleia** var. Amfíklia. Stereá Ellás, C Greece
Amfíklia see Amfíkleia
115 D17 **Amfilochía** var. Amfilokhía. Dytikí Ellás, C Greece
Amfilokhía see Amfilochía
114 H13 **Amfípoli** anc. Amphipolis. site of ancient city Kentrikí Makedonía, NE Greece
115 F18 **Ámfissa** Stereá Ellás, C Greece
123 Q10 **Amga** Respublika Sakha (Yakutiya), NE Russian Federation
123 Q11 **Amga** ≈ NE Russian Federation
163 R7 **Amgalang** var. Xin Barag Zuoqi. Nei Mongol Zizhiqu, N China
123 V5 **Amguema** ≈ NE Russian Federation
123 S12 **Amgun'** ≈ SE Russian Federation
80 J12 **Amhara** ◆ region N Ethiopia
13 P15 **Amherst** Nova Scotia, SE Canada
18 M11 **Amherst** Massachusetts, NE USA
18 D10 **Amherst** New York, NE USA
24 M4 **Amherst** Texas, SW USA
21 U6 **Amherst** Virginia, NE USA
Amherst see Kyaikkami
14 C18 **Amherstburg** Ontario, S Canada
21 Q6 **Amherstdale** West Virginia, NE USA
14 K15 **Amherst Island** island Ontario, SE Canada
28 J3 **Amidon** North Dakota, N USA
103 O3 **Amiens** anc. Ambianum, Samarobriva. Somme, N France
139 P8 **'Amij, Wādī** var. Wadi 'Amiq. dry watercourse W Iraq
136 L17 **Amik Ovasi** ◇ S Turkey
76 K7 **Amílcar Cabral** ✈ Sal, NE Cape Verde
139 R10 **Amīlḥayt, Wādī** see Umm al Ḥayt, Wādī
Amíndaion/Amindeo see Amýntaio
155 C21 **Amindivi Islands** island group Lakshadweep, India, N Indian Ocean
139 U6 **Amín Ḥabīb** E Iraq
83 E20 **Aminuis** Omaheke, E Namibia
142 J7 **Amīrābād** Īlām, NW Iran
Amirante Bank see Amirante Ridge
173 N6 **Amirante Basin** undersea feature W Indian Ocean
173 N6 **Amirante Islands** var. Amirantes Group. island group C Seychelles
Amirantes Group see Amirante Islands
173 N7 **Amirante Ridge** var. Amirante Bank. undersea feature W Indian Ocean
Amirantes Group see Amirante Islands
173 N6 **Amirante Trench** undersea feature W Indian Ocean
9 U13 **Amisk Lake** ◎ Saskatchewan, C Canada
Amistad, Presa de la see Amistad Reservoir
25 O12 **Amistad Reservoir** var. Presa de la Amistad. ⬚ Mexico/USA
Amisus see Samsun
22 K8 **Amite** var. Amite City. Louisiana, S USA
Amite City see Amite
27 T12 **Amity** Arkansas, C USA
154 H11 **Amla** prev. Amulla. Madhya Pradesh, C India
38 I17 **Amlia Island** island Aleutian Islands, Alaska, USA
97 H18 **Amlwch** NW Wales, UK
Amman see Portalegre
138 H10 **'Ammān** var. Amman; anc. Philadelphia, Bibl. Rabbah Ammon, Rabbath Ammon. ● (Jordan) 'Ammān, NW Jordan
138 H10 **'Ammān** off. Muḥāfaẓat 'Ammān; prev. Al 'Aşimah. ◇ governorate NW Jordan
'Ammān, Muḥāfaẓat see 'Ammān
93 N14 **Ämmänsaari** Oulu, E Finland

◆ Country
● Country Capital
◇ Dependent Territory
○ Dependent Territory Capital
◉ Administrative Regions
✈ International Airport
▲ Mountain
▲ Mountain Range
℟ Volcano
≈ River
◎ Lake
⬚ Reservoir

Ammarnäs – Antananarivo

92 H13 **Ammarnäs** Västerbotten, N Sweden
197 O15 **Ammassalik** *var.* Angmagssalik. Tunu, S Greenland
101 K24 **Ammer** ≈ SE Germany
101 K24 **Ammersee** ◎ SE Germany
98 J13 **Ammerzoden** Gelderland, C Netherlands
Ammóchostos *see* Gazimağusa
Ammóchostos, Kólpos *see* Gazimağusa Körfezi
Amnok-kang *see* Yalu
Amoea *see* Portalegre
Amoentai *see* Amuntai
Amoerang *see* Amurang
143 O4 **Āmol** *var.* Amul. Māzandarān, N Iran
115 K21 **Amorgós** Amorgós, Kykládes, Greece, Aegean Sea
115 K22 **Amorgós** *island* Kykládes, Greece, Aegean Sea
23 N3 **Amory** Mississippi, S USA
12 I13 **Amos** Québec, SE Canada
95 G15 **Åmot** Buskerud, S Norway
95 E15 **Åmot** Telemark, S Norway
95 J15 **Åmotfors** Värmland, C Sweden
76 L10 **Amourj** Hodh ech Chargui, SE Mauritania
Amoy *see* Xiamen
172 H7 **Ampanihy** Toliara, SW Madagascar
155 L25 **Ampara** *var.* Amparai. Eastern Province, E Sri Lanka
172 J4 **Amparafaravola** Toamasina, E Madagascar
Amparai *see* Ampara
60 M9 **Amparo** São Paulo, S Brazil
172 J5 **Ampasimanolotra** Toamasina, E Madagascar
57 H17 **Ampato, Nevado** ▲ S Peru
101 L23 **Amper** ≈ SE Germany
64 M9 **Ampère Seamount** *undersea feature* E Atlantic Ocean
Amphipolis *see* Amfípoli
167 X10 **Amphitrite Group** *island group* N Paracel Islands
171 T16 **Amplawas** *var.* Emplawas. Pulau Babar, E Indonesia
105 U7 **Amposta** Cataluña, NE Spain
15 V7 **Amqui** Québec, SE Canada
141 O14 **ʿAmrān** W Yemen
Amraoti *see* Amrāvati
154 H12 **Amrāvati** *prev.* Amraoti. Mahārāshtra, C India
154 C11 **Amreli** Gujarāt, W India
108 H6 **Amriswil** Thurgau, NE Switzerland
138 H5 **ʿAmrīt** *ruins* Ṭarṭūs, W Syria
152 H7 **Amritsar** Punjab, N India
152 J10 **Amroha** Uttar Pradesh, N India
100 G7 **Amrum** *island* NW Germany
93 I15 **Åmsele** Västerbotten, N Sweden
98 I10 **Amstelveen** Noord-Holland, C Netherlands
98 I10 **Amsterdam** ● (Netherlands) Noord-Holland, C Netherlands
18 K10 **Amsterdam** New York, NE USA
173 Q11 **Amsterdam Fracture Zone** *tectonic feature* S Indian Ocean
173 R11 **Amsterdam Island** *island* NE French Southern and Antarctic Territories
109 U4 **Amstetten** Niederösterreich, N Austria
78 J11 **Am Timan** Salamat, SE Chad
146 L12 **Amu-Buxoro Kanali** *var.* Aral-Bukhorskiy Kanal. *canal* C Uzbekistan
139 O1 **ʿĀmūdah** *var.* Amude. Al Ḥasakah, N Syria
147 O15 **Amu Darya** *Rus.* Amudar'ya, *Taj.* Dar"yoi Amu, *Turkm.* Amyderya, *Uzb.* Amudaryo; *anc.* Oxus. ≈ C Asia
Amu-Dar'ya *see* Amyderya
Amudar'ya/Amudaryo/ Amu, Dar"yoi *see* Amu Darya
Amude *see* ʿĀmūdah
140 L3 **ʿAmūd, Jabal al** ▲ NW Saudi Arabia
38 J17 **Amukta Island** *island* Aleutian Islands, Alaska, USA
38 I17 **Amukta Pass** *strait* Aleutian Islands, Alaska, USA
Amul *see* Āmol
Amulla *see* Amla
Amundsen Basin *see* Fram Basin
195 X3 **Amundsen Bay** *bay* Antarctica
195 P10 **Amundsen Coast** *physical region* Antarctica
8 I6 **Amundsen Gulf** *gulf* Northwest Territories, N Canada
193 O14 **Amundsen Plain** *undersea feature* S Pacific Ocean
195 Q9 **Amundsen-Scott** *US research station* Antarctica
194 J11 **Amundsen Sea** *sea* S Pacific Ocean
94 M12 **Amungen** ◎ C Sweden
169 U13 **Amuntai** *prev.* Amoentai. Borneo, C Indonesia
129 W6 **Amur** *Chin.* Heilong Jiang. ≈ China/Russian Federation
171 Q11 **Amurang** *prev.* Amoerang. Sulawesi, C Indonesia
105 O3 **Amurrio** País Vasco, N Spain
123 S13 **Amursk** Khabarovskiy Kray, SE Russian Federation
123 Q12 **Amurskaya Oblast'** ◐ *province* SE Russian Federation
80 G7 **ʿAmur, Wadi** ≈ NE Sudan
115 C17 **Amvrakikós Kólpos** *gulf* W Greece
Amvrosiyevka *see* Amvrosiyivka
117 X8 **Amvrosiyivka** *Rus.* Amvrosiyevka. Donets'ka Oblast', SE Ukraine
146 M14 **Amyderya** *Rus.* Amu-Dar'ya. Lebap Welaýaty, NE Turkmenistan
Amyderya *see* Amu Darya
114 E13 **Amýntaio** *var.* Amindeo; *prev.* Amíndaion. Dytikí Makedonía, N Greece
14 B6 **Amyot** Ontario, S Canada
191 U10 **Anaa** *atoll* Îles Tuamotu, C French Polynesia
Anabanoea *see* Anabanua
171 N14 **Anabanua** *prev.* Anabanoea. Sulawesi, C Indonesia
189 R8 **Anabar** NE Nauru
123 N8 **Anabar** ≈ NE Russian Federation
An Abhainn Mhór *see* Blackwater
55 O6 **Anaco** Anzoátegui, NE Venezuela
33 Q10 **Anaconda** Montana, NW USA
32 H7 **Anacortes** Washington, NW USA
26 M11 **Anadarko** Oklahoma, C USA
114 N12 **Ana Dere** ≈ NW Turkey
104 G8 **Anadia** Aveiro, N Portugal
Anadolu Dağları *see* Doğu Karadeniz Dağları
123 V6 **Anadyr'** Chukotskiy Avtonomnyy Okrug, NE Russian Federation
123 V6 **Anadyr'** ≈ NE Russian Federation
Anadyr, Gulf of *see* Anadyrskiy Zaliv
129 X4 **Anadyrskiy Khrebet** *var.* Chukot Range. ▲▲ NE Russian Federation
123 W6 **Anadyrskiy Zaliv** *Eng.* Gulf of Anadyr. *gulf* NE Russian Federation
115 K22 **Anáfi** *anc.* Anaphe. *island* Kykládes, Greece, Aegean Sea
107 J15 **Anagni** Lazio, C Italy
ʿĀnah *see* ʿAnnah
35 T15 **Anaheim** California, W USA
10 L15 **Anahim Lake** British Columbia, SW Canada
38 B8 **Anahola** Kaua'i, Hawai'i, USA, C Pacific Ocean
41 O7 **Anáhuac** Nuevo León, NE Mexico
25 X11 **Anahuac** Texas, SW USA
155 G22 **Anai Mudi** ▲ S India
Anaiza *see* ʿUnayzah
155 M15 **Anakāpalle** Andhra Pradesh, E India
191 W15 **Anakena, Playa de** *beach* Easter Island, Chile, E Pacific Ocean
39 Q7 **Anaktuvuk Pass** Alaska, USA
39 Q6 **Anaktuvuk River** ≈ Alaska, USA
172 J3 **Analalava** Mahajanga, NW Madagascar
44 F6 **Ana María, Golfo de** *gulf* N Caribbean Sea
Anambas Islands *see* Anambas, Kepulauan
169 N8 **Anambas, Kepulauan** *var.* Anambas Islands. *island group* W Indonesia
77 U17 **Anambra** ◐ *state* SE Nigeria
29 N4 **Anamoose** North Dakota, N USA
29 Y13 **Anamosa** Iowa, C USA
136 H17 **Anamur** Mersin, S Turkey
136 H17 **Anamur Burnu** *headland* S Turkey
154 O12 **Ānandadur** Orissa, E India
155 H18 **Anantapur** Andhra Pradesh, S India
152 H5 **Anantnāg** *var.* Islamabad. Jammu and Kashmir, NW India
Ananyev *see* Anan'yiv
117 O9 **Anan'yiv** *Rus.* Ananyev. Odes'ka Oblast', SW Ukraine
126 J14 **Anapa** Krasnodarskiy Kray, SW Russian Federation
Anaphe *see* Anáfi
59 K18 **Anápolis** Goiás, C Brazil
143 R10 **Anār** Kermān, C Iran
Anár *see* Inari
143 P7 **Anārak** Eşfahān, C Iran
Anar Dara *see* Anār Darreh
148 J7 **Anār Darreh** *var.* Anar Dara. Farāh, W Afghanistan
Anárjohka *see* Inarijoki
23 X9 **Anastasia Island** *island* Florida, SE USA
188 K7 **Anatahan** *island* C Northern Mariana Islands
128 M6 **Anatolia** *plateau* C Turkey
86 F14 **Anatolian Plate** *tectonic feature* Asia/Europe
114 H13 **Anatolikí Makedonía kai Thráki** *Eng.* Macedonia East and Thrace. ◐ *region* NE Greece
Anatom *see* Aneityum
62 L8 **Añatuya** Santiago del Estero, N Argentina
An Baile Meánach *see* Ballymena
An Bhearú *see* Barrow
An Bhóinn *see* Boyne
An Blascaod Mór *see* Great Blasket Island
An Cabhán *see* Cavan
An Caisleán Nua *see* Newcastle
An Caisleán Riabhach *see* Castlerea, Ireland
An Caisleán Riabhach *see* Castlereagh
56 C13 **Ancash** *off.* Departamento de Ancash. ◐ *department* W Peru
Ancash, Departamento de *see* Ancash
An Cathair *see* Caher
102 J8 **Ancenis** Loire-Atlantique, NW France
An Chanáil Ríoga *see* Royal Canal
An Cheacha *see* Caha Mountains
39 R11 **Anchorage** Alaska, USA
39 R12 **Anchorage** ✈ Alaska, USA
39 Q13 **Anchor Point** Alaska, USA
An Chorr Chríochach *see* Cookstown
65 M24 **Anchorstack Point** *headland* W Tristan da Cunha
An Clár *see* Clare
An Clochán *see* Clifden
An Clochán Liath *see* Dunglow
23 U12 **Anclote Keys** *island group* Florida, SE USA
An Cóbh *see* Cobh
57 J17 **Ancohuma, Nevado de** ▲ W Bolivia
An Comar *see* Comber
57 D14 **Ancón** Lima, W Peru
106 J12 **Ancona** Marche, C Italy
Ancuabe *see* Ancuabi
82 Q13 **Ancuabi** *var.* Ancuabe. Cabo Delgado, NE Mozambique
63 F17 **Ancud** *prev.* San Carlos de Ancud. Los Lagos, S Chile
63 G17 **Ancud, Golfo de** *gulf* S Chile
Ancyra *see* Ankara
163 V8 **Anda** Heilongjiang, NE China
57 G16 **Andahuaylas** Apurímac, S Peru
An Daingean *see* Dingle
153 R15 **Andāl** West Bengal, NE India
94 E9 **Åndalsnes** Møre og Romsdal, S Norway
104 K13 **Andalucía** *Eng.* Andalusia. ◐ *autonomous community* S Spain
23 P7 **Andalusia** Alabama, S USA
Andalusia *see* Andalucía
151 Q21 **Andaman and Nicobar Islands** *var.* Andamans and Nicobars. ◐ *union territory* India, NE Indian Ocean
173 T4 **Andaman Basin** *undersea feature* NE Indian Ocean
151 P19 **Andaman Islands** *island group* India, NE Indian Ocean
Andamans and Nicobars *see* Andaman and Nicobar Islands
173 T4 **Andaman Sea** *sea* NE Indian Ocean
57 K19 **Andamarca** Oruro, C Bolivia
182 H5 **Andamooka** South Australia
141 Y9 **ʿAndām, Wādī** *seasonal river* NE Oman
172 J3 **Andapa** Antsirañana, NE Madagascar
149 R4 **Andarāb** *var.* Banow. Baghlān, NE Afghanistan
Andarbag *see* Andarbogh
147 S13 **Andarbogh** *Rus.* Andarbag, Anderbak. S Tajikistan
109 Z5 **Andau** Burgenland, E Austria
108 I10 **Andeer** Graubünden, S Switzerland
92 H9 **Andenes** Nordland, C Norway
99 J20 **Andenne** Namur, SE Belgium
77 S11 **Andéramboukane** Gao, E Mali
Anderbak *see* Andarbogh
99 G18 **Anderlecht** Brussels, C Belgium
99 G21 **Anderlues** Hainaut, S Belgium
108 G9 **Andermatt** Uri, C Switzerland
101 E17 **Andernach** *anc.* Antunnacum. Rheinland-Pfalz, SW Germany
188 D15 **Andersen Air Force Base** *air base* NE Guam
39 R9 **Anderson** Alaska, USA
35 N4 **Anderson** California, W USA
31 P13 **Anderson** Indiana, N USA
27 R8 **Anderson** Missouri, C USA
21 P11 **Anderson** South Carolina, SE USA
25 V10 **Anderson** Texas, SW USA
95 K20 **Anderstorp** Jönköping, S Sweden
54 D9 **Andes** Antioquia, W Colombia
47 P7 **Andes** ▲▲ W South America
29 P12 **Andes, Lake** ◎ South Dakota, N USA
92 H9 **Andfjorden** *fjord* E Norwegian Sea
155 H16 **Andhra Pradesh** ◐ *state* E India
98 J8 **Andijk** Noord-Holland, NW Netherlands
147 S10 **Andijon** *Rus.* Andizhan. Andijon Viloyati, E Uzbekistan
147 S10 **Andijon Viloyati** *Rus.* Andizhanskaya Oblast'. ◐ *province* E Uzbekistan
Andikíthira *see* Antikýthira
172 J4 **Andilamena** Toamasina, C Madagascar
142 L8 **Andimeshk** *var.* Andimishk; *prev.* Salehābād. Khūzestān, SW Iran
Andimishk *see* Andimeshk
Andipáros *see* Antíparos
Andipaxi *see* Antípaxoi
Andipsara *see* Antípsara
136 L16 **Andırın** Kahramanmaraş, S Turkey
158 J8 **Andirlangar** Xinjiang Uygur Zizhiqu, NW China
Andírrion *see* Antírrio
Ándissa *see* Ántissa
Andizhan *see* Andijon
Andizhanskaya Oblast' *see* Andijon Viloyati
149 N2 **Andkhvoy** Fāryāb, N Afghanistan
105 Q2 **Andoain** País Vasco, N Spain
163 Y15 **Andong** *Jap.* Antō. E South Korea
109 R4 **Andorf** Oberösterreich, N Austria
105 S7 **Andorra** Aragón, NE Spain
105 V4 **Andorra** *off.* Principality of Andorra, *Cat.* Valls d'Andorra, *Fr.* Vallée d'Andorre. ◆ *monarchy* SW Europe
Andorra *see* Andorra la Vella
105 V4 **Andorra la Vella** *var.* Andorra, *Fr.* Andorre la Vielle, *Sp.* Andorra la Vieja. ● (Andorra) C Andorra
Andorra la Vieja *see* Andorra la Vella
Andorra, Principality of *see* Andorra
Andorra, Valls d'/Andorre, Vallée d' *see* Andorra
Andorre la Vielle *see* Andorra la Vella
97 M22 **Andover** S England, UK
27 N6 **Andover** Kansas, C USA
92 G10 **Andøya** *island* C Norway
60 I8 **Andradina** São Paulo, S Brazil
105 X9 **Andratx** Mallorca, Spain, W Mediterranean Sea
39 N10 **Andreafsky River** ≈ Alaska, USA
38 H17 **Andreanof Islands** *island group* Aleutian Islands, Alaska, USA
124 H16 **Andreapol'** Tverskaya Oblast', W Russian Federation
Andreas, Cape *see* Zafer Burnu
Andreevka *see* Kabanbay
21 N10 **Andrews** North Carolina, SE USA
21 T13 **Andrews** South Carolina, SE USA
24 M7 **Andrews** Texas, SW USA
173 N5 **Andrew Tablemount** *var.* Gora Andryu. *undersea feature* W Indian Ocean
Andreyevka *see* Kabanbay
107 N17 **Andria** Puglia, SE Italy
113 K16 **Andrijevica** E Montenegro
115 E20 **Andrítsaina** Pelopónnisos, S Greece
An Droichead Nua *see* Newbridge
Andropov *see* Rybinsk
115 J19 **Ándros** Ándros, Kykládes, Greece, Aegean Sea
115 J20 **Ándros** *island* Kykládes, Greece, Aegean Sea
19 O7 **Androscoggin River** ≈ Maine/New Hampshire, NE USA
44 F3 **Andros Island** *island* NW Bahamas
127 R7 **Androsovka** Samarskaya Oblast', W Russian Federation
44 G3 **Andros Town** Andros Island, NW Bahamas
155 D21 **Āndrott Island** *island* Lakshadweep, India, N Indian Ocean
117 N5 **Andrushivka** Zhytomyrs'ka Oblast', N Ukraine
111 K17 **Andrychów** Małopolskie, S Poland
Andryu, Gora *see* Andrew Tablemount
92 I10 **Andselv** Troms, N Norway
79 O17 **Andudu** Orientale, NE Dem. Rep. Congo
105 N13 **Andújar** *anc.* Illiturgis. Andalucía, SW Spain
82 C12 **Andulo** Bié, W Angola
103 Q14 **Anduze** Gard, S France
An Earagail *see* Errigal Mountain
95 L19 **Aneby** Jönköping, S Sweden
Anécho *see* Aného
77 Q9 **Anéfis** Kidal, NE Mali
45 U8 **Anegada** *island* NE British Virgin Islands
61 B25 **Anegada, Bahía** *bay* E Argentina
45 U9 **Anegada Passage** *passage* Anguilla/British Virgin Islands
77 R17 **Aného** *var.* Anécho; *prev.* Petit-Popo. S Togo
197 D17 **Aneityum** *var.* Anatom; *prev.* Kéamu. *island* S Vanuatu
117 N10 **Anenii Noi** *Rus.* Novyye Aneny. C Moldova
186 F7 **Anepmete** New Britain, E Papua New Guinea
105 U4 **Aneto** ▲ NE Spain
146 F13 **Änew** *Rus.* Annau. Ahal Welaýaty, C Turkmenistan
Änewetak *see* Enewetak Atoll
77 Y8 **Aney** Agadez, NE Niger
An Fheoir *see* Nore
122 L12 **Angara** ≈ C Russian Federation
122 M13 **Angarsk** Irkutskaya Oblast', S Russian Federation
Angaur *see* Ngeaur
93 G17 **Änge** Västernorrland, C Sweden
Ángel *see* Úhlava
40 D4 **Ángel de la Guarda, Isla** *island* NW Mexico
171 O3 **Angeles** *off.* Angeles City. Luzon, N Philippines
Angeles City *see* Angeles
Angel Falls *see* Ángel, Salto
95 J22 **Ängelholm** Skåne, S Sweden
61 A17 **Angélica** Santa Fe, C Argentina
25 W8 **Angelina River** ≈ Texas, SW USA
55 Q9 **Ángel, Salto** *Eng.* Angel Falls. *waterfall* E Venezuela
95 M15 **Ängelsberg** Västmanland, C Sweden
35 P8 **Angels Camp** California, W USA
109 W7 **Anger** Steiermark, SE Austria
Angerapp *see* Ozersk
Angerburg *see* Węgorzewo
93 H15 **Ångermanälven** ≈ N Sweden
100 P11 **Angermünde** Brandenburg, NE Germany
102 K7 **Angers** *anc.* Juliomagus. Maine-et-Loire, NW France
15 W7 **Angers** ≈ Québec, SE Canada
93 J16 **Ångesön** *island* N Sweden
Angistro *see* Ágkistro
115 H13 **Angitis** ≈ NE Greece
167 R13 **Ângk Tasaôm** *prev.* Angtassom. Takêv, S Cambodia
185 C25 **Anglem, Mount** ▲ Stewart Island, Southland, SW New Zealand
97 I18 **Anglesey** *cultural region* NW Wales, UK
97 I18 **Anglesey** *island* NW Wales, UK
102 I15 **Anglet** Pyrénées-Atlantiques, SW France
25 W12 **Angleton** Texas, SW USA
Anglia *see* England
14 H9 **Angliers** Québec, SE Canada
Anglo-Egyptian Sudan *see* Sudan
Angmagssalik *see* Ammassalik
167 Q7 **Ang Nam Ngum** ◎ C Laos
79 N16 **Ango** Orientale, N Dem. Rep. Congo
83 Q15 **Angoche** Nampula, E Mozambique
63 G14 **Angol** Araucanía, C Chile
31 Q11 **Angola** Indiana, N USA
82 A9 **Angola** *off.* Republic of Angola; *prev.* People's Republic of Angola, Portuguese West Africa. ◆ *republic* SW Africa
65 P15 **Angola Basin** *undersea feature* E Atlantic Ocean
Angola, People's Republic of *see* Angola
Angola, Republic of *see* Angola
39 X13 **Angoon** Admiralty Island, Alaska, USA
147 O14 **Angor** Surkhondaryo Viloyati, S Uzbekistan
Angora *see* Ankara
186 C6 **Angoram** East Sepik, NW Papua New Guinea
40 H8 **Angostura** Sinaloa, C Mexico
Angostura *see* Ciudad Bolívar
41 U17 **Angostura, Presa de la** ▣ SE Mexico
28 J11 **Angostura Reservoir** ▣ South Dakota, N USA
102 L11 **Angoulême** *anc.* Iculisma. Charente, W France
102 K11 **Angoumois** *cultural region* W France
64 O2 **Angra do Heroísmo** Terceira, Azores, Portugal, NE Atlantic Ocean
60 O10 **Angra dos Reis** Rio de Janeiro, SE Brazil
Angra Pequena *see* Lüderitz
147 Q10 **Angren** Toshkent Viloyati, E Uzbekistan
Angtassom *see* Ângk Tasaôm
167 O10 **Ang Thong** *var.* Angthong. Ang Thong, C Thailand
Angthong *see* Ang Thong
79 M16 **Angu** Orientale, N Dem. Rep. Congo
105 S5 **Angües** Aragón, NE Spain
45 U9 **Anguilla** ◇ *UK dependent territory* E West Indies
45 V9 **Anguilla** *island* E West Indies
44 F4 **Anguilla Cays** *islets* SW Bahamas
Angul *see* Anugul
161 N1 **Anguli Nur** ◎ E China
79 O18 **Angumu** Orientale, E Dem. Rep. Congo
14 G14 **Angus** Ontario, S Canada
96 J10 **Angus** *cultural region* E Scotland, UK
59 K19 **Anhangüera** Goiás, S Brazil
99 I21 **Anhée** Namur, S Belgium
95 I21 **Anholt** *island* C Denmark
160 M11 **Anhua** *var.* Dongping. Hunan, S China
161 P8 **Anhui** *var.* Anhui Sheng, Anhwei, Wan. ◐ *province* E China
AnhuiSheng/Anhwei Wan *see* Anhui
39 O11 **Aniak** Alaska, USA
39 O12 **Aniak River** ≈ Alaska, USA
An Iarmhí *see* Westmeath
189 R8 **Anibare** E Nauru
189 R8 **Anibare Bay** *bay* E Nauru, W Pacific Ocean
Anicium *see* le Puy
115 K22 **Ánidro** *island* Kykládes, Greece, Aegean Sea
77 R15 **Anié** C Togo
77 Q15 **Anié** ≈ C Togo
102 J16 **Anie, Pic d'** ▲ SW France
127 Y7 **Anikhovka** Orenburgskaya Oblast', W Russian Federation
14 G9 **Anima Nipissing Lake** ◎ Ontario, S Canada
37 O16 **Animas** New Mexico, SW USA
37 P16 **Animas Peak** ▲ New Mexico, SW USA
37 P16 **Animas Valley** *valley* New Mexico, SW USA
116 F13 **Anina** *Ger.* Steierdorf, *Hung.* Stájerlakanina; *prev.* Ştaierdorf-Anina, Steierdorf-Anina, Steyerlak-Anina. Caraş-Severin, SW Romania
29 U14 **Anita** Iowa, C USA
123 U14 **Aniva, Mys** *cape* Ostrov Sakhalin, SE Russian Federation
187 S15 **Aniwa** *island* S Vanuatu
93 M19 **Anjalankoski** Etelä-Suomi, S Finland
ʿAnjar *see* Aanjar
Anjiangying *see* Luanping
14 B8 **Anjigami Lake** ◎ Ontario, S Canada
164 K14 **Anjō** *var.* Anzyô. Aichi, Honshū, SW Japan
102 J8 **Anjou** *cultural region* NW France
172 I13 **Anjouan** *var.* Nzwani, Johanna Island. *island* SE Comoros
172 J4 **Anjozorobe** Antananarivo, C Madagascar
163 W13 **Anju** W North Korea
98 M5 **Anjum** *Fris.* Eanjum. Friesland, N Netherlands
172 G6 **Ankaboa, Tanjona** *headland* W Madagascar
160 L7 **Ankang** *prev.* Xing'an. Shaanxi, C China
136 I12 **Ankara** *prev.* Angora; *anc.* Ancyra. ● (Turkey) Ankara, C Turkey
136 H12 **Ankara** ◐ *province* C Turkey
95 N19 **Ankarsrum** Kalmar, S Sweden
172 H6 **Ankazoabo** Toliara, SW Madagascar
172 I4 **Ankazobe** Antananarivo, C Madagascar
29 V14 **Ankeny** Iowa, C USA
167 V11 **An Khê** Gia Lai, C Vietnam
100 O9 **Anklam** Mecklenburg-Vorpommern, NE Germany
80 K13 **Ānkober** Amhara, N Ethiopia
77 O17 **Ankobra** ≈ S Ghana
79 N22 **Ankoro** Katanga, SE Dem. Rep. Congo
99 L24 **Anlier, Forêt d'** *forest* SE Belgium
160 I13 **Anlong** Guizhou, S China
An Longfort *see* Longford
167 R11 **Ânlong Vêng** Siĕmréab, NW Cambodia
An Lorgain *see* Lurgan
161 N8 **Anlu** Hubei, C China
An Mhí *see* Meath
An Mhuir Cheilteach *see* Celtic Sea
An Muileann gCearr *see* Mullingar
93 F16 **Ann** Jämtland, C Sweden
126 M8 **Anna** Voronezhskaya Oblast', W Russian Federation
30 L17 **Anna** Illinois, N USA
25 U5 **Anna** Texas, SW USA
74 L5 **Annaba** *prev.* Bône. NE Algeria
An Nabatīyah at Taḥtā *see* Nabatîyé
101 N17 **Annaberg-Buchholz** Sachsen, E Germany
109 T9 **Annabichl** ✈ (Klagenfurt) Kärnten, S Austria
140 M5 **An Nafūd** *desert* NW Saudi Arabia
139 P6 **ʿAnnah** *var.* ʿĀnah. NW Iraq
139 P6 **An Nāḥiyah** W Iraq
139 T10 **An Najaf** *var.* Najaf. S Iraq
21 V5 **Anna, Lake** ▣ Virginia, NE USA
97 F16 **Annalee** ≈ N Ireland
167 S9 **Annamitique, Chaîne** ▲▲ C Laos
97 J14 **Annan** S Scotland, UK
29 U8 **Annandale** Minnesota, N USA
21 W4 **Annandale** Virginia, NE USA
189 Q7 **Anna Point** *headland* N Nauru
21 X3 **Annapolis** *state capital* Maryland, NE USA
188 A10 **Anna, Pulo** *island* S Palau
153 O10 **Annapurna** ▲ C Nepal
An Nāqūrah *see* En Nâqoûra
31 R10 **Ann Arbor** Michigan, N USA
An Nás *see* Naas
139 W12 **An Nāṣirīyah** *var.* Nasiriya. SE Iraq
139 W11 **An Naṣr** E Iraq
Annau *see* Änew
121 O13 **An Nawfalīyah** *var.* Al Nūwfalīyah. N Libya
19 P10 **Ann, Cape** *headland* Massachusetts, NE USA
180 I10 **Annean, Lake** ◎ Western Australia
Anneciacum *see* Annecy
103 T11 **Annecy** *anc.* Anneciacum. Haute-Savoie, E France
103 T11 **Annecy, Lac d'** ◎ E France
103 T10 **Annemasse** Haute-Savoie, E France
39 Z14 **Annette Island** *island* Alexander Archipelago, Alaska, USA
An Nhon *see* Binh Đinh
An Nīl al Abyaḍ *see* White Nile
An Nīl al Azraq *see* Blue Nile
23 Q3 **Anniston** Alabama, S USA
79 A19 **Annobón** *island* W Equatorial Guinea
103 R12 **Annonay** Ardèche, E France
44 K12 **Annotto Bay** C Jamaica
141 R5 **An Nuʿayrīyah** *var.* Nariya. Ash Sharqīyah, NE Saudi Arabia
182 M9 **Annuello** Victoria, SE Australia
139 Q10 **An Nukhayb** S Iraq
139 U9 **An Nuʿmānīyah** E Iraq
Áno Arkhánai *see* Archánes
115 J25 **Anógeia** *cont.* Anogia, *var.* Anóyia. Kriti, Greece, E Mediterranean Sea
Anogia *see* Anógeia
29 V8 **Anoka** Minnesota, N USA
An Ómaigh *see* Omagh
172 I1 **Anorontany, Tanjona** *headland* N Madagascar
172 J5 **Anosibe An'Ala** Toamasina, E Madagascar
Anóyia *see* Anógeia
An Pointe *see* Warrenpoint
161 P9 **Anqing** Anhui, E China
161 Q5 **Anqiu** Shandong, E China
An Ráth *see* Ráthluirc
An Ribhéar *see* Kenmare River
An Ros *see* Rush
99 K19 **Ans** Liège, E Belgium
Anşāb *see* Nişāb
171 W12 **Ansas** Papua, E Indonesia
101 J20 **Ansbach** Bayern, SE Germany
An Sciobairín *see* Skibbereen
An Scoil *see* Skull
An Seancheann *see* Old Head of Kinsale
45 Y5 **Anse-Bertrand** Grande Terre, N Guadeloupe
172 H17 **Anse Boileau** Mahé, NE Seychelles
45 S11 **Anse La Raye** NW Saint Lucia
54 D9 **Anserma** Caldas, W Colombia
109 T4 **Ansfelden** Oberösterreich, N Austria
163 U12 **Anshan** Liaoning, NE China
160 J12 **Anshun** Guizhou, S China
61 F17 **Ansina** Tacuarembó, C Uruguay
29 O15 **Ansley** Nebraska, C USA
25 P6 **Anson** Texas, SW USA
77 Q10 **Ansongo** Gao, E Mali
An Srath Bán *see* Strabane
21 R5 **Ansted** West Virginia, NE USA
171 Y13 **Ansudu** Papua, E Indonesia
57 G15 **Anta** Cusco, S Peru
57 G16 **Antabamba** Apurímac, C Peru
Antafalva *see* Kovačica
136 L17 **Antakya** *anc.* Antioch, Antiochia. Hatay, S Turkey
172 K3 **Antalaha** Antsirañana, NE Madagascar
136 F17 **Antalya** *prev.* Adalia; *anc.* Attaleia, *Bibl.* Attalia. Antalya, SW Turkey
136 F17 **Antalya** ◐ *province* SW Turkey
136 F16 **Antalya** ✈ Antalya, SW Turkey
121 U10 **Antalya Basin** *undersea feature* E Mediterranean Sea
Antalya, Gulf of *see* Antalya Körfezi
136 F16 **Antalya Körfezi** *var.* Gulf of Adalia, *Eng.* Gulf of Antalya. *gulf* SW Turkey
172 J5 **Antanambao Manampotsy** Toamasina, E Madagascar
172 I5 **Antananarivo** *prev.* Tananarive. ● (Madagascar) Antananarivo, C Madagascar
172 I4 **Antananarivo** ◐ *province* C Madagascar
172 J5 **Antananarivo** ✈ Antananarivo, C Madagascar

◆ Country ● Country Capital ◇ Dependent Territory ○ Dependent Territory Capital ◐ Administrative Regions ✈ International Airport ▲ Mountain ▲▲ Mountain Range Volcano ≈ River ◎ Lake ▣ Reservoir

An tAonach – Arenas de San Pedro

An tAonach see Nenagh
194-195 Antarctica continent
194 I5 Antarctic Peninsula peninsula Antarctica
61 J15 Antas, Rio das ≈ S Brazil
189 U16 Ant Atoll atoll Caroline Islands, E Micronesia
An Teampall Mór see Templemore
Antep see Gaziantep
104 M15 Antequera anc. Anticaria, Antiquaria. Andalucía, S Spain
Antequera see Oaxaca
37 S5 Antero Reservoir ⊠ Colorado, C USA
26 M7 Anthony Kansas, C USA
37 R16 Anthony New Mexico, SW USA
182 D5 Anthony, Lake salt lake South Australia
74 E8 Anti-Atlas ⛰ SW Morocco
103 U15 Antibes anc. Antipolis. Alpes-Maritimes, SE France
103 U15 Antibes, Cap d' headland SE France
Anticaria see Antequera
13 Q11 Anticosti, Île d' Eng. Anticosti Island. island Québec, E Canada
Anticosti Island see Anticosti, Île d'
102 K3 Antifer, Cap d' headland N France
30 L6 Antigo Wisconsin, N USA
13 Q15 Antigonish Nova Scotia, SE Canada
64 P11 Antigua Fuerteventura, Islas Canarias, NE Atlantic Ocean
45 X10 Antigua island S Antigua and Barbuda, Leeward Islands
Antigua see Antigua Guatemala
45 W9 Antigua and Barbuda ◆ island state E West Indies
42 C6 Antigua Guatemala var. Antigua. Sacatepéquez, SW Guatemala
41 P11 Antiguo Morelos var. Antiguo-Morelos. Tamaulipas, C Mexico
115 F19 Antíkyras, Kólpos gulf C Greece
115 G24 Antikýthira var. Andikíthira. island S Greece
138 I7 Anti-Lebanon var. Jebel esh Sharqi, Ar. Al Jabal ash Sharqī, Fr. Anti-Liban. ⛰ Lebanon/Syria
Anti-Liban see Anti-Lebanon
115 M22 Antimácheia Kos, Dodekánisa, Greece
115 I22 Antímilos island Kykládes, Greece, Aegean Sea
36 L6 Antimony Utah, W USA
An tInbhear Mór see Arklow
30 M10 Antioch Illinois, N USA
Antioch see Antakya
102 I10 Antioche, Pertuis d' inlet W France
Antiochia see Antakya
54 D8 Antioquia Antioquia, C Colombia
54 E8 Antioquia off. Departamento de Antioquia. ◐ province C Colombia
Antioquia, Departamento de see Antioquia
115 J21 Antíparos var. Andipáros. island Kykládes, Greece, Aegean Sea
115 B17 Antípaxoi var. Andipaxi. island Iónioi Nísoi, Greece, C Mediterranean Sea
122 J8 Antipayuta Yamalo-Nenetskiy Avtonomnyy Okrug, N Russian Federation
192 L12 Antipodes Islands island group S New Zealand
Antipolis see Antibes
115 J18 Antípsara var. Andípsara. island E Greece
Antiquaria see Antequera
15 N10 Antique, Lac ◎ Québec, SE Canada
115 E18 Antírrio var. Andirrion. Dytikí Ellás, C Greece
115 K16 Ántissa var. Ándissa. Lésvos, E Greece
An tIúr see Newry
Antivari see Bar
56 C6 Antizana ▲ N Ecuador
27 Q13 Antlers Oklahoma, C USA
93 J14 Antnäs Norrbotten, N Sweden
Antō see Andong
62 G5 Antofagasta Antofagasta, N Chile
62 G6 Antofagasta off. Región de Antofagasta. ◐ region N Chile
Antofagasta, Región de see Antofagasta
62 I7 Antofalla, Salar de salt lake NW Argentina
99 D20 Antoing Hainaut, SW Belgium
43 S16 Antón Coclé, C Panama
24 M5 Anton Texas, SW USA
37 T11 Anton Chico New Mexico, SW USA
60 K12 Antonina Paraná, S Brazil
103 O5 Antony Hauts-de-Seine, N France
Antratsit see Antratsyt
117 Y8 Antratsyt Rus. Antratsit. Luhans'ka Oblast', E Ukraine
97 G15 Antrim Ir. Aontroim. NE Northern Ireland, UK
97 G14 Antrim Ir. Aontroim. cultural region NE Northern Ireland, UK
97 G14 Antrim Mountains ⛰ NE Northern Ireland, UK
172 H5 Antsalova Mahajanga, W Madagascar
Antserana see Antsiranana
An tSionainn see Shannon
172 J2 Antsiranana var. Antserana; prev. Antsirane, Diégo-Suarez. Antsiranana, N Madagascar
172 J2 Antsiranana ◐ province N Madagascar
Antsirane see Antsiranana
An tSiúir see Suir
118 I7 Antsla Ger. Anzen. Võrumaa, SE Estonia
An tSláine see Slaney
172 J3 Antsohihy Mahajanga, NW Madagascar
63 G14 Antuco, Volcán 🌋 C Chile
169 W10 Antu, Gunung ▲ Borneo, N Indonesia
An Tullach see Tullow
An-tung see Dandong
Antunnacum see Andernach
Antwerp see Antwerpen
99 G16 Antwerpen Eng. Antwerp, Fr. Anvers. Antwerpen, N Belgium
99 H16 Antwerpen Eng. Antwerp. ◐ province N Belgium
An Uaimh see Navan
154 N12 Anugul var. Angul. Orissa, E India
152 F9 Anūpgarh Rājasthān, NW India
154 K10 Anūppur Madhya Pradesh, C India
155 K24 Anuradhapura North Central Province, C Sri Lanka
Anvers see Antwerpen
194 G4 Anvers Island island Antarctica
39 N11 Anvik Alaska, USA
39 N10 Anvik River ≈ Alaska, USA
38 F17 Anvil Peak ▲ Semisopochnoi Island, Alaska, USA
159 P7 Anxi var. Yuanquan. Gansu, N China
182 F8 Anxious Bay bay South Australia
161 O5 Anyang Henan, C China
159 S11 A'nyêmaqên Shan ⛰ C China
118 H12 Anykščiai Utena, E Lithuania
161 P13 Anyuan var. Xinshan. Jiangxi, S China
123 T7 Anyuysk Chukotskiy Avtonomnyy Okrug, NE Russian Federation
123 T7 Anyuyskiy Khrebet ⛰ NE Russian Federation
54 D8 Anza Antioquia, C Colombia
Anzen see Antsla
107 I16 Anzio Lazio, C Italy
55 O6 Anzoátegui off. Estado Anzoátegui. ◐ state NE Venezuela
Anzoátegui, Estado see Anzoátegui
147 P12 Anzob W Tajikistan
Anzyō see Anjō
Aoba see Ambae
165 X13 Aoga-shima island Izu-shotō, SE Japan
Aohan Qi see Xinhui
Aoiz see Agoiz
186 M9 Aola var. Tenaghau. Guadalcanal, C Solomon Islands
166 M15 Ao Luk Nua Krabi, SW Thailand
Aomen see Macao
172 N8 Aomori Aomori, Honshū, C Japan
172 N8 Aomori off. Aomori-ken. ◐ prefecture Honshū, C Japan
Aomori-ken see Aomori
Aontroim see Antrim
115 C15 Aóos var. Vijosa, Vijosë, Alb. Lumi i Vjosës. ≈ Albania/Greece see also Vjosës, Lumi i
Aóos see Vjosës, Lumi i
191 Q7 Aorai, Mont ▲ Tahiti, W French Polynesia
185 E19 Aoraki prev. Aorangi, Mount Cook. ▲ South Island, New Zealand
167 R13 Aôral, Phnum prev. Phnom Aural. ▲ W Cambodia
Aorangi see Aoraki
185 L15 Aorangi Mountains ⛰ North Island, New Zealand
184 H13 Aorere ≈ South Island, New Zealand
106 A7 Aosta anc. Augusta Praetoria. Valle d'Aosta, NW Italy
77 O11 Aougoundou, Lac ◎ S Mali
76 K9 Aoukâr var. Aouker. plateau C Mauritania
78 J13 Aouk, Bahr ≈ Central African Republic/Chad
Aouker see Aoukâr
74 B11 Aousard SE Western Sahara
164 H12 Aoya Tottori, Honshū, SW Japan
Aoyang see Shanggao
78 H5 Aozou Borkou-Ennedi-Tibesti, N Chad
26 M11 Apache Oklahoma, C USA
36 L14 Apache Junction Arizona, SW USA
24 J9 Apache Mountains ⛰ Texas, SW USA
36 M16 Apache Peak ▲ Arizona, SW USA
116 H10 Apahida Cluj, NW Romania
23 T9 Apalachee Bay bay Florida, SE USA
23 T3 Apalachee River ≈ Georgia, SE USA
23 S10 Apalachicola Florida, SE USA
23 S10 Apalachicola Bay bay Florida, SE USA
23 R9 Apalachicola River ≈ Florida, SE USA
Apam see Apan
Apamama see Abemama
41 P14 Apan var. Apam. Hidalgo, C Mexico
42 J8 Apanás, Lago de ◎ NW Nicaragua
54 H14 Apaporis, Río ≈ Brazil/Colombia
185 C23 Aparima ≈ South Island, New Zealand
171 O1 Aparri Luzon, N Philippines
112 J9 Apatin Vojvodina, NW Serbia
124 J4 Apatity Murmanskaya Oblast', NW Russian Federation
55 X9 Apatou NW French Guiana
40 M14 Apatzingán var. Apatzingán de la Constitución. Michoacán de Ocampo, SW Mexico
Apatzingán de la Constitución see Apatzingán
171 X12 Apauwar Papua, E Indonesia
Apaxtla see Apaxtla de Castrejón
41 O15 Apaxtla de Castrejón var. Apaxtla. Guerrero, S Mexico
118 J7 Ape Alūksne, NE Latvia
98 L11 Apeldoorn Gelderland, E Netherlands
Apennines see Appennino
Apenrade see Aabenraa
57 L17 Apere, Río ≈ C Bolivia
55 W11 Apetina Sipaliwini, SE Surinam
21 U9 Apex North Carolina, SE USA
79 M16 Api Orientale, N Dem. Rep. Congo
152 M9 Api ▲ NW Nepal
192 H16 Āpia ● (Samoa) Upolu, SE Samoa
Apia see Abaiang
60 K11 Apiaí São Paulo, S Brazil
170 M16 Api, Gunung ▲ Pulau Sangeang, S Indonesia
187 N9 Apio Maramasike Island, N Solomon Islands
41 O15 Apipilulco Guerrero, S Mexico
41 P14 Apizaco Tlaxcala, S Mexico
104 I4 A Pobla de Trives Cast. Puebla de Trives. Galicia, NW Spain
55 U9 Apoera Sipaliwini, NW Surinam
115 O23 Apolakkiá Ródos, Dodekánisa, Greece, Aegean Sea
101 L16 Apolda Thüringen, C Germany
192 H16 Apolima Strait strait C Pacific Ocean
182 M13 Apollo Bay Victoria, SE Australia
Apollonia see Sozopol
57 J16 Apolo La Paz, W Bolivia
57 J16 Apolobamba, Cordillera ⛰ Bolivia/Peru
171 Q8 Apo, Mount 🌋 Mindanao, S Philippines
23 W11 Apopka Florida, SE USA
23 W11 Apopka, Lake ◎ Florida, SE USA
59 J19 Aporé, Rio ≈ SW Brazil
30 K2 Apostle Islands island group Wisconsin, N USA
Apostolas Andreas, Cape see Zafer Burnu
61 F14 Apóstoles Misiones, NE Argentina
Apostólou Andréa, Akrotíri see Zafer Burnu
117 S9 Apostolove Rus. Apostolovo. Dnipropetrovs'ka Oblast', E Ukraine
Apostolovo see Apostolove
17 S10 Appalachian Mountains ⛰ E USA
95 K14 Äppelbo Dalarna, C Sweden
98 N7 Appelscha Fris. Appelskea. Friesland, N Netherlands
Appelskea see Appelscha
106 G11 Appennino Eng. Apennines. ⛰ Italy/San Marino
107 L17 Appennino Napoletano ⛰ C Italy
108 I7 Appenzell Appenzell, NW Switzerland
108 H7 Appenzell ◐ canton NE Switzerland
55 V12 Appikalo Sipaliwini, S Surinam
98 O5 Appingedam Groningen, NE Netherlands
25 X8 Appleby Texas, SW USA
97 L15 Appleby-in-Westmorland Cumbria, NW England, UK
30 K10 Apple River ≈ Illinois, N USA
30 I5 Apple River ≈ Wisconsin, N USA
25 W9 Apple Springs Texas, SW USA
29 S8 Appleton Minnesota, N USA
30 M7 Appleton Wisconsin, N USA
27 S5 Appleton City Missouri, C USA
35 U14 Apple Valley California, W USA
29 V9 Apple Valley Minnesota, N USA
21 U6 Appomattox Virginia, NE USA
188 B16 Apra Harbour harbour W Guam
188 B16 Apra Heights W Guam
106 F6 Aprica, Passo dell' pass N Italy
107 M15 Apricena anc. Hadria Picena. Puglia, SE Italy
126 L14 Apsheronsk Krasnodarskiy Kray, SW Russian Federation
Apsheronskiy Poluostrov see Abşeron Yarımadası
103 S15 Apt anc. Apta Julia. Vaucluse, SE France
Apta Julia see Apt
38 H12 'Apua Point var. Apua Point. headland Hawai'i, USA, C Pacific Ocean
60 I10 Apucarana Paraná, S Brazil
Apulia see Puglia
54 K8 Apure off. Estado Apure. ◐ state C Venezuela
Apure, Estado see Apure
54 J7 Apure, Río ≈ W Venezuela
57 F16 Apurímac off. Departamento de Apurímac. ◐ department C Peru
Apurímac, Departamento de see Apurímac
57 F15 Apurímac, Río ≈ S Peru
116 G10 Apuseni, Munţii ⛰ W Romania
Aqaba/'Aqaba see Al 'Aqabah
138 F15 Aqaba, Gulf of var. Gulf of Elat, Ar. Khalīj al 'Aqabah; anc. Sinus Aelaniticus. gulf NE Red Sea
139 R7 'Aqabah C Iraq
'Aqabah, Khalīj al see Aqaba, Gulf of
149 O2 Āqchah var. Āqcheh. Jowzjān, N Afghanistan
Āqcheh see Āqchah
Aqköl see Akkol'
Aqmola see Astana
Aqmola Oblysy see Akmola
158 L10 Aqqikkol Hu ◎ NW China
Aqqystaū see Akkystau
'Aqrah see Ākrē
Aqsay see Aksay
Aqshataū see Akchatau
Aqsū see Aksu
Aqsūat see Aksuat
Aqtas see Aktas
Aqtaū see Aktau
Aqtöbe see Aktobe
Aqtöbe Oblysy see Aktyubinsk
Aqtoghay see Aktogay
Aquae Augustae see Dax
Aquae Calidae see Bath
Aquae Flaviae see Chaves
Aquae Grani see Aachen
Aquae Panoniae see Baden
Aquae Sextiae see Aix-en-Provence
Aquae Solis see Bath
Aquae Tarbelicae see Dax
36 J11 Aquarius Mountains ⛰ Arizona, SW USA
62 O5 Aquidabán, Río ≈ E Paraguay
59 H20 Aquidauana Mato Grosso do Sul, S Brazil
40 L15 Aquila Michoacán de Ocampo, S Mexico
Aquila/Aquila degli Abruzzi see L'Aquila
25 T8 Aquilla Texas, SW USA
44 L9 Aquin S Haiti
Aquisgranum see Aachen
102 J13 Aquitaine ◐ region SW France
Aqzhar see Akzhar
153 P13 Āra prev. Arrah. Bihār, N India
105 S4 Ara ≈ NE Spain
23 P2 Arab Alabama, S USA
Araba see Álava
138 G12 'Arabah, Wādī al Heb. Ha'Arava. ◐ dry watercourse Israel/Jordan
117 U12 Arabats'ka Strilka, Kosa spit S Ukraine
117 U12 Arabats'ka Zatoka gulf S Ukraine
'Arab, Baḥr al see Arab, Bahr el
80 C12 Arab, Bahr el var. Baḥr al 'Arab. ≈ S Sudan
56 E7 Arabela, Río ≈ N Peru
173 O4 Arabian Basin undersea feature N Arabian Sea
Arabian Desert see Sahara el Sharqîya
141 N9 Arabian Peninsula peninsula SW Asia
85 P15 Arabian Plate tectonic feature Africa/Asia/Europe
141 W14 Arabian Sea sea NW Indian Ocean
Arabicus, Sinus see Red Sea
'Arabī, Khalīj al see Gulf, The
Arabistan see Khūzestān
'Arabīyah as Su'ūdīyah, Al Mamlakah al see Saudi Arabia
'Arabīyah Jumhūrīyah, Miṣr al see Egypt
138 I9 'Arab, Jabal al ▲ S Syria
Arab Republic of Egypt see Egypt
139 Y12 'Arab, Shaṭṭ al Eng. Shatt al Arab, Per. Arvand Rūd. ≈ Iran/Iraq
136 I11 Araç Kastamonu, N Turkey
59 P16 Aracaju state capital Sergipe, E Brazil
54 F5 Aracataca Magdalena, N Colombia
58 P13 Aracati Ceará, E Brazil
60 J8 Araçatuba São Paulo, S Brazil
136 I11 Araç Çayı ≈ N Turkey
104 J13 Aracena Andalucía, S Spain
115 F20 Árachnaío ⛰ S Greece
115 D16 Árachthos var. Arta, prev. Árakhthos; anc. Arachthus. ≈ W Greece
Arachthus see Árachthos
59 N19 Araçuaí Minas Gerais, SE Brazil
138 F11 'Arad Southern, S Israel
116 F11 Arad Arad, W Romania
116 F11 Arad ◐ county W Romania
78 J9 Arada Biltine, NE Chad
143 P18 'Arādah Abū Ẓaby, S United Arab Emirates
Aradhippou see Aradíppou
121 Q3 Aradíppou var. Aradhippou. SE Cyprus
174 K6 Arafura Sea Ind. Laut Arafuru. sea W Pacific Ocean
174 L6 Arafura Shelf undersea feature C Arafura Sea
Arafuru, Laut see Arafura Sea
59 J18 Aragarças Goiás, C Brazil
Aragats, Gora see Aragats Lerr
137 T12 Aragats Lerr Rus. Gora Aragats. ▲ W Armenia
32 E14 Arago, Cape headland Oregon, NW USA
105 R6 Aragón ◐ autonomous community E Spain
105 Q4 Aragón ≈ NE Spain
107 J24 Aragona Sicilia, Italy, C Mediterranean Sea
105 Q7 Aragoncillo ▲ C Spain
54 L5 Aragua off. Estado Aragua. ◐ state N Venezuela
55 N6 Aragua de Barcelona Anzoátegui, NE Venezuela
55 O5 Aragua de Maturín Monagas, NE Venezuela
Aragua, Estado see Aragua
59 K15 Araguaia, Río var. Araguaya. ≈ C Brazil
59 K19 Araguari Minas Gerais, SE Brazil
58 J11 Araguari, Rio ≈ SW Brazil
Araguaya see Araguaia, Río
104 K14 Arahal Andalucía, S Spain
165 N11 Arai Niigata, Honshū, C Japan
Árainn see Inishmore
Árainn Mhór see Aran Island
Ara Jovis see Aranjuez
74 J11 Arak C Algeria
171 Y15 Arak Papua, E Indonesia
142 M7 Arāk prev. Sultānābād. Markazī, W Iran
188 D10 Arakabesan island Palau Islands, N Palau
55 S7 Arakaka NW Guyana
166 K6 Arakan State var. Rakhine State. ◐ state W Burma (Myanmar)
166 K5 Arakan Yoma ⛰ W Burma (Myanmar)
165 O10 Arakawa Niigata, Honshū, C Japan
Árakhthos see Árachthos
Araks/Arak's see Aras
158 H7 Aral Xinjiang Uygur Zizhiqu, NW China
Aral see Aralsk, Kazakhstan
Aral see Vose', Tajikistan
Aral-Bukhorskiy Kanal see Amu-Buxoro Kanali
137 T12 Aralık Iğdır, E Turkey
146 H5 Aral Sea Kaz. Aral Tengizi, Rus. Aral'skoye More, Uzb. Orol Dengizi. inland sea Kazakhstan/Uzbekistan
144 L13 Aral'sk Kaz. Aral. Kzylorda, SW Kazakhstan
Aral'skoye More/Aral Tengizi see Aral Sea
41 O10 Aramberri Nuevo León, NE Mexico
186 B8 Aramia ≈ SW Papua New Guinea
143 N6 Ārān var. Golārā. Eşfahān, C Iran
105 N5 Aranda de Duero Castilla-León, N Spain
112 M12 Aranđelovac prev. Arandjelovac. Serbia, C Serbia
Arandjelovac see Aranđelovac
97 J19 Aran Fawddwy ▲ NW Wales, UK
97 C14 Aran Island Ir. Árainn Mhór. island NW Ireland
97 A18 Aran Islands island group W Ireland
105 N9 Aranjuez anc. Ara Jovis. Madrid, C Spain
83 E20 Aranos Hardap, SE Namibia
25 U14 Aransas Bay inlet Texas, SW USA
25 T14 Aransas Pass Texas, SW USA
191 O3 Aranuka prev. Nanouki. atoll Tungaru, W Kiribati
167 Q11 Aranyaprathet Prachin Buri, S Thailand
Aranyosasztal see Zlatý Stôl
Aranyosgyéres see Câmpia Turzii
Aranyosmarót see Zlaté Moravce
164 C14 Arao Kumamoto, Kyūshū, SW Japan
77 O8 Araouane Tombouctou, N Mali
26 L10 Arapaho Oklahoma, C USA
29 N16 Arapahoe Nebraska, C USA
57 I16 Arapa, Laguna ◎ SE Peru
185 K14 Arapawa Island island C New Zealand
61 E17 Arapey Grande, Río ≈ N Uruguay
59 P16 Arapiraca Alagoas, E Brazil
140 M3 'Ar'ar Al Ḥudūd ash Shamālīyah, NW Saudi Arabia
54 G15 Araracuara Caquetá, S Colombia
61 K15 Araranguá Santa Catarina, S Brazil
60 L8 Araraquara São Paulo, S Brazil
59 O13 Araras Ceará, E Brazil
58 I14 Araras Pará, N Brazil
60 L9 Araras São Paulo, S Brazil
60 H11 Araras, Serra das ⛰ S Brazil
137 U12 Ararat S Armenia
182 M12 Ararat Victoria, SE Australia
Ararat, Mount see Büyükağrı Dağı
140 M3 'Ar'ar, Wādī wadi Iraq/Saudi Arabia
129 N7 Aras Arm. Arak's, Az. Araz Nehri, Per. Rūd-e Aras, Rus. Araks; prev. Araxes. ≈ SW Asia
105 R9 Aras de Alpuente País Valenciano, E Spain
137 S13 Aras Güneyi Dağları ⛰ NE Turkey
Aras, Rūd-e see Aras
191 U9 Aratika atoll Îles Tuamotu, C French Polynesia
Aratürük see Yiwu
54 I8 Arauca Arauca, NE Colombia
54 I8 Arauca off. Intendencia de Arauca. ◐ province NE Colombia
Arauca, Intendencia de see Arauca
63 G15 Araucanía off. Región de la Araucanía. ◐ region C Chile
Araucanía, Región de la see Araucanía
54 L7 Arauca, Río ≈ Colombia/Venezuela
63 F14 Arauco Bío Bío, C Chile
63 F14 Arauco, Golfo de gulf S Chile
54 H8 Arauquita Arauca, C Colombia
Arausio see Orange
152 F13 Arāvali Range ⛰ N India
186 J7 Arawa Bougainville Island, NE Papua New Guinea
185 C20 Arawata ≈ South Island, New Zealand
186 F7 Arawe Islands island group E Papua New Guinea
59 L20 Araxá Minas Gerais, SE Brazil
Araxes see Aras
55 O5 Araya Sucre, N Venezuela
Araz Nehri see Aras
105 R4 Arba ≈ N Spain
81 I15 Ārba Minch' Southern, S Ethiopia
139 U4 Arbat NE Iraq
107 D19 Arbatax Sardegna, Italy, C Mediterranean Sea
Arbe see Rab
Arbela see Arbīl
139 S3 Arbīl var. Erbil, Irbīl, Kurd. Hawlēr; anc. Arbela. N Iraq
95 M16 Arboga Västmanland, C Sweden
95 M16 Arbogaån ≈ C Sweden
103 S9 Arbois Jura, E France
54 D6 Arboletes Antioquia, NW Colombia
9 X15 Arborg Manitoba, S Canada
94 N12 Arbrå Gävleborg, C Sweden
96 K10 Arbroath anc. Aberbrothock. E Scotland, UK
35 N6 Arbuckle California, W USA
27 N12 Arbuckle Mountains ⛰ Oklahoma, C USA
162 I5 Arbulag var. Mandal. Hövsgöl, N Mongolia
Arbuzinka see Arbyzynka
117 Q8 Arbyzynka Rus. Arbuzinka. Mykolayivs'ka Oblast', S Ukraine
103 U12 Arc ≈ E France
102 J13 Arcachon Gironde, SW France
102 J13 Arcachon, Bassin d' inlet SW France
18 E10 Arcade New York, NE USA
23 W14 Arcadia Florida, SE USA
22 H5 Arcadia Louisiana, S USA
30 J7 Arcadia Wisconsin, N USA
Arcae Remorum see Châlons-en-Champagne
44 L9 Arcahaie C Haiti
34 K3 Arcata California, W USA
35 U6 Arc Dome ▲ Nevada, W USA
107 J16 Arce Lazio, C Italy
41 O15 Arcelia Guerrero, S Mexico
99 M15 Arcen Limburg, SE Netherlands
115 J25 Archánes var. Áno Arkhánai, Epáno Archánes; prev. Epáno Arkhánai. Kríti, Greece, E Mediterranean Sea
Archangel see Arkhangel'sk
Archangel Bay see Chëshskaya Guba
115 O23 Archángelos var. Arhangelos, Arkhángelos. Ródos, Dodekánisa, Greece, Aegean Sea
114 F7 Archar ≈ NW Bulgaria
31 R11 Archbold Ohio, N USA
105 R12 Archena Murcia, SE Spain
25 R5 Archer City Texas, SW USA
104 M14 Archidona Andalucía, S Spain
65 B25 Arch Islands island group SW Falkland Islands
106 G13 Arcidosso Toscana, C Italy
103 Q5 Arcis-sur-Aube Aube, N France
182 F3 Arckaringa Creek seasonal river South Australia
106 G7 Arco Trentino-Alto Adige, N Italy
33 Q14 Arco Idaho, NW USA
30 M14 Arcola Illinois, N USA
105 P6 Arcos de Jalón Castilla-León, N Spain
104 K15 Arcos de la Frontera Andalucía, S Spain
104 G5 Arcos de Valdevez Viana do Castelo, N Portugal
59 P15 Arcoverde Pernambuco, E Brazil
102 H5 Arcovest, Pointe de l' headland NW France
Arctic Mid Oceanic Ridge see Nansen Cordillera
197 R8 Arctic Ocean ocean
8 G7 Arctic Red River ≈ Northwest Territories/ Yukon Territory, NW Canada
Arctic Red River see Tsiigehtchic
39 S6 Arctic Village Alaska, USA
194 H1 Arctowski Polish research station South Shetland Islands, Antarctica
114 I12 Arda var. Ardhas, Gk. Ardas. ≈ Bulgaria/Greece see also Ardas
Arda see Ardas
142 L2 Ardabīl var. Ardebil. Ardabīl, NW Iran
142 L2 Ardabīl off. Ostān-e Ardabīl. ◐ province NW Iran
Ardabīl, Ostān-e see Ardabīl
137 R11 Ardahan Ardahan, NE Turkey
137 S11 Ardahan ◐ province Ardahan, Turkey Asia
143 P8 Ardakān Yazd, C Iran
94 E12 Årdalstangen Sogn Og Fjordane, S Norway
137 R11 Ardanuç Artvin, NE Turkey
114 L12 Ardas var. Ardhas, Bul. Arda. ≈ Bulgaria/Greece see also Arda
Ardas see Arda
138 I13 Arḍ aş Şawwān var. Ardh es Suwwān. plain S Jordan
127 P5 Ardatov Respublika Mordoviya, W Russian Federation
14 G12 Ardbeg Ontario, S Canada
Ardeal see Transylvania
Ardebil see Ardabīl
103 Q13 Ardèche ◐ department E France
103 Q13 Ardèche ≈ C France
97 F17 Ardee Ir. Baile Átha Fhirdhia. Louth, NE Ireland
103 Q3 Ardennes ◐ department NE France
99 J23 Ardennes physical region Belgium/France
137 Q11 Ardeşen Rize, NE Turkey
143 O7 Ardestān var. Ardistan. Eşfahān, C Iran
108 J9 Ardez Graubünden, SE Switzerland
Ardhas see Arda/Ardas
Ardh es Suwwān see Arḍ aş Şawwān
Ardila see Ardila, Ribeira de
104 I12 Ardila, Ribeira de Sp. Ardilla. ≈ Portugal/Spain see also Ardilla
Ardila, Ribeira de see Ardilla
9 T17 Ardill Saskatchewan, S Canada
104 I12 Ardilla Port. Ribeira de Ardila. ≈ Portugal/Spain see also Ardila, Ribeira de
40 M11 Ardilla, Cerro la ▲ C Mexico
114 J12 Ardino Kŭrdzhali, S Bulgaria
Ardistan see Ardestān
183 P9 Ardlethan New South Wales, SE Australia
Ard Mhacha see Armagh
23 P1 Ardmore Alabama, S USA
27 N13 Ardmore Oklahoma, C USA
20 J10 Ardmore Tennessee, S USA
96 G10 Ardnamurchan, Point of headland N Scotland, UK
Árdni see Arnøya
99 C17 Ardooie West-Vlaanderen, W Belgium
182 I9 Ardrossan South Australia
116 H9 Ardusat Hung. Erdőszáda. Maramureş, N Romania
93 F16 Åre Jämtland, C Sweden
79 P16 Arebi Orientale, NE Dem. Rep. Congo
45 T5 Arecibo C Puerto Rico
171 V13 Aredo Papua, E Indonesia
59 P14 Areia Branca Rio Grande do Norte, E Brazil
119 O14 Arekhawsk Rus. Orekhovsk. Vitsyebskaya Voblasts', N Belarus
Arel see Arlon
Arelas/Arelate see Arles
Arenal, Embalse de see Arenal Laguna
42 L12 Arenal Laguna var. Embalse de Arenal. ◎ NW Costa Rica
42 L13 Arenal, Volcán 🌋 NW Costa Rica
34 K6 Arena, Point headland California, W USA
59 H17 Arenápolis Mato Grosso, W Brazil
40 G10 Arena, Punta headland W Mexico
104 L8 Arenas de San Pedro Castilla-León, N Spain

◆ Country
● Country Capital
◇ Dependent Territory
○ Dependent Territory Capital
◐ Administrative Regions
✈ International Airport
▲ Mountain
⛰ Mountain Range
🌋 Volcano
≈ River
◎ Lake
⊠ Reservoir

ARENAS, PUNTA DE – ASHWABAY, MOUNT

63 I24 Arenas, Punta de *headland* S Argentina
61 B20 Arenaza Buenos Aires, E Argentina
95 F17 Arendal Aust-Agder, S Norway
99 J16 Arendonk Antwerpen, N Belgium
43 T15 Arenosa Panamá, N Panama
Arensburg *see* Kuressaare
105 W5 Arenys de Mar Cataluña, NE Spain
106 C9 Arenzano Liguria, NW Italy
115 F22 Areópoli *prev.* Areópolis. Pelopónnisos, S Greece
Areópolis *see* Areópoli
57 H18 Arequipa Arequipa, SE Peru
57 G17 Arequipa *off.* Departamento de Arequipa. ⬖ *department* Arequia SW Peru
Arequipa, Departamento de *see* Arequipa
61 B19 Arequito Santa Fe, C Argentina
104 M7 Arévalo Castilla-León, N Spain
106 H12 Arezzo *anc.* Arretium. Toscana, C Italy
105 Q4 Arga ≈ N Spain
Argaeus *see* Erciyes Daği
115 G17 Argalastí Thessalía, C Greece
105 O10 Argamasilla de Alba Castilla-La Mancha, C Spain
158 L8 Argan Xinjiang Uygur Zizhiqu, NW China
105 O8 Arganda Madrid, C Spain
104 H8 Arganil Coimbra, N Portugal
171 P6 Argao Cebu, C Philippines
153 V15 Argartala Tripura, NE India
123 N9 Arga-Sala ≈ Respublika Sakha (Yakutiya),NE Russian Federation
103 P17 Argelès-sur-Mer Pyrénées-Orientales, S France
103 T15 Argens ≈ SE France
106 H9 Argenta Emilia-Romagna, N Italy
102 K5 Argentan Orne, N France
103 N12 Argentat Corrèze, C France
106 A9 Argentera Piemonte, NE Italy
103 N5 Argenteuil Val-d'Oise, N France
62 K13 Argentina *off.* Republic of Argentina. ◆ *republic* S South America
Argentina Basin *see* Argentine Basin
Argentina, Republic of *see* Argentina
Argentine Abyssal Plain *see* Argentine Plain
65 I19 Argentine Basin *var.* Argentina Basin. *undersea feature* SW Atlantic Ocean
65 I20 Argentine Plain *var.* Argentine Abyssal Plain. *undersea feature* SW Atlantic Ocean
Argentine Rise *see* Falkland Plateau
63 H22 Argentino, Lago ◎ S Argentina
102 K8 Argenton-Château Deux-Sèvres, W France
102 M9 Argenton-sur-Creuse Indre, C France
Argentoratum *see* Strasbourg
116 I12 Argeş ⬖ *county* S Romania
116 K14 Argeş ≈ S Romania
149 O8 Arghandāb, Daryā-ye ≈ SE Afghanistan
Arghastān *see* Arghestān
149 O8 Arghestān *Pash.* Arghastān. ≈ SE Afghanistan
Argirocastro *see* Gjirokastër
80 E7 Argo Northern, N Sudan
173 P7 Argo Fracture Zone *tectonic feature* C Indian Ocean
115 F20 Argolikós Kólpos *gulf* S Greece
103 R4 Argonne *physical region* NE France
115 F20 Árgos Pelopónnisos, S Greece
139 S1 Argōsh N Iraq
115 D14 Árgos Orestikó Dytikí Makedonía, N Greece
115 B19 Argostóli *var.* Argostólion. Kefallonía, Iónia Nisiá, Greece, C Mediterranean Sea
Argostólion *see* Argostóli
Argovie *see* Aargau
35 O14 Arguello, Point *headland* California, W USA
127 P16 Argun Chechenskaya Respublika, SW Russian Federation
157 T2 Argun *Chin.* Ergun He, *Rus.* Argun'. ≈ China/ Russian Federation
77 T12 Argungu Kebbi, NW Nigeria
Arguut *see* Guchin-Us
181 N3 Argyle, Lake *salt lake* Western Australia
96 G12 Argyll *cultural region* W Scotland, UK
Argyrokastron *see* Gjirokastër
162 I7 Arhangay ⬖ *province* C Mongolia
Arhangelos *see* Archángelos
95 P14 Arholma Stockholm, C Sweden
95 G22 Århus *var.* Aarhus. Århus, C Denmark
95 G22 Århus ⬖ *county* C Denmark
139 T1 Arī E Iraq
Aria *see* Herāt
83 F22 Ariamsvlei Karas, SE Namibia
107 L17 Ariano Irpino Campania, S Italy
54 F11 Ariari, Río ≈ C Colombia
151 K19 Ari Atoll *atoll* C Maldives
77 P11 Aribinda N Burkina
62 G2 Arica *hist.* San Marcos de Arica. Tarapacá, N Chile
54 H16 Arica Amazonas, S Colombia
62 G2 Arica ✕ Tarapacá, N Chile
114 E13 Aridaía *var.* Aridea, Aridhaía. Dytikí Makedonía, N Greece
Aridea *see* Aridaía
172 I15 Aride, Île *island* Inner Islands, NE Seychelles
Aridhaía *see* Aridaía
103 N17 Ariège ⬖ *department* S France
102 M16 Ariège *var.* la Riege. ≈ Andorra/France
116 H11 Arieş ≈ W Romania
149 U10 Ārifwāla Punjab, E Pakistan
Ariguaní *see* El Difícil
138 G11 Arīhā Al Karak, W Jordan
138 I3 Arīḩā *var.* Arīhā. Idlib, W Syria
Arīhā *see* Arīḩā
Arīhā *see* Jericho
37 W4 Arikaree River ≈ Colorado/ Nebraska, C USA
112 L13 Arilje Serbia, W Serbia
45 U14 Arima Trinidad, Trinidad and Tobago
Arime *see* Al 'Arīmah
Ariminum *see* Rimini
59 H16 Arinos, Rio ≈ W Brazil
40 M14 Ario de Rosales *var.* Ario de Rosáles. Michoacán de Ocampo, SW Mexico
Ario de Rosáles *see* Ario de Rosales
118 F12 Ariogala Kaunas, C Lithuania
47 T7 Aripuanã ≈ W Brazil
59 E15 Ariquemes Rondônia, W Brazil
121 W13 'Arīsh, Wādi el ≈ NE Egypt
54 K6 Arismendi Barinas, C Venezuela
10 J14 Aristazabal Island *island* SW Canada
60 F13 Aristóbulo del Valle Misiones, NE Argentina
172 I5 Arivonimamo ✕ (Antananarivo) Antananarivo, C Madagascar
Arixang *see* Wenquan
105 Q6 Ariza Aragón, NE Spain
62 I6 Arizaro, Salar de *salt lake* NW Argentina
105 O2 Arizgoiti *var* Basauri. País Vasco, N Spain
62 K13 Arizona San Luis, C Argentina
36 J12 Arizona *off.* State of Arizona, *also known as* Copper State, Grand Canyon State. ⬖ *state* SW USA
40 G4 Arizpe Sonora, NW Mexico
95 J16 Årjäng Värmland, C Sweden
143 P8 Arjenān Yazd, C Iran
92 I13 Arjeplog Norrbotten, N Sweden
54 E5 Arjona Bolívar, N Colombia
105 N13 Arjona Andalucía, S Spain
123 S10 Arka Khabarovskiy Kray, E Russian Federation
22 L2 Arkabutla Lake ⊠ Mississippi, S USA
127 O7 Arkadak Saratovskaya Oblast', W Russian Federation
27 T13 Arkadelphia Arkansas, C USA
115 J25 Arkalochóri; *prev.* Arkalokhórion. Kríti, Greece, E Mediterranean Sea
Arkalohori/Arkalokhórion *see* Arkalochóri
145 O10 Arkalyk *Kaz.* Arqalyq. Kostanay, N Kazakhstan
27 U10 Arkansas *off.* State of Arkansas, *also known as* The Land of Opportunity. ⬖ *state* S USA
27 W14 Arkansas City Arkansas, C USA
27 O7 Arkansas City Kansas, C USA
16 K11 Arkansas River ≈ C USA
182 J5 Arkaroola South Australia
Arkhángelos *see* Archángelos
124 L8 Arkhangel'sk *Eng.* Archangel. Arkhangel'skaya Oblast', NW Russian Federation
124 L9 Arkhangel'skaya Oblast' ⬖ *province* NW Russian Federation
127 O14 Arkhangel'skoye Stavropol'skiy Kray, SW Russian Federation
123 R14 Arkhara Amurskaya Oblast', S Russian Federation
97 G19 Arklow *Ir.* An tInbhear Mór. SE Ireland
115 M20 Arkoi *island* Dodekánisa, Greece, Aegean Sea
27 R11 Arkoma Oklahoma, C USA
100 O7 Arkona, Kap *cape* NE Germany
95 N17 Arkösund Östergötland, S Sweden
122 J6 Arkticheskogo Instituta, Ostrova *island* N Russian Federation
95 O15 Arlanda ✕ (Stockholm) Stockholm, C Sweden
146 C11 Arlandag *Rus.* Gora Arlan. ▲ W Turkmenistan
Arlan, Gora *see* Arlandag
105 O5 Arlanza ≈ N Spain
105 N5 Arlanzón ≈ N Spain
103 R15 Arles *var.* Arles-sur-Rhône; *anc.* Arelas, Arelate. Bouches-du-Rhône, SE France
Arles-sur-Rhône *see* Arles
103 O17 Arles-sur-Tech Pyrénées-Orientales, S France
29 U9 Arlington Minnesota, N USA
29 R15 Arlington Nebraska, C USA
32 J11 Arlington Oregon, NW USA
29 R10 Arlington South Dakota, N USA
20 E10 Arlington Tennessee, S USA
25 T6 Arlington Texas, SW USA
21 W4 Arlington Virginia, NE USA
32 H7 Arlington Washington, NW USA
30 M10 Arlington Heights Illinois, N USA
77 U8 Arlit Agadez, C Niger
99 L24 Arlon *Dut.* Aarlen, *Ger.* Arel, *Lat.* Orolaunum. Luxembourg, SE Belgium
27 R7 Arma Kansas, C USA
97 F16 Armagh *Ir.* Ard Mhacha. S Northern Ireland, UK
97 F16 Armagh *cultural region* S Northern Ireland, UK
102 K15 Armagnac *cultural region* S France
103 Q7 Armançon ≈ C France
60 K10 Armando Laydner, Represa ⊠ S Brazil
115 M24 Armathía *island* SE Greece
137 T12 Armavir *prev.* Hokhtemberyan, *Rus.* Oktemberyan. SW Armenia
126 M14 Armavir Krasnodarskiy Kray, SW Russian Federation
54 E10 Armenia Quindío, W Colombia
137 T12 Armenia *off.* Republic of Armenia, *var.* Ajastan, *Arm.* Hayastani Hanrapetut'yun; *prev.* Armenian Soviet Socialist Republic. ◆ *republic* SW Asia
Armenian Soviet Socialist Republic *see* Armenia
Armenia, Republic of *see* Armenia
Armenierstadt *see* Gherla
103 O1 Armentières Nord, N France
40 K14 Armería Colima, SW Mexico
183 T5 Armidale New South Wales, SE Australia
29 P11 Armour South Dakota, N USA
61 B18 Armstrong Santa Fe, C Argentina
9 N16 Armstrong British Columbia, SW Canada
12 D11 Armstrong Ontario, S Canada
29 U11 Armstrong Iowa, C USA
25 S16 Armstrong Texas, SW USA
117 S11 Armyans'k *Rus.* Armyansk. Respublika Krym, S Ukraine
115 H14 Arnaia *Cont.* Arnea. Kentrikí Makedonía, N Greece
121 N2 Arnaoúti, Akrotíri *var.* Arnaoútis, Cape Arnaouti. *cape* W Cyprus
Arnaouti, Cape/Arnaoútis *see* Arnaoúti, Akrotíri
12 L4 Arnaud ≈ Québec, E Canada
103 Q8 Arnay-le-Duc Côte d'Or, C France
Arnea *see* Arnaía
105 Q4 Arnedo La Rioja, N Spain
95 I14 Årnes Akershus, S Norway
26 K9 Arnett Oklahoma, C USA
98 L12 Arnhem Gelderland, SE Netherlands
181 Q2 Arnhem Land *physical region* Northern Territory, N Australia
106 F11 Arno ≈ C Italy
Arno *see* Arno Atoll
189 W7 Arno Atoll *var.* Arno. *atoll* Ratak Chain, NE Marshall Islands
182 H8 Arno Bay South Australia
35 Q8 Arnold California, W USA
27 X5 Arnold Missouri, C USA
29 N15 Arnold Nebraska, C USA
109 R10 Arnoldstein *Slvn.* Pod Klošter. Kärnten, S Austria
103 N9 Arnon ≈ C France
45 P14 Arnos Vale ✕ (Kingstown) Saint Vincent, SE Saint Vincent and the Grenadines
92 I8 Arnøya *Lapp.* Árdni. *island* N Norway
14 L12 Arnprior Ontario, SE Canada
101 G15 Arnsberg Nordrhein-Westfalen, W Germany
101 K16 Arnstadt Thüringen, C Germany
Arnswalde *see* Choszczno
54 K5 Aroa Yaracuy, N Venezuela
83 E21 Aroab Karas, SE Namibia
Ároania *see* Chelmós
191 O6 Aroa, Pointe *headland* Moorea, W French Polynesia
Aroe Islands *see* Aru, Kepulauan
101 H15 Arolsen Niedersachsen, C Germany
106 C7 Arona Piemonte, NE Italy
19 R3 Aroostook River ≈ Canada/USA
Arop Island *see* Long Island
38 M12 Aropuk Lake ◎ Alaska, USA
191 P4 Arorae *atoll* Tungaru, W Kiribati
190 G16 Arorangi Rarotonga, S Cook Islands
108 I9 Arosa Graubünden, S Switzerland
104 F4 Arousa, Ría de *estuary* E Atlantic Ocean
184 P8 Arowhana ▲ North Island, New Zealand
137 V12 Arp'a *Az.* Arpaçay. ≈ Armenia/Azerbaijan
137 S11 Arpaçay Kars, NE Turkey
Arpaçay *see* Arp'a
Arqalyq *see* Arkalyk
149 N14 Arra ≈ SW Pakistan
Arrabona *see* Győr
Arrah *see* Āra
Ar Rahad *see* Er Rahad
139 R9 Ar Raḩḩālīyah C Iraq
60 Q10 Arraial do Cabo Rio de Janeiro, SE Brazil
104 H11 Arraiolos Évora, S Portugal
139 R8 Ar Ramādī *var.* Ramadi, Rumadiya. SW Iraq
138 J6 Ar Rāmī Ḩimş, C Syria
Ar Rams *see* Rams
138 H9 Ar Ramthā *var.* Ramtha. Irbid, N Jordan
96 H13 Arran, Isle of *island* SW Scotland, UK
138 L3 Ar Raqqah *var.* Rakka; *anc.* Nicephorium. Ar Raqqah, N Syria
138 L3 Ar Raqqah *off.* Muḩāfaz̧at al Raqqah, *var.* Raqqah, *Fr.* Rakka. ⬖ *governorate* N Syria
103 O2 Arras *anc.* Nemetocenna. Pas-de-Calais, N France
105 P3 Arrasate *Cast.* Mondragón. País Vasco, N Spain
138 G12 Ar Rashādīyah Aţ ţafilah W Jordan
138 I5 Ar Rastan *var.* Rastâne. Ḩimş, W Syria
139 X12 Ar Raţāwī E Iraq
102 L15 Arrats ≈ S France
141 N10 Ar Rawḑah Makkah, S Saudi Arabia
141 Q15 Ar Rawḑah S Yemen
142 K11 Ar Rawḑatayn *var.* Raudhatain. N Kuwait
143 N16 Ar Rayyān *var.* Al Rayyan. C Qatar
102 L17 Arreau Hautes-Pyrénées, S France
64 Q11 Arrecife *var.* Arrecife de Lanzarote, Puerto Arrecife. Lanzarote, Islas Canarias, NE Atlantic Ocean
Arrecife de Lanzarote *see* Arrecife
43 P6 Arrecife Edinburgh *reef* NE Nicaragua
61 C19 Arrecifes Buenos Aires, E Argentina
102 F6 Arrée, Monts d' ▲ NW France
Ar Refā'ī *see* Ar Rifā'ī
Arretium *see* Arezzo
Arriaca *see* Guadalajara
109 S9 Arriach Kärnten, S Austria
41 T16 Arriaga Chiapas, SE Mexico
41 N12 Arriaga San Luis Potosí, C Mexico
139 W10 Ar Rifā'ī *var.* Ar Refā'ī. SE Iraq
139 V12 Ar Riḩāb *salt flat* S Iraq
104 L2 Arriondas Asturias, N Spain
141 Q7 Ar Riyāḑ *Eng.* Riyadh. ● (Saudi Arabia) Ar Riyāḑ, C Saudi Arabia
141 O8 Ar Riyāḑ *off.* Minţaqat ar Riyāḑ. ⬖ *province* C Saudi Arabia
141 S15 Ar Riyān S Yemen
Arrö *see* Ærø
61 H18 Arroio Grande Rio Grande do Sul, S Brazil
102 K15 Arros ≈ S France
103 Q9 Arroux ≈ C France
25 R5 Arrowhead, Lake ⊠ Texas, SW USA
182 L5 Arrowsmith, Mount *hill* New South Wales, SE Australia
185 D21 Arrowtown Otago, South Island, New Zealand
61 D17 Arroyo Barú Entre Ríos, E Argentina
104 J10 Arroyo de la Luz Extremadura, W Spain
63 J16 Arroyo de la Ventana Río Negro, SE Argentina
35 P13 Arroyo Grande California, W USA
Ar Ru'ays *see* Ar Ruways
141 R11 Ar Rub 'al Khālī *Eng.* Empty Quarter, Great Sandy Desert. *desert* SW Asia
139 V13 Ar Rudaymah S Iraq
61 A16 Arrufó Santa Fe, C Argentina
138 I7 Ar Ruḩaybah *var.* Ruhaybeh, *Fr.* Rouhaïbé. Dimashq, W Syria
139 V15 Ar Rukhaymīyah *well* S Iraq
139 U11 Ar Rumaythah *var.* Rumaitha. S Iraq
141 X8 Ar Rustāq *var.* Rostak, Rustaq. N Oman
139 N8 Ar Ruţbah *var.* Rutba. SW Iraq
140 M3 Ar Rūthiyah *spring/well* NW Saudi Arabia
ar-Ruwaida *see* Ar Ruwayḑah
141 O8 Ar Ruwayḑah *var.* ar-Ruwaida. Jīzān, C Saudi Arabia
143 N15 Ar Ruways *var.* Al Ruweis, Ar Ru'ays, Ruwais. N Qatar
143 O17 Ar Ruways *var.* Ar Ru'ays. Abū Z̧aby, W United Arab Emirates
Års *see* Aars
Arsanias *see* Murat Nehri
123 S15 Arsen'yev Primorskiy Kray, SE Russian Federation
155 G19 Arsikere Karnātaka, W India
127 R3 Arsk Respublika Tatarstan, W Russian Federation
94 N10 Årskogen Gävleborg, C Sweden
121 O3 Ársos C Cyprus
94 N13 Årsunda Gävleborg, C Sweden
115 C17 Árta *anc.* Ambracia. Ípeiros, W Greece
105 Y9 Artà Mallorca, Spain, W Mediterranean Sea
Arta *see* Árachthos
137 T12 Artashat S Armenia
40 M15 Arteaga Michoacán de Ocampo, SW Mexico
123 S15 Artem Primorskiy Kray, SE Russian Federation
44 C4 Artemisa La Habana, W Cuba
117 W7 Artemivs'k Donets'ka Oblast', E Ukraine
122 K13 Artemovsk Krasnoyarskiy Kray, S Russian Federation
105 U5 Artesa de Segre Cataluña, NE Spain
37 U14 Artesia New Mexico, SW USA
25 Q14 Artesia Wells Texas, SW USA
108 G8 Arth Schwyz, C Switzerland
14 F15 Arthur Ontario, S Canada
30 M14 Arthur Illinois, N USA
28 L14 Arthur Nebraska, C USA
29 Q5 Arthur North Dakota, N USA
185 B21 Arthur ≈ South Island, New Zealand
18 B13 Arthur, Lake ⊠ Pennsylvania, NE USA
183 N15 Arthur River ≈ Tasmania, SE Australia
185 G18 Arthur's Pass Canterbury, South Island, New Zealand
185 G17 Arthur's Pass *pass* South Island, New Zealand
44 I3 Arthur's Town Cat Island, C Bahamas
44 M9 Artibonite, Rivière de l' ≈ C Haiti
61 E16 Artigas *prev.* San Eugenio, San Eugenio del Cuareim. Artigas, N Uruguay
61 E16 Artigas ⬖ *department* N Uruguay
194 H1 Artigas *Uruguayan research station* Antarctica
137 T11 Art'ik W Armenia
187 O16 Art, Île *island* Îles Belep, W New Caledonia
103 O2 Artois *cultural region* N France
136 L12 Artova Tokat, N Turkey
105 Y9 Artrutx, Cap d' *var.* Cabo Dartuch. *cape* Menorca, Spain, W Mediterranean Sea
Artsiz *see* Artsyz
117 N11 Artsyz *Rus.* Artsiz. Odes'ka Oblast', SW Ukraine
158 E7 Artux Xinjiang Uygur Zizhiqu, NW China
137 R11 Artvin Artvin, NE Turkey
137 R11 Artvin ⬖ *province* NE Turkey
146 G14 Artyk Ahal Welaýaty, C Turkmenistan
79 Q16 Aru Orientale, NE Dem. Rep. Congo
81 E17 Arua NW Uganda
104 I4 A Rúa de Valdeorras *var.* La Rúa. Galicia, NW Spain
Aruângua *see* Luangwa
45 O15 Aruba *var.* Oruba. ◇ *Dutch autonomous region* S West Indies
47 Q4 Aruba *island* Aruba, Lesser Antilles
Aru Islands *see* Aru, Kepulauan
171 W15 Aru, Kepulauan *Eng.* Aru Islands; *prev.* Aroe Islands. *island group* E Indonesia
153 W10 Arunāchal Pradesh *prev.* North East Frontier Agency, North East Frontier Agency of Assam. ⬖ *state* NE India
Arun Qi *see* Naji
155 H23 Aruppukkottai Tamil Nādu, SE India
81 I20 Arusha Arusha, N Tanzania
81 I21 Arusha ⬖ *region* E Tanzania
81 I20 Arusha ✕ Arusha, N Tanzania
54 C9 Arusí, Punta *headland* NW Colombia
155 J23 Aruvi Aru ≈ NW Sri Lanka
79 M17 Aruwimi *var.* Ituri (upper course). ≈ NE Dem. Rep. Congo
Árva *see* Orava
37 T4 Arvada Colorado, C USA
Arvand Rūd *see* 'Arab, Shaţţ al
162 J8 Arvayheer Övörhangay, C Mongolia
9 O10 Arviat *prev.* Eskimo Point. Nunavut, C Canada
93 I14 Arvidsjaur Norrbotten, N Sweden
95 J15 Arvika Värmland, C Sweden
92 J8 Årviksand Troms, N Norway
35 S13 Arvin California, W USA
163 S8 Arxan Nei Mongol Zizhiqu, N China
145 P7 Arykbalyk *Kaz.* Aryqbalyq. Severnyy Kazakhstan, N Kazakhstan
Aryqbalyq *see* Arykbalyk
145 P17 Arys' *Kaz.* Arys. Yuzhnyy Kazakhstan, S Kazakhstan
Arys *see* Arys'
Arys *see* Orzysz
Arys Köli *see* Arys, Ozero
145 O14 Arys, Ozero *Kaz.* Arys Köli. ◎ C Kazakhstan
107 D16 Arzachena Sardegna, Italy, C Mediterranean Sea
127 O4 Arzamas Nizhegorodskaya Oblast', W Russian Federation
141 V13 Arzāt S Oman
104 H3 Arzúa Galicia, NW Spain
111 A16 Aš *Ger.* Asch. Karlovarský Kraj, W Czech Republic
95 H15 Ås Akershus, S Norway
Åsa *see* Asaa
95 H20 Asaa *var.* Åsa. Nordjylland, N Denmark
83 E21 Asab Karas, S Namibia
77 U16 Asaba Delta, S Nigeria
149 S4 Asadābād *var.* Asadābād; *prev.* Chaghasarāy. Konar, E Afghanistan
Asadābād *see* Asadābād
138 K3 Asad, Buḩayrat al ◎ N Syria
63 H20 Asador, Pampa del *plain* S Argentina
165 P14 Asahi Chiba, Honshū, S Japan
164 M11 Asahi Toyama, Honshū, SW Japan
165 T13 Asahi-dake ▲ Hokkaidō, N Japan
165 T3 Asahikawa Hokkaidō, N Japan
147 S10 Asaka *Rus.* Assake; *prev.* Leninsk. Andijon Viloyati, E Uzbekistan
77 P17 Asamankese SE Ghana
188 B15 Asan W Guam
188 B15 Asan Point *headland* W Guam
153 R15 Āsānsol West Bengal, NE India
80 K12 Āsayita Afar, NE Ethiopia
171 T12 Asbakin Papua, E Indonesia
Asben *see* Aïr, Massif de l'
15 Q12 Asbestos Québec, SE Canada
29 Y13 Asbury Iowa, C USA
18 K15 Asbury Park New Jersey, NE USA
41 Z12 Ascensión, Bahía de la *bay* NW Caribbean Sea
40 I3 Ascensión Chihuahua, N Mexico
65 M14 Ascension Fracture Zone *tectonic feature* C Atlantic Ocean
65 G14 Ascension Island ◇ *dependency of St.Helena* C Atlantic Ocean
65 N16 Ascension Island *island* C Atlantic Ocean
Asch *see* Aš
109 S3 Aschach an der Donau Oberösterreich, N Austria
101 H18 Aschaffenburg Bayern, SW Germany
101 F14 Ascheberg Nordrhein-Westfalen, W Germany
101 L14 Aschersleben Sachsen-Anhalt, C Germany
106 G12 Asciano Toscana, C Italy
106 J13 Ascoli Piceno *anc.* Asculum Picenum. Marche, C Italy
107 M17 Ascoli Satriano *anc.* Asculub, Ausculum Apulum. Puglia, SE Italy
108 G11 Ascona Ticino, S Switzerland
Asculub *see* Ascoli Satriano
Asculum Picenum *see* Ascoli Piceno
80 L11 Āseb *var.* Assab, *Amh.* Āseb. SE Eritrea
95 M20 Åseda Kronoberg, S Sweden
127 T6 Asekeyevo Orenburgskaya Oblast', W Russian Federation
81 J14 Āsela *var.* Asella, Aselle, Asselle. Oromo, C Ethiopia
93 H15 Åsele Västerbotten, N Sweden
Asella/Aselle *see* Āsela
94 K12 Åsen Dalarna, C Sweden
114 J11 Asenovgrad *prev.* Stanimaka. Plovdiv, C Bulgaria
171 O13 Asera Sulawesi, C Indonesia
95 E17 Åseral Vest-Agder, S Norway
118 J3 Aseri *var.* Asserin, *Ger.* Asserin. Ida-Virumaa, NE Estonia
40 J10 Aserradero Durango, W Mexico
146 F13 Aşgabat *prev.* Ashgabat, Ashkhabad, Poltoratsk. ● (Turkmenistan) Ahal Welaýaty, C Turkmenistan
146 F13 Aşgabat ✕ Ahal Welaýaty, C Turkmenistan
95 H16 Åsgårdstrand Vestfold, S Norway
Ashara *see* Al 'Ashārah
23 T6 Ashburn Georgia, SE USA
185 G19 Ashburton Canterbury, South Island, New Zealand
185 G19 Ashburton ≈ South Island, New Zealand
180 H8 Ashburton River ≈ Western Australia
145 V10 Ashchysu ≈ E Kazakhstan
10 M16 Ashcroft British Columbia, SW Canada
138 E10 Ashdod *anc.* Azotos, *Lat.* Azotus. Central, W Israel
27 S14 Ashdown Arkansas, C USA
21 T9 Asheboro North Carolina, SE USA
9 X15 Ashern Manitoba, S Canada
21 P10 Asheville North Carolina, SE USA
12 E8 Asheweig ≈ Ontario, C Canada
27 V9 Ash Flat Arkansas, C USA
183 T4 Ashford New South Wales, SE Australia
97 P22 Ashford SE England, UK
36 K11 Ash Fork Arizona, SW USA
Ashgabat *see* Aşgabat
27 T7 Ash Grove Missouri, C USA
165 O12 Ashikaga *var.* Asikaga. Tochigi, Honshū, S Japan
165 Q8 Ashiro Iwate, Honshū, C Japan
164 F15 Ashizuri-misaki Shikoku, SW Japan
Ashkelon *see* Ashqelon
Ashkhabad *see* Aşgabat
23 Q4 Ashland Alabama, S USA
26 K7 Ashland Kansas, C USA
21 P5 Ashland Kentucky, S USA
19 S2 Ashland Maine, NE USA
22 M1 Ashland Mississippi, S USA
27 U4 Ashland Missouri, C USA
29 S15 Ashland Nebraska, C USA
31 T12 Ashland Ohio, N USA
32 G15 Ashland Oregon, NW USA
21 W6 Ashland Virginia, NE USA
30 K3 Ashland Wisconsin, N USA
20 I8 Ashland City Tennessee, S USA
183 S4 Ashley New South Wales, SE Australia
29 O7 Ashley North Dakota, N USA
173 W7 Ashmore and Cartier Islands ◇ *Australian external territory* E Indian Ocean
119 I14 Ashmyany *Rus.* Oshmyany. Hrodzyenskaya Voblasts', W Belarus
18 K12 Ashokan Reservoir ⊠ New York, NE USA
165 U4 Ashoro Hokkaidō, NE Japan
138 E10 Ashqelon *var.* Ashkelon. Southern, C Israel
Ashraf *see* Behshahr
139 O3 Ash Shadādah *var.* Ash Shaddādah, Jisr ash Shadadi, Shaddādi, Shedadi, Tell Shedadi. Al Ḩasakah, NE Syria
Ash Shaddādah *see* Ash Shadādah
139 Y12 Ash Shāfī E Iraq
139 R4 Ash Shakk *var.* Shaykh. C Iraq
Ash Shām *see* Dimashq
Ash Sham/Ash Shām *see* Dimashq
139 T10 Ash Shāmīyah *var.* Shamiya. C Iraq
139 Y13 Ash Shāmīyah *var.* Al Bādiyah al Janūbīyah. *desert* S Iraq
139 T11 Ash Shanāfīyah *var.* Ash Shināfīyah. S Iraq
138 G13 Ash Sharāh *var.* Esh Sharā. ▲ W Jordan
143 R16 Ash Shāriqah *Eng.* Sharjah. Ash Shāriqah, NE United Arab Emirates
143 R16 Ash Shāriqah *var.* Sharjah. ✕ Ash Shāriqah, NE United Arab Emirates
140 I4 Ash Sharmah *var.* Šarma. Tabūk, NW Saudi Arabia
139 R4 Ash Sharqāţ NW Iraq
141 S10 Ash Sharqīyah *off.* Al Minţaqah ash Sharqīyah, *Eng.* Eastern Region. ⬖ *province* E Saudi Arabia
Ash Sharqiyah *see* Al 'Ubaylah
139 W11 Ash Shaţrah *var.* Shatra. SE Iraq
138 G13 Ash Shawbak Ma'ān, W Jordan
138 L5 Ash Shaykh Ibrāhīm Ḩimş, C Syria
141 O17 Ash Shaykh 'Uthmān SW Yemen
141 S15 Ash Shiḩr SE Yemen
Ash Shināfīyah *see* Ash Shanāfīyah
141 V12 Ash Shişar *var.* Shisur. SW Oman
139 S13 Ash Shubrūm *well* S Iraq
141 R10 Ash Shuqqān *desert* E Saudi Arabia
75 O9 Ash Shuwayrif *var.* Ash Shwayrif. N Libya
Ash Shwayrif *see* Ash Shuwayrif
31 U10 Ashtabula Ohio, N USA
29 Q5 Ashtabula, Lake ⊠ North Dakota, N USA
137 T12 Ashtarak W Armenia
142 M6 Āshtīān *var.* Āshtiyān. Markazī, W Iran
Āshtiyān *see* Āshtīān
33 R13 Ashton Idaho, NW USA
13 O10 Ashuanipi Lake ◎ Newfoundland and Labrador, E Canada
15 P6 Ashuapmushuan ≈ Québec, SE Canada
23 Q3 Ashville Alabama, S USA
31 S14 Ashville Ohio, N USA
30 K3 Ashwabay, Mount *hill* Wisconsin, N USA

◆ Country
● Country Capital
◇ Dependent Territory
○ Dependent Territory Capital
⬖ Administrative Regions
✕ International Airport
▲ Mountain
▲▲ Mountain Range
Volcano
≈ River
◎ Lake
⊠ Reservoir

◆ Country   ◇ Dependent Territory   ◈ Administrative Regions   ▲ Mountain   ⋒ Volcano   ◎ Lake
● Country Capital   ○ Dependent Territory Capital   ✈ International Airport   ▲ Mountain Range   ◢ River   ☒ Reservoir

AVASFELSŐFALU – BAGO CITY

Avasfelsőfalu *see* Negreşti-Oaş
38 *L17* **Avatanak Island** *island* Aleutian Islands, Alaska, USA
190 *B16* **Avatele** S Niue
190 *H16* **Avatiu** Rarotonga, S Cook Islands
190 *H15* **Avatiu Harbour** *harbour* Rarotonga, S Cook Islands
Avdeyevka *see* Avdiyivka
114 *J13* **Ávdira** Anatolikí Makedonía kai Thráki, NE Greece
117 *X8* **Avdiyivka** *Rus.* Avdeyevka. Donets'ka Oblast', SE Ukraine
Avdzaga *see* Gurvanbulag
Avdzaga *see* Gurvanbulag
104 *G6* **Ave** ≈ N Portugal
104 *G7* **Aveiro** *anc.* Talabriga. Aveiro, W Portugal
104 *G7* **Aveiro** ◈ *district* N Portugal
Avela *see* Ávila
99 *D18* **Avelgem** West-Vlaanderen, W Belgium
61 *D20* **Avellaneda** Buenos Aires, E Argentina
107 *L17* **Avellino** *anc.* Abellinum. Campania, S Italy
35 *Q12* **Avenal** California, W USA
Avenio *see* Avignon
94 *E8* **Averoya** *island* S Norway
107 *K17* **Aversa** Campania, S Italy
33 *N9* **Avery** Idaho, NW USA
25 *W5* **Avery** Texas, SW USA
Aves, Islas de *see* Las Aves, Islas
Avesnes *see* Avesnes-sur-Helpe
103 *Q2* **Avesnes-sur-Helpe** *var.* Avesnes. Nord, N France
64 *G12* **Aves Ridge** *undersea feature* SE Caribbean Sea
95 *M14* **Avesta** Dalarna, C Sweden
103 *O14* **Aveyron** ◈ *department* S France
103 *N14* **Aveyron** ≈ S France
107 *J15* **Avezzano** Abruzzo, C Italy
115 *D16* **Avgó** ▲ C Greece
Avgustov *see* Augustów
Avgustovskiy Kanal *see* Augustowski, Kanał
96 *J9* **Aviemore** N Scotland, UK
185 *F21* **Aviemore, Lake** ◎ South Island, New Zealand
103 *R15* **Avignon** *anc.* Avenio. Vaucluse, SE France
104 *M7* **Ávila** *var.* Avila; *anc.* Abela, Abula, Abyla, Avela. Castilla-León, C Spain
104 *L8* **Ávila** ◈ *province* Castilla-León, C Spain
104 *K2* **Avilés** Asturias, NW Spain
118 *J4* **Avinurme** *Ger.* Awwinorm. Ida-Virumaa, NE Estonia
104 *H10* **Avis** Portalegre, C Portugal
avlum *see* Aulum
182 *M11* **Avoca** Victoria, SE Australia
29 *T14* **Avoca** Iowa, C USA
182 *M11* **Avoca River** ≈ Victoria, SE Australia
107 *L25* **Avola** Sicilia, Italy, C Mediterranean Sea
18 *F10* **Avon** New York, NE USA
29 *P12* **Avon** South Dakota, N USA
97 *M23* **Avon** ≈ S England, UK
97 *L20* **Avon** ≈ C England, UK
36 *K13* **Avondale** Arizona, SW USA
23 *X13* **Avon Park** Florida, SE USA
102 *J5* **Avranches** Manche, N France
103 *O3* **Avre** ≈ N France
Avveel *see* Ivalojoki
186 *M6* **Avuavu** *var.* Kolotambu. Guadalcanal, C Solomon Islands
Avveel *see* Ivalo
Avvil *see* Ivalo
77 *O17* **Awaaso** *var.* Awaso. SW Ghana
141 *X8* **Awābī** *var.* Al 'Awābī. NE Oman
184 *L9* **Awakino** Waikato, North Island, New Zealand
142 *M15* **'Awālī** C Bahrain
99 *K19* **Awans** Liège, E Belgium
184 *I2* **Awanui** Northland, North Island, New Zealand
148 *M14* **Awārān** Baluchistān, SW Pakistan
81 *K16* **Awara Plain** *plain* NE Kenya
80 *M13* **Āwarē** Somali, E Ethiopia
138 *M6* **'Awāriḍ, Wādī** *dry watercourse* E Syria
185 *B20* **Awarua Point** *headland* South Island, New Zealand
81 *J14* **Āwasa** Southern, S Ethiopia
80 *K13* **Āwash** Afar, NE Ethiopia
80 *K12* **Āwash** *var.* Hawash. ≈ C Ethiopia
Awaso *see* Awaaso
158 *H7* **Awat** Xinjiang Uygur Zizhiqu, NW China
185 *J15* **Awatere** ≈ South Island, New Zealand
75 *O10* **Awbārī** SW Libya
75 *N9* **Awbāri, Idhān** *var.* Edeyen d'Oubari. *desert* Algeria/Libya
80 *M12* **Awdal** *off* Gobolka Awdal. ◈ N Somalia
80 *C13* **Aweil** Northern Bahr el Ghazal, SW Sudan
96 *H11* **Awe, Loch** ◎ W Scotland, UK
77 *U16* **Awka** Anambra, SW Nigeria
39 *O6* **Awuna River** ≈ Alaska, USA
Awwinorm *see* Avinurme
Ax *see* Dax
Axarfjördhur *see* Öxarfjördhur
103 *N17* **Axat** Aude, S France
99 *F16* **Axel** Zeeland, SW Netherlands
197 *P9* **Axel Heiberg Island** *var.* Axel Heiburg. *island* Nunavut, N Canada
Axel Heiburg *see* Axel Heiberg Island
77 *O17* **Axim** S Ghana
114 *F13* **Axiós** *var.* Vardar. ≈ Greece/FYR Macedonia *see also* Vardar
Axiós *see* Vardar
103 *N17* **Ax-les-Thermes** Ariège, S France
120 *D11* **Ayachi, Jbel** ▲ C Morocco
61 *D22* **Ayacucho** Buenos Aires, E Argentina
57 *F15* **Ayacucho** Ayacucho, S Peru
57 *E16* **Ayacucho** *off.* Departamento de Ayacucho. ◈ *department* SW Peru
Ayacucho, Departamento de *see* Ayacucho
145 *W11* **Ayagoz** *var.* Ayaguz, *Kaz.* Ayaköz; *prev.* Sergiopol. Vostochnyy Kazakhstan, E Kazakhstan
113 *V12* **Ayagoz** *var.* Ayaguz, *Kaz.* Ayakoz. ≈ E Kazakhstan
Ayaguz *see* Ayagoz
Ayakagytma *see* Oyoqog'itma
Ayakkuduk *see* Oyoqquduq
158 *L10* **Ayakkum Hu** ◎ NW China
Ayakoz *see* Ayagoz
Ayaköz *see* Ayagoz
104 *H14* **Ayamonte** Andalucía, S Spain
123 *S11* **Ayan** Khabarovskiy Kray, E Russian Federation
136 *J10* **Ayancık** Sinop, N Turkey
55 *S9* **Ayanganna Mountain** ▲ C Guyana
77 *U16* **Ayangba** Kogi, C Nigeria
123 *U7* **Ayanka** Koryakskiy Avtonomnyy Okrug, E Russian Federation
54 *E7* **Ayapel** Córdoba, NW Colombia
136 *H12* **Ayaş** Ankara, N Turkey
57 *I16* **Ayaviri** Puno, S Peru
149 *P3* **Āybak** *var.* Aibak, Haibak; *prev.* Samangān. Samangān, NE Afghanistan
147 *N10* **Aydarko'l Ko'li** *Rus.* Ozero Aydarkul'. ◎ C Uzbekistan
Aydarkul', Ozero *see* Aydarko'l Ko'li
21 *W10* **Ayden** North Carolina, SE USA
136 *C15* **Aydın** *var.* Aïdin; *anc.* Tralles Aydin. Aydın, SW Turkey
136 *C15* **Aydın** *var.* Aïdin. ◈ *province* SW Turkey
136 *I17* **Aydıncık** Mersin, S Turkey
136 *C15* **Aydın Dağları** ▲▲ W Turkey
158 *L6* **Aydingkol Hu** ◎ NW China
127 *X7* **Aydyrlinskiy** Orenburgskaya Oblast', W Russian Federation
105 *S4* **Ayerbe** Aragón, NE Spain
Ayers Rock *see* Uluru
Ayeyarwady *see* Irrawaddy
Ayiá *see* Agiá
Ayia Napa *see* Agía Nápa
Ayia Phyla *see* Agía Fýlaxis
Ayiásos/Ayiássos *see* Agiassós
Áyios Evstrátios *see* Ágios Efstrátios
Áyios Kírikos *see* Ágios Kírykos
Áyios Nikólaos *see* Ágios Nikólaos
80 *I11* **Āykel** Amhara, N Ethiopia
123 *N9* **Aykhal** Respublika Sakha (Yakutiya), NE Russian Federation
14 *J12* **Aylen Lake** ◎ Ontario, SE Canada
97 *N21* **Aylesbury** SE England, UK
105 *O6* **Ayllón** Castilla-León, N Spain
14 *F17* **Aylmer** Ontario, S Canada
14 *L12* **Aylmer** Québec, SE Canada
15 *R12* **Aylmer, Lac** ◎ Québec, SE Canada
8 *L9* **Aylmer Lake** ◎ Northwest Territories, NW Canada
145 *V14* **Aynabulak** *cont.* Ajnabulak. Almaty, SE Kazakhstan
138 *K2* **'Ayn al 'Arab** Ḥalab, N Syria
Aynayn *see* 'Aynīn
139 *V12* **'Ayn Ḥamūd** S Iraq
147 *P12* **Ayní** *prev.* Varzimanor Ayni. W Tajikistan
140 *M10* **'Aynīn** *var.* Aynayn. *spring/well* SW Saudi Arabia
21 *U12* **Aynor** South Carolina, SE USA
139 *Q7* **'Ayn Zāzūh** C Iraq
153 *N12* **Ayodhya** Uttar Pradesh, N India
123 *S6* **Ayon, Ostrov** *island* NE Russian Federation
105 *R11* **Ayora** País Valenciano, E Spain
77 *Q11* **Ayorou** Tillabéri, W Niger
79 *E16* **Ayos** Centre, S Cameroon
76 *L5* **'Ayoûn 'Abd el Mâlek** *well* N Mauritania
76 *K10* **'Ayoûn el 'Atroûs** *var.* Aïoun el Atrous, Aïoun el Atroûss. Hodh el Gharbi, SE Mauritania
96 *I13* **Ayr** W Scotland, UK
96 *I13* **Ayr** ≈ W Scotland, UK
96 *I13* **Ayrshire** *cultural region* SW Scotland, UK
Aysen *see* Aisén
80 *L12* **Āysha** Somali, E Ethiopia
144 *L14* **Ayteke Bi** *Kaz.* Zhangaqazaly; *prev.* Novokazalinsk. Kzylorda, SW Kazakhstan
146 *K8* **Aytim** Nawoiy Viloyati, N Uzbekistan
181 *W4* **Ayton** Queensland, NE Australia
114 *M9* **Aytos** Burgas, E Bulgaria
171 *T11* **Ayu, Kepulauan** *island group* E Indonesia
A Yun Pa *see* Cheo Reo
169 *V11* **Ayu, Tanjung** *cape* Borneo, N Indonesia
41 *P16* **Ayutlá** *var.* Ayutla de los Libres. Guerrero, S Mexico
40 *K13* **Ayutla** Jalisco, C Mexico
Ayutla de los Libres *see* Ayutlá
167 *O11* **Ayutthaya** *var.* Phra Nakhon Si Ayutthaya. Phra Nakhon Si Ayutthaya, C Thailand
136 *B13* **Ayvalık** Balıkesir, W Turkey
99 *L20* **Aywaille** Liège, E Belgium
141 *R13* **'Aywat aş Şay'ar, Wādī** *seasonal river* N Yemen
Azaffal *see* Azeffâl
105 *T9* **Azahar, Costa del** *coastal region* E Spain
105 *S6* **Azaila** Aragón, NE Spain
104 *F10* **Azambuja** Lisboa, C Portugal
153 *N13* **Āzamgarh** Uttar Pradesh, N India
77 *O9* **Azaouâd** *desert* C Mali
77 *S10* **Azaouagh, Vallée de l'** *var.* Azaouak. ≈ W Niger
Azaouak *see* Azaouagh, Vallée de l'
61 *F14* **Azara** Misiones, NE Argentina
Azaran *see* Hashtrūd
Azärbaycan/Azärbaycan Respublikasi *see* Azerbaijan
Āzarbāyjān-e Bākhtarı *see* Āzarbāyjān-e Gharbī
142 *I4* **Āzarbāyjān-e Gharbī** *off.* Ostān-e Āzarbāyjān-e Gharbī, *Eng.* West Azerbaijan; *prev.* Āzarbāyjān-e Bākhtarı. NW Iran
Āzarbāyjān-e Gharbī, Ostān-e *see* Āzarbāyjān-e Gharbī
Azarbayjan-e Khavari *see* Āzarbāyjān-e Sharqī
Āzarbāyjān-e Khāvarī *see* Āzarbāyjān-e Sharqī
142 *J3* **Āzarbāyjān-e Sharqī** *off* Ostān-e Azarbāyjān-e Sharqī, *Eng* East Azerbaijan; *prev.* Azarbayjan-e Khavari. ◈ *province*
142 *J3* **Āzarbāyjān-e Sharqī** *off.* Ostān-e Āzarbāyjān-e Sharqī, *Eng.* East Azerbaijan; *prev.* Āzarbāyjān-e Khāvarī. ◈ *province* NW Iran
Āzarbāyjān-e Sharqī, Ostān-e *see* Āzarbāyjān-e Sharqī
77 *W13* **Azare** Bauchi, N Nigeria
119 *M19* **Azarychy** *Rus.* Ozarichi. Homyel'skaya Voblasts', SE Belarus
102 *L8* **Azay-le-Rideau** Indre-et-Loire, C France
138 *I2* **A'zāz** Ḥalab, NW Syria
76 *H7* **Azeffâl** *var.* Azaffal. *desert* Mauritania/Western Sahara
137 *V12* **Azerbaijan** *off.* Azerbaijani Republic, *Az.* Azärbaycan, Azärbaycan Respublikasi; *prev.* Azerbaijan SSR. ◆ *republic* SE Asia
Azerbaijani Republic *see* Azerbaijan
Azerbaijan SSR *see* Azerbaijan
145 *T7* **Azhbulat, Ozero** ◎ NE Kazakhstan
74 *F7* **Azilal** C Morocco
Azimabad *see* Patna
19 *O6* **Aziscohos Lake** ⊠ Maine, NE USA
Azizbekov *see* Vayk'
Azizie *see* Telish
Aziziya *see* Al 'Azīzīyah
127 *T4* **Aznakayevo** Respublika Tatarstan, W Russian Federation
56 *C8* **Azogues** Cañar, S Ecuador
64 *N2* **Azores** *var.* Açores, Ilhas dos Açores, *Port.* Arquipélago dos Açores. *island group* Portugal, NE Atlantic Ocean
64 *L8* **Azores-Biscay Rise** *undersea feature* E Atlantic Ocean
Azotos/Azotus *see* Ashdod
78 *K11* **Azoum, Bahr** *seasonal river* SE Chad
126 *L12* **Azov** Rostovskaya Oblast', SW Russian Federation
126 *J13* **Azov, Sea of** *Rus.* Azovskoye More, *Ukr.* Azovs'ke More. *sea* NE Black Sea
Azovs'ke More/Azovskoye More *see* Azov, Sea of
138 *I10* **Azraq, Wāḥat al** *oasis* N Jordan
Āzro *see* Āzrow
74 *G6* **Azrou** C Morocco
149 *R5* **Āzrow** *var.* Āzro. Lowgar, E Afghanistan
37 *P8* **Aztec** New Mexico, SW USA
36 *M13* **Aztec Peak** ▲ Arizona, SW USA
45 *N9* **Azua** *var.* Azua de Compostela. S Dominican Republic
Azua de Compostela *see* Azua
104 *K12* **Azuaga** Extremadura, W Spain
56 *B8* **Azuay** ◈ *province* W Ecuador
164 *C13* **Azuchi-Ō-shima** *island* SW Japan
105 *O11* **Azuer** ≈ C Spain
43 *S17* **Azuero, Península de** *peninsula* S Panama
62 *I6* **Azufre, Volcán** *var.* Volcán Lastarria. ▲ N Chile
116 *J12* **Azuga** Prahova, SE Romania
61 *C22* **Azul** Buenos Aires, E Argentina
62 *I8* **Azul, Cerro** ▲ NW Argentina
56 *E12* **Azul, Cordillera** ▲▲ C Peru
165 *P11* **Azuma-san** ▲ Honshū, C Japan
103 *V15* **Azur, Côte d'** *coastal region* SE France
191 *Z3* **Azur Lagoon** ◎ Kiritimati, E Kiribati
'Azza *see* Gaza
Az Zāb al Kabīr *see* Great Zab
138 *H7* **Az Zabdānī** *var.* Zabadani. Dimashq, W Syria
141 *W8* **Az Ẓāhirah** *desert* NW Oman
141 *S6* **Aẓ Ẓahrān** *Eng.* Dhahran. Ash Sharqīyah, NE Saudi Arabia
141 *R6* **Aẓ Ẓahrān al Khubar** *var.* Dhahran Al Khobar. ✈ Ash Sharqīyah, NE Saudi Arabia
Az Zaqāzīq *see* Zagazig
138 *H10* **Az Zarqā'** *var.* Zarqa. Az Zarqā', NW Jordan
138 *I11* **Az Zarqā'** *off.* Muḥāfaẓat az Zarqā', *var.* Zarqa. ◈ *governorate* N Jordan
75 *O7* **Az Zāwiyah** *var.* Zawia. NW Libya
141 *N15* **Az Zaydīyah** W Yemen
74 *I11* **Azzel Matti, Sebkha** *var.* Sebkra Azz el Matti. *salt flat* C Algeria
141 *P6* **Az Zilfī** Ar Riyāḍ, N Saudi Arabia
139 *Y13* **Az Zubayr** *var.* Al Zubair. SE Iraq
Az Zuqur *see* Jabal Zuuqar, Jazīrat

B

187 *X15* **Ba** *prev.* Mba. Viti Levu, W Fiji
Ba *see* Da Rāng, Sông
171 *P17* **Baa** Pulau Rote, C Indonesia
138 *H7* **Baalbek** *var.* Ba'labakk; *anc.* Heliopolis. E Lebanon
108 *G8* **Baar** Zug, N Switzerland
81 *L17* **Baardheere** *var.* Bardere, *It.* Bardera. Gedo, SW Somalia
80 *Q12* **Baargaal** Bari, NE Somalia
99 *I15* **Baarle-Hertog** Antwerpen, N Belgium
99 *I15* **Baarle-Nassau** Noord-Brabant, S Netherlands
98 *J11* **Baarn** Utrecht, C Netherlands
162 *H9* **Baatsagaan** *var.* Bayansayr. Bayanhongor, C Mongolia
114 *D13* **Baba** *var.* Buševa, *Gk.* Varnoús. ▲▲ FYR Macedonia/Greece
76 *H10* **Bababé** Brakna, W Mauritania
136 *G10* **Baba Burnu** *headland* NW Turkey
117 *N13* **Babadag** Tulcea, SE Romania
137 *X10* **Babadağ Dağı** ▲ NE Azerbaijan
146 *H14* **Babadayhan** *Rus.* Babadaykhan; *prev.* Kirovsk. Ahal Welaýaty, C Turkmenistan
Babadaykhan *see* Babadayhan
146 *G14* **Babadurmaz** Ahal Welaýaty, C Turkmenistan
114 *M12* **Babaeski** Kırklareli, NW Turkey
139 *T4* **Bāba Gurguṛ** N Iraq
56 *B7* **Babahoyo** *prev.* Bodegas. Los Ríos, C Ecuador
149 *P5* **Bābā, Kūh-e** ▲▲ C Afghanistan
171 *N12* **Babana** Sulawesi, C Indonesia
Babao *see* Qilian
171 *Q12* **Babar, Kepulauan** *island group* E Indonesia
171 *T12* **Babar, Pulau** *island* Kepulauan Babar, E Indonesia
152 *G4* **Bābāsar Pass** *pass* India/Pakistan
Babashy, Gory *see* Babaşy
146 *C9* **Babaşy** *Rus.* Gory Babashy. ▲▲ W Turkmenistan
168 *M13* **Babat** Sumatera, W Indonesia
81 *H21* **Babati** Manyara, NE Tanzania
124 *J13* **Babayevo** Vologodskaya Oblast', NW Russian Federation
127 *Q15* **Babayurt** Respublika Dagestan, SW Russian Federation
33 *P6* **Babb** Montana, NW USA
29 *X4* **Babbitt** Minnesota, N USA
188 *E9* **Babeldaob** *var.* Babelthuap. *island* N Palau
Babeldaop *see* Babeldaob
141 *N17* **Bab el Mandeb** *strait* Gulf of Aden/Red Sea
Babelthuap *see* Babeldaob
111 *K17* **Babia Góra** *var.* Babia Hora. ▲ Poland/Slovakia
Babia Hora *see* Babia Góra
Babian Jiang *see* Black River
Babichi *see* Babichy
119 *N19* **Babichy** *Rus.* Babichi. Homyel'skaya Voblasts', SE Belarus
112 *I10* **Babina Greda** Vukovar-Srijem, E Croatia
10 *K13* **Babine Lake** ◎ British Columbia, SW Canada
143 *O4* **Bābol** *var.* Babul, Balfrush, Barfrush; *prev.* Barfurush. Māzandarān, N Iran
143 *O4* **Bābolsar** *var.* Babulsar; *prev.* Meshed-i-Sar. Māzandarān, N Iran
36 *L16* **Baboquivari Peak** ▲ Arizona, SW USA
79 *G15* **Baboua** Nana-Mambéré, W Central African Republic
119 *M17* **Babruysk** *Rus.* Bobruysk. Mahilyowskaya Voblasts', E Belarus
Babu *see* Hezhou
Babul *see* Bābol
Babulsar *see* Bābolsar
113 *O19* **Babuna** ≈ C FYR Macedonia
113 *O19* **Babuna** ▲ C FYR Macedonia
148 *K7* **Bābūs, Dasht-e** *Pash.* Bebas, Dasht-i. ▲▲ W Afghanistan
171 *O1* **Babuyan Channel** *channel* N Philippines
171 *O1* **Babuyan Island** *island* N Philippines
139 *T9* **Babylon** *site of ancient city* C Iraq
112 *J9* **Bač** *Ger.* Batsch. Vojvodina, NW Serbia
58 *M13* **Bacabal** Maranhão, E Brazil
41 *Y14* **Bacalar** Quintana Roo, SE Mexico
41 *Y14* **Bacalar Chico, Boca** *strait* SE Mexico
171 *Q12* **Bacan, Kepulauan** *island group* E Indonesia
171 *S12* **Bacan, Pulau** *prev.* Batjan. *island* Maluku, E Indonesia
116 *L10* **Bacău** *Hung.* Bákó. Bacău, NE Romania
116 *K11* **Bacău** ◈ *county* E Romania
Bắc Bộ, Vinh *see* Tongking, Gulf of
167 *T5* **Bắc Can** *var* Bach Thong. Bắc Thai, N Vietnam
103 *T5* **Baccarat** Meurthe-et-Moselle, NE France
183 *N12* **Bacchus Marsh** Victoria, SE Australia
40 *H4* **Bacerac** Sonora, NW Mexico
116 *L10* **Băceşti** Vaslui, E Romania
167 *T6* **Bắc Giang** Hà Bắc, N Vietnam
54 *I5* **Bachaquero** Zulia, NW Venezuela
Bacher *see* Pohorje
118 *M13* **Bacheykava** *Rus.* Bocheykovo. Vitsyebskaya Voblasts', N Belarus
40 *I5* **Bachíniva** Chihuahua, N Mexico
Bach Thong *see* Bắc Can
158 *G8* **Bachu** Xinjiang Uygur Zizhiqu, NW China
9 *N8* **Back** ≈ Nunavut, N Canada
112 *K10* **Bačka Palanka** *prev.* Palanka. Serbia, NW Serbia
112 *K8* **Bačka Topola** *Hung.* Topolya; *prev. Hung.* Bácstopolya. Vojvodina, N Serbia
95 *J17* **Bäckefors** Västra Götaland, S Sweden
Bäckermühle Schulzenmühle *see* Żywiec
95 *L16* **Bäckhammar** Värmland, C Sweden
112 *K9* **Bački Petrovac** *Hung.* Petrőcz; *prev.* Petrovac, Petrowácz. Vojvodina, NW Serbia
101 *I21* **Backnang** Baden-Württemberg, SW Germany
167 *S15* **Bac Liêu** *var.* Vinh Loi. Minh Hai, S Vietnam
167 *T6* **Bắc Ninh** Ha Bắc, N Vietnam
40 *G4* **Bacoachi** Sonora, NW Mexico
171 *P6* **Bacolod** *off.* Bacolod City. Negros, C Philippines
Bacolod City *see* Bacolod
171 *O4* **Baco, Mount** ▲ Mindoro, N Philippines
111 *K25* **Bácsalmás** Bács-Kiskun, S Hungary
Bácsjózseffalva *see* Žednik
111 *J24* **Bács-Kiskun** *off.* Bács-Kiskun Megye. ◈ *county* S Hungary
Bács-Kiskun Megye *see* Bács-Kiskun
Bácsszenttamás *see* Srbobran
Bácstopolya *see* Bačka Topola
Bactra *see* Balkh
Bada *see* Xilin
155 *F21* **Badagara** Kerala, SW India
101 *M24* **Bad Aibling** Bayern, SE Germany
162 *I13* **Badain Jaran Shamo** *desert* N China
104 *I11* **Badajoz** *anc.* Pax Augusta. Extremadura, W Spain
104 *J11* **Badajoz** ◈ *province* Extremadura, W Spain
149 *S2* **Badakhshān** ◈ *province* NE Afghanistan
105 *W6* **Badalona** *anc.* Baetulo. Cataluña, E Spain
154 *O11* **Bādāmpāhārh** Orissa, E India
152 *K8* **Badarīnāth** ▲ N India
169 *O10* **Badas, Kepulauan** *island group* W Indonesia
109 *S6* **Bad Aussee** Salzburg, E Austria
31 *S8* **Bad Axe** Michigan, N USA
101 *G16* **Bad Berleburg** Nordrhein-Westfalen, W Germany
101 *L17* **Bad Blankenburg** Thüringen, C Germany
Bad Borseck *see* Borsec
101 *G18* **Bad Camberg** Hessen, W Germany
100 *L8* **Bad Doberan** Mecklenburg-Vorpommern, N Germany
101 *N14* **Bad Düben** Sachsen, E Germany
109 *X4* **Baden** *var.* Baden bei Wien; *anc.* Aquae Panoniae, Thermae Pannonicae. Niederösterreich, NE Austria
108 *F9* **Baden** Aargau, N Switzerland
101 *G21* **Baden-Baden** *anc.* Aurelia Aquensis. Baden-Württemberg, SW Germany
Baden bei Wien *see* Baden
101 *G22* **Baden-Württemberg** *Fr.* Bade-Wurtemberg. ◈ *state* SW Germany
112 *A10* **Baderna** Istra, NW Croatia
Bade-Wurtemberg *see* Baden-Württemberg
101 *H20* **Bad Fredrichshall** Baden-Württemberg, S Germany
100 *P11* **Bad Freienwalde** Brandenburg, NE Germany
109 *Q8* **Badgastein** *var.* Gastein. Salzburg, NW Austria
Badger State *see* Wisconsin
148 *L4* **Bādghīs** ◈ *province* NW Afghanistan
109 *T5* **Bad Hall** Oberösterreich, N Austria
101 *J14* **Bad Harzburg** Niedersachsen, C Germany
101 *I16* **Bad Hersfeld** Hessen, C Germany
98 *I10* **Badhoevedorp** Noord-Holland, C Netherlands
109 *Q8* **Bad Hofgastein** Salzburg, NW Austria
Bad Homburg *see* Bad Homburg vor der Höhe
101 *G18* **Bad Homburg vor der Höhe** *var.* Bad Homburg. Hessen, W Germany
101 *E17* **Bad Honnef** Nordrhein-Westfalen, W Germany
149 *Q17* **Badīn** Sind, SE Pakistan
21 *S10* **Badin Lake** ⊠ North Carolina, SE USA
40 *I8* **Badiraguato** Sinaloa, C Mexico
109 *R6* **Bad Ischl** Oberösterreich, N Austria
Badjawa *see* Bajawa
Badje-Sohppar *see* Övre Soppero
101 *J18* **Bad Kissingen** Bayern, SE Germany
Bad Königswart *see* Lázně Kynžvart
101 *F19* **Bad Kreuznach** Rheinland-Pfalz, SW Germany
101 *F24* **Bad Krozingen** Baden-Württemberg, SW Germany
101 *G16* **Bad Laasphe** Nordrhein-Westfalen, W Germany
28 *J6* **Badlands** *physical region* North Dakota, N USA
101 *K16* **Bad Langensalza** Thüringen, C Germany
109 *T3* **Bad Leonfelden** Oberösterreich, N Austria
101 *I20* **Bad Mergentheim** Baden-Württemberg, SW Germany
101 *H17* **Bad Nauheim** Hessen, W Germany
101 *E17* **Bad Neuenahr-Arhweiler** Rheinland-Pfalz, W Germany
Bad Neustadt *see* Bad Neustadt an der Saale
101 *J18* **Bad Neustadt an der Saale** *var.* Bad Neustadt. Berlin, C Germany
Badnur *see* Betūl
100 *H13* **Bad Oeynhausen** Nordrhein-Westfalen, NW Germany
100 *J9* **Bad Oldesloe** Schleswig-Holstein, N Germany
77 *Q16* **Badou** C Togo
Bad Polzin *see* Połczyn-Zdrój
100 *H13* **Bad Pyrmont** Niedersachsen, C Germany
109 *X9* **Bad Radkersburg** Steiermark, SE Austria
139 *V8* **Badrah** E Iraq
Badrah *see* Tarialan
101 *N24* **Bad Reichenhall** Bayern, SE Germany
140 *K8* **Badr Ḥunayn** Al Madīnah, W Saudi Arabia
28 *M10* **Bad River** ≈ South Dakota, N USA
30 *K4* **Bad River** ≈ Wisconsin, N USA
100 *H13* **Bad Salzuflen** Nordrhein-Westfalen, NW Germany
101 *J16* **Bad Salzungen** Thüringen, C Germany
109 *V8* **Bad Sankt Leonhard im Lavanttal** Kärnten, S Austria
100 *K9* **Bad Schwartau** Schleswig-Holstein, N Germany
101 *L24* **Bad Tölz** Bayern, SE Germany
181 *U1* **Badu Island** *island* Queensland, NE Australia
155 *K25* **Badulla** Uva Province, C Sri Lanka
109 *X5* **Bad Vöslau** Niederösterreich, NE Austria
101 *I24* **Bad Waldsee** Baden-Württemberg, S Germany
35 *U11* **Badwater Basin** *depression* California, W USA
101 *J20* **Bad Windsheim** Bayern, C Germany
101 *J23* **Bad Wörishofen** Bayern, S Germany
100 *G10* **Bad Zwischenahn** Niedersachsen, NW Germany
104 *M13* **Baena** Andalucía, S Spain
Baeterrae/Baeterrae Septimanorum *see* Béziers
Baetic Cordillera/Baetic Mountains *see* Béticos, Sistemas
Baetulo *see* Badalona
57 *K18* **Baeza** Napo, NE Ecuador
105 *N13* **Baeza** Andalucía, S Spain
79 *D15* **Bafang** Ouest, W Cameroon
76 *H12* **Bafatá** C Guinea-Bissau
149 *U5* **Baffa** North-West Frontier Province, NW Pakistan
197 *O11* **Baffin Basin** *undersea feature* N Labrador Sea
197 *N12* **Baffin Bay** *bay* Canada/Greenland
25 *T15* **Baffin Bay** *inlet* Texas, SW USA
196 *M12* **Baffin Island** *island* Nunavut, NE Canada
79 *E15* **Bafia** Centre, C Cameroon
77 *R14* **Bafilo** NE Togo
76 *J12* **Bafing** ≈ W Africa
76 *J12* **Bafoulabé** Kayes, W Mali
79 *D15* **Bafoussam** Ouest, W Cameroon
143 *R9* **Bāfq** Yazd, C Iran
136 *L10* **Bafra** Samsun, N Turkey
136 *L10* **Bafra Burnu** *headland* N Turkey
143 *S12* **Bāft** Kermān, S Iran
79 *N18* **Bafwabalinga** Orientale, NE Dem. Rep. Congo
79 *N18* **Bafwaboli** Orientale, NE Dem. Rep. Congo
79 *N17* **Bafwasende** Orientale, NE Dem. Rep. Congo
42 *K13* **Bagaces** Guanacaste, NW Costa Rica
153 *O12* **Bagaha** Bihār, N India
155 *F16* **Bāgalkot** Karnātaka, W India
81 *J22* **Bagamoyo** Pwani, E Tanzania
Bagan Datok *see* Bagan Datuk
168 *J8* **Bagan Datuk** *var.* Bagan Datok. Perak, Peninsular Malaysia
171 *R7* **Baganga** Mindanao, S Philippines
168 *J9* **Bagansiapiapi** *var.* Pasirpangarayan. Sumatera, W Indonesia
162 *M8* **Baganuur** *var* Nüürst. Töv, C Mongolia
Bagaria *see* Bagheria
77 *T11* **Bagaroua** Tahoua, W Niger
79 *I20* **Bagata** Bandundu, W Dem. Rep. Congo
Bagdad *see* Baghdād
123 *O13* **Bagdarin** Respublika Buryatiya, S Russian Federation
61 *G17* **Bagé** Rio Grande do Sul, S Brazil
Bagenalstown *see* Muine Bheag
Bagerhat *see* Bagherhat
103 *P16* **Bages et de Sigean, Étang de** ◎ S France
33 *W17* **Baggs** Wyoming, C USA
154 *F11* **Bāgh** Madhya Pradesh, C India
139 *T8* **Baghdād** *var.* Bagdad, *Eng.* Baghdad. ● (Iraq) C Iraq
139 *T8* **Baghdād** ✈ C Iraq
Baghdad *see* Baghdād
153 *T16* **Bagherhat** *var.* Bagerhat. Khulna, S Bangladesh
107 *J23* **Bagheria** *var.* Bagaria. Sicilia, Italy, C Mediterranean Sea
143 *S10* **Bāghīn** Kermān, C Iran
149 *Q3* **Baghlān** Baghlān, NE Afghanistan
149 *Q3* **Baghlān** *var.* Baghlān. ◈ *province* NE Afghanistan
Baghlān *see* Baghlān
148 *M7* **Bāghrān** Helmand, S Afghanistan
29 *T4* **Bagley** Minnesota, N USA
106 *H10* **Bagnacavallo** Emilia-Romagna, C Italy
102 *K16* **Bagnères-de-Bigorre** Hautes-Pyrénées, S France
102 *L17* **Bagnères-de-Luchon** Hautes-Pyrénées, S France
106 *F11* **Bagni di Lucca** Toscana, C Italy
106 *H11* **Bagno di Romagna** Emilia-Romagna, C Italy
103 *R14* **Bagnols-sur-Cèze** Gard, S France
162 *M14* **Bag Nur** ◎ N China
171 *P6* **Bago** *off.* Bago City. Negros, C Philippines
Bago *see* Pegu
Bago City *see* Bago

◆ Country ● Country Capital ◇ Dependent Territory ○ Dependent Territory Capital ◈ Administrative Regions ✈ International Airport ▲ Mountain ▲▲ Mountain Range Volcano ≈ River ◎ Lake ⊠ Reservoir

76 *M13* **Bagoé** ⟿ Ivory Coast/Mali
Bagrāme *see* Bagrāmī
149 *R5* **Bagrāmī** *var.* Bagrāme.
Kābol, E Afghanistan
119 *B14* **Bagrationovsk**
Ger. Preussisch Eylau.
Kaliningradskaya Oblast',
W Russian Federation
Bagrax *see* Bohu
Bagrax Hu *see* Bosten Hu
56 *C10* **Bagua** Amazonas, NE Peru
171 *O2* **Baguio** *off.* Baguio City.
Luzon, N Philippines
Baguio City *see* Baguio
77 *V9* **Bagzane, Monts** ▲ N Niger
Bāhah, Minṭaqat al *see* Al
Bāhah
Bahama Islands *see* Bahamas
44 *H3* **Bahamas** *off.* Commonwealth
of the Bahamas. ◆ *island state*
N West Indies
0 *L13* **Bahamas** *var.* Bahama
Islands. *island group* N West
Indies
**Bahamas, Commonwealth
of the** *see* Bahamas
153 *S15* **Baharampur** *prev.*
Berhampore. West Bengal,
NE India
146 *E12* **Baharly** *var.* Bäherden,
Rus. Bakharden;
prev. Bakharden.
Ahal Welaýaty,
C Turkmenistan
149 *U10* **Bahāwalnagar** Punjab,
E Pakistan
149 *T11* **Bahāwalpur** Punjab,
E Pakistan
136 *L16* **Bahçe** Osmaniye, S Turkey
160 *J8* **Ba He** ⟿ C China
Bäherden *see* Baharly
59 *N16* **Bahia** *off.* Estado da Bahia.
◆ *state* E Brazil
61 *B24* **Bahía Blanca** Buenos Aires,
E Argentina
40 *L15* **Bahía Bufadero** Michoacán
de Ocampo, SW Mexico
63 *J19* **Bahía Bustamante** Chubut,
SE Argentina
40 *D5* **Bahía de los Ángeles** Baja
California, NW Mexico
40 *C6* **Bahía de Tortugas** Baja
California Sur, W Mexico
Bahia, Estado de *see* Bahia
42 *J4* **Bahía, Islas de la** *Eng.* Bay
Islands. *island group* N Honduras
40 *E5* **Bahía Kino** Sonora,
NW Mexico
40 *E9* **Bahía Magdalena** *var.* Puerto
Magdalena. Baja California
Sur, W Mexico
54 *C8* **Bahía Solano** *var.* Ciudad
Mutis, Solano. Chocó,
W Colombia
80 *I11* **Bahir Dar** *var.* Bahr Dar,
Bahrdar Giyorgis. Amhara,
N Ethiopia
141 *X8* **Bahlā'** *var.* Bahlah, Bahlat.
NW Oman
Bāhla *see* Bālān
Bahlah/Bahlat *see* Bahlā'
152 *M11* **Bahraich** Uttar Pradesh,
N India
143 *M14* **Bahrain** *off.* State of Bahrain,
Dawlat al Bahrayn, *Ar.* Al
Baḥrayn, *prev.* Bahrein;
anc. Tylos, Tyros.
◆ *monarchy* SW Asia
142 *M14* **Bahrain** ✈ C Bahrain
142 *M15* **Bahrain, Gulf of** *gulf* Persian
Gulf, NW Arabian Sea
Bahrain, State of *see* Bahrain
138 *I7* **Baḥrat Mallāḥah** ◎ W Syria
Bahrayn, Dawlat al *see*
Bahrain
Bahr Dar/Bahrdar Giyorgis
see Bahir Dar
Bahrein *see* Bahrain
81 *E16* **Bahr el Gabel** ◆ *state* S Sudan
80 *E13* **Bahr ez Zaref** ⟿ C Sudan
67 *R8* **Bahr Kameur** ⟿ N Central
African Republic
Bahr Tabariya, Sea of *see*
Tiberias, Lake
143 *W15* **Bāhū Kalāt** Sīstān va
Balūchestān, SE Iran
118 *N13* **Bahushewsk** *Rus.* Bogushëvsk.
Vitsyebskaya Voblasts',
NE Belarus
Bai *see* Tagow Bāy
116 *G13* **Baia de Aramă** Mehedinţi,
SW Romania
116 *G11* **Baia de Criş** Ger. Altenburg,
Hung. Körösbánya.
Hunedoara, SW Romania
83 *A16* **Baia dos Tigres** Namibe,
SW Angola
82 *A13* **Baía Farta** Benguela,
W Angola
116 *H9* **Baia Mare** *Ger.* Frauenbach,
Hung. Nagybánya;
prev. Neustadt.
Maramureş,
NW Romania
116 *H8* **Baia Sprie** *Ger.* Mittelstadt,
Hung. Felsőbánya.
Maramureş, NW Romania
78 *G13* **Baïbokoum** Logone-Oriental,
SW Chad
160 *F12* **Baicao Ling** ▲ SW China
163 *U9* **Baicheng** *var.* Pai-ch'eng;
prev. T'aon-an. Jilin, NE China
158 *I6* **Baicheng** *var.* Bay. Xinjiang
Uygur Zizhiqu, NW China
116 *J13* **Băicoi** Prahova, SE Romania
Baidoa *see* Baydhabo
15 *U6* **Baie-Comeau** Québec,
SE Canada
15 *T7* **Baie-des-Bacon** Québec,
SE Canada
15 *S8* **Baie-des-Rochers** Québec,
SE Canada
15 *U6* **Baie-des-Sables** Québec,
SE Canada
12 *K11* **Baie-du-Poste** Québec,
SE Canada
172 *H17* **Baie Lazare** Mahé,
NE Seychelles
45 *Y5* **Baie-Mahault** Basse Terre,
C Guadeloupe
15 *R9* **Baie-St-Paul** Québec,
SE Canada
15 *V5* **Baie-Trinité** Québec,
SE Canada
13 *T11* **Baie Verte** Newfoundland and
Labrador, SE Canada
Baiguan *see* Shangyu
Baihe *see* Erdaobaihe
139 *U11* **Bā'ij al Mahdī** S Iraq

Baiji *see* Bayjī
Baikal, Lake *see* Baykal, Ozero
Bailādila *see* Kirandul
Baile an Chaistil *see*
Ballycastle
Baile an Róba *see* Ballinrobe
Baile an tSratha *see* Ballintra
Baile Átha an Rí *see* Athenry
Baile Átha Buí *see* Athboy
35 *W13* **Baker** California, W USA
22 *J8* **Baker** Louisiana, S USA
33 *Y9* **Baker** Montana, NW USA
32 *L12* **Baker** Oregon, NW USA
192 *L7* **Baker and Howland Islands**
◇ *US unincorporated territory*
W Polynesia
36 *L12* **Baker Butte** ▲ Arizona,
SW USA
39 *X15* **Baker Island** *island* Alexander
Archipelago, Alaska, USA
9 *N9* **Baker Lake** Nunavut,
N Canada
9 *N9* **Baker Lake** ◎ Nunavut,
N Canada
32 *H6* **Baker, Mount** ▲ Washington,
NW USA
35 *R13* **Bakersfield** California,
W USA
24 *M9* **Bakersfield** Texas, SW USA
21 *P9* **Bakersville** North Carolina,
SE USA
Bakhābi *see* Bū Khābī
Bakharden *see* Baharly
Bakhardok *see* Bokurdak
143 *U5* **Bākharz, Kuhhā-ye** ▲
NE Iran
152 *D13* **Bākhāsar** Rājasthān,
NW India
Bakhchisaray *see*
Bakhchysaray
117 *T13* **Bakhchysaray**
Rus. Bakhchisaray.
Respublika Krym, S Ukraine
117 *R3* **Bakhmach** Chernihivs'ka
Oblast', N Ukraine
Bākhtarān *see* Kermānshāh
143 *Q11* **Bakhtegān, Daryācheh-ye**
◎ C Iran
145 *X12* **Bakhty** Vostochnyy
Kazakhstan, E Kazakhstan
137 *Z11* **Baku** *Eng.* Baku.
● (Azerbaijan) E Azerbaijan
80 *M12* **Baki** Awdal, N Somalia
137 *Z11* **Baki** ✈ E Azerbaijan
136 *C13* **Bakır Çayı** ⟿ W Turkey
92 *L1* **Bakkafjördhur** Austurland,
NE Iceland
92 *L1* **Bakkaflói** *sea area*
N Norwegian Sea
81 *I15* **Bako** Southern, S Ethiopia
76 *L15* **Bako** NW Ivory Coast
Bákó *see* Bacău
81 *H23* **Bakony** *Eng.* Bakony
Mountains, *Ger.* Bakonywald.
▲▲ W Hungary
**Bakony Mountains/
Bakonywald** *see* Bakony
81 *M16* **Bakool** *off.* Gobolka Bakool.
◆ *region* W Somalia
Bakool, Gobolka *see* Bakool
76 *L15* **Bakoumba** Mbomou,
SE Central African Republic
127 *N15* **Baksan** Kabardino-
Balkarskaya Respublika,
SW Russian Federation
119 *I16* **Bakshty** Hrodzyenskaya
Voblasts', W Belarus
Baku *see* Baki
194 *K12* **Bakutis Coast** *physical region*
Antarctica
145 *O15* **Bakwanga** *see* Mbuji-Mayi
145 *O15* **Bakyrly** Yuzhnyy Kazakhstan,
S Kazakhstan
14 *H13* **Bala** Ontario, S Canada
136 *I13* **Bala** Ankara, C Turkey
97 *J19* **Bala** NW Wales, UK
170 *L7* **Balabac Island** *island*
W Philippines
Balabac, Selat *see* Balabac
Strait
169 *V5* **Balabac Strait**
var. Selat Balabac.
strait Malaysia/Philippines
Ba'labakk *see* Baalbek
187 *P16* **Balabio, Île** *island* Province
Nord, W New Caledonia
114 *I14* **Balaci** Teleorman, S Romania
139 *S7* **Balad** N Iraq
123 *R12* **Balakhta** Khabarovskiy Kray,
SE Russian Federation
139 *V7* **Balad Rūz** E Iraq
154 *J11* **Bālāghāt** Madhya Pradesh,
C India
155 *F14* **Bālāghāt Range** ▲▲ W India
103 *X14* **Balagne** *physical region* Corse,
France, C Mediterranean Sea
105 *U5* **Balaguer** Cataluña, NE Spain
105 *S3* **Balaïtous** *var.* Pic de
Balaïtous. ▲ France/Spain
Balaïtous, Pic de *see* Balaïtous
Balák *see* Balkanabat
127 *O3* **Balakhna** Nizhegorodskaya
Oblast', W Russian Federation
123 *Q4* **Balakhta** Krasnoyarskiy Kray,
S Russian Federation
182 *I9* **Balaklava** South Australia
117 *V6* **Balakliya** *Rus.* Balakleya.
Kharkivs'ka Oblast', E Ukraine
127 *Q7* **Balakovo** Saratovskaya
Oblast', W Russian Federation
83 *Q7* **Balama** Cabo Delgado,
N Mozambique
169 *U9* **Balambangan, Pulau** *island*
East Malaysia
148 *L3* **Bālā Morghāb** Laghmān,
NW Afghanistan
152 *E11* **Bālān** *prev.* Bāhla. Rājasthān,
NW India
116 *J10* **Bălan** *Hung.* Balánbánya.
Harghita, C Romania
Balánbánya *see* Bălan
171 *O3* **Balanga** Luzon, N Philippines
154 *M12* **Bālāngīr** *prev.* Bolangir.
Orissa, E India
127 *N8* **Balashov** Saratovskaya
Oblast', W Russian Federation
Balasore *see* Bāleshwar
111 *K21* **Balassagyarmat** Nógrád,
N Hungary
29 *S10* **Balaton** Minnesota, N USA
111 *H24* **Balaton** *var.* Lake Balaton,
Ger. Plattensee. ◎ W Hungary
111 *I23* **Balatonfüred** *var.* Füred.
Veszprém, W Hungary
Balaton, Lake *see* Balaton
116 *I11* **Bălăuşeri** *Ger.* Bladenmarkt,
Hung. Balavásár. Mureş,
C Romania

145 *V12* **Bakanas** *Kaz.* Baqanas.
⟿ E Kazakhstan
149 *R4* **Bakharz, Kuhhā-ye**
NE Afghanistan
145 *U14* **Bakbakty** *Kaz.* Baqbaqty.
Almaty, SE Kazakhstan
122 *J12* **Bakchar** Tomskaya Oblast',
C Russian Federation
76 *I11* **Bakel** E Senegal
35 *W13* **Baker** California, W USA
22 *J8* **Baker** Louisiana, S USA
33 *Y9* **Baker** Montana, NW USA
32 *L12* **Baker** Oregon, NW USA
192 *L7* **Baker and Howland Islands**
◇ *US unincorporated territory*
W Polynesia
36 *L12* **Baker Butte** ▲ Arizona,
SW USA
39 *X15* **Baker Island** *island* Alexander
Archipelago, Alaska, USA
9 *N9* **Baker Lake** Nunavut,
N Canada
9 *N9* **Baker Lake** ◎ Nunavut,
N Canada
32 *H6* **Baker, Mount** ▲ Washington,
NW USA
35 *R13* **Bakersfield** California,
W USA
24 *M9* **Bakersfield** Texas, SW USA
21 *P9* **Bakersville** North Carolina,
SE USA
Bakhābi *see* Bū Khābī
Bakharden *see* Baharly
Bakhardok *see* Bokurdak
143 *U5* **Bākharz, Kuhhā-ye** ▲
NE Iran
152 *D13* **Bākhāsar** Rājasthān,
NW India
Bakhchisaray *see*
Bakhchysaray
117 *T13* **Bakhchysaray**
Rus. Bakhchisaray.
Respublika Krym, S Ukraine
117 *R3* **Bakhmach** Chernihivs'ka
Oblast', N Ukraine
Bākhtarān *see* Kermānshāh
143 *Q11* **Bakhtegān, Daryācheh-ye**
◎ C Iran
145 *X12* **Bakhty** Vostochnyy
Kazakhstan, E Kazakhstan
137 *Z11* **Baku** *Eng.* Baku.
● (Azerbaijan) E Azerbaijan
80 *M12* **Baki** Awdal, N Somalia
137 *Z11* **Baki** ✈ E Azerbaijan
136 *C13* **Bakır Çayı** ⟿ W Turkey
92 *L1* **Bakkafjördhur** Austurland,
NE Iceland
92 *L1* **Bakkaflói** *sea area*
N Norwegian Sea
81 *I15* **Bako** Southern, S Ethiopia
76 *L15* **Bako** NW Ivory Coast
Bákó *see* Bacău
81 *H23* **Bakony** *Eng.* Bakony
Mountains, *Ger.* Bakonywald.
▲▲ W Hungary
**Bakony Mountains/
Bakonywald** *see* Bakony
81 *M16* **Bakool** *off.* Gobolka Bakool.
◆ *region* W Somalia
Bakool, Gobolka *see* Bakool
76 *L15* **Bakoumba** Mbomou,
SE Central African Republic
127 *N15* **Baksan** Kabardino-
Balkarskaya Respublika,
SW Russian Federation
119 *I16* **Bakshty** Hrodzyenskaya
Voblasts', W Belarus
Baku *see* Baki
194 *K12* **Bakutis Coast** *physical region*
Antarctica
145 *O15* **Bakwanga** *see* Mbuji-Mayi
145 *O15* **Bakyrly** Yuzhnyy Kazakhstan,
S Kazakhstan
14 *H13* **Bala** Ontario, S Canada
136 *I13* **Bala** Ankara, C Turkey
97 *J19* **Bala** NW Wales, UK
170 *L7* **Balabac Island** *island*
W Philippines
Balabac, Selat *see* Balabac
Strait
169 *V5* **Balabac Strait**
var. Selat Balabac.
strait Malaysia/Philippines
Ba'labakk *see* Baalbek
187 *P16* **Balabio, Île** *island* Province
Nord, W New Caledonia
114 *I14* **Balaci** Teleorman, S Romania
139 *S7* **Balad** N Iraq
123 *R12* **Balakhta** Khabarovskiy Kray,
SE Russian Federation
139 *V7* **Balad Rūz** E Iraq
154 *J11* **Bālāghāt** Madhya Pradesh,
C India
155 *F14* **Bālāghāt Range** ▲▲ W India
103 *X14* **Balagne** *physical region* Corse,
France, C Mediterranean Sea
105 *U5* **Balaguer** Cataluña, NE Spain
105 *S3* **Balaïtous** *var.* Pic de
Balaïtous. ▲ France/Spain
Balaïtous, Pic de *see* Balaïtous
Balák *see* Balkanabat
127 *O3* **Balakhna** Nizhegorodskaya
Oblast', W Russian Federation
123 *Q4* **Balakhta** Krasnoyarskiy Kray,
S Russian Federation
182 *I9* **Balaklava** South Australia
117 *V6* **Balakliya** *Rus.* Balakleya.
Kharkivs'ka Oblast', E Ukraine
127 *Q7* **Balakovo** Saratovskaya
Oblast', W Russian Federation
83 *Q7* **Balama** Cabo Delgado,
N Mozambique
169 *U9* **Balambangan, Pulau** *island*
East Malaysia
148 *L3* **Bālā Morghāb** Laghmān,
NW Afghanistan
152 *E11* **Bālān** *prev.* Bāhla. Rājasthān,
NW India
116 *J10* **Bălan** *Hung.* Balánbánya.
Harghita, C Romania
Balánbánya *see* Bălan
171 *O3* **Balanga** Luzon, N Philippines
154 *M12* **Bālāngīr** *prev.* Bolangir.
Orissa, E India
127 *N8* **Balashov** Saratovskaya
Oblast', W Russian Federation
Balasore *see* Bāleshwar
111 *K21* **Balassagyarmat** Nógrád,
N Hungary
29 *S10* **Balaton** Minnesota, N USA
111 *H24* **Balaton** *var.* Lake Balaton,
Ger. Plattensee. ◎ W Hungary
111 *I23* **Balatonfüred** *var.* Füred.
Veszprém, W Hungary
Balaton, Lake *see* Balaton
116 *I11* **Bălăuşeri** *Ger.* Bladenmarkt,
Hung. Balavásár. Mureş,
C Romania

Balavásár *see* Bălăuşeri
105 *Q11* **Balazote** Castilla-La Mancha,
C Spain
Balázsfalva *see* Blaj
119 *F14* **Balbieriškis** Kaunas,
S Lithuania
186 *J7* **Balbi, Mount** ▲ Bougainville
Island, NE Papua New Guinea
58 *F11* **Balbina, Represa**
◎ NW Brazil
43 *T15* **Balboa** Panamá, C Panama
97 *G17* **Balbriggan** *Ir.* Baile Brigín.
E Ireland
81 *N17* **Balcad** Shabeellaha Dhexe,
C Somalia
61 *D23* **Balcarce** Buenos Aires,
E Argentina
9 *U16* **Balcarres** Saskatchewan,
S Canada
114 *O8* **Balchik** Dobrich, NE Bulgaria
185 *E24* **Balclutha** Otago, South Island,
New Zealand
25 *Q12* **Balcones Escarpment**
escarpment Texas, SW USA
18 *F14* **Bald Eagle Creek**
⟿ Pennsylvania, NE USA
Baldenburg *see* Biały Bór
21 *V12* **Bald Head Island** *island*
North Carolina, SE USA
27 *W10* **Bald Knob** Arkansas, C USA
30 *K17* **Bald Knob** *hill* Illinois, N USA
118 *G9* **Baldone** *Ger.* Baldohn. Rīga,
W Latvia
Baldohn *see* Baldone
22 *I9* **Baldwin** Louisiana, S USA
31 *P7* **Baldwin** Michigan, N USA
27 *Q4* **Baldwin City** Kansas, C USA
39 *N8* **Baldwin Peninsula** *headland*
Alaska, USA
18 *H9* **Baldwinsville** New York,
NE USA
23 *N2* **Baldwyn** Mississippi, S USA
9 *W15* **Baldy Mountain** ▲ Manitoba,
S Canada
33 *T7* **Baldy Mountain** ▲ Montana,
NW USA
37 *O13* **Baldy Peak** ▲ Arizona,
SW USA
Bâle *see* Basel
Balearic Plain *see* Algerian
Basin
Baleares *see* Illes Baleares
105 *X11* **Baleares, Islas** *Eng.* Balearic
Islands. *island group* Spain,
W Mediterranean Sea
Baleares Major *see* Mallorca
Balearic Islands *see* Baleares,
Islas
Balearis Minor *see* Menorca
169 *S9* **Baleh, Batang** ⟿ East
Malaysia
12 *J8* **Baleine, Grande Rivière de
la** ⟿ Québec, E Canada
12 *K7* **Baleine, Petite Rivière de la**
⟿ Québec, E Canada
12 *K7* **Baleine, Petite Rivière de la**
⟿ Québec, E Canada
13 *N6* **Baleine, Rivière à la**
⟿ Québec, E Canada
99 *J16* **Balen** Antwerpen, N Belgium
171 *O3* **Baler** Luzon, N Philippines
154 *P11* **Bāleshwar** *prev.* Balasore.
Orissa, E India
77 *S12* **Baléyara** Tillabéri, W Niger
127 *T1* **Balezino** Udmurtskaya
Respublika, NW Russian
Federation
42 *J4* **Balfate** Colón, N Honduras
9 *O17* **Balfour** British Columbia,
SW Canada
29 *N3* **Balfour** North Dakota, N USA
Balfrush *see* Bābol
122 *L14* **Balgazyn** Respublika Tyva,
S Russian Federation
9 *U16* **Balgonie** Saskatchewan,
S Canada
Bâlgrad *see* Alba Iulia
81 *J19* **Balguda** *spring/well* S Kenya
158 *K6* **Balguntay** Xinjiang Uygur
Zizhiqu, NW China
141 *R16* **Balḥāf** S Yemen
152 *F13* **Bāli** Rājasthān, N India
169 *U17* **Bali** ◆ *province* S Indonesia
169 *T17* **Bali** *island* C Indonesia
111 *K16* **Balice** ✈ (Kraków)
Małopolskie, S Poland
171 *Y14* **Baliem, Sungai** ⟿ Papua,
E Indonesia
136 *C12* **Balıkesir** Balıkesir, W Turkey
136 *C12* **Balıkesir** ◆ *province*
NW Turkey
138 *L3* **Balīkh, Nahr** ⟿ N Syria
169 *V12* **Balikpapan** Borneo,
C Indonesia
Bali Laut *see* Bali Sea
171 *N9* **Balimbing** Tawitawi,
SW Philippines
186 *B8* **Balimo** Western, SW Papua
New Guinea
101 *H23* **Balingen** Baden-
Württemberg, SW Germany
116 *F11* **Balinţ** *Hung.* Bálinc. Timiş,
W Romania
171 *O1* **Balintang Channel** *channel*
N Philippines
138 *K3* **Bālis** Ḥalab, N Syria
169 *T16* **Bali Sea** *Ind* Bali Laut. *sea*
C Indonesia
98 *K7* **Balk** Friesland,
N Netherlands
116 *M9* **Bălţi** *Rus.* Bel'tsy. N Moldova
118 *B10* **Baltic Port** *see* Paldiski
Baltic Sea *Ger.* Ostee,
Rus. Baltiskoye More. *sea*
N Europe
21 *X3* **Baltimore** Maryland, NE USA
31 *T13* **Baltimore** Ohio, N USA
21 *X3* **Baltimore-Washington**
✈ Maryland, NE USA
Baltischport/Baltiski *see*
Paldiski
Baltiskoye More *see* Baltic
Sea
119 *A14* **Baltiysk** *Ger.* Pillau.
Kaliningradskaya Oblast',
W Russian Federation
118 *E12* **Baltoji Voke** Vilnius,
SE Lithuania
143 *T15* **Bāluchestān va Sīstān** *see*
Balūchestān va Sīstān
148 *M12* **Baluchistān** *var.* Balochistān,
Beluchistan. ◆ *province*
SW Pakistan
145 *T13* **Balkhash, Ozero**
Eng. Lake Balkhash,
Kaz. Balqash. ◎ SE Kazakhstan
Balud Masbate, N Philippines
169 *T9* **Balui, Batang** ⟿ East
Malaysia
153 *S13* **Bālurghat** West Bengal,
NE India
180 *M12* **Balladonia** Western Australia

97 *C16* **Ballaghaderreen** *Ir.* Bealach
an Doirín. C Ireland
92 *H10* **Ballangen** *Lapp.* Bálák.
Nordland, NW Norway
96 *H11* **Ballantrae** W Scotland, UK
183 *N13* **Ballarat** Victoria, SE Australia
180 *K11* **Ballard, Lake** *salt lake*
Western Australia
Ballari *see* Bellary
76 *L11* **Ballé** Koulikoro, W Mali
40 *D7* **Ballenas, Bahía de** *bay*
W Mexico
40 *D5* **Ballenas, Canal de** *channel*
NW Mexico
40 *J7* **Balleza** *var.* San Pablo Balleza.
Chihuahua, N Mexico
195 *R17* **Balleny Islands** *island group*
Antarctica
97 *C16* **Ballina** *Ir.* Béal an Átha.
W Ireland
153 *O13* **Ballia** Uttar Pradesh, N India
183 *V4* **Ballina** New South Wales,
SE Australia
97 *D16* **Ballinamore** *Ir.* Béal an Átha
Móir. NW Ireland
97 *D18* **Ballinasloe** *Ir.* Béal Átha na
Sluaighe. W Ireland
25 *P8* **Ballinger** Texas, SW USA
97 *C17* **Ballinrobe** *Ir.* Baile an Róba.
W Ireland
97 *A21* **Ballinskelligs Bay** *Ir.* Bá na
Scealg. *inlet* SW Ireland
97 *D15* **Ballintra** *Ir.* Baile an tSratha.
NW Ireland
103 *T7* **Ballon d'Alsace** ▲ NE France
Ballon de Guebwiller *see*
Grand Ballon
113 *K21* **Ballsh** *var.* Ballshi. Fier,
SW Albania
Ballshi *see* Ballsh
98 *K4* **Ballum** Friesland,
N Netherlands
97 *F16* **Ballybay** *Ir.* Béal Átha Beithe.
N Ireland
97 *E14* **Ballybofey** *Ir.* Bealach Féich.
N Ireland
97 *G14* **Ballycastle** *Ir.* Baile an
Chaistil. N Northern Ireland,
UK
97 *G15* **Ballyclare** *Ir.* Bealach Cláir.
E Northern Ireland, UK
97 *E16* **Ballyconnell** *Ir.* Béal Átha
Conaill. N Ireland
97 *C17* **Ballyhaunis** *Ir.* Béal Átha
hAmhnais. W Ireland
97 *G14* **Ballymena** *Ir.* An Baile
Meánach. NE Northern
Ireland, UK
97 *F14* **Ballymoney** *Ir.* Baile
Monaidh. NE Northern
Ireland, UK
97 *G15* **Ballynahinch** *Ir.* Baile na
hInse. SE Northern Ireland,
UK
97 *D16* **Ballysadare** *Ir.* Baile Easa
Dara. NW Ireland
97 *D16* **Ballyshannon** *Ir.* Béal Átha
Seanaidh. NW Ireland
63 *H19* **Balmaceda** Aisén, S Chile
63 *G23* **Balmaceda, Cerro** ▲ S Chile
111 *N22* **Balmazújváros** Hajdú-Bihar,
E Hungary
108 *E10* **Balmhorn** ▲ SW Switzerland
182 *L12* **Balmoral** Victoria,
SE Australia
24 *K9* **Balmorhea** Texas, SW USA
Balneario Claromecó *see*
Claromecó
82 *B13* **Balombo** *Port.* Norton de
Matos, Vila Norton de Matos.
Benguela, W Angola
82 *B13* **Balombo** ⟿ W Angola
181 *X10* **Balonne River**
⟿ Queensland, E Australia
152 *E13* **Bālotra** Rājasthān, N India
145 *V14* **Balpyk Bi** *prev.* Kirovskiy,
Kaz. Kirov. Almaty,
SE Kazakhstan
Balqā'/Balqā', Muḥāfaẓat al
see Al Balqā'
Balqash *see* Balkhash
Balqash *see* Balkhash, Ozero
152 *M12* **Balrāmpur** Uttar Pradesh,
N India
182 *M9* **Balranald** New South Wales,
SE Australia
116 *H14* **Balş** Olt, S Romania
14 *H11* **Balsam Creek** Ontario,
S Canada
30 *I5* **Balsam Lake** Wisconsin,
N USA
14 *I14* **Balsam Lake** ◎ Ontario,
SE Canada
59 *N14* **Balsas** Maranhão, E Brazil
40 *M15* **Balsas, Río** *var.* Río Mexcala.
⟿ S Mexico
43 *W16* **Balsas, Río** SE Panama
119 *O18* **Bal'shavik** *Rus.* Bol'shevik.
Homyel'skaya Voblasts',
SE Belarus
95 *O15* **Bålsta** Uppsala, C Sweden
108 *E7* **Balsthal** Solothurn,
NW Switzerland
117 *O8* **Balta** Odes'ka Oblast',
SW Ukraine
105 *N5* **Baltanás** Castilla-León,
N Spain
61 *E16* **Baltasar Brum** Artigas,
N Uruguay

118 *J8* **Balvi** Balvi, NE Latvia
147 *W7* **Balykchy** *Kir.* Ysyk-Köl;
prev. Issyk-Kul', Rybach'ye.
Issyk-Kul'skaya Oblast',
C Kyrgyzstan
56 *B7* **Balzar** Guayas, W Ecuador
108 *J8* **Balzers** S Liechtenstein
143 *T12* **Bam** Kermān, SE Iran
77 *Y13* **Bama** Borno, NE Nigeria
76 *L12* **Bamako** ● (Mali) Capital
District, SW Mali
77 *P10* **Bamba** Gao, C Mali
42 *M8* **Bambana, Río**
⟿ NE Nicaragua
79 *J15* **Bambari** Ouaka, C Central
African Republic
181 *W5* **Bambaroo** Queensland,
NE Australia
101 *K19* **Bamberg** Bayern, SE Germany
21 *R14* **Bamberg** South Carolina,
SE USA
79 *M16* **Bambesa** Orientale,
N Dem. Rep. Congo
76 *G11* **Bambey** W Senegal
79 *H16* **Bambio** Sangha-Mbaéré,
SW Central African Republic
83 *I24* **Bamboesberge** ▲ S South
Africa
79 *D14* **Bamenda** Nord-Ouest,
W Cameroon
10 *K17* **Bamfield** Vancouver Island,
British Columbia, SW Canada
Bami *see* Bamy
149 *P4* **Bāmiān** *var.* Bāmīān.
Bāmiān, NE Afghanistan
149 *O4* **Bāmiān** ◆ *province*
C Afghanistan
79 *J14* **Bamingui** Bamingui-
Bangoran, C Central African
Republic
79 *J13* **Bamingui** ⟿ N Central
African Republic
78 *J13* **Bamingui-Bangoran**
◆ *prefecture* N Central African
Republic
143 *V13* **Bampūr** Sīstān va Balūchestān,
SE Iran
186 *C8* **Bamu** ⟿ SW Papua New
Guinea
146 *E12* **Bamy** *Rus.* Bami. Ahal
Welaýaty, C Turkmenistan
81 *N17* **Banaadir** *off.* Gobolka
Banaadir. ◆ *region* S Somalia
Banaadir, Gobolka *see*
Banaadir
191 *N3* **Banaba** *var.* Ocean Island.
island Tungaru, W Kiribati
59 *O14* **Banabuíu, Açude**
⊟ E Brazil
57 *O19* **Bañados del Izozog** *salt lake*
SE Bolivia
97 *D18* **Banagher** *Ir.* Beannchar.
C Ireland
79 *M17* **Banalia** Orientale, N Dem.
Rep. Congo
76 *L12* **Banamba** Koulikoro, W Mali
40 *G4* **Banámichi** Sonora,
NW Mexico
181 *Y9* **Banana** Queensland,
E Australia
191 *Z2* **Banana** *prev.* Main Camp.
Kiritimati, E Kiribati
59 *K16* **Banana, Ilha do** *island*
C Brazil
23 *Y12* **Banana River** *lagoon* Florida,
SE USA
151 *Q22* **Banaras** *see* Vārānasi
Banaras *see* Vārānasi
114 *N13* **Banarlı** Tekirdağ, NW Turkey
152 *H12* **Banas** ⟿ N India
25 *Z11* **Banās, Rās** *cape* E Egypt
112 *N10* **Banatski Karlovac**
Vojvodina, NE Serbia
141 *P16* **Banā, Wādī** *dry watercourse*
SW Yemen
136 *E14* **Banaz** Uşak, W Turkey
136 *E14* **Banaz Çayı** ⟿ W Turkey
159 *P14* **Banbar** *var.* Coka. Xizang
Zizhiqu, W China
97 *G15* **Banbridge** *Ir.* Droichead na
Banna. SE Northern Ireland,
UK
Ban Bua Yai *see* Bua Yai
97 *M21* **Banbury** S England, UK
167 *O7* **Ban Chiang Dao** Chiang Mai,
NW Thailand
96 *K9* **Banchory** NE Scotland, UK
14 *J13* **Bancroft** Ontario, SE Canada
33 *R15* **Bancroft** Idaho, NW USA
29 *U11* **Bancroft** Iowa, C USA
154 *J9* **Bānda** Madhya Pradesh,
C India
152 *L13* **Bānda** Uttar Pradesh, N India
168 *F7* **Bandaaceh** *var.* Banda Atjeh;
prev. Koetaradja, Kutaradja,
Kutaraja. Sumatera,
W Indonesia
Banda Atjeh *see* Bandaaceh
171 *S14* **Banda, Kepulauan** *island
group* E Indonesia
Banda, Laut *see* Banda Sea
77 *N17* **Bandama** *var.* Bandama
Fleuve. ⟿ S Ivory Coast
77 *N15* **Bandama Blanc** ⟿ C Ivory
Coast
Bandama Fleuve *see*
Bandama
Bandar 'Abbās *see* Bandar-e
'Abbās
153 *W16* **Bandarban** Chittagong,
SE Bangladesh
81 *Q13* **Bandarbeyla** *var.* Bender
Beila, Bender Beyla. Bari,
NE Somalia
143 *R14* **Bandar-e 'Abbās** *var.* Bandar
'Abbās; *prev.* Gombroon.
Hormozgān, S Iran
142 *M3* **Bandar-e Anzalī** Gīlān,
NW Iran
143 *N12* **Bandar-e Būshehr**
var. Bushehr, *Eng.* Bushire.
Būshehr, S Iran
142 *M11* **Bandar-e Gonāveh**
var. Ganāveh; *prev.* Gonāveh.
Būshehr, SW Iran
143 *T15* **Bandar-e Jāsk** Hormozgān,
SE Iran
143 *S15* **Bandar-e Kangān** *var.* Kangān.
Būshehr, S Iran
143 *R14* **Bandar-e Khamīr**
Hormozgān, S Iran
143 *Q14* **Bandar-e Lengeh** *var.*
Bandar-e Lengeh, Lingeh.
Hormozgān, S Iran
Bandar-e Lengeh *see* Bandar-
e Langeh

◆ Country ◇ Dependent Territory ◆ Administrative Regions ▲ Mountain ⩘ Volcano ◎ Lake
● Country Capital ○ Dependent Territory Capital ✈ International Airport ▲▲ Mountain Range ⟿ River ⊟ Reservoir

BANDAR-E MĀHSHAHR – BARSINGHAUSEN

142 L10 **Bandar-e Māhshahr** *var.* Māh-Shahr; *prev.* Bandar-e Ma'shūr. Khūzestān, SW Iran
Bandar-e Ma'shūr *see* Bandar-e Māhshahr
143 O14 **Bandar-e Nakhīlū** Hormozgān, S Iran
Bandar-e Shāh *see* Bandar-e Torkaman
143 P4 **Bandar-e Torkaman** *var.* Bandar-e Torkeman, Bandar-e Torkman; *prev.* Bandar-e Shāh. Golestān, N Iran
Bandar-e Torkeman/ Bandar-e Torkman *see* Bandar-e Torkaman
Bandar Kassim *see* Boosaaso
168 M15 **Bandar Lampung** *var.* Bandarlampung, Tanjungkarang-Telukbetung; *prev.* Tandjoengkarang, Tanjungkarang, Teloekbetoeng, Telukbetung. Sumatera, W Indonesia
Bandarlampung *see* Bandar Lampung
Bandar Maharani *see* Muar
Bandar Masulipatnam *see* Machilīpatnam
Bandar Penggaram *see* Batu Pahat
169 T7 **Bandar Seri Begawan** *prev.* Brunei Town. ● (Brunei) N Brunei
169 T7 **Bandar Seri Begawan** ✕ N Brunei
171 R15 **Banda Sea** *var.* Laut Banda. *sea* E Indonesia
104 H5 **Bande** Galicia, NW Spain
59 G15 **Bandeirantes** Mato Grosso, W Brazil
59 N20 **Bandeira, Pico da** ▲ SE Brazil
83 K19 **Bandelierkop** Limpopo, NE South Africa
62 L8 **Bandera** Santiago del Estero, N Argentina
25 Q11 **Bandera** Texas, SW USA
40 J13 **Banderas, Bahía de** *bay* W Mexico
77 O11 **Bandiagara** Mopti, C Mali
152 I12 **Bāndīkūi** Rājasthān, N India
136 C11 **Bandırma** *var.* Penderma. Balıkesir, NW Turkey
Bandjarmasin *see* Banjarmasin
Bandoeng *see* Bandung
97 C21 **Bandon** *Ir.* Droicheadna Bandan. SW Ireland
32 E14 **Bandon** Oregon, NW USA
167 R8 **Ban Dong Bang** Nong Khai, E Thailand
167 Q6 **Ban Donkon** Oudômxai, N Laos
172 J14 **Bandrélé** SE Mayotte
79 H20 **Bandundu** *prev.* Banningville. Bandundu, W Dem. Rep. Congo
79 I21 **Bandundu** *off.* Région de Bandundu. ◈ *region* W Dem. Rep. Congo
Bandundu, Région de *see* Bandundu
169 O16 **Bandung** *prev.* Bandoeng. Jawa, C Indonesia
116 L15 **Băneasa** Constanța, SW Romania
142 J4 **Bāneh** Kordestān, N Iran
44 I7 **Banes** Holguín, E Cuba
9 P16 **Banff** Alberta, SW Canada
96 K8 **Banff** NE Scotland, UK
96 K8 **Banff** *cultural region* NE Scotland, UK
Bánffyhunyad *see* Huedin
77 N14 **Banfora** SW Burkina
155 H19 **Bangalore** *state capital* Karnātaka, S India
153 S16 **Bangaon** West Bengal, NE India
79 L15 **Bangassou** Mbomou, SE Central African Republic
186 D7 **Bangeta, Mount** ▲ C Papua New Guinea
171 P12 **Banggai, Kepulauan** *island group* C Indonesia
171 Q12 **Banggai, Pulau** *island* Kepulauan Banggai, N Indonesia
171 X13 **Banggelapa** Papua, E Indonesia
Banggi *see* Banggi, Pulau
169 V6 **Banggi, Pulau** *var.* Banggi. *island* East Malaysia
121 P13 **Banghāzī** *Eng.* Bengazi, Benghazi, *It.* Bengasi. NE Libya
Bang Hieng *see* Xé Banghiang
169 O13 **Bangka-Belitung** *off.* Propinsi Bangka-Belitung. ◈ *province* W Indonesia
Propinsi Bangka-Belitung *see* Bangka-Belitung
169 P11 **Bangkai, Tanjung** *var.* Bankai. *cape* Borneo, N Indonesia
169 S16 **Bangkalan** Pulau Madura, C Indonesia
169 N12 **Bangka, Pulau** *island* W Indonesia
169 N13 **Bangka, Selat** *strait* Sumatera, W Indonesia
169 N13 **Bangka, Selat** *var.* Selat Likupang. *strait* Sulawesi, N Indonesia
168 J11 **Bangkinang** Sumatera, W Indonesia
168 K12 **Bangko** Sumatera, W Indonesia
Bangkok *see* Krung Thep
Bangkok, Bight of *see* Krung Thep, Ao
153 T14 **Bangladesh** *off.* People's Republic of Bangladesh; *prev.* East Pakistan. ◆ *republic* S Asia
Bangladesh, People's Republic of *see* Bangladesh
167 V13 **Ba Ngoi** Khanh Hoa, S Vietnam
152 K5 **Bangong Co** *var.* Pangong Tso. ◎ China/India *see also* Pangong Tso
Bangong Co *see* Pangong Tso
97 I18 **Bangor** NW Wales, UK
97 G15 **Bangor** *Ir.* Beannchar. E Northern Ireland, UK
19 R6 **Bangor** Maine, NE USA
18 I14 **Bangor** Pennsylvania, NE USA
67 R8 **Bangoran** ≈ S Central African Republic
Bang Phra *see* Trat
Bang Pla Soi *see* Chon Buri
25 Q8 **Bangs** Texas, SW USA
167 N13 **Bang Saphan** *var.* Bang Saphan Yai. Prachuap Khiri Khan, SW Thailand
Bang Saphan Yai *see* Bang Saphan
36 I8 **Bangs, Mount** ▲ Arizona, SW USA
93 E15 **Bangsund** Nord-Trøndelag, C Norway
171 O2 **Bangued** Luzon, N Philippines
79 I15 **Bangui** ● (Central African Republic) Ombella-Mpoko, SW Central African Republic
79 I15 **Bangui** ✕ Ombella-Mpoko, SW Central African Republic
83 N16 **Bangula** Southern, S Malawi
Bangwaketse *see* Southern
82 K12 **Bangweulu, Lake** *var.* Lake Bengweulu. ◎ N Zambia
Banhā *see* Benha
Ban Hat Yai *see* Hat Yai
167 Q7 **Ban Hin Heup** Viangchan, C Laos
Ban Houayxay/Ban Houei Sai *see* Houayxay
167 O12 **Ban Hua Hin** *var.* Hua Hin. Prachuap Khiri Khan, SW Thailand
79 L14 **Bani** Haute-Kotto, E Central African Republic
45 O9 **Baní** S Dominican Republic
77 N12 **Bani** ≈ S Mali
Banias *see* Bāniyās
77 S11 **Bani Bangou** Tillabéri, SW Niger
76 M12 **Banifing** *var.* Ngorolaka. ≈ Burkina/Mali
77 R13 **Banikoara** N Benin
Banī Mazār *see* Beni Mazâr
114 K8 **Baniski Lom** ≈ N Bulgaria
21 U7 **Banister River** ≈ Virginia, NE USA
Banī Suwayf *see* Beni Suef
75 O8 **Banī Walīd** NW Libya
138 H5 **Bāniyās** *var.* Banias, Baniyas, Paneas. Ṭarṭūs, W Syria
113 K14 **Banja** Serbia, W Serbia
Banjak, Kepulauan *see* Banyak, Kepulauan
112 J12 **Banja Koviljača** Serbia, W Serbia
112 G11 **Banja Luka** ◈ Republika Srpska, NW Bosnia and Herzegovina
169 T13 **Banjarmasin** *prev.* Bandjarmasin. Borneo, C Indonesia
76 F11 **Banjul** *prev.* Bathurst. ● (Gambia) W Gambia
76 F11 **Banjul** ✕ W Gambia
Bank *see* Bankä
137 Y13 **Bankä** *Rus.* Bank. SE Azerbaijan
167 S11 **Ban Kadian** *var.* Ban Kadiene. Champasak, S Laos
Ban Kadiene *see* Ban Kadian
Bankai *see* Bangkai, Tanjung
166 M14 **Ban Kam Phuam** Phangnga, SW Thailand
Ban Kantang *see* Kantang
77 O11 **Bankass** Mopti, S Mali
95 L19 **Bankeryd** Jönköping, S Sweden
83 K16 **Banket** Mashonaland West, N Zimbabwe
167 T11 **Ban Khamphô** Attapu, S Laos
23 O4 **Bankhead Lake** ⊠ Alabama, S USA
77 Q11 **Bankilaré** Tillabéri, SW Niger
Banks, Îles *see* Banks Islands
10 I14 **Banks Island** *island* British Columbia, SW Canada
187 R12 **Banks Islands** *Fr.* Îles Banks. *island group* N Vanuatu
23 U8 **Banks Lake** ◎ Georgia, SE USA
32 K8 **Banks Lake** ⊠ Washington, NW USA
185 I19 **Banks Peninsula** *peninsula* South Island, New Zealand
183 Q15 **Banks Strait** *strait* SW Tasman Sea
Ban Kui Nua *see* Kui Buri
153 R16 **Bānkura** West Bengal, NE India
167 S8 **Ban Lakxao** *var.* Lak Sao. Bolikhamxai, C Laos
167 O16 **Ban Lam Phai** Songkhla, SW Thailand
Ban Mae Sot *see* Mae Sot
Ban Mae Suai *see* Mae Suai
Ban Mak Khaeng *see* Udon Thani
166 M3 **Banmauk** Sagaing, N Burma (Myanmar)
Banmo *see* Bhamo
167 T10 **Ban Mun-Houamuang** S Laos
97 F14 **Bann** *var.* Lower Bann, Upper Bann. ≈ N Northern Ireland, UK
167 S10 **Ban Nadou** Salavan, S Laos
167 S9 **Ban Nakala** Savannakhét, S Laos
167 Q8 **Ban Nakha** Viangchan, C Laos
167 S9 **Ban Nakham** Khammouan, S Laos
167 P7 **Ban Namoun** Xaignabouli, N Laos
167 O17 **Ban Nang Sata** Yala, SW Thailand
167 N15 **Ban Na San** Surat Thani, SW Thailand
167 R7 **Ban Nasi** Xiangkhoang, N Laos
44 I3 **Bannerman Town** Eleuthera Island, C Bahamas
35 V15 **Banning** California, W USA
Banningville *see* Bandundu
167 S11 **Ban Nongsim** Champasak, S Laos
149 S7 **Bannu** *prev.* Edwardesabad. North-West Frontier Province, NW Pakistan
Bañolas *see* Banyoles
56 C7 **Baños** Tungurahua, C Ecuador
Bánovce *see* Bánovce nad Bebravou
111 I19 **Bánovce nad Bebravou** *var.* Bánovce, *Hung.* Bán. Trenčiansky Kraj, W Slovakia
112 I12 **Banovići** ◈ Federacija Bosna I Hercegovina, E Bosnia and Herzegovina
Banow *see* Andarāb
Ban Pak Phanang *see* Pak Phanang
167 O7 **Ban Pan Nua** Lampang, NW Thailand
167 Q9 **Ban Phai** Khon Kaen, E Thailand
167 T9 **Ban Phou A Douk** Khammouan, C Laos
167 Q8 **Ban Phu** Uthai Thani, W Thailand
167 O11 **Ban Pong** Ratchaburi, W Thailand
190 I3 **Banraeaba** Tarawa, W Kiribati
167 N10 **Ban Sai Yok** Kanchanaburi, W Thailand
Ban Sattahip/Ban Sattahipp *see* Sattahip
Ban Sichon *see* Sichon
Ban Si Racha *see* Siracha
111 J19 **Banská Bystrica** *Ger.* Neusohl, *Hung.* Besztercebánya. Banskobystricky Kraj, C Slovakia
111 K20 **Banskobystrický Kraj** ◈ *region* C Slovakia
167 R8 **Ban Sôppheung** Bolikhamxai, C Laos
Ban Sop Prap *see* Sop Prap
152 G15 **Bānswāra** Rājasthān, N India
167 N15 **Ban Ta Khun** Surat Thani, SW Thailand
Ban Takua Pa *see* Takua Pa
167 S8 **Ban Talak** Khammouan, C Laos
77 R15 **Bantè** W Benin
167 N16 **Banten** *off.* Propinsi Banten. ◈ *province* W Indonesia
Propinsi Banten *see* Banten
167 Q8 **Ban Thabôk** Bolikhamxai, C Laos
167 T9 **Ban Tôp** Savannakhét, S Laos
97 B21 **Bantry** *Ir.* Beanntraí. Cork, SW Ireland
97 A21 **Bantry Bay** *Ir.* Bá Bheanntraí. *bay* SW Ireland
155 F19 **Bantvāl** *var.* Bantwāl. Karnātaka, E India
Bantwāl *see* Bantvāl
114 N9 **Banya** Burgas, E Bulgaria
168 G10 **Banyak, Kepulauan** *prev.* Kepulauan Banjak. *island group* NW Indonesia
105 U8 **Banya, La** *headland* E Spain
79 E14 **Banyo** Adamaoua, NW Cameroon
105 X4 **Banyoles** *var.* Bañolas. Cataluña, NE Spain
167 N16 **Ban Yong Sata** Trang, SW Thailand
195 X14 **Banzare Coast** *physical region* Antarctica
173 Q14 **Banzare Seamounts** *undersea feature* Indian Ocean
Banzart *see* Bizerte
163 Q12 **Baochang** *var.* Taibus Qi. Nei Mongol Zizhiqu, N China
161 O3 **Baoding** *var.* Pao-ting; *prev.* Tsingyuan. Hebei, E China
Baoebaoe *see* Baubau
Baoi, Oileán *see* Dursey Island
160 J6 **Baoji** *var.* Pao-chi, Paoki. Shaanxi, C China
163 U9 **Baokang** *var.* Hoqin Zuoyi Zhongji. Nei Mongol Zizhiqu, N China
186 L8 **Baolo** Santa Isabel, N Solomon Islands
167 U13 **Bao Lôc** Lâm Đông, S Vietnam
163 Z7 **Baoqing** Heilongjiang, NE China
Baoqing *see* Shaoyang
79 H15 **Baoro** Nana-Mambéré, W Central African Republic
160 E12 **Baoshan** *var.* Pao-shan. Yunnan, SW China
163 N13 **Baotou** *var.* Pao-t'ou, Paotow. Nei Mongol Zizhiqu, N China
76 K12 **Baoulé** ≈ W Mali
76 L14 **Baoulé** ≈ S Mali
Bao Yèn *see* Phô Rang
103 O2 **Bapaume** Pas-de-Calais, N France
14 J13 **Baptiste Lake** ◎ Ontario, SE Canada
Bapu *see* Meigu
Baqanas *see* Bakanas
Baqbaqty *see* Bakbakty
159 P14 **Baqên** *var.* Dartang. Xizang Zizhiqu, W China
138 F14 **Bāqir, Jabal** ▲ S Jordan
139 T7 **Ba'qūbah** *var.* Qubba. C Iraq
62 H5 **Baquedano** Antofagasta, N Chile
Baquerizo Moreno *see* Puerto Baquerizo Moreno
113 J18 **Bar** *It.* Antivari. S Montenegro
116 M6 **Bar** Vinnyts'ka Oblast', C Ukraine
80 E10 **Bara** Northern Kordofan, C Sudan
81 M18 **Baraawe** *It.* Brava. Shabeellaha Hoose, S Somalia
152 M12 **Bāra Banki** Uttar Pradesh, N India
30 L8 **Baraboo** Wisconsin, N USA
30 K8 **Baraboo Range** *hill range* Wisconsin, N USA
Baracaldo *see* San Vicente de Barakaldo
15 Y6 **Barachois** Québec, SE Canada
44 J7 **Baracoa** Guantánamo, E Cuba
61 C19 **Baradero** Buenos Aires, E Argentina
183 R6 **Baradine** New South Wales, SE Australia
Baraf Daja Islands *see* Damar, Kepulauan
154 M12 **Baragarh** Orissa, E India
81 I17 **Baragoi** Rift Valley, W Kenya
45 N9 **Barahona** SW Dominican Republic
153 W13 **Barail Range** ▲▲ NE India
80 I9 **Baraka** *var.* Barka, *Ar.* Khawr Barakah. *seasonal river* Eritrea/Sudan
80 G10 **Barakat** Gezira, C Sudan
Barakī *see* Barakī Barak
149 Q6 **Barakī Barak** *var.* Barakī, Baraki Rajan. Lowgar, E Afghanistan
Baraki Rajan *see* Barakī Barak
154 N11 **Bārākot** Orissa, E India
55 S7 **Barama River** ≈ N Guyana
155 E14 **Bārāmati** Mahārāshtra, W India
152 H5 **Bāramūla** Jammu and Kashmir, NW India
119 N14 **Baran'** Vitsyebskaya Voblasts', NE Belarus
152 I14 **Bārān** Rājasthān, N India
139 U4 **Barānān, Shākh-i** ▲▲ E Iraq
119 I17 **Baranavichy** *Pol.* Baranowicze, *Rus.* Baranovichi. Brestskaya Voblasts', SW Belarus
123 T6 **Baranikha** Chukotskiy Avtonomnyy Okrug, NE Russian Federation
116 M4 **Baranivka** Zhytomyrs'ka Oblast', N Ukraine
39 W14 **Baranof Island** *island* Alexander Archipelago, Alaska, USA
Baranovichi/Baranowicze *see* Baranavichy
111 N15 **Baranów Sandomierski** Podkarpackie, SE Poland
111 I26 **Baranya** *off.* Baranya Megye. ◈ *county* S Hungary
Baranya Megye *see* Baranya
153 R13 **Barāri** Bihār, NE India
22 L10 **Barataria Bay** *bay* Louisiana, S USA
Barat Daya, Kepulauan *see* Damar, Kepulauan
118 L12 **Baravukha** *Rus.* Borovukha. Vitsyebskaya Voblasts', N Belarus
54 E11 **Baraya** Huila, C Colombia
59 M21 **Barbacena** Minas Gerais, SE Brazil
54 B13 **Barbacoas** Nariño, SW Colombia
54 L6 **Barbacoas** Aragua, N Venezuela
45 Z13 **Barbados** ◆ *island state* SE West Indies
47 S3 **Barbados** *island* Barbados
105 U11 **Barbaria, Cap de** *var.* Cabo de Berberia. *cape* Formentera, E Spain
114 N13 **Barbaros** Tekirdağ, NW Turkey
74 A11 **Barbas, Cap** *headland* S Western Sahara
105 T5 **Barbastro** Aragón, NE Spain
104 K16 **Barbate** ≈ SW Spain
104 K16 **Barbate de Franco** Andalucía, S Spain
83 K21 **Barberton** Mpumalanga, NE South Africa
31 U12 **Barberton** Ohio, N USA
102 K12 **Barbezieux-St-Hilaire** Charente, W France
54 G9 **Barbosa** Boyacá, C Colombia
21 N7 **Barbourville** Kentucky, S USA
45 W9 **Barbuda** *island* N Antigua and Barbuda
181 W8 **Barcaldine** Queensland, E Australia
Barcarozsnyó *see* Râșnov
104 I11 **Barcarrota** Extremadura, W Spain
Barcău *see* Berettyó
Barce *see* Al Marj
107 L23 **Barcellona** *var.* Barcellona Pozzo di Gotto. Sicilia, Italy, C Mediterranean Sea
Barcellona Pozzo di Gotto *see* Barcellona
105 W6 **Barcelona** *anc.* Barcino, Barcinona. Cataluña, E Spain
55 N5 **Barcelona** Anzoátegui, NE Venezuela
105 S5 **Barcelona** ◈ *province* Cataluña, NE Spain
105 W6 **Barcelona** ✕ Cataluña, E Spain
103 U14 **Barcelonnette** Alpes-de-Haute-Provence, SE France
58 E12 **Barcelos** Amazonas, N Brazil
104 G5 **Barcelos** Braga, N Portugal
110 I10 **Barcin** *Ger.* Bartschin. Kujawski-pomorskie, C Poland
Barcino/Barcinona *see* Barcelona
Barcoo *see* Cooper Creek
111 H26 **Barcs** Somogy, SW Hungary
137 W11 **Bärdä** *Rus.* Barda. C Azerbaijan
Barda *see* Bärdä
78 H5 **Bardaï** Borkou-Ennedi-Tibesti, N Chad
139 R2 **Bardaraṣh** N Iraq
139 Q7 **Bardasah** SW Iraq
153 S16 **Barddhamān** West Bengal, NE India
111 N18 **Bardejov** *Ger.* Bartfeld, *Hung.* Bártfa. Presovský Kraj, E Slovakia
105 R4 **Bárdenas Reales** *physical region* N Spain
Bardera/Bardere *see* Baardheere
Bardesīr *see* Bardsīr
92 K3 **Bardharbunga** C Iceland
Bardhë, Drini i *see* Beli Drim
106 E9 **Bardi** Emilia-Romagna, C Italy
106 A8 **Bardonecchia** Piemonte, W Italy
97 H19 **Bardsey Island** *island* NW Wales, UK
143 S11 **Bardsīr** *var.* Bardesīr, Mashīz. Kermān, C Iran
20 L6 **Bardstown** Kentucky, S USA
Barduli *see* Barletta
20 G7 **Bardwell** Kentucky, S USA
152 K11 **Bareilly** *var.* Bareli. Uttar Pradesh, N India
Bareli *see* Bareilly
98 H13 **Barendrecht** Zuid-Holland, SW Netherlands
102 M3 **Barentin** Seine-Maritime, N France
92 N3 **Barentsburg** Spitsbergen, W Svalbard
Barentsevo More/Barents Havet *see* Barents Sea
92 O3 **Barentsøya** *island* E Svalbard
197 T11 **Barents Plain** *undersea feature* N Barents Sea
125 P3 **Barents Sea** *Nor.* Barents Havet, *Rus.* Barentsevo More. *sea* Arctic Ocean
197 U14 **Barents Trough** *undersea feature* SW Barents Sea
80 J9 **Barentu** W Eritrea
102 J3 **Barfleur** Manche, N France
102 J3 **Barfleur, Pointe de** *headland* N France
Barfrush/Barfurush *see* Bābol
158 H14 **Barga** Xizang Zizhiqu, W China
105 N9 **Bargas** Castilla-La Mancha, C Spain
81 I15 **Bargē** Southern, S Ethiopia
106 A9 **Barge** Piemonte, NE Italy
153 U16 **Barguna** Barisal, S Bangladesh
Bärguşad *see* Vorotan
123 N13 **Barguzin** Respublika Buryatiya, S Russian Federation
153 O13 **Barhaj** Uttar Pradesh, N India
183 N10 **Barham** New South Wales, SE Australia
152 J12 **Barhan** Uttar Pradesh, N India
19 S7 **Bar Harbor** Mount Desert Island, Maine, NE USA
153 R14 **Barharwa** Jhārkhand, NE India
153 P15 **Barhi** Jhārkhand, N India
107 O17 **Bari** *var.* Bari delle Puglie; *anc.* Barium. Puglia, SE Italy
80 P12 **Bari** *off.* Gobolka Bari. ◈ *region* NE Somalia
167 T14 **Ba Ria** *var.* Châu Thanh. Ba Ria-Vung Tau, S Vietnam
Bāridah *see* Al Bāridah
Bari delle Puglie *see* Bari
Bari, Gobolka *see* Bari
Barikot *see* Barīkowṭ
149 T4 **Barīkowṭ** *var.* Barikot. Konar, NE Afghanistan
42 C4 **Barillas** *var.* Santa Cruz Barillas. Huehuetenango, NW Guatemala
54 J6 **Barinas** Barinas, W Venezuela
54 I7 **Barinas** *off.* Estado Barinas; *prev.* Zamora. ◈ *state* C Venezuela
Barinas, Estado *see* Barinas
54 I6 **Barinitas** Barinas, NW Venezuela
154 P11 **Bāripada** Orissa, E India
60 K9 **Bariri** São Paulo, S Brazil
75 W11 **Bârîs** S Egypt
152 G14 **Bari Sādri** Rājasthān, N India
153 U16 **Barisal** Barisal, S Bangladesh
153 U16 **Barisal** ◈ *division* S Bangladesh
168 I10 **Barisan, Pegunungan** ▲▲ Sumatera, W Indonesia
169 T12 **Barito, Sungai** ≈ Borneo, C Indonesia
Barium *see* Bari
Bârjâs *see* Porjus
Barka *see* Baraka
Barka *see* Al Marj
160 H8 **Barkam** Sichuan, C China
118 J9 **Barkava** Madona, C Latvia
10 M15 **Barkerville** British Columbia, SW Canada
14 J12 **Bark Lake** ◎ Ontario, SE Canada
20 H7 **Barkley, Lake** ⊠ Kentucky/ Tennessee, S USA
10 K17 **Barkley Sound** *inlet* British Columbia, W Canada
83 J24 **Barkly East** *Afr.* Barkly-Oos. Eastern Cape, SE South Africa
Barkly-Oos *see* Barkly East
181 S4 **Barkly Tableland** *plateau* Northern Territory/ Queensland, N Australia
Barkly-Wes *see* Barkly West
83 H22 **Barkly West** *Afr.* Barkly-Wes. Northern Cape, N South Africa
159 O5 **Barkol** *var.* Barkol Kazak Zizhixian. Xinjiang Uygur Zizhiqu, NW China
159 O5 **Barkol Hu** ◎ NW China
Barkol Kazak Zizhixian *see* Barkol
30 J3 **Bark Point** *headland* Wisconsin, N USA
25 P11 **Barksdale** Texas, SW USA
Bar Kunar *see* Asmār
116 L11 **Bârlad** *prev.* Birlad. Vaslui, E Romania
116 M11 **Bârlad** *prev.* Birlad. ≈ E Romania
76 D9 **Barlavento, Ilhas de** *var.* Windward Islands. *island group* N Cape Verde
103 R5 **Bar-le-Duc** *var.* Bar-sur-Ornain. Meuse, NE France
180 K11 **Barlee, Lake** ◎ Western Australia
180 H8 **Barlee Range** ▲▲ Western Australia
107 N16 **Barletta** *anc.* Barduli. Puglia, SE Italy
110 E10 **Barlinek** *Ger.* Berlinchen. Zachodnio-pomorskie, NW Poland
27 S11 **Barling** Arkansas, C USA
171 U12 **Barma** Papua, E Indonesia
183 Q9 **Barmedman** New South Wales, SE Australia
Barmen-Elberfeld *see* Wuppertal
152 D12 **Bārmer** Rājasthān, NW India
182 K9 **Barmera** South Australia
97 I19 **Barmouth** NW Wales, UK
154 F10 **Barnagar** Madhya Pradesh, C India
152 H9 **Barnāla** Punjab, NW India
97 L15 **Barnard Castle** N England, UK
183 O6 **Barnato** New South Wales, SE Australia
112 I13 **Barnaul** Altayskiy Kray, C Russian Federation
109 V8 **Bärnbach** Steiermark, SE Austria
18 K16 **Barnegat** New Jersey, NE USA
23 S4 **Barnesville** Georgia, SE USA
29 R6 **Barnesville** Minnesota, N USA
31 U13 **Barnesville** Ohio, N USA
98 K11 **Barneveld** *var.* Barnveld. Gelderland, C Netherlands
25 O9 **Barnhart** Texas, SW USA
27 P8 **Barnsdall** Oklahoma, C USA
97 M17 **Barnsley** N England, UK
19 Q12 **Barnstable** Massachusetts, NE USA
97 I23 **Barnstaple** SW England, UK
Barnveld *see* Barneveld
21 Q14 **Barnwell** South Carolina, SE USA
77 U15 **Baro** Niger, C Nigeria
67 U8 **Baro** *var.* Baro Wenz. ≈ Ethiopia/Sudan
Baro *see* Baro Wenz
Baroda *see* Vadodara
149 U2 **Baroghil Pass** *var.* Kowtal-e Barowghīl. *pass* Afghanistan/Pakistan
119 Q17 **Baron'ki** *Rus.* Boron'ki. Mahilyowskaya Voblasts', E Belarus
182 J9 **Barossa Valley** *valley* South Australia
Baroui *see* Salisbury
81 H14 **Baro Wenz** *var.* Baro, Nahr Barū. ≈ Ethiopia/Sudan
Baro Wenz *see* Baro
Barowghīl, Kowtal-e *see* Baroghil Pass
153 U12 **Barpeta** Assam, NE India
31 S7 **Barques, Pointe Aux** *headland* Michigan, N USA
54 I5 **Barquisimeto** Lara, NW Venezuela
59 N16 **Barra** Bahia, E Brazil
96 E9 **Barra** *island* NW Scotland, UK
183 T5 **Barraba** New South Wales, SE Australia
60 L9 **Barra Bonita** São Paulo, S Brazil
64 J12 **Barracuda Fracture Zone** *var.* Fifteen Twenty Fracture Zone. *tectonic feature* SW Atlantic Ocean
64 G11 **Barracuda Ridge** *undersea feature* N Atlantic Ocean
43 N12 **Barra del Colorado** Limón, NE Costa Rica
43 N9 **Barra de Río Grande** Región Autónoma Atlántico Sur, E Nicaragua
82 A11 **Barra do Cuanza** Luanda, NW Angola
60 O9 **Barra do Piraí** Rio de Janeiro, SE Brazil
61 D16 **Barra do Quaraí** Rio Grande do Sul, SE Brazil
59 G14 **Barra do São Manuel** Pará, N Brazil
83 N19 **Barra Falsa, Ponta da** *headland* S Mozambique
96 E10 **Barra Head** *headland* NW Scotland, UK
60 O9 **Barra Mansa** Rio de Janeiro, SE Brazil
57 D14 **Barranca** Lima, W Peru
54 F8 **Barrancabermeja** Santander, N Colombia
54 H4 **Barrancas** La Guajira, N Colombia
54 J6 **Barrancas** Barinas, NW Venezuela
55 Q6 **Barrancas** Monagas, NE Venezuela
54 F6 **Barranco de Loba** Bolívar, N Colombia
104 I12 **Barrancos** Beja, S Portugal
62 N7 **Barranqueras** Chaco, N Argentina
54 E4 **Barranquilla** Atlántico, N Colombia
83 N20 **Barra, Ponta da** *headland* S Mozambique
105 P11 **Barrax** Castilla-La Mancha, C Spain
19 N11 **Barre** Massachusetts, NE USA
18 M7 **Barre** Vermont, NE USA
59 M17 **Barreiras** Bahia, E Brazil
104 F11 **Barreiro** Setúbal, W Portugal
65 C26 **Barren Island** *island* S Falkland Islands
20 K7 **Barren River Lake** ⊠ Kentucky, S USA
60 L7 **Barretos** São Paulo, S Brazil
9 P14 **Barrhead** Alberta, SW Canada
14 G14 **Barrie** Ontario, S Canada
9 N16 **Barrière** British Columbia, SW Canada
14 H8 **Barrière, Lac** ◎ Québec, SE Canada
182 L6 **Barrier Range** *hill range* New South Wales, SE Australia
42 G3 **Barrier Reef** *reef* E Belize
188 C16 **Barrigada** C Guam
Barrington Island *see* Santa Fe, Isla
183 T7 **Barrington Tops** ▲ New South Wales, SE Australia
183 O4 **Barringun** New South Wales, SE Australia
59 K18 **Barro Alto** Goiás, S Brazil
59 N14 **Barro Duro** Piauí, NE Brazil
30 I5 **Barron** Wisconsin, N USA
14 J12 **Barron** ≈ Ontario, SE Canada
61 H15 **Barros Cassal** Rio Grande do Sul, S Brazil
45 P14 **Barrouallie** Saint Vincent, W Saint Vincent and the Grenadines
39 O4 **Barrow** Alaska, USA
97 E20 **Barrow** *Ir.* An Bhearú. ≈ SE Ireland
181 Q6 **Barrow Creek Roadhouse** Northern Territory, N Australia
97 J16 **Barrow-in-Furness** NW England, UK
180 G7 **Barrow Island** *island* Western Australia
39 O4 **Barrow, Point** *headland* Alaska, USA
9 V14 **Barrows** Manitoba, S Canada
97 J22 **Barry** S Wales, UK
14 J12 **Barry's Bay** Ontario, SE Canada
144 K14 **Barsakel'mes, Ostrov** *island* SW Kazakhstan
Baršć Łužyca *see* Forst
147 S14 **Barsem** S Tajikistan
145 V11 **Barshatas** Vostochnyy Kazakhstan, E Kazakhstan
155 F14 **Bārsi** Mahārāshtra, W India
100 I13 **Barsinghausen** Niedersachsen, C Germany

◆ Country
● Country Capital
◇ Dependent Territory
○ Dependent Territory Capital
◈ Administrative Regions
✕ International Airport
▲ Mountain
▲▲ Mountain Range
Volcano
≈ River
◎ Lake
⊠ Reservoir

147 X8 **Barskoon** Issyk-Kul'skaya Oblast', E Kyrgyzstan
100 F10 **Barssel** Niedersachsen, NW Germany
35 U14 **Barstow** California, W USA
24 L8 **Barstow** Texas, SW USA
103 R6 **Bar-sur-Aube** Aube, NE France
Bar-sur-Ornain see Bar-le-Duc
103 Q6 **Bar-sur-Seine** Aube, N France
147 S13 **Bartang** S Tajikistan
147 T13 **Bartang** var. S Tajikistan
Bartenstein see Bartoszyce
Bártfa/Bartfeld see Bardejov
100 N7 **Barth** Mecklenburg-Vorpommern, NE Germany
27 W13 **Bartholomew, Bayou** ⚡ Arkansas/Louisiana, S USA
55 T8 **Bartica** N Guyana
136 H10 **Bartın** Bartın, NW Turkey
136 H10 **Bartın** ◆ province NW Turkey
181 W4 **Bartle Frere** ▲ Queensland, E Australia
27 P8 **Bartlesville** Oklahoma, C USA
29 P14 **Bartlett** Nebraska, C USA
20 E10 **Bartlett** Tennessee, S USA
25 T9 **Bartlett** Texas, SW USA
36 L13 **Bartlett Reservoir** ⬚ Arizona, SW USA
19 N6 **Barton** Vermont, NE USA
110 L7 **Bartoszyce** Ger. Bartenstein. Warmińsko-mazurskie, NE Poland
23 W12 **Bartow** Florida, SE USA
Bartschin see Barcin
168 J10 **Barumun, Sungai** ⚡ Sumatera, W Indonesia
Barü, Nahr see Baro Wenz
169 S17 **Barung, Nusa** island S Indonesia
168 H9 **Barus** Sumatera, NW Indonesia
162 I9 **Baruunbayan-Ulaan** var. Höövör. Övörhangay, C Mongolia
Baruunsuu see Tsogttsetsiy
163 P8 **Baruun-Urt** Sühbaatar, E Mongolia
43 P15 **Barú, Volcán** var. Volcán de Chiriquí. ▲ W Panama
99 K21 **Barvaux** Luxembourg, SE Belgium
42 M13 **Barva, Volcán** ▲ NW Costa Rica
117 W6 **Barvinkove** Kharkivs'ka Oblast', E Ukraine
154 G11 **Barwäh** Madhya Pradesh, C India
Bärwalde Neumark see Mieszkowice
154 F11 **Barwäni** Madhya Pradesh, C India
183 P5 **Barwon River** ⚡ New South Wales, SE Australia
119 L15 **Barysaw** Rus. Borisov. Minskaya Voblasts', C Belarus
127 Q6 **Barysh** Ul'yanovsk Oblast', W Russian Federation
117 Q4 **Baryshivka** Kyyivs'ka Oblast', N Ukraine
79 J17 **Basankusu** Equateur, NW Dem. Rep. Congo
117 N11 **Basarabeasca** Rus. Bessarabka. SE Moldova
116 M14 **Basarabi** Constanța, SW Romania
40 H6 **Basaseachic** Chihuahua, NW Mexico
Basauri see Arizgoiti
61 D18 **Basavilbaso** Entre Ríos, E Argentina
79 F21 **Bas-Congo** off. Région du Bas-Congo; prev. Bas-Zaïre. ◆ region SW Dem. Rep. Congo
Bas-Zaïre, Région du see Bas-Congo
108 E6 **Basel** Fr. Bâle. Basel-Stadt, NW Switzerland
108 E7 **Basel** Eng. Basle, Fr. Bâle. ◆ canton NW Switzerland
143 T14 **Bashäkerd, Kühhä-ye** ▲ SE Iran
9 Q15 **Bashaw** Alberta, SW Canada
146 K16 **Bashbedeng** Mary Welayaty, S Turkmenistan
83 J24 **Bashee** ⚡ S South Africa
161 T15 **Bashi Channel** Chin. Pa-shih Hai-hsia. channel Philippines/Taiwan
Bashkara see Bashkortostan, Respublika
122 F11 **Bashkortostan, Respublika** prev. Bashkiria. ◆ autonomous republic W Russian Federation
127 N6 **Bashmakovo** Penzenskaya Oblast', W Russian Federation
146 J10 **Bashsakarba** Lebap Welayaty, NE Turkmenistan
117 R9 **Bashtanka** Mykolayivs'ka Oblast', S Ukraine
22 H8 **Basile** Louisiana, S USA
107 M18 **Basilicata** ◆ region S Italy
33 V13 **Basin** Wyoming, C USA
97 N22 **Basingstoke** S England, UK
143 U8 **Başiran** Khoräsän-e Janübï, E Iran
112 B10 **Baška** It. Bescanuova. Primorje-Gorski Kotar, NW Croatia
137 L15 **Başkale** Van, SE Turkey
14 L10 **Baskatong, Réservoir** ⬚ Québec, SE Canada
137 O14 **Baskil** Elazığ, E Turkey
Basle see Basel
154 H9 **Bäsoda** Madhya Pradesh, C India
79 L17 **Basoko** Orientale, N Dem. Rep. Congo
Basque Country, The see País Vasco
Bassa see Al Başrah
103 U5 **Bas-Rhin** ◆ department NE France
Bassam see Grand-Bassam
9 Q16 **Bassano** Alberta, SW Canada
106 H7 **Bassano del Grappa** Veneto, NE Italy
77 Q15 **Bassar** var. Bassari. NW Togo
Bassari see Bassar
172 L9 **Bassas da India** island group W Madagascar
108 D7 **Bassecourt** Jura, W Switzerland
166 K8 **Bassein** var. Pathein. Irrawaddy, SW Burma (Myanmar)
79 J15 **Basse-Kotto** ◆ prefecture S Central African Republic

105 V5 **Bassella** Cataluña, NE Spain
102 J5 **Basse-Normandie** Eng. Lower Normandy. ◆ region N France
45 Q11 **Basse-Pointe** N Martinique
76 H12 **Basse Santa Su** E Gambia
Basse-Saxe see Niedersachsen
45 X6 **Basse-Terre** ○ (Guadeloupe) Basse Terre, SW Guadeloupe
45 V10 **Basseterre** ● (Saint Kitts and Nevis) Saint Kitts, Saint Kitts and Nevis
45 X6 **Basse Terre** island W Guadeloupe
29 O13 **Bassett** Nebraska, C USA
21 S7 **Bassett** Virginia, NE USA
37 N15 **Bassett Peak** ▲ Arizona, SW USA
76 M10 **Bassikounou** Hodh ech Chargui, SE Mauritania
77 R15 **Bassila** W Benin
Bass, Îlots de see Marotiri
31 O11 **Bass Lake** Indiana, N USA
183 O14 **Bass Strait** strait SE Australia
100 H11 **Bassum** Niedersachsen, NW Germany
29 X3 **Basswood Lake** ⬚ Canada/USA
95 J21 **Båstad** Skåne, S Sweden
139 U2 **Bastah** N Iraq
153 N12 **Basti** Uttar Pradesh, N India
103 X14 **Bastia** Corse, France, C Mediterranean Sea
99 L23 **Bastogne** Luxembourg, SE Belgium
22 I5 **Bastrop** Louisiana, S USA
25 T11 **Bastrop** Texas, SW USA
93 J15 **Bastuträsk** Västerbotten, N Sweden
119 J19 **Bastyn'** Rus. Bostyn'. Brestskaya Voblasts', SW Belarus
Basuo see Dongfang
Basutoland see Lesotho
119 O15 **Basya** ⚡ E Belarus
117 V8 **Basyl'kivka** Dnipropetrovs'ka Oblast', E Ukraine
Bas-Zaïre see Bas-Congo
79 D17 **Bata** NW Equatorial Guinea
79 D17 **Bata** ✕ S Equatorial Guinea
Batae Coritanorum see Leicester
123 Q8 **Batagay** Respublika Sakha (Yakutiya), NE Russian Federation
123 P8 **Batagay-Alyta** Respublika Sakha (Yakutiya), NE Russian Federation
112 L10 **Batajnica** Vojvodina, N Serbia
136 H15 **Bataklık Gölü** ⬚ S Turkey
114 H11 **Batak, Yazovir** ⬚ SW Bulgaria
152 H1 **Batala** Punjab, N India
104 F9 **Batalha** Leiria, C Portugal
79 N17 **Batama** Orientale, NE Dem. Rep. Congo
123 Q10 **Batamay** Respublika Sakha (Yakutiya), NE Russian Federation
160 F9 **Batang** var. Bazhong. Sichuan, C China
79 I14 **Batangafo** Ouham, NW Central African Republic
171 P8 **Batangas** off. Batangas City. Luzon, N Philippines
Batangas City see Batangas
Bätania see Battonya
171 Q10 **Batan Islands** island group N Philippines
171 P14 **Baubau** see Baranoa
18 E10 **Batavia** New York, NE USA
Batavia see Jakarta
173 T9 **Batavia Seamount** undersea feature E Indian Ocean
126 L12 **Bataysk** Rostovskaya Oblast', SW Russian Federation
14 B9 **Batchawana** ⚡ Ontario, S Canada
14 B9 **Batchawana Bay** Ontario, S Canada
167 Q12 **Bätdâmbâng** prev. Battambang. Bätdâmbâng, NW Cambodia
79 G20 **Batéké, Plateaux** plateau S Congo
183 S11 **Batemans Bay** New South Wales, SE Australia
21 Q13 **Batesburg** South Carolina, SE USA
28 K12 **Batesland** South Dakota, N USA
27 V10 **Batesville** Arkansas, C USA
31 O14 **Batesville** Indiana, N USA
22 L2 **Batesville** Mississippi, S USA
25 S13 **Batesville** Texas, SW USA
44 L13 **Bath** E Jamaica
97 L22 **Bath** hist. Akermanceaster; anc. Aquae Calidae, Aquae Solis. SW England, UK
19 Q8 **Bath** Maine, NE USA
18 F11 **Bath** New York, NE USA
Bath see Berkeley Springs
78 I10 **Batha** ◆ prefecture C Chad
78 I10 **Batha** seasonal river C Chad
Batha, Préfecture du see Batha
141 Y8 **Batha', Wädi al** dry watercourse E Saudi Arabia
152 H9 **Bathinda** Punjab, NW India
98 M11 **Bathmen** Overijssel, E Netherlands
45 Z14 **Bathsheba** E Barbados
183 R8 **Bathurst** New South Wales, SE Australia
Bathurst see Banjul
13 O13 **Bathurst** New Brunswick, SE Canada
154 H9 **Bathurst, Cape** headland Northwest Territories, NW Canada
196 L8 **Bathurst Inlet** Nunavut, N Canada
196 L8 **Bathurst Inlet** inlet Nunavut, N Canada
181 N1 **Bathurst Island** island Northern Territory, N Australia
197 O9 **Bathurst Island** island Parry Islands, Nunavut, N Canada
77 O14 **Batié** SW Burkina
Batinah see Al Bätinah
141 Y9 **Bätin, Wädi al** dry watercourse SW Asia
15 P9 **Batiscan** ⚡ Québec, SE Canada
136 F16 **Batı Toroslar** ▲ SW Turkey
169 X11 **Batjan** see Bacan, Pulau
147 R11 **Batken** Batkenskaya Oblast', SW Kyrgyzstan
Batken Oblasty see Batkenskaya Oblast'

147 Q11 **Batkenskaya Oblast'** Kir. Batken Oblasty. ◆ province SW Kyrgyzstan
Batle y Ordóñez see José Batlle y Ordóñez
183 Q10 **Batlow** New South Wales, SE Australia
137 Q15 **Batman** var. İluh. Batman, SE Turkey
137 Q15 **Batman** ◆ province SE Turkey
74 L6 **Batna** NE Algeria
163 O7 **Batnorov** var. Dundbürd. Hentiy, E Mongolia
Batoe see Batu, Kepulauan
22 J8 **Baton Rouge** state capital Louisiana, S USA
79 G15 **Batouri** Est, E Cameroon
138 G13 **Baträ', Jibäl al** ▲ S Jordan
138 G6 **Batroûn** var. Al Batrün. N Lebanon
Batsch see Bač
119 M17 **Batsevichy** Rus. Batsevichi. Mahilyowskaya Voblasts', E Belarus
92 M7 **Båtsfjord** Finnmark, N Norway
163 N7 **Batshireet** var. Eg. Hentiy, ◆ province N Mongolia
162 L7 **Batsümber** var. Mandal. Töv, C Mongolia
155 L24 **Batticaloa** Eastern Province, E Sri Lanka
99 L19 **Battice** Liège, E Belgium
107 L18 **Battipaglia** Campania, S Italy
9 R15 **Battle** ⚡ Alberta/Saskatchewan, SW Canada
Battle Born State see Nevada
31 Q10 **Battle Creek** Michigan, N USA
27 T7 **Battlefield** Missouri, C USA
9 S15 **Battleford** Saskatchewan, S Canada
29 S6 **Battle Lake** Minnesota, N USA
35 U3 **Battle Mountain** Nevada, W USA
111 M25 **Battonya** Rom. Bätania. Békés, SE Hungary
162 J7 **Battsengel** var. Jargalant. ◆ province C Mongolia
168 D11 **Batu, Kepulauan** prev. Batoe. island group W Indonesia
137 Q10 **Bat'umi** W Georgia
168 K10 **Batu Pahat** prev. Bandar Penggaram. Johor, Peninsular Malaysia
171 O12 **Baturebe** Sulawesi, N Indonesia
122 J12 **Baturino** Tomskaya Oblast', C Russian Federation
117 R4 **Baturyn** Chernihivs'ka Oblast', N Ukraine
138 F10 **Bat Yam** Tel Aviv, C Israel
127 Q4 **Batyrevo** Chuvashskaya Respublika, W Russian Federation
Batys Qazaqstan Oblysy see Zapadnyy Kazakhstan
102 F5 **Batz, Île de** island NW France
169 Q10 **Bau** Sarawak, East Malaysia
171 N2 **Bauang** Luzon, N Philippines
171 P14 **Baubau** var. Baoebaoe. Pulau Buton, C Indonesia
77 W13 **Bauchi** Bauchi, NE Nigeria
77 W14 **Bauchi** ◆ state C Nigeria
102 N7 **Baud** Morbihan, NW France
29 T2 **Baudette** Minnesota, N USA
193 S9 **Bauer Basin** undersea feature E Pacific Ocean
187 R14 **Bauer Field** var. Port Vila. ✕ (Port-Vila) Éfaté, C Vanuatu
13 T9 **Bauld, Cape** cape Newfoundland and Labrador, E Canada
103 T8 **Baume-les-Dames** Doubs, E France
101 I15 **Baunatal** Hessen, C Germany
107 D18 **Baunei** Sardegna, Italy, C Mediterranean Sea
57 M15 **Baures, Río** ⚡ N Bolivia
60 K9 **Bauru** São Paulo, S Brazil
Baushar see Bawshar
118 O4 **Bauska** Ger. Bauske. Bauska, S Latvia
Bauske see Bauska
101 Q15 **Bautzen** Lus. Budyšin. Sachsen, E Germany
145 Q16 **Bauyrzhan Momyshuly** Kaz. Baüyrzhan Momyshuly; prev. Burnoye. Zhambyl, S Kazakhstan
Bauzanum see Bolzano
Bavaria see Bayern
109 N7 **Bavarian Alps** Ger. Bayrische Alpen. ▲ Austria/Germany
Bavière see Bayern
40 H9 **Bavispe, Río** ⚡ NW Mexico
127 T5 **Bavly** Respublika Tatarstan, W Russian Federation
169 P13 **Bawal, Pulau** island N Indonesia
169 T12 **Bawan** Borneo, C Indonesia
183 O12 **Baw Baw, Mount** ▲ Victoria, SE Australia
169 S15 **Bawean, Pulau** island S Indonesia
75 W9 **Bawîti** N Egypt
77 Q13 **Bawku** N Ghana
167 N7 **Bawlakè** Kayah State, C Burma (Myanmar)
169 H11 **Bawo Ofuloa** Pulau Tanahmasa, W Indonesia
141 P8 **Bawshar** var. Baushar. NE Oman
Ba Xian see Bazhou
158 M8 **Baxkorgan** Xinjiang Uygur Zizhiqu, W China
23 V6 **Baxley** Georgia, SE USA
159 R15 **Baxoi** var. Baima. Xizang Zizhiqu, W China
29 W14 **Baxter** Iowa, C USA
29 U6 **Baxter** Minnesota, N USA
27 R8 **Baxter Springs** Kansas, C USA
81 M17 **Bay** off. Gobolka Bay. ◆ region SW Somalia
Bay see Baicheng
44 H7 **Bayamo** Granma, E Cuba
45 U5 **Bayamón** E Puerto Rico
163 W8 **Bayan** Heilongjiang, NE China
170 L16 **Bayan** prev. Bajan. Pulau Lombok, C Indonesia
162 M8 **Bayan** var. Maaniit. Töv, C Mongolia

Bayan see Hölönbuyr
Bayan Hölönbuyr, Dornod, Mongolia
Bayan see Ihhet
Bayan Ihhet, Dornogovi, Mongolia
Bayan see Bayan-Uul, Govī-Altay, Mongolia
Bayan see Bayanhutag, Hentiy, Mongolia
Bayan see Bürentogtoh, Hövsgöl, Mongolia
152 I12 **Bayana** Räjasthän, N India
149 N5 **Bäyän, Band-e** ▲ C Afghanistan
162 H8 **Bayanbulag** Bayanhongor, C Mongolia
158 J5 **Bayanbulak** Xinjiang Uygur Zizhiqu, W China
162 J11 **Bayandalay** var. Dalay. Ömnögovi, S Mongolia
163 O9 **Bayandelger** var. Shireet. Sühbaatar, SE Mongolia
162 I5 **Bayandzürh** var. Altraga. Hövsgöl, N Mongolia
Bayan Gol see Dengkou
Bayangol see Bugat
162 I9 **Bayangovi** var. Örgön. Bayanhongor, C Mongolia
159 R12 **Bayan Har Shan** var. Bayan Khar. ▲ C China
162 G6 **Bayanhayrhan** Dzavhan, N Mongolia
162 G6 **Bayanhayrhan** var Altanbulag. Dzavhan, N Mongolia
162 I8 **Bayanhongor** Bayanhongor, C Mongolia
162 H9 **Bayanhongor** ◆ province C Mongolia
162 K14 **Bayan Hot** var. Alxa Zuoqi. Nei Mongol Zizhiqu, N China
162 K14 **Bayan Hot** var. Alxa Zuoqi. Nei Mongol Zizhiqu, N China
162 O8 **Bayanhushuu** var. Bayan. Hentiy, C Mongolia
163 T9 **Bayan Huxu** var. Horqin Zuoyi Zhongqi. Nei Mongol Zizhiqu, N China
Bayan Khar see Bayan Har Shan
168 J7 **Bayan Lepas** ✕ (George Town) Pinang, Peninsular Malaysia
162 I10 **Bayanlig** var. Hatansuudal. Bayanhongor, C Mongolia
162 K13 **Bayan Mod** Nei Mongol Zizhiqu, N China
163 N8 **Bayanmönh** var. Ulaan-Ereg. Hentiy, E Mongolia
Bayan Nuru see Xar Burd
162 E5 **Bayannuur** var. Tsul-Ulaan. Bulgan, N Mongolia
162 I9 **Bayan-Ölgiy,** W Mongolia
163 N12 **Bayan Obo** Nei Mongol Zizhiqu, N China
43 V15 **Bayano, Lago** ⬚ E Panama
162 C5 **Bayan-Ölgiy** ◆ province NW Mongolia
162 H9 **Bayan-Öndör** var. Bulgan. Bayanhongor, C Mongolia
162 H9 **Bayan-Öndör** var. Bulgan. Bayanhongor, C Mongolia
162 K8 **Bayan-Öndör** var. Bumbat. Övörhangay, C Mongolia
162 K8 **Bayan-Öndör** var. Övörhangay, C Mongolia
162 L8 **Bayan-Önjüül** var. Ihhayrhan. Töv, C Mongolia
163 O7 **Bayan-Ovoo** var. Javhlant. Hentiy, E Mongolia
162 L11 **Bayan-Ovoo** var. Ergenetsogt. Ömnögovi, S Mongolia
162 L11 **Bayan-Ovoo** var. Erdenetsogt. Ömnögovi, S Mongolia
Bayan-Ovoo see Altay
Bayan-Ovoo see Altay
159 Q9 **Bayan Shan** ▲ C China
162 J9 **Bayanteeg** Övörhangay, C Mongolia
162 G5 **Bayantes** var. Altay. Dzavhan, N Mongolia
Bayantöhöm see Büren
162 M8 **Bayantsagaan** var. Dzogsool. Töv, C Mongolia
163 P7 **Bayantümen** var. Tsagaanders. Dornod, NE Mongolia
Bayan-Uhaa see Ih-Uul
163 R10 **Bayan Ul** var. Xi Ujimqin Qi. Nei Mongol Zizhiqu, N China
Bayan-Ulaan see Dzüünbayan-Ulaan
Bayan-Ulaan see Dzüünbayan-Ulaan
163 O7 **Bayan-Uul** var. Javarthushuu. Dornod, NE Mongolia
162 F7 **Bayan-Uul** var. Bayan. Govī-Altay, W Mongolia
162 M8 **Bayanuur** var. Tsul-Ulaan. Töv, C Mongolia
172 J3 **Bayat** Çorum, N Turkey
171 P6 **Bayawan** Negros, C Philippines
143 R10 **Bayäz** Kermän, C Iran
171 Q6 **Baybay** Leyte, C Philippines
21 X10 **Bayboro** North Carolina, SE USA
137 P12 **Bayburt** Bayburt, NE Turkey
137 P12 **Bayburt** ◆ province NE Turkey
31 R8 **Bay City** Michigan, N USA
25 V12 **Bay City** Texas, SW USA
Baydarata Bay see Baydaratskaya Guba
122 J7 **Baydaratskaya Guba** var. Baydarata Bay. bay N Russian Federation
81 M16 **Baydhabo** var. Baydhowa, Isha Baydhabo, It. Baidoa. Bay, SW Somalia
Baydhowa see Baydhabo
101 N21 **Bayerischer Wald** ▲ SE Germany
101 K21 **Bayern** Eng. Bavaria, Fr. Bavière. ◆ state SE Germany
147 V9 **Bayetovo** Narynskaya Oblast', C Kyrgyzstan
102 K4 **Bayeux** anc. Augustodurum. Calvados, N France

14 E15 **Bayfield** Ontario, S Canada
145 O15 **Baygakum** Kaz. Bäygequm. Kyzylorda, S Kazakhstan
Bäygequm see Baygakum
136 C14 **Bayındır** İzmir, SW Turkey
138 H12 **Bäyir** var. Bâ'ir. Ma'än, S Jordan
139 R5 **Bayji** var. Baiji. N Iraq
Baykadam see Saudakent
123 N13 **Baykal, Ozero** Eng. Lake Baikal. ⬚ S Russian Federation
123 M14 **Baykal'sk** Irkutskaya Oblast', S Russian Federation
137 R15 **Baykan** Siirt, SE Turkey
123 L11 **Baykit** Evenkiyskiy Avtonomnyy Okrug, C Russian Federation
145 N12 **Baykonur** var Baykonyr. Karaganda, C Kazakhstan
Baykonur see Baykonyr
144 M14 **Baykonyr** var Baykonur, Kaz Bayqongyr; prev. Leninsk. Kyzylorda, S Kazakhstan
Baykonyr see Baykonur
158 E7 **Baykurt** Xinjiang Uygur Zizhiqu, W China
14 I9 **Bay, Lac** ⬚ Québec, SE Canada
127 W6 **Baymak** Respublika Bashkortostan, W Russian Federation
23 O8 **Bay Minette** Alabama, S USA
143 O17 **Baynünah** desert W United Arab Emirates
184 O8 **Bay of Plenty** off. Bay of Plenty Region. ◆ region North Island, New Zealand
Bay of Plenty Region see Bay of Plenty
191 Z3 **Bay of Wrecks** bay Kiritimati, E Kiribati
Bayonnaise Rocks see Beyonēsu-retsugan
102 I15 **Bayonne** anc. Lapurdum. Pyrénées-Atlantiques, SW France
22 H4 **Bayou D'Arbonne Lake** ⬚ Louisiana, S USA
23 N9 **Bayou La Batre** Alabama, S USA
Bayou State see Mississippi
Bayqadam see Saudakent
Bayqongyr see Baykonyr
146 J14 **Baýramaly** var. Bayramaly; prev. Bayram-Ali. Mary Welayaty, S Turkmenistan
101 L19 **Bayreuth** var. Baireuth. Bayern, SE Germany
Bayrische Alpen see Bavarian Alps
Bayrüt see Beyrouth
22 L9 **Bay Saint Louis** Mississippi, S USA
Baysän see Bet She'an
Bayshint see Öndörshireet
22 M6 **Bay Springs** Mississippi, S USA
Bay State see Massachusetts
Baysun see Boysun
14 H13 **Baysville** Ontario, S Canada
141 N15 **Bayt al Faqïh** W Yemen
158 M4 **Baytik Shan** ▲ China/Mongolia
Bayt Lahm see Bethlehem
169 V11 **Bayur, Tanjung** cape Borneo, N Indonesia
121 N14 **Bay'al Kabïr, Wädï** dry watercourse NW Libya
Bayyrqum see Bairkum
105 P14 **Baza** Andalucía, S Spain
137 X10 **Bazardüzü Dağ** Rus. Gora Bazardyuzyu. ▲ N Azerbaijan
Bazardüzü Dağı see Bazardyuzyu, Gora
83 N18 **Bazaruto, Ilha do** island SE Mozambique
102 K14 **Bazas** Gironde, SW France
105 O14 **Baza, Sierra de** ▲ S Spain
160 J8 **Bazhong** var Bazhou. Sichuan, C China
Bazhong see Batang
161 P3 **Bazhou** Ba Xian. Hebei, E China
Bazhou see Bazhong
14 M9 **Bazin** ⚡ Québec, SE Canada
Bazin see Pezinok
139 Q7 **Bäziyah** C Iraq
138 H6 **Bcharré** var. Bcharreh, Bsharri. NE Lebanon
Bcharreh see Bcharré

30 J13 **Bear Creek** ⚡ Illinois, N USA
195 Q10 **Beardmore Glacier** glacier Antarctica
27 U13 **Bearden** Arkansas, C USA
30 K13 **Beardstown** Illinois, N USA
28 L14 **Bear Hill** ▲ Nebraska, C USA
Bear Island see Bjørnøya
14 H12 **Bear Lake** Ontario, S Canada
36 M1 **Bear Lake** ⬚ Idaho/Utah, NW USA
39 U11 **Bear, Mount** ▲ Alaska, USA
102 J16 **Béarn** cultural region SW France
194 J11 **Bear Peninsula** peninsula Antarctica
152 I7 **Beäs** ⚡ India/Pakistan
105 P3 **Beasain** País Vasco, N Spain
105 O12 **Beas de Segura** Andalucía, S Spain
45 N10 **Beata, Cabo** headland SW Dominican Republic
45 N10 **Beata, Isla** island SW Dominican Republic
64 F11 **Beata Ridge** undersea feature N Caribbean Sea
29 R7 **Beatrice** Nebraska, C USA
83 L16 **Beatrice** Mashonaland East, NE Zimbabwe
9 N11 **Beatton** ⚡ British Columbia, W Canada
9 N11 **Beatton River** British Columbia, W Canada
35 V10 **Beatty** Nevada, W USA
21 N6 **Beattyville** Kentucky, S USA
173 X16 **Beau Bassin** W Mauritius
103 R15 **Beaucaire** Gard, S France
14 I8 **Beauchastel, Lac** ⬚ Québec, SE Canada
14 I10 **Beauchêne, Lac** ⬚ Québec, SE Canada
65 J24 **Beauchene Island** island S Falkland Islands
182 M12 **Beaufort** Victoria, SE Australia
21 X11 **Beaufort** North Carolina, SE USA
21 R15 **Beaufort** South Carolina, SE USA
38 M11 **Beaufort Sea** sea Arctic Ocean
Beaufort-Wes see Beaufort West
83 G25 **Beaufort West** Afr. Beaufort-Wes. Western Cape, SW South Africa
103 N7 **Beaugency** Loiret, C France
19 R1 **Beau Lake** ⬚ Maine, NE USA
96 I8 **Beauly** N Scotland, UK
99 G21 **Beaumont** Hainaut, S Belgium
185 E23 **Beaumont** Otago, South Island, New Zealand
22 M7 **Beaumont** Mississippi, S USA
25 X10 **Beaumont** Texas, SW USA
102 M15 **Beaumont-de-Lomagne** Tarn-et-Garonne, S France
102 L6 **Beaumont-sur-Sarthe** Sarthe, NW France
103 R8 **Beaune** Côte d'Or, C France
102 J8 **Beaupréau** Maine-et-Loire, NW France
15 R9 **Beaupré** Québec, SE Canada
99 I22 **Beauraing** Namur, SE Belgium
103 R12 **Beaurepaire** Isère, E France
9 Y16 **Beauséjour** Manitoba, S Canada
103 N4 **Beauvais** anc. Bellovacum, Caesaromagus. Oise, N France
9 S13 **Beauval** Saskatchewan, C Canada
102 I9 **Beauvoir-sur-Mer** Vendée, NW France
39 R8 **Beaver** Alaska, USA
26 J8 **Beaver** Oklahoma, C USA
18 B14 **Beaver** Pennsylvania, NE USA
36 L5 **Beaver** Utah, W USA
10 L9 **Beaver** ⚡ British Columbia/Yukon Territory, W Canada
9 S13 **Beaver** ⚡ Saskatchewan, C Canada
29 N17 **Beaver City** Nebraska, C USA
10 G6 **Beaver Creek** Yukon Territory, W Canada
31 R14 **Beavercreek** Ohio, S USA
39 S8 **Beaver Creek** ⚡ Alaska, USA
28 H3 **Beaver Creek** ⚡ Kansas/Nebraska, C USA
28 J5 **Beaver Creek** ⚡ Montana/North Dakota, N USA
29 Q8 **Beaver Creek** ⚡ Nebraska, C USA
25 Q4 **Beaver Creek** ⚡ Texas, SW USA
31 O8 **Beaver Dam** Wisconsin, N USA
30 M8 **Beaver Dam Lake** ⬚ Wisconsin, N USA
18 B14 **Beaver Falls** Pennsylvania, NE USA
33 O7 **Beaverhead Mountains** ▲ Idaho/Montana, NW USA
33 Q12 **Beaverhead River** ⚡ Montana, NW USA
65 A25 **Beaver Island** island W Falkland Islands
31 P5 **Beaver Island** island Michigan, N USA
9 N13 **Beaverlodge** Alberta, W Canada
18 H14 **Beaver River** ⚡ New York, NE USA
26 J9 **Beaver River** ⚡ Oklahoma, C USA
18 B13 **Beaver River** ⚡ Pennsylvania, NE USA
65 A25 **Beaver Settlement** Beaver Island, E Falkland Islands
Beaver State see Oregon
14 H14 **Beaverton** Ontario, S Canada
32 G11 **Beaverton** Oregon, NW USA
152 G12 **Beäwar** Räjasthän, N India
60 K9 **Bebas, Dasht-i** see Bäbüs, Dasht-e
60 L8 **Bebedouro** São Paulo, S Brazil
101 I16 **Bebra** Hessen, C Germany
41 W12 **Becal** Campeche, SE Mexico
15 O11 **Bécancour** ⚡ Québec, SE Canada
97 Q19 **Beccles** E England, UK
112 L9 **Bečej** Ger. Altbetsche, Hung. Óbecse, Rácz-Becse; prev. Magyar-Becse, Stari Bečej. Vojvodina, N Serbia
104 I3 **Becerreá** Galicia, NW Spain
74 H7 **Béchar** prev. Colomb-Béchar. W Algeria
39 O14 **Becharof Lake** ⬚ Alaska, USA

◆ Country ◇ Dependent Territory ▲ Administrative Regions ▲ Mountain 🌋 Volcano ⬚ Lake
● Country Capital ○ Dependent Territory Capital ✕ International Airport ▲▲ Mountain Range ⚡ River ⬚ Reservoir

224

BECHET – BERDSK

116 H15 **Bechet** var. Bechetu. Dolj, SW Romania
Bechetu see Bechet
21 R6 **Beckley** West Virginia, NE USA
101 G14 **Beckum** Nordrhein-Westfalen, W Germany
25 X7 **Beckville** Texas, SW USA
35 X4 **Becky Peak** ▲ Nevada, W USA
116 I9 **Beclean** Hung. Bethlen; prev. Betlen. Bistriţa-Năsăud, N Romania
Bécs see Wien
111 H18 **Bečva** Ger. Betschau, Pol. Beczwa. ≈ E Czech Republic
Beczwa see Bečva
103 P15 **Bédarieux** Hérault, S France
120 B10 **Beddouza, Cap** headland W Morocco
80 I13 **Bedelē** Oromo, C Ethiopia
147 Y8 **Bedel Pass** Rus. Pereval Bedel. pass China/Kyrgyzstan
Bedel, Pereval see Bedel Pass
95 H22 **Beder** Århus, C Denmark
97 N20 **Bedford** E England, UK
31 O15 **Bedford** Indiana, N USA
29 U16 **Bedford** Iowa, C USA
20 L4 **Bedford** Kentucky, S USA
18 D15 **Bedford** Pennsylvania, NE USA
21 T6 **Bedford** Virginia, NE USA
97 N20 **Bedfordshire** cultural region E England, UK
127 N5 **Bednodem'yanovsk** Penzenskaya Oblast', W Russian Federation
98 N5 **Bedum** Groningen, NE Netherlands
27 V11 **Beebe** Arkansas, C USA
Beechy Group see Chichijima-rettō
45 T9 **Beef Island** ✈ (Road Town)Tortola, E British Virgin Islands
Beehive State see Utah
99 L18 **Beek** Limburg, SE Netherlands
99 L18 **Beek** ✈ (Maastricht) Limburg, SE Netherlands
99 K14 **Beek-en-Donk** Noord-Brabant, S Netherlands
138 F13 **Be'er Menuha** var Be'er Menukha. Southern, S Israel
Be'erMenukha see Be'er Menuha
99 D16 **Beernem** West-Vlaanderen, NW Belgium
99 I16 **Beerse** Antwerpen, N Belgium
Beersheba see Be'ér Sheva'
138 E11 **Be'ér Sheva'** var. Beersheba, Ar. Bir es Saba. Southern, S Israel
98 J13 **Beesd** Gelderland, C Netherlands
99 M16 **Beesel** Limburg, SE Netherlands
83 J21 **Beestekraal** North-West, N South Africa
194 J7 **Beethoven Peninsula** peninsula Alexander Island, Antarctica
Beetstersweach see Beetsterzwaag
98 M6 **Beetsterzwaag** Fris. Beetstersweach. Friesland, N Netherlands
25 S13 **Beeville** Texas, SW USA
79 J18 **Befale** Equateur, NW Dem. Rep. Congo
Befandriana see Befandriana Avaratra
172 J3 **Befandriana Avaratra** var. Befandriana, Befandriana Nord. Mahajanga, NW Madagascar
Befandriana Nord see Befandriana Avaratra
79 K18 **Befori** Equateur, N Dem. Rep. Congo
172 I7 **Befotaka** Fianarantsoa, S Madagascar
183 R11 **Bega** New South Wales, SE Australia
102 G5 **Bégard** Côtes d'Armor, NW France
112 M9 **Begejski Kanal** canal Vojvodina, NE Serbia
94 G13 **Begna** ≈ S Norway
Begoml' see Byahoml'
Begovat see Bekobod
153 Q13 **Begusarai** Bihār, NE India
143 R9 **Behābād** Yazd, C Iran
Behagle see Laï
55 Z10 **Béhague, Pointe** headland E French Guiana
Behar see Bihār
142 M10 **Behbahān** var. Behbehān. Khūzestān, SW Iran
Behbehān see Behbahān
44 G3 **Behring Point** Andros Island, W Bahamas
143 P4 **Behshahr** prev. Ashraf. Māzandarān, N Iran
163 V6 **Bei'an** Heilongjiang, NE China
Beibunar see Sredishte
Beibu Wan see Tongking, Gulf of
Beida see Al Bayḍā'
80 H13 **Beigi** Oromo, C Ethiopia
160 L16 **Beihai** Guangxi Zhuangzu Zizhiqu, S China
159 Q10 **Bei Hulsan Hu** ◎ C China
161 N13 **Bei Jiang** ≈ S China
161 O2 **Beijing** var. Pei-ching, Eng. Peking; prev. Pei-p'ing. ● Beijing Shi, E China
161 P2 **Beijing** ✈ Beijing Shi, E China
Beijing see Beijing Shi, China
161 O2 **Beijing Shi** var. Beijing, Jing, Pei-ching, Eng. Peking; prev. Pei-p'ing. ◈ municipality E China
76 G8 **Beïla** Trarza, W Mauritania
98 N7 **Beilen** Drenthe, NE Netherlands
160 L15 **Beiliu** var Lingcheng. Guangxi Zhuangzu Zizhiqu, S China
159 O12 **Beilu He** ≈ W China
Beilul see Beylul
163 U12 **Beining** prev. Beizhen. Liaoning, NE China
96 H8 **Beinn Dearg** ▲ N Scotland, UK
Beinn MacDuibh see Ben Macdui
160 I12 **Beipan Jiang** ≈ S China
163 T12 **Beipiao** Liaoning, NE China
83 N17 **Beira** Sofala, C Mozambique
83 N17 **Beira** ✈ Sofala, C Mozambique
104 I7 **Beira Alta** former province N Portugal
104 H9 **Beira Baixa** former province C Portugal
104 G8 **Beira Litoral** former province N Portugal
Beirut see Beyrouth
Beisān see Bet She'an
9 Q16 **Beiseker** Alberta, SW Canada
Beitai Ding see Wutai Shan
83 K19 **Beitbridge** Matabeleland South, S Zimbabwe
116 G10 **Beiuş** Hung. Belényes. Bihor, NW Romania
Beizhen see Beining
104 H12 **Beja** anc. Pax Julia. Beja, SE Portugal
74 M5 **Béja** var. Bājah. N Tunisia
104 G13 **Beja** ◈ district S Portugal
120 I9 **Béjaïa** var. Bejaïa, Fr. Bougie; anc. Saldae. NE Algeria
Bejaïa see Béjaïa
104 K8 **Béjar** Castilla-León, N Spain
Bejraburi see Phetchaburi
Bekaa Valley see El Beqaa
Bekabad see Bekobod
Békás see Bicaz
169 O15 **Bekasi** Jawa, C Indonesia
Bek-Budi see Qarshi
Bekdaş/Bekdash see Garabogaz
147 T10 **Bek-Dzhar** Oshskaya Oblast', SW Kyrgyzstan
111 N24 **Békés** Rom. Bichiş. Békés, SE Hungary
111 M24 **Békés** off. Békés Megye. ◈ county SE Hungary
111 M24 **Békéscsaba** Rom. Bichiş-Ciaba. Békés, SE Hungary
Békés Megye see Békés
139 S2 **Bēkhma** E Iraq
172 H7 **Bekily** Toliara, S Madagascar
165 W4 **Bekkai** Hokkaidō, NE Japan
147 Q11 **Bekobod** Rus. Bekabad; prev. Begovat. Toshkent Viloyati, E Uzbekistan
127 O7 **Bekovo** Penzenskaya Oblast', W Russian Federation
Bel see Beliu
152 M13 **Bela** Uttar Pradesh, N India
149 N15 **Bela** Baluchistān, SW Pakistan
79 F15 **Bélabo** Est, C Cameroon
112 N10 **Bela Crkva** Ger. Weisskirchen, Hung. Fehértemplom. Vojvodina, W Serbia
173 Y16 **Bel Air** var. Rivière Sèche. E Mauritius
104 L12 **Belalcázar** Andalucía, S Spain
113 P15 **Bela Palanka** Serbia, SE Serbia
119 H16 **Belarus** off. Republic of Belarus, var. Belorussia, Latv. Baltkrievija; prev. Belorussian SSR, Rus. Belorusskaya SSR. ◆ republic E Europe
Belarus, Republic of see Belarus
Belau see Palau
59 H21 **Bela Vista** Mato Grosso do Sul, SW Brazil
83 L21 **Bela Vista** Maputo, S Mozambique
168 I8 **Belawan** Sumatera, W Indonesia
Běla Woda see Weisswasser
127 U4 **Belaya** ≈ W Russian Federation
123 R7 **Belaya Gora** Respublika Sakha (Yakutiya), NE Russian Federation
126 M11 **Belaya Kalitiva** Rostovskaya Oblast', SW Russian Federation
125 R14 **Belaya Kholunitsa** Kirovskaya Oblast', NW Russian Federation
Belaya Tserkov' see Bila Tserkva
77 V11 **Belbédji** Zinder, S Niger
110 K13 **Bełchatów** var. Belchatow. Łódzski, C Poland
Belchatow see Bełchatów
Belcher, Îles see Belcher Islands
12 H7 **Belcher Islands** Fr. Îles Belcher. island group Nunavut, SE Canada
105 S6 **Belchite** Aragón, NE Spain
29 O2 **Belcourt** North Dakota, N USA
31 P9 **Belding** Michigan, N USA
127 U5 **Belebey** Respublika Bashkortostan, W Russian Federation
81 N16 **Beledweyne** var. Belet Huen, It. Belet Uen. Hiiraan, C Somalia
146 B10 **Belek** Balkan Welaýaty, W Turkmenistan
58 L12 **Belém** var. Pará. state capital Pará, N Brazil
65 I14 **Belém Ridge** undersea feature C Atlantic Ocean
62 I7 **Belén** Catamarca, NW Argentina
54 E6 **Belén** Boyacá, C Colombia
42 J11 **Belén** Rivas, SW Nicaragua
62 O5 **Belén** Concepción, C Paraguay
61 D16 **Belén** Salto, N Uruguay
37 R12 **Belen** New Mexico, SW USA
61 D20 **Belén de Escobar** Buenos Aires, E Argentina
114 J7 **Belene** Pleven, N Bulgaria
114 J7 **Belene, Ostrov** island N Bulgaria
43 R15 **Belén, Río** ≈ C Panama
Belényes see Beiuş
Embalse de Belesar see Belesar, Encoro de
104 H3 **Belesar, Encoro de** Sp. Embalse de Belesar. ⊠ NW Spain
Belet Huen/Belet Uen see Beledweyne
126 J5 **Belëv** Tul'skaya Oblast', W Russian Federation
19 R7 **Belfast** Maine, NE USA
97 G15 **Belfast** Ir. Béal Feirste. ● E Northern Ireland, UK
97 G15 **Belfast** ✈ E Northern Ireland, UK
97 G15 **Belfast Lough** Ir. Loch Lao. inlet E Northern Ireland, UK
28 K5 **Belfield** North Dakota, N USA
103 U7 **Belfort** Territoire-de-Belfort, E France
Belgard see Białogard
155 E17 **Belgaum** Karnātaka, W India
Belgian Congo see Congo (Democratic Republic of)
195 T3 **Belgica Mountains** ▲▲ Antarctica
België/Belgique see Belgium
99 F20 **Belgium** off. Kingdom of Belgium, Dut. België, Fr. Belgique. ◆ monarchy NW Europe
Belgium, Kingdom of see Belgium
126 J8 **Belgorod** Belgorodskaya Oblast', W Russian Federation
Belgorod-Dnestrovskiy see Bilhorod-Dnistrovs'kyy
126 J8 **Belgorodskaya Oblast'** ◈ province W Russian Federation
Belgrad see Beograd
29 T8 **Belgrade** Minnesota, N USA
33 S11 **Belgrade** Montana, NW USA
Belgrade see Beograd
Belgrano, Cabo see Meredith, Cape
195 N5 **Belgrano II** Argentinian research station Antarctica
21 X9 **Belhaven** North Carolina, SE USA
107 I23 **Belice** anc. Hypsas. ≈ Sicilia, Italy, C Mediterranean Sea
Belice see Belize/Belize City
113 M16 **Beli Drim** Alb. Drini i Bardhë. ≈ Albania/Serbia
Beligrad see Berat
188 C8 **Beliliou** prev. Peleliu. island S Palau
114 L8 **Beli Lom, Yazovir** ⊠ NE Bulgaria
112 I8 **Beli Manastir** Hung. Pélmonostor; prev. Monostor. Osijek-Baranja, NE Croatia
102 J13 **Bélin-Béliet** Gironde, SW France
79 F17 **Bélinga** Ogooué-Ivindo, NE Gabon
21 S4 **Belington** West Virginia, NE USA
127 O6 **Belinskiy** Penzenskaya Oblast', W Russian Federation
169 N12 **Belinyu** Pulau Bangka, W Indonesia
169 O13 **Belitung, Pulau** island W Indonesia
116 F10 **Beliu** Hung. Bel. Arad, W Romania
114 I9 **Beli Vit** ≈ NW Bulgaria
42 G2 **Belize** Sp. Belice; prev. British Honduras, Colony of Belize. ◆ commonwealth republic Central America
42 F2 **Belize** Sp. Belice. ◈ district NE Belize
42 G2 **Belize** ≈ Belize/Guatemala
Belize see Belize City
42 G2 **Belize City** Sp. Belice. Belize, NE Belize
42 G2 **Belize City** ✈ Belize, NE Belize
Belize, Colony of see Belize
Beljak see Villach
39 N16 **Belkofski** Alaska, USA
123 O6 **Bel'kovskiy, Ostrov** island Novosibirskiye Ostrova, NE Russian Federation
14 J8 **Bell** ≈ Québec, SE Canada
10 J15 **Bella Bella** British Columbia, SW Canada
102 M10 **Bellac** Haute-Vienne, C France
10 K15 **Bella Coola** British Columbia, SW Canada
106 D6 **Bellagio** Lombardia, N Italy
31 P6 **Bellaire** Michigan, N USA
106 D6 **Bellano** Lombardia, N Italy
155 G17 **Bellary** var. Ballari. Karnātaka, S India
183 S5 **Bellata** New South Wales, SE Australia
61 D16 **Bella Unión** Artigas, N Uruguay
61 C14 **Bella Vista** Corrientes, NE Argentina
62 J7 **Bella Vista** Tucumán, N Argentina
62 P4 **Bella Vista** Amambay, C Paraguay
56 B10 **Bellavista** Cajamarca, N Peru
56 D11 **Bellavista** San Martín, N Peru
183 U6 **Bellbrook** New South Wales, SE Australia
27 V5 **Belle** Missouri, C USA
21 Q5 **Belle** West Virginia, NE USA
31 R13 **Bellefontaine** Ohio, N USA
18 F14 **Bellefonte** Pennsylvania, NE USA
28 J9 **Belle Fourche** South Dakota, N USA
28 J9 **Belle Fourche Reservoir** ⊠ South Dakota, N USA
28 K9 **Belle Fourche River** ≈ South Dakota/Wyoming, N USA
103 S10 **Bellegarde-sur-Valserine** Ain, E France
23 Y14 **Belle Glade** Florida, SE USA
102 G8 **Belle Île** island NW France
13 T9 **Belle Isle** island Belle Isle, Newfoundland and Labrador, E Canada
13 S10 **Belle Isle, Strait of** strait Newfoundland and Labrador, E Canada
Bellenz see Bellinzona
29 W14 **Belle Plaine** Iowa, C USA
29 V9 **Belle Plaine** Minnesota, N USA
14 I9 **Belleterre** Québec, SE Canada
14 J15 **Belleville** Ontario, SE Canada
103 R10 **Belleville** Rhône, E France
30 K15 **Belleville** Illinois, N USA
27 N3 **Belleville** Kansas, C USA
29 Z13 **Bellevue** Iowa, C USA
29 S15 **Bellevue** Nebraska, C USA
31 S11 **Bellevue** Ohio, N USA
25 S5 **Bellevue** Texas, SW USA
32 H8 **Bellevue** Washington, NW USA
55 Y11 **Bellevue de l'Inini, Montagnes** ▲▲ S French Guiana
103 S11 **Belley** Ain, E France
Bellin see Kangirsuk
183 V6 **Bellingen** New South Wales, SE Australia
97 L14 **Bellingham** N England, UK
32 H6 **Bellingham** Washington, NW USA
Belling Hausen Mulde see Southeast Pacific Basin
194 H2 **Bellingshausen** Russian research station South Shetland Islands, Antarctica
Bellingshausen see Motu One
Bellingshausen Abyssal Plain see Bellingshausen Plain
196 R14 **Bellingshausen Plain** var. Bellingshausen Abyssal Plain. undersea feature SE Pacific Ocean
194 I8 **Bellingshausen Sea** sea Antarctica
98 P6 **Bellingwolde** Groningen, NE Netherlands
108 H11 **Bellinzona** Ger. Bellenz. Ticino, S Switzerland
25 T8 **Bellmead** Texas, SW USA
54 E8 **Bello** Antioquia, W Colombia
61 B21 **Bellocq** Buenos Aires, E Argentina
Bello Horizonte see Belo Horizonte
186 L10 **Bellona** var. Mungiki. island S Solomon Islands
Bellovacum see Beauvais
182 D7 **Bell, Point** headland South Australia
20 F9 **Bells** Tennessee, S USA
25 U5 **Bells** Texas, SW USA
92 N3 **Bellsund** inlet SW Svalbard
106 H6 **Belluno** Veneto, NE Italy
62 L11 **Bell Ville** Córdoba, C Argentina
83 E26 **Bellville** Western Cape, SW South Africa
25 U11 **Bellville** Texas, SW USA
104 L12 **Belmez** Andalucía, S Spain
29 V12 **Belmond** Iowa, C USA
18 E11 **Belmont** New York, NE USA
21 R10 **Belmont** North Carolina, SE USA
59 O18 **Belmonte** Bahia, E Brazil
104 I8 **Belmonte** Castelo Branco, C Portugal
105 P10 **Belmonte** Castilla-La Mancha, C Spain
42 G2 **Belmopan** ● (Belize) Cayo, C Belize
97 B16 **Belmullet** Ir. Béal an Mhuirhead. Mayo, W Ireland
99 E20 **Belœil** Hainaut, SW Belgium
123 R13 **Belogorsk** Amurskaya Oblast', SE Russian Federation
Belogorsk see Bilohirs'k
114 F7 **Belogradchik** Vidin, NW Bulgaria
172 H8 **Beloha** Toliara, S Madagascar
59 M20 **Belo Horizonte** prev. Bello Horizonte. state capital Minas Gerais, SE Brazil
26 M3 **Beloit** Kansas, C USA
30 L9 **Beloit** Wisconsin, N USA
Belokorovichi see Bilokorovychi
124 J8 **Belomorsk** Respublika Kareliya, NW Russian Federation
124 J8 **Belomorsko-Baltiyskiy Kanal** Eng. White Sea-Baltic Canal, White Sea Canal. canal NW Russian Federation
153 V15 **Belonia** Tripura, NE India
Beloozersk see Byelaazyorsk
Belopol'ye see Bilopillya
105 O4 **Belorado** Castilla-León, N Spain
126 L14 **Belorechensk** Krasnodarskiy Kray, SW Russian Federation
127 W5 **Beloretsk** Respublika Bashkortostan, W Russian Federation
Belorussia/Belorussian SSR see Belarus
Belorusskaya Gryada see Byelaruskaya Hrada
Belorusskaya SSR see Belarus
Beloshchel'ye see Nar'yan-Mar
114 N8 **Beloslav** Varna, E Bulgaria
Belostok see Białystok
Belo-sur-Tsiribihina see Belo Tsiribihina
172 H5 **Belo Tsiribihina** var. Belo-sur-Tsiribihina. Toliara, W Madagascar
Belovár see Bjelovar
Belovezhskaya, Pushcha see Białowieska, Puszcza/Byelavyezhskaya, Pushcha
114 H10 **Belovo** Pazardzhik, C Bulgaria
Belovodsk see Bilovods'k
122 H9 **Beloyarskiy** Khanty-Mansiyskiy Avtonomnyy Okrug, N Russian Federation
124 K7 **Beloye More** Eng. White Sea. sea NW Russian Federation
124 K13 **Beloye, Ozero** ◎ NW Russian Federation
114 J10 **Belozem** Plovdiv, C Bulgaria
124 K13 **Belozërsk** Vologodskaya Oblast', NW Russian Federation
108 D8 **Belp** Bern, W Switzerland
108 D8 **Belp** ✈ (Bern) Bern, C Switzerland
107 L24 **Belpasso** Sicilia, Italy, C Mediterranean Sea
31 U14 **Belpre** Ohio, N USA
98 M8 **Belterwijde** ◎ N Netherlands
27 R4 **Belton** Missouri, C USA
21 P11 **Belton** South Carolina, SE USA
25 T9 **Belton** Texas, SW USA
25 S9 **Belton Lake** ⊠ Texas, SW USA
Bel'tsy see Bălţi
97 E16 **Belturbet** Ir. Béal Tairbirt. Cavan, N Ireland
Beluchistan see Baluchistān
145 Z9 **Belukha, Gora** ▲ Kazakhstan/Russian Federation
107 M20 **Belvedere Marittimo** Calabria, SW Italy
30 L10 **Belvidere** Illinois, N USA
18 J14 **Belvidere** New Jersey, NE USA
Bely see Belyy
127 V8 **Belyayevka** Orenburgskaya Oblast', W Russian Federation
Belynichi see Byalynichy
124 H17 **Belyy** var. Bely, Beyj. Tverskaya Oblast', W Russian Federation
126 I6 **Belyye Berega** Bryanskaya Oblast', W Russian Federation
122 J6 **Belyy, Ostrov** island N Russian Federation
122 J11 **Belyy Yar** Tomskaya Oblast', C Russian Federation
100 N13 **Belzig** Brandenburg, NE Germany
22 K4 **Belzoni** Mississippi, S USA
172 H4 **Bemaraha** var. Plateau du Bemaraha. ▲▲ W Madagascar
Bemaraha, Plateau du see Bemaraha
82 B10 **Bembe** Uíge, NW Angola
77 S14 **Bembèrèkè** var. Bimbéréké. N Benin
104 K12 **Bembézar** ≈ SW Spain
104 J3 **Bembibre** Castilla-León, N Spain
29 T4 **Bemidji** Minnesota, N USA
98 L12 **Bemmel** Gelderland, SE Netherlands
171 T13 **Bemu** Pulau Seram, E Indonesia
Benāb see Bonāb
105 T5 **Benabarre** var. Benavarn. Aragón, NE Spain
Benaco see Garda, Lago di
79 L20 **Bena-Dibele** Kasai Oriental, C Dem. Rep. Congo
105 R9 **Benageber, Embalse de** ⊠ E Spain
183 O11 **Benalla** Victoria, SE Australia
104 M14 **Benamejí** Andalucía, S Spain
Benares see Vārānasi
Benavarn see Benabarre
104 F10 **Benavente** Santarém, C Portugal
104 K5 **Benavente** Castilla-León, N Spain
25 S15 **Benavides** Texas, SW USA
96 F8 **Benbecula** island NW Scotland, UK
Bencovazzo see Benkovac
32 H13 **Bend** Oregon, NW USA
182 K7 **Benda Range** ▲▲ South Australia
183 T6 **Bendemeer** New South Wales, SE Australia
Bender see Tighina
Bender Beila/Bender Beyla see Bandarbeyla
Bender Cassim see Bender Cassim/Bender Qaasim
Bendery see Tighina
183 N11 **Bendigo** Victoria, SE Australia
118 E10 **Bēne** Dobele, SW Latvia
98 K13 **Beneden-Leeuwen** Gelderland, C Netherlands
101 L24 **Benediktenwand** ▲ S Germany
Benemérita de San Cristóbal see San Cristóbal
77 N12 **Bénéna** Ségou, S Mali
172 I7 **Benenitra** Toliara, S Madagascar
Beneschau see Benešov
Beneški Zaliv see Venice, Gulf of
111 D17 **Benešov** Ger. Beneschau. Středočeský Kraj, W Czech Republic
123 Q5 **Benetta, Ostrov** island Novosibirskiye Ostrova, NE Russian Federation
107 L17 **Benevento** anc. Beneventum, Malventum. Campania, S Italy
Beneventum see Benevento
173 S3 **Bengal, Bay of** bay N Indian Ocean
79 M17 **Bengamisa** Orientale, N Dem. Rep. Congo
Bengasi see Banghāzī
Bengazi see Banghāzī
161 P7 **Bengbu** var. Peng-pu. Anhui, E China
32 L9 **Benge** Washington, NW USA
Benghazi see Banghāzī
168 K10 **Bengkalis** Pulau Bengkalis, W Indonesia
168 K10 **Bengkalis, Pulau** island W Indonesia
169 Q10 **Bengkayang** Borneo, C Indonesia
Bengkoeloe see Bengkulu
168 K14 **Bengkulu** prev. Bengkoeloe, Benkoelen, Benkulen. Sumatera, W Indonesia
168 K13 **Bengkulu** off. Propinsi Bengkulu; prev. Bengkoeloe, Benkoelen, Benkulen. ◈ province W Indonesia
Bengkulu, Propinsi see Bengkulu
82 A11 **Bengo** ◈ province W Angola
95 J16 **Bengtsfors** Västra Götaland, S Sweden
82 B13 **Benguela** var. Benguella. Benguela, W Angola
83 A14 **Benguela** ◈ province W Angola
Benguella see Benguela
Bengweulu, Lake see Bangweulu, Lake
121 V13 **Benha** var. Banhā. N Egypt
192 F6 **Benham Seamount** undersea feature W Philippine Sea
96 H6 **Ben Hope** ▲ N Scotland, UK
79 P18 **Beni** Nord Kivu, NE Dem. Rep. Congo
57 L15 **Beni** var. El Beni. ◈ department N Bolivia
74 H8 **Beni Abbès** W Algeria
105 T8 **Benicarló** País Valenciano, E Spain
105 T9 **Benicasim** cat Benicàssim. País Valenciano, E Spain
Benicàssim see Benicasim
105 T12 **Benidorm** País Valenciano, SE Spain
75 W9 **Beni Mazâr** var. Banī Mazār. C Egypt
121 C11 **Beni-Mellal** C Morocco
77 R14 **Benin** off. Republic of Benin; prev. Dahomey. ◆ republic W Africa
77 S17 **Benin, Bight of** gulf W Africa
77 U16 **Benin City** Edo, SW Nigeria
Benin, Republic of see Benin
57 K16 **Beni, Río** ≈ N Bolivia
120 F10 **Beni Saf** var. Beni-Saf. NW Algeria
Beni-Saf see Beni Saf
80 H12 **Benishangul** ◈ region W Ethiopia
105 T11 **Benissa** País Valenciano, E Spain
121 V14 **Beni Suef** var. Banī Suwayf. N Egypt
9 V15 **Benito** Manitoba, S Canada
Benito see Uolo, Río
61 C23 **Benito Juárez** Buenos Aires, E Argentina
41 P14 **Benito Juaréz Internacional** ✈ (México) México, S Mexico
25 P5 **Benjamin** Texas, SW USA
58 B13 **Benjamin Constant** Amazonas, N Brazil
40 F4 **Benjamín Hill** Sonora, NW Mexico
63 F19 **Benjamín, Isla** island Archipiélago de los Chonos, S Chile
164 Q4 **Benkei-misaki** headland Hokkaidō, NE Japan
28 L17 **Benkelman** Nebraska, C USA
96 I7 **Ben Klibreck** ▲ N Scotland, UK
Benkoelen see Bengkulu
Benkoelen/Bengkoeloe see Bengkulu
112 D13 **Benkovac** It. Bencovazzo. Zadar, SW Croatia
Benkulen see Bengkulu
96 I11 **Ben Lawers** ▲ C Scotland, UK
96 J9 **Ben Macdui** var. Beinn MacDuibh. ▲ C Scotland, UK
96 G11 **Ben More** ▲ W Scotland, UK
96 I11 **Ben More** ▲ C Scotland, UK
96 H7 **Ben More Assynt** ▲ N Scotland, UK
185 E20 **Benmore, Lake** ◎ South Island, New Zealand
98 L12 **Bennekom** Gelderland, SE Netherlands
21 T11 **Bennettsville** South Carolina, SE USA
96 H10 **Ben Nevis** ▲ N Scotland, UK
184 M9 **Benneydale** Waikato, North Island, New Zealand
Bennichab see Bennichchâb
76 H8 **Bennichchâb** var. Bennichab. Inchiri, W Mauritania
18 L10 **Bennington** Vermont, NE USA
185 E20 **Ben Ohau Range** ▲▲ South Island, New Zealand
83 J21 **Benoni** Gauteng, NE South Africa
172 J2 **Be, Nosy** var. Nossi-Bé. island NW Madagascar
Bénoué see Benue
42 F2 **Benque Viejo del Carmen** Cayo, W Belize
101 G19 **Bensheim** Hessen, W Germany
37 N16 **Benson** Arizona, SW USA
29 S8 **Benson** Minnesota, N USA
21 U10 **Benson** North Carolina, SE USA
171 N15 **Benteng** Pulau Selayar, C Indonesia
83 A14 **Bentiaba** Namibe, SW Angola
181 T4 **Bentinck Island** island Wellesley Islands, Queensland, N Australia
80 E13 **Bentiu** Wahda, S Sudan
138 G8 **Bent Jbaïl** var. Bint Jubayl. S Lebanon
9 Q15 **Bentley** Alberta, SW Canada
61 I15 **Bento Gonçalves** Rio Grande do Sul, S Brazil
27 U12 **Benton** Arkansas, C USA
30 L16 **Benton** Illinois, N USA
20 H7 **Benton** Kentucky, S USA
22 G5 **Benton** Louisiana, S USA
27 Y7 **Benton** Missouri, C USA
20 M10 **Benton** Tennessee, S USA
31 O10 **Benton Harbor** Michigan, N USA
27 S9 **Bentonville** Arkansas, C USA
77 V16 **Benue** ◈ state SE Nigeria
78 F13 **Benue** Fr. Bénoué. ≈ Cameroon/Nigeria
163 V12 **Benxi** prev. Pen-ch'i, Penhsihu, Penki. Liaoning, NE China
112 K10 **Beočin** Vojvodina, N Serbia
Beodericsworth see Bury St Edmunds
112 M11 **Beograd** Eng. Belgrade, Ger. Belgrad; anc. Singidunum. ● (Serbia) Serbia, N Serbia
112 L11 **Beograd** Eng. Belgrade. ✈ Serbia, N Serbia
112 L11 **Beograd** ✈ Serbia, N Serbia and Montenegro
76 M16 **Béoumi** C Ivory Coast
35 V3 **Beowawe** Nevada, W USA
164 E14 **Beppu** Ōita, Kyūshū, SW Japan
187 X15 **Beqa** prev. Mbengga. island W Fiji
45 Y14 **Bequia** island C Saint Vincent and the Grenadines
113 L16 **Berane** prev. Ivangrad. E Montenegro
113 L21 **Berat** var. Berati, SCr. Beligrad. Berat, C Albania
113 L21 **Berat** ◈ district C Albania
Berătău see Berettyó
Berati see Berat
Beraun see Berounka, Czech Republic
Beraun see Beroun, Czech Republic
171 U13 **Berau, Teluk** var. MacCluer Gulf. bay Papua, E Indonesia
80 G8 **Berber** River Nile, NE Sudan
80 N12 **Berbera** Sahil, NW Somalia
79 H16 **Berbérati** Mambéré-Kadéï, SW Central African Republic
Berberia, Cabo de see Barbaria, Cap de
55 T9 **Berbice River** ≈ NE Guyana
Berchid see Berrechid
103 N2 **Berck-Plage** Pas-de-Calais, N France
25 T13 **Berclair** Texas, SW USA
117 W10 **Berda** ≈ SE Ukraine
Berdichev see Berdychiv
123 P10 **Berdigestyakh** Respublika Sakha (Yakutiya), NE Russian Federation
122 J12 **Berdsk** Novosibirskaya Oblast', C Russian Federation

◆ Country
● Country Capital
◇ Dependent Territory
○ Dependent Territory Capital
◈ Administrative Regions
✈ International Airport
▲ Mountain
▲▲ Mountain Range
Volcano
≈ River
◎ Lake
⊠ Reservoir

Berdyans'k – Bikin

117 W10 **Berdyans'k** *Rus.* Berdyansk; *prev.* Osipenko. Zaporiz'ka Oblast', SE Ukraine
117 W10 **Berdyans'ka Kosa** *spit* SE Ukraine
117 V10 **Berdyans'ka Zatoka** *gulf* S Ukraine
117 N5 **Berdychiv** *Rus.* Berdichev. Zhytomyrs'ka Oblast', N Ukraine
20 M6 **Berea** Kentucky, S USA
Beregovo/Beregszász *see* Berehove
116 G8 **Berehove** *Cz.* Berehovo, *Hung.* Beregszász, *Rus.* Beregovo. Zakarpats'ka Oblast', W Ukraine
Berehovo *see* Berehove
186 D9 **Bereina** Central, S Papua New Guinea
146 C11 **Bereket** *prev. Rus.* Gazandzhyk, Kazandzhik, *Turkm.* Gazanjyk. Balkan Welaýaty, W Turkmenistan
45 O12 **Berekua** S Dominica
77 O16 **Berekum** W Ghana
75 Y11 **Berenice** *var.* Minâ Baranîs. SE Egypt
9 O14 **Berens** ≈ Manitoba/Ontario, C Canada
9 X14 **Berens River** Manitoba, C Canada
29 R12 **Beresford** South Dakota, N USA
116 J4 **Berestechko** Volyns'ka Oblast', NW Ukraine
116 M11 **Bereşti** Galaţi, E Romania
117 U6 **Berestova** ≈ E Ukraine
Beretău *see* Berettyó
111 N23 **Berettyó** *Rom.* Barcău; *prev.* Berătău, Beretău. ≈ Hungary/Romania
111 N23 **Berettyóújfalu** Hajdú-Bihar, E Hungary
Berëza/Bereza Kartuska *see* Byaroza
117 Q4 **Berezan'** Kyyivs'ka Oblast', N Ukraine
117 Q10 **Berezanka** Mykolayivs'ka Oblast', S Ukraine
116 J6 **Berezhany** *Pol.* Brzeżany. Ternopil's'ka Oblast', W Ukraine
Berezina *see* Byerezino
Berezino *see* Byerazino
117 P10 **Berezivka** *Rus.* Berezovka. Odes'ka Oblast', SW Ukraine
117 Q2 **Berezna** Chernihivs'ka Oblast', NE Ukraine
116 L3 **Berezne** Rivnens'ka Oblast', NW Ukraine
117 R9 **Bereznehuvate** Mykolayivs'ka Oblast', S Ukraine
125 N10 **Bereznik** Arkhangel'skaya Oblast', NW Russian Federation
125 U13 **Berezniki** Permskaya Oblast', NW Russian Federation
Berëzovka *see* Byarozawka, Belarus
Berezovka *see* Berezivka, Ukraine
122 H9 **Berezovo** Khanty-Mansiyskiy Avtonomnyy Okrug, N Russian Federation
127 O9 **Berezovskaya** Volgogradskaya Oblast', SW Russian Federation
123 S13 **Berezovyy** Khabarovskiy Kray, E Russian Federation
83 E25 **Berg** ≈ W South Africa
Berg *see* Berg bei Rohrbach
105 V4 **Berga** Cataluña, NE Spain
95 N20 **Berga** Kalmar, S Sweden
136 B13 **Bergama** İzmir, W Turkey
106 E7 **Bergamo** *anc.* Bergomum. Lombardia, N Italy
105 P3 **Bergara** País Vasco, N Spain
109 S3 **Berg bei Rohrbach** *var.* Berg. Oberösterreich, N Austria
100 O6 **Bergen** Mecklenburg-Vorpommern, NE Germany
101 I11 **Bergen** Niedersachsen, NW Germany
98 H8 **Bergen** Noord-Holland, NW Netherlands
94 C13 **Bergen** Hordaland, S Norway
Bergen *see* Mons
55 W9 **Berg en Dal** Brokopondo, C Surinam
99 G15 **Bergen op Zoom** Noord-Brabant, S Netherlands
102 L13 **Bergerac** Dordogne, SW France
99 J16 **Bergeyk** Noord-Brabant, S Netherlands
101 D16 **Bergheim** Nordrhein-Westfalen, W Germany
55 X10 **Bergi** Sipaliwini, E Surinam
101 E16 **Bergisch Gladbach** Nordrhein-Westfalen, W Germany
101 F14 **Bergkamen** Nordrhein-Westfalen, W Germany
95 N21 **Bergkvara** Kalmar, S Sweden
Bergomum *see* Bergamo
98 K13 **Bergse Maas** ≈ S Netherlands
95 P15 **Bergshamra** Stockholm, C Sweden
94 N10 **Bergsjö** Gävleborg, C Sweden
93 J14 **Bergsviken** Norrbotten, N Sweden
98 L6 **Bergum** *Fris.* Burgum. Friesland, N Netherlands
98 M6 **Bergumer Meer** ◎ N Netherlands
94 N12 **Bergviken** ◎ C Sweden
168 M11 **Berhala, Selat** *strait* Sumatera, W Indonesia
Berhampore *see* Baharampur
99 J17 **Beringen** Limburg, NE Belgium
39 T12 **Bering Glacier** *glacier* Alaska, USA
Beringov Proliv *see* Bering Strait
192 L2 **Bering Sea** *sea* N Pacific Ocean
38 L9 **Bering Strait** *Rus.* Beringov Proliv. *strait* Bering Sea/ Chukchi Sea
Berislav *see* Beryslav
105 O15 **Berja** Andalucía, S Spain
94 H9 **Berkåk** Sør-Trøndelag, S Norway
98 N11 **Berkel** ≈ Germany/Netherlands
35 N8 **Berkeley** California, W USA
65 E24 **Berkeley Sound** *sound* NE Falkland Islands
21 V2 **Berkeley Springs** *var.* Bath. West Virginia, NE USA
195 N6 **Berkner Island** *island* Antarctica
114 G8 **Berkovitsa** Montana, NW Bulgaria
97 M22 **Berkshire** *former county* S England, UK
99 H17 **Berlaar** Antwerpen, N Belgium
Berlanga *see* Berlanga de Duero
105 P6 **Berlanga de Duero** *var.* Berlanga. Castilla-León, N Spain
0 I16 **Berlanga Rise** *undersea feature* E Pacific Ocean
99 F17 **Berlare** Oost-Vlaanderen, NW Belgium
104 E9 **Berlenga, Ilha da** *island* C Portugal
92 M7 **Berlevåg** *Lapp.* Bearalváhki. Finnmark, N Norway
100 O12 **Berlin** ● Berlin, NE Germany
21 Z4 **Berlin** Maryland, NE USA
19 O7 **Berlin** New Hampshire, NE USA
18 D16 **Berlin** Pennsylvania, NE USA
30 L7 **Berlin** Wisconsin, N USA
100 O12 **Berlin** ◈ *state* NE Germany
Berlinchen *see* Barlinek
31 U12 **Berlin Lake** ⊠ Ohio, N USA
183 R11 **Bermagui** New South Wales, SE Australia
40 L8 **Bermejillo** Durango, C Mexico
62 L5 **Bermejo, Río** ≈ N Argentina
62 I10 **Bermejo, Río** ≈ W Argentina
62 M6 **Bermejo (viejo), Río** ≈ N Argentina
105 P2 **Bermeo** País Vasco, N Spain
104 K6 **Bermillo de Sayago** Castilla-León, N Spain
106 E6 **Bermina, Pizzo** *Rmsch.* Piz Bernina. ▲ Italy/Switzerland *see also* Bernina, Piz
Bermina, Pizzo *see* Bernina, Piz
64 A12 **Bermuda** *var.* Bermuda Islands, Bermudas; *prev.* Somers Islands. ◇ *UK crown colony* NW Atlantic Ocean
1 N11 **Bermuda** *var.* Great Bermuda, Long Island, Main Island. *island* Bermuda
Bermuda Islands *see* Bermuda
Bermuda-New England Seamount Arc *see* New England Seamounts
1 N11 **Bermuda Rise** *undersea feature* C Sargasso Sea
Bermudas *see* Bermuda
108 D8 **Bern** *Fr.* Berne. ● (Switzerland) Bern, W Switzerland
108 D9 **Bern** *Fr.* Berne. ◈ *canton* W Switzerland
37 R11 **Bernalillo** New Mexico, SW USA
14 H12 **Bernard Lake** ◎ Ontario, S Canada
61 B18 **Bernardo de Irigoyen** Santa Fe, NE Argentina
18 J14 **Bernardsville** New Jersey, NE USA
63 K14 **Bernasconi** La Pampa, C Argentina
100 O12 **Bernau** Brandenburg, NE Germany
102 L4 **Bernay** Eure, N France
101 L14 **Bernburg** Sachsen-Anhalt, C Germany
109 X5 **Berndorf** Niederösterreich, NE Austria
31 Q12 **Berne** Indiana, N USA
Berne *see* Bern
108 D10 **Berner Alpen** *var.* Berner Oberland, *Eng.* Bernese Oberland. ▲▲ SW Switzerland
Berner Oberland/Bernese Oberland *see* Berner Alpen
109 Y2 **Bernhardsthal** Niederösterreich, N Austria
22 H4 **Bernice** Louisiana, S USA
27 Y8 **Bernie** Missouri, C USA
180 G9 **Bernier Island** *island* Western Australia
Bernina Pass *see* Bernina, Passo del
108 J10 **Bernina, Passo del** *Eng.* Bernina Pass. *pass* SE Switzerland
108 J10 **Bernina, Piz** *It.* Pizzo Bernina. ▲ Italy/Switzerland *see also* Bermina, Pizzo
Bernina, Piz *see* Bermina, Pizzo
99 E20 **Bernissart** Hainaut, SW Belgium
101 E18 **Bernkastel-Kues** Rheinland-Pfalz, W Germany
Beroea *see* Ḩalab
172 H6 **Beroroha** Toliara, SW Madagascar
Béroubouay *see* Gbéroubouè
111 C17 **Beroun** *Ger.* Beraun. Středočeský Kraj, W Czech Republic
111 C16 **Berounka** *Ger.* Beraun. ≈ W Czech Republic
113 Q18 **Berovo** E FYR Macedonia
74 F6 **Berrechid** *var.* Berchid. W Morocco
103 R15 **Berre, Étang de** ◎ SE France
103 S15 **Berre-l'Étang** Bouches-du-Rhône, SE France
182 K9 **Berri** South Australia
31 O10 **Berrien Springs** Michigan, N USA
183 O10 **Berrigan** New South Wales, SE Australia
103 N9 **Berry** *cultural region* C France
35 N7 **Berryessa, Lake** ◎ California, W USA
44 G2 **Berry Islands** *island group* N Bahamas
27 T9 **Berryville** Arkansas, C USA
21 V3 **Berryville** Virginia, NE USA
83 D21 **Berseba** Karas, S Namibia
117 O8 **Bershad'** Vinnyts'ka Oblast', C Ukraine
28 L3 **Berthold** North Dakota, N USA
37 T3 **Berthoud** Colorado, C USA
37 S4 **Berthoud Pass** *pass* Colorado, C USA
79 F15 **Bertoua** Est, E Cameroon
25 S10 **Bertram** Texas, SW USA
63 G22 **Bertrand, Cerro** ▲ S Argentina
99 J23 **Bertrix** Luxembourg, SE Belgium
191 P3 **Beru** *var.* Peru. *atoll* Tungaru, W Kiribati
Beruni *see* Beruniy
146 I9 **Beruniy** *var.* Biruni, *Rus.* Beruni. Qoraqalpog'iston Respublikasi, W Uzbekistan
58 F13 **Beruri** Amazonas, NW Brazil
18 H14 **Berwick** Pennsylvania, NE USA
96 K12 **Berwick** *cultural region* SE Scotland, UK
96 L12 **Berwick-upon-Tweed** N England, UK
117 S10 **Beryslav** *Rus.* Berislav. Khersons'ka Oblast', S Ukraine
Berytus *see* Beyrouth
172 H4 **Besalampy** Mahajanga, W Madagascar
103 T8 **Besançon** *anc.* Besontium, Vesontio. Doubs, E France
103 P10 **Besbre** ≈ C France
Bescanuova *see* Baška
Besdan *see* Bezdan
Besed' *see* Byesyedz'
147 R10 **Beshariq** *Rus.* Besharyk; *prev.* Kirovo. Farg'ona Viloyati, E Uzbekistan
Besharyk *see* Beshariq
146 L9 **Beshbuloq** *Rus.* Beshulak. Navoiy Viloyati, N Uzbekistan
Beshenkovichi *see* Byeshankovichy
146 M13 **Beshkent** Qashqadaryo Viloyati, S Uzbekistan
Beshulak *see* Beshbuloq
112 L10 **Beška** Vojvodina, N Serbia
Beskra *see* Biskra
127 O16 **Beslan** Respublika Severnaya Osetiya, SW Russian Federation
113 P16 **Besna Kobila** ▲ SE Serbia
137 N16 **Besni** Adıyaman, S Turkey
Besontium *see* Besançon
121 Q2 **Beşparmak Dağları** *Eng.* Kyrenia Mountains. ▲▲ N Cyprus
Bessarabka *see* Basarabeasca
92 O2 **Bessels, Kapp** *headland* C Svalbard
23 P4 **Bessemer** Alabama, S USA
30 K3 **Bessemer** Michigan, N USA
21 Q10 **Bessemer City** North Carolina, SE USA
102 M10 **Bessines-sur-Gartempe** Haute-Vienne, C France
99 K15 **Best** Noord-Brabant, S Netherlands
25 N9 **Best** Texas, SW USA
125 O11 **Bestuzhevo** Arkhangel'skaya Oblast', NW Russian Federation
123 M11 **Bestyakh** Respublika Sakha (Yakutiya), NE Russian Federation
Beszterce *see* Bistriţa
Besztercebánya *see* Banská Bystrica
172 I5 **Betafo** Antananarivo, C Madagascar
104 H2 **Betanzos** Galicia, NW Spain
104 G2 **Betanzos, Ría de** *estuary* NW Spain
79 G15 **Bétaré Oya** Est, E Cameroon
105 S9 **Bétera** País Valenciano, E Spain
77 R15 **Bétérou** C Benin
83 K21 **Bethal** Mpumalanga, NE South Africa
30 K15 **Bethalto** Illinois, N USA
83 D21 **Bethanie** *var.* Bethanien, Bethany. Karas, S Namibia
Bethanien *see* Bethanie
27 S2 **Bethany** Missouri, C USA
27 N10 **Bethany** Oklahoma, C USA
Bethany *see* Bethanie
39 N12 **Bethel** Alaska, USA
19 P7 **Bethel** Maine, NE USA
21 W9 **Bethel** North Carolina, SE USA
18 B15 **Bethel Park** Pennsylvania, NE USA
21 W3 **Bethesda** Maryland, NE USA
83 J22 **Bethlehem** Free State, C South Africa
18 I14 **Bethlehem** Pennsylvania, NE USA
138 F10 **Bethlehem** *Ar.* Bayt Laḩm, *Heb.* Bet Leḥem. C West Bank
Bethlen *see* Beclean
83 I24 **Bethulie** Free State, C South Africa
103 O1 **Béthune** Pas-de-Calais, N France
102 M3 **Béthune** ≈ N France
104 M14 **Béticos, Sistemas** *var.* Sistema Penibético, *Eng.* Baetic Cordillera, Baetic Mountains. ▲▲ S Spain
54 I6 **Betijoque** Trujillo, NW Venezuela
59 M20 **Betim** Minas Gerais, SE Brazil
190 H3 **Betio** Tarawa, W Kiribati
172 H7 **Betioky** Toliara, S Madagascar
Bet Leḥem *see* Bethlehem
Betlen *see* Beclean
167 O17 **Betong** Yala, SW Thailand
79 I16 **Bétou** La Likouala, N Congo
145 P14 **Betpak-Dala** *Kaz.* Betpaqdala. *plateau* S Kazakhstan
Betpaqdala *see* Betpak-Dala
172 H7 **Betroka** Toliara, S Madagascar
Betschau *see* Bečva
138 G9 **Bet She'an** *Ar.* Baysān, Beisān; *anc.* Scythopolis. Northern, N Israel
15 T6 **Betsiamites** Québec, SE Canada
15 T6 **Betsiamites** ≈ Québec, SE Canada
172 I4 **Betsiboka** ≈ N Madagascar
99 M25 **Bettembourg** Luxembourg, S Luxembourg
99 M23 **Bettendorf** Diekirch, NE Luxembourg
29 Z14 **Bettendorf** Iowa, C USA
75 R13 **Bette, Pic** *var.* Bikkū Bittī, *It.* Picco Bette. ▲ S Libya
Bette, Picco *see* Bette, Pic
153 P12 **Bettiah** Bihār, N India
39 Q7 **Bettles** Alaska, USA
95 N17 **Bettna** Södermanland, C Sweden
154 H11 **Betūl** *prev.* Badnur. Madhya Pradesh, C India
154 H9 **Betwa** ≈ C India
101 F16 **Betzdorf** Rheinland-Pfalz, W Germany
82 C9 **Béu** Uíge, NW Angola
31 P6 **Beulah** Michigan, N USA
28 L5 **Beulah** North Dakota, N USA
98 M8 **Beulakerwijde** ◎ N Netherlands
98 L13 **Beuningen** Gelderland, SE Netherlands
Beuthen *see* Bytom
103 N7 **Beuvron** ≈ C France
99 F16 **Beveren** Oost-Vlaanderen, N Belgium
21 T9 **B. Everett Jordan Reservoir** *var.* Jordan Lake. ⊠ North Carolina, SE USA
97 N17 **Beverley** E England, UK
Beverley *see* Beverly
99 J17 **Beverlo** Limburg, NE Belgium
19 P11 **Beverly** Massachusetts, NE USA
32 J9 **Beverly** *var.* Beverley. Washington, NW USA
35 S15 **Beverly Hills** California, W USA
101 I14 **Beverungen** Nordrhein-Westfalen, C Germany
98 H9 **Beverwijk** Noord-Holland, W Netherlands
108 C10 **Bex** Vaud, W Switzerland
97 P23 **Bexhill** *var.* Bexhill-on-Sea. SE England, UK
Bexhill-on-Sea *see* Bexhill
136 E17 **Bey Dağları** ▲▲ SW Turkey
Beyj *see* Belyy
136 E10 **Beykoz** Istanbul, NW Turkey
76 K15 **Beyla** SE Guinea
137 X12 **Beyläqan** *prev.* Zhdanov. SW Azerbaijan
80 L10 **Beylul** *var.* Beilul. SE Eritrea
144 H14 **Beyneu** *Kaz.* Beyneū. Mangistau, SW Kazakhstan
Beyneū *see* Beyneu
165 X14 **Beyonësu-retsugan** *Eng.* Bayonnaise Rocks. *island group* SE Japan
136 G12 **Beypazarı** Ankara, NW Turkey
155 F21 **Beypore** Kerala, SW India
138 G7 **Beyrouth** *var.* Bayrūt, *Eng.* Beirut; *anc.* Berytus. ● (Lebanon) W Lebanon
138 G7 **Beyrouth** ✈ W Lebanon
136 G15 **Beyşehir** Konya, SW Turkey
136 G15 **Beyşehir Gölü** ◎ C Turkey
108 J7 **Bezau** Vorarlberg, NW Austria
112 J8 **Bezdan** *Ger.* Besdan, *Hung.* Bezdán. Vojvodina, NW Serbia
Bezdezh *see* Byezdzyezh
124 G15 **Bezhanitsy** Pskovskaya Oblast', W Russian Federation
124 K15 **Bezhetsk** Tverskaya Oblast', W Russian Federation
103 P16 **Béziers** *anc.* Baeterrae, Baeterrae Septimanorum, Julia Beterrae. Hérault, S France
Bezmein *see* Abadan
Bezwada *see* Vijayawāda
154 P12 **Bhadrak** *var.* Bhadrakh. Orissa, E India
Bhadrakh *see* Bhadrak
155 F19 **Bhadra Reservoir** ⊠ SW India
155 F18 **Bhadrāvati** Karnātaka, SW India
153 R14 **Bhāgalpur** Bihār, NE India
Bhairab *see* Bhairab Bazar
153 U14 **Bhairab Bazar** *var.* Bhairab. Dhaka, C Bangladesh
153 O11 **Bhairahawā** Western, S Nepal
149 S8 **Bhakkar** Punjab, E Pakistan
153 P11 **Bhaktapur** Central, C Nepal
167 N3 **Bhamo** *var.* Banmo. Kachin State, N Burma (Myanmar)
Bhāmragad *see* Bhāmragarh
154 K13 **Bhāmragarh** *var.* Bhāmragad. Mahārāshtra, C India
154 J12 **Bhandāra** Mahārāshtra, C India
Bhārat *see* India
152 J12 **Bharatpur** *prev.* Bhurtpore. Rājasthān, N India
154 D11 **Bharūch** Gujarāt, W India
155 E18 **Bhatkal** Karnātaka, W India
153 O13 **Bhatni** *var.* Bhatni Junction. Uttar Pradesh, N India
Bhatni Junction *see* Bhatni
153 S16 **Bhātpāra** West Bengal, NE India
149 U7 **Bhaun** Punjab, E Pakistan
Bhaunagar *see* Bhāvnagar
154 M13 **Bhavānipātna** Orissa, E India
155 H21 **Bhavānisāgar Reservoir** ⊠ S India
154 D11 **Bhāvnagar** *prev.* Bhaunagar. Gujarāt, W India
Bheanntraí, Bá *see* Bantry Bay
Bheara, Béal an *see* Gweebarra Bay
154 K12 **Bhilai** Chhattīsgarh, C India
152 G13 **Bhīlwāra** Rājasthān, N India
155 E14 **Bhīma** ≈ S India
155 K16 **Bhīmavaram** Andhra Pradesh, E India
154 I7 **Bhind** Madhya Pradesh, C India
152 E13 **Bhīnmāl** Rājasthān, N India
Bhir *see* Bīd
154 D13 **Bhiwandi** Mahārāshtra, W India
152 H10 **Bhiwāni** Haryāna, N India
152 L13 **Bhognīpur** Uttar Pradesh, N India
153 U16 **Bhola** Barisal, S Bangladesh
154 H10 **Bhopāl** *state capital* Madhya Pradesh, C India
155 J14 **Bhopālpatnam** Chhattīsgarh, C India
155 E14 **Bhor** Mahārāshtra, W India
154 O12 **Bhubaneshwar** *prev.* Bhubaneswar, Bhuvaneshwar. *state capital* Orissa, E India
Bhubaneswar *see* Bhubaneshwar
154 B9 **Bhuj** Gujarāt, W India
Bhuket *see* Phuket
Bhurtpore *see* Bharatpur
154 G12 **Bhusāwal** *prev.* Bhusaval. Mahārāshtra, C India
153 T12 **Bhutan** *off.* Kingdom of Bhutan, *var.* Druk-yul. ◆ *monarchy* S Asia
Bhutan, Kingdom of *see* Bhutan
Bhuvaneshwar *see* Bhubaneshwar
143 T15 **Biābān, Kūh-e** ▲▲ S Iran
77 V18 **Biafra, Bight of** *var.* Bight of Bonny. *bay* W Africa
171 W12 **Biak** Papua, E Indonesia
171 W12 **Biak, Pulau** *island* E Indonesia
110 P12 **Biała Podlaska** Lubelskie, E Poland
110 F7 **Białogard** *Ger.* Belgard. Zachodnio-pomorskie, NW Poland
110 P10 **Białowieska, Puszcza** *Bel.* Byelavyezhskaya Pushcha, *Rus.* Belovezhskaya Pushcha. *physical region* Belarus/Poland *see also* Byelavyezhskaya, Pushcha
Białowieska, Puszcza *see* Byelavyezhskaya Pushcha
110 G8 **Biały Bór** *Ger.* Baldenburg. Zachodnio-pomorskie, NW Poland
110 P9 **Białystok** *Rus.* Belostok, Bielostok. Podlaskie, NE Poland
107 L24 **Biancavilla** *prev.* Inessa. Sicilia, Italy, C Mediterranean Sea
Bianco, Monte *see* Blanc, Mont
Bianjing *see* Xunke
76 L15 **Biankouma** W Ivory Coast
167 R7 **Bia, Phou** *var.* Pou Bia. ▲ C Laos
Bia, Pou *see* Bia, Phou
143 R5 **Biārjmand** Semnān, N Iran
105 P4 **Biarra** ≈ NE Spain
102 I15 **Biarritz** Pyrénées-Atlantiques, SW France
108 H10 **Biasca** Ticino, S Switzerland
61 E16 **Biassini** Salto, N Uruguay
Biasteri *see* Laguardia
165 S3 **Bibai** Hokkaidō, NE Japan
83 B15 **Bibala** *Port.* Vila Arriaga. Namibe, SW Angola
104 I4 **Bibéi** ≈ NW Spain
Biberach *see* Biberach an der Riss
101 I23 **Biberach an der Riss** *var.* Biberach, *Ger.* Biberach an der Riß. Baden-Württemberg, S Germany
108 E7 **Biberist** Solothurn, NW Switzerland
77 O16 **Bibiani** SW Ghana
112 C13 **Bibinje** Zadar, SW Croatia
Biblical Gebal *see* Jbaïl
116 I5 **Bibrka** *Pol.* Bóbrka, *Rus.* Bobrka. L'vivs'ka Oblast', NW Ukraine
117 N10 **Bîc** ≈ S Moldova
113 M18 **Bicaj** Kukës, NE Albania
116 K10 **Bicaz** *Hung.* Békás. Neamţ, NE Romania
183 Q16 **Bicheno** Tasmania, SE Australia
Bichiş *see* Békés
Bichiş-Ciaba *see* Békéscsaba
Bichitra *see* Phichit
137 P8 **Bichvint'a** *Rus.* Pitsunda. NW Georgia
15 T7 **Bic, Île du** *island* Québec, SE Canada
32 J10 **Bickleton** Washington, NW USA
36 L6 **Bicknell** Utah, W USA
171 S11 **Bicoli** Pulau Halmahera, E Indonesia
111 J22 **Bicske** Fejér, C Hungary
155 F14 **Bīd** *prev.* Bhir. Mahārāshtra, W India
77 U15 **Bida** Niger, C Nigeria
155 H15 **Bīdar** Karnātaka, C India
141 Y8 **Bidbid** NE Oman
19 P9 **Biddeford** Maine, NE USA
98 L9 **Biddinghuizen** Flevoland, C Netherlands
33 X11 **Biddle** Montana, NW USA
97 J23 **Bideford** SW England, UK
82 D13 **Bié** ◈ *province* C Angola
35 O2 **Bieber** California, W USA
110 O9 **Biebrza** ≈ NE Poland
165 T3 **Biei** Hokkaidō, NE Japan
108 D8 **Biel** *Fr.* Bienne. Bern, W Switzerland
100 G13 **Bielefeld** Nordrhein-Westfalen, NW Germany
108 D8 **Bieler See** *Fr.* Lac de Bienne. ◎ W Switzerland
Bielitz/Bielitz-Biala *see* Bielsko-Biała
106 C7 **Biella** Piemonte, N Italy
Bielostok *see* Białystok
111 J17 **Bielsko-Biała** *Ger.* Bielitz, Bielitz-Biala. Śląskie, S Poland
110 P10 **Bielsk Podlaski** Białystok, E Poland
Bien Bien *see* Điện Biên
Biên Đông *see* South China Sea
9 V17 **Bienfait** Saskatchewan, S Canada
167 T14 **Biên Hoa** Đông Nai, S Vietnam
Bienne *see* Biel
Bienne, Lac de *see* Bieler See
12 K8 **Bienville, Lac** ◎ Québec, C Canada
82 D13 **Bié, Planalto do** *var.* Bié Plateau. *plateau* C Angola
Bié Plateau *see* Bié, Planalto do
108 B9 **Bière** Vaud, W Switzerland
98 O4 **Bierum** Groningen, NE Netherlands
98 I13 **Biesbos** *var.* Biesbosch. *wetland* S Netherlands
Biesbosch *see* Biesbos
99 H21 **Biesme** Namur, S Belgium
101 H21 **Bietigheim-Bissingen** Baden-Württemberg, SW Germany
99 I23 **Bièvre** Namur, SE Belgium
79 D18 **Bifoun** Moyen-Ogooué, NW Gabon
165 T2 **Bifuka** Hokkaidō, NE Japan
136 C11 **Biga** Çanakkale, NW Turkey
136 C13 **Bigadiç** Balıkesir, W Turkey
26 J7 **Big Basin** *basin* Kansas, C USA
185 B20 **Big Bay** *bay* South Island, New Zealand
31 O5 **Big Bay de Noc** ◎ Michigan, N USA
31 N3 **Big Bay Point** *headland* Michigan, N USA
33 R10 **Big Belt Mountains** ▲▲ Montana, NW USA
29 N10 **Big Bend Dam** *dam* South Dakota, N USA
24 K12 **Big Bend National Park** *national park* Texas, S USA
22 K5 **Big Black River** ≈ Mississippi, S USA
27 O3 **Big Blue River** ≈ Kansas/ Nebraska, C USA
24 M10 **Big Canyon** ≈ Texas, SW USA
33 N12 **Big Creek** Idaho, NW USA
23 N8 **Big Creek Lake** ⊠ Alabama, S USA
23 X15 **Big Cypress Swamp** *wetland* Florida, SE USA
39 S9 **Big Delta** Alaska, USA
30 K6 **Big Eau Pleine Reservoir** ⊠ Wisconsin, N USA
19 P5 **Bigelow Mountain** ▲ Maine, NE USA
162 G9 **Biger** *var* Jargalant. Govĭ-Altay, W Mongolia
29 U3 **Big Falls** Minnesota, N USA
33 P8 **Bigfork** Montana, NW USA
29 U3 **Big Fork River** ≈ Minnesota, N USA
9 S15 **Biggar** Saskatchewan, S Canada
180 L3 **Bigge Island** *island* Western Australia
35 O5 **Biggs** California, W USA
32 I11 **Biggs** Oregon, NW USA
14 K13 **Big Gull Lake** ◎ Ontario, SE Canada
37 P16 **Big Hachet Peak** ▲ New Mexico, SW USA
33 P11 **Big Hole River** ≈ Montana, NW USA
33 V13 **Bighorn Basin** *basin* Wyoming, C USA
33 U11 **Bighorn Lake** ◎ Montana/ Wyoming, NW USA
33 W13 **Bighorn Mountains** ▲▲ Wyoming, C USA
36 J13 **Big Horn Peak** ▲ Arizona, SW USA
33 V11 **Bighorn River** ≈ Montana/ Wyoming, NW USA
9 S7 **Big Island** *island* Nunavut, NE Canada
39 O16 **Big Koniuji Island** *island* Shumagin Islands, Alaska, USA
25 N9 **Big Lake** Texas, SW USA
19 T5 **Big Lake** ◎ Maine, NE USA
30 I3 **Big Manitou Falls** *waterfall* Wisconsin, N USA
35 R2 **Big Mountain** ▲ Nevada, W USA
108 G10 **Bignasco** Ticino, S Switzerland
29 R16 **Big Nemaha River** ≈ Nebraska, C USA
76 G12 **Bignona** SW Senegal
Bigorra *see* Tarbes
Bigosovo *see* Bihosava
35 S10 **Big Pine** California, W USA
35 Q14 **Big Pine Mountain** ▲ California, W USA
27 V6 **Big Piney Creek** ≈ Missouri, C USA
65 M24 **Big Point** *headland* N Tristan da Cunha
31 P8 **Big Rapids** Michigan, N USA
30 K6 **Big Rib River** ≈ Wisconsin, N USA
14 L14 **Big Rideau Lake** ◎ Ontario, SE Canada
9 T14 **Big River** Saskatchewan, C Canada
27 X5 **Big River** ≈ Missouri, C USA
31 N7 **Big Sable Point** *headland* Michigan, N USA
33 S7 **Big Sandy** Montana, NW USA
25 W6 **Big Sandy** Texas, SW USA
37 V5 **Big Sandy Creek** ≈ Colorado, C USA
29 Q16 **Big Sandy Creek** ≈ Nebraska, C USA
29 V5 **Big Sandy Lake** ◎ Minnesota, N USA
36 J11 **Big Sandy River** ≈ Arizona, SW USA
21 P5 **Big Sandy River** ≈ S USA
23 V6 **Big Satilla Creek** ≈ Georgia, SE USA
29 R12 **Big Sioux River** ≈ Iowa/ South Dakota, N USA
35 U7 **Big Smoky Valley** *valley* Nevada, W USA
25 N7 **Big Spring** Texas, SW USA
19 Q5 **Big Squaw Mountain** ▲ Maine, NE USA
21 O7 **Big Stone Gap** Virginia, NE USA
29 Q8 **Big Stone Lake** ◎ Minnesota/ South Dakota, N USA
22 K4 **Big Sunflower River** ≈ Mississippi, S USA
33 T11 **Big Timber** Montana, NW USA
12 D8 **Big Trout Lake** Ontario, C Canada
14 I12 **Big Trout Lake** ◎ Ontario, SE Canada
35 O2 **Big Valley Mountains** ▲▲ California, W USA
25 Q13 **Big Wells** Texas, SW USA
14 H11 **Bigwood** Ontario, S Canada
112 D11 **Bihać** ◈ NW Bosnia and Herzegovina
153 P14 **Bihār** *prev.* Behar. ◈ *state* N India
Bihār *see* Bihār Sharīf
81 F20 **Biharamulo** Kagera, NW Tanzania
153 R13 **Bihārīganj** Bihār, NE India
153 P14 **Bihār Sharīf** *var.* Bihār. Bihār, N India
116 F10 **Bihor** ◈ *county* NW Romania
165 U4 **Bihoro** Hokkaidō, NE Japan
118 K11 **Bihosava** *Rus.* Bigosovo. Vitsyebskaya Voblasts', NW Belarus
Bijagós Archipelago *see* Bijagós, Arquipélago dos
76 G13 **Bijagós, Arquipélago dos** *var.* Bijagos Archipelago. *island group* W Guinea-Bissau
155 F16 **Bijāpur** Karnātaka, C India
142 K5 **Bījār** Kordestān, W Iran
112 J11 **Bijeljina** ◈ Republika Srpska, NE Bosnia and Herzegovina
113 K15 **Bijelo Polje** E Montenegro
160 E11 **Bijiang** Yunnan, SW China
160 I11 **Bijie** Guizhou, S China
152 J10 **Bijnor** Uttar Pradesh, N India
152 F11 **Bikāner** Rājasthān, NW India
189 V3 **Bikar Atoll** *var.* Pikaar. *atoll* Ratak Chain, N Marshall Islands
190 H3 **Bikeman** *atoll* Tungaru, W Kiribati
190 I3 **Bikenebu** Tarawa, W Kiribati
123 S14 **Bikin** Khabarovskiy Kray, SE Russian Federation

◆ Country
● Country Capital
◇ Dependent Territory
○ Dependent Territory Capital
◈ Administrative Regions
✈ International Airport
▲ Mountain
▲▲ Mountain Range
Volcano
◎ Lake
≈ River
⊠ Reservoir

◆ Country ● Country Capital ◇ Dependent Territory ○ Dependent Territory Capital ◐ Administrative Regions ✈ International Airport ▲ Mountain ▲▲ Mountain Range Volcano ~ River ◎ Lake ⊠ Reservoir

BLUE MOUNTAIN PEAK – BORDEN PENINSULA

44 H10 **Blue Mountain Peak** ▲ E Jamaica
183 S8 **Blue Mountains** ▲▲ New South Wales, SE Australia
32 L11 **Blue Mountains** ▲▲ Oregon/Washington, NW USA
80 G12 **Blue Nile** ◈ *state* E Sudan
80 H12 **Blue Nile** *var.* Abai, Bahr el, Azraq, *Amh.* Ābay Wenz, *Ar.* An Nīl al Azraq. ≈ Ethiopia/Sudan
8 J7 **Bluenose Lake** ◎ Nunavut, NW Canada
27 O3 **Blue Rapids** Kansas, C USA
23 S1 **Blue Ridge** Georgia, SE USA
17 S11 **Blue Ridge** *var.* Blue Ridge Mountains. ▲▲ North Carolina/Virginia, USA
23 S1 **Blue Ridge Lake** ⊠ Georgia, SE USA
Blue Ridge Mountains *see* Blue Ridge
9 N15 **Blue River** British Columbia, SW Canada
27 O12 **Blue River** ≈ Oklahoma, C USA
27 R4 **Blue Springs** Missouri, C USA
21 R6 **Bluestone Lake** ⊠ West Virginia, NE USA
185 C25 **Bluff** Southland, South Island, New Zealand
37 O8 **Bluff** Utah, W USA
21 P8 **Bluff City** Tennessee, S USA
65 E24 **Bluff Cove** East Falkland, Falkland Islands
25 S7 **Bluff Dale** Texas, SW USA
183 N15 **Bluff Hill Point** *headland* Tasmania, SE Australia
31 Q12 **Bluffton** Indiana, N USA
31 R12 **Bluffton** Ohio, N USA
25 T7 **Blum** Texas, SW USA
101 G24 **Blumberg** Baden-Württemberg, SW Germany
60 K13 **Blumenau** Santa Catarina, S Brazil
29 N9 **Blunt** South Dakota, N USA
32 H15 **Bly** Oregon, NW USA
39 R13 **Blying Sound** *sound* Alaska, USA
97 M14 **Blyth** N England, UK
35 Y16 **Blythe** California, W USA
27 Y9 **Blytheville** Arkansas, C USA
117 V7 **Blyznyuky** Kharkivs'ka Oblast', E Ukraine
95 G16 **Bø** Telemark, S Norway
76 I15 **Bo** S Sierra Leone
171 O4 **Boac** Marinduque, N Philippines
42 K10 **Boaco** Boaco, S Nicaragua
42 J10 **Boaco** ◈ *department* C Nicaragua
79 I15 **Boali** Ombella-Mpoko, SW Central African Republic
Boalsert *see* Bolsward
31 V12 **Boardman** Ohio, N USA
32 J11 **Boardman** Oregon, NW USA
14 F13 **Boat Lake** ◎ Ontario, S Canada
58 F10 **Boa Vista** *state capital* Roraima, NW Brazil
76 D9 **Boa Vista** *island* Ilhas de Barlavento, E Cape Verde
23 Q2 **Boaz** Alabama, S USA
160 L15 **Bobai** Guangxi Zhuangzu Zizhiqu, S China
172 J1 **Bobaomby, Tanjona** *Fr.* Cap d'Ambre. *headland* N Madagascar
155 M14 **Bobbili** Andhra Pradesh, E India
106 D9 **Bobbio** Emilia-Romagna, C Italy
14 I14 **Bobcaygeon** Ontario, SE Canada
Bober *see* Bóbr
103 O5 **Bobigny** Seine-St-Denis, N France
77 N13 **Bobo-Dioulasso** SW Burkina
110 G8 **Bobolice** *Ger.* Bublitz. Zachodnio-pomorskie, NW Poland
83 J19 **Bobonong** Central, E Botswana
171 R11 **Bobopayo** Pulau Halmahera, E Indonesia
114 G10 **Bobovdol** Kyustendil, W Bulgaria
119 M15 **Bobr** Minskaya Voblasts', NW Belarus
119 M15 **Bobr** ≈ C Belarus
111 E14 **Bóbr** *Eng.* Bobrawa, *Ger.* Bober. ≈ SW Poland
Bobrawa *see* Bóbr
Bobrik *see* Bobryk
Bobrinets *see* Bobrynets'
Bobrka/Bóbrka *see* Bibrka
126 L8 **Bobrov** Voronezhskaya Oblast', W Russian Federation
117 Q4 **Bobrovytsya** Chernihivs'ka Oblast', N Ukraine
Bobruysk *see* Babruysk
119 J19 **Bobryk** *Rus.* Bobrik. ≈ SW Belarus
117 Q8 **Bobrynets'** *Rus.* Bobrinets. Kirovohrads'ka Oblast', C Ukraine
14 K14 **Bobs Lake** ◎ Ontario, SE Canada
54 I6 **Bobures** Zulia, NW Venezuela
42 H1 **Boca Bacalar Chico** *headland* N Belize
112 G11 **Bočac** ◈ Republika Srpska, NW Bosnia and Herzegovina
41 R14 **Boca del Río** Veracruz-Llave, S Mexico
55 O4 **Boca de Pozo** Nueva Esparta, NE Venezuela
59 C15 **Boca do Acre** Amazonas, N Brazil
55 N12 **Boca Mavaca** Amazonas, S Venezuela
79 G14 **Bocaranga** Ouham-Pendé, W Central African Republic
23 Z15 **Boca Raton** Florida, SE USA
43 P14 **Bocas del Toro** Bocas del Toro, NW Panama
43 P15 **Bocas del Toro** *off.* Provincia de Bocas del Toro. ◈ *province* NW Panama
43 P15 **Bocas del Toro, Archipiélago de** *island group* NW Panama
Bocas del Toro, Provincia de *see* Bocas del Toro
42 L7 **Bocay** Jinotega, N Nicaragua
105 N6 **Boceguillas** Castilla-León, N Spain
Bocheykovo *see* Bacheykava
111 L17 **Bochnia** Małopolskie, SE Poland
99 K16 **Bocholt** Limburg, NE Belgium
101 D14 **Bocholt** Nordrhein-Westfalen, W Germany
101 E15 **Bochum** Nordrhein-Westfalen, W Germany
103 Y15 **Bocognano** Corse, France, C Mediterranean Sea
54 I6 **Boconó** Trujillo, NW Venezuela
116 F12 **Bocşa** *Ger.* Bokschen, *Hung.* Boksánbánya. Caraş-Severin, SW Romania
79 H15 **Boda** Lobaye, SW Central African Republic
94 L12 **Böda** Dalarna, C Sweden
95 O20 **Böda** Kalmar, S Sweden
95 L19 **Bodafors** Jönköping, S Sweden
123 O12 **Bodaybo** Irkutskaya Oblast', E Russian Federation
22 G5 **Bodcau, Bayou** *var.* Bodcau Creek. ≈ Louisiana, S USA
Bodcau Creek *see* Bodcau, Bayou
44 D8 **Bodden Town** *var.* Boddentown. Grand Cayman, SW Cayman Islands
Boddentown *see* Bodden Town
101 K14 **Bode** ≈ C Germany
34 L7 **Bodega Head** *headland* California, W USA
Bodegas *see* Babahoyo
98 H11 **Bodegraven** Zuid-Holland, C Netherlands
78 H8 **Bodélé** *depression* W Chad
92 J13 **Boden** Norrbotten, N Sweden
Bodensee *see* Constance, Lake, C Europe
65 M15 **Bode Verde Fracture Zone** *tectonic feature* E Atlantic Ocean
155 H14 **Bodhan** Andhra Pradesh, C India
Bodī *see* Jinst
155 H22 **Bodināyakkanūr** Tamil Nādu, SE India
108 H10 **Bodio** Ticino, S Switzerland
Bodjonegoro *see* Bojonegoro
97 I24 **Bodmin** SW England, UK
97 I24 **Bodmin Moor** *moorland* SW England, UK
92 G12 **Bodø** Nordland, C Norway
59 H20 **Bodoquena, Serra da** ▲▲ SW Brazil
136 B16 **Bodrum** Muğla, SW Turkey
Bodzafordulő *see* Întorsura Buzăului
99 L14 **Boekel** Noord-Brabant, SE Netherlands
Boeloekoemba *see* Bulukumba
103 Q11 **Boën** Loire, E France
79 K18 **Boende** Equateur, C Dem. Rep. Congo
25 R11 **Boerne** Texas, SW USA
Beroee *see* Buru, Pulau
Boetoeng *see* Buton, Pulau
22 I5 **Boeuf River** ≈ Arkansas/Louisiana, S USA
76 H14 **Boffa** Guinée-Maritime, W Guinea
Bó Finne, Inis *see* Inishbofin
Boga *see* Bogë
166 L9 **Bogale** Irrawaddy, SW Burma (Myanmar)
22 L8 **Bogalusa** Louisiana, S USA
77 Q12 **Bogandé** C Burkina
79 I15 **Bogangolo** Ombella-Mpoko, C Central African Republic
183 Q7 **Bogan River** ≈ New South Wales, SE Australia
25 W5 **Bogata** Texas, SW USA
111 D14 **Bogatynia** *Ger.* Reichenau. Dolnośląskie, SW Poland
136 K13 **Boğazlıyan** Yozgat, C Turkey
79 J17 **Bogbonga** Equateur, NW Dem. Rep. Congo
158 J14 **Bogcang Zangbo** ≈ W China
162 I9 **Bogd** *var.* Horiult. Bayanhongor, C Mongolia
162 J10 **Bogd** *var.* Hovd. Övörhangay, C Mongolia
158 L5 **Bogda Feng** ▲ NW China
114 I9 **Bogdan** ▲ C Bulgaria
113 Q20 **Bogdanci** SE FYR Macedonia
158 M5 **Bogda Shan** *var.* Po-ko-to Shan. ▲▲ NW China
113 K17 **Bogë** *var.* Boga. Shkodër, N Albania
Bogendorf *see* Łuków
95 G23 **Bogense** Fyn, C Denmark
183 T3 **Boggabilla** New South Wales, SE Australia
183 S6 **Boggabri** New South Wales, SE Australia
186 D6 **Bogia** Madang, N Papua New Guinea
97 N23 **Bognor Regis** SE England, UK
Bogodukhov *see* Bohodukhiv
181 V15 **Bogong, Mount** ▲ Victoria, SE Australia
169 O16 **Bogor** *Dut.* Buitenzorg. Jawa, C Indonesia
126 L5 **Bogoroditsk** Tul'skaya Oblast', W Russian Federation
127 O3 **Bogorodsk** Nizhegorodskaya Oblast', W Russian Federation
Bogorodskoje *see* Bogorodskoye
123 S12 **Bogorodskoye** Khabarovskiy Kray, SE Russian Federation
125 R15 **Bogorodskoye** *var.* Bogorodskoje. Kirovskaya Oblast', NW Russian Federation
54 F10 **Bogotá** *prev.* Santa Fe, Santa Fe de Bogotá. ● (Colombia) Cundinamarca, C Colombia
153 T14 **Bogra** Rajshahi, N Bangladesh
Bogschan *see* Boldu
122 L12 **Boguchany** Krasnoyarskiy Kray, C Russian Federation
126 M9 **Boguchar** Voronezhskaya Oblast', W Russian Federation
76 H10 **Bogué** Brakna, SW Mauritania
22 K8 **Bogue Chitto** ≈ Louisiana/Mississippi, S USA
Bogushëvsk *see* Bahushewsk
Boguslav *see* Bohuslav
44 K12 **Bog Walk** C Jamaica
161 Q3 **Bo Hai** *var.* Gulf of Chihli. *gulf* NE China
161 R3 **Bohai Haixia** *strait* NE China
161 Q3 **Bohai Wan** *bay* NE China
111 C17 **Bohemia** *Cz.* Čechy, *Ger.* Böhmen. *cultural and historical region* W Czech Republic
111 B18 **Bohemian Forest** *Cz.* Ceský Les, Šumava, *Ger.* Böhmerwald. ▲▲ C Europe
Bohemian-Moravian Highlands *see* Českomoravská Vrchovina
77 R16 **Bohicon** S Benin
109 S11 **Bohinjska Bistrica** *Ger.* Wocheiner Feistritz. NW Slovenia
Bohkká *see* Pokka
Böhmen *see* Bohemia
Böhmerwald *see* Bohemian Forest
Böhmisch-Krumau *see* Český Krumlov
Böhmisch-Leipa *see* Česká Lípa
Böhmisch-Mährische Höhe *see* Českomoravská Vrchovina
Böhmisch-Trübau *see* Česká Třebová
117 U5 **Bohodukhiv** *Rus.* Bogodukhov. Kharkivs'ka Oblast', E Ukraine
171 Q6 **Bohol** *island* C Philippines
171 Q7 **Bohol Sea** *var.* Mindanao Sea. *sea* S Philippines
116 I7 **Bohorodchany** Ivano-Frankivs'ka Oblast', W Ukraine
Böhöt *see* Öndörshil
158 K6 **Bohu** *var.* Bagrax. Xinjiang Uygur Zizhiqu, NW China
111 I17 **Bohumín** *Ger.* Oderberg; *prev.* Neuoderberg, Nový Bohumín. Moravskoslezský Kraj, E Czech Republic
117 P6 **Bohuslav** *Rus.* Boguslav. Kyyivs'ka Oblast', N Ukraine
58 F11 **Boiaçu** Roraima, N Brazil
107 K16 **Boiano** Molise, C Italy
15 R8 **Boilleau** Québec, SE Canada
59 O17 **Boipeba, Ilha de** *island* SE Brazil
104 G3 **Boiro** Galicia, NW Spain
31 Q5 **Bois Blanc Island** *island* Michigan, N USA
29 R7 **Bois de Sioux River** ≈ Minnesota, N USA
33 N14 **Boise** *var.* Boise City. *state capital* Idaho, NW USA
26 G8 **Boise City** Oklahoma, C USA
Boise City *see* Boise
33 N14 **Boise River, Middle Fork** ≈ Idaho, NW USA
Bois, Lac des *see* Woods, Lake of the
Bois-le-Duc *see* 's-Hertogenbosch
9 W17 **Boissevain** Manitoba, S Canada
15 T7 **Boisvert, Pointe au** *headland* Québec, SE Canada
100 K10 **Boizenburg** Mecklenburg-Vorpommern, N Germany
Bojador *see* Boujdour
113 K18 **Bojana** *Alb.* Bunë. ≈ Albania/Montenegro *see also* Bunë
Bojana *see* Bunë
143 S3 **Bojnūrd** *var.* Bujnurd. Khorāsān-e Shemālī, N Iran
169 R16 **Bojonegoro** *prev.* Bodjonegoro. Jawa, C Indonesia
189 T1 **Bokaak Atoll** *var.* Bokak, Taongi. *atoll* Ratak Chain, NE Marshall Islands
Bokak *see* Bokaak Atoll
146 K6 **Bo'kantov Tog'lari** *Rus* Gory Bukantau. N Uzbekistan
146 K8 **Bo'kantov Tog'lari** *Rus.* Gory Bukantau. ▲ N Uzbekistan
153 Q15 **Bokāro** Jhārkhand, N India
79 I18 **Bokatola** Equateur, NW Dem. Rep. Congo
76 H13 **Boké** W Guinea
Bokhara *see* Buxoro
183 Q4 **Bokhara River** ≈ New South Wales/Queensland, SE Australia
95 C16 **Boknafjorden** *fjord* S Norway
78 H11 **Bokoro** Chari-Baguirmi, W Chad
79 K19 **Bokota** Equateur, NW Dem. Rep. Congo
167 N13 **Bokpyin** Tenasserim, S Burma (Myanmar)
Boksánbánya/Bokschen *see* Bocşa
83 F21 **Bokspits** Kgalagadi, SW Botswana
79 K18 **Bokungu** Equateur, C Dem. Rep. Congo
146 F12 **Bokurdak** *Rus.* Bakhardok. Ahal Welaýaty, C Turkmenistan
78 G10 **Bol** Lac, W Chad
76 G13 **Bolama** SW Guinea-Bissau
Bolangir *see* Balāngīr
Bolanos *see* Bolanos, Mount, Guam
Bolaños *see* Bolaños de Calatrava, Spain
105 N11 **Bolaños de Calatrava** *var.* Bolaños. Castilla-La Mancha, C Spain
188 B17 **Bolanos, Mount** *var.* Bolanos. ▲ S Guam
40 L12 **Bolaños, Río** ≈ C Mexico
115 M14 **Bolayır** Çanakkale, NW Turkey
102 L3 **Bolbec** Seine-Maritime, N France
116 L13 **Boldu** *var.* Bogschan. Buzău, SE Romania
146 H8 **Boldumsaz** *prev.* Kalinin, Kalininsk, Porsy. Daşoguz Welaýaty, N Turkmenistan
158 I4 **Bole** *var.* Bortala. Xinjiang Uygur Zizhiqu, NW China
77 O15 **Bole** NW Ghana
79 J19 **Boleko** Equateur, W Dem. Rep. Congo
111 E14 **Bolesławiec** *Ger.* Bunzlau. Dolnośląskie, SW Poland
127 R4 **Bolgar** *prev.* Kuybyshev. Respublika Tatarstan, W Russian Federation
77 P14 **Bolgatanga** N Ghana
Bolgrad *see* Bolhrad
117 N12 **Bolhrad** *Rus.* Bolgrad. Odes'ka Oblast', SW Ukraine
163 Y8 **Boli** Heilongjiang, NE China
79 I19 **Bolia** Bandundu, W Dem. Rep. Congo
93 J14 **Boliden** Västerbotten, N Sweden
171 T13 **Bolifar** Pulau Seram, E Indonesia
171 N2 **Bolinao** Luzon, N Philippines
54 C12 **Bolívar** Cauca, SW Colombia
27 T6 **Bolivar** Missouri, C USA
20 F10 **Bolivar** Tennessee, S USA
54 F7 **Bolívar** *off.* Departmento de Bolívar. ◈ *province* N Colombia
56 A13 **Bolívar** ◈ *province* C Ecuador
55 N9 **Bolívar** *off.* Estado Bolívar. ◈ *state* SE Venezuela
Bolívar, Departmento de *see* Bolívar
Bolívar, Estado *see* Bolívar
25 X12 **Bolivar Peninsula** *headland* Texas, SW USA
54 I6 **Bolívar, Pico** ▲ W Venezuela
57 K17 **Bolivia** *off.* Republic of Bolivia. ◆ *republic* W South America
Bolivia, Republic of *see* Bolivia
112 O13 **Boljevac** Serbia, E Serbia
Bolkenhain *see* Bolków
126 J5 **Bolkhov** Orlovskaya Oblast', W Russian Federation
111 F14 **Bolków** *Ger.* Bolkenhain. Dolnośląskie, SW Poland
182 K3 **Bollards Lagoon** South Australia
103 R14 **Bollène** Vaucluse, SE France
94 N12 **Bollnäs** Gävleborg, C Sweden
181 W10 **Bollon** Queensland, C Australia
192 L12 **Bollons Tablemount** *undersea feature* S Pacific Ocean
93 H17 **Bollstabruk** Västernorrland, C Sweden
Bollulos de Par del Condado *see* Bollullos Par del Condado
104 J14 **Bollullos Par del Condado** *var.* Bolluilos de Par del Condado. Andalucía, S Spain
95 K21 **Bolmen** ◎ S Sweden
137 T10 **Bolnisi** S Georgia
79 H19 **Bolobo** Bandundu, W Dem. Rep. Congo
106 G10 **Bologna** Emilia-Romagna, N Italy
124 I15 **Bologoye** Tverskaya Oblast', W Russian Federation
79 J18 **Bolomba** Equateur, NW Dem. Rep. Congo
41 X13 **Bolónchén de Rejón** *var.* Bolonchén de Rejón. Campeche, SE Mexico
114 J13 **Boloústra, Ákrotírio** *cape* NE Greece
167 L8 **Bolovens, Plateau des** *plateau* S Laos
106 H13 **Bolsena** Lazio, C Italy
107 G14 **Bolsena, Lago di** ◎ C Italy
126 B3 **Bol'shakovo** *Ger.* Kreuzingen; *prev.* Gross-Skaisgirren. Kaliningradskaya Oblast', W Russian Federation
Bol'shaya Berëstovitsa *see* Vyalikaya Byerastavitsa
127 S7 **Bol'shaya Chernigovka** Samarskaya Oblast', W Russian Federation
127 S7 **Bol'shaya Glushitsa** Samarskaya Oblast', W Russian Federation
144 H9 **Bol'shaya Khobda** *Kaz.* Ülkenqobda. ≈ Kazakhstan/Russian Federation
126 M12 **Bol'shaya Martynovka** Rostovskaya Oblast', SW Russian Federation
122 K12 **Bol'shaya Murta** Krasnoyarskiy Kray, C Russian Federation
125 V4 **Bol'shaya Rogovaya** ≈ NW Russian Federation
125 U7 **Bol'shaya Synya** ≈ NW Russian Federation
145 V9 **Bol'shaya Vladimirovka** Vostochnyy Kazakhstan, E Kazakhstan
123 V11 **Bol'sheretsk** Kamchatskaya Oblast', E Russian Federation
127 W3 **Bol'sheust'ikinskoye** Respublika Bashkortostan, W Russian Federation
Bol'shevik *see* Bal'shavik
122 L5 **Bol'shevik, Ostrov** *island* Severnaya Zemlya, N Russian Federation
125 U4 **Bol'shezemel'skaya Tundra** *physical region* NW Russian Federation
144 J13 **Bol'shiye Barsuki, Peski** *desert* SW Kazakhstan
123 T7 **Bol'shoy Anyuy** ≈ NE Russian Federation
123 N7 **Bol'shoy Begichev, Ostrov** *island* NE Russian Federation
123 S15 **Bol'shoye Kamen'** Primorskiy Kray, SE Russian Federation
127 O4 **Bol'shoye Murashkino** Nizhegorodskaya Oblast', W Russian Federation
127 W4 **Bol'shoy Iremel'** ▲ W Russian Federation
127 R7 **Bol'shoy Irgiz** ≈ W Russian Federation
123 Q6 **Bol'shoy Lyakhovskiy, Ostrov** *island* NE Russian Federation
123 Q11 **Bol'shoy Nimnyr** Respublika Sakha (Yakutiya), NE Russian Federation
Bol'shoy Rozhan *see* Vyaliki Rozhan
144 E10 **Bol'shoy Uzen'** *Kaz.* Ülkenözen. ≈ Kazakhstan/Russian Federation
40 K6 **Bolson de Mapimi** ▲▲ NW Mexico
98 K6 **Bolsward** *Fris.* Boalsert. Friesland, N Netherlands
105 T4 **Boltaña** Aragón, NE Spain
14 G15 **Bolton** Ontario, S Canada
97 K17 **Bolton** *prev.* Bolton-le-Moors. NW England, UK
21 V12 **Bolton** North Carolina, SE USA
Bolton-le-Moors *see* Bolton
136 G11 **Bolu** Bolu, NW Turkey
136 G11 **Bolu** ◈ *province* NW Turkey
186 G9 **Bolubolu** Goodenough Island, S Papua New Guinea
92 H1 **Bolungarvík** Vestfirdhir, NW Iceland
159 O10 **Boluntay** Qinghai, W China
159 P8 **Boluozhuanjing**, Aksay Kazakzu Zizhixian. Gansu, N China
136 F14 **Bolvadin** Afyon, W Turkey
114 M10 **Bolyarovo** *prev.* Pashkeni. Yambol, E Bulgaria
106 G6 **Bolzano** *Ger.* Bozen; *anc.* Bauzanum. Trentino-Alto Adige, N Italy
79 F22 **Boma** Bas-Congo, W Dem. Rep. Congo
183 R12 **Bombala** New South Wales, SE Australia
104 F10 **Bombarral** Leiria, C Portugal
Bombay *see* Mumbai
171 U13 **Bomberai, Semenanjung** *cape* Papua, E Indonesia
81 F18 **Bombo** S Uganda
162 I8 **Bömbögör** *var.* Dzadgay. Bayanhongor, C Mongolia
79 I17 **Bomboma** Equateur, NW Dem. Rep. Congo
59 I14 **Bom Futuro** Pará, N Brazil
159 Q15 **Bomi** *var.* Bowo, Zhamo. Xizang Zizhiqu, W China
79 N17 **Bomili** Orientale, NE Dem. Rep. Congo
59 N17 **Bom Jesus da Lapa** Bahia, E Brazil
60 Q8 **Bom Jesus do Itabapoana** Rio de Janeiro, SE Brazil
95 C15 **Bømlafjorden** *fjord* S Norway
95 B15 **Bømlo** *island* S Norway
12 Q12 **Bomnak** Amurskaya Oblast', SE Russian Federation
79 I17 **Bomongo** Equateur, NW Dem. Rep. Congo
61 K14 **Bom Retiro** Santa Catarina, S Brazil
79 L15 **Bomu** *var.* Mbomou, Mbomu, M'Bomu. ≈ Central African Republic/Dem. Rep. Congo
142 J3 **Bonāb** *var.* Benāb, Bunab. Āzarbāyjān-e Sharqī, N Iran
45 Q16 **Bonaire** *island* E Netherlands Antilles
39 U11 **Bona, Mount** ▲ Alaska, USA
183 Q12 **Bonang** Victoria, SE Australia
42 L7 **Bonanza** Región Autónoma Atlántico Norte, NE Nicaragua
37 O4 **Bonanza** Utah, W USA
45 O9 **Bonao** C Dominican Republic
180 L3 **Bonaparte Archipelago** *island group* Western Australia
32 K6 **Bonaparte, Mount** ▲ Washington, NW USA
39 N11 **Bonasila Dome** ▲ Alaska, USA
92 H11 **Bonnåsjøen** Nordland, C Norway
45 T15 **Bonasse** Trinidad, Trinidad and Tobago
15 X7 **Bonaventure** Québec, SE Canada
15 X7 **Bonaventure** ≈ Québec, SE Canada
13 V11 **Bonavista** Newfoundland, Newfoundland and Labrador, SE Canada
13 U11 **Bonavista Bay** *inlet* NW Atlantic Ocean
79 E19 **Bonda** Ogooué-Lolo, C Gabon
127 N6 **Bondari** Tambovskaya Oblast', W Russian Federation
106 G9 **Bondeno** Emilia-Romagna, C Italy
30 L4 **Bond Falls Flowage** ⊠ Michigan, N USA
79 L16 **Bondo** Orientale, N Dem. Rep. Congo
171 N17 **Bondokodi** Pulau Sumba, S Indonesia
77 O15 **Bondoukou** E Ivory Coast
Bondoukui/Bondoukuy *see* Boundoukui
169 T17 **Bondowoso** Jawa, C Indonesia
33 S14 **Bondurant** Wyoming, C USA
Bône *see* Annaba
Bone *see* Watampone
30 I5 **Bone Lake** ◎ Wisconsin, N USA
171 P14 **Bonelipu** Pulau Buton, C Indonesia
171 O15 **Bonerate, Kepulauan** *var.* Macan. *island group* C Indonesia
29 O12 **Bonesteel** South Dakota, N USA
62 I8 **Bonete, Cerro** ▲ N Argentina
171 O14 **Bone, Teluk** *bay* Sulawesi, C Indonesia
108 D6 **Bonfol** Jura, NW Switzerland
153 U12 **Bongaigaon** Assam, NE India
79 K17 **Bongandanga** Equateur, NW Dem. Rep. Congo
78 L13 **Bongo, Massif des** *var.* Chaîne des Mongos. ▲▲ NE Central African Republic
78 G12 **Bongor** Mayo-Kébbi, SW Chad
77 N16 **Bongouanou** E Ivory Coast
167 V11 **Bông Sơn** *var.* Hoai Nhơn. Binh Đinh, C Vietnam
25 U5 **Bonham** Texas, SW USA
Bonhard *see* Bonyhád
103 U6 **Bonhomme, Col du** *pass* NE France
103 Y16 **Bonifacio** Corse, France, C Mediterranean Sea
Bonifacio, Bocche de/Bonifacio, Bouches de *see* Bonifacio, Strait of
103 Y16 **Bonifacio, Strait of** *Fr.* Bouches de Bonifacio, *It.* Bocche di Bonifacio. *strait* C Mediterranean Sea
23 Q8 **Bonifay** Florida, SE USA
Bonin Islands *see* Ogasawara-shotō
192 H5 **Bonin Trench** *undersea feature* NW Pacific Ocean
23 W15 **Bonita Springs** Florida, SE USA
42 I5 **Bonito, Pico** ▲ N Honduras
101 E17 **Bonn** Nordrhein-Westfalen, W Germany
14 J12 **Bonnechere** Ontario, SE Canada
14 J12 **Bonnechere** ≈ Ontario, SE Canada
33 N7 **Bonners Ferry** Idaho, NW USA
27 R4 **Bonner Springs** Kansas, C USA
102 L6 **Bonnétable** Sarthe, NW France
27 X6 **Bonne Terre** Missouri, C USA
10 J5 **Bonnet Plume** ≈ Yukon Territory, NW Canada
102 M6 **Bonneval** Eure-et-Loir, C France
103 T10 **Bonneville** Haute-Savoie, E France
36 J3 **Bonneville Salt Flats** *salt flat* Utah, W USA
77 U18 **Bonny** Rivers, S Nigeria
Bonny, Bight of *see* Biafra, Bight of
37 W4 **Bonny Reservoir** ⊠ Colorado, C USA
9 R14 **Bonnyville** Alberta, SW Canada
107 C18 **Bono** Sardegna, Italy, C Mediterranean Sea
Bononia *see* Vidin, Bulgaria
Bononia *see* Boulogne-sur-Mer, France
107 B18 **Bonorva** Sardegna, Italy, C Mediterranean Sea
30 M15 **Bonpas Creek** ≈ Illinois, N USA
190 I3 **Bonriki** Tarawa, W Kiribati
183 T4 **Bonshaw** New South Wales, SE Australia
76 I16 **Bonthe** SW Sierra Leone
171 N2 **Bontoc** Luzon, N Philippines
25 Y9 **Bon Wier** Texas, SW USA
111 J25 **Bonyhád** *Ger.* Bonhard. Tolna, S Hungary
Bonzabaai *see* Bonza Bay
83 J25 **Bonza Bay** *Afr.* Bonzabaai. Eastern Cape, S South Africa
182 D7 **Bookabie** South Australia
182 H6 **Bookaloo** South Australia
37 P5 **Book Cliffs** *cliff* Colorado/Utah, W USA
25 P1 **Booker** Texas, SW USA
76 K15 **Boola** SE Guinea
183 O8 **Booligal** New South Wales, SE Australia
99 G17 **Boom** Antwerpen, N Belgium
43 N6 **Boom** *var.* Boon. Región Autónoma Atlántico Norte, NE Nicaragua
183 S3 **Boomi** New South Wales, SE Australia
Boon *see* Boom
29 V13 **Boone** Iowa, C USA
21 Q8 **Boone** North Carolina, SE USA
27 S11 **Booneville** Arkansas, C USA
21 N6 **Booneville** Kentucky, S USA
23 N2 **Booneville** Mississippi, S USA
21 V3 **Boonsboro** Maryland, NE USA
162 H9 **Böön Tsagaan Nuur** ◎ S Mongolia
34 L6 **Boonville** California, W USA
31 N16 **Boonville** Indiana, N USA
27 U4 **Boonville** Missouri, C USA
18 I9 **Boonville** New York, NE USA
80 M12 **Boorama** Awdal, NW Somalia
183 O6 **Booroondarra, Mount** *hill* New South Wales, SE Australia
183 N9 **Booroorban** New South Wales, SE Australia
183 R9 **Boorowa** New South Wales, SE Australia
99 H17 **Boortmeerbeek** Vlaams Brabant, C Belgium
80 P11 **Boosaaso** *var.* Bandar Kassim, Bender Qaasim, Bosaso, *It.* Bender Cassim. Bari, N Somalia
19 Q8 **Boothbay Harbor** Maine, NE USA
Boothia Felix *see* Boothia Peninsula
9 N6 **Boothia, Gulf of** *gulf* Nunavut, NE Canada
8 M6 **Boothia Peninsula** *prev.* Boothia Felix. *peninsula* Nunavut, NE Canada
79 E18 **Booué** Ogooué-Ivindo, NE Gabon
101 J21 **Bopfingen** Baden-Württemberg, S Germany
101 F18 **Boppard** Rheinland-Pfalz, W Germany
62 M4 **Boquerón** *off.* Departamento de Boquerón. ◈ *department* W Paraguay
Boquerón, Departamento de *see* Boquerón
43 P15 **Boquete** *var.* Bajo Boquete. Chiriquí, W Panama
40 J6 **Boquilla, Presa de la** ⊠ N Mexico
40 L5 **Boquillas** *var.* Boquillas del Carmen. Coahuila de Zaragoza, NE Mexico
Boquillas del Carmen *see* Boquillas
112 P12 **Bor** Serbia, E Serbia
81 F15 **Bor** Jonglei, S Sudan
95 L20 **Bor** Jönköping, S Sweden
136 J15 **Bor** Niğde, S Turkey
191 S10 **Bora-Bora** *island* Îles Sous le Vent, W French Polynesia
167 Q9 **Borabu** Maha Sarakham, E Thailand
33 P13 **Borah Peak** ▲ Idaho, NW USA
145 U16 **Boralday** *prev.* Burunday. Almaty, SE Kazakhstan
144 G13 **Borankul** *prev.* Opornyy. Mangistau, SW Kazakhstan
95 J19 **Borås** Västra Götaland, S Sweden
143 N11 **Borāzjān** *var.* Borazjān. Būshehr, S Iran
Borazjān *see* Borāzjān
58 G13 **Borba** Amazonas, N Brazil
104 H11 **Borba** Évora, S Portugal
Borbetomagus *see* Worms
55 O7 **Borbón** Bolívar, E Venezuela
59 Q15 **Borborema, Planalto da** *plateau* NE Brazil
116 M14 **Borcea, Braţul** ≈ S Romania
Borchalo *see* Marneuli
195 R15 **Borchgrevink Coast** *physical region* Antarctica
137 Q11 **Borçka** Artvin, NE Turkey
98 N11 **Borculo** Gelderland, E Netherlands
182 G10 **Borda, Cape** *headland* South Australia
102 K13 **Bordeaux** *anc.* Burdigala. Gironde, SW France
9 T15 **Borden** Saskatchewan, S Canada
14 D8 **Borden Lake** ◎ Ontario, S Canada
9 N4 **Borden Peninsula** *peninsula* Baffin Island, Nunavut, NE Canada

◆ Country ● Country Capital ◇ Dependent Territory ○ Dependent Territory Capital ◈ Administrative Regions ✈ International Airport ▲ Mountain ▲▲ Mountain Range ⋀ Volcano ≈ River ◎ Lake ⊠ Reservoir

182 *K11* **Bordertown** South Australia
92 *H2* **Bordheyri** Vestfirdhir, NW Iceland
95 *B18* **Bordhoy** *Dan.* Bordø. *island* NE Faeroe Islands
106 *B11* **Bordighera** Liguria, NW Italy
74 *K5* **Bordj-Bou-Arreridj** *var.* Bordj Bou Arreridj, Bordj Bou Arréridj. N Algeria
74 *L10* **Bordj Omar Driss** E Algeria
143 *N13* **Bord Khūn** Hormozgān, S Iran
Bordø *see* Bordhoy
147 *V7* **Bordunskiy** Chuyskaya Oblast', N Kyrgyzstan
95 *M17* **Borensberg** Östergötland, S Sweden
Borgå *see* Porvoo
92 *L2* **Borgarfjördhur** Austurland, NE Iceland
92 *H3* **Borgarnes** Vesturland, W Iceland
93 *G14* **Børgefjelt** ▲▲ C Norway
98 *O7* **Borger** Drenthe, NE Netherlands
25 *N2* **Borger** Texas, SW USA
95 *N20* **Borgholm** Kalmar, S Sweden
107 *N22* **Borgia** Calabria, SW Italy
99 *J18* **Borgloon** Limburg, NE Belgium
195 *P2* **Borg Massif** ▲▲ Antarctica
22 *L9* **Borgne, Lake** ◎ Louisiana, S USA
106 *C7* **Borgomanero** Piemonte, NE Italy
106 *G10* **Borgo Panigale** ✈ (Bologna) Emilia-Romagna, N Italy
107 *J15* **Borgorose** Lazio, C Italy
106 *A9* **Borgo San Dalmazzo** Piemonte, N Italy
106 *G11* **Borgo San Lorenzo** Toscana, C Italy
106 *C7* **Borgosesia** Piemonte, NE Italy
106 *E9* **Borgo Val di Taro** Emilia-Romagna, C Italy
106 *G6* **Borgo Valsugana** Trentino-Alto Adige, N Italy
Borhoyn Tal *see* Dzamïn-Üüd
167 *R8* **Borikhan** *var.* Borikhane. Bolikhamxai, C Laos
Borikhane *see* Borikhan
Borislav *see* Boryslav
127 *N8* **Borisoglebsk** Voronezhskaya Oblast', W Russian Federation
Borisov *see* Barysaw
Borisovgrad *see* Pŭrvomay
Borispol' *see* Boryspil'
172 *I3* **Boriziny** Mahajanga, NW Madagascar
105 *Q5* **Borja** Aragón, NE Spain
Borjas Blancas *see* Les Borges Blanques
137 *S10* **Borjomi** *Rus.* Borzhomi. C Georgia
118 *L12* **Borkavichy** *Rus.* Borkovichi. Vitsyebskaya Voblasts', N Belarus
101 *H16* **Borken** Hessen, C Germany
101 *E14* **Borken** Nordrhein-Westfalen, W Germany
92 *H10* **Borkenes** Troms, N Norway
78 *H7* **Borkou-Ennedi-Tibesti** *off.* Préfecture du Borkou-Ennedi-Tibesti. ⬖ *prefecture* N Chad
Borkou-Ennedi-Tibesti, Préfecture du *see* Borkou-Ennedi-Tibesti
Borkovichi *see* Borkavichy
100 *E9* **Borkum** *island* NW Germany
81 *K17* **Bor, Lagh** *var.* Lak Bor. *dry watercourse* NE Kenya
Bor, Lak *see* Bor, Lagh
95 *M14* **Borlänge** Dalarna, C Sweden
106 *C9* **Bormida** ≈ NW Italy
106 *F6* **Bormio** Lombardia, N Italy
101 *M16* **Borna** Sachsen, E Germany
98 *O10* **Borne** Overijssel, E Netherlands
99 *F17* **Bornem** Antwerpen, N Belgium
169 *S10* **Borneo** *island* Brunei/Indonesia/Malaysia
101 *E16* **Bornheim** Nordrhein-Westfalen, W Germany
95 *L24* **Bornholm** ⬖ *county* E Denmark
95 *L24* **Bornholm** *island* E Denmark
77 *Y13* **Borno** ⬖ *state* NE Nigeria
104 *K15* **Bornos** Andalucía, S Spain
162 *L7* **Bornuur** Töv, C Mongolia
117 *O4* **Borodyanka** Kyyivs'ka Oblast', N Ukraine
158 *I5* **Borohoro Shan** ▲▲ NW China
77 *O13* **Boromo** SW Burkina
35 *T13* **Boron** California, W USA
Borongo *see* Black Volta
Boron'ki *see* Baron'ki
Borosjenő *see* Ineu
Borossebes *see* Sebiș
76 *L15* **Borotou** NW Ivory Coast
117 *W6* **Borova** Kharkivs'ka Oblast', E Ukraine
114 *H8* **Borovan** Vratsa, NW Bulgaria
124 *I14* **Borovichi** Novgorodskaya Oblast', W Russian Federation
Borovlje *see* Ferlach
112 *J9* **Borovo** Vukovar-Srijem, NE Croatia
145 *Q7* **Borovoye** *Kaz.* Būrabay. Akmola, N Kazakhstan
126 *K4* **Borovsk** Kaluzhskaya Oblast', W Russian Federation
145 *N7* **Borovskoy** Kostanay, N Kazakhstan
Borovukha *see* Baravukha
95 *L23* **Borrby** Skåne, S Sweden
181 *R3* **Borroloola** Northern Territory, N Australia
116 *F9* **Borș** Bihor, NW Romania
116 *I9* **Borșa** *Hung.* Borsa. Maramureș, N Romania
116 *J10* **Borsec** *Ger.* Bad Borseck, *Hung.* Borszék. Harghita, C Romania
92 *K8* **Børselv** *Lapp.* Bissojohka. Finnmark, N Norway
113 *L23* **Borsh** *var.* Borshi. Vlorë, S Albania
Borshchev *see* Borshchiv
116 *K7* **Borshchiv** *Pol.* Borszczów, *Rus.* Borshchev. Ternopil's'ka Oblast', W Ukraine
Borshi *see* Borsh
111 *L20* **Borsod-Abaúj-Zemplén** *off.* Borsod-Abaúj-Zemplén Megye. ⬖ *county* NE Hungary
Borsod-Abaúj-Zemplén Megye *see* Borsod-Abaúj-Zemplén
99 *E15* **Borssele** Zeeland, SW Netherlands
Borszczów *see* Borshchiv
Borszék *see* Borsec
Bortala *see* Bole
103 *O12* **Bort-les-Orgues** Corrèze, C France
Bor u České Lípy *see* Nový Bor
Bor-Udzüür *see* Altay
Bor-Üdzüür *see* Altay
143 *N9* **Borūjen** Chahār Maḩall va Bakhtīārī, C Iran
142 *L7* **Borūjerd** *var.* Burujird. Lorestān, W Iran
116 *H6* **Boryslav** *Pol.* Borysław, *Rus.* Borislav. L'vivs'ka Oblast', NW Ukraine
Borysław *see* Boryslav
117 *P4* **Boryspil'** *Rus.* Borispol'. Kyyivs'ka Oblast', N Ukraine
117 *P4* **Boryspil'** *Rus.* Borispol'. ✈ (Kyyiv) Kyyivs'ka Oblast', N Ukraine
Borzhomi *see* Borjomi
117 *R3* **Borzna** Chernihivs'ka Oblast', NE Ukraine
123 *O14* **Borzya** Chitinskaya Oblast', S Russian Federation
107 *B18* **Bosa** Sardegna, Italy, C Mediterranean Sea
112 *F10* **Bosanska Dubica** *var.* Kozarska Dubica. ⬖ Republika Srpska, NW Bosnia and Herzegovina
112 *G10* **Bosanska Gradiška** *var.* Gradiška. ⬖ Republika Srpska, N Bosnia and Herzegovina
112 *F10* **Bosanska Kostajnica** *var.* Srpska Kostajnica. ⬖ Republika Srpska, NW Bosnia and Herzegovina
112 *E11* **Bosanska Krupa** *var.* Krupa, Krupa na Uni. ⬖ Federacija Bosna I Hercegovina, NW Bosnia and Herzegovina
112 *H10* **Bosanski Brod** *var.* Srpski Brod. ⬖ Republika Srpska, N Bosnia and Herzegovina
112 *E10* **Bosanski Novi** *var.* Novi Grad. ⬖ Republika Srpska, NW Bosnia and Herzegovina
112 *E11* **Bosanski Petrovac** *var.* Petrovac. ⬖ Federacija Bosna I Hercegovina, NW Bosnia and Herzegovina
112 *I10* **Bosanski Šamac** *var.* Šamac. ⬖ Republika Srpska, N Bosnia and Herzegovina
112 *E12* **Bosansko Grahovo** *var.* Grahovo, Hrvatsko Grahovi. ⬖ Federacija Bosna I Hercegovina, W Bosnia and Herzegovina
Bosaso *see* Boosaaso
186 *B7* **Bosavi, Mount** 🌋 W Papua New Guinea
160 *J14* **Bose** Guangxi Zhuangzu Zizhiqu, S China
161 *Q5* **Boshan** Shandong, E China
113 *P16* **Bosilegrad** *prev.* Bosiljgrad. Serbia, SE Serbia
Bosiljgrad *see* Bosilegrad
Bösing *see* Pezinok
98 *H12* **Boskoop** Zuid-Holland, C Netherlands
111 *G18* **Boskovice** *Ger.* Boskowitz. Jihomoravský Kraj, SE Czech Republic
Boskowitz *see* Boskovice
112 *I10* **Bosna** ≈ N Bosnia and Herzegovina
113 *G14* **Bosna I Hercegovina, Federacija** ⬖ *republic* Bosnia and Herzegovina
112 *H12* **Bosnia and Herzegovina** *off.* Republic of Bosnia and Herzegovina. ◆ *republic* SE Europe
Bosnia and Herzegovina, Republic of *see* Bosnia and Herzegovina
79 *J16* **Bosobolo** Equateur, NW Dem. Rep. Congo
165 *O14* **Bōsō-hantō** *peninsula* Honshū, S Japan
Bosora *see* Buṣrá ash Shām
Bosphorus/Bosporus *see* İstanbul Boğazı
Bosporus Cimmerius *see* Kerch Strait
Bosporus Thracius *see* İstanbul Boğazı
Bosra *see* Buṣrá ash Shām
79 *H14* **Bossangoa** Ouham, C Central African Republic
Bossé Bangou *see* Bossey Bangou
79 *I15* **Bossembélé** Ombella-Mpoko, C Central African Republic
79 *H15* **Bossentélé** Ouham-Pendé, W Central African Republic
77 *R12* **Bossey Bangou** *var.* Bossé Bangou. Tillabéri, SW Niger
22 *G5* **Bossier City** Louisiana, S USA
83 *D20* **Bossiesvlei** Hardap, S Namibia
77 *Y11* **Bosso** Diffa, SE Niger
61 *F15* **Bossoroca** Rio Grande do Sul, S Brazil
158 *J10* **Bostan** Xinjiang Uygur Zizhiqu, W China
142 *K3* **Bostānābād** Āžarbāyjān-e Sharqī, N Iran
158 *K6* **Bosten Hu** *var.* Bagrax Hu. ◎ NW China
97 *O18* **Boston** *prev.* St.Botolph's Town. E England, UK
19 *O11* **Boston** *state capital* Massachusetts, NE USA
146 *I9* **Bo'ston** *Rus.* Bustan. Qoraqalpog'iston Respublikasi, W Uzbekistan
10 *M17* **Boston Bar** British Columbia, SW Canada
27 *T10* **Boston Mountains** ▲▲ Arkansas, C USA
15 *P8* **Bostonnais** ≈ Québec, SE Canada
Bostyn' *see* Bastyn'
112 *J10* **Bosut** ≈ E Croatia
154 *C11* **Botād** Gujarāt, W India
183 *T9* **Botany Bay** *inlet* New South Wales, SE Australia
83 *G18* **Boteti** *var.* Botletle. ≈ N Botswana
114 *J9* **Botev** ▲ C Bulgaria
114 *H9* **Botevgrad** *prev.* Orkhaniye. Sofiya, W Bulgaria
93 *J16* **Bothnia, Gulf of** *Fin.* Pohjanlahti, *Swe.* Bottniska Viken. *gulf* N Baltic Sea
183 *P17* **Bothwell** Tasmania, SE Australia
104 *H5* **Boticas** Vila Real, N Portugal
55 *W10* **Boti-Pasi** Sipaliwini, C Surinam
Botletle *see* Boteti
127 *P16* **Botlikh** Chechenskaya Respublika, SW Russian Federation
117 *N10* **Botna** ≈ E Moldova
147 *P12* **Botogot', Tizmasi** *Rus.* Khrebet Babatag. ▲▲ Tajikistan/Uzbekistan
116 *I9* **Botoșani** *Hung.* Botosány. Botoșani, NE Romania
116 *K8* **Botoșani** ⬖ *county* NE Romania
Botosány *see* Botoșani
161 *P4* **Botou** *prev.* Bozhen. Hebei, E China
99 *M20* **Botrange** ▲ E Belgium
107 *O21* **Botricello** Calabria, SW Italy
83 *I23* **Botshabelo** Free State, C South Africa
93 *J15* **Botsmark** Västerbotten, N Sweden
83 *G19* **Botswana** *off.* Republic of Botswana. ◆ *republic* S Africa
Botswana, Republic of *see* Botswana
29 *N2* **Bottineau** North Dakota, N USA
Bottniska Viken *see* Bothnia, Gulf of
60 *L9* **Botucatu** São Paulo, S Brazil
76 *M16* **Bouaflé** C Ivory Coast
77 *N16* **Bouaké** *var.* Bwake. C Ivory Coast
79 *G14* **Bouar** Nana-Mambéré, W Central African Republic
74 *H7* **Bouarfa** NE Morocco
111 *B19* **Boubín** ▲ SW Czech Republic
79 *I14* **Bouca** Ouham, W Central African Republic
15 *T5* **Boucher** ≈ Québec, SE Canada
103 *R15* **Bouches-du-Rhône** ⬖ *department* SE France
74 *C9* **Bou Craa** *var.* Bu Craa. NW Western Sahara
77 *O9* **Boû Djébéha** *oasis* C Mali
108 *C8* **Boudry** Neuchâtel, W Switzerland
180 *L2* **Bougainville, Cape** *cape* Western Australia
65 *E24* **Bougainville, Cape** *headland* East Falkland, Falkland Islands
Bougainville, Détroit de *see* Bougainville Strait
186 *J7* **Bougainville Island** *island* NE Papua New Guinea
186 *I8* **Bougainville Strait** *strait* N Solomon Islands
187 *Q13* **Bougainville Strait** *Fr.* Détroit de Bougainville. *strait* C Vanuatu
120 *I9* **Bougaroun, Cap** *headland* NE Algeria
77 *R8* **Boughessa** Kidal, NE Mali
Bougie *see* Béjaïa
76 *L13* **Bougouni** Sikasso, SW Mali
99 *J24* **Bouillon** Luxembourg, SE Belgium
74 *K5* **Bouira** *var.* Bouïra. N Algeria
74 *D8* **Bou-Izakarn** SW Morocco
74 *B9* **Boujdour** *var.* Bojador. W Western Sahara
74 *G5* **Boukhalef** ✈ (Tanger) N Morocco
Boukombé *see* Boukoumbé
77 *R14* **Boukoumbé** *var.* Boukombé. C Benin
76 *G6* **Boû Lanouâr** Dakhlet Nouâdhibou, W Mauritania
37 *T4* **Boulder** Colorado, C USA
33 *R10* **Boulder** Montana, NW USA
35 *X12* **Boulder City** Nevada, W USA
181 *T7* **Boulia** Queensland, C Australia
15 *N10* **Boullé** ≈ Québec, SE Canada
102 *J9* **Boulogne** ≈ NW France
Boulogne *see* Boulogne-sur-Mer
102 *L16* **Boulogne-sur-Gesse** Haute-Garonne, S France
103 *N1* **Boulogne-sur-Mer** *var.* Boulogne; *anc.* Bononia, Gesoriacum, Gessoriacum. Pas-de-Calais, N France
77 *Q12* **Boulsa** C Burkina
77 *W11* **Boultoum** Zinder, C Niger
187 *Y14* **Bouma** Taveuni, N Fiji
79 *G16* **Boumba** ≈ SE Cameroon
76 *J9* **Boûmdeïd** *var.* Boumdeït. Assaba, S Mauritania
Boumdeït *see* Boûmdeïd
115 *C17* **Boumistós** ▲ W Greece
77 *O15* **Bouna** NE Ivory Coast
19 *P4* **Boundary Bald Mountain** ▲ Maine, NE USA
35 *S8* **Boundary Peak** ▲ Nevada, W USA
76 *M14* **Boundiali** N Ivory Coast
79 *G19* **Boundji** Cuvette, C Congo
77 *O13* **Boundoukui** *var.* Bondoukui, Bondoukuy. W Burkina
36 *L2* **Bountiful** Utah, W USA
Bounty Basin *see* Bounty Trough
191 *Q16* **Bounty Bay** *bay* Pitcairn Island, C Pacific Ocean
192 *L12* **Bounty Islands** *island group* S New Zealand
175 *Q13* **Bounty Trough** *var.* Bounty Basin. *undersea feature* S Pacific Ocean
187 *P17* **Bourail** Province Sud, C New Caledonia
27 *V5* **Bourbeuse River** ≈ Missouri, C USA
103 *Q9* **Bourbon-Lancy** Saône-et-Loire, C France
31 *N11* **Bourbonnais** Illinois, N USA
103 *O10* **Bourbonnais** *cultural region* C France
103 *S7* **Bourbonne-les-Bains** Haute-Marne, N France
Bourbon Vendée *see* la Roche-sur-Yon
74 *M8* **Bourdj Messaouda** E Algeria
77 *Q10* **Bourem** Gao, C Mali
Bourg *see* Bourg-en-Bresse
103 *N11* **Bourganeuf** Creuse, C France
Bourgas *see* Burgas
Bourge-en-Bresse *see* Bourg-en-Bresse
103 *S10* **Bourg-en-Bresse** *var.* Bourg, Bourge-en-Bresse. Ain, E France
103 *O8* **Bourges** *anc.* Avaricum. Cher, C France
103 *T11* **Bourget, Lac du** ◎ E France
103 *P8* **Bourgogne** *Eng.* Burgundy. ⬖ *region* E France
103 *S11* **Bourgoin-Jallieu** Isère, E France
103 *R14* **Bourg-St-Andéol** Ardèche, E France
103 *U11* **Bourg-St-Maurice** Savoie, E France
108 *C11* **Bourg St. Pierre** Valais, SW Switzerland
76 *H8* **Boû Rjeïmât** *well* W Mauritania
183 *P5* **Bourke** New South Wales, SE Australia
97 *M24* **Bournemouth** S England, UK
99 *M23* **Bourscheid** Diekirch, NE Luxembourg
74 *K6* **Bou Saâda** *var.* Bou Saada. N Algeria
36 *I13* **Bouse Wash** ≈ Arizona, SW USA
103 *N10* **Boussac** Creuse, C France
102 *M16* **Boussens** Haute-Garonne, S France
78 *H12* **Bousso** *prev.* Fort-Bretonnet. Chari-Baguirmi, S Chad
76 *H9* **Boutilimit** Trarza, SW Mauritania
65 *D21* **Bouvet Island** ◇ *Norwegian dependency* S Atlantic Ocean
77 *U11* **Bouza** Tahoua, SW Niger
109 *R10* **Bovec** *Ger.* Flitsch, *It.* Plezzo. NW Slovenia
98 *J8* **Bovenkarspel** Noord-Holland, NW Netherlands
29 *V5* **Bovey** Minnesota, N USA
32 *M9* **Bovill** Idaho, NW USA
24 *L4* **Bovina** Texas, SW USA
107 *M17* **Bovino** Puglia, SE Italy
61 *C17* **Bovril** Entre Ríos, E Argentina
28 *L2* **Bowbells** North Dakota, N USA
9 *Q16* **Bow City** Alberta, SW Canada
29 *O8* **Bowdle** South Dakota, N USA
181 *X6* **Bowen** Queensland, NE Australia
192 *L2* **Bowers Ridge** *undersea feature* S Bering Sea
25 *S5* **Bowie** Texas, SW USA
9 *R17* **Bow Island** Alberta, SW Canada
Bowkān *see* Būkān
20 *J7* **Bowling Green** Kentucky, S USA
27 *V3* **Bowling Green** Missouri, C USA
31 *R11* **Bowling Green** Ohio, N USA
21 *W5* **Bowling Green** Virginia, NE USA
28 *J6* **Bowman** North Dakota, N USA
9 *Q7* **Bowman Bay** *bay* NW Atlantic Ocean
194 *I5* **Bowman Coast** *physical region* Antarctica
28 *J7* **Bowman-Haley Lake** ⊠ North Dakota, N USA
195 *Z11* **Bowman Island** *island* Antarctica
Bowo *see* Bomi
183 *S9* **Bowral** New South Wales, SE Australia
186 *E8* **Bowutu Mountains** ▲▲ C Papua New Guinea
83 *I16* **Bowwood** Southern, S Zambia
28 *I12* **Box Butte Reservoir** ⊠ Nebraska, C USA
28 *J10* **Box Elder** South Dakota, N USA
95 *M18* **Boxholm** Östergötland, S Sweden
Bo Xian/Boxian *see* Bozhou
161 *Q4* **Boxing** Shandong, E China
99 *L14* **Boxmeer** Noord-Brabant, SE Netherlands
99 *J14* **Boxtel** Noord-Brabant, S Netherlands
136 *J10* **Boyabat** Sinop, N Turkey
54 *F9* **Boyacá** *off.* Departamento de Boyacá. ⬖ *province* C Colombia
Boyacá, Departamento de *see* Boyacá
117 *O4* **Boyarka** Kyyivs'ka Oblast', N Ukraine
22 *H7* **Boyce** Louisiana, S USA
33 *U11* **Boyd** Montana, NW USA
25 *S6* **Boyd** Texas, SW USA
21 *V8* **Boydton** Virginia, NE USA
Boyer Ahmadī va Kohkīlūyeh *see* Kohgīlūyeh va Būyer Aḩmad
29 *T13* **Boyer River** ≈ Iowa, C USA
21 *W8* **Boykins** Virginia, NE USA
9 *Q13* **Boyle** Alberta, SW Canada
97 *D16* **Boyle** *Ir.* Mainistirna Búille. C Ireland
97 *F17* **Boyne** *Ir.* An Bhóinn. ≈ E Ireland
31 *Q5* **Boyne City** Michigan, N USA
23 *Z14* **Boynton Beach** Florida, SE USA
147 *O13* **Boysun** *Rus.* Baysun. Surkhondaryo Viloyati, S Uzbekistan
Bozau *see* Întorsura Buzăului
136 *B12* **Bozcaada** *Island* Çanakkale, NW Turkey
136 *C14* **Boz Dağları** ▲▲ W Turkey
33 *S11* **Bozeman** Montana, NW USA
Bozen *see* Bolzano
79 *J16* **Bozene** Equateur, NW Dem. Rep. Congo
Bozhen *see* Botou
161 *P7* **Bozhou** *var.* Boxian, Bo Xian. Anhui, E China
136 *H16* **Bozkır** Konya, S Turkey
136 *K13* **Bozok Yaylasī** *plateau* C Turkey
79 *H14* **Bozoum** Ouham-Pendé, W Central African Republic
137 *N16* **Bozova** Sanlıurfa, S Turkey
Bozrah *see* Buṣrá ash Shām
136 *E12* **Bozüyük** Bilecik, NW Turkey
106 *B9* **Bra** Piemonte, NW Italy
194 *G4* **Brabant Island** *island* Antarctica
99 *I20* **Brabant Walloon** ⬖ *province* C Belgium
113 *F15* **Brač** *var.* Brach, *It.* Brazza; *anc.* Brattia. *island* S Croatia
Bracara Augusta *see* Braga
107 *H15* **Bracciano** Lazio, C Italy
107 *H14* **Bracciano, Lago di** ◎ C Italy
14 *H13* **Bracebridge** Ontario, S Canada
Brach *see* Brač
93 *G17* **Bräcke** Jämtland, C Sweden
25 *P12* **Brackettville** Texas, SW USA
97 *N22* **Bracknell** S England, UK
61 *K14* **Braço do Norte** Santa Catarina, S Brazil
116 *G11* **Brad** *Hung.* Brád. Hunedoara, SW Romania
107 *N18* **Bradano** ≈ S Italy
23 *V13* **Bradenton** Florida, SE USA
14 *H14* **Bradford** Ontario, S Canada
97 *L17* **Bradford** N England, UK
27 *W10* **Bradford** Arkansas, C USA
18 *D12* **Bradford** Pennsylvania, NE USA
27 *T15* **Bradley** Arkansas, C USA
25 *P7* **Bradshaw** Texas, SW USA
25 *Q9* **Brady** Texas, SW USA
25 *Q9* **Brady Creek** ≈ Texas, SW USA
95 *G22* **Brædstrup** Vejle, C Denmark
96 *J10* **Braemar** NE Scotland, UK
116 *K8* **Brăești** Botoșani, NW Romania
104 *G5* **Braga** *anc.* Bracara Augusta. Braga, NW Portugal
104 *G5* **Braga** ⬖ *district* N Portugal
116 *J15* **Bragadiru** Teleorman, S Romania
61 *C20* **Bragado** Buenos Aires, E Argentina
104 *J5* **Bragança** *Eng.* Braganza; *anc.* Julio Briga. Bragança, NE Portugal
104 *I5* **Bragança** ⬖ *district* N Portugal
60 *N9* **Bragança Paulista** São Paulo, S Brazil
Braganza *see* Bragança
Bragin *see* Brahin
29 *V7* **Braham** Minnesota, N USA
Brahe *see* Brda
Brahestad *see* Raahe
119 *O20* **Brahin** *Rus.* Bragin. Homyel'skaya Voblasts', SE Belarus
153 *U15* **Brahmanbaria** Chittagong, E Bangladesh
154 *O12* **Brāhmani** ≈ E India
154 *N13* **Brahmapur** Orissa, E India
129 *S10* **Brahmaputra** *var.* Padma, Tsangpo, *Ben.* Jamuna, *Chin.* Yarlung Zangbo Jiang, *Ind.* Bramaputra, Dihang, Siang. ≈ S Asia
97 *H19* **Braich y Pwll** *headland* NW Wales, UK
183 *R10* **Braidwood** New South Wales, SE Australia
30 *M11* **Braidwood** Illinois, N USA
116 *M13* **Brăila** Brăila, E Romania
116 *L13* **Brăila** ⬖ *county* SE Romania
99 *G19* **Braine-l'Alleud** Brabant Walloon, C Belgium
99 *F19* **Braine-le-Comte** Hainaut, SW Belgium
29 *U6* **Brainerd** Minnesota, N USA
99 *J19* **Braives** Liège, E Belgium
83 *H23* **Brak** ≈ C South Africa
Brak *see* Birāk
99 *E18* **Brakel** Oost-Vlaanderen, SW Belgium
98 *J13* **Brakel** Gelderland, C Netherlands
76 *H9* **Brakna** ⬖ *region* S Mauritania
95 *J17* **Brålanda** Västra Götaland, S Sweden
Bramaputra *see* Brahmaputra
95 *F23* **Bramming** Ribe, W Denmark
14 *G15* **Brampton** Ontario, S Canada
100 *F12* **Bramsche** Niedersachsen, NW Germany
116 *J12* **Bran** *Ger.* Törzburg, *Hung.* Törcsvár. Brașov, S Romania
29 *W8* **Branch** Minnesota, N USA
21 *R14* **Branchville** South Carolina, SE USA
47 *Y6* **Branco, Cabo** *headland* E Brazil
58 *F11* **Branco, Rio** ≈ N Brazil
108 *J8* **Brand** Vorarlberg, W Austria
83 *B18* **Brandberg** ▲ NW Namibia
95 *H14* **Brandbu** Oppland, S Norway
95 *F22* **Brande** Ringkøbing, W Denmark
Brandebourg *see* Brandenburg
100 *M12* **Brandenburg** *var.* Brandenburg an der Havel. Brandenburg, NE Germany
20 *K5* **Brandenburg** Kentucky, S USA
100 *N12* **Brandenburg** *off.* Freie und Hansestadt Hamburg, *Fr.* Brandebourg. ⬖ *state* NE Germany
Brandenburg an der Havel *see* Brandenburg
83 *I23* **Brandfort** Free State, C South Africa
9 *W16* **Brandon** Manitoba, S Canada
23 *V12* **Brandon** Florida, SE USA
22 *L6* **Brandon** Mississippi, S USA
97 *A20* **Brandon Mountain** *Ir.* Cnoc Bréanainn. ▲ SW Ireland
Brandsen *see* Coronel Brandsen
95 *I14* **Brandval** Hedmark, S Norway
83 *F24* **Brandvlei** Northern Cape, W South Africa
23 *U9* **Branford** Florida, SE USA
110 *K7* **Braniewo** *Ger.* Braunsberg. Warmińsko-mazurskie, N Poland
194 *H3* **Bransfield Strait** *strait* Antarctica
37 *U8* **Branson** Colorado, C USA
27 *T8* **Branson** Missouri, C USA
14 *G16* **Brantford** Ontario, S Canada
102 *L12* **Brantôme** Dordogne, SW France
182 *L12* **Branxholme** Victoria, SE Australia
Brasil *see* Brazil
59 *C16* **Brasiléia** Acre, W Brazil
59 *K18* **Brasília** ● (Brazil) Distrito Federal, C Brazil
Brasil, República Federativa do *see* Brazil
Braslav *see* Braslaw
118 *J12* **Braslaw** *Pol.* Brasław, *Rus.* Braslav. Vitsyebskaya Voblasts', N Belarus
116 *J12* **Brașov** *Ger.* Kronstadt, *Hung.* Brassó; *prev.* Orașul Stalin. Brașov, C Romania
116 *I12* **Brașov** ⬖ *county* C Romania
77 *U18* **Brass** Bayelsa, S Nigeria
99 *H16* **Brasschaat** *var.* Brasschaet. Antwerpen, N Belgium
Brasschaet *see* Brasschaat
169 *V8* **Brassey, Banjaran** *var.* Brassey Range. ▲▲ East Malaysia
Brassey Range *see* Brassey, Banjaran
Brassó *see* Brașov
23 *T1* **Brasstown Bald** ▲ Georgia, SE USA
113 *K22* **Brataj** Vlorë, SW Albania
114 *J10* **Bratan** *var.* Morozov. ▲ C Bulgaria
111 *F21* **Bratislava** *Ger.* Pressburg, *Hung.* Pozsony. ● (Slovakia) Bratislavský Kraj, W Slovakia
111 *H21* **Bratislavský Kraj** ⬖ *region* W Slovakia
114 *H10* **Bratiya** ▲ C Bulgaria
122 *M12* **Bratsk** Irkutskaya Oblast', C Russian Federation
117 *Q8* **Brats'ke** Mykolayivs'ka Oblast', S Ukraine
122 *M13* **Bratskoye Vodokhranilishche** *Eng.* Bratsk Reservoir. ⊠ S Russian Federation
Bratsk Reservoir *see* Bratskoye Vodokhranilishche
Brattia *see* Brač
94 *D9* **Brattvåg** Møre og Romsdal, S Norway
112 *K12* **Bratunac** ⬖ Republika Srpska, E Bosnia and Herzegovina
114 *J10* **Bratya Daskalovi** *prev.* Grozdovo. Stara Zagora, C Bulgaria
109 *U2* **Braunau** ≈ N Austria
Braunau *see* Braunau am Inn
109 *Q4* **Braunau am Inn** *var.* Braunau. Oberösterreich, N Austria
Braunsberg *see* Braniewo
100 *J13* **Braunschweig** *Eng./Fr.* Brunswick. Niedersachsen, N Germany
Brava *see* Baraawe
105 *Y6* **Brava, Costa** *coastal region* NE Spain
43 *V16* **Brava, Punta** *headland* E Panama
95 *N17* **Bråviken** *inlet* S Sweden
56 *B10* **Bravo, Cerro** ▲ N Peru
Bravo del Norte, Río/Bravo, Río *see* Grande, Rio
35 *X17* **Brawley** California, W USA
97 *G18* **Bray** *Ir.* Bré. E Ireland
59 *G16* **Brazil** *off.* Federative Republic of Brazil, *Port.* República Federativa do Brasil, *Sp.* Brasil; *prev.* United States of Brazil. ◆ *federal republic* South America
65 *K15* **Brazil Basin** *var.* Brazilian Basin, Brazil'skaya Kotlovina. *undersea feature* W Atlantic Ocean
Brazil, Federative Republic of *see* Brazil
Brazilian Basin *see* Brazil Basin
Brazilian Highlands *see* Central, Planalto
Brazil'skaya Kotlovina *see* Brazil Basin
Brazil, United States of *see* Brazil
25 *U10* **Brazos River** ≈ Texas, SW USA
Brazza *see* Brač
79 *G21* **Brazzaville** ● (Congo) Capital District, S Congo
79 *G21* **Brazzaville** ✈ Le Pool, S Congo
112 *J11* **Brčko** ⬖ Republika Srpska, NE Bosnia and Herzegovina
110 *H8* **Brda** *Ger.* Brahe. ≈ N Poland
Bré *see* Bray
185 *A23* **Breaksea Sound** *sound* South Island, New Zealand
184 *L4* **Bream Bay** *bay* North Island, New Zealand
184 *L4* **Bream Head** *headland* North Island, New Zealand
Bréanainn, Cnoc *see* Brandon Mountain
45 *S6* **Brea, Punta** *headland* W Puerto Rico
22 *I9* **Breaux Bridge** Louisiana, S USA
116 *J13* **Breaza** Prahova, SE Romania
169 *P16* **Brebes** Jawa, C Indonesia
96 *K10* **Brechin** E Scotland, UK
99 *H15* **Brecht** Antwerpen, N Belgium
37 *S4* **Breckenridge** Colorado, C USA
29 *R6* **Breckenridge** Minnesota, N USA
25 *R6* **Breckenridge** Texas, SW USA
97 *J21* **Brecknock** *cultural region* SE Wales, UK
63 *G25* **Brecknock, Península** *headland* S Chile
111 *G19* **Břeclav** *Ger.* Lundenburg. Jihomoravský Kraj, SE Czech Republic
97 *J21* **Brecon** E Wales, UK
97 *J21* **Brecon Beacons** ▲▲ S Wales, UK
99 *I14* **Breda** Noord-Brabant, S Netherlands
95 *K20* **Bredaryd** Jönköping, S Sweden

◆ Country
● Country Capital
◇ Dependent Territory
○ Dependent Territory Capital
⬖ Administrative Regions
✈ International Airport
▲ Mountain
▲▲ Mountain Range
🌋 Volcano
≈ River
◎ Lake
⊠ Reservoir

BREDASDORP – BUHL

83 F26 **Bredasdorp** Western Cape, SW South Africa
93 H16 **Bredbyn** Västernorrland, N Sweden
122 F11 **Bredy** Chelyabinskaya Oblast', C Russian Federation
99 K17 **Bree** Limburg, NE Belgium
67 T15 **Breede** ≈ S South Africa
98 I7 **Breezand** Noord-Holland, NW Netherlands
113 P18 **Bregalnica** ≈ E FYR Macedonia
108 I6 **Bregenz** *anc.* Brigantium. Vorarlberg, W Austria
108 J7 **Bregenzer Wald** ▲▲ W Austria
114 F6 **Bregovo** Vidin, NW Bulgaria
102 H5 **Bréhat, Île de** *island* NW France
92 H2 **Breidhafjördhur** *bay* W Iceland
92 L3 **Breidhdalsvík** Austurland, E Iceland
108 H9 **Breil** *Ger.* Brigels. Graubünden, S Switzerland
92 J8 **Breivikbotn** Finnmark, N Norway
94 I9 **Brekken** Sør-Trøndelag, S Norway
94 G7 **Brekstad** Sør-Trøndelag, S Norway
94 B10 **Bremangerlandet** *island* S Norway
Brême *see* Bremen
100 H11 **Bremen** *Fr.* Brême. Bremen, NW Germany
23 R3 **Bremen** Georgia, SE USA
31 O11 **Bremen** Indiana, N USA
100 H10 **Bremen** *off.* Freie Hansestadt Bremen, *Fr.* Brême. ⬖ *state* N Germany
100 G9 **Bremerhaven** Bremen, NW Germany
Bremersdorp *see* Manzini
32 G8 **Bremerton** Washington, NW USA
100 H10 **Bremervörde** Niedersachsen, NW Germany
25 U9 **Bremond** Texas, SW USA
25 U10 **Brenham** Texas, SW USA
108 M8 **Brenner** Tirol, W Austria
Brenner, Col du/Brennero, Passo del *see* Brenner Pass
108 M8 **Brenner Pass** *var.* Brenner Sattel, *Fr.* Col du Brenner, *Ger.* Brennerpass, *It.* Passo del Brennero. *pass* Austria/Italy
Brennerpass *see* Brenner Pass
Brenner Sattel *see* Brenner Pass
108 G10 **Brenno** ≈ SW Switzerland
106 F7 **Breno** Lombardia, N Italy
23 O5 **Brent** Alabama, S USA
106 H7 **Brenta** ≈ NE Italy
97 P21 **Brentwood** E England, UK
18 L14 **Brentwood** Long Island, New York, NE USA
106 F7 **Brescia** *anc.* Brixia. Lombardia, N Italy
99 D15 **Breskens** Zeeland, SW Netherlands
Breslau *see* Wrocław
106 H5 **Bressanone** *Ger.* Brixen. Trentino-Alto Adige, N Italy
96 M2 **Bressay** *island* NE Scotland, UK
102 K9 **Bressuire** Deux-Sèvres, W France
119 F20 **Brest** *Pol.* Brześć nad Bugiem, *Rus.* Brest-Litovsk; *prev.* Brześć Litewski. Brestskaya Voblasts', SW Belarus
102 F5 **Brest** Finistère, NW France
Brest-Litovsk *see* Brest
112 A10 **Brestova** Istra, NW Croatia
Brestskaya Oblast' *see* Brestskaya Voblasts'
119 G19 **Brestskaya Voblasts'** *prev.Rus.* Brestskaya Oblast'. ⬖ *province* SW Belarus
102 G6 **Bretagne** *Eng.* Brittany, *Lat.* Britannia Minor. ⬖ *region* NW France
116 G12 **Bretea-Română** *Hung.* Oláhbrettye; *prev.* Bretea-Romînă. Hunedoara, W Romania
Bretea-Romînă *see* Bretea-Română
103 O3 **Breteuil** Oise, N France
102 I10 **Breton, Pertuis** *inlet* W France
22 L10 **Breton Sound** *sound* Louisiana, S USA
184 K2 **Brett, Cape** *headland* North Island, New Zealand
101 G21 **Bretten** Baden-Württemberg, SW Germany
99 K15 **Breugel** Noord-Brabant, S Netherlands
106 B6 **Breuil-Cervinia** *It.* Cervinia. Valle d'Aosta, NW Italy
98 I11 **Breukelen** Utrecht, C Netherlands
21 P10 **Brevard** North Carolina, SE USA
38 L9 **Brevig Mission** Alaska, USA
95 G16 **Brevik** Telemark, S Norway
183 P5 **Brewarrina** New South Wales, SE Australia
19 R6 **Brewer** Maine, NE USA
29 T11 **Brewster** Minnesota, N USA
29 N14 **Brewster** Nebraska, C USA
31 U12 **Brewster** Ohio, N USA
Brewster, Kap *see* Kangikajik
183 O8 **Brewster, Lake** ◎ New South Wales, SE Australia
23 P7 **Brewton** Alabama, S USA
Brezhnev *see* Naberezhnyye Chelny
109 W12 **Brežice** *Ger.* Rann. E Slovenia
114 G9 **Breznik** Pernik, W Bulgaria
111 K19 **Brezno** *Ger.* Bries, Briesen, *Hung.* Breznóbánya; *prev.* Brezno nad Hronom. Banskobystrický Kraj, C Slovakia
Breznóbánya/Brezno nad Hronom *see* Brezno
116 I12 **Brezoi** Vâlcea, SW Romania
114 J10 **Brezovo** *prev.* Abrashlare. Plovdiv, C Bulgaria
79 K14 **Bria** Haute-Kotto, C Central African Republic
103 U13 **Briançon** *anc.* Brigantio. Hautes-Alpes, SE France
36 K7 **Brian Head** ▲ Utah, W USA
97 O17 **Briare** Loiret, C France
183 V2 **Bribie Island** *island* Queensland, E Australia
43 O14 **Bribrí** Limón, E Costa Rica
116 L8 **Briceni** *var.* Brinceni, *Rus.* Brichany. N Moldova
Bricgstow *see* Bristol
Brichany *see* Briceni
99 M24 **Bridel** Luxembourg, C Luxembourg
97 J22 **Bridgend** S Wales, UK
14 I14 **Bridgenorth** Ontario, SE Canada
23 Q1 **Bridgeport** Alabama, S USA
35 R8 **Bridgeport** California, W USA
18 L13 **Bridgeport** Connecticut, NE USA
31 N15 **Bridgeport** Illinois, N USA
28 J14 **Bridgeport** Nebraska, C USA
25 S6 **Bridgeport** Texas, SW USA
21 S3 **Bridgeport** West Virginia, NE USA
25 S5 **Bridgeport, Lake** ⊠ Texas, SW USA
33 U11 **Bridger** Montana, NW USA
18 I17 **Bridgeton** New Jersey, NE USA
180 J14 **Bridgetown** Western Australia
45 Y14 **Bridgetown** ● (Barbados) SW Barbados
183 P17 **Bridgewater** Tasmania, SE Australia
13 P16 **Bridgewater** Nova Scotia, SE Canada
19 P12 **Bridgewater** Massachusetts, NE USA
29 Q11 **Bridgewater** South Dakota, N USA
21 U5 **Bridgewater** Virginia, NE USA
19 P8 **Bridgton** Maine, NE USA
97 K23 **Bridgwater** SW England, UK
97 K22 **Bridgwater Bay** *bay* SW England, UK
97 O16 **Bridlington** E England, UK
97 O16 **Bridlington Bay** *bay* E England, UK
183 P15 **Bridport** Tasmania, SE Australia
97 K24 **Bridport** S England, UK
103 O5 **Brie** *cultural region* N France
Brieg *see* Brzeg
Briel *see* Brielle
98 G12 **Brielle** *var.* Briel, Bril, *Eng.* The Brill. Zuid-Holland, SW Netherlands
108 E9 **Brienz** Bern, C Switzerland
108 E9 **Brienzer See** ◎ SW Switzerland
Bries/Briesen *see* Brezno
Brietzig *see* Brzesko
103 S4 **Briey** Meurthe-et-Moselle, NE France
108 E10 **Brig** *Fr.* Brigue, *It.* Briga. Valais, SW Switzerland
Briga *see* Brig
101 G24 **Brigach** ≈ S Germany
18 K17 **Brigantine** New Jersey, NE USA
Brigantio *see* Briançon
Brigantium *see* Bregenz
Brigels *see* Breil
25 S9 **Briggs** Texas, SW USA
36 L1 **Brigham City** Utah, W USA
14 J15 **Brighton** Ontario, SE Canada
97 O23 **Brighton** SE England, UK
37 T4 **Brighton** Colorado, C USA
30 K15 **Brighton** Illinois, N USA
103 T16 **Brignoles** Var, SE France
Brigue *see* Brig
105 O7 **Brihuega** Castilla-La Mancha, C Spain
112 A10 **Brijuni** *It.* Brioni. *island group* NW Croatia
76 G12 **Brikama** W Gambia
Bril *see* Brielle
Brill, The *see* Brielle
101 G15 **Brilon** Nordrhein-Westfalen, W Germany
Brinceni *see* Briceni
107 Q18 **Brindisi** *anc.* Brundisium, Brundusium. Puglia, SE Italy
27 W11 **Brinkley** Arkansas, C USA
Brioni *see* Brijuni
103 P12 **Brioude** *anc.* Brivas. Haute-Loire, C France
Briovera *see* St-Lô
183 U2 **Brisbane** *state capital* Queensland, E Australia
183 V2 **Brisbane** ✈ Queensland, E Australia
25 P2 **Briscoe** Texas, SW USA
106 H10 **Brisighella** Emilia-Romagna, C Italy
108 G11 **Brissago** Ticino, S Switzerland
97 K22 **Bristol** *anc.* Bricgstow. SW England, UK
18 M12 **Bristol** Connecticut, NE USA
23 R9 **Bristol** Florida, SE USA
19 N9 **Bristol** New Hampshire, NE USA
29 Q8 **Bristol** South Dakota, N USA
21 P8 **Bristol** Tennessee, S USA
18 M8 **Bristol** Vermont, NE USA
39 N14 **Bristol Bay** *bay* Alaska, USA
97 I22 **Bristol Channel** *inlet* England/Wales, UK
35 W14 **Bristol Lake** ◎ California, W USA
27 P10 **Bristow** Oklahoma, C USA
86 C10 **Britain** *var.* Great Britain. *island* UK
Britannia Minor *see* Bretagne
10 L12 **British Columbia** *Fr.* Colombie-Britannique. ⬖ *province* SW Canada
British Guiana *see* Guyana
British Honduras *see* Belize
173 Q7 **British Indian Ocean Territory** ◇ *UK dependent territory* C Indian Ocean
86 B9 **British Isles** *island group* NW Europe
10 I1 **British Mountains** ▲▲ Yukon Territory, NW Canada
British North Borneo *see* Sabah
British Solomon Islands Protectorate *see* Solomon Islands
45 S8 **British Virgin Islands** *var.* Virgin Islands. ◇ *UK dependent territory* E West Indies
83 J21 **Brits** North-West, N South Africa
83 H24 **Britstown** Northern Cape, W South Africa
14 F12 **Britt** Ontario, S Canada
29 V12 **Britt** Iowa, C USA
Brittany *see* Bretagne
29 Q7 **Britton** South Dakota, N USA
Briva Curretia *see* Brive-la-Gaillarde
Briva Isarae *see* Pontoise
Brivas *see* Brioude
Brive *see* Brive-la-Gaillarde
102 M12 **Brive-la-Gaillarde** *prev.* Brive; *anc.* Briva Curretia. Corrèze, C France
105 O4 **Briviesca** Castilla-León, N Spain
Brixen *see* Bressanone
Brixia *see* Brescia
145 S15 **Brlik** *var.* Novotroickoje, Novotroitskoye. Zhambyl, SE Kazakhstan
Brněnský Kraj *see* Jihomoravský Kraj
111 G18 **Brno** *Ger.* Brünn. Jihomoravský Kraj, SE Czech Republic
96 G7 **Broad Bay** *bay* NW Scotland, UK
25 X8 **Broaddus** Texas, SW USA
183 O12 **Broadford** Victoria, SE Australia
96 G9 **Broadford** N Scotland, UK
96 J13 **Broad Law** ▲ S Scotland, UK
23 U3 **Broad River** ≈ Georgia, SE USA
21 N8 **Broad River** ≈ North Carolina/South Carolina, SE USA
181 Y8 **Broadsound Range** ▲▲ Queensland, E Australia
33 X11 **Broadus** Montana, NW USA
21 U4 **Broadway** Virginia, NE USA
118 E9 **Brocēni** Saldus, SW Latvia
9 U11 **Brochet** Manitoba, C Canada
9 U10 **Brochet, Lac** ◎ Manitoba, C Canada
15 S5 **Brochet, Lac au** ◎ Québec, SE Canada
101 K14 **Brocken** ▲ C Germany
19 O12 **Brockton** Massachusetts, NE USA
14 L14 **Brockville** Ontario, SE Canada
18 D13 **Brockway** Pennsylvania, NE USA
Brod/Bród *see* Slavonski Brod
9 N5 **Brodeur Peninsula** *peninsula* Baffin Island, Nunavut, NE Canada
96 H13 **Brodick** W Scotland, UK
Brod na Savi *see* Slavonski Brod
110 K9 **Brodnica** *Ger.* Buddenbrock. Kujawski-pomorskie, C Poland
112 G10 **Brod-Posavina** *off.* Brodsko-Posavska Županija. ⬖ *province* NE Croatia
Brodsko-Posavska Županija *see* Brod-Posavina
116 J5 **Brody** L'vivs'ka Oblast', NW Ukraine
98 I10 **Broek-in-Waterland** Noord-Holland, C Netherlands
32 L13 **Brogan** Oregon, NW USA
110 N10 **Brok** Mazowieckie, C Poland
27 P9 **Broken Arrow** Oklahoma, C USA
183 T9 **Broken Bay** *bay* New South Wales, SE Australia
29 N15 **Broken Bow** Nebraska, C USA
27 R13 **Broken Bow** Oklahoma, C USA
27 R12 **Broken Bow Lake** ⊠ Oklahoma, C USA
182 L6 **Broken Hill** New South Wales, SE Australia
173 S10 **Broken Ridge** *undersea feature* S Indian Ocean
186 C6 **Broken Water Bay** *bay* W Bismarck Sea
55 W10 **Brokopondo** Brokopondo, NE Surinam
55 W10 **Brokopondo** ⬖ *district* C Surinam
Bromberg *see* Bydgoszcz
95 L22 **Bromölla** Skåne, S Sweden
97 L20 **Bromsgrove** W England, UK
95 G20 **Brønderslev** Nordjylland, N Denmark
106 D8 **Broni** Lombardia, N Italy
10 K11 **Bronlund Peak** ▲ British Columbia, W Canada
93 F14 **Brønnøysund** Nordland, C Norway
23 V10 **Bronson** Florida, SE USA
31 Q11 **Bronson** Michigan, N USA
25 X8 **Bronson** Texas, SW USA
107 L24 **Bronte** Sicilia, Italy, C Mediterranean Sea
25 P8 **Bronte** Texas, SW USA
25 Y9 **Brookeland** Texas, SW USA
170 M7 **Brooke's Point** Palawan, W Philippines
27 T3 **Brookfield** Missouri, C USA
22 K7 **Brookhaven** Mississippi, S USA
32 E16 **Brookings** Oregon, NW USA
29 R10 **Brookings** South Dakota, N USA
29 W14 **Brooklyn** Iowa, C USA
29 U8 **Brooklyn Park** Minnesota, N USA
21 U7 **Brookneal** Virginia, NE USA
9 R16 **Brooks** Alberta, SW Canada
25 V11 **Brookshire** Texas, SW USA
38 L8 **Brooks Mountain** ▲ Alaska, USA
38 M11 **Brooks Range** ▲▲ Alaska, USA
31 O12 **Brookston** Indiana, N USA
23 V11 **Brooksville** Florida, SE USA
23 N4 **Brooksville** Mississippi, S USA
180 J13 **Brookton** Western Australia
31 Q14 **Brookville** Indiana, N USA
18 D13 **Brookville** Pennsylvania, NE USA
31 Q14 **Brookville Lake** ⊠ Indiana, N USA
180 K5 **Broome** Western Australia
37 S4 **Broomfield** Colorado, C USA
Broos *see* Orăştie
96 J7 **Brora** N Scotland, UK
96 I7 **Brora** ≈ N Scotland, UK
95 F23 **Brørup** Ribe, W Denmark
95 L23 **Brösarp** Skåne, S Sweden
116 J9 **Brosteni** Suceava, NE Romania
102 M6 **Brou** Eure-et-Loir, C France
Broucsella *see* Brussel/Bruxelles
Broughton Bay *see* Tongjosŏn-man
9 R5 **Broughton Island** Nunavut, NE Canada
138 G7 **Broummana** C Lebanon
22 I9 **Broussard** Louisiana, S USA
98 E13 **Brouwersdam** *dam* SW Netherlands
98 E13 **Brouwershaven** Zeeland, SW Netherlands
117 P4 **Brovary** Kyyivs'ka Oblast', N Ukraine
95 G20 **Brovst** Nordjylland, N Denmark
31 S8 **Brown City** Michigan, N USA
24 M6 **Brownfield** Texas, SW USA
33 Q7 **Browning** Montana, NW USA
33 R6 **Brown, Mount** ▲ Montana, NW USA
0 M9 **Browns Bank** *undersea feature* NW Atlantic Ocean
31 O14 **Brownsburg** Indiana, N USA
18 J16 **Browns Mills** New Jersey, NE USA
44 J12 **Browns Town** C Jamaica
31 P15 **Brownstown** Indiana, N USA
29 R8 **Browns Valley** Minnesota, N USA
20 K7 **Brownsville** Kentucky, S USA
20 F9 **Brownsville** Tennessee, S USA
25 T17 **Brownsville** Texas, SW USA
55 W10 **Brownsweg** Brokopondo, C Surinam
29 U9 **Brownton** Minnesota, N USA
19 R5 **Brownville Junction** Maine, NE USA
25 R8 **Brownwood** Texas, SW USA
25 R8 **Brownwood Lake** ⊠ Texas, SW USA
104 I9 **Brozas** Extremadura, W Spain
119 M18 **Brozha** Mahilyowskaya Voblasts', E Belarus
103 O2 **Bruay-en-Artois** Pas-de-Calais, N France
103 P2 **Bruay-sur-l'Escaut** Nord, N France
14 F13 **Bruce Peninsula** *peninsula* Ontario, S Canada
20 H9 **Bruceton** Tennessee, S USA
25 T9 **Bruceville** Texas, SW USA
101 G21 **Bruchsal** Baden-Württemberg, SW Germany
109 Q7 **Bruck** Salzburg, NW Austria
Bruck *see* Bruck an der Mur
109 Y4 **Bruck an der Leitha** Niederösterreich, NE Austria
109 V7 **Bruck an der Mur** *var.* Bruck. Steiermark, C Austria
101 M24 **Bruckmühl** Bayern, SE Germany
168 E7 **Brueuh, Pulau** *island* NW Indonesia
Bruges *see* Brugge
108 F6 **Brugg** Aargau, NW Switzerland
99 C16 **Brugge** *Fr.* Bruges. West-Vlaanderen, NW Belgium
109 R9 **Bruggen** Kärnten, S Austria
101 E16 **Brühl** Nordrhein-Westfalen, W Germany
99 F14 **Bruinisse** Zeeland, SW Netherlands
169 R9 **Bruit, Pulau** *island* East Malaysia
14 K10 **Brûlé, Lac** ◎ Québec, SE Canada
30 M4 **Brule River** ≈ Michigan/Wisconsin, N USA
99 H23 **Brûly** Namur, S Belgium
59 N17 **Brumado** Bahia, E Brazil
98 M11 **Brummen** Gelderland, E Netherlands
94 H13 **Brumunddal** Hedmark, S Norway
23 Q6 **Brundidge** Alabama, S USA
Brundisium/Brundusium *see* Brindisi
33 N15 **Bruneau River** ≈ Idaho, NW USA
Bruneck *see* Brunico
169 T8 **Brunei** *off.* Sultanate of Brunei, *Mal.* Negara Brunei Darussalam. ◆ *monarchy* SE Asia
169 T7 **Brunei Bay** *var.* Teluk Brunei. *bay* N Brunei
Brunei, Sultanate of *see* Brunei
Brunei, Teluk *see* Brunei Bay
Brunei Town *see* Bandar Seri Begawan
106 H5 **Brunico** *Ger.* Bruneck. Trentino-Alto Adige, N Italy
Brünn *see* Brno
185 G17 **Brunner, Lake** ◎ South Island, New Zealand
99 M18 **Brunssum** Limburg, SE Netherlands
23 W7 **Brunswick** Georgia, SE USA
19 Q8 **Brunswick** Maine, NE USA
21 V3 **Brunswick** Maryland, NE USA
27 T3 **Brunswick** Missouri, C USA
31 T11 **Brunswick** Ohio, N USA
Brunswick *see* Braunschweig
63 H24 **Brunswick, Península** *headland* S Chile
111 H17 **Bruntál** *Ger.* Freudenthal. Moravskoslezský Kraj, E Czech Republic
195 N3 **Brunt Ice Shelf** *ice shelf* Antarctica
Brusa *see* Bursa
37 U3 **Brush** Colorado, C USA
42 M5 **Brus Laguna** Gracias a Dios, E Honduras
60 K13 **Brusque** Santa Catarina, S Brazil
Brussa *see* Bursa
99 E18 **Brussel** *var.* Brussels, *Fr.* Bruxelles, *Ger.* Brüssel; *anc.* Broucsella. ● (Belgium) Brussels, C Belgium *see also* Bruxelles
Brussel *see* Bruxelles
Brüssel/Brussels *see* Brussel/Bruxelles
Brussels Brussel/Bruxelles
117 O5 **Brusyliv** Zhytomyrs'ka Oblast', N Ukraine
183 Q12 **Bruthen** Victoria, SE Australia
Bruttium *see* Calabria
Brüx *see* Most
99 E18 **Bruxelles** *var.* Brussels, *Dut.* Brussel, *Ger.* Brüssel; *anc.* Broucsella. ● Brussels, C Belgium *see also* Brussel
Bruxelles *see* Brussel
54 J7 **Bruzual** Apure, W Venezuela
31 Q11 **Bryan** Ohio, N USA
25 U10 **Bryan** Texas, SW USA
194 J4 **Bryan Coast** *physical region* Antarctica
122 L11 **Bryanka** Krasnoyarskiy Kray, C Russian Federation
117 Y7 **Bryanka** Luhans'ka Oblast', E Ukraine
182 J8 **Bryan, Mount** ▲ South Australia
126 I6 **Bryansk** Bryanskaya Oblast', W Russian Federation
126 H6 **Bryanskaya Oblast'** ⬖ *province* W Russian Federation
194 J5 **Bryant, Cape** *headland* Antarctica
27 U8 **Bryant Creek** ≈ Missouri, C USA
36 K8 **Bryce Canyon** *canyon* Utah, W USA
119 O15 **Bryli** *Rus.* Bryli. Mahilyowskaya Voblasts', E Belarus
95 C17 **Bryne** Rogaland, S Norway
25 R6 **Bryson** Texas, SW USA
21 N10 **Bryson City** North Carolina, SE USA
14 K11 **Bryson, Lac** ◎ Québec, SE Canada
126 K13 **Bryukhovetskaya** Krasnodarskiy Kray, SW Russian Federation
111 H15 **Brzeg** *Ger.* Brieg; *anc.* Civitas Altae Ripae. Opolskie, S Poland
111 G14 **Brzeg Dolny** *Ger.* Dyhernfurth. Dolnośląskie, SW Poland
Brześć Litewski/Brześć nad Bugiem *see* Brest
111 L17 **Brzesko** *Ger.* Brietzig. Małopolskie, SE Poland
Brzeżany *see* Berezhany
110 K12 **Brzeziny** Łódzkie, C Poland
Brzostowica Wielka *see* Vyalikaya Byerastavitsa
111 O17 **Brzozów** Podkarpackie, SE Poland
Bsharrī/Bsherri *see* Bcharré
187 X14 **Bua** Vanua Levu, N Fiji
95 J20 **Bua** Halland, S Sweden
82 M13 **Bua** ≈ C Malawi
Bua *see* Čiovo
81 L18 **Bu'aale** *It.* Buale. Jubbada Dhexe, SW Somalia
Buache, Mount *see* Mutunte, Mount
189 Q8 **Buada Lagoon** *lagoon* Nauru, C Pacific Ocean
186 M8 **Buala** Santa Isabel, E Solomon Islands
Buale *see* Bu'aale
190 H1 **Buariki** *atoll* Tungaru, W Kiribati
167 Q10 **Bua Yai** *var.* Ban Bua Yai. Nakhon Ratchasima, E Thailand
75 P8 **Bu'ayrāt al Ḩasūn** *var.* Buwayrāt al Hasūn. C Libya
76 H13 **Buba** S Guinea-Bissau
171 P11 **Bubaa** Sulawesi, N Indonesia
81 D20 **Bubanza** NW Burundi
83 K18 **Bubi** *prev.* Bubye. ≈ S Zimbabwe
142 L11 **Būbīyan, Jazīrat** *island* E Kuwait
Bublitz *see* Bobolice
Bubye *see* Bubi
187 Y13 **Buca** *prev.* Mbutha. Vanua Levu, N Fiji
136 F16 **Bucak** Burdur, SW Turkey
54 G8 **Bucaramanga** Santander, N Colombia
107 M18 **Buccino** Campania, S Italy
116 K9 **Bucecea** Botoşani, NE Romania
116 J6 **Buchach** *Pol.* Buczacz. Ternopil's'ka Oblast', W Ukraine
183 Q12 **Buchan** Victoria, SE Australia
76 J17 **Buchanan** *prev.* Grand Bassa. SW Liberia
23 R3 **Buchanan** Georgia, SE USA
31 O11 **Buchanan** Michigan, N USA
21 T6 **Buchanan** Virginia, NE USA
25 R10 **Buchanan Dam** Texas, SW USA
25 R10 **Buchanan, Lake** ⊠ Texas, SW USA
96 L8 **Buchan Ness** *headland* NE Scotland, UK
13 T12 **Buchans** Newfoundland and Labrador, SE Canada
Bucharest *see* Bucureşti
101 H20 **Buchen** Baden-Württemberg, SW Germany
100 I10 **Buchholz in der Nordheide** Niedersachsen, NW Germany
108 F7 **Buchs** Aargau, N Switzerland
108 I8 **Buchs** Sankt Gallen, NE Switzerland
100 H13 **Bückeburg** Niedersachsen, NW Germany
36 K14 **Buckeye** Arizona, SW USA
Buckeye State *see* Ohio
21 S4 **Buckhannon** West Virginia, NE USA
25 T9 **Buckholts** Texas, SW USA
96 K8 **Buckie** NE Scotland, UK
14 M12 **Buckingham** Québec, SE Canada
21 U6 **Buckingham** Virginia, NE USA
97 N21 **Buckinghamshire** *cultural region* SE England, UK
39 N8 **Buckland** Alaska, USA
182 G7 **Buckleboo** South Australia
26 K7 **Bucklin** Kansas, C USA
27 T3 **Bucklin** Missouri, C USA
36 I12 **Buckskin Mountains** ▲▲ Arizona, SW USA
19 R7 **Bucksport** Maine, NE USA
82 A9 **Buco Zau** Cabinda, NW Angola
Bu Craa *see* Bou Craa
116 K14 **Bucureşti** *Eng.* Bucharest, *Ger.* Bukarest, *prev.* Altenburg; *anc.* Cetatea Damboviţei. ● (Romania) Bucureşti, S Romania
31 S12 **Bucyrus** Ohio, N USA
Buczacz *see* Buchach
94 E9 **Bud** Møre og Romsdal, S Norway
25 S11 **Buda** Texas, SW USA
119 O18 **Buda-Kashalyova** *Rus.* Buda-Koshelëvo. Homyel'skaya Voblasts', SE Belarus
Buda-Koshelëvo *see* Buda-Kashalyova
166 L4 **Budalin** Sagaing, C Burma (Myanmar)
111 J22 **Budapest** *off.* Budapest Főváros, *SCr.* Budimpešta. ● (Hungary) Pest, N Hungary
Budapest Főváros *see* Budapest
152 K11 **Budaun** Uttar Pradesh, N India
141 O9 **Budayyi'ah** *oasis* C Saudi Arabia
195 Y12 **Budd Coast** *physical region* Antarctica
Buddenbrock *see* Brodnica
107 C17 **Budduso** Sardegna, Italy, C Mediterranean Sea
97 I23 **Bude** SW England, UK
22 J7 **Bude** Mississippi, S USA
Budějovický Kraj *see* Jihočeský Kraj
99 K16 **Budel** Noord-Brabant, SE Netherlands
100 I8 **Büdelsdorf** Schleswig-Holstein, N Germany
127 O14 **Budënnovsk** Stavropol'skiy Kray, SW Russian Federation
116 K14 **Budeşti** Călăraşi, SE Romania
Budge-Budge *see* Baj Baj
Budgewoi *see* Budgewoi Lake
183 T8 **Budgewoi Lake** *var.* Budgewoi. New South Wales, SE Australia
92 I2 **Búdhardalur** Vesturland, W Iceland
Budimpešta *see* Budapest
79 J16 **Budjala** Equateur, NW Dem. Rep. Congo
106 G10 **Budrio** Emilia-Romagna, C Italy
Budslav *see* Budslaw
119 K14 **Budslaw** *Rus.* Budslav. Minskaya Voblasts', N Belarus
Budua *see* Budva
169 R9 **Budu, Tanjung** *cape* East Malaysia
113 J17 **Budva** *It.* Budua. W Montenegro
Budweis *see* České Budějovice
Budyšin *see* Bautzen
79 D16 **Buea** Sud-Ouest, SW Cameroon
103 S13 **Buëch** ≈ SE France
18 J17 **Buena** New Jersey, NE USA
62 K12 **Buena Esperanza** San Luis, C Argentina
54 C11 **Buenaventura** Valle del Cauca, W Colombia
40 I4 **Buenaventura** Chihuahua, N Mexico
57 M18 **Buena Vista** Santa Cruz, C Bolivia
40 G10 **Buenavista** Baja California Sur, W Mexico
37 S5 **Buena Vista** Colorado, C USA
23 S5 **Buena Vista** Georgia, SE USA
21 T6 **Buena Vista** Virginia, NE USA
44 F5 **Buena Vista, Bahia de** *bay* N Cuba
35 R13 **Buena Vista Lake Bed** ◎ California, W USA
105 P8 **Buendía, Embalse de** ⊠ C Spain
63 F16 **Bueno, Río** ≈ S Chile
62 N12 **Buenos Aires** *hist.* Santa Maria del Buen Aire. ● (Argentina) Buenos Aires, E Argentina
43 O15 **Buenos Aires** Puntarenas, SE Costa Rica
61 C20 **Buenos Aires** *off.* Provincia de Buenos Aires. ⬖ *province* E Argentina
63 H19 **Buenos Aires, Lago** *var.* Lago General Carrera. ◎ Argentina/Chile
Buenos Aires, Provincia de *see* Buenos Aires
54 C13 **Buesaco** Nariño, SW Colombia
29 U8 **Buffalo** Minnesota, N USA
26 T6 **Buffalo** Missouri, C USA
18 D10 **Buffalo** New York, NE USA
27 K8 **Buffalo** Oklahoma, C USA
28 J7 **Buffalo** South Dakota, N USA
25 V8 **Buffalo** Texas, SW USA
33 W12 **Buffalo** Wyoming, C USA
29 U11 **Buffalo Center** Iowa, C USA
24 M3 **Buffalo Lake** ⊠ Texas, SW USA
30 K7 **Buffalo Lake** ⊠ Wisconsin, N USA
9 S12 **Buffalo Narrows** Saskatchewan, C Canada
27 U9 **Buffalo River** ≈ Arkansas, C USA
29 R5 **Buffalo River** ≈ Minnesota, N USA
20 I10 **Buffalo River** ≈ Tennessee, S USA
30 J6 **Buffalo River** ≈ Wisconsin, N USA
44 L12 **Buff Bay** E Jamaica
23 T3 **Buford** Georgia, SE USA
28 J3 **Buford** North Dakota, N USA
33 Y17 **Buford** Wyoming, C USA
116 J14 **Buftea** Ilfov, S Romania
84 I9 **Bug** *Bel.* Zakhodni Buh, *Eng.* Western Bug, *Rus.* Zapadnyy Bug, *Ukr.* Zakhidnyy Buh. ≈ E Europe
54 D11 **Buga** Valle del Cauca, W Colombia
Buga *see* Dörvöljin
103 O17 **Bugarach, Pic du** ▲ S France
162 F8 **Bugat** *var.* Bayangol. Govĭ-Altay, SW Mongolia
146 B12 **Bugdaýly** *Rus.* Bugdayly. Balkan Welaýaty, W Turkmenistan
Bugdayly *see* Bugdaýly
Buggs Island Lake *see* John H. Kerr Reservoir
Bughotu *see* Santa Isabel
171 O14 **Bugingkalo** Sulawesi, C Indonesia
64 P6 **Bugio** *island* Madeira, Portugal, NE Atlantic Ocean
92 M8 **Bugøynes** Finnmark, N Norway
125 Q3 **Bugrino** Nenetskiy Avtonomnyy Okrug, NW Russian Federation
127 T5 **Bugul'ma** Respublika Tatarstan, W Russian Federation
Bügür *see* Luntai
127 T6 **Buguruslan** Orenburgskaya Oblast', W Russian Federation
159 R9 **Buh He** ≈ C China
101 F22 **Bühl** Baden-Württemberg, SW Germany
33 O15 **Buhl** Idaho, NW USA

◆ Country
● Country Capital
◇ Dependent Territory
○ Dependent Territory Capital
⬖ Administrative Regions
✈ International Airport
▲ Mountain
▲▲ Mountain Range
Volcano
≈ River
◎ Lake
⊠ Reservoir

BUHUŞI – BZĪMAH

116 K10 **Buhuşi** Bacău, E Romania
Buie d'Istria *see* Buje
97 J20 **Builth Wells** E Wales, UK
186 J8 **Buin** Bougainville Island, NE Papua New Guinea
108 J9 **Buin, Piz** ▲ Austria/Switzerland
127 Q4 **Buinsk** Chuvashskaya Respublika, W Russian Federation
127 Q4 **Buinsk** Respublika Tatarstan, W Russian Federation
163 R8 **Buir Nur** *Mong.* Buyr Nuur. ◎ China/Mongolia *see also* Buyr Nuur
Buir Nur *see* Buyr Nuur
98 M5 **Buitenpost** *Fris.* Bûtenpost. Friesland, N Netherlands
Buitenzorg *see* Bogor
83 F19 **Buitepos** Omaheke, E Namibia
105 N7 **Buitrago del Lozoya** Madrid, C Spain
Buj *see* Buy
104 M13 **Bujalance** Andalucía, S Spain
113 O17 **Bujanovac** Kosovo, SE Serbia
105 S6 **Bujaraloz** Aragón, NE Spain
112 A9 **Buje** *It.* Buie d'Istria. Istra, NW Croatia
Bujnurd *see* Bojnūrd
81 D21 **Bujumbura** *prev.* Usumbura. ● (Burundi) W Burundi
81 D20 **Bujumbura** ✈ W Burundi
159 N11 **Buka Daban** *var.* Bukadaban Feng. ▲ C China
Bukadaban Feng *see* Buka Daban
186 J6 **Buka Island** *island* NE Papua New Guinea
81 F18 **Bukakata** S Uganda
79 N24 **Bukama** Katanga, SE Dem. Rep. Congo
142 J4 **Būkān** *var.* Bowkān. Āžarbāyjān-e Gharbī, NW Iran
Bukantau, Gory *see* Bo'kantov Tog'lari
Bukantau, Gory *see* Bo'kantov Tog'lari
Bukarest *see* Bucureşti
79 O19 **Bukavu** *prev.* Costermansville. Sud Kivu, E Dem. Rep. Congo
81 F21 **Bukene** Tabora, NW Tanzania
141 W8 **Bū Khābī** *var.* Bakhābī. NW Oman
Bukhara *see* Buxoro
Bukharskaya Oblast' *see* Buxoro Viloyati
168 M14 **Bukitkemuning** Sumatera, W Indonesia
168 I11 **Bukittinggi** *prev.* Fort de Kock. Sumatera, W Indonesia
111 L21 **Bükk** ▲▲ NE Hungary
81 F19 **Bukoba** Kagera, NW Tanzania
113 N20 **Bukovo** S FYR Macedonia
108 G6 **Bülach** Zürich, NW Switzerland
Būlaevo *see* Bulayevo
Bulag *see* Tünel, Hövsgöl, Mongolia
Bulag *see* Möngönmorĭt, Töv, Mongolia
Bulagiyn Denj *see* Bulgan
183 U7 **Bulahdelah** New South Wales, SE Australia
171 P4 **Bulan** Luzon, N Philippines
137 N11 **Bulancak** Giresun, N Turkey
152 J10 **Bulandshahr** Uttar Pradesh, N India
137 R14 **Bulanık** Muş, E Turkey
127 V7 **Bulanovo** Orenburgskaya Oblast', W Russian Federation
83 J17 **Bulawayo** *var.* Buluwayo. Bulawayo, SW Zimbabwe
83 J17 **Bulawayo** ✈ Matabeleland North, SW Zimbabwe
145 Q6 **Bulayevo** *Kaz.* Būlaevo. Severnyy Kazakhstan, N Kazakhstan
136 D15 **Buldan** Denizli, SW Turkey
154 G12 **Buldāna** Mahārāshtra, C India
38 E16 **Buldir Island** *island* Aleutian Islands, Alaska, USA
Buldur *see* Burdur
162 I8 **Bulgan** *var.* Bulagiyn Denj. Arhangay, C Mongolia
162 D7 **Bulgan** *var.* Jargalant. Bayan-Ölgiy, W Mongolia
162 K6 **Bulgan** Bulgan, N Mongolia
162 F7 **Bulgan** *var.* Bürenhayrhan. Hovd, W Mongolia
162 J10 **Bulgan** Ömnögovĭ, S Mongolia
162 J7 **Bulgan** ⬖ *province* N Mongolia
Bulgan Bayan-Öndör, Bayanhongor, Mongolia
Bulgan *see* Bayan-Öndör
Bulgan *see* Darvi, Hovd, Mongolia
Bulgan Tsagaan-Üür, Hövsgöl, Mongolia
Bulgan *see* Bayan-Öndör
114 H10 **Bulgaria** *off.* Republic of Bulgaria, *Bul.* Bŭlgariya; *prev.* People's Republic of Bulgaria. ◆ *republic* SE Europe
Bulgaria, People's Republic of *see* Bulgaria
Bulgaria, Republic of *see* Bulgaria
Bŭlgariya *see* Bulgaria
114 L9 **Bŭlgarka** ▲ E Bulgaria
171 S11 **Buli** Pulau Halmahera, E Indonesia
171 S11 **Buli, Teluk** *bay* Pulau Halmahera, E Indonesia
160 J13 **Buliu He** ≈ S China
Bullange *see* Büllingen
Bulla, Ostrov *see* Xärä Zirä Adası
104 M11 **Bullaque** ≈ C Spain
105 Q13 **Bullas** Murcia, SE Spain
80 M12 **Bullaxaar** Woqooyi Galbeed, NW Somalia
108 C9 **Bulle** Fribourg, SW Switzerland
185 G15 **Buller** ≈ South Island, New Zealand
183 P12 **Buller, Mount** ▲ Victoria, SE Australia
36 H11 **Bullhead City** Arizona, SW USA
99 N21 **Büllingen** *Fr.* Bullange. Liège, E Belgium
Bullion State *see* Missouri
21 T14 **Bull Island** *island* South Carolina, SE USA
182 M4 **Bulloo River Overflow** *wetland* New South Wales, SE Australia
184 M12 **Bulls** Manawatu-Wanganui, North Island, New Zealand
21 T14 **Bulls Bay** *bay* South Carolina, SE USA
27 U9 **Bull Shoals Lake** ▣ Arkansas/Missouri, C USA
181 Q2 **Bulman** Northern Territory, N Australia
162 I6 **Bulnayn Nuruu** ▲▲ N Mongolia
171 O11 **Bulowa, Gunung** ▲ Sulawesi, N Indonesia
Bulqiza *see* Bulqizë
113 L19 **Bulqizë** *var.* Bulqiza. Dibër, C Albania
Bulsar *see* Valsād
171 N14 **Bulukumba** *prev.* Boeloekoemba. Sulawesi, C Indonesia
79 I21 **Bulungu** Bandundu, SW Dem. Rep. Congo
147 O11 **Bulungh'ur** *Rus.* Bulungur; *prev.* Krasnogvardeysk. Samarqand Viloyati, C Uzbekistan
Bulungur *see* Bulungh'ur
Buluwayo *see* Bulawayo
79 K17 **Bumba** Equateur, N Dem. Rep. Congo
121 R12 **Bumbah, Khalīj al** *gulf* N Libya
Bumbat *see* Bayan-Öndör
81 F19 **Bumbire Island** *island* N Tanzania
169 V8 **Bum Bun, Pulau** *island* East Malaysia
81 J17 **Buna** North Eastern, NE Kenya
25 Y10 **Buna** Texas, SW USA
Bunab *see* Bonāb
Bunai *see* M'bunai
147 S13 **Bunay** S Tajikistan
180 I13 **Bunbury** Western Australia
97 E14 **Buncrana** *Ir.* Bun Cranncha. NW Ireland
Bun Cranncha *see* Buncrana
181 Z9 **Bundaberg** Queensland, E Australia
183 T5 **Bundarra** New South Wales, SE Australia
100 G13 **Bünde** Nordrhein-Westfalen, NW Germany
152 H13 **Būndi** Rājasthān, N India
Bun Dobhráin *see* Bundoran
97 D15 **Bundoran** *Ir.* Bun Dobhráin. NW Ireland
113 K18 **Bunë** *SCr.* Bojana. ≈ Albania/Montenegro *see also* Bojana
Bunë *see* Bojana
171 Q8 **Bunga** ≈ Mindanao, S Philippines
168 I12 **Bungalaut, Selat** *strait* W Indonesia
167 R8 **Bung Kan** Nong Khai, E Thailand
181 N4 **Bungle Bungle Range** ▲▲ Western Australia
82 C10 **Bungo** Uíge, NW Angola
81 G18 **Bungoma** Western, W Kenya
164 F15 **Bungo-suidō** *strait* SW Japan
164 E14 **Bungo-Takada** Ōita, Kyūshū, SW Japan
100 K8 **Bungsberg** *hill* N Germany
Bungur *see* Bunyu
79 P17 **Bunia** Orientale, NE Dem. Rep. Congo
35 U6 **Bunker Hill** ▲ Nevada, W USA
22 I7 **Bunkie** Louisiana, S USA
23 X10 **Bunnell** Florida, SE USA
105 S10 **Buñol** País Valenciano, E Spain
98 K11 **Bunschoten** Utrecht, C Netherlands
136 K14 **Bünyan** Kayseri, C Turkey
169 W8 **Bunyu** *var.* Bungur. Borneo, N Indonesia
169 W8 **Bunyu, Pulau** *island* N Indonesia
Bunzlau *see* Bolesławiec
Buoddobohki *see* Patoniva
123 P7 **Buorkhaya Guba** *bay* N Russian Federation
171 Z15 **Bupul** Papua, E Indonesia
81 K19 **Bura** Coast, SE Kenya
80 P12 **Buraan** Bari, N Somalia
Būrabay *see* Borovoye
Buraida *see* Buraydah
Buraimi *see* Al Buraymī
145 Y11 **Buran** Vostochnyy Kazakhstan, E Kazakhstan
158 G15 **Burang** Xizang Zizhiqu, W China
Burao *see* Burco
138 H8 **Burāq** Dar'ā, S Syria
141 O6 **Buraydah** *var.* Buraida. Al Qaşīm, N Saudi Arabia
35 S15 **Burbank** California, W USA
31 N11 **Burbank** Illinois, N USA
183 Q8 **Burcher** New South Wales, SE Australia
80 N13 **Burco** *var.* Burao, Bur'o. Togdheer, NW Somalia
162 K8 **Bürd** *var.* Ongon. Övörhangay, C Mongolia
146 L13 **Burdalyk** Lebap Welaýaty, E Turkmenistan
181 W6 **Burdekin River** ≈ Queensland, NE Australia
27 O7 **Burden** Kansas, C USA
Burdigala *see* Bordeaux
136 E15 **Burdur** *var.* Buldur. Burdur, SW Turkey
136 E15 **Burdur** *var.* Buldur. ⬖ *province* SW Turkey
136 E15 **Burdur Gölü** *salt lake* SW Turkey
65 H21 **Burdwood Bank** *undersea feature* SW Atlantic Ocean
80 I12 **Burē** Amhara, N Ethiopia
80 H13 **Burē** Oromo, C Ethiopia
93 J15 **Bureå** Västerbotten, N Sweden
162 K7 **Büreghangay** *var.* Darhan. Bulgan, C Mongolia
101 G14 **Büren** Nordrhein-Westfalen, W Germany
162 L8 **Büren** *var* Bayantöhöm. Töv, C Mongolia
162 K6 **Bürengiyn Nuruu** ▲▲ N Mongolia
Bürenhayrhan *see* Bulgan
162 I6 **Bürentogtoh** *var.* Bayan. Hövsgol, C Mongolia
Būrewāla *see* Mandi Būrewāla
92 J9 **Burfjord** Troms, N Norway
100 L13 **Burg** *var.* Burg an der Ihle, Burg bei Magdeburg. Sachsen-Anhalt, C Germany
Burg an der Ihle *see* Burg
114 N10 **Burgas** *var.* Bourgas. Burgas, E Bulgaria
114 M10 **Burgas** ⬖ *province* E Bulgaria
114 N9 **Burgas** ✈ Burgas, E Bulgaria
114 N10 **Burgaski Zaliv** *gulf* E Bulgaria
114 M10 **Burgasko Ezero** *lagoon* E Bulgaria
21 V11 **Burgaw** North Carolina, SE USA
Burg bei Magdeburg *see* Burg
108 E8 **Burgdorf** Bern, NW Switzerland
109 Y7 **Burgenland** *off.* Land Burgenland. ⬖ *state* SE Austria
13 S13 **Burgeo** Newfoundland, Newfoundland and Labrador, SE Canada
83 I24 **Burgersdorp** Eastern Cape, SE South Africa
83 K20 **Burgersfort** Mpumalanga, NE South Africa
101 N23 **Burghausen** Bayern, SE Germany
139 O5 **Burghūth, Sabkhat al** ◎ E Syria
101 M20 **Burglengenfeld** Bayern, SE Germany
41 P9 **Burgos** Tamaulipas, C Mexico
105 N4 **Burgos** Castilla-León, N Spain
105 N4 **Burgos** ⬖ *province* Castilla-León, N Spain
Burgstadlberg *see* Hradiště
95 P20 **Burgsvik** Gotland, SE Sweden
Burgum *see* Bergum
Burgundy *see* Bourgogne
159 Q11 **Burhan Budai Shan** ▲▲ C China
136 B12 **Burhaniye** Balıkesir, W Turkey
154 G12 **Burhānpur** Madhya Pradesh, C India
127 W7 **Buribay** Respublika Bashkortostan, W Russian Federation
43 O17 **Burica, Punta** *headland* Costa Rica/Panama
167 Q10 **Buriram** *var.* Buri Ram, Puriramya. Buri Ram, E Thailand
Buri Ram *see* Buriram
105 S10 **Burjassot** País Valenciano, E Spain
81 N16 **Burka Giibi** Hiiraan, C Somalia
147 X8 **Burkan** ≈ E Kyrgyzstan
25 R4 **Burkburnett** Texas, SW USA
29 O12 **Burke** South Dakota, N USA
10 K15 **Burke Channel** *channel* British Columbia, W Canada
194 J10 **Burke Island** *island* Antarctica
20 L7 **Burkesville** Kentucky, S USA
181 T4 **Burketown** Queensland, NE Australia
25 Q8 **Burkett** Texas, SW USA
25 Y9 **Burkeville** Texas, SW USA
21 V7 **Burkeville** Virginia, NE USA
77 O12 **Burkina** *off.* Burkina Faso; *prev.* Upper Volta. ◆ *republic* W Africa
Burkina Faso *see* Burkina
194 L13 **Burks, Cape** *headland* Antarctica
14 H12 **Burk's Falls** Ontario, S Canada
101 H23 **Burladingen** Baden-Württemberg, S Germany
25 T7 **Burleson** Texas, SW USA
33 P15 **Burley** Idaho, NW USA
144 G8 **Burlin** Zapadnyy Kazakhstan, NW Kazakhstan
14 G16 **Burlington** Ontario, S Canada
37 W4 **Burlington** Colorado, C USA
29 Y15 **Burlington** Iowa, C USA
27 P5 **Burlington** Kansas, C USA
21 T9 **Burlington** North Carolina, SE USA
28 M3 **Burlington** North Dakota, N USA
18 L7 **Burlington** Vermont, NE USA
30 M9 **Burlington** Wisconsin, N USA
27 Q1 **Burlington Junction** Missouri, C USA
166 M4 **Burma** *off.* Union of Myanmar. ◆ *military dictatorship* SE Asia
10 L17 **Burnaby** British Columbia, SW Canada
117 O12 **Burnas, Ozero** ◎ SW Ukraine
25 S10 **Burnet** Texas, SW USA
35 O3 **Burney** California, W USA
183 O16 **Burnie** Tasmania, SE Australia
97 L17 **Burnley** NW England, UK
Burnoye *see* Bauyrzhan Momyshuly
153 R15 **Burnpur** West Bengal, NE India
32 K14 **Burns** Oregon, NW USA
26 K11 **Burns Flat** Oklahoma, C USA
20 M7 **Burnside** Kentucky, S USA
8 K8 **Burnside** ≈ Nunavut, NW Canada
32 L15 **Burns Junction** Oregon, NW USA
10 L13 **Burns Lake** British Columbia, SW Canada
29 V9 **Burnsville** Minnesota, N USA
21 P9 **Burnsville** North Carolina, SE USA
21 R4 **Burnsville** West Virginia, NE USA
14 I13 **Burnt River** ≈ Ontario, SE Canada
14 I11 **Burntroot Lake** ◎ Ontario, SE Canada
9 W12 **Burntwood** ≈ Manitoba, C Canada
Bur'o *see* Burco
158 L2 **Burqin** Xinjiang Uygur Zizhiqu, NW China
182 J8 **Burra** South Australia
183 S9 **Burragorang, Lake** ▣ New South Wales, SE Australia
96 K5 **Burray** *island* NE Scotland, UK
113 L19 **Burrel** *var.* Burreli. Dibër, C Albania
Burreli *see* Burrel
183 R8 **Burrendong Reservoir** ▣ New South Wales, SE Australia
183 R5 **Burren Junction** New South Wales, SE Australia
105 T9 **Burriana** País Valenciano, E Spain
183 R10 **Burrinjuck Reservoir** ▣ New South Wales, SE Australia
36 J12 **Burro Creek** ≈ Arizona, SW USA
40 M5 **Burro, Serranías del** ▲▲ NW Mexico
62 K7 **Burruyacú** Tucumán, N Argentina
136 E12 **Bursa** *var.* Brussa, *prev.* Brusa; *anc.* Prusa. Bursa, NW Turkey
136 D12 **Bursa** *var.* Brusa, Brussa. ⬖ *province* NW Turkey
75 Y9 **Bûr Safâga** *var.* Būr Safājah. E Egypt
Būr Safājah *see* Bûr Safâga
Būr Sa'īd *see* Port Said
81 O14 **Bur Tinle** Nugaal, C Somalia
31 Q5 **Burt Lake** ◎ Michigan, N USA
118 H7 **Burtnieks** *var.* Burtnieks Ezers. ◎ N Latvia
Burtnieks Ezers *see* Burtnieks
31 Q9 **Burton** Michigan, N USA
Burton on Trent *see* Burton upon Trent
97 M19 **Burton upon Trent** *var.* Burton on Trent, Burton-upon-Trent. C England, UK
93 J15 **Burträsk** Västerbotten, N Sweden
145 S14 **Burubaytal** *prev.* Burylbaytal. Zhambyl, SE Kazakhstan
Burujird *see* Borūjerd
Burultokay *see* Fuhai
141 R15 **Burūm** SE Yemen
Burunday *see* Boralday
81 D21 **Burundi** *off.* Republic of Burundi; *prev.* Kingdom of Burundi, Urundi. ◆ *republic* C Africa
Burundi, Kingdom of *see* Burundi
Burundi, Republic of *see* Burundi
171 R13 **Buru, Pulau** *prev.* Boeroe. *island* E Indonesia
77 T17 **Burutu** Delta, S Nigeria
10 G7 **Burwash Landing** Yukon Territory, W Canada
29 O14 **Burwell** Nebraska, C USA
97 L17 **Bury** NW England, UK
123 N13 **Buryatiya, Respublika** *prev.* Buryatskaya ASSR. ⬖ *autonomous republic* S Russian Federation
Buryatskaya ASSR *see* Buryatiya, Respublika
Burylbaytal *see* Burubaytal
117 S3 **Buryn'** Sums'ka Oblast', NE Ukraine
97 P20 **Bury St Edmunds** *hist.* Beodericsworth. E England, UK
114 G8 **Bŭrziya** ≈ NW Bulgaria
106 D9 **Busalla** Liguria, NW Italy
Busan *see* Pusan
139 N5 **Buşayrah** Dayr az Zawr, E Syria
Buševa *see* Baba
143 N12 **Būshehr** *off.* Ostān-e Būshehr. ⬖ *province* SW Iran
Būshehr/Bushire *see* Bandar-e Būshehr
Būshehr, Ostān-e *see* Būshehr
25 N2 **Bushland** Texas, SW USA
30 J12 **Bushnell** Illinois, N USA
Busi *see* Biševo
81 G18 **Busia** SE Uganda
Busiasch *see* Buziaş
79 K16 **Businga** Equateur, NW Dem. Rep. Congo
79 J18 **Busira** ≈ NW Dem. Rep. Congo
116 I5 **Bus'k** *Rus.* Busk. L'vivs'ka Oblast', W Ukraine
95 E14 **Buskerud** ⬖ *county* S Norway
113 F14 **Buško Jezero** ▣ SW Bosnia and Herzegovina
111 M15 **Busko-Zdrój** Świętokrzyskie, C Poland
Busra *see* Al Başrah, Iraq
Buşrá *see* Buşrá ash Shām, Syria
138 H9 **Buşrá ash Shām** *var.* Bosora, Bosra, Bozrah, Buşrá. Dar'ā, S Syria
180 I13 **Busselton** Western Australia
81 C14 **Busseri** ≈ W Sudan
106 E9 **Busseto** Emilia-Romagna, C Italy
106 A8 **Bussoleno** Piemonte, NE Italy
Bussora *see* Al Başrah
98 J10 **Bussum** Noord-Holland, C Netherlands
41 N7 **Bustamante** Nuevo León, NE Mexico
63 I23 **Bustamante, Punta** *headland* S Argentina
Bustan *see* Bo'ston
116 J12 **Buşteni** Prahova, SE Romania
106 D7 **Busto Arsizio** Lombardia, N Italy
147 Q10 **Bŭston** *Rus.* Buston. NW Tajikistan
100 H8 **Büsum** Schleswig-Holstein, N Germany
79 M16 **Buta** Orientale, N Dem. Rep. Congo
81 E20 **Butare** *prev.* Astrida. S Rwanda
191 O2 **Butaritari** *atoll* Tungaru, W Kiribati
Butawal *see* Butwal
96 H13 **Bute** *cultural region* SW Scotland, UK
162 K6 **Büteeliyn Nuruu** ▲▲ N Mongolia
10 L16 **Bute Inlet** *fjord* British Columbia, W Canada
96 H12 **Bute, Island of** *island* SW Scotland, UK
79 P18 **Butembo** Nord Kivu, NE Dem. Rep. Congo
Bûtenpost *see* Buitenpost
107 K25 **Butera** Sicilia, Italy, C Mediterranean Sea
99 M20 **Bütgenbach** Liège, E Belgium
Butha Qi *see* Zalantun
166 J5 **Buthidaung** Arakan State, W Burma (Myanmar)
61 I16 **Butiá** Rio Grande do Sul, S Brazil
81 F17 **Butiaba** NW Uganda
23 N6 **Butler** Alabama, S USA
23 S5 **Butler** Georgia, SE USA
31 Q11 **Butler** Indiana, N USA
27 R5 **Butler** Missouri, C USA
18 B14 **Butler** Pennsylvania, NE USA
194 K5 **Butler Island** *island* Antarctica
21 U8 **Butner** North Carolina, SE USA
171 P14 **Buton, Pulau** *var.* Pulau Butung; *prev.* Boetoeng. *island* C Indonesia
Bütow *see* Bytów
113 L23 **Butrintit, Liqeni i** ◎ S Albania
23 N3 **Buttahatchee River** ≈ Alabama/Mississippi, S USA
33 Q10 **Butte** Montana, NW USA
29 O12 **Butte** Nebraska, C USA
168 J7 **Butterworth** Pinang, Peninsular Malaysia
83 J25 **Butterworth** *var.* Gcuwa. Eastern Cape, SE South Africa
13 O3 **Button Islands** *island group* Nunavut, NE Canada
35 R13 **Buttonwillow** California, W USA
171 Q7 **Butuan** *off.* Butuan City. Mindanao, S Philippines
Butuan City *see* Butuan
Butung, Pulau *see* Buton, Pulau
Butuntum *see* Bitonto
126 M8 **Buturlinovka** Voronezhskaya Oblast', W Russian Federation
153 O11 **Butwal** *var.* Butawal. Western, C Nepal
101 G17 **Butzbach** Hessen, W Germany
100 L9 **Bützow** Mecklenburg-Vorpommern, N Germany
80 N13 **Buuhoodle** Togdheer, N Somalia
81 N16 **Buulobarde** *var.* Buulo Berde. Hiiraan, C Somalia Africa
Buulo Berde *see* Buulobarde
80 P12 **Buuraha Cal Miskaat** ▲▲ NE Somalia
81 L19 **Buur Gaabo** Jubbada Hoose, S Somalia
99 M22 **Buurgplaatz** ▲ N Luxembourg
162 H8 **Buutsagaan** *var.* Buyant. Bayanhongor, C Mongolia
Buwayrāt al Hasūn *see* Bu'ayrāt al Ḩasūn
146 L11 **Buxoro** *var.* Bokhara, *Rus.* Bukhara. Buxoro Viloyati, C Uzbekistan
146 J11 **Buxoro Viloyati** *Rus.* Bukharskaya Oblast'. ⬖ *province* C Uzbekistan
100 I10 **Buxtehude** Niedersachsen, NW Germany
97 L18 **Buxton** C England, UK
124 M14 **Buy** *var.* Buj. Kostromskaya Oblast', NW Russian Federation
Buyanbat *see* Jargalant
162 D6 **Buyant** Bayan-Ölgiy, W Mongolia
Buyant *see* Buutsagaan, Bayanhongor, Mongolia
Buyant *see* Galshar
Buyant Otgon, Dzavhan, Mongolia
Buyant *see* Galshar, Hentiy, Mongolia
163 N10 **Buyant-Uhaa** Dornogovĭ, SE Mongolia
162 M7 **Buyant Ukha** ✈ (Ulaanbaatar) Töv, N Mongolia
127 Q16 **Buynaksk** Respublika Dagestan, SW Russian Federation
119 L20 **Buynavichy** *Rus.* Buynovichi. Homyel'skaya Voblasts', SE Belarus
Buynovichi *see* Buynavichy
76 L16 **Buyo** SW Ivory Coast
76 L16 **Buyo, Lac de** ▣ W Ivory Coast
163 R7 **Buyr Nuur** *var.* Buir Nur. ◎ China/Mongolia *see also* Buir Nur
Buyr Nuur *see* Buir Nur
137 T13 **Büyükağrı Dağı** *var.* Aghri Dagh, Agri Dagi, Koh I Noh, Masis, *Eng.* Great Ararat, Mount Ararat. ▲ E Turkey
137 R15 **Büyük Çayı** ≈ NE Turkey
114 O13 **Büyük Çekmece** Istanbul, NW Turkey
114 N12 **Büyükkarıştıran** Kırklareli, NW Turkey
115 L14 **Büyükkemikli Burnu** *cape* NW Turkey
136 E15 **Büyükmenderes Nehri** ≈ SW Turkey
Büyükzap Suyu *see* Great Zab
102 M9 **Buzançais** Indre, C France
116 K13 **Buzău** Buzău, SE Romania
116 K13 **Buzău** ⬖ *county* SE Romania
116 L12 **Buzău** ≈ E Romania
75 S11 **Buzaymah** *var.* Bzīmah. SE Libya
164 E13 **Buzen** Fukuoka, Kyūshū, SW Japan
116 F12 **Buziaş** *Ger.* Busiasch, *Hung.* Buziásfürdő; *prev.* Buziás. Timiş, W Romania
Buziás *see* Buziaş
Buziásfürdő *see* Buziaş
83 M18 **Búzi, Rio** ≈ C Mozambique
117 Q10 **Buz'kyy Lyman** *bay* S Ukraine
145 O8 **Buzuluk** Akmola, C Kazakhstan
127 T6 **Buzuluk** Orenburgskaya Oblast', W Russian Federation
127 N8 **Buzuluk** ≈ SW Russian Federation
19 P12 **Buzzards Bay** Massachusetts, NE USA
19 P13 **Buzzards Bay** *bay* Massachusetts, NE USA
83 G16 **Bwabata** Caprivi, NE Namibia
186 H10 **Bwagaoia** Misima Island, SE Papua New Guinea
Bwake *see* Bouaké
187 R13 **Bwatnapne** Pentecost, C Vanuatu
119 K14 **Byahoml'** *Rus.* Begoml'. Vitsyebskaya Voblasts', N Belarus
114 J8 **Byala** Ruse, N Bulgaria
114 N9 **Byala** *prev.* Ak-Dere. Varna, E Bulgaria
Byala Reka *see* Erythropótamos
114 H8 **Byala Slatina** Vratsa, NW Bulgaria
119 N15 **Byalynichy** *Rus.* Belynichi. Mahilyowskaya Voblasts', E Belarus
Byan Tumen *see* Choybalsan
119 G19 **Byaroza** *Pol.* Bereza Kartuska, *Rus.* Berëza. Brestskaya Voblasts', SW Belarus
119 H16 **Byarozawka** *Rus.* Berëzovka. Hrodzyenskaya Voblasts', W Belarus
Bybles *see* Jbaïl
111 O14 **Bychawa** Lubelskie, SE Poland
Bychikha *see* Bychykha
118 N11 **Bychykha** *Rus.* Bychikha. Vitsyebskaya Voblasts', NE Belarus
111 I14 **Byczyna** *Ger.* Pitschen. Opolskie, S Poland
110 I10 **Bydgoszcz** *Ger.* Bromberg. Kujawski-pomorskie, C Poland
119 H19 **Byelaazyorsk** *Rus.* Beloozersk. Brestskaya Voblasts', SW Belarus
119 I17 **Byelaruskaya Hrada** *Rus.* Belorusskaya Gryada. *ridge* N Belarus
119 G18 **Byelavyezhskaya Pushcha** *Pol.* Puszcza Białowieska, *Rus.* Belovezhskaya Pushcha. *forest* Belarus/Poland *see also* Białowieska, Puszcza
Byelavyezhskaya, Pushcha *see* Białowieska, Puszcza
119 H15 **Byenyakoni** *Rus.* Benyakoni. Hrodzyenskaya Voblasts', W Belarus
119 M16 **Byerazino** *Rus.* Berezino. Minskaya Voblasts', C Belarus
118 L13 **Byerazino** *Rus.* Berezino. Vitsyebskaya Voblasts', N Belarus
119 L14 **Byerezino** *Rus.* Berezina. ≈ C Belarus
118 M13 **Byeshankovichy** *Rus.* Beshenkovichi. Vitsyebskaya Voblasts', N Belarus
31 U13 **Byesville** Ohio, N USA
119 P18 **Byesyedz'** *Rus.* Besed'. ≈ SE Belarus
119 H19 **Byezdzyezh** *Rus.* Bezdezh. Brestskaya Voblasts', SW Belarus
93 J15 **Bygdeå** Västerbotten, N Sweden
94 F12 **Bygdin** ◎ S Norway
93 J15 **Bygdsiljum** Västerbotten, N Sweden
95 E17 **Bygland** Aust-Agder, S Norway
95 E17 **Byglandsfjord** Aust-Agder, S Norway
119 N16 **Bykhaw** *Rus.* Bykhov. Mahilyowskaya Voblasts', E Belarus
Bykhov *see* Bykhaw
127 P9 **Bykovo** Volgogradskaya Oblast', SW Russian Federation
123 P7 **Bykovskiy** Respublika Sakha (Yakutiya), NE Russian Federation
195 R12 **Byrd Glacier** *glacier* Antarctica
14 K10 **Byrd, Lac** ◎ Québec, SE Canada
183 P5 **Byrock** New South Wales, SE Australia
30 L10 **Byron** Illinois, N USA
183 V4 **Byron Bay** New South Wales, SE Australia
183 V4 **Byron, Cape** *cape* New South Wales, E Australia
63 F21 **Byron, Isla** *island* S Chile
Byron Island *see* Nikunau
65 B24 **Byron Sound** *sound* NW Falkland Islands
122 M6 **Byrranga, Gora** ▲▲ N Russian Federation
93 J14 **Byske** Västerbotten, N Sweden
111 K18 **Bystrá** ▲ N Slovakia
111 F18 **Bystřice nad Pernštejnem** *Ger.* Bistritz ober Pernstein. Vysočina, C Czech Republic
Bystrovka *see* Kemin
111 G16 **Bystrzyca Kłodzka** *Ger.* Habelschwerdt. Wałbrzych, SW Poland
111 I18 **Bytča** Žilinský Kraj, N Slovakia
119 L15 **Bytcha** *Rus.* Bytcha. Minskaya Voblasts', NE Belarus
Byten' *see* Bytsyen'
Byteń/Byten' *see* Bytsyen'
111 J16 **Bytom** *Ger.* Beuthen. Śląskie, S Poland
110 H7 **Bytów** *Ger.* Bütow. Pomorskie, N Poland
119 H18 **Bytsyen'** *Pol.* Byteń, *Rus.* Byten'. Brestskaya Voblasts', SW Belarus
81 E19 **Byumba** *var.* Biumba. N Rwanda
Byuzmeyin *see* Abadan
119 O20 **Byval'ki** Homyel'skaya Voblasts', SE Belarus
95 O20 **Byxelkrok** Kalmar, S Sweden
Byzantium *see* İstanbul
Bzīmah *see* Buzaymah

◆ Country ● Country Capital ◇ Dependent Territory ○ Dependent Territory Capital ⬖ Administrative Regions ✈ International Airport ▲ Mountain ▲▲ Mountain Range Volcano ≈ River ◎ Lake ▣ Reservoir

Caacupé – Canarias, Islas

C

62 O6 Caacupé Cordillera, S Paraguay
62 P6 Caaguazú off. Departamento de Caaguazú. ◆ department C Paraguay
Caaguazú, Departamento de see Caaguazú
82 C13 Caála var. Kaala, Port. Vila Robert Williams. Huambo, C Angola
62 P7 Caazapá Caazapá, S Paraguay
62 P7 Caazapá off. Departamento de Caazapá. ◆ department SE Paraguay
Caazapá, Departamento de see Caazapá
81 P15 Cabaad, Raas headland C Somalia
55 N10 Cabadisocaña Amazonas, S Venezuela
44 F5 Cabaiguán Sancti Spíritus, C Cuba
Caballeria, Cabo see Cavalleria, Cap de
37 Q14 Caballo Reservoir ⊠ New Mexico, SW USA
40 L6 Caballos Mesteños, Llano de los plain N Mexico
104 L2 Cabañaquinta Asturias, N Spain
42 B9 Cabañas ◆ department E El Salvador
171 O3 Cabanatuan off. Cabanatuan City. Luzon, N Philippines
Cabanatuan City see Cabanatuan
15 T8 Cabano Québec, SE Canada
104 L11 Cabeza del Buey Extremadura, W Spain
45 V5 Cabezas de San Juan headland E Puerto Rico
105 N2 Cabezón de la Sal Cantabria, N Spain
Cabhán see Cavan
61 B23 Cabildo Buenos Aires, E Argentina
Cabillonum see Chalon-sur-Saône
54 H5 Cabimas Zulia, NW Venezuela
82 A9 Cabinda var. Kabinda. Cabinda, NW Angola
82 A9 Cabinda var. Kabinda. ◆ province NW Angola
33 N7 Cabinet Mountains ▲ Idaho/Montana, NW USA
82 B11 Cabiri Bengo, NW Angola
63 J20 Cabo Blanco Santa Cruz, SE Argentina
82 P13 Cabo Delgado off. Província de Cabo Delgado. ◆ province NE Mozambique
14 L9 Cabonga, Réservoir ⊠ Québec, SE Canada
27 V7 Cabool Missouri, C USA
183 V2 Caboolture Queensland, E Australia
Cabora Bassa, Lake see Cahora Bassa, Albufeira de
40 F3 Caborca Sonora, NW Mexico
Cabo San Lucas see San Lucas
27 V11 Cabot Arkansas, C USA
14 F12 Cabot Head headland Ontario, S Canada
13 R13 Cabot Strait strait E Canada
Cabo Verde, Ilhas do see Cape Verde
104 M14 Cabra Andalucía, S Spain
107 B19 Cabras Sardegna, Italy, C Mediterranean Sea
188 A15 Cabras Island island W Guam
45 O8 Cabrera N Dominican Republic
104 J4 Cabrera ≈ NW Spain
105 X10 Cabrera, Illa de anc. Capraria. island Islas Baleares, Spain, W Mediterranean Sea
105 Q15 Cabrera, Sierra ▲ S Spain
9 S16 Cabri Saskatchewan, S Canada
105 R10 Cabriel ≈ E Spain
54 M7 Cabruta Guárico, C Venezuela
171 N2 Cabugao Luzon, N Philippines
54 G10 Cabuyaro Meta, C Colombia
60 I13 Caçador Santa Catarina, S Brazil
42 G8 Cacaguatique, Cordillera var. Cordillera. ▲ NE El Salvador
112 L13 Čačak Serbia, C Serbia
55 Y10 Cacao NE French Guiana
61 H16 Caçapava do Sul Rio Grande do Sul, S Brazil
21 U3 Cacapon River ≈ West Virginia, NE USA
107 J23 Caccamo Sicilia, Italy, C Mediterranean Sea
107 A17 Caccia, Capo headland Sardegna, Italy, C Mediterranean Sea
146 H15 Çäçe var. Chäche, Rus. Chaacha. Ahal Welaýaty, S Turkmenistan
59 G18 Cáceres Mato Grosso, W Brazil
104 J10 Cáceres Ar. Qazris. Extremadura, W Spain
104 J9 Cáceres ◆ province Extremadura, W Spain
Cachacrou see Scotts Head Village
61 C21 Cacharí Buenos Aires, E Argentina
26 L12 Cache Oklahoma, C USA
10 M16 Cache Creek British Columbia, SW Canada
35 N6 Cache Creek ≈ California, W USA
37 S3 Cache La Poudre River ≈ Colorado, C USA
Cacheo see Cacheu
27 W11 Cache River ≈ Arkansas, C USA
30 L17 Cache River ≈ Illinois, N USA
76 G12 Cacheu var. Cacheo. W Guinea-Bissau
59 I15 Cachimbo Pará, NE Brazil
59 H15 Cachimbo, Serra do ▲ C Brazil
82 D13 Cachingues Bié, C Angola
54 G7 Cáchira Norte de Santander, N Colombia
61 H16 Cachoeira do Sul Rio Grande do Sul, S Brazil
59 O20 Cachoeiro de Itapemirim Espírito Santo, SE Brazil
82 E12 Cacolo Lunda Sul, NE Angola
83 C14 Caconda Huíla, C Angola
82 A9 Cacongo Cabinda, NW Angola
35 U9 Cactus Peak ▲ Nevada, W USA
82 A11 Cacuaco Luanda, NW Angola
83 B14 Cacula Huíla, SW Angola
67 R12 Caculuvar ≈ SW Angola
59 O19 Caçumba, Ilha island SE Brazil
55 N10 Cacuri Amazonas, S Venezuela
81 N17 Cadale Shabeellaha Dhexe, E Somalia
105 X4 Cadaqués Cataluña, NE Spain
111 J18 Čadca Hung. Csaca. Žilinský Kraj, N Slovakia
27 P13 Caddo Oklahoma, C USA
25 R6 Caddo Texas, SW USA
25 X6 Caddo Lake ⊠ Louisiana/Texas, SW USA
27 S12 Caddo Mountains ▲ Arkansas, C USA
41 O8 Cadereyta Nuevo León, NE Mexico
97 J19 Cader Idris ▲ NW Wales, UK
182 F3 Cadibarrawirracanna, Lake salt lake South Australia
14 I7 Cadillac Québec, SE Canada
9 T17 Cadillac Saskatchewan, S Canada
102 K13 Cadillac Gironde, SW France
31 P7 Cadillac Michigan, N USA
105 V4 Cadí, Torre de ▲ NE Spain
171 P5 Cadiz off. Cadiz City. Negros, C Philippines
104 J15 Cádiz anc. Gades, Gadier, Gadir, Gadire. Andalucía, SW Spain
20 H7 Cadiz Kentucky, S USA
31 U13 Cadiz Ohio, N USA
104 K15 Cádiz ◆ province Andalucía, SW Spain
104 I15 Cádiz, Bahía de bay SW Spain
Cadiz City see Cadiz
104 H15 Cádiz, Golfo de Eng. Gulf of Cadiz. gulf Portugal/Spain
Cadiz, Gulf of see Cádiz, Golfo de
35 X14 Cadiz Lake ◎ California, W USA
182 E2 Cadney Homestead South Australia
Cadurcum see Cahors
83 F17 Caecae North-West, NW Botswana
102 K4 Caen Calvados, N France
Caene/Caenepolis see Qena
Caerdydd see Cardiff
Caer Glou see Gloucester
Caer Gybi see Holyhead
Caerleon see Chester
Caer Luel see Carlisle
97 I18 Caernarfon var. Caernarvon, Carnarvon. NW Wales, UK
97 H18 Caernarfon Bay bay NW Wales, UK
97 I19 Caernarvon cultural region NW Wales, UK
Caernarvon see Caernarfon
Caesaraugusta see Zaragoza
Caesarea Mazaca see Kayseri
Caesarobriga see Talavera de la Reina
Caesarodunum see Tours
Caesaromagus see Beauvais
Caesena see Cesena
59 N17 Caetité Bahia, E Brazil
62 J6 Cafayate Salta, N Argentina
171 O2 Cagayan ≈ Luzon, N Philippines
171 Q7 Cagayan de Oro off. Cagayan de Oro City. Mindanao, S Philippines
Cagayan de Oro City see Cagayan de Oro
170 M8 Cagayan de Tawi Tawi island S Philippines
171 N6 Cagayan Islands island group C Philippines
31 O14 Cagles Mill Lake ⊠ Indiana, N USA
106 I12 Cagli Marche, C Italy
107 C20 Cagliari anc. Caralis. Sardegna, Italy, C Mediterranean Sea
107 C20 Cagliari, Golfo di gulf Sardegna, Italy, C Mediterranean Sea
103 U15 Cagnes-sur-Mer Alpes-Maritimes, SE France
54 L5 Cagua Aragua, N Venezuela
171 O1 Cagua, Mount ▲ Luzon, N Philippines
54 F13 Caguán, Río ≈ SW Colombia
45 U6 Caguas E Puerto Rico
146 C9 Çagyl Rus. Chagyl. Balkan Welaýaty, NW Turkmenistan
23 P5 Cahaba River ≈ Alabama, S USA
42 E5 Cahabón, Río ≈ C Guatemala
83 A15 Cahama Cunene, SW Angola
97 B21 Caha Mountains Ir. An Cheacha. ▲ SW Ireland
97 D20 Caher Ir. An Cathair. S Ireland
97 A21 Caherciveen Ir. Cathair Saidhbhín. SW Ireland
30 K15 Cahokia Illinois, N USA
83 L15 Cahora Bassa, Albufeira de var. Lake Cabora Bassa. ⊠ NW Mozambique
97 G20 Cahore Point Ir. Rinn Chathóir. headland SE Ireland
102 M14 Cahors anc. Cadurcum. Lot, S France
56 D9 Cahuapanas, Río ≈ N Peru
116 M12 Cahul Rus. Kagul. S Moldova
Cahul, Lacul see Kahul, Ozero
83 N16 Caia Sofala, C Mozambique
59 J19 Caiapó, Serra do ▲ C Brazil
44 F5 Caibarién Villa Clara, C Cuba
55 O5 Caicara Monagas, NE Venezuela
54 L5 Caicara de Orinoco Bolívar, C Venezuela
59 P14 Caicó Rio Grande do Norte, E Brazil
44 M6 Caicos Islands island group W Turks and Caicos Islands
44 L5 Caicos Passage strait Bahamas/Turks and Caicos Islands
161 O9 Caidian prev. Hanyang. Hubei, C China
Caiffa see Hefa
180 M12 Caiguna Western Australia
Caillí, Ceann see Hag's Head
40 J11 Caimanero, Laguna del var. Laguna del Camaronero. lagoon E Pacific Ocean
117 N10 Căinari Rus. Kaynary. C Moldova
57 L19 Caine, Río ≈ C Bolivia
Caiphas see Hefa
195 N4 Caird Coast physical region Antarctica
96 J9 Cairn Gorm ▲ C Scotland, UK
96 J9 Cairngorm Mountains ▲ C Scotland, UK
39 P12 Cairn Mountain ▲ Alaska, USA
181 W4 Cairns Queensland, NE Australia
121 V13 Cairo Ar. Al Qāhirah, var. El Qâhira. ● (Egypt) N Egypt
23 T8 Cairo Georgia, SE USA
30 L17 Cairo Illinois, N USA
75 V8 Cairo ✈ C Egypt
Caiseal see Cashel
Caisleán an Bharraigh see Castlebar
Caisleán na Finne see Castlefinn
96 J6 Caithness cultural region N Scotland, UK
83 D15 Caiundo Cuando Cubango, S Angola
56 C11 Cajamarca prev. Caxamarca. Cajamarca, NW Peru
56 B11 Cajamarca off. Departamento de Cajamarca. ◆ department N Peru
Cajamarca, Departamento de see Cajamarca
103 N14 Cajarc Lot, S France
42 G6 Cajón, Represa El ⊠ NW Honduras
58 N12 Caju, Ilha do island NE Brazil
159 R10 Caka Yanhu ◎ C China
112 E7 Čakovec Ger. Csakathurn, Hung. Csáktornya; prev. Ger. Tschakathurn. Medimurje, N Croatia
77 V17 Calabar Cross River, S Nigeria
14 K13 Calabogie Ontario, SE Canada
54 L6 Calabozo Guárico, C Venezuela
107 N20 Calabria anc. Bruttium. ◆ region SW Italy
104 M16 Calaburra, Punta de headland S Spain
116 G14 Calafat Dolj, SW Romania
Calafate see El Calafate
105 Q4 Calahorra La Rioja, N Spain
103 N1 Calais Pas-de-Calais, N France
19 T5 Calais Maine, NE USA
Calais, Pas de see Dover, Strait of
Calalen see Kallalen
62 H4 Calama Antofagasta, N Chile
Calamianes see Calamian Group
170 M5 Calamian Group var. Calamianes. island group W Philippines
105 R7 Calamocha Aragón, NE Spain
29 N14 Calamus River ≈ Nebraska, C USA
116 G12 Călan Ger. Kalan, Hung. Pusztakalán. Hunedoara, SW Romania
105 S7 Calanda Aragón, NE Spain
168 F9 Calang Sumatera, W Indonesia
171 N4 Calapan Mindoro, N Philippines
Călăras see Călăraşi
116 M9 Călăraşi var. Călăras, Rus. Kalarash. C Moldova
116 L14 Călăraşi Călăraşi, SE Romania
116 K14 Călăraşi ◆ county SE Romania
54 E10 Calarca Quindío, W Colombia
105 Q12 Calasparra Murcia, SE Spain
107 I23 Calatafimi Sicilia, Italy, C Mediterranean Sea
105 Q6 Calatayud Aragón, NE Spain
171 O4 Calauag Luzon, N Philippines
35 P8 Calaveras River ≈ California, W USA
171 N4 Calavite, Cape headland Mindoro, N Philippines
171 Q8 Calbayog off. Calbayog City. Samar, C Philippines
Calbayog City see Calbayog
22 G9 Calcasieu Lake ◎ Louisiana, S USA
22 H8 Calcasieu River ≈ Louisiana, S USA
56 B6 Calceta Manabí, W Ecuador
61 B16 Calchaquí Santa Fe, C Argentina
62 J6 Calchaquí, Río ≈ NW Argentina
58 J10 Calçoene Amapá, NE Brazil
153 S16 Calcutta ✈ West Bengal, N India
Calcutta see Kolkata
54 E9 Caldas off. Departamento de Caldas. ◆ province W Colombia
104 F10 Caldas da Rainha Leiria, W Portugal
Caldas, Departamento de see Caldas
104 G3 Caldas de Reis var. Caldas de Reyes. Galicia, NW Spain
Caldas de Reyes see Caldas de Reis
58 F13 Caldeirão Amazonas, NW Brazil
62 G7 Caldera Atacama, N Chile
42 L14 Caldera Puntarenas, W Costa Rica
105 N10 Calderina ▲ C Spain
137 T13 Çaldıran Van, E Turkey
32 M14 Caldwell Idaho, NW USA
27 N8 Caldwell Kansas, C USA
14 G15 Caledon Ontario, S Canada
83 I23 Caledon var. Mohokare. ≈ Lesotho/South Africa
42 G1 Caledonia Corozal, N Belize
14 G16 Caledonia Ontario, S Canada
29 X11 Caledonia Minnesota, N USA
105 X5 Calella var. Calella de la Costa. Cataluña, NE Spain
Calella de la Costa see Calella
23 P4 Calera Alabama, S USA
63 I19 Caleta Olivia Santa Cruz, SE Argentina
35 X17 Calexico California, W USA
97 H16 Calf of Man island SW Isle of Man
9 Q16 Calgary Alberta, SW Canada
9 Q16 Calgary ✈ Alberta, SW Canada
37 U5 Calhan Colorado, C USA
64 O5 Calheta Madeira, Portugal, NE Atlantic Ocean
23 R2 Calhoun Georgia, SE USA
20 I6 Calhoun Kentucky, S USA
22 M3 Calhoun City Mississippi, S USA
21 P12 Calhoun Falls South Carolina, SE USA
54 D11 Cali Valle del Cauca, W Colombia
27 V9 Calico Rock Arkansas, C USA
155 F21 Calicut var. Kozhikode. Kerala, SW India
35 Y9 Caliente Nevada, W USA
27 U5 California Missouri, C USA
18 B15 California Pennsylvania, NE USA
35 Q12 California off. State of California, also known as El Dorado, The Golden State. ◆ state W USA
35 P11 California Aqueduct aqueduct California, W USA
35 T13 California City California, W USA
40 F6 California, Golfo de Eng. Gulf of California; prev. Sea of Cortez. gulf W Mexico
California, Gulf of see California, Golfo de
137 Y13 Cälilabad Rus. Dzhalilabad; prev. Astrakhan-Bazar. S Azerbaijan
116 I12 Călimăneşti Vâlcea, SW Romania
116 J9 Călimani, Munţii ▲ N Romania
Calinisc see Cupcina
35 X17 Calipatria California, W USA
Calisia see Kalisz
34 M7 Calistoga California, W USA
83 G25 Calitzdorp Western Cape, SW South Africa
41 W12 Calkiní Campeche, E Mexico
182 K4 Callabonna Creek var. Tilcha Creek. seasonal river New South Wales/South Australia
182 J4 Callabonna, Lake ◎ South Australia
102 G5 Callac Côtes d'Armor, NW France
35 U5 Callaghan, Mount ▲ Nevada, W USA
Callain see Callan
97 E19 Callan Ir. Callain. S Ireland
14 H11 Callander Ontario, S Canada
96 I11 Callander C Scotland, UK
98 H7 Callantsoog Noord-Holland, NW Netherlands
57 D14 Callao Callao, W Peru
57 D15 Callao off. Departamento del Callao. ◆ constitutional province W Peru
Callao, Departamento del see Callao
56 F11 Callaria, Río ≈ E Peru
Callatis see Mangalia
9 Q13 Calling Lake Alberta, W Canada
Callosa de Ensarriá see Callosa d'En Sarrià
105 T11 Callosa d'En Sarrià var. Callosa de Ensarriá. País Valenciano, E Spain
105 S12 Callosa de Segura País Valenciano, E Spain
29 X11 Calmar Iowa, C USA
Calmar see Kalmar
43 R16 Calobre Veraguas, C Panama
23 X14 Caloosahatchee River ≈ Florida, SE USA
183 V2 Caloundra Queensland, E Australia
Calp see Calpe
105 T11 Calpe Cat. Calp. País Valenciano, E Spain
41 P14 Calpulalpan Tlaxcala, S Mexico
107 K25 Caltagirone Sicilia, Italy, C Mediterranean Sea
107 J24 Caltanissetta Sicilia, Italy, C Mediterranean Sea
82 E11 Caluango Lunda Norte, NE Angola
82 C12 Calucinga Bié, W Angola
82 B12 Calulo Cuanza Sul, NW Angola
83 B14 Caluquembe Huíla, W Angola
80 Q11 Caluula Bari, NE Somalia
102 K4 Calvados ◆ department N France
186 I10 Calvados Chain, The island group SE Papua New Guinea
25 U9 Calvert Texas, SW USA
20 H7 Calvert City Kentucky, S USA
103 X14 Calvi Corse, France, C Mediterranean Sea
40 L12 Calvillo Aguascalientes, C Mexico
83 F24 Calvinia Northern Cape, W South Africa
104 K8 Calvitero ▲ W Spain
101 G22 Calw Baden-Württemberg, SW Germany
Calydon see Kalydón
105 N11 Calzada de Calatrava Castilla-La Mancha, C Spain
Cama see Kama
82 C11 Camabatela Cuanza Norte, NW Angola
64 Q5 Camacha Porto Santo, Madeira, Portugal, NE Atlantic Ocean
14 L8 Camachigama, Lac ◎ Québec, SE Canada
40 M9 Camacho Zacatecas, C Mexico
82 D13 Camacupa var. General Machado, Port. Vila General Machado. Bié, C Angola
54 L7 Camaguán Guárico, C Venezuela
44 G6 Camagüey prev. Puerto Príncipe. Camagüey, C Cuba
44 G5 Camagüey, Archipiélago de island group C Cuba
40 D5 Camalli, Sierra de ▲ NW Mexico
57 G18 Camana var. Camaná. Arequipa, SW Peru
29 Z14 Camanche Iowa, C USA
35 P8 Camanche Reservoir ⊠ California, W USA
61 I16 Camaquã Rio Grande do Sul, S Brazil
61 H16 Camaquã, Rio ≈ S Brazil
64 P6 Câmara de Lobos Madeira, Portugal, NE Atlantic Ocean
103 U16 Camarat, Cap headland SE France
41 O8 Camargo Tamaulipas, C Mexico
103 R15 Camargue physical region SE France
104 F2 Camariñas Galicia, NW Spain
Camaronero, Laguna del see Caimanero, Laguna del
63 J18 Camarones Chaco, S Argentina
63 J18 Camarones, Bahía bay S Argentina
104 J14 Camas Andalucía, S Spain
167 S15 Ca Mau var. Quan Long. Minh Hai, S Vietnam
82 E11 Camaxilo Lunda Norte, NE Angola
104 G3 Cambados Galicia, NW Spain
Cambay, Gulf of see Khambhāt, Gulf of
Camberia see Chambéry
97 N22 Camberley SE England, UK
167 R12 Cambodia off. Kingdom of Cambodia, var. Democratic Kampuchea, Roat Kampuchea, Cam. Kampuchea; prev. People's Democratic Republic of Kampuchea. ◆ republic SE Asia
Cambodia, Kingdom of see Cambodia
102 I16 Cambo-les-Bains Pyrénées-Atlantiques, SW France
103 P2 Cambrai Flem. Kambryk, prev. Cambray; anc. Cameracum. Nord, N France
Cambray see Cambrai
104 H2 Cambre Galicia, NW Spain
35 O12 Cambria California, W USA
97 J20 Cambrian Mountains ▲ C Wales, UK
14 G16 Cambridge Ontario, S Canada
44 I12 Cambridge W Jamaica
184 M8 Cambridge Waikato, North Island, New Zealand
97 O20 Cambridge Lat. Cantabrigia. E England, UK
32 M12 Cambridge Idaho, NW USA
30 K11 Cambridge Illinois, N USA
21 Y4 Cambridge Maryland, NE USA
19 O11 Cambridge Massachusetts, NE USA
29 V7 Cambridge Minnesota, N USA
29 N16 Cambridge Nebraska, C USA
31 U13 Cambridge Ohio, NE USA
8 L7 Cambridge Bay Victoria Island, Nunavut, NW Canada
97 O20 Cambridgeshire cultural region E England, UK
105 U6 Cambrils de Mar Cataluña, NE Spain
Cambundi-Catembo see Nova Gaia
137 N11 Çam Burnu headland N Turkey
183 S9 Camden New South Wales, SE Australia
23 O6 Camden Alabama, S USA
27 U14 Camden Arkansas, C USA
21 Y3 Camden Delaware, NE USA
19 R7 Camden Maine, NE USA
18 I16 Camden New Jersey, NE USA
18 I9 Camden New York, NE USA
21 R12 Camden South Carolina, SE USA
20 H8 Camden Tennessee, S USA
25 X9 Camden Texas, SW USA
39 S5 Camden Bay bay S Beaufort Sea
27 U6 Camdenton Missouri, C USA
Camellia State see Alabama
18 M7 Camels Hump ▲ Vermont, NE USA
117 N8 Camenca Rus. Kamenka. N Moldova
Cameracum see Cambrai
22 G9 Cameron Louisiana, S USA
25 T9 Cameron Texas, SW USA
30 J5 Cameron Wisconsin, N USA
10 M12 Cameron ≈ British Columbia, W Canada
185 A24 Cameron Mountains ▲ South Island, New Zealand
79 D15 Cameroon off. Republic of Cameroon, Fr. Cameroun. ◆ republic W Africa
79 D15 Cameroon Mountain ▲ SW Cameroon
Cameroon, Republic of see Cameroon
Cameroon Ridge see Camerounaise, Dorsale
Cameroun see Cameroon
79 E14 Camerounaise, Dorsale Eng. Cameroon Ridge. ridge NW Cameroon
136 B15 Çamiçi Gölü ◎ SW Turkey
171 N3 Camiling Luzon, N Philippines
23 T7 Camilla Georgia, SE USA
104 G5 Caminha Viana do Castelo, N Portugal
35 P7 Camino California, W USA
107 J24 Cammarata Sicilia, Italy, C Mediterranean Sea
42 K10 Camoapa Boaco, S Nicaragua
58 O13 Camocim Ceará, E Brazil
106 D10 Camogli Liguria, NW Italy
181 S5 Camooweal Queensland, C Australia
55 Y11 Camopi E French Guiana
151 Q22 Camorta island Nicobar Islands, India, NE Indian Ocean
42 I6 Campamento Olancho, C Honduras
61 D19 Campana Buenos Aires, E Argentina
63 F21 Campana, Isla island S Chile
104 K11 Campanario Extremadura, W Spain
107 L17 Campania Eng. Champagne. ◆ region S Italy
27 Y8 Campbell Missouri, C USA
185 K15 Campbell, Cape headland South Island, New Zealand
14 J14 Campbellford Ontario, SE Canada
31 R13 Campbell Hill hill Ohio, N USA
192 K13 Campbell Island island S New Zealand
175 P13 Campbell Plateau undersea feature SW Pacific Ocean
10 K17 Campbell River Vancouver Island, British Columbia, SW Canada
20 L6 Campbellsville Kentucky, S USA
13 O13 Campbellton New Brunswick, SE Canada
183 S9 Campbelltown New South Wales, SE Australia
183 P16 Campbell Town Tasmania, SE Australia
96 G13 Campbeltown W Scotland, UK
41 W13 Campeche Campeche, SE Mexico
41 W14 Campeche ◆ state SE Mexico
41 T14 Campeche, Bahía de Eng. Bay of Campeche. bay E Mexico
Campeche, Banco de see Campeche Bank
64 C11 Campeche Bank Sp. Banco de Campeche, Sonda de Campeche. undersea feature S Gulf of Mexico
Campeche, Bay of see Campeche, Bahía de
Campeche, Sonda de see Campeche Bank
44 H7 Campechuela Granma, E Cuba
182 M13 Camperdown Victoria, SE Australia
167 U6 Cẩm Pha Quang Ninh, N Vietnam
116 H10 Câmpia Turzii Ger. Jerischmarkt, Hung. Aranyosgyéres; prev. Cimpia Turzii, Ghiriş, Gyéres. Cluj, NW Romania
104 K12 Campillo de Llerena Extremadura, W Spain
104 L15 Campillos Andalucía, S Spain
116 J13 Câmpina prev. Cîmpina. Prahova, SE Romania
59 Q15 Campina Grande Paraíba, E Brazil
60 L9 Campinas São Paulo, S Brazil
38 L10 Camp Kulowiye Saint Lawrence Island, Alaska, USA
79 D17 Campo var. Kampo. Sud, SW Cameroon
Campo see Ntem
59 N15 Campo Alegre de Lourdes Bahia, E Brazil
107 L16 Campobasso Molise, C Italy
107 H24 Campobello di Mazara Sicilia, Italy, C Mediterranean Sea
Campo Criptana see Campo de Criptana
105 O10 Campo de Criptana var. Campo Criptana. Castilla-La Mancha, C Spain
59 I16 Campo de Diauarum var. Pôsto Diuarum. Mato Grosso, W Brazil
54 E5 Campo de la Cruz Atlántico, N Colombia
105 P11 Campo de Montiel physical region C Spain
Campo dos Goitacazes see Campos
60 H12 Campo Erê Santa Catarina, S Brazil
62 L7 Campo Gallo Santiago del Estero, N Argentina
59 I20 Campo Grande state capital Mato Grosso do Sul, SW Brazil
60 K12 Campo Largo Paraná, S Brazil
58 N13 Campo Maior Piauí, E Brazil
104 I10 Campo Maior Portalegre, C Portugal
60 H10 Campo Mourão Paraná, S Brazil
60 Q9 Campos var. Campo dos Goitacazes. Rio de Janeiro, SE Brazil
59 L17 Campos Belos Goiás, S Brazil
60 N9 Campos do Jordão São Paulo, S Brazil
60 I13 Campos Novos Santa Catarina, S Brazil
59 O14 Campos Sales Ceará, E Brazil
25 Q9 Camp San Saba Texas, SW USA
21 N6 Campton Kentucky, S USA
116 I13 Câmpulung prev. Câmpulung-Muşcel, Cîmpulung. Argeş, S Romania
116 J9 Câmpulung Moldovenesc var. Cîmpulung Moldovenesc, Ger. Kimpolung, Hung. Hosszúmezjő. Suceava, NE Romania
Câmpulung-Muşcel see Câmpulung
Campus Stellae see Santiago
36 L12 Camp Verde Arizona, SW USA
25 P11 Camp Wood Texas, SW USA
167 V13 Cam Ranh Khanh Hoa, S Vietnam
9 Q15 Camrose Alberta, SW Canada
Camulodunum see Colchester
136 B12 Çan Çanakkale, NW Turkey
18 L12 Canaan Connecticut, NE USA
9 O13 Canada ◆ commonwealth republic N North America
197 P6 Canada Basin undersea feature Arctic Ocean
61 B18 Cañada de Gómez Santa Fe, C Argentina
197 P6 Canada Plain undersea feature Arctic Ocean
61 A18 Cañada Rosquín Santa Fe, C Argentina
25 P1 Canadian Texas, SW USA
16 K12 Canadian River ≈ SW USA
8 L12 Canadian Shield physical region Canada
63 I18 Cañadón Grande, Sierra ▲ S Argentina
55 P9 Canaima Bolívar, SE Venezuela
136 B11 Çanakkale var. Dardanelli; prev. Chanak, Kale Sultanie. Çanakkale, W Turkey
136 B12 Çanakkale ◆ province NW Turkey
136 B11 Çanakkale Boğazı Eng. Dardanelles. strait NW Turkey
187 Q17 Canala Province Nord, C New Caledonia
59 A15 Canamari Amazonas, W Brazil
18 G10 Canandaigua New York, NE USA
18 F10 Canandaigua Lake ◎ New York, NE USA
40 G3 Cananea Sonora, NW Mexico
56 B8 Cañar ◆ province C Ecuador
64 N10 Canarias, Islas Eng. Canary Islands. ◆ autonomous community Islas Canarias, Spain Europe, NE Atlantic Ocean

232
◆ Country ● Country Capital ◇ Dependent Territory ○ Dependent Territory Capital ◆ Administrative Regions ✈ International Airport ▲ Mountain ▲ Mountain Range Volcano ≈ River ◎ Lake ⊠ Reservoir

CANARIES BASIN – CARTHAGE

Canaries Basin *see* Canary Basin
44 C6 **Canarreos, Archipiélago de los** *island group* W Cuba
Canary Islands *see* Canarias, Islas
66 K3 **Canary Basin** *var.* Canaries Basin, Monaco Basin. *undersea feature* E Atlantic Ocean
42 L13 **Cañas** Guanacaste, NW Costa Rica
18 I10 **Canastota** New York, NE USA
40 K9 **Canatlán** Durango, C Mexico
104 J9 **Cañaveral** Extremadura, W Spain
23 Y11 **Canaveral, Cape** *headland* Florida, SE USA
59 O18 **Canavieiras** Bahia, E Brazil
43 R16 **Cañazas** Veraguas, W Panama
106 H6 **Canazei** Trentino-Alto Adige, N Italy
183 P6 **Canbelego** New South Wales, SE Australia
183 R10 **Canberra** ● (Australia) Australian Capital Territory, SE Australia
183 R10 **Canberra** ✈ Australian Capital Territory, SE Australia
35 P2 **Canby** California, W USA
29 S9 **Canby** Minnesota, N USA
103 N2 **Canche** ≈ N France
102 L13 **Cancon** Lot-et-Garonne, SW France
41 Z11 **Cancún** Quintana Roo, SE Mexico
104 K2 **Candás** Asturias, N Spain
102 J7 **Cande** Maine-et-Loire, NW France
41 W14 **Candelaria** Campeche, SE Mexico
24 J11 **Candelaria** Texas, SW USA
41 W15 **Candelaria, Río** ≈ Guatemala/Mexico
104 L8 **Candeleda** Castilla-León, N Spain
Candia *see* Irákleio
41 P8 **Cándido Aguilar** Tamaulipas, C Mexico
39 N8 **Candle** Alaska, USA
9 T14 **Candle Lake** Saskatchewan, C Canada
18 L13 **Candlewood, Lake** ⊠ Connecticut, NE USA
29 O3 **Cando** North Dakota, N USA
Canea *see* Chaniá
45 O12 **Canefield** ✈ (Roseau) SW Dominica
61 F20 **Canelones** *prev.* Guadalupe. Canelones, S Uruguay
61 E20 **Canelones** ⬖ *department* S Uruguay
Canendiyú *see* Canindeyú
63 F14 **Cañete** Bío Bío, C Chile
105 Q9 **Cañete** Castilla-La Mancha, C Spain
Cañete *see* San Vicente de Cañete
27 P8 **Caney** Kansas, C USA
27 P8 **Caney River** ≈ Kansas/Oklahoma, C USA
105 S3 **Canfranc-Estación** Aragón, NE Spain
83 E14 **Cangamba** *Port.* Vila de Aljustrel. Moxico, E Angola
82 C12 **Cangandala** Malanje, NW Angola
104 G4 **Cangas** Galicia, NW Spain
104 J2 **Cangas del Narcea** Asturias, N Spain
104 L2 **Cangas de Onís** Asturias, N Spain
161 S11 **Cangnan** *var.* Lingxi. Zhejiang, SE China
82 C10 **Cangola** Uíge, NW Angola
83 E14 **Cangombe** Moxico, E Angola
63 H21 **Cangrejo, Cerro** ▲ S Argentina
61 H17 **Canguçu** Rio Grande do Sul, S Brazil
161 P3 **Cangzhou** Hebei, E China
12 M7 **Caniapiscau** ≈ Québec, E Canada
12 M8 **Caniapiscau, Réservoir de** ⊠ Québec, C Canada
107 J24 **Canicattì** Sicilia, Italy, C Mediterranean Sea
136 L11 **Canik Dağları** ▲▲ N Turkey
105 P14 **Caniles** Andalucía, S Spain
59 B16 **Canindé** Acre, W Brazil
62 P6 **Canindeyú** *var.* Canendiyú, Canindiyú. ⬖ *department* E Paraguay
Canindiyú *see* Canindeyú
194 J10 **Canisteo Peninsula** *peninsula* Antarctica
18 F11 **Canisteo River** ≈ New York, NE USA
40 M10 **Cañitas** *var.* Cañitas de Felipe Pescador. Zacatecas, C Mexico
Cañitas de Felipe Pescador *see* Cañitas
105 P15 **Canjáyar** Andalucía, S Spain
136 I12 **Çankırı** *var.* Chankiri; *anc.* Gangra, Germanicopolis. Çankın, N Turkey
136 I11 **Çankiri** *var.* Chankiri. ⬖ *province* N Turkey
171 P6 **Canlaon Volcano** △ Negros, C Philippines
9 P16 **Canmore** Alberta, SW Canada
96 F9 **Canna** *island* NW Scotland, UK
155 F20 **Cannanore** *var.* Kananur, Kannur. Kerala, SW India
31 O17 **Cannelton** Indiana, N USA
103 U15 **Cannes** Alpes-Maritimes, SE France
39 R5 **Canning River** ≈ Alaska, USA
106 C6 **Cannobio** Piemonte, NE Italy
97 L19 **Cannock** C England, UK
28 M6 **Cannonball River** ≈ North Dakota, N USA
29 W9 **Cannon Falls** Minnesota, N USA
18 I11 **Cannonsville Reservoir** ⊠ New York, NE USA
183 R12 **Cann River** Victoria, SE Australia
61 I16 **Canoas** Rio Grande do Sul, S Brazil
61 I14 **Canoas, Rio** ≈ S Brazil
14 I12 **Canoe Lake** ◎ Ontario, SE Canada
60 J12 **Canoinhas** Santa Catarina, S Brazil
37 T6 **Canon City** Colorado, C USA
55 P8 **Caño Negro** Bolívar, SE Venezuela
173 X15 **Canonniers Point** *headland* N Mauritius
23 W6 **Canoochee River** ≈ Georgia, SE USA
9 V15 **Canora** Saskatchewan, S Canada
45 Y14 **Canouan** *island* S Saint Vincent and the Grenadines
13 R15 **Canso** Nova Scotia, SE Canada
104 M3 **Cantabria** ⬖ *autonomous community* N Spain
104 K3 **Cantábrica, Cordillera** ▲▲ N Spain
Cantabrigia *see* Cambridge
103 O12 **Cantal** ⬖ *department* C France
105 N6 **Cantalejo** Castilla-León, N Spain
103 O12 **Cantal, Monts du** ▲▲ C France
104 G8 **Cantanhede** Coimbra, C Portugal
Cantaño *see* Cataño
55 O6 **Cantaura** Anzoátegui, NE Venezuela
116 M11 **Cantemir** *Rus.* Kantemir. S Moldova
97 Q22 **Canterbury** *hist.* Cantwaraburh; *anc.* Durovernum, *Lat.* Cantuaria. SE England, UK
185 F19 **Canterbury** *off.* Canterbury Region. ⬖ *region* South Island, New Zealand
185 H20 **Canterbury Bight** *bight* South Island, New Zealand
185 H19 **Canterbury Plains** *plain* South Island, New Zealand
Canterbury Region *see* Canterbury
167 S14 **Cần Thơ** Cần Thơ, S Vietnam
104 K13 **Cantillana** Andalucía, S Spain
59 N15 **Canto do Buriti** Piauí, NE Brazil
23 S2 **Canton** Georgia, SE USA
30 K12 **Canton** Illinois, N USA
22 L5 **Canton** Mississippi, S USA
27 V2 **Canton** Missouri, C USA
18 J7 **Canton** New York, NE USA
21 O10 **Canton** North Carolina, SE USA
31 U12 **Canton** Ohio, N USA
26 L9 **Canton** Oklahoma, C USA
18 G12 **Canton** Pennsylvania, NE USA
29 R11 **Canton** South Dakota, N USA
25 V7 **Canton** Texas, SW USA
Canton *see* Guangzhou
Canton Island *see* Kanton
26 L9 **Canton Lake** ⊠ Oklahoma, C USA
106 D7 **Cantù** Lombardia, N Italy
Cantuaria/Cantwaraburh *see* Canterbury
39 R10 **Cantwell** Alaska, USA
59 O16 **Canudos** Bahia, E Brazil
47 T7 **Canumã, Rio** ≈ N Brazil
Canusium *see* Puglia, Canosa di
24 G7 **Canutillo** Texas, SW USA
25 N3 **Canyon** Texas, SW USA
33 S12 **Canyon** Wyoming, C USA
32 K13 **Canyon City** Oregon, NW USA
33 R10 **Canyon Ferry Lake** ◎ Montana, NW USA
25 S11 **Canyon Lake** ⊠ Texas, SW USA
167 T5 **Cao Băng** *var.* Caobang. Cao Băng, N Vietnam
Caobang *see* Cao Băng
160 J12 **Caodu He** ≈ S China
167 S14 **Cao Lanh** Đông Thap, S Vietnam
82 C11 **Caombo** Malanje, NW Angola
Caorach, Cuan na g *see* Sheep Haven
Caozhou *see* Heze
171 Q12 **Capalulu** Pulau Mangole, E Indonesia
54 K8 **Capanaparo, Río** ≈ Colombia/Venezuela
58 L12 **Capanema** Pará, NE Brazil
60 L10 **Capão Bonito** São Paulo, S Brazil
60 I13 **Capão Doce, Morro do** ▲ S Brazil
54 I4 **Capatárida** Falcón, N Venezuela
102 I15 **Capbreton** Landes, SW France
Cap-Breton, Île du *see* Cape Breton Island
15 W6 **Cap-Chat** Québec, SE Canada
15 P11 **Cap-de-la-Madeleine** Québec, SE Canada
103 N13 **Capdenac** Aveyron, S France
183 Q15 **Cape Barren Island** *island* Furneaux Group, Tasmania, SE Australia
65 O18 **Cape Basin** *undersea feature* S Atlantic Ocean
13 R14 **Cape Breton Island** *Fr.* Île du Cap-Breton. *island* Nova Scotia, SE Canada
23 Y11 **Cape Canaveral** Florida, SE USA
21 Y6 **Cape Charles** Virginia, NE USA
77 P17 **Cape Coast** *prev.* Cape Coast Castle. S Ghana
Cape Coast Castle *see* Cape Coast
19 Q12 **Cape Cod Bay** *bay* Massachusetts, NE USA
23 W15 **Cape Coral** Florida, SE USA
181 R4 **Cape Crawford Roadhouse** Northern Territory, N Australia
9 Q7 **Cape Dorset** Baffin Island, Nunavut, NE Canada
21 N8 **Cape Fear River** ≈ North Carolina, SE USA
27 Y7 **Cape Girardeau** Missouri, C USA
21 T14 **Cape Island** *island* South Carolina, SE USA
186 A6 **Capella** ▲ NW Papua New Guinea
98 H12 **Capelle aan den IJssel** Zuid-Holland, SW Netherlands
83 C15 **Capelongo** Huíla, C Angola
18 J17 **Cape May** New Jersey, NE USA
18 J17 **Cape May Court House** New Jersey, NE USA
Cape Palmas *see* Harper
8 I16 **Cape Parry** Northwest Territories, N Canada
65 P19 **Cape Rise** *undersea feature* SW Indian Ocean
Cape Saint Jacques *see* Vung Tau
Capesterre *see* Capesterre-Belle-Eau
45 Y6 **Capesterre-Belle-Eau** *var.* Capesterre. Basse Terre, S Guadeloupe
83 D26 **Cape Town** *var.* Ekapa, *Afr.* Kaapstad, Kapstad. ● (South Africa-legislative capital) Western Cape, SW South Africa
83 E26 **Cape Town** ✈ Western Cape, SW South Africa
76 D9 **Cape Verde** *off.* Republic of Cape Verde, *Port.* Cabo Verde, Ilhas do Cabo Verde. ◆ *republic* E Atlantic Ocean
64 L11 **Cape Verde Basin** *undersea feature* E Atlantic Ocean
66 K5 **Cape Verde Islands** *island group* E Atlantic Ocean
64 L10 **Cape Verde Plain** *undersea feature* E Atlantic Ocean
Cape Verde Plateau/Cape Verde Rise *see* Cape Verde Terrace
Cape Verde, Republic of *see* Cape Verde
64 L11 **Cape Verde Terrace** *var.* Cape Verde Plateau, Cape Verde Rise. *undersea feature* E Atlantic Ocean
181 V2 **Cape York Peninsula** *peninsula* Queensland, N Australia
44 M8 **Cap-Haïtien** *var.* Le Cap. N Haiti
43 T15 **Capira** Panamá, C Panama
14 K8 **Capitachouane** ≈ Québec, SE Canada
14 L8 **Capitachouane, Lac** ◎ Québec, SE Canada
37 T13 **Capitan** New Mexico, SW USA
194 G3 **Capitán Arturo Prat** *Chilean research station* South Shetland Islands, Antarctica
37 S13 **Capitan Mountains** ▲▲ New Mexico, SW USA
62 M3 **Capitán Pablo Lagerenza** *var.* Mayor Pablo Lagerenza. Chaco, N Paraguay
37 T13 **Capitan Peak** ▲ New Mexico, SW USA
188 H5 **Capitol Hill** Saipan, S Northern Mariana Islands
60 I9 **Capivara, Represa** ⊠ S Brazil
61 J16 **Capivari** Rio Grande do Sul, S Brazil
113 H15 **Čapljina** ⬖ S Bosnia and Herzegovina
83 M15 **Capoche** *var.* Kapoche. ≈ Mozambique/Zambia
Capo Delgado, Provincia de *see* Cabo Delgado
107 K17 **Capodichino** ✈ (Napoli) Campania, S Italy
Capodistria *see* Koper
106 E12 **Capraia, Isola di** *island* Arcipelago Toscano, C Italy
107 B16 **Caprara, Punta** *var.* Punta dello Scorno. *headland* Isola Asinara, W Italy
Capraria *see* Cabrera, Illa de
14 F10 **Capreol** Ontario, S Canada
107 K18 **Capri** Campania, S Italy
175 S9 **Capricorn Tablemount** *undersea feature* W Pacific Ocean
107 J18 **Capri, Isola di** *island* S Italy
83 G16 **Caprivi** ⬖ *district* NE Namibia
Caprivi Concession *see* Caprivi Strip
83 F16 **Caprivi Strip** *Ger.* Caprivizipfel; *prev.* Caprivi Concession. *cultural region* NE Namibia
Caprivizipfel *see* Caprivi Strip
25 O5 **Cap Rock Escarpment** *cliffs* Texas, SW USA
15 R10 **Cap-Rouge** Québec, SE Canada
Cap Saint-Jacques *see* Vung Tau
38 F12 **Captain Cook** Hawai'i, USA, C Pacific Ocean
183 R10 **Captains Flat** New South Wales, SE Australia
102 K14 **Captieux** Gironde, SW France
107 K17 **Capua** Campania, S Italy
54 F14 **Caquetá** *off.* Departamento del Caquetá. ⬖ *province* S Colombia
Caquetá, Departamento del *see* Caquetá
54 E13 **Caquetá, Río** *var.* Rio Japurá, Yapurá. ≈ Brazil/Colombia *see also* Japurá, Rio
Caquetá, Río *see* Japurá, Rio
CAR *see* Central African Republic
Cara *see* Kara
57 I16 **Carabaya, Cordillera** ▲▲ E Peru
54 K5 **Carabobo** *off.* Estado Carabobo. ⬖ *state* N Venezuela
Carabobo, Estado *see* Carabobo
116 I14 **Caracal** Olt, S Romania
58 F10 **Caracaraí** Rondônia, W Brazil
54 L5 **Caracas** ● (Venezuela) Distrito Federal, N Venezuela
54 I5 **Carache** Trujillo, N Venezuela
60 N10 **Caraguatatuba** São Paulo, S Brazil
48 I7 **Carajás, Serra dos** ▲▲ N Brazil
Caralis *see* Cagliari
54 E9 **Caramanta** Antioquia, W Colombia
171 P4 **Caramoan** Catanduanes Island, N Philippines
Caramurat *see* Mihail Kogălniceanu
116 F12 **Caransebeş** *Ger.* Karansebesch, *Hung.* Karánsebes. Caraş-Severin, SW Romania
Carapella *see* Carapelle
107 M16 **Carapelle** *var.* Carapella. ≈ SE Italy
55 O9 **Carapo** Bolívar, SE Venezuela
13 P13 **Caraquet** New Brunswick, SE Canada
Caras *see* Caraz
116 F12 **Caraşova** *Hung.* Krassóvár. Caraş-Severin, SW Romania
116 F12 **Caraş-Severin** ⬖ *county* SW Romania
42 M5 **Caratasca, Laguna de** *lagoon* NE Honduras
58 C13 **Carauari** Amazonas, NW Brazil
Caravaca *see* Caravaca de la Cruz
105 Q12 **Caravaca de la Cruz** *var.* Caravaca. Murcia, SE Spain
106 E7 **Caravaggio** Lombardia, N Italy
107 C18 **Caravai, Passo di** *pass* Sardegna, Italy, C Mediterranean Sea
59 O19 **Caravelas** Bahia, E Brazil
56 C12 **Caraz** *var.* Caras. Ancash, W Peru
61 H14 **Carazinho** Rio Grande do Sul, S Brazil
42 J11 **Carazo** ⬖ *department* SW Nicaragua
Carballiño *see* O Carballiño
104 G2 **Carballo** Galicia, NW Spain
9 W16 **Carberry** Manitoba, S Canada
40 F4 **Carbó** Sonora, NW Mexico
107 C20 **Carbonara, Capo** *headland* Sardegna, Italy, C Mediterranean Sea
37 Q5 **Carbondale** Colorado, C USA
30 L17 **Carbondale** Illinois, N USA
27 Q4 **Carbondale** Kansas, C USA
18 I13 **Carbondale** Pennsylvania, NE USA
13 V12 **Carbonear** Newfoundland, Newfoundland and Labrador, SE Canada
105 Q9 **Carboneras de Guadazaón** *var.* Carboneras de Guadazón. Castilla-La Mancha, C Spain
Carboneras de Guadazón *see* Carboneras de Guadazaón
23 O3 **Carbon Hill** Alabama, S USA
107 B20 **Carbonia** *var.* Carbonia Centro. Sardegna, Italy, C Mediterranean Sea
Carbonia Centro *see* Carbonia
105 S10 **Carcaixent** País Valenciano, E Spain
Carcaso *see* Carcassonne
65 B24 **Carcass Island** *island* NW Falkland Islands
103 O16 **Carcassonne** *anc.* Carcaso. Aude, S France
105 R12 **Carche** ▲ S Spain
56 A13 **Carchi** ⬖ *province* N Ecuador
10 I8 **Carcross** Yukon Territory, W Canada
Cardamomes, Chaîne des *see* Krâvanh, Chuŏr Phnum
155 G22 **Cardamom Hills** ▲▲ SW India
Cardamom Mountains *see* Krâvanh, Chuŏr Phnum
104 M12 **Cardeña** Andalucía, S Spain
44 D4 **Cárdenas** Matanzas, W Cuba
41 O11 **Cárdenas** San Luis Potosí, C Mexico
41 U15 **Cárdenas** Tabasco, SE Mexico
63 H21 **Cardiel, Lago** ◎ S Argentina
97 K22 **Cardiff** *Wel.* Caerdydd. ⬖ S Wales, UK
97 J22 **Cardiff-Wales** ✈ S Wales, UK
97 I21 **Cardigan** *Wel.* Aberteifi. SW Wales, UK
97 I20 **Cardigan** *cultural region* W Wales, UK
97 I20 **Cardigan Bay** *bay* W Wales, UK
19 N8 **Cardigan, Mount** ▲ New Hampshire, NE USA
14 M13 **Cardinal** Ontario, SE Canada
105 V5 **Cardona** Cataluña, NE Spain
61 E19 **Cardona** Soriano, SW Uruguay
105 V4 **Cardoner** ≈ NE Spain
9 Q17 **Cardston** Alberta, SW Canada
181 W5 **Cardwell** Queensland, NE Australia
116 G8 **Carei** *Ger.* Gross-Karol, Karol, *Hung.* Nagykároly; *prev.* Careii-Mari. Satu Mare, NW Romania
Careii-Mari *see* Carei
58 F13 **Careiro** Amazonas, NW Brazil
102 J4 **Carentan** Manche, N France
104 M2 **Cares** ≈ N Spain
33 P14 **Carey** Idaho, NW USA
31 S12 **Carey** Ohio, N USA
25 P4 **Carey** Texas, SW USA
180 L11 **Carey, Lake** ◎ Western Australia
173 O8 **Cargados Carajos Bank** *undersea feature* C Indian Ocean
102 G6 **Carhaix-Plouguer** Finistère, NW France
61 A22 **Carhué** Buenos Aires, E Argentina
55 O5 **Cariaco** Sucre, NE Venezuela
107 O20 **Cariati** Calabria, SW Italy
2 H17 **Caribbean Plate** *tectonic feature*
44 I11 **Caribbean Sea** *sea* W Atlantic Ocean
9 N15 **Cariboo Mountains** ▲▲ British Columbia, SW Canada
9 W9 **Caribou** Manitoba, C Canada
19 S2 **Caribou** Maine, NE USA
9 P10 **Caribou Mountains** ▲▲ Alberta, SW Canada
Caribrod *see* Dimitrovgrad
40 I6 **Carichic** Chihuahua, N Mexico
103 R3 **Carignan** Ardennes, N France
183 Q5 **Carinda** New South Wales, SE Australia
105 R6 **Cariñena** Aragón, NE Spain
107 I23 **Carini** Sicilia, Italy, C Mediterranean Sea
107 K17 **Carinola** Campania, S Italy
Carinthi *see* Kärnten
55 O5 **Caripe** Monagas, NE Venezuela
55 P5 **Caripito** Monagas, NE Venezuela
15 W7 **Carleton** Québec, SE Canada
31 S10 **Carleton** Michigan, N USA
13 O14 **Carleton, Mount** ▲ New Brunswick, SE Canada
14 L13 **Carleton Place** Ontario, SE Canada
35 V3 **Carlin** Nevada, W USA
30 K14 **Carlinville** Illinois, N USA
97 K14 **Carlisle** *anc.* Caer Luel, Luguvallium, Luguvallum. NW England, UK
27 V11 **Carlisle** Arkansas, C USA
31 N15 **Carlisle** Indiana, N USA
29 V14 **Carlisle** Iowa, C USA
21 N5 **Carlisle** Kentucky, S USA
18 F15 **Carlisle** Pennsylvania, NE USA
21 Q11 **Carlisle** South Carolina, SE USA
38 J17 **Carlisle Island** *island* Aleutian Islands, Alaska, USA
27 R7 **Carl Junction** Missouri, C USA
107 A20 **Carloforte** Sardegna, Italy, C Mediterranean Sea
Carlopago *see* Karlobag
61 B21 **Carlos Casares** Buenos Aires, E Argentina
61 E18 **Carlos Reyles** Durazno, C Uruguay
61 A21 **Carlos Tejedor** Buenos Aires, E Argentina
97 F19 **Carlow** *Ir.* Ceatharlach. SE Ireland
97 F19 **Carlow** *Ir.* Cheatharlach. ⬖ *county* SE Ireland
96 F7 **Carloway** NW Scotland, UK
35 U17 **Carlsbad** California, W USA
37 U15 **Carlsbad** New Mexico, SW USA
Carlsbad *see* Karlovy Vary
129 N13 **Carlsberg Ridge** *undersea feature* S Arabian Sea
Carlsruhe *see* Karlsruhe
29 W6 **Carlton** Minnesota, N USA
9 V17 **Carlyle** Saskatchewan, S Canada
30 L15 **Carlyle** Illinois, N USA
30 L15 **Carlyle Lake** ⊠ Illinois, N USA
10 H7 **Carmacks** Yukon Territory, W Canada
106 B9 **Carmagnola** Piemonte, NW Italy
9 X16 **Carman** Manitoba, S Canada
Carmana/Carmania *see* Kermān
97 I21 **Carmarthen** SW Wales, UK
97 I21 **Carmarthen** *cultural region* SW Wales, UK
97 I22 **Carmarthen Bay** *inlet* SW Wales, UK
103 N14 **Carmaux** Tarn, S France
35 N11 **Carmel** California, W USA
31 O13 **Carmel** Indiana, N USA
18 L13 **Carmel** New York, NE USA
97 H18 **Carmel Head** *headland* NW Wales, UK
42 E2 **Carmelita** Petén, N Guatemala
61 D19 **Carmelo** Colonia, SW Uruguay
41 V14 **Carmen** *var.* Ciudad del Carmen. Campeche, SE Mexico
61 A25 **Carmen de Patagones** Buenos Aires, E Argentina
40 F8 **Carmen, Isla** *island* W Mexico
40 M5 **Carmen, Sierra del** ▲▲ NW Mexico
30 M16 **Carmi** Illinois, N USA
35 O7 **Carmichael** California, W USA
Carmiel *see* Karmi'él
25 U11 **Carmine** Texas, SW USA
104 K14 **Carmona** Andalucía, S Spain
Carmona *see* Uíge
Carnaro *see* Kvarner
180 G9 **Carnarvon** Western Australia
14 I13 **Carnarvon** Ontario, SE Canada
83 G24 **Carnarvon** Northern Cape, W South Africa
Carnarvon *see* Caernarfon
180 K9 **Carnarvon Range** ▲▲ Western Australia
Carn Domhnach *see* Carndonagh
96 E13 **Carndonagh** *Ir.* Carn Domhnach. NW Ireland
9 V17 **Carnduff** Saskatchewan, S Canada
26 L11 **Carnegie** Oklahoma, C USA
180 L9 **Carnegie, Lake** *salt lake* Western Australia
193 U8 **Carnegie Ridge** *undersea feature* E Pacific Ocean
96 H9 **Carn Eige** ▲ N Scotland, UK
182 F5 **Carnes** South Australia
194 J12 **Carney Island** *island* Antarctica
18 H16 **Carneys Point** New Jersey, NE USA
Carniche, Alpi *see* Karnische Alpen
151 Q21 **Car Nicobar** *island* Nicobar Islands, India, NE Indian Ocean
79 H15 **Carnot** Mambéré-Kadéï, W Central African Republic
182 F10 **Carnot, Cape** *headland* South Australia
96 K11 **Carnoustie** E Scotland, UK
97 F20 **Carnsore Point** *Ir.* Ceann an Chairn. *headland* SE Ireland
8 H7 **Carnwath** ≈ Northwest Territories, NW Canada
31 R8 **Caro** Michigan, N USA
23 Z15 **Carol City** Florida, SE USA
59 L14 **Carolina** Maranhão, E Brazil
45 U5 **Carolina** E Puerto Rico
21 V12 **Carolina Beach** North Carolina, SE USA
Caroline Island *see* Millennium Island
189 N15 **Caroline Islands** *island group* C Micronesia
129 Z14 **Caroline Plate** *tectonic feature*
192 H7 **Caroline Ridge** *undersea feature* E Philippine Sea
Carolopois *see* Châlons-en-Champagne
45 V14 **Caroni Arena Dam** ⊠ Trinidad, Trinidad and Tobago
Caronie, Monti *see* Nebrodi, Monti
55 P7 **Caroní, Río** ≈ E Venezuela
45 U14 **Caroni River** ≈ Trinidad, Trinidad and Tobago
Caronium *see* A Coruña
54 J5 **Carora** Lara, N Venezuela
86 F12 **Carpathian Mountains** *var.* Carpathians, *Cz./Pol.* Karpaty, *Ger.* Karpaten. ▲▲ E Europe
Carpathians *see* Carpathian Mountains
Carpathos/Carpathus *see* Kárpathos
116 H12 **Carpaţii Meridionali** *var.* Alpi Transilvaniei, Carpaţii Sudici, *Eng.* South Carpathians, Transylvanian Alps, *Ger.* Südkarpaten, Transsylvanische Alpen, *Hung.* Déli-Kárpátok, Erdélyi-Havasok. ▲▲ C Romania
Carpaţii Sudici *see* Carpaţii Meridionali
174 L7 **Carpentaria, Gulf of** *gulf* N Australia
Carpentoracte *see* Carpentras
103 R14 **Carpentras** *anc.* Carpentoracte. Vaucluse, SE France
106 F9 **Carpi** Emilia-Romagna, N Italy
116 E11 **Cărpiniş** *Hung.* Gyertyámos. Timiş, W Romania
35 R14 **Carpinteria** California, W USA
23 S9 **Carrabelle** Florida, SE USA
Carraig Aonair *see* Fastnet Rock
Carraig Fhearghais *see* Carrickfergus
Carraig Mhachaire Rois *see* Carrickmacross
Carraig na Siúire *see* Carrick-on-Suir
Carrantual *see* Carrauntoohil
106 E10 **Carrara** Toscana, C Italy
61 F20 **Carrasco** ✈ (Montevideo) Canelones, S Uruguay
105 P9 **Carrascosa del Campo** Castilla-La Mancha, C Spain
54 H4 **Carrasquero** Zulia, NW Venezuela
183 O9 **Carrathool** New South Wales, SE Australia
Carrauntohil *see* Carrauntoohil
97 B21 **Carrauntoohil** *Ir.* Carrantual, Carrauntohil, Corrán Tuathail. ▲ SW Ireland
45 Y15 **Carriacou** *island* N Grenada
97 G15 **Carrickfergus** *Ir.* Carraig Fhearghais. NE Northern Ireland, UK
97 F16 **Carrickmacross** *Ir.* Carraig Mhachaire Rois. N Ireland
97 D16 **Carrick-on-Shannon** *Ir.* Cora Droma Rúisc. NW Ireland
97 E20 **Carrick-on-Suir** *Ir.* Carraig na Siúire. S Ireland
182 I7 **Carrieton** South Australia
40 L7 **Carrillo** Chihuahua, N Mexico
29 O4 **Carrington** North Dakota, N USA
104 M4 **Carrión** ≈ N Spain
104 M4 **Carrión de los Condes** Castilla-León, N Spain
25 P13 **Carrizo Springs** Texas, SW USA
37 S13 **Carrizozo** New Mexico, SW USA
29 T13 **Carroll** Iowa, C USA
23 N4 **Carrollton** Alabama, S USA
23 R3 **Carrollton** Georgia, SE USA
30 K14 **Carrollton** Illinois, N USA
20 L4 **Carrollton** Kentucky, S USA
31 R8 **Carrollton** Michigan, N USA
27 T3 **Carrollton** Missouri, C USA
31 U12 **Carrollton** Ohio, N USA
25 T6 **Carrollton** Texas, SW USA
9 U14 **Carrot** ≈ Saskatchewan, S Canada
9 U14 **Carrot River** Saskatchewan, C Canada
18 J7 **Carry Falls Reservoir** ⊠ New York, NE USA
136 L11 **Çarşamba** Samsun, N Turkey
28 L6 **Carson** North Dakota, N USA
35 Q6 **Carson City** *state capital* Nevada, W USA
35 R6 **Carson River** ≈ Nevada, W USA
35 S5 **Carson Sink** *salt flat* Nevada, W USA
9 Q16 **Carstairs** Alberta, SW Canada
Carstensz, Puntjak *see* Jaya, Puncak
54 E5 **Cartagena** *var.* Cartagena de los Indes. Bolívar, NW Colombia
105 R13 **Cartagena** *anc.* Carthago Nova. Murcia, SE Spain
54 E13 **Cartagena de Chaira** Caquetá, S Colombia
Cartagena de los Indes *see* Cartagena
54 D10 **Cartago** Valle del Cauca, W Colombia
43 N14 **Cartago** Cartago, C Costa Rica
42 M14 **Cartago** *off.* Provincia de Cartago. ⬖ *province* C Costa Rica
Cartago, Provincia de *see* Cartago
25 O11 **Carta Valley** Texas, SW USA
104 F10 **Cartaxo** Santarém, C Portugal
104 I14 **Cartaya** Andalucía, S Spain
Carteret Islands *see* Tulun Islands
29 S15 **Carter Lake** Iowa, C USA
23 S3 **Cartersville** Georgia, SE USA
185 M14 **Carterton** Wellington, North Island, New Zealand
30 J13 **Carthage** Illinois, N USA
22 L5 **Carthage** Mississippi, S USA
27 R7 **Carthage** Missouri, C USA
18 I8 **Carthage** New York, NE USA

◆ Country
● Country Capital
◇ Dependent Territory
○ Dependent Territory Capital
⬖ Administrative Regions
✈ International Airport
▲ Mountain
▲▲ Mountain Range
△ Volcano
≈ River
◎ Lake
⊠ Reservoir

CARTHAGE – CERRIKU

21 T10 **Carthage** North Carolina, SE USA
20 K8 **Carthage** Tennessee, S USA
25 X7 **Carthage** Texas, SW USA
74 M5 **Carthage** ✈ (Tunis) N Tunisia
Carthago Nova *see* Cartagena
14 E10 **Cartier** Ontario, S Canada
13 S8 **Cartwright** Newfoundland and Labrador, E Canada
55 P9 **Caruana de Montaña** Bolívar, SE Venezuela
59 Q15 **Caruaru** Pernambuco, E Brazil
55 P5 **Carúpano** Sucre, NE Venezuela
Carusbur *see* Cherbourg
58 M12 **Carutapera** Maranhão, E Brazil
27 Y9 **Caruthersville** Missouri, C USA
103 O1 **Carvin** Pas-de-Calais, N France
58 E12 **Carvoeiro** Amazonas, NW Brazil
104 E10 **Carvoeiro, Cabo** *cape* C Portugal
21 U9 **Cary** North Carolina, SE USA
182 M3 **Caryapundy Swamp** *wetland* New South Wales/Queensland, SE Australia
65 E24 **Carysfort, Cape** *headland* East Falkland, Falkland Islands
74 F6 **Casablanca** *Ar.* Dar-el-Beida. NW Morocco
60 M8 **Casa Branca** São Paulo, S Brazil
36 L14 **Casa Grande** Arizona, SW USA
106 C8 **Casale Monferrato** Piemonte, NW Italy
106 E8 **Casalpusterlengo** Lombardia, N Italy
54 H10 **Casanare** *off.* Intendencia de Casanare. ⬖ *province* C Colombia
Casanare, Intendencia de *see* Casanare
55 P5 **Casanay** Sucre, NE Venezuela
24 K11 **Casa Piedra** Texas, SW USA
107 Q19 **Casarano** Puglia, SE Italy
42 J11 **Casares** Carazo, W Nicaragua
105 R10 **Casas Ibáñez** Castilla-La Mancha, C Spain
61 I14 **Casca** Rio Grande do Sul, S Brazil
172 I17 **Cascade** Mahé, NE Seychelles
33 N13 **Cascade** Idaho, NW USA
29 Y13 **Cascade** Iowa, C USA
33 R9 **Cascade** Montana, NW USA
185 B20 **Cascade Point** *headland* South Island, New Zealand
32 G13 **Cascade Range** ⛰ Oregon/Washington, NW USA
33 N12 **Cascade Reservoir** ⊡ Idaho, NW USA
0 E8 **Cascadia Basin** *undersea feature* NE Pacific Ocean
104 E11 **Cascais** Lisboa, C Portugal
15 W7 **Cascapédia** ⁓ Québec, SE Canada
59 I22 **Cascavel** Ceará, E Brazil
60 G11 **Cascavel** Paraná, S Brazil
106 I13 **Cascia** Umbria, C Italy
106 F11 **Cascina** Toscana, C Italy
19 Q8 **Casco Bay** *bay* Maine, NE USA
194 J7 **Case Island** *island* Antarctica
106 B8 **Caselle** ✈ (Torino) Piemonte, NW Italy
107 K17 **Caserta** Campania, S Italy
15 N8 **Casey** Québec, SE Canada
30 M14 **Casey** Illinois, N USA
195 Y12 **Casey** *Australian research station* Antarctica
195 W3 **Casey Bay** *bay* Antarctica
80 Q11 **Caseyr, Raas** *cape* NE Somalia
97 D20 **Cashel** *Ir.* Caiseal. S Ireland
54 G6 **Casigua** Zulia, W Venezuela
61 B19 **Casilda** Santa Fe, C Argentina
Casim *see* General Toshevo
183 V4 **Casino** New South Wales, SE Australia
Casinum *see* Cassino
111 E17 **Čáslav** *Ger.* Tschaslau. Střední Čechy, C Czech Republic
56 C13 **Casma** Ancash, C Peru
167 S7 **Ca, Sông** ⁓ N Vietnam
107 K17 **Casoria** Campania, S Italy
105 T6 **Caspe** Aragón, NE Spain
33 X15 **Casper** Wyoming, C USA
84 M10 **Caspian Depression** *Kaz.* Kaspiy Mangy Oypaty, *Rus.* Prikaspiyskaya Nizmennost'. *depression* Kazakhstan/Russian Federation
130 D10 **Caspian Sea** *Az.* Xäzär Dänizi, *Kaz.* Kaspiy Tengizi, *Per.* Baḥr-e Khazar, Daryā-ye Khazar, *Rus.* Kaspiyskoye More. *inland sea* Asia/Europe
83 L14 **Cassacatiza** Tete, NW Mozambique
Cassai *see* Kasai
82 F13 **Cassamba** Moxico, E Angola
107 N20 **Cassano allo Ionio** Calabria, SE Italy
31 S8 **Cass City** Michigan, N USA
Cassel *see* Kassel
14 M13 **Casselman** Ontario, SE Canada
29 R5 **Casselton** North Dakota, N USA
59 M16 **Cássia** *var.* Santa Rita de Cassia. Bahia, E Brazil
10 J9 **Cassiar** British Columbia, W Canada
10 K10 **Cassiar Mountains** ⛰ British Columbia, W Canada
83 C15 **Cassinga** Huíla, SW Angola
107 J16 **Cassino** *prev.* San Germano; *anc.* Casinum. Lazio, C Italy
29 T4 **Cass Lake** Minnesota, N USA
29 T4 **Cass Lake** ◎ Minnesota, N USA
31 P10 **Cassopolis** Michigan, N USA
31 S8 **Cass River** ⁓ Michigan, N USA
27 S8 **Cassville** Missouri, C USA
Castamoni *see* Kastamonu
58 L12 **Castanhal** Pará, NE Brazil
104 G8 **Castanheira de Pêra** Leiria, C Portugal
41 N7 **Castaños** Coahuila de Zaragoza, NE Mexico
108 I10 **Castasegna** Graubünden, SE Switzerland
106 D8 **Casteggio** Lombardia, N Italy
107 K23 **Castelbuono** Sicilia, Italy, C Mediterranean Sea
107 K15 **Castel di Sangro** Abruzzo, C Italy
106 H7 **Castelfranco Veneto** Veneto, NE Italy
102 K14 **Casteljaloux** Lot-et-Garonne, SW France
107 L18 **Castellabate** *var.* Santa Maria di Castellabate. Campania, S Italy
107 I23 **Castellammare del Golfo** Sicilia, Italy, C Mediterranean Sea
107 H22 **Castellammare, Golfo di** *gulf* Sicilia, Italy, C Mediterranean Sea
103 U15 **Castellane** Alpes-de-Haute-Provence, SE France
107 O18 **Castellaneta** Puglia, SE Italy
106 E9 **Castel l'Arquato** Emilia-Romagna, C Italy
61 E21 **Castelli** Buenos Aires, E Argentina
Castelló de la Plana *see* Castellón de la Plana
105 S8 **Castellón** ⬖ *province* País Valenciano, E Spain
Castellón *see* Castellón de la Plana
105 T9 **Castellón de la Plana** *Cat.* Castelló de la Plana, Castellón. País Valenciano, E Spain
105 S7 **Castellote** Aragón, NE Spain
103 N16 **Castelnaudary** Aude, S France
102 L16 **Castelnau-Magnoac** Hautes-Pyrénées, S France
106 F10 **Castelnovo ne' Monti** Emilia-Romagna, C Italy
Castelnuovo *see* Herceg-Novi
104 H9 **Castelo Branco** Castelo Branco, C Portugal
104 H8 **Castelo Branco** ⬖ *district* C Portugal
104 I10 **Castelo de Vide** Portalegre, C Portugal
104 G9 **Castelo do Bode, Barragem do** ⊡ C Portugal
106 G10 **Castel San Pietro Terme** Emilia-Romagna, C Italy
107 B17 **Castelsardo** Sardegna, Italy, C Mediterranean Sea
102 M14 **Castelsarrasin** Tarn-et-Garonne, S France
107 I24 **Casteltermini** Sicilia, Italy, C Mediterranean Sea
107 H24 **Castelvetrano** Sicilia, Italy, C Mediterranean Sea
182 L12 **Casterton** Victoria, SE Australia
102 J15 **Castets** Landes, SW France
106 H12 **Castiglione del Lago** Umbria, C Italy
106 F13 **Castiglione della Pescaia** Toscana, C Italy
106 F8 **Castiglione delle Stiviere** Lombardia, N Italy
104 M9 **Castilla-La Mancha** ⬖ *autonomous community* NE Spain
104 L5 **Castilla-León** *var.* Castillia y Leon. ⬖ *autonomous community* NW Spain
105 N10 **Castilla Nueva** *cultural region* C Spain
105 N6 **Castilla Vieja** *cultural region* N Spain
Castillia y Leon *see* Castilla-León
Castillo de Locubim *see* Castillo de Locubín
105 N14 **Castillo de Locubín** *var.* Castillo de Locubim. Andalucía, S Spain
102 K13 **Castillon-la-Bataille** Gironde, SW France
63 I19 **Castillo, Pampa del** *plain* S Argentina
61 G19 **Castillos** Rocha, SE Uruguay
97 B16 **Castlebar** *Ir.* Caisleán an Bharraigh. W Ireland
97 F16 **Castleblayney** *Ir.* Baile na Lorgan. N Ireland
45 O11 **Castle Bruce** E Dominica
36 M5 **Castle Dale** Utah, W USA
36 I14 **Castle Dome Peak** ▲ Arizona, SW USA
97 J14 **Castle Douglas** S Scotland, UK
97 E14 **Castlefinn** *Ir.* Caisleán na Finne. NW Ireland
97 M17 **Castleford** N England, UK
9 O17 **Castlegar** British Columbia, SW Canada
64 B12 **Castle Harbour** *inlet* Bermuda, NW Atlantic Ocean
21 V12 **Castle Hayne** North Carolina, SE USA
97 B20 **Castleisland** *Ir.* Oileán Ciarraí. SW Ireland
183 N12 **Castlemaine** Victoria, SE Australia
37 R5 **Castle Peak** ▲ Colorado, C USA
33 O13 **Castle Peak** ▲ Idaho, NW USA
184 N13 **Castlepoint** Wellington, North Island, New Zealand
97 D17 **Castlerea** *Ir.* An Caisleán Riabhach. W Ireland
97 G15 **Castlereagh** *Ir.* An Caisleán Riabhach. N Northern Ireland, UK
183 R6 **Castlereagh River** ⁓ New South Wales, SE Australia
37 T5 **Castle Rock** Colorado, C USA
30 K7 **Castle Rock Lake** ⊡ Wisconsin, N USA
65 G25 **Castle Rock Point** *headland* S Saint Helena
97 I16 **Castletown** SE Isle of Man
29 R9 **Castlewood** South Dakota, N USA
9 R15 **Castor** Alberta, SW Canada
14 M13 **Castor** ⁓ Ontario, SE Canada
27 X7 **Castor River** ⁓ Missouri, C USA
Castra Albiensium *see* Castres
Castra Regina *see* Regensburg
103 N15 **Castres** *anc.* Castra Albiensium. Tarn, S France
98 H9 **Castricum** Noord-Holland, W Netherlands
45 S11 **Castries** ● (Saint Lucia) N Saint Lucia
60 J11 **Castro** Paraná, S Brazil
63 F17 **Castro** Los Lagos, W Chile
104 H7 **Castro Daire** Viseu, N Portugal
104 M13 **Castro del Río** Andalucía, S Spain
Castrogiovanni *see* Enna
104 H14 **Castro Marim** Faro, S Portugal
104 J2 **Castropol** Asturias, N Spain
105 O2 **Castro-Urdiales** *var.* Castro Urdiales. Cantabria, N Spain
104 G13 **Castro Verde** Beja, S Portugal
107 N19 **Castrovillari** Calabria, SW Italy
35 N10 **Castroville** California, W USA
25 R12 **Castroville** Texas, SW USA
104 K11 **Castuera** Extremadura, W Spain
61 F19 **Casupá** Florida, S Uruguay
185 A22 **Caswell Sound** *sound* South Island, New Zealand
137 Q13 **Çat** Erzurum, NE Turkey
42 K6 **Catacamas** Olancho, C Honduras
56 A10 **Catacaos** Piura, NW Peru
22 I7 **Catahoula Lake** ◎ Louisiana, S USA
137 S15 **Çatak** Van, SE Turkey
137 S15 **Çatak Çayi** ⁓ SE Turkey
114 O12 **Çatalca** İstanbul, NW Turkey
114 O12 **Çatalca Yarimadasi** *physical region* NW Turkey
62 H6 **Catalina** Antofagasta, N Chile
Catalonia *see* Cataluña
105 U5 **Cataluña** *Cat.* Catalunya, *Eng.* Catalonia. ⬖ *autonomous community* N Spain
Catalunya *see* Cataluña
62 I7 **Catamarca** *off.* Provincia de Catamarca. ⬖ *province* NW Argentina
Catamarca *see* San Fernando del Valle de Catamarca
Catamarca, Provincia de *see* Catamarca
83 M16 **Catandica** Manica, C Mozambique
171 P4 **Catanduanes Island** *island* N Philippines
60 K8 **Catanduva** São Paulo, S Brazil
107 L24 **Catania** Sicilia, Italy, C Mediterranean Sea
107 M24 **Catania, Golfo di** *gulf* Sicilia, Italy, C Mediterranean Sea
45 U5 **Cataño** *var.* Cantaño. E Puerto Rico
107 O21 **Catanzaro** Calabria, SW Italy
107 O22 **Catanzaro Marina** *var.* Marina di Catanzaro. Calabria, S Italy
Marina di Catanzaro *see* Catanzaro Marina
25 Q14 **Catarina** Texas, SW USA
171 Q5 **Catarman** Samar, C Philippines
105 S10 **Catarroja** País Valenciano, E Spain
21 R11 **Catawba River** ⁓ North Carolina/South Carolina, SE USA
171 Q5 **Catbalogan** Samar, C Philippines
14 I14 **Catchacoma** Ontario, SE Canada
41 S15 **Catemaco** Veracruz-Llave, SE Mexico
Cathair na Mart *see* Westport
Cathair Saidhbhín *see* Caherciveen
31 P5 **Cat Head Point** *headland* Michigan, N USA
23 Q2 **Cathedral Caverns** *cave* Alabama, S USA
35 V16 **Cathedral City** California, W USA
24 K10 **Cathedral Mountain** ▲ Texas, SW USA
32 G10 **Cathlamet** Washington, NW USA
76 G13 **Catió** S Guinea-Bissau
55 O10 **Catisimiña** Bolívar, SE Venezuela
44 J3 **Cat Island** *island* C Bahamas
12 B9 **Cat Lake** Ontario, S Canada
21 P5 **Catlettsburg** Kentucky, S USA
185 D24 **Catlins** ⁓ South Island, New Zealand
35 R1 **Catnip Mountain** ▲ Nevada, W USA
41 Z11 **Catoche, Cabo** *headland* SE Mexico
27 P9 **Catoosa** Oklahoma, C USA
41 N10 **Catorce** San Luis Potosí, C Mexico
63 I14 **Catriel** Río Negro, C Argentina
62 K13 **Catriló** La Pampa, C Argentina
58 F11 **Catrimani** Roraima, N Brazil
58 E10 **Catrimani, Rio** ⁓ N Brazil
18 K11 **Catskill** New York, NE USA
18 K11 **Catskill Creek** ⁓ New York, NE USA
18 J11 **Catskill Mountains** ⛰ New York, NE USA
18 D11 **Cattaraugus Creek** ⁓ New York, NE USA
Cattaro *see* Kotor
Cattaro, Bocche di *see* Kotorska, Boka
107 I24 **Cattolica Eraclea** Sicilia, Italy, C Mediterranean Sea
83 B14 **Catumbela** ⁓ W Angola
83 N14 **Catur** Niassa, N Mozambique
82 C10 **Cauale** ⁓ NE Angola
171 O2 **Cauayan** Luzon, N Philippines
54 C12 **Cauca** *off.* Departamento del Cauca. ⬖ *province* SW Colombia
47 P5 **Cauca** ⁓ SE Venezuela
Cauca, Departamento del *see* Cauca
58 P13 **Caucaia** Ceará, E Brazil
54 E7 **Cauca, Río** ⁓ N Colombia
54 E7 **Caucasia** Antioquia, NW Colombia
137 Q8 **Caucasus** *Rus.* Kavkaz. ⛰ Georgia/Russian Federation
62 I10 **Caucete** San Juan, W Argentina
105 R11 **Caudete** Castilla-La Mancha, C Spain
103 P2 **Caudry** Nord, N France
82 D11 **Caungula** Lunda Norte, NE Angola
62 G13 **Cauquenes** Maule, C Chile
55 N8 **Caura, Río** ⁓ C Venezuela
15 V7 **Causapscal** Québec, SE Canada
117 N10 **Căuşeni** *Rus.* Kaushany. E Moldova
102 M14 **Caussade** Tarn-et-Garonne, S France
102 K17 **Cauterets** Hautes-Pyrénées, S France
10 J15 **Caution, Cape** *headland* British Columbia, SW Canada
44 H7 **Cauto** ⁓ E Cuba
Cauvery *see* Kāveri
102 L3 **Caux, Pays de** *physical region* N France
107 L18 **Cava de' Tirreni** Campania, S Italy
104 G6 **Cávado** ⁓ N Portugal
Cavaia *see* Kavajë
103 R15 **Cavaillon** Vaucluse, SE France
103 U16 **Cavalaire-sur-Mer** Var, SE France
106 G6 **Cavalese** *Ger.* Gablös. Trentino-Alto Adige, N Italy
29 Q2 **Cavalier** North Dakota, N USA
76 L17 **Cavalla** *var.* Cavally, Cavally Fleuve. ⁓ Ivory Coast/Liberia
105 Y8 **Cavalleria, Cap de** *var.* Cabo Caballería. *cape* Menorca, Spain, W Mediterranean Sea
184 K2 **Cavalli Islands** *island group* N New Zealand
Cavally/Cavally Fleuve *see* Cavalla
97 E16 **Cavan** *Ir.* Cabhán. N Ireland
97 E16 **Cavan** *Ir.* An Cabhán. ⬖ *county* N Ireland
106 H8 **Cavarzere** Veneto, NE Italy
27 W9 **Cave City** Arkansas, C USA
20 K7 **Cave City** Kentucky, S USA
65 M25 **Cave Point** *headland* S Tristan da Cunha
21 N5 **Cave Run Lake** ⊡ Kentucky, S USA
58 K11 **Caviana de Fora, Ilha** *var.* Ilha Caviana. *island* N Brazil
Caviana, Ilha *see* Caviana de Fora, Ilha
113 I16 **Cavtat** *It.* Ragusavecchia. Dubrovnik-Neretva, SE Croatia
Cawnpore *see* Kānpur
Caxamarca *see* Cajamarca
58 A13 **Caxias** Amazonas, W Brazil
58 N13 **Caxias** Maranhão, E Brazil
61 I15 **Caxias do Sul** Rio Grande do Sul, S Brazil
42 J4 **Caxinas, Punta** *headland* N Honduras
82 B11 **Caxito** Bengo, NW Angola
136 F14 **Çay** Afyon, W Turkey
40 L15 **Cayacal, Punta** *var.* Punta Mongrove. *headland* S Mexico
56 C6 **Cayambe** Pichincha, N Ecuador
56 C6 **Cayambe** ▲ N Ecuador
21 R12 **Cayce** South Carolina, SE USA
55 Y10 **Cayenne** ○ (French Guiana) NE French Guiana
55 Y10 **Cayenne** ✈ NE French Guiana
44 K10 **Cayes** *var.* Les Cayes. SW Haiti
45 U6 **Cayey** C Puerto Rico
45 U6 **Cayey, Sierra de** ⛰ E Puerto Rico
103 N14 **Caylus** Tarn-et-Garonne, S France
44 E8 **Cayman Brac** *island* E Cayman Islands
44 D8 **Cayman Islands** ◇ *UK dependent territory* W West Indies
64 D11 **Cayman Trench** *undersea feature* NW Caribbean Sea
47 O3 **Cayman Trough** *undersea feature* NW Caribbean Sea
80 O13 **Caynabo** Sool, N Somalia
42 F3 **Cayo** ⬖ *district* SW Belize
Cayo *see* San Ignacio
43 N9 **Cayos Guerrero** *reef* E Nicaragua
43 O9 **Cayos King** *reef* E Nicaragua
44 E4 **Cay Sal** *islet* SW Bahamas
14 G16 **Cayuga** Ontario, S Canada
25 V8 **Cayuga** Texas, SW USA
18 G10 **Cayuga Lake** ◎ New York, NE USA
104 K13 **Cazalla de la Sierra** Andalucía, S Spain
116 L14 **Căzăneşti** Ialomiţa, SE Romania
102 M16 **Cazères** Haute-Garonne, S France
112 E10 **Cazin** ⬖ Federacija Bosna I Hercegovina, NW Bosnia and Herzegovina
82 G13 **Cazombo** Moxico, E Angola
105 O13 **Cazorla** Andalucía, S Spain
Cazza *see* Sušac
104 L4 **Cea** ⁓ NW Spain
Ceadâr-Lunga *see* Ciadîr-Lunga
Ceanannas *see* Kells
Ceann Toirc *see* Kanturk
58 O13 **Ceará** *off.* Estado do Ceará. ⬖ *state* C Brazil
Ceará *see* Fortaleza
Ceara Abyssal Plain *see* Ceará Plain
Ceará, Estado do *see* Ceará
59 Q14 **Ceará Mirim** Rio Grande do Norte, E Brazil
64 J13 **Ceará Plain** *var.* Ceara Abyssal Plain. *undersea feature* W Atlantic Ocean
64 I13 **Ceará Ridge** *undersea feature* C Atlantic Ocean
Ceatharlach *see* Carlow
43 Q17 **Cébaco, Isla** *island* SW Panama
40 K7 **Ceballos** Durango, C Mexico
61 G19 **Cebollatí** Rocha, E Uruguay
61 G19 **Cebollatí, Río** ⁓ E Uruguay
105 P5 **Cebollera** ▲ N Spain
104 M8 **Cebreros** Castilla-León, N Spain
171 P6 **Cebu** *off.* Cebu City. Cebu, C Philippines
171 P6 **Cebu** *island* C Philippines
Cebu City *see* Cebu
107 J16 **Ceccano** Lazio, C Italy
Čechy *see* Bohemia
106 F12 **Cecina** Toscana, C Italy
26 K4 **Cedar Bluff Reservoir** ⊡ Kansas, C USA
30 M8 **Cedarburg** Wisconsin, N USA
36 J7 **Cedar City** Utah, W USA
25 T11 **Cedar Creek** Texas, SW USA
28 L7 **Cedar Creek** ⁓ North Dakota, N USA
25 U7 **Cedar Creek Reservoir** ⊡ Texas, SW USA
29 W13 **Cedar Falls** Iowa, C USA
31 N8 **Cedar Grove** Wisconsin, N USA
21 Y6 **Cedar Island** *island* Virginia, NE USA
23 U11 **Cedar Key** Cedar Keys, Florida, SE USA
23 U11 **Cedar Keys** *island group* Florida, SE USA
9 V14 **Cedar Lake** ◎ Manitoba, C Canada
14 I11 **Cedar Lake** ◎ Ontario, SE Canada
24 M6 **Cedar Lake** ◎ Texas, SW USA
29 X13 **Cedar Rapids** Iowa, C USA
29 X14 **Cedar River** ⁓ Iowa/Minnesota, C USA
29 O14 **Cedar River** ⁓ Nebraska, C USA
31 P8 **Cedar Springs** Michigan, N USA
23 R3 **Cedartown** Georgia, SE USA
27 O7 **Cedar Vale** Kansas, C USA
35 Q2 **Cedarville** California, W USA
104 H1 **Cedeira** Galicia, NW Spain
42 H8 **Cedeño** Choluteca, S Honduras
41 N10 **Cedral** San Luis Potosí, C Mexico
42 I6 **Cedros** Francisco Morazán, C Honduras
40 M9 **Cedros** Zacatecas, C Mexico
40 B5 **Cedros, Isla** *island* W Mexico
193 R5 **Cedros Trench** *undersea feature* E Pacific Ocean
182 E7 **Ceduna** South Australia
110 D10 **Cedynia** *Ger.* Zehden. Zachodnio-pomorskie, W Poland
80 P12 **Ceelaayo** Sanaag, N Somalia
81 O16 **Ceel Buur** *It.* El Bur. Galguduud, C Somalia
81 N15 **Ceel Dheere** *var.* Ceel Dher, *It.* El Dere. Galguduud, C Somalia
Ceel Dher *see* Ceel Dheere
81 P14 **Ceel Xamure** Mudug, E Somalia
80 O12 **Ceerigaabo** *var.* Erigabo, Erigavo. Sanaag, N Somalia
107 J23 **Cefalù** *anc.* Cephaloedium. Sicilia, Italy, C Mediterranean Sea
105 N6 **Cega** ⁓ N Spain
111 K23 **Cegléd** *prev.* Czegléd. Pest, C Hungary
113 N18 **Čegrane** W FYR Macedonia
105 Q13 **Cehegín** Murcia, SE Spain
136 K12 **Çekerek** Yozgat, N Turkey
146 B13 **Çekiçler** *Rus.* Chekishlyar, *Turkm.* Chekichler. Balkan Welaýaty, W Turkmenistan
107 J15 **Celano** Abruzzo, C Italy
104 H4 **Celanova** Galicia, NW Spain
42 F6 **Celaque, Cordillera de** ⛰ W Honduras
41 N13 **Celaya** Guanajuato, C Mexico
Celebes *see* Sulawesi
192 F7 **Celebes Basin** *undersea feature* SE South China Sea
192 F7 **Celebes Sea** *Ind.* Laut Sulawesi. *sea* Indonesia/Philippines
41 W12 **Celestún** Yucatán, E Mexico
31 Q12 **Celina** Ohio, N USA
20 L8 **Celina** Tennessee, S USA
25 U5 **Celina** Texas, SW USA
112 G11 **Čelinac Donji** ⬖ Republika Srpska, N Bosnia and Herzegovina
109 V10 **Celje** *Ger.* Cilli. C Slovenia
111 G23 **Celldömölk** Vas, W Hungary
100 J12 **Celle** *var.* Zelle. Niedersachsen, N Germany
99 D19 **Celles** Hainaut, SW Belgium
104 I7 **Celorico da Beira** Guarda, N Portugal
Celovec *see* Klagenfurt
64 M7 **Celtic Sea** *Ir.* An Mhuir Cheilteach. *sea* SW British Isles
64 N7 **Celtic Shelf** *undersea feature* E Atlantic Ocean
114 L13 **Çeltik Gölu** ◎ NW Turkey
146 J17 **Çemenibit** *prev. Rus.* Chemenibit. Mary Welaýaty, S Turkmenistan
113 M14 **Čemerno** ⛰ C Serbia
105 Q12 **Cenajo, Embalse del** ⊡ S Spain
171 V13 **Cenderawasih, Teluk** *var.* Teluk Irian, Teluk Sarera. *bay* W Pacific Ocean
105 P4 **Cenicero** La Rioja, N Spain
106 E9 **Ceno** ⁓ NW Italy
102 K13 **Cenon** Gironde, SW France
14 K13 **Centennial Lake** ◎ Ontario, SE Canada
Centennial State *see* Colorado
37 S7 **Center** Colorado, C USA
29 Q13 **Center** Nebraska, C USA
28 M5 **Center** North Dakota, N USA
25 X8 **Center** Texas, SW USA
29 W8 **Center City** Minnesota, N USA
36 L5 **Centerfield** Utah, W USA
20 K9 **Center Hill Lake** ⊡ Tennessee, S USA
29 X13 **Center Point** Iowa, C USA
25 R11 **Center Point** Texas, SW USA
29 W16 **Centerville** Iowa, C USA
27 W7 **Centerville** Missouri, C USA
29 R12 **Centerville** South Dakota, N USA
20 I9 **Centerville** Tennessee, S USA
25 V9 **Centerville** Texas, SW USA
40 M5 **Centinela, Picacho del** ▲ NE Mexico
106 G9 **Cento** Emilia-Romagna, N Italy
Centrafricaine, République *see* Central African Republic
39 S8 **Central** Alaska, USA
37 P15 **Central** New Mexico, SW USA
83 H18 **Central** ⬖ *district* E Botswana
138 E10 **Central** ⬖ *district* C Israel
81 I19 **Central** ⬖ *province* C Kenya
82 M13 **Central** ⬖ *region* C Malawi
153 P12 **Central** ⬖ *zone* C Nepal
186 E9 **Central** ⬖ *province* S Papua New Guinea
63 I21 **Central** ⬖ *department* C Paraguay
186 E9 **Central** *off.* Central Province. ⬖ *province* S Solomon Islands
83 J14 **Central** ⬖ *province* C Zambia
117 P11 **Central** ✈ (Odesa) Odes'ka Oblast', SW Ukraine
Central *see* Centre
79 H14 **Central African Republic** *var.* République Centrafricaine, *abbrev.* CAR; *prev.* Ubangi-Shari, Oubangui-Chari, Territoire de l'Oubangui-Chari. ◆ *republic* C Africa
192 C6 **Central Basin Trough** *undersea feature* W Pacific Ocean
Central Borneo *see* Kalimantan Tengah
149 P12 **Central Brāhui Range** ⛰ W Pakistan
Central Celebes *see* Sulawesi Tengah
29 Y13 **Central City** Iowa, C USA
20 I6 **Central City** Kentucky, S USA
29 P15 **Central City** Nebraska, C USA
48 D6 **Central, Cordillera** ⛰ W Bolivia
54 D11 **Central, Cordillera** ⛰ W Colombia
42 M13 **Central, Cordillera** ⛰ C Costa Rica
45 N9 **Central, Cordillera** ⛰ C Dominican Republic
43 R16 **Central, Cordillera** ⛰ C Panama
45 S6 **Central, Cordillera** ⛰ Puerto Rico
42 H7 **Central District** *var.* Tegucigalpa. ⬖ *district* C Honduras
Central Group *see* Inner Islands
30 L15 **Centralia** Illinois, N USA
27 U4 **Centralia** Missouri, C USA
32 G9 **Centralia** Washington, NW USA
Central Indian Ridge *see* Mid-Indian Ridge
Central Java *see* Jawa Tengah
Central Kalimantan *see* Kalimantan Tengah
148 L14 **Central Makrān Range** ⛰ W Pakistan
192 K7 **Central Pacific Basin** *undersea feature* C Pacific Ocean
59 M19 **Central, Planalto** *var.* Brazilian Highlands. ⛰ E Brazil
32 F15 **Central Point** Oregon, NW USA
155 K25 **Central Province** ⬖ *province* C Sri Lanka
Central Province *see* Central
Central Provinces and Berar *see* Madhya Pradesh
186 B6 **Central Range** ⛰ NW Papua New Guinea
Central Russian Upland *see* Srednerusskaya Vozvyshennost'
Central Siberian Plateau/Central Siberian Uplands *see* Srednesibirskoye Ploskogor'ye
104 K8 **Central, Sistema** ⛰ C Spain
Central Sulawesi *see* Sulawesi Tengah
35 N3 **Central Valley** California, W USA
35 P8 **Central Valley** *valley* California, W USA
23 Q3 **Centre** Alabama, S USA
79 E15 **Centre** *Eng.* Central. ⬖ *province* C Cameroon
102 M8 **Centre** ⬖ *region* N France
173 Y16 **Centre de Flacq** E Mauritius
55 Y9 **Centre Spatial Guyanais** *space station* N French Guiana
23 O5 **Centreville** Alabama, S USA
21 X3 **Centreville** Maryland, NE USA
22 J7 **Centreville** Mississippi, S USA
Centum Cellae *see* Civitavecchia
160 M14 **Cenxi** Guangxi Zhuangzu Zizhiqu, S China
Ceos *see* Tziá
Cephaloedium *see* Cefalù
112 I9 **Čepin** *Hung.* Csepén. Osijek-Baranja, E Croatia
Ceram *see* Seram, Pulau
171 R13 **Ceram Sea** *Ind.* Laut Seram. *sea* E Indonesia
192 G8 **Ceram Trough** *undersea feature* W Pacific Ocean
Cerasus *see* Giresun
36 I10 **Cerbat Mountains** ⛰ Arizona, SW USA
103 P17 **Cerbère, Cap** *headland* S France
104 F13 **Cercal do Alentejo** Setúbal, S Portugal
111 A18 **Čerchov** *Ger.* Czerkow. ▲ W Czech Republic
103 O13 **Cère** ⁓ C France
61 A16 **Ceres** Santa Fe, C Argentina
59 K18 **Ceres** Goiás, C Brazil
Ceresio *see* Lugano, Lago di
103 O17 **Céret** Pyrénées-Orientales, S France
54 E6 **Cereté** Córdoba, NW Colombia
172 I17 **Cerf, Île au** *island* Inner Islands, NE Seychelles
99 G22 **Cerfontaine** Namur, S Belgium
Cergy-Pontoise *see* Pontoise
107 N16 **Cerignola** Puglia, SE Italy
Cerigo *see* Kýthira
103 O9 **Cérilly** Allier, C France
136 D10 **Çerkezköy** Tekirdağ, NW Turkey
109 T12 **Cerknica** *Ger.* Zirknitz. SW Slovenia
109 S11 **Cerkno** W Slovenia
116 F10 **Cermei** *Hung.* Csermő. Arad, W Romania
137 O15 **Çermik** Diyarbakır, SE Turkey
112 I10 **Cerna** Vukovar-Srijem, E Croatia
Cernăuţi *see* Chernivtsi
116 M14 **Cernavodă** Constanţa, SW Romania
103 U7 **Cernay** Haut-Rhin, NE France
Černice *see* Schwarzach
41 O8 **Cerralvo** Nuevo León, NE Mexico
40 G9 **Cerralvo, Isla** *island* W Mexico
107 L16 **Cerreto Sannita** Campania, S Italy
113 L20 **Cërrik** *var.* Cerriku. Elbasan, C Albania
Cerriku *see* Cërrik

◆ Country ● Country Capital ◇ Dependent Territory ○ Dependent Territory Capital ⬖ Administrative Regions ✈ International Airport ▲ Mountain ⛰ Mountain Range Volcano ⁓ River ◎ Lake ⊡ Reservoir

CERRITOS – CHATKAL RANGE

41 O11 **Cerritos** San Luis Potosí, C Mexico
60 K11 **Cerro Azul** Paraná, S Brazil
61 F18 **Cerro Chato** Treinta y Tres, E Uruguay
61 F19 **Cerro Colorado** Florida, S Uruguay
56 E13 **Cerro de Pasco** Pasco, C Peru
61 G14 **Cêrro Largo** Rio Grande do Sul, S Brazil
61 G18 **Cerro Largo** ◐ *department* NE Uruguay
42 E7 **Cerrón Grande, Embalse** ▣ N El Salvador
63 I14 **Cerros Colorados, Embalse** ◎ W Argentina
105 V5 **Cervera** Cataluña, NE Spain
104 M3 **Cervera del Pisuerga** Castilla-León, N Spain
105 Q5 **Cervera del Río Alhama** La Rioja, N Spain
107 H15 **Cerveteri** Lazio, C Italy
106 H10 **Cervia** Emilia-Romagna, N Italy
106 J7 **Cervignano del Friuli** Friuli-Venezia Giulia, NE Italy
107 L17 **Cervinara** Campania, S Italy
Cervinia *see* Breuil-Cervinia
106 B6 **Cervino, Monte** *var.* Matterhorn. ▲ Italy/Switzerland *see also* Matterhorn
Cervino, Monte *see* Matterhorn
103 Y14 **Cervione** Corse, France, C Mediterranean Sea
104 I1 **Cervo** Galicia, NW Spain
54 F5 **Cesar** *off.* Departamento del Cesar. ◐ *province* N Colombia
Cesar, Departamento del *see* Cesar
106 H10 **Cesena** *anc.* Caesena. Emilia-Romagna, N Italy
106 I10 **Cesenatico** Emilia-Romagna, N Italy
118 H8 **Cēsis** *Ger.* Wenden. Cēsis, C Latvia
111 D15 **Česká Lípa** *Ger.* Böhmisch-Leipa. Liberecký Kraj, N Czech Republic
Česká Republika *see* Czech Republic
111 F17 **Česká Třebová** *Ger.* Böhmisch-Trübau. Pardubický Kraj, C Czech Republic
111 D19 **České Budějovice** *Ger.* Budweis. Jihočeský Kraj, S Czech Republic
111 D19 **České Velenice** Jihočeský Kraj, S Czech Republic
111 E18 **Českomoravská Vrchovina** *var.* Českomoravská Vysočina, *Eng.* Bohemian-Moravian Highlands, *Ger.* Böhmisch-Mährische Höhe. ▲▲ S Czech Republic
Českomoravská Vysočina *see* Českomoravská Vrchovina
111 C19 **Český Krumlov** *var.* Böhmisch-Krumau, *Ger.* Krummau. Jihočeský Kraj, S Czech Republic
Český Les *see* Bohemian Forest
112 F8 **Česma** ≈ N Croatia
136 A14 **Çeşme** İzmir, W Turkey
Cess *see* Cestos
183 T8 **Cessnock** New South Wales, SE Australia
76 K17 **Cestos** *var.* Cess. ≈ S Liberia
118 I9 **Cesvaine** Madona, E Latvia
116 G14 **Cetate** Dolj, SW Romania
Cetatea Albă *see* Bilhorod-Dnistrovs'kyy
Cetatea Damboviței *see* București
113 J17 **Cetinje** *It.* Cettigne. S Montenegro
107 N20 **Cetraro** Calabria, S Italy
Cette *see* Sète
188 A17 **Cetti Bay** *bay* SW Guam
Cettigne *see* Cetinje
104 L17 **Ceuta** *var.* Sebta. Ceuta, Spain, N Africa
88 C16 **Ceuta** *enclave* Spain, N Africa
106 B9 **Ceva** Piemonte, NE Italy
103 P14 **Cévennes** ▲▲ S France
108 G10 **Cevio** Ticino, S Switzerland
136 K16 **Ceyhan** Adana, S Turkey
136 K17 **Ceyhan Nehri** ≈ S Turkey
137 P17 **Ceylanpınar** Şanlıurfa, SE Turkey
Ceylon *see* Sri Lanka
173 R6 **Ceylon Plain** *undersea feature* N Indian Ocean
Ceyre to the Caribs *see* Marie-Galante
103 Q14 **Cèze** ≈ S France
Chaacha *see* Çäçe
127 P6 **Chaadayevka** Penzenskaya Oblast', W Russian Federation
167 O12 **Cha-Am** Phetchaburi, SW Thailand
143 W15 **Chābahār** *var.* Chāh Bahār, Chahbar. Sīstān va Balūchestān, SE Iran
Chabaricha *see* Khabarikha
61 B19 **Chabas** Santa Fe, C Argentina
103 T10 **Chablais** *physical region* E France
61 B20 **Chacabuco** Buenos Aires, E Argentina
42 K8 **Chacagón, Cerro** ▲ N Nicaragua
56 C10 **Chachapoyas** Amazonas, NW Peru
Chäche *see* Çäçe
119 O18 **Chachersk** *Rus.* Chechersk. Homyel'skaya Voblasts', SE Belarus
119 N16 **Chachevichy** *Rus.* Chechevichi. Mahilyowskaya Voblasts', E Belarus
61 B14 **Chaco** *off.* Provincia de Chaco. ◐ *province* NE Argentina
Chaco *see* Gran Chaco
62 M6 **Chaco Austral** *physical region* N Argentina
62 M3 **Chaco Boreal** *physical region* N Paraguay
62 M6 **Chaco Central** *physical region* N Argentina
39 Y15 **Chacon, Cape** *headland* Prince of Wales Island, Alaska, USA
Chaco, Provincia de *see* Chaco
78 H9 **Chad** *off.* Republic of Chad, *Fr.* Tchad. ◆ *republic* C Africa
122 K14 **Chadan** Respublika Tyva, S Russian Federation
21 U12 **Chadbourn** North Carolina, SE USA
83 L14 **Chadiza** Eastern, E Zambia
67 Q7 **Chad, Lake** *Fr.* Lac Tchad. ◎ C Africa
Chad, Republic of *see* Chad
28 J12 **Chadron** Nebraska, C USA
Chadyr-Lunga *see* Ciadîr-Lunga
163 W14 **Chaeryŏng** SW North Korea
105 P17 **Chafarinas, Islas** *island group* S Spain
27 Y7 **Chaffee** Missouri, C USA
148 L12 **Chāgai Hills** *var.* Chāh Gay. ▲▲ Afghanistan/Pakistan
123 Q11 **Chagda** Respublika Sakha (Yakutiya), NE Russian Federation
Chaghasarāy *see* Asadābād
149 N5 **Chaghcharān** *var.* Chakhcharan, Cheghcheran, Qala Āhangarān. Ghowr, C Afghanistan
103 R9 **Chagny** Saône-et-Loire, C France
173 Q7 **Chagos Archipelago** *var.* Oil Islands. *island group* British Indian Ocean Territory
129 O15 **Chagos Bank** *undersea feature* C Indian Ocean
129 O14 **Chagos-Laccadive Plateau** *undersea feature* N Indian Ocean
173 Q7 **Chagos Trench** *undersea feature* N Indian Ocean
43 T14 **Chagres, Río** ≈ C Panama
45 U14 **Chaguanas** Trinidad, Trinidad and Tobago
54 M6 **Chaguaramas** Guárico, N Venezuela
Chagyl *see* Çagyl
Chahārmahāl and Bakhtiyārī *see* Chahār Maḩāll va Bakhtīārī
142 M9 **Chahār Maḩāll va Bakhtīārī** *off.* Ostān-e Chahār Maḩāll va Bakhtīārī, *var.* Chahārmahāl and Bakhtiyārī. ◐ *province* SW Iran
Chahār Maḩāll va Bakhtīārī, Ostān-e *see* Chahār Maḩāll va Bakhtīārī
Chāh Bahār/Chahbar *see* Chābahār
143 V13 **Chāh Derāz** Sīstān va Balūchestān, SE Iran
Chāh Gay *see* Chāgai Hills
167 P10 **Chai Badan** Lop Buri, C Thailand
153 Q16 **Chāībāsa** Jhārkhand, N India
79 E19 **Chaillu, Massif du** ▲▲ C Gabon
167 O10 **Chai Nat** *var.* Chainat, Jainat, Jayanath. Chai Nat, C Thailand
Chainat *see* Chai Nat
65 M14 **Chain Fracture Zone** *tectonic feature* E Atlantic Ocean
173 N5 **Chain Ridge** *undersea feature* W Indian Ocean
Chairn, Ceann an *see* Carnsore Point
158 L5 **Chaiwopu** Xinjiang Uygur Zizhiqu, W China
167 Q10 **Chaiyaphum** *var.* Jayabum. Chaiyaphum, C Thailand
62 N10 **Chajarí** Entre Ríos, E Argentina
42 C5 **Chajul** Quiché, W Guatemala
83 K16 **Chakari** Mashonaland West, N Zimbabwe
148 J9 **Chakhānsūr** Nīmrūz, SW Afghanistan
Chakhānsūr *see* Nīmrūz
Chakhcharan *see* Chaghcharān
149 V8 **Chak Jhumra** *var.* Jhumra. Punjab, E Pakistan
146 I16 **Chaknakdysonga** Ahal Welaýaty, S Turkmenistan
153 P16 **Chakradharpur** Jhārkhand, N India
152 J8 **Chakrāta** Uttaranchal, N India
149 U7 **Chakwāl** Punjab, NE Pakistan
57 F17 **Chala** Arequipa, SW Peru
102 K12 **Chalais** Charente, W France
108 D10 **Chalais** Valais, SW Switzerland
115 J20 **Chalándri** *var.* Halandri; *prev.* Khalándrion. *prehistoric site* Sýros, Kykládes, Greece, Aegean Sea
188 H6 **Chalan Kanoa** Saipan, S Northern Mariana Islands
188 C16 **Chalan Pago** C Guam
Chalap Dalam/Chalap Dalan *see* Chehel Abdālān, Kūh-e
42 F7 **Chalatenango** Chalatenango, N El Salvador
42 A9 **Chalatenango** ◐ *department* NW El Salvador
83 P15 **Chalaua** Nampula, NE Mozambique
81 I16 **Chalbi Desert** *desert* N Kenya
42 D7 **Chalchuapa** Santa Ana, W El Salvador
Chalcidice *see* Chalkidikí
Chalcis *see* Chalkída
Chālderān *see* Siāh Chashmeh
103 N6 **Châlette-sur-Loing** Loiret, C France
15 X8 **Chaleur Bay** *Fr.* Baie des Chaleurs. *bay* New Brunswick/Québec, E Canada
Chaleurs, Baie des *see* Chaleur Bay
57 G16 **Chalhuanca** Apurímac, S Peru
154 F12 **Chālisgaon** Mahārāshtra, C India
115 N23 **Chálki** *island* Dodekánisa, Greece, Aegean Sea
115 F16 **Chalkiádes** Thessalía, C Greece
115 H18 **Chalkída** *var.* Halkida, *prev.* Khalkís; *anc.* Chalcis. Evvoia, E Greece
115 G14 **Chalkidikí** *var.* Khalkidhikí; *anc.* Chalcidice. *peninsula* NE Greece
185 A24 **Chalky Inlet** *inlet* South Island, New Zealand
39 S7 **Chalkyitsik** Alaska, USA
102 I9 **Challans** Vendée, NW France
57 K19 **Challapata** Oruro, SW Bolivia
192 H6 **Challenger Deep** *undersea feature* W Pacific Ocean
Challenger Deep *see* Mariana Trench
193 S11 **Challenger Fracture Zone** *tectonic feature* SE Pacific Ocean
192 K11 **Challenger Plateau** *undersea feature* E Tasman Sea
33 P13 **Challis** Idaho, NW USA
22 L9 **Chalmette** Louisiana, S USA
124 J11 **Chalna** Respublika Kareliya, NW Russian Federation
103 Q5 **Châlons-en-Champagne** *prev.* Châlons-sur-Marne, *hist.* Arcae Remorum; *anc.* Carolopois. Marne, NE France
Châlons-sur-Marne *see* Châlons-en-Champagne
103 R9 **Chalon-sur-Saône** *anc.* Cabillonum. Saône-et-Loire, C France
Chaltel, Cerro *see* Fitzroy, Monte
102 M11 **Châlus** Haute-Vienne, C France
143 N4 **Chālūs** Māzandarān, N Iran
101 N20 **Cham** Bayern, SE Germany
108 F7 **Cham** Zug, N Switzerland
37 R8 **Chama** New Mexico, SW USA
Cha Mai *see* Thung Song
83 E22 **Chamaites** Karas, S Namibia
149 O9 **Chaman** Baluchistān, SW Pakistan
37 R9 **Chama, Rio** ≈ New Mexico, SW USA
152 I6 **Chamba** Himāchal Pradesh, N India
81 I25 **Chamba** Ruvuma, S Tanzania
150 H12 **Chambal** ≈ C India
9 U16 **Chamberlain** Saskatchewan, S Canada
29 O11 **Chamberlain** South Dakota, N USA
19 R3 **Chamberlain Lake** ◎ Maine, NE USA
39 S5 **Chamberlin, Mount** ▲ Alaska, USA
37 O11 **Chambers** Arizona, SW USA
18 F16 **Chambersburg** Pennsylvania, NE USA
31 N5 **Chambers Island** *island* Wisconsin, N USA
103 T11 **Chambéry** *anc.* Camberia. Savoie, E France
82 L12 **Chambeshi** Northern, NE Zambia
82 L12 **Chambeshi** ≈ NE Zambia
74 M6 **Chambi, Jebel** *var.* Jabal ash Sha'nabī. ▲ W Tunisia
15 Q7 **Chambord** Québec, SE Canada
139 U11 **Chamcham** S Iraq
139 T4 **Chamchamāl** N Iraq
Chamdmanī *see* Altanshiree
40 J14 **Chamela** Jalisco, SW Mexico
42 G5 **Chamelecón, Río** ≈ NW Honduras
62 J9 **Chamical** La Rioja, C Argentina
115 L23 **Chamilí** *island* Kykládes, Greece, Aegean Sea
167 Q13 **Châmnar** Kaôh Kông, SW Cambodia
152 K9 **Chamoli** Uttaranchal, N India
103 U11 **Chamonix-Mont-Blanc** Haute-Savoie, E France
154 L11 **Chāmpa** Chhattīsgarh, C India
10 H8 **Champagne** Yukon Territory, W Canada
103 Q5 **Champagne** *cultural region* N France
Champagne *see* Campania
103 Q5 **Champagne-Ardenne** ◐ *region* N France
103 S9 **Champagnole** Jura, E France
30 M13 **Champaign** Illinois, N USA
167 S10 **Champasak** Champasak, S Laos
103 U6 **Champ de Feu** ▲ NE France
13 O7 **Champdoré, Lac** ◎ Québec, NE Canada
42 B6 **Champerico** Retalhuleu, SW Guatemala
108 C11 **Champéry** Valais, SW Switzerland
18 L6 **Champlain** New York, NE USA
18 L9 **Champlain Canal** *canal* New York, NE USA
15 P13 **Champlain, Lac** ◎ Québec, Canada/USA *see also* Champlain, Lake
18 L7 **Champlain, Lake** ◎ Canada/USA *see also* Champlain, Lac
103 S7 **Champlitte** Haute-Saône, E France
41 W13 **Champotón** Campeche, SE Mexico
104 G10 **Chamusca** Santarém, C Portugal
119 O20 **Chamyarysy** *Rus.* Chemerisy. Homyel'skaya Voblasts', SE Belarus
127 P5 **Chamzinka** Respublika Mordoviya, W Russian Federation
Chanáil Mhór, An *see* Grand Canal
Chanak *see* Çanakkale
62 G7 **Chañaral** Atacama, N Chile
104 H13 **Chança, Rio** *var.* Chanza. ≈ Portugal/Spain
57 D14 **Chancay** Lima, W Peru
Chan-chiang/Chanchiang *see* Zhanjiang
62 G13 **Chanco** Maule, Chile South America
39 R7 **Chandalar** Alaska, USA
39 R6 **Chandalar River** ≈ Alaska, USA
152 L10 **Chandan Chauki** Uttar Pradesh, N India
153 S16 **Chandannagar** *prev.* Chandernagore. West Bengal, E India
152 K10 **Chandausi** Uttar Pradesh, N India
22 M10 **Chandeleur Islands** *island group* Louisiana, S USA
22 M9 **Chandeleur Sound** *sound* N Gulf of Mexico
Chandernagore *see* Chandannagar
152 I8 **Chandīgarh** *state capital* Punjab, N India
153 Q16 **Chāndil** Jhārkhand, NE India
182 D2 **Chandler** South Australia
15 Y7 **Chandler** Québec, SE Canada
36 L14 **Chandler** Arizona, SW USA
27 O10 **Chandler** Oklahoma, C USA
25 V7 **Chandler** Texas, SW USA
39 Q6 **Chandler River** ≈ Alaska, USA
56 H13 **Chandles, Río** ≈ E Peru
163 N9 **Chandmanī** Dornogovĭ, SE Mongolia
162 H9 **Chandmanī** *var* Talshand. Govĭ-Altayĭ, C Mongolia
162 E7 **Chandmanī** *var.* Urdgol. Hovd, W Mongolia
14 J13 **Chandos Lake** ◎ Ontario, SE Canada
153 U15 **Chandpur** Chittagong, C Bangladesh
154 I13 **Chandrapur** Mahārāshtra, C India
83 J15 **Changa** Southern, S Zambia
Chang'an *see* Rong'an
Changan *see* Xi'an
155 G23 **Changanācheri** Kerala, SW India
83 M19 **Changane** ≈ S Mozambique
83 M16 **Changara** Tete, NW Mozambique
163 X11 **Changbai** *var.* Changbai Chosenzu Zizhixian. Jilin, NE China
Changbai Chosenzu Zizhixian *see* Changbai
163 X11 **Changbai Shan** ▲▲ NE China
163 V10 **Changchun** *var.* Ch'angch'un, Ch'ang-ch'un; *prev.* Hsinking. *province capital* Jilin, NE China
Ch'angch'un/Ch'ang-ch'un *see* Changchun
160 M10 **Changde** Hunan, S China
161 S13 **Changhua** *Jap.* Shōka. C Taiwan
168 L10 **Changi** ✈ (Singapore) E Singapore
158 L5 **Changji** Xinjiang Uygur Zizhiqu, NW China
160 L17 **Changjiang** *var.* Changjiang Lizu Zizhixian, Shiliu. Hainan, S China
157 O13 **Chang Jiang** *var.* Yangtze Kiang, *Eng.* Yangtze. ≈ C China
157 R11 **Chang Jiang** *var.* Yangtze Kiang, *Eng.* Yangtze. ≈ C China
161 S8 **Changjiang Kou** *delta* E China
Changjiang Lizu Zizhixian *see* Changjiang
Changkiakow *see* Zhangjiakou
167 F12 **Chang, Ko** *island* S Thailand
161 Q2 **Changli** Hebei, E China
163 V10 **Changling** Jilin, NE China
Changning *see* Xunwu
161 N11 **Changsha** *var.* Ch'angsha, Ch'ang-sha. *province capital* Hunan, S China
Ch'angsha/Ch'ang-sha *see* Changsha
161 Q10 **Changshan** Zhejiang, SE China
163 V14 **Changshan Qundao** *island group* NE China
161 S8 **Changshu** *var.* Ch'ang-shu. Jiangsu, E China
Ch'ang-shu *see* Changshu
163 V11 **Changtu** Liaoning, NE China
43 P14 **Changuinola** Bocas del Toro, NW Panama
159 N9 **Changweiliang** Qinghai, W China
160 K6 **Changwu** *var.* Zhaoren. Shaanxi, C China
163 U13 **Changxing Dao** *island* N China
160 M9 **Changyang** *var.* Longzhouping. Hubei, C China
163 W14 **Changyŏn** SW North Korea
161 N5 **Changzhi** Shanxi, C China
161 R8 **Changzhou** Jiangsu, E China
115 H24 **Chaniá** *var.* Hania, Khaniá, *Eng.* Canea; *anc.* Cydonia. Kríti, Greece, E Mediterranean Sea
62 J5 **Chañi, Nevado de** ▲ NW Argentina
115 H24 **Chanión, Kólpos** *gulf* Kríti, Greece, E Mediterranean Sea
Chankiri *see* Çankırı
30 M11 **Channahon** Illinois, N USA
155 H20 **Channapatna** Karnātaka, E India
97 K26 **Channel Islands** *Fr.* Iles Normandes. *island group* S English Channel
35 R16 **Channel Islands** *island group* California, W USA
13 S13 **Channel-Port aux Basques** Newfoundland, Newfoundland and Labrador, SE Canada
Channel, The *see* English Channel
97 Q23 **Channel Tunnel** *tunnel* France/UK
24 M2 **Channing** Texas, SW USA
Chantabun/Chantaburi *see* Chanthaburi
104 H3 **Chantada** Galicia, NW Spain
167 P12 **Chanthaburi** *var.* Chantabun, Chantaburi. Chantaburi, S Thailand
103 O4 **Chantilly** Oise, N France
139 V12 **Chanūn as Sa'ūdī** S Iraq
27 Q6 **Chanute** Kansas, C USA
Chanza *see* Chança, Rio
Ch'ao-an/Chaochow *see* Chaozhou
161 P8 **Chao Hu** ◎ E China
167 P11 **Chao Phraya, Mae Nam** ≈ C Thailand
Chaor He *see* Qulin Gol
Chaouèn *see* Chefchaouen
161 P14 **Chaoyang** Guangdong, S China
163 T12 **Chaoyang** Liaoning, NE China
Chaoyang *see* Jiayin, Heilongjiang, China
Chaoyang *see* Huinan, Jilin China
161 Q14 **Chaozhou** *var.* Chaoan, Chao'an, Ch'ao-an; *prev.* Chaochow. Guangdong, SE China
58 N13 **Chapadinha** Maranhão, E Brazil
12 K12 **Chapais** Québec, SE Canada
40 L13 **Chapala** Jalisco, SW Mexico
40 L13 **Chapala, Lago de** ◎ C Mexico
146 F13 **Chapan, Gora** ▲ C Turkmenistan
57 M18 **Chapare, Río** ≈ C Bolivia
54 E11 **Chaparral** Tolima, C Colombia
144 F9 **Chapayevo** Zapadnyy Kazakhstan, NW Kazakhstan
123 O11 **Chapayevo** Respublika Sakha (Yakutiya), NE Russian Federation
127 R6 **Chapayevsk** Samarskaya Oblast', W Russian Federation
60 H13 **Chapecó** Santa Catarina, S Brazil
60 I13 **Chapecó, Rio** ≈ S Brazil
20 J9 **Chapel Hill** Tennessee, S USA
44 J12 **Chapelton** C Jamaica
14 C8 **Chapleau** Ontario, SE Canada
14 D7 **Chapleau** ≈ Ontario, S Canada
9 T16 **Chaplin** Saskatchewan, S Canada
126 M6 **Chaplygin** Lipetskaya Oblast', W Russian Federation
117 S11 **Chaplynka** Khersons'ka Oblast', S Ukraine
9 O6 **Chapman, Cape** *headland* Nunavut, NE Canada
25 T15 **Chapman Ranch** Texas, SW USA
Chapman's *see* Okwa
21 P5 **Chapmanville** West Virginia, NE USA
28 K15 **Chappell** Nebraska, C USA
Chapra *see* Chhapra
56 D9 **Chapuli, Río** ≈ N Peru
76 I6 **Châr** *well* N Mauritania
123 P12 **Chara** Chitinskaya Oblast', S Russian Federation
123 O11 **Chara** ≈ C Russian Federation
54 G8 **Charala** Santander, C Colombia
41 N10 **Charcas** San Luis Potosí, C Mexico
25 T13 **Charco** Texas, SW USA
194 H7 **Charcot Island** *island* Antarctica
64 M8 **Charcot Seamounts** *undersea feature* E Atlantic Ocean
Chardara *see* Shardara
145 P17 **Chardarinskoye Vodokhranilishche** ▣ S Kazakhstan
31 U11 **Chardon** Ohio, N USA
44 K9 **Chardonnières** SW Haiti
Chardzhev *see* Türkmenabat
Chardzhevskaya Oblast *see* Lebap Welaýaty
Chardzhou/Chardzhui *see* Türkmenabat
102 L11 **Charente** ◐ *department* W France
102 J11 **Charente** ≈ W France
102 J10 **Charente-Maritime** ◐ *department* W France
137 U12 **Ch'arents'avan** C Armenia
78 I12 **Chari** *var.* Shari. ≈ Central African Republic/Chad
78 G11 **Chari-Baguirmi** *off.* Préfecture du Chari-Baguirmi. ◐ *prefecture* SW Chad
Chari-Baguirmi, Préfecture du *see* Chari-Baguirmi
149 Q4 **Chārīkār** Parvān, NE Afghanistan
29 V15 **Chariton** Iowa, C USA
27 U3 **Chariton River** ≈ Missouri, C USA
55 T7 **Charity** NW Guyana
31 R7 **Charity Island** *island* Michigan, N USA
Chärjew *see* Türkmenabat
Chärjew Oblasty *see* Lebap Welaýaty
Charkhlik/Charkhliq *see* Ruoqiang
99 G20 **Charleroi** Hainaut, S Belgium
9 V12 **Charles** Manitoba, C Canada
15 R10 **Charlesbourg** Québec, SE Canada
21 Y7 **Charles, Cape** *headland* Virginia, NE USA
29 W12 **Charles City** Iowa, C USA
21 W6 **Charles City** Virginia, NE USA
103 O5 **Charles de Gaulle** ✈ (Paris) Seine-et-Marne, N France
12 K1 **Charles Island** *island* Nunavut, NE Canada
Charles Island *see* Santa María, Isla
30 K9 **Charles Mound** *hill* Illinois, N USA
185 A22 **Charles Sound** *sound* South Island, New Zealand
185 G15 **Charleston** West Coast, South Island, New Zealand
27 S11 **Charleston** Arkansas, C USA
30 M14 **Charleston** Illinois, N USA
22 L3 **Charleston** Mississippi, S USA
27 Z7 **Charleston** Missouri, C USA
21 T15 **Charleston** South Carolina, SE USA
21 Q5 **Charleston** *state capital* West Virginia, NE USA
14 L14 **Charleston Lake** ◎ Ontario, SE Canada
35 W11 **Charleston Peak** ▲ Nevada, W USA
45 W10 **Charlestown** Nevis, Saint Kitts and Nevis
31 P16 **Charlestown** Indiana, N USA
18 M9 **Charlestown** New Hampshire, NE USA
21 V3 **Charles Town** West Virginia, NE USA
181 W9 **Charleville** Queensland, E Australia
103 R3 **Charleville-Mézières** Ardennes, N France
31 P5 **Charlevoix** Michigan, N USA
31 Q6 **Charlevoix, Lake** ◎ Michigan, N USA
39 T9 **Charley River** ≈ Alaska, USA
64 J6 **Charlie-Gibbs Fracture Zone** *tectonic feature* N Atlantic Ocean
103 Q10 **Charlieu** Loire, E France
31 Q9 **Charlotte** Michigan, N USA
21 R10 **Charlotte** North Carolina, SE USA
20 I8 **Charlotte** Tennessee, S USA
25 R13 **Charlotte** Texas, SW USA
21 R10 **Charlotte** ✈ North Carolina, SE USA
45 T9 **Charlotte Amalie** *prev.* Saint Thomas. ○ (Virgin Islands (US)) Saint Thomas, N Virgin Islands (US)
21 U7 **Charlotte Court House** Virginia, NE USA
23 W14 **Charlotte Harbor** *inlet* Florida, SE USA
Charlotte Island *see* Abaiang
95 J15 **Charlottenberg** Värmland, C Sweden
Charlottenhof *see* Aegviidu
21 U5 **Charlottesville** Virginia, NE USA
13 Q14 **Charlottetown** *province capital* Prince Edward Island, Prince Edward Island, SE Canada
Charlotte Town *see* Roseau
Charlotte Town *see* Gouyave
45 Z16 **Charlotteville** Tobago, Trinidad and Tobago
182 M11 **Charlton** Victoria, SE Australia
12 H10 **Charlton Island** *island* Northwest Territories, C Canada
103 T6 **Charmes** Vosges, NE France
119 F19 **Charnawchytsy** *Rus.* Chernavchitsy. Brestskaya Voblasts', SW Belarus
15 R10 **Charny** Québec, SE Canada
149 T5 **Chārsadda** North-West Frontier Province, NW Pakistan
Charshanga/Charshangngy/Charshangy *see* Köýtendag
Charsk *see* Shar
181 W6 **Charters Towers** Queensland, NE Australia
15 R12 **Chartierville** Québec, SE Canada
102 M6 **Chartres** *anc.* Autricum, Civitas Carnutum. Eure-et-Loir, C France
145 W15 **Charyn** *Kaz.* Sharyn. Almaty, SE Kazakhstan
Charyn *see* Sharyn
61 D21 **Chascomús** Buenos Aires, E Argentina
9 N16 **Chase** British Columbia, SW Canada
21 U7 **Chase City** Virginia, NE USA
19 S4 **Chase, Mount** ▲ Maine, NE USA
118 M13 **Chashniki** *Rus.* Chashniki. Vitsyebskaya Voblasts', N Belarus
115 D15 **Chásia** ▲▲ C Greece
29 V9 **Chaska** Minnesota, N USA
185 D25 **Chaslands Mistake** *headland* South Island, New Zealand
125 R11 **Chasovo** Respublika Komi, NW Russian Federation
Chasovo *see* Vazhgort
124 H14 **Chastova** Novgorodskaya Oblast', NW Russian Federation
143 R3 **Chāt** Golestān, N Iran
Chatak *see* Chhatak
Chatang *see* Zhanang
39 R9 **Chatanika** Alaska, USA
39 R9 **Chatanika River** ≈ Alaska, USA
147 T8 **Chat-Bazar** Talasskaya Oblast', NW Kyrgyzstan
45 Y14 **Chateaubelair** Saint Vincent, W Saint Vincent and the Grenadines
102 J7 **Châteaubriant** Loire-Atlantique, NW France
103 Q8 **Château-Chinon** Nièvre, C France
108 C10 **Château d'Oex** Vaud, W Switzerland
102 L7 **Château-du-Loir** Sarthe, NW France
102 M6 **Châteaudun** Eure-et-Loir, C France
102 K7 **Château-Gontier** Mayenne, NW France
15 O13 **Châteauguay** Québec, SE Canada
102 F6 **Châteaulin** Finistère, NW France
103 N9 **Châteaumeillant** Cher, C France
102 K11 **Châteauneuf-sur-Charente** Charente, W France
102 M7 **Château-Renault** Indre-et-Loire, C France
103 N9 **Châteauroux** *prev.* Indreville. Indre, C France
103 T5 **Château-Salins** Moselle, NE France
103 P4 **Château-Thierry** Aisne, N France
99 H21 **Châtelet** Hainaut, S Belgium
Châtelherault *see* Châtellerault
102 L9 **Châtellerault** *var.* Châtelherault. Vienne, W France
29 X10 **Chatfield** Minnesota, N USA
13 O14 **Chatham** New Brunswick, SE Canada
14 D17 **Chatham** Ontario, S Canada
97 P22 **Chatham** SE England, UK
30 K14 **Chatham** Illinois, N USA
21 T7 **Chatham** Virginia, NE USA
63 F22 **Chatham, Isla** *island* S Chile
175 R12 **Chatham Island** *island* Chatham Islands, New Zealand
Chatham Island *see* San Cristóbal, Isla
Chatham Island Rise *see* Chatham Rise
175 R12 **Chatham Islands** *island group* New Zealand, SW Pacific Ocean
175 Q12 **Chatham Rise** *var.* Chatham Island Rise. *undersea feature* S Pacific Ocean
39 X13 **Chatham Strait** *strait* Alaska, USA
Chathóir, Rinn *see* Cahore Point
102 M9 **Châtillon-sur-Indre** Indre, C France
103 Q7 **Châtillon-sur-Seine** Côte d'Or, C France
147 S8 **Chatkal** *Uzb.* Chotqol. ≈ Kyrgyzstan/Uzbekistan
147 R9 **Chatkal Range** *Rus.* Chatkal'skiy Khrebet. ▲▲ Kyrgyzstan/Uzbekistan

◆ Country ● Country Capital ◇ Dependent Territory ○ Dependent Territory Capital ◐ Administrative Regions ✈ International Airport ▲ Mountain ▲▲ Mountain Range Volcano ≈ River ◎ Lake ▣ Reservoir

Chatkal'skiy Khrebet – Chincoteague

Chatkal'skiy Khrebet see Chatkal Range
23 N7 Chatom Alabama, S USA
Chatrapur see Chhatrapur
143 S10 Chatrūd Kermān, C Iran
23 S2 Chatsworth Georgia, SE USA
Chāttagām see Chittagong
23 S8 Chattahoochee Florida, SE USA
23 R8 Chattahoochee River ≈ SE USA
20 L10 Chattanooga Tennessee, S USA
147 V10 Chatyr-Kël', Ozero ◎ C Kyrgyzstan
147 W9 Chatyr-Tash Narynskaya Oblast', C Kyrgyzstan
15 R12 Chaudière ≈ Québec, SE Canada
167 S14 Châu Đốc var. Chauphu, Chau Phu. An Giang, S Vietnam
152 D13 Chauhtan prev. Chohtan. Rājasthān, NW India
166 L5 Chauk Magwe, W Burma (Myanmar)
103 R6 Chaumont prev. Chaumont-en-Bassigny. Haute-Marne, N France
Chaumont-en-Bassigny see Chaumont
123 T5 Chaunskaya Guba bay NE Russian Federation
103 P3 Chauny Aisne, N France
Châu Ô see Binh Sơn
Chau Phu see Châu Đốc
102 I5 Chausey, Îles island group N France
Chausy see Chavusy
18 C11 Chautauqua Lake ◎ New York, NE USA
ChâuThanh see Ba Ria
102 L9 Chauvigny Vienne, W France
124 L6 Chavan'ga Murmanskaya Oblast', NW Russian Federation
14 K10 Chavannes, Lac ◎ Québec, SE Canada
Chavantes, Represa de see Xavantes, Represa de
61 D15 Chavarría Corrientes, NE Argentina
127 P4 Chuvash Respubliki var. Chuvashskaya Respublika, Eng. Chuvashia. ⬖ autonomous republic W Russian Federation
104 I5 Chaves anc. Aquae Flaviae. Vila Real, N Portugal
Chávez, Isla see Santa Cruz, Isla
82 G13 Chavuma North Western, NW Zambia
119 O16 Chavusy Rus. Chausy. Mahilyowskaya Voblasts', E Belarus
Chayan see Shayan
147 U8 Chayek Narynskaya Oblast', C Kyrgyzstan
139 T6 Chāy Khānah E Iraq
125 T16 Chaykovskiy Permskaya Oblast', NW Russian Federation
167 T12 Chbar Môndól Kiri, E Cambodia
23 Q4 Cheaha Mountain ▲ Alabama, S USA
Cheatharlach see Carlow
21 S2 Cheat River ≈ NE USA
111 A16 Cheb Ger. Eger. Karlovarský Kraj, W Czech Republic
127 Q3 Cheboksary Chavash Respubliki, W Russian Federation
31 Q5 Cheboygan Michigan, N USA
Chechaouèn see Chefchaouen
Chechenia see Chechenskaya Respublika
127 O15 Chechenskaya Respublika Eng. Chechenia, Chechnia, Rus. Chechnya. ⬖ autonomous republic SW Russian Federation
67 N4 Chech, Erg desert Algeria/Mali
Chechevichi see Chachevichy
Che-chiang see Zhejiang
Chechnia/Chechnya see Chechenskaya Respublika
163 Y15 Chech'ŏn Jap. Teisen. N South Korea
111 L15 Chęciny Świętokrzyskie, S Poland
27 Q10 Checotah Oklahoma, C USA
13 R15 Chedabucto Bay inlet Nova Scotia, E Canada
166 J7 Cheduba Island island W Burma (Myanmar)
37 T5 Cheesman Lake ⊠ Colorado, C USA
195 S16 Cheetham, Cape headland Antarctica
74 G5 Chefchaouen var. Chaouèn, Chechaouèn, Sp. Xauen. N Morocco
Chefoo see Yantai
38 M12 Chefornak Alaska, USA
123 R13 Chegdomyn Khabarovskiy Kray, SE Russian Federation
76 M4 Chegga Tiris Zemmour, NE Mauritania
Cheghcheran see Chaghcharān
32 G9 Chehalis Washington, NW USA
32 G9 Chehalis River ≈ Washington, NW USA
148 M6 Chehel Abdālān, Kūh-e var. Chalap Dalam, Pash. Chalap Dalan. ▲ C Afghanistan
115 D14 Cheimadítis, Límni var. Límni Cheimadítis. ◎ N Greece
Cheimadítis, Límni see Cheimadítis, Límni
103 U15 Cheiron, Mont ▲ SE France
163 X17 Cheju Jap. Saishū. S South Korea
163 Y17 Cheju ✈ S South Korea
163 Y17 Cheju-do Jap. Saishū; prev. Quelpart. island S South Korea
163 X17 Cheju-haehyŏp strait S South Korea
Chekiang see Zhejiang
Chekichler/Chekishlyar see Çekiçler
188 F8 Chelab Babeldaob, N Palau
147 N11 Chelak Rus. Chelek. Samarqand Viloyati, C Uzbekistan
32 J7 Chelan, Lake ⊠ Washington, NW USA
Chelek see Chelak
Cheleken see Hazar
Chélif/Chéliff see Chelif, Oued
74 J5 Chelif, Oued var. Chélif, Chéliff, Chellif, Shellif. ≈ N Algeria
Chelkar see Shalkar
Chelkar Ozero see Shalkar, Ozero
Chellif see Chelif, Oued
111 P14 Chełm Rus. Kholm. Lubelskie, SE Poland
110 I9 Chełmno Ger. Culm, Kulm. Kujawski-pomorskie, C Poland
115 E19 Chelmós var Aroania. ▲ S Greece
14 F10 Chelmsford Ontario, S Canada
97 P21 Chelmsford E England, UK
110 J9 Chełmża Ger. Culmsee, Kulmsee. Kujawski-pomorskie, C Poland
27 Q8 Chelsea Oklahoma, C USA
18 M8 Chelsea Vermont, NE USA
97 L21 Cheltenham C England, UK
105 R9 Chelva País Valenciano, E Spain
122 G11 Chelyabinsk Chelyabinskaya Oblast', C Russian Federation
122 F1 Chelyabinskaya Oblast' ⬖ province C Russian Federation
123 N5 Chelyuskin, Mys cape N Russian Federation
41 Y12 Chemax Yucatán, SE Mexico
83 N16 Chemba Sofala, C Mozambique
82 J13 Chembe Luapula, NE Zambia
Chemenibit see Çemenibit
Chemerisy see Chamyarysy
116 K7 Chemerivtsi Khmel'nyts'ka Oblast', W Ukraine
102 J8 Chemillé Maine-et-Loire, NW France
173 X17 Chemin Grenier S Mauritius
101 N16 Chemnitz prev. Karl-Marx-Stadt. Sachsen, E Germany
Chemulpo see Inch'ŏn
32 H14 Chemult Oregon, NW USA
18 G12 Chemung River ≈ New York/Pennsylvania, NE USA
149 U8 Chenāb ≈ India/Pakistan
39 S9 Chena Hot Springs Alaska, USA
18 I11 Chenango River ≈ New York, NE USA
168 J7 Chenderoh, Tasik ◎ Peninsular Malaysia
15 Q11 Chêne, Rivière du ≈ Québec, SE Canada
32 L8 Cheney Washington, NW USA
26 M6 Cheney Reservoir ⊠ Kansas, C USA
Chengchiatun see Liaoyuan
Ch'eng-chou/Chengchow see Zhengzhou
161 P1 Chengde var. Jehol. Hebei, E China
160 I9 Chengdu var. Chengtu, Ch'eng-tu. province capital Sichuan, C China
161 Q14 Chenghai Guangdong, S China
Chenghsien see Zhengzhou
160 H13 Chengjiang Yunnan, SW China
Chengjiang see Taihe
160 L17 Chengmai var. Jinjiang. Hainan, S China
Chengtu/Ch'eng-tu see Chengdu
159 W12 Chengxian var. Cheng Xiang. Gansu, C China
Cheng Xiang see Chengxian
Chengyang see Juxian
Chengzhong see Ningming
Chenkiang see Zhenjiang
155 J19 Chennai prev. Madras. state capital Tamil Nādu, S India
155 J19 Chennai ✈ Tamil Nādu, S India
103 R8 Chenôve Côte d'Or, C France
Chenstokhov see Częstochowa
160 L11 Chenxi var. Chenyang. Hunan, S China
Chen Xian/Chenxian/Chen Xiang see Chenzhou
Chenyang see Chenxi
161 N12 Chenzhou var. Chenxian, Chen Xian, Chen Xiang. Hunan, S China
167 U12 Cheo Reo var. A Yun Pa. Gia Lai, S Vietnam
114 I11 Chepelare Smolyan, S Bulgaria
114 I11 Chepelarska Reka ≈ S Bulgaria
56 B11 Chepén La Libertad, C Peru
62 J10 Chepes La Rioja, C Argentina
161 O15 Chep Lap Kok ✈ (Hong Kong) S China
161 O15 Chep Lap Kok ✈ S China
43 U14 Chepo Panamá, C Panama
Chepping Wycombe see High Wycombe
125 R14 Cheptsa ≈ NW Russian Federation
30 K3 Chequamegon Point headland Wisconsin, N USA
103 O8 Cher ⬖ department C France
102 M8 Cher ≈ C France
Cherangani Hills see Cherangany Hills
81 H17 Cherangany Hills var. Cherangani Hills. ▲▲ W Kenya
21 S11 Cheraw South Carolina, SE USA
102 I3 Cherbourg anc. Carusbur. Manche, N France
127 R5 Cherdakly Ul'yanovskaya Oblast', W Russian Federation
125 U12 Cherdyn' Permskaya Oblast', NW Russian Federation
124 J14 Cherekha ≈ W Russian Federation
122 M13 Cheremkhovo Irkutskaya Oblast', S Russian Federation
Cheren see Keren
124 K14 Cherepovets Vologodskaya Oblast', NW Russian Federation
125 O11 Cherevkovo Arkhangel'skaya Oblast', NW Russian Federation
74 I6 Chergui, Chott ech salt lake NW Algeria
Cherikov see Cherykaw
117 P6 Cherkas'ka Oblast' var. Cherkasy, Rus. Cherkasskaya Oblast'. ⬖ province C Ukraine
Cherkasskaya Oblast' see Cherkas'ka Oblast'
Cherkassy see Cherkasy
117 Q6 Cherkasy Rus. Cherkassy. Cherkas'ka Oblast', C Ukraine
Cherkasy see Cherkas'ka Oblast'
126 M15 Cherkessk Karachayevo-Cherkesskaya Respublika, SW Russian Federation
122 H12 Cherlak Omskaya Oblast', C Russian Federation
122 H12 Cherlakskiy Omskaya Oblast', C Russian Federation
125 U13 Chermoz Permskaya Oblast', NW Russian Federation
Chernavchitsy see Charnawchytsy
125 T3 Chernaya Nenetskiy Avtonomnyy Okrug, NW Russian Federation
125 T4 Chernaya ≈ NW Russian Federation
Chernigov see Chernihiv
Chernigovskaya Oblast' see Chernihivs'ka Oblast'
117 Q2 Chernihiv Rus. Chernigov. Chernihivs'ka Oblast', NE Ukraine
Chernihiv see Chernihivs'ka Oblast'
117 V9 Chernihivka Zaporiz'ka Oblast', SE Ukraine
117 P2 Chernihivs'ka Oblast' var. Chernihiv, Rus. Chernigovskaya Oblast'. ⬖ province NE Ukraine
114 I9 Cherni Osŭm ≈ N Bulgaria
116 J8 Chernivets'ka Oblast' var. Chernivtsi, Rus. Chernovitskaya Oblast'. ⬖ province W Ukraine
114 I9 Cherni Vit ≈ NW Bulgaria
114 G10 Cherni Vrŭkh ▲ W Bulgaria
116 K8 Chernivtsi Ger. Czernowitz, Rom. Cernăuţi, Rus. Chernovtsy. Chernivets'ka Oblast', W Ukraine
116 M7 Chernivtsi Vinnyts'ka Oblast', C Ukraine
Chernivtsi see Chernivets'ka Oblast'
Chernobyl' see Chornobyl'
Cherno More see Black Sea
Chernomorskoye see Chornomors'ke
145 T7 Chernoretskoye Pavlodar, NE Kazakhstan
Chernovitskaya Oblast' see Chernivets'ka Oblast'
Chernovtsy see Chernivtsi
145 U8 Chernoye Pavlodar, NE Kazakhstan
Chernoye More see Black Sea
125 U16 Chernushka Permskaya Oblast', NW Russian Federation
117 N4 Chernyakhiv Rus. Chernyakhov. Zhytomyrs'ka Oblast', N Ukraine
Chernyakhov see Chernyakhiv
119 C14 Chernyakhovsk Ger. Insterburg. Kaliningradskaya Oblast', W Russian Federation
126 K8 Chernyanka Belgorodskaya Oblast', W Russian Federation
125 V5 Chernyshëva, Gryada ▲▲ NW Russian Federation
144 J14 Chernyshëva, Zaliv gulf SW Kazakhstan
123 O10 Chernyshevskiy Respublika Sakha (Yakutiya), NE Russian Federation
127 P13 Chërnyye Zemli plain SW Russian Federation
Chërnyy Irtysh see Ertix He, China/Kazakhstan
Chërnyy Irtysh see Kara Irtysh, Kazakhstan
127 V7 Chernyy Otrog Orenburgskaya Oblast', W Russian Federation
29 T12 Cherokee Iowa, C USA
26 M8 Cherokee Oklahoma, C USA
25 R9 Cherokee Texas, SW USA
21 O8 Cherokee Lake ⊠ Tennessee, S USA
Cherokees, Lake O' The see Grand Lake O' The Cherokees
44 H1 Cherokee Sound Great Abaco, N Bahamas
153 V13 Cherrapunji Meghālaya, NE India
28 L9 Cherry Creek ≈ South Dakota, N USA
18 J16 Cherry Hill New Jersey, NE USA
27 Q7 Cherryvale Kansas, C USA
21 Q10 Cherryville North Carolina, SE USA
Cherski Range see Cherskogo, Khrebet
123 T6 Cherskiy Respublika Sakha (Yakutiya), NE Russian Federation
123 R8 Cherskogo, Khrebet var. Cherski Range. ▲▲ NE Russian Federation
Cherso see Cres
126 L10 Chertkovo Rostovskaya Oblast', SW Russian Federation
Cherven' see Chervyen'
114 H8 Cherven Bryag Pleven, N Bulgaria
116 M4 Chervonoarmiys'k Zhytomyrs'ka Oblast', N Ukraine
Chervonograd see Chervonohrad
116 I4 Chervonohrad Rus. Chervonograd. L'vivs'ka Oblast', NW Ukraine
117 W6 Chervonooskil's'ke Vodoskhovyshche Rus. Krasnooskol'skoye Vodokhranilishche. ⊠ NE Ukraine
Chervonoye, Ozero see Chyrvonaye, Vozyera
117 S4 Chervonozavods'ke Poltavs'ka Oblast', C Ukraine
119 L16 Chervyen' Rus. Cherven'. Minskaya Voblasts', C Belarus
119 P16 Cherykaw Rus. Cherikov. Mahilyowskaya Voblasts', E Belarus
31 R9 Chesaning Michigan, N USA
21 X5 Chesapeake Bay inlet NE USA
Chesha Bay see Chëshskaya Guba
Cheshevlya see Tsyeshawlya
97 K18 Cheshire cultural region C England, UK
125 P5 Chëshskaya Guba var. Archangel Bay, Chesha Bay, Dvina Bay. bay NW Russian Federation
14 F14 Chesley Ontario, S Canada
21 Q10 Chesnee South Carolina, SE USA
97 K18 Chester Wel. Caerleon, hist. Legaceaster, Lat. Deva, Devana Castra. C England, UK
35 O4 Chester California, W USA
30 K16 Chester Illinois, N USA
33 S7 Chester Montana, NW USA
18 I16 Chester Pennsylvania, NE USA
21 R1 Chester South Carolina, SE USA
25 X9 Chester Texas, SW USA
21 W6 Chester Virginia, NE USA
21 R11 Chester West Virginia, NE USA
97 M18 Chesterfield C England, UK
21 S11 Chesterfield South Carolina, SE USA
21 W6 Chesterfield Virginia, NE USA
192 J9 Chesterfield, Îles island group NW New Caledonia
9 O9 Chesterfield Inlet Nunavut, NW Canada
9 O9 Chesterfield Inlet inlet Nunavut, N Canada
21 Y3 Chester River ≈ Delaware/Maryland, NE USA
21 X3 Chestertown Maryland, NE USA
19 R4 Chesuncook Lake ◎ Maine, NE USA
30 J5 Chetek Wisconsin, N USA
13 R14 Chéticamp Nova Scotia, SE Canada
27 Q8 Chetopa Kansas, C USA
41 Y14 Chetumal var. Payo Obispo. Quintana Roo, SE Mexico
Chetumal, Bahia/Chetumal, Bahía de see Chetumal Bay
42 G1 Chetumal Bay var. Bahia Chetumal, Bahía de Chetumal. bay Belize/Mexico
10 M13 Chetwynd British Columbia, W Canada
38 M11 Chevak Alaska, USA
36 M12 Chevelon Creek ≈ Arizona, SW USA
185 J17 Cheviot Canterbury, South Island, New Zealand
96 L13 Cheviot Hills hill range England/Scotland, UK
96 L13 Cheviot, The ▲ NE England, UK
14 M11 Chevreuil, Lac du ◎ Québec, SE Canada
81 I16 Ch'ew Bahir var. Lake Stefanie. ◎ Ethiopia/Kenya
32 L7 Chewelah Washington, NW USA
26 K10 Cheyenne Oklahoma, C USA
33 Z17 Cheyenne state capital Wyoming, C USA
26 L5 Cheyenne Bottoms ◎ Kansas, C USA
16 J8 Cheyenne River ≈ South Dakota/Wyoming, N USA
37 W5 Cheyenne Wells Colorado, C USA
108 C9 Cheyres Vaud, W Switzerland
Chezdi-Oşorheiu see Târgu Secuiesc
153 P13 Chhapra prev. Chapra. Bihār, N India
153 V13 Chhatak var. Chatak. Sylhet, NE Bangladesh
154 J9 Chhatarpur Madhya Pradesh, C India
154 N13 Chhatrapur prev. Chatrapur. Orissa, E India
154 K2 Chhattīsgarh ⬖ state E India
154 L12 Chhattīsgarh plain C India
154 I11 Chhindwāra Madhya Pradesh, C India
153 T12 Chhukha SW Bhutan
161 S14 Chiai var. Chia-i, Chiayi, Kiayi, Jiayi, Jap. Kagi. C Taiwan
Chia-i see Chiai
Chia-mu-ssu see Jiamusi
83 B15 Chiange Port. Vila de Almoster. Huíla, SW Angola
Chiang-hsi see Jiangxi
161 S12 Chiang Kai-shek ✈ (T'aipei) N Taiwan
167 P8 Chiang Khan Loei, E Thailand
167 O7 Chiang Mai var. Chiangmai, Chiengmai, Kiangmai. Chiang Mai, NW Thailand
167 O7 Chiang Mai ✈ Chiang Mai, NW Thailand
Chiangmai see Chiang Mai
167 O6 Chiang Rai var. Chianpai, Chienrai, Muang Chiang Rai. Chiang Rai, NW Thailand
Chiang-su see Jiangsu
Chianning/Chian-ning see Nanjing
Chianpai see Chiang Rai
106 G12 Chianti cultural region C Italy
Chiapa see Chiapa de Corzo
41 U16 Chiapa de Corzo var. Chiapa. Chiapas, SE Mexico
41 V16 Chiapas ⬖ state SE Mexico
106 J12 Chiaravalle Marche, C Italy
107 N22 Chiaravalle Centrale Calabria, SW Italy
106 E7 Chiari Lombardia, N Italy
108 H12 Chiasso Ticino, S Switzerland
137 S9 Chiat'ura C Georgia
41 P15 Chiautla var. Chiautla de Tapia. Puebla, S Mexico
Chiautla de Tapia see Chiautla
106 D10 Chiavari Liguria, NW Italy
106 E6 Chiavenna Lombardia, N Italy
Chiayi see Chiai
Chiazza see Piazza Armerina
165 O14 Chiba var. Tiba. Chiba, Honshū, S Japan
165 O13 Chiba off. Chiba-ken, var. Tiba. ⬖ prefecture Honshū, S Japan
83 M18 Chibabava Sofala, C Mozambique
Chiba-ken see Chiba
161 O10 Chibi prev. Puqi. Hubei, C China
83 B15 Chibia Port. João de Almeida, Vila João de Almeida. Huíla, SW Angola
83 M18 Chiboma Sofala, C Mozambique
82 J12 Chibondo Luapula, N Zambia
82 K11 Chibote Luapula, NE Zambia
12 K12 Chibougamau Québec, SE Canada
164 H11 Chiburi-jima island Oki-shotō, SW Japan
83 M20 Chibuto Gaza, S Mozambique
31 N11 Chicago Illinois, N USA
31 N11 Chicago Heights Illinois, N USA
15 W6 Chic-Chocs, Monts Eng. Shickshock Mountains. ▲▲ Québec, SE Canada
39 W13 Chichagof Island island Alexander Archipelago, Alaska, USA
57 K20 Chichas, Cordillera de ▲▲ SW Bolivia
41 X12 Chichén-Itzá, Ruinas ruins Yucatán, SE Mexico
97 N23 Chichester SE England, UK
42 C5 Chichicastenango Quiché, W Guatemala
42 I9 Chichigalpa Chinandega, NW Nicaragua
Ch'i-ch'i-ha-erh see Qiqihar
165 X16 Chichijima-rettō Eng. Beechy Group. island group SE Japan
54 K4 Chichiriviche Falcón, N Venezuela
39 R11 Chickaloon Alaska, USA
20 L10 Chickamauga Lake ⊠ Tennessee, S USA
23 N7 Chickasawhay River ≈ Mississippi, S USA
26 M11 Chickasha Oklahoma, C USA
39 T9 Chicken Alaska, USA
104 J16 Chiclana de la Frontera Andalucía, S Spain
56 B11 Chiclayo Lambayeque, NW Peru
35 N5 Chico California, W USA
83 L15 Chicoa Tete, NW Mozambique
83 M20 Chicomo Gaza, S Mozambique
18 M11 Chicopee Massachusetts, NE USA
63 I19 Chico, Río ≈ SE Argentina
63 I21 Chico, Río ≈ S Argentina
27 W14 Chicot, Lake ◎ Arkansas, C USA
15 R7 Chicoutimi Québec, SE Canada
15 Q8 Chicoutimi ≈ Québec, SE Canada
83 L19 Chicualacuala Gaza, SW Mozambique
83 B14 Chicuma Benguela, C Angola
155 J21 Chidambaram Tamil Nādu, SE India
196 K13 Chidley, Cape cape Newfoundland and Labrador, E Canada
101 N24 Chiemsee ◎ SE Germany
Chiengmai see Chiang Mai
Chienrai see Chiang Rai
106 B8 Chieri Piemonte, NW Italy
106 F8 Chiese ≈ N Italy
107 K14 Chieti var. Teate. Abruzzo, C Italy
99 E19 Chièvres Hainaut, SW Belgium
163 S12 Chifeng var. Ulanhad. Nei Mongol Zizhiqu, N China
82 F13 Chifumage ≈ E Angola
82 M13 Chifunda Eastern, NE Zambia
145 S14 Chiganak var. Čiganak. Zhambyl, SE Kazakhstan
39 P15 Chiginagak, Mount ▲ Alaska, USA
Chigirin see Chyhyryn
41 P13 Chignahuapan Puebla, S Mexico
39 O15 Chignik Alaska, USA
83 M19 Chigombe ≈ S Mozambique
54 D7 Chigorodó Antioquia, NW Colombia
83 M19 Chigubo Gaza, S Mozambique
Chihertey see Altay
Chih-fu see Yantai
Chihli see Hebei
Chihli, Gulf of see Bo Hai
40 J6 Chihuahua Chihuahua, NW Mexico
40 I6 Chihuahua ⬖ state N Mexico
145 O15 Chiili Kzylorda, S Kazakhstan
26 M7 Chikaskia River ≈ Kansas/Oklahoma, C USA
155 H19 Chik Ballāpur Karnātaka, W India
124 G15 Chikhachevo Pskovskaya Oblast', W Russian Federation
155 F19 Chikmagalūr Karnātaka, W India
129 V7 Chikoy ≈ C Russian Federation
83 J15 Chikumbi Lusaka, C Zambia
82 M13 Chikwa Eastern, NE Zambia
Chikwana see Chikwawa
83 N15 Chikwawa var. Chikwana. Southern, S Malawi
155 J16 Chilakalūrupet Andhra Pradesh, E India
146 L14 Chilan Lebap Welaýaty, E Turkmenistan
Chilapa see Chilapa de Alvarez
41 P16 Chilapa de Alvarez var. Chilapa. Guerrero, S Mexico
155 J25 Chilaw North Western Province, W Sri Lanka
57 D15 Chilca Lima, W Peru
23 Q4 Childersburg Alabama, S USA
25 P4 Childress Texas, SW USA
63 G14 Chile off. Republic of Chile. ◆ republic SW South America
47 R10 Chile Basin undersea feature E Pacific Ocean
63 H20 Chile Chico Aisén, W Chile
62 I9 Chilecito La Rioja, NW Argentina
62 H12 Chilecito Mendoza, W Argentina
83 L14 Chilembwe Eastern, E Zambia
Chile, Republic of see Chile
193 S11 Chile Rise undersea feature SE Pacific Ocean
117 N13 Chilia Braţul ≈ SE Romania
Chilia-Nouă see Kiliya
145 V15 Chilik Almaty, SE Kazakhstan
145 V15 Chilik ≈ SE Kazakhstan
154 O13 Chilika Lake var. Chilka Lake. ◎ E India
82 J13 Chililabombwe Copperbelt, C Zambia
Chi-lin see Jilin
Chilka Lake see Chilika Lake
10 H9 Chilkoot Pass pass British Columbia, W Canada
Chill Ala, Cuan see Killala Bay
62 G13 Chillán Bío Bío, C Chile
61 C22 Chillar Buenos Aires, E Argentina
Chill Chiaráin, Cuan see Kilkieran Bay
30 K12 Chillicothe Illinois, N USA
27 S3 Chillicothe Missouri, C USA
31 S14 Chillicothe Ohio, N USA
25 Q4 Chillicothe Texas, SW USA
10 M17 Chilliwack British Columbia, SW Canada
Chill Mhantáin, Ceann see Wicklow Head
Chill Mhantáin, Sléibhte see Wicklow Mountains
108 C10 Chillon Vaud, W Switzerland
Chil'mamedkum, Peski/Chilmämetgum see Çilmämmetgum
63 F17 Chiloé, Isla de var. Isla Grande de Chiloé. island W Chile
32 H15 Chiloquin Oregon, NW USA
41 O16 Chilpancingo var. Chilpancingo de los Bravos. Guerrero, S Mexico
Chilpancingo de los Bravos see Chilpancingo
97 N21 Chiltern Hills hill range S England, UK
30 M7 Chilton Wisconsin, N USA
82 F11 Chiluage Lunda Sul, NE Angola
82 N12 Chilumba prev. Deep Bay. Northern, N Malawi
161 T12 Chilung var. Keelung, Jap. Kirun, Kirun'; prev. Sp. Santissima Trinidad. N Taiwan
83 N15 Chilwa, Lake var. Lago Chirua, Lake Shirwa. ◎ SE Malawi
167 R10 Chi, Mae Nam ≈ E Thailand
42 C6 Chimaltenango Chimaltenango, C Guatemala
42 A2 Chimaltenango off. Departamento de Chimaltenango. ⬖ department S Guatemala
Chimaltenango, Departamento de see Chimaltenango
43 V15 Chimán Panamá, E Panama
83 M17 Chimanimani prev. Mandidzudzure, Melsetter. Manicaland, E Zimbabwe
99 G22 Chimay Hainaut, S Belgium
37 S10 Chimayo New Mexico, SW USA
Chimbay see Chimboy
56 A13 Chimborazo ⬖ province C Ecuador
56 C7 Chimborazo ⛰ C Ecuador
56 C12 Chimbote Ancash, W Peru
146 H7 Chimboy Rus. Chimbay. Qoraqalpog'iston Respublikasi, NW Uzbekistan
186 D7 Chimbu ⬖ province C Papua New Guinea
54 F6 Chimichagua Cesar, N Colombia
Chimishliya see Cimişlia
Chimkent see Shymkent
Chimkentskaya Oblast' see Yuzhnyy Kazakhstan
28 I14 Chimney Rock rock Nebraska, C USA
83 M17 Chimoio Manica, C Mozambique
82 K11 Chimpembe Northern, NE Zambia
41 O8 China Nuevo León, NE Mexico
156 M9 China off. People's Republic of China, Chin. Chung-hua Jen-min Kung-ho-kuo, Zhonghua Renmin Gongheguo; prev. Chinese Empire. ◆ republic E Asia
19 Q7 China Lake ◎ Maine, NE USA
42 F8 Chinameca San Miguel, E El Salvador
Chi-nan/Chinan see Jinan
42 H9 Chinandega Chinandega, NW Nicaragua
42 H9 Chinandega ⬖ department NW Nicaragua
China, People's Republic of see China
China, Republic of see Taiwan
24 J11 Chinati Mountains ▲▲ Texas, SW USA
Chinaz see Chinoz
57 E15 Chincha Alta Ica, SW Peru
9 N11 Chinchaga ≈ Alberta, SW Canada
Chin-chiang see Quanzhou
Chinchilla see Chinchilla de Monte Aragón
105 Q11 Chinchilla de Monte Aragón var. Chinchilla. Castilla-La Mancha, C Spain
54 D10 Chinchiná Caldas, W Colombia
105 O8 Chinchón Madrid, C Spain
41 Z14 Chinchorro, Banco island SE Mexico
Chin-chou/Chinchow see Jinzhou
21 Z5 Chincoteague Assateague Island, Virginia, NE USA

236
◆ Country ● Country Capital ◇ Dependent Territory ○ Dependent Territory Capital ⬖ Administrative Regions ✈ International Airport ▲ Mountain ▲▲ Mountain Range ⛰ Volcano ≈ River ◎ Lake ⊠ Reservoir

CHINDE – CÎMPULUNG

83 O17 **Chinde** Zambézia, NE Mozambique
163 X17 **Chin-do** *Jap.* Chin-tō. *island* SW South Korea
159 R13 **Chindu** *var.* Chuqung. Qinghai, C China
166 M2 **Chindwin** ≈ N Burma (Myanmar)
Chinese Empire *see* China
Chinghai *see* Qinghai, China
Ch'ing Hai *see* Qinghai Hu, China
Chingildi *see* Shengeldi
Chingildi *see* Shengeldi
144 H9 **Chingirlau** *Kaz.* Shyngghyrlaū. Zapadnyy Kazakhstan, W Kazakhstan
82 J13 **Chingola** Copperbelt, C Zambia
Ching-Tao/Ch'ing-tao *see* Qingdao
82 C13 **Chinguar** Huambo, C Angola
76 I7 **Chinguețți** *var.* Chinguetti. Adrar, C Mauritania
163 Z16 **Chinhae** *Jap.* Chinkai. S South Korea
166 K4 **Chin Hills** ▲▲ W Burma (Myanmar)
83 K16 **Chinhoyi** *prev.* Sinoia. Mashonaland West, N Zimbabwe
Chinhsien *see* Jinzhou
39 Q14 **Chiniak, Cape** *headland* Kodiak Island, Alaska, USA
14 G10 **Chiniguchi Lake** ◎ Ontario, S Canada
149 U8 **Chinīot** Punjab, NE Pakistan
163 Y16 **Chinju** *Jap.* Shinshū. S South Korea
Chinkai *see* Chinhae
78 M13 **Chinko** ≈ E Central African Republic
37 O9 **Chinle** Arizona, SW USA
161 R13 **Chinmen Tao** *var.* Jinmen Dao, Quemoy. *island* W Taiwan
Chinnchâr *see* Shinshār
Chinnereth *see* Tiberias, Lake
164 C12 **Chino** *var.* Tino. Nagano, Honshū, S Japan
102 L8 **Chinon** Indre-et-Loire, C France
33 T7 **Chinook** Montana, NW USA
Chinook State *see* Washington
192 L4 **Chinook Trough** *undersea feature* N Pacific Ocean
36 K11 **Chino Valley** Arizona, SW USA
147 P10 **Chinoz** *Rus.* Chinaz. Toshkent Viloyati, E Uzbekistan
82 L12 **Chinsali** Northern, NE Zambia
166 K5 **Chin State** ◈ *state* W Burma (Myanmar)
Chinsura *see* Chunchura
Chin-tō *see* Chin-do
54 E6 **Chinú** Córdoba, NW Colombia
99 K24 **Chiny, Forêt de** *forest* SE Belgium
83 M15 **Chioco** Tete, NW Mozambique
106 H8 **Chioggia** *anc.* Fossa Claudia. Veneto, NE Italy
114 H12 **Chionótrypa** ▲ NE Greece
115 L18 **Chíos** *var.* Hios, Khíos, *It.* Scio, *Turk.* Sakiz-Adasi. Chíos, E Greece
115 K18 **Chíos** *var.* Khíos. *island* E Greece
83 M14 **Chipata** *prev.* Fort Jameson. Eastern, E Zambia
83 C14 **Chipindo** Huíla, C Angola
23 R8 **Chipley** Florida, SE USA
155 D15 **Chiplūn** Mahārāshtra, W India
81 H22 **Chipogolo** Dodoma, C Tanzania
23 R8 **Chipola River** ≈ Florida, SE USA
97 L22 **Chippenham** S England, UK
30 J6 **Chippewa Falls** Wisconsin, N USA
30 J4 **Chippewa, Lake** ⊠ Wisconsin, N USA
31 Q8 **Chippewa River** ≈ Michigan, N USA
30 I6 **Chippewa River** ≈ Wisconsin, N USA
Chipping Wycombe *see* High Wycombe
114 G8 **Chiprovtsi** Montana, NW Bulgaria
19 T4 **Chiputneticook Lakes** *lakes* Canada/USA
56 D13 **Chiquián** Ancash, W Peru
41 Y11 **Chiquilá** Quintana Roo, SE Mexico
42 E6 **Chiquimula** Chiquimula, SE Guatemala
42 A3 **Chiquimula** *off.* Departamento de Chiquimula. ◈ *department* SE Guatemala
Chiquimula, Departamento de *see* Chiquimula
42 D7 **Chiquimulilla** Santa Rosa, S Guatemala
54 F9 **Chiquinquirá** Boyacá, C Colombia
155 J17 **Chīrāla** Andhra Pradesh, E India
149 N4 **Chīras** Ghowr, N Afghanistan
152 H11 **Chirāwa** Rājasthān, N India
Chirchik *see* Chirchiq
147 Q9 **Chirchiq** *Rus.* Chirchik. Toshkent Viloyati, E Uzbekistan
147 P10 **Chirchiq** ≈ E Uzbekistan
Chire *see* Shire
83 L18 **Chiredzi** Masvingo, SE Zimbabwe
25 X8 **Chireno** Texas, SW USA
77 X7 **Chirfa** Agadez, NE Niger
37 O16 **Chiricahua Mountains** ▲▲ Arizona, SW USA
37 O16 **Chiricahua Peak** ▲ Arizona, SW USA
54 F6 **Chiriguaná** Cesar, N Colombia
39 P15 **Chirikof Island** *island* Alaska, USA
43 P16 **Chiriquí** *off.* Provincia de Chiriquí. ◈ *province* SW Panama
43 P17 **Chiriquí, Golfo de** *Eng.* Chiriqui Gulf. *gulf* SW Panama
43 P15 **Chiriquí Grande** Bocas del Toro, W Panama
Chiriqui Gulf *see* Chiriquí, Golfo de
43 P15 **Chiriquí, Laguna de** *lagoon* NW Panama
Chiriquí, Provincia de *see* Chiriquí
43 O16 **Chiriquí Viejo, Río** ≈ W Panama
Chiriquí, Volcán de *see* Barú, Volcán
83 N15 **Chiromo** Southern, S Malawi
114 J10 **Chirpan** Stara Zagora, C Bulgaria
43 N14 **Chirripó Atlántico, Río** ≈ E Costa Rica
Chirripó, Cerro *see* Chirripó Grande, Cerro
Chirripó del Pacífico, Río *see* Chirripó, Río
43 N14 **Chirripó Grande, Cerro** *var.* Cerro Chirripó. ▲ SE Costa Rica
43 N13 **Chirripó, Río** *var.* Río Chirripó del Pacífico. ≈ NE Costa Rica
Chirua, Lago *see* Chilwa, Lake
83 J15 **Chirundu** Southern, S Zambia
29 W8 **Chisago City** Minnesota, N USA
83 J14 **Chisamba** Central, C Zambia
39 T10 **Chisana** Alaska, USA
82 I13 **Chisasa** North Western, NW Zambia
12 I9 **Chisasibi** Québec, C Canada
42 D4 **Chisec** Alta Verapaz, C Guatemala
127 U5 **Chishmy** Respublika Bashkortostan, W Russian Federation
29 V4 **Chisholm** Minnesota, N USA
160 I11 **Chishui He** ≈ C China
Chisimaio/Chisimayu *see* Kismaayo
117 N10 **Chişinău** *Rus.* Kishinev. ● (Moldova) C Moldova
117 N10 **Chişinău** ✕ S Moldova
Chişinău-Criş *see* Chişineu-Criş
116 F10 **Chişineu-Criş** *Hung.* Kisjenő; *prev.* Chişinău-Criş. Arad, W Romania
83 K14 **Chisomo** Central, C Zambia
106 A8 **Chisone** ≈ NW Italy
24 K12 **Chisos Mountains** ▲▲ Texas, SW USA
149 U10 **Chishtiān Mandi** Punjab, E Pakistan
39 T10 **Chistochina** Alaska, USA
127 R4 **Chistopol'** Respublika Tatarstan, W Russian Federation
145 O8 **Chistopol'ye** Severnyy Kazakhstan, N Kazakhstan
123 O13 **Chita** Chitinskaya Oblast', S Russian Federation
83 B16 **Chitado** Cunene, SW Angola
Chitaldroog/Chitaldrug *see* Chitradurga
83 C15 **Chitanda** ≈ S Angola
Chitangwiza *see* Chitungwiza
82 F10 **Chitato** Lunda Norte, NE Angola
83 C14 **Chitembo** Bié, C Angola
39 T11 **Chitina** Alaska, USA
39 T11 **Chitina River** ≈ Alaska, USA
123 O12 **Chitinskaya Oblast'** ◈ *province* S Russian Federation
82 M11 **Chitipa** Northern, NW Malawi
165 S4 **Chitose** *var.* Titose. Hokkaidō, NE Japan
155 G18 **Chitradurga** *prev.* Chitaldroog, Chitaldrug. Karnātaka, W India
149 T3 **Chitrāl** North-West Frontier Province, NW Pakistan
43 S16 **Chitré** Herrera, S Panama
153 V16 **Chittagong** *Ben.* Chāttagām. Chittagong, SE Bangladesh
153 U16 **Chittagong** ◈ *division* E Bangladesh
153 Q15 **Chittaranjan** West Bengal, NE India
152 G14 **Chittaurgarh** Rājasthān, N India
155 I19 **Chittoor** Andhra Pradesh, E India
155 G21 **Chittūr** Kerala, SW India
83 K16 **Chitungwiza** *prev.* Chitangwiza. Mashonaland East, NE Zimbabwe
62 H4 **Chíuchíu** Antofagasta, N Chile
82 F12 **Chiumbe** *var.* Tshiumbe. ≈ Angola/Dem. Rep. Congo
83 F15 **Chiume** Moxico, E Angola
83 K13 **Chiundaponde** Northern, NE Zambia
106 H13 **Chiusi** Toscana, C Italy
54 J5 **Chivacoa** Yaracuy, N Venezuela
106 B8 **Chivasso** Piemonte, NW Italy
83 L17 **Chivhu** *prev.* Enkeldoorn. Midlands, C Zimbabwe
61 C20 **Chivilcoy** Buenos Aires, E Argentina
82 N12 **Chiweta** Northern, N Malawi
42 D4 **Chixoy, Río** *var.* Río Negro, Río Salinas. ≈ Guatemala/Mexico
82 H13 **Chizela** North Western, NW Zambia
125 O5 **Chizha** Nenetskiy Avtonomnyy Okrug, NW Russian Federation
161 Q9 **Chizhou** *var.* Guichi. Anhui, E China
164 I12 **Chizu** Tottori, Honshū, SW Japan
Chkalov *see* Orenburg
74 J5 **Chlef** *var.* Ech Cheliff, Ech Chleff; *prev.* Al-Asnam, El Asnam, Orléansville. NW Algeria
115 G18 **Chlómo** ▲ C Greece
111 M15 **Chmielnik** Świętokrzyskie, C Poland
167 S11 **Chŏâm Khsant** Preăh Vihéar, N Cambodia
62 G10 **Choapa, Río** *var.* Choapo. ≈ C Chile
Choapas *see* Las Choapas
Choapo *see* Choapa, Río
Choarta *see* Chwārtā
67 T13 **Chobe** ≈ N Botswana
14 K8 **Chochocouane** ≈ Québec, SE Canada
110 E13 **Chocianów** *Ger.* Kotzenan. Dolnośląskie, SW Poland
54 C9 **Chocó** *off.* Departamento del Chocó. ◈ *province* W Colombia
Chocó, Departamento del *see* Chocó
35 X16 **Chocolate Mountains** ▲▲ California, W USA
21 W9 **Chocowinity** North Carolina, SE USA
27 N10 **Choctaw** Oklahoma, C USA
23 Q8 **Choctawhatchee Bay** *bay* Florida, SE USA
23 Q8 **Choctawhatchee River** ≈ Florida, SE USA
163 V14 **Chŏ-do** *island* SW North Korea
Chodorów *see* Khodoriv
111 A16 **Chodov** *Ger.* Chodau. Karlovarský Kraj, W Czech Republic
110 G10 **Chodzież** Wielkopolskie, C Poland
63 J15 **Choele Choel** Río Negro, C Argentina
83 L14 **Chofombo** Tete, NW Mozambique
Chohtan *see* Chauhtan
9 U14 **Choiceland** Saskatchewan, C Canada
186 K8 **Choiseul** *var.* Lauru. *island* NW Solomon Islands
63 M23 **Choiseul Sound** *sound* East Falkland, Falkland Islands
40 H7 **Choix** Sinaloa, C Mexico
110 D10 **Chojna** Zachodnio-pomorskie, W Poland
110 H8 **Chojnice** *Ger.* Konitz. Pomorskie, N Poland
111 F14 **Chojnów** *Ger.* Hainau, Haynau. Dolnośląskie, SW Poland
167 Q10 **Chok Chai** Nakhon Ratchasima, C Thailand
80 I12 **Ch'ok'ē** *var.* Choke Mountains. ▲▲ NW Ethiopia
25 R13 **Choke Canyon Lake** ⊠ Texas, SW USA
Choke Mountains *see* Ch'ok'ē
145 T15 **Chokpar** *Kaz.* Shoqpar. Zhambyl, S Kazakhstan
147 W7 **Chok-Tal** *var.* Choktal. Issyk-Kul'skaya Oblast', E Kyrgyzstan
Choktal *see* Chok-Tal
Chókué *see* Chokwè
123 R7 **Chokurdakh** Respublika Sakha (Yakutiya), NE Russian Federation
83 L20 **Chokwè** *var.* Chókué. Gaza, S Mozambique
188 F8 **Chol** Babeldaob, N Palau
160 E8 **Chola Shan** ▲▲ C China
102 J8 **Cholet** Maine-et-Loire, NW France
63 H17 **Cholila** Chubut, W Argentina
Cholo *see* Thyolo
147 V8 **Cholpon** Narynskaya Oblast', C Kyrgyzstan
147 X7 **Cholpon-Ata** Issyk-Kul'skaya Oblast', E Kyrgyzstan
41 P14 **Cholula** Puebla, S Mexico
42 I8 **Choluteca** Choluteca, S Honduras
42 H8 **Choluteca** ◈ *department* S Honduras
42 G6 **Choluteca, Río** ≈ SW Honduras
83 I15 **Choma** Southern, S Zambia
153 T11 **Chomo Lhari** ▲ NW Bhutan
167 N7 **Chom Thong** Chiang Mai, NW Thailand
111 B15 **Chomutov** *Ger.* Komotau. Ústecký Kraj, NW Czech Republic
123 N11 **Chona** ≈ C Russian Federation
163 X15 **Ch'ŏnan** *Jap.* Tenan. W South Korea
167 P11 **Chon Buri** *prev.* Bang Pla Soi. Chon Buri, S Thailand
56 B6 **Chone** Manabí, W Ecuador
Chong'an *see* Wuyishan
163 W13 **Ch'ŏngch'ŏn-gang** ≈ W North Korea
163 Y11 **Ch'ŏngjin** NE North Korea
163 W13 **Chŏngju** W North Korea
161 S8 **Chongming Dao** *island* E China
160 J10 **Chongqing** *var.* Ch'ung-ching, Ch'ung-ch'ing, Chungking, Pahsien, Tchongking, Yuzhou. Chongqing Shi, C China
Chŏngup *see* Chŏnju
161 O10 **Chongyang** *var.* Tiancheng. Hubei, C China
160 J15 **Chongzuo** Guangxi Zhuangzu Zizhiqu, S China
163 Y16 **Chŏnju** *prev.* Chŏngup, *Jap.* Seiyu. SW South Korea
163 Y15 **Chŏnju** *Jap.* Zenshū. SW South Korea
Chonnacht *see* Connaught
Chonogol *see* Erdenetsagaan
63 F19 **Chonos, Archipiélago de los** *island group* S Chile
42 K10 **Chontales** ◈ *department* S Nicaragua
167 T13 **Chơn Thanh** Sông Be, S Vietnam
158 K17 **Cho Oyu** *var.* Qowowuyag. ▲ China/Nepal
116 G7 **Chop** *Cz.* Cop, *Hung.* Csap. Zakarpats'ka Oblast', W Ukraine
21 Y3 **Choptank River** ≈ Maryland, NE USA
115 J22 **Chóra** *prev.* Íos. Íos, Kykládes, Greece, Aegean Sea
115 H25 **Chóra Sfakíon** *var.* Sfákia. Kríti, Greece, E Mediterranean Sea
Chorcaí, Cuan *see* Cork Harbour
43 P15 **Chorcha, Cerro** ▲ W Panama
Chorku *see* Chorkŭh
147 R11 **Chorkŭh** *Rus.* Chorku. N Tajikistan
97 K17 **Chorley** NW England, UK
Chorne More *see* Black Sea
117 R5 **Chornobay** Cherkas'ka Oblast', C Ukraine
117 O3 **Chornobyl'** *Rus.* Chernobyl'. Kyyivs'ka Oblast', N Ukraine
117 R12 **Chornomors'ke** *Rus.* Chernomorskoye. Respublika Krym, S Ukraine
117 R4 **Chornukhy** Poltavs'ka Oblast', C Ukraine
Chorokh/Chorokhi *see* Çoruh Nehri
110 O9 **Choroszcz** Podlaskie, NE Poland
116 K6 **Chortkiv** *Rus.* Chortkov. Ternopil's'ka Oblast', W Ukraine
Chortkov *see* Chortkiv
Chorum *see* Çorum
110 M9 **Chorzele** Mazowieckie, C Poland
111 J16 **Chorzów** *Ger.* Königshütte; *prev.* Królewska Huta. Śląskie, S Poland
163 W12 **Ch'osan** N North Korea
Chośebuz *see* Cottbus
Chōsen-kaikyō *see* Korea Strait
164 P14 **Chōshi** *var.* Tyôsi. Chiba, Honshū, S Japan
63 H14 **Chos Malal** Neuquén, W Argentina
Chosŏn-minjujuŭi-inmin-kanghwaguk *see* North Korea
110 E9 **Choszczno** *Ger.* Arnswalde. Zachodnio-pomorskie, NW Poland
153 O15 **Chota Nāgpur** *plateau* N India
33 R8 **Choteau** Montana, NW USA
Chotqol *see* Chatkal
14 M8 **Chouart** ≈ Québec, SE Canada
76 I7 **Choûm** Adrar, C Mauritania
27 Q9 **Chouteau** Oklahoma, C USA
21 X8 **Chowan River** ≈ North Carolina, SE USA
35 Q10 **Chowchilla** California, W USA
163 Q7 **Choybalsan** *var.* Hulstay. Dornod, NE Mongolia
163 P7 **Choybalsan** *prev.* Byan Tumen. Dornod, E Mongolia
162 M9 **Choyr** Govĭ Sumber, C Mongolia
185 I19 **Christchurch** Canterbury, South Island, New Zealand
97 M24 **Christchurch** S England, UK
185 I18 **Christchurch** ✕ Canterbury, South Island, New Zealand
44 J12 **Christiana** C Jamaica
83 H22 **Christiana** Free State, C South Africa
115 J23 **Christiána** *var.* Christiani. *island* Kykládes, Greece, Aegean Sea
Christiani *see* Christiána
Christiania *see* Oslo
14 G13 **Christian Island** *island* Ontario, S Canada
191 P16 **Christian, Point** *headland* Pitcairn Island, Pitcairn Islands
38 M11 **Christian River** ≈ Alaska, USA
Christiansand *see* Kristiansand
21 S7 **Christiansburg** Virginia, NE USA
95 G23 **Christiansfeld** Sønderjylland, SW Denmark
Christianshåb *see* Qasigiannguit
39 X14 **Christian Sound** *inlet* Alaska, USA
45 T9 **Christiansted** Saint Croix, S Virgin Islands (US)
Christiansund *see* Kristiansund
25 R13 **Christine** Texas, SW USA
173 U7 **Christmas Island** ◇ *Australian external territory* E Indian Ocean
129 T17 **Christmas Island** *island* E Indian Ocean
Christmas Island *see* Kiritimati
192 M7 **Christmas Ridge** *undersea feature* C Pacific Ocean
30 L16 **Christopher** Illinois, N USA
25 P9 **Christoval** Texas, SW USA
111 F17 **Chrudim** Pardubický Kraj, C Czech Republic
115 K25 **Chrysí** *island* SE Greece
121 N2 **Chrysochoú, Kólpos** *var.* Khrysokhou Bay. *bay* E Mediterranean Sea
114 I13 **Chrysoúpoli** *var.* Hrisoupoli; *prev.* Khrisoúpolis. Anatolikí Makedonía kai Thráki, NE Greece
111 K16 **Chrzanów** *var.* Chrzanow, *Ger.* Zaumgarten. Śląskie, S Poland
129 Q7 **Chu** *Kaz.* Shū. ≈ Kazakhstan/Kyrgyzstan
42 C5 **Chuacús, Sierra de** ▲▲ W Guatemala
153 S15 **Chuadanga** Khulna, W Bangladesh
Chuan *see* Sichuan
Ch'uan-chou *see* Quanzhou
39 O11 **Chuathbaluk** Alaska, USA
Chubek *see* Moskva
63 I17 **Chubut** *off.* Provincia de Chubut. ◈ *province* S Argentina
Chubut, Provincia de *see* Chubut
63 I17 **Chubut, Río** ≈ SE Argentina
43 V15 **Chucanti, Cerro** ▲ E Panama
Ch'u-chiang *see* Shaoguan
43 W15 **Chucunaque, Río** ≈ E Panama
Chudin *see* Chudzin
116 M5 **Chudniv** Zhytomyrs'ka Oblast', N Ukraine
124 H13 **Chudovo** Novgorodskaya Oblast', W Russian Federation
Chudskoye Ozero *see* Peipus, Lake
119 J18 **Chudzin** *Rus.* Chudin. Brestskaya Voblasts', SW Belarus
39 Q13 **Chugach Islands** *island group* Alaska, USA
39 S11 **Chugach Mountains** ▲▲ Alaska, USA
164 G12 **Chūgoku-sanchi** ▲▲ Honshū, SW Japan
Chugqênsumdo *see* Jigzhi
Chuguyev *see* Chuhuyiv
117 V5 **Chuhuyiv** *var.* Chuguyev. Kharkivs'ka Oblast', E Ukraine
61 H19 **Chuí** Rio Grande do Sul, S Brazil
Chuí *see* Chuy
145 S15 **Chu-Iliyskiye Gory** *Kaz.* Shū-Ile Taūlary. ▲▲ S Kazakhstan
Chukai *see* Cukai
Chukchi Avtonomnyy Okrug *see* Chukotskiy Avtonomnyy Okrug
Chukchi Peninsula *see* Chukotskiy Poluostrov
197 R6 **Chukchi Plain** *undersea feature* Arctic Ocean
197 R6 **Chukchi Plateau** *undersea feature* Arctic Ocean
197 R4 **Chukchi Sea** *Rus.* Chukotskoye More. *sea* Arctic Ocean
125 N14 **Chukhloma** Kostromskaya Oblast', NW Russian Federation
Chukotka *see* Chukotskiy Avtonomnyy Okrug
Chukot Range *see* Anadyrskiy Khrebet
123 V6 **Chukotskiy Avtonomnyy Okrug** *var.* Chukchi Avtonomnyy Okrug, Chukotka. ◈ *autonomous district* NE Russian Federation
123 W5 **Chukotskiy, Mys** *cape* NE Russian Federation
123 V5 **Chukotskiy Poluostrov** *Eng.* Chukchi Peninsula. *peninsula* NE Russian Federation
Chukotskoye More *see* Chukchi Sea
Chukurkak *see* Chuqurqoq
Chulakkurgan *see* Sholakkorgan
35 U17 **Chula Vista** California, W USA
123 Q12 **Chul'man** Respublika Sakha (Yakutiya), NE Russian Federation
56 B9 **Chulucanas** Piura, NW Peru
122 J12 **Chulym** ≈ C Russian Federation
152 K6 **Chumar** Jammu and Kashmir, N India
114 K9 **Chumerna** ▲ C Bulgaria
123 R12 **Chumikan** Khabarovskiy Kray, E Russian Federation
167 Q9 **Chum Phae** Khon Kaen, C Thailand
167 N13 **Chumphon** *var.* Jumporn. Chumphon, SW Thailand
167 O9 **Chumsaeng** *var.* Chum Saeng. Nakhon Sawan, C Thailand
Chum Saeng *see* Chumsaeng
122 L12 **Chuna** ≈ C Russian Federation
161 R9 **Chun'an** *var.* Qiandaohu; *prev.* Pailing. Zhejiang, SE China
161 S13 **Chunan** N Taiwan
Chuncheng *see* Yangchun
163 Y14 **Ch'unch'ŏn** *Jap.* Shunsen. N South Korea
153 S16 **Chunchura** *prev.* Chinsura. West Bengal, NE India
145 W15 **Chundzha** Almaty, SE Kazakhstan
Ch'ung-ch'ing/Ch'ung-ching *see* Chongqing
Chung-hua Jen-min Kung-ho-kuo *see* China
163 Y15 **Ch'ungju** *Jap.* Chūshū. C South Korea
Chungking *see* Chongqing
161 T14 **Chungyang Shanmo** *Chin.* Taiwan Shan. ▲▲ C Taiwan
149 V9 **Chūniān** Punjab, E Pakistan
122 L12 **Chunskiy** Irkutskaya Oblast', S Russian Federation
122 M11 **Chunya** ≈ C Russian Federation
124 J6 **Chupa** Respublika Kareliya, NW Russian Federation
125 P8 **Chuprovo** Respublika Komi, NW Russian Federation
57 G17 **Chuquibamba** Arequipa, SW Peru
62 H4 **Chuquicamata** Antofagasta, N Chile
57 L21 **Chuquisaca** ◈ *department* S Bolivia
Chuquisaca *see* Sucre
Chuqung *see* Chindu
146 I8 **Chuqurqoq** *Rus.* Chukurkak. Qoraqalpog'iston Respublikasi, NW Uzbekistan
127 T2 **Chur** Udmurtskaya Respublika, NW Russian Federation
108 I9 **Chur** *Fr.* Coire, *It.* Coira, *Rmsch.* Cuera, Quera; *anc.* Curia Rhaetorum. Graubünden, E Switzerland
123 Q10 **Churapcha** Respublika Sakha (Yakutiya), NE Russian Federation
9 V16 **Churchbridge** Saskatchewan, S Canada
21 O8 **Church Hill** Tennessee, S USA
9 X9 **Churchill** Manitoba, C Canada
9 X10 **Churchill** ≈ Manitoba/Saskatchewan, C Canada
13 P9 **Churchill** ≈ Newfoundland and Labrador, E Canada
9 Y9 **Churchill, Cape** *headland* Manitoba, C Canada
13 P9 **Churchill Falls** Newfoundland and Labrador, E Canada
9 S12 **Churchill Lake** ◎ Saskatchewan, C Canada
19 Q3 **Churchill Lake** ⊠ Maine, NE USA
194 I5 **Churchill Peninsula** *peninsula* Antarctica
22 H8 **Church Point** Louisiana, S USA
29 O3 **Churchs Ferry** North Dakota, N USA
146 G12 **Churchuri** Ahal Welaýaty, C Turkmenistan
21 T5 **Churchville** Virginia, NE USA
152 G10 **Chūru** Rājasthān, NW India
54 J4 **Churuguara** Falcón, N Venezuela
167 U11 **Chư Sê** Gia Lai, C Vietnam
144 J12 **Chushkakul, Gory** ▲▲ SW Kazakhstan
Chūshū *see* Ch'ungju
37 O9 **Chuska Mountains** ▲▲ Arizona/New Mexico, SW USA
Chu, Sông *see* Sam, Nam
125 V14 **Chusovoy** Permskaya Oblast', NW Russian Federation
147 R10 **Chust** Namangan Viloyati, E Uzbekistan
Chust *see* Khust
15 U6 **Chute-aux-Outardes** Québec, SE Canada
117 U5 **Chutove** Poltavs'ka Oblast', C Ukraine
189 O15 **Chuuk** *var.* Truk. ◈ *state* C Micronesia
189 P15 **Chuuk Islands** *var.* Hogoley Islands; *prev.* Truk Islands. *island group* Caroline Islands, C Micronesia
Chuvashia *see* Chuvash Respubliki
Chuvashskaya Respublika *see* Chuvash Respubliki
Chuwārtah *see* Chwārtā
Chu Xian/Chuxian *see* Chuzhou
160 G13 **Chuxiong** Yunnan, SW China
147 V7 **Chuy** Chuyskaya Oblast', N Kyrgyzstan
61 H19 **Chuy** *var.* Chuí. Rocha, E Uruguay
123 O11 **Chuya** Respublika Sakha (Yakutiya), NE Russian Federation
Chüy Oblasty *see* Chuyskaya Oblast'
147 U8 **Chuyskaya Oblast'** *Kir.* Chüy Oblasty. ◈ *province* N Kyrgyzstan
161 Q7 **Chuzhou** *var.* Chuxian, Chu Xian. Anhui, E China
139 U3 **Chwārtā** *var.* Choarta, Chuwārtah. NE Iraq
119 N16 **Chyhirynskaye Vodaskhovishcha** ⊠ E Belarus
117 R6 **Chyhyryn** *Rus.* Chigirin. Cherkas'ka Oblast', N Ukraine
119 J18 **Chyrvonaya Slabada** *Rus.* Krasnaya Slabada, Krasnaya Sloboda. Minskaya Voblasts', S Belarus
119 J18 **Chyrvonaya Slabada** *Rus.* Krasnaya Slabada, Krasnaya Sloboda. Minskaya Voblasts', S Belarus
119 L19 **Chyrvonaye, Vozyera** *Rus.* Ozero Chervonoye. ◎ SE Belarus
117 N11 **Ciadîr-Lunga** *var.* Ceadâr-Lunga, *Rus.* Chadyr-Lunga. S Moldova
169 P16 **Ciamis** *prev.* Tjiamis. Jawa, C Indonesia
107 I16 **Ciampino** ✕ Lazio, C Italy
169 N16 **Cianjur** *prev.* Tjiandjoer. Jawa, C Indonesia
60 H10 **Cianorte** Paraná, S Brazil
Ciarraí *see* Kerry
112 N13 **Ćićevac** Serbia, E Serbia
187 Z14 **Cicia** *prev.* Thithia. *island* Lau Group, E Fiji
105 P4 **Cidacos** ≈ N Spain
136 I10 **Cide** Kastamonu, N Turkey
110 L10 **Ciechanów** *prev.* Zichenau. Mazowieckie, C Poland
110 O10 **Ciechanowiec** *Ger.* Rudelstadt. Podlaskie, E Poland
110 J10 **Ciechocinek** Kujawsko-pomorskie, C Poland
44 F6 **Ciego de Ávila** Ciego de Ávila, C Cuba
54 F4 **Ciénaga** Magdalena, N Colombia
54 E6 **Ciénaga de Oro** Córdoba, NW Colombia
44 E5 **Cienfuegos** Cienfuegos, C Cuba
104 F4 **Cíes, Illas** *island group* NW Spain
111 P16 **Cieszanów** Podkarpackie, SE Poland
111 J17 **Cieszyn** *Cz.* Těšín, *Ger.* Teschen. Śląskie, S Poland
105 R12 **Cieza** Murcia, SE Spain
136 F13 **Çifteler** Eskişehir, W Turkey
105 P7 **Cifuentes** Castilla-La Mancha, C Spain
Čiganak *see* Chiganak
105 P9 **Cigüela** ≈ C Spain
136 H14 **Cihanbeyli** Konya, C Turkey
136 H14 **Cihanbeyli Yaylası** *plateau* C Turkey
104 L10 **Cíjara, Embalse de** ⊠ C Spain
169 P16 **Cikalong** Jawa, S Indonesia
169 N16 **Cikawung** Jawa, S Indonesia
187 Y13 **Cikobia** *prev.* Thikombia. *island* N Fiji
169 P17 **Cilacap** *prev.* Tjilatjap. Jawa, C Indonesia
173 O16 **Cilaos** C Réunion
137 S11 **Çıldır** Ardahan, NE Turkey
137 S11 **Çıldır Gölü** ◎ NE Turkey
160 M10 **Cili** Hunan, S China
Cilician Gates *see* Gülek Boğazı
121 V10 **Cilicia Trough** *undersea feature* E Mediterranean Sea
Cill Airne *see* Killarney
Cill Chainnigh *see* Kilkenny
Cill Chaoi *see* Kilkee
Cill Choca *see* Kilcock
Cill Dara *see* Kildare
105 N3 **Cilleruelo de Bezana** Castilla-León, N Spain
Cilli *see* Celje
Cill Mhantáin *see* Wicklow
Cill Rois *see* Kilrush
146 C11 **Çilmämmetgum** *Rus.* Peski Chil'mamedkum, *Turkm.* Chilmämetgum. *desert* Balkan Welaýaty, W Turkmenistan
137 Z11 **Çiloy Adası** *Rus.* Ostrov Zhiloy. *island* E Azerbaijan
26 J6 **Cimarron** Kansas, C USA
37 T9 **Cimarron** New Mexico, SW USA
26 M9 **Cimarron River** ≈ Kansas/Oklahoma, C USA
117 N11 **Cimişlia** *Rus.* Chimishliya. S Moldova
Cimpia Turzii *see* Câmpia Turzii
Cimpina *see* Câmpina
Cimpulung *see* Câmpulung

◆ Country
● Country Capital
◇ Dependent Territory
○ Dependent Territory Capital
◈ Administrative Regions
✕ International Airport
▲ Mountain
▲▲ Mountain Range
Volcano
≈ River
◎ Lake
⊠ Reservoir

CÎMPULUNG MOLDOVENESC – CONCA

Cîmpulung Moldovenesc *see* Câmpulung Moldovenesc
137 *P15* **Çınar** Dıyarbakır, SE Turkey
54 *J8* **Cinaruco, Río** ≈ Colombia/Venezuela
Cina Selatan, Laut *see* South China Sea
105 *T5* **Cinca** ≈ NE Spain
112 *G13* **Cincar** ▲ SW Bosnia and Herzegovina
31 *Q15* **Cincinnati** Ohio, N USA
21 *M4* **Cincinnati** ✈ Kentucky, S USA
Cinco de Outubro *see* Xá-Muteba
136 *C15* **Çine** Aydın, SW Turkey
99 *J21* **Ciney** Namur, SE Belgium
104 *H6* **Cinfães** Viseu, N Portugal
106 *J12* **Cingoli** Marche, C Italy
41 *U16* **Cintalapa** *var.* Cintalapa de Figueroa. Chiapas, SE Mexico
Cintalapa de Figueroa *see* Cintalapa
103 *X14* **Cinto, Monte** ▲ Corse, France, C Mediterranean Sea
Cintra *see* Sintra
105 *Q5* **Cintruénigo** Navarra, N Spain
Cionn tSáile *see* Kinsale
116 *K13* **Ciorani** Prahova, SE Romania
113 *E14* **Čiovo** *It.* Bua. *island* S Croatia
Cipiúr *see* Kippure
63 *I15* **Cipolletti** Río Negro, C Argentina
120 *L7* **Circeo, Capo** *headland* C Italy
39 *S8* **Circle** *var.* Circle City. Alaska, USA
33 *X8* **Circle** Montana, NW USA
Circle City *see* Circle
31 *S14* **Circleville** Ohio, N USA
36 *K6* **Circleville** Utah, W USA
169 *P16* **Cirebon** *prev.* Tjirebon. Jawa, S Indonesia
97 *L21* **Cirencester** *anc.* Corinium, Corinium Dobunorum. C England, UK
Cirkvenica *see* Crikvenica
107 *O20* **Ciro** Calabria, SW Italy
107 *O20* **Cirò Marina** Calabria, S Italy
102 *K14* **Ciron** ≈ SW France
Cirquenizza *see* Crikvenica
25 *R7* **Cisco** Texas, SW USA
116 *I12* **Cisnădie** *Ger.* Heltau, *Hung.* Nagydisznód. Sibiu, SW Romania
63 *G18* **Cisnes, Río** ≈ S Chile
25 *T11* **Cistern** Texas, SW USA
104 *L3* **Cistierna** Castilla-León, N Spain
Citharista *see* la Ciotat
Citlaltépetl *see* Orizaba, Volcán Pico de
55 *X10* **Citron** NW French Guiana
23 *N7* **Citronelle** Alabama, S USA
35 *O7* **Citrus Heights** California, W USA
106 *H7* **Cittadella** Veneto, NE Italy
106 *H13* **Città della Pieve** Umbria, C Italy
106 *H12* **Città di Castello** Umbria, C Italy
107 *I14* **Cittaducale** Lazio, C Italy
107 *N22* **Cittanova** Calabria, SW Italy
Cittavecchia *see* Stari Grad
116 *G10* **Ciucea** *Hung.* Csucsa. Cluj, NW Romania
116 *M13* **Ciucurova** Tulcea, SE Romania
Ciudad Acuña *see* Villa Acuña
41 *N15* **Ciudad Altamirano** Guerrero, S Mexico
42 *G7* **Ciudad Barrios** San Miguel, NE El Salvador
54 *I7* **Ciudad Bolívar** Barinas, NW Venezuela
55 *N7* **Ciudad Bolívar** *prev.* Angostura. Bolívar, E Venezuela
40 *K6* **Ciudad Camargo** Chihuahua, N Mexico
40 *E8* **Ciudad Constitución** Baja California Sur, W Mexico
Ciudad Cortés *see* Cortés
41 *V17* **Ciudad Cuauhtémoc** Chiapas, SE Mexico
42 *J9* **Ciudad Darío** *var.* Dario. Matagalpa, W Nicaragua
Ciudad de Dolores Hidalgo *see* Dolores Hidalgo
42 *C6* **Ciudad de Guatemala** *Eng.* Guatemala City; *prev.* Santiago de los Caballeros. ● (Guatemala) Guatemala, C Guatemala
Ciudad del Carmen *see* Carmen
62 *Q6* **Ciudad del Este** *prev.* Cuidad Presidente Stroessner, Presidente Stroessner, Puerto Presidente Stroessner. Alto Paraná, SE Paraguay
62 *K5* **Ciudad de Libertador General San Martín** *var.* Libertador General San Martín. Jujuy, C Argentina
Ciudad Delicias *see* Delicias
41 *O11* **Ciudad del Maíz** San Luis Potosí, C Mexico
Ciudad de México *see* México
54 *J7* **Ciudad de Nutrias** Barinas, NW Venezuela
Ciudad de Panama *see* Panamá
55 *P7* **Ciudad Guayana** *prev.* San Tomé de Guayana, Santo Tomé de Guayana. Bolívar, NE Venezuela
40 *K14* **Ciudad Guzmán** Jalisco, SW Mexico
41 *V17* **Ciudad Hidalgo** Chiapas, SE Mexico
41 *N14* **Ciudad Hidalgo** Michoacán de Ocampo, SW Mexico
40 *J3* **Ciudad Juárez** Chihuahua, N Mexico
40 *L8* **Ciudad Lerdo** Durango, C Mexico
41 *Q11* **Ciudad Madero** *var.* Villa Cecilia. Tamaulipas, C Mexico
41 *P11* **Ciudad Mante** Tamaulipas, C Mexico
42 *F2* **Ciudad Melchor de Mencos** *var.* Melchor de Mencos. Petén, NE Guatemala
41 *P8* **Ciudad Miguel Alemán** Tamaulipas, C Mexico
Ciudad Mutis *see* Bahía Solano
40 *G6* **Ciudad Obregón** Sonora, NW Mexico
54 *I5* **Ciudad Ojeda** Zulia, NW Venezuela
55 *P7* **Ciudad Piar** Bolívar, E Venezuela
Ciudad Porfirio Díaz *see* Piedras Negras
Ciudad Quesada *see* Quesada
105 *N11* **Ciudad Real** Castilla-La Mancha, C Spain
105 *N11* **Ciudad Real** ◈ *province* Castilla-La Mancha, C Spain
104 *J7* **Ciudad-Rodrigo** Castilla-León, N Spain
42 *A6* **Ciudad Tecún Umán** San Marcos, SW Guatemala
Ciudad Trujillo *see* Santo Domingo
41 *P12* **Ciudad Valles** San Luis Potosí, C Mexico
41 *O10* **Ciudad Victoria** Tamaulipas, C Mexico
42 *C6* **Ciudad Vieja** Suchitepéquez, S Guatemala
116 *L8* **Ciuhuru** *var.* Reuţel. ≈ N Moldova
105 *Z8* **Ciutadella** *var.* Ciutadella de Menorca. Menorca, Spain, W Mediterranean Sea
Ciutadella Ciutadella de Menorca *see* Ciutadella
136 *L11* **Civa Burnu** *headland* N Turkey
106 *J7* **Cividale del Friuli** Friuli-Venezia Giulia, NE Italy
107 *H14* **Civita Castellana** Lazio, C Italy
106 *J12* **Civitanova Marche** Marche, C Italy
Civitas Altae Ripae *see* Brzeg
Civitas Carnutum *see* Chartres
Civitas Eburovicum *see* Évreux
Civitas Nemetum *see* Speyer
107 *G15* **Civitavecchia** *anc.* Centum Cellae, Trajani Portus. Lazio, C Italy
102 *L10* **Civray** Vienne, W France
136 *E14* **Çivril** Denizli, W Turkey
161 *O5* **Cixian** Hebei, E China
137 *R16* **Cizre** Şırnak, SE Turkey
35 *W16* **Coachella** California, W USA
35 *W16* **Coachella Canal** *canal* California, W USA
40 *I9* **Coacoyole** Durango, C Mexico
25 *N7* **Coahoma** Texas, SW USA
10 *K8* **Coal** ≈ Yukon Territory, NW Canada
40 *L14* **Coalcomán** *var.* Coalcomán de Matamoros. Michoacán de Ocampo, S Mexico
Coalcomán de Matamoros *see* Coalcomán
39 *T8* **Coal Creek** Alaska, USA
9 *Q17* **Coaldale** Alberta, SW Canada
27 *P12* **Coalgate** Oklahoma, C USA
35 *P11* **Coalinga** California, W USA
10 *L9* **Coal River** British Columbia, W Canada
21 *Q6* **Coal River** ≈ West Virginia, NE USA
36 *M2* **Coalville** Utah, W USA
58 *E13* **Coari** Amazonas, N Brazil
104 *I7* **Côa, Rio** ≈ N Portugal
59 *D14* **Coari, Rio** ≈ NW Brazil
81 *J20* **Coast** ◈ *province* SE Kenya
Coast *see* Pwani
10 *G12* **Coast Mountains** *Fr.* Chaîne Côtière. ▲▲ Canada/USA
16 *C7* **Coast Ranges** ▲▲ W USA
96 *I12* **Coatbridge** S Scotland, UK
42 *B6* **Coatepeque** Quezaltenango, SW Guatemala
18 *H16* **Coatesville** Pennsylvania, NE USA
15 *Q13* **Coaticook** Québec, SE Canada
9 *P9* **Coats Island** *island* Nunavut, NE Canada
195 *O4* **Coats Land** *physical region* Antarctica
41 *T14* **Coatzacoalcos** *var.* Quetzalcoalco; *prev.* Puerto México. Veracruz-Llave, E Mexico
41 *S14* **Coatzacoalcos, Río** ≈ SE Mexico
116 *M15* **Cobadin** Constanţa, SW Romania
14 *H9* **Cobalt** Ontario, S Canada
42 *D5* **Cobán** Alta Verapaz, C Guatemala
183 *O6* **Cobar** New South Wales, SE Australia
18 *F12* **Cobb Hill** ▲ Pennsylvania, NE USA
0 *D8* **Cobb Seamount** *undersea feature* E Pacific Ocean
14 *K12* **Cobden** Ontario, SE Canada
97 *D21* **Cobh** *Ir.* An Cóbh; *prev.* Cove of Cork, Queenstown. SW Ireland
57 *J14* **Cobija** Pando, NW Bolivia
Coblence/Coblenz *see* Koblenz
18 *J10* **Cobleskill** New York, NE USA
14 *I15* **Cobourg** Ontario, SE Canada
181 *P1* **Cobourg Peninsula** *headland* Northern Territory, N Australia
183 *O10* **Cobram** Victoria, SE Australia
82 *N13* **Cóbuè** Niassa, N Mozambique
101 *K18* **Coburg** Bayern, SE Germany
19 *Q5* **Coburn Mountain** ▲ Maine, NE USA
Coca *see* Puerto Francisco de Orellana
57 *H18* **Cocachacra** Arequipa, SW Peru
59 *J17* **Cocalinho** Mato Grosso, W Brazil
Cocanada *see* Kākināda
105 *S11* **Cocentaina** País Valenciano, E Spain
57 *L18* **Cochabamba** *hist.* Oropeza. Cochabamba, C Bolivia
57 *K18* **Cochabamba** ◈ *department* C Bolivia
57 *L18* **Cochabamba, Cordillera de** ▲▲ C Bolivia
101 *E18* **Cochem** Rheinland-Pfalz, W Germany
37 *R6* **Cochetopa Hills** ▲▲ Colorado, C USA
155 *G22* **Cochin** *var.* Kochi. Kerala, SW India
44 *D5* **Cochinos, Bahía de** *Eng.* Bay of Pigs. *bay* SE Cuba
37 *O16* **Cochise Head** ▲ Arizona, SW USA
23 *U5* **Cochran** Georgia, SE USA
9 *P16* **Cochrane** Alberta, SW Canada
12 *G12* **Cochrane** Ontario, S Canada
63 *G20* **Cochrane** Aisén, S Chile
9 *U10* **Cochrane** ≈ Manitoba/Saskatchewan, C Canada
Cochrane, Lago *see* Pueyrredón, Lago
Cocibolca *see* Nicaragua, Lago de
Cockade State *see* Maryland
44 *M6* **Cockburn Harbour** South Caicos, S Turks and Caicos Islands
14 *C11* **Cockburn Island** *island* Ontario, S Canada
44 *J3* **Cockburn Town** San Salvador, E Bahamas
21 *X2* **Cockeysville** Maryland, NE USA
181 *N12* **Cocklebiddy** Western Australia
44 *I12* **Cockpit Country, The** *physical region* W Jamaica
43 *S16* **Coclé** *off.* Provincia de Coclé. ◈ *province* C Panama
43 *S15* **Coclé del Norte** Colón, C Panama
Coclé, Provincia de *see* Coclé
23 *Y12* **Cocoa** Florida, SE USA
23 *Y12* **Cocoa Beach** Florida, SE USA
79 *D17* **Cocobeach** Estuaire, NW Gabon
44 *G5* **Coco, Cayo** *island* C Cuba
151 *Q19* **Coco Channel** *strait* Andaman Sea/Bay of Bengal
173 *N6* **Coco-de-Mer Seamounts** *undersea feature* W Indian Ocean
36 *K10* **Coconino Plateau** *plain* Arizona, SW USA
43 *N6* **Coco, Río** *var.* Río Wanki, Segoviao Wangkí. ≈ Honduras/Nicaragua
173 *T7* **Cocos Basin** *undersea feature* E Indian Ocean
188 *B17* **Cocos Island** *island* S Guam
Cocos Island Ridge *see* Cocos Ridge
129 *S17* **Cocos Islands** *island group* E Indian Ocean
173 *T8* **Cocos (Keeling) Islands** ◇ *Australian external territory* E Indian Ocean
0 *G15* **Cocos Plate** *tectonic feature*
193 *T7* **Cocos Ridge** *var.* Cocos Island Ridge. *undersea feature* E Pacific Ocean
40 *K13* **Cocula** Jalisco, SW Mexico
107 *D17* **Coda Cavallo, Capo** *headland* Sardegna, Italy, C Mediterranean Sea
58 *E13* **Codajás** Amazonas, N Brazil
Codazzi *see* Agustín Codazzi
19 *Q12* **Cod, Cape** *headland* Massachusetts, NE USA
185 *B25* **Codfish Island** *island* SW New Zealand
106 *H9* **Codigoro** Emilia-Romagna, N Italy
13 *P5* **Cod Island** *island* Newfoundland and Labrador, E Canada
116 *J12* **Codlea** *Ger.* Zeiden, *Hung.* Feketehalom. Braşov, C Romania
58 *M13* **Codó** Maranhão, E Brazil
106 *E8* **Codogno** Lombardia, N Italy
116 *M10* **Codrii** *hill range* C Moldova
45 *W9* **Codrington** Barbuda, Antigua and Barbuda
106 *J7* **Codroipo** Friuli-Venezia Giulia, NE Italy
28 *M12* **Cody** Nebraska, C USA
33 *U12* **Cody** Wyoming, C USA
21 *P7* **Coeburn** Virginia, NE USA
54 *E10* **Coello** Tolima, W Colombia
Coemba *see* Cuemba
181 *V2* **Coen** Queensland, NE Australia
101 *E14* **Coesfeld** Nordrhein-Westfalen, W Germany
32 *M8* **Coeur d'Alene** Idaho, NW USA
32 *M8* **Coeur d'Alene Lake** ⊠ Idaho, NW USA
98 *O8* **Coevorden** Drenthe, NE Netherlands
10 *H6* **Coffee Creek** Yukon Territory, W Canada
30 *L15* **Coffeen Lake** ⊠ Illinois, N USA
22 *L3* **Coffeeville** Mississippi, S USA
27 *Q8* **Coffeyville** Kansas, C USA
182 *G9* **Coffin Bay** South Australia
182 *F9* **Coffin Bay Peninsula** *peninsula* South Australia
183 *V5* **Coffs Harbour** New South Wales, SE Australia
105 *R10* **Cofrentes** País Valenciano, E Spain
Cogîlnic *see* Kohyl'nyk
102 *K11* **Cognac** *anc.* Compniacum. Charente, W France
106 *B7* **Cogne** Valle d'Aosta, NW Italy
103 *U16* **Cogolin** Var, SE France
105 *O7* **Cogolludo** Castilla-La Mancha, C Spain
Cohalm *see* Rupea
92 *K8* **Čohkarášša** *var.* Cuokkarašša. ▲ N Norway
Čohkkiras *see* Jukkasjärvi
18 *F11* **Cohocton River** ≈ New York, NE USA
18 *L10* **Cohoes** New York, NE USA
183 *N10* **Cohuna** Victoria, SE Australia
43 *P17* **Coiba, Isla de** *island* SW Panama
63 *H23* **Coig, Río** ≈ S Argentina
63 *G19* **Coihaique** *var.* Coyhaique. Aisén, S Chile
155 *G21* **Coimbatore** Tamil Nādu, S India
104 *G8* **Coimbra** *anc.* Conimbria, Conimbriga. Coimbra, W Portugal
104 *G8* **Coimbra** ◈ *district* N Portugal
104 *L15* **Coín** Andalucía, S Spain
57 *J20* **Coipasa, Laguna** ◎ W Bolivia
57 *J20* **Coipasa, Salar de** *salt lake* W Bolivia
Coira/Coire *see* Chur
Coirib, Loch *see* Corrib, Lough
54 *K6* **Cojedes** *off.* Estado Cojedes. ◈ *state* N Venezuela
Cojedes, Estado *see* Cojedes
42 *F7* **Cojutepeque** Cuscatlán, C El Salvador
Coka *see* Banbar
33 *S16* **Cokeville** Wyoming, C USA
182 *M13* **Colac** Victoria, SE Australia
59 *O20* **Colatina** Espírito Santo, SE Brazil
27 *O13* **Colbert** Oklahoma, C USA
100 *L12* **Colbitz-Letzinger Heide** *heathland* N Germany
26 *I3* **Colby** Kansas, C USA
57 *H17* **Colca, Río** ≈ SW Peru
97 *P21* **Colchester** *hist.* Colneceaste; *anc.* Camulodunum. E England, UK
19 *N13* **Colchester** Connecticut, NE USA
38 *M16* **Cold Bay** Alaska, USA
9 *R14* **Cold Lake** Alberta, SW Canada
9 *R13* **Cold Lake** ◎ Alberta/Saskatchewan, S Canada
29 *U8* **Cold Spring** Minnesota, N USA
25 *W10* **Coldspring** Texas, SW USA
9 *N17* **Coldstream** British Columbia, SW Canada
96 *L13* **Coldstream** SE Scotland, UK
14 *H13* **Coldwater** Ontario, S Canada
26 *K7* **Coldwater** Kansas, C USA
31 *Q10* **Coldwater** Michigan, N USA
25 *N1* **Coldwater Creek** ≈ Oklahoma/Texas, SW USA
22 *K2* **Coldwater River** ≈ Mississippi, S USA
183 *O9* **Coleambally** New South Wales, SE Australia
19 *O6* **Colebrook** New Hampshire, NE USA
27 *T5* **Cole Camp** Missouri, C USA
39 *T6* **Coleen River** ≈ Alaska, USA
9 *P17* **Coleman** Alberta, SW Canada
25 *Q8* **Coleman** Texas, SW USA
Çölemerik *see* Hakkâri
83 *K22* **Colenso** KwaZulu/Natal, E South Africa
182 *L12* **Coleraine** Victoria, SE Australia
97 *F14* **Coleraine** *Ir.* Cúil Raithin. N Northern Ireland, UK
185 *G18* **Coleridge, Lake** ◎ South Island, New Zealand
83 *H24* **Colesberg** Northern Cape, C South Africa
22 *H7* **Colfax** Louisiana, S USA
32 *L9* **Colfax** Washington, NW USA
30 *J6* **Colfax** Wisconsin, N USA
63 *I19* **Colhué Huapí, Lago** ◎ S Argentina
45 *Z6* **Colibris, Pointe des** *headland* Grande Terre, E Guadeloupe
106 *D6* **Colico** Lombardia, N Italy
99 *E14* **Colijnsplaat** Zeeland, SW Netherlands
40 *L14* **Colima** Colima, S Mexico
40 *K14* **Colima** ◈ *state* SW Mexico
40 *L14* **Colima, Nevado de** ⟁ C Mexico
59 *M14* **Colinas** Maranhão, E Brazil
96 *F10* **Coll** *island* W Scotland, UK
105 *N7* **Collado Villalba** *var.* Villalba. Madrid, C Spain
183 *R4* **Collarenebri** New South Wales, SE Australia
37 *P5* **Collbran** Colorado, C USA
106 *G12* **Colle di Val d'Elsa** Toscana, C Italy
39 *R9* **College** Alaska, USA
32 *K10* **College Place** Washington, NW USA
25 *U10* **College Station** Texas, SW USA
183 *P4* **Collerina** New South Wales, SE Australia
180 *I13* **Collie** Western Australia
180 *L4* **Collier Bay** *bay* Western Australia
21 *F10* **Collierville** Tennessee, S USA
106 *F11* **Collina, Passo della** *pass* C Italy
14 *G14* **Collingwood** Ontario, S Canada
184 *I13* **Collingwood** Tasman, South Island, New Zealand
22 *L7* **Collins** Mississippi, S USA
30 *K15* **Collinsville** Illinois, N USA
27 *P9* **Collinsville** Oklahoma, C USA
20 *H10* **Collinwood** Tennessee, S USA
Collipo *see* Leiria
63 *G14* **Collipulli** Araucanía, C Chile
97 *D16* **Collooney** *Ir.* Cúil Mhuine. NW Ireland
29 *R10* **Colman** South Dakota, N USA
103 *U6* **Colmar** *Ger.* Kolmar. Haut-Rhin, NE France
104 *M15* **Colmenar** Andalucía, S Spain
Colmenar *see* Colmenar de Oreja
105 *O9* **Colmenar de Oreja** *var.* Colmenar. Madrid, C Spain
105 *N7* **Colmenar Viejo** Madrid, C Spain
25 *X9* **Colmesneil** Texas, SW USA
Cöln *see* Köln
Colneceaste *see* Colchester
40 *C3* **Colnet** Baja California, NW Mexico
59 *G15* **Colniza** Mato Grosso, W Brazil
Cologne *see* Köln
42 *B6* **Colomba** Quezaltenango, SW Guatemala
Colomb-Béchar *see* Béchar
54 *E11* **Colombia** Huila, C Colombia
54 *G10* **Colombia** *off.* Republic of Colombia. ◆ *republic* N South America
64 *E12* **Colombian Basin** *undersea feature* SW Caribbean Sea
Colombia, Republic of *see* Colombia
Colombie-Britannique *see* British Columbia
15 *T6* **Colombier** Québec, SE Canada
155 *J25* **Colombo** ● (Sri Lanka) Western Province, W Sri Lanka
155 *J25* **Colombo** ✈ Western Province, SW Sri Lanka
29 *N11* **Colome** South Dakota, N USA
61 *B19* **Colón** Buenos Aires, E Argentina
61 *D18* **Colon** Entre Ríos, E Argentina
44 *D5* **Colón** Matanzas, C Cuba
43 *T14* **Colón** *prev.* Aspinwall. Colón, C Panama
42 *K5* **Colón** ◈ *department* NE Honduras
43 *S15* **Colón** *off.* Provincia de Colón. ◈ *province* N Panama
57 *A16* **Colón, Archipiélago de** *var.* Islas de los Galápagos, *Eng.* Galapagos Islands, Tortoise Islands. *island group* Ecuador, E Pacific Ocean
44 *K5* **Colonel Hill** Crooked Island, SE Bahamas
40 *B3* **Colonett, Cabo** *headland* NW Mexico
188 *G14* **Colonia** Yap, W Micronesia
61 *D19* **Colonia** ◈ *department* SW Uruguay
Colonia *see* Kolonia, Micronesia
Colonia *see* Colonia del Sacramento, Uruguay
Colonia Agrippina *see* Köln
61 *D20* **Colonia del Sacramento** *var.* Colonia. Colonia, SW Uruguay
62 *L8* **Colonia Dora** Santiago del Estero, N Argentina
Colonia Julia Fanestris *see* Fano
21 *W5* **Colonial Beach** Virginia, NE USA
21 *V6* **Colonial Heights** Virginia, NE USA
Colón, Provincia de *see* Colón
193 *S7* **Colón Ridge** *undersea feature* E Pacific Ocean
96 *F12* **Colonsay** *island* W Scotland, UK
57 *K22* **Colorada, Laguna** ◎ SW Bolivia
37 *R6* **Colorado** *off.* State of Colorado, *also known as* Centennial State, Silver State. ◈ *state* C USA
63 *H22* **Colorado, Cerro** ▲ S Argentina
25 *O7* **Colorado City** Texas, SW USA
36 *M7* **Colorado Plateau** *plateau* W USA
61 *A24* **Colorado, Río** ≈ E Argentina
43 *N12* **Colorado, Río** ≈ NE Costa Rica
Colorado, Río *see* Colorado River
16 *F12* **Colorado River** *var.* Río Colorado. ≈ Mexico/USA
16 *K14* **Colorado River** ≈ Texas, SW USA
35 *W15* **Colorado River Aqueduct** *aqueduct* California, W USA
44 *A4* **Colorados, Archipiélago de los** *island group* NW Cuba
62 *J9* **Colorados, Desagües de los** ◎ W Argentina
37 *T5* **Colorado Springs** Colorado, C USA
40 *L11* **Colotlán** Jalisco, SW Mexico
57 *L19* **Colquechaca** Potosí, C Bolivia
23 *S7* **Colquitt** Georgia, SE USA
29 *R11* **Colton** South Dakota, N USA
32 *M10* **Colton** Washington, NW USA
35 *P8* **Columbia** California, W USA
30 *K16* **Columbia** Illinois, N USA
20 *L7* **Columbia** Kentucky, S USA
22 *I6* **Columbia** Louisiana, S USA
21 *W3* **Columbia** Maryland, NE USA
22 *L7* **Columbia** Mississippi, S USA
27 *U4* **Columbia** Missouri, C USA
21 *Y9* **Columbia** North Carolina, SE USA
18 *G16* **Columbia** Pennsylvania, NE USA
21 *Q12* **Columbia** *state capital* South Carolina, SE USA
20 *I9* **Columbia** Tennessee, S USA
0 *F9* **Columbia** ≈ Canada/USA
32 *K9* **Columbia Basin** *basin* Washington, NW USA
197 *Q10* **Columbia, Cape** *headland* Ellesmere Island, Nunavut, NE Canada
31 *Q12* **Columbia City** Indiana, N USA
21 *W3* **Columbia, District of** ◈ *federal district* NE USA
33 *P7* **Columbia Falls** Montana, NW USA
9 *O15* **Columbia Icefield** *ice field* Alberta/British Columbia, S Canada
9 *O15* **Columbia, Mount** ▲ Alberta/British Columbia, SW Canada
9 *N15* **Columbia Mountains** ▲▲ British Columbia, SW Canada
23 *P4* **Columbiana** Alabama, S USA
31 *V12* **Columbiana** Ohio, N USA
32 *M14* **Columbia Plateau** *plateau* Idaho/Oregon, NW USA
29 *P7* **Columbia Road Reservoir** ⊠ South Dakota, N USA
65 *K16* **Columbia Seamount** *undersea feature* C Atlantic Ocean
83 *D25* **Columbine, Cape** *headland* SW South Africa
105 *U9* **Columbretes, Islas** *island group* E Spain
23 *R5* **Columbus** Georgia, SE USA
31 *P14* **Columbus** Indiana, N USA
27 *R7* **Columbus** Kansas, C USA
23 *N4* **Columbus** Mississippi, S USA
33 *U11* **Columbus** Montana, NW USA
29 *Q15* **Columbus** Nebraska, C USA
37 *Q16* **Columbus** New Mexico, SW USA
21 *P10* **Columbus** North Carolina, SE USA
28 *K2* **Columbus** North Dakota, N USA
31 *S13* **Columbus** *state capital* Ohio, N USA
25 *U11* **Columbus** Texas, SW USA
30 *L8* **Columbus** Wisconsin, N USA
31 *R12* **Columbus Grove** Ohio, N USA
29 *Y15* **Columbus Junction** Iowa, C USA
44 *J3* **Columbus Point** *headland* Cat Island, C Bahamas
35 *T8* **Columbus Salt Marsh** *salt marsh* Nevada, W USA
35 *N6* **Colusa** California, W USA
32 *L7* **Colville** Washington, NW USA
184 *M5* **Colville, Cape** *headland* North Island, New Zealand
184 *M5* **Colville Channel** *channel* North Island, New Zealand
39 *P6* **Colville River** ≈ Alaska, USA
97 *J18* **Colwyn Bay** N Wales, UK
106 *H9* **Comacchio** *var.* Commachio; *anc.* Comactium. Emilia-Romagna, N Italy
106 *H9* **Comacchio, Valli di** *lagoon* Adriatic Sea, N Mediterranean Sea
Comactium *see* Comacchio
41 *V17* **Comalapa** Chiapas, SE Mexico
41 *U15* **Comalcalco** Tabasco, SE Mexico
63 *H16* **Comallo** Río Negro, SW Argentina
26 *M12* **Comanche** Oklahoma, C USA
25 *R8* **Comanche** Texas, SW USA
194 *H2* **Comandante Ferraz** *Brazilian research station* Antarctica
62 *N6* **Comandante Fontana** Formosa, N Argentina
63 *I22* **Comandante Luis Peidra Buena** Santa Cruz, S Argentina
59 *O18* **Comandatuba** Bahia, SE Brazil
116 *K11* **Comăneşti** *Hung.* Kománfalva. Bacău, SW Romania
57 *M19* **Comarapa** Santa Cruz, C Bolivia
116 *J13* **Comarnic** Prahova, SE Romania
42 *H6* **Comayagua** Comayagua, W Honduras
42 *H6* **Comayagua** ◈ *department* W Honduras
42 *I6* **Comayagua, Montañas de** ▲▲ C Honduras
21 *R15* **Combahee River** ≈ South Carolina, SE USA
62 *G10* **Combarbalá** Coquimbo, C Chile
103 *S7* **Combeaufontaine** Haute-Saône, E France
97 *G15* **Comber** *Ir.* An Comar. E Northern Ireland, UK
99 *K20* **Comblain-au-Pont** Liège, E Belgium
102 *I6* **Combourg** Ille-et-Vilaine, NW France
44 *M9* **Comendador** *prev.* Elías Piña. W Dominican Republic
Comer See *see* Como, Lago di
25 *R11* **Comfort** Texas, SW USA
153 *V15* **Comilla** *Ben.* Kumillā. Chittagong, E Bangladesh
99 *B18* **Comines** Hainaut, W Belgium
121 *O15* **Comino** *Malt.* Kemmuna. *island* C Malta
107 *D18* **Comino, Capo** *headland* Sardegna, Italy, C Mediterranean Sea
107 *K25* **Comiso** Sicilia, Italy, C Mediterranean Sea
41 *V16* **Comitán** *var.* Comitán de Domínguez. Chiapas, SE Mexico
Comitán de Domínguez *see* Comitán
Commachio *see* Comacchio
Commander Islands *see* Komandorskiye Ostrova
103 *O10* **Commentry** Allier, C France
23 *T2* **Commerce** Georgia, SE USA
27 *R8* **Commerce** Oklahoma, C USA
25 *V5* **Commerce** Texas, SW USA
37 *T4* **Commerce City** Colorado, C USA
103 *S5* **Commercy** Meuse, NE France
55 *W9* **Commewijne** *var.* Commewyne. ◈ *district* NE Surinam
Commewyne *see* Commewijne
15 *P8* **Commissaires, Lac des** ◎ Québec, SE Canada
64 *A12* **Commissioner's Point** *headland* W Bermuda
9 *O7* **Committee Bay** *bay* Nunavut, N Canada
106 *D7* **Como** *anc.* Comum. Lombardia, N Italy
63 *J19* **Comodoro Rivadavia** Chubut, SE Argentina
106 *D6* **Como, Lago di** *var.* Lario, *Eng.* Lake Como, *Ger.* Comer See. ◎ N Italy
Como, Lake *see* Como, Lago di
40 *E7* **Comondú** Baja California Sur, W Mexico
116 *F12* **Comorâşte** *Hung.* Komornok. Caraş-Severin, SW Romania
Comores, République Fédérale Islamique des *see* Comoros
155 *G24* **Comorin, Cape** *headland* SE India
172 *M8* **Comoro Basin** *undersea feature* SW Indian Ocean
172 *K14* **Comoro Islands** *island group* W Indian Ocean
172 *H13* **Comoros** *off.* Federal Islamic Republic of the Comoros, *Fr.* République Fédérale Islamique des Comores. ◆ *republic* W Indian Ocean
Comoros, Federal Islamic Republic of the *see* Comoros
10 *L17* **Comox** Vancouver Island, British Columbia, SW Canada
103 *O4* **Compiègne** Oise, N France
Complutum *see* Alcalá de Henares
Compniacum *see* Cognac
40 *K12* **Compostela** Nayarit, C Mexico
Compostella *see* Santiago
60 *L11* **Comprida, Ilha** *island* S Brazil
117 *N11* **Comrat** *Rus.* Komrat. S Moldova
25 *O11* **Comstock** Texas, SW USA
31 *P9* **Comstock Park** Michigan, N USA
193 *N3* **Comstock Seamount** *undersea feature* N Pacific Ocean
Comum *see* Como
159 *N17* **Cona** Xizang Zizhiqu, W China
76 *H14* **Conakry** ● (Guinea) SW Guinea
76 *H14* **Conakry** ✈ SW Guinea
Conamara *see* Connemara
Conca *see* Cuenca

◆ Country
● Country Capital
◇ Dependent Territory
○ Dependent Territory Capital
◈ Administrative Regions
✈ International Airport
▲ Mountain
▲▲ Mountain Range
⟁ Volcano
≈ River
◎ Lake
⊠ Reservoir

CONCAN – COWANSVILLE

25 Q12 **Concan** Texas, SW USA
102 F6 **Concarneau** Finistère, NW France
83 O17 **Conceição** Sofala, C Mozambique
59 K15 **Conceição do Araguaia** Pará, NE Brazil
58 F10 **Conceição do Maú** Roraima, W Brazil
61 D14 **Concepción** *var.* Concepcion. Corrientes, NE Argentina
62 J8 **Concepción** Tucumán, N Argentina
57 O17 **Concepción** Santa Cruz, E Bolivia
62 G13 **Concepción** Bío Bío, C Chile
54 E14 **Concepción** Putumayo, S Colombia
62 O5 **Concepción** *var.* Villa Concepción. Concepción, C Paraguay
62 O5 **Concepción** *off.* Departamento de Concepción. ◈ *department* E Paraguay
Concepción *see* La Concepción
Concepción de la Vega *see* La Vega
41 N9 **Concepción del Oro** Zacatecas, C Mexico
61 D18 **Concepción del Uruguay** Entre Ríos, E Argentina
Concepción, Departamento de *see* Concepción
42 K11 **Concepción, Volcán** ⛰ SW Nicaragua
44 J4 **Conception Island** *island* C Bahamas
35 P14 **Conception, Point** *headland* California, W USA
54 H6 **Concha** Zulia, W Venezuela
60 L9 **Conchas** São Paulo, S Brazil
37 U11 **Conchas Dam** New Mexico, SW USA
37 U10 **Conchas Lake** ⊠ New Mexico, SW USA
102 M5 **Conches-en-Ouche** Eure, N France
37 N12 **Concho** Arizona, SW USA
40 J5 **Conchos, Río** ≈ NW Mexico
41 O8 **Conchos, Río** ≈ C Mexico
108 C8 **Concise** Vaud, W Switzerland
35 N8 **Concord** California, W USA
19 O9 **Concord** *state capital* New Hampshire, NE USA
21 R10 **Concord** North Carolina, SE USA
61 D17 **Concordia** Entre Ríos, E Argentina
60 I13 **Concórdia** Santa Catarina, S Brazil
54 D9 **Concordia** Antioquia, W Colombia
40 J10 **Concordia** Sinaloa, C Mexico
57 I19 **Concordia** Tacna, SW Peru
27 N3 **Concordia** Kansas, C USA
27 S4 **Concordia** Missouri, C USA
167 S7 **Con Cuông** Nghê An, N Vietnam
167 T15 **Côn Đao** *var.* Con Son. *island* S Vietnam
Condate *see* Rennes, Ille-et-Vilaine, France
Condate *see* St-Claude, Jura, France
Condate *see* Montereau-Faut-Yonne, Seine-St-Denis, France
29 P8 **Conde** South Dakota, N USA
42 J8 **Condega** Estelí, NW Nicaragua
103 P2 **Condé-sur-l'Escaut** Nord, N France
102 K5 **Condé-sur-Noireau** Calvados, N France
Condivincum *see* Nantes
183 P8 **Condobolin** New South Wales, SE Australia
102 L15 **Condom** Gers, S France
32 J11 **Condon** Oregon, NW USA
54 D9 **Condoto** Chocó, W Colombia
23 P7 **Conecuh River** ≈ Alabama/Florida, SE USA
106 H7 **Conegliano** Veneto, NE Italy
61 C19 **Conesa** Buenos Aires, E Argentina
14 F15 **Conestogo** ≈ Ontario, S Canada
Confluentes *see* Koblenz
102 L10 **Confolens** Charente, W France
36 J4 **Confusion Range** ▲▲ Utah, W USA
62 N6 **Confuso, Río** ≈ C Paraguay
21 R12 **Congaree River** ≈ South Carolina, SE USA
Công Hoa Xa Hôi Chu Nghia Viêt Nam *see* Vietnam
160 K12 **Congjiang** *var.* Bingmei. Guizhou, S China
79 G18 **Congo** *off.* Republic of the Congo, *Fr.* Moyen-Congo; *prev.* Middle Congo. ◆ *republic* C Africa
79 K19 **Congo** *off.* Democratic Republic of Congo; *prev.* Zaire, Belgian Congo, Congo (Kinshasa). ◆ *republic* C Africa
67 T11 **Congo** *var.* Kongo, *Fr.* Zaire. ≈ C Africa
Congo *see* Zaire (province) Angola
68 G12 **Congo Basin** *drainage basin* W Dem. Rep. Congo
67 Q11 **Congo Canyon** *var.* Congo Seavalley, Congo Submarine Canyon. *undersea feature* E Atlantic Ocean
Congo Cone *see* Congo Fan
Congo/Congo (Kinshasa) *see* Congo (Democratic Republic of)
65 P15 **Congo Fan** *var.* Congo Cone. *undersea feature* E Atlantic Ocean
Congo Seavalley *see* Congo Canyon
Congo Submarine Canyon *see* Congo Canyon
Coni *see* Cuneo
63 H18 **Cónico, Cerro** ▲ SW Argentina
Conimbria/Conimbriga *see* Coimbra
Conjeeveram *see* Kānchīpuram
9 R13 **Conklin** Alberta, C Canada
24 M1 **Conlen** Texas, SW USA
Con, Loch *see* Conn, Lough
Connacht *see* Connaught
97 B17 **Connaught** *var.* Connacht, *Ir.* Chonnacht, Cúige. *province* W Ireland
31 V10 **Conneaut** Ohio, N USA
18 L13 **Connecticut** *off.* State of Connecticut, *also known as* Blue Law State, Constitution State, Land of Steady Habits, Nutmeg State. ◈ *state* NE USA
19 N8 **Connecticut** ≈ Canada/USA
19 O6 **Connecticut Lakes** *lakes* New Hampshire, NE USA
32 K9 **Connell** Washington, NW USA
97 B17 **Connemara** *Ir.* Conamara. *physical region* W Ireland
31 Q14 **Connersville** Indiana, N USA
97 B16 **Conn, Lough** *Ir.* Loch Con. ◎ W Ireland
35 X6 **Connors Pass** *pass* Nevada, W USA
181 X7 **Connors Range** ▲▲ Queensland, E Australia
56 E7 **Cononaco, Río** ≈ E Ecuador
29 W13 **Conrad** Iowa, C USA
33 R7 **Conrad** Montana, NW USA
25 W10 **Conroe** Texas, SW USA
25 V10 **Conroe, Lake** ⊠ Texas, SW USA
61 C17 **Conscripto Bernardi** Entre Ríos, E Argentina
59 M20 **Conselheiro Lafaiete** Minas Gerais, SE Brazil
Consentia *see* Cosenza
97 L14 **Consett** N England, UK
44 B5 **Consolación del Sur** Pinar del Río, W Cuba
Con Son *see* Côn Đao
9 R15 **Consort** Alberta, SW Canada
Constance *see* Konstanz
108 I6 **Constance, Lake** *Ger.* Bodensee. ◎ C Europe
104 G9 **Constância** Santarém, C Portugal
117 N14 **Constanța** *var.* Küstendje, *Eng.* Constanza, *Ger.* Konstanza, *Turk.* Küstence. Constanța, SE Romania
116 L14 **Constanța** ◈ *county* SE Romania
Constantia *see* Coutances
Constantia *see* Konstanz
104 K13 **Constantina** Andalucía, S Spain
74 L5 **Constantine** *var.* Qacentina, *Ar.* Qoussantina. NE Algeria
39 O14 **Constantine, Cape** *headland* Alaska, USA
Constantinople *see* İstanbul
Constantiola *see* Oltenișa
Constanz *see* Konstanz
Constanza *see* Constanța
62 G13 **Constitución** Maule, C Chile
61 D17 **Constitución** Salto, N Uruguay
Constitution State *see* Connecticut
105 N10 **Consuegra** Castilla-La Mancha, C Spain
181 X9 **Consuelo Peak** ▲ Queensland, E Australia
56 E11 **Contamana** Loreto, N Peru
Contrasto, Colle del *see* Contrasto, Portella del
107 K23 **Contrasto, Portella del** *var.* Colle del Contrasto. *pass* Sicilia, Italy, C Mediterranean Sea
54 G8 **Contratación** Santander, C Colombia
102 M8 **Contres** Loir-et-Cher, C France
107 O17 **Conversano** Puglia, SE Italy
27 U11 **Conway** Arkansas, C USA
19 O8 **Conway** New Hampshire, NE USA
21 U13 **Conway** South Carolina, SE USA
25 N2 **Conway** Texas, SW USA
27 U11 **Conway, Lake** ⊠ Arkansas, C USA
27 N7 **Conway Springs** Kansas, C USA
97 J18 **Conwy** N Wales, UK
23 T3 **Conyers** Georgia, SE USA
Coo *see* Kos
182 F4 **Coober Pedy** South Australia
182 P2 **Cooinda** Northern Territory, N Australia
182 B6 **Cook** South Australia
29 W4 **Cook** Minnesota, N USA
191 N6 **Cook, Baie de** *bay* Moorea, W French Polynesia
10 J16 **Cook, Cape** *headland* Vancouver Island, British Columbia, SW Canada
37 Q15 **Cookes Peak** ▲ New Mexico, SW USA
20 L8 **Cookeville** Tennessee, S USA
175 P9 **Cook Fracture Zone** *tectonic feature* S Pacific Ocean
Cook, Grand Récif de *see* Cook, Récif de
39 Q12 **Cook Inlet** *inlet* Alaska, USA
191 X2 **Cook Island** *island* Line Islands, E Kiribati
190 J14 **Cook Islands** ◇ *territory in free association with New Zealand* S Pacific Ocean
Mount Cook *see* Aoraki
187 O15 **Cook, Récif de** *var.* Grand Récif de Cook. *reef* S New Caledonia
14 G14 **Cookstown** Ontario, S Canada
97 F15 **Cookstown** *Ir.* An Chorr Chríochach. C Northern Ireland, UK
185 K14 **Cook Strait** *var.* Raukawa. *strait* New Zealand
181 W3 **Cooktown** Queensland, NE Australia
183 P6 **Coolabah** New South Wales, SE Australia
182 J11 **Coola Coola Swamp** *wetland* South Australia
183 S7 **Coolah** New South Wales, SE Australia
183 P9 **Coolamon** New South Wales, SE Australia
183 T4 **Coolatai** New South Wales, SE Australia
180 K12 **Coolgardie** Western Australia
36 L14 **Coolidge** Arizona, SW USA
25 U8 **Coolidge** Texas, SW USA
183 Q11 **Cooma** New South Wales, SE Australia
Coomassie *see* Kumasi
183 R6 **Coonabarabran** New South Wales, SE Australia
182 J10 **Coonalpyn** South Australia
183 R6 **Coonamble** New South Wales, SE Australia
Coondapoor *see* Kundāpura
155 G21 **Coonoor** Tamil Nādu, SE India
29 U14 **Coon Rapids** Iowa, C USA
29 V8 **Coon Rapids** Minnesota, N USA
25 V5 **Cooper** Texas, SW USA
181 U9 **Cooper Creek** *var.* Barcoo, Cooper's Creek. *seasonal river* Queensland/South Australia
39 R12 **Cooper Landing** Alaska, USA
21 T14 **Cooper River** ≈ South Carolina, SE USA
Cooper's Creek *see* Cooper Creek
44 H1 **Coopers Town** Great Abaco, N Bahamas
18 J10 **Cooperstown** New York, NE USA
29 P4 **Cooperstown** North Dakota, N USA
31 P9 **Coopersville** Michigan, N USA
182 D7 **Coorabie** South Australia
23 Q3 **Coosa River** ≈ Alabama/Georgia, S USA
32 E14 **Coos Bay** Oregon, NW USA
183 Q9 **Cootamundra** New South Wales, SE Australia
97 E16 **Cootehill** *Ir.* Muinchille. N Ireland
Čop *see* Chop
57 J17 **Copacabana** La Paz, W Bolivia
63 H14 **Copahué, Volcán** ⛰ C Chile
41 U16 **Copainalá** Chiapas, SE Mexico
32 F8 **Copalis Beach** Washington, NW USA
42 F6 **Copán** ◈ *department* W Honduras
Copán *see* Copán Ruinas
25 T14 **Copano Bay** *bay* NW Gulf of Mexico
42 F6 **Copán Ruinas** *var.* Copán. Copán, W Honduras
Copenhagen *see* København
107 Q19 **Copertino** Puglia, SE Italy
62 H7 **Copiapó** Atacama, N Chile
62 G8 **Copiapó, Bahía** *bay* N Chile
62 G7 **Copiapó, Río** ≈ N Chile
114 M12 **Çöpköy** Edirne, NW Turkey
182 I5 **Copley** South Australia
106 H9 **Copparo** Emilia-Romagna, C Italy
55 V10 **Coppename Rivier** *var.* Koppename. ≈ C Surinam
25 S9 **Copperas Cove** Texas, SW USA
82 J13 **Copperbelt** ◈ *province* C Zambia
39 S11 **Copper Center** Alaska, USA
8 K8 **Coppermine** ≈ Northwest Territories/Nunavut, N Canada
Coppermine *see* Kugluktuk
39 T11 **Copper River** ≈ Alaska, USA
Copper State *see* Arizona
116 I11 **Copșa Mică** *Ger.* Kleinkopisch, *Hung.* Kiskapus. Sibiu, C Romania
158 J14 **Coqên** Xizang Zizhiqu, W China
Coquilhatville *see* Mbandaka
32 E14 **Coquille** Oregon, NW USA
62 G9 **Coquimbo** Coquimbo, N Chile
62 G9 **Coquimbo** *off.* Región de Coquimbo. ◈ *region* C Chile
Coquimbo, Región de *see* Coquimbo
116 I15 **Corabia** Olt, S Romania
57 F17 **Coracora** Ayacucho, SW Peru
Cora Droma Rúisc *see* Carrick-on-Shannon
44 K9 **Corail** SW Haiti
183 V4 **Coraki** New South Wales, SE Australia
180 G8 **Coral Bay** Western Australia
23 Y16 **Coral Gables** Florida, SE USA
9 P8 **Coral Harbour** Southampton Island, Northwest Territories, NE Canada
192 I9 **Coral Sea** *sea* SW Pacific Ocean
174 M7 **Coral Sea Basin** *undersea feature* N Coral Sea
192 H9 **Coral Sea Islands** ◇ *Australian external territory* SW Pacific Ocean
182 M12 **Corangamite, Lake** ◎ Victoria, SE Australia
Corantijn Rivier *see* Courantyne River
18 B14 **Coraopolis** Pennsylvania, NE USA
107 N17 **Corato** Puglia, SE Italy
103 O17 **Corbières** ▲▲ S France
103 P8 **Corbigny** Nièvre, C France
21 N7 **Corbin** Kentucky, S USA
104 L14 **Corbones** ≈ SW Spain
Corcaigh *see* Cork
35 R11 **Corcoran** California, W USA
47 T14 **Corcovado, Golfo** *gulf* S Chile
63 G18 **Corcovado, Volcán** ⛰ S Chile
104 F3 **Corcubión** Galicia, NW Spain
Corcyra Nigra *see* Korčula
60 Q9 **Cordeiro** Rio de Janeiro, SE Brazil
23 T6 **Cordele** Georgia, SE USA
26 L11 **Cordell** Oklahoma, C USA
103 N14 **Cordes** Tarn, S France
62 O6 **Cordillera** *off.* Departamento de la Cordillera. ◈ *department* C Paraguay
Cordillera *see* Cacaguatique, Cordillera
Cordillera, Departamento de la *see* Cordillera
182 K1 **Cordillo Downs** South Australia
62 K10 **Córdoba** Córdoba, C Argentina
41 R14 **Córdoba** Veracruz-Llave, E Mexico
104 M13 **Córdoba** *var.* Cordoba, *Eng.* Cordova; *anc.* Corduba. Andalucía, SW Spain
62 K11 **Córdoba** *off.* Provincia de Córdoba. ◈ *province* C Argentina
54 D7 **Córdoba** *off.* Departamento de Córdoba. ◈ *province* NW Colombia
104 L13 **Córdoba** ◈ *province* Andalucía, S Spain
Córdoba, Departamento de *see* Córdoba
Córdoba, Provincia de *see* Córdoba
62 K10 **Córdoba, Sierras de** ▲▲ C Argentina
23 O3 **Cordova** Alabama, S USA
39 S12 **Cordova** Alaska, USA
Cordova/Cordoba *see* Córdoba
Corduba *see* Córdoba
Corentyne River *see* Courantyne River
Corfu *see* Kérkyra
104 J9 **Coria** Extremadura, W Spain
104 J14 **Coria del Río** Andalucía, S Spain
183 S8 **Coricudgy, Mount** ▲ New South Wales, SE Australia
107 N20 **Corigliano Calabro** Calabria, SW Italy
Corinium/Corinium Dobunorum *see* Cirencester
23 N1 **Corinth** Mississippi, S USA
Corinth *see* Kórinthos
Corinth Canal *see* Dióryga Korinthou
Corinth, Gulf of/Corinthiacus Sinus *see* Korinthiakós Kólpos
Corinthus *see* Kórinthos
42 I9 **Corinto** Chinandega, NW Nicaragua
97 C21 **Cork** *Ir.* Corcaigh. S Ireland
97 C21 **Cork** *Ir.* Corcaigh. ◈ *county* SW Ireland
97 C21 **Cork** ✈ Cork, SW Ireland
97 D21 **Cork Harbour** *Ir.* Cuan Chorcaí. *inlet* SW Ireland
107 I23 **Corleone** Sicilia, Italy, C Mediterranean Sea
114 N13 **Çorlu** Tekirdağ, NW Turkey
114 N12 **Çorlu Çayı** ≈ NW Turkey
Cormaiore *see* Courmayeur
9 V13 **Cormorant** Manitoba, C Canada
23 T2 **Cornelia** Georgia, SE USA
60 J10 **Cornélio Procópio** Paraná, S Brazil
55 V9 **Corneliskondre** Sipaliwini, N Surinam
30 J5 **Cornell** Wisconsin, N USA
13 S12 **Corner Brook** Newfoundland, Newfoundland and Labrador, E Canada
Corner Rise Seamounts *see* Corner Seamounts
64 I9 **Corner Seamounts** *var* Corner Rise Seamounts. *undersea feature* NW Atlantic Ocean
116 M9 **Cornești** *Rus.* Korneshty. C Moldova
Corneto *see* Tarquinia
Cornhusker State *see* Nebraska
27 X8 **Corning** Arkansas, C USA
35 N5 **Corning** California, W USA
29 U15 **Corning** Iowa, C USA
18 G11 **Corning** New York, NE USA
Corn Islands *see* Maíz, Islas del
107 J14 **Corno Grande** ▲ C Italy
15 N13 **Cornwall** Ontario, SE Canada
97 H25 **Cornwall** *cultural region* SW England, UK
97 G25 **Cornwall, Cape** *headland* SW England, UK
54 J4 **Coro** *prev.* Santa Ana de Coro. Falcón, NW Venezuela
57 J18 **Corocoro** La Paz, W Bolivia
57 K17 **Coroico** La Paz, W Bolivia
184 M5 **Coromandel** Waikato, North Island, New Zealand
155 K20 **Coromandel Coast** *coast* E India
184 M5 **Coromandel Peninsula** *peninsula* North Island, New Zealand
184 M6 **Coromandel Range** ▲▲ North Island, New Zealand
171 N5 **Coron** Busuanga Island, W Philippines
35 T15 **Corona** California, W USA
37 T12 **Corona** New Mexico, SW USA
9 U17 **Coronach** Saskatchewan, S Canada
35 U17 **Coronado** California, W USA
43 N15 **Coronado, Bahía de** *bay* S Costa Rica
9 R15 **Coronation** Alberta, SW Canada
8 K7 **Coronation Gulf** *gulf* Nunavut, N Canada
194 I1 **Coronation Island** *island* Antarctica
39 X14 **Coronation Island** *island* Alexander Archipelago, Alaska, USA
61 B18 **Coronda** Santa Fe, C Argentina
63 F14 **Coronel** Bío Bío C Chile
61 D20 **Coronel Brandsen** *var.* Brandsen. Buenos Aires, E Argentina
62 K4 **Coronel Cornejo** Salta, N Argentina
61 B24 **Coronel Dorrego** Buenos Aires, E Argentina
62 P6 **Coronel Oviedo** Caaguazú, SE Paraguay
61 B23 **Coronel Pringles** Buenos Aires, E Argentina
61 B23 **Coronel Suárez** Buenos Aires, E Argentina
61 E22 **Coronel Vidal** Buenos Aires, E Argentina
55 V9 **Coronie** ◈ *district* NW Surinam
57 G17 **Coropuna, Nevado** ▲ S Peru
Çorovoda *see* Çorovodë
113 L22 **Çorovodë** *var.* Corovoda. Berat, S Albania
183 P11 **Corowa** New South Wales, SE Australia
42 G1 **Corozal** Corozal, N Belize
54 E6 **Corozal** Sucre, NW Colombia
42 G1 **Corozal** ◈ *district* N Belize
25 T14 **Corpus Christi** Texas, SW USA
25 T14 **Corpus Christi Bay** *inlet* Texas, SW USA
25 R14 **Corpus Christi, Lake** ⊠ Texas, SW USA
63 F16 **Corral** Los Lagos, C Chile
105 O9 **Corral de Almaguer** Castilla-La Mancha, C Spain
104 K6 **Corrales** Castilla-León, N Spain
37 R11 **Corrales** New Mexico, SW USA
Corrán Tuathail *see* Carrauntoohil
106 F9 **Correggio** Emilia-Romagna, C Italy
59 M16 **Corrente** Piauí, E Brazil
59 I19 **Correntes, Rio** ≈ SW Brazil
103 N12 **Corrèze** ◈ *department* C France
97 C17 **Corrib, Lough** *Ir.* Loch Coirib. ◎ W Ireland
61 C14 **Corrientes** Corrientes, NE Argentina
61 D15 **Corrientes** *off.* Provincia de Corrientes. ◈ *province* NE Argentina
44 A5 **Corrientes, Cabo** *headland* W Cuba
40 I13 **Corrientes, Cabo** *headland* SW Mexico
Corrientes, Provincia de *see* Corrientes
61 C16 **Corrientes, Río** ≈ NE Argentina
56 E8 **Corrientes, Río** ≈ Ecuador/Peru
25 W9 **Corrigan** Texas, SW USA
55 U9 **Corriverton** E Guyana
Corriza *see* Korçë
183 Q11 **Corryong** Victoria, SE Australia
103 F2 **Corse** *Eng.* Corsica. ◈ *region* France, C Mediterranean Sea
101 X13 **Corse** *Eng.* Corsica. *island* France, C Mediterranean Sea
103 Y12 **Corse, Cap** *headland* Corse, France, C Mediterranean Sea
103 X15 **Corse-du-Sud** ◈ *department* Corse, France, C Mediterranean Sea
29 P11 **Corsica** South Dakota, N USA
Corsica *see* Corse
25 U7 **Corsicana** Texas, SW USA
103 Y15 **Corte** Corse, France, C Mediterranean Sea
63 G16 **Corte Alto** Los Lagos, S Chile
104 I13 **Cortegana** Andalucía, S Spain
43 N15 **Cortés** *var.* Ciudad Cortés. Puntarenas, SE Costa Rica
42 G5 **Cortés** ◈ *department* NW Honduras
37 P8 **Cortez** Colorado, C USA
Cortez, Sea of *see* California, Golfo de
106 H6 **Cortina d'Ampezzo** Veneto, NE Italy
18 H11 **Cortland** New York, NE USA
31 V11 **Cortland** Ohio, N USA
106 H12 **Cortona** Toscana, C Italy
76 H13 **Corubal, Rio** ≈ E Guinea-Bissau
104 G10 **Coruche** Santarém, C Portugal
Çoruh *see* Rize
137 R11 **Çoruh Nehri** *Geor.* Chorokh, *Rus.* Chorokhi. ≈ Georgia/Turkey
136 K12 **Çorum** *var.* Chorum. Çorum, N Turkey
136 J12 **Çorum** *var.* Chorum. ◈ *province* N Turkey
59 H19 **Corumbá** Mato Grosso do Sul, S Brazil
14 D16 **Corunna** Ontario, S Canada
Corunna *see* A Coruña
32 F12 **Corvallis** Oregon, NW USA
64 M1 **Corvo** *var.* Ilha do Corvo. *island* Azores, Portugal, NE Atlantic Ocean
Corvo, Ilha do *see* Corvo
31 O16 **Corydon** Indiana, N USA
29 V16 **Corydon** Iowa, C USA
Cos *see* Kos
40 I9 **Cosalá** Sinaloa, C Mexico
41 R15 **Cosamaloapan** *var.* Cosamaloapan de Carpio. Veracruz-Llave, E Mexico
Cosamaloapan de Carpio *see* Cosamaloapan
107 N21 **Cosenza** *anc.* Consentia. Calabria, SW Italy
31 T13 **Coshocton** Ohio, N USA
42 H9 **Cosigüina, Punta** *headland* NW Nicaragua
29 T9 **Cosmos** Minnesota, N USA
103 O8 **Cosne-sur-Loire** Nièvre, C France
108 B9 **Cossonay** Vaud, W Switzerland
Cossyra *see* Pantelleria
47 R4 **Costa, Cordillera de la** *var.* Cordillera de Venezuela. ▲▲ N Venezuela
42 K13 **Costa Rica** *off.* Republic of Costa Rica. ◆ *republic* Central America
Costa Rica, Republic of *see* Costa Rica
43 N15 **Costeña, Fila** ▲▲ S Costa Rica
Costermansville *see* Bukavu
116 I14 **Costești** Argeș, SW Romania
37 S8 **Costilla** New Mexico, SW USA
35 O7 **Cosumnes River** ≈ California, W USA
101 O16 **Coswig** Sachsen, E Germany
101 M14 **Coswig** Sachsen-Anhalt, E Germany
Cosyra *see* Pantelleria
171 Q7 **Cotabato** Mindanao, S Philippines
56 C5 **Cotacachi** ▲ N Ecuador
57 L21 **Cotagaita** Potosí, S Bolivia
103 V15 **Côte d'Azur** *prev.* Nice. ✈ (Nice) Alpes-Maritimes, SE France
Côte d'Ivoire *see* Ivory Coast
Côte d'Ivoire, République de la *see* Ivory Coast
103 R7 **Côte d'Or** ◈ *department* E France
103 R8 **Côte d'Or** *cultural region* C France
Côte Française des Somalis *see* Djibouti
102 J4 **Cotentin** *peninsula* N France
102 G6 **Côtes d'Armor** *prev.* Côtes-du-Nord. ◈ *department* NW France
Côtes-du-Nord *see* Côtes d'Armor
Cöthen *see* Köthen
Côtière, Chaine *see* Coast Mountains
40 M13 **Cotija** *var.* Cotija de la Paz. Michoacán de Ocampo, SW Mexico
Cotija de la Paz *see* Cotija
77 R16 **Cotonou** *var.* Kotonu. S Benin
77 R16 **Cotonou** ✈ S Benin
56 B6 **Cotopaxi** *prev.* León. ◈ *province* C Ecuador
56 C6 **Cotopaxi** ⛰ N Ecuador
Cotrone *see* Crotone
97 L21 **Cotswold Hills** *var.* Cotswolds. *hill range* S England, UK
Cotswolds *see* Cotswold Hills
32 F13 **Cottage Grove** Oregon, NW USA
21 S14 **Cottageville** South Carolina, SE USA
101 P14 **Cottbus** *Lus.* Chośebuz; *prev.* Kottbus. Brandenburg, E Germany
27 U9 **Cotter** Arkansas, C USA
106 A9 **Cottian Alps** *Fr.* Alpes Cottiennes, *It.* Alpi Cozie. ▲▲ France/Italy
Cottiennes, Alpes *see* Cottian Alps
Cotton State, The *see* Alabama
22 G4 **Cotton Valley** Louisiana, S USA
36 L12 **Cottonwood** Arizona, SW USA
32 M10 **Cottonwood** Idaho, NW USA
29 S9 **Cottonwood** Minnesota, N USA
25 Q7 **Cottonwood** Texas, SW USA
27 O5 **Cottonwood Falls** Kansas, C USA
36 L3 **Cottonwood Heights** Utah, W USA
29 S10 **Cottonwood River** ≈ Minnesota, N USA
45 O9 **Cotuí** C Dominican Republic
25 Q13 **Cotulla** Texas, SW USA
Cotyora *see* Ordu
102 I11 **Coubre, Pointe de la** *headland* W France
18 E12 **Coudersport** Pennsylvania, NE USA
15 S9 **Coudres, Île aux** *island* Québec, SE Canada
182 G11 **Couedic, Cape de** *headland* South Australia
Couentrey *see* Coventry
102 I6 **Couesnon** ≈ NW France
32 H10 **Cougar** Washington, NW USA
102 L10 **Couhé** Vienne, W France
32 K8 **Coulee City** Washington, NW USA
195 Q15 **Coulman Island** *island* Antarctica
103 P5 **Coulommiers** Seine-et-Marne, N France
14 K11 **Coulonge** ≈ Québec, SE Canada
14 K11 **Coulonge Est** ≈ Québec, SE Canada
35 Q9 **Coulterville** California, W USA
38 M9 **Council** Alaska, USA
32 M12 **Council** Idaho, NW USA
29 S15 **Council Bluffs** Iowa, C USA
27 O5 **Council Grove** Kansas, C USA
27 O5 **Council Grove Lake** ⊠ Kansas, C USA
32 G7 **Coupeville** Washington, NW USA
55 U12 **Courantyne River** *var.* Corantijn Rivier, Corentyne River. ≈ Guyana/Surinam
99 G21 **Courcelles** Hainaut, S Belgium
108 C7 **Courgenay** Jura, NW Switzerland
126 B2 **Courland Lagoon** *Ger.* Kurisches Haff, *Rus.* Kurskiy Zaliv. *lagoon* Lithuania/Russian Federation
118 B12 **Courland Spit** *Lith.* Kuršių Nerija, *Rus.* Kurshskaya Kosa. *spit* Lithuania/Russian Federation
106 A6 **Courmayeur** *prev.* Cormaiore. Valle d'Aosta, NW Italy
108 D7 **Courroux** Jura, NW Switzerland
10 K17 **Courtenay** Vancouver Island, British Columbia, SW Canada
21 W7 **Courtland** Virginia, NE USA
25 V10 **Courtney** Texas, SW USA
30 J4 **Court Oreilles, Lac** ◎ Wisconsin, N USA
Courtrai *see* Kortrijk
99 H19 **Court-Saint-Étienne** Walloon Brabant, C Belgium
22 G6 **Coushatta** Louisiana, S USA
172 I16 **Cousin** *island* Inner Islands, NE Seychelles
172 I16 **Cousine** *island* Inner Islands, NE Seychelles
102 J4 **Coutances** *anc.* Constantia. Manche, N France
102 K12 **Coutras** Gironde, SW France
45 U14 **Couva** Trinidad, Trinidad and Tobago
108 B8 **Couvet** Neuchâtel, W Switzerland
99 H22 **Couvin** Namur, S Belgium
116 K12 **Covasna** *Ger.* Kowasna, *Hung.* Kovászna. Covasna, E Romania
116 J11 **Covasna** ◈ *county* E Romania
14 E12 **Cove Island** *island* Ontario, S Canada
34 M5 **Covelo** California, W USA
97 M20 **Coventry** *anc.* Couentrey. C England, UK
Cove of Cork *see* Cobh
21 U5 **Covesville** Virginia, NE USA
104 I8 **Covilhã** Castelo Branco, E Portugal
23 T3 **Covington** Georgia, SE USA
31 N13 **Covington** Indiana, N USA
20 M3 **Covington** Kentucky, S USA
22 K8 **Covington** Louisiana, S USA
31 Q13 **Covington** Ohio, N USA
20 F9 **Covington** Tennessee, S USA
21 S6 **Covington** Virginia, NE USA
183 Q8 **Cowal, Lake** *seasonal lake* New South Wales, SE Australia
9 W15 **Cowan** Manitoba, S Canada
18 F12 **Cowanesque River** ≈ New York/Pennsylvania, NE USA
180 L12 **Cowan, Lake** ◎ Western Australia
15 P13 **Cowansville** Québec, SE Canada

◆ Country
● Country Capital
◇ Dependent Territory
○ Dependent Territory Capital
◈ Administrative Regions
✈ International Airport
▲ Mountain
▲▲ Mountain Range
⛰ Volcano
≈ River
◎ Lake
⊠ Reservoir

COWELL – DABU

182 H8 **Cowell** South Australia
97 M23 **Cowes** S England, UK
27 Q10 **Coweta** Oklahoma, C USA
0 D6 **Cowie Seamount** *undersea feature* NE Pacific Ocean
32 G10 **Cowlitz River** ~ Washington, NW USA
21 Q11 **Cowpens** South Carolina, SE USA
183 R8 **Cowra** New South Wales, SE Australia
Coxen Hole *see* Roatán
59 I19 **Coxim** Mato Grosso do Sul, S Brazil
59 I19 **Coxim, Rio** ~ SW Brazil
Coxin Hole *see* Roatán
153 V17 **Cox's Bazar** Chittagong, S Bangladesh
76 H14 **Coyah** Conakry, W Guinea
40 K5 **Coyame** Chihuahua, N Mexico
24 L9 **Coyanosa Draw** ~ Texas, SW USA
Coyhaique *see* Coihaique
42 C7 **Coyolate, Río** ~ S Guatemala
Coyote State, The *see* South Dakota
40 I10 **Coyotitán** Sinaloa, C Mexico
41 O16 **Coyuca** *var.* Coyuca de Benítez. Guerrero, S Mexico
41 N15 **Coyuca** *var.* Coyuca de Catalán. Guerrero, S Mexico
Coyuca de Benítez/Coyuca de Catalán *see* Coyuca
29 N15 **Cozad** Nebraska, C USA
Cozie, Alpi *see* Cottian Alps
Cozmeni *see* Kitsman'
40 E3 **Cozón, Cerro** ▲ NW Mexico
41 Z12 **Cozumel** Quintana Roo, E Mexico
41 Z12 **Cozumel, Isla** *island* SE Mexico
32 K8 **Crab Creek** ~ Washington, NW USA
44 H12 **Crab Pond Point** *headland* W Jamaica
Cracovia/Cracow *see* Kraków
83 I25 **Cradock** Eastern Cape, S South Africa
39 Y14 **Craig** Prince of Wales Island, Alaska, USA
37 Q3 **Craig** Colorado, C USA
97 F15 **Craigavon** C Northern Ireland, UK
21 T5 **Craigsville** Virginia, NE USA
101 J21 **Crailsheim** Baden-Württemberg, S Germany
116 H14 **Craiova** Dolj, SW Romania
10 K12 **Cranberry Junction** British Columbia, SW Canada
18 J8 **Cranberry Lake** ◎ New York, NE USA
9 V13 **Cranberry Portage** Manitoba, C Canada
9 P17 **Cranbrook** British Columbia, SW Canada
30 M5 **Crandon** Wisconsin, N USA
32 K14 **Crane** Oregon, NW USA
24 M9 **Crane** Texas, SW USA
Crane *see* The Crane
25 S8 **Cranfills Gap** Texas, SW USA
19 O12 **Cranston** Rhode Island, NE USA
Cranz *see* Zelenogradsk
59 L15 **Craolândia** Tocantins, E Brazil
102 J7 **Craon** Mayenne, NW France
195 V16 **Crary, Cape** *headland* Antarctica
Crasna *see* Kraszna
32 G14 **Crater Lake** ◎ Oregon, NW USA
33 P14 **Craters of the Moon National Monument** *national park* Idaho, NW USA
59 O14 **Crateús** Ceará, E Brazil
Crathis *see* Crati
107 N20 **Crati** *anc.* Crathis. ~ S Italy
9 U16 **Craven** Saskatchewan, S Canada
54 I8 **Cravo Norte** Arauca, E Colombia
28 J12 **Crawford** Nebraska, C USA
25 T8 **Crawford** Texas, SW USA
9 O17 **Crawford Bay** British Columbia, SW Canada
65 M19 **Crawford Seamount** *undersea feature* S Atlantic Ocean
31 O13 **Crawfordsville** Indiana, N USA
23 S9 **Crawfordville** Florida, SE USA
97 O23 **Crawley** SE England, UK
33 S10 **Crazy Mountains** ▲▲ Montana, NW USA
9 T11 **Cree** ~ Saskatchewan, C Canada
37 R7 **Creede** Colorado, C USA
40 I6 **Creel** Chihuahua, N Mexico
9 S11 **Cree Lake** ◎ Saskatchewan, C Canada
9 V13 **Creighton** Saskatchewan, C Canada
29 Q13 **Creighton** Nebraska, C USA
103 O4 **Creil** Oise, N France
106 E8 **Crema** Lombardia, N Italy
106 E8 **Cremona** Lombardia, N Italy
Creole State *see* Louisiana
112 M10 **Crepaja** *Hung.* Cserépalja. Vojvodina, N Serbia
103 O4 **Crépy-en-Valois** Oise, N France
112 B10 **Cres** *It.* Cherso. Primorje-Gorski Kotar, NW Croatia
112 A11 **Cres** *It.* Cherso; *anc.* Crexa. *island* W Croatia
32 H14 **Crescent** Oregon, NW USA
34 K1 **Crescent City** California, W USA
23 W10 **Crescent City** Florida, SE USA
167 X10 **Crescent Group** *island group* C Paracel Islands
23 W10 **Crescent Lake** ◎ Florida, SE USA
29 X11 **Cresco** Iowa, C USA
61 B18 **Crespo** Entre Ríos, E Argentina
54 E5 **Crespo** ✈ (Cartagena) Bolívar, NW Colombia
103 R13 **Crest** Drôme, E France
37 R5 **Crested Butte** Colorado, C USA
31 S12 **Crestline** Ohio, N USA
9 O17 **Creston** British Columbia, SW Canada
29 U15 **Creston** Iowa, C USA
33 V16 **Creston** Wyoming, C USA
37 S7 **Crestone Peak** ▲ Colorado, C USA
23 P8 **Crestview** Florida, SE USA
121 R10 **Cretan Trough** *undersea feature* Aegean Sea, C Mediterranean Sea
29 R16 **Crete** Nebraska, C USA
Crete *see* Kríti
103 O5 **Créteil** Val-de-Marne, N France
Crete, Sea of/Creticum, Mare *see* Kritikó Pélagos
105 X4 **Creus, Cap de** *cape* NE Spain
103 N10 **Creuse** ◈ *department* C France
102 L9 **Creuse** ~ C France
103 T4 **Creutzwald** Moselle, NE France
105 S12 **Crevillente** País Valenciano, E Spain
97 L18 **Crewe** C England, UK
21 V7 **Crewe** Virginia, NE USA
Crexa *see* Cres
43 Q15 **Cricamola, Río** ~ NW Panama
61 K14 **Criciúma** Santa Catarina, S Brazil
96 J11 **Crieff** C Scotland, UK
112 B10 **Crikvenica** *It.* Cirquenizza; *prev.* Cirkvenica, Crjkvenica. Primorje-Gorski Kotar, NW Croatia
Crimea/Crimean Oblast *see* Krym, Respublika
101 M16 **Crimmitschau** *var.* Krimmitschau. Sachsen, E Germany
116 G11 **Crişcior** *Hung.* Kristyor. Hunedoara, W Romania
21 Y5 **Crisfield** Maryland, NE USA
23 P3 **Crisp Point** *headland* Michigan, N USA
59 L19 **Cristalina** Goiás, C Brazil
44 J7 **Cristal, Sierra del** ▲▲ E Cuba
43 T14 **Cristóbal** Colón, C Panama
54 F4 **Cristóbal Colón, Pico** ▲ N Colombia
Cristur/Cristuru Săcuiesc *see* Cristuru Secuiesc
116 I11 **Cristuru Secuiesc** *prev.* Cristur, Cristuru Săcuiesc, *Ger.* Kreutz, Sitaş Cristuru, *Hung.* Székelykeresztúr, Szitás-Keresztúr. Harghita, C Romania
116 F10 **Crişul Alb** *var.* Weisse Kreisch, *Ger.* Weisse Körös, *Hung* Fehér-Körös. ~ Hungary/Romania
116 F10 **Crişul Negru** *Ger.* Schwarze Körös, *Hung.* Fekete-Körös. ~ Hungary/Romania
116 G10 **Crişul Repede** *var.* Schnelle Kreisch, *Ger.* Schnelle Körös, *Hung.* Sebes-Körös. ~ Hungary/Romania
117 N10 **Criuleni** *Rus.* Kriulyany. C Moldova
Crivadia Vulcanului *see* Vulcan
Crjkvenica *see* Crikvenica
113 O17 **Crna Gora** ▲▲ FYR Macedonia/Serbia
Crna Gora *see* Montenegro
113 O20 **Crna Reka** ~ S FYR Macedonia
Crni Drim *see* Black Drin
109 V10 **Crni Vrh** ▲ NE Slovenia
109 V13 **Črnomelj** *Ger.* Tschernembl. SE Slovenia
97 A17 **Croagh Patrick** *Ir.* Cruach Phádraig. ▲ W Ireland
112 D9 **Croatia** *off.* Republic of Croatia, *Ger.* Kroatien, *SCr.* Hrvatska. ◆ *republic* SE Europe
Croatia, Republic of *see* Croatia
Croce, Picco di *see* Wilde Kreuzspitze
15 P8 **Croche** ~ Québec, SE Canada
169 V7 **Crocker, Banjaran** *var.* Crocker Range. ▲▲ East Malaysia
Crocker Range *see* Crocker, Banjaran
25 V9 **Crockett** Texas, SW USA
67 V14 **Crocodile** *var.* Krokodil. ~ N South Africa
Crocodile *see* Limpopo
20 I7 **Crofton** Kentucky, S USA
29 Q12 **Crofton** Nebraska, C USA
Croia *see* Krujë
103 R16 **Croisette, Cap** *headland* SE France
102 G8 **Croisic, Pointe du** *headland* NW France
103 S13 **Croix Haute, Col de la** *pass* E France
15 U5 **Croix, Pointe à la** *headland* Québec, SE Canada
14 F13 **Croker, Cape** *headland* Ontario, S Canada
181 P1 **Croker Island** *island* Northern Territory, N Australia
96 I8 **Cromarty** N Scotland, UK
99 M21 **Crombach** Liège, E Belgium
97 Q18 **Cromer** E England, UK
185 D22 **Cromwell** Otago, South Island, New Zealand
185 H16 **Cronadun** West Coast, South Island, New Zealand
39 O11 **Crooked Creek** Alaska, USA
44 K5 **Crooked Island** *island* SE Bahamas
44 J5 **Crooked Island Passage** *channel* SE Bahamas
32 I13 **Crooked River** ~ Oregon, NW USA
29 R4 **Crookston** Minnesota, N USA
28 I10 **Crooks Tower** ▲ South Dakota, N USA
31 T14 **Crooksville** Ohio, N USA
183 R9 **Crookwell** New South Wales, SE Australia
14 L14 **Crosby** Ontario, SE Canada
97 K17 **Crosby** *var.* Great Crosby. NW England, UK
29 U6 **Crosby** Minnesota, N USA
28 K2 **Crosby** North Dakota, N USA
25 O5 **Crosbyton** Texas, SW USA
77 V16 **Cross** ~ Cameroon/Nigeria
23 U10 **Cross City** Florida, SE USA
Crossen *see* Krosno Odrzańskie
27 V14 **Crossett** Arkansas, C USA
97 K15 **Cross Fell** ▲ N England, UK
9 P16 **Crossfield** Alberta, SW Canada
21 Q12 **Cross Hill** South Carolina, SE USA
19 U6 **Cross Island** *island* Maine, NE USA
9 X13 **Cross Lake** Manitoba, C Canada
22 F5 **Cross Lake** ⊠ Louisiana, S USA
36 I12 **Crossman Peak** ▲ Arizona, SW USA
25 Q7 **Cross Plains** Texas, SW USA
77 V17 **Cross River** ◈ *state* SE Nigeria
20 L9 **Crossville** Tennessee, S USA
31 S8 **Croswell** Michigan, N USA
14 K13 **Crotch Lake** ◎ Ontario, SE Canada
Croton/Crotona *see* Crotone
107 O21 **Crotone** *var.* Cotrone; *anc.* Croton, Crotona. Calabria, SW Italy
33 V11 **Crow Agency** Montana, NW USA
183 U7 **Crowdy Head** *headland* New South Wales, SE Australia
25 Q4 **Crowell** Texas, SW USA
183 O6 **Crowl Creek** *seasonal river* New South Wales, SE Australia
22 H9 **Crowley** Louisiana, S USA
35 S9 **Crowley, Lake** ⊠ California, W USA
27 X10 **Crowleys Ridge** *hill range* Arkansas, C USA
31 N11 **Crown Point** Indiana, N USA
37 P10 **Crownpoint** New Mexico, SW USA
33 R10 **Crow Peak** ▲ Montana, NW USA
9 P17 **Crowsnest Pass** *pass* Alberta/British Columbia, SW Canada
29 T6 **Crow Wing River** ~ Minnesota, N USA
97 O22 **Croydon** SE England, UK
Crozer, Mount *see* Finkol, Mount
173 P11 **Crozet Basin** *undersea feature* S Indian Ocean
173 O12 **Crozet Islands** *island group* French Southern and Antarctic Territories
173 N12 **Crozet Plateau** *var.* Crozet Plateaus. *undersea feature* SW Indian Ocean
Crozet Plateaus *see* Crozet Plateau
102 E6 **Crozon** Finistère, NW France
Cruacha Dubha, Na *see* Macgillycuddy's Reeks
Cruach Phádraig *see* Croagh Patrick
116 M14 **Crucea** Constanţa, SE Romania
44 E5 **Cruces** Cienfuegos, C Cuba
107 O20 **Crucoli Torretta** Calabria, SW Italy
41 P9 **Cruillas** Tamaulipas, C Mexico
64 K9 **Cruiser Tablemount** *undersea feature* E Atlantic Ocean
61 G14 **Cruz Alta** Rio Grande do Sul, S Brazil
44 G8 **Cruz, Cabo** *headland* S Cuba
60 N9 **Cruzeiro** São Paulo, S Brazil
60 H10 **Cruzeiro do Oeste** Paraná, S Brazil
59 A15 **Cruzeiro do Sul** Acre, W Brazil
23 U11 **Crystal Bay** *bay* Florida, SE USA NE Gulf of Mexico Atlantic Ocean
182 I8 **Crystal Brook** South Australia
9 X17 **Crystal City** Manitoba, S Canada
27 X5 **Crystal City** Missouri, C USA
25 P13 **Crystal City** Texas, SW USA
30 M4 **Crystal Falls** Michigan, N USA
23 Q8 **Crystal Lake** Florida, SE USA
31 O6 **Crystal Lake** ◎ Michigan, N USA
23 V11 **Crystal River** Florida, SE USA
37 Q5 **Crystal River** ~ Colorado, C USA
22 K6 **Crystal Springs** Mississippi, S USA
Csaca *see* Čadca
Csakathurn/Csáktornya *see* Čakovec
Csap *see* Chop
Csepén *see* Čepin
Cserépalja *see* Crepaja
Csermő *see* Cermei
Csíkszereda *see* Miercurea-Ciuc
111 L24 **Csongrád** Csongrád, SE Hungary
111 L24 **Csongrád** *off.* Csongrád Megye. ◈ *county* SE Hungary
Csongrád Megye *see* Csongrád
111 H22 **Csorna** Győr-Moson-Sopron, NW Hungary
Csucsa *see* Ciucea
111 G25 **Csurgó** Somogy, SW Hungary
Csurog *see* Čurug
54 L5 **Cúa** Miranda, N Venezuela
82 C11 **Cuale** Malanje, NW Angola
67 T12 **Cuando** *var.* Kwando. ~ S Africa
83 E15 **Cuando Cubango** *var.* Kuando-Kubango. ◈ *province* SE Angola
83 E16 **Cuangar** Cuando Cubango, S Angola
82 D11 **Cuango** Lunda Norte, NE Angola
82 C10 **Cuango** Uíge, NW Angola
82 C10 **Cuango** *var.* Kwango. ~ Angola/Dem. Rep. Congo *see also* Kwango
Cuango *see* Kwango
Cuan, Loch *see* Strangford Lough
82 C12 **Cuanza** *var.* Kwanza. ~ C Angola
82 B11 **Cuanza Norte** *var.* Kuanza Norte. ◈ *province* NE Angola
82 B12 **Cuanza Sul** *var.* Kuanza Sul. ◈ *province* NE Angola
61 E16 **Cuareim, Río** *var.* Rio Quaraí. ~ Brazil/Uruguay *see also* Quaraí, Rio
Cuareim, Río *see* Quaraí, Rio
83 D15 **Cuatir** ~ S Angola
40 M7 **Cuatro Ciénegas** *var.* Cuatro Ciénegas de Carranza. Coahuila de Zaragoza, NE Mexico
Cuatro Ciénegas de Carranza *see* Cuatro Ciénegas
40 I6 **Cuauhtémoc** Chihuahua, N Mexico
41 P14 **Cuautla** Morelos, S Mexico
104 H12 **Cuba** Beja, S Portugal
27 W6 **Cuba** Missouri, C USA
37 R10 **Cuba** New Mexico, SW USA
44 E6 **Cuba** *off.* Republic of Cuba. ◆ *republic* W West Indies
47 O2 **Cuba** *island* W West Indies
82 B13 **Cubal** Benguela, W Angola
83 C15 **Cubango** *var.* Kuvango, *Port.* Vila Artur de Paiva, Vila da Ponte. Huíla, SW Angola
83 D16 **Cubango** *var.* Kavango, Kavengo, Kubango, Okavango, Okavanggo. ~ S Africa *see also* Okavango
Cubango *see* Okavango
54 H8 **Cubará** Boyacá, N Colombia
Cuba, Republic of *see* Cuba
136 I12 **Çubuk** Ankara, N Turkey
83 D14 **Cuchi** Cuando Cubango, C Angola
42 C5 **Cuchumatanes, Sierra de los** ▲▲ W Guatemala
Cuculaya, Rio *see* Kukalaya, Rio
82 E12 **Cucumbi** *prev.* Trás-os-Montes. Lunda Sul, NE Angola
54 G7 **Cúcuta** *var.* San José de Cúcuta. Norte de Santander, N Colombia
31 N9 **Cudahy** Wisconsin, N USA
155 J21 **Cuddalore** Tamil Nādu, SE India
155 I18 **Cuddapah** Andhra Pradesh, S India
104 M6 **Cuéllar** Castilla-León, N Spain
82 D13 **Cuemba** *var.* Coemba. Bié, C Angola
56 B8 **Cuenca** Azuay, S Ecuador
105 Q9 **Cuenca** *anc.* Conca. Castilla-La Mancha, C Spain
105 P9 **Cuenca** ◈ *province* Castilla-La Mancha, C Spain
40 L9 **Cuencamé** *var.* Cuencamé de Ceniceros. Durango, C Mexico
Cuencamé de Ceniceros *see* Cuencamé
105 Q8 **Cuenca, Serrania de** ▲▲ C Spain
Cuera *see* Chur
105 P5 **Cuerda del Pozo, Embalse de la** ⊠ N Spain
41 O14 **Cuernavaca** Morelos, S Mexico
25 T12 **Cuero** Texas, SW USA
44 I7 **Cueto** Holguín, E Cuba
41 Q13 **Cuetzalán** *var.* Cuetzalán del Progreso. Puebla, S Mexico
Cuetzalán del Progreso *see* Cuetzalán
105 Q14 **Cuevas de Almanzora** Andalucía, S Spain
Cuevas de Vinromá *see* Les Coves de Vinromá
116 H12 **Cugir** *Hung.* Kudzsir. Alba, SW Romania
59 H18 **Cuiabá** *prev.* Cuyabá. *state capital* Mato Grosso, SW Brazil
59 H19 **Cuiabá, Rio** ~ SW Brazil
41 R15 **Cuicatlán** *var.* San Juan Bautista Cuicatlán. Oaxaca, SE Mexico
191 W16 **Cuidado, Punta** *headland* Easter Island, Chile, E Pacific Ocean
Cuidad Presidente Stroessner *see* Ciudad del Este
Cúige *see* Connaught
Cúige Laighean *see* Leinster
Cúige Mumhan *see* Munster
Cuihua *see* Daguan
98 L13 **Cuijck** Noord-Brabant, SE Netherlands
Cúil an tSúdaire *see* Portarlington
42 D7 **Cuilapa** Santa Rosa, S Guatemala
42 B5 **Cuilco, Río** ~ W Guatemala
Cúil Mhuine *see* Collooney
Cúil Raithin *see* Coleraine
83 C14 **Cuima** Huambo, C Angola
83 E16 **Cuito** *var.* Kwito. ~ SE Angola
83 E15 **Cuíto Cuanavale** Cuando Cubango, E Angola
41 N14 **Cuitzeo, Lago de** ◎ C Mexico
27 W4 **Cuivre River** ~ Missouri, C USA
Çuka *see* Çukë
168 L8 **Cukai** *var.* Chukai, Kemaman. Terengganu, Peninsular Malaysia
113 L23 **Çukë** *var.* Çuka. Vlorë, S Albania
Cularo *see* Grenoble
33 Y7 **Culbertson** Montana, NW USA
28 M16 **Culbertson** Nebraska, C USA
183 P10 **Culcairn** New South Wales, SE Australia
45 W5 **Culebra** *var.* Dewey. E Puerto Rico
45 W6 **Culebra, Isla de** *island* E Puerto Rico
37 T8 **Culebra Peak** ▲ Colorado, C USA
104 J5 **Culebra, Sierra de la** ▲▲ NW Spain
98 J12 **Culemborg** Gelderland, C Netherlands
137 V14 **Culfa** *Rus.* Dzhul'fa. SW Azerbaijan
183 P4 **Culgoa River** ~ New South Wales/Queensland, SE Australia
40 I9 **Culiacán** *var.* Culiacán Rosales, Culiacán-Rosales. Sinaloa, C Mexico
Culiacán-Rosales/Culiacán Rosales *see* Culiacán
105 P14 **Cúllar-Baza** Andalucía, S Spain
105 S10 **Cullera** País Valenciano, E Spain
23 P3 **Cullman** Alabama, S USA
108 B10 **Cully** Vaud, W Switzerland
Culm *see* Chełmno
Culmsee *see* Chełmża
21 V4 **Culpeper** Virginia, NE USA
185 I17 **Culverden** Canterbury, South Island, New Zealand
55 N5 **Cumaná** Sucre, NE Venezuela
55 O5 **Cumanacoa** Sucre, NE Venezuela
54 C13 **Cumbal, Nevado de** *elevation* S Colombia
21 O7 **Cumberland** Kentucky, S USA
21 U2 **Cumberland** Maryland, NE USA
21 V6 **Cumberland** Virginia, NE USA
187 P12 **Cumberland, Cape** *var.* Cape Nahoi. *headland* Espiritu Santo, N Vanuatu
9 V14 **Cumberland House** Saskatchewan, C Canada
23 W8 **Cumberland Island** *island* Georgia, SE USA
20 L7 **Cumberland, Lake** ⊠ Kentucky, S USA
9 R5 **Cumberland Peninsula** *peninsula* Baffin Island, Nunavut, NE Canada
2 N9 **Cumberland Plateau** *plateau* E USA
30 L1 **Cumberland Point** *headland* Michigan, N USA
21 O7 **Cumberland River** ~ Kentucky/Tennessee, S USA
9 S6 **Cumberland Sound** *inlet* Baffin Island, Nunavut, NE Canada
96 I12 **Cumbernauld** S Scotland, UK
97 K15 **Cumbria** *cultural region* NW England, UK
97 K15 **Cumbrian Mountains** ▲▲ NW England, UK
23 S2 **Cumming** Georgia, SE USA
Cummin in Pommern *see* Kamień Pomorski
182 G9 **Cummins** South Australia
96 I13 **Cumnock** W Scotland, UK
40 G4 **Cumpas** Sonora, NW Mexico
136 H16 **Çumra** Konya, C Turkey
63 G15 **Cunco** Araucanía, C Chile
54 E9 **Cundinamarca** *off.* Departamento de Cundinamarca. ◈ *province* C Colombia
Cundinamarca, Departamento de *see* Cundinamarca
41 U15 **Cunduacán** Tabasco, SE Mexico
83 C16 **Cunene** ◈ *province* S Angola
83 A16 **Cunene** *var.* Kunene. ~ Angola/Namibia *see also* Kunene
Cunene *see* Kunene
106 A9 **Cuneo** *Fr.* Coni. Piemonte, NW Italy
83 E15 **Cunjamba** Cuando Cubango, E Angola
181 V10 **Cunnamulla** Queensland, E Australia
Čunusavvon *see* Junosuando
Cuokkarašša *see* Čohkarášša
106 B7 **Cuorgne** Piemonte, NE Italy
96 K11 **Cupar** E Scotland, UK
116 L8 **Cupcina** *Rus.* Kupchino; *prev.* Calinisc, Kalinisk. N Moldova
54 C8 **Cupica** Chocó, W Colombia
54 C8 **Cupica, Golfo de** *gulf* W Colombia
112 N13 **Ćuprija** Serbia, E Serbia
Cura *see* Villa de Cura
45 P16 **Curaçao** *island* Netherlands Antilles
56 H13 **Curanja, Río** ~ E Peru
56 F7 **Curaray, Río** ~ Ecuador/Peru
116 K14 **Curcani** Călăraşi, SE Romania
182 H4 **Curdimurka** South Australia
103 P7 **Cure** ~ C France
173 Y16 **Curepipe** C Mauritius
55 R6 **Curiapo** Delta Amacuro, NE Venezuela
Curia Rhaetorum *see* Chur
62 G12 **Curicó** Maule, C Chile
Curieta *see* Krk
172 I15 **Curieuse** *island* Inner Islands, NE Seychelles
59 C16 **Curitiba** Acre, W Brazil
60 K12 **Curitiba** *prev.* Curytiba. *state capital* Paraná, S Brazil
60 J13 **Curitibanos** Santa Catarina, S Brazil
183 S6 **Curlewis** New South Wales, SE Australia
182 J6 **Curnamona** South Australia
83 A15 **Curoca** ~ SW Angola
183 T6 **Currabubula** New South Wales, SE Australia
59 Q14 **Currais Novos** Rio Grande do Norte, E Brazil
35 W7 **Currant** Nevada, W USA
35 W6 **Currant Mountain** ▲ Nevada, W USA
44 H2 **Current** Eleuthera Island, C Bahamas
27 W8 **Current River** ~ Arkansas/Missouri, C USA
182 M14 **Currie** Tasmania, SE Australia
21 Y8 **Currituck** North Carolina, SE USA
21 Y8 **Currituck Sound** *sound* North Carolina, SE USA
39 R11 **Curry** Alaska, USA
Curtbunar *see* Tervel
116 I13 **Curtea de Argeş** *var.* Curtea-de-Arges. Argeş, S Romania
Curtea-de-Arges *see* Curtea de Argeş
116 E10 **Curtici** *Ger.* Kurtitsch, *Hung.* Kürtös. Arad, W Romania
28 M16 **Curtis** Nebraska, C USA
104 H2 **Curtis-Estación** Galicia, NW Spain
183 O14 **Curtis Group** *island group* Tasmania, SE Australia
181 Y8 **Curtis Island** *island* Queensland, SE Australia
58 K11 **Curuá, Ilha do** *island* NE Brazil
47 U7 **Curuá, Rio** ~ N Brazil
59 A14 **Curuçá, Rio** ~ NW Brazil
112 L9 **Čurug** *Hung.* Csurog. Vojvodina, N Serbia
61 D16 **Curuzú Cuatiá** Corrientes, NE Argentina
59 M19 **Curvelo** Minas Gerais, SE Brazil
18 E14 **Curwensville** Pennsylvania, NE USA
30 M3 **Curwood, Mount** ▲ Michigan, N USA
Curytiba *see* Curitiba
Curzola *see* Korčula
42 A10 **Cuscatlán** ◈ *department* C El Salvador
57 H15 **Cusco** *var.* Cuzco. Cusco, C Peru
57 H15 **Cusco** *off.* Departamento de Cusco, *var.* Cuzco. ◈ *department* C Peru
Cusco, Departamento de *see* Cusco
27 O9 **Cushing** Oklahoma, C USA
25 W8 **Cushing** Texas, SW USA
40 I6 **Cusihuiriachic** Chihuahua, N Mexico
103 P10 **Cusset** Allier, C France
23 S6 **Cusseta** Georgia, SE USA
28 J10 **Custer** South Dakota, N USA
Cüstrin *see* Kostrzyn
33 Q7 **Cut Bank** Montana, NW USA
Cutch, Gulf of *see* Kachchh, Gulf of
23 S6 **Cuthbert** Georgia, SE USA
9 S15 **Cut Knife** Saskatchewan, S Canada
23 Y16 **Cutler Ridge** Florida, SE USA
22 K10 **Cut Off** Louisiana, S USA
63 I15 **Cutral-Có** Neuquén, C Argentina
107 O21 **Cutro** Calabria, SW Italy
183 O4 **Cuttaburra Channels** *seasonal river* New South Wales, SE Australia
154 O12 **Cuttack** Orissa, E India
83 C15 **Cuvelai** Cunene, SW Angola
79 G18 **Cuvette** *var.* Région de la Cuvette. ◈ *province* C Congo
Cuvette, Région de la *see* Cuvette
173 V9 **Cuvier Basin** *undersea feature* E Indian Ocean
173 U9 **Cuvier Plateau** *undersea feature* E Indian Ocean
82 B12 **Cuvo** ~ W Angola
100 H9 **Cuxhaven** Niedersachsen, NW Germany
Cuyabá *see* Cuiabá
Cuyuni, Río *see* Cuyuni River
55 S8 **Cuyuni River** *var.* Río Cuyuni. ~ Guyana/Venezuela
Cuzco *see* Cusco
97 K22 **Cwmbran** *Wel.* Cwmbrân. SW Wales, UK
Cwmbrân *see* Cwmbran
28 K15 **C. W. McConaughy, Lake** ⊠ Nebraska, C USA
81 D20 **Cyangugu** SW Rwanda
110 D11 **Cybinka** *Ger.* Ziebingen. Lubuskie, W Poland
Cyclades *see* Kykládes
Cydonia *see* Chaniá
Cymru *see* Wales
20 M5 **Cynthiana** Kentucky, S USA
9 S17 **Cypress Hills** ▲ Alberta/Saskatchewan, SW Canada
Cypro-Syrian Basin *see* Cyprus Basin
121 U11 **Cyprus** *off.* Republic of Cyprus, *Gk.* Kypros, *Turk.* Kıbrıs, Kıbrıs Cumhuriyeti. ◆ *republic* E Mediterranean Sea
84 L14 **Cyprus** *Gk.* Kypros, *Turk.* Kıbrıs. *island* E Mediterranean Sea
121 W11 **Cyprus Basin** *var.* Cypro-Syrian Basin. *undersea feature* E Mediterranean Sea
Cyprus, Republic of *see* Cyprus
Cythera *see* Kýthira
Cythnos *see* Kýthnos
110 F9 **Czaplinek** *Ger.* Tempelburg. Zachodnio-pomorskie, NW Poland
Czarna Woda *see* Wda
110 G8 **Czarne** Pomorskie, N Poland
110 G10 **Czarnków** Wielkopolskie, C Poland
111 E17 **Czech Republic** *Cz.* Česká Republika. ◆ *republic* C Europe
Czegléd *see* Cegléd
110 G12 **Czempiń** Wielkopolskie, C Poland
Czenstochau *see* Częstochowa
Czerkow *see* Čerchov
Czernowitz *see* Chernivtsi
110 I8 **Czersk** Pomorskie, N Poland
111 J15 **Częstochowa** *Ger.* Czenstochau, Tschenstochau, *Rus.* Chenstokhov. Śląskie, S Poland
110 F10 **Człopa** *Ger.* Schloppe. Zachodnio-pomorskie, NW Poland
110 H8 **Człuchów** *Ger.* Schlochau. Pomorskie, NW Poland

D

163 V9 **Da'an** *var.* Dalai. Jilin, NE China
15 S10 **Daaquam** Québec, SE Canada
Daawo, Webi *see* Dawa Wenz
54 I4 **Dabajuro** Falcón, NW Venezuela
77 N15 **Dabakala** NE Ivory Coast
163 S11 **Daban** *var* Bairin Youqi. Nei Mongol Zizhiqu, N China
111 K23 **Dabas** Pest, C Hungary
160 L8 **Daba Shan** ▲▲ C China
Dabba *see* Daocheng
140 J5 **Dabbāgh, Jabal** ▲ NW Saudi Arabia
54 D8 **Dabeiba** Antioquia, NW Colombia
154 E11 **Dabhoi** Gujarāt, W India
161 P8 **Dabie Shan** ▲▲ C China
76 J13 **Dabola** C Guinea
77 N17 **Dabou** S Ivory Coast
162 M15 **Dabqig** *var.* Uxin Qi. Nei Mongol Zizhiqu, N China
110 P8 **Dąbrowa Białostocka** Podlaskie, NE Poland
111 M16 **Dąbrowa Tarnowska** Małopolskie, S Poland
119 M20 **Dabryn'** *Rus.* Dobryn'. Homyel'skaya Voblasts', SE Belarus
159 P10 **Dabsan Hu** ◎ C China
161 Q13 **Dabu** *var.* Huliao. Guangdong, S China

◆ Country
● Country Capital
◇ Dependent Territory
○ Dependent Territory Capital
◈ Administrative Regions
✈ International Airport
▲ Mountain
▲▲ Mountain Range
Volcano
~ River
◎ Lake
⊠ Reservoir

DĂBULENI – DAWS

116 *H15* **Dăbuleni** Dolj, SW Romania
Dacca *see* Dhaka
101 *L23* **Dachau** Bayern, SE Germany
Dachuan *see* Dazhou
Dacia Bank *see* Dacia Seamount
64 *M10* **Dacia Seamount** *var.* Dacia Bank. *undersea feature* E Atlantic Ocean
37 *T3* **Dacono** Colorado, C USA
Đăc Tô *see* Đak Tô
Dacura *see* Dákura
23 *W12* **Dade City** Florida, SE USA
152 *L10* **Ḍaḍeldhurā** *var.* Dandeldhura. Far Western, W Nepal
23 *Q5* **Dadeville** Alabama, S USA
Dadong *see* Donggang
103 *N15* **Dadou** ≈ S France
154 *D12* **Dādra and Nagar Haveli** ◈ *union territory* W India
149 *P14* **Dādu** Sind, SE Pakistan
167 *U11* **Da Du Bơloc** Kon Tum, C Vietnam
160 *G9* **Dadu He** ≈ C China
Daegu *see* Taegu
Daerah Istimewa Aceh *see* Aceh
171 *P4* **Daet** Luzon, N Philippines
160 *I11* **Dafang** Guizhou, S China
Dafeng *see* Shanglin
153 *W11* **Dafla Hills** ▲▲ NE India
9 *U15* **Dafoe** Saskatchewan, S Canada
76 *G10* **Dagana** N Senegal
Dagana *see* Massakory, Chad
Dagana *see* Dahana, Tajikistan
Dagcagoin *see* Zoigê
118 *K11* **Dagda** Krāslava, SE Latvia
Dagden *see* Hiiumaa
Dagden-Sund *see* Soela Väin
127 *P16* **Dagestan, Respublika** *prev.* Dagestanskaya ASSR, *Eng.* Daghestan. ◈ *autonomous republic* SW Russian Federation
Dagestanskaya ASSR *see* Dagestan, Respublika
127 *R17* **Dagestanskiye Ogni** Respublika Dagestan, SW Russian Federation
Dagezhen *see* Fengning
185 *A23* **Dagg Sound** *sound* South Island, New Zealand
Daghestan *see* Dagestan, Respublika
141 *Y8* **Daghmar** NE Oman
Dağliq Quarabağ *see* Nagorno-Karabakh
Dagö *see* Hiiumaa
54 *D11* **Dagua** Valle del Cauca, W Colombia
160 *H11* **Daguan** *var.* Cuihua. Yunnan, SW China
171 *N3* **Dagupan** *off.* Dagupan City. Luzon, N Philippines
Dagupan City *see* Dagupan
159 *N16* **Dagzê** *var.* Dêqên. Xizang Zizhiqu, W China
147 *Q13* **Dahana** *Rus.* Dagana, Dakhana. SW Tajikistan
163 *V10* **Dahei Shan** ▲▲ N China
163 *T7* **Da Hinggan Ling** *Eng.* Great Khingan Range. ▲▲ NE China
Dahlac Archipelago *see* Dahlak Archipelago
80 *K9* **Dahlak Archipelago** *var.* Dahlac Archipelago. *island group* E Eritrea
23 *T2* **Dahlonega** Georgia, SE USA
101 *O14* **Dahme** Brandenburg, E Germany
100 *O13* **Dahme** ≈ E Germany
141 *O14* **Dahm, Ramlat** *desert* NW Yemen
154 *E10* **Dāhod** *prev.* Dohad. Gujarāt, W India
Dahomey *see* Benin
158 *G10* **Dahongliutan** Xinjiang Uygur Zizhiqu, NW China
Dahra *see* Dara
139 *R2* **Dahūk** *var.* Dohuk, *Kurd.* Dihōk. N Iraq
116 *J15* **Daia** Giurgiu, S Romania
165 *P12* **Daigo** Ibaraki, Honshū, S Japan
163 *O13* **Dai Hai** ◎ N China
Daihoku *see* T'aipei
186 *M8* **Dai Island** *island* N Solomon Islands
149 *O6* **Dāikondī** ◈ *province* C Afghanistan
166 *M8* **Daik-u** Pegu, SW Burma (Myanmar)
138 *H9* **Dā'īl** Dar'ā, S Syria
167 *U12* **Đai Lanh** Khanh Hoa, S Vietnam
161 *Q13* **Daimao Shan** ▲▲ SE China
105 *N11* **Daimiel** Castilla-La Mancha, C Spain
115 *F22* **Daimoniá** Pelopónnisos, S Greece
Dainan *see* T'ainan
25 *W6* **Daingerfield** Texas, SW USA
Daingin, Bá an *see* Dingle Bay
159 *R13* **Dainkognubma** Xizang Zizhiqu, W China
164 *K14* **Daiō-zaki** *headland* Honshū, SW Japan
Dairbhre *see* Valencia Island
61 *B22* **Daireaux** Buenos Aires, E Argentina
Dairen *see* Dalian
75 *W9* **Dairûṭ** *var.* Dayrūṭ. C Egypt
25 *X10* **Daisetta** Texas, SW USA
192 *G5* **Daitō-jima** *island group* SW Japan
192 *G5* **Daitō Ridge** *undersea feature* N Philippine Sea
161 *N3* **Daixian** *var.* Dai Xian. Shanxi, C China
Dai Xian *see* Daixian
Daiyue *see* Shanyin
161 *Q12* **Daiyun Shan** ▲▲ SE China
44 *M8* **Dajabón** NW Dominican Republic
160 *G8* **Dajin Chuan** ≈ C China
148 *J6* **Dak** ◎ W Afghanistan
76 *F11* **Dakar** ● (Senegal) W Senegal
76 *F11* **Dakar** ✈ W Senegal
167 *U10* **Đak Glây** Kon Tum, C Vietnam
Dakhana *see* Dahana
153 *U16* **Dakhin Shahbazpur Island** *island* S Bangladesh
Dakhla *see* Ad Dakhla
76 *F7* **Dakhlet Nouâdhibou** ◈ *region* NW Mauritania
Đak Lap *see* Kiên Đưc
Đak Nông *see* Gia Nghia
77 *U11* **Dakoro** Maradi, S Niger
29 *U12* **Dakota City** Iowa, C USA
29 *R13* **Dakota City** Nebraska, C USA
113 *M17* **Đakovica** *var.* Djakovica, *Alb.* Gjakovë. Kosovo, S Serbia
112 *I10* **Đakovo** *var.* Djakovo, *Hung.* Diakovár. Osijek-Baranja, E Croatia
Dakshin *see* Deccan
167 *U11* **Đak Tô** *var.* Đăc Tô. Kon Tum, C Vietnam
43 *N7* **Dákura** *var.* Dacura. Región Autónoma Atlántico Norte, NE Nicaragua
95 *I14* **Dal** Akershus, S Norway
82 *E12* **Dala** Lunda Sul, E Angola
108 *J8* **Dalaas** Vorarlberg, W Austria
76 *I13* **Dalaba** W Guinea
Dalai *see* Da'an
162 *I12* **Dalain Hob** *var.* Ejin Qi. Nei Mongol Zizhiqu, N China
Dalai Nor *see* Hulun Nur
163 *Q11* **Dalai Nur** *salt lake* N China
Dala-Jarna *see* Järna
95 *M14* **Dalälven** ≈ C Sweden
136 *C16* **Dalaman** Muğla, SW Turkey
136 *C16* **Dalaman** ✈ Muğla, SW Turkey
136 *D16* **Dalaman Çayı** ≈ SW Turkey
162 *K11* **Dalandzadgad** Ömnögovĭ, S Mongolia
95 *D17* **Dalane** *physical region* S Norway
189 *Z2* **Dalap-Uliga-Djarrit** *var.* Delap-Uliga-Darrit, D-U-D. *island group* Ratak Chain, SE Marshall Islands
94 *J12* **Dalarna** *prev.* Kopparberg. ◈ *county* C Sweden
94 *L13* **Dalarna** *prev. Eng.* Dalecarlia. *cultural region* C Sweden
95 *P16* **Dalarö** Stockholm, C Sweden
167 *U13* **Đa Lat** Lâm Đồng, S Vietnam
Dalay *see* Bayandalay
148 *L12* **Dālbandin** *var.* Dāl Bandin. Baluchistān, SW Pakistan
Dāl Bandin *see* Dālbandin
95 *J17* **Dalbosjön** *lake bay* S Sweden
181 *Y10* **Dalby** Queensland, E Australia
94 *D13* **Dale** Hordaland, S Norway
94 *C12* **Dale** Sogn Og Fjordane, S Norway
32 *K12* **Dale** Oregon, NW USA
25 *T11* **Dale** Texas, SW USA
Dalecarlia *see* Dalarna
21 *W4* **Dale City** Virginia, NE USA
20 *L8* **Dale Hollow Lake** ▣ Kentucky/Tennessee, S USA
98 *O8* **Dalen** Drenthe, NE Netherlands
95 *E15* **Dalen** Telemark, S Norway
166 *K14* **Daletme** Chin State, W Burma (Myanmar)
23 *Q7* **Daleville** Alabama, S USA
98 *M9* **Dalfsen** Overijssel, E Netherlands
24 *M1* **Dalhart** Texas, SW USA
13 *O13* **Dalhousie** New Brunswick, SE Canada
152 *I6* **Dalhousie** Himāchal Pradesh, N India
160 *F12* **Dali** *var.* Xiaguan. Yunnan, SW China
Dali *see* Idálion
163 *U14* **Dalian** *var.* Dairen, Dalien, Lüda, Ta-lien, *Rus.* Dalny. Liaoning, NE China
105 *O15* **Dalías** Andalucía, S Spain
Dalien *see* Dalian
Dalijan *see* Delījān
112 *J9* **Dalj** *Hung.* Dalja. Osijek-Baranja, E Croatia
Dalja *see* Dalj
32 *F12* **Dallas** Oregon, NW USA
25 *U6* **Dallas** Texas, SW USA
25 *T7* **Dallas-Fort Worth** ✈ Texas, SW USA
154 *K12* **Dalli Rājhara** Chhattīsgarh, C India
39 *X15* **Dall Island** *island* Alexander Archipelago, Alaska, USA
38 *M12* **Dall Lake** ◎ Alaska, USA
Dállogilli *see* Korpilombolo
77 *S12* **Dallol Bosso** *seasonal river* W Niger
141 *U7* **Dalmā** *island* W United Arab Emirates
113 *E14* **Dalmacija** *Eng.* Dalmatia, *Ger.* Dalmatien, *It.* Dalmazia. *cultural region* S Croatia
Dalmatia/Dalmatien/ Dalmazia *see* Dalmacija
Dalmatien *see* Dalmacija
123 *S15* **Dal'negorsk** Primorskiy Kray, SE Russian Federation
Dalny *see* Dalian
76 *M16* **Daloa** C Ivory Coast
160 *J11* **Dalou Shan** ▲▲ S China
181 *X7* **Dalrymple Lake** ◎ Queensland, E Australia
14 *H14* **Dalrymple Lake** ◎ Ontario, S Canada
181 *X7* **Dalrymple, Mount** ▲ Queensland, E Australia
93 *K20* **Dalsbruk** *Fin.* Taalintehdas. Länsi-Soumi, W Finland
95 *K19* **Dalsjöfors** Västra Götaland, S Sweden
95 *J17* **Dals Långed** *var.* Långed. Västra Götaland, S Sweden
153 *O15* **Dāltenganj** *prev.* Daltonganj. Jhārkhand, N India
23 *R2* **Dalton** Georgia, SE USA
Daltonganj *see* Dāltenganj
195 *X14* **Dalton Iceberg Tongue** *ice feature* Antarctica
92 *J1* **Dalvík** Nordhurland Eystra, N Iceland
Dálvvadis *see* Jokkmokk
35 *N8* **Daly City** California, W USA
181 *P2* **Daly River** ≈ Northern Territory, N Australia
181 *Q3* **Daly Waters** Northern Territory, N Australia
119 *F20* **Damachava** *var.* Damachova, *Pol.* Domaczewo, *Rus.* Domachëvo. Brestskaya Voblasts', SW Belarus
Damachova *see* Damachava
77 *W11* **Damagaram Takaya** Zinder, S Niger
154 *D12* **Damān** Damān and Diu, W India
154 *B12* **Damān and Diu** ◈ *union territory* W India
75 *V7* **Damanhûr** *anc.* Hermopolis Parva. N Egypt
161 *O1* **Damaqun Shan** ▲▲ E China
79 *I15* **Damara** Ombella-Mpoko, S Central African Republic
83 *D18* **Damaraland** *physical region* C Namibia
171 *S15* **Damar, Kepulauan** *var.* Baraf Daja Islands, Kepulauan Barat Daya. *island group* C Indonesia
168 *J8* **Damar Laut** Perak, Peninsular Malaysia
171 *S15* **Damar, Pulau** *island* Maluku, E Indonesia
Damas *see* Dimashq
77 *Y12* **Damasak** Borno, NE Nigeria
Damasco *see* Dimashq
21 *Q8* **Damascus** Virginia, NE USA
Damascus *see* Dimashq
77 *X13* **Damaturu** Yobe, NE Nigeria
171 *R9* **Damau** Pulau Kaburuang, N Indonesia
143 *O5* **Damāvand, Qolleh-ye** ▲ N Iran
82 *B10* **Damba** Uíge, NW Angola
114 *M12* **Dambaslar** Tekirdağ, NW Turkey
116 *J13* **Dâmbovița** *prev.* Dîmbovița. ◈ *county* SE Romania
116 *J13* **Dâmbovița** *prev.* Dîmbovița. ≈ S Romania
173 *Y15* **D'Ambre, Île** *island* NE Mauritius
155 *K24* **Dambulla** Central Province, C Sri Lanka
44 *K9* **Dame-Marie** SW Haiti
44 *J9* **Dame Marie, Cap** *headland* SW Haiti
143 *Q4* **Dāmghān** Semnān, N Iran
Damietta *see* Dumyât
138 *G10* **Dāmiyā** Al Balqā', NW Jordan
146 *G11* **Damla** Daşoguz Welaýaty, N Turkmenistan
Dammām *see* Ad Dammān
100 *G12* **Damme** Niedersachsen, NW Germany
153 *R15* **Dāmodar** ≈ NE India
154 *J9* **Damoh** Madhya Pradesh, C India
77 *P15* **Damongo** NW Ghana
138 *G7* **Damoûr** *var.* Ad Dāmūr. W Lebanon
171 *N11* **Dampal, Teluk** *bay* Sulawesi, C Indonesia
180 *H7* **Dampier** Western Australia
180 *H6* **Dampier Archipelago** *island group* Western Australia
141 *U14* **Damqawt** *var.* Damqut. E Yemen
159 *O13* **Dam Qu** ≈ C China
Damqut *see* Damqawt
167 *R13* **Dâmrei, Chuŏr Phnum** *Fr.* Chaîne de l'Éléphant. ▲▲ SW Cambodia
108 *C7* **Damvant** Jura, NW Switzerland
Damwâld *see* Damwoude
98 *L5* **Damwoude** *Fris.* Damwâld. Friesland, N Netherlands
159 *N15* **Damxung** *var.* Gongtang. Xizang Zizhiqu, W China
80 *K11* **Danakil Desert** *var.* Afar Depression, Danakil Plain. *desert* E Africa
Danakil Plain *see* Danakil Desert
35 *R8* **Dana, Mount** ▲ California, W USA
76 *L16* **Danané** W Ivory Coast
167 *U10* **Đă Năng** *prev.* Tourane. Quang Nam-Đa Năng, C Vietnam
160 *G9* **Danba** *var.* Zhanggu, *Tib.* Rongzhag. Sichuan, C China
Danborg *see* Daneborg
18 *L13* **Danbury** Connecticut, NE USA
25 *W12* **Danbury** Texas, SW USA
35 *X15* **Danby Lake** ◎ California, W USA
194 *H4* **Danco Coast** *physical region* Antarctica
82 *B11* **Dande** ≈ NW Angola
Dandeldhura *see* Ḍaḍeldhurā
155 *E17* **Dandeli** Karnātaka, W India
183 *O12* **Dandenong** Victoria, SE Australia
163 *V13* **Dandong** *var.* Tan-tung; *prev.* An-tung. Liaoning, NE China
197 *Q14* **Daneborg** *var.* Danborg. ◈ Tunu, N Greenland
25 *V12* **Danevang** Texas, SW USA
Dänew *see* Galkynyş
Danfeng *see* Shizong
14 *L12* **Danford Lake** Québec, SE Canada
19 *T4* **Danforth** Maine, NE USA
37 *P3* **Danforth Hills** ▲▲ Colorado, C USA
Dangara *see* Danghara
159 *V12* **Dangchang** Gansu, C China
159 *P8* **Dangchengwan** *var.* Subei, Subei Mongolzu Zizhixian. Gansu, N China
82 *B10* **Dange** Uíge, NW Angola
Dangerous Archipelago *see* Tuamotu, Îles
83 *E26* **Danger Point** *headland* SW South Africa
147 *Q13* **Danghara** *Rus.* Dangara. SW Tajikistan
159 *P8* **Danghe Nanshan** ▲▲ W China
80 *I12* **Dangila** *var.* Dānglā. Amhara, NW Ethiopia
159 *P8* **Dangjin Shankou** *pass* N China
Dangla *see* Tanggula Shan, China
Dang La *see* Tanggula Shankou, China
Dānglā *see* Dangila, Ethiopia
Dangme Chu *see* Manās
153 *Y11* **Dāngori** Assam, NE India
Dang Raek, Phanom/ Dangrek, Chaîne des *see* Dângrêk, Chuŏr Phnum
167 *S11* **Dângrêk, Chuŏr Phnum** *var.* Phanom Dang Raek, Phanom Dong Rak, *Fr.* Chaîne des Dangrek. ▲▲ Cambodia/Thailand
42 *G3* **Dangriga** *prev.* Stann Creek. Stann Creek, E Belize
161 *P6* **Dangshan** Anhui, E China
33 *T15* **Daniel** Wyoming, C USA
83 *H22* **Daniëlskuil** Northern Cape, N South Africa
19 *N12* **Danielson** Connecticut, NE USA
124 *M15* **Danilov** Yaroslavskaya Oblast', W Russian Federation
127 *O9* **Danilovka** Volgogradskaya Oblast', SW Russian Federation
Danish West Indies *see* Virgin Islands (US)
160 *L7* **Dan Jiang** ≈ C China
160 *M7* **Danjiangkou Shuiku** ▣ C China
141 *W8* **Ḍank** *var.* Dhank. NW Oman
152 *J7* **Dankhar** Himāchal Pradesh, N India
126 *L6* **Dankov** Lipetskaya Oblast', W Russian Federation
42 *J7* **Danlí** El Paraíso, S Honduras
Danmark *see* Denmark
Danmarksstraedet *see* Denmark Strait
95 *O14* **Dannemora** Uppsala, C Sweden
18 *L6* **Dannemora** New York, NE USA
100 *K11* **Dannenberg** Niedersachsen, N Germany
184 *N12* **Dannevirke** Manawatu-Wanganui, North Island, New Zealand
21 *U8* **Dan River** ≈ Virginia, NE USA
167 *P8* **Dan Sai** Loei, C Thailand
18 *F10* **Dansville** New York, NE USA
Dantzig *see* Gdańsk
86 *E12* **Danube** *Bul.* Dunav, *Cz.* Dunaj, *Ger.* Donau, *Hung.* Duna, *Rom.* Dunărea. ≈ C Europe
Danubian Plain *see* Dunavska Ravnina
166 *L8* **Danubyu** Irrawaddy, SW Burma (Myanmar)
Danum *see* Doncaster
19 *P11* **Danvers** Massachusetts, NE USA
27 *T11* **Danville** Arkansas, C USA
31 *N13* **Danville** Illinois, N USA
31 *O14* **Danville** Indiana, N USA
29 *Y15* **Danville** Iowa, C USA
20 *M6* **Danville** Kentucky, S USA
18 *G14* **Danville** Pennsylvania, NE USA
21 *T6* **Danville** Virginia, NE USA
Danxian/Dan Xian *see* Danzhou
160 *L17* **Danzhou** *prev.* Danxian, Dan Xian, Nada. Hainan, S China
Danzhou *see* Yichuan
Danzig *see* Gdańsk
Danziger Bucht *see* Danzig, Gulf of
110 *J6* **Danzig, Gulf of** *var.* Gulf of Gdańsk, *Ger.* Danziger Bucht, *Pol.* Zakota Gdańska, *Rus.* Gdan'skaya Bukhta. *gulf* N Poland
160 *F10* **Daocheng** *var.* Jinzhou, *Tib.* Dabba. Sichuan, C China
Daojiang *see* Daoxian
Daokou *see* Huaxian
104 *H7* **Dão, Rio** ≈ N Portugal
Daosa *see* Dausa
77 *Y7* **Dao Timmi** Agadez, NE Niger
160 *M13* **Daoxian** *var.* Daojiang. Hunan, S China
77 *Q14* **Dapaong** N Togo
23 *N8* **Daphne** Alabama, S USA
171 *P7* **Dapitan** Mindanao, S Philippines
159 *P9* **Da Qaidam** Qinghai, C China
163 *V8* **Daqing** *var.* Sartu. Heilongjiang, NE China
163 *O13* **Daqing Shan** ▲▲ N China
163 *T11* **Daqin Tal** *var.* Naiman Qi. Nei Mongol Zizhiqu, N China
Daqm *see* Duqm
160 *G8* **Da Qu** *var.* Do Qu. ≈ C China
139 *T5* **Dāqūq** *var.* Tāwūq. N Iraq
76 *G10* **Dara** *var.* Dahra. NW Senegal
138 *H9* **Dar'ā** *var.* Der'a, *Fr.* Déraa. Dar'ā, SW Syria
138 *H8* **Dar'ā** *off.* Muḥāfaẓat Dar'ā, *var.* Dará, Der'a, Derrá. ◈ *governorate* S Syria
Dará *see* Dar'ā
143 *Q12* **Dārāb** Fārs, S Iran
116 *K8* **Darabani** Botoşani, NW Romania
Daraj *see* Dirj
Dar'ā, Muḥāfaẓat *see* Dar'ā
142 *M8* **Dārān** Eşfahān, W Iran
167 *U12* **Da Răng, Sông** *var.* Ba. ≈ S Vietnam
Daraut-Kurgan *see* Daroot-Korgon
77 *W13* **Darazo** Bauchi, E Nigeria
139 *S3* **Darband** N Iraq
139 *V4* **Darband-i Khān, Sadd** *dam* NE Iraq
139 *N1* **Darbāsīyah** *var.* Derbisīye. Al Ḥasakah, N Syria
118 *C11* **Darbėnai** Klaipėda, NW Lithuania
153 *Q13* **Darbhanga** Bihār, N India
38 *M9* **Darby, Cape** *headland* Alaska, USA
112 *I9* **Darda** *Hung.* Dárda. Osijek-Baranja, E Croatia
Dárda *see* Darda
27 *T11* **Dardanelle** Arkansas, C USA
27 *S11* **Dardanelle, Lake** ▣ Arkansas, C USA
Dardanelles *see* Çanakkale Boğazı
Dardanelli *see* Çanakkale
Dardo *see* Kangding
Dar-el-Beida *see* Casablanca
136 *M14* **Darende** Malatya, C Turkey
81 *J22* **Dar es Salaam** Dar es Salaam, E Tanzania
81 *J22* **Dar es Salaam** ✈ Pwani, E Tanzania
185 *H18* **Darfield** Canterbury, South Island, New Zealand
106 *F7* **Darfo** Lombardia, N Italy
80 *B10* **Darfur** *var.* Darfur Massif. *cultural region* W Sudan
Darfur Massif *see* Darfur
Darganata/Dargan-Ata *see* Birata
143 *T3* **Dargaz** *var.* Darreh Gaz; *prev.* Moḥammadābād. Khorāsān-Razavī, NE Iran
139 *U4* **Dargazayn** NE Iraq
183 *P12* **Dargo** Victoria, SE Australia
162 *L6* **Darhan** Darhan Uul, N Mongolia
163 *N8* **Darhan** Hentiy, C Mongolia
Darhan *see* Büreghangay
Darhan Muminggan Lianheqi *see* Bailingmiao
162 *L6* **Darhan Uul** ◈ *province* N Mongolia
23 *W7* **Darien** Georgia, SE USA
43 *W16* **Darién** *off.* Provincia del Darién. ◈ *province* SE Panama
Darién, Golfo del *see* Darien, Gulf of
43 *X14* **Darien, Gulf of** *Sp.* Golfo del Darién. *gulf* S Caribbean Sea
Darien, Isthmus of *see* Panama, Istmo de
Darién, Provincia del *see* Darién
42 *K9* **Dariense, Cordillera** ▲▲ C Nicaragua
43 *W15* **Darién, Serranía del** ▲▲ Colombia/Panama
163 *P10* **Darīganga** *var.* Ovoot. Sühbaatar, SE Mongolia
Dario *see* Ciudad Darío
Dariorigum *see* Vannes
Dariv *see* Darvi
Darj *see* Dirj
Darjeeling *see* Darjiling
153 *S12* **Darjiling** *prev.* Darjeeling. West Bengal, NE India
Darkehnen *see* Ozersk
159 *S12* **Darlag** *var.* Gümai. Qinghai, C China
183 *T3* **Darling Downs** *hill range* Queensland, E Australia
28 *M2* **Darling, Lake** ▣ North Dakota, N USA
180 *I12* **Darling Range** ▲▲ Western Australia
182 *L8* **Darling River** ≈ New South Wales, SE Australia
97 *M15* **Darlington** N England, UK
21 *T12* **Darlington** South Carolina, SE USA
30 *K9* **Darlington** Wisconsin, N USA
110 *G7* **Darłowo** Zachodnio-pomorskie, NW Poland
101 *G19* **Darmstadt** Hessen, SW Germany
75 *S7* **Darnah** *var.* Dérna. NE Libya
103 *S6* **Darney** Vosges, NE France
182 *M7* **Darnick** New South Wales, SE Australia
195 *Y6* **Darnley, Cape** *cape* Antarctica
105 *R7* **Daroca** Aragón, NE Spain
147 *S11* **Daroot-Korgon** *var.* Daraut-Kurgan. Oshskaya Oblast', SW Kyrgyzstan
61 *A23* **Darragueira** *var.* Darregueira. Buenos Aires, E Argentina
Darregueira *see* Darragueira
Darreh Gaz *see* Dargaz
142 *K7* **Darreh Shahr** *var.* Darreh-ye Shahr. Īlām, W Iran
Darreh-ye Shahr *see* Darreh Shahr
32 *I7* **Darrington** Washington, NW USA
25 *P1* **Darrouzett** Texas, SW USA
153 *S15* **Darsana** *var.* Darshana. Khulna, N Bangladesh
Darshana *see* Darsana
100 *M7* **Darss** *peninsula* NE Germany
100 *M7* **Darsser Ort** *cape* NE Germany
97 *J24* **Dart** ≈ SW England, UK
Dartang *see* Baqên
97 *P22* **Dartford** SE England, UK
182 *L12* **Dartmoor** Victoria, SE Australia
97 *I24* **Dartmoor** *moorland* SW England, UK
13 *Q15* **Dartmouth** Nova Scotia, SE Canada
97 *J24* **Dartmouth** SW England, UK
15 *Y6* **Dartmouth** ≈ Québec, SE Canada
183 *Q11* **Dartmouth Reservoir** ◎ Victoria, SE Australia
Dartuch, Cabo *see* Artrutx, Cap d'
186 *C9* **Daru** Western, SW Papua New Guinea
112 *G9* **Daruvar** *Hung.* Daruvár. Bjelovar-Bilogora, NE Croatia
Daruvár *see* Daruvar
Darvaza *see* Derweze, Turkmenistan
Darvaza *see* Darvoza, Uzbekistan
Darvazskiy Khrebet *see* Darvoz, Qatorkŭhi
Darvel Bay *see* Lahad Datu, Teluk
Darvel, Teluk *see* Lahad Datu, Teluk
162 *F8* **Darvi** *var.* Dariv. Govĭ-Altay, W Mongolia
162 *F7* **Darvi** *var.* Bulgan. Hovd, W Mongolia
148 *L9* **Darvīshān** *var.* Darweshan, Garmser. Helmand, S Afghanistan
147 *O10* **Darvoza** *Rus.* Darvaza. Jizzax Viloyati, C Uzbekistan
147 *R13* **Darvoz, Qatorkŭhi** *Rus.* Darvazskiy Khrebet. ▲▲ C Tajikistan
Darweshan *see* Darvīshān
63 *J15* **Darwin** Río Negro, S Argentina
181 *O1* **Darwin** *prev.* Palmerston, Port Darwin. *territory capital* Northern Territory, N Australia
65 *D24* **Darwin** *var.* Darwin Settlement. East Falkland, Falkland Islands
62 *H8* **Darwin, Cordillera** ▲▲ N Chile
Darwin Settlement *see* Darwin
57 *B17* **Darwin, Volcán** ⛰ Galapagos Islands, Ecuador, E Pacific Ocean
149 *S8* **Darya Khān** Punjab, E Pakistan
145 *O15* **Dar'yalyktakyr, Ravnina** *plain* S Kazakhstan
143 *T11* **Dārzīn** Kermān, S Iran
Dashennongjia *see* Shennong Ding
Dashhowuz *see* Daşoguz
Dashhowuz Welayaty *see* Daşoguz Welaýaty
162 *K7* **Dashinchilen** *var.* Süüj. Bulgan, C Mongolia
119 *O16* **Dashkawka** *Rus.* Dashkovka. Mahilyowskaya Voblasts', E Belarus
Dashkhovuz *see* Daşoguz Welaýaty
Dashkhovuzskiy Velayat *see* Daşoguz Welaýaty
Dashköpri *see* Daşköpri
Dashkovka *see* Dashkawka
148 *J15* **Dasht** ≈ SW Pakistan
Dasht-i *see* Bābūs, Dasht-e
Dashtidzhum *see* Dashtijum
147 *R13* **Dashtijum** *Rus.* Dashtidzhum. SW Tajikistan
149 *W7* **Daska** Punjab, NE Pakistan
146 *J16* **Daşköpri** *var.* Dashköpri, *Rus.* Tashkepri. Mary Welaýaty, S Turkmenistan
146 *H8* **Daşoguz** *Rus.* Dashkhovuz, *Turkm.* Dashhowuz; *prev.* Tashauz. Daşoguz Welaýaty, N Turkmenistan
146 *E9* **Daşoguz Welaýaty** *var.* Dashhowuz Welayaty, *Rus.* Dashkhovuz, Dashkhovuzskiy Velayat. ◈ *province* N Turkmenistan
Đa, Sông *see* Black River
77 *R15* **Dassa** *var.* Dassa-Zoumé. S Benin
Dassa-Zoumé *see* Dassa
29 *U8* **Dassel** Minnesota, N USA
152 *H3* **Dastegil Sar** ▲ N India
136 *C16* **Datça** Muğla, SW Turkey
165 *R4* **Date** Hokkaidō, NE Japan
154 *I8* **Datia** *prev.* Duttia. Madhya Pradesh, C India
Dåtnejaevrie *see* Tunnsjøen
159 *T10* **Datong** *var.* Qiaotou. Qinghai, C China
161 *N2* **Datong** *var.* Tatung, Ta-t'ung. Shanxi, C China
Datong *see* Tong'an
159 *S8* **Datong He** ≈ C China
159 *S9* **Datong Shan** ▲▲ C China
169 *O10* **Datu, Tanjung** *cape* Indonesia/Malaysia
Datu, Teluk *see* Lahad Datu, Teluk
Daua *see* Dawa Wenz
172 *H16* **Dauban, Mount** ▲ Silhouette, NE Seychelles
149 *T7* **Dāūd Khel** Punjab, E Pakistan
119 *G15* **Daugai** Alytus, S Lithuania
Daugava *see* Western Dvina
118 *J11* **Daugavpils** *Ger.* Dünaburg; *prev. Rus.* Dvinsk. Daugvapils, SE Latvia
Dauka *see* Dawkah
Daulatabad *see* Malāyer
101 *D18* **Daun** Rheinland-Pfalz, W Germany
155 *E14* **Daund** *prev.* Dhond. Mahārāshtra, W India
166 *M12* **Daung Kyun** *island* S Burma (Myanmar)
9 *W15* **Dauphin** Manitoba, S Canada
103 *S13* **Dauphiné** *cultural region* E France
23 *N9* **Dauphin Island** *island* Alabama, S USA
9 *X15* **Dauphin River** Manitoba, S Canada
77 *V12* **Daura** Katsina, N Nigeria
152 *H12* **Dausa** *prev.* Daosa. Rājasthān, N India
Dauwa *see* Dawwah
137 *Y10* **Däväçi** *Rus.* Divichi. NE Azerbaijan
155 *F18* **Dāvangere** Karnātaka, W India
171 *Q8* **Davao** *off.* Davao City. Mindanao, S Philippines
Davao City *see* Davao
171 *Q8* **Davao Gulf** *gulf* Mindanao, S Philippines
15 *Q11* **Daveluyville** Québec, SE Canada
29 *Z14* **Davenport** Iowa, C USA
32 *L8* **Davenport** Washington, NW USA
43 *P16* **David** Chiriquí, W Panama
15 *O11* **David** ≈ Québec, SE Canada
29 *R15* **David City** Nebraska, C USA
David-Gorodok *see* Davyd-Haradok
9 *T16* **Davidson** Saskatchewan, S Canada
21 *R10* **Davidson** North Carolina, SE USA
26 *K12* **Davidson** Oklahoma, C USA
39 *S6* **Davidson Mountains** ▲▲ Alaska, USA
172 *M8* **Davie Ridge** *undersea feature* W Indian Ocean
182 *A1* **Davies, Mount** ▲ South Australia
35 *O7* **Davis** California, W USA
27 *N12* **Davis** Oklahoma, C USA
195 *Y7* **Davis** *Australian research station* Antarctica
194 *H3* **Davis Coast** *physical region* Antarctica
18 *C16* **Davis, Mount** ▲ Pennsylvania, NE USA
24 *K9* **Davis Mountains** ▲▲ Texas, SW USA
195 *Z9* **Davis Sea** *sea* Antarctica
65 *O20* **Davis Seamounts** *undersea feature* S Atlantic Ocean
196 *M13* **Davis Strait** *strait* Baffin Bay/Labrador Sea
127 *U5* **Davlekanovo** Respublika Bashkortostan, W Russian Federation
108 *J9* **Davos** *Rmsch.* Tavau. Graubünden, E Switzerland
119 *J20* **Davyd-Haradok** *Pol.* Dawidgródek, *Rus.* David-Gorodok. Brestskaya Voblasts', SW Belarus
163 *U12* **Dawa** Liaoning, NE China
141 *O11* **Dawāsir, Wādī ad** *dry watercourse* S Saudi Arabia
81 *K15* **Dawa Wenz** *var.* Daua, Webi Daawo. ≈ E Africa
Dawaymah, Birkat ad *see* Umm al Baqar, Hawr
Dawei *see* Tavoy
119 *K14* **Dawhinava** *Rus.* Dolginovo. Minskaya Voblasts', N Belarus
Dawidgródek *see* Davyd-Haradok
141 *V12* **Dawkah** *var.* Dauka. SW Oman
Dawlat Qaṭar *see* Qatar
24 *M3* **Dawn** Texas, SW USA
Dawo *see* Maqên
140 *M11* **Daws** Al BāḤah, SW Saudi Arabia

◆ Country
● Country Capital
◇ Dependent Territory
○ Dependent Territory Capital
◈ Administrative Regions
✈ International Airport
▲ Mountain
▲▲ Mountain Range
⛰ Volcano
≈ River
◎ Lake
▣ Reservoir

DAWSON – DEVON

10 *H5* **Dawson** *var.* Dawson City. Yukon Territory, NW Canada
23 *S6* **Dawson** Georgia, SE USA
29 *S9* **Dawson** Minnesota, N USA
Dawson City *see* Dawson
9 *N13* **Dawson Creek** British Columbia, W Canada
10 *H7* **Dawson Range** ▲▲ Yukon Territory, W Canada
181 *Y9* **Dawson River** ≋ Queensland, E Australia
10 *J15* **Dawsons Landing** British Columbia, SW Canada
20 *I7* **Dawson Springs** Kentucky, S USA
23 *S2* **Dawsonville** Georgia, SE USA
160 *G8* **Dawu** *var.* Xianshui. Sichuan, C China
Dawu *see* Maqên
Dawukou *see* Shizuishan
141 *Y10* **Dawwah** *var.* Dauwa. W Oman
102 *J15* **Dax** *var.* Ax; *anc.* Aquae Augustae, Aquae Tarbelicae. Landes, SW France
Daxian *see* Dazhou
Daxue *see* Wencheng
160 *G9* **Daxue Shan** ▲▲ C China
Dayan *see* Lijiang
160 *G12* **Dayao** *var.* Jinbi. Yunnan, SW China
Dayishan *see* Gaoyou
183 *N12* **Daylesford** Victoria, SE Australia
35 *U10* **Daylight Pass** *pass* California, W USA
61 *D17* **Daymán, Río** ≋ N Uruguay
Dayong *see* Zhangjiajie
Dayr *see* Ad Dayr
138 *G10* **Dayr 'Allā** *var.* Deir 'Alla. Al Balqā', N Jordan
139 *N4* **Dayr az Zawr** *var.* Deir ez Zor. Dayr az Zawr, E Syria
138 *M5* **Dayr az Zawr** *off.* Muḩāfaẓat Dayr az Zawr, *var.* Dayr Az-Zor. ◈ *governorate* E Syria
Dayr az Zawr, Muḩāfaẓat *see* Dayr az Zawr
Dayr Az-Zor *see* Dayr az Zawr
Dayrūṭ *see* Dairûṭ
9 *Q15* **Daysland** Alberta, SW Canada
31 *R14* **Dayton** Ohio, N USA
20 *L10* **Dayton** Tennessee, S USA
25 *W11* **Dayton** Texas, SW USA
32 *L10* **Dayton** Washington, NW USA
23 *X10* **Daytona Beach** Florida, SE USA
169 *U12* **Dayu** Borneo, C Indonesia
161 *O13* **Dayu Ling** ▲▲ S China
161 *R7* **Da Yunhe** *Eng.* Grand Canal. *canal* E China
161 *S11* **Dayu Shan** *island* SE China
160 *K8* **Dazhou** *prev.* Dachuan, Daxian. Sichuan, C China
160 *J9* **Dazhu** *var.* Zhuyang. Sichuan, C China
160 *J9* **Dazu** *var.* Longgang. Chongqing Shi, C China
83 *H24* **De Aar** Northern Cape, C South Africa
194 *K5* **Deacon, Cape** *headland* Antarctica
39 *R5* **Deadhorse** Alaska, USA
33 *T12* **Dead Indian Peak** ▲ Wyoming, C USA
23 *R9* **Dead Lake** ◎ Florida, SE USA
44 *J4* **Deadman's Cay** Long Island, C Bahamas
138 *G11* **Dead Sea** *var.* Bahret Lut, Lacus Asphaltites, *Ar.* Al Baḩr al Mayyit, Baḩrat Lūt, *Heb.* Yam HaMelaḥ. *salt lake* Israel/Jordan
28 *J9* **Deadwood** South Dakota, N USA
97 *Q22* **Deal** SE England, UK
83 *I22* **Dealesville** Free State, C South Africa
161 *P10* **De'an** *var.* Puting. Jiangxi, S China
62 *K9* **Deán Funes** Córdoba, C Argentina
194 *L12* **Dean Island** *island* Antarctica
Deanuvuotna *see* Tanafjorden
31 *S10* **Dearborn** Michigan, N USA
27 *R3* **Dearborn** Missouri, C USA
Deargget *see* Tärendö
32 *K9* **Deary** Idaho, NW USA
32 *M9* **Deary** Washington, NW USA
10 *J10* **Dease** ≋ British Columbia, W Canada
10 *J10* **Dease Lake** British Columbia, W Canada
35 *U11* **Death Valley** California, W USA
35 *U11* **Death Valley** *valley* California, W USA
92 *L9* **Deatnu** *Fin.* Tenojoki, *Nor.* Tana. ≋ Finland/Norway *see also* Tenojoki
92 *M8* **Deatnu** *Fin.* Tenojoki, *Nor.* Tana. ≋ Finland/Norway
Deatnu Tenojoki
102 *L4* **Deauville** Calvados, N France
117 *X7* **Debal'tseve** *Rus.* Debal'tsevo. Donets'ka Oblast', SE Ukraine
Debal'tsevo *see* Debal'tseve
113 *M19* **Debar** *Ger.* Dibra, *Turk.* Debre. W FYR Macedonia
39 *O9* **Debauch Mountain** ▲ Alaska, USA
De Behagle *see* Laï
25 *X7* **De Berry** Texas, SW USA
127 *T2* **Debesy** Udmurtskaya Respublika, NW Russian Federation
111 *N16* **Dębica** Podkarpackie, SE Poland
De Bildt *see* De Bilt
98 *J11* **De Bilt** *var.* De Bildt. Utrecht, C Netherlands
123 *T9* **Debin** Magadanskaya Oblast', E Russian Federation
110 *N13* **Dęblin** *Rus.* Ivangorod. Lubelskie, E Poland
110 *D10* **Dębno** Zachodnio-pomorskie, NW Poland
39 *S10* **Deborah, Mount** ▲ Alaska, USA
33 *N8* **De Borgia** Montana, NW USA
Debra Birhan *see* Debre Birhan
Debra Marcos *see* Debre Mark'os
Debra Tabor *see* Debre Tabor
Debre *see* Debar
80 *J13* **Debre Birhan** *var.* Debra Birhan. Amhara, N Ethiopia
111 *N22* **Debrecen** *Ger.* Debreczin, *Rom.* Debreţin; *prev.* Debreczen. Hajdú-Bihar, E Hungary
Debreczen/Debreczin *see* Debrecen
80 *I12* **Debre Mark'os** *var.* Debra Marcos. Amhara, N Ethiopia
113 *N19* **Debrešte** SW FYR Macedonia
80 *J11* **Debre Tabor** *var.* Debra Tabor. Amhara, N Ethiopia
Debreţin *see* Debrecen
80 *J13* **Debre Zeyt** Oromo, C Ethiopia
113 *L16* **Dečani** Kosovo, S Serbia
23 *P2* **Decatur** Alabama, S USA
23 *S3* **Decatur** Georgia, SE USA
30 *L13* **Decatur** Illinois, N USA
31 *Q12* **Decatur** Indiana, N USA
22 *M5* **Decatur** Mississippi, S USA
29 *S14* **Decatur** Nebraska, C USA
25 *S6* **Decatur** Texas, SW USA
20 *H9* **Decaturville** Tennessee, S USA
103 *O13* **Decazeville** Aveyron, S France
155 *H17* **Deccan** *Hind.* Dakshin. *plateau* C India
14 *J8* **Decelles, Réservoir** ⊠ Québec, SE Canada
12 *K2* **Déception** Québec, NE Canada
160 *G11* **Dechang** *var.* Dezhou. Sichuan, C China
111 *C15* **Děčín** *Ger.* Tetschen. Ústecký Kraj, NW Czech Republic
103 *P9* **Decize** Nièvre, C France
98 *I6* **De Cocksdorp** Noord-Holland, NW Netherlands
29 *X11* **Decorah** Iowa, C USA
Dedeagaç/Dedeagach *see* Alexandroúpoli
188 *C15* **Dededo** N Guam
98 *N9* **Dedemsvaart** Overijssel, E Netherlands
19 *O11* **Dedham** Massachusetts, NE USA
63 *H19* **Dedo, Cerro** ▲ SW Argentina
77 *O13* **Dédougou** W Burkina
124 *G15* **Dedovichi** Pskovskaya Oblast', W Russian Federation
Dedu *see* Wudalianchi
155 *J24* **Deduru Oya** ≋ W Sri Lanka
83 *N14* **Dedza** Central, S Malawi
83 *N14* **Dedza Mountain** ▲ C Malawi
96 *K9* **Dee** ≋ NE Scotland, UK
97 *J19* **Dee** *Wel.* Afon Dyfrdwy. ≋ England/Wales, UK
Deep Bay *see* Chilumba
21 *T3* **Deep Creek Lake** ⊠ Maryland, NE USA
36 *J4* **Deep Creek Range** ▲▲ Utah, W USA
27 *P10* **Deep Fork** ≋ Oklahoma, C USA
14 *J11* **Deep River** Ontario, SE Canada
21 *T10* **Deep River** ≋ North Carolina, SE USA
183 *U4* **Deepwater** New South Wales, SE Australia
31 *S14* **Deer Creek Lake** ◎ Ohio, N USA
23 *Z15* **Deerfield Beach** Florida, SE USA
39 *N8* **Deering** Alaska, USA
38 *M16* **Deer Island** *island* Alaska, USA
19 *S7* **Deer Isle** *island* Maine, NE USA
13 *S11* **Deer Lake** Newfoundland and Labrador, SE Canada
99 *D18* **Deerlijk** West-Vlaanderen, W Belgium
33 *Q10* **Deer Lodge** Montana, NW USA
32 *L8* **Deer Park** Washington, NW USA
29 *U5* **Deer River** Minnesota, N USA
Deés *see* Dej
Defeng *see* Liping
31 *R11* **Defiance** Ohio, N USA
23 *Q8* **De Funiak Springs** Florida, SE USA
95 *L23* **Degeberga** Skåne, S Sweden
104 *H12* **Degebe, Ribeira** ≋ S Portugal
80 *M13* **Degeh Bur** Somali, E Ethiopia
15 *U9* **Dégelis** Québec, SE Canada
77 *U17* **Degema** Rivers, S Nigeria
95 *L16* **Degerfors** Örebro, C Sweden
193 *R14* **De Gerlache Seamounts** *undersea feature* SE Pacific Ocean
101 *N21* **Deggendorf** Bayern, SE Germany
80 *I11* **Degoma** Amhara, N Ethiopia
De Gordyk *see* Gorredijk
27 *T12* **De Gray Lake** ⊠ Arkansas, C USA
180 *J6* **De Grey River** ≋ Western Australia
126 *M10* **Degtevo** Rostovskaya Oblast', SW Russian Federation
143 *X13* **Dehak** Sīstān va Balūchestān, SE Iran
143 *R9* **Deh 'Alī** Kermān, C Iran
Dehbārez *see* Rūdān
143 *P10* **Deh Bīd** Fārs, C Iran
142 *M10* **Deh Dasht** Kohkīlūyeh va Būyer AḤmad, SW Iran
75 *N8* **Dehibat** SE Tunisia
Dehli *see* Delhi
142 *K8* **Dehlorān** Īlām, W Iran
147 *N13* **Dehqonobod** *Rus.* Dekhkanabad. Qashqadaryo Viloyati, S Uzbekistan
152 *J9* **Dehra Dūn** Uttararanchal, N India
153 *O14* **Dehri** Bihār, N India
148 *K10* **Deh Shū** *var.* Deshu. Helmand, S Afghanistan
163 *W9* **Dehui** Jilin, NE China
99 *D17* **Deinze** Oost-Vlaanderen, NW Belgium
Deir 'Alla *see* Dayr 'Allā
Deir ez Zor *see* Dayr az Zawr
Deirgeirt, Loch *see* Derg, Lough
116 *H9* **Dej** *Hung.* Dés; *prev.* Deés. Cluj, NW Romania
95 *K15* **Deje** Värmland, C Sweden
171 *Y15* **De Jongs, Tanjung** *headland* Papua, SE Indonesia
De Jouwer *see* Joure
30 *M10* **De Kalb** Illinois, N USA
22 *M5* **De Kalb** Mississippi, S USA
25 *W5* **De Kalb** Texas, SW USA
Dekéleia *see* Dhekéleia
79 *K20* **Dekese** Kasai Occidental, C Dem. Rep. Congo
Dekhkanabad *see* Dehqonobod
79 *I14* **Dékoa** Kémo, C Central African Republic
98 *H6* **De Koog** Noord-Holland, NW Netherlands
30 *M9* **Delafield** Wisconsin, N USA
61 *C23* **De La Garma** Buenos Aires, E Argentina
14 *K10* **Delahey, Lac** ◎ Québec, SE Canada
80 *E11* **Delami** Southern Kordofan, C Sudan
23 *X11* **De Land** Florida, SE USA
35 *R12* **Delano** California, W USA
29 *V8* **Delano** Minnesota, N USA
36 *K6* **Delano Peak** ▲ Utah, W USA
Delap-Uliga-Darrit *see* Dalap-Uliga-Djarrit
148 *L7* **Delārām** Nīmrūz, SW Afghanistan
38 *F17* **Delarof Islands** *island group* Aleutian Islands, Alaska, USA
30 *M9* **Delavan** Wisconsin, N USA
31 *S13* **Delaware** Ohio, N USA
18 *I17* **Delaware** *off.* State of Delaware, ***also known as*** Blue Hen State, Diamond State, First State. ◈ *state* NE USA
18 *I17* **Delaware Bay** *bay* NE USA
24 *J8* **Delaware Mountains** ▲▲ Texas, SW USA
18 *I12* **Delaware River** ≋ NE USA
27 *Q3* **Delaware River** ≋ Kansas, C USA
18 *J14* **Delaware Water Gap** *valley* New Jersey/Pennsylvania, NE USA
101 *G14* **Delbrück** Nordrhein-Westfalen, W Germany
9 *Q15* **Delburne** Alberta, SW Canada
172 *M12* **Del Cano Rise** *undersea feature* SW Indian Ocean
113 *Q18* **Delčevo** NE FYR Macedonia
Delcommune, Lac *see* Nzilo, Lac
98 *O10* **Delden** Overijssel, E Netherlands
183 *R12* **Delegate** New South Wales, SE Australia
De Lemmer *see* Lemmer
108 *D7* **Delémont** *Ger.* Delsberg. Jura, NW Switzerland
25 *R7* **De Leon** Texas, SW USA
115 *F18* **Delfoí** Stereá Ellás, C Greece
98 *G12* **Delft** Zuid-Holland, W Netherlands
155 *J23* **Delft** *island* NW Sri Lanka
98 *O5* **Delfzijl** Groningen, NE Netherlands
0 *E9* **Delgada Fan** *undersea feature* NE Pacific Ocean
42 *F7* **Delgado** San Salvador, SW El Salvador
82 *Q12* **Delgado, Cabo** *headland* N Mozambique
162 *G8* **Delger** *var.* Taygan. Govĭ-Altay, C Mongolia
163 *O9* **Delgereh** *var.* Hongor. Dornogovĭ, SE Mongolia
162 *J8* **Delgerhaan** *var.* Hujirt. Töv, C Mongolia
162 *K9* **Delgerhangay** *var.* Hashaat. Dundgovĭ, C Mongolia
162 *L9* **Delgertsogt** *var.* Amardalay. Dundgovĭ, C Mongolia
162 *L9* **Delgertsogt** *var* Amardalay. Dundgovĭ, C Mongolia
80 *E6* **Delgo** Northern, N Sudan
159 *R10* **Delhi** *var.* Delingha. Qinghai, C China
152 *I10* **Delhi** *var.* Dehli, *Hind.* Dilli, *hist.* Shahjahanabad. *union territory capital* Delhi, N India
22 *J5* **Delhi** Louisiana, S USA
18 *J11* **Delhi** New York, NE USA
152 *I10* **Delhi** ◈ *union territory* NW India
136 *J17* **Deli Burnu** *headland* S Turkey
136 *J12* **Delice Çayı** ≋ C Turkey
55 *X10* **Délices** C French Guiana
40 *J6* **Delicias** *var.* Ciudad Delicias. Chihuahua, N Mexico
143 *N7* **Delījān** *var.* Dalijan, Dilijan. Markazī, W Iran
112 *P12* **Deli Jovan** ▲▲ E Serbia
Déli-Kárpátok *see* Carpaţii Meridionali
8 *I8* **Délįne** *prev.* Fort Franklin. Northwest Territories, NW Canada
Delingha *see* Delhi
15 *Q7* **Delisle** Québec, SE Canada
9 *T15* **Delisle** Saskatchewan, S Canada
101 *M15* **Delitzsch** Sachsen, E Germany
33 *Q12* **Dell** Montana, NW USA
24 *I7* **Dell City** Texas, SW USA
103 *U7* **Delle** Territoire-de-Belfort, E France
36 *J9* **Dellenbaugh, Mount** ▲ Arizona, SW USA
29 *R11* **Dell Rapids** South Dakota, N USA
21 *Y4* **Delmar** Maryland, NE USA
18 *K11* **Delmar** New York, NE USA
100 *G11* **Delmenhorst** Niedersachsen, NW Germany
112 *C9* **Delnice** Primorje-Gorski Kotar, NW Croatia
37 *R7* **Del Norte** Colorado, C USA
39 *N6* **De Long Mountains** ▲▲ Alaska, USA
183 *P16* **Deloraine** Tasmania, SE Australia
9 *W17* **Deloraine** Manitoba, S Canada
31 *O12* **Delphi** Indiana, N USA
31 *Q12* **Delphos** Ohio, N USA
23 *Z15* **Delray Beach** Florida, SE USA
25 *O12* **Del Rio** Texas, SW USA
Delsberg *see* Delémont
94 *N11* **Delsbo** Gävleborg, C Sweden
37 *P6* **Delta** Colorado, C USA
36 *K5* **Delta** Utah, W USA
77 *T17* **Delta** ◈ *state* S Nigeria
55 *Q6* **Delta Amacuro** *off.* Territorio Delta Amacuro. ◈ *federal district* NE Venezuela
Delta Amacuro, Territorio *see* Delta Amacuro
39 *S9* **Delta Junction** Alaska, USA
23 *X11* **Deltona** Florida, SE USA
183 *T5* **Delungra** New South Wales, SE Australia
162 *D6* **Delüün** *var.* Rashaant. Bayan-Ölgiy, W Mongolia
154 *C12* **Delvāda** Gujarāt, W India
61 *B21* **Del Valle** Buenos Aires, E Argentina
Delvina *see* Delvinë
115 *C15* **Delvináki** *var.* Dhelvinákion; *prev.* Pogónion. Ípeiros, W Greece
113 *L23* **Delvinë** *var.* Delvina, *It.* Delvino. Vlorë, S Albania
Delvino *see* Delvinë
116 *I7* **Delyatyn** Ivano-Frankivs'ka Oblast', W Ukraine
127 *U5* **Dëma** ≋ W Russian Federation
105 *O5* **Demanda, Sierra de la** ▲▲ W Spain
39 *T5* **Demarcation Point** *headland* Alaska, USA
79 *K21* **Demba** Kasai Occidental, C Dem. Rep. Congo
172 *H13* **Dembéni** Grande Comore, NW Comoros
79 *M15* **Dembia** Mbomou, SE Central African Republic
Dembidollo *see* Dembī Dolo
80 *H13* **Dembī Dolo** *var.* Dembidollo. Oromo, C Ethiopia
152 *K6* **Demchok** China/India
152 *L6* **Demchok** *var.* Dêmqog. *disputed region* China/India *see also* Dêmqog
Demchok *see* Dêmqog
98 *I12* **De Meern** Utrecht, C Netherlands
99 *I17* **Demer** ≋ C Belgium
64 *H12* **Demerara Plain** *undersea feature* W Atlantic Ocean
64 *H12* **Demerara Plateau** *undersea feature* W Atlantic Ocean
55 *T9* **Demerara River** ≋ NE Guyana
126 *H3* **Demidov** Smolenskaya Oblast', W Russian Federation
37 *Q15* **Deming** New Mexico, SW USA
32 *H6* **Deming** Washington, NW USA
58 *E10* **Demini, Rio** ≋ NW Brazil
136 *D13* **Demirci** Manisa, W Turkey
113 *P19* **Demir Kapija** *prev.* Železna Vrata. SE FYR Macedonia
114 *N11* **Demirköy** Kırklareli, NW Turkey
100 *N9* **Demmin** Mecklenburg-Vorpommern, NE Germany
23 *O5* **Demopolis** Alabama, S USA
31 *N11* **Demotte** Indiana, N USA
158 *F13* **Dêmqog** *var.* Demchok. China/India
152 *L6* **Dêmqog** *var.* Demchok. *disputed region* China/India *see also* Demchok
Dêmqog *see* Demchok
Dêmqog *see* Demchok
171 *Y13* **Demta** Papua, E Indonesia
121 *K11* **Dem'yanka** ≋ C Russian Federation
124 *H15* **Demyansk** Novgorodskaya Oblast', W Russian Federation
122 *H10* **Dem'yanskoye** Tyumenskaya Oblast', C Russian Federation
103 *P2* **Denain** Nord, N France
39 *S10* **Denali** Alaska, USA
Denali *see* McKinley, Mount
81 *M14* **Denan** Somali, E Ethiopia
Denau *see* Denow
97 *J18* **Denbigh** *Wel.* Dinbych. NE Wales, UK
97 *J18* **Denbigh** *cultural region* N Wales, UK
98 *I6* **Den Burg** Noord-Holland, NW Netherlands
99 *F18* **Dender** *Fr.* Dendre. ≋ W Belgium
99 *F18* **Denderleeuw** Oost-Vlaanderen, NW Belgium
99 *F17* **Dendermonde** *Fr.* Termonde. Oost-Vlaanderen, NW Belgium
Dendre *see* Dender
194 *I9* **Dendtler Island** *island* Antarctica
98 *P10* **Denekamp** Overijssel, E Netherlands
77 *W12* **Dengas** Zinder, S Niger
Dêngkagoin *see* Têwo
162 *L13* **Dengkou** *var.* Bayan Gol. Nei Mongol Zizhiqu, N China
159 *Q14* **Dêngqên** *var.* Gyamotang. Xizang Zizhiqu, W China
Deng Xian *see* Dengzhou
160 *M7* **Dengzhou** *prev.* Deng Xian. Henan, C China
Dengzhou *see* Penglai
Den Haag *see* 's-Gravenhage
180 *H10* **Denham** Western Australia
98 *N9* **Den Ham** Overijssel, E Netherlands
44 *J12* **Denham, Mount** ▲ C Jamaica
22 *J8* **Denham Springs** Louisiana, S USA
98 *I7* **Den Helder** Noord-Holland, NW Netherlands
105 *T11* **Dénia** País Valenciano, E Spain
189 *Q8* **Denig** W Nauru
183 *N10* **Deniliquin** New South Wales, SE Australia
29 *T14* **Denison** Iowa, C USA
25 *U5* **Denison** Texas, SW USA
144 *L8* **Denisovka** *prev.* Ordzhonikidze. Kostanay, N Kazakhstan
136 *D15* **Denizli** Denizli, SW Turkey
136 *D15* **Denizli** ◈ *province* SW Turkey
Denjong *see* Sikkim
183 *S7* **Denman** New South Wales, SE Australia
195 *Y10* **Denman Glacier** *glacier* Antarctica
21 *R14* **Denmark** South Carolina, SE USA
95 *G23* **Denmark** *off.* Kingdom of Denmark, *Dan.* Danmark; *anc.* Hafnia. ◆ *monarchy* N Europe
Denmark, Kingdom of *see* Denmark
92 *H1* **Denmark Strait** *var.* Danmarksstraedet. *strait* Greenland/Iceland
45 *T11* **Dennery** E Saint Lucia
98 *I7* **Den Oever** Noord-Holland, NW Netherlands
147 *O13* **Denow** *Rus.* Denau. Surkhondaryo Viloyati, S Uzbekistan
169 *U17* **Denpasar** *prev.* Paloe. Bali, C Indonesia
116 *E12* **Denta** Timiş, W Romania
21 *Y3* **Denton** Maryland, NE USA
25 *T6* **Denton** Texas, SW USA
186 *G9* **D'Entrecasteaux Islands** *island group* SE Papua New Guinea
37 *T4* **Denver** *state capital* Colorado, C USA
37 *T4* **Denver** ✈ Colorado, C USA
24 *L6* **Denver City** Texas, SW USA
152 *J9* **Deoband** Uttar Pradesh, N India
Deoghar *see* Devghar
154 *E13* **Deolāli** Mahārāshtra, W India
154 *I10* **Deori** Madhya Pradesh, C India
153 *O12* **Deoria** Uttar Pradesh, N India
99 *A17* **De Panne** West-Vlaanderen, W Belgium
Departamento del Quindío *see* Quindío
Departamento de Narino, *see* Narino
54 *M5* **Dependencia Federal** *off.* Territorio Dependencia Federal. ◈ *federal dependency* N Venezuela
Dependencia Federal, Territorio *see* Dependencia Federal
30 *M7* **De Pere** Wisconsin, N USA
18 *D10* **Depew** New York, NE USA
99 *E17* **De Pinte** Oost-Vlaanderen, NW Belgium
25 *V5* **Deport** Texas, SW USA
123 *Q8* **Deputatskiy** Respublika Sakha (Yakutiya), NE Russian Federation
Dêqên *see* Dagzê
27 *S13* **De Queen** Arkansas, C USA
22 *G8* **De Quincy** Louisiana, S USA
81 *J20* **Dera** *spring/well* S Kenya
Der'a *see* Dar'ā
Déraa *see* Dar'ā
Der'a/Derá/Déraa *see* Dar'ā
149 *S10* **Dera Ghāzi Khān** *var.* Dera Ghāzikhān. Punjab, C Pakistan
Dera Ghāzikhān *see* Dera Ghāzi Khān
149 *S8* **Dera Ismāīl Khān** North-West Frontier Province, C Pakistan
113 *L16* **Đeravica** ▲ S Serbia
116 *L6* **Derazhnya** Khmel'nyts'ka Oblast', W Ukraine
127 *R17* **Derbent** Respublika Dagestan, SW Russian Federation
147 *N13* **Derbent** Surkhondaryo Viloyati, S Uzbekistan
Derbisīye *see* Darbāsīyah
79 *M15* **Derbissaka** Mbomou, SE Central African Republic
180 *L4* **Derby** Western Australia
97 *M19* **Derby** C England, UK
27 *N7* **Derby** Kansas, C USA
97 *L18* **Derbyshire** *cultural region* C England, UK
112 *O11* **Đerdap** *physical region* E Serbia
Derelí *see* Gónnoi
162 *L9* **Deren** *var.* Tsant. Dundgovĭ, C Mongolia
171 *W13* **Derew** ≋ Papua, E Indonesia
127 *R8* **Dergachi** Saratovskaya Oblast', W Russian Federation
Dergachi *see* Derhachi
97 *C19* **Derg, Lough** *Ir.* Loch Deirgeirt. ◎ W Ireland
117 *V5* **Derhachi** *Rus.* Dergachi. Kharkivs'ka Oblast', E Ukraine
22 *G8* **De Ridder** Louisiana, S USA
137 *P16* **Derik** Mardin, SE Turkey
83 *E20* **Derm** Hardap, C Namibia
144 *M14* **Dermentobe** *prev.* Dyurment'yube. Kzyl-Orda, S Kazakhstan
27 *W14* **Dermott** Arkansas, C USA
Dérna *see* Darnah
Dernberg, Cape *see* Dolphin Head
22 *J11* **Dernieres, Isles** *island group* Louisiana, S USA
102 *I4* **Déroute, Passage de la** *strait* Channel Islands/France
Derrá *see* Dar'ā
Derry *see* Londonderry
Dertona *see* Tortona
Dertosa *see* Tortosa
80 *H8* **Derudeb** Red Sea, NE Sudan
112 *H10* **Derventa** ◈ Republika Srpska, N Bosnia and Herzegovina
183 *O16* **Derwent Bridge** Tasmania, SE Australia
183 *O17* **Derwent, River** ≋ Tasmania, SE Australia
146 *F10* **Derweze** *Rus.* Darvaza. Ahal Welaýaty, C Turkmenistan
Deržavinsk *see* Derzhavinsk
145 *O9* **Derzhavinsk** *var.* Deržavinsk. ◈ Akmola, C Kazakhstan
Dés *see* Dej
57 *J18* **Desaguadero** Puno, S Peru
57 *J18* **Desaguadero, Río** ≋ Bolivia/Peru
191 *W9* **Désappointement, Îles du** *island group* Îles Tuamotu, C French Polynesia
27 *W11* **Des Arc** Arkansas, C USA
14 *C10* **Desbarats** Ontario, S Canada
62 *H13* **Descabezado Grande, Volcán** ⩘ C Chile
40 *B2* **Descanso** Baja California, NW Mexico
102 *L9* **Descartes** Indre-et-Loire, C France
9 *T13* **Deschambault Lake** ◎ Saskatchewan, C Canada
Deschnaer Koppe *see* Velká Deštná
32 *I11* **Deschutes River** ≋ Oregon, NW USA
80 *J12* **Desē** *var.* Desse, *It.* Dessie. Amhara, N Ethiopia
63 *I20* **Deseado, Río** ≋ S Argentina
106 *F8* **Desenzano del Garda** Lombardia, N Italy
36 *K3* **Deseret Peak** ▲ Utah, W USA
64 *P6* **Deserta Grande** *island* Madeira, Portugal, NE Atlantic Ocean
64 *P6* **Desertas, Ilhas** *island group* Madeira, Portugal, NE Atlantic Ocean
35 *X16* **Desert Center** California, W USA
35 *V15* **Desert Hot Springs** California, W USA
14 *K10* **Désert, Lac** ◎ Québec, SE Canada
36 *J2* **Desert Peak** ▲ Utah, W USA
31 *R11* **Deshler** Ohio, N USA
Deshu *see* Deh Shū
Desiderii Fanum *see* St-Dizier
106 *D7* **Desio** Lombardia, N Italy
115 *E15* **Deskáti** *var.* Dheskáti. Dytikí Makedonía, N Greece
28 *L2* **Des Lacs River** ≋ North Dakota, N USA
27 *X6* **Desloge** Missouri, C USA
9 *Q12* **Desmarais** Alberta, W Canada
29 *Q10* **De Smet** South Dakota, N USA
29 *V14* **Des Moines** *state capital* Iowa, C USA
17 *N9* **Des Moines River** ≋ C USA
117 *P4* **Desna** ≋ Russian Federation/Ukraine
116 *G14* **Desnăţui** ≋ S Romania
63 *F24* **Desolación, Isla** *island* S Chile
29 *V14* **De Soto** Iowa, C USA
23 *Q4* **De Soto Falls** *waterfall* Alabama, S USA
83 *I25* **Despatch** Eastern Cape, S South Africa
105 *N12* **Despeñaperros, Desfiladero de** *pass* S Spain
31 *N10* **Des Plaines** Illinois, N USA
115 *J21* **Despotikó** *island* Kykládes, Greece, Aegean Sea
112 *N12* **Despotovac** Serbia, E Serbia
101 *M14* **Dessau** Sachsen-Anhalt, E Germany
Desse *see* Desē
99 *J16* **Dessel** Antwerpen, N Belgium
Dessie *see* Desē
Destêrro *see* Florianópolis
23 *P9* **Destin** Florida, SE USA
Deštná *see* Velká Deštná
193 *T10* **Desventurados, Islas de los** *island group* W Chile
103 *N1* **Desvres** Pas-de-Calais, N France
116 *E12* **Deta** *Ger.* Detta. Timiş, W Romania
101 *H14* **Detmold** Nordrhein-Westfalen, W Germany
31 *S10* **Detroit** Michigan, N USA
25 *W5* **Detroit** Texas, SW USA
31 *S10* **Detroit** ≋ Canada/USA
29 *S6* **Detroit Lakes** Minnesota, N USA
31 *S10* **Detroit Metropolitan** ✈ Michigan, N USA
Detta *see* Deta
167 *S10* **Det Udom** Ubon Ratchathani, E Thailand
111 *K20* **Detva** *Hung.* Gyeva. Bankobýstricky Kraj, C Slovakia
154 *G13* **Deūlgaon Rāja** Mahārāshtra, C India
99 *L15* **Deurne** Noord-Brabant, SE Netherlands
99 *H16* **Deurne** ✈ (Antwerpen) Antwerpen, N Belgium
Deutsch-Brod *see* Havlíčkův Brod
Deutschendorf *see* Poprad
Deutsch-Eylau *see* Iława
109 *Y6* **Deutschkreutz** Burgenland, E Austria
Deutsch Krone *see* Wałcz
Deutschland/Deutschland, Bundesrepublik *see* Germany
109 *V9* **Deutschlandsberg** Steiermark, SE Austria
Deutsch-Südwestafrika *see* Namibia
109 *Y3* **Deutsch-Wagram** Niederösterreich, E Austria
Deux-Ponts *see* Zweibrücken
14 *I11* **Deux Rivieres** Ontario, SE Canada
102 *K9* **Deux-Sèvres** ◈ *department* W France
116 *G11* **Deva** *Ger.* Diemrich, *Hung.* Déva. Hunedoara, W Romania
Déva *see* Deva
Deva *see* Chester
Devana *see* Aberdeen
Devana Castra *see* Chester
Đevđelija *see* Gevgelija
136 *L12* **Deveci Dağları** ▲▲ N Turkey
137 *P15* **Devegeçidi Barajī** ⊠ SE Turkey
136 *K15* **Develi** Kayseri, C Turkey
98 *M11* **Deventer** Overijssel, E Netherlands
15 *O10* **Devenyns, Lac** ◎ Québec, SE Canada
96 *K8* **Deveron** ≋ NE Scotland, UK
153 *R14* **Devghar** *prev.* Deoghar. Jhārkhand, NE India
27 *R10* **Devil's Den** *plateau* Arkansas, C USA
35 *R7* **Devils Gate** *pass* California, W USA
30 *J2* **Devils Island** *island* Apostle Islands, Wisconsin, N USA
Devil's Island *see* Diable, Île du
29 *P3* **Devils Lake** North Dakota, N USA
31 *R10* **Devils Lake** ◎ Michigan, N USA
29 *O3* **Devils Lake** ◎ North Dakota, N USA
35 *W13* **Devils Playground** *desert* California, W USA
25 *O11* **Devils River** ≋ Texas, SW USA
33 *Y12* **Devils Tower** ▲ Wyoming, C USA
114 *I11* **Devin** *prev.* Dovlen. Smolyan, S Bulgaria
25 *R12* **Devine** Texas, SW USA
152 *H13* **Devli** Rājasthān, N India
Devne *see* Devnya
114 *N8* **Devnya** *prev.* Devne. Varna, E Bulgaria
31 *U14* **Devola** Ohio, N USA
Devoll *see* Devollit, Lumi i
113 *M21* **Devollit, Lumi i** *var.* Devoll. ≋ SE Albania
9 *Q14* **Devon** Alberta, SW Canada

◆ Country
● Country Capital
◇ Dependent Territory
○ Dependent Territory Capital
◈ Administrative Regions
✈ International Airport
▲ Mountain
▲▲ Mountain Range
⩘ Volcano
≋ River
◎ Lake
⊠ Reservoir

97 J23 **Devon** *cultural region* SW England, UK
197 N10 **Devon Island** *prev.* North Devon Island. *island* Parry Islands, Nunavut, NE Canada
183 O16 **Devonport** Tasmania, SE Australia
136 H11 **Devrek** Zonguldak, N Turkey
154 G10 **Dewās** Madhya Pradesh, C India
De Westereen *see* Zwaagwesteinde
27 P8 **Dewey** Oklahoma, C USA
Dewey *see* Culebra
98 M8 **De Wijk** Drenthe, NE Netherlands
27 W12 **De Witt** Arkansas, C USA
29 Z14 **De Witt** Iowa, C USA
29 R16 **De Witt** Nebraska, C USA
97 M17 **Dewsbury** N England, UK
161 Q10 **Dexing** Jiangxi, S China
27 Y8 **Dexter** Missouri, C USA
37 U14 **Dexter** New Mexico, SW USA
160 I8 **Deyang** Sichuan, C China
182 C4 **Dey-Dey, Lake** *salt lake* South Australia
143 S7 **Deyhūk** Yazd, E Iran
Deynau *see* Galkynyş
142 L8 **Dezful** var. Dizful. Khūzestān, SW Iran
129 X4 **Dezhneva, Mys** *headland* NE Russian Federation
161 P4 **Dezhou** Shandong, E China
Dezhou *see* Dechang
Dezh Shāhpūr *see* Marīvān
Dhaalu Atoll *see* South Nilandhe Atoll
Dhahran *see* Aẓ Ẓahrān
Dhahran Al Khobar *see* Aẓ Ẓahrān al Khubar
153 U14 **Dhaka** *prev.* Dacca. ● (Bangladesh) Dhaka, C Bangladesh
153 T15 **Dhaka** ◆ *division* C Bangladesh
Dhali *see* Idálion
141 O15 **Dhamār** W Yemen
154 K12 **Dhamtari** Chhattīsgarh, C India
153 Q15 **Dhanbād** Jhārkhand, NE India
152 L10 **Dhangaḍhi** *var.* Dhangarhi. Far Western, W Nepal
Dhangarhi *see* Dhangaḍhi
Dhank *see* Ḍank
153 R12 **Dhankuṭā** Eastern, E Nepal
152 I6 **Dhaola Dhār** ▲ NE India
154 F10 **Dhār** Madhya Pradesh, C India
153 R12 **Dharan** *var.* Dharan Bazar. Eastern, E Nepal
Dharan Bazar *see* Dharān
155 H21 **Dhārāpuram** Tamil Nādu, S India
155 H20 **Dharmapuri** Tamil Nādu, SE India
155 H18 **Dharmavaram** Andhra Pradesh, E India
154 M11 **Dharmjaygarh** Chhattīsgarh, C India
Dharmsāla *see* Dharmshāla
152 I7 **Dharmshāla** *prev.* Dharmsāla. Himāchal Pradesh, N India
155 F17 **Dhārwād** *prev.* Dharwar. Karnātaka, SW India
Dharwar *see* Dhārwād
Dhaulagiri *see* Dhawalāgiri
153 O10 **Dhawalāgiri** *var* Dhaulagiri. ▲ C Nepal
81 L18 **Dheere Laaq** *var.* Lak Dera, *It.* Lach Dera. *seasonal river* Kenya/Somalia
121 Q3 **Dhekeleia Sovereign Base Area** UK military installation E Cyprus
121 Q3 **Dhekélia** *Eng.* Dhekelia, *Gk.* Dekéleia. *UK air base* SE Cyprus
see **Dhekéleia**
Dhelvinákion *see* Delviniáki
113 M22 **Dhëmbelit, Majae** ▲ S Albania
154 O12 **Dhenkanāl** Orissa, E India
Dheskáti *see* Deskáti
138 G11 **Dhībān** Ma'dabā, NW Jordan
Dhidhimótikhon *see* Didymóteicho
Dhíkti Ori *see* Díkti
138 I12 **Dhirwah, Wādī adh** *dry watercourse* C Jordan
Dhístomon *see* Dístomo
Dhodhekánisos *see* Dodekánisa
Dhodhóni *see* Dodóni
Dhofar *see* Ẓufār
Dhomokós *see* Domokós
Dhond *see* Daund
155 H17 **Dhone** Andhra Pradesh, C India
154 B11 **Dhorāji** Gujarāt, W India
Dhráma *see* Dráma
154 C10 **Dhrāngadhra** Gujarāt, W India
Dhrepanon, Akrotírio *see* Drépano, Akrotírio
153 T13 **Dhuburi** Assam, NE India
154 F12 **Dhule** *prev.* Dhulia. Mahārāshtra, C India
Dhulia *see* Dhule
Dhún Dealgan, Cuan *see* Dundalk Bay
Dhún Droma, Cuan *see* Dundrum Bay
Dhún na nGall, Bá *see* Donegal Bay
Dhū Shaykh *see* Qazānīyah
80 Q13 **Dhuudo** Bari, NE Somalia
81 N15 **Dhuusa Marreeb** *var.* Dusa Marreb, *It.* Dusa Mareb. Galguduud, C Somalia
115 J24 **Día** *island* SE Greece
55 Y9 **Diable, Île du** *var.* Devil's Island. *island* N French Guiana
15 N12 **Diable, Rivière du** ♣ Québec, SE Canada
35 N8 **Diablo, Mount** ▲ California, W USA
35 O9 **Diablo Range** ▲ California, W USA
24 I8 **Diablo, Sierra** ▲ Texas, SW USA
45 O11 **Diablotins, Morne** ▲ N Dominica
77 N11 **Diafarabé** Mopti, C Mali
77 N11 **Diaka** ♣ SW Mali
Diakovár *see* Đakovo
76 I12 **Dialakoto** S Senegal
61 B18 **Diamante** Entre Ríos, E Argentina

62 I12 **Diamante, Río** ♣ C Argentina
59 M19 **Diamantina** Minas Gerais, SE Brazil
59 N17 **Diamantina, Chapada** ▲ E Brazil
173 U11 **Diamantina Fracture Zone** *tectonic feature* E Indian Ocean
181 T8 **Diamantina River** ♣ Queensland/South Australia
38 D9 **Diamond Head** *headland* O'ahu, Hawai'i, USA
37 P2 **Diamond Peak** ▲ Colorado, C USA
35 W5 **Diamond Peak** ▲ Nevada, W USA
Diamond State *see* Delaware
76 J11 **Diamou** Kayes, SW Mali
95 I23 **Dianalund** Vestsjælland, C Denmark
65 G25 **Diana's Peak** ▲ C Saint Helena
160 M16 **Dianbai** *var.* Shuidong. Guangdong, S China
160 G13 **Dian Chi** ◎ SW China
106 B10 **Diano Marina** Liguria, NW Italy
163 V11 **Diaobingshan** *var.* Tiefa. Liaoning, NE China
77 R13 **Diapaga** E Burkina
107 J15 **Diavolo, Passo del** *pass* C Italy
61 B18 **Díaz** Santa Fe, C Argentina
141 W6 **Dibā al Ḩiṣn** *var.* Dibāh, Dibba. Ash Shariqah, NE United Arab Emirates
139 S3 **Dibaga** N Iraq
Dibāh *see* Dibā al Ḩiṣn
79 L22 **Dibaya** Kasai Occidental, S Dem. Rep. Congo
195 W15 **Dibble Iceberg Tongue** *ice feature* Antarctica
113 L19 **Dibër** ◆ *district* E Albania
83 I20 **Dibete** Central, SE Botswana
25 W9 **Diboll** Texas, SW USA
Dibra *see* Debar
153 X11 **Dibrugarh** Assam, NE India
54 G4 **Dibulla** La Guajira, N Colombia
25 O5 **Dickens** Texas, SW USA
19 R2 **Dickey** Maine, NE USA
30 K9 **Dickeyville** Wisconsin, N USA
28 K5 **Dickinson** North Dakota, N USA
0 E6 **Dickins Seamount** *undersea feature* NE Pacific Ocean
27 O13 **Dickson** Oklahoma, C USA
20 I9 **Dickson** Tennessee, S USA
Dicle *see* Tigris
Dicsőszentmárton *see* Târnăveni
98 M12 **Didam** Gelderland, E Netherlands
163 Y8 **Didao** Heilongjiang, NE China
76 L12 **Didiéni** Koulikoro, W Mali
Didimo *see* Dídymo
81 K17 **Didimtu** *spring/well* NE Kenya
67 U9 **Dindinga Hills** ▲ S Sudan
9 Q16 **Didsbury** Alberta, SW Canada
152 G11 **Didwāna** Rājasthān, N India
115 G20 **Dídymo** *var.* Didimo. ▲ S Greece
114 L12 **Didymóteicho** *var.* Dhidhimótikhon, Didimotiho. Anatolikí Makedonía kaí Thráki, NE Greece
103 S13 **Die** Drôme, E France
77 O13 **Diébougou** SW Burkina
Diedenhofen *see* Thionville
9 S16 **Diefenbaker, Lake** ◎ Saskatchewan, S Canada
62 H7 **Diego de Almagro** Atacama, N Chile
63 F23 **Diego de Almagro, Isla** *island* S Chile
61 A20 **Diego de Alvear** Santa Fe, C Argentina
173 Q7 **Diego Garcia** *island* S British Indian Ocean Territory
Diégo-Suarez *see* Antsiranana
99 M23 **Diekirch** Diekirch, C Luxembourg
99 L23 **Diekirch** ◆ *district* C Luxembourg
76 K11 **Diéma** Kayes, W Mali
101 H15 **Diemel** ♣ W Germany
98 I10 **Diemen** Noord-Holland, C Netherlands
Diemrich *see* Deva
167 R6 **Điện Biên**, Điện Biên, Dien Bien Phu. Lai Châu, N Vietnam
Điện Biên Phu *see* Điện Biên
136 E15 **Diên Châu** Nghệ An, N Vietnam
98 N11 **Diepenbeek** Limburg, NE Belgium
98 N11 **Diepenheim** Overijssel, E Netherlands
98 M10 **Diepenveen** Overijssel, E Netherlands
100 G12 **Diepholz** Niedersachsen, NW Germany
102 M3 **Dieppe** Seine-Maritime, N France
98 M12 **Dieren** Gelderland, E Netherlands
99 J17 **Diest** Vlaams Brabant, C Belgium
108 F7 **Dietikon** Zürich, NW Switzerland
103 R13 **Dieulefit** Drôme, E France
103 T5 **Dieuze** Moselle, NE France
119 H15 **Dieveniškės** Vilnius, SE Lithuania
98 N7 **Diever** Drenthe, NE Netherlands
101 F17 **Diez** Rheinland-Pfalz, W Germany
77 Y12 **Diffa** Diffa, SE Niger
77 Y10 **Diffa** ◆ *department* SE Niger
99 L25 **Differdange** Luxembourg, SW Luxembourg
13 O16 **Digby** Nova Scotia, SE Canada
26 J5 **Dighton** Kansas, C USA
103 T14 **Digne** *var.* Digne-les-Bains. Alpes-de-Haute-Provence, SE France
Digne-les-Bains *see* Digne
Digoel *see* Digul, Sungai

103 Q10 **Digoin** Saône-et-Loire, C France
171 Q8 **Digos** Mindanao, S Philippines
149 Q16 **Digri** Sind, SE Pakistan
171 Y14 **Digul Barat, Sungai** ♣ Papua, E Indonesia
171 Y15 **Digul, Sungai** *prev.* Digoel. ♣ Papua, E Indonesia
171 Z14 **Digul Timur, Sungai** ♣ Papua, E Indonesia
153 X10 **Dihāng** ♣ NE India
Dihang *see* Brahmaputra
Dihōk *see* Dahūk
81 L17 **Diinsoor** Bay, S Somalia
99 H17 **Dijlah** *see* Tigris
99 H17 **Dijle** ♣ C Belgium
103 R8 **Dijon** *anc.* Dibio. Côte d'Or, C France
93 H14 **Dikanäs** Västerbotten, N Sweden
80 L12 **Dikhil** SW Djibouti
136 B13 **Dikili** Izmir, W Turkey
99 B17 **Diksmuide** *var.* Dixmuide, *Fr.* Dixmude. West-Vlaanderen, W Belgium
122 K7 **Dikson** Taymyrskiy (Dolgano-Nenetskiy) Avtonomnyy Okrug, N Russian Federation
115 K25 **Díkti** *var.* Dhíkti Ori. ▲ Kríti, Greece, E Mediterranean Sea
77 Z13 **Dikwa** Borno, NE Nigeria
81 J15 **Dīla** Southern, S Ethiopia
99 G18 **Dilbeek** Vlaams Brabant, C Belgium
171 Q16 **Dili** *var.* Dilli, Dilly. ● (East Timor) N East Timor
77 Y11 **Dilia** *var.* Dillia. ♣ SE Niger
167 U13 **Di Linh** Lâm Đồng, S Vietnam
101 G16 **Dillenburg** Hessen, W Germany
25 Q13 **Dilley** Texas, SW USA
Dilli *see* Dili, East Timor
Dilli *see* Delhi, India
Dillia *see* Dilia
80 E11 **Dilling** *var.* Ad Dalanj. Southern Kordofan, C Sudan
101 D20 **Dillingen** Saarland, SW Germany
101 J22 **Dillingen an der Donau** *var.* Dillingen. Bayern, S Germany
39 O13 **Dillingham** Alaska, USA
33 Q12 **Dillon** Montana, NW USA
21 T12 **Dillon** South Carolina, SE USA
31 T13 **Dillon Lake** ◎ Ohio, N USA
Dilly *see* Dili
Dilman *see* Salmās
79 K24 **Dilolo** Katanga, S Dem. Rep. Congo
115 J20 **Dílos** *island* Kykládes, Greece, Aegean Sea
141 Y11 **Dil', Ra's ad** *headland* E Oman
108 G9 **Disentis** *Rmsch.* Mustér. Graubünden, S Switzerland
39 O10 **Dishna River** ♣ Alaska, USA
108 B12 **Disko Bugt** *see* Qeqertarsuup Tunua
195 X4 **Dismal Mountains** ▲ Antarctica
28 M14 **Dismal River** ♣ Nebraska, C USA
99 L19 **Dison** Liège, E Belgium
153 V12 **Dispur** *capital* Assam, NE India
15 R11 **Disraeli** Québec, SE Canada
115 F18 **Dístomo** *prev.* Dhístomon. Stereá Elláos, C Greece
59 L14 **Distrito Federal** *Eng.* Federal District. ◆ *federal district* C Brazil
41 P14 **Distrito Federal** ◆ *federal district* S Mexico
54 L4 **Distrito Federal** *off.* Territorio Distrito Federal. ◆ *federal district* N Venezuela
Distrito Federal, Territorio *see* Distrito Federal
116 J10 **Ditrău** *Hung.* Ditró. Harghita, C Romania
Ditró *see* Ditrău
154 B12 **Diu** Damān and Diu, W India
103 S13 **Divača** SW Slovenia
102 K5 **Dives** ♣ N France
33 Q11 **Divide** Montana, NW USA
116 F12 **Divin** *see* Divin
83 N18 **Divinhe** Sofala, E Mozambique
59 L20 **Divinópolis** Minas Gerais, SE Brazil
127 N13 **Divnoye** Stavropol'skiy Kray, SW Russian Federation
76 M17 **Divo** S Ivory Coast
121 J21 **Dinant** Namur, S Belgium
136 E15 **Dinar** Afyon, SW Turkey
112 F13 **Dinara** ▲ W Croatia
112 F13 **Dinara** *var.* Dinaric Alps. ▲ Bosnia and Herzegovina/Croatia
137 N16 **Divriği** Sivas, C Turkey
149 S10 **Diwāniyah** *see* Ad Dīwānīyah
35 N7 **Dixon** California, W USA
30 L10 **Dixon** Illinois, N USA
20 I6 **Dixon** Kentucky, S USA
27 V6 **Dixon** Missouri, C USA
37 S9 **Dixon** New Mexico, SW USA
9 Y15 **Dixon Entrance** *strait* Canada/USA
18 D14 **Dixonville** Pennsylvania, NE USA
137 T13 **Diyadin** Ağrı, E Turkey
139 V5 **Diyālá, Nahr** *var.* Rudkhaneh-ye Sīrvān, Sīrwan. ♣ Iran/Iraq *see also* Sīrvān, Rudkhaneh-ye
Diyālá, Nahr *see* Sīrvān, Rudkhaneh-ye
137 P15 **Diyarbakır** *var.* Diarbekr; *anc.* Amida. Diyarbakır, SE Turkey
137 P15 **Diyarbakır** ◆ *province* SE Turkey

101 J21 **Dinkelsbühl** Bayern, S Germany
101 D14 **Dinslaken** Nordrhein-Westfalen, W Germany
35 R11 **Dinuba** California, W USA
21 W7 **Dinwiddie** Virginia, NE USA
98 N13 **Dinxperlo** Gelderland, E Netherlands
Dio *see* Díon
26 M12 **Dioïla** Koulikoro, W Mali
115 F14 **Díon** *var* Dio; *anc.* Dium. *site of ancient city* Kentrikí Makedonía, N Greece
115 G19 **Dióryga Korinthou** *Eng.* Corinth Canal. *canal* S Greece
76 G12 **Dioubloulou** SW Senegal
77 N11 **Dioura** Mopti, W Mali
76 G11 **Diourbel** W Senegal
152 L10 **Dipāyal** Far Western, W Nepal
121 R1 **Dipkarpaz** *Gk.* Rizokárpason, Rizokárpason. NE Cyprus
149 R17 **Diplo** Sind, SE Pakistan
171 P7 **Dipolog** *var.* Dipolog City. Mindanao, S Philippines
Dipolog City *see* Dipolog
185 C23 **Dipton** Southland, South Island, New Zealand
77 O10 **Diré** Tombouctou, C Mali
80 L13 **Dirē Dawa** Dirē Dawa, E Ethiopia
115 H18 **Dirfís** *var.* Dírfis. ▲ Évvoia, C Greece
Dírfis *see* Dirfís
75 N9 **Dirj** *var.* Daraj, Darj. W Libya
181 X11 **Dirk Hartog Island** *island* Western Australia
181 X11 **Dirranbandi** Queensland, E Australia
81 O16 **Dirri** Galguduud, C Somalia
37 Q13 **Dirty Devil River** ♣ Utah, W USA
32 E10 **Disappointment, Cape** *headland* Washington, NW USA
180 L8 **Disappointment, Lake** *salt lake* Western Australia
183 R12 **Disaster Bay** *bay* New South Wales, SE Australia
44 J11 **Discovery Bay** C Jamaica
182 K13 **Discovery Bay** *inlet* SW Australia
67 Y15 **Discovery II Fracture Zone** *tectonic feature* SW Indian Ocean
Discovery Seamount/ Discovery Seamounts *see* Discovery Tablemount
65 O19 **Discovery Tablemount** *var.* Discovery Seamount, Discovery Seamounts. *undersea feature* SW Indian Ocean

126 K3 **Dmitriyevsk** *see* Makiyivka
39 O10 **Dishna River** ...

126 K3 **Dmitriyevka** Moskovskaya Oblast', W Russian Federation
126 J6 **Dmitrovich** *see* Dzmitravichy
195 X4 **Dmitrovsk-Orlovskiy** Orlovskaya Oblast', W Russian Federation
117 R3 **Dmytrivka** Chernihivs'ka Oblast', N Ukraine
117 R3 **Dmytrivka** Chernihivs'ka Oblast', N Ukraine
Dnepr *see* Dnieper
Dneprodzerzhinsk *see* Dniprodzerzhyns'k
Dneprodzerzhinskoye Vodokhranilishche *see* Dniprodzerzhyns'ke Vodoskhovyshche
Dnepropetrovsk *see* Dnipropetrovs'k
Dnepropetrovskaya Oblast' *see* Dnipropetrovs'ka Oblast'
Dneprorudnoye *see* Dniprorudne
Dneprovskiy Liman *see* Dnipros'kyy Lyman
Dneprovsko-Bugskiy Kanal *see* Dnyaprowska-Buhski, Kanal
Dnestr *see* Dniester
Dnestrovskiy Liman *see* Dnistrovs'kyy Lyman
86 H11 **Dnieper** *Bel.* Dnyapro, *Rus.* Dnepr, *Ukr.* Dnipro. ♣ E Europe
117 P3 **Dnieper Lowland** *Bel.* Prydnyaprowskaya Nizina, *Ukr.* Prydniprovs'ka Nyzovyna. *lowlands* Belarus/Ukraine
116 M8 **Dniester** *Rom.* Nistru, *Rus.* Dnestr, *Ukr.* Dnister; *anc.* Tyras. ♣ Moldova/Ukraine
Dnipro *see* Dnieper
117 T7 **Dniprodzerzhyns'k** *Rus.* Dneprodzerzhinsk; *prev.* Kamenskoye. Dnipropetrovs'ka Oblast', E Ukraine
117 T7 **Dniprodzerzhyns'ke Vodoskhovyshche** *Rus.* Dneprodzerzhinskoye Vodokhranilishche. ◎ C Ukraine
117 U7 **Dnipropetrovs'k** *Rus.* Dnepropetrovsk; *prev.* Yekaterinoslav. Dnipropetrovs'ka Oblast', E Ukraine
117 T7 **Dnipropetrovs'k** ✈ Dnipropetrovs'ka Oblast', E Ukraine
117 T7 **Dnipropetrovs'ka Oblast'** *var.* Dnipropetrovs'k, *Rus.* Dnepropetrovskaya Oblast'. ◆ *province* E Ukraine
117 U9 **Dniprorudne** *Rus.* Dneprorudnoye. Zaporiz'ka Oblast', SE Ukraine
117 Q11 **Dnipros'kyy Lyman** *Rus.* Dneprovskiy Liman. *bay* S Ukraine
117 O10 **Dnistrovs'kyy Lyman** *Rus.* Dnestrovskiy Liman. *inlet* S Ukraine
124 G14 **Dno** Pskovskaya Oblast', W Russian Federation
119 H20 **Dnyaprowska-Buhski, Kanal** *Rus.* Dneprovsko-Bugskiy Kanal. *canal* SW Belarus

Djakovica *see* Đakovica
Djakovo *see* Đakovo
79 G20 **Djambala** Plateaux, S Congo
79 I20 **Djambi** *see* Hari, Batang
Djambi *see* Jambi
74 M9 **Djanet** E Algeria
74 M11 **Djanet** *prev.* Fort Charlet. SE Algeria
Djaul *see* Dyaul Island
Djawa *see* Jawa
Djéblé *see* Jablah
76 M12 **Dioïla** Koulikoro, W Mali
115 F14 ...
74 I10 **Djédaa** Batha, C Chad
74 J6 **Djelfa** *var.* El Djelfa. N Algeria
79 M14 **Djéma** Haut-Mbomou, E Central African Republic
Djember *see* Jember
Djeneponto *see* Jeneponto
77 N12 **Djenné** *var.* Jenné. Mopti, C Mali
Djérablous *see* Jarābulus
76 G11 **Djerba** *see* Jerba, Île de
79 F15 **Djérem** ♣ C Cameroon
77 P11 **Djibo** N Burkina
80 L12 **Djibouti** *var.* Jibuti. ● (Djibouti) E Djibouti
80 L12 **Djibouti** *off.* Republic of Djibouti, *var.* Jibuti; *prev.* French Somaliland, French Territory of the Afars and Issas, Côte Française des Somalis, Fr. Territoire Français des Afars et des Issas. ◆ *republic* E Africa
80 L12 **Djibouti** ✈ E Djibouti
Djibouti, Republic of *see* Djibouti
Djidjel/Djidjelli *see* Jijel
55 W10 **Djoemoe** Sipaliwini, C Surinam
77 Y8 **Dirkou** Agadez, NE Niger
55 W10 **Djoemoe** Sipaliwini, C Surinam
79 K21 **Djoku-Punda** Kasai Occidental, S Dem. Rep. Congo
79 K18 **Djolu** Equateur, N Dem. Rep. Congo
79 F17 **Djoua** ♣ Congo/Gabon
79 F16 **Djougou** W Benin
78 I8 **Djourab, Erg du** *desert* N Chad
79 P17 **Djugu** Orientale, NE Dem. Rep. Congo
92 L3 **Djúpivogur** Austurland, SE Iceland
94 L13 **Djura** Dalarna, C Sweden
Djurdjevac *see* Đurđevac
83 G18 **D'Kar** Ghanzi, NW Botswana
197 U6 **Dmitriya Lapteva, Proliv** *strait* N Russian Federation
126 J7 **Dmitriyev-L'govskiy** Kurskaya Oblast', W Russian Federation
Dmitriyevsk *see* Makiyivka

13 O14 **Doaktown** New Brunswick, SE Canada
78 H13 **Doba** Logone-Oriental, S Chad
118 E9 **Dobele** *Ger.* Doblen. Dobele, W Latvia
101 N16 **Döbeln** Sachsen, E Germany
171 U12 **Doberai, Jazirah** *Dut.* Vogelkop. *peninsula* Papua, E Indonesia
110 F10 **Dobiegniew** *Ger.* Lubuskie, Woldenberg Neumark. Lubuskie, W Poland
Doblen *see* Dobele
81 K18 **Dobli** *spring/well* SW Somalia
112 H11 **Doboj** ◆ Republiks Srpska, N Bosnia and Herzegovina
110 L8 **Dobre Miasto** *Ger.* Guttstadt. Warmińsko-mazurskie, NE Poland
114 N7 **Dobrich** *Rom.* Bazargic; *prev.* Tolbukhin. Dobrich, NE Bulgaria
114 N7 **Dobrich** ◆ *province* NE Bulgaria
126 M8 **Dobrinka** Lipetskaya Oblast', W Russian Federation
126 M7 **Dobrinka** Volgogradskaya Oblast', SW Russian Federation
Dobrla Vas *see* Eberndorf
111 I15 **Dobrodzień** *Ger.* Guttentag. Opolskie, S Poland
Dobrogea *see* Dobruja
117 W7 **Dobropillya** *Rus.* Dobropol'ye. Donets'ka Oblast', SE Ukraine
Dobropol'ye *see* Dobropillya
117 P8 **Dobrovelychkivka** Kirovohrads'ka Oblast', C Ukraine
Dobrudja/Dobrudzha *see* Dobruja
114 O7 **Dobruja** *var.* Dobrudja, *Bul.* Dobrudzha, *Rom.* Dobrogea. *physical region* Bulgaria/Romania
119 P19 **Dobrush** Homyel'skaya Voblasts', SE Belarus
125 U14 **Dobryanka** Permskaya Oblast', NW Russian Federation
117 O2 **Dobryanka** Chernihivs'ka Oblast', N Ukraine
Dobryn' *see* Dabryn'
21 R8 **Dobson** North Carolina, SE USA
59 N20 **Doce, Rio** ♣ SE Brazil
93 I16 **Docksta** Västernorrland, C Sweden
41 N10 **Doctor Arroyo** Nuevo León, NE Mexico
62 L4 **Doctor Pedro P. Peña** Boquerón, W Paraguay
171 S11 **Dodaga** Pulau Halmahera, E Indonesia
155 G21 **Dodda Betta** ▲ S India
115 M22 **Dodekánisa** *var.* Dodekanese, Sporádes; *Eng.* Dodecanese; *prev.* Dhodhekánisos, Dodekánisos. *island group* SE Greece
Dodekanisos *see* Dodekánisa
26 J6 **Dodge City** Kansas, C USA
30 K9 **Dodgeville** Wisconsin, N USA
97 H25 **Dodman Point** *headland* SW England, UK
81 J14 **Dodola** Oromo, C Ethiopia
81 H22 **Dodoma** ● (Tanzania) Dodoma, C Tanzania
81 H22 **Dodoma** ◆ *region* C Tanzania
115 C16 **Dodóni** *var.* Dhodhóni. *site of ancient city* Ípeiros, W Greece
33 U7 **Dodson** Montana, NW USA
25 P3 **Dodson** Texas, SW USA
98 M12 **Doesburg** Gelderland, E Netherlands
98 N12 **Doetinchem** Gelderland, E Netherlands
158 L12 **Dogai Coring** *var.* Lake Montcalm. ◎ W China
137 N15 **Doğanşehir** Malatya, C Turkey
84 E9 **Dogger Bank** *undersea feature* C North Sea
23 S10 **Dog Island** *island* Florida, SE USA
14 C2 **Dog Lake** ◎ Ontario, S Canada
106 B9 **Dogliani** Piemonte, NE Italy
164 H11 **Dōgo** *island* Oki-shotō, SW Japan
77 S12 **Dogondoutchi** Dosso, SW Niger
Dogrular *see* Pravda
137 T13 **Doğubayazıt** Ağrı, E Turkey
137 P12 **Doğu Karadeniz Dağları** *var.* Anadolu Dağları. ▲ NE Turkey
158 K16 **Dogxung Zangbo** ♣ W China
Doha *see* Ad Dawḩah
Doha *see* Ad Dawḩah
Dohad *see* Dāhod
Dohuk *see* Dahūk
159 N16 **Doilungdêqên** *var.* Namka. Xizang Zizhiqu, W China
114 F12 **Doïráni, Límni** *var.* Limni Doïranis, *Bul.* Ezero Doyranko. ◎ N Greece
Doire *see* Londonderry
59 H22 **Doische** Namur, S Belgium
59 P15 **Dois de Julho** ✈ (Salvador) Bahia, NE Brazil
60 H10 **Dois Vizinhos** Paraná, S Brazil
139 T3 **Dokan** *var.* Dūkān. E Iraq
94 H13 **Dokka** Oppland, S Norway
98 L5 **Dokkum** Friesland, N Netherlands
98 L5 **Dokkumer Ee** ♣ N Netherlands
76 K13 **Doko** Haute-Guinée, NE Guinea
Dokshitsy *see* Dokshytsy
118 K13 **Dokshytsy** *Rus.* Dokshitsy. Vitsyebskaya Voblasts', N Belarus
117 X8 **Dokuchayevs'k** *var.* Dokuchayevsk. Donets'ka Oblast', SE Ukraine
Dokuchayevsk *see* Dokuchayevs'k

Legend:
◆ Country | ◇ Dependent Territory | ● Administrative Regions | ▲ Mountain | ♣ Volcano | ◎ Lake
● Country Capital | ○ Dependent Territory Capital | ✈ International Airport | ▲ Mountain Range | ♣ River | ▣ Reservoir

DOLAK, PULAU – DUBOVKA

Dolak, Pulau see Yos Sudarso, Pulau
29 P9 **Doland** South Dakota, N USA
63 J18 **Dolavón** Chaco, S Argentina
15 P6 **Dolbeau** Québec, SE Canada
102 I5 **Dol-de-Bretagne** Ille-et-Vilaine, NW France
64 J13 **Doldrums Fracture Zone** *tectonic feature* W Atlantic Ocean
103 S8 **Dôle** Jura, E France
97 J19 **Dolgellau** NW Wales, UK
Dolginovo see Dawhinava
Dolgi, Ostrov see Dolgiy, Ostrov
125 U2 **Dolgiy, Ostrov** var. Ostrov Dolgi. *island* NW Russian Federation
162 J9 **Dölgöön** Övörhangay, C Mongolia
107 C20 **Dolianova** Sardegna, Italy, C Mediterranean Sea
Dolina see Dolyna
123 T13 **Dolinsk** Ostrov Sakhalin, Sakhalinskaya Oblast', SE Russian Federation
Dolinskaya see Dolyns'ka
79 F21 **Dolisie** prev. Loubomo. Le Niari, S Congo
116 G14 **Dolj** ❖ *county* SW Romania
98 P5 **Dollard** *bay* NW Germany
194 J5 **Dolleman Island** *island* Antarctica
114 I8 **Dolni Dŭbnik** Pleven, N Bulgaria
114 F8 **Dolni Lom** Vidin, NW Bulgaria
Dolnja Lendava see Lendava
114 K9 **Dolno Panicherevo** var. Panicherevo. Sliven, C Bulgaria
129 F14 **Dolnośląskie** ❖ *province* SW Poland
111 K18 **Dolný Kubín** *Hung.* Alsókubin. Žilinský Kraj, N Slovakia
106 H8 **Dolo** Veneto, NE Italy
Dolomites/Dolomiti see Dolomitiche, Alpi
106 H6 **Dolomitiche, Alpi** var. Dolomiti, *Eng.* Dolomites. ▲▲ NE Italy
Dolonnur see Duolun
Doloon see Tsogt-Ovoo
61 E21 **Dolores** Buenos Aires, E Argentina
42 E3 **Dolores** Petén, N Guatemala
171 Q5 **Dolores** Samar, C Philippines
105 S12 **Dolores** País Valenciano, E Spain
61 D19 **Dolores** Soriano, SW Uruguay
41 N12 **Dolores Hidalgo** var. Ciudad de Dolores Hidalgo. Guanajuato, C Mexico
8 J7 **Dolphin and Union Strait** *strait* Northwest Territories/ Nunavut, N Canada
65 D23 **Dolphin, Cape** *headland* East Falkland, Falkland Islands
44 H12 **Dolphin Head** *hill* W Jamaica
83 B21 **Dolphin Head** var. Cape Dernberg. *headland* SW Namibia
110 G12 **Dolsk** *Ger.* Dolzig. Weilkopolskie, C Poland
167 S8 **Đô Lương** Nghê An, N Vietnam
116 I6 **Dolyna** *Rus.* Dolina. Ivano-Frankivs'ka Oblast', W Ukraine
117 R8 **Dolyns'ka** *Rus.* Dolinskaya. Kirovohrads'ka Oblast', S Ukraine
Dolzig see Dolsk
Domachëvo/Domaczewo see Damachava
117 P9 **Domanivka** Mykolayivs'ka Oblast', S Ukraine
153 S13 **Domar** Rajshahi, N Bangladesh
108 I9 **Domat/Ems** Graubünden, SE Switzerland
111 A18 **Domažlice** *Ger.* Taus. Plzeňský Kraj, W Czech Republic
127 X8 **Dombarovskiy** Orenburgskaya Oblast', W Russian Federation
94 G10 **Dombås** Oppland, S Norway
83 M17 **Dombe** Manica, C Mozambique
82 A13 **Dombe Grande** Benguela, C Angola
103 R10 **Dombes** *physical region* E France
111 I25 **Dombóvár** Tolna, S Hungary
99 D14 **Domburg** Zeeland, SW Netherlands
58 L13 **Dom Eliseu** Pará, NE Brazil
Domel Island see Letsôk-aw Kyun
103 O11 **Dôme, Puy de** ▲ C France
36 H13 **Dome Rock Mountains** ▲▲ Arizona, SW USA
Domesnes, Cape see Kolkasrags
62 G8 **Domeyko** Atacama, N Chile
62 H5 **Domeyko, Cordillera** ▲▲ N Chile
102 K5 **Domfront** Orne, N France
171 X13 **Dom, Gunung** ▲ Papua, E Indonesia
45 X11 **Dominica** *off.* Commonwealth of Dominica. ◆ *republic* E West Indies
47 S3 **Dominica** *island* Dominica
Dominica Channel see Martinique Passage
Dominica, Commonwealth of see Dominica
43 N15 **Dominical** Puntarenas, SE Costa Rica
45 Q8 **Dominican Republic** ◆ *republic* C West Indies
45 X11 **Dominica Passage** *passage* E Caribbean Sea
99 K14 **Dommel** 〜 S Netherlands
81 O14 **Domo** Somali, E Ethiopia
126 L4 **Domodedovo** ✕ (Moskva) Moskovskaya Oblast', W Russian Federation
106 C6 **Domodossola** Piemonte, NE Italy
115 F17 **Domokós** var. Dhomokós. Stereá Ellás, C Greece
172 I14 **Domoni** Anjouan, SE Comoros
61 G16 **Dom Pedrito** Rio Grande do Sul, S Brazil
Dompoe see Dompu
170 M16 **Dompu** prev. Dompoe. Sumbawa, C Indonesia
Domschale see Domžale
62 H13 **Domuyo, Volcán** ▲ W Argentina
109 U11 **Domžale** *Ger.* Domschale. C Slovenia
127 O10 **Don** var. Duna, Tanais. 〜 SW Russian Federation
96 K9 **Don** 〜 NE Scotland, UK
182 M11 **Donald** Victoria, SE Australia
22 J9 **Donaldsonville** Louisiana, S USA
23 S8 **Donalsonville** Georgia, SE USA
Donau see Danube
101 G23 **Donaueschingen** Baden-Württemberg, SW Germany
101 K22 **Donaumoos** *wetland* S Germany
101 K22 **Donauwörth** Bayern, S Germany
109 U7 **Donawitz** Steiermark, SE Austria
117 X7 **Donbass** *industrial region* Russian Federation/Ukraine
104 K11 **Don Benito** Extremadura, W Spain
97 M17 **Doncaster** *anc.* Danum. N England, UK
44 K12 **Don Christophers Point** *headland* C Jamaica
55 V9 **Donderkamp** Sipaliwini, NW Surinam
82 B12 **Dondo** Cuanza Norte, NW Angola
171 O12 **Dondo** Sulawesi, N Indonesia
83 N17 **Dondo** Sofala, C Mozambique
155 K26 **Dondra Head** *headland* S Sri Lanka
Donduşani see Donduşeni
116 M8 **Donduşeni** var. Donduşani, *Rus.* Dondyushany. N Moldova
Dondyushany see Donduşeni
97 D15 **Donegal** *Ir.* Dún na nGall. Donegal, NW Ireland
97 D14 **Donegal** *Ir.* Dún na nGall. ❖ *county* NW Ireland
97 C15 **Donegal Bay** *Ir.* Bá Dhún na nGall. *bay* NW Ireland
84 K10 **Donets** 〜 Russian Federation/Ukraine
117 X8 **Donets'k** *Rus.* Donetsk; *prev.* Stalino. Donets'ka Oblast', E Ukraine
117 W8 **Donets'k** ✕ Donets'ka Oblast', E Ukraine
Donets'k see Donets'ka Oblast'
117 W8 **Donets'ka Oblast'** var. Donets'k, *Rus.* Donetskaya Oblast'; *prev. Rus.* Stalins'kaya Oblast'. ❖ *province* SE Ukraine
Donetskaya Oblast' see Donets'ka Oblast'
67 P8 **Donga** 〜 Cameroon/Nigeria
157 O13 **Dongchuan** Yunnan, SW China
99 I14 **Dongen** Noord-Brabant, S Netherlands
160 K17 **Dongfang** var. Basuo. Hainan, S China
163 Z7 **Dongfanghong** Heilongjiang, NE China
163 W11 **Dongfeng** Jilin, NE China
Đông Phu see Đông Xoai
171 N12 **Donggala** Sulawesi, C Indonesia
163 V13 **Donggang** var Dadong, prev Donggou. Liaoning, NE China
Donggou see Donggang
161 O14 **Dongguan** Guangdong, S China
167 T9 **Đông Ha** Quang Tri, C Vietnam
Dong Hai see East China Sea
161 M16 **Donghai Dao** *island* S China
162 I12 **Dong He** *Mong.* Narin Gol. 〜 N China
Donghe see Wangcang
167 T9 **Đông Hơi** Quang Binh, C Vietnam
108 H10 **Dongio** Ticino, S Switzerland
Dongkan see Binhai
160 L11 **Dongkou** Hunan, S China
Dongliao see Liaoyuan
Dong-nai see Đông Nai, Sông
167 U13 **Đông Nai, Sông** var. Dong-nai, Dong Noi, Donnai. 〜 S Vietnam
161 N14 **Dongnan Qiuling** *plateau* SE China
163 Y9 **Dongning** Heilongjiang, NE China
Dong Noi see Đông Nai, Sông
83 C14 **Dongo** Huíla, C Angola
80 E7 **Dongola** var. Donqola, Dunqulah. Northern, N Sudan
79 I17 **Dongou** La Likouala, NE Congo
Dongping see Anhua
Dong Rak, Phanom see Dângrêk, Chuŏr Phnum
161 Q14 **Dongshan Dao** *island* SE China
Dongsha Qundao see Tungsha Tao
Dongsheng see Ordos
161 R7 **Dongtai** Jiangsu, E China
161 N10 **Dongting Hu** var. Tung-t'ing Hu. ◎ S China
161 P10 **Dongxiang** var. Xiaogang. Jiangxi, S China
167 T13 **Đông Xoai** var. Đông Phu. Sông Be, S Vietnam
161 Q4 **Dongying** Shandong, E China
27 X8 **Doniphan** Missouri, C USA
Donja Łužica see Niederlausitz
10 G7 **Donjek** 〜 Yukon Territory, W Canada
112 E11 **Donji Lapac** Lika-Senj, W Croatia
112 H8 **Donji Miholjac** Osijek-Baranja, NE Croatia
112 P12 **Donji Milanovac** Serbia, E Serbia
112 G12 **Donji Vakuf** var. Srbobran. ❖ Federacija Bosna I Hercegovina, C Bosnia and Herzegovina
98 M6 **Donkerbroek** Friesland, N Netherlands
167 P11 **Don Muang** ✕ (Krung Thep) Nonthaburi, C Thailand
25 S17 **Donna** Texas, SW USA
15 Q10 **Donnacona** Québec, SE Canada
Donnai see Đông Nai, Sông
29 Y16 **Donnellson** Iowa, C USA
9 O13 **Donnelly** Alberta, W Canada
35 P6 **Donner Pass** *Pass* California, W USA
101 F19 **Donnersberg** ▲ W Germany
Donoso see Miguel de la Borda
105 P2 **Donostia-San Sebastián** País Vasco, N Spain
115 K21 **Donoúsa** *island* Kykládes, Greece, Aegean Sea
Donoússa see Donoúsa
35 P8 **Don Pedro Reservoir** ⊠ California, W USA
Donqola see Dongola
126 L5 **Donskoy** Tul'skaya Oblast', W Russian Federation
81 L16 **Doolow** Somali, E Ethiopia
39 Q7 **Doonerak, Mount** ▲ Alaska, USA
98 J12 **Doorn** Utrecht, C Netherlands
Doornik see Tournai
31 N6 **Door Peninsula** *peninsula* Wisconsin, N USA
80 P13 **Dooxo Nugaaleed** var. Nogal Valley. *valley* E Somalia
Do Qu see Da Qu
106 B7 **Dora Baltea** *anc.* Duria Major. 〜 NW Italy
180 K7 **Dora, Lake** *salt lake* Western Australia
106 A8 **Dora Riparia** *anc.* Duria Minor. 〜 NW Italy
Dorbiljin see Emin
Dorbod/Dorbod Mongolzu Zizhixian see Taikang
Dorbod Mongolzu Zizhixian see Taikang
113 N18 **Đorče Petrov** var. Djorče Petrov, Gorče Petrov. N Macedonia
14 F16 **Dorchester** Ontario, S Canada
97 L24 **Dorchester** *anc.* Durnovaria. S England, UK
9 P7 **Dorchester, Cape** *headland* Baffin Island, Nunavut, NE Canada
83 D19 **Dordabis** Khomas, C Namibia
102 L12 **Dordogne** ❖ *department* SW France
103 N12 **Dordogne** 〜 W France
98 H13 **Dordrecht** var. Dordt, Dort. Zuid-Holland, SW Netherlands
Dordt see Dordrecht
103 P11 **Dore** 〜 C France
9 S13 **Doré Lake** Saskatchewan, C Canada
103 O12 **Dore, Monts** ▲▲ C France
101 M23 **Dorfen** Bayern, SE Germany
107 D18 **Dorgali** Sardegna, Italy, C Mediterranean Sea
159 N11 **Dorgê Co** var. Elsen Nur. ◎ C China
159 N11 **Dorgê Co** var. Elsen Nur. ◎ C China
162 E6 **Dörgön** Hovd, W Mongolia
162 F7 **Dörgön Nuur** ◎ NW Mongolia
77 Q12 **Dori** N Burkina
83 E24 **Doring** 〜 S South Africa
101 E16 **Dormagen** Nordrhein-Westfalen, W Germany
103 P4 **Dormans** Marne, N France
108 E6 **Dornach** Solothurn, NW Switzerland
Dorna Watra see Vatra Dornei
108 J7 **Dornbirn** Vorarlberg, W Austria
96 I7 **Dornoch** N Scotland, UK
96 J7 **Dornoch Firth** *inlet* N Scotland, UK
163 P7 **Dornod** ❖ *province* E Mongolia
163 N10 **Dornogovi** ❖ *province* SE Mongolia
77 P10 **Doro** Tombouctou, S Mali
116 L14 **Dorobanţu** Călăraşi, S Romania
111 J22 **Dorog** Komárom-Esztergom, N Hungary
126 I4 **Dorogobuzh** Smolenskaya Oblast', W Russian Federation
116 K8 **Dorohoi** Botoşani, NE Romania
93 H15 **Dorotea** Västerbotten, N Sweden
Dorpat see Tartu
180 G10 **Dorre Island** *island* Western Australia
183 U5 **Dorrigo** New South Wales, SE Australia
35 N1 **Dorris** California, W USA
14 H13 **Dorset** Ontario, SE Canada
97 K23 **Dorset** *cultural region* S England, UK
101 E14 **Dorsten** Nordrhein-Westfalen, W Germany
Dort see Dordrecht
101 F15 **Dortmund** Nordrhein-Westfalen, W Germany
100 F12 **Dortmund-Ems-Kanal** *canal* W Germany
136 L17 **Dörtyol** Hatay, S Turkey
142 L7 **Do Rūd** var. Dow Rūd, Durud. Lorestān, W Iran
79 O15 **Doruma** Orientale, N Dem. Rep. Congo
15 O12 **Dorval** ✕ (Montréal) Québec, SE Canada
162 F7 **Dörvöljin** var. Buga. Dzavhan, W Mongolia
45 T5 **Dos Bocas, Lago** ⊠ C Puerto Rico
104 K14 **Dos Hermanas** Andalucía, S Spain
Dospad Dagh see Rhodope Mountains
35 P10 **Dos Palos** California, W USA
114 I11 **Dospat** Smolyan, S Bulgaria
114 H11 **Dospat, Yazovir** ⊠ SW Bulgaria
100 M11 **Dosse** 〜 NE Germany
77 S12 **Dosso** Dosso, SW Niger
77 S12 **Dosso** ❖ *department* SW Niger
144 G12 **Dossor** Atyrau, SW Kazakhstan
147 O10 **Do'stlik** Jizzakh Viloyati, C Uzbekistan
147 Q10 **Do'stlik** Jizzax Viloyati, C Uzbekistan
147 V9 **Dostuk** Narynskaya Oblast', C Kyrgyzstan
145 X13 **Dostyk** *prev.* Druzhba. Almaty, SE Kazakhstan
23 R7 **Dothan** Alabama, S USA
39 T9 **Dot Lake** Alaska, USA
118 F12 **Dotnuva** Kaunas, C Lithuania
99 D19 **Dottignies** Hainaut, W Belgium
103 P2 **Douai** *prev.* Douay; *anc.* Duacum. Nord, N France
14 L9 **Douaire, Lac** ◎ Québec, SE Canada
79 D16 **Douala** var. Duala. Littoral, W Cameroon
79 D16 **Douala** ✕ Littoral, W Cameroon
102 F6 **Douarnenez** Finistère, NW France
102 E6 **Douarnenez, Baie de** *bay* NW France
Douay see Douai
25 O6 **Double Mountain Fork Brazos River** 〜 Texas, SW USA
23 O3 **Double Springs** Alabama, S USA
103 T8 **Doubs** ❖ *department* E France
108 C8 **Doubs** 〜 France/Switzerland
185 A22 **Doubtful Sound** *sound* South Island, New Zealand
184 J2 **Doubtless Bay** *bay* North Island, New Zealand
25 X9 **Doucette** Texas, SW USA
102 K8 **Doué-la-Fontaine** Maine-et-Loire, NW France
77 O11 **Douentza** Mopti, S Mali
38 L9 **Douglas** East Falkland, Falkland Islands
97 I16 **Douglas** ○ (Isle of Man) E Isle of Man
83 H23 **Douglas** Northern Cape, C South Africa
39 X13 **Douglas** Alexander Archipelago, Alaska, USA
37 O17 **Douglas** Arizona, SW USA
23 U7 **Douglas** Georgia, SE USA
33 Y15 **Douglas** Wyoming, C USA
21 O7 **Douglas Cape** *headland* Alaska, N USA
10 J14 **Douglas Channel** *channel* British Columbia, W Canada
182 G3 **Douglas Creek** *seasonal river* South Australia
31 P5 **Douglas Lake** ◎ Michigan, N USA
21 O9 **Douglas Lake** ⊠ Tennessee, S USA
39 Q13 **Douglas, Mount** ▲ Alaska, USA
194 I6 **Douglas Range** ▲▲ Alexander Island, Antarctica
121 P9 **Doukáto, Ákra** *headland* Lefkáda, W Greece
103 O2 **Doullens** Somme, N France
Douma see Dūmā
79 F15 **Doumé** Est, E Cameroon
99 E21 **Dour** Hainaut , S Belgium
59 K18 **Dourada, Serra** ▲▲ S Brazil
59 I21 **Dourados** Mato Grosso do Sul, S Brazil
103 N5 **Dourdan** Essonne, N France
104 O6 **Douro** *Port.* Duero. 〜 Portugal/Spain
104 I6 **Douro** *Sp.* Duero. 〜 Portugal/Spain *see also* Duero
Douro Duero
104 G6 **Douro Litoral** *former province* N Portugal
Douvres see Dover
102 K15 **Douze** 〜 SW France
183 P17 **Dover** Tasmania, SE Australia
97 Q22 **Dover** *Fr.* Douvres, *Lat.* Dubris Portus. SE England, UK
21 Y3 **Dover** *state capital* Delaware, NE USA
19 P9 **Dover** New Hampshire, NE USA
18 J14 **Dover** New Jersey, NE USA
31 U12 **Dover** Ohio, N USA
20 H8 **Dover** Tennessee, S USA
97 Q23 **Dover, Strait of** var. Straits of Dover, *Fr.* Pas de Calais. *strait* England, UK/France
Dover, Straits of see Dover, Strait of
Dovlen see Devin
94 G11 **Dovre** Oppland, S Norway
94 G10 **Dovrefjell** *plateau* S Norway
Dovsk see Dowsk
83 M14 **Dowa** Central, C Malawi
31 O10 **Dowagiac** Michigan, N USA
143 N10 **Dow Gonbadān** var. Do Gonbadān, Gonbadān. Kohkīlūyeh va Būyer AḤmad, SW Iran
148 M2 **Dowlatābād** Fāryāb, N Afghanistan
97 G16 **Down** *cultural region* SE Northern Ireland, UK
33 R16 **Downey** Idaho, NW USA
35 P5 **Downieville** California, W USA
97 G16 **Downpatrick** *Ir.* Dún Pádraig. SE Northern Ireland, UK
26 M3 **Downs** Kansas, C USA
18 J12 **Downsville** New York, NE USA
Dow Rūd see Do Rūd
29 V12 **Dows** Iowa, C USA
119 O17 **Dowsk** *Rus.* Dovsk. Homyel'skaya Voblasts', SE Belarus
35 Q4 **Doyle** California, W USA
18 I15 **Doylestown** Pennsylvania, NE USA
Doyransko, Ezero see Doïrani, Límni
114 I8 **Doyrentsi** Lovech, N Bulgaria
164 G11 **Dōzen** *island* Oki-shotō, SW Japan
14 K9 **Dozois, Réservoir** ⊠ Québec, SE Canada
74 D9 **Drâa** *seasonal river* S Morocco
Drâa, Hammada du see Dra, Hamada du
Drabble see José Enrique Rodó
117 Q5 **Drabiv** Cherkas'ka Oblast', C Ukraine
Drable see José Enrique Rodó
103 S13 **Drac** 〜 E France
Drač/Draç see Durrës
60 I8 **Dracena** São Paulo, S Brazil
98 M6 **Drachten** Friesland, N Netherlands
92 H11 **Drag** *Lapp.* Ájluokta. Nordland, C Norway
116 L14 **Dragalina** Călăraşi, SE Romania
116 I14 **Draganesti-Olt** Olt, S Romania
116 J14 **Drăgăneşti-Vlaşca** Teleorman, S Romania
116 I13 **Drăgăşani** Vâlcea, SW Romania
114 G9 **Dragoman** Sofiya, W Bulgaria
115 L25 **Dragonáda** *island* SE Greece
Dragonera, Isla see Sa Dragonera
45 T14 **Dragon's Mouths, The** *strait* Trinidad and Tobago/Venezuela
95 J23 **Dragør** København, E Denmark
114 F10 **Dragovishtitsa** Kyustendil, W Bulgaria
103 U15 **Draguignan** Var, SE France
74 E9 **Dra, Hamada du** var. Hammada du Drâa, Haut Plateau du Dra. *plateau* W Algeria
Dra, Haut Plateau du see Dra, Hamada du
119 H19 **Drahichyn** *Pol.* Drohiczyn Poleski, *Rus.* Drogichin. Brestskaya Voblasts', SW Belarus
29 N4 **Drake** North Dakota, N USA
83 K23 **Drakensberg** ▲▲ Lesotho/ South Africa
194 F3 **Drake Passage** *passage* Atlantic Ocean/Pacific Ocean
114 L8 **Dralfa** Tŭrgovishte, N Bulgaria
114 I12 **Dráma** var. Dhráma. Anatolikí Makedonía kai Thráki, NE Greece
Dramburg see Drawsko Pomorskie
95 H15 **Drammen** Buskerud, S Norway
95 H15 **Drammensfjorden** *fjord* S Norway
92 H1 **Drangajökull** ▲ NW Iceland
95 F16 **Drangedal** Telemark, S Norway
92 I2 **Drangsnes** Vestfirdhir, NW Iceland
Drann see Dravinja
109 T10 **Drau** var. Drava, *Eng.* Drave, *Hung.* Dráva. 〜 C Europe *see also* Drava
Drau see Drava
84 I11 **Drava** var. Drau, *Eng.* Drave, *Hung.* Dráva. 〜 C Europe *see also* Drau
Drava see Drau
Dráva/Drave see Drau/Drava
109 W10 **Dravinja** *Ger.* Drann. 〜 NE Slovenia
109 V9 **Dravograd** *Ger.* Unterdrauburg; *prev.* Spodnji Dravograd. N Slovenia
110 F10 **Drawa** 〜 NW Poland
110 F9 **Drawno** Zachodnio-pomorskie, NW Poland
110 F9 **Drawsko Pomorskie** *Ger.* Dramburg. Zachodnio-pomorskie, NW Poland
29 R3 **Drayton** North Dakota, N USA
9 P14 **Drayton Valley** Alberta, SW Canada
186 B6 **Dreikikir** East Sepik, NW Papua New Guinea
Dreikirchen see Teiuş
98 N7 **Drenthe** ❖ *province* NE Netherlands
115 H15 **Drépano, Akrotírio** var. Akrotírio Dhrepanon. *cape* N Greece
Drepanum see Trapani
14 D17 **Dresden** Ontario, S Canada
101 O16 **Dresden** Sachsen, E Germany
20 G8 **Dresden** Tennessee, S USA
118 M11 **Dretun'** *Rus.* Dretun'. Vitsyebskaya Voblasts', N Belarus
102 M5 **Dreux** *anc.* Drocae, Durocasses. Eure-et-Loir, C France
94 I11 **Drevsjø** Hedmark, S Norway
22 K3 **Drew** Mississippi, S USA
110 F10 **Drezdenko** *Ger.* Driesen. Lubuskie, W Poland
98 J12 **Driebergen** var. Driebergen-Rijsenburg. Utrecht, C Netherlands
Driebergen-Rijsenburg see Driebergen
Driesen see Drezdenko
97 N16 **Driffield** E England, UK
65 D25 **Driftwood Point** *headland* East Falkland, Falkland Islands
33 S14 **Driggs** Idaho, NW USA
Drin see Drinit, Lumi
112 K12 **Drina** 〜 Bosnia and Herzegovina/Serbia
Drin, Gulf of see Drinit, Gjiri i
113 K18 **Drinit, Gjiri i** var. Pellg i Drinit, *Eng.* Gulf of Drin. *gulf* NW Albania
113 L17 **Drinit, Lumi** var. Drin. 〜 NW Albania
Drinit, Pellg i see Drinit, Gjiri i
Drinit të Zi, Lumi i see Black Drin
113 L22 **Dríno** var. Drino, Drínos Pótamos, *Alb.* Lumi i Drinos. 〜 Albania/Greece
Drínos, Lumi i/Drínos Pótamos see Dríno
25 S11 **Dripping Springs** Texas, SW USA
25 Q15 **Driscoll** Texas, SW USA
22 H5 **Driskill Mountain** ▲ Louisiana, S USA
Drissa see Drysa
94 G10 **Driva** 〜 S Norway
112 E13 **Drniš** *It.* Šibenik-Knin. Šibenik-Knin, S Croatia
95 H15 **Drøbak** Akershus, S Norway
116 G13 **Drobeta-Turnu Severin** *prev.* Turnu Severin. Mehedinţi, SW Romania
Drocae see Dreux
116 M8 **Drochia** *Rus.* Drokiya. N Moldova
97 F17 **Drogheda** *Ir.* Droichead Átha. NE Ireland
Drogichin see Drahichyn
Drogobych see Drohobych
Drohiczyn Poleski see Drahichyn
116 H6 **Drohobych** *Pol.* Drohobycz, *Rus.* Drogobych. L'vivs'ka Oblast', NW Ukraine
Drohobycz see Drohobych
Droichead Átha see Drogheda
Droicheadna Bandan see Bandon
Droichead na Banna see Banbridge
Droim Mór see Dromore
Drokiya see Drochia
103 R13 **Drôme** ❖ *department* E France
103 S13 **Drôme** 〜 E France
97 G15 **Dromore** *Ir.* Droim Mór. SE Northern Ireland, UK
106 A9 **Dronero** Piemonte, NE Italy
102 L12 **Dronne** 〜 SW France
195 Q3 **Dronning Maud Land** *physical region* Antarctica
98 K6 **Dronrijp** *Fris.* Dronryp. Friesland, N Netherlands
Dronryp see Dronrijp
98 L9 **Dronten** Flevoland, C Netherlands
Drontheim see Trondheim
102 L13 **Dropt** 〜 SW France
149 T4 **Drosh** North-West Frontier Province, NW Pakistan
Drossen see Ośno Lubuskie
Drug see Durg
Drujba see Pitnak
118 I12 **Drūkšiai** ◎ NE Lithuania
Druk-yul see Bhutan
9 Q16 **Drumheller** Alberta, SW Canada
33 Q10 **Drummond** Montana, NW USA
31 R4 **Drummond Island** *island* Michigan, N USA
Drummond Island see Tabiteuea
21 X7 **Drummond, Lake** ◎ Virginia, NE USA
15 P12 **Drummondville** Québec, SE Canada
39 T11 **Drum, Mount** ▲ Alaska, USA
27 O9 **Drumright** Oklahoma, C USA
99 J14 **Drunen** Noord-Brabant, S Netherlands
Druskienniki see Druskininkai
119 F15 **Druskininkai** *Pol.* Druskienniki. Alytus, S Lithuania
98 K13 **Druten** Gelderland, SE Netherlands
118 K11 **Druya** Vitsyebskaya Voblasts', NW Belarus
117 S2 **Druzhba** Sums'ka Oblast', NE Ukraine
Druzhba see Dostyk, Kazakhstan
Druzhba see Pitnak, Uzbekistan
123 R7 **Druzhina** Respublika Sakha (Yakutiya), NE Russian Federation
117 X7 **Druzhkivka** Donets'ka Oblast', E Ukraine
112 E12 **Drvar** ❖ Federacija Bosna I Hercegovina, W Bosnia and Herzegovina
113 G15 **Drvenik** Split-Dalmacija, SE Croatia
114 K9 **Dryanovo** Gabrovo, N Bulgaria
26 G7 **Dry Cimarron River** 〜 Kansas/Oklahoma, C USA
12 B11 **Dryden** Ontario, C Canada
24 M11 **Dryden** Texas, SW USA
195 Q14 **Drygalski Ice Tongue** *ice feature* Antarctica
118 L11 **Drysa** *Rus.* Drissa. 〜 N Belarus
23 V17 **Dry Tortugas** *island* Florida, SE USA
79 D15 **Dschang** Ouest, W Cameroon
54 J5 **Duaca** Lara, N Venezuela
Duacum see Douai
Duala see Douala
45 N9 **Duarte, Pico** ▲ C Dominican Republic
140 J5 **Dubā** Tabūk, NW Saudi Arabia
Dubai see Dubayy
117 N9 **Dubăsari** *Rus.* Dubossary. NE Moldova
117 N9 **Dubăsari Reservoir** ⊠ NE Moldova
8 M10 **Dubawnt** 〜 Nunavut, NW Canada
8 L9 **Dubawnt Lake** ◎ Northwest Territories/Nunavut, N Canada
30 L6 **Du Bay, Lake** ⊠ Wisconsin, N USA
141 U7 **Dubayy** *Eng.* Dubai. Dubayy, NE United Arab Emirates
141 W7 **Dubayy** *Eng.* Dubai. ✕ Dubayy, NE United Arab Emirates
183 R7 **Dubbo** New South Wales, SE Australia
108 G7 **Dübendorf** Zürich, NW Switzerland
97 F18 **Dublin** *Ir.* Baile Átha Cliath; *anc.* Eblana. ● (Ireland) Dublin, E Ireland
23 U5 **Dublin** Georgia, SE USA
25 R7 **Dublin** Texas, SW USA
97 G18 **Dublin** *Ir.* Baile Átha Cliath; *anc.* Eblana. ❖ *county* E Ireland
97 G18 **Dublin Airport** ✕ Dublin, E Ireland
189 V12 **Dublon** var Tonoas. *island* Chuuk Islands, C Micronesia
126 K2 **Dubna** Moskovskaya Oblast', W Russian Federation
111 G19 **Dubňany** *Ger.* Dubnian. Jihomoravský Kraj, SE Czech Republic
Dubnian see Dubňany
111 I19 **Dubnica nad Váhom** *Hung.* Máriatölgyes; *prev.* Dubnicz. Trenčiansky Kraj, W Slovakia
Dubnicz see Dubnica nad Váhom
116 K4 **Dubno** Rivnens'ka Oblast', NW Ukraine
33 R13 **Dubois** Idaho, NW USA
18 D13 **Du Bois** Pennsylvania, NE USA
33 T14 **Dubois** Wyoming, C USA
Dubossary see Dubăsari
127 O10 **Dubovka** Volgogradskaya Oblast', SW Russian Federation

◆ Country ● Country Capital ◇ Dependent Territory ○ Dependent Territory Capital ❖ Administrative Regions ✕ International Airport ▲ Mountain ▲▲ Mountain Range ▲ Volcano 〜 River ◎ Lake ⊠ Reservoir

DUBRÉKA – EASTER ISLAND

76 H14 **Dubréka** Guinée-Maritime, SW Guinea
14 B7 **Dubreuilville** Ontario, S Canada
Dubris Portus *see* Dover
119 L20 **Dubrova** *Rus.* Dubrova. Homyel'skaya Voblasts', SE Belarus
Dubrovačko-Neretvanska Županija *see* Dubrovnik-Neretva
126 I5 **Dubrovka** Bryanskaya Oblast', W Russian Federation
113 H16 **Dubrovnik** *It.* Ragusa. Dubrovnik-Neretva, SE Croatia
113 I16 **Dubrovnik** ✈ Dubrovnik-Neretva, SE Croatia
113 F16 **Dubrovnik-Neretva** *off.* Dubrovačko-Neretvanska Županija. ◆ *province* SE Croatia
Dubrovno *see* Dubrowna
116 L2 **Dubrovytsya** Rivnens'ka Oblast', NW Ukraine
119 O14 **Dubrowna** *Rus.* Dubrovno. Vitsyebskaya Voblasts', N Belarus
29 Z13 **Dubuque** Iowa, C USA
118 E12 **Dubysa** ⚞ C Lithuania
167 U11 **Đưc Cơ** Gia Lai, C Vietnam
191 V12 **Duc de Gloucester, Îles du** *Eng.* Duke of Gloucester Islands. *island group* C French Polynesia
111 C15 **Duchcov** *Ger.* Dux. Ústecký Kraj, NW Czech Republic
37 N3 **Duchesne** Utah, W USA
191 P17 **Ducie Island** *atoll* E Pitcairn Islands
9 W15 **Duck Bay** Manitoba, S Canada
23 X17 **Duck Key** *island* Florida Keys, Florida, SE USA
9 T14 **Duck Lake** Saskatchewan, S Canada
9 V15 **Duck Mountain** ▲▲ Manitoba, S Canada
20 I9 **Duck River** ⚞ Tennessee, S USA
20 M10 **Ducktown** Tennessee, S USA
167 U10 **Đưc Phô** Quang Ngai, C Vietnam
Đưc Tho *see* Lin Camh
167 U13 **Đưc Trong** *var.* Liên Nghia. Lâm Đông, S Vietnam
D-U-D *see* Dalap-Uliga-Djarrit
99 M25 **Dudelange** *var.* Forge du Sud, *Ger.* Dudelingen. Luxembourg, S Luxembourg
Dudelingen *see* Dudelange
101 J15 **Duderstadt** Niedersachsen, C Germany
153 N15 **Dūdhi** Uttar Pradesh, N India
122 K8 **Dudinka** Taymyrskiy (Dolgano-Nenetskiy) Avtonomnyy Okrug, N Russian Federation
97 L20 **Dudley** C England, UK
154 G13 **Dudna** ⚞ C India
76 L16 **Duékoué** W Ivory Coast
104 M5 **Dueñas** Castilla-León, N Spain
104 K4 **Duerna** ⚞ NW Spain
105 O6 **Duero** *Port.* Douro. ⚞ Portugal/Spain *see also* Douro
Duero *see* Douro
Duero *see* Douro
Duesseldorf *see* Düsseldorf
21 P12 **Due West** South Carolina, SE USA
195 P11 **Dufek Coast** *physical region* Antarctica
99 H17 **Duffel** Antwerpen, C Belgium
35 S2 **Duffer Peak** ▲ Nevada, W USA
187 Q9 **Duff Islands** *island group* E Solomon Islands
Dufour, Pizzo/Dufour, Punta *see* Dufour Spitze
108 E12 **Dufour Spitze** *It.* Pizzo Dufour, Punta Dufour. ▲ Italy/Switzerland
112 D9 **Duga Resa** Karlovac, C Croatia
22 H5 **Dugdemona River** ⚞ Louisiana, S USA
154 J12 **Duggīpar** Mahārāshtra, C India
112 B13 **Dugi Otok** *var.* Isola Grossa, *It.* Isola Lunga. *island* W Croatia
113 F14 **Dugopolje** Split-Dalmacija, S Croatia
160 L8 **Du He** ⚞ C China
54 M11 **Duida, Cerro** *elevation* S Venezuela
Duinekerke *see* Dunkerque
101 E15 **Duisburg** *prev.* Duisburg-Hamborn. Nordrhein-Westfalen, W Germany
Duisburg-Hamborn *see* Duisburg
99 F14 **Duiveland** *island* SW Netherlands
98 M12 **Duiven** Gelderland, E Netherlands
139 W10 **Dujaylah, Hawr ad** ◎ S Iraq
160 H9 **Dujiangyan** *var.* Guanxian, Guan Xian. Sichuan, C China
81 L18 **Dujuuma** Shabeellaha Hoose, S Somalia
Dūkān *see* Dokan
39 Z14 **Duke Island** *island* Alexander Archipelago, Alaska, USA
Dukelský Priesmy/Dukelský Průsmyk *see* Dukla Pass
Duke of Gloucester Islands *see* Duc de Gloucester, Îles du
81 F14 **Duk Faiwil** Jonglei, SE Sudan
141 T7 **Dukhān** C Qatar
Dukhan Heights *see* Dukhān, Jabal
143 N16 **Dukhān, Jabal** *var.* Dukhan Heights. *hill range* S Qatar
127 Q7 **Dukhovnitskoye** Saratovskaya Oblast', W Russian Federation
126 H4 **Dukhovshchina** Smolenskaya Oblast', W Russian Federation
Dukielska, Przełęcz *see* Dukla Pass
111 N17 **Dukla** Podkarpackie, SE Poland
Duklai Hág *see* Dukla Pass
111 N18 **Dukla Pass** *Cz.* Dukelský Průsmyk, *Ger.* Dukla-Pass, *Hung.* Duklai Hág, *Pol.* Przełęcz Dukielska, *Slvk.* Dukelský Priesmy. *pass* Poland/Slovakia
Dukla-Pass *see* Dukla Pass
Dukou *see* Panzhihua
118 I12 **Dūkštas** Utena, E Lithuania
Dulaan *see* Herlenbayan-Ulaan
159 R10 **Dulan** *var.* Qagan Us. Qinghai, C China
37 R8 **Dulce** New Mexico, SW USA
43 N16 **Dulce, Golfo** *gulf* S Costa Rica
Dulce, Golfo *see* Izabal, Lago de
42 K6 **Dulce Nombre de Culmí** Olancho, C Honduras
62 L9 **Dulce, Río** ⚞ C Argentina
123 Q9 **Dulgalakh** ⚞ NE Russian Federation
114 M8 **Dŭlgopol** Varna, E Bulgaria
153 V14 **Dullabchara** Assam, NE India
20 D3 **Dulles** ✈ (Washington DC)Virginia, NE USA
101 E14 **Dülmen** Nordrhein-Westfalen, W Germany
114 M7 **Dulovo** Silistra, NE Bulgaria
29 W5 **Duluth** Minnesota, N USA
138 H7 **Dūmā** *Fr.* Douma. Dimashq, SW Syria
171 O8 **Dumagasa Point** *headland* Mindanao, S Philippines
171 P6 **Dumaguete** *var.* Dumaguete City. Negros, C Philippines
Dumaguete City *see* Dumaguete
168 J10 **Dumai** Sumatera, W Indonesia
183 T4 **Dumaresq River** ⚞ New South Wales/Queensland, SE Australia
27 W13 **Dumas** Arkansas, C USA
25 N1 **Dumas** Texas, SW USA
138 I7 **Dumayr** Dimashq, W Syria
96 I12 **Dumbarton** W Scotland, UK
96 I12 **Dumbarton** *cultural region* C Scotland, UK
187 Q17 **Dumbéa** Province Sud, S New Caledonia
111 K19 **Ďumbier** *Ger.* Djumbir, *Hung.* Gyömbér. ▲ C Slovakia
116 I11 **Dumbrăveni** *Ger.* Elisabethstedt, *Hung.* Erzsébetváros; *prev.* Ebesfalva, Eppeschdorf, Ibaşfalău. Sibiu, C Romania
116 L12 **Dumbrăveni** Vrancea, E Romania
97 J14 **Dumfries** S Scotland, UK
97 J14 **Dumfries** *cultural region* SW Scotland, UK
153 R15 **Dumka** Jhārkhand, NE India
Dümmer *see* Dümmersee
100 G12 **Dümmersee** *var.* Dümmer. ◎ NW Germany
14 J11 **Dumoine** ⚞ Québec, SE Canada
14 J10 **Dumoine, Lac** ◎ Québec, SE Canada
195 V16 **Dumont d'Urville** *French research station* Antarctica
195 W15 **Dumont d'Urville Sea** *sea* S Pacific Ocean
14 K11 **Dumont, Lac** ◎ Québec, SE Canada
75 W7 **Dumyât** *Eng.* Damietta. N Egypt
Duna *see* Danube, C Europe
Düna *see* Western Dvina
Duna *see* Don, Russian Federation
Dünaburg *see* Daugavpils
111 J24 **Dunaföldvár** Tolna, C Hungary
Dunaj *see* Wien, Austria
Dunaj *see* Danube, C Europe
111 L18 **Dunajec** ⚞ S Poland
111 H21 **Dunajská Streda** *Hung.* Dunaszerdahely. Trnavský Kraj, W Slovakia
Dunapentele *see* Dunaújváros
Dunărea *see* Danube
116 M13 **Dunărea Veche, Braţul** ⚞ SE Romania
117 N13 **Dunării, Delta** *delta* SE Romania
Dunaszerdahely *see* Dunajská Streda
111 J23 **Dunaújváros** *prev.* Dunapentele, Sztálinváros. Fejér, C Hungary
Dunav *see* Danube
114 J8 **Dunavska Ravnina** *Eng.* Danubian Plain. *lowlands* N Bulgaria
114 G7 **Dunavtsi** Vidin, NW Bulgaria
123 S15 **Dunay** Primorskiy Kray, SE Russian Federation
Dunayevtsy *see* Dunayivtsi
116 L7 **Dunayivtsi** *Rus.* Dunayevtsy. Khmel'nyts'ka Oblast', NW Ukraine
185 F22 **Dunback** Otago, South Island, New Zealand
10 L17 **Duncan** Vancouver Island, British Columbia, SW Canada
37 O15 **Duncan** Arizona, SW USA
26 M12 **Duncan** Oklahoma, C USA
Duncan Island *see* Pinzón, Isla
151 Q20 **Duncan Passage** *strait* Andaman Sea/Bay of Bengal
96 K6 **Duncansby Head** *headland* N Scotland, UK
14 G12 **Dunchurch** Ontario, S Canada
118 D7 **Dundaga** Talsi, NW Latvia
14 G14 **Dundalk** Ontario, S Canada
97 F16 **Dundalk** *Ir.* Dún Dealgan. Louth, NE Ireland
21 X3 **Dundalk** Maryland, NE USA
97 F16 **Dundalk Bay** *Ir.* Cuan Dhún Dealgan. *bay* NE Ireland
14 G16 **Dundas** Ontario, S Canada
180 L12 **Dundas, Lake** *salt lake* Western Australia
Dundbürd *see* Batnorov
Dún Dealgan *see* Dundalk
15 N13 **Dundee** Québec, SE Canada
83 K22 **Dundee** KwaZulu/Natal, E South Africa
96 K11 **Dundee** E Scotland, UK
31 R10 **Dundee** Michigan, N USA
25 R5 **Dundee** Texas, SW USA
194 H3 **Dundee Island** *island* Antarctica
162 L9 **Dundgovĭ** ◆ *province* C Mongolia
97 G16 **Dundrum Bay** *Ir.* Cuan Dhún Droma. *inlet* NW Irish Sea
9 T15 **Dundurn** Saskatchewan, S Canada
162 J10 **Dund-Us** Hovd, W Mongolia
Dund-Us *see* Hovd
Dund-Us *see* Dund-Us
185 F23 **Dunedin** Otago, South Island, New Zealand
183 R7 **Dunedoo** New South Wales, SE Australia
97 D14 **Dunfanaghy** *Ir.* Dún Fionnachaidh. NW Ireland
96 J12 **Dunfermline** C Scotland, UK
Dún Fionnachaidh *see* Dunfanaghy
149 V10 **Dunga Bunga** Punjab, E Pakistan
97 F15 **Dungannon** *Ir.* Dún Geanainn. C Northern Ireland, UK
Dun Garbháin *see* Dungarvan
152 F15 **Dūngarpur** Rājasthān, N India
97 E21 **Dungarvan** *Ir.* Dun Garbháin. Waterford, S Ireland
101 N21 **Dungau** *cultural region* SE Germany
Dún Geanainn *see* Dungannon
97 P23 **Dungeness** *headland* SE England, UK
63 I23 **Dungeness, Punta** *headland* S Argentina
Dungloe *see* Dunglow
97 D14 **Dunglow** *var.* Dungloe, *Ir.* An Clochán Liath. Donegal, NW Ireland
183 T7 **Dungog** New South Wales, SE Australia
79 O16 **Dungu** Orientale, NE Dem. Rep. Congo
168 L8 **Dungun** *var.* Kuala Dungun. Terengganu, Peninsular Malaysia
80 I6 **Dungûnab** Red Sea, NE Sudan
15 P13 **Dunham** Québec, SE Canada
Dunheved *see* Launceston
Dunholme *see* Durham
163 X10 **Dunhua** Jilin, NE China
159 P8 **Dunhuang** Gansu, N China
182 L12 **Dunkeld** Victoria, SE Australia
103 O1 **Dunkerque** *Eng.* Dunkirk, *Flem.* Duinekerke; *prev.* Dunquerque. Nord, N France
97 K23 **Dunkery Beacon** ▲ SW England, UK
18 C11 **Dunkirk** New York, NE USA
Dunkirk *see* Dunkerque
77 P17 **Dunkwa** SW Ghana
97 G18 **Dún Laoghaire** *Eng.* Dunleary; *prev.* Kingstown. E Ireland
29 S14 **Dunlap** Iowa, C USA
20 L10 **Dunlap** Tennessee, S USA
Dunleary *see* Dún Laoghaire
Dún Mánmhaí *see* Dunmanway
97 B21 **Dunmanway** *Ir.* Dún Mánmhaí. Cork, SW Ireland
18 I13 **Dunmore** Pennsylvania, NE USA
21 U10 **Dunn** North Carolina, SE USA
Dún na nGall *see* Donegal
23 V11 **Dunnellon** Florida, SE USA
96 J6 **Dunnet Head** *headland* N Scotland, UK
29 N14 **Dunning** Nebraska, C USA
65 B24 **Dunnose Head Settlement** West Falkland, Falkland Islands
14 G17 **Dunnville** Ontario, S Canada
Dún Pádraig *see* Downpatrick
Dunquerque *see* Dunkerque
Dunqulah *see* Dongola
96 L12 **Duns** SE Scotland, UK
29 N2 **Dunseith** North Dakota, N USA
35 N2 **Dunsmuir** California, W USA
97 N21 **Dunstable** *Lat.* Durocobrivae. E England, UK
185 D21 **Dunstan Mountains** ▲▲ South Island, New Zealand
103 O9 **Dun-sur-Auron** Cher, C France
185 F21 **Duntroon** Canterbury, South Island, New Zealand
149 T10 **Dunyāpur** Punjab, E Pakistan
163 U5 **Duobukur He** ⚞ NE China
163 R12 **Duolun** *var.* Dolonnur. Nei Mongol Zizhiqu, N China
114 G10 **Dupnitsa** *prev.* Marek, Stanke Dimitrov. Kyustendil, W Bulgaria
28 L8 **Dupree** South Dakota, N USA
33 Q7 **Dupuyer** Montana, NW USA
141 Y11 **Duqm** *var.* Daqm. E Oman
63 F23 **Duque de York, Isla** *island* S Chile
181 N4 **Durack Range** ▲▲ Western Australia
136 K10 **Durağan** Sinop, N Turkey
103 S15 **Durance** ⚞ SE France
31 R9 **Durand** Michigan, N USA
30 I6 **Durand** Wisconsin, N USA
40 K10 **Durango** *var.* Victoria de Durango. Durango, W Mexico
105 P3 **Durango** País Vasco, N Spain
37 Q8 **Durango** Colorado, C USA
40 J9 **Durango** ◆ *state* C Mexico
114 O7 **Durankulak** *Rom.* Răcari; *prev.* Blatnitsa, Duranulac. Dobrich, NE Bulgaria
22 L4 **Durant** Mississippi, S USA
27 P13 **Durant** Oklahoma, C USA
Duranulac *see* Durankulak
105 N6 **Duratón** ⚞ N Spain
61 E19 **Durazno** *var.* San Pedro de Durazno. Durazno, C Uruguay
61 E19 **Durazno** ◆ *department* C Uruguay
Durazzo *see* Durrës
83 K23 **Durban** *var.* Port Natal. KwaZulu/Natal, E South Africa
83 K23 **Durban** ✈ KwaZulu/Natal, E South Africa
118 C9 **Durbe** *Ger.* Durben. Liepāja, W Latvia
Durben *see* Durbe
99 K21 **Durbuy** Luxembourg, SE Belgium
105 N15 **Dúrcal** Andalucía, S Spain
112 F8 **Đurđevac** *Ger.* Sankt Georgen, *Hung.* Szentgyörgy; *prev.* Djurdjevac, Gjurgjevac. Koprivnica-Križevci, N Croatia
113 K15 **Đurđevica Tara** N Montenegro
97 L24 **Durdle Door** *natural arch* S England, UK
158 L3 **Düre** Xinjiang Uygur Zizhiqu, W China
101 D16 **Düren** *anc.* Marcodurum. Nordrhein-Westfalen, W Germany
154 K12 **Durg** *prev.* Drug. Chhattīsgarh, C India
153 U13 **Durgapur** Dhaka, N Bangladesh
153 R15 **Durgāpur** West Bengal, NE India
14 F14 **Durham** Ontario, S Canada
97 M14 **Durham** *hist.* Dunholme. N England, UK
21 U9 **Durham** North Carolina, SE USA
97 L15 **Durham** *cultural region* N England, UK
168 J10 **Duri** Sumatera, W Indonesia
Duria Major *see* Dora Baltea
Duria Minor *see* Dora Riparia
Durlas *see* Thurles
141 P8 **Ḑurmā** Ar Riyāḑ, C Saudi Arabia
113 J15 **Durmitor** ▲ N Montenegro
96 H6 **Durness** N Scotland, UK
109 Y3 **Dürnkrut** Niederösterreich, E Austria
Durnovaria *see* Dorchester
Durobrivae *see* Rochester
Durocasses *see* Dreux
Durocobrivae *see* Dunstable
Durocortorum *see* Reims
Durostorum *see* Silistra
Durovernum *see* Canterbury
113 K20 **Durrës** *var.* Durrësi, Dursi, *It.* Durazzo, *SCr.* Drač, *Turk.* Draç. Durrës, W Albania
113 K19 **Durrës** ◆ *district* W Albania
Durrësi *see* Durrës
97 A21 **Dursey Island** *Ir.* Oileán Baoi. *island* SW Ireland
Dursi *see* Durrës
Duru *see* Wuchuan
Durud *see* Do Rūd
114 P12 **Durusu** İstanbul, NW Turkey
114 O12 **Durusu Gölü** ◎ NW Turkey
138 I9 **Durūz, Jabal ad** ▲ SW Syria
184 K13 **D'Urville Island** *island* C New Zealand
171 X12 **D'Urville, Tanjung** *cape* Papua, E Indonesia
146 H14 **Dushak** *Rus.* Dushak. Ahal Welaýaty, S Turkmenistan
Dusa Mareb/Dusa Marreb *see* Dhuusa Marreeb
118 I11 **Dusetos** Utena, NE Lithuania
Dushak *see* Dushak
160 K12 **Dushan** Guizhou, S China
147 P13 **Dushanbe** *var.* Dyushambe; *prev.* Stalinabad, *Taj.* Stalinobod. ● (Tajikistan) W Tajikistan
147 P13 **Dushanbe** ✈ W Tajikistan
137 T9 **Dushet'i** E Georgia
18 H13 **Dushore** Pennsylvania, NE USA
185 A23 **Dusky Sound** *sound* South Island, New Zealand
101 E15 **Düsseldorf** *var.* Duesseldorf. Nordrhein-Westfalen, W Germany
147 P14 **Dŭstí** *Rus.* Dusti. SW Tajikistan
194 I9 **Dustin Island** *island* Antarctica
Dutch East Indies *see* Indonesia
Dutch Guiana *see* Surinam
38 L17 **Dutch Harbor** Unalaska Island, Alaska, USA
36 J3 **Dutch Mount** ▲ Utah, W USA
Dutch New Guinea *see* Papua
Dutch West Indies *see* Netherlands Antilles
83 H20 **Dutlwe** Kweneng, S Botswana
67 V16 **Du Toit Fracture Zone** *tectonic feature* SW Indian Ocean
125 U8 **Dutovo** Respublika Komi, NW Russian Federation
77 V13 **Dutsan Wai** *var.* Dutsen Wai. Kaduna, C Nigeria
77 W13 **Dutse** Jigawa, N Nigeria
Dutsen Wai *see* Dutsan Wai
Duttia *see* Datia
14 E17 **Dutton** Ontario, S Canada
36 L7 **Dutton, Mount** ▲ Utah, W USA
162 E7 **Duut** Hovd, W Mongolia
14 K11 **Duval, Lac** ◎ Québec, SE Canada
127 W3 **Duvan** Respublika Bashkortostan, W Russian Federation
138 L9 **Duwaykhilat Satīh ar Ruwayshid** *seasonal river* SE Jordan
Dux *see* Duchcov
160 J13 **Duyang Shan** ▲▲ S China
167 T14 **Duyên Hai** Tra Vinh, S Vietnam
160 K12 **Duyun** Guizhou, S China
136 G11 **Düzce** Düzce, NW Turkey
136 K14 **Düzce** ◆ *province* NW Turkey
Duzdab *see* Zāhedān
Duzenkyr, Khrebet *see* Duzkyr, Khrebet
146 I16 **Duzkyr, Khrebet** *prev.* Khrebet Duzenkyr. ▲▲ S Turkmenistan
Dvina Bay *see* Chëshskaya Guba
Dvinsk *see* Daugavpils
124 L7 **Dvinskaya Guba** *bay* NW Russian Federation
112 E10 **Dvor** Sisak-Moslavina, C Croatia
117 W5 **Dvorichna** Kharkivs'ka Oblast', E Ukraine
111 F16 **Dvůr Králové nad Labem** *Ger.* Königinhof an der Elbe. Královéhradecký Kraj, N Czech Republic
154 A10 **Dwārka** Gujarāt, W India
30 M12 **Dwight** Illinois, N USA
98 N8 **Dwingeloo** Drenthe, NE Netherlands
33 N10 **Dworshak Reservoir** ▣ Idaho, NW USA
Dyal *see* Dyaul Island
Dyanev *see* Galkynyş
Dyatlovo *see* Dzyatlava
186 G5 **Dyaul Island** *var.* Djaul, Dyal. *island* NE Papua New Guinea
20 G8 **Dyer** Tennessee, S USA
9 S5 **Dyer, Cape** *headland* Baffin Island, Nunavut, NE Canada
20 F8 **Dyersburg** Tennessee, S USA
29 Y13 **Dyersville** Iowa, C USA
97 I21 **Dyfed** *cultural region* SW Wales, UK
Dyfrdwy, Afon *see* Dee
Dyhernfurth *see* Brzeg Dolny
111 E19 **Dyje** *var.* Thaya. ⚞ Austria/Czech Republic *see also* Thaya
Dyje *see* Thaya
117 T5 **Dykanska** Poltavs'ka Oblast', C Ukraine
127 N16 **Dykhtau** ▲ SW Russian Federation
111 A16 **Dyleń** *Ger.* Tillenberg. ▲ NW Czech Republic
110 K9 **Dylewska Góra** ▲ N Poland
117 O4 **Dymer** Kyyivs'ka Oblast', N Ukraine
117 W7 **Dymytrov** *Rus.* Dimitrov. Donets'ka Oblast', SE Ukraine
111 O17 **Dynów** Podkarpackie, SE Poland
29 X13 **Dysart** Iowa, C USA
Dysna *see* Dzisna
115 H18 **Dýstos, Límni** *var.* Limni Distos. ◎ Évvoia, C Greece
115 D18 **Dytikí Ellás** *Eng.* Greece West. ◆ *region* C Greece
115 C14 **Dytikí Makedonía** *Eng.* Macedonia West. ◆ *region* N Greece
Dyurment'yube *see* Dermentobe
127 U4 **Dyurtyuli** Respublika Bashkortostan, W Russian Federation
Dyushambe *see* Dushanbe
162 K7 **Dzaamar** *var.* Bat-Öldziyt. Töv, C Mongolia
Dzaanhushuu *see* Ihtamir
Dza Chu *see* Mekong
Dzadgay *see* Bömbögör
162 H8 **Dzag** Bayanhongor, C Mongolia
Dzalaa *see* Shinejinst
163 O11 **Dzamïn-Üüd** *var.* Borhoyn Tal. Dornogovĭ, SE Mongolia
172 J14 **Dzaoudzi** E Mayotte
Dzaudzhikau *see* Vladikavkaz
162 G7 **Dzavhan** ◆ *province* NW Mongolia
162 G7 **Dzavhan Gol** ⚞ NW Mongolia
162 G6 **Dzavhanmandal** *var.* Nuga. Dzavhan, W Mongolia
Dzegstey *see* Ögiynuur
162 E7 **Dzereg** *var* Altanteel. Hovd, W Mongolia
127 O3 **Dzerzhinsk** Nizhegorodskaya Oblast', W Russian Federation
Dzerzhinsk *see* Dzyarzhynsk Belarus
Dzerzhinsk *see* Dzerzhyns'k
Dzerzhinskiy *see* Nar'yan-Mar
145 W13 **Dzerzhinskoye** *var.* Dzerzhinskoye. Taldykorgan, SE Kazakhstan
Dzerzhinskoye *see* Tokzhaylau
Dzerzhinskoye *see* Dzerzhinskoye
117 X7 **Dzerzhyns'k** *Rus.* Dzerzhinsk. Donets'ka Oblast', SE Ukraine
116 M5 **Dzerzhyns'k** Zhytomyrs'ka Oblast', N Ukraine
Dzhetygara *see* Zhitikara
Dzhailgan *see* Jayilgan
145 N14 **Dzhalagash** *Kaz.* Zhalashash. Kzylorda, S Kazakhstan
147 T10 **Dzhalal-Abad** *Kir.* Jalal-Abad. Dzhalal-Abadskaya Oblast', W Kyrgyzstan
147 S9 **Dzhalal-Abadskaya Oblast'** *Kir.* Jalal-Abad Oblasty. ◆ *province* W Kyrgyzstan
Dzhalilabad *see* Cälilabad
Dzhambeyty *see* Zhympity
Dzhambulskaya Oblast' *see* Zhambyl
Dzhanibek *see* Zhanibek
Dzhankel'dy *see* Jongeldi
117 T12 **Dzhankoy** Respublika Krym, S Ukraine
145 V14 **Dzhansugurov** *Kaz.* Zhansügirov. Almaty, SE Kazakhstan
147 R9 **Dzhany-Bazar** *var.* Yangibazar. Dzhalal-Abadskaya Oblast', W Kyrgyzstan
Dzhanybek *see* Zhanibek
123 P8 **Dzhardzhan** Respublika Sakha (Yakutiya), NE Russian Federation
Dzharkurgan *see* Jarqo'rg'on
117 S11 **Dzharylhats'ka Zatoka** *gulf* S Ukraine
Dzhayilgan *see* Jayilgan
Dzhebel *see* Jebel
147 T14 **Dzhelandy** SE Tajikistan
147 Y7 **Dzhergalan** *Kir.* Jyrgalan. Issyk-Kul'skaya Oblast', NE Kyrgyzstan
Dzhetygara *see* Zhitikara
Dzhetysay *see* Zhetysay
Dzhezkazgan *see* Zhezkazgan
Dzhigirbent *see* Jigerbent
Dzhirgatal' *see* Jirgatol
Dzhizak *see* Jizzax
Dzhizakskaya Oblast' *see* Jizzax Viloyati
123 P8 **Dzhugdzhur, Khrebet** ▲▲ E Russian Federation
Dzhul'fa *see* Culfa
Dzhuma *see* Juma
145 W14 **Dzhungarskiy Alatau** ▲▲ China/Kazakhstan
144 M14 **Dzhusaly** *Kaz.* Zholsaly. Kzylorda, SW Kazakhstan
146 J12 **Dzhynlykum, Peski** *desert* E Turkmenistan
110 L9 **Działdowo** Warmińsko-Mazurskie, C Poland
111 L16 **Działoszyce** Świętokrzyskie, C Poland
41 X11 **Dzidzantún** Yucatán, E Mexico
111 G15 **Dzierżoniów** *Ger.* Reichenbach. Dolnośląskie, SW Poland
41 X11 **Dzilam de Bravo** Yucatán, E Mexico
118 L12 **Dzisna** *Rus.* Disna. Vitsyebskaya Voblasts', N Belarus
118 K12 **Dzisna** *Lith.* Dysna, *Rus.* Disna. ⚞ Belarus/Lithuania
119 G20 **Dzivin** *Rus.* Divin. Brestskaya Voblasts', SW Belarus
119 M15 **Dzmitravichy** *Rus.* Dmitrovichi. Minskaya Voblasts', C Belarus
Dzogsool *see* Bayantsagaan
162 I5 **Dzöölön** *var.* Rinchinlhumbe. Hövsgöl, N Mongolia
129 S8 **Dzungaria** *var.* Sungaria, Zungaria. *physical region* W China
Dzungarian Basin *see* Junggar Pendi
Dzür *see* Tes
162 J8 **Dzüünbayan-Ulaan** *var* Bayan-Ulaan. Övörhangay, C Mongolia
162 J8 **Dzüünbayan-Ulaan** *var.* Bayan-Ulaan. Övörhangay, C Mongolia
Dzüünbulag *see* Matad, Dornod, Mongolia
Dzüünbulag *see* Uulbayan, Sühbaatar, Mongolia
162 L8 **Dzuunmod** Töv, C Mongolia
Dzuunmod *see* Ider
Dzüün Soyonï Nuruu *see* Eastern Sayans
Dzüyl *see* Tonhil
Dzvina *see* Western Dvina
119 J16 **Dzyarzhynsk Belarus** *Rus.* Dzerzhinsk; *prev.* Kaydanovo. Minskaya Voblasts', C Belarus
119 H17 **Dzyatlava** *Pol.* Zdzięciół, *Rus.* Dyatlovo. Hrodzyenskaya Voblasts', W Belarus

E

E *see* Hubei
Éadan Doire *see* Edenderry
37 W6 **Eads** Colorado, C USA
37 O13 **Eagar** Arizona, SW USA
39 T8 **Eagle** Alaska, USA
13 S8 **Eagle** ⚞ Newfoundland and Labrador, E Canada
10 I3 **Eagle** ⚞ Yukon Territory, NW Canada
29 T7 **Eagle Bend** Minnesota, N USA
28 M8 **Eagle Butte** South Dakota, N USA
29 V12 **Eagle Grove** Iowa, C USA
19 R2 **Eagle Lake** Maine, NE USA
25 U11 **Eagle Lake** Texas, SW USA
12 A11 **Eagle Lake** ◎ Ontario, S Canada
35 P3 **Eagle Lake** ◎ California, W USA
19 R3 **Eagle Lake** ◎ Maine, NE USA
29 Y3 **Eagle Mountain** ▲ Minnesota, N USA
25 T6 **Eagle Mountain Lake** ▣ Texas, SW USA
37 S9 **Eagle Nest Lake** ▣ New Mexico, SW USA
25 P13 **Eagle Pass** Texas, SW USA
65 C25 **Eagle Passage** *passage* SW Atlantic Ocean
35 R8 **Eagle Peak** ▲ California, W USA
35 Q2 **Eagle Peak** ▲ California, W USA
37 P13 **Eagle Peak** ▲ New Mexico, SW USA
10 I4 **Eagle Plain** Yukon Territory, NW Canada
32 G15 **Eagle Point** Oregon, NW USA
186 P10 **Eagle Point** *headland* SE Papua New Guinea
39 R11 **Eagle River** Alaska, USA
30 M2 **Eagle River** Michigan, N USA
30 L4 **Eagle River** Wisconsin, N USA
21 S6 **Eagle Rock** Virginia, NE USA
36 J13 **Eagletail Mountains** ▲▲ Arizona, SW USA
167 U12 **Ea Hleo** Đăc Lăc, S Vietnam
167 U12 **Ea Kar** Đăc Lăc, S Vietnam
Eanjum *see* Anjum
Eanodat *see* Enontekiö
12 B10 **Ear Falls** Ontario, C Canada
27 X10 **Earle** Arkansas, C USA
35 R12 **Earlimart** California, W USA
20 I6 **Earlington** Kentucky, S USA
14 H8 **Earlton** Ontario, S Canada
29 T13 **Early** Iowa, C USA
96 J11 **Earn** ⚞ N Scotland, UK
185 C21 **Earnslaw, Mount** ▲ South Island, New Zealand
24 M4 **Earth** Texas, SW USA
21 P11 **Easley** South Carolina, SE USA
East *see* Est
East Açores Fracture Zone *see* East Azores Fracture Zone
97 P19 **East Anglia** *physical region* E England, UK
15 Q12 **East Angus** Québec, SE Canada
East Antarctica *see* Greater Antarctica
18 E10 **East Aurora** New York, NE USA
East Australian Basin *see* Tasman Basin
East Azerbaijan *see* Āzarbāyjān-e Sharqī
East Azerbaijan *see* Āzarbāyjān-e Sharqī
64 L9 **East Azores Fracture Zone** *var.* East Açores Fracture Zone. *tectonic feature* E Atlantic Ocean
22 M11 **East Bay** *bay* Louisiana, S USA
25 V11 **East Bernard** Texas, SW USA
29 V8 **East Bethel** Minnesota, N USA
East Borneo *see* Kalimantan Timur
97 P23 **Eastbourne** SE England, UK
15 R11 **East-Broughton** Québec, SE Canada
44 M6 **East Caicos** *island* E Turks and Caicos Islands
184 R7 **East Cape** *headland* North Island, New Zealand
174 M4 **East Caroline Basin** *undersea feature* SW Pacific Ocean
192 P4 **East China Sea** *Chin.* Dong Hai. *sea* W Pacific Ocean
97 P19 **East Dereham** E England, UK
30 J9 **East Dubuque** Illinois, N USA
9 S17 **Eastend** Saskatchewan, S Canada
193 S10 **Easter Fracture Zone** *tectonic feature* E Pacific Ocean
Easter Island *see* Pascua, Isla de

◆ Country ● Country Capital ◇ Dependent Territory ○ Dependent Territory Capital ◆ Administrative Regions ✈ International Airport ▲ Mountain ▲▲ Mountain Range ⚠ Volcano ⚞ River ◎ Lake ▣ Reservoir

EASTERN – ELESHNITSA

81 J18 **Eastern** ◈ province Kenya
153 Q12 **Eastern** ◈ zone E Nepal
82 L13 **Eastern** ◈ province E Zambia
83 H24 **Eastern Cape** off. Eastern Cape Province, Afr. Oos-Kaap. ◈ province SE South Africa
Eastern Cape Province see Eastern Cape
Eastern Desert see Sahara el Sharqîya
81 F15 **Eastern Equatoria** ◈ state SE Sudan
Eastern Euphrates see Murat Nehri
155 J17 **Eastern Ghats** ▲▲ SE India
186 E7 **Eastern Highlands** ◈ province C Papua New Guinea
155 K25 **Eastern Province** ◈ province E Sri Lanka
Eastern Region see Ash Sharqīyah
122 L13 **Eastern Sayans** Mong. Dzüün Soyonï Nuruu, Rus. Vostochnyy Sayan. ▲▲ Mongolia/Russian Federation
Eastern Scheldt see Oosterschelde
Eastern Sierra Madre see Sierra Madre Oriental
Eastern Transvaal see Mpumalanga
9 W14 **Easterville** Manitoba, C Canada
Easterwâlde see Oosterwolde
63 M23 **East Falkland** var. Isla Soledad. island E Falkland Islands
19 P12 **East Falmouth** Massachusetts, NE USA
East Fayu see Fayu
East Flanders see Oost-Vlaanderen
39 S6 **East Fork Chandalar River** ≈ Alaska, USA
29 U12 **East Fork Des Moines River** ≈ Iowa/Minnesota, C USA
East Frisian Islands see Ostfriesische Inseln
18 K10 **East Glenville** New York, NE USA
29 R4 **East Grand Forks** Minnesota, N USA
97 O23 **East Grinstead** SE England, UK
18 M12 **East Hartford** Connecticut, NE USA
18 M13 **East Haven** Connecticut, NE USA
173 T9 **East Indiaman Ridge** undersea feature E Indian Ocean
129 V16 **East Indies** island group SE Asia
East Java see Jawa Timur
31 Q6 **East Jordan** Michigan, N USA
East Kalimantan see Kalimantan Timur
East Kazakhstan see Vostochnyy Kazakhstan
96 I12 **East Kilbride** S Scotland, UK
25 R7 **Eastland** Texas, SW USA
31 Q9 **East Lansing** Michigan, N USA
35 X11 **East Las Vegas** Nevada, W USA
97 M23 **Eastleigh** S England, UK
31 V12 **East Liverpool** Ohio, N USA
83 J25 **East London** Afr. Oos-Londen; prev. Emonti, Port Rex. Eastern Cape, S South Africa
96 K12 **East Lothian** cultural region SE Scotland, UK
12 I10 **Eastmain** Québec, E Canada
12 J10 **Eastmain** ≈ Québec, C Canada
15 P13 **Eastman** Québec, SE Canada
23 U6 **Eastman** Georgia, SE USA
175 O3 **East Mariana Basin** undersea feature W Pacific Ocean
30 K11 **East Moline** Illinois, N USA
186 H7 **East New Britain** ◈ province E Papua New Guinea
29 T15 **East Nishnabotna River** ≈ Iowa, C USA
197 V12 **East Novaya Zemlya Trough** var. Novaya Zemlya Trough. undersea feature W Kara Sea
East Nusa Tenggara see Nusa Tenggara Timur
21 X4 **Easton** Maryland, NE USA
18 I14 **Easton** Pennsylvania, NE USA
193 R16 **East Pacific Rise** undersea feature E Pacific Ocean
East Pakistan see Bangladesh
31 V12 **East Palestine** Ohio, N USA
30 L12 **East Peoria** Illinois, N USA
23 S3 **East Point** Georgia, SE USA
19 U6 **Eastport** Maine, NE USA
27 Z8 **East Prairie** Missouri, C USA
19 O12 **East Providence** Rhode Island, NE USA
20 L11 **East Ridge** Tennessee, S USA
97 N16 **East Riding** cultural region N England, UK
18 F9 **East Rochester** New York, NE USA
30 K15 **East Saint Louis** Illinois, N USA
65 K21 **East Scotia Basin** undersea feature SE Scotia Sea
129 Y8 **East Sea** var. Sea of Japan, Rus. Yapanskoye More. Sea NW Pacific Ocean see also Japan, Sea of
186 B6 **East Sepik** ◈ province NW Papua New Guinea
173 N4 **East Sheba Ridge** undersea feature W Arabian Sea
East Siberian Sea see Vostochno-Sibirskoye More
18 I14 **East Stroudsburg** Pennsylvania, NE USA
East Tasmanian Rise/East Tasmania Plateau/East Tasmania Rise see East Tasman Plateau
192 I12 **East Tasman Plateau** var. East Tasmanian Rise, East Tasmania Plateau, East Tasmania Rise. undersea feature SW Tasman Sea
64 L7 **East Thulean Rise** undersea feature N Atlantic Ocean
171 R16 **East Timor** var. Loro Sae; prev. Portuguese Timor, Timor Timur. ◆ country S Indonesia
21 Y6 **Eastville** Virginia, NE USA
35 R7 **East Walker River** ≈ California/Nevada, W USA
182 D1 **Eateringinna Creek** ≈ South Australia
37 T3 **Eaton** Colorado, C USA
15 Q12 **Eaton** ≈ Québec, SE Canada
9 S16 **Eatonia** Saskatchewan, S Canada
31 Q10 **Eaton Rapids** Michigan, N USA
23 U4 **Eatonton** Georgia, SE USA
32 H9 **Eatonville** Washington, NW USA
30 J6 **Eau Claire** Wisconsin, N USA
12 J7 **Eau Claire, Lac à l'** ◎ Québec, SE Canada
Eau Claire, Lac À L' see St. Clair, Lake
30 L6 **Eau Claire River** ≈ Wisconsin, N USA
188 J16 **Eauripik Atoll** atoll Caroline Islands, C Micronesia
192 H7 **Eauripik Rise** undersea feature W Pacific Ocean
102 K15 **Eauze** Gers, S France
41 P11 **Ébano** San Luis Potosí, C Mexico
97 K21 **Ebbw Vale** SE Wales, UK
79 E17 **Ebebiyín** NE Equatorial Guinea
95 H22 **Ebeltoft** Århus, C Denmark
109 X5 **Ebenfurth** Niederösterreich, E Austria
18 D14 **Ebensburg** Pennsylvania, NE USA
109 S5 **Ebensee** Oberösterreich, N Austria
101 H20 **Eberbach** Baden-Württemberg, SW Germany
121 U8 **Eber Gölü** salt lake C Turkey
109 U9 **Eberndorf** Slvn. Dobrla Vas. Kärnten, S Austria
109 R4 **Eberschwang** Oberösterreich, N Austria
100 O11 **Eberswalde-Finow** Brandenburg, E Germany
Ebesfalva see Dumbrăveni
165 T4 **Ebetsu** var. Ebetu. Hokkaidō, NE Japan
Ebetu see Ebetsu
Ebinayon see Evinayong
158 I4 **Ebinur Hu** ◎ NW China
138 I3 **Ebla** Ar. Tell Mardīkh. site of ancient city Idlib, NW Syria
Eblana see Dublin
108 H7 **Ebnat** Sankt Gallen, NE Switzerland
107 L18 **Eboli** Campania, S Italy
79 E16 **Ebolowa** Sud, S Cameroon
79 N21 **Ebombo** Kasai Oriental, C Dem. Rep. Congo
189 T9 **Ebon Atoll** var. Epoon. atoll Ralik Chain, S Marshall Islands
Ebora see Évora
Eboracum see York
Eborodunum see Yverdon
101 J19 **Ebrach** Bayern, C Germany
109 X5 **Ebreichsdorf** Niederösterreich, E Austria
105 S6 **Ebro** ≈ NE Spain
105 N3 **Ebro, Embalse del** ⊠ N Spain
120 G7 **Ebro Fan** undersea feature W Mediterranean Sea
Eburacum see York
Ebusus see Ibiza
Ebusus see Eivissa
99 F20 **Écaussinnes-d'Enghien** Hainaut, SW Belgium
Ecbatana see Hamadān
21 Q6 **Eccles** West Virginia, NE USA
115 L14 **Eceabat** Çanakkale, NW Turkey
171 O2 **Echague** Luzon, N Philippines
Ech Cheliff/Ech Chleff see Chlef
Echeng see Ezhou
115 C18 **Echinádes** island group W Greece
114 J12 **Echínos** var. Ehinos, Ekhínos. Anatolikí Makedonía kai Thráki, NE Greece
164 J12 **Echizen-misaki** headland Honshū, SW Japan
Echmiadzin see Vagharshapat
8 J8 **Echo Bay** Northwest Territories, NW Canada
35 Y11 **Echo Bay** Nevada, W USA
36 L9 **Echo Cliffs** cliff Arizona, SW USA
14 C10 **Echo Lake** ◎ Ontario, S Canada
35 Q7 **Echo Summit** ▲ California, W USA
14 L8 **Échouani, Lac** ◎ Québec, SE Canada
99 L17 **Echt** Limburg, SE Netherlands
101 H22 **Echterdingen** ✈ (Stuttgart) Baden-Württemberg, SW Germany
99 N24 **Echternach** Grevenmacher, E Luxembourg
183 N11 **Echuca** Victoria, SE Australia
104 L14 **Ecija** anc. Astigi. Andalucía, SW Spain
Eckengraf see Viesīte
100 I7 **Eckernförde** Schleswig-Holstein, N Germany
100 J7 **Eckernförder Bucht** inlet N Germany
102 L7 **Écommoy** Sarthe, NW France
14 L10 **Écorce, Lac de l'** ◎ Québec, SE Canada
15 Q8 **Écorces, Rivière aux** ≈ Québec, SE Canada
56 C7 **Ecuador** off. Republic of Ecuador. ◆ republic NW South America
Ecuador, Republic of see Ecuador
80 L10 **Ed** var. Edd. SE Eritrea
95 I17 **Ed** Älvsborg, S Sweden
98 I9 **Edam** Noord-Holland, C Netherlands
96 K4 **Eday** island NE Scotland, UK
25 S17 **Edcouch** Texas, SW USA
Edd see Ed
80 C11 **Ed Da'ein** Southern Darfur, W Sudan
80 G11 **Ed Damazin** var. Ad Damazīn. Blue Nile, E Sudan
80 G8 **Ed Damer** var. Ad Dāmir, Ad Damar. River Nile, NE Sudan
80 E8 **Ed Debba** Northern, N Sudan
80 F10 **Ed Dueim** var. Ad Duwaym, Ad Duwēm. White Nile, C Sudan
183 Q16 **Eddystone Point** headland Tasmania, SE Australia
97 I25 **Eddystone Rocks** rocks SW England, UK
29 W15 **Eddyville** Iowa, C USA
20 H7 **Eddyville** Kentucky, S USA
98 L12 **Ede** Gelderland, C Netherlands
77 T16 **Ede** Osun, SW Nigeria
79 D16 **Edéa** Littoral, SW Cameroon
111 M20 **Edelény** Borsod-Abaúj-Zemplén, NE Hungary
183 R12 **Eden** New South Wales, SE Australia
21 T8 **Eden** North Carolina, SE USA
25 P9 **Eden** Texas, SW USA
97 K14 **Eden** ≈ NW England, UK
83 I23 **Edenburg** Free State, C South Africa
185 D24 **Edendale** Southland, South Island, New Zealand
97 E18 **Edenderry** Ir. Éadan Doire. Offaly, C Ireland
182 L11 **Edenhope** Victoria, SE Australia
21 X8 **Edenton** North Carolina, SE USA
101 G16 **Eder** ≈ NW Germany
101 H15 **Edersee** ◎ W Germany
114 E13 **Édessa** var. Édhessa. Kentrikí Makedonía, N Greece
Edessa see Şanlıurfa
Edfu see Idfu
29 P16 **Edgar** Nebraska, C USA
19 P13 **Edgartown** Martha's Vineyard, Massachusetts, NE USA
39 X13 **Edgecumbe, Mount** ▲ Baranof Island, Alaska, USA
21 Q13 **Edgefield** South Carolina, SE USA
29 P6 **Edgeley** North Dakota, N USA
28 I11 **Edgemont** South Dakota, N USA
92 O3 **Edgeøya** island S Svalbard
27 Q4 **Edgerton** Kansas, C USA
29 S10 **Edgerton** Minnesota, N USA
21 X3 **Edgewood** Maryland, NE USA
25 V6 **Edgewood** Texas, SW USA
Édhessa see Édessa
29 V9 **Edina** Minnesota, N USA
27 U2 **Edina** Missouri, C USA
25 S17 **Edinburg** Texas, SW USA
65 M24 **Edinburgh** var. Settlement of Edinburgh. O (Tristan da Cunha) NW Tristan da Cunha
96 J12 **Edinburgh** ● S Scotland, UK
31 P14 **Edinburgh** Indiana, N USA
96 J12 **Edinburgh** ✈ S Scotland, UK
116 L8 **Edineț** var. Edineţi, Rus. Yedintsy. NW Moldova
Edineţi see Edineț
Edingen see Enghien
136 B9 **Edirne** Eng. Adrianople, anc Adrianopolis, Hadrianopolis. Edirne, NW Turkey
136 B11 **Edirne** ◈ province NW Turkey
18 K15 **Edison** New Jersey, NE USA
21 S15 **Edisto Island** South Carolina, SE USA
21 R14 **Edisto River** ≈ South Carolina, SE USA
33 S10 **Edith, Mount** ▲ Montana, NW USA
27 N10 **Edmond** Oklahoma, C USA
32 H8 **Edmonds** Washington, NW USA
9 Q14 **Edmonton** province capital Alberta, SW Canada
20 K7 **Edmonton** Kentucky, S USA
9 Q14 **Edmonton** ✈ Alberta, SW Canada
29 P3 **Edmore** North Dakota, N USA
13 N13 **Edmundston** New Brunswick, SE Canada
25 U12 **Edna** Texas, SW USA
39 X14 **Edna Bay** Kosciusko Island, Alaska, USA
77 U16 **Edo** ◈ state S Nigeria
106 F6 **Edolo** Lombardia, N Italy
64 L6 **Edoras Bank** undersea feature C Atlantic Ocean
96 G7 **Edrachillis Bay** bay NW Scotland, UK
136 B12 **Edremit** Balıkesir, NW Turkey
136 B12 **Edremit Körfezi** gulf NW Turkey
95 P14 **Edsbro** Stockholm, C Sweden
95 N18 **Edsbruk** Kalmar, S Sweden
94 M12 **Edsbyn** Gävleborg, C Sweden
9 O14 **Edson** Alberta, SW Canada
62 K13 **Eduardo Castex** La Pampa, C Argentina
58 F12 **Eduardo Gomes** ✈ (Manaus) Amazonas, NW Brazil
Edwardesabad see Bannu
67 U9 **Edward, Lake** var. Albert Edward Nyanza, Edward Nyanza, Lac Idi Amin, Lake Rutanzige. ◎ Uganda/Dem. Rep. Congo
Edward Nyanza see Edward, Lake
22 K5 **Edwards** Mississippi, S USA
25 O10 **Edwards Plateau** plain Texas, SW USA
30 J11 **Edwards River** ≈ Illinois, N USA
30 K15 **Edwardsville** Illinois, N USA
195 X4 **Edward VIII Gulf** bay Antarctica
195 O13 **Edward VII Peninsula** peninsula Antarctica
10 J11 **Edziza, Mount** ▲ British Columbia, W Canada
23 H16 **Edzo** prev. Rae-Edzo. Northwest Territories, NW Canada
39 N12 **Eek** Alaska, USA
99 D16 **Eeklo** var. Eekloo. Oost-Vlaanderen, NW Belgium
Eekloo see Eeklo
39 N12 **Eek River** ≈ Alaska, USA
98 N6 **Eelde** Drenthe, NE Netherlands
34 L5 **Eel River** ≈ California, W USA
31 P12 **Eel River** ≈ Indiana, N USA
Eems see Ems
98 O4 **Eemshaven** Groningen, NE Netherlands
98 O5 **Eems Kanaal** canal NE Netherlands
98 M11 **Eerbeek** Gelderland, E Netherlands
99 C17 **Eernegem** West-Vlaanderen, W Belgium
99 J15 **Eersel** Noord-Brabant, S Netherlands
Eesti Vabariik see Estonia
187 R14 **Éfaté** var. Efate, Fr. Vaté; prev. Sandwich Island. island C Vanuatu
Efate see Éfaté
109 S4 **Eferding** Oberösterreich, N Austria
30 M15 **Effingham** Illinois, N USA
117 N15 **Eforie-Nord** Constanţa, SE Romania
117 N15 **Eforie Sud** Constanţa, E Romania
Efyrnwy, Afon see Vyrnwy
Eg see Batshireet
107 G23 **Egadi, Isole** island group S Italy
35 X6 **Egan Range** ▲▲ Nevada, W USA
14 K12 **Eganville** Ontario, SE Canada
Ege Denizi see Aegean Sea
39 O14 **Egegik** Alaska, USA
111 L21 **Eger** Ger. Erlau. Heves, NE Hungary
Eger see Cheb
Eger see Ohre
173 P8 **Egeria Fracture Zone** tectonic feature W Indian Ocean
95 C17 **Egersund** Rogaland, S Norway
108 J7 **Egg** Vorarlberg, NW Austria
101 H14 **Egge-gebirge** ▲▲ C Germany
109 Q4 **Eggelsberg** Oberösterreich, N Austria
109 W2 **Eggenburg** Niederösterreich, NE Austria
101 N22 **Eggenfelden** Bayern, SE Germany
18 J17 **Egg Harbor City** New Jersey, NE USA
65 G25 **Egg Island** island W Saint Helena
183 N14 **Egg Lagoon** Tasmania, SE Australia
99 I20 **Éghezée** Namur, C Belgium
92 L2 **Egilsstadhir** Austurland, E Iceland
Egina see Aígina
Egindibulaq see Yegindybulak
Egio see Aígio
103 N12 **Égletons** Corrèze, C France
98 H9 **Egmond aan Zee** Noord-Holland, NW Netherlands
Egmont see Taranaki, Mount
184 J10 **Egmont, Cape** cape North Island, New Zealand
Egoli see Johannesburg
Eğri Palanka see Kriva Palanka
95 G23 **Egtved** Vejle, C Denmark
123 U5 **Egvekinot** Chukotskiy Avtonomnyy Okrug, NE Russian Federation
75 V9 **Egypt** off. Arab Republic of Egypt, Ar. Jumhūrīyah Miṣr al 'Arabīyah, prev. United Arab Republic; anc. Aegyptus. ◆ republic NE Africa
30 L17 **Egypt, Lake Of** ⊠ Illinois, N USA
162 I14 **Ehen Hudag** var Alx Youqi. Nei Mongol Zizhiqu, N China
164 F14 **Ehime** off. Ehime-ken. ◈ prefecture Shikoku, SW Japan
Ehime-ken see Ehime
101 I23 **Ehingen** Baden-Württemberg, S Germany
Ehinos see Echínos
21 R14 **Ehrhardt** South Carolina, SE USA
108 L7 **Ehrwald** Tirol, W Austria
191 W6 **Eiao** island Îles Marquises, NE French Polynesia
105 P2 **Eibar** País Vasco, N Spain
98 O11 **Eibergen** Gelderland, E Netherlands
109 V9 **Eibiswald** Steiermark, SE Austria
109 P8 **Eichham** ▲ SW Austria
101 J15 **Eichsfeld** hill range C Germany
101 K21 **Eichstätt** Bayern, SE Germany
100 H8 **Eider** ≈ N Germany
94 E13 **Eidfjord** Hordaland, S Norway
94 D13 **Eidfjorden** fjord S Norway
94 F9 **Eidsvåg** Møre og Romsdal, S Norway
95 I14 **Eidsvoll** Akershus, S Norway
92 N2 **Eidsvollfjellet** ▲ NW Svalbard
Eier-Berg see Suur Munamägi
101 D18 **Eifel** plateau W Germany
108 E9 **Eiger** ▲ C Switzerland
96 G10 **Eigg** island W Scotland, UK
155 D24 **Eight Degree Channel** channel India/Maldives
44 G1 **Eight Mile Rock** Grand Bahama Island, N Bahamas
194 J9 **Eights Coast** physical region Antarctica
180 K6 **Eighty Mile Beach** beach Western Australia
99 L18 **Eijsden** Limburg, SE Netherlands
95 G15 **Eikeren** ◎ S Norway
Eil see Eyl
Eilat see Elat
183 O12 **Eildon** Victoria, SE Australia
183 O12 **Eildon, Lake** ◎ Victoria, SE Australia
80 E8 **Eilei** Northern Kordofan, C Sudan
101 N15 **Eilenburg** Sachsen, E Germany
Eil Malk see Mecherchar
94 H13 **Eina** Oppland, S Norway
101 I14 **Einbeck** Niedersachsen, C Germany
99 K15 **Eindhoven** Noord-Brabant, S Netherlands
108 G8 **Einsiedeln** Schwyz, NE Switzerland
Eipel see Ipel'
Éire see Ireland
Éireann, Muir see Irish Sea
Eirik Outer Ridge see Eirik Ridge
64 I6 **Eirik Ridge** var. Eirik Outer Ridge. undersea feature E Labrador Sea
92 I3 **Eiríksjökull** ▲ C Iceland
59 B14 **Eirunepé** Amazonas, N Brazil
99 L17 **Eisden** Limburg, NE Belgium
83 F18 **Eiseb** ≈ Botswana/Namibia
Eisen see Yŏngch'ŏn
101 J16 **Eisenach** Thüringen, C Germany
Eisenburg see Vasvár
109 U6 **Eisenerz** Steiermark, SE Austria
100 Q13 **Eisenhüttenstadt** Brandenburg, E Germany
109 U10 **Eisenkappel** Slvn. Železna Kapela. Kärnten, S Austria
Eisenmarkt see Hunedoara
109 Y5 **Eisenstadt** Burgenland, E Austria
Eishū see Yŏngju
119 H15 **Eišiškes** Vilnius, SE Lithuania
101 L15 **Eisleben** Sachsen-Anhalt, C Germany
190 I3 **Eita** Tarawa, W Kiribati
Eitape see Aitape
105 V11 **Eivissa** var. Iviza, Cast. Ibiza; anc. Ebusus. Ibiza, Spain, W Mediterranean Sea
Eivissa see Ibiza
105 R4 **Ejea de los Caballeros** Aragón, NE Spain
40 E8 **Ejido Insurgentes** Baja California Sur, W Mexico
Ejin Qi see Dalain Hob
Ejmiadzin/Ejmiatsin see Vagharshapat
77 P16 **Ejura** C Ghana
41 R16 **Ejutla** var. Ejutla de Crespo. Oaxaca, SE Mexico
Ejutla de Crespo see Ejutla
33 Y10 **Ekalaka** Montana, NW USA
Ekapa see Cape Town
Ekaterinodar see Krasnodar
93 L20 **Ekenäs** Fin. Tammisaari. Etelä-Suomi, SW Finland
146 B13 **Ekerem** Rus. Okarem. Balkan Welaýaty, W Turkmenistan
184 M13 **Eketahuna** Manawatu-Wanganui, North Island, New Zealand
Ekhínos see Echínos
Ostan-e Khorāsān-e Shemālī see Khorāsān-e Shemālī
123 U5 **Ekiatapskiy Khrebet** ▲▲ NE Russian Federation
145 T8 **Ekibastuz** Pavlodar, NE Kazakhstan
123 R13 **Ekimchan** Amurskaya Oblast', SE Russian Federation
95 O15 **Ekoln** ◎ C Sweden
80 I7 **Ekowit** Red Sea, NE Sudan
95 L19 **Eksjö** Jönköping, S Sweden
93 I15 **Ekträsk** Västerbotten, N Sweden
39 O13 **Ekuk** Alaska, USA
12 F9 **Ekwan** ≈ Ontario, C Canada
39 O13 **Ekwok** Alaska, USA
166 M6 **Ela** Mandalay, C Burma (Myanmar)
El Aaiun see El Ayoun
81 N15 **El Ābrēd** Somali, E Ethiopia
115 F22 **Elafónisos** island S Greece
115 F22 **Elafonísou, Porthmós** strait S Greece
El-Aïoun see El Ayoun
75 U8 **El 'Alamein** var. Al 'Alamayn. N Egypt
41 Q12 **El Alazán** Veracruz-Llave, C Mexico
57 J18 **El Alto** var. La Paz. ✈ (La Paz) La Paz, W Bolivia
Elam see Īlām
El Amparo see El Amparo de Apure
54 I8 **El Amparo de Apure** var. El Amparo. Apure, C Venezuela
171 R13 **Elara** Pulau Ambelau, E Indonesia
El Araïch/El Araïche see Larache
40 D6 **El Arco** Baja California, NW Mexico
75 X7 **El 'Arîsh** var. Al 'Arīsh. NE Egypt
115 L25 **Elása** island SE Greece
El Asnam see Chlef
Elassón see Elassóna
115 E15 **Elassóna** prev. Elassón. Thessalía, C Greece
105 N2 **El Astillero** Cantabria, N Spain
138 F14 **Elat** var. Eilat, Elath. Southern, S Israel
Elat, Gulf of see Aqaba, Gulf of
Elath see Elat, Israel
Elath see Al 'Aqabah, Jordan
115 C17 **Eláti** ▲ Lefkáda, Iónioi Nísoi, Greece, C Mediterranean Sea
188 L16 **Elato Atoll** atoll Caroline Islands, C Micronesia
80 C7 **El'Atrun** Northern Darfur, NW Sudan
74 H6 **El Ayoun** var. El Aaiun, El-Aïoun, La Youne. NE Morocco
137 N14 **Elâzığ** var. Elâzig, Elâziz. Elâzığ, E Turkey
137 O14 **Elâzığ** var. Elâzig, Elâziz. ◈ province C Turkey
Elâzig/Elâziz see Elâzığ
23 Q7 **Elba** Alabama, S USA
106 E13 **Elba, Isola d'** island Archipelago Toscano, C Italy
123 S13 **El'ban** Khabarovskiy Kray, E Russian Federation
54 F6 **El Banco** Magdalena, N Colombia
El Barco see O Barco
104 L8 **El Barco de Ávila** Castilla-León, N Spain
El Barco de Valdeorras see O Barco
138 H7 **El Barouk, Jabal** ▲ C Lebanon
113 L20 **Elbasan** var. Elbasani. Elbasan, C Albania
113 L20 **Elbasan** ◈ district C Albania
Elbasani see Elbasan
54 K6 **El Baúl** Cojedes, C Venezuela
86 D11 **Elbe** Cz. Labe. ≈ Czech Republic/Germany
100 L13 **Elbe-Havel-Kanal** canal E Germany
100 K9 **Elbe-Lübeck-Kanal** canal N Germany
El Beni see Beni
138 H7 **El Beqaa** var. Al Biqā', Bekaa Valley. valley E Lebanon
25 R6 **Elbert** Texas, SW USA
37 R5 **Elbert, Mount** ▲ Colorado, C USA
23 U3 **Elberton** Georgia, SE USA
100 K11 **Elbe-Seiten-Kanal** canal N Germany
102 M4 **Elbeuf** Seine-Maritime, N France
Elbing see Elbląg
136 M15 **Elbistan** Kahramanmaraş, S Turkey
110 K7 **Elbląg** var. Elblag, Ger. Elbing. Warmińsko-Mazurskie, NE Poland
43 N10 **El Bluff** Región Autónoma Atlántico Sur, SE Nicaragua
63 H17 **El Bolsón** Río Negro, W Argentina
105 P11 **El Bonillo** Castilla-La Mancha, C Spain
El Bordo see Patía
El Boulaida/El Boulaïda see Blida
9 T16 **Elbow** Saskatchewan, S Canada
29 S7 **Elbow Lake** Minnesota, N USA
127 N16 **El'brus** var. Gora El'brus. ▲ SW Russian Federation
El'brus, Gora see El'brus
126 M15 **El'brusskiy** Karachayevo-Cherkesskaya Respublika, SW Russian Federation
81 D14 **El Buhayrat** var. Lakes State. ◈ state S Sudan
El Bur see Ceel Buur
98 L10 **Elburg** Gelderland, E Netherlands
105 O6 **El Burgo de Osma** Castilla-León, C Spain
Elburz Mountains see Alborz, Reshteh-ye Kūhhā-ye
35 V17 **El Cajon** California, W USA
63 H22 **El Calafate** var. Calafate. Santa Cruz, S Argentina
55 Q8 **El Callao** Bolívar, E Venezuela
25 U12 **El Campo** Texas, SW USA
54 I7 **El Cantón** Barinas, W Venezuela
35 Q8 **El Capitan** ▲ California, W USA
54 H5 **El Carmelo** Zulia, NW Venezuela
62 J5 **El Carmen** Jujuy, NW Argentina
54 E5 **El Carmen de Bolívar** Bolívar, NW Colombia
55 O8 **El Casabe** Bolívar, SE Venezuela
42 M12 **El Castillo de La Concepción** Río San Juan, SE Nicaragua
El Cayo see San Ignacio
35 X17 **El Centro** California, W USA
55 N6 **El Chaparro** Anzoátegui, NE Venezuela
105 S12 **Elche** Cat. Elx; anc. Ilici, Lat. Illicis. País Valenciano, E Spain
105 Q12 **Elche de la Sierra** Castilla-La Mancha, C Spain
41 U15 **El Chichónal, Volcán** ⛰ SE Mexico
40 C2 **El Chinero** Baja California, NW Mexico
181 R1 **Elcho Island** island Wessel Islands, Northern Territory, N Australia
63 H18 **El Corcovado** Chubut, SW Argentina
105 R12 **Elda** País Valenciano, E Spain
100 M10 **Elde** ≈ NE Germany
98 L12 **Elden** Gelderland, E Netherlands
81 J16 **El Der** spring/well S Ethiopia
El Dere see Ceel Dheere
40 E3 **El Desemboque** Sonora, NW Mexico
54 F5 **El Difícil** var. Ariguaní. Magdalena, N Colombia
123 R10 **El'dikan** Respublika Sakha (Yakutiya), NE Russian Federation
El Djazaïr see Alger
El Djelfa see Djelfa
29 X15 **Eldon** Iowa, C USA
27 U5 **Eldon** Missouri, C USA
54 E13 **El Doncello** Caquetá, S Colombia
29 W13 **Eldora** Iowa, C USA
60 G12 **Eldorado** Misiones, NE Argentina
40 I9 **El Dorado** Sinaloa, C Mexico
27 U14 **El Dorado** Arkansas, C USA
30 M17 **Eldorado** Illinois, N USA
27 O6 **El Dorado** Kansas, C USA
26 K12 **Eldorado** Oklahoma, C USA
25 O9 **Eldorado** Texas, SW USA
55 Q8 **El Dorado** Bolívar, E Venezuela
54 F10 **El Dorado** ✈ (Bogotá) Cundinamarca, C Colombia
El Dorado see California
27 O6 **El Dorado Lake** ⊠ Kansas, C USA
27 S6 **El Dorado Springs** Missouri, C USA
81 H18 **Eldoret** Rift Valley, W Kenya
29 Z14 **Eldridge** Iowa, C USA
95 J21 **Eldsberga** Halland, S Sweden
25 R4 **Electra** Texas, SW USA
37 Q7 **Electra Lake** ⊠ Colorado, C USA
38 B8 **'Ele'ele** var. Eleele. Kaua'i, Hawai'i, USA
Eleele see 'Ele'ele
Elefantes see Olifants
115 H19 **Elefsína** prev. Elevsís. Attikí, C Greece
115 G19 **Eléftheres** anc. Eleutherae. site of ancient city Attikí/Stereá Ellás, C Greece
114 I13 **Eleftheroúpoli** prev. Elevtheroúpolis. Anatolikí Makedonía kai Thráki, NE Greece
74 F10 **El Eglab** ▲ SW Algeria
118 F10 **Eleja** Jelgava, C Latvia
Elek see Ilek
119 G14 **Elektrėnai** Vilnius, SE Lithuania
126 L3 **Elektrostal'** Moskovskaya Oblast', W Russian Federation
81 H15 **Elemi Triangle** disputed region Kenya/Sudan
54 G16 **El Encanto** Amazonas, S Colombia
37 R14 **Elephant Butte Reservoir** ⊠ New Mexico, SW USA
Éléphant, Chaîne de l' see Dâmrei, Chuŏr Phnum
194 G2 **Elephant Island** island South Shetland Islands, Antarctica
Elephant River see Olifants
El Escorial see San Lorenzo de El Escorial
Élesd see Aleşd
114 F11 **Eleshnitsa** ≈ W Bulgaria

◆ Country ● Country Capital ◇ Dependent Territory O Dependent Territory Capital ◈ Administrative Regions ✈ International Airport ▲ Mountain ▲▲ Mountain Range ⛰ Volcano ≈ River ◎ Lake ⊠ Reservoir

Eleşkirt – Erdao Jiang

137 S13 **Eleşkirt** Ağrı, E Turkey
42 F5 **El Estor** Izabal, E Guatemala
Eleutherae see Eléftheres
44 I2 **Eleuthera Island** *island* N Bahamas
37 S5 **Elevenmile Canyon Reservoir** ⊠ Colorado, C USA
27 W8 **Eleven Point River** ≈ Arkansas/Missouri, C USA
Elevsís see Elefsína
Elevtheroúpolis see Eleftheroúpoli
75 W8 **El Faiyûm** *var.* Al Fayyūm. N Egypt
80 B10 **El Fasher** *var.* Al Fāshir. Northern Darfur, W Sudan
75 W8 **El Fashn** *var.* Al Fashn. C Egypt
El Ferrol/El Ferrol del Caudillo see Ferrol
39 W13 **Elfin Cove** Chichagof Island, Alaska, USA
105 W4 **El Fluvià** ≈ NE Spain
40 H7 **El Fuerte** Sinaloa, W Mexico
80 D11 **El Fula** Western Kordofan, C Sudan
El Gedaref see Gedaref
80 A10 **El Geneina** *var.* Ajjinena, Al-Genain, Al Junaynah. Western Darfur, W Sudan
96 J8 **Elgin** NE Scotland, UK
30 M10 **Elgin** Illinois, N USA
29 P14 **Elgin** Nebraska, C USA
35 Y9 **Elgin** Nevada, W USA
28 L6 **Elgin** North Dakota, N USA
26 M12 **Elgin** Oklahoma, C USA
25 T10 **Elgin** Texas, SW USA
123 R9 **El'ginskiy** Respublika Sakha (Yakutiya), NE Russian Federation
75 W8 **El Giza** *var.* Al Jīzah, Gîza, Gizeh. N Egypt
74 J8 **El Goléa** *var.* Al Golea. C Algeria
40 D2 **El Golfo de Santa Clara** Sonora, NW Mexico
81 G18 **Elgon, Mount** ▲ E Uganda
105 T4 **El Grado** Aragón, NE Spain
94 I10 **Elgpiggen** ▲ S Norway
40 L6 **El Guaje, Laguna** ⊠ NE Mexico
54 H6 **El Guayabo** Zulia, W Venezuela
77 O6 **El Gueṭṭâra** *oasis* N Mali
76 J6 **El Ḥammâmi** *desert* N Mauritania
76 M5 **El Ḥank** *cliff* N Mauritania
El Haseke see Al Ḥasakah
80 H10 **El Hawata** Gedaref, E Sudan
El Higo see Higos
171 T16 **Eliase** Pulau Selaru, E Indonesia
Elías Piña see Comendador
25 R6 **Eliasville** Texas, SW USA
Elichpur see Achalpur
37 V13 **Elida** New Mexico, SW USA
115 F18 **Elikónas** ▲ C Greece
67 T10 **Elila** ≈ W Dem. Rep. Congo
39 N9 **Elim** Alaska, USA
Elimberrum see Auch
Eliocroca see Lorca
61 B16 **Elisa** Santa Fe, C Argentina
Elisabethstedt see Dumbrăveni
Élisabethville see Lubumbashi
127 O13 **Elista** Respublika Kalmykiya, SW Russian Federation
182 I9 **Elizabeth** South Australia
21 Q3 **Elizabeth** West Virginia, NE USA
19 Q9 **Elizabeth, Cape** *headland* Maine, NE USA
21 Y8 **Elizabeth City** North Carolina, SE USA
21 P8 **Elizabethton** Tennessee, S USA
30 M17 **Elizabethtown** Illinois, N USA
20 K6 **Elizabethtown** Kentucky, S USA
18 L7 **Elizabethtown** New York, NE USA
21 U11 **Elizabethtown** North Carolina, SE USA
18 G15 **Elizabethtown** Pennsylvania, NE USA
74 E6 **El-Jadida** *prev.* Mazagan. W Morocco
El Jafr see Jafr, Qā' al
80 F11 **El Jebelein** White Nile, E Sudan
110 N8 **Ełk** *Ger.* Lyck. Warmińsko-mazurskie, NE Poland
110 O8 **Ełk** ≈ NE Poland
29 Y12 **Elkader** Iowa, C USA
80 G9 **El Kamlin** Gezira, C Sudan
33 N11 **Elk City** Idaho, NW USA
26 K10 **Elk City** Oklahoma, C USA
27 P7 **Elk City Lake** ⊠ Kansas, C USA
34 M5 **Elk Creek** California, W USA
28 J10 **Elk Creek** ≈ South Dakota, N USA
74 M5 **El Kef** *var.* Al Kāf, Le Kef. NW Tunisia
74 F7 **El Kelâa Srarhna** *var.* Kal al Sraghna. C Morocco
El Kerak see Al Karak
9 P17 **Elkford** British Columbia, SW Canada
El Khalil see Hebron
80 E7 **El Khandaq** Northern, N Sudan
75 W10 **El Khârga** *var.* Al Khārijah. C Egypt
31 P11 **Elkhart** Indiana, N USA
26 H7 **Elkhart** Kansas, C USA
25 V8 **Elkhart** Texas, SW USA
30 M7 **Elkhart Lake** ◎ Wisconsin, N USA
El Khartûm see Khartoum
37 Q3 **Elkhead Mountains** ▲▲ Colorado, C USA
18 I12 **Elk Hill** ▲ Pennsylvania, NE USA
138 G8 **El Khiyam** , *var.* Al Khiyām. S Lebanon
29 S15 **Elkhorn** Nebraska, C USA
30 M9 **Elkhorn** Wisconsin, N USA
29 R14 **Elkhorn River** ≈ Nebraska, C USA
127 O16 **El'khotovo** Respublika Severnaya Osetiya, SW Russian Federation
114 L10 **Elkhovo** *prev.* Kizilagach. Yambol, E Bulgaria
21 R8 **Elkin** North Carolina, SE USA
21 S4 **Elkins** West Virginia, NE USA
195 X3 **Elkins, Mount** ▲ Antarctica
14 G8 **Elk Lake** Ontario, S Canada
31 P6 **Elk Lake** ◎ Michigan, N USA
18 F12 **Elkland** Pennsylvania, NE USA
35 W3 **Elko** Nevada, W USA
9 R14 **Elk Point** Alberta, SW Canada
29 R12 **Elk Point** South Dakota, N USA
29 V8 **Elk River** Minnesota, N USA
20 J10 **Elk River** ≈ Alabama/Tennessee, S USA
21 R4 **Elk River** ≈ West Virginia, NE USA
20 I7 **Elkton** Kentucky, S USA
21 Y2 **Elkton** Maryland, NE USA
29 R10 **Elkton** South Dakota, N USA
20 I10 **Elkton** Tennessee, S USA
21 U5 **Elkton** Virginia, NE USA
El Kuneitra see Al Qunayṭirah
81 L15 **El Kure** Somali, E Ethiopia
80 D12 **El Lagowa** Western Kordofan, C Sudan
39 S12 **Ellamar** Alaska, USA
Ellás see Greece
23 S6 **Ellaville** Georgia, SE USA
197 P9 **Ellef Ringnes Island** *island* Nunavut, N Canada
29 V10 **Ellendale** Minnesota, N USA
29 P7 **Ellendale** North Dakota, N USA
36 M6 **Ellen, Mount** ▲ Utah, W USA
32 I9 **Ellensburg** Washington, NW USA
18 K12 **Ellenville** New York, NE USA
Ellep see Lib
21 T10 **Ellerbe** North Carolina, SE USA
197 P10 **Ellesmere Island** *island* Queen Elizabeth Islands, Nunavut, N Canada
185 H19 **Ellesmere, Lake** ◎ South Island, New Zealand
97 K18 **Ellesmere Port** C England, UK
31 O14 **Ellettsville** Indiana, N USA
99 E19 **Ellezelles** Hainaut, SW Belgium
8 L7 **Ellice** ≈ Nunavut, NE Canada
Ellice Islands see Tuvalu
Ellichpur see Achalpur
21 W3 **Ellicott City** Maryland, NE USA
23 S2 **Ellijay** Georgia, SE USA
27 W7 **Ellington** Missouri, C USA
26 L5 **Ellinwood** Kansas, C USA
83 J24 **Elliot** Eastern Cape, SE South Africa
14 D10 **Elliot Lake** Ontario, S Canada
181 X6 **Elliot, Mount** ▲ Queensland, E Australia
21 T5 **Elliott Knob** ▲ Virginia, NE USA
26 K4 **Ellis** Kansas, C USA
182 F8 **Elliston** South Australia
22 M7 **Ellisville** Mississippi, S USA
105 V5 **El Llobregat** ≈ NE Spain
96 L9 **Ellon** NE Scotland, UK
Ellore see Elūru
21 S13 **Elloree** South Carolina, SE USA
26 M4 **Ellsworth** Kansas, C USA
19 S7 **Ellsworth** Maine, NE USA
30 I6 **Ellsworth** Wisconsin, N USA
26 M11 **Ellsworth, Lake** ⊠ Oklahoma, C USA
194 K9 **Ellsworth Land** *physical region* Antarctica
194 L9 **Ellsworth Mountains** ▲▲ Antarctica
101 J21 **Ellwangen** Baden-Württemberg, S Germany
18 B14 **Ellwood City** Pennsylvania, NE USA
108 H8 **Elm** Glarus, NE Switzerland
32 G9 **Elma** Washington, NW USA
121 V13 **El Maḥalla el Kubra** *var.* Al Maḥallah al Kubrá, Mahalla el Kubra. N Egypt
74 E9 **El Mahbas** *var.* Mahbés. SW Western Sahara
63 H17 **El Maitén** Chubut, W Argentina
136 E16 **Elmalı** Antalya, SW Turkey
80 G10 **El Manaqil** Gezira, C Sudan
54 M12 **El Mango** Amazonas, S Venezuela
75 W7 **El Manṣûra** *var.* Al Manṣūrah, Manṣūra. N Egypt
55 P8 **El Manteco** Bolívar, E Venezuela
29 O16 **Elm Creek** Nebraska, C USA
El Mediyya see Médéa
77 V9 **Elméki** Agadez, C Niger
108 K7 **Elmen** Tirol, W Austria
18 I16 **Elmer** New Jersey, NE USA
138 G6 **El Mina** *var.* Al Mīnā'. N Lebanon
75 W9 **El Minya** *var.* Al Minyā, Minya. C Egypt
14 F15 **Elmira** Ontario, S Canada
18 G11 **Elmira** New York, NE USA
36 K13 **El Mirage** Arizona, SW USA
29 O7 **Elm Lake** ⊠ South Dakota, N USA
El Moján see San Rafael
105 N7 **El Molar** Madrid, C Spain
76 L7 **El Mrâyer** *well* C Mauritania
76 L5 **El Mreiti** *well* N Mauritania
76 L8 **El Mreyyé** *desert* E Mauritania
29 P8 **Elm River** ≈ North Dakota/South Dakota, N USA
100 I9 **Elmshorn** Schleswig-Holstein, N Germany
80 D12 **El Muglad** Western Kordofan, C Sudan
El Muwaqqar see Al Muwaqqar
14 G14 **Elmvale** Ontario, S Canada
30 K12 **Elmwood** Illinois, N USA
26 J8 **Elmwood** Oklahoma, C USA
103 P17 **Elne** *anc.* Illiberis. Pyrénées-Orientales, S France
54 F11 **El Nevado, Cerro** *elevation* C Colombia
171 N5 **El Nido** Palawan, W Philippines
62 I12 **El Nihuil** Mendoza, W Argentina
75 W7 **El Nouzha** ✕ (Alexandria) N Egypt
80 E10 **El Obeid** *var.* Al Obayyid, Al Ubayyiḍ. Northern Kordofan, C Sudan
41 O13 **El Oro** México, S Mexico
56 B8 **El Oro** ◈ *province* SW Ecuador
61 B19 **Elortondo** Santa Fe, C Argentina
54 J8 **Elorza** Apure, C Venezuela
El Ouâdi see El Oued
74 L7 **El Oued** *var.* Al Oued, El Ouâdi, El Wad. NE Algeria
36 L15 **Eloy** Arizona, SW USA
55 Q7 **El Palmar** Bolívar, E Venezuela
40 K8 **El Palmito** Durango, W Mexico
55 P7 **El Pao** Bolívar, E Venezuela
54 K5 **El Pao** Cojedes, N Venezuela
42 J7 **El Paraíso** El Paraíso, S Honduras
42 I7 **El Paraíso** ◈ *department* SE Honduras
30 L12 **El Paso** Illinois, N USA
24 G8 **El Paso** Texas, SW USA
24 G8 **El Paso** ✕ Texas, SW USA
105 U7 **El Perello** Cataluña, NE Spain
55 P5 **El Pilar** Sucre, NE Venezuela
42 F7 **El Pital, Cerro** ▲ El Salvador/Honduras
35 Q9 **El Portal** California, W USA
40 J3 **El Porvenir** Chihuahua, N Mexico
43 U14 **El Porvenir** San Blas, N Panama
105 W6 **El Prat de Llobregat** Cataluña, NE Spain
42 H5 **El Progreso** Yoro, NW Honduras
42 A2 **El Progreso** *off.* Departamento de El Progreso. ◈ *department* C Guatemala
El Progreso see Guastatoya
El Progreso, Departamento de see El Progreso
104 L9 **El Puente del Arzobispo** Castilla-La Mancha, C Spain
104 J15 **El Puerto de Santa María** Andalucía, S Spain
62 I8 **El Puesto** Catamarca, NW Argentina
El Qâhira see Cairo
75 V10 **El Qaṣr** *var.* Al Qaṣr. C Egypt
El Qatrani see Al Qaṭrānah
40 I10 **El Quelite** Sinaloa, C Mexico
62 G8 **Elqui, Río** ≈ N Chile
El Q'unayṭirah see Al Qunayṭirah
El Quneitra see Al Qunayṭirah
El Quseir see Al Quṣayr
El Quweira see Al Quwayrah
141 O15 **El-Rahaba** ✕ (Ṣan'ā') W Yemen
42 M10 **El Rama** Región Autónoma Atlántico Sur, SE Nicaragua
43 W16 **El Real** *var.* El Real de Santa María. Darién, SE Panama
El Real de Santa María see El Real
26 M10 **El Reno** Oklahoma, C USA
40 K9 **El Rodeo** Durango, C Mexico
104 J13 **El Ronquillo** Andalucía, S Spain
9 S16 **Elrose** Saskatchewan, S Canada
30 K8 **Elroy** Wisconsin, N USA
25 S17 **Elsa** Texas, SW USA
75 W8 **El Ṣaff** *var.* Aṣ Ṣaff. N Egypt
40 J10 **El Salto** Durango, C Mexico
42 D8 **El Salvador** *off.* Republica de El Salvador. ◆ *republic* Central America
El Salvador, Republica de see El Salvador
54 K7 **El Samán de Apure** Apure, C Venezuela
14 D7 **Elsas** Ontario, S Canada
40 F3 **El Sásabe** *var.* Aduana del Sásabe. Sonora, NW Mexico
Elsass see Alsace
40 J5 **El Sáuz** Chihuahua, N Mexico
27 W4 **Elsberry** Missouri, C USA
45 F9 **El Seibo** *var.* Santa Cruz de El Seibo, Santa Cruz del Seibo. E Dominican Republic
42 B7 **El Semillero Barra Nahualate** Escuintla, SW Guatemala
Elsene see Ixelles
Elsen Nur see Dorgê Co
Elsen Nur see Dorgê Co
36 L6 **Elsinore** Utah, W USA
Elsinore see Helsingør
99 L18 **Elsloo** Limburg, SE Netherlands
60 G13 **El Soberbio** Misiones, NE Argentina
55 N6 **El Socorro** Guárico, C Venezuela
54 L5 **El Sombrero** Guárico, N Venezuela
98 L10 **Elspeet** Gelderland, E Netherlands
98 L12 **Elst** Gelderland, E Netherlands
101 O15 **Elsterwerda** Brandenburg, E Germany
40 J4 **El Sueco** Chihuahua, N Mexico
El Suweida see As Suwaydā'
El Suweis see Suez
54 D12 **El Tambo** Cauca, SW Colombia
175 T13 **Eltanin Fracture Zone** *tectonic feature* SE Pacific Ocean
105 X5 **El Ter** ≈ NE Spain
184 K11 **Eltham** Taranaki, North Island, New Zealand
55 O6 **El Tigre** Anzoátegui, NE Venezuela
El Tigrito see San José de Guanipa
54 J5 **El Tocuyo** Lara, N Venezuela
127 Q10 **El'ton** Volgogradskaya Oblast', SW Russian Federation
32 K10 **Eltopia** Washington, NW USA
El Toro see Mare de Déu del Toro
61 A18 **El Trébol** Santa Fe, C Argentina
40 J13 **El Tuito** Jalisco, SW Mexico
75 X8 **El Ṭûr** *var.* Aṭ Ṭūr. NE Egypt
155 K16 **Elūru** *prev.* Ellore. Andhra Pradesh, E India
118 H13 **Elva** *Ger.* Elwa. Tartumaa, SE Estonia
37 R9 **El Vado Reservoir** ⊠ New Mexico, SW USA
43 S15 **El Valle** Coclé, C Panama
104 I11 **Elvas** Portalegre, C Portugal
54 K7 **El Venado** Apure, C Venezuela
105 V6 **El Vendrell** Cataluña, NE Spain
94 I13 **Elverum** Hedmark, S Norway
42 I9 **El Viejo** Chinandega, NW Nicaragua
54 G7 **El Viejo, Cerro** ▲ C Colombia
54 H6 **El Vigía** Mérida, NW Venezuela
105 Q4 **El Villar de Arnedo** La Rioja, N Spain
59 A14 **Elvira** Amazonas, W Brazil
Elwa see Elva
El Wad see El Oued
81 K17 **El Wak** North Eastern, NE Kenya
33 R7 **Elwell, Lake** ⊠ Montana, NW USA
31 P13 **Elwood** Indiana, N USA
27 R3 **Elwood** Kansas, C USA
29 N16 **Elwood** Nebraska, C USA
Elx see Elche
97 O20 **Ely** E England, UK
29 X4 **Ely** Minnesota, N USA
35 X6 **Ely** Nevada, W USA
El Yopal see Yopal
31 T11 **Elyria** Ohio, N USA
45 S9 **El Yunque** ▲ E Puerto Rico
101 F23 **Elz** ≈ SW Germany
187 R14 **Emae** *island* Shepherd Islands, C Vanuatu
118 I5 **Emajõgi** *Ger.* Embach. ≈ SE Estonia
Emāmrūd see Shāhrūd
149 Q2 **Emām Ṣāḥeb** *var.* Emam Saheb, Hazarat Imam. Kunduz, NE Afghanistan
Emam Saheb see Emām Ṣāḥeb
Emāmshahr see Shāhrūd
95 M20 **Emån** ≈ S Sweden
144 J11 **Emba** *Kaz.* Embi. Aktyubinsk, W Kazakhstan
144 H12 **Emba** *Kaz.* Zhem. ≈ W Kazakhstan
Embach see Emajõgi
62 K5 **Embarcación** Salta, N Argentina
30 M15 **Embarras River** ≈ Illinois, N USA
Embi see Emba
81 I19 **Embu** Eastern, C Kenya
100 E10 **Emden** Niedersachsen, NW Germany
160 H9 **Emei Shan** ▲ Sichuan, C China
29 Q4 **Emerado** North Dakota, N USA
181 X8 **Emerald** Queensland, E Australia
Emerald Isle see Montserrat
57 J15 **Emero, Río** ≈ W Bolivia
9 Y17 **Emerson** Manitoba, S Canada
29 T15 **Emerson** Iowa, C USA
29 R13 **Emerson** Nebraska, C USA
36 M5 **Emery** Utah, W USA
Emesa see Ḥimṣ
136 E13 **Emet** Kütahya, W Turkey
186 B8 **Emeti** Western, SW Papua New Guinea
35 V3 **Emigrant Pass** *pass* Nevada, W USA
78 I6 **Emi Koussi** ▲ N Chad
Emilia see Emilia-Romagna
41 V15 **Emiliano Zapata** Chiapas, SE Mexico
106 E9 **Emilia-Romagna** *prev.* Emilia; *anc.* Æmilia. ◈ *region* N Italy
158 J3 **Emin** *var.* Dorbiljin. Xinjiang Uygur Zizhiqu, NW China
149 W8 **Eminābād** Punjab, E Pakistan
21 L5 **Eminence** Kentucky, S USA
27 W7 **Eminence** Missouri, C USA
114 N9 **Emine, Nos** *headland* E Bulgaria
158 J3 **Emin He** ≈ NW China
186 G4 **Emirau Island** *island* N Papua New Guinea
136 F13 **Emirdağ** Afyon, W Turkey
95 M21 **Emmaboda** Kalmar, S Sweden
118 E5 **Emmaste** Hiiumaa, W Estonia
18 I15 **Emmaus** Pennsylvania, NE USA
183 U4 **Emmaville** New South Wales, SE Australia
108 E9 **Emme** ≈ W Switzerland
98 L8 **Emmeloord** Flevoland, N Netherlands
98 O8 **Emmen** Drenthe, NE Netherlands
108 F8 **Emmen** Luzern, C Switzerland
101 F23 **Emmendingen** Baden-Württemberg, SW Germany
98 P8 **Emmer-Compascuum** Drenthe, NE Netherlands
101 D14 **Emmerich** Nordrhein-Westfalen, W Germany
29 U12 **Emmetsburg** Iowa, C USA
32 M14 **Emmett** Idaho, NW USA
38 M10 **Emmonak** Alaska, USA
Emona see Ljubljana
Emonti see East London
24 L12 **Emory Peak** ▲ Texas, SW USA
40 F6 **Empalme** Sonora, NW Mexico
83 L23 **Empangeni** KwaZulu/Natal, E South Africa
61 C14 **Empedrado** Corrientes, NE Argentina
192 K3 **Emperor Seamounts** *undersea feature* NW Pacific Ocean
192 L3 **Emperor Trough** *undersea feature* N Pacific Ocean
35 R4 **Empire** Nevada, W USA
Empire State of the South see Georgia
Emplawas see Amplawas
106 F11 **Empoli** Toscana, C Italy
27 P5 **Emporia** Kansas, C USA
21 W7 **Emporia** Virginia, NE USA
18 E13 **Emporium** Pennsylvania, NE USA
Empty Quarter see Ar Rub 'al Khālī
100 E10 **Ems** *Dut.* Eems. ≈ NW Germany
100 F13 **Emsdetten** Nordrhein-Westfalen, NW Germany
Ems-Hunte Canal see Küstenkanal
100 F10 **Ems-Jade-Kanal** *canal* NW Germany
100 F11 **Emsland** *cultural region* NW Germany
182 D3 **Emu Junction** South Australia
163 T3 **Emur He** ≈ NE China
55 R8 **Enachu Landing** NW Guyana
93 F16 **Enafors** Jämtland, C Sweden
94 N11 **Enånger** Gävleborg, C Sweden
96 G7 **Enard Bay** *bay* NW Scotland, UK
Enareträsk see Inarijärvi
171 X14 **Enarotali** Papua, E Indonesia
138 E12 **En 'Avedat** *var.* En'Avedat. *well* S Israel
En'Avedat see En 'Avedat
165 T2 **Enbetsu** Hokkaidō, NE Japan
61 H16 **Encantadas, Serra das** ▲▲ S Brazil
40 E7 **Encantado, Cerro** ▲ NW Mexico
62 P7 **Encarnación** Itapúa, S Paraguay
40 M12 **Encarnación de Díaz** Jalisco, SW Mexico
77 O17 **Enchi** SW Ghana
25 Q14 **Encinal** Texas, SW USA
35 U17 **Encinitas** California, W USA
25 S16 **Encino** Texas, SW USA
54 H6 **Encontrados** Zulia, NW Venezuela
182 I10 **Encounter Bay** *inlet* South Australia
61 F15 **Encruzilhada** Rio Grande do Sul, S Brazil
61 H16 **Encruzilhada do Sul** Rio Grande do Sul, S Brazil
111 M20 **Encs** Borsod-Abaúj-Zemplén, NE Hungary
193 P3 **Endeavour Seamount** *undersea feature* N Pacific Ocean
181 V1 **Endeavour Strait** *strait* Queensland, NE Australia
171 O16 **Endeh** Flores, S Indonesia
95 G23 **Endelave** *island* C Denmark
191 T4 **Enderbury Island** *atoll* Phoenix Islands, C Kiribati
9 N16 **Enderby** British Columbia, SW Canada
195 W4 **Enderby Land** *physical region* Antarctica
173 N14 **Enderby Plain** *undersea feature* S Indian Ocean
29 Q6 **Enderlin** North Dakota, N USA
Endersdorf see Jędrzejów
28 K16 **Enders Reservoir** ⊠ Nebraska, C USA
18 H11 **Endicott** New York, NE USA
39 P7 **Endicott Mountains** ▲▲ Alaska, USA
118 I5 **Endla Raba** *wetland* C Estonia
117 T9 **Enerhodar** Zaporiz'ka Oblast', SE Ukraine
57 F14 **Ene, Río** ≈ C Peru
189 N4 **Enewetak Atoll** *var.* Ānewetak, Eniwetok. *atoll* Ralik Chain, W Marshall Islands
114 L13 **Enez** Edirne, NW Turkey
21 W8 **Enfield** North Carolina, SE USA
186 B7 **Enga** ◈ *province* W Papua New Guinea
45 Q9 **Engaño, Cabo** *headland* E Dominican Republic
164 U3 **Engaru** Hokkaidō, NE Japan
138 F11 **'En Gedi** Southern, E Israel
108 F9 **Engelberg** Unterwalden, C Switzerland
21 Y9 **Engelhard** North Carolina, SE USA
127 P8 **Engel's** Saratovskaya Oblast', W Russian Federation
101 G24 **Engen** Baden-Württemberg, SW Germany
Engeten see Aiud
168 K15 **Enggano, Pulau** *island* W Indonesia
80 J8 **Enghershatu** ▲ N Eritrea
99 F19 **Enghien** *Dut.* Edingen. Hainaut, SW Belgium
27 V12 **England** Arkansas, C USA
97 M20 **England** *Lat.* Anglia. *cultural region* England, UK
14 H8 **Englehart** Ontario, S Canada
37 T4 **Englewood** Colorado, C USA
31 O16 **English** Indiana, N USA
39 Q13 **English Bay** Alaska, USA
English Bazar see Ingrāj Bāzār
97 N25 **English Channel** *var.* The Channel, *Fr.* la Manche. *channel* NW Europe
194 J7 **English Coast** *physical region* Antarctica
105 S11 **Enguera** País Valenciano, E Spain
118 E8 **Engure** Tukums, W Latvia
118 E8 **Engures Ezers** ◎ NW Latvia
137 R9 **Enguri** *Rus.* Inguri. ≈ NW Georgia
Engyum see Gangi
26 M9 **Enid** Oklahoma, C USA
22 L3 **Enid Lake** ⊠ Mississippi, S USA
189 Y2 **Enigu** *island* Ratak Chain, SE Marshall Islands
Enikale Strait see Kerch Strait
147 Z8 **Enil'chek** Issyk-Kul'skaya Oblast', E Kyrgyzstan
115 F17 **Enipéfs** ≈ C Greece
165 S4 **Eniwa** Hokkaidō, NE Japan
Eniwetok see Enewetak Atoll
Enjiang see Yongfeng
Enkeldoorn see Chivhu
98 J8 **Enkhuizen** Noord-Holland, NW Netherlands
109 Q4 **Enknach** ≈ N Austria
95 N15 **Enköping** Uppsala, C Sweden
107 K24 **Enna** *var.* Castrogiovanni, Henna. Sicilia, Italy, C Mediterranean Sea
80 D11 **En Nahud** Western Kordofan, C Sudan
138 F8 **En Nâqoûra** *var.* An Nāqūrah. SW Lebanon
En Nazira see Naẓerat
78 K8 **Ennedi** *plateau* E Chad
101 E15 **Ennepetal** Nordrhein-Westfalen, W Germany
183 P4 **Enngonia** New South Wales, SE Australia
97 C19 **Ennis** *Ir.* Inis. Clare, W Ireland
33 R11 **Ennis** Montana, NW USA
25 U7 **Ennis** Texas, SW USA
97 F20 **Enniscorthy** *Ir.* Inis Córthaidh. Wexford, SE Ireland
97 E15 **Enniskillen** *var.* Inniskilling, *Ir.* Inis Ceithleann. SW Northern Ireland, UK
97 B19 **Ennistimon** *Ir.* Inis Díomáin. Clare, W Ireland
109 T4 **Enns** Oberösterreich, N Austria
109 T4 **Enns** ≈ C Austria
93 O16 **Eno** Pohjois-Karjala, SE Finland
24 M5 **Enochs** Texas, SW USA
93 N17 **Enonkoski** Isä-Suomi, E Finland
92 K10 **Enontekiö** *Lapp.* Eanodat. Lappi, N Finland
21 Q11 **Enoree** South Carolina, SE USA
21 P11 **Enoree River** ≈ South Carolina, SE USA
18 M6 **Enosburg Falls** Vermont, NE USA
171 N13 **Enrekang** Sulawesi, C Indonesia
45 N10 **Enriquillo** SW Dominican Republic
45 N9 **Enriquillo, Lago** ◎ SW Dominican Republic
98 L9 **Ens** Flevoland, N Netherlands
98 P11 **Enschede** Overijssel, E Netherlands
40 B2 **Ensenada** Baja California, NW Mexico
101 E20 **Ensheim** ✕ (Saarbrücken) Saarland, W Germany
160 L9 **Enshi** Hubei, C China
164 L14 **Enshū-nada** *gulf* SW Japan
23 O8 **Ensley** Florida, SE USA
Enso see Svetogorsk
81 F18 **Entebbe** S Uganda
81 F18 **Entebbe** ✕ C Uganda
101 M18 **Entenbühl** ▲ Czech Republic/Germany
98 N10 **Enter** Overijssel, E Netherlands
23 Q7 **Enterprise** Alabama, S USA
32 L11 **Enterprise** Oregon, NW USA
36 J7 **Enterprise** Utah, W USA
32 J8 **Entiat** Washington, NW USA
105 P15 **Entinas, Punta de las** *headland* S Spain
108 F8 **Entlebuch** Luzern, W Switzerland
108 F8 **Entlebuch** *valley* C Switzerland
63 I22 **Entrada, Punta** *headland* S Argentina
103 O13 **Entraygues-sur-Truyère** Aveyron, S France
187 O14 **Entrecasteaux, Récifs d'** *reef* N New Caledonia
61 C17 **Entre Ríos** *off.* Provincia de Entre Ríos. ◈ *province* NE Argentina
42 K7 **Entre Ríos, Cordillera** ▲▲ Honduras/Nicaragua
Entre Ríos, Provincia de see Entre Ríos
104 G9 **Entroncamento** Santarém, C Portugal
77 U16 **Enugu** Enugu, S Nigeria
77 U16 **Enugu** ◈ *state* SE Nigeria
123 V5 **Enurmino** Chukotskiy Avtonomnyy Okrug, NE Russian Federation
54 E9 **Envigado** Antioquia, W Colombia
59 B15 **Envira** Amazonas, W Brazil
Enyélé see Enyellé
79 I16 **Enyellé** *var.* Enyélé. La Likouala, NE Congo
101 H21 **Enz** ≈ SW Germany
165 N13 **Enzan** Yamanashi, Honshū, S Japan
104 I2 **Eo** ≈ NW Spain
Eochaill see Youghal
Eochaille, Cuan see Youghal Bay
107 K22 **Eolie, Isole** *var.* Isole Lipari, *Eng.* Aeolian Islands, Lipari Islands. *island group* S Italy
189 U12 **Eot** *island* Chuuk, C Micronesia
Epáno Archánes/Epáno Arkhánai see Archánes
115 G14 **Epanomí** Kentrikí Makedonía, N Greece
98 M10 **Epe** Gelderland, E Netherlands
77 S16 **Epe** Lagos, S Nigeria
79 I17 **Epéna** La Likouala, NE Congo
Eperies/Eperjes see Prešov
103 Q4 **Épernay** *anc.* Sparnacum. Marne, N France
36 L5 **Ephraim** Utah, W USA
18 H15 **Ephrata** Pennsylvania, NE USA
32 J8 **Ephrata** Washington, NW USA
187 R14 **Epi** *var.* Épi. *island* C Vanuatu
Épi see Epi
105 R6 **Épila** Aragón, NE Spain
103 T6 **Épinal** Vosges, NE France
Epiphania see Ḥamāh
Epirus see Ípeiros
121 P3 **Episkopí** SW Cyprus
Episkopi Bay see Episkopí, Kólpos
121 P3 **Episkopí, Kólpos** *var.* Episkopi Bay. *bay* SE Cyprus
Epitoli see Tshwane
Epoon see Ebon Atoll
Eporedia see Ivrea
Eppeschdorf see Dumbrăveni
101 H21 **Eppingen** Baden-Württemberg, SW Germany
83 E18 **Epukiro** Omaheke, E Namibia
29 Y13 **Epworth** Iowa, C USA
143 O10 **Eqlīd** *var.* Iqlid. Fārs, C Iran
Equality State see Wyoming
79 J18 **Equateur** *off.* Région de l' Equateur. ◈ *region* N Dem. Rep. Congo
Equateur, Région de l' see Equateur
151 K22 **Equatorial Channel** *channel* S Maldives
79 B17 **Equatorial Guinea** *off.* Equatorial Guinea, Republic of. ◆ *republic* C Africa
Equatorial Guinea, Republic of see Equatorial Guinea
121 V11 **Eratosthenes Tablemount** *undersea feature* E Mediterranean Sea
Erautini see Johannesburg
136 L12 **Erbaa** Tokat, N Turkey
101 E19 **Erbeskopf** ▲ W Germany
Erbil see Arbīl
121 P2 **Ercan** ✕ (Nicosia) N Cyprus
Ercegnovi see Herceg-Novi
137 T14 **Erçek Gölü** ◎ E Turkey
137 S14 **Erciş** Van, E Turkey
136 K14 **Erciyes Dağı** *anc.* Argaeus. ▲ C Turkey
111 J22 **Érd** *Ger.* Hanselbeck. Pest, C Hungary
163 X11 **Erdaobaihe** *prev.* Baihe. Jilin, NE China
159 O12 **Erdaogou** Qinghai, W China
163 X11 **Erdao Jiang** ≈ NE China

◆ Country
● Country Capital
◇ Dependent Territory
○ Dependent Territory Capital
◈ Administrative Regions
✕ International Airport
▲ Mountain
▲▲ Mountain Range
Volcano
≈ River
◎ Lake
⊠ Reservoir

ERDĂT-SÂNGEORZ – FÅBORG

Erdăt-Sângeorz see Sângeorgiu de Pădure
136 C11 **Erdek** Balıkesir, NW Turkey
Erdély see Transylvania
Erdélyi-Havasok see Carpaţii Meridionali
136 J17 **Erdemli** Mersin, S Turkey
163 O10 **Erdene** var. Ulaan-Uul. Dornogovĭ, SE Mongolia
162 H9 **Erdene** var. Sangiyn Dalay. Govĭ-Altay, C Mongolia
162 E6 **Erdenebüren** var. Har-Us. Hovd, W Mongolia
162 K9 **Erdenedalay** var. Sangiyn Dalay. Dundgovĭ, C Mongolia
162 G7 **Erdenehayrhan** var. Altan. Dzavhan, W Mongolia
162 J7 **Erdenemandal** var. Öldziyt. Arhangay, C Mongolia
162 K6 **Erdenet** Orhon, N Mongolia
163 Q9 **Erdenetsagaan** var. Chonogol. Sühbaatar, E Mongolia
162 I8 **Erdenetsogt** Bayanhongor, C Mongolia
Erdenetsogt see Bayan-Ovoo
78 K7 **Erdi** plateau NE Chad
78 L7 **Erdi Ma** desert NE Chad
101 M23 **Erding** Bayern, SE Germany
Erdőszáda see Ardusat
Erdőszentgyörgy see Sângeorgiu de Pădure
102 I7 **Erdre** ≈ NW France
195 R13 **Erebus, Mount** ⛰ Ross Island, Antarctica
61 H14 **Erechim** Rio Grande do Sul, S Brazil
163 O7 **Ereen Davaanï Nuruu** ▲▲ NE Mongolia
163 Q6 **Ereentsav** Dornod, NE Mongolia
136 I16 **Ereğli** Konya, S Turkey
136 I15 **Eğridir Gölü** ◎ W Turkey
115 A15 **Ereíkoussa** island Iónioi Nísoi, Greece, C Mediterranean Sea
163 O11 **Erenhot** var. Erlian. Nei Mongol Zizhiqu, NE China
104 M6 **Eresma** ≈ N Spain
115 K17 **Eresós** var. Eressós. Lésvos, E Greece
Eressós see Eresós
Ereymentaū see Yermentau
99 K21 **Érezée** Luxembourg, SE Belgium
74 G7 **Erfoud** SE Morocco
101 D16 **Erft** ≈ W Germany
101 K16 **Erfurt** Thüringen, C Germany
137 P15 **Ergani** Dıyarbakır, SE Turkey
Ergel see Hatanbulag
136 C10 **Ergene Çayi** var. Ergene Irmaği. ≈ NW Turkey
Ergene Irmaği see Ergene Çayi
Ergenetsogt see Bayan-Ovoo
118 I9 **Ērgļi** Madona, C Latvia
78 H11 **Erguig, Bahr** ≈ SW Chad
163 S5 **Ergun** var. Labudalin; prev. Ergun Youqi. Nei Mongol Zizhiqu, N China
Ergun He see Argun
Ergun Youqi see Ergun
Ergun Zuoqi see Genhe
160 F12 **Er Hai** ⊠ SW China
104 K4 **Ería** ≈ NW Spain
80 H8 **Eriba** Kassala, NE Sudan
96 I6 **Eriboll, Loch** inlet NW Scotland, UK
65 Q18 **Erica Seamount** undersea feature SW Indian Ocean
107 H23 **Erice** Sicilia, Italy, C Mediterranean Sea
104 E10 **Ericeira** Lisboa, C Portugal
96 H10 **Ericht, Loch** ◎ C Scotland, UK
26 J11 **Erick** Oklahoma, C USA
18 B11 **Erie** Pennsylvania, NE USA
18 E9 **Erie Canal** canal New York, NE USA
Érié, Lac see Erie, Lake
31 T10 **Erie, Lake** Fr. Lac Érié. ◎ Canada/USA
Erigabo see Ceerigaabo
77 N8 **'Erîgât** desert N Mali
Erigavo see Ceerigaabo
92 P2 **Erik Eriksenstretet** strait E Svalbard
9 X15 **Eriksdale** Manitoba, S Canada
189 V6 **Erikub Atoll** var. Ādkup. atoll Ratak Chain, C Marshall Islands
102 G4 **Er, Îles d'** Island group NW France
Erimanthos see Erýmanthos
165 T6 **Erimo** Hokkaidō, NE Japan
165 T6 **Erimo-misaki** headland Hokkaidō, NE Japan
20 H8 **Erin** Tennessee, S USA
96 E9 **Eriskay** island NW Scotland, UK
Erithraí see Erythrés
80 I9 **Eritrea** off. State of Eritrea, Ērtra. ◆ transitional government E Africa
Eritrea, State of see Eritrea
Erivan see Yerevan
101 D16 **Erkelenz** Nordrhein-Westfalen, W Germany
95 P15 **Erken** ◎ C Sweden
101 K19 **Erlangen** Bayern, S Germany
160 G9 **Erlang Shan** ▲ C China
Erlau see Eger
109 V5 **Erlauf** ≈ NE Austria
181 Q8 **Erldunda Roadhouse** Northern Territory, N Australia
Erlian see Erenhot
27 T15 **Erling, Lake** ⊠ Arkansas, USA
109 O8 **Erlsbach** Tirol, W Austria
Ermak see Aksu
98 K10 **Ermelo** Gelderland, C Netherlands
83 K21 **Ermelo** Mpumalanga, NE South Africa
136 H17 **Ermenek** Karaman, S Turkey
Érmihályfalva see Valea lui Mihai
115 G20 **Ermióni** Pelopónnisos, S Greece
115 J20 **Ermoúpoli** var. Hermoupolis; prev. Ermoúpolis. Sýyros, Kykládes, Greece, Aegean Sea
Ermoúpolis see Ermoúpoli
Ernabella see Pukatja
155 G22 **Ernākulam** Kerala, SW India
102 J6 **Ernée** Mayenne, NW France
61 H14 **Ernestina, Barragem** ⊠ S Brazil
54 E4 **Ernesto Cortissoz** ✈ (Barranquilla) Atlántico, N Colombia
155 H21 **Erode** Tamil Nādu, SE India
Eroj see Iroj
83 C19 **Erongo** ◈ district W Namibia
99 F21 **Erquelinnes** Hainaut, S Belgium
74 G7 **Er-Rachidia** var. Ksar al Soule. E Morocco
80 E11 **Er Rahad** var. Ar Rahad. Northern Kordofan, C Sudan
Er Ramle see Ramla
83 O15 **Errego** Zambézia, NE Mozambique
105 Q2 **Errenteria** Cast. Rentería. País Vasco, N Spain
Er Rif/Er Riff see Rif
97 D14 **Errigal Mountain** Ir. An Earagail. ▲ N Ireland
97 A15 **Erris Head** Ir. Ceann Iorrais. headland W Ireland
187 S15 **Erromango** island S Vanuatu
Error Guyot see Error Tablemount
173 O4 **Error Tablemount** var. Error Guyot. undersea feature W Indian Ocean
80 G11 **Er Roseires** Blue Nile, E Sudan
Erseka see Ersekë
113 M22 **Ersekë** var. Erseka, Kolonjë. Korçë, SE Albania
Érsekújvár see Nové Zámky
29 S4 **Erskine** Minnesota, N USA
103 V6 **Erstein** Bas-Rhin, NE France
108 G9 **Erstfeld** Uri, C Switzerland
158 M3 **Ertai** Xinjiang Uygur Zizhiqu, NW China
126 M7 **Ertil'** Voronezhskaya Oblast', W Russian Federation
Ertis see Irtysh, C Asia
Ertis see Irtyshsk, Kazakhstan
158 K2 **Ertix He** Rus. Chërnyy Irtysh. ≈ China/Kazakhstan
Ērtra see Eritrea
21 P9 **Erwin** North Carolina, SE USA
Erydropótamos see Erythropótamos
115 E19 **Erýmanthos** var. Erimanthos. ▲ S Greece
115 G19 **Erythrés** prev. Erithraí. Stereá Ellás, C Greece
114 L12 **Erythropótamos** Bul. Byala Reka, var. Erydropótamos. ≈ Bulgaria/Greece
160 F12 **Eryuan** var. Yuhu. Yunnan, SW China
109 U6 **Erzbach** ≈ W Austria
Erzerum see Erzurum
101 N17 **Erzgebirge** Cz. Krušné Hory, Eng. Ore Mountains. ▲ Czech Republic/Germany see also Krušné Hory
Erzgebirge see Krušné Hory
122 L14 **Erzin** Respublika Tyva, S Russian Federation
137 O13 **Erzincan** var. Erzinjan. Erzincan, E Turkey
137 N13 **Erzincan** var. Erzinjan. ◈ province NE Turkey
Erzinjan see Erzincan
Erzsébetváros see Dumbrăveni
137 Q13 **Erzurum** prev. Erzerum. Erzurum, NE Turkey
137 Q12 **Erzurum** prev. Erzerum. ◈ province NE Turkey
186 G9 **Esa'ala** Normanby Island, SE Papua New Guinea
165 T2 **Esashi** Hokkaidō, NE Japan
165 Q9 **Esashi** var. Esasi. Iwate, Honshū, C Japan
165 Q5 **Esasho** Hokkaidō, N Japan
Esasi see Esashi
95 F23 **Esbjerg** Ribe, W Denmark
Esbo see Espoo
36 L7 **Escalante** Utah, W USA
36 M7 **Escalante River** ≈ Utah, W USA
14 L12 **Escalier, Réservoir l'** ⊠ Québec, SE Canada
40 K7 **Escalón** Chihuahua, N Mexico
104 M8 **Escalona** Castilla-La Mancha, C Spain
23 O8 **Escambia River** ≈ Florida, SE USA
31 N5 **Escanaba** Michigan, N USA
31 N4 **Escanaba River** ≈ Michigan, N USA
105 R8 **Escandón, Puerto de** pass E Spain
41 W14 **Escárcega** Campeche, SE Mexico
171 O1 **Escarpada Point** headland Luzon, N Philippines
23 N8 **Escatawpa River** ≈ Alabama/Mississippi, S USA
103 P2 **Escaut** ≈ N France
Escaut see Scheldt
99 M25 **Esch-sur-Alzette** Luxembourg, S Luxembourg
101 J15 **Eschwege** Hessen, C Germany
101 D16 **Eschweiler** Nordrhein-Westfalen, W Germany
Esclaves, Grand Lac des see Great Slave Lake
45 O8 **Escocesa, Bahía** bay N Dominican Republic
43 W15 **Escocés, Punta** headland NE Panama
35 U17 **Escondido** California, W USA
42 M10 **Escondido, Río** ≈ SE Nicaragua
15 S7 **Escoumins, Rivière des** ≈ Québec, SE Canada
37 O13 **Escudilla Mountain** ▲ Arizona, SW USA
40 J11 **Escuinapa** var. Escuinapa de Hidalgo. Sinaloa, C Mexico
Escuinapa de Hidalgo see Escuinapa
42 C6 **Escuintla** Escuintla, S Guatemala
41 V17 **Escuintla** Chiapas, SE Mexico
42 A2 **Escuintla** off. Departamento de Escuintla. ◈ department S Guatemala
Escuintla, Departamento de see Escuintla
15 W7 **Escuminac** ≈ Québec, SE Canada
79 D16 **Eséka** Centre, SW Cameroon
136 I12 **Esenboğa** ✈ (Ankara) Ankara, C Turkey
136 D17 **Eşen Çayı** ≈ SW Turkey
146 B13 **Esenguly** Rus. Gasan-Kuli. Balkan Welaýaty, W Turkmenistan
105 T4 **Ésera** ≈ NE Spain
143 N8 **Eşfahān** Eng. Isfahan; anc. Aspadana. Eşfahān, C Iran
143 O7 **Eşfahān** off. Ostān-e Eşfahān. ◈ province C Iran
Eşfahān, Ostān-e see Eşfahān
105 N5 **Esgueva** ≈ N Spain
149 Q3 **Eshkamesh** Takhār, NE Afghanistan
149 T2 **Eshkāshem** Badakhshān, NE Afghanistan
83 L23 **Eshowe** KwaZulu/Natal, E South Africa
143 T5 **'Eshqābād** Khorāsān, NE Iran
Esh Sham see Dimashq
Esh Sharā see Ash Sharāh
Esik see Yesik
Esil see Yesil'
Esil see Ishim, Kazakhstan/Russian Federation
183 V2 **Esk** Queensland, E Australia
184 O11 **Eskdale** Hawke's Bay, North Island, New Zealand
Eski Dzhumaya see Türgovishte
92 L2 **Eskifjördhur** Austurland, E Iceland
139 S3 **Eski Kaļak** var. Askī Kalak, Kalak. N Iraq
95 N16 **Eskilstuna** Södermanland, C Sweden
8 H6 **Eskimo Lakes** ◎ Northwest Territories, NW Canada
9 O10 **Eskimo Point** headland Nunavut, E Canada
Eskimo Point see Arviat
139 Q2 **Eski Mosul** N Iraq
147 T10 **Eski-Nookat** var. Iski-Nauket. Oshskaya Oblast', SW Kyrgyzstan
136 F12 **Eskişehir** var. Eskishehr. Eskişehir, W Turkey
136 F13 **Eskişehir** var. Eski shehr. ◈ province NW Turkey
Eskishehr see Eskişehir
104 K5 **Esla** ≈ NW Spain
142 J6 **Eslāmābād** var. Eslāmābād-e Gharb; prev. Harunabad, Shāhābād. Kermānshāhān, W Iran
Eslāmābād-e Gharb see Eslāmābād
148 J4 **Eslām Qal'eh** Pash. Islam Qala. Herāt, W Afghanistan
95 K23 **Eslöv** Skåne, S Sweden
143 S12 **Esmā'īlābād** Kermān, S Iran
143 U8 **Esmā'īlābād** Khorāsān, E Iran
136 D14 **Eşme** Uşak, W Turkey
44 G6 **Esmeralda** Camagüey, E Cuba
63 F21 **Esmeralda, Isla** island S Chile
56 B5 **Esmeraldas** Esmeraldas, N Ecuador
56 B5 **Esmeraldas** ◈ province NW Ecuador
Esna see Isna
14 B6 **Esnagi Lake** ◎ Ontario, S Canada
143 V14 **Espakeh** Sīstān va Balūchestān, SE Iran
103 O13 **Espalion** Aveyron, S France
España see Spain
14 E11 **Espanola** Ontario, S Canada
37 S10 **Espanola** New Mexico, SW USA
57 C18 **Española, Isla** var. Hood Island. island Galapagos Islands, Ecuador, E Pacific Ocean
104 M13 **Espejo** Andalucía, S Spain
94 C13 **Espeland** Hordaland, S Norway
100 G12 **Espelkamp** Nordrhein-Westfalen, NW Germany
38 M8 **Espenberg, Cape** headland Alaska, USA
180 L13 **Esperance** Western Australia
186 L9 **Esperance, Cape** headland Guadacanal, C Solomon Islands
57 P18 **Esperancita** Santa Cruz, E Bolivia
61 B17 **Esperanza** Santa Fe, C Argentina
40 G6 **Esperanza** Sonora, NW Mexico
24 H9 **Esperanza** Texas, SW USA
194 H3 **Esperanza** Argentinian research station Antarctica
104 E12 **Espichel, Cabo** cape S Portugal
54 E10 **Espinal** Tolima, C Colombia
48 K10 **Espinhaço, Serra do** ▲▲ SE Brazil
104 G6 **Espinho** Aveiro, N Portugal
59 N18 **Espinosa** Minas Gerais, SE Brazil
103 U15 **Espinouse** ▲▲ S France
60 Q8 **Espírito Santo** off. Estado do Espírito Santo. ◈ state E Brazil
Espírito Santo, Estado do see Espírito Santo
187 P13 **Espiritu Santo** var. Santo. island W Vanuatu
41 Z13 **Espíritu Santo, Bahía del** bay SE Mexico
40 F9 **Espíritu Santo, Isla del** island W Mexico
41 Y12 **Espita** Yucatán, SE Mexico
15 Y7 **Espoir, Cap d'** headland Québec, SE Canada
Esponsede/Esponsende see Esposende
93 L20 **Espoo** Swe. Esbo. Etelä-Suomi, S Finland
104 G5 **Esposende** var. Esponsede, Esponsende. Braga, N Portugal
83 M18 **Espungabera** Manica, SW Mozambique
63 H17 **Esquel** Chubut, SW Argentina
10 L17 **Esquimalt** Vancouver Island, British Columbia, SW Canada
61 C16 **Esquina** Corrientes, NE Argentina
42 E6 **Esquipulas** Chiquimula, SE Guatemala
42 K9 **Esquipulas** Matagalpa, C Nicaragua
94 I8 **Essandjøen** ◎ S Norway
74 E7 **Essaouira** prev. Mogador. W Morocco
Es Seo see Osijek
Es Semara see Smara
99 G15 **Essen** Antwerpen, N Belgium
101 E15 **Essen** var. Essen an der Ruhr. Nordrhein-Westfalen, W Germany
Essen an der Ruhr see Essen
74 I5 **Es Senia** ✈ (Oran) NW Algeria
55 T8 **Essequibo Islands** island group N Guyana
55 T11 **Essequibo River** ≈ C Guyana
14 C18 **Essex** Ontario, S Canada
29 T16 **Essex** Iowa, C USA
97 P21 **Essex** cultural region E England, UK
31 R8 **Essexville** Michigan, N USA
101 H22 **Esslingen** var. Esslingen am Neckar. Baden-Württemberg, SW Germany
Esslingen am Neckar see Esslingen
103 N6 **Essonne** ◈ department N France
Es Suweida see As Suwaydā'
79 F16 **Est** Eng. East. ◈ province SE Cameroon
104 I1 **Estaca de Bares, Punta da** point NW Spain
24 M5 **Estacado, Llano** plain New Mexico/Texas, SW USA
63 K25 **Estados, Isla de los** prev. Eng. Staten Island. island S Argentina
Estado Vargas see Vargas
143 P12 **Eşţahbān** Fārs, S Iran
14 F11 **Estaire** Ontario, S Canada
59 P16 **Estância** Sergipe, E Brazil
37 S12 **Estancia** New Mexico, SW USA
104 G7 **Estarreja** Aveiro, N Portugal
102 M17 **Estats, Pic d'** Sp. Pico d'Estats. ▲ France/Spain
Estats, Pico d' see Estats, Pic d'
83 K23 **Estcourt** KwaZulu/Natal, E South Africa
106 H8 **Este** anc. Ateste. Veneto, NE Italy
42 J9 **Estelí** Estelí, NW Nicaragua
42 J9 **Estelí** ◈ department NW Nicaragua
105 Q4 **Estella** Bas. Lizarra. Navarra, N Spain
29 R9 **Estelline** South Dakota, N USA
25 P4 **Estelline** Texas, SW USA
104 L14 **Estepa** Andalucía, S Spain
104 L16 **Estepona** Andalucía, S Spain
39 R9 **Ester** Alaska, USA
9 V16 **Esterhazy** Saskatchewan, S Canada
37 S3 **Estes Park** Colorado, C USA
9 V17 **Estevan** Saskatchewan, S Canada
29 T11 **Estherville** Iowa, C USA
21 R15 **Estill** South Carolina, SE USA
103 Q6 **Estissac** Aube, N France
15 T9 **Est, Lac de l'** ◎ Québec, SE Canada
Estland see Estonia
9 S16 **Eston** Saskatchewan, S Canada
118 G5 **Estonia** off. Republic of Estonia, Est. Eesti Vabariik, Ger. Estland, Latv. Igaunija; prev. Estonian SSR, Rus. Estonskaya SSR. ◆ republic NE Europe
Estonian SSR see Estonia
Estonia, Republic of see Estonia
Estonskaya SSR see Estonia
104 E11 **Estoril** Lisboa, W Portugal
59 L14 **Estreito** Maranhão, E Brazil
104 I8 **Estrela, Serra da** ▲▲ C Portugal
40 D3 **Estrella, Punta** headland NW Mexico
104 F10 **Estremadura** cultural and historical region W Portugal
Estremadura see Extremadura
104 H11 **Estremoz** Évora, S Portugal
79 D18 **Estuaire** off. Province de l'Estuaire, var. L'Estuaire. ◈ province NW Gabon
Estuaire, Province de l' see Estuaire
Eszék see Osijek
111 I22 **Esztergom** Ger. Gran; anc. Strigonium. Komárom-Esztergom, N Hungary
152 K11 **Etah** Uttar Pradesh, N India
189 R17 **Etal Atoll** atoll Mortlock Islands, C Micronesia
99 K24 **Étalle** Luxembourg, SE Belgium
103 N6 **Étampes** Essonne, N France
182 J1 **Etamunbanie, Lake** salt lake South Australia
103 N1 **Étaples** Pas-de-Calais, N France
152 K12 **Etāwah** Uttar Pradesh, N India
15 R10 **Etchemin** ≈ Québec, SE Canada
Etchmiadzin see Vagharshapat
40 G7 **Etchojoa** Sonora, NW Mexico
93 L19 **Etelä-Suomi** ◈ province S Finland
83 B16 **Etengua** Kunene, NW Namibia
99 K25 **Éthe** Luxembourg, SE Belgium
9 W15 **Ethelbert** Manitoba, S Canada
80 H12 **Ethiopia** off. Federal Democratic Republic of Ethiopia; prev. Abyssinia, People's Democratic Republic of Ethiopia. ◆ republic E Africa
Ethiopia, Federal Democratic Republic of see Ethiopia
80 I13 **Ethiopian Highlands** var. Ethiopian Plateau. plateau N Ethiopia
Ethiopian Plateau see Ethiopian Highlands
Ethiopia, People's Democratic Republic of see Ethiopia
34 M2 **Etna** California, W USA
18 B14 **Etna** Pennsylvania, NE USA
94 G12 **Etna** ≈ S Norway
107 L24 **Etna, Monte** Eng. Mount Etna. ⛰ Sicilia, Italy, C Mediterranean Sea
Etna, Mount see Etna, Monte
95 C15 **Etne** Hordaland, S Norway
Etoliko see Aitolikó
39 Y14 **Etolin Island** island Alexander Archipelago, Alaska, USA
38 L12 **Etolin Strait** strait Alaska, USA
83 C17 **Etosha Pan** salt lake N Namibia
79 G18 **Etoumbi** Cuvette Ouest, NW Congo
20 M10 **Etowah** Tennessee, S USA
23 S2 **Etowah River** ≈ Georgia, SE USA
146 B13 **Etrek** var. Gyzyletrek, Rus. Kizyl-Atrek. Balkan Welaýaty, W Turkmenistan
146 C13 **Etrek** Per. Rūd-e Atrak, Rus. Atrak, Atrek. ≈ Iran/Turkmenistan
102 L3 **Étretat** Seine-Maritime, N France
114 H9 **Etropole** Sofiya, W Bulgaria
Etsch see Adige
Et Tafila see Aţ Ţafīlah
99 M23 **Ettelbrück** Diekirch, C Luxembourg
189 V12 **Etten** atoll Chuuk Islands, C Micronesia
99 H14 **Etten-Leur** Noord-Brabant, S Netherlands
76 G7 **Et Tîdra** var. Ile Tîdra. island Dakhlet Nouâdhibou, NW Mauritania
101 G21 **Ettlingen** Baden-Württemberg, SW Germany
102 M2 **Eu** Seine-Maritime, N France
193 W16 **'Eua** prev. Middleburg Island. island Tongatapu Group, SE Tonga
193 W15 **Eua Iki** island Tongatapu Group, S Tonga
Euboea see Évvoia
181 O12 **Eucla** Western Australia
31 U11 **Euclid** Ohio, N USA
27 W14 **Eudora** Arkansas, C USA
27 Q4 **Eudora** Kansas, C USA
182 J9 **Eudunda** South Australia
23 R6 **Eufaula** Alabama, S USA
27 Q11 **Eufaula** Oklahoma, C USA
27 Q11 **Eufaula Lake** var. Eufaula Reservoir. ⊠ Oklahoma, C USA
Eufaula Reservoir see Eufaula Lake
32 F13 **Eugene** Oregon, NW USA
40 B6 **Eugenia, Punta** headland W Mexico
183 Q8 **Eugowra** New South Wales, SE Australia
104 I2 **Eume** ≈ NW Spain
104 H2 **Eume, Embalse do** ⊠ NW Spain
Eumolpias see Plovdiv
59 O18 **Eunápolis** Bahia, SE Brazil
22 H8 **Eunice** Louisiana, S USA
37 W15 **Eunice** New Mexico, SW USA
99 M19 **Eupen** Liège, E Belgium
130 B10 **Euphrates** Ar. Al-Furāt, Turk. Firat Nehri. ≈ SW Asia
138 L3 **Euphrates Dam** dam N Syria
22 M4 **Eupora** Mississippi, S USA
93 K19 **Eura** Länsi-Soumi, SW Finland
93 K19 **Eurajoki** Länsi-Soumi, SW Finland
0-1 **Eurasian Plate** tectonic feature
102 L4 **Eure** ◈ department N France
102 M4 **Eure** ≈ N France
102 M6 **Eure-et-Loir** ◈ department C France
34 K3 **Eureka** California, W USA
27 P6 **Eureka** Kansas, C USA
33 O6 **Eureka** Montana, NW USA
35 V5 **Eureka** Nevada, W USA
29 O7 **Eureka** South Dakota, N USA
36 L4 **Eureka** Utah, W USA
32 K10 **Eureka** Washington, NW USA
27 S9 **Eureka Springs** Arkansas, C USA
182 K6 **Eurinilla Creek** seasonal river South Australia
183 O11 **Euroa** Victoria, SE Australia
172 M9 **Europa** island W Madagascar
104 L3 **Europa, Picos de** ▲▲ N Spain
104 L16 **Europa Point** headland S Gibraltar
84-85 **Europe** continent
98 F12 **Europoort** Zuid-Holland, W Netherlands
Euskadi see País Vasco
101 D17 **Euskirchen** Nordrhein-Westfalen, W Germany
23 W11 **Eustis** Florida, SE USA
182 M9 **Euston** New South Wales, SE Australia
23 N5 **Eutaw** Alabama, S USA
100 K8 **Eutin** Schleswig-Holstein, N Germany
10 K14 **Eutsuk Lake** ⊠ British Columbia, SW Canada
Euxine Sea see Black Sea
83 C16 **Evale** Cunene, SW Angola
37 T3 **Evans** Colorado, C USA
9 P14 **Evansburg** Alberta, SW Canada
29 X13 **Evansdale** Iowa, C USA
183 V4 **Evans Head** New South Wales, SE Australia
12 J11 **Evans, Lac** ◎ Québec, SE Canada
37 S5 **Evans, Mount** ▲ Colorado, C USA
31 N10 **Evanston** Illinois, N USA
33 S17 **Evanston** Wyoming, C USA
14 D11 **Evansville** Manitoulin Island, Ontario, S Canada
31 N16 **Evansville** Indiana, N USA
30 L9 **Evansville** Wisconsin, N USA
25 S8 **Evant** Texas, SW USA
143 P13 **Evaz** Fārs, S Iran
29 W4 **Eveleth** Minnesota, N USA
182 E3 **Evelyn Creek** seasonal river South Australia
181 Q2 **Evelyn, Mount** ▲ Northern Territory, N Australia
122 K10 **Evenkiyskiy Avtonomnyy Okrug** ◈ autonomous district N Russian Federation
183 R13 **Everard, Cape** headland Victoria, SE Australia
182 F6 **Everard, Lake** salt lake South Australia
182 C2 **Everard Ranges** ▲▲ South Australia
153 R11 **Everest, Mount** Chin. Qomolangma Feng, Nep. Sagarmāthā. ▲ China/Nepal
18 E15 **Everett** Pennsylvania, NE USA
32 H7 **Everett** Washington, NW USA
99 E17 **Evergem** Oost-Vlaanderen, NW Belgium
23 X16 **Everglades City** Florida, SE USA
23 Y16 **Everglades, The** wetland Florida, SE USA
23 P7 **Evergreen** Alabama, S USA
37 T4 **Evergreen** Colorado, C USA
Evergreen State see Washington
97 L21 **Evesham** C England, UK
103 T10 **Évian-les-Bains** Haute-Savoie, E France
93 K16 **Evijärvi** Länsi-Soumi, W Finland
79 D17 **Evinayong** var. Ebinayon, Evinayoung. C Equatorial Guinea
Evinayoung see Evinayong
115 E18 **Évinos** ≈ C Greece
95 E17 **Evje** Aust-Agder, S Norway
Evmolpia see Plovdiv
104 H11 **Évora** anc. Ebora, Lat. Liberalitas Julia. Évora, C Portugal
104 G11 **Évora** ◈ district S Portugal
102 M4 **Évreux** anc. Civitas Eburovicum. Eure, N France
102 K6 **Évron** Mayenne, NW France
114 L13 **Évros** Bul. Maritsa, Turk. Meriç; anc. Hebrus. ≈ SE Europe see also Maritsa/Meriç
Évros see Meriç
Évros see Maritsa
115 F21 **Evrótas** ≈ S Greece
103 O5 **Évry** Essonne, N France
25 O8 **E. V. Spence Reservoir** ⊠ Texas, SW USA
115 I18 **Évvoia** Lat. Euboea. island C Greece
38 D9 **'Ewa Beach** var. Ewa Beach. O'ahu, Hawai'i, USA
Ewa Beach see 'Ewa Beach
32 L9 **Ewan** Washington, NW USA
44 K12 **Ewarton** C Jamaica
81 J18 **Ewaso Ng'iro** var. Nyiro. ≈ C Kenya
29 P13 **Ewing** Nebraska, C USA
194 J5 **Ewing Island** island Antarctica
65 P17 **Ewing Seamount** undersea feature E Atlantic Ocean
158 L6 **Ewirgol** Xinjiang Uygur Zizhiqu, W China
79 G19 **Ewo** Cuvette, W Congo
27 S3 **Excelsior Springs** Missouri, C USA
97 J23 **Exe** ≈ SW England, UK
194 L12 **Executive Committee Range** ▲▲ Antarctica
14 E16 **Exeter** Ontario, S Canada
97 J24 **Exeter** anc. Isca Damnoniorum. SW England, UK
35 R11 **Exeter** California, W USA
19 P10 **Exeter** New Hampshire, NE USA
Exin see Kcynia
29 T14 **Exira** Iowa, C USA
97 J23 **Exmoor** moorland SW England, UK
21 Y6 **Exmore** Virginia, NE USA
180 G8 **Exmouth** Western Australia
97 J24 **Exmouth** SW England, UK
180 G8 **Exmouth Gulf** gulf Western Australia
173 V8 **Exmouth Plateau** undersea feature E Indian Ocean
115 J20 **Exompourgo** ancient monument Tínos, Kykládes, Greece, Aegean Sea
104 I10 **Extremadura** var. Estremadura. ◈ autonomous community W Spain
78 F12 **Extrême-Nord** Eng. Extreme North. ◈ province N Cameroon
Extreme North see Extrême-Nord
44 I3 **Exuma Cays** islets C Bahamas
44 I3 **Exuma Sound** sound C Bahamas
81 H20 **Eyasi, Lake** ◎ N Tanzania
95 F17 **Eydehavn** Aust-Agder, S Norway
96 L12 **Eyemouth** SE Scotland, UK
96 G7 **Eye Peninsula** peninsula NW Scotland, UK
80 Q13 **Eyl** It. Eil. Nugaal, E Somalia
103 N11 **Eymoutiers** Haute-Vienne, C France
Eyo (lower course) see Uolo, Río
29 X10 **Eyota** Minnesota, N USA
182 H2 **Eyre Basin, Lake** salt lake South Australia
182 I1 **Eyre Creek** seasonal river Northern Territory/South Australia
174 L9 **Eyre, Lake** salt lake South Australia
185 C22 **Eyre Mountains** ▲▲ South Island, New Zealand
182 H3 **Eyre North, Lake** salt lake South Australia
182 G7 **Eyre Peninsula** peninsula South Australia
182 H4 **Eyre South, Lake** salt lake South Australia
95 B18 **Eysturoy** Dan. Østerø. island N Faeroe Islands
61 D20 **Ezeiza** ✈ (Buenos Aires) Buenos Aires, E Argentina
Ezeres see Ezeriş
116 F12 **Ezeriş** Hung. Ezeres. Caraş-Severin, W Romania
161 O9 **Ezhou** prev. Echeng. Hubei, C China
125 R11 **Ezhva** Respublika Komi, NW Russian Federation
136 B12 **Ezine** Çanakkale, NW Turkey
Ezo see Hokkaidō
Ezra/Ezraa see Izra'

F

191 P7 **Faaa** Tahiti, W French Polynesia
191 P7 **Faaa** ✈ (Papeete) Tahiti, W French Polynesia
95 H24 **Faaborg** var. Fåborg. Fyn, C Denmark
151 K19 **Faadhippolhu Atoll** var. Fadiffolu, Lhaviyani Atoll. atoll N Maldives
191 U10 **Faaite** atoll Îles Tuamotu, C French Polynesia
191 Q8 **Faaone** Tahiti, W French Polynesia
24 H8 **Fabens** Texas, SW USA
94 H12 **Fåberg** Oppland, S Norway
Fåborg see Faaborg

◆ Country ● Country Capital ◇ Dependent Territory ○ Dependent Territory Capital ◈ Administrative Regions ✈ International Airport ▲ Mountain ▲▲ Mountain Range ⛰ Volcano ≈ River ◎ Lake ⊠ Reservoir
248

FABRIANO – FICCE

106 *I12* **Fabriano** Marche, C Italy
145 *U16* **Fabrichnyy** Almaty, SE Kazakhstan
54 *F10* **Facatativá** Cundinamarca, C Colombia
77 *X9* **Fachi** Agadez, C Niger
188 *B16* **Facpi Point** *headland* W Guam
18 *I13* **Factoryville** Pennsylvania, NE USA
78 *K8* **Fada** Borkou-Ennedi-Tibesti, E Chad
77 *Q13* **Fada-Ngourma** E Burkina
123 *N6* **Faddeya, Zaliv** *bay* N Russian Federation
123 *Q5* **Faddeyevskiy, Ostrov** *island* Novosibirskiye Ostrova, NE Russian Federation
141 *W12* **Fadhī** S Oman
Fadiffolu *see* Faadhippolhu Atoll
106 *H10* **Faenza** *anc.* Faventia. Emilia-Romagna, N Italy
64 *M5* **Faeroe-Iceland Ridge** *undersea feature* NW Norwegian Sea
64 *M5* **Faeroe Islands** *Dan.* Færøerne, *Faer.* Føroyar. ◇ *Danish external territory* N Atlantic Ocean
86 *C8* **Faeroe Islands** *island group* N Atlantic Ocean
Færøerne *see* Faeroe Islands
64 *N6* **Faeroe-Shetland Trough** *undersea feature* NE Atlantic Ocean
104 *H6* **Fafe** Braga, N Portugal
80 *K13* **Fafen Shet'** ~ E Ethiopia
193 *V15* **Fafo** *island* Tongatapu Group, S Tonga
192 *I16* **Fagaloa Bay** *bay* Upolu, E Samoa
192 *H15* **Fagamālo** Savai'i, N Samoa
116 *I12* **Făgăraş** *Ger.* Fogarasch, *Hung.* Fogaras. Braşov, C Romania
95 *M20* **Fagerhult** Kalmar, S Sweden
94 *G13* **Fagernes** Oppland, S Norway
92 *I9* **Fagernes** Troms, N Norway
95 *M14* **Fagersta** Västmanland, C Sweden
77 *W13* **Faggo** *var.* Foggo. Bauchi, N Nigeria
Faghman *see* Fughmah
Fagibina, Lake *see* Faguibine, Lac
63 *J25* **Fagnano, Lago** ◎ S Argentina
99 *G22* **Fagne** *hill range* S Belgium
77 *N10* **Faguibine, Lac** *var.* Lake Fagibina. ◎ NW Mali
Fahaheel *see* Al Fuḩayḩīl
Fahlun *see* Falun
143 *U12* **Fahraj** Kermān, SE Iran
64 *P5* **Faial** Madeira, Portugal, NE Atlantic Ocean
64 *N2* **Faial** *var.* Ilha do Faial. *island* Azores, Portugal, NE Atlantic Ocean
Faial, Ilha do *see* Faial
108 *G10* **Faido** Ticino, S Switzerland
Faifo *see* Hôi An
Failaka Island *see* Faylakah
190 *G12* **Faioa, Île** *island* N Wallis and Futuna
181 *W8* **Fairbairn Reservoir** ⊠ Queensland, E Australia
39 *R9* **Fairbanks** Alaska, USA
21 *U12* **Fair Bluff** North Carolina, SE USA
31 *R14* **Fairborn** Ohio, N USA
23 *S3* **Fairburn** Georgia, SE USA
30 *M12* **Fairbury** Illinois, N USA
29 *Q17* **Fairbury** Nebraska, C USA
29 *T9* **Fairfax** Minnesota, N USA
27 *O8* **Fairfax** Oklahoma, C USA
21 *R14* **Fairfax** South Carolina, SE USA
35 *N8* **Fairfield** California, W USA
33 *O14* **Fairfield** Idaho, NW USA
30 *M16* **Fairfield** Illinois, N USA
29 *X15* **Fairfield** Iowa, C USA
33 *R8* **Fairfield** Montana, NW USA
31 *Q14* **Fairfield** Ohio, N USA
25 *U8* **Fairfield** Texas, SW USA
27 *T7* **Fair Grove** Missouri, C USA
19 *P12* **Fairhaven** Massachusetts, NE USA
23 *N8* **Fairhope** Alabama, S USA
96 *L4* **Fair Isle** *island* NE Scotland, UK
185 *F20* **Fairlie** Canterbury, South Island, New Zealand
29 *U11* **Fairmont** Minnesota, N USA
29 *Q16* **Fairmont** Nebraska, C USA
21 *S3* **Fairmont** West Virginia, NE USA
31 *P13* **Fairmount** Indiana, N USA
18 *H10* **Fairmount** New York, NE USA
29 *R7* **Fairmount** North Dakota, N USA
37 *S5* **Fairplay** Colorado, C USA
18 *F9* **Fairport** New York, NE USA
9 *O12* **Fairview** Alberta, W Canada
26 *L9* **Fairview** Oklahoma, C USA
36 *L4* **Fairview** Utah, W USA
35 *T6* **Fairview Peak** ▲ Nevada, W USA
188 *H14* **Fais** *atoll* Caroline Islands, W Micronesia
149 *U8* **Faisalābād** *prev.* Lyallpur. Punjab, NE Pakistan
Faisaliya *see* Fayşalīyah
28 *L8* **Faith** South Dakota, N USA
153 *N12* **Faizābād** Uttar Pradesh, N India
Faizabad/Faizābād *see* Feyẓābād
45 *S9* **Fajardo** E Puerto Rico
139 *R9* **Fajj, Wādī al** *dry watercourse* S Iraq
140 *K4* **Fajr, Bi'r** *well* NW Saudi Arabia
191 *W10* **Fakahina** *atoll* Îles Tuamotu, C French Polynesia
190 *L10* **Fakaofo Atoll** *island* SE Tokelau
191 *U10* **Fakarava** *atoll* Îles Tuamotu, C French Polynesia
127 *T2* **Fakel** Udmurtskaya Respublika, NW Russian Federation
97 *P19* **Fakenham** E England, UK
171 *U13* **Fakfak** Papua, E Indonesia
153 *T12* **Fakīragrām** Assam, NE India
114 *M10* **Fakiyska Reka** ~ SE Bulgaria
95 *J24* **Fakse** Storstrøm, SE Denmark
95 *J24* **Fakse Bugt** *bay* SE Denmark
95 *J24* **Fakse Ladeplads** Storstrøm, SE Denmark
163 *V11* **Faku** Liaoning, NE China
76 *J14* **Falaba** N Sierra Leone
102 *K5* **Falaise** Calvados, N France
114 *H12* **Falakró** ▲▲ NE Greece
189 *T12* **Falalu** *island* Chuuk, C Micronesia
166 *L4* **Falam** Chin State, W Burma (Myanmar)
143 *N8* **Falāvarjān** Eşfahān, C Iran
116 *M11* **Fălciu** Vaslui, E Romania
54 *I4* **Falcón** *off.* Estado Falcón. ◆ *state* NW Venezuela
106 *J12* **Falconara Marittima** Marche, C Italy
Falcone, Capo del *see* Falcone, Punta del
107 *A16* **Falcone, Punta del** *var.* Capo del Falcone. *headland* Sardegna, Italy, C Mediterranean Sea
Falcón, Estado *see* Falcón
9 *Y16* **Falcon Lake** Manitoba, S Canada
Falcon Lake *see* Falcón, Presa/Falcon Reservoir
41 *O7* **Falcón, Presa** *var.* Falcon Lake, Falcon Reservoir. ⊠ *see also* Falcon Reservoir
Falcón, Presa *see* Falcon Reservoir
25 *Q16* **Falcon Reservoir** *var.* Falcon Lake, Presa Falcón. ⊠ *see also* Falcón, Presa
Falcon Reservoir *see* Falcón, Presa
190 *L10* **Fale** *island* Fakaofo Atoll, SE Tokelau
192 *F15* **Faleālupo** Savai'i, NW Samoa
190 *B10* **Falefatu** *island* Funafuti Atoll, C Tuvalu
192 *G15* **Fālelima** Savai'i, NW Samoa
95 *N18* **Falerum** Östergötland, S Sweden
Faleshty *see* Făleşti
116 *M9* **Făleşti** *Rus.* Faleshty. NW Moldova
25 *S15* **Falfurrias** Texas, SW USA
9 *O13* **Falher** Alberta, W Canada
Falkenau an der Eger *see* Sokolov
95 *J21* **Falkenberg** Halland, S Sweden
Falkenberg *see* Niemodlin
Falkenburg in Pommern *see* Złocieniec
100 *N12* **Falkensee** Brandenburg, NE Germany
96 *J12* **Falkirk** C Scotland, UK
65 *I20* **Falkland Escarpment** *undersea feature* SW Atlantic Ocean
63 *K24* **Falkland Islands** *var.* Falklands, Islas Malvinas. ◇ *UK dependent territory* SW Atlantic Ocean
47 *W14* **Falkland Islands** *island group* SW Atlantic Ocean
65 *I20* **Falkland Plateau** *var.* Argentine Rise. *undersea feature* SW Atlantic Ocean
Falklands *see* Falkland Islands
63 *M23* **Falkland Sound** *var.* Estrecho de San Carlos. *strait* C Falkland Islands
Falknov nad Ohří *see* Sokolov
115 *H21* **Falkonéra** *island* S Greece
95 *K18* **Falköping** Västra Götaland, S Sweden
139 *U8* **Fallāḩ** E Iraq
35 *U16* **Fallbrook** California, W USA
189 *U12* **Falleallej Pass** *passage* Chuuk Islands, C Micronesia
93 *J14* **Fällfors** Västerbotten, N Sweden
194 *I6* **Fallières Coast** *physical region* Antarctica
100 *I11* **Fallingbostel** Niedersachsen, NW Germany
33 *X9* **Fallon** Montana, NW USA
35 *S5* **Fallon** Nevada, W USA
19 *O12* **Fall River** Massachusetts, NE USA
27 *P6* **Fall River Lake** ⊠ Kansas, C USA
35 *O3* **Fall River Mills** California, W USA
21 *W4* **Falls Church** Virginia, NE USA
29 *S17* **Falls City** Nebraska, C USA
25 *S12* **Falls City** Texas, SW USA
Falluja *see* Al Fallūjah
77 *S12* **Falmey** Dosso, SW Niger
45 *W10* **Falmouth** Antigua, Antigua and Barbuda
44 *J11* **Falmouth** W Jamaica
97 *H25* **Falmouth** SW England, UK
20 *M4* **Falmouth** Kentucky, S USA
19 *P13* **Falmouth** Massachusetts, NE USA
21 *W5* **Falmouth** Virginia, NE USA
189 *U12* **Falos** *island* Chuuk, C Micronesia
83 *E26* **False Bay** *Afr.* Valsbaai. *bay* SW South Africa
155 *K17* **False Divi Point** *headland* E India
38 *M16* **False Pass** Unimak Island, Alaska, USA
154 *P12* **False Point** *headland* E India
105 *U6* **Falset** Cataluña, NE Spain
95 *I25* **Falster** *island* SE Denmark
116 *K9* **Fălticeni** *Hung.* Falticsén. Suceava, NE Romania
Falticsén *see* Fălticeni
94 *M13* **Falun** *var.* Fahlun. Kopparberg, C Sweden
Famagusta *see* Gazimağusa
Famagusta Bay *see* Gazimağusa Körfezi
62 *I8* **Famatina** La Rioja, NW Argentina
99 *J21* **Famenne** *physical region* SE Belgium
113 *D22* **Fan** *var.* Fani. ~ N Albania
77 *X15* **Fan** ~ E Nigeria
76 *M12* **Fana** Koulikoro, SW Mali
115 *K19* **Fána** *ancient harbour* Chíos, SE Greece
189 *V13* **Fanan** *island* Chuuk, C Micronesia
189 *U12* **Fanapanges** *island* Chuuk, C Micronesia
115 *L20* **Fanári, Ákrotírio** *cape* Ikaría, Dodekánisa, Greece, Aegean Sea
45 *Q13* **Fancy** Saint Vincent, Saint Vincent and the Grenadines
172 *I5* **Fandriana** Fianarantsoa, SE Madagascar
167 *O6* **Fang** Chiang Mai, NW Thailand
80 *E13* **Fangak** Jonglei, SE Sudan
191 *W10* **Fangatau** *atoll* Îles Tuamotu, C French Polynesia
191 *X12* **Fangataufa** *island* Îles Tuamotu, SE French Polynesia
193 *V15* **Fanga Uta** *bay* S Tonga
161 *N7* **Fangcheng** Henan, C China
Fangcheng *see* Fangchenggang
160 *K15* **Fangchenggang** *var.* Fangcheng Gezu Zizhixian; *prev.* Fangcheng. Guangxi Zhuangzu Zizhiqu, S China
Fangcheng Gezu Zizhixian *see* Fangchenggang
161 *S15* **Fangshan** S Taiwan
163 *X8* **Fangzheng** Heilongjiang, NE China
Fani *see* Fan
119 *K16* **Fanipal'** *Rus.* Fanipol'. Minskaya Voblasts', C Belarus
Fanipol' *see* Fanipal'
25 *T13* **Fannin** Texas, SW USA
Fanning Island *see* Tabuaeran
94 *G8* **Fannrem** Sør-Trøndelag, S Norway
106 *I11* **Fano** *anc.* Colonia Julia Fanestris, Fanum Fortunae. Marche, C Italy
95 *E23* **Fanø** *island* W Denmark
167 *R5* **Fan Si Pan** ▲ N Vietnam
Fanum Fortunae *see* Fano
Fao *see* Al Fāw
141 *W7* **Faq'** *var.* Al Faqa. Dubayy, E United Arab Emirates
Farab *see* Farap
194 *H5* **Faraday** *UK research station* Antarctica
185 *G16* **Faraday, Mount** ▲ South Island, New Zealand
79 *P16* **Faradje** Orientale, NE Dem. Rep. Congo
Faradofay *see* Tôlanaro
172 *I7* **Farafangana** Fianarantsoa, SE Madagascar
148 *J7* **Farāh** *var.* Farah, Fararud. Farāh, W Afghanistan
148 *K7* **Farāh** ◆ *province* W Afghanistan
148 *J7* **Farāh Rūd** ~ W Afghanistan
188 *K7* **Farallon de Medinilla** *island* C Northern Mariana Islands
188 *J2* **Farallon de Pajaros** *var.* Uracas. *island* N Northern Mariana Islands
76 *J14* **Faranah** Haute-Guinée, S Guinea
146 *K12* **Farab** *Rus.* Farab. Lebap Welaýaty, NE Turkmenistan
Fararud *see* Farāh
140 *M13* **Farasān, Jazā'ir** *island group* SW Saudi Arabia
172 *I5* **Faratsiho** Antananarivo, C Madagascar
188 *K15* **Faraulep Atoll** *atoll* Caroline Islands, C Micronesia
99 *H20* **Farciennes** Hainaut, S Belgium
105 *O14* **Fardes** ~ S Spain
191 *S10* **Fare** Huahine, W French Polynesia
97 *M23* **Fareham** S England, UK
39 *P11* **Farewell** Alaska, USA
184 *H13* **Farewell, Cape** *headland* South Island, New Zealand
Farewell, Cape *see* Nunap Isua
184 *I13* **Farewell Spit** *spit* South Island, New Zealand
95 *I17* **Färgelanda** Älvsborg, S Sweden
Farghona, Wodii/Farghona Valley *see* Fergana Valley
Farghona Wodiysi *see* Fergana Valley
23 *V8* **Fargo** Georgia, SE USA
29 *R5* **Fargo** North Dakota, N USA
147 *S10* **Farg'ona** *Rus.* Fergana; *prev.* Novyy Margilan. Farg'ona Viloyati, E Uzbekistan
147 *R10* **Farg'ona Viloyati** *Rus.* Ferganskaya Oblast'. ◆ *province* E Uzbekistan
29 *V10* **Faribault** Minnesota, N USA
152 *J11* **Farīdābād** Haryāna, N India Asia
152 *H8* **Farīdkot** Punjab, NW India
153 *T15* **Faridpur** Dhaka, C Bangladesh
121 *P14* **Fārigh, Wādī al** ~ N Libya
172 *I4* **Farihy Alaotra** ◎ C Madagascar
94 *M11* **Färila** Gävleborg, C Sweden
104 *E9* **Farilhões** *island* C Portugal
76 *G12* **Farim** NW Guinea-Bissau
Farish *see* Forish
141 *T11* **Fāris, Qalamat** *well* SE Saudi Arabia
95 *N21* **Färjestaden** Kalmar, S Sweden
149 *R2* **Farkhār** Takhār, NE Afghanistan
147 *Q14* **Farkhor** *Rus.* Parkhar. SW Tajikistan
116 *F12* **Fârliug** *prev.* Fîrliug, *Hung.* Furluk. Caraş-Severin, SW Romania
115 *M21* **Farmakonísi** *island* Dodekánisa, Greece, Aegean Sea
30 *M13* **Farmer City** Illinois, N USA
31 *N14* **Farmersburg** Indiana, N USA
25 *U6* **Farmersville** Texas, SW USA
22 *H5* **Farmerville** Louisiana, S USA
29 *X16* **Farmington** Iowa, C USA
19 *Q6* **Farmington** Maine, NE USA
29 *V9* **Farmington** Minnesota, N USA
27 *X6* **Farmington** Missouri, C USA
19 *O9* **Farmington** New Hampshire, NE USA
37 *P9* **Farmington** New Mexico, SW USA
36 *L2* **Farmington** Utah, W USA
21 *W9* **Farmville** North Carolina, SE USA
21 *U6* **Farmville** Virginia, NE USA
97 *N22* **Farnborough** S England, UK
97 *N22* **Farnham** S England, UK
10 *J7* **Faro** Yukon Territory, W Canada
104 *G14* **Faro** Faro, S Portugal
95 *Q18* **Fårö** Gotland, SE Sweden
104 *G14* **Faro** ◆ *district* S Portugal
78 *F13* **Faro** ~ Cameroon/Nigeria
104 *G14* **Faro** ✈ Faro, S Portugal
Faro, Punta del *see* Peloro, Capo
95 *Q18* **Fårösund** Gotland, SE Sweden
173 *N7* **Farquhar Group** *island group* S Seychelles
18 *B13* **Farrell** Pennsylvania, NE USA
152 *K11* **Farrukhābād** Uttar Pradesh, N India
143 *P11* **Fārs** *off.* Ostān-e Fārs; *anc.* Persis. ◆ *province* S Iran
115 *F16* **Fársala** Thessalía, C Greece
143 *R4* **Farsīān** Golestán, N Iran
95 *G21* **Farsø** Nordjylland, N Denmark
Fārs, Ostān-e *see* Fārs
95 *D18* **Farsund** Vest-Agder, S Norway
141 *U14* **Fartak, Ra's** *headland* E Yemen
60 *H13* **Fartura, Serra da** ▲▲ S Brazil
Farvel, Kap *see* Nunap Isua
24 *L4* **Farwell** Texas, SW USA
194 *I9* **Farwell Island** *island* Antarctica
152 *L9* **Far Western** ◆ *zone* W Nepal
148 *M3* **Fāryāb** ◆ *province* N Afghanistan
143 *P12* **Fasā** Fārs, S Iran
141 *U12* **Fasad, Ramlat** *desert* SW Oman
107 *P17* **Fasano** Puglia, SE Italy
92 *L3* **Fáskrúdhsfjördhur** Austurland, E Iceland
117 *O5* **Fastiv** *Rus.* Fastov. Kyyivs'ka Oblast', NW Ukraine
97 *B22* **Fastnet Rock** *Ir.* Carraig Aonair. *island* SW Ireland
Fastov *see* Fastiv
190 *C9* **Fatato** *island* Funafuti Atoll, C Tuvalu
152 *K12* **Fatehgarh** Uttar Pradesh, N India
149 *U6* **Fatehjang** Punjab, E Pakistan
152 *G11* **Fatehpur** Rājasthān, N India
152 *L13* **Fatehpur** Uttar Pradesh, N India
126 *J7* **Fatezh** Kurskaya Oblast', W Russian Federation
76 *G11* **Fatick** W Senegal
104 *G9* **Fátima** Santarém, W Portugal
136 *M11* **Fatsa** Ordu, N Turkey
Fatshan *see* Foshan
190 *D12* **Fatua, Pointe** *var.* Pointe Nord. *headland* Île Futuna, S Wallis and Futuna
191 *X7* **Fatu Hiva** *island* Îles Marquises, NE French Polynesia
Fatunda *see* Fatundu
79 *H21* **Fatundu** *var.* Fatunda. Bandundu, W Dem. Rep. Congo
29 *O8* **Faulkton** South Dakota, N USA
116 *L13* **Făurei** *prev.* Filimon Sîrbu. Brăila, SE Romania
92 *G12* **Fauske** Nordland, C Norway
9 *P13* **Faust** Alberta, W Canada
99 *L23* **Fauvillers** Luxembourg, SE Belgium
107 *J24* **Favara** Sicilia, Italy, C Mediterranean Sea
Faventia *see* Faenza
107 *G23* **Favignana, Isola** *island* Isole Egadi, S Italy
12 *D8* **Fawn** ~ Ontario, SE Canada
Faxa Bay *see* Faxaflói
92 *H3* **Faxaflói** *Eng.* Faxa Bay. *bay* W Iceland
78 *I7* **Faya** *prev.* Faya-Largeau, Largeau. Borkou-Ennedi-Tibesti, N Chad
Faya-Largeau *see* Faya
187 *Q16* **Fayaoué** Province des Îles Loyauté, C New Caledonia
138 *M5* **Fayḑāt** *hill range* E Syria
23 *O3* **Fayette** Alabama, S USA
29 *X12* **Fayette** Iowa, C USA
22 *J6* **Fayette** Mississippi, S USA
27 *U4* **Fayette** Missouri, C USA
27 *S9* **Fayetteville** Arkansas, C USA
21 *U10* **Fayetteville** North Carolina, SE USA
20 *J10* **Fayetteville** Tennessee, S USA
25 *U11* **Fayetteville** Texas, SW USA
21 *R5* **Fayetteville** West Virginia, NE USA
141 *R4* **Faylakah** *var.* Failaka Island. *island* E Kuwait
139 *T10* **Fayşalīyah** *var.* Faisaliya. S Iraq
189 *P15* **Fayu** *var.* East Fayu. *island* Hall Islands, C Micronesia
152 *G8* **Fāzilka** Punjab, NW India
Fdérick *see* Fdérik
76 *I6* **Fdérik** *var.* Fdérick, *Fr.* Fort Gouraud. Tiris Zemmour, NW Mauritania
Feabhail, Loch *see* Foyle, Lough
97 *B20* **Feale** ~ SW Ireland
21 *V12* **Fear, Cape** *headland* Bald Head Island, North Carolina, SE USA
35 *O6* **Feather River** ~ California, W USA
185 *M14* **Featherston** Wellington, North Island, New Zealand
102 *L3* **Fécamp** Seine-Maritime, N France
Fédala *see* Mohammedia
61 *D17* **Federación** Entre Ríos, E Argentina
61 *D17* **Federal** Entre Ríos, E Argentina
77 *T15* **Federal Capital District** ◆ *capital territory* C Nigeria
Federal Capital Territory *see* Australian Capital Territory
Federal District *see* Distrito Federal
21 *Y4* **Federalsburg** Maryland, NE USA
74 *M6* **Fedjaj, Chott el** *var.* Chott el Fejaj, Shaṭṭ al Fijāj. *salt lake* C Tunisia
94 *B13* **Fedje** *island* S Norway
144 *M7* **Fedorovka** Kostanay, N Kazakhstan
127 *U6* **Fedorovka** Respublika Bashkortostan, W Russian Federation
Fëdory *see* Fyadory
117 *U11* **Fedotova Kosa** *spit* SE Ukraine
189 *V13* **Fefan** *atoll* Chuuk Islands, C Micronesia
111 *O21* **Fehérgyarmat** Szabolcs-Szatmár-Bereg, E Hungary
Fehér-Körös *see* Crişul Alb
Fehértemplom *see* Bela Crkva
Fehérvölgy *see* Albac
100 *L7* **Fehmarn** *island* N Germany
95 *H25* **Fehmarn Belt** *Dan.* Femern Bælt, *Ger.* Fehmarnbelt. *strait* Denmark /Germany *see also* Femern Bælt
Fehmarnbelt Fehmarn Belt/Femer Bælt
109 *X8* **Fehring** Steiermark, SE Austria
59 *B15* **Feijó** Acre, W Brazil
184 *M12* **Feilding** Manawatu-Wanganui, North Island, New Zealand
Feira *see* Feira de Santana
59 *O17* **Feira de Santana** *var.* Feira. Bahia, E Brazil
109 *X7* **Feistritz** ~ SE Austria
Feistritz *see* Ilirska Bistrica
161 *P8* **Feixi** *var.* Shangpai; *prev.* Shangpaihe. Anhui, E China
Fejaj, Chott el *see* Fedjaj, Chott el
111 *I23* **Fejér** *off.* Fejér Megye. ◆ *county* W Hungary
Fejér Megye *see* Fejér
95 *I24* **Fejø** *island* SE Denmark
136 *K15* **Feke** Adana, S Turkey
Feketehalom *see* Codlea
Fekete-Körös *see* Crişul Negru
105 *Y9* **Felanitx** Mallorca, Spain, W Mediterranean Sea
109 *T3* **Feldaist** ~ N Austria
109 *W8* **Feldbach** Steiermark, SE Austria
101 *F24* **Feldberg** ▲ SW Germany
116 *J12* **Feldioara** *Ger.* Marienburg, *Hung.* Földvár. Braşov, C Romania
108 *I7* **Feldkirch** *anc.* Clunia. Vorarlberg, W Austria
109 *S9* **Feldkirchen in Kärnten** *Slvn.* Trg. Kärnten, S Austria
Félegyháza *see* Kiskunfélegyháza
192 *H16* **Feleolo** ✈ (Āpia) Upolu, C Samoa
104 *H6* **Felgueiras** Porto, N Portugal
Felicitas Julia *see* Lisboa
172 *J16* **Félicité** *island* Inner Islands, NE Seychelles
151 *K20* **Felidhu Atoll** *atoll* C Maldives
41 *Y13* **Felipe Carrillo Puerto** Quintana Roo, SE Mexico
97 *Q21* **Felixstowe** E England, UK
103 *N11* **Felletin** Creuse, C France
Fellin *see* Viljandi
Felsőbánya *see* Baia Sprie
Felsőmuzslya *see* Mužlja
Felsővisó *see* Vişeu de Sus
35 *N10* **Felton** California, W USA
106 *H7* **Feltre** Veneto, NE Italy
95 *H25* **Femer Bælt** *Dan.* Fehmarn Belt, *Ger.* Fehmarnbelt. *strait* Denmark/Germany SW Baltic Sea *see also* Fehmarn Belt
Femern Bælt Fehmarn Belt
95 *I24* **Femø** *island* SE Denmark
94 *I10* **Femunden** ◎ S Norway
104 *H2* **Fene** Galicia, NW Spain
14 *I14* **Fenelon Falls** Ontario, SE Canada
189 *U13* **Feneppi** *atoll* Chuuk Islands, C Micronesia
137 *O11* **Fener Burnu** *headland* N Turkey
115 *J14* **Fengári** ▲ Samothráki, E Greece
163 *V13* **Fengcheng** *var.* Feng-cheng, Fenghwangcheng. Liaoning, NE China
Feng-cheng *see* Fengcheng
160 *K11* **Fenggang** *var.* Longquan. Guizhou, S China
161 *S9* **Fenghua** Zhejiang, SE China
Fenghwangcheng *see* Fengcheng
Fengjiaba *see* Wangcang
160 *L9* **Fengjie** *var.* Yong'an. Sichuan, C China
160 *M14* **Fengkai** *var.* Jiangkou. Guangdong, S China
161 *T13* **Fenglin** *Jap.* Hōrin. C Taiwan
161 *P1* **Fengning** *prev.* Dagezhen. Hebei, E China
160 *E13* **Fengqing** *var.* Fengshan. Yunnan, SW China
161 *O6* **Fengqiu** Henan, C China
161 *Q2* **Fengrun** Hebei, E China
Fengshan *see* Luoyuan
Fengshan *see* Fengqing
163 *T4* **Fengshui Shan** ▲ NE China
161 *P14* **Fengshun** Guangdong, S China
Fengtien *see* Shenyang, China
Fengtien *see* Liaoning, China
160 *J7* **Fengxian** *var.* Feng Xian; *prev.* Shuangshipu. Shaanxi, C China
Feng Xian *see* Fengxian
Fengxiang *see* Luobei
Fengyizhen *see* Maoxian
163 *P13* **Fengzhen** Nei Mongol Zizhiqu, N China
160 *M6* **Fen He** ~ C China
153 *V15* **Feni** Chittagong, E Bangladesh
186 *I6* **Feni Islands** *island group* NE Papua New Guinea
38 *H17* **Fenimore Pass** *strait* Aleutian Islands, Alaska, USA
84 *B9* **Feni Ridge** *undersea feature* N Atlantic Ocean
Fennern *see* Vändra
30 *J9* **Fennimore** Wisconsin, N USA
172 *J4* **Fenoarivo** Toamasina, E Madagascar
95 *I24* **Fensmark** Storstrøm, SE Denmark
97 *O19* **Fens, The** *wetland* E England, UK
31 *R9* **Fenton** Michigan, N USA
190 *K10* **Fenua Fala** *island* SE Tokelau
190 *F12* **Fenuafo'ou, Île** *island* E Wallis and Futuna
190 *L10* **Fenua Loa** *island* Fakaofo Atoll, E Tokelau
160 *M4* **Fenyang** Shanxi, C China
117 *U13* **Feodosiya** *var.* Kefe, *It.* Kaffa; *anc.* Theodosia. Respublika Krym, S Ukraine
94 *I10* **Feragen** ◎ S Norway
74 *L5* **Fer, Cap de** *headland* NE Algeria
31 *O16* **Ferdinand** Indiana, N USA
Ferdinand *see* Montana, Bulgaria
Ferdinand *see* Mihail Kogălniceanu, Romania
Ferdinandsberg *see* Oţelu Roşu
143 *T7* **Ferdows** *var.* Firdaus; *prev.* Tūn. Khorāsān-Razavī, E Iran
103 *Q5* **Fère-Champenoise** Marne, N France
Ferencz-Jósef Csúcs *see* Gerlachovský štít
107 *J16* **Ferentino** Lazio, C Italy
114 *L13* **Féres** Anatolikí Makedonía kai Thráki, NE Greece
Fergana *see* Farg'ona
147 *S10* **Fergana Valley** *var.* Farghona Valley, *Rus.* Ferganskaya Dolina, *Taj.* Wodii Farghona, *Uzb.* Farghona Wodiysi. *basin* Tajikistan/Uzbekistan
Ferganskaya Dolina *see* Fergana Valley
Ferganskaya Oblast' *see* Farg'ona Viloyati
147 *U9* **Ferganskiy Khrebet** ▲▲ C Kyrgyzstan
14 *F15* **Fergus** Ontario, S Canada
29 *S6* **Fergus Falls** Minnesota, N USA
186 *G9* **Fergusson Island** *var.* Kaluwawa. *island* SE Papua New Guinea
111 *K22* **Ferihegy** ✈ (Budapest) Budapest, C Hungary
Ferizaj *see* Uroševac
77 *N14* **Ferkessédougou** N Ivory Coast
109 *T10* **Ferlach** *Slvn.* Borovlje. Kärnten, S Austria
97 *E16* **Fermanagh** *cultural region* SW Northern Ireland, UK
106 *J13* **Fermo** *anc.* Firmum Picenum. Marche, C Italy
104 *J6* **Fermoselle** Castilla-León, N Spain
97 *D20* **Fermoy** *Ir.* Mainistir Fhear Maí. SW Ireland
23 *W8* **Fernandina Beach** Amelia Island, Florida, SE USA
57 *A17* **Fernandina, Isla** *var.* Narborough Island. *island* Galapagos Islands, Ecuador, E Pacific Ocean
47 *Y5* **Fernando de Noronha** *island* E Brazil
Fernando Po/Fernando Póo *see* Bioco, Isla de
60 *J7* **Fernandópolis** São Paulo, S Brazil
104 *M13* **Fernán Núñez** Andalucía, S Spain
83 *Q14* **Fernão Veloso, Baia de** *bay* NE Mozambique
34 *K3* **Ferndale** California, W USA
32 *H6* **Ferndale** Washington, NW USA
9 *P17* **Fernie** British Columbia, SW Canada
35 *R5* **Fernley** Nevada, W USA
Ferozepore *see* Firozpur
107 *N18* **Ferrandina** Basilicata, S Italy
106 *G9* **Ferrara** *anc.* Forum Alieni. Emilia-Romagna, N Italy
120 *F9* **Ferrat, Cap** *headland* NW Algeria
107 *D20* **Ferrato, Capo** *headland* Sardegna, Italy, C Mediterranean Sea
104 *G12* **Ferreira do Alentejo** Beja, S Portugal
56 *B11* **Ferreñafe** Lambayeque, W Peru
108 *C12* **Ferret** Valais, SW Switzerland
102 *I13* **Ferret, Cap** *headland* W France
22 *I6* **Ferriday** Louisiana, S USA
Ferro *see* Hierro
107 *D16* **Ferro, Capo** *headland* Sardegna, Italy, C Mediterranean Sea
104 *H2* **Ferrol** *var.* El Ferrol; *prev.* El Ferrol del Caudillo. Galicia, NW Spain
56 *B12* **Ferrol, Península de** *peninsula* W Peru
36 *M5* **Ferron** Utah, W USA
21 *S7* **Ferrum** Virginia, NE USA
23 *O8* **Ferry Pass** Florida, SE USA
Ferryville *see* Menzel Bourguiba
29 *S4* **Fertile** Minnesota, N USA
Fertő *see* Neusiedler See
98 *L5* **Ferwerd** *Fris.* Ferwert. Friesland, N Netherlands
Ferwert *see* Ferwerd
74 *G6* **Fès** *Eng.* Fez. N Morocco
79 *I22* **Feshi** Bandundu, SW Dem. Rep. Congo
29 *O4* **Fessenden** North Dakota, N USA
Festenberg *see* Twardogóra
27 *X5* **Festus** Missouri, C USA
116 *M14* **Feteşti** Ialomiţa, SE Romania
136 *D17* **Fethiye** Muğla, SW Turkey
96 *M1* **Fetlar** *island* NE Scotland, UK
95 *I15* **Fetsund** Akershus, S Norway
12 *L5* **Feuilles, Lac aux** ◎ Québec, E Canada
12 *L5* **Feuilles, Rivière aux** ~ Québec, E Canada
99 *M23* **Feulen** Diekirch, C Luxembourg
103 *Q11* **Feurs** Loire, E France
95 *F18* **Fevik** Aust-Agder, S Norway
123 *R13* **Fevral'sk** Amurskaya Oblast', SE Russian Federation
149 *S2* **Feyẓābād** *var.* Faizabad, Faizābād, Feyzābād, Fyzabad. Badakhshān, NE Afghanistan
Feyzābād *see* Feyẓābād
Fez *see* Fès
97 *J19* **Ffestiniog** NW Wales, UK
Fhóid Duibh, Cuan an *see* Blacksod Bay
62 *I8* **Fiambalá** Catamarca, NW Argentina
172 *I6* **Fianarantsoa** Fianarantsoa, C Madagascar
172 *H6* **Fianarantsoa** ◆ *province* SE Madagascar
78 *G12* **Fianga** Mayo-Kébbi, SW Chad
Ficce *see* Fichē

◆ Country ● Country Capital ◇ Dependent Territory ○ Dependent Territory Capital ◆ Administrative Regions ✈ International Airport ▲ Mountain ▲▲ Mountain Range Volcano ~ River ◎ Lake ⊠ Reservoir

80 *J12* **Fichê** *It.* Ficce. C Ethiopia
101 *N17* **Fichtelberg** ▲ Czech Republic/Germany
101 *M18* **Fichtelgebirge** ▲▲ SE Germany
101 *M19* **Fichtelnaab** ♒ SE Germany
106 *E9* **Fidenza** Emilia-Romagna, N Italy
113 *K21* **Fier** *var.* Fieri. Fier, SW Albania
113 *K21* **Fier** ♦ *district* W Albania
Fieri *see* Fier
Fierza *see* Fierzë
113 *L17* **Fierzë** *var.* Fierza. Shkodër, N Albania
113 *L17* **Fierzës, Liqeni i** ⊜ N Albania
108 *F10* **Fiesch** Valais, SW Switzerland
106 *G11* **Fiesole** Toscana, C Italy
138 *G12* **Fifah** Aṭ Ṭafīlah, W Jordan
96 *K11* **Fife** *var.* Kingdom of Fife. *cultural region* E Scotland, UK
Fife, Kingdom of *see* Fife
96 *K11* **Fife Ness** *headland* E Scotland, UK
Fifteen Twenty Fracture Zone *see* Barracuda Fracture Zone
103 *N13* **Figeac** Lot, S France
95 *N19* **Figeholm** Kalmar, SE Sweden
Figig *see* Figuig
83 *J18* **Figtree** Matabeleland South, SW Zimbabwe
104 *F8* **Figueira da Foz** Coimbra, W Portugal
105 *X4* **Figueres** Cataluña, E Spain
74 *H7* **Figuig** *var.* Figig. E Morocco
Fijäjj, Shaṭṭ al *see* Fedjaj, Chott el
187 *Y15* **Fiji** *off.* Sovereign Democratic Republic of Fiji, *Fij.* Viti. ♦ *republic* SW Pacific Ocean
192 *K9* **Fiji** *island group* SW Pacific Ocean
175 *Q8* **Fiji Plate** *tectonic feature*
Fiji, Sovereign Democratic Republic of *see* Fiji
105 *P14* **Filabres, Sierra de los** ▲▲ SE Spain
83 *K18* **Filabusi** Matabeleland South, S Zimbabwe
42 *K13* **Filadelfia** Guanacaste, W Costa Rica
111 *K20* **Fiľakovo** *Hung.* Fülek. Banskobýstricky Kraj, C Slovakia
195 *N5* **Filchner Ice Shelf** *ice shelf* Antarctica
14 *J11* **Fildegrand** ♒ Québec, SE Canada
94 *E12* **Fillefjell** ▲ S Norway
33 *O15* **Filer** Idaho, NW USA
Filevo *see* Vŭrbitsa
116 *H14* **Filiaşi** Dolj, SW Romania
115 *B16* **Filiátes** Ípeiros, W Greece
115 *D21* **Filiatrá** Pelopónnisos, S Greece
107 *K22* **Filicudi, Isola** *island* Isole Eolie, S Italy
141 *Y10* **Filim** E Oman
Filimon Sîrbu *see* Făurei
77 *S11* **Filingué** Tillabéri, W Niger
114 *K13* **Filiouri** ♒ NE Greece
Filiouri *see* Líssos
114 *I13* **Filippoi** *anc.* Philippi. *site of ancient city* Anatolikí Makedonía kai Thráki, NE Greece
95 *L15* **Filipstad** Värmland, C Sweden
108 *I9* **Filisur** Graubünden, S Switzerland
35 *R14* **Fillmore** California, W USA
36 *K5* **Fillmore** Utah, W USA
14 *J10* **Fils, Lac du** ⊜ Québec, SE Canada
136 *H11* **Filyos Çayı** ♒ N Turkey
195 *Q1* **Fimbul Ice Shelf** *ice shelf* Antarctica
195 *Q2* **Fimbulheimen** *physical region* Antarctica
106 *G9* **Finale Emilia** Emilia-Romagna, C Italy
106 *C10* **Finale Ligure** Liguria, NW Italy
105 *P14* **Fiñana** Andalucía, S Spain
172 *I6* **Finandrahana** Fianarantsoa, SE Madagascar
21 *S6* **Fincastle** Virginia, NE USA
99 *M25* **Findel** ✈ (Luxembourg) Luxembourg, C Luxembourg
96 *J9* **Findhorn** ♒ N Scotland, UK
31 *R12* **Findlay** Ohio, N USA
18 *G11* **Finger Lakes** ⊜ New York, NE USA
83 *L14* **Fingoè** Tete, NW Mozambique
136 *E17* **Finike** Antalya, SW Turkey
102 *F6* **Finistère** ♦ *department* NW France
186 *D7* **Finisterre Range** ▲▲ N Papua New Guinea
181 *Q8* **Finke** Northern Territory, N Australia
109 *S10* **Finkenstein** Kärnten, S Austria
189 *Y15* **Finkol, Mount** *var.* Mount Crozer. ▲ Kosrae, E Micronesia
93 *L17* **Finland** *off.* Republic of Finland, *Fin.* Suomen Tasavalta, Suomi. ♦ *republic* N Europe
124 *F12* **Finland, Gulf of** *Est.* Soome Laht, *Fin.* Suomenlahti, *Ger.* Finnischer Meerbusen, *Rus.* Finskiy Zaliv, *Swe.* Finska Viken. *gulf* E Baltic Sea
Finland, Republic of *see* Finland
10 *L11* **Finlay** ♒ British Columbia, W Canada
183 *O10* **Finley** New South Wales, SE Australia
29 *Q4* **Finley** North Dakota, N USA
Finnischer Meerbusen *see* Finland, Gulf of
92 *K9* **Finnmark** ♦ *county* N Norway
92 *K9* **Finnmarksvidda** *physical region* N Norway
92 *I9* **Finnsnes** Troms, N Norway
186 *E7* **Finschhafen** Morobe, C Papua New Guinea
94 *E13* **Finse** Hordaland, S Norway
Finska Viken/Finskiy Zaliv *see* Finland, Gulf of
95 *M17* **Finspång** Östergötland, S Sweden
108 *F10* **Finsteraarhorn** ▲ Switzerland
101 *O14* **Finsterwalde** Brandenburg, E Germany

185 *A23* **Fiordland** *physical region* South Island, New Zealand
106 *E9* **Fiorenzuola d'Arda** Emilia-Romagna, C Italy
Firat Nehri *see* Euphrates
Firdaus *see* Ferdows
18 *M14* **Fire Island** *island* New York, NE USA
106 *G11* **Firenze** *Eng.* Florence; *anc.* Florentia. Toscana, C Italy
106 *G10* **Firenzuola** Toscana, C Italy
14 *C6* **Fire River** Ontario, S Canada
Firliug *see* Fârliug
61 *B19* **Firmat** Santa Fe, C Argentina
103 *Q12* **Firminy** Loire, E France
Firmum Picenum *see* Fermo
152 *J12* **Firozābād** Uttar Pradesh, N India
152 *G8* **Firozpur** *var.* Ferozepore. Punjab, NW India
143 *O12* **Fīrūzābād** Fārs, S Iran
Fischamend *see* Fischamend Markt
109 *Y4* **Fischamend Markt** *var.* Fischamend. Niederösterreich, NE Austria
109 *W6* **Fischbacher Alpen** ▲▲ E Austria
Fischhausen *see* Primorsk
83 *D21* **Fish** *var.* Vis. ♒ S Namibia
83 *F24* **Fish** *Afr.* Vis. ♒ SW South Africa
9 *X15* **Fisher Branch** Manitoba, S Canada
9 *X15* **Fisher River** Manitoba, S Canada
19 *N13* **Fishers Island** *island* New York, NE USA
37 *U8* **Fishers Peak** ▲ Colorado, C USA
9 *P9* **Fisher Strait** *strait* Nunavut, N Canada
97 *H21* **Fishguard** *Wel.* Abergwaun. SW Wales, UK
19 *R2* **Fish River Lake** ⊜ Maine, NE USA
194 *K6* **Fiske, Cape** *headland* Antarctica
103 *P4* **Fismes** Marne, N France
104 *F3* **Fisterra, Cabo** *cape* NW Spain
19 *N11* **Fitchburg** Massachusetts, NE USA
96 *L3* **Fitful Head** *headland* NE Scotland, UK
95 *C14* **Fitjar** Hordaland, S Norway
192 *H16* **Fito** ▲ Upolu, C Samoa
23 *U6* **Fitzgerald** Georgia, SE USA
180 *M5* **Fitzroy Crossing** Western Australia
63 *G21* **Fitzroy, Monte** *var.* Cerro Chaltel. ▲ S Argentina
181 *Y8* **Fitzroy River** ♒ Queensland, E Australia
180 *L5* **Fitzroy River** ♒ Western Australia
14 *E12* **Fitzwilliam Island** *island* Ontario, S Canada
107 *J15* **Fiuggi** Lazio, C Italy
Fiume *see* Rijeka
107 *H15* **Fiumicino** Lazio, C Italy
Fiumicino *see* Leonardo da Vinci
106 *E10* **Fivizzano** Toscana, C Italy
79 *O21* **Fizi** Sud Kivu, E Dem. Rep. Congo
92 *I11* **Fjällåsen** Norrbotten, N Sweden
95 *G20* **Fjerritslev** Nordjylland, N Denmark
F.J.S. *see* Franz Josef Strauss
95 *L16* **Fjugesta** Örebro, C Sweden
Fladstrand *see* Frederikshavn
37 *V5* **Flagler** Colorado, C USA
23 *X10* **Flagler Beach** Florida, SE USA
36 *L11* **Flagstaff** Arizona, SW USA
65 *H24* **Flagstaff Bay** *bay* N Saint Helena, C Atlantic Ocean
19 *P5* **Flagstaff Lake** ⊜ Maine, NE USA
94 *E13* **Flåm** Sogn Og Fjordane, S Norway
15 *O8* **Flamand** ♒ Québec, SE Canada
30 *J5* **Flambeau River** ♒ Wisconsin, N USA
97 *O16* **Flamborough Head** *headland* E England, UK
100 *N13* **Fläming** *hill range*
16 *H8* **Flaming Gorge Reservoir** ⊜ Utah/Wyoming, NW USA
99 *B18* **Flanders** *Dut.* Vlaanderen, *Fr.* Flandre. *cultural region* Belgium/France
Flandre *see* Flanders
29 *R10* **Flandreau** South Dakota, N USA
96 *D6* **Flannan Isles** *island group* NW Scotland, UK
28 *M6* **Flasher** North Dakota, N USA
93 *G15* **Flåsjön** ⊜ N Sweden
39 *O11* **Flat** Alaska, USA
92 *H1* **Flateyri** Vestfirdhir, NW Iceland
33 *P8* **Flathead Lake** ⊜ Montana, NW USA
173 *Y15* **Flat Island** *island* N Mauritius
25 *T11* **Flatonia** Texas, SW USA
185 *M14* **Flat Point** *headland* North Island, New Zealand
27 *X4* **Flat River** Missouri, C USA
31 *P8* **Flat River** ♒ Michigan, N USA
31 *P14* **Flatrock River** ♒ Indiana, N USA
32 *E6* **Flattery, Cape** *headland* Washington, NW USA
64 *B12* **Flatts Village** *var.* The Flatts Village. C Bermuda
108 *H7* **Flawil** Sankt Gallen, NE Switzerland
97 *N22* **Fleet** S England, UK
97 *K16* **Fleetwood** NW England, UK
18 *H15* **Fleetwood** Pennsylvania, NE USA
31 *R9* **Flekkefjord** Vest-Agder, S Norway
21 *N5* **Flemingsburg** Kentucky, S USA
18 *J15* **Flemington** New Jersey, NE USA
64 *I7* **Flemish Cap** *undersea feature* NW Atlantic Ocean
95 *N16* **Flen** Södermanland, C Sweden

100 *I6* **Flensburg** Schleswig-Holstein, N Germany
100 *J6* **Flensburger Förde** *inlet* Denmark/Germany
102 *K5* **Flers** Orne, N France
95 *C14* **Flesland** ✈ (Bergen) Hordaland, S Norway
21 *P10* **Fletcher** North Carolina, SE USA
31 *R6* **Fletcher Pond** ⊜ Michigan, N USA
102 *L15* **Fleurance** Gers, S France
88 *B8* **Fleurier** Neuchâtel, W Switzerland
99 *H20* **Fleurus** Hainaut, S Belgium
103 *N7* **Fleury-les-Aubrais** Loiret, C France
98 *K10* **Flevoland** ♦ *province* C Netherlands
Flickertail State *see* North Dakota
108 *H9* **Flims** Glarus, NE Switzerland
182 *F8* **Flinders Island** *island* Investigator Group, South Australia
183 *P14* **Flinders Island** *island* Furneaux Group, Tasmania, SE Australia
182 *I6* **Flinders Ranges** ▲▲ South Australia
181 *U5* **Flinders River** ♒ Queensland, NE Australia
9 *V13* **Flin Flon** Manitoba, C Canada
97 *K18* **Flint** NE Wales, UK
31 *R9* **Flint** Michigan, N USA
97 *J18* **Flint** *cultural region* NE Wales, UK
27 *O7* **Flint Hills** *hill range* Kansas, C USA
191 *Y6* **Flint Island** *island* Line Islands, E Kiribati
23 *S4* **Flint River** ♒ Georgia, SE USA
31 *R9* **Flint River** ♒ Michigan, N USA
21 *T15* **Folly Beach** South Carolina, SE USA
189 *X12* **Flipper Point** *headland* C Wake Island
94 *I13* **Flisa** Hedmark, S Norway
94 *J13* **Flisa** ♒ S Norway
122 *J5* **Fliseggskiy, Mys** *headland* Novaya Zemlya, NW Russian Federation
Flitsch *see* Bovec
105 *U6* **Flix** Cataluña, NE Spain
95 *J19* **Floda** Älvsborg, S Sweden
101 *O16* **Flöha** ♒ E Germany
25 *O4* **Flomot** Texas, SW USA
29 *V5* **Floodwood** Minnesota, N USA
30 *M15* **Flora** Illinois, N USA
103 *P14* **Florac** Lozère, S France
23 *Q8* **Florala** Alabama, S USA
103 *S4* **Florange** Moselle, NE France
Floreana, Isla *see* Santa María, Isla
23 *O2* **Florence** Alabama, S USA
36 *L14* **Florence** Arizona, SW USA
37 *T6* **Florence** Colorado, C USA
27 *O5* **Florence** Kansas, C USA
20 *M4* **Florence** Kentucky, S USA
32 *E13* **Florence** Oregon, NW USA
21 *T12* **Florence** South Carolina, SE USA
25 *S9* **Florence** Texas, SW USA
54 *E13* **Florencia** Caquetá, S Colombia
99 *H21* **Florennes** Namur, S Belgium
Florentia *see* Firenze
63 *J18* **Florentino Ameghino, Embalse** ⊜ S Argentina
99 *J24* **Florenville** Luxembourg, SE Belgium
42 *E3* **Flores** Petén, N Guatemala
61 *E19* **Flores** ♦ *department* S Uruguay
171 *O16* **Flores** *island* Nusa Tenggara, C Indonesia
64 *M1* **Flores** *island* Azores, Portugal, NE Atlantic Ocean
Floreshty *see* Floreşti
Flores, Lago de *see* Petén Itzá, Lago
171 *N15* **Flores, Laut** *see* Flores Sea
116 *M8* **Floreşti** *Rus.* Floreshty. N Moldova
25 *S12* **Floresville** Texas, SW USA
59 *N14* **Floriano** Piauí, E Brazil
61 *K14* **Florianópolis** *prev.* Destêrro. *state capital* Santa Catarina, S Brazil
44 *G6* **Florida** Camagüey, C Cuba
61 *F19* **Florida** Florida, S Uruguay
61 *F19* **Florida** ♦ *department* S Uruguay
23 *U9* **Florida** *off.* State of Florida, *also known as* Peninsular State, Sunshine State. ♦ *state* SE USA
20 *J6* **Floridablanca** Santander, N Colombia
23 *Y17* **Florida Bay** *bay* Florida, SE USA
54 *G8* **Floridablanca** Santander, N Colombia
23 *Y17* **Florida Keys** *island group* Florida, SE USA
37 *Q16* **Florida Mountains** ▲▲ New Mexico, SW USA
64 *D10* **Florida, Straits of** *strait* Atlantic Ocean/Gulf of Mexico
114 *D13* **Flórina, var.** Phlórina. Dytikí Makedonía, N Greece
94 *C11* **Florø** Sogn Og Fjordane, S Norway
115 *L22* **Floúda, Ákrotírio** *cape* Astypálaia, Kykládes, Greece, Aegean Sea
21 *S7* **Floyd** Virginia, NE USA
25 *N4* **Floydada** Texas, SW USA
Flüela Wisshorn *see* Flüelapass
98 *K7* **Fluessen** ⊜ N Netherlands
105 *S5* **Flumen** ♒ NE Spain
107 *C20* **Flumendosa** ♒ Sardegna, Italy, C Mediterranean Sea
31 *R9* **Flushing** Michigan, N USA
Flushing *see* Vlissingen
25 *O6* **Fluvanna** Texas, SW USA
186 *B8* **Fly** ♒ Indonesia/Papua New Guinea
194 *I10* **Flying Fish, Cape** *cape* Thurston Island, Antarctica
95 *Y15* **Flylän** *see* Vlieland
193 *Y15* **Foa** *island* Ha'apai Group, C Tonga

9 *U15* **Foam Lake** Saskatchewan, S Canada
113 *J14* **Foča** SE Bosnia and Herzegovina
116 *L12* **Focşani** Vrancea, E Romania
Fogaras/Fogarasch *see* Făgăraş
107 *M16* **Foggia** Puglia, SE Italy
Foggo *see* Faggo
76 *D10* **Fogo Island** *island* Newfoundland and Labrador, SW Cape Verde
13 *U11* **Fogo Island** *island* Newfoundland and Labrador, E Canada
109 *U7* **Fohnsdorf** Steiermark, SE Austria
100 *G7* **Föhr** *island* NW Germany
104 *F14* **Fóia** ▲ S Portugal
14 *I10* **Foins, Lac aux** ⊜ Québec, SE Canada
103 *N17* **Foix** Ariège, S France
126 *I5* **Fokino** Bryanskaya Oblast', W Russian Federation
123 *S15* **Fokino** Primorskiy Kray, SE Russian Federation
Fola, Cnoc *see* Bloody Foreland
94 *K13* **Folarskardnuten** ▲ S Norway
92 *G11* **Folda** *fjord* C Norway
93 *F14* **Foldereid** Nord-Trøndelag, C Norway
115 *J22* **Folégandros** *island* Kykládes, Greece, Aegean Sea
23 *O9* **Foley** Alabama, S USA
29 *U7* **Foley** Minnesota, N USA
14 *E7* **Foleyet** Ontario, S Canada
95 *D14* **Folgefonni** *glacier* S Norway
106 *I13* **Foligno** Umbria, C Italy
97 *Q23* **Folkestone** SE England, UK
23 *W8* **Folkston** Georgia, SE USA
94 *H10* **Folldal** Hedmark, S Norway
25 *P1* **Follett** Texas, SW USA
106 *F13* **Follonica** Toscana, C Italy
21 *T15* **Folly Beach** South Carolina, SE USA
35 *O7* **Folsom** California, W USA
116 *M12* **Folteşti** Galaţi, E Romania
172 *H14* **Fomboni** Mohéli, S Comoros
18 *K10* **Fonda** New York, NE USA
9 *S10* **Fond-du-Lac** Saskatchewan, C Canada
30 *M8* **Fond du Lac** Wisconsin, N USA
9 *T10* **Fond-du-Lac** ♒ Saskatchewan, C Canada
190 *C9* **Fongafale** *var.* Funafuti. ● (Tuvalu) Funafuti Atoll, C Tuvalu
190 *G8* **Fongafale** *atoll* C Tuvalu
107 *C18* **Fonni** Sardegna, Italy, C Mediterranean Sea
189 *V12* **Fono** *island* Chuuk, C Micronesia
54 *G4* **Fonseca** La Guajira, N Colombia
Fonseca, Golfo de *see* Fonseca, Gulf of
42 *H8* **Fonseca, Gulf of** *Sp.* Golfo de Fonseca. *gulf* C Central America
103 *O6* **Fontainebleau** Seine-et-Marne, N France
63 *G19* **Fontana, Lago** ⊜ W Argentina
21 *N10* **Fontana Lake** ⊜ North Carolina, SE USA
107 *L24* **Fontanarossa** ✈ (Catania) Sicilia, Italy, C Mediterranean Sea
9 *N11* **Fontas** ♒ British Columbia, W Canada
58 *D12* **Fonte Boa** Amazonas, N Brazil
102 *J10* **Fontenay-le-Comte** Vendée, NW France
33 *T16* **Fontenelle Reservoir** ⊜ Wyoming, C USA
193 *Y14* **Fonualei** *island* Vava'u Group, N Tonga
111 *H24* **Fonyód** Somogy, W Hungary
Foochow *see* Fuzhou
39 *Q10* **Foraker, Mount** ▲ Alaska, USA
187 *R14* **Forari** Éfaté, C Vanuatu
103 *U4* **Forbach** Moselle, NE France
183 *Q8* **Forbes** New South Wales, SE Australia
77 *T17* **Forcados** Delta, S Nigeria
103 *S14* **Forcalquier** Alpes-de-Haute-Provence, SE France
101 *N18* **Forchheim** Bayern, SE Germany
35 *R13* **Ford City** California, W USA
94 *D11* **Førde** Sogn Og Fjordane, S Norway
31 *N4* **Ford River** ♒ Michigan, N USA
183 *O4* **Fords Bridge** New South Wales, SE Australia
20 *J6* **Fordsville** Kentucky, S USA
27 *U13* **Fordyce** Arkansas, C USA
76 *I14* **Forécariah** SW Guinea
197 *O14* **Forel, Mont** ▲ SE Greenland
9 *R17* **Foremost** Alberta, SW Canada
14 *D16* **Forest** Ontario, S Canada
22 *L5* **Forest** Mississippi, S USA
31 *S12* **Forest** Ohio, N USA
29 *V11* **Forest City** Iowa, C USA
21 *Q10* **Forest City** North Carolina, SE USA
32 *G11* **Forest Grove** Oregon, NW USA
21 *P5* **Forest Gay** West Virginia, NE USA
29 *V8* **Forest Lake** Minnesota, N USA
23 *S3* **Forest Park** Georgia, SE USA
29 *Q3* **Forest River** ♒ North Dakota, N USA
15 *T6* **Forestville** Québec, SE Canada
103 *Q11* **Forez, Monts du** ▲ C France
96 *K10* **Forfar** E Scotland, UK
28 *J8* **Forgan** Oklahoma, C USA
Forge du Sud *see* Dudelange
101 *J22* **Forią** ♒ C Poland
147 *N10* **Forish** *Rus.* Farish. Jizzax Viloyati, C Uzbekistan
20 *F9* **Forked Deer River** ♒ Tennessee, S USA
32 *F7* **Forks** Washington, NW USA
14 *M8* **Fortier** ♒ Québec, SE Canada
106 *H10* **Forlì** *anc.* Forum Livii. Emilia-Romagna, N Italy
97 *K17* **Formby** NW England, UK

105 *V11* **Formentera** *anc.* Ophiusa, *Lat.* Frumentum. *island* Islas Baleares, Spain, W Mediterranean Sea
Formentor, Cabo de *see* Formentor, Cap de
105 *Y9* **Formentor, Cap de** *var.* Cabo de Formentor, Cape Formentor. *cape* Mallorca, Spain, W Mediterranean Sea
Formentor, Cape de *see* Formentor, Cap de
107 *J16* **Formia** Lazio, C Italy
62 *O7* **Formosa** Formosa, NE Argentina
62 *M6* **Formosa** *off.* Provincia de Formosa. ♦ *province* NE Argentina
Formosa *see* Taiwan
Formosa/Formo'sa *see* Taiwan
59 *I17* **Formosa, Serra** ▲▲ C Brazil
Formosa, Provincia de *see* Formosa
Formosa Strait *see* Taiwan Strait
95 *H21* **Fornæs** *headland* C Denmark
95 *H15* **Fornebu** ✈ (Oslo) Akershus, S Norway
25 *U6* **Forney** Texas, SW USA
106 *E9* **Fornovo di Taro** Emilia-Romagna, C Italy
117 *T14* **Foros** Respublika Krym, S Ukraine
Føroyar *see* Faeroe Islands
96 *J8* **Forres** NE Scotland, UK
27 *X11* **Forrest City** Arkansas, C USA
39 *Y15* **Forrester Island** *island* Alexander Archipelago, Alaska, USA
25 *N7* **Forsan** Texas, SW USA
181 *V5* **Forsayth** Queensland, NE Australia
95 *L19* **Forserum** Jönköping, S Sweden
95 *K15* **Forshaga** Värmland, C Sweden
101 *Q14* **Forst** *Lus.* Barść Łużyca. Brandenburg, E Germany
183 *U7* **Forster-Tuncurry** New South Wales, SE Australia
23 *T4* **Forsyth** Georgia, SE USA
27 *T8* **Forsyth** Missouri, C USA
33 *W10* **Forsyth** Montana, NW USA
56 *L13* **Fortaleza** Pando, N Bolivia
58 *P13* **Fortaleza** *prev.* Ceará. *state capital* Ceará, NE Brazil
59 *D16* **Fortaleza** Rondônia, W Brazil
56 *C13* **Fortaleza, Río** ♒ W Peru
Fort-Archambault *see* Sarh
21 *U3* **Fort Ashby** West Virginia, NE USA
96 *I9* **Fort Augustus** N Scotland, UK
Fort-Bayard *see* Zhanjiang
33 *S8* **Fort Benton** Montana, NW USA
35 *Q1* **Fort Bidwell** California, W USA
34 *L5* **Fort Bragg** California, W USA
31 *N16* **Fort Branch** Indiana, N USA
Fort-Bretonnet *see* Bousso
33 *T17* **Fort Bridger** Wyoming, C USA
Fort-Cappolani *see* Tidjikja
Fort-Carnot *see* Ikongo
Fort Charlet *see* Djanet
Fort-Chimo *see* Kuujjuaq
9 *R10* **Fort Chipewyan** Alberta, C Canada
27 *R10* **Fort Cobb Lake** *see* Fort Cobb Reservoir
26 *L11* **Fort Cobb Reservoir** *var.* Fort Cobb Lake. ⊜ Oklahoma, C USA
37 *T3* **Fort Collins** Colorado, C USA
14 *K12* **Fort-Coulonge** Québec, SE Canada
Fort-Crampel *see* Kaga Bandoro
Fort-Dauphin *see* Tôlanaro
24 *K10* **Fort Davis** Texas, SW USA
37 *O10* **Fort Defiance** Arizona, SW USA
45 *Q12* **Fort-de-France** *prev.* Fort-Royal. ● (Martinique) W Martinique
45 *P12* **Fort-de-France, Baie de** *bay* W Martinique
Fort de Kock *see* Bukittinggi
23 *P6* **Fort Deposit** Alabama, S USA
29 *U13* **Fort Dodge** Iowa, C USA
13 *S10* **Forteau** Québec, E Canada
106 *E11* **Forte dei Marmi** Toscana, C Italy
14 *H17* **Fort Erie** Ontario, S Canada
180 *H7* **Fortescue River** ♒ Western Australia
19 *S2* **Fort Fairfield** Maine, NE USA
Fort-Foureau *see* Kousséri
12 *A11* **Fort Frances** Ontario, S Canada
Fort Franklin *see* Déline
Fort-Français *see* Fréjus
143 *Q15* **Forūr, Jazīreh-ye** *island* S Iran
94 *H7* **Fosen** *physical region* S Norway
161 *N14* **Foshan** *var.* Fatshan, Fo-shan, Namhoi. Guangdong, S China
Fo-shan *see* Foshan
106 *B9* **Fossano** Piemonte, NW Italy
99 *H21* **Fosses-la-Ville** Namur, S Belgium
32 *J12* **Fossil** Oregon, NW USA
106 *I11* **Fossombrone** Marche, C Italy
26 *K10* **Foss Reservoir** *var.* Foss Lake. ⊜ Oklahoma, C USA
29 *S4* **Fosston** Minnesota, N USA
183 *O13* **Foster** Victoria, SE Australia
9 *T12* **Foster Lakes** ⊜ Saskatchewan, C Canada
31 *S12* **Fostoria** Ohio, N USA
79 *D19* **Fougamou** Ngounié, C Gabon
102 *J6* **Fougères** Ille-et-Vilaine, NW France
96 *K2* **Foula** *island* NE Scotland, UK
65 *D24* **Foul Bay** *bay* East Falkland, Falkland Islands

Fort-Lamy *see* Ndjamena
23 *Z15* **Fort Lauderdale** Florida, SE USA
21 *R11* **Fort Lawn** South Carolina, SE USA
8 *H10* **Fort Liard** *var.* Liard. Northwest Territories, W Canada
44 *M8* **Fort-Liberté** NE Haiti
21 *N9* **Fort Loudoun Lake** ⊜ Tennessee, S USA
37 *T3* **Fort Lupton** Colorado, C USA
9 *R12* **Fort MacKay** Alberta, C Canada
9 *Q17* **Fort Macleod** *var.* MacLeod. Alberta, SW Canada
29 *Y16* **Fort Madison** Iowa, C USA
Fort Manning *see* Mchinji
25 *P9* **Fort McKavett** Texas, SW USA
9 *R12* **Fort McMurray** Alberta, C Canada
8 *G7* **Fort McPherson** *var.* McPherson. Northwest Territories, NW Canada
21 *R11* **Fort Mill** South Carolina, SE USA
Fort-Millot *see* Ngouri
37 *U3* **Fort Morgan** Colorado, C USA
23 *W14* **Fort Myers** Florida, SE USA
23 *W15* **Fort Myers Beach** Florida, SE USA
10 *M10* **Fort Nelson** British Columbia, W Canada
10 *M10* **Fort Nelson** ♒ British Columbia, W Canada
Fort Norman *see* Tulita
23 *Q2* **Fort Payne** Alabama, S USA
33 *W7* **Fort Peck** Montana, NW USA
33 *V8* **Fort Peck Lake** ⊜ Montana, NW USA
23 *Y13* **Fort Pierce** Florida, SE USA
29 *N10* **Fort Pierre** South Dakota, N USA
81 *E18* **Fort Portal** SW Uganda
8 *J10* **Fort Providence** *var.* Providence. Northwest Territories, W Canada
9 *U16* **Fort Qu'Appelle** Saskatchewan, S Canada
Fort-Repoux *see* Akjoujt
8 *K10* **Fort Resolution** *var.* Resolution. Northwest Territories, W Canada
33 *T13* **Fortress Mountain** ▲ Wyoming, C USA
Fort Rosebery *see* Mansa
Fort Rousset *see* Owando
Fort-Royal *see* Fort-de-France
12 *I10* **Fort Rupert** *prev.* Rupert House. Québec, SE Canada
8 *H13* **Fort St. James** British Columbia, W Canada
9 *N12* **Fort St. John** British Columbia, W Canada
Fort Sandeman *see* Zhob
9 *Q14* **Fort Saskatchewan** Alberta, SW Canada
27 *R6* **Fort Scott** Kansas, C USA
12 *E6* **Fort Severn** Ontario, C Canada
27 *R10* **Fort Shawnee** Ohio, N USA
144 *E14* **Fort-Shevchenko** Mangistau, W Kazakhstan
Fort-Sibut *see* Sibut
Fort Simpson *var.* Simpson. Northwest Territories, W Canada
8 *I10* **Fort Smith** Northwest Territories, W Canada
27 *R10* **Fort Smith** Arkansas, C USA
37 *T13* **Fort Stanton** New Mexico, SW USA
24 *L9* **Fort Stockton** Texas, SW USA
37 *U12* **Fort Sumner** New Mexico, SW USA
26 *K8* **Fort Supply** Oklahoma, C USA
26 *K8* **Fort Supply Lake** ⊜ Oklahoma, C USA
29 *O10* **Fort Thompson** South Dakota, N USA
Fort-Trinquet *see* Bir Mogrein
105 *R12* **Fortuna** Murcia, SE Spain
34 *J1* **Fortuna** California, W USA
28 *J2* **Fortuna** North Dakota, N USA
23 *T5* **Fort Valley** Georgia, SE USA
9 *P11* **Fort Vermilion** Alberta, W Canada
Fort Victoria *see* Masvingo
31 *P13* **Fortville** Indiana, N USA
23 *P9* **Fort Walton Beach** Florida, SE USA
31 *P12* **Fort Wayne** Indiana, N USA
96 *H10* **Fort William** N Scotland, UK
25 *T6* **Fort Worth** Texas, SW USA
28 *M7* **Fort Yates** North Dakota, N USA
39 *S7* **Fort Yukon** Alaska, USA
Forum Alieni *see* Ferrara
Forum Julii *see* Fréjus
Forum Livii *see* Forlì

♦ Country ◇ Dependent Territory ◈ Administrative Regions ▲ Mountain 𝔙 Volcano ⊜ Lake
● Country Capital ○ Dependent Territory Capital ✈ International Airport ▲▲ Mountain Range ♒ River ▩ Reservoir

FOULNESS ISLAND – GABLONZ AN DER NEISSE

97 P21 **Foulness Island** *island* SE England, UK
185 F15 **Foulwind, Cape** *headland* South Island, New Zealand
79 E15 **Foumban** Ouest, NW Cameroon
172 H13 **Foumbouni** Grande Comore, NW Comoros
195 N8 **Foundation Ice Stream** *glacier* Antarctica
37 T6 **Fountain** Colorado, C USA
36 L4 **Fountain Green** Utah, W USA
21 P11 **Fountain Inn** South Carolina, SE USA
27 S11 **Fourche LaFave River** ≈ Arkansas, C USA
33 Z13 **Four Corners** Wyoming, C USA
103 Q2 **Fourmies** Nord, N France
38 J17 **Four Mountains, Islands of** *island group* Aleutian Islands, Alaska, USA
173 P17 **Fournaise, Piton de la** ▲ SE Réunion
14 J8 **Fournière, Lac** ◎ Québec, SE Canada
115 L20 **Foúrnoi** *island* Dodekánisa, Greece, Aegean Sea
64 K13 **Four North Fracture Zone** *tectonic feature* W Atlantic Ocean
Fouron-Saint-Martin *see* Sint-Martens-Voeren
30 L3 **Fourteen Mile Point** *headland* Michigan, N USA
Fou-shan *see* Fushun
76 I13 **Fouta Djallon** *var.* Futa Jallon. ▲▲ W Guinea
185 C25 **Foveaux Strait** *strait* S New Zealand
35 Q11 **Fowler** California, W USA
37 U6 **Fowler** Colorado, C USA
31 N12 **Fowler** Indiana, N USA
182 D7 **Fowlers Bay** *bay* South Australia
25 R13 **Fowlerton** Texas, SW USA
142 M3 **Fowman** *var.* Fuman, Fumen. Gīlān, NW Iran
65 C25 **Fox Bay East** West Falkland, Falkland Islands
65 C25 **Fox Bay West** West Falkland, Falkland Islands
14 J14 **Foxboro** Ontario, SE Canada
9 O14 **Fox Creek** Alberta, W Canada
64 G5 **Foxe Basin** *sea* Nunavut, N Canada
64 G5 **Foxe Channel** *channel* Nunavut, N Canada
95 I16 **Foxen** ◎ C Sweden
9 Q7 **Foxe Peninsula** *peninsula* Baffin Island, Nunavut, NE Canada
185 E19 **Fox Glacier** West Coast, South Island, New Zealand
38 L17 **Fox Islands** *island* Aleutian Islands, Alaska, USA
30 M10 **Fox Lake** Illinois, N USA
9 V12 **Fox Mine** Manitoba, C Canada
35 R3 **Fox Mountain** ▲ Nevada, W USA
65 E25 **Fox Point** *headland* East Falkland, Falkland Islands
30 M11 **Fox River** ≈ Illinois/ Wisconsin, N USA
30 L7 **Fox River** ≈ Wisconsin, N USA
184 L13 **Foxton** Manawatu-Wanganui, North Island, New Zealand
9 S16 **Fox Valley** Saskatchewan, S Canada
9 W16 **Foxwarren** Manitoba, S Canada
97 E14 **Foyle, Lough** *Ir.* Loch Feabhail. *inlet* N Ireland
194 H5 **Foyn Coast** *physical region* Antarctica
104 I2 **Foz** Galicia, NW Spain
60 I12 **Foz do Areia, Represa de** ▣ S Brazil
59 A16 **Foz do Breu** Acre, W Brazil
83 A16 **Foz do Cunene** Namibe, SW Angola
60 G12 **Foz do Iguaçu** Paraná, S Brazil
58 C12 **Foz do Mamoriá** Amazonas, NW Brazil
105 T6 **Fraga** Aragón, NE Spain
44 F5 **Fragoso, Cayo** *island* C Cuba
61 G18 **Fraile Muerto** Cerro Largo, NE Uruguay
99 H21 **Fraire** Namur, S Belgium
99 L21 **Fraiture, Baraque de** *hill* SE Belgium
Frakštát *see* Hlohovec
197 S10 **Fram Basin** *var.* Amundsen Basin. *undersea feature* Arctic Ocean
99 F20 **Frameries** Hainaut, S Belgium
19 O11 **Framingham** Massachusetts, NE USA
60 L7 **Franca** São Paulo, S Brazil
187 O15 **Français, Récif des** *reef* W New Caledonia
107 K14 **Francavilla al Mare** Abruzzi, C Italy
107 P18 **Francavilla Fontana** Puglia, SE Italy
102 M8 **France** *off.* French Republic, *It./Sp.* Francia; *prev.* Gaul, Gaule, *Lat.* Gallia. ◆ *republic* W Europe
45 O8 **Francés Viejo, Cabo** *headland* NE Dominican Republic
79 F19 **Franceville** *var.* Massoukou, Masuku. Haut-Ogooué, E Gabon
79 F19 **Franceville** ✈ Haut-Ogooué, E Gabon
Francfort *see* Frankfurt am Main
103 T8 **Franche-Comté** ◐ *region* E France
Francia *see* France
29 O11 **Francis Case, Lake** ▣ South Dakota, N USA
60 H12 **Francisco Beltrão** Paraná, S Brazil
Francisco I. Madero *see* Villa Madero
61 A21 **Francisco Madero** Buenos Aires, E Argentina
42 H6 **Francisco Morazán** *prev.* Tegucigalpa. ◐ *department* C Honduras
83 J18 **Francistown** North East, NE Botswana
Franconian Forest *see* Frankenwald
Franconian Jura *see* Fränkische Alb
98 K6 **Franeker** *Fris.* Frjentsjer. Friesland, N Netherlands
Frankenalb *see* Fränkische Alb
101 H16 **Frankenberg** Hessen, C Germany
101 J20 **Frankenhöhe** *hill range* C Germany
31 R8 **Frankenmuth** Michigan, N USA
101 F20 **Frankenstein** *hill* W Germany
Frankenstein/Frankenstein in Schlesien *see* Ząbkowice Śląskie
101 G20 **Frankenthal** Rheinland-Pfalz, W Germany
101 L18 **Frankenwald** *Eng.* Franconian Forest. ▲▲ C Germany
44 J12 **Frankfield** C Jamaica
14 J14 **Frankford** Ontario, SE Canada
31 O13 **Frankfort** Indiana, N USA
27 O3 **Frankfort** Kansas, C USA
20 L5 **Frankfort** *state capital* Kentucky, S USA
Frankfort on the Main *see* Frankfurt am Main
Frankfurt *see* Frankfurt am Main, Germany
Frankfurt *see* Słubice, Poland
101 G18 **Frankfurt am Main** *var.* Frankfurt, *Fr.* Francfort; *prev. Eng.* Frankfort on the Main. Hessen, SW Germany
100 Q12 **Frankfurt an der Oder** Brandenburg, E Germany
101 L21 **Fränkische Alb** *var.* Frankenalb, *Eng.* Franconian Jura. ▲▲ S Germany
101 I18 **Fränkische Saale** ≈ C Germany
101 L19 **Fränkische Schweiz** *hill range* C Germany
23 R4 **Franklin** Georgia, SE USA
31 P14 **Franklin** Indiana, N USA
20 J7 **Franklin** Kentucky, S USA
22 I9 **Franklin** Louisiana, S USA
29 O17 **Franklin** Nebraska, C USA
21 N10 **Franklin** North Carolina, SE USA
18 C13 **Franklin** Pennsylvania, NE USA
20 J9 **Franklin** Tennessee, S USA
25 U9 **Franklin** Texas, SW USA
21 X7 **Franklin** Virginia, NE USA
21 T4 **Franklin** West Virginia, NE USA
30 M9 **Franklin** Wisconsin, N USA
8 I6 **Franklin Bay** *inlet* Northwest Territories, N Canada
32 K7 **Franklin D. Roosevelt Lake** ▣ Washington, NW USA
35 W4 **Franklin Lake** ◎ Nevada, W USA
185 B22 **Franklin Mountains** ▲▲ South Island, New Zealand
39 R5 **Franklin Mountains** ▲▲ Alaska, USA
39 N4 **Franklin, Point** *headland* Alaska, USA
183 O17 **Franklin River** ≈ Tasmania, SE Australia
22 K8 **Franklinton** Louisiana, S USA
21 U9 **Franklinton** North Carolina, SE USA
Frankstadt *see* Frenštát pod Radhoštěm
25 V7 **Frankston** Texas, SW USA
33 U12 **Frannie** Wyoming, C USA
15 U5 **Franquelin** Québec, SE Canada
15 U5 **Franquelin** ≈ Québec, SE Canada
83 C18 **Fransfontein** Kunene, NW Namibia
93 H17 **Fränsta** Västernorrland, C Sweden
122 J3 **Frantsa-Iosifa, Zemlya** *Eng.* Franz Josef Land. *island group* N Russian Federation
185 E18 **Franz Josef Glacier** West Coast, South Island, New Zealand
Franz Josef Land *see* Frantsa-Iosifa, Zemlya
Franz-Josef Spitze *see* Gerlachovský štít
101 L23 **Franz Josef Strauss** *abbrev.* F.J.S.. ✈ (München) Bayern, SE Germany
107 A19 **Frasca, Capo della** *headland* Sardegna, Italy, C Mediterranean Sea
107 I15 **Frascati** Lazio, C Italy
9 N14 **Fraser** ≈ British Columbia, SW Canada
83 G24 **Fraserburg** Western Cape, SW South Africa
96 L8 **Fraserburgh** NE Scotland, UK
181 Z9 **Fraser Island** *var.* Great Sandy Island. *island* Queensland, E Australia
10 L14 **Fraser Lake** British Columbia, SW Canada
10 L15 **Fraser Plateau** *plateau* British Columbia, SW Canada
184 P10 **Frasertown** Hawke's Bay, North Island, New Zealand
99 E19 **Frasnes-lez-Buissenal** Hainaut, SW Belgium
108 I7 **Frastanz** Vorarlberg, NW Austria
14 B8 **Frater** Ontario, S Canada
Frauenbach *see* Baia Mare
Frauenburg *see* Saldus, Latvia
Frauenburg *see* Frombork, Poland
108 H6 **Frauenfeld** Thurgau, NE Switzerland
109 Z5 **Frauenkirchen** Burgenland, E Austria
61 D19 **Fray Bentos** Río Negro, W Uruguay
61 F19 **Fray Marcos** Florida, S Uruguay
29 S6 **Frazee** Minnesota, N USA
104 M5 **Frechilla** Castilla-León, N Spain
30 I4 **Frederic** Wisconsin, N USA
95 G23 **Fredericia** Vejle, C Denmark
21 W3 **Frederick** Maryland, NE USA
26 L12 **Frederick** Oklahoma, C USA
29 P7 **Frederick** South Dakota, N USA
29 X13 **Fredericksburg** Iowa, C USA
25 R10 **Fredericksburg** Texas, SW USA
21 W5 **Fredericksburg** Virginia, NE USA
39 X13 **Frederick Sound** *sound* Alaska, USA
27 X6 **Fredericktown** Missouri, C USA
60 H13 **Frederico Westphalen** Rio Grande do Sul, S Brazil
13 O15 **Fredericton** *province capital* New Brunswick, SE Canada
95 I22 **Frederiksborg** *off* Frederiksborgs Amt. ◐ *county* E Denmark
Frederiksborgs Amt *see* Frederiksborg
Frederikshåb *see* Paamiut
95 H19 **Frederikshavn** *prev.* Fladstrand. Nordjylland, N Denmark
95 J22 **Frederikssund** Frederiksborg, E Denmark
45 T9 **Frederiksted** Saint Croix, S Virgin Islands (US)
95 I22 **Frederiksværk** *var.* Frederiksværk og Hanehoved. Frederiksborg, E Denmark
Frederiksværk og Hanehoved *see* Frederiksværk
54 E9 **Fredonia** Antioquia, W Colombia
36 K8 **Fredonia** Arizona, SW USA
27 P7 **Fredonia** Kansas, C USA
18 C11 **Fredonia** New York, NE USA
35 P4 **Fredonyer Pass** *pass* California, W USA
93 I15 **Fredrika** Västerbotten, N Sweden
95 L14 **Fredriksberg** Dalarna, C Sweden
Fredrikshald *see* Halden
Fredrikshamn *see* Hamina
95 H16 **Fredrikstad** Østfold, S Norway
30 K16 **Freeburg** Illinois, N USA
18 K15 **Freehold** New Jersey, NE USA
18 H14 **Freeland** Pennsylvania, NE USA
182 J5 **Freeling Heights** ▲ South Australia
35 Q7 **Freel Peak** ▲ California, W USA
9 Z9 **Freels, Cape** *headland* Newfoundland, Newfoundland and Labrador, E Canada
29 Q11 **Freeman** South Dakota, N USA
44 G1 **Freeport** Grand Bahama Island, N Bahamas
30 L10 **Freeport** Illinois, N USA
25 W12 **Freeport** Texas, SW USA
44 G1 **Freeport** ✈ Grand Bahama Island, N Bahamas
25 R14 **Freer** Texas, SW USA
83 I22 **Free State** *off.* Free State Province; *prev.* Orange Free State, *Afr.* Oranje Vrystaat. ◐ *province* C South Africa
Free State *see* Maryland
Free State Province *see* Free State
76 G15 **Freetown** ● (Sierra Leone) W Sierra Leone
172 J16 **Frégate** *island* Inner Islands, NE Seychelles
104 J12 **Fregenal de la Sierra** Extremadura, W Spain
182 C2 **Fregon** South Australia
102 H5 **Fréhel, Cap** *headland* NW France
94 F8 **Frei** Møre og Romsdal, S Norway
101 O16 **Freiberg** Sachsen, E Germany
101 O16 **Freiberger Mulde** ≈ E Germany
Freiburg *see* Freiburg im Breisgau, Germany
Freiburg *see* Fribourg, Switzerland
101 F23 **Freiburg im Breisgau** *var.* Freiburg, *Fr.* Fribourg-en-Brisgau. Baden-Württemberg, SW Germany
Freiburg in Schlesien *see* Świebodzice
Freie Hansestadt Bremen *see* Bremen
Freie und Hansestadt Hamburg *see* Brandenburg
101 L22 **Freising** Bayern, SE Germany
109 T3 **Freistadt** Oberösterreich, N Austria
Freistadtl *see* Hlohovec
101 O16 **Freital** Sachsen, E Germany
Freiwaldau *see* Jeseník
104 J6 **Freixo de Espada à Cinta** Bragança, N Portugal
103 U15 **Fréjus** *anc.* Forum Julii. Var, SE France
180 I13 **Fremantle** Western Australia
35 N9 **Fremont** California, W USA
31 Q11 **Fremont** Indiana, N USA
29 W15 **Fremont** Iowa, C USA
31 P8 **Fremont** Michigan, N USA
29 R15 **Fremont** Nebraska, C USA
31 S11 **Fremont** Ohio, N USA
33 T14 **Fremont Peak** ▲ Wyoming, C USA
36 M6 **Fremont River** ≈ Utah, W USA
21 O9 **French Broad River** ≈ Tennessee, S USA
21 N5 **Frenchburg** Kentucky, S USA
18 C12 **French Creek** ≈ Pennsylvania, NE USA
32 K15 **Frenchglen** Oregon, NW USA
55 Y10 **French Guiana** *var.* Guiana, Guyane. ◇ *French overseas department* N South America
French Guinea *see* Guinea
31 O15 **French Lick** Indiana, N USA
185 J14 **French Pass** Marlborough, South Island, New Zealand
191 T11 **French Polynesia** ◇ *French overseas territory* C Polynesia
French Republic *see* France
14 F11 **French River** ≈ Ontario, S Canada
French Somaliland *see* Djibouti
173 P12 **French Southern and Antarctic Territories** *Fr.* Terres Australes et Antarctiques Françaises. ◇ *French overseas territory* S Indian Ocean
French Sudan *see* Mali
French Territory of the Afars and Issas *see* Djibouti
French Togoland *see* Togo
74 J6 **Frenda** NW Algeria
111 I18 **Frenštát pod Radhoštěm** *Ger.* Frankstadt. Moravskoslezský Kraj, E Czech Republic
76 M17 **Fresco** S Ivory Coast
195 U16 **Freshfield, Cape** *headland* Antarctica
40 L10 **Fresnillo** Zacatecas, C Mexico
Fresnillo de González Echeverría *see* Fresnillo
35 Q10 **Fresno** California, W USA
Freu, Cabo del *see* Freu, Cap des
105 Y9 **Freu, Cap des** *var.* Cabo del Freu. *cape* Mallorca, Spain, W Mediterranean Sea
101 G22 **Freudenstadt** Baden-Württemberg, SW Germany
Freudenthal *see* Bruntál
183 Q17 **Freycinet Peninsula** *peninsula* Tasmania, SE Australia
76 H14 **Fria** Guinée-Maritime, W Guinea
83 A17 **Fria, Cape** *headland* NW Namibia
35 Q10 **Friant** California, W USA
62 K8 **Frías** Catamarca, N Argentina
108 D9 **Fribourg** *Ger.* Freiburg. Fribourg, W Switzerland
108 C9 **Fribourg** *Ger.* Freiburg. ◐ *canton* W Switzerland
Fribourg-en-Brisgau *see* Freiburg im Breisgau
32 G7 **Friday Harbor** San Juan Islands, Washington, NW USA
Friedau *see* Ormož
101 K23 **Friedberg** Bayern, S Germany
101 H18 **Friedberg** Hessen, W Germany
Friedeberg Neumark *see* Strzelce Krajeńskie
Friedek-Mistek *see* Frýdek-Místek
Friedland *see* Pravdinsk
101 I24 **Friedrichshafen** Baden-Württemberg, S Germany
Friedrichstadt *see* Jaunjelgava
29 Q16 **Friend** Nebraska, C USA
Friendly Islands *see* Tonga
55 V9 **Friendship** Coronie, N Surinam
30 L7 **Friendship** Wisconsin, N USA
109 T8 **Friesach** Kärnten, S Austria
Friesche Eilanden *see* Frisian Islands
101 F22 **Friesenheim** Baden-Württemberg, SW Germany
Friesische Inseln *see* Frisian Islands
98 K6 **Friesland** ◐ *province* N Netherlands
60 Q10 **Frio, Cabo** *headland* SE Brazil
24 M3 **Friona** Texas, SW USA
42 L12 **Frío, Río** ≈ N Costa Rica
25 R13 **Frio River** ≈ Texas, SW USA
99 M25 **Frisange** Luxembourg, S Luxembourg
Frisches Haff *see* Vistula Lagoon
36 J6 **Frisco Peak** ▲ Utah, W USA
84 F9 **Frisian Islands** *Dut.* Friesche Eilanden, *Ger.* Friesische Inseln. *island group* N Europe
18 L12 **Frissell, Mount** ▲ Connecticut, NE USA
95 J19 **Fristad** Västra Götaland, S Sweden
25 N2 **Fritch** Texas, SW USA
95 J19 **Fritsla** Västra Götaland, S Sweden
101 H16 **Fritzlar** Hessen, C Germany
106 H6 **Friuli-Venezia Giulia** ◐ *region* NE Italy
Frjentsjer *see* Franeker
196 L13 **Frobisher Bay** *inlet* Baffin Island, Nunavut, NE Canada
Frobisher Bay *see* Iqaluit
9 S12 **Frobisher Lake** ◎ Saskatchewan, C Canada
94 G7 **Frohavet** *sound* C Norway
Frohenbruck *see* Veselí nad Lužnicí
109 V7 **Frohnleiten** Steiermark, SE Austria
99 G22 **Froidchapelle** Hainaut, S Belgium
127 O9 **Frolovo** Volgogradskaya Oblast', SW Russian Federation
110 K7 **Frombork** *Ger.* Frauenburg. Warmińsko-Mazurskie, NE Poland
97 L22 **Frome** SW England, UK
182 I4 **Frome Creek** *seasonal river* South Australia
182 J6 **Frome Downs** South Australia
182 J5 **Frome, Lake** *salt lake* South Australia
Fronicken *see* Wronki
104 H10 **Fronteira** Portalegre, C Portugal
40 M7 **Frontera** Coahuila de Zaragoza, NE Mexico
41 U14 **Frontera** Tabasco, SE Mexico
40 G3 **Fronteras** Sonora, NW Mexico
103 Q16 **Frontignan** Hérault, S France
54 D8 **Frontino** Antioquia, NW Colombia
21 V4 **Front Royal** Virginia, NE USA
107 J16 **Frosinone** *anc.* Frusino. Lazio, C Italy
107 K16 **Frosolone** Molise, C Italy
25 U7 **Frost** Texas, SW USA
21 U2 **Frostburg** Maryland, NE USA
23 X13 **Frostproof** Florida, SE USA
Frostviken *see* Kvarnbergsvattnet
95 M15 **Frövi** Örebro, C Sweden
94 F7 **Frøya** *island* W Norway
37 P5 **Fruita** Colorado, C USA
28 J9 **Fruitdale** South Dakota, N USA
23 W11 **Fruitland Park** Florida, SE USA
Frumentum *see* Formentera
147 S11 **Frunze** Batkenskaya Oblast', SW Kyrgyzstan
Frunze *see* Bishkek
117 O9 **Frunzivka** Odes'ka Oblast', SW Ukraine
Frusino *see* Frosinone
108 E9 **Frutigen** Bern, W Switzerland
111 I17 **Frýdek-Místek** *Ger.* Friedek-Mistek. Moravskoslezský Kraj, E Czech Republic
193 V16 **Fua'amotu** Tongatapu, S Tonga
190 A9 **Fuafatu** *island* Funafuti Atoll, C Tuvalu
190 A9 **Fuagea** *island* Funafuti Atoll, C Tuvalu
190 B8 **Fualifeke** *atoll* C Tuvalu
190 A8 **Fualopa** *island* Funafuti Atoll, C Tuvalu
151 K22 **Fuammulah** *var.* Gnaviyani Atoll. *atoll* S Maldives
161 R11 **Fu'an** Fujian, SE China
Fu-chien *see* Fujian
Fu-chou *see* Fuzhou
164 G13 **Fuchū** *var.* Hutyû. Hiroshima, Honshū, SW Japan
160 M13 **Fuchuan** Guangxi Zhuangzu Zizhiqu, S China
165 R8 **Fudai** Iwate, Honshū, C Japan
161 S11 **Fuding** *var* Tongshan. Fujian, SE China
81 J20 **Fudua** *spring/well* S Kenya
104 M16 **Fuengirola** Andalucía, S Spain
104 J12 **Fuente de Cantos** Extremadura, W Spain
104 J11 **Fuente del Maestre** Extremadura, W Spain
104 L12 **Fuente Obejuna** Andalucía, S Spain
104 L6 **Fuentesaúco** Castilla-León, N Spain
62 O3 **Fuerte Olimpo** *var.* Olimpo. Alto Paraguay, NE Paraguay
40 H8 **Fuerte, Río** ≈ C Mexico
64 Q11 **Fuerteventura** *island* Islas Canarias, Spain, NE Atlantic Ocean
141 S14 **Fughmah** *var.* Faghman, Fugma. C Yemen
92 M2 **Fuglehuken** *headland* W Svalbard
Fuglø *see* Fugloy
95 B18 **Fugloy** *Dan.* Fuglø. *island* NE Faeroe Islands
197 T15 **Fugløya Bank** *undersea feature* E Norwegian Sea
Fugma *see* Fughmah
81 K16 **Fugugo** *spring/well* NE Kenya
158 L2 **Fuhai** *var.* Burultokay. Xinjiang Uygur Zizhiqu, NW China
161 P10 **Fu He** ≈ S China
Fuhkien *see* Fujian
100 J9 **Fuhlsbüttel** ✈ (Hamburg) Hamburg, N Germany
101 L14 **Fuhne** ≈ C Germany
Fu-hsin *see* Fuxin
Fujairah *see* Al Fujayrah
164 M14 **Fuji** *var.* Huzi. Shizuoka, Honshū, S Japan
161 Q12 **Fujian** *var.* Fu-chien, Fuhkien, Fukien, Min, Fujian Sheng. ◐ *province* SE China
160 I9 **Fu Jiang** ≈ C China
Fujian Sheng *see* Fujian
164 M14 **Fujieda** *var.* Huzieda. Shizuoka, Honshū, S Japan
Fuji, Mount/Fujiyama *see* Fuji-san
163 Y7 **Fujin** Heilongjiang, NE China
164 M13 **Fujinomiya** *var.* Huzinomiya. Shizuoka, Honshū, S Japan
164 N13 **Fuji-san** *var.* Fujiyama, *Eng.* Mount Fuji. ▲ Honshū, SE Japan
165 N14 **Fujisawa** *var.* Huzisawa. Kanagawa, Honshū, S Japan
165 T3 **Fukagawa** *var.* Hukagawa. Hokkaidō, NE Japan
158 L5 **Fukang** Xinjiang Uygur Zizhiqu, W China
165 P7 **Fukaura** Aomori, Honshū, C Japan
193 W15 **Fukave** *island* Tongatapu Group, S Tonga
Fukien *see* Fujian
164 J13 **Fukuchiyama** *var.* Hukutiyama. Kyōto, Honshū, SW Japan
164 A14 **Fukue** *var.* Hukue. Nagasaki, Fukue-jima, SW Japan
164 A13 **Fukue-jima** *island* Gotō-rettō, SW Japan
164 K12 **Fukui** *var.* Hukui. Fukui, Honshū, SW Japan
164 K12 **Fukui** *off.* Fukui-ken, *var.* Hukui. ◐ *prefecture* Honshū, SW Japan
Fukui-ken *see* Fukui
164 D13 **Fukuoka** *var.* Hukuoka, *hist.* Najima. Fukuoka, Kyūshū, SW Japan
164 D13 **Fukuoka** *off.* Fukuoka-ken, *var.* Hukuoka. ◐ *prefecture* Kyūshū, SW Japan
Fukuoka-ken *see* Fukuoka
165 Q6 **Fukushima** Hokkaidō, NE Japan
165 Q12 **Fukushima** *off.* Fukushima-ken, *var.* Hukusima. ◐ *prefecture* Honshū, C Japan
Fukushima-ken *see* Fukushima
164 G13 **Fukuyama** *var.* Hukuyama. Hiroshima, Honshū, SW Japan
76 G13 **Fulacunda** C Guinea-Bissau
129 P8 **Fūlādī, Kūh-e** ▲ E Afghanistan
187 Z15 **Fulaga** *island* Lau Group, E Fiji
101 I17 **Fulda** Hessen, C Germany
29 S10 **Fulda** Minnesota, N USA
101 I16 **Fulda** ≈ C Germany
Fülek *see* Fil'akovo
Fulin *see* Hanyuan
160 K10 **Fuling** Sichuan, C China
35 T15 **Fullerton** California, SE USA
29 P15 **Fullerton** Nebraska, C USA
108 M8 **Fulpmes** Tirol, W Austria
20 G8 **Fulton** Kentucky, S USA
23 N2 **Fulton** Mississippi, S USA
27 V4 **Fulton** Missouri, C USA
18 H9 **Fulton** New York, NE USA
Fuman/Fumen *see* Fowman
103 R3 **Fumay** Ardennes, N France
102 M13 **Fumel** Lot-et-Garonne, SW France
190 B10 **Funafara** *atoll* C Tuvalu
190 C9 **Funafuti** ✈ Funafuti Atoll, C Tuvalu
Funafuti *see* Fongafale
190 F8 **Funafuti Atoll** *atoll* C Tuvalu
Funan *see* Fusui
190 B9 **Funangongo** *atoll* C Tuvalu
93 F17 **Funäsdalen** Jämtland, C Sweden
64 O6 **Funchal** Madeira, Portugal, NE Atlantic Ocean
64 P5 **Funchal** ✈ Madeira, Portugal, NE Atlantic Ocean
54 F5 **Fundación** Magdalena, N Colombia
104 I8 **Fundão** *var.* Fundão. Castelo Branco, C Portugal
Fundão *see* Fundão
13 O16 **Fundy, Bay of** *bay* Canada/USA
Fünen *see* Fyn
54 C13 **Fúnes** Nariño, SW Colombia
Fünfkirchen *see* Pécs
83 M19 **Funhalouro** Inhambane, S Mozambique
161 R6 **Funing** Jiangsu, E China
160 I14 **Funing** *var.* Xinhua. Yunnan, SW China
160 M7 **Funiu Shan** ▲▲ C China
77 U13 **Funtua** Katsina, N Nigeria
161 R12 **Fuqing** Fujian, SE China
83 M14 **Furancungo** Tete, NW Mozambique
116 I15 **Furculeşti** Teleorman, S Romania
Füred *see* Balatonfüred
165 W4 **Füren-ko** ◎ Hokkaidō, NE Japan
143 R12 **Fūrg** Fārs, S Iran
Furluk *see* Fârliug
Fürmanov/Furmanovka *see* Moyynkum
Furmanovo *see* Zhalpaktal
59 L20 **Furnas, Represa de** ▣ SE Brazil
183 Q14 **Furneaux Group** *island group* Tasmania, SE Australia
Furnes *see* Veurne
160 J10 **Furong Jiang** ≈ S China
138 I5 **Furqlus** Ḩimş, W Syria
100 F12 **Fürstenau** Niedersachsen, NW Germany
109 X8 **Fürstenfeld** Steiermark, SE Austria
101 L23 **Fürstenfeldbruck** Bayern, S Germany
100 P12 **Fürstenwalde** Brandenburg, NE Germany
101 K20 **Fürth** Bayern, S Germany
109 W3 **Furth bei Göttweig** Niederösterreich, NW Austria
165 R3 **Furubira** Hokkaidō, NE Japan
94 L12 **Furudal** Dalarna, C Sweden
164 L12 **Furukawa** Gifu, Honshū, SW Japan
165 Q10 **Furukawa** *var.* Hurukawa. Miyagi, Honshū, C Japan
54 F10 **Fusagasugá** Cundinamarca, C Colombia
Fusan *see* Pusan
Fushë-Arëzi/Fushë-Arrësi *see* Fushë-Arrëz
113 L18 **Fushë-Arrëz** *var.* Fushë-Arëzi, Fushë-Arrësi. Shkodër, N Albania
Fushë-Kruja *see* Fushë-Krujë
113 K19 **Fushë-Krujë** *var.* Fushë-Kruja. Durrës, C Albania
163 V12 **Fushun** *var.* Fou-shan, Fu-shun. Liaoning, NE China
Fu-shun *see* Fushun
Fusin *see* Fuxin
108 G10 **Fusio** Ticino, S Switzerland
163 X11 **Fusong** Jilin, NE China
101 K24 **Füssen** Bayern, S Germany
160 K15 **Fusui** *prev.* Funan. Guangxi Zhuangzu Zizhiqu, S China
Futa Jallon *see* Fouta Djallon
63 G18 **Futaleufú** Los Lagos, S Chile
112 K10 **Futog** Vojvodina, NW Serbia
165 O14 **Futtsu** *var.* Huttu. Chiba, Honshū, S Japan
187 S15 **Futuna** *island* S Vanuatu
190 D12 **Futuna, Île** *island* S Wallis and Futuna
161 Q11 **Futun Xi** ≈ SE China
160 L5 **Fuxian** *var.* Fu Xian. Shaanxi, C China
Fuxian *see* Wafangdian
Fu Xian *see* Fuxian
160 G13 **Fuxian Hu** ▣ SW China
163 U12 **Fuxin** *var.* Fou-hsin, Fu-hsin, Fusin. Liaoning, NE China
Fuxing *see* Wangmo
161 P7 **Fuyang** Anhui, E China
161 O4 **Fuyang He** ≈ E China
163 U7 **Fuyu** Heilongjiang, NE China
163 Z6 **Fuyuan** Heilongjiang, NE China
Fuyu/Fu-yü *see* Songyuan
158 M3 **Fuyun** *var.* Koktokay. Xinjiang Uygur Zizhiqu, NW China
111 L22 **Füzesabony** Heves, E Hungary
161 R12 **Fuzhou** *var.* Foochow, Fu-chou. *province capital* Fujian, SE China
137 W13 **Füzuli** *Rus.* Fizuli. SW Azerbaijan
119 I20 **Fyadory** *Rus.* Fëdory. Brestskaya Voblasts', SW Belarus
95 G24 **Fyn** *off.* Fyns Amt, *var.* Fünen. ◐ *county* C Denmark
95 G23 **Fyn** *Ger.* Fünen. *island* C Denmark
96 H12 **Fyne, Loch** *inlet* W Scotland, UK
Fyns Amt *see* Fyn
95 E16 **Fyresvatnet** ◎ S Norway
FYR Macedonia/FYROM *see* Macedonia, FYR
Fyzabad *see* Feyẓābād

G

Gaafu Alifu Atoll *see* North Huvadhu Atoll
81 O14 **Gaalkacyo** *var.* Galka'yo, *It.* Galcaio. Mudug, C Somalia
146 J11 **Gabakly** *Rus.* Kabakly. Lebap Welaýaty, NE Turkmenistan
114 H8 **Gabare** Vratsa, NW Bulgaria
102 K15 **Gabas** ≈ SW France
Gabasumdo *see* Tongde
35 T7 **Gabbs** Nevada, W USA
82 B12 **Gabela** Cuanza Sul, W Angola
Gaberones *see* Gaborone
189 X14 **Gabert** *island* Caroline Islands, E Micronesia
74 M7 **Gabès** *var.* Qābis. E Tunisia
74 M6 **Gabès, Golfe de** *Ar.* Khalīj Qābis. *gulf* E Tunisia
Gablonz an der Neisse *see* Jablonec nad Nisou

◆ Country
● Country Capital
◇ Dependent Territory
○ Dependent Territory Capital
◐ Administrative Regions
✈ International Airport
▲ Mountain
▲▲ Mountain Range
Volcano
≈ River
◎ Lake
▣ Reservoir

GABLÖS – GEAVVÚ

Gablös *see* Cavalese
79 *E18* **Gabon** *off.* Gabonese Republic. ◆ *republic* C Africa
Gabonese Republic *see* Gabon
83 *I20* **Gaborone** *prev.* Gaberones. ● (Botswana) South East, SE Botswana
83 *I20* **Gaborone** ✈ South East, SE Botswana
104 *K8* **Gabriel y Galán, Embalse de** ▣ W Spain
143 *U15* **Gābrīk, Rūd-e** ↝ SE Iran
114 *J9* **Gabrovo** Gabrovo, N Bulgaria
114 *J9* **Gabrovo** ◈ *province* N Bulgaria
76 *H12* **Gabú** *prev.* Nova Lamego. E Guinea-Bissau
29 *O6* **Gackle** North Dakota, N USA
113 *I15* **Gacko** Repulika Srpska, S Bosnia and Herzegovina
155 *F17* **Gadag** Karnātaka, W India
93 *G15* **Gäddede** Jämtland, C Sweden
159 *S12* **Gadê** Qinghai, C China
Gades/Gadier/Gadir/Gadire *see* Cádiz
105 *P15* **Gádor, Sierra de** ▲▲ S Spain
149 *S15* **Gadra** Sind, SE Pakistan
23 *Q3* **Gadsden** Alabama, S USA
36 *H15* **Gadsden** Arizona, SW USA
Gadyach *see* Hadyach
79 *H15* **Gadzi** Mambéré-Kadéï, SW Central African Republic
116 *J13* **Găeşti** Dâmboviţa, S Romania
107 *J17* **Gaeta** Lazio, C Italy
107 *J17* **Gaeta, Golfo di** *var.* Gulf of Gaeta. *gulf* C Italy
Gaeta, Gulf of *see* Gaeta, Golfo di
188 *L14* **Gaferut** *atoll* Caroline Islands, W Micronesia
21 *Q10* **Gaffney** South Carolina, SE USA
Gäfle *see* Gävle
Gäfleborg *see* Gävleborg
74 *M6* **Gafsa** *var.* Qafşah. W Tunisia
Gafurov *see* Ghafurov
147 *O10* **Gagarin** Jizzax Viloyati, C Uzbekistan
101 *G21* **Gaggenau** Baden-Württemberg, SW Germany
188 *F16* **Gagil Tamil** *var.* Gagil-Tomil. *island* Caroline Islands, W Micronesia
Gagil-Tomil *see* Gagil Tamil
127 *O4* **Gagino** Nizhegorodskaya Oblast', W Russian Federation
107 *Q19* **Gagliano del Capo** Puglia, SE Italy
94 *L13* **Gagnef** Dalarna, C Sweden
76 *M17* **Gagnoa** C Ivory Coast
13 *N10* **Gagnon** Québec, E Canada
Gago Coutinho *see* Lumbala N'Guimbo
137 *P8* **Gagra** NW Georgia
31 *S13* **Gahanna** Ohio, N USA
143 *R13* **Gahkom** Hormozgān, S Iran
Gahnpa *see* Ganta
57 *Q19* **Gaíba, Laguna** ◎ E Bolivia
153 *T13* **Gaibanda** *var.* Gaibandah. Rajshahi, NW Bangladesh
Gaibandah *see* Gaibanda
Gaibhlte, Cnoc Mór na n *see* Galtymore Mountain
109 *R9* **Gail** ↝ S Austria
101 *I21* **Gaildorf** Baden-Württemberg, S Germany
103 *N15* **Gaillac** *var.* Gaillac-sur-Tarn. Tarn, S France
Gaillac-sur-Tarn *see* Gaillac
Gaillimh *see* Galway
Gaillimhe, Cuan na *see* Galway Bay
109 *Q9* **Gailtaler Alpen** ▲▲ S Austria
63 *J17* **Gaimán** Chaco, S Argentina
20 *K8* **Gainesboro** Tennessee, S USA
23 *V10* **Gainesville** Florida, SE USA
23 *T2* **Gainesville** Georgia, SE USA
27 *U8* **Gainesville** Missouri, C USA
25 *T5* **Gainesville** Texas, SW USA
109 *X5* **Gainfarn** Niederösterreich, NE Austria
97 *N18* **Gainsborough** E England, UK
182 *G6* **Gairdner, Lake** *salt lake* South Australia
Gaissane *see* Gáissát
92 *L8* **Gáissát** *var.* Gaissane. ▲▲ N Norway
43 *T15* **Gaital, Cerro** ▲ C Panama
21 *W3* **Gaithersburg** Maryland, NE USA
163 *U13* **Gaizhou** Liaoning, NE China
Gaizina Kalns *see* Gaiziņakalns
118 *H7* **Gaiziņakalns** *var.* Gaizina Kalns. ▲ E Latvia
Gajac *see* Villeneuve-sur-Lot
39 *S10* **Gakona** Alaska, USA
Galaassiya *see* Galaosiyo
Galāğil *see* Jalājil
Galam, Pulau *see* Gelam, Pulau
62 *J6* **Galán, Cerro** ▲ NW Argentina
111 *H21* **Galanta** *Hung.* Galánta. Trnavský Kraj, W Slovakia
146 *L11* **Galaosiyo** *Rus.* Galaassiya. Buxoro Viloyati, C Uzbekistan
57 *B17* **Galápagos** *off.* Provincia de Galápagos. ◈ *province* W Ecuador, E Pacific Ocean
193 *P8* **Galapagos Fracture Zone** *tectonic feature* E Pacific Ocean
Galapagos Islands *see* Colón, Archipiélago de
Galápagos, Islas de los *see* Colón, Archipiélago de
Galápagos, Provincia de *see* Galápagos
193 *S9* **Galapagos Rise** *undersea feature* E Pacific Ocean
96 *K13* **Galashiels** SE Scotland, UK
116 *M12* **Galaţi** *Ger.* Galatz. Galaţi, E Romania
116 *L12* **Galaţi** ◈ *county* E Romania
107 *Q19* **Galatina** Puglia, SE Italy
107 *Q19* **Galatone** Puglia, SE Italy
Galatz *see* Galaţi
21 *R8* **Galax** Virginia, NE USA
146 *J16* **Galaýmor** *Rus.* Kala-i-Mor. Mary Welaýaty, S Turkmenistan
Galcaio *see* Gaalkacyo
64 *P11* **Gáldar** Gran Canaria, Islas Canarias, NE Atlantic Ocean
94 *F11* **Galdhøpiggen** ▲ S Norway
40 *I4* **Galeana** Chihuahua, N Mexico
41 *O9* **Galeana** Nuevo León, NE Mexico
60 *P9* **Galeão** ✈ (Rio de Janeiro) Rio de Janeiro, SE Brazil
171 *R10* **Galela** Pulau Halmahera, E Indonesia
39 *O9* **Galena** Alaska, USA
30 *K10* **Galena** Illinois, N USA
27 *R7* **Galena** Kansas, C USA
27 *T8* **Galena** Missouri, C USA
45 *V15* **Galeota Point** *headland* Trinidad, Trinidad and Tobago
105 *P13* **Galera** Andalucía, S Spain
45 *Y16* **Galera Point** *headland* Trinidad, Trinidad and Tobago
56 *A5* **Galera, Punta** *headland* NW Ecuador
30 *K12* **Galesburg** Illinois, N USA
30 *J7* **Galesville** Wisconsin, N USA
18 *F12* **Galeton** Pennsylvania, NE USA
116 *H9* **Gâlgău** *Hung.* Galgó; *prev.* Gilgău. Sălaj, NW Romania
Galgó *see* Gâlgău
Galgóc *see* Hlohovec
81 *N15* **Galguduud** *off.* Gobolka Galguduud. ◈ *region* E Somalia
Galguduud, Gobolka *see* Galguduud
137 *Q9* **Gali** W Georgia
125 *N14* **Galich** Kostromskaya Oblast', NW Russian Federation
114 *H7* **Galiche** Vratsa, NW Bulgaria
104 *H3* **Galicia** *anc.* Gallaecia. ◈ *autonomous community* NW Spain
64 *M8* **Galicia Bank** *undersea feature* E Atlantic Ocean
Galilee *see* HaGalil
181 *W7* **Galilee, Lake** ◎ Queensland, NE Australia
Galilee, Sea of *see* Tiberias, Lake
106 *E11* **Galileo Galilei** ✈ (Pisa) Toscana, C Italy
31 *S12* **Galion** Ohio, N USA
Galka'yo *see* Gaalkacyo
146 *K12* **Galkynyş** *prev. Rus.* Deynau, Dyanev, *Turkm.* Dänew. Lebap Welaýaty, NE Turkmenistan
80 *H11* **Gallabat** Gedaref, E Sudan
Gallaecia *see* Galicia
147 *O11* **G'allaorol** Jizzakh Viloyati, C Uzbekistan
147 *O11* **G'allaorol** Jizzax Viloyati, C Uzbekistan
106 *C7* **Gallarate** Lombardia, NW Italy
27 *S2* **Gallatin** Missouri, C USA
20 *J8* **Gallatin** Tennessee, S USA
33 *R11* **Gallatin Peak** ▲ Montana, NW USA
33 *R12* **Gallatin River** ↝ Montana/Wyoming, NW USA
155 *J26* **Galle** *prev.* Point de Galle. Southern Province, SW Sri Lanka
105 *S5* **Gállego** ↝ NE Spain
193 *Q8* **Gallego Rise** *undersea feature* E Pacific Ocean
Gallegos *see* Río Gallegos
63 *H23* **Gallegos, Río** ↝ Argentina/Chile
Gallia *see* France
22 *K10* **Galliano** Louisiana, S USA
114 *G13* **Gallikós** ↝ N Greece
37 *S12* **Gallinas Peak** ▲ New Mexico, SW USA
54 *H3* **Gallinas, Punta** *headland* NE Colombia
37 *T11* **Gallinas River** ↝ New Mexico, SW USA
107 *Q19* **Gallipoli** Puglia, SE Italy
Gallipoli *see* Gelibolu
Gallipoli Peninsula *see* Gelibolu Yarımadası
31 *T15* **Gallipolis** Ohio, N USA
92 *J12* **Gällivare** *Lapp.* Váhtjer. Norrbotten, N Sweden
109 *T4* **Gallneukirchen** Oberösterreich, N Austria
93 *G17* **Gällö** Jämtland, C Sweden
105 *Q7* **Gallo** ↝ C Spain
107 *I23* **Gallo, Capo** *headland* Sicilia, Italy, C Mediterranean Sea
37 *P13* **Gallo Mountains** ▲▲ New Mexico, SW USA
18 *G8* **Galloo Island** *island* New York, NE USA
97 *H15* **Galloway, Mull of** *headland* S Scotland, UK
37 *P10* **Gallup** New Mexico, SW USA
105 *R5* **Gallur** Aragón, NE Spain
Gâlma *see* Guelma
162 *H7* **Galshar** *var.* Buyant. Dzavhan, C Mongolia
163 *N9* **Galshar** *var.* Buyant. Hentiy, C Mongolia
162 *I6* **Galt** *var.* Ider. Hövsgöl, C Mongolia
35 *O8* **Galt** California, W USA
74 *C10* **Galtat-Zemmour** C Western Sahara
95 *G22* **Galten** Århus, C Denmark
97 *D20* **Galtymore Mountain** *Ir.* Cnoc Mór na nGaibhlte. ▲ S Ireland
97 *D20* **Galty Mountains** *Ir.* Na Gaibhlte. ▲▲ S Ireland
30 *K11* **Galva** Illinois, N USA
25 *X12* **Galveston** Texas, SW USA
25 *W11* **Galveston Bay** *inlet* Texas, SW USA
25 *W12* **Galveston Island** *island* Texas, SW USA
61 *B18* **Gálvez** Santa Fe, C Argentina
97 *C18* **Galway** *Ir.* Gaillimh. Galway, W Ireland
97 *B18* **Galway** *Ir.* Gaillimh. ◈ *county* W Ireland
97 *B18* **Galway Bay** *Ir.* Cuan na Gaillimhe. *bay* W Ireland
83 *F18* **Gam** Otjozondjupa, NE Namibia
164 *L14* **Gamagōri** Aichi, Honshū, SW Japan
54 *F7* **Gamarra** Cesar, N Colombia
Gámas *see* Kaamanen
158 *L17* **Gamba** Xizang Zizhiqu, W China
Gamba *see* Zamtang
77 *P14* **Gambaga** NE Ghana
80 *G13* **Gambēla** W Ethiopia
81 *H14* **Gambēla** ◈ *region* W Ethiopia
38 *K10* **Gambell** Saint Lawrence Island, Alaska, USA
76 *E12* **Gambia** *off.* Republic of The Gambia, The Gambia. ◆ *republic* W Africa
76 *I12* **Gambia** *Fr.* Gambie. ↝ W Africa
64 *K12* **Gambia Plain** *undersea feature* E Atlantic Ocean
Gambia, Republic of The *see* Gambia
Gambia, The *see* Gambia
Gambie *see* Gambia
31 *T13* **Gambier** Ohio, N USA
191 *Y13* **Gambier, Îles** *island group* E French Polynesia
182 *G10* **Gambier Islands** *island group* South Australia
79 *H19* **Gamboma** Plateaux, E Congo
79 *G16* **Gamboula** Mambéré-Kadéï, SW Central African Republic
37 *P10* **Gamerco** New Mexico, SW USA
137 *V12* **Gamış Dağı** ▲ W Azerbaijan
Gamlakarleby *see* Kokkola
95 *N18* **Gamleby** Kalmar, S Sweden
Gammelstad *see* Gammelstaden
93 *J14* **Gammelstaden** *var* Gammelstad. Norrbotten, N Sweden
Gammouda *see* Sidi Bouzid
155 *J25* **Gampaha** Western Province, W Sri Lanka
155 *K25* **Gampola** Central Province, C Sri Lanka
167 *S5* **Gâm, Sông** ↝ N Vietnam
92 *L7* **Gamvik** Finnmark, N Norway
150 *H13* **Gan** Addu Atoll, C Maldives
Gan *see* Gansu
Gan *see* Jiangxi
Ganaane *see* Juba
37 *O10* **Ganado** Arizona, SW USA
25 *U12* **Ganado** Texas, SW USA
14 *L14* **Gananoque** Ontario, SE Canada
Ganāveh *see* Bandar-e Gonāveh
137 *V11* **Gäncä** *Rus.* Gyandzha; *prev.* Kirovabad, Yelisavetpol. W Azerbaijan
Ganchi *see* Ghonchí
Gand *see* Gent
82 *B13* **Ganda** *var.* Mariano Machado, *Port.* Vila Mariano Machado. Benguela, W Angola
79 *L22* **Gandajika** Kasai Oriental, S Dem. Rep. Congo
153 *O12* **Gandak** *Nep.* Nārāyāni. ↝ India/Nepal
13 *U11* **Gander** Newfoundland, Newfoundland and Labrador, SE Canada
13 *U11* **Gander** ✈ Newfoundland, Newfoundland and Labrador, E Canada
100 *G11* **Ganderkesee** Niedersachsen, NW Germany
105 *T7* **Gandesa** Cataluña, NE Spain
154 *B10* **Gāndhīdhām** Gujarāt, W India
154 *D10* **Gāndhīnagar** *state capital* Gujarāt, W India
154 *F9* **Gāndhi Sāgar** ◎ C India
105 *T11* **Gandía** País Valenciano, E Spain
159 *O10* **Gang** Qinghai, W China
152 *G9* **Gangānagar** Rājasthān, NW India
152 *I12* **Gangāpur** Rājasthān, N India
153 *S17* **Gangā Sāgar** West Bengal, NE India
Gangavathi *see* Gangāwati
155 *G17* **Gangāwati** *var.* Gangavathi. Karnātaka, C India
159 *S9* **Gangca** *var.* Shaliuhe. Qinghai, C China
158 *H14* **Gangdisê Shan** *Eng.* Kailas Range. ▲▲ W China
103 *Q15* **Ganges** Hérault, S France
153 *P13* **Ganges** *Ben.* Padma. ↝ Bangladesh/India *see also* Padma
Ganges *see* Padma
Ganges Cone *see* Ganges Fan
173 *S3* **Ganges Fan** *var.* Ganges Cone. *undersea feature* N Bay of Bengal
153 *U17* **Ganges, Mouths of the** *delta* Bangladesh/India
107 *K23* **Gangi** *anc.* Engyum. Sicilia, Italy, C Mediterranean Sea
152 *K8* **Gangotri** Uttaranchal, N India
Gangra *see* Çankırı
153 *S11* **Gangtok** *state capital* Sikkim, N India
159 *W11* **Gangu** Gansu, C China
163 *U5* **Gan He** ↝ NE China
171 *S12* **Gani** Pulau Halmahera, E Indonesia
161 *O12* **Gan Jiang** ↝ S China
163 *U11* **Ganjig** *var* Horqin Zuoyi Houqi. Nei Mongol Zizhiqu, N China
146 *H15* **Gannaly** Ahal Welaýaty, S Turkmenistan
163 *U7* **Gannan** Heilongjiang, NE China
103 *P10* **Gannat** Allier, C France
33 *T14* **Gannett Peak** ▲ Wyoming, C USA
29 *O10* **Gannvalley** South Dakota, N USA
Ganqu *see* Lhünzhub
109 *Y3* **Gänserndorf** Niederösterreich, NE Austria
Gansos, Lago dos *see* Goose Lake
159 *T9* **Gansu** *var.* Gan, Gansu Sheng, Kansu. ◈ *province* N China
Gansu Sheng *see* Gansu
76 *K16* **Ganta** *var.* Gahnpa. NE Liberia
182 *H11* **Gantheaume, Cape** *headland* South Australia
Gantsevichi *see* Hantsavichy
161 *Q6* **Ganyu** *var.* Qingkou. Jiangsu, E China
144 *D12* **Ganyushkino** Atyrau, SW Kazakhstan
161 *O12* **Ganzhou** Jiangxi, S China
Ganzhou *see* Zhangye
77 *Q10* **Gao** Gao, E Mali
77 *R10* **Gao** ◈ *region* SE Mali
161 *O10* **Gao'an** Jiangxi, S China
Gaocheng *see* Litang
Gaoleshan *see* Xianfeng
Gaongjiang *see* Yudu
161 *N5* **Gaoping** Shanxi, C China
159 *S8* **Gaotai** Gansu, N China
Gaoth Dobhair *see* Gweedore
77 *O14* **Gaoua** SW Burkina
76 *I13* **Gaoual** N Guinea
Gaoxiong *see* Kaohsiung
161 *R7* **Gaoyou** *var.* Dayishan. Jiangsu, E China
161 *R7* **Gaoyou Hu** ◎ E China
160 *M15* **Gaozhou** Guangdong, S China
103 *T13* **Gap** *anc.* Vapincum. Hautes-Alpes, SE France
146 *E9* **Gaplaňgyr Platosy** *Rus.* Plato Kaplangky. *ridge* Turkmenistan/Uzbekistan
158 *G13* **Gar** *var.* Gar Xincun. Xizang Zizhiqu, W China
Garabekevyul *see* Garabekewül
146 *L13* **Garabekewül** *Rus.* Garabekevyul, Karabekaul. Lebap Welaýaty, E Turkmenistan
146 *K15* **Garabil Belentligi** *Rus.* Vozvyshennost' Karabil'. ▲▲ S Turkmenistan
146 *A8* **Garabogaz** *Rus.* Bekdash. Balkan Welaýaty, NW Turkmenistan
146 *B9* **Garabogaz Aylagy** *Rus.* Zaliv Kara-Bogaz-Gol. *bay* NW Turkmenistan
146 *A9* **Garabogazköl** *Rus.* Kara-Bogaz-Gol. Balkan Welaýaty, E Turkmenistan
146 *A9* **Garabogazköl** *Rus.* Kara-Bogazkol. Balkan Welaýaty, NW Turkmenistan
43 *V16* **Garachiné** Darién, SE Panama
43 *V16* **Garachiné, Punta** *headland* SE Panama
146 *K12* **Garagan** *Rus.* Karagan. Ahal Welaýaty, C Turkmenistan
54 *G10* **Garagoa** Boyacá, C Colombia
146 *A11* **Garagöl'** *Rus.* Karagel'. Balkan Welaýaty, W Turkmenistan
146 *F12* **Garagum** *var.* Garagumy, Qara Qum, *Eng.* Black Sand Desert, Kara Kum; *prev.* Peski Karakumy. *desert* C Turkmenistan
146 *E12* **Garagum Kanaly** *var.* Kara Kum Canal, *Rus.* Karagumskiy Kanal, Karakumskiy Kanal. *canal* C Turkmenistan
Garagumy *see* Garagum
183 *S4* **Garah** New South Wales, SE Australia
64 *O11* **Garajonay** ▲ Gomera, Islas Canarias, NE Atlantic Ocean
114 *M8* **Gara Khitrino** Shumen, NE Bulgaria
76 *L13* **Garalo** Sikasso, SW Mali
Garam *see* Hron
146 *L14* **Garamätnyýaz** *Rus.* Karamet-Niyaz. Lebap Welaýaty, E Turkmenistan
Garamszentkereszt *see* Žiar nad Hronom
77 *Q13* **Garango** S Burkina
59 *Q15* **Garanhuns** Pernambuco, E Brazil
188 *H5* **Garapan** Saipan, S Northern Mariana Islands
Gárasavvon *see* Karesuando
Gárassavon *see* Kaaresuvanto
78 *J13* **Garba** Bamingui-Bangoran, N Central African Republic
Garba *see* Jiulong
81 *L16* **Garbahaarrey** *It.* Garba Harre. Gedo, SW Somalia
Garba Harre *see* Garbahaarrey
81 *J18* **Garba Tula** Eastern, C Kenya
27 *N9* **Garber** Oklahoma, C USA
34 *L4* **Garberville** California, W USA
Garbo *see* Lhozhag
100 *I12* **Garbsen** Niedersachsen, N Germany
60 *K9* **Garça** São Paulo, S Brazil
104 *L10* **García de Solá, Embalse de** ▣ C Spain
103 *Q14* **Gard** ◈ *department* S France
103 *Q14* **Gard** ↝ S France
106 *F7* **Garda, Lago di** *var.* Benaco, *Eng.* Lake Garda, *Ger.* Gardasee. ◎ NE Italy
Garda, Lake *see* Garda, Lago di
Gardan Divāl *see* Gardan Dīwāl
149 *Q5* **Gardan Dīwāl** *var.* Gardan Divāl. Vardak, C Afghanistan
103 *S15* **Gardanne** Bouches-du-Rhône, SE France
Gardasee *see* Garda, Lago di
100 *L12* **Gardelegen** Sachsen-Anhalt, C Germany
14 *B10* **Garden** ↝ Ontario, S Canada
23 *X6* **Garden City** Georgia, SE USA
26 *I6* **Garden City** Kansas, C USA
27 *S5* **Garden City** Missouri, C USA
25 *N8* **Garden City** Texas, SW USA
23 *P3* **Gardendale** Alabama, S USA
31 *P5* **Garden Island** *island* Michigan, N USA
22 *M11* **Garden Island Bay** *bay* Louisiana, S USA
31 *O5* **Garden Peninsula** *peninsula* Michigan, N USA
The Garden State *see* New Jersey
95 *I14* **Gardermoen** Akershus, S Norway
Gardeyz/Gardez *see* Gardīz
93 *G14* **Gardiken** ◎ N Sweden
19 *Q7* **Gardiner** Maine, NE USA
33 *S12* **Gardiner** Montana, NW USA
19 *N13* **Gardiners Island** *island* New York, NE USA
149 *Q6* **Gardīz** *var.* Gardeyz, Gardez, Gordiaz. Paktīā, E Afghanistan
Gardner Island *see* Nikumaroro
19 *T6* **Gardner Lake** ◎ Maine, NE USA
35 *Q6* **Gardnerville** Nevada, W USA
Gardo *see* Qardho
106 *F7* **Gardone Val Trompia** Lombardia, N Italy
Garegegasnjárga *see* Karigasniemi
38 *F17* **Gareloi Island** *island* Aleutian Islands, Alaska, USA
Gares *see* Puente la Reina
106 *B10* **Garessio** Piemonte, NE Italy
32 *M9* **Garfield** Washington, NW USA
31 *U11* **Garfield Heights** Ohio, N USA
Gargaliani *see* Gargaliánoi
115 *D21* **Gargaliánoi** *var.* Gargaliani. Pelopónnisos, S Greece
107 *N15* **Gargàno, Promontorio del** *headland* SE Italy
108 *J8* **Gargellen** Graubünden, W Switzerland
93 *I14* **Gargnäs** Västerbotten, N Sweden
118 *C11* **Gargždai** Klaipėda, W Lithuania
154 *J13* **Garhchiroli** Mahārāshtra, C India
153 *O15* **Garhwa** Jhārkhand, N India
171 *V13* **Gariau** Papua, E Indonesia
83 *E24* **Garies** Northern Cape, W South Africa
107 *K17* **Garigliano** ↝ C Italy
81 *K19* **Garissa** Coast, E Kenya
21 *V11* **Garland** North Carolina, SE USA
25 *T6* **Garland** Texas, SW USA
36 *L1* **Garland** Utah, W USA
106 *D8* **Garlasco** Lombardia, N Italy
119 *F14* **Garliava** Kaunas, S Lithuania
Garm *see* Gharm
142 *M9* **Garm, Āb-e** *var.* Rūd-e Khersān. ↝ SW Iran
101 *K25* **Garmisch-Partenkirchen** Bayern, S Germany
143 *O5* **Garmsār** *prev.* Qishlaq. Semnān, N Iran
Garmser *see* Darvīshān
29 *V12* **Garner** Iowa, C USA
21 *U9* **Garner** North Carolina, SE USA
27 *Q5* **Garnett** Kansas, C USA
99 *M25* **Garnich** Luxembourg, SW Luxembourg
182 *M8* **Garnpung, Lake** *salt lake* New South Wales, SE Australia
Garoe *see* Garoowe
Garoet *see* Garut
153 *U13* **Gāro Hills** *hill range* NE India
102 *K13* **Garonne** *anc.* Garumna. ↝ S France
80 *P13* **Garoowe** *var.* Garoe. Nugaal, N Somalia
78 *F12* **Garoua** *var.* Garua. Nord, N Cameroon
79 *G14* **Garoua Boulaï** Est, E Cameroon
77 *O10* **Garou, Lac** ◎ C Mali
95 *L16* **Garphyttan** Örebro, C Sweden
29 *R11* **Garretson** South Dakota, N USA
31 *Q11* **Garrett** Indiana, N USA
33 *Q10* **Garrison** Montana, NW USA
28 *M4* **Garrison** North Dakota, N USA
25 *X8* **Garrison** Texas, SW USA
28 *L4* **Garrison Dam** *dam* North Dakota, N USA
104 *J9* **Garrovillas** Extremadura, W Spain
Garrygala *see* Magtymguly
8 *L8* **Garry Lake** ◎ Nunavut, N Canada
Gars *see* Gars am Kamp
109 *W3* **Gars am Kamp** *var.* Gars. Niederösterreich, NE Austria
81 *K20* **Garsen** Coast, S Kenya
Garshy *see* Garşy
11 *F10* **Garson** Ontario, S Canada
109 *T5* **Garsten** Oberösterreich, N Austria
Gartar *see* Qianning
102 *M10* **Gartempe** ↝ C France
Gartog *see* Markam
Garua *see* Garoua
83 *D21* **Garub** Karas, SW Namibia
Garumna *see* Garonne
169 *P16* **Garut** *prev.* Garoet. Jawa, C Indonesia
185 *C20* **Garvie Mountains** ▲▲ South Island, New Zealand
110 *N12* **Garwolin** Mazowieckie, E Poland
25 *U12* **Garwood** Texas, SW USA
Gar Xincun *see* Gar
146 *A9* **Garşy** *var.* Garshy, *Rus.* Karshi. Balkan Welaýaty, NW Turkmenistan
31 *N11* **Gary** Indiana, N USA
25 *X7* **Gary** Texas, SW USA
158 *G13* **Gar Zangbo** ↝ W China
160 *F8* **Garzê** Sichuan, C China
54 *E12* **Garzón** Huila, S Colombia
Gasan-Kuli *see* Esenguly
31 *P13* **Gas City** Indiana, N USA
102 *K15* **Gascogne** *Eng.* Gascony. *cultural region* S France
26 *V5* **Gasconade River** ↝ Missouri, C USA
Gascony *see* Gascogne
180 *H9* **Gascoyne Junction** Western Australia
173 *V8* **Gascoyne Plain** *undersea feature* E Indian Ocean
180 *H9* **Gascoyne River** ↝ Western Australia
192 *J11* **Gascoyne Tablemount** *undersea feature* N Tasman Sea
67 *U6* **Gash** *var.* Nahr al Qāsh. ↝ W Sudan
149 *X3* **Gasherbrum** ▲ NE Pakistan
Gas Hu *see* Gas Hure Hu
77 *X12* **Gashua** Yobe, NE Nigeria
159 *N9* **Gas Hure Hu** *var.* Gas Hu. ◎ C China
186 *G7* **Gasmata** New Britain, E Papua New Guinea
23 *V14* **Gasparilla Island** *island* Florida, SE USA
169 *O13* **Gaspar, Selat** *strait* W Indonesia
15 *Y6* **Gaspé** Québec, SE Canada
15 *Z6* **Gaspé, Cap de** *headland* Québec, SE Canada
15 *X6* **Gaspé, Péninsule de** *var.* Péninsule de la Gaspésie. *peninsula* Québec, SE Canada
Gaspésie, Péninsule de la *see* Gaspé, Péninsule de
77 *W15* **Gassol** Taraba, E Nigeria
Gastein *see* Badgastein
21 *R10* **Gastonia** North Carolina, SE USA
21 *V8* **Gaston, Lake** ◎ North Carolina/Virginia, SE USA
115 *D19* **Gastoúni** Dytikí Ellás, S Greece
63 *I17* **Gastre** Chubut, S Argentina
Gat *see* Ghāt
105 *P15* **Gata, Cabo de** *cape* S Spain
Gata, Cape *see* Gátas, Akrotíri
105 *T11* **Gata de Gorgos** País Valenciano, E Spain
116 *E12* **Gătaia** *Ger.* Gataja, *Hung.* Gátalja; *prev.* Gáttája. Timiş, W Romania
Gataja/Gátalja *see* Gătaia
121 *P3* **Gátas, Akrotíri** *var.* Cape Gata. *cape* S Cyprus
104 *J8* **Gata, Sierra de** ▲▲ W Spain
124 *G13* **Gatchina** Leningradskaya Oblast', NW Russian Federation
21 *P8* **Gate City** Virginia, NE USA
97 *M14* **Gateshead** NE England, UK
21 *X8* **Gatesville** North Carolina, SE USA
25 *S8* **Gatesville** Texas, SW USA
14 *L12* **Gatineau** Québec, SE Canada
14 *L11* **Gatineau** ↝ Ontario/Québec, SE Canada
21 *N9* **Gatlinburg** Tennessee, S USA
Gatooma *see* Kadoma
Gáttája *see* Gătaia
43 *T14* **Gatún, Lago** ▣ C Panama
59 *N14* **Gaturiano** Piauí, NE Brazil
97 *O22* **Gatwick** ✈ (London) SE England, UK
187 *Y14* **Gau** *prev.* Ngau. *island* C Fiji
187 *R12* **Gaua** *var.* Santa Maria. *Island* Banks Island, N Vanuatu
104 *L16* **Gaucín** Andalucía, S Spain
Gauhāti *see* Guwāhāti
118 *I8* **Gauja** *Ger.* Aa. ↝ Estonia/Latvia
118 *I7* **Gaujiena** Alūksne, NE Latvia
94 *H9* **Gauldalen** *valley* S Norway
21 *R5* **Gauley River** ↝ West Virginia, NE USA
Gaul/Gaule *see* France
99 *D19* **Gaurain-Ramecroix** Hainaut, SW Belgium
95 *F15* **Gaustatoppen** ▲ S Norway
83 *J21* **Gauteng** *off.* Gauteng Province; *prev.* Pretoria-Witwatersrand-Vereeniging. ◈ *province* NE South Africa
Gauteng *see* Germiston, South Africa
Gauteng *see* Johannesburg, South Africa
Gauteng Province *see* Gauteng
137 *U11* **Gavarr** *prev.* Kamo. C Armenia
143 *P14* **Gāvbandī** Hormozgān, S Iran
115 *H25* **Gavdopoúla** *island* SE Greece
115 *H26* **Gávdos** *island* SE Greece
102 *K16* **Gave de Pau** *var.* Gave-de-Pay. ↝ SW France
Gave-de-Pay *see* Gave de Pau
102 *J16* **Gave d'Oloron** ↝ SW France
99 *E18* **Gavere** Oost-Vlaanderen, NW Belgium
94 *N13* **Gävle** *var.* Gäfle; *prev.* Gefle. Gävleborg, C Sweden
94 *M11* **Gävleborg** *var.* Gäfleborg, Gefleborg. ◈ *county* C Sweden
94 *O13* **Gävlebukten** *bay* C Sweden
124 *L16* **Gavrilov-Yam** Yaroslavskaya Oblast', W Russian Federation
182 *I9* **Gawler** South Australia
182 *G7* **Gawler Ranges** *hill range* South Australia
Gawso *see* Goaso
162 *H11* **Gaxun Nur** ◎ N China
153 *P14* **Gaya** Bihār, N India
77 *S13* **Gaya** Dosso, SW Niger
Gaya *see* Kyjov
31 *Q6* **Gaylord** Michigan, N USA
29 *U9* **Gaylord** Minnesota, N USA
181 *Y9* **Gayndah** Queensland, E Australia
125 *T12* **Gayny** Permskaya Oblast', NW Russian Federation
Gaysin *see* Haysyn
Gayvorno *see* Hayvoron
138 *E11* **Gaza** *Ar.* Ghazzah, *Heb.* 'Azza. NE Gaza Strip
83 *L20* **Gaza** *off.* Província de Gaza. ◈ *province* SW Mozambique
Gaz-Achak *see* Gazojak
147 *Q9* **G'azalkent** *Rus.* Gazalkent. Toshkent Viloyati, E Uzbekistan
Gazalkent *see* G'azalkent
Gazandzhyk/Gazanjyk *see* Bereket
77 *V12* **Gazaoua** Maradi, S Niger
Gaza, Província de *see* Gaza
138 *E11* **Gaza Strip** *Ar.* Qita Ghazzah. *disputed region* SW Asia
Gazgan *see* G'ozg'on
Gazgan *see* G'ozg'on
136 *M16* **Gaziantep** *var.* Gazi Antep; *prev.* Aintab, Antep. Gaziantep, S Turkey
136 *M17* **Gaziantep** *var.* Gazi Antep. ◈ *province* S Turkey
Gazi Antep *see* Gaziantep
114 *M13* **Gaziköy** Tekirdağ, NW Turkey
121 *Q2* **Gazimağusa** *var.* Famagusta, *Gk.* Ammóchostos. E Cyprus
121 *Q2* **Gazimağusa Körfezi** *var.* Famagusta Bay, *Gk.* Kólpos Ammóchostos. *bay* E Cyprus
146 *K11* **Gazli** Buxoro Viloyati, C Uzbekistan
146 *I9* **Gazojak** *Rus.* Gaz-Achak. Lebap Welaýaty, NE Turkmenistan
79 *K15* **Gbadolite** Equateur, NW Dem. Rep. Congo
76 *K16* **Gbanga** *var.* Gbarnga. N Liberia
Gbarnga *see* Gbanga
77 *S14* **Gbéroubouè** *var.* Béroubouay. N Benin
77 *W16* **Gboko** Benue, S Nigeria
Gcuwa *see* Butterworth
110 *J7* **Gdańsk** *Fr.* Dantzig, *Ger.* Danzig. Pomorskie, N Poland
Gdan'skaya Bukhta/Gdańsk, Gulf of *see* Danzig, Gulf of
Gdańska, Zakota *see* Danzig, Gulf of
Gdingen *see* Gdynia
124 *F13* **Gdov** Pskovskaya Oblast', W Russian Federation
110 *I6* **Gdynia** *Ger.* Gdingen. Pomorskie, N Poland
26 *M10* **Geary** Oklahoma, C USA
Geavvú *see* Kevo

◆ Country ● Country Capital ◇ Dependent Territory ○ Dependent Territory Capital ◈ Administrative Regions ✈ International Airport ▲ Mountain ▲▲ Mountain Range ⩚ Volcano ↝ River ◎ Lake ▣ Reservoir

GÊBA, RIO – GLÅMA

76 H12 **Gêba, Rio** ≈ C Guinea-Bissau
136 E11 **Gebze** Kocaeli, NW Turkey
80 H10 **Gedaref** *var.* Al Qaḑārif, El Gedaref. Gedaref, E Sudan
80 H10 **Gedaref** ◈ *state* E Sudan
80 B11 **Gedid Ras el Fil** Southern Darfur, W Sudan
99 I23 **Gedinne** Namur, SE Belgium
136 E13 **Gediz** Kütahya, W Turkey
136 C14 **Gediz Nehri** ≈ W Turkey
81 N14 **Gedlegubē** Somali, E Ethiopia
81 L17 **Gedo** *off.* Gobolka Gedo. ◈ *region* SW Somalia
Gedo, Gobolka *see* Gedo
95 I25 **Gedser** Storstrøm, SE Denmark
99 I16 **Geel** *var.* Gheel. Antwerpen, N Belgium
183 N13 **Geelong** Victoria, SE Australia
Ge'e'mu *see* Golmud
99 I14 **Geertruidenberg** Noord-Brabant, S Netherlands
100 H10 **Geeste** ≈ NW Germany
100 J10 **Geesthacht** Schleswig-Holstein, N Germany
183 P17 **Geeveston** Tasmania, SE Australia
Gefle *see* Gävle
Gefleborg *see* Gävleborg
158 G13 **Gê'gyai** Xizang Zizhiqu, W China
77 X12 **Geidam** Yobe, NE Nigeria
9 T11 **Geikie** ≈ Saskatchewan, C Canada
94 F13 **Geilo** Buskerud, S Norway
94 E10 **Geiranger** Møre og Romsdal, S Norway
101 I22 **Geislingen** *var.* Geislingen an der Steige. Baden-Württemberg, SW Germany
Geislingen an der Steige *see* Geislingen
81 F20 **Geita** Mwanza, NW Tanzania
95 G15 **Geithus** Buskerud, S Norway
160 H14 **Gejiu** *var.* Kochiu. Yunnan, S China
Gëkdepe *see* Gökdepe
146 E9 **Geklengkui, Solonchak** *var.* Solonchak Goklenkuy. *salt marsh* NW Turkmenistan
81 D14 **Gel** ≈ W Sudan
107 K25 **Gela** *prev.* Terranova di Sicilia. Sicilia, Italy, C Mediterranean Sea
159 N13 **Gêladaindong** ▲ C China
159 N13 **Gêladaindong** ▲ C China
81 N14 **Geladī** SE Ethiopia
169 P13 **Gelam, Pulau** *var.* Pulau Galam. *island* N Indonesia
Gelaozu Miaozu Zhizhixian *see* Wuchuan
98 L11 **Gelderland** *prev. Eng.* Guelders. ◈ *province* E Netherlands
98 J13 **Geldermalsen** Gelderland, C Netherlands
101 D14 **Geldern** Nordrhein-Westfalen, W Germany
99 K15 **Geldrop** Noord-Brabant, SE Netherlands
99 L17 **Geleen** Limburg, SE Netherlands
126 K14 **Gelendzhik** Krasnodarskiy Kray, SW Russian Federation
Gelib *see* Jilib
136 B11 **Gelibolu** *Eng.* Gallipoli. Çanakkale, NW Turkey
115 L14 **Gelibolu Yarımadası** *Eng.* Gallipoli Peninsula. *peninsula* NW Turkey
81 O14 **Gellinsor** Mudug, C Somalia
101 H18 **Gelnhausen** Hessen, C Germany
101 E14 **Gelsenkirchen** Nordrhein-Westfalen, W Germany
83 C20 **Geluk** Hardap, SW Namibia
99 H20 **Gembloux** Namur, Belgium
79 J16 **Gemena** Equateur, NW Dem. Rep. Congo
99 L14 **Gemert** Noord-Brabant, SE Netherlands
136 E11 **Gemlik** Bursa, NW Turkey
Gem of the Mountains *see* Idaho
106 J6 **Gemona del Friuli** Friuli-Venezia Giulia, NE Italy
Gem State *see* Idaho
Genalē Wenz *see* Juba
169 R10 **Genali, Danau** ◎ Borneo, N Indonesia
99 G19 **Genappe** Walloon Brabant, C Belgium
137 P14 **Genç** Bingöl, E Turkey
Genck *see* Genk
98 M9 **Genemuiden** Overijssel, E Netherlands
63 K14 **General Acha** La Pampa, C Argentina
61 C21 **General Alvear** Buenos Aires, E Argentina
62 I12 **General Alvear** Mendoza, W Argentina
61 B20 **General Arenales** Buenos Aires, E Argentina
61 D21 **General Belgrano** Buenos Aires, E Argentina
194 H3 **General Bernardo O'Higgins** *Chilean research station* Antarctica
41 O8 **General Bravo** Nuevo León, NE Mexico
62 M7 **General Capdevila** Chaco, N Argentina
General Carrera, Lago *see* Buenos Aires, Lago
41 N9 **General Cepeda** Coahuila de Zaragoza, NE Mexico
63 K15 **General Conesa** Río Negro, E Argentina
61 G18 **General Enrique Martínez** Treinta y Tres, E Uruguay
62 L3 **General Eugenio A. Garay** *var.* Fortín General Eugenio Garay; *prev.* Yrendagüé. Nueva Asunción NW Paraguay
61 C18 **General Galarza** Entre Ríos, E Argentina
61 E22 **General Guido** Buenos Aires, E Argentina
General José F.Uriburu *see* Zárate
61 E22 **General Juan Madariaga** Buenos Aires, E Argentina
41 O16 **General Juan N Alvarez** ✈ (Acapulco) Guerrero, S Mexico
61 B22 **General La Madrid** Buenos Aires, E Argentina
61 E21 **General Lavalle** Buenos Aires, E Argentina
General Machado *see* Camacupa
62 I8 **General Manuel Belgrano, Cerro** ▲ W Argentina
41 O8 **General Mariano Escobero** ✈ (Monterrey) Nuevo León, NE Mexico
61 B20 **General O'Brien** Buenos Aires, E Argentina
62 K13 **General Pico** La Pampa, C Argentina
62 M7 **General Pinedo** Chaco, N Argentina
61 B20 **General Pinto** Buenos Aires, E Argentina
61 E22 **General Pirán** Buenos Aires, E Argentina
43 N15 **General, Río** ≈ S Costa Rica
63 I15 **General Roca** Río Negro, C Argentina
171 Q8 **General Santos** *off.* General Santos City. Mindanao, S Philippines
General Santos City *see* General Santos
41 O9 **General Terán** Nuevo León, NE Mexico
114 N7 **General Toshevo** *Rom.* I.G.Duca; *prev.* Casim, Kasimköj. Dobrich, NE Bulgaria
61 B20 **General Viamonte** Buenos Aires, E Argentina
61 A20 **General Villegas** Buenos Aires, E Argentina
Gênes *see* Genova
18 E11 **Genesee River** ≈ New York/Pennsylvania, NE USA
30 K11 **Geneseo** Illinois, N USA
18 F10 **Geneseo** New York, NE USA
57 L14 **Geneshuaya, Río** ≈ N Bolivia
23 Q8 **Geneva** Alabama, S USA
30 M10 **Geneva** Illinois, N USA
29 Q16 **Geneva** Nebraska, C USA
18 G10 **Geneva** New York, NE USA
31 U10 **Geneva** Ohio, NE USA
Geneva *see* Genève
108 B10 **Geneva, Lake** *Fr.* Lac de Genève, Lac Léman, *var.* le Léman, *Ger.* Genfer See. ◎ France/Switzerland
108 A10 **Genève** *Eng.* Geneva, *Ger.* Genf, *It.* Ginevra. Genève, SW Switzerland
108 A11 **Genève** *Eng.* Geneva, *Ger.* Genf, *It.* Ginevra. ◈ *canton* SW Switzerland
108 A10 **Genève** *var.* Geneva. ✈ Vaud, SW Switzerland
Genève, Lac de *see* Geneva, Lake
Genf *see* Genève
Genfer See *see* Geneva, Lake
163 T5 **Genhe** *prev.* Ergun Zuoqi. Nei Mongol Zizhiqu, N China
163 S5 **Gen He** ≈ NE China
Genichesk *see* Heniches'k
104 L14 **Genil** ≈ S Spain
99 K18 **Genk** *var.* Genck. Limburg, NE Belgium
164 C13 **Genkai-nada** *gulf* Kyūshū, SW Japan
107 C19 **Gennargentu, Monti del** ▲▲ Sardegna, Italy, C Mediterranean Sea
99 M14 **Gennep** Limburg, SE Netherlands
30 M10 **Genoa** Illinois, N USA
29 Q15 **Genoa** Nebraska, C USA
Genoa *see* Genova
Genoa, Gulf of *see* Genova, Golfo di
106 D10 **Genova** *Eng.* Genoa; *anc.* Genua, *Fr.* Gênes. Liguria, NW Italy
106 D10 **Genova, Golfo di** *Eng.* Gulf of Genoa. *gulf* NW Italy
57 C17 **Genovesa, Isla** *var.* Tower Island. *island* Galapagos Islands, Ecuador, E Pacific Ocean
Genshū *see* Wŏnju
99 E17 **Gent** *Eng.* Ghent, *Fr.* Gand. Oost-Vlaanderen, NW Belgium
169 N16 **Genteng** Jawa, C Indonesia
100 M12 **Genthin** Sachsen-Anhalt, E Germany
27 R9 **Gentry** Arkansas, C USA
Genua *see* Genova
107 I15 **Genzano di Roma** Lazio, C Italy
Geokchay *see* Göyçay
Geok-Tepe *see* Gökdepe
122 I3 **Georga, Zemlya** *Eng.* George Land. *island* Zemlya Frantsa-Iosifa, N Russian Federation
83 G26 **George** Western Cape, S South Africa
29 S11 **George** Iowa, C USA
13 O5 **George** ≈ Newfoundland and Labrador/Québec, E Canada
45 T11 **George F L Charles** *prev.* Vigie. ✈ (Castries) NE Saint Lucia
65 C25 **George Island** *island* S Falkland Islands
183 R10 **George, Lake** ◎ New South Wales, SE Australia
81 E18 **George, Lake** ◎ SW Uganda
23 W10 **George, Lake** ◎ Florida, SE USA
18 L8 **George, Lake** ⊠ New York, NE USA
George Land *see* Georga, Zemlya
Georgenburg *see* Jurbarkas
George River *see* Kangiqsualujjuaq
64 G8 **Georges Bank** *undersea feature* W Atlantic Ocean
185 A21 **George Sound** *sound* South Island, New Zealand
65 F15 **Georgetown** ○ (Ascension Island) NW Ascension Island
181 V5 **Georgetown** Queensland, NE Australia
183 P15 **George Town** Tasmania, SE Australia
44 I4 **George Town** Great Exuma Island, C Bahamas
44 D8 **George Town** *var.* Georgetown. ○ (Cayman Islands) Grand Cayman, SW Cayman Islands
76 H12 **Georgetown** E Gambia
55 T8 **Georgetown** ● (Guyana) N Guyana
168 J7 **George Town** *var.* Penang, Pinang. Pinang, Peninsular Malaysia
45 Y14 **Georgetown** Saint Vincent, Saint Vincent and the Grenadines
21 Y4 **Georgetown** Delaware, NE USA
23 R6 **Georgetown** Georgia, SE USA
20 M5 **Georgetown** Kentucky, S USA
21 T13 **Georgetown** South Carolina, SE USA
25 S10 **Georgetown** Texas, SW USA
55 T8 **Georgetown** ✈ N Guyana
Georgetown *see* George Town
195 U16 **George V Coast** *physical region* Antarctica
194 J7 **George VI Ice Shelf** *ice shelf* Antarctica
194 J6 **George VI Sound** *sound* Antarctica
195 T15 **George V Land** *physical region* Antarctica
25 S14 **George West** Texas, SW USA
137 R9 **Georgia** *off.* Republic of Georgia, *Geor.* Sak'art'velo, *Rus.* Gruzinskaya SSR, Gruziya. ◆ *republic* SW Asia
23 S5 **Georgia** *off.* State of Georgia, *also known as* Empire State of the South, Peach State. ◈ *state* SE USA
14 F12 **Georgian Bay** *lake bay* Ontario, S Canada
Georgia, Republic of *see* Georgia
10 L17 **Georgia, Strait of** *strait* British Columbia, W Canada
Georgi Dimitrov *see* Kostenets
Georgi Dimitrov, Yazovir *see* Koprinka, Yazovir
114 M9 **Georgi Traykov, Yazovir** ⊠ NE Bulgaria
Georgiu-Dezh *see* Liski
145 W10 **Georgiyevka** Semipalatinsk, E Kazakhstan
Georgiyevka *see* Korday
127 N15 **Georgiyevsk** Stavropol'skiy Kray, SW Russian Federation
100 G13 **Georgsmarienhütte** Niedersachsen, NW Germany
195 O1 **Georg von Neumayer** *German research station* Antarctica
101 M16 **Gera** Thüringen, E Germany
101 K16 **Gera** ≈ C Germany
99 E19 **Geraardsbergen** Oost-Vlaanderen, SW Belgium
115 F21 **Geráki** Pelopónnisos, S Greece
27 W5 **Gerald** Missouri, C USA
47 I8 **Geral de Goiás, Serra** ▲▲ E Brazil
185 G20 **Geraldine** Canterbury, South Island, New Zealand
180 H11 **Geraldton** Western Australia
12 E11 **Geraldton** Ontario, S Canada
60 J12 **Geral, Serra** ▲▲ S Brazil
103 U6 **Gérardmer** Vosges, NE France
Gerasa *see* Jarash
Gerdauen *see* Zheleznodorozhnyy
39 Q11 **Gerdine, Mount** ▲ Alaska, USA
136 H11 **Gerede** Bolu, N Turkey
136 H11 **Gerede Çayī** ≈ N Turkey
148 M8 **Gereshk** Helmand, SW Afghanistan
101 L24 **Geretsried** Bayern, S Germany
105 P14 **Gérgal** Andalucía, S Spain
28 I14 **Gering** Nebraska, C USA
35 R3 **Gerlach** Nevada, W USA
Gerlachfalvi Csúcs/Gerlachovka *see* Gerlachovský štít
111 L18 **Gerlachovský štít** *var.* Gerlachovka, *Ger.* Gerlsdorfer Spitze, *Hung.* Gerlachfalvi Csúcs; *prev.* Stalinov Štít, *Ger.* Franz-Josef Spitze, *Hung.* Ferencz-József Csúcs. ▲ N Slovakia
108 E8 **Gerlafingen** Solothurn, NW Switzerland
Gerlsdorfer Spitze *see* Gerlachovský štít
139 V3 **Germak** E Iraq
German East Africa *see* Tanzania
Germanicopolis *see* Çankırı
Germanicum, Mare/German Ocean *see* North Sea
Germanovichi *see* Hyermanavichy
German Southwest Africa *see* Namibia
20 E10 **Germantown** Tennessee, S USA
101 I15 **Germany** *off.* Federal Republic of Germany, Bundesrepublik Deutschland, *Ger.* Deutschland. ◆ *federal republic* N Europe
Germany, Federal Republic of *see* Germany
101 L23 **Germering** Bayern, SE Germany
83 J21 **Germiston** *var.* Gauteng. Gauteng, NE South Africa
Gernika *see* Gernika-Lumo
105 P2 **Gernika-Lumo** *var.* Gernika, Guernica, Guernica y Lumo. País Vasco, N Spain
164 L12 **Gero** Gifu, Honshū, SW Japan
115 F22 **Geroliménas** Pelopónnisos, S Greece
Gerona *see* Girona
99 H21 **Gerpinnes** Hainaut, S Belgium
102 L15 **Gers** ◈ *department* S France
102 L14 **Gers** ≈ S France
Gerunda *see* Girona
158 I13 **Gêrzê** *var.* Luring. Xizang Zizhiqu, W China
136 K10 **Gerze** Sinop, N Turkey
Gesoriacum *see* Boulogne-sur-Mer
Gessoriacum *see* Boulogne-sur-Mer
99 J21 **Gesves** Namur, SE Belgium
93 J20 **Geta** Åland, SW Finland
105 N8 **Getafe** Madrid, C Spain
95 J21 **Getinge** Halland, S Sweden
18 F16 **Gettysburg** Pennsylvania, NE USA
29 N8 **Gettysburg** South Dakota, N USA
194 K12 **Getz Ice Shelf** *ice shelf* Antarctica
137 S15 **Gevaş** Van, SE Turkey
Gevgeli *see* Gevgelija
113 Q20 **Gevgelija** *var.* Đevđelija, Djevdjelija, *Turk.* Gevgeli. SE Macedonia
103 T10 **Gex** Ain, E France
92 I3 **Geysir** *physical region* SW Iceland
136 F11 **Geyve** Sakarya, NW Turkey
80 G10 **Gezira** ◈ *state* E Sudan
109 V3 **Gföhl** Niederösterreich, N Austria
83 H22 **Ghaap Plateau** *Afr.* Ghaapplato. *plateau* C South Africa
Ghaapplato *see* Ghaap Plateau
Ghaba *see* Al Ghābah
138 J8 **Ghāb, Tall** ▲ SE Syria
139 Q9 **Ghadaf, Wādī al** *dry watercourse* C Iraq
Ghadamès *see* Ghadāmis
74 M9 **Ghadāmis** *var.* Ghadamès, Rhadames. W Libya
141 Y10 **Ghadan** E Oman
75 O10 **Ghaddūwah** C Libya
147 Q11 **Ghafurov** *Rus.* Gafurov; *prev.* Sovetabad. NW Tajikistan
153 N12 **Ghāghara** ≈ S Asia
149 P13 **Ghaibi Dero** Sind, SE Pakistan
141 Y10 **Ghalat** E Oman
139 W11 **Ghamūkah, Hawr** ◎ S Iraq
77 P15 **Ghana** *off.* Republic of Ghana. ◆ *republic* W Africa
141 X12 **Ghānah** *spring/well* S Oman
Ghanongga *see* Ranongga
Ghansi/Ghansiland *see* Ghanzi
83 F18 **Ghanzi** *var.* Khanzi. Ghanzi, W Botswana
83 G19 **Ghanzi** *var.* Ghansi, Ghansiland, Khanzi. ◈ *district* C Botswana
67 T14 **Ghanzi** *var.* Knanzi. ≈ Botswana/South Africa
Ghap'an *see* Kapan
138 F13 **Gharandal** Al'Aqabah, SW Jordan
Gharbt, Jabal al *see* Liban, Jebel
74 K7 **Ghardaïa** N Algeria
139 U14 **Gharibīyah, Sha'īb al** ≈ S Iraq
147 R12 **Gharm** *Rus.* Garm. C Tajikistan
149 P17 **Gharo** Sind, SE Pakistan
139 W10 **Gharrāf, Shaṭṭ al** ≈ S Iraq
Gharvān *see* Gharyān
75 O7 **Gharyān** *var.* Gharvān. NW Libya
74 M11 **Ghāt** *var.* Gat. SW Libya
Ghawdex *see* Gozo
141 U8 **Ghayathi** Abū Ẓaby, W United Arab Emirates
Ghazāl, Baḥr al *see* Ghazal, Bahr el
78 H9 **Ghazal, Bahr el** *var.* Soro. *seasonal river* C Chad
80 E13 **Ghazal, Bahr el** *var.* Baḥr al Ghazāl. ≈ S Sudan
74 H6 **Ghazaouet** NW Algeria
152 J10 **Ghāziābād** Uttar Pradesh, N India
153 O13 **Ghāzīpur** Uttar Pradesh, N India
149 Q6 **Ghaznī** *var.* Ghazni. Ghaznī, E Afghanistan
149 P7 **Ghaznī** ◈ *province* SE Afghanistan
Ghazzah *see* Gaza
Gheel *see* Geel
Ghelīzāne *see* Relizane
Ghent *see* Gent
Gheorghe Brațul *see* Sfântu Gheorghe, Brațul
Gheorghe Gheorghiu-Dej *see* Onești
116 J10 **Gheorgheni** *prev.* Gheorghieni, Sîn-Miclăuș, *Ger.* Niklasmarkt, *Hung.* Gyergyószentmiklós. Harghita, C Romania
Gheorghieni *see* Gheorgheni
116 H10 **Gherla** *Ger.* Neuschliss, *Hung.* Szamosújvár; *prev.* Armenierstadt. Cluj, NW Romania
Gheweifat *see* Ghuwayfāt
Ghilan *see* Gīlān
107 C18 **Ghilarza** Sardegna, Italy, C Mediterranean Sea
Ghilizane *see* Relizane
Ghimbi *see* Gīmbī
Ghiriş *see* Câmpia Turzii
103 Y15 **Ghisonaccia** Corse, France, C Mediterranean Sea
147 Q11 **Ghonchī** *Rus.* Ganchi. NW Tajikistan
Ghor *see* Ghowr
153 T13 **Ghoraghat** Rajshahi, NW Bangladesh
149 R13 **Ghotki** Sind, SE Pakistan
148 M5 **Ghowr** *var.* Ghor. ◈ *province* C Afghanistan
147 T13 **Ghŭdara** *var.* Gudara, *Rus.* Kudara. SE Tajikistan
153 R13 **Ghugri** ≈ N India
147 S14 **Ghund** *Rus.* Gunt. ≈ SE Tajikistan
Ghurdaqah *see* Hurghada
148 J5 **Ghūrīān** Herāt, W Afghanistan
141 T8 **Ghuwayfāt** *var.* Gheweifat. Abū Ẓaby, W United Arab Emirates
121 O14 **Ghuzayyil, Sabkhat** *salt lake* N Libya
126 J3 **Ghzatsk** Smolenskaya Oblast', W Russian Federation
115 G17 **Giáltra** Évvoia, C Greece
Giamame *see* Jamaame
167 U13 **Gia Nghia** *var.* Đak Nông. Đắc Lắc, S Vietnam
114 F13 **Giannitsá** *var.* Yiannitsá. Kentrikí Makedonía, N Greece
107 F14 **Giannutri, Isola di** *island* Archipelago Toscano, C Italy
96 F13 **Giant's Causeway** *Ir.* Clochán an Aifir. *lava flow* N Northern Ireland, UK
167 S15 **Gia Rai** Minh Hai, S Vietnam
107 L24 **Giarre** Sicilia, Italy, C Mediterranean Sea
44 I7 **Gibara** Holguín, E Cuba
29 O16 **Gibbon** Nebraska, C USA
32 K11 **Gibbon** Oregon, NW USA
33 P11 **Gibbonsville** Idaho, NW USA
64 A13 **Gibb's Hill** *hill* S Bermuda
92 I9 **Gibostad** Troms, N Norway
104 I14 **Gibraleón** Andalucía, S Spain
104 L16 **Gibraltar** ○ (Gibraltar) S Gibraltar
104 L16 **Gibraltar** ◇ *UK dependent territory* SW Europe
Gibraltar, Détroit de/Gibraltar, Estrecho de *see* Gibraltar, Strait of
104 J17 **Gibraltar, Strait of** *Fr.* Détroit de Gibraltar, *Sp.* Estrecho de Gibraltar. *strait* Atlantic Ocean/Mediterranean Sea
31 S11 **Gibsonburg** Ohio, N USA
30 M13 **Gibson City** Illinois, N USA
180 L8 **Gibson Desert** *desert* Western Australia
10 L17 **Gibsons** British Columbia, SW Canada
149 N12 **Gīdār** Baluchistān, SW Pakistan
155 I17 **Giddalūr** Andhra Pradesh, E India
25 U10 **Giddings** Texas, SW USA
27 Y8 **Gideon** Missouri, C USA
81 I15 **Gīdolē** Southern, S Ethiopia
118 H13 **Giedraičiai** Utena, E Lithuania
103 O7 **Gien** Loiret, C France
101 G17 **Giessen** Hessen, W Germany
98 O6 **Gieten** Drenthe, NE Netherlands
23 Y13 **Gifford** Florida, SE USA
9 O5 **Gifford** ≈ Baffin Island, Nunavut, NE Canada
100 J12 **Gifhorn** Niedersachsen, N Germany
9 P13 **Gift Lake** Alberta, W Canada
164 L13 **Gifu** *var.* Gihu. Gifu, Honshū, SW Japan
164 K13 **Gifu** *off.* Gifu-ken, *var.* Gihu. ◈ *prefecture* Honshū, SW Japan
Gifu-ken *see* Gifu
126 M13 **Gigant** Rostovskaya Oblast', SW Russian Federation
40 E8 **Giganta, Sierra de la** ▲▲ W Mexico
54 E12 **Gigante** Huila, S Colombia
114 I7 **Gigen** Pleven, N Bulgaria
Giggiga *see* Jijiga
96 G12 **Gigha Island** *island* SW Scotland, UK
107 E14 **Giglio, Isola del** *island* Archipelago Toscano, C Italy
Gihu *see* Gifu
146 L11 **G'ijduvon** *Rus.* Gizhduvon. Buxoro Viloyati, C Uzbekistan
104 L2 **Gijón** *var.* Xixón. Asturias, NW Spain
81 D20 **Gikongoro** SW Rwanda
36 K14 **Gila Bend** Arizona, SW USA
36 J14 **Gila Bend Mountains** ▲▲ Arizona, SW USA
37 N14 **Gila Mountains** ▲▲ Arizona, SW USA
36 I15 **Gila Mountains** ▲▲ Arizona, SW USA
142 M4 **Gīlān** *off.* Ostān-e Gīlān, *var.* Ghilan, Guilan. ◈ *province* NW Iran
Gilani *see* Gnjilane
Gīlān, Ostān-e *see* Gīlān
36 L14 **Gila River** ≈ Arizona, SW USA
29 W4 **Gilbert** Minnesota, N USA
Gilbert Islands *see* Tungaru
10 L16 **Gilbert, Mount** ▲ British Columbia, SW Canada
181 U4 **Gilbert River** ≈ Queensland, NE Australia
0 C6 **Gilbert Seamounts** *undersea feature* NE Pacific Ocean
33 S7 **Gildford** Montana, NW USA
83 P15 **Gilé** Zambézia, NE Mozambique
30 K4 **Gile Flowage** ◎ Wisconsin, N USA
182 G7 **Giles, Lake** *salt lake* South Australia
75 U12 **Gilf Kebir Plateau** *Ar.* Haḍabat al Jilf al Kabīr. *plateau* SW Egypt
183 R6 **Gilgandra** New South Wales, SE Australia
Gilgău *see* Gâlgău
81 I19 **Gilgil** Rift Valley, SW Kenya
183 S4 **Gil Gil Creek** ≈ New South Wales, SE Australia
149 V3 **Gilgit** Jammu and Kashmir, NE Pakistan
149 V3 **Gilgit** ≈ N Pakistan
9 X11 **Gillam** Manitoba, C Canada
95 J22 **Gilleleje** Frederiksborg, E Denmark
30 K14 **Gillespie** Illinois, N USA
27 W13 **Gillett** Arkansas, C USA
33 X12 **Gillette** Wyoming, C USA
97 P22 **Gillingham** SE England, UK
195 X6 **Gillock Island** *island* Antarctica
173 O16 **Gillot** ✈ (St-Denis) N Réunion
65 H25 **Gill Point** *headland* E Saint Helena
30 M12 **Gilman** Illinois, N USA
25 W6 **Gilmer** Texas, SW USA
Gilolo *see* Halmahera, Pulau
81 G14 **Gīlo Wenz** ≈ SW Ethiopia
35 O10 **Gilroy** California, W USA
123 Q12 **Gilyuy** ≈ SE Russian Federation
99 I14 **Gilze** Noord-Brabant, S Netherlands
165 R16 **Gima** Okinawa, Kume-jima, SW Japan
80 H13 **Gīmbī** *It.* Ghimbi. Oromo, C Ethiopia
45 T12 **Gimie, Mount** ▲ C Saint Lucia
9 X16 **Gimli** Manitoba, S Canada
Gimma *see* Jīma
95 O14 **Gimo** Uppsala, C Sweden
102 L15 **Gimone** ≈ S France
Gimpoe *see* Gimpu
171 N12 **Gimpu** *prev.* Gimpoe. Sulawesi, C Indonesia
182 F5 **Gina** South Australia
Ginevra *see* Genève
99 J19 **Gingelom** Limburg, NE Belgium
180 I12 **Gingin** Western Australia
171 Q7 **Gingoog** Mindanao, S Philippines
81 K14 **Gīnīr** Oromo, C Ethiopia
Giohar *see* Jawhar
107 O17 **Gióia del Colle** Puglia, SE Italy
107 M22 **Gioia, Golfo di** *gulf* S Italy
Giona *see* Gkióna
115 I16 **Gioúra** *island* Vóreioi Sporádes, Greece, Aegean Sea
107 O17 **Giovinazzo** Puglia, SE Italy
Gipeswic *see* Ipswich
Gipuzkoa *see* Guipúzcoa
Giran *see* Ilan
30 K14 **Girard** Illinois, N USA
27 R7 **Girard** Kansas, C USA
25 O6 **Girard** Texas, SW USA
54 E10 **Girardot** Cundinamarca, C Colombia
172 M7 **Giraud Seamount** *undersea feature* SW Indian Ocean
83 A15 **Giraul** ≈ SW Angola
96 L9 **Girdle Ness** *headland* NE Scotland, UK
137 N11 **Giresun** *var.* Kerasunt; *anc.* Cerasus, Pharnacia. Giresun, NE Turkey
137 N12 **Giresun** *var.* Kerasunt. ◈ *province* NE Turkey
137 N12 **Giresun Dağları** ▲▲ N Turkey
75 X10 **Girga** *var.* Girgeh, Jirjā. C Egypt
Girgeh *see* Girga
Girgenti *see* Agrigento
153 Q15 **Girīdīh** Jhārkhand, NE India
183 P6 **Girilambone** New South Wales, SE Australia
Girin *see* Jilin
121 W10 **Girne** *Gk.* Kerýneia, Kyrenia. N Cyprus
Giron *see* Kiruna
105 X5 **Girona** *var.* Gerona; *anc.* Gerunda. Cataluña, NE Spain
105 W5 **Gerona** ◈ *province* Cataluña, NE Spain
102 J12 **Gironde** ◈ *department* SW France
102 J11 **Gironde** *estuary* SW France
105 V5 **Gironella** Cataluña, NE Spain
103 N15 **Girou** ≈ S France
97 H14 **Girvan** W Scotland, UK
24 M9 **Girvin** Texas, SW USA
184 Q9 **Gisborne** Gisborne, North Island, New Zealand
184 P9 **Gisborne** *off.* Gisborne District. ◈ *unitary authority* North Island, New Zealand
Gisborne District *see* Gisborne
Giseifu *see* Ŭijŏngbu
Gisenye *see* Gisenyi
81 D19 **Gisenyi** *var.* Gisenye. NW Rwanda
95 K20 **Gislaved** Jönköping, S Sweden
103 N4 **Gisors** Eure, N France
Gissar *see* Hisor
147 P12 **Gissar Range** *Rus.* Gissarskiy Khrebet. ▲▲ Tajikistan/Uzbekistan
Gissarskiy Khrebet *see* Gissar Range
99 B16 **Gistel** West-Vlaanderen, W Belgium
108 F9 **Giswil** Unterwalden, C Switzerland
115 B16 **Gitánes** *ancient monument* Ípeiros, W Greece
81 E20 **Gitarama** C Rwanda
81 E20 **Gitega** C Burundi
Githio *see* Gýtheio
108 H11 **Giubiasco** Ticino, S Switzerland
106 K13 **Giulianova** Abruzzi, C Italy
Giulie, Alpi *see* Julian Alps
Giumri *see* Gyumri
116 M13 **Giurgeni** Ialomița, SE Romania
116 J15 **Giurgiu** Giurgiu, S Romania
116 J14 **Giurgiu** ◈ *county* SE Romania
95 F22 **Give** Vejle, C Denmark
103 R2 **Givet** Ardennes, N France
103 R11 **Givors** Rhône, E France
83 K19 **Giyani** Limpopo, NE South Africa
80 I13 **Giyon** Oromo, C Ethiopia
Giza/Gizeh *see* El Gîza
75 V8 **Giza, Pyramids of** *ancient monument* N Egypt
Gizhduvon *see* G'ijduvon
123 U8 **Gizhiga** Magadanskaya Oblast', E Russian Federation
123 T9 **Gizhiginskaya Guba** *bay* E Russian Federation
186 K8 **Gizo** Gizo, NW Solomon Islands
110 N7 **Giżycko** Warmińsko-Mazurskie, NE Poland
Gízymałów *see* Hrymayliv
Gjakovë *see* Đakovica
94 F12 **Gjende** ◎ S Norway
95 F17 **Gjerstad** Aust-Agder, S Norway
Gjilan *see* Gnjilane
Gjinokastër *see* Gjirokastër
113 L23 **Gjirokastër** *var.* Gjirokastra; *prev.* Gjinokastër, *Gk.* Argyrokastron, *It.* Argirocastro. Gjirokastër, S Albania
113 L22 **Gjirokastër** ◈ *district* S Albania
Gjirokastra *see* Gjirokastër
94 H13 **Gjøvik** Oppland, S Norway
113 J22 **Gjuhëzës, Kepi i** *headland* SW Albania
Gjurgjevac *see* Đurđevac
115 E18 **Gkióna** *var.* Giona. ▲ C Greece
121 R3 **Gkréko, Akrotíri** *var.* Cape Greco, Pidálion. *cape* E Cyprus
99 I18 **Glabbeek-Zuurbemde** Vlaams Brabant, C Belgium
13 R14 **Glace Bay** Cape Breton Island, Nova Scotia, SE Canada
9 O16 **Glacier** British Columbia, SW Canada
39 W12 **Glacier Bay** *inlet* Alaska, USA
32 I7 **Glacier Peak** ▲ Washington, NW USA
21 Q7 **Glade Spring** Virginia, NE USA
43 W7 **Gladewater** Texas, SW USA
181 Y8 **Gladstone** Queensland, E Australia
182 I8 **Gladstone** South Australia
9 X16 **Gladstone** Manitoba, S Canada
31 O5 **Gladstone** Michigan, N USA
27 R4 **Gladstone** Missouri, C USA
31 Q7 **Gladwin** Michigan, N USA
95 J15 **Glafsfjorden** ◎ C Sweden
92 H2 **Glåma** *physical region* NW Iceland
94 I12 **Glåma** *var.* Glommen. ≈ S Norway

◆ Country
● Country Capital
◇ Dependent Territory
○ Dependent Territory Capital
◈ Administrative Regions
✈ International Airport
▲ Mountain
▲▲ Mountain Range
Volcano
≈ River
◎ Lake
⊠ Reservoir

◆ Country ◇ Dependent Territory ◆ Administrative Regions ▲ Mountain ☒ Volcano ☺ Lake
● Country Capital ○ Dependent Territory Capital ✈ International Airport ▲ Mountain Range ⚑ River ☒ Reservoir

Govĭ-Sumber – Gregory Lake

162 M8 **Govĭ-Sumber** ◈ *province* C Mongolia
Govurdak *see* Govurdak
18 D11 **Gowanda** New York, NE USA
148 J10 **Gowd-e Zereh, Dasht-e** *var.* Guad-i-Zirreh. *marsh* SW Afghanistan
14 F8 **Gowganda** Ontario, S Canada
14 G8 **Gowganda Lake** ◎ Ontario, S Canada
29 U13 **Gowrie** Iowa, C USA
147 N14 **Govurdak** *Rus.* Govurdak; *prev.* Guardak. Lebap Welaýaty, E Turkmenistan
61 C15 **Goya** Corrientes, NE Argentina
Goyania *see* Goiânia
Goyaz *see* Goiás
137 X11 **Göyçay** *Rus.* Geokchay. C Azerbaijan
146 D10 **Goymat** *Rus.* Koymat. Balkan Welaýaty, NW Turkmenistan
146 D10 **Goymatdag, Gory** *Rus.* Gory Koymatdag. *hill range* Balkan Welaýaty, NW Turkmenistan
136 F12 **Göynük** Bolu, NW Turkey
165 R9 **Goyō-san** ▲ Honshū, C Japan
78 K11 **Goz Beïda** Ouaddaï, SE Chad
146 M10 **G'ozg'on** *Rus.* Gazgan. Navoy Viloyati, C Uzbekistan
146 M10 **G'ozg'on** *Rus.* Gazgan. Nawoiy Viloyati, C Uzbekistan
158 H11 **Gozha Co** ◎ W China
121 O15 **Gozo** *var.* Ghawdex. *island* N Malta
80 H9 **Göz Regeb** Kassala, NE Sudan
83 H25 **Graaff-Reinet** Eastern Cape, S South Africa
Graasten *see* Gråsten
76 L17 **Grabo** SW Ivory Coast
112 P11 **Grabovica** Serbia, E Serbia
110 I13 **Grabów nad Prosną** Wielkopolskie, C Poland
108 I8 **Grabs** Sankt Gallen, NE Switzerland
112 D12 **Gračac** Zadar, SW Croatia
112 I11 **Gračanica** Federacija Bosna I Hercegovina, NE Bosnia and Herzegovina
14 L11 **Gracefield** Québec, SE Canada
99 K19 **Grâce-Hollogne** Liège, E Belgium
23 R8 **Graceville** Florida, SE USA
29 R8 **Graceville** Minnesota, N USA
42 G6 **Gracias** Lempira, W Honduras
Gracias *see* Lempira
42 L5 **Gracias a Dios** ◈ *department* E Honduras
43 O6 **Gracias a Dios, Cabo de** *headland* Honduras/Nicaragua
64 O2 **Graciosa** *var.* Ilha Graciosa. *island* Azores, Portugal, NE Atlantic Ocean
64 Q11 **Graciosa** *island* Islas Canarias, Spain, NE Atlantic Ocean
Graciosa, Ilha *see* Graciosa
112 I11 **Gradačac** Federacija Bosna I Hercegovina, N Bosnia and Herzegovina
59 J15 **Gradaús, Serra dos** ▲▲ C Brazil
104 L3 **Gradefes** Castilla-León, N Spain
Gradiška *see* Bosanska Gradiška
Gradizhsk *see* Hradyz'k
106 J7 **Grado** Friuli-Venezia Giulia, NE Italy
104 K2 **Grado** Asturias, N Spain
113 P19 **Gradsko** C FYR Macedonia
37 V11 **Grady** New Mexico, SW USA
Grad Zagreb *see* Zagreb
29 T12 **Graettinger** Iowa, C USA
101 M23 **Grafing** Bayern, SE Germany
25 S6 **Graford** Texas, SW USA
183 V5 **Grafton** New South Wales, SE Australia
29 Q3 **Grafton** North Dakota, N USA
21 S3 **Grafton** West Virginia, NE USA
21 T9 **Graham** North Carolina, SE USA
25 R6 **Graham** Texas, SW USA
Graham Bell Island *see* Greem-Bell, Ostrov
10 I13 **Graham Island** *island* Queen Charlotte Islands, British Columbia, SW Canada
19 S6 **Graham Lake** ◎ Maine, NE USA
194 H4 **Graham Land** *physical region* Antarctica
37 N15 **Graham, Mount** ▲ Arizona, SW USA
Grahamstad *see* Grahamstown
83 I25 **Grahamstown** *Afr.* Grahamstad. Eastern Cape, S South Africa
Grahovo *see* Bosansko Grahovo
68 C12 **Grain Coast** *coastal region* S Liberia
169 S17 **Grajagan, Teluk** *bay* Jawa, S Indonesia
59 L14 **Grajaú** Maranhão, E Brazil
58 M13 **Grajaú, Rio** ≈ NE Brazil
110 O8 **Grajewo** Podlaskie, NE Poland
95 F24 **Gram** Sønderjylland, SW Denmark
103 N13 **Gramat** Lot, S France
22 H5 **Grambling** Louisiana, S USA
115 C14 **Grámmos** ▲▲ Albania/Greece
96 I9 **Grampian Mountains** ▲▲ C Scotland, UK
182 L12 **Grampians, The** ▲▲ Victoria, SE Australia
98 O9 **Gramsbergen** Overijssel, E Netherlands
113 L21 **Gramsh** *var.* Gramshi. Elbasan, C Albania
Gramshi *see* Gramsh
Gran *see* Esztergom
Gran *see* Hron
54 F11 **Granada** Meta, C Colombia
42 J10 **Granada** Granada, SW Nicaragua
105 N14 **Granada** Andalucía, S Spain
37 W6 **Granada** Colorado, C USA
42 J11 **Granada** ◈ *department* SW Nicaragua
105 N14 **Granada** ◈ *province* Andalucía, S Spain
63 I21 **Gran Antiplanicie Central** *plain* S Argentina
97 E17 **Granard** Longford, C Ireland
63 J20 **Gran Bajo** *basin* S Argentina
63 J15 **Gran Bajo del Gualicho** *basin* E Argentina
63 I21 **Gran Bajo de San Julián** *basin* SE Argentina
25 S7 **Granbury** Texas, SW USA
15 P12 **Granby** Québec, SE Canada
27 S8 **Granby** Missouri, C USA
37 S3 **Granby, Lake** ⊠ Colorado, C USA
64 O12 **Gran Canaria** *var.* Grand Canary. *island* Islas Canarias, Spain, NE Atlantic Ocean
47 T11 **Gran Chaco** *var.* Chaco. *lowland plain* South America
45 R14 **Grand Anse** SW Grenada
Grand-Anse *see* Portsmouth
44 G1 **Grand Bahama Island** *island* N Bahamas
Grand Balé *see* Tui
103 U7 **Grand Ballon** *Ger.* Ballon de Guebwiller. ▲ NE France
13 T13 **Grand Bank** Newfoundland, Newfoundland and Labrador, SE Canada
64 I7 **Grand Banks of Newfoundland** *undersea feature* NW Atlantic Ocean
Grand Bassa *see* Buchanan
77 N17 **Grand-Bassam** *var.* Bassam. SE Ivory Coast
14 E16 **Grand Bend** Ontario, S Canada
76 L17 **Grand-Bérébi** *var.* Grand-Béréby. SW Ivory Coast
Grand-Béréby *see* Grand-Bérébi
45 X11 **Grand-Bourg** Marie-Galante, SE Guadeloupe
44 M6 **Grand Caicos** *var.* Middle Caicos. *island* C Turks and Caicos Islands
14 K12 **Grand Calumet, Île du** *island* Québec, SE Canada
97 E18 **Grand Canal** *Ir.* An Chanáil Mhór. *canal* C Ireland
Grand Canal *see* Da Yunhe
Grand Canary *see* Gran Canaria
36 K10 **Grand Canyon** Arizona, SW USA
36 J9 **Grand Canyon** *canyon* Arizona, SW USA
Grand Canyon State *see* Arizona
44 D8 **Grand Cayman** *island* SW Cayman Islands
9 R14 **Grand Centre** Alberta, SW Canada
76 L17 **Grand Cess** SE Liberia
108 D12 **Grand Combin** ▲ S Switzerland
32 K8 **Grand Coulee** Washington, NW USA
32 J8 **Grand Coulee** *valley* Washington, NW USA
45 X5 **Grand Cul-de-Sac Marin** *bay* N Guadeloupe
Grand Duchy of Luxembourg *see* Luxembourg
63 I22 **Grande, Bahía** *bay* S Argentina
9 N14 **Grande Cache** Alberta, W Canada
103 U12 **Grande Casse** ▲ E France
172 G12 **Grande Comore** *var.* Njazidja, Great Comoro. *island* NW Comoros
61 G18 **Grande, Cuchilla** *hill range* E Uruguay
45 S5 **Grande de Añasco, Río** ≈ W Puerto Rico
Grande de Chiloé, Isla *see* Chiloé, Isla de
58 J12 **Grande de Gurupá, Ilha** *river island* NE Brazil
57 K21 **Grande de Lipez, Río** ≈ SW Bolivia
45 U6 **Grande de Loíza, Río** ≈ E Puerto Rico
45 T5 **Grande de Manatí, Río** ≈ C Puerto Rico
42 L9 **Grande de Matagalpa, Río** ≈ C Nicaragua
40 K12 **Grande de Santiago, Río** *var.* Santiago. ≈ C Mexico
43 O15 **Grande de Térraba, Río** *var.* Río Térraba. ≈ SE Costa Rica
12 J9 **Grande Deux, Réservoir la** ⊠ Québec, E Canada
60 O10 **Grande, Ilha** *island* SE Brazil
9 O13 **Grande Prairie** Alberta, W Canada
74 I8 **Grand Erg Occidental** *desert* W Algeria
74 L9 **Grand Erg Oriental** *desert* Algeria/Tunisia
57 M18 **Grande, Río** ≈ C Bolivia
59 J20 **Grande, Rio** ≈ S Brazil
2 F15 **Grande, Rio** *var.* Río Bravo, *Sp.* Río Bravo del Norte, Bravo del Norte. ≈ Mexico/USA
15 Y7 **Grande-Rivière** Québec, SE Canada
15 Y6 **Grande Rivière** ≈ Québec, SE Canada
44 M8 **Grande-Rivière-du-Nord** N Haiti
62 K9 **Grande, Salina** *var.* Gran Salitral. *salt lake* C Argentina
15 S7 **Grandes-Bergeronnes** Québec, SE Canada
47 W6 **Grande, Serra** ▲ W Brazil
40 K4 **Grande, Sierra** ▲▲ N Mexico
103 S12 **Grandes Rousses** ▲▲ E France
63 K17 **Grandes, Salinas** *salt lake* E Argentina
45 Y5 **Grande Terre** *island* E West Indies
15 X5 **Grande-Vallée** Québec, SE Canada
45 Y5 **Grande Vigie, Pointe de la** *headland* Grande Terre, N Guadeloupe
13 N14 **Grand Falls** New Brunswick, SE Canada
13 T11 **Grand Falls** Newfoundland, Newfoundland and Labrador, SE Canada
24 L9 **Grandfalls** Texas, SW USA
21 P9 **Grandfather Mountain** ▲ North Carolina, SE USA
26 L13 **Grandfield** Oklahoma, C USA
9 N17 **Grand Forks** British Columbia, SW Canada
29 R4 **Grand Forks** North Dakota, N USA
31 O9 **Grand Haven** Michigan, N USA
Grandichi *see* Hrandzichy
29 P15 **Grand Island** Nebraska, C USA
31 O3 **Grand Island** *island* Michigan, N USA
22 K10 **Grand Isle** Louisiana, S USA
65 A23 **Grand Jason** *island* Jason Islands, NW Falkland Islands
37 P5 **Grand Junction** Colorado, C USA
20 F10 **Grand Junction** Tennessee, S USA
14 J9 **Grand-Lac-Victoria** Québec, SE Canada
14 J9 **Grand lac Victoria** ◎ Québec, SE Canada
77 N17 **Grand-Lahou** *var.* Grand Lahu. S Ivory Coast
Grand Lahu *see* Grand-Lahou
37 S3 **Grand Lake** Colorado, C USA
13 S11 **Grand Lake** ◎ Newfoundland, Newfoundland and Labrador, E Canada
22 G9 **Grand Lake** ◎ Louisiana, S USA
31 R5 **Grand Lake** ◎ Michigan, N USA
31 Q13 **Grand Lake** ⊠ Ohio, N USA
27 R9 **Grand Lake O' The Cherokees** *var.* Lake O' The Cherokees. ⊠ Oklahoma, C USA
31 Q9 **Grand Ledge** Michigan, N USA
102 I8 **Grand-Lieu, Lac de** ◎ NW France
19 U6 **Grand Manan Channel** *channel* Canada/USA
13 O15 **Grand Manan Island** *island* New Brunswick, SE Canada
29 Y4 **Grand Marais** Minnesota, N USA
15 P10 **Grand-Mère** Québec, SE Canada
37 P5 **Grand Mesa** ▲▲ Colorado, C USA
108 C10 **Grand Muveran** ▲ W Switzerland
104 G12 **Grândola** Setúbal, S Portugal
Grand Paradis *see* Gran Paradiso
187 O15 **Grand Passage** *passage* N New Caledonia
77 R16 **Grand-Popo** S Benin
29 Z3 **Grand Portage** Minnesota, N USA
25 T6 **Grand Prairie** Texas, SW USA
9 W14 **Grand Rapids** Manitoba, C Canada
31 P9 **Grand Rapids** Michigan, N USA
29 V5 **Grand Rapids** Minnesota, N USA
14 L10 **Grand-Remous** Québec, SE Canada
14 F15 **Grand River** ≈ Ontario, S Canada
31 P9 **Grand River** ≈ Michigan, N USA
27 T3 **Grand River** ≈ Missouri, C USA
28 M7 **Grand River** ≈ South Dakota, N USA
45 Q11 **Grand' Rivière** N Martinique
32 F11 **Grand Ronde** Oregon, NW USA
32 L11 **Grand Ronde River** ≈ Oregon/Washington, NW USA
Grand-Saint-Bernard, Col du *see* Great Saint Bernard Pass
25 V6 **Grand Saline** Texas, SW USA
55 X10 **Grand-Santi** W French Guiana
Grandsee *see* Grandson
172 J16 **Grand Sœur** *island* Les Sœurs, NE Seychelles
108 B9 **Grandson** *prev.* Grandsee. Vaud, W Switzerland
33 S14 **Grand Teton** ▲ Wyoming, C USA
31 P5 **Grand Traverse Bay** *lake bay* Michigan, N USA
45 N6 **Grand Turk** ○ (Turks and Caicos Islands) Grand Turk Island, S Turks and Caicos Islands
45 N6 **Grand Turk Island** *island* SE Turks and Caicos Islands
103 S13 **Grand Veymont** ▲ E France
9 W15 **Grandview** Manitoba, S Canada
27 R4 **Grandview** Missouri, C USA
36 I10 **Grand Wash Cliffs** *cliff* Arizona, SW USA
14 J8 **Granet, Lac** ◎ Québec, SE Canada
95 L14 **Grangärde** Dalarna, C Sweden
44 H12 **Grange Hill** W Jamaica
96 J12 **Grangemouth** C Scotland, UK
25 T10 **Granger** Texas, SW USA
32 J10 **Granger** Washington, NW USA
33 T17 **Granger** Wyoming, C USA
Granges *see* Grenchen
95 L14 **Grängesberg** Kopparberg, C Sweden
33 N11 **Grangeville** Idaho, NW USA
10 K13 **Granisle** British Columbia, SW Canada
30 K15 **Granite City** Illinois, N USA
29 S9 **Granite Falls** Minnesota, N USA
21 Q9 **Granite Falls** North Carolina, SE USA
36 K12 **Granite Mountain** ▲ Arizona, SW USA
33 T12 **Granite Peak** ▲ Montana, NW USA
35 T2 **Granite Peak** ▲ Nevada, W USA
36 J3 **Granite Peak** ▲ Utah, W USA
Granite State *see* New Hampshire
107 H24 **Granitola, Capo** *headland* Sicilia, Italy, C Mediterranean Sea
185 H15 **Granity** West Coast, South Island, New Zealand
Gran Lago *see* Nicaragua, Lago de
63 J18 **Gran Laguna Salada** ◎ S Argentina
Gran Malvina *see* West Falkland
95 L18 **Gränna** Jönköping, S Sweden
105 W5 **Granollers** *var.* Granollérs. Cataluña, NE Spain
Granollérs *see* Granollers
106 A7 **Gran Paradiso** *Fr.* Grand Paradis. ▲ NW Italy
Gran Pilastro *see* Hochfeiler
Gran Salitral *see* Grande, Salina
Gran San Bernardo, Passo di *see* Great Saint Bernard Pass
Gran Santiago *see* Santiago
107 J14 **Gran Sasso d'Italia** ▲▲ C Italy
100 N11 **Gransee** Brandenburg, NE Germany
28 L15 **Grant** Nebraska, C USA
27 R1 **Grant City** Missouri, C USA
97 N19 **Grantham** E England, UK
65 D24 **Grantham Sound** *sound* East Falkland, Falkland Islands
194 K13 **Grant Island** *island* Antarctica
45 Z14 **Grantley Adams** ✈ (Bridgetown) SE Barbados
35 S7 **Grant, Mount** ▲ Nevada, W USA
96 J9 **Grantown-on-Spey** N Scotland, UK
35 W8 **Grant Range** ▲▲ Nevada, W USA
37 Q11 **Grants** New Mexico, SW USA
30 I4 **Grantsburg** Wisconsin, N USA
32 F15 **Grants Pass** Oregon, NW USA
36 K3 **Grantsville** Utah, W USA
21 R4 **Grantsville** West Virginia, NE USA
102 I5 **Granville** Manche, N France
9 V12 **Granville Lake** ◎ Manitoba, C Canada
25 V8 **Grapeland** Texas, SW USA
25 T6 **Grapevine** Texas, SW USA
83 K20 **Graskop** Mpumalanga, NE South Africa
95 P14 **Gräsö** Uppsala, C Sweden
93 I19 **Gräsö** *island* C Sweden
103 U15 **Grasse** Alpes-Maritimes, SE France
18 E14 **Grassflat** Pennsylvania, NE USA
33 U9 **Grassrange** Montana, NW USA
18 J6 **Grass River** ≈ New York, NE USA
35 P6 **Grass Valley** California, W USA
183 N14 **Grassy** Tasmania, SE Australia
28 K4 **Grassy Butte** North Dakota, N USA
21 R5 **Grassy Knob** ▲ West Virginia, NE USA
95 G24 **Gråsten** *var.* Graasten. Sønderjylland, SW Denmark
95 J18 **Grästorp** Västra Götaland, S Sweden
Gratianopolis *see* Grenoble
109 V8 **Gratwein** Steiermark, SE Austria
Gratz *see* Graz
108 I9 **Graubünden** *Fr.* Grisons, *It.* Grigioni. ◈ *canton* SE Switzerland
Graudenz *see* Grudziądz
103 N15 **Graulhet** Tarn, S France
105 T4 **Graus** Aragón, NE Spain
61 I16 **Gravataí** Rio Grande do Sul, S Brazil
98 L13 **Grave** Noord-Brabant, SE Netherlands
9 T17 **Gravelbourg** Saskatchewan, S Canada
103 N1 **Gravelines** Nord, N France
Graven *see* Grez-Doiceau
14 H13 **Gravenhurst** Ontario, S Canada
33 O10 **Grave Peak** ▲ Idaho, NW USA
102 I11 **Grave, Pointe de** *headland* W France
183 S4 **Gravesend** New South Wales, SE Australia
97 P22 **Gravesend** SE England, UK
107 N17 **Gravina di Puglia** Puglia, SE Italy
103 S8 **Gray** Haute-Saône, E France
23 T4 **Gray** Georgia, SE USA
195 V16 **Gray, Cape** *headland* Antarctica
32 F9 **Grayland** Washington, NW USA
39 N10 **Grayling** Alaska, USA
31 Q6 **Grayling** Michigan, N USA
32 F9 **Grays Harbor** *inlet* Washington, NW USA
21 O5 **Grayson** Kentucky, S USA
37 S4 **Grays Peak** ▲ Colorado, C USA
30 M16 **Grayville** Illinois, N USA
109 V8 **Graz** *prev.* Gratz. Steiermark, SE Austria
104 L15 **Grazalema** Andalucía, S Spain
113 P15 **Grdelica** Serbia, SE Serbia
44 H1 **Great Abaco** *var.* Abaco Island. *island* N Bahamas
Great Admiralty Island *see* Manus Island
Great Alfold *see* Great Hungarian Plain
Great Ararat *see* Büyükağrı Dağı
181 U8 **Great Artesian Basin** *lowlands* Queensland, C Australia
181 O12 **Great Australian Bight** *bight* S Australia
64 E11 **Great Bahama Bank** *undersea feature* E Gulf of Mexico
184 M4 **Great Barrier Island** *island* N New Zealand
181 X4 **Great Barrier Reef** *reef* Queensland, NE Australia
18 L11 **Great Barrington** Massachusetts, NE USA
0 F10 **Great Basin** *basin* W USA
8 I8 **Great Bear Lake** *Fr.* Grand Lac de l'Ours. ◎ Northwest Territories, NW Canada
Great Belt *see* Storebælt
26 L5 **Great Bend** Kansas, C USA
Great Bermuda *see* Bermuda
97 A20 **Great Blasket Island** *Ir.* An Blascaod Mór. *island* SW Ireland
Great Britain *see* Britain
151 Q23 **Great Channel** *channel* Andaman Sea/Indian Ocean
166 J10 **Great Coco Island** *island* SW Burma (Myanmar)
Great Comoro *see* Grande Comore
Great Crosby *see* Crosby
21 X7 **Great Dismal Swamp** *wetland* North Carolina/Virginia, SE USA
33 V16 **Great Divide Basin** *basin* Wyoming, C USA
181 W7 **Great Dividing Range** ▲▲ NE Australia
14 D12 **Great Duck Island** *island* Ontario, S Canada
Great Elder Reservoir *see* Waconda Lake
195 V8 **Greater Antarctica** *var.* East Antarctica. *physical region* Antarctica
44 G8 **Greater Antilles** *island group* West Indies
129 V16 **Greater Sunda Islands** *var.* Sunda Islands. *island group* Indonesia
184 I1 **Great Exhibition Bay** *inlet* North Island, New Zealand
44 H4 **Great Exuma Island** *island* C Bahamas
33 R8 **Great Falls** Montana, NW USA
21 R11 **Great Falls** South Carolina, SE USA
84 F9 **Great Fisher Bank** *undersea feature* C North Sea
Great Glen *see* Mor, Glen
Great Grimsby *see* Grimsby
44 I4 **Great Guana Cay** *island* C Bahamas
64 I5 **Great Hellefiske Bank** *undersea feature* N Atlantic Ocean
111 L24 **Great Hungarian Plain** *var.* Great Alfold, Plain of Hungary, *Hung.* Alföld. *plain* SE Europe
44 L7 **Great Inagua** *var.* Inagua Islands. *island* S Bahamas
Great Indian Desert *see* Thar Desert
83 G25 **Great Karoo** *var.* Great Karroo, High Veld, *Afr.* Groot Karoo, Hoë Karoo. *plateau region* S South Africa
Great Karroo *see* Great Karoo
Great Kei *see* Groot-Kei
Great Khingan Range *see* Da Hinggan Ling
14 E11 **Great La Cloche Island** *island* Ontario, S Canada
183 P16 **Great Lake** ◎ Tasmania, SE Australia
Great Lake *see* Tônlé Sap
9 R15 **Great Lakes** *lakes* Ontario, Canada/USA
Great Lakes State *see* Michigan
97 L20 **Great Malvern** W England, UK
184 M5 **Great Mercury Island** *island* N New Zealand
Great Meteor Seamount *see* Great Meteor Tablemount
64 K10 **Great Meteor Tablemount** *var.* Great Meteor Seamount. *undersea feature* E Atlantic Ocean
31 Q14 **Great Miami River** ≈ Ohio, N USA
151 Q24 **Great Nicobar** *island* Nicobar Islands, India, NE Indian Ocean
67 T4 **Great Oasis, The** *var.* Khârga Oasis. *oasis* S Egypt
97 O19 **Great Ouse** *var.* Ouse. ≈ E England, UK
183 Q17 **Great Oyster Bay** *bay* Tasmania, SE Australia
44 I13 **Great Pedro Bluff** *headland* W Jamaica
21 T12 **Great Pee Dee River** ≈ North Carolina/South Carolina, SE USA
129 W9 **Great Plain of China** *plain* E China
0 F12 **Great Plains** *var.* High Plains. *plains* Canada/USA
37 W6 **Great Plains Reservoirs** ⊠ Colorado, C USA
19 Q13 **Great Point** *headland* Nantucket Island, Massachusetts, NE USA
68 I13 **Great Rift Valley** *var.* Rift Valley. *depression* Asia/Africa
81 I23 **Great Ruaha** ≈ S Tanzania
18 K10 **Great Sacandaga Lake** ⊠ New York, NE USA
108 C12 **Great Saint Bernard Pass** *Fr.* Col du Grand-Saint-Bernard, *It.* Passo del Gran San Bernardo. *pass* Italy/Switzerland
44 F1 **Great Sale Cay** *island* N Bahamas
Great Salt Desert *see* Kavīr, Dasht-e
36 K1 **Great Salt Lake** *salt lake* Utah, W USA
36 J3 **Great Salt Lake Desert** *plain* Utah, W USA
26 M8 **Great Salt Plains Lake** ⊠ Oklahoma, C USA
75 T9 **Great Sand Sea** *desert* Egypt/Libya
180 L6 **Great Sandy Desert** *desert* Western Australia
Great Sandy Desert *see* Ar Rub 'al Khālī
Great Sandy Island *see* Fraser Island
187 Y13 **Great Sea Reef** *reef* Vanua Levu, N Fiji
38 H17 **Great Sitkin Island** *island* Aleutian Islands, Alaska, USA
8 J10 **Great Slave Lake** *Fr.* Grand Lac des Esclaves. ◎ Northwest Territories, NW Canada
21 O10 **Great Smoky Mountains** ▲▲ North Carolina/Tennessee, SE USA
10 L11 **Great Snow Mountain** ▲ British Columbia, W Canada
64 A12 **Great Sound** *sound* Bermuda, NW Atlantic Ocean
180 M10 **Great Victoria Desert** *desert* South Australia/Western Australia
194 H2 **Great Wall** *Chinese research station* South Shetland Islands, Antarctica
19 T7 **Great Wass Island** *island* Maine, NE USA
97 Q19 **Great Yarmouth** *var.* Yarmouth. E England, UK
139 S1 **Great Zab** *Ar.* Az Zāb al Kabīr, *Kurd.* Zē-i Bādīnān, *Turk.* Büyükzap Suyu. ≈ Iraq/Turkey
95 I17 **Grebbestad** Västra Götaland, S Sweden
Grebenka *see* Hrebinka
42 M13 **Grecia** Alajuela, C Costa Rica
61 E18 **Greco** Río Negro, W Uruguay
Greco, Cape *see* Gkréko, Akrotíri
104 L8 **Gredos, Sierra de** ▲▲ W Spain
18 F9 **Greece** New York, NE USA
115 E17 **Greece** *off.* Hellenic Republic, *Gk.* Ellás; *anc.* Hellas. ◆ *republic* SE Europe
Greece Central *see* Stereá Ellás
Greece West *see* Dytikí Ellás
37 T3 **Greeley** Colorado, C USA
29 P14 **Greeley** Nebraska, C USA
122 K3 **Greem-Bell, Ostrov** *Eng.* Graham Bell Island. *island* Zemlya Frantsa-Iosifa, N Russian Federation
30 M6 **Green Bay** Wisconsin, N USA
31 N6 **Green Bay** *lake bay* Michigan/Wisconsin, N USA
21 S5 **Greenbrier River** ≈ West Virginia, NE USA
29 S2 **Greenbush** Minnesota, N USA
183 R12 **Green Cape** *headland* New South Wales, SE Australia
31 O14 **Greencastle** Indiana, N USA
18 F16 **Greencastle** Pennsylvania, NE USA
27 T2 **Green City** Missouri, C USA
21 O9 **Greeneville** Tennessee, S USA
35 O11 **Greenfield** California, W USA
31 P14 **Greenfield** Indiana, N USA
29 U15 **Greenfield** Iowa, C USA
18 M11 **Greenfield** Massachusetts, NE USA
27 S7 **Greenfield** Missouri, C USA
31 S14 **Greenfield** Ohio, N USA
20 G8 **Greenfield** Tennessee, S USA
30 M9 **Greenfield** Wisconsin, N USA
27 T9 **Green Forest** Arkansas, C USA
37 T7 **Greenhorn Mountain** ▲ Colorado, C USA
Green Island *see* Lü Tao
186 I6 **Green Islands** *var.* Nissan Islands. *island group* NE Papua New Guinea
9 S14 **Green Lake** Saskatchewan, C Canada
30 L8 **Green Lake** ◎ Wisconsin, N USA
197 O14 **Greenland** *Dan.* Grønland, *Inuit* Kalaallit Nunaat. ◇ *Danish external territory* NE North America
84 D4 **Greenland** *island* NE North America
197 R13 **Greenland Plain** *undersea feature* N Greenland Sea
197 R14 **Greenland Sea** *sea* Arctic Ocean
37 R4 **Green Mountain Reservoir** ⊠ Colorado, C USA
18 M8 **Green Mountains** ▲▲ Vermont, NE USA
Green Mountain State *see* Vermont
96 H12 **Greenock** W Scotland, UK
39 T5 **Greenough, Mount** ▲ Alaska, USA
186 A6 **Green River** Sandaun, NW Papua New Guinea
37 N5 **Green River** Utah, W USA
33 U17 **Green River** Wyoming, C USA
16 H9 **Green River** ≈ W USA
30 K11 **Green River** ≈ Illinois, N USA
20 J7 **Green River** ≈ Kentucky, C USA
28 K5 **Green River** ≈ North Dakota, N USA
37 N6 **Green River** ≈ Utah, W USA
33 T16 **Green River** ≈ Wyoming, C USA
20 L7 **Green River Lake** ⊠ Kentucky, S USA
23 O5 **Greensboro** Alabama, S USA
23 U3 **Greensboro** Georgia, SE USA
21 T9 **Greensboro** North Carolina, SE USA
31 P14 **Greensburg** Indiana, N USA
26 K6 **Greensburg** Kansas, C USA
20 L7 **Greensburg** Kentucky, S USA
18 C15 **Greensburg** Pennsylvania, NE USA
37 O13 **Greens Peak** ▲ Arizona, SW USA
21 V12 **Green Swamp** *wetland* North Carolina, SE USA
21 O4 **Greenup** Kentucky, S USA
36 M16 **Green Valley** Arizona, SW USA
76 K17 **Greenville** *var.* Sino, Sinoe. SE Liberia
23 P6 **Greenville** Alabama, S USA
23 T8 **Greenville** Florida, SE USA
23 S4 **Greenville** Georgia, SE USA
30 L15 **Greenville** Illinois, N USA
20 I7 **Greenville** Kentucky, S USA
19 Q5 **Greenville** Maine, NE USA
31 P9 **Greenville** Michigan, N USA
22 J4 **Greenville** Mississippi, S USA
21 W9 **Greenville** North Carolina, SE USA
31 Q13 **Greenville** Ohio, N USA
19 O12 **Greenville** Rhode Island, NE USA
21 P11 **Greenville** South Carolina, SE USA
25 U6 **Greenville** Texas, SW USA
31 T12 **Greenwich** Ohio, N USA
27 S11 **Greenwood** Arkansas, C USA
31 O14 **Greenwood** Indiana, N USA
22 K4 **Greenwood** Mississippi, S USA
21 P12 **Greenwood** South Carolina, SE USA
21 Q12 **Greenwood, Lake** ⊠ South Carolina, SE USA
21 P11 **Greer** South Carolina, SE USA
27 V10 **Greers Ferry Lake** ⊠ Arkansas, C USA
27 S13 **Greeson, Lake** ⊠ Arkansas, C USA
29 O12 **Gregory** South Dakota, N USA
182 J3 **Gregory, Lake** *salt lake* South Australia
180 J9 **Gregory Lake** ◎ Western Australia

◆ Country ● Country Capital ◇ Dependent Territory ○ Dependent Territory Capital ◈ Administrative Regions ✈ International Airport ▲ Mountain ▲▲ Mountain Range Ѫ Volcano ≈ River ◎ Lake ⊠ Reservoir

GREGORY RANGE – GUINGAMP

181 *V5* **Gregory Range** ▲▲ Queensland, E Australia
Greifenberg/Greifenberg in Pommern *see* Gryfice
Greifenhagen *see* Gryfino
100 *O8* **Greifswald** Mecklenburg-Vorpommern, NE Germany
100 *O8* **Greifswalder Bodden** *bay* NE Germany
109 *U4* **Grein** Oberösterreich, N Austria
101 *M17* **Greiz** Thüringen, C Germany
Gremicha/Gremiha *see* Gremikha
124 *M4* **Gremikha** ***var.*** Gremicha, Gremiha. Murmanskaya Oblast', NW Russian Federation
125 *V14* **Gremyachinsk** Permskaya Oblast', NW Russian Federation
Grenå *see* Grenaa
95 *H21* **Grenaa** ***var.*** Grenå. Århus, C Denmark
22 *L3* **Grenada** Mississippi, S USA
45 *W15* **Grenada** ◆ *commonwealth republic* SE West Indies
47 *S4* **Grenada** *island* Grenada
47 *R4* **Grenada Basin** *undersea feature* W Atlantic Ocean
22 *L3* **Grenada Lake** ⊠ Mississippi, S USA
45 *Y14* **Grenadines, The** *island group* Grenada/St Vincent and the Grenadines
108 *D7* **Grenchen** ***Fr.*** Granges. Solothurn, NW Switzerland
183 *Q9* **Grenfell** New South Wales, SE Australia
9 *V16* **Grenfell** Saskatchewan, S Canada
92 *J1* **Grenivík** Nordhurland Eystra, N Iceland
103 *S12* **Grenoble** ***anc.*** Cularo, Gratianopolis. Isère, E France
28 *J2* **Grenora** North Dakota, N USA
92 *N8* **Grense-Jakobselv** Finnmark, N Norway
45 *S14* **Grenville** E Grenada
32 *G11* **Gresham** Oregon, NW USA
Gresk *see* Hresk
106 *B7* **Gressoney-St-Jean** Valle d'Aosta, NW Italy
22 *K9* **Gretna** Louisiana, S USA
21 *T7* **Gretna** Virginia, NE USA
98 *F13* **Grevelingen** *inlet* S North Sea
100 *F13* **Greven** Nordrhein-Westfalen, NW Germany
115 *D15* **Grevená** Dytikí Makedonía, N Greece
101 *D16* **Grevenbroich** Nordrhein-Westfalen, W Germany
99 *N24* **Grevenmacher** Grevenmacher, E Luxembourg
99 *M24* **Grevenmacher** ◐ *district* E Luxembourg
100 *K9* **Grevesmülhen** Mecklenburg-Vorpommern, N Germany
185 *H16* **Grey** ≈ South Island, New Zealand
33 *V12* **Greybull** Wyoming, C USA
33 *U13* **Greybull River** ≈ Wyoming, C USA
65 *A24* **Grey Channel** *sound* Falkland Islands
Greyerzer See *see* Gruyère, Lac de la
13 *T10* **Grey Islands** *island group* Newfoundland and Labrador, E Canada
18 *L10* **Greylock, Mount** ▲ Massachusetts, NE USA
185 *G17* **Greymouth** West Coast, South Island, New Zealand
181 *U10* **Grey Range** ▲▲ New South Wales/Queensland, E Australia
97 *G18* **Greystones** ***Ir.*** Na Clocha Liatha. E Ireland
185 *M14* **Greytown** Wellington, North Island, New Zealand
83 *K23* **Greytown** KwaZulu/Natal, E South Africa
Greytown *see* San Juan del Norte
99 *H19* **Grez-Doiceau** ***Dut.*** Graven. Walloon Brabant, C Belgium
115 *J19* **Griá, Ákrotirio** *headland* Ándros, Kykládes, Greece, Aegean Sea
127 *N8* **Gribanovskiy** Voronezhskaya Oblast', W Russian Federation
78 *I13* **Gribingui** ≈ N Central African Republic
35 *O6* **Gridley** California, W USA
83 *G23* **Griekwastad** Northern Cape, C South Africa
23 *S4* **Griffin** Georgia, SE USA
183 *O9* **Griffith** New South Wales, SE Australia
14 *F13* **Griffith Island** *island* Ontario, S Canada
21 *W10* **Grifton** North Carolina, SE USA
Grigioni *see* Graubünden
119 *H14* **Grigiškes** Vilnius, SE Lithuania
117 *N10* **Grigoriopol** C Moldova
147 *X7* **Grigor'yevka** Issyk-Kul'skaya Oblast', E Kyrgyzstan
193 *U8* **Grijalva Ridge** *undersea feature* E Pacific Ocean
41 *U15* **Grijalva, Río** ***var.*** Tabasco. ≈ Guatemala/Mexico
98 *N5* **Grijpskerk** Groningen, NE Netherlands
83 *C22* **Grillenthal** Karas, SW Namibia
79 *J15* **Grimari** Ouaka, C Central African Republic
Grimaylov *see* Hrymayliv
99 *G18* **Grimbergen** Vlaams Brabant, C Belgium
183 *N15* **Grim, Cape** *headland* Tasmania, SE Australia
100 *N8* **Grimmen** Mecklenburg-Vorpommern, NE Germany
14 *G16* **Grimsby** Ontario, S Canada
97 *O17* **Grimsby** ***prev.*** Great Grimsby. E England, UK
92 *J1* **Grímsey** ***var.*** Grimsey. *island* N Iceland
Grimsey *see* Grímsey
9 *O12* **Grimshaw** Alberta, W Canada
95 *F18* **Grimstad** Aust-Agder, S Norway
92 *H4* **Grindavík** Reykjanes, W Iceland
108 *F9* **Grindelwald** Bern, S Switzerland
95 *F23* **Grindsted** Ribe, W Denmark
29 *W14* **Grinnell** Iowa, C USA
109 *U10* **Grintovec** ▲ N Slovenia
182 *H1* **Griselda, Lake** *salt lake* South Australia
Grisons *see* Graubünden
95 *P14* **Grisslehamn** Stockholm, C Sweden
29 *T15* **Griswold** Iowa, C USA
102 *M1* **Griz Nez, Cap** *headland* N France
112 *P13* **Grljan** Serbia, E Serbia
112 *E11* **Grmeč** ▲▲ NW Bosnia and Herzegovina
99 *H16* **Grobbendonk** Antwerpen, N Belgium
Grobin *see* Grobiņa
118 *C10* **Grobiņa** ***Ger.*** Grobin. Liepāja, W Latvia
83 *K20* **Groblersdal** Mpumalanga, NE South Africa
83 *G23* **Groblershoop** Northern Cape, W South Africa
Gródek Jagielloński *see* Horodok
109 *Q6* **Grödig** Salzburg, W Austria
111 *H15* **Grodków** Opolskie, S Poland
Grodnenskaya Oblast' *see* Hrodzyenskaya Voblasts'
Grodno *see* Hrodna
110 *L12* **Grodzisk Mazowiecki** Mazowieckie, C Poland
110 *F12* **Grodzisk Wielkopolski** Weilkopolskie, C Poland
Grodzyanka *see* Hradzyanka
98 *O12* **Groenlo** Gelderland, E Netherlands
83 *E22* **Groenrivier** Karas, SE Namibia
25 *U8* **Groesbeck** Texas, SW USA
98 *L13* **Groesbeek** Gelderland, SE Netherlands
102 *G7* **Groix, Îles de** *island group* NW France
110 *M12* **Grójec** Mazowieckie, C Poland
65 *K15* **Gröll Seamount** *undersea feature* C Atlantic Ocean
100 *E13* **Gronau** ***var.*** Gronau in Westfalen. Nordrhein-Westfalen, NW Germany
Gronau in Westfalen *see* Gronau
93 *F15* **Grong** Nord-Trøndelag, C Norway
95 *N22* **Grönhögen** Kalmar, S Sweden
98 *N5* **Groningen** Groningen, NE Netherlands
55 *W9* **Groningen** Saramacca, N Surinam
98 *N5* **Groningen** ◐ *province* NE Netherlands
Grønland *see* Greenland
108 *H11* **Grono** Graubünden, S Switzerland
95 *M20* **Grönskåra** Kalmar, S Sweden
25 *O2* **Groom** Texas, SW USA
35 *W9* **Groom Lake** ◎ Nevada, W USA
83 *H25* **Groot** ≈ S South Africa
181 *S2* **Groote Eylandt** *island* Northern Territory, N Australia
98 *M6* **Grootegast** Groningen, NE Netherlands
83 *D17* **Grootfontein** Otjozondjupa, N Namibia
83 *E22* **Groot Karasberge** ▲▲ S Namibia
Groot Karoo *see* Great Karoo
83 *J25* **Groot-Kei** ***Eng.*** Great Kei. ≈ S South Africa
45 *T10* **Gros Islet** N Saint Lucia
44 *L8* **Gros-Morne** NW Haiti
13 *S11* **Gros Morne** ▲ Newfoundland, Newfoundland and Labrador, E Canada
103 *R9* **Grosne** ≈ C France
45 *S12* **Gros Piton** ▲ SW Saint Lucia
Grossa, Isola *see* Dugi Otok
Grossbetschkerek *see* Zrenjanin
Grosse Isper *see* Grosse Ysper
Grosse Kokel *see* Târnava Mare
101 *M21* **Grosse Laaber** ***var.*** Grosse Laber. ≈ SE Germany
Grosse Laber *see* Grosse Laaber
Grosse Morava *see* Velika Morava
101 *O15* **Grossenhain** Sachsen, E Germany
109 *Y4* **Grossenzersdorf** Niederösterreich, NE Austria
101 *O21* **Grosser Arber** ▲ SE Germany
101 *K17* **Grosser Beerberg** ▲ C Germany
101 *G18* **Grosser Feldberg** ▲ W Germany
109 *O8* **Grosser Löffler** ***It.*** Monte Lovello. ▲ Austria/Italy
109 *N8* **Grosser Möseler** ***var.*** Mesule. ▲ Austria/Italy
100 *J8* **Grosser Plöner See** ◎ N Germany
101 *O21* **Grosser Rachel** ▲ SE Germany
Grosser Sund *see* Suur Väin
15 *V6* **Grosses-Roches** Québec, SE Canada
109 *P8* **Grosses Weiesbachhorn** ***var.*** Wiesbachhorn. ▲ W Austria
106 *F13* **Grosseto** Toscana, C Italy
101 *M22* **Grosse Vils** ≈ SE Germany
109 *U4* **Grosse Ysper** ***var.*** Grosse Isper. ≈ N Austria
101 *G19* **Gross-Gerau** Hessen, W Germany
109 *U3* **Gross Gerungs** Niederösterreich, N Austria
109 *P8* **Grossglockner** ▲ W Austria
Grosskanizsa *see* Nagykanizsa
Gross-Karol *see* Carei
Grosskikinda *see* Kikinda
109 *W9* **Grossklein** Steiermark, SE Austria
Grosskoppe *see* Velká Deštná
Grossmeseritsch *see* Velké Meziříčí
Grossmichel *see* Michalovce
101 *H19* **Grossostheim** Bayern, C Germany
109 *X7* **Grosspetersdorf** Burgenland, SE Austria
109 *T5* **Grossraming** Oberösterreich, C Austria
101 *P14* **Grossräschen** Brandenburg, E Germany
Grossrauschenbach *see* Revúca
Gross-Sankt-Johannis *see* Suure-Jaani
Gross-Schlatten *see* Abrud
109 *V2* **Gross-Siegharts** Niederösterreich, N Austria
Gross-Skaisgirren *see* Bol'shakovo
Gross-Steffelsdorf *see* Rimavská Sobota
Gross Strehlitz *see* Strzelce Opolskie
109 *O8* **Grossvenediger** ▲ W Austria
Grosswardein *see* Oradea
Gross Wartenberg *see* Syców
109 *U11* **Grosuplje** C Slovenia
99 *H17* **Grote Nete** ≈ N Belgium
94 *E10* **Grotli** Oppland, S Norway
19 *N13* **Groton** Connecticut, NE USA
29 *P8* **Groton** South Dakota, N USA
107 *P18* **Grottaglie** Puglia, SE Italy
107 *L17* **Grottaminarda** Campania, S Italy
106 *K13* **Grottammare** Marche, C Italy
21 *U5* **Grottoes** Virginia, NE USA
Grou *see* Grouw
13 *N10* **Groulx, Monts** ▲▲ Québec, E Canada
14 *E7* **Groundhog** ≈ Ontario, S Canada
36 *J1* **Grouse Creek** Utah, W USA
36 *J1* **Grouse Creek Mountains** ▲▲ Utah, W USA
98 *L6* **Grouw** ***Fris.*** Grou. Friesland, N Netherlands
27 *R8* **Grove** Oklahoma, C USA
31 *S13* **Grove City** Ohio, N USA
18 *B13* **Grove City** Pennsylvania, NE USA
23 *O6* **Grove Hill** Alabama, S USA
33 *S15* **Grover** Wyoming, C USA
35 *P13* **Grover City** California, W USA
25 *Y11* **Groves** Texas, SW USA
19 *O7* **Groveton** New Hampshire, NE USA
25 *W9* **Groveton** Texas, SW USA
36 *J15* **Growler Mountains** ▲▲ Arizona, SW USA
Grozdovo *see* Bratya Daskalovi
127 *P16* **Groznyy** Chechenskaya Respublika, SW Russian Federation
Grubeshov *see* Hrubieszów
112 *G9* **Grubišno Polje** Bjelovar-Bilogora, NE Croatia
Grudovo *see* Sredets
110 *J9* **Grudziądz** ***Ger.*** Graudenz. Kujawsko-pomorskie, C Poland
25 *R17* **Grulla** ***var.*** La Grulla. Texas, SW USA
40 *K14* **Grullo** Jalisco, SW Mexico
67 *V10* **Grumeti** ≈ N Tanzania
95 *K16* **Grums** Värmland, C Sweden
109 *S5* **Grünau im Almtal** Oberösterreich, N Austria
101 *H17* **Grünberg** Hessen, W Germany
Grünberg/Grünberg in Schlesien *see* Zielona Góra
92 *H3* **Grundarfjördhur** Vestfirdhir, W Iceland
21 *P7* **Grundy** Virginia, NE USA
29 *W13* **Grundy Center** Iowa, C USA
Grüneberg *see* Zielona Góra
25 *N1* **Gruver** Texas, SW USA
108 *C9* **Gruyère, Lac de la** ***Ger.*** Greyerzer See. ◎ SW Switzerland
108 *C9* **Gruyères** Fribourg, W Switzerland
118 *E11* **Gruzdīai** Šiauliai, N Lithuania
Gruzinskaya SSR/Gruziya *see* Georgia
Gryada Akkyr *see* Akgyr Erezi
126 *L7* **Gryazi** Lipetskaya Oblast', W Russian Federation
124 *M14* **Gryazovets** Vologodskaya Oblast', NW Russian Federation
111 *M17* **Grybów** Małopolskie, SE Poland
94 *M13* **Grycksbo** Dalarna, C Sweden
110 *E8* **Gryfice** ***Ger.*** Greifenberg, Greifenberg in Pommern. Zachodnio-pomorskie, NW Poland
110 *D9* **Gryfino** ***Ger.*** Greifenhagen. Zachodnio-pomorskie, NW Poland
92 *H9* **Gryllefjord** Troms, N Norway
95 *L15* **Grythyttan** Örebro, C Sweden
108 *D10* **Gstaad** Bern, W Switzerland
43 *P14* **Guabito** Bocas del Toro, NW Panama
44 *G7* **Guacanayabo, Golfo de** *gulf* S Cuba
40 *I7* **Guachochi** Chihuahua, N Mexico
104 *J11* **Guadajira** ≈ SW Spain
104 *M13* **Guadajoz** ≈ S Spain
40 *L13* **Guadalajara** Jalisco, C Mexico
105 *O8* **Guadalajara** ***Ar.*** Wad Al-Hajarah; ***anc.*** Arriaca. Castilla-La Mancha, C Spain
105 *O7* **Guadalajara** ◐ *province* Castilla-La Mancha, C Spain
104 *K12* **Guadalcanal** Andalucía, S Spain
186 *L10* **Guadalcanal** ***off.*** Guadalcanal Province. ◐ *province* C Solomon Islands
186 *M9* **Guadalcanal** *island* C Solomon Islands
Guadalcanal Province *see* Guadalcanal
105 *O12* **Guadalén** ≈ S Spain
105 *R13* **Guadalentín** ≈ SE Spain
104 *K15* **Guadalete** ≈ SW Spain
105 *O13* **Guadalimar** ≈ S Spain
105 *P12* **Guadalmena** ≈ S Spain
104 *L11* **Guadalmez** ≈ W Spain
105 *S7* **Guadalope** ≈ E Spain
104 *K13* **Guadalquivir** ≈ W Spain
104 *J14* **Guadalquivir, Marismas del** ***var.*** Las Marismas. *wetland* SW Spain
40 *M11* **Guadalupe** Zacatecas, C Mexico
57 *E16* **Guadalupe** Ica, W Peru
104 *L10* **Guadalupe** Extremadura, W Spain
36 *L14* **Guadalupe** Arizona, SW USA
35 *P13* **Guadalupe** California, W USA
Guadalupe *see* Canelones
40 *J3* **Guadalupe Bravos** Chihuahua, N Mexico
40 *A4* **Guadalupe, Isla** *island* NW Mexico
37 *U15* **Guadalupe Mountains** ▲▲ New Mexico/Texas, SW USA
24 *J8* **Guadalupe Peak** ▲ Texas, SW USA
25 *R11* **Guadalupe River** ≈ SW USA
104 *K10* **Guadalupe, Sierra de** ▲▲ W Spain
40 *K9* **Guadalupe Victoria** Durango, C Mexico
40 *I8* **Guadalupe y Calvo** Chihuahua, N Mexico
105 *N7* **Guadarrama** Madrid, C Spain
105 *N7* **Guadarrama** ≈ C Spain
104 *M7* **Guadarrama, Puerto de** *pass* C Spain
105 *N9* **Guadarrama, Sierra de** ▲▲ C Spain
105 *Q9* **Guadazaón** ≈ C Spain
45 *X10* **Guadeloupe** ◇ *French overseas department* E West Indies
47 *S3* **Guadeloupe** *island group* E West Indies
45 *W10* **Guadeloupe Passage** *passage* E Caribbean Sea
104 *H13* **Guadiana** ≈ Portugal/Spain
105 *O13* **Guadiana Menor** ≈ S Spain
105 *Q8* **Guadiela** ≈ C Spain
105 *O14* **Guadix** Andalucía, S Spain
Guad-i-Zirreh *see* Gowd-e Zereh, Dasht-e
193 *T12* **Guafo Fracture Zone** *tectonic feature* SE Pacific Ocean
63 *F18* **Guafo, Isla** *island* S Chile
42 *I6* **Guaimaca** Francisco Morazán, C Honduras
54 *J12* **Guainía** ***off.*** Comisaría del Guainía. ◐ *province* E Colombia
Guainía, Comisaría del *see* Guainía
54 *K12* **Guainía, Río** ≈ Colombia/Venezuela
55 *O9* **Guaiquinima, Cerro** *elevation* SE Venezuela
60 *G10* **Guaíra** Paraná, S Brazil
60 *L7* **Guaíra** São Paulo, S Brazil
62 *O7* **Guairá** ***off.*** Departamento del Guairá. ◐ *department* S Paraguay
Guairá, Departamento del *see* Guairá
Guaire *see* Gorey
63 *F18* **Guaiteca, Isla** *island* S Chile
44 *G6* **Guajaba, Cayo** *headland* C Cuba
59 *D16* **Guajará-Mirim** Rondônia, W Brazil
Guajira *see* La Guajira
Guajira, Departamento de La *see* La Guajira
54 *H3* **Guajira, Península de la** *peninsula* N Colombia
42 *J6* **Gualaco** Olancho, C Honduras
34 *L7* **Gualala** California, W USA
42 *E5* **Gualán** Zacapa, C Guatemala
61 *C19* **Gualeguay** Entre Ríos, E Argentina
61 *D18* **Gualeguaychú** Entre Ríos, E Argentina
61 *C18* **Gualeguay, Río** ≈ E Argentina
63 *K16* **Gualicho, Salina del** *salt lake* E Argentina
188 *B15* **Guam** ◇ *US unincorporated territory* W Pacific Ocean
63 *F19* **Guamblin, Isla** *island* Archipiélago de los Chonos, S Chile
61 *A22* **Guaminí** Buenos Aires, E Argentina
40 *H8* **Guamúchil** Sinaloa, C Mexico
54 *H4* **Guana** ***var.*** Misión de Guana. Zulia, NW Venezuela
44 *C4* **Guanabacoa** La Habana, W Cuba
42 *K13* **Guanacaste** ***off.*** Provincia de Guanacaste. ◐ *province* NW Costa Rica
42 *K12* **Guanacaste, Cordillera de** ▲▲ NW Costa Rica
Guanacaste, Provincia de *see* Guanacaste
40 *J8* **Guanaceví** Durango, C Mexico
44 *A5* **Guanahacabibes, Golfo de** *gulf* W Cuba
42 *K4* **Guanaja, Isla de** *island* Islas de la Bahía, N Honduras
44 *C4* **Guanajay** La Habana, W Cuba
41 *N12* **Guanajuato** Guanajuato, C Mexico
40 *M12* **Guanajuato** ◐ *state* C Mexico
54 *J6* **Guanare** Portuguesa, N Venezuela
54 *K7* **Guanare, Río** ≈ W Venezuela
54 *J6* **Guanarito** Portuguesa, NW Venezuela
160 *M3* **Guancen Shan** ▲▲ C China
62 *I9* **Guandacol** La Rioja, W Argentina
44 *A5* **Guane** Pinar del Río, W Cuba
161 *N14* **Guangdong** ***var.*** Guangdong Sheng, Kuang-tung, Kwangtung, Yue. ◐ *province* S China
Guangdong Sheng *see* Guangdong
Guanghua *see* Laohekou
Guangju *see* Kwangju
160 *I13* **Guangnan** ***var.*** Liancheng. Yunnan, SW China
161 *N8* **Guangshui** ***prev.*** Yingshan. Hubei, C China
Guangxi *see* Guangxi Zhuangzu Zizhiqu
160 *K14* **Guangxi Zhuangzu Zizhiqu** ***var.*** Guangxi, Gui, Kuang-hsi, Kwangsi, ***Eng.*** Kwangsi Chuang Autonomous Region. ◐ *autonomous region* S China
160 *J8* **Guangyuan** ***var.*** Kuang-yuan, Kwangyuan. Sichuan, C China
161 *N14* **Guangzhou** ***var.*** Kwangchow, ***Eng.*** Canton. *province capital* Guangdong, S China
59 *N19* **Guanhães** Minas Gerais, SE Brazil
160 *I12* **Guanling** ***var.*** Guanling Buyeizu Miaozu Zizhixian. Guizhou, S China
Guanling Buyeizu Miaozu Zizhixian *see* Guanling
55 *N5* **Guanta** Anzoátegui, NE Venezuela
44 *J8* **Guantánamo** Guantánamo, SE Cuba
44 *J8* **Guantánamo, Bahia de** ***Eng.*** Guantanamo Bay. *US military base* SE Cuba
Guantanamo Bay *see* Guantánamo, Bahia de
Guanxian/Guan Xian *see* Dujiangyan
161 *Q6* **Guanyun** ***var*** Yishan. Jiangsu, E China
54 *C12* **Guapí** Cauca, SW Colombia
43 *N13* **Guápiles** Limón, NE Costa Rica
61 *I15* **Guaporé** Rio Grande do Sul, S Brazil
47 *S8* **Guaporé, Rio** ***var.*** Río Iténez. ≈ Bolivia/Brazil ***see also*** Río Iténez
Guaporé, Rio *see* Iténez, Río
56 *B7* **Guaranda** Bolívar, C Ecuador
60 *H11* **Guaraniaçu** Paraná, S Brazil
59 *O20* **Guarapari** Espírito Santo, SE Brazil
60 *I12* **Guarapuava** Paraná, S Brazil
60 *J8* **Guararapes** São Paulo, S Brazil
105 *S4* **Guara, Sierra de** ▲▲ NE Spain
60 *N10* **Guaratinguetá** São Paulo, S Brazil
104 *I7* **Guarda** Guarda, N Portugal
104 *I7* **Guarda** ◐ *district* N Portugal
Guardak *see* Govurdak
104 *M3* **Guardo** Castilla-León, N Spain
104 *K11* **Guareña** Extremadura, W Spain
60 *J11* **Guaricana, Pico** ▲ S Brazil
54 *L6* **Guárico** ***off.*** Estado Guárico. ◐ *state* N Venezuela
Guárico, Estado *see* Guárico
44 *J7* **Guarico, Punta** *headland* E Cuba
54 *L7* **Guárico, Río** ≈ C Venezuela
60 *M10* **Guarujá** São Paulo, SE Brazil
61 *L22* **Guarulhos** ✕ (São Paulo) São Paulo, S Brazil
43 *R17* **Guarumal** Veraguas, S Panama
Guasapa *see* Guasopa
40 *H8* **Guasave** Sinaloa, C Mexico
54 *I8* **Guasdualito** Apure, C Venezuela
55 *Q7* **Guasipati** Bolívar, E Venezuela
186 *I9* **Guasopa** ***var.*** Guasapa. Woodlark Island, SE Papua New Guinea
106 *F9* **Guastalla** Emilia-Romagna, C Italy
42 *D6* **Guastatoya** ***var.*** El Progreso. El Progreso, C Guatemala
42 *D5* **Guatemala** ***off.*** Republic of Guatemala. ◆ *republic* Central America
42 *A2* **Guatemala** ***off.*** Departamento de Guatemala. ◐ *department* S Guatemala
193 *S7* **Guatemala Basin** *undersea feature* E Pacific Ocean
Guatemala City *see* Ciudad de Guatemala
Guatemala, Departamento de *see* Guatemala
Guatemala, Republic of *see* Guatemala
45 *V14* **Guatuaro Point** *headland* Trinidad, Trinidad and Tobago
186 *B8* **Guavi** ≈ SW Papua New Guinea
54 *G13* **Guaviare** ***off.*** Comisaría Guaviare. ◐ *province* S Colombia
Guaviare, Comisaría *see* Guaviare
54 *J11* **Guaviare, Río** ≈ E Colombia
61 *E15* **Guaviravi** Corrientes, NE Argentina
54 *G12* **Guayabero, Río** ≈ SW Colombia
45 *U6* **Guayama** E Puerto Rico
42 *J7* **Guayambre, Río** ≈ S Honduras
Guayanas, Macizo de las *see* Guiana Highlands
45 *V6* **Guayanés, Punta** *headland* E Puerto Rico
42 *J6* **Guayape, Río** ≈ C Honduras
56 *B7* **Guayaquil** ***var.*** Santiago de Guayaquil. Guayas, SW Ecuador
Guayaquil *see* Simon Bolivar
56 *A8* **Guayaquil, Golfo de** ***var.*** Gulf of Guayaquil. *gulf* SW Ecuador
Guayaquil, Gulf of *see* Guayaquil, Golfo de
56 *A7* **Guayas** ◐ *province* W Ecuador
62 *N7* **Guaycurú, Río** ≈ NE Argentina
40 *F6* **Guaymas** Sonora, NW Mexico
45 *U5* **Guaynabo** E Puerto Rico
80 *H12* **Guba** Benishangul, W Ethiopia
146 *H8* **Gubadag** ***Turkm.*** Tel'man; ***prev.*** Tel'mansk. Daşoguz Welaýaty, N Turkmenistan
125 *T1* **Guba Dolgaya** Nenetskiy Avtonomnyy Okrug, NW Russian Federation
125 *V13* **Gubakha** Permskaya Oblast', NW Russian Federation
106 *I12* **Gubbio** Umbria, C Italy
100 *Q13* **Guben** ***var.*** Wilhelm-Pieck-Stadt. Brandenburg, E Germany
Guben *see* Gubin
110 *D12* **Gubin** ***Ger.*** Guben. Lubuskie, W Poland
126 *K8* **Gubkin** Belgorodskaya Oblast', W Russian Federation
162 *J9* **Guchin-Us** ***var.*** Arguut. Övörhangay, C Mongolia
Gudara *see* Ghŭdara
105 *S8* **Gúdar, Sierra de** ▲▲ E Spain
137 *P8* **Gudaut'a** NW Georgia
94 *G12* **Gudbrandsdalen** *valley* S Norway
95 *G21* **Gudenå** ***var.*** Gudenaa. ≈ C Denmark
Gudenaa *see* Gudenå
127 *P16* **Gudermes** Chechenskaya Respublika, SW Russian Federation
155 *J18* **Gūdūr** Andhra Pradesh, E India
146 *B13* **Gudurolum** Balkan Welaýaty, W Turkmenistan
94 *D13* **Gudvangen** Sogn Og Fjordane, S Norway
103 *U7* **Guebwiller** Haut-Rhin, NE France
Guéckédou *see* Guékédou
14 *K8* **Guéguen, Lac** ◎ Québec, SE Canada
76 *J15* **Guékédou** ***var.*** Guéckédou. Guinée-Forestière, S Guinea
41 *R16* **Guelatao** Oaxaca, SE Mexico
Guelders *see* Gelderland
78 *G11* **Guélengdeng** Mayo-Kébbi, W Chad
74 *L5* **Guelma** ***var.*** Gâlma. NE Algeria
74 *D8* **Guelmime** ***var.*** Goulimime. SW Morocco
14 *G15* **Guelph** Ontario, S Canada
102 *I7* **Gueméné-Penfao** Loire-Atlantique, NW France
102 *I7* **Guer** Morbihan, NW France
78 *I11* **Guéra** ***off.*** Préfecture du Guéra. ◐ *prefecture* S Chad
102 *H8* **Guérande** Loire-Atlantique, NW France
Guéra, Préfecture du *see* Guéra
78 *K9* **Guéréda** Biltine, E Chad
103 *N10* **Guéret** Creuse, C France
Guernica/Guernica y Lumo *see* Gernika-Lumo
33 *Z15* **Guernsey** Wyoming, C USA
97 *K25* **Guernsey** *island* Channel Islands, NW Europe
76 *J10* **Guérou** Assaba, S Mauritania
25 *R16* **Guerra** Texas, SW USA
41 *O15* **Guerrero** ◐ *state* S Mexico
40 *D6* **Guerrero Negro** Baja California Sur, NW Mexico
103 *P9* **Gueugnon** Saône-et-Loire, C France
76 *M17* **Guéyo** S Ivory Coast
107 *L15* **Guglionesi** Molise, C Italy
188 *K5* **Guguan** *island* C Northern Mariana Islands
Guhrau *see* Góra
Gui *see* Guangxi Zhuangzu Zizhiqu
Guiana *see* French Guiana
47 *V4* **Guiana Basin** *undersea feature* W Atlantic Ocean
48 *G6* **Guiana Highlands** ***var.*** Macizo de las Guayanas. ▲▲ N South America
Guiba *see* Juba
102 *I7* **Guichen** Ille-et-Vilaine, NW France
Guichi *see* Chizhou
61 *E18* **Guichón** Paysandú, W Uruguay
77 *U12* **Guidan-Roumji** Maradi, S Niger
Guidder *see* Guider
159 *T10* **Guide** ***var.*** Heyin. Qinghai, C China
78 *F12* **Guider** ***var.*** Guidder. Nord, N Cameroon
76 *I11* **Guidimaka** ◐ *region* S Mauritania
77 *W12* **Guidimouni** Zinder, S Niger
76 *G10* **Guier, Lac de** ***var.*** Lac de Guiers. ◎ N Senegal
Guiers, Lac de *see* Guier, Lac de
160 *L14* **Guigang** ***var.*** Guixian, Gui Xian. Guangxi Zhuangzu Zizhiqu, S China
76 *L16* **Guiglo** W Ivory Coast
54 *L5* **Güigüe** Carabobo, N Venezuela
83 *M20* **Guijá** Gaza, S Mozambique
42 *E7* **Güija, Lago de** ◎ El Salvador/Guatemala
160 *L14* **Gui Jiang** ***var.*** Gui Shui. ≈ S China
104 *K8* **Guijuelo** Castilla-León, N Spain
Guilan *see* Gīlān
97 *N22* **Guildford** SE England, UK
19 *R5* **Guildford** Maine, NE USA
19 *O7* **Guildhall** Vermont, NE USA
103 *R13* **Guilherand** Ardèche, E France
160 *L13* **Guilin** ***var.*** Kuei-lin, Kweilin. Guangxi Zhuangzu Zizhiqu, S China
12 *J6* **Guillaume-Delisle, Lac** ◎ Québec, NE Canada
103 *U13* **Guillestre** Hautes-Alpes, SE France
104 *H6* **Guimarães** ***var.*** Guimaráes. Braga, N Portugal
Guimaráes *see* Guimarães
58 *D11* **Guimarães Rosas, Pico** ▲ NW Brazil
23 *N3* **Guin** Alabama, S USA
Güina *see* Wina
76 *I14* **Guinea** ***off.*** Republic of Guinea, ***var.*** Guinée; ***prev.*** French Guinea, People's Revolutionary Republic of Guinea. ◆ *republic* W Africa
64 *N13* **Guinea Basin** *undersea feature* E Atlantic Ocean
76 *E12* **Guinea-Bissau** ***off.*** Republic of Guinea-Bissau, ***Fr.*** Guinée-Bissau, ***Port.*** Guiné-Bissau; ***prev.*** Portuguese Guinea. ◆ *republic* W Africa
Guinea-Bissau, Republic of *see* Guinea-Bissau
66 *K7* **Guinea Fracture Zone** *tectonic feature* E Atlantic Ocean
64 *O13* **Guinea, Gulf of** ***Fr.*** Golfe de Guinée. *gulf* E Atlantic Ocean
Guinea, People's Revolutionary Republic of *see* Guinea
Guinea, Republic of *see* Guinea
Guiné-Bissau *see* Guinea-Bissau
Guinée *see* Guinea
Guinée-Bissau *see* Guinea-Bissau
Guinée, Golfe de *see* Guinea, Gulf of
44 *C4* **Güines** La Habana, W Cuba
102 *G5* **Guingamp** Côtes d'Armor, NW France

◆ Country
● Country Capital
◇ Dependent Territory
○ Dependent Territory Capital
◐ Administrative Regions
✕ International Airport
▲ Mountain
▲▲ Mountain Range
Volcano
≈ River
◎ Lake
⊠ Reservoir

Guipúzcoa – Halīl Rūd

105 P3 Guipúzcoa Basq. Gipuzkoa. ⬖ province País Vasco, N Spain
44 C5 Güira de Melena La Habana, W Cuba
74 G8 Guir, Hamada du desert Algeria/Morocco
55 P5 Güiria Sucre, NE Venezuela
Gui Shui see Gui Jiang
104 H2 Guitiriz Galicia, NW Spain
77 N17 Guitri S Ivory Coast
171 Q5 Guiuan Samar, C Philippines
Gui Xian/Guixian see Guigang
160 J12 Guiyang var. Kuei-Yang, Kuei-yang, Kueyang, Kweiyang; prev. Kweichu. province capital Guizhou, S China
160 J12 Guizhou var. Guizhou Sheng, Kuei-chou, Kweichow, Qian. ⬖ province S China
Guizhou Sheng see Guizhou
102 J13 Gujan-Mestras Gironde, SW France
154 B10 Gujarāt var. Gujerat. ⬖ state W India
149 V6 Gūjar Khān Punjab, E Pakistan
Gujerat see Gujarāt
149 V7 Gujrānwāla Punjab, NE Pakistan
149 V7 Gujrāt Punjab, E Pakistan
146 B8 Gulandag Rus. Gory Kulandag. ▲▲ Balkan Welaýaty, W Turkmenistan
159 U9 Gulang Gansu, C China
183 R6 Gulargambone New South Wales, SE Australia
155 G15 Gulbarga Karnātaka, C India
118 J8 Gulbene Ger. Alt-Schwanenburg. Gulbene, NE Latvia
147 U10 Gul'cha Kir. Gülchö. Oshskaya Oblast', SW Kyrgyzstan
Gülchö see Gul'cha
173 T10 Gulden Draak Seamount undersea feature E Indian Ocean
136 J16 Gülek Boğazı var. Cilician Gates. pass S Turkey
186 D8 Gulf ⬖ province S Papua New Guinea
23 O9 Gulf Breeze Florida, SE USA
Gulf of Liaotung see Liaodong Wan
23 V13 Gulfport Florida, SE USA
22 M9 Gulfport Mississippi, S USA
23 O9 Gulf Shores Alabama, S USA
141 T5 Gulf, The var. Persian Gulf, Ar. Khalīj al 'Arabī, Per. Khalīj-e Fars. Gulf SW Asia see also Persian Gulf
183 R7 Gulgong New South Wales, SE Australia
160 I11 Gulin Sichuan, C China
171 U14 Gulir Pulau Kasiui, E Indonesia
Gulistan see Guliston
147 P10 Guliston Rus. Gulistan. Sirdaryo Viloyati, E Uzbekistan
163 T6 Guliya Shan ▲ NE China
Gulja see Yining
39 S11 Gulkana Alaska, USA
9 S17 Gull Lake Saskatchewan, S Canada
31 P10 Gull Lake ◎ Michigan, N USA
29 T6 Gull Lake ◎ Minnesota, N USA
95 L16 Gullspång Västra Götaland, S Sweden
136 B15 Güllük Körfezi prev Akbük Limanı. bay W Turkey
152 H5 Gulmarg Jammu and Kashmir, NW India
Gulpaigan see Golpāyegān
99 L18 Gulpen Limburg, SE Netherlands
Gul'shad see Gul'shad
145 S13 Gul'shad var. Gul'shad. Karaganda, E Kazakhstan
81 F17 Gulu N Uganda
114 K10 Gŭlŭbovo Stara Zagora, C Bulgaria
114 I7 Gulyantsi Pleven, N Bulgaria
Gulyaypole see Hulyaypole
Guma see Pishan
Gümai see Darlag
79 K16 Gumba Equateur, NW Dem. Rep. Congo
Gumbinnen see Gusev
81 H24 Gumbiro Ruvuma, S Tanzania
146 B11 Gumdag prev. Kum-Dag. Balkan Welaýaty, W Turkmenistan
77 W12 Gumel Jigawa, N Nigeria
105 N5 Gumiel de Hizán Castilla-León, N Spain
153 P16 Gumla Jhārkhand, N India
Gumma see Gunma
101 F16 Gummersbach Nordrhein-Westfalen, W Germany
77 T13 Gummi Zamfara, NW Nigeria
Gumpolds see Humpolec
153 N13 Gumti var. Gomati. 〰 N India
Gümülcine/Gümüljina see Komotiní
Gümüşane see Gümüşhane
137 O12 Gümüşhane var. Gümüşane, Gumushkhane. Gümüşhane, NE Turkey
137 O12 Gümüşhane var. Gümüşane, Gumushkhane. ⬖ province NE Turkey
Gumushkhane see Gümüşhane
171 V14 Gumzai Pulau Kola, E Indonesia
154 H9 Guna Madhya Pradesh, C India
Gunabad see Gonābād
Gunan see Qijiang
Gunbad-i-Qawus see Gonbad-e Kāvūs
183 O9 Gunbar New South Wales, SE Australia
183 O9 Gun Creek seasonal river New South Wales, SE Australia
183 Q10 Gundagai New South Wales, SE Australia
79 K17 Gundji Equateur, N Dem. Rep. Congo
155 G20 Gundlupet Karnātaka, W India
136 G16 Gündoğmuş Antalya, S Turkey
137 O14 Güney Doğu Toroslar ▲▲ SE Turkey
79 J21 Gungu Bandundu, SW Dem. Rep. Congo
127 P17 Gunib Respublika Dagestan, SW Russian Federation
112 J11 Gunja Vukovar-Srijem, E Croatia
31 P9 Gun Lake ◎ Michigan, N USA
165 N12 Gunma off. Gunma-ken, var. Gumma. ⬖ prefecture Honshū, S Japan
Gunma-ken see Gunma
197 P15 Gunnbjørn Fjeld var. Gunnbjörns Bjerge. ▲ C Greenland
Gunnbjörns Bjerge see Gunnbjørn Fjeld
183 S6 Gunnedah New South Wales, SE Australia
173 Y15 Gunner's Quoin island N Mauritius
37 R6 Gunnison Colorado, C USA
36 L5 Gunnison Utah, W USA
37 P5 Gunnison River 〰 Colorado, C USA
21 X2 Gunpowder River 〰 Maryland, NE USA
Güns see Kőszeg
Gunsan see Kunsan
109 S4 Gunskirchen Oberösterreich, N Austria
Gunt see Ghund
155 H17 Guntakal Andhra Pradesh, C India
23 Q2 Guntersville Alabama, S USA
23 Q2 Guntersville Lake ⊠ Alabama, S USA
109 X4 Guntramsdorf Niederösterreich, E Austria
155 J16 Guntūr var. Guntur. Andhra Pradesh, SE India
168 H10 Gunungsitoli Pulau Nias, W Indonesia
155 M14 Gunupur Orissa, E India
101 J23 Günz 〰 S Germany
Gunzan see Kunsan
101 J22 Günzburg Bayern, S Germany
101 K21 Gunzenhausen Bayern, S Germany
Guolüezhen see Lingbao
Guovdageaidnu see Kautokeino
161 P7 Guoyang Anhui, E China
116 G11 Gurahonț Hung. Honctő. Arad, W Romania
Gurahumora see Gura Humorului
116 K9 Gura Humorului Ger. Gurahumora. Suceava, NE Romania
146 H8 Gurbansoltan Eje Prev. Ýylanly, Rus. Il'yaly. Daşoguz Welaýaty, N Turkmenistan
146 H8 Gurbansoltan Eje prev. Ýylanly, Rus. Il'yaly. Daşoguz Welaýaty, N Turkmenistan
158 K4 Gurbantünggüt Shamo desert W China
152 H7 Gurdāspur Punjab, N India
27 T13 Gurdon Arkansas, C USA
Gurdzhaani see Gurjaani
Gurgan see Gorgān
152 I10 Gurgaon Haryāna, N India
59 M15 Gurguéia, Rio 〰 NE Brazil
55 Q7 Guri, Embalse de ⊠ E Venezuela
137 V10 Gurjaani Rus. Gurdzhaani. E Georgia
109 T8 Gurk Kärnten, S Austria
109 T9 Gurk Slvn. Krka. 〰 S Austria
Gurkfeld see Krško
114 K9 Gurkovo prev. Kolupchii. Stara Zagora, C Bulgaria
109 S9 Gurktaler Alpen ▲▲ S Austria
146 H8 Gurlan Rus. Gurlen. Xorazm Viloyati, W Uzbekistan
Gurlen see Gurlan
83 M16 Guro Manica, C Mozambique
136 M14 Gürün Sivas, C Turkey
59 K16 Gurupi Tocantins, C Brazil
58 L12 Gurupi, Rio 〰 NE Brazil
152 E14 Guru Sikhar ▲ NW India
162 H8 Gurvanbulag var. Höviyn Am. Bayanhongor, C Mongolia
162 K7 Gurvanbulag var. Avdzaga. Bulgan, C Mongolia
162 K7 Gurvanbulag var. Avdzaga. Bulgan, C Monogolia
162 I11 Gurvantes var. Urt. Ömnögovĭ, S Mongolia
Gur'yev/Gur'yevskaya Oblast' see Atyrau
77 U13 Gusau Zamfara, NW Nigeria
126 C3 Gusev Ger. Gumbinnen. Kaliningradskaya Oblast', W Russian Federation
146 J17 Gushgy Rus. Kushka. 〰 Mary Welaýaty, S Turkmenistan
Gushgy see Serhetabat
Gushiago see Gushiegu
77 Q14 Gushiegu var. Gushiago. NE Ghana
165 S17 Gushikawa Okinawa, Okinawa, SW Japan
113 L16 Gusinje E Montenegro
126 M4 Gus'-Khrustal'nyy Vladimirskaya Oblast', W Russian Federation
107 B19 Guspini Sardegna, Italy, C Mediterranean Sea
109 X8 Güssing Burgenland, SE Austria
109 V6 Gusswerk Steiermark, E Austria
92 O2 Gustav Adolf Land physical region NE Svalbard
195 X5 Gustav Bull Mountains ▲▲ Antarctica
39 W13 Gustavus Alaska, USA
92 O1 Gustav V Land physical region NE Svalbard
35 P9 Gustine California, W USA
25 R8 Gustine Texas, SW USA
100 M9 Güstrow Mecklenburg-Vorpommern, NE Germany
95 N18 Gusum Östergötland, S Sweden
Guta/Gúta see Kolárovo
Gutenstein see Ravne na Koroškem
101 G14 Gütersloh Nordrhein-Westfalen, W Germany
27 N10 Guthrie Oklahoma, C USA
25 P5 Guthrie Texas, SW USA
29 U14 Guthrie Center Iowa, C USA
41 Q13 Gutiérrez Zamora Veracruz-Llave, E Mexico
Gutta see Kolárovo
29 Y12 Guttenberg Iowa, C USA
Guttentag see Dobrodzień
Guttstadt see Dobre Miasto
162 G8 Guulin Govĭ-Altay, C Mongolia
153 V12 Guwāhāti prev. Gauhāti. Assam, NE India
139 R3 Guwēr var. Al Kuwayr, Al Quwayr, Quwair. N Iraq
146 A10 Guwlumaýak Rus. Kuuli-Mayak. Balkan Welaýaty, NW Turkmenistan
55 R9 Guyana off. Cooperative Republic of Guyana; prev. British Guiana. ◆ republic N South America
Guyana, Cooperative Republic of see Guyana
21 P5 Guyandotte River 〰 West Virginia, NE USA
Guyane see French Guiana
Guyi see Sanjiang
26 H8 Guymon Oklahoma, C USA
146 K12 Guynuk Lebap Welaýaty, NE Turkmenistan
Guyong see Jiangle
21 O9 Guyot, Mount ▲ North Carolina/Tennessee, SE USA
183 U5 Guyra New South Wales, SE Australia
159 W10 Guyuan Ningxia, N China
Guzar see G'uzor
Guzar see G'uzor
121 P2 Güzelyurt Gk. Mórfou, Morphou. W Cyprus
121 N2 Güzelyurt Körfezi var. Morfou Bay, Morphou Bay, Gk. Kólpos Mórfou. bay W Cyprus
Guzhou see Rongjiang
40 I3 Guzmán Chihuahua, N Mexico
147 N13 G'uzor Rus. Guzar. Qashqadaryo Viloyati, S Uzbekistan
147 N13 G'uzor Rus. Guzar. Qashqadaryo Viloyati, S Uzbekistan
119 B14 Gvardeysk Ger. Tapaiu. Kaliningradskaya Oblast', W Russian Federation
Gvardeyskoye see Hvardiys'ke
183 R5 Gwabegar New South Wales, SE Australia
148 J16 Gwādar var. Gwadur. Baluchistān, SW Pakistan
148 J16 Gwādar East Bay bay SW Pakistan
148 J16 Gwādar West Bay bay SW Pakistan
Gwadur see Gwādar
83 J17 Gwai Matabeleland North, W Zimbabwe
154 I7 Gwalior Madhya Pradesh, C India
83 J18 Gwanda Matabeleland South, SW Zimbabwe
79 N15 Gwane Orientale, N Dem. Rep. Congo
83 I17 Gwayi 〰 W Zimbabwe
110 G8 Gwda var. Głda, Ger. Küddow. 〰 NW Poland
97 C14 Gweebarra Bay Ir. Béal an Bheara. inlet W Ireland
97 D14 Gweedore Ir. Gaoth Dobhair. Donegal, NW Ireland
Gwelo see Gweru
97 K21 Gwent cultural region S Wales, UK
83 K17 Gweru prev. Gwelo. Midlands, C Zimbabwe
29 Q7 Gwinner North Dakota, N USA
77 Y13 Gwoza Borno, NE Nigeria
Gwy see Wye
183 R4 Gwydir River 〰 New South Wales, SE Australia
97 I19 Gwynedd var. Gwyneth. cultural region NW Wales, UK
Gwyneth see Gwynedd
159 O16 Gyaca var. Ngarrab. Xizang Zizhiqu, W China
Gya'gya see Saga
Gyaijêpozhanggê see Zhidoi
Gyaisi see Jiulong
115 M22 Gyalí var. Yialí. island Dodekánisa, Greece, Aegean Sea
Gyamotang see Dêngqên
Gyandzha see Gäncä
Gyangkar see Dinggyê
158 M16 Gyangzê Xizang Zizhiqu, W China
158 L14 Gyaring Co ◎ W China
159 Q12 Gyaring Hu ◎ C China
115 I20 Gyáros var. Yioúra. island Kykládes, Greece, Aegean Sea
122 J7 Gyda Yamalo-Nenetskiy Avtonomnyy Okrug, N Russian Federation
122 J7 Gydanskiy Poluostrov Eng. Gyda Peninsula. peninsula N Russian Federation
Gyda Peninsula see Gydanskiy Poluostrov
Gyêgu see Yushu
Gyéres see Câmpia Turzii
Gyergyószentmiklós see Gheorgheni
Gyergyótölgyes see Tulgheş
Gyertyámos see Cărpiniş
Gyeva see Detva
Gyigang see Zayü
Gyixong see Gonggar
95 I23 Gyldenløveshøy hill range C Denmark
181 Z10 Gympie Queensland, E Australia
166 L7 Gyobingauk Pegu, SW Burma (Myanmar)
111 M23 Gyomaendrőd Békés, SE Hungary
Gyömbér see Ďumbier
111 L22 Gyöngyös Heves, NE Hungary
111 H22 Győr Ger. Raab, Lat. Arrabona. Győr-Moson-Sopron, NW Hungary
111 G22 Győr-Moson-Sopron off. Győr-Moson-Sopron Megye. ⬖ county NW Hungary
Győr-Moson-Sopron Megye see Győr-Moson-Sopron
9 X15 Gypsumville Manitoba, S Canada
12 M4 Gyrfalcon Islands island group Northwest Territories, NE Canada
95 N14 Gysinge Gävleborg, C Sweden
115 F22 Gýtheio var. Githio; prev. Ýthion. Pelopónnisos, S Greece
146 L13 Gyuichbirleshik Lebap Welaýaty, E Turkmenistan
111 N24 Gyula Rom. Jula. Békés, SE Hungary
Gyulafehérvár see Alba Iulia
Gyulovo see Roza
137 T11 Gyumri var. Giumri, Rus. Kumayri; prev. Aleksandropol', Leninakan. W Armenia
146 D13 Gyunuzyndag, Gora ▲ Balkan Welaýaty, W Turkmenistan
146 J15 Gyzylbaydak Rus. Krasnoye Znamya. Mary Welaýaty, S Turkmenistan
Gyzyletrek see Etrek
146 D10 Gyzylgaýa Rus. Kizyl-Kaya. Balkan Welaýaty, NW Turkmenistan
146 A10 Gyzylsuw Rus. Kizyl-Su. Balkan Welaýaty, W Turkmenistan
Gyzyrlabat see Serdar
126 J3 Gzhatsk Smolenskaya Oblast', W Russian Federation

H

153 T12 Ha W Bhutan
Haabai see Ha'apai Group
99 H17 Haacht Vlaams Brabant, C Belgium
109 T4 Haag Niederösterreich, NE Austria
194 L8 Haag Nunataks ▲▲ Antarctica
92 N2 Haakon VII Land physical region NW Svalbard
98 O11 Haaksbergen Overijssel, E Netherlands
99 E14 Haamstede Zeeland, SW Netherlands
193 Y15 Ha'ano island Ha'apai Group, C Tonga
193 Y15 Ha'apai Group var. Haabai. island group C Tonga
93 L15 Haapajärvi Oulu, C Finland
93 L17 Haapamäki Länsi-Soumi, C Finland
93 L15 Haapavesi Oulu, C Finland
191 N7 Haapiti Moorea, W French Polynesia
118 F4 Haapsalu Ger. Hapsal. Läänemaa, W Estonia
Ha'Arava see 'Arabah, Wādī al
95 G24 Haarby var. Hårby. Fyn, C Denmark
98 H10 Haarlem prev. Harlem. Noord-Holland, W Netherlands
185 D19 Haast West Coast, South Island, New Zealand
185 C20 Haast 〰 South Island, New Zealand
185 D20 Haast Pass pass South Island, New Zealand
193 W16 Ha'atua 'Eau, E Tonga
149 P15 Hab 〰 SW Pakistan
141 W7 Haba var. Al Haba. Dubayy, NE United Arab Emirates
158 K2 Habahe var. Kaba. Xinjiang Uygur Zizhiqu, NW China
141 U13 Ḩabarūt var. Habrut. SW Oman
81 J18 Habaswein North Eastern, NE Kenya
99 L24 Habay-la-Neuve Luxembourg, SE Belgium
139 S8 Ḩabbānīyah, Buḩayrat ◎ C Iraq
Habelschwerdt see Bystrzyca Kłodzka
153 V14 Habiganj Sylhet, NE Bangladesh
163 Q12 Habirag Nei Mongol Zizhiqu, N China
95 L19 Habo Västra Götaland, S Sweden
123 V14 Habomai Islands island group Kuril'skiye Ostrova, SE Russian Federation
165 S2 Haboro Hokkaidō, NE Japan
153 S16 Habra West Bengal, NE India
Habrut see Ḩabarūt
143 P17 Ḩabshān Abū Ẓaby, C United Arab Emirates
54 E14 Hacha Putumayo, S Colombia
165 X13 Hachijō Tōkyō, Hachijō-jima, SE Japan
165 X13 Hachijō-jima island Izu-shotō, SE Japan
164 L12 Hachiman Gifu, Honshū, SW Japan
165 P7 Hachimori Akita, Honshū, C Japan
165 R7 Hachinohe Aomori, Honshū, C Japan
93 G17 Hackås Jämtland, C Sweden
18 K14 Hackensack New Jersey, NE USA
Hadama see Nazrēt
141 W13 Ḩadbaram S Oman
139 U13 Ḩaddānīyah well S Iraq
96 K12 Haddington SE Scotland, UK
141 Z8 Ḩadd, Ra's al headland NE Oman
Haded see Xadeed
77 W12 Hadejia Jigawa, N Nigeria
77 W12 Hadejia 〰 N Nigeria
138 F9 Ḩadera var. Khadera. Haifa, C Israel
Hadersleben see Haderslev
95 G24 Haderslev Ger. Hadersleben. Sønderjylland, SW Denmark
151 J21 Hadhdhunmathi Atoll atoll S Maldives
Hadhramaut see Ḩaḑramawt
141 W17 Hadīboh Suquṭrā, SE Yemen
158 K9 Hadilik Xinjiang Uygur Zizhiqu, W China
136 H16 Hadım Konya, S Turkey
140 K7 Hadīyah Al Madīnah, W Saudi Arabia
8 L5 Hadley Bay bay Victoria Island, Nunavut, N Canada
167 S6 Ha Đông var. Hadong. Ha Tây, N Vietnam
Hadong see Ha Đông
141 R15 Ḩaḑramawt Eng. Hadhramaut. ▲▲ S Yemen
Hadria see Adria
Hadrianopolis see Edirne
Hadria Picena see Apricena
95 G22 Hadsten Århus, C Denmark
95 G21 Hadsund Nordjylland, N Denmark
117 S4 Hadyach Rus. Gadyach. Poltavs'ka Oblast', NE Ukraine
112 I13 Hadžići Federacija Bosna I Hercegovina, SE Bosnia and Herzegovina
163 W14 Haeju S North Korea
Haerbin/Haerhpin/Ha-erh-pin see Harbin
141 P5 Ḩafar al Bāṭin Ash Sharqīyah, N Saudi Arabia
9 T15 Hafford Saskatchewan, S Canada
136 M13 Hafik Sivas, N Turkey
149 V8 Hāfizābād Punjab, E Pakistan
92 H4 Hafnarfjördhur Reykjanes, W Iceland
Hafnia see Denmark
Hafnia see København
Hafren see Severn
Hafun see Xaafuun
Hafun, Ras see Xaafuun, Raas
80 G10 Hag 'Abdullah Sinnar, E Sudan
81 K18 Hagadera North Eastern, E Kenya
138 G8 HaGalil Eng. Galilee. ▲▲ N Israel
14 G10 Hagar Ontario, S Canada
155 G18 Hagari var. Vedāvati. 〰 W India
188 B16 Hagåtña var. Agana, var. Agaña. ○ (Guam) NW Guam
100 M13 Hagelberg hill NE Germany
39 N14 Hagemeister Island island Alaska, USA
101 F15 Hagen Nordrhein-Westfalen, W Germany
100 K10 Hagenow Mecklenburg-Vorpommern, N Germany
10 K15 Hagensborg British Columbia, SW Canada
80 I13 Hägere Hiywet var. Agere Hiywet, Ambo. Oromo, C Ethiopia
33 O15 Hagerman Idaho, NW USA
37 U14 Hagerman New Mexico, SW USA
21 V2 Hagerstown Maryland, NE USA
14 G16 Hagersville Ontario, S Canada
102 J15 Hagetmau Landes, SW France
95 K14 Hagfors Värmland, C Sweden
93 G16 Häggenås Jämtland, C Sweden
164 E12 Hagi Yamaguchi, Honshū, SW Japan
167 S5 Ha Giang Ha Giang, N Vietnam
Hagios Evstrátios see Ágios Efstrátios
HaGolan see Golan Heights
103 T4 Hagondange Moselle, NE France
97 B18 Hag's Head Ir. Ceann Caillí. headland W Ireland
102 I3 Hague, Cap de la headland N France
103 V5 Haguenau Bas-Rhin, NE France
165 X16 Hahajima-rettō island group SE Japan
15 R8 Há Há, Lac ◎ Québec, SE Canada
172 H13 Hahaya ✈ (Moroni) Grande Comore, NW Comoros
22 K9 Hahnville Louisiana, S USA
83 E22 Haib Karas, S Namibia
Haibak see Āybak
149 N15 Haibo 〰 SW Pakistan
Haibowan see Wuhai
163 U12 Haicheng Liaoning, NE China
Haicheng see Haiyuan
167 T6 Hai Dương Hai Hưng, N Vietnam
Haida see Nový Bor
Haidarabad see Hyderābād
Haidenschaft see Ajdovščina
138 F9 Haifa ⬖ district NW Israel
Haifa see Ḩefa
Haifa, Bay of see Ḩefa, Mifraẓ
161 P14 Haifeng Guangdong, S China
Haifong see Hai Phong
161 P3 Hai He 〰 E China
Haikang see Leizhou
160 L17 Haikou var. Hai-k'ou, Hoihow, Fr. Hoï-Hao. province capital Hainan, S China
Hai-k'ou see Haikou
140 M6 Ḩā'il Ḩā'il, NW Saudi Arabia
141 N5 Ḩā'il off. Minṭaqah Ḩā'il. ⬖ province N Saudi Arabia
Hai-la-erh see Hailar
163 S6 Hailar var. Hai-la-erh; prev. Hulun. Nei Mongol Zizhiqu, N China
163 S6 Hailar He 〰 NE China
33 P14 Hailey Idaho, NW USA
14 H9 Haileybury Ontario, S Canada
163 X9 Hailin Heilongjiang, NE China
Ḩā'il, Minṭaqah see Ḩā'il
Hailong see Meihekou
93 K14 Hailuoto Swe. Karlö. island W Finland
Haima see Haymā'
Haimen see Taizhou
160 M17 Hainan var. Hainan Sheng, Qiong. ⬖ province S China
160 K17 Hainan Dao island S China
Hainan Sheng see Hainan
Hainan Strait see Qiongzhou Haixia
Hainasch see Ainaži
Hainau see Chojnów
99 E20 Hainaut ⬖ province SW Belgium
Hainburg see Hainburg an der Donau
109 Z4 Hainburg an der Donau var. Hainburg. Niederösterreich, NE Austria
39 W12 Haines Alaska, USA
32 L12 Haines Oregon, NW USA
23 W12 Haines City Florida, SE USA
10 H8 Haines Junction Yukon Territory, W Canada
109 W4 Hainfeld Niederösterreich, NE Austria
101 N16 Hainichen Sachsen, E Germany
Hai Ninh see Mong Cai
167 T6 Hai Phong var. Haifong, Haiphong. N Vietnam
Haiphong see Hai Phong
161 S12 Haitan Dao island SE China
44 K8 Haiti off. Republic of Haiti. ◆ republic C West Indies
Haiti, Republic of see Haiti
35 T11 Haiwee Reservoir ⊠ California, W USA
80 I7 Haiya Red Sea, NE Sudan
159 T10 Haiyan var. Sanjiaocheng. Qinghai, W China
160 M13 Haiyang Shan ▲▲ S China
159 V10 Haiyuan Ningxia, N China
Hajda see Nový Bor
111 M22 Hajdú-Bihar off. Hajdú-Bihar Megye. ⬖ county E Hungary
Hajdú-Bihar Megye see Hajdú-Bihar
111 N22 Hajdúböszörmény Hajdú-Bihar, E Hungary
111 N22 Hajdúhadház Hajdú-Bihar, E Hungary
111 N21 Hajdúnánás Hajdú-Bihar, E Hungary
111 N22 Hajdúszoboszló Hajdú-Bihar, E Hungary
142 I3 Ḩājī Ebrāhīm, Kūh-e ▲ Iran/Iraq
165 O9 Hajiki-zaki headland Sado, C Japan
Hajine see Abū Ḩardān
153 P13 Hājīpur Bihār, N India
141 N14 Ḩajjah W Yemen
139 U11 Ḩajjama S Iraq
143 R12 Ḩājjīābād Hormozgān, C Iran
139 U14 Ḩājj, Thaqb al well S Iraq
113 L16 Hajla ▲▲ E Montenegro
110 P10 Hajnówka Ger. Hermhausen. Podlaskie, NE Poland
166 K4 Haka Chin State, W Burma (Myanmar)
Hakapehi see Punaauia
Hakâri see Hakkâri
137 T16 Hakkâri var. Çölemerik, Hakâri. Hakkâri, SE Turkey
137 T16 Hakkâri var. Hakkari. ⬖ province SE Turkey
Hakkari see Hakkâri
92 J12 Hakkas Norrbotten, N Sweden
164 J14 Hakken-zan ▲ Honshū, SW Japan
165 R4 Hakkōda-san ▲ Honshū, C Japan
165 T2 Hako-dake ▲ Hokkaidō, NE Japan
165 R5 Hakodate Hokkaidō, NE Japan
164 L11 Hakui Ishikawa, Honshū, SW Japan
190 B16 Hakupu SE Niue
164 L12 Haku-san ▲ Honshū, SW Japan
Hal see Halle
149 Q15 Hāla Sind, SE Pakistan
138 J3 Ḩalab Eng. Aleppo, Fr. Alep; anc. Beroea. Ḩalab, NW Syria
138 J3 Ḩalab off. Muḩāfaẓat Ḩalab, var. Aleppo, Halab. ⬖ governorate NW Syria
138 J3 Ḩalab ✈ Ḩalab, NW Syria
Halab see Ḩalab
141 O8 Ḩalabān var. Halibān. Ar Riyāḑ, C Saudi Arabia
139 V4 Ḩalabja NE Iraq
Ḩalab, Muḩāfaẓat see Ḩalab
146 L13 Halaç Rus. Khalach. Lebap Welaýaty, E Turkmenistan
190 A16 Halagigie Point headland W Niue
75 Z11 Halaib SE Egypt
190 G12 Halalo Île Uvea, N Wallis and Futuna
Halandri see Chalándri
141 X13 Ḩalānīyāt, Juzur al var. Jazā'ir Bin Ghalfān, Eng. Kuria Muria Islands. island group S Oman
141 W13 Ḩalānīyāt, Khalīj al Eng. Kuria Muria Bay. bay S Oman
Halas see Kiskunhalas
38 G11 Hālawa var. Halawa. Hawai'i, USA, C Pacific Ocean
Halawa see Hālawa
38 F9 Hālawa, Cape var. Cape Halawa. headland Moloka'i, Hawai'i, USA
Cape Halawa see Hālawa, Cape
Halban see Tsetserleg
101 K14 Halberstadt Sachsen-Anhalt, C Germany
184 M12 Halcombe Manawatu-Wanganui, North Island, New Zealand
95 I16 Halden prev. Fredrikshald. Østfold, S Norway
100 L13 Haldensleben Sachsen-Anhalt, C Germany
Háldi see Halti
153 S17 Haldia West Bengal, NE India
152 K10 Haldwāni Uttaranchal, N India
163 P9 Haldzan var. Hatavch. Sühbaatar
38 F10 Haleakalā crater Maui, Hawai'i, USA
25 N4 Hale Center Texas, SW USA
99 J18 Halen Limburg, NE Belgium
23 O2 Haleyville Alabama, S USA
77 O17 Half Assini SW Ghana
35 R8 Half Dome ▲ California, W USA
185 C25 Halfmoon Bay var. Oban. Stewart Island, Southland, New Zealand
182 E5 Half Moon Lake salt lake South Australia
163 S8 Halhgol var. Tsagaannuur. Dornod, E Mongolia
163 R7 Halhgol Dornod, E Mongolia
Haliacmon see Aliákmonas
Halibān see Ḩalabān
14 I13 Haliburton Ontario, SE Canada
14 I12 Haliburton Highlands var. Madawaska Highlands. hill range Ontario, SE Canada
13 Q15 Halifax province capital Nova Scotia, SE Canada
97 L17 Halifax N England, UK
21 W8 Halifax North Carolina, SE USA
21 U7 Halifax Virginia, NE USA
13 Q15 Halifax ✈ Nova Scotia, SE Canada
143 T13 Halīl Rūd seasonal river SE Iran

◆ Country ● Country Capital ◇ Dependent Territory ○ Dependent Territory Capital ⬖ Administrative Regions ✈ International Airport ▲ Mountain ▲▲ Mountain Range ⛰ Volcano 〰 River ◎ Lake ⊠ Reservoir

ḤALĪMAH – HATZFELD

138 I6 **Ḥalīmah** ▲ Lebanon/Syria
162 G8 **Haliun** Govĭ-Altay, W Mongolia
118 I3 **Haljala** *Ger.* Halljal. Lääne-Virumaa, N Estonia
39 Q4 **Halkett, Cape** *headland* Alaska, USA
Halkida *see* Chalkída
96 J6 **Halkirk** N Scotland, UK
15 X7 **Hall** ≈ Québec, SE Canada
Hall *see* Schwäbisch Hall
93 H15 **Hälla** Västerbotten, N Sweden
96 J6 **Halladale** ≈ N Scotland, UK
95 J21 **Halland** ◈ *county* S Sweden
23 Z15 **Hallandale** Florida, SE USA
95 K22 **Hallandsås** *physical region* S Sweden
9 P6 **Hall Beach** Nunavut, N Canada
99 G19 **Halle** *Fr.* Hal. Vlaams Brabant, C Belgium
101 M15 **Halle** *var.* Halle an der Saale. Sachsen-Anhalt, C Germany
Halle an der Saale *see* Halle
35 W3 **Halleck** Nevada, W USA
95 L15 **Hällefors** Örebro, C Sweden
95 N16 **Hälleforsnäs** Södermanland, C Sweden
109 Q6 **Hallein** Salzburg, N Austria
101 L15 **Halle-Neustadt** Sachsen-Anhalt, C Germany
25 U12 **Hallettsville** Texas, SW USA
195 N4 **Halley** *UK research station* Antarctica
28 L4 **Halliday** North Dakota, N USA
37 S2 **Halligan Reservoir** ⊠ Colorado, C USA
100 G7 **Halligen** *island group* N Germany
94 G13 **Hallingdal** *valley* S Norway
38 J12 **Hall Island** *island* Alaska, USA
Hall Island *see* Maiana
189 P15 **Hall Islands** *island group* C Micronesia
118 H6 **Halliste** ≈ S Estonia
Halljal *see* Haljala
93 I15 **Hällnäs** Västerbotten, N Sweden
29 R2 **Hallock** Minnesota, N USA
9 S6 **Hall Peninsula** *peninsula* Baffin Island, Nunavut, NE Canada
20 F9 **Halls** Tennessee, S USA
95 M16 **Hallsberg** Örebro, C Sweden
181 N5 **Halls Creek** Western Australia
182 L12 **Halls Gap** Victoria, SE Australia
95 N15 **Hallstahammar** Västmanland, C Sweden
109 R6 **Hallstatt** Salzburg, W Austria
109 R6 **Hallstatter See** ◎ C Austria
95 P14 **Hallstavik** Stockholm, C Sweden
25 X7 **Hallsville** Texas, SW USA
103 P1 **Halluin** Nord, N France
Halmahera, Laut *see* Halmahera Sea
171 R11 **Halmahera, Pulau** *prev.* Djailolo, Gilolo, Jailolo. *island* E Indonesia
171 S12 **Halmahera Sea** *Ind.* Laut Halmahera. *sea* E Indonesia
95 J21 **Halmstad** Halland, S Sweden
119 N15 **Halowchyn** *Rus.* Golovchin. Mahilyowskaya Voblasts', E Belarus
95 H20 **Hals** Nordjylland, N Denmark
94 F8 **Halsa** Møre og Romsdal, S Norway
119 I15 **Hal'shany** *Rus.* Gol'shany. Hrodzyenskaya Voblasts', W Belarus
Hälsingborg *see* Helsingborg
29 R5 **Halstad** Minnesota, N USA
27 N6 **Halstead** Kansas, C USA
99 G15 **Halsteren** Noord-Brabant, S Netherlands
93 L16 **Halsua** Länsi-Soumi, W Finland
101 E14 **Haltern** Nordrhein-Westfalen, W Germany
92 J9 **Halti** *var.* Haltiatunturi, *Lapp.* Háldi. ▲ Finland/Norway
Haltiatunturi *see* Halti
116 J6 **Halych** Ivano-Frankivs'ka Oblast', W Ukraine
Halycus *see* Platani
103 P3 **Ham** Somme, N France
Hama *see* Ḥamāh
164 F12 **Hamada** Shimane, Honshū, SW Japan
142 L6 **Hamadān** *anc.* Ecbatana. Hamadān, W Iran
142 L6 **Hamadān** *off.* Ostān-e Hamadān. ◈ *province* W Iran
Hamadān, Ostān-e *see* Hamadān
138 I5 **Ḥamāh** *var.* Hama; *anc.* Epiphania, *Bibl.* Hamath. Ḥamāh, W Syria
138 I5 **Ḥamāh** *off.* Muḥāfaẓat Ḥamāh, *var.* Hama. ◈ *governorate* C Syria
Ḥamāh, Muḥāfaẓat *see* Ḥamāh
165 S3 **Hamamasu** Hokkaidō, NE Japan
164 L14 **Hamamatsu** *var.* Hamamatu. Shizuoka, Honshū, S Japan
Hamamatu *see* Hamamatsu
165 W14 **Hamanaka** Hokkaidō, NE Japan
164 L14 **Hamana-ko** ◎ Honshū, S Japan
94 I13 **Hamar** *prev.* Storhammer. Hedmark, S Norway
141 U10 **Ḥamārīr al Kidan, Qalamat** *well* E Saudi Arabia
164 I12 **Hamasaka** Hyōgo, Honshū, SW Japan
Hamath *see* Ḥamāh
165 T1 **Hamatonbetsu** Hokkaidō, NE Japan
155 K26 **Hambantota** Southern Province, SE Sri Lanka
Hambourg *see* Hamburg
100 J9 **Hamburg** Hamburg, N Germany
27 V14 **Hamburg** Arkansas, C USA
29 S16 **Hamburg** Iowa, C USA
18 D10 **Hamburg** New York, NE USA
100 I10 **Hamburg** *Fr.* Hambourg. ◈ *state* N Germany
148 K5 **Hamdam Āb, Dasht-e** *Pash.* Dasht-i Hamdamab. ▲▲ W Afghanistan
Hamdamab, Dasht-i *see* Hamdam Āb, Dasht-e
18 M13 **Hamden** Connecticut, NE USA
140 K6 **Ḥamḍ, Wādī al** *dry watercourse* W Saudi Arabia
93 K18 **Hämeenkyrö** Länsi-Suomi, W Finland
93 L19 **Hämeenlinna** *Swe.* Tavastehus. Etelä-Suomi, S Finland
HaMela h, Yam *see* Dead Sea
Hamelin *see* Hameln
100 I13 **Hameln** *Eng.* Hamelin. Niedersachsen, N Germany
180 I8 **Hamersley Range** ▲▲ Western Australia
163 Y12 **Hamgyŏng-sanmaek** ▲▲ N North Korea
163 X13 **Hamhŭng** C North Korea
159 O6 **Hami** *var.* Ha-mi, *Uigh.* Kumul, Qomul. Xinjiang Uygur Zizhiqu, NW China
Ha-mi *see* Hami
139 X10 **Ḥāmid Amīn** E Iraq
141 W11 **Hamīdān, Khawr** *oasis* SE Saudi Arabia
138 H5 **Ḥamīdīyah** *var.* Hamîdîyé. Ṭarṭūs, W Syria
114 L12 **Hamidiye** Edirne, NW Turkey
Hamîdîyé *see* Ḥamīdīyah
182 L12 **Hamilton** Victoria, SE Australia
64 B12 **Hamilton** ○ (Bermuda) C Bermuda
14 G16 **Hamilton** Ontario, S Canada
184 M7 **Hamilton** Waikato, North Island, New Zealand
96 I12 **Hamilton** S Scotland, UK
23 N3 **Hamilton** Alabama, S USA
38 M10 **Hamilton** Alaska, USA
30 J13 **Hamilton** Illinois, N USA
27 S3 **Hamilton** Missouri, C USA
33 P10 **Hamilton** Montana, NW USA
25 S8 **Hamilton** Texas, SW USA
14 G16 **Hamilton** ✈ Ontario, SE Canada
64 I6 **Hamilton Bank** *undersea feature* SE Labrador Sea
182 E1 **Hamilton Creek** *seasonal river* South Australia
13 R8 **Hamilton Inlet** *inlet* Newfoundland and Labrador, E Canada
27 T12 **Hamilton, Lake** ⊠ Arkansas, C USA
35 W6 **Hamilton, Mount** ▲ Nevada, W USA
75 S8 **Ḥamīm, Wādī al** ≈ NE Libya
93 N19 **Hamina** *Swe.* Fredrikshamn. Kymi, S Finland
9 W16 **Hamiota** Manitoba, S Canada
152 L13 **Hamīrpur** Uttar Pradesh, N India
Hamïs Musait *see* Khamīs Mushayṭ
21 T11 **Hamlet** North Carolina, SE USA
25 P6 **Hamlin** Texas, SW USA
21 P5 **Hamlin** West Virginia, NE USA
31 O7 **Hamlin Lake** ◎ Michigan, N USA
101 F14 **Hamm** *var.* Hamm in Westfalen. Nordrhein-Westfalen, W Germany
Ḥammāmāt, Khalīj al *see* Hammamet, Golfe de
75 N5 **Hammamet, Golfe de** *Ar.* Khalīj al Ḥammāmāt. *gulf* NE Tunisia
139 R3 **Ḥammān al 'Alīl** N Iraq
139 X12 **Ḥammār, Hawr al** ◎ SE Iraq
93 J20 **Hammarland** Åland, SW Finland
93 H16 **Hammarstrand** Jämtland, C Sweden
93 O17 **Hammaslahti** Pohjois-Karjala, SE Finland
99 F17 **Hamme** Oost-Vlaanderen, NW Belgium
100 H10 **Hamme** ≈ NW Germany
95 G22 **Hammel** Århus, C Denmark
101 I18 **Hammelburg** Bayern, C Germany
99 H18 **Hamme-Mille** Walloon Brabant, C Belgium
100 H10 **Hamme-Oste-Kanal** *canal* NW Germany
93 G16 **Hammerdal** Jämtland, C Sweden
92 K8 **Hammerfest** Finnmark, N Norway
101 D14 **Hamminkeln** Nordrhein-Westfalen, W Germany
Hamm in Westfalen *see* Hamm
26 K10 **Hammon** Oklahoma, C USA
31 N11 **Hammond** Indiana, N USA
22 K8 **Hammond** Louisiana, S USA
99 K20 **Hamoir** Liège, E Belgium
99 J21 **Hamois** Namur, SE Belgium
99 K16 **Hamont** Limburg, NE Belgium
185 F22 **Hampden** Otago, South Island, New Zealand
19 R6 **Hampden** Maine, NE USA
97 M23 **Hampshire** *cultural region* S England, UK
13 O15 **Hampton** New Brunswick, SE Canada
27 U14 **Hampton** Arkansas, C USA
29 V12 **Hampton** Iowa, C USA
19 P10 **Hampton** New Hampshire, NE USA
21 R14 **Hampton** South Carolina, SE USA
21 P8 **Hampton** Tennessee, S USA
21 X7 **Hampton** Virginia, NE USA
94 L11 **Hamra** Gävleborg, C Sweden
80 D10 **Hamrat esh Sheikh** Northern Kordofan, C Sudan
139 S5 **Ḥamrīn, Jabal** ▲ N Iraq
121 P16 **Hamrun** C Malta
167 U14 **Ham Thuân Nam** Binh Thuân, S Vietnam
Hāmūn, Daryācheh-ye *see* Şāberī, Hāmūn-e/Sīstān, Daryācheh-ye
Hamwih *see* Southampton
38 G10 **Hāna** *var.* Hana. Maui, Hawai'i, USA
Hana *see* Hāna
21 S14 **Hanahan** South Carolina, SE USA
38 B8 **Hanalei** Kaua'i, Hawai'i, USA
167 U10 **Ha Nam** Quang Nam-fa Năng, C Vietnam
165 Q9 **Hanamaki** Iwate, Honshū, C Japan
38 F10 **Hanamanioa, Cape** *headland* Maui, Hawai'i, USA
190 B16 **Hanan** ✈ (Alofi) SW Niue
101 H18 **Hanau** Hessen, W Germany
162 M11 **Hanbogd** *var.* Ih Bulag. Ömnögovĭ, S Mongolia
8 L9 **Hanbury** ≈ Northwest Territories, NW Canada
Hâncești *see* Hîncești
10 M15 **Hanceville** British Columbia, SW Canada
23 P3 **Hanceville** Alabama, S USA
Hancewicze *see* Hantsavichy
160 L6 **Hancheng** Shaanxi, C China
21 V2 **Hancock** Maryland, NE USA
30 M3 **Hancock** Michigan, N USA
29 S8 **Hancock** Minnesota, N USA
18 I12 **Hancock** New York, NE USA
80 Q12 **Handa** Bari, NE Somalia
161 O5 **Handan** *var.* Han-tan. Hebei, E China
95 P16 **Handen** Stockholm, C Sweden
81 J22 **Handeni** Tanga, E Tanzania
37 Q7 **Handies Peak** ▲ Colorado, C USA
111 J19 **Handlová** *Ger.* Krickerhäu, *Hung.* Nyitrabánya; *prev.* Krigerhaj. Trenčiansky Kraj, C Slovakia
165 O13 **Haneda** ✈ (Tōkyō) Tōkyō, Honshū, S Japan
138 F13 **HaNegev** *Eng.* Negev. *desert* S Israel
Hanfeng *see* Kaixian
35 Q11 **Hanford** California, W USA
191 V16 **Hanga Roa** Easter Island, Chile, E Pacific Ocean
162 I7 **Hangay** *var.* Hunt. Arhangay, C Mongolia
162 H7 **Hangayn Nuruu** ▲▲ C Mongolia
Hang-chou/Hangchow *see* Hangzhou
95 K20 **Hånger** Jönköping, S Sweden
Hangö *see* Hanko
161 R9 **Hangzhou** *var.* Hang-chou, Hangchow. *province capital* Zhejiang, SE China
162 J4 **Hanh** *var.* Turt. Hövsgöl, N Mongolia
162 F5 **Hanhöhiy Uul** ▲▲ NW Mongolia
162 K10 **Hanhongor** *var.* Ögöömör. Ömnögovĭ, S Mongolia
146 I14 **Hanhowuz** *Rus.* Khauz-Khan. Ahal Welaýaty, S Turkmenistan
146 I14 **Hanhowuz Suw Howdany** *Rus.* Khauzkhanskoye Vodokhranilishche. ◎ S Turkmenistan
146 I14 **Hanhowuz Suw Howdany** *Rus.* Khauzkhanskoye Vodoranilishche. ⊠ S Turkmenistan
137 P15 **Hani** Diyarbakır, SE Turkey
Hania *see* Chaniá
141 R11 **Ḥanīsh al Kabīr, Jazīrat al** *island* SW Yemen
Hanka, Lake *see* Khanka, Lake
93 M17 **Hankasalmi** Länsi-Suomi, C Finland
29 R7 **Hankinson** North Dakota, N USA
93 K20 **Hanko** *Swe.* Hangö. Etelä-Suomi, SW Finland
Han-kou/Han-k'ou/Hankow *see* Wuhan
36 M6 **Hanksville** Utah, W USA
152 K6 **Hanle** Jammu and Kashmir, NW India
185 I17 **Hanmer Springs** Canterbury, South Island, New Zealand
9 R16 **Hanna** Alberta, SW Canada
27 V3 **Hannibal** Missouri, C USA
180 M3 **Hann, Mount** ▲ Western Australia
100 I12 **Hannover** *Eng.* Hanover. Niedersachsen, NW Germany
99 J19 **Hannut** Liège, C Belgium
95 L22 **Hanöbukten** *bay* S Sweden
167 T6 **Ha Nôi** *Eng.* Hanoi, *Fr.* Hanoï. ● (Vietnam) N Vietnam
14 F14 **Hanover** Ontario, S Canada
31 P15 **Hanover** Indiana, N USA
18 G16 **Hanover** Pennsylvania, NE USA
21 W6 **Hanover** Virginia, NE USA
Hanover *see* Hannover
63 G23 **Hanover, Isla** *island* S Chile
Hanselbeck *see* Érd
195 X5 **Hansen Mountains** ▲▲ Antarctica
160 M8 **Han Shui** ≈ C China
152 H10 **Hānsi** Haryāna, NW India
95 F20 **Hanstholm** Viborg, NW Denmark
Han-tan *see* Handan
158 H6 **Hantengri Feng** *var.* Pik Khan-Tengri. ▲ China/Kazakhstan *see also* Khan-Tengri, Pik
119 I18 **Hantsavichy** *Pol.* Hancewicze, *Rus.* Gantsevichi. Brestskaya Voblasts', SW Belarus
9 Q6 **Hantzsch** ≈ Baffin Island, Nunavut, NE Canada
152 G9 **Hanumāngarh** Rājasthān, NW India
183 O9 **Hanwood** New South Wales, SE Australia
Hanyang *see* Wuhan
Hanyang *see* Caidian
160 H10 **Hanyuan** *var.* Fulin. Sichuan, C China
Hanyuan *see* Xihe
160 J7 **Hanzhong** Shaanxi, C China
191 W11 **Hao** *atoll* Îles Tuamotu, C French Polynesia
153 S16 **Hāora** *prev.* Howrah. West Bengal, NE India
78 K8 **Haouach, Ouadi** *dry watercourse* E Chad
92 K13 **Haparanda** Norrbotten, N Sweden
25 N3 **Happy** Texas, SW USA
34 M1 **Happy Camp** California, W USA
13 Q9 **Happy Valley-Goose Bay** *prev.* Goose Bay. Newfoundland and Labrador, E Canada
Hapsal *see* Haapsalu
152 J10 **Hāpur** Uttar Pradesh, N India
138 F12 **HaQatan, HaMakhtesh** ≈ S Israel
140 I4 **Ḥaql** Tabūk, NW Saudi Arabia
171 U14 **Har** Pulau Kai Besar, E Indonesia
Haraat *see* Tsagaandelger
141 R8 **Ḥaraḍ** *var.* Haradh. Ash Sharqīyah, E Saudi Arabia
Haradh *see* Ḥaraḍ
118 N12 **Haradok** *Rus.* Gorodok. Vitsyebskaya Voblasts', N Belarus
92 J13 **Harads** Norrbotten, N Sweden
119 G19 **Haradzyets** *Rus.* Gorodets. Brestskaya Voblasts', SW Belarus
119 J17 **Haradzyeya** *Rus.* Gorodeya. Minskaya Voblasts', C Belarus
191 V10 **Haraiki** *atoll* Îles Tuamotu, C French Polynesia
165 Q11 **Haramachi** Fukushima, Honshū, E Japan
118 M12 **Harany** *Rus.* Gorany. Vitsyebskaya Voblasts', N Belarus
83 L16 **Harare** *prev.* Salisbury. ● (Zimbabwe) Mashonaland East, NE Zimbabwe
83 L16 **Harare** ✈ Mashonaland East, NE Zimbabwe
78 J10 **Haraz-Djombo** Batha, C Chad
119 O16 **Harbavichy** *Rus.* Gorbovichi. Mahilyowskaya Voblasts', E Belarus
76 J16 **Harbel** W Liberia
163 W8 **Harbin** *var.* Haerbin, Ha-erh-pin, Kharbin; *prev.* Haerhpin, Pingkiang, Pinkiang. *province capital* Heilongjiang, NE China
31 S7 **Harbor Beach** Michigan, N USA
13 T13 **Harbour Breton** Newfoundland, Newfoundland and Labrador, E Canada
65 D25 **Harbours, Bay of** *bay* East Falkland, Falkland Islands
Hårby *see* Haarby
36 I13 **Harcuvar Mountains** ▲▲ Arizona, SW USA
108 I7 **Hard** Vorarlberg, NW Austria
154 H11 **Harda Khas** Madhya Pradesh, C India
95 D14 **Hardanger** *physical region* S Norway
95 D14 **Hardangerfjorden** *fjord* S Norway
94 E13 **Hardangerjøkulen** *glacier* S Norway
95 E14 **Hardangervidda** *plateau* S Norway
83 D20 **Hardap** ◈ *district* S Namibia
21 R15 **Hardeeville** South Carolina, SE USA
98 L5 **Hardegarijp** *Fris.* Hurdegaryp. Friesland, N Netherlands
98 O9 **Hardenberg** Overijssel, E Netherlands
183 Q9 **Harden-Murrumburrah** New South Wales, SE Australia
98 K10 **Harderwijk** Gelderland, C Netherlands
30 J14 **Hardin** Illinois, N USA
33 V11 **Hardin** Montana, NW USA
23 R5 **Harding, Lake** ⊠ Alabama/Georgia, SE USA
20 J6 **Hardinsburg** Kentucky, S USA
98 I13 **Hardinxveld-Giessendam** Zuid-Holland, C Netherlands
9 R15 **Hardisty** Alberta, SW Canada
152 L12 **Hardoi** Uttar Pradesh, N India
Hardwar *see* Haridwār
23 U4 **Hardwick** Georgia, SE USA
27 W9 **Hardy** Arkansas, C USA
94 D10 **Hareid** Møre og Romsdal, S Norway
8 H7 **Hare Indian** ≈ Northwest Territories, NW Canada
99 D18 **Harelbeke** *var.* Harlebeke. West-Vlaanderen, W Belgium
Harem *see* Ḥārim
100 E11 **Haren** Niedersachsen, NW Germany
98 N6 **Haren** Groningen, NE Netherlands
80 L13 **Hārer** E Ethiopia
95 P14 **Harg** Uppsala, C Sweden
Hargeisa *see* Hargeysa
80 M13 **Hargeysa** *var.* Hargeisa. Woqooyi Galbeed, NW Somalia
116 J10 **Harghita** ◈ *county* NE Romania
25 S17 **Hargill** Texas, SW USA
162 J8 **Harhorin** Övörhangay, C Mongolia
159 Q9 **Har Hu** ◎ C China
Hariana *see* Haryāna
141 P15 **Ḥarīb** W Yemen
168 M12 **Hari, Batang** *prev.* Djambi. ≈ Sumatera, W Indonesia
152 J9 **Haridwār** *prev.* Hardwar. Uttaranchal, N India
155 F18 **Harihar** Karnātaka, W India
185 F18 **Harihari** West Coast, South Island, New Zealand
138 I3 **Ḥārim** *var.* Harem. Idlib, W Syria
98 F13 **Haringvliet** *channel* SW Netherlands
98 F13 **Haringvlietdam** *dam* SW Netherlands
149 U5 **Harīpur** North-West Frontier Province, NW Pakistan
148 J4 **Harīrūd** *var.* Tedzhen, *Turkm.* Tejen. ≈ Afghanistan/Iran *see also* Tejen
Harīrūd *see* Tejen
94 J11 **Härjåhågnen** *Swe.* Härjahågnen, *var* Härjehågna. ▲ Norway/Sweden
Härjahågnen *see* Østrehogna
Härjahågnen *see* Härjåhågnen
93 K18 **Harjavalta** Länsi-Suomi, W Finland
Härjehågna *see* Østrehogna
Härjehågna *see* Härjåhågnen
118 G4 **Harjumaa** *var.* Harju Maakond. ◈ *province* NW Estonia
Harju Maakond *see* Harjumaa
21 X11 **Harkers Island** North Carolina, SE USA
139 S1 **Harki** N Iraq
29 T14 **Harlan** Iowa, C USA
21 O7 **Harlan** Kentucky, S USA
29 N17 **Harlan County Lake** ⊠ Nebraska, C USA
116 L9 **Hârlău** *var.* Hîrlău. Iaşi, NE Romania
Harlebeke *see* Harelbeke
33 U7 **Harlem** Montana, NW USA
Harlem *see* Haarlem
95 G22 **Harlev** Århus, C Denmark
98 K6 **Harlingen** *Fris.* Harns. Friesland, N Netherlands
25 T17 **Harlingen** Texas, SW USA
97 O21 **Harlow** E England, UK
33 T10 **Harlowton** Montana, NW USA
94 N11 **Harmånger** Gävleborg, C Sweden
98 I11 **Harmelen** Utrecht, C Netherlands
29 X11 **Harmony** Minnesota, N USA
32 J14 **Harney Basin** *basin* Oregon, NW USA
0 F9 **Harney Basin** ▲▲ Oregon, NW USA
32 J14 **Harney Lake** ◎ Oregon, NW USA
28 J10 **Harney Peak** ▲ South Dakota, N USA
93 H17 **Härnösand** *var.* Hernösand. Västernorrland, C Sweden
Harns *see* Harlingen
162 F6 **Har Nuur** ◎ NW Mongolia
105 P4 **Haro** La Rioja, N Spain
40 F6 **Haro, Cabo** *headland* NW Mexico
94 D9 **Harøy** *island* S Norway
97 N21 **Harpenden** E England, UK
76 L18 **Harper** *var.* Cape Palmas. NE Liberia
26 M7 **Harper** Kansas, C USA
32 L13 **Harper** Oregon, NW USA
25 Q10 **Harper** Texas, SW USA
35 U13 **Harper Lake** *salt flat* California, W USA
39 T9 **Harper, Mount** ▲ Alaska, USA
95 J21 **Harplinge** Halland, S Sweden
36 J13 **Harquahala Mountains** ▲▲ Arizona, SW USA
141 T15 **Ḥarrah** SE Yemen
12 H11 **Harricana** ≈ Québec, SE Canada
20 M9 **Harriman** Tennessee, S USA
13 R11 **Harrington Harbour** Québec, E Canada
64 B12 **Harrington Sound** *bay* Bermuda, NW Atlantic Ocean
96 F8 **Harris** *physical region* NW Scotland, UK
27 X10 **Harrisburg** Arkansas, C USA
30 M17 **Harrisburg** Illinois, N USA
28 I14 **Harrisburg** Nebraska, C USA
32 F12 **Harrisburg** Oregon, NW USA
18 G15 **Harrisburg** *state capital* Pennsylvania, NE USA
182 F6 **Harris, Lake** ◎ South Australia
23 W11 **Harris, Lake** ◎ Florida, SE USA
83 J22 **Harrismith** Free State, E South Africa
27 T9 **Harrison** Arkansas, C USA
31 Q7 **Harrison** Michigan, N USA
28 I12 **Harrison** Nebraska, C USA
39 Q5 **Harrison Bay** *inlet* Alaska, USA
22 I6 **Harrisonburg** Louisiana, S USA
21 U4 **Harrisonburg** Virginia, NE USA
13 R7 **Harrison, Cape** *cape* Newfoundland and Labrador, E Canada
27 R5 **Harrisonville** Missouri, C USA
Harris Ridge *see* Lomonosov Ridge
192 M3 **Harris Seamount** *undersea feature* N Pacific Ocean
96 F8 **Harris, Sound of** *strait* NW Scotland, UK
31 R6 **Harrisville** Michigan, N USA
21 R3 **Harrisville** West Virginia, NE USA
20 M6 **Harrodsburg** Kentucky, S USA
97 M16 **Harrogate** N England, UK
25 Q4 **Harrold** Texas, SW USA
27 S5 **Harry S. Truman Reservoir** ⊠ Missouri, C USA
100 G13 **Harsewinkel** Nordrhein-Westfalen, W Germany
116 M14 **Hârşova** *prev.* Hîrşova. Constanța, SE Romania
92 H10 **Harstad** Troms, N Norway
31 O8 **Hart** Michigan, N USA
24 M4 **Hart** Texas, SW USA
10 I5 **Hart** ≈ Yukon Territory, NW Canada
83 F23 **Hartbees** ≈ C South Africa
109 X7 **Hartberg** Steiermark, SE Austria
182 I10 **Hart, Cape** *headland* South Australia
95 E14 **Hårteigen** ▲ S Norway
23 Q7 **Hartford** Alabama, S USA
27 R11 **Hartford** Arkansas, C USA
18 M12 **Hartford** *state capital* Connecticut, NE USA
20 J6 **Hartford** Kentucky, S USA
31 P10 **Hartford** Michigan, N USA
29 R11 **Hartford** South Dakota, N USA
30 M8 **Hartford** Wisconsin, N USA
31 P13 **Hartford City** Indiana, N USA
29 Q13 **Hartington** Nebraska, C USA
13 N14 **Hartland** New Brunswick, SE Canada
97 H23 **Hartland Point** *headland* SW England, UK
97 M15 **Hartlepool** N England, UK
29 T12 **Hartley** Iowa, C USA
24 M1 **Hartley** Texas, SW USA
32 J15 **Hart Mountain** ▲ Oregon, NW USA
173 U10 **Hartog Ridge** *undersea feature* W Indian Ocean
93 M18 **Hartola** Etelä-Suomi, S Finland
67 U14 **Harts** *var.* Hartz. ≈ N South Africa
23 P2 **Hartselle** Alabama, S USA
23 S3 **Hartsfield Atlanta** ✈ Georgia, SE USA
27 Q11 **Hartshorne** Oklahoma, C USA
21 S12 **Hartsville** South Carolina, SE USA
20 K8 **Hartsville** Tennessee, S USA
27 U7 **Hartville** Missouri, C USA
23 U2 **Hartwell** Georgia, SE USA
21 O11 **Hartwell Lake** ⊠ Georgia/South Carolina, SE USA
Hartz *see* Harts
Harunabad *see* Eslāmābād
Har-Us *see* Erdenebüren
162 E6 **Harus Nuur** ◎ NW Mongolia
30 M10 **Harvard** Illinois, N USA
29 P16 **Harvard** Nebraska, C USA
37 R5 **Harvard, Mount** ▲ Colorado, C USA
31 N11 **Harvey** Illinois, N USA
29 N4 **Harvey** North Dakota, N USA
97 Q21 **Harwich** E England, UK
152 H10 **Haryāna** *var.* Hariana. ◈ *state* N India
141 Y9 **Ḥaryān, Ṭawī al** *spring/well* NE Oman
101 J14 **Harz** ▲▲ C Germany
Ḥasakah, Muḥāfaẓat al *see* Al Ḥasakah
165 Q9 **Hasama** Miyagi, Honshū, C Japan
136 J15 **Hasan Dağı** ▲ C Turkey
139 T9 **Ḥasan Ibn Ḥassūn** C Iraq
149 R6 **Ḥasan Khēl** *var.* Ahmad Khel. Paktīā, SE Afghanistan
100 F12 **Hase** ≈ NW Germany
Haselberg *see* Krasnoznamensk
100 F12 **Haselünne** Niedersachsen, NW Germany
Hashaat *see* Delgerhangay
Hashemite Kingdom of Jordan *see* Jordan
139 V8 **Hāshimah** E Iraq
142 K3 **Hashtrūd** *var.* Azaran. Āẕarbāyjān-e Khāvarī, N Iran
141 W13 **Ḥāsik** S Oman
149 U10 **Hāsilpur** Punjab, E Pakistan
27 Q10 **Haskell** Oklahoma, C USA
25 Q6 **Haskell** Texas, SW USA
114 M11 **Hasköy** Edirne, NW Turkey
95 L24 **Hasle** Bornholm, E Denmark
97 N23 **Haslemere** SE England, UK
102 I16 **Hasparren** Pyrénées-Atlantiques, SW France
Hassakeh *see* Al Ḥasakah
155 G19 **Hassan** Karnātaka, W India
36 J13 **Hassayampa River** ≈ Arizona, SW USA
101 J18 **Hassberge** *hill range* C Germany
94 N10 **Hassela** Gävleborg, C Sweden
99 J18 **Hasselt** Limburg, NE Belgium
98 M9 **Hasselt** Overijssel, E Netherlands
Hassetché *see* Al Ḥasakah
101 J18 **Hassfurt** Bayern, C Germany
74 L9 **Hassi Bel Guebbour** E Algeria
74 L8 **Hassi Messaoud** E Algeria
95 K22 **Hässleholm** Skåne, S Sweden
Hasta Colonia/Hasta Pompeia *see* Asti
183 O13 **Hastings** Victoria, SE Australia
184 O11 **Hastings** Hawke's Bay, North Island, New Zealand
97 P23 **Hastings** SE England, UK
31 P9 **Hastings** Michigan, N USA
29 W9 **Hastings** Minnesota, N USA
29 P16 **Hastings** Nebraska, C USA
95 K22 **Hästveda** Skåne, S Sweden
92 J8 **Hasvik** Finnmark, N Norway
37 V6 **Haswell** Colorado, C USA
163 N11 **Hatanbulag** *var.* Ergel. Dornogovĭ, SE Mongolia
Hatansuudal *see* Bayanlig
163 P9 **Hatavch** *var.* Hatavch. Sühbaatar, E Mongolia
Hatavch *see* Hatavch
Hatavch *see* Haldzan
136 K17 **Hatay** ◈ *province* S Turkey
37 R15 **Hatch** New Mexico, SW USA
36 K7 **Hatch** Utah, W USA
20 F9 **Hatchie River** ≈ Tennessee, S USA
116 G12 **Haţeg** *Ger.* Wallenthal, *Hung.* Hátszeg; *prev.* Hatzeg, Hötzing. Hunedoara, SW Romania
165 O17 **Hateruma-jima** *island* Yaeyama-shotō, SW Japan
183 N8 **Hatfield** New South Wales, SE Australia
162 I5 **Hatgal** Hövsgöl, N Mongolia
153 V16 **Hathazari** Chittagong, SE Bangladesh
141 T13 **Hathūt, Hiṣā'** *oasis* NE Yemen
167 R14 **Ha Tiên** Kiên Giang, S Vietnam
167 T8 **Ha Tinh** Ha Tinh, N Vietnam
138 F12 **Hatira, Haré** *hill range* S Israel
167 R6 **Hat Lot** *var* Mai Son. Son La, N Vietnam
45 P16 **Hato Airport** ✈ (Willemstad) Curaçao, SW Netherlands Antilles
54 H9 **Hato Corozal** Casanare, C Colombia
Hato del Volcán *see* Volcán
45 P9 **Hato Mayor** E Dominican Republic
Hatra *see* Al Ḥaḍr
Hatria *see* Adria
Hátszeg *see* Haţeg
143 R16 **Ḥattā** Dubayy, NE United Arab Emirates
182 L9 **Hattah** Victoria, SE Australia
98 M9 **Hattem** Gelderland, E Netherlands
21 Z10 **Hatteras** Hatteras Island, North Carolina, SE USA
21 Rr10 **Hatteras, Cape** *headland* North Carolina, SE USA
21 Z9 **Hatteras Island** *island* North Carolina, SE USA
64 F10 **Hatteras Plain** *undersea feature* W Atlantic Ocean
93 G14 **Hattfjelldal** Troms, N Norway
22 M7 **Hattiesburg** Mississippi, S USA
29 Q4 **Hatton** North Dakota, N USA
Hatton Bank *see* Hatton Ridge
64 L6 **Hatton Ridge** *var.* Hatton Bank. *undersea feature* N Atlantic Ocean
191 W6 **Hatutu** *island* Îles Marquises, NE French Polynesia
111 K22 **Hatvan** Heves, NE Hungary
167 O16 **Hat Yai** *var.* Ban Hat Yai. Songkhla, SW Thailand
Hatzeg *see* Haţeg
Hatzfeld *see* Jimbolia

◆ Country ● Country Capital ◇ Dependent Territory ○ Dependent Territory Capital ◈ Administrative Regions ✈ International Airport ▲ Mountain ▲▲ Mountain Range ⩙ Volcano ≈ River ◎ Lake ⊠ Reservoir

HAUD – HESSTON

80 *N13* **Haud** *plateau* Ethiopia/Somalia
95 *D18* **Hauge** Rogaland, S Norway
95 *C15* **Haugesund** Rogaland, S Norway
109 *X2* **Haugsdorf** Niederösterreich, NE Austria
184 *M9* **Hauhungaroa Range** ▲▲ North Island, New Zealand
95 *E15* **Haukeligrend** Telemark, S Norway
93 *L14* **Haukipudas** Oulu, C Finland
93 *M17* **Haukivesi** ◎ SE Finland
93 *M17* **Haukivuori** Isä-Suomi, E Finland
Hauptkanal *see* Havelländ Grosse
187 *N10* **Hauraha** San Cristobal, SE Solomon Islands
184 *L5* **Hauraki Gulf** *gulf* North Island, N New Zealand
185 *B24* **Hauroko, Lake** ◎ South Island, New Zealand
167 *S14* **Hâu, Sông** ≈ S Vietnam
92 *N12* **Hautajärvi** Lappi, NE Finland
74 *F7* **Haut Atlas** ***Eng.*** High Atlas. ▲▲ C Morocco
79 *M17* **Haut-Congo** ***off.*** Région du Haut-Congo, ***prev*** Haut-Zaïre. ◈ *region* NE Dem. Rep. Congo
103 *Y14* **Haute-Corse** ◈ *department* Corse, France, C Mediterranean Sea
102 *L16* **Haute-Garonne** ◈ *department* S France
79 *K14* **Haute-Kotto** ◈ *prefecture* E Central African Republic
103 *P12* **Haute-Loire** ◈ *department* C France
103 *R6* **Haute-Marne** ◈ *department* N France
102 *M3* **Haute-Normandie** ◈ *region* N France
15 *U6* **Hauterive** Québec, SE Canada
103 *T13* **Hautes-Alpes** ◈ *department* SE France
103 *S7* **Haute-Saône** ◈ *department* E France
103 *T10* **Haute-Savoie** ◈ *department* E France
99 *M20* **Hautes Fagnes** ***Ger.*** Hohes Venn. ▲▲ E Belgium
102 *K16* **Hautes-Pyrénées** ◈ *department* S France
99 *L23* **Haute Sûre, Lac de la** ⊠ NW Luxembourg
102 *M11* **Haute-Vienne** ◈ *department* C France
19 *S8* **Haut, Isle au** *island* Maine, NE USA
79 *M14* **Haut-Mbomou** ◈ *prefecture* SE Central African Republic
103 *Q2* **Hautmont** Nord, N France
79 *F19* **Haut-Ogooué** ***off.*** Province du Haut-Ogooué, ***var.*** Le Haut-Ogooué. ◈ *province* SE Gabon
Haut-Ogooué, Le *see* Haut-Ogooué
Haut-Ogooué, Province du *see* Haut-Ogooué
103 *U7* **Haut-Rhin** ◈ *department* NE France
74 *I6* **Hauts Plateaux** *plateau* Algeria/Morocco
Haut-Zaïre *see* Haut-Congo
38 *D9* **Hau'ula** ***var.*** Hauula. O'ahu, Hawai'i, USA
Hauula *see* Hau'ula
101 *O22* **Hauzenberg** Bayern, SE Germany
30 *K13* **Havana** Illinois, N USA
Havana *see* La Habana
97 *N23* **Havant** S England, UK
35 *Y14* **Havasu, Lake** ⊠ Arizona/California, W USA
95 *J23* **Havdrup** Roskilde, E Denmark
100 *N10* **Havel** ≈ NE Germany
99 *J21* **Havelange** Namur, SE Belgium
100 *M11* **Havelberg** Sachsen-Anhalt, NE Germany
149 *U5* **Haveliān** North-West Frontier Province, NW Pakistan
100 *N12* **Havelländ Grosse** ***var.*** Hauptkanal. *canal* NE Germany
14 *J14* **Havelock** Ontario, SE Canada
185 *J14* **Havelock** Marlborough, South Island, New Zealand
21 *X11* **Havelock** North Carolina, SE USA
184 *O11* **Havelock North** Hawke's Bay, North Island, New Zealand
98 *M8* **Havelte** Drenthe, NE Netherlands
27 *N6* **Haven** Kansas, C USA
97 *H21* **Haverfordwest** SW Wales, UK
97 *P20* **Haverhill** E England, UK
19 *O10* **Haverhill** Massachusetts, NE USA
93 *G17* **Haverö** Västernorrland, C Sweden
111 *I17* **Havířov** Moravskoslezský Kraj, E Czech Republic
111 *E17* **Havlíčkův Brod** ***Ger.*** Deutsch-Brod; ***prev.*** Německý Brod. Vysočina, C Czech Republic
92 *K7* **Havøysund** Finnmark, N Norway
99 *F20* **Havré** Hainaut, S Belgium
33 *T7* **Havre** Montana, NW USA
Havre *see* le Havre
13 *P11* **Havre-St-Pierre** Québec, E Canada
136 *B10* **Havsa** Edirne, NW Turkey
38 *G11* **Hawi** ***var.*** Hawi. Hawaii, USA
38 *D8* **Hawai'i** ***off.*** State of Hawai'i, ***also known as*** Aloha State, Paradise of the Pacific, ***var.*** Hawaii. ◈ *state* USA, C Pacific Ocean
38 *G12* **Hawai'i** ***var.*** Hawaii. *island* Hawaiian Islands, USA, C Pacific Ocean
192 *M5* **Hawaiian Islands** ***prev.*** Sandwich Islands. *island group* Hawaii, USA
192 *L5* **Hawaiian Ridge** *undersea feature* N Pacific Ocean
193 *N6* **Hawaiian Trough** *undersea feature* N Pacific Ocean
29 *R12* **Hawarden** Iowa, C USA
Hawash *see* Āwash
139 *P6* **Hawbayn al Gharbīyah** C Iraq
185 *D21* **Hawea, Lake** ◎ South Island, New Zealand
184 *K11* **Hawera** Taranaki, North Island, New Zealand
20 *J5* **Hawesville** Kentucky, S USA
38 *G11* **Hāwī** ***var.*** Hawi. Hawai'i, USA, C Pacific Ocean
Hawi *see* Hāwī
Hawi *see* Hawi
96 *K13* **Hawick** SE Scotland, UK
139 *S4* **Ḩawījah** C Iraq
139 *Y10* **Ḩawīzah, Hawr al** ◎ S Iraq
185 *E21* **Hawkdun Range** ▲▲ South Island, New Zealand
184 *P10* **Hawke Bay** *bay* North Island, New Zealand
182 *I6* **Hawker** South Australia
184 *N11* **Hawke's Bay** ***off.*** Hawkes Bay Region. ◈ *region* North Island, New Zealand
149 *O16* **Hawkes Bay** *bay* SE Pakistan
Hawkes Bay Region *see* Hawke's Bay
15 *N12* **Hawkesbury** Ontario, SE Canada
Hawkeye State *see* Iowa
23 *T5* **Hawkinsville** Georgia, SE USA
14 *B7* **Hawk Junction** Ontario, S Canada
21 *N10* **Haw Knob** ▲ North Carolina/Tennessee, SE USA
21 *Q9* **Hawksbill Mountain** ▲ North Carolina, SE USA
33 *Z16* **Hawk Springs** Wyoming, C USA
Hawlēr *see* Arbīl
29 *S5* **Hawley** Minnesota, N USA
25 *P7* **Hawley** Texas, SW USA
141 *R14* **Ḩawrā'** C Yemen
139 *P7* **Ḩawrān, Wadi** *dry watercourse* W Iraq
21 *T9* **Haw River** ≈ North Carolina, SE USA
139 *U5* **Hawshqūrah** E Iraq
35 *S7* **Hawthorne** Nevada, W USA
37 *W3* **Haxtun** Colorado, C USA
183 *N9* **Hay** New South Wales, SE Australia
9 *O10* **Hay** ≈ W Canada
171 *S13* **Haya** Pulau Seram, E Indonesia
165 *R9* **Hayachine-san** ▲ Honshū, C Japan
103 *S4* **Hayange** Moselle, NE France
HaYarden *see* Jordan
Hayastani Hanrapetut'yun *see* Armenia
Hayasui-seto *see* Hōyo-kaikyō
39 *N9* **Haycock** Alaska, USA
36 *M14* **Hayden** Arizona, SW USA
37 *Q3* **Hayden** Colorado, C USA
28 *M10* **Hayes** South Dakota, N USA
9 *X13* **Hayes** ≈ Manitoba, C Canada
9 *P12* **Hayes** ≈ Nunavut, NE Canada
28 *M16* **Hayes Center** Nebraska, C USA
39 *S10* **Hayes, Mount** ▲ Alaska, USA
21 *N11* **Hayesville** North Carolina, SE USA
35 *X10* **Hayford Peak** ▲ Nevada, W USA
34 *M3* **Hayfork** California, W USA
Hayir, Qasr al *see* Ḩayr al Gharbī, Qaşr al
Haylaastay *see* Sühbaatar
14 *I12* **Hay Lake** ◎ Ontario, SE Canada
141 *X11* **Haymā'** ***var.*** Haima. C Oman
136 *H13* **Haymana** Ankara, C Turkey
138 *J7* **Ḩaymūr, Jabal** ▲▲ W Syria
Haynau *see* Chojnów
22 *G4* **Haynesville** Louisiana, S USA
23 *P6* **Hayneville** Alabama, S USA
114 *M12* **Hayrabolu** Tekirdağ, NW Turkey
136 *C10* **Hayrabolu Deresi** ≈ NW Turkey
138 *J6* **Ḩayr al Gharbī, Qaşr al** ***var.*** Qasr al Hayir, Qasr al Hir al Gharbi. *ruins* Ḩimş, C Syria
138 *L5* **Ḩayr ash Sharqī, Qaşr al** ***var.*** Qasr al Hir Ash Sharqī. *ruins* Ḩimş, C Syria
162 *J7* **Hayrhan** ***var.*** Uubulan. Arhangay, C Mongolia
162 *J9* **Hayrhandulaan** ***var.*** Mardzad. Övörhangay, C Mongolia
8 *J10* **Hay River** Northwest Territories, W Canada
26 *K4* **Hays** Kansas, C USA
28 *K12* **Hay Springs** Nebraska, C USA
65 *H25* **Haystack, The** ▲ NE Saint Helena
27 *N7* **Haysville** Kansas, C USA
117 *O7* **Haysyn** ***Rus.*** Gaysin. Vinnyts'ka Oblast', C Ukraine
27 *Y9* **Hayti** Missouri, C USA
29 *Q9* **Hayti** South Dakota, N USA
117 *O8* **Hayvoron** ***Rus.*** Gayvorno. Kirovohrads'ka Oblast', C Ukraine
35 *N9* **Hayward** California, W USA
30 *J4* **Hayward** Wisconsin, N USA
97 *O23* **Haywards Heath** SE England, UK
146 *A11* **Hazar** ***prev. Rus.*** Cheleken. Balkan Welaýaty, W Turkmenistan
143 *S11* **Hazārān, Kūh-e** ***var.*** Kūh-e ā Hazr. ▲ SE Iran
Hazarat Imam *see* Emām Şāḩeb
21 *O7* **Hazard** Kentucky, S USA
137 *O15* **Hazar Gölü** ◎ C Turkey
153 *P15* **Hazārībāg** ***var.*** Hazāribāgh. Jhārkhand, N India
Hazāribāgh *see* Hazārībāg
103 *O1* **Hazebrouck** Nord, N France
30 *K9* **Hazel Green** Wisconsin, N USA
192 *K9* **Hazel Holme Bank** *undersea feature* S Pacific Ocean
10 *K13* **Hazelton** British Columbia, SW Canada
29 *N6* **Hazelton** North Dakota, N USA
35 *R5* **Hazen** Nevada, W USA
28 *L5* **Hazen** North Dakota, N USA
38 *L12* **Hazen Bay** *bay* E Bering Sea
139 *S5* **Hazīm, Bi'r** *well* C Iraq
23 *V6* **Hazlehurst** Georgia, SE USA
22 *K6* **Hazlehurst** Mississippi, S USA
18 *K15* **Hazlet** New Jersey, NE USA
146 *I9* **Hazorasp** ***Rus.*** Khazarosp. Xorazm Viloyati, W Uzbekistan
147 *R13* **Hazratishoh, Qatorkŭhi** ***var.*** Khrebet Khazretishi, ***Rus.*** Khrebet Khozretishi. ▲▲ S Tajikistan
Hazr, Kūh-e ā *see* Hazārān, Kūh-e
149 *U6* **Hazro** Punjab, E Pakistan
23 *R7* **Headland** Alabama, S USA
182 *C6* **Head of Bight** *headland* South Australia
33 *N10* **Headquarters** Idaho, NW USA
34 *M7* **Healdsburg** California, W USA
27 *N13* **Healdton** Oklahoma, C USA
183 *O12* **Healesville** Victoria, SE Australia
39 *R10* **Healy** Alaska, USA
173 *R13* **Heard and McDonald Islands** ◇ *Australian external territory* S Indian Ocean
173 *R13* **Heard Island** *island* Heard and McDonald Islands, S Indian Ocean
25 *U9* **Hearne** Texas, SW USA
12 *F12* **Hearst** Ontario, S Canada
194 *J5* **Hearst Island** *island* Antarctica
Heart of Dixie *see* Alabama
28 *L5* **Heart River** ≈ North Dakota, N USA
31 *T13* **Heath** Ohio, N USA
183 *N11* **Heathcote** Victoria, SE Australia
97 *N22* **Heathrow** ✈ (London) SE England, UK
21 *X5* **Heathsville** Virginia, NE USA
27 *R11* **Heavener** Oklahoma, C USA
25 *R15* **Hebbronville** Texas, SW USA
163 *Q13* **Hebei** ***var.*** Hebei Sheng, Hopeh, Hopei, Ji; ***prev.*** Chihli. ◈ *province* E China
Hebei Sheng *see* Hebei
36 *M3* **Heber City** Utah, W USA
27 *V10* **Heber Springs** Arkansas, C USA
161 *N5* **Hebi** Henan, C China
32 *F11* **Hebo** Oregon, NW USA
96 *F9* **Hebrides, Sea of the** *sea* NW Scotland, UK
13 *P5* **Hebron** Newfoundland and Labrador, E Canada
31 *N11* **Hebron** Indiana, N USA
29 *Q17* **Hebron** Nebraska, C USA
28 *L5* **Hebron** North Dakota, N USA
138 *F11* **Hebron** ***var.*** Al Khalīl, El Khalil, ***Heb.*** Hevron; ***anc.*** Kiriath-Arba. S West Bank
Hebrus *see* Évros/Maritsa/Meriç
95 *N14* **Heby** Västmanland, C Sweden
10 *I14* **Hecate Strait** *strait* British Columbia, W Canada
41 *W12* **Hecelchakán** Campeche, SE Mexico
160 *K13* **Hechi** ***var.*** Jinchengjiang. Guangxi Zhuangzu Zizhiqu, S China
101 *H23* **Hechingen** Baden-Württemberg, S Germany
99 *K17* **Hechtel** Limburg, NE Belgium
160 *J9* **Hechuan** ***var.*** Heyang. Chongqing Shi, C China
29 *P7* **Hecla** South Dakota, N USA
29 *T9* **Hector** Minnesota, N USA
93 *F17* **Hede** Jämtland, C Sweden
Hede *see* Sheyang
95 *M14* **Hedemora** Dalarna, C Sweden
92 *K13* **Hedenäset** Norrbotten, N Sweden
95 *G23* **Hedensted** Vejle, C Denmark
95 *N14* **Hedesunda** Gävleborg, C Sweden
95 *N14* **Hedesundafjord** ◎ C Sweden
25 *O3* **Hedley** Texas, SW USA
94 *I12* **Hedmark** ◈ *county* S Norway
165 *T16* **Hedo-misaki** *headland* Okinawa, SW Japan
29 *X15* **Hedrick** Iowa, C USA
99 *L16* **Heel** Limburg, SE Netherlands
189 *Y12* **Heel Point** *point* Wake Island
98 *H9* **Heemskerk** Noord-Holland, W Netherlands
98 *M10* **Heerde** Gelderland, E Netherlands
98 *L7* **Heerenveen** ***Fris.*** It Hearrenfean. Friesland, N Netherlands
98 *I8* **Heerhugowaard** Noord-Holland, NW Netherlands
92 *O3* **Heer Land** *physical region* C Svalbard
99 *M18* **Heerlen** Limburg, SE Netherlands
99 *J19* **Heers** Limburg, NE Belgium
Heerwegen *see* Polkowice
98 *K13* **Heesch** Noord-Brabant, S Netherlands
99 *K15* **Heeze** Noord-Brabant, SE Netherlands
138 *F8* **Ḥefa** ***var.*** Haifa, ***hist.*** Caiffa, Caiphas; ***anc.*** Sycaminum. Haifa, N Israel
138 *F8* **Ḥefa, Mifraẕ** ***Eng.*** Bay of Haifa. *bay* N Israel
161 *Q8* **Hefei** ***var.*** Hofei, ***hist.*** Luchow. *province capital* Anhui, E China
23 *R3* **Heflin** Alabama, S USA
163 *X7* **Hegang** Heilongjiang, NE China
164 *L10* **Hegura-jima** *island* SW Japan
Heguri-jima *see* Heigun-tō
Hei *see* Heilongjiang
100 *H8* **Heide** Schleswig-Holstein, N Germany
101 *G20* **Heidelberg** Baden-Württemberg, SW Germany
83 *J21* **Heidelberg** Gauteng, NE South Africa
22 *M6* **Heidelberg** Mississippi, S USA
Heidenheim *see* Heidenheim an der Brenz
101 *J22* **Heidenheim an der Brenz** ***var.*** Heidenheim. Baden-Württemberg, S Germany
109 *U2* **Heidenreichstein** Niederösterreich, N Austria
164 *F14* **Heigun-tō** ***var.*** Heguri-jima. *island* SW Japan
163 *W5* **Heihe** ***prev.*** Ai-hun. Heilongjiang, NE China
162 *S8* **Hei He** ≈ C China
Hei-ho *see* Nagqu
83 *J22* **Heilbron** Free State, N South Africa
101 *H21* **Heilbronn** Baden-Württemberg, SW Germany
Heiligenbeil *see* Mamonovo
109 *Q8* **Heiligenblut** Tirol, W Austria
100 *K7* **Heiligenhafen** Schleswig-Holstein, N Germany
Heiligenkreuz *see* Žiar nad Hronom
101 *J15* **Heiligenstadt** Thüringen, C Germany
163 *W8* **Heilongjiang** ***var.*** Hei, Heilongjiang Sheng, Hei-lung-chiang, Heilungkiang. ◈ *province* NE China
Heilong Jiang *see* Amur
Heilongjiang Sheng *see* Heilongjiang
98 *H9* **Heiloo** Noord-Holland, NW Netherlands
Heilsberg *see* Lidzbark Warmiński
Hei-lung-chiang/Heilungkiang *see* Heilongjiang
Heimaæy *see* Heimaey
92 *I4* **Heimaey** ***var.*** Heimaæy. *island* S Iceland
94 *H8* **Heimdal** Sør-Trøndelag, S Norway
Heinaste *see* Ainaži
93 *N17* **Heinävesi** Isä-Suomi, E Finland
99 *M22* **Heinerscheid** Diekirch, N Luxembourg
98 *M10* **Heino** Overijssel, E Netherlands
93 *M18* **Heinola** Etelä-Suomi, S Finland
101 *C16* **Heinsberg** Nordrhein-Westfalen, W Germany
163 *U12* **Heishan** Liaoning, NE China
160 *H8* **Heishui** ***var.*** Luhua. Sichuan, C China
99 *H17* **Heist-op-den-Berg** Antwerpen, C Belgium
Heitō *see* P'ingtung
171 *X15* **Heitske** Papua, E Indonesia
Hejanah *see* Al Hījānah
Hejaz *see* Al Ḩijāz
160 *M14* **He Jiang** ≈ S China
Hejiayan *see* Lüeyang
158 *K6* **Hejing** Xinjiang Uygur Zizhiqu, NW China
Héjjasfalva *see* Vânători
Heka *see* Hoika
137 *N14* **Hekimhan** Malatya, C Turkey
92 *J4* **Hekla** ▲ S Iceland
Hekou *see* Yanshan, Jiangxi, China
Hekou *see* Yajiang, Sichuan, China
110 *J6* **Hel** ***Ger.*** Hela. Pomorskie, N Poland
Hela *see* Hel
93 *F17* **Helagsfjället** ▲ C Sweden
159 *W8* **Helan** ***var.*** Xigang. Ningxia, N China
162 *K14* **Helan Shan** ▲▲ N China
99 *M16* **Helden** Limburg, SE Netherlands
27 *X12* **Helena** Arkansas, C USA
33 *R10* **Helena** *state capital* Montana, NW USA
96 *H12* **Helensburgh** W Scotland, UK
184 *K5* **Helensville** Auckland, North Island, New Zealand
95 *L20* **Helgasjön** ◎ S Sweden
100 *G8* **Helgoland** ***Eng.*** Heligoland. *island* NW Germany
Helgoland Bay *see* Helgoländer Bucht
100 *G8* **Helgoländer Bucht** ***var.*** Helgoland Bay, Heligoland Bight. *bay* NW Germany
Heligoland *see* Helgoland
Heligoland Bight *see* Helgoländer Bucht
Heliopolis *see* Baalbek
92 *I4* **Hella** Sudhurland, SW Iceland
Hellas *see* Greece
143 *N11* **Ḩelleh, Rūd-e** ≈ S Iran
98 *N10* **Hellendoorn** Overijssel, E Netherlands
Hellenic Republic *see* Greece
121 *Q10* **Hellenic Trough** *undersea feature* Aegean Sea, C Mediterranean Sea
94 *E10* **Hellesylt** Møre og Romsdal, S Norway
98 *F13* **Hellevoetsluis** Zuid-Holland, SW Netherlands
105 *Q12* **Hellín** Castilla-La Mancha, C Spain
115 *H19* **Hellinikon** ✈ (Athína) Attikí, C Greece
32 *M12* **Hells Canyon** *valley* Idaho/Oregon, NW USA
148 *L9* **Helmand** ◈ *province* S Afghanistan
148 *K10* **Helmand, Daryā-ye** ***var.*** Rūd-e Hīrmand. ≈ Afghanistan/Iran ***see also*** Hīrmand, Rūd-e
Helmand, Daryā-ye *see* Hīrmand, Rūd-e
Helmantica *see* Salamanca
101 *K15* **Helme** ≈ C Germany
99 *L15* **Helmond** Noord-Brabant, S Netherlands
96 *J7* **Helmsdale** N Scotland, UK
100 *K13* **Helmstedt** Niedersachsen, N Germany
163 *Y10* **Helong** Jilin, NE China
36 *M4* **Helper** Utah, W USA
100 *O10* **Helpter Berge** *hill* NE Germany
95 *J22* **Helsingborg** ***prev.*** Hälsingborg. Skåne, S Sweden
Helsingfors *see* Helsinki
95 *J22* **Helsingør** ***Eng.*** Elsinore. Frederiksborg, E Denmark
93 *M20* **Helsinki** ***Swe.*** Helsingfors. ● (Finland) Etelä-Suomi, S Finland
97 *H25* **Helston** SW England, UK
Heltau *see* Cisnădie
61 *C17* **Helvecia** Santa Fe, C Argentina
97 *K15* **Helvellyn** ▲ NW England, UK
Helvetia *see* Switzerland
75 *W8* **Helwân** ***var.*** Hilwân, Hulwan, Hulwân. N Egypt
97 *N21* **Hemel Hempstead** E England, UK
35 *U16* **Hemet** California, W USA
28 *J13* **Hemingford** Nebraska, C USA
21 *T13* **Hemingway** South Carolina, SE USA
92 *G13* **Hemnesberget** Nordland, C Norway
25 *Y8* **Hemphill** Texas, SW USA
25 *V11* **Hempstead** Texas, SW USA
95 *P20* **Hemse** Gotland, SE Sweden
94 *F13* **Hemsedal** *valley* S Norway
159 *T11* **Henan** ***var.*** Henan Mongolzu Zizhixian, Yêgainnyin. Qinghai, C China
161 *N6* **Henan** ***var.*** Henan Sheng, Honan, Yu. ◈ *province* C China
184 *L4* **Hen and Chickens** *island group* N New Zealand
105 *O7* **Henares** ≈ C Spain
165 *P7* **Henashi-zaki** *headland* Honshū, C Japan
102 *I16* **Hendaye** Pyrénées-Atlantiques, SW France
136 *F11* **Hendek** Sakarya, NW Turkey
61 *B21* **Henderson** Buenos Aires, E Argentina
20 *I5* **Henderson** Kentucky, S USA
35 *X11* **Henderson** Nevada, W USA
21 *V8* **Henderson** North Carolina, SE USA
20 *G10* **Henderson** Tennessee, S USA
25 *W7* **Henderson** Texas, SW USA
30 *J12* **Henderson Creek** ≈ Illinois, N USA
186 *M9* **Henderson Field** ✈ (Honiara) Guadalcanal, C Solomon Islands
191 *O17* **Henderson Island** *atoll* N Pitcairn Islands
21 *O10* **Hendersonville** North Carolina, SE USA
20 *J8* **Hendersonville** Tennessee, S USA
143 *O14* **Hendorābī, Jazīreh-ye** *island* S Iran
55 *V10* **Hendrik Top** ***var.*** Hendriktop. *elevation* C Surinam
Hendriktop *see* Hendrik Top
Hendū Kosh *see* Hindu Kush
14 *L12* **Heney, Lac** ◎ Québec, SE Canada
Hengchow *see* Hengyang
161 *S15* **Hengchun** S Taiwan
159 *R16* **Hengduan Shan** ▲▲ SW China
98 *N12* **Hengelo** Gelderland, E Netherlands
98 *O10* **Hengelo** Overijssel, E Netherlands
Hengnan *see* Hengyang
161 *N11* **Hengshan** Hunan, S China
160 *L4* **Hengshan** Shaanxi, C China
161 *O4* **Hengshui** Hebei, E China
161 *N12* **Hengyang** ***var.*** Hengnan, Heng-yang; ***prev.*** Hengchow. Hunan, S China
Heng-yang *see* Hengyang
117 *U11* **Heniches'k** ***Rus.*** Genichesk. Khersons'ka Oblast', S Ukraine
21 *Z4* **Henlopen, Cape** *headland* Delaware, NE USA
Henna *see* Enna
94 *M10* **Hennan** Gävleborg, C Sweden
102 *G7* **Hennebont** Morbihan, NW France
30 *L11* **Hennepin** Illinois, N USA
26 *M9* **Hennessey** Oklahoma, C USA
100 *N12* **Hennigsdorf** ***var.*** Hennigsdorf bei Berlin. Brandenburg, NE Germany
Hennigsdorf bei Berlin *see* Hennigsdorf
19 *N9* **Henniker** New Hampshire, NE USA
25 *S5* **Henrietta** Texas, SW USA
Henrique de Carvalho *see* Saurimo
30 *L12* **Henry** Illinois, N USA
21 *Y7* **Henry, Cape** *headland* Virginia, NE USA
27 *P10* **Henryetta** Oklahoma, C USA
194 *M7* **Henry Ice Rise** *ice cap* Antarctica
33 *R13* **Henrys Fork** ≈ Idaho, NW USA
14 *E15* **Hensall** Ontario, S Canada
100 *J9* **Henstedt-Ulzburg** Schleswig-Holstein, N Germany
Hentiy *see* Batshireet
162 *M7* **Hentiyn Nuruu** ▲▲ N Mongolia
183 *P10* **Henty** New South Wales, SE Australia
166 *L8* **Henzada** Irrawaddy, SW Burma (Myanmar)
Heping *see* Huishui
101 *G19* **Heppenheim** Hessen, W Germany
32 *J11* **Heppner** Oregon, NW USA
160 *L15* **Hepu** ***var.*** Lianzhou. Guangxi Zhuangzu Zizhiqu, S China
Heracleum *see* Irákleio
92 *J2* **Heradhsvötn** ≈ C Iceland
Herakleion *see* Irákleio
148 *K5* **Herāt** ***var.*** Herat; ***anc.*** Aria. Herāt, W Afghanistan
148 *J5* **Herāt** ◈ *province* W Afghanistan
103 *P14* **Hérault** ◈ *department* S France
103 *P15* **Hérault** ≈ S France
9 *T16* **Herbert** Saskatchewan, S Canada
185 *F22* **Herbert** Otago, South Island, New Zealand
38 *J17* **Herbert Island** *island* Aleutian Islands, Alaska, USA
Herbertshöhe *see* Kokopo
15 *Q7* **Hérbertville** Québec, SE Canada
101 *G17* **Herborn** Hessen, W Germany
113 *I17* **Herceg-Novi** ***It.*** Castelnuovo; ***prev.*** Ercegnovi. SW Montenegro
9 *X10* **Herchmer** Manitoba, C Canada
186 *E8* **Hercules Bay** *bay* E Papua New Guinea
92 *K2* **Herdhubreidh** ▲ C Iceland
42 *M13* **Heredia** Heredia, C Costa Rica
42 *M12* **Heredia** ***off.*** Provincia de Heredia. ◈ *province* N Costa Rica
Heredia, Provincia de *see* Heredia
97 *K21* **Hereford** W England, UK
24 *M3* **Hereford** Texas, SW USA
15 *Q13* **Hereford, Mont** ▲ Québec, SE Canada
97 *K21* **Herefordshire** *cultural region* W England, UK
191 *U11* **Hereheretue** *atoll* Îles Tuamotu, C French Polynesia
105 *N10* **Herencia** Castilla-La Mancha, C Spain
99 *H18* **Herent** Vlaams Brabant, C Belgium
99 *I16* **Herentals** ***var.*** Herenthals. Antwerpen, N Belgium
Herenthals *see* Herentals
99 *H17* **Herenthout** Antwerpen, N Belgium
95 *J23* **Herfølge** Roskilde, E Denmark
100 *G13* **Herford** Nordrhein-Westfalen, NW Germany
27 *O5* **Herington** Kansas, C USA
108 *H7* **Herisau** ***Fr.*** Hérisau. Appenzell Ausser Rhoden, NE Switzerland
Hérisau *see* Herisau
Héristal *see* Herstal
99 *J18* **Herk-de-Stad** Limburg, NE Belgium
Herkulesbad/Herkulesfürdő *see* Băile Herculane
162 *M8* **Herlenbayan-Ulaan** ***var.*** Dulaan. Hentiy, C Mongolia
Herlen Gol/Herlen He *see* Kerulen
35 *Q4* **Herlong** California, W USA
97 *L26* **Herm** *island* Channel Islands
109 *R9* **Hermagor** ***Slvn.*** Šmohor. Kärnten, S Austria
29 *S7* **Herman** Minnesota, N USA
96 *L1* **Herma Ness** *headland* NE Scotland, UK
27 *V4* **Hermann** Missouri, C USA
181 *Q8* **Hermannsburg** Northern Territory, N Australia
Hermannstadt *see* Sibiu
94 *E12* **Hermansverk** Sogn Og Fjordane, S Norway
138 *H6* **Hermel** ***var.*** Hirmil. NE Lebanon
Hermhausen *see* Hajnówka
183 *P6* **Hermidale** New South Wales, SE Australia
55 *X9* **Herminadorp** Sipaliwini, NE Surinam
32 *K11* **Hermiston** Oregon, NW USA
27 *T6* **Hermitage** Missouri, C USA
186 *D4* **Hermit Islands** *island group* N Papua New Guinea
25 *O7* **Hermleigh** Texas, SW USA
138 *G7* **Hermon, Mount** ***Ar.*** Jabal ash Shaykh. ▲ S Syria
Hermopolis Parva *see* Damanhûr
28 *J10* **Hermosa** South Dakota, N USA
40 *F5* **Hermosillo** Sonora, NW Mexico
Hermoupolis *see* Ermoúpoli
111 *N20* **Hernád** ***var.*** Hornád, ***Ger.*** Kundert. ≈ Hungary/Slovakia
61 *C18* **Hernández** Entre Ríos, E Argentina
23 *V11* **Hernando** Florida, SE USA
22 *L1* **Hernando** Mississippi, S USA
105 *Q2* **Hernani** País Vasco, N Spain
99 *F19* **Herne** Vlaams Brabant, C Belgium
101 *E14* **Herne** Nordrhein-Westfalen, W Germany
95 *F22* **Herning** Ringkøbing, W Denmark
Hernösand *see* Härnösand
121 *U11* **Herodotus Basin** *undersea feature* E Mediterranean Sea
121 *Q12* **Herodotus Trough** *undersea feature* C Mediterranean Sea
29 *T11* **Heron Lake** Minnesota, N USA
Herowābād *see* Khalkhāl
95 *G16* **Herre** Telemark, S Norway
29 *N7* **Herreid** South Dakota, N USA
101 *H22* **Herrenberg** Baden-Württemberg, S Germany
104 *L14* **Herrera** Andalucía, S Spain
43 *R17* **Herrera** ***off.*** Provincia de Herrera. ◈ *province* S Panama
104 *L10* **Herrera del Duque** Extremadura, W Spain
104 *M4* **Herrera de Pisuerga** Castilla-León, N Spain
Herrera, Provincia de *see* Herrera
41 *Z13* **Herrero, Punta** *headland* SE Mexico
183 *P16* **Herrick** Tasmania, SE Australia
30 *L17* **Herrin** Illinois, N USA
20 *M6* **Herrington Lake** ⊠ Kentucky, S USA
95 *K18* **Herrljunga** Västra Götaland, S Sweden
103 *N16* **Hers** ≈ S France
10 *I1* **Herschel Island** *island* Yukon Territory, NW Canada
99 *I17* **Herselt** Antwerpen, C Belgium
18 *G15* **Hershey** Pennsylvania, NE USA
99 *K19* **Herstal** ***Fr.*** Héristal. Liège, E Belgium
97 *O21* **Hertford** E England, UK
21 *X8* **Hertford** North Carolina, SE USA
97 *O21* **Hertfordshire** *cultural region* E England, UK
181 *Z9* **Hervey Bay** Queensland, E Australia
101 *O14* **Herzberg** Brandenburg, E Germany
99 *E18* **Herzele** Oost-Vlaanderen, NW Belgium
101 *K20* **Herzogenaurach** Bayern, SE Germany
109 *W4* **Herzogenburg** Niederösterreich, NE Austria
Herzogenbusch *see* 's-Hertogenbosch
103 *N2* **Hesdin** Pas-de-Calais, N France
160 *K14* **Heshan** Guangxi Zhuangzu Zizhiqu, S China
159 *X10* **Heshui** ***var.*** Xihuachi. Gansu, C China
99 *M25* **Hespérange** Luxembourg, SE Luxembourg
35 *U14* **Hesperia** California, W USA
37 *P7* **Hesperus Mountain** ▲ Colorado, C USA
10 *J6* **Hess** ≈ Yukon Territory, NW Canada
Hesse *see* Hessen
101 *J21* **Hesselberg** ▲ S Germany
95 *I22* **Hesselo** *island* E Denmark
101 *H17* **Hessen** ***Eng./Fr.*** Hesse. ◈ *state* C Germany
192 *L6* **Hess Tablemount** *undersea feature* C Pacific Ocean
27 *N6* **Hesston** Kansas, C USA

◆ Country
● Country Capital
◇ Dependent Territory
○ Dependent Territory Capital
◈ Administrative Regions
✈ International Airport
▲ Mountain
▲▲ Mountain Range
⛰ Volcano
≈ River
◎ Lake
⊠ Reservoir

HESTKJØLTOPPEN – HÔNG HÀ, SÔNG

93 G15 **Hestkjøltoppen** ▲ C Norway
97 K18 **Heswall** NW England, UK
153 P12 **Hetaudā** Central, C Nepal
Hétfalu see Săcele
28 K7 **Hettinger** North Dakota, N USA
101 L14 **Hettstedt** Sachsen-Anhalt, C Germany
92 P3 **Heuglin, Kapp** headland SE Svalbard
187 N10 **Heuru** San Cristobal, SE Solomon Islands
99 J17 **Heusden** Limburg, NE Belgium
98 J13 **Heusden** Noord-Brabant, S Netherlands
102 K3 **Hève, Cap de la** headland N France
99 H18 **Heverlee** Vlaams Brabant, C Belgium
111 L22 **Heves** Heves, NE Hungary
111 L22 **Heves** off. Heves Megye. ◆ county NE Hungary
Heves Megye see Heves
Hevron see Hebron
45 Y13 **Hewanorra** ✈ (Saint Lucia) S Saint Lucia
Hexian see Hezhou
160 L6 **Heyang** Shaanxi, C China
Heyang see Hechuan
Heydebrech see Kędzierzyn-Kozle
Heydekrug see Šilutė
Heyin see Guide
97 K16 **Heysham** NW England, UK
161 O14 **Heyuan** Guangdong, S China
182 L12 **Heywood** Victoria, SE Australia
180 K3 **Heywood Islands** island group Western Australia
161 O6 **Heze** var. Caozhou. Shandong, E China
159 U11 **Hezheng** Gansu, C China
160 M13 **Hezhou** var. Babu; prev. Hexian. Guangxi Zhuangzu Zizhiqu, S China
159 U11 **Hezuo** Gansu, C China
23 Z16 **Hialeah** Florida, SE USA
27 Q3 **Hiawatha** Kansas, C USA
36 M4 **Hiawatha** Utah, W USA
29 V4 **Hibbing** Minnesota, N USA
183 N17 **Hibbs, Point** headland Tasmania, SE Australia
Hibernia see Ireland
20 F8 **Hickman** Kentucky, S USA
21 Q9 **Hickory** North Carolina, SE USA
21 Q9 **Hickory, Lake** ◎ North Carolina, SE USA
184 Q7 **Hicks Bay** Gisborne, North Island, New Zealand
25 S8 **Hico** Texas, SW USA
165 T4 **Hidaka** Hokkaidō, NE Japan
164 I12 **Hidaka** Hyōgo, Honshū, SW Japan
165 T5 **Hidaka-sanmyaku** ▲▲ Hokkaidō, NE Japan
41 O6 **Hidalgo** var. Villa Hidalgo. Coahuila de Zaragoza, NE Mexico
41 N8 **Hidalgo** Nuevo León, NE Mexico
41 O10 **Hidalgo** Tamaulipas, C Mexico
41 O13 **Hidalgo** ◆ state C Mexico
40 J7 **Hidalgo del Parral** var. Parral. Chihuahua, N Mexico
100 N7 **Hiddensee** island NE Germany
80 G6 **Hidiglib, Wadi** ≈ NE Sudan
109 U6 **Hieflau** Salzburg, E Austria
187 P16 **Hienghène** Province Nord, C New Caledonia
Hierosolyma see Jerusalem
64 N12 **Hierro** var. Ferro. island Islas Canarias, Spain, NE Atlantic Ocean
164 G13 **Higashi-Hiroshima** var. Higasihirosima. Hiroshima, Honshū, SW Japan
164 C12 **Higashi-suidō** strait SW Japan
Higasihirosima see Higashi-Hiroshima
25 P1 **Higgins** Texas, SW USA
31 P7 **Higgins Lake** ◎ Michigan, N USA
27 S4 **Higginsville** Missouri, C USA
High Atlas see Haut Atlas
30 M5 **High Falls Reservoir** ▣ Wisconsin, N USA
44 K12 **Highgate** C Jamaica
25 X11 **High Island** Texas, SW USA
31 O5 **High Island** island Michigan, N USA
30 K15 **Highland** Illinois, N USA
31 N10 **Highland Park** Illinois, N USA
21 O10 **Highlands** North Carolina, SE USA
9 O11 **High Level** Alberta, W Canada
29 O9 **Highmore** South Dakota, N USA
171 N3 **High Peak** ▲ Luzon, N Philippines
High Plains see Great Plains
21 S9 **High Point** North Carolina, SE USA
18 J13 **High Point** hill New Jersey, NE USA
9 P13 **High Prairie** Alberta, W Canada
9 Q16 **High River** Alberta, SW Canada
21 S9 **High Rock Lake** ▣ North Carolina, SE USA
23 V9 **High Springs** Florida, SE USA
High Veld see Great Karoo
97 J24 **High Willhays** ▲ SW England, UK
97 N22 **High Wycombe** prev. Chepping Wycombe, Chipping Wycombe. SE England, UK
41 P12 **Higos** var. El Higo. Veracruz-Llave, E Mexico
102 I16 **Higuer, Cap** headland NE Spain
45 R5 **Higüero, Punta** headland W Puerto Rico
45 P9 **Higüey** var. Salvaleón de Higüey. E Dominican Republic
190 G11 **Hihifo** ✈ (Matā'utu) Île Uvea, N Wallis and Futuna
81 N16 **Hiiraan** off. Gobolka Hiiraan. ◆ region C Somalia
Hiiraan, Gobolka see Hiiraan
118 E4 **Hiiumaa** var. Hiiumaa Maakond. ◆ province W Estonia
118 D4 **Hiiumaa** Ger. Dagden, Swe. Dagö. island W Estonia
Hiiumaa Maakond see Hiiumaa
Hijanah see Al Hījānah
105 S6 **Híjar** Aragón, NE Spain
191 V10 **Hikueru** atoll Îles Tuamotu, C French Polynesia
184 K3 **Hikurangi** Northland, North Island, New Zealand
184 Q8 **Hikurangi** ▲ North Island, New Zealand
192 L11 **Hikurangi Trench** var. Hikurangi Trough. undersea feature SW Pacific Ocean
Hikurangi Trough see Hikurangi Trench
190 B15 **Hikutavake** NW Niue
121 Q12 **Hilāl, Ra's al** headland N Libya
61 A24 **Hilario Ascasubi** Buenos Aires, E Argentina
101 K17 **Hildburghausen** Thüringen, C Germany
101 E15 **Hilden** Nordrhein-Westfalen, W Germany
100 I13 **Hildesheim** Niedersachsen, N Germany
33 T9 **Hilger** Montana, NW USA
Hili see Hilli
Hilla see Al Ḩillah
45 O14 **Hillaby, Mount** ▲ N Barbados
95 K19 **Hillared** Älvsborg, S Sweden
195 R12 **Hillary Coast** physical region Antarctica
42 G2 **Hill Bank** Orange Walk, N Belize
33 O14 **Hill City** Idaho, NW USA
26 K3 **Hill City** Kansas, C USA
29 V5 **Hill City** Minnesota, N USA
28 J10 **Hill City** South Dakota, N USA
65 C24 **Hill Cove Settlement** West Falkland, Falkland Islands
98 H10 **Hillegom** Zuid-Holland, W Netherlands
95 J22 **Hillerød** Frederiksborg, E Denmark
36 M7 **Hillers, Mount** ▲ Utah, W USA
153 S13 **Hilli** var. Hili. Rajshahi, NW Bangladesh
29 R11 **Hills** Minnesota, N USA
30 L14 **Hillsboro** Illinois, N USA
27 N5 **Hillsboro** Kansas, C USA
27 X5 **Hillsboro** Missouri, C USA
19 N10 **Hillsboro** New Hampshire, NE USA
37 Q14 **Hillsboro** New Mexico, SW USA
29 R4 **Hillsboro** North Dakota, N USA
31 R14 **Hillsboro** Ohio, N USA
32 G11 **Hillsboro** Oregon, NW USA
25 T8 **Hillsboro** Texas, SW USA
30 K8 **Hillsboro** Wisconsin, N USA
23 Y14 **Hillsboro Canal** canal Florida, SE USA
45 Y15 **Hillsborough** Carriacou, N Grenada
97 G15 **Hillsborough** E Northern Ireland, UK
21 U9 **Hillsborough** North Carolina, SE USA
31 Q10 **Hillsdale** Michigan, N USA
183 O8 **Hillston** New South Wales, SE Australia
21 R7 **Hillsville** Virginia, NE USA
96 L2 **Hillswick** NE Scotland, UK
Hill Tippera see Tripura
38 H11 **Hilo** Hawai'i, USA, C Pacific Ocean
18 F9 **Hilton** New York, NE USA
14 C10 **Hilton Beach** Ontario, S Canada
21 R16 **Hilton Head Island** South Carolina, SE USA
21 R16 **Hilton Head Island** island South Carolina, SE USA
99 J15 **Hilvarenbeek** Noord-Brabant, S Netherlands
98 J11 **Hilversum** Noord-Holland, C Netherlands
Hilwān see Helwan
152 J7 **Himāchal Pradesh** ◆ state NW India
Himalaya/Himalaya Shan see Himalayas
152 M9 **Himalayas** var. Himalaya, Chin. Himalaya Shan. ▲▲ S Asia
171 P6 **Himamaylan** Negros, C Philippines
93 K15 **Himanka** Länsi-Soumi, W Finland
Himara see Himarë
113 L23 **Himarë** var. Himara. Vlorë, S Albania
138 M2 **Ḩimār, Wādī al** dry watercourse N Syria
154 D9 **Himatnagar** Gujarāt, W India
109 Y4 **Himberg** Niederösterreich, E Austria
164 I13 **Himeji** var. Himezi. Hyōgo, Honshū, SW Japan
164 E14 **Hime-jima** island SW Japan
Himezi see Himeji
164 L13 **Himi** Toyama, Honshū, SW Japan
109 S9 **Himmelberg** Kärnten, S Austria
138 I5 **Ḩimş** var. Homs; anc. Emesa. Ḩimş, C Syria
138 K6 **Ḩimş** off. Muḩāfaẓat Ḩims, var. Homs. ◆ governorate C Syria
138 I5 **Ḩimş, Buḩayrat** var. Buhayrat Qattīnah. ◎ W Syria
171 R7 **Hinatuan** Mindanao, S Philippines
117 N10 **Hînceşti** var. Hânceşti; prev. Kotovsk. C Moldova
44 M9 **Hinche** C Haiti
181 X5 **Hinchinbrook Island** island Queensland, NE Australia
39 S12 **Hinchinbrook Island** island Alaska, USA
97 M19 **Hinckley** C England, UK
29 V7 **Hinckley** Minnesota, N USA
36 K5 **Hinckley** Utah, W USA
18 J9 **Hinckley Reservoir** ▣ New York, NE USA
152 I12 **Hindaun** Rājasthān, N India
Hindenburg/Hindenburg in Oberschlesien see Zabrze
Hindiya see Al Hindīyah
21 O6 **Hindman** Kentucky, S USA
182 L10 **Hindmarsh, Lake** ◎ Victoria, SE Australia
185 G19 **Hinds** Canterbury, South Island, New Zealand
185 G19 **Hinds** ≈ South Island, New Zealand
95 H23 **Hindsholm** island C Denmark
149 S4 **Hindu Kush** Per. Hendū Kosh. ▲▲ Afghanistan/Pakistan
155 H19 **Hindupur** Andhra Pradesh, E India
9 O12 **Hines Creek** Alberta, W Canada
23 W6 **Hinesville** Georgia, SE USA
154 I12 **Hinganghāt** Mahārāshtra, C India
149 N15 **Hingol** ≈ SW Pakistan
154 H13 **Hingoli** Mahārāshtra, C India
137 R13 **Hınıs** Erzurum, E Turkey
92 O2 **Hinlopenstretet** strait N Svalbard
92 G10 **Hinnøya** Lapp. Iinnasuolu. island C Norway
108 H10 **Hinterrhein** ≈ SW Switzerland
9 O14 **Hinton** Alberta, SW Canada
26 M10 **Hinton** Oklahoma, C USA
21 R6 **Hinton** West Virginia, NE USA
Hios see Chíos
41 N8 **Hipolito** Coahuila de Zaragoza, NE Mexico
Hipponium see Vibo Valentia
164 B13 **Hirado** Nagasaki, Hirado-shima, SW Japan
164 B13 **Hirado-shima** island SW Japan
165 P16 **Hirakubo-saki** headland Ishigaki-jima, SW Japan
154 M11 **Hīrākud Reservoir** ▣ E India
Hir al Gharbi, Qasr al see Ḩayr al Gharbī, Qaşr al
165 Q16 **Hirara** Okinawa, Miyako-jima, SW Japan
164 G12 **Hirata** Shimane, Honshū, SW Japan
136 I13 **Hirfanlı Barajı** ▣ C Turkey
155 G18 **Hiriyūr** Karnātaka, W India
Hîrlău see Hârlău
148 K10 **Hirmand, Rūd-e** var. Daryā-ye Helmand. ≈ Afghanistan/Iran see also Helmand, Daryā-ye
Hirmand, Rūd-e see Helmand, Daryā-ye
Hirmil see Hermel
165 T5 **Hiroo** Hokkaidō, NE Japan
165 Q7 **Hirosaki** Aomori, Honshū, C Japan
164 G13 **Hiroshima** var. Hirosima. Hiroshima, Honshū, SW Japan
164 F13 **Hiroshima** off. Hiroshima-ken, var. Hirosima. ◆ prefecture Honshū, SW Japan
Hiroshima-ken see Hiroshima
Hirosima see Hiroshima
Hirschberg/Hirschberg im Riesengebirge/Hirschberg in Schlesien see Jelenia Góra
103 Q3 **Hirson** Aisne, N France
Hîrşova see Hârşova
95 G19 **Hirtshals** Nordjylland, N Denmark
152 H10 **Hisār** Haryāna, NW India
162 K7 **Hishig Öndör** var. Maanĭt. Bulgan, C Mongolia
186 E9 **Hisiu** Central, SW Papua New Guinea
147 P13 **Hisor** Rus. Gissar. W Tajikistan
Hispalis see Sevilla
Hispana/Hispania see Spain
44 M7 **Hispaniola** island Dominion Republic/Haiti
64 F11 **Hispaniola Basin** var. Hispaniola Trough. undersea feature SW Atlantic Ocean
Hispaniola Trough see Hispaniola Basin
Histonium see Vasto
139 R7 **Hīt** SW Iraq
165 P14 **Hita** Ōita, Kyūshū, SW Japan
165 P12 **Hitachi** var. Hitati. Ibaraki, Honshū, S Japan
165 P12 **Hitachi-Ōta** var. Hitatiôta. Ibaraki, Honshū, S Japan
Hitati see Hitachi
Hitatiôta see Hitachi-Ōta
97 O21 **Hitchin** E England, UK
191 Q7 **Hitiaa** Tahiti, W French Polynesia
164 D15 **Hitoyoshi** var. Hitoyosi. Kumamoto, Kyūshū, SW Japan
Hitoyosi see Hitoyoshi
94 F7 **Hitra** prev. Hitteren. island S Norway
Hitteren see Hitra
187 Q11 **Hiu** island Torres Islands, N Vanuatu
165 O11 **Hiuchiga-take** ▲ Honshū, C Japan
191 X7 **Hiva Oa** island Îles Marquises, N French Polynesia
20 M10 **Hiwassee Lake** ▣ North Carolina, SE USA
20 M10 **Hiwassee River** ≈ SE USA
95 H20 **Hjallerup** Nordjylland, N Denmark
95 M16 **Hjälmaren** Eng. Lake Hjalmar. ◎ C Sweden
Hjalmar, Lake see Hjälmaren
95 C14 **Hjellestad** Hordaland, S Norway
95 D16 **Hjelmeland** Rogaland, S Norway
94 G10 **Hjerkinn** Oppland, S Norway
95 L18 **Hjo** Västra Götaland, S Sweden
95 G19 **Hjørring** Nordjylland, N Denmark
167 O1 **Hkakabo Razi** ▲ Burma (Myanmar)/China
167 N1 **Hkring Bum** ▲ N Burma (Myanmar)
83 L21 **Hlathikulu** var. Hlatikulu. S Swaziland
Hlatikulu see Hlathikulu
Hliboka see Hlyboka
111 F17 **Hlinsko** var. Hlinsko v Čechách. Pardubický Kraj, C Czech Republic
Hlinsko v Čechách see Hlinsko
117 S6 **Hlobyne** Rus. Globino. Poltavs'ka Oblast', NE Ukraine
111 H20 **Hlohovec** Ger. Freistadtl, Hung. Galgóc; prev. Frakštát. Trnavský Kraj, W Slovakia
83 J23 **Hlotse** var. Leribe. NW Lesotho
111 I17 **Hlučín** Ger. Hultschin, Pol. Hulczyn. Moravskoslezský Kraj, E Czech Republic
117 S2 **Hlukhiv** Rus. Glukhov. Sums'ka Oblast', NE Ukraine
119 K21 **Hlushkavichy** Rus. Glushkevichi. Homyel'skaya Voblasts', SE Belarus
119 L18 **Hlusk** Rus. Glusk, Glussk. Mahilyowskaya Voblasts', E Belarus
116 K8 **Hlyboka** Ger. Hliboka, Rus. Glybokaya. Chernivets'ka Oblast', W Ukraine
118 K13 **Hlybokaye** Rus. Glubokoye. Vitsyebskaya Voblasts', N Belarus
77 Q16 **Ho** SE Ghana
167 S6 **Hoa Binh** Hoa Binh, N Vietnam
83 E20 **Hoachanas** Hardap, C Namibia
Hoai Nhơn see Bông Sơn
167 T8 **Hoa Lac** Quang Binh, C Vietnam
167 S5 **Hoang Liên Sơn** ▲▲ N Vietnam
83 B17 **Hoanib** ≈ NW Namibia
33 S15 **Hoback Peak** ▲ Wyoming, C USA
183 P17 **Hobart** prev. Hobarton, Hobart Town. state capital Tasmania, SE Australia
26 L11 **Hobart** Oklahoma, C USA
183 P17 **Hobart** ✈ Tasmania, SE Australia
Hobarton/Hobart Town see Hobart
37 W14 **Hobbs** New Mexico, SW USA
194 L12 **Hobbs Coast** physical region Antarctica
23 Z14 **Hobe Sound** Florida, SE USA
Hobicaurikány see Uricani
54 E12 **Hobo** Huila, S Colombia
99 G16 **Hoboken** Antwerpen, N Belgium
158 K3 **Hoboksar** var. Hoboksar Mongol Zizhixian. Xinjiang Uygur Zizhiqu, NW China
Hoboksar Mongol Zizhixian see Hoboksar
95 G21 **Hobro** Nordjylland, N Denmark
21 X10 **Hobucken** North Carolina, SE USA
95 O20 **Hoburgen** headland SE Sweden
81 P15 **Hobyo** It. Obbia. Mudug, E Somalia
109 R8 **Hochalmspitze** ▲ SW Austria
109 Q4 **Hochburg** Oberösterreich, N Austria
108 F8 **Hochdorf** Luzern, N Switzerland
109 N8 **Hochfeiler** It. Gran Pilastro. ▲ Austria/Italy
167 T14 **Hô Chi Minh** var. Ho Chi Minh City; prev. Saigon. S Vietnam
Ho Chi Minh City see Hô Chi Minh
108 I7 **Höchst** Vorarlberg, NW Austria
Höchstadt see Höchstadt an der Aisch
101 K19 **Höchstadt an der Aisch** var. Höchstadt. Bayern, C Germany
108 L9 **Hochwilde** It. L'Altissima. ▲ Austria/Italy
109 S7 **Hochwildstelle** ▲ C Austria
31 T14 **Hocking River** ≈ Ohio, N USA
Hoctúm see Hoctún
41 X12 **Hoctún** var. Hoctúm. Yucatán, E Mexico
Hodeida see Al Ḩudaydah
20 K6 **Hodgenville** Kentucky, S USA
9 T17 **Hodgeville** Saskatchewan, S Canada
76 L9 **Hodh ech Chargui** ◆ region E Mauritania
Hodh el Garbi see Hodh el Gharbi
76 J10 **Hodh el Gharbi** var. Hodh el Garbi. ◆ region S Mauritania
111 L25 **Hódmezővásárhely** Csongrád, SE Hungary
74 J6 **Hodna, Chott El** var. Chott el-Hodna, Ar. Shatt al-Hodna. salt lake N Algeria
Hodna, Chott el-/Hodna, Shatt al- see Hodna, Chott El
111 G19 **Hodonín** Ger. Göding. Jihomoravský Kraj, SE Czech Republic
Hödrögö see Nömrög
Hodság/Hodschag see Odžaci
39 R7 **Hodzana River** ≈ Alaska, USA
Hoei see Huy
99 H19 **Hoeilaart** Vlaams Brabant, C Belgium
Hoë Karoo see Great Karoo
98 F12 **Hoek van Holland** Eng. Hook of Holland. Zuid-Holland, W Netherlands
98 L11 **Hoenderloo** Gelderland, E Netherlands
99 L18 **Hoensbroek** Limburg, SE Netherlands
163 Y11 **Hoeryŏng** NE North Korea
99 K18 **Hoeselt** Limburg, NE Belgium
98 K11 **Hoevelaken** Gelderland, C Netherlands
Hoey see Huy
101 M18 **Hof** Bayern, SE Germany
Höfdhakaupstadhur see Skagaströnd
Hofei see Hefei
101 G18 **Hofheim am Taunus** Hessen, W Germany
Hofmarkt see Odorheiu Secuiesc
92 L3 **Höfn** Austurland, SE Iceland
94 N13 **Hofors** Gävleborg, C Sweden
92 J6 **Hofsjökull** glacier C Iceland
92 J1 **Hofsós** Nordhurland Vestra, N Iceland
164 E13 **Hōfu** Yamaguchi, Honshū, SW Japan
Hofuf see Al Hufūf
95 J22 **Höganäs** Skåne, S Sweden
183 P14 **Hogan Group** island group Tasmania, SE Australia
23 R4 **Hogansville** Georgia, SE USA
39 P8 **Hogatza River** ≈ Alaska, USA
28 I14 **Hogback Mountain** ▲ Nebraska, C USA
95 G14 **Høgevarde** ▲ S Norway
Högfors see Karkkila
31 P5 **Hog Island** island Michigan, N USA
21 Y6 **Hog Island** island Virginia, NE USA
Hogoley Islands see Chuuk Islands
95 N20 **Högsby** Kalmar, S Sweden
36 K1 **Hogup Mountains** ▲▲ Utah, W USA
101 E17 **Hohe Acht** ▲ W Germany
Hohenelbe see Vrchlabí
108 I7 **Hohenems** Vorarlberg, W Austria
Hohenmauth see Vysoké Mýto
Hohensalza see Inowrocław
Hohenstadt see Zábřeh
Hohenstein in Ostpreussen see Olsztynek
20 I9 **Hohenwald** Tennessee, S USA
101 L17 **Hohenwarte-stausee** ▣ C Germany
Hohes Venn see Hautes Fagnes
109 Q8 **Hohe Tauern** ▲▲ W Austria
163 O13 **Hohhot** var. Huhehot, Huhohaote, Mong. Kukukhoto; prev. Kweisui, Kwesui. Nei Mongol Zizhiqu, N China
162 F7 **Hohmorit** var. Sayn-Ust. Govĭ-Altay, W Mongolia
103 U6 **Hohneck** ▲ NE France
77 Q16 **Hohoe** E Ghana
164 E12 **Hōhoku** Yamaguchi, Honshū, SW Japan
159 O11 **Hoh Sai Hu** ◎ C China
159 N11 **Hoh Xil Hu** ◎ C China
158 L11 **Hoh Xil Shan** ▲▲ W China
167 U10 **Hôi An** prev. Faifo. Quang Nam-Đa Nâng, C Vietnam
Hoï-Hao/Hoihow see Haikou
159 S11 **Hoika** prev. Heka. Qinghai, W China
81 F17 **Hoima** W Uganda
26 L5 **Hoisington** Kansas, C USA
146 D12 **Hojagala** Rus. Khodzhakala. Balkan Welaýaty, W Turkmenistan
146 M13 **Hojambaz** Rus. Khodzhambas. Lebap Welaýaty, E Turkmenistan
95 H23 **Højby** Fyn, C Denmark
95 F24 **Højer** Sønderjylland, SW Denmark
164 E14 **Hōjō** var. Hôzyô. Ehime, Shikoku, SW Japan
184 J3 **Hokianga Harbour** inlet SE Tasman Sea
185 F17 **Hokitika** West Coast, South Island, New Zealand
165 U4 **Hokkai-dō** ◆ territory Hokkaidō, NE Japan
165 T3 **Hokkaidō** prev. Ezo, Yeso, Yezo. island NE Japan
95 G15 **Hokksund** Buskerud, S Norway
143 S4 **Hokmābād** KhorāsānRazavī, N Iran
Hokō see P'ohang
Hoko-guntō/Hoko-shotō see P'enghu Liehtao
Hoktemberyan see Armavir
94 F13 **Hol** Buskerud, S Norway
117 R11 **Hola Prystan'** Rus. Golaya Pristan. Khersons'ka Oblast', S Ukraine
95 I23 **Holbæk** Vestsjælland, E Denmark
Holboo see Santmargats
183 P10 **Holbrook** New South Wales, SE Australia
37 N11 **Holbrook** Arizona, SW USA
27 S5 **Holden** Missouri, C USA
36 K5 **Holden** Utah, W USA
27 O11 **Holdenville** Oklahoma, C USA
29 O16 **Holdrege** Nebraska, C USA
35 X3 **Hole in the Mountain Peak** ▲ Nevada, W USA
155 G20 **Hole Narsipur** Karnātaka, W India
111 H18 **Holešov** Ger. Holleschau. Zlínský Kraj, E Czech Republic
45 N14 **Holetown** prev. Jamestown. W Barbados
31 Q12 **Holgate** Ohio, N USA
44 I7 **Holguín** Holguín, SE Cuba
23 V12 **Holiday** Florida, SE USA
39 O12 **Holitna River** ≈ Alaska, USA
94 J13 **Höljes** Värmland, C Sweden
109 X3 **Hollabrunn** Niederösterreich, NE Austria
36 L3 **Holladay** Utah, W USA
9 X16 **Holland** Manitoba, S Canada
31 O9 **Holland** Michigan, N USA
25 T9 **Holland** Texas, SW USA
Holland see Netherlands
22 K4 **Hollandale** Mississippi, S USA
Hollandia see Jayapura
Hollandsch Diep see Hollands Diep
99 H14 **Hollands Diep** var. Hollandsch Diep. channel SW Netherlands
Holleschau see Holešov
25 R5 **Holliday** Texas, SW USA
18 E15 **Hollidaysburg** Pennsylvania, NE USA
21 S6 **Hollins** Virginia, NE USA
26 J12 **Hollis** Oklahoma, C USA
35 O10 **Hollister** California, W USA
27 T8 **Hollister** Missouri, C USA
93 M19 **Hollola** Etelä-Suomi, S Finland
98 K4 **Hollum** Friesland, N Netherlands
95 J23 **Höllviksnäs** Skåne, S Sweden
37 W6 **Holly** Colorado, C USA
31 R9 **Holly** Michigan, N USA
21 S14 **Holly Hill** South Carolina, SE USA
21 W11 **Holly Ridge** North Carolina, SE USA
22 L1 **Holly Springs** Mississippi, S USA
23 Z15 **Hollywood** Florida, SE USA
8 J6 **Holman** Victoria Island, Northwest Territories, N Canada
92 I2 **Hólmavík** Vestfirdhir, NW Iceland
30 J7 **Holmen** Wisconsin, N USA
23 R8 **Holmes Creek** ≈ Alabama/Florida, SE USA
95 H16 **Holmestrand** Vestfold, S Norway
93 J16 **Holmön** island N Sweden
95 E22 **Holmsland Klit** beach W Denmark
93 J16 **Holmsund** Västerbotten, N Sweden
95 Q18 **Holmudden** headland SE Sweden
138 F10 **Holon** var Kholon. Tel Aviv, C Israel
163 P7 **Hölönbuyr** var. Bayan. Dornod, E Mongolia
163 P7 **Hölönbuyr** var. Bayan. Dornod, E Mongolia
117 P8 **Holovanivs'k** Rus. Golovanevsk. Kirovohrads'ka Oblast', C Ukraine
95 F21 **Holstebro** Ringkøbing, W Denmark
95 F23 **Holsted** Ribe, W Denmark
29 T13 **Holstein** Iowa, C USA
Holsteinborg/Holsteinsborg/Holstenborg/Holstensborg see Sisimiut
21 O8 **Holston River** ≈ Tennessee, S USA
31 Q9 **Holt** Michigan, N USA
98 N10 **Holten** Overijssel, E Netherlands
27 P3 **Holton** Kansas, C USA
27 U5 **Holts Summit** Missouri, C USA
35 X17 **Holtville** California, W USA
98 L5 **Holwerd** Fris. Holwert. Friesland, N Netherlands
Holwert see Holwerd
39 O11 **Holy Cross** Alaska, USA
37 R4 **Holy Cross, Mount Of The** ▲ Colorado, C USA
97 I18 **Holyhead** Wel. Caer Gybi. NW Wales, UK
97 H18 **Holy Island** island NW Wales, UK
96 L12 **Holy Island** island NE England, UK
37 W3 **Holyoke** Colorado, C USA
18 M11 **Holyoke** Massachusetts, NE USA
101 I14 **Holzminden** Niedersachsen, C Germany
81 G19 **Homa Bay** Nyanza, W Kenya
Homāyūnshahr see Khomeynīshahr
77 P11 **Hombori** Mopti, S Mali
101 E20 **Homburg** Saarland, SW Germany
9 R5 **Home Bay** bay Baffin Bay, Nunavut, NE Canada
Homenau see Humenné
39 Q13 **Homer** Alaska, USA
22 H4 **Homer** Louisiana, S USA
18 H10 **Homer** New York, NE USA
23 V7 **Homerville** Georgia, SE USA
23 Y16 **Homestead** Florida, SE USA
27 O9 **Hominy** Oklahoma, C USA
94 H8 **Hommelvik** Sør-Trøndelag, S Norway
95 C16 **Hommersåk** Rogaland, S Norway
155 H15 **Homnābād** Karnātaka, C India
22 J7 **Homochitto River** ≈ Mississippi, S USA
83 N20 **Homoine** Inhambane, SE Mozambique
112 O12 **Homoljske Planine** ▲▲ E Serbia
Homonna see Humenné
Homs see Al Khums, Libya
Homs see Ḩimş
119 P19 **Homyel'** Rus. Gomel'. Homyel'skaya Voblasts', SE Belarus
118 L12 **Homyel'** Vitsyebskaya Voblasts', N Belarus
119 L19 **Homyel'skaya Voblasts'** prev. Rus. Gomel'skaya Oblast'. ◆ province SE Belarus
Honan see Luoyang, China
Honan see Henan, China
164 U4 **Honbetsu** Hokkaidō, NE Japan
Honctő see Gurahonț
54 E9 **Honda** Tolima, C Colombia
83 D24 **Hondeklip** Afr. Hondeklipbaai. Northern Cape, W South Africa
Hondeklipbaai see Hondeklip
9 Q13 **Hondo** Alberta, W Canada
164 C15 **Hondo** Kumamoto, Shimo-jima, SW Japan
25 Q12 **Hondo** Texas, SW USA
42 G1 **Hondo** ≈ Central America
Hondo see Honshū
42 G6 **Honduras** off. Republic of Honduras. ◆ republic Central America
Honduras, Golfo de see Honduras, Gulf of
42 H4 **Honduras, Gulf of** Sp. Golfo de Honduras. gulf W Caribbean Sea
Honduras, Republic of see Honduras
9 V12 **Hone** Manitoba, C Canada
21 P12 **Honea Path** South Carolina, SE USA
95 H14 **Hønefoss** Buskerud, S Norway
31 S12 **Honey Creek** ≈ Ohio, N USA
25 V5 **Honey Grove** Texas, SW USA
35 Q4 **Honey Lake** ◎ California, W USA
102 L4 **Honfleur** Calvados, N France
Hon Gai see Hông Gai
161 O8 **Hong'an** prev. Huang'an. Hubei, C China
Hongay see Hông Gai
167 T6 **Hông Gai** var. Hon Gai, Hongay. Quang Ninh, N Vietnam
161 O15 **Honghai Wan** bay N South China Sea
Hông Hà, Sông see Red River

◆ Country
● Country Capital
◇ Dependent Territory
○ Dependent Territory Capital
◆ Administrative Regions
✈ International Airport
▲ Mountain
▲▲ Mountain Range
Volcano
≈ River
◎ Lake
▣ Reservoir

HONG HE – HUIXTLA

161 O7 **Hong He** ≈ C China
161 N9 **Hong Hu** ◎ C China
160 L11 **Hongjiang** Hunan, S China
Hongjiang *see* Wangcang
161 O15 **Hong Kong** *Chin.* Xianggang. Hong Kong, S China
160 L4 **Hongliu He** ≈ C China
159 P8 **Hongliuwan** *var.* Aksay, Aksay Kazakzu Zizhixian. Gansu, N China
159 P7 **Hongliuyuan** Gansu, N China
Hongor *see* Delgereh
161 S8 **Hongqiao** ✈ (Shanghai) Shanghai Shi, E China
160 K14 **Hongshui He** ≈ S China
160 M5 **Hongtong** Shanxi, C China
164 J15 **Hongū** Wakayama, Honshū, SW Japan
Honguedo, Détroit d' *see* Honguedo Passage
15 Y5 **Honguedo Passage** *var.* Honguedo Strait, *Fr.* Détroit d'Honguedo. *strait* Québec, E Canada
Honguedo Strait *see* Honguedo Passage
Hongwan *see* Hongwansi
159 S8 **Hongwansi** *var.* Sunan, Sunan Yugurzu Zizhixian; *prev.* Hongwan. Gansu, N China
163 X13 **Hongwŏn** E North Korea
160 H7 **Hongyuan** *var.* Qiongxi; *prev.* Hurama. Sichuan, C China
161 Q7 **Hongze Hu** *var.* Hung-tse Hu. ◎ E China
186 L9 **Honiara** ● (Solomon Islands) Guadalcanal, C Solomon Islands
165 P8 **Honjō** *var.* Honzyô. Akita, Honshū, C Japan
93 K18 **Honkajoki** Länsi-Soumi, SW Finland
92 K7 **Honningsvåg** Finnmark, N Norway
95 I19 **Hönö** Västra Götaland, S Sweden
38 G11 **Honoka'a** *var.* Honokaa. Hawai'i, USA, C Pacific Ocean
38 G11 **Honoka'a** Hawaii, USA
Honokaa *see* Honoka'a
38 D9 **Honolulu** *state capital* O'ahu, Hawai'i, USA
38 H11 **Honomú** *var.* Honomu. Hawai'i, USA, C Pacific Ocean
105 P10 **Honrubia** Castilla-La Mancha, C Spain
164 M12 **Honshū** *var.* Hondo, Honsyû. *island* SW Japan
Honsyû *see* Honshū
Honte *see* Westerschelde
Honzyô *see* Honjō
8 K8 **Hood** ≈ Nunavut, NW Canada
Hood Island *see* Española, Isla
32 H11 **Hood, Mount** ▲ Oregon, NW USA
32 H11 **Hood River** Oregon, NW USA
98 H10 **Hoofddorp** Noord-Holland, W Netherlands
99 G15 **Hoogerheide** Noord-Brabant, S Netherlands
98 N8 **Hoogeveen** Drenthe, NE Netherlands
98 O6 **Hoogezand-Sappemeer** Groningen, NE Netherlands
98 J8 **Hoogkarspel** Noord-Holland, NW Netherlands
98 N5 **Hoogkerk** Groningen, NE Netherlands
98 G13 **Hoogvliet** Zuid-Holland, SW Netherlands
26 I8 **Hooker** Oklahoma, C USA
97 E21 **Hook Head** *Ir.* Rinn Duáin. *headland* SE Ireland
Hook of Holland *see* Hoek van Holland
Hoolt *see* Tögrög
39 W13 **Hoonah** Chichagof Island, Alaska, USA
38 L11 **Hooper Bay** Alaska, USA
31 N13 **Hoopeston** Illinois, N USA
95 K22 **Höör** Skåne, S Sweden
98 I9 **Hoorn** Noord-Holland, NW Netherlands
18 L10 **Hoosic River** ≈ New York, NE USA
Hoosier State *see* Indiana
35 Y11 **Hoover Dam** *dam* Arizona/Nevada, W USA
Höövör *see* Baruunbayan-Ulaan
137 Q11 **Hopa** Artvin, NE Turkey
18 J14 **Hopatcong** New Jersey, NE USA
10 M17 **Hope** British Columbia, SW Canada
39 R12 **Hope** Alaska, USA
27 T14 **Hope** Arkansas, C USA
31 P14 **Hope** Indiana, N USA
29 Q5 **Hope** North Dakota, N USA
13 Q7 **Hopedale** Newfoundland and Labrador, NE Canada
Hopeh/Hopei *see* Hebei
180 K13 **Hope, Lake** *salt lake* Western Australia
41 X13 **Hopelchén** Campeche, SE Mexico
21 U11 **Hope Mills** North Carolina, SE USA
183 O7 **Hope, Mount** New South Wales, SE Australia
92 P4 **Hopen** *island* SE Svalbard
197 Q4 **Hope, Point** *headland* Alaska, USA
12 M3 **Hopes Advance, Cap** *cape* Québec, NE Canada
182 L10 **Hopetoun** Victoria, SE Australia
83 H23 **Hopetown** Northern Cape, W South Africa
21 W6 **Hopewell** Virginia, NE USA
109 O7 **Hopfgarten im Brixental** Tirol, W Austria
181 N8 **Hopkins Lake** *salt lake* Western Australia
182 M12 **Hopkins River** ≈ Victoria, SE Australia
20 I7 **Hopkinsville** Kentucky, S USA
34 M6 **Hopland** California, W USA
95 G24 **Hoptrup** Sønderjylland, SW Denmark
Hoqin Zuoyi Zhongji *see* Baokang
32 F9 **Hoquiam** Washington, NW USA
29 R6 **Horace** North Dakota, N USA
137 R12 **Horasan** Erzurum, NE Turkey
101 G22 **Horb am Neckar** Baden-Württemberg, S Germany
95 K23 **Hörby** Skåne, S Sweden
43 P16 **Horconcitos** Chiriquí, W Panama
95 C14 **Hordaland** ◈ *county* S Norway
116 H13 **Horezu** Vâlcea, SW Romania
108 G7 **Horgen** Zürich, N Switzerland
Horgo *see* Tariat
Hörin *see* Fenglin
163 O13 **Horinger** Nei Mongol Zizhiqu, N China
Horiult *see* Bogd
9 U17 **Horizon** Saskatchewan, S Canada
192 K9 **Horizon Bank** *undersea feature* S Pacific Ocean
192 L10 **Horizon Deep** *undersea feature* W Pacific Ocean
95 L14 **Hörken** Örebro, S Sweden
119 O15 **Horki** *Rus.* Gorki. Mahilyowskaya Voblasts', E Belarus
195 O10 **Horlick Mountains** ▲▲ Antarctica
117 X7 **Horlivka** *Rom.* Adâncata, *Rus.* Gorlovka. Donets'ka Oblast', E Ukraine
143 V11 **Ḩormak** Sīstān va Balūchestān, SE Iran
143 R13 **Hormozgān** *off.* Ostān-e Hormozgān. ◈ *province* S Iran
Hormozgān, Ostān-e *see* Hormozgān
Hormoz, Tangeh-ye *see* Hormuz, Strait of
141 W6 **Hormuz, Strait of** *var.* Strait of Ormuz, *Per.* Tangeh-ye Hormoz. *strait* Iran/Oman
109 W2 **Horn** Niederösterreich, NE Austria
95 M18 **Horn** Östergötland, S Sweden
8 J9 **Horn** ≈ Northwest Territories, NW Canada
Hornád *see* Hernád
8 I6 **Hornaday** ≈ Northwest Territories, NW Canada
92 H13 **Hornavan** ◎ N Sweden
65 C24 **Hornby Mountains** *hill range* West Falkland, Falkland Islands
Horn, Cape *see* Hornos, Cabo de
97 O18 **Horncastle** E England, UK
95 N14 **Horndal** Dalarna, C Sweden
93 I16 **Hörnefors** Västerbotten, N Sweden
18 F11 **Hornell** New York, NE USA
Horné Nové Mesto *see* Kysucké Nové Mesto
12 F12 **Hornepayne** Ontario, S Canada
94 D10 **Hornindalsvatnet** ◎ S Norway
101 G22 **Hornisgrinde** ▲ SW Germany
22 M9 **Horn Island** *island* Mississippi, S USA
Hornja Łužica *see* Oberlausitz
63 J26 **Hornos, Cabo de** *Eng.* Cape Horn. *cape* S Chile
117 S10 **Hornostayivka** Khersons'ka Oblast', S Ukraine
183 T9 **Hornsby** New South Wales, SE Australia
97 O16 **Hornsea** E England, UK
94 O11 **Hornslandet** *peninsula* C Sweden
95 H22 **Hornslet** Århus, C Denmark
92 O4 **Hornsundtind** ▲ S Svalbard
Horochów *see* Horokhiv
116 J7 **Horodenka** *Rus.* Gorodenka. Ivano-Frankivs'ka Oblast', W Ukraine
117 Q2 **Horodnya** *Rus.* Gorodnya. Chernihivs'ka Oblast', NE Ukraine
116 K6 **Horodok** Khmel'nyts'ka Oblast', W Ukraine
116 H5 **Horodok** *Pol.* Gródek Jagielloński, *Rus.* Gorodok, Gorodok Yagellonski. L'vivs'ka Oblast', NW Ukraine
117 Q6 **Horodyshche** *Rus.* Gorodishche. Cherkas'ka Oblast', C Ukraine
165 T3 **Horokanai** Hokkaidō, NE Japan
116 J4 **Horokhiv** *Pol.* Horochów, *Rus.* Gorokhov. Volyns'ka Oblast', NW Ukraine
165 T4 **Horoshiri-dake** *var.* Horosiri Dake. ▲ Hokkaidō, N Japan
Horosiri Dake *see* Horoshiri-dake
111 C17 **Hořovice** *Ger.* Horowitz. Střední Čechy, W Czech Republic
Horowitz *see* Hořovice
Horqin Zuoyi Houqi *see* Ganjig
Horqin Zuoyi Zhongqi *see* Bayan Huxu
62 O5 **Horqueta** Concepción, C Paraguay
55 O12 **Horqueta Minas** Amazonas, S Venezuela
95 J20 **Horred** Älvsborg, S Sweden
151 J19 **Horsburgh Atoll** *atoll* N Maldives
20 K7 **Horse Cave** Kentucky, S USA
37 V6 **Horse Creek** ≈ Colorado, C USA
27 S6 **Horse Creek** ≈ Missouri, C USA
18 G11 **Horseheads** New York, NE USA
37 P13 **Horse Mount** ▲ New Mexico, SW USA
95 G22 **Horsens** Vejle, C Denmark
65 F25 **Horse Pasture Point** *headland* W Saint Helena
33 N13 **Horseshoe Bend** Idaho, NW USA
36 L13 **Horseshoe Reservoir** ⊠ Arizona, SW USA
64 M9 **Horseshoe Seamounts** *undersea feature* E Atlantic Ocean
182 L11 **Horsham** Victoria, SE Australia
97 O23 **Horsham** SE England, UK
99 M15 **Horst** Limburg, SE Netherlands
64 N2 **Horta** Faial, Azores, Portugal, NE Atlantic Ocean
95 H16 **Horten** Vestfold, S Norway
111 M23 **Hortobágy-Berettyó** ≈ E Hungary
27 Q3 **Horton** Kansas, C USA
8 I7 **Horton** ≈ Northwest Territories, NW Canada
95 I23 **Hørve** Vestsjælland, E Denmark
95 L22 **Hörvik** Blekinge, S Sweden
138 E11 **Ḩorvot Ḩaluza** *var* Khorvot Khalutsa. *ruins* Southern, S Israel
14 E7 **Horwood Lake** ◎ Ontario, S Canada
116 K4 **Horyn'** *Rus.* Goryn. ≈ NW Ukraine
81 I14 **Hosa'ina** *var.* Hosseina, *It.* Hosanna. Southern, S Ethiopia
Hosanna *see* Hosa'ina
101 H18 **Hösbach** Bayern, C Germany
Hose Mountains *see* Hose, Pegunungan
169 T9 **Hose, Pegunungan** *var.* Hose Mountains. ▲▲ East Malaysia
148 L15 **Hoshāb** Baluchistān, SW Pakistan
154 H10 **Hoshangābād** Madhya Pradesh, C India
116 L4 **Hoshcha** Rivnens'ka Oblast', NW Ukraine
152 I7 **Hoshiārpur** Punjab, NW India
Hōshööt *see* Öldziyt
99 M23 **Hosingen** Diekirch, NE Luxembourg
186 G7 **Hoskins** New Britain, E Papua New Guinea
155 G17 **Hospet** Karnātaka, C India
104 K4 **Hospital de Orbigo** Castilla-León, N Spain
Hospitalet *see* L'Hospitalet de Llobregat
92 N13 **Hossa** Oulu, E Finland
Hosseina *see* Hosa'ina
Hosszúmezjő *see* Câmpulung Moldovenesc
63 I25 **Hoste, Isla** *island* S Chile
117 O4 **Hostomel'** *Rus.* Gostomel'. Kyyivs'ka Oblast', N Ukraine
155 H20 **Hosūr** Tamil Nādu, SE India
167 N8 **Hot** Chiang Mai, NW Thailand
158 G10 **Hotan** *var.* Khotan, *Chin.* Ho-t'ien. Xinjiang Uygur Zizhiqu, NW China
158 H9 **Hotan He** ≈ NW China
83 G22 **Hotazel** Northern Cape, N South Africa
37 Q5 **Hotchkiss** Colorado, C USA
35 V7 **Hot Creek Range** ▲▲ Nevada, W USA
Hote *see* Hoti
171 T13 **Hoti** *var.* Hote. Pulau Seram, E Indonesia
Ho-t'ien *see* Hotan
Hotin *see* Khotyn
93 H15 **Hoting** Jämtland, C Sweden
162 L14 **Hotong Qagan Nur** ◎ N China
162 J8 **Hotont** Arhangay, C Mongolia
27 T12 **Hot Springs** Arkansas, C USA
28 J11 **Hot Springs** South Dakota, N USA
21 S5 **Hot Springs** Virginia, NE USA
35 Q4 **Hot Springs Peak** ▲ California, W USA
27 T12 **Hot Springs Village** Arkansas, C USA
Hotspur Bank *see* Hotspur Seamount
65 J16 **Hotspur Seamount** *var.* Hotspur Bank. *undersea feature* C Atlantic Ocean
8 J8 **Hottah Lake** ◎ Northwest Territories, NW Canada
44 K9 **Hotte, Massif de la** ▲▲ SW Haiti
99 K21 **Hotton** Luxembourg, SE Belgium
Hötzing *see* Haţeg
187 P17 **Houaïlou** Province Nord, C New Caledonia
74 K5 **Houari Boumediène** ✈ (Alger) N Algeria
167 P6 **Houayxay** *var.* Ban Houayxay. Bokèo, N Laos
103 N5 **Houdan** Yvelines, N France
99 F20 **Houdeng-Goegnies** *var.* Houdeng-Gœgnies. Hainaut, S Belgium
102 K14 **Houeillès** Lot-et-Garonne, SW France
99 L22 **Houffalize** Luxembourg, SE Belgium
30 M3 **Houghton** Michigan, N USA
31 Q7 **Houghton Lake** Michigan, N USA
31 Q7 **Houghton Lake** ◎ Michigan, N USA
19 T3 **Houlton** Maine, NE USA
160 M5 **Houma** Shanxi, C China
193 U15 **Houma** 'Eua, C Tonga
193 Y16 **Houma** Tongatapu, S Tonga
22 J10 **Houma** Louisiana, S USA
196 V16 **Houma Taloa** *headland* Tongatapu, S Tonga
77 O13 **Houndé** SW Burkina
102 J12 **Hourtin-Carcans, Lac d'** ◎ SW France
36 J5 **House Range** ▲▲ Utah, W USA
10 K13 **Houston** British Columbia, SW Canada
39 R11 **Houston** Alaska, USA
29 X10 **Houston** Minnesota, N USA
22 M3 **Houston** Mississippi, S USA
27 V7 **Houston** Missouri, C USA
25 W11 **Houston** Texas, SW USA
25 W11 **Houston** ✈ Texas, SW USA
98 J12 **Houten** Utrecht, C Netherlands
99 K17 **Houthalen** Limburg, NE Belgium
99 I22 **Houyet** Namur, SE Belgium
95 H22 **Hov** Århus, C Denmark
95 L17 **Hova** Västra Götaland, S Sweden
162 E6 **Hovd** *var.* Khovd, Kobdo; *prev.* Jirgalanta. Hovd, W Mongolia
162 E6 **Hovd** *var.* Dund-Us. Hovd, W Mongolia
162 E7 **Hovd** ◈ *province* W Mongolia
Hovd *see* Bogd
162 C5 **Hovd Gol** ≈ NW Mongolia
97 O23 **Hove** SE England, UK
29 N8 **Hoven** South Dakota, N USA
116 I8 **Hoverla, Hora** *Rus.* Gora Goverla. ▲ W Ukraine
Höviyn Am *see* Gurvanbulag
95 M21 **Hovmantorp** Kronoberg, S Sweden
163 N11 **Hövsgöl** Dornogovĭ, SE Mongolia
162 I5 **Hövsgöl** ◈ *province* N Mongolia
Hövsgöl, Lake *see* Hövsgöl Nuur
162 J5 **Hövsgöl Nuur** *var.* Lake Hovsgol. ◎ N Mongolia
78 L9 **Howa, Ouadi** *var.* Wādi Howar. ≈ Chad/Sudan *see also* Howar, Wādi
Howa, Ouadi *see* Howar, Wādi
27 P7 **Howard** Kansas, C USA
29 Q10 **Howard** South Dakota, N USA
25 N10 **Howard Draw** *valley* Texas, SW USA
29 U8 **Howard Lake** Minnesota, N USA
80 B8 **Howar, Wādi** *var.* Ouadi Howa. ≈ Chad/Sudan *see also* Howa, Ouadi
Howar, Wādi *see* Howa, Ouadi
25 U5 **Howe** Texas, SW USA
183 R12 **Howe, Cape** *cape* New South Wales/Victoria, SE Australia
31 R9 **Howell** Michigan, N USA
28 L9 **Howes** South Dakota, N USA
83 K23 **Howick** KwaZulu/Natal, E South Africa
Howrah *see* Hāora
27 W9 **Hoxie** Arkansas, C USA
26 J3 **Hoxie** Kansas, C USA
101 I14 **Höxter** Nordrhein-Westfalen, W Germany
158 K6 **Hoxud** Xinjiang Uygur Zizhiqu, NW China
96 J5 **Hoy** *island* N Scotland, UK
43 S17 **Hoya, Cerro** ▲ S Panama
94 D12 **Høyanger** Sogn Og Fjordane, S Norway
101 P15 **Hoyerswerda** *Lus.* Wojerecy. Sachsen, E Germany
164 R14 **Hōyo-kaikyō** *var.* Hayasui-seto. *strait* SW Japan
104 J8 **Hoyos** Extremadura, W Spain
29 W4 **Hoyt Lakes** Minnesota, N USA
87 V2 **Hoyvík** Streymoy, N Faeroe Islands
137 O14 **Hozat** Tunceli, E Turkey
Hôzyô *see* Hōjō
111 F16 **Hradec Králové** *Ger.* Königgrätz. Královéhradecký Kraj, N Czech Republic
Hradecký Kraj *see* Královéhradecký Kraj
111 B16 **Hradiště** *Ger.* Burgstadlberg. ▲ NW Czech Republic
117 R6 **Hradyz'k** *Rus.* Gradizhsk. Poltavs'ka Oblast', NE Ukraine
119 M16 **Hradzyanka** *Rus.* Grodzyanka. Mahilyowskaya Voblasts', E Belarus
119 F16 **Hrandzichy** *Rus.* Grandichi. Hrodzyenskaya Voblasts', W Belarus
111 H18 **Hranice** *Ger.* Mährisch-Weisskirchen. Olomoucký Kraj, E Czech Republic
112 I13 **Hrasnica** Federacija Bosna I Hercegovina, SE Bosnia and Herzegovina
109 V11 **Hrastnik** C Slovenia
137 U12 **Hrazdan** *Rus.* Razdan. C Armenia
137 T12 **Hrazdan** *var.* Zanga, *Rus.* Razdan. ≈ C Armenia
117 R5 **Hrebinka** *Rus.* Grebenka. Poltavs'ka Oblast', NE Ukraine
119 K17 **Hresk** *Rus.* Gresk. Minskaya Voblasts', C Belarus
Hrisoupoli *see* Chrysoúpoli
119 F16 **Hrodna** *Pol.* Grodno. Hrodzyenskaya Voblasts', W Belarus
119 F16 **Hrodzyenskaya Voblasts'** *prev. Rus.* Grodnenskaya Oblast'. ◈ *province* W Belarus
111 J21 **Hron** *Ger.* Gran, *Hung.* Garam. ≈ C Slovakia
111 Q14 **Hrubieszów** *Rus.* Grubeshov. Lubelskie, E Poland
112 F13 **Hrvace** Split-Dalmacija, SE Croatia
Hrvatska *see* Croatia
112 F10 **Hrvatska Kostajnica** *var.* Kostajnica. Sisak-Moslavina, C Croatia
Hrvatsko Grahovi *see* Bosansko Grahovo
116 K6 **Hrymayliv** *Pol.* Gizymałów, *Rus.* Grimaylov. Ternopil's'ka Oblast', W Ukraine
167 N4 **Hsenwi** Shan State, E Burma (Myanmar)
Hsia-men *see* Xiamen
Hsiang-t'an *see* Xiangtan
Hsi Chiang *see* Xi Jiang
167 N6 **Hsihseng** Shan State, C Burma (Myanmar)
161 S13 **Hsinchu** N Taiwan
Hsing-K'ai Hu *see* Khanka, Lake
Hsi-ning/Hsining *see* Xining
Hsinking *see* Changchun
Hsin-yang *see* Xinyang
161 S14 **Hsinying** *var.* Sinying, *Jap.* Shinei. C Taiwan
167 N4 **Hsipaw** Shan State, C Burma (Myanmar)
Hsu-chou *see* Xuzhou
161 S13 **Hsüeh Shan** ▲ N Taiwan
Hu *see* Shanghai Shi
161 Q7 **Huaiyin** Jiangsu, E China
83 B18 **Huab** ≈ W Namibia
57 M21 **Huacaya** Chuquisaca, S Bolivia
57 J19 **Huachacalla** Oruro, SW Bolivia
159 X9 **Huachi** *var.* Rouyuanchengzi. Gansu, C China
57 N16 **Huachi, Laguna** ◎ N Bolivia
57 D14 **Huacho** Lima, W Peru
163 Y7 **Huachuan** Heilongjiang, NE China
163 P12 **Huade** Nei Mongol Zizhiqu, N China
163 W10 **Huadian** Jilin, NE China
56 E13 **Huagaruncho, Cordillera** ▲▲ C Peru
Hua Hin *see* Ban Hua Hin
191 S10 **Huahine** *island* Îles Sous le Vent, W French Polynesia
Huahua, Rio *see* Wawa, Río
167 R8 **Huai** ≈ E Thailand
161 Q7 **Huai'an** *var.* Qingjiang; *prev.* Huaiyin. Jiangsu, E China
161 P6 **Huaibei** Anhui, E China
Huaide *see* Gongzhuling
157 T10 **Huai He** ≈ C China
160 L11 **Huaihua** Hunan, S China
161 N14 **Huaiji** Guangdong, S China
161 O2 **Huailai** *var.* Shacheng. Hebei, E China
161 P7 **Huainan** *var.* Huai-nan, Hwainan. Anhui, E China
Huai-nan *see* Huainan
161 N2 **Huairen** Shanxi, C China
161 O7 **Huaiyang** Henan, C China
Huaiyin *see* Huai'an
167 N16 **Huai Yot** Trang, SW Thailand
41 Q15 **Huajuapan** *var.* Huajuapan de León. Oaxaca, SE Mexico
Huajuapan de León *see* Huajuapan
41 O9 **Hualahuises** Nuevo León, NE Mexico
36 I11 **Hualapai Mountains** ▲▲ Arizona, SW USA
36 I11 **Hualapai Peak** ▲ Arizona, SW USA
62 J7 **Hualfín** Catamarca, N Argentina
161 T13 **Hualien** *var.* Hwalien, *Jap.* Karen. C Taiwan
56 E10 **Huallaga, Río** ≈ N Peru
56 C11 **Huamachuco** La Libertad, C Peru
41 Q14 **Huamantla** Tlaxcala, S Mexico
82 C13 **Huambo** *Port.* Nova Lisboa. Huambo, C Angola
82 B13 **Huambo** ◈ *province* C Angola
41 P15 **Huamuxtitlán** Guerrero, S Mexico
163 Y8 **Huachuan** Heilongjiang, NE China
63 H17 **Huancache, Sierra** ▲▲ SW Argentina
57 I17 **Huancané** Puno, SE Peru
57 F16 **Huancapi** Ayacucho, C Peru
57 E15 **Huancavelica** Huancavelica, SW Peru
57 E15 **Huancavelica** *off.* Departamento de Huancavelica. ◈ *department* W Peru
Huancavelica, Departamento de *see* Huancavelica
57 E14 **Huancayo** Junín, C Peru
57 K20 **Huanchaca, Cerro** ▲ S Bolivia
56 C12 **Huandoy, Nevado** ▲ W Peru
Huang'an *see* Hong'an
161 O8 **Huangchuan** Henan, C China
161 O9 **Huanggang** Hubei, C China
Huang Hai *see* Yellow Sea
157 Q8 **Huang He** *var.* Yellow River. ≈ C China
161 Q4 **Huanghe Kou** *delta* E China
160 L5 **Huangling** Shaanxi, C China
161 O9 **Huangpi** Hubei, C China
163 P13 **Huangqi Hai** ◎ N China
161 Q9 **Huangshan** *var.* Tunxi. Anhui, E China
161 Q9 **Huang Shan** *tourist site* Anhui, E China
161 O9 **Huangshi** *var.* Huang-shih, Hwangshih. Hubei, C China
Huang-shih *see* Huangshi
160 L5 **Huangtu Gaoyuan** *plateau* C China
61 B22 **Huanguelén** Buenos Aires, E Argentina
161 S10 **Huangyan** Zhejiang, SE China
159 T10 **Huangyuan** Qinghai, C China
159 T10 **Huangzhong** *var.* Lushar. Qinghai, C China
163 W12 **Huanren** *var.* Huanren Manzu Zizhixian. Liaoning, NE China
Huanren Manzu Zizhixian *see* Huanren
57 F15 **Huanta** Ayacucho, C Peru
56 E13 **Huánuco** Huánuco, C Peru
56 D13 **Huánuco** *off.* Departamento de Huánuco. ◈ *department* C Peru
Huánuco, Departamento de *see* Huánuco
57 K19 **Huanuni** Oruro, W Bolivia
159 X9 **Huanxian** Gansu, C China
161 S12 **Huap'ing Yu** *island* N Taiwan
62 H3 **Huara** Tarapacá, N Chile
57 D14 **Huaral** Lima, W Peru
Huarás *see* Huaraz
56 D13 **Huaraz** *var.* Huarás. Ancash, W Peru
57 I16 **Huari Huari, Río** ≈ S Peru
56 C13 **Huarmey** Ancash, W Peru
40 H4 **Huásabas** Sonora, NW Mexico
56 D8 **Huasaga, Río** ≈ Ecuador/Peru
167 O15 **Hua Sai** Nakhon Si Thammarat, SW Thailand
56 D12 **Huascarán, Nevado** ▲ W Peru
62 G8 **Huasco** Atacama, N Chile
62 G8 **Huasco, Río** ≈ C Chile
159 S11 **Huashikia** Qinghai, W China
40 G7 **Huatabampo** Sonora, NW Mexico
159 W10 **Huating** Gansu, C China
167 S7 **Huatt, Phou** ▲ N Vietnam
41 Q14 **Huatusco** *var.* Huatusco de Chicuellar. Veracruz-Llave, C Mexico
Huatusco de Chicuellar *see* Huatusco
41 P13 **Huauchinango** Puebla, S Mexico
Huaunta *see* Wounta
41 R15 **Huautla** *var.* Huautla de Jiménez. Oaxaca, SE Mexico
Huautla de Jiménez *see* Huautla
161 O5 **Huaxian** *var.* Daokou, Hua Xian. Henan, C China
Hua Xian *see* Huaxian
Huazangsi *see* Tianzhu
29 V13 **Hubbard** Iowa, C USA
25 U8 **Hubbard** Texas, SW USA
25 Q6 **Hubbard Creek Lake** ⊠ Texas, SW USA
31 R6 **Hubbard Lake** ◎ Michigan, N USA
160 M9 **Hubei** *var.* E, Hubei Sheng, Hupeh, Hupei. ◈ *province* C China
Hubei Sheng *see* Hubei
109 P8 **Huben** Tirol, W Austria
31 R13 **Huber Heights** Ohio, N USA
155 F17 **Hubli** Karnātaka, SW India
163 X12 **Huch'ang** N North Korea
97 M18 **Hucknall** C England, UK
97 L17 **Huddersfield** N England, UK
95 O16 **Huddinge** Stockholm, C Sweden
94 N11 **Hudiksvall** Gävleborg, C Sweden
29 W13 **Hudson** Iowa, C USA
19 O11 **Hudson** Massachusetts, NE USA
31 Q11 **Hudson** Michigan, N USA
30 H6 **Hudson** Wisconsin, N USA
9 V14 **Hudson Bay** Saskatchewan, S Canada
12 G6 **Hudson Bay** *bay* NE Canada
195 T16 **Hudson, Cape** *headland* Antarctica
Hudson, Détroit d' *see* Hudson Strait
27 Q9 **Hudson, Lake** ⊠ Oklahoma, C USA
18 K9 **Hudson River** ≈ New Jersey/New York, NE USA
10 M12 **Hudson's Hope** British Columbia, W Canada
12 L2 **Hudson Strait** *Fr.* Détroit d'Hudson. *strait* Northwest Territories/Québec, NE Canada
Ḩudūd ash Shamālīyah, Minţaqat al *see* Al Ḩudūd ash Shamālīyah
Hudur *see* Xuddur
167 U9 **Huê** Th,a Thiên-Huê, C Vietnam
104 J7 **Huebra** ≈ W Spain
24 H8 **Hueco Mountains** ▲▲ Texas, SW USA
116 G10 **Huedin** *Hung.* Bánffyhunyad. Cluj, NW Romania
40 J10 **Huehuento, Cerro** ▲ C Mexico
42 B5 **Huehuetenango** Huehuetenango, W Guatemala
42 B4 **Huehuetenango** *off.* Departamento de Huehuetenango. ◈ *department* W Guatemala
Huehuetenango, Departamento de *see* Huehuetenango
40 L11 **Huejuquilla** Jalisco, SW Mexico
41 P12 **Huejutla** *var.* Huejutla de Reyes. Hidalgo, C Mexico
Huejutla de Reyes *see* Huejutla
102 G6 **Huelgoat** Finistère, NW France
105 O13 **Huelma** Andalucía, S Spain
104 I14 **Huelva** *anc.* Onuba. Andalucía, SW Spain
104 I13 **Huelva** ◈ *province* Andalucía, SW Spain
104 J13 **Huelva** ≈ SW Spain
105 Q14 **Huercal-Overa** Andalucía, S Spain
37 Q9 **Huerfano Mountain** ▲ New Mexico, SW USA
37 T7 **Huerfano River** ≈ Colorado, C USA
105 S12 **Huertas, Cabo** *cape* SE Spain
105 R6 **Huerva** ≈ N Spain
105 S4 **Huesca** *anc.* Osca. Aragón, NE Spain
105 T4 **Huesca** ◈ *province* Aragón, NE Spain
105 P13 **Huéscar** Andalucía, S Spain
41 N15 **Huetamo** *var.* Huetamo de Núñez. Michoacán de Ocampo, SW Mexico
Huetamo de Núñez *see* Huetamo
105 P8 **Huete** Castilla-La Mancha, C Spain
23 P4 **Hueytown** Alabama, S USA
28 L16 **Hugh Butler Lake** ⊠ Nebraska, C USA
181 V6 **Hughenden** Queensland, NE Australia
182 A6 **Hughes** South Australia
39 P8 **Hughes** Alaska, USA
27 X11 **Hughes** Arkansas, C USA
25 W6 **Hughes Springs** Texas, SW USA
37 V5 **Hugo** Colorado, C USA
27 Q13 **Hugo** Oklahoma, C USA
27 Q13 **Hugo Lake** ⊠ Oklahoma, C USA
26 H7 **Hugoton** Kansas, C USA
Huhehot/Huhohaote *see* Hohhot
Huhttán *see* Kvikkjokk
161 R13 **Hui'an** *var.* Luocheng. Fujian, SE China
184 O9 **Huiarau Range** ▲▲ North Island, New Zealand
83 D22 **Huib-Hoch Plateau** *plateau* S Namibia
41 O13 **Huichapán** Hidalgo, C Mexico
Huicheng *see* Shexian
163 W13 **Hŭich'ŏn** C North Korea
83 B15 **Huíla** ◈ *province* SW Angola
54 E12 **Huila** *off.* Departamento del Huila. ◈ *province* S Colombia
Huila, Departamento del *see* Huila
54 D11 **Huila, Nevado del** *elevation* C Colombia
83 B15 **Huíla Plateau** *plateau* S Angola
160 G12 **Huili** Sichuan, C China
161 P4 **Huimin** Shandong, E China
163 W11 **Huinan** *var.* Chaoyang. Jilin, NE China
62 K12 **Huinca Renancó** Córdoba, C Argentina
159 V10 **Huining** *var.* Huishi. Gansu, C China
Huishi *see* Huining
160 J12 **Huishui** *var.* Heping. Guizhou, S China
102 L6 **Huisne** ≈ NW France
98 L12 **Huissen** Gelderland, SE Netherlands
159 N11 **Huiten Nur** ◎ C China
93 K19 **Huittinen** Länsi-Soumi, SW Finland
41 O15 **Huitzuco** *var.* Huitzuco de los Figueroa. Guerrero, S Mexico
Huitzuco de los Figueroa *see* Huitzuco
159 V11 **Huixian** *var.* Hui Xian. Gansu, C China
Hui Xian *see* Huixian
41 V17 **Huixtla** Chiapas, SE Mexico

◆ Country ● Country Capital ◇ Dependent Territory ○ Dependent Territory Capital ◈ Administrative Regions ✈ International Airport ▲ Mountain ▲▲ Mountain Range Volcano ≈ River ◎ Lake ⊠ Reservoir

103 O17 **Ille-sur-Têt** *var.* Ille-sur-la-Têt. Pyrénées-Orientales, S France
Illi *see* Ile/Ili He
Illiberis *see* Elne
117 P11 **Illichivs'k** *Rus.* Il'ichevsk. Odes'ka Oblast', SW Ukraine
Illicis *see* Elche
102 M6 **Illiers-Combray** Eure-et-Loir, C France
30 K12 **Illinois** *off.* State of Illinois, *also known as* Prairie State, Sucker State. ◆ *state* C USA
30 J13 **Illinois River** ⚉ Illinois, N USA
117 N6 **Illintsi** Vinnyts'ka Oblast', C Ukraine
74 M10 **Illizi** SE Algeria
27 Y7 **Illmo** Missouri, C USA
Illurco *see* Lorca
Illuro *see* Mataró
Illyrisch-Feistritz *see* Ilirska Bistrica
101 K16 **Ilm** ⚉ C Germany
101 K17 **Ilmenau** Thüringen, C Germany
124 H14 **Il'men', Ozero** ⊚ NW Russian Federation
57 H18 **Ilo** Moquegua, SW Peru
171 O6 **Iloilo** *off.* Iloilo City. Panay Island, C Philippines
Iloilo City *see* Iloilo
112 K10 **Ilok** *Hung.* Újlak. Vojvodina, NW Serbia
93 O16 **Ilomantsi** Pohjois-Karjala, SE Finland
42 F8 **Ilopango, Lago de** *volcanic lake* C El Salvador
77 T15 **Ilorin** Kwara, W Nigeria
117 X8 **Ilovays'ka** *Rus.* Ilovaysk. Donets'ka Oblast', SE Ukraine
Ilovaysk *see* Ilovays'k
127 O10 **Ilovlya** Volgogradskaya Oblast', SW Russian Federation
127 O10 **Ilovlya** ⚉ SW Russian Federation
126 K14 **Il'skiy** Krasnodarskiy Kray, SW Russian Federation
182 B2 **Iltur** South Australia
171 Y13 **Ilugwa** Papua, E Indonesia
Iluh *see* Batman
118 I11 **Ilūkste** Daugavpils, SE Latvia
171 Y13 **Ilur** Pulau Gorong, E Indonesia
32 F10 **Ilwaco** Washington, NW USA
Il'yaly *see* Gurbansoltan Eje
Il'yaly *see* Gurbansoltan Eje
Ilyasbaba Burnu *see* Tekke Burnu
125 U9 **Ilych** ⚉ NW Russian Federation
101 O21 **Ilz** ⚉ SE Germany
111 M14 **Iłża** Radom, SE Poland
164 G13 **Imabari** *var.* Imaharu. Ehime, Shikoku, SW Japan
Imaharu *see* Imabari
165 O12 **Imaichi** *var.* Imaiti. Tochigi, Honshū, S Japan
Imaiti *see* Imaichi
164 K12 **Imajō** Fukui, Honshū, SW Japan
139 R9 **Imām Ibn Hāshim** C Iraq
139 T11 **Imām 'Abd Allāh** S Iraq
124 J4 **Imandra, Ozero** ⊚ NW Russian Federation
164 F15 **Imano-yama** ▲ Shikoku, SW Japan
164 C13 **Imari** Saga, Kyūshū, SW Japan
Imarssuak Mid-Ocean Seachannel *see* Imarssuak Seachannel
64 J6 **Imarssuak Seachannel** *var.* Imarssuak Mid-Ocean Seachannel. *channel* N Atlantic Ocean
93 N18 **Imatra** Kymi, SE Finland
164 K13 **Imazu** Shiga, Honshū, SW Japan
56 C6 **Imbabura** ◆ *province* N Ecuador
55 R9 **Imbaimadai** W Guyana
61 K14 **Imbituba** Santa Catarina, S Brazil
27 W9 **Imboden** Arkansas, C USA
Imbros *see* Gökçeada
Imeni 26 Bakinskikh Komissarov *see* 26 Bakı Komissarı
Imeni 26 Bakinskikh Komissarov *see* Uzboý
125 N13 **Imeni Babushkina** Vologodskaya Oblast', NW Russian Federation
126 J7 **Imeni Karla Libknekhta** Kurskaya Oblast', W Russian Federation
Imeni Mollanepesa *see* Mollanepes Adyndaky
Imeni S. A. Nіyazova *see* S. A.Nyýazow Adyndaky
Imeni Sverdlova Rudnik *see* Sverdlovs'k
188 E9 **Imeong** Babeldaob, N Palau
81 L14 **Ìmī** Somali, E Ethiopia
115 M21 **Imia** *Turk.* Kardak. *island* Dodekánisa, Greece, Aegean Sea
Imishli *see* İmişli
137 X12 **İmişli** *Rus.* Imishli. C Azerbaijan
163 X14 **Imjin-gang** ⚉ North Korea/ South Korea
35 S3 **Imlay** Nevada, W USA
31 S9 **Imlay City** Michigan, N USA
23 X15 **Immokalee** Florida, SE USA
77 U17 **Imo** ◆ *state* SE Nigeria
106 G12 **Imola** Emilia-Romagna, N Italy
186 A5 **Imonda** Sandaun, NW Papua New Guinea
Imoschi *see* Imotski
113 G14 **Imotski** *It.* Imoschi. Split-Dalmacija, SE Croatia
59 L14 **Imperatriz** Maranhão, NE Brazil
106 B10 **Imperia** Liguria, NW Italy
57 E15 **Imperial** Lima, W Peru
35 X17 **Imperial** California, W USA
28 L16 **Imperial** Nebraska, C USA
24 M9 **Imperial** Texas, SW USA
35 Y17 **Imperial Dam** *dam* California, W USA
79 I17 **Impfondo** La Likouala, NE Congo
153 X14 **Imphal** *state capital* Manipur, NE India
128 P9 **Imphy** Nièvre, C France
106 G11 **Impruneta** Toscana, C Italy

115 K15 **İmroz** *var.* Gökçeada. Çanakkale, NW Turkey
İmroz Adası *see* Gökçeada
108 L7 **Imst** Tirol, W Austria
40 F3 **Imuris** Sonora, NW Mexico
164 M13 **Ina** Nagano, Honshū, S Japan
65 M18 **Inaccessible Island** *island* W Tristan da Cunha
115 F20 **Ínachos** ⚉ S Greece
188 H6 **I Naftan, Puntan** *headland* Saipan, S Northern Mariana Islands
Inagua Islands *see* Little Inagua
Inagua Islands *see* Great Inagua
154 G10 **Indore** Madhya Pradesh, C India
185 H15 **Inangahua** West Coast, South Island, New Zealand
57 I14 **Iñapari** Madre de Dios, E Peru
188 B17 **Inarajan** SE Guam
92 L10 **Inari** *Lapp.* Anár, Aanaar. Lappi, N Finland
92 L10 **Inarijärvi** *Lapp.* Aanaarjävri, *Swe.* Enareträsk. ⊚ N Finland
92 L9 **Inarijoki** *Lapp.* Anárjohka. ⚉ Finland/Norway
Inău *see* Ineu
165 P11 **Inawashiro-ko** *var.* Inawasiro Ko. ⊚ Honshū, C Japan
Inawasiro Ko *see* Inawashiro-ko
105 X9 **Inca** Mallorca, Spain, W Mediterranean Sea
62 H7 **Inca de Oro** Atacama, N Chile
115 J15 **İnce Burnu** *cape* NW Turkey
136 K9 **İnce Burnu** *headland* N Turkey
136 I17 **İncekum Burnu** *headland* S Turkey
76 G7 **Inchiri** ◆ *region* NW Mauritania
163 X15 **Inch'ŏn** *off.* Inch'ŏn-gwangyŏksi, *Jap.* Jinsen; *prev.* Chemulpo. NW South Korea
161 X15 **Inch'ŏn** ✈ (Sŏul) NW South Korea
Inch'ŏn-gwangyŏksi *see* Inch'ŏn
83 M17 **Inchope** Manica, C Mozambique
Incoronata *see* Kornat
103 Y15 **Incudine, Monte** ▲ Corse, France, C Mediterranean Sea
60 M10 **Indaiatuba** São Paulo, S Brazil
93 H17 **Indal** Västernorrland, C Sweden
93 H17 **Indalsälven** ⚉ C Sweden
40 K8 **Inde** Durango, C Mexico
Indefatigable Island *see* Santa Cruz, Isla
35 S10 **Independence** California, W USA
29 X13 **Independence** Iowa, C USA
27 P7 **Independence** Kansas, C USA
20 M4 **Independence** Kentucky, S USA
27 R4 **Independence** Missouri, C USA
21 R8 **Independence** Virginia, NE USA
30 J7 **Independence** Wisconsin, N USA
197 R12 **Independence Fjord** *fjord* N Greenland
Independence Island *see* Malden Island
35 W2 **Independence Mountains** ▲ Nevada, W USA
57 K18 **Independencia** Cochabamba, C Bolivia
57 E16 **Independencia, Bahía de la** *bay* W Peru
Independencia, Monte *see* Adam, Mount
116 M12 **Independenţa** Galaţi, SE Romania
Inderagiri *see* Indragiri, Sungai
Ìnderbor *see* Inderborskiy
144 F11 **Inderborskiy** *Kaz.* Inderbor. Atyrau, W Kazakhstan
151 I14 **India** *off.* Republic of India, *var.* Indian Union, Union of India, *Hind.* Bhārat. ◆ *republic* S Asia
India *see* Indija
18 D14 **Indiana** Pennsylvania, NE USA
31 N13 **Indiana** *off.* State of Indiana, *also known as* Hoosier State. ◆ *state* N USA
31 O14 **Indianapolis** *state capital* Indiana, N USA
9 O10 **Indian Cabins** Alberta, W Canada
42 G1 **Indian Church** Orange Walk, N Belize
Indian Desert *see* Thar Desert
9 U16 **Indian Head** Saskatchewan, S Canada
31 O4 **Indian Lake** ⊚ Michigan, N USA
18 K9 **Indian Lake** ⊚ New York, NE USA
31 R13 **Indian Lake** ⊠ Ohio, N USA
172-173 **Indian Ocean** *ocean*
29 V15 **Indianola** Iowa, C USA
22 K4 **Indianola** Mississippi, S USA
36 J6 **Indian Peak** ▲ Utah, W USA
23 Y13 **Indian River** *lagoon* Florida, SE USA
35 W10 **Indian Springs** Nevada, W USA
23 Y14 **Indiantown** Florida, SE USA
Indian Union *see* India
59 K19 **Indiara** Goiás, S Brazil
India, Republic of *see* India
India, Union of *see* India
54 K11 **Inírida, Río** ⚉ E Colombia
127 N7 **Inis** *see* Ennis
Inis Ceithleann *see* Enniskillen
Inis Córthaidh *see* Enniscorthy
112 L10 **Indija** *Hung.* India; *prev.* Indjija. Vojvodina, N Serbia
39 V16 **Indio** California, W USA
42 M12 **Indio, Río** ⚉ SE Nicaragua
152 I10 **Indira Gandhi International** ✈ (Delhi) N India
151 Q23 **Indira Point** *headland* Andaman and Nicobar Islands, India, NE Indian Ocean
129 Q13 **Indo-Australian Plate** *tectonic feature*
173 N11 **Indomed Fracture Zone** *tectonic feature* SW Indian Ocean
170 L12 **Indonesia** *off.* Republic of Indonesia, *Ind.* Republik Indonesia; *prev.* Dutch East Indies, Netherlands East Indies, United States of Indonesia. ◆ *republic* SE Asia
Indonesian Borneo *see* Kalimantan
Indonesia, Republic of *see* Indonesia
Indonesia, Republik *see* Indonesia
Indonesia, United States of *see* Indonesia
168 L11 **Indragiri, Sungai** *var.* Batang Kuantan, Inderagiri. ⚉ Sumatera, W Indonesia
169 P15 **Indramayu** *prev.* Indramajoe, Indramaju. Jawa, C Indonesia
155 K14 **Indrāvati** ⚉ S India
103 N9 **Indre** ◆ *department* C France
102 M8 **Indre** ⚉ C France
94 D13 **Indre Ålvik** Hordaland, S Norway
102 L8 **Indre-et-Loire** ◆ *department* C France
Indreville *see* Châteauroux
152 G3 **Indus** *Tib.* Sênggê Khabab; *prev.* Yin-tu Ho. ⚉ S Asia
Indus Cone *see* Indus Fan
173 P3 **Indus Fan** *var.* Indus Cone. *undersea feature* N Arabian Sea
149 P17 **Indus, Mouths of the** *delta* S Pakistan
83 I24 **Indwe** Eastern Cape, SE South Africa
136 I10 **İnebolu** Kastamonu, N Turkey
77 P8 **I-n-Échaï** *oasis* C Mali
114 M13 **İnecik** Tekirdağ, NW Turkey
136 E12 **İnegöl** Bursa, NW Turkey
Inessa *see* Biancavilla
116 F10 **Ineu** *Hung.* Borosjenő; *prev.* Inău. Arad, W Romania
Ineu, Vârful *see* Ineu
116 J9 **Ineu, Vârful** *var.* Ineul; *prev.* Vîrful Ineu. ▲ N Romania
21 P6 **Inez** Kentucky, S USA
74 E8 **Inezgane** ✈ (Agadir) W Morocco
41 T17 **Inferior, Laguna** *lagoon* S Mexico
40 M15 **Infiernillo, Presa del** ⊠ S Mexico
104 L2 **Infiesto** Asturias, N Spain
93 L20 **Ingå** *Fin.* Inkoo. Etelä-Suomi, S Finland
77 U10 **Ingal** *var.* I-n-Gall. Agadez, C Niger
99 C18 **Ingelmunster** West-Vlaanderen, W Belgium
79 I18 **Ingende** Équateur, W Dem. Rep. Congo
62 L5 **Ingeniero Guillermo Nueva Juárez** Formosa, N Argentina
63 H16 **Ingeniero Jacobacci** Río Negro, C Argentina
14 G14 **Ingersoll** Ontario, S Canada
Ingettolgoy *see* Selenge
181 W5 **Ingham** Queensland, NE Australia
146 M11 **Ingichka** Samarqand Viloyati, C Uzbekistan
97 L17 **Ingleborough** ▲ N England, UK
25 T14 **Ingleside** Texas, SW USA
184 K10 **Inglewood** Taranaki, North Island, New Zealand
35 S15 **Inglewood** California, W USA
101 L21 **Ingolstadt** Bayern, S Germany
33 V9 **Ingomar** Montana, NW USA
13 R14 **Ingonish Beach** Cape Breton Island, Nova Scotia, SE Canada
153 S14 **Ingrāj Bāzār** *prev.* English Bazar. West Bengal, NE India
195 X7 **Ingrid Christensen Coast** *physical region* Antarctica
74 K14 **I-n-Guezzam** S Algeria
Ingulets *see* Inhulets'
Inguri *see* Enguri
Ingushetia/Ingushetiya, Respublika *see* Ingushskaya Respublika
127 O15 **Ingushskaya Respublika** *var.* Respublika Ingushetiya, *Eng.* Ingushetia. ◆ *autonomous republic* SW Russian Federation
83 N20 **Inhambane** Inhambane, SE Mozambique
83 N20 **Inhambane** *off.* Província de Inhambane. ◆ *province* S Mozambique
Inhambane, Província de *see* Inhambane
83 N17 **Inhaminga** Sofala, C Mozambique
83 N20 **Inharrime** Inhambane, SE Mozambique
83 M18 **Inhassoro** Inhambane, SE Mozambique
117 S9 **Inhulets'** *Rus.* Ingulets. Dnipropetrovs'ka Oblast', E Ukraine
117 S10 **Inhulets'** *Rus.* Ingulets. ⚉ S Ukraine
127 P6 **Inza** Ul'yanovskaya Oblast', W Russian Federation
127 W5 **Inzer** Respublika Bashkortostan, W Russian Federation
127 N7 **Inzhavino** Tambovskaya Oblast', W Russian Federation
115 C16 **Ioánnina** *var.* Janina, Yannina. Ípeiros, W Greece
164 B17 **Iō-jima** *var.* Iwojima. *island* Nansei-shotō, SW Japan
124 L4 **Iokan'ga** ⚉ NW Russian Federation
97 B18 **Inishbofin** *Ir.* Inis Bó Finne. *island* W Ireland
97 A17 **Inishbofin** *Ir.* Inis Bó Finne. *island* W Ireland
97 B18 **Inisheer** *var.* Inis Thiar, *Ir.* Inis Oírr. *island* W Ireland
Inishere *see* Inisheer
97 B18 **Inishmaan** *Ir.* Inis Meáin. *island* W Ireland
83 A16 **Iona** Namibe, SW Angola
96 F11 **Iona** *island* W Scotland, UK
116 M15 **Ion Corvin** Constanţa, SE Romania
35 P7 **Ione** California, W USA
116 I13 **Ioneşti** Vâlcea, SW Romania
31 Q9 **Ionia** Michigan, N USA
Ionia Basin *see* Ionian Basin
121 O10 **Ionian Basin** *var.* Ionia Basin. *undersea feature* Ionian Sea, C Mediterranean Sea
115 B17 **Iónia Nisiá** *var.* Iónioi Nísoi, *Eng.* Ionian Islands. *island group* W Greece
121 O10 **Ionian Sea** *Gk.* Iónio Pélagos, *It.* Mar Ionio. *sea* C Mediterranean Sea
115 B17 **Iónioi Nisoi** *Eng.* Ionian Islands. ◆ *region* W Greece
Iónioi Nísoi *see* Iónia Nisiá
Ionio, Mar/Iónio Pélagos *see* Ionian Sea
137 U10 **Iori** *var.* Qabırrı. ⚉ Azerbaijan/Georgia
Iorrais, Ceann *see* Erris Head
115 J22 **Íos** *var.* Nio. *island* Kykládes, Greece, Aegean Sea
Íos *see* Chóra
22 G9 **Iowa** Louisiana, S USA
29 V13 **Iowa** *off.* State of Iowa, *also known as* Hawkeye State. ◆ *state* C USA
29 Y14 **Iowa City** Iowa, C USA
29 V13 **Iowa Falls** Iowa, C USA
25 R4 **Iowa Park** Texas, SW USA
29 X14 **Iowa River** ⚉ Iowa, C USA
119 M19 **Ipa** ⚉ SE Belaeus
59 N20 **Ipatinga** Minas Gerais, SE Brazil
127 N13 **Ipatovo** Stavropol'skiy Kray, SW Russian Federation
115 C16 **Ípeiros** *Eng.* Epirus. ◆ *region* W Greece
Ipek *see* Peć
111 J27 **Ipel'** *var.* Ipoly, *Ger.* Eipel. ⚉ Hungary/Slovakia
54 C13 **Ipiales** Nariño, SW Colombia
189 V14 **Ipis** *atoll* Chuuk Islands, C Micronesia
59 A14 **Ipixuna** Amazonas, W Brazil
168 J8 **Ipoh** Perak, Peninsular Malaysia
Ipoly *see* Ipel'
187 S15 **Ipota** Erromango, S Vanuatu
79 K14 **Ippy** Ouaka, C Central African Republic
114 L13 **Ipsala** Edirne, NW Turkey
183 V3 **Ipswich** Queensland, E Australia
97 Q20 **Ipswich** *hist.* Gipeswic. E England, UK
29 O8 **Ipswich** South Dakota, N USA
119 P18 **Iputs'** ⚉ Belarus/Russian Federation
9 R7 **Iqaluit** *var.* Frobisher Bay. *province capital* Baffin Island, Nunavut, NE Canada
159 P9 **Iqe** Qinghai, W China
159 P9 **Iqe He** ⚉ C China
Iqlid *see* Eqlid
62 G8 **Iquique** Tarapacá, N Chile
56 G8 **Iquitos** Loreto, N Peru
79 K14 **Ira Banda** Haute-Kotto, E Central African Republic
165 P16 **Irabu-jima** *island* Miyako-shotō, SW Japan
55 Y9 **Iracoubo** N French Guiana
60 H13 **Iraí** Rio Grande do Sul, S Brazil
114 G12 **Irákleia** Kentrikí Makedonía, N Greece
115 J21 **Irákleia** *island* Kykládes, Greece, Aegean Sea
115 J25 **Irákleio** *var.* Herakleion, *Eng.* Candia; *prev.* Iráklion. Kríti, Greece, E Mediterranean Sea
115 F15 **Irákleio** *anc.* Heracleum. *castle* Kentrikí Makedonía, N Greece
115 J25 **Irákleio** ✈ Kríti, Greece, E Mediterranean Sea
Iráklion *see* Irákleio
143 O7 **Iran** *off.* Islamic Republic of Iran; *prev.* Persia. ◆ *republic* SW Asia
58 F13 **Iranduba** Amazonas, NW Brazil
Iranian Plate *tectonic feature*
143 Q9 **Iranian Plateau** *var.* Plateau of Iran. *plateau* N Iran
Iran, Islamic Republic of *see* Iran
169 U9 **Iran, Pegunungan** ▲ Indonesia/Malaysia
Iran, Plateau of *see* Iranian Plateau
143 W13 **Īrānshahr** Sīstān va Balūchestān, SE Iran
55 P5 **Irapa** Sucre, NE Venezuela
41 N13 **Irapuato** Guanajuato, C Mexico
139 R7 **Iraq** *off.* Republic of Iraq, *Ar.* 'Irāq. ◆ *republic* SW Asia
'Irāq *see* Iraq
Iraq, Republic of *see* Iraq
60 J12 **Irati** Paraná, S Brazil
105 R3 **Irati** ⚉ N Spain
125 T8 **Iṙayël'** Respublika Komi, NW Russian Federation
43 N13 **Irazú, Volcán** ▲ C Costa Rica
118 D7 **Irbe Strait** *Est.* Kura Kurk, *Latv.* Irbes Šaurums, Irbenskiy Zaliv; *prev. Est.* Irbe Väin. *strait* Estonia/Latvia
Irbe Väin *see* Irbe Strait
138 G9 **Irbid** N Jordan
138 G9 **Irbid** *off.* Muḥāfaẓat Irbid. ◆ *governorate* N Jordan
Irbid, Muḥāfaẓat *see* Irbid
Irbil *see* Arbīl
109 S6 **Irdning** Steiermark, SE Austria
79 I18 **Irebu** Équateur, W Dem. Rep. Congo
97 D17 **Ireland** *off.* Republic of Ireland, *Ir.* Éire. ◆ *republic* NW Europe
84 C9 **Ireland** *Lat.* Hibernia. *island* Ireland/UK
64 A12 **Ireland Island North** *island* W Bermuda
64 A12 **Ireland Island South** *island* W Bermuda
Ireland, Republic of *see* Ireland
125 V15 **Iren'** ⚉ NW Russian Federation
185 A22 **Irene, Mount** ▲ South Island, New Zealand
79 M18 **Irga** S Dem. Rep. Congo
Irgalem *see* Yirga 'Alem
144 L11 **Irgiz** Aktyubinsk, C Kazakhstan
Irian *see* New Guinea
Irian Barat *see* Papua
Irian Jaya *see* Papua
Irian Jaya *see* Papua
Cendrawasih, Teluk *see* Cenderawasih, Teluk
78 K9 **Iriba** Biltine, NE Chad
127 X7 **Iriklinskoye Vodokhranilishche** ⊠ W Russian Federation
81 H23 **Iringa** Iringa, C Tanzania
81 H23 **Iringa** ◆ *region* S Tanzania
165 O16 **Iriomote-jima** *island* Sakishima-shotō, SW Japan
42 L4 **Iriona** Colón, NE Honduras
47 U7 **Iriri** N Brazil
58 I13 **Iriri, Rio** ⚉ C Brazil
35 W9 **Irish, Mount** ▲ Nevada, W USA
97 H17 **Irish Sea** *Ir.* Muir Éireann. *sea* C British Isles
139 U12 **Irjal ash Shaykhīyah** S Iraq
147 U11 **Irkeshtam** Oshskaya Oblast', SW Kyrgyzstan
122 M13 **Irkutsk** Irkutskaya Oblast', S Russian Federation
122 M12 **Irkutskaya Oblast'** ◆ *province* S Russian Federation
Irlir, Gora *see* Irlir Tog'i
146 K8 **Irlir Tog'i** *var.* Gora Irlir. ▲ N Uzbekistan
Irminger Basin *see* Reykjanes Basin
21 H2 **Irmo** South Carolina, SE USA
102 E6 **Iroise** *sea* NW France
189 X2 **Iroj** *var.* Eroj. *island* Ratak Chain, SE Marshall Islands
182 H7 **Iron Baron** South Australia
14 C10 **Iron Bridge** Ontario, S Canada
20 H10 **Iron City** Tennessee, S USA
14 I13 **Irondale** ⚉ Ontario, SE Canada
182 H7 **Iron Knob** South Australia
30 M5 **Iron Mountain** Michigan, N USA
30 M4 **Iron River** Michigan, N USA
30 J3 **Iron River** Wisconsin, N USA
27 X6 **Ironton** Missouri, C USA
31 S15 **Ironton** Ohio, N USA
30 K4 **Ironwood** Michigan, N USA
12 H12 **Iroquois Falls** Ontario, S Canada
31 N12 **Iroquois River** ⚉ Illinois/ Indiana, N USA
164 M15 **Irō-zaki** *headland* Honshū, S Japan
Irpen' *see* Irpin'
9 R7 **Irpin'** *Rus.* Irpen'. Kyyivs'ka Oblast', N Ukraine
117 O4 **Irpin'** *Rus.* Irpen'. ⚉ N Ukraine
141 Q16 **'Irqah** SW Yemen
166 K8 **Irrawaddy** *var.* Ayeyarwady. ◆ *division* SW Burma (Myanmar)
166 L6 **Irrawaddy** *var.* Ayeyarwady. ⚉ W Burma (Myanmar)
166 K8 **Irrawaddy, Mouths of the** *delta* SW Burma (Myanmar)
117 N4 **Irsha** ⚉ N Ukraine
116 H7 **Irshava** Zakarpats'ka Oblast', W Ukraine
107 N18 **Irsina** Basilicata, S Italy
Irtish *see* Irtysh
129 R5 **Irtysh** *var.* Irtish, *Kaz.* Ertis. ⚉ C Asia
145 X7 **Irtyshsk** *Kaz.* Ertis. Pavlodar, NE Kazakhstan
79 I17 **Irumu** Orientale, E Dem. Rep. Congo
105 Q3 **Irún** País Vasco, N Spain
105 P2 **Iruña** *see* Pamplona
96 I13 **Irvine** W Scotland, UK
21 N6 **Irvine** Kentucky, S USA
25 T6 **Irving** Texas, SW USA
20 K5 **Irvington** Kentucky, S USA
Isaak *see* Iisaku
28 L8 **Isabel** South Dakota, N USA
186 L8 **Isabel** *off.* Isabel Province. ◆ *province* N Solomon Islands
171 O8 **Isabela** Basilan Island, SW Philippines
45 S5 **Isabela** W Puerto Rico
45 N8 **Isabela, Cabo** *headland* NW Dominican Republic
57 A18 **Isabela, Isla** *var.* Albemarle Island. *island* Galapagos Islands, Ecuador, E Pacific Ocean
40 I12 **Isabela, Isla** *island* C Mexico
42 K9 **Isabela, Cordillera** ▲ NW Nicaragua
35 S12 **Isabella Lake** ⊠ California, W USA
31 N2 **Isabelle, Point** *headland* Michigan, N USA
Isabel Province *see* Isabel
Isabel Segunda *see* Vieques
116 M13 **Isaccea** Tulcea, E Romania
92 H1 **Ísafjarðardjúp** *inlet* NW Iceland
92 H1 **Ísafjörður** Vestfirðir, NW Iceland
164 C14 **Isahaya** Nagasaki, Kyūshū, SW Japan
149 S7 **Isa Khel** Punjab, E Pakistan
172 H7 **Isalo** *var.* Massif de L'Isalo. ▲ SW Madagascar
79 K20 **Isandja** Kasai Occidental, C Dem. Rep. Congo
187 R15 **Isangel** Tanna, S Vanuatu
79 M18 **Isangi** C Dem. Rep. Congo
147 Q7 **Isar** ⚉ Austria/Germany
101 M23 **Isar-Kanal** *canal* SE Germany
Isbarta *see* Isparta
Isca Damnoniorum *see* Exeter
107 K17 **Ischia** *var.* Isola d'Ischea; *anc.* Aenaria. Campania, S Italy
107 K17 **Ischia, Isola d'** *island* S Italy
54 B12 **Iscuandé** *var.* Santa Bárbara. Nariño, SW Colombia
164 H14 **Ise** Mie, Honshū, SW Japan
100 J12 **Ise** ⚉ N Germany
95 I23 **Isefjord** *fjord* E Denmark
192 M14 **Iselin Seamount** *undersea feature* S Pacific Ocean
Isenhof *see* Püssi
106 D7 **Iseo, Lago d'** ⊚ N Italy
103 U12 **Iseran, Col de l'** *pass* E France

ISÈRE – JAMES BAY

103 S11 **Isère** ⬖ *department* E France
103 S12 **Isère** ≈ E France
101 F15 **Iserlohn** Nordrhein-Westfalen, W Germany
107 K16 **Isernia** *var.* Æsernia. Molise, C Italy
165 N12 **Isesaki** Gunma, Honshū, S Japan
129 Q5 **Iset'** ≈ C Russian Federation
77 S15 **Iseyin** Oyo, W Nigeria
Isfahan *see* Eşfahān
147 Q11 **Isfana** Batkenskaya Oblast', SW Kyrgyzstan
147 R11 **Isfara** N Tajikistan
149 O4 **Isfi Maidān** Ghowr, N Afghanistan
92 O3 **Isfjorden** *fjord* W Svalbard
Isgender *see* Kul'mach
Isha Baydhabo *see* Baydhabo
125 V11 **Isherim, Gora** ▲ NW Russian Federation
127 Q5 **Isheyevka** Ul'yanovskaya Oblast', W Russian Federation
165 P16 **Ishigaki** Okinawa, Ishigaki-jima, SW Japan
165 P16 **Ishigaki-jima** *island* Sakishima-shotō, SW Japan
165 R3 **Ishikari-wan** *bay* Hokkaidō, NE Japan
165 S16 **Ishikawa** *var.* Isikawa. Okinawa, Okinawa, SW Japan
164 K11 **Ishikawa** *off.* Ishikawa-ken, *var.* Isikawa. ⬖ *prefecture* Honshū, SW Japan
Ishikawa-ken *see* Ishikawa
122 H11 **Ishim** Tyumenskaya Oblast', C Russian Federation
129 R6 **Ishim** *Kaz.* Esil. ≈ Kazakhstan/Russian Federation
127 V6 **Ishimbay** Respublika Bashkortostan, W Russian Federation
145 O9 **Ishimskoye** Akmola, C Kazakhstan
165 Q10 **Ishinomaki** *var.* Isinomaki. Miyagi, Honshū, C Japan
165 P13 **Ishioka** *var.* Isioka. Ibaraki, Honshū, S Japan
Ishkashim *see* Ishkoshim
Ishkashimskiy Khrebet *see* Ishkoshim, Qatorkŭhi
147 S15 **Ishkoshim** *Rus.* Ishkashim. S Tajikistan
147 S15 **Ishkoshim, Qatorkŭhi** *Rus.* Ishkashimskiy Khrebet. ▲▲ SE Tajikistan
31 N4 **Ishpeming** Michigan, N USA
147 N11 **Ishtikhon** *Rus.* Ishtykhan. Samarqand Viloyati, C Uzbekistan
Ishtykhan *see* Ishtikhon
153 T15 **Ishurdi** *var* Iswardi. Rajshahi, W Bangladesh
61 G17 **Isidoro Noblia** Cerro Largo, NE Uruguay
102 J4 **Isigny-sur-Mer** Calvados, N France
Isikawa *see* Ishikawa
136 C11 **Işıklar Dağı** ▲▲ NW Turkey
107 C19 **Isili** Sardegna, Italy, C Mediterranean Sea
122 H12 **Isil'kul'** Omskaya Oblast', C Russian Federation
Isinomaki *see* Ishinomaki
Isioka *see* Ishioka
81 I18 **Isiolo** Eastern, C Kenya
79 O16 **Isiro** Orientale, NE Dem. Rep. Congo
92 P2 **Isispynten** *headland* NE Svalbard
123 P11 **Isit** Respublika Sakha (Yakutiya), NE Russian Federation
149 O2 **Iskabad Canal** *canal* N Afghanistan
147 Q9 **Iskandar** *Rus.* Iskander. Toshkent Viloyati, E Uzbekistan
Iskander *see* Iskandar
Iskăr *see* Iskŭr
121 Q2 **İskele** *var.* Trikomo, *Gk.* Tríkomon. E Cyprus
136 K17 **İskenderun** *Eng.* Alexandretta. Hatay, S Turkey
138 H2 **İskenderun Körfezi** *Eng.* Gulf of Alexandretta. *gulf* S Turkey
136 J11 **İskilip** Çorum, N Turkey
Iski-Nauket *see* Eski-Nookat
114 J11 **Iskra** *prev.* Popovo. Khaskovska Oblast, S Bulgaria
114 G10 **Iskŭr** *var.* Iskăr. ≈ NW Bulgaria
114 H10 **Iskŭr, Yazovir** *prev.* Yazovir Stalin. ⊠ W Bulgaria
41 S15 **Isla** Veracruz-Llave, SE Mexico
119 J15 **Islach** *Rus.* Isloch'. ≈ C Belarus
104 H14 **Isla Cristina** Andalucía, S Spain
Isla de León *see* San Fernando
149 U6 **Islāmābād** ● (Pakistan) Federal Capital Territory Islāmābād, NE Pakistan
149 V6 **Islāmābād** ✈ Federal Capital Territory Islāmābād, NE Pakistan
Islamabad *see* Anantnāg
149 R17 **Islāmkot** Sind, SE Pakistan
23 Y17 **Islamorada** Florida Keys, Florida, SE USA
153 P14 **Islāmpur** Bihār, N India
Islam Qala *see* Eslām Qal'eh
18 K16 **Island Beach** *spit* New Jersey, NE USA
19 S4 **Island Falls** Maine, NE USA
Island/Ísland *see* Iceland
182 H6 **Island Lagoon** ◎ South Australia
9 Y13 **Island Lake** ◎ Manitoba, C Canada
29 W5 **Island Lake Reservoir** ⊠ Minnesota, N USA
77 O8 **I-n-Sâkâne, 'Erg** *desert* N Mali
33 R13 **Island Park** Idaho, NW USA
19 N6 **Island Pond** Vermont, NE USA
184 K2 **Islands, Bay of** *inlet* North Island, New Zealand
103 R7 **Is-sur-Tille** Côte d'Or, C France
42 J3 **Islas de la Bahía** ⬖ *department* N Honduras
65 L20 **Islas Orcadas Rise** *undersea feature* S Atlantic Ocean
96 F12 **Islay** *island* SW Scotland, UK
116 I15 **Islaz** Teleorman, S Romania
29 V7 **Isle** Minnesota, N USA
102 M12 **Isle** ≈ W France
97 I16 **Isle of Man** ◇ *UK crown dependency* NW Europe
21 X7 **Isle of Wight** Virginia, NE USA
97 M24 **Isle of Wight** *cultural region* S England, UK
191 Y3 **Isles Lagoon** ◎ Kiritimati, E Kiribati
37 R11 **Isleta Pueblo** New Mexico, SW USA
Isloch' *see* Islach
61 E19 **Ismael Cortinas** Flores, S Uruguay
Ismailia *see* Ismâ'ilîya
75 W7 **Ismâ'ilîya** *var.* Ismailia. N Egypt
Ismailly *see* İsmayıllı
137 X11 **İsmayıllı** *Rus.* Ismailly. N Azerbaijan
Ismid *see* İzmit
75 X10 **Isna** *var.* Esna. SE Egypt
93 K18 **Isojoki** Länsi-Soumi, W Finland
82 M12 **Isoka** Northern, NE Zambia
Isola d'Ischea *see* Ischia
Isola d'Istria *see* Izola
Isonzo *see* Soča
15 U4 **Isoukustouc** ≈ Québec, SE Canada
136 F15 **Isparta** *var.* Isbarta. Isparta, SW Turkey
136 F15 **Isparta** *var.* Isbarta. ⬖ *province* SW Turkey
114 M7 **Isperikh** *prev.* Kemanlar. Razgrad, N Bulgaria
107 L26 **Ispica** Sicilia, Italy, C Mediterranean Sea
148 J14 **Ispikān** Baluchistān, SW Pakistan
137 Q12 **İspir** Erzurum, NE Turkey
138 E12 **Israel** *off.* State of Israel, *var.* Medinat Israel, *Heb.* Yisrael, Yisra'el. ◆ *republic* SW Asia
Israel, State of *see* Israel
Issa *see* Vis
55 S9 **Issano** C Guyana
76 M16 **Issia** SW Ivory Coast
Issiq Köl *see* Issyk-Kul', Ozero
103 P11 **Issoire** Puy-de-Dôme, C France
103 N9 **Issoudun** *anc.* Uxellodunum. Indre, C France
81 H22 **Issuna** Singida, C Tanzania
Issyk *see* Yesik
Issyk-Kul' *see* Balykchy
147 X7 **Issyk-Kul', Ozero** *var.* Issiq Köl, *Kir.* Ysyk-Köl. ◎ E Kyrgyzstan
147 X7 **Issyk-Kul'skaya Oblast'** *Kir.* Ysyk-Köl Oblasty. ⬖ *province* E Kyrgyzstan
149 Q7 **Īstādeh-ye Moqor, Āb-e-** *var.* Āb-i-Istāda. ◎ SE Afghanistan
136 D11 **İstanbul** *Bul.* Tsarigrad, *Eng.* Istanbul, *prev.* Constantinople; *anc.* Byzantium. Istanbul, NW Turkey
114 P12 **İstanbul** ⬖ *province* NW Turkey
114 P12 **İstanbul Boğazı** *var.* Bosporus Thracius, *Eng.* Bosphorus, Bosporus, *Turk.* Karadeniz Boğazi. *strait* NW Turkey
Istarska Županija *see* Istra
115 G19 **Isthmía** Pelopónnisos, S Greece
115 G17 **Istiaía** Évvoia, C Greece
54 D9 **Istmina** Chocó, W Colombia
23 W13 **Istokpoga, Lake** ◎ Florida, SE USA
112 A9 **Istra** *off.* Istarska Županija. ⬖ *province* NW Croatia
112 I10 **Istra** *Eng.* Istria, *Ger.* Istrien. *cultural region* NW Croatia
103 R15 **Istres** Bouches-du-Rhône, SE France
Istria/Istrien *see* Istra
Iswardi *see* Ishurdi
127 V7 **Isyangulovo** Respublika Bashkortostan, W Russian Federation
62 O6 **Itá** Central, S Paraguay
59 O17 **Itaberaba** Bahia, E Brazil
59 M20 **Itabira** *prev.* Presidente Vargas. Minas Gerais, SE Brazil
59 O18 **Itabuna** Bahia, E Brazil
59 J18 **Itacaiu** Mato Grosso, S Brazil
58 G12 **Itacoatiara** Amazonas, N Brazil
54 D9 **Itagüí** Antioquia, W Colombia
60 D13 **Itá Ibaté** Corrientes, NE Argentina
60 G11 **Itaipú, Represa de** ⊠ Brazil/Paraguay
58 H13 **Itaituba** Pará, NE Brazil
60 K13 **Itajaí** Santa Catarina, S Brazil
Italia/Italiana, Republica/Italian Republic, The *see* Italy
Italian Somaliland *see* Somalia
25 T7 **Italy** Texas, SW USA
106 G12 **Italy** *off.* The Italian Republic, *It.* Italia, Repubblica Italiana. ◆ *republic* S Europe
59 O19 **Itamaraju** Bahia, E Brazil
59 C14 **Itamarati** Amazonas, W Brazil
59 M19 **Itambé, Pico de** ▲ SE Brazil
164 J13 **Itami** ✈ (Ōsaka) Ōsaka, Honshū, SW Japan
115 H15 **Ítamos** ▲ N Greece
153 W11 **Itānagar** *state capital* Arunāchal Pradesh, NE India
Itany *see* Litani
59 N19 **Itaobim** Minas Gerais, SE Brazil
59 P15 **Itaparica, Represa de** ⊠ E Brazil
58 M13 **Itapecuru-Mirim** Maranhão, E Brazil
60 Q8 **Itaperuna** Rio de Janeiro, SE Brazil
59 O18 **Itapetinga** Bahia, E Brazil
60 L10 **Itapetininga** São Paulo, S Brazil
60 K10 **Itapeva** São Paulo, S Brazil
47 W6 **Itapicuru, Rio** ≈ NE Brazil
58 O13 **Itapipoca** Ceará, E Brazil
60 M9 **Itapira** São Paulo, S Brazil
60 K8 **Itápolis** São Paulo, S Brazil
60 K10 **Itaporanga** São Paulo, S Brazil
62 P7 **Itapúa** *off.* Departamento de Itapúa. ⬖ *department* SE Paraguay
Itapúa, Departamento de *see* Itapúa
59 E15 **Itapuã do Oeste** Rondônia, W Brazil
61 E15 **Itaqui** Rio Grande do Sul, S Brazil
60 K10 **Itararé** São Paulo, S Brazil
60 K10 **Itararé, Rio** ≈ S Brazil
154 H11 **Itārsi** Madhya Pradesh, C India
25 T7 **Itasca** Texas, SW USA
Itassi *see* Vieille Case
60 D13 **Itatí** Corrientes, NE Argentina
60 K10 **Itatinga** São Paulo, S Brazil
115 F18 **Itéas, Kólpos** *gulf* C Greece
57 N15 **Iténez, Río** *var.* Rio Guaporé. ≈ Bolivia/Brazil *see also* Rio Guaporé
Iténez, Río *see* Guaporé, Rio
54 H11 **Iteviate, Río** ≈ C Colombia
100 I13 **Ith** *hill range* C Germany
31 Q8 **Ithaca** Michigan, N USA
18 H11 **Ithaca** New York, NE USA
115 C18 **Itháki** *island* Iónia Nísiá, Greece, C Mediterranean Sea
Itháki *see* Vathy
It Hearrenfean *see* Heerenveen
79 L17 **Itimbiri** ≈ N Dem. Rep. Congo
Itinomiya *see* Ichinomiya
Itinoseki *see* Ichinoseki
39 Q5 **Itkilik River** ≈ Alaska, USA
164 M11 **Itoigawa** Niigata, Honshū, C Japan
15 R6 **Itomamo, Lac** ◎ Québec, SE Canada
165 S17 **Itoman** Okinawa, SW Japan
102 M5 **Iton** ≈ N France
57 M16 **Itonamas Río** ≈ NE Bolivia
Itoupé, Mont *see* Sommet Tabulaire
Itseqqortoormiit *see* Ittoqqortoormiit
22 K4 **Itta Bena** Mississippi, S USA
107 B17 **Ittiri** Sardegna, Italy, C Mediterranean Sea
197 Q14 **Ittoqqortoormiit** *var.* Itseqqortoormiit, *Dan.* Scoresbysund, *Eng.* Scoresby Sound. Tunu, C Greenland
60 M10 **Itu** São Paulo, S Brazil
54 D8 **Ituango** Antioquia, NW Colombia
59 A14 **Ituí, Rio** ≈ NW Brazil
79 O20 **Itula** Sud Kivu, E Dem. Rep. Congo
59 K19 **Itumbiara** Goiás, C Brazil
55 T9 **Ituni** E Guyana
41 X13 **Iturbide** Campeche, SE Mexico
Ituri *see* Aruwimi
123 V13 **Iturup, Ostrov** *island* Kuril'skiye Ostrova, SE Russian Federation
60 L7 **Ituverava** São Paulo, S Brazil
59 C15 **Ituxi, Rio** ≈ W Brazil
61 E14 **Ituzaingó** Corrientes, NE Argentina
101 K18 **Itz** ≈ C Germany
100 I9 **Itzehoe** Schleswig-Holstein, N Germany
23 N2 **Iuka** Mississippi, S USA
60 I11 **Ivaiporã** Paraná, S Brazil
60 I11 **Ivaí, Rio** ≈ S Brazil
92 L10 **Ivalo** *Lapp.* Avveel, Avvil. Lappi, N Finland
92 L10 **Ivalojoki** *Lapp.* Avveel. ≈ N Finland
119 H20 **Ivanava** *Pol.* Janów, Janów Poleski, *Rus.* Ivanovo. Brestskaya Voblasts', SW Belarus
Ivangorod *see* Dęblin
Ivangrad *see* Berane
183 N7 **Ivanhoe** New South Wales, SE Australia
29 S9 **Ivanhoe** Minnesota, N USA
14 D8 **Ivanhoe** ≈ Ontario, S Canada
112 E8 **Ivanić-Grad** Sisak-Moslavina, N Croatia
117 T10 **Ivanivka** Khersons'ka Oblast', S Ukraine
117 P10 **Ivanivka** Odes'ka Oblast', SW Ukraine
113 L14 **Ivanjica** Serbia, C Serbia
112 G11 **Ivanjska** *var* Potkozarje. Republika Srpska, NW Bosnia and Herzegovina
111 H21 **Ivanka** ✈ (Bratislava) Bratislavský Kraj, W Slovakia
117 O3 **Ivankiv** *Rus.* Ivankov. Kyyivs'ka Oblast', N Ukraine
Ivankov *see* Ivankiv
39 O15 **Ivanof Bay** Alaska, USA
116 J7 **Ivano-Frankivs'k** *Ger.* Stanislau, *Pol.* Stanisławów, *Rus.* Ivano-Frankovsk; *prev.* Stanislav. Ivano-Frankivs'ka Oblast', W Ukraine
Ivano-Frankivs'k *see* Ivano-Frankivs'ka Oblast'
116 I7 **Ivano-Frankivs'ka Oblast'** *var.* Ivano-Frankivs'k, *Rus.* Ivano-Frankovskaya Oblast'; *prev.* Stanislavskaya Oblast'. ⬖ *province* W Ukraine
Ivano-Frankovsk *see* Ivano-Frankivs'k
Ivano-Frankovskaya Oblast' *see* Ivano-Frankivs'ka Oblast'
124 M16 **Ivanovo** Ivanovskaya Oblast', W Russian Federation
Ivanovo *see* Ivanava
124 M16 **Ivanovskaya Oblast'** ⬖ *province* W Russian Federation
35 X12 **Ivanpah Lake** ◎ California, W USA
112 E7 **Ivanščica** ▲▲ NE Croatia
114 M8 **Ivanski** Shumen, NE Bulgaria
127 R7 **Ivanteyevka** Saratovskaya Oblast', W Russian Federation
Ivantsevichi/Ivatsevichi *see* Ivatsevichy
116 I4 **Ivanychi** Volyns'ka Oblast', NW Ukraine
119 H18 **Ivatsevichy** *Pol.* Iwacewicze, *Rus.* Ivantsevichi, Ivatsevichi. Brestskaya Voblasts', SW Belarus
114 L12 **Ivaylovgrad** Khaskovska Oblast, S Bulgaria
114 K11 **Ivaylovgrad, Yazovir** ⊠ S Bulgaria
122 G9 **Ivdel'** Sverdlovskaya Oblast', C Russian Federation
Ivenets *see* Ivyanyets
116 L12 **Iveşti** Galaţi, E Romania
Ivgovuotna *see* Lyngen
Ivigtut *see* Ivittuut
79 F18 **Ivindo** ≈ Congo/Gabon
59 I21 **Ivinheima** Mato Grosso do Sul, SW Brazil
196 M15 **Ivittuut** *var.* Ivigtut. Kitaa, S Greenland
Iviza *see* Ibiza
Iviza *see* Eivissa
172 I6 **Ivohibe** Fianarantsoa, SE Madagascar
Ivoire, Côte d' *see* Ivory Coast
76 L15 **Ivory Coast** *off.* Republic of the Ivory Coast, *Fr.* Côte d'Ivoire, République de la Côte d'Ivoire. ◆ *republic* W Africa
68 C12 **Ivory Coast** *Fr.* Côte d'Ivoire. *coastal region* S Ivory Coast
Ivory Coast, Republic of the *see* Ivory Coast
95 L22 **Ivösjön** ◎ S Sweden
106 B7 **Ivrea** *anc.* Eporedia. Piemonte, NW Italy
12 J2 **Ivujivik** Québec, NE Canada
119 J16 **Ivyanyets** *Rus.* Ivenets. Minskaya Voblasts', C Belarus
Iv'ye *see* Iwye
Iwacewicze *see* Ivatsevichy
165 R8 **Iwaizumi** Iwate, Honshū, NE Japan
165 P12 **Iwaki** Fukushima, Honshū, N Japan
164 F13 **Iwakuni** Yamaguchi, Honshū, SW Japan
165 S4 **Iwamizawa** Hokkaidō, NE Japan
165 R4 **Iwanai** Hokkaidō, NE Japan
165 Q10 **Iwanuma** Miyagi, Honshū, C Japan
164 L14 **Iwata** Shizuoka, Honshū, S Japan
165 R8 **Iwate** Iwate, Honshū, N Japan
165 R8 **Iwate** *off.* Iwate-ken. ⬖ *prefecture* Honshū, C Japan
Iwate-ken *see* Iwate
77 S16 **Iwo** Oyo, SW Nigeria
Iwojima *see* Iō-jima
119 I16 **Iwye** *Pol.* Iwje, *Rus.* Iv'ye. Hrodzyenskaya Voblasts', W Belarus
42 C4 **Ixcán, Río** ≈ Guatemala/Mexico
99 G18 **Ixelles** *Dut.* Elsene. Brussels, C Belgium
57 J16 **Ixiamas** La Paz, NW Bolivia
41 O13 **Ixmiquilpan** *var.* Ixmiquilpán. Hidalgo, C Mexico
Ixmiquilpán *see* Ixmiquilpan
83 K23 **Ixopo** KwaZulu/Natal, E South Africa
Ixtaccíhuatal, Volcán *see* Iztaccíhuati, Volcán
40 M16 **Ixtapa** Guerrero, S Mexico
41 S16 **Ixtepec** Oaxaca, SE Mexico
40 K12 **Ixtlán** *var.* Ixtlán del Río. Nayarit, C Mexico
Ixtlán del Río *see* Ixtlán
122 H11 **Iyevlevo** Tyumenskaya Oblast', C Russian Federation
164 F14 **Iyo** Ehime, Shikoku, SW Japan
164 E14 **Iyo-nada** *sea* S Japan
42 E4 **Izabal** *off.* Departamento de Izabal. ⬖ *department* E Guatemala
Izabal, Departamento de *see* Izabal
42 F5 **Izabal, Lago de** *prev.* Golfo Dulce. ◎ E Guatemala
143 O9 **Īzad Khvāst** Fārs, C Iran
41 X12 **Izamal** Yucatán, SE Mexico
127 Q16 **Izberbash** Respublika Dagestan, SW Russian Federation
99 C18 **Izegem** *prev.* Iseghem. West-Vlaanderen, W Belgium
142 M9 **Īzeh** Khūzestān, SW Iran
165 T16 **Izena-jima** *island* Nansei-shotō, SW Japan
114 N10 **Izgrev** Burgas, E Bulgaria
127 T2 **Izhevsk** *prev.* Ustinov. Udmurtskaya Respublika, NW Russian Federation
125 S7 **Izhma** Respublika Komi, NW Russian Federation
125 S7 **Izhma** ≈ NW Russian Federation
141 X8 **Izkī** NE Oman
Izmail *see* Izmayil
117 N13 **Izmayil** *Rus.* Izmail. Odes'ka Oblast', SW Ukraine
136 B14 **İzmir** *prev.* Smyrna. İzmır, W Turkey
136 C14 **İzmir** *prev.* Smyrna. ⬖ *province* W Turkey
136 E11 **İzmit** *var.* Ismid; *anc.* Astacus. Kocaeli, NW Turkey
104 M14 **Iznájar** Andalucía, S Spain
104 M14 **Iznajar, Embalse de** ⊠ S Spain
105 N14 **Iznalloz** Andalucía, S Spain
136 E11 **İznik** Bursa, NW Turkey
136 E12 **İznik Gölü** ◎ NW Turkey
126 M14 **Izobil'nyy** Stavropol'skiy Kray, SW Russian Federation
109 S13 **Izola** *It.* Isola d'Istria. SW Slovenia
138 H9 **Izra'** *var.* Ezra, Ezraa. Dar'ā, S Syria
41 P14 **Iztaccíhuati, Volcán** *var.* Volcán Ixtaccíhuatal. ⛰ S Mexico
42 C7 **Iztapa** Escuintla, SE Guatemala
Izúcar de Matamoros *see* Matamoros
165 N14 **Izu-hantō** *peninsula* Honshū, S Japan
164 C12 **Izuhara** Nagasaki, Tsushima, SW Japan
164 J14 **Izumiōtsu** Ōsaka, Honshū, SW Japan
164 I14 **Izumi-Sano** Ōsaka, Honshū, SW Japan
164 G12 **Izumo** Shimane, Honshū, SW Japan
192 H5 **Izu Trench** *undersea feature* NW Pacific Ocean
122 K6 **Izvestiy TsIK, Ostrova** *island* N Russian Federation
114 G10 **Izvor** Pernik, W Bulgaria
116 L5 **Izyaslav** Khmel'nyts'ka Oblast', W Ukraine
117 W6 **Izyum** Kharkivs'ka Oblast', E Ukraine

J

93 M18 **Jaala** Kymi, S Finland
140 J5 **Jabal ash Shifā** *desert* NW Saudi Arabia
141 U8 **Jabal az̧ Z̧annah** *var.* Jebel Dhanna. Abū Z̧aby, W United Arab Emirates
138 E11 **Jabalīya** *var.* Jabāliyah. NE Gaza Strip
Jabāliyah *see* Jabalīya
105 N11 **Jabalón** ≈ C Spain
154 J10 **Jabalpur** *prev.* Jubbulpore. Madhya Pradesh, C India
141 N15 **Jabal Zuuqar, Jazīrat** *var.* Az Zuqur. *island* SW Yemen
Jabat *see* Jabwot
138 J3 **Jabbūl, Sabkhat al** *sabkha* NW Syria
181 P1 **Jabiru** Northern Territory, N Australia
138 H4 **Jablah** *var.* Jeble, *Fr.* Djéblé. Al Lādhiqīyah, W Syria
112 C11 **Jablanac** Lika-Senj, W Croatia
113 H14 **Jablanica** Federacija Bosna I Hercegovina, SW Bosnia and Herzegovina
113 M20 **Jablanica** *Alb.* Mali i Jabllanicës, *var.* Malet e Jabllanicës. ▲ Albania/FYR Macedonia *see also* Jabllanicës, Mali i
Jabllanicës, Malet e *see* Jablanica/Jabllanicës, Mali i
113 M20 **Jabllanicës, Mali i**, *Mac.* Jablanica. ▲ Albania/FYR Macedonia *see also* Jablanica
111 E15 **Jablonec nad Nisou** *Ger.* Gablonz an der Neisse. Liberecký Kraj, N Czech Republic
Jabłonków/Jablunkau *see* Jablunkov
110 J9 **Jabłonowo Pomorskie** Kujawski-pomorskie, C Poland
111 J17 **Jablunkov** *Ger.* Jablunkau, *Pol.* Jabłonków. Moravskoslezský Kraj, E Czech Republic
59 Q15 **Jaboatão** Pernambuco, E Brazil
60 L8 **Jaboticabal** São Paulo, S Brazil
189 U7 **Jabwot** *var.* Jabat, Jebat, Jōwat. *island* Ralik Chain, S Marshall Islands
105 S4 **Jaca** Aragón, NE Spain
42 B4 **Jacaltenango** Huehuetenango, W Guatemala
59 G14 **Jacaré-a-Canga** Pará, NE Brazil
60 N10 **Jacareí** São Paulo, S Brazil
59 I18 **Jaciara** Mato Grosso, W Brazil
59 E15 **Jaciparaná** Rondônia, W Brazil
19 P5 **Jackman** Maine, NE USA
35 X1 **Jackpot** Nevada, W USA
20 M8 **Jacksboro** Tennessee, S USA
25 S6 **Jacksboro** Texas, SW USA
23 N7 **Jackson** Alabama, S USA
35 P7 **Jackson** California, W USA
23 T4 **Jackson** Georgia, SE USA
21 O6 **Jackson** Kentucky, S USA
22 J8 **Jackson** Louisiana, S USA
31 Q10 **Jackson** Michigan, N USA
29 T11 **Jackson** Minnesota, N USA
22 K5 **Jackson** *state capital* Mississippi, S USA
27 Y7 **Jackson** Missouri, C USA
21 W8 **Jackson** North Carolina, SE USA
31 T15 **Jackson** Ohio, NE USA
20 G9 **Jackson** Tennessee, S USA
33 S14 **Jackson** Wyoming, C USA
185 C19 **Jackson Bay** *bay* South Island, New Zealand
186 E9 **Jackson Field** ✈ (Port Moresby) Central/National Capital District, S Papua New Guinea
185 C20 **Jackson Head** *headland* South Island, New Zealand
23 S8 **Jackson, Lake** ◎ Florida, SE USA
33 S13 **Jackson Lake** ◎ Wyoming, C USA
194 J6 **Jackson, Mount** ▲ Antarctica
37 U3 **Jackson Reservoir** ◎ Colorado, C USA
23 Q3 **Jacksonville** Alabama, S USA
27 V11 **Jacksonville** Arkansas, C USA
23 W8 **Jacksonville** Florida, SE USA
30 K14 **Jacksonville** Illinois, N USA
21 W11 **Jacksonville** North Carolina, SE USA
25 W7 **Jacksonville** Texas, SW USA
23 X9 **Jacksonville Beach** Florida, SE USA
44 L9 **Jacmel** *var.* Jaquemel. S Haiti
Jacob *see* Nkayi
149 Q12 **Jacobābād** Sind, SE Pakistan
55 T11 **Jacobs Ladder Falls** *waterfall* S Guyana
45 O11 **Jaco, Pointe** *headland* N Dominica
15 Q9 **Jacques-Cartier** ≈ Québec, SE Canada
13 P11 **Jacques-Cartier, Détroit de** *var.* Jacques-Cartier Passage. *strait* Gulf of St. Lawrence/St. Lawrence River
15 W6 **Jacques-Cartier, Mont** ▲ Québec, SE Canada
Jacques-Cartier Passage *see* Jacques-Cartier, Détroit de
61 H16 **Jacuí, Rio** ≈ S Brazil
60 L11 **Jacupiranga** São Paulo, S Brazil
100 G10 **Jade** ≈ NW Germany
100 G10 **Jadebusen** *bay* NW Germany
Jadotville *see* Likasi
Jadransko More/Jadransko Morje *see* Adriatic Sea
105 O7 **Jadraque** Castilla-La Mancha, C Spain
95 I22 **Jægerspris** Frederiksborg, E Denmark
56 C10 **Jaén** Cajamarca, N Peru
105 N13 **Jaén** Andalucía, SW Spain
105 N13 **Jaén** ⬖ *province* Andalucía, S Spain
95 C17 **Jæren** *physical region* S Norway
155 J23 **Jaffna** Northern Province, N Sri Lanka
155 K23 **Jaffna Lagoon** *lagoon* N Sri Lanka
19 N10 **Jaffrey** New Hampshire, NE USA
138 H13 **Jafr, Qā' al** *var.* El Jafr. *salt pan* S Jordan
152 J9 **Jagādhri** Haryāna, N India
118 H4 **Jägala** *var.* Jägala Jõgi, *Ger.* Jaggowal. ≈ NW Estonia
Jägala Jõgi *see* Jägala
Jagannath *see* Puri
155 L14 **Jagdalpur** Chhattīsgarh, C India
163 U5 **Jagdaqi** Nei Mongol Zizhiqu, N China
Jägerndorf *see* Krnov
Jaggowal *see* Jägala
139 O2 **Jaghjaghah, Nahr** ≈ N Syria
112 N13 **Jagodina** *prev.* Svetozarevo. Serbia, C Serbia
112 K12 **Jagodnja** ▲▲ W Serbia
101 I20 **Jagst** ≈ SW Germany
155 I14 **Jagtiāl** Andhra Pradesh, C India
61 H18 **Jaguarão** Rio Grande do Sul, S Brazil
61 H18 **Jaguarão, Rio** *var.* Río Yaguarón. ≈ Brazil/Uruguay
60 K11 **Jaguariaíva** Paraná, S Brazil
44 D5 **Jagüey Grande** Matanzas, W Cuba
153 P14 **Jahānābād** Bihār, N India
Jahra *see* Al Jahrā'
143 P12 **Jahrom** *var.* Jahrum. Fārs, S Iran
Jahrum *see* Jahrom
Jailolo *see* Halmahera, Pulau
Jainat *see* Chai Nat
Jainti *see* Jayanti
152 H12 **Jaipur** *prev.* Jeypore. *state capital* Rājasthān, N India
153 T14 **Jaipur Hat** Rajshahi, NW Bangladesh
152 D11 **Jaisalmer** Rājasthān, NW India
154 O12 **Jājapur** Orissa, E India
143 R4 **Jājarm** Khorāsān-e Shemālī, NE Iran
112 G12 **Jajce** Federacija Bosna I Hercegovina, W Bosnia and Herzegovina
Jajī *see* 'Alī Kheyl
83 D17 **Jakalsberg** Otjozondjupa, N Namibia
169 O15 **Jakarta** *prev.* Djakarta, *Dut.* Batavia. ● (Indonesia) Jawa, C Indonesia
10 I8 **Jakes Corner** Yukon Territory, W Canada
152 H9 **Jākhal** Haryāna, NW India
Jakobeny *see* Iacobeni
93 K16 **Jakobstad** *Fin.* Pietarsaari. Länsi-Suomi, W Finland
Jakobstadt *see* Jēkabpils
113 O18 **Jakupica** ▲▲ C FYR Macedonia
37 W15 **Jal** New Mexico, SW USA
141 P7 **Jalājil** *var.* Ğalāğīl. Ar Riyāḑ, C Saudi Arabia
149 S5 **Jalālābād** *var.* Jalalabad, Jelalabad. Nangarhār, E Afghanistan
Jalal-Abad *see* Dzhalal-Abad
Jalal-Abad Oblasty *see* Dzhalal-Abadskaya Oblast'
149 V7 **Jalālpur** Punjab, E Pakistan
149 T11 **Jalālpur Pīrwāla** Punjab, E Pakistan
152 H8 **Jalandhar** *prev.* Jullundur. Punjab, N India
42 J7 **Jalán, Río** ≈ S Honduras
42 E6 **Jalapa** Jalapa, C Guatemala
42 J7 **Jalapa** Nueva Segovia, NW Nicaragua
42 A3 **Jalapa** *off.* Departamento de Jalapa. ⬖ *department* SE Guatemala
Jalapa, Departamento de *see* Jalapa
42 E6 **Jalapa, Río** ≈ SE Guatemala
143 X13 **Jālaq** Sīstān va Balūchestān, SE Iran
93 K17 **Jalasjärvi** Länsi-Soumi, W Finland
149 O8 **Jaldak** Zābol, SE Afghanistan
60 J7 **Jales** São Paulo, S Brazil
154 P11 **Jaleshwar** *var.* Jaleswar. Orissa, NE India
Jaleswar *see* Jaleshwar
154 F12 **Jalgaon** Mahārāshtra, C India
139 W12 **Jalībah** S Iraq
139 W13 **Jalīb Shahāb** S Iraq
77 X15 **Jalingo** Taraba, E Nigeria
40 K13 **Jalisco** ⬖ *state* SW Mexico
154 G13 **Jālna** Mahārāshtra, W India
Jalomitsa *see* Ialomiţa
105 R5 **Jalón** ≈ N Spain
152 E13 **Jālor** Rājasthān, N India
112 K11 **Jalovik** Serbia, W Serbia
40 L12 **Jalpa** Zacatecas, C Mexico
153 S12 **Jalpāiguri** West Bengal, NE India
41 O12 **Jalpán** *var.* Jalpan. Querétaro de Arteaga, C Mexico
Jalpan *see* Jalpán
67 P2 **Jalta** *island* N Tunisia
75 S9 **Jālū** *var.* Jūlā. NE Libya
189 U8 **Jaluit Atoll** *var.* Jālwōj. *atoll* Ralik Chain, S Marshall Islands
Jālwōj *see* Jaluit Atoll
81 L18 **Jamaame** *It.* Giamame; *prev.* Margherita. Jubbada Hoose, S Somalia
77 W13 **Jamaare** ≈ NE Nigeria
44 G9 **Jamaica** ◆ *island state* W West Indies
47 P3 **Jamaica** *island* W West Indies
44 I9 **Jamaica Channel** *channel* Haiti/Jamaica
153 T14 **Jamalpur** Dhaka, N Bangladesh
153 Q14 **Jamālpur** Bihār, NE India
168 L9 **Jamaluang** *var.* Jemaluang. Johor, Peninsular Malaysia
59 I14 **Jamanxim, Rio** ≈ C Brazil
56 B8 **Jambeli, Canal de** *channel* S Ecuador
99 I20 **Jambes** Namur, SE Belgium
168 L12 **Jambi** *var.* Telanaipura; *prev.* Djambi. Sumatera, W Indonesia
168 K12 **Jambi** *off.* Propinsi Jambi, *var.* Djambi. ⬖ *province* W Indonesia
Jambi, Propinsi *see* Jambi
Jamdena *see* Yamdena, Pulau
12 H8 **James Bay** *bay* Ontario/Québec, E Canada

◆ Country ● Country Capital ◇ Dependent Territory ○ Dependent Territory Capital ⬖ Administrative Regions ✈ International Airport ▲ Mountain ▲▲ Mountain Range ⛰ Volcano ≈ River ◎ Lake ⊠ Reservoir

63 F19 **James, Isla** *island* Archipiélago de los Chonos, S Chile

181 Q8 **James Ranges** ▲ Northern Territory, C Australia

29 P8 **James River** ♒ North Dakota/South Dakota, N USA

21 X7 **James River** ♒ Virginia, NE USA

194 H4 **James Ross Island** *island* Antarctica

182 I8 **Jamestown** South Australia

65 G25 **Jamestown** ○ (Saint Helena) NW Saint Helena

35 P8 **Jamestown** California, W USA

20 L7 **Jamestown** Kentucky, S USA

18 D11 **Jamestown** New York, NE USA

29 P5 **Jamestown** North Dakota, N USA

20 L8 **Jamestown** Tennessee, S USA *see* Holetown

15 N10 **Jamet** ♒ Québec, SE Canada

41 Q17 **Jamiltepec** *var.* Santiago Jamiltepec. Oaxaca, SE Mexico

95 F20 **Jammerbugten** *bay* Skagerrak, E North Sea

152 H6 **Jammu** *prev.* Jummoo. *state capital* Jammu and Kashmir, NW India

152 I5 **Jammu and Kashmir** *var.* Jammu-Kashmir, Kashmir. ◆ *state* NW India

149 V4 **Jammu and Kashmir** *disputed region* India/Pakistan
Jammu-Kashmir *see* Jammu and Kashmir

154 B10 **Jāmnagar** *prev.* Navanagar. Gujarāt, W India

149 S11 **Jāmpur** Punjab, E Pakistan

93 L18 **Jämsä** Länsi-Suomi, C Finland

93 L18 **Jämsänkoski** Länsi-Suomi, C Finland

153 Q16 **Jamshedpur** Jhārkhand, NE India

94 K9 **Jämtland** ◆ *county* C Sweden

153 Q14 **Jamūi** Bihār, NE India

153 T14 **Jamuna** ♒ N Bangladesh
Jamuna *see* Brahmaputra
Jamundá *see* Nhamundá, Rio

54 D11 **Jamundí** Valle del Cauca, SW Colombia

153 Q12 **Janakpur** Central, C Nepal

59 N18 **Janaúba** Minas Gerais, SE Brazil

58 K11 **Janaucu, Ilha** *island* NE Brazil

143 Q7 **Jandaq** Eşfahān, C Iran

64 Q11 **Jandía, Punta de** *headland* Fuerteventura, Islas Canarias, Spain, NE Atlantic Ocean

59 B14 **Jandiatuba, Rio** ♒ NW Brazil

105 N12 **Jándula** ♒ S Spain

29 V10 **Janesville** Minnesota, N USA

30 L9 **Janesville** Wisconsin, N USA

149 N13 **Jangal** Baluchistān, SW Pakistan

83 N20 **Jangamo** Inhambane, SE Mozambique

155 J14 **Jangaon** Andhra Pradesh, C India

153 S14 **Jangīpur** West Bengal, NE India
Janina *see* Ioánnina
Janischken *see* Joniškis

112 J11 **Janja** NE Bosnia and Herzegovina
Jankovac *see* Jánoshalma

197 Q15 **Jan Mayen** ◇ *Norwegian dependency* N Atlantic Ocean

84 D5 **Jan Mayen** *island* N Atlantic Ocean

197 R15 **Jan Mayen Fracture Zone** *tectonic feature* Greenland Sea/Norwegian Sea

197 R15 **Jan Mayen Ridge** *undersea feature* Greenland Sea/Norwegian Sea

40 H3 **Janos** Chihuahua, N Mexico

111 K25 **Jánoshalma** *SCr.* Jankovac. Bács-Kiskun, S Hungary
Janów *see* Ivanava, Belarus

110 H10 **Janowiec Wielkopolski** *Ger.* Janowitz. Kujawski-pomorskie, C Poland
Janowitz *see* Janowiec Wielkopolski
Janow/Janów *see* Jonava, Lithuania

111 O15 **Janów Lubelski** Lubelski, E Poland
Janów Poleski *see* Ivanava

83 H25 **Jansenville** Eastern Cape, S South Africa

59 M18 **Januária** Minas Gerais, SE Brazil
Janūbīyah, Al Bādiyah al *see* Ash Shāmīyah

102 I7 **Janzé** Ille-et-Vilaine, NW France

154 F10 **Jaora** Madhya Pradesh, C India

131 Y9 **Japan** *var.* Nippon, *Jap.* Nihon. ◆ *monarchy* E Asia

129 Y9 **Japan** *island group* E Asia

192 H4 **Japan Basin** *undersea feature* N Sea of Japan

129 Y8 **Japan, Sea of** *var.* East Sea, *Rus.* Yaponskoye More. *sea* NW Pacific Ocean *see also* East Sea

192 H4 **Japan Trench** *undersea feature* NW Pacific Ocean

59 A15 **Japiim** *var.* Máncio Lima. Acre, W Brazil

58 D12 **Japurá** Amazonas, N Brazil

58 C12 **Japurá, Rio** *var.* Río Caquetá, Yapurá. ♒ Brazil/Colombia *see also* Caquetá, Río
Japurá, Rio *see* Caquetá, Río

43 W17 **Jaqué** Darién, SE Panama
Jaqueme *see* Jacmel
Jarablos *see* Jarābulus

138 K2 **Jarābulus** *var.* Jarablos, Jerablus, *Fr.* Djérablous. Halab, N Syria

60 K13 **Jaraguá do Sul** Santa Catarina, S Brazil

104 K9 **Jaraicejo** Extremadura, W Spain

104 K9 **Jaraíz de la Vera** Extremadura, W Spain

105 O7 **Jarama** ♒ C Spain

104 J20 **Jaramillo** Santa Cruz, SE Argentina
Jarandilla de la Vega *see* Jarandilla de la Vera

104 K8 **Jarandilla de la Vera** *var.* Jarandilla de la Vega. Extremadura, W Spain

149 V9 **Jaranwāla** Punjab, E Pakistan

138 G9 **Jarash** *var.* Jerash; *anc.* Gerasa. Irbid, NW Jordan

94 N13 **Järbo** Gävleborg, C Sweden
Jardan *see* Yordan

44 F7 **Jardines de la Reina, Archipiélago de los** *island group* C Cuba

162 I8 **Jargalang** Bayanhongor, C Mongolia

162 K6 **Jargalant** Bulgan, N Mongolia

162 G7 **Jargalant** *var.* Buyanbat. Govĭ-Altay, W Mongolia

162 I6 **Jargalant** *var.* Orgil. Hövsgöl, C Mongolia
Jargalant *see* Battsengel
Jargalant *see* Bulgan
Jargalant *see* Biger

58 I11 **Jari, Shatt al** *see* Jerid, Chott el

141 N7 **Jari, Rio** *var.* Jary.

94 L13 **Jarīr, Wādī al** *dry watercourse* C Saudi Arabia
Jarja *see* Yur'ya

95 O16 **Järna** *var.* Dala-Jarna. Dalarna, C Sweden

102 K11 **Järna** Stockholm, C Sweden

110 H12 **Jarnac** Charente, W France

111 F16 **Jarocin** Wielkopolskie, C Poland

111 O16 **Jaroměř** *Ger.* Jermer. Královéhradecký Kraj, N Czech Republic

93 F16 **Jarosław** *Ger.* Jaroslau, *Rus.* Yaroslav. Podkarpackie, SE Poland
Jaroslau *see* Jarosław

147 O14 **Järpen** Jämtland, C Sweden

139 P2 **Jarqo'rg'on** *Rus.* Dzharkurgan. Surkhondaryo Viloyati, S Uzbekistan

162 K14 **Jarrāh, Wadi** *dry watercourse* NE Syria
Jars, Plain of *see* Xiangkhoang, Plateau de

59 E16 **Jartai Yanchi** ⊚ N China

118 I4 **Jaru** Rondônia, W Brazil
Jarud Qi *see* Lubei

118 G5 **Järva-Jaani** *Ger.* Sankt-Johannis. Järvamaa, N Estonia

118 H4 **Järvakandi** *Ger.* Jerwakant. Raplamaa, NW Estonia

93 L19 **Järvamaa** *var.* Järva Maakond. ◆ *province* N Estonia
Järva Maakond *see* Järvamaa

14 G17 **Järvenpää** Uusimaa, S Finland

177 R8 **Jarvis** Ontario, S Canada

94 M11 **Jarvis Island** ◇ *US unincorporated territory* C Pacific Ocean

112 M9 **Järvsö** Gävleborg, C Sweden
Jary *see* Jari, Rio

112 D12 **Jaša Tomić** Vojvodina, NE Serbia

138 I11 **Jasenice** Zadar, SW Croatia

77 Q16 **Jashshat al 'Adlah, Wādī al** *dry watercourse* C Jordan

146 F6 **Jasikan** E Ghana

Jāsk *var.* Bandar-e Jāsk. Hormozgān, S Iran

Jasliq *Rus.* Zhaslyk. Qoraqalpoghiston Respublikasi, NW Uzbekistan

111 N17 **Jasło** Podkarpackie, SE Poland

9 U16 **Jasmin** Saskatchewan, S Canada

65 A23 **Jason Islands** *island group* NW Falkland Islands

194 I4 **Jason Peninsula** *peninsula* Antarctica

31 N15 **Jasonville** Indiana, N USA

9 O15 **Jasper** Alberta, SW Canada

14 L13 **Jasper** Ontario, SE Canada

23 S9 **Jasper** Alabama, S USA

27 T9 **Jasper** Arkansas, C USA

23 U8 **Jasper** Florida, SE USA

31 N16 **Jasper** Indiana, N USA

29 R11 **Jasper** Minnesota, N USA

27 S7 **Jasper** Missouri, C USA

20 K10 **Jasper** Tennessee, S USA

25 Y9 **Jasper** Texas, SW USA

9 O15 **Jasper National Park** *national park* Alberta/British Columbia, SW Canada
Jassy *see* Iaşi

113 N14 **Jastrebac** ▲ SE Serbia

112 D9 **Jastrebarsko** Grad Zagreb, N Croatia
Jastrow *see* Jastrowie

110 G9 **Jastrowie** *Ger.* Jastrow. Wielkopolskie, C Poland

111 J17 **Jastrzębie-Zdrój** Śląskie, S Poland

111 L22 **Jászapáti** Jász-Nagykun-Szolnok, E Hungary

111 L22 **Jászberény** Jász-Nagykun-Szolnok, E Hungary

111 L23 **Jász-Nagykun-Szolnok** *off.* Jász-Nagykun-Szolnok Megye. ◆ *county* E Hungary
Jász-Nagykun-Szolnok Megye *see* Jász-Nagykun-Szolnok

59 J20 **Jataí** Goiás, C Brazil

58 G12 **Jatapu, Serra do** ▲ N Brazil

41 W16 **Jatate, Río** ♒ SE Mexico

149 P17 **Jāti** Sind, SE Pakistan

44 F6 **Jatibonico** Sancti Spíritus, C Cuba

169 O16 **Jatiluhur, Danau** ⊚ Jawa, S Indonesia

169 R13 **Jati, Sungai** ♒ Borneo, N Indonesia

149 S11 **Jattoi** Punjab, E Pakistan

59 L20 **Jaú** São Paulo, S Brazil

58 F11 **Jauaperi, Rio** ♒ N Brazil

99 J19 **Jauche** Walloon Brabant, C Belgium
Jauer *see* Jawor

149 U7 **Jauharābād** Punjab, E Pakistan

57 E14 **Jauja** Junín, C Peru

41 O10 **Jaumave** Tamaulipas, C Mexico

118 H10 **Jaunjelgava** *Ger.* Friedrichstadt. Aizkraukle, S Latvia

118 I8 **Jaunlatgale** *see* Pytalovo

118 E9 **Jaunpils** Tukums, C Latvia

153 P13 **Jaunpur** Uttar Pradesh, N India

29 N8 **Java** South Dakota, N USA
Java Sea *see* Jawa, Laut

105 R9 **Javalambre** ▲ E Spain

173 V7 **Java Ridge** *undersea feature* E Indian Ocean

169 Q15 **Java Sea** *Ind.* Laut Jawa. *sea* W Indonesia

173 U7 **Java Trench** *var.* Sunda Trench. *undersea feature* E Indian Ocean

143 Q10 **Javazm** *var.* Jowzam. Kermān, C Iran

105 T11 **Jávea** *Cat.* Xàbia. País Valenciano, E Spain
Javhlant *see* Bayan-Ovoo

63 G20 **Javier, Isla** *island* S Chile

113 L14 **Javor** ▲ Bosnia and Herzegovina/Serbia

111 K20 **Javorie** *Hung.* Jávoros. ▲ S Slovakia
Jávoros *see* Javorie

93 J14 **Jävre** Norrbotten, N Sweden

192 E8 **Jawa, Eng.** Java; *prev.* Djawa. *island* C Indonesia

169 O16 **Jawa Barat** *off.* Propinsi Jawa Barat, *Eng.* West Java. ◆ *province* S Indonesia
Jawa Barat, Propinsi *see* Jawa Barat

Jawa, Laut *see* Java Sea

139 R3 **Jawān** NW Iraq

169 P16 **Jawa Tengah** *off.* Propinsi Jawa Tengah, *Eng.* Central Java. ◆ *province* S Indonesia
Jawa Tengah, Propinsi *see* Jawa Tengah

169 R16 **Jawa Timur** *off.* Propinsi Jawa Timur, *Eng.* East Java. ◆ *province* S Indonesia
Jawa Timur, Propinsi *see* Jawa Timur

81 N17 **Jawhar** *var.* Jowhar, *It.* Giohar. Shabeellaha Dhexe, S Somalia

111 F14 **Jawor** *Ger.* Jauer. Dolnośląskie, SW Poland
Jaworów *see* Yavoriv

111 J16 **Jaworzno** Śląskie, S Poland
Jaxartes *see* Syr Darya

27 R9 **Jay** Oklahoma, C USA
Jayabum *see* Chaiyaphum
Jayanath *see* Chai Nat

153 T12 **Jayanti** *prev.* Jainti. West Bengal, NE India

171 X14 **Jaya, Puncak** *prev.* Puntjak Carstensz, Puntjak Sukarno. ▲ Papua, E Indonesia

171 Z13 **Jayapura** *var.* Djajapura, *Dut.* Hollandia; *prev.* Kotabaru, Sukarnapura. Papua, E Indonesia

147 S12 **Jayhawker State** *see* Kansas

155 L14 **Jaypur** *var.* Jeypore, Jeypur. Orissa, E India

25 O6 **Jayton** Texas, SW USA

143 U13 **Jaz Mūriān, Hāmūn-e** ⊚ SE Iran

138 M4 **Jazrah** Ar Raqqah, C Syria

138 G6 **Jba'ī** *var.* Jebeil, Jubayl, Jubeil; *anc.* Biblical Gebal, Bybles. W Lebanon

25 O7 **J. B. Thomas, Lake** ⊡ Texas, SW USA
Jdaïdé *see* Judaydah

35 X12 **Jean** Nevada, W USA

22 I9 **Jeanerette** Louisiana, S USA

44 L8 **Jean-Rabel** NW Haiti

143 T12 **Jebāl Bārez, Kūh-e** ▲ SE Iran

77 T15 **Jebba** Kwara, W Nigeria
Jebeil *see* Jba'ī

116 E12 **Jebel** *Hung.* Széphely; *prev. Hung.* Zsebely. Timiş, W Romania

146 B11 **Jebel** *Rus.* Dzhebel. Balkan Welaýaty, W Turkmenistan
Jebel, Bahr el *see* White Nile
Jebel Dhanna *see* Jabal aẓ Zannah
Jeble *see* Jablah

96 K13 **Jedburgh** SE Scotland, UK
Jedda *see* Jiddah

111 L15 **Jędrzejów** *Ger.* Endersdorf. Świętokrzyskie, C Poland

100 K12 **Jeetze** *var.* Jeetzel. ♒ C Germany
Jeetzel *see* Jeetze

29 U14 **Jefferson** Iowa, C USA

21 Q8 **Jefferson** North Carolina, SE USA

25 X6 **Jefferson** Texas, SW USA

30 M9 **Jefferson** Wisconsin, N USA

27 U5 **Jefferson City** *state capital* Missouri, C USA

21 N9 **Jefferson City** Tennessee, S USA

33 R10 **Jefferson City** Montana, NW USA

35 U7 **Jefferson, Mount** ▲ Nevada, W USA

32 H12 **Jefferson, Mount** ▲ Oregon, NW USA

20 L5 **Jeffersontown** Kentucky, S USA

31 P16 **Jeffersonville** Indiana, N USA

33 V15 **Jeffrey City** Wyoming, C USA

77 T13 **Jega** Kebbi, NW Nigeria
Jehol *see* Chengde

62 P5 **Jejuí-Guazú, Río** ♒ E Paraguay

118 I10 **Jēkabpils** *Ger.* Jakobstadt. S Latvia

23 W7 **Jekyll Island** *island* Georgia, SE USA

169 N14 **Jelai, Sungai** ♒ Borneo, N Indonesia
Jelalabad *see* Jalālābād

111 H14 **Jelcz-Laskowice** Dolnośląskie, SW Poland

111 E14 **Jelenia Góra** *Ger.* Hirschberg, Hirschberg im Riesengebirge, Hirschberg in Riesengebirge, Hirschberg in Schlesien. Dolnośląskie, SW Poland

112 L13 **Jelica** ▲ C Serbia

20 M8 **Jellico** Tennessee, S USA

95 G23 **Jelling** Vejle, C Denmark

169 N9 **Jemaja, Pulau** *island* W Indonesia
Jemappes *see* Jemmapes

99 E20 **Jemappes** Hainaut, S Belgium

169 S17 **Jember** *prev.* Djember. Jawa, C Indonesia

99 I20 **Jemeppe-sur-Sambre** Namur, S Belgium

37 R10 **Jemez Pueblo** New Mexico, SW USA

158 K2 **Jeminay** Xinjiang Uygur Zizhiqu, NW China

189 U5 **Jemo Island** *atoll* Ratak Chain, C Marshall Islands

169 U11 **Jempang, Danau** ⊚ Borneo, N Indonesia

101 L16 **Jena** Thüringen, C Germany

22 I6 **Jena** Louisiana, S USA

108 I8 **Jenaz** Graubünden, SE Switzerland

109 N7 **Jenbach** Tirol, W Austria

171 N15 **Jeneponto** *prev.* Djeneponto. Sulawesi, C Indonesia

138 F9 **Jenin** N West Bank

21 P7 **Jenkins** Kentucky, S USA

27 P9 **Jenks** Oklahoma, C USA
Jenné *see* Djenné

109 X8 **Jennersdorf** Burgenland, SE Austria

22 I8 **Jennings** Louisiana, S USA

9 N7 **Jenny Lind Island** *island* Nunavut, N Canada

23 Y13 **Jensen Beach** Florida, SE USA

9 P6 **Jens Munk Island** *island* Nunavut, NE Canada

59 O17 **Jequié** Bahia, E Brazil

59 O18 **Jequitinhonha, Rio** ♒ E Brazil

74 H6 **Jerada** NE Morocco

75 N7 **Jerba, Île de** *var.* Djerba, Jazīrat Jarbah. *island* E Tunisia

44 K9 **Jérémie** SW Haiti

40 L11 **Jerez de García Salinas** *var.* Jerez de García Salinas, Mexico
Jerez *see* Jerez de la Frontera, Spain

40 L11 **Jerez de García Salinas** *var.* Jeréz. Zacatecas, C Mexico

104 J15 **Jeréz de la Frontera** *var.* Jerez; *prev.* Xeres. Andalucía, SW Spain

104 J12 **Jeréz de los Caballeros** Extremadura, W Spain
Jergucati *see* Jorgucat

138 G10 **Jericho** *Ar.* Arīḥā, *Heb.* Yeriḥo. E West Bank

74 M7 **Jerid, Chott el** *var.* Shaṭṭ al Jarīd. *salt lake* SW Tunisia

183 O10 **Jerilderie** New South Wales, SE Australia
Jerischmarkt *see* Câmpia Turzii

92 K11 **Jerisjärvi** ⊚ NW Finland
Jermak *see* Aksu
Jermentau *see* Yermentau
Jermer *see* Jaroměř

36 K11 **Jerome** Arizona, SW USA

33 O15 **Jerome** Idaho, NW USA

97 L26 **Jersey** *island* NW Europe

18 K14 **Jersey City** New Jersey, NE USA

18 F13 **Jersey Shore** Pennsylvania, NE USA

30 K11 **Jerseyville** Illinois, N USA

183 S10 **Jervis Bay** New South Wales, SE Australia

183 S10 **Jervis Bay Territory** ◇ *territory* SE Australia
Jerwakant *see* Järvakandi

111 E18 **Jesenice** *Ger.* Assling. NW Slovenia

111 H16 **Jeseník** *Ger.* Freiwaldau. Olomoucký Kraj, E Czech Republic
Jesero *see* Iesi

106 I8 **Jesolo** *var.* Iesolo. Veneto, NE Italy
Jesselton *see* Kota Kinabalu

95 I14 **Jessheim** Akershus, S Norway

153 T15 **Jessore** Khulna, S Bangladesh

23 W6 **Jesup** Georgia, SE USA

41 S15 **Jesús Carranza** Veracruz-Llave, SE Mexico

62 P5 **Jesús María** Córdoba, C Argentina

26 K6 **Jetmore** Kansas, C USA

103 Q2 **Jeumont** Nord, N France

95 H14 **Jevnaker** Oppland, S Norway

25 V9 **Jewett** Texas, SW USA

19 N12 **Jewett City** Connecticut, NE USA

113 L17 **Jezërcës, Maja e** ▲ N Albania

111 B18 **Jezerní Hora** ▲ SW Czech Republic

154 F10 **Jhābua** Madhya Pradesh, C India

152 H14 **Jhālāwār** Rājasthān, N India
Jhang/Jhang Sadar *see* Jhang Sadr

149 U9 **Jhang Sadr** *var.* Jhang, Jhang Sadar. Punjab, NE Pakistan

152 J13 **Jhānsi** Uttar Pradesh, N India

153 O16 **Jhārkhand** ◆ *state* NE India

154 M13 **Jhārsuguda** Orissa, E India

149 V7 **Jhelum** Punjab, NE Pakistan

129 P9 **Jhelum** ♒ E Pakistan
Jhenaidaha *see* Jhenida

153 T15 **Jhenida** *var.* Jhenaidaha. Dhaka, W Bangladesh

149 P16 **Jhimpir** Sind, SE Pakistan

149 R16 **Jhind** *see* Jind

152 H11 **Jhumra** *var.* Chak Jhumra. N India

158 M5 **Jhunjhunūn** Rājasthān, N India

18 I14 **Jim Thorpe** Pennsylvania, NE USA
Jin *see* Shanxi
Jin *see* Tianjin Shi

153 S14 **Jiāganj** West Bengal, NE India
Jiāi *see* Qionghai

160 J7 **Jialing Jiang** ♒ C China

161 Y7 **Jiamusi** *var.* Chia-mu-ssu, Kiamusze. Heilongjiang, NE China
Jin'an *see* Songpan
Jinbi *see* Dayao

161 O11 **Ji'an** Jiangxi, S China

163 W12 **Ji'an** Jilin, NE China

163 T13 **Jianchang** Liaoning, NE China
Jiancheng *see* Wuding

160 F11 **Jianchuan** *var.* Jinhuan. Yunnan, SW China

158 M4 **Jianjunmiao** Xinjiang Uygur Zizhiqu, NW China

160 K11 **Jiangkou** *var.* Shuangjiang. Guizhou, S China
Jiangkou *see* Fengkai

161 Q12 **Jiangle** *var.* Guyong. Fujian, SE China

161 N15 **Jiangmen** Guangdong, S China
Jiangna *see* Yanshan

161 Q10 **Jiangshan** Zhejiang, SE China

161 Q7 **Jiangsu** *var.* Chiang-su, Jiangsu Sheng, Kiangsu, Su. ◆ *province* E China
Jiangsu *see* Nanjing
Jiangsu Sheng *see* Jiangsu

161 O11 **Jiangxi** *var.* Chiang-hsi, Gan, Jiangxi Sheng, Kiangsi. ◆ *province* S China
Jiangxi Sheng *see* Jiangxi

160 I8 **Jiangyou** *prev.* Zhongba. Sichuan, C China

161 N9 **Jianli** *var.* Rongcheng. Hubei, C China

23 Y13 **Jian'ou** Fujian, SE China

163 S12 **Jianping** *var.* Yebaishou. Liaoning, NE China
Jianshe *see* Baiyu

160 L9 **Jianshi** *var.* Yezhou. Hubei, C China

161 V11 **Jian Xi** ♒ SE China

161 Q11 **Jianyang** Fujian, SE China

160 I9 **Jianyang** *var.* Jiancheng. Sichuan, C China

163 X10 **Jiaohe** Jilin, NE China
Jiaojiang *see* Taizhou

161 R5 **Jiaozhou** *prev.* Jiaoxian. Shandong, E China

161 N6 **Jiaozuo** Henan, C China

112 I15 **Jiashan** *see* Mingguang

158 F8 **Jiashi** *var.* Payzawat. Xinjiang Uygur Zizhiqu, NW China

161 S9 **Jiaxing** Zhejiang, SE China
Jiayi *see* Chiai

163 X6 **Jiayin** *var.* Chaoyang. Heilongjiang, NE China

159 N8 **Jiayuguan** Gansu, N China

146 J10 **Jibhalanta** *see* Uliastay

116 H9 **Jibou** Fr. Zsibó. Sălaj, NW Romania

141 Z9 **Jibsh, Ra's al** *headland* E Oman

141 E15 **Jiddah** *Eng.* Jedda. ● (Saudi Arabia) Makkah, W Saudi Arabia

141 W11 **Jiddat al Ḥarāsīs** *desert* C Oman

160 M4 **Jiexiu** Shanxi, C China

104 P14 **Jieyang** Guangdong, S China

119 F14 **Jieznas** Kaunas, S Lithuania

138 F10 **Jifa'** *Bi'r* var. Jif'yah, Bi'r. Al Quds ash Sharīf, *Heb.* Yerushalayim; *anc.* Hierosolyma. ● (Israel) Jerusalem, NE Israel

141 P15 **Jif'yah, Bi'r** *var.* Jifa'; Bi'r. *well* C Yemen

77 W13 **Jigawa** ◆ *state* N Nigeria

146 J10 **Jigerbent** *Rus.* Dzhigirbent. Lebap Welaýaty, NE Turkmenistan

44 I7 **Jiguaní** Granma, E Cuba

159 T12 **Jigzhi** *var.* Chügqênsumdo. Qinghai, C China

111 E18 **Jihlava** *Ger.* Iglau, *Pol.* Iglawa. Vysočina, S Czech Republic

111 E18 **Jihlava** *var.* Igel, *Ger.* Iglawa. ♒ Vysočina, C Czech Republic

111 C18 **Jihočeský Kraj** *prev.* Budějovický Kraj. ◇ *region* Czech Republic

111 G19 **Jihomoravský Kraj** *prev.* Brněnský Kraj. ◇ *region* SE Czech Republic

74 L5 **Jijel** *var.* Djidjel; *prev.* Djidjelli. NE Algeria

116 L9 **Jijia** ♒ N Romania

80 L13 **Jijiga** *It.* Giggiga. Somali, E Ethiopia

104 K16 **Jimena de la Frontera** Andalucía, S Spain

40 K7 **Jiménez** Chihuahua, N Mexico

41 N5 **Jiménez** Coahuila de Zaragoza, NE Mexico

41 N7 **Jiménez** *var.* Santander Jiménez. Tamaulipas, C Mexico

40 L10 **Jiménez del Teul** Zacatecas, C Mexico

77 Y14 **Jimeta** Adamawa, E Nigeria

158 M5 **Jimsar** Xinjiang Uygur Zizhiqu, NW China

153 S14 **Jiānganj** West Bengal, NE India

160 J7 **Jialing Jiang** ♒ C China

74 M9 **Jimani** W Dominican Republic

116 E11 **Jimbolia** *Ger.* Hatzfeld, *Hung.* Zsombolya. Timiş, W Romania

80 I13 **Jima** *var.* Jimma, *It.* Gimma. Oromo, C Ethiopia
Jimma *see* Jima

163 Y8 **Jixi** Heilongjiang, NE China

163 Y7 **Jixian** Heilongjiang, NE China

160 M5 **Jixian** *var.* Ji Xian. Shanxi, C China
Ji Xian *see* Jixian

141 N13 **Jīzān** var. Qīzān. Jīzān, SW Saudi Arabia

141 N13 **Jīzān** *var.* Mintaqat Jīzān. ◆ *province* SW Saudi Arabia
Jizān, Minṭaqat *see* Jīzān

140 K6 **Jizl, Wādī al** *dry watercourse* W Saudi Arabia

164 H12 **Jizō-zaki** *headland* Honshū, SW Japan

147 O11 **Jizzax** *Rus.* Dzhizak. Jizzax Viloyati, C Uzbekistan

147 N11 **Jizzax Viloyati** *Rus.* Dzhizakskaya Oblast'. ◇ *province* C Uzbekistan

60 I13 **Joaçaba** Santa Catarina, S Brazil

76 F11 **Joal-Fadiout** *prev.* Joal. W Senegal

76 E10 **João Barrosa** Boa Vista, E Cape Verde
João Belo *see* Xai-Xai

59 Q15 **João Pessoa** *prev.* Paraíba. *state capital* Paraíba, E Brazil

25 X7 **Joaquin** Texas, SW USA

160 K11 **Jindřichův Hradec** *Ger.* Neuhaus. Jihočeský Kraj, S Czech Republic
Jing *see* Beijing Shi
Jing *see* Jinghe, China

159 X10 **Jingchuan** Gansu, C China

161 Q10 **Jingdezhen** Jiangxi, S China

161 P3 **Jinggangshan** Jiangxi, S China

158 I4 **Jinghai** Tianjin Shi, E China
Jinghe *var.* Jing. Xinjiang Uygur Zizhiqu, NW China

160 K6 **Jing He** ♒ C China

160 F15 **Jinghong** *var.* Yunjinghong. Yunnan, SW China

160 M9 **Jingmen** Hubei, C China

163 X10 **Jingpo Hu** ⊚ NE China

160 M8 **Jing Shan** ▲ C China

159 V9 **Jingtai** *var.* Yitiaoshan. Gansu, C China

160 J14 **Jingxi** *var.* Xinjing. Guangxi Zhuangzu Zizhiqu, S China
Jing Xian *see* Jingzhou

163 W11 **Jingyu** Jilin, NE China

159 V10 **Jingyuan** Gansu, C China

160 M9 **Jingzhou** *prev.* Shashi, Shashih, Shasi. Hubei, C China

160 L12 **Jingzhou** *var.* Jing, Jingzhou Miaouzu Dongzu Zizhixian, Quyang. Hunan, S China
Jingzhou Miaouzu Dongzu Zizhixian *see* Jingzhou
Jinhe *see* Jinghe

161 R10 **Jinhua** Zhejiang, SE China

163 P13 **Jining** Nei Mongol Zizhiqu, N China

161 P5 **Jining** Shandong, E China

81 G18 **Jinja** S Uganda

161 R13 **Jinjiang** *var.* Qingyang. Fujian, SE China

161 O11 **Jin Jiang** ♒ S China
Jinjiang *see* Chengmai

171 V15 **Jin, Kepulauan** *island group* E Indonesia

42 J9 **Jinotega** Jinotega, NW Nicaragua

42 K7 **Jinotega** ◆ *department* N Nicaragua

42 J11 **Jinotepe** Carazo, SW Nicaragua

160 L13 **Jinping** *var.* Sanjiang. Guizhou, S China

160 H14 **Jinping** *var.* Jinhe. Yunnan, SW China
Jinsen *see* Inch'ŏn

160 M10 **Jinshi** Hunan, S China
Jinshi *see* Xinning

162 I9 **Jinst** *var.* Bodĭ. Bayanhongor, C Mongolia

159 R7 **Jinta** Gansu, N China

161 Q12 **Jin Xi** ♒ SE China
Jinxi *see* Huludao

163 U14 **Jinxian** Liaoning, NE China

161 P6 **Jinxiang** Shandong, SE China

161 P8 **Jinzhai** *var.* Meishan. Anhui, E China

161 N4 **Jinzhong** *var.* Yuci. Shanxi, C China

163 T12 **Jinzhou** *var.* Chin-chou, Chinchow; *prev.* Chinhsien. Liaoning, NE China

138 H12 **Jinz, Qā' al** ⊚ C Jordan

56 A7 **Jipijapa** Manabí, W Ecuador

42 F8 **Jiquilisco** Usulután, S El Salvador

147 S12 **Jirgatol** *Rus.* Dzhirgatal'. C Tajikistan
Jirjā *see* Girga

111 B15 **Jírkov** *Ger.* Görkau. Ústecký Kraj, NW Czech Republic
Jiroft *see* Sabzvārān

160 L11 **Jishou** Hunan, S China
Jisr ash Shadadi *see* Ash Shadādah

116 I14 **Jitaru** Olt, S Romania
Jitschin *see* Jičín

116 H14 **Jiu** *Ger.* Schil, Schyl, *Hung.* Zsil, Zsily. ♒ S Romania

161 R11 **Jiufeng Shan** ▲ SE China

161 P11 **Jiujiang** Jiangxi, S China

161 O10 **Jiuling Shan** ▲ S China

160 G16 **Jiulong** *var.* Garba, *Tib.* Gyaisi. Sichuan, C China

161 Q13 **Jiulong Jiang** ♒ SE China

161 Q12 **Jiulong Xi** ♒ SE China

159 R8 **Jiuquan** *var.* Suzhou. Gansu, C China

163 S10 **Jiuquan** *see* Hainan, S China

163 W10 **Jiutai** Jilin, NE China

160 K13 **Jiuwan Dashan** ▲ S China

160 I7 **Jiuzhaigou** *prev.* Nanping. Sichuan, C China

161 I16 **Jiwani** Baluchistān, SW Pakistan

161 O5 **Jixi** Heilongjiang, NE China

62 K6 **Joaquín V. González** Salta, N Argentina
Joazeiro see Juazeiro
Job'urg see Johannesburg
109 O7 **Jochberger Ache** ↗ W Austria
Jo-ch'iang see Ruoqiang
92 K12 **Jock** Norrbotten, N Sweden
42 I5 **Jocón** Yoro, N Honduras
105 O13 **Jódar** Andalucía, S Spain
152 F12 **Jodhpur** Rājasthān, NW India
99 I19 **Jodoigne** Walloon Brabant, C Belgium
93 O16 **Joensuu** Itä-Suomi, SE Finland
37 W4 **Joes** Colorado, C USA
191 Z3 **Joe's Hill** hill Kiritimati, NE Kiribati
165 N11 **Jōetsu** var. Zyôetu. Niigata, Honshū, C Japan
83 M18 **Jofane** Inhambane, S Mozambique
153 R12 **Jogbani** Bihār, NE India
118 I5 **Jõgeva** Ger. Laisholm. Jõgevamaa, E Estonia
118 I4 **Jõgevamaa** off. Jõgeva Maakond. ◆ province E Estonia
Jõgeva Maakond see Jõgevamaa
155 E18 **Jog Falls** Waterfall Karnātaka, W India
143 S4 **Joghatāy** Khorāsān, NE Iran
153 U12 **Jogighopa** Assam, NE India
152 I7 **Jogindarnagar** Himāchal Pradesh, N India
Jogjakarta see Yogyakarta
164 L11 **Jōhana** Toyama, Honshū, SW Japan
Johanna Island see Anjouan
83 J21 **Johannesburg** var. Egoli, Erautini, Gauteng, abbrev. Job'urg. Gauteng, NE South Africa
35 T13 **Johannesburg** California, W USA
83 I21 **Johannesburg** ✕ Gauteng, NE South Africa
Johannisburg see Pisz
149 P14 **Johi** Sind, SE Pakistan
55 T13 **Johi Village** S Guyana
32 K13 **John Day** Oregon, NW USA
32 I11 **John Day River** ↗ Oregon, NW USA
18 L14 **John F Kennedy** ✕ (New York) Long Island, New York, NE USA
21 V8 **John H. Kerr Reservoir** var. Buggs Island Lake, Kerr Lake. ◻ North Carolina/ Virginia, SE USA
37 V6 **John Martin Reservoir** ◻ Colorado, C USA
96 K6 **John o'Groats** N Scotland, UK
27 P5 **John Redmond Reservoir** ◻ Kansas, C USA
39 Q7 **John River** ↗ Alaska, USA
26 H6 **Johnson** Kansas, C USA
18 M7 **Johnson** Vermont, NE USA
18 D13 **Johnsonburg** Pennsylvania, NE USA
18 H11 **Johnson City** New York, NE USA
21 P8 **Johnson City** Tennessee, S USA
25 R10 **Johnson City** Texas, SW USA
35 S12 **Johnsondale** California, W USA
10 I8 **Johnsons Crossing** Yukon Territory, W Canada
21 T13 **Johnsonville** South Carolina, SE USA
21 Q13 **Johnston** South Carolina, SE USA
192 M6 **Johnston Atoll** ◇ US unincorporated territory C Pacific Ocean
175 Q3 **Johnston Atoll** atoll C Pacific Ocean
30 L17 **Johnston City** Illinois, N USA
180 K12 **Johnston, Lake** salt lake Western Australia
31 S13 **Johnstown** Ohio, N USA
18 D15 **Johnstown** Pennsylvania, NE USA
168 L10 **Johor** var. Johore. ◆ state Peninsular Malaysia
Johor Baharu see Johor Bahru
168 K10 **Johor Bahru** var. Johor Baharu, Johore Bahru. Johor, Peninsular Malaysia
Johore see Johor
Johore Bahru see Johor Bahru
118 K3 **Jõhvi** Ger. Jewe. Ida-Virumaa, NE Estonia
103 P7 **Joigny** Yonne, C France
Joinville see Joinville
60 K12 **Joinville** var. Joinville. Santa Catarina, S Brazil
103 R6 **Joinville** Haute-Marne, N France
194 H3 **Joinville Island** island Antarctica
41 O15 **Jojutla** var. Jojutla de Juárez. Morelos, S Mexico
Jojutla de Juárez see Jojutla
92 I12 **Jokkmokk** Lapp. Dálvvadis. Norrbotten, N Sweden
92 L2 **Jökulsá á Dal** ↗ E Iceland
92 K2 **Jökulsá á Fjöllum** ↗ NE Iceland
Jokyakarta see Yogyakarta
30 M11 **Joliet** Illinois, N USA
15 O11 **Joliette** Québec, SE Canada
171 O8 **Jolo** Jolo Island, SW Philippines
94 D11 **Jølstervatnet** ◻ S Norway
169 S16 **Jombang** prev. Djombang. Jawa, S Indonesia
159 R14 **Jomda** Xizang Zizhiqu, W China
56 A6 **Jome, Punta de** headland W Ecuador
118 G13 **Jonava** Ger. Janow, Pol. Janów. Kaunas, C Lithuania
146 L11 **Jondor** Rus. Zhondor. Buxoro Viloyati, C Uzbekistan
159 V11 **Jonê** Gansu, C China
27 X9 **Jonesboro** Arkansas, C USA
23 S4 **Jonesboro** Georgia, SE USA
30 L17 **Jonesboro** Illinois, N USA
22 H5 **Jonesboro** Louisiana, S USA
21 P8 **Jonesboro** Tennessee, S USA
19 T6 **Jonesport** Maine, NE USA
0 J4 **Jones Sound** channel Nunavut, N Canada
22 I6 **Jonesville** Louisiana, S USA
31 Q10 **Jonesville** Michigan, N USA
21 Q11 **Jonesville** South Carolina, SE USA

146 K10 **Jongeldi** Rus. Dzhankel'dy. Buxoro Viloyati, C Uzbekistan
81 F14 **Jonglei** Jonglei, SE Sudan
81 F14 **Jonglei** var. Jonglei. ◆ state SE Sudan
81 F14 **Jonglei Canal** canal S Sudan
118 F11 **Joniškėlis** Panevėžys, N Lithuania
118 F10 **Joniškis** Ger. Janischken. Šiauliai, N Lithuania
95 L19 **Jönköping** Jönköping, S Sweden
95 K20 **Jönköping** ◇ county S Sweden
15 Q7 **Jonquière** Québec, SE Canada
41 V15 **Jonuta** Tabasco, SE México
102 K12 **Jonzac** Charente-Maritime, W France
27 R7 **Joplin** Missouri, C USA
33 W8 **Jordan** Montana, NW USA
138 H12 **Jordan** off. Hashemite Kingdom of Jordan, Ar. Al Mamlaka al Urduniya al Hashemiyah, Al Urdunn; prev. Transjordan. ◆ monarchy SW Asia
138 G9 **Jordan** Ar. Urdunn, Heb. HaYarden. ↗ SW Asia
Jordan Lake see B. Everett Jordan Reservoir
111 K17 **Jordanów** Małopolskie, S Poland
32 M15 **Jordan Valley** Oregon, NW USA
138 G9 **Jordan Valley** valley N Israel
57 D15 **Jorge Chávez International** var. Lima. ✕ (Lima) Lima, W Peru
113 L23 **Jorgucat** var. Jergucati, Jorgucati. Gjirokastër, S Albania
Jorgucati see Jorgucat
153 X12 **Jorhāt** Assam, NE India
93 J14 **Jörn** Västerbotten, N Sweden
37 R14 **Jornada Del Muerto** valley New Mexico, SW USA
93 N17 **Joroinen** Isä-Suomi, E Finland
95 C16 **Jørpeland** Rogaland, S Norway
77 W14 **Jos** Plateau, C Nigeria
171 Q8 **Jose Abad Santos** var. Trinidad. Mindanao, S Philippines
61 F19 **José Batlle y Ordóñez** var. Batlle y Ordóñez. Florida, C Uruguay
63 H18 **José de San Martín** Chubut, S Argentina
61 E19 **José Enrique Rodó** var. Rodó, José E.Rodo; prev. Drabble, Drable. Soriano, SW Uruguay
José E.Rodo see José Enrique Rodó
Josefsdorf see Žabalj
44 C4 **José Martí** ✕ (La Habana) Cuidad de La Habana, N Cuba
61 F19 **José Pedro Varela** var. José P.Varela. Lavalleja, S Uruguay
181 N2 **Joseph Bonaparte Gulf** gulf N Australia
37 N11 **Joseph City** Arizona, SW USA
13 O9 **Joseph, Lake** ◻ Newfoundland and Labrador, E Canada
14 G13 **Joseph, Lake** ◻ Ontario, S Canada
186 C6 **Josephstaal** Madang, N Papua New Guinea
José P.Varela see José Pedro Varela
59 J14 **José Rodrigues** Pará, N Brazil
152 K9 **Joshimath** Uttaranchal, N India
25 T7 **Joshua** Texas, SW USA
35 V15 **Joshua Tree** California, W USA
77 V14 **Jos Plateau** plateau C Nigeria
102 H6 **Josselin** Morbihan, NW France
Jos Sudar see Yos Sudarso, Pulau
94 E11 **Jostedalsbreen** glacier S Norway
94 F12 **Jotunheimen** ▲ S Norway
138 G7 **Joûnié** var. Junīyah. W Lebanon
25 R13 **Jourdanton** Texas, SW USA
98 L7 **Joure** Fris. De Jouwer. Friesland, N Netherlands
93 M18 **Joutsa** Länsi-Suomi, C Finland
93 N18 **Joutseno** Etelä-Suomi, SE Finland
92 M12 **Joutsijärvi** Lappi, NE Finland
108 A9 **Joux, Lac de** ◻ W Switzerland
44 D5 **Jovellanos** Matanzas, N Cuba
153 V13 **Jowai** Meghālaya, NE India
143 O12 **Jowkān** Fārs, S Iran
Jowhar see Jawhar
Jowzam see Javazm
149 N2 **Jowzjān** ◆ province N Afghanistan
Józseffalva see Žabalj
J.Storm Thurmond Reservoir see Clark Hill Lake
45 T6 **Juana Díaz** C Puerto Rico
40 L9 **Juan Aldama** Zacatecas, C Mexico
0 E9 **Juan de Fuca Plate** tectonic feature
32 F7 **Juan de Fuca, Strait of** strait Canada/USA
Juan Fernandez Islands see Juan Fernández, Islas
193 S11 **Juan Fernández, Islas** Eng. Juan Fernandez Islands. island group W Chile
55 O4 **Juangriego** Nueva Esparta, NE Venezuela
56 D11 **Juanjuí** var. Juanjuy. San Martín, C Peru
Juanjuy see Juanjuí
93 N16 **Juankoski** Kuopio, C Finland
61 E20 **Juan L. Lacaze** var. Juan Lacaze, prev. Sauce. Colonia, SW Uruguay
Juan Lacaze see Juan L. Lacaze
62 L5 **Juan Solá** Salta, N Argentina
63 F21 **Juan Stuven, Isla** island S Chile
59 H16 **Juara** Mato Grosso, W Brazil
41 N7 **Juárez** var. Villa Juárez. Coahuila de Zaragoza, NE Mexico
40 C2 **Juárez, Sierra de** ▲ NW Mexico
59 O15 **Juazeiro** prev. Joazeiro. Bahia, E Brazil

59 P14 **Juazeiro do Norte** Ceará, E Brazil
81 F15 **Juba** var. Jūbā. Bahr el Gabel, S Sudan
81 L17 **Juba** Amh. Genalē Wenz, It. Guiba, Som. Ganaane, Webi Jubba. ↗ Ethiopia/Somalia
194 H2 **Jubany** Argentinian research station Antarctica
Jubayl see Jbail
81 L18 **Jubbada Dhexe** off. Gobolka Jubbada Dhexe. ◆ region SW Somalia
Jubbada Dhexe, Gobolka see Jubbada Dhexe
81 K18 **Jubbada Hoose** ◆ region SW Somalia
Jubba, Webi see Juba
Jubbulpore see Jabalpur
Jubeil see Jbail
74 B7 **Juby, Cap** headland NW Morocco
105 R10 **Júcar** var. Jucar. ↗ C Spain
40 L12 **Juchipila** Zacatecas, C Mexico
41 S16 **Juchitán** var. Juchitán de Zaragosa. Oaxaca, SE Mexico
Juchitán de Zaragosa see Juchitán
138 G11 **Judaea** cultural region Israel/ West Bank
138 F11 **Judaean Hills** Heb. Haré Yehuda. hill range SE Israel
138 H8 **Judaydah** Fr. Jdaidé. Dimashq, W Syria
139 P11 **Judayyidat Hāmir** S Iraq
109 U8 **Judenburg** Steiermark, C Austria
33 T8 **Judith River** ↗ Montana, NW USA
27 V11 **Judsonia** Arkansas, C USA
141 P14 **Jufrah, Wādī al** dry watercourse NW Yemen
Jugar see Sêrxü
Jugoslavija see Serbia
42 K6 **Juigalpa** Chontales, S Nicaragua
161 T13 **Juishui** C Taiwan
100 E9 **Juist** island NW Germany
59 M21 **Juiz de Fora** Minas Gerais, SE Brazil
62 J5 **Jujuy** off. Provincia de Jujuy. ◆ province N Argentina
Jujuy see San Salvador de Jujuy
Jujuy, Provincia de see Jujuy
92 J11 **Jukkasjärvi** Lapp. Čohkkiras. Norrbotten, N Sweden
Jula see Gyula, Hungary
Jūlā see Jālū, Libya
37 W2 **Julesburg** Colorado, C USA
57 I17 **Juliaca** Puno, SE Peru
181 U6 **Julia Creek** Queensland, C Australia
35 V17 **Julian** California, W USA
98 H7 **Julianadorp** Noord-Holland, NW Netherlands
109 S11 **Julian Alps** Ger. Julische Alpen, It. Alpi Giulie, Slvn. Julijske Alpe. ▲ Italy/Slovenia
55 V11 **Juliana Top** ▲ C Surinam
Julianehåb see Qaqortoq
Julijske Alpe see Julian Alps
40 J6 **Julimes** Chihuahua, N Mexico
Julio Briga see Bragança
Juliobriga see Logroño
61 G15 **Júlio de Castilhos** Rio Grande do Sul, S Brazil
Juliomagus see Angers
Julische Alpen see Julian Alps
Jullundur see Jalandhar
147 N11 **Juma** Rus. Dzhuma. Samarqand Viloyati, C Uzbekistan
161 Q3 **Juma He** ↗ E China
81 L18 **Jumboo** Jubbada Hoose, S Somalia
35 Y11 **Jumbo Peak** ▲ Nevada, W USA
105 R12 **Jumilla** Murcia, SE Spain
153 N10 **Jumla** Mid Western, NW Nepal
Jummoo see Jammu
Jumna see Yamuna
Jumporn see Chumphon
30 M10 **Jump River** ↗ Wisconsin, N USA
154 B11 **Jūnāgadh** var. Junagarh. Gujarāt, W India
Junagarh see Jūnāgadh
161 Q6 **Junan** var. Shizilu. Shandong, E China
62 G12 **Juncal, Cerro** ▲ C Chile
25 Q10 **Junction** Texas, SW USA
36 K6 **Junction** Utah, W USA
27 O4 **Junction City** Kansas, C USA
32 F13 **Junction City** Oregon, NW USA
60 M10 **Jundiaí** São Paulo, S Brazil
39 X12 **Juneau** state capital Alaska, USA
30 M8 **Juneau** Wisconsin, N USA
105 U6 **Juneda** Cataluña, NE Spain
183 Q9 **Junee** New South Wales, SE Australia
35 R8 **June Lake** California, W USA
Jungbunzlau see Mladá Boleslav
158 L4 **Junggar Pendi** Eng. Dzungarian Basin. basin NW China
99 N24 **Junglinster** Grevenmacher, C Luxembourg
18 F14 **Juniata River** ↗ Pennsylvania, NE USA
61 B20 **Junín** Buenos Aires, E Argentina
57 E14 **Junín** Junín, C Peru
57 F14 **Junín** off. Departamento de Junín. ◆ department C Peru
63 H18 **Junín de los Andes** Neuquén, W Argentina
Junín, Departamento de see Junín
57 D14 **Junín, Lago de** ◻ C Peru
Junīyah see Joûnié
Junkseylon see Phuket
160 I11 **Junlian** Sichuan, C China
25 O11 **Juno** Texas, SW USA
29 W3 **Junosuando** Lapp. Cunusavvon. Norrbotten, N Sweden
93 H16 **Junsele** Västernorrland, C Sweden
32 L13 **Juntura** Oregon, NW USA
93 N14 **Juntusranta** Oulu, E Finland

118 H11 **Juodupė** Panevėžys, NE Lithuania
119 H14 **Juozapinės Kalnas** ▲ SE Lithuania
99 K19 **Juprelle** Liège, E Belgium
80 D13 **Jur** ↗ C Sudan
103 S9 **Jura** ◆ department E France
108 C7 **Jura** ◆ canton NW Switzerland
108 B8 **Jura** ▲ Jura Mountains
96 G12 **Jura** island SW Scotland, UK
54 C8 **Juradó** Chocó, NW Colombia
Jura Mountains see Jura
96 G12 **Jura, Sound of** strait W Scotland, UK
139 V15 **Juraybīyāt, Bi'r** well S Iraq
118 E13 **Jurbarkas** Ger. Georgenburg, Jurburg. Tauragé, W Lithuania
99 F20 **Jurbise** Hainaut, SW Belgium
Jurburg see Jurbarkas
118 F9 **Jūrmala** Rīga, C Latvia
58 D13 **Juruá** Amazonas, NW Brazil
48 F7 **Juruá, Rio** var. Río Yuruá. ↗ Brazil/Peru
59 G16 **Juruena** Mato Grosso, W Brazil
59 G16 **Juruena, Rio** ↗ W Brazil
165 Q6 **Jūsan-kō** ◻ Honshū, C Japan
25 O6 **Justiceburg** Texas, SW USA
113 N17 **Justinianopolis** see Kırşehir
62 K11 **Justo Daract** San Luis, C Argentina
42 A3 **Jutiapa** Jutiapa, S Guatemala
42 A3 **Jutiapa** off. Departamento de Jutiapa. ◆ department SE Guatemala
Jutiapa, Departamento de see Jutiapa
42 J6 **Juticalpa** Olancho, C Honduras
82 I13 **Jutila** North Western, NW Zambia
Jutland see Jylland
84 F8 **Jutland Bank** undersea feature SE North Sea
93 N16 **Juuka** Pohjois-Karjala, E Finland
93 N17 **Juva** Isä-Suomi, E Finland
Juvavum see Salzburg
44 A6 **Juventud, Isla de la** var. Isla de Pinos, Eng. Isle of Youth; prev. The Isle of the Pines. island W Cuba
161 Q5 **Juxian** var. Chengyang, Ju Xian. Shandong, E China
Ju Xian see Juxian
191 P6 **Juye** Shandong, E China
113 O15 **Južna Morava** Ger. Südliche Morava. ↗ SE Serbia
83 H20 **Jwaneng** Southern, S Botswana Africa
95 I23 **Jyderup** Vestsjælland, E Denmark
95 F22 **Jylland** Eng. Jutland. peninsula W Denmark
Jyrgalan see Dzhergalan
93 M17 **Jyväskylä** Länsi-Suomi, C Finland

K

38 D9 **Ka'a'awa** var. Kaaawa. Hawai'i, O'ahu, USA, C Pacific Ocean
Kaaawa see Ka'a'awa
81 G16 **Kaabong** NE Uganda
79 G16 **Kadéï** ↗ Cameroon/Central African Republic
Kadhimain see Al Kāẓimīyah
114 M13 **Kadıköy Baraji** ◻ NW Turkey
182 I8 **Kadina** South Australia
136 H15 **Kadınhanı** Konya, C Turkey
76 M14 **Kadiolo** Sikasso, S Mali
136 L16 **Kadirli** Osmaniye, S Turkey
114 G11 **Kadiytsa** Mac. Kadijica. ▲ Bulgaria/FYR Macedonia
28 L9 **Kadoka** South Dakota, N USA
127 N5 **Kadom** Ryazanskaya Oblast', W Russian Federation
83 K16 **Kadoma** prev. Gatooma. Mashonaland West, C Zimbabwe
80 E12 **Kadugli** Southern Kordofan, S Sudan
77 V14 **Kaduna** Kaduna, C Nigeria
77 V15 **Kaduna** ◆ state C Nigeria
124 K14 **Kaduy** Vologodskaya Oblast', NW Russian Federation
154 E13 **Kadwa** ↗ W India
123 S9 **Kadykchan** Magadanskaya Oblast', E Russian Federation
125 T7 **Kadzherom** Respublika Komi, NW Russian Federation
147 X8 **Kadzhi-Say** Kir. Kajisay. Issyk-Kul'skaya Oblast', NE Kyrgyzstan
76 I10 **Kaédi** Gorgol, S Mauritania
78 G12 **Kaélé** Extrême-Nord, N Cameroon
145 W13 **Kaakpak** Kaz. Qabanbay; prev. Andreyevka, Kaz. Andreevka. Almaty, SE Kazakhstan
184 J2 **Kaeo** Northland, North Island, New Zealand
163 X14 **Kaesŏng** var. Kaesŏng-si. N North Korea
Kaesŏng-si see Kaesŏng
Kaewieng see Kavieng
79 L24 **Kafakumba** Shaba, S Dem. Rep. Congo
77 V14 **Kafan** see Kapan
77 V14 **Kafanchan** Kaduna, C Nigeria
Kaffa see Feodosiya
79 G17 **Kafia** Sud Kivu, E Dem. Rep. Congo
115 I19 **Kafiréos, Stenó** strait Évvoia/ Kykládes, Greece, Aegean Sea
Kafirnigan see Kofarnihon
Kafo see Kafu
75 W7 **Kafr ash Shaykh/Kafrel Sheik** see Kafr el Sheikh
138 M6 **Kabd aş Şārim** hill range E Syria
81 F17 **Kafu** var. Kafo. ↗ W Uganda
82 J15 **Kafue** Lusaka, SE Zambia
83 J15 **Kafue** ↗ C Zambia
82 J14 **Kafue Flats** plain C Zambia
165 K12 **Kaga** Ishikawa, Honshū, SW Japan
79 J14 **Kaga Bandoro** prev. Fort-Crampel. Nana-Grébizi, C Central African Republic

81 E18 **Kagadi** W Uganda
38 H17 **Kagalaska Island** island Aleutian Islands, Alaska, USA
Kagan see Kogon
Kaganovichabad see Kolkhozobod
149 Q5 **Kābol** var. Kabul, Pash. Kābul. ◆ (Afghanistan) Kābul, E Afghanistan
149 Q5 **Kābol** Eng. Kabul, Pash. Kābul. ◆ province E Afghanistan
149 Q5 **Kābol** ✕ Kābul, E Afghanistan
149 R5 **Kabul** var. Darya-ye Kābul. see also Kābul, Darya-ye ↗ Afghanistan/Pakistan
Kabul see Kābol
Kabul see Kābul, Darya-ye
149 S5 **Kābul, Darya-ye** var. Kabul. ↗ Afghanistan/Pakistan see also Kabul
Kābul, Darya-ye see Kabul
79 O25 **Kaburuang, Pulau** island Kepulauan Talaud, N Indonesia
171 R9 **Kabwe** Central, C Zambia
80 G8 **Kabushiya** River Nile, NE Sudan
83 J14 **Kabwe** Central, C Zambia
186 E7 **Kabwum** Morobe, C Papua New Guinea
113 N17 **Kačanik** Kosovo, S Serbia
118 F13 **Kačerginė** Kaunas, C Lithuania
117 S13 **Kacha** Respublika Krym, S Ukraine
154 A10 **Kachchh, Gulf of** var. Gulf of Cutch, Gulf of Kutch. gulf W India
154 I11 **Kachchhīdhāna** Madhya Pradesh, C India
149 Q11 **Kachchh, Rann of** var. Rann of Kachh, Rann of Kutch. salt marsh India/Pakistan
39 Q13 **Kachemak Bay** bay Alaska, USA
Kachh, Rann of see Kachchh, Rann of
77 V14 **Kachia** Kaduna, C Nigeria
167 N2 **Kachin State** ◆ state N Burma (Myanmar)
145 T7 **Kachiry** Pavlodar, NE Kazakhstan
137 Q11 **Kaçkar Dağları** ▲ NE Turkey
155 C21 **Kadamatt Island** island Lakshadweep, India, N Indian Ocean
111 B15 **Kadaň** Ger. Kaaden. Ústecký Kraj, NW Czech Republic
1667 N11 **Kadan Kyun** prev. King Island. island Mergui Archipelago, S Burma (Myanmar)
187 X15 **Kadavu** prev. Kandavu. island S Fiji
187 X15 **Kadavu Passage** channel S Fiji
79 G16 **Kadéï** ↗ Cameroon/Central African Republic

81 E18 **Kagadi** W Uganda
38 H17 **Kagalaska Island** island Aleutian Islands, Alaska, USA
Kagan see Kogon
Kaganovichabad see Kolkhozobod
164 H14 **Kagawa** off. Kagawa-ken. ◆ prefecture Shikoku, SW Japan
Kagawa-ken see Kagawa
154 J13 **Kagaznagar** Andhra Pradesh, C India
93 J14 **Kåge** Västerbotten, N Sweden
81 E19 **Kagera** var. Ziwa Magharibi, It. West Lake. ◆ region NW Tanzania
81 E19 **Kagera** var. Akagera. ↗ Rwanda/Tanzania see also Akagera
76 L5 **Kâghet** var. Karet. physical region N Mauritania
Kagi see Chiai
137 S12 **Kağızman** Kars, NE Turkey
188 I6 **Kagman Point** headland Saipan, S Northern Mariana Islands
164 C16 **Kagoshima** var. Kagosima. Kagoshima, Kyūshū, SW Japan
164 C16 **Kagoshima** off. Kagoshima-ken, var. Kagosima. ◇ prefecture Kyūshū, SW Japan
Kagoshima-ken see Kagoshima
Kagosima see Kagoshima
Kagul see Cahul
Kagul, Ozero see Kahul, Ozero
38 B8 **Kahala Point** headland Kaua'i, Hawai'i, USA
81 F21 **Kahama** Shinyanga, NW Tanzania
117 P5 **Kaharlyk** Rus. Kagarlyk. Kyyivs'ka Oblast', N Ukraine
169 T13 **Kahayan, Sungai** ↗ Borneo, C Indonesia
79 I22 **Kahemba** Bandundu, SW Dem. Rep. Congo
185 A23 **Kaherekoau Mountains** ▲ South Island, New Zealand
143 W14 **Kahīrī** var. Kūhīrī. Sīstān va Balūchestān, SE Iran
101 L16 **Kahla** Thüringen, C Germany
101 G15 **Kahler Asten** ▲ W Germany
149 Q4 **Kahmard, Darya-ye** prev. Darya-i-surkhab. ↗ NE Afghanistan
143 T13 **Kahnūj** Kermān, SE Iran
27 V1 **Kahoka** Missouri, C USA
38 E10 **Kaho'olawe** var. Kahoolawe. island Hawaiian Islands, Hawai'i, USA
Kahoolawe see Kaho'olawe
136 M16 **Kahramanmaraş** var. Kahraman Maraş, Maraş, Marash. Kahramanmaraş, S Turkey
136 L15 **Kahramanmaraş** var. Kahraman Maraş, Maraş, Marash. ◆ province C Turkey
Kahraman Maraş see Kahramanmaraş
Kahramanmaras see Kahramanmaraş
137 N15 **Kâhta** Adıyaman, S Turkey
38 D8 **Kahuku** O'ahu, Hawai'i, USA
38 D8 **Kahuku Point** headland O'ahu, Hawai'i, USA
116 M12 **Kahul, Ozero** var. Lacul Cahul, Rus. Ozero Kagul. ◻ Moldova/Ukraine
143 V11 **Kahūrak** Sīstān va Balūchestān, SE Iran
184 G13 **Kahurangi Point** headland South Island, New Zealand
149 V6 **Kahūta** Punjab, E Pakistan
77 S14 **Kaiama** Kwara, W Nigeria
186 D7 **Kaiapit** Morobe, C Papua New Guinea
185 I18 **Kaiapoi** Canterbury, South Island, New Zealand
36 K9 **Kaibab Plateau** plain Arizona, SW USA
171 U14 **Kai Besar, Pulau** island Kepulauan Kai, E Indonesia
36 L9 **Kaibito Plateau** plain Arizona, SW USA
158 K6 **Kaidu He** var. Karaxahar. ↗ NW China
55 S10 **Kaieteur Falls** waterfall C Guyana
Kaifeng Henan, C China
181 J3 **Kaihu** Northland, North Island, New Zealand
Kaihua see Wenshan
171 U14 **Kai Kecil, Pulau** island Kepulauan Kai, E Indonesia
169 U16 **Kai, Kepulauan** prev. Kei Islands. island group Maluku, SE Indonesia
184 J3 **Kaikohe** Northland, North Island, New Zealand
185 J16 **Kaikoura** Canterbury, South Island, New Zealand
185 J16 **Kaikoura Peninsula** peninsula South Island, New Zealand
Kailas Range see Gangdisê Shan
160 K12 **Kaili** Guizhou, S China
38 F10 **Kailua** Maui, Hawaii, USA
38 F10 **Kailua** Maui, Hawaii, USA, C Pacific Ocean
Kailua see Kalaoa
38 F10 **Kailua-Kona** var. Kona. Hawai'i, USA, C Pacific Ocean
186 B7 **Kaim** ↗ W Papua New Guinea
171 X14 **Kaimana** Papua, E Indonesia
184 M7 **Kaimai Range** ▲ North Island, New Zealand
114 E13 **Kaïmaktsalán** ▲ Greece/FYR Macedonia
185 C20 **Kaimanawa Mountains** ▲ North Island, New Zealand
118 E4 **Käina** Ger. Keinis; prev. Keina. Hiiumaa, W Estonia
109 V7 **Kainach** ↗ SE Austria
164 H14 **Kainan** Tokushima, Shikoku, SW Japan
164 H15 **Kainan** Wakayama, Honshū, SW Japan
77 T14 **Kainji Dam** dam W Nigeria
Kainji Lake see Kainji Reservoir

◆ Country ● Country Capital ◇ Dependent Territory ○ Dependent Territory Capital ◆ Administrative Regions ✕ International Airport ▲ Mountain ▲ Mountain Range ℞ Volcano ↗ River ◻ Lake ◻ Reservoir

KAINJI RESERVOIR – KANIN KAMEN’

77 *T14* **Kainji Reservoir** *var.* Kainji Lake. ⊠ W Nigeria
186 *D8* **Kaintiba** *var.* Kamina. Gulf, S Papua New Guinea
92 *K12* **Kainulaisjärvi** Norrbotten, N Sweden
184 *K5* **Kaipara Harbour** *harbour* North Island, New Zealand
152 *I10* **Kairāna** Uttar Pradesh, N India
74 *M6* **Kairouan** *var.* Al Qayrawān. E Tunisia
Kaisaria *see* Kayseri
101 *F20* **Kaiserslautern** Rheinland-Pfalz, SW Germany
118 *G13* **Kaišiadorys** Kąunas, S Lithuania
184 *I2* **Kaitaia** Northland, North Island, New Zealand
185 *E24* **Kaitangata** Otago, South Island, New Zealand
152 *I9* **Kaithal** Haryāna, NW India
Kaitong *see* Tongyu
169 *N13* **Kait, Tanjung** *cape* Sumatera, W Indonesia
38 *E9* **Kaiwi Channel** *channel* Hawai'i, USA, C Pacific Ocean
160 *K9* **Kaixian** *var.* Hanfeng. Sichuan, C China
163 *V11* **Kaiyuan** *var.* K'ai-yüan. Liaoning, NE China
160 *H14* **Kaiyuan** Yunnan, SW China
K'ai-yüan *see* Kaiyuan
39 *O9* **Kaiyuh Mountains** ▲▲ Alaska, USA
93 *M15* **Kajaani** *Swe.* Kajana. Oulu, C Finland
149 *N7* **Kajakī, Band-e** ◎ C Afghanistan
Kajan *see* Kayan, Sungai
Kajana *see* Kajaani
137 *V13* **K'ajaran** *Rus.* Kadzharan. SE Armenia
Kajisay *see* Kadzhi-Say
113 *O20* **Kajmakčalan** ▲ S FYR Macedonia
Kajnar *see* Kaynar
149 *N6* **Kajrān** Dāikondī, C Afghanistan
149 *N5* **Kaj Rūd** ≈ C Afghanistan
146 *G14* **Kaka** *Rus.* Kaakhka. Ahal Welaýaty, S Turkmenistan
12 *C12* **Kakabeka Falls** Ontario, S Canada
83 *F23* **Kakamas** Northern Cape, W South Africa
81 *H18* **Kakamega** Western, W Kenya
112 *H13* **Kakanj** Federacija Bosna I Hercegovina, C Bosnia and Herzegovina
185 *F22* **Kakanui Mountains** ▲▲ South Island, New Zealand
184 *K11* **Kakaramea** Taranaki, North Island, New Zealand
76 *J16* **Kakata** C Liberia
184 *M11* **Kakatahi** Manawatu-Wanganui, North Island, New Zealand
113 *M23* **Kakavi** Gjirokastër, S Albania
147 *O14* **Kakaydi** Surkhondaryo Viloyati, S Uzbekistan
164 *F13* **Kake** Hiroshima, Honshū, SW Japan
39 *X13* **Kake** Kupreanof Island, Alaska, USA
171 *P14* **Kakea** Pulau Wowoni, C Indonesia
164 *M14* **Kakegawa** Shizuoka, Honshū, S Japan
165 *V16* **Kakeromajima** Kagoshima, SW Japan
143 *T6* **Kākhak** Khorāsān, E Iran
118 *L11* **Kakhanavichy** *Rus.* Kokhanovichi. Vitsyebskaya Voblasts', N Belarus
39 *P13* **Kakhonak** Alaska, USA
117 *S10* **Kakhovka** Khersons'ka Oblast', S Ukraine
117 *U9* **Kakhovs'ke Vodoskhovyshche** *Rus.* Kakhovskoye Vodokhranilishche. ⊠ SE Ukraine
Kakhovskoye Vodokhranilishche *see* Kakhovs'ke Vodoskhovyshche
117 *T11* **Kakhovs'kyy Kanal** *canal* S Ukraine
Kakia *see* Khakhea
155 *L16* **Kākināda** *prev.* Cocanada. Andhra Pradesh, E India
Käkisalmi *see* Priozersk
164 *I13* **Kakogawa** Hyōgo, Honshū, SW Japan
81 *F18* **Kakoge** C Uganda
145 *O7* **Kak, Ozero** ◎ N Kazakhstan
Ka-Krem *see* Malyy Yenisey
Kakshaal-Too, Khrebet *see* Kokshaal-Tau
39 *S5* **Kaktovik** Alaska, USA
165 *Q11* **Kakuda** Miyagi, Honshū, C Japan
165 *Q8* **Kakunodate** Akita, Honshū, C Japan
Kalaallit Nunaat *see* Greenland
149 *T7* **Kālābāgh** Punjab, E Pakistan
171 *Q16* **Kalabahi** Pulau Alor, S Indonesia
188 *I5* **Kalabera** Saipan, S Northern Mariana Islands
83 *G14* **Kalabo** Western, W Zambia
126 *M9* **Kalach** Voronezhskaya Oblast', W Russian Federation
127 *N10* **Kalach-na-Donu** Volgogradskaya Oblast', SW Russian Federation
166 *K5* **Kaladan** ≈ W Burma (Myanmar)
14 *K14* **Kaladar** Ontario, SE Canada
38 *G13* **Ka Lae** *var.* South Cape, South Point. *headland* Hawai'i, USA, C Pacific Ocean
83 *G19* **Kalahari Desert** *desert* Southern Africa
38 *B8* **Kalāheo** *var.* Kalaheo. Kaua'i, Hawai'i, USA
Kalaheo *see* Kalāheo
Kalaikhum *see* Qal'aikhum
Kala-i-Mor *see* Galaýmor
93 *K15* **Kalajoki** Oulu, W Finland
Kalak *see* Eski Kaļak
Kal al Sraghna *see* El Kelâa Srarhna
32 *G10* **Kalama** Washington, NW USA
Kalámai *see* Kalámata
115 *G14* **Kalamariá** Kentrikí Makedonía, N Greece
115 *C15* **Kalamás** *var.* Thiamis, *prev* Thýamis. ≈ W Greece
115 *E21* **Kalámata** *prev.* Kalámai. Pelopónnisos, S Greece
31 *P10* **Kalamazoo** Michigan, N USA
31 *P9* **Kalamazoo River** ≈ Michigan, N USA
Kalambaka *see* Kalampáka
117 *S13* **Kalamits'ka Zatoka** *Rus.* Kalamitskiy Zaliv. *gulf* S Ukraine
Kalamitskiy Zaliv *see* Kalamits'ka Zatoka
115 *H18* **Kálamos** Attikí, C Greece
115 *C18* **Kálamos** *island* Iónioi Nísia, Greece, C Mediterranean Sea
115 *D15* **Kalampáka** *var.* Kalambaka. Thessalía, C Greece
Kalan *see* Călan, Romania
Kalan *see* Tunceli, Turkey
117 *S11* **Kalanchak** Khersons'ka Oblast', S Ukraine
38 *G11* **Kalaoa** *var.* Kailua. Hawai'i, USA, C Pacific Ocean
171 *O15* **Kalaotoa, Pulau** *island* W Indonesia
155 *J24* **Kala Oya** ≈ NW Sri Lanka
Kalarash *see* Călăraşi
93 *H17* **Kälarne** Jämtland, C Sweden
143 *V15* **Kalar Rūd** ≈ SE Iran
169 *R9* **Kalasin** *var.* Muang Kalasin. Kalasin, E Thailand
149 *O11* **Kalāt** *var.* Kelat, Khelat. Baluchistān, SW Pakistan
Kalāt *see* Qalāt
115 *J14* **Kalathriá, Ákrotirio** *headland* Samothráki, NE Greece
193 *W17* **Kalau** *island* Tongatapu Group, SE Tonga
38 *E9* **Kalaupapa** Moloka'i, Hawai'i, USA
127 *N13* **Kalaus** ≈ SW Russian Federation
Kalávrita *see* Kalávryta
115 *E19* **Kalávryta** *var.* Kalávrita. Dytikí Ellás, S Greece
141 *Y10* **Kalbān** W Oman
180 *H11* **Kalbarri** Western Australia
145 *X10* **Kalbinskiy Khrebet** *Kaz.* Qalba Zhotasy. ▲▲ E Kazakhstan
144 *G10* **Kaldygayty** ≈ W Kazakhstan
136 *I12* **Kalecik** Ankara, N Turkey
79 *O19* **Kalehe** Sud Kivu, E Dem. Rep. Congo
79 *P22* **Kalemie** *prev.* Albertville. Katanga, SE Dem. Rep. Congo
166 *L4* **Kalemyo** Sagaing, W Burma (Myanmar)
82 *H12* **Kalene Hill** North Western, NW Zambia
Kale Sultanie *see* Çanakkale
124 *I7* **Kalevala** Respublika Kareliya, NW Russian Federation
166 *L4* **Kalewa** Sagaing, C Burma (Myanmar)
Kalgan *see* Zhangjiakou
39 *Q12* **Kalgin Island** *island* Alaska, USA
180 *L12* **Kalgoorlie** Western Australia
Kali *see* Sārda
115 *E17* **Kaliakoúda** ▲ C Greece
114 *O8* **Kaliakra, Nos** *cape* NE Bulgaria
115 *F19* **Kaliánoi** Pelopónnisos, S Greece
115 *N24* **Kalí Límni** ▲ Kárpathos, SE Greece
79 *N20* **Kalima** Maniema, E Dem. Rep. Congo
169 *S11* **Kalimantan** *Eng.* Indonesian Borneo. *geopolitcal region* Borneo, C Indonesia
169 *Q11* **Kalimantan Barat** *off.* Propinsi Kalimantan Berat, *Eng.* West Borneo, West Kalimantan. ⬖ *province* N Indonesia
Kalimantan Barat, Propinsi *see* Kalimantan Barat
169 *T13* **Kalimantan Selatan** *off.* Propinsi Kalimantan Selatan, *Eng.* South Borneo, South Kalimantan. ⬖ *province* N Indonesia
Kalimantan Selatan, Propinsi *see* Kalimantan Selatan
169 *R12* **Kalimantan Tengah** *off.* Propinsi Kalimantan Tengah, *Eng.* Central Borneo, Central Kalimantan. ⬖ *province* N Indonesia
Kalimantan Tengah, Propinsi *see* Kalimantan Tengah
169 *U10* **Kalimantan Timur** *off.* Propinsi Kalimantan Timur, *Eng.* East Borneo, East Kalimantan. ⬖ *province* N Indonesia
Kalimantan Timur, Propinsi *see* Kalimantan Timur
Kálimnos *see* Kálymnos
153 *S12* **Kālimpang** West Bengal, NE India
Kalinin *see* Tver'
Kalinin *see* Boldumsaz
Kalininabad *see* Kalininobod
126 *B3* **Kaliningrad** Kaliningradskaya Oblast', W Russian Federation
Kaliningrad *see* Kaliningradskaya Oblast'
126 *A3* **Kaliningradskaya Oblast'** *var.* Kaliningrad. ⬖ *province and enclave* W Russian Federation
Kalinino *see* Tashir
147 *P14* **Kalininobod** *Rus.* Kalininabad. SW Tajikistan
127 *O8* **Kalininsk** Saratovskaya Oblast', W Russian Federation
Kalininsk *see* Boldumsaz
Kalinisk *see* Cupcina
119 *M19* **Kalinkavichy** *Rus.* Kalinkovichi. Homyel'skaya Voblasts', SE Belarus
Kalinkovichi *see* Kalinkavichy
81 *G18* **Kaliro** SE Uganda
Kalisch/Kalish *see* Kalisz
33 *O7* **Kalispell** Montana, NW USA
110 *I13* **Kalisz** *Ger.* Kalisch, *Rus.* Kalish; *anc.* Calisia. Wielkopolskie, C Poland
110 *F9* **Kalisz Pomorski** *Ger.* Kallies. Zachodnio-pomorskie, NW Poland
126 *M10* **Kalitva** ≈ SW Russian Federation
81 *F21* **Kaliua** Tabora, C Tanzania
92 *K13* **Kalix** Norrbotten, N Sweden
92 *K12* **Kalixälven** ≈ N Sweden
92 *J11* **Kalixfors** Norrbotten, N Sweden
145 *T8* **Kalkaman** Pavlodar, NE Kazakhstan
Kalkandelen *see* Tetovo
181 *O4* **Kalkarindji** Northern Territory, N Australia
31 *P6* **Kalkaska** Michigan, N USA
93 *F16* **Kall** Jämtland, C Sweden
189 *X2* **Kallalen** *var.* Calalen. *island* Ratak Chain, SE Marshall Islands
118 *J5* **Kallaste** *Ger.* Krasnogor. Tartumaa, SE Estonia
93 *N16* **Kallavesi** ◎ SE Finland
115 *F17* **Kallídromo** ▲▲ C Greece
Kallies *see* Kalisz Pomorski
95 *M22* **Kallinge** Blekinge, S Sweden
115 *L16* **Kalloní** Lésvos, E Greece
93 *F16* **Kallsjön** ◎ C Sweden
95 *N21* **Kalmar** *var.* Calmar. Kalmar, S Sweden
95 *M19* **Kalmar** *var.* Calmar. ⬖ *county* S Sweden
95 *N20* **Kalmarsund** *strait* S Sweden
148 *L16* **Kalmat, Khor** *Eng.* Kalmat Lagoon. *lagoon* SW Pakistan
Kalmat Lagoon *see* Kalmat, Khor
117 *X9* **Kal'mius** ≈ E Ukraine
99 *H15* **Kalmthout** Antwerpen, N Belgium
Kalmykia/Kalmykiya-Khal'mg Tangch, Respublika *see* Kalmykiya, Respublika
127 *O12* **Kalmykiya, Respublika** *var.* Respublika Kalmykiya-Khal'mg Tangch, *Eng.* Kalmykia; *prev.* Kalmytskaya ASSR. ⬖ *autonomous republic* SW Russian Federation
Kalmytskaya ASSR *see* Kalmykiya, Respublika
118 *F9* **Kalnciems** Jelgava, C Latvia
114 *L10* **Kalnitsa** ≈ SE Bulgaria
111 *J24* **Kalocsa** Bács-Kiskun, S Hungary
114 *J9* **Kalofer** Plovdiv, C Bulgaria
38 *E10* **Kalohi Channel** *channel* C Pacific Ocean
83 *I16* **Kalomo** Southern, S Zambia
29 *X14* **Kalona** Iowa, C USA
115 *K22* **Kalotási, Ákrotirio** *cape* Amorgós, Kykládes, Greece, Aegean Sea
152 *J8* **Kalpa** Himāchal Pradesh, N India
115 *C15* **Kalpáki** Ípeiros, W Greece
155 *C22* **Kalpeni Island** *island* Lakshadweep, India, N Indian Ocean
152 *K13* **Kālpi** Uttar Pradesh, N India
158 *G7* **Kalpin** Xinjiang Uygur Zizhiqu, NW China
149 *P16* **Kalri Lake** ◎ SE Pakistan
143 *R5* **Kāl Shūr** ≈ N Iran
39 *N11* **Kalskag** Alaska, USA
Kalsø *see* Kalsoy
95 *B18* **Kalsoy** *Dan.* Kalsø. *island* N Faeroe Islands
39 *O9* **Kaltag** Alaska, USA
108 *H7* **Kaltbrunn** Sankt Gallen, NE Switzerland
Kaltdorf *see* Pruszków
77 *X14* **Kaltungo** Gombe, E Nigeria
126 *K4* **Kaluga** Kaluzhskaya Oblast', W Russian Federation
155 *J26* **Kalu Ganga** ≈ S Sri Lanka
82 *J13* **Kalulushi** Copperbelt, C Zambia
180 *M2* **Kalumburu** Western Australia
95 *H23* **Kalundborg** Vestsjælland, E Denmark
82 *K11* **Kalungwishi** ≈ N Zambia
149 *T8* **Kalūr Kot** Punjab, E Pakistan
116 *I6* **Kalush** *Pol.* Kałusz. Ivano-Frankivs'ka Oblast', W Ukraine
Kałusz *see* Kalush
110 *N11* **Kałuszyn** Mazowieckie, C Poland
155 *J26* **Kalutara** Western Province, SW Sri Lanka
Kaluwawa *see* Fergusson Island
126 *I5* **Kaluzhskaya Oblast'** ⬖ *province* W Russian Federation
119 *E14* **Kalvarija** *Pol.* Kalwaria. Marijampol˙e, S Lithuania
93 *K15* **Kälviä** Länsi-Soumi, W Finland
109 *U6* **Kalwang** Steiermark, E Austria
Kalwaria *see* Kalvarija
154 *D13* **Kalyān** Mahārāshtra, W India
124 *K16* **Kalyazin** Tverskaya Oblast', W Russian Federation
115 *D18* **Kalydón** *anc.* Calydon. *site of ancient city* Dytikí Ellás, C Greece
115 *M21* **Kálymnos** *var.* Kálimnos. Kálymnos, Dodekánisa, Greece, Aegean Sea
115 *M21* **Kálymnos** *var.* Kálimnos. *island* Dodekánisa, Greece, Aegean Sea
117 *O5* **Kalynivka** Kyyivs'ka Oblast', N Ukraine
117 *N6* **Kalynivka** Vinnyts'ka Oblast', C Ukraine
42 *M10* **Kama** *var.* Cama. Región Autónoma Atlántico Sur, SE Nicaragua
165 *R9* **Kamaishi** *var.* Kamaisi. Iwate, Honshū, C Japan
Kamaisi *see* Kamaishi
118 *H11* **Kamajai** Panevėžys, NE Lithuania
118 *H13* **Kamajai** Utena, E Lithuania
149 *U9* **Kamālia** Punjab, NE Pakistan
83 *I14* **Kamalondo** North Western, NW Zambia
136 *I13* **Kaman** Kirşehir, C Turkey
79 *O20* **Kamanyola** Sud Kivu, E Dem. Rep. Congo
141 *N14* **Kamarān** *island* W Yemen
55 *R9* **Kamarang** W Guyana
Kāmāreddi/Kamareddy *see* Rāmāreddi
Kama Reservoir *see* Kamskoye Vodokhranilishche
148 *K13* **Kamarod** Baluchistān, SW Pakistan
171 *P14* **Kamaru** Pulau Buton, C Indonesia
147 *N12* **Kamashi** Qashqadaryo Viloyati, S Uzbekistan
77 *S13* **Kamba** Kebbi, NW Nigeria
Kambaeng Petch *see* Kamphaeng Phet
180 *L12* **Kambalda** Western Australia
149 *P13* **Kambar** *var.* Qambar. Sind, SE Pakistan
Kambara *see* Kabara
76 *I14* **Kambia** W Sierra Leone
Kambos *see* Kámpos
79 *N25* **Kambove** Katanga, SE Dem. Rep. Congo
Kambryk *see* Cambrai
123 *V10* **Kamchatka** ≈ E Russian Federation
Kamchatka *see* Kamchatka, Poluostrov
Kamchatka Basin *see* Komandorskaya Basin
123 *U10* **Kamchatka, Poluostrov** *Eng.* Kamchatka. *peninsula* E Russian Federation
123 *V10* **Kamchatskaya Oblast'** ⬖ *province* E Russian Federation
123 *V10* **Kamchatskiy Zaliv** *gulf* E Russian Federation
114 *N9* **Kamchiya** ≈ E Bulgaria
114 *L9* **Kamchiya, Yazovir** ◎ E Bulgaria
Kamdesh *see* Kāmdeysh
149 *T4* **Kāmdeysh** *var.* Kamdesh. Nūrestān, E Afghanistan
118 *M13* **Kamen'** *Rus.* Kamen'. Vitsyebskaya Voblasts', N Belarus
Kamenets *see* Kamyanyets
Kamenets-Podol'skaya Oblast' *see* Khmel'nyts'ka Oblast'
Kamenets-Podol'skiy *see* Kam"yanets'-Podil's'kyy
113 *Q18* **Kamenica** NE Macedonia
112 *A11* **Kamenjak, Rt** *headland* NW Croatia
144 *F8* **Kamenka** Zapadnyy Kazakhstan, NW Kazakhstan
125 *O6* **Kamenka** Arkhangel'skaya Oblast', NW Russian Federation
126 *6* **Kamenka** Penzenskaya Oblast', W Russian Federation
127 *L8* **Kamenka** Voronezhskaya Oblast', W Russian Federation
Kamenka *see* Camenca
Kamenka *see* Kam"yanka
Kamenka-Bugskaya *see* Kam"yanka-Buz'ka
Kamenka Dneprovskaya *see* Kam"yanka-Dniprovs'ka
Kamen Kashirskiy *see* Kamin'-Kashyrs'kyy
126 *L15* **Kamennomostskiy** Respublika Adygeya, SW Russian Federation
126 *L11* **Kamenolomni** Rostovskaya Oblast', SW Russian Federation
127 *P8* **Kamenskiy** Saratovskaya Oblast', W Russian Federation
Kamenskoye *see* Dniprodzerzhyns'k
126 *L11* **Kamensk-Shakhtinskiy** Rostovskaya Oblast', SW Russian Federation
101 *P15* **Kamenz** Sachsen, E Germany
164 *J13* **Kameoka** Kyōto, Honshū, SW Japan
126 *M3* **Kameshkovo** Vladimirskaya Oblast', W Russian Federation
164 *C11* **Kami-Agata** Nagasaki, Tsushima, SW Japan
33 *N10* **Kamiah** Idaho, NW USA
Kamień Koszyrski *see* Kamin'-Kashyrs'kyy
110 *H9* **Kamień Krajeński** *Ger.* Kamin in Westpreussen. Kujawski-pomorskie, C Poland
111 *F15* **Kamienna Góra** *Ger.* Landeshut, Landeshut in Schlesien. Dolnośląskie, SW Poland
110 *D8* **Kamień Pomorski** *Ger.* Cummin in Pommern. Zachodnio-pomorskie, NW Poland
165 *R5* **Kamiiso** Hokkaidō, NE Japan
79 *L22* **Kamiji** Kasai Oriental, S Dem. Rep. Congo
165 *T3* **Kamikawa** Hokkaidō, NE Japan
164 *B15* **Kami-Koshiki-jima** *island* SW Japan
79 *M23* **Kamina** Shaba, S Dem. Rep. Congo
Kamina *see* Kaintiba
42 *C6* **Kaminaljuyú** *ruins* Guatemala, C Guatemala
Kamin in Westpreussen *see* Kamień Krajeński
116 *J2* **Kamin'-Kashyrs'kyy** *Pol.* Kamień Koszyrski, *Rus.* Kamen Kashirskiy. Volyns'ka Oblast', NW Ukraine
165 *Q5* **Kaminokuni** Hokkaidō, NE Japan
165 *P10* **Kaminoyama** Yamagata, Honshū, C Japan
39 *Q13* **Kamishak Bay** *bay* Alaska, USA
165 *U4* **Kami-Shihoro** Hokkaidō, NE Japan
Kamishli *see* Al Qāmishlī
Kamissar *see* Kamsar
164 *C11* **Kami-Tsushima** Nagasaki, Tsushima, SW Japan
79 *O20* **Kamituga** Sud Kivu, E Dem. Rep. Congo
164 *B17* **Kamiyaku** Kagoshima, Yaku-shima, SW Japan
9 *N16* **Kamloops** British Columbia, SW Canada
107 *G25* **Kamma** Sicilia, Italy, C Mediterranean Sea
192 *K4* **Kammu Seamount** *undersea feature* N Pacific Ocean
109 *U11* **Kamnik** *Ger.* Stein. C Slovenia
Kamniške Alpe *see* Kamniško-Savinjske Alpe
109 *T10* **Kamniško-Savinjske Alpe** *var.* Kamniške Alpe, Sanntaler Alpen, *Ger* Steiner Alpen. ▲▲ N Slovenia
Kamo *see* Gavarr
165 *O14* **Kamogawa** Chiba, Honshū, S Japan
149 *W8* **Kāmoke** Punjab, E Pakistan
82 *L13* **Kamoto** Eastern, E Zambia
109 *V3* **Kamp** ≈ N Austria
81 *F18* **Kampala** ● (Uganda) S Uganda
168 *K11* **Kampar, Sungai** ≈ Sumatera, W Indonesia
98 *L9* **Kampen** Overijssel, E Netherlands
79 *N20* **Kampene** Maniema, E Dem. Rep. Congo
29 *Q9* **Kampeska, Lake** ◎ South Dakota, N USA
167 *O9* **Kamphaeng Phet** *var.* Kambaeng Petch. Kamphaeng Phet, W Thailand
Kampo *see* Campo, Cameroon
Kampo *see* Ntem, Cameroon/Equatorial Guinea
167 *S12* **Kâmpóng Cham** *prev.* Kompong Cham. Kâmpóng Cham, C Cambodia
167 *R12* **Kâmpóng Chhnăng** *prev.* Kompong. Kâmpóng Chhnăng, C Cambodia
167 *R12* **Kâmpóng Khleăng** *prev.* Kompong Kleang. Siĕmréab, NW Cambodia
167 *Q14* **Kâmpóng Saôm** *prev.* Kompong Som, Sihanoukville. Kâmpóng Saôm, SW Cambodia
167 *R13* **Kâmpóng Spoe** *prev.* Kompong Speu. Kâmpóng Spœ, S Cambodia
121 *O2* **Kámpos** *var.* Kambos. NW Cyprus
167 *R14* **Kâmpôt** Kâmpôt, SW Cambodia
Kamptee *see* Kāmthi
77 *O14* **Kampti** SW Burkina
Kampuchea *see* Cambodia
Kampuchea, Democratic *see* Cambodia
Kampuchea, People's Democratic Republic of *see* Cambodia
169 *Q9* **Kampung Sirik** Sarawak, East Malaysia
9 *V15* **Kamsack** Saskatchewan, S Canada
76 *H13* **Kamsar** *var.* Kamissar. Guinée-Maritime, W Guinea
127 *R4* **Kamskoye Ust'ye** Respublika Tatarstan, W Russian Federation
125 *U14* **Kamskoye Vodokhranilishche** *var.* Kama Reservoir. ⊠ NW Russian Federation
154 *I12* **Kāmthi** *prev.* Kamptee. Mahārāshtra, C India
Kamuela *see* Waimea
165 *R3* **Kamuenai** Hokkaidō, NE Japan
165 *T5* **Kamui-dake** ⛰ Hokkaidō, NE Japan
165 *R3* **Kamui-misaki** *headland* Hokkaidō, NE Japan
43 *O15* **Kámuk, Cerro** ▲ SE Costa Rica
116 *K7* **Kam"yanets'-Podil's'kyy** *Rus.* Kamenets-Podol'skiy. Khmel'nyts'ka Oblast', W Ukraine
117 *Q6* **Kam"yanka** *Rus.* Kamenka. Cherkas'ka Oblast', C Ukraine
116 *I5* **Kam"yanka-Buz'ka** *Rus.* Kamenka-Bugskaya. L'vivs'ka Oblast', NW Ukraine
117 *T9* **Kam"yanka-Dniprovs'ka** *Rus.* Kamenka Dneprovskaya. Zaporiz'ka Oblast', SE Ukraine
119 *F19* **Kamyanyets** *Rus.* Kamenets. Brestskaya Voblasts', SW Belarus
127 *P9* **Kamyshin** Volgogradskaya Oblast', SW Russian Federation
127 *Q13* **Kamyzyak** Astrakhanskaya Oblast', SW Russian Federation
12 *K8* **Kanaaupscow** ≈ Québec, C Canada
36 *K8* **Kanab** Utah, W USA
36 *K9* **Kanab Creek** ≈ Arizona/Utah, SW USA
187 *Y14* **Kanacea** *prev.* Kanathea. Taveuni, N Fiji
38 *G17* **Kanaga Island** *island* Aleutian Islands, Alaska, USA
38 *G17* **Kanaga Volcano** ▲ Kanaga Island, Alaska, USA
164 *N14* **Kanagawa** *off.* Kanagawa-ken. ⬖ *prefecture* Honshū, S Japan
Kanagawa-ken *see* Kanagawa
13 *Q8* **Kanairiktok** ≈ Newfoundland and Labrador, E Canada
Kanaky *see* New Caledonia
79 *K22* **Kananga** *prev.* Luluabourg. Kasai Occidental, S Dem. Rep. Congo
Kananur *see* Cannanore
Kanara *see* Karnātaka
36 *J7* **Kanarraville** Utah, W USA
127 *Q4* **Kanash** Chuvashskaya Respublika, W Russian Federation
Kanathea *see* Kanacea
21 *Q4* **Kanawha River** ≈ West Virginia, NE USA
164 *L13* **Kanayama** Gifu, Honshū, SW Japan
164 *L11* **Kanazawa** Ishikawa, Honshū, SW Japan
166 *M4* **Kanbalu** Sagaing, C Burma (Myanmar)
166 *L8* **Kanbe** Yangon, SW Burma (Myanmar)
167 *O11* **Kanchanaburi** Kanchanaburi, W Thailand
Kanchanjańghā *see* Kangchenjunga
Kānchenjunga *see* Kangchenjunga
145 *V11* **Kanchingiz, Khrebet** ▲▲ E Kazakhstan
155 *J19* **Kānchīpuram** *prev.* Conjeeveram. Tamil Nādu, SE India
149 *N8* **Kandahār** *Per.* Qandahār. Kandahār, S Afghanistan
149 *N9* **Kandahār** *Per.* Qandahār. ⬖ *province* SE Afghanistan
Kandalakša *see* Kandalaksha
124 *I5* **Kandalaksha** *var.* Kandalakša, *Fin.* Kantalahti. Murmanskaya Oblast', NW Russian Federation
Kandalaksha Gulf/Kandalakshskaya Guba *see* Kandalakshskiy Zaliv
124 *K6* **Kandalakshskiy Zaliv** *var.* Kandalakshskaya Guba, *Eng.* Kandalaksha Gulf. *bay* NW Russian Federation
Kandalangodi *see* Kandalengoti
83 *G17* **Kandalengoti** *var.* Kandalangodi. Ngamiland, NW Botswana
169 *U13* **Kandangan** Borneo, C Indonesia
Kandau *see* Kandava
118 *E8* **Kandava** *Ger.* Kandau. Tukums, W Latvia
Kandavu *see* Kadavu
77 *R14* **Kandé** *var.* Kanté. NE Togo
101 *F23* **Kandel** ▲ SW Germany
186 *C7* **Kandep** Enga, W Papua New Guinea
149 *R12* **Kandh kot** Sind, SE Pakistan
77 *S13* **Kandi** N Benin
149 *P14* **Kandiāro** Sind, SE Pakistan
136 *F11* **Kandıra** Kocaeli, NW Turkey
183 *S8* **Kandos** New South Wales, SE Australia
148 *M16* **Kandrāch** *var.* Kanrach. Baluchistān, SW Pakistan
172 *I4* **Kandreho** Mahajanga, C Madagascar
186 *F7* **Kandrian** New Britain, E Papua New Guinea
Kandukur *see* Kondukūr
155 *K25* **Kandy** Central Province, C Sri Lanka
144 *I10* **Kandyagash** *Kaz.* Qandyaghash; *prev.* Oktyab'rsk. Aktyubinsk, W Kazakhstan
18 *D12* **Kane** Pennsylvania, NE USA
64 *I11* **Kane Fracture Zone** *tectonic feature* NW Atlantic Ocean
Kanëka *see* Kanëvka
78 *G9* **Kanem** *off.* Préfecture du Kanem. ⬖ *prefecture* W Chad
Kanem, Préfecture du *see* Kanem
38 *D9* **Kāne'ohe** *var.* Kaneohe. O'ahu, Hawai'i, USA
Kanestron, Akra *see* Palioúri, Ákrotírio
Kanëv *see* Kaniv
124 *M5* **Kanëvka** *var.* Kanëka. Murmanskaya Oblast', NW Russian Federation
126 *K13* **Kanevskaya** Krasnodarskiy Kray, SW Russian Federation
Kanevskoye Vodokhranilishche *see* Kanivs'ke Vodoskhovyshche
165 *P9* **Kaneyama** Yamagata, Honshū, C Japan
83 *G20* **Kang** Kgalagadi, C Botswana
76 *L13* **Kangaba** Koulikoro, SW Mali
136 *M13* **Kangal** Sivas, C Turkey
143 *O13* **Kangan** Būshehr, S Iran
Kangān *see* Bandar-e Kangān
168 *J6* **Kangar** Perlis, Peninsular Malaysia
76 *L13* **Kangaré** Sikasso, S Mali
182 *F10* **Kangaroo Island** *island* South Australia
93 *M17* **Kangasniemi** Isä-Suomi, E Finland
142 *K6* **Kangāvar** *var.* Kangāwar. Kermānshāhān, W Iran
Kangāwar *see* Kangāvar
153 *S11* **Kangchenjunga** *var.* Kānchenjunga, *Nep.* Kanchanjańghā. ▲ NE India
160 *G9* **Kangding** *var.* Lucheng, *Tib.* Dardo. Sichuan, C China
169 *U16* **Kangean, Kepulauan** *island group* S Indonesia
169 *T16* **Kangean, Pulau** *island* Kepulauan Kangean, S Indonesia
67 *U8* **Kangen** *var.* Kengen. ≈ SE Sudan
197 *N14* **Kangerlussuaq** *Dan.* Sondre Strømfjord. ✈ Kitaa, W Greenland
197 *Q15* **Kangertittivaq** *Dan.* Scoresby Sund. *fjord* E Greenland
167 *O2* **Kangfang** Kachin State, N Burma (Myanmar)
163 *X12* **Kanggye** N North Korea
197 *P15* **Kangikajik** *var.* Kap Brewster. *headland* E Greenland
13 *N5* **Kangiqsualujjuaq** *prev.* George River, Port-Nouveau-Québec. Québec, E Canada
12 *L2* **Kangiqsujuaq** *prev.* Maricourt, Wakeham Bay. Québec, NE Canada
12 *M4* **Kangirsuk** *prev.* Bellin, Payne. Québec, E Canada
Kangle *see* Wanzai
158 *M16* **Kangmar** Xizang Zizhiqu, W China
158 *J15* **Kangmar** Xizang Zizhiqu, W China
163 *Y14* **Kangnŭng** *Jap.* Kōryō. NE South Korea
79 *D18* **Kango** Estuaire, NW Gabon
152 *I7* **Kāngra** Himāchal Pradesh, NW India
153 *Q16* **Kangsabati Reservoir** ⊠ N India
159 *O17* **Kangto** ▲ China/India
159 *W12* **Kangxian** *var.* Kang Xian, Zuitai, Zuitaizi. Gansu, C China
Kang Xian *see* Kangxian
76 *M15* **Kani** NW Ivory Coast
166 *L4* **Kani** Sagaing, C Burma (Myanmar)
79 *M23* **Kaniama** Katanga, S Dem. Rep. Congo
Kanibadam *see* Konibodom
169 *V6* **Kanibongan** Sabah, East Malaysia
185 *F17* **Kaniere** West Coast, South Island, New Zealand
185 *G17* **Kaniere, Lake** ◎ South Island, New Zealand
188 *E17* **Kanifaay** Yap, W Micronesia
125 *O4* **Kanin Kamen'** ▲▲ NW Russian Federation

◆ Country
● Country Capital
◇ Dependent Territory
○ Dependent Territory Capital
⬖ Administrative Regions
✈ International Airport
▲ Mountain
▲▲ Mountain Range
⛰ Volcano
≈ River
◎ Lake
⊠ Reservoir

125 N3 **Kanin Nos** Nenetskiy Avtonomnyy Okrug, NW Russian Federation
125 N3 **Kanin Nos, Mys** *cape* NW Russian Federation
125 O5 **Kanin, Poluostrov** *peninsula* NW Russian Federation
139 V8 **Käni Sakht** E Iraq
139 T3 **Käni Sulaymän** N Iraq
165 Q6 **Kanita** Aomori, Honshū, C Japan
117 Q5 **Kaniv** *Rus.* Kanëv. Cherkas'ka Oblast', C Ukraine
182 K11 **Kaniva** Victoria, SE Australia
117 Q5 **Kanivs'ke Vodoskhovyshche** *Rus.* Kanevskoye Vodokhranilishche. ☒ C Ukraine
112 L8 **Kanjiža** *Ger.* Altkanischa, *Hung.* Magyarkanizsa, Ökanizsa; *prev.* Stara Kanjiža. Vojvodina, N Serbia
93 K18 **Kankaanpää** Länsi-Soumi, SW Finland
30 M12 **Kankakee** Illinois, N USA
31 O11 **Kankakee River** ☒ Illinois/ Indiana, N USA
76 K14 **Kankan** Haute-Guinée, E Guinea
154 K13 **Känker** Chhattīsgarh, C India
76 J10 **Kankossa** Assaba, S Mauritania
169 N12 **Kanmaw Kyun** *var.* Kisseraing, Kithareng. *island* Mergui Archipelago, S Burma (Myanmar)
164 F12 **Kanmuri-yama** ▲ Kyūshū, SW Japan
21 R10 **Kannapolis** North Carolina, SE USA
93 L16 **Kannonkoski** Länsi-Soumi, C Finland
Kannur *see* Cannanore
93 K15 **Kannus** Länsi-Soumi, W Finland
77 V13 **Kano** Kano, N Nigeria
77 V13 **Kano** ◆ *state* N Nigeria
77 V13 **Kano** ✈ Kano, N Nigeria
164 G14 **Kan'onji** *var.* Kanonzi. Kagawa, Shikoku, SW Japan
Kanonzi *see* Kan'onji
26 M5 **Kanopolis Lake** ☒ Kansas, C USA
36 K5 **Kanosh** Utah, W USA
169 R9 **Kanowit** Sarawak, East Malaysia
164 C16 **Kanoya** Kagoshima, Kyūshū, SW Japan
152 L13 **Känpur** *Eng.* Cawnpore. Uttar Pradesh, N India
Kanrach *see* Kandrāch
164 I14 **Kansai** ✈ (Ōsaka) Ōsaka, Honshū, SW Japan
27 R9 **Kansas** Oklahoma, C USA
26 L5 **Kansas** ◆ *state* of Kansas, *also known as* Jayhawker State, Sunflower State. ◆ *state* C USA
27 R4 **Kansas City** Kansas, C USA
27 R4 **Kansas City** Missouri, C USA
27 R3 **Kansas City** ✈ Kansas, C USA
27 P4 **Kansas River** ☒ Kansas, C USA
122 L14 **Kansk** Krasnoyarskiy Kray, S Russian Federation
Kansu *see* Gansu
147 V7 **Kant** Chuyskaya Oblast', N Kyrgyzstan
Kantalahti *see* Kandalaksha
167 N16 **Kantang** *var.* Ban Kantang. Trang, SW Thailand
115 H25 **Kántanos** Krίti, Greece, E Mediterranean Sea
77 R12 **Kantchari** E Burkina
Kanté *see* Kandé
Kantemir *see* Cantemir
126 L9 **Kantemirovka** Voronezhskaya Oblast', W Russian Federation
167 R11 **Kantharalak** Si Sa Ket, E Thailand
Kantipur *see* Kathmandu
39 Q9 **Kantishna River** ☒ Alaska, USA
191 S3 **Kanton** *var.* Abariringa, Canton Island; *prev.* Mary Island. *atoll* Phoenix Islands, C Kiribati
97 C20 **Kanturk** *Ir.* Ceann Toirc. Cork, SW Ireland
55 T11 **Kanuku Mountains** ▲ S Guyana
165 O12 **Kanuma** Tochigi, Honshū, S Japan
83 H20 **Kanye** Southern, SE Botswana
83 H17 **Kanyu** Ngamiland, C Botswana
166 M7 **Kanyutkwin** Pegu, C Burma (Myanmar)
79 M24 **Kanzenze** Shaba, SE Dem. Rep. Congo
193 Y15 **Kao** *island* Kotu Group, W Tonga
161 S14 **Kaohsiung** *var.* Gaoxiong, *Jap.* Takao, Takow. S Taiwan
161 S14 **Kaohsiung** ✈ S Taiwan
Kaokaona *see* Kirakira
83 B17 **Kaoko Veld** ▲ N Namibia
76 G11 **Kaolack** *var.* Kaolak. W Senegal
Kaolak *see* Kaolack
186 M8 **Kaolo** San Jorge, N Solomon Islands
83 H14 **Kaoma** Western, W Zambia
38 B8 **Kapa'a** *var.* Kapaa. Kaua'i, Hawai'i, USA, C pacific Ocean
Kapaa *see* Kapa'a
113 J16 **Kapa Moračka** ▲ C Montenegro
137 V13 **Kapan** *Rus.* Kafan; *prev.* Ghap'an. SE Armenia
82 L13 **Kapandashila** Northern, NE Zambia
79 L23 **Kapanga** Katanga, S Dem. Rep. Congo
145 U15 **Kapchagay** *Kaz.* Kapshaghay. Almaty, SE Kazakhstan
145 V15 **Kapchagayskoye Vodokhranilishche** *Kaz.* Qapshagay Böyeni. ☒ SE Kazakhstan
99 F15 **Kapelle** Zeeland, SW Netherlands
99 G16 **Kapellen** Antwerpen, N Belgium
95 P15 **Kapellskär** Stockholm, C Sweden

81 H18 **Kapenguria** Rift Valley, W Kenya
109 V6 **Kapfenberg** Steiermark, C Austria
83 J14 **Kapiri Mposhi** Central, C Zambia
149 R4 **Käpïsä** ◆ *province* E Afghanistan
12 G10 **Kapiskau** ☒ Ontario, C Canada
184 K13 **Kapiti Island** *island* C New Zealand
78 K9 **Kapka, Massif du** ▲ E Chad
Kaplamada *see* Kaubalatmada, Gunung
22 H9 **Kaplan** Louisiana, S USA
Kaplangky, Plato *see* Gaplaňgyr Platosy
111 D19 **Kaplice** *Ger.* Kaplitz. Jihočeský Kraj, S Czech Republic
Kaplitz *see* Kaplice
Kapoche *see* Capoche
171 T12 **Kapocol** Papua, E Indonesia
167 N14 **Kapoe** Ranong, SW Thailand
81 G15 **Kapoeta** Eastern Equatoria, SE Sudan
111 I25 **Kapos** ☒ S Hungary
111 H25 **Kaposvár** Somogy, SW Hungary
94 H13 **Kapp** Oppland, S Norway
100 I7 **Kappeln** Schleswig-Holstein, N Germany
Kaproncza *see* Koprivnica
109 P7 **Kaprun** Salzburg, C Austria
Kapshaghay *see* Kapchagay
Kapstad *see* Cape Town
171 Y13 **Kaptiau** Papua, E Indonesia
119 L19 **Kaptsevichy** *Rus.* Koptsevichi. Homyel'skaya Voblasts', SE Belarus
Kapuas Hulu, Banjaran/ Kapuas Hulu, Pegunungan *see* Kapuas Mountains
169 S10 **Kapuas Mountains** *Ind.* Banjaran Kapuas Hulu, Pegunungan Kapuas Hulu. ▲ Indonesia/Malaysia
169 P11 **Kapuas, Sungai** ☒ Borneo, N Indonesia
169 T13 **Kapuas, Sungai** *prev.* Kapoeas. ☒ Borneo, C Indonesia
182 J9 **Kapunda** South Australia
152 H8 **Kapūrthala** Punjab, N India
12 G12 **Kapuskasing** Ontario, S Canada
14 D6 **Kapuskasing** ☒ Ontario, S Canada
127 P11 **Kapustin Yar** Astrakhanskaya Oblast', SW Russian Federation
82 K11 **Kaputa** Northern, NE Zambia
111 G22 **Kapuvár** Győr-Moson-Sopron, NW Hungary
Kapydzhik, Gora *see* Qazangödağ
119 J17 **Kapyl'** *Rus.* Kopyl'. Minskaya Voblasts', C Belarus
43 N9 **Kara** *var.* Cara. Región Autónoma Atlántico Sur, E Nicaragua
77 R14 **Kara** *var.* Lama-Kara. NE Togo
77 Q14 **Kara** ☒ N Togo
147 U7 **Kara-Balta** Chuyskaya Oblast', N Kyrgyzstan
144 L7 **Karabalyk** *Kaz.* Komsomol, *var.* Komsomolets. Kostanay, N Kazakhstan
144 G11 **Karabau** Atyrau, W Kazakhstan
146 E7 **Karabaur', Uval** *Kaz.* Korabavur Pastligi, *Uzb.* Qorabowur Kirlari. *physical region* Kazakhstan/Uzbekistan
Karabekaul *see* Garabekewül
Karabil', Vozvyshennost' *see* Garabil Belentligi
Kara-Bogaz-Gol *see* Garabogazköl
Kara-Bogaz-Gol, Zaliv *see* Garabogaz Aylagy
Kara-Bogazkol *see* Garabogazköl
145 R15 **Karaboget** *Kaz.* Qaraböget. Zhambyl, S Kazakhstan
136 H11 **Karabük** Karabük, NW Turkey
136 H11 **Karabük** ◆ *province* NW Turkey
122 L12 **Karabula** Krasnoyarskiy Kray, C Russian Federation
145 V14 **Karabulak** *Kaz.* Qarabulaq. Taldykorgan, SE Kazakhstan
145 Y11 **Karabulak** *Kaz.* Qarabulaq. Vostochnyy Kazakhstan, E Kazakhstan
145 Q17 **Karabulak** *Kaz.* Qarabulaq. Yuzhnyy Kazakhstan, S Kazakhstan
136 C17 **Kara Burnu** *headland* SW Turkey
144 K10 **Karabutak** *Kaz.* Qarabutaq. Aktyubinsk, W Kazakhstan
136 D12 **Karacabey** Bursa, NW Turkey
114 O12 **Karaçali** ☒Istanbul, NW Turkey
114 M12 **Karacaoğlan** Kırklareli, NW Turkey
Karachay-Cherkessia *see* Karachayevo-Cherkesskaya Respublika
126 L15 **Karachayevo-Cherkesskaya Respublika** *Eng.* Karachay-Cherkessia. ◆ *autonomous republic* SW Russian Federation
126 M15 **Karachayevsk** Karachayevo-Cherkesskaya Respublika, SW Russian Federation
126 J6 **Karachev** Bryanskaya Oblast', W Russian Federation
149 O16 **Karāchi** Sind, SE Pakistan
149 O16 **Karāchi** ✈ Sind, S Pakistan
155 E15 **Karād** Mahārāshtra, W India
143 N7 **Karadağ** ▲ S Turkey
147 T10 **Karadar'ya** *Uzb.* Qoradaryo. ☒ Kyrgyzstan/Uzbekistan
Karadeniz *see* Black Sea
Karadeniz Boğazi *see* İstanbul Boğazı
146 B13 **Karadepe** Balkan Welaýaty, W Turkmenistan
Karadzhar *see* Qorajar
Karaferiye *see* Véroia

Karagan *see* Garagan
145 R10 **Karaganda** *Kaz.* Qaraghandy. Karaganda, C Kazakhstan
145 R10 **Karaganda** *off.* Karagandinskaya Oblast', *Kaz.* Qaraghandy Oblysy. ◆ *province* C Kazakhstan
Karagandinskaya Oblast' *see* Karaganda
145 T10 **Karagayly** *Kaz.* Qaraghayly. Karaganda, C Kazakhstan
Karagel' *see* Garagöl'
123 U9 **Karaginskiy, Ostrov** *island* E Russian Federation
197 T1 **Karaginskiy Zaliv** *bay* E Russian Federation
137 P13 **Karagöl Dağları** ▲ NE Turkey
Karagumskiy Kanal *see* Garagum Kanaly
114 L13 **Karahisar** Edirne, NW Turkey
127 V3 **Karaidel'** Respublika Bashkortostan, W Russian Federation
127 V3 **Karaidel'skiy Respublika** Bashkortostan, W Russian Federation
114 L13 **Karaidemir Barajı** ☒ NW Turkey
155 J21 **Kāraikāl** Pondicherry, SE India
155 I22 **Kāraikkudi** Tamil Nādu, SE India
145 Y11 **Kara Irtysh** *Rus.* Chërnyy Irtysh. ☒ NE Kazakhstan
143 N13 **Karaj** Tehrän, N Iran
168 K8 **Karak** Pahang, Peninsular Malaysia
Karak *see* Al Karak
147 V13 **Kara-Kabak** Oshskaya Oblast', SW Kyrgyzstan
Kara-Kala *see* Magtymguly
Karakala *see* Oqqal'a
Karakalpakstan, Respublika *see* Qoraqalpog'iston Respublikasi
Karakalpakya *see* Qoraqalpog'iston
Karakax He *see* Moyu
158 O10 **Karakax He** ☒ NW China
121 X8 **Karakaya Baraji** ☒ C Turkey
171 Q9 **Karakelang, Pulau** *island* N Indonesia
Karakilisse *see* Ağrı
Karak, Muḩāfaẓat al *see* Al Karak
147 Y7 **Karakol** *prev.* Przheval'sk. Issyk-Kul'skaya Oblast', NE Kyrgyzstan
147 X8 **Karakol** *var.* Karakolka. Issyk-Kul'skaya Oblast', NE Kyrgyzstan
Karakolka *see* Karakol
149 W2 **Karakoram Highway** *road* China/Pakistan
149 Z3 **Karakoram Pass** *Chin.* Karakoram Shankou. *pass* C Asia
152 I3 **Karakoram Range** ▲ C Asia
Karakoram Shankou *see* Karakoram Pass
Karaköse *see* Ağrı
145 P14 **Kara-Koyyn, Ozero** *Kaz.* Qaraqoyyn. ☒ C Kazakhstan
83 F19 **Karakubis** Ghanzi, W Botswana
147 T9 **Kara-Kul'** *Kir.* Kara-Köl. Dzhalal-Abadskaya Oblast', W Kyrgyzstan
Karakul' *see* Qarokŭl
Kara-Kul'dzha Oshskaya Oblast', SW Kyrgyzstan
147 U10 **Kara-Kul'dzha** Oshskaya Oblast', SW Kyrgyzstan
127 T3 **Karakulino** Udmurtskaya Respublika, NW Russian Federation
Karakul', Ozero *see* Qarokŭl
Kara Kum *see* Garagum
Kara Kum Canal/ Karakumskiy Kanal *see* Garagum Kanaly
Karakumy, Peski *see* Garagum
83 E17 **Karakuwisa** Okavango, NE Namibia
122 M13 **Karam** Irkutskaya Oblast', C Russian Federation
Karamai *see* Karamay
169 T14 **Karamain, Pulau** *island* N Indonesia
136 I16 **Karaman** Karaman, S Turkey
136 I16 **Karaman** ◆ *province* S Turkey
114 M8 **Karamandere** ☒ NE Bulgaria
158 J4 **Karamay** *var.* Karamai, Kelamayi; *prev. Chin.* K'o-la-ma-i. Xinjiang Uygur Zizhiqu, NW China
169 U14 **Karambu** Borneo, C Indonesia
185 H14 **Karamea** West Coast, South Island, New Zealand
185 H14 **Karamea** ☒ South Island, New Zealand
185 G15 **Karamea Bight** *gulf* South Island, New Zealand
Karamet-Niyaz *see* Garamätnyýaz
158 K10 **Karamiran He** ☒ NW China
147 S11 **Karamyk** Oshskaya Oblast', SW Kyrgyzstan
169 U17 **Karangasem** Bali, S Indonesia
154 H12 **Kāranja** Mahārāshtra, C India
152 F9 **Karanpur** *var.* Karanpura. Rājasthān, NW India
Karánsebes/Karansebesch *see* Caransebeş
145 T14 **Karaoy** *Kaz.* Qaraoy. Almaty, SE Kazakhstan
114 N7 **Karapelit** *Rom.* Stejarul. Dobrich, NE Bulgaria
136 I15 **Karapınar** Konya, C Turkey
83 D22 **Karas** ◆ *district* S Namibia
147 N3 **Kara-Say** Issyk-Kul'skaya Oblast', NE Kyrgyzstan
83 E22 **Karasburg** Karas, S Namibia
92 K9 **Kárášjohka** *var.* Karašjokka. ☒ N Norway
92 L9 **Karasjok** *Fin.* Kaarasjoki, *Lapp.* Kárášjohka. Finnmark, N Norway
Karašjokka *see* Kárášjohka
Kara Strait *see* Karskiye Vorota, Proliv
145 N8 **Karasu** *Kaz.* Qarasū. Kostanay, N Kazakhstan

136 F11 **Karasu** Sakarya, NW Turkey
Kara Su *see* Mesta/Néstos
Karasubazar *see* Bilohirs'k
122 I12 **Karasuk** Novosibirskaya Oblast', C Russian Federation
145 U13 **Karatal** *Kaz.* Qaratal. ◆ SE Kazakhstan
136 K17 **Karataş** Adana, S Turkey
145 Q16 **Karatau** *Kaz.* Qarataū. Zhambyl, S Kazakhstan
Karatau *see* Karatau, Khrebet
145 P16 **Karatau, Khrebet** *var.* Karatau, *Kaz.* Qarataū. ▲ S Kazakhstan
144 G13 **Karaton** *Kaz.* Qaraton. Atyrau, W Kazakhstan
164 C13 **Karatsu** *var.* Karatu. Saga, Kyūshū, SW Japan
Karatu *see* Karatsu
122 K8 **Karaul** Taymyrskiy (Dolgano-Nenetskiy) Avtonomnyy Okrug, N Russian Federation
Karaulbazar *see* Qorowulbozor
Karauzyak *see* Qorao'zak
115 D16 **Karáva** ▲ C Greece
115 F22 **Karavás** Kýthira, S Greece
113 J20 **Karavastasë, Laguna e** *var.* Kënet' e Karavastas, Kravasta Lagoon. *lagoon* W Albania
Karavastasë, Laguna e *see* Karavastasë, Kënet' e
118 I5 **Karavere** Tartumaa, E Estonia
115 L23 **Karavonísia** *island* Kykládes, Greece, Aegean Sea
169 O15 **Karawang** *prev.* Krawang. Jawa, C Indonesia
109 T10 **Karawanken** *Slvn.* Karavanke. ▲ Austria/Serbia
Karaxahar *see* Kaidu He
137 R13 **Karayazı** Erzurum, NE Turkey
145 Q12 **Karazhal** Karaganda, C Kazakhstan
139 S9 **Karbalā'** *var.* Kerbala, Kerbela. S Iraq
95 L17 **Kärböle** Gävleborg, C Sweden
111 M23 **Karcag** Jász-Nagykun-Szolnok, E Hungary
Kardak *see* Imia
114 N7 **Kardam** Dobrich, NE Bulgaria
115 M22 **Kardámaina** Kos, Dodekánisa, Greece, Aegean Sea
115 L18 **Kardámyla** *var.* Kardhámila, Kardhámila. Chίos, E Greece
Kardeljevo *see* Ploče
Kardh *see* Qardho
Kardhámila *see* Kardámyla
115 E16 **Karditsa** *var.* Kardhítsa. Thessalía, C Greece
Kardhítsa *see* Karditsa
118 E4 **Kärdla** *Ger.* Kertel. Hiiumaa, W Estonia
Kärdžali *see* Kŭrdzhali
119 I16 **Karelichy** *Pol.* Korelicze, *Rus.* Korelichi. Hrodzyenskaya Voblasts', W Belarus
124 I10 **Kareliya, Respublika** *prev.* Karel'skaya ASSR, *Eng.* Karelia. ◆ *autonomous republic* NW Russian Federation
Karel'skaya ASSR *see* Kareliya, Respublika
92 J10 **Karesuando** *Fin.* Kaaresuanto, *Lapp.* Gárasavvon. Norrbotten, N Sweden
Karet *see* Kâghet
Kareyz-e-Elyäs/Kärez Iliäs *see* Käriz-e Elyäs
122 J11 **Kargasok** Tomskaya Oblast', C Russian Federation
122 I12 **Kargat** Novosibirskaya Oblast', C Russian Federation
136 J11 **Kargı** Çorum, N Turkey
152 I5 **Kargil** Jammu and Kashmir, NW India
Kargilyovka *see* Karlovac
124 L11 **Kargopol'** Arkhangel'skaya Oblast', NW Russian Federation
110 G12 **Kargowa** *Ger.* Unruhstadt. Lubuskie, W Poland
77 X13 **Kari** Bauchi, E Nigeria
114 M8 **Kariadere** ☒ NE Bulgaria
83 J15 **Kariba** Mashonaland West, N Zimbabwe
83 J16 **Kariba, Lake** ☒ Zambia/Zimbabwe
83 C19 **Karibib** Erongo, C Namibia
92 L9 **Karigasniemi** *Lapp.* Garegegasnjárga. Lappi, N Finland
184 J2 **Karikari, Cape** *headland* North Island, New Zealand
Karīmābād *see* Hunza
169 P12 **Karimata, Kepulauan** *island group* N Indonesia
169 P12 **Karimata, Pulau** *island* Kepulauan Karimata, N Indonesia
169 O11 **Karimata, Selat** *strait* W Indonesia
155 I14 **Karīmnagar** Andhra Pradesh, C India
186 C7 **Karimui** Chimbu, C Papua New Guinea
169 Q15 **Karimunjawa, Pulau** *island* S Indonesia
80 N11 **Karin** Woqooyi Galbeed, N Somalia
Kariot *see* Ikaría
93 L20 **Karis** *Fin.* Karjaa. Etelä-Suomi, SW Finland
Káristos *see* Kárystos
137 S12 **Kars** *var.* Qars. Kars, NE Turkey
137 S12 **Kars** *var.* Qars. ◆ *province* NE Turkey
145 O12 **Karsakpay** *Kaz.* Qarsaqbay. Karaganda, C Kazakhstan
Karjaa *see* Karis
93 L15 **Kärsämäki** Oulu, C Finland
118 K9 **Kārsava** *Ger.* Karsau; *prev. Rus.* Korsovka. Ludza, E Latvia
Karshi *see* Garşy
143 K8 **Karkheh, Rūd-e** ☒ SW Iran
115 H22 **Karkinágri** *var.* Karkinagrio. Ikaría, Dodekánisa, Greece, Aegean Sea
Karkinítska Zatoka *see* Karkinits'ka Zatoka
Karshinskaya Step *see* Qarshi Cho'li

117 R12 **Karkinits'ka Zatoka** *Rus.* Karkinitskiy Zaliv. *gulf* S Ukraine
Karkinitskiy Zaliv *see* Karkinits'ka Zatoka
93 L19 **Karkkila** *Swe.* Högfors. Uusimaa, S Finland
93 M19 **Kärkölä** Etelä-Suomi, S Finland
182 G9 **Karkoo** South Australia
118 D5 **Kärla** *Ger.* Kergel. Saaremaa, W Estonia
110 F7 **Karlino** *Ger.* Körlin an der Persante. Zachodnio-pomorskie, NW Poland
137 Q13 **Karlıova** Bingöl, E Turkey
117 U6 **Karlivka** Poltavs'ka Oblast', C Ukraine
Karl-Marx-Stadt *see* Chemnitz
Karló *see* Hailuoto
112 C11 **Karlobag** *It.* Carlopago. Lika-Senj, W Croatia
112 D9 **Karlovac** *Ger.* Karlstadt, *Hung.* Károlyváros. N Croatia
112 C10 **Karlovac** *off.* Karlovačka Županija. ◆ *province* C Croatia
Karlovačka Županija *see* Karlovac
118 I5 **Karlovo** *prev.* Levskigrad. Plovdiv, C Bulgaria
114 J9 **Karlovo** *prev.* Levskigrad. Plovdiv, C Bulgaria
111 A16 **Karlovy Vary** *Ger.* Karlsbad; *prev. Eng.* Carlsbad. Karlovarský Kraj, W Czech Republic
111 A16 **Karlovarský Kraj** ◆ *region* W Czech Republic
115 M19 **Karlovási** *var.* Neon Karlovási, Neon Karlovásion. Sámos, Greece, Aegean Sea
115 M19 **Karlovási** *var.* Néon Karlovási, Néon Karlovásion. Sámos, Dodekánisa, Greece, Aegean Sea
114 J9 **Karlovo** *prev.* Levskigrad. Plovdiv, C Bulgaria
95 L17 **Karlsborg** Västra Götaland, S Sweden
Karlsburg *see* Alba Iulia
95 L22 **Karlshamn** Blekinge, S Sweden
95 L16 **Karlskoga** Örebro, C Sweden
95 M22 **Karlskrona** Blekinge, S Sweden
101 G21 **Karlsruhe** *var.* Carlsruhe. Baden-Württemberg, SW Germany
95 K16 **Karlstad** Värmland, C Sweden
29 R3 **Karlstad** Minnesota, N USA
101 J18 **Karlstadt** Bayern, C Germany
118 E4 **Kärmlä** *Ger.* Kertel. Hiiumaa, W Estonia
39 Q14 **Karluk** Kodiak Island, Alaska, USA
Karluk *see* Qarluq
119 O17 **Karma** *Rus.* Korma. Homyel'skaya Voblasts', SE Belarus
155 F14 **Karmāla** Mahārāshtra, W India
146 M11 **Karmana** Navoiy Viloyati, C Uzbekistan
138 G8 **Karmi'él** *var.* Carmiel. Northern, N Israel
95 B16 **Karmøy** *island* S Norway
152 I9 **Karnāl** Haryāna, N India
153 W15 **Karnaphuli Reservoir** ☒ NE India
155 F17 **Karnātaka** *var.* Kanara; *prev.* Maisur, Mysore. ◆ *state* W India
25 S13 **Karnes City** Texas, SW USA
109 P9 **Karnische Alpen** *It.* Alpi Carniche. ▲ Austria/Italy
109 Q9 **Kärnten** *off.* Land Kärten, *Eng.* Carinthi, *Slvn.* Koroška. ◆ *state* S Austria
114 M9 **Karnobat** Burgas, E Bulgaria
83 K16 **Karoi** Mashonaland West, N Zimbabwe
Karol *see* Carei
143 U4 **Károly-Fehérvár** *see* Alba Iulia
82 M12 **Karonga** Northern, N Malawi
147 W10 **Karool-Tëbë** Narynskaya Oblast', C Kyrgyzstan
182 J7 **Karoonda** South Australia
149 S9 **Karor Lāl Esan** Punjab, E Pakistan
149 T11 **Karor Pacca** *var.* Kahror, *var.* Kahror Pakka. Punjab, E Pakistan
171 N12 **Karosa** *var.* Karosa. Sulawesi, C Indonesia
Karosa *see* Karosa
Karpaten *see* Carpathian Mountains
Karies *see* Karyés
115 L22 **Karpáthio Pélagos** *sea* Dodekánisa, Greece, Aegean Sea
115 N24 **Kárpathos** Kárpathos, SE Greece
115 N24 **Kárpathos** *It.* Scarpanto; *anc.* Carpathos, Carpathus. *island* SE Greece
115 N24 **Karpathos Strait** *see* Karpathou, Stenó
115 N24 **Karpathou, Stenó** *var.* Karpathos Strait, Scarpanto Strait. *strait* Dodekánisa, Greece, Aegean Sea E Greece
Karpaty *see* Carpathian Mountains
115 E17 **Karpenísi** *prev.* Karpenísion. Sterea Ellás, C Greece
Karpenísion *see* Karpenísi
125 O8 **Karpogory** Arkhangel'skaya Oblast', NW Russian Federation
180 I7 **Karratha** Western Australia
137 S12 **Kars** *var.* Qars. Kars, NE Turkey
137 S12 **Kars** *var.* Qars. ◆ *province* NE Turkey
145 O12 **Karsakpay** *Kaz.* Qarsaqbay. Karaganda, C Kazakhstan
93 L15 **Kärsämäki** Oulu, C Finland
118 K9 **Kārsava** *Ger.* Karsau; *prev. Rus.* Korsovka. Ludza, E Latvia

84 I5 **Karskiye Vorota, Proliv** *Eng.* Kara Strait. *strait* N Russian Federation
122 J6 **Karskoye More** *Eng.* Kara Sea. *sea* Arctic Ocean
93 L17 **Karstula** Länsi-Soumi, C Finland
127 Q5 **Karsun** Ul'yanovskaya Oblast', W Russian Federation
122 F11 **Kartaly** Chelyabinskaya Oblast', C Russian Federation
18 E13 **Karthaus** Pennsylvania, NE USA
110 I7 **Kartuzy** Pomorskie, NW Poland
165 R8 **Karumai** Iwate, Honshū, C Japan
181 U4 **Karumba** Queensland, NE Australia
92 K13 **Karungi** Norrbotten, N Sweden
92 K13 **Karunki** Lappi, N Finland
155 H21 **Karūr** Tamil Nādu, SE India
93 K17 **Karvia** Länsi-Soumi, SW Finland
111 J17 **Karviná** *Ger.* Karwin, *Pol.* Karwina; *prev.* Karvinná. Moravskoslezský Kraj, E Czech Republic
155 E17 **Kārwār** Karnātaka, W India
108 M7 **Karwendelgebirge** ▲ Austria/Germany
Karwin/Karwina *see* Karviná
115 I14 **Karyés** *var.* Karies. Ágion Óros, N Greece
115 I19 **Kárystos** *var.* Káristos. Évvoia, C Greece
136 E17 **Kaş** Antalya, SW Turkey
39 Y14 **Kasaan** Prince of Wales Island, Alaska, USA
164 I13 **Kasai** Hyōgo, Honshū, SW Japan
79 K21 **Kasai** *var.* Cassai, Kassai. ☒ Angola/Dem. Rep. Congo
79 K22 **Kasai Occidental** *off.* Région ◆ *region* S Dem. Rep. Congo
Kasai Occidental, Région *see* Kasai Occidental
79 L24 **Kasai Oriental** *off.* Région ◆ *region* C Dem. Rep. Congo
Kasai Oriental, Région *see* Kasai Oriental
79 L24 **Kasaji** Katanga, S Dem. Rep. Congo
82 L12 **Kasama** Northern, N Zambia
Kasan *see* Koson
83 H16 **Kasane** North-West, NE Botswana
81 E23 **Kasanga** Rukwa, W Tanzania
79 G21 **Kasangulu** Bas-Congo, W Dem. Rep. Congo
Kasansay *see* Kosonsoy
155 E20 **Kāsaragod** Kerala, SW India
118 P13 **Kasari** *var.* Kasari Jõgi, *W* Estonia
Kasari Jõgi *see* Kasari
8 L11 **Kasba Lake** ☒ Northwest Territories, Nunavut N Canada
164 B16 **Kaseda** Kagoshima, Kyūshū, SW Japan
83 I14 **Kasempa** North Western, NW Zambia
79 O24 **Kasenga** Katanga, SE Dem. Rep. Congo
79 P17 **Kasese** *var.* Kasenyi. Orientale, NE Dem. Rep. Congo
79 O19 **Kasese** Maniema, E Dem. Rep. Congo
81 E18 **Kasese** SW Uganda
152 J11 **Kāsganj** Uttar Pradesh, N India
143 U4 **Kashaf Rūd** ☒ NE Iran
143 N7 **Käshän** Eṣfahān, C Iran
126 M10 **Kashary** Rostovskaya Oblast', SW Russian Federation
39 O12 **Kashegelok** Alaska, USA
158 E7 **Kashgar** *see* Kashi
158 E7 **Kashi** *Chin.* Kaxgar, K'o-shih, *Uigh.* Kashgar. Xinjiang Uygur Zizhiqu, NW China
164 J14 **Kashihara** *var.* Kashiwara. Nara, Honshū, SW Japan
165 P13 **Kashima-nada** *gulf* S Japan
124 K15 **Kashin** Tverskaya Oblast', W Russian Federation
152 K10 **Kāshipur** Uttaranchal, N India
126 L4 **Kashira** Moskovskaya Oblast', W Russian Federation
165 N11 **Kashiwazaki** *var.* Kasiwazaki. Niigata, Honshū, C Japan
Kashkadar'inskaya Oblast' *see* Qashqadaryo Viloyati
143 T5 **Kashmar** *var.* Turshiz; *prev.* Solṭānābād, Torshiz. Khorāsān, NE Iran
Kashmir *see* Jammu and Kashmir
149 R12 **Kashmor** Sind, SE Pakistan
149 S5 **Kashmünd Ghar** *Eng.* Kashmund Range. ▲ E Afghanistan
Kashmund Range *see* Kashmünd Ghar
Kasi *see* Vārānasi
153 O12 **Kasia** Uttar Pradesh, N India
39 N12 **Kasigluk** Alaska, USA
39 N11 **Kasilof** Alaska, USA
Kasimköj *see* General Toshevo
126 M4 **Kasimov** Ryazanskaya Oblast', W Russian Federation
79 P18 **Kasindi** Nord Kivu, E Dem. Rep. Congo
82 M12 **Kasitu** ☒ N Malawi
Kasiwazaki *see* Kashiwazaki
30 L14 **Kaskaskia River** ☒ Illinois, N USA
93 J17 **Kaskinen** *Swe.* Kaskö. Länsi-Soumi, SW Finland
Kaskö *see* Kaskinen
9 O17 **Kas Kong** *see* Kông, Kaôh
9 O17 **Kaslo** British Columbia, SW Canada
Käsmark *see* Kežmarok
169 T12 **Kasongan** Borneo, C Indonesia
79 N21 **Kasongo** Maniema, E Dem. Rep. Congo

◆ Country ◇ Dependent Territory ◆ Administrative Regions ▲ Mountain ☒ Volcano ☒ Lake
● Country Capital ○ Dependent Territory Capital ✈ International Airport ▲ Mountain Range ☒ River ☒ Reservoir

Kasongo-Lunda – Kerby

79 H22 **Kasongo-Lunda** Bandundu, SW Dem. Rep. Congo
115 M24 **Kásos** *island* S Greece
Kasos Strait *see* Kasou, Stenó
115 M25 **Kasou, Stenó** *var.* Kasos Strait. *strait* Dodekánisa/Kríti, Greece, Aegean Sea
137 T10 **Kaspi** C Georgia
114 M8 **Kaspichan** Shumen, NE Bulgaria
Kaspīy Mangy Oypaty *see* Caspian Depression
127 Q16 **Kaspiysk** Respublika Dagestan, SW Russian Federation
Kaspiyskiy *see* Lagan'
Kaspiyskoye More/Kaspiy Tengizi *see* Caspian Sea
Kassa *see* Košice
Kassai *see* Kasai
80 I9 **Kassala** Kassala, E Sudan
80 H9 **Kassala** ⬖ *state* NE Sudan
115 G15 **Kassándra** *prev.* Pallíni; *anc.* Pallene. *peninsula* NE Greece
115 G15 **Kassándras, Akrotírio** *cape* N Greece
115 H15 **Kassándras, Kólpos** *var.* Kólpos Toronaíos. *gulf* N Greece
139 Y11 **Kassārah** E Iraq
101 I15 **Kassel** *prev.* Cassel. Hessen, C Germany
74 M6 **Kasserine** *var.* Al Qaşrayn. W Tunisia
14 J14 **Kasshabog Lake** ◎ Ontario, SE Canada
139 O5 **Kassīr, Sabkhat al** ◎ E Syria
29 W10 **Kasson** Minnesota, N USA
115 C17 **Kassópeia** *Var.* Kassópi. *site of ancient city* Ípeiros, W Greece
Kassópi *see* Kassópeia
115 N24 **Kastállou, Akrotírio** *headland* Kárpathos, SE Greece
136 I11 **Kastamonu** *var.* Castamoni, Kastamuni. Kastamonu, N Turkey
136 I10 **Kastamonu** *var.* Kastamuni. ⬖ *province* N Turkey
Kastamuni *see* Kastamonu
115 E14 **Kastaneá** Kentrikí Makedonía, N Greece
Kastélli *see* Kíssamos
Kastellórizon *see* Megísti
95 N21 **Kastlösa** Kalmar, S Sweden
115 D14 **Kastoría** Dytikí Makedonía, N Greece
126 K7 **Kastornoye** Kurskaya Oblast', W Russian Federation
115 I21 **Kástro** Sífnos, Kykládes, Greece, Aegean Sea
95 J23 **Kastrup** ✈ (København) København, E Denmark
119 Q17 **Kastsyukovichy** *Rus.* Kostyukovichi. Mahilyowskaya Voblasts', E Belarus
119 O18 **Kastsyukowka** *Rus.* Kostyukovka. Homyel'skaya Voblasts', SE Belarus
164 D13 **Kasuga** Fukuoka, Kyūshū, SW Japan
164 L13 **Kasugai** Aichi, Honshū, SW Japan
81 E21 **Kasulu** Kigoma, W Tanzania
164 I12 **Kasumi** Hyōgo, Honshū, SW Japan
127 R17 **Kasumkent** Respublika Dagestan, SW Russian Federation
82 M13 **Kasungu** Central, C Malawi
149 W9 **Kasūr** Punjab, E Pakistan
83 G15 **Kataba** Western, W Zambia
19 R4 **Katahdin, Mount** ▲ Maine, NE USA
79 M20 **Katako-Kombe** Kasai Oriental, C Dem. Rep. Congo
39 T12 **Katalla** Alaska, USA
Katana *see* Qaṭanā
79 L24 **Katanga** *off.* Région du Katanga, *prev* Shaba. ⬖ *region* SE Dem. Rep. Congo
122 M11 **Katanga** ≈ C Russian Federation
Katanga, Région du *see* Katanga
154 J11 **Katāngi** Madhya Pradesh, C India
180 J13 **Katanning** Western Australia
181 P8 **Kata Tjuta** *var.* Mount Olga. ▲ Northern Territory, C Australia
Katawaz *see* Zarghūn Shahr
151 Q22 **Katchall Island** *island* Nicobar Islands, India, NE Indian Ocean
115 F14 **Kateríni** Kentrikí Makedonía, N Greece
117 P7 **Katerynopil'** Cherkas'ka Oblast', C Ukraine
166 M3 **Katha** Sagaing, N Burma (Myanmar)
181 P2 **Katherine** Northern Territory, N Australia
154 B11 **Kāthiāwār Peninsula** *peninsula* W India
153 P11 **Kathmandu** *prev.* Kantipur. ● (Nepal) Central, C Nepal
152 H7 **Kathua** Jammu and Kashmir, NW India
76 L12 **Kati** Koulikoro, SW Mali
153 R13 **Katihār** Bihār, NE India
184 N7 **Katikati** Bay of Plenty, North Island, New Zealand
83 H16 **Katima Mulilo** Caprivi, NE Namibia
77 N15 **Katiola** C Ivory Coast
191 V10 **Katiu** *atoll* Îles Tuamotu, C French Polynesia
117 N12 **Katlabukh, Ozero** ◎ SW Ukraine
39 P14 **Katmai, Mount** ▲ Alaska, USA
154 J9 **Katni** Madhya Pradesh, C India
115 D19 **Káto Achaïa** *var.* Kato Ahaia, Káto Akhaía. Dytikí Ellás, S Greece
Kato Ahaia/Káto Akhaía *see* Káto Achaïa
121 P2 **Kato Lakatámeia** *var.* Kato Lakatamia. C Cyprus
Kato Lakatamia *see* Kato Lakatámeia
79 N22 **Katompi** Katanga, SE Dem. Rep. Congo
83 K14 **Katondwe** Lusaka, C Zambia
114 H12 **Káto Nevrokópi** *prev.* Káto Nevrokópion. Anatolikí Makedonía kai Thráki, NE Greece
Káto Nevrokópion *see* Káto Nevrokópi
81 E18 **Katonga** ≈ S Uganda
115 F15 **Káto Ólympos** ▲▲ C Greece
115 D17 **Katoúna** Dytikí Ellás, C Greece
115 E19 **Káto Vlasiá** Dytikí Makedonía, S Greece
111 J16 **Katowice** *Ger.* Kattowitz. Śląskie, S Poland
153 S15 **Kātoya** West Bengal, NE India
136 E16 **Katrançik Dağı** ▲▲ SW Turkey
95 N16 **Katrineholm** Södermanland, C Sweden
96 I11 **Katrine, Loch** ◎ C Scotland, UK
77 V12 **Katsina** Katsina, N Nigeria
77 U12 **Katsina** ⬖ *state* N Nigeria
67 P8 **Katsina Ala** ≈ S Nigeria
164 C13 **Katsumoto** Nagasaki, Iki, SW Japan
165 P13 **Katsuta** *var.* Katuta. Ibaraki, Honshū, S Japan
165 O14 **Katsuura** *var.* Katuura. Chiba, Honshū, S Japan
164 K12 **Katsuyama** *var.* Katuyama. Fukui, Honshū, SW Japan
164 H12 **Katsuyama** Okayama, Honshū, SW Japan
Kattakurgan *see* Kattaqo'rg'on
147 N11 **Kattaqo'rg'on** *Rus.* Kattakurgan. Samarqand Viloyati, C Uzbekistan
115 O23 **Kattavía** Ródos, Dodekánisa, Greece, Aegean Sea
95 I21 **Kattegat** *Dan.* Kattegatt. *strait* N Europe
Kattegatt *see* Kattegat
95 P19 **Katthammarsvik** Gotland, SE Sweden
Kattowitz *see* Katowice
122 J13 **Katun'** ≈ S Russian Federation
Katuta *see* Katsuta
Katuura *see* Katsuura
Katuyama *see* Katsuyama
Katwijk *see* Katwijk aan Zee
98 G11 **Katwijk aan Zee** *var.* Katwijk. Zuid-Holland, W Netherlands
38 B8 **Kaua'i** *var.* Kauai. *island* Hawaiian Islands, Hawai'i, USA, C PacificOcean
Kauai *see* Kaua'i
38 C8 **Kaua'i Channel** *var.* Kauai Channel. *channel* Hawai'i, USA, C Pacific Ocean
Kauai Channel *see* Kaua'i Channel
171 R13 **Kaubalatmada, Gunung** *var.* Kaplamada. ▲ Pulau Buru, E Indonesia
191 U10 **Kauehi** *atoll* Îles Tuamotu, C French Polynesia
Kauen *see* Kaunas
101 K24 **Kaufbeuren** Bayern, S Germany
25 U7 **Kaufman** Texas, SW USA
101 I15 **Kaufungen** Hessen, C Germany
93 K17 **Kauhajoki** Länsi-Soumi, W Finland
93 K16 **Kauhava** Länsi-Soumi, W Finland
30 M7 **Kaukauna** Wisconsin, N USA
92 L11 **Kaukonen** Lappi, N Finland
38 A8 **Kaulakahi Channel** *channel* Hawai'i, USA, C Pacific Ocean
38 E9 **Kaunakakai** Moloka'i, Hawai'i, USA, C Pacific Ocean
38 F12 **Kaunā Point** *var.* Kauna Point. *headland* Hawai'i, USA, C Pacific Ocean
Kauna Point *see* Kaunā Point
118 F13 **Kaunas** *Ger.* Kauen, *Pol.* Kowno; *prev. Rus.* Kovno. Kaunas, C Lithuania
118 F13 **Kaunas** ⬖ *province* C Lithuania
186 C6 **Kaup** East Sepik, NW Papua New Guinea
77 U12 **Kaura Namoda** Zamfara, NW Nigeria
Kaushany *see* Căuşeni
93 K16 **Kaustinen** Länsi-Soumi, W Finland
99 M23 **Kautenbach** Diekirch, NE Luxembourg
92 K10 **Kautokeino** *Lapp.* Guovdageaidnu. Finnmark, N Norway
Kavadar *see* Kavadarci
113 P19 **Kavadarci** *Turk.* Kavadar. C Macedonia
Kavaja *see* Kavajë
113 K20 **Kavajë** *It.* Cavaia, Kavaja. Tiranë, W Albania
114 M13 **Kavak Çayı** ≈ NW Turkey
Kavakli *see* Topolovgrad
114 I13 **Kavála** *prev.* Kaválla. Anatolikí Makedonía kai Thráki, NE Greece
114 I13 **Kaválas, Kólpos** *gulf* Aegean Sea, NE Mediterranean Sea
155 J17 **Kāvali** Andhra Pradesh, E India
Kaválla *see* Kavála
Kavango *see* Cubango/Okavango
155 C21 **Kavaratti** Lakshadweep, SW India
114 O8 **Kavarna** Dobrich, NE Bulgaria
118 G12 **Kavarskas** Utena, E Lithuania
76 I13 **Kavendou** ▲ C Guinea
Kavengo *see* Cubango/Okavango
155 F20 **Kāveri** *var.* Cauvery. ≈ S India
186 G5 **Kavieng** *var.* Kaewieng. New Ireland, NE Papua New Guinea
83 H16 **Kavimba** North-West, NE Botswana
83 I15 **Kavingu** Southern, S Zambia
143 Q6 **Kavīr, Dasht-e** *var.* Great Salt Desert. *salt pan* N Iran
Kavirondo Gulf *see* Winam Gulf
Kavkaz *see* Caucasus
95 K23 **Kävlinge** Skåne, S Sweden
82 G12 **Kavungo** Moxico, E Angola
165 Q8 **Kawabe** Akita, Honshū, C Japan
165 R9 **Kawai** Iwate, Honshū, C Japan
38 A8 **Kawaihoa Point** *headland* Ni'ihau, Hawai'i, USA, C Pacific Ocean
184 K3 **Kawakawa** Northland, North Island, New Zealand
82 I13 **Kawama** North Western, NW Zambia
82 K11 **Kawambwa** Luapula, N Zambia
154 K11 **Kawardha** Chhattīsgarh, C India
14 I14 **Kawartha Lakes** ◎ Ontario, SE Canada
165 O13 **Kawasaki** Kanagawa, Honshū, S Japan
171 R12 **Kawassi** Pulau Obi, E Indonesia
165 R6 **Kawauchi** Aomori, Honshū, C Japan
184 L5 **Kawau Island** *island* N New Zealand
184 N10 **Kaweka Range** ▲▲ North Island, New Zealand
Kawelecht *see* Puhja
184 O8 **Kawerau** Bay of Plenty, North Island, New Zealand
184 L8 **Kawhia** Waikato, North Island, New Zealand
184 K8 **Kawhia Harbour** *inlet* North Island, New Zealand
35 V8 **Kawich Peak** ▲ Nevada, W USA
35 V9 **Kawich Range** ▲▲ Nevada, W USA
14 G12 **Kawigamog Lake** ◎ Ontario, S Canada
171 P9 **Kawio, Kepulauan** *island group* N Indonesia
167 N9 **Kawkareik** Karen State, S Burma (Myanmar)
27 O8 **Kaw Lake** ⊠ Oklahoma, C USA
166 M3 **Kawlin** Sagaing, N Burma (Myanmar)
Kawm Umbū *see* Kôm Ombo
Kawthule State *see* Karen State
Kaxgar *see* Kashi
158 D7 **Kaxgar He** ≈ NW China
158 J5 **Kax He** ≈ NW China
77 P12 **Kaya** C Burkina
167 N6 **Kayah State** ⬖ *state* C Burma (Myanmar)
39 T12 **Kayak Island** *island* Alaska, USA
114 M11 **Kayalıköy Barajı** ⊠ NW Turkey
155 G23 **Kāyankulam** Kerala, SW India
166 M8 **Kayan** Yangon, SW Burma (Myanmar)
Kayangel Islands *see* Ngcheangel
169 V9 **Kayan, Sungai** *prev.* Kajan. ≈ Borneo, C Indonesia
144 F14 **Kaydak, Sor** *salt flat* SW Kazakhstan
Kaydanovo *see* Dzyarzhynsk Belarus
37 N9 **Kayenta** Arizona, SW USA
76 J11 **Kayes** Kayes, W Mali
76 J11 **Kayes** ⬖ *region* SW Mali
Kayin State *see* Karen State
145 U10 **Kaynar** *var.* Kajnar. Vostochnyy Kazakhstan, E Kazakhstan
Kaynary *see* Căinari
83 H15 **Kayoya** Western, W Zambia
Kayrakkum *see* Qayroqqum
Kayrakkumskoye Vodokhranilishche *see* Qayroqqum, Obanbori
136 K14 **Kayseri** *var.* Kaisaria; *anc.* Caesarea Mazaca, Mazaca. Kayseri, C Turkey
136 K14 **Kayseri** *var.* Kaisaria. ⬖ *province* C Turkey
36 L2 **Kaysville** Utah, W USA
Kayyngdy *see* Kaindy
14 L11 **Kazabazua** Québec, SE Canada
14 L12 **Kazabazua** ≈ Québec, SE Canada
123 Q7 **Kazach'ye** Respublika Sakha (Yakutiya), NE Russian Federation
Kazakdar'ya *see* Qozoqdaryo
146 E9 **Kazakhlyshor, Solonchak** *var.* Solonchak Shorkazakhly. *salt marsh* NW Turkmenistan
Kazakhskaya SSR/Kazakh Soviet Socialist Republic *see* Kazakhstan
145 R9 **Kazakhskiy Melkosopochnik** *Eng.* Kazakh Uplands, Kirghiz Steppe, *Kaz.* Saryarqa. *uplands* C Kazakhstan
144 L12 **Kazakhstan** *off.* Republic of Kazakhstan, *var.* Kazakstan, *Kaz.* Qazaqstan, Qazaqstan Respublikasy; *prev.* Kazakh Soviet Socialist Republic, *Rus.* Kazakhskaya SSR. ◆ *republic* C Asia
Kazakhstan, Republic of *see* Kazakhstan
Kazakh Uplands *see* Kazakhskiy Melkosopochnik
Kazakstan *see* Kazakhstan
144 L14 **Kazalinsk** Kzyl-Orda, S Kazakhstan
127 R4 **Kazan'** Respublika Tatarstan, W Russian Federation
8 M10 **Kazan** ≈ Nunavut, NW Canada
127 R4 **Kazan'** ✈ Respublika Tatarstan, W Russian Federation
Kazandzhik *see* Bereket
117 R8 **Kazanka** Mykolayivs'ka Oblast', S Ukraine
Kazanketken *see* Qozonketkan
Kazanlik *see* Kazanlŭk
114 J9 **Kazanlŭk** *prev.* Kazanlik. Stara Zagorat, C Bulgaria
165 Y16 **Kazan-rettō** *Eng.* Volcano Islands. *island group* SE Japan
117 V12 **Kazantip, Mys** *headland* S Ukraine
147 U9 **Kazarman** Narynskaya Oblast', C Kyrgyzstan
Kazatin *see* Kozyatyn
Kazbegi *see* Qazbegi
Kazbegi *see* Kazbek
137 T9 **Kazbek** *var.* Kazbegi, *Geor.* Mqinvartsveri. ▲ N Georgia
82 M13 **Kazembe** Eastern, NE Zambia
143 N11 **Kāzerūn** Fārs, S Iran
125 R12 **Kazhym** Respublika Komi, NW Russian Federation
Kazi Ahmad *see* Qāzi Ahmad
Kazi Magomed *see* Qazimämmäd
136 H16 **Kazımkarabekir** Karaman, S Turkey
111 M20 **Kazincbarcika** Borsod-Abaúj-Zemplén, NE Hungary
119 H17 **Kazlowshchyna** *Pol.* Kozłowszczyzna, *Rus.* Kozlovshchina. Hrodzyenskaya Voblasts', W Belarus
119 E14 **Kazlų Rūda** Marijampolė, S Lithuania
144 E9 **Kaztalovka** Zapadnyy Kazakhstan, W Kazakhstan
79 K22 **Kazumba** Kasai Occidental, S Dem. Rep. Congo
165 Q8 **Kazuno** Akita, Honshū, C Japan
Kazvin *see* Qazvīn
118 J12 **Kaz'yany** *Rus.* Koz'yany. Vitsyebskaya Voblasts', NW Belarus
122 H9 **Kazym** ≈ N Russian Federation
110 H10 **Kcynia** *Ger.* Exin. Kujawsko-pomorskie, C Poland
Kéa *see* Tziá
38 H11 **Kea'au** *var.* Keaau. Hawai'i, USA, C Pacific Ocean
Keaau *see* Kea'au
38 F11 **Keāhole Point** *var.* Keahole Point. *headland* Hawai'i, USA, C Pacific Ocean
38 G12 **Kealakekua** Hawai'i, USA, C Pacific Ocean
38 H11 **Kea, Mauna** ▲ Hawaii, USA
37 N10 **Keams** Arizona, SW USA
Kéamu *see* Aneityum
29 O16 **Kearney** Nebraska, C USA
36 L3 **Kearns** Utah, W USA
115 H20 **Kéas, Stenó** *strait* SE Greece
137 O14 **Keban Barajı** *dam* C Turkey
137 O14 **Keban Barajı** ⊠ C Turkey
77 S13 **Kebbi** ⬖ *state* NW Nigeria
76 G10 **Kébémèr** NW Senegal
74 M7 **Kebili** *var.* Qibilī. C Tunisia
138 H4 **Kebir, Nahr el** ≈ NW Syria
80 A10 **Kebkabiya** Northern Darfur, W Sudan
92 I11 **Kebnekaise** ▲ N Sweden
81 M14 **K'ebrī Dehar** Somali, E Ethiopia
148 K15 **Kech** ≈ SW Pakistan
10 K10 **Kechika** ≈ British Columbia, W Canada
111 K23 **Kecskemét** Bács-Kiskun, C Hungary
168 J6 **Kedah** ⬖ *state* Peninsular Malaysia
118 F12 **Kėdainiai** Kaunas, C Lithuania
Kedder *see* Kehra
13 N13 **Kedgwick** New Brunswick, SE Canada
169 R16 **Kediri** Jawa, C Indonesia
171 Y13 **Kedir Sarmi** Papua, E Indonesia
163 V7 **Kedong** Heilongjiang, NE China
76 I12 **Kédougou** SE Senegal
122 I11 **Kedrovyy** Tomskaya Oblast', C Russian Federation
111 H16 **Kędzierzyn-Kozle** *Ger.* Heydebrech. Opolskie, S Poland
8 H8 **Keele** ≈ Northwest Territories, NW Canada
10 K6 **Keele Peak** ▲ Yukon Territory, NW Canada
Keelung *see* Chilung
19 N10 **Keene** New Hampshire, NE USA
99 H17 **Keerbergen** Vlaams Brabant, C Belgium
83 E21 **Keetmanshoop** Karas, S Namibia
12 A11 **Keewatin** Ontario, S Canada
29 V4 **Keewatin** Minnesota, N USA
Kefallinía *see* Kefallonía
115 B18 **Kefallonía** *var.* Kefallinía. *island* Iónioi Nísoi, Greece, C Mediterranean Sea
115 M22 **Kéfalos** Kos, Dodekánisa, Greece, Aegean Sea
171 Q17 **Kefamenanu** Timor, C Indonesia
138 F10 **Kefar Sava** *var.* Kfar Saba. Central, C Israel
Kefe *see* Feodosiya
77 V15 **Keffi** Nassarawa, C Nigeria
92 H4 **Keflavík** Reykjanes, W Iceland
92 H4 **Keflavík** ✈ (Reykjavík) Reykjanes, W Iceland
Kegalee *see* Kegalla
155 J25 **Kegalla** *var.* Kegalee, Kegalle. Sabaragamuwa Province, C Sri Lanka
Kegalle *see* Kegalla
Kegayli *see* Kegeyli
Kegel *see* Keila
145 W16 **Kegen** Almaty, SE Kazakhstan
146 H7 **Kegeyli** *Rus.* Kegayli. Qoraqalpoghiston Respublikasi, W Uzbekistan
101 F22 **Kehl** Baden-Württemberg, SW Germany
118 H3 **Kehra** *Ger.* Kedder. Harjumaa, NW Estonia
117 U6 **Kehychivka** Kharkivs'ka Oblast', E Ukraine
97 L17 **Keighley** N England, UK
Kei Islands *see* Kai, Kepulauan
Keijō *see* Sŏul
118 G3 **Keila** *Ger.* Kegel. Harjumaa, NW Estonia
Keilberg *see* Klínovec
83 F23 **Keimoes** Northern Cape, W South Africa
Keina/Keinis *see* Käina
Keishū *see* Kyŏngju
77 T11 **Keïta** Tahoua, C Niger
78 J12 **Kéita, Bahr** *var.* Doka. ≈ S Chad
93 M16 **Keitele** ◎ C Finland
182 K10 **Keith** South Australia
96 K8 **Keith** NE Scotland, UK
26 K3 **Keith Sebelius Lake** ⊠ Kansas, C USA
32 G11 **Keizer** Oregon, NW USA
38 A8 **Kekaha** Kaua'i, Hawai'i, USA
147 U10 **Këk-Art** *prev.* Alaykel', Alay-Kuu. Oshskaya Oblast', SW Kyrgyzstan
147 W10 **Këk-Aygyr** *var.* Keyaygyr. Narynskaya Oblast', C Kyrgyzstan
147 V9 **Këk-Dzhar** Narynskaya Oblast', C Kyrgyzstan
14 L8 **Kekek** ≈ Québec, SE Canada
185 K15 **Kekerengu** Canterbury, South Island, New Zealand
111 L21 **Kékes** ▲ N Hungary
171 P17 **Kekneno, Gunung** ▲ Timor, S Indonesia
147 S9 **Këk-Tash** *Kir.* Kök-Tash. Dzhalal-Abadskaya Oblast', W Kyrgyzstan
81 M15 **K'elafo** Somali, E Ethiopia
169 U10 **Kelai, Sungai** ≈ Borneo, N Indonesia
Kelamayi *see* Karamay
Kelang *see* Klang
168 K7 **Kelantan** ⬖ *state* Peninsular Malaysia
Kelantan *see* Kelantan, Sungai
168 K7 **Kelantan, Sungai** *var.* Kelantan. ≈ Peninsular Malaysia
Kelat *see* Kalāt
Këlcyra *see* Këlcyrë
113 L22 **Këlcyrë** *var.* Këlcyra. Gjirokastër, S Albania
Kelifskiy Uzboy *see* Kelifskiy Uzboýy
146 L14 **Kelifskiy Uzboýy** *Rus.* Kelifskiy Uzboy. *salt marsh* Lebap Welaýaty, E Turkmenistan
137 O12 **Kelkit** Gümüşhane, NE Turkey
136 M12 **Kelkit Çayı** ≈ N Turkey
79 G18 **Kéllé** Cuvette-Quest, W Congo
77 W11 **Kéllé** Zinder, S Niger
145 P7 **Kellerovka** Severnyy Kazakhstan, N Kazakhstan
8 I5 **Kellett, Cape** *headland* Banks Island, Northwest Territories, NW Canada
31 S11 **Kelleys Island** *island* Ohio, N USA
33 N8 **Kellogg** Idaho, NW USA
92 M12 **Kelloselkä** Lappi, N Finland
97 F17 **Kells** *Ir.* Ceanannas. Meath, E Ireland
118 E12 **Kelmė** Šiaulai, C Lithuania
99 M19 **Kelmis** *var.* La Calamine. Liège, E Belgium
78 H12 **Kélo** Tandjilé, SW Chad
83 I14 **Kelongwa** North Western, NW Zambia
9 N17 **Kelowna** British Columbia, SW Canada
9 X12 **Kelsey** Manitoba, C Canada
34 M6 **Kelseyville** California, W USA
96 K13 **Kelso** SE Scotland, UK
32 G10 **Kelso** Washington, NW USA
195 W15 **Keltie, Cape** *headland* Antarctica
Keltsy *see* Kielce
168 L9 **Keluang** *var.* Kluang. Johor, Peninsular Malaysia
168 M11 **Kelume** Pulau Lingga, W Indonesia
9 U15 **Kelvington** Saskatchewan, S Canada
124 J7 **Kem'** Respublika Kareliya, NW Russian Federation
124 I7 **Kem'** ≈ NW Russian Federation
137 O13 **Kemah** Erzincan, E Turkey
137 N13 **Kemaliye** Erzincan, C Turkey
Kemaman *see* Cukai
Kemanlar *see* Isperikh
10 K14 **Kemano** British Columbia, SW Canada
Kemarat *see* Khemmarat
171 P12 **Kembani** Pulau Peleng, N Indonesia
136 F17 **Kemer** Antalya, SW Turkey
122 J12 **Kemerovo** *prev.* Shcheglovsk. Kemerovskaya Oblast', C Russian Federation
122 K12 **Kemerovskaya Oblast'** ⬖ *province* S Russian Federation
92 L13 **Kemi** Lappi, NW Finland
92 M12 **Kemijärvi** *Swe.* Kemiträsk. Lappi, N Finland
92 M12 **Kemijärvi** ◎ N Finland
92 L13 **Kemijoki** ≈ NW Finland
147 V7 **Kemin** *prev.* Bystrovka. Chuyskaya Oblast', N Kyrgyzstan
92 L13 **Keminmaa** Lappi, NW Finland
Kemins Island *see* Nikumaroro
Kemiö *see* Kimito
Kemiträsk *see* Kemijärvi
127 P5 **Kemlya** Respublika Mordoviya, W Russian Federation
99 B18 **Kemmel** West-Vlaanderen, W Belgium
33 S16 **Kemmerer** Wyoming, C USA
Kemmuna *see* Comino
79 I14 **Kémo** ⬖ *prefecture* S Central African Republic
25 U7 **Kemp** Texas, SW USA
93 L14 **Kempele** Oulu, C Finland
101 D15 **Kempen** Nordrhein-Westfalen, W Germany
25 Q5 **Kemp, Lake** ◎ Texas, SW USA
195 W5 **Kemp Land** *physical region* Antarctica
25 S9 **Kempner** Texas, SW USA
44 H3 **Kemp's Bay** Andros Island, W Bahamas
183 U6 **Kempsey** New South Wales, SE Australia
101 J24 **Kempten** Bayern, S Germany
15 N9 **Kempt, Lac** ◎ Québec, SE Canada
183 P17 **Kempton** Tasmania, SE Australia
154 J9 **Ken** ≈ C India
39 R12 **Kenai** Alaska, USA
0 D5 **Kenai Mountains** ▲▲ Alaska, USA
39 R12 **Kenai Peninsula** *peninsula* Alaska, USA
21 V11 **Kenansville** North Carolina, SE USA
146 A10 **Kenar** *prev. Rus.* Ufra. Balkan Welaýaty, NW Turkmenistan
121 U13 **Kenâyis, Râs el-** *headland* N Egypt
97 K16 **Kendal** NW England, UK
23 Y16 **Kendall** Florida, SE USA
9 O8 **Kendall, Cape** *headland* Nunavut, E Canada
18 J15 **Kendall Park** New Jersey, NE USA
31 Q11 **Kendallville** Indiana, N USA
171 P14 **Kendari** Sulawesi, C Indonesia
169 Q13 **Kendawangan** Borneo, C Indonesia
154 O12 **Kendrāpāra** *var.* Kendrāparha. Orissa, E India
Kendrāparha *see* Kendrāpāra
154 O11 **Kendujhargarh** *prev.* Keonjihargarh. Orissa, E India
25 S13 **Kenedy** Texas, SW USA
Kënekesir *see* Kënekesir
76 J15 **Kenema** SE Sierra Leone
29 P16 **Kenesaw** Nebraska, C USA
Këneurgench *see* Këneurgench
79 H21 **Kenge** Bandundu, SW Dem. Rep. Congo
Kengen *see* Kangen
167 O5 **Keng Tung** *var.* Kentung. Shan State, E Burma (Myanmar)
83 F23 **Kenhardt** Northern Cape, W South Africa
76 J12 **Kéniéba** Kayes, W Mali
Kenimekh *see* Konimex
169 U7 **Keningau** Sabah, East Malaysia
74 F6 **Kénitra** *prev.* Port-Lyautey. NW Morocco
21 V9 **Kenly** North Carolina, SE USA
97 B21 **Kenmare** *Ir.* Neidín. Kerry, S Ireland
28 L2 **Kenmare** North Dakota, N USA
97 A21 **Kenmare River** *Ir.* An Ribhéar. *inlet* NE Atlantic Ocean
18 D10 **Kenmore** New York, NE USA
25 W8 **Kennard** Texas, SW USA
29 N10 **Kennebec** South Dakota, N USA
19 Q7 **Kennebec River** ≈ Maine, NE USA
19 P9 **Kennebunk** Maine, NE USA
39 R13 **Kennedy Entrance** *strait* Alaska, USA
166 L3 **Kennedy Peak** ▲ W Burma (Myanmar)
22 K9 **Kenner** Louisiana, S USA
180 I8 **Kenneth Range** ▲▲ Western Australia
27 Y9 **Kennett** Missouri, C USA
18 I16 **Kennett Square** Pennsylvania, NE USA
32 K10 **Kennewick** Washington, NW USA
12 E11 **Kenogami** ≈ Ontario, S Canada
15 Q7 **Kénogami, Lac** ◎ Québec, SE Canada
14 G8 **Kenogami Lake** Ontario, S Canada
14 F7 **Kenogamissi Lake** ◎ Ontario, S Canada
10 I6 **Keno Hill** Yukon Territory, NW Canada
12 A11 **Kenora** Ontario, S Canada
31 N9 **Kenosha** Wisconsin, N USA
13 P14 **Kensington** Prince Edward Island, SE Canada
26 L3 **Kensington** Kansas, C USA
32 I11 **Kent** Oregon, NW USA
24 J9 **Kent** Texas, SW USA
32 H8 **Kent** Washington, NW USA
97 P22 **Kent** *cultural region* SE England, UK
145 P16 **Kentau** Yuzhnyy Kazakhstan, S Kazakhstan
183 P14 **Kent Group** *island group* Tasmania, SE Australia
31 N12 **Kentland** Indiana, N USA
31 R12 **Kenton** Ohio, N USA
8 K7 **Kent Peninsula** *peninsula* Nunavut, N Canada
115 F14 **Kentrikí Makedonía** *Eng.* Macedonia Central. ⬖ *region* N Greece
20 J6 **Kentucky** *off.* Commonwealth of Kentucky, *also known as* Bluegrass State. ⬖ *state* C USA
20 H8 **Kentucky Lake** ⊠ Kentucky/Tennessee, S USA
Kentung *see* Keng Tung
13 P15 **Kentville** Nova Scotia, SE Canada
22 K8 **Kentwood** Louisiana, S USA
31 P9 **Kentwood** Michigan, N USA
81 H17 **Kenya** *off.* Republic of Kenya. ◆ *republic* E Africa
Kenya, Mount *see* Kirinyaga
Kenya, Republic of *see* Kenya
168 L7 **Kenyir, Tasik** *var.* Tasek Kenyir. ◎ Peninsular Malaysia
29 W10 **Kenyon** Minnesota, N USA
29 Y16 **Keokuk** Iowa, C USA
Keonjihargarh *see* Kendujhargarh
Kéos *see* Tziá
29 X16 **Keosauqua** Iowa, C USA
29 X15 **Keota** Iowa, C USA
21 O11 **Keowee, Lake** ⊠ South Carolina, SE USA
124 I7 **Kepa** *var.* Kepe. Respublika Kareliya, NW Russian Federation
Kepe *see* Kepa
189 O13 **Kepirohi Falls** *waterfall* Pohnpei, E Micronesia
185 B22 **Kepler Mountains** ▲▲ South Island, New Zealand
111 I14 **Kępno** Wielkopolskie, C Poland
65 C24 **Keppel Island** *island* N Falkland Islands
Keppel Island *see* Niuatoputapu
65 C23 **Keppel Sound** *sound* N Falkland Islands
136 D12 **Kepsut** Balıkesir, NW Turkey
168 M11 **Kepulauan Riau** *off.* Propinsi Kepulauan Riau. ⬖ *province* NW Indonesia
171 V13 **Kerai** Papua, E Indonesia
Kerak *see* Al Karak
155 F22 **Kerala** ⬖ *state* S India
165 R16 **Kerama-rettō** *island group* SW Japan
183 N10 **Kerang** Victoria, SE Australia
Kerasunt *see* Giresun
115 H19 **Keratéa** *var.* Keratea. Attikí, C Greece
Keratea *see* Keratéa
93 M19 **Kerava** *Swe.* Kervo. Etelä-Suomi, S Finland
Kerbala/Kerbela *see* Karbalā'
32 F15 **Kerby** Oregon, NW USA

◆ Country
● Country Capital
◇ Dependent Territory
○ Dependent Territory Capital
⬖ Administrative Regions
✈ International Airport
▲ Mountain
▲▲ Mountain Range
⋀ Volcano
≈ River
◎ Lake
⊠ Reservoir

KERCH – KIENGE

117 W12 Kerch Rus. Kerch'. Respublika Krym, SE Ukraine
Kerch' see Kerch
Kerchens'ka Protska/Kerchenskiy Proliv see Kerch Strait
117 V13 Kerchens'kyy Pivostriv peninsula S Ukraine
121 V4 Kerch Strait var. Bosporus Cimmerius, Enikale Strait, Rus. Kerchenskiy Proliv, Ukr. Kerchens'ka Protska. strait Black Sea/Sea of Azov
152 K8 Kerdārnāth Uttaranchal, N India
Kerdilio see Kerdýlio
114 H13 Kerdýlio var. Kerdilio. ▲ N Greece
186 D8 Kerema Gulf, S Papua New Guinea
Keremitlik see Lyulyakovo
136 I9 Kerempe Burnu headland N Turkey
80 J9 Keren var. Cheren. C Eritrea
25 U7 Kerens Texas, SW USA
184 M6 Kerepehi Waikato, North Island, New Zealand
145 P10 Kerey, Ozero ◎ C Kazakhstan
Kergel see Kärla
173 Q12 Kerguelen island C French Southern and Antarctic Territories
173 Q13 Kerguelen Plateau undersea feature S Indian Ocean
115 C20 Kerí Zákynthos, Iónioi Nísoi, Greece, C Mediterranean Sea
81 H19 Kericho Rift Valley, W Kenya
184 K2 Kerikeri Northland, North Island, New Zealand
93 O17 Kerimäki Isä-Suomi, E Finland
168 K12 Kerinci, Gunung ▲ Sumatera, W Indonesia
Keriya see Yutian
158 H9 Keriya He ≈ NW China
98 I9 Kerkbuurt Noord-Holland, C Netherlands
98 J13 Kerkdriel Gelderland, C Netherlands
75 N6 Kerkenah, Îles de var. Kerkenna Islands, Ar. Juzur Qarqannah. island group E Tunisia
Kerkenna Islands see Kerkenah, Îles de
115 M20 Kerketévs ▲ Sámos, Dodekánisa, Greece, Aegean Sea
29 T8 Kerkhoven Minnesota, N USA
Kerki see Atamyrat
Kerkichi see Kerkiçi
146 M14 Kerkiçi Rus. Kerkichi. Lebap Welaýaty, E Turkmenistan
115 F16 Kerkíneo prehistoric site Thessalía, C Greece
114 G12 Kerkíni, Límni var. Kerkinitis Límni. ◎ N Greece
Kérkira see Kérkyra
99 M18 Kerkrade Limburg, SE Netherlands
Kerkuk see Kirkūk
115 B16 Kérkyra var. Kérkira, Eng. Corfu. Kérkyra, Iónioi Nísoi, Greece, C Mediterranean Sea
115 B16 Kerkyra ✈ Kérkyra, Iónioi Nísoi, Greece, C Mediterranean Sea
115 A16 Kérkyra var. Kérkira, Eng. Corfu. island Iónioi Nísoi, Greece, C Mediterranean Sea
192 K10 Kermadec Islands island group New Zealand, SW Pacific Ocean
175 R10 Kermadec Ridge undersea feature SW Pacific Ocean
175 R11 Kermadec Trench undersea feature SW Pacific Ocean
143 S10 Kermān var. Kirman; anc. Carmana. Kermān, C Iran
143 R11 Kermān off. Ostān-e Kermān, var. Kirman; anc. Carmania. ◈ province SE Iran
143 U12 Kermān, Biābān-e desert SE Iran
Kermān, Ostān-e see Kermān
142 K6 Kermānshāh var. Qahremānshahr; prev. Bākhtarān. Kermānshāhān, W Iran
143 Q9 Kermānshāh Yazd, C Iran
142 J6 Kermānshāh off. Ostān-e Kermānshāhān; prev. Bākhtarān. ◈ province W Iran
Kermānshāhān, Ostān-e see Kermānshāh
114 L10 Kermen Sliven, C Bulgaria
24 L8 Kermit Texas, SW USA
21 P6 Kermit West Virginia, NE USA
21 S9 Kernersville North Carolina, SE USA
35 S12 Kern River ≈ California, W USA
35 S12 Kernville California, W USA
115 K21 Kéros island Kykládes, Greece, Aegean Sea
76 K14 Kérouané Haute-Guinée, SE Guinea
101 D16 Kerpen Nordrhein-Westfalen, W Germany
146 I11 Kerpichli Lebap Welaýaty, NE Turkmenistan
24 M1 Kerrick Texas, SW USA
Kerr Lake see John H. Kerr Reservoir
9 S15 Kerrobert Saskatchewan, S Canada
25 Q11 Kerrville Texas, SW USA
97 B20 Kerry Ir. Ciarraí. ◈ county SW Ireland
21 S11 Kershaw South Carolina, SE USA
Kertel see Kärdla
95 H23 Kerteminde Fyn, C Denmark
163 Q7 Kerulen Chin. Herlen He, Mong. Herlen Gol. ≈ China/Mongolia
Kervo see Kerava
Kerýneia see Girne
12 H11 Kesagami Lake ◎ Ontario, SE Canada
93 O17 Kesälahti Pohjois-Karjala, SE Finland
136 B11 Keşan Edirne, NW Turkey
165 R9 Kesennuma Miyagi, Honshū, C Japan
163 V7 Keshan Heilongjiang, NE China
30 M6 Keshena Wisconsin, N USA
136 I13 Keskin Kırıkkale, C Turkey
Késmárk see Kežmarok
124 I6 Kesten'ga var. Kest Enga. Respublika Kareliya, NW Russian Federation
Kest Enga see Kesten'ga
98 K12 Kesteren Gelderland, C Netherlands
14 H14 Keswick Ontario, S Canada
97 K15 Keswick NW England, UK
111 H24 Keszthely Zala, SW Hungary
122 K11 Ket' ≈ C Russian Federation
77 R17 Keta SE Ghana
169 Q12 Ketapang Borneo, C Indonesia
127 O12 Ketchenery prev. Sovetskoye. Respublika Kalmykiya, SW Russian Federation
39 Y14 Ketchikan Revillagigedo Island, Alaska, USA
33 O14 Ketchum Idaho, NW USA
Kete/Kete Krakye see Kete-Krachi
77 Q15 Kete-Krachi var. Kete, Kete Krakye. E Ghana
98 L9 Ketelmeer channel E Netherlands
149 P17 Keti Bandar Sind, SE Pakistan
145 W16 Ketmen', Khrebet ▲▲ SE Kazakhstan
77 S16 Kétou SE Benin
110 M7 Kętrzyn Ger. Rastenburg. Warmińsko-Mazurskie, NE Poland
97 N20 Kettering C England, UK
31 R14 Kettering Ohio, N USA
18 F13 Kettle Creek ≈ Pennsylvania, NE USA
32 L7 Kettle Falls Washington, NW USA
14 D16 Kettle Point headland Ontario, S Canada
29 V6 Kettle River ≈ Minnesota, N USA
186 B7 Ketu ≈ W Papua New Guinea
18 G10 Keuka Lake ◎ New York, NE USA
Keupriya see Primorsko
93 L17 Keuruu Länsi-Soumi, C Finland
Kevevára see Kovin
92 L9 Kevo Lapp. Geavvú. Lappi, N Finland
44 M6 Kew North Caicos, N Turks and Caicos Islands
30 K11 Kewanee Illinois, N USA
31 N7 Kewaunee Wisconsin, N USA
30 M3 Keweenaw Bay ◎ Michigan, N USA
31 N2 Keweenaw Peninsula peninsula Michigan, N USA
31 N2 Keweenaw Point peninsula Michigan, N USA
29 N12 Keya Paha River ≈ Nebraska/South Dakota, N USA
Keyaygyr see Këk-Aygyr
23 Z16 Key Biscayne Florida, SE USA
26 G8 Keyes Oklahoma, C USA
23 Y17 Key Largo Key Largo, Florida, SE USA
21 U3 Keyser West Virginia, NE USA
27 O9 Keystone Lake ⊠ Oklahoma, C USA
36 L16 Keystone Peak ▲ Arizona, SW USA
Keystone State see Pennsylvania
21 U7 Keysville Virginia, NE USA
27 T3 Keytesville Missouri, C USA
23 W17 Key West Florida Keys, Florida, SE USA
127 T1 Kez Udmurtskaya Respublika, NW Russian Federation
Kezdivásárhely see Târgu Secuiesc
122 M12 Kezhma Krasnoyarskiy Kray, C Russian Federation
111 L18 Kežmarok Ger. Käsmark, Hung. Késmárk. Prešovský Kraj, E Slovakia
Kfar Saba see Kefar Sava
83 F20 Kgalagadi ◈ district SW Botswana
83 I20 Kgatleng ◈ district SE Botswana
188 F8 Kgkeklau Babeldaob, N Palau
125 R6 Khabarikha var. Chabaricha. Respublika Komi, NW Russian Federation
123 S14 Khabarovsk Khabarovskiy Kray, SE Russian Federation
123 R11 Khabarovskiy Kray ◈ territory E Russian Federation
141 W7 Khabb Abū Ẓaby, E United Arab Emirates
Khabour, Nahr al see Khābūr, Nahr al
Khabura see Al Khābūrah
139 N2 Khābūr, Nahr al var. Nahr al Khabour. ≈ Syria/Turkey
Khachmas see Xaçmaz
80 B12 Khadari ≈ W Sudan
Khadera see Hadera
141 X12 Khādhil var. Khudal. SE Oman
155 E14 Khadki prev. Kirkee. Mahārāshtra, W India
126 L14 Khadyzhensk Krasnodarskiy Kray, SW Russian Federation
114 N9 Khadzhiyska Reka ≈ E Bulgaria
117 P10 Khadzhybeys'kyy Lyman ◎ SW Ukraine
138 K3 Khafsah Ḥalab, N Syria
152 M13 Khāga Uttar Pradesh, N India
153 Q13 Khagaria Bihār, NE India
149 Q13 Khairpur Sind, SE Pakistan
122 K13 Khakasiya, Respublika prev. Khakasskaya Avtonomnaya Oblast', Eng. Khakassia. ◈ autonomous republic C Russian Federation
Khakassia/Khakasskaya Avtonomnaya Oblast' see Khakasiya, Respublika
167 N9 Kha Khaeng, Khao ▲ W Thailand
83 G20 Khakhea var. Kakia. Southern, S Botswana
Khalach see Halaç
Khalándrion see Chalándri
Khalij-e Fars see Gulf, The
127 W7 Khalilovo Orenburgskaya Oblast', W Russian Federation
Khalkabad see Xalqobod
142 L3 Khalkhāl prev. Herowābād. Ardabīl, NW Iran
Khalkidhikí see Chalkidikí
Khalkís see Chalkída
125 W3 Khal'mer-Yu Respublika Komi, NW Russian Federation
119 M14 Khalopyenichy Rus. Kholopenichi. Minskaya Voblasts', NE Belarus
Khalturin see Orlov
141 Y10 Khalūf var. Al Khaluf. E Oman
154 K10 Khamaria Madhya Pradesh, C India
154 D11 Khambhāt Gujarāt, W India
154 C12 Khambhāt, Gulf of Eng. Gulf of Cambay. gulf W India
167 U10 Khâm Đưc Quang Nam-Đa Năng, C Vietnam
154 G12 Khāmgaon Mahārāshtra, C India
141 O14 Khamir var. Khamr. W Yemen
141 N12 Khamīs Mushayt var. Hamīs Musait. 'Asīr, SW Saudi Arabia
123 P10 Khampa Respublika Sakha (Yakutiya), NE Russian Federation
Khamr see Khamir
83 C19 Khan ≈ W Namibia
149 Q2 Khānābād Kunduz, NE Afghanistan
Khân Abou Châmâte/Khan Abou Ech Cham see Khān Abū Shāmāt
138 I7 Khān Abū Shāmāt var. Khân Abou Châmâte, Khan Abou Ech Cham. Dimashq, W Syria
Khān al Baghdādī see Al Baghdādī
Khān al Maḩāwīl see Al Maḩāwīl
139 T7 Khān al Mashāhidah C Iraq
139 T10 Khān al Muşallá S Iraq
139 U6 Khānaqīn E Iraq
139 T11 Khān ar Ruḩbah S Iraq
139 Q8 Khān as Sūr N Iraq
139 T8 Khān Āzād C Iraq
154 N13 Khandaparha prev. Khandpara. Orissa, E India
Khandpara see Khandaparha
149 T2 Khandūd var. Khandud, Wakhan. Badakhshān, NE Afghanistan
Khandud see Khandūd
154 G11 Khandwa Madhya Pradesh, C India
123 R10 Khandyga Respublika Sakha (Yakutiya), NE Russian Federation
149 T10 Khānewāl Punjab, NE Pakistan
149 S10 Khāngarh Punjab, E Pakistan
Khanh Hung see Soc Trăng
Khaniá see Chaniá
Khanka see Xonqa
163 Z8 Khanka, Lake var. Hsing-K'ai Hu, Lake Hanka, Chin. Xingkai Hu, Rus. Ozero Khanka. ◎ China/Russian Federation
Khanka, Ozero see Khanka, Lake
Khankendi see Xankändi
Khanlar see Xanlar
123 O9 Khannya ≈ NE Russian Federation
149 S12 Khānpur Punjab, SE Pakistan
149 S12 Khānpur Punjab, E Pakistan
138 I4 Khān Shaykhūn var. Khan Sheikhun. Idlib, NW Syria
Khan Sheikhun see Khān Shaykhūn
145 S15 Khantau Zhambyl, S Kazakhstan
145 W16 Khan Tengri, Pik ▲ SE Kazakhstan
Khan-Tengri, Pik see Hantengri Feng
167 S9 Khanthabouli var. Savannakhét. S Laos
127 V8 Khanty-Mansiysk prev. Ostyako-Voguls'k. Khanty-Mansiyskiy Avtonomnyy Okrug, C Russian Federation
125 V8 Khanty-Mansiyskiy Avtonomnyy Okrug ◈ autonomous district C Russian Federation
139 R4 Khānūqah C Iraq
138 E11 Khān Yūnis var. Khān Yūnus. S Gaza Strip
Khān Yūnus see Khān Yūnis
Khanzi see Ghanzi
139 U5 Khān Zūr E Iraq
167 N10 Khao Laem Reservoir ⊠ W Thailand
123 O14 Khapcheranga Chitinskaya Oblast', S Russian Federation
127 Q12 Kharabali Astrakhanskaya Oblast', SW Russian Federation
153 R16 Kharagpur West Bengal, NE India
139 V11 Kharā'ib 'Abd al Karīm S Iraq
143 Q8 Kharānaq Yazd, C Iran
Kharbin see Harbin
146 H13 Khardzhagaz Ahal Welaýaty, C Turkmenistan
Khārga Oasis see Great Oasis, The
154 F11 Khargon Madhya Pradesh, C India
149 V7 Khāriān Punjab, NE Pakistan
117 X8 Kharisyz'k Donets'ka Oblast', E Ukraine
117 V5 Kharkiv Rus. Khar'kov. Kharkivs'ka Oblast', NE Ukraine
117 V5 Kharkiv ✈ Kharkivs'ka Oblast', E Ukraine
Kharkiv see Kharkivs'ka Oblast'
117 U5 Kharkivs'ka Oblast' var. Kharkiv, Rus. Khar'kovskaya Oblast'. ◈ province E Ukraine
Khar'kov see Kharkiv
Khar'kovskaya Oblast' see Kharkivs'ka Oblast'
124 L3 Kharlovka Murmanskaya Oblast', NW Russian Federation
114 K11 Kharmanli Khaskovo, S Bulgaria
114 K11 Kharmanliyska Reka ≈ S Bulgaria
124 M13 Kharovsk Vologodskaya Oblast', NW Russian Federation
80 F9 Khartoum var. El Khartûm, Khartum. ● (Sudan) Khartoum, C Sudan
80 F9 Khartoum ◈ state NE Sudan
80 F9 Khartoum ✈ Khartoum, C Sudan
80 F9 Khartoum North Khartoum, C Sudan
117 X8 Khartsyz'k Rus. Khartsyzsk. Donets'ka Oblast', SE Ukraine
Khartsyzsk see Khartsyz'k
Khartum see Khartoum
Khasab see Al Khaşab
123 S15 Khasan Primorskiy Kray, SE Russian Federation
127 P16 Khasavyurt Respublika Dagestan, SW Russian Federation
143 W12 Khāsh prev. Vāsht. Sīstān va Balūchestān, SE Iran
148 K8 Khāsh, Dasht-e Eng. Khash Desert. desert SW Afghanistan
Khash Desert see Khāsh, Dasht-e
Khashim Al Qirba/Khashm al Qirbah see Khashm el Girba
80 H9 Khashm el Girba var. Khashim Al Qirba, Khashm al Qirbah. Kassala, E Sudan
138 G14 Khashsh, Jabal al ▲▲ S Jordan
137 S10 Khashuri C Georgia
153 V13 Khāsi Hills hill range NE India
114 K11 Khaskovo Khaskovo, S Bulgaria
114 K11 Khaskovo ◈ province S Bulgaria
122 M7 Khatanga ≈ N Russian Federation
Khatanga, Gulf of see Khatangskiy Zaliv
123 N7 Khatangskiy Zaliv var. Gulf of Khatanga. bay N Russian Federation
141 W7 Khatmat al Malāḩah N Oman
143 S16 Khaṭmat al Malāḩah Ash Shāriqah, E United Arab Emirates
123 V7 Khatyrka Chukotskiy Avtonomnyy Okrug, NE Russian Federation
Khauz-Khan see Hanhowuz
Khauzkhanskoye Vodokhranilishche see Hanhowuz Suw Howdany
Khauzkhanskoye Vodoranilishche see Hanhowuz Suw Howdany
Khavaling see Khovaling
Khavast see Xovos
139 W10 Khawrah, Nahr al ≈ S Iraq
Khawr Barakah see Baraka
141 W7 Khawr Fakkān var. Khor Fakkan. Ash Shāriqah, NE United Arab Emirates
140 L6 Khaybar Al Madīnah, NW Saudi Arabia
Khaybar, Kowtal-e see Khyber Pass
147 S11 Khaydarkan var. Khaydarken. Batkenskaya Oblast', SW Kyrgyzstan
Khaydarken see Khaydarkan
125 U2 Khaypudyrskaya Guba bay NW Russian Federation
139 S1 Khayrūzuk E Iraq
Khazar, Baḩr-e/Khazar, Daryā-ye see Caspian Sea
Khazarosp see Hazorasp
Khazretishi, Khrebet see Hazratishoh, Qatorkŭhi
Khelat see Kalāt
74 F6 Khemisset NW Morocco
167 R10 Khemmarat var. Kemarat. Ubon Ratchathani, E Thailand
74 L6 Khenchela var. Khenchla. NE Algeria
Khenchla see Khenchela
74 G7 Khénifra C Morocco
Kherān, Rūd-e see Garm, Āb-e
117 R10 Kherson Khersons'ka Oblast', S Ukraine
Kherson see Khersons'ka Oblast'
117 S14 Khersones, Mys Rus. Mys Khersonesskiy. headland S Ukraine
Khersonesskiy, Mys see Khersones, Mys
117 R10 Khersons'ka Oblast' var. Kherson, Rus. Khersonskaya Oblast'. ◈ province S Ukraine
Khersonskaya Oblast' see Khersons'ka Oblast'
122 L8 Kheta ≈ N Russian Federation
167 S8 Khe Ve Quang Binh, C Vietnam
149 U7 Khewra Punjab, E Pakistan
Khiam see El Khiyam
124 J4 Khibiny ▲▲ NW Russian Federation
126 K3 Khimki Moskovskaya Oblast', W Russian Federation
147 S12 Khingov Rus. Obi-Khingou. ≈ C Tajikistan
Khíos see Chíos
149 R15 Khipro Sind, SE Pakistan
139 S10 Khirr, Wādī al dry watercourse S Iraq
114 I10 Khisarya Plovdiv, C Bulgaria
Khiva/Khiwa see Xiva
167 N9 Khlong Khlung Kamphaeng Phet, W Thailand
167 N15 Khlong Thom Krabi, SW Thailand
167 P12 Khlung Chantaburi, S Thailand
Khmel'nik see Khmil'nyk
Khmel'nitskaya Oblast' see Khmel'nyts'ka Oblast'
Khmel'nitskiy see Khmel 'nyts'kyy
116 K5 Khmel'nyts'ka Oblast' var. Khmel'nyts'kyy, Rus. Khmel'nitskaya Oblast'; prev. Kamenets-Podol'skaya Oblast'. ◈ province NW Ukraine
116 L6 Khmel 'nyts'kyy Rus. Khmel'nitskiy; prev. Proskurov. Khmel'nyts'ka Oblast', W Ukraine
Khmel'nyts'kyy see Khmel'nyts'ka Oblast'
116 M6 Khmil'nyk Rus. Khmel'nik. Vinnyts'ka Oblast', C Ukraine
144 I10 Khobda prev. Novoalekseyevka. Aktyubinsk, W Kazakhstan
137 R9 Khobi W Georgia
119 P15 Khodasy Rus. Khodosy. Mahilyowskaya Voblasts', E Belarus
116 I6 Khodoriv Pol. Chodorów, Rus. Khodorov. L'vivs'ka Oblast', NW Ukraine
Khodorov see Khodoriv
Khodosy see Khodasy
Khodzhakala see Hojagala
146 M13 Khodzhambas Rus. Khodzhambas. Lebap Welaýaty, E Turkmenistan
Khodzhambas see Hojambaz
Khodzhambas see Khodzhambas
Khodzhent see Khŭjand
Khodzheyli see Xo'jayli
Khoi see Khvoy
Khojend see Khŭjand
Khokand see Qo'qon
126 L8 Khokhol'skiy Voronezhskaya Oblast', W Russian Federation
167 P10 Khok Samrong Lop Buri, C Thailand
149 P2 Kholm var. Tashqurghan, Pash. Khulm. Balkh, N Afghanistan
124 H15 Kholm Novgorodskaya Oblast', W Russian Federation
Kholm see Chełm
Kholmech' see Kholmyech
123 T13 Kholmsk Ostrov Sakhalin, Sakhalinskaya Oblast', SE Russian Federation
119 O19 Kholmyech Rus. Kholmech'. Homyel'skaya Voblasts', SE Belarus
Kholon see Holon
Kholopenichi see Khalopyenichy
83 D19 Khomas ◈ district C Namibia
83 D19 Khomas Hochland var. Khomasplato. plateau C Namibia
Khomasplato see Khomas Hochland
Khomein see Khomeyn
142 M7 Khomeyn var. Khomein, Khumain. Markazī, W Iran
143 N8 Khomeynīshahr prev. Homāyūnshahr. Eşfahān, C Iran
Khoms see Al Khums
Khong Sedone see Muang Khôngxédôn
167 Q9 Khon Kaen var. Muang Khon Kaen. Khon Kaen, E Thailand
Khonqa see Xonqa
167 Q9 Khon San Khon Kaen, E Thailand
123 R8 Khonuu Respublika Sakha (Yakutiya), NE Russian Federation
127 N8 Khopër var. Khoper. ≈ SW Russian Federation
Khoper see Khopër
123 S14 Khor Khabarovskiy Kray, SE Russian Federation
143 U9 Khorāsān-e Janūbī off. Ostan-e Khorāsān-e Janūbī. ◈ province E Iran
143 S3 Khorāsān-e Shemālī off. Ostan-e Khorāsān-e Shemālī. ◈ province NE Iran
143 U5 Khorāsān-Razavī off. Ostan-e Khorāsān-Razavī. ◈ province NE Iran
Khorat see Nakhon Ratchasima
154 O13 Khordha prev. Khurda. Orissa, E India
125 U4 Khorey-Ver Nenetskiy Avtonomnyy Okrug, NW Russian Federation
Khorezmskaya Oblast' see Xorazm Viloyati
Khor Fakkan see Khawr Fakkān
145 W15 Khorgos Almaty, SE Kazakhstan
123 N13 Khorinsk Respublika Buryatiya, S Russian Federation
83 C18 Khorixas Kunene, NW Namibia
141 O17 Khormaksar var. Aden. ✈ ('Adan) SW Yemen
Khormal see Khurmāl
Khormuj see Khvormūj
Khorog see Khorugh
117 S5 Khorol Poltavs'ka Oblast', NE Ukraine
142 L7 Khorramābād var. Khurramabad. Lorestān, W Iran
142 K10 Khorramshahr var. Khurramshahr, Muhammerah; prev. Mohammerah. Khūzestān, SW Iran
147 S14 Khorugh Rus. Khorog. S Tajikistan
Khorvot Khalutsa see Horvot Haluza
127 Q12 Khosheutovo Astrakhanskaya Oblast', SW Russian Federation
Khotan see Hotan
Khotimsk see Khotsimsk
Khotin see Khotyn
119 R16 Khotsimsk Rus. Khotimsk. Mahilyowskaya Voblasts', E Belarus
116 K7 Khotyn Rom. Hotin, Rus. Khotin. Chernivets'ka Oblast', W Ukraine
74 F7 Khouribga C Morocco
147 Q13 Khovaling Rus. Khavaling. SW Tajikistan
Khovd see Hovd
149 R6 Khowst Khowst, E Afghanistan
149 S6 Khowst ◈ province E Afghanistan
Khoy see Khvoy
119 N20 Khoyniki Rus. Khoyniki. Homyel'skaya Voblasts', SE Belarus
Khozretishi, Khrebet see Hazratishoh, Qatorkŭhi
Khrebet Babatag see Bototog', Tizmasi
Khrisoúpolis see Chrysoúpoli
144 J10 Khromtau Kaz. Khromtaū. Aktyubinsk, W Kazakhstan
Khromtaū see Khromtau
Khrysokhou Bay see Chrysochoú, Kólpos
117 O7 Khrystynivka Cherkas'ka Oblast', C Ukraine
167 R10 Khuang Nai Ubon Ratchathani, E Thailand
Khudal see Khādhil
Khudat see Xudat
149 W9 Khudiān Punjab, E Pakistan
Khudzhand see Khŭjand
147 O13 Khufar Surkhondaryo Viloyati, S Uzbekistan
83 G21 Khuis Kgalagadi, SW Botswana
147 Q11 Khŭjand var. Khodzhent, Khojend, Rus. Khudzhand; prev. Leninabad, Taj. Leninobod. N Tajikistan
167 R11 Khukhan Si Sa Ket, E Thailand
Khulm see Kholm
153 T16 Khulna Khulna, SW Bangladesh
153 T16 Khulna ◈ division SW Bangladesh
Khumain see Khomeyn
Khums see Al Khums
149 W2 Khunjerāb Pass pass China/Pakistan
Khūnjerāb Pass see Kunjirap Daban
153 P16 Khunti Jhārkhand, N India
167 N7 Khun Yuam Mae Hong Son, NW Thailand
Khurais see Khurayş
141 R7 Khurayş var. Khurais. Ash Sharqīyah, C Saudi Arabia
Khurda see Khordha
152 J11 Khurja Uttar Pradesh, N India
139 V4 Khurmāl var. Khormal. NE Iraq
Khurramabad see Khorramābād
Khurramshahr see Khorramshahr
149 U7 Khushāb Punjab, NE Pakistan
116 H8 Khust Cz. Chust, var. Husté, Hung. Huszt. Zakarpats'ka Oblast', W Ukraine
80 D11 Khuwei Western Kordofan, C Sudan
149 O13 Khuzdār Baluchistān, SW Pakistan
142 L9 Khūzestān off. Ostān-e Khūzestān, var. Khuzistan, prev. Arabistan; anc. Susiana. ◈ province SW Iran
Khūzestān, Ostān-e see Khūzestān
Khuzistan see Khūzestān
149 R2 Khvājeh Ghār var. Khwajaghar, Khwaja-i-Ghar. Takhār, NE Afghanistan
127 Q7 Khvalynsk Saratovskaya Oblast', W Russian Federation
143 N12 Khvormūj var. Khormuj. Būshehr, S Iran
142 I2 Khvoy var. Khoi, Khoy. Āžarbāyjān-e Bākhtarī, NW Iran
Khwajaghar/Khwaja-i-Ghar see Khvājeh Ghār
149 S5 Khyber Pass var. Kowtal-e Khaybar. pass Afghanistan/Pakistan
186 L8 Kia Santa Isabel, N Solomon Islands
183 S10 Kiama New South Wales, SE Australia
79 O22 Kiambi Katanga, SE Dem. Rep. Congo
27 Q12 Kiamichi Mountains ▲▲ Oklahoma, C USA
27 Q12 Kiamichi River ≈ Oklahoma, C USA
14 M10 Kiamika, Réservoir ⊠ Québec, SE Canada
Kiamusze see Jiamusi
39 N7 Kiana Alaska, USA
Kiangmai see Chiang Mai
Kiang-ning see Nanjing
Kiangsi see Jiangxi
Kiangsu see Jiangsu
93 M14 Kiantajärvi ◎ E Finland
115 F19 Kiáto prev. Kiáton. Pelopónnisos, S Greece
Kiáton see Kiáto
Kiayi see Chiai
95 F22 Kibæk Ringkøbing, W Denmark
67 T9 Kibali var. Uele (upper course). ≈ NE Dem. Rep. Congo
79 E20 Kibangou Le Niari, SW Congo
Kibarty see Kybartai
92 M8 Kiberg Finnmark, N Norway
79 N20 Kibombo Maniema, E Dem. Rep. Congo
81 E20 Kibondo Kigoma, NW Tanzania
81 J15 Kibre Mengist var. Adola. Oromo, C Ethiopia
Kıbrıs see Cyprus
Kıbrıs/Kıbrıs Cumhuriyeti see Cyprus
81 E20 Kibungo var. Kibungu. SE Rwanda
Kibungu see Kibungo
113 N19 Kičevo SW FYR Macedonia
125 P13 Kichmengskiy Gorodok Vologodskaya Oblast', NW Russian Federation
30 J8 Kickapoo River ≈ Wisconsin, N USA
9 P16 Kicking Horse Pass pass Alberta/British Columbia, SW Canada
77 R9 Kidal Kidal, C Mali
77 Q8 Kidal ◈ region NE Mali
171 Q7 Kidapawan Mindanao, S Philippines
97 L20 Kidderminster C England, UK
76 I11 Kidira E Senegal
184 O11 Kidnappers, Cape headland North Island, New Zealand
100 J8 Kiel Schleswig-Holstein, N Germany
111 L15 Kielce Rus. Keltsy. Świętokrzyskie, C Poland
100 K7 Kieler Bucht bay N Germany
100 J7 Kieler Förde inlet N Germany
167 U13 Kiên Đưc var. Đak Lap. Đắc Lắc, S Vietnam
79 N24 Kienge Katanga, SE Dem. Rep. Congo

◆ Country
● Country Capital
◇ Dependent Territory
○ Dependent Territory Capital
◈ Administrative Regions
✈ International Airport
▲ Mountain
▲▲ Mountain Range
⊼ Volcano
≈ River
◎ Lake
⊠ Reservoir

100 Q12 **Kietz** Brandenburg, NE Germany
Kiev see Kyyiv
Kiev Reservoir see Kyyivs'ke Vodoskhovyshche
76 J10 **Kiffa** Assaba, S Mauritania
115 H19 **Kifisiá** Attikí, C Greece
115 F18 **Kifisós** ✦ C Greece
139 U5 **Kifrī** N Iraq
81 D20 **Kigali** ● (Rwanda) C Rwanda
81 E20 **Kigali** ✕ C Rwanda
137 P13 **Kiği** Bingöl, E Turkey
81 E21 **Kigoma** Kigoma, W Tanzania
81 E21 **Kigoma** ✦ region W Tanzania
38 F10 **Kihei** var. Kihei. Maui, Hawaii, USA
38 F10 **Kihei** var. Kihei. Maui, Hawai'i, USA, C Pacific Ocean
Kihei see Kihei
93 K17 **Kihniö** Länsi-Suomi, W Finland
118 F6 **Kihnu** var. Kihnu Saar, Ger. Kühnö. island SW Estonia
Kihnu Saar see Kihnu
38 A8 **Kii Landing** Ni'ihau, Hawai'i, USA
93 L14 **Kiiminki** Oulu, C Finland
164 J14 **Kii-Nagashima** var. Nagashima. Mie, Honshū, SW Japan
164 J14 **Kii-sanchi** ▲ Honshū, SW Japan
92 L11 **Kiistala** Lappi, N Finland
164 I15 **Kii-suidō** strait S Japan
165 V16 **Kikai-shima** island Nansei-shotō, SW Japan
112 M8 **Kikinda** Ger. Grosskikinda, Hung. Nagykikinda; prev. Velika Kikinda. Vojvodina, N Serbia
Kikládhes see Kykládes
165 Q5 **Kikonai** Hokkaidō, NE Japan
186 C8 **Kikori** Gulf, S Papua New Guinea
186 C8 **Kikori** ✦ W Papua New Guinea
165 O14 **Kikuchi** var. Kikuti. Kumamoto, Kyūshū, SW Japan
Kikuti see Kikuchi
127 N8 **Kikvidze** Volgogradskaya Oblast', SW Russian Federation
14 I10 **Kikwissi, Lac** ⊚ Québec, SE Canada
79 I21 **Kikwit** Bandundu, W Dem. Rep. Congo
95 K15 **Kil** Värmland, C Sweden
94 N12 **Kilafors** Gävleborg, C Sweden
38 B8 **Kilauea** Kauai, Hawaii, USA, C Pacific Ocean
38 B8 **Kilauea** var. Kilauea. Kaua'i, Hawai'i, USA, C Pacific Ocean
38 H12 **Kilauea Caldera** crater Hawai'i, USA, C Pacific Ocean
Kilauea Caldera see Kīlauea Caldera
109 V4 **Kilb** Niederösterreich, C Austria
39 O12 **Kilbuck Mountains** ▲ Alaska, USA
163 Y12 **Kilchu** NE North Korea
97 F18 **Kilcock** Ir. Cill Choca. Kildare, E Ireland
183 V2 **Kilcoy** Queensland, E Australia
97 F18 **Kildare** Ir. Cill Dara. Kildare, E Ireland
97 F18 **Kildare** Ir. Cill Dara. ✦ county E Ireland
124 K2 **Kil'din, Ostrov** island NW Russian Federation
25 W7 **Kilgore** Texas, SW USA
Kilien Mountains see Qilian Shan
114 K9 **Kilifarevo** Veliko Tūrnovo, N Bulgaria
81 K20 **Kilifi** Coast, SE Kenya
189 U9 **Kili Island** var. Köle. island Ralik Chain, S Marshall Islands
149 V2 **Kilik Pass** pass Afghanistan/China
Kilimane see Quelimane
81 I21 **Kilimanjaro** ✦ region E Tanzania
81 I20 **Kilimanjaro** var. Uhuru Peak. ▲ NE Tanzania
Kilimbangara see Kolombangara
Kilinailau Islands see Tulun Islands
81 K23 **Kilindoni** Pwani, E Tanzania
118 H6 **Kilingi-Nõmme** Ger. Kurkund. Pärnumaa, SW Estonia
137 M15 **Kilis** Kilis, S Turkey
136 M16 **Kilis** ✦ province S Turkey
117 N12 **Kiliya** Rom. Chilia-Nouă. Odes'ka Oblast', SW Ukraine
97 B19 **Kilkee** Ir. Cill Chaoi. Clare, W Ireland
97 E19 **Kilkenny** Ir. Cill Chainnigh. Kilkenny, S Ireland
97 E19 **Kilkenny** Ir. Cill Chainnigh. ✦ county S Ireland
97 B18 **Kilkieran Bay** Ir. Cuan Chill Chiaráin. bay W Ireland
114 G13 **Kilkís** Kentrikí Makedonía, N Greece
97 C15 **Killala Bay** Ir. Cuan Chill Ala. inlet NW Ireland
9 R15 **Killam** Alberta, SW Canada
183 U3 **Killarney** Queensland, E Australia
9 W17 **Killarney** Manitoba, S Canada
14 E11 **Killarney** Ontario, S Canada
97 B20 **Killarney** Ir. Cill Airne. Kerry, SW Ireland
28 K4 **Killdeer** North Dakota, N USA
28 J4 **Killdeer Mountains** ▲ North Dakota, N USA
45 V15 **Killdeer River** ✦ Trinidad, Trinidad and Tobago
25 S9 **Killeen** Texas, SW USA
39 P6 **Killik River** ✦ Alaska, USA
9 T7 **Killinek Island** island Nunavut, NE Canada
115 C19 **Killínis, Akrotírio** cape S Greece
97 D15 **Killybegs** Ir. Na Cealla Beaga. NW Ireland
Kilmain see Quelimane
96 I13 **Kilmarnock** W Scotland, UK
21 X6 **Kilmarnock** Virginia, NE USA
125 S16 **Kil'mez'** Kirovskaya Oblast', NW Russian Federation
127 S2 **Kil'mez'** Udmurtskaya Respublika, NW Russian Federation

125 R16 **Kil'mez'** ✦ NW Russian Federation
67 V11 **Kilombero** ✦ S Tanzania
92 J10 **Kilpisjärvi** Lappi, N Finland
97 B19 **Kilrush** Ir. Cill Rois. Clare, W Ireland
Kilwa see Kilwa Kivinje
81 J24 **Kilwa Kivinje** var. Kilwa. Lindi, SE Tanzania
81 J24 **Kilwa Masoko** Lindi, SE Tanzania
171 T13 **Kilwo** Pulau Seram, E Indonesia
114 P12 **Kilyos** 4Istanbul, NW Turkey
37 V8 **Kim** Colorado, C USA
169 U7 **Kimanis, Teluk** bay Sabah, East Malaysia
182 H8 **Kimba** South Australia
28 I15 **Kimball** Nebraska, C USA
29 O11 **Kimball** South Dakota, N USA
79 I21 **Kimbao** Bandundu, SW Dem. Rep. Congo
186 F7 **Kimbe** New Britain, E Papua New Guinea
186 G7 **Kimbe Bay** inlet New Britain, E Papua New Guinea
9 P17 **Kimberley** British Columbia, SW Canada
83 H23 **Kimberley** Northern Cape, C South Africa
180 M4 **Kimberley Plateau** plateau Western Australia
33 P15 **Kimberly** Idaho, NW USA
163 Y12 **Kimch'aek** prev. Sŏngjin. E North Korea
163 Y15 **Kimch'ŏn** C South Korea
163 Z16 **Kim Hae** var. Pusan. ✕ (Pusan) SE South Korea
93 K20 **Kimito** Swe. Kemiö. Länsi-Suomi, SW Finland
165 R4 **Kimobetsu** Hokkaidō, NE Japan
115 I21 **Kímolos** island Kykládes, Greece, Aegean Sea
115 I21 **Kímolou Sífnou, Stenó** strait Kykládes, Greece, Aegean Sea
126 L5 **Kimovsk** Tul'skaya Oblast', W Russian Federation
163 X15 **Kimpo** ✕ NW South Korea
Kimpolung see Câmpulung Moldovenesc
124 K16 **Kimry** Tverskaya Oblast', W Russian Federation
79 H21 **Kimvula** Bas-Congo, SW Dem. Rep. Congo
169 U6 **Kinabalu, Gunung** ▲ East Malaysia
Kinabatangan see Kinabatangan, Sungai
169 V7 **Kinabatangan, Sungai** var. Kinabatangan. ✦ East Malaysia
115 L21 **Kínaros** island Kykládes, Greece, Aegean Sea
9 O15 **Kinbasket Lake** ⊠ British Columbia, SW Canada
96 I7 **Kinbrace** N Scotland, UK
14 E14 **Kincardine** Ontario, S Canada
96 K10 **Kincardine** cultural region E Scotland, UK
79 K21 **Kinda** Kasai Occidental, SE Dem. Rep. Congo
79 M24 **Kinda** Katanga, SE Dem. Rep. Congo
166 L3 **Kindat** Sagaing, N Burma (Myanmar)
109 V6 **Kindberg** Steiermark, C Austria
22 H8 **Kinder** Louisiana, S USA
98 H13 **Kinderdijk** Zuid-Holland, SW Netherlands
97 M17 **Kinder Scout** ▲ C England, UK
9 S16 **Kindersley** Saskatchewan, S Canada
76 I14 **Kindia** Guinée-Maritime, SW Guinea
64 B11 **Kindley Field** air base E Bermuda
29 R6 **Kindred** North Dakota, N USA
79 N20 **Kindu** prev. Kindu-Port-Empain. Maniema, C Dem. Rep. Congo
Kindu-Port-Empain see Kindu
127 S6 **Kinel'** Samarskaya Oblast', W Russian Federation
125 N15 **Kineshma** Ivanovskaya Oblast', W Russian Federation
140 K10 **King Abdul Aziz** ✕ (Makkah) Makkah, W Saudi Arabia
21 X6 **King and Queen Court House** Virginia, NE USA
King Charles Islands see Kong Karls Land
King Christian IX Land see Kong Christian IX Land
King Christian X Land see Kong Christian X Land
35 O11 **King City** California, W USA
27 R2 **King City** Missouri, C USA
38 M16 **King Cove** Alaska, USA
26 M10 **Kingfisher** Oklahoma, C USA
King Frederik VI Coast see Kong Frederik VI Kyst
King Frederik VIII Land see Kong Frederik VIII Land
65 B24 **King George Bay** bay West Falkland, Falkland Islands
194 G3 **King George Island** var. King George Land. island Shetland Islands, Antarctica
12 I6 **King George Islands** island group Northwest Territories, C Canada
King George Land see King George Island
124 G13 **Kingisepp** Leningradskaya Oblast', NW Russian Federation
Kingisepp see Kuressaare
183 N14 **King Island** island Tasmania, SE Australia
10 J15 **King Island** island British Columbia, SW Canada
King Island see Kadan Kyun
Kingissepp see Kuressaare
141 Q7 **King Khalid** ✕ (Ar Riyāḍ) Ar Riyāḍ, C Saudi Arabia
35 S2 **King Lear Peak** ▲ Nevada, W USA
195 Y8 **King Leopold and Queen Astrid Land** physical region Antarctica
180 M4 **King Leopold Ranges** ▲ Western Australia

36 I11 **Kingman** Arizona, SW USA
26 M6 **Kingman** Kansas, C USA
192 L7 **Kingman Reef** ✦ US territory C Pacific Ocean
79 N20 **Kingombe** Maniema, E Dem. Rep. Congo
182 F5 **Kingoonya** South Australia
194 J10 **King Peninsula** peninsula Antarctica
39 P13 **King Salmon** Alaska, USA
35 Q6 **Kings Beach** California, W USA
35 R11 **Kingsburg** California, W USA
182 I10 **Kingscote** South Australia
King's County see Offaly
194 H2 **King Sejong** South Korean research station Antarctica
183 T9 **Kingsford Smith** ✕ (Sydney) New South Wales, SE Australia
9 P17 **Kingsgate** British Columbia, SW Canada
23 W8 **Kingsland** Georgia, SE USA
29 S13 **Kingsley** Iowa, C USA
97 O19 **King's Lynn** var. Bishop's Lynn, Kings Lynn, Lynn, Lynn Regis. E England, UK
Kings Lynn see King's Lynn
21 Q10 **Kings Mountain** North Carolina, SE USA
180 K4 **King Sound** sound Western Australia
37 N2 **Kings Peak** ▲ Utah, W USA
21 O8 **Kingsport** Tennessee, S USA
35 R11 **Kings River** ✦ California, W USA
183 P17 **Kingston** Tasmania, SE Australia
14 G14 **Kingston** Ontario, SE Canada
44 K13 **Kingston** ● (Jamaica) E Jamaica
185 C22 **Kingston** Otago, South Island, New Zealand
19 P12 **Kingston** Massachusetts, NE USA
27 S3 **Kingston** Missouri, C USA
18 K12 **Kingston** New York, NE USA
31 S14 **Kingston** Ohio, N USA
19 O13 **Kingston** Rhode Island, NE USA
20 M9 **Kingston** Tennessee, S USA
35 W12 **Kingston Peak** ▲ California, W USA
182 J11 **Kingston Southeast** South Australia
97 N17 **Kingston upon Hull** var. Hull. NE England, UK
97 N22 **Kingston upon Thames** SE England, UK
45 U14 **Kingstown** ● (Saint Vincent and the Grenadines) Saint Vincent, Saint Vincent and the Grenadines
Kingstown see Dún Laoghaire
23 T13 **Kingstree** South Carolina, SE USA
64 L8 **Kings Trough** undersea feature E Atlantic Ocean
24 C18 **Kingsville** Ontario, S Canada
25 S15 **Kingsville** Texas, SW USA
21 W6 **King William** Virginia, NE USA
8 M7 **King William Island** island Nunavut, N Canada Arctic Ocean
83 I25 **King William's Town** var. King, Kingwilliamstown. Eastern Cape, S South Africa
Kingwilliamstown see King William's Town
21 T3 **Kingwood** West Virginia, NE USA
136 C13 **Kınık** İzmir, W Turkey
79 G21 **Kinkala** Le Pool, S Congo
165 R10 **Kinka-san** headland Honshū, C Japan
184 M8 **Kinleith** Waikato, North Island, New Zealand
95 J19 **Kinna** Älvsborg, S Sweden
96 L8 **Kinnaird Head** var. Kinnairds Head. headland NE Scotland, UK
Kinnairds Head see Kinnaird Head
95 K20 **Kinnared** Halland, S Sweden
148 Yam see Tiberias, Lake
155 K24 **Kinniyai** Eastern Province, NE Sri Lanka
93 L16 **Kinnula** Länsi-Suomi, C Finland
14 I8 **Kinojévis** ✦ Québec, SE Canada
164 I14 **Kino-kawa** ✦ Honshū, SW Japan
9 U11 **Kinoosao** Saskatchewan, C Canada
99 L17 **Kinrooi** Limburg, NE Belgium
96 J11 **Kinross** C Scotland, UK
96 J11 **Kinross** cultural region C Scotland, UK
97 C21 **Kinsale** Ir. Cionn tSáile. Cork, SW Ireland
95 D14 **Kinsarvik** Hordaland, S Norway
79 G21 **Kinshasa** prev. Léopoldville. ● Kinshasa, W Dem. Rep. Congo
79 G21 **Kinshasa** off. Ville de Kinshasa, var. Kinshasa City. ✦ region (Dem. Rep. Congo) SW Dem. Rep. Congo
79 G21 **Kinshasa** ✕ Kinshasa, SW Dem. Rep. Congo
Kinshasa City see Kinshasa
117 O19 **Kins'ka** ✦ SE Ukraine
26 K6 **Kinsley** Kansas, C USA
21 W10 **Kinston** North Carolina, SE USA
77 R14 **Kintampo** W Ghana
182 B1 **Kintore, Mount** ▲ South Australia
96 I13 **Kintyre** peninsula W Scotland, UK
96 H13 **Kintyre, Mull of** headland W Scotland, UK
166 M4 **Kin-u** Sagaing, C Burma (Myanmar)
12 G2 **Kinushseo** ✦ Ontario, C Canada
11 P13 **Kinuso** Alberta, W Canada
154 I13 **Kinwat** Mahārāshtra, C India
81 F16 **Kinyeti** ▲ S Sudan
101 I17 **Kinzig** ✦ SW Germany
12 H10 **Kipawa, Lac** ⊚ Québec, SE Canada

81 G24 **Kipengere Range** ▲ SW Tanzania
81 E23 **Kipili** Rukwa, W Tanzania
81 K20 **Kipini** Coast, SE Kenya
9 V16 **Kipling** Saskatchewan, S Canada
38 M13 **Kipnuk** Alaska, USA
97 F18 **Kippure** Ir. Cipúr. ▲ E Ireland
79 N25 **Kipushi** Katanga, SE Dem. Rep. Congo
187 N10 **Kirakira** var. Kaokaona. San Cristobal, SE Solomon Islands
155 K14 **Kirandul** var. Bailādila. Chhattisgarh, C India
155 I21 **Kiranur** Tamil Nādu, SE India
119 N21 **Kiraw** Rus. Kirov. Homyel'skaya Voblasts', SE Belarus
119 M17 **Kirawsk** Rus. Kirovsk; prev. Startsy. Mahilyowskaya Voblasts', E Belarus
118 F5 **Kirbla** Läänemaa, W Estonia
25 Y9 **Kirbyville** Texas, SE USA
114 J12 **Kircasalih** Edirne, NW Turkey
109 W8 **Kirchbach** var. Kirchbach in Steiermark. Steiermark, SE Austria
Kirchbach in Steiermark see Kirchbach
108 H7 **Kirchberg** Sankt Gallen, NE Switzerland
109 S5 **Kirchdorf an der Krems** Oberösterreich, N Austria
Kirchheim see Kirchheim unter Teck
101 I22 **Kirchheim** var. Kirchheim. Baden-Württemberg, SW Germany
Kirdzhali see Kŭrdzhali
123 N13 **Kirenga** ✦ S Russian Federation
123 N12 **Kirensk** Irkutskaya Oblast', C Russian Federation
Kirghizia see Kyrgyzstan
145 S16 **Kirghiz Range** Rus. Kirgizskiy Khrebet; prev. Alexander Range. ▲ Kazakhstan/Kyrgyzstan
Kirghiz SSR see Kyrgyzstan
Kirghiz Steppe see Kazakhskiy Melkosopochnik
Kirgizskaya SSR see Kyrgyzstan
Kirgizskiy Khrebet see Kirghiz Range
71 I19 **Kiri** Bandundu, W Dem. Rep. Congo
191 R3 **Kiribati** off. Republic of Kiribati. ✦ republic C Pacific Ocean
Kiribati, Republic of see Kiribati
136 L17 **Kırıkhan** Hatay, S Turkey
136 I13 **Kırıkkale** Kırıkkale, C Turkey
136 C10 **Kırıkkale** ✦ province C Turkey
124 L13 **Kirillov** Vologodskaya Oblast', NW Russian Federation
Kirin see Jilin
81 I18 **Kirinyaga** prev. Mount Kenya. ▲ C Kenya
124 H13 **Kirishi** var. Kirisi. Leningradskaya Oblast', NW Russian Federation
164 C16 **Kirishima-yama** ▲ Kyūshū, SW Japan
Kirisi see Kirishi
191 Y2 **Kiritimati** ✕ Kiritimati, E Kiribati
191 Y2 **Kiritimati** prev. Christmas Island. atoll Line Islands, E Kiribati
186 G9 **Kiriwina Island** Eng. Trobriand Island. island SE Papua New Guinea
186 G9 **Kiriwina Islands** var. Trobriand Islands. island group S Papua New Guinea
96 K12 **Kirkcaldy** E Scotland, UK
97 I14 **Kirkcudbright** S Scotland, U
97 I14 **Kirkcudbright** cultural region S Scotland, UK
Kirkee see Khadki
95 I14 **Kirkenær** Hedmark, S Norway
92 M8 **Kirkenes** Fin. Kirkkoniemi. Finnmark, N Norway
92 J4 **Kirkjubæjarklaustur** Suðurland, S Iceland
Kirk-Kilissa see Kırklareli
Kirkkoniemi see Kirkenes
93 L20 **Kirkkonummi** Swe. Kyrkslätt. Uusimaa, S Finland
14 G7 **Kirkland Lake** Ontario, S Canada
136 C9 **Kırklareli** prev. Kirk-Kilissa. Kırklareli, NW Turkey
136 I13 **Kırklareli** ✦ province NW Turkey
185 F20 **Kirkliston Range** ▲ South Island, New Zealand
14 D10 **Kirkpatrick Lake** ⊚ Ontario, S Canada
195 Q11 **Kirkpatrick, Mount** ▲ Antarctica
27 U2 **Kirksville** Missouri, C USA
139 T4 **Kirkūk** var. Karkūk, Kerkuk. N Iraq
139 U7 **Kir Kush** E Iraq
96 K5 **Kirkwall** NE Scotland, UK
83 H25 **Kirkwood** Eastern Cape, S South Africa
27 X5 **Kirkwood** Missouri, C USA
Kirman see Kermān
Kir of Moab see Al Karak
Kir Moab see Al Karak
126 I5 **Kirov** Kaluzhskaya Oblast', W Russian Federation
125 R14 **Kirov** prev. Vyatka. Kirovskaya Oblast', NW Russian Federation
Kirov see Balpyk Bi
76 K12 **Kita** Kayes, W Mali
197 N14 **Kitaa** ✦ province W Greenland
165 Q4 **Kitahiyama** Hokkaidō, NE Japan
165 P12 **Kita-Ibaraki** Ibaraki, Honshū, S Japan
165 X16 **Kita-Iō-jima** island SE Japan
165 Q9 **Kitakami** Iwate, Honshū, C Japan
165 P11 **Kitakata** Fukushima, Honshū, C Japan
164 D13 **Kitakyūshū** var. Kitakyūshū. Fukuoka, Kyūshū, SW Japan
Kitakyūsyū see Kitakyūshū

81 H18 **Kitale** Rift Valley, W Kenya
165 U3 **Kitami** Hokkaidō, NE Japan
165 T2 **Kitami-sanchi** ▲ Hokkaidō, NE Japan
37 W5 **Kit Carson** Colorado, C USA
180 M12 **Kitchener** Western Australia
14 F16 **Kitchener** Ontario, S Canada
93 O17 **Kitee** Itä-Suomi, SE Finland
81 G16 **Kitgum** N Uganda
Kithareng see Kanmaw Kyun
Kíthira see Kýthira
Kíthnos see Kýthnos
10 J13 **Kitimat** British Columbia, SW Canada
92 L11 **Kitinen** ✦ N Finland
147 N12 **Kitob** Rus. Kitab. Qashqadaryo Viloyati, S Uzbekistan
116 K7 **Kitsman'** Ger. Kotzman, Rom. Cozmeni, Rus. Kitsman. Chernivets'ka Oblast', W Ukraine
164 E14 **Kitsuki** var. Kituki. Ōita, SW Japan
18 C14 **Kittanning** Pennsylvania, NE USA
19 P10 **Kittery** Maine, NE USA
92 L11 **Kittilä** Lappi, N Finland
109 Z4 **Kittsee** Burgenland, E Austria
81 J19 **Kitui** Eastern, S Kenya
Kituki see Kitsuki
81 G22 **Kitunda** Tabora, C Tanzania
10 K13 **Kitwanga** British Columbia, SW Canada
82 J13 **Kitwe** var. Kitwe-Nkana. Copperbelt, C Zambia
Kitwe-Nkana see Kitwe
109 O7 **Kitzbühel** Tirol, W Austria
109 O7 **Kitzbüheler Alpen** ▲ W Austria
101 J19 **Kitzingen** Bayern, SE Germany
153 Q14 **Kiul** Bihār, NE India
186 A7 **Kiunga** Western, SW Papua New Guinea
93 H16 **Kiuruvesi** Kuopio, C Finland
38 M7 **Kivalina** Alaska, USA
92 L13 **Kivalo** ridge C Finland
116 J3 **Kivertsi** Pol. Kiwerce, Rus. Kivertsy. Volyns'ka Oblast', NW Ukraine
Kivertsy see Kivertsi
93 L16 **Kivijärvi** Länsi-Suomi, C Finland
95 L23 **Kivik** Skåne, S Sweden
118 J3 **Kiviõli** Ida-Virumaa, NE Estonia
Kivu, Lac see Kivu, Lake
67 U10 **Kivu, Lake** Fr. Lac Kivu. ⊚ Rwanda/Dem. Rep. Congo
186 C9 **Kiwai Island** island SW Papua New Guinea
39 N8 **Kiwalik** Alaska, USA
Kiwerce see Kivertsi
122 J13 **Kiselevsk** Kemerovskaya Oblast', S Russian Federation
153 R13 **Kishanganj** Bihār, NE India
152 G12 **Kishangarh** Rājasthān, N India
Kishegyes see Mali Iđoš
77 S15 **Kishi** Oyo, W Nigeria
Kishinev see Chişinău
Kishiözen see Malyy Uzen'
164 I14 **Kishiwada** var. Kisiwada. Ōsaka, Honshū, SW Japan
143 P14 **Kish, Jazīreh-ye** island S Iran
145 R7 **Kishkenekol'** prev. Kzyltu, Kaz. Qyzyltü. Kokshetau, N Kazakhstan
152 I6 **Kishtwār** Jammu and Kashmir, NW India
81 H19 **Kisii** Nyanza, SW Kenya
81 J23 **Kisiju** Pwani, E Tanzania
Kisiwada see Kishiwada
Kisjenő see Chişineu-Criş
38 E17 **Kiska Island** island Aleutian Islands, Alaska, USA
186 E9 **Kiskapus** var. Copşa Mică SE Papua New Guinea
111 M22 **Kiskörei-víztároló** ☐ E Hungary
111 L24 **Kiskunfélegyháza** var. Félegyháza. Bács-Kiskun, C Hungary
111 K25 **Kiskunhalas** var. Halas. Bács-Kiskun, S Hungary
111 K24 **Kiskunmajsa** Bács-Kiskun, S Hungary
127 N15 **Kislovodsk** Stavropol'skiy Kray, SW Russian Federation
81 L18 **Kismaayo** var. Chisimayu, Kismayu, It. Chisimaio. Jubbada Hoose, S Somalia
Kismayu see Kismaayo
164 M13 **Kiso-sanmyaku** ▲ Honshū, S Japan
115 H24 **Kíssamos** prev Kastélli. Kríti, Greece, E Mediterranean Sea
Kisseraing see Kanmaw Kyun
76 K13 **Kissidougou** Guinée-Forestière, S Guinea
23 X12 **Kissimmee** Florida, SE USA
23 X12 **Kissimmee, Lake** ⊚ Florida, SE USA
23 X13 **Kissimmee River** ✦ Florida, SE USA
9 V13 **Kississing Lake** ⊚ Manitoba, C Canada
111 L24 **Kistelek** Csongrád, SE Hungary
Kistna see Krishna
111 M23 **Kisújszállás** Jász-Nagykun-Szolnok, E Hungary
164 G12 **Kisuki** Shimane, Honshū, SW Japan
81 H18 **Kisumu** prev. Port Florence. Nyanza, W Kenya
Kisutzaneustadtl see Kysucké Nové Mesto

81 J24 **Kiswere** Lindi, SE Tanzania
Kiszucaújhely see Kysucké Nové Mesto
76 K12 **Kita** Kayes, W Mali
111 B15 **Kláštérec nad Ohří** Ger. Klösterle an der Eger. Ústecký Kraj, NW Czech Republic
82 J14 **Kitwe** var. Kitwe-Nkana.
165 P13 **Kita-Ibaraki**
145 O9 **Kiyma** Akmola, C Kazakhstan
125 V13 **Kizel** Permskaya Oblast', NW Russian Federation
125 O12 **Kizema** var. Kizëma. Arkhangel'skaya Oblast', NW Russian Federation
Kizëma see Kizema
136 H12 **Kızılcahamam** Ankara, N Turkey
136 J10 **Kızıl Irmak** ✦ C Turkey
137 P16 **Kızıl Kum** see Kyzyl Kum
137 P16 **Kızıltepe** Mardin, SE Turkey
Ki Zil Uzen see Qezel Owzan, Rūd-e
127 Q16 **Kizilyurt** Respublika Dagestan, SW Russian Federation
127 Q15 **Kizlyar** Respublika Dagestan, SW Russian Federation
127 S3 **Kizner** Udmurtskaya Respublika, NW Russian Federation
Kizyl-Arvat see Serdar
Kizyl-Atrek see Etrek
Kizyl-Kaya see Gyzylgaýa
95 H16 **Kjerkøy** island S Norway
92 L7 **Kjøllefjord** Finnmark, N Norway
95 B18 **Kjølsäs** Nordland, C Norway
169 N12 **Klabat, Teluk** bay Pulau Bangka, W Indonesia
112 I12 **Kladanj** ✦ Federeracija Bosna I Hercegovina, E Bosnia and Herzegovina
171 X16 **Kladar** Papua, E Indonesia
111 C16 **Kladno** Střední Čechy, NW Czech Republic
112 P11 **Kladovo** Serbia, E Serbia
167 P22 **Klæng** Rayong, S Thailand
109 T9 **Klagenfurt** Slvn. Celovec. Kärnten, S Austria
118 C11 **Klaipėda** Ger. Memel. Klaipėda, NW Lithuania
118 C11 **Klaipėda** ✦ province W Lithuania
95 B18 **Klaksvík** Dan. Klaksvig. Bordhoy, N Faeroe Islands
32 H16 **Klamath** California, W USA
32 H16 **Klamath Falls** Oregon, W USA
34 M1 **Klamath Mountains** ▲ California/Oregon, W USA
34 L2 **Klamath River** ✦ California/Oregon, W USA
168 K4 **Klang** var. Kelang; prev. Port Swettenham. Selangor, Peninsular Malaysia
Klang see Kelang
95 I14 **Klarälven** ✦ Norway/Sweden
111 B18 **Klatovy** Ger. Klattau. Plzeňský Kraj, W Czech Republic
Klattau see Klatovy
Klausenburg see Cluj-Napoca
9 Y14 **Klawock** Prince of Wales Island, Alaska, USA
98 P8 **Klazienaveen** Drenthe, NE Netherlands
Kleck see Klyetsk

KŁECKO – KONTICH

110 H11 **Kłecko** Wielkopolskie, C Poland
110 I11 **Kleczew** Wielkopolskie, C Poland
10 L15 **Kleena Kleene** British Columbia, SW Canada
83 D20 **Klein Aub** Hardap, C Namibia
Kleine Donau *see* Mosoni-Duna
101 O14 **Kleine Elster** ∼ E Germany
Kleine Kokel *see* Târnava Mică
99 I16 **Kleine Nete** ∼ N Belgium
Kleines Ungarisches Tiefland *see* Little Alföld
83 E22 **Klein Karas** Karas, S Namibia
Kleinkopisch *see* Copşa Mică
Klein-Marien *see* Väike-Maarja
Kleinschlatten *see* Zlatna
83 D23 **Kleinsee** Northern Cape, W South Africa
Kleinwardein *see* Kisvárda
115 C16 **Kleisoúra** Ípeiros, W Greece
95 C17 **Klepp** Rogaland, S Norway
83 I22 **Klerksdorp** North-West, N South Africa
126 I5 **Kletnya** Bryanskaya Oblast', W Russian Federation
Kletsk *see* Klyetsk
101 D14 **Kleve** *Eng.* Cleves, *Fr.* Clèves; *prev.* Cleve. Nordrhein-Westfalen, W Germany
113 J16 **Kličevo** C Montenegro
119 M16 **Klichaw** *Rus.* Klichev. Mahilyowskaya Voblasts', E Belarus
Klichev *see* Klichaw
119 Q16 **Klimavichy** *Rus.* Klimovichi. Mahilyowskaya Voblasts', E Belarus
114 M7 **Kliment** Shumen, NE Bulgaria
Klimovichi *see* Klimavichy
93 G14 **Klimpfjäll** Västerbotten, N Sweden
126 K3 **Klin** Moskovskaya Oblast', W Russian Federation
113 M16 **Klina** Kosovo, S Serbia
111 B15 **Klínovec** *Ger.* Keilberg. ▲ NW Czech Republic
95 P19 **Klintehamn** Gotland, SE Sweden
127 R8 **Klintsovka** Saratovskaya Oblast', W Russian Federation
126 H6 **Klintsy** Bryanskaya Oblast', W Russian Federation
95 K22 **Klippan** Skåne, S Sweden
92 G13 **Klippen** Västerbotten, N Sweden
121 P2 **Klírou** W Cyprus
114 I9 **Klisura** Plovdiv, C Bulgaria
95 F20 **Klitmøller** Viborg, NW Denmark
112 F11 **Ključ** ◈ Federacija Bosna I Hercegovina, NW Bosnia and Herzegovina
111 J14 **Kłobuck** Śląskie, S Poland
110 J11 **Kłodawa** Wielkopolskie, C Poland
111 G16 **Kłodzko** *Ger.* Glatz. Dolnośląskie, SW Poland
95 I14 **Kløfta** Akershus, S Norway
112 P12 **Klokočevac** Serbia, E Serbia
118 G3 **Klooga** *Ger.* Lodensee. Harjumaa, NW Estonia
99 F15 **Kloosterzande** Zeeland, SW Netherlands
113 L19 **Klos** *var.* Klosi. Dibër, C Albania
Klosi *see* Klos
Klösterle an der Eger *see* Klášterec nad Ohří
109 X3 **Klosterneuburg** Niederösterreich, NE Austria
108 J9 **Klosters** Graubünden, SE Switzerland
108 G7 **Kloten** Zürich, N Switzerland
108 G7 **Kloten** ✈ (Zürich) Zürich, N Switzerland
100 K12 **Klötze** Sachsen-Anhalt, C Germany
12 K3 **Klotz, Lac** ◎ Québec, NE Canada
101 O15 **Klotzsche** ✈ (Dresden) Sachsen, E Germany
10 H7 **Kluane Lake** ◎ Yukon Territory, W Canada
Kluang *see* Keluang
111 I14 **Kluczbork** *Ger.* Kreuzburg, Kreuzburg in Oberschlesien. Opolskie, S Poland
39 W12 **Klukwan** Alaska, USA
Klyastitsy *see* Klyastsitsy
118 L11 **Klyastsitsy** *Rus.* Klyastitsy. Vitsyebskaya Voblasts', N Belarus
127 T5 **Klyavlino** Samarskaya Oblast', W Russian Federation
84 K9 **Klyaz'in** ∼ W Russian Federation
127 N3 **Klyaz'ma** ∼ W Russian Federation
119 J17 **Klyetsk** *Pol.* Kleck, *Rus.* Kletsk. Minskaya Voblasts', SW Belarus
147 S8 **Klyuchevka** Talasskaya Oblast', NW Kyrgyzstan
123 V10 **Klyuchevskaya Sopka, Vulkan** ⛰ E Russian Federation
95 D17 **Knaben** Vest-Agder, S Norway
95 K21 **Knäred** Halland, S Sweden
97 M16 **Knaresborough** N England, UK
114 H8 **Knezha** Vratsa, NW Bulgaria
25 O9 **Knickerbocker** Texas, SW USA
28 K5 **Knife River** ∼ North Dakota, N USA
10 K16 **Knight Inlet** *inlet* British Columbia, W Canada
39 S12 **Knight Island** *island* Alaska, USA
97 K20 **Knighton** E Wales, UK
35 O7 **Knights Landing** California, W USA
112 E13 **Knin** Šibenik-Knin, S Croatia
25 Q12 **Knippal** Texas, SW USA
109 U7 **Knittelfeld** Steiermark, C Austria
95 O15 **Knivsta** Uppsala, C Sweden
113 P14 **Knjaževac** Serbia, E Serbia
27 S4 **Knob Noster** Missouri, C USA
99 D15 **Knokke-Heist** West-Vlaanderen, NW Belgium
95 H20 **Knøsen** *hill* N Denmark
Knosós *see* Knossos
115 J25 **Knossos** *Gk.* Knosós. *prehistoric site* Kríti, Greece, E Mediterranean Sea
25 N7 **Knott** Texas, SW USA
194 K5 **Knowles, Cape** *headland* Antarctica
31 O11 **Knox** Indiana, N USA
29 O3 **Knox** North Dakota, N USA
18 C13 **Knox** Pennsylvania, NE USA
189 X8 **Knox Atoll** *var.* Nadikdik, Narikrik. *atoll* Ratak Chain, SE Marshall Islands
10 H13 **Knox, Cape** *headland* Graham Island, British Columbia, SW Canada
25 P5 **Knox City** Texas, SW USA
195 Y11 **Knox Coast** *physical region* Antarctica
31 T12 **Knox Lake** ⊞ Ohio, N USA
23 T5 **Knoxville** Georgia, SE USA
30 K12 **Knoxville** Illinois, N USA
29 W15 **Knoxville** Iowa, C USA
21 N9 **Knoxville** Tennessee, S USA
197 P11 **Knud Rasmussen Land** *physical region* N Greenland
Knüll *see* Knüllgebirge
101 I16 **Knüllgebirge** *var.* Knüll. ▲▲ C Germany
Knyazhevo *see* Sredishte
Knyazhitsy *see* Knyazhytsy
119 O15 **Knyazhytsy** *Rus.* Knyazhitsy. Mahilyowskaya Voblasts', E Belarus
83 G26 **Knysna** Western Cape, SW South Africa
Koartac *see* Quaqtaq
169 N13 **Koba** Pulau Bangka, W Indonesia
164 D16 **Kobayashi** *var.* Kobayasi. Miyazaki, Kyūshū, SW Japan
Kobayasi *see* Kobayashi
Kobdo *see* Hovd
164 I13 **Kōbe** Hyōgo, Honshū, SW Japan
Kobelyaki *see* Kobelyaky
117 T6 **Kobelyaky** *Rus.* Kobelyaki. Poltavs'ka Oblast', NE Ukraine
95 J22 **København** *Eng.* Copenhagen; *anc.* Hafnia. ● (Denmark) Sjælland, København, E Denmark
95 J23 **København** *off.* Københavns Amt. ◈ *county* E Denmark
Københavns Amt *see* København
76 K10 **Kobenni** Hodh el Gharbi, S Mauritania
171 T13 **Kobi** Pulau Seram, E Indonesia
101 F17 **Koblenz** *prev.* Coblenz, *Fr.* Coblence; *anc.* Confluentes. Rheinland-Pfalz, W Germany
108 F6 **Koblenz** Aargau, N Switzerland
124 J14 **Kabozha** Novgorodskaya Oblast', W Russian Federation
Kobrin *see* Kobryn
171 V15 **Kobroor, Pulau** *island* Kepulauan Aru, E Indonesia
119 G19 **Kobryn** *Pol.* Kobryn, *Rus.* Kobrin. Brestskaya Voblasts', SW Belarus
39 O7 **Kobuk** Alaska, USA
39 O7 **Kobuk River** ∼ Alaska, USA
137 Q10 **K'obulet'i** W Georgia
123 P10 **Kobyay** Respublika Sakha (Yakutiya), NE Russian Federation
136 E11 **Kocaeli** ◈ *province* NW Turkey
113 P18 **Kočani** NE FYR Macedonia
112 K12 **Koceljevo** Serbia, W Serbia
109 U12 **Kočevje** *Ger.* Gottschee. S Slovenia
153 T12 **Koch Bihār** West Bengal, NE India
122 M9 **Kochechum** ∼ N Russian Federation
101 I20 **Kocher** ∼ SW Germany
125 T13 **Kochevo** Komi-Permyatskiy Avtonomnyy Okrug, NW Russian Federation
164 G14 **Kōchi** *var.* Kôti. Kōchi, Shikoku, SW Japan
164 G14 **Kōchi** *off.* Kōchi-ken, *var.* Kôti. ◈ *prefecture* Shikoku, SW Japan
Kochi *see* Cochin
Kōchi-ken *see* Kōchi
Kochiu *see* Gejiu
Kochkor *see* Kochkorka
147 V8 **Kochkorka** *Kir.* Kochkor. Narynskaya Oblast', C Kyrgyzstan
125 V5 **Kochmes** Respublika Komi, NW Russian Federation
127 P15 **Kochubey** Respublika Dagestan, SW Russian Federation
115 I17 **Kochýlas** ▲ Skýros, Vóreioi Sporádes, Greece, Aegean Sea
110 O13 **Kock** Lubelskie, E Poland
81 J19 **Kodacho** *spring/well* S Kenya
155 K24 **Koddiyar Bay** *bay* NE Sri Lanka
39 Q14 **Kodiak** Kodiak Island, Alaska, USA
39 Q14 **Kodiak Island** *island* Alaska, USA
154 B12 **Kodīnār** Gujarāt, W India
124 M9 **Kodino** Arkhangel'skaya Oblast', NW Russian Federation
122 M12 **Kodinsk** Krasnoyarskiy Kray, C Russian Federation
80 F12 **Kodok** Upper Nile, SE Sudan
117 N8 **Kodyma** Odes'ka Oblast', SW Ukraine
Koedoes *see* Kudus
99 B17 **Koekelare** West-Vlaanderen, W Belgium
Koeln *see* Köln
Koepang *see* Kupang
Ko-erh-mu *see* Golmud
99 J17 **Koersel** Limburg, NE Belgium
83 E21 **Koës** Karas, SE Namibia
Koetai *see* Mahakam, Sungai
Koetaradja *see* Bandaaceh
36 I14 **Kofa Mountains** ▲▲ Arizona, SW USA
171 Y15 **Kofarau** Papua, E Indonesia
147 P13 **Kofarnihon** *Rus.* Kofarnikhon; *prev.* Ordzhonikidzeabad, *Taj* Orjonikidzeobod, Yangi-Bazar. W Tajikistan
147 P14 **Kofarnihon** *Rus.* Kafirnigan. ∼ SW Tajikistan
Kofarnikhon *see* Kofarnihon
114 M11 **Kofçaz** Kırklareli, NW Turkey
115 J25 **Kófinas** ▲ Kríti, Greece, E Mediterranean Sea
121 P3 **Kofínou** *var.* Kophinou. S Cyprus
109 V8 **Köflach** Steiermark, SE Austria
77 Q17 **Koforidua** SE Ghana
164 H12 **Kōfu** Tottori, Honshū, SW Japan
164 M13 **Kōfu** *var.* Kôhu. Yamanashi, Honshū, S Japan
81 F22 **Koga** Tabora, C Tanzania
Kogălniceanu *see* Mihail Kogălniceanu
13 P6 **Kogaluk** ∼ Newfoundland and Labrador, E Canada
12 J4 **Kogaluk** ∼ Québec, NE Canada
122 I10 **Kogalym** Khanty-Mansiyskiy Avtonomnyy Okrug, C Russian Federation
95 J23 **Køge** Roskilde, E Denmark
95 J23 **Køge Bugt** *bay* E Denmark
77 U16 **Kogi** ◈ *state* C Nigeria
146 L11 **Kogon** *Rus.* Kagan. Buxoro Viloyati, C Uzbekistan
163 Y17 **Kōgŭm-do** *island* S South Korea
Kőhalom *see* Rupea
149 T6 **Kohāt** North-West Frontier Province, NW Pakistan
142 L10 **Kohgīlūyeh va Būyer Aḩmad** *off.* Ostān-e Kohkīlūyeh va Būyer Aḩmadī, *var.* Boyer Ahmadī va Kohkīlūyeh. ◈ *province* SW Iran
118 G4 **Kohila** *Ger.* Koil. Raplamaa, NW Estonia
153 X13 **Kohīma** *state capital* Nāgāland, E India
Koh I Noh *see* Büyükağrı Dağı
Kohkīlūyeh va Būyer Aḩmadī, Ostān-e *see* Kohgīlūyeh va Būyer Aḩmad
Kohsān *see* Kūhestān
118 J3 **Kohtla-Järve** Ida-Virumaa, NE Estonia
Kōhu *see* Kōfu
117 N10 **Kohyl'nyk** *Rom.* Cogîlnic. ∼ Moldova/Ukraine
165 N11 **Koide** Niigata, Honshū, C Japan
10 G7 **Koidern** Yukon Territory, W Canada
76 J15 **Koidu** E Sierra Leone
118 I4 **Koigi** Järvamaa, C Estonia
Koil *see* Kohila
172 H13 **Koimbani** Grande Comore, NW Comoros
139 T3 **Koi Sanjaq** *var.* Koysanjaq, Küysanjaq. N Iraq
93 O16 **Koitere** ◎ E Finland
Koivisto *see* Primorsk
163 Z16 **Kōje-do** *Jap.* Kyōsai-tō. *island* S South Korea
80 J13 **K'ok'a Hāyk'** ◎ C Ethiopia
Kokand *see* Qo'qon
182 F6 **Kokatha** South Australia
146 M10 **Ko'kcha** *Rus.* Kokcha. Boxoro Viloyati, C Uzbekistan
146 M10 **Ko'kcha** *Rus.* Kokcha. Buxoro Viloyati, C Uzbekistan
Kokcha *see* Ko'kcha
Kokcha *see* Ko'kcha
Kokchetav *see* Kokshetau
93 K18 **Kokemäenjoki** ∼ SW Finland
171 W14 **Kokenau** *var.* Kokonau. Papua, E Indonesia
83 E22 **Kokerboom** Karas, SE Namibia
119 N14 **Kokhanava** *Rus.* Kokhanovo. Vitsyebskaya Voblasts', NE Belarus
Kokhanovichi *see* Kakhanavichy
Kokhanovo *see* Kokhanava
Kök-Janggak *see* Kok-Yangak
93 K16 **Kokkola** *Swe.* Karleby; *prev. Swe.* Gamlakarleby. Länsi-Soumi, W Finland
118 H9 **Koknese** Aizkraukle, C Latvia
77 T13 **Koko** Kebbi, W Nigeria
186 E9 **Kokoda** Northern, S Papua New Guinea
76 K12 **Kokofata** Kayes, W Mali
39 N6 **Kokolik River** ∼ Alaska, USA
31 O13 **Kokomo** Indiana, N USA
Kokonau *see* Kokenau
Koko Nor *see* Qinghai Hu, China
Koko Nor *see* Qinghai, China
186 H6 **Kokopo** *var.* Kopopo; *prev.* Herbertshöhe. New Britain, E Papua New Guinea
145 X10 **Kokpekti** *Kaz.* Kökpekti. Semipalatinsk, E Kazakhstan
145 X11 **Kokpekti** ∼ E Kazakhstan
Kökpekti *see* Kokpekti
39 P9 **Kokrines** Alaska, USA
39 P9 **Kokrines Hills** ▲▲ Alaska, USA
145 P17 **Koksaray** Yuzhnyy Kazakhstan, S Kazakhstan
147 X9 **Kokshaal-Tau** *Rus.* Khrebet Kakshaal-Too. ▲▲ China/Kyrgyzstan
145 P7 **Kokshetau** *Kaz.* Kökshetaū; *prev.* Kokchetav. Kokshetau, N Kazakhstan
Kökshetaū *see* Kokshetau
99 A17 **Koksijde** West-Vlaanderen, W Belgium
12 M5 **Koksoak** ∼ Québec, E Canada
83 K24 **Kokstad** KwaZulu/Natal, E South Africa
145 V14 **Koksu** *Kaz.* Rūdnīchnyy. Almaty, SE Kazakhstan
145 W15 **Koktal** *Kaz.* Köktal. Almaty, SE Kazakhstan
145 Q12 **Koktas** ∼ C Kazakhstan
Kök-Tash *see* Këk-Tash
Koktokay *see* Fuyun
147 T9 **Kok-Yangak** *Kir.* Kök-Janggak. Dzhalal-Abadskaya Oblast', W Kyrgyzstan
158 F9 **Kokyar** Xinjiang Uygur Zizhiqu, W China
149 O13 **Kolāchi** *var.* Kulachi. ∼ SW Pakistan
76 J15 **Kolahun** N Liberia
171 O14 **Kolaka** Sulawesi, C Indonesia
Kolam *see* Quilon
K'o-la-ma-i *see* Karamay
Kola Peninsula *see* Kol'skiy Poluostrov
155 H19 **Kolār** Karnātaka, E India
155 H19 **Kolār Gold Fields** Karnātaka, E India
92 K11 **Kolari** Lappi, NW Finland
111 I21 **Kolárovo** *Ger.* Gutta; *prev.* Guta, *Hung.* Gúta. Nitriansky Kraj, SW Slovakia
113 K16 **Kolašin** E Montenegro
152 F11 **Kolāyat** Rājasthān, NW India
95 N15 **Kolbäck** Västmanland, C Sweden
Kolbcha *see* Kowbcha
197 Q15 **Kolbeinsey Ridge** *undersea feature* Denmark Strait/Norwegian Sea
Kolberg *see* Kołobrzeg
95 H15 **Kolbotn** Akershus, S Norway
111 N16 **Kolbuszowa** Podkarpackie, SE Poland
126 L3 **Kol'chugino** Vladimirskaya Oblast', W Russian Federation
76 H12 **Kolda** S Senegal
95 G23 **Kolding** Vejle, C Denmark
79 K20 **Kole** Kasai Oriental, SW Dem. Rep. Congo
79 M17 **Kole** Orientale, N Dem. Rep. Congo
Kōle *see* Kili Island
84 F6 **Kölen** ▲▲ Norway/Sweden
Kolepom, Pulau *see* Yos Sudarso, Pulau
118 H3 **Kolga Laht** *Ger.* Kolko-Wiek. *bay* N Estonia
125 Q3 **Kolguyev, Ostrov** *island* NW Russian Federation
155 E16 **Kolhāpur** Mahārāshtra, SW India
151 K21 **Kolhumadulu Atoll** *atoll* S Maldives
93 O16 **Koli** *var.* Kolinkylä. Pohjois-Karjala, E Finland
39 O13 **Koliganek** Alaska, USA
111 E16 **Kolín** *Ger.* Kolin. Střední Čechy, C Czech Republic
Kolinkylä *see* Koli
190 E12 **Koliu** Île Futuna, W Wallis and Futuna
118 E7 **Kolka** Talsi, NW Latvia
118 E7 **Kolkasrags** *prev. Eng.* Cape Domesnes. *cape* NW Latvia
153 S16 **Kolkata** *prev.* Calcutta. *state capital* West Bengal, NE India
Kolkhozabad *see* Kolkhozobod
147 P14 **Kolkhozobod** *Rus.* Kolkhozabad; *prev.* Kaganovichabad, Tugalan. SW Tajikistan
Kolki/Kołki *see* Kolky
Kolko-Wiek *see* Kolga Laht
116 K3 **Kolky** *Pol.* Kołki, *Rus.* Kolki. Volyns'ka Oblast', NW Ukraine
Kollam *see* Quilon
155 G20 **Kollegāl** Karnātaka, W India
98 M5 **Kollum** Friesland, N Netherlands
Kolmar *see* Colmar
101 E16 **Köln** *var.* Koeln, *Eng./Fr.* Cologne, *prev.* Cöln; *anc.* Colonia Agrippina, Oppidum Ubiorum. Nordrhein-Westfalen, W Germany
110 N9 **Kolno** Podlaskie, NE Poland
110 J12 **Koło** Wielkopolskie, C Poland
38 B8 **Kōloa** *var.* Koloa. Kaua'i, Hawai'i, USA
Koloa *see* Kōloa
110 E7 **Kołobrzeg** *Ger.* Kolberg. Zachodnio-pomorskie, NW Poland
126 H4 **Kolodnya** Smolenskaya Oblast', W Russian Federation
190 E13 **Kolofau, Mont** ⛰ Île Alofi, S Wallis and Futuna
125 O14 **Kologriv** Kostromskaya Oblast', NW Russian Federation
76 L12 **Kolokani** Koulikoro, W Mali
77 N13 **Koloko** W Burkina
186 K8 **Kolombangara** *var.* Kilimbangara, Nduke. *island* New Georgia Islands, NW Solomon Islands
Kolomea *see* Kolomyya
126 L4 **Kolomna** Moskovskaya Oblast', W Russian Federation
116 J7 **Kolomyya** *Ger.* Kolomea. Ivano-Frankivs'ka Oblast', W Ukraine
76 M13 **Kolondiéba** Sikasso, SW Mali
193 V15 **Kolonga** Tongatapu, S Tonga
189 U16 **Kolonia** *var.* Colonia. Pohnpei, E Micronesia
Kolonja *see* Kolonjë
113 K21 **Kolonjë** *var.* Kolonja. Fier, C Albania
Kolonjë *see* Ersekë
Kolotambu *see* Avuavu
193 U15 **Kolovai** Tongatapu, S Tonga
Kolozsvár *see* Cluj-Napoca
112 C9 **Kolpa** *Ger.* Kulpa, *SCr.* Kupa. ∼ Croatia/Slovenia
122 J11 **Kolpashevo** Tomskaya Oblast', C Russian Federation
124 H13 **Kolpino** Leningradskaya Oblast', NW Russian Federation
100 M10 **Kölpinsee** ◎ NE Germany
146 K8 **Koʻlquduq** *Rus.* Kulkuduk. Navoiy Viloyati, N Uzbekistan
146 K8 **Koʻlquduq** *Rus.* Kulkuduk. Nawoiy Viloyati, N Uzbekistan
124 K5 **Kol'skiy Poluostrov** *Eng.* Kola Peninsula. *peninsula* NW Russian Federation
127 T6 **Koltubanovskiy** Orenburgskaya Oblast', W Russian Federation
112 L11 **Kolubara** ∼ C Serbia
Kolupchii *see* Gurkovo
110 K13 **Koluszki** Łódźskie, C Poland
125 T6 **Kolva** ∼ NW Russian Federation
93 E14 **Kolvereid** Nord-Trøndelag, W Norway
148 L15 **Kolwa** Balūchistān, SW Pakistan
79 M24 **Kolwezi** Katanga, S Dem. Rep. Congo
123 S7 **Kolyma** ∼ NE Russian Federation
Kolyma Lowland *see* Kolymskaya Nizmennost'
Kolyma Range/Kolymskiy, Khrebet *see* Kolymskoye Nagor'ye
123 S7 **Kolymskaya Nizmennost'** *Eng.* Kolyma Lowland. *lowlands* NE Russian Federation
123 S7 **Kolymskoye** Respublika Sakha (Yakutiya), NE Russian Federation
123 U8 **Kolymskoye Nagor'ye** *var.* Khrebet Kolymskiy, *Eng.* Kolyma Range. ▲▲ E Russian Federation
123 V5 **Kolyuchinskaya Guba** *bay* NE Russian Federation
145 W15 **Kol'zhat** Almaty, SE Kazakhstan
114 G8 **Kom** ▲ NW Bulgaria
80 I13 **Koma** Oromo, C Ethiopia
77 X12 **Komadugu Gana** ∼ NE Nigeria
164 M13 **Komagane** Nagano, Honshū, S Japan
79 P17 **Komanda** Orientale, NE Dem. Rep. Congo
197 U1 **Komandorskaya Basin** *var.* Kamchatka Basin. *undersea feature* SW Bering Sea
125 Pp9 **Komandorskiye Ostrova** *Eng.* Commander Islands. *island group* E Russian Federation
Kománfalva *see* Comănești
111 I22 **Komárno** *Ger.* Komorn, *Hung.* Komárom. Nitriansky Kraj, SW Slovakia
111 I22 **Komárom** Komárom-Esztergom, NW Hungary
Komárom *see* Komárno
111 I22 **Komárom-Esztergom** *off.* Komárom-Esztergom Megye. ◈ *county* N Hungary
Komárom-Esztergom Megye *see* Komárom-Esztergom
164 K11 **Komatsu** *var.* Komatu. Ishikawa, Honshū, SW Japan
Komatu *see* Komatsu
83 D17 **Kombat** Otjozondjupa, N Namibia
Kombissiguiri *see* Kombissiri
77 P13 **Kombissiri** *var.* Kombissiguiri. C Burkina
188 E10 **Komebail Lagoon** *lagoon* N Palau
81 F20 **Kome Island** *island* N Tanzania
Komeyo *see* Wandai
117 P10 **Kominternivs'ke** Odes'ka Oblast', SW Ukraine
125 R12 **Komi-Permyatskiy Avtonomnyy Okrug** ◈ *autonomous district* W Russian Federation
125 R8 **Komi, Respublika** ◈ *autonomous republic* NW Russian Federation
111 I25 **Komló** Baranya, SW Hungary
Kommunarsk *see* Alchevs'k
147 S12 **Kommunizm, Qullai** ▲ E Tajikistan
186 B7 **Komo** Southern Highlands, W Papua New Guinea
170 M16 **Komodo, Pulau** *island* Nusa Tenggara, S Indonesia
77 N15 **Komoé** *var.* Komoé Fleuve. ∼ E Ivory Coast
Komoé Fleuve *see* Komoé
75 X11 **Kôm Ombo** *var.* Kawm Umbū. SE Egypt
79 F20 **Komono** La Lékoumou, SW Congo
171 Y16 **Komoran** Papua, E Indonesia
171 Y16 **Komoran, Pulau** *island* E Indonesia
Komorn *see* Komárno
Komornok *see* Comorâște
Komosolabad *see* Komsomolobod
Komotau *see* Chomutov
114 K13 **Komotiní** *var.* Gümüljina, *Turk.* Gümülcine. Anatolikí Makedonía kai Thráki, NE Greece
113 K16 **Komovi** ▲▲ E Montenegro
117 R8 **Kompaniyivka** Kirovohrads'ka Oblast', C Ukraine
Kompong *see* Kâmpóng Chhnăng
Kompong Cham *see* Kâmpóng Cham
Kompong Kleang *see* Kâmpóng Khleăng
Kompong Som *see* Kâmpóng Saôm
Kompong Speu *see* Kâmpóng Spoe
Komrat *see* Comrat
Komsomol *see* Komsomol'skiy
122 K14 **Komsomolets, Ostrov** *island* Severnaya Zemlya, N Russian Federation
144 F13 **Komsomolets, Zaliv** *lake gulf* SW Kazakhstan
Komsomol/Komsomolets *see* Karabalyk, Kostanay, Kazakhstan
147 Q12 **Komsomolobod** *Rus.* Komosolabad. C Tajikistan
124 M16 **Komsomol'sk** Ivanovskaya Oblast', W Russian Federation
117 S6 **Komsomol's'k** Poltavs'ka Oblast', C Ukraine
146 M11 **Komsomol'sk** Navoiy Viloyati, N Uzbekistan
144 G12 **Komsomol'skiy** *Kaz.* Komsomol. Atyrau, W Kazakhstan
125 W4 **Komsomol'skiy** Respublika Komi, NW Russian Federation
123 S13 **Komsomol'sk-na-Amure** Khabarovskiy Kray, SE Russian Federation
Komsomol'sk-na-Ustyurte *see* Kubla-Ustyurt
144 K10 **Komsomol'skoye** Aktyubinsk, NW Kazakhstan
127 Q8 **Komsomol'skoye** Saratovskaya Oblast', W Russian Federation
145 P10 **Kon** ∼ C Kazakhstan
Kona *see* Kailua-Kona
124 K16 **Konakovo** Tverskaya Oblast', W Russian Federation
149 S4 **Konar** *Per.* Konarhā, *Pash.* Kunar. ◈ *province* E Afghanistan
143 V15 **Konārak** Sīstān va Balūchestān, SE Iran
Konarhā *see* Konar
27 O11 **Konawa** Oklahoma, C USA
122 H10 **Konda** ∼ C Russian Federation
154 L13 **Kondagaon** Chhattīsgarh, C India
14 K10 **Kondiaronk, Lac** ◎ Québec, SE Canada
180 J13 **Kondinin** Western Australia
81 H21 **Kondoa** Dodoma, C Tanzania
127 P6 **Kondol'** Penzenskaya Oblast', W Russian Federation
114 N10 **Kondolovo** Burgas, E Bulgaria
171 Z16 **Kondomirat** Papua, E Indonesia
124 J10 **Kondopoga** Respublika Kareliya, NW Russian Federation
149 Q2 **Kondoz** *var.* Kondoz, Kundūz, Qondūz, *Per.* Kondūz. Kunduz, NE Afghanistan
149 Q2 **Kondoz** *Pash.* Kunduz. ◈ *province* NE Afghanistan
Kondoz *see* Kondoz
155 J17 **Kondukūr** *var.* Kandukur. Andhra Pradesh, E India
Kondūz *see* Kondoz
187 P16 **Koné** Province Nord, W New Caledonia
146 E13 **Kënekesir** *Rus.* Kënekesir. Balkan Welaýaty, W Turkmenistan
146 G8 **Këneurgench** *var.* Köneürgench, *Rus.* Këneurgench; *prev.* Kunya-Urgench. Daşoguz Welaýaty, N Turkmenistan
Köneürgench *see* Këneurgench
77 N15 **Kong** N Ivory Coast
39 S5 **Kongakut River** ∼ Alaska, USA
197 O14 **Kong Christian IX Land** *Eng.* King Christian IX Land. *physical region* SE Greenland
197 P13 **Kong Christian X Land** *Eng.* King Christian X Land. *physical region* E Greenland
197 N13 **Kong Frederik IX Land** *physical region* SW Greenland
197 Q12 **Kong Frederik VIII Land** *Eng.* King Frederik VIII Land. *physical region* NE Greenland
197 N15 **Kong Frederik VI Kyst** *Eng.* King Frederik VI Coast. *physical region* SE Greenland
167 P13 **Kong, Kaôh** *prev.* Kas Kong. *island* SW Cambodia
92 P2 **Kong Karls Land** *Eng.* King Charles Islands. *island group* SE Svalbard
81 G14 **Kong Kong** ∼ SE Sudan
Kongo *see* Congo (river)
83 G16 **Kongola** Caprivi, NE Namibia
79 N21 **Kongolo** Katanga, E Dem. Rep. Congo
81 F14 **Kongor** Jonglei, SE Sudan
197 Q14 **Kong Oscar Fjord** *fjord* E Greenland
77 P12 **Kongoussi** N Burkina
95 G15 **Kongsberg** Buskerud, S Norway
92 Q2 **Kongsøya** *island* Kong Karls Land, E Svalbard
95 I14 **Kongsvinger** Hedmark, S Norway
Kongtong *see* Pingliang
167 T11 **Kông, Tônle** *var.* Xê Kong. ∼ Cambodia/Laos
158 E8 **Kongur Shan** ▲ NW China
81 I22 **Kongwa** Dodoma, C Tanzania
Kong, Xê *see* Kông, Tônle
Konia *see* Konya
147 R11 **Konibodom** *Rus.* Kanibadam. N Tajikistan
111 K15 **Koniecpol** Śląskie, S Poland
Konieh *see* Konya
Königgrätz *see* Hradec Králové
Königinhof an der Elbe *see* Dvůr Králové nad Labem
101 K23 **Königsbrunn** Bayern, S Germany
Königshütte *see* Chorzów
101 O24 **Königssee** ◎ SE Germany
109 S8 **Königstuhl** ▲ S Austria
109 U3 **Königswiesen** Oberösterreich, N Austria
101 E17 **Königswinter** Nordrhein-Westfalen, W Germany
146 M11 **Konimex** *Rus.* Kenimekh. Navoiy Viloyati, N Uzbekistan
110 I12 **Konin** *Ger.* Kuhnau. Weilkopolskie, C Poland
Koninkrijk der Nederlanden *see* Netherlands
113 L24 **Konispol** *var.* Konispoli. Vlorë, S Albania
Konispoli *see* Konispol
115 C15 **Kónitsa** Ípeiros, W Greece
Konitz *see* Chojnice
108 D8 **Köniz** Bern, W Switzerland
113 H14 **Konjic** ◈ Federacija Bosna I Hercegovina, S Bosnia and Herzegovina
92 J10 **Könkämäälven** ∼ Finland/Sweden
155 D14 **Konkan** *plain* W India
83 D22 **Konkiep** ∼ S Namibia
76 I14 **Konkouré** ∼ W Guinea
77 O11 **Konna** Mopti, S Mali
186 H6 **Konogaiang, Mount** ▲ New Ireland, NE Papua New Guinea
186 H5 **Konogogo** New Ireland, NE Papua New Guinea
108 E9 **Konolfingen** Bern, W Switzerland
77 P16 **Konongo** C Ghana
186 H5 **Konos** New Ireland, NE Papua New Guinea
124 M12 **Konosha** Arkhangel'skaya Oblast', NW Russian Federation
117 R3 **Konotop** Sums'ka Oblast', NE Ukraine
158 L7 **Konqi He** ∼ NW China
111 L14 **Końskie** Śiętokrzyskie, C Poland
Konstantinovka *see* Kostyantynivka
126 M11 **Konstantinovsk** Rostovskaya Oblast', SW Russian Federation
101 H24 **Konstanz** *var.* Constanz, *Eng.* Constance, *hist.* Kostnitz; *anc.* Constantia. Baden-Württemberg, S Germany
Konstanza *see* Constanța
77 T14 **Kontagora** Niger, W Nigeria
78 E13 **Kontcha** Nord, N Cameroon
99 G17 **Kontich** Antwerpen, N Belgium

◆ Country ● Country Capital ◇ Dependent Territory ○ Dependent Territory Capital ◈ Administrative Regions ✈ International Airport ▲ Mountain ▲▲ Mountain Range ⛰ Volcano ∼ River ◎ Lake ⊞ Reservoir

KONTIOLAHTI – KRASNOVISHERSK

93 O16 **Kontiolahti** Itä-Suomi, SE Finland
93 M15 **Kontiomäki** Oulu, C Finland
167 U11 **Kon Tum** *var.* Kontum. Kon Tum, C Vietnam
Kontum *see* Kon Tum
Konur *see* Sulakyurt
136 H15 **Konya** *var.* Konieh, *prev.* Konia; *anc.* Iconium. Konya, C Turkey
136 H15 **Konya** *var.* Konia, Konieh. ◈ *province* C Turkey
Konya Reservoir *see* Shivāji Sāgar
145 T13 **Konyrat** *var.* Kounradskiy, *Kaz.* Qongyrat. Karaganda, SE Kazakhstan
145 W15 **Konyrolen** Almaty, SE Kazakhstan
81 I19 **Konza** Eastern, S Kenya
98 I9 **Koog aan den Zaan** Noord-Holland, C Netherlands
182 E7 **Koonibba** South Australia
31 O11 **Koontz Lake** Indiana, N USA
171 U12 **Koor** Papua, E Indonesia
183 R9 **Koorawatha** New South Wales, SE Australia
118 J5 **Koosa** Tartumaa, E Estonia
33 N7 **Kootenai** *var.* Kootenay. ≈ Canada/USA *see also* Kootenay
9 P17 **Kootenay** ≈ Canada/USA
Kootenay *see* Kootenai
83 F24 **Kootjieskolk** Northern Cape, W South Africa
113 M15 **Kopaonik** ▲▲ S Serbia
Kopar *see* Koper
92 K1 **Kópasker** Nordhurland Eystra, N Iceland
92 H4 **Kópavogur** Reykjanes, W Iceland
145 U13 **Kopbirlik** *prev.* Kīrov, Kirova. Almaty, SE Kazakhstan
109 S13 **Koper** *It.* Capodistria; *prev.* Kopar. SW Slovenia
95 C16 **Kopervik** Rogaland, S Norway
Köpetdag Gershi/Kopetdag, Khrebet *see* Koppeh Dāgh
Kophinou *see* Kofínou
182 G8 **Kopi** South Australia
153 W12 **Kopili** ≈ NE India
95 M15 **Köping** Västmanland, C Sweden
113 K17 **Koplik** *var.* Kopliku. Shkodër, NW Albania
Kopliku *see* Koplik
Kopopo *see* Kokopo
94 I11 **Koppang** Hedmark, S Norway
Kopparberg *see* Dalarna
143 S3 **Koppeh Dāgh** *Rus.* Khrebet Kopetdag, *Turkm.* Köpetdag Gershi. ▲▲ Iran/Turkmenistan
Koppename *see* Coppename Rivier
95 J15 **Koppom** Värmland, C Sweden
Kopreinitz *see* Koprivnica
114 K9 **Koprinka, Yazovir** *prev.* Yazovir Georgi Dimitrov. ⊠ C Bulgaria
112 F7 **Koprivnica** *Ger.* Kopreinitz, *Hung.* Kaproncza. Koprivnica-Kri»zevci, N Croatia
112 F8 **Koprivnica-Križevci** *off.* Koprivničko-Križevačka Županija. ◈ *province* N Croatia
111 I17 **Kopřivnice** *Ger.* Nesselsdorf. Moravskoslezský Kraj, E Czech Republic
Koprivničko-Križevačka Županija *see* Koprivnica-Križevci
Köprülü *see* Veles
Koptsevichi *see* Kaptsevichy
Kopyl' *see* Kapyl'
119 O14 **Kopys'** *Rus.* Kopys'. Vitsyebskaya Voblasts', NE Belarus
113 M18 **Korab** ▲ Albania/FYR Macedonia
Korabavur Pastligi *see* Karabaur', Uval
81 M14 **K'orahē** Somali, E Ethiopia
115 L16 **Kórakas, Ákrotírio** *cape* Lésvos, E Greece
112 D9 **Korana** ≈ C Croatia
155 L14 **Korāput** Orissa, E India
Korat *see* Nakhon Ratchasima
167 Q9 **Korat Plateau** *plateau* E Thailand
139 T1 **Kōrāwa, Sar-i** ▲ NE Iraq
154 L11 **Korba** Chhattīsgarh, C India
101 H15 **Korbach** Hessen, C Germany
Korça *see* Korçë
113 M21 **Korçë** *var.* Korça, *Gk.* Korytsa, *It.* Corriza; *prev.* Koritsa. Korçë, SE Albania
113 M21 **Korçë** ◈ *district* SE Albania
113 G15 **Korčula** *It.* Curzola. Dubrovnik-Neretva, S Croatia
113 F15 **Korčula** *It.* Curzola; *anc.* Corcyra Nigra. *island* S Croatia
113 F15 **Korčulanski Kanal** *channel* S Croatia
145 T6 **Korday** *prev.* Georgiyevka. Zhambyl, SE Kazakhstan
142 J5 **Kordestān** *off.* Ostān-e Kordestān, *var.* Kurdestan. ◈ *province* W Iran
Kordestān, Ostān-e *see* Kordestān
143 P4 **Kord Kūy** *var.* Kurd Kui. Golestān, N Iran
163 V13 **Korea Bay** *bay* China/North Korea
Korea, Democratic People's Republic of *see* North Korea
171 T15 **Koreare** Pulau Yamdena, E Indonesia
Korea, Republic of *see* South Korea
163 Z17 **Korea Strait** *Jap.* Chōsen-kaikyō, *Kor.* Taehan-haehyŏp. *channel* Japan/South Korea
Korelichi/Korelicze *see* Karelichy
80 J11 **Korem** ◈ Tigrai, N Ethiopia
77 U11 **Korén Adoua** ≈ C Niger
126 I7 **Korenevo** Kurskaya Oblast', W Russian Federation
126 L13 **Korenovsk** Krasnodarskiy Kray, SW Russian Federation
116 L4 **Korets'** *Pol.* Korzec, *Rus.* Korets. Rivnens'ka Oblast', NW Ukraine
Korets *see* Korets'
194 L7 **Korff Ice Rise** *ice cap* Antarctica
145 Q10 **Korgalzhyn** *var.* Kurgal'dzhino, Kurgal'dzhinsky, *Kaz.* Qorgazhyn. Akmola, C Kazakhstan
92 G13 **Korgen** Troms, N Norway
147 R9 **Korgon-Dĕbĕ** Dzhalal-Abadskaya Oblast', W Kyrgyzstan
76 M14 **Korhogo** N Ivory Coast
115 F19 **Korinthiakós Kólpos** *Eng.* Gulf of Corinth; *anc.* Corinthiacus Sinus. *gulf* C Greece
115 F19 **Kórinthos** *anc.* Corinthus *Eng.* Corinth. Pelopónnisos, S Greece
113 M18 **Koritnik** ▲ S Serbia
Koritsa *see* Korçë
165 P11 **Kōriyama** Fukushima, Honshū, C Japan
136 E16 **Korkuteli** Antalya, SW Turkey
158 K6 **Korla** *Chin.* K'u-erh-lo. Xinjiang Uygur Zizhiqu, NW China
122 J10 **Korliki** Khanty-Mansiyskiy Avtonomnyy Okrug, C Russian Federation
Körlin an der Persante *see* Karlino
Korma *see* Karma
14 D8 **Kormak** Ontario, S Canada
Kormakíti, Akrotíri/Kormakiti, Cape/Kormakítis *see* Koruçam Burnu
111 G23 **Körmend** Vas, W Hungary
139 T5 **Kōrmōr** E Iraq
112 C13 **Kornat** *It.* Incoronata. *island* W Croatia
Korneshty *see* Corneşti
109 X3 **Korneuburg** Niederösterreich, NE Austria
145 P7 **Korneyevka** Severnyy Kazakhstan, N Kazakhstan
95 I17 **Kornsjø** Østfold, S Norway
77 O11 **Koro** Mopti, S Mali
187 Y14 **Koro** *island* C Fiji
186 B7 **Koroba** Southern Highlands, W Papua New Guinea
126 K8 **Korocha** Belgorodskaya Oblast', W Russian Federation
136 H12 **Köroğlu Dağları** ▲▲ C Turkey
183 V6 **Korogoro Point** *headland* New South Wales, SE Australia
81 J21 **Korogwe** Tanga, E Tanzania
182 L13 **Koroit** Victoria, SE Australia
187 X15 **Korolevu** Viti Levu, W Fiji
190 I17 **Koromiri** *island* S Cook Islands
171 Q8 **Koronadal** Mindanao, S Philippines
114 G13 **Koróneia, Límni** *var.* Límni Korónia. ◎ N Greece
115 E22 **Koróni** Pelopónnisos, S Greece
Korónia, Límni *see* Koróneia, Límni
110 I9 **Koronowo** *Ger.* Krone an der Brahe. Kujawski-pomorskie, C Poland
117 R2 **Korop** Chernihivs'ka Oblast', N Ukraine
115 H19 **Koropí** Attikí, C Greece
188 C8 **Koror** *var.* Oreor. ● (Palau) Oreor, N Palau
Koror *see* Oreor
111 L23 **Körös** ≈ E Hungary
Kőrös *see* Križevci
Körösbánya *see* Baia de Criş
187 Y14 **Koro Sea** *sea* C Fiji
Koroška *see* Kärnten
117 N3 **Korosten'** Zhytomyrs'ka Oblast', NW Ukraine
Korostyshev *see* Korostyshiv
117 N4 **Korostyshiv** *Rus.* Korostyshev. Zhytomyrs'ka Oblast', N Ukraine
125 V3 **Korotaikha** ≈ NW Russian Federation
122 J9 **Korotchayevo** Yamalo-Nenetskiy Avtonomnyy Okrug, N Russian Federation
78 I8 **Koro Toro** Borkou-Ennedi-Tibesti, N Chad
39 N16 **Korovin Island** *island* Shumagin Islands, Alaska, USA
187 X14 **Korovou** Viti Levu, W Fiji
93 M17 **Korpilahti** Länsi-Suomi, C Finland
92 K12 **Korpilombolo** *Lapp.* Dállogilli. Norrbotten, N Sweden
123 T13 **Korsakov** Ostrov Sakhalin, Sakhalinskaya Oblast', SE Russian Federation
93 J16 **Korsholm** *Fin.* Mustasaari. Länsi-Suomi, W Finland
95 I23 **Korsør** Vestsjælland, E Denmark
Korsovka *see* Kārsava
117 P6 **Korsun'-Shevchenkivs'kyy** *Rus.* Korsun'-Shevchenkovskiy. Cherkas'ka Oblast', C Ukraine
Korsun'-Shevchenkovskiy *see* Korsun'-Shevchenkivs'kyy
99 C17 **Kortemark** West-Vlaanderen, W Belgium
99 H18 **Kortenberg** Vlaams Brabant, C Belgium
99 K18 **Kortessem** Limburg, NE Belgium
99 E14 **Kortgene** Zeeland, SW Netherlands
80 F8 **Korti** Northern, N Sudan
99 C18 **Kortrijk** *Fr.* Courtrai. West-Vlaanderen, W Belgium
121 O2 **Koruçam Burnu** *var.* Cape Kormakiti, Kormakítis, *Gk.* Akrotíri Kormakití. *cape* N Cyprus
183 O13 **Korumburra** Victoria, SE Australia
Koryak Range *see* Koryakskoye Nagor'ye
123 V8 **Koryakskiy Avtonomnyy Okrug** ◈ *autonomous district* E Russian Federation
Koryakskiy Khrebet *see* Koryakskoye Nagor'ye
123 V7 **Koryakskoye Nagor'ye** *var.* Koryakskiy Khrebet, *Eng.* Koryak Range. ▲▲ NE Russian Federation
125 P11 **Koryazhma** Arkhangel'skaya Oblast', NW Russian Federation
Kōryō *see* Kangnŭng
Korytsa *see* Korçë
117 Q2 **Koryukivka** Chernihivs'ka Oblast', N Ukraine
Korzec *see* Korets'
115 N21 **Kos** Kos, Dodekánisa, Greece, Aegean Sea
115 M21 **Kos** *It.* Coo; *anc.* Cos. *island* Dodekánisa, Greece, Aegean Sea
125 T12 **Kosa** Permskaya Oblast', NW Russian Federation
125 T13 **Kosa** ≈ NW Russian Federation
164 B12 **Kō-saki** *headland* Nagasaki, Tsushima, SW Japan
163 X13 **Kosan** SE North Korea
119 H18 **Kosava** *Rus.* Kosovo. Brestskaya Voblasts', SW Belarus
Kosch *see* Kose
144 G12 **Koschagyl** *Kaz.* Qosshaghyl. Atyrau, W Kazakhstan
110 G12 **Kościan** *Ger.* Kosten. Wielkopolskie, C Poland
110 I7 **Kościerzyna** Pomorskie, NW Poland
22 L4 **Kosciusko** Mississippi, S USA
Kosciusko, Mount *see* Kosciuszko, Mount
183 R11 **Kosciuszko, Mount** *prev.* Mount Kosciusko. ▲ New South Wales, SE Australia
118 H4 **Kose** *Ger.* Kosch. Harjumaa, NW Estonia
114 G6 **Koshava** Vidin, NW Bulgaria
147 U9 **Kosh-Dĕbĕ** *var.* Koshtebĕ. Narynskaya Oblast', C Kyrgyzstan
K'o-shih *see* Kashi
164 B12 **Koshikijima-rettō** *var.* Kosikizima Rettô. *island group* SW Japan
145 W13 **Koshkarkol', Ozero** ◎ SE Kazakhstan
30 L9 **Koshkonong, Lake** ◎ Wisconsin, N USA
Koshoba *see* Goşabo
Koshoba *see* Goşoba
164 M12 **Kōshoku** *var.* Kôsyoku. Nagano, Honshū, S Japan
Koshtebĕ *see* Kosh-Dĕbĕ
Kōshū *see* Kwangju
111 N19 **Košice** *Ger.* Kaschau, *Hung.* Kassa. Košický Kraj, E Slovakia
111 M20 **Košický Kraj** ◈ E Slovakia
Kosikizima Rettô *see* Koshikijima-rettō
153 R12 **Kosi Reservoir** ⊠ E Nepal
116 J8 **Kosiv** Ivano-Frankivs'ka Oblast', W Ukraine
145 O11 **Koskol'** Karaganda, C Kazakhstan
125 Q9 **Koslan** Respublika Komi, NW Russian Federation
Köslin *see* Koszalin
146 M12 **Koson** *Rus.* Kasan. Qashqadaryo Viloyati, S Uzbekistan
163 Y13 **Kosŏng** SE North Korea
147 S9 **Kosonsoy** *Rus.* Kasansay. Namangan Viloyati, E Uzbekistan
113 M16 **Kosovo** *prev.* Autonomous Province of Kosovo and Metohija. ◈ *province* S Serbia
Kosovo *see* Kosava
Kosovo and Metohija, Autonomous Province of *see* Kosovo
113 N16 **Kosovo Polje** Kosovo, S Serbia
113 O16 **Kosovska Kamenica** Kosovo, SE Serbia
113 M16 **Kosovska Mitrovica** *Alb.* Mitrovicë; *prev.* Mitrovica, Titova Mitrovica. Kosovo, S Serbia
189 X17 **Kosrae** ◈ *state* E Micronesia
189 Y14 **Kosrae** *prev.* Kusaie. *island* Caroline Islands, E Micronesia
25 U9 **Kosse** Texas, SW USA
109 P6 **Kössen** Tirol, W Austria
76 M16 **Kossou, Lac de** ◎ C Ivory Coast
Kossukavak *see* Krumovgrad
Kostajnica *see* Hrvatska Kostajnica
Kostamus *see* Kostomuksha
144 M7 **Kostanay** *var.* Kostanai, *Kaz.* Qostanay. Kustanay, N Kazakhstan
144 L8 **Kostanay** *var.* Kostanayskaya Oblast', *Kaz.* Qostanay Oblysy. ◈ *province* N Kazakhstan
Kostanayskaya Oblast' *see* Kostanay
Kosten *see* Kościan
114 H10 **Kostenets** *prev.* Georgi Dimitrov. Sofiya, W Bulgaria
80 F10 **Kosti** White Nile, C Sudan
Kostnitz *see* Konstanz
124 H7 **Kostomuksha** *Fin.* Kostamus. Respublika Kareliya, NW Russian Federation
116 K3 **Kostopil'** *Rus.* Kostopol'. Rivnens'ka Oblast', NW Ukraine
Kostopol' *see* Kostopil'
124 M15 **Kostroma** Kostromskaya Oblast', NW Russian Federation
125 N14 **Kostroma** ≈ NW Russian Federation
125 N14 **Kostromskaya Oblast'** ◈ *province* NW Russian Federation
110 D11 **Kostrzyn** *Ger.* Cüstrin, Küstrin. Lubuskie, W Poland
110 H11 **Kostrzyn** Wielkopolskie, C Poland
117 X7 **Kostyantynivka** *Rus.* Konstantinovka. Donets'ka Oblast', SE Ukraine
Kostyukovichi *see* Kastsyukovichy
Kostyukovka *see* Kastsyukowka
Kōsyoku *see* Kōshoku
125 U6 **Kos'yu** Respublika Komi, NW Russian Federation
125 U6 **Kos'yu** ≈ NW Russian Federation
110 F7 **Koszalin** *Ger.* Köslin. Zachodnio-pomorskie, NW Poland
111 F22 **Kőszeg** *Ger.* Güns. Vas, W Hungary
152 H13 **Kota** *prev.* Kotah. Rājasthān, N India
Kota Baharu *see* Kota Bharu
Kota Bahru *see* Kota Bharu
169 U13 **Kotabaru** Pulau Laut, C Indonesia
168 K12 **Kota Baru** Sumatera, W Indonesia
Kotabaru *see* Jayapura
168 K6 **Kota Bharu** *var.* Kota Baharu, Kota Bahru. Kelantan, Peninsular Malaysia
Kotaboemi *see* Kotabumi
168 M14 **Kotabumi** *prev.* Kotaboemi. Sumatera, W Indonesia
149 S10 **Kot Addu** Punjab, E Pakistan
Kotah *see* Kota
169 U7 **Kota Kinabalu** *prev.* Jesselton. Sabah, East Malaysia
169 U7 **Kota Kinabalu** ✈ Sabah, East Malaysia
92 M12 **Kotala** Lappi, N Finland
Kotamobagoe *see* Kotamobagu
171 Q11 **Kotamobagu** *prev.* Kotamobagoe. Sulawesi, C Indonesia
155 L14 **Kotapad** *var.* Kotapārh. Orissa, E India
Kotapārh *see* Kotapad
166 N17 **Ko Ta Ru Tao** *island* SW Thailand
169 R13 **Kotawaringin, Teluk** *bay* Borneo, C Indonesia
149 Q13 **Kot Dīji** Sind, SE Pakistan
152 K9 **Kotdwāra** Uttaranchal, N India
125 Q14 **Kotel'nich** Kirovskaya Oblast', NW Russian Federation
127 N12 **Kotel'nikovo** Volgogradskaya Oblast', SW Russian Federation
123 Q6 **Kotel'nyy, Ostrov** *island* Novosibirskiye Ostrova, N Russian Federation
117 T5 **Kotel'va** Poltavs'ka Oblast', C Ukraine
101 M14 **Köthen** *var.* Cöthen. Sachsen-Anhalt, C Germany
Kōti *see* Kōchi
81 G17 **Kotido** NE Uganda
93 N19 **Kotka** Kymi, S Finland
125 P11 **Kotlas** Arkhangel'skaya Oblast', NW Russian Federation
38 M10 **Kotlik** Alaska, USA
77 Q17 **Kotoka** ✈ (Accra) S Ghana
Kotonu *see* Cotonou
113 J17 **Kotor** *It.* Cattaro. SW Montenegro
Kotor *see* Kotoriba
112 F7 **Kotoriba** *Hung.* Kotor. Medimurje, N Croatia
113 I17 **Kotorska, Boka** *It.* Bocche di Cattaro. *bay* SW Montenegro
112 H11 **Kotorsko** ◈ Republika Srpska, N Bosnia and Herzegovina
112 G11 **Kotor Varoš** ◈ Republika Srpska, N Bosnia and Herzegovina
Koto Sho/Kotosho *see* Lan Yü
126 M7 **Kotovsk** Tambovskaya Oblast', W Russian Federation
117 O9 **Kotovs'k** *Rus.* Kotovsk. Odes'ka Oblast', SW Ukraine
Kotovsk *see* Hînceşti
119 G16 **Kotra** *Rus.* Kotra. ≈ W Belarus
149 P16 **Kotri** Sind, SE Pakistan
109 Q9 **Kötschach** Kärnten, S Austria
155 K15 **Kottagūdem** Andhra Pradesh, E India
155 F21 **Kottappadi** Kerala, SW India
155 G23 **Kottayam** Kerala, SW India
Kottbus *see* Cottbus
Kotte *see* Sri Jayawardanapura
79 K15 **Kotto** ≈ Central African Republic/Dem. Rep. Congo
193 X15 **Kotu Group** *island group* W Tonga
Koturdepe *see* Goturdepe
122 M9 **Kotuy** ≈ N Russian Federation
83 M16 **Kotwa** Mashonaland East, NE Zimbabwe
39 N7 **Kotzebue** Alaska, USA
38 M7 **Kotzebue Sound** *inlet* Alaska, USA
Kotzenan *see* Chocianów
Kotzman *see* Kitsman'
77 R14 **Kouandé** NW Benin
79 J15 **Kouango** Ouaka, S Central African Republic
77 O13 **Koudougou** C Burkina
98 K7 **Koudum** Friesland, N Netherlands
115 L25 **Koufonísi** *island* SE Greece
115 K21 **Koufonísi** *island* Kykládes, Greece, Aegean Sea
38 M8 **Kougarok Mountain** ▲ Alaska, USA
79 E20 **Kouilou** ≈ S Congo
121 O3 **Koúklia** SW Cyprus
79 E19 **Koulamoutou** Ogooué-Lolo, C Gabon
76 L12 **Koulikoro** Koulikoro, SW Mali
76 L11 **Koulikoro** ◈ *region* SW Mali
187 P16 **Koumac** Province Nord, W New Caledonia
165 N12 **Koumi** Nagano, Honshū, S Japan
78 I13 **Koumra** Moyen-Chari, S Chad
Kounadougou *see* Koundougou
76 M15 **Kounahiri** C Ivory Coast
76 I12 **Koundâra** Moyenne-Guinée, NW Guinea
77 N13 **Koundougou** *var.* Kounadougou. C Burkina
76 H11 **Koungheul** C Senegal
Kounradskiy *see* Konyrat
25 X10 **Kountze** Texas, SW USA
77 Q13 **Koupéla** C Burkina
77 N13 **Kouri** Sikasso, SW Mali
55 Y9 **Kourou** N French Guiana
114 J12 **Kouroú** ≈ NE Greece
76 K14 **Kouroussa** Haute-Guinée, C Guinea
Kousseir *see* Al Quşayr
78 G11 **Kousséri** *prev.* Fort-Foureau. Extrême-Nord, NE Cameroon
Kouteifé *see* Al Quţayfah
76 M13 **Koutiala** Sikasso, S Mali
76 M14 **Kouto** NW Ivory Coast
93 M19 **Kouvola** Kymi, S Finland
79 G18 **Kouyou** ≈ C Congo
112 M10 **Kovačica** *Hung.* Antafalva; *prev.* Kovacsicza. Vojvodina, N Serbia
Kovacsicza *see* Kovačica
Kővárhosszúfalu *see* Satulung
Kovászna *see* Covasna
124 I4 **Kovdor** Murmanskaya Oblast', NW Russian Federation
124 I5 **Kovdozero, Ozero** ◎ NW Russian Federation
116 J3 **Kovel'** *Pol.* Kowel. Volyns'ka Oblast', NW Ukraine
112 M11 **Kovin** *Hung.* Keveára; *prev.* Temes-Kubin. Vojvodina, NE Serbia
Kovno *see* Kaunas
127 N3 **Kovrov** Vladimirskaya Oblast', W Russian Federation
127 O5 **Kovylkino** Respublika Mordoviya, W Russian Federation
110 J11 **Kowal** Kujawsko-pomorskie, C Poland
110 J9 **Kowalewo Pomorskie** *Ger.* Schönsee. Kujawskio-pomorskie, N Poland
Kowasna *see* Covasna
119 M16 **Kowbcha** *Rus.* Kolbcha. Mahilyowskaya Voblasts', E Belarus
Koweit *see* Kuwait
Kowel *see* Kovel'
185 F17 **Kowhitirangi** West Coast, South Island, New Zealand
161 O15 **Kowloon** Hong Kong, S China
Kowno *see* Kaunas
158 L3 **Kok Kuduk** *spring/well* N China
159 N7 **Kox Kuduk** *spring/well* NW China
136 D16 **Köyceğiz** Muğla, SW Turkey
125 N6 **Koyda** Arkhangel'skaya Oblast', NW Russian Federation
Koymat *see* Goymat
Koymatdag, Gory *see* Goymatdag, Gory
151 E15 **Koyna Reservoir** ⊠ W India
165 P9 **Koyoshi-gawa** ≈ Honshū, C Japan
Koysanjaq *see* Koi Sanjaq
Koytash *see* Qo'ytosh
Koytash *see* Qo'ytosh
146 M14 **Köytendag** *prev. Rus.* Charshanga, Charshangy, *Turkm.* Charshangngy. Lebap Welaýaty, E Turkmenistan
39 N9 **Koyuk** Alaska, USA
39 N9 **Koyuk River** ≈ Alaska, USA
39 O9 **Koyukuk** Alaska, USA
39 O9 **Koyukuk River** ≈ Alaska, USA
136 J13 **Kozaklı** Nevşehir, C Turkey
136 K16 **Kozan** Adana, S Turkey
115 E14 **Kozáni** Dytikí Makedonía, N Greece
112 F10 **Kozara** ▲▲ NW Bosnia and Herzegovina
Kozarska Dubica *see* Bosanska Dubica
117 P3 **Kozelets'** *Rus.* Kozelets. Chernihivs'ka Oblast', NE Ukraine
Kozelets *see* Kozelets'
117 S6 **Kozel'shchyna** Poltavs'ka Oblast', C Ukraine
126 J5 **Kozel'sk** Kaluzhskaya Oblast', W Russian Federation
Kozhikode *see* Calicut
125 U6 **Kozhim** Respublika Komi, NW Russian Federation
125 V9 **Kozhimiz, Gora** ▲ NW Russian Federation
124 L9 **Kozhozero, Ozero** ◎ NW Russian Federation
125 T7 **Kozhva** Respublika Komi, NW Russian Federation
125 T7 **Kozhva** ≈ NW Russian Federation
110 N13 **Kozienice** Mazowieckie, C Poland
109 S13 **Kozina** SW Slovenia
114 H7 **Kozloduy** Vratsa, NW Bulgaria
127 Q3 **Kozlovka** Chuvashskaya Respublika, W Russian Federation
Kozlovshchina/Kozlowszczyzna *see* Kazlowshchyna
127 P3 **Koz'modem'yansk** Respublika Mariy El, W Russian Federation
116 J6 **Kozova** Ternopil's'ka Oblast', W Ukraine
113 P20 **Kožuf** ▲ S Macedonia
165 N15 **Kōzu-shima** *island* E Japan
Koz'yany *see* Kaz'yany
117 N5 **Kozyatyn** *Rus.* Kazatin. Vinnyts'ka Oblast', C Ukraine
77 Q16 **Kpalimé** *var.* Palimé. SW Togo
77 Q16 **Kpandu** E Ghana
99 F15 **Krabbendijke** Zeeland, SW Netherlands
167 N15 **Krabi** *var.* Muang Krabi. Krabi, SW Thailand
167 N13 **Kra Buri** Ranong, SW Thailand
167 S12 **Krâchéh** *prev.* Kratie. Krâchéh, E Cambodia
Kradnovodskiy Zaliv *see* Krasnovodskiy Zaliv
95 G17 **Kragerø** Telemark, S Norway
112 M13 **Kragujevac** Serbia, C Serbia
Krainburg *see* Kranj
166 N13 **Kra, Isthmus of** *isthmus* Malaysia/Thailand
112 D12 **Krajina** *cultural region* SW Croatia
Krakatau, Pulau *see* Rakata, Pulau
Krakau *see* Kraków
111 L16 **Kraków** *Eng.* Cracow, *Ger.* Krakau; *anc.* Cracovia. Małopolskie, S Poland
100 L9 **Krakower See** ◎ NE Germany
167 Q11 **Krâlănh** Siĕmréab, NW Cambodia
45 Q16 **Kralendijk** Bonaire, E Netherlands Antilles
112 B10 **Kraljevica** *It.* Porto Re. Primorje-Gorski Kotar, NW Croatia
112 M13 **Kraljevo** *prev.* Rankovićevo. Serbia, C Serbia
185 B16 **Kralovarský Kraj** ◈ W Czech Republic
111 E16 **Královehradecký Kraj** *prev.* Hradecký Kraj. ◈ *region* N Czech Republic
Kralup an der Moldau *see* Kralupy nad Vltavou
111 C16 **Kralupy nad Vltavou** *Ger.* Kralup an der Moldau. Střední Čechy, NW Czech Republic
117 W7 **Kramators'k** *Rus.* Kramatorsk. Donets'ka Oblast', SE Ukraine
Kramatorsk *see* Kramators'k
93 H17 **Kramfors** Västernorrland, C Sweden
Kranéa *see* Kraniá
108 M7 **Kranebitten** ✈ (Innsbruck) Tirol, W Austria
115 D15 **Kraniá** *var* Kranéa. Dytikí Makedonía, N Greece
115 G20 **Kranídi** Pelopónnisos, S Greece
109 T11 **Kranj** *Ger.* Krainburg. NW Slovenia
115 F16 **Krannón** *battleground* Thessalía, C Greece
Kranz *see* Zelenogradsk
112 D7 **Krapina** Krapina-Zagorje, N Croatia
112 E8 **Krapina** ≈ N Croatia
112 D8 **Krapina-Zagorje** *off.* Krapinsko-Zagorska Županija. ◈ *province* N Croatia
114 L7 **Krapinets** ≈ NE Bulgaria
Krapinsko-Zagorska Županija *see* Krapina-Zagorje
111 I15 **Krapkowice** *Ger.* Krappitz. Opolskie, SW Poland
Krappitz *see* Krapkowice
125 O12 **Krasavino** Vologodskaya Oblast', NW Russian Federation
122 H6 **Krasino** Novaya Zemlya, Arkhangel'skaya Oblast', N Russian Federation
123 S15 **Kraskino** Primorskiy Kray, SE Russian Federation
118 J11 **Krāslava** Krāslava, SE Latvia
119 M14 **Krasnaluki** *Rus.* Krasnoluki. Vitsyebskaya Voblasts', N Belarus
119 P17 **Krasnapollye** *Rus.* Krasnopol'ye. Mahilyowskaya Voblasts', E Belarus
126 L15 **Krasnaya Polyana** Krasnodarskiy Kray, SW Russian Federation
Krasnaya Slabada/Krasnaya Sloboda *see* Chyrvonaya Slabada
Krasnaya Slabada / Krasnaya Sloboda *see* Chyrvonaya Slabada
119 J15 **Krasnaye** *Rus.* Krasnoye. Minskaya Voblasts', C Belarus
111 O14 **Kraśnik** *Ger.* Kratznick. Lubelskie, E Poland
117 O9 **Krasni Okny** Odes'ka Oblast', SW Ukraine
127 P8 **Krasnoarmeysk** Saratovskaya Oblast', W Russian Federation
Krasnoarmeysk *see* Tayynsha
Krasnoarmeysk *see* Krasnoarmiys'k/Tayynsha
123 T6 **Krasnoarmeyskiy** Chukotskiy Avtonomnyy Okrug, NE Russian Federation
117 W7 **Krasnoarmiys'k** *Rus.* Krasnoarmeysk. Donets'ka Oblast', SE Ukraine
125 P11 **Krasnoborsk** Arkhangel'skaya Oblast', NW Russian Federation
126 K14 **Krasnodar** *prev.* Ekaterinodar, Yekaterinodar. Krasnodarskiy Kray, SW Russian Federation
126 K13 **Krasnodarskiy Kray** ◈ *territory* SW Russian Federation
117 Z7 **Krasnodon** Luhans'ka Oblast', E Ukraine
Krasnogor *see* Kallaste
127 T2 **Krasnogorskoye** *Latv.* Sarkaņi. Udmurtskaya Respublika, NW Russian Federation
Krasnograd *see* Krasnohrad
Krasnogvardeysk *see* Bulungh'ur
126 M13 **Krasnogvardeyskoye** Stavropol'skiy Kray, SW Russian Federation
Krasnogvardeyskoye *see* Krasnohvardiys'ke
117 U6 **Krasnohrad** *Rus.* Krasnograd. Kharkivs'ka Oblast', E Ukraine
117 S12 **Krasnohvardiys'ke** *Rus.* Krasnogvardeyskoye. Respublika Krym, S Ukraine
123 P14 **Krasnokamensk** Chitinskaya Oblast', S Russian Federation
125 U14 **Krasnokamsk** Permskaya Oblast', W Russian Federation
127 U8 **Krasnokholm** Orenburgskaya Oblast', W Russian Federation
117 U5 **Krasnokuts'k** *Rus.* Krasnokutsk. Kharkivs'ka Oblast', E Ukraine
Krasnokutsk *see* Krasnokuts'k
126 L7 **Krasnolesnyy** Voronezhskaya Oblast', W Russian Federation
Krasnoluki *see* Krasnaluki
Krasnoosol'skoye Vodokhranilishche *see* Chervonooskil's'ke Vodoskhovyshche
117 S11 **Krasnoperekops'k** *Rus.* Krasnoperekopsk. Respublika Krym, S Ukraine
Krasnoperekopsk *see* Krasnoperekops'k
117 U4 **Krasnopillya** Sums'ka Oblast', NE Ukraine
Krasnopol'ye *see* Krasnapollye
124 L5 **Krasnoshchel'ye** Murmanskaya Oblast', NW Russian Federation
127 O5 **Krasnoslobodsk** Respublika Mordoviya, W Russian Federation
127 T2 **Krasnoslobodsk** Volgogradskaya Oblast', SW Russian Federation
Krasnostav *see* Krasnystaw
127 V5 **Krasnousol'skiy** Respublika Bashkortostan, W Russian Federation
125 U12 **Krasnovishersk** Permskaya Oblast', NW Russian Federation

◆ Country
● Country Capital
◇ Dependent Territory
○ Dependent Territory Capital
◈ Administrative Regions
✈ International Airport
▲ Mountain
▲▲ Mountain Range
⧋ Volcano
≈ River
◎ Lake
⊠ Reservoir

KRASNOVODSK – KUPYANSK

Krasnovodsk *see* Turkmenbaşy
146 A10 **Krasnovodskiy Zaliv** *prev. Rus.* Kradnovodskiy Zaliv, *Turkm.* Krasnowodsk Aylagy. *lake gulf* W Turkmenistan
Krasnovodskiy Zaliv *see* Türkmenbasy Aylagy
146 B10 **Krasnovodskoye Plato** *Turkm.* Krasnowodsk Platosy. *plateau* Krasnowodsk Platosy, NW Turkmenistan
Krasnowodsk Aylagy *see* Türkmenbasy Aylagy
Krasnowodsk Aylagy *see* Krasnovodskiy Zaliv
Krasnowodsk Platosy *see* Krasnovodskoye Plato
122 K12 **Krasnoyarsk** Krasnoyarskiy Kray, S Russian Federation
127 X7 **Krasnoyarskiy** Orenburgskaya Oblast', W Russian Federation
122 K11 **Krasnoyarskiy Kray** ◆ *territory* C Russian Federation
Krasnoye *see* Krasnaye
Krasnoye Znamya *see* Gyzylbaydak
125 R11 **Krasnozatonskiy** Respublika Komi, NW Russian Federation
118 D13 **Krasnoznamensk** *prev.* Lasdehnen, *Ger.* Haselberg. Kaliningradskaya Oblast', W Russian Federation
126 K3 **Krasnoznamensk** Moskovskaya Oblast', W Russian Federation
117 R11 **Krasnoznam"yans'kyy Kanal** *canal* S Ukraine
111 P14 **Krasnystaw** *Rus.* Krasnostav. Lubelskie, SE Poland
126 H4 **Krasnyy** Smolenskaya Oblast', W Russian Federation
127 P2 **Krasnyye Baki** Nizhegorodskaya Oblast', W Russian Federation
127 Q13 **Krasnyye Barrikady** Astrakhanskaya Oblast', SW Russian Federation
124 K15 **Krasnyy Kholm** Tverskaya Oblast', W Russian Federation
127 Q8 **Krasnyy Kut** Saratovskaya Oblast', W Russian Federation
Krasnyy Liman *see* Krasnyy Lyman
117 Y7 **Krasnyy Luch** *prev.* Krindachevka. Luhans'ka Oblast', E Ukraine
117 X6 **Krasnyy Lyman** *Rus.* Krasnyy Liman. Donets'ka Oblast', SE Ukraine
127 R3 **Krasnyy Steklovar** Respublika Mariy El, W Russian Federation
127 P8 **Krasnyy Tekstil'shchik** Saratovskaya Oblast', W Russian Federation
127 R13 **Krasnyy Yar** Astrakhanskaya Oblast', SW Russian Federation
Krassóvár *see* Caraşova
116 L5 **Krasyliv** Khmel'nyts'ka Oblast', W Ukraine
111 O21 **Kraszna** *Rom.* Crasna. ⚟ Hungary/Romania
Kratie *see* Krâchéh
113 P17 **Kratovo** NE FYR Macedonia
Kratznick *see* Kraśnik
171 Y13 **Krau** Papua, E Indonesia
167 Q13 **Krâvanh, Chuŏr Phnum** *Eng.* Cardamom Mountains, *Fr.* Chaîne des Cardamomes. ▲ W Cambodia
Kravasta Lagoon *see* Karavastasë, Laguna e
Krawang *see* Karawang
127 Q15 **Kraynovka** Respublika Dagestan, SW Russian Federation
118 D12 **Kražiai** Šiaulai, C Lithuania
27 P11 **Krebs** Oklahoma, C USA
101 D15 **Krefeld** Nordrhein-Westfalen, W Germany
Kreisstadt *see* Krosno Odrzańskie
115 D17 **Kremastón, Technití Límni** ⊠ C Greece
Kremenchug *see* Kremenchuk
Kremenchugskoye Vodokhranilishche/ Kremenchuk Reservoir *see* Kremenchuts'ke Vodoskhovyshche
117 S6 **Kremenchuk** *Rus.* Kremenchug. Poltavs'ka Oblast', NE Ukraine
117 R6 **Kremenchuts'ke Vodoskhovyshche** *Eng.* Kremenchuk Reservoir, *Rus.* Kremenchugskoye Vodokhranilishche. ⊠ C Ukraine
116 K5 **Kremenets'** *Pol.* Krzemieniec, *Rus.* Kremenets. Ternopil's'ka Oblast', W Ukraine
Kremennaya *see* Kreminna
117 X6 **Kreminna** *Rus.* Kremennaya. Luhans'ka Oblast', E Ukraine
37 R4 **Kremmling** Colorado, C USA
109 V3 **Krems** ⚟ NE Austria
Krems *see* Krems an der Donau
109 W3 **Krems an der Donau** *var.* Krems. Niederösterreich, N Austria
Kremsier *see* Kroměříž
109 S4 **Kremsmünster** Oberösterreich, N Austria
38 M17 **Krenitzin Islands** *island* Aleutian Islands, Alaska, USA
Kresena *see* Kresna
114 G11 **Kresna** *var.* Kresena. Blagoevgrad, SW Bulgaria
112 O12 **Krespoljin** Serbia, E Serbia
25 N4 **Kress** Texas, SW USA
123 V6 **Kresta, Zaliv** *bay* E Russian Federation
115 D20 **Kréstena** *prev.* Selinoús. Dytikí Ellás, S Greece
124 H14 **Kresttsy** Novgorodskaya Oblast', W Russian Federation
Kretikon Delagos *see* Kritikó Pélagos
118 C11 **Kretinga** *Ger.* Krottingen. Klaipėda, NW Lithuania
Kreutz *see* Cristuru Secuiesc
Kreuz *see* Križevci
Kreuz *see* Risti
Kreuzburg/Kreuzburg in Oberschlesien *see* Kluczbork
Kreuzingen *see* Bol'shakovo
108 H6 **Kreuzlingen** Thurgau, NE Switzerland
101 K25 **Kreuzspitze** ▲ S Germany
101 F16 **Kreuztal** Nordrhein-Westfalen, W Germany
119 I15 **Kreva** *Rus.* Krevo. Hrodzyenskaya Voblasts', W Belarus
Krevo *see* Kreva
Kría Vrísi *see* Krýa Vrýsi
79 D16 **Kribi** Sud, SW Cameroon
Krichëv *see* Krychaw
Krickerhäu/Kriegerhaj *see* Handlová
109 W6 **Krieglach** Steiermark, E Austria
108 F8 **Kriens** Luzern, W Switzerland
Krievija *see* Russian Federation
Krimmitschau *see* Crimmitschau
98 H12 **Krimpen aan den IJssel** Zuid-Holland, SW Netherlands
Krindachevka *see* Krasnyy Luch
115 G25 **Kríos, Ákrotírio** *headland* Kríti, Greece, E Mediterranean Sea
155 J16 **Krishna** *prev.* Kistna. ⚟ C India
155 H20 **Krishnagiri** Tamil Nādu, SE India
155 K17 **Krishna, Mouths of the** *delta* SE India
153 S15 **Krishnanagar** West Bengal, N India
155 G20 **Krishnarājāsāgara Reservoir** ⊠ W India
95 N19 **Kristdala** Kalmar, S Sweden
Kristiania *see* Oslo
95 E18 **Kristiansand** *var.* Christiansand. Vest-Agder, S Norway
95 L22 **Kristianstad** Skåne, S Sweden
94 F8 **Kristiansund** *var.* Christiansund. Møre og Romsdal, S Norway
Kristiinankaupunki *see* Kristinestad
93 I14 **Kristineberg** Västerbotten, N Sweden
95 L16 **Kristinehamn** Värmland, C Sweden
93 J17 **Kristinestad** *Fin.* Kristiinankaupunki. Länsi-Soumi, W Finland
Kristyor *see* Crişcior
115 J25 **Kríti** *Eng.* Crete. ◆ *region* Greece, Aegean Sea
115 J24 **Kríti** *Eng.* Crete. *island* Greece, Aegean Sea
115 J23 **Kritikó Pélagos** *var.* Kretikon Delagos, *Eng.* Sea of Crete; *anc.* Mare Creticum. *sea* Greece, Aegean Sea
Kriulyany *see* Criuleni
112 I12 **Krivaja** ⚟ NE Bosnia and Herzegovina
Krivaja *see* Mali Iđoš
113 P17 **Kriva Palanka** *Turk.* Eğri Palanka. NE Macedonia
Krivichi *see* Kryvychy
114 H8 **Krivodol** Vratsa, NW Bulgaria
126 M10 **Krivorozh'ye** Rostovskaya Oblast', SW Russian Federation
Krivoshin *see* Kryvoshyn
Krivoy Rog *see* Kryvyy Rih
112 F7 **Križevci** *Ger.* Kreuz, *Hung.* Kőrös. Varaždin, NE Croatia
112 B10 **Krk** *It.* Veglia. Primorje-Gorski Kotar, NW Croatia
112 B10 **Krk** *It.* Veglia; *anc.* Curieta. *island* NW Croatia
109 V12 **Krka** ⚟ SE Slovenia
Krka *see* Gurk
109 R11 **Krn** ▲ NW Slovenia
111 H16 **Krnov** *Ger.* Jägerndorf. Moravskoslezský Kraj, E Czech Republic
Kroatien *see* Croatia
95 G14 **Krøderen** Buskerud, S Norway
95 G14 **Krøderen** ◎ S Norway
Kroi *see* Krui
95 N17 **Krokek** Östergötland, S Sweden
Krokodil *see* Crocodile
93 G16 **Krokom** Jämtland, C Sweden
117 S2 **Krolevets'** *Rus.* Krolevets. Sums'ka Oblast', NE Ukraine
Krolevets *see* Krolevets'
Królewska Huta *see* Chorzów
111 H18 **Kroměříž** *Ger.* Kremsier. Zlínský Kraj, E Czech Republic
98 I9 **Krommenie** Noord-Holland, C Netherlands
126 J6 **Kromy** Orlovskaya Oblast', W Russian Federation
101 L18 **Kronach** Bayern, E Germany
Krone an der Brahe *see* Koronowo
167 Q13 **Krŏng Kaôh Kŏng** Kaôh Kŏng, SW Cambodia
95 K21 **Kronoberg** ◆ *county* S Sweden
123 V10 **Kronotskiy Zaliv** *bay* E Russian Federation
195 O2 **Kronprinsesse Märtha Kyst** *physical region* Antarctica
195 V3 **Kronprins Olav Kyst** *physical region* Antarctica
124 G12 **Kronshtadt** Leningradskaya Oblast', NW Russian Federation
Kronstadt *see* Braşov
83 I22 **Kroonstad** Free State, C South Africa
123 O12 **Kropotkin** Irkutskaya Oblast', C Russian Federation
126 L14 **Kropotkin** Krasnodarskiy Kray, SW Russian Federation
110 J11 **Krośniewice** Łódzskie, C Poland
111 N17 **Krosno** *Ger.* Krossen. Podkarpackie, SE Poland
110 E12 **Krosno Odrzańskie** *Ger.* Crossen, Kreisstadt. Lubuskie, W Poland
Krossen *see* Krosno
Krotoschin *see* Krotoszyn
110 H13 **Krotoszyn** *Ger.* Krotoschin. Wielkopolskie, C Poland
Krottingen *see* Kretinga
Krousón *see* Krousónas
115 J25 **Krousónas** *prev.* Krousón, Kroussón. Kríti, Greece, E Mediterranean Sea
Kroussón *see* Krousónas
Krrabë *see* Krrabë
113 L20 **Krrabë** *var.* Krraba. Tiranë, C Albania
113 L17 **Krrabit, Mali i** ▲ N Albania
109 W12 **Krško** *Ger.* Gurkfeld; *prev.* Videm-Krško. E Slovenia
83 K19 **Kruger National Park** *national park* Northern, N South Africa
83 J21 **Krugersdorp** Gauteng, NE South Africa
38 D16 **Krugloi Point** *headland* Agattu Island, Alaska, USA
Krugloye *see* Kruhlaye
119 N15 **Kruhlaye** *Rus.* Krugloye. Mahilyowskaya Voblasts', E Belarus
168 L15 **Krui** *var.* Kroi. Sumatera, SW Indonesia
99 G16 **Kruibeke** Oost-Vlaanderen, N Belgium
83 G25 **Kruidfontein** Western Cape, SW South Africa
99 F15 **Kruiningen** Zeeland, SW Netherlands
Kruja *see* Krujë
113 L19 **Krujë** *var.* Kruja, *It.* Croia. Durrës, C Albania
Krulevshchina/ Krulewshchyna *see* Krulyewshchyna
118 K13 **Krulyewshchyna** *Rus.* Krulevshchina, Krulewshchyna. Vitsyebskaya Voblasts', N Belarus
25 T6 **Krum** Texas, SW USA
101 J23 **Krumbach** Bayern, S Germany
113 M17 **Krumë** Kukës, NE Albania
Krummau *see* Český Krumlov
114 K12 **Krumovgrad** *prev.* Kossukavak. Yambol, E Bulgaria
114 K12 **Krumovitsa** ⚟ S Bulgaria
114 L10 **Krumovo** Yambol, E Bulgaria
167 O11 **Krung Thep** *var.* Krung Thep Mahanakhon, *Eng.* Bangkok. ● (Thailand) Bangkok, C Thailand
167 O11 **Krung Thep, Ao** *var.* Bight of Bangkok. *bay* S Thailand
Krung Thep Mahanakhon *see* Krung Thep
Krupa/Krupa na Uni *see* Bosanska Krupa
119 M15 **Krupki** *Rus.* Krupki. Minskaya Voblasts', C Belarus
95 G24 **Kruså** *var.* Krusaa. Sønderjylland, SW Denmark
Krusaa *see* Kruså
113 N14 **Kruševac** Serbia, C Serbia
113 N19 **Kruševo** SW FYR Macedonia
111 A15 **Krušné Hory** *Eng.* Ore Mountains, *Ger.* Erzgebirge. ▲ Czech Republic/Germany *see also* Erzgebirge
Krušné Hory *see* Erzgebirge
39 W13 **Kruzof Island** *island* Alexander Archipelago, Alaska, USA
114 F13 **Krýa Vrýsi** *var.* Kría Vrísi. Kentrikí Makedonía, N Greece
119 P16 **Krychaw** *Rus.* Krichëv. Mahilyowskaya Voblasts', E Belarus
64 K11 **Krylov Seamount** *undersea feature* E Atlantic Ocean
Krym *see* Krym, Respublika
117 S13 **Krym, Respublika** *var.* Krym, *Eng.* Crimea, Crimean Oblast; *prev. Rus.* Krymskaya ASSR, Krymskaya Oblast'. ◆ *province* SE Ukraine
126 K14 **Krymsk** Krasnodarskiy Kray, SW Russian Federation
Krymskaya ASSR/ Krymskaya Oblast' *see* Krym, Respublika
117 T13 **Kryms'ki Hory** ▲ S Ukraine
117 T13 **Kryms'kyy Pivostriv** *peninsula* S Ukraine
111 M18 **Krynica** *Ger.* Tannenhof. Małopolskie, S Poland
117 P8 **Kryve Ozero** Odes'ka Oblast', SW Ukraine
119 I18 **Kryvoshyn** *Rus.* Krivoshin. Brestskaya Voblasts', SW Belarus
119 K14 **Kryvychy** *Rus.* Krivichi. Minskaya Voblasts', C Belarus
117 S8 **Kryvyy Rih** *Rus.* Krivoy Rog. Dnipropetrovs'ka Oblast', SE Ukraine
117 N8 **Kryzhopil'** Vinnyts'ka Oblast', C Ukraine
Krzemieniec *see* Kremenets'
111 J14 **Krzepice** Śląskie, S Poland
110 F10 **Krzyż Wielkopolskie** Wielkopolskie, W Poland
Ksar al Kabir *see* Ksar-el-Kebir
Ksar al Soule *see* Er-Rachidia
74 J5 **Ksar El Boukhari** N Algeria
74 G5 **Ksar-el-Kebir** *var.* Alcázar, Ksar al Kabir, Ksar-el-Kébir, *Ar.* Al-Kasr al-Kebir, Al-Qsar al-Kbir, *Sp.* Alcazarquivir. NW Morocco
Ksar-el-Kébir *see* Ksar-el-Kebir
110 H12 **Książ Wielkopolski** *Ger.* Xions. Weilkopolskie, W Poland
127 O3 **Kstovo** Nizhegorodskaya Oblast', W Russian Federation
169 T8 **Kuala Belait** W Brunei
Kuala Dungun *see* Dungun
169 S10 **Kualakerian** Borneo, C Indonesia
169 S12 **Kualakuayan** Borneo, C Indonesia
168 K8 **Kuala Lipis** Pahang, Peninsular Malaysia
168 K9 **Kuala Lumpur** ● (Malaysia) Kuala Lumpur, Peninsular Malaysia
168 K9 **Kuala Lumpur International** ✈ Selangor, Peninsular Malaysia
Kuala Pelabohan Kelang *see* Pelabuhan Klang
169 U7 **Kuala Penyu** Sabah, East Malaysia
38 E9 **Kualapu'u** *var.* Kualapuu. Moloka'i, Hawai'i, USA
Kualapuu *see* Kualapu'u
168 L7 **Kuala Terengganu** *var.* Kuala Trengganu. Terengganu, Peninsular Malaysia
168 L11 **Kualatungkal** Sumatera, W Indonesia
171 P11 **Kuandang** Sulawesi, N Indonesia
163 V12 **Kuandian** *var.* Kuandian Manzu Zizhixian. Liaoning, NE China
Kuandian Manzu Zizhixian *see* Kuandian
Kuando-Kubango *see* Cuando Cubango
Kuang-chou *see* Guangzhou
Kuang-hsi *see* Guangxi Zhuangzu Zizhiqu
Kuang-tung *see* Guangdong
Kuang-yuan *see* Guangyuan
Kuantan, Batang *see* Indragiri, Sungai
Kuanza Norte *see* Cuanza Norte
Kuanza Sul *see* Cuanza Sul
Kuanzhou *see* Qingjian
Kuba *see* Quba
Kubango *see* Cubango/Okavango
141 X8 **Kubārah** NW Oman
93 H16 **Kubbe** Västernorrland, C Sweden
80 A11 **Kubbum** Southern Darfur, W Sudan
124 L13 **Kubenskoye, Ozero** ◎ NW Russian Federation
146 G6 **Komsomol'sk-Ustyurt** *Rus.* Komsomol'sk-na-Ustyurte. Qoraqalpoghiston Respublikasi, NW Uzbekistan
164 G15 **Kubokawa** Kōchi, Shikoku, SW Japan
114 L7 **Kubrat** *prev.* Balbunar. Razgrad, N Bulgaria
112 O13 **Kučajske Planine** ▲ E Serbia
165 T1 **Kuccharo-ko** ◎ Hokkaidō, N Japan
112 O11 **Kučevo** Serbia, NE Serbia
Kuchan *see* Qūchān
169 Q10 **Kuching** *prev.* Sarawak. Sarawak, East Malaysia
169 Q10 **Kuching** ✈ Sarawak, East Malaysia
164 B17 **Kuchinoerabu-jima** *island* Nansei-shotō, SW Japan
164 C14 **Kuchinotsu** Nagasaki, Kyūshū, SW Japan
109 Q6 **Kuchl** Salzburg, NW Austria
148 L9 **Kūchnay Darweyshān** Helmand, S Afghanistan
Kuchurgan *see* Kuchurhan
117 O9 **Kuchurhan** *Rus.* Kuchurgan. ⚟ NE Ukraine
Kuçova *see* Kuçovë
113 L21 **Kuçovë** *var.* Kuçova; *prev.* Qyteti Stalin. Berat, C Albania
136 D11 **Küçük Çekmece** İstanbul, NW Turkey
164 F14 **Kudamatsu** *var.* Kudamatu. Yamaguchi, Honshū, SW Japan
Kudamatu *see* Kudamatsu
Kudara *see* Ghŭdara
169 V6 **Kudat** Sabah, East Malaysia
Kūddow *see* Gwda
155 G17 **Kūdligi** Karnātaka, W India
Kudowa *see* Kudowa-Zdrój
111 F16 **Kudowa-Zdrój** *Ger.* Kudowa. Wałbrzych, SW Poland
117 P9 **Kudryavtsivka** Mykolayivs'ka Oblast', S Ukraine
169 R16 **Kudus** *prev.* Koedoes. Jawa, C Indonesia
125 T13 **Kudymkar** Permskaya Oblast', NW Russian Federation
Kudzsir *see* Cugir
Kuei-chou *see* Guizhou
Kuei-lin *see* Guilin
Kuei-Yang/Kuei-yang *see* Guiyang
K'u-erh-lo *see* Korla
Kueyang *see* Guiyang
Kufa *see* Al Kūfah
136 E14 **Küfiçayı** ⚟ C Turkey
109 O6 **Kufstein** Tirol, W Austria
145 V14 **Kugaly** *Kaz.* Qoghaly. Almaty, SE Kazakhstan
8 K8 **Kugluktuk** *var.* Qurlurtuuq; *prev.* Coppermine. Nunavut, NW Canada
143 Y13 **Kūhak** Sīstān va Balūchestān, SE Iran
143 R9 **Kūhbonān** Kermān, C Iran
148 J5 **Kūhestān** *var.* Kohsān. Herāt, W Afghanistan
Kūhīrī *see* Kahīrī
93 N15 **Kuhmo** Oulu, E Finland
93 L18 **Kuhmoinen** Länsi-Soumi, C Finland
Kuhnau *see* Konin
Kūhnö *see* Kihnu
143 O8 **Kūhpāyeh** Eşfahān, C Iran
167 O12 **Kui Buri** *var.* Ban Kui Nua. Prachuap Khiri Khan, SW Thailand
Kuibyshev *see* Kuybyshevskoye Vodokhranilishche
82 D13 **Kuito** *Port.* Silva Porto. Bié, C Angola
39 X14 **Kuiu Island** *island* Alexander Archipelago, Alaska, USA
92 L13 **Kuivaniemi** Oulu, C Finland
77 V14 **Kujama** Kaduna, C Nigeria
110 I10 **Kujawsko-pomorskie** ◆ *province* C Poland
165 R8 **Kuji** *var.* Kuzi. Iwate, Honshū, C Japan
Kujto, Ozero *see* Kuyto, Ozero
Kujū-renzan *see* Kujū-san
164 D14 **Kujū-san** *var.* Kujū-renzan. ▲ Kyūshū, SW Japan
43 N7 **Kukalaya, Rio** *var.* Rio Cuculaya, Rio Kukulaya. ⚟ NE Nicaragua
113 O16 **Kukavica** *var.* Vlajna. ▲ SE Serbia
113 M18 **Kukës** *var.* Kukësi. Kukës, NE Albania
113 L18 **Kukës** ◆ *district* NE Albania
Kukësi *see* Kukës
186 D8 **Kukipi** Gulf, S Papua New Guinea
127 S3 **Kukmor** Respublika Tatarstan, W Russian Federation
Kukong *see* Shaoguan
39 N6 **Kukpowruk River** ⚟ Alaska, USA
38 M6 **Kukpuk River** ⚟ Alaska, USA
Kūkūdağ *see* Gogi, Mount
Kukukhoto *see* Hohhot
Kukulaya, Rio *see* Kukalaya, Rio
189 W12 **Kuku Point** *headland* NW Wake Island
146 G11 **Kukurtli** Ahal Welaýaty, C Turkmenistan
Kūl *see* Kūl, Rūd-e
114 F7 **Kula** Vidin, NW Bulgaria
112 K9 **Kula** Vojvodina, NW Serbia
136 D14 **Kula** Manisa, W Turkey
149 S8 **Kulāchi** North-West Frontier Province, NW Pakistan
Kulachi *see* Kolāchi
144 F11 **Kulagino** *Kaz.* Külagīno. Atyrau, W Kazakhstan
Külagīno *see* Kulagino
168 L10 **Kulai** Johor, Peninsular Malaysia
114 M7 **Kulak** ⚟ NE Bulgaria
153 T11 **Kula Kangri** *var.* Kulhakangri. ▲ Bhutan/China
144 E13 **Kulaly, Ostrov** *island* SW Kazakhstan
145 S16 **Kulan** *Kaz.* Qulan; *prev.* Lugovoy, Lugovoye. Zhambyl, S Kazakhstan
147 V9 **Kulanak** Narynskaya Oblast', C Kyrgyzstan
Gory Kulandag *see* Gulandag
153 V14 **Kulaura** Sylhet, NE Bangladesh
118 D9 **Kuldīga** *Ger.* Goldingen. Kuldīga, W Latvia
Kuldja *see* Yining
Kul'dzhuktau, Gory *see* QuljuqtovTog'lari
127 N4 **Kulebaki** Nizhegorodskaya Oblast', W Russian Federation
112 E11 **Kulen Vakuf** *var.* Spasovo. ◆ Federacija Bosna I Hercegovina, NW Bosnia and Herzegovina
181 Q9 **Kulgera Roadhouse** Northern Territory, N Australia
Kulhakangri *see* Kula Kangri
127 T1 **Kuliga** Udmurtskaya Respublika, NW Russian Federation
Kulkuduk *see* Ko'lquduq
Kulkuduk *see* Ko'lquduq
118 G4 **Kullamaa** Läänemaa, W Estonia
197 O12 **Kullorsuaq** *var.* Kuvdlorssuak. ◆ Kitaa, C Greenland
29 O6 **Kulm** North Dakota, N USA
Kulm *see* Chełmno
146 D12 **Kul'mach** *prev. Turkm.* Isgender. Balkan Welaýaty, W Turkmenistan
101 L18 **Kulmbach** Bayern, SE Germany
Kulmsee *see* Chełmża
147 Q14 **Kŭlob** *Rus.* Kulyab. SW Tajikistan
92 M13 **Kuloharju** Lappi, N Finland
125 N7 **Kuloy** Arkhangel'skaya Oblast', NW Russian Federation
125 N7 **Kuloy** ⚟ NW Russian Federation
137 Q14 **Kulp** Dıyarbakır, SE Turkey
Kulpa *see* Kolpa
77 P14 **Kulpawn** ⚟ N Ghana
143 R13 **Kūl, Rūd-e** *var.* Kūl. ⚟ S Iran
144 G12 **Kul'sary** *Kaz.* Qulsary. Atyrau, W Kazakhstan
153 R15 **Kulti** West Bengal, NE India
93 G14 **Kultsjön** ◎ N Sweden
136 I14 **Kulu** Konya, W Turkey
123 S9 **Kulu** ⚟ E Russian Federation
122 I13 **Kulunda** Altayskiy Kray, S Russian Federation
145 T7 **Kulunda Steppe** *Kaz.* Qulyndy Zhazyghy, *Rus.* Kulundinskaya Ravnina. *grassland* Kazakhstan/ Russian Federation
Kulundinskaya Ravnina *see* Kulunda Steppe
182 M9 **Kulwin** Victoria, SE Australia
Kulyab *see* Kŭlob
117 Q3 **Kulykivka** Chernihivs'ka Oblast', N Ukraine
Kum *see* Qom
164 F14 **Kuma** Ehime, Shikoku, SW Japan
127 P14 **Kuma** ⚟ SW Russian Federation
165 O12 **Kumagaya** Saitama, Honshū, S Japan
165 Q5 **Kumaishi** Hokkaidō, NE Japan
169 R13 **Kumai, Teluk** *bay* Borneo, C Indonesia
127 Y7 **Kumak** Orenburgskaya Oblast', W Russian Federation
164 C14 **Kumamoto** Kumamoto, Kyūshū, SW Japan
164 D15 **Kumamoto** *off.* Kumamoto-ken. ◆ *prefecture* Kyūshū, SW Japan
Kumamoto-ken *see* Kumamoto
164 J15 **Kumano** Mie, Honshū, SW Japan
Kumanova *see* Kumanovo
113 O17 **Kumanovo** *Turk.* Kumanova. N Macedonia
185 G17 **Kumara** West Coast, South Island, New Zealand
180 J8 **Kumarina Roadhouse** Western Australia
153 T15 **Kumarkhali** Khulna, W Bangladesh
77 P16 **Kumasi** *prev.* Coomassie. C Ghana
Kumayri *see* Gyumri
79 D15 **Kumba** Sud-Ouest, W Cameroon
114 N13 **Kumbağ** Tekirdağ, NW Turkey
155 J21 **Kumbakonam** Tamil Nādu, SE India
Kum-Dag *see* Gumdag
165 R16 **Kume-jima** *island* Nansei-shotō, SW Japan
127 V6 **Kumertau** Respublika Bashkortostan, W Russian Federation
Kumillā *see* Comilla
35 R4 **Kumiva Peak** ▲ Nevada, W USA
159 N7 **Kumkuduk** Xinjiang Uygur Zizhiqu, W China
159 N8 **Kum Kuduk** *spring/well* NW China
Kumkurgan *see* Qumqo'rg'on
95 M16 **Kumla** Örebro, C Sweden
136 E17 **Kumluca** Antalya, SW Turkey
100 N9 **Kummerower See** ◎ NE Germany
77 X14 **Kumo** Gombi, E Nigeria
145 O13 **Kumola** ⚟ C Kazakhstan
167 N1 **Kumon Range** ▲ N Burma (Myanmar)
83 F22 **Kums** Karas, SE Namibia
155 E18 **Kumta** Karnātaka, W India
158 L6 **Kümük** Xinjiang Uygur Zizhiqu, W China
38 H12 **Kumukahi, Cape** *headland* Hawai'i, USA, C Pacific Ocean
127 Q17 **Kumukh** Respublika Dagestan, SW Russian Federation
Kumul *see* Hami
127 N9 **Kumylzhenskaya** Volgogradskaya Oblast', SW Russian Federation
141 W6 **Kumzār** N Oman
Kunar *see* Konar
Kunashiri *see* Kunashir, Ostrov
123 U14 **Kunashir, Ostrov** *var.* Kunashiri. *island* Kuril'skiye Ostrova, SE Russian Federation
118 I3 **Kunda** Lääne-Virumaa, NE Estonia
152 M13 **Kunda** Uttar Pradesh, N India
155 E19 **Kundāpura** *var.* Coondapoor. Karnātaka, W India
79 O24 **Kundelungu, Monts** ▲ S Dem. Rep. Congo
Kundert *see* Hernád
186 D7 **Kundiawa** Chimbu, W Papua New Guinea
Kundla *see* Sāvarkundla
168 L10 **Kundur, Pulau** *island* W Indonesia
Kunduz *see* Kondoz
Kunduz/Kundūz *see* Kondoz
Kuneitra *see* Al Qunayţirah
83 B18 **Kunene** ◆ *district* NE Namibia
83 A16 **Kunene** *var.* Cunene. ⚟ Angola/Namibia *see also* Cunene
Kunene *see* Cunene
Künes *see* Xinyuan
158 J5 **Künes He** ⚟ NW China
95 I19 **Kungälv** Västra Götaland, S Sweden
147 W7 **Kungei Ala-Tau** *Rus.* Khrebet Kyungëy Ala-Too, *Kir.* Küngöy Ala-Too. ▲ Kazakhstan/Kyrgyzstan
Küngöy Ala-Too *see* Kungei Ala-Tau
Kungrad *see* Qo'ng'irot
95 J19 **Kungsbacka** Halland, S Sweden
95 I18 **Kungshamn** Västra Götaland, S Sweden
95 M16 **Kungsör** Västmanland, C Sweden
79 J16 **Kungu** Equateur, NW Dem. Rep. Congo
125 V15 **Kungur** Permskaya Oblast', NW Russian Federation
166 L9 **Kungyangon** Yangon, SW Burma (Myanmar)
111 M22 **Kunhegyes** Jász-Nagykun-Szolnok, E Hungary
167 O5 **Kunhing** Shan State, E Burma (Myanmar)
158 D9 **Kunjirap Daban** *var.* Khūnjerāb Pass. *pass* China/Pakistan
Kunjirap Daban Khunjerāb Pass
Kunlun Mountains *see* Kunlun Shan
158 H10 **Kunlun Shan** *Eng.* Kunlun Mountains. ▲ NW China
159 P11 **Kunlun Shankou** *pass* C China
160 G13 **Kunming** *var.* K'un-ming; *prev.* Yunnan. *province capital* Yunnan, SW China
K'un-ming *see* Kunming
Kuno *see* Kunoy
95 B18 **Kunoy** *Dan.* Kunø. *island* N Faeroe Islands
163 X16 **Kunsan** *var.* Gunsan, *Jap.* Gunzan. W South Korea
111 L24 **Kunszentmárton** Jász-Nagykun-Szolnok, E Hungary
111 J23 **Kunszentmiklós** Bács-Kiskun, C Hungary
181 N3 **Kununurra** Western Australia
Kunyang *see* Pingyang
Kunya-Urgench *see* Köneürgench
Kunyé *see* Pins, Île des
169 T11 **Kunyi** Borneo, C Indonesia
101 I20 **Künzelsau** Baden-Württemberg, S Germany
161 S10 **Kuocang Shan** ▲ SE China
124 H5 **Kuoloyarvi** *var.* Luolajarvi. Murmanskaya Oblast', NW Russian Federation
93 N16 **Kuopio** Kuopio, C Finland
93 N17 **Kuopio** ◆ *province* C Finland
93 K17 **Kuortane** Länsi-Soumi, W Finland
93 M18 **Kuortti** Isäsuomi, E Finland
Kupa *see* Kolpa
171 P17 **Kupang** *prev.* Koepang. Timor, C Indonesia
39 Q5 **Kuparuk River** ⚟ Alaska, USA
Kupchino *see* Cupcina
186 E9 **Kupiano** Central, S Papua New Guinea
180 M4 **Kupingarri** Western Australia
122 I12 **Kupino** Novosibirskaya Oblast', C Russian Federation
118 H11 **Kupiškis** Panevėžys, NE Lithuania
114 L13 **Küplü** Edirne, NW Turkey
39 X13 **Kupreanof Island** *island* Alexander Archipelago, Alaska, USA
39 O16 **Kupreanof Point** *headland* Alaska, USA
112 G13 **Kupres** ◆ Federacija Bosna I Hercegovina, SW Bosnia and Herzegovina
117 W5 **Kup"yans'k** *Rus.* Kupyansk. Kharkivs'ka Oblast', E Ukraine
Kupyansk *see* Kup"yans'k

◆ Country ● Country Capital ◇ Dependent Territory ○ Dependent Territory Capital ◆ Administrative Regions ✈ International Airport ▲ Mountain ▲ Mountain Range ⛰ Volcano ⚟ River ◎ Lake ⊠ Reservoir

KUP"YANS'K-VUZLOVYY – LACQ

117 *W5* **Kup"yans'k-Vuzlovyy** Kharkivs'ka Oblast', E Ukraine
158 *I6* **Kuqa** Xinjiang Uygur Zizhiqu, NW China
Kür *see* Kura
137 *W11* **Kura** *Az.* Kür, *Geor.* Mtkvari, *Turk.* Kura Nehri. ≈ SW Asia
55 *R8* **Kuracki** NW Guyana
Kura Kurk *see* Irbe Strait
147 *Q10* **Kurama Range** *Rus.* Kuraminskiy Khrebet. ⛰ Tajikistan/Uzbekistan
Kuraminskiy Khrebet *see* Kurama Range
Kura Nehri *see* Kura
119 *J14* **Kuranyets** *Rus.* Kurenets. Minskaya Voblasts', C Belarus
164 *H13* **Kurashiki** *var.* Kurasiki. Okayama, Honshū, SW Japan
154 *L10* **Kurasia** Chhattīsgarh, C India
Kurasiki *see* Kurashiki
164 *H12* **Kurayoshi** *var.* Kurayosi. Tottori, Honshū, SW Japan
Kurayosi *see* Kurayoshi
163 *X6* **Kurbin He** ≈ NE China
145 *X10* **Kurchum** *Kaz.* Kürshim. Vostochnyy Kazakhstan, E Kazakhstan
145 *Y10* **Kurchum** ≈ E Kazakhstan
137 *X11* **Kürdämir** *Rus.* Kyurdamir. C Azerbaijan
Kurdestan *see* Kordestān
139 *S1* **Kurdistan** *cultural region* SW Asia
Kurd Kui *see* Kord Kūy
155 *F15* **Kurduvādi** Mahārāshtra, W India
114 *J11* **Kŭrdzhali** *var.* Kirdzhali, Kărdžali. Kŭrdzhali, S Bulgaria
114 *K11* **Kŭrdzhali** ◈ *province* S Bulgaria
114 *J11* **Kŭrdzhali, Yazovir** ▦ S Bulgaria
164 *F13* **Kure** Hiroshima, Honshū, SW Japan
192 *K5* **Kure Atoll** *var.* Ocean Island. *atoll* Hawaiian Islands, Hawaii, USA
136 *J10* **Küre Dağları** ⛰ N Turkey
146 *C11* **Kurendag** *rus* Gora Kyuren. ▲ W Turkmenistan
Kurenets *see* Kuranyets
118 *E6* **Kuressaare** *Ger.* Arensburg; *prev.* Kingissepp. Saaremaa, W Estonia
122 *K9* **Kureyka** Krasnoyarskiy Kray, N Russian Federation
122 *K9* **Kureyka** ≈ N Russian Federation
Kurgal'dzhino/ Kurgal'dzhinsky *see* Korgalzhyn
122 *G11* **Kurgan** Kurganskaya Oblast', C Russian Federation
126 *L14* **Kurganinsk** Krasnodarskiy Kray, SW Russian Federation
122 *G11* **Kurganskaya Oblast'** ◈ *province* C Russian Federation
Kurgan-Tyube *see* Qŭrghonteppa
191 *O2* **Kuria** *prev.* Woodle Island. *island* Tungaru, W Kiribati
Kuria Muria Bay *see* Ḥalānīyāt, Khalīj al
Kuria Muria Islands *see* Ḥalāniyāt, Juzur al
153 *T13* **Kurigram** Rajshahi, N Bangladesh
93 *K17* **Kurikka** Länsi-Soumi, W Finland
192 *I3* **Kurile Basin** *undersea feature* NW Pacific Ocean
Kurile Islands *see* Kuril'skiye Ostrova
Kurile-Kamchatka Depression *see* Kurile Trench
192 *J3* **Kurile Trench** *var.* Kurile-Kamchatka Depression. *undersea feature* NW Pacific Ocean
127 *Q9* **Kurilovka** Saratovskaya Oblast', W Russian Federation
123 *U13* **Kuril'sk** Kuril'skiye Ostrova, Sakhalinskaya Oblats', SE Russian Federation
122 *G11* **Kuril'skiye Ostrova** *Eng.* Kurile Islands. *island group* SE Russian Federation
42 *M9* **Kurinwas, Río** ≈ E Nicaragua
Kurisches Haff *see* Courland Lagoon
Kurkund *see* Kilingi-Nõmme
126 *M4* **Kurlovskiy** Vladimirskaya Oblast', W Russian Federation
80 *G12* **Kurmuk** Blue Nile, SE Sudan
Kurna *see* Al Qurnah
155 *H17* **Kurnool** *var.* Karnul. Andhra Pradesh, S India
164 *M11* **Kurobe** Toyama, Honshū, SW Japan
165 *Q7* **Kuroishi** *var.* Kuroisi. Aomori, Honshū, C Japan
Kuroisi *see* Kuroishi
165 *O12* **Kuroiso** Tochigi, Honshū, S Japan
165 *Q4* **Kuromatsunai** Hokkaidō, NE Japan
164 *B17* **Kuro-shima** *island* SW Japan
185 *F21* **Kurow** Canterbury, South Island, New Zealand
127 *N15* **Kursavka** Stavropol'skiy Kray, SW Russian Federation
118 *E11* **Kuršėnai** Šiauliai, N Lithuania
Kürshim *see* Kurchum
Kurshskaya Kosa/Kuršių Nerija *see* Courland Spit
126 *J7* **Kursk** Kurskaya Oblast', W Russian Federation
126 *I7* **Kurskaya Oblast'** ◈ *province* W Russian Federation
Kurskiy Zaliv *see* Courland Lagoon
113 *N15* **Kuršumlija** Serbia, S Serbia
137 *R15* **Kurtalan** Siirt, SE Turkey
Kurtbunar *see* Tervel
Kurt-Dere *see* Vŭlchidol
Kurtitsch/Kürtös *see* Curtici
Kurtty *see* Kurtty
145 *U15* **Kurtty** *var.* Kurtty. ≈ SE Kazakhstan
93 *L18* **Kuru** Länsi-Suomi, W Finland
80 *C13* **Kuru** ≈ W Sudan
114 *M13* **Kuru Dağı** ⛰ NW Turkey
158 *L7* **Kuruktag** ⛰ NW China
83 *G22* **Kuruman** Northern Cape, N South Africa
67 *T14* **Kuruman** ≈ W South Africa
164 *D14* **Kurume** Fukuoka, Kyūshū, SW Japan
123 *N13* **Kurumkan** Respublika Buryatiya, S Russian Federation
155 *J25* **Kurunegala** North Western Province, C Sri Lanka
55 *T10* **Kurupukari** C Guyana
125 *U10* **Kur"ya** Respublika Komi, NW Russian Federation
144 *E15* **Kuryk** *var.* Yeraliyev. Mangistau, SW Kazakhstan
136 *B15* **Kuşadası** Aydın, SW Turkey
115 *M19* **Kuşadası Körfezi** *gulf* SW Turkey
164 *A17* **Kusagaki-guntō** *island* SW Japan
Kusaie *see* Kosrae
145 *T12* **Kusak** ≈ C Kazakhstan
Kusary *see* Qusar
167 *P7* **Ku Sathan, Doi** ▲ NW Thailand
164 *J13* **Kusatsu** *var.* Kusatu. Shiga, Honshū, SW Japan
Kusatu *see* Kusatsu
138 *F11* **Kuseifa** Southern, C Israel
136 *C12* **Kuş Gölü** ◎ NW Turkey
126 *L12* **Kushchevskaya** Krasnodarskiy Kray, SW Russian Federation
164 *D16* **Kushima** *var.* Kusima. Miyazaki, Kyūshū, SW Japan
164 *I15* **Kushimoto** Wakayama, Honshū, SW Japan
165 *V4* **Kushiro** *var.* Kusiro. Hokkaidō, NE Japan
148 *K4* **Kūshk** Herāt, W Afghanistan
Kushka *see* Serhetabat
Kushka *see* Gushgy
145 *N8* **Kushmurun** *Kaz.* Qusmuryn. Kostanay, N Kazakhstan
145 *N8* **Kushmurun, Ozero** *Kaz.* Qusmuryn. ◎ N Kazakhstan
127 *U4* **Kushnarenkovo** Respublika Bashkortostan, W Russian Federation
Kushrabat *see* Qoʻshrabot
Kushrabat *see* Qoʻshrabot
153 *T15* **Kushtia** *var.* Kustia. Khulna, W Bangladesh
Kusima *see* Kushima
Kusiro *see* Kushiro
38 *M13* **Kuskokwim Bay** *bay* Alaska, USA
39 *P11* **Kuskokwim Mountains** ⛰ Alaska, USA
39 *N12* **Kuskokwim River** ≈ Alaska, USA
108 *G7* **Küsnacht** Zürich, N Switzerland
165 *V4* **Kussharo-ko** *var.* Kussyaro. ◎ Hokkaidō, NE Japan
Küssnacht *see* Küssnacht am Rigi
108 *F8* **Küssnacht am Rigi** *var.* Küssnacht. Schwyz, C Switzerland
Kussyaro *see* Kussharo-ko
Kustanay *see* Kostanay
Küstence/Küstendje *see* Constanța
100 *F11* **Küstenkanal** *var.* Ems-Hunte Canal. *canal* NW Germany
Kustia *see* Kushtia
Küstrin *see* Kostrzyn
171 *R11* **Kusu** Pulau Halmahera, E Indonesia
170 *L16* **Kuta** Pulau Lombok, S Indonesia
139 *T4* **Kutabān** N Iraq
136 *E13* **Kütahya** *prev.* Kutaia. Kütahya, W Turkey
136 *E13* **Kütahya** *var.* Kutaia. ◈ *province* W Turkey
Kutai *see* Mahakam, Sungai
Kutaia *see* Kütahya
137 *R9* **K'ut'aisi** W Georgia
Kūt al 'Amārah *see* Al Kūt
Kut al Hai/Kūt al Ḥayy *see* Al Ḥayy
Kut al Imara *see* Al Kūt
123 *Q11* **Kutana** Respublika Sakha (Yakutiya), NE Russian Federation
Kutaradja/Kutaraja *see* Bandaaceh
165 *R4* **Kutchan** Hokkaidō, NE Japan
Kutch, Gulf of *see* Kachchh, Gulf of
Kutch, Rann of *see* Kachchh, Rann of
112 *F9* **Kutina** Sisak-Moslavina, NE Croatia
112 *H9* **Kutjevo** Po»zega-Slavonija, NE Croatia
111 *E17* **Kutná Hora** *Ger.* Kuttenberg. Střední Čechy, C Czech Republic
110 *K12* **Kutno** Łódzkie, C Poland
Kuttenberg *see* Kutná Hora
79 *I20* **Kutu** Bandundu, W Dem. Rep. Congo
153 *V17* **Kutubdia Island** *island* SE Bangladesh
80 *B10* **Kutum** Northern Darfur, W Sudan
147 *Y7* **Kuturgu** Issyk-Kul'skaya Oblast', E Kyrgyzstan
12 *M5* **Kuujjuaq** *prev.* Fort-Chimo. Québec, E Canada
12 *I7* **Kuujjuarapik** Québec, C Canada
Kuuli-Mayak *see* Guwlumaýak
118 *I6* **Kuulse magi** ▲ S Estonia
92 *N13* **Kuusamo** Oulu, E Finland
93 *M19* **Kuusankoski** Kymi, S Finland
127 *W7* **Kuvandyk** Orenburgskaya Oblast', W Russian Federation
Kuvango *see* Cubango
Kuvasay *see* Quvasoy
Kuvdlorssuak *see* Kullorsuaq
124 *I16* **Kuvshinovo** Tverskaya Oblast', W Russian Federation
141 *Q4* **Kuwait** *off.* State of Kuwait, *var.* Dawlat al Kuwait, Koweit, Kuweit. ◆ *monarchy* SW Asia
Kuwait *see* Al Kuwayt
Kuwait Bay *see* Kuwayt, Jūn al
Kuwait City *see* Al Kuwayt
Kuwait, Dawlat al *see* Kuwait
Kuwait, State of *see* Kuwait
Kuwajleen *see* Kwajalein Atoll
164 *K13* **Kuwana** Mie, Honshū, SW Japan
139 *X9* **Kuwayt** E Iraq
142 *K11* **Kuwayt, Jūn al** *var.* Kuwait Bay. *bay* E Kuwait
Kuweit *see* Kuwait
117 *P10* **Kuyal'nyts'kyy Lyman** ◎ SW Ukraine
122 *I12* **Kuybyshev** Novosibirskaya Oblast', C Russian Federation
Kuybyshev *see* Bolgar, Respublika Tatarstan, Russian Federation
Kuybyshev *see* Samara
117 *W9* **Kuybysheve** *Rus.* Kuybyshevo. Zaporiz'ka Oblast', SE Ukraine
Kuybyshevo *see* Kuybysheve
Kuybyshev Reservoir *see* Kuybyshevskoye Vodokhranilishche
Kuybyshevskaya Oblast' *see* Samarskaya Oblast'
Kuybyshevskiy *see* Novoishimskiy
127 *R4* **Kuybyshevskoye Vodokhranilishche** *var.* Kuibyshev, *Eng.* Kuybyshev Reservoir. ▦ W Russian Federation
123 *S9* **Kuydusun** Respublika Sakha (Yakutiya), NE Russian Federation
125 *U16* **Kuyeda** Permskaya Oblast', NW Russian Federation
Küysanjaq *see* Koi Sanjaq
124 *I7* **Kuyto, Ozero** *var.* Ozero Kujto. ◎ NW Russian Federation
158 *J4* **Kuytun** Xinjiang Uygur Zizhiqu, NW China
122 *M13* **Kuytun** Irkutskaya Oblast', S Russian Federation
55 *S12* **Kuyuwini Landing** S Guyana
Kuzi *see* Kuji
38 *M9* **Kuzitrin River** ≈ Alaska, USA
127 *P6* **Kuznetsk** Penzenskaya Oblast', W Russian Federation
116 *K3* **Kuznetsovs'k** Rivnens'ka Oblast', NW Ukraine
124 *K6* **Kuzomen'** Murmanskaya Oblast', NW Russian Federation
165 *R8* **Kuzumaki** Iwate, Honshū, C Japan
95 *H24* **Kværndrup** Fyn, C Denmark
92 *H9* **Kvaløya** *island* N Norway
92 *K8* **Kvalsund** Finnmark, N Norway
94 *G11* **Kvam** Oppland, S Norway
127 *X7* **Kvarkeno** Orenburgskaya Oblast', W Russian Federation
93 *G15* **Kvarnbergsvattnet** *var.* Frostviken. ◎ N Sweden
112 *A11* **Kvarner** *var.* Carnaro, *It.* Quarnero. *gulf* W Croatia
112 *B11* **Kvarnerić** *channel* W Croatia
39 *O14* **Kvichak Bay** *bay* Alaska, USA
92 *H12* **Kvikkjokk** *Lapp.* Huhttán. Norrbotten, N Sweden
95 *D17* **Kvina** ≈ S Norway
95 *F16* **Kvitseid** Telemark, S Norway
92 *Q1* **Kvitøya** *island* NE Svalbard
79 *H20* **Kwa** ≈ W Dem. Rep. Congo
77 *Q15* **Kwadwokurom** C Ghana
186 *M8* **Kwailibesi** Malaita, N Solomon Islands
189 *S6* **Kwajalein Atoll** *var.* Kuwajleen. *atoll* Ralik Chain, C Marshall Islands
55 *W9* **Kwakoegron** Brokopondo, N Surinam
81 *J21* **Kwale** Coast, S Kenya
77 *U17* **Kwale** Delta, S Nigeria
79 *H20* **Kwamouth** Bandundu, W Dem. Rep. Congo
Kwando *see* Cuando
Kwangchow *see* Guangzhou
Kwangchu *see* Kwangju
163 *X16* **Kwangju** *off.* Kwangju-gwangyŏksi, *var.* Guangju, Kwangchu, *Jap.* Kōshū. SW South Korea
Kwangju-gwangyŏksi *see* Kwangju
79 *H20* **Kwango** *Port.* Cuango. ≈ Angola/Dem. Rep. Congo *see also* Cuango
Kwango *see* Cuango
Kwangsi/Kwangsi Chuang Autonomous Region *see* Guangxi Zhuangzu Zizhiqu
Kwangtung *see* Guangdong
Kwangyuan *see* Guangyuan
81 *F17* **Kwania, Lake** ◎ C Uganda
Kwanza *see* Cuanza
77 *S15* **Kwara** ◈ *state* SW Nigeria
83 *K22* **KwaZulu/Natal** *off.* KwaZulu/Natal Province; *prev.* Natal. ◈ *province* E South Africa
KwaZulu/Natal Province *see* KwaZulu/Natal
Kweichow *see* Guizhou
Kweichu *see* Guiyang
Kweilin *see* Guilin
Kweisui *see* Hohhot
Kweiyang *see* Guiyang
83 *K17* **Kwekwe** *prev.* Que Que. Midlands, C Zimbabwe
83 *G20* **Kweneng** ◈ *district* S Botswana
Kwesui *see* Hohhot
39 *N12* **Kwethluk** Alaska, USA
39 *N12* **Kwethluk River** ≈ Alaska, USA
110 *J8* **Kwidzyń** *Ger.* Marienwerder. Pomorskie, N Poland
38 *M13* **Kwigillingok** Alaska, USA
186 *E9* **Kwikila** Central, S Papua New Guinea
79 *I20* **Kwilu** ≈ W Dem. Rep. Congo
Kwito *see* Cuito
171 *U12* **Kwoka, Gunung** ▲ Papua, E Indonesia
78 *I12* **Kyabé** Moyen-Chari, S Chad
183 *O11* **Kyabram** Victoria, SE Australia
166 *M9* **Kyaikkami** *prev.* Amherst. Mon State, S Burma (Myanmar)
166 *L9* **Kyaiklat** Irrawaddy, SW Burma (Myanmar)
166 *M8* **Kyaikto** Mon State, S Burma (Myanmar)
123 *N14* **Kyakhta** Respublika Buryatiya, S Russian Federation
182 *G8* **Kyancutta** South Australia
167 *T8* **Ky Anh** Ha Tinh, N Vietnam
166 *L5* **Kyaukpadaung** Mandalay, C Burma (Myanmar)
166 *J6* **Kyaukpyu** Arakan State, W Burma (Myanmar)
166 *M5* **Kyaukse** Mandalay, C Burma (Myanmar)
166 *L8* **Kyaunggon** Irrawaddy, SW Burma (Myanmar)
119 *E14* **Kybartai** *Pol.* Kibarty. Marijampolė, S Lithuania
152 *I7* **Kyelang** Himāchal Pradesh, NW India
111 *G19* **Kyjov** *Ger.* Gaya. Jihomoravský Kraj, SE Czech Republic
115 *J21* **Kykládes** *var.* Kikládhes, *Eng.* Cyclades. *island group* SE Greece
25 *S11* **Kyle** Texas, SW USA
96 *G9* **Kyle of Lochalsh** N Scotland, UK
101 *D18* **Kyll** ≈ W Germany
115 *F19* **Kyllíni** *var.* Killini. ⛰ S Greece
115 *H18* **Kými** Évvoia, C Greece
93 *L19* **Kymi** ◈ *province* SE Finland
115 *H18* **Kýmis, Ákrotírio** *cape* Évvoia, C Greece
93 *M19* **Kymijoki** ≈ S Finland
115 *H18* **Kýmis, Akrotírio** *headland* C Greece
125 *W14* **Kyn** Permskaya Oblast', NW Russian Federation
183 *N12* **Kyneton** Victoria, SE Australia
81 *G17* **Kyoga, Lake** *var.* Lake Kioga. ◎ C Uganda
164 *J12* **Kyōga-misaki** *headland* Honshū, SW Japan
183 *V4* **Kyogle** New South Wales, SE Australia
163 *W15* **Kyŏnggi-man** *bay* NW South Korea
163 *Z16* **Kyŏngju** *Jap.* Keishū. SE South Korea
Kyŏngsŏng *see* Sŏul
Kyōsai-tō *see* Kŏje-do
81 *F19* **Kyotera** S Uganda
164 *J13* **Kyōto** Kyōto, Honshū, SW Japan
164 *J13* **Kyōto** *off.* Kyōto-fu, *var.* Kyōto Hu. ◈ *urban prefecture* Honshū, SW Japan
Kyōto-fu/Kyōto Hu *see* Kyōto
115 *D21* **Kyparissía** *var.* Kiparissía. Pelopónnisos, S Greece
115 *D20* **Kyparissiakós Kólpos** *gulf* S Greece
Kyperounda *see* Kyperoúnta
121 *P3* **Kyperoúnta** *var.* Kyperounda. C Cyprus
Kypros *see* Cyprus
115 *H16* **Kyrá Panagía** *island* Vóreies Sporádes, Greece, Aegean Sea
Kyrenia *see* Girne
Kyrenia Mountains *see* Beşparmak Dağları
Kyrgyz Republic *see* Kyrgyzstan
147 *U9* **Kyrgyzstan** *off.* Kyrgyz Republic, *var.* Kirghizia; *prev.* Kirgizskaya SSR, Kirghiz SSR, Republic of Kyrgyzstan. ◆ *republic* C Asia
Kyrgyzstan, Republic of *see* Kyrgyzstan
Kyriat Gat *see* Qiryat Gat
100 *M11* **Kyritz** Brandenburg, NE Germany
94 *G8* **Kyrksæterøra** Sør-Trøndelag, S Norway
Kyrkslätt *see* Kirkkonummi
125 *U8* **Kyrta** Respublika Komi, NW Russian Federation
111 *J18* **Kysucké Nové Mesto** *prev.* Horné Nové Mesto, *Ger.* Kisutzaneustadtl, Oberneustadtl, *Hung.* Kiszucaújhely. Žilinský Kraj, N Slovakia
117 *N12* **Kytay, Ozero** ◎ SW Ukraine
115 *F23* **Kýthira** *var.* Kíthira, *It.* Cerigo, *Lat.* Cythera. Kńythira, S Greece
115 *F23* **Kýthira** *var.* Kíthira, *It.* Cerigo, *Lat.* Cythera. *island* S Greece
115 *I20* **Kýthnos** Kńythnos, Kykládes, Greece, Aegean Sea
115 *I20* **Kýthnos** *var.* Kíthnos, Thermiá, *It.* Termia; *anc.* Cythnos. *island* Kykládes, Greece, Aegean Sea
115 *I20* **Kýthnou, Stenó** *strait* Kykládes, Greece, Aegean Sea
Kyungëy Ala-Too, Khrebet *see* Kungei Ala-Tau
Kyurdamir *see* Kürdämir
164 *D15* **Kyūshū** *var.* Kyûsyû. *island* SW Japan
192 *H6* **Kyushu-Palau Ridge** *var.* Kyusyu-Palau Ridge. *undersea feature* W Pacific Ocean
114 *F10* **Kyustendil** *anc.* Pautalia. Kyustendil, W Bulgaria
114 *G11* **Kyustendil** ◈ *province* W Bulgaria
Kyûsyû *see* Kyūshū
Kyusyu-Palau Ridge *see* Kyushu-Palau Ridge
123 *P8* **Kyusyur** Respublika Sakha (Yakutiya), NE Russian Federation
183 *P10* **Kywong** New South Wales, SE Australia
117 *P4* **Kyyiv** *Eng.* Kiev, *Rus.* Kiyev. ● (Ukraine) Kyyivs'ka Oblast', N Ukraine
Kyyiv *see* Kyyivs'ka Oblast'
117 *O4* **Kyyivs'ka Oblast'** *var.* Kyyiv, *Rus.* Kiyevskaya Oblast'. ◈ *province* N Ukraine
117 *P3* **Kyyivs'ke Vodoskhovyshche** *Eng.* Kiev Reservoir, *Rus.* Kiyevskoye Vodokhranilishche. ▦ N Ukraine
93 *L16* **Kyyjärvi** Länsi-Soumi, C Finland
122 *K14* **Kyzyl** Respublika Tyva, C Russian Federation
147 *S8* **Kyzyl-Adyr** *var.* Kirovskoye. Talasskaya Oblast', NW Kyrgyzstan
145 *V14* **Kyzylagash** Almaty, SE Kazakhstan
146 *C13* **Kyzylbair** Balkan Welaýaty, W Turkmenistan
Kyzyl-Dzhiik, Pereval *see* Uzbel Shankou
145 *S7* **Kyzylkak, Ozero** ◎ NE Kazakhstan
145 *X11* **Kyzylkesek** Vostochnyy Kazakhstan, E Kazakhstan
147 *S10* **Kyzyl-Kiya** *Kir.* Kyzyl-Kyya. Batkenskaya Oblast', SW Kyrgyzstan
144 *L11* **Kyzylkol', Ozero** ◎ C Kazakhstan
122 *K14* **Kyzyl Kum** *var.* Kizil Kum, Qizil Qum, *Uzb.* Qizilqum. *desert* Kazakhstan/Uzbekistan
Kyzyl-Kyya *see* Kyzyl-Kiya
145 *N15* **Kyzylorda** *var.* Kzyl-Orda, Qizil Orda, Qyzylorda; *prev.* Perovsk. Kyzylorda, S Kazakhstan
144 *L14* **Kyzylorda** *off.* Kyzylordinskaya Oblast', *Kaz.* Qyzylorda Oblysy. ◈ *province* S Kazakhstan
Kyzylordinskaya Oblast' *see* Kyzylorda
Kyzylrabat *see* Qizilravot
Kyzylrabot *see* Qizilrabot
Kyzylsu *see* Kyzyl-Suu
147 *X7* **Kyzyl-Suu** *prev.* Pokrovka. Issyk-Kul'skaya Oblast', NE Kyrgyzstan
147 *S12* **Kyzyl-Suu** *var.* Kyzylsu. ≈ Kyrgyzstan/Tajikistan
147 *X8* **Kyzyl-Tuu** Issyk-Kul'skaya Oblast', E Kyrgyzstan
145 *Q12* **Kyzylzhar** *Kaz.* Qyzylzhar. Karaganda, C Kazakhstan
145 *N15* **Kzyl-Orda** Kzyl-Orda, S Kazakhstan
144 *L14* **Kzylorda** ◈ *province* S Kazakhstan
Kzyl-Orda *see* Kyzylorda
Kzyltu *see* Kishkenekol'

L

109 *X2* **Laa an der Thaya** Niederösterreich, NE Austria
63 *K15* **La Adela** La Pampa, SE Argentina
Laagen *see* Numedalslågen
109 *S5* **Laakirchen** Oberösterreich, N Austria
Laaland *see* Lolland
104 *I11* **La Albuera** Extremadura, W Spain
105 *O7* **La Alcarria** *physical region* C Spain
104 *K14* **La Algaba** Andalucía, S Spain
105 *P9* **La Almarcha** Castilla-La Mancha, C Spain
105 *R6* **La Almunia de Doña Godina** Aragón, NE Spain
41 *N5* **La Amistad, Presa** ▦ NW Mexico
118 *F4* **Läänemaa** *var.* Lääne Maakond. ◈ *province* NW Estonia
Lääne Maakond *see* Läänemaa
118 *I3* **Lääne-Virumaa** *off* Lääne-Viru Maakond. ◈ *province* NE Estonia
Lääne-Viru Maakond *see* Lääne-Virumaa
62 *J9* **La Antigua, Salina** *salt lake* W Argentina
99 *E17* **Laarne** Oost-Vlaanderen, NW Belgium
80 *O13* **Laas Caanood** Sool, N Somalia
41 *O9* **La Ascensión** Nuevo León, NE Mexico
80 *N12* **Laas Dhaareed** Sanaag, N Somalia
55 *O4* **La Asunción** Nueva Esparta, NE Venezuela
Laatokka *see* Ladozhskoye, Ozero
100 *I13* **Laatzen** Niedersachsen, NW Germany
38 *E9* **Laʻau Point** *var.* Laau Point. *headland* Molokaʻi, Hawaiʻi, USA
Laau Point *see* Laʻau Point
42 *D6* **La Aurora** ✈ (Ciudad de Guatemala) Guatemala, C Guatemala
74 *C9* **Laâyoune** *var.* Aaiún. ● (Western Sahara) NW Western Sahara
126 *L14* **Laba** ≈ SW Russian Federation
40 *M6* **La Babia** Coahuila de Zaragoza, NE Mexico
15 *R7* **La Baie** Québec, SE Canada
171 *P16* **Labala** Pulau Lomblen, S Indonesia
62 *K8* **La Banda** Santiago del Estero, N Argentina
La Banda Oriental *see* Uruguay
104 *K4* **La Bañeza** Castilla-León, N Spain
40 *M13* **La Barca** Jalisco, SW Mexico
40 *K14* **La Barra de Navidad** Jalisco, C Mexico
187 *Y13* **Labasa** *prev.* Lambasa. Vanua Levu, N Fiji
102 *H8* **la Baule-Escoublac** Loire-Atlantique, NW France
76 *I13* **Labé** NW Guinea
Labe *see* Elbe
15 *N11* **Labelle** Québec, SE Canada
23 *X14* **La Belle** Florida, SE USA
10 *H7* **Laberge, Lake** ◎ Yukon Territory, W Canada
Labes *see* Łobez
Labiau *see* Polessk
112 *A10* **Labin** *It.* Albona. Istra, NW Croatia
126 *L14* **Labinsk** Krasnodarskiy Kray, SW Russian Federation
105 *X5* **La Bisbal d'Empordà** Cataluña, NE Spain
119 *P16* **Labkovichy** *Rus.* Lobkovichi. Mahilyowskaya Voblasts', E Belarus
15 *S4* **La Blache, Lac de** ◎ Québec, SE Canada
171 *P4* **Labo** Luzon, N Philippines
Laboehanbadjo *see* Labuhanbajo
Laborca *see* Laborec
111 *N18* **Laborec** *Hung.* Laborca. ≈ E Slovakia
108 *D11* **La Borgne** ≈ S Switzerland
45 *T12* **Laborie** SW Saint Lucia
79 *F21* **La Bouenza** ◈ *province* S Congo
102 *J14* **Labouheyre** Landes, SW France
62 *L12* **Laboulaye** Córdoba, C Argentina
13 *Q7* **Labrador** *cultural region* Newfoundland and Labrador, SW Canada
64 *I6* **Labrador Basin** *var.* Labrador Sea Basin. *undersea feature* Labrador Sea
13 *N9* **Labrador City** Newfoundland and Labrador, E Canada
13 *Q5* **Labrador Sea** *sea* NW Atlantic Ocean
Labrador Sea Basin *see* Labrador Basin
Labrang *see* Xiahe
54 *G9* **Labranzagrande** Boyacá, C Colombia
59 *D14* **Lábrea** Amazonas, N Brazil
45 *U15* **La Brea** Trinidad, Trinidad and Tobago
15 *S6* **Labrieville** Québec, SE Canada
102 *K14* **Labrit** Landes, SW France
108 *C9* **La Broye** ≈ SW Switzerland
103 *N15* **Labruguière** Tarn, S France
168 *M11* **Labu** Pulau Singkep, W Indonesia
169 *T7* **Labuan** *var.* Victoria. Labuan, East Malaysia
169 *T7* **Labuan** ◈ *federal territory* East Malaysia
Labuan *see* Labuan, Pulau
169 *T7* **Labuan, Pulau** *var.* Labuan. *island* East Malaysia
Labudalin *see* Ergun
171 *N16* **Labuhanbajo** *prev.* Laboehanbadjo. Flores, S Indonesia
168 *J9* **Labuhanbilik** Sumatera, N Indonesia
168 *G8* **Labuhanhaji** Sumatera, W Indonesia
Labuk *see* Labuk, Sungai
Labuk Bay *see* Labuk, Teluk
169 *V7* **Labuk, Sungai** *var.* Labuk. ≈ East Malaysia
169 *W6* **Labuk, Teluk** *var.* Labuk Bay, Telukan Labuk. *bay* S Sulu Sea
Labuk, Telukan *see* Labuk, Teluk
166 *K9* **Labutta** Irrawaddy, SW Burma (Myanmar)
122 *I8* **Labytnangi** Yamalo-Nenetskiy Avtonomnyy Okrug, N Russian Federation
113 *K19* **Laç** *var.* Laci. Lezhë, C Albania
78 *F10* **Lac** *off.* Préfecture du Lac. ◈ *prefecture* W Chad
57 *K19* **Lacajahuira, Rio** ≈ W Bolivia
La Calamine *see* Kelmis
62 *G11* **La Calera** Valparaíso, C Chile
13 *P11* **Lac-Allard** Québec, E Canada
104 *L13* **La Campana** Andalucía, S Spain
102 *J12* **Lacanau** Gironde, SW France
42 *C2* **Lacandón, Sierra del** ⛰ Guatemala/Mexico
La Cañiza *see* A Cañiza
41 *W16* **Lacantún, Río** ≈ SE Mexico
103 *Q3* **la Capelle** Aisne, N France
112 *K10* **Laćarak** Vojvodina, NW Serbia
62 *L11* **La Carlota** Córdoba, C Argentina
104 *L13* **La Carlota** Andalucía, S Spain
105 *N12* **La Carolina** Andalucía, S Spain
103 *O15* **Lacaune** Tarn, S France
15 *P7* **Lac-Bouchette** Québec, SE Canada
Laccadive Islands/Laccadive Minicoy and Amindivi Islands, the *see* Lakshadweep
9 *Y16* **Lac du Bonnet** Manitoba, S Canada
30 *L4* **Lac du Flambeau** Wisconsin, N USA
15 *P8* **Lac-Édouard** Québec, SE Canada
42 *I4* **La Ceiba** Atlántida, N Honduras
54 *E9* **La Ceja** Antioquia, W Colombia
182 *J11* **Lacepede Bay** *bay* South Australia
32 *G9* **Lacey** Washington, NW USA
103 *P12* **la Chaise-Dieu** Haute-Loire, C France
114 *G13* **Lachanás** Kentrikí Makedonía, N Greece
124 *L11* **Lacha, Ozero** ◎ NW Russian Federation
103 *O8* **la Charité-sur-Loire** Nièvre, C France
103 *N9* **la Châtre** Indre, C France
108 *C8* **La Chaux-de-Fonds** Neuchâtel, W Switzerland
Lach Dera *see* Dheere Laaq
108 *G8* **Lachen** Schwyz, C Switzerland
183 *Q8* **Lachlan River** ≈ New South Wales, SE Australia
43 *T15* **La Chorrera** Panamá, C Panama
15 *V7* **Lac-Humqui** Québec, SE Canada
15 *N12* **Lachute** Québec, SE Canada
Lachyn *see* Laçın
Laci *see* Laç
137 *W13* **Laçın** *Rus.* Lachyn. SW Azerbaijan
103 *S16* **la Ciotat** *anc.* Citharista. Bouches-du-Rhône, SE France
18 *D10* **Lackawanna** New York, NE USA
9 *Q13* **Lac La Biche** Alberta, SW Canada
Lac la Martre *see* Wha Ti
Lac la Martre *see* Wha Ti
15 *R12* **Lac-Mégantic** *var.* Mégantic. Québec, SE Canada
Lacobriga *see* Lagos
40 *G5* **La Colorada** Sonora, NW Mexico
9 *Q15* **Lacombe** Alberta, SW Canada
30 *L12* **Lacon** Illinois, N USA
43 *P16* **La Concepción** *var.* Concepción. Chiriquí, W Panama
54 *H5* **La Concepción** Zulia, NW Venezuela
107 *C19* **Laconi** Sardegna, Italy, C Mediterranean Sea
19 *O9* **Laconia** New Hampshire, NE USA
61 *H19* **La Coronilla** Rocha, E Uruguay
La Coruña *see* A Coruña
103 *O11* **la Courtine** Creuse, C France
Lac, Préfecture du *see* Lac
102 *J16* **Lacq** Pyrénées-Atlantiques, SW France

◆ Country ● Country Capital ◇ Dependent Territory ○ Dependent Territory Capital ◈ Administrative Regions ✈ International Airport ▲ Mountain ⛰ Mountain Range ☗ Volcano ≈ River ◎ Lake ▦ Reservoir

275

La Croche – Långshyttan

15 P9 La Croche Québec, SE Canada
29 X3 la Croix, Lac ◎ Canada/USA
26 K5 La Crosse Kansas, C USA
21 V7 La Crosse Virginia, NE USA
32 L9 La Crosse Washington, NW USA
30 J7 La Crosse Wisconsin, N USA
54 C13 La Cruz Nariño, SW Colombia
42 K12 La Cruz Guanacaste, NW Costa Rica
40 I10 La Cruz Sinaloa, W Mexico
61 F19 La Cruz Florida, S Uruguay
42 M9 La Cruz de Río Grande Región Autónoma Atlántico Sur, E Nicaragua
54 J4 La Cruz de Taratara Falcón, N Venezuela
15 Q10 Lac-St-Charles Québec, SE Canada
40 M6 La Cuesta Coahuila de Zaragoza, NE Mexico
57 A17 La Cumbra, Volcán ⛰ Galapagos Islands, Ecuador, E Pacific Ocean
152 J5 Ladākh Range ▲▲ NE India
26 I5 Ladder Creek ≈ Kansas, C USA
45 X10 la Désirade atoll E Guadeloupe
Lādhiqīyah, Muḥāfaẓat al see Al Lādhiqīyah
83 F25 Ladismith Western Cape, SW South Africa
152 G11 Lādnūn Rājasthān, NW India
Ladoga, Lake see Ladozhskoye, Ozero
115 F19 Ládon ≈ S Greece
54 E9 La Dorada Caldas, C Colombia
124 H11 Ladozhskoye, Ozero Eng. Lake Ladoga, Fin. Laatokka. ◎ NW Russian Federation
37 R12 Ladron Peak ▲ New Mexico, SW USA
124 J11 Ladva-Vetka Respublika Kareliya, NW Russian Federation
183 Q15 Lady Barron Tasmania, SE Australia
14 G9 Lady Evelyn Lake ◎ Ontario, S Canada
23 W11 Lady Lake Florida, SE USA
10 L17 Ladysmith Vancouver Island, British Columbia, SW Canada
83 J22 Ladysmith KwaZulu/Natal, E South Africa
30 J5 Ladysmith Wisconsin, N USA
145 P9 Ladyzhenka Akmola, C Kazakhstan
186 E7 Lae Morobe, W Papua New Guinea
189 R6 Lae Atoll atoll Ralik Chain, W Marshall Islands
40 C3 La Encantada, Cerro de ▲ NW Mexico
94 E12 Lærdalsøyri Sogn Og Fjordane, S Norway
55 N11 La Esmeralda Amazonas, S Venezuela
95 H20 Læso Island N Denmark
42 F7 La Esperanza Intibucá, SW Honduras
30 K8 La Farge Wisconsin, N USA
23 R5 Lafayette Alabama, S USA
37 T4 Lafayette Colorado, C USA
23 R2 La Fayette Georgia, SE USA
31 O13 Lafayette Indiana, N USA
22 I9 Lafayette Louisiana, S USA
20 K8 Lafayette Tennessee, S USA
19 N7 Lafayette, Mount ▲ New Hampshire, NE USA
La Fe see Santa Fé
103 P3 la Fère Aisne, N France
102 L6 la Ferté-Bernard Sarthe, NW France
102 K5 la Ferté-Macé Orne, N France
103 N7 la Ferté-St-Aubin Loiret, C France
103 P5 la Ferté-sous-Jouarre Seine-et-Marne, N France
77 V15 Lafia Nassarawa, C Nigeria
77 T15 Lafiagi Kwara, W Nigeria
9 T17 Lafleche Saskatchewan, S Canada
102 K7 la Flèche Sarthe, NW France
109 X7 Lafnitz Hung. Lapines. ≈ Austria/Hungary
187 P17 La Foa Province Sud, S New Caledonia
20 M8 La Follette Tennessee, S USA
15 N12 Lafontaine Québec, SE Canada
22 K10 Lafourche, Bayou ≈ Louisiana, S USA
62 K6 La Fragua Santiago del Estero, N Argentina
54 H7 La Fría Táchira, NW Venezuela
104 J7 La Fuente de San Esteban Castilla-León, N Spain
186 C7 Lagaip ≈ W Papua New Guinea
61 B15 La Gallareta Santa Fe, C Argentina
127 Q14 Lagan' prev. Kaspiyskiy. Respublika Kalmykiya, SW Russian Federation
95 L20 Lagan Kronoberg, S Sweden
95 K21 Lågan ≈ S Sweden
92 L2 Lagarfljót var. Lögurinn. ◎ E Iceland
37 R7 La Garita Mountains ▲▲ Colorado, C USA
171 O2 Lagawe Luzon, N Philippines
78 F13 Lagdo Nord, N Cameroon
78 F13 Lagdo, Lac de ◎ N Cameroon
100 H13 Lage Nordrhein-Westfalen, W Germany
94 H12 Lågen ≈ S Norway
61 J14 Lages Santa Catarina, S Brazil
Lágesvuotna see Laksefjorden
149 R4 Laghmān ◐ province E Afghanistan
74 J6 Laghouat N Algeria
105 Q10 La Gineta Castilla-La Mancha, C Spain
115 E21 Lagkáda var. Langada. Pelopónnisos, S Greece
114 G13 Lagkadás var. Langades, Langadhás. Kentrikí Makedonía, N Greece
115 E20 Lagkádia var. Langádhia, cont. Langadia. Pelopónnisos, S Greece
54 F6 La Gloria Cesar, N Colombia
41 O7 La Gloria Nuevo León, NE Mexico
92 N3 Lågneset headland W Svalbard
104 G14 Lagoa Faro, S Portugal
La Goagira see La Guajira
Lago Agrio see Nueva Loja
61 I14 Lagoa Vermelha Rio Grande do Sul, S Brazil
137 V10 Lagodekhi SE Georgia
42 C7 La Gomera Escuintla, S Guatemala
Lagone see Logone
107 M19 Lagonegro Basilicata, S Italy
63 G16 Lago Ranco Los Lagos, S Chile
77 S16 Lagos Lagos, SW Nigeria
104 F14 Lagos anc. Lacobriga. Faro, S Portugal
77 S16 Lagos ◐ state SW Nigeria
40 M12 Lagos de Moreno Jalisco, SW Mexico
Lagosta see Lastovo
74 A12 Lagouira SW Western Sahara
92 O1 Lågøya island N Svalbard
32 L11 La Grande Oregon, NW USA
103 Q14 la Grande-Combe Gard, S France
12 K9 La Grande Rivière var. Fort George. ≈ Québec, SE Canada
23 R4 La Grange Georgia, SE USA
31 P11 Lagrange Indiana, N USA
20 L5 La Grange Kentucky, S USA
27 V2 La Grange Missouri, C USA
21 V10 La Grange North Carolina, SE USA
25 U11 La Grange Texas, SW USA
105 N7 La Granja Castilla-León, N Spain
55 Q9 La Gran Sabana grassland E Venezuela
54 H7 La Grita Táchira, NW Venezuela
La Grulla see Grulla
15 R11 La Guadeloupe Québec, SE Canada
64 F12 La Guaira Distrito Federal, N Venezuela
54 G4 La Guajira off. Departamento de La Guajira, var. Guajira, La Goagira. ◐ province NE Colombia
188 I4 Laguna Lichan, Punta headland Saipan, S Northern Mariana Islands
105 P4 Laguardia Basq Biasteri. País Vasco, N Spain
18 K14 La Guardia ✈ (New York) Long Island, New York, NE USA
La Guardia/Laguardia see A Guarda
La Gudiña see A Gudiña
103 O9 la Guerche-sur-l'Aubois Cher, C France
103 O13 Laguiole Aveyron, S France
83 F26 L'Agulhas var. Agulhas. Western Cape, SW South Africa
61 K14 Laguna Santa Catarina, S Brazil
37 Q11 Laguna New Mexico, SW USA
35 T16 Laguna Beach California, W USA
35 Y17 Laguna Dam dam Arizona/California, W USA
40 L7 Laguna El Rey Coahuila de Zaragoza, N Mexico
35 V17 Laguna Mountains ▲▲ California, W USA
61 B17 Laguna Paiva Santa Fe, C Argentina
62 H3 Lagunas Tarapacá, N Chile
56 E9 Lagunas Loreto, N Peru
57 M20 Lagunillas Santa Cruz, SE Bolivia
54 H6 Lagunillas Mérida, NW Venezuela
44 C4 La Habana var. Havana. ● (Cuba) Ciudad de La Habana, W Cuba
169 W7 Lahad Datu Sabah, East Malaysia
169 W7 Lahad Datu, Teluk var. Telukan Lahad Datu, Teluk Darvel, Teluk Datu; prev. Darvel Bay. bay Sabah, East Malaysia, C Pacific Ocean
Lahad Datu, Telukan see Lahad Datu, Teluk
38 F10 Lahaina Maui, Hawai'i, USA
168 L14 Lahat Sumatera, W Indonesia
La Haye see 's-Gravenhage
Lahej see Laḥij
62 G9 La Higuera Coquimbo, N Chile
141 S13 Lahī, Ḥisā' al spring/well NE Yemen
141 O16 Laḥij var. Laḥj, Eng. Lahej. SW Yemen
142 M3 Lāhījān Gīlān, NW Iran
119 I19 Lahishyn Pol. Lohiszyn, Rus. Logishin. Brestskaya Voblasts', SW Belarus
Laḥj see Laḥij
101 F18 Lahn ≈ W Germany
Lähn see Wleń
95 J21 Laholm Halland, S Sweden
95 J21 Laholmsbukten bay S Sweden
35 R6 Lahontan Reservoir ⊠ Nevada, W USA
149 W8 Lahore Punjab, NE Pakistan
149 W8 Lahore ✈ Punjab, E Pakistan
55 Q6 La Horqueta Delta Amacuro, NE Venezuela
119 K15 Lahoysk Rus. Logoysk. Minskaya Voblasts', C Belarus
101 F22 Lahr Baden-Württemberg, S Germany
93 M19 Lahti Swe. Lahtis. Etelä-Suomi, S Finland
Lahtis see Lahti
40 M14 La Huacana Michoacán de Ocampo, SW Mexico
40 K14 La Huerta Jalisco, SW Mexico
78 H12 Laï prev. Behagle, De Behagle. Tandjilé, S Chad
Laibach see Ljubljana
167 Q5 Lai Châu Lai Châu, N Vietnam
Laichow Bay see Laizhou Wan
38 D9 Lā'ie var. Laie. O'ahu, Hawai'i, USA
Laie see Lā'ie
102 L5 l'Aigle Orne, N France
103 Q7 Laignes Côte d'Or, C France
93 K17 Laihia Länsi-Soumi, W Finland
Laila see Laylā
83 F25 Laingsburg Western Cape, SW South Africa
109 U2 Lainsitz Cz. Lužnice. ≈ Austria/Czech Republic
96 I7 Lairg N Scotland, UK
81 I17 Laisamis Eastern, N Kenya
Laisberg see Leisi
127 R4 Laishevo Respublika Tatarstan, W Russian Federation
Laisholm see Jõgeva
92 H13 Laisvall Norrbotten, N Sweden
93 K19 Laitila Länsi-Soumi, SW Finland
161 P5 Laiwu Shandong, E China
161 R4 Laixi var. Shuiji. Shandong, E China
161 R4 Laiyang Shandong, E China
161 O3 Laiyuan Hebei, E China
161 R4 Laizhou var. Ye Xian. Shandong, E China
161 Q4 Laizhou Wan var. Laichow Bay. bay E China
37 S8 La Jara Colorado, C USA
61 I15 Lajeado Rio Grande do Sul, S Brazil
112 L12 Lajkovac Serbia, C Serbia
111 K23 Lajosmizse Bács-Kiskun, C Hungary
Lajta see Leitha
40 I6 La Junta Chihuahua, N Mexico
37 V7 La Junta Colorado, C USA
92 J13 Lakaträsk Norrbotten, N Sweden
Lak Dera see Dheere Laaq
Lakeamu see Lakekamu
29 P12 Lake Andes South Dakota, N USA
22 H9 Lake Arthur Louisiana, S USA
187 Z15 Lakeba prev. Lakemba. island Lau Group, E Fiji
187 Z14 Lakeba Passage channel E Fiji
29 S10 Lake Benton Minnesota, N USA
23 V9 Lake Butler Florida, SE USA
183 P8 Lake Cargelligo New South Wales, SE Australia
22 G9 Lake Charles Louisiana, S USA
27 X9 Lake City Arkansas, C USA
37 Q7 Lake City Colorado, C USA
23 V9 Lake City Florida, SE USA
29 U13 Lake City Iowa, C USA
31 P7 Lake City Michigan, N USA
29 W9 Lake City Minnesota, N USA
21 T13 Lake City South Carolina, SE USA
29 Q7 Lake City South Dakota, N USA
20 M8 Lake City Tennessee, S USA
10 L17 Lake Cowichan Vancouver Island, British Columbia, SW Canada
29 U10 Lake Crystal Minnesota, N USA
25 T6 Lake Dallas Texas, SW USA
97 K15 Lake District physical region NW England, UK
18 D10 Lake Erie Beach New York, NE USA
29 T11 Lakefield Minnesota, N USA
25 V6 Lake Fork Reservoir ⊠ Texas, SW USA
30 M9 Lake Geneva Wisconsin, N USA
18 L9 Lake George New York, NE USA
9 R7 Lake Harbour Baffin Island, Nunavut, NE Canada
36 I12 Lake Havasu City Arizona, SW USA
25 W12 Lake Jackson Texas, SW USA
186 D8 Lakekamu var. Lakeamu. ≈ S Papua New Guinea
180 K13 Lake King Western Australia
23 V12 Lakeland Florida, SE USA
23 U7 Lakeland Georgia, SE USA
181 W4 Lakeland Downs Queensland, NE Australia
9 P16 Lake Louise Alberta, SW Canada
Lakemba see Lakeba
29 V11 Lake Mills Iowa, C USA
39 Q10 Lake Minchumina Alaska, USA
Lakemti see Nek'emtē
186 A7 Lake Murray Western, SW Papua New Guinea
31 R9 Lake Orion Michigan, N USA
190 B16 Lakepa NE Niue
29 T11 Lake Park Iowa, C USA
18 K7 Lake Placid New York, NE USA
18 K9 Lake Pleasant New York, NE USA
34 M6 Lakeport California, W USA
29 Q10 Lake Preston South Dakota, N USA
22 J5 Lake Providence Louisiana, S USA
185 E20 Lake Pukaki Canterbury, South Island, New Zealand
183 Q12 Lakes Entrance Victoria, SE Australia
37 N12 Lakeside Arizona, SW USA
35 V17 Lakeside California, W USA
23 S9 Lakeside Florida, SE USA
28 K13 Lakeside Nebraska, C USA
32 E13 Lakeside Oregon, NW USA
21 W6 Lakeside Virginia, NE USA
Lakes State see El Buhayrat
Lake State see Michigan
185 F20 Lake Tekapo Canterbury, South Island, New Zealand
21 O10 Lake Toxaway North Carolina, SE USA
29 T13 Lake View Iowa, C USA
32 I16 Lakeview Oregon, NW USA
25 O3 Lakeview Texas, SW USA
27 W14 Lake Village Arkansas, C USA
23 W12 Lake Wales Florida, SE USA
37 T4 Lakewood Colorado, C USA
18 K15 Lakewood New Jersey, NE USA
18 C11 Lakewood New York, NE USA
31 T11 Lakewood Ohio, N USA
23 Y13 Lakewood Park Florida, SE USA
23 Z14 Lake Worth Florida, SE USA
152 H4 Lake Wular ◎ NE India
124 H11 Lakhdenpokh'ya Respublika Kareliya, NW Russian Federation
152 L11 Lakhimpur Uttar Pradesh, N India
154 J11 Lakhnādon Madhya Pradesh, C India
Lakhnau see Lucknow
154 A9 Lakhpat Gujarāt, W India
119 K19 Lakhva Rus. Lakhva. Brestskaya Voblasts', SW Belarus
26 I6 Lakin Kansas, C USA
149 S7 Lakki Marwat North-West Frontier Province, NW Pakistan
115 F21 Lakonía historical region S Greece
115 F22 Lakonikós Kólpos gulf S Greece
76 M17 Lakota S Ivory Coast
29 U11 Lakota Iowa, C USA
29 P3 Lakota North Dakota, N USA
Lak Sao see Ban Lakxao
92 L8 Laksefjorden Lapp. Lágesvuotna. fjord N Norway
92 K8 Lakselv Lapp. Leavdnja. Finnmark, N Norway
155 B21 Lakshadweep prev. the Laccadive Minicoy and Amindivi Islands. ◐ union territory India, N Indian Ocean
155 C22 Lakshadweep Eng. Laccadive Islands. island group India, N Indian Ocean
153 S17 Lakshmikāntapur West Bengal, NE India
112 G11 Laktaši ◐ Republika Srpska, N Bosnia and Herzegovina
149 V7 Lāla Mūsa Punjab, NE Pakistan
la Laon see Laon
114 M11 Lalapaşa Edirne, NW Turkey
83 P14 Lalaua Nampula, N Mozambique
105 S9 L'Alcora var. Alcora. País Valenciano, E Spain
105 S10 L'Alcúdia var. L'Alcudia. País Valenciano, E Spain
79 F20 La Lékoumou ◐ province SW Congo
42 E8 La Libertad La Libertad, SW El Salvador
42 E3 La Libertad Petén, N Guatemala
42 H6 La Libertad Comayagua, SW Honduras
40 E4 La Libertad var. Puerto Libertad. Sonora, NW Mexico
42 K10 La Libertad Chontales, S Nicaragua
42 A9 La Libertad ◐ department SW El Salvador
56 B11 La Libertad ◐ department W Peru
62 G11 La Ligua Valparaíso, C Chile
139 U5 La'lī Khān E Iraq
79 H16 La Likouala ◐ province NE Congo
104 H3 Lalín Galicia, NW Spain
102 L13 Lalinde Dordogne, SW France
104 K16 La Línea var. La Línea de la Concepción. Andalucía, S Spain
La Línea de la Concepción see La Línea
152 J14 Lalitpur Uttar Pradesh, N India
153 P11 Lalitpur Central, C Nepal
152 K10 Lālkua Uttarachal, N India
153 T12 Lalmanirhat Rājshāhi, N Bangladesh
9 R12 La Loche Saskatchewan, C Canada
102 M6 la Loupe Eure-et-Loir, C France
99 G20 La Louvière Hainaut, S Belgium
L'Altissima see Hochwilde
104 L14 La Luisiana Andalucía, S Spain
37 S14 La Luz New Mexico, SW USA
107 D16 la Maddalena Sardegna, Italy, C Mediterranean Sea
62 J7 La Madrid Tucumán, N Argentina
Lama-Kara see Kara
15 S8 La Malbaie Québec, SE Canada
167 T10 Lamam Xékong, S Laos
105 P10 La Mancha physical region C Spain
la Manche see English Channel
187 R13 Lamap Malekula, C Vanuatu
37 W6 Lamar Colorado, C USA
27 S7 Lamar Missouri, C USA
21 S12 Lamar South Carolina, SE USA
107 C19 La Marmora, Punta ▲ Sardegna, Italy, C Mediterranean Sea
8 I9 La Martre, Lac ◎ Northwest Territories, NW Canada
56 D10 Lamas San Martín, N Peru
42 I5 La Masica Atlántida, NW Honduras
103 R12 Lamastre Ardèche, E France
La Matepec see Santa Ana, Volcán de
44 I7 La Maya Santiago de Cuba, E Cuba
109 S5 Lambach Oberösterreich, N Austria
168 I11 Lambak Pulau Pini, W Indonesia
102 H5 Lamballe Côtes d'Armor, NW France
79 D18 Lambaréné Moyen-Ogooué, W Gabon
Lambasa see Labasa
56 B11 Lambayeque Lambayeque, W Peru
56 A10 Lambayeque off. Departamento de Lambayeque. ◐ department NW Peru
Lambayeque, Departamento de see Lambayeque
97 G17 Lambay Island Ir. Reachrainn. island E Ireland
186 G6 Lambert, Cape headland New Britain, E Papua New Guinea
195 W6 Lambert Glacier glacier Antarctica
29 T10 Lamberton Minnesota, N USA
27 X4 Lambert-Saint Louis ✈ Missouri, C USA
31 R11 Lambertville Michigan, N USA
18 J15 Lambertville New Jersey, NE USA
171 N12 Lambogo Sulawesi, N Indonesia
106 D8 Lambro ≈ N Italy
33 W11 Lame Deer Montana, NW USA
104 H6 Lamego Viseu, N Portugal
187 Q14 Lamen Bay Épi, C Vanuatu
45 X6 Lamentin Basse Terre, N Guadeloupe
Lamentin see le Lamentin
182 K10 Lameroo South Australia
54 F10 La Mesa Cundinamarca, C Colombia
35 U17 La Mesa California, W USA
37 R16 La Mesa New Mexico, SW USA
25 N6 Lamesa Texas, SW USA
107 N21 Lamezia Terme Calabria, SE Italy
115 F17 Lamía Stereá Ellás, C Greece
171 O8 Lamitan Basilan Island, SW Philippines
187 Y14 Lamiti Gau, C Fiji
171 T11 Lamlam Papua, E Indonesia
188 B16 Lamlam, Mount ▲ SW Guam
109 Q6 Lammer ≈ E Austria
185 E23 Lammerlaw Range ▲▲ South Island, New Zealand
95 L20 Lammhult Kronoberg, S Sweden
93 L18 Lammi Etelä-Suomi, S Finland
189 U11 Lamoil island Chuuk, C Micronesia
35 W3 Lamoille Nevada, W USA
18 M7 Lamoille River ≈ Vermont, NE USA
30 J13 La Moine River ≈ Illinois, N USA
171 P4 Lamon Bay bay Luzon, N Philippines
29 V16 Lamoni Iowa, C USA
33 R13 Lamont California, W USA
27 N8 Lamont Oklahoma, C USA
54 E13 La Montañita var. Montañita. Caquetá, S Colombia
43 N8 La Mosquitia var. Miskito Coast, Eng. Mosquito Coast. coastal region E Nicaragua
102 I9 la Mothe-Achard Vendée, NW France
188 L15 Lamotrek Atoll atoll Caroline Islands, C Micronesia
29 P6 La Moure North Dakota, N USA
167 O8 Lampang var. Muang Lampang. Lampang, NW Thailand
167 R9 Lam Pao Reservoir ⊠ E Thailand
25 S9 Lampasas Texas, SW USA
25 S9 Lampasas River ≈ Texas, SW USA
41 N7 Lampazos var. Lampazos de Naranjo. Nuevo León, NE Mexico
Lampazos de Naranjo see Lampazos
115 E19 Lámpeia Dytikí Ellás, S Greece
101 G19 Lampertheim Hessen, W Germany
97 I20 Lampeter SW Wales, UK
167 O7 Lamphun var. Lampun, Muang Lamphun. Lamphun, NW Thailand
9 X10 Lamprey Manitoba, C Canada
Lampun see Lamphun
168 M15 Lampung off. Propinsi Lampung. ◐ province SW Indonesia
Lampung, Propinsi see Lampung
126 K6 Lamskoye Lipetskaya Oblast', W Russian Federation
81 K20 Lamu Coast, SE Kenya
43 N14 La Muerte, Cerro ▲ C Costa Rica
103 S13 la Mure Isère, E France
37 S10 Lamy New Mexico, SW USA
119 J18 Lan' Rus. Lan'. ≈ C Belarus
38 E10 Lāna'i var. Lanai. island Hawai'i, USA, C Pacific Ocean
38 E10 Lāna'i City var. Lanai City. Lanai, Hawai'i, USA, C Pacific Ocean
Lanai City see Lāna'i City
99 L18 Lanaken Limburg, NE Belgium
171 Q7 Lanao, Lake var. Lake Sultan Alonto. ◎ Mindanao, S Philippines
96 J12 Lanark S Scotland, UK
96 I13 Lanark cultural region C Scotland, UK
104 L9 La Nava de Ricomalillo Castilla-La Mancha, C Spain
166 M13 Lanbi Kyun prev. Sullivan Island. island Mergui Archipelago, S Burma (Myanmar)
Lancang Jiang see Mekong
97 K17 Lancashire cultural region N England, UK
15 N13 Lancaster Ontario, SE Canada
97 K16 Lancaster NW England, UK
35 T14 Lancaster California, W USA
20 M6 Lancaster Kentucky, S USA
27 U1 Lancaster Missouri, C USA
19 O7 Lancaster New Hampshire, NE USA
18 D10 Lancaster New York, NE USA
31 T14 Lancaster Ohio, N USA
18 H16 Lancaster Pennsylvania, NE USA
21 R11 Lancaster South Carolina, SE USA
25 U7 Lancaster Texas, SW USA
21 X5 Lancaster Virginia, NE USA
30 J9 Lancaster Wisconsin, N USA
197 N10 Lancaster Sound sound Nunavut, N Canada
Lan-chou/Lan-chow/Lanchow see Lanzhou
107 K14 Lanciano Abruzzo, C Italy
111 O16 Łańcut Podkarpackie, SE Poland
169 Q11 Landak, Sungai ≈ Borneo, N Indonesia
Landao see Lantau Island
Landau see Landau an der Isar
Landau see Landau in der Pfalz
101 N22 Landau an der Isar var. Landau. Bayern, SE Germany
101 F20 Landau in der Pfalz var. Landau. Rheinland-Pfalz, SW Germany
Land Burgenland see Burgenland
108 K8 Landeck Tirol, W Austria
99 J19 Landen Vlaams Brabant, C Belgium
33 U15 Lander Wyoming, C USA
102 F5 Landerneau Finistère, NW France
95 K20 Landeryd Halland, S Sweden
102 J15 Landes ◐ department SW France
Landeshut/Landeshut in Schlesien see Kamienna Góra
105 R9 Landete Castilla-La Mancha, C Spain
99 M18 Landgraaf Limburg, SE Netherlands
102 F5 Landivisiau Finistère, NW France
Land Kärten see Kärnten
Land of Enchantment see New Mexico
The Land of Opportunity see Arkansas
Land of Steady Habits see Connecticut
Land of the Midnight Sun see Alaska
108 I8 Landquart Graubünden, SE Switzerland
108 J9 Landquart ≈ Austria/Switzerland
21 P10 Landrum South Carolina, SE USA
Landsberg see Gorzów Wielkopolski, Lubuskie, Poland
Landsberg see Górowo Iławeckie, Warmińsko-Mazurskie, NE Poland
101 K23 Landsberg am Lech Bayern, S Germany
Landsberg an der Warthe see Gorzów Wielkopolski
97 G25 Land's End headland SW England, UK
101 M22 Landshut Bayern, SE Germany
Landskron see Lanškroun
95 J22 Landskrona Skåne, S Sweden
98 I10 Landsmeer Noord-Holland, C Netherlands
95 J19 Landvetter ✈ (Göteborg) Västra Götaland, S Sweden
Landwarów see Lentvaris
23 R5 Lanett Alabama, S USA
108 C8 La Neuveville var. Neuveville, Ger. Neuenstadt. Neuchâtel, W Switzerland
95 G21 Langå var. Langaa. Århus, C Denmark
Langaa see Langå
158 G14 La'nga Co ◎ W China
Langada see Lagkáda
Langades/Langadhás see Lagkadás
Langádhia/ see Lagkádia
147 T14 Langar Rus. Lyangar. SE Tajikistan
146 M10 Langar Rus. Lyangar. Navoiy Viloyati, C Uzbekistan
142 M3 Langarūd Gīlān, NW Iran
9 V16 Langbank Saskatchewan, S Canada
29 P2 Langdon North Dakota, N USA
103 P12 Langeac Haute-Loire, C France
102 L8 Langeais Indre-et-Loire, C France
80 I8 Langeb, Wadi ≈ NE Sudan
Långed see Dals Långed
95 G25 Langeland island S Denmark
99 B18 Langemark West-Vlaanderen, W Belgium
101 G18 Langen Hessen, W Germany
101 J22 Langenau Baden-Württemberg, S Germany
9 V16 Langenburg Saskatchewan, S Canada
108 L8 Längenfeld Tirol, W Austria
101 E16 Langenfeld Nordrhein-Westfalen, W Germany
100 I12 Langenhagen Niedersachsen, N Germany
100 I12 Langenhagen ✈ (Hannover) Niedersachsen, NW Germany
109 W3 Langenlois Niederösterreich, NE Austria
108 E7 Langenthal Bern, NW Switzerland
109 W6 Langenwang Steiermark, E Austria
109 X3 Langenzersdorf Niederösterreich, E Austria
100 F9 Langeoog island NW Germany
95 H23 Langeskov Fyn, C Denmark
95 G16 Langesund Telemark, S Norway
95 G17 Langesundsfjorden fjord S Norway
94 D10 Langevågen Møre og Romsdal, S Norway
161 P3 Langfang Hebei, E China
94 E9 Langfjorden fjord S Norway
29 Q8 Langford South Dakota, N USA
168 I10 Langgapayung Sumatera, W Indonesia
106 E9 Langhirano Emilia-Romagna, C Italy
97 K14 Langholm S Scotland, UK
92 I3 Langjökull glacier C Iceland
168 I6 Langkawi, Pulau island Peninsular Malaysia
166 M14 Langkha Tuk, Khao ▲ SW Thailand
14 L8 Langlade Québec, SE Canada
10 M17 Langley British Columbia, SW Canada
167 S7 Lang Mô Thanh Hoa, N Vietnam
Langnau see Langnau im Emmental
108 E8 Langnau im Emmental var. Langnau. Bern, W Switzerland
103 Q13 Langogne Lozère, S France
102 K13 Langon Gironde, SW France
La Ngounié see Ngounié
92 G10 Langøya island C Norway
158 G14 Langqên Zangbo ≈ China/India
104 K2 Langreo var. Sama de Langreo. Asturias, N Spain
103 S7 Langres Haute-Marne, N France
103 R8 Langres, Plateau de plateau C France
168 H8 Langsa Sumatera, W Indonesia
93 H16 Långsele Västernorrland, C Sweden
162 L12 Lang Shan ▲▲ N China
95 M14 Långshyttan Dalarna, C Sweden

◆ Country ● Country Capital ◇ Dependent Territory ○ Dependent Territory Capital ◐ Administrative Regions ✈ International Airport ▲ Mountain ▲▲ Mountain Range ⛰ Volcano ≈ River ◎ Lake ⊠ Reservoir

LANG SƠN – LEAMHCÁN

167 T5 **Lang Sơn** var. Langson. Lang Sơn, N Vietnam
Langson see Lang Sơn
167 N14 **Lang Suan** Chumphon, SW Thailand
93 J14 **Långträsk** Norrbotten, N Sweden
25 N11 **Langtry** Texas, SW USA
103 P16 **Languedoc** cultural region S France
103 P15 **Languedoc-Roussillon** ◐ region S France
27 X10 **L'Anguille River** ≈ Arkansas, C USA
93 I16 **Långviksmon** Västernorrland, N Sweden
101 K22 **Langweid** Bayern, S Germany
160 J8 **Langzhong** Sichuan, C China
Lan Hsü see Lan Yü
9 U15 **Lanigan** Saskatchewan, S Canada
116 K5 **Lanivtsi** Ternopil's'ka Oblast', W Ukraine
137 Y13 **Länkäran** Rus. Lenkoran'. S Azerbaijan
102 L16 **Lannemezan** Hautes-Pyrénées, S France
102 G5 **Lannion** Côtes d'Armor, NW France
14 M11 **L'Annonciation** Québec, SE Canada
105 V5 **L'Anoia** ≈ NE Spain
18 I15 **Lansdale** Pennsylvania, NE USA
14 L14 **Lansdowne** Ontario, SE Canada
152 K9 **Lansdowne** Uttaranchal, N India
30 M3 **L'Anse** Michigan, N USA
15 S7 **L'Anse-St-Jean** Québec, SE Canada
29 Y11 **Lansing** Iowa, C USA
27 R4 **Lansing** Kansas, C USA
31 Q9 **Lansing** state capital Michigan, N USA
93 K18 **Länsi-Suomi** ◐ province W Finland
92 J12 **Lansjärv** Norrbotten, N Sweden
111 G17 **Lanškroun** Ger. Landskron. Pardubický Kraj, E Czech Republic
167 N16 **Lanta, Ko** island S Thailand
161 O15 **Lantau Island** Cant. Tai Yue Shan, Chin. Landao. island Hong Kong, S China
Lantian see Lianyuan
Lan-ts'ang Chiang see Mekong
Lantung, Gulf of see Liaodong Wan
171 O11 **Lanu** Sulawesi, N Indonesia
107 D19 **Lanusei** Sardegna, Italy, C Mediterranean Sea
102 H7 **Lanvaux, Landes de** physical region NW France
163 W8 **Lanxi** Heilongjiang, NE China
161 R10 **Lanxi** Zhejiang, SE China
La Nyanga see Nyanga
161 T15 **Lan Yü** var. Huoshao Tao, var. Hungt'ou, Lan Hsü, Lanyü, Eng. Orchid Island; prev. Kotosho, Koto Sho. island SE Taiwan
Lanyü see Lan Yü
64 P11 **Lanzarote** island Islas Canarias, Spain, NE Atlantic Ocean
159 V10 **Lanzhou** var. Lan-chou, Lanchow, Lan-chow; prev. Kaolan. province capital Gansu, C China
106 B8 **Lanzo Torinese** Piemonte, NE Italy
171 O11 **Laoag** Luzon, N Philippines
171 Q5 **Laoang** Samar, C Philippines
167 R5 **Lao Cai** Lao Cai, N Vietnam
Laodicea/Laodicea ad Mare see Al Lādhiqīyah
Laoet see Laut, Pulau
163 T11 **Laoha He** ≈ NE China
160 M8 **Laohekou** var. Guanghua. Hubei, C China
Laoi, An see Lee
97 E19 **Laois** prev. Leix, Queen's County. ◐ county C Ireland
Laojunmiao see Yumen
163 W12 **Lao Ling** ⛰ N China
64 Q11 **La Oliva** var. Oliva. Fuerteventura, Islas Canarias, Spain, NE Atlantic Ocean
Lao, Loch see Belfast Lough
Laolong see Longchuan
Lao Mangnai see Mangnai
103 P3 **Laon** var. la Laon; anc. Laudunum. Aisne, N France
Lao People's Democratic Republic see Laos
54 M3 **La Orchila, Isla** island N Venezuela
64 O11 **La Orotava** Tenerife, Islas Canarias, Spain, NE Atlantic Ocean
57 E14 **La Oroya** Junín, C Peru
167 Q7 **Laos** off. Lao People's Democratic Republic. ◆ republic SE Asia
161 R5 **Laoshan Wan** bay E China
163 Y10 **Laoye Ling** ⛰ NE China
60 J12 **Lapa** Paraná, S Brazil
103 P10 **Lapalisse** Allier, C France
54 F9 **La Palma** Cundinamarca, C Colombia
42 F7 **La Palma** Chalatenango, N El Salvador
43 W16 **La Palma** Darién, SE Panama
64 N11 **La Palma** island Islas Canarias, Spain, NE Atlantic Ocean
104 J14 **La Palma del Condado** Andalucía, S Spain
61 F18 **La Paloma** Durazno, C Uruguay
61 G20 **La Paloma** Rocha, E Uruguay
61 A21 **La Pampa** off. Provincia de La Pampa. ◐ province C Argentina
La Pampa, Provincia de see La Pampa
55 P8 **La Paragua** Bolívar, E Venezuela
119 O16 **Lapatsichy** Rus. Lopatichi. Mahilyowskaya Voblasts', E Belarus
61 C16 **La Paz** Entre Ríos, E Argentina
62 I11 **La Paz** Mendoza, C Argentina
57 J18 **La Paz** var. La Paz de Ayacucho. ● (Bolivia-legislative and administrative capital) La Paz, W Bolivia
42 H6 **La Paz** La Paz, SW Honduras
40 F9 **La Paz** Baja California Sur, NW Mexico
61 F20 **La Paz** Canelones, S Uruguay
57 J16 **La Paz** ◐ department W Bolivia
42 B9 **La Paz** ◐ department S El Salvador
42 G7 **La Paz** ◐ department SW Honduras
La Paz see El Alto
La Paz see Robles
La Paz see La Paz Centro
40 F9 **La Paz, Bahía de** bay W Mexico
42 I10 **La Paz Centro** var. La Paz. León, W Nicaragua
La Paz de Ayacucho see La Paz
54 J15 **La Pedrera** Amazonas, SE Colombia
31 S9 **Lapeer** Michigan, N USA
40 K6 **La Perla** Chihuahua, N Mexico
165 T1 **La Perouse Strait** Jap. Sōya-kaikyō, Rus. Proliv Laperuza. strait Japan/Russian Federation
63 I14 **La Perra, Salitral de** salt lake C Argentina
Laperuza, Proliv see La Perouse Strait
41 Q10 **La Pesca** Tamaulipas, C Mexico
40 M13 **La Piedad Cavadas** Michoacán de Ocampo, C Mexico
Lapines see Lafnitz
93 M16 **Lapinlahti** Kuopio, C Finland
Lápithos see Lapta
22 K9 **Laplace** Louisiana, S USA
45 X12 **La Plaine** SE Dominica
173 P16 **La Plaine-des-Palmistes** C Réunion
92 K11 **Lapland** Fin. Lappi, Swe. Lappland. cultural region N Europe
28 M8 **La Plant** South Dakota, N USA
61 D20 **La Plata** Buenos Aires, E Argentina
54 D12 **La Plata** Huila, SW Colombia
21 W4 **La Plata** Maryland, NE USA
La Plata see Sucre
45 U6 **la Plata, Río de** ≈ C Puerto Rico
105 W4 **La Pobla de Lillet** Cataluña, NE Spain
105 U4 **La Pobla de Segur** Cataluña, NE Spain
15 S9 **La Pocatière** Québec, SE Canada
104 L3 **La Pola de Gordón** Castilla-León, N Spain
31 O11 **La Porte** Indiana, N USA
18 H13 **Laporte** Pennsylvania, NE USA
29 X13 **La Porte City** Iowa, C USA
62 J8 **La Posta** Catamarca, C Argentina
40 E8 **La Poza Grande** Baja California Sur, W Mexico
93 K16 **Lappajärvi** Länsi-Soumi, W Finland
93 L16 **Lappajärvi** ◎ W Finland
93 N18 **Lappeenranta** Swe. Villmanstrand. Etelä-Suomi, SE Finland
93 J17 **Lappfjärd** Fin. Lapväärtti. Länsi-Soumi, W Finland
92 L12 **Lappi** Swe. Lappland. ◐ province N Finland
Lappi/Lappland see Lapland
Lappland see Lappi
Lappo see Lapua
61 C23 **Laprida** Buenos Aires, E Argentina
25 P13 **La Pryor** Texas, SW USA
136 B11 **Lâpseki** Çanakkale, NW Turkey
121 P2 **Lapta** Gk. Lápithos. NW Cyprus
Laptev Sea see Laptevykh, More
122 N6 **Laptevykh, More** Eng. Laptev Sea. sea Arctic Ocean
93 K16 **Lapua** Swe. Lappo. Länsi-Soumi, W Finland
105 P3 **La Puebla de Arganzón** País Vasco, N Spain
104 L14 **La Puebla de Cazalla** Andalucía, S Spain
104 M9 **La Puebla de Montalbán** Castilla-La Mancha, C Spain
54 I6 **La Puerta** Trujillo, NW Venezuela
Lapurdum see Bayonne
40 E7 **La Purísima** Baja California Sur, W Mexico
Lapväärtti see Lappfjärd
110 O10 **Łapy** Podlaskie, NE Poland
80 D6 **Laqiya Arba'in** Northern, NW Sudan
62 J4 **La Quiaca** Jujuy, N Argentina
107 J14 **L'Aquila** var. Aquila, Aquila degli Abruzzi. Abruzzo, C Italy
143 Q13 **Lār** Fārs, S Iran
54 J5 **Lara** off. Estado Lara. ◐ state NW Venezuela
104 G2 **Laracha** Galicia, NW Spain
74 G5 **Larache** var. al Araïch, El Araïch, prev. El Araïche; anc. Lixus. NW Morocco
Lara, Estado see Lara
103 T14 **Laragne-Montéglin** Hautes-Alpes, SE France
104 M13 **La Rambla** Andalucía, S Spain
33 Y17 **Laramie** Wyoming, C USA
33 X15 **Laramie Mountains** ⛰ Wyoming, C USA
33 Y16 **Laramie River** ≈ Wyoming, C USA
60 H12 **Laranjeiras do Sul** Paraná, S Brazil
Larantoeka see Larantuka
171 P16 **Larantuka** prev. Larantoeka. Flores, C Indonesia
171 U15 **Larat** Pulau Larat, E Indonesia
171 U15 **Larat, Pulau** island Kepulauan Tanimbar, E Indonesia
95 P19 **Lärbro** Gotland, SE Sweden
106 A9 **Larche, Col de** pass France/Italy
14 H8 **Larder Lake** Ontario, S Canada
105 O2 **Laredo** Cantabria, N Spain
25 Q15 **Laredo** Texas, SW USA
40 H9 **La Reforma** Sinaloa, W Mexico
98 N11 **Laren** Gelderland, E Netherlands
98 J11 **Laren** Noord-Holland, C Netherlands
102 K13 **la Réole** Gironde, SW France
La Réunion see Réunion
Largeau see Faya
103 U13 **l'Argentière-la-Bessée** Hautes-Alpes, SE France
149 O4 **Lar Gerd** var. Largird. Balkh, N Afghanistan
Largird see Lar Gerd
23 V12 **Largo** Florida, SE USA
37 Q9 **Largo, Canon** valley New Mexico, SW USA
44 D6 **Largo, Cayo** island W Cuba
23 Z17 **Largo, Key** island Florida Keys, Florida, SE USA
96 H12 **Largs** W Scotland, UK
102 I16 **la Rhune** var. Larrún. ▲ France/Spain see also Larrún
la Rhune see Larrún
la Riege see Ariège
29 Q4 **Larimore** North Dakota, N USA
107 L15 **Larino** Molise, C Italy
Lario see Como, Lago di
62 J9 **La Rioja** La Rioja, NW Argentina
62 I9 **La Rioja** off. Provincia de La Rioja. ◐ province NW Argentina
105 O4 **La Rioja** ◐ autonomous community N Spain
La Rioja, Provincia de see La Rioja
115 F16 **Lárisa** var. Larissa. Thessalía, C Greece
Larissa see Lárisa
149 Q13 **Lārkāna** var. Larkhana. Sind, SE Pakistan
Larkhana see Lārkāna
Larnaca see Lárnaka
121 Q3 **Lárnaka** var. Larnaca, Larnax. SE Cyprus
121 Q3 **Lárnaka** ✈ SE Cyprus
Larnax see Lárnaka
97 G14 **Larne** Ir. Latharna. E Northern Ireland, UK
26 L5 **Larned** Kansas, C USA
104 L3 **La Robla** Castilla-León, N Spain
104 J10 **La Roca de la Sierra** Extremadura, W Spain
99 K22 **La Roche-en-Ardenne** Luxembourg, SE Belgium
102 L11 **la Rochefoucauld** Charente, W France
102 J10 **la Rochelle** anc. Rupella. Charente-Maritime, W France
102 I9 **la Roche-sur-Yon** prev. Bourbon Vendée, Napoléon-Vendée. Vendée, NW France
105 Q10 **La Roda** Castilla-La Mancha, C Spain
104 L14 **La Roda de Andalucía** Andalucía, S Spain
45 P9 **La Romana** E Dominican Republic
9 T13 **La Ronge** Saskatchewan, C Canada
9 U13 **La Ronge, Lac** ◎ Saskatchewan, C Canada
22 K10 **Larose** Louisiana, S USA
42 M7 **La Rosita** Región Autónoma Atlántico Norte, NE Nicaragua
181 Q3 **Larrimah** Northern Territory, N Australia
62 N11 **Larroque** Entre Ríos, E Argentina
105 Q2 **Larrún** Fr. la Rhune. ▲ France/Spain see also la Rhune
Larrún see la Rhune
195 X6 **Lars Christensen Coast** physical region Antarctica
39 Q14 **Larsen Bay** Kodiak Island, Alaska, USA
194 I5 **Larsen Ice Shelf** ice shelf Antarctica
8 M6 **Larsen Sound** sound Nunavut, N Canada
La Rúa see A Rúa de Valdeorras
102 K16 **Laruns** Pyrénées-Atlantiques, SW France
95 G16 **Larvik** Vestfold, S Norway
La-sa see Lhasa
171 S13 **Lasahata** Pulau Seram, E Indonesia
Lasahau see Lasihao
37 O6 **La Sal** Utah, W USA
14 C17 **La Salle** Ontario, S Canada
30 L11 **La Salle** Illinois, N USA
45 O9 **Las Americas** ✈ (Santo Domingo) S Dominican Republic
79 G17 **La Sangha** ◐ province N Congo
37 V6 **Las Animas** Colorado, C USA
108 D10 **La Sarine** var. Sarine. ≈ SW Switzerland
108 B9 **La Sarraz** Vaud, W Switzerland
12 H12 **La Sarre** Québec, SE Canada
54 L3 **Las Aves, Islas** var. Islas de Aves. island group N Venezuela
55 N7 **Las Bonitas** Bolívar, C Venezuela
104 K15 **Las Cabezas de San Juan** Andalucía, S Spain
61 G19 **Lascano** Rocha, E Uruguay
62 I5 **Lascar, Volcán** 🌋 N Chile
41 T15 **Las Choapas** var. Choapas. Veracruz-Llave, SE Mexico
37 R15 **Las Cruces** New Mexico, SW USA
Lasdehnen see Krasnoznamensk
105 V4 **La See d'Urgel** var. La Seu d'Urgell, Seo de Urgel. Cataluña, NE Spain
La Selle see Selle, Pic de la
62 G9 **La Serena** Coquimbo, C Chile
104 K11 **La Serena** physical region W Spain
La Seu d'Urgell see La See d'Urgel
103 T16 **La Seyne-sur-Mer** Var, SE France
61 D21 **Las Flores** Buenos Aires, E Argentina
62 H9 **Las Flores** San Juan, W Argentina
9 S14 **Lashburn** Saskatchewan, S Canada
62 I11 **Las Heras** Mendoza, W Argentina
148 M8 **Lashkar Gāh** var. Lash-Kar-Gar'. Helmand, S Afghanistan
Lash-Kar-Gar' see Lashkar Gāh
171 P14 **Lasihao** var. Lasahau. Pulau Muna, C Indonesia
107 N21 **La Sila** ⛰ SW Italy
63 H23 **La Silueta, Cerro** ▲ S Chile
42 L9 **La Sirena** Región Autónoma Atlántico Sur, E Nicaragua
110 J13 **Łask** Łódzkie, C Poland
109 V11 **Laško** Ger. Tüffer. C Slovenia
63 H14 **Las Lajas** Neuquén, W Argentina
63 H15 **Las Lajas, Cerro** ▲ W Argentina
62 M6 **Las Lomitas** Formosa, N Argentina
41 V16 **Las Margaritas** Chiapas, SE Mexico
Las Marismas see Guadalquivir, Marismas del
54 M6 **Las Mercedes** Guárico, N Venezuela
42 F6 **Las Minas, Cerro** ▲ W Honduras
105 O11 **La Solana** Castilla-La Mancha, C Spain
45 Q14 **La Soufrière** ▲ Saint Vincent, Saint Vincent and the Grenadines
102 M10 **la Souterraine** Creuse, C France
62 N7 **Las Palmas** Chaco, N Argentina
43 Q16 **Las Palmas** Veraguas, W Panama
64 P12 **Las Palmas** var. Las Palmas de Gran Canaria. Gran Canaria, Islas Canarias, Spain, NE Atlantic Ocean
64 P12 **Las Palmas** ◐ province Islas Canarias, Spain, NE Atlantic Ocean
64 Q12 **Las Palmas** ✈ Gran Canaria, Islas Canarias, Spain, NE Atlantic Ocean
Las Palmas de Gran Canaria see Las Palmas
40 D6 **Las Palomas** Baja California Sur, W Mexico
105 P10 **Las Pedroñeras** Castilla-La Mancha, C Spain
106 E10 **La Spezia** Liguria, NW Italy
61 F20 **Las Piedras** Canelones, S Uruguay
63 J18 **Las Plumas** Chubut, S Argentina
61 B18 **Las Rosas** Santa Fe, C Argentina
Lassa see Lhasa
35 O4 **Lassen Peak** ▲ California, W USA
194 K6 **Lassiter Coast** physical region Antarctica
109 V9 **Lassnitz** ≈ SE Austria
15 O12 **L'Assomption** Québec, SE Canada
15 N11 **L'Assomption** ≈ Québec, SE Canada
43 S17 **Las Tablas** Los Santos, S Panama
Lastarria, Volcán see Azufre, Volcán
37 V4 **Last Chance** Colorado, C USA
Last Frontier, The see Alaska
9 U16 **Last Mountain Lake** ◎ Saskatchewan, S Canada
62 H9 **Las Tórtolas, Cerro** ▲ W Argentina
61 C14 **Las Toscas** Santa Fe, C Argentina
79 F19 **Lastoursville** Ogooué-Lolo, E Gabon
113 F16 **Lastovo** It. Lagosta. island SW Croatia
113 F16 **Lastovski Kanal** channel SW Croatia
40 E6 **Las Tres Vírgenes, Volcán** 🌋 W Mexico
40 F4 **Las Trincheras** Sonora, NW Mexico
55 N8 **Las Trincheras** Bolívar, E Venezuela
44 H7 **Las Tunas** var. Victoria de las Tunas. Las Tunas, E Cuba
La Suisse see Switzerland
40 I5 **Las Varas** Chihuahua, N Mexico
40 J12 **Las Varas** Nayarit, C Mexico
62 L10 **Las Varillas** Córdoba, E Argentina
35 X11 **Las Vegas** Nevada, W USA
37 T10 **Las Vegas** New Mexico, SW USA
187 P10 **Lata** Nendö, Solomon Islands
13 R10 **La Tabatière** Québec, E Canada
56 C6 **Latacunga** Cotopaxi, C Ecuador
194 I7 **Latady Island** island Antarctica
54 E14 **La Tagua** Putumayo, S Colombia
Latakia see Al Lādhiqīyah
92 J10 **Lätäseno** ≈ NW Finland
14 H9 **Latchford** Ontario, S Canada
14 J13 **Latchford Bridge** Ontario, SE Canada
193 Y14 **Late** island Vava'u Group, N Tonga
153 P15 **Lātehār** Jhārkhand, N India
15 R7 **Laterrière** Québec, SE Canada
102 J13 **la Teste** Gironde, SW France
25 V8 **Latexo** Texas, SW USA
18 L10 **Latham** New York, NE USA
Latharna see Larne
108 B9 **La Thielle** var. Thièle. ≈ W Switzerland
27 R3 **Lathrop** Missouri, C USA
107 I16 **Latina** prev. Littoria. Lazio, C Italy
41 R14 **La Tinaja** Veracruz-Llave, S Mexico
106 J7 **Latisana** Friuli-Venezia Giulia, NE Italy
Latium see Lazio
115 K25 **Lató** site of ancient city Kríti, Greece, E Mediterranean Sea
187 Q17 **La Tontouta** ✈ (Noumea) Province Sud, S New Caledonia
55 N4 **La Tortuga, Isla** var. Isla Tortuga. island N Venezuela
108 C10 **La Tour-de-Peilz** var. La Tour de Peilz. Vaud, SW Switzerland
La Tour de Peilz see La Tour-de-Peilz
103 S11 **la Tour-du-Pin** Isère, E France
102 J11 **la Tremblade** Charente-Maritime, W France
102 L10 **la Trimouille** Vienne, W France
42 J9 **La Trinidad** Estelí, NW Nicaragua
41 V16 **La Trinitaria** Chiapas, SE Mexico
45 Q11 **la Trinité** E Martinique
15 U7 **La Trinité-des-Monts** Québec, SE Canada
18 C15 **Latrobe** Pennsylvania, NE USA
183 P13 **La Trobe River** ≈ Victoria, SE Australia
Lattakia/Lattaquié see Al Lādhiqīyah
171 S13 **Latu** Pulau Seram, E Indonesia
15 P9 **La Tuque** Québec, SE Canada
155 G14 **Lātūr** Mahārāshtra, C India
118 G8 **Latvia** off. Republic of Latvia, Ger. Lettland, Latv. Latvija, Latvijas Republika; prev. Latvian SSR, Rus. Latviyskaya SSR. ◆ republic NE Europe
Latvian SSR/Latvija/Latvijas Republika/Latviyskaya SSR see Latvia
Latvia, Republic of see Latvia
186 H7 **Lau** New Britain, E Papua New Guinea
175 R9 **Lau Basin** undersea feature S Pacific Ocean
101 O15 **Lauchhammer** Brandenburg, E Germany
Laudunum see Laon
Laudus see St-Lô
Lauenburg/Lauenburg in Pommern see Lębork
101 L20 **Lauf an der Pegnitz** Bayern, SE Germany
108 D7 **Laufen** Basel, NW Switzerland
109 P5 **Lauffen** Salzburg, NW Austria
92 I2 **Laugarbakki** Nordhurland Vestra, N Iceland
92 I4 **Laugarvatn** Sudhurland, SW Iceland
31 O3 **Laughing Fish Point** headland Michigan, N USA
187 Z14 **Lau Group** island group E Fiji
Lauis see Lugano
93 M17 **Laukaa** Länsi-Soumi, C Finland
118 D12 **Laukuva** Tauragė, W Lithuania
Laun see Louny
183 P16 **Launceston** Tasmania, SE Australia
97 I24 **Launceston** anc. Dunheved. SW England, UK
54 C13 **La Unión** Nariño, SW Colombia
42 H8 **La Unión** La Unión, SE El Salvador
42 I6 **La Unión** Olancho, C Honduras
40 M15 **La Unión** Guerrero, S Mexico
41 Y14 **La Unión** Quintana Roo, E Mexico
105 S13 **La Unión** Murcia, SE Spain
54 L7 **La Unión** Barinas, C Venezuela
42 B10 **La Unión** ◐ department E El Salvador
38 H11 **Laupāhoehoe** var. Laupahoehoe. Hawai'i, USA, C Pacific Ocean
Laupahoehoe see Laupāhoehoe
101 I23 **Laupheim** Baden-Württemberg, S Germany
181 W3 **Laura** Queensland, NE Australia
189 X2 **Laura** atoll Majuro Atoll, SE Marshall Islands
Laurana see Lovran
54 L8 **La Urbana** Bolívar, C Venezuela
21 Y4 **Laurel** Delaware, NE USA
23 V14 **Laurel** Florida, SE USA
21 W3 **Laurel** Maryland, NE USA
22 M6 **Laurel** Mississippi, S USA
33 U11 **Laurel** Montana, NW USA
29 R13 **Laurel** Nebraska, C USA
18 H15 **Laureldale** Pennsylvania, NE USA
18 C16 **Laurel Hill** ridge Pennsylvania, NE USA
29 T12 **Laurens** Iowa, C USA
21 P11 **Laurens** South Carolina, SE USA
Laurentian Highlands see Laurentian Mountains
15 P10 **Laurentian Mountains** var. Laurentian Highlands, Fr. Les Laurentides. plateau Newfoundland and Labrador/Québec, Canada
15 O12 **Laurentides** Québec, SE Canada
Laurentides, Les see Laurentian Mountains
107 M19 **Lauria** Basilicata, S Italy
194 I1 **Laurie Island** island Antarctica
21 T11 **Laurinburg** North Carolina, SE USA
30 M2 **Laurium** Michigan, N USA
Lauru see Choiseul
108 B9 **Lausanne** It. Losanna. Vaud, SW Switzerland
101 Q16 **Lausche** var. Luže. ▲ Czech Republic/Germany see also Luže
Lausche see Luže
101 Q16 **Lausitzer Bergland** var. Lausitzer Gebirge, Cz. Gory Lużyckie, Lužické Hory', Eng. Lusatian Mountains. ⛰ E Germany
Lausitzer Gebirge see Lausitzer Bergland
Lausitzer Neisse see Neisse
103 T12 **Lautaret, Col du** pass SE France
63 G15 **Lautaro** Araucanía, C Chile
101 F21 **Lauter** ≈ W Germany
108 I7 **Lauterach** Vorarlberg, NW Austria
101 I17 **Lauterbach** Hessen, C Germany
108 E9 **Lauterbrunnen** Bern, C Switzerland
169 U14 **Laut Kecil, Kepulauan** island group N Indonesia
187 X14 **Lautoka** Viti Levu, W Fiji
169 O8 **Laut, Pulau** prev. Laoet. island Borneo, C Indonesia
169 V14 **Laut, Pulau** island Kepulauan Natuna, W Indonesia
169 U13 **Laut, Selat** strait Borneo, C Indonesia
168 H8 **Laut Tawar, Danau** ◎ Sumatera, NW Indonesia
189 V14 **Lauvergne Island** island Chuuk, C Micronesia
98 M5 **Lauwers Meer** ◎ N Netherlands
98 M4 **Lauwersoog** Groningen, NE Netherlands
102 M14 **Lauzerte** Tarn-et-Garonne, S France
25 U13 **Lavaca Bay** bay Texas, SW USA
25 U12 **Lavaca River** ≈ Texas, SW USA
15 O12 **Laval** Québec, SE Canada
102 J6 **Laval** Mayenne, NW France
15 T6 **Laval** ≈ Québec, SE Canada
105 S9 **La Vall d'Uixó** var. Vall d'Uxó. País Valenciano, E Spain
105 S9 **La Vall D'Uixó** var. Vall D'Uxó. País Valenciano, E Spain
61 F19 **Lavalleja** ◐ department S Uruguay
15 O12 **Lavaltrie** Québec, SE Canada
186 M10 **Lavanggu** Rennell, S Solomon Islands
143 O14 **Lāvān, Jazīreh-ye** island S Iran
109 U8 **Lavant** ≈ S Austria
118 G5 **Lavassaare** Ger. Lawassaar. Pärnumaa, SW Estonia
104 L3 **La Vecilla de Curueño** Castilla-León, N Spain
45 N8 **La Vega** var. Concepción de la Vega. C Dominican Republic
La Vela see La Vela de Coro
54 J4 **La Vela de Coro** var. La Vela. Falcón, N Venezuela
103 N17 **Lavelanet** Ariège, S France
107 M17 **Lavello** Basilicata, S Italy
36 J8 **La Verkin** Utah, W USA
26 J8 **Laverne** Oklahoma, C USA
25 S12 **La Vernia** Texas, SW USA
93 K18 **Lavia** Länsi-Soumi, SW Finland
14 I12 **Lavieille, Lake** ◎ Ontario, SE Canada
94 C12 **Lavik** Sogn Og Fjordane, S Norway
La Vila Joíosa see Villajoyosa
33 U10 **Lavina** Montana, NW USA
194 H5 **Lavoisier Island** island Antarctica
23 U2 **Lavonia** Georgia, SE USA
103 R13 **la Voulte-sur-Rhône** Ardèche, E France
123 W5 **Lavrentiya** Chukotskiy Avtonomnyy Okrug, NE Russian Federation
115 H20 **Lávrio** prev. Lávrion. Attikí, C Greece
Lávrion see Lávrio
83 L22 **Lavumisa** prev. Gollel. SE Swaziland
149 T4 **Lawarai Pass** pass N Pakistan
Lawassaar see Lavassaare
141 P16 **Lawdar** SW Yemen
25 Q7 **Lawn** Texas, SW USA
195 Y4 **Law Promontory** headland Antarctica
77 O14 **Lawra** NW Ghana
185 E23 **Lawrence** Otago, South Island, New Zealand
31 P14 **Lawrence** Indiana, N USA
27 Q4 **Lawrence** Kansas, C USA
19 O10 **Lawrence** Massachusetts, NE USA
20 L5 **Lawrenceburg** Kentucky, S USA
20 I10 **Lawrenceburg** Tennessee, S USA
23 T3 **Lawrenceville** Georgia, SE USA
31 N15 **Lawrenceville** Illinois, N USA
21 V7 **Lawrenceville** Virginia, NE USA
27 S3 **Lawson** Missouri, C USA
26 L12 **Lawton** Oklahoma, C USA
140 I4 **Lawz, Jabal al** ▲ NW Saudi Arabia
95 L16 **Laxå** Örebro, C Sweden
125 T5 **Laya** ≈ NW Russian Federation
57 I19 **La Yarada** Tacna, SW Peru
141 S15 **Layjūn** C Yemen
141 Q9 **Laylā** var. Laila. Ar Riyāḍ, C Saudi Arabia
23 P4 **Lay Lake** ⊠ Alabama, S USA
45 P14 **Layou** Saint Vincent, Saint Vincent and the Grenadines
La Youne see El Ayoun
192 L5 **Laysan Island** island Hawaiian Islands, Hawaii, USA
36 L2 **Layton** Utah, W USA
34 L5 **Laytonville** California, N USA
172 H17 **Lazare, Pointe** headland Mahé, NE Seychelles
123 T12 **Lazarev** Khabarovskiy Kray, SE Russian Federation
112 L12 **Lazarevac** Serbia, C Serbia
65 N22 **Lazarev Sea** sea Antarctica
40 M15 **Lázaro Cárdenas** Michoacán de Ocampo, SW Mexico
119 F15 **Lazdijai** Alytus, S Lithuania
107 H15 **Lazio** anc. Latium. ◐ region C Italy
111 A16 **Lázně Kynžvart** Ger. Bad Königswart. Karlovarský Kraj, W Czech Republic
Lazovsk see Sîngerei
167 R12 **Leach** Poŭthĭsăt, W Cambodia
27 X9 **Leachville** Arkansas, C USA
28 I9 **Lead** South Dakota, N USA
9 S16 **Leader** Saskatchewan, S Canada
19 S6 **Lead Mountain** ▲ Maine, NE USA
37 R5 **Leadville** Colorado, C USA
9 V12 **Leaf Rapids** Manitoba, C Canada
22 M7 **Leaf River** ≈ Mississippi, S USA
25 W11 **League City** Texas, SW USA
92 K8 **Leaibevuotna** Nor. Olderfjord. Finnmark, N Norway
23 N7 **Leakesville** Mississippi, S USA
25 Q11 **Leakey** Texas, SW USA
Leal see Lihula
83 G15 **Lealui** Western, W Zambia
Leamhcán see Lucan

◆ Country
● Country Capital
◇ Dependent Territory
○ Dependent Territory Capital
◐ Administrative Regions
✈ International Airport
▲ Mountain
⛰ Mountain Range
🌋 Volcano
≈ River
◎ Lake
⊠ Reservoir

LEAMINGTON – LEWIS SMITH LAKE

14 C18 **Leamington** Ontario, S Canada
Leamington/Leamington Spa *see* Royal Leamington Spa
Leammi *see* Lemmenjoki
25 S10 **Leander** Texas, SW USA
60 F13 **Leandro N. Alem** Misiones, NE Argentina
97 A20 **Leane, Lough** *Ir.* Loch Léin. ◎ SW Ireland
180 G8 **Learmouth** Western Australia
Leau *see* Zoutleeuw
L'Eau d'Heure *see* Plate Taille, Lac de la
190 D12 **Leava** Île Futuna, S Wallis and Futuna
Leavdnja *see* Lakselv
27 R3 **Leavenworth** Kansas, C USA
32 I8 **Leavenworth** Washington, NW USA
92 L8 **Leavvajohka** *var.* Levvajok. Finnmark, N Norway
27 R4 **Leawood** Kansas, C USA
110 H6 **Łeba** *Ger.* Leba. Pomorskie, N Poland
110 I6 **Łeba** *Ger.* Leba. ≈ N Poland
Leba *see* Łeba
101 D20 **Lebach** Saarland, SW Germany
łeba, Jezioro *see* Łebsko, Jezioro
171 P8 **Lebak** Mindanao, S Philippines
31 O13 **Lebanon** Indiana, N USA
20 L6 **Lebanon** Kentucky, S USA
27 U6 **Lebanon** Missouri, C USA
19 N9 **Lebanon** New Hampshire, NE USA
32 G12 **Lebanon** Oregon, NW USA
18 H15 **Lebanon** Pennsylvania, NE USA
20 J8 **Lebanon** Tennessee, S USA
21 P7 **Lebanon** Virginia, NE USA
138 G6 **Lebanon** *off.* Republic of Lebanon, *Ar.* Al Lubnān, *Fr.* Liban. ◆ *republic* SW Asia
20 K6 **Lebanon Junction** Kentucky, S USA
Lebanon, Mount *see* Liban, Jebel
Lebanon, Republic of *see* Lebanon
146 J10 **Lebap** Lebapskiy Velayat, NE Turkmenistan
Lebapskiy Velayat *see* Lebap Welaýaty
146 J11 **Lebap Welaýaty** *Rus* Lebapskiy Velayat; *prev. Rus.* Chardzhevskaya Oblast, *Turkm.* Chärjew Oblasty. ⬖ *province* E Turkmenistan
Lebasee *see* Łebsko, Jezioro
99 F17 **Lebbeke** Oost-Vlaanderen, NW Belgium
35 S14 **Lebec** California, W USA
Lebedin *see* Lebedyn
123 Q11 **Lebedinyy** Respublika Sakha (Yakutiya), NE Russian Federation
126 L6 **Lebedyan'** Lipetskaya Oblast', W Russian Federation
117 T4 **Lebedyn** *Rus.* Lebedin. Sums'ka Oblast', NE Ukraine
12 I12 **Lebel-sur-Quévillon** Québec, SE Canada
92 L8 **Lebesby** Finnmark, N Norway
102 M9 **le Blanc** Indre, C France
79 L15 **Lebo** Orientale, N Dem. Rep. Congo
27 P5 **Lebo** Kansas, C USA
110 H6 **Lębork** *var.* Lębórk, *Ger.* Lauenburg, Lauenburg in Pommern. Pomorskie, N Poland
103 O17 **le Boulou** Pyrénées-Orientales, S France
108 A9 **Le Brassus** Vaud, W Switzerland
104 J15 **Lebrija** Andalucía, S Spain
110 G6 **Łebsko, Jezioro** *Ger.* Lebasee; *prev.* Jezioro Łeba. ◎ N Poland
63 F14 **Lebu** Bío Bío, C Chile
Lebyazh'ye *see* Akku
104 F6 **Leça da Palmeira** Porto, N Portugal
103 U15 **le Cannet** Alpes-Maritimes, SE France
Le Cap *see* Cap-Haïtien
103 P2 **le Cateau-Cambrésis** Nord, N France
107 Q18 **Lecce** Puglia, SE Italy
106 D7 **Lecco** Lombardia, N Italy
29 V10 **Le Center** Minnesota, N USA
108 J7 **Lech** Vorarlberg, W Austria
101 K22 **Lech** ≈ Austria/Germany
115 D19 **Lechainá** *var.* Lehena, Lekhainá. Dytikí Ellás, S Greece
102 J11 **le Château d'Oléron** Charente-Maritime, W France
103 R3 **le Chesne** Ardennes, N France
103 R13 **le Cheylard** Ardèche, E France
108 K7 **Lechtaler Alpen** ⛰ W Austria
100 H6 **Leck** Schleswig-Holstein, N Germany
14 L9 **Lecointre, Lac** ◎ Québec, SE Canada
22 H7 **Lecompte** Louisiana, S USA
103 Q9 **le Creusot** Saône-et-Loire, C France
Lecumberri *see* Lekunberri
110 P13 **Łęczna** Lublin, E Poland
110 J12 **Łęczyca** *Ger.* Lentschiza, *Rus.* Lenchitsa. Łódzkie, C Poland
100 F10 **Leda** ≈ NW Germany
109 Y9 **Ledava** ≈ NE Slovenia
99 F17 **Lede** Oost-Vlaanderen, NW Belgium
104 K6 **Ledesma** Castilla-León, N Spain
45 Q12 **le Diamant** SW Martinique
172 J16 **Le Digue** *island* Inner Islands, NE Seychelles
103 Q10 **le Donjon** Allier, C France
102 M10 **le Dorat** Haute-Vienne, C France
Ledo Salinarius *see* Lons-le-Saunier
9 Q14 **Leduc** Alberta, SW Canada
123 V7 **Ledyanaya, Gora** ▲ E Russian Federation
97 C21 **Lee** *Ir.* An Laoi. ≈ SW Ireland
29 U5 **Leech Lake** ◎ Minnesota, N USA
26 K10 **Leedey** Oklahoma, C USA
97 M17 **Leeds** N England, UK
23 P4 **Leeds** Alabama, S USA
29 O3 **Leeds** North Dakota, N USA
98 N6 **Leek** Groningen, NE Netherlands
99 K15 **Leende** Noord-Brabant, SE Netherlands
100 F10 **Leer** Niedersachsen, NW Germany
98 J13 **Leerdam** Zuid-Holland, C Netherlands
98 K12 **Leersum** Utrecht, C Netherlands
23 W11 **Leesburg** Florida, SE USA
21 V3 **Leesburg** Virginia, NE USA
27 R4 **Lees Summit** Missouri, C USA
22 G7 **Leesville** Louisiana, S USA
25 S12 **Leesville** Texas, SW USA
31 U13 **Leesville Lake** ⊠ Ohio, N USA
Leesville Lake *see* Smith Mountain Lake
183 P9 **Leeton** New South Wales, SE Australia
98 L6 **Leeuwarden** *Fris.* Ljouwert. Friesland, N Netherlands
180 I14 **Leeuwin, Cape** *headland* Western Australia
35 R8 **Lee Vining** California, W USA
45 V8 **Leeward Islands** *island group* E West Indies
Leeward Islands *see* Sotavento, Ilhas de
Leeward Islands *see* Vent, Îles Sous le
79 G20 **Léfini** ≈ SE Congo
115 C17 **Lefkáda** *prev.* Levkás. Lefkáda, Iónioi Nísoi, Greece, C Mediterranean Sea
115 B17 **Lefkáda** *It.* Santa Maura, *prev.* Levkás; *anc.* Leucas. *island* Iónioi Nísoi, Greece, C Mediterranean Sea
115 H25 **Lefká Óri** ⛰ Kríti, Greece, E Mediterranean Sea
115 B16 **Lefkímmi** *var.* Levkímmi. Kérkyra, Iónia Nisiá, Greece, C Mediterranean Sea
Lefkosía/Lefkoşa *see* Nicosia
25 O2 **Lefors** Texas, SW USA
45 R12 **le François** E Martinique
180 L12 **Lefroy, Lake** *salt lake* Western Australia
Legaceaster *see* Chester
105 N8 **Leganés** Madrid, C Spain
Leghorn *see* Livorno
110 M11 **Legionowo** Mazowieckie, C Poland
99 K24 **Léglise** Luxembourg, SE Belgium
106 G8 **Legnago** Lombardia, NE Italy
106 D7 **Legnano** Veneto, NE Italy
111 F14 **Legnica** *Ger.* Liegnitz. Dolnośląskie, SW Poland
35 Q9 **Le Grand** California, W USA
103 Q15 **le Grau-du-Roi** Gard, S France
183 U3 **Legume** New South Wales, SE Australia
102 L4 **le Havre** *Eng.* Havre; *prev.* le Havre-de-Grâce. Seine-Maritime, N France
le Havre-de-Grâce *see* le Havre
Lehena *see* Lechainá
36 L3 **Lehi** Utah, W USA
18 I14 **Lehighton** Pennsylvania, NE USA
29 O6 **Lehr** North Dakota, N USA
38 A8 **Lehua Island** *island* Hawaiian Islands, Hawai'i, USA
149 S9 **Leiāh** Punjab, NE Pakistan
109 W9 **Leibnitz** Steiermark, SE Austria
97 M19 **Leicester** *Lat.* Batae Coritanorum. C England, UK
97 M19 **Leicestershire** *cultural region* C England, UK
Leicheng *see* Leizhou
98 H11 **Leiden** *prev.* Leyden; *anc.* Lugdunum Batavorum. Zuid-Holland, W Netherlands
98 H11 **Leiderdorp** Zuid-Holland, W Netherlands
98 G11 **Leidschendam** Zuid-Holland, W Netherlands
99 D18 **Leie** *Fr.* Lys. ≈ Belgium/France
Leifear *see* Lifford
184 L4 **Leigh** Auckland, North Island, New Zealand
97 K17 **Leigh** NW England, UK
182 I5 **Leigh Creek** South Australia
23 O2 **Leighton** Alabama, S USA
97 M21 **Leighton Buzzard** E England, UK
Léim an Bhradáin *see* Leixlip
Léim An Mhadaidh *see* Limavady
Léime, Ceann *see* Loop Head, Ireland
Léime, Ceann *see* Slyne Head, Ireland
101 G20 **Leimen** Baden-Württemberg, SW Germany
100 I13 **Leine** ≈ NW Germany
101 J15 **Leinefelde** Thüringen, C Germany
Léin, Loch *see* Leane, Lough
97 D19 **Leinster** *Ir.* Cúige Laighean. *cultural region* E Ireland
97 F19 **Leinster, Mount** *Ir.* Stua Laighean. ▲ SE Ireland
119 F15 **Leipalingis** Alytus, S Lithuania
92 J12 **Leipojärvi** Norrbotten, N Sweden
31 R12 **Leipsic** Ohio, N USA
Leipsic *see* Leipzig
115 M20 **Leipsoí** *island* Dodekánisa, Greece, Aegean Sea
101 M15 **Leipzig** *Pol.* Lipsk, *hist.* Leipsic; *anc.* Lipsia. Sachsen, E Germany
101 M15 **Leipzig Halle** ✈ Sachsen, E Germany
104 G9 **Leiria** *anc.* Collipo. Leiria, C Portugal
104 F9 **Leiria** ⬖ *district* C Portugal
95 C15 **Leirvik** Hordaland, S Norway
118 E5 **Leisi** *Ger.* Laisberg. Saaremaa, W Estonia
104 J3 **Leitariegos, Puerto de** *pass* NW Spain
20 J6 **Leitchfield** Kentucky, S USA
109 Y5 **Leitha** *Hung.* Lajta. ≈ Austria/Hungary
Leitir Ceanainn *see* Letterkenny
97 D16 **Leitrim** *Ir.* Liatroim. ⬖ *county* NW Ireland
Leivádia *see* Livádeia
Leix *see* Laois
97 F18 **Leixlip** *Eng.* Salmon Leap, *Ir.* Léim an Bhradáin. Kildare, E Ireland
64 N8 **Leixões** Porto, N Portugal
161 N12 **Leiyang** Hunan, S China
160 L16 **Leizhou** *var.* Haikang, Leicheng. Guangdong, S China
160 L16 **Leizhou Bandao** *var.* Luichow Peninsula. *peninsula* S China
98 H13 **Lek** ≈ SW Netherlands
114 I13 **Lekánis** ⛰ NE Greece
172 H13 **Le Kartala** ▲ Grande Comore, NW Comoros
Le Kef *see* El Kef
79 G20 **Lékéti, Monts de la** ⛰ S Congo
Lekhainá *see* Lechainá
114 H8 **Lekhchevo** Montana, NW Bulgaria
92 G11 **Leknes** Nordland, C Norway
79 E21 **Le Kouilou** ⬖ *province* SW Congo
94 L13 **Leksand** Dalarna, C Sweden
124 H8 **Leksozero, Ozero** ◎ NW Russian Federation
105 Q3 **Lekunberri** *var.* Lecumberri. Navarra, N Spain
171 S11 **Lelai, Tanjung** *headland* Pulau Halmahera, N Indonesia
45 Q12 **le Lamentin** *var.* Lamentin. C Martinique
45 Q12 **le Lamentin** ✈ (Fort-de-France) C Martinique
31 P6 **Leland** Michigan, N USA
22 J4 **Leland** Mississippi, S USA
95 J16 **Lelång** *var.* Lelången. ◎ S Sweden
Lelången *see* Lelång
Lel'chitsy *see* Lyel'chytsy
le Léman *see* Geneva, Lake
Leli *see* Tianlin
25 O3 **Lelia Lake** Texas, SW USA
113 I14 **Lelija** ▲ SE Bosnia and Herzegovina
108 C8 **Le Locle** Neuchâtel, W Switzerland
189 Y14 **Lelu** Kosrae, E Micronesia
Lelu *see* Lelu Island
189 Y14 **Lelu Island** *var.* Lelu. *island* Kosrae, E Micronesia
55 W9 **Lelydorp** Wanica, N Surinam
98 K9 **Lelystad** Flevoland, C Netherlands
63 K25 **Le Maire, Estrecho de** *strait* S Argentina
168 L10 **Lemang** Pulau Rangsang, W Indonesia
186 I7 **Lemankoa** Buka Island, NE Papua New Guinea
Léman, Lac *see* Geneva, Lake
102 L6 **le Mans** Sarthe, NW France
29 S12 **Le Mars** Iowa, C USA
109 S3 **Lembach im Mühlkreis** Oberösterreich, N Austria
101 G23 **Lemberg** ▲ SW Germany
Lemberg *see* L'viv
Lemdiyya *see* Médéa
121 P3 **Lemesós** *var.* Limassol. SW Cyprus
100 H13 **Lemgo** Nordrhein-Westfalen, W Germany
33 P13 **Lemhi Range** ⛰ Idaho, NW USA
9 S6 **Lemieux Islands** *island group* Nunavut, NE Canada
171 O11 **Lemito** Sulawesi, N Indonesia
92 L10 **Lemmenjoki** *Lapp.* Leammi. ≈ NE Finland
98 L7 **Lemmer** *Fris.* De Lemmer. Friesland, N Netherlands
28 L7 **Lemmon** South Dakota, N USA
36 M15 **Lemmon, Mount** ▲ Arizona, SW USA
Lemnos *see* Límnos
31 O14 **Lemon, Lake** ◎ Indiana, N USA
102 J5 **le Mont St-Michel** *castle* Manche, N France
35 Q11 **Lemoore** California, W USA
189 T13 **Lemotol Bay** *bay* Chuuk Islands, C Micronesia
45 Y5 **le Moule** *var.* Moule. Grande Terre, NE Guadeloupe
Lemovices *see* Limoges
Le Moyen-Ogooué *see* Moyen-Ogooué
12 M6 **le Moyne, Lac** ◎ Québec, E Canada
93 L18 **Lempäälä** Länsi-Suomi, W Finland
42 E7 **Lempa, Río** ≈ Central America
42 F7 **Lempira** *prev.* Gracias. ⬖ *department* SW Honduras
Lemsalu *see* Limbaži
107 N17 **Le Murge** ⛰ SE Italy
125 V6 **Lemva** ≈ NW Russian Federation
95 F21 **Lemvig** Ringkøbing, W Denmark
166 K8 **Lemyethna** Irrawaddy, SW Burma (Myanmar)
30 K10 **Lena** Illinois, N USA
129 V4 **Lena** ≈ NE Russian Federation
173 N13 **Lena Tablemount** *undersea feature* S Indian Ocean
Lenchitsa *see* Łęczyca
59 N17 **Lençóis** Bahia, E Brazil
60 K9 **Lençóis Paulista** São Paulo, S Brazil
109 Y9 **Lendava** *Hung.* Lendva, *Ger.* Unterlimbach; *prev.* Dolnja Lendava. NE Slovenia
83 F20 **Lendepas** Hardap, SE Namibia
124 H9 **Lendery** Respublika Kareliya, NW Russian Federation
Lendum *see* Lens
Lendva *see* Lendava
27 R4 **Lenexa** Kansas, C USA
109 Q5 **Lengau** Oberösterreich, N Austria
145 Q17 **Lenger** Yuzhnyy Kazakhstan, S Kazakhstan
Lenghu *see* Lenghuzhen
159 O9 **Lenghuzhen** *var.* Lenghu. Qinghai, C China
159 T9 **Lenglong Ling** ▲ N China
108 D7 **Lengnau** Bern, W Switzerland
Lengshuitan *see* Yongzhou
95 M20 **Lenhovda** Kronoberg, S Sweden
79 E20 **Le Niari** ⬖ *province* SW Congo
Lenīn *see* Uzynkol'
Lenin *see* Akdepe
Leninabad *see* Khŭjand
Leninakan *see* Gyumri
Lenina, Pik *see* Lenin Peak
117 V12 **Lenine** *Rus.* Lenino. Respublika Krym, S Ukraine
Leningor *see* Leninogorsk
147 Q13 **Leningrad** *Rus.* Leningradskiy; *prev.* Mŭ'minobod, *Rus.* Muminabad. SW Tajikistan
Leningrad *see* Sankt-Peterburg
126 L13 **Leningradskaya** Krasnodarskiy Kray, SW Russian Federation
195 S16 **Leningradskaya** *Russian research station* Antarctica
124 H12 **Leningradskaya Oblast'** ⬖ *province* NW Russian Federation
Leningradskiy *see* Leningrad
Lenino *see* Lyenina
Lenino *see* Lenine
Leninobod *see* Khŭjand
145 X9 **Leninogorsk** *Kaz.* Leningor. Vostochnyy Kazakhstan, E Kazakhstan
127 T5 **Leninogorsk** Respublika Tatarstan, W Russian Federation
147 T12 **Lenin Peak** *Rus.* Pik Lenina, *Taj.* Qullai Lenin. ▲ Kyrgyzstan/Tajikistan
147 S8 **Leninpol'** Talasskaya Oblast', NW Kyrgyzstan
Lenin, Qullai *see* Lenin Peak
127 P11 **Leninsk** Volgogradskaya Oblast', SW Russian Federation
Leninsk *see* Baykonyr
Leninsk *see* Akdepe
Leninsk *see* Asaka
145 T8 **Leninskiy** Pavlodar, E Kazakhstan
122 I13 **Leninsk-Kuznetskiy** Kemerovskaya Oblast', S Russian Federation
125 P15 **Leninskoye** Kirovskaya Oblast', NW Russian Federation
Leninskoye *see* Uzynkol'
Lenin-Turkmenski *see* Türkmenabat
Leninváros *see* Tiszaújváros
Lenkoran' *see* Länkäran
101 F15 **Lenne** ≈ W Germany
101 G16 **Lennestadt** Nordrhein-Westfalen, W Germany
29 R11 **Lennox** South Dakota, N USA
63 J25 **Lennox, Isla** *Eng.* Lennox Island. *island* S Chile
Lennox Island *see* Lennox, Isla
21 Q9 **Lenoir** North Carolina, SE USA
20 M9 **Lenoir City** Tennessee, S USA
108 C7 **Le Noirmont** Jura, NW Switzerland
14 L9 **Lenôtre, Lac** ◎ Québec, SE Canada
29 U15 **Lenox** Iowa, C USA
103 O2 **Lens** *anc.* Lendum, Lentium. Pas-de-Calais, N France
123 O11 **Lensk** Respublika Sakha (Yakutiya), NE Russian Federation
111 F24 **Lenti** Zala, SW Hungary
Lentia *see* Linz
93 N14 **Lentiira** Oulu, E Finland
107 L25 **Lentini** *anc.* Leontini. Sicilia, Italy, C Mediterranean Sea
Lentium *see* Lens
Lentschiza *see* Łęczyca
93 N15 **Lentua** ◎ E Finland
119 H14 **Lentvaris** *Pol.* Landwarów. Vilnius, SE Lithuania
108 F7 **Lenzburg** Aargau, N Switzerland
109 R5 **Lenzing** Oberösterreich, N Austria
77 P13 **Léo** SW Burkina
109 V7 **Leoben** Steiermark, C Austria
Leobschütz *see* Głubczyce
44 L9 **Léogâne** S Haiti
171 O11 **Leok** Sulawesi, N Indonesia
29 O7 **Leola** South Dakota, N USA
97 K20 **Leominster** W England, UK
19 N11 **Leominster** Massachusetts, NE USA
102 I15 **Léon** Landes, SW France
40 M12 **León** *var.* León de los Aldamas. Guanajuato, C Mexico
42 I10 **León** León, NW Nicaragua
104 L4 **León** Castilla-León, NW Spain
29 V16 **Leon** Iowa, C USA
42 I9 **León** ⬖ *department* W Nicaragua
104 K4 **León** ⬖ *province* Castilla-León, NW Spain
León *see* Cotopaxi
25 V9 **Leona** Texas, SW USA
180 K11 **Leonara** Western Australia
25 U5 **Leonard** Texas, SW USA
107 H15 **Leonardo da Vinci** *prev.* Fiumicino. ✈ (Roma) Lazio, C Italy
21 X5 **Leonardtown** Maryland, NE USA
25 Q13 **Leona River** ≈ Texas, SW USA
41 Z11 **Leona Vicario** Quintana Roo, SE Mexico
101 H21 **Leonberg** Baden-Württemberg, SW Germany
62 M3 **León, Cerro** ▲ NW Paraguay
León de los Aldamas *see* León
109 T4 **Leonding** Oberösterreich, N Austria
107 I14 **Leonessa** Lazio, C Italy
107 K24 **Leonforte** Sicilia, Italy, C Mediterranean Sea
183 O13 **Leongatha** Victoria, SE Australia
115 F21 **Leonídio** *var.* Leonídi. Pelopónnisos, S Greece
Leonídi *see* Leonídio
104 J4 **León, Montes de** ⛰ NW Spain
25 S8 **Leon River** ≈ Texas, SW USA
Leontini *see* Lentini
Léopold II, Lac *see* Mai-Ndombe, Lac
99 J17 **Leopoldsburg** Limburg, NE Belgium
Léopoldville *see* Kinshasa
26 I5 **Leoti** Kansas, C USA
116 M11 **Leova** *Rus.* Leovo. SW Moldova
Leovo *see* Leova
102 G8 **le Palais** Morbihan, NW France
27 X10 **Lepanto** Arkansas, C USA
169 N13 **Lepar, Pulau** *island* W Indonesia
104 I14 **Lepe** Andalucía, S Spain
Lepel' *see* Lyepyel'
83 I19 **Lephepe** Kweneng, SE Botswana
161 Q10 **Leping** Jiangxi, S China
Lépontiennes, Alpes/Lepontine, Alpi *see* Lepontine Alps
108 G10 **Lepontine Alps** *Fr.* Alpes Lépontiennes, *It.* Alpi Lepontine. ⛰ Italy/Switzerland
79 G20 **Le Pool** ⬖ *province* S Congo
173 O16 **Le Port** NW Réunion
103 N1 **le Portel** Pas-de-Calais, N France
93 N17 **Leppävirta** Itä-Suomi, C Finland
45 Q11 **le Prêcheur** NW Martinique
Lepsi *see* Lepsy
145 V13 **Lepsy** *Kaz.* Lepsi. Taldykorgan, SE Kazakhstan
145 V13 **Lepsy** *Kaz.* Lepsi. ≈ SE Kazakhstan
Le Puglie *see* Puglia
103 Q12 **le Puy** *prev.* le Puy-en-Velay, *hist.* Anicium, Podium Anicensis. Haute-Loire, C France
le Puy-en-Velay *see* le Puy
45 X11 **le Raizet** *var.* Le Raizet. ✈ (Pointe-à-Pitre) Grande Terre, C Guadeloupe
107 J24 **Lercara Friddi** Sicilia, Italy, C Mediterranean Sea
78 G12 **Léré** Mayo-Kébbi, SW Chad
Leribe *see* Hlotse
106 E10 **Lerici** Liguria, NW Italy
54 I14 **Lérida** Vaupés, SE Colombia
Lérida *see* Lleida
105 N5 **Lerma** Castilla-León, N Spain
40 M13 **Lerma, Río** ≈ C Mexico
Lerna *see* Lérni
115 F20 **Lérni** *var.* Lerna. *prehistoric site* Pelopónnisos, S Greece
45 R11 **le Robert** E Martinique
115 M21 **Léros** *island* Dodekánisa, Greece, Aegean Sea
30 L13 **Le Roy** Illinois, N USA
27 Q6 **Le Roy** Kansas, C USA
29 W11 **Le Roy** Minnesota, N USA
18 E10 **Le Roy** New York, NE USA
Lerrnayin Gharabakh *see* Nagorno-Karabakh
95 J19 **Lerum** Älvsborg, S Sweden
96 M2 **Lerwick** NE Scotland, UK
45 Y6 **les Abymes** *var.* Abymes. Grande Terre, C Guadeloupe
les Albères *see* Albères, Chaîne des
102 M4 **les Andelys** Eure, N France
45 Q12 **les Anses-d'Arlets** SW Martinique
105 U6 **Les Borges Blanques** *var.* Borjas Blancas. Cataluña, NE Spain
Lesbos *see* Lésvos
Les Cayes *see* Cayes
31 Q4 **Les Cheneaux Islands** *island* Michigan, N USA
105 T8 **Les Coves de Vinromá** *Cast.* Cuevas de Vinromá. País Valenciano, E Spain
103 T12 **les Écrins** ▲ E France
108 C10 **Le Sépey** Vaud, W Switzerland
15 T7 **Les Escoumins** Québec, SE Canada
Les Gonaïves *see* Gonaïves
160 H9 **Leshan** Sichuan, C China
108 D11 **Les Haudères** Valais, SW Switzerland
102 J9 **les Herbiers** Vendée, NW France
Lesh/Leshi *see* Lezhë
125 O8 **Leshukonskoye** Arkhangel'skaya Oblast', NW Russian Federation
Lesina *see* Hvar
107 M15 **Lesina, Lago di** ◎ SE Italy
114 K13 **Lesítse** ⛰ NE Greece
94 G10 **Lesja** Oppland, S Norway
95 L15 **Lesjöfors** Värmland, C Sweden
111 O18 **Lesko** Podkarpackie, SE Poland
113 O15 **Leskovac** Serbia, SE Serbia
113 M22 **Leskovik** *var.* Leskoviku. Korçë, S Albania
Leskoviku *see* Leskovik
33 P14 **Leslie** Idaho, NW USA
31 Q10 **Leslie** Michigan, N USA
Leśna/Lesnaya *see* Lyasnaya
Lesnaya *see* Lyasnaya
102 F5 **Lesneven** Finistère, NW France
112 J11 **Lešnica** Serbia, W Serbia
125 S13 **Lesnoy** Kirovskaya Oblast', NW Russian Federation
122 G10 **Lesnoy** Sverdlovskaya Oblast', C Russian Federation
122 K12 **Lesosibirsk** Krasnoyarskiy Kray, C Russian Federation
83 J23 **Lesotho** *off.* Kingdom of Lesotho; *prev.* Basutoland. ◆ *monarchy* S Africa
Lesotho, Kingdom of *see* Lesotho
102 J12 **Lesparre-Médoc** Gironde, SW France
108 C8 **Les Ponts-de-Martel** Neuchâtel, W Switzerland
103 P1 **Lesquin** ✈ Nord, N France
102 I9 **les Sables-d'Olonne** Vendée, NW France
109 S7 **Lessach** *var.* Lessachbach. ≈ E Austria
Lessachbach *see* Lessach
45 W11 **les Saintes** *var.* Îles des Saintes. *island group* S Guadeloupe
74 L5 **Les Salines** ✈ (Annaba) NE Algeria
99 J22 **Lesse** ≈ SE Belgium
95 M21 **Lessebo** Kronoberg, S Sweden
194 M10 **Lesser Antarctica** *var.* West Antarctica. *physical region* Antarctica
45 P15 **Lesser Antilles** *island group* E West Indies
137 T10 **Lesser Caucasus** *Rus.* Malyy Kavkaz. ⛰ SW Asia
Lesser Khingan Range *see* Xiao Hinggan Ling
9 P13 **Lesser Slave Lake** ◎ Alberta, W Canada
99 E19 **Lessines** Hainaut, SW Belgium
103 R16 **les Stes-Maries-de-la-Mer** Bouches-du-Rhône, SE France
14 G15 **Lester B. Pearson** *var.* Toronto. ✈ (Toronto) Ontario, S Canada
29 U9 **Lester Prairie** Minnesota, N USA
93 L16 **Lestijärvi** Länsi-Soumi, W Finland
L'Estuaire *see* Estuaire
29 U9 **Le Sueur** Minnesota, N USA
108 B8 **Les Verrières** Neuchâtel, W Switzerland
115 L17 **Lésvos** *anc.* Lesbos. *island* E Greece
110 G12 **Leszno** *Ger.* Lissa. Wielkopolskie, C Poland
83 L20 **Letaba** Northern, NE South Africa
173 P17 **Le Tampon** SW Réunion
97 O21 **Letchworth** E England, UK
111 G25 **Letenye** Zala, SW Hungary
9 Q17 **Lethbridge** Alberta, SW Canada
55 S11 **Lethem** S Guyana
83 H18 **Letiahau** ≈ W Botswana
54 J18 **Leticia** Amazonas, S Colombia
171 S16 **Leti, Kepulauan** *island group* E Indonesia
83 I18 **Letlhakane** Central, C Botswana
83 H20 **Letlhakeng** Kweneng, SE Botswana
114 J8 **Letnitsa** Lovech, N Bulgaria
103 N1 **le Touquet-Paris-Plage** Pas-de-Calais, N France
166 L8 **Letpadan** Pegu, SW Burma (Myanmar)
166 K6 **Letpan** Arakan State, W Burma (Myanmar)
102 M2 **le Tréport** Seine-Maritime, N France
166 M12 **Letsôk-aw Kyun** *var.* Letsutan Island; *prev.* Domel Island. *island* Mergui Archipelago, S Burma (Myanmar)
Letsutan Island *see* Letsôk-aw Kyun
97 E14 **Letterkenny** *Ir.* Leitir Ceanainn. Donegal, NW Ireland
Lettland *see* Latvia
116 M6 **Letychiv** Khmel'nyts'ka Oblast', W Ukraine
Lëtzebuerg *see* Luxembourg
116 H14 **Leu** Dolj, SW Romania
Leucas *see* Lefkáda
103 P17 **Leucate** Aude, S France
103 P17 **Leucate, Étang de** ◎ S France
108 E10 **Leuk** Valais, SW Switzerland
108 E10 **Leukerbad** Valais, SW Switzerland
Leusden *see* Leusden-Centrum
98 K11 **Leusden-Centrum** *var.* Leusden. Utrecht, C Netherlands
Leutschau *see* Levoča
99 H18 **Leuven** *Fr.* Louvain, *Ger.* Löwen. Vlaams Brabant, C Belgium
99 I20 **Leuze** Namur, C Belgium
Leuze *see* Leuze-en-Hainaut
99 E19 **Leuze-en-Hainaut** *var.* Leuze. Hainaut, SW Belgium
Léva *see* Levice
36 L4 **Levan** Utah, W USA
93 E16 **Levanger** Nord-Trøndelag, C Norway
106 D10 **Levanto** Liguria, W Italy
107 H23 **Levanzo, Isola di** *island* Isole Egadi, S Italy
127 Q17 **Levashi** Respublika Dagestan, SW Russian Federation
24 M5 **Levelland** Texas, SW USA
39 P13 **Levelock** Alaska, USA
101 E16 **Leverkusen** Nordrhein-Westfalen, W Germany
111 J21 **Levice** *Ger.* Lewentz, *Hung.* Léva, Lewenz. Nitriansky Kraj, SW Slovakia
106 G6 **Levico Terme** Trentino-Alto Adige, N Italy
115 E20 **Levídi** Pelopónnisos, S Greece
103 P14 **le Vigan** Gard, S France
184 L13 **Levin** Manawatu-Wanganui, North Island, New Zealand
15 R10 **Lévis** *var.* Levis. Québec, SE Canada
Levis *see* Lévis
21 P6 **Levisa Fork** ≈ Kentucky/Virginia, S USA
115 L21 **Levítha** *island* Kykládes, Greece, Aegean Sea
18 L14 **Levittown** Long Island, New York, NE USA
18 J15 **Levittown** Pennsylvania, NE USA
Levkás *see* Lefkáda
Levkímmi *see* Lefkímmi
111 L19 **Levoča** *Ger.* Leutschau, *Hung.* Lőcse. Prešovský Kraj, E Slovakia
Lévrier, Baie du *see* Nouâdhibou, Dakhlet
103 N9 **Levroux** Indre, C France
114 J8 **Levski** Pleven, N Bulgaria
Levskigrad *see* Karlovo
126 L6 **Lev Tolstoy** Lipetskaya Oblast', W Russian Federation
187 X14 **Levuka** Ovalau, C Fiji
Levvajok *see* Leavvajohka
166 L6 **Lewe** Mandalay, C Burma (Myanmar)
Lewentz/Lewenz *see* Levice
97 O23 **Lewes** SE England, UK
21 Z4 **Lewes** Delaware, NE USA
29 Q12 **Lewis And Clark Lake** ⊠ Nebraska/South Dakota, N USA
18 G14 **Lewisburg** Pennsylvania, NE USA
20 J10 **Lewisburg** Tennessee, S USA
21 S6 **Lewisburg** West Virginia, NE USA
96 F6 **Lewis, Butt of** *headland* NW Scotland, UK
96 F7 **Lewis, Isle of** *island* NW Scotland, UK
35 U4 **Lewis, Mount** ▲ Nevada, W USA
185 H16 **Lewis Pass** *pass* South Island, New Zealand
33 P7 **Lewis Range** ⛰ Montana, NW USA
23 O3 **Lewis Smith Lake** ⊠ Alabama, S USA

◆ Country ● Country Capital ◇ Dependent Territory ○ Dependent Territory Capital ⬖ Administrative Regions ✈ International Airport ▲ Mountain ⛰ Mountain Range Volcano ≈ River ◎ Lake ⊠ Reservoir

32 M10 **Lewiston** Idaho, NW USA
19 P7 **Lewiston** Maine, NE USA
29 X10 **Lewiston** Minnesota, N USA
18 D9 **Lewiston** New York, NE USA
36 L1 **Lewiston** Utah, W USA
30 K13 **Lewiston** Illinois, N USA
33 T9 **Lewistown** Montana, NW USA
27 T14 **Lewisville** Arkansas, C USA
25 T6 **Lewisville** Texas, SW USA
25 T6 **Lewisville, Lake** ☒ Texas, SW USA
Le Woleu-Ntem see Woleu-Ntem
23 U3 **Lexington** Georgia, SE USA
20 M5 **Lexington** Kentucky, S USA
22 L4 **Lexington** Mississippi, S USA
27 S4 **Lexington** Missouri, C USA
29 N16 **Lexington** Nebraska, C USA
20 S9 **Lexington** North Carolina, SE USA
27 N11 **Lexington** Oklahoma, C USA
21 R12 **Lexington** South Carolina, SE USA
20 G9 **Lexington** Tennessee, S USA
25 T10 **Lexington** Texas, SW USA
21 T6 **Lexington** Virginia, NE USA
21 X5 **Lexington Park** Maryland, NE USA
Leyden see Leiden
102 J14 **Leyre** ♒ SW France
171 Q5 **Leyte** island C Philippines
171 Q6 **Leyte Gulf** gulf E Philippines
111 O16 **Leżajsk** Podkarpackie, SE Poland
Lezha see Lezhë
113 K18 **Lezhë** var. Lezha; prev. Lesh, Leshi. Lezhë, NW Albania
113 K18 **Lezhë** ◆ district NW Albania
103 O16 **Lézignan-Corbières** Aude, S France
126 J7 **L'gov** Kurskaya Oblast', W Russian Federation
159 P15 **Lhari** Xizang Zizhiqu, W China
159 N16 **Lhasa** var. La-sa, Lassa. Xizang Zizhiqu, W China
159 O15 **Lhasa He** ♒ W China
Lhaviyani Atoll see Faadhippolhu Atoll
158 K16 **Lhazê** var Quxar. Xizang Zizhiqu, W China
158 K17 **Lhazhong** Xizang Zizhiqu, W China
168 H7 **Lhoksukon** Sumatera, W Indonesia
159 Q15 **Lhorong** var. Zito. Xizang Zizhiqu, W China
105 W6 **L'Hospitalet de Llobregat** var. Hospitalet. Cataluña, NE Spain
153 R11 **Lhotse** ▲ China/Nepal
159 N17 **Lhozhag** var. Garbo. Xizang Zizhiqu, W China
159 O16 **Lhünzê** var. Xingba. Xizang Zizhiqu, W China
159 N15 **Lhünzhub** var. Ganqu. Xizang Zizhiqu, W China
167 N8 **Li** Lamphun, NW Thailand
115 L21 **Liádi** var Livádi. island Kykládes, Greece, Aegean Sea
Liancheng see Lianjiang
Liancheng see Qinglong
Liancheng see Guangnan
Lianfeng see Liangcheng
161 P12 **Liangcheng** var. Lianfeng. Fujian, SE China
160 K9 **Liangping** var. Liangshan. Sichuan, C China
Liangshan see Liangping
Liangzhou see Wuwei
161 O9 **Lianjiang** Fujian, SE China
161 R12 **Lianjiang** Fujian, SE China
160 L15 **Lianjiang** var Liancheng. Guangdong, S China
Lianjiang see Xingguo
161 O13 **Lianping** var. Yuanshan. Guangdong, S China
Lianshan see Huludao
Lian Xian see Lianzhou
160 M11 **Lianyuan** prev. Lantian. Hunan, S China
161 Q6 **Lianyungang** var. Xinpu. Jiangsu, E China
161 N13 **Lianzhou** var. Linxian; prev. Lian Xian. Guangdong, S China
Lianzhou see Hepu
Liao see Liaoning
161 P5 **Liaocheng** Shandong, E China
163 U13 **Liaodong Bandao** var. Liaotung Peninsula. peninsula NE China
163 T13 **Liaodong Wan** Eng. Gulf of Lantung. Gulf of Liaotung. gulf NE China
163 U11 **Liao He** ♒ NE China
163 U12 **Liaoning** var. Liao, Liaoning Sheng, Shengking, hist. Fengtien, Shenking. ◆ province NE China
Liaoning Sheng see Liaoning
Liaotung Peninsula see Liaodong Bandao
163 V12 **Liaoyang** var. Liao-yang. Liaoning, NE China
Liao-yang see Liaoyang
163 V11 **Liaoyuan** var. Dongliao, Shuang-liao, Jap. Chengchiatun. Jilin, NE China
163 U12 **Liaozhong** Liaoning, NE China
Liaqatabad see Piplán
10 M10 **Liard** ♒ W Canada
Liard see Fort Liard
10 L10 **Liard River** British Columbia, W Canada
149 O15 **Liāri** Baluchistān, SW Pakistan
Liatroim see Leitrim
189 S6 **Lib** var. Ellep. island Ralik Chain, C Marshall Islands
Liban see Lebanon
138 H6 **Liban, Jebel** Ar. Jabal al Gharbit, Jabal Lubnān, al Lubnān. Fr. Mont Liban. ▲▲ C Lebanon
Libau see Liepāja
33 N7 **Libby** Montana, NW USA
79 I16 **Libenge** Equateur, NW Dem. Rep. Congo
26 I7 **Liberal** Kansas, C USA
27 R7 **Liberal** Missouri, C USA
Liberalitas Julia see Évora
111 D15 **Liberec** Ger. Reichenberg. Liberecký Kraj, N Czech Republic
111 D15 **Liberecký Kraj** ◆ region N Czech Republic
42 K12 **Liberia** Guanacaste, NW Costa Rica

76 K17 **Liberia** off. Republic of Liberia. ◆ republic W Africa
Liberia, Republic of see Liberia
61 D16 **Libertad** Corrientes, NE Argentina
61 E20 **Libertad** San José, S Uruguay
54 I7 **Libertad** Barinas, NW Venezuela
54 K6 **Libertad** Cojedes, N Venezuela
62 G12 **Libertador** off. Región del Libertador General Bernardo O'Higgins. ◆ region C Chile
Libertador General Bernardo O'Higgins, Región del see Libertador
Libertador General San Martín see Ciudad de Libertador General San Martín
20 L6 **Liberty** Kentucky, S USA
22 J7 **Liberty** Mississippi, S USA
27 R4 **Liberty** Missouri, C USA
18 J12 **Liberty** New York, NE USA
21 T9 **Liberty** North Carolina, SE USA
Libian Desert see Libyan Desert
99 J23 **Libin** Luxembourg, SE Belgium
Lībīyah, Aş Şaḩrā' al see Libyan Desert
160 K13 **Libo** var. Yuping. Guizhou, S China
113 L23 **Libohovë** var. Libohova. Gjirokastër, S Albania
81 K18 **Liboi** North Eastern, E Kenya
102 K13 **Libourne** Gironde, SW France
99 K23 **Libramont** Luxembourg, SE Belgium
113 M20 **Librazhd** var. Librazhdi. Elbasan, E Albania
Librazhdi see Librazhd
79 C18 **Libreville** ● (Gabon) Estuaire, NW Gabon
75 P10 **Libya** off. Socialist People's Libyan Arab Jamahiriya, Ar. Al Jamāhīrīyah al 'Arabīyah al Lībīyah ash Sha'bīyah al Ishtirākīy; prev. Libyan Arab Republic. ◆ islamic state N Africa
Libyan Arab Republic see Libya
75 T11 **Libyan Desert** var. Libian Desert, Ar. Aş Şaḩrā' al Lībīyah. desert N Africa
75 T8 **Libyan Plateau** var. Aḑ Diffah. plateau Egypt/Libya
62 G12 **Licantén** Maule, C Chile
107 J25 **Licata** anc. Phintias. Sicilia, Italy, C Mediterranean Sea
137 P14 **Lice** Diyarbakır, SE Turkey
97 L19 **Lichfield** C England, UK
83 N14 **Lichinga** Niassa, N Mozambique
109 V3 **Lichtenau** Niederösterreich, N Austria
83 I21 **Lichtenburg** North-West, N South Africa
101 K18 **Lichtenfels** Bayern, SE Germany
98 O12 **Lichtenvoorde** Gelderland, E Netherlands
Lichtenwald see Sevnica
99 C17 **Lichtervelde** West-Vlaanderen, W Belgium
160 L9 **Lichuan** Hubei, C China
27 W7 **Licking** Missouri, C USA
20 M4 **Licking River** ♒ Kentucky, S USA
112 C11 **Lički Osik** Lika-Senj, C Croatia
Ličko-Senjska Županija see Lika-Senj
107 K19 **Licosa, Punta** headland S Italy
119 H16 **Lida** Rus. Lida. Hrodzyenskaya Voblasts', W Belarus
93 H17 **Liden** Västernorrland, C Sweden
29 R7 **Lidgerwood** North Dakota, N USA
Lidhorikíon see Lidoríki
95 K21 **Lidhult** Kronoberg, S Sweden
95 K17 **Lidingö** Stockholm, C Sweden
95 K17 **Lidköping** Västra Götaland, S Sweden
Lido di Iesolo see Lido di Jesolo
106 I8 **Lido di Jesolo** var. Lido di Iesolo. Veneto, NE Italy
107 H15 **Lido di Ostia** Lazio, C Italy
115 E18 **Lidoríki** prev. Lidhorikíon, Lidokhórikion. Stereá Ellás, C Greece
110 K9 **Lidzbark** Warmińsko-Mazurskie, NE Poland
110 L7 **Lidzbark Warmiński** Ger. Heilsberg. Olsztyn, N Poland
109 U3 **Liebenau** Oberösterreich, N Austria
181 P7 **Liebig, Mount** ▲ Northern Territory, C Australia
109 V8 **Lieboch** Steiermark, SE Austria
108 I8 **Liechtenstein** off. Principality of Liechtenstein. ◆ principality C Europe
Liechtenstein, Principality of see Liechtenstein
99 F18 **Liedekerke** Vlaams Brabant, C Belgium
99 K19 **Liège** Dut. Luik, Ger. Lüttich. Liège, E Belgium
99 K20 **Liège** Dut. Luik. ◆ province E Belgium
Liegnitz see Legnica
93 O16 **Lieksa** Pohjois-Karjala, E Finland
118 F10 **Lielvārde** Ger. Latvia/Lithuania
118 G9 **Lielvārde** Ogre, C Latvia
10 U13 **Liên Hương** var. Tuy Phong. Bình Thuận, S Vietnam
Liên Nghia see Đức Trong
109 P9 **Lienz** Tirol, W Austria
118 B10 **Liepāja** Ger. Libau. Liepāja, W Latvia
99 H17 **Lier** Fr. Lierre. Antwerpen, N Belgium
99 L21 **Lierneux** Liège, E Belgium
Lierre see Lier
101 D18 **Lieser** ♒ W Germany
109 U7 **Liesing** ♒ E Austria
108 E6 **Liestal** Basel-Land, N Switzerland
Lietuva see Lithuania

Lievenhof see Līvāni
103 O2 **Liévin** Pas-de-Calais, N France
14 M9 **Lièvre, Rivière du** ♒ Québec, SE Canada
109 T6 **Liezen** Steiermark, C Austria
97 E14 **Lifford** Ir. Leifear. Donegal, NW Ireland
187 Q16 **Lifou** island Îles Loyauté, E New Caledonia
193 Y15 **Lifuka** island Ha'apai Group, C Tonga
171 P4 **Ligao** Luzon, N Philippines
Liger see Loire
183 Q4 **Lighthouse Reef** reef E Belize
183 Q4 **Lightning Ridge** New South Wales, SE Australia
103 N9 **Lignières** Cher, C France
103 S5 **Ligny-en-Barrois** Meuse, NE France
83 P15 **Ligonha** ♒ NE Mozambique
31 P11 **Ligonier** Indiana, N USA
81 I25 **Ligunga** Ruvuma, S Tanzania
106 D9 **Ligure, Appennino** Eng. Ligurian Mountains. ▲▲ NW Italy
Ligure, Mar see Ligurian Sea
Ligurian Mountains see Ligure, Appennino
120 K6 **Ligurian Sea** Fr. Mer Ligurienne, It. Mar Ligure. sea N Mediterranean Sea
Ligurienne, Mer see Ligurian Sea
186 H5 **Lihir Group** island group NE Papua New Guinea
38 B8 **Lihir** North Eastern, E Kenya
38 B8 **Lihue** var. Lihue. Kaua'i, Hawai'i, USA North America
38 B8 **Lihue** var. Lihue. Kauai, Hawaii, USA
118 F5 **Lihula** Ger. Leal. Läänemaa, W Estonia
124 I2 **Liinakhamari** var. Linacmamari. Murmanskaya Oblast', NW Russian Federation
160 F11 **Lijiang** var. Dayan, Lijiang Naxizu Zizhixian. Yunnan, SW China
Lijiang Naxizu Zizhixian see Lijiang
112 C11 **Lika-Senj** off. Ličko-Senjska Županija. ◆ province W Croatia
153 P15 **Likasi** prev. Jadotville. Shaba, SE Dem. Rep. Congo
79 L16 **Likati** Orientale, N Dem. Rep. Congo
10 M15 **Likely** British Columbia, SW Canada
153 Y11 **Likhapāni** Assam, NE India
124 J16 **Likhoslavl'** Tverskaya Oblast', W Russian Federation
189 U5 **Likiep Atoll** atoll Ratak Chain, C Marshall Islands
95 D18 **Liknes** Vest-Agder, S Norway
79 H18 **Likouala** ♒ N Congo
79 H18 **Likouala aux Herbes** ♒ E Congo
190 B16 **Liku** E Niue
Likupang, Selat see Bangka, Selat
27 Y8 **Lilbourn** Missouri, C USA
103 X14 **L'Île-Rousse** Corse, France, C Mediterranean Sea
109 W5 **Lilienfeld** Niederösterreich, NE Austria
161 N11 **Lili** Oman
95 J18 **Lilla Edet** Älvsborg, S Sweden
103 P1 **Lille** var. l'Isle, Dut. Rijssel, Flem. Ryssel, prev. Lisle; anc. Insula. Nord, N France
95 G24 **Lillebælt** var. Lille Bælt, Eng. Little Belt. strait S Denmark
Lille Bælt see Lillebælt
102 L3 **Lillebonne** Seine-Maritime, N France
94 H12 **Lillehammer** Oppland, S Norway
103 O1 **Lillers** Pas-de-Calais, N France
95 F18 **Lillesand** Aust-Agder, S Norway
95 I15 **Lillestrøm** Akershus, S Norway
93 F18 **Lillhärdal** Jämtland, C Sweden
21 U10 **Lillington** North Carolina, SE USA
105 O9 **Lillo** Castilla-La Mancha, C Spain
10 M16 **Lillooet** British Columbia, SW Canada
83 M14 **Lilongwe** ● (Malawi) Central, W Malawi
83 M14 **Lilongwe** ✈ Central, W Malawi
83 M14 **Lilongwe** ♒ W Malawi
171 P7 **Liloy** Mindanao, S Philippines
Lilybaeum see Marsala
182 J7 **Lilydale** South Australia
183 P16 **Lilydale** Tasmania, SE Australia
113 J14 **Lim** ♒ SE Europe
57 D15 **Lima** ● (Peru) Lima, W Peru
94 K13 **Lima** Dalarna, C Sweden
31 Q12 **Lima** Ohio, N USA
57 D14 **Lima** ◆ department W Peru
Lima see Jorge Chávez International
111 L17 **Limanowa** Małopolskie, S Poland
104 G5 **Lima, Rio** Sp. Limia. ♒ Portugal/Spain see also Limia
Lima, Rio Limia
95 J19 **Limandsberg** Örebro, S Sweden
163 S10 **Lindong** var. Bairin Zuoqi. Nei Mongol Zizhiqu, N China
115 O23 **Líndos** var. Líndhos. Ródos, Dodekánisa, Greece, Aegean Sea
14 J14 **Lindsay** Ontario, SE Canada
35 R11 **Lindsay** California, W USA
33 X3 **Lindsay** Montana, NW USA
27 N11 **Lindsay** Oklahoma, C USA
95 N21 **Lindsdal** Kalmar, S Sweden
Lindum/Lindum Colonia see Lincoln
191 W3 **Line Islands** island group K Kiribati
95 J19 **Linnévo** see Linova

99 L16 **Limburg** ◆ province SE Netherlands
101 F17 **Limburg an der Lahn** Hessen, W Germany
94 K13 **Limedsforsen** Dalarna, C Sweden
60 L9 **Limeira** São Paulo, S Brazil
97 C19 **Limerick** Ir. Luimneach, SW Ireland
97 C20 **Limerick** Ir. Luimneach. ◆ county SW Ireland
19 S2 **Limestone** Maine, NE USA
25 U9 **Limestone, Lake** ☒ Texas, SW USA
39 P12 **Lime Village** Alaska, USA
95 F20 **Limfjorden** fjord N Denmark
95 J23 **Limhamn** Skåne, S Sweden
104 H5 **Limia** Port. Rio Lima. ♒ Portugal/Spain see also Lima, Rio
Limia Lima, Rio
93 L14 **Liminka** Oulu, C Finland
115 J18 **Límni** Vathéos see Sámos
115 G17 **Límni** Évvoia, C Greece
33 Z15 **Limni Distos** see Dýstos, Límni
18 G15 **Linglestown** Pennsylvania, NE USA
Limni Doïranis see Doïrani, Límni
Limni Kerkinitis see Kerkíni, Límni
115 J15 **Límnos** anc. Lemnos. island E Greece
102 M11 **Limoges** anc. Augustoritum Lemovicensium, Lemovices. Haute-Vienne, C France
43 O13 **Limón** var. Puerto Limón. Limón, E Costa Rica
42 K4 **Limón** Colón, NE Honduras
37 U5 **Limon** Colorado, C USA
43 N13 **Limón** off. Provincia de Limón. ◆ province E Costa Rica
Limón, Provincia de see Limón
Limonum see Poitiers
103 N15 **Limousin** ◆ region C France
103 N16 **Limoux** Aude, S France
83 J20 **Limpopo** off. Limpopo Province; prev. Northern, Northern Transvaal. ◆ province NE South Africa
83 L19 **Limpopo** var. Crocodile. ♒ S Africa
Limpopo Province see Limpopo
160 K17 **Limu Ling** ▲▲ S China
113 M20 **Lin** var. Lini. Elbasan, E Albania
Linacmamari see Liinakhamari
Liinakhamari Liinakhamari
62 G13 **Linares** Maule, C Chile
54 C13 **Linares** Nariño, SW Colombia
41 O9 **Linares** Nuevo León, NE Mexico
105 N12 **Linares** Andalucía, S Spain
107 G15 **Linaro, Capo** headland C Italy
106 D8 **Linate** ✈ (Milano) Lombardia, N Italy
167 T8 **Lin Camh** prev. Đức Tho. Ha Tinh, N Vietnam
160 F13 **Lincang** Yunnan, SW China
Lincheng see Lingao
161 P11 **Linchuan** prev. Linchuan. Jiangxi, S China
61 B20 **Lincoln** Buenos Aires, E Argentina
185 H19 **Lincoln** Canterbury, South Island, New Zealand
97 N18 **Lincoln** anc. Lindum, Lindum Colonia. E England, UK
35 O5 **Lincoln** California, W USA
30 L13 **Lincoln** Illinois, N USA
26 M4 **Lincoln** Kansas, C USA
19 S5 **Lincoln** Maine, NE USA
27 T5 **Lincoln** Missouri, C USA
29 R16 **Lincoln** state capital Nebraska, C USA
32 F11 **Lincoln City** Oregon, NW USA
167 X10 **Lincoln Island** island E Paracel Islands
197 Q11 **Lincoln Sea** sea Arctic Ocean
97 N18 **Lincolnshire** cultural region E England, UK
21 R10 **Lincolnton** North Carolina, SE USA
25 V7 **Lindale** Texas, SW USA
101 I25 **Lindau** var. Lindau am Bodensee. Bayern, S Germany
Lindau am Bodensee see Lindau
83 K16 **Lions Den** Mashonaland West, N Zimbabwe
14 F13 **Lion's Head** Ontario, S Canada
123 P9 **Linden** ● NE Russian Federation
55 T9 **Linden** E Guyana
23 O6 **Linden** Alabama, S USA
20 H9 **Linden** Tennessee, S USA
25 X6 **Linden** Texas, SW USA
18 J16 **Lindenwold** New Jersey, NE USA
95 M15 **Lindesberg** Örebro, S Sweden
95 D18 **Lindesnes** headland S Norway
81 K24 **Lindi** Lindi, SE Tanzania
81 J24 **Lindi** ◆ region SE Tanzania
79 N17 **Lindi** ♒ NE Dem. Rep. Congo
163 O9 **Lindian** Heilongjiang, N China
185 E21 **Lindis Pass** pass South Island, New Zealand
83 I22 **Lindley** Free State, C South Africa
95 J19 **Lindome** Västra Götaland, S Sweden

155 F18 **Linganamakki Reservoir** ☒ SW India
160 L17 **Lingao** var. Lincheng. Hainan, S China
171 N3 **Lingayen** Luzon, N Philippines
160 M6 **Lingbao** var. Guolüezhen. Henan, C China
94 N12 **Lingbo** Gävleborg, C Sweden
Lingcheng see Beiliu
Lingen see Bandar-e Langeh
100 E12 **Lingen** var. Lingen an der Ems. Niedersachsen, NW Germany
Lingen an der Ems see Lingen
168 M11 **Lingga, Kepulauan** island group W Indonesia
168 L11 **Lingga, Pulau** island Kepulauan Lingga, W Indonesia
14 J14 **Lingham Lake** ☒ Ontario, SE Canada
94 M13 **Linghed** Dalarna, C Sweden
Lingheng see Lingshan
18 G15 **Lingle** Wyoming, C USA
160 L15 **Lingshan** var Lingheng. Guangxi Zhuangzu Zizhiqu, S China
160 L17 **Lingshui** var. Lingshui Lizu Zizhixian. Hainan, S China
Lingshui Lizu Zizhixian see Lingshui
155 G16 **Lingsugūr** Karnātaka, C India
159 W8 **Lingwu** Ningxia, N China
Lingxi see Yongshun
Lingxi see Cangnan
Lingxian/Ling Xian see Yanling
163 S15 **Lingyuan** Liaoning, NE China
163 U14 **Linhai** Heilongjiang, NE China
161 S10 **Linhai** var. Taizhou. Zhejiang, SE China
59 O20 **Linhares** Espírito Santo, SE Brazil
162 M13 **Linhe** Nei Mongol Zizhiqu, N China
Lini see Lin
94 K13 **Liniks, Chiyā-ē** ▲ N Iraq
95 M18 **Linköping** Östergötland, S Sweden
163 Y8 **Linkou** Heilongjiang, NE China
118 F11 **Linkuva** Šiauliai, N Lithuania
27 S16 **Linn** Missouri, C USA
27 T2 **Linn** Texas, SW USA
96 H10 **Linnhe, Loch** inlet W Scotland, UK
119 G19 **Linova** Rus. Linëvo. Brestskaya Voblasts', SW Belarus
161 O5 **Linqing** Shandong, E China
161 N6 **Linruzhen** Henan, C China
60 L9 **Lins** São Paulo, S Brazil
93 F17 **Linsell** Jämtland, C Sweden
160 J9 **Linshui** Sichuan, C China
44 K12 **Linstead** C Jamaica
159 U11 **Lintan** Gansu, N China
159 V11 **Lintao** Gansu, C China
15 S12 **Lintère** ♒ Québec, SE Canada
108 H8 **Linth** ♒ NW Switzerland
108 H8 **Linthal** Glarus, NE Switzerland
31 N15 **Linton** Indiana, N USA
29 N6 **Linton** North Dakota, N USA
163 R11 **Linxi** Nei Mongol Zizhiqu, N China
159 U11 **Linxia** var. Linxia Huizu Zizhizhou. Gansu, C China
Linxia Huizu Zizhizhou see Linxia
Linxian see Lianzhou
161 P4 **Linyi** Shandong, E China
160 M6 **Linyi** Shanxi, C China
109 T4 **Linz** anc. Lentia. Oberösterreich, N Austria
159 S8 **Linze** var. Shahepu. Gansu, N China
44 J13 **Lionel Town** C Jamaica
103 Q16 **Lion, Golfe du** Eng. Gulf of Lion, Gulf of Lions; anc. Sinus Gallicus. gulf S France
Lion, Gulf of/Lions, Gulf of see Lion, Golfe du

116 F11 **Lipova** Hung. Lippa. Arad, W Romania
Lipovets see Lypovets'
Lippa see Lipova
101 E14 **Lippe** ♒ W Germany
Lippehne see Lipiany
101 G14 **Lippstadt** Nordrhein-Westfalen, W Germany
25 P1 **Lipscomb** Texas, SW USA
Lipsia/Lipsk see Leipzig
Liptau-Sankt-Nikolaus/ Liptószentmiklós see Liptovský Mikuláš
111 K19 **Liptovský Mikuláš** Ger. Liptau-Sankt-Nikolaus, Hung. Liptószentmiklós. Žilinský Kraj, N Slovakia
183 O13 **Liptrap, Cape** headland Victoria, SE Australia
160 L13 **Lipu** Guangxi Zhuangzu Zizhiqu, S China
141 X12 **Liqbi** S Oman
81 G17 **Lira** N Uganda
57 F15 **Lircay** Huancavelica, C Peru
107 K17 **Liri** ♒ C Italy
144 M8 **Lisakovsk** Kustanay, NW Kazakhstan
79 K17 **Lisala** Equateur, N Dem. Rep. Congo
104 F11 **Lisboa** Eng. Lisbon; Cz. anc. Felicitas Julia, Olisipo. ● (Portugal) Lisboa, W Portugal
104 F10 **Lisboa** Eng. Lisbon. ◆ district C Portugal
19 N7 **Lisbon** New Hampshire, NE USA
29 Q6 **Lisbon** North Dakota, N USA
19 Q8 **Lisbon Falls** Maine, NE USA
97 G15 **Lisburn** Ir. Lios na gCearrbhach. E Northern Ireland, UK
38 L6 **Lisburne, Cape** headland Alaska, USA
97 B19 **Liscannor Bay** Ir. Bá Lios Ceannúir. inlet W Ireland
113 Q18 **Lisec** ▲ E FYR Macedonia
160 F13 **Lishe Jiang** ♒ SW China
160 M4 **Lishi** Shanxi, C China
163 V10 **Lishu** Jilin, NE China
161 R10 **Lishui** Zhejiang, SE China
192 L5 **Lisianski Island** island Hawaiian Islands, Hawaii, USA
102 L4 **Lisieux** anc. Noviomagus. Calvados, N France
126 L8 **Liski** prev. Georgiu-Dezh. Voronezhskaya Oblast', W Russian Federation
182 M12 **Lismore** Victoria, SE Australia
97 D20 **Lismore** Ir. Lios Mór. S Ireland
Lissa see Vis
Lissa see Leszno
98 H11 **Lisse** Zuid-Holland, W Netherlands
114 K13 **Líssos** var. Filiouri. ♒ NE Greece
95 D18 **Lista** peninsula S Norway
95 D18 **Listafjorden** fjord S Norway
195 R13 **Lister, Mount** ▲ Antarctica
126 M8 **Listopadovka** Voronezhskaya Oblast', W Russian Federation
11 T15 **Listowel** Ontario, S Canada
97 B20 **Listowel** Ir. Lios Tuathail. Kerry, SW Ireland
160 L14 **Litang** Guangxi Zhuangzu Zizhiqu, S China
160 F9 **Litang** var. Gaocheng. Sichuan, C China
160 F10 **Litang Qu** ♒ C China
55 X12 **Litani, var. Itany. ♒ French Guiana/Surinam
138 G8 **Litani, Nahr el** var. Nahr el Litant. ♒ C Lebanon
Litant, Nahr al see Litani, Nahr el
Litauen see Lithuania
30 K14 **Litchfield** Illinois, N USA
29 U8 **Litchfield** Minnesota, N USA
36 K13 **Litchfield Park** Arizona, SW USA
183 S8 **Lithgow** New South Wales, SE Australia
115 I26 **Líthino, Ákrotírio** headland Kríti, Greece, E Mediterranean Sea
118 D12 **Lithuania** off. Republic of Lithuania, Ger. Litauen, Lith. Lietuva, Pol. Litwa, Rus. Litva; prev. Lithuanian SSR, Rus. Litovskaya SSR. ◆ republic NE Europe
Lithuanian SSR see Lithuania
Lithuania, Republic of see Lithuania
109 U11 **Litija** Ger. Littai. C Slovenia
18 H15 **Lititz** Pennsylvania, NE USA
115 F15 **Litóchoro** var. Litohoro, Litókhoron. Kentrikí Makedonía, N Greece
Litohoro/Litókhoron see Litóchoro
111 C15 **Litoměřice** Ústecký Kraj, NW Czech Republic
111 F17 **Litomyšl** Pardubický Kraj, C Czech Republic
111 F17 **Litovel** Ger. Littau. Olomoucký Kraj, E Czech Republic
123 S13 **Litovko** Khabarovskiy Kray, SE Russian Federation
Litovskaya SSR see Lithuania
Littai see Litija
Littau see Litovel
44 G1 **Little Abaco** var. Abaco Island. island N Bahamas
111 I21 **Little Alföld** Ger. Kleines Ungarisches Tiefland, Hung. Kisalföld, Slvk. Podunajská Rovina. plain Hungary/Slovakia
151 Q20 **Little Andaman** island Andaman Islands, India, E Indian Ocean
26 M5 **Little Arkansas River** ♒ Kansas, C USA
184 L4 **Little Barrier Island** island N New Zealand
Little Belt see Lillebælt
38 M11 **Little Black River** ♒ Alaska, USA

Little Blue River – Lörrach

27 O2 **Little Blue River** ≈ Kansas/Nebraska, C USA
44 D8 **Little Cayman** *island* E Cayman Islands
9 X11 **Little Churchill** ≈ Manitoba, C Canada
166 J10 **Little Coco Island** *island* SW Burma (Myanmar)
36 L10 **Little Colorado River** ≈ Arizona, SW USA
14 E11 **Little Current** Manitoulin Island, Ontario, S Canada
12 E11 **Little Current** ≈ Ontario, S Canada
38 L8 **Little Diomede Island** *island* Alaska, USA
44 I4 **Little Exuma** *island* C Bahamas
29 U7 **Little Falls** Minnesota, N USA
18 J10 **Little Falls** New York, NE USA
24 M5 **Littlefield** Texas, SW USA
29 V3 **Littlefork** Minnesota, N USA
29 V3 **Little Fork River** ≈ Minnesota, N USA
9 N16 **Little Fort** British Columbia, SW Canada
9 Y14 **Little Grand Rapids** Manitoba, C Canada
97 N23 **Littlehampton** SE England, UK
35 T2 **Little Humboldt River** ≈ Nevada, W USA
44 K6 **Little Inagua** *var.* Inagua Islands. *island* S Bahamas
21 Q4 **Little Kanawha River** ≈ West Virginia, NE USA
83 F25 **Little Karoo** *plateau* S South Africa
39 O16 **Little Koniuji Island** *island* Shumagin Islands, Alaska, USA
44 H12 **Little London** W Jamaica
13 R10 **Little Mecatina** *Fr.* Rivière du Petit Mécatina. ≈ Newfoundland and Labrador/Québec, E Canada
96 F8 **Little Minch, The** *strait* NW Scotland, UK
27 T13 **Little Missouri River** ≈ Arkansas, USA
28 J7 **Little Missouri River** ≈ NW USA
28 J3 **Little Muddy River** ≈ North Dakota, N USA
151 Q22 **Little Nicobar** *island* Nicobar Islands, India, NE Indian Ocean
27 R6 **Little Osage River** ≈ Missouri, C USA
97 P20 **Little Ouse** ≈ E England, UK
149 V2 **Little Pamir** *Pash.* Pāmīr-e Khord, *Rus.* Malyy Pamir. ▲▲ Afghanistan/Tajikistan
21 U12 **Little Pee Dee River** ≈ North Carolina/South Carolina, SE USA
27 V10 **Little Red River** ≈ Arkansas, C USA
Little Rhody *see* Rhode Island
185 I19 **Little River** Canterbury, South Island, New Zealand
21 U12 **Little River** South Carolina, SE USA
27 Y9 **Little River** ≈ Arkansas/Missouri, C USA
27 R13 **Little River** ≈ Arkansas/Oklahoma, USA
23 T7 **Little River** ≈ Georgia, SE USA
22 H6 **Little River** ≈ Louisiana, S USA
25 T10 **Little River** ≈ Texas, SW USA
27 V12 **Little Rock** *state capital* Arkansas, C USA
31 N8 **Little Sable Point** *headland* Michigan, N USA
103 U11 **Little Saint Bernard Pass** *Fr.* Col du Petit St-Bernard, *It.* Colle del Piccolo San Bernardo. *pass* France/Italy
36 K7 **Little Salt Lake** ◎ Utah, W USA
180 K8 **Little Sandy Desert** *desert* Western Australia
29 S13 **Little Sioux River** ≈ Iowa, C USA
38 E17 **Little Sitkin Island** *island* Aleutian Islands, Alaska, USA
9 O13 **Little Smoky** Alberta, W Canada
9 O14 **Little Smoky** ≈ Alberta, W Canada
37 P3 **Little Snake River** ≈ Colorado, C USA
64 A12 **Little Sound** *bay* Bermuda, NW Atlantic Ocean
37 T4 **Littleton** Colorado, C USA
19 N7 **Littleton** New Hampshire, NE USA
18 D11 **Little Valley** New York, NE USA
30 M15 **Little Wabash River** ≈ Illinois, N USA
14 D10 **Little White River** ≈ Ontario, S Canada
28 M12 **Little White River** ≈ South Dakota, N USA
25 R5 **Little Wichita River** ≈ Texas, SW USA
142 I4 **Little Zab** *Ar.* Nahraz Zāb aş Şaghīr, *Kurd.* Zē-i Kōya, *Per.* Rūdkhāneh-ye Zāb-e Kūchek. ≈ Iran/Iraq
79 D15 **Littoral** ◈ *province* W Cameroon
Littoria *see* Latina
Litva/Litwa *see* Lithuania
111 B15 **Litvínov** Ústecký Kraj, NW Czech Republic
116 M6 **Lityn** Vinnyts'ka Oblast', C Ukraine
Liu-chou/Liuchow *see* Liuzhou
163 W11 **Liuhe** Jilin, NE China
83 Q15 **Liúpo** Nampula, NE Mozambique
83 G14 **Liuwa Plain** *plain* W Zambia
160 L13 **Liuzhou** *var.* Liu-chou, Liuchow. Guangxi Zhuangzu Zizhiqu, S China
116 H8 **Livada** *Hung.* Sárköz. Satu Mare, NW Romania
115 J20 **Liváda, Ákrotírio** *headland* Tínos, Kykládes, Greece, Aegean Sea
115 F18 **Livádeia** *prev.* Leivádia. Stereá Ellás, C Greece
Livádi *see* Liádi
Livanátai *see* Livanátes
115 G18 **Livanátes** *prev.* Livanátai. Stereá Ellás, C Greece
118 I10 **Līvāni** *Ger.* Lievenhof. Preiļi, SE Latvia
65 E25 **Lively Island** *island* SE Falkland Islands
65 D25 **Lively Sound** *sound* SE Falkland Islands
39 R8 **Livengood** Alaska, USA
106 I7 **Livenza** ≈ NE Italy
35 O6 **Live Oak** California, W USA
23 U9 **Live Oak** Florida, SE USA
35 O9 **Livermore** California, W USA
20 I6 **Livermore** Kentucky, S USA
19 Q7 **Livermore Falls** Maine, NE USA
24 J10 **Livermore, Mount** ▲ Texas, SW USA
13 P16 **Liverpool** Nova Scotia, SE Canada
97 K17 **Liverpool** NW England, UK
183 S7 **Liverpool Range** ▲▲ New South Wales, SE Australia
42 F4 **Lívingston** Izabal, E Guatemala
96 J12 **Livingston** C Scotland, UK
23 N5 **Livingston** Alabama, S USA
35 P9 **Livingston** California, W USA
22 J8 **Livingston** Louisiana, S USA
33 S11 **Livingston** Montana, NW USA
20 L8 **Livingston** Tennessee, S USA
25 W9 **Livingston** Texas, SW USA
83 I16 **Livingstone** *var.* Maramba. Southern, S Zambia
185 B22 **Livingstone Mountains** ▲▲ South Island, New Zealand
80 K13 **Livingstone Mountains** ▲▲ S Tanzania
82 N12 **Livingstonia** Northern, N Malawi
194 G4 **Livingston Island** *island* Antarctica
25 W9 **Livingston, Lake** ⊠ Texas, SW USA
112 F13 **Livno** ◈ Federicija Bosna I Hercegovina, SW Bosnia and Herzegovina
126 K7 **Livny** Orlovskaya Oblast', W Russian Federation
93 M14 **Livojoki** ≈ C Finland
31 R10 **Livonia** Michigan, N USA
106 E11 **Livorno** *Eng.* Leghorn. Toscana, C Italy
Livramento *see* Santana do Livramento
141 U8 **Līwā** *var.* Al Liwā'. *oasis region* S United Arab Emirates
81 I24 **Liwale** Lindi, SE Tanzania
159 W9 **Liwangbu** Ningxia, N China
83 N15 **Liwonde** Southern, S Malawi
159 V11 **Lixian** Gansu, C China
160 H8 **Lixian** *var.* Li Xian, Zagunao. Sichuan, C China
Li Xian *see* Lixian
Li Xian *see* Lixian
Lixian Jiang *see* Black River
115 B18 **Lixoúri** *prev.* Lixoúrion. Kefallinía, Iónia Nisiá, Greece, C Mediterranean Sea
Lixoúrion *see* Lixoúri
Lixus *see* Larache
33 U15 **Lizard Head Peak** ▲ Wyoming, C USA
97 H25 **Lizard Point** *headland* SW England, UK
Lizarra *see* Estella
112 L12 **Ljig** Serbia, C Serbia
Ljouwert *see* Leeuwarden
Ljubelj *see* Loibl Pass
109 U11 **Ljubljana** *Ger.* Laibach, *It.* Lubiana; *anc.* Aemona, Emona. ● (Slovenia) C Slovenia
109 T11 **Ljubljana** ✈ C Slovenia
113 N17 **Ljuboten** ▲ S Serbia
95 P19 **Ljugarn** Gotland, SE Sweden
84 G7 **Ljungan** ≈ N Sweden
93 F17 **Ljungan** ≈ C Sweden
95 K21 **Ljungby** Kronoberg, S Sweden
95 M17 **Ljungsbro** Östergötland, S Sweden
95 I18 **Ljungskile** Västra Götaland, S Sweden
94 M11 **Ljusdal** Gävleborg, C Sweden
94 M11 **Ljusnan** ≈ C Sweden
94 N12 **Ljusne** Gävleborg, C Sweden
95 P15 **Ljusterö** Stockholm, C Sweden
109 X9 **Ljutomer** *Ger.* Luttenberg. NE Slovenia
63 G15 **Llaima, Volcán** ⛰ S Chile
105 X4 **Llançà** *var.* Llansá. Cataluña, NE Spain
97 J21 **Llandovery** C Wales, UK
97 J20 **Llandrindod Wells** E Wales, UK
97 J18 **Llandudno** N Wales, UK
97 I21 **Llanelli** *prev.* Llanelly. SW Wales, UK
Llanelly *see* Llanelli
104 M2 **Llanes** Asturias, N Spain
97 K19 **Llangollen** NE Wales, UK
25 R10 **Llano** Texas, SW USA
25 Q10 **Llano River** ≈ Texas, SW USA
54 I9 **Llanos** *physical region* Colombia/Venezuela
63 G16 **Llanquihue, Lago** ◎ S Chile
Llansá *see* Llançà
105 U5 **Lleida** *Cast.* Lérida; *anc.* Ilerda. Cataluña, NE Spain
105 U5 **Lérida** ◈ *province* Cataluña, NE Spain
104 K12 **Llerena** Extremadura, W Spain
105 S9 **Lliria** País Valenciano, E Spain
105 W4 **Llivia** Cataluña, NE Spain
105 O3 **Llodio** País Vasco, N Spain
105 X5 **Lloret de Mar** Cataluña, NE Spain
Llorri *see* Tossal de l'Orri
10 L11 **Lloyd George, Mount** ▲ British Columbia, W Canada
9 R14 **Lloydminster** Alberta/Saskatchewan, SW Canada
105 X9 **Llucmajor** Mallorca, Spain, W Mediterranean Sea
36 L6 **Loa** Utah, W USA
169 S8 **Loagan Bunut** ◎ East Malaysia
38 G12 **Loa, Mauna** ▲ Hawaii, USA
Loanda *see* Luanda
79 J22 **Loange** ≈ S Dem. Rep. Congo
79 E21 **Loango** Le Kouilou, S Congo
106 B10 **Loano** Liguria, NW Italy
62 H4 **Loa, Río** ≈ N Chile
83 I20 **Lobatse** *var.* Lobatsi. Kgatleng, SE Botswana
Lobatsi *see* Lobatse
101 Q15 **Löbau** Sachsen, E Germany
79 H16 **Lobaye** ◈ *prefecture* SW Central African Republic
79 I16 **Lobaye** ≈ SW Central African Republic
99 G21 **Lobbes** Hainaut, S Belgium
61 D23 **Lobería** Buenos Aires, E Argentina
110 F8 **Łobez** *Ger.* Labes. Zacodniopomorskie, NW Poland
82 A13 **Lobito** Benguela, W Angola
Lobkovichi *see* Labkovichy
Lob Nor *see* Lop Nur
171 V13 **Lobo** Papua, E Indonesia
104 J11 **Lobón** Extremadura, W Spain
61 D20 **Lobos** Buenos Aires, E Argentina
40 E4 **Lobos, Cabo** *headland* NW Mexico
40 F6 **Lobos, Isla** *island* NW Mexico
Lobositz *see* Lovosice
Lobsens *see* Łobżenica
Loburi *see* Lop Buri
110 H9 **Łobżenica** *Ger.* Lobsens. Wielkopolskie, C Poland
108 G11 **Locarno** *Ger.* Luggarus. Ticino, S Switzerland
96 E9 **Lochboisdale** NW Scotland, UK
98 N11 **Lochem** Gelderland, E Netherlands
102 M8 **Loches** Indre-et-Loire, C France
Loch Garman *see* Wexford
96 H12 **Lochgilphead** W Scotland, UK
96 H7 **Lochinver** N Scotland, UK
96 F8 **Lochmaddy** NW Scotland, UK
96 J10 **Lochnagar** ▲ C Scotland, UK
99 E17 **Lochristi** Oost-Vlaanderen, NW Belgium
96 H9 **Lochy, Loch** ◎ N Scotland, UK
182 G8 **Lock** South Australia
97 J14 **Lockerbie** S Scotland, UK
27 S13 **Lockesburg** Arkansas, C USA
183 P10 **Lockhart** New South Wales, SE Australia
25 S11 **Lockhart** Texas, SW USA
18 F13 **Lock Haven** Pennsylvania, NE USA
25 N4 **Lockney** Texas, SW USA
100 O12 **Löcknitz** ≈ NE Germany
18 E9 **Lockport** New York, NE USA
167 T13 **Lôc Ninh** Sông Be, S Vietnam
107 N23 **Locri** Calabria, SW Italy
Locse *see* Levoča
27 T2 **Locust Creek** ≈ Missouri, C USA
23 P3 **Locust Fork** ≈ Alabama, S USA
27 Q9 **Locust Grove** Oklahoma, C USA
94 E11 **Lodalskåpa** ▲ S Norway
183 N10 **Loddon River** ≈ Victoria, SE Australia
Lodensee *see* Klooga
103 P15 **Lodève** *anc.* Luteva. Hérault, S France
124 I12 **Lodeynoye Pole** Leningradskaya Oblast', NW Russian Federation
33 V11 **Lodge Grass** Montana, NW USA
28 J15 **Lodgepole Creek** ≈ Nebraska/Wyoming, C USA
149 T11 **Lodhrān** Punjab, E Pakistan
106 D8 **Lodi** Lombardia, NW Italy
35 O8 **Lodi** California, W USA
31 T12 **Lodi** Ohio, N USA
92 H10 **Lødingen** Nordland, C Norway
79 L20 **Lodja** Kasai Oriental, C Dem. Rep. Congo
37 O3 **Lodore, Canyon of** *canyon* Colorado, C USA
105 Q4 **Lodosa** Navarra, N Spain
81 H16 **Lodwar** Rift Valley, NW Kenya
110 K13 **Łódź** *Rus.* Lodz. Łódzkie, C Poland
110 E12 **Łódzkie** ◈ *province* C Poland
167 P8 **Loei** *var.* Loey, Muang Loei. Loei, C Thailand
98 I11 **Loenen** Utrecht, C Netherlands
167 R9 **Loeng Nok Tha** Yasothon, E Thailand
83 F24 **Loeriesfontein** Northern Cape, W South Africa
Loewoek *see* Luwuk
Loey *see* Loei
76 J16 **Lofa** ≈ N Liberia
109 P6 **Lofer** Salzburg, C Austria
92 F11 **Lofoten** *var.* Lofoten Islands. *island group* C Norway
Lofoten Islands *see* Lofoten
95 N18 **Loftahammar** Kalmar, S Sweden
127 O10 **Log** Volgogradskaya Oblast', SW Russian Federation
77 S12 **Loga** Dosso, SW Niger
29 S14 **Logan** Iowa, C USA
26 K3 **Logan** Kansas, C USA
31 T14 **Logan** Ohio, N USA
36 L1 **Logan** Utah, W USA
21 P6 **Logan** West Virginia, NE USA
35 Y10 **Logandale** Nevada, W USA
19 O11 **Logan International** ✈ (Boston) Massachusetts, NE USA
9 N15 **Logan Lake** British Columbia, SW Canada
23 Q4 **Logan Martin Lake** ⊠ Alabama, S USA
10 G8 **Logan, Mount** ▲ Yukon Territory, W Canada
32 I7 **Logan, Mount** ▲ Washington, NW USA
33 P7 **Logan Pass** *pass* Montana, NW USA
31 O12 **Logansport** Indiana, N USA
22 F6 **Logansport** Louisiana, S USA
Logar *see* Lowgar
67 R11 **Loge** ≈ NW Angola
Logishin *see* Lahishyn
Log na Coille *see* Lugnaquillia Mountain
78 G11 **Logone** *var.* Lagone. ≈ Cameroon/Chad
78 G13 **Logone-Occidental** *off.* Préfecture du Logone-Occidental. ◈ *prefecture* SW Chad
78 H13 **Logone Occidental** ≈ SW Chad
Logone-Occidental, Préfecture du *see* Logone-Occidental
78 G13 **Logone-Oriental** *off.* Préfecture du Logone-Oriental. ◈ *prefecture* SW Chad
78 H13 **Logone Oriental** ≈ SW Chad
Logone Oriental *see* Pendé
Logone-Oriental, Préfecture du *see* Logone-Oriental
L'Ogooué-Ivindo *see* Ogooué-Ivindo
L'Ogooué-Lolo *see* Ogooué-Lolo
L'Ogooué-Maritime *see* Ogooué-Maritime
Logoysk *see* Lahoysk
105 P4 **Logroño** *anc.* Vareia, *Lat.* Juliobriga. La Rioja, N Spain
104 L10 **Logrosán** Extremadura, W Spain
95 G20 **Løgstør** Nordjylland, N Denmark
95 H22 **Løgten** Århus, C Denmark
95 F24 **Løgumkloster** Sønderjylland, SW Denmark
Lögurinn *see* Lagarfljót
153 P15 **Lohārdaga** Jhārkhand, N India
152 H10 **Lohāru** Haryāna, N India
101 D15 **Lohausen** ✈ (Düsseldorf) Nordrhein-Westfalen, W Germany
189 O14 **Lohd** Pohnpei, E Micronesia
92 L12 **Lohiniva** Lappi, N Finland
Lohiszyn *see* Lahishyn
93 L20 **Lohja** *var.* Lojo. Etelä-Suomi, S Finland
169 V11 **Lohjanan** Borneo, C Indonesia
25 Q9 **Lohn** Texas, SW USA
100 G12 **Lohne** Niedersachsen, NW Germany
Lohr *see* Lohr am Main
101 I18 **Lohr am Main** *var.* Lohr. Bayern, C Germany
109 T10 **Loibl Pass** *Ger.* Loiblpass, *Slvn.* Ljubelj. *pass* Austria/Slovenia
Loiblpass *see* Loibl Pass
167 N6 **Loi-Kaw** Kayah State, C Burma (Myanmar)
93 K19 **Loimaa** Länsi-Soumi, SW Finland
103 O6 **Loing** ≈ C France
167 R6 **Loi, Phou** ▲ N Laos
102 L7 **Loir** ≈ C France
103 Q11 **Loire** ◈ *department* E France
102 M7 **Loire** *var.* Liger. ≈ C France
102 I7 **Loire-Atlantique** ◈ *department* NW France
103 O7 **Loiret** ◈ *department* C France
102 M8 **Loir-et-Cher** ◈ *department* C France
101 L24 **Loisach** ≈ SE Germany
56 B9 **Loja** Loja, S Ecuador
104 M14 **Loja** Andalucía, S Spain
56 B9 **Loja** ◈ *province* S Ecuador
Lojo *see* Lohja
116 J4 **Lokachi** Volyns'ka Oblast', NW Ukraine
79 M20 **Lokandu** Maniema, C Dem. Rep. Congo
92 M11 **Lokan Tekojärvi** ◎ NE Finland
137 Z11 **Lökbatan** *Rus.* Lokbatan. E Azerbaijan
Lokbatan *see* Lökbatan
99 F17 **Lokeren** Oost-Vlaanderen, NW Belgium
Lokhvitsa *see* Lokhvytsya
117 S4 **Lokhvytsya** *Rus.* Lokhvitsa. Poltavs'ka Oblast', NE Ukraine
81 H17 **Lokichar** Rift Valley, NW Kenya
81 G16 **Lokichokio** Rift Valley, NW Kenya
81 H16 **Lokitaung** Rift Valley, NW Kenya
92 M11 **Lokka** Lappi, N Finland
94 G8 **Løkken Verk** Sør-Trøndelag, S Norway
124 G16 **Loknya** Pskovskaya Oblast', W Russian Federation
77 V15 **Loko** Nassarawa, C Nigeria
77 U15 **Lokoja** Kogi, C Nigeria
81 H17 **Lokori** Rift Valley, W Kenya
77 R16 **Lokossa** S Benin
118 I3 **Loksa** *Ger.* Loxa. Harjumaa, NW Estonia
9 T7 **Loks Land** *island* Nunavut, NE Canada
80 C13 **Lol** ≈ S Sudan
76 K15 **Lola** Guinée-Forestière, SE Guinea
35 Q5 **Lola, Mount** ▲ California, W USA
81 H20 **Loliondo** Arusha, NE Tanzania
95 H25 **Lolland** *prev.* Laaland. *island* S Denmark
186 G6 **Lolobau Island** *island* E Papua New Guinea
79 E16 **Lolodorf** Sud, SW Cameroon
114 G7 **Lom** *prev.* Lom-Palanka. Montana, NW Bulgaria
114 G7 **Lom** ≈ NW Bulgaria
79 M19 **Lomami** ≈ C Dem. Rep. Congo
57 F17 **Lomas** Arequipa, SW Peru
63 I23 **Lomas, Bahía** *bay* S Chile
61 D20 **Lomas de Zamora** Buenos Aires, E Argentina
61 D20 **Loma Verde** Buenos Aires, E Argentina
180 K4 **Lombadina** Western Australia
106 E6 **Lombardia** *Eng.* Lombardy. ◈ *region* N Italy
Lombardy *see* Lombardia
102 M15 **Lombez** Gers, S France
171 Q16 **Lomblen, Pulau** *island* Nusa Tenggara, S Indonesia
173 W7 **Lombok Basin** *undersea feature* E Indian Ocean
170 L16 **Lombok, Pulau** *island* Nusa Tenggara, C Indonesia
77 Q16 **Lomé** ● (Togo) S Togo
77 Q16 **Lomé** ✈ S Togo
79 L19 **Lomela** Kasai Oriental, C Dem. Rep. Congo
25 R9 **Lometa** Texas, SW USA
79 F16 **Lomié** Est, SE Cameroon
30 M8 **Lomira** Wisconsin, N USA
95 K23 **Lomma** Skåne, S Sweden
99 J16 **Lommel** Limburg, N Belgium
96 I11 **Lomond, Loch** ◎ C Scotland, UK
197 R9 **Lomonosov Ridge** *var.* Harris Ridge, *Rus.* Khrebet Homonsova. *undersea feature* Arctic Ocean
Lomonsova, Khrebet *see* Lomonosov Ridge
Lom-Palanka *see* Lom
Lomphat *see* Lumphăt
35 P14 **Lompoc** California, W USA
167 P9 **Lom Sak** *var.* Muang Lom Sak. Phetchabun, C Thailand
110 N9 **Łomża** *Rus.* Lomzha. Podlaskie, NE Poland
Lomzha *see* Łomża
Lonaula *see* Lonāvale
155 D14 **Lonāvale** *prev.* Lonaula. Mahārāshtra, W India
63 G15 **Loncoche** Araucanía, C Chile
63 H14 **Loncopue** Neuquén, W Argentina
99 G17 **Londerzeel** Vlaams Brabant, C Belgium
Londinium *see* London
14 E16 **London** Ontario, S Canada
191 Y2 **London** Kiritimati, E Kiribati
97 O22 **London** *anc.* Augusta, *Lat.* Londinium. ● (UK) SE England, UK
21 N7 **London** Kentucky, S USA
31 S13 **London** Ohio, NE USA
25 Q10 **London** Texas, SW USA
97 O22 **London City** ✈ SE England, UK
97 E14 **Londonderry** *var.* Derry, *Ir.* Doire. NW Northern Ireland, UK
97 F14 **Londonderry** *cultural region* NW Northern Ireland, UK
180 M2 **Londonderry, Cape** *cape* Western Australia
63 H25 **Londonderry, Isla** *island* S Chile
43 O7 **Londres, Cayos** *reef* NE Nicaragua
60 I10 **Londrina** Paraná, S Brazil
27 N13 **Lone Grove** Oklahoma, C USA
14 E12 **Lonely Island** *island* Ontario, S Canada
35 T8 **Lone Mountain** ▲ Nevada, W USA
25 V6 **Lone Oak** Texas, SW USA
35 T11 **Lone Pine** California, W USA
Lone Star State *see* Texas
83 D14 **Longa** Cuando Cubango, C Angola
82 B12 **Longa** ≈ W Angola
83 E15 **Longa** ≈ SE Angola
Long'an *see* Pingwu
197 S4 **Longa, Proliv** *Eng.* Long Strait. *strait* NE Russian Federation
44 J13 **Long Bay** *bay* W Jamaica
21 V13 **Long Bay** *bay* North Carolina/South Carolina, E USA
35 T16 **Long Beach** California, W USA
22 M9 **Long Beach** Mississippi, S USA
18 L14 **Long Beach** Long Island, New York, NE USA
32 F9 **Long Beach** Washington, NW USA
18 K16 **Long Beach Island** *island* New Jersey, NE USA
65 M25 **Longbluff** *headland* SW Tristan da Cunha
23 U13 **Longboat Key** *island* Florida, SE USA
18 K15 **Long Branch** New Jersey, NE USA
44 J5 **Long Cay** *island* SE Bahamas
Longcheng *see* Xiaoxian
161 P14 **Longchuan** *var.* Laolong. Guangdong, S China
Longchuan *see* Nanhua
Longchuan Jiang *see* Shweli
32 K12 **Long Creek** Oregon, NW USA
159 W10 **Longde** Ningxia, N China
183 P16 **Longford** Tasmania, SE Australia
97 D17 **Longford** *Ir.* An Longfort. Longford, C Ireland
97 E17 **Longford** *Ir.* An Longfort. ◈ *county* C Ireland
Longgang *see* Dazu
163 W11 **Longang Shan** ▲▲ NE China
161 P1 **Longhua** Hebei, E China
169 U11 **Longiram** Borneo, C Indonesia
44 J4 **Long Island** *island* C Bahamas
12 H8 **Long Island** *island* Northwest Territories, C Canada
186 D7 **Long Island** *var.* Arop Island. *island* N Papua New Guinea
18 L14 **Long Island** *island* New York, NE USA
Long Island *see* Bermuda
18 M14 **Long Island Sound** *sound* NE USA
163 U7 **Longjiang** Heilongjiang, NE China
160 K13 **Long Jiang** ≈ S China
163 Y10 **Longjing** *var.* Yanji. Jilin, NE China
161 R4 **Longkou** Shandong, E China
12 E11 **Longlac** Ontario, S Canada
19 S1 **Long Lake** ◎ Maine, NE USA
31 R5 **Long Lake** ◎ Michigan, N USA
31 O6 **Long Lake** ◎ Michigan, N USA
29 N6 **Long Lake** ◎ North Dakota, N USA
30 J4 **Long Lake** ⊠ Wisconsin, N USA
99 K23 **Longlier** Luxembourg, SE Belgium
160 I13 **Longlin** *var.* Longlin Gezu Zizhixian, Xinzhou. Guangxi Zhuangzu Zizhiqu, S China
Longlin Gezu Zizhixian *see* Longlin
37 T3 **Longmont** Colorado, C USA
157 P10 **Longnan** *var.* Wudu. Gansu, C China
29 N13 **Long Pine** Nebraska, C USA
Longping *see* Luodian
14 F17 **Long Point** *headland* Ontario, S Canada
14 K15 **Long Point** *headland* Ontario, SE Canada
184 P10 **Long Point** *headland* North Island, New Zealand
30 L2 **Long Point** *headland* Michigan, N USA
14 G17 **Long Point Bay** *lake bay* Ontario, S Canada
29 T7 **Long Prairie** Minnesota, N USA
Longquan *see* Fenggang
13 S11 **Long Range Mountains** *hill range* Newfoundland, Newfoundland and Labrador, E Canada
65 H25 **Long Range Point** *headland* SE Saint Helena
181 V8 **Longreach** Queensland, E Australia
160 H7 **Longriba** Sichuan, C China
160 L10 **Longshan** *var.* Min'an. Hunan, S China
37 S3 **Longs Peak** ▲ Colorado, C USA
Long Strait *see* Longa, Proliv
102 K8 **Longué** Maine-et-Loire, NW France
13 P11 **Longue-Pointe** Québec, E Canada
103 S4 **Longuyon** Meurthe-et-Moselle, NE France
25 W7 **Longview** Texas, SW USA
32 G10 **Longview** Washington, NW USA
65 H25 **Longwood** C Saint Helena
25 P7 **Longworth** Texas, SW USA
103 S3 **Longwy** Meurthe-et-Moselle, NE France
159 V11 **Longxi** Gansu, C China
Longxian *see* Wengyuan
167 S14 **Long Xuyên** *var.* Longxuyen. An Giang, S Vietnam
Longxuyen *see* Long Xuyên
161 Q13 **Longyan** Fujian, SE China
92 O3 **Longyearbyen** ○ (Svalbard) Spitsbergen, W Svalbard
160 J15 **Longzhou** Guangxi Zhuangzu Zizhiqu, S China
Longzhouping *see* Changyang
100 F12 **Löningen** Niedersachsen, NW Germany
27 V11 **Lonoke** Arkansas, C USA
95 L21 **Lönsboda** Skåne, S Sweden
103 S9 **Lons-le-Saunier** *anc.* Ledo Salinarius. Jura, E France
31 O15 **Loogootee** Indiana, N USA
31 Q9 **Looking Glass River** ≈ Michigan, N USA
21 X11 **Lookout, Cape** *cape* North Carolina, SE USA
39 O6 **Lookout Ridge** *ridge* Alaska, USA
181 N11 **Loongana** Western Australia
99 I14 **Loon op Zand** Noord-Brabant, S Netherlands
97 A19 **Loop Head** *Ir.* Ceann Léime. *promontory* W Ireland
109 V4 **Loosdorf** Niederösterreich, NE Austria
158 G10 **Lop** Xinjiang Uygur Zizhiqu, NW China
112 J11 **Lopare** ◈ Republika Srpska, NE Bosnia and Herzegovina
Lopatichi *see* Lapatsichy
127 Q15 **Lopatin** Respublika Dagestan, SW Russian Federation
127 P7 **Lopatino** Penzenskaya Oblast', W Russian Federation
167 P10 **Lop Buri** *var.* Loburi. Lop Buri, C Thailand
25 R16 **Lopeno** Texas, SW USA
79 C18 **Lopez, Cap** *cape* W Gabon
98 I12 **Lopik** Utrecht, C Netherlands
Lop Nor *see* Lop Nur
158 M7 **Lop Nur** *var.* Lob Nor, Lop Nor, Lo-pu Po. *seasonal lake* NW China
Lopnur *see* Yuli
79 K17 **Lopori** ≈ NW Dem. Rep. Congo
98 O5 **Loppersum** Groningen, NE Netherlands
92 I8 **Lopphavet** *sound* N Norway
Lo-pu Po *see* Lop Nur
Lora *see* Lowrah
182 F3 **Lora Creek** *seasonal river* South Australia
104 K13 **Lora del Río** Andalucía, S Spain
148 M11 **Lora, Hāmūn-i** *wetland* SW Pakistan
31 T11 **Lorain** Ohio, N USA
25 O7 **Loraine** Texas, SW USA
31 R13 **Loramie, Lake** ⊠ Ohio, N USA
105 Q13 **Lorca** *Ar.* Lurka; *anc.* Eliocroca, *Lat.* Illurco. Murcia, S Spain
192 I10 **Lord Howe Island** *island* E Australia
Lord Howe Island *see* Ontong Java Atoll
175 O10 **Lord Howe Rise** *undersea feature* SW Pacific Ocean
192 J10 **Lord Howe Seamounts** *undersea feature* W Pacific Ocean
37 P15 **Lordsburg** New Mexico, SW USA
186 E5 **Lorengau** *var.* Lorungau. Manus Island, N Papua New Guinea
25 N5 **Lorenzo** Texas, SW USA
142 K7 **Lorestān** *off.* Ostān-e Lorestān, *var.* Luristan. ◈ *province* W Iran
Lorestān, Ostān-e *see* Lorestān
57 M17 **Loreto** Beni, N Bolivia
106 J12 **Loreto** Marche, C Italy
40 F8 **Loreto** Baja California Sur, W Mexico
40 M11 **Loreto** Zacatecas, C Mexico
56 E9 **Loreto** *off.* Departamento de Loreto. ◈ *department* NE Peru
Loreto, Departamento de *see* Loreto
81 K18 **Lorian Swamp** *swamp* E Kenya
54 E6 **Lorica** Córdoba, NW Colombia
102 G7 **Lorient** *prev.* l'Orient. Morbihan, NW France
l'Orient *see* Lorient
111 K22 **Lőrinci** Heves, NE Hungary
14 G11 **Loring** Ontario, S Canada
33 V6 **Loring** Montana, NW USA
103 R13 **Loriol-sur-Drôme** Drôme, E France
21 U12 **Loris** South Carolina, SE USA
57 I18 **Loriscota, Laguna** ◎ S Peru
183 N13 **Lorne** Victoria, SE Australia
96 G11 **Lorn, Firth of** *inlet* W Scotland, UK
Loro Sae *see* East Timor
101 F24 **Lörrach** Baden-Württemberg, S Germany

◆ Country
● Country Capital
◇ Dependent Territory
○ Dependent Territory Capital
◈ Administrative Regions
✈ International Airport
▲ Mountain
▲▲ Mountain Range
⛰ Volcano
≈ River
◎ Lake
⊠ Reservoir

LORRAINE – LUPIRE

103 T5 **Lorraine** ◐ *region* NE France
Lorrungau *see* Lorengau
94 L11 **Los** Gävleborg, C Sweden
35 P14 **Los Alamos** California, W USA
37 S10 **Los Alamos** New Mexico, SW USA
42 F5 **Los Amates** Izabal, E Guatemala
63 G14 **Los Ángeles** Bío Bío, C Chile
35 S15 **Los Angeles** California, W USA
35 S15 **Los Angeles** ✈ California, W USA
35 T13 **Los Angeles Aqueduct** *aqueduct* California, W USA
Losanna *see* Lausanne
63 H20 **Los Antiguos** Santa Cruz, SW Argentina
189 Q16 **Losap Atoll** *atoll* C Micronesia
35 P10 **Los Banos** California, W USA
104 K16 **Los Barrios** Andalucía, S Spain
62 L5 **Los Blancos** Salta, N Argentina
42 L12 **Los Chiles** Alajuela, NW Costa Rica
105 O2 **Los Corrales de Buelna** Cantabria, N Spain
25 T17 **Los Fresnos** Texas, SW USA
35 N9 **Los Gatos** California, W USA
110 O11 **Łosice** Mazowieckie, C Poland
112 B11 **Lošinj** *Ger.* Lussin, *It.* Lussino. *island* W Croatia
Los Jardines *see* Ngetik Atoll
63 G15 **Los Lagos** Los Lagos, C Chile
63 F17 **Los Lagos** *off.* Región de los Lagos. ◐ *region* C Chile
los Lagos, Región de *see* Los Lagos
Loslau *see* Wodzisław Śląski
64 N11 **Los Llanos** *var.* Los Llanos de Aridane. La Palma, Islas Canarias, Spain, NE Atlantic Ocean
Los Llanos de Aridane *see* Los Llanos
37 R11 **Los Lunas** New Mexico, SW USA
63 I16 **Los Menucos** Río Negro, C Argentina
40 H8 **Los Mochis** Sinaloa, C Mexico
35 N4 **Los Molinos** California, W USA
104 M9 **Los Navalmorales** Castilla-La Mancha, C Spain
25 S15 **Los Olmos Creek** ≈ Texas, SW USA
Losonc/Losontz *see* Lučenec
167 S5 **Lô, Sông** *var.* Panlong Jiang. ≈ China/Vietnam
44 B5 **Los Palacios** Pinar del Río, W Cuba
104 K14 **Los Palacios y Villafranca** Andalucía, S Spain
37 R12 **Los Pinos Mountains** ▲▲ New Mexico, SW USA
37 R11 **Los Ranchos de Albuquerque** New Mexico, SW USA
40 M14 **Los Reyes** Michoacán de Ocampo, SW Mexico
56 B7 **Los Ríos** ◐ *province* C Ecuador
64 O11 **Los Rodeos** ✈ (Santa Cruz de Tenerife) Tenerife, Islas Canarias, Spain, NE Atlantic Ocean
54 L4 **Los Roques, Islas** *island group* N Venezuela
43 S17 **Los Santos** Los Santos, S Panama
43 S17 **Los Santos** *off.* Provincia de Los Santos. ◐ *province* S Panama
Los Santos *see* Los Santos de Maimona
104 J12 **Los Santos de Maimona** *var.* Los Santos. Extremadura, W Spain
Los Santos, Provincia de *see* Los Santos
98 P10 **Losser** Overijssel, E Netherlands
96 J8 **Lossiemouth** NE Scotland, UK
61 B14 **Los Tábanos** Santa Fe, C Argentina
54 J4 **Los Taques** Falcón, N Venezuela
14 G11 **Lost Channel** Ontario, S Canada
54 L5 **Los Teques** Miranda, N Venezuela
35 Q12 **Lost Hills** California, W USA
36 I7 **Lost Peak** ▲ Utah, W USA
33 P11 **Lost Trail Pass** *pass* Montana, NW USA
186 G9 **Losuia** Kiriwina Island, SE Papua New Guinea
62 G10 **Los Vilos** Coquimbo, C Chile
105 N10 **Los Yébenes** Castilla-La Mancha, C Spain
103 N13 **Lot** ◐ *department* S France
103 N13 **Lot** ≈ S France
63 F14 **Lota** Bío Bío, C Chile
81 G15 **Lotagipi Swamp** *wetland* Kenya/Sudan
102 K14 **Lot-et-Garonne** ◐ *department* SW France
83 K21 **Lothair** Mpumalanga, NE South Africa
33 R7 **Lothair** Montana, NW USA
79 L20 **Loto** Kasai Oriental, C Dem. Rep. Congo
108 E10 **Lötschbergtunnel** *tunnel* Valais, SW Switzerland
25 T9 **Lott** Texas, SW USA
124 H3 **Lotta** *var.* Lutto. ≈ Finland/Russian Federation
184 Q7 **Lottin Point** *headland* North Island, New Zealand
Loualaba *see* Lualaba
167 P6 **Louangnamtha** *var.* Luong Nam Tha. Louang Namtha, N Laos
167 Q7 **Louangphabang** *var.* Louangphrabang, Luang Prabang. Louangphabang, N Laos
Louangphrabang *see* Louangphabang
194 H5 **Loubet Coast** *physical region* Antarctica
Loubomo *see* Dolisie
Louch *see* Loukhi
102 H6 **Loudéac** Côtes d'Armor, NW France
160 M11 **Loudi** Hunan, S China
79 F21 **Loudima** La Bouenza, S Congo
20 M9 **Loudon** Tennessee, S USA
31 T12 **Loudonville** Ohio, N USA
102 L8 **Loudun** Vienne, W France
102 K7 **Loué** Sarthe, NW France
76 G10 **Louga** NW Senegal
97 M19 **Loughborough** C England, UK
97 C18 **Loughrea** *Ir.* Baile Locha Riach. Galway, W Ireland
103 S9 **Louhans** Saône-et-Loire, C France
21 P5 **Louisa** Kentucky, S USA
21 V5 **Louisa** Virginia, NE USA
21 V9 **Louisburg** North Carolina, SE USA
25 U12 **Louise** Texas, SW USA
15 P11 **Louiseville** Québec, SE Canada
27 W3 **Louisiana** Missouri, C USA
22 G8 **Louisiana** *off.* State of Louisiana, *also known as* Creole State, Pelican State. ◐ *state* S USA
83 K19 **Louis Trichardt** Northern, NE South Africa
23 V4 **Louisville** Georgia, SE USA
30 M15 **Louisville** Illinois, N USA
20 K5 **Louisville** Kentucky, S USA
22 M4 **Louisville** Mississippi, S USA
29 S15 **Louisville** Nebraska, C USA
192 L11 **Louisville Ridge** *undersea feature* S Pacific Ocean
124 J6 **Loukhi** *var.* Louch. Respublika Kareliya, NW Russian Federation
79 H19 **Loukoléla** Cuvette, E Congo
104 G14 **Loulé** Faro, S Portugal
111 C16 **Louny** *Ger.* Laun. Ústecký Kraj, NW Czech Republic
29 O15 **Loup City** Nebraska, C USA
29 P15 **Loup River** ≈ Nebraska, C USA
15 S9 **Loup, Rivière du** ≈ Québec, SE Canada
12 K7 **Loups Marins, Lacs des** ◎ Québec, NE Canada
102 K16 **Lourdes** Hautes-Pyrénées, S France
Lourenço Marques *see* Maputo
104 F11 **Loures** Lisboa, C Portugal
104 F10 **Lourinhã** Lisboa, C Portugal
115 C16 **Loúros** ≈ W Greece
104 G8 **Lousã** Coimbra, N Portugal
160 M10 **Lou Shui** ≈ C China
183 O5 **Louth** New South Wales, SE Australia
97 O18 **Louth** E England, UK
97 F17 **Louth** *Ir.* Lú. ◐ *county* NE Ireland
115 H15 **Loutrá** Kentrikí Makedonía, N Greece
115 G19 **Loutráki** Pelopónnisos, S Greece
Louvain *see* Leuven
99 H19 **Louvain-la Neuve** Walloon Brabant, C Belgium
14 J8 **Louvicourt** Québec, SE Canada
102 M4 **Louviers** Eure, N France
30 K14 **Lou Yaeger, Lake** ⊠ Illinois, N USA
93 J15 **Lövånger** Västerbotten, N Sweden
124 J14 **Lovat'** ≈ NW Russian Federation
113 J17 **Lovćen** ▲ SW Montenegro
114 I8 **Lovech** Lovech, N Bulgaria
114 I9 **Lovech** ◐ *province* N Bulgaria
25 V9 **Lovelady** Texas, SW USA
37 T3 **Loveland** Colorado, C USA
33 U12 **Lovell** Wyoming, C USA
Lovello, Monte *see* Grosser Löffler
35 S4 **Lovelock** Nevada, W USA
106 E7 **Lovere** Lombardia, N Italy
30 L10 **Loves Park** Illinois, N USA
26 M2 **Lovewell Reservoir** ⊠ Kansas, C USA
93 M19 **Loviisa** *Swe.* Lovisa. Etelä-Suomi, S Finland
37 V15 **Loving** New Mexico, SW USA
21 U6 **Lovingston** Virginia, NE USA
37 V14 **Lovington** New Mexico, SW USA
Lovisa *see* Loviisa
111 C15 **Lovosice** *Ger.* Lobositz. Ústecký Kraj, NW Czech Republic
124 K4 **Lovozero** Murmanskaya Oblast', NW Russian Federation
124 K4 **Lovozero, Ozero** ◎ NW Russian Federation
112 B9 **Lovran** *It.* Laurana. Primorje-Gorski Kotar, NW Croatia
116 E11 **Lovrin** *Ger.* Lowrin. Timiş, W Romania
82 E10 **Lóvua** Lunda Norte, NE Angola
82 G12 **Lóvua** Moxico, E Angola
65 D25 **Low Bay** *bay* East Falkland, Falkland Islands
9 P9 **Low, Cape** *headland* Nunavut, E Canada
33 N10 **Lowell** Idaho, NW USA
19 O10 **Lowell** Massachusetts, NE USA
Löwen *see* Leuven
Löwenberg in Schlesien *see* Lwówek Śląski
Lower Austria *see* Niederösterreich
Lower Bann *see* Bann
Lower California *see* Baja California
Lower Danube *see* Niederösterreich
185 L14 **Lower Hutt** Wellington, North Island, New Zealand
39 N11 **Lower Kalskag** Alaska, USA
35 O1 **Lower Klamath Lake** ◎ California, W USA
35 Q2 **Lower Lake** ◎ California/Nevada, W USA
97 E15 **Lower Lough Erne** ◎ SW Northern Ireland, UK
Lower Lusatia *see* Niederlausitz
Lower Normandy *see* Basse-Normandie
10 K9 **Lower Post** British Columbia, W Canada
29 T4 **Lower Red Lake** ◎ Minnesota, N USA
Lower Rhine *see* Neder Rijn
Lower Saxony *see* Niedersachsen
97 Q19 **Lowestoft** E England, UK
149 Q5 **Lowgar** *var.* Logar. ◐ *province* E Afghanistan
182 H7 **Low Hill** South Australia
110 K12 **Łowicz** Łódzkie, C Poland
33 N13 **Lowman** Idaho, NW USA
149 P8 **Lowrah** *var.* Lora. ≈ SE Afghanistan
Lowrin *see* Lovrin
183 N17 **Low Rocky Point** *headland* Tasmania, SE Australia
18 I8 **Lowville** New York, NE USA
Loxa *see* Loksa
182 K9 **Loxton** South Australia
81 G21 **Loya** Tabora, C Tanzania
30 K6 **Loyal** Wisconsin, N USA
18 G13 **Loyalsock Creek** ≈ Pennsylvania, NE USA
35 Q5 **Loyalton** California, W USA
Lo-yang *see* Luoyang
187 Q16 **Loyauté, Îles** *island group* S New Caledonia
Loyev *see* Loyew
119 O20 **Loyew** *Rus.* Loyev. Homyel'skaya Voblasts', SE Belarus
125 S13 **Loyno** Kirovskaya Oblast', NW Russian Federation
103 P13 **Lozère** ◐ *department* S France
103 Q14 **Lozère, Mont** ▲ S France
112 J11 **Loznica** Serbia, W Serbia
117 V7 **Lozova** *Rus.* Lozovaya. Kharkivs'ka Oblast', E Ukraine
Lozovaya *see* Lozova
105 N7 **Lozoyuela** Madrid, C Spain
Lu *see* Shandong
Lú *see* Louth
82 F12 **Luacano** Moxico, E Angola
79 N21 **Lualaba** *Fr.* Loualaba. ≈ SE Dem. Rep. Congo
83 H14 **Luampa** Western, NW Zambia
83 H15 **Luampa Kuta** Western, W Zambia
161 P8 **Lu'an** Anhui, E China
104 K2 **Luanco** Asturias, N Spain
82 A11 **Luanda** *var.* Loanda, *Port.* São Paulo de Loanda. ● Luanda, NW Angola
82 A11 **Luanda** ◐ *province* (Angola) NW Angola
82 A11 **Luanda** ✈ Luanda, NW Angola
82 D12 **Luando** ≈ C Angola
Luang *see* Tapi, Mae Nam
83 G14 **Luanginga** *var.* Luanguinga. ≈ Angola/Zambia
167 N15 **Luang, Khao** ▲ SW Thailand
Luang Prabang *see* Louangphabang
167 P8 **Luang Prabang Range** *Th.* Thiukhaoluang Phrahang. ▲▲ Laos/Thailand
167 N16 **Luang, Thale** *lagoon* S Thailand
Luangua, Rio *see* Luangwa
82 E11 **Luangue** ≈ NE Angola
Luanguinga *see* Luanginga
83 K15 **Luangwa** *var.* Aruângua. Lusaka, C Zambia
83 K14 **Luangwa** , *var.* Rio Luangua. ≈ Mozambique/Zambia
161 Q2 **Luan He** ≈ E China
190 G11 **Luaniva, Île** *island* E Wallis and Futuna
161 P2 **Luanping** *var.* Anjiangying. Hebei, E China
82 J13 **Luanshya** Copperbelt, C Zambia
62 K13 **Luan Toro** La Pampa, C Argentina
161 Q2 **Luanxian** *var.* Luan Xian. Hebei, E China
Luan Xian *see* Luanxian
82 J12 **Luapula** ◐ *province* N Zambia
79 O25 **Luapula** ≈ Dem. Rep. Congo/Zambia
104 J2 **Luarca** Asturias, N Spain
169 R10 **Luar, Danau** ◎ Borneo, N Indonesia
79 L25 **Luashi** Katanga, S Dem. Rep. Congo
82 G12 **Luau** *Port.* Vila Teixeira de Sousa. Moxico, NE Angola
79 C16 **Luba** *prev.* San Carlos. Isla de Bioco, NW Equatorial Guinea
42 F4 **Lubaantun** *ruins* Toledo, S Belize
111 P16 **Lubaczów** *var.* Lúbaczów. Podkarpackie, SE Poland
Lubale *see* Lubalo
82 E11 **Lubalo** Lunda Norte, NE Angola
82 E11 **Lubalo** *var.* Lubale. ≈ Angola/Dem. Rep. Congo
118 J9 **Lubāna** Madona, E Latvia
Lubānas Ezers *see* Lubāns
171 N4 **Lubang Island** *island* N Philippines
83 B15 **Lubango** *Port.* Sá da Bandeira. Huíla, SW Angola
118 J9 **Lubāns** *var.* Lubānas Ezers. ◎ E Latvia
79 M21 **Lubao** Kasai Oriental, C Dem. Rep. Congo
110 O13 **Lubartów** *Ger.* Qumälisch. Lublin, E Poland
100 G13 **Lübbecke** Nordrhein-Westfalen, NW Germany
100 O13 **Lübben** Brandenburg, E Germany
101 P14 **Lübbenau** Brandenburg, E Germany
25 N5 **Lubbock** Texas, SW USA
Lubcz *see* Lyubcha
19 U6 **Lubec** Maine, NE USA
100 K9 **Lübeck** Schleswig-Holstein, N Germany
100 K8 **Lübecker Bucht** *bay* N Germany
79 M21 **Lubefu** Kasai Oriental, C Dem. Rep. Congo
163 T10 **Lubei** *var.* Jarud Qi. Nei Mongol Zizhiqu, N China
111 O14 **Lubelska, Wyżyna** *plateau* SE Poland
110 O13 **Lubelskie** ◐ *province* E Poland
Lubembe *see* Luembe
Lüben *see* Lubin
144 H9 **Lubenka** Zapadnyy Kazakhstan, W Kazakhstan
79 P18 **Lubero** Nord Kivu, E Dem. Rep. Congo
79 L22 **Lubi** ≈ S Dem. Rep. Congo
Lubiana *see* Ljubljana
110 J11 **Lubień Kujawski** Kujawsko-pomorskie, C Poland
67 T11 **Lubilandji** ≈ S Dem. Rep. Congo
110 F13 **Lubin** *Ger.* Lüben. Dolnośląskie, SW Poland
111 O14 **Lublin** *Rus.* Lyublin. Lubelskie, E Poland
111 J15 **Lubliniec** Śląskie, S Poland
Lubnān, Jabal *see* Liban, Jebel
117 R5 **Lubny** Poltavs'ka Oblast', NE Ukraine
Luboml *see* Lyuboml'
110 G11 **Luboń** *Ger.* Peterhof. Wielkolpolskie, C Poland
110 D12 **Lubsko** *Ger.* Sommerfeld. Lubuskie, W Poland
79 N24 **Lubudi** Katanga, SE Dem. Rep. Congo
168 L13 **Lubuklinggau** Sumatera, W Indonesia
79 N25 **Lubumbashi** *prev.* Élisabethville. Shaba, SE Dem. Rep. Congo
83 I14 **Lubungu** Central, C Zambia
110 E12 **Lubuskie** ◐ *province* W Poland
Lubuskie *see* Dobiegniew
79 N18 **Lubutu** Maniema, E Dem. Rep. Congo
Luca *see* Lucca
82 C11 **Lucala** ≈ W Angola
14 E16 **Lucan** Ontario, S Canada
97 F18 **Lucan** *Ir.* Leamhcán. Dublin, E Ireland
Lucanian Mountains *see* Lucano, Appennino
107 M18 **Lucano, Appennino** *Eng.* Lucanian Mountains. ▲▲ S Italy
82 F11 **Lucapa** *var.* Lukapa. Lunda Norte, NE Angola
29 V15 **Lucas** Iowa, C USA
61 C18 **Lucas González** Entre Ríos, E Argentina
65 C25 **Lucas Point** *headland* West Falkland, Falkland Islands
31 S15 **Lucasville** Ohio, N USA
106 F11 **Lucca** *anc.* Luca. Toscana, C Italy
44 H12 **Lucea** W Jamaica
97 H15 **Luce Bay** *inlet* SW Scotland, UK
22 M8 **Lucedale** Mississippi, S USA
171 O4 **Lucena** *off.* Lucena City. Luzon, N Philippines
104 M14 **Lucena** Andalucía, S Spain
Lucena City *see* Lucena
105 S8 **Lucena del Cid** País Valenciano, E Spain
111 D15 **Lučenec** *Ger.* Losontz, *Hung.* Losonc. Banskobystrický Kraj, C Slovakia
Lucentum *see* Alicante
107 M16 **Lucera** Puglia, SE Italy
Lucerna/Lucerne *see* Luzern
Lucerne, Lake of *see* Vierwaldstätter See
40 J4 **Lucero** Chihuahua, N Mexico
123 S14 **Luchegorsk** Primorskiy Kray, SE Russian Federation
105 Q13 **Luchena** ≈ SE Spain
Lucheng *see* Kangding
82 N13 **Luchenga** *var.* Luchulingo. ≈ N Mozambique
Luchesa *see* Luchosa
Luchin *see* Luchyn
118 N13 **Luchosa** *Rus.* Luchesa. ≈ N Belarus
100 K11 **Lüchow** Mecklenburg-Vorpommern, N Germany
Luchow *see* Hefei
Luchulingo *see* Lucheringo
119 N17 **Luchyn** *Rus.* Luchin. Homyel'skaya Voblasts', SE Belarus
55 U11 **Lucie Rivier** ≈ W Surinam
182 K11 **Lucindale** South Australia
83 A14 **Lucira** Namibe, SW Angola
Luck *see* Luts'k
101 O14 **Luckau** Brandenburg, E Germany
100 N13 **Luckenwalde** Brandenburg, E Germany
14 E15 **Lucknow** Ontario, S Canada
152 L12 **Lucknow** *var.* Lakhnau. *state capital* Uttar Pradesh, N India
102 J10 **Luçon** Vendée, NW France
44 I7 **Lucrecia, Cabo** *headland* E Cuba
82 F13 **Lucusse** Moxico, E Angola
Lüda *see* Dalian
114 M9 **Luda Kamchiya** ≈ E Bulgaria
Ludasch *see* Luduş
114 I10 **Luda Yana** ≈ C Bulgaria
112 F7 **Ludbreg** Varaždin, N Croatia
29 P7 **Ludden** North Dakota, N USA
101 F15 **Lüdenscheid** Nordrhein-Westfalen, W Germany
83 C21 **Lüderitz** *prev.* Angra Pequena. Karas, SW Namibia
152 H8 **Ludhiāna** Punjab, N India
31 O7 **Ludington** Michigan, N USA
97 K20 **Ludlow** W England, UK
35 W14 **Ludlow** California, W USA
28 J7 **Ludlow** South Dakota, N USA
18 M9 **Ludlow** Vermont, NE USA
114 L7 **Ludogorie** *physical region* NE Bulgaria
23 W6 **Ludowici** Georgia, SE USA
Ludsan *see* Ludza
116 I10 **Luduş** *Ger.* Ludasch, *Hung.* Marosludas. Mureş, C Romania
95 M14 **Ludvika** Dalarna, C Sweden
101 H21 **Ludwigsburg** Baden-Württemberg, SW Germany
100 O13 **Ludwigsfelde** Brandenburg, NE Germany
101 G20 **Ludwigshafen** *var.* Ludwigshafen am Rhein. Rheinland-Pfalz, W Germany
Ludwigshafen am Rhein *see* Ludwigshafen
101 L20 **Ludwigskanal** *canal* SE Germany
100 L10 **Ludwigslust** Mecklenburg-Vorpommern, N Germany
118 K10 **Ludza** *Ger.* Ludsan. Ludza, E Latvia
79 K21 **Luebo** Kasai Occidental, SW Dem. Rep. Congo
25 Q6 **Lueders** Texas, SW USA
79 N20 **Lueki** Maniema, C Dem. Rep. Congo
82 F10 **Luembe** *var.* Lubembe. ≈ Angola/Dem. Rep. Congo
82 E13 **Luena** *var.* Lwena, *Port.* Luso. Moxico, E Angola
79 M24 **Luena** Katanga, SE Dem. Rep. Congo
82 K12 **Luena** Northern, NE Zambia
82 F13 **Luena** ≈ E Angola
83 F16 **Luengue** ≈ SE Angola
67 V13 **Luenha** ≈ W Mozambique
83 G15 **Lueti** ≈ Angola/Zambia
160 J7 **Lüeyang** *var.* Hejiayan. Shaanxi, C China
161 P14 **Lufeng** Guangdong, S China
79 N24 **Lufira** ≈ SE Dem. Rep. Congo
79 N25 **Lufira, Lac de Retenue de la** *var.* Lac Tshangalele. ◎ SE Dem. Rep. Congo
25 W8 **Lufkin** Texas, SW USA
82 L11 **Lufubu** ≈ N Zambia
124 G14 **Luga** Leningradskaya Oblast', NW Russian Federation
124 G13 **Luga** ≈ NW Russian Federation
Luganer See *see* Lugano, Lago di
108 H11 **Lugano** *Ger.* Lauis. Ticino, S Switzerland
108 H12 **Lugano, Lago di** *var.* Ceresio, *Ger.* Luganer See. ◎ S Switzerland
Lugansk *see* Luhans'k
187 Q13 **Luganville** Espiritu Santo, C Vanuatu
Lugdunum *see* Lyon
Lugdunum Batavorum *see* Leiden
83 O15 **Lugela** Zambézia, NE Mozambique
83 O16 **Lugela** ≈ C Mozambique
82 P13 **Lugenda, Rio** ≈ N Mozambique
Luggarus *see* Locarno
Lugh Ganana *see* Luuq
97 G19 **Lugnaquillia Mountain** *Ir.* Log na Coille. ▲ E Ireland
106 H10 **Lugo** Emilia-Romagna, N Italy
104 I3 **Lugo** *anc.* Lugus Augusti. Galicia, NW Spain
104 I3 **Lugo** ◐ *province* Galicia, NW Spain
21 R12 **Lugoff** South Carolina, SE USA
116 F12 **Lugoj** *Ger.* Lugosch, *Hung.* Lugos. Timiş, W Romania
Lugos/Lugosch *see* Lugoj
Lugovoy/Lugovoye *see* Kulan
158 I13 **Lugu** Xizang Zizhiqu, W China
Lugus Augusti *see* Lugo
Luguvallium/Luguvallum *see* Carlisle
117 Y7 **Luhans'k** *Rus.* Lugansk; *prev.* Voroshilovgrad. Luhans'ka Oblast', E Ukraine
117 Y7 **Luhans'k** ✈ Luhans'ka Oblast', E Ukraine
Luhans'k *see* Luhans'ka Oblast'
117 X6 **Luhans'ka Oblast'** *var.* Luhans'k; *prev.* Voroshilovgrad, *Rus.* Voroshilovgradskaya Oblast'. ◐ *province* E Ukraine
161 Q7 **Luhe** Jiangsu, E China
171 S13 **Luhu** Pulau Seram, E Indonesia
Luhua *see* Heishui
160 G8 **Luhuo** *var.* Xindu, *Tib.* Zhaggo. Sichuan, C China
116 M3 **Luhyny** Zhytomyrs'ka Oblast', N Ukraine
83 G15 **Lui** ≈ W Zambia
83 G16 **Luiana** ≈ SE Angola
83 L15 **Luia, Rio** *var.* Ruya. ≈ Mozambique/Zimbabwe
Luichow Peninsula *see* Leizhou Bandao
Luik *see* Liège
82 C13 **Luimbale** Huambo, C Angola
Luimneach *see* Limerick
106 D6 **Luino** Lombardia, N Italy
82 E13 **Luio** ≈ E Angola
92 L11 **Luiro** ≈ NE Finland
79 N25 **Luishia** Katanga, SE Dem. Rep. Congo
59 M19 **Luislândia do Oeste** Minas Gerais, SE Brazil
40 K5 **Luis L. León, Presa** ⊠ N Mexico
Luis Muñoz Marin *see* San Juan
195 N5 **Luitpold Coast** *physical region* Antarctica
79 K22 **Luiza** Kasai Occidental, S Dem. Rep. Congo
61 D20 **Luján** Buenos Aires, E Argentina
79 N24 **Lukafu** Katanga, SE Dem. Rep. Congo
Lukapa *see* Lucapa
112 I11 **Lukavac** ◐ Federacija Bosna I Hercegovina, NE Bosnia and Herzegovina
79 I20 **Lukenie** ≈ C Dem. Rep. Congo
79 H19 **Lukolela** Equateur, W Dem. Rep. Congo
119 M14 **Lukom'skaye, Vozyera** *Rus.* Ozero Lukoml'skoye. ◎ N Belarus
Lukoml'skoye, Ozero *see* Lukom'skaye, Vozyera
114 I8 **Lukovit** Lovech, N Bulgaria
110 O12 **Łuków** *Ger.* Bogendorf. Lubelskie, E Poland
127 O4 **Lukoyanov** Nizhegorodskaya Oblast', W Russian Federation
79 N22 **Lukuga** ≈ SE Dem. Rep. Congo
79 F21 **Lukula** Bas-Congo, SW Dem. Rep. Congo
83 G14 **Lukulu** Western, NW Zambia
189 R17 **Lukunor Atoll** *atoll* Mortlock Islands, C Micronesia
82 K12 **Lukwesa** Luapula, NE Zambia
93 J14 **Luleå** Norrbotten, N Sweden
92 J13 **Luleälven** ≈ N Sweden
136 C10 **Lüleburgaz** Kırklareli, NW Turkey
160 M4 **Lüliang Shan** ▲▲ C China
79 O21 **Lulimba** Maniema, E Dem. Rep. Congo
22 K9 **Luling** Louisiana, S USA
25 T11 **Luling** Texas, SW USA
79 I18 **Lulonga** ≈ NW Dem. Rep. Congo
79 K22 **Lulua** ≈ S Dem. Rep. Congo
Luluabourg *see* Kananga
192 L17 **Luma** Ta'ū, E American Samoa
169 S17 **Lumajang** Jawa, C Indonesia
158 G12 **Lumajangdong Co** ◎ W China
82 G13 **Lumbala Kaquengue** Moxico, E Angola
83 F14 **Lumbala N'Guimbo** *var.* Nguimbo, Gago Coutinho, *Port.* Vila Gago Coutinho. Moxico, E Angola
21 T11 **Lumber River** ≈ North Carolina/South Carolina, SE USA
Lumber State *see* Maine
22 L8 **Lumberton** Mississippi, S USA
21 U11 **Lumberton** North Carolina, SE USA
105 R4 **Lumbier** Navarra, N Spain
83 Q15 **Lumbo** Nampula, NE Mozambique
124 M4 **Lumbovka** Murmanskaya Oblast', NW Russian Federation
104 J7 **Lumbrales** Castilla-León, N Spain
153 W13 **Lumding** Assam, NE India
82 F12 **Lumege** *var.* Lumeje. Moxico, E Angola
Lumeje *see* Lumege
99 J17 **Lummen** Limburg, NE Belgium
93 J20 **Lumparland** Åland, SW Finland
167 T11 **Lumphăt** *prev.* Lomphat. Rôtânôkiri, NE Cambodia
9 U16 **Lumsden** Saskatchewan, S Canada
185 C23 **Lumsden** Southland, South Island, New Zealand
169 N14 **Lumut, Tanjung** *cape* Sumatera, W Indonesia
157 P4 **Lün** Töv, C Mongolia
116 I13 **Lunca Corbului** Argeş, S Romania
95 K23 **Lund** Skåne, S Sweden
35 X6 **Lund** Nevada, W USA
82 D11 **Lunda Norte** ◐ *province* NE Angola
82 E12 **Lunda Sul** ◐ *province* NE Angola
82 M13 **Lundazi** Eastern, NE Zambia
95 G16 **Lunde** Telemark, S Norway
Lundenburg *see* Břeclav
95 C17 **Lundevatnet** ◎ S Norway
Lundi *see* Runde
97 I23 **Lundy** *island* SW England, UK
100 J10 **Lüneburg** Niedersachsen, N Germany
100 J11 **Lüneburger Heide** *heathland* NW Germany
103 Q15 **Lunel** Hérault, S France
101 F14 **Lünen** Nordrhein-Westfalen, W Germany
13 P16 **Lunenburg** Nova Scotia, SE Canada
21 V7 **Lunenburg** Virginia, NE USA
103 T5 **Lunéville** Meurthe-et-Moselle, NE France
83 I14 **Lunga** ≈ C Zambia
Lunga, Isola *see* Dugi Otok
158 H12 **Lungdo** Xizang Zizhiqu, W China
158 I14 **Lunggar** Xizang Zizhiqu, W China
76 I15 **Lungi** ✈ (Freetown) W Sierra Leone
Lungkiang *see* Qiqihar
Lungleh *see* Lunglei
153 W15 **Lunglei** *prev.* Lungleh. Mizoram, NE India
158 L15 **Lungsang** Xizang Zizhiqu, W China
82 E13 **Lungué-Bungo** *var.* Lungwebungu. ≈ Angola/Zambia *see also* Lungwebungu
Lungué-Bungo *see* Lungwebungu
83 G14 **Lungwebungu** *var.* Lungué-Bungo. ≈ Angola/Zambia *see also* Lungué-Bungo
Lungwebungu *see* Lungué-Bungo
152 F12 **Lūni** Rājasthān, N India
152 F12 **Lūni** ≈ N India
Luninets *see* Luninyets
35 S7 **Luning** Nevada, W USA
Łuniniec *see* Luninyets
127 P6 **Lunino** Penzenskaya Oblast', W Russian Federation
119 J19 **Luninyets** *Pol.* Łuniniec, *Rus.* Luninets. Brestskaya Voblasts', SW Belarus
152 F10 **Lūnkaransar** Rājasthān, NW India
119 G17 **Lunna** *Pol.* Łunna, *Rus.* Lunna. Hrodzyenskaya Voblasts', W Belarus
76 I15 **Lunsar** W Sierra Leone
83 K14 **Lunsemfwa** ≈ C Zambia
158 J6 **Luntai** *var.* Bügür. Xinjiang Uygur Zizhiyu, NW China
98 K11 **Lunteren** Gelderland, C Netherlands
109 U5 **Lunz am See** Niederösterreich, C Austria
163 Y7 **Luobei** *var.* Fengxiang. Heilongjiang, NE China
Luocheng *see* Hui'an
Luocheng *see* Luoding
160 J13 **Luodian** *var.* Longping. Guizhou, S China
160 M15 **Luoding** *var.* Luocheng. Guangdong, S China
161 N7 **Luohe** Henan, C China
160 M6 **Luo He** ≈ C China
160 L5 **Luo He** ≈ C China
Luolajarvi *see* Kuoloyarvi
Luong Nam Tha *see* Louangnamtha
160 L13 **Luoqing Jiang** ≈ S China
161 O8 **Luoshan** Henan, C China
161 O12 **Luoxiao Shan** ▲▲ S China
161 N6 **Luoyang** *var.* Honan, Lo-yang. Henan, C China
161 R12 **Luoyuan** *var.* Fengshan. Fujian, SE China
79 F21 **Luozi** Bas-Congo, W Dem. Rep. Congo
83 J17 **Lupane** Matabeleland North, W Zimbabwe
160 I12 **Lupanshui** *prev.* Shuicheng. Guizhou, S China
169 R10 **Lupar, Batang** ≈ East Malaysia
Lupatia *see* Altamura
116 G12 **Lupeni** *Hung.* Lupény. Hunedoara, SW Romania
Lupény *see* Lupeni
82 N13 **Lupiliche** Niassa, N Mozambique
83 E14 **Lupire** Cuando Cubango, E Angola

◆ Country
● Country Capital
◇ Dependent Territory
○ Dependent Territory Capital
◐ Administrative Regions
✈ International Airport
▲ Mountain
▲▲ Mountain Range
Volcano
≈ River
◎ Lake
⊠ Reservoir

M

◆ Country ◇ Dependent Territory ▲ Administrative Regions ▲ Mountain ⩕ Volcano ⊚ Lake
● Country Capital ○ Dependent Territory Capital ✈ International Airport ▲ Mountain Range ☙ River ▨ Reservoir

MAESEYCK – MALOENDA

Maeseyck *see* Maaseik
167 *N9* **Mae Sot** *var.* Ban Mae Sot. Tak, W Thailand
Maestricht *see* Maastricht
167 *O7* **Mae Suai** *var.* Ban Mae Suai. Chiang Rai, NW Thailand
167 *O7* **Mae Tho, Doi** ▲ NW Thailand
172 *I4* **Maevatanana** Mahajanga, C Madagascar
187 *R13* **Maéwo** *prev.* Aurora. *island* C Vanuatu
171 *S11* **Mafa** Pulau Halmahera, E Indonesia
83 *I23* **Mafeteng** W Lesotho
99 *J21* **Maffe** Namur, SE Belgium
183 *P12* **Maffra** Victoria, SE Australia
81 *K23* **Mafia** *island* E Tanzania
81 *J23* **Mafia Channel** *sea waterway* E Tanzania
83 *I21* **Mafikeng** North-West, N South Africa
60 *J12* **Mafra** Santa Catarina, S Brazil
104 *F10* **Mafra** Lisboa, C Portugal
143 *Q17* **Mafraq** Abū Ẓaby, C United Arab Emirates
Mafraq/Muḥāfaẓat al Mafraq *see* Al Mafraq
123 *T10* **Magadan** Magadanskaya Oblast', E Russian Federation
123 *T9* **Magadanskaya Oblast'** ⬗ *province* E Russian Federation
108 *G11* **Magadino** Ticino, S Switzerland
63 *G23* **Magallanes** *var.* Región de Magallanes y de la Antártica Chilena. ⬗ *region* S Chile
Magallanes *see* Punta Arenas
Magallanes, Estrecho de *see* Magellan, Strait of
Magallanes y de la Antártica Chilena, Región de *see* Magallanes
14 *I10* **Maganasipi, Lac** ◎ Québec, SE Canada
54 *F6* **Magangué** Bolívar, N Colombia
Magareva *see* Mangareva
77 *V12* **Magaria** Zinder, S Niger
186 *F10* **Magarida** Central, SW Papua New Guinea
171 *O2* **Magat** ≈ Luzon, N Philippines
27 *T11* **Magazine Mountain** ▲ Arkansas, C USA
76 *I15* **Magburaka** C Sierra Leone
123 *Q13* **Magdagachi** Amurskaya Oblast', SE Russian Federation
62 *O12* **Magdalena** Buenos Aires, E Argentina
57 *M15* **Magdalena** Beni, N Bolivia
40 *F4* **Magdalena** Sonora, NW Mexico
37 *Q13* **Magdalena** New Mexico, SW USA
54 *F5* **Magdalena** *off.* Departamento del Magdalena. ⬗ *province* N Colombia
40 *E9* **Magdalena, Bahía** *bay* W Mexico
Magdalena, Departamento del *see* Magdalena
63 *G19* **Magdalena, Isla** *island* Archipiélago de los Chonos, S Chile
40 *D8* **Magdalena, Isla** *island* W Mexico
47 *P6* **Magdalena, Río** ≈ C Colombia
40 *F4* **Magdalena, Río** ≈ NW Mexico
Magdalen Islands *see* Madeleine, Îles de la
100 *L13* **Magdeburg** Sachsen-Anhalt, C Germany
22 *L6* **Magee** Mississippi, S USA
169 *Q16* **Magelang** Jawa, C Indonesia
192 *K7* **Magellan Rise** *undersea feature* C Pacific Ocean
63 *H24* **Magellan, Strait of** *Sp.* Estrecho de Magallanes. *strait* Argentina/Chile
106 *D7* **Magenta** Lombardia, NW Italy
Magerøy *see* Magerøya
92 *K7* **Magerøya** *var.* Magerøy, *Lapp.* Máhkarávju. *island* N Norway
164 *C17* **Mage-shima** *island* Nansei-shotō, SW Japan
108 *G11* **Maggia** Ticino, S Switzerland
108 *G10* **Maggia** ≈ SW Switzerland
Maggiore, Lago *see* Maggiore, Lake
106 *C6* **Maggiore, Lake** *It.* Lago Maggiore. ◎ Italy/Switzerland
44 *I12* **Maggotty** W Jamaica
76 *I10* **Maghama** Gorgol, S Mauritania
97 *F14* **Maghera** *Ir.* Machaire Rátha. C Northern Ireland, UK
97 *F15* **Magherafelt** *Ir.* Machaire Fíolta. C Northern Ireland, UK
188 *H6* **Magicienne Bay** *bay* Saipan, S Northern Mariana Islands
105 *O13* **Magina** ▲ S Spain
81 *H24* **Magingo** Ruvuma, S Tanzania
112 *H11* **Maglaj** ⬗ Federacija Bosna I Hercegovina, N Bosnia and Herzegovina
107 *Q19* **Maglie** Puglia, SE Italy
36 *L2* **Magna** Utah, W USA
Magnesia *see* Manisa
14 *G12* **Magnetawan** ≈ Ontario, S Canada
27 *T14* **Magnolia** Arkansas, C USA
22 *K7* **Magnolia** Mississippi, S USA
25 *V10* **Magnolia** Texas, SW USA
Magnolia State *see* Mississippi
95 *J15* **Magnor** Hedmark, S Norway
187 *Y14* **Mago** *prev.* Mango. *island* Lau Group, E Fiji
83 *L15* **Màgoé** Tete, NW Mozambique
15 *Q13* **Magog** Québec, SE Canada
83 *J15* **Magoye** Southern, S Zambia
41 *Q12* **Magozal** Veracruz-Llave, C Mexico
14 *B7* **Magpie** ≈ Ontario, S Canada
9 *Q17* **Magrath** Alberta, SW Canada
105 *R10* **Magro** ≈ E Spain
76 *I9* **Magṭa' Laḥjar** *var.* Magta Lahjar, Magṭa' Lahjar, Magtá Lahjar. Brakna, SW Mauritania
146 *D12* **Magtymguly** *prev.* Garrygala, *Rus.* Kara-Kala. Balkan Welaýaty, W Turkmenistan
83 *L20* **Magude** Maputo, S Mozambique
77 *Y12* **Magumeri** Borno, NE Nigeria
189 *O14* **Magur Islands** *island group* Caroline Islands, C Micronesia
Magway *see* Magwe
166 *L6* **Magwe** *var.* Magway. Magwe, W Burma (Myanmar)
166 *L6* **Magwe** *var.* Magway. ⬗ *division* C Burma (Myanmar)
Magyar-Becse *see* Bečej
Magyarkanizsa *see* Kanjiža
Magyarország *see* Hungary
Magyarzsombor *see* Zimbor
142 *J4* **Mahābād** *var.* Mehabad; *prev.* Sāūjbulāgh. Āžarbāyjān-e Gharbī, NW Iran
172 *H5* **Mahabo** Toliara, W Madagascar
Maha Chai *see* Samut Sakhon
155 *D14* **Mahād** Mahārāshtra, W India
81 *N17* **Mahadday Weyne** Shabeellaha Dhexe, C Somalia
79 *Q17* **Mahagi** Orientale, NE Dem. Rep. Congo
Mahāil *see* Muhāyil
172 *I4* **Mahajamba** *seasonal river* NW Madagascar
152 *G10* **Mahājan** Rājasthān, NW India
172 *I3* **Mahajanga** *var.* Majunga. Mahajanga, NW Madagascar
172 *I3* **Mahajanga** ⬗ *province* W Madagascar
172 *I3* **Mahajanga** ✈ Mahajanga, NW Madagascar
169 *U10* **Mahakam, Sungai** *var.* Koetai, Kutai. ≈ Borneo, C Indonesia
83 *I19* **Mahalapye** *var.* Mahalatswe. Central, SE Botswana
Mahalatswe *see* Mahalapye
Mahalla el Kubra *see* El Maḥalla el Kubra
171 *O13* **Mahalona** Sulawesi, C Indonesia
Mahameru *see* Semeru, Gunung
143 *S11* **Mahān** Kermān, E Iran
154 *N12* **Mahanādi** ≈ E India
172 *J5* **Mahanoro** Toamasina, E Madagascar
153 *P13* **Mahārājganj** Bihār, N India
154 *G13* **Mahārāshtra** ⬗ *state* W India
172 *I4* **Mahavavy** *seasonal river* N Madagascar
155 *K24* **Mahaweli Ganga** ≈ C Sri Lanka
Mahbés *see* El Mahbas
155 *J15* **Mahbūbābād** Andhra Pradesh, E India
155 *H16* **Mahbūbnagar** Andhra Pradesh, C India
140 *M8* **Mahd adh Dhahab** Al Madīnah, W Saudi Arabia
55 *S9* **Mahdia** C Guyana
75 *N6* **Mahdia** *var.* Al Mahdīyah, Mehdia. NE Tunisia
155 *F20* **Mahe** *Fr.* Mahé; *prev.* Mayyali. Pondicherry, SW India
172 *I16* **Mahé** ✈ Mahé, NE Seychelles
172 *H16* **Mahé** *island* Inner Islands, NE Seychelles
Mahé *see* Mahe
173 *Y17* **Mahebourg** SE Mauritius
152 *L10* **Mahendranagar** Far Western, W Nepal
81 *I23* **Mahenge** Morogoro, SE Tanzania
185 *F22* **Maheno** Otago, South Island, New Zealand
154 *D9* **Mahesāna** Gujarāt, W India
154 *F11* **Maheshwar** Madhya Pradesh, C India
151 *F14* **Mahi** ≈ N India
184 *Q10* **Mahia Peninsula** *peninsula* North Island, New Zealand
119 *O16* **Mahilyow** *Rus.* Mogilëv. Mahilyowskaya Voblasts', E Belarus
119 *M16* **Mahilyowskaya Voblasts'** *prev. Rus.* Mogilëvskaya Oblast'. ⬗ *province* E Belarus
191 *P7* **Mahina** Tahiti, W French Polynesia
185 *E23* **Mahinerangi, Lake** ◎ South Island, New Zealand
Máhkarávju *see* Magerøya
83 *L22* **Mahlabatini** KwaZulu/Natal, E South Africa
166 *L5* **Mahlaing** Mandalay, C Burma (Myanmar)
109 *X8* **Mahldorf** Steiermark, SE Austria
Mahmūd-e 'Erāqī *see* Maḥmūd-e Rāqī
149 *R4* **Maḥmūd-e Rāqī** *var.* Mahmūd-e 'Erāqī. Kāpīsā, NE Afghanistan
Mahmudiya *see* Al Maḥmūdīyah
29 *S5* **Mahnomen** Minnesota, N USA
152 *K14* **Mahoba** Uttar Pradesh, N India
105 *Z9* **Mahón** *Cat.* Maó, *Eng.* Port Mahon; *anc.* Portus Magonis. Menorca, Spain, W Mediterranean Sea
18 *D14* **Mahoning Creek Lake** ⊠ Pennsylvania, NE USA
105 *Q10* **Mahora** Castilla-La Mancha, C Spain
Mähren *see* Moravia
Mährisch-Budwitz *see* Moravské Budějovice
Mährisch-Kromau *see* Moravský Krumlov
Mährisch-Neustadt *see* Uničov
Mährisch-Schönberg *see* Šumperk
Mährisch-Trübau *see* Moravská Třebová
Mährisch-Weisskirchen *see* Hranice
Māh-Shahr *see* Bandar-e Māhshahr
79 *N19* **Mahulu** Maniema, E Dem. Rep. Congo
154 *C12* **Mahuva** Gujarāt, W India
114 *N11* **Mahya Dağı** ▲ NW Turkey
105 *T6* **Maials** *var.* Mayals. Cataluña, NE Spain
191 *O2* **Maiana** *prev.* Hall Island. *atoll* Tungaru, W Kiribati
191 *S11* **Maiao** *var.* Tapuaemanu, Tubuai-Manu. *island* Îles du Vent, W French Polynesia
54 *H4* **Maicao** La Guajira, N Colombia
Mai Ceu/Mai Chio *see* Maych'ew
103 *U8* **Maîche** Doubs, E France
97 *N22* **Maidenhead** S England, UK
9 *S15* **Maidstone** Saskatchewan, S Canada
97 *P22* **Maidstone** SE England, UK
77 *Y13* **Maiduguri** Borno, NE Nigeria
108 *I8* **Maienfeld** Sankt Gallen, NE Switzerland
116 *J12* **Măieruş** *Hung.* Szászmagyarós. Braşov, C Romania
Maigh Chromtha *see* Macroom
Maigh Eo *see* Mayo
55 *N9* **Maigualida, Sierra** ▲▲ S Venezuela
154 *K9* **Maihar** Madhya Pradesh, C India
154 *K11* **Maikala Range** ▲▲ C India
67 *T10* **Maiko** ≈ W Dem. Rep. Congo
Mailand *see* Milano
152 *L11* **Mailāni** Uttar Pradesh, N India
149 *U10* **Māilsi** Punjab, E Pakistan
147 *R8* **Maimak** Talasskaya Oblast', NW Kyrgyzstan
Maimāna *see* Meymaneh
Maimansingh *see* Mymensingh
171 *V13* **Maimawa** Papua, E Indonesia
Maimuna *see* Al Maymūnah
101 *G18* **Main** ≈ C Germany
115 *F22* **Maïna** *ancient monument* Pelopónnisos, S Greece
115 *E20* **Maínalo** ▲▲ S Greece
101 *L22* **Mainburg** Bayern, SE Germany
Main Camp *see* Banana
14 *E12* **Main Channel** *lake channel* Ontario, S Canada
79 *I20* **Mai-Ndombe, Lac** *prev.* Lac Léopold II. ◎ W Dem. Rep. Congo
101 *K20* **Main-Donau-Kanal** *canal* SE Germany
19 *R6* **Maine** *off.* State of Maine, *also known as* Lumber State, Pine Tree State. ⬗ *state* NE USA
102 *K6* **Maine** *cultural region* NW France
102 *J7* **Maine-et-Loire** ⬗ *department* NW France
19 *Q9* **Maine, Gulf of** *gulf* NE USA
77 *X12* **Maïné-Soroa** Diffa, SE Niger
167 *N2* **Maingkwan** *var.* Mungkawn. Kachin State, N Burma (Myanmar)
Main Island *see* Bermuda
Mainistir Fhear Maí *see* Fermoy
Mainistirna Búille *see* Boyle
Mainistir na Corann *see* Midleton
Mainistir na Féile *see* Abbeyfeale
96 *J5* **Mainland** *island* N Scotland, UK
96 *L2* **Mainland** *island* NE Scotland, UK
159 *P16* **Mainling** *var.* Tungdor. Xizang Zizhiqu, W China
152 *K12* **Mainpuri** Uttar Pradesh, N India
103 *N5* **Maintenon** Eure-et-Loir, C France
172 *H4* **Maintirano** Mahajanga, W Madagascar
93 *M15* **Mainua** Oulu, C Finland
101 *G18* **Mainz** *Fr.* Mayence. Rheinland-Pfalz, SW Germany
76 *I9* **Maio** *var.* Vila do Maio. Maio, S Cape Verde
76 *E10* **Maio** *var.* Mayo. *island* Ilhas de Sotavento, SE Cape Verde
62 *G12* **Maipo, Río** ≈ C Chile
62 *H12* **Maipo, Volcán** 🌋 W Argentina
61 *E22* **Maipú** Buenos Aires, E Argentina
62 *I11* **Maipú** Mendoza, E Argentina
62 *H11* **Maipú** Santiago, C Chile
106 *A9* **Maira** ≈ NW Italy
108 *I10* **Maira** *It.* Mera. ≈ Italy/Switzerland
153 *V12* **Mairābari** Assam, NE India
44 *K7* **Maisí** Guantánamo, E Cuba
118 *H13* **Maišiagala** Vilnius, SE Lithuania
153 *V17* **Maiskhal Island** *island* SE Bangladesh
167 *N13* **Mai Sombun** Chumphon, SW Thailand
Mai Son *see* Hat Lot
Maisur *see* Karnātaka, India
Maisur *see* Mysore, India
183 *T8* **Maitland** New South Wales, SE Australia
182 *I9* **Maitland** South Australia
14 *F15* **Maitland** ≈ Ontario, S Canada
195 *R1* **Maitri** *Indian research station* Antarctica
159 *N15* **Maizhokunggar** Xizang Zizhiqu, W China
43 *O10* **Maíz, Islas del** *var.* Corn Islands. *island group* SE Nicaragua
164 *J12* **Maizuru** Kyōto, Honshū, SW Japan
54 *F6* **Majagual** Sucre, N Colombia
41 *Z13* **Majahual** Quintana Roo, E Mexico
Mājeej *see* Mejit Island
171 *N13* **Majene** *prev.* Madjene. Sulawesi, C Indonesia
43 *V15* **Majé, Serranía de** ▲▲ E Panama
112 *I11* **Majevica** ▲▲ NE Bosnia and Herzegovina
81 *H15* **Majī** Southern, S Ethiopia
141 *X7* **Majīs** NW Oman
Majorca *see* Mallorca
105 *X9* **Major, Puig** ▲ Mallorca, Spain, W Mediterranean Sea
Mājro *see* Majuro Atoll
Majunga *see* Mahajanga
189 *Y3* **Majuro** ✈ Majuro Atoll, SE Marshall Islands
189 *Y2* **Majuro Atoll** *var.* Mājro. *atoll* Ratak Chain, SE Marshall Islands
189 *X2* **Majuro Lagoon** *lagoon* Majuro Atoll, SE Marshall Islands
76 *H11* **Maka** C Senegal
79 *F20* **Makabana** Le Niari, SW Congo
38 *D9* **Mākaha** *var.* Makaha. O'ahu, Hawai'i, USA
38 *B8* **Makahū'ena Point** *var.* Makahuena Point. *headland* Kaua'i, Hawai'i, USA
38 *D9* **Makakilo City** O'ahu, Hawai'i, USA
83 *H18* **Makalamabedi** Central, C Botswana
Makale *see* Mek'elē
158 *K17* **Makalu** *Chin.* Makaru Shan. ▲ China/Nepal
81 *G23* **Makampi** Mbeya, S Tanzania
145 *X12* **Makanchi** *Kaz.* Maqanshy. Vostochnyy Kazakhstan, E Kazakhstan
42 *M8* **Makantaka** Región Autónoma Atlántico Norte, NE Nicaragua
190 *B16* **Makapu Point** *headland* W Niue
185 *C24* **Makarewa** Southland, South Island, New Zealand
117 *O4* **Makariv** Kyyivs'ka Oblast', N Ukraine
185 *D20* **Makarora** ≈ South Island, New Zealand
123 *T13* **Makarov** Ostrov Sakhalin, Sakhalinskaya Oblast', SE Russian Federation
197 *R9* **Makarov Basin** *undersea feature* Arctic Ocean
192 *I5* **Makarov Seamount** *undersea feature* W Pacific Ocean
113 *F15* **Makarska** *It.* Macarsca. Split-Dalmacija, SE Croatia
Makaru Shan *see* Makalu
125 *O15* **Makar'yev** Kostromskaya Oblast', NW Russian Federation
82 *L11* **Makasa** Northern, NE Zambia
Makasar *see* Makassar
Makasar, Selat *see* Makassar Straits
170 *M14* **Makassar** *var.* Macassar, Makasar; *prev.* Ujungpandang. Sulawesi, C Indonesia
192 *F7* **Makassar Straits** *Ind.* Makasar Selat. *strait* C Indonesia
144 *G12* **Makat** *Kaz.* Maqat. Atyrau, SW Kazakhstan
191 *T10* **Makatea** *island* Îles Tuamotu, C French Polynesia
139 *U7* **Makātū** E Iraq
172 *H6* **Makay** *var.* Massif du Makay. ▲▲ SW Madagascar
Makay, Massif du *see* Makay
114 *J12* **Makaza** *pass* Bulgaria/Greece
Makedonija *see* Macedonia, FYR
190 *B16* **Makefu** W Niue
191 *V10* **Makemo** *atoll* Îles Tuamotu, C French Polynesia
76 *I15* **Makeni** C Sierra Leone
Makenzen *see* Orlyak
Makeyevka *see* Makiyivka
127 *Q16* **Makhachkala** *prev.* Petrovsk-Port. Respublika Dagestan, SW Russian Federation
144 *F11* **Makhambet** Atyrau, W Kazakhstan
Makharadze *see* Ozurget'i
139 *W13* **Makhfar Al Buṣayyah** S Iraq
139 *R4* **Makhmūr** N Iraq
138 *I11* **Makhrūq, Wadi al** *dry watercourse* E Jordan
139 *R4* **Makḥūl, Jabal** ▲▲ C Iraq
141 *R13* **Makhyah, Wādī** *dry watercourse* N Yemen
171 *V13* **Maki** Papua, E Indonesia
185 *G21* **Makikihi** Canterbury, South Island, New Zealand
191 *O2* **Makin** *prev.* Pitt Island. *atoll* Tungaru, W Kiribati
81 *I20* **Makindu** Eastern, S Kenya
145 *Q8* **Makinsk** Akmola, N Kazakhstan
187 *N10* **Makira** *off.* Makira Province. ⬗ *province* SE Solomon Islands
Makira *see* San Cristobal
Makira Province *see* Makira
117 *X8* **Makiyivka** *Rus.* Makeyevka; *prev.* Dmitriyevsk. Donets'ka Oblast', E Ukraine
140 *L10* **Makkah** *Eng.* Mecca. Makkah, W Saudi Arabia
140 *M10* **Makkah** *var.* Minṭaqat Makkah. ⬗ *province* W Saudi Arabia
Makkah, Minṭaqat *see* Makkah
13 *R7* **Makkovik** Newfoundland and Labrador, NE Canada
98 *K6* **Makkum** Friesland, N Netherlands
111 *M25* **Makó** *Rom.* Macău. Csongrád, SE Hungary
Mako *see* Makung
14 *G9* **Makobe Lake** ◎ Ontario, S Canada
79 *F18* **Makokou** Ogooué-Ivindo, NE Gabon
81 *G23* **Makongolosi** Mbeya, S Tanzania
81 *E19* **Makota** SW Uganda
79 *G18* **Makoua** Cuvette, C Congo
110 *M10* **Maków Mazowiecki** Mazowieckie, C Poland
111 *K17* **Maków Podhalański** Małopolskie, S Poland
143 *V14* **Makran** *cultural region* Iran/Pakistan
152 *G12* **Makrāna** Rājasthān, N India
143 *U15* **Makran Coast** *coastal region* SE Iran
119 *F20* **Makrany** *Rus.* Mokrany. Brestskaya Voblasts', SW Belarus
Makrinoros *see* Makrynóros
115 *H20* **Makrónisosi** *island* Kykládes, Greece, Aegean Sea
115 *D17* **Makrynóros** *var.* Makrinoros. ▲▲ C Greece
115 *G19* **Makryplági** ▲ C Greece
Maksamaa *see* Maxmo
Maksatha *see* Maksatikha
Maksaticha *see* Maksatikha
124 *J15* **Maksatikha** *var.* Maksatha, Maksaticha. Tverskaya Oblast', W Russian Federation
154 *G10* **Maksi** Madhya Pradesh, C India
142 *I1* **Mākū** Āžarbāyjān-e Gharbī, NW Iran
153 *Y11* **Mākum** Assam, NE India
Makun *see* Makung
161 *R14* **Makung** *prev.* Mako, Makun. W Taiwan
164 *B16* **Makurazaki** Kagoshima, Kyūshū, SW Japan
77 *V15* **Makurdi** Benue, C Nigeria
38 *L17* **Makushin Volcano** ▲ Unalaska Island, Alaska, USA
83 *K16* **Makwiro** Mashonaland West, N Zimbabwe
57 *D15* **Mala** Lima, W Peru
Mala *see* Mallow, Ireland
Mala *see* Malaita, Solomon Islands
93 *I14* **Malå** Västerbotten, N Sweden
190 *G12* **Mala'atoli** Île Uvea, E Wallis and Futuna
171 *P8* **Malabang** Mindanao, S Philippines
155 *E21* **Malabār Coast** *coast* SW India
79 *C16* **Malabo** *prev.* Santa Isabel. ● (Equatorial Guinea) Isla de Bioco, NW Equatorial Guinea
79 *C16* **Malabo** ✈ Isla de Bioco, N Equatorial Guinea
Malaca *see* Málaga
Malacca *see* Melaka
168 *I7* **Malacca, Strait of** *Ind.* Selat Malaka. *strait* Indonesia/Malaysia
Malacka *see* Malacky
111 *G20* **Malacky** *Hung.* Malacka. Bratislavský Kraj, W Slovakia
33 *R16* **Malad City** Idaho, NW USA
117 *Q4* **Mala Divytsya** Chernihivs'ka Oblast', N Ukraine
119 *J15* **Maladzyechna** *Pol.* Molodeczno, *Rus.* Molodechno. Minskaya Voblasts', C Belarus
190 *D12* **Malaee** Île Futuna, N Wallis and Futuna
54 *G8* **Málaga** Santander, C Colombia
104 *M15* **Málaga** *anc.* Malaca. Andalucía, S Spain
37 *V15* **Malaga** New Mexico, SW USA
104 *L15* **Málaga** ⬗ *province* Andalucía, S Spain
104 *M15* **Málaga** ✈ Andalucía, S Spain
Malagasy Republic *see* Madagascar
105 *N10* **Malagón** Castilla-La Mancha, C Spain
97 *G18* **Malahide** *Ir.* Mullach Íde. Dublin, E Ireland
187 *N9* **Malaita** *off.* Malaita Province. ⬗ *province* N Solomon Islands
187 *N8* **Malaita** *var.* Mala. *island* N Solomon Islands
Malaita Province *see* Malaita
80 *F13* **Malakal** Upper Nile, S Sudan
112 *C10* **Mala Kapela** ▲▲ NW Croatia
25 *V7* **Malakoff** Texas, SW USA
Malakula *see* Malekula
149 *V7* **Malakwāl** *var.* Mālikwāla. Punjab, E Pakistan
186 *E7* **Malalamai** Madang, W Papua New Guinea
171 *O13* **Malamala** Sulawesi, C Indonesia
169 *S17* **Malang** Jawa, C Indonesia
83 *O14* **Malanga** Niassa, N Mozambique
Malange *see* Malanje
92 *I9* **Malangen** *sound* N Norway
82 *C11* **Malanje** *var.* Malange. Malanje, NW Angola
82 *C11* **Malanje** *var.* Malange. ⬗ *province* N Angola
148 *M16* **Malān, Rās** *cape* SW Pakistan
77 *S13* **Malanville** NE Benin
Malapane *see* Ozimek
155 *F21* **Malappuram** Kerala, SW India
43 *T17* **Mala, Punta** *headland* S Panama
95 *N16* **Mälaren** ◎ C Sweden
62 *H13* **Malargüe** Mendoza, W Argentina
14 *J8* **Malartic** Québec, SE Canada
119 *F20* **Malaryta** *Pol.* Maloryta, *Rus.* Malorita. Brestskaya Voblasts', SW Belarus
63 *J19* **Malaspina** Chubut, SE Argentina
39 *U12* **Malaspina Glacier** *glacier* Alaska, USA
137 *N15* **Malatya** *anc.* Melitene. Malatya, SE Turkey
136 *M14* **Malatya** ⬗ *province* C Turkey
Malavate *see* Pédima
117 *Q7* **Mala Vyska** *Rus.* Malaya Viska. Kirovohrads'ka Oblast', S Ukraine
83 *M14* **Malawi** *off.* Republic of Malaŵi; *prev.* Nyasaland, Nyasaland Protectorate. ◆ *republic* S Africa
Malawi, Lake *see* Nyasa, Lake
Malaŵi, Republic of *see* Malawi
93 *J17* **Malax** *Fin.* Maalahti. Länsi-Soumi, W Finland
124 *H14* **Malaya Vishera** Novgorodskaya Oblast', W Russian Federation
Malaya Viska *see* Mala Vyska
171 *Q7* **Malaybalay** Mindanao, S Philippines
142 *L6* **Malāyer** *prev.* Daulatabad. Hamadān, W Iran
168 *J7* **Malay Peninsula** *peninsula* Malaysia/Thailand
168 *L7* **Malaysia** *var.* Federation of Malaysia; *prev.* the separate territories of Federation of Malaya, Sarawak and Sabah (North Borneo) and Singapore. ◆ *monarchy* SE Asia
Malaysia, Federation of *see* Malaysia
137 *R14* **Malazgirt** Muş, E Turkey
15 *R8* **Malbaie** ≈ Québec, SE Canada
77 *T12* **Malbaza** Tahoua, S Niger
110 *J7* **Malbork** *Ger.* Marienburg, Marienburg in Westpreussen. Pomorskie, N Poland
100 *N9* **Malchin** Mecklenburg-Vorpommern, N Germany
100 *M9* **Malchiner See** ◎ NE Germany
99 *D16* **Maldegem** Oost-Vlaanderen, NW Belgium
98 *L13* **Malden** Gelderland, SE Netherlands
19 *O11* **Malden** Massachusetts, NE USA
27 *Y8* **Malden** Missouri, C USA
191 *X4* **Malden Island** *prev.* Independence Island. *atoll* E Kiribati
173 *Q6* **Maldives** *off.* Maldivian Divehi, Republic of Maldives. ◆ *republic* N Indian Ocean
Maldives, Republic of *see* Maldives
Maldivian Divehi *see* Maldives
97 *P21* **Maldon** E England, UK
61 *G20* **Maldonado** Maldonado, S Uruguay
61 *G20* **Maldonado** ⬗ *department* S Uruguay
41 *P17* **Maldonado, Punta** *headland* S Mexico
106 *G6* **Malè** Trentino-Alto Adige, N Italy
151 *K19* **Male'** *Div.* Maale. ● (Maldives) Male' Atoll, C Maldives
76 *K13* **Maléa** *var.* Maléya. NE Guinea
Maléas, Ákra *see* Agriliá, Akrotírio
115 *G22* **Maléas, Akrotírio** *cape* S Greece
151 *K19* **Male' Atoll** *var.* Kaafu Atoll. *atoll* C Maldives
Malebo, Pool *see* Stanley Pool
154 *E12* **Mālegaon** Mahārāshtra, W India
81 *F15* **Malek** Jonglei, S Sudan
187 *Q13* **Malekula** *var.* Malakula; *prev.* Mallicolo. *island* W Vanuatu
189 *Y15* **Malem** Kosrae, E Micronesia
83 *O15* **Malema** Nampula, N Mozambique
79 *N23* **Malemba-Nkulu** Katanga, SE Dem. Rep. Congo
124 *K9* **Malen'ga** Respublika Kareliya, NW Russian Federation
95 *M20* **Målerås** Kalmar, S Sweden
103 *O6* **Malesherbes** Loiret, C France
115 *G18* **Malesína** Stereá Ellás, E Greece
Maléya *see* Maléa
127 *O15* **Malgobek** Chechenskaya Respublika, SW Russian Federation
105 *X5* **Malgrat de Mar** Cataluña, NE Spain
80 *C9* **Malha** Northern Darfur, W Sudan
139 *Q5* **Malḥāt** C Iraq
32 *K14* **Malheur Lake** ◎ Oregon, NW USA
32 *L14* **Malheur River** ≈ Oregon, NW USA
76 *I13* **Mali** NW Guinea
77 *O9* **Mali** *off.* Republic of Mali, *Fr.* République du Mali; *prev.* French Sudan, Sudanese Republic. ◆ *republic* W Africa
171 *Q16* **Maliana** W East Timor
167 *O2* **Mali Hka** ≈ N Burma (Myanmar)
Mali Idjoš *see* Mali Iđoš
112 *K8* **Mali Iđoš** *var.* Mali Idjoš, *Hung.* Kishegyes; *prev.* Krivaja. Vojvodina, N Serbia
112 *K9* **Mali Kanal** *canal* N Serbia
171 *P12* **Maliku** Sulawesi, N Indonesia
Malik, Wadi al *see* Milk, Wadi el
Mālikwāla *see* Malakwāl
167 *N11* **Mali Kyun** *var.* Tavoy Island. *island* Mergui Archipelago, S Burma (Myanmar)
95 *M19* **Målilla** Kalmar, S Sweden
112 *B11* **Mali Lošinj** *It.* Lussinpiccolo. Primorje-Gorski Kotar, W Croatia
Malin *see* Malyn
171 *P7* **Malindang, Mount** ▲ Mindanao, S Philippines
81 *K20* **Malindi** Coast, SE Kenya
Malines *see* Mechelen
96 *E13* **Malin Head** *Ir.* Cionn Mhálanna. *headland* NW Ireland
171 *O11* **Malino, Gunung** ▲ Sulawesi, N Indonesia
113 *M21* **Maliq** *var.* Maliqi. Korçë, SE Albania
Maliqi *see* Maliq
Mali, Republic of *see* Mali
Mali, République du *see* Mali
171 *Q8* **Malita** Mindanao, S Philippines
154 *G12* **Malkāpur** Mahārāshtra, C India
136 *B10* **Malkara** Tekirdağ, NW Turkey
119 *J19* **Mal'kavichy** *Rus.* Mal'kovichi. Brestskaya Voblasts', SW Belarus
Malkiye *see* Al Mālikīyah
114 *L11* **Malko Sharkovo, Yazovir** ⊠ SE Bulgaria
114 *N11* **Malko Tŭrnovo** Burgas, E Bulgaria
Mal'kovichi *see* Mal'kavichy
183 *R12* **Mallacoota** Victoria, SE Australia
96 *G10* **Mallaig** N Scotland, UK
182 *I9* **Mallala** South Australia
75 *W9* **Mallawi** C Egypt
105 *R5* **Mallén** Aragón, NE Spain
106 *F5* **Malles Venosta** *Ger.* Mals im Vinschgau. Trentino-Alto Adige, N Italy
Mallicolo *see* Malekula
109 *Q8* **Mallnitz** Salzburg, S Austria
105 *W9* **Mallorca** *Eng.* Majorca; *anc.* Baleares Major. *island* Islas Baleares, Spain, W Mediterranean Sea
97 *C20* **Mallow** *Ir.* Mala. SW Ireland
93 *E15* **Malm** Nord-Trøndelag, C Norway
95 *L19* **Malmbäck** Jönköping, S Sweden
92 *J12* **Malmberget** *Lapp.* Malmivaara. Norrbotten, N Sweden
99 *M20* **Malmédy** Liège, E Belgium
83 *E25* **Malmesbury** Western Cape, SW South Africa
Malmivaara *see* Malmberget
95 *N16* **Malmköping** Södermanland, C Sweden
95 *K23* **Malmö** Skåne, S Sweden
95 *K23* **Malmo** ✈ Skåne, S Sweden
45 *Q16* **Malmok** *headland* Bonaire, S Netherlands Antilles
95 *M18* **Malmslätt** Östergötland, S Sweden
125 *R16* **Malmyzh** Kirovskaya Oblast', NW Russian Federation
187 *Q13* **Malo** *island* W Vanuatu
126 *J7* **Maloarkhangel'sk** Orlovskaya Oblast', W Russian Federation
Maļoeļap *see* Maloelap Atoll
189 *V6* **Maloelap Atoll** *var.* Maļoeļap. *atoll* E Marshall Islands
Maloenda *see* Malunda

◆ Country ● Country Capital ◇ Dependent Territory ○ Dependent Territory Capital ⬗ Administrative Regions ✈ International Airport ▲ Mountain ▲▲ Mountain Range 🌋 Volcano ≈ River ◎ Lake ⊠ Reservoir

283

MALOJA – MARACAIBO

108 *I10* **Maloja** Graubünden, S Switzerland
82 *L12* **Malole** Northern, NE Zambia
171 *O3* **Malolos** Luzon, N Philippines
18 *K6* **Malone** New York, NE USA
79 *K25* **Malonga** Katanga, S Dem. Rep. Congo
111 *L17* **Małopolskie** ◐ *province* SE Poland
Malorita/Maloryta *see* Malaryta
124 *K9* **Maloshuyka** Arkhangel'skaya Oblast', NW Russian Federation
114 *G10* **Mal'ovitsa** ▲ W Bulgaria
145 *V15* **Malovodnoye** Almaty, SE Kazakhstan
94 *C10* **Måløy** Sogn Og Fjordane, S Norway
126 *K4* **Maloyaroslavets** Kaluzhskaya Oblast', W Russian Federation
122 *G7* **Malozemel'skaya Tundra** *physical region* NW Russian Federation
104 *J10* **Malpartida de Cáceres** Extremadura, W Spain
104 *K9* **Malpartida de Plasencia** Extremadura, W Spain
106 *C7* **Malpensa** ✕ (Milano) Lombardia, N Italy
76 *J6* **Malqteïr** *desert* N Mauritania
Mals im Vinschgau *see* Malles Venosta
118 *J10* **Malta** Rēzekne, SE Latvia
33 *V7* **Malta** Montana, NW USA
120 *M11* **Malta** *off.* Republic of Malta. ◆ *republic* C Mediterranean Sea
109 *R8* **Malta** *var.* Maltabach. ≈ S Austria
120 *M11* **Malta** *island* Malta, C Mediterrnean Sea
Maltabach *see* Malta
Malta, Canale di *see* Malta Channel
120 *M11* **Malta Channel** *It.* Canale di Malta. *strait* Italy/Malta
83 *D20* **Maltahöhe** Hardap, SW Namibia
Malta, Republic of *see* Malta
97 *N16* **Malton** N England, UK
171 *R13* **Maluku** *off.* Propinsi Maluku, *Dut.* Molukken, *Eng.* Moluccas. ◐ *province* E Indonesia
171 *R13* **Maluku** *Dut.* Molukken, *Eng.* Moluccas; *prev.* Spice Islands. *island group* E Indonesia
Maluku, Laut *see* Molucca Sea
Maluku, Propinsi *see* Maluku
171 *R11* **Maluku Utara** *off.* Propinsi Maluku Utara. ◐ *province* E Indonesia
Maluku Utara, Propinsi *see* Maluku Utara
77 *V13* **Malumfashi** Katsina, N Nigeria
171 *N13* **Malunda** *prev.* Maloenda. Sulawesi, C Indonesia
94 *K13* **Malung** Dalarna, C Sweden
94 *K13* **Malungsfors** Dalarna, C Sweden
186 *M8* **Maluu** *var.* Malu'u. Malaita, N Solomon Islands
Malu'u *see* Maluu
155 *D16* **Mālvan** Mahārāshtra, W India
Malventum *see* Benevento
27 *U12* **Malvern** Arkansas, C USA
29 *S15* **Malvern** Iowa, C USA
44 *I13* **Malvern** ▲ W Jamaica
Malvinas, Islas *see* Falkland Islands
117 *N4* **Malyn** *Rus.* Malin. Zhytomyrs'ka Oblast', N Ukraine
127 *O11* **Malyye Derbety** Respublika Kalmykiya, SW Russian Federation
Malyy Kavkaz *see* Lesser Caucasus
123 *Q6* **Malyy Lyakhovskiy, Ostrov** *island* NE Russian Federation
Malyy Pamir *see* Little Pamir
122 *N5* **Malyy Taymyr, Ostrov** *island* Severnaya Zemlya, N Russian Federation
144 *E10* **Malyy Uzen'** *Kaz.* Kishiözen. ≈ Kazakhstan/Russian Federation
122 *L14* **Malyy Yenisey** *var.* Ka-Krem. ≈ S Russian Federation
127 *S3* **Mamadysh** Respublika Tatarstan, W Russian Federation
117 *N14* **Mamaia** Constanța, E Romania
187 *W14* **Mamanuca Group** *island group* Yasawa Group, W Fiji
146 *L13* **Mamash** Lebap Welaýaty, E Turkmenistan
79 *O17* **Mambasa** Orientale, NE Dem. Rep. Congo
171 *X13* **Mamberamo, Sungai** ≈ Papua, E Indonesia
79 *G15* **Mambéré** ≈ SW Central African Republic
79 *G15* **Mambéré-Kadéï** ◐ *prefecture* SW Central African Republic
Mambij *see* Manbij
79 *H18* **Mambili** ≈ W Congo
83 *N18* **Mambone** *var.* Nova Mambone. Inhambane, E Mozambique
171 *O4* **Mamburao** Mindoro, N Philippines
172 *I16* **Mamelles** *island* Inner Islands, NE Seychelles
99 *M25* **Mamer** Luxembourg, SW Luxembourg
102 *L6* **Mamers** Sarthe, NW France
79 *D15* **Mamfe** Sud-Ouest, W Cameroon
145 *P6* **Mamlyutka** Severnyy Kazakhstan, N Kazakhstan
36 *M15* **Mammoth** Arizona, SW USA
33 *S12* **Mammoth Hot Springs** Wyoming, C USA
Mamoedjoe *see* Mamuju
119 *A14* **Mamonovo** *Ger.* Heiligenbeil. Kaliningradskaya Oblast', W Russian Federation
57 *L14* **Mamoré, Rio** ≈ Bolivia/Brazil
76 *I14* **Mamou** W Guinea
22 *H8* **Mamou** Louisiana, S USA
172 *I14* **Mamoudzou** ○ (Mayotte) C Mayotte
172 *I3* **Mampikony** Mahajanga, N Madagascar
77 *P16* **Mampong** C Ghana
110 *M7* **Mamry, Jezioro** *Ger.* Mauersee. ◎ NE Poland
171 *N13* **Mamuju** *prev.* Mamoedjoe. Sulawesi, S Indonesia
83 *F19* **Mamuno** Ghanzi, W Botswana
113 *K19* **Mamuras** *var.* Mamurasi, Mamurras. Lezhë, C Albania
Mamurasi/Mamurras *see* Mamuras
76 *L16* **Man** W Ivory Coast
55 *X9* **Mana** NW French Guiana
56 *A6* **Manabí** ◐ *province* W Ecuador
42 *G4* **Manabique, Punta** *var.* Cabo Tres Puntas. *headland* E Guatemala
54 *G11* **Manacacías, Río** ≈ C Colombia
58 *F13* **Manacapuru** Amazonas, N Brazil
105 *Y9* **Manacor** Mallorca, Spain, W Mediterranean Sea
171 *Q11* **Manado** *prev.* Menado. Sulawesi, C Indonesia
188 *H5* **Managaha** *island* S Northern Mariana Islands
99 *G20* **Manage** Hainaut, S Belgium
42 *J10* **Managua** ● (Nicaragua) Managua, W Nicaragua
42 *J10* **Managua** ◐ *department* W Nicaragua
42 *J10* **Managua** ✕ Managua, W Nicaragua
42 *J10* **Managua, Lago de** *var.* Xolotlán. ◎ W Nicaragua
Manaḩ *see* Bilād Manaḩ
18 *K16* **Manahawkin** New Jersey, NE USA
184 *K11* **Manaia** Taranaki, North Island, New Zealand
172 *J6* **Manakara** Fianarantsoa, SE Madagascar
152 *J7* **Manāli** Himāchal Pradesh, NW India
129 *U12* **Ma, Nam** *Vtn.* Sông Mã. ≈ Laos/Vietnam
Manama *see* Al Manāmah
186 *D6* **Manam Island** *island* N Papua New Guinea
67 *Y13* **Mananara** ≈ SE Madagascar
182 *M9* **Manangatang** Victoria, SE Australia
172 *J6* **Mananjary** Fianarantsoa, SE Madagascar
76 *L14* **Manankoro** Sikasso, SW Mali
76 *J12* **Manantali, Lac de** ⊠ W Mali
Manáos *see* Manaus
185 *B23* **Manapouri** Southland, South Island, New Zealand
185 *B23* **Manapouri, Lake** ◎ South Island, New Zealand
58 *F13* **Manaquiri** Amazonas, NW Brazil
Manar *see* Mannar
158 *K5* **Manas** Xinjiang Uygur Zizhiqu, NW China
153 *U12* **Manās** *var.* Dangme Chu. ≈ Bhutan/India
153 *P10* **Manāsalu** *var.* Manaslu. ▲ C Nepal
147 *R8* **Manas, Gora** ▲ Kyrgyzstan/Uzbekistan
158 *K3* **Manas Hu** ◎ NW China
Manaslu *see* Manāsalu
37 *S8* **Manassa** Colorado, C USA
21 *W4* **Manassas** Virginia, NE USA
45 *T5* **Manatí** C Puerto Rico
186 *E8* **Manau** Northern, S Papua New Guinea
54 *H4* **Manaure** La Guajira, N Colombia
58 *F12* **Manaus** *prev.* Manáos. *state capital* Amazonas, NW Brazil
136 *G17* **Manavgat** Antalya, SW Turkey
184 *M13* **Manawatu** ≈ North Island, New Zealand
184 *L11* **Manawatu-Wanganui** *off.* Manawatu-Wanganui Region. ◐ *region* North Island, New Zealand
Manawatu-Wanganui Region *see* Manawatu-Wanganui
171 *R7* **Manay** Mindanao, S Philippines
138 *K2* **Manbij** *var.* Mambij, *Fr.* Membidj. Ḩalab, N Syria
105 *N13* **Mancha Real** Andalucía, S Spain
102 *I4* **Manche** ◐ *department* N France
97 *L17* **Manchester** *Lat.* Mancunium. NW England, UK
23 *S5* **Manchester** Georgia, SE USA
29 *Y13* **Manchester** Iowa, C USA
21 *N7* **Manchester** Kentucky, S USA
19 *O10* **Manchester** New Hampshire, NE USA
20 *K10* **Manchester** Tennessee, S USA
18 *M9* **Manchester** Vermont, NE USA
97 *L18* **Manchester** ✕ NW England, UK
149 *P15* **Manchhar Lake** ◎ SE Pakistan
Man-chou-li *see* Manzhouli
129 *X7* **Manchurian Plain** *plain* NE China
Máncio Lima *see* Japiim
Mancunium *see* Manchester
148 *J15* **Mand** Baluchistān, SW Pakistan
Mand *see* Mand, Rūd-e
81 *H25* **Manda** Iringa, SW Tanzania
172 *H6* **Mandabe** Toliara, W Madagascar
162 *M10* **Mandah** *var.* Töhöm. Dornogovĭ, SE Mongolia
95 *E18* **Mandal** Vest-Agder, S Norway
Mandal *see* Arbulag, Hövsgöl, Mongolia
Mandal *see* Batsümber, Töv, Mongolia
166 *L5* **Mandalay** Mandalay, C Burma (Myanmar)
166 *M6* **Mandalay** ◐ *division* C Burma (Myanmar)
162 *L9* **Mandalgovĭ** Dundgovĭ, C Mongolia
139 *V7* **Mandalī** E Iraq
162 *K10* **Mandal-Ovoo** *var.* Sharhulsan. Ömnögovĭ, S Mongolia
95 *E18* **Mandalselva** ≈ S Norway
163 *P11* **Mandalt** *var.* Sonid Zuoqi. Nei Mongol Zizhiqu, N China
28 *M5* **Mandan** North Dakota, N USA
Mandargiri Hill *see* Mandār Hill
153 *R14* **Mandār Hill** *prev.* Mandargiri Hill. Bihār, NE India
170 *M13* **Mandar, Teluk** *bay* Sulawesi, C Indonesia
107 *C19* **Mandas** Sardegna, Italy, C Mediterranean Sea
Mandasor *see* Mandsaur
81 *L16* **Mandera** North Eastern, NE Kenya
33 *V13* **Manderson** Wyoming, C USA
44 *J12* **Mandeville** C Jamaica
22 *K9* **Mandeville** Louisiana, S USA
152 *I7* **Mandi** Himāchal Pradesh, NW India
76 *K14* **Mandiana** E Guinea
149 *U10* **Mandi Būrewāla** *var.* Būrewāla. Punjab, E Pakistan
152 *G9* **Mandi Dabwāli** Haryāna, NW India
Mandidzudzure *see* Chimanimani
83 *M15* **Mandié** Manica, NW Mozambique
83 *N14* **Mandimba** Niassa, N Mozambique
57 *Q19* **Mandioré, Laguna** ◎ E Bolivia
154 *J10* **Mandla** Madhya Pradesh, C India
83 *M20* **Mandlakazi** *var.* Manjacaze. Gaza, S Mozambique
95 *E24* **Mandø** *var.* Manø. *island* W Denmark
Mandoúdhion/Mandoudi *see* Mantoúdi
115 *G19* **Mándra** Attikí, C Greece
172 *I7* **Mandrare** ≈ S Madagascar
114 *M10* **Mandra, Yazovir** *salt lake* SE Bulgaria
107 *L23* **Mandrazzi, Portella** *pass* Sicilia, Italy, C Mediterranean Sea
172 *J3* **Mandritsara** Mahajanga, N Madagascar
143 *O13* **Mand, Rūd-e** *var.* Mand. ≈ S Iran
154 *F9* **Mandsaur** *prev.* Mandasor. Madhya Pradesh, C India
154 *F11* **Māndu** Madhya Pradesh, C India
169 *W8* **Mandul, Pulau** *island* N Indonesia
83 *G15* **Mandundu** Western, W Zambia
180 *I13* **Mandurah** Western Australia
107 *P18* **Manduria** Puglia, SE Italy
155 *G20* **Mandya** Karnātaka, C India
77 *P12* **Mané** C Burkina
106 *E8* **Manerbio** Lombardia, NW Italy
Manevichi *see* Manevychi
116 *K3* **Manevychi** *Pol.* Maniewicze, *Rus.* Manevichi. Volyns'ka Oblast', NW Ukraine
107 *N16* **Manfredonia** Puglia, SE Italy
107 *N16* **Manfredonia, Golfo di** *gulf* Adriatic Sea, N Mediterranean Sea
77 *P13* **Manga** C Burkina
59 *L16* **Mangabeiras, Chapada das** ▲▲ E Brazil
79 *J20* **Mangai** Bandundu, W Dem. Rep. Congo
190 *L17* **Mangaia** *island group* S Cook Islands
184 *M9* **Mangakino** Waikato, North Island, New Zealand
116 *M15* **Mangalia** *anc.* Callatis. Constanța, SE Romania
78 *J11* **Mangalmé** Guéra, SE Chad
155 *E19* **Mangalore** Karnātaka, W India
191 *Y13* **Mangareva** *var.* Magareva. *island* Îles Tuamotu, SE French Polynesia
83 *I23* **Mangaung** Free State, C South Africa
Mangaung *see* Bloemfontein
154 *K9* **Mangawān** Madhya Pradesh, C India
184 *M11* **Mangaweka** Manawatu-Wanganui, North Island, New Zealand
184 *N11* **Mangaweka** ▲ North Island, New Zealand
79 *P17* **Mangbwalu** Orientale, NE Dem. Rep. Congo
101 *L24* **Mangfall** ≈ SE Germany
169 *P13* **Manggar** Pulau Belitung, W Indonesia
166 *M2* **Mangin Range** ▲▲ N Burma (Myanmar)
139 *R1* **Mangish** N Iraq
144 *F15* **Mangistau** *Kaz.* Mangqystaū Oblysy; *prev.* Mangyshlaskaya. ◐ *province* SW Kazakhstan
Mangit *see* Mang'it
146 *H8* **Mang'it** *Rus.* Mangit. Qoraqalpog'iston Respublikasi, W Uzbekistan
54 *A13* **Manglares, Cabo** *headland* SW Colombia
149 *V6* **Mangla Reservoir** ⊠ NE Pakistan
159 *N9* **Mangnai** *var.* Lao Mangnai. Qinghai, C China
Mango *see* Mago, Fiji
Mango *see* Sansanné-Mango, Togo
Mangoche *see* Mangochi
83 *N14* **Mangochi** *var.* Mangoche; *prev.* Fort Johnston. Southern, SE Malawi
77 *N14* **Mangodara** SW Burkina
172 *H6* **Mangoky** ≈ W Madagascar
171 *Q12* **Mangole, Pulau** *island* Kepulauan Sula, E Indonesia
184 *J2* **Mangonui** Northland, North Island, New Zealand
Mangqystaū Oblysy *see* Mangistau
Mangqystaū Shyghanaghy *see* Mangyshlakskiy Zaliv
Mangshi *see* Luxi
104 *H7* **Mangualde** Viseu, N Portugal
61 *H18* **Mangueira, Lagoa** ◎ S Brazil
77 *X6* **Manguéni, Plateau du** ▲▲ NE Niger
163 *T4* **Mangui** Nei Mongol Zizhiqu, N China
26 *K11* **Mangum** Oklahoma, C USA
79 *O18* **Manguredjipa** Nord Kivu, E Dem. Rep. Congo
83 *L16* **Mangwendi** Mashonaland East, E Zimbabwe
144 *F15* **Mangyshlak, Plato** *plateau* SW Kazakhstan
144 *E14* **Mangyshlakskiy Zaliv** *Kaz.* Mangqystaū Shyghanaghy. *gulf* SW Kazakhstan
Mangyshlaskaya *see* Mangistau
162 *E7* **Manhan** *var.* Tögrög. Hovd, W Mongolia
Manhan *see* Alag-Erdene
27 *O4* **Manhattan** Kansas, C USA
99 *L21* **Manhay** Luxembourg, SE Belgium
83 *L21* **Manhiça** *prev.* Vila de Manhiça. Maputo, S Mozambique
83 *L21* **Manhoca** Maputo, S Mozambique
59 *N20* **Manhuaçu** Minas Gerais, SE Brazil
54 *H10* **Maní** Casanare, C Colombia
143 *R11* **Mānī** Kermān, C Iran
83 *M17* **Manica** *var.* Vila de Manica. Manica, W Mozambique
83 *M17* **Manica** *off.* Província de Manica. ◐ *province* W Mozambique
83 *L17* **Manicaland** ◐ *province* E Zimbabwe
Manica, Província de *see* Manica
15 *U5* **Manic Deux, Réservoir** ⊠ Québec, SE Canada
Manich *see* Manych
59 *F14* **Manicoré** Amazonas, N Brazil
13 *N11* **Manicouagan** Québec, SE Canada
13 *N11* **Manicouagan** ≈ Québec, SE Canada
15 *U6* **Manicouagan, Péninsule de** *peninsula* Québec, SE Canada
13 *N11* **Manicouagan, Réservoir** ◎ Québec, E Canada
15 *T4* **Manic Trois, Réservoir** ⊠ Québec, SE Canada
79 *M20* **Maniema** *off.* Région du Maniema. ◐ *region* E Dem. Rep. Congo
Maniema, Région du *see* Maniema
Maniewicze *see* Manevychi
160 *F8* **Maniganggo** Sichuan, C China
9 *Y15* **Manigotagan** Manitoba, S Canada
153 *R13* **Manihāri** Bihār, N India
191 *U9* **Manihi** *island* Îles Tuamotu, C French Polynesia
190 *L13* **Manihiki** *atoll* N Cook Islands
175 *U8* **Manihiki Plateau** *undersea feature* C Pacific Ocean
196 *M14* **Maniitsoq** *var.* Manîtsoq, *Dan.* Sukkertoppen. ◐ Kitaa, S Greenland
153 *T15* **Manikganj** Dhaka, C Bangladesh
152 *M14* **Mānikpur** Uttar Pradesh, N India
171 *N4* **Manila** *off.* City of Manila. ● (Philippines) Luzon, N Philippines
27 *Y9* **Manila** Arkansas, C USA
Manila, City of *see* Manila
189 *N16* **Manila Reef** *reef* W Micronesia
183 *T6* **Manilla** New South Wales, SE Australia
192 *P6* **Maniloa** *island* Tongatapu Group, S Tonga
123 *U8* **Manily** Koryakskiy Avtonomnyy Okrug, E Russian Federation
171 *V12* **Manim, Pulau** *island* E Indonesia
168 *I11* **Maninjau, Danau** ◎ Sumatera, W Indonesia
153 *W13* **Manipur** ◐ *state* NE India
153 *X14* **Manipur Hills** *hill range* E India
136 *C14* **Manisa** *var.* Manissa, *prev.* Saruhan; *anc.* Magnesia. Manisa, W Turkey
136 *C13* **Manisa** *var.* Manissa. ◐ *province* W Turkey
Manissa *see* Manisa
31 *O7* **Manistee** Michigan, N USA
31 *P7* **Manistee River** ≈ Michigan, N USA
31 *O4* **Manistique** Michigan, N USA
31 *P4* **Manistique Lake** ◎ Michigan, N USA
9 *W13* **Manitoba** ◐ *province* S Canada
9 *X16* **Manitoba, Lake** ◎ Manitoba, S Canada
9 *X17* **Manitou** Manitoba, S Canada
31 *N2* **Manitou Island** *island* Michigan, N USA
14 *H11* **Manitou Lake** ◎ Ontario, SE Canada
12 *G15* **Manitoulin Island** *island* Ontario, S Canada
37 *T5* **Manitou Springs** Colorado, C USA
14 *G12* **Manitouwabing Lake** ◎ Ontario, S Canada
12 *E12* **Manitouwadge** Ontario, S Canada
12 *G15* **Manitowaning** Manitoulin Island, Ontario, S Canada
14 *B7* **Manitowik Lake** ◎ Ontario, S Canada
31 *N7* **Manitowoc** Wisconsin, N USA
Manîtsoq *see* Maniitsoq
139 *O7* **Mānī', Wādī al** *dry watercourse* W Iraq
12 *J14* **Maniwaki** Québec, SE Canada
171 *W13* **Maniwori** Papua, E Indonesia
54 *E10* **Manizales** Caldas, W Colombia
112 *F11* **Manjača** ▲▲ NW Bosnia and Herzegovina
Manjacaze *see* Mandlakazi
180 *J14* **Manjimup** Western Australia
109 *V4* **Mank** Niederösterreich, C Austria
79 *I17* **Mankanza** Equateur, NW Dem. Rep. Congo
153 *N12* **Mankāpur** Uttar Pradesh, N India
26 *M3* **Mankato** Kansas, C USA
29 *U10* **Mankato** Minnesota, N USA
117 *O7* **Man'kivka** Cherkas'ka Oblast', C Ukraine
76 *M15* **Mankono** C Ivory Coast
9 *T17* **Mankota** Saskatchewan, S Canada
155 *K23* **Mankulam** Northern Province, N Sri Lanka
162 *L10* **Manlay** *var.* Üydzen. Ömnögovĭ, S Mongolia
39 *Q9* **Manley Hot Springs** Alaska, USA
18 *H10* **Manlius** New York, NE USA
105 *W5* **Manlleu** Cataluña, NE Spain
29 *V11* **Manly** Iowa, C USA
154 *E13* **Manmād** Mahārāshtra, W India
182 *J7* **Mannahill** South Australia
155 *J23* **Mannar** *var.* Manar. Northern Province, NW Sri Lanka
155 *I24* **Mannar, Gulf of** *gulf* India/Sri Lanka
155 *J23* **Mannar Island** *island* N Sri Lanka
Mannersdorf *see* Mannersdorf am Leithagebirge
109 *Y5* **Mannersdorf am Leithagebirge** *var.* Mannersdorf. Niederösterreich, E Austria
109 *Y6* **Mannersdorf an der Rabnitz** Burgenland, E Austria
101 *G20* **Mannheim** Baden-Württemberg, SW Germany
9 *O12* **Manning** Alberta, W Canada
29 *T14* **Manning** Iowa, C USA
28 *K5* **Manning** North Dakota, N USA
21 *S13* **Manning** South Carolina, SE USA
191 *Y2* **Manning, Cape** *headland* Kiritimati, NE Kiribati
21 *S3* **Mannington** West Virginia, NE USA
182 *A1* **Mann Ranges** ▲▲ South Australia
107 *C19* **Mannu** ≈ Sardegna, Italy, C Mediterranean Sea
9 *R14* **Mannville** Alberta, SW Canada
76 *J15* **Mano** ≈ Liberia/Sierra Leone
Manø *see* Mandø
39 *O13* **Manokotak** Alaska, USA
171 *V12* **Manokwari** Papua, E Indonesia
79 *N22* **Manono** Shabo, SE Dem. Rep. Congo
25 *T10* **Manor** Texas, SW USA
97 *D16* **Manorhamilton** *Ir.* Cluainín. Leitrim, NW Ireland
103 *S15* **Manosque** Alpes-de-Haute-Provence, SE France
12 *L11* **Manouane, Lac** ◎ Québec, SE Canada
163 *W12* **Manp'o** *var.* Manp'ojin. NW North Korea
Manp'ojin *see* Manp'o
191 *T4* **Manra** *prev.* Sydney Island. *atoll* Phoenix Islands, C Kiribati
105 *V5* **Manresa** Cataluña, NE Spain
152 *H9* **Mānsa** Punjab, NW India
82 *J12* **Mansa** *prev.* Fort Rosebery. Luapula, N Zambia
76 *G12* **Mansa Konko** C Gambia
15 *Q11* **Manseau** Québec, SE Canada
149 *U5* **Mānsehra** North-West Frontier Province, NW Pakistan
9 *Q9* **Mansel Island** *island* Nunavut, NE Canada
183 *O12* **Mansfield** Victoria, SE Australia
97 *M18* **Mansfield** C England, UK
27 *S11* **Mansfield** Arkansas, C USA
22 *G6* **Mansfield** Louisiana, S USA
19 *O12* **Mansfield** Massachusetts, NE USA
31 *T12* **Mansfield** Ohio, N USA
18 *G12* **Mansfield** Pennsylvania, NE USA
18 *M7* **Mansfield, Mount** ▲ Vermont, NE USA
59 *M16* **Mansidão** Bahia, E Brazil
102 *L11* **Mansle** Charente, W France
76 *G12* **Mansôa** C Guinea-Bissau
47 *V8* **Manso, Rio** ≈ C Brazil
Manṣûra *see* El Manṣûra
Mansurabad *see* Mehrān, Rūd-e
56 *A6* **Manta** Manabí, W Ecuador
56 *A6* **Mania, Bahía de** *bay* W Ecuador
57 *F14* **Mantaro, Río** ≈ C Peru
35 *O8* **Manteca** California, W USA
54 *J7* **Mantecal** Apure, C Venezuela
31 *N11* **Manteno** Illinois, N USA
21 *Y9* **Manteo** Roanoke Island, North Carolina, SE USA
Mantes-Gassicourt *see* Mantes-la-Jolie
103 *N5* **Mantes-la-Jolie** *prev.* Mantes-Gassicourt, Mantes-sur-Seine; *anc.* Medunta. Yvelines, N France
Mantes-sur-Seine *see* Mantes-la-Jolie
36 *L5* **Manti** Utah, W USA
Mantinea *see* Mantíneia
115 *F20* **Mantíneia** *anc.* Mantinea. *site of ancient city* Pelopónnisos, S Greece
59 *M21* **Mantiqueira, Serra da** ▲▲ S Brazil
29 *W10* **Mantorville** Minnesota, N USA
115 *G17* **Mantoúdi** *var.* Mandoudi; *prev.* Mandoúdhion. Évvoia, C Greece
Mantoue *see* Mantova
106 *F8* **Mantova** *Eng.* Mantua, *Fr.* Mantoue. Lombardia, NW Italy
93 *M19* **Mäntsälä** Etelä-Suomi, S Finland
93 *L17* **Mänttä** Länsi-Suomi, W Finland
Mantua *see* Mantova
125 *O14* **Manturovo** Kostromskaya Oblast', NW Russian Federation
93 *M18* **Mäntyharju** Isä-Suomi, SE Finland
92 *M13* **Mäntyjärvi** Lappi, N Finland
190 *L16* **Manuae** *island* S Cook Islands
191 *Q10* **Manuae** *atoll* Îles Sous le Vent, W French Polynesia
192 *L16* **Manua Islands** *island group* E American Samoa
40 *L5* **Manuel Benavides** Chihuahua, N Mexico
61 *D21* **Manuel J. Cobo** Buenos Aires, E Argentina
58 *M12* **Manuel Luís, Recife** *reef* E Brazil
61 *F15* **Manuel Viana** Rio Grande do Sul, S Brazil
59 *I14* **Manuel Zinho** Pará, N Brazil
191 *V11* **Manuhangi** *atoll* Îles Tuamotu, C French Polynesia
185 *E22* **Manuherikia** ≈ South Island, New Zealand
171 *P13* **Manui, Pulau** *island* N Indonesia
Manukau *see* Manurewa
184 *L6* **Manukau Harbour** *harbour* North Island, New Zealand
191 *Z2* **Manulu Lagoon** ◎ Kiritimati, E Kiribati
182 *J7* **Manunda Creek** *seasonal river* South Australia
57 *K15* **Manupari, Río** ≈ N Bolivia
184 *L6* **Manurewa** *var.* Manukau. Auckland, North Island, New Zealand
57 *K15* **Manurimi, Río** ≈ NW Bolivia
186 *D5* **Manus** ◐ *province* N Papua New Guinea
186 *D5* **Manus Island** *var.* Great Admiralty Island. *island* N Papua New Guinea
171 *T16* **Manuwui** Pulau Babar, E Indonesia
29 *Q3* **Manvel** North Dakota, N USA
33 *Z14* **Manville** Wyoming, C USA
22 *G6* **Many** Louisiana, S USA
81 *H21* **Manyara, Lake** ◎ NE Tanzania
126 *L12* **Manych** *var.* Manich. ≈ SW Russian Federation
127 *N13* **Manych-Gudilo, Ozero** *salt lake* SW Russian Federation
83 *H14* **Manyinga** North Western, NW Zambia
105 *O11* **Manzanares** Castilla-La Mancha, C Spain
44 *H7* **Manzanillo** Granma, E Cuba
40 *K14* **Manzanillo** Colima, SW Mexico
40 *K14* **Manzanillo, Bahía** *bay* SW Mexico
37 *S11* **Manzano Mountains** ▲▲ New Mexico, SW USA
37 *R12* **Manzano Peak** ▲ New Mexico, SW USA
163 *R6* **Manzhouli** *var.* Man-chou-li. Nei Mongol Zizhiqu, N China
Manzil Bū Ruqaybah *see* Menzel Bourguiba
139 *X9* **Manzilīyah** E Iraq
83 *L21* **Manzini** *prev.* Bremersdorp. C Swaziland
83 *L21* **Manzini** ✕ (Mbabane) C Swaziland
78 *G10* **Mao** Kanem, W Chad
45 *N8* **Mao** NW Dominican Republic
Maó *see* Mahón
Maoemere *see* Maumere
159 *W9* **Maojing** Gansu, N China
171 *Y14* **Maoke, Pegunungan** *Dut.* Sneeuw-gebergte, *Eng.* Snow Mountains. ▲▲ Papua, E Indonesia
Maol Réidh, Caoc *see* Mweelrea
160 *M15* **Maoming** Guangdong, S China
160 *H8* **Maoxian** *var.* Mao Xian; *prev.* Fengyizhen. Sichuan, C China
Mao Xian *see* Maoxian
83 *L19* **Mapai** Gaza, SW Mozambique
158 *H15* **Mapam Yumco** ◎ W China
83 *I15* **Mapanza** Southern, S Zambia
54 *J4* **Mapararí** Falcón, N Venezuela
41 *U17* **Mapastepec** Chiapas, SE Mexico
169 *V9* **Mapat, Pulau** *island* N Indonesia
171 *Y15* **Mapi** Papua, E Indonesia
171 *V11* **Mapia, Kepulauan** *island group* E Indonesia
40 *L8* **Mapimí** Durango, C Mexico
83 *N19* **Mapinhane** Inhambane, SE Mozambique
55 *N7* **Mapire** Monagas, NE Venezuela
9 *S17* **Maple Creek** Saskatchewan, S Canada
31 *Q9* **Maple River** ≈ Michigan, N USA
29 *P7* **Maple River** ≈ North Dakota/South Dakota, N USA
29 *S13* **Mapleton** Iowa, C USA
29 *U10* **Mapleton** Minnesota, N USA
29 *R5* **Mapleton** North Dakota, N USA
32 *F13* **Mapleton** Oregon, NW USA
36 *L3* **Mapleton** Utah, W USA
192 *K5* **Mapmaker Seamounts** *undersea feature* N Pacific Ocean
186 *B6* **Maprik** East Sepik, NW Papua New Guinea
83 *L21* **Maputo** *prev.* Lourenço Marques. ● (Mozambique) Maputo, S Mozambique
83 *L21* **Maputo** ◐ *province* S Mozambique
67 *V14* **Maputo** ≈ S Mozambique
83 *L21* **Maputo** ✕ Maputo, S Mozambique
Maqanshy *see* Makanchi
Maqat *see* Makat
113 *K19* **Maqë** ≈ NW Albania
113 *M19* **Maqellarë** Dibër, C Albania
159 *S12* **Maqên** *var.* Dawo; *prev.* Dawu. Qinghai, C China
159 *S11* **Maqen Kangri** ▲ C China
159 *U12* **Maqu** *var.* Nyinma. Gansu, C China
104 *M9* **Maqueda** Castilla-La Mancha, C Spain
82 *B9* **Maquela do Zombo** Uíge, NW Angola
63 *I16* **Maquinchao** Río Negro, C Argentina
29 *Z13* **Maquoketa** Iowa, C USA
29 *Y13* **Maquoketa River** ≈ Iowa, C USA
14 *F13* **Mar** Ontario, S Canada
95 *F14* **Mår** ◎ S Norway
81 *G19* **Mara** ◐ *region* N Tanzania
58 *D12* **Maraã** Amazonas, NW Brazil
191 *P8* **Maraa** Tahiti, W French Polynesia
191 *O8* **Maraa, Pointe** *headland* Tahiti, W French Polynesia
59 *K14* **Marabá** Pará, NE Brazil
54 *H5* **Maracaibo** Zulia, NW Venezuela

◆ Country
● Country Capital
◇ Dependent Territory
○ Dependent Territory Capital
◐ Administrative Regions
✕ International Airport
▲ Mountain
▲▲ Mountain Range
⩕ Volcano
≈ River
◎ Lake
⊠ Reservoir

MARACAIBO, GULF OF – MASCOTA

Maracaibo, Gulf of see Venezuela, Golfo de
54 H5 **Maracaibo, Lago de** var. Lake Maracaibo. *inlet* NW Venezuela
Maracaibo, Lake see Maracaibo, Lago de
58 K10 **Maracá, Ilha de** *island* NE Brazil
59 H20 **Maracaju, Serra de** ▲▲ S Brazil
58 I11 **Maracanaquará, Planalto** ▲▲ NE Brazil
54 L5 **Maracay** Aragua, N Venezuela
Marada see Marādah
75 R9 **Marādah** var. Marada. N Libya
77 U12 **Maradi** Maradi, S Niger
77 U11 **Maradi** ◐ *department* S Niger
81 E21 **Maragarazi** var. Muragarazi. ≈ Burundi/Tanzania
Maragha see Marāgheh
142 J3 **Marāgheh** var. Maragha. Āžarbāyjān-e Khāvarī, NW Iran
141 P7 **Marāh** var. Marrāt. Ar Riyāḍ, C Saudi Arabia
55 N11 **Marahuaca, Cerro** ▲ S Venezuela
27 R5 **Marais des Cygnes River** ≈ Kansas/Missouri, C USA
58 L11 **Marajó, Baía de** *bay* N Brazil
59 K12 **Marajó, Ilha de** *island* N Brazil
191 O2 **Marakei** *atoll* Tungaru, W Kiribati
Marakesh see Marrakech
81 I18 **Maralal** Rift Valley, C Kenya
83 G21 **Maralaleng** Kgalagadi, S Botswana
145 U8 **Maraldy, Ozero** ◎ NE Kazakhstan
182 C5 **Maralinga** South Australia
Máramarossziget see Sighetu Marmaţiei
187 N9 **Maramasike** var. Small Malaita. *island* N Solomon Islands
Maramba see Livingstone
194 H3 **Marambio** *Argentinian research station* Antarctica
116 H9 **Maramureş** ◐ *county* NW Romania
36 L15 **Marana** Arizona, SW USA
105 P7 **Maranchón** Castilla-La Mancha, C Spain
142 J2 **Marand** var. Merend. Āžarbāyjān-e Sharqī, NW Iran
Marandellas see Marondera
58 L13 **Maranhão** off. Estado do Maranhão. ◐ *state* E Brazil
104 H10 **Maranhão, Barragem do** ⊠ C Portugal
Maranhão, Estado do see Maranhão
149 O11 **Mārān, Koh-i** ▲ SW Pakistan
106 J7 **Marano, Laguna di** *lagoon* NE Italy
56 E9 **Marañón, Río** ≈ N Peru
102 J10 **Marans** Charente-Maritime, W France
83 M20 **Marão** Inhambane, S Mozambique
185 B23 **Mararoa** ≈ South Island, New Zealand
Maraş/Marash see Kahramanmaraş
107 M19 **Maratea** Basilicata, S Italy
104 G11 **Marateca** Setúbal, S Portugal
115 B20 **Marathiá, Akrotírio** *headland* Zákynthos, Iónia Nisiá, Greece, C Mediterranean Sea
12 E12 **Marathon** Ontario, S Canada
23 Y17 **Marathon** Florida Keys, Florida, SE USA
24 L10 **Marathon** Texas, SW USA
Marathón see Marathónas
115 H19 **Marathónas** prev. Marathón. Attikí, C Greece
169 W9 **Maratua, Pulau** *island* N Indonesia
59 O18 **Maraú** Bahia, SE Brazil
143 R3 **Marāveh Tappeh** Golestān, N Iran
24 L11 **Maravillas Creek** ≈ Texas, SW USA
186 D8 **Marawaka** Eastern Highlands, C Papua New Guinea
171 Q7 **Marawi** Mindanao, S Philippines
137 Y11 **Märäzä** Rus. Maraza. E Azerbaijan
Maraza see Märäzä
Marbat see Mirbāţ
104 L16 **Marbella** Andalucía, S Spain
180 J7 **Marble Bar** Western Australia
36 L9 **Marble Canyon** *canyon* Arizona, SW USA
25 S10 **Marble Falls** Texas, SW USA
27 Y7 **Marble Hill** Missouri, C USA
33 T15 **Marbleton** Wyoming, C USA
Marburg see Marburg an der Lahn
Marburg see Maribor
101 H16 **Marburg an der Lahn** hist. Marburg. Hessen, W Germany
111 H23 **Marcal** ≈ W Hungary
42 G7 **Marcala** La Paz, SW Honduras
111 H24 **Marcali** Somogy, SW Hungary
83 A16 **Marca, Ponta da** *headland* SW Angola
59 I16 **Marcelândia** Mato Grosso, W Brazil
27 T3 **Marceline** Missouri, C USA
60 I13 **Marcelino Ramos** Rio Grande do Sul, S Brazil
55 Y12 **Marcel, Mont** ▲ S French Guiana
97 O19 **March** E England, UK
109 Z3 **March** var. Morava. ≈ C Europe **see also** Morava
March see Morava
106 I12 **Marche** Eng. Marches. ◐ *region* C Italy
103 N11 **Marche** *cultural region* C France
99 J21 **Marche-en-Famenne** Luxembourg, SE Belgium
104 K14 **Marchena** Andalucía, S Spain
57 B17 **Marchena, Isla** var. Bindloe Island. *island* Galapagos Islands, Ecuador, E Pacific Ocean
Marches see Marche
99 J20 **Marchin** Liège, E Belgium
181 S1 **Marchinbar Island** *island* Wessel Islands, Northern Territory, N Australia
62 L9 **Mar Chiquita, Laguna** ◎ C Argentina
103 Q10 **Marcigny** Saône-et-Loire, C France
23 W16 **Marco** Florida, SE USA
Marcodurum see Düren
59 O15 **Marcolândia** Pernambuco, E Brazil
106 I8 **Marco Polo** ✕ (Venezia) Veneto, NE Italy
Marcounda see Markounda
Marcq see Mark
116 M8 **Mărculeşti** Rus. Markuleshty. N Moldova
29 S12 **Marcus** Iowa, C USA
39 S11 **Marcus Baker, Mount** ▲ Alaska, USA
192 I5 **Marcus Island** var. Minami Tori Shima. *island* E Japan
18 K8 **Marcy, Mount** ▲ New York, NE USA
149 T5 **Mardān** North-West Frontier Province, N Pakistan
63 N14 **Mar del Plata** Buenos Aires, E Argentina
137 Q16 **Mardin** Mardin, SE Turkey
137 Q16 **Mardin** ◐ *province* SE Turkey
137 Q16 **Mardin Dağları** ▲▲ SE Turkey
Mardzad see Hayrhandulaan
187 R17 **Maré** *island* Îles Loyauté, E New Caledonia
Marea Neagră see Black Sea
105 Z8 **Mare de Déu del Toro** var. El Toro. ▲ Menorca, Spain, W Mediterranean Sea
181 W4 **Mareeba** Queensland, NE Australia
96 G8 **Maree, Loch** ◎ N Scotland, UK
Mareeq see Mereeg
Marek see Dupnitsa
76 J11 **Maréna** Kayes, W Mali
191 I2 **Marenanuka** *atoll* Tungaru, W Kiribati
29 X14 **Marengo** Iowa, C USA
102 J11 **Marennes** Charente-Maritime, W France
107 G23 **Marettimo, Isola** *island* Isole Egadi, S Italy
24 K10 **Marfa** Texas, SW USA
57 P17 **Marfil, Laguna** ◎ E Bolivia
Marganets see Marhanets'
25 Q4 **Margaret** Texas, SW USA
180 I14 **Margaret River** Western Australia
186 C7 **Margarima** Southern Highlands, W Papua New Guinea
55 N4 **Margarita, Isla de** *island* N Venezuela
115 I25 **Margarítes** Kríti, Greece, E Mediterranean Sea
97 Q22 **Margate** prev. Mergate. SE England, UK
23 Z15 **Margate** Florida, SE USA
Margelan see Marg'ilon
103 P13 **Margeride, Montagnes de la** ▲▲ C France
Margherita see Jamaame
107 N16 **Margherita di Savoia** Puglia, SE Italy
Margherita, Lake see Ābaya Hāyk'
81 E18 **Margherita Peak** Fr. Pic Marguerite. ▲ Uganda/Dem. Rep. Congo
149 O4 **Marghī** Bāmīān, N Afghanistan
116 G9 **Marghita** Hung. Margitta. Bihor, NW Romania
Margilan see Marg'ilon
147 S10 **Marg'ilon** var. Margelan, Rus. Margilan. Farg'ona Viloyati, E Uzbekistan
116 K8 **Marginea** Suceava, NE Romania
Margitta see Marghita
148 K9 **Mārgow, Dasht-e** *desert* SW Afghanistan
99 L18 **Margraten** Limburg, SE Netherlands
10 M15 **Marguerite** British Columbia, SW Canada
15 V3 **Marguerite** ≈ Québec, SE Canada
194 I6 **Marguerite Bay** *bay* Antarctica
Marguerite, Pic see Margherita Peak
117 T9 **Marhanets'** Rus. Marganets. Dnipropetrovs'ka Oblast', E Ukraine
186 B9 **Mari** Western, SW Papua New Guinea
191 Y12 **Maria** *atoll* Groupe Actéon, SE French Polynesia
191 R12 **Maria** *island* Îles Australes, SW French Polynesia
40 I12 **María Cleofas, Isla** *island* C Mexico
62 H4 **María Elena** var. Oficina María Elena. Antofagasta, N Chile
95 G21 **Mariager** Århus, C Denmark
61 C22 **María Ignacia** Buenos Aires, E Argentina
183 P17 **Maria Island** *island* Tasmania, SE Australia
40 H12 **María Madre, Isla** *island* C Mexico
40 I12 **María Magdalena, Isla** *island* C Mexico
192 H6 **Mariana Islands** *island group* Guam/Northern Mariana Islands
175 N3 **Mariana Trench** var. Challenger Deep. *undersea feature* W Pacific Ocean
153 X12 **Mariāni** Assam, NE India
27 X11 **Marianna** Arkansas, C USA
23 R8 **Marianna** Florida, SE USA
172 J16 **Marianne** *island* Inner Islands, NE Seychelles
95 M19 **Mariannelund** Jönköping, S Sweden
61 D15 **Mariano I. Loza** Corrientes, NE Argentina
Mariano Machado see Ganda
111 A16 **Mariánské Lázně** Ger. Marienbad. Karlovarský Kraj, W Czech Republic
Máriaradna see Radna
33 S7 **Marias River** ≈ Montana, NW USA
Maria-Theresiopel see Subotica
Máriatölgyes see Dubnica nad Váhom
184 H1 **Maria van Diemen, Cape** *headland* North Island, New Zealand
109 V5 **Mariazell** Steiermark, E Austria
141 P15 **Mar'ib** W Yemen
95 I25 **Maribo** Storstrøm, S Denmark
109 W9 **Maribor** Ger. Marburg. NE Slovenia
35 R13 **Maricopa** California, W USA
Maricourt see Kangiqsujuaq
81 D15 **Maridi** Western Equatoria, SW Sudan
194 M11 **Marie Byrd Land** *physical region* Antarctica
193 P14 **Marie Byrd Seamount** *undersea feature* N Amundsen Sea
45 X11 **Marie-Galante** var. Ceyre to the Caribs. *island* SE Guadeloupe
45 Y6 **Marie-Galante, Canal de** *channel* S Guadeloupe
93 J20 **Mariehamn** Fin. Maarianhamina. Åland, SW Finland
44 C4 **Mariel** La Habana, W Cuba
99 H22 **Mariembourg** Namur, S Belgium
Marienbad see Mariánské Lázně
Marienburg see Alūksne, Latvia
Marienburg see Malbork, Poland
Marienburg see Feldioara, Romania
Marienburg in Westpreussen see Malbork
Marienhausen see Viļaka
83 D20 **Mariental** Hardap, SW Namibia
18 D13 **Marienville** Pennsylvania, NE USA
Marienwerder see Kwidzyń
58 C12 **Marié, Rio** ≈ NW Brazil
95 K17 **Mariestad** Västra Götaland, S Sweden
23 S3 **Marietta** Georgia, SE USA
31 U14 **Marietta** Ohio, N USA
27 N13 **Marietta** Oklahoma, C USA
81 H18 **Marigat** Rift Valley, W Kenya
103 S16 **Marignane** Bouches-du-Rhône, SE France
Marignano see Melegnano
45 O11 **Marigot** NE Dominica
122 K12 **Mariinsk** Kemerovskaya Oblast', S Russian Federation
127 Q3 **Mariinskiy Posad** Respublika Mariy El, W Russian Federation
119 E14 **Marijampolė** prev. Kapsukas. Marijampolė, S Lithuania
114 G12 **Marikostenovo** Blagoevgrad, SW Bulgaria
60 J9 **Marília** São Paulo, S Brazil
82 D11 **Marimba** Malanje, NW Angola
139 T1 **Marī Mīlā** E Iraq
104 G4 **Marín** Galicia, NW Spain
35 N10 **Marina** California, W USA
Mar'ina Gorka see Mar"ina Horka
119 L17 **Mar"ina Horka** Rus. Mar'ina Gorka. Minskaya Voblasts', C Belarus
171 O4 **Marinduque** *island* C Philippines
31 S9 **Marine City** Michigan, N USA
31 N6 **Marinette** Wisconsin, N USA
60 I10 **Maringá** Paraná, S Brazil
83 N16 **Maringuè** Sofala, C Mozambique
104 F9 **Marinha Grande** Leiria, C Portugal
107 I15 **Marino** Lazio, C Italy
59 A15 **Mário Lobão** Acre, W Brazil
23 O5 **Marion** Alabama, S USA
27 Y11 **Marion** Arkansas, C USA
30 L17 **Marion** Illinois, N USA
31 P13 **Marion** Indiana, N USA
29 X13 **Marion** Iowa, C USA
27 O5 **Marion** Kansas, C USA
20 H6 **Marion** Kentucky, S USA
21 P9 **Marion** North Carolina, SE USA
31 S12 **Marion** Ohio, N USA
21 T12 **Marion** South Carolina, SE USA
21 Q7 **Marion** Virginia, NE USA
27 O5 **Marion Lake** ⊠ Kansas, C USA
21 S13 **Marion, Lake** ⊠ South Carolina, SE USA
27 S8 **Marionville** Missouri, C USA
55 N7 **Maripa** Bolívar, E Venezuela
55 X11 **Maripasoula** W French Guiana
35 Q9 **Mariposa** California, W USA
61 G19 **Mariscala** Lavalleja, S Uruguay
62 M4 **Mariscal Estigarribia** Boquerón, NW Paraguay
56 C6 **Mariscal Sucre** var. Quito. ✕ (Quito) Pichincha, C Ecuador
30 K16 **Marissa** Illinois, N USA
103 U14 **Maritime Alps** Fr. Alpes Maritimes, It. Alpi Marittime. ▲▲ France/Italy
Maritimes, Alpes see Maritime Alps
Maritime Territory see Primorskiy Kray
114 K11 **Maritsa** var. Marica, Gk. Évros, Turk. Meriç; anc. Hebrus. ≈ SW Europe **see also** Évros/Meriç
Maritsa see Simeonovgrad
Maritsa see Évros
Maritsa see Meriç
Marittime, Alpi see Maritime Alps
Maritzburg see Pietermaritzburg
117 X9 **Mariupol'** prev. Zhdanov. Donets'ka Oblast', SE Ukraine
55 Q6 **Mariusa, Caño** ≈ NE Venezuela
142 J5 **Marīvān** prev. Dezh Shāhpūr. Kordestān, W Iran
127 R3 **Mariyets** Respublika Mariy El, W Russian Federation
118 G4 **Märjamaa** Ger. Merjama. Raplamaa, NW Estonia
99 I15 **Mark** Fr. Marcq. ≈ Belgium/Netherlands
81 N17 **Marka** var. Merca. Shabeellaha Hoose, S Somalia
145 Z10 **Markakol', Ozero** Kaz. Marqaköl. ◎ E Kazakhstan
76 M12 **Markala** Ségou, W Mali
159 S15 **Markam** var. Gartog. Xizang Zizhiqu, W China
95 K21 **Markaryd** Kronoberg, S Sweden
142 L7 **Markazī** off. Ostān-e Markazī. ◐ *province* W Iran
Markazī, Ostān-e see Markazī
14 F14 **Markdale** Ontario, S Canada
27 X10 **Marked Tree** Arkansas, C USA
98 N11 **Markelo** Overijssel, E Netherlands
98 J9 **Markermeer** ◎ C Netherlands
97 N20 **Market Harborough** C England, UK
97 N18 **Market Rasen** E England, UK
123 O10 **Markha** ≈ NE Russian Federation
12 H16 **Markham** Ontario, S Canada
25 V12 **Markham** Texas, SW USA
186 E7 **Markham** ≈ C Papua New Guinea
195 Q11 **Markham, Mount** ▲ Antarctica
110 M11 **Marki** Mazowieckie, C Poland
158 F8 **Markit** Xinjiang Uygur Zizhiqu, NW China
117 Y5 **Markivka** Rus. Markovka. Luhans'ka Oblast', E Ukraine
35 Q7 **Markleeville** California, W USA
98 L8 **Marknesse** Flevoland, N Netherlands
79 H14 **Markounda** var. Marcounda. Ouham, NW Central African Republic
Markovka see Markivka
123 U7 **Markovo** Chukotskiy Avtonomnyy Okrug, NE Russian Federation
127 P8 **Marks** Saratovskaya Oblast', W Russian Federation
22 K2 **Marks** Mississippi, S USA
22 I7 **Marksville** Louisiana, S USA
101 I19 **Marktheidenfeld** Bayern, C Germany
101 J24 **Marktoberdorf** Bayern, S Germany
101 M18 **Marktredwitz** Bayern, E Germany
Markt-Übelbach see Übelbach
27 V3 **Mark Twain Lake** ⊠ Missouri, C USA
Markuleshty see Mărculeşti
101 E14 **Marl** Nordrhein-Westfalen, W Germany
182 E2 **Marla** South Australia
181 Y8 **Marlborough** Queensland, E Australia
97 M22 **Marlborough** S England, UK
185 I15 **Marlborough** off. Marlborough District. ◐ *unitary authority* South Island, New Zealand
Marlborough District see Marlborough
103 P3 **Marle** Aisne, N France
31 S8 **Marlette** Michigan, N USA
25 T9 **Marlin** Texas, SW USA
21 S5 **Marlinton** West Virginia, NE USA
26 M12 **Marlow** Oklahoma, C USA
155 E17 **Marmagao** Goa, W India
Marmanda see Marmande
102 L13 **Marmande** anc. Marmanda. Lot-et-Garonne, SW France
136 C11 **Marmara** Balıkesir, NW Turkey
136 D11 **Marmara Denizi** Eng. Sea of Marmara. *sea* NW Turkey
114 N13 **Marmaraereğlisi** Tekirdağ, NW Turkey
Marmara, Sea of see Marmara Denizi
136 C16 **Marmaris** Muğla, SW Turkey
28 J6 **Marmarth** North Dakota, N USA
21 Q5 **Marmet** West Virginia, NE USA
106 H5 **Marmolada, Monte** ▲ N Italy
104 M13 **Marmolejo** Andalucía, S Spain
14 J14 **Marmora** Ontario, SE Canada
39 Q14 **Marmot Bay** *bay* Alaska, USA
103 Q4 **Marne** ◐ *department* N France
103 Q4 **Marne** ≈ N France
137 U10 **Marneuli** prev. Borchalo, Sarvani. S Georgia
78 I13 **Maro** Moyen-Chari, S Chad
54 L12 **Maroa** Amazonas, S Venezuela
172 J3 **Maroantsetra** Toamasina, NE Madagascar
191 W11 **Marokau** *atoll* Îles Tuamotu, C French Polynesia
172 J5 **Marolambo** Toamasina, E Madagascar
172 J2 **Maromokotro** ▲ N Madagascar
83 L16 **Marondera** prev. Marandellas. Mashonaland East, NE Zimbabwe
55 X9 **Maroni** Dut. Marowijne. ≈ French Guiana/Surinam
183 V2 **Maroochydore-Mooloolaba** Queensland, E Australia
171 N14 **Maros** Sulawesi, C Indonesia
116 H11 **Maros** var. Mureş, Mureşul, Ger. Marosch, Mieresch. ≈ Hungary/Romania **see also** Mureş
Marosch see Maros/Mureş
Maroshevíz see Toplița
Marosillye see Ilia
Marosludas see Luduş
Marosújvár/Marosújvárakna see Ocna Mureş
Marosvásárhely see Târgu Mureş
191 V14 **Marotiri** var. Îlots de Bass, Morotiri. *island group* Îles Australes, SW French Polynesia
78 G12 **Maroua** Extrême-Nord, N Cameroon
55 X12 **Marouini Rivier** ≈ SE Surinam
172 I3 **Marovoay** Mahajanga, NW Madagascar
55 W9 **Marowijne** ◐ *district* NE Surinam
Marowijne see Maroni
Marqaköl see Markakol', Ozero
193 P8 **Marquesas Fracture Zone** *tectonic feature* E Pacific Ocean
Marquesas Islands see Marquises, Îles
23 W17 **Marquesas Keys** *island group* Florida, SE USA
29 Y12 **Marquette** Iowa, C USA
31 N3 **Marquette** Michigan, N USA
103 N1 **Marquise** Pas-de-Calais, N France
191 X7 **Marquises, Îles** Eng. Marquesas Islands. *island group* N French Polynesia
183 Q6 **Marra Creek** ≈ New South Wales, SE Australia
80 B10 **Marra Hills** *plateau* W Sudan
80 B11 **Marra, Jebel** ▲ W Sudan
74 E7 **Marrakech** var. Marakesh, Eng. Marrakesh; prev. Morocco. W Morocco
Marrakesh see Marrakech
Marrāt see Marāh
183 N15 **Marrawah** Tasmania, SE Australia
182 I4 **Marree** South Australia
81 L17 **Marrehan** ▲▲ SW Somalia
83 N17 **Marromeu** Sofala, C Mozambique
104 J17 **Marroquí, Punta** *headland* SW Spain
183 N8 **Marrowie Creek** *seasonal river* New South Wales, SE Australia
83 O14 **Marrupa** Niassa, N Mozambique
182 D1 **Marryat** South Australia
75 Y10 **Marsa 'Alam** SE Egypt
75 R8 **Marsá al Burayqah** var. Al Burayqah. N Libya
81 J17 **Marsabit** Eastern, N Kenya
107 H23 **Marsala** anc. Lilybaeum. Sicilia, Italy, C Mediterranean Sea
121 P16 **Marsaxlokk Bay** *bay* SE Malta
65 G15 **Mars Bay** *bay* Ascension Island, C Atlantic Ocean
101 H15 **Marsberg** Nordrhein-Westfalen, W Germany
9 R15 **Marsden** Saskatchewan, S Canada
98 H7 **Marsdiep** *strait* NW Netherlands
103 R16 **Marseille** Eng. Marseilles; anc. Massilia. Bouches-du-Rhône, SE France
Marseille-Marigrane see Provence
30 M11 **Marseilles** Illinois, N USA
Marseilles see Marseille
76 J16 **Marshall** W Liberia
39 N11 **Marshall** Alaska, USA
27 U9 **Marshall** Arkansas, C USA
31 N14 **Marshall** Illinois, N USA
31 Q10 **Marshall** Michigan, N USA
29 S9 **Marshall** Minnesota, N USA
27 T4 **Marshall** Missouri, C USA
21 O9 **Marshall** North Carolina, SE USA
25 X6 **Marshall** Texas, SW USA
189 S4 **Marshall Islands** off. Republic of the Marshall Islands. ◆ *republic* W Pacific Ocean
175 Q3 **Marshall Islands** *island group* W Pacific Ocean
Marshall Islands, Republic of the see Marshall Islands
192 K6 **Marshall Seamounts** *undersea feature* SW Pacific Ocean
29 W13 **Marshalltown** Iowa, C USA
19 P12 **Marshfield** Massachusetts, NE USA
27 T7 **Marshfield** Missouri, C USA
30 K6 **Marshfield** Wisconsin, N USA
44 H1 **Marsh Harbour** Great Abaco, W Bahamas
19 S3 **Mars Hill** Maine, NE USA
21 P9 **Mars Hill** North Carolina, SE USA
22 H10 **Marsh Island** *island* Louisiana, S USA
21 S11 **Marshville** North Carolina, SE USA
15 W5 **Marsoui** Québec, SE Canada
15 R8 **Mars, Rivière à** ≈ Québec, SE Canada
95 O15 **Märsta** Stockholm, C Sweden
95 H24 **Marstal** Fyn, C Denmark
95 I19 **Marstrand** Västra Götaland, S Sweden
25 U8 **Mart** Texas, SW USA
166 M9 **Martaban** var. Moktama. Mon State, S Burma (Myanmar)
166 L9 **Martaban, Gulf of** *gulf* S Burma (Myanmar)
107 Q19 **Martano** Puglia, SE Italy
Martapoera see Martapura
169 T13 **Martapura** prev. Martapoera. Borneo, C Indonesia
99 L23 **Martelange** Luxembourg, SE Belgium
114 L7 **Marten** Ruse, N Bulgaria
14 H10 **Marten River** Ontario, S Canada
9 T15 **Martensville** Saskatchewan, S Canada
Marteskirch see Târnăveni
Martes Tolosane see Martres-Tolosane
115 K25 **Mártha** Kríti, Greece, E Mediterranean Sea
183 Q6 **Marthaguy Creek** ≈ New South Wales, SE Australia
19 P13 **Martha's Vineyard** *island* Massachusetts, NE USA
108 C11 **Martigny** Valais, SW Switzerland
103 R16 **Martigues** Bouches-du-Rhône, SE France
111 J19 **Martin** Ger. Sankt Martin, Hung. Turócszentmárton; prev. Turčiansky Svätý Martin. Žilinský Kraj, N Slovakia
28 L11 **Martin** South Dakota, N USA
20 G8 **Martin** Tennessee, S USA
105 S7 **Martín** ≈ E Spain
107 P18 **Martina Franca** Puglia, SE Italy
185 M14 **Martinborough** Wellington, North Island, New Zealand
25 S11 **Martindale** Texas, SW USA
35 N8 **Martinez** California, W USA
23 V3 **Martinez** Georgia, SE USA
41 Q13 **Martínez de La Torre** Veracruz-Llave, E Mexico
45 Y12 **Martinique** ◇ *French overseas department* E West Indies
1 O15 **Martinique** *island* E West Indies
Martinique Channel see Martinique Passage
45 X12 **Martinique Passage** var. Dominica Channel, Martinique Channel. *channel* Dominica/Martinique
23 Q5 **Martin Lake** ⊠ Alabama, S USA
115 G18 **Martíno** prev. Martínon. Stereá Ellás, C Greece
Martínon see Martíno
194 J11 **Martin Peninsula** *peninsula* Antarctica
39 S5 **Martin Point** *headland* Alaska, USA
109 V3 **Martinsberg** Niederösterreich, NE Austria
21 V3 **Martinsburg** West Virginia, NE USA
31 V13 **Martins Ferry** Ohio, N USA
Martinskirch see Târnăveni
31 O14 **Martinsville** Indiana, N USA
21 S8 **Martinsville** Virginia, NE USA
65 K16 **Martin Vaz, Ilhas** *island group* E Brazil
Martök see Martuk
184 M12 **Marton** Manawatu-Wanganui, North Island, New Zealand
105 N13 **Martos** Andalucía, S Spain
102 M16 **Martres-Tolosane** var. Martes Tolosane. Haute-Garonne, S France
92 M11 **Martti** Lappi, NE Finland
144 I9 **Martuk** Kaz. Martök. Aktyubinsk, NW Kazakhstan
137 U12 **Martuni** E Armenia
58 L11 **Marudá** Pará, E Brazil
169 V6 **Marudu, Teluk** *bay* East Malaysia
149 O8 **Ma'rūf** Kandahār, SE Afghanistan
164 H13 **Marugame** Kagawa, Shikoku, SW Japan
185 H16 **Maruia** ≈ South Island, New Zealand
98 M6 **Marum** Groningen, NE Netherlands
187 R13 **Marum, Mount** ▲ Ambrym, C Vanuatu
79 P23 **Marungu** ▲▲ SE Dem. Rep. Congo
191 Y12 **Marutea** *atoll* Groupe Actéon, C French Polynesia
143 O11 **Marv Dasht** var. Mervdasht. Fārs, S Iran
103 P13 **Marvejols** Lozère, S France
27 X12 **Marvell** Arkansas, C USA
36 L6 **Marvine, Mount** ▲ Utah, W USA
139 Q7 **Marwānīyah** C Iraq
152 F13 **Mārwār** var. Marwar Junction. Rājasthān, N India
Marwar Junction see Mārwār
9 R14 **Marwayne** Alberta, SW Canada
146 I14 **Mary** prev. Merv. Mary Welaýaty, S Turkmenistan
Mary see Mary Welaýaty
181 Z9 **Maryborough** Queensland, E Australia
182 M11 **Maryborough** Victoria, SE Australia
Maryborough see Port Laoise
83 G23 **Marydale** Northern Cape, W South Africa
117 W8 **Mar"yinka** Donets'ka Oblast', E Ukraine
Mary Island see Kanton
21 W4 **Maryland** off. State of Maryland, **also known as** America in Miniature, Cockade State, Free State, Old Line State. ◐ *state* NE USA
Maryland, State of see Maryland
25 P7 **Maryneal** Texas, SW USA
97 J15 **Maryport** NW England, UK
13 U13 **Marystown** Newfoundland, Newfoundland and Labrador, SE Canada
36 K6 **Marysvale** Utah, W USA
35 O6 **Marysville** California, W USA
27 O3 **Marysville** Kansas, C USA
31 S13 **Marysville** Michigan, N USA
31 S9 **Marysville** Ohio, NE USA
32 H7 **Marysville** Washington, NW USA
27 R2 **Maryville** Missouri, C USA
21 N9 **Maryville** Tennessee, S USA
146 I15 **Mary Welaýaty** var. Mary, Rus. Maryyskiy Velayat. ◐ *province* S Turkmenistan
Maryyskiy Velayat see Mary Welaýaty
Marzūq see Murzuq
42 J11 **Masachapa** var. Puerto Masachapa. Managua, W Nicaragua
81 G19 **Masai Mara National Reserve** *reserve* C Kenya
81 I21 **Masai Steppe** *grassland* NW Tanzania
81 F19 **Masaka** SW Uganda
169 T15 **Masalembo Besar, Pulau** *island* S Indonesia
137 Y13 **Masallı** Rus. Masally. S Azerbaijan
Masally see Masallı
171 N13 **Masamba** Sulawesi, C Indonesia
Masampo see Masan
163 Y16 **Masan** prev. Masampo. S South Korea
Masandam Peninsula see Musandam Peninsula
81 J25 **Masasi** Mtwara, SE Tanzania
Masawa see Massawa
42 J10 **Masaya** Masaya, W Nicaragua
42 J10 **Masaya** ◐ *department* W Nicaragua
171 P5 **Masbate** Masbate, N Philippines
171 P5 **Masbate** *island* C Philippines
74 I6 **Mascara** var. Mouaskar. NW Algeria
173 O7 **Mascarene Basin** *undersea feature* W Indian Ocean
173 O9 **Mascarene Islands** *island group* W Indian Ocean
173 N9 **Mascarene Plain** *undersea feature* W Indian Ocean
173 O7 **Mascarene Plateau** *undersea feature* W Indian Ocean
194 H5 **Mascart, Cape** *headland* Adelaide Island, Antarctica
62 J10 **Mascasín, Salinas de** *salt lake* C Argentina
40 K13 **Mascota** Jalisco, C Mexico

◆ Country
● Country Capital
◇ Dependent Territory
○ Dependent Territory Capital
◐ Administrative Regions
✕ International Airport
▲ Mountain
▲▲ Mountain Range
Volcano
≈ River
◎ Lake
⊠ Reservoir

Mascouche – McConnellsburg

15 O12 **Mascouche** Québec, SE Canada
124 J9 **Masel'gskaya** Respublika Kareliya, NW Russian Federation
83 J23 **Maseru** ● (Lesotho)
83 J23 **Maseru** ✈ W Lesotho
Mashaba *see* Mashava
160 K14 **Mashan** *var.* Baishan. Guangxi Zhuangzu Zizhiqu, S China
83 K17 **Mashava** *prev.* Mashaba. Masvingo, SE Zimbabwe
143 U4 **Mashhad** *var.* Meshed. Khorāsān-Razavī, NE Iran
165 S3 **Mashike** Hokkaidō, NE Japan
Mashīz *see* Bardsīr
149 N14 **Mashkai** ≈ SW Pakistan
143 X13 **Māshkel** *var.* Rūd-i Māshkel, Rūd-e Māshkīd. ≈ Iran/Pakistan
148 K12 **Māshkel, Hāmūn-i** *salt marsh* SW Pakistan
Māshkel, Rūd-i/Māshkīd, Rūd-e *see* Māshkel
83 K15 **Mashonaland Central** ⬖ *province* N Zimbabwe
83 K16 **Mashonaland East** ⬖ *province* NE Zimbabwe
83 J16 **Mashonaland West** ⬖ *province* NW Zimbabwe
Mashtagi *see* Maştağa
141 S14 **Masīlah, Wādī al** *dry watercourse* SE Yemen
79 I21 **Masi-Manimba** Bandundu, SW Dem. Rep. Congo
81 F17 **Masindi** W Uganda
81 I19 **Masinga Reservoir** ⊠ S Kenya
Masīra *see* Maşīrah, Jazīrat
Masira, Gulf of *see* Maşīrah, Khalīj
141 Y10 **Maşīrah, Jazīrat** *var.* Masīra. *island* E Oman
141 Y10 **Maşīrah, Khalīj** *var.* Gulf of Masira. *bay* E Oman
Masis *see* Büyükağrı Dağı
79 O19 **Masisi** Nord Kivu, E Dem. Rep. Congo
Masjed-e Soleymān *see* Masjed Soleymān
142 L9 **Masjed Soleymān** *var.* Masjed-e Soleymān, Masjid-i Sulaiman. Khūzestān, SW Iran
Masjid-i Sulaiman *see* Masjed Soleymān
Maskat *see* Masqaţ
139 Q7 **Maskhān** C Iraq
141 X8 **Maskin** *var.* Miskin. NW Oman
97 B17 **Mask, Lough** *Ir.* Loch Measca. ◎ W Ireland
114 N10 **Maslen Nos** *headland* E Bulgaria
172 K3 **Masoala, Tanjona** *headland* NE Madagascar
Masohi *see* Amahai
31 Q9 **Mason** Michigan, N USA
31 R14 **Mason** Ohio, N USA
25 Q10 **Mason** Texas, SW USA
21 P4 **Mason** West Virginia, NE USA
185 B25 **Mason Bay** *bay* Stewart Island, New Zealand
30 K13 **Mason City** Illinois, N USA
29 V12 **Mason City** Iowa, C USA
Mā, Sông *see* Ma, Nam
18 B16 **Masontown** Pennsylvania, NE USA
141 Y8 **Masqaţ** *var.* Maskat, *Eng.* Muscat. ● (Oman) NE Oman
106 E10 **Massa** Toscana, C Italy
18 M11 **Massachusetts** *off.* Commonwealth of Massachusetts, *also known as* Bay State, Old Bay State, Old Colony State. ⬖ *state* NE USA
19 P11 **Massachusetts Bay** *bay* Massachusetts, NE USA
35 R2 **Massacre Lake** ◎ Nevada, W USA
107 O18 **Massafra** Puglia, SE Italy
108 G11 **Massagno** Ticino, S Switzerland
78 G11 **Massaguet** Chari-Baguirmi, W Chad
Massakori *see* Massakory
78 G10 **Massakory** *var.* Massakori; *prev.* Dagana. Chari-Baguirmi, W Chad
78 H11 **Massalassef** Chari-Baguirmi, SW Chad
106 F13 **Massa Marittima** Toscana, C Italy
82 B11 **Massangano** Cuanza Norte, NW Angola
83 M18 **Massangena** Gaza, S Mozambique
80 J9 **Massawa** *var.* Masawa, *Amh.* Mits'iwa. E Eritrea
80 K9 **Massawa Channel** *channel* E Eritrea
18 J6 **Massena** New York, NE USA
78 H11 **Massenya** Chari-Baguirmi, SW Chad
10 I13 **Masset** Graham Island, British Columbia, SW Canada
102 L16 **Masseube** Gers, S France
14 E11 **Massey** Ontario, S Canada
103 P12 **Massiac** Cantal, C France
103 P12 **Massif Central** *plateau* C France
Massif de L'Isalo *see* Isalo
Massilia *see* Marseille
31 U12 **Massillon** Ohio, N USA
77 N12 **Massina** Ségou, W Mali
83 N19 **Massinga** Inhambane, SE Mozambique
83 L20 **Massingir** Gaza, SW Mozambique
195 Z10 **Masson Island** *island* Antarctica
Massoukou *see* Franceville
137 Z11 **Maştağa** *Rus.* Mashtagi, Mastaga. E Azerbaijan
Mastanli *see* Momchilgrad
184 M13 **Masterton** Wellington, North Island, New Zealand
18 M14 **Mastic** Long Island, New York, NE USA
149 O10 **Mastung** Baluchistān, SW Pakistan
119 J20 **Mastva** *Rus.* Mostva. ≈ SW Belarus
119 G17 **Masty** *Rus.* Mosty. Hrodzyenskaya Voblasts', W Belarus
164 F12 **Masuda** Shimane, Honshū, SW Japan
92 J11 **Masugnsbyn** Norrbotten, N Sweden
Masuku *see* Franceville
83 K17 **Masvingo** *prev.* Fort Victoria, Nyanda, Victoria. Masvingo, SE Zimbabwe
83 K18 **Masvingo** *prev.* Victoria. ⬖ *province* SE Zimbabwe
138 H5 **Maşyāf** *Fr.* Misiaf. Ḩamāh, C Syria
110 E9 **Maszewo** Zachodniopomorskie, NW Poland
83 I17 **Matabeleland North** ⬖ *province* W Zimbabwe
83 J18 **Matabeleland South** ⬖ *province* S Zimbabwe
82 O13 **Mataca** Niassa, N Mozambique
14 G8 **Matachewan** Ontario, S Canada
163 Q8 **Matad** *var.* Dzüünbulag. Dornod, E Mongolia
79 F22 **Matadi** Bas-Congo, W Dem. Rep. Congo
25 O4 **Matador** Texas, SW USA
42 J9 **Matagalpa** Matagalpa, C Nicaragua
42 K9 **Matagalpa** ⬖ *department* W Nicaragua
12 I12 **Matagami** Québec, S Canada
25 U13 **Matagorda** Texas, SW USA
25 U13 **Matagorda Bay** *inlet* Texas, SW USA
25 U14 **Matagorda Island** *island* Texas, SW USA
25 V13 **Matagorda Peninsula** *headland* Texas, SW USA
191 Q8 **Mataiea** Tahiti, W French Polynesia
191 T9 **Mataiva** *atoll* Îles Tuamotu, C French Polynesia
183 O7 **Matakana** New South Wales, SE Australia
184 N7 **Matakana Island** *island* NE New Zealand
83 C15 **Matala** Huíla, SW Angola
190 G12 **Matala'a Pointe** *headland* Île Uvea, N Wallis and Futuna
155 K25 **Matale** Central Province, C Sri Lanka
190 E12 **Matalesina, Pointe** *headland* Île Alofi, W Wallis and Futuna
76 I10 **Matam** NE Senegal
184 M8 **Matamata** Waikato, North Island, New Zealand
77 V12 **Matamey** Zinder, S Niger
40 L8 **Matamoros** Coahuila de Zaragoza, NE Mexico
41 P15 **Matamoros** *var.* Izúcar de Matamoros. Puebla, S Mexico
41 Q8 **Matamoros** Tamaulipas, C Mexico
75 S13 **Ma'ţan as Sārah** SE Libya
82 J12 **Matanda** Luapula, N Zambia
81 J24 **Matandu** ≈ S Tanzania
15 V6 **Matane** Québec, SE Canada
15 V6 **Matane** ≈ Québec, SE Canada
77 S12 **Matankari** Dosso, SW Niger
39 R11 **Matanuska River** ≈ Alaska, USA
54 G7 **Matanza** Santander, N Colombia
44 D4 **Matanzas** Matanzas, NW Cuba
15 V7 **Matapédia** ≈ Québec, SE Canada
15 V6 **Matapédia, Lac** ◎ Québec, SE Canada
190 B17 **Mata Point** *headland* SE Niue
190 D12 **Matapu, Pointe** *headland* Île Futuna, W Wallis and Futuna
62 G12 **Mataquito, Río** ≈ C Chile
155 K26 **Matara** Southern Province, S Sri Lanka
115 D18 **Matarágka** *var.* Mataránga. Dytikí Ellás, C Greece
171 K16 **Mataram** Pulau Lombok, C Indonesia
Mataránga *see* Matarágka
181 Q3 **Mataranka** Northern Territory, N Australia
105 W6 **Mataró** *anc.* Illuro. Cataluña, E Spain
184 O8 **Matata** Bay of Plenty, North Island, New Zealand
192 K16 **Matātula, Cape** *headland* Tutuila, W American Samoa
185 D24 **Mataura** Southland, South Island, New Zealand
185 D24 **Mataura** ≈ South Island, New Zealand
Mata Uta *see* Matā'utu
192 H16 **Matāutu** Upolu, C Samoa
190 G11 **Matā'utu** *var.* Mata Uta. ○ (Wallis and Futuna) Île Uvea, Wallis and Futuna
190 G12 **Matā'utu, Baie de** *bay* Île Uvea, Wallis and Futuna
191 P7 **Mataval, Baie de** *bay* Tahiti, W French Polynesia
190 I16 **Matavera** Rarotonga, S Cook Islands
191 V16 **Mataveri** Easter Island, Chile, E Pacific Ocean
191 V17 **Mataveri** ✈ (Easter Island) Easter Island, Chile, E Pacific Ocean
184 P9 **Matawai** Gisborne, North Island, New Zealand
15 O10 **Matawin** ≈ Québec, SE Canada
145 V13 **Matay** Almaty, SE Kazakhstan
14 K8 **Matchi-Manitou, Lac** ◎ Québec, SE Canada
41 O10 **Matehuala** San Luis Potosí, C Mexico
45 V13 **Matelot** Trinidad, Trinidad and Tobago
83 M15 **Matenge** Tete, NW Mozambique
107 O18 **Matera** Basilicata, S Italy
111 O21 **Mátészalka** Szabolcs-Szatmár-Bereg, E Hungary
93 H17 **Matfors** Västernorrland, C Sweden
102 K11 **Matha** Charente-Maritime, W France
0 F15 **Mathematicians Seamounts** *undersea feature* E Pacific Ocean
21 X6 **Mathews** Virginia, NE USA
25 S14 **Mathis** Texas, SW USA
152 J11 **Mathura** *prev.* Muttra. Uttar Pradesh, N India
Mathurai *see* Madurai
171 R7 **Mati** Mindanao, S Philippines
Matianus *see* Orūmīyeh, Daryācheh-ye
Matiara *see* Matiāri
149 Q15 **Matiāri** *var.* Matiara. Sind, SE Pakistan
41 S16 **Matías Romero** Oaxaca, SE Mexico
43 O13 **Matina** Limón, E Costa Rica
14 D10 **Matinenda Lake** ◎ Ontario, S Canada
19 R8 **Matinicus Island** *island* Maine, NE USA
Matisco/Matisco Ædourum *see* Mâcon
149 Q16 **Mātli** Sind, SE Pakistan
97 M18 **Matlock** C England, UK
59 F18 **Mato Grosso** *prev.* Vila Bela da Santissima Trindade. Mato Grosso, W Brazil
59 G17 **Mato Grosso** *off.* Estado de Mato Grosso; *prev.* Matto Grosso. ⬖ *state* W Brazil
60 H8 **Mato Grosso do Sul** *off.* Estado de Mato Grosso do Sul. ⬖ *state* S Brazil
Mato Grosso do Sul, Estado de *see* Mato Grosso do Sul
Mato Grosso, Estado de *see* Mato Grosso
59 I18 **Mato Grosso, Planalto de** *plateau* C Brazil
83 L21 **Matola** Maputo, S Mozambique
104 G6 **Matosinhos** *prev.* Matozinhos. Porto, NW Portugal
Matou *see* Pingguo
55 Z10 **Matoury** NE French Guiana
Matozinhos *see* Matosinhos
111 L21 **Mátra** ▲▲ N Hungary
141 Y8 **Maţraḩ** *var.* Mutrah. NE Oman
116 L12 **Mătrașești** Vrancea, E Romania
108 M8 **Matrei am Brenner** Tirol, W Austria
109 P8 **Matrei in Osttirol** Tirol, W Austria
76 I15 **Matru** SW Sierra Leone
75 U7 **Maţrûḩ** *var.* Mersa Maţrûḩ; *anc.* Paraetonium. NW Egypt
165 U16 **Matsubara** *var.* Matubara. Kagoshima, Tokuno-shima, SW Japan
164 G12 **Matsue** *var.* Matsuye, Matue. Shimane, Honshū, SW Japan
165 Q6 **Matsumae** Hokkaidō, NE Japan
164 M12 **Matsumoto** *var.* Matumoto. Nagano, Honshū, S Japan
164 K14 **Matsusaka** *var.* Matsuzaka, Matusaka. Mie, Honshū, SW Japan
161 S12 **Matsu Tao** *Chin.* Mazu Dao. *island* NW Taiwan
Matsutō *see* Mattō
164 F14 **Matsuyama** *var.* Matuyama. Ehime, Shikoku, SW Japan
Matsuye *see* Matsue
Matsuzaka *see* Matsusaka
164 M14 **Matsuzaki** Shizuoka, Honshū, S Japan
14 F8 **Mattagami** ≈ Ontario, S Canada
14 F8 **Mattagami Lake** ◎ Ontario, S Canada
62 K12 **Mattaldi** Córdoba, C Argentina
21 Y9 **Mattamuskeet, Lake** ◎ North Carolina, SE USA
21 W6 **Mattaponi River** ≈ Virginia, NE USA
14 I11 **Mattawa** Ontario, SE Canada
14 I11 **Mattawa** ≈ Ontario, SE Canada
19 S5 **Mattawamkeag** Maine, NE USA
19 S4 **Mattawamkeag Lake** ◎ Maine, NE USA
108 D11 **Matterhorn** *It.* Monte Cervino. ▲ Italy/Switzerland *see also* Cervino, Monte
32 L12 **Matterhorn** *var.* Sacajawea Peak. ▲ Oregon, NW USA
35 W1 **Matterhorn** ▲ Nevada, W USA
Matterhorn *see* Cervino, Monte
35 R8 **Matterhorn Peak** ▲ California, W USA
109 Y5 **Mattersburg** Burgenland, E Austria
108 E11 **Matter Vispa** ≈ S Switzerland
55 R7 **Matthews Ridge** N Guyana
44 K7 **Matthew Town** Great Inagua, S Bahamas
109 Q4 **Mattighofen** Oberösterreich, NW Austria
107 N16 **Mattinata** Puglia, SE Italy
141 T9 **Maţţī, Sabkhat** *sabkha* Saudi Arabia/United Arab Emirates
18 M14 **Mattituck** Long Island, New York, NE USA
164 L11 **Mattō** *var.* Matsutō. Ishikawa, Honshū, SW Japan
Matto Grosso *see* Mato Grosso
30 M14 **Mattoon** Illinois, N USA
57 L16 **Mattos, Río** ≈ C Bolivia
Mattu *see* Metu
169 R9 **Matu** Sarawak, East Malaysia
Matubara *see* Matsubara
57 E14 **Matucana** Lima, W Peru
Matue *see* Matsue
187 Y15 **Matuku** *island* S Fiji
112 B9 **Matulji** Primorje-Gorski Kotar, NW Croatia
Matumoto *see* Matsumoto
55 P5 **Maturín** Monagas, NE Venezuela
Matusaka *see* Matsusaka
Matuyama *see* Matsuyama
126 K11 **Matveyev Kurgan** Rostovskaya Oblast', SW Russian Federation
127 O8 **Matyshevo** Volgogradskaya Oblast', SW Russian Federation
153 O13 **Mau** *var.* Maunāth Bhanjan. Uttar Pradesh, N India
83 O14 **Maúa** Niassa, N Mozambique
102 M17 **Maubermé, Pic de** *var.* Tuc de Moubermé, *Sp.* Pico Mauberme; *prev.* Tuc de Maubermé. ▲ France/Spain *see also* Moubermé, Tuc de
Maubermé, Pic de *see* Moubermé, Tuc de
Mauberme, Pico *see* Maubermé, Pic de/Moubermé, Tuc de
Maubermé, Tuc de *see* Maubermé, Pic de/Moubermé, Tuc de
103 Q2 **Maubeuge** Nord, N France
166 L8 **Maubin** Irrawaddy, SW Burma (Myanmar)
152 L13 **Maudaha** Uttar Pradesh, N India
183 N9 **Maude** New South Wales, SE Australia
195 P3 **Maudheimvidda** *physical region* Antarctica
65 N22 **Maud Rise** *undersea feature* S Atlantic Ocean
109 Q4 **Mauerkirchen** Oberösterreich, NW Austria
Mauersee *see* Mamry, Jezioro
188 K2 **Maug Islands** *island group* N Northern Mariana Islands
103 Q15 **Mauguio** Hérault, S France
193 N5 **Maui** *island* Hawai'i, USA, C Pacific Ocean
190 M16 **Mauke** *atoll* S Cook Islands
62 G13 **Maule** *var.* Región del Maule. ⬖ *region* C Chile
102 J9 **Mauléon** Deux-Sèvres, W France
102 J16 **Mauléon-Licharre** Pyrénées-Atlantiques, SW France
Maule, Región del *see* Maule
62 G13 **Maule, Río** ≈ C Chile
63 G17 **Maullín** Los Lagos, S Chile
Maulmain *see* Moulmein
31 R11 **Maumee** Ohio, N USA
31 Q12 **Maumee River** ≈ Indiana/Ohio, N USA
27 U11 **Maumelle** Arkansas, C USA
27 T11 **Maumelle, Lake** ⊠ Arkansas, C USA
171 O16 **Maumere** *prev.* Maoemere. Flores, S Indonesia
83 G17 **Maun** North-West, C Botswana
Maunāth Bhanjan *see* Mau
Maunawai *see* Waimea
190 H16 **Maungaroa** ▲ Rarotonga, S Cook Islands
184 K3 **Maungatapere** Northland, North Island, New Zealand
184 K4 **Maungaturoto** Northland, North Island, New Zealand
191 R10 **Maupiti** *var.* Maurua. *island* Îles Sous le Vent, W French Polynesia
152 K14 **Mau Rānīpur** Uttar Pradesh, N India
22 K9 **Maurepas, Lake** ◎ Louisiana, S USA
103 T16 **Maures** ▲▲ SE France
103 O12 **Mauriac** Cantal, C France
Maurice *see* Mauritius
65 J20 **Maurice Ewing Bank** *undersea feature* SW Atlantic Ocean
182 C4 **Maurice, Lake** *salt lake* South Australia
18 I17 **Maurice River** ≈ New Jersey, NE USA
25 Y10 **Mauriceville** Texas, SW USA
98 K12 **Maurik** Gelderland, C Netherlands
76 H8 **Mauritania** *off.* Islamic Republic of Mauritania, *Ar.* Mūrītānīyah. ◆ *republic* W Africa
Mauritania, Islamic Republic of *see* Mauritania
173 W15 **Mauritius** *off.* Republic of Mauritius, *Fr.* Maurice. ◆ *republic* W Indian Ocean
128 M17 **Mauritius** *island* W Indian Ocean
Mauritius, Republic of *see* Mauritius
173 N9 **Mauritius Trench** *undersea feature* W Indian Ocean
102 H6 **Mauron** Morbihan, NW France
103 N13 **Maurs** Cantal, C France
Maurua *see* Maupiti
Maury Mid-Ocean Channel *see* Maury Seachannel
64 L6 **Maury Seachannel** *var.* Maury Mid-Ocean Channel. *undersea feature* N Atlantic Ocean
30 K6 **Mauston** Wisconsin, N USA
109 R8 **Mauterndorf** Salzburg, NW Austria
109 T4 **Mauthausen** Oberösterreich, N Austria
109 Q9 **Mauthen** Kärnten, S Austria
83 F15 **Mavinga** Cuando Cubango, SE Angola
83 M17 **Mavita** Manica, W Mozambique
115 K22 **Mavrópetra, Akrotírio** *cape* Santoríni, Kykládes, Greece, Aegean Sea
115 F16 **Mavrovoúni** ▲ C Greece
184 Q8 **Mawhai Point** *headland* North Island, New Zealand
166 L3 **Mawlaik** Sagaing, C Burma (Myanmar)
Mawlamyine *see* Moulmein
141 N14 **Mawr, Wādī** *dry watercourse* NW Yemen
195 X5 **Mawson** *Australian research station* Antarctica
195 X5 **Mawson Coast** *physical region* Antarctica
28 M4 **Max** North Dakota, N USA
41 W12 **Maxcanú** Yucatán, SE Mexico
Maxesibebi *see* Mount Ayliff
109 Q5 **Maxglan** ✈ (Salzburg) Salzburg, W Austria
93 K16 **Maxmo** *Fin.* Maksamaa. Länsi-Soumi, W Finland
21 T11 **Maxton** North Carolina, SE USA
25 R8 **May** Texas, SW USA
186 B6 **May** ≈ NW Papua New Guinea
123 R10 **Maya** ≈ E Russian Federation
151 Q19 **Māyābandar** Andaman and Nicobar Islands, India, E Indian Ocean
Mayadin *see* Al Mayādīn
44 L5 **Mayaguana** *island* SE Bahamas
44 L5 **Mayaguana Passage** *passage* SE Bahamas
45 S6 **Mayagüez** W Puerto Rico
45 R6 **Mayagüez, Bahía de** *bay* W Puerto Rico
Mayals *see* Maials
79 G20 **Mayama** Le Pool, SE Congo
37 V8 **Maya, Mesa De** ▲ Colorado, C USA
143 R4 **Mayamey** Semnān, N Iran
42 F3 **Maya Mountains** *Sp.* Montañas Mayas. ▲▲ Belize/Guatemala
44 I7 **Mayarí** Holguín, E Cuba
Mayas, Montañas *see* Maya Mountains
18 I17 **May, Cape** *headland* New Jersey, NE USA
80 J11 **Maych'ew** *var.* Mai Chio, *It.* Mai Ceu. Tigray, N Ethiopia
138 I2 **Maydān Ikbiz** Ḩalab, N Syria
Maydān Shahr *see* Meydān Shahr
80 O12 **Maydh** Sanaag, N Somalia
Maydī *see* Mīdī
Mayebashi *see* Maebashi
Mayence *see* Mainz
102 K6 **Mayenne** Mayenne, NW France
102 J6 **Mayenne** ⬖ *department* NW France
102 J7 **Mayenne** ≈ N France
36 K12 **Mayer** Arizona, SW USA
22 J4 **Mayersville** Mississippi, S USA
9 P14 **Mayerthorpe** Alberta, SW Canada
21 S12 **Mayesville** South Carolina, SE USA
185 G19 **Mayfield** Canterbury, South Island, New Zealand
33 N14 **Mayfield** Idaho, NW USA
20 G7 **Mayfield** Kentucky, S USA
36 L5 **Mayfield** Utah, W USA
Mayhan *see* Sant
37 T14 **Mayhill** New Mexico, SW USA
145 T9 **Maykain** *Kaz.* Mayqayyng. Pavlodar, NE Kazakhstan
126 L14 **Maykop** Respublika Adygeya, SW Russian Federation
Maylibash *see* Maylybas
Mayli-Say *see* Mayluu-Suu
147 T9 **Mayluu-Suu** *prev.* Mayli-Say, *Kir.* Mayly-Say. Dzhalal-Abadskaya Oblast', W Kyrgyzstan
144 L14 **Maylybas** *prev.* Maylibash. Kzylorda, S Kazakhstan
Mayly-Say *see* Mayluu-Suu
Maymana *see* Meymaneh
166 M5 **Maymyo** Mandalay, C Burma (Myanmar)
123 V7 **Mayn** ≈ NE Russian Federation
127 Q5 **Mayna** Ul'yanovskaya Oblast', W Russian Federation
21 N8 **Maynardville** Tennessee, S USA
14 J13 **Maynooth** Ontario, SE Canada
10 I6 **Mayo** Yukon Territory, NW Canada
23 U9 **Mayo** Florida, SE USA
97 B16 **Mayo** *Ir.* Maigh Eo. ⬖ *county* W Ireland
Mayo *see* Maio
78 G12 **Mayo-Kébbi** *off.* Préfecture du Mayo-Kébbi, *var.* Mayo-Kébi. ⬖ *prefecture* SW Chad
Mayo-Kébbi, Préfecture du *see* Mayo-Kébbi
Mayo-Kébi *see* Mayo-Kébbi
79 F19 **Mayoko** Le Niari, SW Congo
171 P4 **Mayon Volcano** ⛰ Luzon, N Philippines
61 A24 **Mayor Buratovich** Buenos Aires, E Argentina
104 L4 **Mayorga** Castilla-León, N Spain
184 N6 **Mayor Island** *island* NE New Zealand
Mayor Pablo Lagerenza *see* Capitán Pablo Lagerenza
173 I14 **Mayotte** ◇ *French territorial collectivity* E Africa
Mayoumba *see* Mayumba
44 J13 **May Pen** C Jamaica
Mayqayyng *see* Maykain
171 O1 **Mayraira Point** *headland* Luzon, N Philippines
109 N8 **Mayrhofen** Tirol, W Austria
186 A6 **May River** East Sepik, NW Papua New Guinea
123 R13 **Mayskiy** Amurskaya Oblast', SE Russian Federation
127 O15 **Mayskiy** Kabardino-Balkarskaya Respublika, SW Russian Federation
145 U9 **Mayskoye** Pavlodar, NE Kazakhstan
18 J17 **Mays Landing** New Jersey, NE USA
21 N4 **Maysville** Kentucky, S USA
27 R2 **Maysville** Missouri, C USA
79 D20 **Mayumba** *var.* Mayoumba. Nyanga, S Gabon
31 S8 **Mayville** Michigan, N USA
18 C11 **Mayville** New York, NE USA
29 Q4 **Mayville** North Dakota, N USA
Mayyali *see* Mahe
Mayyit, Al Baḩr al *see* Dead Sea
83 J15 **Mazabuka** Southern, S Zambia
Mazaca *see* Kayseri
Mazagan *see* El-Jadida
32 J7 **Mazama** Washington, NW USA
103 O15 **Mazamet** Tarn, S France
143 O4 **Māzandarān** *off.* Ostān-e Māzandarān. ⬖ *province* N Iran
Māzandarān, Ostān-e *see* Māzandarān
156 F7 **Mazar** Xinjiang Uygur Zizhiqu, NW China
107 H24 **Mazara del Vallo** Sicilia, Italy, C Mediterranean Sea
149 O2 **Mazār-e Sharīf** *var.* Mazār-i Sharif. Balkh, N Afghanistan
Mazār-i Sharif *see* Mazār-e Sharīf
105 R13 **Mazarrón** Murcia, SE Spain
105 R14 **Mazarrón, Golfo de** *gulf* SE Spain
55 S9 **Mazaruni River** ≈ N Guyana
42 B6 **Mazatenango** Suchitepéquez, SW Guatemala
40 I10 **Mazatlán** Sinaloa, C Mexico
36 L12 **Mazatzal Mountains** ▲▲ Arizona, SW USA
118 D10 **Mažeikiai** Telšiai, NW Lithuania
118 D7 **Mazirbe** Talsi, NW Latvia
40 G5 **Mazocahui** Sonora, NW Mexico
57 I18 **Mazocruz** Puno, S Peru
Mazoe, Rio *see* Mazowe
79 N21 **Mazomeno** Maniema, E Dem. Rep. Congo
159 Q6 **Mazong Shan** ▲ N China
83 L16 **Mazowe** *var.* Rio Mazoe. ≈ Mozambique/Zimbabwe
110 M11 **Mazowieckie** ⬖ *province* C Poland
Mazra'a *see* Al Mazra'ah
138 G6 **Mazraat Kfar Debiâne** C Lebanon
118 H7 **Mazsalaca** *Est.* Väike-Salatsi, *Ger.* Salisburg. Valmiera, N Latvia
Mazu Dao *see* Matsu Tao
110 L9 **Mazury** *physical region* NE Poland
119 M20 **Mazyr** *Rus.* Mozyr'. Homyel'skaya Voblasts', SE Belarus
107 K25 **Mazzarino** Sicilia, Italy, C Mediterranean Sea
Mba *see* Ba
83 L21 **Mbabane** ● (Swaziland) NW Swaziland
Mbacké *see* Mbaké
77 N16 **Mbahiakro** E Ivory Coast
79 I16 **Mbaïki** *var.* M'Baiki. Lobaye, SW Central African Republic
M'Baiki *see* Mbaïki
79 F14 **Mbakaou, Lac de** ◎ C Cameroon
76 G11 **Mbaké** *var.* Mbacké. W Senegal
82 L11 **Mbala** *prev.* Abercorn. Northern, NE Zambia
83 J18 **Mbalabala** *prev.* Balla Balla. Matabeleland South, SW Zimbabwe
81 G18 **Mbale** E Uganda
79 E16 **Mbalmayo** *var.* M'Balmayo. Centre, S Cameroon
M'Balmayo *see* Mbalmayo
81 H25 **Mbamba Bay** Ruvuma, S Tanzania
79 I18 **Mbandaka** *prev.* Coquilhatville. Equateur, NW Dem. Rep. Congo
82 B9 **M'Banza Congo** *var.* Mbanza Congo; *prev.* São Salvador, São Salvador do Congo. Dem. Rep. Congo, NW Angola
79 G21 **Mbanza-Ngungu** Bas-Congo, W Dem. Rep. Congo
67 V11 **Mbarangandu** ≈ E Tanzania
81 E19 **Mbarara** SW Uganda
79 L15 **Mbari** ≈ SE Central African Republic
81 I24 **Mbarika Mountains** ▲▲ S Tanzania
83 J24 **Mbashe** ≈ S South Africa
78 F13 **Mbé** Nord, N Cameroon
81 J24 **Mbemkuru** *var.* Mbwemkuru. ≈ S Tanzania
Mbengga *see* Beqa
172 H13 **Mbéni** Grande Comore, NW Comoros
83 K18 **Mberengwa** Midlands, S Zimbabwe
81 G24 **Mbeya** Mbeya, SW Tanzania
81 G23 **Mbeya** ⬖ *region* S Tanzania
79 E19 **Mbigou** Ngounié, C Gabon
Mbilua *see* Vella Lavella
79 F19 **Mbinda** Le Niari, SW Congo
79 D17 **Mbini** W Equatorial Guinea
Mbini *see* Uolo, Río
83 L18 **Mbizi** Masvingo, SE Zimbabwe
81 G23 **Mbogo** Mbeya, W Tanzania
79 N15 **Mboki** Haut-Mbomou, SE Central African Republic
79 G18 **Mbomo** Cuvette, NW Congo
79 L15 **Mbomou** ⬖ *prefecture* SE Central African Republic
Mbomou/M'Bomu/Mbomu *see* Bomu
76 F11 **Mbour** W Senegal
76 I10 **Mbout** Gorgol, S Mauritania
79 J14 **Mbrès** *var.* Mbrés. Nana-Grébizi, C Central African Republic
Mbrés *see* Mbrès
79 L22 **Mbuji-Mayi** *prev.* Bakwanga. Kasai Oriental, S Dem. Rep. Congo
81 H21 **Mbulu** Manyara, N Tanzania
186 E5 **M'bunai** *var.* Bunai. Manus Island, N Papua New Guinea
62 N8 **Mburucuyá** Corrientes, NE Argentina
Mbutha *see* Buca
Mbwemkuru *see* Mbemkuru
81 G21 **Mbwikwe** Singida, C Tanzania
13 O15 **McAdam** New Brunswick, SE Canada
25 O5 **McAdoo** Texas, SW USA
35 V2 **McAfee Peak** ▲ Nevada, W USA
27 P11 **McAlester** Oklahoma, C USA
25 S17 **McAllen** Texas, SW USA
21 S11 **McBee** South Carolina, SE USA
9 N14 **McBride** British Columbia, SW Canada
24 M9 **McCamey** Texas, SW USA
33 R15 **McCammon** Idaho, NW USA
35 X11 **McCarran** ✈ (Las Vegas) Nevada, W USA
39 T11 **McCarthy** Alaska, USA
30 M5 **McCaslin Mountain** *hill* Wisconsin, N USA
25 O2 **McClellan Creek** ≈ Texas, SW USA
21 T14 **McClellanville** South Carolina, SE USA
8 L6 **McClintock Channel** *channel* Nunavut, N Canada
195 R12 **McClintock, Mount** ▲ Antarctica
35 N2 **McCloud** California, W USA
35 N3 **McCloud River** ≈ California, W USA
35 Q9 **McClure, Lake** ⊠ California, W USA
197 O8 **McClure Strait** *strait* Northwest Territories, N Canada
29 N4 **McClusky** North Dakota, N USA
21 T11 **McColl** South Carolina, SE USA
22 K7 **McComb** Mississippi, S USA
18 E16 **McConnellsburg** Pennsylvania, NE USA

◆ Country
● Country Capital
◇ Dependent Territory
○ Dependent Territory Capital
⬖ Administrative Regions
✈ International Airport
▲ Mountain
▲▲ Mountain Range
⛰ Volcano
≈ River
◎ Lake
⊠ Reservoir

McConnelsville – Meriden

31 T14 **McConnelsville** Ohio, N USA
28 M17 **McCook** Nebraska, C USA
21 P13 **McCormick** South Carolina, SE USA
9 W16 **McCreary** Manitoba, S Canada
27 W11 **McCrory** Arkansas, C USA
25 T10 **McDade** Texas, SW USA
23 O8 **McDavid** Florida, SE USA
35 T1 **McDermitt** Nevada, W USA
23 S4 **McDonough** Georgia, SE USA
36 L12 **McDowell Mountains** ▲▲ Arizona, SW USA
20 H8 **McEwen** Tennessee, S USA
35 R12 **McFarland** California, W USA
Mcfarlane, Lake see Macfarlane, Lake
27 P12 **McGee Creek Lake** ⊠ Oklahoma, C USA
27 W13 **McGehee** Arkansas, C USA
35 X5 **Mcgill** Nevada, W USA
14 K11 **McGillivray, Lac** ◎ Québec, SE Canada
39 P10 **McGrath** Alaska, USA
25 T8 **McGregor** Texas, SW USA
33 O12 **McGuire, Mount** ▲ Idaho, NW USA
83 M14 **Mchinji** prev. Fort Manning. Central, W Malawi
28 M7 **McIntosh** South Dakota, N USA
9 S7 **McKeand** ≈ Baffin Island, Nunavut, NE Canada
191 R4 **McKean Island** island Phoenix Islands, C Kiribati
30 J13 **McKee Creek** ≈ Illinois, N USA
18 C15 **Mckeesport** Pennsylvania, NE USA
21 V7 **McKenney** Virginia, NE USA
20 G8 **McKenzie** Tennessee, S USA
185 B20 **McKerrow, Lake** ◎ South Island, New Zealand
39 Q10 **McKinley, Mount** var. Denali. ▲ Alaska, USA
39 R10 **McKinley Park** Alaska, USA
34 K3 **McKinleyville** California, W USA
25 U6 **McKinney** Texas, SW USA
26 I5 **McKinney, Lake** ◎ Kansas, C USA
28 M7 **McLaughlin** South Dakota, N USA
25 O2 **McLean** Texas, SW USA
30 M16 **Mcleansboro** Illinois, N USA
9 O13 **McLennan** Alberta, W Canada
14 L9 **McLennan, Lac** ◎ Québec, SE Canada
10 M13 **McLeod Lake** British Columbia, W Canada
27 N10 **McLoud** Oklahoma, C USA
32 G15 **McLoughlin, Mount** ▲ Oregon, NW USA
37 U15 **McMillan, Lake** ⊠ New Mexico, SW USA
32 G11 **McMinnville** Oregon, NW USA
20 K9 **McMinnville** Tennessee, S USA
195 R13 **McMurdo** US research station Antarctica
37 N13 **Mcnary** Arizona, SW USA
24 H9 **McNary** Texas, SW USA
27 N5 **McPherson** Kansas, C USA
McPherson see Fort McPherson
23 U6 **McRae** Georgia, SE USA
29 P4 **McVille** North Dakota, N USA
83 J25 **Mdantsane** Eastern Cape, SE South Africa
167 T6 **Me** Ninh Binh, N Vietnam
26 J7 **Meade** Kansas, C USA
39 O5 **Meade River** ≈ Alaska, USA
35 Y11 **Mead, Lake** ⊠ Arizona/ Nevada, W USA
24 M5 **Meadow** Texas, SW USA
9 S14 **Meadow Lake** Saskatchewan, C Canada
35 Y10 **Meadow Valley Wash** ≈ Nevada, W USA
22 J7 **Meadville** Mississippi, S USA
18 B12 **Meadville** Pennsylvania, NE USA
14 F14 **Meaford** Ontario, S Canada
Meáin, Inis see Inishmaan
104 G8 **Mealhada** Aveiro, N Portugal
13 R8 **Mealy Mountains** ▲▲ Newfoundland and Labrador, E Canada
9 O10 **Meander River** Alberta, W Canada
32 E11 **Meares, Cape** headland Oregon, NW USA
47 V6 **Mearim, Rio** ≈ NE Brazil
Measca, Loch see Mask, Lough
97 F17 **Meath** Ir. An Mhí. ◈ county E Ireland
9 T14 **Meath Park** Saskatchewan, S Canada
103 O5 **Meaux** Seine-et-Marne, N France
21 T9 **Mebane** North Carolina, SE USA
171 U12 **Mebo, Gunung** ▲ Papua, E Indonesia
94 I8 **Mebonden** Sør-Trøndelag, S Norway
82 A10 **Mebridege** ≈ NW Angola
35 W16 **Mecca** California, W USA
Mecca see Makkah
29 Y14 **Mechanicsville** Iowa, C USA
18 L10 **Mechanicville** New York, NE USA
99 H17 **Mechelen** Eng. Mechlin, Fr. Malines. Antwerpen, C Belgium
188 C8 **Mecherchar** var. Eil Malk. island Palau Islands, Palau
101 D17 **Mechernich** Nordrhein-Westfalen, W Germany
126 L12 **Mechetinskaya** Rostovskaya Oblast', SW Russian Federation
114 J11 **Mechka** ≈ S Bulgaria
Mechlin see Mechelen
61 D23 **Mechongué** Buenos Aires, E Argentina
115 L14 **Mecidiye** Edirne, NW Turkey
101 I24 **Meckenbeuren** Baden-Württemberg, S Germany
100 L8 **Mecklenburger Bucht** bay N Germany
100 M10 **Mecklenburgische Seenplatte** wetland NE Germany
100 L9 **Mecklenburg-Vorpommern** ◈ state NE Germany
83 Q15 **Meconta** Nampula, NE Mozambique
111 I25 **Mecsek** ▲▲ SW Hungary
83 P14 **Mecubúri** ≈ N Mozambique
83 Q14 **Mecúfi** Cabo Delgado, NE Mozambique
82 O13 **Mecula** Niassa, N Mozambique
168 I8 **Medan** Sumatera, E Indonesia
61 A24 **Médanos** var. Medanos. Buenos Aires, E Argentina
61 C19 **Médanos** Entre Ríos, E Argentina
155 K24 **Medawachchiya** North Central Province, N Sri Lanka
106 C8 **Mede** Lombardia, N Italy
74 J5 **Médéa** var. El Mediyya, Lemdiyya. N Algeria
Medeba see Ma'dabā
54 E8 **Medellín** Antioquia, NW Colombia
100 H9 **Medem** ≈ NW Germany
98 J8 **Medemblik** Noord-Holland, NW Netherlands
75 N7 **Médenine** var. Madanīyīn. SE Tunisia
76 G9 **Mederdra** Trarza, SW Mauritania
Medeshamstede see Peterborough
42 F4 **Medesto Mendez** Izabal, NE Guatemala
19 O11 **Medford** Massachusetts, NE USA
27 N8 **Medford** Oklahoma, C USA
32 G15 **Medford** Oregon, NW USA
30 K6 **Medford** Wisconsin, N USA
39 P10 **Medfra** Alaska, USA
116 M14 **Medgidia** Constanța, SE Romania
Medgyes see Mediaș
43 O5 **Media Luna, Arrecifes de la** reef E Honduras
60 G11 **Medianeira** Paraná, S Brazil
29 Y15 **Mediapolis** Iowa, C USA
116 I11 **Mediaș** Ger. Mediasch, Hung. Medgyes. Sibiu, C Romania
41 S15 **Medias Aguas** Veracruz-Llave, SE Mexico
Mediasch see Mediaș
106 G10 **Medicina** Emilia-Romagna, C Italy
33 X16 **Medicine Bow** Wyoming, C USA
37 S2 **Medicine Bow Mountains** ▲▲ Colorado/Wyoming, C USA
33 X16 **Medicine Bow River** ≈ Wyoming, C USA
9 R17 **Medicine Hat** Alberta, SW Canada
26 L7 **Medicine Lodge** Kansas, C USA
26 L7 **Medicine Lodge River** ≈ Kansas/Oklahoma, C USA
112 E7 **Medimurje** off. Međimurska Županija. ◈ province N Croatia
Međimurska Županija see Međimurje
54 G10 **Medina** Cundinamarca, C Colombia
18 E9 **Medina** New York, NE USA
29 O5 **Medina** North Dakota, N USA
31 T11 **Medina** Ohio, N USA
25 Q11 **Medina** Texas, SW USA
Medina see Al Madīnah
105 P6 **Medinaceli** Castilla-León, N Spain
104 L6 **Medina del Campo** Castilla-León, N Spain
104 L5 **Medina de Ríoseco** Castilla-León, N Spain
Médina Gonassé see Médina Gounas
76 H12 **Médina Gounas** var. Médina Gonassé. S Senegal
25 S12 **Medina River** ≈ Texas, SW USA
104 K16 **Medina Sidonia** Andalucía, S Spain
Medinat Israel see Israel
119 H14 **Medininkai** Vilnius, SE Lithuania
153 R16 **Medinīpur** West Bengal, NE India
Mediolanum see Saintes, France
Mediolanum see Milano, Italy
Mediomatrica see Metz
121 Q11 **Mediterranean Ridge** undersea feature C Mediterranean Sea
121 O16 **Mediterranean Sea** Fr. Mer Méditerranée. sea Africa/Asia/Europe
Méditerranée, Mer see Mediterranean Sea
79 N17 **Medje** Orientale, NE Dem. Rep. Congo
Medjerda, Oued see Mejerda
114 G7 **Medkovets** Montana, NW Bulgaria
93 J15 **Medle** Västerbotten, N Sweden
127 W7 **Mednogorsk** Orenburgskaya Oblast', W Russian Federation
123 W9 **Mednyy, Ostrov** island E Russian Federation
102 J12 **Médoc** cultural region SW France
159 Q16 **Mêdog** Xizang Zizhiqu, W China
28 J5 **Medora** North Dakota, N USA
79 E17 **Médouneu** Woleu-Ntem, N Gabon
106 I7 **Meduna** ≈ NE Italy
Medunta see Mantes-la-Jolie
Medvedica see Medveditsa
124 J16 **Medveditsa** var. Medvedica. ≈ W Russian Federation
127 O9 **Medveditsa** ≈ SW Russian Federation
112 E8 **Medvednica** ▲▲ NE Croatia
125 R15 **Medvedok** Kirovskaya Oblast', NW Russian Federation
123 S6 **Medvezh'i, Ostrova** island group NE Russian Federation
124 J9 **Medvezh'yegorsk** Respublika Kareliya, NW Russian Federation
109 T11 **Medvode** Ger. Zwischenwässern. NW Slovenia
126 J4 **Medyn'** Kaluzhskaya Oblast', W Russian Federation
180 J10 **Meekatharra** Western Australia
37 Q4 **Meeker** Colorado, C USA
13 T12 **Meelpaeg Lake** ◎ Newfoundland, Newfoundland and Labrador, E Canada
Meemu Atoll see Mulaku Atoll
Meenen see Menen
101 M16 **Meerane** Sachsen, E Germany
101 D15 **Meerbusch** Nordrhein-Westfalen, W Germany
98 I12 **Meerkerk** Zuid-Holland, C Netherlands
99 L18 **Meerssen** var. Mersen. Limburg, SE Netherlands
152 J10 **Meerut** Uttar Pradesh, N India
33 U13 **Meeteetse** Wyoming, C USA
99 K17 **Meeuwen** Limburg, NE Belgium
81 J16 **Mēga** Oromo, C Ethiopia
81 J16 **Mēga Escarpment** escarpment S Ethiopia
Megála Kalívia see Megála Kalývia
115 E16 **Megála Kalývia** var. Megála Kalívia. Thessalía, C Greece
115 H14 **Megáli Panagiá** var. Megáli Panayía. Kentrikí Makedonía, N Greece
Megáli Panayía see Megáli Panagiá
Megáli Préspa, Límni see Prespa, Lake
114 K12 **Megálo Livádi** ▲ Bulgaria/Greece
115 E20 **Megalópoli** prev. Megalópolis. Pelopónnisos, S Greece
Megalópolis see Megalópoli
171 U12 **Megamo** Papua, E Indonesia
115 C18 **Meganísi** island Iónia Nisiá, Greece, C Mediterranean Sea
Meganom, Mys see Mehanom, Mys
Mégantic see Lac-Mégantic
15 R12 **Mégantic, Mont** ▲ Québec, SE Canada
115 G19 **Mégara** Attikí, C Greece
25 R5 **Megargel** Texas, SW USA
98 K13 **Megen** Noord-Brabant, S Netherlands
153 U13 **Meghālaya** ◈ state NE India
153 U16 **Meghna** ≈ S Bangladesh
137 V14 **Meghri** Rus. Megri. SE Armenia
115 Q23 **Megísti** var. Kastellórizon. island SE Greece
Megri see Meghri
Mehabad see Mahābād
116 F13 **Mehadia** Hung. Mehádia. Caraș-Severin, SW Romania
Mehádia see Mehadia
92 L7 **Mehamn** Finnmark, N Norway
117 U13 **Mehanom, Mys** Rus. Mys Meganom. headland S Ukraine
149 P14 **Mehar** Sind, SE Pakistan
180 J8 **Meharry, Mount** ▲ Western Australia
Mehdia see Mahdia
116 G14 **Mehedinți** ◈ county SW Romania
153 S15 **Meherpur** Khulna, W Bangladesh
21 W8 **Meherrin River** ≈ North Carolina/Virginia, SE USA
Meheso see Mī'ēso
191 T11 **Mehetia** island Îles du Vent, W French Polynesia
118 K6 **Mehikoorma** Tartumaa, E Estonia
Me Hka see Nmai Hka
143 N5 **Mehrabad** ✕ (Tehrān) Tehrān, N Iran
142 J7 **Mehrān** Īlām, W Iran
143 Q14 **Mehrān, Rūd-e** prev. Mansurabad. ≈ W Iran
143 Q9 **Mehrīz** Yazd, C Iran
149 R5 **Mehtar Lām** var. Mehtarlām, Meterlam, Methariam, Metharlam. Laghmān, E Afghanistan
Mehtarlām see Mehtar Lām
103 N8 **Mehun-sur-Yèvre** Cher, C France
79 G14 **Meiganga** Adamaoua, NE Cameroon
160 H10 **Meigu** var. Bapu. Sichuan, C China
163 W11 **Meihekou** var. Hailong. Jilin, NE China
99 L15 **Meijel** Limburg, SE Netherlands
Meijiang see Ningdu
166 M5 **Meiktila** Mandalay, C Burma (Myanmar)
Meilbhe, Loch see Melvin, Lough
108 G7 **Meilen** Zürich, N Switzerland
Meilu see Wuchuan
161 T12 **Meinhua Yu** island N Taiwan
101 J17 **Meiningen** Thüringen, C Germany
108 F9 **Meiringen** Bern, S Switzerland
Meishan see Jinzhai
101 O15 **Meissen** Ger. Meißen. Sachsen, E Germany
Meißen see Meissen
101 I15 **Meissner** ▲ C Germany
99 K25 **Meix-devant-Virton** Luxembourg, SE Belgium
Meixian see Meizhou
Meixing see Xinjin
161 P13 **Meizhou** var. Meixian, Mei Xian. Guangdong, S China
67 P2 **Mejerda** var. Oued Medjerda, Wādī Majardah. ≈ Algeria/ Tunisia see also Medjerda, Oued
42 F7 **Mejicanos** San Salvador, C El Salvador
Méjico see Mexico
62 G5 **Mejillones** Antofagasta, N Chile
189 V5 **Mejit Island** var. Mājeej. island Ratak Chain, NE Marshall Islands
79 F17 **Mékambo** Ogooué-Ivindo, NE Gabon
80 J10 **Mek'elē** var. Makale. Tigray, N Ethiopia
74 I10 **Mekerrhane, Sebkha** var. Sebkha Meqerghane, Sebkra Mekerrhane. salt flat C Algeria
Mekerrhane, Sebkra see Mekerrhane, Sebkha
76 G10 **Mékhé** NW Senegal
146 G14 **Mekhinli** Ahal Welaýaty, C Turkmenistan
15 P9 **Mékinac, Lac** ◎ Québec, SE Canada
Meklong see Samut Songhram
74 G6 **Meknès** N Morocco
129 U12 **Mekong** var. Lan-ts'ang Chiang, Cam. Mékôngk, Chin. Lancang Jiang, Lao. Mènam Khong, Th. Mae Nam Khong, Tib. Dza Chu, Vtn. Sông Tiên Giang. ≈ SE Asia
Mékôngk see Mekong
167 T15 **Mekong, Mouths of the** delta S Vietnam
38 L12 **Mekoryuk** Nunivak Island, Alaska, USA
77 R14 **Mékrou** ≈ N Benin
168 K9 **Melaka** var. Malacca. Melaka, Peninsular Malaysia
168 L9 **Melaka** var. Malacca. ◈ state Peninsular Malaysia
Melaka, Selat see Malacca, Strait of
175 O6 **Melanesia** island group W Pacific Ocean
175 P5 **Melanesian Basin** undersea feature W Pacific Ocean
171 R9 **Melanguane** Pulau Karakelang, N Indonesia
169 R11 **Melawi, Sungai** ≈ Borneo, N Indonesia
183 N12 **Melbourne** state capital Victoria, SE Australia
27 V9 **Melbourne** Arkansas, C USA
23 Y12 **Melbourne** Florida, SE USA
29 W14 **Melbourne** Iowa, C USA
92 G10 **Melbu** Nordland, C Norway
Melchor de Mencos see Ciudad Melchor de Mencos
63 F19 **Melchor, Isla** island Archipiélago de los Chonos, S Chile
40 M9 **Melchor Ocampo** Zacatecas, C Mexico
14 C11 **Meldrum Bay** Manitoulin Island, Ontario, S Canada
Meleda see Mljet
106 D8 **Melegnano** prev. Marignano. Lombardia, N Italy
Melekeiok see Melekeok
188 F9 **Melekeok** var. Melekeiok. Babeldaob, N Palau
112 L9 **Melenci** Hung. Melencze. Vojvodina, N Serbia
Melencze see Melenci
127 N4 **Melenki** Vladimirskaya Oblast', W Russian Federation
127 V6 **Meleuz** Respublika Bashkortostan, W Russian Federation
12 L6 **Mélèzes, Rivière aux** ≈ Québec, C Canada
78 I11 **Melfi** Guéra, S Chad
107 M17 **Melfi** Basilicata, S Italy
9 U14 **Melfort** Saskatchewan, S Canada
104 H4 **Melgaço** Viana do Castelo, N Portugal
105 N4 **Melgar de Fernamental** Castilla-León, N Spain
74 L6 **Melghir, Chott** var. Chott Melrhir. salt lake E Algeria
94 H8 **Melhus** Sør-Trøndelag, S Norway
104 H3 **Melide** Galicia, NW Spain
Meligalá see Meligalás
115 E21 **Meligalás** prev. Meligalá. Pelopónnisos, S Greece
60 L12 **Mel, Ilha do** island S Brazil
120 E10 **Melilla** anc. Rusaddir, Russadir. Melilla, Spain, N Africa
71 N1 **Melilla** enclave Spain, N Africa
63 G18 **Melimoyu, Monte** ▲ S Chile
169 V11 **Melintang, Danau** ◎ Borneo, N Indonesia
117 U7 **Melioratyvne** Dnipropetrovs'ka Oblast', E Ukraine
62 G11 **Melipilla** Santiago, C Chile
115 I25 **Mélissa, Akrotírio** cape Kríti, Greece, E Mediterranean Sea
11 W17 **Melita** Manitoba, S Canada
Melita see Mljet
Melitene see Malatya
107 M23 **Melito di Porto Salvo** Calabria, SW Italy
117 U10 **Melitopol'** Zaporiz'ka Oblast', SE Ukraine
109 V4 **Melk** Niederösterreich, NE Austria
95 K15 **Mellan-Fryken** ◎ C Sweden
99 E17 **Melle** Oost-Vlaanderen, NW Belgium
100 G13 **Melle** Niedersachsen, NW Germany
95 J17 **Mellerud** Västra Götaland, S Sweden
102 K10 **Melle-sur-Bretonne** Deux-Sèvres, W France
29 P8 **Mellette** South Dakota, N USA
121 O15 **Mellieha** E Malta
80 B10 **Mellit** Northern Darfur, W Sudan
75 N7 **Mellita** ✕ SE Tunisia
63 G21 **Mellizo Sur, Cerro** ▲ S Chile
100 G9 **Mellum** island NW Germany
83 L22 **Melmoth** KwaZulu/Natal, E South Africa
111 D16 **Mělník** Ger. Melnik. Středočeský Kraj, NW Czech Republic
122 J12 **Mel'nikovo** Tomskaya Oblast', C Russian Federation
61 G18 **Melo** Cerro Largo, NE Uruguay
Melodunum see Melun
Melrhir, Chott see Melghir, Chott
183 P7 **Melrose** New South Wales, SE Australia
182 I7 **Melrose** South Australia
29 T7 **Melrose** Minnesota, N USA
33 Q11 **Melrose** Montana, NW USA
37 V12 **Melrose** New Mexico, SW USA
108 I8 **Mels** Sankt Gallen, NE Switzerland
Melsetter see Chimanimani
33 V9 **Melstone** Montana, NW USA
101 I16 **Melsungen** Hessen, C Germany
92 L12 **Meltaus** Lappi, NW Finland
97 N19 **Melton Mowbray** C England, UK
82 Q13 **Meluco** Cabo Delgado, NE Mozambique
103 O5 **Melun** anc. Melodunum. Seine-et-Marne, N France
80 F12 **Melut** Upper Nile, SE Sudan
27 P5 **Melvern Lake** ⊠ Kansas, C USA
9 V16 **Melville** Saskatchewan, S Canada
Melville Bay/Melville Bugt see Qimusseriarsuaq
45 O11 **Melville Hall** ✕ (Dominica) NE Dominica
181 O1 **Melville Island** island Northern Territory, N Australia
197 O8 **Melville Island** island Parry Islands, Northwest Territories, NW Canada
9 W9 **Melville, Lake** ◎ Newfoundland and Labrador, E Canada
9 O7 **Melville Peninsula** peninsula Nunavut, NE Canada
Melville Sound see Viscount Melville Sound
25 Q9 **Melvin** Texas, SW USA
97 D15 **Melvin, Lough** Ir. Loch Meilbhe. ◎ S Northern Ireland, UK/Ireland
169 S12 **Memala** Borneo, C Indonesia
113 L22 **Memaliaj** Gjirokastër, S Albania
83 Q14 **Memba** Nampula, NE Mozambique
83 Q14 **Memba, Baia de** inlet NE Mozambique
Membidj see Manbij
Memel see Neman, NE Europe
Memel see Klaipeda, Lithuania
101 J23 **Memmingen** Bayern, S Germany
27 U1 **Memphis** Missouri, C USA
20 E10 **Memphis** Tennessee, S USA
25 P3 **Memphis** Texas, SW USA
20 E10 **Memphis** ✕ Tennessee, S USA
15 Q13 **Memphrémagog, Lac** var. Lake Memphremagog. ◎ Canada/USA see also Lake Memphremagog
19 N6 **Memphremagog, Lake** var. Lac Memphrémagog. ◎ Canada/USA see also Memphrémagog, Lac
117 Q2 **Mena** Chernihivs'ka Oblast', NE Ukraine
27 S12 **Mena** Arkansas, C USA
Menaam see Menaldum
Menado see Manado
106 D6 **Menaggio** Lombardia, N Italy
29 T6 **Menahga** Minnesota, N USA
77 R10 **Ménaka** Goa, E Mali
98 K5 **Menaldum** Fris. Menaam. Friesland, N Netherlands
Mènam Khong see Mekong
74 E7 **Menara** ✕ (Marrakech) C Morocco
25 Q9 **Menard** Texas, SW USA
193 Q12 **Menard Fracture Zone** tectonic feature E Pacific Ocean
30 M7 **Menasha** Wisconsin, N USA
Mencezi Garagum see Merkezi Garagumy
Mencezi Garagum see Merkezi Garagumy
193 U9 **Mendaña Fracture Zone** tectonic feature E Pacific Ocean
169 S13 **Mendawai, Sungai** ≈ Borneo, C Indonesia
103 P13 **Mende** anc. Mimatum. Lozère, S France
81 J14 **Mendebo** ▲▲ C Ethiopia
80 J9 **Mendefera** prev. Adi Ugri. S Eritrea
197 S7 **Mendeleyev Ridge** undersea feature Arctic Ocean
127 T3 **Mendeleyevsk** Respublika Tatarstan, W Russian Federation
101 F15 **Menden** Nordrhein-Westfalen, W Germany
22 L6 **Mendenhall** Mississippi, S USA
38 L13 **Mendenhall, Cape** headland Nunivak Island, Alaska, USA
41 P9 **Méndez** var. Villa de Méndez. Tamaulipas, C Mexico
80 H13 **Mendī** Oromo C Ethiopia
186 C7 **Mendi** Southern Highlands, W Papua New Guinea
97 K22 **Mendip Hills** var. Mendips. hill range S England, UK
Mendips see Mendip Hills
34 L6 **Mendocino** California, W USA
34 J3 **Mendocino, Cape** headland California, W USA
0 B8 **Mendocino Fracture Zone** tectonic feature NE Pacific Ocean
35 P10 **Mendota** California, W USA
30 L11 **Mendota** Illinois, N USA
30 K8 **Mendota, Lake** ◎ Wisconsin, N USA
62 I11 **Mendoza** Mendoza, W Argentina
62 I12 **Mendoza** off. Provincia de Mendoza. ◈ province W Argentina
Mendoza, Provincia de see Mendoza
108 H12 **Mendrisio** Ticino, S Switzerland
168 L10 **Mendung** Pulau Mendol, W Indonesia
54 I5 **Mene de Mauroa** Falcón, NW Venezuela
54 I5 **Mene Grande** Zulia, NW Venezuela
136 B14 **Menemen** İzmir, W Turkey
99 C18 **Menen** var. Meenen, Fr. Menin. West-Vlaanderen, W Belgium
163 Q8 **Menengiyn Tal** plain E Mongolia
189 R9 **Meneng Point** headland SW Nauru
92 L10 **Menesjärvi** Lapp. Menešjávri. Lappi, N Finland
Menešjávri see Menesjärvi
107 I24 **Menfi** Sicilia, Italy, C Mediterranean Sea
161 P7 **Mengcheng** Anhui, E China
160 F15 **Menghai** Yunnan, SW China
160 F15 **Mengla** Yunnan, SW China
65 F24 **Menguera Point** headland East Falkland, Falkland Islands
160 M13 **Mengzhu Ling** ▲▲ S China
160 H14 **Mengzi** Yunnan, SW China
114 H13 **Menikio** var. Menoíkio. ▲ NE Greece
Menin see Menen
182 L7 **Menindee** New South Wales, SE Australia
182 L7 **Menindee Lake** ◎ New South Wales, SE Australia
182 J10 **Meningie** South Australia
103 O5 **Mennecy** Essonne, N France
29 Q12 **Menno** South Dakota, N USA
114 H13 **Menoíkio** ▲▲ NE Greece
Menoíkio see Meníkio
31 N5 **Menominee** Michigan, N USA
30 M5 **Menominee River** ≈ Michigan/Wisconsin, N USA
30 M8 **Menomonee Falls** Wisconsin, N USA
30 I6 **Menomonie** Wisconsin, N USA
83 D14 **Menongue** var. Vila Serpa Pinto, Port. Serpa Pinto. Cuando Cubango, C Angola
120 H8 **Menorca** Eng. Minorca; anc. Balearis Minor. island Islas Baleares, Spain, W Mediterranean Sea
105 S13 **Menor, Mar** lagoon SE Spain
39 S10 **Mentasta Lake** ◎ Alaska, USA
39 S10 **Mentasta Mountains** ▲▲ Alaska, USA
168 I13 **Mentawai, Kepulauan** island group W Indonesia
168 I12 **Mentawai, Selat** strait W Indonesia
168 M12 **Mentok** Pulau Bangka, W Indonesia
103 V15 **Menton** It. Mentone. Alpes-Maritimes, SE France
24 K8 **Mentone** Texas, SW USA
Mentone see Menton
31 U11 **Mentor** Ohio, N USA
169 U10 **Menyapa, Gunung** ▲ Borneo, N Indonesia
159 T9 **Menyuan** var. Menyuan Huizu Zizhixian. Qinghai, C China
Menyuan Huizu Zizhixian see Menyuan
74 M5 **Menzel Bourguiba** var. Manzil Bū Ruqaybah; prev. Ferryville. N Tunisia
136 M15 **Menzelet Barajı** ⊠ C Turkey
127 T4 **Menzelinsk** Respublika Tatarstan, W Russian Federation
180 K11 **Menzies** Western Australia
195 V6 **Menzies, Mount** ▲ Antarctica
40 J6 **Meoqui** Chihuahua, N Mexico
83 N14 **Meponda** Niassa, NE Mozambique
98 M8 **Meppel** Drenthe, NE Netherlands
100 E12 **Meppen** Niedersachsen, NW Germany
Meqerghane, Sebkha see Mekerrhane, Sebkha
105 T6 **Mequinenza, Embalse de** ⊠ NE Spain
30 M8 **Mequon** Wisconsin, N USA
Mera see Maira
182 D3 **Meramangye, Lake** salt lake South Australia
27 W5 **Meramec River** ≈ Missouri, C USA
Meran see Merano
168 K13 **Merangin** ≈ Sumatera, W Indonesia
106 G5 **Merano** Ger. Meran. Trentino-Alto Adige, N Italy
168 K8 **Merapuh Lama** Pahang, Peninsular Malaysia
106 D7 **Merate** Lombardia, N Italy
169 U13 **Meratus, Pegunungan** ▲▲ Borneo, N Indonesia
171 Y16 **Merauke, Sungai** ≈ Papua, E Indonesia
182 L9 **Merbein** Victoria, SE Australia
99 F21 **Merbes-le-Château** Hainaut, S Belgium
Merca see Marka
54 C13 **Mercaderes** Cauca, SW Colombia
Mercara see Madikeri
35 P9 **Merced** California, W USA
61 C20 **Mercedes** Buenos Aires, E Argentina
61 D15 **Mercedes** Corrientes, NE Argentina
62 J11 **Mercedes** prev. Villa Mercedes. San Luis, C Argentina
61 D19 **Mercedes** Soriano, SW Uruguay
25 S17 **Mercedes** Texas, SW USA
35 R9 **Merced Peak** ▲ California, W USA
35 P9 **Merced River** ≈ California, W USA
18 B13 **Mercer** Pennsylvania, NE USA
99 G18 **Merchtem** Vlaams Brabant, C Belgium
15 O13 **Mercier** Québec, SE Canada
25 Q9 **Mercury** Texas, SW USA
184 M5 **Mercury Islands** island group N New Zealand
19 O9 **Meredith** New Hampshire, NE USA
65 B25 **Meredith, Cape** var. Cabo Belgrano. headland West Falkland, Falkland Islands
37 V6 **Meredith, Lake** ◎ Colorado, C USA
25 N2 **Meredith, Lake** ⊠ Texas, SW USA
81 O16 **Mereeg** var. Mareeq, It. Meregh. Galguduud, E Somalia
117 V5 **Merefa** Kharkivs'ka Oblast', E Ukraine
Meregh see Mereeg
99 E17 **Merelbeke** Oost-Vlaanderen, NW Belgium
Merend see Marand
167 T12 **Mereuch** Môndól Kiri, E Cambodia
Mergate see Margate
144 F9 **Mergenevo** Zapadnyy Kazakhstan, NW Kazakhstan
167 N12 **Mergui** Tenasserim, S Burma (Myanmar)
166 M12 **Mergui Archipelago** island group S Burma (Myanmar)
114 L12 **Meriç** Edirne, NW Turkey
114 L12 **Meriç** Bul. Maritsa, Gk. Évros; anc. Hebrus. ≈ SE Europe see also Évros/Maritsa
41 X12 **Mérida** Yucatán, SW Mexico
104 J11 **Mérida** anc. Augusta Emerita. Extremadura, W Spain
54 I6 **Mérida** Mérida, W Venezuela
54 H7 **Mérida** off. Estado Mérida. ◈ state W Venezuela
Mérida, Estado see Mérida
18 M13 **Meriden** Connecticut, NE USA

◆ Country ◇ Dependent Territory ◈ Administrative Regions ▲ Mountain Volcano ◎ Lake
● Country Capital ○ Dependent Territory Capital ✕ International Airport ▲▲ Mountain Range ≈ River ⊠ Reservoir

Meridian – Milton

22 M5 Meridian Mississippi, S USA
25 S8 Meridian Texas, SW USA
102 J13 Mérignac Gironde, SW France
102 J13 Mérignac ✕ (Bordeaux) Gironde, SW France
93 J18 Merikarvia Länsi-Soumi, SW Finland
183 R12 Merimbula New South Wales, SE Australia
182 L9 Meringur Victoria, SE Australia
Merín, Laguna see Mirim Lagoon
97 I19 Merioneth cultural region W Wales, UK
188 A11 Merir island Palau Islands, N Palau
188 B17 Merizo SW Guam
Merjama see Märjamaa
145 S16 Merke Zhambyl, S Kazakhstan
25 P7 Merkel Texas, SW USA
146 E12 Merkezi Garagumy var. Mencezi Garagum, Rus. Tsentral'nyye Nizmennyye Garagumy. desert C Turkmenistan
146 E12 Merkezi Garagumy var. Mencezi Garagum, Rus. Tsentral'nyye Nizmennyye Garagumy. desert C Turkmenistan
119 F15 Merkinė Alytus, S Lithuania
99 G16 Merksem Antwerpen, N Belgium
99 I15 Merksplas Antwerpen, N Belgium
Merkulovichi see Myerkulavichy
119 G15 Merkys ≈ S Lithuania
32 F15 Merlin Oregon, NW USA
61 C20 Merlo Buenos Aires, E Argentina
138 G8 Meron, Haré ▲ N Israel
74 K6 Merouane, Chott salt lake NE Algeria
80 F7 Merowe Northern, N Sudan
180 J12 Merredin Western Australia
97 I14 Merrick ▲ S Scotland, UK
32 H16 Merrill Oregon, NW USA
30 L5 Merrill Wisconsin, N USA
31 N11 Merrillville Indiana, N USA
19 O10 Merrimack River ≈ Massachusetts/New Hampshire, NE USA
28 L12 Merriman Nebraska, C USA
9 N17 Merritt British Columbia, SW Canada
23 Y12 Merritt Island Florida, SE USA
23 Y11 Merritt Island island Florida, SE USA
28 M12 Merritt Reservoir ⊠ Nebraska, C USA
183 S7 Merriwa New South Wales, SE Australia
183 O8 Merriwagga New South Wales, SE Australia
22 G8 Merryville Louisiana, S USA
80 K9 Mersa Fatma E Eritrea
102 M7 Mer St-Aubin Loir-et-Cher, C France
Mersa Maṭrûḥ see Maṭrûḥ
99 M24 Mersch Luxembourg, C Luxembourg
101 M15 Merseburg Sachsen-Anhalt, C Germany
Mersen see Meerssen
97 K18 Mersey ≈ NW England, U K
136 J17 Mersin Mersin, S Turkey
136 I17 Mersin prev. İçel, Ichili. ❖ province S Turkey
168 L9 Mersing Johor, Peninsular Malaysia
118 E8 Mērsrags Talsi, NW Latvia
152 G12 Merta var. Merta City. Rājasthān, N India
Merta City see Merta
152 F12 Merta Road Rājasthān, N India
97 J21 Merthyr Tydfil S Wales, UK
104 H13 Mértola Beja, S Portugal
144 G14 Mertvyy Kultuk, Sor salt flat SW Kazakhstan
195 V16 Mertz Glacier glacier Antarctica
99 M24 Mertzig Diekirch, C Luxembourg
25 O9 Mertzon Texas, SW USA
103 N4 Méru Oise, N France
81 I18 Meru Eastern, C Kenya
81 I20 Meru, Mount ▲ NE Tanzania
Merv see Mary
Mervdasht see Marv Dasht
136 K11 Merzifon Amasya, N Turkey
101 D20 Merzig Saarland, SW Germany
36 L14 Mesa Arizona, SW USA
29 V4 Mesabi Range ▲▲ Minnesota, N USA
54 H6 Mesa Bolívar Mérida, NW Venezuela
107 Q18 Mesagne Puglia, SE Italy
39 P12 Mesa Mountain ▲ Alaska, USA
115 J25 Mesará lowland Kríti, Greece, E Mediterranean Sea
37 S14 Mescalero New Mexico, SW USA
101 G15 Meschede Nordrhein-Westfalen, W Germany
137 Q12 Mescit Dağları ▲▲ NE Turkey
189 V13 Mesegon island Chuuk, C Micronesia
Meseritz see Międzyrzecz
54 F11 Mesetas Meta, C Colombia
Meshchera Lowland see Meshcherskaya Nizina
126 M4 Meshcherskaya Nizina Eng. Meshchera Lowland. basin W Russian Federation
126 J5 Meshchovsk Kaluzhskaya Oblast', W Russian Federation
125 R9 Meshchura Respublika Komi, NW Russian Federation
Meshed see Mashhad
Meshed-i-Sar see Bābolsar
80 E13 Meshra'er Req Warab, S Sudan
37 R15 Mesilla New Mexico, SW USA
108 H10 Mesocco Ger. Misox. Ticino, S Switzerland
115 D18 Mesolóngi prev. Mesolóngion. Dytikí Ellás, W Greece
Mesolóngion see Mesolóngi
14 E8 Mesomikenda Lake ◎ Ontario, S Canada
61 D15 Mesopotamia var. Mesopotamia Argentina. physical region NE Argentina
Mesopotamia Argentina see Mesopotamia
35 Y10 Mesquite Nevada, W USA
82 Q13 Messalo, Rio var. Mualo. ≈ NE Mozambique
Messana/Messene see Messina
99 L25 Messancy Luxembourg, SE Belgium
107 M23 Messina var. Messana, Messene; anc. Zancle. Sicilia, Italy, C Mediterranean Sea
Messina see Musina
Messina, Strait of see Messina, Stretto di
107 M23 Messina, Stretto di Eng. Strait of Messina. strait SW Italy
115 E21 Messíni Pelopónnisos, S Greece
115 E21 Messinía peninsula S Greece
115 E22 Messiniakós Kólpos gulf S Greece
122 J8 Messoyakha ≈ N Russian Federation
114 H11 Mesta Gk. Néstos, Turk. Kara Su. ≈ Bulgaria/Greece see also Néstos
Mesta see Néstos
Mestghanem see Mostaganem
137 R8 Mestia var. Mestiya. N Georgia
Mestiya see Mestia
115 K18 Mestón, Akrotírio cape Chíos, E Greece
106 H8 Mestre Veneto, NE Italy
59 M16 Mestre, Espigão ▲▲ E Brazil
169 N14 Mesuji ≈ Sumatera, W Indonesia
Mesule see Grosser Möseler
10 J10 Meszah Peak ▲ British Columbia, W Canada
54 G11 Meta off. Departamento del Meta. ❖ province C Colombia
15 Q8 Metabetchouane ≈ Québec, SE Canada
Meta, Departamento del see Meta
9 S7 Meta Incognita Peninsula peninsula Baffin Island, Nunavut, NE Canada
22 K9 Metairie Louisiana, S USA
32 M6 Metaline Falls Washington, NW USA
62 K6 Metán Salta, N Argentina
82 N13 Metangula Niassa, N Mozambique
42 E7 Metapán Santa Ana, NW El Salvador
54 K9 Meta, Río ≈ Colombia/Venezuela
106 I11 Metauro ≈ C Italy
80 H11 Metema Amhara, N Ethiopia
115 D15 Metéora religious building Thessalía, C Greece
65 O20 Meteor Rise undersea feature SW Indian Ocean
186 G5 Meteran New Hanover, NE Papua New Guinea
Meterlam see Mehtar Lām
115 G20 Methanon peninsula S Greece
Methariam/Metharlam see Mehtar Lām
32 J6 Methow River ≈ Washington, NW USA
19 O10 Methuen Massachusetts, NE USA
185 G19 Methven Canterbury, South Island, New Zealand
Metis see Metz
113 G15 Metković Dubrovnik-Neretva, SE Croatia
39 Y14 Metlakatla Annette Island, Alaska, USA
109 V13 Metlika Ger. Möttling. SE Slovenia
109 T8 Metnitz Kärnten, S Austria
27 W12 Meto, Bayou ≈ Arkansas, C USA
168 M15 Metro Sumatera, W Indonesia
30 M17 Metropolis Illinois, N USA
Metropolitan see Santiago
35 N8 Metropolitan Oakland ✕ California, W USA
115 D15 Métsovo prev. Métsovon. Ípeiros, C Greece
Métsovon see Métsovo
23 V5 Metter Georgia, SE USA
99 H21 Mettet Namur, S Belgium
101 D20 Mettlach Saarland, SW Germany
Mettu see Metu
80 H13 Metu var. Mattu, Mettu. Oromo, C Ethiopia
169 T10 Metulang Borneo, N Indonesia
138 G8 Metulla Northern, N Israel
103 T4 Metz anc. Divodurum Mediomatricum, Mediomatrica, Metis. Moselle, NE France
101 H22 Metzingen Baden-Württemberg, S Germany
168 G8 Meulaboh Sumatera, W Indonesia
99 D18 Meulebeke West-Vlaanderen, W Belgium
103 U6 Meurthe ≈ NE France
103 S5 Meurthe-et-Moselle ❖ department NE France
103 S4 Meuse ❖ department NE France
84 F10 Meuse Dut. Maas. ≈ W Europe see also Maas
Meuse see Maas
Mexcala, Río see Balsas, Río
25 U8 Mexia Texas, SW USA
58 K11 Mexiana, Ilha island NE Brazil
40 C1 Mexicali Baja California, NW Mexico
Mexicanos, Estados Unidos see Mexico
41 O14 México var. Ciudad de México, Eng. Mexico City. ● (Mexico) México, C Mexico
27 V4 Mexico Missouri, C USA
18 H9 Mexico New York, NE USA
40 L7 Mexico off. United Mexican States, var. Méjico, México, Sp. Estados Unidos Mexicanos. ◆ federal republic N Central America
41 O13 México ❖ state S Mexico
México see Mexico
0 J13 Mexico Basin var. Sigsbee Deep. undersea feature C Gulf of Mexico
Mexico City see México
México, Golfo de see Mexico, Gulf of
44 B4 Mexico, Gulf of Sp. Golfo de México. gulf W Atlantic Ocean
Meyadine see Al Mayādīn
149 Q5 Meydān Shahr var. Maydān Shahr. Vardak, E Afghanistan
39 Y14 Meyers Chuck Etolin Island, Alaska, USA
148 M3 Meymaneh var. Maimāna, Maymana. Fāryāb, NW Afghanistan
143 N7 Meymeh Eṣfahān, C Iran
123 V7 Meynypil'gyno Chukotskiy Avtonomnyy Okrug, NE Russian Federation
108 A10 Meyrin Genève, SW Switzerland
166 L7 Mezaligon Irrawaddy, SW Burma (Myanmar)
41 O15 Mezcala Guerrero, S Mexico
114 H8 Mezdra Vratsa, NW Bulgaria
103 P16 Mèze Hérault, S France
125 O6 Mezen' Arkhangel'skaya Oblast', NW Russian Federation
125 P8 Mezen' ≈ NW Russian Federation
Mezen, Bay of see Mezenskaya Guba
103 Q13 Mézenc, Mont ▲ C France
125 O8 Mezenskaya Guba var. Bay of Mezen. bay NW Russian Federation
Mezha see Myazha
122 H6 Mezhdusharskiy, Ostrov island Novaya Zemlya, N Russian Federation
Mezhëvo see Myezhava
127 W5 Mezhgor'ye Respublika Bashkortostan, W Russian Federation
Mezhgor'ye see Mizhhir"ya
117 V8 Mezhova Dnipropetrovs'ka Oblast', E Ukraine
10 J12 Meziadin Junction British Columbia, W Canada
111 G16 Mezileské Sedlo var. Przełęcz Międzyleska. pass Czech Republic/Poland
102 L14 Mézin Lot-et-Garonne, SW France
111 M24 Mezőberény Békés, SE Hungary
111 M25 Mezőhegyes Békés, SE Hungary
111 M25 Mezőkovácsháza Békés, SE Hungary
111 M21 Mezőkövesd Borsod-Abaúj-Zemplén, NE Hungary
Mezőtelegd see Tileagd
111 M23 Mezőtúr Jász-Nagykun-Szolnok, E Hungary
40 K10 Mezquital Durango, C Mexico
106 G6 Mezzolombardo Trentino-Alto Adige, N Italy
82 L13 Mfuwe Northern, N Zambia
121 O15 Mġarr Gozo, N Malta
126 H6 Mglin Bryanskaya Oblast', W Russian Federation
Mhálanna, Cionn see Malin Head
154 G10 Mhow Madhya Pradesh, C India
Miadzioł Nowy see Myadzyel
171 O6 Miagao Panay Island, C Philippines
41 R17 Miahuatlán var. Miahuatlán de Porfirio Díaz. Oaxaca, SE Mexico
Miahuatlán de Porfirio Díaz see Miahuatlán
104 K10 Miajadas Extremadura, W Spain
Miajlar see Myājlār
36 M14 Miami Arizona, SW USA
23 Z16 Miami Florida, SE USA
27 R8 Miami Oklahoma, C USA
25 O2 Miami Texas, SW USA
23 Z16 Miami ✕ Florida, SE USA
23 Z16 Miami Beach Florida, SE USA
23 Y15 Miami Canal canal Florida, SE USA
31 R14 Miamisburg Ohio, N USA
149 U10 Miān Channūn Punjab, E Pakistan
142 J4 Miāndowāb var. Mianduab, Miyāndoāb. Āẕarbāyjān-e Gharbī, NW Iran
172 H5 Miandrivazo Toliara, C Madagascar
Mianduab see Miāndowāb
142 K3 Miāneh var. Miyāneh. Āẕarbāyjān-e Sharqī, NW Iran
149 O16 Miāni Hōr lagoon S Pakistan
160 G10 Mianning Sichuan, C China
149 T7 Miānwāli Punjab, NE Pakistan
160 J7 Mianxian var. Mian Xian. Shaanxi, C China
Mian Xian see Mianxian
160 I8 Mianyang Sichuan, C China
Mianyang see Xiantao
161 R3 Miaodao Qundao island group E China
161 S13 Miaoli N Taiwan
122 F11 Miass Chelyabinskaya Oblast', C Russian Federation
110 G8 Miastko Ger. Rummelsburg in Pommern. Pomorskie, N Poland
Miava see Myjava
9 O15 Mica Creek British Columbia, SW Canada
160 J7 Micang Shan ▲▲ C China
Mi Chai see Nong Khai
111 O19 Michalovce Ger. Grossmichel, Hung. Nagymihály. Košický Kraj, E Slovakia
99 M20 Michel, Baraque hill E Belgium
39 S5 Michelson, Mount ▲ Alaska, USA
45 P9 Miches E Dominican Republic
30 M4 Michigamme, Lake ◎ Michigan, N USA
30 M4 Michigamme Reservoir ⊠ Michigan, N USA
31 N4 Michigamme River ≈ Michigan, N USA
31 O7 Michigan off. State of Michigan, also known as Great Lakes State, Lake State, Wolverine State. ◆ state N USA
31 O11 Michigan City Indiana, N USA
31 O8 Michigan, Lake ◎ N USA
31 P2 Michipicoten Bay lake bay Ontario, N Canada
14 A8 Michipicoten Island island Ontario, S Canada
14 B7 Michipicoten River Ontario, S Canada
Michurin see Tsarevo
126 M6 Michurinsk Tambovskaya Oblast', W Russian Federation
Mico, Punta/Mico, Punto see Monkey Point
42 L10 Mico, Río ≈ SE Nicaragua
45 T12 Micoud SE Saint Lucia
189 N16 Micronesia off. Federated States of Micronesia. ◆ federation W Pacific Ocean
175 P4 Micronesia island group W Pacific Ocean
Micronesia, Federated States of see Micronesia
169 O9 Midai, Pulau island Kepulauan Natuna, W Indonesia
Mid-Atlantic Cordillera see Mid-Atlantic Ridge
65 M17 Mid-Atlantic Ridge var. Mid-Atlantic Cordillera, Mid-Atlantic Rise, Mid-Atlantic Swell. undersea feature Atlantic Ocean
Mid-Atlantic Rise/Mid-Atlantic Swell see Mid-Atlantic Ridge
99 E15 Middelburg Zeeland, SW Netherlands
83 H24 Middelburg Eastern Cape, S South Africa
83 K21 Middelburg Mpumalanga, NE South Africa
95 G23 Middelfart Fyn, C Denmark
98 G13 Middelharnis Zuid-Holland, SW Netherlands
99 B16 Middelkerke West-Vlaanderen, W Belgium
98 I9 Middenbeemster Noord-Holland, C Netherlands
98 I8 Middenmeer Noord-Holland, NW Netherlands
35 Q2 Middle Alkali Lake ◎ California, W USA
193 S6 Middle America Trench undersea feature E Pacific Ocean
151 P19 Middle Andaman island Andaman Islands, India, NE Indian Ocean
Middle Atlas see Moyen Atlas
21 R3 Middlebourne West Virginia, NE USA
23 W9 Middleburg Florida, SE USA
Middleburg Island see 'Eua
Middle Caicos see Grand Caicos
25 N8 Middle Concho River ≈ Texas, SW USA
Middle Congo see Congo (Republic of)
39 R6 Middle Fork Chandalar River ≈ Alaska, USA
39 Q7 Middle Fork Koyukuk River ≈ Alaska, USA
33 O12 Middle Fork Salmon River ≈ Idaho, NW USA
9 T15 Middle Lake Saskatchewan, S Canada
28 L13 Middle Loup River ≈ Nebraska, C USA
185 E22 Middlemarch Otago, South Island, New Zealand
31 T15 Middleport Ohio, N USA
29 U14 Middle Raccoon River ≈ Iowa, C USA
29 R3 Middle River ≈ Minnesota, N USA
21 N8 Middlesboro Kentucky, S USA
97 M15 Middlesbrough N England, UK
42 G3 Middlesex Stann Creek, C Belize
97 N22 Middlesex cultural region SE England, UK
13 P15 Middleton Nova Scotia, SE Canada
20 F10 Middleton Tennessee, S USA
30 L9 Middleton Wisconsin, N USA
39 S13 Middleton Island island Alaska, USA
34 M7 Middletown California, W USA
21 Y2 Middletown Delaware, NE USA
18 K15 Middletown New Jersey, NE USA
18 K13 Middletown New York, NE USA
31 R14 Middletown Ohio, N USA
18 G15 Middletown Pennsylvania, NE USA
141 N14 Mīdī var. Maydī. NW Yemen
103 O16 Midi, Canal du canal S France
102 K17 Midi de Bigorre, Pic du ▲ S France
102 K17 Midi d'Ossau, Pic du ▲ SW France
173 R7 Mid-Indian Basin undersea feature N Indian Ocean
173 P7 Mid-Indian Ridge var. Central Indian Ridge. undersea feature C Indian Ocean
103 N14 Midi-Pyrénées ❖ region S France
25 N8 Midkiff Texas, SW USA
14 G13 Midland Ontario, S Canada
31 R8 Midland Michigan, N USA
28 M10 Midland South Dakota, N USA
24 M8 Midland Texas, SW USA
83 K17 Midlands ❖ province C Zimbabwe
97 D21 Midleton Ir. Mainistir na Corann. SW Ireland
25 T7 Midlothian Texas, SW USA
96 K12 Midlothian cultural region S Scotland, UK
172 I7 Midongy Fianarantsoa, S Madagascar
102 K15 Midou ≈ SW France
192 J6 Mid-Pacific Mountains var. Mid-Pacific Seamounts. undersea feature NW Pacific Ocean
Mid-Pacific Seamounts see Mid-Pacific Mountains
171 Q7 Midsayap Mindanao, S Philippines
36 L3 Midway Utah, W USA
192 L5 Midway Islands ◇ US territory C Pacific Ocean
33 X14 Midwest Wyoming, C USA
27 N10 Midwest City Oklahoma, C USA
152 M10 Mid Western ❖ zone W Nepal
98 P5 Midwolda Groningen, NE Netherlands
137 Q16 Midyat Mardin, SE Turkey
114 F8 Midzhur SCr. Midžor. ▲ Bulgaria/Serbia see also Midžor
Midzhur see Midžor
113 Q14 Midžor Bul. Midzhur. ▲ Bulgaria/Serbia see also Midzhur
Midžor see Midzhur
164 K14 Mie off. Mie-ken. ❖ prefecture Honshū, SW Japan
111 L16 Miechów Małopolskie, S Poland
110 F11 Międzychód Ger. Mitteldorf. Wielkopolskie, C Poland
Międzyleska, Przełęcz see Mezileské Sedlo
110 O12 Międzyrzec Podlaski Lubelskie, E Poland
110 E11 Międzyrzecz Ger. Meseritz. Lubuskie, W Poland
Mie-ken see Mie
102 L16 Miélan Gers, S France
111 N16 Mielec Podkarpackie, SE Poland
95 L21 Mien ◎ S Sweden
41 O8 Mier Tamaulipas, C Mexico
116 J11 Miercurea-Ciuc Ger. Szeklerburg, Hung. Csíkszereda. Harghita, C Romania
Mieresch see Maros/Mureş
Mieres del Camín see Mieres del Camino
104 K2 Mieres del Camino var. Mieres del Camín. Asturias, NW Spain
99 K15 Mierlo Noord-Brabant, SE Netherlands
41 O10 Mier y Noriega Nuevo León, NE Mexico
Mies see Stříbro
80 K13 Mī'ēso var. Meheso, Miesso. Oromo, C Ethiopia
Miesso see Mī'ēso
110 D10 Mieszkowice Ger. Bärwalde Neumark. Zachodnio-pomorskie, W Poland
18 G14 Mifflinburg Pennsylvania, NE USA
18 F14 Mifflintown Pennsylvania, NE USA
41 R15 Miguel Alemán, Presa ⊠ SE Mexico
40 L9 Miguel Asua var. Miguel Auza. Zacatecas, C Mexico
Miguel Auza see Miguel Asua
43 S15 Miguel de la Borda var. Donoso. Colón, C Panama
41 N13 Miguel Hidalgo ✕ (Guadalajara) Jalisco, SW Mexico
40 H7 Miguel Hidalgo, Presa ⊠ W Mexico
116 J14 Mihăileşti Giurgiu, S Romania
116 M14 Mihail Kogălniceanu var. Kogălniceanu; prev. Caramurat, Ferdinand. Constanţa, SE Romania
117 N14 Mihai Viteazu Constanţa, SE Romania
136 G12 Mihalıççık Eskişehir, NW Turkey
164 G13 Mihara Hiroshima, Honshū, SW Japan
165 N14 Mihara-yama ⛰ Miyako-jima, SE Japan
105 S8 Mijares ≈ E Spain
98 I11 Mijdrecht Utrecht, C Netherlands
165 S4 Mikasa Hokkaidō, NE Japan
Mikashevichi see Mikashevichy
119 K19 Mikashevichy Pol. Mikaszewicze, Rus. Mikashevichi. Brestskaya Voblasts', SW Belarus
Mikaszewicze see Mikashevichy
126 L5 Mikhaylov Ryazanskaya Oblast', W Russian Federation
Mikhaylovgrad see Montana
195 Z8 Mikhaylov Island island Antarctica
145 T6 Mikhaylovka Pavlodar, N Kazakhstan
127 N9 Mikhaylovka Volgogradskaya Oblast', SW Russian Federation
Mikhaylovka see Mykhaylivka
81 K24 Mikindani Mtwara, SE Tanzania
93 N18 Mikkeli Swe. Sankt Michel. Itä-Suomi, SE Finland
110 M8 Mikołajki Ger. Nikolaiken. Warmińsko-Mazurskie, NE Poland
Míkonos see Mýkonos
114 I9 Mikre Lovech, N Bulgaria
114 C13 Mikrí Préspa, Límni ◎ N Greece
125 P4 Mikulkin, Mys cape NW Russian Federation
81 I23 Mikumi Morogoro, SE Tanzania
125 R10 Mikun' Respublika Komi, NW Russian Federation
164 K13 Mikuni Fukui, Honshū, SW Japan
165 X13 Mikura-jima island E Japan
29 V7 Milaca Minnesota, N USA
62 J10 Milagro La Rioja, C Argentina
56 B7 Milagro Guayas, SW Ecuador
31 P4 Milakokia Lake ◎ Michigan, N USA
30 J1 Milan Illinois, N USA
31 R10 Milan Michigan, N USA
27 T2 Milan Missouri, C USA
37 Q11 Milan New Mexico, SW USA
20 G9 Milan Tennessee, S USA
Milan see Milano
95 F15 Miland Telemark, S Norway
83 N15 Milange Zambézia, NE Mozambique
106 D8 Milano Eng. Milan, Ger. Mailand; anc. Mediolanum. Lombardia, N Italy
25 U10 Milano Texas, SW USA
136 C15 Milas Muğla, SW Turkey
119 K21 Milashavichy Rus. Milashevichi. Homyel'skaya Voblasts', SE Belarus
Milashevichi see Milashavichy
119 I18 Milavidy Rus. Milovidy. Brestskaya Voblasts', SW Belarus
107 L23 Milazzo anc. Mylae. Sicilia, Italy, C Mediterranean Sea
29 R8 Milbank South Dakota, N USA
19 T7 Milbridge Maine, NE USA
100 L11 Milde ≈ C Germany
14 F14 Mildmay Ontario, S Canada
182 L9 Mildura Victoria, SE Australia
137 X12 Mil Düzü Rus. Mil'skaya Ravnina, Mil'skaya Step'. physical region C Azerbaijan
160 H13 Mile var. Miyang. Yunnan, SW China
Mile see Mili Atoll
181 Y10 Miles Queensland, E Australia
25 P8 Miles Texas, SW USA
33 X9 Miles City Montana, NW USA
9 U17 Milestone Saskatchewan, S Canada
107 N22 Mileto Calabria, SW Italy
107 K16 Miletto, Monte ▲ C Italy
18 M13 Milford Connecticut, NE USA
21 Y3 Milford var. Milford City. Delaware, NE USA
29 T11 Milford Iowa, C USA
19 S6 Milford Maine, NE USA
29 R16 Milford Nebraska, C USA
19 O10 Milford New Hampshire, NE USA
18 J13 Milford Pennsylvania, NE USA
25 T7 Milford Texas, SW USA
36 K6 Milford Utah, W USA
Milford see Milford Haven
Milford City see Milford
97 H21 Milford Haven prev. Milford. SW Wales, UK
27 O4 Milford Lake ⊠ Kansas, C USA
185 B21 Milford Sound Southland, South Island, New Zealand
185 B21 Milford Sound inlet South Island, New Zealand
Milhau see Millau
Milh, Bahr al see Razāzah, Buḥayrat ar
139 T10 Milḥ, Wādī al dry watercourse S Iraq
189 W8 Mili Atoll var. Mile. atoll Ratak Chain, SE Marshall Islands
110 H13 Milicz Dolnośląskie, SW Poland
107 L25 Militello in Val di Catania Sicilia, Italy, C Mediterranean Sea
9 R17 Milk River Alberta, SW Canada
44 J13 Milk River ≈ C Jamaica
33 W7 Milk River ≈ Montana, NW USA
80 D9 Milk, Wadi el var. Wadi al Malik. ≈ C Sudan
99 L14 Mill Noord-Brabant, SE Netherlands
103 P14 Millau var. Milhau; anc. Æmilianum. Aveyron, S France
14 I14 Millbrook Ontario, SE Canada
23 U4 Milledgeville Georgia, SE USA
12 C12 Mille Lacs, Lac des ◎ Ontario, S Canada
29 V6 Mille Lacs Lake ◎ Minnesota, N USA
23 V4 Millen Georgia, SE USA
191 Y5 Millennium Island prev. Caroline Island, Thornton Island. atoll Line Islands, E Kiribati
29 O9 Miller South Dakota, N USA
30 K5 Miller Dam Flowage ◎ Wisconsin, N USA
39 U12 Miller, Mount ▲ Alaska, USA
126 L10 Millerovo Rostovskaya Oblast', SW Russian Federation
37 N17 Miller Peak ▲ Arizona, SW USA
31 T12 Millersburg Ohio, N USA
18 G15 Millersburg Pennsylvania, NE USA
185 D23 Millers Flat Otago, South Island, New Zealand
25 Q8 Millersview Texas, SW USA
106 B10 Millesimo Piemonte, NE Italy
12 C12 Milles Lacs, Lac des ◎ Ontario, SW Canada
25 Q13 Millett Texas, SW USA
103 N11 Millevaches, Plateau de plateau C France
182 K12 Millicent South Australia
98 M13 Millingen aan den Rijn Gelderland, SE Netherlands
20 E10 Millington Tennessee, S USA
19 R4 Millinocket Maine, NE USA
19 R4 Millinocket Lake ◎ Maine, NE USA
195 Z11 Mill Island island Antarctica
183 T3 Millmerran Queensland, E Australia
109 R9 Millstatt Kärnten, S Austria
97 B19 Milltown Malbay Ir. Sráid na Cathrach. W Ireland
18 J17 Millville New Jersey, NE USA
27 S13 Millwood Lake ⊠ Arkansas, C USA
Milne Bank see Milne Seamounts
186 G10 Milne Bay ❖ province SE Papua New Guinea
64 J8 Milne Seamounts var. Milne Bank. undersea feature N Atlantic Ocean
29 Q6 Milnor North Dakota, N USA
19 R5 Milo Maine, NE USA
115 I22 Mílos island Kykládes, Greece, Aegean Sea
Mílos see Pláka
110 H11 Miłosław Wielkopolskie, C Poland
113 K19 Milot var. Miloti. Lezhë, C Albania
Miloti see Milot
117 Z5 Milove Luhans'ka Oblast', E Ukraine
Milovidy see Milavidy
182 L4 Milparinka New South Wales, SE Australia
35 N9 Milpitas California, W USA
Mil'skaya Ravnina/Mil'skaya Step' see Mil Düzü
14 G15 Milton Ontario, S Canada
185 E24 Milton Otago, South Island, New Zealand
21 Y4 Milton Delaware, NE USA
23 P8 Milton Florida, SE USA
18 G14 Milton Pennsylvania, NE USA
18 L7 Milton Vermont, NE USA

◆ Country ◇ Dependent Territory ❖ Administrative Regions ▲ Mountain ⛰ Volcano ◎ Lake
● Country Capital ○ Dependent Territory Capital ✕ International Airport ▲▲ Mountain Range ≈ River ⊠ Reservoir
288

MILTON-FREEWATER – MOÍRES

32 K11 **Milton-Freewater** Oregon, NW USA
97 N21 **Milton Keynes** SE England, UK
27 N3 **Miltonvale** Kansas, C USA
161 N10 **Miluo** Hunan, S China
30 M9 **Milwaukee** Wisconsin, N USA
Milyang *see* Miryang
Mimatum *see* Mende
37 Q15 **Mimbres Mountains** ⛰ New Mexico, SW USA
182 D2 **Mimili** South Australia
102 J14 **Mimizan** Landes, SW France
Mimmaya *see* Minmaya
79 E19 **Mimongo** Ngounié, C Gabon
Min *see* Fujian
35 T7 **Mina** Nevada, W USA
143 S14 **Mīnāb** Hormozgān, SE Iran
Mînâ Baranîs *see* Berenice
149 R9 **Mīna Bāzār** Baluchistān, SW Pakistan
165 X17 **Minami-Iō-jima** *Eng.* San Augustine. *island* SE Japan
165 R5 **Minami-Kayabe** Hokkaidō, NE Japan
164 C17 **Minamitane** Kagoshima, Tanega-shima, SW Japan
Minami Tori Shima *see* Marcus Island
Min'an *see* Longshan
62 J4 **Mina Pirquitas** Jujuy, NW Argentina
173 O3 **Mīnā' Qābūs** NE Oman
61 F19 **Minas** Lavalleja, S Uruguay
13 P15 **Minas Basin** *bay* Nova Scotia, SE Canada
61 F17 **Minas de Corrales** Rivera, NE Uruguay
44 A5 **Minas de Matahambre** Pinar del Río, W Cuba
104 J13 **Minas de Ríotinto** Andalucía, S Spain
60 K7 **Minas Gerais** *off.* Estado de Minas Gerais. ◐ *state* E Brazil
Minas Gerais, Estado de *see* Minas Gerais
42 E5 **Minas, Sierra de las** ⛰ E Guatemala
41 T15 **Minatitlán** Veracruz-Llave, E Mexico
166 L6 **Minbu** Magwe, W Burma (Myanmar)
149 V10 **Minchinābād** Punjab, E Pakistan
63 G17 **Minchinmávida, Volcán** 🌋 S Chile
96 G7 **Minch, The** *var.* North Minch. *strait* NW Scotland, UK
106 F8 **Mincio** *anc.* Mincius. ∽ N Italy
Mincius *see* Mincio
26 M11 **Minco** Oklahoma, C USA
171 Q7 **Mindanao** *island* S Philippines
Mindanao Sea *see* Bohol Sea
101 J23 **Mindel** ∽ S Germany
101 J23 **Mindelheim** Bayern, S Germany
Mindello *see* Mindelo
76 C9 **Mindelo** *var.* Mindello; *prev.* Porto Grande. São Vicente, N Cape Verde
14 I13 **Minden** Ontario, SE Canada
100 H13 **Minden** *anc.* Minthun. Nordrhein-Westfalen, NW Germany
22 G5 **Minden** Louisiana, S USA
29 O16 **Minden** Nebraska, C USA
35 Q6 **Minden** Nevada, W USA
182 L8 **Mindona Lake** *seasonal lake* New South Wales, SE Australia
171 O4 **Mindoro** *island* N Philippines
171 N5 **Mindoro Strait** *strait* W Philippines
159 S9 **Mine** Gansu, N China
97 J23 **Minehead** SW England, UK
97 E21 **Mine Head** *Ir.* Mionn Ard. *headland* S Ireland
59 J19 **Mineiros** Goiás, C Brazil
25 V6 **Mineola** Texas, SW USA
25 S13 **Mineral** Texas, SW USA
127 N15 **Mineral'nyye Vody** Stavropol'skiy Kray, SW Russian Federation
30 K9 **Mineral Point** Wisconsin, N USA
25 S6 **Mineral Wells** Texas, SW USA
36 K6 **Minersville** Utah, W USA
31 U12 **Minerva** Ohio, N USA
107 N17 **Minervino Murge** Puglia, SE Italy
103 O16 **Minervois** *physical region* S France
158 I10 **Minfeng** *var.* Niya. Xinjiang Uygur Zizhiqu, NW China
79 O25 **Minga** Katanga, SE Dem. Rep. Congo
137 W11 **Mingäçevir** *Rus.* Mingechaur, Mingechevir. C Azerbaijan
137 W11 **Mingäçevir Su Anbarı** *Rus.* Mingechaurskoye Vodokhranilishche, Mingechevirskoye Vodokhranilishche. ⊞ NW Azerbaijan
166 L8 **Mingaladon** ✈ (Yangon) Yangon, SW Burma (Myanmar)
13 P11 **Mingan** Québec, E Canada
149 U5 **Mingāora** *var.* Mingora, Mongora. North-West Frontier Province, N Pakistan
146 K8 **Mingbuloq** *Rus.* Mynbulak. Navoiy Viloyati, N Uzbekistan
146 K9 **Mingbuloq Botig'I** *Rus.* Vpadina Mynbulak. *depression* N Uzbekistan
Mingechaur/Mingechevir *see* Mingäçevir
Mingechaurskoye Vodokhranilishche/ Mingechevirskoye Vodokhranilishche *see* Mingäçevir Su Anbarı
161 Q7 **Mingguang** *prev.* Jiashan. Anhui, SE China
166 L4 **Mingin** Sagaing, C Burma (Myanmar)
105 Q10 **Minglanilla** Castilla-La Mancha, C Spain
31 V13 **Mingo Junction** Ohio, N USA
Mingora *see* Mingāora
163 V7 **Mingshui** Heilongjiang, NE China
Mingtekl Daban *see* Mintaka Pass
83 Q14 **Minguri** Nampula, NE Mozambique
Mingzhou *see* Suide
159 U10 **Minhe** *var.* Shangchuankou. Qinghai, C China
166 L6 **Minhla** Magwe, W Burma (Myanmar)
167 S14 **Minh Lương** Kiên Giang, S Vietnam
104 G5 **Minho** *former province* N Portugal
104 G5 **Minho, Rio** *Sp.* Miño. ∽ Portugal/Spain *see also* Miño
Minho, Rio *see* Miño
155 C24 **Minicoy Island** *island* SW India
33 P15 **Minidoka** Idaho, NW USA
118 C11 **Minija** ∽ W Lithuania
180 G9 **Minilya** Western Australia
14 E8 **Minisinakwa Lake** ◎ Ontario, S Canada
45 T12 **Ministre Point** *headland* S Saint Lucia
9 V15 **Minitonas** Manitoba, S Canada
Minius *see* Miño
161 R12 **Min Jiang** ∽ SE China
160 H10 **Min Jiang** ∽ C China
182 H9 **Minlaton** South Australia
165 Q6 **Minmaya** *var.* Mimmaya. Aomori, Honshū, C Japan
77 U14 **Minna** Niger, C Nigeria
165 P16 **Minna-jima** *island* Sakishima-shotō, SW Japan
27 N4 **Minneapolis** Kansas, C USA
29 U9 **Minneapolis** Minnesota, N USA
29 V8 **Minneapolis-Saint Paul** ✈ Minnesota, N USA
11 W16 **Minnedosa** Manitoba, S Canada
26 J7 **Minneola** Kansas, C USA
29 S7 **Minnesota** *off.* State of Minnesota, *also known as* Gopher State, New England of the West, North Star State. ◐ *state* N USA
29 S9 **Minnesota River** ∽ Minnesota/South Dakota, N USA
29 V9 **Minnetonka** Minnesota, N USA
29 O3 **Minnewaukan** North Dakota, N USA
182 F7 **Minnipa** South Australia
104 H2 **Miño** Galicia, NW Spain
104 G5 **Miño** *var.* Mino, Minius, *Port.* Rio Minho. ∽ Portugal/ Spain *see also* Minho, Rio
Miño *see* Minho, Rio
30 L4 **Minocqua** Wisconsin, N USA
30 L12 **Minonk** Illinois, N USA
Minorca *see* Menorca
28 M3 **Minot** North Dakota, N USA
159 U8 **Minqin** Gansu, N China
119 J16 **Minsk** ● (Belarus) Minskaya Voblasts', C Belarus
119 L16 **Minsk** ✈ Minskaya Voblasts', C Belarus
Minskaya Oblast' *see* Minskaya Voblasts'
119 K16 **Minskaya Voblasts'** *prev. Rus.* Minskaya Oblast'. ◐ *province* C Belarus
119 J16 **Minskaya Wzvyshsha** ⛰ C Belarus
110 N12 **Mińsk Mazowiecki** *var.* Nowo-Minsk. Mazowieckie, C Poland
31 Q13 **Minster** Ohio, N USA
79 F15 **Minta** Centre, C Cameroon
149 W2 **Mintaka Pass** *Chin.* Mingtekl Daban. *pass* China/Pakistan
115 D20 **Mínthi** ⛰ S Greece
Minthun *see* Minden
13 O14 **Minto** New Brunswick, SE Canada
10 H6 **Minto** Yukon Territory, W Canada
39 R9 **Minto** Alaska, USA
29 Q3 **Minto** North Dakota, N USA
12 K6 **Minto, Lac** ◎ Québec, C Canada
195 R16 **Minto, Mount** ▲ Antarctica
9 U17 **Minton** Saskatchewan, S Canada
189 R15 **Minto Reef** *atoll* Caroline Islands, C Micronesia
37 R4 **Minturn** Colorado, C USA
107 J16 **Minturno** Lazio, C Italy
122 K13 **Minusinsk** Krasnoyarskiy Kray, S Russian Federation
108 G11 **Minusio** Ticino, S Switzerland
79 E17 **Minvoul** Woleu-Ntem, N Gabon
141 R13 **Minwakh** N Yemen
159 V11 **Minxian** *var.* Min Xian. Gansu, C China
Min Xian *see* Minxian
Minya *see* El Minya
31 R6 **Mio** Michigan, N USA
Mionn Ard *see* Mine Head
158 L5 **Miquan** Xinjiang Uygur Zizhiqu, NW China
119 I17 **Mir** Hrodzyenskaya Voblasts', W Belarus
106 H8 **Mira** Veneto, NE Italy
104 G13 **Mira, Rio** ∽ S Portugal
12 K15 **Mirabel** *var.* Montreal. ✈ (Montréal) Québec, SE Canada
60 Q8 **Miracema** Rio de Janeiro, SE Brazil
54 G9 **Miraflores** Boyacá, C Colombia
40 G10 **Miraflores** Baja California Sur, W Mexico
44 L9 **Miragoâne** S Haiti
155 E16 **Miraj** Mahārāshtra, W India
61 E23 **Miramar** Buenos Aires, E Argentina
103 R15 **Miramas** Bouches-du-Rhône, SE France
102 K12 **Mirambeau** Charente-Maritime, W France
102 L13 **Miramont-de-Guyenne** Lot-et-Garonne, SW France
115 L25 **Mirampéllou Kólpos** *gulf* Kríti, Greece, E Mediterranean Sea
158 L8 **Miran** Xinjiang Uygur Zizhiqu, NW China
54 M5 **Miranda** *off.* Estado Miranda. ◐ *state* N Venezuela
Miranda de Corvo *see* Miranda do Corvo
105 O3 **Miranda de Ebro** La Rioja, N Spain
104 G8 **Miranda do Corvo** *var.* Miranda de Corvo. Coimbra, N Portugal
104 J6 **Miranda do Douro** Bragança, N Portugal
Miranda, Estado *see* Miranda
102 L15 **Mirande** Gers, S France
104 I6 **Mirandela** Bragança, N Portugal
25 R15 **Mirando City** Texas, SW USA
106 G9 **Mirandola** Emilia-Romagna, N Italy
60 I8 **Mirandópolis** São Paulo, S Brazil
60 K8 **Mirassol** São Paulo, S Brazil
104 J3 **Miravalles** ▲ NW Spain
42 L12 **Miravalles, Volcán** 🌋 NW Costa Rica
141 W13 **Mirbāṭ** *var.* Marbat. S Oman
44 M9 **Mirebalais** C Haiti
103 T6 **Mirecourt** Vosges, NE France
103 N16 **Mirepoix** Ariège, S France
Mirgorod *see* Myrhorod
139 W10 **Mīr Ḥājī Khalīl** E Iraq
169 T8 **Miri** Sarawak, East Malaysia
77 W12 **Miria** Zinder, S Niger
182 F5 **Mirikata** South Australia
54 K4 **Mirimire** Falcón, N Venezuela
61 H18 **Mirim Lagoon** *var.* Lake Mirim, *Sp.* Laguna Merín. *lagoon* Brazil/Uruguay
Mirim, Lake *see* Mirim Lagoon
Mírina *see* Mýrina
172 H14 **Miringoni** Mohéli, S Comoros
143 W11 **Mīrjāveh** Sīstān va Balūchestān, SE Iran
195 Z9 **Mirny** *Russian research station* Antarctica
124 M10 **Mirnyy** Arkhangel'skaya Oblast', NW Russian Federation
123 O10 **Mirnyy** Respublika Sakha (Yakutiya), NE Russian Federation
Mironovka *see* Myronivka
110 F9 **Mirosławiec** Zachodnio-pomorskie, NW Poland
Mirovo *see* Vrattsa
100 N10 **Mirow** Mecklenburg-Vorpommern, N Germany
152 G6 **Mīrpur** Jammu and Kashmir, NW India
Mīrpur *see* New Mīrpur
149 P17 **Mīrpur Batoro** Sind, SE Pakistan
149 Q16 **Mīrpur Khās** Sind, SE Pakistan
149 P17 **Mīrpur Sakro** Sind, SE Pakistan
143 T14 **Mīr Shahdād** Hormozgān, S Iran
Mirtoan Sea *see* Mirtóo Pélagos
115 G21 **Mirtóo Pélagos** *Eng.* Mirtoan Sea; *anc.* Myrtoum Mare. *sea* S Greece
163 Z16 **Miryang** *var.* Milyang, *Jap.* Mitsuō. SE South Korea
Mirzachirla *see* Murzechirla
164 E14 **Misaki** Ehime, Shikoku, SW Japan
41 Q13 **Misantla** Veracruz-Llave, E Mexico
165 R7 **Misawa** Aomori, Honshū, C Japan
57 G14 **Mishagua, Río** ∽ C Peru
163 Z8 **Mishan** Heilongjiang, NE China
31 O11 **Mishawaka** Indiana, N USA
39 N6 **Misheguk Mountain** ▲ Alaska, USA
165 N14 **Mishima** *var.* Misima. Shizuoka, Honshū, S Japan
164 E12 **Mi-shima** *island* SW Japan
127 V4 **Mishkino** Respublika Bashkortostan, W Russian Federation
153 Y10 **Mishmi Hills** *hill range* NE India
161 N11 **Mi Shui** ∽ S China
Misiaf *see* Maṣyāf
107 J23 **Misilmeri** Sicilia, Italy, C Mediterranean Sea
Misima *see* Mishima
Misión de Guana *see* Guana
60 F13 **Misiones** *off.* Provincia de Misiones. ◐ *province* NE Argentina
62 P8 **Misiones** *off.* Departamento de las Misiones. ◐ *department* S Paraguay
Misiones, Departamento de las *see* Misiones
Misiones, Provincia de *see* Misiones
Misión San Fernando *see* San Fernando
Miskin *see* Maskin
Miskito Coast *see* La Mosquitia
43 O7 **Miskitos, Cayos** *island group* NE Nicaragua
111 M21 **Miskolc** Borsod-Abaúj-Zemplén, NE Hungary
171 T12 **Misool, Pulau** *island* Maluku, E Indonesia
Misox *see* Mesocco
29 Y3 **Misquah Hills** *hill range* Minnesota, N USA
75 P7 **Miṣrātah** *var.* Misurata. NW Libya
75 P7 **Miṣrātah, Râs** *headland* N Libya
14 C7 **Missanabie** Ontario, S Canada
58 E10 **Missão Catrimani** Roraima, N Brazil
14 D6 **Missinaibi** ∽ Ontario, S Canada
14 C7 **Missinaibi Lake** ◎ Ontario, S Canada
9 T13 **Missinipe** Saskatchewan, C Canada
28 M11 **Mission** South Dakota, N USA
25 S17 **Mission** Texas, SW USA
12 F10 **Missisa Lake** ◎ Ontario, C Canada
18 M6 **Missisquoi Bay** *lake bay* Canada/USA
14 C10 **Mississagi** ∽ Ontario, S Canada
14 G15 **Mississauga** Ontario, S Canada
31 P12 **Mississinewa Lake** ⊞ Indiana, N USA
31 P12 **Mississinewa River** ∽ Indiana/Ohio, N USA
22 K4 **Mississippi** *off.* State of Mississippi, *also known as* Bayou State, Magnolia State. ◐ *state* SE USA
14 K13 **Mississippi** ∽ Ontario, SE Canada
0 J11 **Mississippi River** ∽ C USA
47 N1 **Mississippi Fan** *undersea feature* N Gulf of Mexico
14 L13 **Mississippi Lake** ◎ Ontario, SE Canada
22 M10 **Mississippi Delta** *delta* Louisiana, S USA
22 M9 **Mississippi Sound** *sound* Alabama/Mississippi, S USA
33 P9 **Missoula** Montana, NW USA
27 T5 **Missouri** *off.* State of Missouri, *also known as* Bullion State, Show Me State. ◐ *state* C USA
25 V11 **Missouri City** Texas, SW USA
0 J10 **Missouri River** ∽ C USA
15 Q6 **Mistassibi** ∽ Québec, SE Canada
15 P6 **Mistassini** Québec, SE Canada
15 P6 **Mistassini** ∽ Québec, SE Canada
12 J11 **Mistassini, Lac** ◎ Québec, SE Canada
109 Y3 **Mistelbach an der Zaya** Niederösterreich, NE Austria
107 L24 **Misterbianco** Sicilia, Italy, C Mediterranean Sea
95 N19 **Misterhult** Kalmar, S Sweden
57 H17 **Misti, Volcán** 🌋 S Peru
Mistras *see* Mystrás
107 K23 **Mistretta** *anc.* Amestratus. Sicilia, Italy, C Mediterranean Sea
164 F12 **Misumi** Shimane, Honshū, SW Japan
Misurata *see* Miṣrātah
83 O14 **Mitande** Niassa, N Mozambique
40 J13 **Mita, Punta de** *headland* C Mexico
55 W12 **Mitaraka, Massif du** ▲ NE South America
Mitau *see* Jelgava
181 X9 **Mitchell** Queensland, E Australia
14 E15 **Mitchell** Ontario, S Canada
28 I13 **Mitchell** Nebraska, C USA
32 J12 **Mitchell** Oregon, NW USA
29 P11 **Mitchell** South Dakota, N USA
23 P5 **Mitchell Lake** ⊞ Alabama, S USA
31 P7 **Mitchell, Lake** ◎ Michigan, N USA
21 P9 **Mitchell, Mount** ▲ North Carolina, SE USA
181 V3 **Mitchell River** ∽ Queensland, NE Australia
97 D20 **Mitchelstown** *Ir.* Baile Mhistéala. SW Ireland
14 M9 **Mitchinamécus, Lac** ◎ Québec, SE Canada
Mitèmboni *see* Mitemele, Río
79 D17 **Mitemele, Río** *var.* Mitèmboni, Temboni, Utamboni. ∽ S Equatorial Guinea
149 S12 **Mithānkot** Punjab, E Pakistan
149 T7 **Mitha Tiwāna** Punjab, E Pakistan
149 R17 **Mithi** Sind, SE Pakistan
Míthimna *see* Míthymna
Mi Tho *see* My Tho
115 L16 **Míthymna** *var.* Míthimna. Lésvos, E Greece
190 L16 **Mitiaro** *island* S Cook Islands
Mitilíni *see* Mytilíni
15 U7 **Mitis** ∽ Québec, SE Canada
41 R16 **Mitla** Oaxaca, SE Mexico
165 P13 **Mito** Ibaraki, Honshū, S Japan
92 N2 **Mitra, Kapp** *headland* W Svalbard
184 M13 **Mitre** ▲ North Island, New Zealand
185 B21 **Mitre Peak** ▲ South Island, New Zealand
39 O15 **Mitrofania Island** *island* Alaska, USA
Mitrovica/Mitrovicë *see* Kosovska Mitrovica, Serbia
Mitrovica/Mitrowitz *see* Sremska Mitrovica, Serbia
172 H12 **Mitsamiouli** Grande Comore, NW Comoros
172 I3 **Mitsinjo** Mahajanga, NW Madagascar
Mits'iwa *see* Massawa
172 H13 **Mitsoudjé** Grande Comore, NW Comoros
Mitspe Ramon *see* Mizpé Ramon
165 T5 **Mitsuishi** Hokkaidō, NE Japan
165 O11 **Mitsuke** *var.* Mituke. Niigata, Honshū, C Japan
Mitsuō *see* Miryang
164 C12 **Mitsushima** Nagasaki, Tsushima, SW Japan
100 G12 **Mittelandkanal** *canal* NW Germany
108 J7 **Mittelberg** Vorarlberg, NW Austria
Mitteldorf *see* Międzychód
Mittelstadt *see* Baia Sprie
Mitterburg *see* Pazin
109 P7 **Mittersill** Salzburg, NW Austria
101 N16 **Mittweida** Sachsen, E Germany
54 J13 **Mitú** Vaupés, SE Colombia
Mituke *see* Mitsuke
Mitumba, Chaîne des/Mitumba Range *see* Mitumba, Monts
79 O22 **Mitumba, Monts** *var.* Chaîne des Mitumba, Mitumba Range. ⛰ E Dem. Rep. Congo
79 N23 **Mitwaba** Katanga, SE Dem. Rep. Congo
79 E18 **Mitzic** Woleu-Ntem, N Gabon
82 K11 **Miueru Wantipa, Lake** ◎ N Zambia
165 N14 **Miura** Kanagawa, Honshū, S Japan
165 Q10 **Miyagi** *off.* Miyagi-ken. ◐ *prefecture* Honshū, C Japan
Miyagi-ken *see* Miyagi
138 M7 **Miyāh, Wādī al** *dry watercourse* E Syria
165 X13 **Miyake** Tōkyō, Miyako-jima, SE Japan
165 R8 **Miyako** Iwate, Honshū, C Japan
165 Q16 **Miyako-jima** *island* Sakishima-shotō, SW Japan
164 D16 **Miyakonojō** *var.* Miyakonzyô. Miyazaki, Kyūshū, SW Japan
Miyakonzyô *see* Miyakonojō
165 Q16 **Miyako-shotō** *island group* SW Japan
144 G11 **Miyaly** Atyrau, W Kazakhstan
Miyāndoāb *see* Mīāndowāb
Miyāneh *see* Mīāneh
Miyang *see* Mile
164 D16 **Miyazaki** Miyazaki, Kyūshū, SW Japan
164 D16 **Miyazaki** *off.* Miyazaki-ken. ◐ *prefecture* Kyūshū, SW Japan
Miyazaki-ken *see* Miyazaki
164 J12 **Miyazu** Kyōto, Honshū, SW Japan
Miyory *see* Myory
164 G12 **Miyoshi** *var.* Miyosi. Hiroshima, Honshū, SW Japan
Miyosi *see* Miyoshi
Miza *see* Mizë
81 H14 **Mīzan Teferī** Southern, S Ethiopia
Mizda *see* Mizdah
75 O8 **Mizdah** *var.* Mizda. NW Libya
113 K20 **Mizë** *var.* Miza. Fier, W Albania
97 A22 **Mizen Head** *Ir.* Carn Uí Néid. *headland* SW Ireland
116 H7 **Mizhhir"ya** *Rus.* Mezhgor'ye. Zakarpats'ka Oblast', W Ukraine
160 L4 **Mizhi** Shaanxi, C China
116 K13 **Mizil** Prahova, SE Romania
114 H7 **Miziya** Vratsa, NW Bulgaria
153 W15 **Mizo Hills** *hill range* E India
153 W15 **Mizoram** ◐ *state* NE India
138 F12 **Mizpé Ramon** *var.* Mitspe Ramon. Southern, S Israel
57 L19 **Mizque** Cochabamba, C Bolivia
57 M19 **Mizque, Río** ∽ C Bolivia
165 Q9 **Mizusawa** Iwate, Honshū, C Japan
95 M18 **Mjölby** Östergötland, S Sweden
95 G15 **Mjøndalen** Buskerud, S Norway
95 J19 **Mjörn** ◎ S Sweden
94 I13 **Mjøsa** *var.* Mjøsen. ◎ S Norway
Mjøsen *see* Mjøsa
81 G21 **Mkalama** Singida, C Tanzania
80 K13 **Mkata** ∽ C Tanzania
83 K14 **Mkushi** Central, C Zambia
83 L22 **Mkuze** KwaZulu/Natal, E South Africa
81 J22 **Mkwaja** Tanga, E Tanzania
111 D16 **Mladá Boleslav** *Ger.* Jungbunzlau. Středočeský Kraj, N Czech Republic
112 M12 **Mladenovac** Serbia, C Serbia
114 L11 **Mladinovo** Khaskovo, S Bulgaria
113 O17 **Mlado Nagoričane** N FYR Macedonia
Mlanje *see* Mulanje
112 N12 **Mlava** ∽ E Serbia
110 L9 **Mława** Mazowieckie, C Poland
113 G16 **Mljet** *It.* Meleda; *anc.* Melita. *island* S Croatia
116 K4 **Mlyniv** Rivnens'ka Oblast', NW Ukraine
83 I21 **Mmabatho** North-West, N South Africa
83 I19 **Mmashoro** Central, E Botswana
44 J7 **Moa** Holguín, E Cuba
76 J15 **Moa** ∽ Guinea/Sierra Leone
37 O6 **Moab** Utah, W USA
181 V1 **Moa Island** *island* Queensland, NE Australia
187 Y15 **Moala** *island* S Fiji
83 L21 **Moamba** Maputo, SW Mozambique
79 F19 **Moanda** *var.* Mouanda. Haut-Ogooué, SE Gabon
83 M15 **Moatize** Tete, NW Mozambique
79 P22 **Moba** Katanga, E Dem. Rep. Congo
Mobay *see* Montego Bay
79 K15 **Mobaye** Basse-Kotto, S Central African Republic
79 K15 **Mobayi-Mbongo** Equateur, NW Dem. Rep. Congo
25 P2 **Mobeetie** Texas, SW USA
27 U3 **Moberly** Missouri, C USA
23 N8 **Mobile** Alabama, S USA
23 N9 **Mobile Bay** *bay* Alabama, S USA
23 N8 **Mobile River** ∽ Alabama, S USA
29 N8 **Mobridge** South Dakota, N USA
Mobutu Sese Seko, Lac *see* Albert, Lake
45 N8 **Moca** N Dominican Republic
83 Q15 **Moçambique** Nampula, NE Mozambique Africa
Moçâmedes *see* Namibe
167 S6 **Môc Châu** Sơn La, N Vietnam
187 Z15 **Moce** *island* Lau Group, E Fiji
Mocha *see* Al Mukhā
193 T11 **Mocha Fracture Zone** *tectonic feature* SE Pacific Ocean
63 F14 **Mocha, Isla** *island* C Chile
56 C12 **Moche, Río** ∽ W Peru
167 S14 **Môc Hoa** Long An, S Vietnam
83 I20 **Mochudi** Kgatleng, SE Botswana
82 Q13 **Mocímboa da Praia** *var.* Vila de Mocímboa da Praia. Cabo Delgado, N Mozambique
94 L13 **Mockfjärd** Dalarna, C Sweden
21 R9 **Mocksville** North Carolina, SE USA
32 F8 **Moclips** Washington, NW USA
82 C13 **Môco** *var.* Morro de Môco. ▲ W Angola
54 D13 **Mocoa** Putumayo, SW Colombia
60 M8 **Mococa** São Paulo, S Brazil
Môco, Morro de *see* Môco
40 H8 **Mocorito** Sinaloa, C Mexico
40 J4 **Moctezuma** Chihuahua, N Mexico
41 N11 **Moctezuma** San Luis Potosí, C Mexico
40 G4 **Moctezuma** Sonora, NW Mexico
41 P12 **Moctezuma, Río** ∽ C Mexico
Mó, Cuan *see* Clew Bay
83 O16 **Mocuba** Zambézia, NE Mozambique
103 U12 **Modane** Savoie, E France
106 F9 **Modena** *anc.* Mutina. Emilia-Romagna, N Italy
36 I7 **Modena** Utah, W USA
35 O9 **Modesto** California, W USA
107 L25 **Modica** *anc.* Motyca. Sicilia, Italy, C Mediterranean Sea
83 J20 **Modimolle** *prev.* Nylstroom. Limpopo, NE South Africa
79 K17 **Modjamboli** Equateur, N Dem. Rep. Congo
109 X4 **Mödling** Niederösterreich, NE Austria
Modohn *see* Madona
Modot *see* Tsenhermandal
171 V14 **Modowi** Papua, E Indonesia
112 I12 **Modračko Jezero** ⊞ NE Bosnia and Herzegovina
112 I10 **Modriča** Republika Srpska, N Bosnia and Herzegovina
183 O13 **Moe** Victoria, SE Australia
Moearatewe *see* Muaratewe
Moei, Mae Nam *see* Thaungyin
94 H13 **Moelv** Hedmark, S Norway
92 I10 **Moen** Troms, N Norway
Möen *see* Møn, Denmark
Moen *see* Weno, Micronesia
Moena *see* Muna, Pulau
36 M10 **Moenkopi Wash** ∽ Arizona, SW USA
185 F22 **Moeraki Point** *headland* South Island, New Zealand
99 F16 **Moerbeke** Oost-Vlaanderen, NW Belgium
99 H14 **Moerdijk** Noord-Brabant, S Netherlands
Moero, Lac *see* Mweru, Lake
101 D15 **Moers** *var.* Mörs. Nordrhein-Westfalen, W Germany
Moesi *see* Musi, Air
Moeskroen *see* Mouscron
96 J13 **Moffat** S Scotland, UK
185 C22 **Moffat Peak** ▲ South Island, New Zealand
79 N19 **Moga** Sud Kivu, E Dem. Rep. Congo
152 H8 **Moga** Punjab, N India
Mogadiscio/Mogadishu *see* Muqdisho
Mogador *see* Essaouira
104 J6 **Mogadouro** Bragança, N Portugal
167 N2 **Mogaung** Kachin State, N Burma (Myanmar)
110 L13 **Mogielnica** Mazowieckie, C Poland
Mogilëv *see* Mahilyow
Mogilev-Podol'skiy *see* Mohyliv-Podil's'kyy
Mogilëvskaya Oblast' *see* Mahilyowskaya Voblasts'
110 I11 **Mogilno** Kujawsko-pomorskie, C Poland
60 L9 **Mogi-Mirim** *var.* Moji-Mirim. São Paulo, S Brazil
83 Q15 **Mogincual** Nampula, NE Mozambique
114 E13 **Moglenítsas** ∽ N Greece
106 H8 **Mogliano Veneto** Veneto, NE Italy
113 M21 **Moglicë** Korçë, SE Albania
123 O13 **Mogocha** Chitinskaya Oblast', S Russian Federation
122 J11 **Mogochin** Tomskaya Oblast', C Russian Federation
80 F13 **Mogogh** Jonglei, SE Sudan
171 U12 **Mogoi** Papua, E Indonesia
166 M4 **Mogok** Mandalay, C Burma (Myanmar)
37 P14 **Mogollon Mountains** ⛰ New Mexico, SW USA
36 M12 **Mogollon Rim** *cliff* Arizona, SW USA
61 E23 **Mogotes, Punta** *headland* E Argentina
42 J8 **Mogotón** ▲ NW Nicaragua
104 I14 **Moguer** Andalucía, S Spain
111 J26 **Mohács** Baranya, SW Hungary
185 C20 **Mohaka** ∽ North Island, New Zealand
28 M2 **Mohall** North Dakota, N USA
Moḥammadābād *see* Dargaz
74 F6 **Mohammedia** *prev.* Fédala. NW Morocco
74 F6 **Mohammed V** ✈ (Casablanca) W Morocco
Mohammerah *see* Khorramshahr
36 H10 **Mohave, Lake** ⊞ Arizona/ Nevada, W USA
36 I12 **Mohave Mountains** ⛰ Arizona, SW USA
36 I15 **Mohawk Mountains** ⛰ Arizona, SW USA
18 J10 **Mohawk River** ∽ New York, NE USA
163 T3 **Mohe** *var.* Xilinji. Heilongjiang, NE China
95 L20 **Moheda** Kronoberg, S Sweden
172 H13 **Mohéli** *var.* Mwali, Mohilla, Mohila, *Fr.* Moili. *island* S Comoros
152 I11 **Mahendragarh** Haryāna, N India
38 K12 **Mohican, Cape** *headland* Nunivak Island, Alaska, USA
Mohila *see* Mohéli
Mohilla *see* Mohéli
Mohn *see* Muhu
101 G15 **Möhne** ∽ W Germany
101 G15 **Möhne-Stausee** ⊞ W Germany
92 P2 **Mohn, Kapp** *headland* NW Svalbard
197 S14 **Mohns Ridge** *undersea feature* Greenland Sea/ Norwegian Sea
57 I17 **Moho** Puno, SE Peru
Mohokare *see* Caledon
95 L17 **Moholm** Västra Götaland, S Sweden
36 J11 **Mohon Peak** ▲ Arizona, SW USA
81 J23 **Mohoro** Pwani, E Tanzania
Mohra *see* Moravice
Mohrungen *see* Morąg
116 M7 **Mohyliv-Podil's'kyy** *Rus.* Mogilev-Podol'skiy. Vinnyts'ka Oblast', C Ukraine
95 D17 **Moi** Rogaland, S Norway
Moili *see* Mohéli
116 K11 **Moinești** *Hung.* Mojnest. Bacău, E Romania
Móinteach Mílic *see* Mountmellick
14 J14 **Moira** ∽ Ontario, SE Canada
92 G13 **Mo i Rana** Nordland, C Norway
153 X14 **Moirāng** Manipur, NE India
115 J25 **Moíres** Kríti, Greece, E Mediterranean Sea

◆ Country
● Country Capital
◇ Dependent Territory
○ Dependent Territory Capital
◐ Administrative Regions
✈ International Airport
▲ Mountain
⛰ Mountain Range
🌋 Volcano
∽ River
◎ Lake
⊞ Reservoir

Mõisaküla – Moosonee

118 H6 **Mõisaküla** Ger. Moiseküll. Viljandimaa, S Estonia
Moiseküll see Mõisaküla
15 W4 **Moisie** Québec, E Canada
15 W3 **Moisie** ∽ Québec, SE Canada
102 M14 **Moissac** Tarn-et-Garonne, S France
78 I13 **Moïssala** Moyen-Chari, S Chad
55 O7 **Moitaco** Bolívar, E Venezuela
95 P15 **Möja** Stockholm, C Sweden
105 Q14 **Mojácar** Andalucía, S Spain
35 T13 **Mojave** California, W USA
35 V13 **Mojave Desert** plain California, W USA
35 V13 **Mojave River** ∽ California, W USA
Moji-Mirim see Mogi-Mirim
113 K15 **Mojkovac** E Montenegro
Mojnest see Moinești
Mōka see Mooka
153 Q13 **Mokāma** prev. Mokameh, Mukama. Bihār, N India
79 O25 **Mokambo** Katanga, SE Dem. Rep. Congo
Mokameh see Mokāma
38 D9 **Mōkapu Point** var Mokapu Point. headland O'ahu, Hawai'i, USA
184 L9 **Mokau** Waikato, North Island, New Zealand
184 L9 **Mokau** ∽ North Island, New Zealand
35 P7 **Mokelumne River** ∽ California, W USA
83 J23 **Mokhotlong** NE Lesotho
Mokil Atoll see Mwokil Atoll
95 N14 **Möklinta** Västmanland, C Sweden
184 L4 **Mokohinau Islands** island group N New Zealand
153 X12 **Mokokchūng** Nāgāland, NE India
78 F12 **Mokolo** Extrême-Nord, N Cameroon
83 J20 **Mokopane** prev. Potgietersrus. Limpopo, NE South Africa
185 D24 **Mokoreta** ∽ South Island, New Zealand
163 X17 **Mokp'o** Jap. Moppo. SW South Korea
113 L16 **Mokra Gora** ▲▲ S Serbia
Mokrany see Makrany
127 O5 **Moksha** ∽ W Russian Federation
Moktama see Martaban
77 T14 **Mokwa** Niger, W Nigeria
99 J16 **Mol** prev. Moll. Antwerpen, N Belgium
107 O17 **Mola di Bari** Puglia, SE Italy
Molai see Moláoi
41 P13 **Molango** Hidalgo, C Mexico
115 F22 **Moláoi** var. Molai. Pelopónnisos, S Greece
41 Z12 **Molas del Norte, Punta** var. Punta Molas. headland SE Mexico
Molas, Punta see Molas del Norte, Punta
105 R11 **Molatón** ▲ C Spain
97 K18 **Mold** NE Wales, UK
Moldau see Vltava, Czech Republic
Moldau see Moldova
Moldavia see Moldova
Moldavian SSR/ Moldavskaya SSR see Moldova
94 E9 **Molde** Møre og Romsdal, S Norway
Moldotau, Khrebet see Moldo-Too, Khrebet
147 V9 **Moldo-Too, Khrebet** prev. Khrebet Moldotau. ▲▲ C Kyrgyzstan
116 L9 **Moldova** off. Republic of Moldova, var. Moldavia; prev. Moldavian SSR, Rus. Moldavskaya SSR. ◆ republic SE Europe
116 K9 **Moldova** Eng. Moldavia, Ger. Moldau. former province NE Romania
116 K9 **Moldova** ∽ N Romania
116 F13 **Moldova Nouă** Ger. Neumoldowa, Hung. Újmoldova. Caraș-Severin, SW Romania
Moldova, Republic of see Moldova
116 F13 **Moldova Veche** Ger. Altmoldowa, Hung. Ómoldova. Caraș-Severin, SW Romania
Moldoveanul see Vârful Moldoveanu
83 I20 **Molepolole** Kweneng, SE Botswana
44 L8 **Môle-St-Nicolas** NW Haiti
118 H13 **Molėtai** Utena, E Lithuania
107 O17 **Molfetta** Puglia, SE Italy
171 P11 **Molibagu** Sulawesi, N Indonesia
62 G12 **Molina** Maule, C Chile
105 Q7 **Molina de Aragón** Castilla-La Mancha, C Spain
105 R13 **Molina de Segura** Murcia, SE Spain
30 J11 **Moline** Illinois, N USA
27 P7 **Moline** Kansas, C USA
79 P23 **Moliro** Katanga, SE Dem. Rep. Congo
107 K16 **Molise** ⬖ region S Italy
95 K15 **Molkom** Värmland, C Sweden
109 Q9 **Möll** ∽ S Austria
Moll see Mol
146 I14 **Mollanepes Adyndaky** Rus. Imeni Mollanepesa. Mary Welaýaty, S Turkmenistan
95 J22 **Mölle** Skåne, S Sweden
57 H18 **Mollendo** Arequipa, SW Peru
105 U5 **Mollerussa** Cataluña, NE Spain
108 H8 **Mollis** Glarus, NE Switzerland
95 J19 **Mölndal** Västra Götaland, S Sweden
95 J19 **Mölnlycke** Västra Götaland, S Sweden
117 U9 **Molochans'k** Rus. Molochansk. Zaporiz'ka Oblast', SE Ukraine
117 U10 **Molochna** Rus. Molochnaya. ∽ S Ukraine
Molochnaya see Molochna
117 U10 **Molochnyy Lyman** bay N Black Sea
Molodechno/Molodeczno see Maladzyechna
195 V3 **Molodezhnaya** Russian research station Antarctica
124 J14 **Mologa** ∽ NW Russian Federation
38 E9 **Moloka'i** var. Molokai. island Hawaiian Islands, Hawai'i, USA
175 X3 **Molokai Fracture Zone** tectonic feature NE Pacific Ocean
124 K15 **Molokovo** Tverskaya Oblast', W Russian Federation
125 Q14 **Moloma** ∽ NW Russian Federation
183 R8 **Molong** New South Wales, SE Australia
83 H21 **Molopo** seasonal river Botswana/South Africa
115 F17 **Mólos** Stereá Ellás, C Greece
171 O11 **Molosipat** Sulawesi, N Indonesia
Molotov see Severodvinsk, Arkhangel'skaya Oblast', Russian Federation
Molotov see Perm', Permskaya Oblast', Russian Federation
79 G17 **Moloundou** Est, SE Cameroon
103 U5 **Molsheim** Bas-Rhin, NE France
11 X13 **Molson Lake** ◎ Manitoba, C Canada
Moluccas see Maluku
171 Q12 **Molucca Sea** Ind. Laut Maluku. sea E Indonesia
Molukken see Maluku
83 O15 **Molumbo** Zambézia, N Mozambique
171 T15 **Molu, Pulau** island Maluku, E Indonesia
83 P16 **Moma** Nampula, NE Mozambique
171 X14 **Momats** ∽ Papua, E Indonesia
42 J11 **Mombacho, Volcán** ⛰ SW Nicaragua
81 K21 **Mombasa** Coast, SE Kenya
81 J21 **Mombasa** ✈ Coast, SE Kenya
Mombetsu see Monbetsu
114 J12 **Momchilgrad** prev. Mastanli. Kŭrdzhali, S Bulgaria
99 F23 **Momignies** Hainaut, S Belgium
54 E6 **Momil** Córdoba, NW Colombia
42 I10 **Momotombo, Volcán** ⛰ W Nicaragua
56 B5 **Mompiche, Ensenada de** bay NW Ecuador
79 K18 **Mompono** Equateur, NW Dem. Rep. Congo
54 F6 **Mompós** Bolívar, NW Colombia
95 J24 **Møn** prev. Möen. island SE Denmark
36 L4 **Mona** Utah, W USA
Mona, Canal de la see Mona Passage
96 E8 **Monach Islands** island group NW Scotland, UK
103 V14 **Monaco** var. Monaco-Ville; anc. Monoecus. ● (Monaco) S Monaco
103 V14 **Monaco** off. Principality of Monaco. ◆ monarchy W Europe
Monaco see München
Monaco Basin see Canary Basin
Monaco, Principality of see Monaco
Monaco-Ville see Monaco
96 I9 **Monadhliath Mountains** ▲▲ N Scotland, UK
55 O6 **Monagas** off. Estado Monagas. ⬖ state NE Venezuela
Monagas, Estado see Monagas
97 F16 **Monaghan** Ir. Muineachán. Monaghan, N Ireland
97 E16 **Monaghan** Ir. Muineachán. ⬖ county N Ireland
43 S16 **Monagrillo** Herrera, S Panama
24 L8 **Monahans** Texas, SW USA
45 Q9 **Mona, Isla** island W Puerto Rico
45 Q9 **Mona Passage** Sp. Canal de la Mona. channel Dominican Republic/Puerto Rico
43 O14 **Mona, Punta** headland E Costa Rica
155 K25 **Monaragala** Uva Province, SE Sri Lanka
33 S9 **Monarch** Montana, NW USA
10 H14 **Monarch Mountain** ▲ British Columbia, SW Canada
Monasterio see Monesterio
Monasterzyska see Monastyrys'ka
Monastir see Bitola
Monastyriska see Monastyrys'ka
117 O7 **Monastyryshche** Cherkas'ka Oblast', C Ukraine
116 J6 **Monastyrys'ka** Pol. Monasterzyska, Rus. Monastyriska. Ternopil's'ka Oblast', W Ukraine
79 E15 **Monatélé** Centre, SW Cameroon
165 U2 **Monbetsu** var. Mombetsu, Monbetu. Hokkaidō, NE Japan
Monbetu see Monbetsu
106 B8 **Moncalieri** Piemonte, NW Italy
104 G4 **Monção** Viana do Castelo, N Portugal
105 Q5 **Moncayo** ▲ N Spain
105 Q5 **Moncayo, Sierra del** ▲▲ N Spain
124 J4 **Monchegorsk** Murmanskaya Oblast', NW Russian Federation
101 D15 **Mönchengladbach** prev. München-Gladbach. Nordrhein-Westfalen, W Germany
104 F14 **Monchique** Faro, S Portugal
104 G14 **Monchique, Serra de** ▲▲ S Portugal
21 S14 **Moncks Corner** South Carolina, SE USA
41 N7 **Monclova** Coahuila de Zaragoza, NE Mexico
Moncorvo see Torre de Moncorvo
13 P14 **Moncton** New Brunswick, SE Canada
104 F8 **Mondego, Cabo** cape N Portugal
104 G8 **Mondego, Rio** ∽ N Portugal
104 I2 **Mondoñedo** Galicia, NW Spain
99 N25 **Mondorf-les-Bains** Grevenmacher, SE Luxembourg
102 M7 **Mondoubleau** Loir-et-Cher, C France
30 J6 **Mondovi** Wisconsin, N USA
106 B9 **Mondovì** Piemonte, NW Italy
Mondragón see Arrasate
107 J17 **Mondragone** Campania, S Italy
109 R5 **Mondsee** ◎ N Austria
115 G22 **Monemvasiá** var. Monemvasia. Pelopónnisos, S Greece
18 B15 **Monessen** Pennsylvania, NE USA
104 J12 **Monesterio** var. Monasterio. Extremadura, W Spain
14 L8 **Monet** Québec, SE Canada
27 S8 **Monett** Missouri, C USA
27 X9 **Monette** Arkansas, C USA
14 G11 **Monetville** Ontario, S Canada
106 J7 **Monfalcone** Friuli-Venezia Giulia, NE Italy
104 H10 **Monforte** Portalegre, C Portugal
104 I4 **Monforte de Lemos** Galicia, NW Spain
79 L16 **Monga** Orientale, N Dem. Rep. Congo
81 I24 **Monga** Lindi, SE Tanzania
81 F15 **Mongalla** Bahr el Gabel, S Sudan
153 U11 **Mongar** E Bhutan
167 U6 **Mong Cai** var. Hai Ninh. Quang Ninh, N Vietnam
180 I11 **Mongers Lake** salt lake Western Australia
186 K8 **Mongga** Kolombangara, NW Solomon Islands
167 O6 **Möng Hpayak** Shan State, E Burma (Myanmar)
Monghyr see Munger
106 B10 **Mongioie, Monte** ▲ NW Italy
Mongla see Mungla
188 C15 **Mongmong** C Guam
167 N6 **Möng Nai** Shan State, E Burma (Myanmar)
78 I11 **Mongo** Guéra, C Chad
76 I14 **Mongo** ∽ N Sierra Leone
163 I8 **Mongolia** Mong. Mongol Uls. ◆ republic E Asia
129 V8 **Mongolia, Plateau of** plateau E Mongolia
Mongolküre see Zhaosu
Mongol Uls see Mongolia
79 E17 **Mongomo** E Equatorial Guinea
162 M7 **Möngönmorĭt** var. Bulag. Töv, C Mongolia
77 Y12 **Mongonu** var. Monguno. Borno, NE Nigeria
Mongora see Mingāora
78 K11 **Mongororo** Ouaddaï, SE Chad
Mongos, Chaîne des see Bongo, Massif des
79 I16 **Mongoumba** Lobaye, SW Central African Republic
Mongrove, Punta see Cayacal, Punta
83 G15 **Mongu** Western, W Zambia
76 I10 **Mônguel** Gorgol, SW Mauritania
Monguno see Mongonu
167 N4 **Möng Yai** Shan State, E Burma (Myanmar)
167 O5 **Möng Yang** Shan State, E Burma (Myanmar)
167 N3 **Möng Yu** Shan State, E Burma (Myanmar)
Mönhbulag see Yösöndzüyl
163 O8 **Mönhhaan** var. Bayasgalant. Sühbaatar, E Mongolia
162 E7 **Mönhhayrhan** var. Tsenher. Hovd, W Mongolia
Mönh Sarĭdag see Munku-Sardyk, Gora
186 P9 **Moni** ∽ S Papau New Guinea
115 I15 **Moní Megístis Lávras** monastery Kentrikí Makedonía, N Greece
115 F18 **Moní Osíou Loúkas** monastery Stereá Ellás, C Greece
54 F9 **Moniquirá** Boyacá, C Colombia
103 Q12 **Monistrol-sur-Loire** Haute-Loire, C France
35 V7 **Monitor Range** ▲▲ Nevada, W USA
115 I14 **Moní Vatopedíou** monastery Kentrikí Makedonía, N Greece
Monkchester see Newcastle upon Tyne
83 N14 **Monkey Bay** Southern, SE Malawi
43 N11 **Monkey Point** var. Punta Mico, Punte Mono, Punto Mico. headland SE Nicaragua
Monkey River see Monkey River Town
42 G3 **Monkey River Town** var. Monkey River. Toledo, SE Belize
14 M13 **Monkland** Ontario, SE Canada
79 J19 **Monkoto** Equateur, NW Dem. Rep. Congo
97 K21 **Monmouth** Wel. Trefynwy. SE Wales, UK
30 J12 **Monmouth** Illinois, N USA
32 F12 **Monmouth** Oregon, NW USA
97 K21 **Monmouth** cultural region SE Wales, UK
98 I10 **Monnickendam** Noord-Holland, C Netherlands
77 R15 **Mono** ∽ C Togo
Monoecus see Monaco
35 R8 **Mono Lake** ◎ California, W USA
115 O23 **Monólithos** Ródos, Dodekánisa, Greece, Aegean Sea
19 Q12 **Monomoy Island** island Massachusetts, NE USA
31 O12 **Monon** Indiana, N USA
29 Y12 **Monona** Iowa, C USA
30 L9 **Monona** Wisconsin, N USA
18 B15 **Monongahela** Pennsylvania, NE USA
18 B16 **Monongahela River** ∽ NE USA
107 P17 **Monopoli** Puglia, SE Italy
Mono, Punte see Monkey Point
111 K23 **Monor** Pest, C Hungary
Monostor see Beli Manastir
78 K8 **Monou** Borkou-Ennedi-Tibesti, NE Chad
105 S12 **Monovar** Cat. Monover. País Valenciano, E Spain
Monover see Monovar
105 R7 **Monreal del Campo** Aragón, NE Spain
107 I23 **Monreale** Sicilia, Italy, C Mediterranean Sea
23 T3 **Monroe** Georgia, SE USA
29 W14 **Monroe** Iowa, C USA
22 I5 **Monroe** Louisiana, S USA
31 S10 **Monroe** Michigan, N USA
18 K13 **Monroe** New York, NE USA
21 S11 **Monroe** North Carolina, SE USA
36 L6 **Monroe** Utah, W USA
32 H7 **Monroe** Washington, NW USA
30 L9 **Monroe** Wisconsin, N USA
27 V3 **Monroe City** Missouri, C USA
31 O15 **Monroe Lake** ⊠ Indiana, N USA
23 O7 **Monroeville** Alabama, S USA
18 C15 **Monroeville** Pennsylvania, NE USA
76 J16 **Monrovia** ● (Liberia) W Liberia
76 J16 **Monrovia** ✈ W Liberia
105 T7 **Monroyo** Aragón, NE Spain
99 F20 **Mons** Dut. Bergen. Hainaut, S Belgium
104 I8 **Monsanto** Castelo Branco, C Portugal
106 H8 **Monselice** Veneto, NE Italy
166 M9 **Mon State** ⬖ state S Burma (Myanmar)
98 G12 **Monster** Zuid-Holland, W Netherlands
95 N20 **Mönsterås** Kalmar, S Sweden
101 F17 **Montabaur** Rheinland-Pfalz, W Germany
106 G8 **Montagnana** Veneto, NE Italy
35 N1 **Montague** California, W USA
25 S5 **Montague** Texas, SW USA
183 S11 **Montague Island** island New South Wales, SE Australia
39 S12 **Montague Island** island Alaska, USA
39 S13 **Montague Strait** strait N Gulf of Alaska
102 J8 **Montaigu** Vendée, NW France
Montaigu see Scherpenheuvel
105 S7 **Montalbán** Aragón, NE Spain
106 G13 **Montalcino** Toscana, C Italy
104 H5 **Montalegre** Vila Real, N Portugal
114 G8 **Montana** prev. Ferdinand, Mikhaylovgrad. Montana, NW Bulgaria
108 D10 **Montana** Valais, SW Switzerland
39 R11 **Montana** Alaska, USA
114 G8 **Montana** ⬖ province NW Bulgaria
33 T9 **Montana** off. State of Montana, also known as Mountain State, Treasure State. ⬖ state NW USA
104 J10 **Montánchez** Extremadura, W Spain
Montañita see La Montañita
15 Q8 **Mont-Apica** Québec, SE Canada
104 G10 **Montargil** Portalegre, C Portugal
104 G10 **Montargil, Barragem de** ⊠ C Portugal
103 O7 **Montargis** Loiret, C France
103 O4 **Montataire** Oise, N France
102 M14 **Montauban** Tarn-et-Garonne, S France
19 N14 **Montauk** Long Island, New York, NE USA
19 N14 **Montauk Point** headland Long Island, New York, NE USA
103 Q7 **Montbard** Côte d'Or, C France
103 U7 **Montbéliard** Doubs, E France
25 W11 **Mont Belvieu** Texas, SW USA
105 U6 **Montblanc** var. Montblanch. Cataluña, NE Spain
Montblanch see Montblanc
103 Q11 **Montbrison** Loire, E France
Montcalm, Lake see Dogai Coring
103 Q9 **Montceau-les-Mines** Saône-et-Loire, C France
103 U12 **Mont Cenis, Col du** pass E France
102 K15 **Mont-de-Marsan** Landes, SW France
103 O3 **Montdidier** Somme, N France
187 Q17 **Mont-Dore** Province Sud, S New Caledonia
20 K10 **Monteagle** Tennessee, S USA
57 M20 **Monteagudo** Chuquisaca, S Bolivia
41 R16 **Monte Albán** ruins Oaxaca, S Mexico
105 R11 **Montealegre del Castillo** Castilla-La Mancha, C Spain
59 N18 **Monte Azul** Minas Gerais, SE Brazil
14 M12 **Montebello** Québec, SE Canada
106 H7 **Montebelluna** Veneto, NE Italy
60 G13 **Montecarlo** Misiones, NE Argentina
61 D16 **Monte Caseros** Corrientes, NE Argentina
60 J13 **Monte Castelo** Santa Catarina, S Brazil
106 F11 **Montecatini Terme** Toscana, C Italy
42 H7 **Montecillos, Cordillera de** ▲▲ W Honduras
62 I12 **Monte Comén** Mendoza, W Argentina
44 M8 **Monte Cristi** var. San Fernando de Monte Cristi. NW Dominican Republic
58 C13 **Monte Cristo** Amazonas, W Brazil
107 E14 **Montecristo, Isola di** island Archipelago Toscano, C Italy
Monte Croce Carnico, Passo di see Plöcken Pass
58 J12 **Monte Dourado** Pará, NE Brazil
40 L11 **Monte Escobedo** Zacatecas, C Mexico
106 I13 **Montefalco** Umbria, C Italy
107 H14 **Montefiascone** Lazio, C Italy
105 N14 **Montefrío** Andalucía, S Spain
44 I11 **Montego Bay** var. Mobay. W Jamaica
Montego Bay see Sangster
104 J8 **Montehermoso** Extremadura, W Spain
104 F10 **Montejunto, Serra de** ▲ C Portugal
Monteleone di Calabria see Vibo Valentia
54 E7 **Montelíbano** Córdoba, NW Colombia
103 R13 **Montélimar** anc. Acunum Acusio, Montilium Adhemari. Drôme, E France
104 K15 **Montellano** Andalucía, S Spain
35 Y2 **Montello** Nevada, W USA
30 L8 **Montello** Wisconsin, N USA
63 J18 **Montemayor, Meseta de** plain SE Argentina
41 O9 **Montemorelos** Nuevo León, NE Mexico
104 G11 **Montemor-o-Novo** Évora, S Portugal
104 G8 **Montemor-o-Velho** var. Montemor-o-Vélho. Coimbra, N Portugal
Montemor-o-Vélho see Montemor-o-Velho
104 H7 **Montemuro, Serra de** ▲ N Portugal
102 K12 **Montendre** Charente-Maritime, W France
61 I15 **Montenegro** Rio Grande do Sul, S Brazil
113 J16 **Montenegro** Serb. Crna Gora. ◆ SW Europe
62 G10 **Monte Patria** Coquimbo, N Chile
45 O9 **Monte Plata** E Dominican Republic
83 P14 **Montepuez** Cabo Delgado, N Mozambique
83 P14 **Montepuez** ∽ N Mozambique
106 G13 **Montepulciano** Toscana, C Italy
62 L6 **Monte Quemado** Santiago del Estero, N Argentina
103 O6 **Montereau-Faut-Yonne** anc. Condate. Seine-St-Denis, N France
35 N11 **Monterey** California, W USA
20 L9 **Monterey** Tennessee, S USA
21 T5 **Monterey** Virginia, NE USA
Monterey see Monterrey
35 N10 **Monterey Bay** bay California, W USA
54 D6 **Montería** Córdoba, NW Colombia
57 N18 **Montero** Santa Cruz, C Bolivia
62 J7 **Monteros** Tucumán, C Argentina
104 I5 **Monterrei** Galicia, NW Spain
41 O8 **Monterrey** var. Monterey. Nuevo León, NE Mexico
32 F9 **Montesano** Washington, NW USA
107 M19 **Montesano sulla Marcellana** Campania, S Italy
107 N16 **Monte Sant' Angelo** Puglia, SE Italy
59 O16 **Monte Santo** Bahia, E Brazil
107 D18 **Monte Santu, Capo di** headland Sardegna, Italy, C Mediterranean Sea
59 M19 **Montes Claros** Minas Gerais, SE Brazil
107 K14 **Montesilvano Marina** Abruzzo, C Italy
23 P4 **Montevallo** Alabama, S USA
106 G12 **Montevarchi** Toscana, C Italy
61 F20 **Montevideo** ● (Uruguay) Montevideo, S Uruguay
29 S9 **Montevideo** Minnesota, N USA
37 S7 **Monte Vista** Colorado, C USA
23 T5 **Montezuma** Georgia, SE USA
29 W14 **Montezuma** Iowa, C USA
26 J6 **Montezuma** Kansas, C USA
103 U12 **Montgenèvre, Col de** pass France/Italy
97 K20 **Montgomery** E Wales, UK
23 Q5 **Montgomery** state capital Alabama, S USA
29 V9 **Montgomery** Minnesota, N USA
18 G13 **Montgomery** Pennsylvania, NE USA
21 Q5 **Montgomery** West Virginia, NE USA
97 K19 **Montgomery** cultural region E Wales, UK
Montgomery see Sāhīwāl
27 V4 **Montgomery City** Missouri, C USA
35 S8 **Montgomery Pass** pass Nevada, W USA
102 K12 **Montguyon** Charente-Maritime, W France
108 C10 **Monthey** Valais, SW Switzerland
27 V13 **Monticello** Arkansas, C USA
23 T4 **Monticello** Florida, SE USA
23 T8 **Monticello** Georgia, SE USA
30 M13 **Monticello** Illinois, N USA
31 O12 **Monticello** Indiana, N USA
29 Y13 **Monticello** Iowa, C USA
20 L7 **Monticello** Kentucky, S USA
29 V8 **Monticello** Minnesota, N USA
22 K7 **Monticello** Mississippi, S USA
27 V2 **Monticello** Missouri, C USA
18 J12 **Monticello** New York, NE USA
37 O7 **Monticello** Utah, W USA
106 F8 **Montichiari** Lombardia, N Italy
102 M12 **Montignac** Dordogne, SW France
99 G21 **Montignies-le-Tilleul** var. Montigny-le-Tilleul. Hainaut, S Belgium
14 J8 **Montigny, Lac de** ◎ Québec, SE Canada
103 S6 **Montigny-le-Roi** Haute-Marne, N France
Montigny-le-Tilleul see Montignies-le-Tilleul
43 R16 **Montijo** Veraguas, S Panama
104 F11 **Montijo** Setúbal, W Portugal
104 J11 **Montijo** Extremadura, W Spain
Montilium Adhemari see Montélimar
104 M13 **Montilla** Andalucía, S Spain
102 L3 **Montivilliers** Seine-Maritime, N France
15 U7 **Mont-Joli** Québec, SE Canada
14 M10 **Mont-Laurier** Québec, SE Canada
15 X5 **Mont-Louis** Québec, SE Canada
103 N17 **Mont-Louis** var. Mont Louis. Pyrénées-Orientales, S France
103 O10 **Montluçon** Allier, C France
15 R10 **Montmagny** Québec, SE Canada
103 S3 **Montmédy** Meuse, NE France
103 P5 **Montmirail** Marne, N France
15 R9 **Montmorency** ∽ Québec, SE Canada
102 M10 **Montmorillon** Vienne, W France
107 J14 **Montorio al Vomano** Abruzzo, C Italy
104 M13 **Montoro** Andalucía, S Spain
33 S16 **Montpelier** Idaho, NW USA
29 P6 **Montpelier** North Dakota, N USA
18 M7 **Montpelier** state capital Vermont, NE USA
103 Q15 **Montpellier** Hérault, S France
102 L12 **Montpon-Ménestérol** Dordogne, SW France
12 K15 **Montréal** Eng. Montreal. Québec, SE Canada
14 C8 **Montreal** ∽ Ontario, S Canada
14 G8 **Montreal** ∽ Ontario, S Canada
Montreal see Mirabel
9 T14 **Montreal Lake** ◎ Saskatchewan, C Canada
14 B9 **Montreal River** Ontario, S Canada
103 N2 **Montreuil** Pas-de-Calais, N France
102 K8 **Montreuil-Bellay** Maine-et-Loire, NW France
108 C10 **Montreux** Vaud, SW Switzerland
108 B9 **Montricher** Vaud, W Switzerland
96 K10 **Montrose** E Scotland, UK
27 W14 **Montrose** Arkansas, C USA
37 Q6 **Montrose** Colorado, C USA
29 Y16 **Montrose** Iowa, C USA
18 H12 **Montrose** Pennsylvania, NE USA
21 X5 **Montross** Virginia, NE USA
15 O12 **Mont-St-Hilaire** Québec, SE Canada
103 S3 **Mont-St-Martin** Meurthe-et-Moselle, NE France
45 V10 **Montserrat** var. Emerald Isle. ◇ UK dependent territory E West Indies
105 V5 **Montserrat** ▲ NE Spain
104 M7 **Montuenga** Castilla-León, N Spain
99 M19 **Montzen** Liège, E Belgium
37 N8 **Monument Valley** valley Arizona/Utah, SW USA
166 L4 **Monywa** Sagaing, C Burma (Myanmar)
106 D7 **Monza** Lombardia, N Italy
83 J15 **Monze** Southern, S Zambia
105 T5 **Monzón** Aragón, NE Spain
25 T9 **Moody** Texas, SW USA
98 L13 **Mook** Limburg, SE Netherlands
165 O12 **Mooka** var. Mōka. Tochigi, Honshū, S Japan
182 K3 **Moomba** South Australia
14 G13 **Moon** ∽ Ontario, S Canada
Moon see Muhu
181 Y10 **Moonie** Queensland, E Australia
193 O5 **Moonless Mountains** undersea feature E Pacific Ocean
182 L13 **Moonlight Head** headland Victoria, SE Australia
Moon-Sund see Väinameri
182 H8 **Moonta** South Australia
Moor see Mór
180 I12 **Moora** Western Australia
98 H12 **Moordrecht** Zuid-Holland, C Netherlands
33 T9 **Moore** Montana, NW USA
27 N11 **Moore** Oklahoma, C USA
25 R12 **Moore** Texas, SW USA
191 S10 **Moorea** island Îles du Vent, W French Polynesia
21 U3 **Moorefield** West Virginia, NE USA
23 X14 **Moore Haven** Florida, SE USA
180 J11 **Moore, Lake** ◎ Western Australia
19 N7 **Moore Reservoir** ⊠ New Hampshire/Vermont, NE USA
44 G1 **Moores Island** island N Bahamas
21 R10 **Mooresville** North Carolina, SE USA
29 R5 **Moorhead** Minnesota, N USA
22 K4 **Moorhead** Mississippi, S USA
99 F18 **Moorsel** Oost-Vlaanderen, C Belgium
99 C18 **Moorslede** West-Vlaanderen, W Belgium
18 L8 **Moosalamoo, Mount** ▲ Vermont, NE USA
101 M22 **Moosburg an der Isar** Bayern, SE Germany
33 S14 **Moose** Wyoming, C USA
12 H11 **Moose** ∽ Ontario, S Canada
12 H10 **Moose Factory** Ontario, S Canada
19 Q4 **Moosehead Lake** ◎ Maine, NE USA
9 U16 **Moose Jaw** Saskatchewan, S Canada
9 V14 **Moose Lake** Manitoba, C Canada
29 W6 **Moose Lake** Minnesota, N USA
19 P6 **Mooselookmeguntic Lake** ◎ Maine, NE USA
39 R12 **Moose Pass** Alaska, USA
19 P5 **Moose River** ∽ Maine, NE USA
18 J9 **Moose River** ∽ New York, NE USA
9 V16 **Moosomin** Saskatchewan, S Canada
12 H10 **Moosonee** Ontario, SE Canada

◆ Country
● Country Capital
◇ Dependent Territory
○ Dependent Territory Capital
⬖ Administrative Regions
✈ International Airport
▲ Mountain
▲▲ Mountain Range
⛰ Volcano
∽ River
◎ Lake
⊠ Reservoir

Moosup – Mozhaysk

19 *N12* **Moosup** Connecticut, NE USA
83 *N16* **Mopeia** Zambézia, NE Mozambique
83 *H18* **Mopipi** Central, C Botswana
Moppo *see* Mokp'o
77 *N11* **Mopti** Mopti, C Mali
77 *O11* **Mopti** ◈ *region* S Mali
57 *H18* **Moquegua** Moquegua, SE Peru
57 *H18* **Moquegua** *off.* Departamento de Moquegua. ◈ *department* S Peru
Moquegua, Departamento de *see* Moquegua
111 *I23* **Mór** *Ger.* Moor. Fejér, C Hungary
78 *G11* **Mora** Extrême-Nord, N Cameroon
104 *G11* **Mora** Évora, S Portugal
105 *N9* **Mora** Castilla-La Mancha, C Spain
94 *L12* **Mora** Dalarna, C Sweden
29 *V7* **Mora** Minnesota, N USA
37 *T10* **Mora** New Mexico, SW USA
113 *J17* **Morača** ≋ S Montenegro
152 *K10* **Morādābād** Uttar Pradesh, N India
105 *U6* **Móra d'Ebre** *var.* Mora de Ebro. Cataluña, NE Spain
Mora de Ebro *see* Móra d'Ebre
105 *S8* **Mora de Rubielos** Aragón, NE Spain
172 *H4* **Morafenobe** Mahajanga, W Madagascar
110 *K8* **Morąg** *Ger.* Mohrungen. Warmińsko-Mazurskie, N Poland
111 *L25* **Mórahalom** Csongrád, S Hungary
105 *N11* **Moral de Calatrava** Castilla-La Mancha, C Spain
63 *G19* **Moraleda, Canal** *strait* SE Pacific Ocean
54 *J3* **Morales** Bolívar, N Colombia
54 *D12* **Morales** Cauca, SW Colombia
42 *F5* **Morales** Izabal, E Guatemala
172 *J5* **Moramanga** Toamasina, E Madagascar
27 *Q6* **Moran** Kansas, C USA
25 *Q7* **Moran** Texas, SW USA
181 *X7* **Moranbah** Queensland, NE Australia
44 *L13* **Morant Bay** E Jamaica
96 *G10* **Morar, Loch** ◎ N Scotland, UK
Morata *see* Goodenough Island
105 *Q12* **Moratalla** Murcia, SE Spain
108 *C8* **Morat, Lac de** *Ger.* Murtensee. ◎ W Switzerland
84 *I11* **Morava** *var.* March. ≋ C Europe *see also* March
Morava *see* March
Morava *see* Moravia, Czech Republic
Morava *see* Velika Morava, Serbia
29 *W15* **Moravia** Iowa, C USA
111 *F18* **Moravia** *Cz.* Morava, *Ger.* Mähren. *cultural region* E Czech Republic
111 *H17* **Moravice** *Ger.* Mohra. ≋ NE Czech Republic
116 *E12* **Moravița** Timiș, SW Romania
111 *G17* **Moravská Třebová** *Ger.* Mährisch-Trübau. Pardubický Kraj, C Czech Republic
111 *E19* **Moravské Budějovice** *Ger.* Mährisch-Budwitz. Vysočina, C Czech Republic
111 *H17* **Moravskoslezský Kraj** *prev.* Ostravský Kraj. ◈ *region* E Czech Republic
111 *F19* **Moravský Krumlov** *Ger.* Mährisch-Kromau. Jihomoravský Kraj, SE Czech Republic
96 *J8* **Moray** *cultural region* N Scotland, UK
96 *J8* **Moray Firth** *inlet* N Scotland, UK
42 *B10* **Morazán** ◈ *department* NE El Salvador
154 *C10* **Morbi** Gujarāt, W India
102 *G7* **Morbihan** ◈ *department* NW France
Mörbisch *see* Mörbisch am See
109 *Y5* **Mörbisch am See** *var.* Mörbisch. Burgenland, E Austria
95 *N21* **Mörbylånga** Kalmar, S Sweden
102 *J14* **Morcenx** Landes, SW France
Morcheh Khort *see* Mürcheh Khvort
163 *T5* **Mordaga** Nei Mongol Zizhiqu, N China
11 *X17* **Morden** Manitoba, S Canada
Mordovia *see* Mordoviya, Respublika
127 *N5* **Mordoviya, Respublika** *prev.* Mordovskaya ASSR, *Eng.* Mordovia, *var.* Mordvinia. ◈ *autonomous republic* W Russian Federation
126 *M7* **Mordovo** Tambovskaya Oblast', W Russian Federation
Mordovskaya ASSR/ Mordvinia *see* Mordoviya, Respublika
Morea *see* Pelopónnisos
28 *K8* **Moreau River** ≋ South Dakota, N USA
97 *K16* **Morecambe** NW England, UK
97 *K16* **Morecambe Bay** *inlet* NW England, UK
183 *S4* **Moree** New South Wales, SE Australia
21 *N5* **Morehead** Kentucky, S USA
21 *X11* **Morehead City** North Carolina, SE USA
27 *Y8* **Morehouse** Missouri, C USA
108 *E10* **Mörel** Valais, SW Switzerland
54 *D13* **Morelia** Caquetá, S Colombia
41 *N14* **Morelia** Michoacán de Ocampo, S Mexico
105 *T7* **Morella** País Valenciano, E Spain
40 *I7* **Morelos** Chihuahua, N Mexico
41 *O15* **Morelos** ◈ *state* S Mexico
154 *H7* **Morena** Madhya Pradesh, C India
104 *L12* **Morena, Sierra** ▲▲ S Spain
37 *O14* **Morenci** Arizona, SW USA
31 *R11* **Morenci** Michigan, N USA
116 *J13* **Moreni** Dâmbovița, S Romania
94 *D9* **Møre og Romsdal** ◈ *county* S Norway
10 *I14* **Moresby Island** *island* Queen Charlotte Islands, British Columbia, SW Canada
183 *W2* **Moreton Island** *island* Queensland, E Australia
103 *O3* **Moreuil** Somme, N France
35 *V7* **Morey Peak** ▲ Nevada, W USA
125 *U4* **More-Yu** ≋ NW Russian Federation
103 *T9* **Morez** Jura, E France
Mórfou *see* Güzelyurt
Morfou Bay/Mórfou, Kólpos *see* Güzelyurt Körfezi
182 *J8* **Morgan** South Australia
23 *S7* **Morgan** Georgia, SE USA
25 *S8* **Morgan** Texas, SW USA
22 *J10* **Morgan City** Louisiana, S USA
20 *H6* **Morganfield** Kentucky, S USA
35 *O10* **Morgan Hill** California, W USA
21 *Q9* **Morganton** North Carolina, SE USA
20 *J7* **Morgantown** Kentucky, S USA
21 *S2* **Morgantown** West Virginia, NE USA
108 *B10* **Morges** Vaud, SW Switzerland
Morghāb, Daryā-ye *see* Murgap
148 *M4* **Morghāb, Daryā-ye** *Rus.* Murgab, Murghab, *Turk.* Murgap, Deryasy Murgap. ≋ Afghanistan/ Turkmenistan *see also* Murgap
96 *I9* **Mor, Glen** *var.* Glen Albyn, Great Glen. *valley* N Scotland, UK
103 *T5* **Morhange** Moselle, NE France
158 *M5* **Mori** *var.* Mori Kazak Zizhixian. Xinjiang Uygur Zizhiqu, NW China
165 *R5* **Mori** Hokkaidō, NE Japan
35 *Y6* **Moriah, Mount** ▲ Nevada, W USA
37 *S11* **Moriarty** New Mexico, SW USA
54 *J12* **Morichal** Guaviare, E Colombia
Mori Kazak Zizhixian *see* Mori
Morin Dawa Daurzu Zizhiqi *see* Nirji
11 *Q14* **Morinville** Alberta, SW Canada
165 *R8* **Morioka** Iwate, Honshū, C Japan
183 *T8* **Morisset** New South Wales, SE Australia
165 *Q8* **Moriyoshi-yama** ▲ Honshū, C Japan
92 *K13* **Morjärv** Norrbotten, N Sweden
127 *R3* **Morki** Respublika Mariy El, W Russian Federation
123 *N10* **Morkoka** ≋ NE Russian Federation
102 *F5* **Morlaix** Finistère, NW France
95 *M20* **Mörlunda** Kalmar, S Sweden
107 *N19* **Mormanno** Calabria, SW Italy
36 *L11* **Mormon Lake** ◎ Arizona, SW USA
35 *Y10* **Mormon Peak** ▲ Nevada, W USA
Mormon State *see* Utah
45 *Y5* **Morne-à-l'Eau** Grande Terre, N Guadeloupe
29 *Y15* **Morning Sun** Iowa, C USA
193 *S12* **Mornington Abyssal Plain** *undersea feature* SE Pacific Ocean
63 *F22* **Mornington, Isla** *island* S Chile
181 *T4* **Mornington Island** *island* Wellesley Islands, Queensland, N Australia
115 *E18* **Mórnos** ≋ C Greece
149 *P14* **Moro** Sind, SE Pakistan
32 *I11* **Moro** Oregon, NW USA
186 *E8* **Morobe** Morobe, C Papua New Guinea
186 *E8* **Morobe** ◈ *province* C Papua New Guinea
31 *N12* **Morocco** Indiana, N USA
74 *E8* **Morocco** *off.* Kingdom of Morocco, *Ar.* Al Mamlakah. ◆ *monarchy* N Africa
Morocco *see* Marrakech
Morocco, Kingdom of *see* Morocco
81 *I22* **Morogoro** Morogoro, E Tanzania
81 *H24* **Morogoro** ◈ *region* SE Tanzania
171 *Q7* **Moro Gulf** *gulf* S Philippines
41 *N13* **Moroleón** Guanajuato, C Mexico
172 *H6* **Morombe** Toliara, W Madagascar
44 *G5* **Morón** Ciego de Ávila, C Cuba
163 *N8* **Mörön** Hentiy, C Mongolia
162 *I6* **Mörön** Hövsgöl, N Mongolia
54 *K5* **Morón** Carabobo, N Venezuela
Morón *see* Morón de la Frontera
56 *D8* **Morona, Río** ≋ N Peru
56 *C8* **Morona Santiago** ◈ *province* E Ecuador
172 *H5* **Morondava** Toliara, W Madagascar
104 *K14* **Morón de la Frontera** *var.* Morón. Andalucía, S Spain
172 *G13* **Moroni** ● (Comoros) Grande Comore, NW Comoros
171 *S10* **Morotai, Pulau** *island* Maluku, E Indonesia
Morotiri *see* Marotiri
81 *H17* **Moroto** NE Uganda
Morozov *see* Bratan
126 *M11* **Morozovsk** Rostovskaya Oblast', SW Russian Federation
97 *L14* **Morpeth** N England, UK
Morphou *see* Güzelyurt
Morphou Bay *see* Güzelyurt Körfezi
28 *I13* **Morrill** Nebraska, C USA
27 *U11* **Morrilton** Arkansas, C USA
9 *Q16* **Morrin** Alberta, SW Canada
184 *M7* **Morrinsville** Waikato, North Island, New Zealand
9 *X16* **Morris** Manitoba, S Canada
30 *M11* **Morris** Illinois, N USA
29 *S8* **Morris** Minnesota, N USA
14 *M13* **Morrisburg** Ontario, SE Canada
197 *R11* **Morris Jesup, Kap** *headland* N Greenland
182 *B1* **Morris, Mount** ▲ South Australia
30 *K10* **Morrison** Illinois, N USA
36 *K13* **Morristown** Arizona, SW USA
18 *J14* **Morristown** New Jersey, NE USA
21 *O8* **Morristown** Tennessee, S USA
42 *L11* **Morrito** Río San Juan, SW Nicaragua
35 *P13* **Morro Bay** California, W USA
95 *L22* **Mörrum** Blekinge, S Sweden
83 *N16* **Morrumbala** Zambézia, NE Mozambique
83 *N20* **Morrumbene** Inhambane, SE Mozambique
95 *F21* **Mors** *island* NW Denmark
Mörs *see* Moers
25 *N1* **Morse** Texas, SW USA
127 *N6* **Morshansk** Tambovskaya Oblast', W Russian Federation
102 *L5* **Mortagne-au-Perche** Orne, N France
102 *J8* **Mortagne-sur-Sèvre** Vendée, NW France
104 *G8* **Mortágua** Viseu, N Portugal
102 *J5* **Mortain** Manche, N France
106 *C8* **Mortara** Lombardia, N Italy
59 *J17* **Mortes, Rio das** ≋ C Brazil
182 *M12* **Mortlake** Victoria, SE Australia
Mortlock Group *see* Takuu Islands
189 *Q17* **Mortlock Islands** *prev.* Nomoi Islands. *island group* C Micronesia
29 *T9* **Morton** Minnesota, N USA
22 *L5* **Morton** Mississippi, S USA
24 *M5* **Morton** Texas, SW USA
32 *H9* **Morton** Washington, NW USA
0 *D7* **Morton Seamount** *undersea feature* NE Pacific Ocean
45 *U15* **Moruga** Trinidad, Trinidad and Tobago
183 *P9* **Morundah** New South Wales, SE Australia
Moruroa *see* Mururoa
183 *S11* **Moruya** New South Wales, SE Australia
103 *Q8* **Morvan** *physical region* C France
185 *G21* **Morven** Canterbury, South Island, New Zealand
183 *O13* **Morwell** Victoria, SE Australia
125 *N6* **Morzhovets, Ostrov** *island* NW Russian Federation
126 *J4* **Mosal'sk** Kaluzhskaya Oblast', W Russian Federation
101 *H20* **Mosbach** Baden-Württemberg, SW Germany
95 *E18* **Mosby** Vest-Agder, S Norway
33 *V9* **Mosby** Montana, NW USA
32 *M9* **Moscow** Idaho, NW USA
20 *F10* **Moscow** Tennessee, S USA
Moscow *see* Moskva
101 *D19* **Mosel** *Fr.* Moselle. ≋ W Europe *see also* Moselle
Mosel *see* Moselle
103 *T4* **Moselle** ◈ *department* NE France
103 *T6* **Moselle** *Ger.* Mosel. ≋ W Europe *see also* Mosel
Moselle *see* Mosel
32 *K9* **Moses Lake** ◎ Washington, NW USA
83 *I18* **Mosetse** Central, E Botswana
92 *H4* **Mosfellsbær** Sudhurland, SW Iceland
185 *F23* **Mosgiel** Otago, South Island, New Zealand
124 *M11* **Mosha** ≋ NW Russian Federation
81 *I20* **Moshi** Kilimanjaro, NE Tanzania
110 *G12* **Mosina** Wielkolpolskie, C Poland
30 *L6* **Mosinee** Wisconsin, N USA
92 *F13* **Mosjøen** Nordland, C Norway
123 *S12* **Moskal'vo** Ostrov Sakhalin, Sakhalinskaya Oblast', SE Russian Fèderation
92 *I13* **Moskosel** Norrbotten, N Sweden
126 *K4* **Moskovskaya Oblast'** ◈ *province* W Russian Federation
Moskovskiy *see* Moskva
126 *J3* **Moskva** *Eng.* Moscow. ● (Russian Federation) Gorod Moskva, W Russian Federation
147 *Q14* **Moskva** *Rus.* Moskovskiy; *prev.* Chubek. SW Tajikistan
126 *L4* **Moskva** ≋ W Russian Federation
83 *I20* **Mosomane** Kgatleng, SE Botswana
Moson and Magyaróvár *see* Mosonmagyaróvár
111 *H21* **Mosoni-Duna** *Ger.* Kleine Donau. ≋ NW Hungary
111 *H21* **Mosonmagyaróvár** *Ger.* Wieselburg-Ungarisch-Altenburg; *prev.* Moson and Magyaróvár, *Ger.* Wieselburg and Ungarisch-Altenburg. Győr-Moson-Sopron, NW Hungary
Mospino *see* Mospyne
117 *X8* **Mospyne** *Rus.* Mospino. Donets'ka Oblast', E Ukraine
54 *B12* **Mosquera** Nariño, SW Colombia
37 *U10* **Mosquero** New Mexico, SW USA
Mosquito Coast *see* La Mosquitia
31 *U11* **Mosquito Creek Lake** ⊞ Ohio, N USA
Mosquito Gulf *see* Mosquitos, Golfo de los
23 *X11* **Mosquito Lagoon** *wetland* Florida, SE USA
43 *N10* **Mosquito, Punta** *headland* E Nicaragua
43 *W14* **Mosquito, Punta** *headland* NE Panama
43 *Q15* **Mosquitos, Golfo de los** *Eng.* Mosquito Gulf. *gulf* N Panama
95 *H16* **Moss** Østfold, S Norway
Mossâmedes *see* Namibe
22 *G8* **Moss Bluff** Louisiana, S USA
185 *C23* **Mossburn** Southland, South Island, New Zealand
83 *G26* **Mosselbaai** *var.* Mosselbai, *Eng.* Mossel Bay. Western Cape, SW South Africa
Mosselbai/Mossel Bay *see* Mosselbaai
79 *F20* **Mossendjo** Le Niari, SW Congo
183 *N8* **Mossgiel** New South Wales, SE Australia
101 *H22* **Mössingen** Baden-Württemberg, S Germany
181 *W4* **Mossman** Queensland, NE Australia
59 *P14* **Mossoró** Rio Grande do Norte, NE Brazil
23 *N9* **Moss Point** Mississippi, S USA
183 *S9* **Moss Vale** New South Wales, SE Australia
32 *G9* **Mossyrock** Washington, NW USA
111 *B15* **Most** *Ger.* Brüx. Ústecký Kraj, NW Czech Republic
162 *E7* **Möst** *var.* Ulaantolgoy. Hovd, W Mongolia
121 *P16* **Mosta** *var.* Musta. C Malta
74 *I5* **Mostaganem** *var.* Mestghanem. NW Algeria
113 *H14* **Mostar** Federacija Bosna I Hercegovina, S Bosnia and Herzegovina
61 *J17* **Mostardas** Rio Grande do Sul, S Brazil
116 *K14* **Mostiștea** ≋ S Romania
Mostva *see* Mastva
Mosty *see* Masty
116 *H5* **Mostys'ka** L'vivs'ka Oblast', W Ukraine
Mosul *see* Al Mawșil
95 *F15* **Møsvatnet** ◎ S Norway
80 *J12* **Mot'a** Amhara, N Ethiopia
79 *H16* **Motaba** ≋ N Congo
105 *O10* **Mota del Cuervo** Castilla-La Mancha, C Spain
104 *L5* **Mota del Marqués** Castilla-León, N Spain
42 *F5* **Motagua, Río** ≋ Guatemala/Honduras
119 *H19* **Motal'** Brestskaya Voblasts', SW Belarus
95 *L17* **Motala** Östergötland, S Sweden
191 *X7* **Motane** *island* Îles Marquises, NE French Polynesia
152 *K13* **Moth** Uttar Pradesh, N India
Mother of Presidents/ Mother of States *see* Virginia
96 *I12* **Motherwell** C Scotland, UK
153 *P12* **Motīhāri** Bihār, N India
105 *Q10* **Motilla del Palancar** Castilla-La Mancha, C Spain
184 *N7* **Motiti Island** *island* NE New Zealand
65 *E25* **Motley Island** *island* SE Falkland Islands
83 *J19* **Motloutse** ≋ E Botswana
41 *V17* **Motozintla de Mendoza** Chiapas, SE Mexico
105 *N15* **Motril** Andalucía, S Spain
116 *G13* **Motru** Gorj, SW Romania
165 *Q4* **Motsuta-misaki** *headland* Hokkaidō, NE Japan
28 *L6* **Mott** North Dakota, N USA
Möttling *see* Metlika
107 *O18* **Mottola** Puglia, SE Italy
184 *P8* **Motu** ≋ North Island, New Zealand
185 *I14* **Motueka** Tasman, South Island, New Zealand
185 *I14* **Motueka** ≋ South Island, New Zealand
Motu Iti *see* Tupai
41 *X12* **Motul** *var.* Motul de Felipe Carrillo Puerto. Yucatán, SE Mexico
Motul de Felipe Carrillo Puerto *see* Motul
191 *U17* **Motu Nui** *island* Easter Island, Chile, E Pacific Ocean
191 *Q10* **Motu One** *var.* Bellingshausen. *atoll* Îles Sous le Vent, W French Polynesia
190 *I16* **Motutapu** *island* E Cook Islands
193 *V15* **Motu Tapu** *island* Tongatapu Group, S Tonga
184 *L5* **Motutapu Island** *island* N New Zealand
Motyca *see* Modica
Mouanda *see* Moanda
Mouaskar *see* Mascara
105 *U3* **Moubermé, Tuc de** *Fr.* Pic de Maubermé, *Sp.* Pico Mauberme; *prev.* Tuc de Maubermé. ▲ France/Spain *see also* Maubermé, Pic de
Moubermé, Tuc de *see* Maubermé, Pic de
45 *N7* **Mouchoir Passage** *passage* SE Turks and Caicos Islands
76 *I9* **Moudjéria** Tagant, SW Mauritania
108 *C9* **Moudon** Vaud, W Switzerland
Mouhoun *see* Black Volta
79 *E19* **Mouila** Ngounié, C Gabon
79 *K14* **Mouka** Haute-Kotto, C Central African Republic
Moukden *see* Shenyang
183 *N10* **Moulamein** New South Wales, SE Australia
Moulamein Creek *see* Billabong Creek
74 *F6* **Moulay-Bousselham** NW Morocco
Moule *see* le Moule
80 *M11* **Moulhoulé** N Djibouti
103 *P9* **Moulins** Allier, C France
166 *M9* **Moulmein** *var.* Maulmain, Mawlamyine. Mon State, S Burma (Myanmar)
166 *L8* **Moulmeingyun** Irrawaddy, SW Burma (Myanmar)
74 *G6* **Moulouya** *var.* Mulucha, Muluya, Mulwiya. *seasonal river* NE Morocco
23 *O2* **Moulton** Alabama, S USA
29 *W16* **Moulton** Iowa, C USA
25 *T11* **Moulton** Texas, SW USA
23 *T7* **Moultrie** Georgia, SE USA
21 *S14* **Moultrie, Lake** ⊞ South Carolina, SE USA
22 *K3* **Mound Bayou** Mississippi, S USA
30 *L17* **Mound City** Illinois, N USA
27 *R6* **Mound City** Kansas, C USA
27 *Q2* **Mound City** Missouri, C USA
29 *N7* **Mound City** South Dakota, N USA
78 *H13* **Moundou** Logone-Occidental, SW Chad
27 *P10* **Mounds** Oklahoma, C USA
21 *R2* **Moundsville** West Virginia, NE USA
167 *Q12* **Moŭng Roessei** Bătdâmbâng, W Cambodia
Moun Hou *see* Black Volta
8 *H8* **Mountain** ≋ Northwest Territories, NW Canada
37 *S12* **Mountainair** New Mexico, SW USA
35 *V1* **Mountain City** Nevada, W USA
21 *Q8* **Mountain City** Tennessee, S USA
27 *U7* **Mountain Grove** Missouri, C USA
27 *U9* **Mountain Home** Arkansas, C USA
33 *N15* **Mountain Home** Idaho, NW USA
25 *Q11* **Mountain Home** Texas, SW USA
29 *W4* **Mountain Iron** Minnesota, N USA
29 *T10* **Mountain Lake** Minnesota, N USA
23 *S3* **Mountain Park** Georgia, SE USA
35 *W12* **Mountain Pass** *pass* California, W USA
27 *T12* **Mountain Pine** Arkansas, C USA
39 *Y14* **Mountain Point** Annette Island, Alaska, USA
Mountain State *see* Montana
Mountain State *see* West Virginia
27 *V7* **Mountain View** Arkansas, C USA
38 *H12* **Mountain View** Hawai'i, USA, C Pacific Ocean
27 *V10* **Mountain View** Missouri, C USA
38 *M11* **Mountain Village** Alaska, USA
21 *R8* **Mount Airy** North Carolina, SE USA
83 *K24* **Mount Ayliff** *Xh.* Maxesibebi. Eastern Cape, SE South Africa
29 *U16* **Mount Ayr** Iowa, C USA
182 *J9* **Mount Barker** South Australia
180 *J14* **Mount Barker** Western Australia
183 *P11* **Mount Beauty** Victoria, SE Australia
14 *E16* **Mount Brydges** Ontario, S Canada
31 *N16* **Mount Carmel** Illinois, N USA
30 *K10* **Mount Carroll** Illinois, N USA
31 *S9* **Mount Clemens** Michigan, N USA
185 *E19* **Mount Cook** Canterbury, South Island, New Zealand
83 *L16* **Mount Darwin** Mashonaland Central, NE Zimbabwe
19 *S7* **Mount Desert Island** *island* Maine, NE USA
23 *W11* **Mount Dora** Florida, SE USA
182 *G5* **Mount Eba** South Australia
25 *W8* **Mount Enterprise** Texas, SW USA
182 *J4* **Mount Fitton** South Australia
83 *J24* **Mount Fletcher** Eastern Cape, SE South Africa
14 *F15* **Mount Forest** Ontario, S Canada
182 *K12* **Mount Gambier** South Australia
181 *W5* **Mount Garnet** Queensland, NE Australia
21 *P6* **Mount Gay** West Virginia, NE USA
31 *S12* **Mount Gilead** Ohio, N USA
186 *C7* **Mount Hagen** Western Highlands, C Papua New Guinea
18 *J16* **Mount Holly** New Jersey, NE USA
21 *R10* **Mount Holly** North Carolina, SE USA
27 *T12* **Mount Ida** Arkansas, C USA
181 *T6* **Mount Isa** Queensland, C Australia
21 *U4* **Mount Jackson** Virginia, NE USA
18 *D12* **Mount Jewett** Pennsylvania, NE USA
18 *L13* **Mount Kisco** New York, NE USA
18 *B15* **Mount Lebanon** Pennsylvania, NE USA
182 *J8* **Mount Lofty Ranges** ▲▲ South Australia
180 *J10* **Mount Magnet** Western Australia
184 *N7* **Mount Maunganui** Bay of Plenty, North Island, New Zealand
97 *E18* **Mountmellick** *Ir.* Móinteach Mílic. Laois, C Ireland
30 *L10* **Mount Morris** Illinois, N USA
31 *R9* **Mount Morris** Michigan, N USA
18 *F10* **Mount Morris** New York, NE USA
18 *B16* **Mount Morris** Pennsylvania, NE USA
30 *K15* **Mount Olive** Illinois, N USA
21 *V10* **Mount Olive** North Carolina, SE USA
21 *N4* **Mount Olivet** Kentucky, S USA
29 *Y15* **Mount Pleasant** Iowa, C USA
31 *Q8* **Mount Pleasant** Michigan, N USA
18 *C15* **Mount Pleasant** Pennsylvania, NE USA
21 *T14* **Mount Pleasant** South Carolina, SE USA
20 *I9* **Mount Pleasant** Tennessee, S USA
25 *W6* **Mount Pleasant** Texas, SW USA
36 *L4* **Mount Pleasant** Utah, W USA
63 *N23* **Mount Pleasant** ✈ (Stanley) East Falkland, Falkland Islands
97 *G25* **Mount's Bay** *inlet* SW England, UK
35 *N2* **Mount Shasta** California, W USA
30 *J13* **Mount Sterling** Illinois, N USA
21 *N5* **Mount Sterling** Kentucky, S USA
18 *E15* **Mount Union** Pennsylvania, NE USA
23 *V6* **Mount Vernon** Georgia, SE USA
30 *L16* **Mount Vernon** Illinois, N USA
20 *M6* **Mount Vernon** Kentucky, S USA
27 *S7* **Mount Vernon** Missouri, C USA
31 *T13* **Mount Vernon** Ohio, N USA
32 *K13* **Mount Vernon** Oregon, NW USA
25 *W6* **Mount Vernon** Texas, SW USA
32 *H7* **Mount Vernon** Washington, NW USA
20 *L5* **Mount Washington** Kentucky, S USA
182 *F8* **Mount Wedge** South Australia
30 *L14* **Mount Zion** Illinois, N USA
181 *Y9* **Moura** Queensland, NE Australia
58 *F12* **Moura** Amazonas, NW Brazil
104 *H12* **Moura** Beja, S Portugal
104 *I12* **Mourão** Évora, S Portugal
76 *L11* **Mourdiah** Koulikoro, W Mali
78 *K7* **Mourdi, Dépression du** *desert lowland* Chad/Sudan
102 *J16* **Mourenx** Pyrénées-Atlantiques, SW France
Mourgana *see* Mourgkána
115 *C15* **Mourgkána** *var.* Mourgana. ▲ Albania/Greece
97 *G16* **Mourne Mountains** *Ir.* Beanna Boirche. ▲▲ SE Northern Ireland, UK
115 *I15* **Moúrtzeflos, Ákrotírio** *headland* Límnos, E Greece
99 *C19* **Mouscron** *Dut.* Moeskroen. Hainaut, W Belgium
Mouse River *see* Souris River
78 *H10* **Moussoro** Kanem, W Chad
103 *T11* **Moûtiers** Savoie, E France
172 *J14* **Moutsamoudou** *var.* Mutsamudu. Anjouan, SE Comoros
74 *K11* **Mouydir, Monts de** ▲▲ S Algeria
79 *F20* **Mouyondzi** La Bouenza, S Congo
115 *E16* **Mouzáki** *prev.* Mouzákion. Thessalía, C Greece
Mouzákion *see* Mouzáki
29 *S13* **Moville** Iowa, C USA
82 *E13* **Moxico** ◈ *province* E Angola
172 *I14* **Moya** Anjouan, SE Comoros
40 *L12* **Moyahua** Zacatecas, C Mexico
81 *J16* **Moyalē** Oromo, C Ethiopia
76 *I15* **Moyamba** W Sierra Leone
74 *G7* **Moyen Atlas** *Eng.* Middle Atlas. ▲▲ N Morocco
78 *H13* **Moyen-Chari** *off.* Préfecture du Moyen-Chari. ◈ *prefecture* S Chad
Moyen-Chari, Préfecture du *see* Moyen-Chari
Moyen-Congo *see* Congo (Republic of)
83 *J24* **Moyeni** *var.* Quthing. SW Lesotho
79 *D18* **Moyen-Ogooué** *off.* Province du Moyen-Ogooué, *var.* Le Moyen-Ogooué. ◈ *province* C Gabon
Moyen-Ogooué, Province du *see* Moyen-Ogooué
103 *S4* **Moyeuvre-Grande** Moselle, NE France
33 *N7* **Moyie Springs** Idaho, NW USA
146 *G6* **Mo'ynoq** *Rus.* Muynak. Qoraqalpog'iston Respublikasi, NW Uzbekistan
81 *F16* **Moyo** NW Uganda
56 *D10* **Moyobamba** San Martín, NW Peru
78 *H10* **Moyto** Chari-Baguirmi, W Chad
158 *G9* **Moyu** *var.* Karakax. Xinjiang Uygur Zizhiqu, NW China
122 *M9* **Moyyero** ≋ N Russian Federation
145 *S15* **Moyynkum** *var.* Furmanovka, *Kaz.* Fūrmanov. Zhambyl, S Kazakhstan
145 *Q15* **Moyynkum, Peski** *Kaz.* Moyynqum. *desert* S Kazakhstan
Moyynqum *see* Moyynkum, Peski
145 *S12* **Moyynty** Karaganda, C Kazakhstan
145 *S12* **Moyynty** ≋ Karaganda, C Kazakhstan
Mozambika, Lakandranon' i *see* Mozambique Channel
83 *M18* **Mozambique** *off.* Republic of Mozambique; *prev.* People's Republic of Mozambique, Portuguese East Africa. ◆ *republic* S Africa
Mozambique Basin *see* Natal Basin
Mozambique, Canal de *see* Mozambique Channel
83 *P17* **Mozambique Channel** *Fr.* Canal de Mozambique, *Mal.* Lakandranon' i Mozambika. *strait* W Indian Ocean
172 *L11* **Mozambique Escarpment** *var.* Mozambique Scarp. *undersea feature* SW Indian Ocean
Mozambique, People's Republic of *see* Mozambique
172 *L10* **Mozambique Plateau** *var.* Mozambique Rise. *undersea feature* SW Indian Ocean
Mozambique, Republic of *see* Mozambique
Mozambique Rise *see* Mozambique Plateau
Mozambique Scarp *see* Mozambique Escarpment
127 *O15* **Mozdok** Respublika Severnaya Osetiya, SW Russian Federation
57 *K17* **Mozetenes, Serranías de** ▲▲ C Bolivia
126 *J4* **Mozhaysk** Moskovskaya Oblast', W Russian Federation

◆ Country
● Country Capital
◇ Dependent Territory
○ Dependent Territory Capital
◈ Administrative Regions
✈ International Airport
▲ Mountain
▲▲ Mountain Range
Volcano
≋ River
◎ Lake
⊞ Reservoir

MOZHGA – MUSTAFĀBĀD

127 T3 **Mozhga** Udmurtskaya Respublika, NW Russian Federation
Mozyr' see Mazyr
79 P22 **Mpala** Katanga, E Dem. Rep. Congo
79 G19 **Mpama** ≈ C Congo
81 E22 **Mpanda** Rukwa, W Tanzania
82 L11 **Mpande** Northern, NE Zambia
83 J18 **Mphoengs** Matabeleland South, SW Zimbabwe
81 F18 **Mpigi** S Uganda
82 L13 **Mpika** Northern, NE Zambia
83 J14 **Mpima** Central, C Zambia
82 J13 **Mpongwe** Copperbelt, C Zambia
82 K11 **Mporokoso** Northern, N Zambia
79 H20 **Mpouya** Plateaux, SE Congo
77 P16 **Mpraeso** C Ghana
82 L11 **Mpulungu** Northern, N Zambia
83 K21 **Mpumalanga** *prev.* Eastern Transvaal, *Afr.* Oos-Transvaal. ⬖ *province* NE South Africa
83 D16 **Mpungu** Okavango, N Namibia
81 I22 **Mpwapwa** Dodoma, C Tanzania
Mqinvartsveri see Kazbek
110 M8 **Mrągowo** *Ger.* Sensburg. Warmińsko-Mazurskie, NE Poland
127 V6 **Mrakovo** Respublika Bashkortostan, W Russian Federation
172 I13 **Mramani** Anjouan, E Comoros
112 F12 **Mrkonjić Grad** ⬖ Republika Srpska, W Bosnia and Herzegovina
110 H9 **Mrocza** Kujawsko-pomorskie, C Poland
124 I14 **Msta** ≈ NW Russian Federation
Mstislavl' see Mstsislaw
119 P15 **Mstsislaw** *Rus.* Mstislavl'. Mahilyowskaya Voblasts', E Belarus
Mtkvari see Kura
Mtoko see Mutoko
126 K6 **Mtsensk** Orlovskaya Oblast', W Russian Federation
81 K24 **Mtwara** Mtwara, SE Tanzania
81 J25 **Mtwara** ⬖ *region* SE Tanzania
100 G14 **Mu** ▲ S Portugal
193 V15 **Mu'a** Tongatapu, S Tonga
Muai To see Mae Hong Son
83 P16 **Mualama** Zambézia, NE Mozambique
Mualo see Messalo, Rio
79 E22 **Muanda** Bas-Congo, SW Dem. Rep. Congo
Muang Chiang Rai see Chiang Rai
167 R6 **Muang Ham** Houaphan, N Laos
167 S8 **Muang Hinboun** Khammouan, C Laos
Muang Kalasin see Kalasin
Muang Khammouan see Thakhèk
167 S11 **Muang Không** Champasak, S Laos
167 S10 **Muang Khôngxédôn** *var.* Khong Sedone. Salavan, S Laos
Muang Khon Kaen see Khon Kaen
167 Q6 **Muang Khoua** Phôngsali, N Laos
Muang Krabi see Krabi
Muang Lampang see Lampang
Muang Lamphun see Lamphun
Muang Loei see Loei
Muang Lom Sak see Lom Sak
Muang Nakhon Sawan see Nakhon Sawan
167 Q6 **Muang Namo** Oudômxai, N Laos
Muang Nan see Nan
167 Q6 **Muang Ngoy** Louangphabang, N Laos
167 Q5 **Muang Ou Tai** Phôngsali, N Laos
Muang Pak Lay see Pak Lay
Muang Pakxan see Pakxan
167 T10 **Muang Pakxong** Champasak, S Laos
167 S9 **Muang Phalan** *var.* Muang Phalane. Savannakhét, S Laos
Muang Phalane see Muang Phalan
Muang Phan see Phan
Muang Phayao see Phayao
Muang Phichit see Phichit
167 T9 **Muang Phin** Savannakhét, S Laos
Muang Phitsanulok see Phitsanulok
Muang Phrae see Phrae
Muang Roi Et see Roi Et
Muang Sakon Nakhon see Sakon Nakhon
Muang Samut Prakan see Samut Prakan
167 P6 **Muang Sing** Louang Namtha, N Laos
Muang Ubon see Ubon Ratchathani
Muang Uthai Thani see Uthai Thani
167 P7 **Muang Vangviang** Viangchan, C Laos
Muang Xaignabouri see Xaignabouli
Muang Xay see Xai
167 S9 **Muang Xépôn** *var.* Sepone. Savannakhét, S Laos
168 K10 **Muar** *var.* Bandar Maharani. Johor, Peninsular Malaysia
168 J9 **Muara** Sumatera, W Indonesia
168 L13 **Muarabeliti** Sumatera, W Indonesia
168 K12 **Muarabungo** Sumatera, W Indonesia
168 L13 **Muaraenim** Sumatera, W Indonesia
169 T11 **Muarajuloi** Borneo, C Indonesia
169 U12 **Muarakaman** Borneo, C Indonesia
168 H12 **Muarasigep** Pulau Siberut, W Indonesia
168 L12 **Muaratembesi** Sumatera, W Indonesia
169 T12 **Muaratewe** *var.* Muarateweh; *prev.* Moearatewe. Borneo, C Indonesia
Muarateweh see Muaratewe
169 U10 **Muarawahau** Borneo, N Indonesia
138 G13 **Mubārak, Jabal** ▲ S Jordan
153 N13 **Mubārakpur** Uttar Pradesh, N India
Mubarek see Muborak
81 F18 **Mubende** SW Uganda
77 Y14 **Mubi** Adamawa, NE Nigeria
146 M12 **Muborak** *Rus.* Mubarek. Qashqadaryo Viloyati, S Uzbekistan
171 U12 **Mubrani** Papua, E Indonesia
67 U12 **Muchinga Escarpment** *escarpment* NE Zambia
127 N7 **Muchkapskiy** Tambovskaya Oblast', W Russian Federation
96 G10 **Muck** *island* W Scotland, UK
82 Q13 **Mucojo** Cabo Delgado, N Mozambique
82 F12 **Muconda** Lunda Sul, NE Angola
54 I10 **Muco, Río** ≈ E Colombia
83 O16 **Mucubela** Zambézia, NE Mozambique
42 J5 **Mucupina, Monte** ▲ N Honduras
136 J14 **Mucur** Kirşehir, C Turkey
143 U8 **Mūd** Khorāsān-e Janūbī, E Iran
163 Y9 **Mudanjiang** *var.* Mu-tan-chiang. Heilongjiang, NE China
163 Y9 **Mudan Jiang** ≈ NE China
136 D11 **Mudanya** Bursa, NW Turkey
28 K8 **Mud Butte** South Dakota, N USA
155 G16 **Muddebihāl** Karnātaka, C India
27 P12 **Muddy Boggy Creek** ≈ Oklahoma, C USA
36 M6 **Muddy Creek** ≈ Utah, W USA
37 V7 **Muddy Creek Reservoir** ⊠ Colorado, C USA
33 W15 **Muddy Gap** Wyoming, C USA
35 Y11 **Muddy Peak** ▲ Nevada, W USA
183 R7 **Mudgee** New South Wales, SE Australia
29 S3 **Mud Lake** ◎ Minnesota, N USA
29 P7 **Mud Lake Reservoir** ⊠ South Dakota, N USA
167 N9 **Mudon** Mon State, S Burma (Myanmar)
81 O14 **Mudug** *off.* Gobolka Mudug. ⬖ *region* NE Somalia
81 O14 **Mudug** *var.* Mudugh. *plain* N Somalia
Mudug, Gobolka see Mudug
Mudugh see Mudug
83 Q15 **Muecate** Nampula, NE Mozambique
82 Q13 **Mueda** Cabo Delgado, NE Mozambique
42 L10 **Muelle de los Bueyes** Región Autónoma Atlántico Sur, SE Nicaragua
Muenchen see München
83 M14 **Muende** Tete, NW Mozambique
25 T5 **Muenster** Texas, SW USA
Muenster see Münster
43 O6 **Muerto, Cayo** *reef* NE Nicaragua
41 T17 **Muerto, Mar** *lagoon* SE Mexico
64 F11 **Muertos Trough** *undersea feature* N Caribbean Sea
83 H14 **Mufaya Kuta** Western, NW Zambia
82 J13 **Mufulira** Copperbelt, C Zambia
161 O10 **Mufu Shan** ▲▲ C China
Mugalzhar Taŭlary see Mugodzhary, Gory
137 Y12 **Muğan Düzü** *Rus.* Muganskaya Ravnina, Muganskaya Step'. *physical region* S Azerbaijan
Muganskaya Ravnina/Muganskaya Step' see Muğan Düzü
106 K8 **Múggia** Friuli-Venezia Giulia, NE Italy
153 N14 **Mughal Sarāi** Uttar Pradesh, N India
Mughla see Muğla
141 W11 **Mughshin** *var.* Muqshin. S Oman
147 S12 **Mughsu** *Rus.* Muksu. ≈ C Tajikistan
164 H14 **Mugi** Tokushima, Shikoku, SW Japan
136 C16 **Muğla** *var.* Mughla. Muğla, SW Turkey
136 C16 **Muğla** *var.* Mughla. ⬖ *province* SW Turkey
144 J11 **Mugodzhary, Gory** *Kaz.* Mugalzhar Taŭlary. ▲▲ W Kazakhstan
83 O15 **Mugulama** Zambézia, NE Mozambique
Muḩāfazat Hims see Ḩimş
Muḩāfazat Ma'dabā see Ma'dabā
139 U9 **Muḩammad** E Iraq
139 R8 **Muḩammadīyah** C Iraq
80 I6 **Muhammad Qol** Red Sea, NE Sudan
75 Y9 **Muhammad, Râs** *headland* E Egypt
Muhammerah see Khorramshahr
Muḩāfazat Al 'Aqabah see Al 'Aqabah
140 M12 **Muhāyil** *var.* Mahāil. 'Asīr, SW Saudi Arabia
139 O7 **Muḩaywīr** W Iraq
101 H21 **Mühlacker** Baden-Württemberg, SW Germany
Mühlbach see Sebeş
Mühldorf see Mühldorf am Inn
101 N23 **Mühldorf am Inn** *var.* Mühldorf. Bayern, SE Germany
101 J15 **Mühlhausen** *var.* Mühlhausen in Thüringen. Thüringen, C Germany
Mühlhausen in Thüringen see Mühlhausen
195 Q2 **Mühlig-Hofmann Mountains** ▲▲ Antarctica
93 L14 **Muhos** Oulu, C Finland
138 K6 **Muḩ, Sabkhat al** ◎ C Syria
118 E5 **Muhu** *Ger.* Mohn, Moon. *island* W Estonia
81 F19 **Muhutwe** Kagera, NW Tanzania
Muhu Väin see Väinameri
98 J10 **Muiden** Noord-Holland, C Netherlands
193 W15 **Mui Hopohoponga** *headland* Tongatapu, S Tonga
Muinchille see Cootehill
Muineachán see Monaghan
97 F19 **Muine Bheag** *Eng.* Bagenalstown. Carlow, SE Ireland
56 B5 **Muisne** Esmeraldas, NW Ecuador
83 P14 **Muite** Nampula, NE Mozambique
41 Z11 **Mujeres, Isla** *island* E Mexico
116 G7 **Mukacheve** *Hung.* Munkács, *Rus.* Mukachevo. Zakarpats'ka Oblast', W Ukraine
Mukachevo see Mukacheve
169 R9 **Mukah** Sarawak, East Malaysia
Mukalla see Al Mukallā
Mukama see Mokāma
Mukāshafa/Mukashshafah see Mukayshīfah
139 S6 **Mukayshīfah** *var.* Mukāshafa, Mukashshafah. N Iraq
167 R9 **Mukdahan** Mukdahan, E Thailand
Mukden see Shenyang
165 Y15 **Mukojima-rettō** *Eng.* Parry group. *island group* SE Japan
146 M14 **Mukry** Lebap Welaýaty, E Turkmenistan
Muksu see Mughsu
153 U14 **Muktagacha** *var.* Muktagachha Dhaka. N Bangladesh
Muktagachha Dhaka see Muktagacha
82 K13 **Mukuku** Central, C Zambia
82 K11 **Mukupa Kaoma** Northern, NE Zambia
81 I18 **Mukutan** Rift Valley, W Kenya
83 F16 **Mukwe** Caprivi, NE Namibia
105 R13 **Mula** Murcia, SE Spain
151 K20 **Mulaku Atoll** *var.* Meemu Atoll. *atoll* C Maldives
83 J15 **Mulalika** Lusaka, C Zambia
163 X8 **Mulan** Heilongjiang, NE China
83 N15 **Mulanje** *var.* Mlanje. Southern, S Malawi
40 H5 **Mulatos** Sonora, NW Mexico
23 P3 **Mulberry Fork** ≈ Alabama, S USA
39 P12 **Mulchatna River** ≈ Alaska, USA
125 W4 **Mul'da** Respublika Komi, NW Russian Federation
101 M14 **Mulde** ≈ E Germany
27 R10 **Muldrow** Oklahoma, C USA
40 E7 **Mulegé** Baja California Sur, W Mexico
108 I10 **Mulegns** Graubünden, S Switzerland
79 M21 **Mulenda** Kasai Oriental, C Dem. Rep. Congo
24 M4 **Muleshoe** Texas, SW USA
83 O15 **Mulevala** Zambézia, NE Mozambique
183 P5 **Mulgoa Creek** *seasonal river* New South Wales, SE Australia
105 O15 **Mulhacén** *var.* Cerro de Mulhacén. ▲ S Spain
Mulhacén, Cerro de see Mulhacén
Mülhausen see Mulhouse
101 E24 **Mülheim** Baden-Württemberg, SW Germany
101 E15 **Mülheim** *var.* Mulheim an der Ruhr. Nordrhein-Westfalen, W Germany
Mulheim an der Ruhr see Mülheim
103 U7 **Mulhouse** *Ger.* Mülhausen. Haut-Rhin, NE France
160 G11 **Muli** *var.* Qiaowa, Muli Zangzu Zizhixian. Sichuan, C China
171 X15 **Muli** *channel* Papua, E Indonesia
163 Y9 **Muling** Heilongjiang, NE China
Muli Zangzu Zizhixian see Muli
Mullach Íde see Malahide
Mullaitivu see Mullaittivu
155 K23 **Mullaittivu** *var.* Mullaitivu. Northern Province, N Sri Lanka
33 N8 **Mullan** Idaho, NW USA
28 M13 **Mullen** Nebraska, C USA
183 Q6 **Mullengudgery** New South Wales, SE Australia
21 Q6 **Mullens** West Virginia, NE USA
Müller-gerbergte see Muller, Pegunungan
169 T10 **Muller, Pegunungan** *Dut.* Müller-gerbergte. ▲▲ Borneo, C Indonesia
31 Q5 **Mullett Lake** ◎ Michigan, N USA
18 J16 **Mullica River** ≈ New Jersey, NE USA
25 R8 **Mullin** Texas, SW USA
97 E17 **Mullingar** *Ir.* An Muileann gCearr. C Ireland
21 T12 **Mullins** South Carolina, SE USA
96 G11 **Mull, Isle of** *island* W Scotland, UK
127 R5 **Mullovka** Ul'yanovskaya Oblast', W Russian Federation
95 K19 **Mullsjö** Västra Götaland, S Sweden
183 V4 **Mullumbimby** New South Wales, SE Australia
83 H15 **Mulobezi** Western, SW Zambia
83 C15 **Mulondo** Huíla, SW Angola
83 G15 **Mulonga Plain** *plain* W Zambia
79 N23 **Mulongo** Katanga, SE Dem. Rep. Congo
149 T10 **Multān** Punjab, E Pakistan
93 L17 **Multia** Länsi-Soumi, C Finland
Mulucha see Moulouya
83 J14 **Mulungushi** Central, C Zambia
83 K14 **Mulungwe** Central, C Zambia
Muluya see Moulouya
27 N7 **Mulvane** Kansas, C USA
183 O10 **Mulwala** New South Wales, SE Australia
Mulwiya see Moulouya
182 K6 **Mulyungarie** South Australia
154 D13 **Mumbai** *prev.* Bombay. *state capital* Mahārāshtra, W India
154 D13 **Mumbai** ✕ Mahārāshtra, W India
83 D14 **Mumbué** Bié, C Angola
186 E8 **Mumeng** Morobe, C Papua New Guinea
171 V12 **Mumi** Papua, E Indonesia
Muminabad/Mŭ'minobod see Leningrad
127 Q13 **Mumra** Astrakhanskaya Oblast', SW Russian Federation
41 X12 **Muna** Yucatán, SE Mexico
123 O9 **Muna** ≈ NE Russian Federation
152 C12 **Munābāo** Rājasthān, NW India
Munamägi see Suur Munamägi
171 O14 **Muna, Pulau** *prev.* Moena. *island* C Indonesia
101 L18 **Münchberg** Bayern, E Germany
101 L23 **München** *var.* Muenchen, *Eng.* Munich, *It.* Monaco. Bayern, SE Germany
München-Gladbach see Mönchengladbach
108 E6 **Münchenstein** Basel-Land, NW Switzerland
10 L10 **Muncho Lake** British Columbia, W Canada
31 P13 **Muncie** Indiana, N USA
18 G13 **Muncy** Pennsylvania, NE USA
9 Q14 **Mundare** Alberta, SW Canada
25 Q5 **Munday** Texas, SW USA
31 N10 **Mundelein** Illinois, N USA
101 I15 **Münden** Niedersachsen, C Germany
105 Q12 **Mundo** ≈ S Spain
82 B12 **Munenga** Cuanza Sul, NW Angola
105 P11 **Munera** Castilla-La Mancha, C Spain
20 E9 **Munford** Tennessee, S USA
20 K7 **Munfordville** Kentucky, S USA
182 D5 **Mungala** South Australia
83 M16 **Mungári** Manica, C Mozambique
79 O16 **Mungbere** Orientale, NE Dem. Rep. Congo
153 Q13 **Munger** *prev.* Monghyr. Bihār, NE India
182 I2 **Mungeranie** South Australia
Mu Nggava see Rennell
169 O10 **Mungguresak, Tanjung** *cape* Borneo, N Indonesia
Mungiki see Bellona
183 R4 **Mungindi** New South Wales, SE Australia
Mungkawn see Maingkwan
153 T16 **Mungla** *var.* Mongla. Khulna, S Bangladesh
82 C13 **Mungo** Huambo, W Angola
188 F16 **Munguuy Bay** *bay* Yap, W Micronesia
82 E13 **Munhango** Bié, C Angola
Munich see München
105 S7 **Muniesa** Aragón, NE Spain
31 O4 **Munising** Michigan, N USA
Munkács see Mukacheve
95 I17 **Munkedal** Västra Götaland, S Sweden
95 K15 **Munkfors** Värmland, C Sweden
122 M14 **Munku-Sardyk, Gora** *var.* Mönh Sarĭdag. ▲ Mongolia/Russian Federation
99 E18 **Munkzwalm** Oost-Vlaanderen, NW Belgium
167 R10 **Mun, Mae Nam** ≈ E Thailand
153 U15 **Munshiganj** Dhaka, C Bangladesh
108 D8 **Münsingen** Bern, W Switzerland
103 U6 **Munster** Haut-Rhin, NE France
100 J11 **Munster** Niedersachsen, NW Germany
100 F13 **Münster** *var.* Muenster, Münster in Westfalen. Nordrhein-Westfalen, W Germany
108 F10 **Münster** Valais, S Switzerland
97 B20 **Munster** *Ir.* Cúige Mumhan. *cultural region* S Ireland
Münsterberg in Schlesien see Ziębice
Münster in Westfalen see Münster
100 E13 **Münsterland** *cultural region* NW Germany
100 F13 **Münster-Osnabruck** ✕ Nordrhein-Westfalen, NW Germany
31 R4 **Munuscong Lake** ◎ Michigan, N USA
83 K17 **Munyati** ≈ C Zimbabwe
109 R3 **Münzkirchen** Oberösterreich, N Austria
92 K11 **Muodoslompolo** Norrbotten, N Sweden
92 M13 **Muojärvi** ◎ NE Finland
167 S6 **Mương Khên** Hoa Binh, N Vietnam
Muong Sai see Xai
167 Q7 **Muong Xiang Ngeun** *var.* Xieng Ngeun. Louangphabang, N Laos
92 K11 **Muonio** Lappi, N Finland
Muonioälv/Muoniojoki see Muonionjoki
92 K11 **Muonionjoki** *var.* Muoniojoki, *Swe.* Muonioälv. ≈ Finland/Sweden
83 N17 **Mupa** ≈ C Mozambique
83 E16 **Mupini** Okavango, NE Namibia
80 F8 **Muqaddam, Wadi** ≈ N Sudan
138 K9 **Muqāţ** Al Mafraq, E Jordan
141 X7 **Muqaz** N Oman
81 N17 **Muqdisho** *Eng.* Mogadishu, *It.* Mogadiscio. ● (Somalia) Banaadir, S Somalia
81 N17 **Muqdisho** ✕ Banaadir, E Somalia
Muqshin see Mughshin
109 T8 **Mur** *SCr.* Mura. ≈ C Europe
109 X9 **Mura** ≈ NE Slovenia
Mura see Mur
137 T14 **Muradiye** Van, E Turkey
Muragarazi see Maragarazi
165 O10 **Murakami** Niigata, Honshū, C Japan
63 G22 **Murallón, Cerro** ▲ S Argentina
81 E20 **Muramvya** C Burundi
81 I19 **Murang'a** *prev.* Fort Hall. Central, SW Kenya
81 H16 **Murangering** Rift Valley, NW Kenya
Murapara see Murupara
140 M5 **Murār, Bi'r al** *well* NW Saudi Arabia
125 Q13 **Murashi** Kirovskaya Oblast', NW Russian Federation
103 O12 **Murat** Cantal, C France
114 N12 **Muratlı** Tekirdağ, NW Turkey
137 R14 **Murat Nehri** *var.* Eastern Euphrates; *anc.* Arsanias. ≈ NE Turkey
107 D20 **Muravera** Sardegna, Italy, C Mediterranean Sea
165 P10 **Murayama** Yamagata, Honshū, C Japan
121 R13 **Muraysah, Ra's al** *headland* N Libya
104 I6 **Murça** Vila Real, N Portugal
80 Q11 **Murcanyo** Bari, NE Somalia
143 N8 **Mūrcheh Khvort** *var.* Morcheh Khort. Eşfahān, C Iran
185 H15 **Murchison** Tasman, South Island, New Zealand
185 B22 **Murchison Mountains** ▲▲ South Island, New Zealand
180 I10 **Murchison River** ≈ Western Australia
105 R13 **Murcia** Murcia, SE Spain
105 Q13 **Murcia** ⬖ *autonomous community* SE Spain
103 O13 **Mur-de-Barrez** Aveyron, S France
182 G8 **Murdinga** South Australia
28 M10 **Murdo** South Dakota, N USA
15 X6 **Murdochville** Québec, SE Canada
109 W9 **Mureck** Steiermark, SE Austria
114 M13 **Mürefte** Tekirdağ, NW Turkey
116 I10 **Mureş** ⬖ *county* N Romania
84 J11 **Mureş** ≈ Hungary/Romania
Mureş see Maros
Mureşul see Maros/Mureş
102 M16 **Muret** Haute-Garonne, S France
27 T13 **Murfreesboro** Arkansas, C USA
21 W8 **Murfreesboro** North Carolina, SE USA
20 J9 **Murfreesboro** Tennessee, S USA
Murgab see Morghāb, Daryā-ye/Murgap
Murgab see Murghob
146 I14 **Murgap** *Rus.* Murgab. Mary Welaýaty, S Turkmenistan
146 J16 **Murgap** *var.* Deryasy Murgap, Murghab, *Pash.* Daryā-ye Morghāb, *Rus.* Murgab. ≈ Afghanistan/Turkmenistan see also Morghāb, Daryā-ye
Murgap see Morghāb, Daryā-ye
Murgap, Deryasy see Morghāb, Daryā-ye/Murgap
114 H9 **Murgash** ▲ W Bulgaria
Murghab see Morghāb, Daryā-ye/Murgap
147 U13 **Murghob** *Rus.* Murgab. SE Tajikistan
147 U13 **Murghob** *Rus.* Murgab. ≈ SE Tajikistan
181 Z10 **Murgon** Queensland, E Australia
190 I16 **Muri** Rarotonga, S Cook Islands
108 F7 **Muri** Aargau, W Switzerland
108 D8 **Muri** *var.* Muri bei Bern. Bern, W Switzerland
104 K3 **Murias de Paredes** Castilla-León, N Spain
Muri bei Bern see Muri
82 F11 **Muriege** Lunda Sul, NE Angola
189 P14 **Murilo Atoll** *atoll* Hall Islands, C Micronesia
Mūrītānīyah see Mauritania
100 N10 **Müritz** *var.* Müritzee. ◎ NE Germany
Müritzee see Müritz
100 L10 **Müritz-Elde-Kanal** *canal* N Germany
184 K6 **Muriwai Beach** Auckland, North Island, New Zealand
92 J13 **Murjek** Norrbotten, N Sweden
124 J3 **Murmansk** Murmanskaya Oblast', NW Russian Federation
124 I4 **Murmanskaya Oblast'** ⬖ *province* NW Russian Federation
197 V14 **Murmansk Rise** *undersea feature* SW Barents Sea
124 J3 **Murmashi** Murmanskaya Oblast', NW Russian Federation
126 M5 **Murmino** Ryazanskaya Oblast', W Russian Federation
101 K24 **Murnau** Bayern, SE Germany
103 X16 **Muro, Capo di** *headland* Corse, France, C Mediterranean Sea
107 M18 **Muro Lucano** Basilicata, S Italy
127 N4 **Murom** Vladimirskaya Oblast', W Russian Federation
122 I11 **Muromtsevo** Omskaya Oblast', C Russian Federation
165 R5 **Muroran** Hokkaidō, NE Japan
104 G3 **Muros** Galicia, NW Spain
104 F3 **Muros e Noia, Ría de** *estuary* NW Spain
164 H15 **Muroto** Kōchi, Shikoku, SW Japan
164 H15 **Muroto-zaki** Shikoku, SW Japan
116 L7 **Murovani Kurylivtsi** Vinnyts'ka Oblast', C Ukraine
110 G11 **Murowana Goślina** Wielkolpolskie, W Poland
32 M14 **Murphy** Idaho, NW USA
21 N10 **Murphy** North Carolina, SE USA
35 P8 **Murphys** California, W USA
30 L17 **Murphysboro** Illinois, N USA
29 V15 **Murray** Iowa, C USA
20 H8 **Murray** Kentucky, S USA
182 J10 **Murray Bridge** South Australia
175 X2 **Murray Fracture Zone** *tectonic feature* NE Pacific Ocean
192 H11 **Murray, Lake** ◎ SW Papua New Guinea
21 P12 **Murray, Lake** ⊠ South Carolina, SE USA
10 K8 **Murray, Mount** ▲ Yukon Territory, NW Canada
Murray Range see Murray Ridge
173 O3 **Murray Ridge** *var.* Murray Range. *undersea feature* N Arabian Sea
183 N10 **Murray River** ≈ SE Australia
182 K10 **Murrayville** Victoria, SE Australia
149 U5 **Murree** Punjab, E Pakistan
101 I21 **Murrhardt** Baden-Württemberg, S Germany
183 O9 **Murrumbidgee River** ≈ New South Wales, SE Australia
83 P15 **Murrupula** Nampula, NE Mozambique
183 T7 **Murrurundi** New South Wales, SE Australia
109 X9 **Murska Sobota** *Ger.* Olsnitz. NE Slovenia
154 G12 **Murtajāpur** *prev.* Murtazapur. Mahārāshtra, C India
77 S16 **Murtala Muhammed** ✕ (Lagos) Ogun, SW Nigeria
Murtazapur see Murtajāpur
108 C8 **Murten** Neuchâtel, W Switzerland
Murtensee see Morat, Lac de
182 L11 **Murtoa** Victoria, SE Australia
92 N13 **Murtovaara** Oulu, E Finland
Murua Island see Woodlark Island
155 D14 **Murud** Mahārāshtra, W India
184 O9 **Murupara** *var.* Murapara. Bay of Plenty, North Island, New Zealand
191 X12 **Mururoa** *var.* Moruroa. *atoll* Îles Tuamotu, SE French Polynesia
Murviedro see Sagunto
154 J9 **Murwāra** Madhya Pradesh, N India
183 V4 **Murwillumbah** New South Wales, SE Australia
146 H11 **Murzechirla** *prev.* Mirzachirla. Ahal Welaýaty, C Turkmenistan
Murzuk see Murzuq
75 O11 **Murzuq** *var.* Marzūq, Murzuk. SW Libya
Murzuq, Edeyin see Murzuq, Idhān
75 N11 **Murzuq, Ḩamādat** *plateau* W Libya
75 O11 **Murzuq, Idhān** *var.* Edeyin Murzuq. *desert* SW Libya
109 W6 **Mürzzuschlag** Steiermark, E Austria
137 Q14 **Muş** *var.* Mush. Muş, E Turkey
137 Q14 **Muş** *var.* Mush. ⬖ *province* E Turkey
118 G11 **Mūša** ≈ Latvia/Lithuania
186 F9 **Musa** ≈ S Papua New Guinea
75 X8 **Mûsa, Gebel** ▲ NE Egypt
Musaiyib see Al Musayyib
Musa Khel see Mūsa Khel Bāzār
149 R9 **Mūsa Khel Bāzār** *var.* Musa Khel. Baluchistān, SW Pakistan
114 H10 **Musala** ▲ W Bulgaria
168 H10 **Musala, Pulau** *island* W Indonesia
83 I15 **Musale** Southern, S Zambia
141 Y9 **Muşalla** NE Oman
141 W6 **Musandam Peninsula** *Ar.* Masandam Peninsula. *peninsula* N Oman
Musay'īd see Umm Sa'īd
Muscat see Masqaţ
Muscat and Oman see Oman
29 Y14 **Muscatine** Iowa, C USA
Muscat Sīb Airport see Seeb
31 O15 **Muscatuck River** ≈ Indiana, N USA
30 K8 **Muscoda** Wisconsin, N USA
185 F19 **Musgrave, Mount** ▲ South Island, New Zealand
181 P9 **Musgrave Ranges** ▲▲ South Australia
Mush see Muş
138 H12 **Mushayyish, Qaşr al** *castle* Ma'ān, C Jordan
79 H20 **Mushie** Bandundu, W Dem. Rep. Congo
168 M13 **Musi, Air** *prev.* Moesi. ≈ Sumatera, W Indonesia
192 M4 **Musicians Seamounts** *undersea feature* N Pacific Ocean
83 K19 **Musina** *prev.* Messina. Limpopo, NE South Africa
54 D8 **Musinga, Alto** ▲ NW Colombia
29 T2 **Muskeg Bay** *lake bay* Minnesota, N USA
31 O8 **Muskegon** Michigan, N USA
31 O8 **Muskegon Heights** Michigan, N USA
31 P8 **Muskegon River** ≈ Michigan, N USA
31 T14 **Muskingum River** ≈ Ohio, N USA
95 P16 **Muskö** Stockholm, C Sweden
Muskogean see Tallahassee
27 Q10 **Muskogee** Oklahoma, C USA
14 H13 **Muskoka, Lake** ◎ Ontario, S Canada
80 H8 **Musmar** Red Sea, NE Sudan
81 K14 **Musofu** Central, C Zambia
81 G19 **Musoma** Mara, N Tanzania
83 L13 **Musoro** Central, C Zambia
186 F4 **Mussau Island** *island* NE Papua New Guinea
98 P7 **Musselkanaal** Groningen, NE Netherlands
33 V9 **Musselshell River** ≈ Montana, NW USA
82 C12 **Mussende** Cuanza Sul, NW Angola
102 L12 **Mussidan** Dordogne, SW France
99 L25 **Musson** Luxembourg, SE Belgium
152 J9 **Mussoorie** Uttaranchal, N India
Musta see Mosta
152 M13 **Mustafābād** Uttar Pradesh, N India

◆ Country
● Country Capital
◇ Dependent Territory
○ Dependent Territory Capital
⬖ Administrative Regions
✕ International Airport
▲ Mountain
▲▲ Mountain Range
⛰ Volcano
≈ River
◎ Lake
⊠ Reservoir

Mustafakemalpaşa – Nan'an

136 *D12* **Mustafakemalpaşa** Bursa, NW Turkey
Mustafa-Pasha *see* Svilengrad
81 *M15* **Mustahīl** Somali, E Ethiopia
24 *M7* **Mustang Draw** *valley* Texas, SW USA
25 *T14* **Mustang Island** *island* Texas, SW USA
Mustasaari *see* Korsholm
Mustér *see* Disentis
63 *I19* **Musters, Lago** ◎ S Argentina
45 *Y14* **Mustique** *island* C Saint Vincent and the Grenadines
118 *I6* **Mustla** Viljandimaa, S Estonia
118 *J4* **Mustvee** *Ger.* Tschorna. Jõgevamaa, E Estonia
42 *L9* **Musún, Cerro** ▲ NE Nicaragua
183 *T7* **Muswellbrook** New South Wales, SE Australia
111 *M18* **Muszyna** Małopolskie, SE Poland
75 *V10* **Mût** *var.* Mut. C Egypt
136 *I17* **Mut** Mersin, S Turkey
109 *V9* **Muta** N Slovenia
190 *B15* **Mutalau** N Niue
Mu-tan-chiang *see* Mudanjiang
82 *I13* **Mutanda** North Western, NW Zambia
59 *O17* **Mutá, Ponta do** *headland* E Brazil
83 *L17* **Mutare** *var.* Mutari; *prev.* Umtali. Manicaland, E Zimbabwe
Mutari *see* Mutare
54 *D8* **Mutatá** Antioquia, NW Colombia
Mutina *see* Modena
83 *L16* **Mutoko** *prev.* Mtoko. Mashonaland East, NE Zimbabwe
81 *J20* **Mutomo** Eastern, S Kenya
Mutrah *see* Maṭraḩ
Mutsamudu *see* Moutsamoudou
79 *M24* **Mutshatsha** Katanga, S Dem. Rep. Congo
165 *R6* **Mutsu** *var.* Mutu. Aomori, Honshū, N Japan
165 *R6* **Mutsu-wan** *bay* N Japan
108 *E6* **Muttenz** Basel-Land, NW Switzerland
185 *A26* **Muttonbird Islands** *island group* SW New Zealand
Muttra *see* Mathura
Mutu *see* Mutsu
83 *O15* **Mutuáli** Nampula, N Mozambique
82 *D13* **Mutumbo** Bié, C Angola
189 *Y14* **Mutunte, Mount** *var.* Mount Buache. ▲ Kosrae, E Micronesia
155 *K24* **Mutur** Eastern Province, E Sri Lanka
92 *L13* **Muurola** Lappi, NW Finland
162 *M14* **Mu Us Shadi** *var.* Ordos Desert; *prev.* Mu Us Shamo. *desert* N China
Mu Us Shamo *see* Mu Us Shadi
82 *B11* **Muxima** Bengo, NW Angola
124 *I8* **Muyezerskiy** Respublika Kareliya, NW Russian Federation
81 *E20* **Muyinga** NE Burundi
42 *K9* **Muy Muy** Matagalpa, C Nicaragua
Muynak *see* Mo'ynoq
79 *N22* **Muyumba** Katanga, SE Dem. Rep. Congo
149 *V5* **Muzaffarābād** Jammu and Kashmir, NE Pakistan
149 *S10* **Muzaffargarh** Punjab, E Pakistan
152 *J9* **Muzaffarnagar** Uttar Pradesh, N India
153 *P13* **Muzaffarpur** Bihār, N India
158 *H6* **Muzat He** ≈ W China
83 *L15* **Muze** Tete, NW Mozambique
122 *H8* **Muzhi** Yamalo-Nenetskiy Avtonomnyy Okrug, N Russian Federation
102 *H7* **Muzillac** Morbihan, NW France
Muzkol, Khrebet *see* Muzqŭl, Qatorkŭhi
112 *L9* **Mužlja** *Hung.* Felsőmuzslya; *prev.* Gornja Mužlja. Vojvodina, N Serbia
54 *F9* **Muzo** Boyacá, C Colombia
83 *J15* **Muzoka** Southern, S Zambia
39 *Y15* **Muzon, Cape** *headland* Dall Island, Alaska, USA
40 *M6* **Múzquiz** Coahuila de Zaragoza, NE Mexico
147 *U13* **Muzqŭl, Qatorkŭhi** *Rus.* Khrebet Muzkol. ▲▲ SE Tajikistan
158 *G10* **Muztag** ▲ NW China
158 *K10* **Muztag** ▲ W China
158 *D8* **Muztagata** ▲ NW China
83 *K17* **Mvuma** *prev.* Umvuma. Midlands, C Zimbabwe
Mwali *see* Mohéli
82 *L13* **Mwanya** Eastern, E Zambia
79 *N23* **Mwanza** Katanga, SE Dem. Rep. Congo
81 *G20* **Mwanza** Mwanza, NW Tanzania
81 *F20* **Mwanza** ◐ *region* N Tanzania
82 *M13* **Mwase Lundazi** Eastern, E Zambia
97 *B17* **Mweelrea** *Ir.* Caoc Maol Réidh. ▲ W Ireland
79 *K21* **Mweka** Kasai Occidental, C Dem. Rep. Congo
82 *K12* **Mwenda** Luapula, N Zambia
79 *L22* **Mwene-Ditu** Kasai Oriental, S Dem. Rep. Congo
83 *L18* **Mwenezi** ≈ S Zimbabwe
79 *O20* **Mwenga** Sud Kivu, E Dem. Rep. Congo
82 *K11* **Mweru, Lake** *var.* Lac Moero. ◎ Dem. Rep. Congo/Zambia
82 *H13* **Mwinilunga** North Western, NW Zambia
189 *V16* **Mwokil Atoll** *prev.* Mokil Atoll. *atoll* Caroline Islands, E Micronesia
Myadel' *see* Myadzyel
118 *J13* **Myadzyel** *Pol.* Miadzioł Nowy, *Rus.* Myadel'. Minskaya Voblasts', N Belarus
152 *C12* **Myājlār** *var.* Miajlar. Rājasthān, NW India
123 *T9* **Myakit** Magadanskaya Oblast', E Russian Federation
23 *W13* **Myakka River** ≈ Florida, SE USA
124 *L14* **Myaksa** Vologodskaya Oblast', NW Russian Federation
183 *U8* **Myall Lake** ◎ New South Wales, SE Australia
166 *L7* **Myanaung** Irrawaddy, SW Burma (Myanmar)
166 *K8* **Myaungmya** Irrawaddy, SW Burma (Myanmar)
118 *N11* **Myazha** *Rus.* Mezha. Vitsyebskaya Voblasts', NE Belarus
119 *O18* **Myerkulavichy** *Rus.* Merkulovichi. Homyel'skaya Voblasts', SE Belarus
119 *N14* **Myezhava** *Rus.* Mezhëvo. Vitsyebskaya Voblasts', NE Belarus
Myggenaes *see* Mykines
166 *L5* **Myingyan** Mandalay, C Burma (Myanmar)
167 *N12* **Myitkyina** Kachin State, N Burma (Myanmar)
166 *M5* **Myittha** Mandalay, C Burma (Myanmar)
111 *H19* **Myjava** *Hung.* Miava. Trenčiansky Kraj, W Slovakia
Myjeldino *see* Myyëldino
117 *U9* **Mykhaylivka** *Rus.* Mikhaylovka. Zaporiz'ka Oblast', SE Ukraine
95 *A18* **Mykines** *Dan.* Myggenaes. *island* W Faeroe Islands
116 *I5* **Mykolayiv** L'vivs'ka Oblast', W Ukraine
117 *Q10* **Mykolayiv** *Rus.* Nikolayev. Mykolayivs'ka Oblast', S Ukraine
117 *Q10* **Mykolayiv** ✈ Mykolayivs'ka Oblast', S Ukraine
Mykolayiv *see* Mykolayivs'ka Oblast'
117 *P9* **Mykolayivka** Odes'ka Oblast', SW Ukraine
117 *S13* **Mykolayivka** Respublika Krym, S Ukraine
117 *P9* **Mykolayivs'ka Oblast'** *var.* Mykolayiv, *Rus.* Nikolayevskaya Oblast'. ◐ *province* S Ukraine
115 *J20* **Mýkonos** Mńykonos, Kykládes, Greece, Aegean Sea
115 *K20* **Mýkonos** *var.* Míkonos. *island* Kykládes, Greece, Aegean Sea
125 *R7* **Myla** Respublika Komi, NW Russian Federation
Mylae *see* Milazzo
93 *M19* **Myllykoski** Etelä-Suomi, S Finland
Mymensing *see* Mymensingh
153 *U14* **Mymensingh** *var.* Maimansingh, Mymensing; *prev.* Nasirābād. Dhaka, N Bangladesh
93 *K19* **Mynämäki** Länsi-Soumi, SW Finland
145 *S14* **Mynaral** *Kaz.* Myngaral. Zhambyl, S Kazakhstan
Mynbulak *see* Mingbuloq
Mynbulak, Vpadina *see* Mingbuloq Botig'I
Myngaral *see* Mynaral
166 *K5* **Myohaung** Arakan State, W Burma (Myanmar)
163 *W13* **Myohyang-sanmaek** ▲▲ C North Korea
164 *M11* **Myōkō-san** ▲ Honshū, S Japan
83 *J15* **Myooye** Central, C Zambia
118 *K12* **Myory** *prev.* Miyory. Vitsyebskaya Voblasts', N Belarus
92 *J4* **Mýrdalsjökull** *glacier* S Iceland
92 *G10* **Myre** Nordland, C Norway
117 *S5* **Myrhorod** *Rus.* Mirgorod. Poltavs'ka Oblast', NE Ukraine
115 *J15* **Mýrina** *var.* Mírina. Límnos, SE Greece
117 *P5* **Myronivka** *Rus.* Mironovka. Kyyivs'ka Oblast', N Ukraine
21 *U13* **Myrtle Beach** South Carolina, SE USA
32 *F14* **Myrtle Creek** Oregon, NW USA
183 *P11* **Myrtleford** Victoria, SE Australia
32 *E14* **Myrtle Point** Oregon, NW USA
115 *K25* **Mýrtos** Kríti, Greece, E Mediterranean Sea
Myrtoum Mare *see* Mirtóo Pélagos
93 *G17* **Myrviken** Jämtland, C Sweden
95 *I15* **Mysen** Østfold, S Norway
124 *L15* **Myshkin** Yaroslavskaya Oblast', NW Russian Federation
111 *K17* **Myślenice** Malopolskie, S Poland
110 *D10* **Myślibórz** Zachodnio-pomorskie, NW Poland
155 *G20* **Mysore** *var.* Maisur. Karnātaka, W India
Mysore *see* Karnātaka
115 *F21* **Mystrás** *var.* Mistras. Pelopónnisos, S Greece
125 *T12* **Mysy** Permskaya Oblast', NW Russian Federation
111 *K15* **Myszków** Ślaskie, S Poland
167 *T14* **My Tho** *var.* Mi Tho. Tiên Giang, S Vietnam
Mytilene *see* Mytilíni
115 *L17* **Mytilíni** *var.* Mitilíni; *anc.* Mytilene. Lésvos, E Greece
126 *K3* **Mytishchi** Moskovskaya Oblast', W Russian Federation
37 *N3* **Myton** Utah, W USA
92 *K2* **Mývatn** ◎ C Iceland
125 *T11* **Myyëldino** *var.* Myjeldino. Respublika Komi, NW Russian Federation
82 *M13* **Mzimba** Northern, NW Malawi
82 *M12* **Mzuzu** Northern, N Malawi

N

101 *M19* **Naab** ≈ SE Germany
98 *G12* **Naaldwijk** Zuid-Holland, W Netherlands
38 *G12* **Nā'ālehu** *var.* Naalehu. Hawai'i, USA, C Pacific Ocean
93 *K19* **Naantali** *Swe.* Nådendal. Länsi-Soumi, SW Finland
98 *J10* **Naarden** Noord-Holland, C Netherlands
109 *U4* **Naarn** ≈ N Austria
97 *F18* **Naas** *Ir.* An Nás, Nás na Ríogh. Kildare, C Ireland
92 *M9* **Näätämöjoki** *Lapp.* Njávdám. ≈ NE Finland
83 *E23* **Nababeep** *var.* Nababiep. Northern Cape, W South Africa
Nababiep *see* Nababeep
Nabadwip *see* Navadwīp
164 *J14* **Nabari** Mie, Honshū, SW Japan
Nabatié *see* Nabatîyé
138 *G8* **Nabatîyé** *var.* An Nabatīyah at Taḩtā, Nabatié, Nabatiyet et Tahta. SW Lebanon
Nabatiyet et Tahta *see* Nabatîyé
187 *X14* **Nabavatu** Vanua Levu, N Fiji
190 *I2* **Nabeina** *island* Tungaru, W Kiribati
127 *T4* **Naberezhnyye Chelny** *prev.* Brezhnev. Respublika Tatarstan, W Russian Federation
39 *T10* **Nabesna** Alaska, USA
39 *T10* **Nabesna River** ≈ Alaska, USA
75 *N5* **Nabeul** *var.* Nābul. NE Tunisia
152 *I9* **Nābha** Punjab, NW India
171 *W13* **Nabire** Papua, E Indonesia
141 *O15* **Nabī Shu'ayb, Jabal an** ▲ W Yemen
138 *F10* **Nablus** *var.* Nābulus, *Heb.* Shekhem; *anc.* Neapolis, *Bibl.* Shechem. N West Bank
187 *X14* **Nabouwalu** Vanua Levu, N Fiji
Nābul *see* Nabeul
Nābulus *see* Nablus
187 *Y13* **Nabuna** Vanua Levu, N Fiji
83 *Q14* **Nacala** Nampula, NE Mozambique
42 *H8* **Nacaome** Valle, S Honduras
Na Cealla Beaga *see* Killybegs
Na-Ch'ii *see* Nagqu
164 *J15* **Nachikatsuura** *var.* Nachi-Katsuura. Wakayama, Honshū, SE Japan
Nachi-Katsuura *see* Nachikatsuura
81 *J24* **Nachingwea** Lindi, SE Tanzania
111 *F16* **Náchod** Královéhradecký Kraj, N Czech Republic
Na Clocha Liatha *see* Greystones
40 *G3* **Naco** Sonora, NW Mexico
25 *X8* **Nacogdoches** Texas, SW USA
40 *G4* **Nacozari de García** Sonora, NW Mexico
Nada *see* Danzhou
77 *O14* **Nadawli** NW Ghana
104 *I3* **Nadela** Galicia, NW Spain
Nådendal *see* Naantali
144 *M7* **Nadezhdinka** *prev.* Nadezhdinskiy. Kostanay, N Kazakhstan
Nadezhdinskiy *see* Nadezhdinka
Nadgan *see* Nadqān, Qalamat
187 *W14* **Nadi** *prev.* Nandi. Viti Levu, W Fiji
187 *X14* **Nadi** *prev.* Nandi. ✈ Viti Levu, W Fiji
154 *D10* **Nadiād** Gujarāt, W India
Nadikdik *see* Knox Atoll
116 *E11* **Nădlac** *Ger.* Nadlak, *Hung.* Nagylak. Arad, W Romania
Nadlak *see* Nădlac
74 *H6* **Nador** *prev.* Villa Nador. NE Morocco
141 *S9* **Nadqān, Qalamat** *var.* Nadgan. *well* E Saudi Arabia
111 *N22* **Nádudvar** Hajdú-Bihar, E Hungary
121 *O15* **Nadur** Gozo, N Malta
187 *X13* **Naduri** *prev.* Nanduri. Vanua Levu, N Fiji
116 *I7* **Nadvirna** *Pol.* Nadwórna, *Rus.* Nadvornaya. Ivano-Frankivs'ka Oblast', W Ukraine
124 *J8* **Nadvoitsy** Respublika Kareliya, NW Russian Federation
Nadvornaya/Nadwórna *see* Nadvirna
122 *I9* **Nadym** Yamalo-Nenetskiy Avtonomnyy Okrug, N Russian Federation
122 *I9* **Nadym** ≈ C Russian Federation
186 *E7* **Nadzab** Morobe, C Papua New Guinea
95 *C17* **Nærbø** Rogaland, S Norway
95 *I24* **Næstved** Storstrøm, SE Denmark
77 *X13* **Nafada** Gombe, E Nigeria
108 *H8* **Näfels** Glarus, NE Switzerland
115 *E18* **Náfpaktos** *var.* Návpaktos. Dytikí Ellás, C Greece
115 *F20* **Náfplio** *prev.* Návplion. Pelopónnisos, S Greece
139 *U6* **Naft Khāneh** E Iraq
149 *N13* **Nāg** Baluchistān, SW Pakistan
171 *P4* **Naga** *off.* Naga City; *prev.* Nueva Caceres. Luzon, N Philippines
Nagaarzê *see* Nagarzê
Naga City *see* Naga
12 *F11* **Nagagami** ≈ Ontario, S Canada
164 *F14* **Nagahama** Ehime, Shikoku, SW Japan
153 *X12* **Nāga Hills** ▲▲ NE India
165 *P10* **Nagai** Yamagata, Honshū, C Japan
Na Gaibhlte *see* Galty Mountains
39 *N16* **Nagai Island** *island* Shumagin Islands, Alaska, USA
153 *X12* **Nāgāland** ◐ *state* NE India
164 *M11* **Nagano** Nagano, Honshū, S Japan
164 *M12* **Nagano** *off.* Nagano-ken. ◐ *prefecture* Honshū, S Japan
Nagano-ken *see* Nagano
165 *N11* **Nagaoka** Niigata, Honshū, C Japan
153 *W12* **Nagaon** *var.* Nowgong. Assam, NE India
155 *J21* **Nāgappattinam** *var.* Negapatam, Negapattinam. Tamil Nādu, SE India
Nagara Nayok *see* Nakhon Nayok
Nagara Panom *see* Nakhon Phanom
Nagara Pathom *see* Nakhon Pathom
Nagara Sridharmaraj *see* Nakhon Si Thammarat
Nagara Svarga *see* Nakhon Sawan
155 *H16* **Nāgārjuna Sāgar** ⊠ E India
42 *I10* **Nagarote** León, SW Nicaragua
158 *M16* **Nagarzê** *var.* Nagaarzê. Xizang Zizhiqu, W China
164 *C14* **Nagasaki** Nagasaki, Kyūshū, SW Japan
164 *C14* **Nagasaki** *off.* Nagasaki-ken. ◐ *prefecture* Kyūshū, SW Japan
Nagasaki-ken *see* Nagasaki
Nagashima *see* Kii-Nagashima
164 *E12* **Nagato** Yamaguchi, Honshū, SW Japan
152 *F11* **Nāgaur** Rājasthān, NW India
154 *F10* **Nāgda** Madhya Pradesh, C India
98 *L8* **Nagele** Flevoland, N Netherlands
155 *H24* **Nāgercoil** Tamil Nādu, SE India
153 *X12* **Nāginimāra** Nāgāland, NE India
Na Gleannta *see* Glenties
165 *T16* **Nago** Okinawa, Okinawa, SW Japan
154 *K9* **Nāgod** Madhya Pradesh, C India
155 *J26* **Nagoda** Southern Province, S Sri Lanka
101 *G22* **Nagold** Baden-Württemberg, SW Germany
137 *V12* **Nagorno-Karabakh** *var.* Nagorno- Karabakhskaya Avtonomnaya Oblast, *Arm.* Lerrnayin Gharabakh, *Az.* Dağliq Quarabağ, *Rus.* Nagornyy Karabakh. *former autonomous region* SW Azerbaijan
Nagorno- Karabakhskaya Avtonomnaya Oblast *see* Nagorno-Karabakh
123 *Q12* **Nagornyy** Respublika Sakha (Yakutiya), NE Russian Federation
Nagornyy Karabakh *see* Nagorno-Karabakh
125 *R13* **Nagorsk** Kirovskaya Oblast', NW Russian Federation
164 *K13* **Nagoya** Aichi, Honshū, SW Japan
154 *I12* **Nāgpur** Mahārāshtra, C India
156 *K10* **Nagqu** *Chin.* Na-Ch'ii; *prev.* Hei-ho. Xizang Zizhiqu, W China
152 *J8* **Nāg Tibba Range** ▲▲ N India
45 *O8* **Nagua** NE Dominican Republic
111 *H25* **Nagyatád** Somogy, SW Hungary
Nagybánya *see* Baia Mare
Nagybecskerek *see* Zrenjanin
Nagydisznód *see* Cisnădie
Nagyenyed *see* Aiud
111 *N21* **Nagykálló** Szabolcs-Szatmár-Bereg, E Hungary
111 *G25* **Nagykanizsa** *Ger.* Grosskanizsa. Zala, SW Hungary
Nagykároly *see* Carei
111 *K22* **Nagykáta** Pest, C Hungary
Nagykikinda *see* Kikinda
111 *K23* **Nagykőrös** Pest, C Hungary
Nagy-Küküllő *see* Târnava Mare
Nagylak *see* Nădlac
Nagymihály *see* Michalovce
Nagyrőce *see* Revúca
Nagysomkút *see* Şomcuta Mare
Nagysurány *see* Šurany
Nagyszalonta *see* Salonta
Nagyszeben *see* Sibiu
Nagyszentmiklós *see* Sânnicolau Mare
Nagyszöllös *see* Vynohradiv
Nagyszombat *see* Trnava
Nagytapolcsány *see* Topoľčany
Nagyvárad *see* Oradea
165 *S17* **Naha** Okinawa, Okinawa, SW Japan
152 *J8* **Nāhan** Himāchal Pradesh, NW India
Nahang, Rūd-e *see* Nihing
Nahariya *see* Nahariyya
138 *F8* **Nahariyya** *var.* Nahariya. Northern, N Israel
142 *L6* **Nahāvand** *var.* Nehavend. Hamadān, W Iran
101 *F19* **Nahe** ≈ SW Germany
Na H-Iarmhidhe *see* Westmeath
189 *O13* **Nahnalaud** ▲ Pohnpei, E Micronesia
Nahoi, Cape *see* Cumberland, Cape
Nahtavárr *see* Nattavaara
63 *H16* **Nahuel Huapí, Lago** ◎ W Argentina
23 *W7* **Nahunta** Georgia, SE USA
40 *J6* **Naica** Chihuahua, N Mexico
9 *U15* **Naicam** Saskatchewan, S Canada
Naiman Qi *see* Daqin Tal
158 *M4* **Naimin Bulak** *spring* NW China
13 *P6* **Nain** Newfoundland and Labrador, NE Canada
143 *P8* **Nā'īn** Eşfahān, C Iran
152 *K10* **Naini Tāl** Uttaranchal, N India
154 *J11* **Nainpur** Madhya Pradesh, C India
96 *J8* **Nairn** N Scotland, UK
96 *I8* **Nairn** *cultural region* NE Scotland, UK
81 *I19* **Nairobi** ● (Kenya) Nairobi Area, S Kenya
81 *I19* **Nairobi** ✈ Nairobi Area, S Kenya
82 *P13* **Nairoto** Cabo Delgado, NE Mozambique
118 *G3* **Naissaar** *island* N Estonia
Naissus *see* Niš
187 *Z14* **Naitaba** *var.* Naitauba; *prev.* Naitamba. *island* Lau Group, E Fiji
Naitamba/Naitauba *see* Naitaba
81 *I19* **Naivasha** Rift Valley, SW Kenya
81 *H19* **Naivasha, Lake** ◎ SW Kenya
Najaf *see* An Najaf
143 *N8* **Najafābād** *var.* Nejafabad. Eşfahān, C Iran
141 *N7* **Najd** *var.* Nejd. *cultural region* C Saudi Arabia
105 *O4* **Nájera** La Rioja, N Spain
105 *P4* **Najerilla** ≈ N Spain
163 *U7* **Naji** *var.* Arun Qi. Nei Mongol Zizhiqu, N China
152 *J9* **Najībābād** Uttar Pradesh, N India
Najima *see* Fukuoka
163 *Y11* **Najin** NE North Korea
139 *T9* **Najm al Ḩassūn** C Iraq
141 *O13* **Najrān** *var.* Abā as Su'ūd. Najrān, S Saudi Arabia
141 *P12* **Najrān** *var.* Minţaqat al Najrān. ◐ *province* S Saudi Arabia
Najrān, Minţaqat al *see* Najrān
165 *T2* **Nakagawa** Hokkaidō, NE Japan
38 *F9* **Nākālele Point** *var.* Nakalele Point. *headland* Maui, Hawai'i, USA
164 *D13* **Nakama** Fukuoka, Kyūshū, SW Japan
Nakambé *see* White Volta
Nakamti *see* Nek'emtē
164 *F15* **Nakamura** Kōchi, Shikoku, SW Japan
186 *H7* **Nakanai Mountains** ▲▲ New Britain, E Papua New Guinea
164 *H11* **Nakano-shima** *island* Oki-shotō, SW Japan
165 *Q6* **Nakasato** Aomori, Honshū, C Japan
165 *T5* **Nakasatsunai** Hokkaidō, NE Japan
165 *W4* **Nakashibetsu** Hokkaidō, NE Japan
81 *F18* **Nakasongola** C Uganda
165 *T1* **Nakatonbetsu** Hokkaidō, NE Japan
164 *L13* **Nakatsugawa** *var.* Nakatugawa. Gifu, Honshū, SW Japan
Nakatugawa *see* Nakatsugawa
Nakdong *see* Naktong-gang
Nakel *see* Nakło nad Notecią
80 *J8* **Nakfa** N Eritrea
Nakhichevan' *see* Naxçıvan
123 *S15* **Nakhodka** Primorskiy Kray, SE Russian Federation
122 *J8* **Nakhodka** Yamalo-Nenetskiy Avtonomnyy Okrug, N Russian Federation
Nakhon Navok *see* Nakhon Nayok
167 *P11* **Nakhon Nayok** *var.* Nagara Nayok, Nakhon Navok. Nakhon Nayok, C Thailand
167 *O11* **Nakhon Pathom** *var.* Nagara Pathom, Nakorn Pathom. Nakhon Pathom, W Thailand
167 *R8* **Nakhon Phanom** *var.* Nagara Panom. Nakhon Phanom, E Thailand
167 *Q10* **Nakhon Ratchasima** *var.* Khorat, Korat. Nakhon Ratchasima, E Thailand
167 *O9* **Nakhon Sawan** *var.* Muang Nakhon Sawan, Nagara Svarga. Nakhon Sawan, W Thailand
167 *N15* **Nakhon Si Thammarat** *var.* Nagara Sridharmaraj, Nakhon Sithamnaraj. Nakhon Si Thammarat, SW Thailand
Nakhon Sithamnaraj *see* Nakhon Si Thammarat
139 *Y11* **Nakhrash** SE Iraq
10 *I9* **Nakina** British Columbia, W Canada
110 *H9* **Nakło nad Notecią** *Ger.* Nakel. Kujawsko-pomorskie, C Poland
39 *P13* **Naknek** Alaska, USA
152 *H8* **Nakodar** Punjab, NW India
82 *M11* **Nakonde** Northern, NE Zambia
Nakorn Pathom *see* Nakhon Pathom
95 *H24* **Nakskov** Storstrøm, SE Denmark
163 *Y15* **Naktong-gang** *var.* Nakdong, *Jap.* Rakutō-kō. ≈ C South Korea
81 *H18* **Nakuru** Rift Valley, SW Kenya
81 *H19* **Nakuru, Lake** ◎ Rift Valley, C Kenya
9 *O17* **Nakusp** British Columbia, SW Canada
149 *N15* **Nāl** ≈ W Pakistan
162 *M7* **Nalayh** Töv, C Mongolia
153 *V12* **Nalbāri** Assam, NE India
63 *G19* **Nalcayec, Isla** *island* Archipiélago de los Chonos, S Chile
127 *N15* **Nal'chik** Kabardino-Balkarskaya Respublika, SW Russian Federation
155 *I16* **Nalgonda** Andhra Pradesh, C India
153 *S14* **Nalhāti** West Bengal, NE India
153 *U14* **Nalitabari** Dhaka, N Bangladesh
155 *I17* **Nallamala Hills** ▲▲ E India
136 *G12* **Nallıhan** Ankara, NW Turkey
104 *K2* **Nalón** ≈ NW Spain
167 *N3* **Nalong** Kachin State, N Burma (Myanmar)
75 *N8* **Nālūt** NW Libya
171 *T14* **Nama** Pulau Manawoka, E Indonesia
189 *Q16* **Nama** *island* C Micronesia
83 *O16* **Namacurra** Zambézia, NE Mozambique
188 *F9* **Namai Bay** *bay* Babeldaob, N Palau
29 *W2* **Namakan Lake** ◎ Canada/USA
143 *O6* **Namak, Daryācheh-ye** *marsh* N Iran
143 *T6* **Namak, Kavīr-e** *salt pan* NE Iran
167 *O6* **Namaklwe** Shan State, E Burma (Myanmar)
Namaksār, Kowl-e/ Namakzār, Daryācheh-ye *see* Namakzar
148 *I5* **Namakzar** *Pash.* Daryācheh-ye Namakzār, Kowl-e Namaksār. *marsh* Afghanistan/Iran
171 *V15* **Namalau** Pulau Jursian, E Indonesia
81 *I20* **Namanga** Rift Valley, S Kenya
147 *S10* **Namangan** Namangan Viloyati, E Uzbekistan
Namanganskaya Oblast' *see* Namangan Viloyati
147 *R10* **Namangan Viloyati** *Rus.* Namanganskaya Oblast'. ◐ *province* E Uzbekistan
83 *Q14* **Namapa** Nampula, NE Mozambique
83 *C21* **Namaqualand** *physical region* S Namibia
81 *G18* **Namasagali** C Uganda
186 *H6* **Namatanai** New Ireland, NE Papua New Guinea
83 *I14* **Nambala** Central, C Zambia
81 *J23* **Nambanje** Lindi, SE Tanzania
83 *G16* **Nambiya** North West, N Botswana
183 *V2* **Nambour** Queensland, E Australia
183 *V6* **Nambucca Heads** New South Wales, SE Australia
159 *N15* **Nam Co** ◎ W China
167 *R5* **Nâm Cum** Lai Châu, N Vietnam
Namdik *see* Namorik Atoll
167 *T6* **Nam Đinh** Nam Ha, N Vietnam
99 *I20* **Namêche** Namur, SE Belgium
30 *J4* **Namekagon Lake** ◎ Wisconsin, N USA
188 *F10* **Namekakl Passage** *passage* Babeldaob, N Palau
Namen *see* Namur
83 *P15* **Nametil** Nampula, NE Mozambique
163 *X14* **Nam-gang** ≈ C North Korea
163 *Y16* **Nam-gang** ≈ S South Korea
163 *Y17* **Namhae-do** *Jap.* Nankai-tō. *island* S South Korea
Namhoi *see* Foshan
83 *C19* **Namib Desert** *desert* W Namibia
83 *A15* **Namibe** *Port.* Moçâmedes, Mossâmedes. Namibe, SW Angola
83 *A15* **Namibe** ◐ *province* SE Angola
83 *C18* **Namibia** *off.* Republic of Namibia, *var.* South West Africa, *Afr.* Suidwes-Afrika, *Ger.* Deutsch-Südwestafrika; *prev.* German Southwest Africa, South-West Africa. ◆ *republic* S Africa
65 *O17* **Namibia Plain** *undersea feature* S Atlantic Ocean
Namibia, Republic of *see* Namibia
165 *Q11* **Namie** Fukushima, Honshū, C Japan
165 *Q7* **Namioka** Aomori, Honshū, C Japan
40 *I5* **Namiquipa** Chihuahua, N Mexico
159 *P15* **Namjagbarwa Feng** ▲ W China
Namka *see* Doilungdêqên
171 *R13* **Namlea** Pulau Buru, E Indonesia
158 *L16* **Namling** Xizang Zizhiqu, W China
Namnetes *see* Nantes
167 *R8* **Nam Ngum** ≈ C Laos
Namo *see* Namu Atoll
183 *R5* **Namoi River** ≈ New South Wales, SE Australia
189 *Q17* **Namoluk Atoll** *atoll* Mortlock Islands, C Micronesia
189 *O15* **Namonuito Atoll** *atoll* Caroline Islands, C Micronesia
189 *T9* **Namorik Atoll** *var.* Namdik. *atoll* Ralik Chain, S Marshall Islands
167 *Q6* **Nam Ou** ≈ N Laos
32 *M14* **Nampa** Idaho, NW USA
76 *M11* **Nampala** Ségou, W Mali
163 *W14* **Namp'o** SW North Korea
83 *P15* **Nampula** Nampula, NE Mozambique
83 *P15* **Nampula** *off.* Província de Nampula. ◐ *province* NE Mozambique
Nampula, Província de *see* Nampula
163 *W13* **Namsan-ni** NW North Korea
Namslau *see* Namysłów
93 *E15* **Namsos** Nord-Trøndelag, C Norway
93 *F14* **Namsskogan** Nord-Trøndelag, C Norway
167 *O6* **Nam Teng** ≈ E Burma (Myanmar)
167 *P6* **Nam Tha** ≈ N Laos
123 *Q10* **Namsty** Respublika Sakha (Yakutiya), NE Russian Federation
167 *N4* **Namtu** Shan State, E Burma (Myanmar)
10 *J15* **Namu** British Columbia, SW Canada
189 *T7* **Namu Atoll** *var.* Namo. *atoll* Ralik Chain, C Marshall Islands
187 *Y15* **Namuka-i-lau** *island* Lau Group, E Fiji
83 *O15* **Namuli, Mont** ▲ NE Mozambique
83 *P14* **Namuno** Cabo Delgado, N Mozambique
99 *I20* **Namur** *Dut.* Namen. Namur, SE Belgium
99 *H21* **Namur** *Dut.* Namen. ◐ *province* S Belgium
83 *D17* **Namutoni** Kunene, N Namibia
163 *Y16* **Namwŏn** *Jap.* Nangen. S South Korea
111 *H14* **Namysłów** *Ger.* Namslau. Opole, SW Poland
167 *P7* **Nan** *var.* Muang Nan. Nan, NW Thailand
79 *G15* **Nana** ≈ W Central African Republic
165 *R5* **Nanae** Hokkaidō, NE Japan
79 *I14* **Nana-Grébizi** ◐ *prefecture* N Central African Republic
10 *L17* **Nanaimo** Vancouver Island, British Columbia, SW Canada
38 *C9* **Nānākuli** *var.* Nanakuli. O'ahu, Hawai'i, USA
79 *G15* **Nana-Mambéré** ◐ *prefecture* W Central African Republic
161 *R13* **Nan'an** Fujian, SE China

◆ Country
● Country Capital
◇ Dependent Territory
○ Dependent Territory Capital
◐ Administrative Regions
✈ International Airport
▲ Mountain
▲▲ Mountain Range
Volcano
≈ River
◎ Lake
⊠ Reservoir

NANANGO – NEGARA BRUNEI DARUSSALAM

183 *U2* **Nanango** Queensland, E Australia
164 *L11* **Nanao** Ishikawa, Honshū, SW Japan
161 *Q14* **Nan'ao Dao** *island* S China
164 *L10* **Nanatsu-shima** *island* SW Japan
56 *F8* **Nanay, Río** ≈ NE Peru
160 *J8* **Nanbu** Sichuan, C China
163 *X7* **Nancha** Heilongjiang, NE China
161 *P10* **Nanchang** *var.* Nan-ch'ang, Nanch'ang-hsien. *province capital* Jiangxi, S China
Nan-ch'ang *see* Nanchang
Nanch'ang-hsien *see* Nanchang
161 *P11* **Nancheng** *var.* Jianchang. Jiangxi, S China
Nan-ching *see* Nanjing
160 *J9* **Nanchong** Sichuan, C China
160 *J10* **Nanchuan** Chongqing Shi, C China
103 *T5* **Nancy** Meurthe-et-Moselle, NE France
185 *A22* **Nancy Sound** *sound* South Island, New Zealand
152 *L9* **Nanda Devi** ▲ NW India
42 *J11* **Nandaime** Granada, SW Nicaragua
160 *K13* **Nandan** Guangxi Zhuangzu Zizhiqu, S China
155 *H14* **Nānded** Mahārāshtra, C India
183 *S5* **Nandewar Range** ▲▲ New South Wales, SE Australia
Nandi *see* Nadi
160 *E13* **Nanding He** ≈ China/Vietnam
Nándorhgy *see* Oţelu Roşu
154 *E11* **Nandurbār** Mahārāshtra, W India
Nanduri *see* Naduri
155 *I17* **Nandyāl** Andhra Pradesh, E India
161 *P11* **Nanfeng** *var.* Qincheng. Jiangxi, S China
Nang *see* Nangxian
79 *E15* **Nanga Eboko** Centre, C Cameroon
Nangah Serawai *see* Nangaserawai
149 *W4* **Nanga Parbat** ▲ India/Pakistan
169 *R11* **Nangapinoh** Borneo, C Indonesia
149 *R5* **Nangarhār** ⬖ *province* E Afghanistan
169 *S11* **Nangaserawai** *var.* Nangah Serawai. Borneo, C Indonesia
169 *Q12* **Nangatayap** Borneo, C Indonesia
Nangen *see* Namwŏn
103 *P5* **Nangis** Seine-et-Marne, N France
163 *X13* **Nangnim-sanmaek** ▲▲ C North Korea
161 *O4* **Nangong** Hebei, E China
159 *Q14* **Nangqên** *var.* Xangda. Qinghai, C China
167 *Q10* **Nang Rong** Buri Ram, E Thailand
159 *O16* **Nangxian** *var.* Nang. Xizang Zizhiqu, W China
Nan Hai *see* South China Sea
160 *L8* **Nan He** ≈ C China
160 *F12* **Nanhua** *var.* Longchuan. Yunnan, SW China
Naniwa *see* Ōsaka
155 *G20* **Nanjangūd** Karnātaka, W India
161 *Q8* **Nanjing** *var.* Nan-ching, Nanking; *prev.* Chianning, Chian-ning, Kiang-ning, Jiangsu. *province capital* Jiangsu, E China
Nankai-tō *see* Namhae-do
161 *O12* **Nankang** *var.* Rongjiang. Jiangxi, S China
Nanking *see* Nanjing
161 *N13* **Nan Ling** ▲▲ S China
160 *L15* **Nanliu Jiang** ≈ S China
189 *P13* **Nan Madol** *ruins* Temwen Island, E Micronesia
160 *K15* **Nanning** *var.* Nan-ning; *prev.* Yung-ning. Guangxi Zhuangzu Zizhiqu, S China
Nan-ning *see* Nanning
196 *M15* **Nanortalik** ⬖ Kitaa, S Greenland
Nanouki *see* Aranuka
160 *H13* **Nanpan Jiang** ≈ S China
152 *M11* **Nānpāra** Uttar Pradesh, N India
161 *Q12* **Nanping** *var.* Nan-p'ing; *prev.* Yenping. Fujian, SE China
Nan-p'ing *see* Nanping
Nanping *see* Jiuzhaigou
Nanpu *see* Pucheng
161 *R12* **Nanri Dao** *island* SE China
165 *S16* **Nansei-shotō** *Eng.* Ryukyu Islands. *island group* SW Japan
Nansei Syotō Trench *see* Ryukyu Trench
197 *T10* **Nansen Basin** *undersea feature* Arctic Ocean
197 *T10* **Nansen Cordillera** *var.* Arctic Mid Oceanic Ridge, Nansen Ridge. *undersea feature* Arctic Ocean
Nansen Ridge *see* Nansen Cordillera
129 *T9* **Nan Shan** ▲▲ C China
Nansha Qundao *see* Spratly Islands
12 *K3* **Nantais, Lac** ◎ Québec, NE Canada
103 *N5* **Nanterre** Hauts-de-Seine, N France
102 *I8* **Nantes** *Bret.* Naoned; *anc.* Condivincum, Namnetes. Loire-Atlantique, NW France
14 *G17* **Nanticoke** Ontario, S Canada
18 *H13* **Nanticoke** Pennsylvania, NE USA
21 *Y4* **Nanticoke River** ≈ Delaware/Maryland, NE USA
9 *Q17* **Nanton** Alberta, SW Canada
161 *S8* **Nantong** Jiangsu, E China
161 *S13* **Nant'ou** W Taiwan
103 *S10* **Nantua** Ain, E France
19 *Q13* **Nantucket** Nantucket Island, Massachusetts, NE USA
19 *Q13* **Nantucket Island** *island* Massachusetts, NE USA
19 *Q13* **Nantucket Sound** *sound* Massachusetts, NE USA
82 *P13* **Nantulo** Cabo Delgado, N Mozambique
189 *O12* **Nanuh** Pohnpei, E Micronesia
190 *D6* **Nanumaga** *atoll* NW Tuvalu
190 *D5* **Nanumea Atoll** *atoll* NW Tuvalu
59 *O19* **Nanuque** Minas Gerais, SE Brazil
171 *R10* **Nanusa, Kepulauan** *island group* N Indonesia
163 *U4* **Nanweng He** ≈ NE China
160 *I10* **Nanxi** Sichuan, C China
161 *N10* **Nanxian** *var.* Nan Xian, Nanzhou. Hunan, S China
Nan Xian *see* Nanxian
161 *N7* **Nanyang** *var.* Nan-yang. Henan, C China
Nan-yang *see* Nanyang
161 *P6* **Nanyang Hu** ◎ E China
165 *P10* **Nan'yō** Yamagata, Honshū, C Japan
81 *I18* **Nanyuki** Central, C Kenya
160 *M8* **Nanzhang** Hubei, C China
Nanzhou *see* Nanxian
105 *T11* **Nao, Cabo de La** *cape* E Spain
12 *M9* **Naococane, Lac** ◎ Québec, E Canada
153 *S14* **Naogaon** Rajshahi, NW Bangladesh
Naokot *see* Naukot
187 *R13* **Naone** Maewo, C Vanuatu
Naoned *see* Nantes
115 *E14* **Náousa** Kentrikí Makedonía, N Greece
35 *N8* **Napa** California, W USA
39 *O11* **Napaimiut** Alaska, USA
39 *N12* **Napakiak** Alaska, USA
122 *J7* **Napalkovo** Yamalo-Nenetskiy Avtonomnyy Okrug, N Russian Federation
12 *I16* **Napanee** Ontario, SE Canada
39 *N12* **Napaskiak** Alaska, USA
167 *S5* **Na Phac** Cao Bằng, N Vietnam
184 *O11* **Napier** Hawke's Bay, North Island, New Zealand
195 *X3* **Napier Mountains** ▲▲ Antarctica
15 *O13* **Napierville** Québec, SE Canada
23 *W15* **Naples** Florida, SE USA
25 *W5* **Naples** Texas, SW USA
Naples *see* Napoli
160 *I14* **Napo** Guangxi Zhuangzu Zizhiqu, S China
56 *C6* **Napo** ⬖ *province* NE Ecuador
29 *O6* **Napoleon** North Dakota, N USA
31 *R11* **Napoleon** Ohio, N USA
Napoléon-Vendée *see* la Roche-sur-Yon
22 *J9* **Napoleonville** Louisiana, S USA
107 *K17* **Napoli** *Eng.* Naples, *Ger.* Neapel; *anc.* Neapolis. Campania, S Italy
107 *J18* **Napoli, Golfo di** *gulf* S Italy
57 *F7* **Napo, Río** ≈ Ecuador/Peru
191 *W9* **Napuka** *island* Îles Tuamotu, C French Polynesia
142 *J3* **Naqadeh** Āžarbāyjān-e Bākhtarī, NW Iran
139 *U6* **Naqnah** E Iraq
Nar *see* Nera
164 *J14* **Nara** Nara, Honshū, SW Japan
76 *L11* **Nara** Koulikoro, W Mali
149 *R14* **Nāra Canal** *irrigation canal* S Pakistan
182 *K11* **Naracoorte** South Australia
183 *P8* **Naradhan** New South Wales, SE Australia
Naradhivas *see* Narathiwat
56 *B8* **Naranjal** Guayas, W Ecuador
57 *Q19* **Naranjos** Santa Cruz, E Bolivia
41 *Q12* **Naranjos** Veracruz-Llave, E Mexico
159 *Q6* **Naran Sebstein Bulag** *spring* NW China
143 *X12* **Narānū** Sīstān va Balūchestān, SE Iran
164 *B14* **Narao** Nagasaki, Nakadōri-jima, SW Japan
155 *J16* **Narasaraopet** Andhra Pradesh, E India
158 *J5* **Narat** Xinjiang Uygur Zizhiqu, W China
167 *P17* **Narathiwat** *var.* Naradhivas. Narathiwat, SW Thailand
37 *V10* **Nara Visa** New Mexico, SW USA
Nārāyāni *see* Gandak
Narbada *see* Narmada
Narbo Martius *see* Narbonne
103 *P16* **Narbonne** *anc.* Narbo Martius. Aude, S France
Narborough Island *see* Fernandina, Isla
104 *J2* **Narcea** ≈ NW Spain
152 *J9* **Narendranagar** Uttaranchal, N India
Nares Abyssal Plain *see* Nares Plain
64 *G11* **Nares Plain** *var.* Nares Abyssal Plain. *undersea feature* NW Atlantic Ocean
Nares Stræde *see* Nares Strait
197 *P10* **Nares Strait** *Dan.* Nares Stræde. *strait* Canada/Greenland
110 *O9* **Narew** ≈ E Poland
155 *F17* **Nargund** Karnātaka, W India
83 *D20* **Narib** Hardap, S Namibia
Narikrik *see* Knox Atoll
Narin Gol *see* Dong He
54 *B13* **Nariño** *off.* Departamento de Nariño. ⬖ *province* SW Colombia
165 *P13* **Narita** Chiba, Honshū, S Japan
165 *P13* **Narita** ✈ (Tōkyō) Chiba, Honshū, S Japan
Nariya *see* An Nu'ayrīyah
162 *F5* **Nariyn Gol** ≈ Mongolia/Russian Federation
162 *J8* **Nariynteel** *var.* Tsagaan-Ovoo. Övörhangay, C Mongolia
152 *J8* **Nārkanda** Himāchal Pradesh, NW India
92 *L13* **Narkaus** Lappi, NW Finland
154 *E11* **Narmada** *var.* Narbada. ≈ C India
152 *H11* **Narnaul** *var.* Nārnaul. Haryāna, N India
107 *I14* **Narni** Umbria, C Italy
107 *J24* **Naro** Sicilia, Italy, C Mediterranean Sea
Narodichi *see* Narodychi
125 *V7* **Narodnaya, Gora** ▲ NW Russian Federation
117 *N3* **Narodychi** *Rus.* Narodichi. Zhytomyrs'ka Oblast', N Ukraine
126 *J4* **Naro-Fominsk** Moskovskaya Oblast', W Russian Federation
81 *H19* **Narok** Rift Valley, SW Kenya
104 *H2* **Narón** Galicia, NW Spain
183 *S11* **Narooma** New South Wales, SE Australia
Narova *see* Narva
Narovlya *see* Narowlya
149 *W8* **Nārowāl** Punjab, E Pakistan
119 *N20* **Narowlya** *Rus.* Narovlya. Homyel'skaya Voblasts', SE Belarus
93 *J17* **Närpes** *Fin.* Närpiö. Länsi-Soumi, W Finland
Närpiö *see* Närpes
183 *S5* **Narrabri** New South Wales, SE Australia
183 *P9* **Narrandera** New South Wales, SE Australia
183 *Q4* **Narran Lake** ◎ New South Wales, SE Australia
183 *Q4* **Narran River** ≈ New South Wales/Queensland, SE Australia
180 *J13* **Narrogin** Western Australia
183 *Q7* **Narromine** New South Wales, SE Australia
21 *R6* **Narrows** Virginia, NE USA
196 *M15* **Narsarsuaq** ✈ Kitaa, S Greenland
154 *I10* **Narsimhapur** Madhya Pradesh, C India
Narsingdi *see* Narsinghdi
153 *U15* **Narsinghdi** *var.* Narsingdi. Dhaka, C Bangladesh
154 *H9* **Narsinghgarh** Madhya Pradesh, C India
163 *Q11* **Nart** Nei Mongol Zizhiqu, N China
Nartës, Gjol i/Nartës, Laguna e *see* Nartës, Liqeni i
113 *J22* **Nartës, Liqeni i** *var.* Gjol i Nartës, Laguna e Nartës. ◎ SW Albania
115 *F17* **Narthákí** ▲ C Greece
127 *O15* **Nartkala** Kabardino-Balkarskaya Respublika, SW Russian Federation
118 *K3* **Narva** Ida-Virumaa, NE Estonia
118 *K4* **Narva** *prev.* Narova. ≈ Estonia/Russian Federation
118 *J3* **Narva Bay** *Est.* Narva Laht, *Ger.* Narwa-Bucht, *Rus.* Narvskiy Zaliv. *bay* Estonia/Russian Federation
Narva Laht *see* Narva Bay
124 *F13* **Narva Reservoir** *Est.* Narva Veehoidla, *Rus.* Narvskoye Vodokhranilishche. ⊠ Estonia/Russian Federation
Narva Veehoidla *see* Narva Reservoir
92 *H10* **Narvik** Nordland, C Norway
Narvskiy Zaliv *see* Narva Bay
Narvskoye Vodokhranilishche *see* Narva Reservoir
Narwa-Bucht *see* Narva Bay
152 *I9* **Narwāna** Haryāna, NW India
125 *R4* **Nar'yan-Mar** *prev.* Beloshchel'ye, Dzerzhinskiy. Nenetskiy Avtonomnyy Okrug, NW Russian Federation
122 *J12* **Narym** Tomskaya Oblast', C Russian Federation
145 *Y10* **Narymskiy Khrebet** *Kaz.* Naryn Zhotasy. ▲▲ E Kazakhstan
147 *W9* **Naryn** Narynskaya Oblast', C Kyrgyzstan
147 *U8* **Naryn** ≈ Kyrgyzstan/Uzbekistan
145 *W16* **Narynkol** *Kaz.* Narynqol. Almaty, SE Kazakhstan
Naryn Oblasty *see* Narynskaya Oblast'
Narynqol *see* Narynkol
147 *V9* **Narynskaya Oblast'** *Kir.* Naryn Oblasty. ⬖ *province* C Kyrgyzstan
Naryn Zhotasy *see* Narymskiy Khrebet
126 *J6* **Naryshkino** Orlovskaya Oblast', W Russian Federation
95 *L14* **Nås** Dalarna, C Sweden
92 *G13* **Nasafjellet** *Lapp.* Násávárre. ▲ C Norway
93 *H16* **Näsåker** Västernorrland, C Sweden
187 *Y14* **Nasau** Koro, C Fiji
116 *I9* **Năsăud** *Ger.* Nussdorf, *Hung.* Naszód. Bistriţa-Năsăud, N Romania
Násávárre *see* Nasafjellet
103 *P13* **Nasbinals** Lozère, S France
Na Sceirí *see* Skerries
Nase *see* Naze
185 *E22* **Naseby** Otago, South Island, New Zealand
143 *R10* **Nāşerīyeh** Kermān, C Iran
25 *X5* **Nash** Texas, SW USA
154 *E13* **Nāshik** *prev.* Nāsik. Mahārāshtra, W India
56 *E7* **Nashiño, Río** ≈ Ecuador/Peru
29 *W12* **Nashua** Iowa, C USA
33 *W7* **Nashua** Montana, NW USA
19 *O10* **Nashua** New Hampshire, NE USA
27 *S13* **Nashville** Arkansas, C USA
23 *U7* **Nashville** Georgia, SE USA
30 *L16* **Nashville** Illinois, N USA
31 *O14* **Nashville** Indiana, N USA
21 *V9* **Nashville** North Carolina, SE USA
20 *J8* **Nashville** *state capital* Tennessee, S USA
20 *J9* **Nashville** ✈ Tennessee, S USA
64 *H10* **Nashville Seamount** *undersea feature* NW Atlantic Ocean
112 *H9* **Našice** Osijek-Baranja, E Croatia
110 *M11* **Nasielsk** Mazowieckie, C Poland
93 *K18* **Näsijärvi** ◎ SW Finland
Nāsik *see* Nāshik
80 *G13* **Nasir** Upper Nile, SE Sudan
149 *Q12* **Nasīrābād** Baluchistān, SW Pakistan
148 *K15* **Nasīrābād** Baluchistān, SW Pakistan
Nasīrābād *see* Mymensingh
Nasir, Buhayrat/Nâṣir,Buḥeiret *see* Nasser, Lake
Nāsiri *see* Ahvāz
Nasiriya *see* An Nāṣirīyah
Nás na Ríogh *see* Naas
107 *L23* **Naso** Sicilia, Italy, C Mediterranean Sea
Nasratabad *see* Zābol
10 *J11* **Nass** ≈ British Columbia, SW Canada
77 *V15* **Nassarawa** Nassarawa, C Nigeria
44 *H2* **Nassau** ● (Bahamas) New Providence, N Bahamas
44 *H2* **Nassau** ✈ New Providence, C Bahamas
190 *J13* **Nassau** *island* N Cook Islands
23 *W8* **Nassau Sound** *sound* Florida, SE USA
108 *L7* **Nassereith** Tirol, W Austria
75 *X11* **Nasser, Lake** ◎ Egypt/Sudan
80 *F5* **Nasser, Lake** *var.* Buhayrat Nasir, Buḥayrat Nāṣir, Buḥeiret Nâṣir. ◎ Egypt/Sudan
95 *L19* **Nässjö** Jönköping, S Sweden
99 *K22* **Nassogne** Luxembourg, SE Belgium
12 *J6* **Nastapoka Islands** *island group* Northwest Territories, C Canada
93 *M19* **Nastola** Etelä-Suomi, S Finland
171 *O4* **Nasugbu** Luzon, N Philippines
94 *N11* **Näsviken** Gävleborg, C Sweden
Naszód *see* Năsăud
83 *I17* **Nata** Central, NE Botswana
54 *E11* **Natagaima** Tolima, C Colombia
59 *Q14* **Natal** *state capital* Rio Grande do Norte, E Brazil
168 *I11* **Natal** Sumatera, N Indonesia
Natal *see* KwaZulu/Natal
173 *L10* **Natal Basin** *var.* Mozambique Basin. *undersea feature* W Indian Ocean
25 *R12* **Natalia** Texas, SW USA
67 *W15* **Natal Valley** *undersea feature* SW Indian Ocean
Natanya *see* Netanya
143 *O7* **Naṭanz** Eşfahān, C Iran
13 *Q11* **Natashquan** Québec, E Canada
13 *Q10* **Natashquan** ≈ Newfoundland and Labrador/Québec, E Canada
22 *J7* **Natchez** Mississippi, S USA
22 *G6* **Natchitoches** Louisiana, S USA
108 *E10* **Naters** Valais, S Switzerland
Nathanya *see* Netanya
92 *O3* **Nathorst Land** *physical region* W Svalbard
186 *E9* **National Capital District** ⬖ *province* S Papua New Guinea
35 *U17* **National City** California, W USA
184 *M10* **National Park** Manawatu-Wanganui, North Island, New Zealand
77 *R14* **Natitingou** NW Benin
40 *B5* **Natividad, Isla** *island* W Mexico
165 *Q10* **Natori** Miyagi, Honshū, C Japan
18 *C14* **Natrona Heights** Pennsylvania, NE USA
81 *H20* **Natron, Lake** ◎ Kenya/Tanzania
Natsrat *see* Naẓerat
166 *L7* **Nattalin** Pegu, C Burma (Myanmar)
92 *J12* **Nattavaara** *Lapp.* Nahtavárr. Norrbotten, N Sweden
109 *S3* **Natternbach** Oberösterreich, N Austria
95 *M22* **Nättraby** Blekinge, S Sweden
169 *P10* **Natuna Besar, Pulau** *island* Kepulauan Natuna, W Indonesia
Natuna Islands *see* Natuna, Kepulauan
169 *O9* **Natuna, Kepulauan** *var.* Natuna Islands. *island group* W Indonesia
169 *N9* **Natuna, Laut** *sea* W Indonesia
21 *N6* **Natural Bridge** *tourist site* Kentucky, C USA
173 *V11* **Naturaliste Fracture Zone** *tectonic feature* E Indian Ocean
174 *J10* **Naturaliste Plateau** *undersea feature* E Indian Ocean
Nau *see* Nov
103 *O14* **Naucelle** Aveyron, S France
83 *D20* **Nauchas** Hardap, C Namibia
108 *K9* **Nauders** Tirol, W Austria
Naugard *see* Nowogard
118 *F12* **Naujamiestis** Panevėžys, C Lithuania
118 *E10* **Naujoji Akmenė** Šiaulai, NW Lithuania
149 *R16* **Naukot** *var.* Naokot. Sind, SE Pakistan
101 *L16* **Naumburg** *var.* Naumburg an der Saale. Sachsen-Anhalt, C Germany
Naumburg am Queis *see* Nowogrodziec
Naumburg an der Saale *see* Naumburg
191 *W15* **Naunau** *ancient monument* Easter Island, Chile, E Pacific Ocean
138 *G10* **Nā'ūr** 'Ammān, W Jordan
189 *Q8* **Nauru** *off.* Republic of Nauru; *prev.* Pleasant Island. ◆ *republic* W Pacific Ocean
175 *P5* **Nauru** *island* W Pacific Ocean
189 *Q9* **Nauru International** ✈ S Nauru
Nauru, Republic of *see* Nauru
Nausari *see* Navsāri
19 *Q12* **Nauset Beach** *beach* Massachusetts, NE USA
Naushahra *see* Nowshera
149 *P14* **Naushahro Firoz** Sind, SE Pakistan
Naushara *see* Nowshera
187 *X14* **Nausori** Viti Levu, W Fiji
56 *F9* **Nauta** Loreto, N Peru
153 *O12* **Nautanwa** Uttar Pradesh, N India
41 *R13* **Nautla** Veracruz-Llave, E Mexico
Nauzad *see* Now Zād
41 *N6* **Nava** Coahuila de Zaragoza, NE Mexico
Navabad *see* Navobod
104 *L6* **Nava del Rey** Castilla-León, N Spain
153 *S15* **Navadwīp** *prev.* Nabadwip. West Bengal, NE India
104 *M9* **Navahermosa** Castilla-La Mancha, C Spain
119 *I16* **Navahrudak** *Pol.* Nowogródek, *Rus.* Novogrudok. Hrodzyenskaya Voblasts', W Belarus
119 *I16* **Navahrudskaye Wzvyshsha** ▲▲ W Belarus
36 *M8* **Navajo Mount** ▲ Utah, W USA
37 *Q9* **Navajo Reservoir** ⊠ New Mexico, SW USA
104 *K9* **Navalmoral de la Mata** Extremadura, W Spain
104 *K10* **Navalvillar de Pelea** Extremadura, W Spain
97 *F17* **Navan** *Ir.* An Uaimh. E Ireland
Navanagar *see* Jāmnagar
118 *L12* **Navapolatsk** *Rus.* Novopolotsk. Vitsyebskaya Voblasts', N Belarus
149 *P6* **Nāvar, Dasht-e** *Pash.* Dasht-i-Nawar. *desert* C Afghanistan
123 *W6* **Navarin, Mys** *cape* NE Russian Federation
63 *J25* **Navarino, Isla** *island* S Chile
105 *Q4* **Navarra** *Eng./Fr.* Navarre. ⬖ *autonomous community* N Spain
Navarre *see* Navarra
105 *P4* **Navarrete** La Rioja, N Spain
61 *C20* **Navarro** Buenos Aires, E Argentina
105 *O12* **Navas de San Juan** Andalucía, S Spain
25 *V10* **Navasota** Texas, SW USA
25 *U9* **Navasota River** ≈ Texas, SW USA
44 *I9* **Navassa Island** ◇ *US unincorporated territory* C West Indies
119 *L19* **Navasyolki** *Rus.* Novosëlki. Homyel'skaya Voblasts', SE Belarus
119 *H17* **Navayel'nya** *Pol.* Nowojelnia, *Rus.* Novoyel'nya. Hrodzyenskaya Voblasts', W Belarus
171 *Y13* **Naver** Papua, E Indonesia
118 *H5* **Navesti** ≈ C Estonia
104 *J2* **Navia** Asturias, N Spain
104 *J2* **Navia** ≈ NW Spain
59 *I21* **Naviraí** Mato Grosso do Sul, SW Brazil
126 *I6* **Navlya** Bryanskaya Oblast', W Russian Federation
187 *X13* **Navoalevu** Vanua Levu, N Fiji
147 *R12* **Navobod** *Rus.* Navabad, Novabad. C Tajikistan
147 *P13* **Navobod** *Rus.* Navabad. W Tajikistan
Navoi *see* Navoiy
146 *M11* **Navoiy** *Rus.* Navoi. Navoiy Viloyati, C Uzbekistan
Navoiyskaya Oblast' *see* Navoiy Viloyati
146 *K8* **Navoiy Viloyati** *Rus.* Navoiyskaya Oblast'. ⬖ *province* N Uzbekistan
40 *G7* **Navojoa** Sonora, NW Mexico
Navolat *see* Navolato
40 *H9* **Navolato** *var.* Navolat. Sinaloa, C Mexico
187 *Q13* **Navonda** Ambae, C Vanuatu
Návpaktos *see* Náfpaktos
Návplion *see* Náfplio
77 *P14* **Navrongo** N Ghana
154 *D12* **Navsāri** *var.* Nausari. Gujarāt, W India
187 *X15* **Navua** Viti Levu, W Fiji
138 *H8* **Nawá** Dar'ā, S Syria
Nawabashah *see* Nawābshāh
153 *S14* **Nawabganj** Rajshahi, NW Bangladesh
153 *S14* **Nawābganj** Uttar Pradesh, N India
149 *Q15* **Nawābshāh** *var.* Nawabashah. Sind, S Pakistan
153 *P14* **Nawāda** Bihār, N India
152 *H11* **Nawalgarh** Rājasthān, N India
Nawāl, Sabkhat an *see* Noual, Sebkhet en
Nawar, Dasht-i- *see* Nāvar, Dasht-e
167 *N4* **Nawnghkio** *var.* Nawngkio. Shan State, C Burma (Myanmar)
Nawngkio *see* Nawnghkio
137 *U13* **Naxçıvan** *Rus.* Nakhichevan'. SW Azerbaijan
160 *I10* **Naxi** Sichuan, C China
115 *K21* **Náxos** *var.* Naxos. Náxos, Kykládes, Greece, Aegean Sea
115 *K21* **Náxos** *island* Kykládes, Greece, Aegean Sea
40 *J11* **Nayarit** ⬖ *state* C Mexico
187 *Y14* **Nayau** *island* Lau Group, E Fiji
143 *S8* **Nāy Band** Yazd, E Iran
165 *T2* **Nayoro** Hokkaidō, NE Japan
104 *F9* **Nazaré** *var.* Nazare. Leiria, C Portugal
Nazare *see* Nazaré
24 *M4* **Nazareth** Texas, SW USA
Nazareth *see* Naẓerat
173 *O8* **Nazareth Bank** *undersea feature* W Indian Ocean
40 *K9* **Nazas** Durango, C Mexico
57 *F16* **Nazca** Ica, S Peru
0 *L17* **Nazca Plate** *tectonic feature*
193 *U9* **Nazca Ridge** *undersea feature* E Pacific Ocean
165 *V15* **Naze** *var.* Nase. Kagoshima, Amami-ōshima, SW Japan
138 *G9* **Naẓerat** *var.* Natsrat, *Ar.* En Nazira, *Eng.* Nazareth. Northern, N Israel
137 *R14* **Nazik Gölü** ◎ E Turkey
136 *C15* **Nazilli** Aydın, SW Turkey
137 *P14* **Nazimiye** Tunceli, E Turkey
Nazinon *see* Red Volta
10 *L15* **Nazko** British Columbia, SW Canada
127 *O16* **Nazran'** Ingushskaya Respublika, SW Russian Federation
80 *J13* **Nazrēt** *var.* Adama, Hadama. Oromo, C Ethiopia
Nazwāh *see* Nizwá
82 *J13* **Nchanga** Copperbelt, C Zambia
82 *J11* **Nchelenge** Luapula, N Zambia
Ncheu *see* Ntcheu
Ndaghamcha, Sebkra de *see* Te-n-Dghâmcha, Sebkhet
81 *G21* **Ndala** Tabora, C Tanzania
82 *B11* **N'Dalatando** *Port.* Salazar, Vila Salazar. Cuanza Norte, NW Angola
77 *S14* **Ndali** C Benin
81 *E18* **Ndeke** SW Uganda
78 *J13* **Ndélé** Bamingui-Bangoran, N Central African Republic
79 *E19* **Ndendé** Ngounié, S Gabon
79 *E20* **Ndindi** Nyanga, S Gabon
78 *G11* **Ndjamena** *var.* N'Djamena; *prev.* Fort-Lamy. ● (Chad) Chari-Baguirmi, W Chad
78 *G11* **Ndjamena** ✈ Chari-Baguirmi, W Chad
N'Djamena *see* Ndjamena
79 *D18* **Ndjolé** Moyen-Ogooué, W Gabon
82 *J13* **Ndola** Copperbelt, C Zambia
Ndrhamcha, Sebkha de *see* Te-n-Dghâmcha, Sebkhet
79 *L15* **Ndu** Orientale, N Dem. Rep. Congo
81 *H21* **Nduguti** Singida, C Tanzania
186 *M9* **Nduindui** Guadalcanal, C Solomon Islands
Nduke *see* Kolombangara
115 *F16* **Néa Anchiálos** *var.* Nea Anhialos, Néa Ankhíalos. Thessalía, C Greece
Nea Anhialos/Néa Ankhíalos *see* Néa Anchiálos
115 *H18* **Néa Artáki** Évvoia, C Greece
97 *F15* **Neagh, Lough** ◎ E Northern Ireland, UK
32 *F7* **Neah Bay** Washington, NW USA
115 *J22* **Nea Kaméni** *island* Kykládes, Greece, Aegean Sea
181 *O8* **Neale, Lake** ◎ Northern Territory, C Australia
182 *G2* **Neales River** *seasonal river* South Australia
115 *G14* **Néa Moudanía** *var.* Néa Moudhaniá. Kentrikí Makedonía, N Greece
Néa Moudhaniá *see* Néa Moudanía
116 *K10* **Neamţ** ⬖ *county* NE Romania
Neapel *see* Napoli
115 *D14* **Neápoli** *prev.* Neápolis. Dytikí Makedonía, N Greece
115 *K25* **Neápoli** Kríti, Greece, E Mediterranean Sea
115 *G22* **Neápoli** Pelopónnisos, S Greece
Neápolis *see* Neápoli, Greece
Neapolis *see* Napoli, Italy
Neapolis *see* Nablus, West Bank
38 *D16* **Near Islands** *island group* Aleutian Islands, Alaska, USA
97 *J21* **Neath** S Wales, UK
114 *H13* **Néa Zíchni** *var.* Néa Zíkhni; *prev.* Néa Zíkhna. Kentrikí Makedonía, NE Greece
Néa Zíkhna/Néa Zíkhni *see* Néa Zíchni
42 *C5* **Nebaj** Quiché, W Guatemala
77 *P13* **Nebbou** S Burkina
Nebitdag *see* Balkanabat
54 *M13* **Neblina, Pico da** ▲ NW Brazil
124 *I13* **Nebolchi** Novgorodskaya Oblast', W Russian Federation
36 *L4* **Nebo, Mount** ▲ Utah, W USA
28 *L14* **Nebraska** *off.* State of Nebraska, *also known as* Blackwater State, Cornhusker State, Tree Planters State. ⬖ *state* C USA
29 *S16* **Nebraska City** Nebraska, C USA
107 *K23* **Nebrodi, Monti** *var.* Monti Caronie. ▲▲ Sicilia, Italy, C Mediterranean Sea
10 *L14* **Nechako** ≈ British Columbia, SW Canada
29 *Q2* **Neche** North Dakota, N USA
25 *V8* **Neches** Texas, SW USA
25 *W8* **Neches River** ≈ Texas, SW USA
101 *H20* **Neckar** ≈ SW Germany
101 *H20* **Neckarsulm** Baden-Württemberg, SW Germany
192 *L5* **Necker Island** *island* C British Virgin Islands
175 *U3* **Necker Ridge** *undersea feature* N Pacific Ocean
61 *D23* **Necochea** Buenos Aires, E Argentina
104 *H2* **Neda** Galicia, NW Spain
115 *E20* **Néda** *var.* Nédas. ≈ S Greece
Nédas *see* Néda
25 *Y11* **Nederland** Texas, SW USA
Nederland *see* Netherlands
98 *K12* **Neder Rijn** *Eng.* Lower Rhine. ≈ C Netherlands
99 *L16* **Nederweert** Limburg, SE Netherlands
95 *G16* **Nedre Tokke** ◎ S Norway
Nedrigaylov *see* Nedryhayliv
117 *S3* **Nedryhayliv** *Rus.* Nedrigaylov. Sums'ka Oblast', NE Ukraine
98 *O11* **Neede** Gelderland, E Netherlands
33 *T13* **Needle Mountain** ▲ Wyoming, C USA
35 *Y14* **Needles** California, W USA
97 *M24* **Needles, The** *rocks* S England, UK
62 *O7* **Ñeembucú** *off.* Departamento de Ñeembucú. ⬖ *department* SW Paraguay
Ñeembucú, Departamento de *see* Ñeembucú
30 *M7* **Neenah** Wisconsin, N USA
9 *W16* **Neepawa** Manitoba, S Canada
99 *K16* **Neerpelt** Limburg, NE Belgium
74 *M6* **Nefta** ✈ W Tunisia
126 *L15* **Neftegorsk** Krasnodarskiy Kray, SW Russian Federation
127 *U3* **Neftekamsk** Respublika Bashkortostan, W Russian Federation
127 *O14* **Neftekumsk** Stavropol'skiy Kray, SW Russian Federation
Neftezavodsk *see* Seýdi
82 *C10* **Negage** *var.* N'Gage. Uíge, NW Angola
Negapatam/Negapattinam *see* Nāgappattinam
169 *T17* **Negara** Bali, Indonesia
169 *T13* **Negara** Borneo, C Indonesia
Negara Brunei Darussalam *see* Brunei

◆ Country
● Country Capital
◇ Dependent Territory
○ Dependent Territory Capital
⬖ Administrative Regions
✈ International Airport
▲ Mountain
▲▲ Mountain Range
⛰ Volcano
≈ River
◎ Lake
⊠ Reservoir

NEGAUNEE – NGALA

31 N4 **Negaunee** Michigan, N USA
81 J15 **Negēlē** *var.* Negelli, *It.* Neghelli. Oromo, C Ethiopia
Negelli *see* Negēlē
Negeri Pahang Darul Makmur *see* Pahang
Negeri Selangor Darul Ehsan *see* Selangor
168 K9 **Negeri Sembilan** *var.* Negri Sembilan. ⬖ *state* Peninsular Malaysia
92 P3 **Negerpynten** *headland* S Svalbard
Negev *see* HaNegev
Neghelli *see* Negēlē
116 I12 **Negoiu** *var.* Negoiul. ▲ S Romania
Negoiul *see* Negoiu
82 P13 **Negomane** *var.* Negomano. Cabo Delgado, N Mozambique
Negomano *see* Negomane
155 J25 **Negombo** Western Province, SW Sri Lanka
Negoreloye *see* Nyeharelaye
112 P12 **Negotin** Serbia, E Serbia
113 P15 **Negotino** C Macedonia
56 A10 **Negra, Punta** *point* NW Peru
104 G3 **Negreira** Galicia, NW Spain
116 L10 **Negrești** Vaslui, E Romania
Negrești *see* Negrești-Oaș
116 H8 **Negrești-Oaș** *Hung.* Avasfelsőfalu; *prev.* Negrești. Satu Mare, NE Romania
44 H12 **Negril** W Jamaica
Negri Sembilan *see* Negeri Sembilan
63 K15 **Negro, Río** ≈ E Argentina
62 N7 **Negro, Río** ≈ NE Argentina
57 N17 **Negro, Río** ≈ E Bolivia
48 F6 **Negro, Rio** ≈ N South America
61 E18 **Negro, Río** ≈ Brazil/Uruguay
62 O5 **Negro, Río** ≈ C Paraguay
Negro, Río *see* Chixoy, Río
Negro, Río *see* Sico Tinto, Río
171 P6 **Negros** *island* C Philippines
116 M15 **Negru Vodă** Constanța, SE Romania
13 P13 **Neguac** New Brunswick, SE Canada
14 B7 **Negwazu, Lake** ◎ Ontario, S Canada
Négyfalu *see* Săcele
32 F10 **Nehalem** Oregon, NW USA
32 F10 **Nehalem River** ≈ Oregon, NW USA
Nehavend *see* Nahāvand
143 V9 **Nehbandān** Khorāsān, E Iran
163 V6 **Nehe** Heilongjiang, NE China
193 Y14 **Neiafu** 'Uta Vava'u, N Tonga
45 N9 **Neiba** *var.* Neyba. SW Dominican Republic
Néid, Carn Uí *see* Mizen Head
92 M9 **Neiden** Finnmark, N Norway
Neidín *see* Kenmare
Néifinn *see* Nephin
103 S10 **Neige, Crêt de la** ▲ E France
173 O16 **Neiges, Piton des** ▲ C Réunion
15 R9 **Neiges, Rivière des** ≈ Québec, SE Canada
160 I10 **Neijiang** Sichuan, C China
30 K6 **Neillsville** Wisconsin, N USA
Nei Monggol Zizhiqu/Nei Mongol *see* Nei Mongol Zizhiqu
163 Q10 **Nei Mongol Gaoyuan** *plateau* NE China
163 O12 **Nei Mongol Zizhiqu** *var.* Nei Mongol, *Eng.* Inner Mongolia, Inner Mongolian Autonomous Region; *prev.* Nei Monggol Zizhiqu. ⬖ *autonomous region* N China
161 O4 **Neiqiu** Hebei, E China
Neiriz *see* Neyrīz
101 Q16 **Neisse** *Pol.* Nisa *Cz.* Lužická Nisa, *Ger.* Lausitzer Neisse, Nysa Łużycka. ≈ C Europe
Neisse *see* Nysa
54 E11 **Neiva** Huila, S Colombia
160 M7 **Neixiang** Henan, C China
Nejafabad *see* Najafābād
9 V9 **Nejanilini Lake** ◎ Manitoba, C Canada
Nejd *see* Najd
80 I13 **Nek'emtē** *var.* Lakemti, Nakamti. Oromo, C Ethiopia
126 M9 **Nekhayevskiy** Volgogradskaya Oblast', SW Russian Federation
30 K7 **Nekoosa** Wisconsin, N USA
Neksø Bornholm *see* Nexø
115 C16 **Nekyomanteío** *ancient monument* Ípeiros, W Greece
104 H7 **Nelas** Viseu, N Portugal
124 H16 **Nelidovo** Tverskaya Oblast', W Russian Federation
29 P13 **Neligh** Nebraska, C USA
123 R11 **Nel'kan** Khabarovskiy Kray, E Russian Federation
92 M10 **Nellim** *var.* Nellimö, *Lapp.* Njellim. Lappi, N Finland
Nellimö *see* Nellim
155 J18 **Nellore** Andhra Pradesh, E India
123 T14 **Nel'ma** Khabarovskiy Kray, SE Russian Federation
61 B17 **Nelson** Santa Fe, C Argentina
9 O17 **Nelson** British Columbia, SW Canada
185 I14 **Nelson** Nelson, South Island, New Zealand
97 L17 **Nelson** NW England, UK
29 P17 **Nelson** Nebraska, C USA
185 J14 **Nelson** ⬖ *unitary authority* South Island, New Zealand
9 X12 **Nelson** ≈ Manitoba, C Canada
183 U8 **Nelson Bay** New South Wales, SE Australia
182 K13 **Nelson, Cape** *headland* Victoria, SE Australia
63 G23 **Nelson, Estrecho** *strait* SE Pacific Ocean
9 W12 **Nelson House** Manitoba, C Canada
30 J4 **Nelson Lake** ◎ Wisconsin, N USA
31 T14 **Nelsonville** Ohio, N USA
27 S2 **Nelsoon River** ≈ Iowa/Missouri, C USA
83 K21 **Nelspruit** Mpumalanga, NE South Africa
76 L10 **Néma** Hodh ech Chargui, SE Mauritania
118 D13 **Neman** *Ger.* Ragnit. Kaliningradskaya Oblast', W Russian Federation
84 I9 **Neman** *Bel.* Nyoman, *Ger.* Memel, *Lith.* Nemunas, *Pol.* Niemen, *Rus.* Neman. ≈ NE Europe
Nemausus *see* Nîmes
115 F19 **Neméa** Pelopónnisos, S Greece
Německý Brod *see* Havlíčkův Brod
14 D7 **Nemegosenda** ≈ Ontario, S Canada
14 D8 **Nemegosenda Lake** ◎ Ontario, S Canada
119 H14 **Nemencinė** Vilnius, SE Lithuania
Nemetocenna *see* Arras
Nemirov *see* Nemyriv
103 O6 **Nemours** Seine-et-Marne, N France
Nemunas *see* Neman
165 W4 **Nemuro** Hokkaidō, NE Japan
165 W4 **Nemuro-hantō** *peninsula* Hokkaidō, NE Japan
165 W3 **Nemuro-kaikyō** *strait* Japan/Russian Federation
165 W4 **Nemuro-wan** *bay* N Japan
116 H5 **Nemyriv** *Rus.* Nemirov. L'vivs'ka Oblast', NW Ukraine
117 N7 **Nemyriv** *Rus.* Nemirov. Vinnyts'ka Oblast', C Ukraine
97 D19 **Nenagh** *Ir.* An tAonach. Tipperary, C Ireland
39 R9 **Nenana** Alaska, USA
39 R9 **Nenana River** ≈ Alaska, USA
187 P10 **Nendö** *var.* Swallow Island. *island* Santa Cruz Islands, E Solomon Islands
97 O19 **Nene** ≈ E England, UK
125 R4 **Nenetskiy Avtonomnyy Okrug** ⬖ *autonomous district* NW Russian Federation
191 W11 **Nengonengo** *atoll* Îles Tuamotu, C French Polynesia
163 V6 **Nenjiang** Heilongjiang, NE China
163 U6 **Nen Jiang** *var.* Nonni. ≈ NE China
189 P16 **Neoch** *atoll* Caroline Islands, C Micronesia
115 D18 **Neochóri** Dytikí Ellás, C Greece
27 Q7 **Neodesha** Kansas, C USA
29 S14 **Neola** Iowa, C USA
Néon Karlovasi/Néon Karlovásion *see* Karlovási
115 E16 **Néo Monastíri** Thessalía, C Greece
Néon Monastiri *see* Néo Monastíri
27 R8 **Neosho** Missouri, C USA
27 Q7 **Neosho River** ≈ Kansas/Oklahoma, C USA
123 N12 **Nepa** ≈ C Russian Federation
153 N10 **Nepal** *off.* Kingdom of Nepal. ◆ *monarchy* S Asia
152 M11 **Nepālganj** Mid Western, SW Nepal
Nepal, Kingdom of *see* Nepal
14 L13 **Nepean** Ontario, SE Canada
36 L4 **Nephi** Utah, W USA
97 B16 **Nephin** *Ir.* Néifinn. ▲ W Ireland
67 T9 **Nepoko** ≈ NE Dem. Rep. Congo
18 K15 **Neptune** New Jersey, NE USA
182 G10 **Neptune Islands** *island group* South Australia
107 I14 **Nera** *anc.* Nar. ≈ C Italy
102 L14 **Nérac** Lot-et-Garonne, SW France
111 D16 **Neratovice** *Ger.* Neratowitz. Středocesky Kraj, C Czech Republic
Neratowitz *see* Neratovice
123 O13 **Nercha** ≈ S Russian Federation
123 O13 **Nerchinsk** Chitinskaya Oblast', S Russian Federation
123 P14 **Nerchinskiy Zavod** Chitinskaya Oblast', S Russian Federation
124 M15 **Nerekhta** Kostromskaya Oblast', NW Russian Federation
118 H10 **Nereta** Aizkraukle, S Latvia
106 K13 **Nereto** Abruzzo, C Italy
113 H15 **Neretva** ≈ Bosnia and Herzegovina/Croatia
115 C17 **Nerikós** *ruins* Lefkáda, Iónia Nisiá, Greece, C Mediterranean Sea
83 F15 **Neriquinha** Cuando Cubango, SE Angola
118 I13 **Neris** *Bel.* Viliya, *Pol.* Wilia; *prev. Pol.* Wilja. ≈ Belarus/Lithuania
Neris *see* Viliya
105 N15 **Nerja** Andalucía, S Spain
124 L16 **Nerl'** ≈ W Russian Federation
105 P12 **Nerpio** Castilla-La Mancha, C Spain
104 J13 **Nerva** Andalucía, S Spain
98 L4 **Nes** Friesland, N Netherlands
94 G13 **Nesbyen** Buskerud, S Norway
92 L2 **Neskaupstadhur** Austurland, E Iceland
92 F13 **Nesna** Nordland, C Norway
26 K5 **Ness City** Kansas, C USA
Nesselsdorf *see* Kopřivnice
108 H7 **Nesslau** Sankt Gallen, NE Switzerland
96 I9 **Ness, Loch** ◎ N Scotland, UK
Nesterov *see* Zhovkva
114 I12 **Néstos** *Bul.* Mesta, *Turk.* Kara Su. ≈ Bulgaria/Greece *see also* Mesta
Néstos *see* Mesta
95 C14 **Nesttun** Hordaland, S Norway
Nesvizh *see* Nyasvizh
138 F9 **Netanya** *var.* Natanya, Nathanya. Central, C Israel
98 I9 **Netherlands** *off.* Kingdom of the Netherlands, *var.* Holland, *Dut.* Koninkrijk der Nederlanden, Nederland. ◆ *monarchy* NW Europe
45 S9 **Netherlands Antilles** *prev.* Dutch West Indies. ◇ *Dutch autonomous region* S Caribbean Sea
Netherlands East Indies *see* Indonesia
Netherlands Guiana *see* Surinam
Netherlands, Kingdom of the *see* Netherlands
Netherlands New Guinea *see* Papua
116 L4 **Netishyn** Khmel'nyts'ka Oblast', W Ukraine
138 E11 **Netivot** Southern, S Israel
107 O21 **Neto** ≈ S Italy
9 Q6 **Nettilling Lake** ◎ Baffin Island, Nunavut, N Canada
29 V3 **Nett Lake** ◎ Minnesota, N USA
107 I16 **Nettuno** Lazio, C Italy
Netum *see* Noto
41 U16 **Netzahualcóyotl, Presa** ⊠ SE Mexico
Netze *see* Noteć
Neu Amerika *see* Puławy
Neubetsche *see* Novi Bečej
Neubidschow *see* Nový Bydžov
Neubistritz *see* Nová Bystřice
100 N9 **Neubrandenburg** Mecklenburg-Vorpommern, NE Germany
101 K22 **Neuburg an der Donau** Bayern, S Germany
108 C8 **Neuchâtel** *Ger.* Neuenburg. Neuchâtel, W Switzerland
108 C8 **Neuchâtel** *Ger.* Neuenburg. ⬖ *canton* W Switzerland
108 C8 **Neuchâtel, Lac de** *Ger.* Neuenburger See. ◎ W Switzerland
Neudorf *see* Spišská Nová Ves
100 L10 **Neue Elde** *canal* N Germany
Neuenburg *see* Neuchâtel
Neuenburg an der Elbe *see* Nymburk
Neuenburger See *see* Neuchâtel, Lac de
108 F7 **Neuenhof** Aargau, N Switzerland
100 H11 **Neuenland** ✈ (Bremen) Bremen, NW Germany
Neuenstadt *see* La Neuveville
101 C18 **Neuerburg** Rheinland-Pfalz, W Germany
99 K24 **Neufchâteau** Luxembourg, SE Belgium
103 S6 **Neufchâteau** Vosges, NE France
102 M3 **Neufchâtel-en-Bray** Seine-Maritime, N France
109 S3 **Neufelden** Oberösterreich, N Austria
Neugradisk *see* Nova Gradiška
Neuhaus *see* Jindřichův Hradec
Neuhäusel *see* Nové Zámky
108 G6 **Neuhausen** *var.* Neuhausen am Rheinfall. Schaffhausen, N Switzerland
Neuhausen am Rheinfall *see* Neuhausen
101 I17 **Neuhof** Hessen, C Germany
Neuhof *see* Zgierz
Neukuhren *see* Pionerskiy
Neu-Langenburg *see* Tukuyu
109 W4 **Neulengbach** Niederösterreich, NE Austria
113 G15 **Neum** ⬖ Federacija Bosna I Hercegovina, S Bosnia and Herzegovina
Neumark *see* Nowy Targ
Neumark *see* Nowe Miasto Lubawskie, Warmińsko-Mazurskie, Poland
Neumarkt *see* Neumarkt im Hausruckkreis, Oberösterreich, Austria
Neumarkt *see* Neumarkt am Wallersee, Salzburg, Austria
Neumarkt *see* Środa Śląska, Dolnośląskie, Poland
Neumarkt *see* Târgu Secuiesc, Covasna, Romania
Neumarkt *see* Târgu Mureș
109 Q5 **Neumarkt am Wallersee** *var.* Neumarkt. Salzburg, NW Austria
109 R4 **Neumarkt im Hausruckkreis** *var.* Neumarkt. Oberösterreich, N Austria
101 L20 **Neumarkt in der Oberpfalz** Bayern, SE Germany
Neumarktl *see* Tržič
Neumoldowa *see* Moldova Nouă
100 J8 **Neumünster** Schleswig-Holstein, N Germany
109 X5 **Neunkirchen** *var.* Neunkirchen am Steinfeld. Niederösterreich, E Austria
101 E20 **Neunkirchen** Saarland, SW Germany
Neunkirchen am Steinfeld *see* Neunkirchen
Neuoderberg *see* Bohumín
63 I15 **Neuquén** Neuquén, SE Argentina
63 H14 **Neuquén** *off.* Provincia de Neuquén. ⬖ *province* W Argentina
Neuquén, Provincia de *see* Neuquén
63 H14 **Neuquén, Río** ≈ W Argentina
Neurode *see* Nowa Ruda
100 N11 **Neuruppin** Brandenburg, NE Germany
Neusalz an der Oder *see* Nowa Sól
Neu Sandec *see* Nowy Sącz
101 K22 **Neusäss** Bayern, S Germany
Neusatz *see* Novi Sad
Neuschliss *see* Gherla
21 N8 **Neuse River** ≈ North Carolina, SE USA
109 Z5 **Neusiedl am See** Burgenland, E Austria
111 G22 **Neusiedler See** *Hung.* Fertő. ◎ Austria/Hungary
Neusohl *see* Banská Bystrica
101 D15 **Neuss** *anc.* Novaesium, Novesium. Nordrhein-Westfalen, W Germany
Neuss *see* Nyon
Neustadt *see* Neustadt bei Coburg, Bayern, Germany
Neustadt *see* Neustadt an der Aisch, Bayern, Germany
Neustadt *see* Prudnik, Opole, Poland
Neustadt *see* Baia Mare, Maramureș, Romania
100 I12 **Neustadt am Rübenberge** Niedersachsen, N Germany
101 J19 **Neustadt an der Aisch** *var.* Neustadt. Bayern, C Germany
Neustadt an der Haardt *see* Neustadt an der Weinstrasse
101 F20 **Neustadt an der Weinstrasse** *prev.* Neustadt an der Haardt, *hist.* Niewenstat; *anc.* Nova Civitas. Rheinland-Pfalz, SW Germany
101 K18 **Neustadt bei Coburg** *var.* Neustadt. Bayern, C Germany
Neustadt bei Pinne *see* Lwówek
Neustadt in Oberschlesien *see* Prudnik
Neustadtl *see* Novo mesto
Neustadtl in Mähren *see* Nové Město na Moravě
Neustettin *see* Szczecinek
108 M8 **Neustift im Stubaital** *var.* Stubaital. Tirol, W Austria
100 N10 **Neustrelitz** Mecklenburg-Vorpommern, NE Germany
Neutitschein *see* Nový Jičín
Neutra *see* Nitra
101 J22 **Neu-Ulm** Bayern, S Germany
Neuveville *see* La Neuveville
103 N12 **Neuvic** Corrèze, C France
Neuwarp *see* Nowe Warpno
100 G9 **Neuwerk** *island* NW Germany
101 E17 **Neuwied** Rheinland-Pfalz, W Germany
Neuzen *see* Terneuzen
124 H12 **Neva** ≈ NW Russian Federation
29 V14 **Nevada** Iowa, C USA
27 R6 **Nevada** Missouri, C USA
35 R5 **Nevada** *off.* State of Nevada, *also known as* Battle Born State, Sagebrush State, Silver State. ⬖ *state* W USA
35 P6 **Nevada City** California, W USA
124 G16 **Nevel'** Pskovskaya Oblast', W Russian Federation
123 T14 **Nevel'sk** Ostrov Sakhalin, Sakhalinskaya Oblast', SE Russian Federation
123 Q13 **Never** Amurskaya Oblast', SE Russian Federation
127 Q6 **Neverkino** Penzenskaya Oblast', W Russian Federation
103 P9 **Nevers** *anc.* Noviodunum. Nièvre, C France
18 J12 **Neversink River** ≈ New York, NE USA
183 Q6 **Nevertire** New South Wales, SE Australia
113 H15 **Nevesinje** ⬖ Republika Srpska, S Bosnia and Herzegovina
118 G12 **Nevėžis** ≈ C Lithuania
126 M14 **Nevinnomyssk** Stavropol'skiy Kray, SW Russian Federation
45 W10 **Nevis** *island* Saint Kitts and Nevis
Nevoso, Monte *see* Veliki Snežnik
Nevrokop *see* Gotse Delchev
136 J14 **Nevşehir** *var.* Nevshehr. Nevşehir, C Turkey
136 J14 **Nevşehir** *var.* Nevshehr. ⬖ *province* C Turkey
Nevshehr *see* Nevşehir
122 G10 **Nev'yansk** Sverdlovskaya Oblast', C Russian Federation
81 J25 **Newala** Mtwara, SE Tanzania
31 P16 **New Albany** Indiana, N USA
22 M2 **New Albany** Mississippi, S USA
29 Y11 **New Albin** Iowa, C USA
55 U8 **New Amsterdam** E Guyana
183 Q4 **New Angledool** New South Wales, SE Australia
21 Y2 **Newark** Delaware, NE USA
18 K14 **Newark** New Jersey, NE USA
18 G10 **Newark** New York, NE USA
31 T13 **Newark** Ohio, N USA
Newark *see* Newark-on-Trent
35 W5 **Newark Lake** ◎ Nevada, W USA
97 N18 **Newark-on-Trent** *var.* Newark. C England, UK
22 M7 **New Augusta** Mississippi, S USA
19 P12 **New Bedford** Massachusetts, NE USA
32 G11 **Newberg** Oregon, NW USA
21 X10 **New Bern** North Carolina, SE USA
20 F8 **Newbern** Tennessee, S USA
31 P4 **Newberry** Michigan, N USA
21 Q12 **Newberry** South Carolina, SE USA
18 F15 **New Bloomfield** Pennsylvania, NE USA
25 X5 **New Boston** Texas, SW USA
25 S11 **New Braunfels** Texas, SW USA
31 Q13 **New Bremen** Ohio, N USA
97 F18 **Newbridge** *Ir.* An Droichead Nua. Kildare, C Ireland
18 B14 **New Brighton** Pennsylvania, NE USA
18 M12 **New Britain** Connecticut, NE USA
186 G7 **New Britain** *island* E Papua New Guinea
192 I8 **New Britain Trench** *undersea feature* W Pacific Ocean
18 J15 **New Brunswick** New Jersey, NE USA
15 V8 **New Brunswick** *Fr.* Nouveau-Brunswick. ⬖ *province* SE Canada
18 K13 **Newburgh** New York, NE USA
97 M22 **Newbury** S England, UK
19 P10 **Newburyport** Massachusetts, NE USA
77 T14 **New Bussa** Niger, W Nigeria
187 O17 **New Caledonia** *var.* Kanaky, *Fr.* Nouvelle-Calédonie. ◇ *French overseas territory* SW Pacific Ocean
187 O15 **New Caledonia** *island* SW Pacific Ocean
175 O10 **New Caledonia Basin** *undersea feature* W Pacific Ocean
183 T8 **Newcastle** New South Wales, SE Australia
13 O14 **Newcastle** New Brunswick, SE Canada
14 I15 **Newcastle** Ontario, SE Canada
83 K22 **Newcastle** KwaZulu/Natal, E South Africa
97 G16 **Newcastle** *Ir.* An Caisleán Nua. SE Northern Ireland, UK
31 P13 **New Castle** Indiana, N USA
20 L5 **New Castle** Kentucky, S USA
27 N11 **Newcastle** Oklahoma, C USA
18 B13 **New Castle** Pennsylvania, NE USA
25 R6 **Newcastle** Texas, SW USA
36 J7 **Newcastle** Utah, W USA
21 S6 **New Castle** Virginia, NE USA
33 Z13 **Newcastle** Wyoming, C USA
45 W10 **Newcastle** ✈ Nevis, Saint Kitts and Nevis
97 L14 **Newcastle** ✈ NE England, UK
Newcastle *see* Newcastle upon Tyne
97 L18 **Newcastle-under-Lyme** C England, UK
97 M14 **Newcastle upon Tyne** *var.* Newcastle, *hist.* Monkchester, *Lat.* Pons Aelii. NE England, UK
181 Q4 **Newcastle Waters** Northern Territory, N Australia
Newchwang *see* Yingkou
18 K13 **New City** New York, NE USA
31 U13 **Newcomerstown** Ohio, N USA
18 G15 **New Cumberland** Pennsylvania, NE USA
21 R1 **New Cumberland** West Virginia, NE USA
152 I10 **New Delhi** ● (India) Delhi, N India
9 O17 **New Denver** British Columbia, SW Canada
28 J9 **Newell** South Dakota, N USA
21 Q13 **New Ellenton** South Carolina, SE USA
22 J6 **Newellton** Louisiana, S USA
28 K6 **New England** North Dakota, N USA
19 P8 **New England** *cultural region* NE USA
New England of the West *see* Minnesota
183 U5 **New England Range** ▲▲ New South Wales, SE Australia
64 G9 **New England Seamounts** *var.* Bermuda-New England Seamount Arc. *undersea feature* W Atlantic Ocean
38 M14 **Newenham, Cape** *headland* Alaska, USA
138 F11 **Newé Zohar** Southern, E Israel
18 D9 **Newfane** New York, NE USA
97 M23 **New Forest** *physical region* S England, UK
13 T12 **Newfoundland** *Fr.* Terre-Neuve. *island* Newfoundland and Labrador, SE Canada
13 R9 **Newfoundland and Labrador** *Fr.* Terre Neuve. ⬖ *province* E Canada
65 J8 **Newfoundland Basin** *undersea feature* NW Atlantic Ocean
64 I8 **Newfoundland Ridge** *undersea feature* NW Atlantic Ocean
64 J8 **Newfoundland Seamounts** *undersea feature* N Sargasso Sea
18 G16 **New Freedom** Pennsylvania, NE USA
186 K9 **New Georgia** *island* New Georgia Islands, NW Solomon Islands
186 K8 **New Georgia Islands** *island group* NW Solomon Islands
186 L8 **New Georgia Sound** *var.* The Slot. *sound* E Solomon Sea
30 L9 **New Glarus** Wisconsin, N USA
13 Q15 **New Glasgow** Nova Scotia, SE Canada
New Goa *see* Panaji
186 A6 **New Guinea** *Dut.* Nieuw Guinea, *Ind.* Irian. *island* Indonesia/Papua New Guinea
192 H8 **New Guinea Trench** *undersea feature* SW Pacific Ocean
32 I6 **Newhalem** Washington, NW USA
39 P13 **Newhalen** Alaska, USA
29 X13 **Newhall** Iowa, C USA
14 F16 **New Hamburg** Ontario, S Canada
19 N9 **New Hampshire** *off.* State of New Hampshire, *also known as* Granite State. ⬖ *state* NE USA
29 W12 **New Hampton** Iowa, C USA
186 G5 **New Hanover** *island* NE Papua New Guinea
97 P23 **Newhaven** SE England, UK
18 M13 **New Haven** Connecticut, NE USA
31 Q12 **New Haven** Indiana, N USA
27 W5 **New Haven** Missouri, C USA
10 K13 **New Hazelton** British Columbia, SW Canada
New Hebrides *see* Vanuatu
175 P9 **New Hebrides Trench** *undersea feature* N Coral Sea
18 H15 **New Holland** Pennsylvania, NE USA
22 I9 **New Iberia** Louisiana, S USA
186 G5 **New Ireland** ⬖ *province* NE Papua New Guinea
186 G5 **New Ireland** *island* NE Papua New Guinea
65 A24 **New Island** *island* W Falkland Islands
18 J15 **New Jersey** *off.* State of New Jersey, *also known as* The Garden State. ⬖ *state* NE USA
18 C14 **New Kensington** Pennsylvania, NE USA
21 W6 **New Kent** Virginia, NE USA
27 O8 **Newkirk** Oklahoma, C USA
21 Q9 **Newland** North Carolina, SE USA
28 L6 **New Leipzig** North Dakota, N USA
14 H9 **New Liskeard** Ontario, S Canada
22 G7 **Newllano** Louisiana, S USA
19 N13 **New London** Connecticut, NE USA
29 Y15 **New London** Iowa, C USA
29 T8 **New London** Minnesota, N USA
27 V3 **New London** Missouri, C USA
30 M7 **New London** Wisconsin, N USA
27 Y8 **New Madrid** Missouri, C USA
180 J8 **Newman** Western Australia
194 M13 **Newman Island** *island* Antarctica
14 H15 **Newmarket** Ontario, S Canada
97 P20 **Newmarket** E England, UK
19 P10 **Newmarket** New Hampshire, NE USA
21 U4 **New Market** Virginia, NE USA
21 R2 **New Martinsville** West Virginia, NE USA
31 U14 **New Matamoras** Ohio, N USA
32 M12 **New Meadows** Idaho, NW USA
26 R12 **New Mexico** *off.* State of New Mexico, *also known as* Land of Enchantment, Sunshine State. ⬖ *state* SW USA
149 V6 **New Mīrpur** *var.* Mīrpur. Sind, SE Pakistan
151 N15 **New Moore Island** *Island* E India
23 S4 **Newnan** Georgia, SE USA
183 P17 **New Norfolk** Tasmania, SE Australia
22 K9 **New Orleans** Louisiana, S USA
22 K9 **New Orleans** ✈ Louisiana, S USA
18 K12 **New Paltz** New York, NE USA
31 U12 **New Philadelphia** Ohio, N USA
184 K10 **New Plymouth** Taranaki, North Island, New Zealand
97 M24 **Newport** S England, UK
97 K22 **Newport** SE Wales, UK
27 W10 **Newport** Arkansas, C USA
31 N13 **Newport** Indiana, N USA
20 M3 **Newport** Kentucky, S USA
29 W9 **Newport** Minnesota, N USA
32 F12 **Newport** Oregon, NW USA
19 O13 **Newport** Rhode Island, NE USA
21 O9 **Newport** Tennessee, S USA
19 N6 **Newport** Vermont, NE USA
32 M7 **Newport** Washington, NW USA
21 X7 **Newport News** Virginia, NE USA
97 N20 **Newport Pagnell** SE England, UK
23 U12 **New Port Richey** Florida, SE USA
29 V9 **New Prague** Minnesota, N USA
44 H3 **New Providence** *island* N Bahamas
97 I20 **New Quay** SW Wales, UK
97 H24 **Newquay** SW England, UK
29 V10 **New Richland** Minnesota, N USA
15 X7 **New-Richmond** Québec, SE Canada
31 R15 **New Richmond** Ohio, N USA
30 I5 **New Richmond** Wisconsin, N USA
42 G1 **New River** ≈ N Belize
55 T12 **New River** ≈ SE Guyana
21 R6 **New River** ≈ West Virginia, NE USA
42 G1 **New River Lagoon** ◎ N Belize
22 J8 **New Roads** Louisiana, S USA
18 L14 **New Rochelle** New York, NE USA
29 O4 **New Rockford** North Dakota, N USA
97 P23 **New Romney** SE England, UK
97 F20 **New Ross** *Ir.* Ros Mhic Thriúin. Wexford, SE Ireland
97 F16 **Newry** *Ir.* An tIúr. SE Northern Ireland, UK
28 M5 **New Salem** North Dakota, N USA
New Sarum *see* Salisbury
29 W14 **New Sharon** Iowa, C USA
New Siberian Islands *see* Novosibirskiye Ostrova
23 X11 **New Smyrna Beach** Florida, SE USA
183 O7 **New South Wales** ⬖ *state* SE Australia
39 O13 **New Stuyahok** Alaska, USA
21 N8 **New Tazewell** Tennessee, S USA
38 M12 **Newtok** Alaska, USA
23 S7 **Newton** Georgia, SE USA
29 W14 **Newton** Iowa, C USA
27 N6 **Newton** Kansas, C USA
19 O11 **Newton** Massachusetts, NE USA
22 M5 **Newton** Mississippi, S USA
18 J14 **Newton** New Jersey, NE USA
21 R9 **Newton** North Carolina, SE USA
25 Y9 **Newton** Texas, SW USA
97 J24 **Newton Abbot** SW England, UK
96 K13 **Newton St Boswells** SE Scotland, UK
97 I14 **Newton Stewart** S Scotland, UK
92 O2 **Newtontoppen** ▲ C Svalbard
97 J20 **Newtown** E Wales, UK
28 K3 **New Town** North Dakota, N USA
97 G15 **Newtownabbey** *Ir.* Baile na Mainistreach. E Northern Ireland, UK
97 G15 **Newtownards** *Ir.* Baile Nua na hArda. SE Northern Ireland, UK
29 U10 **New Ulm** Minnesota, N USA
28 K10 **New Underwood** South Dakota, N USA
25 V10 **New Waverly** Texas, SW USA
18 K14 **New York** New York, NE USA
18 G10 **New York** ⬖ *state* NE USA
35 X13 **New York Mountains** ▲▲ California, W USA
184 K12 **New Zealand** ◆ *commonwealth republic* SW Pacific Ocean
95 M24 **Nexø** *var.* Neksø. Bornholm, E Denmark
125 O15 **Neya** Kostromskaya Oblast', NW Russian Federation
Neyba *see* Neiba
143 Q12 **Neyrīz** *var.* Neiriz, Niriz. Fārs, S Iran
143 T4 **Neyshābūr** *var.* Nishapur. Khorāsān-Razavi, NE Iran
155 J21 **Neyveli** Tamil Nādu, SE India
Nezhin *see* Nizhyn
33 N10 **Nezperce** Idaho, NW USA
22 H8 **Nezpique, Bayou** ≈ Louisiana, S USA
77 Y13 **Ngadda** ≈ NE Nigeria
N'Gage *see* Negage
185 G16 **Ngahere** West Coast, South Island, New Zealand
77 Z12 **Ngala** Borno, NE Nigeria

◆ Country ● Country Capital ◇ Dependent Territory ○ Dependent Territory Capital ⬖ Administrative Regions ✈ International Airport ▲ Mountain ▲▲ Mountain Range Volcano ≈ River ◎ Lake ⊠ Reservoir

NGAMRING – NOMUKA GROUP

158 *K16* **Ngamring** Xizang Zizhiqu, W China
81 *K19* **Ngangerabeli Plain** *plain* SE Kenya
158 *I14* **Ngangla Ringco** ◎ W China
158 *G13* **Nganglong Kangri** ▲ W China
158 *K15* **Ngangzê Co** ◎ W China
79 *F14* **Ngaoundéré** *var.* N'Gaoundéré. Adamaoua, N Cameroon
N'Gaoundéré *see* Ngaoundéré
81 *E20* **Ngara** Kagera, NW Tanzania
188 *F8* **Ngardmau Bay** *bay* Babeldaob, N Palau
188 *F7* **Ngaregur** *island* Palau Islands, N Palau
Ngarrab *see* Gyaca
184 *L7* **Ngaruawahia** Waikato, North Island, New Zealand
184 *N11* **Ngaruroro** ≈ North Island, New Zealand
190 *I16* **Ngatangiia** Rarotonga, S Cook Islands
184 *M6* **Ngatea** Waikato, North Island, New Zealand
166 *L8* **Ngathainggyaung** Irrawaddy, SW Burma (Myanmar)
Ngatik *see* Ngetik Atoll
Ngau *see* Gau
Ngawa *see* Aba
188 *C7* **Ngcheangel** *var.* Kayangel Islands. *island* Palau Islands, N Palau
188 *E10* **Ngchemiangel** Babeldaob, N Palau
188 *C8* **Ngeaur** *var.* Angaur. *island* Palau Islands, S Palau
188 *E10* **Ngerkeai** Babeldaob, N Palau
188 *F9* **Ngermechau** Babeldaob, N Palau
188 *C8* **Ngeruktabel** *prev.* Urukthapel. *island* Palau Islands, S Palau
188 *F8* **Ngetbong** Babeldaob, N Palau
189 *T17* **Ngetik Atoll** *var.* Ngatik; *prev.* Los Jardines. *atoll* Caroline Islands, E Micronesia
188 *E10* **Ngetkip** Babeldaob, N Palau
Nghia Dan *see* Thai Hoa
83 *C16* **N'Giva** *var.* Ondjiva, *Port.* Vila Pereira de Eça. Cunene, S Angola
79 *G20* **Ngo** Plateaux, SE Congo
167 *S7* **Ngoc Lac** Thanh Hoa, N Vietnam
79 *G17* **Ngoko** ≈ Cameroon/Congo
81 *H19* **Ngorengore** Rift Valley, SW Kenya
159 *Q11* **Ngoring Hu** ◎ C China
Ngorolaka *see* Banifing
81 *H20* **Ngorongoro Crater** *crater* N Tanzania
79 *D19* **Ngounié** *off.* Province de la Ngounié, *var.* La Ngounié. ◐ *province* S Gabon
79 *D19* **Ngounié** ≈ Congo/Gabon
Ngounié, Province de la *see* Ngounié
78 *H10* **Ngoura** *var.* NGoura. Chari-Baguirmi, W Chad
NGoura *see* Ngoura
78 *G10* **Ngouri** *var.* NGouri; *prev.* Fort-Millot. Lac, W Chad
NGouri *see* Ngouri
77 *Y10* **Ngourti** Diffa, E Niger
77 *Y11* **Nguigmi** *var.* N'Guigmi. Diffa, SE Niger
N'Guigmi *see* Nguigmi
Nguimbo *see* Lumbala N'Guimbo
188 *F15* **Ngulu Atoll** *atoll* Caroline Islands, W Micronesia
187 *R14* **Nguna** *island* C Vanuatu
N'Gunza *see* Sumbe
169 *U17* **Ngurah Rai** ✕ (Bali) Bali, S Indonesia
77 *W12* **Nguru** Yobe, NE Nigeria
Ngwaketze *see* Southern
83 *I16* **Ngweze** ≈ S Zambia
83 *M17* **Nhamatanda** Sofala, C Mozambique
58 *G12* **Nhamundá, Rio** *var.* Jamundá, Yamundá. ≈ N Brazil
60 *J7* **Nhandeara** São Paulo, S Brazil
82 *D12* **Nharêa** *var.* N'Harea, Nhareia. Bié, W Angola
N'Harea *see* Nharêa
Nhareia *see* Nharêa
167 *V12* **Nha Trang** Khanh Hoa, S Vietnam
182 *L11* **Nhill** Victoria, SE Australia
83 *L22* **Nhlangano** *prev.* Goedgegun. SW Swaziland
181 *S1* **Nhulunbuy** Northern Territory, N Australia
77 *N10* **Niafounké** Tombouctou, W Mali
31 *N5* **Niagara** Wisconsin, N USA
14 *H16* **Niagara** ≈ Ontario, S Canada
14 *G15* **Niagara Escarpment** *hill range* Ontario, S Canada
14 *H16* **Niagara Falls** Ontario, S Canada
18 *D9* **Niagara Falls** New York, NE USA
14 *H16* **Niagara Falls** *waterfall* Canada/USA
76 *K12* **Niagassola** *var.* Nyagassola. Haute-Guinée, NE Guinea
77 *R12* **Niamey** ● (Niger) Niamey, SW Niger
77 *R12* **Niamey** ✕ Niamey, SW Niger
77 *R14* **Niamtougou** N Togo
79 *O16* **Niangara** Orientale, NE Dem. Rep. Congo
77 *O10* **Niangay, Lac** ◎ E Mali
77 *N14* **Niangoloko** SW Burkina
27 *U6* **Niangua River** ≈ Missouri, C USA
79 *O17* **Nia-Nia** Orientale, NE Dem. Rep. Congo
19 *N13* **Niantic** Connecticut, NE USA
163 *U7* **Nianzishan** Heilongjiang, NE China
168 *H10* **Nias, Pulau** *island* W Indonesia
82 *O13* **Niassa** *off.* Província do Niassa. ◐ *province* N Mozambique
Niassa, Província do *see* Niassa
191 *U10* **Niau** *island* Îles Tuamotu, C French Polynesia
95 *G20* **Nibe** Nordjylland, N Denmark
189 *Q8* **Nibok** N Nauru
118 *C10* **Nīca** Liepāja, W Latvia
Nicaea *see* Nice
42 *J9* **Nicaragua** *off.* Republic of Nicaragua. ◆ *republic* Central America
42 *K11* **Nicaragua, Lago de** *var.* Cocibolca, Gran Lago, *Eng.* Lake Nicaragua. ◎ S Nicaragua
Nicaragua, Lake *see* Nicaragua, Lago de
64 *D11* **Nicaraguan Rise** *undersea feature* NW Caribbean Sea
Nicaragua, Republic of *see* Nicaragua
Nicaria *see* Ikaría
107 *N21* **Nicastro** Calabria, SW Italy
103 *V15* **Nice** *It.* Nizza; *anc.* Nicaea. Alpes-Maritimes, SE France
Nice *see* Côte d'Azur
Nicephorium *see* Ar Raqqah
12 *M9* **Nichicun, Lac** ◎ Québec, E Canada
164 *D16* **Nichinan** *var.* Nitinan. Miyazaki, Kyūshū, SW Japan
44 *E4* **Nicholas Channel** *channel* N Cuba
Nicholas II Land *see* Severnaya Zemlya
149 *U2* **Nicholas Range** *Pash.* Selselehye Kuhe Vākhān, *Taj.* Qatorkūhi Vakhon. ⛰ Afghanistan/Tajikistan
20 *M6* **Nicholasville** Kentucky, S USA
44 *G2* **Nicholls Town** Andros Island, NW Bahamas
21 *U12* **Nichols** South Carolina, SE USA
55 *U9* **Nickerie** ◐ *district* NW Surinam
55 *V9* **Nickerie Rivier** ≈ NW Surinam
151 *P22* **Nicobar Islands** *island group* India, E Indian Ocean
116 *L9* **Nicolae Bălcescu** Botoşani, NE Romania
15 *P11* **Nicolet** Québec, SE Canada
15 *Q12* **Nicolet** ≈ Québec, SE Canada
31 *Q4* **Nicolet, Lake** ◎ Michigan, N USA
29 *U10* **Nicollet** Minnesota, N USA
61 *F19* **Nico Pérez** Florida, S Uruguay
Nicopolis *see* Nikopol, Bulgaria
Nicopolis *see* Nikópoli, Greece
121 *P2* **Nicosia** *Gk.* Lefkosía, *Turk.* Lefkoşa. ● (Cyprus) C Cyprus
107 *K24* **Nicosia** Sicilia, Italy, C Mediterranean Sea
107 *N22* **Nicotera** Calabria, SW Italy
42 *K13* **Nicoya** Guanacaste, W Costa Rica
42 *L14* **Nicoya, Golfo de** *gulf* W Costa Rica
42 *L14* **Nicoya, Península de** *peninsula* NW Costa Rica
Nictheroy *see* Niterói
118 *B12* **Nida** *Ger.* Nidden. Klaipėda, SW Lithuania
111 *L15* **Nida** ≈ S Poland
Nidaros *see* Trondheim
108 *D8* **Nidau** Bern, W Switzerland
101 *H17* **Nidda** ≈ W Germany
Nidden *see* Nida
95 *F17* **Nidelva** ≈ S Norway
110 *L9* **Nidzica** *Ger.* Niedenburg. Warmińsko Mazurskie, NE Poland
100 *H6* **Niebüll** Schleswig-Holstein, N Germany
Niedenburg *see* Nidzica
99 *N25* **Niederanven** Luxembourg, C Luxembourg
103 *V4* **Niederbronn-les-Bains** Bas-Rhin, NE France
Niederdonau *see* Niederösterreich
109 *S7* **Niedere Tauern** ⛰ C Austria
101 *P14* **Niederlausitz** *Eng.* Lower Lusatia, *Lus.* Donja Łužica. *physical region* E Germany
109 *U5* **Niederösterreich** *off.* Land Niederösterreich, *Eng.* Lower Austria, *Ger.* Niederdonau; *prev.* Lower Danube. ◐ *state* NE Austria
Niederösterreich, Land *see* Niederösterreich
100 *G12* **Niedersachsen** *Eng.* Lower Saxony, *Fr.* Basse-Saxe. ◐ *state* NW Germany
79 *D17* **Niefang** *var.* Sevilla de Niefang. NW Equatorial Guinea
83 *G23* **Niekerkshoop** Northern Cape, W South Africa
99 *G17* **Niel** Antwerpen, N Belgium
Niélé *see* Niellé
76 *M14* **Niellé** *var.* Niélé. N Ivory Coast
79 *O22* **Niemba** Katanga, E Dem. Rep. Congo
111 *G15* **Niemcza** *Ger.* Nimptsch. Dolnośląskie, SW Poland
Niemen *see* Neman
92 *J13* **Niemisel** Norrbotten, N Sweden
111 *H15* **Niemodlin** *Ger.* Falkenberg. Opolskie, SW Poland
76 *M13* **Niéna** Sikasso, SW Mali
100 *H12* **Nienburg** Niedersachsen, N Germany
100 *N13* **Nieplitz** ≈ NE Germany
111 *L16* **Niepołomice** Malopolskie, S Poland
101 *D14* **Niers** ≈ Germany/Netherlands
101 *Q15* **Niesky** *Lus.* Niska. Sachsen, E Germany
Nieśwież *see* Nyasvizh
Nieuport *see* Nieuwpoort
98 *O8* **Nieuw-Amsterdam** Drenthe, NE Netherlands
55 *W9* **Nieuw Amsterdam** Commewijne, NE Surinam
99 *M14* **Nieuw-Bergen** Limburg, SE Netherlands
98 *O7* **Nieuw-Buinen** Drenthe, NE Netherlands
98 *J12* **Nieuwegein** Utrecht, C Netherlands
98 *P6* **Nieuwe Pekela** Groningen, NE Netherlands
98 *P5* **Nieuweschans** Groningen, NE Netherlands
Nieuw Guinea *see* New Guinea
98 *I11* **Nieuwkoop** Zuid-Holland, C Netherlands
98 *M9* **Nieuwleusen** Overijssel, S Netherlands
98 *J11* **Nieuw-Loosdrecht** Noord-Holland, C Netherlands
55 *U9* **Nieuw Nickerie** Nickerie, NW Surinam
98 *P5* **Nieuwolda** Groningen, NE Netherlands
99 *B17* **Nieuwpoort** *var.* Nieuport. West-Vlaanderen , W Belgium
99 *G14* **Nieuw-Vossemeer** Noord-Brabant, S Netherlands
98 *P7* **Nieuw-Weerdinge** Drenthe, NE Netherlands
40 *L10* **Nieves** Zacatecas, C Mexico
64 *O11* **Nieves, Pico de las** ▲ Gran Canaria, Islas Canarias, Spain, NE Atlantic Ocean
103 *P8* **Nièvre** ◐ *department* C France
Niewenstat *see* Neustadt an der Weinstrasse
136 *J15* **Niğde** Niğde, C Turkey
136 *J15* **Niğde** ◐ *province* C Turkey
83 *J21* **Nigel** Gauteng, NE South Africa
77 *V10* **Niger** *off.* Republic of Niger. ◆ *republic* W Africa
77 *T14* **Niger** ◐ *state* C Nigeria
67 *P8* **Niger** ≈ W Africa
Niger Cone *see* Niger Fan
67 *P9* **Niger Delta** *delta* S Nigeria
67 *P9* **Niger Fan** *var.* Niger Cone. *undersea feature* E Atlantic Ocean
77 *T13* **Nigeria** *off.* Federal Republic of Nigeria. ◆ *federal republic* W Africa
Nigeria, Federal Republic of *see* Nigeria
77 *T17* **Niger, Mouths of the** *delta* S Nigeria
Niger, Republic of *see* Niger
185 *C24* **Nightcaps** Southland, South Island, New Zealand
14 *F7* **Night Hawk Lake** ◎ Ontario, S Canada
65 *M19* **Nightingale Island** *island* S Tristan da Cunha, S Atlantic Ocean
38 *M12* **Nightmute** Alaska, USA
114 *G13* **Nigríta** Kentrikí Makedonía, NE Greece
148 *J15* **Nihing** *Per.* Rūd-e Nahang. ≈ Iran/Pakistan
191 *V10* **Nihiru** *atoll* Îles Tuamotu, C French Polynesia
Nihommatsu *see* Nihonmatsu
Nihon *see* Japan
165 *P11* **Nihonmatsu** *var.* Nihommatsu, Nihonmatu. Fukushima, Honshū, C Japan
Nihonmatu *see* Nihonmatsu
62 *I12* **Nihuil, Embalse del** ◎ W Argentina
165 *O10* **Niigata** Niigata, Honshū, C Japan
165 *O11* **Niigata** *off.* Niigata-ken. ◐ *prefecture* Honshū, C Japan
Niigata-ken *see* Niigata
165 *G14* **Niihama** Ehime, Shikoku, SW Japan
38 *A8* **Ni'ihau** *var.* Niihau. *island* Hawai'i, USA, C Pacific Ocean
165 *X12* **Nii-jima** *island* E Japan
165 *H12* **Niimi** Okayama, Honshū, SW Japan
165 *O10* **Niitsu** *var.* Niitu. Niigata, Honshū, C Japan
Niitu *see* Niitsu
105 *P15* **Nijar** Andalucía, S Spain
98 *K11* **Nijkerk** Gelderland, C Netherlands
99 *H16* **Nijlen** Antwerpen, N Belgium
98 *L13* **Nijmegen** *Ger.* Nimwegen; *anc.* Noviomagus. Gelderland, SE Netherlands
98 *N10* **Nijverdal** Overijssel, E Netherlands
190 *G16* **Nikao** Rarotonga, S Cook Islands
Nikaria *see* Ikaría
124 *I2* **Nikel'** Murmanskaya Oblast', NW Russian Federation
171 *Q17* **Nikiniki** Timor, S Indonesia
129 *Q15* **Nikitin Seamount** *undersea feature* E Indian Ocean
77 *S14* **Nikki** E Benin
Niklasmarkt *see* Gheorgheni
39 *P10* **Nikolai** Alaska, USA
Nikolaiken *see* Mikołajki
Nikolainkaupunki *see* Vaasa
Nikolayev *see* Mykolayiv
145 *O6* **Nikolayevka** Severnyy Kazakhstan, N Kazakhstan
Nikolayevka *see* Zhetigen
127 *P9* **Nikolayevsk** Volgogradskaya Oblast', SW Russian Federation
Nikolayevskaya Oblast' *see* Mykolayivs'ka Oblast'
123 *S12* **Nikolayevsk-na-Amure** Khabarovskiy Kray, SE Russian Federation
127 *P6* **Nikol'sk** Penzenskaya Oblast', W Russian Federation
125 *O13* **Nikol'sk** Vologodskaya Oblast', NW Russian Federation
Nikol'sk *see* Ussuriysk
38 *K17* **Nikolski** Umnak Island, Alaska, USA
Nikol'skiy *see* Satpayev
127 *V7* **Nikol'skoye** Orenburgskaya Oblast', W Russian Federation
Nikol'sk-Ussuriyskiy *see* Ussuriysk
114 *J7* **Nikopol** *anc.* Nicopolis. Pleven, N Bulgaria
117 *S9* **Nikopol'** Dnipropetrovs'ka Oblast', SE Ukraine
115 *C17* **Nikópoli** *anc.* Nicopolis. *site of ancient city* Ípeiros, W Greece
136 *M12* **Niksar** Tokat, N Turkey
143 *V14* **Nīkshahr** Sīstān va Balūchestān, SE Iran
113 *J16* **Nikšić** C Montenegro
191 *R4* **Nikumaroro** ; *prev.* Gardner Island. *atoll* Phoenix Islands, C Kiribati
191 *P3* **Nikunau** *var.* Nukunau; *prev.* Byron Island. *atoll* Tungaru, W Kiribati
155 *G21* **Nilambūr** Kerala, SW India
35 *X16* **Niland** California, W USA
80 *G8* **Nile** *former province* NW Uganda
67 *T3* **Nile** *Ar.* Nahr an Nīl. ≈ N Africa
75 *W7* **Nile Delta** *delta* N Egypt
67 *T3* **Nile Fan** *undersea feature* E Mediterranean Sea
31 *O11* **Niles** Michigan, N USA
31 *V11* **Niles** Ohio, N USA
155 *F20* **Nīleswaram** Kerala, SW India
14 *K10* **Nilgaut, Lac** ◎ Québec, SE Canada
149 *O6* **Nīlī** Dāikondī, C Afghanistan
158 *I5* **Nilka** Xinjiang Uygur Zizhiqu, NW China
Nīl, Nahr an *see* Nile
93 *N16* **Nilsiä** Itä-Suomi, C Finland
154 *F9* **Nimach** Madhya Pradesh, C India
152 *G14* **Nimbāhera** Rājasthān, N India
76 *L15* **Nimba, Monts** *var.* Nimba Mountains. ⛰ W Africa
Nimba Mountains *see* Nimba, Monts
Nimburg *see* Nymburk
103 *Q15* **Nîmes** *anc.* Nemausus, Nismes. Gard, S France
152 *H11* **Nīm ka Thāna** Rājasthān, N India
183 *R11* **Nimmitabel** New South Wales, SE Australia
Nimptsch *see* Niemcza
195 *R11* **Nimrod Glacier** *glacier* Antarctica
Nimroze *see* Nīmrūz
148 *K8* **Nīmrūz** *var.* Nimroze; *prev.* Chakhānsūr. ◐ *province* SW Afghanistan
81 *F16* **Nimule** Eastern Equatoria, S Sudan
Nimwegen *see* Nijmegen
155 *C23* **Nine Degree Channel** *channel* India/Maldives
18 *G9* **Ninemile Point** *headland* New York, NE USA
173 *S8* **Ninetyeast Ridge** *undersea feature* E Indian Ocean
183 *P13* **Ninety Mile Beach** *beach* Victoria, SE Australia
184 *I2* **Ninety Mile Beach** *beach* North Island, New Zealand
21 *P12* **Ninety Six** South Carolina, SE USA
163 *Y9* **Ning'an** Heilongjiang, NE China
161 *S9* **Ningbo** *var.* Ning-po, Yin-hsien; *prev.* Ninghsien. Zhejiang, SE China
161 *U12* **Ningde** Fujian, SE China
161 *P12* **Ningdu** *var.* Meijiang. Jiangxi, S China
Ning'er *see* Pu'er
186 *A7* **Ningerum** Western, SW Papua New Guinea
161 *R9* **Ningguo** Anhui, E China
161 *S9* **Ninghai** Zhejiang, SE China
Ning-hsia *see* Ningxia
Ninghsien *see* Ningbo
160 *J15* **Ningming** *var.* Chengzhong. Guangxi Zhuangzu Zizhiqu, S China
160 *H11* **Ningnan** *var.* Pisha. Sichuan, C China
Ning-po *see* Ningbo
Ningsia/Ningsia Hui/ Ningsia Hui Autonomous Region *see* Ningxia
160 *J5* **Ningxia** *off.* Ningxia Huizu Zizhiqu, *var.* Ning-hsia, Ningsia, *Eng.* Ningsia Hui, Ningsia Hui Autonomous Region. ◐ *autonomous region* N China
Ningxia Huizu Zizhiqu *see* Ningxia
159 *X10* **Ningxian** Gansu, N China
167 *T7* **Ninh Binh** Ninh Binh, N Vietnam
167 *V12* **Ninh Hoa** Khanh Hoa, S Vietnam
186 *C4* **Ninigo Group** *island group* N Papua New Guinea
39 *Q12* **Ninilchik** Alaska, USA
27 *N7* **Ninnescah River** ≈ Kansas, C USA
195 *U16* **Ninnis Glacier** *glacier* Antarctica
165 *R8* **Ninohe** Iwate, Honshū, C Japan
99 *F18* **Ninove** Oost-Vlaanderen, C Belgium
171 *O4* **Ninoy Aquino** ✕ (Manila) Luzon, N Philippines
Nio *see* Íos
29 *P12* **Niobrara** Nebraska, C USA
28 *M12* **Niobrara River** ≈ Nebraska/ Wyoming, C USA
79 *I20* **Nioki** Bandundu, W Dem. Rep. Congo
76 *M11* **Niono** Ségou, C Mali
76 *K11* **Nioro** *var.* Nioro du Sahel. Kayes, W Mali
76 *G11* **Nioro du Rip** SW Senegal
Nioro du Sahel *see* Nioro
102 *K10* **Niort** Deux-Sèvres, W France
172 *H14* **Nioumachoua** Mohéli, S Comoros
186 *C7* **Nipa** Southern Highlands, W Papua New Guinea
9 *U14* **Nipawin** Saskatchewan, S Canada
12 *D12* **Nipigon** Ontario, S Canada
12 *D11* **Nipigon, Lake** ◎ Ontario, S Canada
9 *S13* **Nipin** ≈ Saskatchewan, C Canada
14 *G11* **Nipissing, Lake** ◎ Ontario, S Canada
35 *P13* **Nipomo** California, W USA
Nippon *see* Japan
138 *K6* **Niqniqīyah, Jabal an** ⛰ C Syria
62 *I9* **Niquivil** San Juan, W Argentina
171 *Y13* **Nirabotong** Papua, E Indonesia
Niriz *see* Neyrīz
163 *U7* **Nirji** *var.* Morin Dawa Daurzu Zizhiqi. Nei Mongol Zizhiqu, N China
155 *I14* **Nirmal** Andhra Pradesh, C India
153 *Q13* **Nirmāli** Bihār, NE India
113 *O14* **Niš** *Eng.* Nish, *Ger.* Nisch; *anc.* Naissus. Serbia, SE Serbia
104 *H9* **Nisa** Portalegre, C Portugal
Nisa *see* Neisse
141 *P4* **Nişab** Al Ḩudūd ash Shamālīyah, N Saudi Arabia
141 *Q15* **Nişāb** *var.* Anşāb. SW Yemen
113 *P14* **Nišava** *Bul.* Nishava. ≈ Bulgaria/Serbia *see also* Nishava
Nišava *see* Nishava
107 *K25* **Niscemi** Sicilia, Italy, C Mediterranean Sea
Nisch/Nish *see* Niš
165 *R4* **Niseko** Hokkaidō, NE Japan
Nishapur *see* Neyshābūr
114 *G9* **Nishava** *var.* Nišava. ≈ Bulgaria/Serbia *see also* Nišava
Nishava *see* Nišava
118 *L11* **Nishcha** ≈ N Belarus
165 *C17* **Nishinoomote** Kagoshima, Tanega-shima, SW Japan
165 *X15* **Nishino-shima** *Eng.* Rosario. *island* Ogasawara-shotō, SE Japan
165 *I13* **Nishiwaki** *var.* Nisiwaki. Hyōgo, Honshū, SW Japan
141 *U14* **Nishtūn** SE Yemen
Nisibin *see* Nusaybin
Nisiros *see* Nísyros
Nisiwaki *see* Nishiwaki
Niska *see* Niesky
113 *O14* **Niška Banja** Serbia, SE Serbia
12 *D6* **Niskibi** ≈ Ontario, C Canada
111 *O15* **Nisko** Podkrapackie, SE Poland
10 *H7* **Nisling** ≈ Yukon Territory, W Canada
99 *H22* **Nismes** Namur, S Belgium
Nismes *see* Nîmes
116 *M10* **Nisporeni** *Rus.* Nisporeny. W Moldova
Nisporeny *see* Nisporeni
95 *K20* **Nissan** ≈ S Sweden
Nissan Islands *see* Green Islands
95 *F16* **Nisser** ◎ S Norway
95 *E21* **Nissum Bredning** *inlet* NW Denmark
29 *U6* **Nisswa** Minnesota, N USA
Nistru *see* Dniester
115 *M22* **Nísyros** *var.* Nisiros. *island* Dodekánisa, Greece, Aegean Sea
118 *H8* **Nītaure** Cēsis, C Latvia
60 *P10* **Niterói** *prev.* Nictheroy. Rio de Janeiro, SE Brazil
14 *F16* **Nith** ≈ Ontario, S Canada
96 *J13* **Nith** ≈ S Scotland, UK
Nitinan *see* Nichinan
111 *I21* **Nitra** *Ger.* Neutra, *Hung.* Nyitra. Nitriansky Kraj, SW Slovakia
111 *I20* **Nitra** *Ger.* Neutra, *Hung.* Nyitra. ≈ W Slovakia
111 *I21* **Nitriansky Kraj** ◐ *region* SW Slovakia
21 *Q5* **Nitro** West Virginia, NE USA
95 *H14* **Nittedal** Akershus, S Norway
Niuatobutabu *see* Niuatoputapu
193 *X13* **Niuatoputapu** *var.* Niuatobutabu; *prev.* Keppel Island. *island* N Tonga
193 *U15* **Niu'Aunofa** *headland* Tongatapu, S Tonga
Niuchwang *see* Yingkou
190 *B16* **Niue** ◇ *self-governing territory in free association with New Zealand* S Pacific Ocean
190 *F10* **Niulakita** *var.* Nurakita. *atoll* S Tuvalu
190 *E6* **Niutao** *atoll* NW Tuvalu
93 *L15* **Nivala** Oulu, C Finland
102 *I15* **Nive** ≈ SW France
99 *G19* **Nivelles** Walloon Brabant, C Belgium
103 *P8* **Nivernais** *cultural region* C France
15 *N8* **Niverville, Lac** ◎ Québec, SE Canada
27 *T7* **Nixa** Missouri, C USA
35 *R5* **Nixon** Nevada, W USA
25 *S12* **Nixon** Texas, SW USA
Niya *see* Minfeng
155 *H14* **Nizāmābād** Andhra Pradesh, C India
155 *H15* **Nizām Sāgar** ◎ C India
125 *N16* **Nizhegorodskaya Oblast'** ◐ *province* W Russian Federation
Nizhnegorskiy *see* Nyzhn'ohirs'kyy
127 *S4* **Nizhnekamsk** Respublika Tatarstan, W Russian Federation
127 *U3* **Nizhnekamskoye Vodokhranilishche** ▣ W Russian Federation
123 *S14* **Nizhneleninskoye** Yevreyskaya Avtonomnaya Oblast', SE Russian Federation
122 *L13* **Nizhneudinsk** Irkutskaya Oblast', S Russian Federation
122 *I10* **Nizhnevartovsk** Khanty-Mansiyskiy Avtonomnyy Okrug, C Russian Federation
123 *Q7* **Nizhneyansk** Respublika Sakha (Yakutiya), NE Russian Federation
127 *Q11* **Nizhniy Baskunchak** Astrakhanskaya Oblast', SW Russian Federation
127 *O6* **Nizhniy Lomov** Penzenskaya Oblast', W Russian Federation
127 *P3* **Nizhniy Novgorod** *prev.* Gor'kiy. Nizhegorodskaya Oblast', W Russian Federation
125 *T8* **Nizhniy Odes** Respublika Komi, NW Russian Federation
Nizhniy Pyandzh *see* Panji Poyon
122 *G10* **Nizhniy Tagil** Sverdlovskaya Oblast', C Russian Federation
125 *T9* **Nizhnyaya-Omra** Respublika Komi, NW Russian Federation
125 *P5* **Nizhnyaya Pesha** Nenetskiy Avtonomnyy Okrug, NW Russian Federation
117 *Q3* **Nizhyn** *Rus.* Nezhin. Chernihivs'ka Oblast', NE Ukraine
136 *M17* **Nizip** Gaziantep, S Turkey
141 *X8* **Nizwá** *var.* Nazwāh. NE Oman
Nizza *see* Nice
106 *C9* **Nizza Monferrato** Piemonte, NE Italy
Njávdám *see* Näätämöjoki
Njazidja *see* Grande Comore
Njellim *see* Nellim
81 *H24* **Njombe** Iringa, S Tanzania
81 *G23* **Njombe** ≈ C Tanzania
Njuk, Ozero *see* Nyuk, Ozero
Njuksenica *see* Nyuksenitsa
92 *I10* **Njunis** ▲ N Norway
93 *H17* **Njurunda** Västernorrland, C Sweden
94 *N11* **Njutånger** Gävleborg, C Sweden
79 *D14* **Nkambe** Nord-Ouest, NW Cameroon
Nkata Bay *see* Nkhata Bay
79 *F21* **Nkayi** *prev.* Jacob. La Bouenza, S Congo
83 *J17* **Nkayi** Matabeleland North, W Zimbabwe
82 *N13* **Nkhata Bay** *var.* Nkata Bay. Northern, N Malawi
81 *E22* **Nkonde** Kigoma, N Tanzania
79 *D15* **Nkongsamba** *var.* N'Kongsamba. Littoral, W Cameroon
N'Kongsamba *see* Nkongsamba
83 *E16* **Nkurenkuru** Okavango, N Namibia
77 *Q15* **Nkwanta** E Ghana
167 *O2* **Nmai Hka** *var.* Me Hka. ≈ N Burma (Myanmar)
Noardwâlde *see* Noordwolde
39 *N7* **Noatak** Alaska, USA
39 *N7* **Noatak River** ≈ Alaska, USA
164 *E15* **Nobeoka** Miyazaki, Kyūshū, SW Japan
27 *N11* **Noble** Oklahoma, C USA
31 *P13* **Noblesville** Indiana, N USA
165 *R5* **Noboribetsu** *var.* Noboribetu. Hokkaidō, NE Japan
Noboribetu *see* Noboribetsu
59 *H18* **Nobres** Mato Grosso, W Brazil
107 *N21* **Nocera Terinese** Calabria, S Italy
41 *Q16* **Nochixtlán** *var.* Asunción Nochixtlán. Oaxaca, SE Mexico
25 *S5* **Nocona** Texas, SW USA
63 *K21* **Nodales, Bahía de los** *bay* S Argentina
27 *Q2* **Nodaway River** ≈ Iowa/ Missouri, C USA
27 *R8* **Noel** Missouri, C USA
40 *H3* **Nogales** Chihuahua, NW Mexico
40 *F3* **Nogales** Sonora, NW Mexico
36 *M17* **Nogales** Arizona, SW USA
Nogal Valley *see* Dooxo Nugaaleed
102 *K15* **Nogaro** Gers, S France
110 *J7* **Nogat** ≈ N Poland
164 *D12* **Nōgata** Fukuoka, Kyūshū, SW Japan
127 *P15* **Nogayskaya Step'** *steppe* SW Russian Federation
102 *M6* **Nogent-le-Rotrou** Eure-et-Loir, C France
103 *O4* **Nogent-sur-Oise** Oise, N France
103 *P6* **Nogent-sur-Seine** Aube, N France
122 *L10* **Noginsk** Evenkiyskiy Avtonomnyy Okrug, N Russian Federation
126 *L3* **Noginsk** Moskovskaya Oblast', W Russian Federation
123 *T12* **Nogliki** Ostrov Sakhalin, Sakhalinskaya Oblast', SE Russian Federation
164 *K12* **Nōgōhaku-san** ▲ Honshū, SW Japan
162 *D5* **Nogoonnuur** Bayan-Ölgiy, NW Mongolia
61 *C18* **Nogoyá** Entre Ríos, E Argentina
111 *K21* **Nógrád** *off.* Nógrád Megye. ◐ *county* N Hungary
Nógrád Megye *see* Nógrád
105 *U5* **Noguera Pallaresa** ≈ NE Spain
105 *U4* **Noguera Ribagorçana** ≈ NE Spain
101 *E19* **Nohfelden** Saarland, SW Germany
38 *A8* **Nohili Point** *headland* Kaua'i, Hawai'i, USA
104 *G3* **Noia** Galicia, NW Spain
103 *N16* **Noire, Montagne** ⛰ S France
15 *P12* **Noire, Rivière** ≈ Québec, SE Canada
14 *J10* **Noire, Rivière** ≈ Québec, SE Canada
Noire, Rivi`ere *see* Black River
102 *G6* **Noires, Montagnes** ⛰ NW France
102 *H8* **Noirmoutier-en-l'Île** Vendée, NW France
102 *H8* **Noirmoutier, Île de** *island* NW France
187 *Q10* **Noka** Nendö, E Solomon Islands
83 *G17* **Nokaneng** North West, NW Botswana
93 *L18* **Nokia** Länsi-Suomi, W Finland
148 *K11* **Nok Kundi** Baluchistān, SW Pakistan
30 *L14* **Nokomis** Illinois, N USA
30 *K5* **Nokomis, Lake** ▣ Wisconsin, N USA
78 *G9* **Nokou** Kanem, W Chad
187 *Q12* **Nokuku** Espiritu Santo, W Vanuatu
95 *J18* **Nol** Västra Götaland, S Sweden
79 *H16* **Nola** Sangha-Mbaéré, SW Central African Republic
25 *P7* **Nolan** Texas, SW USA
125 *R15* **Nolinsk** Kirovskaya Oblast', NW Russian Federation
Nolsø *see* Nólsoy
95 *B19* **Nólsoy** *Dan.* Nolsø. *island* E Faeroe Islands
186 *B7* **Nomad** Western, SW Papau New Guinea
164 *B16* **Noma-zaki** Kyūshū, SW Japan
40 *K10* **Nombre de Dios** Durango, C Mexico
42 *I5* **Nombre de Dios, Cordillera** ⛰ N Honduras
38 *M9* **Nome** Alaska, USA
29 *Q6* **Nome** North Dakota, N USA
38 *M9* **Nome, Cape** *headland* Alaska, USA
162 *K11* **Nomgon** *var.* Sangiyn Dalay. Ömnögovĭ, S Mongolia
14 *M11* **Nominingue, Lac** ◎ Québec, SE Canada
Nomoi Islands *see* Mortlock Islands
164 *B16* **Nomo-zaki** *headland* Kyūshū, SW Japan
162 *G6* **Nömrög** *var.* Hödrögö. Dzavhan, N Mongolia
193 *X15* **Nomuka** *island* Nomuka Group, C Tonga
193 *X15* **Nomuka Group** *island group* W Tonga

◆ Country
● Country Capital
◇ Dependent Territory
○ Dependent Territory Capital
◐ Administrative Regions
✕ International Airport
▲ Mountain
⛰ Mountain Range
⋏ Volcano
≈ River
◎ Lake
▣ Reservoir

NOMWIN ATOLL – NOUAL, SEBKHET EN

189 Q15 **Nomwin Atoll** *atoll* Hall Islands, C Micronesia
8 L10 **Nonacho Lake** ◎ Northwest Territories, NW Canada
Nondaburi *see* Nonthaburi
39 P12 **Nondalton** Alaska, USA
163 V16 **Nong'an** Jilin, NE China
169 P10 **Nong Bua Khok** Nakhon Ratchasima, C Thailand
167 Q9 **Nong Bua Lamphu** Udon Thani, E Thailand
167 R7 **Nông Hèt** Xiangkhoang, N Laos
Nongkaya *see* Nong Khai
167 Q8 **Nong Khai** *var.* Mi Chai, Nongkaya. Nong Khai, E Thailand
167 N14 **Nong Met** Surat Thani, SW Thailand
83 L22 **Nongoma** KwaZulu/Natal, E South Africa
167 P9 **Nong Phai** Phetchabun, C Thailand
153 U13 **Nongstoin** Meghālaya, NE India
83 C19 **Nonidas** Erongo, N Namibia
Nonni *see* Nen Jiang
40 I7 **Nonoava** Chihuahua, N Mexico
191 O3 **Nonouti** *prev.* Sydenham Island. *atoll* Tungaru, W Kiribati
167 O11 **Nonthaburi** *var.* Nondaburi, Nontha Buri. Nonthaburi, C Thailand
Nontha Buri *see* Nonthaburi
102 L11 **Nontron** Dordogne, SW France
181 P1 **Noonamah** Northern Territory, N Australia
28 K2 **Noonan** North Dakota, N USA
99 E14 **Noord-Beveland** *var.* North Beveland. *island* SW Netherlands
99 J14 **Noord-Brabant** *Eng.* North Brabant. ⬖ *province* S Netherlands
98 H7 **Noorder Haaks** *spit* NW Netherlands
98 H9 **Noord-Holland** *Eng.* North Holland. ⬖ *province* NW Netherlands
Noordhollandsch Kanaal *see* Noordhollands Kanaal
98 H8 **Noordhollands Kanaal** *var.* Noordhollandsch Kanaal. *canal* NW Netherlands
Noord-Kaap *see* Northern Cape
98 L8 **Noordoostpolder** *island* N Netherlands
45 P16 **Noordpunt** *headland* Curaçao, C Netherlands Antilles
98 I8 **Noord-Scharwoude** Noord-Holland, NW Netherlands
Noordwes *see* North-West
98 G11 **Noordwijk aan Zee** Zuid-Holland, W Netherlands
98 H11 **Noordwijkerhout** Zuid-Holland, W Netherlands
98 M7 **Noordwolde** *Fris.* Noardwâlde. Friesland, N Netherlands
Noordzee *see* North Sea
98 H10 **Noordzee-Kanaal** *canal* NW Netherlands
93 K18 **Noormarkku** *Swe.* Norrmark. Länsi-Soumi, SW Finland
39 N8 **Noorvik** Alaska, USA
10 J17 **Nootka Sound** *inlet* British Columbia, W Canada
82 A9 **Nóqui** Dem. Rep. Congo, W Angola
95 L15 **Nora** Örebro, C Sweden
147 Q13 **Norak** *Rus.* Nurek. W Tajikistan
13 I13 **Noranda** Québec, SE Canada
29 W12 **Nora Springs** Iowa, C USA
95 M14 **Norberg** Västmanland, C Sweden
14 K13 **Norcan Lake** ◎ Ontario, SE Canada
197 R12 **Nord** Avannaarsua, N Greenland
78 F13 **Nord** *Eng.* North. ⬖ *province* N Cameroon
103 P2 **Nord** ⬖ *department* N France
92 P1 **Nordaustlandet** *island* NE Svalbard
95 G24 **Nordborg** *Ger.* Nordburg. Sønderjylland, SW Denmark
Nordburg *see* Nordborg
95 F23 **Nordby** Ribe, W Denmark
9 P15 **Nordegg** Alberta, SW Canada
100 E9 **Norden** Niedersachsen, NW Germany
100 G10 **Nordenham** Niedersachsen, NW Germany
122 M6 **Nordenshel'da, Arkhipelag** *island group* N Russian Federation
92 O3 **Nordenskiold Land** *physical region* W Svalbard
100 E9 **Norderney** *island* NW Germany
100 J9 **Norderstedt** Schleswig-Holstein, N Germany
94 D11 **Nordfjord** *fjord* S Norway
94 C11 **Nordfjord** *physical region* S Norway
94 D11 **Nordfjordeid** Sogn Og Fjordane, S Norway
92 G11 **Nordfold** Nordland, C Norway
Nordfriesische Inseln *see* North Frisian Islands
100 H7 **Nordfriesland** *cultural region* N Germany
101 K15 **Nordhausen** Thüringen, C Germany
25 T13 **Nordheim** Texas, SW USA
94 C13 **Nordhordland** *physical region* S Norway
100 E12 **Nordhorn** Niedersachsen, NW Germany
92 I1 **Nordhurfjördhur** Vestfirdhir, NW Iceland
92 J1 **Nordhurland Eystra** ⬖ *region* N Iceland
92 I2 **Nordhurland Vestra** ⬖ *region* N Iceland
172 H16 **Nord, Île du** *island* Inner Islands, NE Seychelles
95 F20 **Nordjylland** *var.* Nordjyllands Amt. ⬖ *county* N Denmark
Nordjyllands Amt *see* Nordjylland
92 K7 **Nordkapp** *Eng.* North Cape. *headland* N Norway
92 O1 **Nordkapp** *headland* N Svalbard
92 L7 **Nordkinn** *headland* N Norway
79 N19 **Nord Kivu** *off.* Région du Nord Kivu. ⬖ *region* E Dem. Rep. Congo
Nord Kivu, Région du *see* Nord Kivu
92 G12 **Nordland** ⬖ *county* C Norway
101 J21 **Nördlingen** Bayern, S Germany
93 I16 **Nordmaling** Västerbotten, N Sweden
95 K15 **Nordmark** Värmland, C Sweden
Nord, Mer du *see* North Sea
94 F8 **Nordmøre** *physical region* S Norway
100 I8 **Nord-Ostee-Kanal** *canal* N Germany
0 J3 **Nordostrundingen** *cape* NE Greenland
79 D14 **Nord-Ouest** *Eng.* North-West. ⬖ *province* NW Cameroon
Nord-Ouest, Territoires du *see* Northwest Territories
103 N2 **Nord-Pas-de-Calais** ⬖ *region* N France
101 F19 **Nordpfälzer Bergland** ⛰ W Germany
Nord, Pointe *see* Fatua, Pointe
187 P16 **Nord, Province** ⬖ *province* C New Caledonia
101 D14 **Nordrhein-Westfalen** *Eng.* North Rhine-Westphalia, *Fr.* Rhénanie du Nord-Westphalie. ⬖ *state* W Germany
Nordsee/Nordsjøen/Nordsøen *see* North Sea
100 H7 **Nordstrand** *island* N Germany
93 E15 **Nord-Trøndelag** ⬖ *county* C Norway
97 E19 **Nore** *Ir.* An Fheoir. ≈ S Ireland
29 Q14 **Norfolk** Nebraska, C USA
21 X7 **Norfolk** Virginia, NE USA
97 P19 **Norfolk** *cultural region* E England, UK
192 K10 **Norfolk Island** ◇ *Australian external territory* SW Pacific Ocean
175 P9 **Norfolk Ridge** *undersea feature* W Pacific Ocean
27 U8 **Norfork Lake** ⊠ Arkansas/Missouri, C USA
98 N6 **Norg** Drenthe, NE Netherlands
Norge *see* Norway
95 D14 **Norheimsund** Hordaland, S Norway
25 S16 **Norias** Texas, SW USA
164 L12 **Norikura-dake** ▲ Honshū, S Japan
122 K8 **Noril'sk** Taymyrskiy (Dolgano-Nenetskiy) Avtonomnyy Okrug, N Russian Federation
14 I13 **Norland** Ontario, SE Canada
21 V8 **Norlina** North Carolina, SE USA
30 L13 **Normal** Illinois, N USA
27 N11 **Norman** Oklahoma, C USA
Norman *see* Tulita
186 G9 **Normanby Island** *island* SE Papua New Guinea
Normandes, Îles *see* Channel Islands
58 G9 **Normandia** Roraima, N Brazil
102 L5 **Normandie** *Eng.* Normandy. *cultural region* N France
102 J5 **Normandie, Collines de** *hill range* NW France
Normandy *see* Normandie
25 V9 **Normangee** Texas, SW USA
21 Q10 **Norman, Lake** ⊠ North Carolina, SE USA
44 K13 **Norman Manley** ✈ (Kingston) E Jamaica
181 U5 **Norman River** ≈ Queensland, NE Australia
181 U4 **Normanton** Queensland, NE Australia
8 I8 **Norman Wells** Northwest Territories, NW Canada
12 H12 **Normétal** Québec, S Canada
163 O7 **Norovlin** *var.* Uldz. Hentiy, NE Mongolia
9 V15 **Norquay** Saskatchewan, S Canada
94 N11 **Norra Dellen** ◎ C Sweden
93 G15 **Norråker** Jämtland, C Sweden
94 N12 **Norrala** Gävleborg, C Sweden
Norra Ny *see* Stöllet
92 G13 **Norra Storjfjället** ▲ N Sweden
92 I13 **Norrbotten** ⬖ *county* N Sweden
95 G23 **Nørre Aaby** *var.* Nørre Åby. Fyn, C Denmark
Nørre Åby *see* Nørre Aaby
95 I24 **Nørre Alslev** Storstrøm, SE Denmark
95 E23 **Nørre Nebel** Ribe, W Denmark
95 G20 **Nørresundby** Nordjylland, N Denmark
21 N8 **Norris Lake** ⊠ Tennessee, S USA
18 I15 **Norristown** Pennsylvania, NE USA
95 N17 **Norrköping** Östergötland, S Sweden
Normark *see* Noormarkku
94 N13 **Norrsundet** Gävleborg, C Sweden
95 P15 **Norrtälje** Stockholm, C Sweden
180 L12 **Norseman** Western Australia
93 I14 **Norsjö** Västerbotten, N Sweden
95 G16 **Norsjø** ◎ S Norway
123 R13 **Norsk** Amurskaya Oblast', SE Russian Federation
Norske Havet *see* Norwegian Sea
187 Q13 **Norsup** Malekula, C Vanuatu
191 V15 **Norte, Cabo** *cape* Easter Island, Chile, E Pacific Ocean
54 F7 **Norte de Santander** *off.* Departamento de Norte de Santander. ⬖ *province* N Colombia
Norte de Santander, Departamento de *see* Norte de Santander
61 E21 **Norte, Punta** *headland* E Argentina
21 R13 **North** South Carolina, SE USA
North *see* Nord
18 L10 **North Adams** Massachusetts, NE USA
113 L17 **North Albanian Alps** *Alb.* Bjeshkët e Namuna, *SCr.* Prokletije. ⛰ SE Europe
97 M15 **Northallerton** N England, UK
180 J12 **Northam** Western Australia
83 J20 **Northam** Northern, N South Africa
1 **North America** *continent*
1 N12 **North American Basin** *undersea feature* W Sargasso Sea
0 C5 **North American Plate** *tectonic feature*
18 M11 **North Amherst** Massachusetts, NE USA
97 N20 **Northampton** C England, UK
97 M20 **Northamptonshire** *cultural region* C England, UK
151 P18 **North Andaman** *island* Andaman Islands, India, NE Indian Ocean
65 D25 **North Arm** East Falkland, Falkland Islands
21 Q13 **North Augusta** South Carolina, SE USA
173 W8 **North Australian Basin** *Fr.* Bassin Nord de l' Australie. *undersea feature* E Indian Ocean
31 R11 **North Baltimore** Ohio, N USA
9 T15 **North Battleford** Saskatchewan, S Canada
14 H11 **North Bay** Ontario, S Canada
12 H6 **North Belcher Islands** *island group* Belcher Islands, Nunavut, C Canada
29 R15 **North Bend** Nebraska, C USA
32 E14 **North Bend** Oregon, NW USA
96 K12 **North Berwick** SE Scotland, UK
North Beveland *see* Noord-Beveland
North Borneo *see* Sabah
183 P5 **North Bourke** New South Wales, SE Australia
North Brabant *see* Noord-Brabant
182 F2 **North Branch Neales** *seasonal river* South Australia
44 M6 **North Caicos** *island* NW Turks and Caicos Islands
26 L10 **North Canadian River** ≈ Oklahoma, C USA
31 U12 **North Canton** Ohio, N USA
13 R13 **North, Cape** *headland* Cape Breton Island, Nova Scotia, SE Canada
184 I1 **North Cape** *headland* North Island, New Zealand
186 G5 **North Cape** *headland* New Ireland, NE Papua New Guinea
North Cape *see* Nordkapp
18 J17 **North Cape May** New Jersey, NE USA
12 C9 **North Caribou Lake** ◎ Ontario, C Canada
21 U10 **North Carolina** *off.* State of North Carolina, *also known as* Old North State, Tar Heel State, Turpentine State. ⬖ *state* SE USA
North Celebes *see* Sulawesi Utara
155 J24 **North Central Province** ⬖ *province* N Sri Lanka
31 S4 **North Channel** *lake channel* Canada/USA
97 G14 **North Channel** *strait* Northern Ireland/Scotland, UK
21 S14 **North Charleston** South Carolina, SE USA
31 N10 **North Chicago** Illinois, N USA
195 Y10 **Northcliffe Glacier** *glacier* Antarctica
31 Q14 **North College Hill** Ohio, N USA
25 O8 **North Concho River** ≈ Texas, SW USA
19 O8 **North Conway** New Hampshire, NE USA
27 V14 **North Crossett** Arkansas, C USA
28 L4 **North Dakota** *off.* State of North Dakota, *also known as* Flickertail State, Peace Garden State, Sioux State. ⬖ *state* N USA
North Devon Island *see* Devon Island
97 O22 **North Downs** *hill range* SE England, UK
18 C11 **North East** Pennsylvania, NE USA
83 I18 **North East** ⬖ *district* NE Botswana
65 G15 **North East Bay** *bay* Ascension Island, C Atlantic Ocean
38 L10 **Northeast Cape** *headland* Saint Lawrence Island, Alaska, USA
81 J17 **North Eastern** ⬖ *province* Kenya
North East Frontier Agency/North East Frontier Agency of Assam *see* Arunāchal Pradesh
65 E25 **North East Island** *island* E Falkland Islands
189 V11 **Northeast Island** *island* Chuuk, C Micronesia
44 L6 **Northeast Point** *headland* Great Inagua, S Bahamas
44 K5 **Northeast Point** *headland* Acklins Island, SE Bahamas
44 L12 **North East Point** *headland* E Jamaica
191 Z2 **Northeast Point** *headland* Kiritimati, E Kiribati
44 H2 **Northeast Providence Channel** *channel* N Bahamas
101 J14 **Northeim** Niedersachsen, C Germany
29 X14 **North English** Iowa, C USA
138 G8 **Northern** ⬖ *district* N Israel
82 M12 **Northern** ⬖ *region* N Malawi
186 F8 **Northern** ⬖ *province* S Papua New Guinea
80 D7 **Northern** ⬖ *state* N Sudan
82 K12 **Northern** ⬖ *province* NE Zambia
Northern *see* Limpopo
80 B13 **Northern Bahr el Ghazal** ⬖ *state* SW Sudan
Northern Border Region *see* Al Ḩudūd ash Shamālīyah
83 F24 **Northern Cape** *off.* Northern Cape Province, *Afr.* Noord-Kaap. ⬖ *province* W South Africa
Northern Cape Province *see* Northern Cape
190 K14 **Northern Cook Islands** *island group* N Cook Islands
80 B8 **Northern Darfur** ⬖ *state* NW Sudan
Northern Dvina *see* Severnaya Dvina
97 F14 **Northern Ireland** *var.* The Six Counties. *cultural region* Northern Ireland, UK
80 D9 **Northern Kordofan** ⬖ *state* C Sudan
187 Z14 **Northern Lau Group** *island group* Lau Group, NE Fiji
188 K3 **Northern Mariana Islands** ◇ *US commonwealth territory* W Pacific Ocean
155 J23 **Northern Province** ⬖ *province* N Sri Lanka
Northern Rhodesia *see* Zambia
Northern Sporades *see* Vóreies Sporádes
182 D1 **Northern Territory** ⬖ *territory* N Australia
Northern Transvaal *see* Limpopo
Northern Ural Hills *see* Severnyye Uvaly
84 I9 **North European Plain** *plain* N Europe
27 V2 **North Fabius River** ≈ Missouri, C USA
65 D24 **North Falkland Sound** *sound* N Falkland Islands
29 V9 **Northfield** Minnesota, N USA
19 O9 **Northfield** New Hampshire, NE USA
175 Q8 **North Fiji Basin** *undersea feature* N Coral Sea
97 Q22 **North Foreland** *headland* SE England, UK
35 P6 **North Fork American River** ≈ California, W USA
39 R7 **North Fork Chandalar River** ≈ Alaska, USA
28 K7 **North Fork Grand River** ≈ North Dakota/South Dakota, N USA
21 O6 **North Fork Kentucky River** ≈ Kentucky, S USA
39 Q7 **North Fork Koyukuk River** ≈ Alaska, USA
39 Q10 **North Fork Kuskokwim River** ≈ Alaska, USA
26 K11 **North Fork Red River** ≈ Oklahoma/Texas, SW USA
26 K3 **North Fork Solomon River** ≈ Kansas, C USA
23 W14 **North Fort Myers** Florida, SE USA
31 P5 **North Fox Island** *island* Michigan, N USA
100 G6 **North Frisian Islands** *var.* Nordfriesische Inseln. *island group* N Germany
197 N9 **North Geomagnetic Pole** *pole* Arctic Ocean
18 M13 **North Haven** Connecticut, NE USA
184 J5 **North Head** *headland* North Island, New Zealand
18 L6 **North Hero** Vermont, NE USA
35 O7 **North Highlands** California, W USA
North Holland *see* Noord-Holland
81 I16 **North Horr** Eastern, N Kenya
151 K21 **North Huvadhu Atoll** *var.* Gaafu Alifu Atoll. *atoll* S Maldives
65 A24 **North Island** *island* W Falkland Islands
184 N9 **North Island** *island* N New Zealand
21 U14 **North Island** *island* South Carolina, SE USA
31 O11 **North Judson** Indiana, N USA
North Kazakhstan *see* Severnyy Kazakhstan
31 V10 **North Kingsville** Ohio, N USA
163 Y13 **North Korea** *off.* Democratic People's Republic of Korea, *Kor.* Chosŏn-minjujuŭi-inmin-kanghwaguk. ◆ *republic* E Asia
153 X11 **North Lakhimpur** Assam, NE India
184 J3 **Northland** *off.* Northland Region. ⬖ *region* North Island, New Zealand
192 K11 **Northland Plateau** *undersea feature* S Pacific Ocean
Northland Region *see* Northland
35 X11 **North Las Vegas** Nevada, W USA
31 O11 **North Liberty** Indiana, N USA
29 X14 **North Liberty** Iowa, C USA
27 V12 **North Little Rock** Arkansas, C USA
28 M13 **North Loup River** ≈ Nebraska, C USA
151 K18 **North Maalhosmadulu Atoll** *var.* North Malosmadulu Atoll, Raa Atoll. *atoll* N Maldives
31 U10 **North Madison** Ohio, N USA
North Malosmadulu Atoll *see* North Maalhosmadulu Atoll
31 P12 **North Manchester** Indiana, N USA
31 P6 **North Manitou Island** *island* Michigan, N USA
29 U10 **North Mankato** Minnesota, N USA
23 Z15 **North Miami** Florida, SE USA
151 K18 **North Miladummadulu Atoll** *atoll* N Maldives
North Minch *see* Minch, The
23 W15 **North Naples** Florida, SE USA
175 P8 **North New Hebrides Trench** *undersea feature* N Coral Sea
23 Y15 **North New River Canal** ≈ Florida, SE USA
151 K20 **North Nilandhe Atoll** *atoll* C Maldives
36 L2 **North Ogden** Utah, W USA
North Ossetia *see* Severnaya Osetiya-Alaniya, Respublika
35 S10 **North Palisade** ▲ California, W USA
189 U11 **North Pass** *passage* Chuuk Islands, C Micronesia
28 M15 **North Platte** Nebraska, C USA
33 X17 **North Platte River** ≈ C USA
65 G14 **North Point** *headland* Ascension Island, C Atlantic Ocean
172 I16 **North Point** *headland* Mahé, NE Seychelles
31 R5 **North Point** *headland* Michigan, N USA
31 S6 **North Point** *headland* Michigan, N USA
39 S9 **North Pole** Alaska, USA
197 R9 **North Pole** *pole* Arctic Ocean
23 O4 **Northport** Alabama, S USA
23 W14 **North Port** Florida, SE USA
32 L6 **Northport** Washington, NW USA
32 L12 **North Powder** Oregon, NW USA
29 U13 **North Raccoon River** ≈ Iowa, C USA
North Rhine-Westphalia *see* Nordrhein-Westfalen
97 M16 **North Riding** *cultural region* N England, UK
96 G5 **North Rona** *island* NW Scotland, UK
96 K4 **North Ronaldsay** *island* NE Scotland, UK
36 L2 **North Salt Lake** Utah, W USA
9 P15 **North Saskatchewan** ≈ Alberta/Saskatchewan, S Canada
35 X5 **North Schell Peak** ▲ Nevada, W USA
North Scotia Ridge *see* South Georgia Ridge
86 D10 **North Sea** *Dan.* Nordsøen, *Dut.* Noordzee, *Fr.* Mer du Nord, *Ger.* Nordsee, *Nor.* Nordsjøen; *prev.* German Ocean, *Lat.* Mare Germanicum. *sea* NW Europe
35 T6 **North Shoshone Peak** ▲ Nevada, W USA
North Siberian Lowland/North Siberian Plain *see* Severo-Sibirskaya Nizmennost'
29 R13 **North Sioux City** South Dakota, N USA
96 K4 **North Sound, The** *sound* N Scotland, UK
183 T4 **North Star** New South Wales, SE Australia
North Star State *see* Minnesota
183 V3 **North Stradbroke Island** *island* Queensland, E Australia
North Sulawesi *see* Sulawesi Utara
North Sumatra *see* Sumatera Utara
14 D17 **North Sydenham** ≈ Ontario, S Canada
18 H9 **North Syracuse** New York, NE USA
184 K9 **North Taranaki Bight** *gulf* North Island, New Zealand
12 H9 **North Twin Island** *island* Nunavut, C Canada
96 E8 **North Uist** *island* NW Scotland, UK
97 L14 **Northumberland** *cultural region* N England, UK
181 Y7 **Northumberland Isles** *island group* Queensland, NE Australia
13 Q14 **Northumberland Strait** *strait* SE Canada
32 G14 **North Umpqua River** ≈ Oregon, NW USA
45 Q13 **North Union** Saint Vincent, Saint Vincent and the Grenadines
10 L17 **North Vancouver** British Columbia, SW Canada
18 K9 **Northville** New York, NE USA
97 Q19 **North Walsham** E England, UK
39 T10 **Northway** Alaska, USA
83 G17 **North-West** ⬖ *district* NW Botswana
83 G21 **North-West** *off.* North-West Province, *Afr.* Noordwes. ⬖ *province* N South Africa
Northwest *see* Nord-Ouest
64 I6 **Northwest Atlantic Mid-Ocean Canyon** *undersea feature* N Atlantic Ocean
180 G8 **North West Cape** *cape* Western Australia
38 J9 **Northwest Cape** *headland* Saint Lawrence Island, Alaska, USA
82 H13 **North Western** ⬖ *province* W Zambia
155 J24 **North Western Province** ⬖ *province* W Sri Lanka
149 U4 **North-West Frontier Province** ⬖ *province* NW Pakistan
96 H8 **North West Highlands** ⛰ N Scotland, UK
192 J4 **Northwest Pacific Basin** *undersea feature* NW Pacific Ocean
191 Y2 **Northwest Point** *headland* Kiritimati, E Kiribati
44 G1 **Northwest Providence Channel** *channel* N Bahamas
North-West Province *see* North-West
13 Q8 **North West River** Newfoundland and Labrador, E Canada
8 J9 **Northwest Territories** *Fr.* Territoires du Nord-Ouest. ⬖ *territory* NW Canada
97 K18 **Northwich** C England, UK
25 Q5 **North Wichita River** ≈ Texas, SW USA
18 J17 **North Wildwood** New Jersey, NE USA
21 R9 **North Wilkesboro** North Carolina, SE USA
19 P8 **North Windham** Maine, NE USA
197 Q6 **Northwind Plain** *undersea feature* Arctic Ocean
29 V11 **Northwood** Iowa, C USA
29 Q4 **Northwood** North Dakota, N USA
97 M15 **North York Moors** *moorland* N England, UK
25 V9 **North Zulch** Texas, SW USA
26 K2 **Norton** Kansas, C USA
31 S13 **Norton** Ohio, N USA
21 P7 **Norton** Virginia, NE USA
39 N9 **Norton Bay** *bay* Alaska, USA
Norton de Matos *see* Balombo
31 O9 **Norton Shores** Michigan, N USA
38 M10 **Norton Sound** *inlet* Alaska, USA
27 Q3 **Nortonville** Kansas, C USA
102 I8 **Nort-sur-Erdre** Loire-Atlantique, NW France
195 N2 **Norvegia, Cape** *headland* Antarctica
18 L13 **Norwalk** Connecticut, NE USA
29 V14 **Norwalk** Iowa, C USA
31 S11 **Norwalk** Ohio, N USA
19 P7 **Norway** Maine, NE USA
31 N5 **Norway** Michigan, N USA
93 E17 **Norway** *off.* Kingdom of Norway, *Nor.* Norge. ◆ *monarchy* N Europe
9 X13 **Norway House** Manitoba, C Canada
Norway, Kingdom of *see* Norway
197 R16 **Norwegian Basin** *undersea feature* NW Norwegian Sea
84 D6 **Norwegian Sea** *var.* Norske Havet. *sea* NE Atlantic Ocean
197 S17 **Norwegian Trench** *undersea feature* NE North Sea
14 F16 **Norwich** Ontario, S Canada
97 Q19 **Norwich** E England, UK
19 N13 **Norwich** Connecticut, NE USA
18 I11 **Norwich** New York, NE USA
29 U9 **Norwood** Minnesota, N USA
31 Q15 **Norwood** Ohio, N USA
14 H11 **Nosbonsing, Lake** ◎ Ontario, S Canada
Nösen *see* Bistriţa
165 T1 **Noshappu-misaki** *headland* Hokkaidō, NE Japan
165 P7 **Noshiro** *var.* Nosiro; *prev.* Noshirominato. Akita, Honshū, C Japan
Noshirominato/Nosiro *see* Noshiro
117 Q3 **Nosivka** *Rus.* Nosovka. Chernihivs'ka Oblast', NE Ukraine
67 T14 **Nosop** *var.* Nossob, Nossop. ≈ Botswana/Namibia
125 S4 **Nosovaya** Nenetskiy Avtonomnyy Okrug, NW Russian Federation
Nosovka *see* Nosivka
143 V11 **Noṣratābād** Sīstān va Balūchestān, E Iran
95 J18 **Nossebro** Västra Götaland, S Sweden
96 K6 **Noss Head** *headland* N Scotland, UK
Nossi-Bé *see* Be, Nosy
83 E20 **Nossob** ≈ E Namibia
Nossob/Nossop *see* Nosop
172 J2 **Nosy Be** ✈ Antsirānana, N Madagascar
172 J6 **Nosy Varika** Fianarantsoa, SE Madagascar
14 L10 **Notawassi** ≈ Québec, SE Canada
14 M9 **Notawassi, Lac** ◎ Québec, SE Canada
36 J5 **Notch Peak** ▲ Utah, W USA
110 G10 **Noteć** *Ger.* Netze. ≈ NW Poland
Nóties Sporádes *see* Dodekánisa
115 J22 **Nótion Aigaíon** *Eng.* Aegean South. ⬖ *region* E Greece
115 H18 **Nótios Evvoïkós Kólpos** *gulf* E Greece
115 B16 **Nótio Stenó Kérkyras** *strait* W Greece
107 L25 **Noto** *anc.* Netum. Sicilia, Italy, C Mediterranean Sea
164 M10 **Noto** Ishikawa, Honshū, SW Japan
95 G15 **Notodden** Telemark, S Norway
107 L25 **Noto, Golfo di** *gulf* Sicilia, Italy, C Mediterranean Sea
164 L10 **Noto-hantō** *peninsula* Honshū, SW Japan
164 L11 **Noto-jima** *island* SW Japan
13 T11 **Notre Dame Bay** *bay* Newfoundland, Newfoundland and Labrador, E Canada
15 P6 **Notre-Dame-de-Lorette** Québec, SE Canada
14 L11 **Notre-Dame-de-Pontmain** Québec, SE Canada
15 T8 **Notre-Dame-du-Lac** Québec, SE Canada
15 Q6 **Notre-Dame-du-Rosaire** Québec, SE Canada
15 U8 **Notre-Dame, Monts** ⛰ Québec, S Canada
77 R16 **Notsé** S Togo
14 G14 **Nottawasaga** ≈ Ontario, S Canada
14 G14 **Nottawasaga Bay** *lake bay* Ontario, S Canada
12 I11 **Nottaway** ≈ Québec, SE Canada
23 S1 **Nottely Lake** ⊠ Georgia, SE USA
95 H16 **Nøtterøy** *island* S Norway
97 M19 **Nottingham** C England, UK
9 E14 **Nottingham Island** *island* Nunavut, NE Canada
97 N18 **Nottinghamshire** *cultural region* C England, UK
21 V7 **Nottoway** Virginia, NE USA
21 V7 **Nottoway River** ≈ Virginia, NE USA
76 G7 **Nouâdhibou** *prev.* Port-Étienne. Dakhlet Nouâdhibou, W Mauritania
76 G7 **Nouâdhibou** ✈ Dakhlet Nouâdhibou, W Mauritania
76 F7 **Nouâdhibou, Dakhlet** *prev.* Baie du Lévrier. *bay* W Mauritania
76 F7 **Nouâdhibou, Râs** *prev.* Cap Blanc. *headland* NW Mauritania
76 G9 **Nouakchott** ● (Mauritania) Nouakchott District, SW Mauritania
76 G9 **Nouakchott** ✈ Trarza, SW Mauritania
120 J11 **Noual, Sebkhet en** *var.* Sabkhat an Nawāl. *salt flat* C Tunisia

◆ Country ● Country Capital ◇ Dependent Territory ○ Dependent Territory Capital ⬖ Administrative Regions ✈ International Airport ▲ Mountain ⛰ Mountain Range ⛰ Volcano ≈ River ◎ Lake ⊠ Reservoir

Nouâmghâr – Nyos, Lake

76 G8 Nouâmghâr var. Nouamrhar. Dakhlet Nouâdhibou, W Mauritania
Nouamrhar see Nouâmghâr
Nouă Sulița see Novoselytsya
187 Q17 Nouméa ○ (New Caledonia) Province Sud, S New Caledonia
79 E15 Noun ≈ C Cameroon
77 N12 Nouna W Burkina
83 H24 Noupoort Northern Cape, C South Africa
Nouveau-Brunswick see New Brunswick
Nouveau-Comptoir see Wemindji
15 T4 Nouvel, Lacs ◎ Québec, SE Canada
15 W7 Nouvelle Québec, SE Canada
15 W7 Nouvelle ≈ Québec, SE Canada
Nouvelle-Calédonie see New Caledonia
Nouvelle Écosse see Nova Scotia
103 R3 Nouzonville Ardennes, N France
147 Q11 Nov Rus. Nau. NW Tajikistan
59 I21 Nova Alvorada Mato Grosso do Sul, SW Brazil
Novabad see Navobod
111 D19 Nová Bystřice Ger. Neubistritz. Jihočeský Kraj, S Czech Republic
116 H13 Novaci Gorj, SW Romania
Nova Civitas see Neustadt an der Weinstrasse
Novaesium see Neuss
60 H10 Nova Esperança Paraná, S Brazil
106 H11 Novafeltria Marche, C Italy
60 Q9 Nova Friburgo Rio de Janeiro, SE Brazil
82 D12 Nova Gaia var. Cambundi-Catembo. Malanje, NE Angola
109 S12 Nova Gorica W Slovenia
112 G10 Nova Gradiška Ger. Neugradisk, Hung. Újgradiska. Brod-Posavina, NE Croatia
60 K7 Nova Granada São Paulo, S Brazil
60 O10 Nova Iguaçu Rio de Janeiro, SE Brazil
117 S10 Nova Kakhovka Rus. Novaya Kakhovka. Khersons'ka Oblast', SE Ukraine
Nová Karvinná see Karviná
Nova Lamego see Gabú
Nova Lisboa see Huambo
112 C11 Novalja Lika-Senj, W Croatia
119 M14 Novalukoml' Rus. Novolukoml'. Vitsyebskaya Voblasts', N Belarus
Nova Mambone see Mambone
83 P16 Nova Nabúri Zambézia, NE Mozambique
117 Q9 Nova Odesa var. Novaya Odessa. Mykolayivs'ka Oblast', S Ukraine
60 H10 Nova Olímpia Paraná, S Brazil
61 I15 Nova Prata Rio Grande do Sul, S Brazil
14 H12 Novar Ontario, S Canada
106 C7 Novara anc. Novaria. Piemonte, NW Italy
Novaria see Novara
117 P7 Novarkanels'k Kirovohrads'ka Oblast', C Ukraine
13 P15 Nova Scotia Fr. Nouvelle Écosse. ⬖ province SE Canada
0 M9 Nova Scotia physical region SE Canada
34 M8 Novato California, W USA
192 M7 Nova Trough undersea feature W Pacific Ocean
116 L7 Nova Ushtsya Khmel'nyts'ka Oblast', W Ukraine
83 M17 Nova Vanduzi Manica, C Mozambique
117 U5 Nova Vodolaha Rus. Novaya Vodolaga. Kharkivs'ka Oblast', E Ukraine
123 O12 Novaya Chara Chitinskaya Oblast', S Russian Federation
122 M12 Novaya Igirma Irkutskaya Oblast', C Russian Federation
Novaya Kakhovka see Nova Kakhovka
144 E10 Novaya Kazanka Zapadnyy Kazakhstan, W Kazakhstan
124 I12 Novaya Ladoga Leningradskaya Oblast', NW Russian Federation
127 R5 Novaya Malykla Ul'yanovskaya Oblast', W Russian Federation
Novaya Odessa see Nova Odesa
123 Q5 Novaya Sibir', Ostrov island Novosibirskiye Ostrova, NE Russian Federation
Novaya Vodolaga see Nova Vodolaha
119 P17 Novaya Yel'nya Rus. Novaya Yel'nya. Mahilyowskaya Voblasts', E Belarus
122 I6 Novaya Zemlya island group N Russian Federation
Novaya Zemlya Trough see East Novaya Zemlya Trough
114 K10 Nova Zagora Sliven, C Bulgaria
105 S12 Novelda País Valenciano, E Spain
111 H19 Nové Mesto nad Váhom Ger. Waagneustadtl, Hung. Vágújhely. Trenčiansky Kraj, W Slovakia
111 F17 Nové Město na Moravě Ger. Neustadtl in Mähren. Vysočina, C Czech Republic
Novesium see Neuss
111 I21 Nové Zámky Ger. Neuhäusel, Hung. Érsekújvár. Nitriansky Kraj, SW Slovakia
Novgorod see Velikiy Novgorod
Novgorod-Severskiy see Novhorod-Sivers'kyy
122 C7 Novgorodskaya Oblast' ⬖ province W Russian Federation
117 R8 Novhorodka Kirovohrads'ka Oblast', C Ukraine
117 R2 Novhorod-Sivers'kyy Rus. Novgorod-Severskiy. Chernihivs'ka Oblast', NE Ukraine
31 R10 Novi Michigan, N USA
Novi see Novi Vinodolski
112 L9 Novi Bečej prev. Új-Becse, Vološinovo, Ger. Neubetsche, Hung. Törökbecse. Vojvodina, N Serbia
25 Q8 Novice Texas, SW USA
112 A9 Novigrad Istra, NW Croatia
Novi Grad see Bosanski Novi
114 G9 Novi Iskŭr Sofiya-Grad, W Bulgaria
106 C9 Novi Ligure Piemonte, NW Italy
99 L22 Noville Luxembourg, SE Belgium
194 I10 Noville Peninsula peninsula Thurston Island, Antarctica
Noviodunum see Soissons, Aisne, France
Noviodunum see Nevers, Nièvre, France
Noviodunum see Nyon, Vaud, Switzerland
Noviomagus see Lisieux, Calvados, France
Noviomagus see Nijmegen, Netherlands
114 M8 Novi Pazar Shumen, NE Bulgaria
113 M15 Novi Pazar Turk. Yenipazar. Serbia, S Serbia
112 K10 Novi Sad Ger. Neusatz, Hung. Újvidék. Vojvodina, N Serbia
117 T6 Novi Sanzhary Poltavs'ka Oblast', C Ukraine
112 H12 Novi Travnik prev. Pučarevo. ⬖ Federacija Bosna I Hercegovina, C Bosnia and Herzegovina
112 B10 Novi Vinodolski var. Novi. Primorje-Gorski Kotar, NW Croatia
58 F12 Novo Airão Amazonas, N Brazil
127 N14 Novoaleksandrovsk Stavropol'skiy Kray, SW Russian Federation
Novoalekseyevka see Khobda
127 N9 Novoanninskiy Volgogradskaya Oblast', SW Russian Federation
58 F13 Novo Aripuanã Amazonas, N Brazil
117 Y6 Novoaydar Luhans'ka Oblast', E Ukraine
117 X9 Novoazovs'k Rus. Novoazovsk. Donets'ka Oblast', E Ukraine
123 R14 Novobureyskiy Amurskaya Oblast', SE Russian Federation
127 Q3 Novocheboksarsk Chavash Respubliki, W Russian Federation
127 R5 Novocheremshansk Ul'yanovskaya Oblast', W Russian Federation
126 L12 Novocherkassk Rostovskaya Oblast', SW Russian Federation
127 R6 Novodevich'ye Samarskaya Oblast', W Russian Federation
124 M8 Novodvinsk Arkhangel'skaya Oblast', NW Russian Federation
Novograd-Volynskiy see Novohrad-Volyns'kyy
Novogrudok see Navahrudak
61 I15 Novo Hamburgo Rio Grande do Sul, S Brazil
59 H16 Novo Horizonte Mato Grosso, W Brazil
60 K8 Novo Horizonte São Paulo, S Brazil
116 M4 Novohrad-Volyns'kyy Rus. Novograd-Volynskiy. Zhytomyrs'ka Oblast', N Ukraine
145 O7 Novoishimskiy prev. Kuybyshevskiy. Severnyy Kazakhstan, N Kazakhstan
Novokazalinsk see Ayteke Bi
126 M8 Novokhopersk Voronezhskaya Oblast', W Russian Federation
127 R6 Novokuybyshevsk Samarskaya Oblast', W Russian Federation
122 J13 Novokuznetsk prev. Stalinsk. Kemerovskaya Oblast', S Russian Federation
195 R1 Novolazarevskaya Russian research station Antarctica
Novolukoml' see Novalukoml'
109 V12 Novo mesto Ger. Rudolfswert; prev. Ger. Neustadtl. SE Slovenia
126 K15 Novomikhaylovskiy Krasnodarskiy Kray, SW Russian Federation
112 L8 Novo Miloševo Vojvodina, N Serbia
Novomirgorod see Novomyrhorod
126 L5 Novomoskovsk Tul'skaya Oblast', W Russian Federation
117 U7 Novomoskovs'k Rus. Novomoskovsk. Dnipropetrovs'ka Oblast', E Ukraine
117 V8 Novomykolayivka Zaporiz'ka Oblast', SE Ukraine
117 Q7 Novomyrhorod Rus. Novomirgorod. Kirovohrads'ka Oblast', S Ukraine
127 N8 Novonikolayevskiy Volgogradskaya Oblast', SW Russian Federation
127 P10 Novonikol'skoye Volgogradskaya Oblast', SW Russian Federation
127 X7 Novoorsk Orenburgskaya Oblast', W Russian Federation
126 M13 Novopokrovskaya Krasnodarskiy Kray, SW Russian Federation
Novopolotsk see Navapolatsk
117 Y5 Novopskov Luhans'ka Oblast', E Ukraine
Novoradomsk see Radomsko
Novo Redondo see Sumbe
127 R8 Novorepnoye Saratovskaya Oblast', W Russian Federation
126 K14 Novorossiysk Krasnodarskiy Kray, SW Russian Federation
Novorossiyskiy/Novorossiyskoye see Akzhar
124 F15 Novorzhev Pskovskaya Oblast', W Russian Federation
Novoselitsa see Novoselytsya
117 S12 Novoselivs'ke Respublika Krym, S Ukraine
Novosëlki see Navasyolki
114 G6 Novo Selo Vidin, NW Bulgaria
113 M14 Novo Selo Serbia, C Serbia
116 K8 Novoselytsya Rom. Nouă Sulița, Rus. Novoselitsa. Chernivets'ka Oblast', W Ukraine
127 U7 Novosergiyevka Orenburgskaya Oblast', W Russian Federation
126 L11 Novoshakhtinsk Rostovskaya Oblast', SW Russian Federation
122 J12 Novosibirsk Novosibirskaya Oblast', C Russian Federation
122 J12 Novosibirskaya Oblast' ⬖ province C Russian Federation
122 M4 Novosibirskiye Ostrova Eng. New Siberian Islands. island group N Russian Federation
126 K6 Novosil' Orlovskaya Oblast', W Russian Federation
124 G16 Novosokol'niki Pskovskaya Oblast', W Russian Federation
127 Q6 Novospasskoye Ul'yanovskaya Oblast', W Russian Federation
Novotroickoje see Brlik
127 X8 Novotroitsk Orenburgskaya Oblast', W Russian Federation
Novotroitskoye see Brlik, Kazakhstan
Novotroitskoye see Novotroyits'ke, Ukraine
117 T11 Novotroyits'ke Rus. Novotroitskoye. Khersons'ka Oblast', S Ukraine
Novoukrainka see Novoukrayinka
117 Q8 Novoukrayinka Rus. Novoukrainka. Kirovohrads'ka Oblast', C Ukraine
127 Q5 Novoul'yanovsk Ul'yanovskaya Oblast', W Russian Federation
127 W8 Novouralets Orenburgskaya Oblast', W Russian Federation
Novo-Urgench see Urganch
116 I4 Novovolyns'k Rus. Novovolynsk. Volyns'ka Oblast', NW Ukraine
117 S9 Novovorontsovka Khersons'ka Oblast', S Ukraine
147 Y7 Novovoznesenovka Issyk-Kul'skaya Oblast', E Kyrgyzstan
125 R14 Novovyatsk Kirovskaya Oblast', NW Russian Federation
Novoyel'nya see Navayel'nya
124 I7 Novoye Yushkozero Respublika Kareliya, NW Russian Federation
117 O6 Novozhyvotiv Vinnyts'ka Oblast', C Ukraine
126 H6 Novozybkov Bryanskaya Oblast', W Russian Federation
112 F9 Novska Sisak-Moslavina, NE Croatia
Nový Bohumín see Bohumín
111 D15 Nový Bor Ger. Haida; prev. Bor u České Lípy, Hajda. Liberecký Kraj, N Czech Republic
111 E16 Nový Bydžov Ger. Neubidschow. Královéhradecký Kraj, N Czech Republic
119 G18 Novy Dvor Rus. Novyy Dvor. Hrodzyenskaya Voblasts', W Belarus
111 I17 Nový Jičín Ger. Neutitschein. Moravskoslezský Kraj, E Czech Republic
118 K12 Novy Pahost Rus. Novyy Pogost. Vitsyebskaya Voblasts', NW Belarus
Novyy Bug see Novyy Buh
117 R9 Novyy Buh Rus. Novyy Bug. Mykolayivs'ka Oblast', S Ukraine
117 Q4 Novyy Bykiv Chernihivs'ka Oblast', N Ukraine
Novyy Dvor see Novy Dvor
Novyye Aneny see Anenii Noi
127 P7 Novyye Burasy Saratovskaya Oblast', W Russian Federation
Novyy Margilan see Farg'ona
126 K8 Novyy Oskol Belgorodskaya Oblast', W Russian Federation
Novyy Pogost see Novy Pahost
127 R2 Novyy Tor"yal Respublika Mariy El, W Russian Federation
123 N12 Novyy Uoyan Respublika Buryatiya, S Russian Federation
122 J9 Novyy Urengoy Yamalo-Nenetskiy Avtonomnyy Okrug, N Russian Federation
Novyy Uzen' see Zhanaozen
111 N16 Nowa Dęba Podkarpackie, SE Poland
111 G15 Nowa Ruda Ger. Neurode. Dolnośląskie, SW Poland
110 F12 Nowa Sól var. Nowasól, Ger. Neusalz an der Oder. Lubuskie, W Poland
Nowasól see Nowa Sól
27 Q8 Nowata Oklahoma, C USA
142 M6 Nowbarān Markazī, W Iran
110 I8 Nowe Kujawski-pomorskie, N Poland
110 K9 Nowe Miasto Lubawskie Ger. Neumark. Warmińsko-Mazurskie, NE Poland
110 L13 Nowe Miasto nad Pilicą Mazowieckie, C Poland
110 D8 Nowe Warpno Ger. Neuwarp. Zachodnio-pomorskie, NW Poland
Nowgong see Nagaon
110 E8 Nowogard var. Nowógard, Ger. Naugard. Zachodnio-pomorskie, NW Poland
110 N9 Nowogród Podlaskie, NE Poland
Nowogródek see Navahrudak
111 E14 Nowogrodziec Ger. Naumburg am Queis. Dolnośląskie, SW Poland
Nowojelnia see Navayel'nya
Nowo-Minsk see Mińsk Mazowiecki
33 V13 Nowood River ≈ Wyoming, C USA
Nowo-Święciany see Švenčionėliai
183 S10 Nowra-Bomaderry New South Wales, SE Australia
149 T5 Nowshera var. Naushahra, Naushara. North-West Frontier Province, NE Pakistan
110 J7 Nowy Dwór Gdański Ger. Tiegenhof. Pomorskie, N Poland
110 L11 Nowy Dwór Mazowiecki Mazowieckie, C Poland
111 M17 Nowy Sącz Ger. Neu Sandec. Małopolskie, S Poland
111 L18 Nowy Targ Ger. Neumark. Małopolskie, S Poland
110 F11 Nowy Tomyśl var. Nowy Tomysl. Wielkopolskie, C Poland
Nowy Tomysl see Nowy Tomyśl
148 M7 Now Zād var. Nauzad. Helmand, S Afghanistan
23 N4 Noxubee River ≈ Alabama/Mississippi, S USA
122 I10 Noyabr'sk Yamalo-Nenetskiy Avtonomnyy Okrug, N Russian Federation
102 L8 Noyant Maine-et-Loire, NW France
39 X14 Noyes Island island Alexander Archipelago, Alaska, USA
103 O3 Noyon Oise, N France
102 I7 Nozay Loire-Atlantique, NW France
82 L12 Nsando Northern, NE Zambia
83 N16 Nsanje Southern, S Malawi
77 Q17 Nsawam SE Ghana
79 E16 Nsimalen ✈ Centre, C Cameroon
82 K12 Nsombo Northern, NE Zambia
82 H13 Ntambu North Western, NW Zambia
83 N14 Ntcheu var. Ncheu. Central, S Malawi
79 D17 Ntem prev. Campo, var. Kampo. ≈ Cameroon/Equatorial Guinea
83 I14 Ntemwa North Western, NW Zambia
Ntlenyana, Mount see Thabana Ntlenyana
79 I19 Ntomba, Lac var. Lac Tumba. ◎ NW Dem. Rep. Congo
115 I19 Ntóro, Kávo prev. Ákrotírio Kafiréas. cape Évvoia, C Greece
81 E19 Ntungamo SW Uganda
81 E18 Ntusi SW Uganda
83 H18 Ntwetwe Pan salt lake NE Botswana
93 M15 Nuasjärvi ◎ C Finland
80 F11 Nuba Mountains ▲▲ C Sudan
68 J9 Nubian Desert desert NE Sudan
116 G10 Nucet Hung. Diófás. Bihor, W Romania
Nu Chiang see Salween
145 U9 Nuclear Testing Ground nuclear site Pavlodar, E Kazakhstan
56 E9 Nucuray, Río ≈ N Peru
25 R14 Nueces River ≈ Texas, SW USA
9 V9 Nueltin Lake ◎ Manitoba/Northwest Territories, C Canada
99 K15 Nuenen Noord-Brabant, S Netherlands
62 G6 Nuestra Señora, Bahía bay N Chile
61 D14 Nuestra Señora Rosario de Caa Catí Corrientes, NE Argentina
54 J9 Nueva Antioquia Vichada, E Colombia
Nueva Caceres see Naga
41 O7 Nueva Ciudad Guerrera Tamaulipas, C Mexico
55 N4 Nueva Esparta off. Estado Nueva Esparta. ⬖ state NE Venezuela
Nueva Esparta, Estado see Nueva Esparta
44 C5 Nueva Gerona Isla de la Juventud, S Cuba
42 H8 Nueva Guadalupe San Miguel, E El Salvador
42 M11 Nueva Guinea Región Autónoma Atlántico Sur, SE Nicaragua
61 D19 Nueva Helvecia Colonia, SW Uruguay
63 J25 Nueva, Isla island S Chile
40 M14 Nueva Italia Michoacán de Ocampo, SW Mexico
56 D6 Nueva Loja var. Lago Agrio. Sucumbíos, NE Ecuador
42 F6 Nueva Ocotepeque prev. Ocotepeque. Ocotepeque, W Honduras
61 D19 Nueva Palmira Colonia, SW Uruguay
41 N6 Nueva Rosita Coahuila de Zaragoza, NE Mexico
42 E7 Nueva San Salvador prev. Santa Tecla. La Libertad, SW El Salvador
42 J8 Nueva Segovia ⬖ department NW Nicaragua
Nueva Tabarca see Plana, Isla
Nueva Villa de Padilla see Nuevo Padilla
61 B21 Nueve de Julio Buenos Aires, E Argentina
44 H6 Nuevitas Camagüey, E Cuba
61 D18 Nuevo Berlín Río Negro, W Uruguay
40 I4 Nuevo Casas Grandes Chihuahua, N Mexico
43 T14 Nuevo Chagres Colón, C Panama
41 W15 Nuevo Coahuila Campeche, E Mexico
63 K17 Nuevo, Golfo gulf S Argentina
41 O7 Nuevo Laredo Tamaulipas, NE Mexico
41 N8 Nuevo León ⬖ state NE Mexico
41 P10 Nuevo Padilla var. Nueva Villa de Padilla. Tamaulipas, C Mexico
56 E6 Nuevo Rocafuerte Orellana, E Ecuador
Nuga see Dzavhanmandal
80 O13 Nugaal off. Gobolka Nugaal. ⬖ region N Somalia
Nugaal, Gobolka see Nugaal
185 E24 Nugget Point headland South Island, New Zealand
186 J5 Nuguria Islands island group E Papua New Guinea
184 P10 Nuhaka Hawke's Bay, North Island, New Zealand
138 M10 Nuhaydayn, Wādī an dry watercourse W Iraq
190 E7 Nui Atoll atoll W Tuvalu
Nu Jiang see Salween
Nûk see Nuuk
182 G7 Nukey Bluff hill South Australia
Nukha see Şäki
123 T9 Nukh Yablonevyy, Gora ▲ E Russian Federation
186 K7 Nukiki Choiseul Island, NW Solomon Islands
186 B6 Nuku Sandaun, NW Papua New Guinea
193 W15 Nuku island Tongatapu Group, NE Tonga
193 U15 Nuku'alofa Tongatapu, S Tonga
193 Y16 Nuku'alofa ● (Tonga) Tongatapu, S Tonga
190 G12 Nukuatea island N Wallis and Futuna
190 F7 Nukufetau Atoll atoll C Tuvalu
190 G12 Nukuhifala island E Wallis and Futuna
191 W7 Nuku Hiva island Îles Marquises, NE French Polynesia
191 W7 Nuku Hiva Island island Îles Marquises, N French Polynesia
190 F9 Nukulaelae Atoll var. Nukulailai. atoll E Tuvalu
Nukulailai see Nukulaelae Atoll
190 G11 Nukuloa island N Wallis and Futuna
186 L6 Nukumanu Islands prev. Tasman Group. island group NE Papua New Guinea
Nukunau see Nikunau
190 J9 Nukunonu Atoll island C Tokelau
190 J9 Nukunonu Village Nukunonu Atoll, C Tokelau
189 S18 Nukuoro Atoll atoll Caroline Islands, S Micronesia
146 H8 Nukus Qoraqalpog'iston Respublikasi, W Uzbekistan
190 G11 Nukutapu island N Wallis and Futuna
39 O9 Nulato Alaska, USA
39 O10 Nulato Hills ▲▲ Alaska, USA
105 T9 Nules País Valenciano, E Spain
Nuling see Sultan Kudarat
182 C6 Nullarbor South Australia
180 M11 Nullarbor Plain plateau South Australia/Western Australia
163 S12 Nulu'erhu Shan ▲▲ N China
77 X14 Numan Adamawa, E Nigeria
165 S3 Numata Hokkaidō, NE Japan
81 C15 Numatinna ≈ W Sudan
95 F14 Numedalen valley S Norway
95 G14 Numedalslågen var. Laagen. ≈ S Norway
93 L19 Nummela Etelä-Suomi, S Finland
183 O11 Numurkah Victoria, SE Australia
196 L16 Nunap Isua var. Uummannarsuaq, Dan. Kap Farvel, Eng. Cape Farewell. cape S Greenland
9 N8 Nunavut ⬖ territory N Canada
54 H9 Nunchia Casanare, C Colombia
97 M20 Nuneaton C England, UK
153 W14 Nungba Manipur, NE India
38 L12 Nunivak Island island Alaska, USA
152 I5 Nun Kun ▲ NW India
98 L10 Nunspeet Gelderland, E Netherlands
107 C18 Nuoro Sardegna, Italy, C Mediterranean Sea
75 R12 Nuqayy, Jabal hill range S Libya
54 C9 Nuquí Chocó, W Colombia
143 O4 Nūr Māzandarān, N Iran
145 Q9 Nura ≈ N Kazakhstan
143 N11 Nūrābād Fārs, C Iran
Nurakita see Niulakita
Nurata see Nurota
Nuratau, Khrebet see Nurota Tizmasi
136 L17 Nur Dağları ▲▲ S Turkey
Nurek see Norak
Nuremberg see Nürnberg
149 S4 Nūrestān ⬖ province C Afghanistan
136 M15 Nurhak Kahramanmaraş, S Turkey
182 J9 Nuriootpa South Australia
127 S5 Nurlat Respublika Tatarstan, W Russian Federation
93 N15 Nurmes Itä-Suomi, E Finland
101 K20 Nürnberg Eng. Nuremberg. Bayern, S Germany
101 K20 Nürnberg ✈ Bayern, SE Germany
146 M10 Nurota Rus. Nurata. Navoiy Viloyati, C Uzbekistan
147 N10 Nurota Tizmasi Rus. Khrebet Nuratau. ▲▲ C Uzbekistan
149 T8 Nūrpur Punjab, E Pakistan
183 P6 Nurri, Mount hill New South Wales, SE Australia
25 T13 Nursery Texas, SW USA
169 V17 Nusa Tenggara Barat off. Propinsi Nusa Tenggara Barat, Eng. West Nusa Tenggara. ⬖ province S Indonesia
Nusa Tenggara Barat, Propinsi see Nusa Tenggara Barat
171 O16 Nusa Tenggara Timur off. Propinsi Nusa Tenggara Timur, Eng. East Nusa Tenggara. ⬖ province S Indonesia
Nusa Tenggara Timur, Propinsi see Nusa Tenggara Timur
171 U14 Nusawulan Papua, E Indonesia
137 Q16 Nusaybin var. Nisibin. Manisa, SE Turkey
39 O14 Nushagak Bay bay Alaska, USA
39 O13 Nushagak Peninsula headland Alaska, USA
39 O13 Nushagak River ≈ Alaska, USA
160 E11 Nu Shan ▲▲ SW China
149 N11 Nushki Baluchistān, SW Pakistan
Nussdorf see Năsăud
112 J9 Nuštar Vukovar-Srijem, E Croatia
99 L18 Nuth Limburg, SE Netherlands
100 N13 Nuthe ≈ NE Germany
Nutmeg State see Connecticut
39 T10 Nutzotin Mountains ▲▲ Alaska, USA
64 I5 Nuuk var. Nûk, Dan. Godthaab, Godthåb. ○ (Greenland) Kitaa, SW Greenland
92 L13 Nuupas Lappi, NW Finland
191 O7 Nuupere, Pointe headland Moorea, W French Polynesia
191 O7 Nuuroa, Pointe headland Tahiti, W French Polynesia
Nüürst see Baganuur
Nuwara see Nuwara Eliya
155 K25 Nuwara Eliya var. Nuwara. Central Province, S Sri Lanka
182 E7 Nuyts Archipelago island group South Australia
83 F17 Nxaunxau North West, NW Botswana
39 N12 Nyac Alaska, USA
122 H9 Nyagan' Khanty-Mansiyskiy Avtonomnyy Okrug, N Russian Federation
Nyagassola see Niagassola
Nyagquka see Yajiang
81 I18 Nyahururu Central, W Kenya
182 M10 Nyah West Victoria, SE Australia
158 M15 Nyainqêntanglha Feng ▲ W China
159 N15 Nyainqêntanglha Shan ▲▲ W China
80 B11 Nyala Southern Darfur, W Sudan
83 M16 Nyamapanda Mashonaland East, NE Zimbabwe
81 H25 Nyamtumbo Ruvuma, S Tanzania
Nyanda see Masvingo
124 M11 Nyandoma Arkhangel'skaya Oblast', NW Russian Federation
83 M16 Nyanga prev. Inyanga. Manicaland, E Zimbabwe
79 D20 Nyanga off. Province de la Nyanga, var. La Nyanga. ⬖ province SW Gabon
79 E20 Nyanga ≈ Congo/Gabon
Nyanga, Province de la see Nyanga
81 F20 Nyantakara Kagera, NW Tanzania
81 G19 Nyanza ⬖ province W Kenya
81 E21 Nyanza-Lac S Burundi
68 J14 Nyasa, Lake var. Lake Malawi; prev. Lago Nyassa. ◎ E Africa
Nyasaland/Nyasaland Protectorate see Malawi
Nyassa, Lago see Nyasa, Lake
119 J17 Nyasvizh Pol. Nieśwież, Rus. Nesvizh. Minskaya Voblasts', C Belarus
166 M8 Nyaunglebin Pegu, SW Burma (Myanmar)
166 M5 Nyaung-u Magwe, C Burma (Myanmar)
95 H24 Nyborg Fyn, C Denmark
95 N21 Nybro Kalmar, S Sweden
119 J16 Nyeharelaye Rus. Negoreloye. Minskaya Voblasts', C Belarus
195 W3 Nye Mountains ▲▲ Antarctica
81 I19 Nyeri Central, C Kenya
118 M11 Nyeshcharda, Vozyera ◎ N Belarus
92 O2 Ny-Friesland physical region N Svalbard
95 L14 Nyhammar Dalarna, C Sweden
160 F7 Nyikog Qu ≈ C China
158 L14 Nyima Xizang Zizhiqu, W China
83 L14 Nyimba Eastern, E Zambia
159 P16 Nyingchi var. Pula. Xizang Zizhiqu, W China
Nyinma see Maqu
111 O21 Nyírbátor Szabolcs-Szatmár-Bereg, E Hungary
111 N21 Nyíregyháza Szabolcs-Szatmár-Bereg, NE Hungary
Nyiro see Ewaso Ng'iro
Nyitra see Nitra
Nyitrabánya see Handlová
93 K16 Nykarleby Fin. Uusikaarlepyy. Länsi-Soumi, W Finland
95 I25 Nykøbing Storstrøm, SE Denmark
95 I22 Nykøbing Vestsjælland, C Denmark
95 F21 Nykøbing Viborg, NW Denmark
95 N17 Nyköping Södermanland, S Sweden
95 L15 Nykroppa Värmland, C Sweden
Nylstroom see Modimolle
183 P7 Nymagee New South Wales, SE Australia
183 V5 Nymboida New South Wales, SE Australia
183 U5 Nymboida River ≈ New South Wales, SE Australia
111 D16 Nymburk var. Neuenburg an der Elbe, Ger. Nimburg. Středočeský Kraj, C Czech Republic
95 O16 Nynäshamn Stockholm, C Sweden
183 Q6 Nyngan New South Wales, SE Australia
Nyoman see Neman
108 A10 Nyon Ger. Neuss; anc. Noviodunum. Vaud, SW Switzerland
79 D16 Nyong ≈ SW Cameroon
103 S14 Nyons Drôme, E France
79 D14 Nyos, Lac Eng. Lake Nyos. ◎ NW Cameroon
Nyos, Lake see Nyos, Lac

◆ Country
● Country Capital
◇ Dependent Territory
○ Dependent Territory Capital
⬖ Administrative Regions
✈ International Airport
▲ Mountain
▲▲ Mountain Range
Volcano
≈ River
◎ Lake
▣ Reservoir

NYROB – OLAVARRÍA

125 U11 **Nyrob** *var.* Nyrov. Permskaya Oblast', NW Russian Federation
Nyrov *see* Nyrob
111 H15 **Nysa** *Ger.* Neisse. Opolskie, S Poland
Nysa Łużycka *see* Neisse
Nyslott *see* Savonlinna
32 M13 **Nyssa** Oregon, NW USA
Nystad *see* Uusikaupunki
95 I25 **Nysted** Storstrøm, SE Denmark
125 U14 **Nytva** Permskaya Oblast', NW Russian Federation
165 P8 **Nyūdō-zaki** *headland* Honshū, C Japan
125 P9 **Nyukhcha** Arkhangel'skaya Oblast', NW Russian Federation
124 H8 **Nyuk, Ozero** *var.* Ozero Njuk. ◎ NW Russian Federation
125 O12 **Nyuksenitsa** *var.* Njuksenica. Vologodskaya Oblast', NW Russian Federation
79 O22 **Nyunzu** Katanga, SE Dem. Rep. Congo
123 O10 **Nyurba** Respublika Sakha (Yakutiya), NE Russian Federation
123 O11 **Nyuya** Respublika Sakha (Yakutiya), NE Russian Federation
146 K12 **Niyazow** *Rus.* Nyyazov. Lebap Welaýaty, NE Turkmenistan
Nyyazov *see* Niyazow
117 T10 **Nyzhni Sirohozy** Khersons'ka Oblast', S Ukraine
117 U12 **Nyzhn'ohirs'kyy** *Rus.* Nizhnegorskiy. Respublika Krym, S Ukraine
NZ *see* New Zealand
81 G21 **Nzega** Tabora, C Tanzania
76 K15 **Nzérékoré** SE Guinea
82 A10 **N'Zeto** *prev.* Ambrizete. Zaire, NW Angola
79 M24 **Nzilo, Lac** *prev.* Lac Delcommune. ◎ SE Dem. Rep. Congo
Nzwani *see* Anjouan

O

29 O11 **Oacoma** South Dakota, N USA
29 N9 **Oahe Dam** *dam* South Dakota, N USA
28 M9 **Oahe, Lake** ⊠ North Dakota/South Dakota, N USA
38 C9 **Oʻahu** *var.* Oahu. *island* Hawaiian Islands, Hawaiʻi, USA
165 V4 **O-Akan-dake** ▲ Hokkaidō, NE Japan
182 K8 **Oakbank** South Australia
19 P13 **Oak Bluffs** Martha's Vineyard, New York, NE USA
36 K4 **Oak City** Utah, W USA
37 R3 **Oak Creek** Colorado, C USA
35 P8 **Oakdale** California, W USA
22 H8 **Oakdale** Louisiana, S USA
29 P7 **Oakes** North Dakota, N USA
22 J4 **Oak Grove** Louisiana, S USA
97 N19 **Oakham** C England, UK
32 H7 **Oak Harbor** Washington, NW USA
21 R5 **Oak Hill** West Virginia, NE USA
35 N8 **Oakland** California, W USA
29 T15 **Oakland** Iowa, C USA
19 Q7 **Oakland** Maine, NE USA
21 T3 **Oakland** Maryland, NE USA
29 R14 **Oakland** Nebraska, C USA
31 N11 **Oak Lawn** Illinois, N USA
33 P16 **Oakley** Idaho, NW USA
26 I4 **Oakley** Kansas, C USA
31 N10 **Oak Park** Illinois, N USA
9 X16 **Oak Point** Manitoba, S Canada
32 G13 **Oakridge** Oregon, NW USA
20 M9 **Oak Ridge** Tennessee, S USA
184 K10 **Oakura** Taranaki, North Island, New Zealand
22 L7 **Oak Vale** Mississippi, S USA
14 G16 **Oakville** Ontario, S Canada
25 V8 **Oakwood** Texas, SW USA
185 F22 **Oamaru** Otago, South Island, New Zealand
96 F13 **Oa, Mull of** *headland* W Scotland, UK
171 O11 **Oan** Sulawesi, N Indonesia
185 J17 **Oaro** Canterbury, South Island, New Zealand
35 X2 **Oasis** Nevada, W USA
195 S15 **Oates Land** *physical region* Antarctica
183 P17 **Oatlands** Tasmania, SE Australia
36 I11 **Oatman** Arizona, SW USA
41 R16 **Oaxaca** *var.* Oaxaca de Juárez; *prev.* Antequera. Oaxaca, SE Mexico
41 Q16 **Oaxaca** ◆ *state* SE Mexico
Oaxaca de Juárez *see* Oaxaca
122 I19 **Ob'** ~ C Russian Federation
14 G9 **Obabika Lake** ◎ Ontario, S Canada
Obagan *see* Ubagan
118 M12 **Obal'** *Rus.* Obol'. Vitsyebskaya Voblasts', N Belarus
79 E16 **Obala** Centre, SW Cameroon
14 C6 **Oba Lake** ◎ Ontario, S Canada
164 J12 **Obama** Fukui, Honshū, SW Japan
96 H11 **Oban** W Scotland, UK
Oban *see* Halfmoon Bay
Obando *see* Puerto Inírida
104 I4 **O Barco** *var.* El Barco, El Barco de Valdeorras, O Barco de Valdeorras. Galicia, NW Spain
O Barco de Valdeorras *see* O Barco
Obbia *see* Hobyo
93 J16 **Obbola** Västerbotten, N Sweden
Obbrovazzo *see* Obrovac
Obchuga *see* Abchuha
Obdorsk *see* Salekhard
Óbecse *see* Bečej
118 I11 **Obeliai** Panevėžys, NE Lithuania
60 F13 **Oberá** Misiones, NE Argentina
108 E8 **Oberburg** Bern, W Switzerland
109 Q9 **Oberdrauburg** Salzburg, S Austria
Oberglogau *see* Głogówek
109 W4 **Ober Grafendorf** Niederösterreich, NE Austria
101 E15 **Oberhausen** Nordrhein-Westfalen, W Germany
Oberhollabrunn *see* Tulln
Oberlaibach *see* Vrhnika
101 Q15 **Oberlausitz** *var.* Hornja Łužica. *physical region* E Germany
26 J2 **Oberlin** Kansas, C USA
22 H8 **Oberlin** Louisiana, S USA
31 T11 **Oberlin** Ohio, N USA
103 U5 **Obernai** Bas-Rhin, NE France
109 R4 **Obernberg am Inn** Oberösterreich, N Austria
Oberndorf *see* Oberndorf am Neckar
101 G23 **Oberndorf am Neckar** *var.* Oberndorf. Baden-Württemberg, SW Germany
109 Q5 **Oberndorf bei Salzburg** Salzburg, W Austria
Oberneustadtl *see* Kysucké Nové Mesto
183 S8 **Oberon** New South Wales, SE Australia
109 Q4 **Oberösterreich** *off.* Land Oberösterreich, *Eng.* Upper Austria. ◆ *state* NW Austria
Oberösterreich, Land *see* Oberösterreich
Oberpahlen *see* Põltsamaa
101 M19 **Oberpfälzer Wald** ▲▲ SE Germany
109 Y6 **Oberpullendorf** Burgenland, E Austria
Oberradkersburg *see* Gornja Radgona
101 G18 **Oberursel** Hessen, W Germany
109 Q8 **Obervellach** Salzburg, S Austria
109 X7 **Oberwart** Burgenland, SE Austria
Oberwischau *see* Vişeu de Sus
109 T7 **Oberwölz** *var.* Oberwölz-Stadt. Steiermark, SE Austria
Oberwölz-Stadt *see* Oberwölz
31 S13 **Obetz** Ohio, N USA
Ob', Gulf of *see* Obskaya Guba
54 G8 **Obia** Santander, C Colombia
58 H12 **Óbidos** Pará, NE Brazil
104 F10 **Óbidos** Leiria, C Portugal
Obidovichi *see* Abidavichy
147 Q13 **Obigarm** W Tajikistan
165 T2 **Obihiro** Hokkaidō, NE Japan
Obi-Khingou *see* Khingov
147 P13 **Obikiik** SW Tajikistan
113 N16 **Obilić** Kosovo, S Serbia
127 O12 **Obil'noye** Respublika Kalmykiya, SW Russian Federation
20 F8 **Obion** Tennessee, S USA
20 F8 **Obion River** ~ Tennessee, S USA
171 S12 **Obi, Pulau** *island* Maluku, E Indonesia
165 S2 **Obira** Hokkaidō, NE Japan
127 N11 **Oblivskaya** Rostovskaya Oblast', SW Russian Federation
123 R14 **Obluch'ye** Yevreyskaya Avtonomnaya Oblast', SE Russian Federation
126 K4 **Obninsk** Kaluzhskaya Oblast', W Russian Federation
114 J8 **Obnova** Pleven, N Bulgaria
79 N15 **Obo** Haut-Mbomou, E Central African Republic
159 T9 **Obo** Qinghai, C China
80 M11 **Obock** E Djibouti
Obol' *see* Obal'
Obolyanka *see* Abalyanka
171 V13 **Obome** Papua, E Indonesia
110 G11 **Oborniki** Wielkolpolskie, W Poland
79 G19 **Obouya** Cuvette, C Congo
126 J8 **Oboyan'** Kurskaya Oblast', W Russian Federation
124 M9 **Obozerskiy** Arkhangel'skaya Oblast', NW Russian Federation
112 L11 **Obrenovac** Serbia, N Serbia
112 D12 **Obrovac** *It.* Obbrovazzo. Zadar, SW Croatia
Obrovo *see* Abrova
35 Q3 **Observation Peak** ▲ California, W USA
122 J8 **Obskaya Guba** *Eng.* Gulf of Ob. *gulf* N Russian Federation
173 N13 **Ob' Tablemount** *undersea feature* S Indian Ocean
173 T10 **Ob' Trench** *undersea feature* E Indian Ocean
77 P16 **Obuasi** S Ghana
117 P5 **Obukhiv** *Rus.* Obukhov. Kyyivs'ka Oblast', N Ukraine
Obukhov *see* Obukhiv
125 U14 **Obva** ~ NW Russian Federation
117 V10 **Obytichna Kosa** *spit* SE Ukraine
117 V10 **Obytichna Zatoka** *gulf* SE Ukraine
105 O3 **Oca** ~ N Spain
23 W10 **Ocala** Florida, SE USA
40 M7 **Ocampo** Coahuila de Zaragoza, NE Mexico
54 G7 **Ocaña** Norte de Santander, N Colombia
105 N9 **Ocaña** Castilla-La Mancha, C Spain
104 H4 **O Carballiño** *Cast.* Carballiño. Galicia, NW Spain
37 T9 **Ocate** New Mexico, SW USA
Ocavango *see* Okavango
57 D14 **Occidental, Cordillera** ▲▲ W Colombia
54 I4 **Occidental, Cordillera** ▲▲ W Colombia
21 Q6 **Oceana** West Virginia, NE USA
21 Z4 **Ocean City** Maryland, NE USA
18 J17 **Ocean City** New Jersey, NE USA
10 K15 **Ocean Falls** British Columbia, SW Canada
Ocean Island *see* Banaba
Ocean Island *see* Kure Atoll
64 J9 **Oceanographer Fracture Zone** *tectonic feature* NW Atlantic Ocean
35 U17 **Oceanside** California, W USA
22 M9 **Ocean Springs** Mississippi, S USA
Ocean State *see* Rhode Island
25 O9 **O C Fisher Lake** ⊠ Texas, SW USA
117 Q10 **Ochakiv** *Rus.* Ochakov. Mykolayivs'ka Oblast', S Ukraine
Ochakov *see* Ochakiv
Ochamchira *see* Och'amch'ire
137 Q9 **Och'amch'ire** *Rus.* Ochamchira. W Georgia
Ochansk *see* Okhansk
125 T15 **Ocher** Permskaya Oblast', NW Russian Federation
115 I19 **Óchi** ▲ Évvoia, C Greece
165 W4 **Ochiishi-misaki** *headland* Hokkaidō, NE Japan
23 S9 **Ochlockonee River** ~ Florida/Georgia, SE USA
44 K12 **Ocho Rios** C Jamaica
Ochrida *see* Ohrid
Ochrida, Lake *see* Ohrid, Lake
101 J19 **Ochsenfurt** Bayern, C Germany
23 U7 **Ocilla** Georgia, SE USA
94 N13 **Ockelbo** Gävleborg, C Sweden
Ocker *see* Oker
95 I19 **Öckerö** Västra Götaland, S Sweden
23 U6 **Ocmulgee River** ~ Georgia, SE USA
116 H11 **Ocna Mureş** *Hung.* Marosújvár; *prev.* Ocna Mureşului, *prev. Hung.* Marosújvárakna. Alba, C Romania
Ocna Mureşului *see* Ocna Mureş
116 H11 **Ocna Sibiului** *Ger.* Salzburg, *Hung.* Vizakna. Sibiu, C Romania
116 H13 **Ocnele Mari** *prev.* Vioara. Vâlcea, S Romania
116 L7 **Ocniţa** *Rus.* Oknitsa. N Moldova
23 U4 **Oconee, Lake** ⊠ Georgia, SE USA
23 U5 **Oconee River** ~ Georgia, SE USA
30 M9 **Oconomowoc** Wisconsin, N USA
30 M6 **Oconto** Wisconsin, N USA
30 M6 **Oconto Falls** Wisconsin, N USA
30 M6 **Oconto River** ~ Wisconsin, N USA
104 I3 **O Corgo** Galicia, NW Spain
41 V16 **Ocosingo** Chiapas, SE Mexico
42 J8 **Ocotal** Nueva Segovia, NW Nicaragua
42 F6 **Ocotepeque** ◆ *department* W Honduras
Ocotepeque *see* Nueva Ocotepeque
40 L13 **Ocotlán** Jalisco, SW Mexico
41 R16 **Ocotlán** *var.* Ocotlán de Morelos. Oaxaca, SE Mexico
Ocotlán de Morelos *see* Ocotlán
41 U16 **Ocozocuautla** Chiapas, SE Mexico
21 Y10 **Ocracoke Island** *island* North Carolina, SE USA
102 I3 **Octeville** Manche, N France
October Revolution Island *see* Oktyabr'skoy Revolyutsii, Ostrov
43 R17 **Ocú** Herrera, S Panama
83 Q14 **Ocua** Cabo Delgado, NE Mozambique
Ocumare *see* Ocumare del Tuy
54 M5 **Ocumare del Tuy** *var.* Ocumare. Miranda, N Venezuela
77 P17 **Oda** SE Ghana
165 G12 **Ōda** *var.* Oda. Shimane, Honshū, SW Japan
92 K3 **Ódadhahraun** *lava flow* C Iceland
165 Q7 **Ōdate** Akita, Honshū, C Japan
165 N14 **Odawara** Kanagawa, Honshū, S Japan
95 D14 **Odda** Hordaland, S Norway
95 G22 **Odder** Århus, C Denmark
Oddur *see* Xuddur
29 T13 **Odebolt** Iowa, C USA
104 H14 **Odeleite** Faro, S Portugal
25 Q4 **Odell** Texas, SW USA
25 T14 **Odem** Texas, SW USA
104 F13 **Odemira** Beja, S Portugal
136 C14 **Ödemiş** İzmir, SW Turkey
Ödenburg *see* Sopron
83 I22 **Odendaalsrus** Free State, C South Africa
Odenpäh *see* Otepää
95 H23 **Odense** Fyn, C Denmark
101 H19 **Odenwald** ▲▲ W Germany
84 H10 **Oder** *Cz./Pol.* Odra. ~ C Europe
Oderberg *see* Bohumín
100 P11 **Oderbruch** *wetland* Germany/Poland
Oderhaff *see* Szczeciński, Zalew
100 O11 **Oder-Havel-Kanal** *canal* NE Germany
Oderhellen *see* Odorheiu Secuiesc
100 P13 **Oder-Spree-Kanal** *canal* NE Germany
Odertal *see* Zdzieszowice
106 I7 **Oderzo** Veneto, NE Italy
177 P10 **Odesa** *Rus.* Odessa. Odes'ka Oblast', SW Ukraine
Odesa *see* Odes'ka Oblast'
95 L18 **Ödeshög** Östergötland, S Sweden
117 O9 **Odes'ka Oblast'** *var.* Odesa, *Rus.* Odesskaya Oblast'. ◆ *province* SW Ukraine
24 M8 **Odessa** Texas, SW USA
32 K8 **Odessa** Washington, NW USA
Odessa *see* Odesa
Odesskaya Oblast' *see* Odes'ka Oblast'
122 H12 **Odesskoye** Omskaya Oblast', C Russian Federation
Odessus *see* Varna
102 F6 **Odet** ~ NW France
104 I14 **Odiel** ~ SW Spain
76 L14 **Odienné** NW Ivory Coast
171 O4 **Odiongan** Tablas Island, C Philippines
116 L12 **Odobeşti** Vrancea, E Romania
110 H13 **Odolanów** *Ger.* Adelnau. Wielkopolskie, C Poland
167 R13 **Ŏdôngk** Kâmpóng Spoe, S Cambodia
25 N6 **O'donnell** Texas, SW USA
98 O7 **Odoorn** Drenthe, NE Netherlands
Odorhei *see* Odorheiu Secuiesc
116 J11 **Odorheiu Secuiesc** *Ger.* Oderhellen, *Hung.* Vámosudvarhely; *prev.* Odorhei, *Ger.* Hofmarkt. Harghita, C Romania
Odra *see* Oder
112 J9 **Odžaci** *Ger.* Hodschag, *Hung.* Hodság. Vojvodina, NW Serbia
59 N14 **Oeiras** Piauí, E Brazil
104 F11 **Oeiras** Lisboa, C Portugal
101 G14 **Oelde** Nordrhein-Westfalen, W Germany
28 J11 **Oelrichs** South Dakota, N USA
101 M17 **Oelsnitz** Sachsen, E Germany
Oels/Oels in Schlesien *see* Oleśnica
29 X12 **Oelwein** Iowa, C USA
Oeniadae *see* Oiniádes
191 N17 **Oeno Island** *atoll* Pitcairn Islands, C Pacific Ocean
Oesel *see* Saaremaa
108 L7 **Oetz** *var.* Ötz. Tirol, W Austria
137 P11 **Of** Trabzon, NE Turkey
30 K15 **O'Fallon** Illinois, N USA
27 W4 **O'Fallon** Missouri, C USA
107 N16 **Ofanto** ~ S Italy
97 D18 **Offaly** *Ir.* Ua Uíbh Fhailí; *prev.* King's County. ◆ *county* C Ireland
101 H18 **Offenbach** *var.* Offenbach am Main. Hessen, W Germany
Offenbach am Main *see* Offenbach
101 F22 **Offenburg** Baden-Württemberg, SW Germany
182 C2 **Officer Creek** *seasonal river* South Australia
Oficina María Elena *see* María Elena
Oficina Pedro de Valdivia *see* Pedro de Valdivia
115 K22 **Ofidoússa** *island* Kykládes, Greece, Aegean Sea
Ofiral *see* Sharm el Sheikh
92 H10 **Ofotfjorden** *fjord* N Norway
192 L16 **Ofu** *island* Manua Islands, E American Samoa
165 R9 **Ōfunato** Iwate, Honshū, C Japan
165 P8 **Oga** Akita, Honshū, C Japan
Ogaadeen *see* Ogaden
165 Q9 **Ogachi** Akita, Honshū, C Japan
165 P9 **Ogachi-tōge** *pass* Honshū, C Japan
81 N14 **Ogaden** *Som.* Ogaadeen. *plateau* Ethiopia/Somalia
165 P8 **Oga-hantō** *peninsula* Honshū, C Japan
165 K13 **Ōgaki** Gifu, Honshū, SW Japan
28 L15 **Ogallala** Nebraska, C USA
168 M14 **Ogan, Air** ~ Sumatera, W Indonesia
165 Y15 **Ogasawara-shotō** *Eng.* Bonin Islands. *island group* SE Japan
14 I9 **Ogascanane, Lac** ◎ Québec, SE Canada
165 R7 **Ogawara-ko** ◎ Honshū, C Japan
77 T15 **Ogbomosho** *var.* Ogmoboso. Oyo, W Nigeria
29 U13 **Ogden** Iowa, C USA
36 L2 **Ogden** Utah, W USA
18 I6 **Ogdensburg** New York, NE USA
23 W5 **Ogeechee River** ~ Georgia, SE USA
Oger *see* Ogre
165 N10 **Ogi** Niigata, Sado, C Japan
10 H5 **Ogilvie** Yukon Territory, NW Canada
10 H4 **Ogilvie** ~ Yukon Territory, NW Canada
10 H5 **Ogilvie Mountains** ▲▲ Yukon Territory, NW Canada
Oginskiy Kanal *see* Ahinski Kanal
162 J7 **Ögiynuur** *var.* Dzegstey. Arhangay, C Mongolia
146 F6 **Ogʻiyon Shoʻrxogi** *wetland* NW Uzbekistan
146 F6 **Ogʻiyon Shoʻrxogi** *wetland* NW Uzbekistan
146 B10 **Oglanly** Balkan Welaýaty, W Turkmenistan
23 T5 **Oglethorpe** Georgia, SE USA
23 T2 **Oglethorpe, Mount** ▲ Georgia, SE USA
106 F7 **Oglio** *anc.* Ollius. ~ N Italy
Ogmoboso *see* Ogbomosho
103 T8 **Ognon** ~ E France
123 R13 **Ogodzha** Amurskaya Oblast', S Russian Federation
77 W16 **Ogoja** Cross River, S Nigeria
12 C10 **Ogoki** ~ Ontario, S Canada
12 D11 **Ogoki Lake** ◎ Ontario, C Canada
Ögöömör *see* Hanhongor
79 F19 **Ogooué** ~ Congo/Gabon
79 E18 **Ogooué-Ivindo** *off.* Province de l'Ogooué-Ivindo, *var.* L'Ogooué-Ivindo. ◆ *province* N Gabon
Ogooué-Ivindo, Province de l' *see* Ogooué-Ivindo
79 E19 **Ogooué-Lolo** *off.* Province de l'Ogooué-Lolo, *var.* L'Ogooué-Lolo. ◆ *province* C Gabon
Ogooué-Lolo, Province de l' *see* Ogooué-Lolo
79 C19 **Ogooué-Maritime** *off.* Province de l'Ogooué-Maritime, *var.* L'Ogooué-Maritime. ◆ *province* W Gabon
Ogooué-Maritime, Province de l' *see* Ogooué-Maritime
165 D14 **Ogōri** Fukuoka, Kyūshū, SW Japan
114 H7 **Ogosta** ~ NW Bulgaria
112 Q9 **Ogražden** *Bul.* Ograzhden. ▲ Bulgaria/FYR Macedonia *see also* Ograzhden
114 G12 **Ograzhden** *Mac.* Orgražden. ▲ Bulgaria/FYR Macedonia *see also* Orgražden
Ograzhden *see* Ogražden
118 G9 **Ogre** *Ger.* Oger. Ogre, C Latvia
118 H9 **Ogre** ~ C Latvia
112 C10 **Ogulin** Karlovac, NW Croatia
77 S16 **Ogun** ◆ *state* SW Nigeria
Ogurdzhaly, Ostrov *see* OgurjalyAdasy
146 A12 **OgurjalyAdasy** *Rus.* Ogurdzhaly, Ostrov. *island* W Turkmenistan
77 U16 **Ogwashi-Uku** Delta, S Nigeria
185 B23 **Ohai** Southland, South Island, New Zealand
147 Q10 **Ohangaron** *Rus.* Akhangaran. Toshkent Viloyati, E Uzbekistan
147 Q10 **Ohangaron** *Rus.* Akhangaran. ~ E Uzbekistan
83 C16 **Ohangwena** ◆ *district* N Namibia
30 M10 **O'Hare** ✈ (Chicago) Illinois, N USA
165 R6 **Ōhata** Aomori, Honshū, C Japan
184 L13 **Ohau** Manawatu-Wanganui, North Island, New Zealand
185 E20 **Ohau, Lake** ◎ South Island, New Zealand
Ohcejohka *see* Utsjoki
99 J20 **Ohey** Namur, SE Belgium
191 X15 **O'Higgins, Cabo** *cape* Easter Island, Chile, E Pacific Ocean
O'Higgins, Lago *see* San Martín, Lago
31 S12 **Ohio** *off.* State of Ohio, *also known as* Buckeye State. ◆ *state* N USA
0 L10 **Ohio River** ~ N USA
Ohlau *see* Oława
101 H16 **Ohm** ~ C Germany
193 W16 **Ohonua** 'Eua, E Tonga
23 V5 **Ohoopee River** ~ Georgia, SE USA
100 L12 **Ohre** *Ger.* Eger. ~ Czech Republic/Germany
Ohri *see* Ohrid
113 M20 **Ohrid** *Turk.* Ochrida, Ohri. SW FYR Macedonia
113 M20 **Ohrid, Lake** *var.* Lake Ochrida, *Alb.* Liqeni i Ohrit, *Mac.* Ohridsko Ezero. ◎ Albania/FYR Macedonia
Ohridsko Ezero/Ohrit, Liqeni i *see* Ohrid, Lake
184 L9 **Ohura** Manawatu-Wanganui, North Island, New Zealand
58 J9 **Oiapoque** Amapá, E Brazil
58 J10 **Oiapoque, Rio** *var.* Fleuve l'Oyapok, Oyapock. ~ Brazil/French Guiana *see also* Oyapok, Fleuve l'
Oiapoque, Rio *see* Oyapok, Fleuve l'
15 O9 **Oies, Île aux** *island* Québec, SE Canada
92 L13 **Oijärvi** Oulu, C Finland
92 L12 **Oikarainen** Lappi, N Finland
188 F10 **Oikuul** Babeldaob, N Palau
18 C13 **Oil City** Pennsylvania, NE USA
18 C12 **Oil Creek** ~ Pennsylvania, NE USA
35 R13 **Oildale** California, W USA
Oileán Ciarral *see* Castleisland
Oil Islands *see* Chagos Archipelago
115 D18 **Oiniádes** *anc.* Oeniadae. *site of ancient city* Dytikí Ellás, W Greece
115 L18 **Oinoússes** *island* E Greece
Oírr, Inis *see* Inisheer
99 J15 **Oirschot** Noord-Brabant, S Netherlands
103 N4 **Oise** ◆ *department* N France
103 P3 **Oise** ~ N France
99 J14 **Oisterwijk** Noord-Brabant, S Netherlands
45 O14 **Oistins** S Barbados
165 E4 **Ōita** Ōita, Kyūshū, SW Japan
165 D14 **Ōita** *off.* Ōita-ken. ◆ *prefecture* Kyūshū, SW Japan
Ōita-ken *see* Ōita
115 E17 **Oíti** ▲ C Greece
165 S4 **Oiwake** Hokkaidō, NE Japan
35 R14 **Ojai** California, W USA
94 K13 **Öje** Dalarna, C Sweden
93 J14 **Öjebyn** Norrbotten, N Sweden
165 B13 **Ojika-jima** *island* SW Japan
40 K5 **Ojinaga** Chihuahua, N Mexico
40 M11 **Ojo Caliente** *var.* Ojocaliente. Zacatecas, C Mexico
Ojocaliente *see* Ojo Caliente
40 D6 **Ojo de Liebre, Laguna** *var.* Laguna Scammon, Scammon Lagoon. *lagoon* W Mexico
62 I7 **Ojos del Salado, Cerro** ▲ W Argentina
105 R7 **Ojos Negros** Aragón, NE Spain
40 M12 **Ojuelos de Jalisco** Aguascalientes, C Mexico
127 N4 **Oka** ~ W Russian Federation
83 D19 **Okahandja** Otjozondjupa, C Namibia
184 L9 **Okahukura** Manawatu-Wanganui, North Island, New Zealand
184 J3 **Okaihau** Northland, North Island, New Zealand
83 D18 **Okakarara** Otjozondjupa, N Namibia
13 P5 **Okak Islands** *island group* Newfoundland and Labrador, E Canada
10 M17 **Okanagan** ~ British Columbia, SW Canada
9 N17 **Okanagan Lake** ◎ British Columbia, SW Canada
Ókanizsa *see* Kanjiža
83 C16 **Okankolo** Otjikoto, N Namibia
32 K6 **Okanogan River** ~ Washington, NW USA
83 D18 **Okaputa** Otjozondjupa, N Namibia
149 V9 **Okāra** Punjab, E Pakistan
26 M10 **Okarche** Oklahoma, C USA
Okarem *see* Ekerem
189 X14 **Okat Harbor** *harbour* Kosrae, E Micronesia
22 M5 **Okatibbee Creek** ~ Mississippi, S USA
83 C17 **Okaukuejo** Kunene, N Namibia
Okavanggo *see* Cubango/Okavango
83 E17 **Okavango** ◆ *district* NW Namibia
83 G17 **Okavango** *var.* Cubango, Kavango, Kavengo, Kubango, Okavanggo, *Port.* Ocavango. ~ S Africa *see also* Cubango
Okavango *see* Cubango
83 G17 **Okavango Delta** *wetland* N Botswana
164 M12 **Okaya** Nagano, Honshū, S Japan
164 H13 **Okayama** Okayama, Honshū, SW Japan
164 H13 **Okayama** *off.* Okayama-ken. ◆ *prefecture* Honshū, SW Japan
Okayama-ken *see* Okayama
164 L14 **Okazaki** Aichi, Honshū, C Japan
110 M12 **Okęcie** ✈ (Warszawa) Mazowieckie, C Poland
23 Y13 **Okeechobee** Florida, SE USA
23 Y14 **Okeechobee, Lake** ◎ Florida, SE USA
26 M9 **Okeene** Oklahoma, C USA
23 V8 **Okefenokee Swamp** *wetland* Georgia, SE USA
97 J24 **Okehampton** SW England, UK
27 P10 **Okemah** Oklahoma, C USA
77 U16 **Okene** Kogi, S Nigeria
100 K13 **Oker** *var.* Ocker. ~ NW Germany
101 J14 **Oker-Stausee** ◎ C Germany
123 T12 **Okha** Ostrov Sakhalin, Sakhalinskaya Oblast', SE Russian Federation
125 U15 **Okhansk** *var.* Ochansk. Permskaya Oblast', NW Russian Federation
123 S10 **Okhotsk** Khabarovskiy Kray, E Russian Federation
192 J2 **Okhotsk, Sea of** *sea* NW Pacific Ocean
117 T4 **Okhtyrka** *Rus.* Akhtyrka. Sums'ka Oblast', NE Ukraine
83 E23 **Okiep** Northern Cape, W South Africa
Oki-guntō *see* Oki-shotō
164 H11 **Oki-kaikyō** *strait* SW Japan
165 P16 **Okinawa** Okinawa, SW Japan
165 S16 **Okinawa** *off.* Okinawa-ken. ◆ *prefecture* Okinawa, SW Japan
165 S16 **Okinawa** *island* SW Japan
Okinawa-ken *see* Okinawa
165 U16 **Okinoerabu-jima** *island* Nansei-shotō, SW Japan
164 F15 **Okino-shima** *island* SW Japan
164 H11 **Oki-shotō** *var.* Oki-guntō. *island group* SW Japan
77 T16 **Okitipupa** Ondo, SW Nigeria
166 L8 **Okkan** Pegu, SW Burma (Myanmar)
27 N10 **Oklahoma** *off.* State of Oklahoma, *also known as* The Sooner State. ◆ *state* C USA
27 N11 **Oklahoma City** *state capital* Oklahoma, C USA
25 Q4 **Oklaunion** Texas, SW USA
23 W10 **Oklawaha River** ~ Florida, SE USA
27 P10 **Okmulgee** Oklahoma, C USA
Oknitsa *see* Ocniţa
22 M3 **Okolona** Mississippi, S USA
165 U2 **Okoppe** Hokkaidō, NE Japan
9 Q16 **Okotoks** Alberta, SW Canada
80 H6 **Oko, Wadi** ~ NE Sudan
79 G19 **Okoyo** Cuvette, W Congo
77 S15 **Okpara** ~ Benin/Nigeria
92 J8 **Øksfjord** Finnmark, N Norway
125 R4 **Oksino** Nenetskiy Avtonomnyy Okrug, NW Russian Federation
92 G13 **Oksskolten** ▲ C Norway
Oksu *see* Oqsu
144 M8 **Oktaybr'skiy** Kostanay, N Kazakhstan
186 B7 **Ok Tedi** Western, W Papua New Guinea
Oktemberyan *see* Armavir
166 M7 **Oktwin** Pegu, C Burma (Myanmar)
127 R6 **Oktyabr'sk** Samarskaya Oblast', W Russian Federation
Oktyab'rsk *see* Kandyagash
125 N12 **Oktyabr'skiy** Arkhangel'skaya Oblast', NW Russian Federation
122 E10 **Oktyabr'skiy** Kamchatskaya Oblast', E Russian Federation
127 T5 **Oktyabr'skiy** Respublika Bashkortostan, W Russian Federation
127 O11 **Oktyabr'skiy** Volgogradskaya Oblast', SW Russian Federation
Oktyabr'skiy *see* Aktsyabrski
127 V7 **Oktyabr'skoye** Orenburgskaya Oblast', W Russian Federation
122 M5 **Oktyabr'skoy Revolyutsii, Ostrov** *Eng.* October Revolution Island. *island* Severnaya Zemlya, N Russian Federation
164 C15 **Ōkuchi** *var.* Ōkuti. Kagoshima, Kyūshū, SW Japan
Okulovka *see* Uglovka
165 Q4 **Okushiri-tō** *var.* Okusiri Tô. *island* NE Japan
Okusiri Tô *see* Okushiri-tō
77 S15 **Okuta** Kwara, W Nigeria
Ōkuti *see* Ōkuchi
83 F19 **Okwa** *var.* Chapman's. ~ Botswana/Namibia
123 T10 **Ola** Magadanskaya Oblast', E Russian Federation
27 T11 **Ola** Arkansas, C USA
Ola *see* Ala
35 T11 **Olacha Peak** ▲ California, W USA
92 J1 **Ólafsfjördhur** Nordhurland Eystra, N Iceland
92 H3 **Ólafsvík** Vesturland, W Iceland
Oláhbrettye *see* Bretea-Română
Oláhszentgyörgy *see* Sângeorz-Băi
Oláh-Toplicza *see* Toplița
35 T11 **Olancha** California, W USA
42 J5 **Olanchito** Yoro, C Honduras
42 J6 **Olancho** ◆ *department* E Honduras
95 O20 **Öland** *island* S Sweden
95 O19 **Ölands norra udde** *headland* S Sweden
95 N22 **Ölands södra udde** *headland* S Sweden
182 K7 **Olary** South Australia
27 R4 **Olathe** Kansas, C USA
61 C22 **Olavarría** Buenos Aires, E Argentina

◆ Country ● Country Capital ◇ Dependent Territory ○ Dependent Territory Capital ◆ Administrative Regions ✈ International Airport ▲ Mountain ▲▲ Mountain Range Volcano ~ River ◎ Lake ⊠ Reservoir

Olav V Land – Oreor

92 O2 **Olav V Land** *physical region* C Svalbard
111 H14 **Oława** *Ger.* Ohlau. Dolnośląskie, SW Poland
107 D17 **Olbia** *prev.* Terranova Pausania. Sardegna, Italy, C Mediterranean Sea
44 G5 **Old Bahama Channel** *channel* Bahamas/Cuba
Old Bay State/Old Colony State *see* Massachusetts
10 H2 **Old Crow** Yukon Territory, NW Canada
Old Dominion *see* Virginia
Oldeberkeap *see* Oldeberkoop
98 M7 **Oldeberkoop** *Fris.* Oldeberkeap. Friesland, N Netherlands
98 L10 **Oldebroek** Gelderland, E Netherlands
98 L8 **Oldemarkt** Overijssel, N Netherlands
94 E11 **Olden** Sogn Og Fjordane, C Norway
100 G10 **Oldenburg** Niedersachsen, NW Germany
100 K8 **Oldenburg** *var.* Oldenburg in Holstein. Schleswig-Holstein, N Germany
Oldenburg in Holstein *see* Oldenburg
98 P10 **Oldenzaal** Overijssel, E Netherlands
Olderfjord *see* Leaibevuotna
18 J8 **Old Forge** New York, NE USA
Old Goa *see* Goa
97 L17 **Oldham** NW England, UK
39 Q14 **Old Harbor** Kodiak Island, Alaska, USA
44 J13 **Old Harbour** C Jamaica
97 C22 **Old Head of Kinsale** *Ir.* An Seancheann. *headland* SW Ireland
20 J8 **Old Hickory Lake** ▣ Tennessee, S USA
Old Line State *see* Maryland
Old North State *see* North Carolina
81 I17 **Ol Doinyo Lengeyo** ▲▲ C Kenya
9 Q16 **Olds** Alberta, SW Canada
19 O7 **Old Speck Mountain** ▲ Maine, NE USA
19 S6 **Old Town** Maine, NE USA
9 T17 **Old Wives Lake** ◎ Saskatchewan, S Canada
162 J7 **Öldziyt** *var.* Höshööt. Arhangay, C Mongolia
162 I8 **Öldziyt** *var.* Ulaan-Uul. Bayanhongor, C Mongolia
162 L10 **Öldziyt** *var.* Rashaant. Dundgovĭ, C Mongolia
162 K8 **Öldziyt** *var.* Sangiyn Dalay. Övörhangay, C Mongolia
Öldziyt *see* Erdenemandal, Arhangay, Mongolia
Öldziyt *see* Sayhandulaan, Dornogovĭ, Mongolia
188 H6 **Oleai** *var.* San Jose. Saipan, S Northern Mariana Islands
18 E11 **Olean** New York, NE USA
110 O7 **Olecko** *Ger.* Treuburg. Warmińsko-Mazurskie, NE Poland
106 C7 **Oleggio** Piemonte, NE Italy
123 P11 **Olëkma** Amurskaya Oblast', SE Russian Federation
123 P12 **Olëkma** ≈ C Russian Federation
123 P11 **Olëkminsk** Respublika Sakha (Yakutiya), NE Russian Federation
117 W7 **Oleksandrivka** Donets'ka Oblast', E Ukraine
117 R7 **Oleksandrivka** *Rus.* Aleksandrovka. Kirovohrads'ka Oblast', C Ukraine
117 Q9 **Oleksandrivka** Mykolayivs'ka Oblast', S Ukraine
117 S7 **Oleksandriya** *Rus.* Aleksandriya. Kirovohrads'ka Oblast', C Ukraine
93 B20 **Ølen** Hordaland, S Norway
124 J4 **Olenegorsk** Murmanskaya Oblast', NW Russian Federation
123 N9 **Olenëk** Respublika Sakha (Yakutiya), NE Russian Federation
123 N9 **Olenëk** ≈ NE Russian Federation
123 O7 **Olenëkskiy Zaliv** *bay* N Russian Federation
124 K6 **Olenitsa** Murmanskaya Oblast', NW Russian Federation
102 I11 **Oléron, Île d'** *island* W France
111 H14 **Oleśnica** *Ger.* Oels, Oels in Schlesien. Dolnośląskie, SW Poland
111 I15 **Olesno** *Ger.* Rosenberg. Opolskie, S Poland
116 M3 **Olevs'k** *Rus.* Olevsk. Zhytomyrs'ka Oblast', N Ukraine
Olevsk *see* Olevs'k
123 S15 **Ol'ga** Primorskiy Kray, SE Russian Federation
Olga, Mount *see* Kata Tjuta
92 P2 **Olgastretet** *strait* E Svalbard
162 D5 **Ölgiy** Bayan-Ölgiy, W Mongolia
95 F23 **Ølgod** Ribe, W Denmark
104 H14 **Olhão** Faro, S Portugal
93 L14 **Olhava** Oulu, C Finland
112 B12 **Olib** *It.* Ulbo. *island* W Croatia
83 B16 **Olifa** Kunene, NW Namibia
83 E20 **Olifants** *var.* Elephant River. ≈ E Namibia
83 E25 **Olifants** *var.* Elefantes. ≈ SW South Africa
83 G22 **Olifantshoek** Northern Cape, N South Africa
188 L15 **Olimarao Atoll** *atoll* Caroline Islands, C Micronesia
Ólimbos *see* Ólympos
Olimpo *see* Fuerte Olimpo
59 Q15 **Olinda** Pernambuco, E Brazil
Olinthos *see* Ólynthos
83 I20 **Oliphants Drift** Kgatleng, SE Botswana
Olisipo *see* Lisboa
Olita *see* Alytus
105 Q4 **Olite** Navarra, N Spain
62 K10 **Oliva** Córdoba, C Argentina
105 T11 **Oliva** País Valenciano, E Spain
Oliva *see* La Oliva
104 I12 **Oliva de la Frontera** Extremadura, W Spain
Olivares *see* Olivares de Júcar
62 H9 **Olivares, Cerro de** ▲ N Chile
105 P9 **Olivares de Júcar** *var.* Olivares. Castilla-La Mancha, C Spain
22 L1 **Olive Branch** Mississippi, S USA
21 O5 **Olive Hill** Kentucky, S USA
35 O6 **Olivehurst** California, W USA
104 G7 **Oliveira de Azeméis** Aveiro, N Portugal
104 I11 **Olivenza** Extremadura, W Spain
9 N17 **Oliver** British Columbia, SW Canada
103 N7 **Olivet** Loiret, C France
29 Q12 **Olivet** South Dakota, N USA
29 T9 **Olivia** Minnesota, N USA
185 C20 **Olivine Range** ▲▲ South Island, New Zealand
108 H10 **Olivone** Ticino, S Switzerland
Ölkeyek *see* Ul'kayak
127 O9 **Ol'khovka** Volgogradskaya Oblast', SW Russian Federation
111 K16 **Olkusz** Małopolskie, S Poland
22 I6 **Olla** Louisiana, S USA
62 I4 **Ollagüe, Volcán** *var.* Oyahue, Volcán Oyahue. ✹ N Chile
189 U13 **Ollan** *island* Chuuk, C Micronesia
188 F7 **Ollei** Babeldaob, N Palau
Ollius *see* Oglio
108 C10 **Ollon** Vaud, W Switzerland
147 Q10 **Olmaliq** *Rus.* Almalyk. Toshkent Viloyati, E Uzbekistan
104 M6 **Olmedo** Castilla-León, N Spain
56 B10 **Olmos** Lambayeque, W Peru
Olmütz *see* Olomouc
30 M15 **Olney** Illinois, N USA
25 R5 **Olney** Texas, SW USA
95 L22 **Olofström** Blekinge, S Sweden
187 N9 **Olomburi** Malaita, N Solomon Islands
111 H17 **Olomouc** *Ger.* Olmütz, *Pol.* Ołomuniec. Olomoucký Kraj, E Czech Republic
111 H18 **Olomoucký Kraj** ◈ *region* E Czech Republic
Ołomuniec *see* Olomouc
122 D7 **Olonets** Respublika Kareliya, NW Russian Federation
171 N3 **Olongapo** *off.* Olongapo City. Luzon, N Philippines
Olongapo City *see* Olongapo
102 J16 **Oloron-Ste-Marie** Pyrénées-Atlantiques, SW France
192 L16 **Olosega** *island* Manua Islands, E American Samoa
105 W4 **Olot** Cataluña, NE Spain
146 K12 **Olot** *Rus.* Alat. Buxoro Viloyati, C Uzbekistan
112 I12 **Olovo** ◈ Federacija Bosna I Hercegovina, E Bosnia and Herzegovina
123 O14 **Olovyannaya** Chitinskaya Oblast', S Russian Federation
123 T7 **Oloy** ≈ NE Russian Federation
101 F16 **Olpe** Nordrhein-Westfalen, W Germany
109 N8 **Olperer** ▲ SW Austria
Olshanka *see* Vil'shanka
Ol'shany *see* Al'shany
Olsnitz *see* Murska Sobota
98 M10 **Olst** Overijssel, E Netherlands
110 L8 **Olsztyn** *Ger.* Allenstein. Warmińsko-Mazurskie, N Poland
110 L8 **Olsztynek** *Ger.* Hohenstein in Ostpreussen. Warmińsko-Mazurskie, N Poland
116 I14 **Olt** ◈ *county* SW Romania
116 I14 **Olt** *var.* Oltul, *Ger.* Alt. ≈ S Romania
108 E7 **Olten** Solothurn, NW Switzerland
116 K14 **Oltenița** *prev. Eng.* Oltenitsa; *anc.* Constantiola. Călărași, SE Romania
Oltenitsa *see* Oltenița
116 H14 **Olteț** ≈ S Romania
24 M4 **Olton** Texas, SW USA
137 R12 **Oltu** Erzurum, NE Turkey
Oltul *see* Olt
146 G7 **Oltynko'l** Qoraqalpog'iston Respublikasi, NW Uzbekistan
161 S15 **Oluan Pi** *Eng.* Cape Olwanpi. *cape* S Taiwan
Olubló *see* Stará L'ubovňa
137 R11 **Olur** Erzurum, NE Turkey
104 L15 **Olvera** Andalucía, S Spain
Ol'viopol' *see* Pervomays'k
Olwanpi, Cape *see* Oluan Pi
115 D20 **Olympia** Dytikí Ellás, S Greece
32 G9 **Olympia** *state capital* Washington, NW USA
182 H5 **Olympic Dam** South Australia
32 F7 **Olympic Mountains** ▲▲ Washington, NW USA
121 O3 **Olympos** *var.* Troodos, *Eng.* Mount Olympus. ▲ C Cyprus
115 F15 **Ólympos** *var.* Ólimbos, *Eng.* Mount Olympus. ▲ N Greece
115 L17 **Ólympos** ▲ Lésvos, E Greece
16 C5 **Olympus, Mount** ▲ Washington, NW USA
Olympus, Mount *see* Ólympos
115 G14 **Ólynthos** *var.* Olinthos; *anc.* Olynthus. *site of ancient city* Kentrikí Makedonía, N Greece
Olynthus *see* Ólynthos
117 Q3 **Olyshivka** Chernihivs'ka Oblast', N Ukraine
123 W8 **Olyutorskiy, Mys** *headland* E Russian Federation
123 V8 **Olyutorskiy Zaliv** *bay* E Russian Federation
186 M10 **Om** ≈ W Papua New Guinea
129 S6 **Om'** ≈ N Russian Federation
158 I13 **Oma** Xizang Zizhiqu, W China
165 R6 **Ōma** Aomori, Honshū, C Japan
125 P6 **Oma** ≈ NW Russian Federation
164 M12 **Ōmachi** *var.* Ōmati. Nagano, Honshū, S Japan
165 Q8 **Ōmagari** Akita, Honshū, C Japan
97 E15 **Omagh** *Ir.* An Ómaigh. W Northern Ireland, UK
29 S15 **Omaha** Nebraska, C USA
83 E19 **Omaheke** ◈ *district* W Namibia
141 W10 **Oman** *off.* Sultanate of Oman, *Ar.* Salṭanat 'Umān; *prev.* Muscat and Oman. ♦ *monarchy* SW Asia
129 O10 **Oman Basin** *var.* Bassin d'Oman. *undersea feature* N Indian Ocean
Oman, Bassin d' *see* Oman Basin
129 N10 **Oman, Gulf of** *Ar.* Khalīj 'Umān. *gulf* N Arabian Sea
Oman, Sultanate of *see* Oman
184 J3 **Omapere** Northland, North Island, New Zealand
185 E20 **Omarama** Canterbury, South Island, New Zealand
112 F11 **Omarska** ◈ Republika Srpska, NW Bosnia and Herzegovina
83 C18 **Omaruru** Erongo, NW Namibia
83 C19 **Omaruru** ≈ W Namibia
83 E17 **Omatako** ≈ NE Namibia
Ōmati *see* Ōmachi
83 E18 **Omawewozonyanda** Omaheke, E Namibia
165 R6 **Ōma-zaki** *headland* Honshū, C Japan
Omba *see* Ambae
Ombai *see* Alor, Pulau
83 C16 **Ombalantu** Omusati, N Namibia
79 H15 **Ombella-Mpoko** ◈ *prefecture* S Central African Republic
Ombetsu *see* Onbetsu
83 B17 **Ombombo** Kunene, NW Namibia
79 D19 **Omboué** Ogooué-Maritime, W Gabon
106 G13 **Ombrone** ≈ C Italy
80 F9 **Omdurman** *var.* Umm Durmān. Khartoum, C Sudan
165 N13 **Ōme** Tōkyō, Honshū, S Japan
106 C6 **Omegna** Piemonte, NE Italy
183 P12 **Omeo** Victoria, SE Australia
138 F11 **'Omer** Southern, C Israel
41 P16 **Ometepec** Guerrero, S Mexico
42 K11 **Ometepe, Isla de** *island* S Nicaragua
Om Hager *see* Om Hajer
80 I10 **Om Hajer** *var.* Om Hager. SW Eritrea
165 J13 **Ōmi-Hachiman** *var.* Ōmihachiman. Shiga, Honshū, SW Japan
Ōmihachiman *see* Ōmi-Hachiman
10 L12 **Omineca Mountains** ▲▲ British Columbia, W Canada
113 F14 **Omiš** *It.* Almissa. Split-Dalmacija, S Croatia
112 B10 **Omišalj** Primorje-Gorski Kotar, NW Croatia
83 D19 **Omitara** Khomas, C Namibia
41 O16 **Omitlán, Río** ≈ S Mexico
39 X14 **Ommaney, Cape** *headland* Baranof Island, Alaska, USA
98 N9 **Ommen** Overijssel, E Netherlands
163 N7 **Ömnödelger** *var.* Bayanbulag. Hentiy, C Mongolia
163 N7 **Ömnödelger** *var.* Bayanbulag. Hentiy, C Mongolia
162 K11 **Ömnögovĭ** ◈ *province* S Mongolia
191 X7 **Omoa** Fatu Hira, NE French Polynesia
Omo Botego *see* Omo Wenz
Ómoldova *see* Moldova Veche
123 T7 **Omolon** Chukotskiy Avtonomnyy Okrug, NE Russian Federation
123 T7 **Omolon** ≈ NE Russian Federation
123 Q8 **Omoloy** ≈ NE Russian Federation
165 P8 **Omono-gawa** ≈ Honshū, C Japan
81 I14 **Omo Wenz** *var.* Omo Botego. ≈ Ethiopia/Kenya
122 H12 **Omsk** Omskaya Oblast', C Russian Federation
122 H11 **Omskaya Oblast'** ◈ *province* C Russian Federation
165 U2 **Ōmu** Hokkaidō, NE Japan
110 M9 **Omulew** ≈ NE Poland
116 J12 **Omul, Vârful** *prev.* Virful Omu. ▲ C Romania
83 D16 **Omundaungilo** Ohangwena, N Namibia
164 C14 **Ōmura** Nagasaki, Kyūshū, SW Japan
83 B17 **Omusati** ◈ *district* N Namibia
164 C14 **Ōmuta** Fukuoka, Kyūshū, SW Japan
125 S14 **Omutninsk** Kirovskaya Oblast', NW Russian Federation
Omu, Virful *see* Omul, Vârful
29 V7 **Onamia** Minnesota, N USA
21 Y5 **Onancock** Virginia, NE USA
14 E10 **Onaping Lake** ◎ Ontario, S Canada
30 M12 **Onarga** Illinois, N USA
15 R6 **Onatchiway, Lac** ◎ Québec, SE Canada
29 S14 **Onawa** Iowa, C USA
165 U5 **Onbetsu** *var.* Ombetsu. Hokkaidō, NE Japan
83 B16 **Oncócua** Cunene, SW Angola
105 S9 **Onda** País Valenciano, E Spain
111 N18 **Ondava** ≈ NE Slovakia
Ondjiva *see* N'Giva
77 T16 **Ondo** Ondo, SW Nigeria
77 T16 **Ondo** ◈ *state* SW Nigeria
163 N8 **Öndörhaan** *var.* Undur Khan; *prev.* Tsetsen Khan. Hentiy, E Mongolia
162 M9 **Öndörshil** *var.* Böhöt. Dundgovĭ, C Mongolia
162 L8 **Öndörshireet** *var.* Bayshint. Töv, C Mongolia
162 I7 **Öndör-Ulaan** *var.* Teel. Arhangay, C Mongolia
83 D18 **Ondundazongonda** Otjozondjupa, N Namibia
151 K21 **One and Half Degree Channel** *channel* S Maldives
187 Z15 **Oneata** *island* Lau Group, E Fiji
124 L9 **Onega** Arkhangel'skaya Oblast', NW Russian Federation
124 L9 **Onega** ≈ NW Russian Federation
Onega Bay *see* Onezhskaya Guba
Onega, Lake *see* Onezhskoye Ozero
18 I10 **Oneida** New York, NE USA
20 M8 **Oneida** Tennessee, S USA
18 H9 **Oneida Lake** ◎ New York, NE USA
29 P13 **O'Neill** Nebraska, C USA
123 V12 **Onekotan, Ostrov** *island* Kuril'skiye Ostrova, SE Russian Federation
23 P3 **Oneonta** Alabama, S USA
18 J11 **Oneonta** New York, NE USA
190 I16 **Oneroa** *island* S Cook Islands
116 K11 **Onești** *Hung.* Onyest; *prev.* Gheorghe Gheorghiu-Dej. Bacău, E Romania
193 V15 **Onevai** *island* Tongatapu Group, S Tonga
108 A11 **Onex** Genève, SW Switzerland
124 K8 **Onezhskaya Guba** *Eng.* Onega Bay. *bay* NW Russian Federation
122 D7 **Onezhskoye Ozero** *Eng.* Lake Onega. ◎ NW Russian Federation
83 C16 **Ongandjera** Omusati, N Namibia
184 N12 **Ongaonga** Hawke's Bay, North Island, New Zealand
Ongi *see* Sayhan-Ovoo, Dundgovĭ, Mongolia
Ongi *see* Uyanga
163 W14 **Ongjin** SW North Korea
155 J17 **Ongole** Andhra Pradesh, E India
Ongon *see* Bürd
Ongtüstik Qazaqstan Oblysy *see* Yuzhnyy Kazakhstan
99 I21 **Onhaye** Namur, S Belgium
166 M8 **Onhne** Pegu, SW Burma (Myanmar)
137 S9 **Oni** N Georgia
29 N9 **Onida** South Dakota, N USA
164 F15 **Onigajō-yama** ▲ Shikoku, SW Japan
172 H7 **Onilahy** ≈ S Madagascar
77 U16 **Onitsha** Anambra, S Nigeria
164 I12 **Ono** Fukui, Honshū, SW Japan
164 I13 **Ono** Hyōgo, Honshū, SW Japan
187 K15 **Ono** *island* SW Fiji
164 E13 **Onoda** Yamaguchi, Honshū, SW Japan
187 Z16 **Ono-i-lau** *island* SE Fiji
164 D13 **Onojō** *var.* Ōnozyô. Fukuoka, Kyūshū, SW Japan
163 O7 **Onon Gol** ≈ N Mongolia
Ononte *see* Orontes
55 N6 **Onoto** Anzoátegui, NE Venezuela
191 O3 **Onotoa** *prev.* Clerk Island. *atoll* Tungaru, W Kiribati
Ōnozyô *see* Ōnojō
95 I19 **Onsala** Halland, S Sweden
83 E23 **Onseepkans** Northern Cape, W South Africa
104 F4 **Ons, Illa de** *island* NW Spain
180 H7 **Onslow** Western Australia
21 W11 **Onslow Bay** *bay* North Carolina, E USA
98 P6 **Onstwedde** Groningen, NE Netherlands
164 C16 **On-take** ▲ Kyūshū, SW Japan
35 T15 **Ontario** California, W USA
32 M13 **Ontario** Oregon, NW USA
12 D10 **Ontario** ◈ *province* S Canada
9 P14 **Ontario, Lake** ◎ Canada/USA
0 L9 **Ontario Peninsula** *peninsula* Canada/USA
Onteniente *see* Ontinyent
105 S11 **Ontinyent** *var.* Onteniente. País Valenciano, E Spain
93 N15 **Ontojärvi** ◎ E Finland
30 L3 **Ontonagon** Michigan, N USA
30 L3 **Ontonagon River** ≈ Michigan, N USA
186 M7 **Ontong Java Atoll** *prev.* Lord Howe Island. *atoll* N Solomon Islands
175 N5 **Ontong Java Rise** *undersea feature* W Pacific Ocean
Onuba *see* Huelva
55 W9 **Onverwacht** Para, N Surinam
Onyest *see* Onești
Oodeypore *see* Udaipur
182 J7 **Oodla Wirra** South Australia
182 F2 **Oodnadatta** South Australia
182 C5 **Ooldea** South Australia
27 Q8 **Oologah Lake** ▣ Oklahoma, C USA
Oos-Kaap *see* Eastern Cape
Oos-Londen *see* East London
99 E17 **Oostakker** Oost-Vlaanderen, NW Belgium
99 D15 **Oostburg** Zeeland, SW Netherlands
98 K9 **Oostelijk-Flevoland** *polder* C Netherlands
99 B16 **Oostende** *Eng.* Ostend, *Fr.* Ostende. West-Vlaanderen, NW Belgium
99 B16 **Oostende** ✈ West-Vlaanderen, NW Belgium
98 L12 **Oosterbeek** Gelderland, SE Netherlands
99 I14 **Oosterhout** Noord-Brabant, S Netherlands
98 O6 **Oostermoers Vaart** *var.* Hunze. ≈ NE Netherlands
99 F14 **Oosterschelde** *Eng.* Eastern Scheldt. *inlet* SW Netherlands
99 E14 **Oosterscheldedam** *dam* SW Netherlands
98 M7 **Oosterwolde** *Fris.* Easterwâlde. Friesland, N Netherlands
98 I9 **Oosthuizen** Noord-Holland, NW Netherlands
99 H16 **Oostmalle** Antwerpen, N Belgium
Oos-Transvaal *see* Mpumalanga
99 E15 **Oost-Souburg** Zeeland, SW Netherlands
99 E17 **Oost-Vlaanderen** *Eng.* East Flanders. ◈ *province* NW Belgium
98 J5 **Oost-Vlieland** Friesland, N Netherlands
98 F12 **Oostvoorne** Zuid-Holland, SW Netherlands
Ootacamund *see* Udagamandalam
98 O10 **Ootmarsum** Overijssel, E Netherlands
10 K14 **Ootsa Lake** ▣ British Columbia, SW Canada
114 L8 **Opaka** Tŭrgovishte, N Bulgaria
79 M18 **Opala** Orientale, C Dem. Rep. Congo
125 Q13 **Oparino** Kirovskaya Oblast', NW Russian Federation
14 H8 **Opasatica, Lac** ◎ Québec, SE Canada
112 B9 **Opatija** *It.* Abbazia. Primorje-Gorski Kotar, NW Croatia
111 N15 **Opatów** Świętokrzyskie, C Poland
111 I17 **Opava** *Ger.* Troppau. Moravskoslezský Kraj, E Czech Republic
111 H16 **Opava** *Ger.* Oppa. ≈ NE Czech Republic
Ópazova *see* Stara Pazova
Ópécska *see* Pecica
14 E8 **Opeepeesway Lake** ◎ Ontario, S Canada
23 R5 **Opelika** Alabama, S USA
22 I8 **Opelousas** Louisiana, S USA
186 G6 **Open Bay** *bay* New Britain, E Papua New Guinea
14 I12 **Opeongo Lake** ◎ Ontario, SE Canada
99 K17 **Opglabbeek** Limburg, NE Belgium
33 W6 **Opheim** Montana, NW USA
39 P10 **Ophir** Alaska, USA
Ophiusa *see* Formentera
79 N18 **Opienge** Orientale, E Dem. Rep. Congo
185 G20 **Opihi** ≈ South Island, New Zealand
12 J9 **Opinaca** ≈ Québec, C Canada
12 J10 **Opinaca, Réservoir** ▣ Québec, E Canada
117 T5 **Opishnya** *Rus.* Oposhnya. Poltavs'ka Oblast', NE Ukraine
98 I8 **Opmeer** Noord-Holland, NW Netherlands
77 V17 **Opobo** Akwa Ibom, S Nigeria
124 F16 **Opochka** Pskovskaya Oblast', W Russian Federation
110 L13 **Opoczno** Lodzkie, C Poland
111 I15 **Opole** *Ger.* Oppeln. Opolskie, S Poland
111 H15 **Opolskie** ◈ *province* S Poland
Opornyy *see* Borankul
104 G4 **O Porriño** *var.* Porriño. Galicia, NW Spain
Oporto *see* Porto
Oposhnya *see* Opishnya
184 P8 **Opotiki** Bay of Plenty, North Island, New Zealand
23 Q7 **Opp** Alabama, S USA
Oppa *see* Opava
94 G9 **Oppdal** Sør-Trøndelag, S Norway
Oppeln *see* Opole
107 N23 **Oppido Mamertina** Calabria, SW Italy
Oppidum Ubiorum *see* Köln
94 F12 **Oppland** ◈ *county* S Norway
118 J12 **Opsa** *Rus.* Opsa. Vitsyebskaya Voblasts', NW Belarus
26 I8 **Optima Lake** ▣ Oklahoma, C USA
184 J11 **Opunake** Taranaki, North Island, New Zealand
191 N6 **Opunohu, Baie d'** *bay* Moorea, W French Polynesia
83 B17 **Opuwo** Kunene, NW Namibia
146 H6 **Oqqal'a** *var.* Akkala, *Rus.* Karakala. Qoraqalpog'iston Respublikasi, NW Uzbekistan
147 V13 **Oqsu** *Rus.* Oksu. ≈ SE Tajikistan
147 P14 **Oqtogh, Qatorkŭhi** *Rus.* Khrebet Aktau. ▲▲ SW Tajikistan
146 M11 **Oqtosh** *Rus.* Aktash. Samarqand Viloyati, C Uzbekistan
147 N11 **Oqtow Tizmasi** *var.* Khrebet Aktau. ▲▲ C Uzbekistan
30 J12 **Oquawka** Illinois, N USA
144 J10 **Or'** *Kaz.* Or. ≈ Kazakhstan/Russian Federation
36 M15 **Oracle** Arizona, SW USA
147 N13 **O'radaryo** *Rus.* Uradar'ya. ≈ S Uzbekistan
147 N13 **O'radaryo** *Rus.* Uradar'ya. ≈ S Uzbekistan
116 F9 **Oradea** *prev.* Oradea Mare, *Ger.* Grosswardein, *Hung.* Nagyvárad. Bihor, NW Romania
Oradea Mare *see* Oradea
113 M17 **Orahovac** *Alb.* Rahovec. Kosovo, S Serbia
112 H9 **Orahovica** Virovitica-Podravina, NE Croatia
152 K13 **Orai** Uttar Pradesh, N India
92 K12 **Orajärvi** Lappi, NW Finland
Or Akiva *see* Or 'Aqiva
Oral *see* Ural'sk
74 I5 **Oran** *var.* Ouahran, Wahran. NW Algeria
183 R8 **Orange** New South Wales, SE Australia
103 R14 **Orange** *anc.* Arausio. Vaucluse, SE France
25 Y10 **Orange** Texas, SW USA
21 V5 **Orange** Virginia, NE USA
21 R13 **Orangeburg** South Carolina, SE USA
58 J9 **Orange, Cabo** *headland* NE Brazil
29 S12 **Orange City** Iowa, C USA
Orange Cone *see* Orange Fan
172 J10 **Orange Fan** *var.* Orange Cone. *undersea feature* SW Indian Ocean
Orange Free State *see* Free State
25 S14 **Orange Grove** Texas, SW USA
18 K13 **Orange Lake** New York, NE USA
23 V10 **Orange Lake** ◎ Florida, SE USA
Orange Mouth/Orangemund *see* Oranjemund
23 W9 **Orange Park** Florida, SE USA
83 E23 **Orange River** *Afr.* Oranjerivier. ≈ S Africa
14 G15 **Orangeville** Ontario, S Canada
36 M5 **Orangeville** Utah, W USA
42 G1 **Orange Walk** Orange Walk, N Belize
42 F1 **Orange Walk** ◈ *district* NW Belize
100 N11 **Oranienburg** Brandenburg, NE Germany
98 O7 **Oranjekanaal** *canal* NE Netherlands
83 D23 **Oranjemund** *var.* Orangemund; *prev.* Orange Mouth. Karas, SW Namibia
Oranjerivier *see* Orange River
45 N16 **Oranjestad** ○ (Aruba) W Aruba
Oranje Vrystaat *see* Free State
Orany *see* Varėna
83 H18 **Orapa** Central, C Botswana
138 F9 **Or 'Aqiva** *var* Or Akiva. Haifa, W Israel
112 I10 **Orašje** ◈ Federacija Bosna I Herecegovina, N Bosnia and Herzegovina
116 G11 **Orăștie** *Ger.* Broos, *Hung.* Szászváros. Hunedoara, W Romania
Orașul Stalin *see* Brașov
111 K18 **Orava** *Hung.* Árva, *Pol.* Orawa. ≈ N Slovakia
Oravainen *see* Oravais
93 K16 **Oravais** *Fin.* Oravainen. Länsi-Soumi, W Finland
Oravicabánya *see* Oravița
116 F13 **Oravița** *Ger.* Orawitza, *Hung.* Oravicabánya. Caraș-Severin, SW Romania
Orawa *see* Orava
185 B24 **Orawia** Southland, South Island, New Zealand
Orawitza *see* Oravița
103 P16 **Orb** ≈ S France
106 C9 **Orba** ≈ NW Italy
158 H12 **Orba Co** ◎ W China
108 B9 **Orbe** Vaud, W Switzerland
107 G14 **Orbetello** Toscana, C Italy
104 K3 **Orbigo** ≈ NW Spain
183 Q12 **Orbost** Victoria, SE Australia
95 O14 **Örbyhus** Uppsala, C Sweden
194 I1 **Orcadas** *Argentinian research station* South Orkney Islands, Antarctica
105 P12 **Orcera** Andalucía, S Spain
33 P9 **Orchard Homes** Montana, NW USA
37 P5 **Orchard Mesa** Colorado, C USA
18 D10 **Orchard Park** New York, NE USA
Orchid Island *see* Lan Yü
115 G18 **Orchómenos** *var.* Orhomenos, Orkhómenos, *prev.* Skripón; *anc.* Orchomenus. Stereá Ellás, C Greece
Orchomenus *see* Orchómenos
106 B7 **Orco** ≈ NW Italy
103 R8 **Or, Côte d'** *physical region* C France
29 O14 **Ord** Nebraska, C USA
119 O15 **Ordats'** *Rus.* Ordat'. Mahilyowskaya Voblasts', E Belarus
36 K8 **Orderville** Utah, W USA
104 H2 **Ordes** Galicia, NW Spain
35 V14 **Ord Mountain** ▲ California, W USA
163 N14 **Ordos** *prev.* Dongsheng. Nei Mongol Zizhiqu, N China
Ordos Desert *see* Mu Us Shadi
188 B16 **Ordot** C Guam
137 N11 **Ordu** *anc.* Cotyora. Ordu, N Turkey
136 M11 **Ordu** ◈ *province* N Turkey
137 V14 **Ordubad** SW Azerbaijan
Orduña *see* Urduña
37 U6 **Ordway** Colorado, C USA
117 T9 **Ordzhonikidze** Dnipropetrovs'ka Oblast', E Ukraine
Ordzhonikidze *see* Denisovka, Kazakhstan
Ordzhonikidze *see* Vladikavkaz, Russian Federation
Ordzhonikidze *see* Yenakiyeve, Ukraine
Ordzhonikidzeabad *see* Kofarnihon
55 U12 **Orealla** E Guyana
113 G15 **Orebić** *It.* Sabbioncello. Dubrovnik-Neretva, S Croatia
95 M16 **Örebro** Örebro, C Sweden
95 L16 **Örebro** ◈ *county* C Sweden
25 W6 **Ore City** Texas, SW USA
30 L10 **Oregon** Illinois, N USA
27 Q2 **Oregon** Missouri, C USA
31 R11 **Oregon** Ohio, N USA
32 H13 **Oregon** *off.* State of Oregon, *also known as* Beaver State, Sunset State, Valentine State, Webfoot State. ◈ *state* NW USA
32 G11 **Oregon City** Oregon, NW USA
Oregon, State of *see* Oregon
95 P14 **Öregrund** Uppsala, C Sweden
Orekhov *see* Orikhiv
126 L3 **Orekhovo-Zuyevo** Moskovskaya Oblast', W Russian Federation
Orekhovsk *see* Arekhawsk
126 J6 **Orël** Orlovskaya Oblast', W Russian Federation
Orel *see* Oril'
56 E11 **Orellana** Loreto, N Peru
56 E6 **Orellana** ◈ *province* NE Ecuador
104 L11 **Orellana, Embalse de** ▣ W Spain
36 L3 **Orem** Utah, W USA
Ore Mountains *see* Erzgebirge/Krušné Hory
127 V7 **Orenburg** *prev.* Chkalov. Orenburgskaya Oblast', W Russian Federation
127 V7 **Orenburg** ✈ Orenburgskaya Oblast', W Russian Federation
127 T7 **Orenburgskaya Oblast'** ◈ *province* W Russian Federation
Orense *see* Ourense
188 C8 **Oreor** *var.* Koror. *island* N Palau

♦ Country
● Country Capital
◇ Dependent Territory
○ Dependent Territory Capital
◈ Administrative Regions
✈ International Airport
▲ Mountain
▲▲ Mountain Range
✹ Volcano
≈ River
◎ Lake
▣ Reservoir

Oreor – Ouidah

Oreor see Koror
185 B24 Orepuki Southland, South Island, New Zealand
114 L12 Orestiáda prev. Orestiás. Anatolikí Makedonía kai Thráki, NE Greece
Orestiás see Orestiáda
Öresund/Øresund see Sound, The
185 C23 Oreti ≈ South Island, New Zealand
184 L5 Orewa Auckland, North Island, New Zealand
65 A25 Orford, Cape headland West Falkland, Falkland Islands
44 B5 Órganos, Sierra de los ▲▲ W Cuba
37 R15 Organ Peak ▲ New Mexico, SW USA
105 N9 Orgaz Castilla-La Mancha, C Spain
Orgeyev see Orhei
Orgil see Jargalant
105 O15 Orgiva var. Orjiva. Andalucía, S Spain
163 O10 Örgön var. Senj. Dornogovĭ, SE Mongolia
Örgön see Bayangovĭ
Orgražden see Ograzhden
117 N9 Orhei var. Orheiu, Rus. Orgeyev. N Moldova
Orheiu see Orhei
105 R3 Orhi var. Orhy, Pico de Orhy, Pic d'Orhy. ▲ France/Spain see also Orhy
Orhi see Orhy
Orhomenos see Orchómenos
162 K6 Orhon ⬖ province N Mongolia
162 L6 Orhon Gol ≈ N Mongolia
102 J16 Orhy var. Orhi, Pico de Orhy, Pic d'Orhy. ▲ France/Spain see also Orhi
Orhy see Orhi
Orhy, Pic d'/Orhy, Pico de see Orhi/Orhy
34 L2 Orick California, W USA
32 L6 Orient Washington, NW USA
48 D6 Oriental, Cordillera ▲▲ Bolivia/Peru
48 D6 Oriental, Cordillera ▲▲ C Colombia
57 H16 Oriental, Cordillera ▲▲ C Peru
63 M15 Oriente Buenos Aires, E Argentina
105 R12 Orihuela País Valenciano, E Spain
117 V9 Orikhiv Rus. Orekhov. Zaporiz'ka Oblast', SE Ukraine
113 K22 Orikum var. Orikumi. Vlorë, SW Albania
Orikumi see Orikum
117 V6 Oril' Rus. Orel. ≈ E Ukraine
14 H14 Orillia Ontario, S Canada
93 M19 Orimattila Etelä-Suomi, S Finland
33 Y15 Orin Wyoming, C USA
47 R4 Orinoco, Río ≈ Colombia/Venezuela
186 C9 Oriomo Western, SW Papua New Guinea
30 K11 Orion Illinois, N USA
29 Q5 Oriska North Dakota, N USA
153 P17 Orissa ⬖ state NE India
Orissaar see Orissaare
118 E5 Orissaare Ger. Orissaar. Saaremaa, W Estonia
107 B19 Oristano Sardegna, Italy, C Mediterranean Sea
107 A19 Oristano, Golfo di gulf Sardegna, Italy, C Mediterranean Sea
54 D13 Orito Putumayo, SW Colombia
93 L18 Orivesi Häme, W Finland
93 N17 Orivesi ◎ Länsi-Suomi, SE Finland
58 H12 Oriximiná Pará, NE Brazil
41 Q14 Orizaba Veracruz-Llave, E Mexico
41 Q14 Orizaba, Volcán Pico de var. Citlaltépetl. ▲ S Mexico
95 I16 Ørje Østfold, S Norway
113 I16 Orjen ▲▲ Bosnia and Herzegovina/Montenegro
Orjiva see Orgiva
Orjonikidzeobod see Kofarnihon
94 G8 Orkanger Sør-Trøndelag, S Norway
94 G8 Orkdalen valley S Norway
95 K22 Örkelljunga Skåne, S Sweden
Orkhaniye see Botevgrad
Orkhómenos see Orchómenos
94 H9 Orkla ≈ S Norway
Orkney see Orkney Islands
65 J22 Orkney Deep undersea feature Scotia Sea/Weddell Sea
96 J4 Orkney Islands var. Orkney, Orkneys. island group N Scotland, UK
Orkneys see Orkney Islands
24 K8 Orla Texas, SW USA
35 N5 Orland California, W USA
23 X11 Orlando Florida, SE USA
23 X12 Orlando ✈ Florida, SE USA
107 K23 Orlando, Capo d' headland Sicilia, Italy, C Mediterranean Sea
Orlau see Orlová
103 N6 Orléanais cultural region C France
103 N7 Orléans anc. Aurelianum. Loiret, C France
34 L2 Orleans California, W USA
19 Q12 Orleans Massachusetts, NE USA
15 R10 Orléans, Île d' island Québec, SE Canada
Orléansville see Chlef
111 F16 Orlice Ger. Adler. ≈ NE Czech Republic
122 L13 Orlik Respublika Buryatiya, S Russian Federation
125 Q14 Orlov prev. Khalturin. Kirovskaya Oblast', NW Russian Federation
111 I17 Orlová Ger. Orlau, Pol. Orłowa. Moravskoslezský Kraj, E Czech Republic
Orlov, Mys see Orlovskiy, Mys
126 I6 Orlovskaya Oblast' ⬖ province W Russian Federation
124 M5 Orlovskiy, Mys var. Mys Orlov. headland NW Russian Federation
Orłowa see Orlová
103 O5 Orly ✈ (Paris) Essonne, N France
119 G16 Orlya Rus. Orlya. Hrodzyenskaya Voblasts', W Belarus
114 M7 Orlyak prev. Makenzen, Trubchular, Rom. Trupcilar. Dobrich, NE Bulgaria
148 L16 Ormāra Baluchistān, SW Pakistan
171 P5 Ormoc off. Ormoc City, var. MacArthur. Leyte, C Philippines
Ormoc City see Ormoc
23 X10 Ormond Beach Florida, SE USA
109 X10 Ormož Ger. Friedau. NE Slovenia
14 J13 Ormsby Ontario, SE Canada
97 K17 Ormskirk NW England, UK
Ormsö see Vormsi
15 N13 Ormstown Québec, SE Canada
Ormuz, Strait of see Hormuz, Strait of
103 T8 Ornans Doubs, E France
102 K5 Orne ⬖ department N France
102 K5 Orne ≈ N France
92 G12 Ørnes Nordland, C Norway
110 L7 Orneta Warmińsko-Mazurskie, NE Poland
95 P16 Ornö Stockholm, C Sweden
37 Q3 Orno Peak ▲ Colorado, C USA
93 I16 Örnsköldsvik Västernorrland, C Sweden
163 X13 Oro E North Korea
45 T6 Orocovis C Puerto Rico
54 H10 Orocué Casanare, E Colombia
77 N13 Orodara SW Burkina
105 S4 Oroel, Peña de ▲ N Spain
33 N10 Orofino Idaho, NW USA
162 I9 Orog Nuur ◎ S Mongolia
35 U14 Oro Grande California, W USA
37 S15 Orogrande New Mexico, SW USA
191 Q7 Orohena, Mont △ Tahiti, W French Polynesia
Orolaunum see Arlon
Orol Dengizi see Aral Sea
189 S15 Oroluk Atoll atoll Caroline Islands, C Micronesia
80 J13 Oromo ⬖ region C Ethiopia
Oromo see Goba
13 O15 Oromocto New Brunswick, SE Canada
191 S4 Orona prev. Hull Island. atoll Phoenix Islands, C Kiribati
191 V17 Orongo ancient monument Easter Island, Chile, E Pacific Ocean
138 I3 Orontes var. Ononte, Nahr el Aassi, Ar. Nahr al 'Āṣī. ≈ SW Asia
104 L9 Oropesa Castilla-La Mancha, C Spain
105 T8 Oropesa País Valenciano, E Spain
Oropeza see Cochabamba
Oroqen Zizhiqi see Alihe
171 P7 Oroquieta var. Oroquieta City. Mindanao, S Philippines
Oroquieta City see Oroquieta
40 J8 Oro, Río del ≈ C Mexico
59 O14 Orós, Açude ⊠ E Brazil
107 D18 Orosei, Golfo di gulf Tyrrhenian Sea, C Mediterranean Sea
111 M24 Orosháza Békés, SE Hungary
Orosirá Rodhópis see Rhodope Mountains
111 I22 Oroszlány Komárom-Esztergom, W Hungary
188 B16 Orote Peninsula peninsula W Guam
123 T9 Orotukan Magadanskaya Oblast', E Russian Federation
35 O5 Oroville California, W USA
32 K6 Oroville Washington, NW USA
35 O5 Oroville, Lake ⊠ California, W USA
0 G15 Orozco Fracture Zone tectonic feature E Pacific Ocean
64 I7 Orphan Knoll undersea feature NW Atlantic Ocean
29 V3 Orr Minnesota, N USA
95 M21 Orrefors Kalmar, S Sweden
182 I7 Orroroo South Australia
31 T12 Orrville Ohio, N USA
94 L12 Orsa Dalarna, C Sweden
Orschowa see Orşova
Orschütz see Orzyc
119 O14 Orsha Rus. Orsha. Vitsyebskaya Voblasts', NE Belarus
127 Q2 Orshanka Respublika Mariy El, W Russian Federation
108 C11 Orsières Valais, SW Switzerland
127 X8 Orsk Orenburgskaya Oblast', W Russian Federation
116 F13 Orşova Ger. Orschowa, Hung. Orsova. Mehedinți, SW Romania
94 D10 Ørsta Møre og Romsdal, S Norway
95 O15 Örsundsbro Uppsala, C Sweden
136 D16 Ortaca Muğla, SW Turkey
107 M16 Orta Nova Puglia, SE Italy
136 I17 Orta Toroslar ▲▲ S Turkey
54 E11 Ortega Tolima, W Colombia
104 H1 Ortegal, Cabo cape NW Spain
Ortelsburg see Szczytno
102 J15 Orthez Pyrénées-Atlantiques, SW France
57 K14 Orthon, Río ≈ N Bolivia
60 J10 Ortigueira Paraná, S Brazil
104 H1 Ortigueira Galicia, NW Spain
106 H5 Ortisei Ger. Sankt-Ulrich. Trentino-Alto Adige, N Italy
40 F6 Ortiz Sonora, NW Mexico
54 L5 Ortiz Guárico, N Venezuela
Ortler see Ortles
106 F5 Ortles Ger. Ortler. ▲ N Italy
107 K14 Ortona Abruzzo, C Italy
29 R8 Ortonville Minnesota, N USA
147 W8 Orto-Tokoy Issyk-Kul'skaya Oblast', NE Kyrgyzstan
93 I15 Orträsk Västerbotten, N Sweden
100 J12 Örtze ≈ NW Germany
Oruba see Aruba
142 I3 Orūmīyeh var. Rizaiyeh, Urmia, Urmiyeh; prev. Reza'iyeh. Āžarbāyjān-e Gharbī, NW Iran
142 J3 Orūmīyeh, Daryācheh-ye var. Matianus, Sha Hi, Urumi Yeh, Eng. Lake Urmia; prev. Daryācheh-ye Rezā'īyeh. ◎ NW Iran
57 K19 Oruro Oruro, W Bolivia
57 J19 Oruro ⬖ department W Bolivia
95 I18 Orust island S Sweden
149 O7 Orūzgān var. Oruzgān, Pash. Ūrūzgān. Urūzgān, C Afghanistan
149 N6 Orūzgān Pash. Orūzgān. ⬖ province C Afghanistan
Orūzgān see Orūzgān
Oruzgān see Orūzgān
106 H13 Orvieto anc. Velsuna. Umbria, C Italy
194 K7 Orville Coast physical region Antarctica
114 H7 Oryakhovo Vratsa, NW Bulgaria
Oryokko see Yalu
117 R5 Orzhytsya Poltavs'ka Oblast', C Ukraine
110 M9 Orzyc Ger. Orschütz. ≈ NE Poland
110 N8 Orzysz Ger. Arys. Warmińsko-Mazurskie, NE Poland
94 I10 Os Hedmark, S Norway
125 U15 Osa Permskaya Oblast', NW Russian Federation
29 W11 Osage Iowa, C USA
27 U5 Osage Beach Missouri, C USA
27 P5 Osage City Kansas, C USA
27 U7 Osage Fork River ≈ Missouri, C USA
27 U5 Osage River ≈ Missouri, C USA
164 J13 Ōsaka hist. Naniwa. Ōsaka, Honshū, SW Japan
164 I13 Ōsaka off. Ōsaka-fu, var. Ōsaka Hu. ⬖ urban prefecture Honshū, SW Japan
Ōsaka-fu/Ōsaka Hu see Ōsaka
145 R10 Osakarovka Karaganda, C Kazakhstan
29 T7 Osakis Minnesota, N USA
43 N16 Osa, Península de peninsula S Costa Rica
60 M10 Osasco São Paulo, S Brazil
27 R5 Osawatomie Kansas, C USA
26 L3 Osborne Kansas, C USA
173 S8 Osborn Plateau undersea feature E Indian Ocean
95 L21 Osby Skåne, S Sweden
Osca see Huesca
92 N2 Oscar II Land physical region W Svalbard
27 Y10 Osceola Arkansas, C USA
29 V15 Osceola Iowa, C USA
27 S6 Osceola Missouri, C USA
29 Q15 Osceola Nebraska, C USA
101 N15 Oschatz Sachsen, E Germany
100 K13 Oschersleben Sachsen-Anhalt, C Germany
31 R7 Oscoda Michigan, N USA
Ösel see Saaremaa
94 H6 Osen Sør-Trøndelag, S Norway
92 I13 Osensjøen ◎ S Norway
164 A14 Ōse-zaki Fukue-jima, SW Japan
147 T10 Osh Oshskaya Oblast', SW Kyrgyzstan
83 C16 Oshakati Oshana, N Namibia
83 C16 Oshana ⬖ district N Namibia
14 H15 Oshawa Ontario, SE Canada
165 R10 Oshika-hantō peninsula Honshū, C Japan
83 C16 Oshikango Ohangwena, N Namibia
Oshikoto see Otjikoto
165 P5 Ō-shima island NE Japan
165 N14 Ō-shima island S Japan
165 Q5 Oshima-hantō ▲▲ Hokkaidō, NE Japan
83 D17 Oshivelo Otjikoto, N Namibia
28 K14 Oshkosh Nebraska, C USA
30 M7 Oshkosh Wisconsin, N USA
Oshmyany see Ashmyany
Osh Oblasty see Oshskaya Oblast'
77 T16 Oshogbo var. Osogbo. Osun, W Nigeria
147 S11 Oshskaya Oblast' Kir. Osh Oblasty. ⬖ province SW Kyrgyzstan
Oshun see Osun
79 J20 Oshwe Bandundu, C Dem. Rep. Congo
Osiek see Osijek
112 I9 Osijek prev. Osiek, Osjek, Ger. Esseg, Hung. Eszék. Osijek-Baranja, E Croatia
112 I9 Osijek-Baranja off. Osječko-Baranjska Županija. ⬖ province E Croatia
106 J12 Osimo Marche, C Italy
122 M12 Osinovka Irkutskaya Oblast', C Russian Federation
Osintorf see Asintorf
112 N11 Osipaonica Serbia, NE Serbia
Osipenko see Berdyans'k
Osipovichi see Asipovichy
Osječko-Baranjska Županija see Osijek-Baranja
Osjek see Osijek
29 W15 Oskaloosa Iowa, C USA
27 Q4 Oskaloosa Kansas, C USA
95 N20 Oskarshamn Kalmar, S Sweden
95 J21 Oskarström Halland, S Sweden
14 M8 Oskélanéo Québec, SE Canada
Öskemen see Ust'-Kamenogorsk
Oskil see Oskol
117 W5 Oskol Ukr. Oskil. ≈ Russian Federation/Ukraine
93 D20 Oslo prev. Christiania, Kristiania. ● (Norway) Oslo, S Norway
93 D20 Oslo ⬖ county S Norway
93 D21 Oslofjorden fjord S Norway
155 G15 Osmānābād Mahārāshtra, C India
136 J11 Osmancık Çorum, N Turkey
136 L16 Osmaniye Osmaniye, S Turkey
136 L16 Osmaniye ⬖ province S Turkey
95 O16 Ösmo Stockholm, C Sweden
118 E3 Osmussaar island W Estonia
100 G13 Osnabrück Niedersachsen, NW Germany
110 D11 Ośno Lubuskie Ger. Drossen. Lubuskie, W Poland
Osogbo see Oshogbo
113 P19 Osogov Mountains var. Osogovske Planine, Osogovski Planina, Mac. Osogovski Planini. ▲▲ Bulgaria/FYR Macedonia
Osogovske Planine/ Osogovski Planina/ Osogovski Planini see Osogov Mountains
165 R6 Osore-yama ▲ Honshū, C Japan
Oşorhei see Târgu Mureş
61 J16 Osório Rio Grande do Sul, S Brazil
63 G16 Osorno Los Lagos, C Chile
104 M4 Osorno Castilla-León, N Spain
9 N17 Osoyoos British Columbia, SW Canada
95 C14 Osøyro Hordaland, S Norway
54 J6 Ospino Portuguesa, N Venezuela
98 K13 Oss Noord-Brabant, S Netherlands
115 F15 Óssa ▲▲ C Greece
104 H11 Ossa ▲ S Portugal
23 X6 Ossabaw Island island Georgia, SE USA
23 X6 Ossabaw Sound sound Georgia, SE USA
183 O16 Ossa, Mount ▲ Tasmania, SE Australia
104 H11 Ossa, Serra d' ▲▲ SE Portugal
77 U16 Osse ≈ S Nigeria
30 J6 Osseo Wisconsin, N USA
109 S9 Ossiacher See ◎ S Austria
18 K13 Ossining New York, NE USA
123 V9 Ossora Koryakskiy Avtonomnyy Okrug, E Russian Federation
Ostān-e Āzarbāyjān-e Sharqī see Āžarbāyjān-e Sharqī
Ostan-e Khorāsān-e Janūbī see Khorāsān-e Janūbī
Ostān-e Khorāsān-e Razavī see Khorāsān-e Razavī
124 I15 Ostashkov Tverskaya Oblast', W Russian Federation
100 H9 Oste ≈ NW Germany
Ostee see Baltic Sea
Ostend/Ostende see Oostende
117 P3 Oster Chernihivs'ka Oblast', N Ukraine
95 O14 Österbybruk Uppsala, C Sweden
95 M19 Österbymo Östergotland, S Sweden
94 K12 Österdalälven ≈ C Sweden
94 I12 Østerdalen valley S Norway
95 L18 Östergötland ⬖ county S Sweden
100 H10 Osterholz-Scharmbeck Niedersachsen, NW Germany
Östermark see Teuva
Östermyra see Seinäjoki
Østerø see Eysturoy
101 J14 Osterode am Harz Niedersachsen, C Germany
Osterode/Osterode in Ostpreussen see Ostróda
94 C13 Osterøy island S Norway
Österreich see Austria
93 G16 Östersund Jämtland, C Sweden
95 N14 Östervåla Västmanland, C Sweden
101 H22 Ostfildern Baden-Württemberg, SW Germany
95 H16 Østfold ⬖ county S Norway
100 E9 Ostfriesische Inseln Eng. East Frisian Islands. island group NW Germany
100 F10 Ostfriesland historical region NW Germany
95 P14 Östhammar Uppsala, C Sweden
Ostia Aterni see Pescara
106 G8 Ostiglia Lombardia, N Italy
95 J14 Östmark Värmland, C Sweden
95 K22 Östra Ringsjön ◎ S Sweden
111 I17 Ostrava Moravskoslezský Kraj, E Czech Republic
Ostravský Kraj see Moravskoslezský Kraj
94 J11 Østrehogna Swe. Härjahågnen, Härjehågna. ▲ Norway/Sweden
110 K8 Ostróda Ger. Osterode, Osterode in Ostpreussen. Warmińsko-Mazurskie, NE Poland
Ostrog/Ostróg see Ostroh
126 L8 Ostrogozhsk Voronezhskaya Oblast', W Russian Federation
116 L4 Ostroh Pol. Ostróg, Rus. Ostrog. Rivnens'ka Oblast', NW Ukraine
110 N9 Ostrołęka Ger. Wiesenhof, Rus. Ostrolenka. Mazowieckie, C Poland
Ostrolenka see Ostrołęka
111 A16 Ostrov Ger. Schlackenwerth. Karlovarský Kraj, W Czech Republic
124 F15 Ostrov Latv. Austrava. Pskovskaya Oblast', W Russian Federation
Ostrovets see Ostrowiec Świętokrzyski
113 M21 Ostrovicës, Mali i ▲ SE Albania
165 Z2 Ostrov Iturup island NE Russian Federation
124 M4 Ostrovnoy Murmanskaya Oblast', NW Russian Federation
114 L7 Ostrovo prev. Golema Ada. Razgrad, N Bulgaria
125 N15 Ostrovskoye Kostromskaya Oblast', NW Russian Federation
Ostrów see Ostrów Wielkopolski
Ostrowiec see Ostrowiec Świętokrzyski
111 M14 Ostrowiec Świętokrzyski var. Ostrowiec, Rus. Ostrovets. Świętokrzyskie, C Poland
110 P13 Ostrów Lubelski Lubelskie, E Poland
110 N10 Ostrów Mazowiecka var. Ostrów Mazowiecki. Mazowieckie, NE Poland
Ostrów Mazowiecki see Ostrów Mazowiecka
Ostrowo see Ostrów Wielkopolski
110 H13 Ostrów Wielkopolski var. Ostrów, Ger. Ostrowo. Wielkopolskie, C Poland
Ostryna see Astryna
110 I13 Ostrzeszów Wielkopolskie, C Poland
107 P18 Ostuni Puglia, SE Italy
Ostyako-Voguls'k see Khanty-Mansiysk
114 I9 Osŭm ≈ N Bulgaria
Osum see Osumit, Lumi i
164 C17 Ōsumi-hantō ▲▲ Kyūshū, SW Japan
164 C17 Ōsumi-kaikyō strait SW Japan
113 L22 Osumit, Lumi i var. Osum. ≈ SE Albania
77 T16 Osun var. Oshun. ⬖ state SW Nigeria
104 L14 Osuna Andalucía, S Spain
60 J8 Osvaldo Cruz São Paulo, S Brazil
Osveya see Asvyeya
18 J7 Oswegatchie River ≈ New York, NE USA
27 Q7 Oswego Kansas, C USA
18 H9 Oswego New York, NE USA
97 K19 Oswestry W England, UK
111 J16 Oświęcim Ger. Auschwitz. Małopolskie, S Poland
185 E22 Otago off. Otago Region. ⬖ region South Island, New Zealand
185 F23 Otago Peninsula peninsula South Island, New Zealand
Otago Region see Otago
165 F13 Ōtake Hiroshima, Honshū, SW Japan
184 L13 Otaki Wellington, North Island, New Zealand
93 M15 Otanmäki Oulu, C Finland
145 T15 Otar Zhambyl, SE Kazakhstan
165 R4 Otaru Hokkaidō, NE Japan
185 C24 Otatara Southland, South Island, New Zealand
185 C24 Otautau Southland, South Island, New Zealand
93 M18 Otava Isä-Suomi, E Finland
111 B18 Otava Ger. Wottawa. ≈ SW Czech Republic
56 C6 Otavalo Imbabura, N Ecuador
83 D17 Otavi Otjozondjupa, N Namibia
165 P12 Ōtawara Tochigi, Honshū, S Japan
83 B16 Otchinjau Cunene, SW Angola
116 F12 Oţelu Roşu Ger. Ferdinandsberg, Hung. Nándorhgy. Caras-Severin, SW Romania
185 E21 Otematata Canterbury, South Island, New Zealand
118 I6 Otepää Ger. Odenpäh. Valgamaa, SE Estonia
162 H7 Otgon var. Buyant. Dzavhan, C Mongolia
32 K9 Othello Washington, NW USA
115 A15 Othonoí island Iónia Nisiá, Greece, C Mediterranean Sea
Othris see Óthrys
115 F17 Óthrys var. Othris. ▲▲ C Greece
77 Q14 Oti ≈ N Togo
40 K10 Otinapa Durango, C Mexico
185 G17 Otira West Coast, South Island, New Zealand
37 V3 Otis Colorado, C USA
12 L10 Otish, Monts ▲▲ Québec, E Canada
83 C17 Otjikondo Kunene, N Namibia
83 C17 Otjikoto var. Oshikoto. ⬖ district N Namibia
83 E18 Otjinene Omaheke, NE Namibia
83 D18 Otjiwarongo Otjozondjupa, N Namibia
83 D18 Otjosondu var. Otjosundu. Otjozondjupa, C Namibia
Otjosundu see Otjosondu
83 D18 Otjozondjupa ⬖ district C Namibia
112 C11 Otočac Lika-Senj, W Croatia
Otog Qi see Ulan
112 J10 Otok Vukovar-Srijem, E Croatia
116 K14 Otopeni ✈ (Bucureşti) Ilfov, S Romania
184 L8 Otorohanga Waikato, North Island, New Zealand
12 D9 Otoskwin ≈ Ontario, C Canada
165 G14 Ōtoyo Kōchi, Shikoku, SW Japan
95 E16 Otra ≈ S Norway
107 R19 Otranto Puglia, SE Italy
Otranto, Canale d' see Otranto, Strait of
107 Q18 Otranto, Strait of It. Canale d'Otranto. strait Albania/Italy
111 H18 Otrokovice Ger. Otrokowitz. Zlínský Kraj, E Czech Republic
Otrokowitz see Otrokovice
31 P10 Otsego Michigan, N USA
31 Q6 Otsego Lake ◎ Michigan, N USA
18 I11 Otselic River ≈ New York, NE USA
164 J14 Ōtsu var. Ōtu. Shiga, Honshū, SW Japan
94 G11 Otta Oppland, S Norway
189 U13 Otta island Chuuk, C Micronesia
94 F11 Otta ≈ S Norway
189 U13 Otta Pass passage Chuuk Islands, C Micronesia
95 J22 Ottarp Skåne, S Sweden
14 L12 Ottawa ● (Canada) Ontario, SE Canada
30 L11 Ottawa Illinois, N USA
27 Q5 Ottawa Kansas, C USA
31 R12 Ottawa Ohio, N USA
14 L12 Ottawa var. Uplands. ✈ Ontario, SE Canada
14 M12 Ottawa Fr. Outaouais. ≈ Ontario/Québec, SE Canada
12 I4 Ottawa Islands island group Nunavut, C Canada
18 L8 Otter Creek ≈ Vermont, NE USA
36 L6 Otter Creek Reservoir ⊠ Utah, W USA
98 L11 Otterlo Gelderland, E Netherlands
94 D9 Otterøya island S Norway
29 S6 Otter Tail Lake ◎ Minnesota, N USA
29 R7 Otter Tail River ≈ Minnesota, C USA
95 H23 Otterup Fyn, C Denmark
99 H19 Ottignies Wallon Brabant, C Belgium
101 L23 Ottobrunn Bayern, SE Germany
29 X15 Ottumwa Iowa, C USA
Ōtu see Ōtsu
83 B16 Otuazuma Kunene, NW Namibia
77 V16 Oturkpo Benue, S Nigeria
193 Y15 Otu Tolu Group island group SE Tonga
182 M13 Otway, Cape headland Victoria, SE Australia
63 H24 Otway, Seno inlet S Chile
Ötz see Oetz
108 L8 Ötztaler Ache ≈ W Austria
108 L9 Ötztaler Alpen It. Alpi Venoste. ▲▲ SW Austria
27 T12 Ouachita, Lake ⊠ Arkansas, C USA
27 R11 Ouachita Mountains ▲▲ Arkansas/Oklahoma, C USA
27 U13 Ouachita River ≈ Arkansas/Louisiana, C USA
Ouadaï see Ouaddaï
76 J7 Ouadâne var. Ouadane. Adrar, C Mauritania
78 K13 Ouadda Haute-Kotto, N Central African Republic
78 J10 Ouaddaï off. Préfecture du Ouaddaï, var. Ouadaï, Wadai. ⬖ prefecture SE Chad
Ouaddaï, Préfecture du see Ouaddaï
77 P13 Ouagadougou var. Wagadugu. ● (Burkina) C Burkina
77 P13 Ouagadougou ✈ C Burkina
77 O12 Ouahigouya NW Burkina
Ouahran see Oran
79 J14 Ouaka ⬖ prefecture C Central African Republic
79 J15 Ouaka ≈ S Central African Republic
Oualam see Ouallam
76 M9 Oualâta var. Oualata. Hodh ech Chargui, SE Mauritania
77 R11 Ouallam var. Oualam. Tillabéri, W Niger
172 H14 Ouanani Mohéli, S Comoros
55 Z10 Ouanary E French Guiana
78 L13 Ouanda Djallé Vakaga, NE Central African Republic
79 N14 Ouando Haut-Mbomou, SE Central African Republic
79 L15 Ouango Mbomou, S Central African Republic
77 N14 Ouangolodougou var. Wangolodougou. N Ivory Coast
172 I13 Ouani Anjouan, SE Comoros
79 M15 Ouara ≈ E Central African Republic
76 K7 Ouarâne desert C Mauritania
15 O11 Ouareau ≈ Québec, SE Canada
74 K7 Ouargla var. Wargla. NE Algeria
74 F8 Ouarzazate S Morocco
77 Q11 Ouatagouna Gao, E Mali
74 G6 Ouazzane var. Ouezzane, Ar. Wazan, Wazzan. N Morocco
Oubangui see Ubangi
Oubangui-Chari see Central African Republic
Oubangui-Chari, Territoire de l' see Central African Republic
Oubari, Edeyen d' see Awbāri, Idhān
98 G13 Oud-Beijerland Zuid-Holland, SW Netherlands
98 F13 Ouddorp Zuid-Holland, SW Netherlands
77 P9 Oudeïka oasis C Mali
98 G13 Oude Maas ≈ SW Netherlands
99 E18 Oudenaarde Fr. Audenarde. Oost-Vlaanderen, SW Belgium
99 H14 Oudenbosch Noord-Brabant, S Netherlands
98 P6 Oude Pekela Groningen, NE Netherlands
Ouderkerk see Ouderkerk aan den Amstel
98 I10 Ouderkerk aan den Amstel var. Ouderkerk. Noord-Holland, C Netherlands
98 I6 Oudeschild Noord-Holland, NW Netherlands
99 G14 Oude-Tonge Zuid-Holland, SW Netherlands
98 I12 Oudewater Utrecht, C Netherlands
Oudjda see Oujda
98 L5 Oudkerk Friesland, N Netherlands
102 J7 Oudon ≈ NW France
98 I9 Oudorp Noord-Holland, NW Netherlands
83 G25 Oudtshoorn Western Cape, SW South Africa
99 I16 Oud-Turnhout Antwerpen, N Belgium
74 F7 Oued-Zem C Morocco
187 P16 Ouégoa Province Nord, C New Caledonia
76 L13 Ouéléssébougou var. Ouolossébougou. Koulikoro, SW Mali
77 N16 Ouellé E Ivory Coast
77 R16 Ouémé ≈ C Benin
77 O13 Ouessa S Burkina
102 D5 Ouessant, Île d' Eng. Ushant. island NW France
79 H17 Ouésso La Sangha, NW Congo
79 D15 Ouest Eng. West. ⬖ province W Cameroon
190 G11 Ouest, Baie de l' bay Îles Wallis, E Wallis and Futuna
15 Y7 Ouest, Pointe de l' headland Québec, SE Canada
Ouezzane see Ouazzane
99 K20 Ouffet Liège, E Belgium
79 H14 Ouham ⬖ prefecture NW Central African Republic
78 I13 Ouham ≈ Central African Republic/Chad
79 G14 Ouham-Pendé ⬖ prefecture W Central African Republic
77 R16 Ouidah Eng. Whydah, var. Wida. S Benin

◆ Country
● Country Capital
◇ Dependent Territory
○ Dependent Territory Capital
⬖ Administrative Regions
✈ International Airport
▲ Mountain
▲▲ Mountain Range
△ Volcano
≈ River
◎ Lake
⊠ Reservoir

OUJDA – PAMIR

74 H6 **Oujda** Ar. Oudjda, Ujda. NE Morocco
76 I7 **Oujeft** Adrar, C Mauritania
93 L15 **Oulainen** Oulu, C Finland
Ould Yanja see Ould Yenjé
76 J10 **Ould Yenjé** var. Ould Yanja. Guidimaka, S Mauritania
93 L14 **Oulu** Swe. Uleåborg. Oulu, C Finland
93 M14 **Oulu** Swe. Uleåborg. ◈ province N Finland
93 L15 **Oulujärvi** Swe. Uleträsk. ◎ C Finland
93 M14 **Oulujoki** Swe. Uleälv. ≈ C Finland
93 L14 **Oulunsalo** Oulu, C Finland
106 A8 **Oulx** Piemonte, NE Italy
78 J9 **Oum-Chalouba** Borkou-Ennedi-Tibesti, NE Chad
76 M16 **Oumé** C Ivory Coast
74 F7 **Oum er Rbia** ≈ C Morocco
78 J10 **Oum-Hadjer** Batha, E Chad
92 K10 **Ounasjoki** ≈ N Finland
78 J7 **Ounianga Kébir** Borkou-Ennedi-Tibesti, N Chad
Ouolossébougou see Ouéléssébougou
Oup see Auob
99 K19 **Oupeye** Liège, E Belgium
99 N21 **Our** ≈ NW Europe
37 Q7 **Ouray** Colorado, C USA
103 R7 **Ource** ≈ C France
104 G9 **Ourém** Santarém, C Portugal
104 H4 **Ourense** Cast. Orense, Lat. Aurium. Galicia, NW Spain
104 I4 **Ourense** Cast. Orense. ◈ province Galicia, NW Spain
59 O15 **Ouricuri** Pernambuco, E Brazil
60 J9 **Ourinhos** São Paulo, S Brazil
104 G13 **Ourique** Beja, S Portugal
59 M20 **Ouro Preto** Minas Gerais, NE Brazil
Ours, Grand Lac de l' see Great Bear Lake
99 K20 **Ourthe** ≈ E Belgium
165 Q9 **Ōu-sanmyaku** ▲▲ Honshū, C Japan
97 M17 **Ouse** ≈ N England, UK
Ouse see Great Ouse
102 H7 **Oust** ≈ NW France
Outaouais see Ottawa
15 T4 **Outardes Quatre, Réservoir** ⊞ Québec, SE Canada
15 T5 **Outardes, Rivière aux** ≈ Québec, SE Canada
96 E8 **Outer Hebrides** var. Western Isles. island group NW Scotland, UK
30 K3 **Outer Island** island Apostle Islands, Wisconsin, N USA
35 S16 **Outer Santa Barbara Passage** passage California, SW USA
104 G3 **Outes** Galicia, NW Spain
83 C18 **Outjo** Kunene, N Namibia
9 T16 **Outlook** Saskatchewan, S Canada
93 N16 **Outokumpu** Itä-Suomi, E Finland
96 M2 **Out Skerries** island group NE Scotland, UK
187 Q16 **Ouvéa** island Îles Loyauté, NE New Caledonia
103 S14 **Ouvèze** ≈ SE France
182 L9 **Ouyen** Victoria, SE Australia
39 Q14 **Ouzinkie** Kodiak Island, Alaska, USA
137 O13 **Ovacık** Tunceli, E Turkey
106 C9 **Ovada** Piemonte, NE Italy
187 X14 **Ovalau** island C Fiji
62 G9 **Ovalle** Coquimbo, N Chile
83 C17 **Ovamboland** physical region N Namibia
54 L10 **Ovana, Cerro** ▲ S Venezuela
104 G7 **Ovar** Aveiro, N Portugal
114 L10 **Ovcharitsa, Yazovir** ⊞ SE Bulgaria
54 E6 **Ovejas** Sucre, NW Colombia
101 E16 **Overath** Nordrhein-Westfalen, W Germany
98 F13 **Overflakkee** island SW Netherlands
99 H19 **Overijse** Vlaams Brabant, C Belgium
98 N10 **Overijssel** ◈ province E Netherlands
98 M9 **Overijssels Kanaal** canal E Netherlands
92 K13 **Överkalix** Norrbotten, N Sweden
27 R4 **Overland Park** Kansas, C USA
99 L14 **Overloon** Noord-Brabant, SE Netherlands
99 K16 **Overpelt** Limburg, NE Belgium
35 Y10 **Overton** Nevada, W USA
25 W7 **Overton** Texas, SW USA
92 K13 **Övertorneå** Norrbotten, N Sweden
95 N18 **Överum** Kalmar, S Sweden
92 G13 **Överuman** ◎ N Sweden
117 P11 **Ovidiopol'** Odes'ka Oblast', SW Ukraine
116 M14 **Ovidiu** Constanța, SE Romania
45 N10 **Oviedo** SW Dominican Republic
104 K2 **Oviedo** anc. Asturias. Asturias, NW Spain
104 K2 **Oviedo** ✕ Asturias, N Spain
Ovilava see Wels
118 D7 **Oviši** Ventspils, W Latvia
146 K10 **Ovminzatovo Tog'lari** ▲▲ N Uzbekistan
146 K10 **Ovminzatovo Tog'lari** Rus. Gory Auminzatau. ▲▲ N Uzbekistan
Övögdiy see Telmen
Ovoot see Darīganga
157 O4 **Övörhangay** ◈ province C Mongolia
94 E12 **Øvre Årdal** Sogn Og Fjordane, S Norway
95 J14 **Övre Fryken** ◎ C Sweden
92 J11 **Övre Soppero** Lapp. Badje-Sohppar. Norrbotten, N Sweden
117 N3 **Ovruch** Zhytomyrs'ka Oblast', N Ukraine
Övt see Bat-Öldziy
185 E24 **Owaka** Otago, South Island, New Zealand
79 H18 **Owando** prev. Fort Rousset. Cuvette, C Congo
164 J14 **Owase** Mie, Honshū, SW Japan
27 P9 **Owasso** Oklahoma, C USA
29 V10 **Owatonna** Minnesota, N USA
173 O4 **Owen Fracture Zone** tectonic feature W Arabian Sea
185 H15 **Owen, Mount** ▲ South Island, New Zealand
185 H15 **Owen River** Tasman, South Island, New Zealand
44 D8 **Owen Roberts** ✕ Grand Cayman, Cayman Islands
20 I6 **Owensboro** Kentucky, S USA
35 T11 **Owens Lake** salt flat California, W USA
14 F14 **Owen Sound** Ontario, S Canada
14 F13 **Owen Sound** ◎ Ontario, S Canada
35 T10 **Owens River** ≈ California, W USA
186 F9 **Owen Stanley Range** ▲▲ S Papua New Guinea
27 V5 **Owensville** Missouri, C USA
20 M4 **Owenton** Kentucky, S USA
77 U17 **Owerri** Imo, S Nigeria
184 M10 **Owhango** Manawatu-Wanganui, North Island, New Zealand
21 N5 **Owingsville** Kentucky, S USA
77 T16 **Owo** Ondo, SW Nigeria
31 R9 **Owosso** Michigan, N USA
35 V1 **Owyhee** Nevada, W USA
32 L14 **Owyhee, Lake** ◎ Oregon, NW USA
32 L15 **Owyhee River** ≈ Idaho/Oregon, NW USA
92 K1 **Öxarfjördhur** var. Axarfjördhur. fjord N Iceland
94 K12 **Oxberg** Dalarna, C Sweden
9 V17 **Oxbow** Saskatchewan, S Canada
95 O17 **Oxelösund** Södermanland, S Sweden
185 H18 **Oxford** Canterbury, South Island, New Zealand
97 M21 **Oxford** Lat. Oxonia. S England, UK
23 Q3 **Oxford** Alabama, S USA
22 L2 **Oxford** Mississippi, S USA
29 N16 **Oxford** Nebraska, C USA
18 I11 **Oxford** New York, NE USA
21 U8 **Oxford** North Carolina, SE USA
31 Q14 **Oxford** Ohio, N USA
18 H16 **Oxford** Pennsylvania, NE USA
9 X12 **Oxford House** Manitoba, C Canada
29 Y13 **Oxford Junction** Iowa, C USA
9 X12 **Oxford Lake** ◎ Manitoba, C Canada
97 M21 **Oxfordshire** cultural region S England, UK
Oxia see Oxyá
41 X12 **Oxkutzcab** Yucatán, SE Mexico
35 R15 **Oxnard** California, W USA
Oxonia see Oxford
14 I12 **Oxtongue** ≈ Ontario, SE Canada
Oxus see Amu Darya
115 E15 **Oxyá** var. Oxia. ▲ C Greece
164 L11 **Oyabe** Toyama, Honshū, SW Japan
Oyahue/Oyahue, Volcán see Ollagüe, Volcán
165 O12 **Oyama** Tochigi, Honshū, S Japan
47 U5 **Oyapock** ≈ E French Guiana
Oyapock see Oiapoque, Rio/Oyapok, Fleuve l'
55 Z10 **Oyapok, Baie de L'** bay Brazil/French Guiana South America W Atlantic Ocean
55 Z11 **Oyapok, Fleuve l'** var. Rio Oiapoque, Oyapock. ≈ Brazil/French Guiana see also Oiapoque, Rio
Oyapok, Fleuve l' see Oiapoque, Rio
79 E17 **Oyem** Woleu-Ntem, N Gabon
9 R16 **Oyen** Alberta, SW Canada
95 I15 **Øyeren** ◎ S Norway
Oygon see Tüdevtey
96 I7 **Oykel** ≈ N Scotland, UK
123 R9 **Oymyakon** Respublika Sakha (Yakutiya), NE Russian Federation
79 H19 **Oyo** Cuvette, C Congo
77 S15 **Oyo** Oyo, W Nigeria
77 S15 **Oyo** ◈ state SW Nigeria
56 D13 **Oyón** Lima, C Peru
103 S10 **Oyonnax** Ain, E France
146 L10 **Oyoqog'itma** Rus. Ayakagytma. Buxoro Viloyati, C Uzbekistan
146 M9 **Oyoqquduq** Rus. Ayakkuduk. Navoiy Viloyati, N Uzbekistan
32 F9 **Oysterville** Washington, NW USA
95 D14 **Øystese** Hordaland, S Norway
145 S16 **Oytal** Zhambyl, S Kazakhstan
147 U10 **Oy-Tal** Oshskaya Oblast', SW Kyrgyzstan
147 T10 **Oy-Tal** ≈ SW Kyrgyzstan
Oyyl see Uil
Ozarichi see Azarychy
23 R7 **Ozark** Alabama, S USA
27 S10 **Ozark** Arkansas, C USA
27 T8 **Ozark** Missouri, C USA
27 T8 **Ozark Plateau** plain Arkansas/Missouri, C USA
27 T6 **Ozarks, Lake of the** ⊞ Missouri, C USA
192 L10 **Ozbourn Seamount** undersea feature W Pacific Ocean
111 L20 **Ózd** Borsod-Abaúj-Zemplén, NE Hungary
112 D11 **Ozeblin** ▲ C Croatia
123 V11 **Ozernovskiy** Kamchatskaya Oblast', E Russian Federation
144 M7 **Ozërnoye** var. Ozërnyy. Kostanay, N Kazakhstan
124 J15 **Ozërnyy** Tverskaya Oblast', W Russian Federation
Ozërnyy see Ozërnoye
115 D18 **Ozerós, Límni** ◎ W Greece
122 F11 **Ozërsk** Chelyabinskaya Oblast', C Russian Federation
119 D14 **Ozersk** prev. Darkehnen, Ger. Angerapp. Kaliningradskaya Oblast', W Russian Federation
126 L4 **Ozery** Moskovskaya Oblast', W Russian Federation
Özgön see Uzgen
107 C17 **Ozieri** Sardegna, Italy, C Mediterranean Sea
111 I15 **Ozimek** Ger. Malapane. Opolskie, SW Poland
127 R8 **Ozinki** Saratovskaya Oblast', W Russian Federation
25 O10 **Ozona** Texas, SW USA
Ozorkov see Ozorków
110 J12 **Ozorków** Rus. Ozorkov. Łódź, C Poland
164 F14 **Ōzu** Ehime, Shikoku, SW Japan
137 R10 **Ozurget'i** prev. Makharadze. W Georgia

P

99 J17 **Paal** Limburg, NE Belgium
196 M14 **Paamiut** var. Pâmiut, Dan. Frederikshåb. S Greenland
167 N8 **Pa-an** Karen State, S Burma (Myanmar)
101 L22 **Paar** ≈ SE Germany
83 E26 **Paarl** Western Cape, SW South Africa
93 L15 **Paavola** Oulu, C Finland
96 E8 **Pabbay** island NW Scotland, UK
153 T15 **Pabna** Rajshahi, W Bangladesh
109 U4 **Pabneukirchen** Oberösterreich, N Austria
118 H13 **Pabradė** Pol. Podbrodzie. Vilnius, SE Lithuania
56 L13 **Pacahuaras, Río** ≈ N Bolivia
Pacaraima, Sierra/Pacaraim, Serra see Pakaraima Mountains
56 B11 **Pacasmayo** La Libertad, W Peru
42 D6 **Pacaya, Volcán de** ⩕ S Guatemala
115 K23 **Pacheía** var Pachía. island Kykládes, Greece, Aegean Sea
Pachía see Pacheía
107 L26 **Pachino** Sicilia, Italy, C Mediterranean Sea
56 F12 **Pachitea, Río** ≈ C Peru
154 I11 **Pachmarhi** Madhya Pradesh, C India
121 P3 **Páchna** var. Pakhna. SW Cyprus
115 H25 **Páchnes** ▲ Kríti, Greece, E Mediterranean Sea
54 F9 **Pacho** Cundinamarca, C Colombia
154 F13 **Pāchora** Mahārāshtra, C India
41 P13 **Pachuca** var. Pachuca de Soto. Hidalgo, C Mexico
Pachuca de Soto see Pachuca
27 W5 **Pacific** Missouri, C USA
192 L14 **Pacific-Antarctic Ridge** undersea feature S Pacific Ocean
32 F8 **Pacific Beach** Washington, NW USA
35 N10 **Pacific Grove** California, W USA
29 S15 **Pacific Junction** Iowa, C USA
192-193 **Pacific Ocean** ocean
129 Z10 **Pacific Plate** tectonic feature
113 J15 **Pačir** ▲ N Montenegro
182 L5 **Packsaddle** New South Wales, SE Australia
32 H9 **Packwood** Washington, NW USA
Padalung see Phatthalung
168 J12 **Padang** Sumatera, W Indonesia
168 L9 **Padang Endau** Pahang, Peninsular Malaysia
Padangpandjang see Padangpanjang
168 I11 **Padangpanjang** prev. Padangpandjang. Sumatera, W Indonesia
168 I10 **Padangsidempuan** prev. Padangsidimpoean. Sumatera, W Indonesia
Padangsidimpoean see Padangsidempuan
124 I9 **Padany** Respublika Kareliya, NW Russian Federation
93 M18 **Padasjoki** Etelä-Suomi, S Finland
57 M22 **Padcaya** Tarija, S Bolivia
101 H14 **Paderborn** Nordrhein-Westfalen, W Germany
Padeşul/Padeş, Vîrful see Padeş, Vârful
116 F12 **Padeş, Vârful** var. Padeşul; prev. Vîrful Padeş. ▲ W Romania
112 L10 **Padinska Skela** Serbia, N Serbia
153 S14 **Padma** var. Ganges. ≈ Bangladesh/India see also Ganges
Padma see Brahmaputra
Padma see Ganges
106 H8 **Padova** Eng. Padua; anc. Patavium. Veneto, NE Italy
82 A10 **Padrão, Ponta do** headland NW Angola
25 T16 **Padre Island** island Texas, SW USA
104 G3 **Padrón** Galicia, NW Spain
118 K13 **Padsvillye** Rus. Podsvil'ye. Vitsyebskaya Voblasts', N Belarus
182 K11 **Padthaway** South Australia
Padua see Padova
20 G7 **Paducah** Kentucky, S USA
25 P4 **Paducah** Texas, SW USA
105 N15 **Padul** Andalucía, S Spain
191 P8 **Paea** Tahiti, W French Polynesia
185 L14 **Paekakariki** Wellington, North Island, New Zealand
163 X11 **Paektu-san** var. Baitou Shan. ▲ China/North Korea
163 V15 **Paengnyŏng-do** island NW South Korea
184 M7 **Paeroa** Waikato, North Island, New Zealand
54 D12 **Páez** Cauca, SW Colombia
121 O3 **Páfos** var. Paphos. W Cyprus
121 O3 **Páfos** ✕ SW Cyprus
83 L19 **Pafuri** Gaza, SW Mozambique
112 C12 **Pag** It. Pago. Lika-Senj, SW Croatia
112 B11 **Pag** It. Pago. island Zadar, C Croatia
171 P7 **Pagadian** Mindanao, S Philippines
168 J13 **Pagai Selatan, Pulau** island Kepulauan Mentawai, W Indonesia
168 J13 **Pagai Utara, Pulau** island Kepulauan Mentawai, W Indonesia
188 K4 **Pagan** island C Northern Mariana Islands
115 G16 **Pagasitikós Kólpos** gulf E Greece
36 L8 **Page** Arizona, SW USA
29 Q5 **Page** North Dakota, N USA
118 D13 **Pagėgiai** Ger. Pogegen. Tauragė, SW Lithuania
21 S11 **Pageland** South Carolina, SE USA
81 G16 **Pager** ≈ NE Uganda
149 Q5 **Paghmān** Kābol, E Afghanistan
Pago see Pag
188 C16 **Pago Bay** bay E Guam, W Pacific Ocean
115 M20 **Pagóndas** var. Pagóndhas. Sámos, Dodekánisa, Greece, Aegean Sea
Pagóndhas see Pagóndas
192 J16 **Pago Pago** ○ (American Samoa) Tutuila, W American Samoa
37 R8 **Pagosa Springs** Colorado, C USA
38 H12 **Pāhala** var. Pahala. Hawai'i, USA, C Pacific Ocean
168 K8 **Pahang** var. Negeri Pahang Darul Makmur. ◈ state Peninsular Malaysia
Pahang see Pahang, Sungai
168 L8 **Pahang, Sungai** var. Pahang, Sungei Pahang. ≈ Peninsular Malaysia
149 S8 **Pahārpur** North-West Frontier Province, NW Pakistan
185 B24 **Pahia Point** headland South Island, New Zealand
184 M13 **Pahiatua** Manawatu-Wanganui, North Island, New Zealand
38 H12 **Pāhoa** var. Pahoa. Hawai'i, USA, C Pacific Ocean
23 Y14 **Pahokee** Florida, SE USA
35 X9 **Pahranagat Range** ▲▲ Nevada, W USA
35 W11 **Pahrump** Nevada, W USA
Pahsien see Chongqing
35 V9 **Pahute Mesa** ▲ Nevada, W USA
167 N7 **Pai** Mae Hong Son, NW Thailand
38 F10 **Pa'ia** var. Paia. Maui, Hawai'i, USA, C Pacific Ocean
Paia see Pa'ia
Pai-ch'eng see Baicheng
118 H4 **Paide** Ger. Weissenstein. Järvamaa, N Estonia
97 J24 **Paignton** SW England, UK
184 K3 **Paihia** Northland, North Island, New Zealand
93 M18 **Päijänne** ◎ S Finland
114 F13 **Páïko** ▲▲ N Greece
57 M17 **Paila, Río** ≈ C Bolivia
167 Q12 **Pailīn** Bătdâmbâng, W Cambodia
Pailing see Chun'an
54 F6 **Pailitas** Cesar, N Colombia
38 F9 **Pailolo Channel** channel Hawai'i, USA, C Pacific Ocean
93 K19 **Paimio** Swe. Pemar. Länsi-Suomi, SW Finland
165 O16 **Paimi-saki** var. Yaeme-saki. headland Iriomote-jima, SW Japan
102 G5 **Paimpol** Côtes d'Armor, NW France
168 J12 **Painan** Sumatera, W Indonesia
63 G23 **Paine, Cerro** ▲ S Chile
31 U11 **Painesville** Ohio, N USA
31 S14 **Paint Creek** ≈ Ohio, N USA
36 L10 **Painted Desert** desert Arizona, SW USA
Paint Hills see Wemindji
30 M4 **Paint River** ≈ Michigan, N USA
25 P8 **Paint Rock** Texas, SW USA
21 O6 **Paintsville** Kentucky, S USA
Paisance see Piacenza
96 I12 **Paisley** W Scotland, UK
32 I15 **Paisley** Oregon, NW USA
105 R10 **País Valenciano** var. Valencia, Cat. València; anc. Valentia. ◈ autonomous community NE Spain
105 O3 **País Vasco** Basq. Euskadi, Eng. The Basque Country, Sp. Provincias Vascongadas. ◈ autonomous community N Spain
56 A9 **Paita** Piura, NW Peru
169 V6 **Paitan, Teluk** bay Sabah, East Malaysia
104 H7 **Paiva, Rio** ≈ N Portugal
92 K12 **Pajala** Norrbotten, N Sweden
104 K3 **Pajares, Puerto de** pass NW Spain
54 G9 **Pajarito** Boyacá, C Colombia
54 G4 **Pajaro** La Guajira, S Colombia
Pakanbaru see Pekanbaru
55 Q10 **Pakaraima Mountains** var. Serra Pacaraim, Sierra Pacaraima. ▲▲ N South America
167 P10 **Pak Chong** Nakhon Ratchasima, C Thailand
123 V8 **Pakhachi** Koryakskiy Avtonomnyy Okrug, E Russian Federation
Pakhna see Páchna
189 U16 **Pakin Atoll** atoll Caroline Islands, E Micronesia
149 Q12 **Pakistan** off. Islamic Republic of Pakistan, var. Islami Jamhuriya e Pakistan. ◆ republic S Asia
Pakistan, Islamic Republic of see Pakistan
Pakistan, Islami Jamhuriya e see Pakistan
167 P8 **Pak Lay** var. Muang Pak Lay. Xaignabouli, C Laos
Paknam see Samut Prakan
166 L5 **Pakokku** Magwe, C Burma (Myanmar)
110 I10 **Pakość** Ger. Pakosch. Kujawski-pomorskie, C Poland
Pakosch see Pakość
149 V10 **Pākpattan** Punjab, E Pakistan
167 O15 **Pak Phanang** var. Ban Pak Phanang. Nakhon Si Thammarat, SW Thailand
112 G9 **Pakrac** Hung. Pakrácz. Požega-Slavonija, NE Croatia
Pakrácz see Pakrac
118 F11 **Pakruojis** Šiauliai, N Lithuania
111 J24 **Paks** Tolna, S Hungary
Pak Sane see Pakxan
Paksé see Pakxé
167 Q10 **Pak Thong Chai** Nakhon Ratchasima, C Thailand
149 R6 **Paktīā** ◈ province SE Afghanistan
149 Q7 **Paktīkā** ◈ province SE Afghanistan
171 N12 **Pakuli** Sulawesi, C Indonesia
81 F17 **Pakwach** NW Uganda
167 R8 **Pakxan** var. Muang Pakxan, Pak Sane. Bolikhamxai, C Laos
167 S10 **Pakxé** var. Paksé. Champasak, S Laos
78 G12 **Pala** Mayo-Kébbi, SW Chad
61 A17 **Palacios** Santa Fe, C Argentina
25 V13 **Palacios** Texas, SW USA
105 X5 **Palafrugell** Cataluña, NE Spain
107 L24 **Palagonia** Sicilia, Italy, C Mediterranean Sea
113 E17 **Palagruža** It. Pelagosa. island SW Croatia
115 G20 **Palaiá Epídavros** Pelopónnisos, S Greece
121 P3 **Palaichóri** var. Palekhori. C Cyprus
115 H25 **Palaiochóra** Kríti, Greece, E Mediterranean Sea
115 A15 **Palaiolastrítsa** religious building Kérkyra, Iónia Nisiá, Greece, C Mediterranean Sea
115 J19 **Palaiópoli** Ándros, Kykládes, Greece, Aegean Sea
103 N5 **Palaiseau** Essonne, N France
Palakkad see Pālghāt
154 N11 **Pāla Laharha** Orissa, E India
83 G19 **Palamakoloi** Ghanzi, C Botswana
115 E16 **Palamás** Thessalía, C Greece
105 X5 **Palamós** Cataluña, NE Spain
118 J5 **Palamuse** Ger. Sankt-Bartholomäi. Jõgevamaa, E Estonia
183 Q14 **Palana** Tasmania, SE Australia
123 U9 **Palana** Koryakskiy Avtonomnyy Okrug, E Russian Federation
118 C11 **Palanga** Ger. Polangen. Klaipėda, NW Lithuania
143 V10 **Palangān, Kūh-e** ▲ E Iran
Palangkaraja see Palangkaraya
169 T12 **Palangkaraya** prev. Palangkaraja. Borneo, C Indonesia
155 H22 **Palani** Tamil Nādu, SE India
Palanka see Bačka Palanka
154 D9 **Pālanpur** Gujarāt, W India
Palantia see Palencia
83 I19 **Palapye** Central, SE Botswana
155 J19 **Pālār** ≈ SE India
104 H3 **Palas de Rei** Galicia, NW Spain
123 T9 **Palatka** Magadanskaya Oblast', E Russian Federation
23 W10 **Palatka** Florida, SE USA
188 B9 **Palau** var. Belau. ◆ republic W Pacific Ocean
129 Y14 **Palau Islands** island group N Palau
192 G16 **Palauli Bay** bay Savai'i, C Samoa, C Pacific Ocean
167 N11 **Palaw** Tenasserim, S Burma (Myanmar)
170 M6 **Palawan** island W Philippines
171 N6 **Palawan Passage** passage W Philippines
192 E7 **Palawan Trough** undersea feature S South China Sea
155 H23 **Pālayankottai** Tamil Nādu, SE India
107 L25 **Palazzola Acreide** anc. Acrae. Sicilia, Italy, C Mediterranean Sea
118 G3 **Paldiski** prev. Baltiski, Eng Baltic Port, Ger. Baltischport. Harjumaa, NW Estonia
112 I13 **Pale** ◈ Republika Srpska, SE Bosnia and Herzegovina
Palekhori see Palaichóri
168 L13 **Palembang** Sumatera, W Indonesia
63 G18 **Palena** Los Lagos, S Chile
63 G18 **Palena, Río** ≈ S Chile
104 M5 **Palencia** anc. Palantia, Pallantia. Castilla-León, NW Spain
104 M3 **Palencia** ◈ province Castilla-León, N Spain
35 X15 **Palen Dry Lake** ◎ California, W USA
41 V15 **Palenque** Chiapas, SE Mexico
41 V15 **Palenque** var. Ruinas de Palenque. ruins Chiapas, SE Mexico
45 O9 **Palenque, Punta** headland S Dominican Republic
Palenque, Ruinas de see Palenque
Palerme see Palermo
107 I23 **Palermo** Fr. Palerme; anc. Panhormus, Panormus. Sicilia, Italy, C Mediterranean Sea
25 V8 **Palestine** Texas, SW USA
25 V7 **Palestine, Lake** ⊞ Texas, SW USA
107 I15 **Palestrina** Lazio, C Italy
166 K5 **Paletwa** Chin State, W Burma (Myanmar)
155 G21 **Pālghāt** var. Palakkad; prev. Pulicat. Kerala, SW India
152 F13 **Pāli** Rājasthān, N India
167 N16 **Palian** Trang, SW Thailand
189 O12 **Palikir** ● (Micronesia) Pohnpei, E Micronesia
Palimé see Kpalimé
107 L19 **Palinuro, Capo** headland S Italy
115 H15 **Palioúri, Ákrotírio** var. Akra Kanestron. headland N Greece
33 R14 **Palisades Reservoir** ⊞ Idaho, NW USA
99 J23 **Paliseul** Luxembourg, SE Belgium
154 C11 **Pālitāna** Gujarāt, W India
118 F4 **Palivere** Läänemaa, W Estonia
41 V14 **Palizada** Campeche, SE Mexico
93 L18 **Pälkäne** Länsi-Suomi, W Finland
155 J22 **Palk Strait** strait India/Sri Lanka
155 J23 **Pallai** Northern Province, NW Sri Lanka
Pallantia see Palencia
106 C6 **Pallanza** Piemonte, NE Italy
127 Q9 **Pallasovka** Volgogradskaya Oblast', SW Russian Federation
Pallene/Pallíni see Kassándra
185 L15 **Palliser Bay** bay North Island, New Zealand
185 L15 **Palliser, Cape** headland North Island, New Zealand
191 U9 **Palliser, Îles** island group Îles Tuamotu, C French Polynesia
82 Q12 **Palma** Cabo Delgado, N Mozambique
105 X9 **Palma** var. Palma de Mallorca. Mallorca, Spain, W Mediterranean Sea
105 X9 **Palma** ✕ Mallorca, Spain, W Mediterranean Sea
105 X10 **Palma, Badia de** bay Mallorca, Spain, W Mediterranean Sea
104 L13 **Palma del Río** Andalucía, S Spain
Palma de Mallorca see Palma
107 J25 **Palma di Montechiaro** Sicilia, Italy, C Mediterranean Sea
106 J7 **Palmanova** Friuli-Venezia Giulia, NE Italy
54 J7 **Palmarito** Apure, C Venezuela
43 N15 **Palmar Sur** Puntarenas, SE Costa Rica
60 I12 **Palmas** Paraná, S Brazil
59 K16 **Palmas** var Palmas do Tocantins. Tocantins, C Brazil
76 L18 **Palmas, Cape** Fr. Palmés, Cap des. headland SW Ivory Coast
Palmas do Tocantins see Palmas
54 D11 **Palmaseca** ✕ (Cali) Valle del Cauca, SW Colombia
107 B21 **Palmas, Golfo di** gulf Sardegna, Italy, C Mediterranean Sea
44 I7 **Palma Soriano** Santiago de Cuba, E Cuba
23 Y12 **Palm Bay** Florida, SE USA
35 T14 **Palmdale** California, W USA
61 H14 **Palmeira das Missões** Rio Grande do Sul, S Brazil
82 A11 **Palmeirinhas, Ponta das** headland NW Angola
39 R11 **Palmer** Alaska, USA
19 N11 **Palmer** Massachusetts, NE USA
25 U7 **Palmer** Texas, SW USA
194 H4 **Palmer** US research station Antarctica
15 R11 **Palmer** ≈ Québec, SE Canada
37 T5 **Palmer Lake** Colorado, C USA
194 J6 **Palmer Land** physical region Antarctica
14 F15 **Palmerston** Ontario, SE Canada
185 F22 **Palmerston** Otago, South Island, New Zealand
190 K15 **Palmerston** island S Cook Islands
Palmerston see Darwin
184 M12 **Palmerston North** Manawatu-Wanganui, North Island, New Zealand
Palmés, Cap des see Palmas, Cape
23 V13 **Palmetto** Florida, SE USA
The Palmetto State see South Carolina
107 M22 **Palmi** Calabria, SW Italy
54 D11 **Palmira** Valle del Cauca, W Colombia
56 F8 **Palmira, Río** ≈ N Peru
61 D19 **Palmitas** Soriano, SW Uruguay
Palmnicken see Yantarnyy
35 V15 **Palm Springs** California, W USA
27 V2 **Palmyra** Missouri, C USA
18 G10 **Palmyra** New York, NE USA
18 G15 **Palmyra** Pennsylvania, NE USA
21 V5 **Palmyra** Virginia, NE USA
Palmyra see Tudmur
192 L7 **Palmyra Atoll** ◇ US privately owned unincorporated territory C Pacific Ocean
154 P12 **Palmyras Point** headland E India
35 N9 **Palo Alto** California, W USA
25 O1 **Palo Duro Creek** ≈ Texas, SW USA
Paloe see Denpasar, Bali, C Indonesia
Paloe see Palu
168 L9 **Paloh** Johor, Peninsular Malaysia
80 F12 **Paloich** Upper Nile, SE Sudan
40 I3 **Palomas** Chihuahua, N Mexico
107 I15 **Palombara Sabina** Lazio, C Italy
105 S13 **Palos, Cabo de** cape SE Spain
104 I14 **Palos de la Frontera** Andalucía, S Spain
60 G11 **Palotina** Paraná, S Brazil
32 M9 **Palouse** Washington, NW USA
32 L9 **Palouse River** ≈ Washington, NW USA
35 Y16 **Palo Verde** California, W USA
57 E16 **Palpa** Ica, W Peru
95 M16 **Pålsboda** Örebro, C Sweden
93 M15 **Paltamo** Oulu, C Finland
171 N12 **Palu** prev. Paloe. Sulawesi, C Indonesia
137 P14 **Palu** Elazığ, E Turkey
152 I11 **Palwal** Haryāna, N India
123 U6 **Palyavaam** ≈ NE Russian Federation
77 Q13 **Pama** SE Burkina
172 J14 **Pamandzi** ✕ (Mamoudzou) Petite-Terre, E Mayotte
Pamangkat see Pemangkat
143 R11 **Pā Mazār** Kermān, C Iran
83 N19 **Pambarra** Inhambane, SE Mozambique
171 X12 **Pamdai** Papua, E Indonesia
103 N16 **Pamiers** Ariège, S France
147 T14 **Pamir** var. Daryā-ye Pāmīr, Taj. Dar"yoi Pomir. ≈ Afghanistan/Tajikistan see also Pāmīr, Daryā-ye

◆ Country
● Country Capital
◇ Dependent Territory
○ Dependent Territory Capital
◈ Administrative Regions
✕ International Airport
▲ Mountain
▲▲ Mountain Range
⩕ Volcano
≈ River
◎ Lake
⊞ Reservoir

PAMIR – PATCHEWOLLOCK

Pamir *see* Pāmīr, Daryā-ye
149 *U1* **Pāmīr, Daryā-ye** *var.* Pamir, ***Taj.*** Dar"yoi Pomir. ≈ Afghanistan/Tajikistan ***see also*** Pamir
Pāmīr, Daryā-ye *see* Pamir
Pāmīr-e Khord *see* Little Pamir
Pamir/Pāmīr, Daryā-ye *see* Pamirs
129 *Q8* **Pamirs** ***Pash.*** Daryā-ye Pāmīr, ***Rus.*** Pamir. ▲▲ C Asia
Pâmiut *see* Paamiut
21 *X10* **Pamlico River** ≈ North Carolina, SE USA
21 *Y10* **Pamlico Sound** *sound* North Carolina, SE USA
25 *O2* **Pampa** Texas, SW USA
Pampa Aullagas, Lago *see* Poopó, Lago
61 *B21* **Pampa Húmeda** *grassland* E Argentina
56 *A10* **Pampa las Salinas** *salt lake* NW Peru
57 *F15* **Pampas** Huancavelica, C Peru
62 *K13* **Pampas** *plain* C Argentina
55 *O4* **Pampatar** Nueva Esparta, NE Venezuela
Pampeluna *see* Pamplona
104 *H8* **Pampilhosa da Serra** ***var.*** Pampilhosa de Serra. Coimbra, N Portugal
173 *Y15* **Pamplemousses** N Mauritius
54 *G7* **Pamplona** Norte de Santander, N Colombia
105 *Q3* **Pamplona** ***Basq.*** Iruña, ***prev.*** Pampeluna; ***anc.*** Pompaelo. Navarra, N Spain
114 *I11* **Pamporovo** ***prev.*** Vasil Kolarov. Smolyan, S Bulgaria
136 *D15* **Pamukkale** Denizli, W Turkey
21 *W5* **Pamunkey River** ≈ Virginia, NE USA
152 *K5* **Pamzal** Jammu and Kashmir, NW India
30 *L14* **Pana** Illinois, N USA
41 *Y11* **Panabá** Yucatán, SE Mexico
35 *Y8* **Panaca** Nevada, W USA
115 *E19* **Panachaikó** ▲▲ S Greece
14 *F11* **Panache Lake** ◎ Ontario, S Canada
114 *I10* **Panagyurishte** Pazardzhik, C Bulgaria
168 *M16* **Panaitan, Pulau** *island* S Indonesia
115 *D18* **Panaitolikó** ▲▲ C Greece
155 *E17* **Panaji** ***var.*** Pangim, Panjim, New Goa. *state capital* Goa, W India
43 *T15* **Panamá** ***var.*** Ciudad de Panama, ***Eng.*** Panama City. ● (Panama) Panamá, C Panama
43 *T14* **Panama** ***off.*** Republic of Panama. ◆ *republic* Central America
43 *U14* **Panamá** ***off.*** Provincia de Panamá. ◈ *province* E Panama
43 *U15* **Panamá, Bahía de** *bay* N Gulf of Panama
193 *T7* **Panama Basin** *undersea feature* E Pacific Ocean
43 *T15* **Panama Canal** *shipping canal* E Panama
23 *R9* **Panama City** Florida, SE USA
43 *T14* **Panama City** ✈ Panamá, C Panama
Panama City *see* Panamá
23 *Q9* **Panama City Beach** Florida, SE USA
43 *T17* **Panamá, Golfo de** ***var.*** Gulf of Panama. *gulf* S Panama
Panama, Gulf of *see* Panamá, Golfo de
Panama, Isthmus of *see* Panama, Istmo de
43 *T15* **Panama, Istmo de** ***Eng.*** Isthmus of Panama; ***prev.*** Isthmus of Darien. *isthmus* E Panama
Panamá, Provincia de *see* Panamá
Panama, Republic of *see* Panama
35 *U11* **Panamint Range** ▲▲ California, W USA
107 *L22* **Panarea, Isola** *island* Isole Eolie, S Italy
106 *G9* **Panaro** ≈ N Italy
171 *P5* **Panay Island** *island* C Philippines
35 *W7* **Pancake Range** ▲▲ Nevada, W USA
112 *M11* **Pančevo** ***Ger.*** Pantschowa, ***Hung.*** Pancsova. Vojvodina, N Serbia
113 *M15* **Pančićev Vrh** ▲ SW Serbia
116 *L12* **Panciu** Vrancea, E Romania
116 *F10* **Pâncota** ***Hung.*** Pankota; ***prev.*** Pîncota. Arad, W Romania
Pancsova *see* Pančevo
83 *N20* **Panda** Inhambane, SE Mozambique
171 *X12* **Pandaidori, Kepulauan** *island group* E Indonesia
25 *N11* **Pandale** Texas, SW USA
169 *P12* **Pandang Tikar, Pulau** *island* N Indonesia
61 *F20* **Pan de Azúcar** Maldonado, S Uruguay
118 *H11* **Pandėlys** Panevėžys, NE Lithuania
155 *F15* **Pandharpur** Mahārāshtra, W India
182 *J1* **Pandie Pandie** South Australia
171 *O12* **Pandiri** Sulawesi, C Indonesia
61 *F20* **Pando** Canelones, S Uruguay
57 *J14* **Pando** ◈ *department* N Bolivia
192 *K9* **Pandora Bank** *undersea feature* W Pacific Ocean
95 *G20* **Pandrup** Nordjylland, N Denmark
79 *J15* **Pandu** Equateur, NW Dem. Rep. Congo
153 *V12* **Pandu** Assam, NE India
Paneas *see* Bāniyās
59 *F15* **Panelas** Mato Grosso, W Brazil
118 *G12* **Panevėžys** Panevėžys, C Lithuania
118 *G11* **Panevėžys** ◈ *province* NW Lithuania
Panfilov *see* Zharkent
127 *N9* **Panfilovo** Volgogradskaya Oblast', SW Russian Federation
79 *N17* **Panga** Orientale, N Dem. Rep. Congo
193 *Y15* **Pangai** Lifuka, C Tonga
114 *H13* **Pangaío** ▲▲ N Greece
79 *G20* **Pangala** Le Pool, S Congo
81 *J22* **Pangani** Tanga, E Tanzania
81 *I21* **Pangani** ≈ NE Tanzania
186 *K8* **Panggoe** Choiseul Island, NW Solomon Islands
79 *N20* **Pangi** Maniema, E Dem. Rep. Congo
Pangim *see* Panaji
168 *H8* **Pangkalanbrandan** Sumatera, W Indonesia
Pangkalanbun *see* Pangkalanbuun
169 *R13* **Pangkalanbuun** ***var.*** Pangkalanbun. Borneo, C Indonesia
169 *N12* **Pangkalpinang** Pulau Bangka, W Indonesia
9 *U17* **Pangman** Saskatchewan, S Canada
Pang-Nga *see* Phang-Nga
9 *S6* **Pangnirtung** Baffin Island, Nunavut, NE Canada
152 *K6* **Pangong Tso** ***var.*** Bangong Co. ◎ China/India ***see also*** Bangong Co
Pangong Tso *see* Bangong Co
36 *K7* **Panguitch** Utah, W USA
186 *J7* **Panguna** Bougainville Island, NE Papua New Guinea
171 *N8* **Pangutaran Group** *island group* Sulu Archipelago, SW Philippines
25 *N2* **Panhandle** Texas, SW USA
Panhormus *see* Palermo
171 *W14* **Paniai, Danau** ◎ Papua, E Indonesia
79 *L21* **Pania-Mutombo** Kasai Oriental, C Dem. Rep. Congo
Panicherevo *see* Dolno Panicherevo
187 *P16* **Panié, Mont** ▲ C New Caledonia
152 *I10* **Pānīpat** Haryāna, N India
147 *Q14* **Panj** ***Rus.*** Pyandzh; ***prev.*** Kirovabad. SW Tajikistan
147 *P15* **Panj** ***Rus.*** Pyandzh. ≈ Afghanistan/Tajikistan
149 *O5* **Panjāb** Bāmīān, C Afghanistan
147 *O12* **Panjakent** ***Rus.*** Pendzhikent. W Tajikistan
148 *L14* **Panjgūr** Baluchistān, SW Pakistan
Panjim *see* Panaji
163 *U12* **Panjin** Liaoning, NE China
147 *P14* **Panji Poyon** ***Rus.*** Nizhniy Pyandzh. SW Tajikistan
149 *S4* **Panjshīr** ◈ *province* NE Afghanistan
149 *Q4* **Panjshīr** ≈ E Afghanistan
Pankota *see* Pâncota
77 *W14* **Pankshin** Plateau, C Nigeria
163 *Y10* **Pan Ling** ▲▲ N China
Panlong Jiang *see* Lô, Sông
154 *J9* **Panna** Madhya Pradesh, C India
99 *M16* **Panningen** Limburg, SE Netherlands
149 *R13* **Pāno Āqil** Sind, SE Pakistan
121 *P3* **Páno Léfkara** S Cyprus
121 *O3* **Páno Panagiá** ***var.*** Pano Panayia. W Cyprus
Pano Panayia *see* Páno Panagiá
Panopolis *see* Akhmîm
29 *U14* **Panora** Iowa, C USA
60 *I8* **Panorama** São Paulo, S Brazil
115 *I24* **Pánormos** Kríti, Greece, E Mediterranean Sea
Panormus *see* Palermo
163 *W11* **Panshi** Jilin, NE China
59 *H19* **Pantanal** ***var.*** Pantanalmato-Grossense. *swamp* SW Brazil
Pantanalmato-Grossense *see* Pantanal
61 *H16* **Pântano Grande** Rio Grande do Sul, S Brazil
171 *Q16* **Pantar, Pulau** *island* Kepulauan Alor, S Indonesia
21 *X9* **Pantego** North Carolina, SE USA
107 *G25* **Pantelleria** ***anc.*** Cossyra, Cosyra. Sicilia, Italy, C Mediterranean Sea
107 *G25* **Pantelleria, Isola di** *island* SW Italy
Pante Macassar/Pante Makassar *see* Pante Makasar
171 *Q16* **Pante Makasar** ***var.*** Pante Macassar, Pante Makassar. W East Timor
152 *K10* **Pantnagar** Uttaranchal, N India
115 *A15* **Pantokrátoras** ▲ Kérkyra, Iónia Nisiá, Greece, C Mediterranean Sea
Pantschowa *see* Pančevo
41 *P11* **Pánuco** Veracruz-Llave, E Mexico
41 *P11* **Pánuco, Río** ≈ C Mexico
160 *I12* **Panxian** Guizhou, S China
168 *I10* **Panyabungan** Sumatera, N Indonesia
77 *W14* **Panyam** Plateau, C Nigeria
157 *N13* **Panzhihua** ***prev.*** Dukou, Tu-k'ou. Sichuan, C China
79 *I22* **Panzi** Bandundu, SW Dem. Rep. Congo
42 *E5* **Panzós** Alta Verapaz, E Guatemala
Pao-chi/Paoki *see* Baoji
Pao-king *see* Shaoyang
107 *N20* **Paola** Calabria, SW Italy
121 *P16* **Paola** E Malta
27 *R5* **Paola** Kansas, C USA
31 *O15* **Paoli** Indiana, N USA
187 *R14* **Paonangisu** Éfaté, C Vanuatu
171 *S13* **Paoni** ***var.*** Pauni. Pulau Seram, E Indonesia
37 *Q5* **Paonia** Colorado, C USA
191 *O7* **Paopao** Moorea, W French Polynesia
Pao-shan *see* Baoshan
Pao-ting *see* Baoding
Pao-t'ou/Paotow *see* Baotou
79 *H14* **Paoua** Ouham-Pendé, W Central African Republic
Pap *see* Pop
111 *H23* **Pápa** Veszprém, W Hungary
42 *J12* **Papagayo, Golfo de** *gulf* NW Costa Rica
38 *H11* **Pāpa'ikou** ***var.*** Papaikou. Hawai'i, USA, C Pacific Ocean
41 *R15* **Papaloapan, Río** ≈ S Mexico
184 *L6* **Papakura** Auckland, North Island, New Zealand
41 *Q13* **Papantla** ***var.*** Papantla de Olarte. Veracruz-Llave, E Mexico
Papantla de Olarte *see* Papantla
191 *P8* **Papara** Tahiti, W French Polynesia
184 *K4* **Paparoa** Northland, North Island, New Zealand
185 *G16* **Paparoa Range** ▲▲ South Island, New Zealand
115 *K20* **Pápas, Akrotírio** *cape* Ikaría, Dodekánisa, Greece, Aegean Sea
96 *L2* **Papa Stour** *island* NE Scotland, UK
184 *L6* **Papatoetoe** Auckland, North Island, New Zealand
185 *E25* **Papatowai** Otago, South Island, New Zealand
96 *K4* **Papa Westray** *island* NE Scotland, UK
191 *T10* **Papeete** ○ (French Polynesia) Tahiti, W French Polynesia
100 *F11* **Papenburg** Niedersachsen, NW Germany
98 *H13* **Papendrecht** Zuid-Holland, SW Netherlands
191 *Q7* **Papenoo** Tahiti, W French Polynesia
191 *Q7* **Papenoo Rivière** ≈ Tahiti, W French Polynesia
191 *N7* **Papetoai** Moorea, W French Polynesia
92 *L3* **Papey** *island* E Iceland
Paphos *see* Páfos
40 *H5* **Papigochic, Río** ≈ NW Mexico
118 *E10* **Papilė** Šiaulai, NW Lithuania
29 *S15* **Papillion** Nebraska, C USA
15 *T5* **Papinachois** ≈ Québec, SE Canada
171 *X13* **Papua** ***var.*** Irian Barat, West Irian, West New Guinea, West Papua; ***prev.*** Dutch New Guinea, Irian Jaya, Netherlands New Guinea. ◈ *province* E Indonesia
Papua and New Guinea, Territory of *see* Papua New Guinea
186 *C9* **Papua, Gulf of** *gulf* S Papua New Guinea
186 *C8* **Papua New Guinea** ***off.*** Independent State of Papua New Guinea; ***prev.*** Territory of Papua and New Guinea. ◆ *commonwealth republic* NW Melanesia
Papua New Guinea, Independent State of *see* Papua New Guinea
192 *H8* **Papua Plateau** *undersea feature* N Coral Sea
112 *G9* **Papuk** ▲▲ NE Croatia
167 *N8* **Papun** Karen State, S Burma (Myanmar)
42 *L14* **Paquera** Puntarenas, W Costa Rica
58 *I13* **Pará** ***off.*** Estado do Pará. ◈ *state* NE Brazil
55 *V9* **Para** ◈ *district* N Surinam
Pará *see* Belém
180 *I8* **Paraburdoo** Western Australia
57 *E16* **Paracas, Península de** *peninsula* W Peru
59 *L19* **Paracatu** Minas Gerais, NE Brazil
192 *E6* **Paracel Islands** ◇ *disputed territory* SE Asia
182 *I6* **Parachilna** South Australia
149 *R6* **Pārachinār** North-West Frontier Province, NW Pakistan
112 *N13* **Paraćin** Serbia, C Serbia
14 *K8* **Paradis** Québec, SE Canada
39 *N11* **Paradise** ***var.*** Paradise Hill. Alaska, USA
35 *O5* **Paradise** California, W USA
35 *X11* **Paradise** Nevada, W USA
Paradise Hill *see* Paradise
37 *R11* **Paradise Hills** New Mexico, SW USA
Paradise of the Pacific *see* Hawai'i
36 *L13* **Paradise Valley** Arizona, SW USA
35 *T2* **Paradise Valley** Nevada, W USA
115 *O22* **Paradisi** ✈ (Ródos) Ródos, Dodekánisa, Greece, Aegean Sea
154 *P12* **Pārādwīp** Orissa, E India
Pará, Estado do *see* Pará
Paraetonium *see* Maṭrûḥ
117 *R4* **Parafiyivka** Chernihivs'ka Oblast', N Ukraine
36 *K7* **Paragonah** Utah, W USA
27 *X9* **Paragould** Arkansas, C USA
47 *X8* **Paraguaçu** ***var.*** Paraguassú. ≈ E Brazil
60 *J9* **Paraguaçu Paulista** São Paulo, S Brazil
54 *H4* **Paraguaipoa** Zulia, NW Venezuela
62 *O6* **Paraguarí** Paraguarí, S Paraguay
62 *O7* **Paraguarí** ***off.*** Departamento de Paraguarí. ◈ *department* S Paraguay
Paraguarí, Departamento de *see* Paraguarí
57 *O16* **Paraguá, Río** ≈ NE Bolivia
55 *O8* **Paragua, Río** ≈ SE Venezuela
Paraguassú *see* Paraguaçu
62 *N5* **Paraguay** ◆ *republic* C South America
47 *U10* **Paraguay** ***var.*** Río Paraguay. ≈ C South America
Paraguay, Río *see* Paraguay
Parahiba/Parahyba *see* Paraíba
59 *P15* **Paraíba** ***off.*** Estado da Paraíba; ***prev.*** Parahiba, Parahyba. ◈ *state* E Brazil
Paraíba *see* João Pessoa
60 *P9* **Paraíba do Sul, Rio** ≈ SE Brazil
Paraíba, Estado da *see* Paraíba
Parainen *see* Pargas
43 *N14* **Paraíso** Cartago, C Costa Rica
41 *U14* **Paraíso** Tabasco, SE Mexico
57 *O17* **Paraiso, Río** ≈ E Bolivia
Parajd *see* Praid
77 *S14* **Parakou** C Benin
115 *F20* **Paralía Tyrou** Pelopónnisos, S Greece
121 *Q2* **Paralímni** E Cyprus
115 *G18* **Paralímni, Límni** ◎ C Greece
55 *W8* **Paramaribo** ● (Surinam) Paramaribo, N Surinam
55 *W9* **Paramaribo** ◈ *district* N Surinam
55 *W9* **Paramaribo** ✈ Paramaribo, N Surinam
Paramithiá *see* Paramythiá
56 *C13* **Paramonga** Lima, W Peru
123 *V12* **Paramushir, Ostrov** *island* SE Russian Federation
115 *C16* **Paramythiá** ***var.*** Paramithiá. Ípeiros, W Greece
62 *M10* **Paraná** Entre Ríos, E Argentina
60 *H11* **Paraná** ***off.*** Estado do Paraná. ◈ *state* S Brazil
47 *U11* **Paraná** ***var.*** Alto Paraná. ≈ C South America
Paraná, Estado do *see* Paraná
60 *K12* **Paranaguá** Paraná, S Brazil
59 *J20* **Paranaíba, Rio** ≈ E Brazil
61 *C19* **Paraná Ibicuy, Río** ≈ E Argentina
59 *H15* **Paranaíta** Mato Grosso, W Brazil
60 *H9* **Paranapanema, Rio** ≈ S Brazil
60 *K11* **Paranapiacaba, Serra do** ▲▲ S Brazil
60 *H9* **Paranavaí** Paraná, S Brazil
143 *N5* **Parandak** Markazī, W Iran
114 *I12* **Paranésti** ***var*** Paranestio. Anatolikí Makedonía kai Thráki, NE Greece
Paranestio *see* Paranésti
191 *W11* **Paraoa** *atoll* Îles Tuamotu, C French Polynesia
184 *L13* **Paraparaumu** Wellington, North Island, New Zealand
57 *N20* **Parapeti, Río** ≈ SE Bolivia
54 *L10* **Paraque, Cerro** ▲ W Venezuela
154 *I11* **Parāsiya** Madhya Pradesh, C India
115 *M23* **Paraspóri, Ákrotírio** *cape* Kárpathos, SE Greece
60 *O10* **Parati** Rio de Janeiro, SE Brazil
59 *K14* **Parauapebas** Pará, N Brazil
103 *Q10* **Paray-le-Monial** Saône-et-Loire, C France
Parbatsar *see* Parvatsar
154 *G13* **Parbhani** Mahārāshtra, C India
100 *L10* **Parchim** Mecklenburg-Vorpommern, N Germany
Parchwitz *see* Prochowice
110 *P13* **Parczew** Lubelskie, E Poland
60 *L8* **Pardo, Rio** ≈ S Brazil
111 *E16* **Pardubice** ***Ger.*** Pardubitz. Pardubický Kraj, C Czech Republic
111 *E17* **Pardubický Kraj** ◈ *region* N Czech Republic
Pardubitz *see* Pardubice
119 *F16* **Parechcha** ***Pol.*** Porzecze, ***Rus.*** Porech'ye. Hrodzyenskaya Voblasts', W Belarus
59 *F17* **Parecis, Chapada dos** ***var.*** Serra dos Parecis. ▲▲ W Brazil
Parecis, Serra dos *see* Parecis, Chapada dos
104 *M4* **Paredes de Nava** Castilla-León, N Spain
189 *U12* **Parem** *island* Chuuk, C Micronesia
189 *O12* **Parem Island** *island* E Micronesia
184 *I1* **Parengarenga Harbour** *inlet* North Island, New Zealand
15 *N8* **Parent** Québec, SE Canada
102 *J14* **Parentis-en-Born** Landes, SW France
Parenzo *see* Poreč
185 *G20* **Pareora** Canterbury, South Island, New Zealand
171 *N14* **Parepare** Sulawesi, C Indonesia
115 *B16* **Párga** Ípeiros, W Greece
93 *K20* **Pargas** ***Swe.*** Parainen. Länsi-Soumi, SW Finland
64 *O5* **Pargo, Ponta do** *headland* Madeira, Portugal, NE Atlantic Ocean
Paria, Golfo de *see* Paria, Gulf of
55 *N6* **Pariaguán** Anzoátegui, NE Venezuela
45 *X17* **Paria, Gulf of** ***var.*** Golfo de Paria. *gulf* Trinidad and Tobago/Venezuela
57 *I15* **Pariamanu, Río** ≈ E Peru
36 *L8* **Paria River** ≈ Utah, W USA
Parichi *see* Parychy
40 *M14* **Paricutín, Volcán** ⛰ C Mexico
43 *P16* **Parida, Isla** *island* SW Panama
55 *T8* **Parika** NE Guyana
93 *O18* **Parikkala** Etelä-Suomi, SE Finland
58 *E10* **Parima, Serra** ***var.*** Sierra Parima. ▲ Brazil/Venezuela ***see also*** Parima, Sierra
55 *N11* **Parima, Sierra** ***var.*** Serra Parima. ▲ Brazil/Venezuela ***see also*** Parima, Serra
57 *F17* **Parinacochas, Laguna** ◎ SW Peru
56 *A9* **Pariñas, Punta** *headland* NW Peru
58 *H12* **Parintins** Amazonas, N Brazil
103 *O5* **Paris** ***anc.*** Lutetia, Lutetia Parisiorum, Parisii. ● (France) Paris, N France
191 *Y2* **Paris** Kiritimati, E Kiribati
27 *S11* **Paris** Arkansas, C USA
33 *S16* **Paris** Idaho, NW USA
31 *N14* **Paris** Illinois, N USA
20 *M5* **Paris** Kentucky, S USA
27 *V3* **Paris** Missouri, C USA
20 *H8* **Paris** Tennessee, S USA
25 *V5* **Paris** Texas, SW USA
Parisii *see* Paris
43 *S16* **Parita** Herrera, S Panama
43 *S16* **Parita, Bahía de** *bay* S Panama
93 *K18* **Parkano** Länsi-Suomi, W Finland
Parkan/Párkány *see* Štúrovo
27 *N6* **Park City** Kansas, C USA
36 *L3* **Park City** Utah, W USA
36 *I12* **Parker** Arizona, SW USA
23 *R9* **Parker** Florida, SE USA
29 *R11* **Parker** South Dakota, N USA
35 *Z14* **Parker Dam** California, W USA
29 *W13* **Parkersburg** Iowa, C USA
21 *Q3* **Parkersburg** West Virginia, NE USA
29 *T7* **Parkers Prairie** Minnesota, N USA
171 *P8* **Parker Volcano** ⛰ Mindanao, S Philippines
181 *W13* **Parkes** New South Wales, SE Australia
30 *K4* **Park Falls** Wisconsin, N USA
Parkhar *see* Farkhor
14 *E16* **Parkhill** Ontario, S Canada
29 *T5* **Park Rapids** Minnesota, N USA
29 *Q3* **Park River** North Dakota, N USA
29 *Q11* **Parkston** South Dakota, N USA
10 *L17* **Parksville** Vancouver Island, British Columbia, SW Canada
37 *S3* **Parkview Mountain** ▲ Colorado, C USA
105 *N8* **Parla** Madrid, C Spain
29 *S8* **Parle, Lac qui** ▣ Minnesota, N USA
155 *G14* **Parli Vaijnāth** Mahārāshtra, C India
106 *F9* **Parma** Emilia-Romagna, N Italy
31 *T11* **Parma** Ohio, N USA
Parnahyba *see* Parnaíba
58 *N13* **Parnaíba** ***var.*** Parnahyba. Piauí, E Brazil
65 *J14* **Parnaíba Ridge** *undersea feature* C Atlantic Ocean
58 *N13* **Parnaíba, Rio** ≈ NE Brazil
115 *F18* **Parnassós** ▲▲ C Greece
185 *J17* **Parnassus** Canterbury, South Island, New Zealand
182 *H10* **Parndana** South Australia
115 *H19* **Párnitha** ▲▲ C Greece
Parnon *see* Párnonas
115 *F21* **Párnonas** ***var.*** Parnon. ▲▲ S Greece
118 *G5* **Pärnu** ***Ger.*** Pernau, ***Latv.*** Pērnava; ***prev. Rus.*** Pernov. Pärnumaa, SW Estonia
118 *G6* **Pärnu** ***var.*** Parnu Jõgi, ***Ger.*** Pernau. ≈ SW Estonia
118 *G5* **Pärnu-Jaagupi** ***Ger.*** Sankt-Jakobi. Pärnumaa, SW Estonia
Parnu Jõgi *see* Pärnu
118 *G5* **Pärnu Laht** ***Ger.*** Pernauer Bucht. *bay* SW Estonia
118 *F5* **Pärnumaa** ***var.*** Pärnu Maakond. ◈ *province* SW Estonia
Pärnu Maakond *see* Pärnumaa
153 *T11* **Paro** W Bhutan
153 *T11* **Paro** ✈ (Thimphu) W Bhutan
185 *G17* **Paroa** West Coast, South Island, New Zealand
163 *X14* **P'aro-ho** ***var.*** Hwach'ŏn-chŏsuji. ▣ N South Korea
115 *J21* **Pároikiá** ***prev.*** Páros. Páros, Kykládes, Greece, Aegean Sea
183 *N6* **Paroo River** *seasonal river* New South Wales/Queensland, SE Australia
Paropamisus Range *see* Sefīd Kūh, Selseleh-ye
Paropamisus Range *see* Safidkūh, Selseleh-ye
115 *J21* **Páros** *island* Kykládes, Greece, Aegean Sea
Páros *see* Pároikiá
36 *K7* **Parowan** Utah, W USA
103 *U13* **Parpaillon** ▲▲ SE France
108 *I9* **Parpan** Graubünden, S Switzerland
62 *G13* **Parral** Maule, C Chile
Parral *see* Hidalgo del Parral
183 *T9* **Parramatta** New South Wales, SE Australia
21 *Y6* **Parramore Island** *island* Virginia, NE USA
40 *M8* **Parras** ***var.*** Parras de la Fuente. Coahuila de Zaragoza, NE Mexico
Parras de la Fuente *see* Parras
42 *M14* **Parrita** Puntarenas, S Costa Rica
Parry group *see* Mukojima-rettō
14 *G13* **Parry Island** *island* Ontario, S Canada
197 *O9* **Parry Islands** *island group* Nunavut, NW Canada
14 *G12* **Parry Sound** Ontario, S Canada
110 *F7* **Parsęta** ***Ger.*** Persante. ≈ NW Poland
28 *L3* **Parshall** North Dakota, N USA
27 *Q7* **Parsons** Kansas, C USA
20 *H9* **Parsons** Tennessee, S USA
21 *T3* **Parsons** West Virginia, NE USA
Parsonstown *see* Birr
100 *P11* **Parsteiner See** ◎ NE Germany
107 *I24* **Partanna** Sicilia, Italy, C Mediterranean Sea
108 *J8* **Partenen** Graubünden, E Switzerland
102 *K9* **Parthenay** Deux-Sèvres, W France
95 *J19* **Partille** Västra Götaland, S Sweden
107 *I23* **Partinico** Sicilia, Italy, C Mediterranean Sea
111 *I20* **Partizánske** ***prev.*** Šimonovany, ***Hung.*** Simony. Trenčiansky Kraj, W Slovakia
58 *H11* **Paru de Oeste, Rio** ≈ N Brazil
182 *K9* **Paruna** South Australia
58 *I11* **Paru, Rio** ≈ N Brazil
149 *Q5* **Parvān** ***Pash.*** Parwān. ◈ *province* E Afghanistan
155 *M14* **Pārvatipuram** Andhra Pradesh, E India
152 *G12* **Parvatsar** ***prev.*** Parbatsar. Rājasthān, N India
Parwān *see* Parvān
158 *I15* **Paryang** Xizang Zizhiqu, W China
119 *M18* **Parychy** ***Rus.*** Parichi. Homyel'skaya Voblasts', SE Belarus
83 *J21* **Parys** Free State, C South Africa
35 *T15* **Pasadena** California, W USA
25 *W11* **Pasadena** Texas, SW USA
56 *B8* **Pasaje** El Oro, SW Ecuador
137 *T9* **P'asanauri** N Georgia
168 *I13* **Pasapuat** Pulau Pagai Utara, W Indonesia
167 *N7* **Pasawng** Kayah State, C Burma (Myanmar)
114 *L13* **Paşayiğit** Edirne, NW Turkey
23 *N9* **Pascagoula** Mississippi, S USA
22 *M8* **Pascagoula River** ≈ Mississippi, S USA
116 *F12* **Paşcani** ***Hung.*** Páskán. Iaşi, NE Romania
109 *T4* **Pasching** Oberösterreich, N Austria
32 *K10* **Pasco** Washington, NW USA
56 *E13* **Pasco** ***off.*** Departamento de Pasco. ◈ *department* C Peru
Pasco, Departamento de *see* Pasco
191 *N11* **Pascua, Isla de** ***var.*** Rapa Nui, Easter Island. *island* E Pacific Ocean
63 *G21* **Pascua, Río** ≈ S Chile
103 *N1* **Pas-de-Calais** ◈ *department* N France
100 *P10* **Pasewalk** Mecklenburg-Vorpommern, NE Germany
9 *T10* **Pasfield Lake** ◎ Saskatchewan, C Canada
Pa-shih Hai-hsia *see* Bashi Channel
Pashkeni *see* Bolyarovo
Pashmakli *see* Smolyan
153 *X10* **Pāsighāt** Arunāchel Pradesh, NE India
137 *Q12* **Pasinler** Erzurum, NE Turkey
Pasi Oloy, Qatorkŭhi *see* Zaalayskiy Khrebet
42 *E3* **Pasión, Río de la** ≈ N Guatemala
168 *J12* **Pasirganting** Sumatera, W Indonesia
Pasirpangarayan *see* Bagansiapiapi
168 *K6* **Pasir Puteh** ***var.*** Pasir Putih. Kelantan, Peninsular Malaysia
Pasir Putih *see* Pasir Puteh
169 *R9* **Pasir, Tanjung** *cape* East Malaysia
95 *N20* **Påskallavik** Kalmar, S Sweden
Páskán *see* Paşcani
Paskevicha, Zaliv *see* Tushybas, Zaliv
110 *K7* **Pasłęk** ***Ger.*** Preußisch Holland. Warmińsko-Mazurskie, NE Poland
110 *K7* **Pasłęka** ***Ger.*** Passarge. ≈ N Poland
148 *K16* **Pasni** Baluchistān, SW Pakistan
63 *I18* **Paso de Indios** Chubut, S Argentina
54 *L7* **Paso del Caballo** Guárico, N Venezuela
61 *E15* **Paso de los Libres** Corrientes, NE Argentina
61 *E18* **Paso de los Toros** Tacuarembó, C Uruguay
Pasoeroean *see* Pasuruan
35 *P12* **Paso Robles** California, W USA
15 *Y7* **Paspébiac** Québec, SE Canada
9 *U14* **Pasquia Hills** ▲▲ Saskatchewan, S Canada
149 *W7* **Pasrūr** Punjab, E Pakistan
30 *M1* **Passage Island** *island* Michigan, N USA
65 *B24* **Passage Islands** *island group* W Falkland Islands
8 *K5* **Passage Point** *headland* Banks Island, Northwest Territories, NW Canada
Passarge *see* Pasłęka
115 *C15* **Passarón** *ancient monument* Ípeiros, W Greece
Passarowitz *see* Požarevac
101 *O22* **Passau** Bayern, SE Germany
22 *M9* **Pass Christian** Mississippi, S USA
107 *L26* **Passero, Capo** *headland* Sicilia, Italy, C Mediterranean Sea
171 *P5* **Passi** Panay Island, C Philippines
61 *H14* **Passo Fundo** Rio Grande do Sul, S Brazil
60 *H13* **Passo Fundo, Barragem de** ▣ S Brazil
61 *H15* **Passo Real, Barragem de** ▣ S Brazil
59 *L20* **Passos** Minas Gerais, NE Brazil
167 *X10* **Passu Keah** *island* S Paracel Islands
118 *J13* **Pastavy** ***Pol.*** Postawy, ***Rus.*** Postavy. Vitsyebskaya Voblasts', NW Belarus
56 *D7* **Pastaza** ◈ *province* E Ecuador
56 *D9* **Pastaza, Río** ≈ Ecuador/Peru
61 *A21* **Pasteur** Buenos Aires, E Argentina
15 *V3* **Pasteur** ≈ Québec, SE Canada
147 *Q12* **Pastigav** ***Rus.*** Pastigov. W Tajikistan
Pastigov *see* Pastigav
54 *C13* **Pasto** Nariño, SW Colombia
38 *M10* **Pastol Bay** *bay* Alaska, USA
37 *O8* **Pastora Peak** ▲ Arizona, SW USA
105 *O8* **Pastrana** Castilla-La Mancha, C Spain
169 *S16* **Pasuruan** ***prev.*** Pasoeroean. Jawa, C Indonesia
118 *F11* **Pasvalys** Panevėžys, N Lithuania
111 *K21* **Pásztó** Nógrád, N Hungary
189 *U12* **Pata** ***var.*** Patta. *atoll* Chuuk Islands, C Micronesia
36 *M16* **Patagonia** Arizona, SW USA
63 *H20* **Patagonia** *semi arid region* Argentina/Chile
Patalung *see* Phatthalung
154 *D9* **Pātan** Gujarāt, W India
154 *J10* **Pātan** Madhya Pradesh, C India
171 *S11* **Patani** Pulau Halmahera, E Indonesia
Patani *see* Pattani
15 *V7* **Patapédia Est** ≈ Québec, SE Canada
116 *K13* **Pătâriagele** ***prev.*** Pătîriagele. Buzău, SE Romania
Patavium *see* Padova
182 *I5* **Patawarta Hill** ▲ South Australia
182 *L10* **Patchewollock** Victoria, SE Australia

◆ Country
● Country Capital
◇ Dependent Territory
○ Dependent Territory Capital
◈ Administrative Regions
✈ International Airport
▲ Mountain
▲▲ Mountain Range
⛰ Volcano
≈ River
◎ Lake
▣ Reservoir

PATEA – PERKIVTSI

184 K11 Patea Taranaki, North Island, New Zealand
184 K11 Patea ≈ North Island, New Zealand
77 U15 Pategi Kwara, C Nigeria
81 K20 Pate Island var. Patta Island. island SE Kenya
105 S10 Paterna País Valenciano, E Spain
109 R9 Paternion Slvn. Špatrjan. Kärnten, S Austria
107 L24 Paternò anc. Hybla, Hybla Major. Sicilia, Italy, C Mediterranean Sea
32 J7 Pateros Washington, NW USA
18 J14 Paterson New Jersey, NE USA
32 J10 Paterson Washington, NW USA
185 C25 Paterson Inlet inlet Stewart Island, New Zealand
98 N6 Paterswolde Drenthe, NE Netherlands
152 H7 Pathānkot Himāchal Pradesh, N India
Pathein see Bassein
33 W15 Pathfinder Reservoir ⊠ Wyoming, C USA
167 O11 Pathum Thani var. Patumdhani, Prathum Thani. Pathum Thani, C Thailand
54 C12 Patía var. El Bordo. Cauca, SW Colombia
152 I9 Patiāla var. Puttiala. Punjab, NW India
54 B12 Patía, Río ≈ SW Colombia
188 D15 Pati Point headland NE Guam
Pātiriagele see Pătâriagele
56 C13 Pativilca Lima, W Peru
166 M1 Pātkai Bum var. Patkai Range. ▲▲ Burma (Myanmar)/India
Patkai Range see Pātkai Bum
115 L20 Pátmos Pátmos, Dodekánisa, Greece, Aegean Sea
115 L20 Pátmos island Dodekánisa, Greece, Aegean Sea
153 P13 Patna var. Azimabad. state capital Bihār, N India
154 M12 Patnāgarh Orissa, E India
171 O5 Patnongon Panay Island, C Philippines
137 S13 Patnos Ağrı, E Turkey
60 H12 Pato Branco Paraná, S Brazil
31 O16 Patoka Lake ◎ Indiana, N USA
92 L9 Patoniva Lapp. Buoddobohki. Lappi, N Finland
113 K21 Patos var. Patosi. Fier, SW Albania
Patos see Patos de Minas
59 K19 Patos de Minas var. Patos. Minas Gerais, NE Brazil
Patosi see Patos
61 I17 Patos, Lagoa dos lagoon S Brazil
62 J9 Patquía La Rioja, C Argentina
115 E19 Pátra Eng. Patras; prev. Pátrai. Dytikí Ellás, S Greece
115 D18 Patraïkós Kólpos gulf S Greece
Pátrai/Patras see Pátra
92 G2 Patreksfjördhur Vestfirdhir, W Iceland
24 M7 Patricia Texas, SW USA
63 F21 Patricio Lynch, Isla island S Chile
Patta see Pata
Patta Island see Pate Island
167 O16 Pattani var. Patani. Pattani, SW Thailand
167 P12 Pattaya Chon Buri, S Thailand
19 S4 Patten Maine, NE USA
35 O9 Patterson California, W USA
22 J10 Patterson Louisiana, S USA
35 R7 Patterson, Mount ▲ California, W USA
31 P4 Patterson, Point headland Michigan, N USA
107 L23 Patti Sicilia, Italy, C Mediterranean Sea
107 L23 Patti, Golfo di gulf Sicilia, Italy
93 L14 Pattijoki Oulu, W Finland
193 Q4 Patton Escarpment undersea feature E Pacific Ocean
27 S2 Pattonsburg Missouri, C USA
0 D6 Patton Seamount undersea feature NE Pacific Ocean
10 J12 Pattullo, Mount ▲ British Columbia, W Canada
42 M5 Patuca, Río ≈ E Honduras
153 U16 Patuakhali var. Patukhali. Barisal, S Bangladesh
Patukhali see Patuakhali
Patumdhani see Pathum Thani
40 M14 Pátzcuaro Michoacán de Ocampo, SW Mexico
42 C6 Patzicía Chimaltenango, S Guatemala
102 K16 Pau Pyrénées-Atlantiques, SW France
102 J12 Pauillac Gironde, SW France
166 L5 Pauk Magwe, W Burma (Myanmar)
8 I6 Paulatuk Northwest Territories, NW Canada
42 K5 Paulayá, Río ≈ NE Honduras
22 M6 Paulding Mississippi, S USA
31 Q12 Paulding Ohio, N USA
29 S12 Paullina Iowa, C USA
59 P15 Paulo Afonso Bahia, E Brazil
38 M16 Pauloff Harbor var. Pavlor Harbour. Sanak Island, Alaska, USA
27 N12 Pauls Valley Oklahoma, C USA
166 L7 Paungde Pegu, C Burma (Myanmar)
Pauni see Paoni
152 K9 Pauri Uttaranchal, N India
Pautalia see Kyustendil
142 J5 Pāveh Kermānshāhān, NW Iran
126 L5 Pavelets Ryazanskaya Oblast', W Russian Federation
106 D8 Pavia anc. Ticinum. Lombardia, N Italy
118 C9 Pāvilosta Liepāja, W Latvia
125 P14 Pavino Kostromskaya Oblast', NW Russian Federation
114 J8 Pavlikeni Veliko Tŭrnovo, N Bulgaria
145 T8 Pavlodar Pavlodar, NE Kazakhstan
145 S9 Pavlodar off. Pavlodarskaya Oblast', Kaz. Pavlodar Oblysy. ❖ province NE Kazakhstan
Pavlodar Oblysy/Pavlodarskaya Oblast' see Pavlodar
Pavlograd see Pavlohrad
117 U7 Pavlohrad Rus. Pavlograd. Dnipropetrovs'ka Oblast', E Ukraine
Pavlor Harbour see Pauloff Harbor
145 R9 Pavlovka Akmola, C Kazakhstan
127 V4 Pavlovka Respublika Bashkortostan, W Russian Federation
127 Q7 Pavlovka Ul'yanovskaya Oblast', W Russian Federation
127 N3 Pavlovo Nizhegorodskaya Oblast', W Russian Federation
126 L9 Pavlovsk Voronezhskaya Oblast', W Russian Federation
126 L13 Pavlovskaya Krasnodarskiy Kray, SW Russian Federation
117 S7 Pavlysh Kirovohrads'ka Oblast', C Ukraine
106 F10 Pavullo nel Frignano Emilia-Romagna, C Italy
27 P8 Pawhuska Oklahoma, C USA
21 U13 Pawleys Island South Carolina, SE USA
167 N6 Pawn ≈ C Burma (Myanmar)
30 K14 Pawnee Illinois, N USA
27 O9 Pawnee Oklahoma, C USA
37 U2 Pawnee Buttes ▲ Colorado, C USA
29 S17 Pawnee City Nebraska, C USA
26 K5 Pawnee River ≈ Kansas, C USA
31 O10 Paw Paw Michigan, N USA
31 O10 Paw Paw Lake Michigan, N USA
19 O12 Pawtucket Rhode Island, NE USA
Pax Augusta see Badajoz
115 I25 Paximádia island SE Greece
Pax Julia see Beja
115 B16 Paxoí island Iónia Nisiá, Greece, C Mediterranean Sea
39 S10 Paxson Alaska, USA
147 O11 Paxtakor Jizzax Viloyati, C Uzbekistan
30 M13 Paxton Illinois, N USA
124 J11 Pay Respublika Kareliya, NW Russian Federation
166 M8 Payagyi Pegu, SW Burma (Myanmar)
108 C9 Payerne Ger. Peterlingen. Vaud, W Switzerland
32 M13 Payette Idaho, NW USA
32 M13 Payette River ≈ Idaho, NW USA
125 V2 Pay-Khoy, Khrebet ▲▲ NW Russian Federation
Payne see Kangirsuk
12 K4 Payne, Lac ◎ Québec, NE Canada
29 T8 Paynesville Minnesota, N USA
169 S8 Payong, Tanjung cape East Malaysia
Payo Obispo see Chetumal
61 D18 Paysandú Paysandú, W Uruguay
61 D17 Paysandú ❖ department W Uruguay
102 I7 Pays de la Loire ❖ region NW France
36 L12 Payson Arizona, SW USA
36 L4 Payson Utah, W USA
125 W4 Payyer, Gora ▲ NW Russian Federation
Payzawat see Jiashi
137 Q11 Pazar Rize, NE Turkey
136 F10 Pazarbaşı Burnu headland NW Turkey
136 M16 Pazarcık Kahramanmaraş, S Turkey
114 I10 Pazardzhik prev. Tatar Pazardzhik. Pazardzhik, SW Bulgaria
64 H11 Pazardzhik ❖ province C Bulgaria
54 H9 Paz de Ariporo Casanare, E Colombia
111 B17 Pazeński-Kraj ❖ region W Czech Republic
112 A10 Pazin Ger. Mitterburg, It. Pisino. Istra, NW Croatia
42 D7 Paz, Río ≈ El Salvador/Guatemala
113 O18 Pčinja ≈ N Macedonia
193 V15 Pea Tongatapu, S Tonga
27 O6 Peabody Kansas, C USA
9 O12 Peace ≈ Alberta/British Columbia, W Canada
Peace Garden State see North Dakota
9 Q10 Peace Point Alberta, C Canada
9 O12 Peace River Alberta, W Canada
23 W13 Peace River ≈ Florida, SE USA
9 N17 Peachland British Columbia, SW Canada
36 J10 Peach Springs Arizona, SW USA
Peach State see Georgia
23 S4 Peachtree City Georgia, SE USA
189 Y13 Peacock Point point SE Wake Island
97 M18 Peak District physical region C England, UK
183 Q7 Peak Hill New South Wales, SE Australia
65 G15 Peak, The ▲ C Ascension Island
105 O13 Peal de Becerro Andalucía, S Spain
189 X11 Peale Island island N Wake Island
37 O6 Peale, Mount ▲ Utah, W USA
39 O4 Peard Bay bay Alaska, USA
23 Q7 Pea River ≈ Alabama/Florida, S USA
25 W11 Pearland Texas, SW USA
38 D9 Pearl City O'ahu, Hawai'i, USA
38 D9 Pearl Harbor inlet O'ahu, Hawai'i, USA, C Pacific Ocean
Pearl Islands see Perlas, Archipiélago de las
Pearl Lagoon see Perlas, Laguna de
22 M5 Pearl River ≈ Louisiana/Mississippi, S USA
25 Q13 Pearsall Texas, SW USA
23 U7 Pearson Georgia, SE USA
25 P4 Pease River ≈ Texas, SW USA
12 F7 Peawanuk Ontario, C Canada
83 P16 Pebane Zambézia, NE Mozambique
65 C23 Pebble Island island N Falkland Islands
65 C23 Pebble Island Settlement Pebble Island, N Falkland Islands
113 L16 Peć Alb. Pejë, Turk. Ipek. Kosovo, S Serbia
25 R8 Pecan Bayou ≈ Texas, SW USA
22 H10 Pecan Island Louisiana, S USA
60 L12 Peças, Ilha das island S Brazil
30 L10 Pecatonica River ≈ Illinois/Wisconsin, N USA
108 G10 Peccia Ticino, S Switzerland
Pechenegi see Pechenihy
Pechenezhskoye Vodokhranilishche see Pecheniz'ke Vodoskhovyshche
124 I2 Pechenga Fin. Petsamo. Murmanskaya Oblast', NW Russian Federation
117 V5 Pechenihy Rus. Pechenegi. Kharkivs'ka Oblast', E Ukraine
117 V5 Pecheniz'ke Vodoskhovyshche Rus. Pechenezhskoye Vodokhranilishche. ⊠ E Ukraine
125 U7 Pechora Respublika Komi, NW Russian Federation
125 R6 Pechora ≈ NW Russian Federation
Pechora Bay see Pechorskaya Guba
Pechora Sea see Pechorskoye More
125 S3 Pechorskaya Guba Eng. Pechora Bay. bay NW Russian Federation
122 H7 Pechorskoye More Eng. Pechora Sea. sea NW Russian Federation
116 E11 Pecica Ger. Petschka, Hung. Ópécska. Arad, W Romania
24 K8 Pecos Texas, SW USA
25 N11 Pecos River ≈ New Mexico/Texas, SW USA
111 I25 Pécs Ger. Fünfkirchen, Lat. Sopianae. Baranya, SW Hungary
43 T17 Pedasí Los Santos, S Panama
Pedde see Pedja
183 O17 Pedder, Lake ◎ Tasmania, SE Australia
44 M10 Pedernales SW Dominican Republic
55 Q5 Pedernales Delta Amacuro, NE Venezuela
25 R10 Pedernales River ≈ Texas, SW USA
62 H6 Pedernales, Salar de salt lake N Chile
Pedhoulas see Pedoulás
55 X11 Pédima var. Malavate. SW French Guiana
182 F1 Pedirka South Australia
171 S11 Pedirwang Pulau Halmahera, E Indonesia
118 I5 Pedja var. Pedja Jõgi, Ger. Pedde. ≈ E Estonia
Pedja Jõgi see Pedja
121 O3 Pedoulás var. Pedhoulas. W Cyprus
59 N18 Pedra Azul Minas Gerais, NE Brazil
104 I3 Pedrafita, Porto de var. Puerto de Piedrafita. pass NW Spain
76 E9 Pedra Lume Sal, NE Cape Verde
43 P16 Pedregal Chiriquí, W Panama
54 J4 Pedregal Falcón, N Venezuela
40 L9 Pedriceña Durango, C Mexico
60 L11 Pedro Barros São Paulo, S Brazil
39 Q13 Pedro Bay Alaska, USA
62 H4 Pedro de Valdivia var. Oficina Pedro de Valdivia. Antofagasta, N Chile
62 P4 Pedro Juan Caballero Amambay, E Paraguay
63 L15 Pedro Luro Buenos Aires, E Argentina
105 O10 Pedro Muñoz Castilla-La Mancha, C Spain
155 J22 Pedro, Point headland NW Sri Lanka
182 K9 Peebinga South Australia
96 J13 Peebles SE Scotland, UK
31 S15 Peebles Ohio, N USA
96 J12 Peebles cultural region SE Scotland, UK
18 K13 Peekskill New York, NE USA
97 I16 Peel W Isle of Man
8 G7 Peel ≈ Northwest Territories/Yukon Territory, NW Canada
8 K5 Peel Point headland Victoria Island, Northwest Territories, NW Canada
8 M5 Peel Sound passage Nunavut, N Canada
100 N9 Peene ≈ NE Germany
99 K17 Peer Limburg, NE Belgium
14 H14 Pefferlaw Ontario, S Canada
185 I18 Pegasus Bay bay South Island, New Zealand
121 O3 Pégeia var. Peyia. SW Cyprus
109 V7 Peggau Steiermark, SE Austria
101 L19 Pegnitz Bayern, SE Germany
101 L19 Pegnitz ≈ SE Germany
105 T11 Pego País Valenciano, E Spain
166 L8 Pegu var. Bago. Pegu, SW Burma (Myanmar)
166 L7 Pegu ❖ division S Burma (Myanmar)
189 N13 Pehleng Pohnpei, E Micronesia
114 M12 Pehlivanköy Kırklareli, NW Turkey
77 R14 Péhonko C Benin
61 B21 Pehuajó Buenos Aires, E Argentina
Pei-ching see Beijing/Beijing Shi
100 J13 Peine Niedersachsen, C Germany
Pei-p'ing see Beijing/Beijing Shi
Peipsi Järv/Peipus-See see Peipus, Lake
118 J5 Peipus, Lake Est. Peipsi Järv, Ger. Peipus-See, Rus. Chudskoye Ozero. ◎ Estonia/Russian Federation
115 H19 Peiraías prev. Piraiévs, Eng. Piraeus. Attikí, C Greece
Peisern see Pyzdry
60 I8 Peixe, Rio do ≈ S Brazil
59 I16 Peixoto de Azevedo Mato Grosso, W Brazil
168 O11 Pejantan, Pulau island W Indonesia
Pejë see Peć
167 R7 Pèk var. Xieng Khouang; prev. Xiangkhoang. Xiangkhoang, N Laos
112 N11 Pek ≈ E Serbia
169 Q16 Pekalongan Jawa, C Indonesia
168 K11 Pekanbaru var. Pakanbaru. Sumatera, W Indonesia
30 L12 Pekin Illinois, N USA
Peking see Beijing/Beijing Shi
Pelabohan Kelang/Pelabuhan Kelang see Pelabuhan Klang
168 J9 Pelabuhan Klang var. Kuala Pelabohan Kelang, Pelabohan Kelang, Pelabuhan Kelang, Port Klang, Port Swettenham. Selangor, Peninsular Malaysia
120 L11 Pelagie, Isole island group SW Italy
Pelagosa see Palagruža
22 L5 Pelahatchie Mississippi, S USA
169 T14 Pelaihari var. Pleihari. Borneo, C Indonesia
103 U14 Pelat, Mont ▲ SE France
116 F12 Peleaga, Vârful prev. Vîrful Peleaga. ▲ W Romania
Peleaga, Vîrful see Peleaga, Vârful
123 O11 Peleduy Respublika Sakha (Yakutiya), NE Russian Federation
14 C18 Pelee Island island Ontario, S Canada
45 Q11 Pelée, Montagne ▲ N Martinique
14 D18 Pelee, Point headland Ontario, S Canada
171 P12 Pelei Pulau Peleng, N Indonesia
Peleliu see Beliliou
171 P12 Peleng, Pulau island Kepulauan Banggai, N Indonesia
23 T7 Pelham Georgia, SE USA
111 E18 Pelhřimov Ger. Pilgram. Vysočina, C Czech Republic
39 W13 Pelican Chichagof Island, Alaska, USA
191 Z3 Pelican Lagoon ◎ Kiritimati, E Kiribati
29 V3 Pelican Lake ◎ Minnesota, N USA
29 U6 Pelican Lake ◎ Minnesota, N USA
30 L5 Pelican Lake ◎ Wisconsin, N USA
44 G1 Pelican Point Grand Bahama Island, N Bahamas
83 B19 Pelican Point headland W Namibia
29 S6 Pelican Rapids Minnesota, N USA
Pelican State see Louisiana
9 U13 Pelikan Narrows Saskatchewan, C Canada
115 L18 Pelinaío ▲ Chíos, E Greece
Pelinnaeum see Pelinnaío
115 E16 Pelinnaío anc. Pelinnaeum. ruins Thessalía, C Greece
113 N20 Pelister ▲ SW FYR Macedonia
113 G15 Pelješac peninsula S Croatia
92 M12 Pelkosenniemi Lappi, NE Finland
29 W15 Pella Iowa, C USA
114 F13 Pélla site of ancient city Kentrikí Makedonía, N Greece
23 Q3 Pell City Alabama, S USA
61 A22 Pellegrini Buenos Aires, E Argentina
92 K12 Pello Lappi, NW Finland
100 G7 Pellworm island N Germany
10 H6 Pelly ≈ Yukon Territory, NW Canada
9 N7 Pelly Bay Nunavut, N Canada
10 I8 Pelly Mountains ▲▲ Yukon Territory, W Canada
Pélmonostor see Beli Manastir
37 P13 Pelona Mountain ▲ New Mexico, SW USA
Peloponnese/Peloponnesus see Pelopónnisos
115 E20 Pelopónnisos Eng. Peloponnese. ❖ region S Greece
115 E20 Pelopónnisos var. Morea, Eng. Peloponnese; anc. Peloponnesus. peninsula S Greece
107 L23 Peloritani, Monti anc. Pelorus and Neptunius. ▲▲ Sicilia, Italy, C Mediterranean Sea
107 M22 Peloro, Capo var. Punta del Faro. headland S Italy
Pelorus and Neptunius see Peloritani, Monti
61 H17 Pelotas Rio Grande do Sul, S Brazil
61 I14 Pelotas, Rio ≈ S Brazil
92 K10 Peltovuoma Lapp. Bealdovuopmi. Lappi, N Finland
19 R4 Pemadumcook Lake ◎ Maine, NE USA
169 Q16 Pemalang Jawa, C Indonesia
169 P10 Pemangkat var. Pamangkat. Borneo, C Indonesia
Pemar see Paimio
168 I9 Pematangsiantar Sumatera, W Indonesia
83 Q14 Pemba prev. Port Amelia, Porto Amélia. Cabo Delgado, NE Mozambique
81 J22 Pemba ❖ region E Tanzania
81 K21 Pemba island E Tanzania
83 Q14 Pemba, Baia de inlet NE Mozambique
81 J21 Pemba Channel channel E Tanzania
180 J14 Pemberton Western Australia
10 M16 Pemberton British Columbia, SW Canada
29 Q2 Pembina North Dakota, N USA
9 P15 Pembina ≈ Alberta, SW Canada
29 Q2 Pembina ≈ Canada/USA
171 X16 Pembre Papua, E Indonesia
14 K12 Pembroke Ontario, SE Canada
97 H21 Pembroke SW Wales, UK
23 W6 Pembroke Georgia, SE USA
21 U11 Pembroke North Carolina, SE USA
21 R7 Pembroke Virginia, NE USA
97 H21 Pembroke cultural region SW Wales, UK
Pembuang, Sungai see Seruyan, Sungai
43 S15 Peña Blanca, Cerro ▲ C Panama
104 K8 Peña de Francia, Sierra de la ▲▲ W Spain
104 G6 Penafiel var. Peñafiel. Porto, N Portugal
105 N6 Peñafiel Castilla-León, N Spain
Peñafiel see Penafiel
105 S8 Peñagolosa ▲ E Spain
105 N7 Peñalara, Pico de ▲ C Spain
171 X16 Penambo, Banjaran var. Banjaran Tama Abu, Penambo Range. ▲▲ Indonesia/Malaysia
Penambo Range see Penambo, Banjaran
41 O10 Peña Nevada, Cerro ▲ C Mexico
Penang see Pinang, Pulau, Peninsular Malaysia
Penang see Pinang
Penang see George Town
60 J8 Penápolis São Paulo, S Brazil
104 L7 Peñaranda de Bracamonte Castilla-León, N Spain
105 S8 Peñarroya ▲ E Spain
104 L12 Peñarroya-Pueblonuevo Andalucía, S Spain
97 K22 Penarth S Wales, UK
104 K1 Peñas, Cabo de cape N Spain
63 F20 Penas, Golfo de gulf S Chile
Pen-ch'i see Benxi
79 H14 Pendé var. Logone Oriental. ≈ Central African Republic/Chad
76 I14 Pendembu E Sierra Leone
29 R13 Pender Nebraska, C USA
Penderma see Bandırma
32 K11 Pendleton Oregon, NW USA
32 M7 Pend Oreille, Lake ◎ Idaho, NW USA
32 M7 Pend Oreille River ≈ Idaho/Washington, NW USA
Pendzhikent see Panjakent
Peneius see Pineiós
104 G8 Penela Coimbra, N Portugal
14 G13 Penetanguishene Ontario, S Canada
151 H15 Penganga ≈ C India
161 T12 P'engchia Yu island N Taiwan
79 M21 Penge Kasai Oriental, C Dem. Rep. Congo
Penghu Archipelago/P'enghu Ch'üntao/Penghu Islands see P'enghu Liehtao
161 R14 P'enghu Liehtao var. P'enghu Ch'üntao, Penghu Islands, Eng. Penghu Archipelago, Pescadores, Jap. Hoko-guntō, Hoko-shotō. island group W Taiwan
Penghu Shuidao/P'enghu Shuitao see Pescadores Channel
161 R4 Penglai var. Dengzhou. Shandong, E China
Peng-pu see Bengbu
Penhsihu see Benxi
Penibético, Sistema see Béticos, Sistemas
104 F10 Peniche Leiria, W Portugal
169 U17 Penida, Nusa island S Indonesia
Peninsular State see Florida
105 T8 Peñíscola País Valenciano, E Spain
40 M13 Pénjamo Guanajuato, C Mexico
Penki see Benxi
102 F7 Penmarch, Pointe de headland NW France
107 L15 Penna, Punta della headland C Italy
107 K14 Penne Abruzzo, C Italy
Penner see Penneru
155 J18 Penneru var. Penner. ≈ C India
182 I10 Penneshaw South Australia
18 C14 Penn Hills Pennsylvania, NE USA
Penninae, Alpes/Pennine, Alpi see Pennine Alps
108 D11 Pennine Alps Fr. Alpes Pennines, It. Alpi Pennine, Lat. Alpes Penninae. ▲▲ Italy/Switzerland
Pennine Chain see Pennines
97 L15 Pennines var. Pennine Chain. ▲▲ N England, UK
Pennines, Alpes see Pennine Alps
21 O8 Pennington Gap Virginia, NE USA
18 I16 Penns Grove New Jersey, NE USA
18 I16 Pennsville New Jersey, NE USA
18 E14 Pennsylvania off. Commonwealth of Pennsylvania, also known as Keystone State. ❖ state NE USA
18 G10 Penn Yan New York, NE USA
124 H16 Peno Tverskaya Oblast', W Russian Federation
19 R7 Penobscot Bay bay Maine, NE USA
19 S5 Penobscot River ≈ Maine, NE USA
182 K12 Penola South Australia
40 K9 Peñón Blanco Durango, C Mexico
182 E7 Penong South Australia
43 S16 Penonomé Coclé, C Panama
190 L13 Penrhyn atoll N Cook Islands
192 M9 Penrhyn Basin undersea feature C Pacific Ocean
183 S9 Penrith New South Wales, SE Australia
97 K15 Penrith NW England, UK
23 O9 Pensacola Florida, SE USA
23 O9 Pensacola Bay bay Florida, SE USA
195 N7 Pensacola Mountains ▲▲ Antarctica
182 L12 Penshurst Victoria, SE Australia
187 R13 Pentecost Fr. Pentecôte. island C Vanuatu
15 V4 Pentecôte ≈ Québec, SE Canada
Pentecôte see Pentecost
15 V4 Pentecôte, Lac ◎ Québec, SE Canada
8 H15 Penticton British Columbia, SW Canada
96 J6 Pentland Firth strait N Scotland, UK
96 J12 Pentland Hills hill range S Scotland, UK
171 Q12 Penu Pulau Taliabu, E Indonesia
155 H18 Penukonda Andhra Pradesh, E India
166 L7 Penwegon Pegu, C Burma (Myanmar)
24 M8 Penwell Texas, SW USA
97 J21 Pen y Fan ▲ SE Wales, UK
97 L16 Pen-y-ghent ▲ N England, UK
127 O6 Penza Penzenskaya Oblast', W Russian Federation
97 G25 Penzance SW England, UK
127 N6 Penzenskaya Oblast' ❖ province W Russian Federation
123 U7 Penzhina ≈ E Russian Federation
123 U9 Penzhinskaya Guba bay E Russian Federation
Penzig see Pieńsk
36 K13 Peoria Arizona, SW USA
30 L12 Peoria Illinois, N USA
30 L12 Peoria Heights Illinois, N USA
31 N11 Peotone Illinois, N USA
18 J11 Pepacton Reservoir ⊠ New York, NE USA
76 I15 Pepel W Sierra Leone
30 I6 Pepin, Lake ⊠ Minnesota/Wisconsin, N USA
99 L20 Pepinster Liège, E Belgium
113 L20 Peqin var. Peqini. Elbasan, C Albania
Peqini see Peqin
40 D7 Pequeña, Punta headland W Mexico
168 J8 Perak ❖ state Peninsular Malaysia
105 R7 Perales del Alfambra Aragón, NE Spain
115 C15 Pérama var. Perama. Ípeiros, W Greece
Perama see Pérama
92 M13 Perä-Posio Lappi, NE Finland
15 Z6 Percé Québec, SE Canada
15 Z6 Percé, Rocher island Québec, S Canada
102 L5 Perche, Collines de ▲▲ N France
109 X4 Perchtoldsdorf Niederösterreich, NE Austria
180 L6 Percival Lakes lakes Western Australia
105 T3 Perdido, Monte ▲ NE Spain
23 O8 Perdido River ≈ Alabama/Florida, S USA
Perece Vela Basin see West Mariana Basin
116 G7 Perechyn Zakarpats'ka Oblast', W Ukraine
54 E10 Pereira Risaralda, W Colombia
60 I7 Pereira Barreto São Paulo, S Brazil
59 G15 Pereirinha Pará, N Brazil
127 N10 Perelazovskiy Volgogradskaya Oblast', SW Russian Federation
127 S7 Perelyub Saratovskaya Oblast', W Russian Federation
31 P7 Pere Marquette River ≈ Michigan, N USA
Peremyshl see Przemyśl
116 I5 Peremyshlyany L'vivs'ka Oblast', W Ukraine
Pereshchepino see Pereshchepyne
116 L9 Pereshchepyne Rus. Pereshchepino. Dnipropetrovs'ka Oblast', E Ukraine
124 L16 Pereslavl'-Zalesskiy Yaroslavskaya Oblast', W Russian Federation
117 Y7 Pereval's'k Luhans'ka Oblast', E Ukraine
127 U7 Perevolotskiy Orenburgskaya Oblast', W Russian Federation
Pereyaslav-Khmel'nitskiy see Pereyaslav-Khmel'nyts'kyy
117 Q5 Pereyaslav-Khmel'nyts'kyy Rus. Pereyaslav-Khmel'nitskiy. Kyyivs'ka Oblast', N Ukraine
109 U4 Perg Oberösterreich, N Austria
61 B19 Pergamino Buenos Aires, E Argentina
106 G6 Pergine Valsugana Ger. Persen. Trentino-Alto Adige, N Italy
29 S6 Perham Minnesota, N USA
93 L16 Perho Länsi-Soumi, W Finland
116 E11 Periam Ger. Perjamosch, Hung. Perjámos. Timiş, W Romania
15 Q6 Péribonca ≈ Québec, SE Canada
12 L11 Péribonca, Lac ◎ Québec, SE Canada
15 Q6 Péribonca, Petite Rivière ≈ Québec, SE Canada
15 Q7 Péribonka Québec, SE Canada
40 I9 Pericos Sinaloa, C Mexico
169 Q10 Perigi Borneo, C Indonesia
102 L12 Périgueux anc. Vesuna. Dordogne, SW France
54 G5 Perijá, Serranía de ▲▲ Columbia/Venezuela
115 H17 Peristéra island Vóreioi Sporádes, Greece, Aegean Sea
63 H20 Perito Moreno Santa Cruz, S Argentina
155 G22 Periyāl var. Periyār. ≈ SW India
Periyār see Periyāl
155 G23 Periyār Lake ◎ S India
Perjámos/Perjamosch see Periam
27 O9 Perkins Oklahoma, C USA
116 L7 Perkivtsi Chernivets'ka Oblast', W Ukraine

◆ Country
● Country Capital
◇ Dependent Territory
○ Dependent Territory Capital
❖ Administrative Regions
✈ International Airport
▲ Mountain
▲▲ Mountain Range
Volcano
≈ River
◎ Lake
⊠ Reservoir

Perlas, Archipiélago de las – Pimenta

43 U15 **Perlas, Archipiélago de las** Eng. Pearl Islands. island group SE Panama
43 O10 **Perlas, Cayos de** reef SE Nicaragua
43 N9 **Perlas, Laguna de** Eng. Pearl Lagoon. lagoon E Nicaragua
43 N10 **Perlas, Punta de** headland E Nicaragua
100 L11 **Perleberg** Brandenburg, N Germany
Perlepe see Prilep
168 I6 **Perlis** ⬖ state Peninsular Malaysia
125 U14 **Perm'** prev. Molotov. Permskaya Oblast', NW Russian Federation
113 M22 **Përmet** var. Përmeti, Prëmet. Gjirokastër, S Albania
Përmeti see Përmet
125 U15 **Permskaya Oblast'** ⬖ province NW Russian Federation
59 P15 **Pernambuco** off. Estado de Pernambuco. ⬖ state E Brazil
Pernambuco see Recife
Pernambuco Abyssal Plain see Pernambuco Plain
Pernambuco, Estado de see Pernambuco
47 Y6 **Pernambuco Plain** var. Pernambuco Abyssal Plain. undersea feature E Atlantic Ocean
65 K15 **Pernambuco Seamounts** undersea feature C Atlantic Ocean
182 H6 **Pernatty Lagoon** salt lake South Australia
Pernau see Pärnu
Pernauer Bucht see Pärnu Laht
Përnava see Pärnu
114 G9 **Pernik** prev. Dimitrovo. Pernik, W Bulgaria
114 G10 **Pernik** ⬖ province W Bulgaria
93 K20 **Perniö** Swe. Bjärnå. Länsi-Soumi, SW Finland
109 X5 **Pernitz** Niederösterreich, E Austria
Pernov see Pärnu
103 O3 **Péronne** Somme, N France
14 L8 **Péronne, Lac** ◎ Québec, SE Canada
106 A8 **Perosa Argentina** Piemonte, NE Italy
41 Q14 **Perote** Veracruz-Llave, E Mexico
Pérouse see Perugia
191 W15 **Pérouse, Bahía de la** bay Easter Island, Chile, E Pacific Ocean
Perovsk see Kyzylorda
103 O17 **Perpignan** Pyrénées-Orientales, S France
113 M20 **Përrenjas** var. Përrenjasi, Prenjas, Prenjasi. Elbasan, E Albania
Përrenjasi see Përrenjas
92 O2 **Perriertoppen** ▲ C Svalbard
25 S6 **Perrin** Texas, SW USA
23 Y16 **Perrine** Florida, SE USA
37 S12 **Perro, Laguna del** ◎ New Mexico, SW USA
102 G5 **Perros-Guirec** Côtes d'Armor, NW France
23 T9 **Perry** Florida, SE USA
23 T5 **Perry** Georgia, SE USA
29 U14 **Perry** Iowa, C USA
18 E10 **Perry** New York, NE USA
27 N9 **Perry** Oklahoma, C USA
27 Q3 **Perry Lake** ⊞ Kansas, C USA
31 R11 **Perrysburg** Ohio, N USA
25 O1 **Perryton** Texas, SW USA
39 O15 **Perryville** Alaska, USA
27 U11 **Perryville** Arkansas, C USA
27 Y6 **Perryville** Missouri, C USA
Persante see Parsęta
Persen see Pergine Valsugana
Pershay see Pyarshai
117 V7 **Pershotravens'k** Dnipropetrovs'ka Oblast', E Ukraine
117 W9 **Pershotravneve** Donets'ka Oblast', E Ukraine
Persia see Iran
141 T5 **Persian Gulf** var. The Gulf, Ar. Khalīj al 'Arabī, Per. Khalīj-e Fars. Gulf SW Asia see also Gulf, The
Persis see Fārs
95 K22 **Perstorp** Skåne, S Sweden
137 O14 **Pertek** Tunceli, C Turkey
183 P16 **Perth** Tasmania, SE Australia
180 I13 **Perth** state capital Western Australia
14 L13 **Perth** Ontario, SE Canada
96 J11 **Perth** C Scotland, UK
96 J10 **Perth** cultural region C Scotland, UK
180 I12 **Perth** ✈ Western Australia
173 V10 **Perth Basin** undersea feature SE Indian Ocean
103 S15 **Pertuis** Vaucluse, SE France
103 Y16 **Pertusato, Capo** headland Corse, France, C Mediterranean Sea
30 L11 **Peru** Illinois, N USA
31 P12 **Peru** Indiana, N USA
57 E13 **Peru** off. Republic of Peru. ◆ republic W South America
Peru see Beru
193 T9 **Peru Basin** undersea feature E Pacific Ocean
193 U8 **Peru-Chile Trench** undersea feature E Pacific Ocean
112 F13 **Perućko Jezero** ◎ S Croatia
106 H13 **Perugia** Fr. Pérouse; anc. Perusia. Umbria, C Italy
Perugia, Lake of see Trasimeno, Lago
61 D15 **Perugorría** Corrientes, NE Argentina
60 M11 **Peruíbe** São Paulo, S Brazil
155 B21 **Perumalpār** reef India, N Indian Ocean
Peru, Republic of see Peru
Perusia see Perugia
99 D20 **Péruwelz** Hainaut, SW Belgium
137 R15 **Pervari** Siirt, SE Turkey
127 O4 **Pervomaysk** Nizhegorodskaya Oblast', W Russian Federation
117 X7 **Pervomays'k** Luhans'ka Oblast', E Ukraine
117 P8 **Pervomays'k** prev. Ol'viopol'. Mykolayivs'ka Oblast', S Ukraine
117 S12 **Pervomays'ke** Respublika Krym, S Ukraine
125 R14 **Pervomayskiy** Kirovskaya Oblast', NW Russian Federation
127 V7 **Pervomayskiy** Orenburgskaya Oblast', W Russian Federation
126 M6 **Pervomayskiy** Tambovskaya Oblast', W Russian Federation
117 V6 **Pervomays'kyy** Kharkivs'ka Oblast', E Ukraine
122 F10 **Pervoural'sk** Sverdlovskaya Oblast', C Russian Federation
123 V11 **Pervyy Kuril'skiy Proliv** strait E Russian Federation
99 I19 **Perwez** Walloon Brabant, C Belgium
106 I11 **Pesaro** anc. Pisaurum. Marche, C Italy
35 N9 **Pescadero** California, W USA
Pescadores see P'enghu Liehtao
161 S14 **Pescadores Channel** var. Penghu Shuidao, P'enghu Shuitao. channel W Taiwan
107 K14 **Pescara** anc. Aternum, Ostia Aterni. Abruzzo, C Italy
107 K15 **Pescara** ≈ C Italy
106 F11 **Pescia** Toscana, C Italy
108 C8 **Peseux** Neuchâtel, W Switzerland
125 P6 **Pesha** ≈ NW Russian Federation
149 T5 **Peshāwar** North-West Frontier Province, N Pakistan
149 T6 **Peshāwar** ✈ North-West Frontier Province, N Pakistan
113 M19 **Peshkopi** var. Peshkopia, Peshkopija. Dibër, NE Albania
Peshkopia/Peshkopija see Peshkopi
114 I11 **Peshtera** Pazardzhik, C Bulgaria
31 N6 **Peshtigo** Wisconsin, N USA
31 N6 **Peshtigo River** ≈ Wisconsin, N USA
Peski see Pyeski
125 S13 **Peskovka** Kirovskaya Oblast', NW Russian Federation
103 S8 **Pesmes** Haute-Saône, E France
104 H6 **Peso da Régua** var. Pêso da Regua. Vila Real, N Portugal
40 F5 **Pesqueira** Sonora, NW Mexico
102 J13 **Pessac** Gironde, SW France
111 J23 **Pest** off. Pest Megye. ⬖ county C Hungary
Pest Megye see Pest
124 J14 **Pestovo** Novgorodskaya Oblast', W Russian Federation
40 M15 **Petacalco, Bahía** bay W Mexico
Petach-Tikva see Petaḥ Tiqwa
138 F10 **Petaḥ Tiqwa** var. Petach-Tikva, Petah Tiqva, Petakh Tikva. Tel Aviv, C Israel
93 L17 **Petäjävesi** Länsi-Soumi, C Finland
Petakh Tikva/Petah Tiqva see Petaḥ Tiqwa
22 M7 **Petal** Mississippi, S USA
115 I19 **Petalioí** island C Greece
115 H19 **Petalión, Kólpos** gulf E Greece
115 J19 **Pétalo** ▲ Ándros, Kykládes, Greece, Aegean Sea
34 M8 **Petaluma** California, W USA
99 L25 **Pétange** Luxembourg, SW Luxembourg
54 M5 **Petare** Miranda, N Venezuela
41 N16 **Petatlán** Guerrero, S Mexico
83 L14 **Petauke** Eastern, E Zambia
14 J12 **Petawawa** Ontario, SE Canada
14 J11 **Petawawa** ≈ Ontario, SE Canada
Petchaburi see Phetchaburi
42 D2 **Petén** off. Departamento del Petén. ⬖ department N Guatemala
Petén, Departamento del see Petén
42 D2 **Petén Itzá, Lago** var. Lago de Flores. ◎ N Guatemala
30 K7 **Petenwell Lake** ⊞ Wisconsin, N USA
14 D6 **Peterbell** Ontario, S Canada
182 I7 **Peterborough** South Australia
14 I14 **Peterborough** Ontario, SE Canada
97 N20 **Peterborough** prev. Medeshamstede. E England, UK
19 N10 **Peterborough** New Hampshire, NE USA
96 L8 **Peterhead** NE Scotland, UK
Peterhof see Luboń
193 Q14 **Peter I Island** ◇ Norwegian dependency Antarctica
194 H9 **Peter I Island** var. Peter I øy. island Antarctica
Peter I øy see Peter I Island
97 M14 **Peterlee** N England, UK
Peterlingen see Payerne
197 P14 **Petermann Bjerg** ▲ C Greenland
9 S12 **Peter Pond Lake** ◎ Saskatchewan, C Canada
39 X13 **Petersburg** Mytkof Island, Alaska, USA
30 K13 **Petersburg** Illinois, N USA
31 N16 **Petersburg** Indiana, N USA
29 Q3 **Petersburg** North Dakota, N USA
25 N5 **Petersburg** Texas, SW USA
21 V7 **Petersburg** Virginia, NE USA
21 T4 **Petersburg** West Virginia, NE USA
100 H12 **Petershagen** Nordrhein-Westfalen, NW Germany
55 S9 **Peters Mine** var. Peter's Mine. N Guyana
107 O21 **Petilia Policastro** Calabria, SW Italy
44 M9 **Pétionville** S Haiti
45 X6 **Petit-Bourg** Basse Terre, C Guadeloupe
15 Y5 **Petit-Cap** Québec, SE Canada
45 Y6 **Petit Cul-de-Sac Marin** bay C Guadeloupe
44 M9 **Petite-Rivière-de-l'Artibonite** C Haiti
173 X16 **Petite Rivière Noire, Piton de la** ▲ C Mauritius
15 R9 **Petite-Rivière-St-François** Québec, SE Canada
44 L9 **Petit-Goâve** S Haiti
Petitjean see Sidi-Kacem
13 N10 **Petit Lac Manicouagan** ◎ Québec, E Canada
19 T7 **Petit Manan Point** headland Maine, NE USA
Petit Mécatina, Rivière du see Little Mecatina
9 N10 **Petitot** ≈ Alberta/British Columbia, W Canada
45 S12 **Petit Piton** ▲ SW Saint Lucia
Petit-Popo see Aného
Petit St-Bernard, Col du see Little Saint Bernard Pass
13 O8 **Petitsikapau Lake** ◎ Newfoundland and Labrador, E Canada
92 L11 **Petkula** Lappi, N Finland
41 X12 **Peto** Yucatán, SE Mexico
62 G10 **Petorca** Valparaíso, C Chile
31 Q5 **Petoskey** Michigan, N USA
138 G14 **Petra** archaeological site Ma'ān, W Jordan
Petra see Wādī Mūsā
115 F14 **Pétras, Sténa** pass N Greece
123 S16 **Petra Velikogo, Zaliv** bay SE Russian Federation
Petrel see Petrer
14 K15 **Petre, Point** headland Ontario, SE Canada
105 S12 **Petrer** var. Petrel. País Valenciano, E Spain
125 U11 **Petretsovo** Permskaya Oblast', NW Russian Federation
114 G12 **Petrich** Blagoevgrad, SW Bulgaria
187 P15 **Petrie, Récif** reef N New Caledonia
37 N11 **Petrified Forest** prehistoric site Arizona, SW USA
Petrikau see Piotrków Trybunalski
Petrikov see Pyetrykaw
116 H12 **Petrila** Hung. Petrilla. Hunedoara, W Romania
Petrilla see Petrila
112 E9 **Petrinja** Sisak-Moslavina, C Croatia
Petroaleksandrovsk see To'rtkok'l
Petrőcz see Bački Petrovac
124 G12 **Petrodvorets** Fin. Pietarhovi. Leningradskaya Oblast', NW Russian Federation
Petrograd see Sankt-Peterburg
Petrokov see Piotrków Trybunalski
54 G6 **Petrólea** Norte de Santander, NE Colombia
14 D16 **Petrolia** Ontario, S Canada
25 S4 **Petrolia** Texas, SW USA
59 O15 **Petrolina** Pernambuco, E Brazil
45 T6 **Petrona, Punta** headland C Puerto Rico
Petropavl see Petropavlovsk
117 V7 **Petropavlivka** Dnipropetrovs'ka Oblast', E Ukraine
145 P6 **Petropavlovsk** Kaz. Petropavl. Severnyy Kazakhstan, N Kazakhstan
123 V11 **Petropavlovsk-Kamchatskiy** Kamchatskaya Oblast', E Russian Federation
60 P9 **Petrópolis** Rio de Janeiro, SE Brazil
116 H12 **Petroşani** var. Petroşeni, Ger. Petroschen, Hung. Petrozsény. Hunedoara, W Romania
Petroschen/Petroşeni see Petroşani
Petroskoi see Petrozavodsk
112 N12 **Petrovac** Serbia, E Serbia
Petrovac see Bosanski Petrovac
113 J17 **Petrovac na Moru** S Montenegro
Petrovac/Petrovácz see Bački Petrovac
117 S8 **Petrove** Kirovohrads'ka Oblast', C Ukraine
113 O18 **Petrovec** C FYR Macedonia
Petrovgrad see Zrenjanin
127 P7 **Petrovsk** Saratovskaya Oblast', W Russian Federation
124 J9 **Petrovskiy Yam** Respublika Kareliya, NW Russian Federation
Petrovsk-Port see Makhachkala
127 P9 **Petrov Val** Volgogradskaya Oblast', SW Russian Federation
124 J11 **Petrozavodsk** Fin. Petroskoi. Respublika Kareliya, NW Russian Federation
Petrozsény see Petroşani
83 D20 **Petrusdal** Hardap, C Namibia
117 T7 **Petrykivka** Dnipropetrovs'ka Oblast', E Ukraine
Petsamo see Pechenga
Petschka see Pecica
Pettau see Ptuj
109 S5 **Pettenbach** Oberösterreich, C Austria
25 S13 **Pettus** Texas, SW USA
122 G12 **Petukhovo** Kurganskaya Oblast', C Russian Federation
Petuna see Songyuan
109 R4 **Peuerbach** Oberösterreich, N Austria
62 G12 **Peumo** Libertador, C Chile
123 T6 **Pevek** Chukotskiy Avtonomnyy Okrug, NE Russian Federation
27 X5 **Pevely** Missouri, C USA
Peyia see Pégeia
102 J15 **Peyrehorade** Landes, SW France
124 J14 **Peza** ≈ NW Russian Federation
103 P16 **Pézenas** Hérault, S France
111 H20 **Pezinok** Ger. Bösing, Hung. Bazin. Bratislavský Kraj, W Slovakia
101 L22 **Pfaffenhofen an der Ilm** Bayern, SE Germany
108 G7 **Pfäffikon** Schwyz, C Switzerland
101 F20 **Pfälzer Wald** hill range W Germany
101 N22 **Pfarrkirchen** Bayern, SE Germany
101 G21 **Pforzheim** Baden-Württemberg, SW Germany
101 H24 **Pfullendorf** Baden-Württemberg, S Germany
108 K8 **Pfunds** Tirol, W Austria
101 G19 **Pfungstadt** Hessen, W Germany
83 L20 **Phalaborwa** Limpopo, NE South Africa
152 E11 **Phalodi** Rājasthān, NW India
152 E12 **Phalsund** Rājasthān, NW India
155 E15 **Phaltan** Mahārāshtra, W India
167 O7 **Phan** var. Muang Phan. Chiang Rai, NW Thailand
167 O14 **Phangan, Ko** island SW Thailand
166 M15 **Phang-Nga** var. Pang-Nga, Phangnga. Phangnga, SW Thailand
Phangnga see Phang-Nga
Phan Rang/Phanrang see Phan Rang-Thap Cham
167 V13 **Phan Rang-Thap Cham** var. Phanrang, Phan Rang, Phan Rang Thap Cham. Ninh Thuận, S Vietnam
167 U13 **Phan Ri** Binh Thuận, S Vietnam
167 U13 **Phan Thiêt** Binh Thuận, S Vietnam
Pharnacia see Giresun
25 S17 **Pharr** Texas, SW USA
Pharus see Hvar
167 N16 **Phatthalung** var. Padalung, Patalung. Phatthalung, SW Thailand
167 O7 **Phayao** var. Muang Phayao. Phayao, NW Thailand
9 U10 **Phelps Lake** ◎ Saskatchewan, C Canada
21 X9 **Phelps Lake** ◎ North Carolina, SE USA
23 R5 **Phenix City** Alabama, S USA
167 T8 **Pheo** Quang Binh, C Vietnam
Phet Buri see Phetchaburi
167 O11 **Phetchaburi** var. Bejraburi, Petchaburi, Phet Buri. Phetchaburi, SW Thailand
167 O9 **Phichit** var. Bichitra, Muang Phichit, Pichit. Phichit, C Thailand
22 M5 **Philadelphia** Mississippi, S USA
18 I7 **Philadelphia** New York, NE USA
18 I16 **Philadelphia** Pennsylvania, NE USA
18 I16 **Philadelphia** ✈ Pennsylvania, NE USA
Philadelphia see 'Ammān
28 L10 **Philip** South Dakota, N USA
99 H22 **Philippeville** Namur, S Belgium
Philippeville see Skikda
21 S3 **Philippi** West Virginia, NE USA
Philippi see Fílippoi
195 Y9 **Philippi Glacier** glacier Antarctica
192 G6 **Philippine Basin** undersea feature W Pacific Ocean
129 X12 **Philippine Plate** tectonic feature
171 O5 **Philippines** off. Republic of the Philippines. ◆ republic SE Asia
129 X13 **Philippines** island group W Pacific Ocean
171 P3 **Philippine Sea** sea W Pacific Ocean
Philippines, Republic of the see Philippines
192 F6 **Philippine Trench** undersea feature W Philippine Sea
83 H23 **Philippolis** Free State, C South Africa
Philippopolis see Plovdiv
Philippopolis see Shahbā', Syria
45 V9 **Philipsburg** Sint Maarten, N Netherlands Antilles
33 P10 **Philipsburg** Montana, NW USA
39 R6 **Philip Smith Mountains** ▲▲ Alaska, USA
152 H8 **Phillaur** Punjab, N India
183 N13 **Phillip Island** island Victoria, SE Australia
25 N2 **Phillips** Texas, SW USA
30 K5 **Phillips** Wisconsin, N USA
26 K3 **Phillipsburg** Kansas, C USA
18 I14 **Phillipsburg** New Jersey, NE USA
21 S7 **Philpott Lake** ⊞ Virginia, NE USA
Phintias see Licata
167 P9 **Phitsanulok** var. Bisnulok, Muang Phitsanulok, Pitsanulok. Phitsanulok, C Thailand
Phlórina see Flórina
Phnom Penh see Phnum Penh
167 S13 **Phnum Penh** var. Phnom Penh. ● (Cambodia) Phnum Penh, S Cambodia
167 S11 **Phnum Tbêng Meanchey** Preăh Vihéar, N Cambodia
36 K13 **Phoenix** state capital Arizona, SW USA
Phoenix Island see Rawaki
191 R3 **Phoenix Islands** island group C Kiribati
18 I15 **Phoenixville** Pennsylvania, NE USA
83 K22 **Phofung** var. Mont-aux-Sources. ▲ N Lesotho
167 Q10 **Phon** Khon Kaen, E Thailand
167 Q5 **Phôngsali** var. Phong Saly. Phôngsali, N Laos
Phong Saly see Phôngsali
167 Q8 **Phônhông** C Laos
167 R5 **Phô Rang** var Bao Yên. Lao Cai, N Vietnam
Phort Láirge, Cuan see Waterford Harbour
167 N10 **Phra Chedi Sam Ong** Kanchanaburi, W Thailand
167 O8 **Phrae** var. Muang Phrae, Prae. Phrae, NW Thailand
Phra Nakhon Si Ayutthaya see Ayutthaya
167 M14 **Phra Thong, Ko** island SW Thailand
Phu Cŭong see Thu Dâu Môt
166 M15 **Phuket** var. Bhuket, Puket, Mal. Ujung Salang; prev. Junkseylon, Salang. Phuket, SW Thailand
166 M15 **Phuket** ✈ Phuket, SW Thailand
166 M15 **Phuket, Ko** island SW Thailand
154 N12 **Phulabāni** prev. Phulbani. Orissa, E India
Phulbani see Phulabāni
167 U9 **Phu Lôc** Th,a Thiên-Huê, C Vietnam
167 S13 **Phumĭ Banam** Prey Vêng, S Cambodia
167 R13 **Phumĭ Choâm** Kâmpóng Spœ, SW Cambodia
167 T11 **Phumĭ Kalêng** Stœng Trêng, NE Cambodia
167 S12 **Phumĭ Kâmpóng Trâbêk** prev. Phum Kompong Trabek. Kâmpóng Thum, C Cambodia
167 Q11 **Phumĭ Koŭk Kduŏch** Bătdâmbâng, NW Cambodia
167 T11 **Phumĭ Labăng** Rôtânôkiri, NE Cambodia
167 S11 **Phumĭ Mlu Prey** Preăh Vihéar, N Cambodia
167 R11 **Phumĭ Moŭng** Siĕmréab, NW Cambodia
167 Q12 **Phumĭ Prâmaôy** Poŭthĭsăt, W Cambodia
167 Q13 **Phumĭ Samĭt** Kaôh Kông, SW Cambodia
167 R11 **Phumĭ Sâmraông** prev. Phum Samrong. Siĕmréab, NW Cambodia
167 S12 **Phumĭ Siĕmbok** Stœng Trêng, N Cambodia
167 S11 **Phumĭ Thalabârĭvăt** Stœng Trêng, N Cambodia
167 R13 **Phumĭ Veal Renh** Kâmpôt, SW Cambodia
167 P13 **Phumĭ Yeay Sên** Kaôh Kông, SW Cambodia
Phum Kompong Trabek see Phumĭ Kâmpóng Trâbêk
Phum Samrong see Phumĭ Sâmraông
167 V11 **Phu My** Binh Đinh, C Vietnam
167 S14 **Phung Hiêp** Cân Thơ, S Vietnam
153 T12 **Phuntsholing** SW Bhutan
167 R15 **Phước Long** Minh Hai, S Vietnam
167 R14 **Phu Quôc, Đao** var. Phu Quoc Island. island S Vietnam
Phu Quoc Island see Phu Quôc, Đao
167 S6 **Phu Tho** Vinh Phu, N Vietnam
Phu Vinh see Tra Vinh
189 T13 **Piaanu Pass** passage Chuuk Islands, C Micronesia
106 E8 **Piacenza** Fr. Paisance; anc. Placentia. Emilia-Romagna, N Italy
107 K14 **Pianella** Abruzzo, C Italy
107 M15 **Pianosa, Isola** island Archipelago Toscano, C Italy
171 U13 **Piar** Papua, E Indonesia
45 U14 **Piarco** var. Port of Spain. ✈ (Port-of-Spain) Trinidad, Trinidad and Tobago
110 M12 **Piaseczno** Mazowieckie, C Poland
116 I15 **Piatra** Teleorman, S Romania
116 L10 **Piatra-Neamţ** Hung. Karácsonkő. Neamţ, NE Romania
Piauhy see Piauí
59 N15 **Piauí** off. Estado do Piauí; prev. Piauhy. ⬖ state E Brazil
Piauí, Estado do see Piauí
106 I7 **Piave** ≈ NE Italy
107 K24 **Piazza Armerina** var. Chiazza. Sicilia, Italy, C Mediterranean Sea
81 G14 **Pibor** Amh. Pibor Wenz. ≈ Ethiopia/Sudan
81 G14 **Pibor Post** Jonglei, SE Sudan
Pibor Wenz see Pibor
Pibrans see Příbram
36 K11 **Picacho Butte** ▲ Arizona, SW USA
40 D4 **Picachos, Cerro** ▲ NW Mexico
103 O4 **Picardie** Eng. Picardy. ⬖ region N France
Picardy see Picardie
22 L8 **Picayune** Mississippi, S USA
Piccolo San Bernardo, Colle di see Little Saint Bernard Pass
PicdeBälaitous see Balaïtous
62 K5 **Pichanal** Salta, N Argentina
147 P12 **Pichandar** W Tajikistan
27 R8 **Picher** Oklahoma, C USA
62 G12 **Pichilemu** Libertador, C Chile
40 F9 **Pichilingue** Baja California Sur, W Mexico
56 B6 **Pichincha** ⬖ province N Ecuador
56 C6 **Pichincha** ▲ N Ecuador
Pichit see Phichit
41 U15 **Pichucalco** Chiapas, SE Mexico
22 L5 **Pickens** Mississippi, S USA
21 O11 **Pickens** South Carolina, SE USA
14 G11 **Pickerel** ≈ Ontario, S Canada
14 H15 **Pickering** Ontario, S Canada
97 N16 **Pickering** N England, UK
31 S13 **Pickerington** Ohio, N USA
12 C10 **Pickle Lake** Ontario, C Canada
29 P12 **Pickstown** South Dakota, N USA
25 V6 **Pickton** Texas, SW USA
23 N1 **Pickwick Lake** ⊞ S USA
64 N2 **Pico** var. Ilha do Pico. island Azores, Portugal, NE Atlantic Ocean
63 J19 **Pico de Salamanca** Chubut, SE Argentina
1 P9 **Pico Fracture Zone** tectonic feature NW Atlantic Ocean
Pico, Ilha do see Pico
59 O14 **Picos** Piauí, E Brazil
63 I20 **Pico Truncado** Santa Cruz, SE Argentina
183 S9 **Picton** New South Wales, SE Australia
14 K15 **Picton** Ontario, SE Canada
185 K14 **Picton** Marlborough, South Island, New Zealand
63 H15 **Piĉun Leufú, Arroyo** ≈ SW Argentina
Pidálion see Gkréko, Akrotíri
155 K25 **Pidurutalagala** ▲ S Sri Lanka
116 K6 **Pidvolochys'k** Ternopil's'ka Oblast', W Ukraine
107 K16 **Piedimonte Matese** Campania, S Italy
27 X7 **Piedmont** Missouri, C USA
21 P11 **Piedmont** South Carolina, SE USA
17 S12 **Piedmont** escarpment E USA
Piedmont see Piemonte
31 U13 **Piedmont Lake** ⊞ Ohio, N USA
104 M11 **Piedrabuena** Castilla-La Mancha, C Spain
Piedrafita, Puerto de see Pedrafita, Porto de
104 L8 **Piedrahita** Castilla-León, N Spain
41 N6 **Piedras Negras** var. Ciudad Porfirio Díaz. Coahuila de Zaragoza, NE Mexico
61 E21 **Piedras, Punta** headland E Argentina
57 I14 **Piedras, Río de las** ≈ E Peru
111 J16 **Piekary Śląskie** Śląskie, S Poland
93 M17 **Pieksämäki** Isä-Suomi, E Finland
109 V5 **Pielach** ≈ NE Austria
93 M16 **Pielavesi** Itä-Suomi, C Finland
93 N16 **Pielinen** var. Pielisjärvi. ◎ E Finland
Pielisjärvi see Pielinen
106 A8 **Piemonte** Eng. Piedmont. ⬖ region NW Italy
111 L18 **Pieniny** ▲▲ S Poland
111 E14 **Pieńsk** Ger. Penzig. Dolnośląskie, SW Poland
29 Q13 **Pierce** Nebraska, C USA
9 R14 **Pierceland** Saskatchewan, C Canada
115 E14 **Piéria** ▲▲ N Greece
29 N10 **Pierre** state capital South Dakota, N USA
102 K16 **Pierrefitte-Nestalas** Hautes-Pyrénées, S France
103 R14 **Pierrelatte** Drôme, E France
15 P11 **Pierreville** Québec, SE Canada
15 O7 **Pierriche** ≈ Québec, SE Canada
111 H20 **Piešt'any** Ger. Pistyan, Hung. Pöstyén. Tranavský Kraj, W Slovakia
109 X5 **Piesting** ≈ E Austria
Pietarhovi see Petrodvorets
Pietari see Sankt-Peterburg
Pietarsaari see Jakobstad
83 K23 **Pietermaritzburg** var. Maritzburg. KwaZulu/Natal, E South Africa
Pietersburg see Polokwane
107 K24 **Pietraperzia** Sicilia, Italy, C Mediterranean Sea
107 N22 **Pietra Spada, Passo della** pass SW Italy
83 K22 **Piet Retief** Mpumalanga, E South Africa
116 J10 **Pietrosul, Vârful** prev. Vîrful Pietrosu. ▲ N Romania
116 I9 **Pietrosul, Vârful** prev. Vîrful Pietrosu. ▲ N Romania
Pietrosu, Vîrful see Pietrosul, Vârful
106 I6 **Pieve di Cadore** Veneto, NE Italy
14 C18 **Pigeon Bay** lake bay Ontario, S Canada
27 X8 **Piggott** Arkansas, C USA
83 L21 **Piggs Peak** NW Swaziland
Pigs, Bay of see Cochinos, Bahía de
61 A23 **Pigüé** Buenos Aires, E Argentina
41 O12 **Piguícas** ▲ C Mexico
193 W15 **Piha Passage** passage S Tonga
Pihkva Järv see Pskov, Lake
93 N18 **Pihlajavesi** ◎ SE Finland
93 J18 **Pihlava** Länsi-Soumi, SW Finland
93 L16 **Pihtipudas** Länsi-Soumi, C Finland
40 L14 **Pihuamo** Jalisco, SW Mexico
189 U11 **Piis Moen** var. Pis. atoll Chuuk Islands, C Micronesia
41 U17 **Pijijiapán** Chiapas, SE Mexico
98 G12 **Pijnacker** Zuid-Holland, W Netherlands
42 H5 **Pijol, Pico** ▲ NW Honduras
Pikaar see Bikar Atoll
124 I13 **Pikalevo** Leningradskaya Oblast', NW Russian Federation
188 M15 **Pikelot** island Caroline Islands, C Micronesia
30 M5 **Pike River** ≈ Wisconsin, N USA
37 T5 **Pikes Peak** ▲ Colorado, C USA
21 P6 **Pikeville** Kentucky, S USA
20 L9 **Pikeville** Tennessee, S USA
Pikinni see Bikini Atoll
79 H18 **Pikounda** La Sangha, C Congo
110 G9 **Piła** Ger. Schneidemühl. Wielkopolskie, C Poland
62 N6 **Pilagá, Riacho** ≈ NE Argentina
61 D20 **Pilar** Buenos Aires, E Argentina
62 N7 **Pilar** var. Villa del Pilar. Ñeembucú, S Paraguay
62 N6 **Pilcomayo, Rio** ≈ C South America
147 R12 **Pildon** Rus. Pil'don. C Tajikistan
Piles see Pylés
Pilgram see Pelhřimov
152 L10 **Pīlībhīt** Uttar Pradesh, N India
110 M13 **Pilica** ≈ C Poland
115 G16 **Pílio** ▲ C Greece
111 J22 **Pilisvörösvár** Pest, N Hungary
65 G15 **Pillar Bay** bay Ascension Island, C Atlantic Ocean
183 P17 **Pillar, Cape** headland Tasmania, SE Australia
Pillau see Baltiysk
183 R5 **Pilliga** New South Wales, SE Australia
44 H8 **Pilón** Granma, E Cuba
Pilos see Pýlos
9 W17 **Pilot Mound** Manitoba, S Canada
21 S8 **Pilot Mountain** North Carolina, SE USA
39 O14 **Pilot Point** Alaska, USA
25 T5 **Pilot Point** Texas, SW USA
32 K11 **Pilot Rock** Oregon, NW USA
38 M11 **Pilot Station** Alaska, USA
Pilsen see Plzeň
111 K18 **Pilsko** ▲ N Slovakia
Pilten see Piltene
118 D8 **Piltene** Ger. Pilten. Ventspils, W Latvia
111 M16 **Pilzno** Podkarpackie, SE Poland
Pilzno see Plzeň
37 N14 **Pima** Arizona, SW USA
58 H13 **Pimenta** Pará, N Brazil

◆ Country
● Country Capital
◇ Dependent Territory
○ Dependent Territory Capital
⬖ Administrative Regions
✈ International Airport
▲ Mountain
▲▲ Mountain Range
Volcano
≈ River
◎ Lake
⊞ Reservoir

59 F16 **Pimenta Bueno** Rondônia, W Brazil
56 B11 **Pimentel** Lambayeque, W Peru
105 S6 **Pina** Aragón, NE Spain
119 I20 **Pina** ≈ SW Belarus
40 E2 **Pinacate, Sierra del** ▲▲ NW Mexico
63 H22 **Pináculo, Cerro** ▲ S Argentina
191 X11 **Pinaki** atoll Îles Tuamotu, E French Polynesia
37 N15 **Pinaleno Mountains** ▲▲ Arizona, SW USA
171 P4 **Pinamalayan** Mindoro, N Philippines
169 Q10 **Pinang** Borneo, C Indonesia
168 J7 **Pinang** var. Penang. ◈ state Peninsular Malaysia
Pinang see George Town
Pinang see Pinang, Pulau, Peninsular Malaysia
168 J7 **Pinang, Pulau** var. Penang; prev. Prince of Wales Island. island Peninsular Malaysia
44 B5 **Pinar del Río** Pinar del Río, W Cuba
114 N11 **Pınarhisar** Kırklareli, NW Turkey
171 O3 **Pinatubo, Mount** ※ Luzon, N Philippines
9 Y16 **Pinawa** Manitoba, S Canada
9 Q17 **Pincher Creek** Alberta, SW Canada
30 L16 **Pinckneyville** Illinois, N USA
Pincota see Pâncota
111 L15 **Pińczów** Świętokrzyskie, C Poland
149 U7 **Pind Dādan Khān** Punjab, E Pakistan
Píndhos/Píndhos Óros see Píndos
149 V8 **Pindi Bhattiān** Punjab, E Pakistan
149 U6 **Pindi Gheb** Punjab, E Pakistan
115 D15 **Píndos** var. Píndhos Óros, Eng. Pindus Mountains; prev. Píndhos. ▲▲ C Greece
Pindus Mountains see Píndos
18 J16 **Pine Barrens** physical region New Jersey, NE USA
27 V12 **Pine Bluff** Arkansas, C USA
23 X11 **Pine Castle** Florida, SE USA
29 V7 **Pine City** Minnesota, N USA
181 P2 **Pine Creek** Northern Territory, N Australia
35 V4 **Pine Creek** ≈ Nevada, W USA
18 F13 **Pine Creek** ≈ Pennsylvania, NE USA
27 Q13 **Pine Creek Lake** ▣ Oklahoma, C USA
33 T15 **Pinedale** Wyoming, C USA
9 X15 **Pine Dock** Manitoba, S Canada
9 Y16 **Pine Falls** Manitoba, S Canada
35 R10 **Pine Flat Lake** ▣ California, W USA
125 N8 **Pinega** Arkhangel'skaya Oblast', NW Russian Federation
125 N8 **Pinega** ≈ NW Russian Federation
15 N12 **Pine Hill** Québec, SE Canada
9 T12 **Pinehouse Lake** ◎ Saskatchewan, C Canada
21 T10 **Pinehurst** North Carolina, SE USA
115 D19 **Pineiós** ≈ S Greece
115 E16 **Pineiós** var. Piniós; anc. Peneius. ≈ C Greece
29 W10 **Pine Island** Minnesota, N USA
23 V15 **Pine Island** island Florida, SE USA
194 K10 **Pine Island Glacier** glacier Antarctica
25 X9 **Pineland** Texas, SW USA
23 V13 **Pinellas Park** Florida, SE USA
10 M13 **Pine Pass** pass British Columbia, W Canada
8 J10 **Pine Point** Northwest Territories, W Canada
28 K12 **Pine Ridge** South Dakota, N USA
29 U6 **Pine River** Minnesota, N USA
31 Q8 **Pine River** ≈ Michigan, N USA
30 M4 **Pine River** ≈ Wisconsin, N USA
106 A8 **Pinerolo** Piemonte, NE Italy
115 I15 **Pínes, Akrotírio** var. Akrotírio Pínnes. headland N Greece
25 W6 **Pines, Lake O' the** ▣ Texas, SW USA
Pines, The Isle of the see Juventud, Isla de la
Pine Tree State see Maine
21 N7 **Pineville** Kentucky, S USA
22 H7 **Pineville** Louisiana, S USA
27 R8 **Pineville** Missouri, C USA
21 R10 **Pineville** North Carolina, SE USA
21 Q6 **Pineville** West Virginia, NE USA
33 V8 **Piney Buttes** physical region Montana, NW USA
160 H14 **Pingbian** var. Pingbian Miaozu Zizhixian, Yuping. Yunnan, SW China
Pingbian Miaozu Zizhixian see Pingbian
157 S9 **Pingdingshan** Henan, C China
161 R4 **Pingdu** Shandong, E China
189 W16 **Pingelap Atoll** atoll Caroline Islands, E Micronesia
160 K14 **Pingguo** var. Matou. Guangxi Zhuangzu Zizhiqu, S China
161 Q13 **Pinghe** var. Xiaoxi. Fujian, SE China
P'ing-hsiang see Pingxiang
161 N10 **Pingjiang** Hunan, S China
Pingkiang see Harbin
160 L8 **Pingli** Shaanxi, C China
159 W10 **Pingliang** var. Kongtong, P'ing-liang. Gansu, C China
P'ing-liang see Pingliang
159 W8 **Pingluo** Ningxia, N China
Pingma see Tiandong
167 O7 **Ping, Mae Nam** ≈ W Thailand
161 Q1 **Pingquan** Hebei, E China
29 P5 **Pingree** North Dakota, N USA
163 W9 **Pingshan** Jilin, NE China
Pingsiang see Pingxiang
161 S14 **P'ingtung** Jap. Heitō. S Taiwan
160 I8 **Pingwu** var. Long'an. Sichuan, C China
160 J15 **Pingxiang** Guangxi Zhuangzu Zizhiqu, S China
161 O11 **Pingxiang** var. P'ing-hsiang; prev. Pingsiang. Jiangxi, S China
161 S11 **Pingyang** var. Kunyang. Zhejiang, SE China
161 P5 **Pingyi** Shandong, E China
161 P5 **Pingyin** Shandong, E China
60 H13 **Pinhalzinho** Santa Catarina, S Brazil
60 I12 **Pinhão** Paraná, S Brazil
61 H17 **Pinheiro Machado** Rio Grande do Sul, S Brazil
104 I7 **Pinhel** Guarda, N Portugal
Piniós see Pineiós
168 I11 **Pini, Pulau** island Kepulauan Batu, W Indonesia
109 Y7 **Pinka** ≈ SE Austria
109 X7 **Pinkafeld** Burgenland, SE Austria
Pinkiang see Harbin
10 M12 **Pink Mountain** British Columbia, W Canada
166 M3 **Pinlebu** Sagaing, N Burma (Myanmar)
38 J12 **Pinnacle Island** island Alaska, USA
180 I12 **Pinnacles, The** tourist site Western Australia
182 K10 **Pinnaroo** South Australia
Pinne see Pniewy
100 I9 **Pinneberg** Schleswig-Holstein, N Germany
115 I15 **Pínnes, Ákrotírio** cape N Greece
Pínnes, Akrotírio see Pínes, Akrotírio
Pinos, Isla de see Juventud, Isla de la
35 R14 **Pinos, Mount** ▲ California, W USA
105 R12 **Pinoso** País Valenciano, E Spain
105 N14 **Pinos-Puente** Andalucía, S Spain
41 Q17 **Pinotepa Nacional** var. Santiago Pinotepa Nacional. Oaxaca, SE Mexico
114 F13 **Pínovo** ▲ N Greece
187 R17 **Pins, Île des** var. Kunyé. island E New Caledonia
119 I20 **Pinsk** Pol. Pińsk. Brestskaya Voblasts', SW Belarus
14 D18 **Pins, Pointe aux** headland Ontario, S Canada
57 B16 **Pinta, Isla** var. Abingdon. island Galapagos Islands, Ecuador, E Pacific Ocean
125 Q12 **Pinyug** Kirovskaya Oblast', NW Russian Federation
57 B17 **Pinzón, Isla** var. Duncan Island. island Galapagos Islands, Ecuador, E Pacific Ocean
35 Y8 **Pioche** Nevada, W USA
106 F13 **Piombino** Toscana, C Italy
0 C9 **Pioneer Fracture Zone** tectonic feature NE Pacific Ocean
122 L5 **Pioner, Ostrov** island Severnaya Zemlya, N Russian Federation
118 A13 **Pionerskiy** Ger. Neukuhren. Kaliningradskaya Oblast', W Russian Federation
110 N13 **Pionki** Mazowieckie, C Poland
184 L9 **Piopio** Waikato, North Island, New Zealand
110 K13 **Piotrków Trybunalski** Ger. Petrikau, Rus. Petrokov. Lodzkie, C Poland
152 F12 **Pīpār Road** Rājasthān, N India
115 I16 **Pipéri** island Vóreioi Sporádes, Greece, Aegean Sea
29 S10 **Pipestone** Minnesota, N USA
12 C9 **Pipestone** ≈ Ontario, C Canada
61 E21 **Pipinas** Buenos Aires, E Argentina
149 T7 **Piplān** prev. Liaqatabad. Punjab, E Pakistan
15 R5 **Pipmuacan, Réservoir** ▣ Québec, SE Canada
Piqan see Shanshan
31 R13 **Piqua** Ohio, N USA
105 P5 **Piqueras, Puerto de** pass N Spain
60 H11 **Piquiri, Rio** ≈ S Brazil
60 L9 **Piracicaba** São Paulo, S Brazil
Piraeus/Piraiévs see Peiraías
60 K10 **Piraju** São Paulo, S Brazil
60 J9 **Pirajuí** São Paulo, S Brazil
63 G21 **Pirámide, Cerro** ▲ S Chile
Piramiva see Pyramíva
109 R13 **Piran** It. Pirano. SW Slovenia
62 N6 **Pirané** Formosa, N Argentina
59 J18 **Piranhas** Goiás, S Brazil
Pirano see Piran
142 I4 **Pīrānshahr** Āžarbāyjān-e Gharbī, NW Iran
59 M19 **Pirapora** Minas Gerais, NE Brazil
60 I9 **Pirapòzinho** São Paulo, S Brazil
61 G19 **Piraraja** Lavalleja, S Uruguay
60 L9 **Pirassununga** São Paulo, S Brazil
45 V6 **Pirata, Monte** ▲ E Puerto Rico
60 I13 **Piratuba** Santa Catarina, S Brazil
114 I9 **Pirdop** prev. Strednogorie. Sofiya, W Bulgaria
191 P7 **Pirea** Tahiti, W French Polynesia
59 K18 **Pirenópolis** Goiás, S Brazil
153 S13 **Pirganj** Rajshahi, NW Bangladesh
Pirgi see Pyrgí
Pírgos see Pýrgos
61 F20 **Piriápolis** Maldonado, S Uruguay
114 G11 **Pirin** ▲▲ SW Bulgaria
Pirineos see Pyrenees
58 N13 **Piripiri** Piauí, E Brazil
118 H4 **Pirita** var. Pirita Jõgi. ≈ NW Estonia
Pirita Jõgi see Pirita
54 J6 **Píritu** Portuguesa, N Venezuela
93 L18 **Pirkkala** Länsi-Suomi, W Finland
101 F20 **Pirmasens** Rheinland-Pfalz, SW Germany
101 P16 **Pirna** Sachsen, E Germany
Piroe see Piru
113 Q15 **Pirot** Serbia, SE Serbia
152 H6 **Pīr Panjāl Range** ▲▲ NE India
43 W16 **Pirre, Cerro** ▲ SE Panama
137 Y11 **Pirsaat** Rus. Pirsagat. ≈ E Azerbaijan
Pirsagat see Pirsaat
143 V11 **Pīr Shūrān, Selseleh-ye** ▲ SE Iran
92 M12 **Pirttikoski** Lappi, N Finland
Pirttikylä see Pörtom
171 R13 **Piru** prev. Piroe. Pulau Seram, E Indonesia
Piryatin see Pyryatyn
Pis see Piis Moen
106 F11 **Pisa** var. Pisae. Toscana, C Italy
Pisae see Pisa
189 V12 **Pisar** atoll Chuuk Islands, C Micronesia
Pisaurum see Pesaro
14 M10 **Piscatosine, Lac** ◎ Québec, SE Canada
109 W7 **Pischeldorf** Steiermark, SE Austria
Pischk see Simeria
107 L19 **Pisciotta** Campania, S Italy
57 E16 **Pisco** Ica, SW Peru
116 G9 **Pişcolt** Hung. Piskolt. Satu Mare, NW Romania
57 E16 **Pisco, Río** ≈ E Peru
111 C18 **Písek** Budějovický Kraj, S Czech Republic
31 R14 **Pisgah** Ohio, N USA
Pisha see Ningnan
158 F9 **Pishan** var. Guma. Xinjiang Uygur Zizhiqu, NW China
117 N8 **Pishchanka** Vinnyts'ka Oblast', C Ukraine
113 K21 **Pishë** Fier, SW Albania
143 X14 **Pishin** Sīstān va Balūchestān, SE Iran
149 O9 **Pishin** North-West Frontier Province, NW Pakistan
149 N11 **Pishin Lora** var. Psein Lora, Pash. Pseyn Bowr. ≈ SW Pakistan
Pishma see Pizhma
Pishpek see Bishkek
171 O14 **Pising** Pulau Kabaena, C Indonesia
Pisino see Pazin
Piski see Simeria
Piskolt see Pişcolt
147 Q9 **Piskom** Rus. Pskem. ≈ E Uzbekistan
Piskom Tizmasi see Pskemskiy Khrebet
35 P13 **Pismo Beach** California, W USA
77 P12 **Pissila** C Burkina
62 H8 **Pissis, Monte** ▲ N Argentina
41 X12 **Piste** Yucatán, E Mexico
107 O18 **Pisticci** Basilicata, S Italy
106 F11 **Pistoia** anc. Pistoria, Pistoriæ. Toscana, C Italy
32 E15 **Pistol River** Oregon, NW USA
Pistoria/Pistoriæ see Pistoia
15 U5 **Pistuacanis** ≈ Québec, SE Canada
Pistyan see Piešt'any
104 M5 **Pisuerga** ≈ N Spain
110 N8 **Pisz** Ger. Johannisburg. Warmińsko-Mazurskie, NE Poland
76 I13 **Pita** NW Guinea
54 D12 **Pitalito** Huila, S Colombia
60 I11 **Pitanga** Paraná, S Brazil
182 M9 **Pitarpunga Lake** salt lake New South Wales, SE Australia
193 P10 **Pitcairn Island** island S Pitcairn Islands
193 P10 **Pitcairn Islands** ◇ UK dependent territory C Pacific Ocean
93 J14 **Piteå** Norrbotten, N Sweden
92 I13 **Piteälven** ≈ N Sweden
116 I13 **Piteşti** Argeş, S Romania
Pithagorio see Pythagóreio
180 I12 **Pithara** Western Australia
103 N6 **Pithiviers** Loiret, C France
152 L9 **Pithorāgarh** Uttaranchal, N India
188 B16 **Piti** W Guam
106 G13 **Pitigliano** Toscana, C Italy
40 F3 **Pitiquito** Sonora, NW Mexico
Pitkäranta see Pitkyaranta
38 M11 **Pitkas Point** Alaska, USA
124 H11 **Pitkyaranta** Fin. Pitkäranta. Respublika Kareliya, NW Russian Federation
96 J10 **Pitlochry** C Scotland, UK
18 I16 **Pitman** New Jersey, NE USA
146 I9 **Pitnak** var. Drujba, Rus. Druzhba. Xorazm Viloyati, W Uzbekistan
112 G8 **Pitomača** Virovitica-Podravina, NE Croatia
35 O2 **Pit River** ≈ California, W USA
63 G15 **Pitrufquén** Araucanía, S Chile
Pitsanulok see Phitsanulok
Pitschen see Byczyna
Pitsunda see Bichvint'a
109 X6 **Pitten** ≈ E Austria
10 J14 **Pitt Island** island British Columbia, W Canada
Pitt Island see Makin
22 M3 **Pittsboro** Mississippi, S USA
21 T9 **Pittsboro** North Carolina, SE USA
27 R7 **Pittsburg** Kansas, C USA
25 W6 **Pittsburg** Texas, SW USA
18 B14 **Pittsburgh** Pennsylvania, NE USA
30 J14 **Pittsfield** Illinois, N USA
19 R6 **Pittsfield** Maine, NE USA
18 L11 **Pittsfield** Massachusetts, NE USA
183 U3 **Pittsworth** Queensland, E Australia
62 I8 **Pituil** La Rioja, NW Argentina
56 A10 **Piura** Piura, NW Peru
56 A9 **Piura** off. Departamento de Piura. ◈ department NW Peru
Piura, Departamento de see Piura
35 S13 **Piute Peak** ▲ California, W USA
113 J15 **Piva** ≈ NW Montenegro
117 V5 **Pivdenne** Kharkivs'ka Oblast', E Ukraine
117 P8 **Pivdennyy Buh** Rus. Yuzhnyy Bug. ≈ S Ukraine
54 F5 **Pivijay** Magdalena, N Colombia
109 T13 **Pivka** prev. Šent Peter, Ger. Sankt Peter, It. San Pietro del Carso. SW Slovenia
117 U13 **Pivnichno-Kryms'kyy Kanal** canal S Ukraine
113 J15 **Pivsko Jezero** ◎ NW Montenegro
111 M18 **Piwniczna** Małopolskie, S Poland
35 R12 **Pixley** California, W USA
125 Q15 **Pizhma** var. Pishma. ≈ NW Russian Federation
13 U13 **Placentia** Newfoundland, Newfoundland and Labrador, SE Canada
Placentia see Piacenza
13 U13 **Placentia Bay** inlet Newfoundland, Newfoundland and Labrador, SE Canada
171 P5 **Placer** Masbate, N Philippines
35 P7 **Placerville** California, W USA
44 F5 **Placetas** Villa Clara, C Cuba
113 Q18 **Plačkovica** ▲▲ E Macedonia
36 L2 **Plain City** Utah, W USA
22 G4 **Plain Dealing** Louisiana, S USA
31 O14 **Plainfield** Indiana, N USA
18 K14 **Plainfield** New Jersey, NE USA
33 O8 **Plains** Montana, NW USA
24 L6 **Plains** Texas, SW USA
29 X10 **Plainview** Minnesota, N USA
29 Q13 **Plainview** Nebraska, C USA
25 N4 **Plainview** Texas, SW USA
26 K4 **Plainville** Kansas, C USA
115 I22 **Pláka** var. Mílos. Mílos, Kykládes, Greece, Aegean Sea
115 J15 **Pláka, Ákrotírio** headland Kríti, Greece, E Mediterranean Sea
115 J15 **Pláka, Akrotírio** headland Límnos, E Greece
113 N19 **Plakenska Planina** ▲▲ SW Macedonia
44 K5 **Plana Cays** islets SE Bahamas
105 S12 **Plana, Isla** var. Nueva Tabarca. island E Spain
59 L18 **Planaltina** Goiás, S Brazil
83 O14 **Planalto Moçambicano** plateau N Mozambique
112 N10 **Plandište** Vojvodina, NE Serbia
100 N13 **Plane** ≈ NE Germany
54 E6 **Planeta Rica** Córdoba, NW Colombia
29 P11 **Plankinton** South Dakota, N USA
30 M11 **Plano** Illinois, N USA
25 U6 **Plano** Texas, SW USA
23 W12 **Plant City** Florida, SE USA
22 J9 **Plaquemine** Louisiana, S USA
104 K9 **Plasencia** Extremadura, W Spain
110 P7 **Plaska** Podlaskie, NE Poland
112 C10 **Plaški** Karlovac, C Croatia
113 N19 **Plasnica** SW FYR Macedonia
13 N14 **Plaster Rock** New Brunswick, SE Canada
107 J24 **Platani** anc. Halycus. ≈ Sicilia, Italy, C Mediterranean Sea
115 G17 **Plataniá** Thessalía, C Greece
115 G24 **Plátanos** Kríti, Greece, E Mediterranean Sea
65 H18 **Plata, Río de la** var. River Plate. estuary Argentina/Uruguay
77 V15 **Plateau** ◈ state C Nigeria
79 G19 **Plateaux** var. Région des Plateaux. ◈ province C Congo
Plateaux, Région des see Plateaux
92 P1 **Platen, Kapp** headland NE Svalbard
Plate, River see Plata, Río de la
99 G22 **Plate Taille, Lac de la** var. L'Eau d'Heure. ◎ SE Belgium
Plathe see Płoty
39 N13 **Platinum** Alaska, USA
54 F5 **Plato** Magdalena, N Colombia
29 O11 **Platte** South Dakota, N USA
27 R3 **Platte City** Missouri, C USA
Plattensee see Balaton
27 R3 **Platte River** ≈ Iowa/Missouri, USA
29 Q15 **Platte River** ≈ Nebraska, C USA
37 T3 **Platteville** Colorado, C USA
30 K9 **Platteville** Wisconsin, N USA
101 N21 **Plattling** Bayern, SE Germany
27 R3 **Plattsburg** Missouri, C USA
18 L6 **Plattsburgh** New York, NE USA
29 S15 **Plattsmouth** Nebraska, C USA
101 M17 **Plauen** var. Plauen im Vogtland. Sachsen, E Germany
Plauen im Vogtland see Plauen
100 M10 **Plauer See** ◎ NE Germany
113 L16 **Plav** E Montenegro
118 I10 **Pļaviņas** Ger. Stockmannshof. Aizkraukle, S Latvia
126 K5 **Plavsk** Tul'skaya Oblast', W Russian Federation
41 Z12 **Playa del Carmen** Quintana Roo, E Mexico
40 J12 **Playa Los Corchos** Nayarit, SW Mexico
37 P16 **Playas Lake** ◎ New Mexico, SW USA
41 S15 **Playa Vicenté** Veracruz-Llave, SE Mexico
167 U11 **Plây Cu** var. Pleiku. Gia Lai, C Vietnam
28 L3 **Plaza** North Dakota, N USA
63 I15 **Plaza Huincul** Neuquén, C Argentina
36 L3 **Pleasant Grove** Utah, W USA
29 V14 **Pleasant Hill** Iowa, C USA
27 R4 **Pleasant Hill** Missouri, C USA
Pleasant Island see Nauru
36 K13 **Pleasant, Lake** ▣ Arizona, SW USA
19 P8 **Pleasant Mountain** ▲ Maine, NE USA
27 R5 **Pleasanton** Kansas, C USA
25 R12 **Pleasanton** Texas, SW USA
185 G20 **Pleasant Point** Canterbury, South Island, New Zealand
19 R5 **Pleasant River** ≈ Maine, NE USA
18 J17 **Pleasantville** New Jersey, NE USA
103 N12 **Pléaux** Cantal, C France
111 B19 **Plechý** var. Plöckenstein. ▲ Austria/Czech Republic
Pleebo see Plibo
Pleihari see Pelaihari
Pleiku see Plây Cu
101 M16 **Pleisse** ≈ E Germany
Plencia see Plentzia
184 O7 **Plenty, Bay of** bay North Island, New Zealand
33 Y6 **Plentywood** Montana, NW USA
105 O2 **Plentzia** var. Plencia. País Vasco, N Spain
102 H5 **Plérin** Côtes d'Armor, NW France
124 M10 **Plesetsk** Arkhangel'skaya Oblast', NW Russian Federation
Pleshchenitsy see Plyeshchanitsy
Pleskau see Pskov
Pleskauer See see Pskov, Lake
Pleskava see Pskov
112 E8 **Pleso International** ✈ (Zagreb) Zagreb, NW Croatia
Pless see Pszczyna
15 Q11 **Plessisville** Québec, SE Canada
110 H12 **Pleszew** Wielkopolskie, C Poland
12 L10 **Plétipi, Lac** ◎ Québec, SE Canada
101 F15 **Plettenberg** Nordrhein-Westfalen, W Germany
114 I8 **Pleven** prev. Plevna. Pleven, N Bulgaria
114 I8 **Pleven** ◈ province N Bulgaria
Plevlja/Plevlje see Pljevlja
Plevna see Pleven
Plezzo see Bovec
Pliberk see Bleiburg
76 L17 **Plibo** var. Pleebo. SE Liberia
121 R11 **Pliny Trench** undersea feature C Mediterranean Sea
118 K13 **Plisa** Rus. Plissa. Vitsyebskaya Voblasts', N Belarus
Plissa see Plisa
112 D11 **Plitvica Selo** Lika-Senj, W Croatia
112 D11 **Plješevica** ▲▲ C Croatia
113 K14 **Pljevlja** prev. Plevlja, Plevlje. N Montenegro
Ploça see Ploçë
Plocce see Ploče
113 K22 **Ploçë** var. Ploça. Vlorë, SW Albania
113 G15 **Ploče** It. Plocce; prev. Kardeljevo. Dubrovnik-Neretva, SE Croatia
110 K11 **Płock** Ger. Plozk. Mazowieckie, C Poland
109 Q10 **Plöcken Pass** Ger. Plöckenpass, It. Passo di Monte Croce Carnico. pass SW Austria
Plöckenpass see Plöcken Pass
Plöckenstein see Plechý
99 B19 **Ploegsteert** Hainaut, W Belgium
102 H6 **Ploërmel** Morbihan, NW France
Ploeşti see Ploieşti
116 K13 **Ploieşti** prev. Ploeşti. Prahova, SE Romania
115 L17 **Plomári** prev. Plomárion. Lésvos, E Greece
Plomárion see Plomári
103 O12 **Plomb du Cantal** ▲ C France
183 V6 **Plomer, Point** headland New South Wales, SE Australia
100 J8 **Plön** Schleswig-Holstein, N Germany
110 L11 **Płońsk** Mazowieckie, C Poland
119 J20 **Plotnitsa** Rus. Plotnitsa. Brestskaya Voblasts', SW Belarus
110 E8 **Płoty** Ger. Plathe. Zachodnio-pomorskie, NW Poland
102 G7 **Plouay** Morbihan, NW France
111 D15 **Ploučnice** Ger. Polzen. ≈ NE Czech Republic
114 I10 **Plovdiv** prev. Eumolpias; anc. Evmolpia, Philippopolis, Lat. Trimontium. Plovdiv, C Bulgaria
114 I11 **Plovdiv** ◈ province C Bulgaria
30 L6 **Plover** Wisconsin, N USA
Plozk see Płock
27 U11 **Plumerville** Arkansas, C USA
19 P12 **Plum Island** island Massachusetts, NE USA
32 M9 **Plummer** Idaho, NW USA
83 J18 **Plumtree** Matabeleland South, SW Zimbabwe
118 D11 **Plungė** Telšiai, W Lithuania
113 J15 **Plužine** NW Montenegro
119 K14 **Plyeshchanitsy** Rus. Pleshchenitsy. Minskaya Voblasts', N Belarus
45 V10 **Plymouth** ○ (Montserrat) SW Montserrat
97 I24 **Plymouth** SW England, UK
31 O11 **Plymouth** Indiana, N USA
19 P12 **Plymouth** Massachusetts, NE USA
19 N8 **Plymouth** New Hampshire, NE USA
21 X9 **Plymouth** North Carolina, SE USA
30 M8 **Plymouth** Wisconsin, N USA
97 J20 **Plynlimon** ▲ C Wales, UK
124 G14 **Plyussa** Pskovskaya Oblast', W Russian Federation
111 B17 **Plzeň** Ger. Pilsen, Pol. Pilzno. Plzeňský Kraj, W Czech Republic
111 B17 **Plzeňský Kraj** ◈ region W Czech Republic
110 F11 **Pniewy** Ger. Pinne. Wielkolpolskie, W Poland
77 P13 **Pô** S Burkina
106 D8 **Po** ≈ N Italy
42 M13 **Poás, Volcán** ※ NW Costa Rica
77 S16 **Pobè** S Benin
123 S8 **Pobeda, Gora** ▲ NE Russian Federation
Pobeda Peak see Pobedy, Pik/Tomur Feng
147 Z7 **Pobedy, Pik** Chin. Tomür Feng. ▲ China/Kyrgyzstan see also Tomür Feng
Pobedy, Pik see Tomur Feng
110 H11 **Pobiedziska** Ger. Pudewitz. Wielkolpolskie, C Poland
Po, Bocche del see Po, Foci del
27 W9 **Pocahontas** Arkansas, C USA
29 U12 **Pocahontas** Iowa, C USA
33 Q15 **Pocatello** Idaho, NW USA
167 S13 **Pochentong** ✈ (Phnum Penh) Phnum Penh, S Cambodia
126 I6 **Pochep** Bryanskaya Oblast', W Russian Federation
126 H4 **Pochinok** Smolenskaya Oblast', W Russian Federation
41 R17 **Pochutla** var. San Pedro Pochutla. Oaxaca, SE Mexico
62 I6 **Pocitos, Salar** var. Salar Quiróm. salt lake NW Argentina
101 O22 **Pocking** Bayern, SE Germany
186 I10 **Pocklington Reef** reef SE Papua New Guinea
59 P15 **Poço da Cruz, Açude** ▣ E Brazil
27 R11 **Pocola** Oklahoma, C USA
21 Y5 **Pocomoke City** Maryland, NE USA
59 L21 **Poços de Caldas** Minas Gerais, NE Brazil
124 H14 **Podberez'ye** Novgorodskaya Oblast', NW Russian Federation
Podbrodzie see Pabradė
125 U8 **Podcher'ye** Respublika Komi, NW Russian Federation
111 E16 **Poděbrady** Ger. Podiebrad. Středočeský Kraj, C Czech Republic
126 L9 **Podgorenskiy** Voronezhskaya Oblast', W Russian Federation
113 J17 **Podgorica** prev. Titograd. ● S Montenegro
113 K17 **Podgorica** ✈ S Montenegro
109 T13 **Podgrad** SW Slovenia
Podiebrad see Poděbrady
116 M5 **Podil's'ka Vysochina** plateau W Ukraine
Podium Anicensis see le Puy
122 L11 **Podkamennaya Tunguska** Eng. Stony Tunguska. ≈ C Russian Federation
111 N17 **Podkarpackie** ◈ province SW Poland
Pod Klošter see Arnoldstein
110 P9 **Podlaskie** ◈ province Mazowieckie, C Poland
127 Q8 **Podlesnoye** Saratovskaya Oblast', W Russian Federation
126 K4 **Podol'sk** Moskovskaya Oblast', W Russian Federation
76 H10 **Podor** N Senegal
125 P12 **Podosinovets** Kirovskaya Oblast', NW Russian Federation
124 I12 **Podporozh'ye** Leningradskaya Oblast', NW Russian Federation
Podravska Slatina see Slatina
112 J13 **Podromanlja** ◈ Republika Srpska, SE Bosnia and Herzegovina
Podsvil'ye see Padsvillye
116 L9 **Podu Iloaiei** prev. Podul Iloaiei. Iaşi, NE Romania
113 N15 **Podujevo** Kosovo, S Serbia
Podul Iloaiei see Podu Iloaiei
Podunajská Rovina see Little Alföld
124 M12 **Podyuga** Arkhangel'skaya Oblast', NW Russian Federation
56 A9 **Poechos, Embalse** ◎ NW Peru
55 W10 **Poeketi** Sipaliwini, E Surinam
100 L8 **Poel** island N Germany
83 M20 **Poelela, Lagoa** ◎ S Mozambique
Poerwodadi see Purwodadi
Poerwokerto see Purwokerto
Poerworedjo see Purworejo
Poetovio see Ptuj
83 E23 **Pofadder** Northern Cape, W South Africa
106 I9 **Po, Foci del** var. Bocche del Po. ≈ NE Italy
116 E12 **Pogăniş** ≈ W Romania
Pogegen see Pagėgiai
106 G12 **Poggibonsi** Toscana, C Italy
107 I14 **Poggio Mirteto** Lazio, C Italy
109 V4 **Pöggstall** Niederösterreich, N Austria
116 L13 **Pogoanele** Buzău, SE Romania
Pogónion see Delvináki
113 M21 **Pogradec** var. Pogradeci. Korçë, SE Albania
Pogradeci see Pogradec
123 S15 **Pogranichnyy** Primorskiy Kray, SE Russian Federation
38 M16 **Pogromni Volcano** ※ Unimak Island, Alaska, USA
163 Z15 **P'ohang** Jap. Hokō. E South Korea
15 T9 **Pohénégamook, Lac** ◎ Québec, SE Canada
93 L20 **Pohja** Swe. Pojo. Etelä-Suomi, SW Finland
Pohjanlahti see Bothnia, Gulf of
189 U16 **Pohnpei** ◈ state E Micronesia
189 O12 **Pohnpei** ✈ Pohnpei, E Micronesia
189 O12 **Pohnpei** prev. Ponape Ascension Island. island E Micronesia
111 F19 **Pohořelice** Ger. Pohrlitz. Jihomoravský Kraj, SE Czech Republic
109 V10 **Pohorje** Ger. Bacher. ▲▲ N Slovenia
117 N6 **Pohrebyshche** Vinnyts'ka Oblast', C Ukraine
Pohrlitz see Pohořelice
161 P9 **Po Hu** ▣ E China
116 G15 **Poiana Mare** Dolj, S Romania
Poictiers see Poitiers
127 N6 **Poim** Penzenskaya Oblast', W Russian Federation
159 N15 **Poindo** Xigzang Zizhiqu, W China
195 Y13 **Poinsett, Cape** cape Antarctica
29 R9 **Poinsett, Lake** ◎ South Dakota, N USA
22 I10 **Point Au Fer Island** island Louisiana, S USA
39 X14 **Point Baker** Prince of Wales Island, Alaska, USA
25 U13 **Point Comfort** Texas, SW USA
Point de Galle see Galle
44 K10 **Pointe à Gravois** headland SW Haiti
22 L10 **Pointe a la Hache** Louisiana, S USA
45 Y6 **Pointe-à-Pitre** Grande Terre, C Guadeloupe

POINTE-AU-PÈRE – PORTO SANTO

15 *U7* **Pointe-au-Père** Québec, SE Canada
15 *V5* **Pointe-aux-Anglais** Québec, SE Canada
45 *T10* **Pointe Du Cap** *headland* N Saint Lucia
79 *E21* **Pointe-Noire** Le Kouilou, S Congo
45 *X6* **Pointe Noire** Basse Terre, W Guadeloupe
79 *E21* **Pointe-Noire** ✈ Le Kouilou, S Congo
45 *U15* **Point Fortin** Trinidad, Trinidad and Tobago
38 *M6* **Point Hope** Alaska, USA
39 *N5* **Point Lay** Alaska, USA
18 *B16* **Point Marion** Pennsylvania, NE USA
18 *K16* **Point Pleasant** New Jersey, NE USA
21 *P4* **Point Pleasant** West Virginia, NE USA
45 *R14* **Point Salines** ✈ (St. George's) SW Grenada
102 *L9* **Poitiers** *prev.* Poictiers; *anc.* Limonum. Vienne, W France
102 *K9* **Poitou** *cultural region* W France
102 *K10* **Poitou-Charentes** ◈ *region* W France
103 *N3* **Poix-de-Picardie** Somme, N France
Pojo *see* Pohja
37 *S10* **Pojoaque** New Mexico, SW USA
152 *E11* **Pokaran** Rājasthān, NW India
183 *R4* **Pokataroo** New South Wales, SE Australia
119 *P18* **Pokats'** *Rus.* Pokot'. ≈ SE Belarus
29 *V5* **Pokegama Lake** ◎ Minnesota, N USA
184 *L6* **Pokeno** Waikato, North Island, New Zealand
153 *O11* **Pokharā** Western, C Nepal
127 *T6* **Pokhvistnevo** Samarskaya Oblast', W Russian Federation
55 *W10* **Pokigron** Sipaliwini, C Surinam
92 *L10* **Pokka** *Lapp.* Bohkká. Lappi, N Finland
79 *N16* **Poko** Orientale, NE Dem. Rep. Congo
Pokot' *see* Pokats'
Po-ko-to Shan *see* Bogda Shan
147 *S7* **Pokrovka** Talasskaya Oblast', NW Kyrgyzstan
Pokrovka *see* Kyzyl-Suu
117 *V8* **Pokrovs'ke** *Rus.* Pokrovskoye. Dnipropetrovs'ka Oblast', E Ukraine
Pokrovskoye *see* Pokrovs'ke
Pola *see* Pula
37 *N10* **Polacca** Arizona, SW USA
104 *L2* **Pola de Laviana** Asturias, N Spain
104 *K2* **Pola de Lena** Asturias, N Spain
104 *L2* **Pola de Siero** Asturias, N Spain
191 *Y3* **Poland** Kiritimati, E Kiribati
110 *H12* **Poland** *off.* Republic of Poland, *var.* Polish Republic, *Pol.* Polska, Rzeczpospolita Polska; *prev. Pol.* Polska Rzeczpospolita Ludowa, The Polish People's Republic. ◆ *republic* C Europe
Poland, Republic of *see* Poland
Polangen *see* Palanga
110 *G7* **Polanów** *Ger.* Pollnow. Zachodnio-pomorskie, NW Poland
136 *H13* **Polatlı** Ankara, C Turkey
118 *L12* **Polatsk** *Rus.* Polotsk. Vitsyebskaya Voblasts', N Belarus
110 *F8* **Połczyn-Zdrój** *Ger.* Bad Polzin. Zachodnio-pomorskie, NW Poland
149 *R5* **Pol-e-'Alam** Lowgar, E Afghanistan
Polekhatum *see* Pulhatyn
149 *Q3* **Pol-e Khomrī** *var.* Pul-i-Khumri. Baghlān, NE Afghanistan
197 *S10* **Pole Plain** *undersea feature* Arctic Ocean
143 *P5* **Pol-e Safīd** *var.* Pol-e-Sefid, Pul-i-Sefid. Māzandarān, N Iran
Pol-e-Sefid *see* Pol-e Safīd
118 *B13* **Polessk** *Ger.* Labiau. Kaliningradskaya Oblast', W Russian Federation
Polesskoye *see* Polis'ke
171 *N13* **Polewali** Sulawesi, C Indonesia
114 *G11* **Polezhan** ▲ SW Bulgaria
78 *F13* **Poli** Nord, N Cameroon
Poli *see* Pólis
107 *M19* **Policastro, Golfo di** *gulf* S Italy
110 *D8* **Police** *Ger.* Politz. Zachodnio-pomorskie, NW Poland
172 *I17* **Police, Pointe** *headland* Mahé, NE Seychelles
115 *L17* **Polichnítos** *var.* Polihnitos, Polikhnitos. Lésvos, E Greece
Poligiros *see* Polýgyros
107 *P17* **Polignano a Mare** Puglia, SE Italy
103 *S9* **Poligny** Jura, E France
Polihnitos *see* Polichnítos
Polikastro/Políkastron *see* Polýkastro
Polikhnitos *see* Polichnítos
114 *K8* **Polikrayshte** Veliko Tŭrnovo, N Bulgaria
171 *O3* **Polillo Islands** *island group* N Philippines
109 *Q9* **Polinik** ▲ SW Austria
115 *J15* **Políochni** *var.* Polýochni. *site of ancient city* Límnos, E Greece
121 *O2* **Pólis** *var.* Poli. W Cyprus
Polish People's Republic, The *see* Poland
Polish Republic *see* Poland
117 *O3* **Polis'ke** *Rus.* Polesskoye. Kyyivs'ka Oblast', N Ukraine
107 *N22* **Polistena** Calabria, SW Italy
Politz *see* Police
Políyiros *see* Polýgyros
29 *V14* **Polk City** Iowa, C USA
110 *F13* **Polkowice** *Ger.* Heerwegen. Dolnośląskie, W Poland
155 *G22* **Pollāchi** Tamil Nādu, SE India
109 *W7* **Pöllau** Steiermark, SE Austria
189 *T13* **Polle** *atoll* Chuuk Islands, C Micronesia
105 *X9* **Pollença** Mallorca, Spain, W Mediterranean Sea
Pollnow *see* Polanów
29 *N7* **Pollock** South Dakota, N USA
92 *L8* **Polmak** Finnmark, N Norway
30 *L10* **Polo** Illinois, N USA
193 *V15* **Poloa** *island* Tongatapu Group, N Tonga
42 *E5* **Polochic, Río** ≈ C Guatemala
Pologi *see* Polohy
117 *V9* **Polohy** *Rus.* Pologi. Zaporiz'ka Oblast', SE Ukraine
83 *K20* **Polokwane** *prev.* Pietersburg. Limpopo, NE South Africa
14 *M10* **Polonais, Lac des** ◎ Québec, SE Canada
61 *G20* **Polonio, Cabo** *headland* E Uruguay
155 *K24* **Polonnaruwa** North Central Province, C Sri Lanka
116 *L5* **Polonne** *Rus.* Polonnoye. Khmel'nyts'ka Oblast', NW Ukraine
Polonnoye *see* Polonne
Polotsk *see* Polatsk
109 *T7* **Pöls** *var.* Pölsbach. ≈ E Austria
Pölsbach *see* Pöls
Polska/Polska, Rzeczpospolita/Polska Rzeczpospolita Ludowa *see* Poland
114 *L10* **Polski Gradets** Stara Zagora, C Bulgaria
114 *K8* **Polsko Kosovo** Ruse, N Bulgaria
33 *P8* **Polson** Montana, NW USA
117 *T6* **Poltava** Poltavs'ka Oblast', NE Ukraine
Poltava *see* Poltavs'ka Oblast'
117 *R5* **Poltavs'ka Oblast'** *var.* Poltava, *Rus.* Poltavskaya Oblast'. ◈ *province* NE Ukraine
Poltavskaya Oblast' *see* Poltavs'ka Oblast'
Poltoratsk *see* Aşgabat
118 *I5* **Põltsamaa** *Ger.* Oberpahlen. Jõgevamaa, E Estonia
118 *I4* **Põltsamaa** *var.* Põltsamaa Jõgi. ≈ C Estonia
Põltsamaa Jõgi *see* Põltsamaa
122 *I8* **Poluy** ≈ N Russian Federation
118 *J6* **Põlva** *Ger.* Pölwe. Põlvamaa, SE Estonia
93 *N16* **Polvijärvi** Itä-Suomi, SE Finland
Pölwe *see* Põlva
115 *I22* **Polýaigos** *island* Kykládes, Greece, Aegean Sea
115 *I22* **Polyaígou Folégandrou, Stenó** *strait* Kykládes, Greece, Aegean Sea
124 *J3* **Polyarnyy** Murmanskaya Oblast', NW Russian Federation
125 *W5* **Polyarnyy Ural** ▲▲ NW Russian Federation
115 *G14* **Polýgyros** *var.* Poligiros, Políyiros. Kentrikí Makedonía, N Greece
114 *F13* **Polýkastro** *var.* Polikastro; *prev.* Políkastron. Kentrikí Makedonía, N Greece
193 *O9* **Polynesia** *island group* C Pacific Ocean
Polýochni *see* Políochni
41 *Y13* **Polyuc** Quintana Roo, E Mexico
109 *V10* **Polzela** C Slovenia
Polzen *see* Ploučnice
56 *D12* **Pomabamba** Ancash, C Peru
185 *D23* **Pomahaka** ≈ South Island, New Zealand
106 *F12* **Pomarance** Toscana, C Italy
104 *G9* **Pombal** Leiria, C Portugal
76 *D9* **Pombas** Santo Antão, NW Cape Verde
83 *N19* **Pomene** Inhambane, SE Mozambique
110 *G8* **Pomerania** *cultural region* Germany/Poland
110 *D7* **Pomeranian Bay** *Ger.* Pommersche Bucht, *Pol.* Zatoka Pomorska. *bay* Germany/Poland
31 *T15* **Pomeroy** Ohio, N USA
32 *L10* **Pomeroy** Washington, NW USA
117 *Q8* **Pomichna** Kirovohrads'ka Oblast', C Ukraine
186 *H7* **Pomio** New Britain, E Papua New Guinea
Pomir, Dar''yoi *see* Pamir/Pāmīr, Daryā-ye
27 *T6* **Pomme de Terre Lake** ▣ Missouri, C USA
29 *S8* **Pomme de Terre River** ≈ Minnesota, N USA
Pommersche Bucht *see* Pomeranian Bay
35 *T15* **Pomona** California, W USA
114 *N9* **Pomorie** Burgas, E Bulgaria
Pomorska, Zatoka *see* Pomeranian Bay
110 *H8* **Pomorskie** ◈ *province* N Poland
125 *Q4* **Pomorskiy Proliv** *strait* NW Russian Federation
125 *T10* **Pomozdino** Respublika Komi, NW Russian Federation
Pompaelo *see* Pamplona
23 *Z15* **Pompano Beach** Florida, SE USA
107 *K18* **Pompei** Campania, S Italy
33 *V10* **Pompeys Pillar** Montana, NW USA
Ponape Ascension Island *see* Pohnpei
29 *R13* **Ponca** Nebraska, C USA
27 *O8* **Ponca City** Oklahoma, C USA
45 *T6* **Ponce** C Puerto Rico
23 *X10* **Ponce de Leon Inlet** *inlet* Florida, SE USA
22 *K8* **Ponchatoula** Louisiana, S USA
26 *M8* **Pond Creek** Oklahoma, C USA
155 *J20* **Pondicherry** *var.* Puduchcheri, *Fr.* Pondichéry. Pondicherry, SE India
151 *I20* **Pondicherry** *var.* Puduchcheri, *Fr.* Pondichéry. ◈ *union territory* India
Pondichéry *see* Pondicherry
197 *N11* **Pond Inlet** Baffin Island, Nunavut, NE Canada
187 *P16* **Ponérihouen** Province Nord, C New Caledonia
104 *J4* **Ponferrada** Castilla-León, NW Spain
184 *N13* **Pongaroa** Manawatu-Wanganui, North Island, New Zealand
167 *Q12* **Pong Nam Ron** Chantaburi, S Thailand
81 *C14* **Pongo** ≈ S Sudan
152 *I7* **Pong Reservoir** ▣ N India
111 *N14* **Poniatowa** Lubelskie, E Poland
167 *R12* **Pônley** Kâmpóng Chhnăng, C Cambodia
155 *I20* **Ponnaiyār** ≈ SE India
9 *Q15* **Ponoka** Alberta, SW Canada
127 *U6* **Ponomarevka** Orenburgskaya Oblast', W Russian Federation
169 *Q17* **Ponorogo** Jawa, C Indonesia
124 *M5* **Ponoy** Murmanskaya Oblast', NW Russian Federation
122 *F6* **Ponoy** ≈ NW Russian Federation
102 *K11* **Pons** Charente-Maritime, W France
Pons *see* Ponts
Pons Aelii *see* Newcastle upon Tyne
Pons Vetus *see* Pontevedra
99 *G20* **Pont-à-Celles** Hainaut, S Belgium
102 *K16* **Pontacq** Pyrénées-Atlantiques, SW France
64 *P3* **Ponta Delgada** São Miguel, Azores, Portugal, NE Atlantic Ocean
64 *P3* **Ponta Delgado** ✈ São Miguel, Azores, Portugal, NE Atlantic Ocean
64 *N2* **Ponta do Pico** ▲ Pico, Azores, Portugal, NE Atlantic Ocean
60 *J11* **Ponta Grossa** Paraná, S Brazil
103 *S5* **Pont-à-Mousson** Meurthe-et-Moselle, NE France
103 *T9* **Pontarlier** Doubs, E France
106 *G11* **Pontassieve** Toscana, C Italy
102 *L4* **Pont-Audemer** Eure, N France
22 *K9* **Pontchartrain, Lake** ◎ Louisiana, S USA
102 *I8* **Pontchâteau** Loire-Atlantique, NW France
103 *R10* **Pont-de-Vaux** Ain, E France
104 *G4* **Ponteareas** Galicia, NW Spain
106 *J6* **Pontebba** Friuli-Venezia Giulia, NE Italy
104 *G4* **Ponte Caldelas** Galicia, NW Spain
107 *J16* **Pontecorvo** Lazio, C Italy
104 *G5* **Ponte da Barca** Viana do Castelo, N Portugal
104 *G5* **Ponte de Lima** Viana do Castelo, N Portugal
106 *F11* **Pontedera** Toscana, C Italy
104 *H10* **Ponte de Sor** Portalegre, C Portugal
104 *H2* **Pontedeume** Galicia, NW Spain
106 *F6* **Ponte di Legno** Lombardia, N Italy
9 *T17* **Ponteix** Saskatchewan, S Canada
59 *N20* **Ponte Nova** Minas Gerais, NE Brazil
59 *G18* **Pontes e Lacerda** Mato Grosso, W Brazil
104 *G4* **Pontevedra** *anc.* Pons Vetus. Galicia, NW Spain
104 *G3* **Pontevedra** ◈ *province* Galicia, NW Spain
104 *G4* **Pontevedra, Ría de** *estuary* NW Spain
30 *M12* **Pontiac** Illinois, N USA
31 *R9* **Pontiac** Michigan, N USA
169 *P11* **Pontianak** Borneo, C Indonesia
107 *I16* **Pontino, Agro** *plain* C Italy
Pontisarae *see* Pontoise
102 *H6* **Pontivy** Morbihan, NW France
102 *F6* **Pont-l'Abbé** Finistère, NW France
103 *N4* **Pontoise** *anc.* Briva Isarae, Cergy-Pontoise, Pontisarae. Val-d'Oise, N France
9 *W13* **Ponton** Manitoba, C Canada
102 *J5* **Pontorson** Manche, N France
22 *M2* **Pontotoc** Mississippi, S USA
25 *R9* **Pontotoc** Texas, SW USA
106 *E10* **Pontremoli** Toscana, C Italy
108 *J10* **Pontresina** Graubünden, S Switzerland
105 *U5* **Ponts** *var.* Pons. Cataluña, NE Spain
103 *R14* **Pont-St-Esprit** Gard, S France
97 *K21* **Pontypool** *Wel.* Pontypŵl. SE Wales, UK
97 *J22* **Pontypridd** S Wales, UK
Pontypŵl *see* Pontypool
43 *R17* **Ponuga** Veraguas, SE Panama
184 *L6* **Ponui Island** *island* N New Zealand
119 *K14* **Ponya** ≈ N Belarus
107 *I17* **Ponza, Isola di** *Island* Isole Ponziane, S Italy
107 *I17* **Ponziane, Isole** *island* C Italy
182 *F7* **Poochera** South Australia
97 *L24* **Poole** S England, UK
25 *S6* **Poolville** Texas, SW USA
Poona *see* Pune
182 *M8* **Pooncarie** New South Wales, SE Australia
183 *N6* **Poopelloe Lake** *seasonal lake* New South Wales, SE Australia
57 *K19* **Poopó** Oruro, C Bolivia
57 *K19* **Poopó, Lago** *var.* Lago Pampa Aullagas. ◎ W Bolivia
184 *L3* **Poor Knights Islands** *island* N New Zealand
39 *P10* **Poorman** Alaska, USA
182 *E3* **Pootnoura** South Australia
147 *R10* **Pop** *Rus.* Pap. Namangan Viloyati, E Uzbekistan
117 *X7* **Popasna** *Rus.* Popasnaya. Luhans'ka Oblast', E Ukraine
Popasnaya *see* Popasna
54 *D12* **Popayán** Cauca, SW Colombia
99 *B18* **Poperinge** West-Vlaanderen, W Belgium
123 *N7* **Popigay** Taymyrskiy (Dolgano-Nenetskiy) Avtonomnyy Okrug, N Russian Federation
123 *N7* **Popigay** ≈ N Russian Federation
117 *O5* **Popil'nya** Zhytomyrs'ka Oblast', N Ukraine
182 *K8* **Popiltah Lake** *seasonal lake* New South Wales, SE Australia
33 *X7* **Poplar** Montana, NW USA
9 *Y14* **Poplar** ≈ Manitoba, C Canada
27 *X8* **Poplar Bluff** Missouri, C USA
33 *X6* **Poplar River** ≈ Montana, NW USA
41 *P14* **Popocatépetl** ⛰ S Mexico
79 *H21* **Popokabaka** Bandundu, SW Dem. Rep. Congo
107 *J15* **Popoli** Abruzzo, C Italy
186 *F9* **Popondetta** Northern, S Papua New Guinea
112 *F9* **Popovača** Sisak-Moslavina, NE Croatia
114 *J10* **Popovitsa** Loveshka Oblast, C Bulgaria
114 *L8* **Popovo** Tŭrgovishte, N Bulgaria
Popovo *see* Iskra
Popper *see* Poprad
30 *M5* **Popple River** ≈ Wisconsin, N USA
111 *L19* **Poprad** *Ger.* Deutschendorf, *Hung.* Poprád. Prešovský Kraj, E Slovakia
111 *L18* **Poprad** *Ger.* Popper, *Hung.* Poprád. ≈ Poland/Slovakia
111 *L19* **Poprad-Tatry** ✈ (Poprad) Prešovský Kraj, E Slovakia
21 *X7* **Poquoson** Virginia, NE USA
149 *O15* **Porāli** ≈ SW Pakistan
184 *N12* **Porangahau** Hawke's Bay, North Island, New Zealand
59 *K17* **Porangatu** Goiás, C Brazil
119 *G18* **Porazava** *Pol.* Porozow, *Rus.* Porozovo. Hrodzyenskaya Voblasts', W Belarus
154 *A11* **Porbandar** Gujarāt, W India
10 *I13* **Porcher Island** *island* British Columbia, SW Canada
104 *M13* **Porcuna** Andalucía, S Spain
14 *F7* **Porcupine** Ontario, S Canada
64 *M6* **Porcupine Bank** *undersea feature* N Atlantic Ocean
9 *V15* **Porcupine Hills** ▲▲ Manitoba/Saskatchewan, S Canada
30 *L3* **Porcupine Mountains** *hill range* Michigan, N USA
64 *M7* **Porcupine Plain** *undersea feature* E Atlantic Ocean
8 *G7* **Porcupine River** ≈ Canada/USA
106 *I7* **Pordenone** *anc.* Portenau. Friuli-Venezia Giulia, NE Italy
54 *H9* **Pore** Casanare, E Colombia
112 *A9* **Poreč** *It.* Parenzo. Istra, NW Croatia
60 *I9* **Porecatu** Paraná, S Brazil
Porech'ye *see* Parechcha
127 *P4* **Poretskoye** Chuvashskaya Respublika, W Russian Federation
77 *Q13* **Porga** N Benin
186 *B7* **Porgera** Enga, W Papua New Guinea
93 *K18* **Pori** *Swe.* Björneborg. Länsi-Soumi, SW Finland
185 *L14* **Porirua** Wellington, North Island, New Zealand
92 *I12* **Porjus** *Lapp.* Bårjås. Norrbotten, N Sweden
124 *G14* **Porkhov** Pskovskaya Oblast', W Russian Federation
55 *O4* **Porlamar** Nueva Esparta, NE Venezuela
102 *I8* **Pornic** Loire-Atlantique, NW France
186 *B7* **Poroma** Southern Highlands, W Papua New Guinea
123 *T13* **Poronaysk** Ostrov Sakhalin, Sakhalinskaya Oblast', SE Russian Federation
115 *G20* **Póros** Póros, S Greece
115 *C19* **Póros** Kefallinía, Iónia Nisiá, Greece, C Mediterranean Sea
115 *G20* **Póros** *island* S Greece
81 *G24* **Poroto Mountains** ▲▲ SW Tanzania
112 *B10* **Porozina** Primorje-Gorski Kotar, NW Croatia
Porozovo/Porozow *see* Porazava
195 *X15* **Porpoise Bay** *bay* Antarctica
65 *G15* **Porpoise Point** *headland* NE Ascension Island
65 *C25* **Porpoise Point** *headland* East Falkland, Falkland Islands
108 *C6* **Porrentruy** Jura, NW Switzerland
106 *F10* **Porretta Terme** Emilia-Romagna, C Italy
Porriño *see* O Porriño
Pors *see* Porsangenfijorden
92 *L7* **Porsangenfijorden** *Lapp.* Pors. *fjord* N Norway
92 *K8* **Porsangerhalvøya** *peninsula* N Norway
95 *G16* **Porsgrunn** Telemark, S Norway
136 *E13* **Porsuk Çayı** ≈ C Turkey
Porsy *see* Boldumsaz
57 *N18* **Portachuelo** Santa Cruz, C Bolivia
182 *I9* **Port Adelaide** South Australia
97 *F15* **Portadown** *Ir.* Port An Dúnáin. S Northern Ireland, UK
31 *P10* **Portage** Michigan, N USA
18 *D15* **Portage** Pennsylvania, NE USA
30 *K8* **Portage** Wisconsin, N USA
30 *M3* **Portage Lake** ◎ Michigan, N USA
9 *X16* **Portage la Prairie** Manitoba, S Canada
31 *R11* **Portage River** ≈ Ohio, N USA
27 *Y8* **Portageville** Missouri, C USA
28 *L2* **Portal** North Dakota, N USA
10 *L17* **Port Alberni** Vancouver Island, British Columbia, SW Canada
14 *E15* **Port Albert** Ontario, S Canada
104 *I10* **Portalegre** *anc.* Ammaia, Amoea. Portalegre, E Portugal
104 *H10* **Portalegre** ◈ *district* C Portugal
37 *V12* **Portales** New Mexico, SW USA
39 *X14* **Port Alexander** Baranof Island, Alaska, USA
83 *I25* **Port Alfred** Eastern Cape, S South Africa
10 *J16* **Port Alice** Vancouver Island, British Columbia, SW Canada
22 *J8* **Port Allen** Louisiana, S USA
Port Amelia *see* Pemba
Port An Dúnáin *see* Portadown
32 *G7* **Port Angeles** Washington, NW USA
44 *L12* **Port Antonio** NE Jamaica
115 *D16* **Pórta Panagiá** *religious building* Thessalía, C Greece
25 *T14* **Port Aransas** Texas, SW USA
97 *E18* **Portarlington** *Ir.* Cúil an tSúdaire. Laois/Offaly, C Ireland
183 *P17* **Port Arthur** Tasmania, SE Australia
25 *Y11* **Port Arthur** Texas, SW USA
96 *G12* **Port Askaig** W Scotland, UK
182 *I7* **Port Augusta** South Australia
44 *M9* **Port-au-Prince** ● (Haiti) C Haiti
44 *M9* **Port-au-Prince** ✈ E Haiti
22 *I8* **Port Barre** Louisiana, S USA
151 *Q19* **Port Blair** Andaman and Nicobar Islands, SE India
25 *X12* **Port Bolivar** Texas, SW USA
105 *X4* **Portbou** Cataluña, NE Spain
77 *N17* **Port Bouet** ✈ (Abidjan) SE Ivory Coast
182 *I8* **Port Broughton** South Australia
14 *F17* **Port Burwell** Ontario, S Canada
12 *G17* **Port Burwell** Québec, NE Canada
182 *M13* **Port Campbell** Victoria, SE Australia
15 *V4* **Port-Cartier** Québec, SE Canada
185 *F23* **Port Chalmers** Otago, South Island, New Zealand
23 *W14* **Port Charlotte** Florida, SE USA
38 *L9* **Port Clarence** Alaska, USA
10 *I13* **Port Clements** Graham Island, British Columbia, SW Canada
31 *S11* **Port Clinton** Ohio, N USA
14 *H17* **Port Colborne** Ontario, S Canada
15 *Y7* **Port-Daniel** Québec, SE Canada
Port Darwin *see* Darwin
183 *O17* **Port Davey** *headland* Tasmania, SE Australia
44 *K8* **Port-de-Paix** NW Haiti
181 *W4* **Port Douglas** Queensland, NE Australia
10 *J13* **Port Edward** British Columbia, SW Canada
83 *K24* **Port Edward** KwaZulu/Natal, SE South Africa
58 *J12* **Portel** Pará, NE Brazil
104 *H12* **Portel** Évora, S Portugal
14 *E14* **Port Elgin** Ontario, S Canada
45 *Y14* **Port Elizabeth** Bequia, Saint Vincent and the Grenadines
83 *I26* **Port Elizabeth** Eastern Cape, S South Africa
96 *G13* **Port Ellen** W Scotland, UK
Portenau *see* Pordenone
97 *H16* **Port Erin** SW Isle of Man
45 *Q13* **Porter Point** *headland* Saint Vincent, Saint Vincent and the Grenadines
185 *G18* **Porters Pass** *pass* South Island, New Zealand
83 *E25* **Porterville** Western Cape, SW South Africa
35 *R12* **Porterville** California, W USA
Port-Étienne *see* Nouâdhibou
182 *L13* **Port Fairy** Victoria, SE Australia
184 *M4* **Port Fitzroy** Great Barrier Island, Auckland, NE New Zealand
Port Florence *see* Kisumu
Port-Francqui *see* Ilebo
79 *C18* **Port-Gentil** Ogooué-Maritime, W Gabon
182 *I7* **Port Germein** South Australia
22 *J6* **Port Gibson** Mississippi, S USA
39 *Q13* **Port Graham** Alaska, USA
77 *U17* **Port Harcourt** Rivers, S Nigeria
10 *J16* **Port Hardy** Vancouver Island, British Columbia, SW Canada
Port Harrison *see* Inukjuak
13 *R14* **Port Hawkesbury** Cape Breton Island, Nova Scotia, SE Canada
180 *I6* **Port Hedland** Western Australia
39 *O15* **Port Heiden** Alaska, USA
97 *I19* **Porthmadog** *var.* Portmadoc. NW Wales, UK
14 *I15* **Port Hope** Ontario, SE Canada
13 *S9* **Port Hope Simpson** Newfoundland and Labrador, E Canada
65 *C24* **Port Howard Settlement** West Falkland, Falkland Islands
31 *T9* **Port Huron** Michigan, N USA
107 *K17* **Portici** Campania, S Italy
137 *Y13* **Port-İliç** *Rus.* Port Il'ich. SE Azerbaijan
Port Il'ich *see* Port-İliç
104 *G14* **Portimão** *var.* Vila Nova de Portimão. Faro, S Portugal
25 *T17* **Port Isabel** Texas, SW USA
18 *J13* **Port Jervis** New York, NE USA
55 *S7* **Port Kaituma** NW Guyana
126 *K12* **Port Katon** Rostovskaya Oblast', SW Russian Federation
183 *S9* **Port Kembla** New South Wales, SE Australia
182 *F8* **Port Kenny** South Australia
Port Klang *see* Pelabuhan Klang
Port Láirge *see* Waterford
183 *S8* **Portland** New South Wales, SE Australia
182 *L13* **Portland** Victoria, SE Australia
184 *K4* **Portland** Northland, North Island, New Zealand
31 *Q13* **Portland** Indiana, N USA
19 *P8* **Portland** Maine, NE USA
31 *Q9* **Portland** Michigan, N USA
29 *Q4* **Portland** North Dakota, N USA
32 *G11* **Portland** Oregon, NW USA
20 *J8* **Portland** Tennessee, S USA
25 *T14* **Portland** Texas, SW USA
32 *G11* **Portland** ✈ Oregon, NW USA
182 *L13* **Portland Bay** *bay* Victoria, SE Australia
44 *K13* **Portland Bight** *bay* S Jamaica
97 *L24* **Portland Bill** *var.* Bill of Portland. *headland* S England, UK
Portland, Bill of *see* Portland Bill
183 *P15* **Portland, Cape** *headland* Tasmania, SE Australia
10 *J12* **Portland Inlet** *inlet* British Columbia, W Canada
184 *P11* **Portland Island** *island* E New Zealand
65 *F15* **Portland Point** *headland* SW Ascension Island
44 *J13* **Portland Point** *headland* C Jamaica
103 *P16* **Port-la-Nouvelle** Aude, S France
Portlaoighise *see* Port Laoise
97 *E18* **Port Laoise** *var.* Portlaoise, *Ir.* Portlaoighise; *prev.* Maryborough. C Ireland
Portlaoise *see* Port Laoise
25 *U13* **Port Lavaca** Texas, SW USA
182 *G9* **Port Lincoln** South Australia
39 *Q14* **Port Lions** Kodiak Island, Alaska, USA
76 *I15* **Port Loko** W Sierra Leone
65 *E24* **Port Louis** East Falkland, Falkland Islands
45 *Y5* **Port-Louis** Grande Terre, N Guadeloupe
173 *X16* **Port Louis** ● (Mauritius) NW Mauritius
Port Louis *see* Scarborough
Port-Lyautey *see* Kénitra
182 *K12* **Port MacDonnell** South Australia
183 *U7* **Port Macquarie** New South Wales, SE Australia
Portmadoc *see* Porthmadog
Port Mahon *see* Mahón
44 *K12* **Port Maria** C Jamaica
10 *K16* **Port McNeill** Vancouver Island, British Columbia, SW Canada
13 *P11* **Port-Menier** Île d'Anticosti, Québec, E Canada
39 *N15* **Port Moller** Alaska, USA
44 *L13* **Port Morant** E Jamaica
44 *K13* **Portmore** C Jamaica
186 *D9* **Port Moresby** ● (Papua New Guinea) Central/National Capital District, SW Papua New Guinea
Port Natal *see* Durban
25 *Y11* **Port Neches** Texas, SW USA
182 *G9* **Port Neill** South Australia
15 *S6* **Portneuf** ≈ Québec, SE Canada
15 *R6* **Portneuf, Lac** ◎ Québec, SE Canada
83 *D23* **Port Nolloth** Northern Cape, W South Africa
18 *J17* **Port Norris** New Jersey, NE USA
Port-Nouveau-Québec *see* Kangiqsualujjuaq
104 *G6* **Porto** *Eng.* Oporto; *anc.* Portus Cale. Porto, NW Portugal
104 *G6* **Porto** *var.* Pôrto. ◈ *district* N Portugal
104 *G6* **Porto** ✈ Porto, W Portugal
Pôrto *see* Porto
61 *I16* **Porto Alegre** *var.* Pôrto Alegre. *state capital* Rio Grande do Sul, S Brazil
Porto Alexandre *see* Tombua
82 *B12* **Porto Amboim** Cuanza Sul, NW Angola
Porto Amélia *see* Pemba
Porto Bello *see* Portobelo
43 *T14* **Portobelo** *var.* Porto Bello, Puerto Bello. Colón, N Panama
60 *G10* **Pôrto Camargo** Paraná, S Brazil
25 *U13* **Port O'Connor** Texas, SW USA
Pôrto de Mós *see* Porto de Moz
58 *J12* **Porto de Moz** *var.* Pôrto de Mós. Pará, NE Brazil
64 *O5* **Porto do Moniz** Madeira, Portugal, NE Atlantic Ocean
59 *H16* **Porto dos Gaúchos** Mato Grosso, W Brazil
Porto Edda *see* Sarandë
107 *J24* **Porto Empedocle** Sicilia, Italy, C Mediterranean Sea
59 *H20* **Porto Esperança** Mato Grosso do Sul, SW Brazil
106 *E13* **Portoferraio** Toscana, C Italy
96 *G6* **Port of Ness** NW Scotland, UK
45 *U14* **Port-of-Spain** ● (Trinidad and Tobago) Trinidad, Trinidad and Tobago
Port of Spain *see* Piarco
103 *X15* **Porto, Golfe de** *gulf* Corse, France, C Mediterranean Sea
Porto Grande *see* Mindelo
106 *I7* **Portogruaro** Veneto, NE Italy
35 *P5* **Portola** California, W USA
187 *Q13* **Port-Olry** Espiritu Santo, C Vanuatu
93 *J17* **Pörtom** *Fin.* Pirttikylä. Länsi-Soumi, W Finland
Port Omna *see* Portumna
59 *G21* **Porto Murtinho** Mato Grosso do Sul, SW Brazil
59 *K16* **Porto Nacional** Tocantins, C Brazil
77 *S16* **Porto-Novo** ● (Benin) S Benin
23 *X10* **Port Orange** Florida, SE USA
32 *G8* **Port Orchard** Washington, NW USA
Porto Re *see* Kraljevica
32 *E15* **Port Orford** Oregon, NW USA
Porto Rico *see* Puerto Rico
106 *J13* **Porto San Giorgio** Marche, C Italy
64 *P5* **Porto Santo** *var.* Vila Baleira. Porto Santo, Madeira, Portugal, NE Atlantic Ocean
64 *Q5* **Porto Santo** ✈ Porto Santo, Madeira, Portugal, NE Atlantic Ocean

◆ Country
● Country Capital
◇ Dependent Territory
○ Dependent Territory Capital
◈ Administrative Regions
✈ International Airport
▲ Mountain
▲▲ Mountain Range
⛰ Volcano
≈ River
◎ Lake
▣ Reservoir

PORTO SANTO – PROVINS

64 P5 **Porto Santo** *var.* Ilha do Porto Santo. *island* Madeira, Portugal, NE Atlantic Ocean
Porto Santo, Ilha do *see* Porto Santo
107 F14 **Porto Santo Stefano** Toscana, C Italy
60 H9 **Porto São José** Paraná, S Brazil
59 O19 **Porto Seguro** Bahia, E Brazil
107 B17 **Porto Torres** Sardegna, Italy, C Mediterranean Sea
59 J23 **Porto União** Santa Catarina, S Brazil
103 Y16 **Porto-Vecchio** Corse, France, C Mediterranean Sea
59 E15 **Porto Velho** *var.* Velho. *state capital* Rondônia, W Brazil
56 A6 **Portoviejo** *var.* Puertoviejo. Manabí, W Ecuador
185 B26 **Port Pegasus** *bay* Stewart Island, New Zealand
14 H15 **Port Perry** Ontario, SE Canada
183 N12 **Port Phillip Bay** *harbour* Victoria, SE Australia
182 I8 **Port Pirie** South Australia
96 G9 **Portree** N Scotland, UK
Port Rex *see* East London
Port Rois *see* Portrush
44 K13 **Port Royal** E Jamaica
21 R15 **Port Royal** South Carolina, SE USA
21 R15 **Port Royal Sound** *inlet* South Carolina, SE USA
97 F14 **Portrush** *Ir.* Port Rois. N Northern Ireland, UK
75 W7 **Port Said** *Ar.* Būr Saʻīd. N Egypt
23 R9 **Port Saint Joe** Florida, SE USA
23 Y11 **Port Saint John** Florida, SE USA
83 K24 **Port St. Johns** Eastern Cape, SE South Africa
103 R16 **Port-St-Louis-du-Rhône** Bouches-du-Rhône, SE France
44 K10 **Port Salut** SW Haiti
65 E24 **Port Salvador** *inlet* East Falkland, Falkland Islands
65 D24 **Port San Carlos** East Falkland, Falkland Islands
13 S10 **Port Saunders** Newfoundland, Newfoundland and Labrador, SE Canada
83 K24 **Port Shepstone** KwaZulu/Natal, E South Africa
45 O11 **Portsmouth** *var.* Grand-Anse. NW Dominica
97 N24 **Portsmouth** S England, UK
19 P10 **Portsmouth** New Hampshire, NE USA
31 S15 **Portsmouth** Ohio, N USA
21 X7 **Portsmouth** Virginia, NE USA
14 E17 **Port Stanley** Ontario, S Canada
Port Stanley *see* Stanley
65 B25 **Port Stephens** *inlet* West Falkland, Falkland Islands
65 B25 **Port Stephens Settlement** West Falkland, Falkland Islands
97 F14 **Portstewart** *Ir.* Port Stíobhaird. N Northern Ireland, UK
Port Stíobhaird *see* Portstewart
80 I7 **Port Sudan** Red Sea, NE Sudan
22 L10 **Port Sulphur** Louisiana, S USA
Port Swettenham *see* Klang/Pelabuhan Klang
97 J22 **Port Talbot** S Wales, UK
92 L11 **Porttipahdan Tekojärvi** ◎ N Finland
32 G7 **Port Townsend** Washington, NW USA
104 H9 **Portugal** *off.* Republic of Portugal. ◆ *republic* SW Europe
105 O2 **Portugalete** País Vasco, N Spain
Portugal, Republic of *see* Portugal
54 J6 **Portuguesa** *off.* Estado Portuguesa. ◈ *state* N Venezuela
Portuguesa, Estado *see* Portuguesa
Portuguese East Africa *see* Mozambique
Portuguese Guinea *see* Guinea-Bissau
Portuguese Timor *see* East Timor
Portuguese West Africa *see* Angola
97 D18 **Portumna** *Ir.* Port Omna. Galway, W Ireland
Portus Cale *see* Porto
Portus Magnus *see* Almería
Portus Magonis *see* Mahón
103 P17 **Port-Vendres** *var.* Port Vendres. Pyrénées-Orientales, S France
182 H9 **Port Victoria** South Australia
187 Q14 **Port-Vila** *var.* Vila. ● (Vanuatu) Éfaté, C Vanuatu
Port Vila *see* Bauer Field
182 I9 **Port Wakefield** South Australia
31 N8 **Port Washington** Wisconsin, N USA
57 J14 **Porvenir** Pando, NW Bolivia
63 I24 **Porvenir** Magallanes, S Chile
61 D18 **Porvenir** Paysandú, W Uruguay
93 M19 **Porvoo** *Swe.* Borgå. Etelä-Suomi, S Finland
Porzecze *see* Parechcha
104 M10 **Porzuna** Castilla-La Mancha, C Spain
61 E14 **Posadas** Misiones, NE Argentina
104 L13 **Posadas** Andalucía, S Spain
Poschega *see* Požega
108 J11 **Poschiavino** ∼ Italy/Switzerland
108 J10 **Poschiavo** *Ger.* Puschlav. Graubünden, S Switzerland
112 D12 **Posedarje** Zadar, SW Croatia
Posen *see* Poznań
124 L14 **Poshekhon'ye** Yaroslavskaya Oblast', W Russian Federation
92 M13 **Posio** Lappi, NE Finland
Poskam *see* Zepu
Posnania *see* Poznań
171 O12 **Poso** Sulawesi, C Indonesia
171 O12 **Poso, Danau** ◎ Sulawesi, C Indonesia
137 R10 **Posof** Ardahan, NE Turkey
25 R6 **Possum Kingdom Lake** ⊠ Texas, SW USA
25 N6 **Post** Texas, SW USA
Postavy/Postawy *see* Pastavy
12 I7 **Poste-de-la-Baleine** Québec, NE Canada
99 M17 **Posterholt** Limburg, SE Netherlands
83 G22 **Postmasburg** Northern Cape, N South Africa
Pôsto Diuarum *see* Campo de Diauarum
59 I16 **Pôsto Jacaré** Mato Grosso, W Brazil
109 T12 **Postojna** *Ger.* Adelsberg, *It.* Postumia. SW Slovenia
Postumia *see* Postojna
29 X12 **Postville** Iowa, C USA
Pöstyén *see* Piešťany
113 G14 **Posušje** ◈ Federacija Bosna I Hercegovina, SW Bosnia and Herzegovina
171 O16 **Pota** Flores, C Indonesia
115 G23 **Potamós** Antikýthira, S Greece
55 S9 **Potaru River** ∼ C Guyana
83 I21 **Potchefstroom** North-West, N South Africa
27 R11 **Poteau** Oklahoma, C USA
25 R12 **Poteet** Texas, SW USA
115 G14 **Poteídaia** *site of ancient city* Kentrikí Makedonía, N Greece
Potentia *see* Potenza
107 M18 **Potenza** *anc.* Potentia. Basilicata, S Italy
185 A24 **Poteriteri, Lake** ◎ South Island, New Zealand
104 M2 **Potes** Cantabria, N Spain
Potgietersrus *see* Mokopane
25 S12 **Poth** Texas, SW USA
32 J9 **Potholes Reservoir** ⊠ Washington, NW USA
137 Q9 **P'ot'i** W Georgia
77 X13 **Potiskum** Yobe, NE Nigeria
Potkozarje *see* Ivanjska
32 M9 **Potlatch** Idaho, NW USA
33 N9 **Pot Mountain** ▲ Idaho, NW USA
113 H14 **Potoci** ◈ Federacija Bosna I Hercegovina, S Bosnia and Herzegovina
21 V3 **Potomac River** ∼ NE USA
57 L20 **Potosí** Potosí, S Bolivia
42 H9 **Potosí** Chinandega, NW Nicaragua
27 W6 **Potosi** Missouri, C USA
57 K21 **Potosí** ◈ *department* SW Bolivia
62 H7 **Potrerillos** Atacama, N Chile
42 H5 **Potrerillos** Cortés, NW Honduras
62 H8 **Potro, Cerro del** ▲ N Chile
100 N12 **Potsdam** Brandenburg, NE Germany
18 J7 **Potsdam** New York, NE USA
109 X5 **Pottendorf** Niederösterreich, E Austria
109 X5 **Pottenstein** Niederösterreich, E Austria
18 I15 **Pottstown** Pennsylvania, NE USA
18 H14 **Pottsville** Pennsylvania, NE USA
155 L25 **Pottuvil** Eastern Province, SE Sri Lanka
149 U6 **Potwar Plateau** *plateau* NE Pakistan
102 J7 **Pouancé** Maine-et-Loire, W France
15 R6 **Poulin de Courval, Lac** ◎ Québec, SE Canada
18 L9 **Poultney** Vermont, NE USA
187 O16 **Poum** Province Nord, W New Caledonia
59 L21 **Pouso Alegre** Minas Gerais, NE Brazil
192 I16 **Poutasi** Upolu, SE Samoa
167 R12 **Poŭthĭsăt** *prev.* Pursat. Poŭthĭsăt, W Cambodia
167 R12 **Poŭthĭsăt, Stœng** *prev.* Pursat. ∼ W Cambodia
102 J9 **Pouzauges** Vendée, NW France
Po, Valle del *see* Po Valley
106 F8 **Po Valley** *It.* Valle del Po. *valley* N Italy
111 I19 **Považská Bystrica** *Ger.* Waagbistritz, *Hung.* Vágbeszterce. Trenčiansky Kraj, W Slovakia
124 J10 **Povenets** Respublika Kareliya, NW Russian Federation
184 Q9 **Poverty Bay** *inlet* North Island, New Zealand
112 K12 **Povlen** ▲▲ W Serbia
104 G6 **Póvoa de Varzim** Porto, NW Portugal
127 N8 **Povorino** Voronezhskaya Oblast', W Russian Federation
Povungnituk *see* Puvirnituq
12 J3 **Povungnituk, Rivière de** ∼ Québec, NE Canada
14 H11 **Powassan** Ontario, S Canada
35 U17 **Poway** California, W USA
33 W14 **Powder River** Wyoming, C USA
33 Y10 **Powder River** ∼ Montana/Wyoming, NW USA
32 L12 **Powder River** ∼ Oregon, NW USA
33 W13 **Powder River Pass** *pass* Wyoming, C USA
33 U12 **Powell** Wyoming, C USA
65 I22 **Powell Basin** *undersea feature* NW Weddell Sea
36 M8 **Powell, Lake** ◎ Utah, W USA
37 R4 **Powell, Mount** ▲ Colorado, C USA
10 L17 **Powell River** British Columbia, SW Canada
31 N5 **Powers** Michigan, N USA
28 K2 **Powers Lake** North Dakota, N USA
21 V6 **Powhatan** Virginia, NE USA
31 V13 **Powhatan Point** Ohio, N USA
97 J20 **Powys** *cultural region* E Wales, UK
187 P17 **Poya** Province Nord, C New Caledonia
161 P10 **Poyang Hu** ◎ S China
30 L7 **Poygan, Lake** ◎ Wisconsin, N USA
109 Y2 **Poysdorf** Niederösterreich, NE Austria
112 N11 **Požarevac** *Ger.* Passarowitz. Serbia, NE Serbia
41 Q13 **Poza Rica** *var.* Poza Rica de Hidalgo. Veracruz-Llave, E Mexico
Poza Rica de Hidalgo *see* Poza Rica
112 L13 **Požega** *prev.* Slavonska Požega, *Ger.* Poschega, *Hung.* Pozsega. Požega-Slavonija, NE Croatia
112 H9 **Požega-Slavonija** *off.* Požeško-Slavonska Županija. ◈ *province* NE Croatia
Požeško-Slavonska Županija *see* Požega-Slavonija
125 U13 **Pozhva** Permskaya Oblast', NW Russian Federation
110 G11 **Poznań** *Ger.* Posen, Posnania. Wielkolpolskie, C Poland
105 O13 **Pozo Alcón** Andalucía, S Spain
62 H3 **Pozo Almonte** Tarapacá, N Chile
104 L12 **Pozoblanco** Andalucía, S Spain
105 Q11 **Pozo Cañada** Castilla-La Mancha, C Spain
62 N5 **Pozo Colorado** Presidente Hayes, C Paraguay
63 J20 **Pozos, Punta** *headland* S Argentina
Pozsega *see* Požega
Pozsony *see* Bratislava
55 N5 **Pozuelos** Anzoátegui, NE Venezuela
107 L26 **Pozzallo** Sicilia, Italy, C Mediterranean Sea
107 K17 **Pozzuoli** *anc.* Puteoli. Campania, S Italy
77 P17 **Pra** ∼ S Ghana
111 C19 **Prachatice** *Ger.* Prachatitz. Jihočeský Kraj, S Czech Republic
Prachatitz *see* Prachatice
167 P11 **Prachin Buri** *var.* Prachinburi. Prachin Buri, C Thailand
Prachinburi *see* Prachin Buri
Prachuab Girikhand *see* Prachuap Khiri Khan
167 O12 **Prachuap Khiri Khan** *var.* Prachuab Girikhand. Prachuap Khiri Khan, SW Thailand
111 H16 **Praděd** *Ger.* Altvater. ▲ NE Czech Republic
54 D11 **Pradera** Valle del Cauca, SW Colombia
103 O17 **Prades** Pyrénées-Orientales, S France
59 O19 **Prado** Bahia, SE Brazil
54 E11 **Prado** Tolima, C Colombia
Prado del Ganso *see* Goose Green
Prae *see* Phrae
95 I24 **Præstø** Storstrøm, SE Denmark
Prag/Praga/Prague *see* Praha
27 O10 **Prague** Oklahoma, C USA
111 D16 **Praha** *Eng.* Prague, *Ger.* Prag, *Pol.* Praga. ● (Czech Republic) Středočeský Kraj, NW Czech Republic
116 J13 **Prahova** ◈ *county* SE Romania
116 J13 **Prahova** ∼ S Romania
76 E10 **Praia** ● (Cape Verde) Santiago, S Cape Verde
83 M21 **Praia do Bilene** Gaza, S Mozambique
83 M20 **Praia do Xai-Xai** Gaza, S Mozambique
116 J10 **Praid** *Hung.* Parajd. Harghita, C Romania
26 J3 **Prairie Dog Creek** ∼ Kansas/Nebraska, C USA
30 J9 **Prairie du Chien** Wisconsin, N USA
27 S9 **Prairie Grove** Arkansas, C USA
31 P10 **Prairie River** ∼ Michigan, N USA
Prairie State *see* Illinois
25 V11 **Prairie View** Texas, SW USA
167 Q10 **Prakhon Chai** Buri Ram, E Thailand
109 R4 **Pram** ∼ N Austria
109 S4 **Prambachkirchen** Oberösterreich, N Austria
118 H2 **Prangli** *island* N Estonia
154 J13 **Prānhita** ∼ C India
172 I15 **Praslin** *island* Inner Islands, NE Seychelles
115 O23 **Prasonísi, Ákrotírio** *cape* Ródos, Dodekánisa, Greece, Aegean Sea
111 I14 **Praszka** Opolskie, S Poland
Pratas Island *see* Tungsha Tao
119 M18 **Pratasy** *Rus.* Protasy. Homyel'skaya Voblasts', SE Belarus
167 Q10 **Prathai** Nakhon Ratchasima, E Thailand
Prathet Thai *see* Thailand
Prathum Thani *see* Pathum Thani
63 F21 **Prat, Isla** *island* S Chile
106 G11 **Prato** Toscana, C Italy
103 O17 **Prats-de-Mollo-la-Preste** Pyrénées-Orientales, S France
26 L6 **Pratt** Kansas, C USA
108 E6 **Pratteln** Basel-Land, NW Switzerland
193 O2 **Pratt Seamount** *undersea feature* N Pacific Ocean
23 P5 **Prattville** Alabama, S USA
Praust *see* Pruszcz Gdański
114 M7 **Pravda** *prev.* Dogrular. Silistra, NE Bulgaria
119 B14 **Pravdinsk** *Ger.* Friedland. Kaliningradskaya Oblast', W Russian Federation
104 K2 **Pravia** Asturias, N Spain
118 L12 **Prazaroki** *Rus.* Prozoroki. Vitsyebskaya Voblasts', N Belarus
Prázsmár *see* Prejmer
167 S11 **Preăh Vihéar** Preăh Vihéar, N Cambodia
116 J12 **Predeal** *Hung.* Predeál. Brașov, C Romania
109 S8 **Predlitz** Steiermark, SE Austria
9 V15 **Preeceville** Saskatchewan, S Canada
Preenkuln *see* Priekule
102 K6 **Pré-en-Pail** Mayenne, NW France
109 T4 **Pregarten** Oberösterreich, N Austria
54 H7 **Pregonero** Táchira, NW Venezuela
118 J10 **Preiļi** *Ger.* Preli. Preiļi, SE Latvia
116 J12 **Prejmer** *Ger.* Tartlau, *Hung.* Prázsmár. Brașov, S Romania
113 J16 **Prekornica** ▲▲ C Montenegro
Preli *see* Preiļi
Prëmet *see* Përmet
100 M12 **Premnitz** Brandenburg, NE Germany
25 S15 **Premont** Texas, SW USA
113 H14 **Prenj** ▲▲ S Bosnia and Herzegovina
Prenjas/Prenjasi *see* Përrenjas
22 L7 **Prentiss** Mississippi, S USA
Preny *see* Prienai
100 O10 **Prenzlau** Brandenburg, NE Germany
123 N11 **Preobrazhenka** Irkutskaya Oblast', C Russian Federation
166 J9 **Preparis Island** *island* SW Burma (Myanmar)
Prerau *see* Přerov
111 H18 **Přerov** *Ger.* Prerau. Olomoucký Kraj, E Czech Republic
Preschau *see* Prešov
14 M14 **Prescott** Ontario, SE Canada
36 K12 **Prescott** Arizona, SW USA
27 T13 **Prescott** Arkansas, C USA
32 L10 **Prescott** Washington, NW USA
30 H6 **Prescott** Wisconsin, N USA
185 A24 **Preservation Inlet** *inlet* South Island, New Zealand
112 O7 **Preševo** Serbia, SE Serbia
29 N10 **Presho** South Dakota, N USA
58 M13 **Presidente Dutra** Maranhão, E Brazil
60 I8 **Presidente Epitácio** São Paulo, S Brazil
62 N5 **Presidente Hayes** *off.* Departamento de Presidente Hayes. ◈ *department* C Paraguay
Presidente Hayes, Departamento de *see* Presidente Hayes
60 I9 **Presidente Prudente** São Paulo, S Brazil
Presidente Stroessner *see* Ciudad del Este
Presidente Vargas *see* Itabira
60 I8 **Presidente Venceslau** São Paulo, S Brazil
193 O10 **President Thiers Seamount** *undersea feature* C Pacific Ocean
24 J11 **Presidio** Texas, SW USA
Preslav *see* Veliki Preslav
111 M19 **Prešov** *var.* Preschau, *Ger.* Eperies, *Hung.* Eperjes. Prešovský Kraj, E Slovakia
111 M19 **Prešovský Kraj** ◈ *region* E Slovakia
113 N20 **Prespa, Lake** *Alb.* Liqen i Prespës, *Gk.* Límni Megáli Préspa, Límni Prespa, *Mac.* Prespansko Ezero, *Serb.* Prespansko Jezero. ◎ SE Europe
Prespa, Limni/Prespansko Ezero/Prespansko Jezero/Prespës, Liqen i *see* Prespa, Lake
19 S2 **Presque Isle** Maine, NE USA
18 B11 **Presque Isle** *headland* Pennsylvania, NE USA
Pressburg *see* Bratislava
77 P17 **Prestea** SW Ghana
111 B17 **Přeštice** *Ger.* Pschestitz. Plzeňský Kraj, W Czech Republic
97 K17 **Preston** NW England, UK
23 S6 **Preston** Georgia, SE USA
33 R16 **Preston** Idaho, NW USA
29 Z13 **Preston** Iowa, C USA
29 X11 **Preston** Minnesota, N USA
21 O6 **Prestonsburg** Kentucky, S USA
96 I13 **Prestwick** W Scotland, UK
Pretoria *see* Tshwane
Pretoria-Witwatersrand-Vereeniging *see* Gauteng
Pretusha *see* Pretushë
113 M21 **Pretushë** *var.* Pretusha. Korçë, SE Albania
Preussisch Eylau *see* Bagrationovsk
Preußisch Holland *see* Pasłęk
Preussisch-Stargard *see* Starogard Gdański
115 C17 **Préveza** Ípeiros, W Greece
37 V3 **Prewitt Reservoir** ⊠ Colorado, C USA
167 S13 **Prey Vêng** Prey Vêng, S Cambodia
144 M12 **Priaral'skiye Karakumy, Peski** *desert* SW Kazakhstan
123 P14 **Priargunsk** Chitinskaya Oblast', S Russian Federation
38 K14 **Pribilof Islands** *island group* Alaska, USA
113 K14 **Priboj** Serbia, W Serbia
111 C17 **Příbram** *Ger.* Pibrans. Středočeský Kraj, W Czech Republic
36 M4 **Price** Utah, W USA
37 N5 **Price River** ∼ Utah, W USA
23 N8 **Prichard** Alabama, S USA
25 R8 **Priddy** Texas, SW USA
105 P8 **Priego** Castilla-La Mancha, C Spain
104 M14 **Priego de Córdoba** Andalucía, S Spain
118 C10 **Priekule** *Ger.* Preenkuln. Liepāja, SW Latvia
118 C12 **Priekulė** *Ger.* Prökuls. Klaipėda, W Lithuania
119 F14 **Prienai** *Pol.* Preny. Kaunas, S Lithuania
83 G23 **Prieska** Northern Cape, C South Africa
32 M7 **Priest Lake** ⊠ Idaho, NW USA
32 M7 **Priest River** Idaho, NW USA
104 M3 **Prieta, Peña** ▲ N Spain
40 J10 **Prieto, Cerro** ▲ C Mexico
111 J19 **Prievidza** *var.* Priewitz, *Ger.* Priwitz, *Hung.* Privigye. Trenčiansky Kraj, W Slovakia
Priewitz *see* Prievidza
112 F10 **Prijedor** ◈ Republika Srpska, NW Bosnia and Herzegovina
113 K14 **Prijepolje** Serbia, W Serbia
Prikaspiyskaya Nizmennost' *see* Caspian Depression
113 O19 **Prilep** *Turk.* Perlepe. S FYR Macedonia
108 B9 **Prilly** Vaud, SW Switzerland
Priluki *see* Pryluky
62 L10 **Primero, Río** ∼ C Argentina
29 S12 **Primghar** Iowa, C USA
112 B9 **Primorje-Gorski Kotar** *off.* Primorsko-Goranska Županija. ◈ *province* NW Croatia
118 A13 **Primorsk** *Ger.* Fischhausen. Kaliningradskaya Oblast', W Russian Federation
124 G12 **Primorsk** *Fin.* Koivisto. Leningradskaya Oblast', NW Russian Federation
123 S14 **Primorskiy Kray** *prev. Eng.* Maritime Territory. ◈ *territory* SE Russian Federation
114 N10 **Primorsko** *prev.* Keupriya. Burgas, E Bulgaria
126 K13 **Primorsko-Akhtarsk** Krasnodarskiy Kray, SW Russian Federation
Primorsko-Goranska Županija *see* Primorje-Gorski Kotar
Primorsk/Primorskoye *see* Prymors'k
117 U13 **Primors'kyy** Respublika Krym, S Ukraine
113 D14 **Primošten** Šibenik-Knin, S Croatia
9 R13 **Primrose Lake** ◎ Saskatchewan, C Canada
9 T14 **Prince Albert** Saskatchewan, S Canada
83 G25 **Prince Albert** Western Cape, SW South Africa
8 J5 **Prince Albert Peninsula** *peninsula* Victoria Island, Northwest Territories, NW Canada
8 J6 **Prince Albert Sound** *inlet* Northwest Territories, N Canada
9 P6 **Prince Charles Island** *island* Nunavut, NE Canada
195 W6 **Prince Charles Mountains** ▲▲ Antarctica
Prince-Édouard, Île-du *see* Prince Edward Island
172 M13 **Prince Edward Fracture Zone** *tectonic feature* SW Indian Ocean
13 P14 **Prince Edward Island** *Fr.* Île-du Prince-Édouard. ◈ *province* SE Canada
13 Q14 **Prince Edward Island** *Fr.* Île-du Prince-Édouard. *island* SE Canada
173 M12 **Prince Edward Islands** *island group* S South Africa
21 X4 **Prince Frederick** Maryland, NE USA
10 M14 **Prince George** British Columbia, SW Canada
21 W6 **Prince George** Virginia, NE USA
197 O8 **Prince Gustaf Adolf Sea** *sea* Nunavut, N Canada
197 Q3 **Prince of Wales, Cape** *headland* Alaska, USA
181 V1 **Prince of Wales Island** *island* Queensland, E Australia
8 L5 **Prince of Wales Island** *island* Queen Elizabeth Islands, Nunavut, NW Canada
39 Y14 **Prince of Wales Island** *island* Alexander Archipelago, Alaska, USA
Prince of Wales Island *see* Pinang, Pulau
8 J5 **Prince of Wales Strait** *strait* Northwest Territories, N Canada
197 O8 **Prince Patrick Island** *island* Parry Islands, Northwest Territories, NW Canada
9 N5 **Prince Regent Inlet** *channel* Nunavut, N Canada
10 J13 **Prince Rupert** British Columbia, SW Canada
Prince's Island *see* Príncipe
21 Y5 **Princess Anne** Maryland, NE USA
195 R1 **Princess Astrid Kyst** *physical region* Antarctica
181 W2 **Princess Charlotte Bay** *bay* Queensland, NE Australia
195 W7 **Princess Elizabeth Land** *physical region* Antarctica
10 J14 **Princess Royal Island** *island* British Columbia, SW Canada
45 U15 **Princes Town** Trinidad, Trinidad and Tobago
9 N17 **Princeton** British Columbia, SW Canada
30 L11 **Princeton** Illinois, N USA
31 N16 **Princeton** Indiana, N USA
29 Z14 **Princeton** Iowa, C USA
20 H7 **Princeton** Kentucky, S USA
29 V8 **Princeton** Minnesota, N USA
27 S1 **Princeton** Missouri, C USA
18 J15 **Princeton** New Jersey, NE USA
21 R6 **Princeton** West Virginia, NE USA
39 S12 **Prince William Sound** *inlet* Alaska, USA
67 P9 **Príncipe** *var.* Príncipe Island, *Eng.* Prince's Island. *island* N Sao Tome and Principe
Príncipe Island *see* Príncipe
32 I13 **Prineville** Oregon, NW USA
28 J11 **Pringle** South Dakota, N USA
25 N1 **Pringle** Texas, SW USA
99 H14 **Prinsenbeek** Noord-Brabant, S Netherlands
98 L6 **Prinses Margriet Kanaal** *canal* N Netherlands
195 T2 **Prinsesse Ragnhild Kyst** *physical region* Antarctica
195 U2 **Prins Harald Kyst** *physical region* Antarctica
92 N2 **Prins Karls Forland** *island* W Svalbard
43 N8 **Prinzapolka** Región Autónoma Atlántico Norte, NE Nicaragua
42 L8 **Prinzapolka, Río** ∼ NE Nicaragua
122 H9 **Priob'ye** Khanty-Mansiyskiy Avtonomnyy Okrug, N Russian Federation
104 H1 **Prior, Cabo** *cape* NW Spain
29 V9 **Prior Lake** Minnesota, N USA
124 H11 **Priozersk** *Fin.* Käkisalmi. Leningradskaya Oblast', NW Russian Federation
119 J20 **Pripet** *Bel.* Prypyats', *Ukr.* Pryp"yat'. ∼ Belarus/Ukraine
119 J20 **Pripet Marshes** *forested and swampy region* Belarus/Ukraine
Prishtinë *see* Priština
126 J8 **Pristen'** Kurskaya Oblast', W Russian Federation
113 N16 **Priština** *Alb.* Prishtinë. Kosovo, S Serbia
100 M10 **Pritzwalk** Brandenburg, NE Germany
103 R13 **Privas** Ardèche, E France
107 I16 **Priverno** Lazio, C Italy
Privigye *see* Prievidza
112 C12 **Privlaka** Zadar, SW Croatia
124 M15 **Privolzhsk** Ivanovskaya Oblast', NW Russian Federation
127 P7 **Privolzhskaya Vozvyshennost'** *var.* Volga Uplands. ▲▲ W Russian Federation
127 P8 **Privolzhskoye** Saratovskaya Oblast', W Russian Federation
Priwitz *see* Prievidza
127 N13 **Priyutnoye** Respublika Kalmykiya, SW Russian Federation
113 M17 **Prizren** *Alb.* Prizreni. Kosovo, S Serbia
Prizreni *see* Prizren
107 I24 **Prizzi** Sicilia, Italy, C Mediterranean Sea
113 P18 **Probištip** NE FYR Macedonia
169 S16 **Probolinggo** Jawa, C Indonesia
Probstberg *see* Wyszków
111 F14 **Prochowice** *Ger.* Parchwitz. Dolnośląskie, SW Poland
29 W5 **Proctor** Minnesota, N USA
25 R8 **Proctor** Texas, SW USA
25 R8 **Proctor Lake** ⊠ Texas, SW USA
155 I18 **Proddatūr** Andhra Pradesh, E India
104 H9 **Proença-a-Nova** *var.* Proença a Nova. Castelo Branco, C Portugal
Proença a Nova *see* Proença-a-Nova
99 I21 **Profondeville** Namur, SE Belgium
41 W11 **Progreso** Yucatán, SE Mexico
123 R14 **Progress** Amurskaya Oblast', SE Russian Federation
127 O15 **Prokhladnyy** Kabardino-Balkarskaya Respublika, SW Russian Federation
Prokletije *see* North Albanian Alps
Prökuls *see* Priekulė
113 O15 **Prokuplje** Serbia, SE Serbia
124 H14 **Proletariy** Novgorodskaya Oblast', W Russian Federation
126 M12 **Proletarsk** Rostovskaya Oblast', SW Russian Federation
126 J8 **Proletarskiy** Belgorodskaya Oblast', W Russian Federation
166 L7 **Prome** *var.* Pyè. Pegu, C Burma (Myanmar)
60 J8 **Promissão** São Paulo, S Brazil
60 J8 **Promissão, Represa de** ⊠ S Brazil
125 V4 **Promyshlennyy** Respublika Komi, NW Russian Federation
119 O16 **Pronya** ∼ E Belarus
10 M11 **Prophet River** British Columbia, W Canada
30 K11 **Prophetstown** Illinois, N USA
Propinsi Kepulauan Riau *see* Kepulauan Riau
59 P16 **Propriá** Sergipe, E Brazil
103 X16 **Propriano** Corse, France, C Mediterranean Sea
Prościejów *see* Prostějov
Proskurov *see* Khmel'nyts'kyy
114 H12 **Prosotsáni** Anatolikí Makedonía kai Thráki, NE Greece
171 Q7 **Prosperidad** Mindanao, S Philippines
32 J10 **Prosser** Washington, NW USA
Prossnitz *see* Prostějov
111 G18 **Prostějov** *Ger.* Prossnitz, *Pol.* Prościejów. Olomoucký Kraj, E Czech Republic
117 V8 **Prosyana** Dnipropetrovs'ka Oblast', E Ukraine
111 L16 **Proszowice** Małopolskie, S Poland
Protasy *see* Pratasy
172 J11 **Protea Seamount** *undersea feature* SW Indian Ocean
115 D21 **Próti** *island* S Greece
114 N8 **Provadiya** Varna, E Bulgaria
103 T14 **Provence** *cultural region* SE France
103 S15 **Provence** *prev.* Marseille-Marignane. ✕ (Marseille) Bouches-du-Rhône, SE France
103 T14 **Provence-Alpes-Côte d'Azur** ◈ *region* SE France
20 H6 **Providence** Kentucky, S USA
19 N12 **Providence** *state capital* Rhode Island, NE USA
36 L1 **Providence** Utah, W USA
Providence *see* Fort Providence
Providence *see* Providence Atoll
67 X10 **Providence Atoll** *var.* Providence. *atoll* S Seychelles
14 D12 **Providence Bay** Manitoulin Island, Ontario, S Canada
23 R6 **Providence Canyon** *valley* Alabama/Georgia, S USA
22 I5 **Providence, Lake** ◎ Louisiana, S USA
35 X13 **Providence Mountains** ▲▲ California, W USA
44 L6 **Providenciales** *island* W Turks and Caicos Islands
19 Q12 **Provincetown** Massachusetts, NE USA
103 P5 **Provins** Seine-et-Marne, N France

◆ Country ● Country Capital ◇ Dependent Territory ○ Dependent Territory Capital ◈ Administrative Regions ✕ International Airport ▲ Mountain ▲▲ Mountain Range ⛰ Volcano ∼ River ◎ Lake ⊠ Reservoir

Provo – Qala Āhangarān

36 L3 **Provo** Utah, W USA
9 R15 **Provost** Alberta, SW Canada
112 G13 **Prozor** ◐ Federacija Bosna I Hercegovina, SW Bosnia and Herzegovina
Prozoroki *see* Prazaroki
60 I11 **Prudentópolis** Paraná, S Brazil
39 R5 **Prudhoe Bay** Alaska, USA
39 R4 **Prudhoe Bay** *bay* Alaska, USA
111 H15 **Prudnik** *Ger.* Neustadt, Neustadt in Oberschlesien. Opole, SW Poland
119 J16 **Prudy** *Rus.* Prudy. Minskaya Voblasts', C Belarus
101 D18 **Prüm** Rheinland-Pfalz, W Germany
101 D18 **Prüm** ≈ W Germany
Prusa *see* Bursa
110 J7 **Pruszcz Gdański** *Ger.* Praust. Pomorskie, N Poland
110 M12 **Pruszków** *Ger.* Kaltdorf. Mazowieckie, C Poland
116 K8 **Prut** *Ger.* Pruth. ≈ E Europe
Pruth *see* Prut
108 L8 **Prutz** Tirol, W Austria
Pružana *see* Pruzhany
119 G19 **Pruzhany** *Pol.* Prużana. Brestskaya Voblasts', SW Belarus
124 I11 **Pryazha** Respublika Kareliya, NW Russian Federation
117 U10 **Pryazovs'ke** Zaporiz'ka Oblast', SE Ukraine
Prychornomor'ska Nyzovyna *see* Black Sea Lowland
Prydniprovs'ka Nyzovyna/ Prydnyaprowskaya Nizina *see* Dnieper Lowland
195 Y7 **Prydz Bay** *bay* Antarctica
117 R4 **Pryluky** *Rus.* Priluki. Chernihivs'ka Oblast', NE Ukraine
117 V10 **Prymors'k** *Rus.* Primorsk; *prev.* Primorskoye. Zaporiz'ka Oblast', SE Ukraine
27 Q9 **Pryor** Oklahoma, C USA
33 U11 **Pryor Creek** ≈ Montana, NW USA
Pryp"yat'/Prypyats' *see* Pripet
110 M10 **Przasnysz** Mazowieckie, C Poland
111 K14 **Przedbórz** Lodzkie, S Poland
111 P17 **Przemyśl** *Rus.* Peremyshl. Podkarpackie, C Poland
111 O16 **Przeworsk** Podkarpackie, SE Poland
Przheval'sk *see* Karakol
110 L13 **Przysucha** Mazowieckie, SE Poland
115 H18 **Psachná** *var.* Psahna, Psakhná. Évvoia, C Greece
Psahna/Psakhná *see* Psachná
115 K18 **Psará** *island* E Greece
115 I16 **Psathoúra** *island* Vóreioi Sporádes, Greece, Aegean Sea
Pschestitz *see* Přeštice
Psein Lora *see* Pishin Lora
117 S5 **Psël** ≈ Russian Federation/Ukraine
115 M21 **Psérimos** *island* Dodekánisa, Greece, Aegean Sea
Pseyn Bowr *see* Pishin Lora
Pskem *see* Piskom
147 R8 **Pskemskiy Khrebet** *Uzb.* Piskom Tizmasi. ▲▲ Kyrgyzstan/Uzbekistan
124 F14 **Pskov** *Ger.* Pleskau, *Latv.* Pleskava. Pskovskaya Oblast', W Russian Federation
118 K6 **Pskov, Lake** *Est.* Pihkva Järv, *Ger.* Pleskauer See, *Rus.* Pskovskoye Ozero. ◎ Estonia/Russian Federation
124 F15 **Pskovskaya Oblast'** ◐ *province* W Russian Federation
Pskovskoye Ozero *see* Pskov, Lake
112 G9 **Psunj** ▲▲ NE Croatia
111 J17 **Pszczyna** *Ger.* Pless. Śląskie, S Poland
Ptačnik/Ptacsnik *see* Vtáčnik
115 D17 **Ptéri** ▲ C Greece
Ptich' *see* Ptsich
115 E14 **Ptolemaïda** *prev.* Ptolemaïs. Dytikí Makedonía, N Greece
Ptolemaïs *see* Ptolemaïda, Greece
Ptolemaïs *see* 'Akko, Israel
119 M19 **Ptsich** *Rus.* Ptich'. Homyel'skaya Voblasts', SE Belarus
119 M18 **Ptsich** *Rus.* Ptich'. ≈ SE Belarus
109 X10 **Ptuj** *Ger.* Pettau; *anc.* Poetovio. NE Slovenia
61 A23 **Puán** Buenos Aires, E Argentina
192 H15 **Pu'apu'a** Savai'i, C Samoa
192 G15 **Puava, Cape** *cape* Savai'i, NW Samoa
56 F12 **Pucallpa** Ucayali, C Peru
57 J17 **Pucarani** La Paz, NW Bolivia
Pučarevo *see* Novi Travnik
157 U12 **Pucheng** Shaanxi, SE China
160 L6 **Pucheng** *var.* Nanpu. Fujian, C China
125 N16 **Puchezh** Ivanovskaya Oblast', W Russian Federation
111 I19 **Púchov** *Hung.* Puhó. Trenčiansky Kraj, W Slovakia
116 J13 **Pucioasa** Dâmbovița, S Romania
110 I6 **Puck** Pomorskie, N Poland
30 L8 **Puckaway Lake** ◎ Wisconsin, N USA
63 G15 **Pucón** Araucanía, S Chile
93 M14 **Pudasjärvi** Oulu, C Finland
148 L8 **Pūdeh Tal, Shelleh-ye** ≈ SW Afghanistan
127 S1 **Pudem** Udmurtskaya Respublika, NW Russian Federation
Pudewitz *see* Pobiedziska
124 K11 **Pudozh** Respublika Kareliya, NW Russian Federation
97 M17 **Pudsey** N England, UK
Puduchcheri *see* Pondicherry
151 H21 **Pudukkottai** Tamil Nādu, SE India
171 Z13 **Pue** Papua, E Indonesia
41 P14 **Puebla** *var.* Puebla de Zaragoza. Puebla, S Mexico
41 P15 **Puebla** ◐ *state* S Mexico
104 L11 **Puebla de Alcocer** Extremadura, W Spain
Puebla de Don Fabrique *see* Puebla de Don Fadrique
105 P13 **Puebla de Don Fadrique** *var.* Puebla de Don Fabrique. Andalucía, S Spain
104 J11 **Puebla de la Calzada** Extremadura, W Spain
104 J5 **Puebla de Sanabria** Castilla-León, N Spain
Puebla de Trives *see* A Pobla de Trives
Puebla de Zaragoza *see* Puebla
37 T6 **Pueblo** Colorado, C USA
37 N10 **Pueblo Colorado Wash** *valley* Arizona, SW USA
61 C16 **Pueblo Libertador** Corrientes, NE Argentina
40 J10 **Pueblo Nuevo** Durango, C Mexico
42 J8 **Pueblo Nuevo** Estelí, NW Nicaragua
54 J3 **Pueblo Nuevo** Falcón, N Venezuela
42 B6 **Pueblo Nuevo Tiquisate** *var.* Tiquisate. Escuintla, SW Guatemala
41 Q11 **Pueblo Viejo, Laguna de** *lagoon* E Mexico
63 J14 **Puelches** La Pampa, C Argentina
104 L14 **Puente-Genil** Andalucía, S Spain
105 Q3 **Puente la Reina** *Bas.* Gares. Navarra, N Spain
104 L12 **Puente Nuevo, Embalse de** ▣ S Spain
57 D14 **Puente Piedra** Lima, W Peru
160 F14 **Pu'er** *var.* Ning'er. Yunnan, SW China
45 V6 **Puerca, Punta** *headland* E Puerto Rico
37 R12 **Puerco, Rio** ≈ New Mexico, SW USA
57 J17 **Puerto Acosta** La Paz, W Bolivia
63 G19 **Puerto Aisén** Aisén, S Chile
41 R17 **Puerto Ángel** Oaxaca, SE Mexico
Puerto Argentino *see* Stanley
41 T17 **Puerto Arista** Chiapas, SE Mexico
43 O16 **Puerto Armuelles** Chiriquí, SW Panama
Puerto Arrecife *see* Arrecife
54 D14 **Puerto Asís** Putumayo, SW Colombia
54 L9 **Puerto Ayacucho** Amazonas, SW Venezuela
57 C18 **Puerto Ayora** Galapagos Islands, Ecuador, E Pacific Ocean
57 C18 **Puerto Baquerizo Moreno** *var.* Baquerizo Moreno. Galapagos Islands, Ecuador, E Pacific Ocean
42 G4 **Puerto Barrios** Izabal, E Guatemala
Puerto Bello *see* Portobelo
54 F8 **Puerto Berrío** Antioquia, C Colombia
54 F9 **Puerto Boyaca** Boyacá, C Colombia
54 K4 **Puerto Cabello** Carabobo, N Venezuela
43 N7 **Puerto Cabezas** *var.* Bilwi. Región Autónoma Atlántico Norte, NE Nicaragua
54 L9 **Puerto Carreño** Vichada, E Colombia
54 E4 **Puerto Colombia** Atlántico, N Colombia
42 H4 **Puerto Cortés** Cortés, NW Honduras
54 J4 **Puerto Cumarebo** Falcón, N Venezuela
Puerto de Cabras *see* Puerto del Rosario
55 Q5 **Puerto de Hierro** Sucre, NE Venezuela
64 O11 **Puerto de la Cruz** Tenerife, Islas Canarias, Spain, NE Atlantic Ocean
64 Q11 **Puerto del Rosario** *var.* Puerto de Cabras. Fuerteventura, Islas Canarias, Spain, NE Atlantic Ocean
63 J20 **Puerto Deseado** Santa Cruz, SE Argentina
40 F8 **Puerto Escondido** Baja California Sur, W Mexico
41 R17 **Puerto Escondido** Oaxaca, SE Mexico
60 G12 **Puerto Esperanza** Misiones, NE Argentina
56 D6 **Puerto Francisco de Orellana** *var.* Coca. Orellana, N Ecuador
54 H10 **Puerto Gaitán** Meta, C Colombia
Puerto Gallegos *see* Río Gallegos
60 G12 **Puerto Iguazú** Misiones, NE Argentina
56 F12 **Puerto Inca** Huánuco, N Peru
54 L11 **Puerto Inírida** *var.* Obando. Guainía, E Colombia
42 K13 **Puerto Jesús** Guanacaste, NW Costa Rica
41 Z11 **Puerto Juárez** Quintana Roo, SE Mexico
55 N5 **Puerto La Cruz** Anzoátegui, NE Venezuela
54 E14 **Puerto Leguízamo** Putumayo, S Colombia
43 N5 **Puerto Lempira** Gracias a Dios, E Honduras
Puerto Libertad *see* La Libertad
54 I11 **Puerto Limón** Meta, E Colombia
54 D13 **Puerto Limón** Putumayo, SW Colombia
Puerto Limón *see* Limón
105 N11 **Puertollano** Castilla-La Mancha, C Spain
63 K17 **Puerto Lobos** Chubut, SE Argentina
54 I3 **Puerto López** La Guajira, N Colombia
105 Q14 **Puerto Lumbreras** Murcia, SE Spain
41 V17 **Puerto Madero** Chiapas, SE Mexico
63 K17 **Puerto Madryn** Chubut, S Argentina
Puerto Magdalena *see* Bahía Magdalena
57 J15 **Puerto Maldonado** Madre de Dios, E Peru
Puerto Masachapa *see* Masachapa
Puerto México *see* Coatzacoalcos
63 G17 **Puerto Montt** Los Lagos, C Chile
41 Z12 **Puerto Morelos** Quintana Roo, SE Mexico
54 L10 **Puerto Nariño** Vichada, E Colombia
63 H23 **Puerto Natales** Magallanes, S Chile
43 X15 **Puerto Obaldía** San Blas, NE Panama
44 H6 **Puerto Padre** Las Tunas, E Cuba
54 L9 **Puerto Páez** Apure, C Venezuela
40 E3 **Puerto Peñasco** Sonora, NW Mexico
55 N5 **Puerto Píritu** Anzoátegui, NE Venezuela
45 N8 **Puerto Plata** *var.* San Felipe de Puerto Plata. N Dominican Republic
45 N8 **Puerto Plata** ✈ N Dominican Republic
Puerto Presidente Stroessner *see* Ciudad del Este
171 N6 **Puerto Princesa** *off.* Puerto Princesa City. Palawan, W Philippines
Puerto Princesa City *see* Puerto Princesa
Puerto Príncipe *see* Camagüey
Puerto Quellón *see* Quellón
60 F13 **Puerto Rico** Misiones, NE Argentina
57 K14 **Puerto Rico** Pando, N Bolivia
54 E12 **Puerto Rico** Caquetá, S Colombia
45 U5 **Puerto Rico** *off.* Commonwealth of Puerto Rico; *prev.* Porto Rico. ◇ *US commonwealth territory* C West Indies
64 F11 **Puerto Rico** *island* C West Indies
Puerto Rico, Commonwealth of *see* Puerto Rico
64 G11 **Puerto Rico Trench** *undersea feature* NE Caribbean Sea
54 I8 **Puerto Rondón** Arauca, E Colombia
Puerto San José *see* San José
63 J21 **Puerto San Julián** *var.* San Julián. Santa Cruz, SE Argentina
63 I22 **Puerto Santa Cruz** *var.* Santa Cruz. Santa Cruz, SE Argentina
Puerto Sauce *see* Juan L. Lacaze
57 Q20 **Puerto Suárez** Santa Cruz, E Bolivia
54 D13 **Puerto Umbría** Putumayo, SW Colombia
40 J13 **Puerto Vallarta** Jalisco, SW Mexico
63 G16 **Puerto Varas** Los Lagos, C Chile
42 M13 **Puerto Viejo** Heredia, NE Costa Rica
Puertoviejo *see* Portoviejo
57 B18 **Puerto Villamil** *var.* Villamil. Galapagos Islands, Ecuador, E Pacific Ocean
54 F8 **Puerto Wilches** Santander, N Colombia
63 H20 **Pueyrredón, Lago** *var.* Lago Cochrane. ◎ S Argentina
127 R7 **Pugachëv** Saratovskaya Oblast', W Russian Federation
127 T3 **Pugachëvo** Udmurtskaya Respublika, NW Russian Federation
32 H8 **Puget Sound** *sound* Washington, NW USA
107 O17 **Puglia** *var.* Le Puglie, *Eng.* Apulia. ◐ *region* SE Italy
107 N17 **Puglia, Canosa di** *anc.* Canusium. Puglia, SE Italy
118 I6 **Puhja** *Ger.* Kawelecht. Tartumaa, SE Estonia
Puhó *see* Púchov
105 V4 **Puigcerdà** Cataluña, NE Spain
Puigmal *see* Puigmal d'Err
103 N17 **Puigmal d'Err** *var.* Puigmal. ▲ S France
76 I16 **Pujehun** S Sierra Leone
Puka *see* Pukë
185 E20 **Pukaki, Lake** ◎ South Island, New Zealand
38 F10 **Pukalani** Maui, Hawai'i, USA
190 J13 **Pukapuka** *atoll* N Cook Islands
191 X9 **Pukapuka** *atoll* Îles Tuamotu, E French Polynesia
Pukari Neem *see* Purekkari Neem
191 X11 **Pukarua** *var.* Pukaruha. *atoll* Îles Tuamotu, E French Polynesia
Pukaruha *see* Pukarua
14 A7 **Pukaskwa** ≈ Ontario, S Canada
9 V15 **Pukatawagan** Manitoba, C Canada
191 X16 **Pukatikei, Maunga** ⛰ Easter Island, Chile, E Pacific Ocean
182 C1 **Pukatja** *var.* Ernabella. South Australia
163 Y12 **Pukch'ŏng** E North Korea
113 L18 **Pukë** *var.* Puka. Shkodër, N Albania
184 L6 **Pukekohe** Auckland, North Island, New Zealand
184 L7 **Pukemiro** Waikato, North Island, New Zealand
190 D12 **Puke, Mont** ▲ Île Futuna, W Wallis and Futuna
Puket *see* Phuket
185 C20 **Puketeraki Range** ▲▲ South Island, New Zealand
184 N13 **Puketoi Range** ▲▲ North Island, New Zealand
185 F21 **Pukeuri Junction** Otago, South Island, New Zealand
119 L16 **Pukhavichy** *Rus.* Pukhovichi. Minskaya Voblasts', C Belarus
Pukhovichi *see* Pukhavichy
124 M10 **Puksoozero** Arkhangel'skaya Oblast', NW Russian Federation
112 A10 **Pula** *It.* Pola; *prev.* Pulj. Istra, NW Croatia
Pula *see* Nyingchi
163 U14 **Pulandian** *var.* Xinjin. Liaoning, NE China
163 T14 **Pulandian Wan** *bay* NE China
189 O15 **Pulap Atoll** *atoll* Caroline Islands, C Micronesia
18 H9 **Pulaski** New York, NE USA
20 I10 **Pulaski** Tennessee, S USA
21 R7 **Pulaski** Virginia, NE USA
171 Y14 **Pulau, Sungai** ≈ Papua, E Indonesia
110 N13 **Puławy** *Ger.* Neu Amerika. Lubelskie, E Poland
146 I16 **Pulhatyn** *Rus.* Polekhatum; *prev.* Pul'-I-Khatum. Ahal Welaýaty, S Turkmenistan
101 E16 **Pulheim** Nordrhein-Westfalen, W Germany
Pulicat *see* Pālghāt
155 J19 **Pulicat Lake** *lagoon* SE India
Pul'-I-Khatum *see* Pulhatyn
Pul-i-Khumri *see* Pol-e Khomrī
Pul-i-Sefid *see* Pol-e Safīd
Pulj *see* Pula
109 W2 **Pulkau** ≈ NE Austria
93 L15 **Pulkkila** Oulu, C Finland
122 C7 **Pul'kovo** ✈ (Sankt-Peterburg) Leningradskaya Oblast', NW Russian Federation
32 M9 **Pullman** Washington, NW USA
108 B10 **Pully** Vaud, SW Switzerland
40 F7 **Púlpita, Punta** *headland* W Mexico
110 M10 **Pułtusk** Mazowieckie, C Poland
158 H10 **Pulu** Xinjiang Uygur Zizhiqu, W China
137 P13 **Pülümür** Tunceli, E Turkey
189 N16 **Pulusuk** *island* Caroline Islands, C Micronesia
189 N16 **Puluwat Atoll** *atoll* Caroline Islands, C Micronesia
25 N11 **Pumpville** Texas, SW USA
191 P7 **Punaauia** *var.* Hakapehi. Tahiti, W French Polynesia
56 B8 **Puná, Isla** *island* SW Ecuador
185 G16 **Punakaiki** West Coast, South Island, New Zealand
153 T11 **Punakha** C Bhutan
57 L18 **Punata** Cochabamba, C Bolivia
155 E14 **Pune** *prev.* Poona. Mahārāshtra, W India
83 M17 **Pungoè, Rio** *var.* Púnguè, Pungwe. ≈ C Mozambique
21 X10 **Pungo River** ≈ North Carolina, SE USA
Púnguè/Pungwe *see* Pungoè, Rio
79 N19 **Punia** Maniema, E Dem. Rep. Congo
62 H8 **Punilla, Sierra de la** ▲▲ W Argentina
161 P14 **Puning** Guangdong, S China
62 G10 **Punitaqui** Coquimbo, C Chile
152 H8 **Punjab** ◐ *state* NW India
149 T9 **Punjab** *prev.* West Punjab, Western Punjab. ◐ *province* E Pakistan
129 Q9 **Punjab Plains** *plain* N India
93 O17 **Punkaharju** *var.* Punkasalmi. Isä-Suomi, E Finland
Punkasalmi *see* Punkaharju
57 I17 **Puno** Puno, SE Peru
57 H17 **Puno** *off.* Departamento de Puno. ◐ *department* S Peru
Puno, Departamento de *see* Puno
61 B24 **Punta Alta** Buenos Aires, E Argentina
63 H24 **Punta Arenas** *prev.* Magallanes. Magallanes, S Chile
45 T6 **Punta, Cerro de** ▲ C Puerto Rico
43 T15 **Punta Chame** Panamá, C Panama
57 G17 **Punta Colorada** Arequipa, SW Peru
40 F9 **Punta Coyote** Baja California Sur, W Mexico
62 G8 **Punta de Díaz** Atacama, N Chile
61 G20 **Punta del Este** Maldonado, S Uruguay
63 K17 **Punta Delgada** Chubut, SE Argentina
55 O5 **Punta de Mata** Monagas, NE Venezuela
55 O4 **Punta de Piedras** Nueva Esparta, NE Venezuela
42 F4 **Punta Gorda** Toledo, SE Belize
43 N11 **Punta Gorda** Región Autónoma Atlántico Sur, SE Nicaragua
23 W14 **Punta Gorda** Florida, SE USA
42 M11 **Punta Gorda, Río** ≈ SE Nicaragua
62 H6 **Punta Negra, Salar de** *salt lake* N Chile
40 D5 **Punta Prieta** Baja California, NW Mexico
42 L13 **Puntarenas** Puntarenas, W Costa Rica
42 L13 **Puntarenas** *off.* Provincia de Puntarenas. ◐ *province* W Costa Rica
Puntarenas, Provincia de *see* Puntarenas
80 P13 **Puntland** *cultural region* NE Somalia
54 J4 **Punto Fijo** Falcón, N Venezuela
105 S4 **Puntón de Guara** ▲ N Spain
18 D14 **Punxsutawney** Pennsylvania, NE USA
93 M14 **Puolanka** Oulu, C Finland
57 J17 **Pupuya, Nevado** ▲ W Bolivia
Puqi *see* Chibi
57 F16 **Puquio** Ayacucho, S Peru
122 J9 **Pur** ≈ N Russian Federation
186 D7 **Purari** ≈ S Papua New Guinea
27 N11 **Purcell** Oklahoma, C USA
9 O16 **Purcell Mountains** ▲▲ British Columbia, SW Canada
105 P14 **Purchena** Andalucía, S Spain
27 S8 **Purdy** Missouri, C USA
118 I2 **Purekkari Neem** *prev.* Pukari Neem. *headland* N Estonia
37 U7 **Purgatoire River** ≈ Colorado, C USA
Purgstall *see* Purgstall an der Erlauf
109 V5 **Purgstall an der Erlauf** *var.* Purgstall. Niederösterreich, NE Austria
154 O13 **Puri** *var.* Jagannath. Orissa, E India
Puriramya *see* Buriram
109 X4 **Purkersdorf** Niederösterreich, NE Austria
98 I9 **Purmerend** Noord-Holland, C Netherlands
151 G16 **Pūrna** ≈ C India
Purnea *see* Pūrnia
153 R13 **Pūrnia** *prev.* Purnea. Bihār, NE India
Pursat *see* Poŭthĭsăt, Poŭthĭsăt, W Cambodia
Pursat *see* Poŭthĭsăt, Stœ̆ng, W, Cambodia
Purulia *see* Puruliya
150 L13 **Puruliya** *prev.* Purulia. West Bengal, NE India
47 G7 **Purus, Rio** *var.* Río Purús. ≈ Brazil/Peru
186 C9 **Purutu Island** *island* SW Papua New Guinea
93 N17 **Puruvesi** ◎ SE Finland
22 L7 **Purvis** Mississippi, S USA
114 J11 **Pŭrvomay** *prev.* Borisovgrad. Plovdiv, C Bulgaria
169 R16 **Purwodadi** *prev.* Poerwodadi. Jawa, C Indonesia
169 P16 **Purwokerto** *prev.* Poerwokerto. Jawa, C Indonesia
169 P16 **Purworejo** *prev.* Poerworedjo. Jawa, C Indonesia
20 H8 **Puryear** Tennessee, S USA
154 H13 **Pusad** Mahārāshtra, C India
163 Z16 **Pusan** *off.* Pusan-gwangyŏksi, *var.* Busan, *Jap.* Fusan. SE South Korea
Pusan *see* Kim Hae
Pusan-gwangyŏksi *see* Pusan
168 H7 **Pusatgajo, Pegunungan** ▲▲ Sumatera, NW Indonesia
Puschlav *see* Poschiavo
Pushkin *see* Tsarskoye Selo
127 Q8 **Pushkino** Saratovskaya Oblast', W Russian Federation
Pushkino *see* Biläsuvar
111 M22 **Püspökladány** Hajdú-Bihar, E Hungary
118 J3 **Püssi** *Ger.* Isenhof. Ida-Virumaa, NE Estonia
116 I5 **Pustomyty** L'vivs'ka Oblast', W Ukraine
124 F16 **Pustoshka** Pskovskaya Oblast', W Russian Federation
Pusztakalán *see* Călan
167 N1 **Putao** *prev.* Fort Hertz. Kachin State, N Burma (Myanmar)
184 M8 **Putaruru** Waikato, North Island, New Zealand
Puteoli *see* Pozzuoli
161 R12 **Putian** Fujian, SE China
107 O17 **Putignano** Puglia, SE Italy
Puting *see* De'an
Putivl' *see* Putyvl'
41 Q16 **Putla** *var.* Putla de Guerrero. Oaxaca, SE Mexico
Putla de Guerrero *see* Putla
19 N12 **Putnam** Connecticut, NE USA
25 Q7 **Putnam** Texas, SW USA
18 M10 **Putney** Vermont, NE USA
111 L20 **Putnok** Borsod-Abaúj-Zemplén, NE Hungary
Putorana, Gory/Putorana Mountains *see* Putorana, Plato
122 L8 **Putorana, Plato** *var.* Gory Putorana, *Eng.* Putorana Mountains. ▲▲ N Russian Federation
168 K9 **Putrajaya** ● (Malaysia) Kuala Lumpur, Peninsular Malaysia
62 H2 **Putre** Tarapacá, N Chile
155 J24 **Puttalam** North Western Province, W Sri Lanka
155 J24 **Puttalam Lagoon** *lagoon* W Sri Lanka
99 H17 **Putte** Antwerpen, C Belgium
94 E10 **Puttegga** ▲ S Norway
98 K11 **Putten** Gelderland, C Netherlands
100 K7 **Puttgarden** Schleswig-Holstein, N Germany
Puttiala *see* Patiāla
101 D20 **Püttlingen** Saarland, SW Germany
54 D14 **Putumayo** *off.* Intendencia del Putumayo. ◐ *province* S Colombia
Putumayo, Intendencia del *see* Putumayo
48 E7 **Putumayo, Río** *var.* Içá, Rio. ≈ NW South America *see also* Içá, Rio
Putumayo, Río *see* Içá, Rio
169 P11 **Putus, Tanjung** *cape* Borneo, N Indonesia
116 J8 **Putyla** Chernivets'ka Oblast', W Ukraine
117 S3 **Putyvl'** *Rus.* Putivl'. Sums'ka Oblast', NE Ukraine
93 M18 **Puula** ◎ SE Finland
93 N18 **Puumala** Isä-Suomi, E Finland
118 I5 **Puurmani** *Ger.* Talkhof. Jõgevamaa, E Estonia
99 G17 **Puurs** Antwerpen, N Belgium
38 F10 **Pu'u 'Ula'ula** *var.* Red Hill. ▲ Maui, Hawai'i, USA
38 A8 **Pu'uwai** *var* Puuwai. Ni'ihau, Hawai'i, USA
12 J4 **Puvirnituq** *prev.* Povungnituk. Québec, NE Canada
32 H8 **Puyallup** Washington, NW USA
161 O5 **Puyang** Henan, C China
161 R9 **Puyang Jiang** *var.* Tsien Tang. ≈ SE China
103 O11 **Puy-de-Dôme** ◐ *department* C France
103 N15 **Puylaurens** Tarn, S France
102 M13 **Puy-l'Evêque** Lot, S France
103 N17 **Puymorens, Col de** *pass* S France
56 C7 **Puyo** Pastaza, C Ecuador
185 A24 **Puysegur Point** *headland* South Island, New Zealand
148 J8 **Pūzak, Hāmūn-e** *Pash.* Hāmūn-i-Puzak. ◎ SW Afghanistan
Puzak, Hāmūn-i- *see* Pūzak, Hāmūn-e
81 J23 **Pwani** *Eng.* Coast. ◐ *region* E Tanzania
79 O23 **Pweto** Katanga, SE Dem. Rep. Congo
97 I19 **Pwllheli** NW Wales, UK
189 O14 **Pwok** Pohnpei, E Micronesia
122 I9 **Pyakupur** ≈ N Russian Federation
124 M6 **Pyalitsa** Murmanskaya Oblast', NW Russian Federation
124 K10 **Pyal'ma** Respublika Kareliya, NW Russian Federation
Pyandzh *see* Panj
124 I6 **Pyaozero, Ozero** ◎ NW Russian Federation
166 L9 **Pyapon** Irrawaddy, SW Burma (Myanmar)
119 J15 **Pyarshai** *Rus.* Pershay. Minskaya Voblasts', C Belarus
122 K8 **Pyasina** ≈ N Russian Federation
114 I10 **Pyasŭchnik, Yazovir** ▣ C Bulgaria
Pyatikhatki *see* P"yatykhatky
117 S7 **P"yatykhatky** *Rus.* Pyatikhatki. Dnipropetrovs'ka Oblast', E Ukraine
166 M6 **Pyawbwe** Mandalay, C Burma (Myanmar)
127 T3 **Pychas** Udmurtskaya Respublika, NW Russian Federation
Pyè *see* Prome
166 K6 **Pyechin** Chin State, W Burma (Myanmar)
119 G17 **Pyeski** *Rus.* Peski. Hrodzyenskaya Voblasts', W Belarus
119 L19 **Pyetrykaw** *Rus.* Petrikov. Homyel'skaya Voblasts', SE Belarus
93 O17 **Pyhäjärvi** ◎ SE Finland
93 M16 **Pyhäjärvi** ◎ C Finland
93 L15 **Pyhäjoki** Oulu, W Finland
93 L15 **Pyhäjoki** ≈ W Finland
93 M15 **Pyhäntä** Oulu, C Finland
93 M16 **Pyhäsalmi** Oulu, C Finland
93 O17 **Pyhäselkä** ◎ SE Finland
93 M19 **Pyhtää** *Swe.* Pyttis. Etelä-Suomi, S Finland
166 M6 **Pyinmana** (Burma (Myanmar)) Mandalay, C Burma (Myanmar)
115 N24 **Pylés** *var.* Piles. Kárpathos, SE Greece
115 D21 **Pýlos** *var.* Pilos. Pelopónnisos, S Greece
18 B12 **Pymatuning Reservoir** ▣ Ohio/Pennsylvania, NE USA
163 X15 **P'yŏngt'aek** NW South Korea
163 V14 **P'yŏngyang** *var.* P'yŏngyang-si, *Eng.* Pyongyang. ● (North Korea) SW North Korea
P'yŏngyang-si *see* P'yŏngyang
35 Q4 **Pyramid Lake** ◎ Nevada, W USA
37 P15 **Pyramid Mountains** ▲▲ New Mexico, SW USA
37 R5 **Pyramid Peak** ▲ Colorado, C USA
115 D17 **Pyramíva** *var.* Piramiva. ▲ C Greece
Pyrenaei Montes *see* Pyrenees
86 B12 **Pyrenees** *Fr.* Pyrénées, *Sp.* Pirineos; *anc.* Pyrenaei Montes. ▲▲ SW Europe
102 J16 **Pyrénées-Atlantiques** ◐ *department* SW France
103 N17 **Pyrénées-Orientales** ◐ *department* S France
115 L19 **Pyrgí** *var.* Pirgi. Chíos, E Greece
115 D20 **Pýrgos** *var.* Pírgos. Dytikí Ellás, S Greece
Pyritz *see* Pyrzyce
115 E19 **Pýrros** ≈ S Greece
117 R4 **Pyryatyn** *Rus.* Piryatin. Poltavs'ka Oblast', NE Ukraine
110 D9 **Pyrzyce** *Ger.* Pyritz. Zachodnio-pomorskie, NW Poland
124 F15 **Pytalovo** *Latv.* Abrene; *prev.* Jaunlatgale. Pskovskaya Oblast', W Russian Federation
115 M20 **Pythagóreio** *var.* Pithagorio. Sámos, Dodekánisa, Greece, Aegean Sea
14 L11 **Pythonga, Lac** ◎ Québec, SE Canada
Pyttis *see* Pyhtää
166 M7 **Pyu** Pegu, C Burma (Myanmar)
166 M8 **Pyuntaza** Pegu, SW Burma (Myanmar)
153 N11 **Pyuthan** Mid Western, W Nepal
110 H12 **Pyzdry** *Ger.* Peisern. Wielkopolskie, C Poland

Q

138 H13 **Qā' al Jafr** ◎ S Jordan
197 O11 **Qaanaaq** *var.* Qânâq, *Dan.* Thule. ◐ Avannaarsua, N Greenland
Qabanbay *see* Kabanbay
138 G7 **Qabb Eliâs** E Lebanon
Qabil *see* Al Qābil
Qabirri *see* Iori
Qābis *see* Gabès
Qābis, Khalīj *see* Gabès, Golfe de
Qabqa *see* Gonghe
141 S14 **Qabr Hūd** C Yemen
Qacentina *see* Constantine
148 L4 **Qādes** Bādghīs, NW Afghanistan
139 T11 **Qādisīyah** S Iraq
143 O4 **Qā'emshahr** *prev.* 'Alīābad, Shāhī. Māzandarān, N Iran
143 U7 **Qā'en** *var.* Qain, Qāyen. Khorāsān-Razavī, E Iran
141 U13 **Qafa** *spring/well* SW Oman
Qafṣah *see* Gafsa
163 Q12 **Qagan Nur** *var.* Xulun Hobot Qagan, Zhengxiangbai Qi. Nei Mongol Zizhiqu, N China
163 V9 **Qagan Nur** ◎ NE China
163 Q11 **Qagan Nur** ◎ N China
Qagan Us *see* Dulan
158 H13 **Qagcaka** Xizang Zizhiqu, W China
Qagchêng *see* Xiangcheng
Qahremānshahr *see* Kermānshāh
159 Q10 **Qaidam He** ≈ C China
156 L8 **Qaidam Pendi** *basin* C China
Qain *see* Qā'en
Qala Āhangarān *see* Chaghcharān

◆ Country ● Country Capital ◇ Dependent Territory ○ Dependent Territory Capital ◐ Administrative Regions ✈ International Airport ▲ Mountain ▲▲ Mountain Range ⛰ Volcano ≈ River ◎ Lake ▣ Reservoir

139 U3 Qaḷā Diza var. Qal 'at Dizah. NE Iraq
Qal'ah Sālih see Qal'at Ṣāliḥ
147 R13 Qal'aikhum Rus. Kalaikhum. S Tajikistan
Qala Nau see Qal'eh-ye Now
141 V17 Qalansīyah Suqutṛā, W Yemen
Qala Panja see Qal'eh-ye Panjeh
Qala Shāhar see Qal'eh Shahr
149 O8 Qalāt Per. Kalāt. Zābol, S Afghanistan
139 W9 Qal'at Aḥmad E Iraq
141 N11 Qal'at Bishah 'Asīr, SW Saudi Arabia
138 H4 Qal'at Burzay Ḥamāh, W Syria
Qal 'at Dīzah see Qaḷā Diza
139 W9 Qal'at Ḥusayn E Iraq
139 V10 Qal'at Majnūnah S Iraq
139 X11 Qal'at Ṣāliḥ var. Qal'ah Sālih. E Iraq
139 V10 Qal'at Sukkar SE Iraq
Qalba Zhotasy see Kalbinskiy Khrebet
143 Q12 Qal'eh Biābān Fārs, S Iran
149 N4 Qal'eh Shahr Pash. Qala Shāhar. Sar-e Pol, N Afghanistan
148 L4 Qal'eh-ye Now var. Qala Nau. Bādghīs, NW Afghanistan
149 T2 Qal'eh-ye Panjeh var. Qala Panja. Badakhshān, NE Afghanistan
Qamar Bay see Qamar, Ghubbat al
141 U14 Qamar, Ghubbat al Eng. Qamar Bay. bay Oman/Yemen
141 V13 Qamar, Jabal al ▲ SW Oman
147 N12 Qamashi Qashqadaryo Viloyati, S Uzbekistan
Qambar see Kambar
159 R14 Qamdo Xizang Zizhiqu, W China
75 R7 Qamīnis NE Libya
Qamishly see Al Qāmishlī
Qānāq see Qaanaaq
Qandahār see Kandahār
80 Q11 Qandala Bari, NE Somalia
Qandyaghash see Kandyagash
138 L2 Qanṭārī Ar Raqqah, N Syria
Qapiçiğ Dağı see Qazangödağ
158 H5 Qapqal var. Qapqal Xibe Zizhixian. Xinjiang Uygur Zizhiqu, NW China
Qapqal Xibe Zizhixian see Qapqal
Qapshagay Böyeni see Kapchagayskoye Vodokhranilishche
Qapugtang see Zadoi
196 M15 Qaqortoq Dan. Julianehåb. ◆ Kitaa, S Greenland
75 U8 Qāra var. Qārah. NW Egypt
139 T4 Qara Anjīr N Iraq
Qarabāgh see Qarah Bāgh
Qaraböget see Karaboget
Qarabulaq see Karabulak
Qarabutaq see Karabutak
Qaraghandy/Qaraghandy Oblysy see Karaganda
Qaraghayly see Karagayly
139 U4 Qara Gol N Iraq
Qārah see Qāra
148 J4 Qarah Bāgh var. Qarabāgh. Herāt, NW Afghanistan
138 G7 Qaraoun, Lac de var. Buḥayrat al Qir'awn. ◎ S Lebanon
Qaraoy see Karaoy
Qaraqoyyn see Karakoyyn, Ozero
Qara Qum see Garagum
Qarasū see Karasu
Qaratal see Karatal
Qarataū see Karatau, Khrebet, Kazakhstan
Qarataū see Karatau, Zhambyl, Kazakhstan
Qaraton see Karaton
80 P13 Qardho Rus. Kardh, It. Gardo. Bari, N Somalia
142 M6 Qareh Chāy ≈ N Iran
142 K2 Qareh Sū ≈ NW Iran
Qariateine see Al Qaryatayn
Qarkilik see Ruoqiang
147 O13 Qarluq Rus. Karluk. Surkhondaryo Viloyati, S Uzbekistan
147 U12 Qarokül Rus. Karakul'. E Tajikistan
147 T12 Qarokül Rus. Ozero Karakul'. ◎ E Tajikistan
Qarqan see Qiemo
158 K9 Qarqan He ≈ NW China
Qarqannah, Juzur see Kerkenah, Îles de
Qarqaraly see Karkaralinsk
149 O1 Qarqin Jowzjān, N Afghanistan
Qars see Kars
Qarsaqbay see Karsakpay
146 M12 Qarshi Rus. Karshi; prev. Bek-Budi. Qashqadaryo Viloyati, S Uzbekistan
146 L12 Qarshi Cho'li Rus. Karshinskaya Step. grassland S Uzbekistan
146 M13 Qarshi Kanali Rus. Karshinskiy Kanal. canal Turkmenistan/Uzbekistan
Qaryatayn see Al Qaryatayn
Qāsh, Nahr al see Gash
146 M12 Qashqadaryo Viloyati Rus. Kashkadar'inskaya Oblast'. ◆ province S Uzbekistan
Qasigianguit see Qasigiannguit
197 N13 Qasigiannguit var. Qasigianguit, Dan. Christianshåb. ◆ Kitaa, C Greenland
Qāsim, Minṭaqat see Al Qaṣīm
Qasr al Hir Ash Sharqī see Ḥayr ash Sharqī, Qaṣr al
139 P8 Qaṣr 'Amīj C Iraq
139 R9 Qaṣr Darwīshah C Iraq
142 J6 Qaṣr-e Shīrīn Kermānshāhān, W Iran
75 V10 Qaṣr Farāfra W Egypt
Qassim see Al Qaṣīm
141 O11 Qaʿṭabah SW Yemen
138 H7 Qaṭanā var. Katana. Dimashq, S Syria
143 N15 Qatar off. State of Qatar, Ar. Dawlat Qatar. ◆ monarchy SW Asia

Qatar, State of see Qatar
Qatrana see Al Qaṭrānah
143 Q12 Qaṭrūyeh Fārs, S Iran
Qattara Depression/Qaṭṭāra, Munkhafaḍ al see Qaṭṭāra, Monkhafad el
75 U8 Qaṭṭāra, Monkhafad el var. Munkhafaḍ al Qaṭṭārah, Eng. Qattara Depression. desert NW Egypt
Qattinah, Buḥayrat see Ḥimṣ, Buḥayrat
Qaydār see Qeydār
Qāyen see Qā'en
147 Q11 Qayroqqum Rus. Kayrakkum. NW Tajikistan
147 Q10 Qayroqqum, Obanbori Rus. Kayrakkumskoye Vodokhranilishche. ◎ NW Tajikistan
137 V13 Qazangödağ Rus. Gora Kapydzhik, Turk. Qapiçiğ Dağı. ▲ SW Azerbaijan
139 U7 Qazānīyah var. Dhū Shaykh. E Iraq
Qazaqstan/Qazaqstan Respublikasy see Kazakhstan
137 T9 Qazbegi Rus. Kazbegi. NE Georgia
149 P15 Qāzi Ahmad var. Kazi Ahmad. Sind, SE Pakistan
137 Y12 Qazimämmäd Rus. Kazi Magomed. SE Azerbaijan
142 M4 Qazvīn var. Kazvin. Qazvīn, N Iran
142 M5 Qazvīn ◆ province N Iran
187 Z13 Qelelevu Lagoon lagoon NE Fiji
75 X10 Qena var. Qinā; anc. Caene, Caenepolis. E Egypt
113 L23 Qeparo Vlorë, S Albania
197 N13 Qeqertarssuaq see Qeqertarsuaq
197 N13 Qeqertarsuaq var. Qeqertarssuaq, Dan. Godhavn. ◆ Kitaa, S Greenland
196 M13 Qeqertarsuaq island W Greenland
197 N13 Qeqertarsuup Tunua Dan. Disko Bugt. inlet S Greenland
142 L4 Qeydār var. Qaydār. Zanjān, NW Iran
142 K5 Qezel Owzan, Rūd-e var. Ki Zil Uzen, Qi Zil Uzun. ≈ NW Iran
161 Q2 Qian'an Hebei, E China
161 Q2 Qian Guizhou
Qiandao Hu see Xin'anjiang Shuiku
Qiandaohu see Chun'an
Qian Gorlo/Qian Gorlos/Qian Gorlos Mongolzu Zizhixian/Qiuanguozhen see Qianguo
163 V9 Qianguo var. Qian Gorlo, Qian Gorlos, Qian Gorlos Mongolzu Zizhixian, Jilin, NE China
161 N9 Qianjiang Hubei, C China
160 K10 Qianjiang Sichuan, C China
160 L14 Qian Jiang ≈ S China
160 G9 Qianning var. Gartar. Sichuan, C China
163 U13 Qian Shan ▲ NE China
160 H10 Qianwei var. Yujin. Sichuan, C China
160 J11 Qianxi Guizhou, S China
Qiaotou see Datong
Qiaowa see Muli
Qibili see Kebili
160 J10 Qijiang var. Gunan. Chongqing Shi, C China
159 N5 Qijiaojing Xinjiang Uygur Zizhiqu, NW China
Qike see Qinghe
149 P9 Qila Saifullāh Baluchistān, SW Pakistan
159 S9 Qilian var. Babao. Qinghai, C China
159 N8 Qilian Shan var. Kilien Mountains. ▲ N China
197 O11 Qimusseriarsuaq Dan. Melville Bugt, Eng. Melville Bay. bay NW Greenland
Qinā see Qena
159 W11 Qin'an Gansu, C China
Qincheng see Nanfeng
163 W7 Qing'an Heilongjiang, NE China
161 R5 Qingdao var. Ching-Tao, Ch'ing-tao, Tsingtao, Tsintao, Ger. Tsingtau. Shandong, E China
163 V8 Qinggang Heilongjiang, NE China
Qinggil see Qinghe
159 P11 Qinghai var. Chinghai, Koko Nor, Qing, Qinghai Sheng, Tsinghai. ◆ province C China
159 S10 Qinghai Hu var. Ch'ing Hai, Tsing Hai, Mong. Koko Nor. ◎ C China
Qinghai Sheng see Qinghai
158 M3 Qinghe var. Qinggil. Xinjiang Uygur Zizhiqu, NW China
160 L4 Qingjian var Kuanzhou, prev Xiuyan. Shaanxi, C China
Qingjiang see Huai'an
160 I12 Qinglong var. Liancheng. Guizhou, S China
161 Q3 Qinglong Hebei, E China
159 R14 Qingshuihe Qinghai, C China
159 X10 Qingyang var. Xifeng. Gansu, C China
161 N14 Qingyuan Guangdong, S China
163 V11 Qingyuan var. Qingyuan Manzu Zizhixian. Liaoning, NE China

Qingyuan Manzu Zizhixian see Qingyuan
158 L13 Qingzang Gaoyuan var. Xizang Gaoyuan, Eng. Plateau of Tibet. plateau W China
161 Q4 Qingzhou prev. Yidu. Shandong, E China
157 R9 Qin He ≈ C China
161 Q2 Qinhuangdao Hebei, E China
160 K7 Qin Ling ▲ C China
161 N5 Qinxian var. Qin Xian. Shanxi, C China
Qin Xian see Qinxian
161 N6 Qinyang Henan, C China
160 K15 Qinzhou Guangxi Zhuangzu Zizhiqu, S China
160 L17 Qionghai prev. Jiaji. Hainan, S China
160 H13 Qionglai Sichuan, C China
160 H8 Qiongshan S China
Qiongxi see Hongyuan
160 L17 Qiongzhou Haixia var. Hainan Strait. strait S China
163 Q3 Qiqihar var. Ch'i-ch'i-ha-erh, Tsitsihar; prev. Lungkiang. Heilongjiang, NE China
Qir see Qīr-va-Kārzīn
158 H10 Qir Xinjiang Uygur Zizhiqu, NW China
Qir'awn, Buḥayrat al see Qaraoun, Lac de
143 P12 Qīr-va-Kārzīn var Qīr. Fārs, S Iran
138 F11 Qiryat Gat var. Kiryat Gat. Southern, C Israel
138 G8 Qiryat Shemona Northern, N Israel
Qishlaq see Garmsār
141 U14 Qishn SE Yemen
138 G9 Qishon, Naḥal ≈ N Israel
Qīta Ghazzah see Gaza Strip
156 K5 Qitai Xinjiang Uygur Zizhiqu, NW China
163 Y8 Qitaihe Heilongjiang, NE China
141 W12 Qitbīt, Wādī dry watercourse S Oman
161 O5 Qixian var. Qi Xian, Zhaoge. Henan, C China
Qi Xian see Qixian
Qīzān see Jīzān
Qizil Orda see Kyzylorda
Qizil Qum/Qizilqum see Kyzyl Kum
147 V14 Qizilrabot Rus. Kyzylrabot. SE Tajikistan
146 J10 Qizilravot Rus. Kyzylrabot. Buxoro Viloyati, C Uzbekistan
139 S4 Qizil Yār N Iraq
Qoghaly see Kugaly
Qogir Feng see K2
143 N6 Qom var. Kum, Qum. Qom, N Iran
143 N6 Qom ◆ province N Iran
Qomisheh see Shahreẕā
Qomolangma Feng see Everest, Mount
142 M7 Qom, Rūd-e ≈ C Iran
Qomsheh see Shahreẕā
Qomul see Hami
Qonduz see Kondoz
146 G7 Qo'ng'irot Rus. Kungrad. Qoraqalpog'iston Respublikasi, NW Uzbekistan
Qongyrat see Konyrat
Qoqek see Tacheng
147 R10 Qo'qon var. Khokand, Rus. Kokand. Farg'ona Voliyati, E Uzbekistan
Qorabowur Kirlari see Karabaur', Uval
Qoradaryo see Karadar'ya
146 G6 Qorajar Rus. Karadzhar. Qoraqalpog'iston Respublikasi, NW Uzbekistan
146 K12 Qorako'l Rus. Karakul'. Buxoro Viloyati, C Uzbekistan
146 H7 Qorao'zak Rus. Karauzyak. Qoraqalpog'iston Respublikasi, NW Uzbekistan
146 E5 Qoraqalpog'iston Rus. Karakalpakya. Qoraqalpog'iston Respublikasi, NW Uzbekistan
146 G7 Qoraqalpog'iston Respublikasi Rus. Respublika Karakalpakstan. ◆ autonomous republic NW Uzbekistan
Qorgazhyn see Korgalzhyn
138 H6 Qornet es Saouda ▲ NE Lebanon
146 L12 Qorowulbozor Rus. Karaulbazar. Buxoro Viloyati, C Uzbekistan
142 K5 Qorveh var. Qerveh, Qurveh. Kordestān, W Iran
147 N11 Qo'shrabot Rus. Kushrabat. Samarqand Viloyati, C Uzbekistan
Qosshaghyl see Koschagyl
Qostanay/Qostanay Oblysy see Kostanay
143 P12 Qoṭbābād Fārs, S Iran
143 R13 Qoṭbābād Hormozgān, S Iran
138 H6 Qoubaiyât var. Al Qubayāt. N Lebanon
Qoussantina see Constantine
Qowowuyag see Cho Oyu
147 O11 Qo'ytosh Rus. Koytash. Jizzax Viloyati, C Uzbekistan
146 H6 Qozoqdaryo Rus. Kazakhdar'inskiy. Qoraqalpog'iston Respublikasi, W Uzbekistan
9 N11 Quabbin Reservoir ☐ Massachusetts, NE USA
183 V6 Quambatook Victoria, SE Australia
28 I5 Quakenbrück Niedersachsen, NW Germany
O12 Quakertown Pennsylvania, NE USA
25 Q4 Quanah, SW USA

167 V10 Quang Ngai var. Quangngai, Quang Nghia. Quang Ngai, C Vietnam
Quangngai see Quang Ngai
Quang Nghia see Quang Ngai
167 T9 Quang Tri var. Trièu Hai. Quang Tri, C Vietnam
Quan Long see Ca Mau
152 L4 Quanshuigou China/India
161 R13 Quanzhou var. Ch'uan-chou, Tsinkiang; prev. Chin-chiang. Fujian, SE China
160 M12 Quanzhou Guangxi Zhuangzu Zizhiqu, S China
9 V16 Qu'Appelle ≈ Saskatchewan, S Canada
12 M3 Quaqtaq prev. Koartac. Québec, NE Canada
61 E16 Quaraí Rio Grande do Sul, S Brazil
59 H24 Quaraí, Rio Sp. Cuareim. ≈ Brazil/Uruguay see also Cuareim, Río
Quaraí, Rio see Cuareim, Río
171 N13 Quarles, Pegunungan ▲ Sulawesi, C Indonesia
Quarnero see Kvarner
107 C20 Quartu Sant' Elena Sardegna, Italy, C Mediterranean Sea
29 X13 Quasqueton Iowa, C USA
173 X16 Quatre Bornes W Mauritius
172 I17 Quatre Bornes Mahé, NE Seychelles
137 X10 Quba var. Kuba. N Azerbaijan
Qubba see Ba'qūbah
143 T3 Qūchān var. Kuchan. Khorāsān-Razavī, NE Iran
183 R10 Queanbeyan New South Wales, SE Australia
11 Q10 Québec prev. Quebec. province capital Québec, SE Canada
14 K10 Québec var. Quebec. ◆ province SE Canada
61 D17 Quebracho Paysandú, W Uruguay
101 K14 Quedlinburg Sachsen-Anhalt, C Germany
138 H10 Queen Alia ✕ ('Ammān). 'Ammān, C Jordan
10 L16 Queen Bess, Mount ▲ British Columbia, SW Canada
10 I14 Queen Charlotte British Columbia, SW Canada
65 B24 Queen Charlotte Bay bay West Falkland, W Falkland Islands
10 H14 Queen Charlotte Islands Fr. Îles de la Reine-Charlotte. island group British Columbia, SW Canada
10 I15 Queen Charlotte Sound sea area British Columbia, W Canada
10 J16 Queen Charlotte Strait strait British Columbia, W Canada
27 U1 Queen City Missouri, C USA
25 X5 Queen City Texas, SW USA
197 O9 Queen Elizabeth Islands Fr. Îles de la Reine-Élisabeth. island group Nunavut, N Canada
195 Y10 Queen Mary Coast physical region Antarctica
39 N13 Queen Mary's Peak ▲ C Tristan da Cunha
196 M8 Queen Maud Gulf gulf Arctic Ocean
195 P11 Queen Maud Mountains ▲ Antarctica
Queen's County see Laois
181 U7 Queensland ◆ state N Australia
192 I9 Queensland Plateau undersea feature N Coral Sea
183 O16 Queenstown Tasmania, SE Australia
185 C22 Queenstown Otago, South Island, New Zealand
83 I24 Queenstown Eastern Cape, S South Africa
Queenstown see Cobh
52 F8 Queets Washington, NW USA
61 D18 Queguay Grande, Río ≈ W Uruguay
59 O16 Queimadas Bahia, E Brazil
82 D11 Quela Malanje, NW Angola
82 D12 Quelimane var. Kilimane, Kilmain, Quilimane. Zambézia, NE Mozambique
63 G18 Quellón var. Puerto Quellón. Los Lagos, S Chile
Quelpart see Cheju-do
37 P12 Quemado New Mexico, SW USA
25 O12 Quemado Texas, SW USA
44 K7 Quemado, Punta de headland E Cuba
Quemoy see Chinmen Tao
62 K13 Quemú Quemú La Pampa, E Argentina
155 E17 Quepem Goa, W India
42 M14 Quepos Puntarenas, S Costa Rica
Que Que see Kwekwe
61 D23 Quequén Buenos Aires, E Argentina
61 C23 Quequén Grande, Río ≈ E Argentina
Quequén Salado, Río ≈ E Argentina
41 N13 Querétaro Querétaro de Arteaga, C Mexico
40 F4 Querobabi Sonora, NW Mexico
42 M13 Quesada var. Ciudad Quesada, San Carlos. Alajuela, N Costa Rica
105 O10 Quesada Andalucía, S Spain
161 O7 Queshan Henan, C China
10 M15 Quesnel British Columbia, SW Canada
37 S9 Questa New Mexico, SW USA
102 H7 Questembert Morbihan, NW France
57 K22 Quetena, Río ≈ SW Bolivia
149 O10 Quetta Baluchistān, SW Pakistan
Quetzalcoalco see Coatzacoalcos
Quetzaltenango see Quezaltenango
42 B6 Quezaltenango var. Quetzaltenango. Quezaltenango, W Guatemala

42 A2 Quezaltenango off. Departamento de Quezaltenango, var. Quetzaltenango. ◆ department SW Guatemala
Quezaltenango, Departamento de see Quezaltenango
42 E6 Quezaltepeque Chiquimula, SE Guatemala
170 M6 Quezon Palawan, W Philippines
161 P5 Qufu Shandong, E China
82 B12 Quibala Cuanza Sul, NW Angola
82 B11 Quibaxe var. Quibaxi. Cuanza Norte, NW Angola
Quibaxi see Quibaxe
54 C8 Quibdó Chocó, W Colombia
102 G7 Quiberon Morbihan, NW France
102 G7 Quiberon, Baie de bay NW France
42 C4 Quiché off. Departamento del Quiché. ◆ department W Guatemala
Quiché, Departamento del see Quiché
99 E21 Quiévrain Hainaut, S Belgium
40 I9 Quila Sinaloa, C Mexico
83 B14 Quilengues Huíla, SW Angola
Quilimane see Quelimane
57 G15 Quillabamba Cusco, C Peru
57 L18 Quillacollo Cochabamba, C Bolivia
62 H4 Quillagua Antofagasta, N Chile
103 N17 Quillan Aude, S France
9 U15 Quill Lakes ◎ Saskatchewan, S Canada
62 G11 Quillota Valparaíso, C Chile
155 G23 Quilon var. Kolam, Kollam. Kerala, SW India
181 V9 Quilpie Queensland, C Australia
149 O4 Quil-Qala Bāmīān, N Afghanistan
62 L7 Quimilí Santiago del Estero, C Argentina
57 O19 Quimome Santa Cruz, E Bolivia
102 F6 Quimper anc. Quimper Corentin. Finistère, NW France
Quimper Corentin see Quimper
102 G7 Quimperlé Finistère, NW France
32 F8 Quinault Washington, NW USA
32 F8 Quinault River ≈ Washington, NW USA
35 P5 Quincy California, W USA
23 S8 Quincy Florida, SE USA
30 I13 Quincy Illinois, N USA
9 O11 Quincy Massachusetts, NE USA
32 J9 Quincy Washington, NW USA
54 E10 Quindío off. Departamento del Quindío. ◆ province C Colombia
54 E10 Quindío, Nevado del ▲ C Colombia
62 J10 Quines San Luis, C Argentina
39 N13 Quinhagak Alaska, USA
76 G13 Quinhámel W Guinea-Bissau
Qui Nhon/Quinhon see Quy Nhon
61 H17 Quinta Rio Grande do Sul, S Brazil
105 O10 Quintanar de la Orden Castilla-La Mancha, C Spain
41 X13 Quintana Roo ◆ state SE Mexico
105 S6 Quinto Aragón, NE Spain
108 G10 Quinto Ticino, S Switzerland
27 Q11 Quinton Oklahoma, C USA
82 A10 Quinzau Dem. Rep. Congo, NW Angola
14 H8 Quinze, Lac des ◎ Québec, SE Canada
83 B15 Quipungo Huíla, C Angola
82 B12 Quirihue Bío Bío, C Chile
82 D12 Quirima Malanje, NW Angola
183 T6 Quirindi New South Wales, SE Australia
55 P5 Quiriquire Monagas, NE Venezuela
14 D10 Quirke Lake ◎ Ontario, S Canada
61 B21 Quiroga Buenos Aires, E Argentina
104 I4 Quiroga Galicia, NW Spain
Quirón, Salar see Pocitos, Salar
56 B9 Quiroz, Río ≈ NW Peru
82 Q13 Quissanga Cabo Delgado, NE Mozambique
83 M20 Quissico Inhambane, S Mozambique
25 O4 Quitaque Texas, SW USA
82 Q13 Quiterajo Cabo Delgado, NE Mozambique
23 T6 Quitman Georgia, SE USA
22 M6 Quitman Mississippi, S USA
25 V6 Quitman Texas, S USA
56 C6 Quito ● (Ecuador) Pichincha, N Ecuador
Quito see Mariscal Sucre
59 P13 Quixadá Ceará, E Brazil
83 Q15 Quixaxe Nampula, NE Mozambique
161 N13 Qujiang var. Maba. Guangdong, S China
160 J9 Qu Jiang ≈ C China
160 H12 Qujing Yunnan, SW China
Qulan see Kulan
146 L10 Quljuqtov Tog'lari Rus. Gory Kul'dzhuktau. ▲ C Uzbekistan
Qulsary see Kulsary
Qulyndy Zhazyghy see Kulunda Steppe
Qum see Qom
159 P11 Qumar He ≈ C China
159 Q12 Qumarlêb var. Yuegaitan. Qinghai, C China
Qumisheh see Shahreẕā
147 O14 Qumqo'rg'on Rus. Kumkurgan. Surkhondaryo Viloyati, S Uzbekistan

Qunaytirah/Qunayṭirah, Muḥāfaẓat al see Al Qunayṭirah
189 V12 Quoi island Chuuk, C Micronesia
9 N8 Quoich ≈ Nunavut, NE Canada
83 E26 Quoin Point headland SW South Africa
182 I7 Quorn South Australia
Qureïn see Al Kuwayt
147 P14 Qŭrghonteppa Rus. Kurgan-Tyube. SW Tajikistan
Qurlurtuuq see Kugluktuk
Qurveh see Qorveh
137 X10 Qusar Rus. Kusary. NE Azerbaijan
Qusair see Quseir
75 Y10 Quseir var. Al Quṣayr, Quṣair. E Egypt
Quṣayr, al see Al Quṣayr
142 I2 Qūshchī Āžarbāyjān-e Gharbī, N Iran
Qusmuryn see Kushmurun, Ozero
Qusmuryn see Kushmurun, Kostanay, Kazakhstan
Quṭayfah/Qutayfe/Quteife see Al Quṭayfah
Quthing see Moyeni
147 S10 Quvasoy Rus. Kuvasay. Farg'ona Viloyati, E Uzbekistan
Quwair see Guwêr
Quxar see Lhazê
159 N16 Qüxü var. Xoi. Xizang Zizhiqu, W China
Quyang see Jingzhou
167 V13 Quy Chanh Ninh Thuận, S Vietnam
167 V11 Quy Nhon var. Quinhon, Qui Nhon. Bình Định, C Vietnam
161 R10 Quzhou var. Qu Xian. Zhejiang, SE China
Qyteti Stalin see Kuçovë
Qyzylorda/Qyzylorda Oblysy see Kyzylorda
Qyzyltū see Kishkenekol'
Qyzylzhar see Kyzylzhar

R

Raa Atoll see North Maalhosmadulu Atoll
109 R4 Raab Oberösterreich, N Austria
109 X8 Raab Austria/Hungary
Raab see Rába
Raab see Győr
109 V2 Raabs an der Thaya Niederösterreich, E Austria
93 L14 Raahe Swe. Brahestad. Oulu, W Finland
98 M10 Raalte Overijssel, E Netherlands
99 I14 Raamsdonksveer Noord-Brabant, S Netherlands
92 L12 Raanujärvi Lappi, NW Finland
96 G9 Raasay island NW Scotland, UK
118 H3 Raasiku Ger. Rasik. Harjumaa, NW Estonia
112 B11 Rab It. Arbe. Primorje-Gorski Kotar, NW Croatia
112 B11 Rab It. Arbe. island NW Croatia
171 N16 Raba Sumbawa, S Indonesia
111 G22 Rába Ger. Raab. ≈ Austria/Hungary
112 A10 Rabac Istra, NW Croatia
104 L2 Rábade Galicia, NW Spain
80 F10 Rabak White Nile, C Sudan
186 G9 Rabaraba Milne Bay, SE Papua New Guinea
102 K16 Rabastens-de-Bigorre Hautes-Pyrénées, S France
121 O14 Rabat W Malta
74 F6 Rabat var. al Dar al Baida. ● (Morocco) NW Morocco
Rabat see Victoria
186 H6 Rabaul New Britain, E Papua New Guinea
Rabbah Ammon/Rabbath Ammon see 'Ammān
28 K8 Rabbit Creek ≈ South Dakota, N USA
14 D10 Rabbit Lake ◎ Ontario, S Canada
187 Y14 Rabi prev. Rambi. island N Fiji
140 K9 Rābigh Makkah, W Saudi Arabia
42 D5 Rabinal Baja Verapaz, C Guatemala
168 J12 Rabi, Pulau island NW Indonesia, East Indies
111 L17 Rabka Małopolskie, S Poland
155 F16 Rabkavi Karnātaka, W India
Rábnita see Râbniţa
124 J7 Rabocheostrovsk Respublika Kareliya, NW Russian Federation
23 U1 Rabun Bald ▲ Georgia, SE USA
75 S11 Rabyānah SE Libya
75 S11 Rabyānah, Ramlat var. Rebiana Sand Sea, Ṣaḥrā' Rabyānah. desert SE Libya
Rabyānah, Ṣaḥrā' see Rabyānah, Ramlat
116 L11 Răcăciuni Bacău, E Romania
Racaka see Riwoqê
107 J24 Racalmuto Sicilia, Italy, C Mediterranean Sea
116 J14 Răcari Dâmbovița, SE Romania
Răcari see Durankulak
116 F12 Răcăşdia Hung. Rakasd. Caraş-Severin, SW Romania
106 B9 Racconigi Piemonte, NE Italy
31 T15 Raccoon Creek ≈ Ohio, N USA
13 V13 Race, Cape cape Newfoundland, Newfoundland and Labrador, E Canada
22 K10 Raceland Louisiana, S USA
19 O17 Race Point headland Massachusetts, NE USA
167 S14 Rach Gia Kiên Giang, S Vietnam
167 S14 Rach Gia, Vinh bay S Vietnam
76 J8 Rachid Tagant, C Mauritania
110 L10 Raciąż Mazowieckie, C Poland
111 I16 Racibórz Ger. Ratibor. Śląskie, S Poland

◆ Country ◇ Dependent Territory ◈ Administrative Regions ▲ Mountain 🌋 Volcano ◎ Lake
● Country Capital ○ Dependent Territory Capital ✕ International Airport ▲ Mountain Range ≈ River ☐ Reservoir

Racine – Red Hill

31 *N9* **Racine** Wisconsin, N USA
14 *D7* **Racine Lake** ◎ Ontario, S Canada
111 *J23* **Ráckeve** Pest, C Hungary
Rácz-Becse *see* Bečej
141 *O15* **Radā'** *var.* Ridā'. W Yemen
113 *O15* **Radan** ▲ SE Serbia
63 *J19* **Rada Tilly** Chubut, SE Argentina
116 *K8* **Rădăuţi** *Ger.* Radautz, *Hung.* Rádóc. Suceava, N Romania
116 *L8* **Rădăuţi-Prut** Botoşani, NE Romania
Radautz *see* Rădăuţi
Radbusa *see* Radbuza
111 *A17* **Radbuza** *Ger.* Radbusa. ≈ SE Czech Republic
20 *K6* **Radcliff** Kentucky, S USA
139 *O2* **Radd, Wādī ar** *dry watercourse* N Syria
95 *H16* **Råde** Østfold, S Norway
109 *V11* **Radeče** *Ger.* Ratschach. C Slovenia
Radein *see* Radenci
116 *J4* **Radekhiv** *Pol.* Radziechów, *Rus.* Radekhov. L'vivs'ka Oblast', W Ukraine
Radekhov *see* Radekhiv
109 *X9* **Radenci** *Ger.* Radein; *prev.* Radinci. NE Slovenia
109 *S9* **Radenthein** Kärnten, S Austria
21 *R7* **Radford** Virginia, NE USA
154 *C9* **Rādhanpur** Gujarāt, W India
Radinci *see* Radenci
127 *Q6* **Radishchevo** Ul'yanovskaya Oblast', W Russian Federation
12 *I9* **Radisson** Québec, E Canada
9 *P16* **Radium Hot Springs** British Columbia, SW Canada
116 *F11* **Radna** *Hung.* Máriaradna. Arad, W Romania
114 *K10* **Radnevo** Stara Zagora, C Bulgaria
97 *J20* **Radnor** *cultural region* E Wales, UK
Radnót *see* Iernut
Rádóc *see* Rădăuţi
101 *H24* **Radolfzell am Bodensee** Baden-Württemberg, S Germany
110 *M13* **Radom** Mazowieckie, C Poland
116 *I14* **Radomireşti** Olt, S Romania
111 *K14* **Radomsko** *Rus.* Novoradomsk. Łódzkie, C Poland
117 *N4* **Radomyshl'** Zhytomyrs'ka Oblast', N Ukraine
113 *P19* **Radoviš** *prev.* Radovište. E Macedonia
Radovište *see* Radoviš
94 *B13* **Radøy** *island* S Norway
109 *R7* **Radstadt** Salzburg, NW Austria
182 *E8* **Radstock, Cape** *headland* South Australia
109 *U10* **Raduha** ▲ N Slovenia
119 *G15* **Radun'** *Rus.* Radun'. Hrodzyenskaya Voblasts', W Belarus
126 *M3* **Raduzhnyy** Vladimirskaya Oblast', W Russian Federation
118 *F11* **Radviliškis** Šiaulai, N Lithuania
9 *U17* **Radville** Saskatchewan, S Canada
140 *K7* **Raḑwá, Jabal** ▲ W Saudi Arabia
111 *P16* **Radymno** Podkarpackie, SE Poland
116 *J5* **Radyvyliv** Rivnens'ka Oblast', NW Ukraine
Radziechów *see* Radekhiv
110 *I11* **Radziejów** Kujawskio-pomorskie, C Poland
110 *O12* **Radzyń Podlaski** Lubelskie, E Poland
8 *J7* **Rae** ≈ Nunavut, NW Canada
152 *M13* **Rāe Bareli** Uttar Pradesh, N India
Rae-Edzo *see* Edzo
21 *T11* **Raeford** North Carolina, SE USA
99 *M19* **Raeren** Liège, E Belgium
9 *N7* **Rae Strait** *strait* Nunavut, N Canada
184 *L11* **Raetihi** Manawatu-Wanganui, North Island, New Zealand
191 *U13* **Raevavae** *var* Raivavae. *island* Îles Australes, SW French Polynesia
Rafa *see* Rafah
62 *M10* **Rafaela** Santa Fe, E Argentina
138 *E11* **Rafah** *var.* Rafa, Rafaḥ, *Heb.* Rafiah, *var.* Raphiah. SW Gaza Strip
79 *L15* **Rafaï** Mbomou, SE Central African Republic
141 *O4* **Rafḥah** Al Ḥudūd ash Shamālīyah, N Saudi Arabia
Rafiah *see* Rafah
143 *R10* **Rafsanjān** Kermān, C Iran
80 *B13* **Raga** Western Bahr el Ghazal, SW Sudan
19 *S8* **Ragged Island** *island* Maine, NE USA
44 *I5* **Ragged Island Range** *island group* S Bahamas
184 *L7* **Raglan** Waikato, North Island, New Zealand
22 *G8* **Ragley** Louisiana, S USA
Ragnit *see* Neman
107 *K25* **Ragusa** Sicilia, Italy, C Mediterranean Sea
Ragusa *see* Dubrovnik
Ragusavecchia *see* Cavtat
171 *P14* **Raha** Pulau Muna, C Indonesia
119 *N17* **Rahachow** *Rus.* Rogachëv. Homyel'skaya Voblasts', SE Belarus
67 *U6* **Rahad** *var.* Nahr ar Rahad. ≈ W Sudan
Rahad, Nahr ar *see* Rahad
Rahaeng *see* Tak
138 *F11* **Rahat** Southern, C Israel
140 *L8* **Rahaţ, Ḥarrat** *lava flow* W Saudi Arabia
149 *S12* **Rahīmyār Khān** Punjab, SE Pakistan
95 *I14* **Råholt** Akershus, S Norway
Rahovec *see* Orahovac
191 *S10* **Raiatea** *island* Îles Sous le Vent, W French Polynesia
155 *H16* **Rāichūr** Karnātaka, C India
Raidestos *see* Tekirdağ
153 *S13* **Rāiganj** West Bengal, NE India
154 *M11* **Raigarh** Chhattīsgarh, C India
183 *O16* **Railton** Tasmania, SE Australia
36 *L8* **Rainbow Bridge** *natural arch* Utah, W USA
23 *Q3* **Rainbow City** Alabama, S USA
9 *N11* **Rainbow Lake** Alberta, W Canada
21 *R5* **Rainelle** West Virginia, NE USA
32 *G10* **Rainier** Oregon, NW USA
32 *H9* **Rainier, Mount** ⛰ Washington, NW USA
23 *Q2* **Rainsville** Alabama, S USA
12 *B11* **Rainy Lake** ◎ Canada/USA
12 *A11* **Rainy River** Ontario, C Canada
Raippaluoto *see* Replot
154 *K12* **Raipur** Chhattīsgarh, C India
154 *H10* **Raisen** Madhya Pradesh, C India
15 *N13* **Raisin** ≈ Ontario, SE Canada
31 *R11* **Raisin, River** ≈ Michigan, N USA
Raivavae *see* Raevavae
149 *W9* **Rāiwind** Punjab, E Pakistan
171 *T12* **Raja Ampat, Kepulauan** *island group* E Indonesia
155 *L16* **Rājahmundry** Andhra Pradesh, E India
155 *I18* **Rājampet** Andhra Pradesh, E India
Rajang *see* Rajang, Batang
169 *S9* **Rajang, Batang** *var.* Rajang. ≈ East Malaysia
149 *S11* **Rājanpur** Punjab, E Pakistan
155 *H23* **Rājapālaiyam** Tamil Nādu, SE India
152 *E12* **Rājasthān** ◐ *state* NW India
153 *T15* **Rajbari** Dhaka, C Bangladesh
153 *R12* **Rajbiraj** Eastern, E Nepal
154 *G9* **Rājgarh** Madhya Pradesh, C India
152 *H10* **Rājgarh** Rājasthān, NW India
153 *P14* **Rājgīr** Bihār, N India
110 *O8* **Rajgród** Podlaskie, NE Poland
154 *L12* **Rājim** Chhattīsgarh, C India
112 *C11* **Rajinac, Mali** ▲ W Croatia
154 *B10* **Rājkot** Gujarāt, W India
153 *R14* **Rājmahal** Jhārkhand, NE India
153 *Q14* **Rājmahāl Hills** *hill range* N India
154 *K12* **Rāj Nāndgaon** Chhattīsgarh, C India
152 *I8* **Rājpura** Punjab, NW India
153 *S14* **Rajshahi** *prev.* Rampur Boalia. Rajshahi, W Bangladesh
153 *S13* **Rajshahi** ◐ *division* NW Bangladesh
190 *K13* **Rakahanga** *atoll* N Cook Islands
185 *H19* **Rakaia** Canterbury, South Island, New Zealand
185 *G19* **Rakaia** ≈ South Island, New Zealand
152 *H3* **Rakaposhi** ▲ N India
Rakasd *see* Răcăşdia
169 *N15* **Rakata, Pulau** *var.* Pulau Krakatau. *island* S Indonesia
141 *U10* **Rakbah, Qalamat ar** *well* SE Saudi Arabia
Rakhine State *see* Arakan State
116 *I8* **Rakhiv** Zakarpats'ka Oblast', W Ukraine
141 *V13* **Rakhyūt** SW Oman
192 *K9* **Rakiraki** Viti Levu, W Fiji
Rakka *see* Ar Raqqah
118 *I4* **Rakke** Lääne-Virumaa, NE Estonia
95 *I16* **Rakkestad** Østfold, S Norway
110 *F12* **Rakoniewice** *Ger.* Rakwitz. Wielkopolskie, C Poland
Rakonitz *see* Rakovník
83 *H18* **Rakops** Central, C Botswana
111 *C16* **Rakovník** *Ger.* Rakonitz. Středočeský Kraj, W Czech Republic
114 *J10* **Rakovski** Plovdiv, C Bulgaria
Rakutō-kō *see* Naktong-gang
118 *I3* **Rakvere** *Ger.* Wesenberg. Lääne-Virumaa, N Estonia
Rakwitz *see* Rakoniewice
22 *L6* **Raleigh** Mississippi, S USA
21 *U9* **Raleigh** *state capital* North Carolina, SE USA
21 *Y11* **Raleigh Bay** *bay* North Carolina, SE USA
21 *U9* **Raleigh-Durham** ✈ North Carolina, SE USA
189 *S6* **Ralik Chain** *island group* Ralik Chain, W Marshall Islands
25 *N5* **Ralls** Texas, SW USA
18 *G13* **Ralston** Pennsylvania, NE USA
141 *O16* **Ramādah** W Yemen
Ramadi *see* Ar Ramādī
105 *N2* **Ramales de la Victoria** Cantabria, N Spain
138 *F10* **Ramallah** C West Bank
61 *C19* **Ramallo** Buenos Aires, E Argentina
155 *H20* **Rāmanagaram** Karnātaka, E India
155 *I23* **Rāmanāthapuram** Tamil Nādu, SE India
154 *N12* **Rāmapur** Orissa, E India
155 *I14* **Rāmāreddi** *var.* Kāmāreddi, Kamareddy. Andhra Pradesh, C India
138 *F10* **Ramat Gan** Tel Aviv, W Israel
103 *T6* **Rambervillers** Vosges, NE France
Rambi *see* Rabi
103 *N5* **Rambouillet** Yvelines, N France
186 *E5* **Rambutyo Island** *island* N Papua New Guinea
153 *Q12* **Ramechhāp** Central, C Nepal
183 *R12* **Rame Head** *headland* Victoria, SE Australia
126 *L4* **Ramenskoye** Moskovskaya Oblast', W Russian Federation
124 *J15* **Rameshki** Tverskaya Oblast', W Russian Federation
153 *P14* **Rāmgarh** Jhārkhand, N India
152 *D11* **Rāmgarh** Rājasthān, NW India
142 *M9* **Rāmhormoz** *var.* Ram Hormuz, Ramuz. Khūzestān, SW Iran
Ram Hormuz *see* Rāmhormoz
Ram, Jebel *see* Ramm, Jabal
138 *F10* **Ramla** *var.* Ramle, Ramleh, *Ar.* Er Ramle. Central, C Israel
Ramle/Ramleh *see* Ramla
138 *F14* **Ramm, Jabal** *var.* Jebel Ram. ▲ SW Jordan
152 *K10* **Rāmnagar** Uttaranchal, N India
95 *N15* **Ramnäs** Västmanland, C Sweden
Râmnicul-Sărat *see* Râmnicu Sărat
116 *L12* **Râmnicu Sărat** *prev.* Râmnicul-Sărat, Rîmnicu-Sărat. Buzău, E Romania
116 *I13* **Râmnicu Vâlcea** *prev.* Rîmnicu Vîlcea. Vâlcea, C Romania
Ramokgwebana *see* Ramokgwebane
83 *J18* **Ramokgwebane** *var.* Ramokgwebana. Central, NE Botswana
126 *L7* **Ramon'** Voronezhskaya Oblast', W Russian Federation
35 *V17* **Ramona** California, W USA
56 *A10* **Ramón, Laguna** ◎ NW Peru
14 *G7* **Ramore** Ontario, S Canada
40 *M11* **Ramos** San Luis Potosí, C Mexico
41 *N8* **Ramos Arizpe** Coahuila de Zaragoza, NE Mexico
40 *J9* **Ramos, Río de** ≈ C Mexico
83 *J21* **Ramotswa** South East, S Botswana
39 *R8* **Rampart** Alaska, USA
8 *H8* **Ramparts** ≈ Northwest Territories, NW Canada
152 *K10* **Rāmpur** Uttar Pradesh, N India
154 *F9* **Rāmpura** Madhya Pradesh, C India
Rampur Boalia *see* Rajshahi
166 *K6* **Ramree Island** *island* W Burma (Myanmar)
141 *W6* **Rams** *var.* Ar Rams. Ra's al Khaymah, NE United Arab Emirates
143 *N4* **Rāmsar** *prev.* Sakhtsar. Māzandarān, N Iran
93 *H16* **Ramsele** Västernorrland, N Sweden
21 *T9* **Ramseur** North Carolina, SE USA
97 *I16* **Ramsey** NE Isle of Man
97 *I16* **Ramsey Bay** *bay* NE Isle of Man
14 *E9* **Ramsey Lake** ◎ Ontario, S Canada
97 *Q22* **Ramsgate** SE England, UK
94 *M10* **Ramsjö** Gävleborg, C Sweden
154 *I12* **Rāmtek** Mahārāshtra, C India
Ramtha *see* Ar Ramthā
Ramuz *see* Rāmhormoz
118 *G12* **Ramygala** Panevėžys, C Lithuania
152 *H14* **Rāna Pratāp Sāgar** ◎ N India
169 *V7* **Ranau** Sabah, East Malaysia
168 *L14* **Ranau, Danau** ◎ Sumatera, W Indonesia
62 *H12* **Rancagua** Libertador, C Chile
99 *G22* **Rance** Hainaut, S Belgium
102 *H6* **Rance** ≈ NW France
60 *J9* **Rancharia** São Paulo, S Brazil
153 *P15* **Rānchi** Jhārkhand, N India
61 *D21* **Ranchos** Buenos Aires, E Argentina
37 *S9* **Ranchos De Taos** New Mexico, SW USA
63 *G16* **Ranco, Lago** ◎ C Chile
95 *C16* **Randaberg** Rogaland, S Norway
29 *U7* **Randall** Minnesota, N USA
107 *L23* **Randazzo** Sicilia, Italy, C Mediterranean Sea
95 *G21* **Randers** Århus, C Denmark
92 *I12* **Randijaure** ◎ N Sweden
21 *T9* **Randleman** North Carolina, SE USA
19 *O11* **Randolph** Massachusetts, NE USA
29 *Q13* **Randolph** Nebraska, C USA
36 *M1* **Randolph** Utah, W USA
100 *P9* **Randow** ≈ NE Germany
95 *H14* **Randsfjorden** ◎ S Norway
92 *K13* **Råneå** Norrbotten, N Sweden
92 *G12* **Ranelva** ≈ C Norway
93 *F15* **Ranemsletta** Nord-Trøndelag, C Norway
76 *H10* **Ranérou** C Senegal
Ráneš *see* Ringvassøya
185 *E22* **Ranfurly** Otago, South Island, New Zealand
167 *P17* **Rangae** Narathiwat, SW Thailand
153 *V16* **Rangamati** Chittagong, SE Bangladesh
184 *I2* **Rangauru Bay** *bay* North Island, New Zealand
19 *P6* **Rangeley** Maine, NE USA
37 *O4* **Rangely** Colorado, C USA
25 *R7* **Ranger** Texas, SW USA
14 *C9* **Ranger Lake** Ontario, S Canada
14 *C9* **Ranger Lake** ◎ Ontario, S Canada
153 *V12* **Rangia** Assam, NE India
185 *I18* **Rangiora** Canterbury, South Island, New Zealand
191 *T9* **Rangiroa** *atoll* Îles Tuamotu, W French Polynesia
184 *N9* **Rangitaiki** ≈ North Island, New Zealand
185 *F19* **Rangitata** ≈ South Island, New Zealand
184 *M12* **Rangitikei** ≈ North Island, New Zealand
184 *L6* **Rangitoto Island** *island* N New Zealand
Rangkasbitoeng *see* Rangkasbitung
169 *N16* **Rangkasbitung** *prev.* Rangkasbitoeng. Jawa, SW Indonesia
167 *P9* **Rang, Khao** ▲ C Thailand
147 *V13* **Rangkŭl** *Rus.* Rangkul'. SE Tajikistan
Rangkul' *see* Rangkŭl
Rangoon *see* Yangon
153 *T13* **Rangpur** Rajshahi, N Bangladesh
155 *F18* **Rānibennur** Karnātaka, W India
153 *R15* **Rāniganj** West Bengal, NE India
149 *Q13* **Rānīpur** Sind, SE Pakistan
Rāniyah *see* Rānya
25 *N9* **Rankin** Texas, SW USA
9 *O9* **Rankin Inlet** Nunavut, C Canada
183 *P8* **Rankins Springs** New South Wales, SE Australia
Rankovićevo *see* Kraljevo
108 *I7* **Rankweil** Vorarlberg, W Austria
Rann *see* Brežice
127 *T8* **Ranneye** Orenburgskaya Oblast', W Russian Federation
96 *I10* **Rannoch, Loch** ◎ C Scotland, UK
191 *U17* **Rano Kau** *var.* Rano Kao. *crater* Easter Island, Chile, E Pacific Ocean
167 *N14* **Ranong** Ranong, SW Thailand
186 *J8* **Ranongga** *var.* Ghanongga. *island* NW Solomon Islands
191 *W16* **Rano Raraku** *ancient monument* Easter Island, Chile, E Pacific Ocean
171 *V12* **Ransiki** Papua, E Indonesia
92 *K12* **Rantajärvi** Norrbotten, N Sweden
93 *N17* **Rantasalmi** Itä-Suomi, SE Finland
169 *U13* **Rantau** Borneo, C Indonesia
168 *L10* **Rantau, Pulau** *var.* Pulau Tebingtinggi. *island* W Indonesia
171 *N13* **Rantepao** Sulawesi, C Indonesia
30 *M13* **Rantoul** Illinois, N USA
93 *L15* **Rantsila** Oulu, C Finland
92 *L13* **Ranua** Lappi, NW Finland
139 *T3* **Rānya** *var.* Rāniyah. NE Iraq
157 *X3* **Raohe** Heilongjiang, NE China
74 *H9* **Raoui, Erg er** *desert* W Algeria
193 *O10* **Rapa** *island* Îles Australes, S French Polynesia
191 *V14* **Rapa Iti** *island* Îles Australes, SW French Polynesia
106 *D10* **Rapallo** Liguria, NW Italy
Rapa Nui *see* Pascua, Isla de
Raphiah *see* Rafah
21 *V5* **Rapidan River** ≈ Virginia, NE USA
28 *J10* **Rapid City** South Dakota, N USA
15 *P8* **Rapide-Blanc** Québec, SE Canada
14 *I8* **Rapide-Deux** Québec, SE Canada
118 *K6* **Räpina** *Ger.* Rappin. Põlvamaa, SE Estonia
118 *G4* **Rapla** *Ger.* Rappel. Raplamaa, NW Estonia
118 *G4* **Raplamaa** *var.* Rapla Maakond. ◐ *province* NW Estonia
Rapla Maakond *see* Raplamaa
21 *X6* **Rappahonnock River** ≈ Virginia, NE USA
Rappel *see* Rapla
108 *G7* **Rapperswil** Sankt Gallen, NE Switzerland
Rappin *see* Räpina
153 *N12* **Rāpti** ≈ N India
57 *K16* **Rapulo, Río** ≈ E Bolivia
Raqqah/Raqqah, Muḩāfaẓat al *see* Ar Raqqah
18 *J8* **Raquette Lake** ◎ New York, NE USA
18 *J6* **Raquette River** ≈ New York, NE USA
191 *V10* **Raraka** *atoll* Îles Tuamotu, C French Polynesia
191 *V10* **Raroia** *atoll* Îles Tuamotu, C French Polynesia
190 *H15* **Rarotonga** ✈ Rarotonga, S Cook Islands, C Pacific Ocean
190 *H16* **Rarotonga** *island* S Cook Islands, C Pacific Ocean
147 *P12* **Rarz** W Tajikistan
Ras al'Ain *see* Ra's al 'Ayn
139 *N2* **Ra's al 'Ayn** *var.* Ras al'Ain. Al Ḥasakah, N Syria
138 *H3* **Ra's al Basīţ** Al Lādhiqīyah, W Syria
Ra's al-Hafğī *see* Ra's al Khafjī
141 *R5* **Ra's al Khafjī** *var.* Ra's al-Hafğī. Ash Sharqīyah, NE Saudi Arabia
Ras al-Khaimah/Ras al Khaimah *see* Ra's al Khaymah
143 *R15* **Ra's al Khaymah** *var.* Ras al Khaimah. Ra's al Khaymah, NE United Arab Emirates
143 *R15* **Ra's al Khaymah** *var.* Ras al-Khaimah. ✈ Ra's al Khaymah, NE United Arab Emirates
138 *G13* **Ra's an Naqb** Ma'ān, S Jordan
61 *B26* **Rasa, Punta** *headland* E Argentina
171 *V12* **Rasawi** Papua, E Indonesia
Râşcani *see* Rîşcani
80 *J10* **Ras Dashen Terara** ▲ N Ethiopia
151 *K19* **Rasdu Atoll** *atoll* C Maldives
118 *E12* **Raseiniai** Kaunas, C Lithuania
75 *X8* **Râs Ghârib** E Egypt
162 *J6* **Rashaant** Hövsgöl, N Mongolia
Rashaant *see* Delüün, Bayan-Ölgiy, Mongolia
Rashaant *see* Öldziyt, Dundgovĭ, Mongolia
75 *V7* **Rashîd** *Eng.* Rosetta. N Egypt
139 *Y11* **Rashīd** E Iraq
142 *M3* **Rasht** *var.* Resht. Gīlān, NW Iran
139 *S2* **Rashwān** N Iraq
Rasik *see* Raasiku
113 *M15* **Raška** Serbia, C Serbia
119 *P15* **Rasna** *Rus.* Ryasna. Mahilyowskaya Voblasts', E Belarus
116 *J12* **Râşnov** *prev.* Rîşno, Rozsnyó, *Hung.* Barcarozsnyó. Braşov, C Romania
118 *L11* **Rasony** *Rus.* Rossony. Vitsyebskaya Voblasts', N Belarus
Ra's Shamrah *see* Ugarit
127 *N7* **Rasskazovo** Tambovskaya Oblast', W Russian Federation
119 *O16* **Rasta** ≈ E Belarus
Rastadt *see* Rastatt
Rastâne *see* Ar Rastān
141 *S6* **Ra's Tannūrah** *Eng.* Ras Tanura. Ash Sharqīyah, NE Saudi Arabia
Ras Tanura *see* Ra's Tannūrah
101 *G21* **Rastatt** *var.* Rastadt. Baden-Württemberg, SW Germany
Rastenburg *see* Kętrzyn
149 *V7* **Rasūlnagar** Punjab, E Pakistan
189 *U6* **Ratak Chain** *island group* Ratak Chain, E Marshall Islands
119 *K15* **Ratamka** *Rus.* Ratomka. Minskaya Voblasts', C Belarus
93 *G17* **Ratan** Jämtland, C Sweden
152 *G11* **Ratangarh** Rājasthān, NW India
Rat Buri *see* Ratchaburi
167 *O11* **Ratchaburi** *var.* Rat Buri. Ratchaburi, W Thailand
29 *W15* **Rathbun Lake** ▣ Iowa, C USA
Ráth Caola *see* Rathkeale
166 *K5* **Rathedaung** Arakan State, W Burma (Myanmar)
100 *M12* **Rathenow** Brandenburg, NE Germany
97 *C19* **Rathkeale** *Ir.* Ráth Caola. Limerick, SW Ireland
96 *F13* **Rathlin Island** *Ir.* Reachlainn. *island* N Northern Ireland, UK
97 *C20* **Ráthluirc** *Ir.* An Ráth. Cork, SW Ireland
Ratibor *see* Racibórz
Ratisbon/Ratisbona/Ratisbonne *see* Regensburg
Rätische Alpen *see* Rhaetian Alps
38 *E17* **Rat Island** *island* Aleutian Islands, Alaska, USA
38 *E17* **Rat Islands** *island group* Aleutian Islands, Alaska, USA
154 *F10* **Ratlām** *prev.* Rutlam. Madhya Pradesh, C India
155 *D15* **Ratnāgiri** Mahārāshtra, W India
155 *K26* **Ratnapura** Sabaragamuwa Province, S Sri Lanka
116 *J2* **Ratne** *Rus.* Ratno. Volyns'ka Oblast', NW Ukraine
Ratno *see* Ratne
Ratomka *see* Ratamka
37 *U8* **Raton** New Mexico, SW USA
139 *O7* **Ratqah, Wādī ar** *dry watercourse* W Iraq
Ratschach *see* Radeče
167 *O16* **Rattaphum** Songkhla, SW Thailand
26 *L6* **Rattlesnake Creek** ≈ Kansas, C USA
94 *L13* **Rättvik** Dalarna, C Sweden
100 *K9* **Ratzeburg** Mecklenburg-Vorpommern, N Germany
100 *K9* **Ratzeburger See** ◎ N Germany
10 *J10* **Ratz, Mount** ▲ British Columbia, SW Canada
61 *D22* **Rauch** Buenos Aires, E Argentina
41 *U16* **Raudales** Chiapas, SE Mexico
Raudhatain *see* Ar Rawḑatayn
Raudnitz an der Elbe *see* Roudnice nad Labem
92 *K1* **Raufarhöfn** Nordhurland Eystra, NE Iceland
94 *H13* **Raufoss** Oppland, S Norway
Raukawa *see* Cook Strait
184 *Q8* **Raukumara** ▲ North Island, New Zealand
192 *K11* **Raukumara Plain** *undersea feature* N Coral Sea
184 *P8* **Raukumara Range** ▲▲ North Island, New Zealand
154 *N11* **Rāurkela** *var.* Raurkela; *prev.* Rourkela. Orissa, E India
95 *F15* **Rauland** Telemark, S Norway
93 *J19* **Rauma** *Swe.* Raumo. Länsi-Soumi, SW Finland
94 *F10* **Rauma** ≈ S Norway
Raumo *see* Rauma
118 *H8* **Rauna** Cēsis, C Latvia
169 *T17* **Raung, Gunung** ▲ Jawa, S Indonesia
Raurkela *see* Rāurkela
95 *J22* **Raus** Skåne, S Sweden
165 *W3* **Rausu** Hokkaidō, NE Japan
165 *W3* **Rausu-dake** ▲ Hokkaidō, NE Japan
93 *M17* **Rautalampi** Itä-Suomi, C Finland
93 *N16* **Rautavaara** Itä-Suomi, C Finland
116 *M9* **Raŭtel** ≈ C Moldova
93 *O18* **Rautjärvi** Etelä-Suomi, SE Finland
Rautu *see* Sosnovo
191 *V11* **Ravahere** *atoll* Îles Tuamotu, C French Polynesia
107 *J25* **Ravanusa** Sicilia, Italy, C Mediterranean Sea
143 *S9* **Rāvar** Kermān, C Iran
147 *Q11* **Ravat** Batkenskaya Oblast', SW Kyrgyzstan
18 *K11* **Ravena** New York, NE USA
106 *H10* **Ravenna** Emilia-Romagna, N Italy
29 *O15* **Ravenna** Nebraska, C USA
31 *U11* **Ravenna** Ohio, N USA
101 *I24* **Ravensburg** Baden-Württemberg, S Germany
181 *W4* **Ravenshoe** Queensland, NE Australia
180 *K13* **Ravensthorpe** Western Australia
21 *Q4* **Ravenswood** West Virginia, NE USA
149 *U9* **Rāvi** ≈ India/Pakistan
112 *C9* **Ravna Gora** Primorje-Gorski Kotar, NW Croatia
109 *U10* **Ravne na Koroškem** *Ger.* Gutenstein. N Slovenia
139 *P6* **Rāwah** W Iraq
191 *T4* **Rawaki** *prev.* Phoenix Island. *atoll* Phoenix Islands, C Kiribati
149 *U6* **Rāwalpindi** Punjab, NE Pakistan
110 *L13* **Rawa Mazowiecka** Łódzkie, C Poland
139 *T2* **Rawāndiz** *var.* Rawandoz, Rawāndūz. N Iraq
Rawandoz/Rawāndūz *see* Rawāndiz
171 *U12* **Rawas** Papua, E Indonesia
139 *O4* **Rawḑah** ◎ E Syria
110 *G13* **Rawicz** *Ger.* Rawitsch. Wielkopolskie, C Poland
Rawitsch *see* Rawicz
180 *M11* **Rawlinna** Western Australia
33 *W16* **Rawlins** Wyoming, C USA
63 *K17* **Rawson** Chubut, SE Argentina
159 *R16* **Rawu** Xizang Zizhiqu, W China
153 *P12* **Raxaul** Bihār, N India
28 *K3* **Ray** North Dakota, N USA
169 *S11* **Raya, Bukit** ▲ Borneo, C Indonesia
155 *I18* **Rāyachoti** Andhra Pradesh, E India
Rāyadrug *see* Rāyagarha
155 *M14* **Rāyagarha** *prev.* Rāyadrug. Orissa, E India
138 *H7* **Rayak** *var.* Rayaq, Riyāq. E Lebanon
Rayaq *see* Rayak
139 *T2* **Rāyat** E Iraq
169 *N12* **Raya, Tanjung** *cape* Pulau Bangka, W Indonesia
13 *R13* **Ray, Cape** *cape* Newfoundland, Newfoundland and Labrador, E Canada
123 *Q13* **Raychikhinsk** Amurskaya Oblast', SE Russian Federation
127 *U5* **Rayevskiy** Respublika Bashkortostan, W Russian Federation
9 *Q17* **Raymond** Alberta, SW Canada
22 *K6* **Raymond** Mississippi, S USA
32 *F9* **Raymond** Washington, NW USA
183 *T8* **Raymond Terrace** New South Wales, SE Australia
25 *T17* **Raymondville** Texas, SW USA
9 *U16* **Raymore** Saskatchewan, S Canada
39 *Q8* **Ray Mountains** ▲▲ Alaska, USA
22 *H9* **Rayne** Louisiana, S USA
41 *O12* **Rayón** San Luis Potosí, C Mexico
40 *G4* **Rayón** Sonora, NW Mexico
167 *P12* **Rayong** Rayong, S Thailand
25 *T5* **Ray Roberts, Lake** ◎ Texas, SW USA
18 *E15* **Raystown Lake** ▣ Pennsylvania, NE USA
141 *V13* **Raysūt** SW Oman
27 *R4* **Raytown** Missouri, C USA
22 *I5* **Rayville** Louisiana, S USA
142 *L5* **Razan** Hamadān, W Iran
139 *S9* **Razāzah, Buḩayrat ar** *var.* Baḩr al Milḩ. ◎ C Iraq
114 *L9* **Razboyna** ▲ E Bulgaria
Razdan *see* Hrazdan
Razdolnoye *see* Rozdol'ne
Razelm, Lacul *see* Razim, Lacul
139 *U2* **Razga** E Iraq
114 *L8* **Razgrad** Razgrad, N Bulgaria
114 *L8* **Razgrad** ◐ *province* NE Bulgaria
117 *N13* **Razim, Lacul** *prev.* Lacul Razelm. *lagoon* NW Black Sea
114 *G11* **Razlog** Blagoevgrad, SW Bulgaria
118 *K10* **Rāznas Ezers** ◎ SE Latvia
102 *E6* **Raz, Pointe du** *headland* NW France
Reachlainn *see* Rathlin Island
Reachrainn *see* Lambay Island
97 *N22* **Reading** S England, UK
18 *H15* **Reading** Pennsylvania, NE USA
48 *C7* **Real, Cordillera** ▲▲ C Ecuador
62 *K12* **Realicó** La Pampa, C Argentina
25 *R15* **Realitos** Texas, SW USA
108 *G9* **Realp** Uri, C Switzerland
167 *Q12* **Reăng Kesei** Bătdâmbâng, W Cambodia
191 *Y11* **Reao** *atoll* Îles Tuamotu, E French Polynesia
Reate *see* Rieti
180 *L11* **Rebecca, Lake** ◎ Western Australia
Rebiana Sand Sea *see* Rabyānah, Ramlat
124 *H8* **Reboly** Respublika Kareliya, NW Russian Federation
165 *S1* **Rebun** Rebun-tō, NE Japan
165 *S1* **Rebun-tō** *island* NE Japan
106 *J12* **Recanati** Marche, C Italy
Rechitsa *see* Rechytsa
109 *Y7* **Rechnitz** Burgenland, SE Austria
119 *J20* **Rechytsa** *Rus.* Rechitsa. Brestskaya Voblasts', SW Belarus
119 *O19* **Rechytsa** *Rus.* Rechitsa. Homyel'skaya Voblasts', SE Belarus
59 *Q15* **Recife** *prev.* Pernambuco. *state capital* Pernambuco, E Brazil
83 *I26* **Recife, Cape** *Afr.* Kaap Recife. *headland* S South Africa
Recife, Kaap *see* Recife, Cape
172 *I16* **Récifs, Îles aux** *island* Inner Islands, NE Seychelles
101 *E14* **Recklinghausen** Nordrhein-Westfalen, W Germany
100 *M8* **Recknitz** ≈ NE Germany
99 *K23* **Recogne** Luxembourg, SE Belgium
61 *C15* **Reconquista** Santa Fe, C Argentina
195 *O6* **Recovery Glacier** *glacier* Antarctica
59 *G15* **Recreio** Mato Grosso, W Brazil
27 *X9* **Rector** Arkansas, C USA
110 *E9* **Recz** *Ger.* Reetz Neumark. Zachodnio-pomorskie, NW Poland
99 *L24* **Redange** *var.* Redange-sur-Attert. Diekirch, W Luxembourg
Redange-sur-Attert *see* Redange
18 *C13* **Redbank Creek** ≈ Pennsylvania, NE USA
13 *S9* **Red Bay** Québec, E Canada
23 *N2* **Red Bay** Alabama, S USA
35 *N4* **Red Bluff** California, W USA
24 *J8* **Red Bluff Reservoir** ◎ New Mexico/Texas, SW USA
30 *K16* **Red Bud** Illinois, N USA
30 *J5* **Red Cedar River** ≈ Wisconsin, N USA
9 *R17* **Redcliff** Alberta, SW Canada
83 *K17* **Redcliff** Midlands, C Zimbabwe
182 *L9* **Red Cliffs** Victoria, SE Australia
29 *P17* **Red Cloud** Nebraska, C USA
22 *L8* **Red Creek** ≈ Mississippi, S USA
9 *P15* **Red Deer** Alberta, SW Canada
9 *Q16* **Red Deer** ≈ Alberta, SW Canada
39 *O11* **Red Devil** Alaska, USA
35 *N3* **Redding** California, W USA
97 *L20* **Redditch** W England, UK
29 *P9* **Redfield** South Dakota, N USA
24 *J12* **Redford** Texas, SW USA
45 *V13* **Redhead** Trinidad, Trinidad and Tobago
182 *I8* **Red Hill** South Australia
Red Hill *see* Pu'u 'Ula'ula

◆ Country ● Country Capital ◇ Dependent Territory ○ Dependent Territory Capital ◐ Administrative Regions ✈ International Airport ▲ Mountain ▲▲ Mountain Range ⛰ Volcano ≈ River ◎ Lake ▣ Reservoir

311

RED HILLS – RINGKØBING AMT

26 K7 **Red Hills** *hill range* Kansas, C USA
13 T12 **Red Indian Lake** ◎ Newfoundland, Newfoundland and Labrador, E Canada
124 J16 **Redkino** Tverskaya Oblast', W Russian Federation
12 A10 **Red Lake** Ontario, C Canada
36 I10 **Red Lake** *salt flat* Arizona, SW USA
29 S4 **Red Lake Falls** Minnesota, N USA
29 R4 **Red Lake River** ≈ Minnesota, N USA
35 U15 **Redlands** California, W USA
18 G16 **Red Lion** Pennsylvania, NE USA
33 U11 **Red Lodge** Montana, NW USA
32 H13 **Redmond** Oregon, NW USA
36 L5 **Redmond** Utah, W USA
32 H8 **Redmond** Washington, NW USA
Rednitz *see* Regnitz
29 T15 **Red Oak** Iowa, C USA
18 K12 **Red Oaks Mill** New York, NE USA
102 I7 **Redon** Ille-et-Vilaine, NW France
45 W10 **Redonda** *island* SW Antigua and Barbuda
104 G4 **Redondela** Galicia, NW Spain
104 H11 **Redondo** Évora, S Portugal
39 Q12 **Redoubt Volcano** ▲ Alaska, USA
9 Y16 **Red River** ≈ Canada/USA
129 U12 **Red River** *var.* Yuan, *Chin.* Yuan Jiang, *Vtn.* Sông Hông Hà. ≈ China/Vietnam
25 W4 **Red River** ≈ S USA
22 H7 **Red River** ≈ Louisiana, S USA
30 M6 **Red River** ≈ Wisconsin, N USA
Red Rock, Lake *see* Red Rock Reservoir
29 W14 **Red Rock Reservoir** *var.* Lake Red Rock. ⊠ Iowa, C USA
80 H7 **Red Sea** ⬖ *state* NE Sudan
75 Y9 **Red Sea** *var.* Sinus Arabicus. *sea* Africa/Asia
21 T11 **Red Springs** North Carolina, SE USA
8 I9 **Redstone** ≈ Northwest Territories, NW Canada
9 V17 **Redvers** Saskatchewan, S Canada
77 P13 **Red Volta** *var.* Nazinon, *Fr.* Volta Rouge. ≈ Burkina/Ghana
9 Q14 **Redwater** Alberta, SW Canada
28 M16 **Red Willow Creek** ≈ Nebraska, C USA
29 W9 **Red Wing** Minnesota, N USA
35 N9 **Redwood City** California, W USA
29 T9 **Redwood Falls** Minnesota, N USA
31 P7 **Reed City** Michigan, N USA
28 K6 **Reeder** North Dakota, N USA
35 R11 **Reedley** California, W USA
33 T11 **Reedpoint** Montana, NW USA
30 K8 **Reedsburg** Wisconsin, N USA
32 E13 **Reedsport** Oregon, NW USA
187 Q9 **Reef Islands** *island group* Santa Cruz Islands, E Solomon Islands
185 H16 **Reefton** West Coast, South Island, New Zealand
20 F8 **Reelfoot Lake** ◎ Tennessee, S USA
97 D17 **Ree, Lough** *Ir.* Loch Rí. ◎ C Ireland
Reengus *see* Rīngas
35 U4 **Reese River** ≈ Nevada, W USA
98 M8 **Reest** ≈ E Netherlands
Reetz Neumark *see* Recz
Reevhtse *see* Røsvatnet
137 N13 **Refahiye** Erzincan, C Turkey
23 N4 **Reform** Alabama, S USA
95 K20 **Reftele** Jönköping, S Sweden
25 T14 **Refugio** Texas, SW USA
110 E8 **Rega** ≈ NW Poland
Regar *see* Tursunzoda
101 O21 **Regen** Bayern, SE Germany
101 M20 **Regen** ≈ SE Germany
101 M21 **Regensburg** *Eng.* Ratisbon, *Fr.* Ratisbonne, *hist.* Ratisbona; *anc.* Castra Regina, Reginum. Bayern, SE Germany
101 M21 **Regenstauf** Bayern, SE Germany
74 I10 **Reggane** C Algeria
98 N9 **Regge** ≈ E Netherlands
Reggio *see* Reggio nell'Emilia
Reggio Calabria *see* Reggio di Calabria
107 M23 **Reggio di Calabria** *var.* Reggio Calabria, *Gk.* Rhegion; *anc.* Regium, Rhegium. Calabria, SW Italy
Reggio Emilia *see* Reggio nell'Emilia
106 F9 **Reggio nell'Emilia** *var.* Reggio Emilia, *abbrev.* Reggio; *anc.* Regium Lepidum. Emilia-Romagna, N Italy
116 I10 **Reghin** *Ger.* Sächsisch-Reen, *Hung.* Szászrégen; *prev.* Reghinul Săsesc, *Ger.* Sächsisch-Regen. Mureş, C Romania
Reghinul Săsesc *see* Reghin
9 U16 **Regina** *province capital* Saskatchewan, S Canada
55 Z10 **Régina** E French Guiana
9 U16 **Regina** ✕ Saskatchewan, S Canada
9 U16 **Regina Beach** Saskatchewan, S Canada
Reginum *see* Regensburg
Région du Haut-Congo *see* Haut-Congo
Registan *see* Rīgestān
60 L11 **Registro** São Paulo, S Brazil
Regium *see* Reggio di Calabria
Regium Lepidum *see* Reggio nell'Emilia
101 K19 **Regnitz** *var.* Rednitz. ≈ SE Germany
40 K10 **Regocijo** Durango, W Mexico
104 H12 **Reguengos de Monsaraz** Évora, S Portugal
101 M18 **Rehau** Bayern, E Germany
83 D19 **Rehoboth** Hardap, C Namibia
21 Z4 **Rehoboth Beach** Delaware, NE USA
Rehoboth/Rehovoth *see* Rehovot
138 F10 **Rehovot** *var.* Rehoboth, Rekhovot, Rehovoth. Central, C Israel
81 J20 **Rei** *spring/well* S Kenya
Reichenau *see* Rychnov nad Kněžnou
Reichenau *see* Bogatynia, Poland
101 M17 **Reichenbach** *var.* Reichenbach im Vogtland. Sachsen, E Germany
Reichenbach *see* Dzierżoniów
Reichenbach im Vogtland *see* Reichenbach
Reichenberg *see* Liberec
181 O11 **Reid** Western Australia
23 V6 **Reidsville** Georgia, SE USA
21 T8 **Reidsville** North Carolina, SE USA
Reifnitz *see* Ribnica
97 O22 **Reigate** SE England, UK
Reikjavik *see* Reykjavík
102 I10 **Ré, Île de** *island* W France
37 N15 **Reiley Peak** ▲ Arizona, SW USA
103 Q4 **Reims** *Eng.* Rheims; *anc.* Durocortorum, Remi. Marne, N France
63 G23 **Reina Adelaida, Archipiélago** *island group* S Chile
45 O16 **Reina Beatrix** ✕ (Oranjestad) C Aruba
108 F7 **Reinach** Aargau, W Switzerland
108 E6 **Reinach** Basel-Land, NW Switzerland
64 O11 **Reina Sofía** ✕ (Tenerife) Tenerife, Islas Canarias, Spain, NE Atlantic Ocean
29 W13 **Reinbeck** Iowa, C USA
100 J10 **Reinbek** Schleswig-Holstein, N Germany
9 U12 **Reindeer** ≈ Saskatchewan, C Canada
9 U11 **Reindeer Lake** ◎ Manitoba/Saskatchewan, C Canada
Reine-Charlotte, Îles de la *see* Queen Charlotte Islands
Reine-Élisabeth, Îles de la *see* Queen Elizabeth Islands
94 F13 **Reineskarvet** ▲ S Norway
184 H1 **Reinga, Cape** *headland* North Island, New Zealand
105 N3 **Reinosa** Cantabria, N Spain
109 R8 **Reisseck** ▲ S Austria
21 W3 **Reisterstown** Maryland, NE USA
Reisui *see* Yŏsu
98 N5 **Reitdiep** ≈ NE Netherlands
191 V10 **Reitoru** *atoll* Îles Tuamotu, C French Polynesia
95 M17 **Rejmyre** Östergötland, S Sweden
Reka *see* Rijeka
Reka Ili *see* Ile/Ili He
95 N16 **Rekarne** Västmanland, C Sweden
Rekhovot *see* Rehovot
8 K9 **Reliance** Northwest Territories, C Canada
33 U16 **Reliance** Wyoming, C USA
74 I5 **Relizane** *var.* Ghelîzâne, Ghilizane. NW Algeria
182 I7 **Remarkable, Mount** ▲ South Australia
54 E8 **Remedios** Antioquia, N Colombia
43 Q16 **Remedios** Veraguas, W Panama
42 D8 **Remedios, Punta** *headland* SW El Salvador
Remi *see* Reims
99 N25 **Remich** Grevenmacher, SE Luxembourg
99 J19 **Remicourt** Liège, E Belgium
14 H8 **Rémigny, Lac** ◎ Québec, SE Canada
55 Z10 **Rémire** NE French Guiana
127 N13 **Remontnoye** Rostovskaya Oblast', SW Russian Federation
171 U14 **Remoon** Pulau Kur, E Indonesia
99 L20 **Remouchamps** Liège, E Belgium
103 R15 **Remoulins** Gard, S France
173 X16 **Rempart, Mont du** *hill* W Mauritius
101 E15 **Remscheid** Nordrhein-Westfalen, W Germany
29 S12 **Remsen** Iowa, C USA
94 I12 **Rena** Hedmark, S Norway
94 I11 **Renåa** ≈ S Norway
Renaix *see* Ronse
118 H7 **Renceni** Valmiera, N Latvia
118 D9 **Renda** Kuldīga, W Latvia
107 N20 **Rende** Calabria, SW Italy
99 K21 **Rendeux** Luxembourg, SE Belgium
Rendina *see* Rentína
30 L16 **Rend Lake** ⊠ Illinois, N USA
186 K9 **Rendova** *island* New Georgia Islands, NW Solomon Islands
100 I8 **Rendsburg** Schleswig-Holstein, N Germany
108 B9 **Renens** Vaud, SW Switzerland
14 K12 **Renfrew** Ontario, SE Canada
96 I12 **Renfrew** *cultural region* SW Scotland, UK
168 L11 **Rengat** Sumatera, W Indonesia
153 W12 **Rengma Hills** ▲▲ NE India
62 H12 **Rengo** Libertador, C Chile
116 M12 **Reni** Odes'ka Oblast', SW Ukraine
80 F11 **Renk** Upper Nile, E Sudan
93 L19 **Renko** Etelä-Suomi, S Finland
98 L12 **Renkum** Gelderland, SE Netherlands
182 K9 **Renmark** South Australia
186 L10 **Rennell** *var.* Mu Nggava. *island* S Solomon Islands
181 Q4 **Renner Springs Roadhouse** Northern Territory, N Australia
102 I6 **Rennes** *Bret.* Roazon; *anc.* Condate. Ille-et-Vilaine, NW France
195 S16 **Rennick Glacier** *glacier* Antarctica
9 Y16 **Rennie** Manitoba, S Canada
35 Q5 **Reno** Nevada, W USA
106 H10 **Reno** ≈ N Italy
35 Q5 **Reno-Cannon** ✕ Nevada, W USA
83 F24 **Renoster** ≈ SW South Africa
15 T5 **Renouard, Lac** ◎ Québec, SE Canada
18 F13 **Renovo** Pennsylvania, NE USA
161 O3 **Renqiu** Hebei, E China
160 I9 **Renshou** Sichuan, C China
31 N12 **Rensselaer** Indiana, N USA
18 L11 **Rensselaer** New York, NE USA
Rentería *see* Errenteria
115 E17 **Rentína** *var.* Rendina. Thessalía, C Greece
29 T9 **Renville** Minnesota, N USA
77 O13 **Réo** W Burkina
15 O12 **Repentigny** Québec, SE Canada
146 K13 **Repetek** Lebap Welaýaty, E Turkmenistan
93 J16 **Replot** *Fin.* Raippaluoto. *island* W Finland
Reppen *see* Rzepin
Reps *see* Rupea
27 T7 **Republic** Missouri, C USA
32 K7 **Republic** Washington, NW USA
27 N3 **Republican River** ≈ Kansas/Nebraska, C USA
Republika Srpska *see* Foča
9 O7 **Repulse Bay** Northwest Territories, N Canada
56 F9 **Requena** Loreto, NE Peru
105 R10 **Requena** País Valenciano, E Spain
103 O14 **Réquista** Aveyron, S France
136 M12 **Reşadiye** Tokat, N Turkey
Reschenpass *see* Resia, Passo di
Reschitza *see* Reşiţa
113 N20 **Resen** *Turk.* Resne. SW FYR Macedonia
60 J11 **Reserva** Paraná, S Brazil
9 V15 **Reserve** Saskatchewan, S Canada
37 P13 **Reserve** New Mexico, SW USA
Reshetilovka *see* Reshetylivka
117 S6 **Reshetylivka** *Rus.* Reshetilovka. Poltavs'ka Oblast', NE Ukraine
Resht *see* Rasht
106 F5 **Resia, Passo di** *Ger.* Reschenpass. *pass* Austria/Italy
Resicabánya *see* Reşiţa
62 N7 **Resistencia** Chaco, NE Argentina
116 F12 **Reşiţa** *Ger.* Reschitza, *Hung.* Resicabánya. Caraş-Severin, W Romania
Resne *see* Resen
197 N9 **Resolute** Cornwallis Island, Nunavut, N Canada
Resolution *see* Fort Resolution
9 T7 **Resolution Island** *island* Nunavut, NE Canada
185 A23 **Resolution Island** *island* SW New Zealand
15 W7 **Restigouche** Québec, SE Canada
9 W17 **Reston** Manitoba, S Canada
14 H11 **Restoule Lake** ◎ Ontario, S Canada
54 F10 **Restrepo** Meta, C Colombia
42 B6 **Retalhuleu** Retalhuleu, SW Guatemala
42 A1 **Retalhuleu** *off.* Departamento de Retalhuleu. ⬖ *department* SW Guatemala
Retalhuleu, Departamento de *see* Retalhuleu
97 N18 **Retford** C England, UK
103 Q3 **Rethel** Ardennes, N France
Rethimno/Réthimnon *see* Réthymno
115 I25 **Réthymno** *prev.* Rethimno, Réthimnon. Kriti, Greece, E Mediterranean Sea
Retiche, Alpi *see* Rhaetian Alps
99 J16 **Retie** Antwerpen, N Belgium
111 J21 **Rétság** Nógrád, N Hungary
109 W2 **Retz** Niederösterreich, NE Austria
173 N15 **Réunion** *off.* La Réunion. ◇ *French overseas department* W Indian Ocean
128 L17 **Réunion** *island* W Indian Ocean
105 U6 **Reus** Cataluña, E Spain
99 J15 **Reusel** Noord-Brabant, S Netherlands
108 F7 **Reuss** ≈ NW Switzerland
Reutel *see* Ciuhuru
101 H22 **Reutlingen** Baden-Württemberg, S Germany
108 L7 **Reutte** Tirol, W Austria
99 M16 **Reuver** Limburg, SE Netherlands
28 K7 **Reva** South Dakota, N USA
Reval/Revel *see* Tallinn
124 J4 **Revda** Murmanskaya Oblast', NW Russian Federation
122 F6 **Revda** Sverdlovskaya Oblast', C Russian Federation
103 N16 **Revel** Haute-Garonne, S France
9 O16 **Revelstoke** British Columbia, SW Canada
43 N13 **Reventazón, Río** ≈ E Costa Rica
106 G9 **Revere** Lombardia, N Italy
39 Y14 **Revillagigedo Island** *island* Alexander Archipelago, Alaska, USA
103 R3 **Revin** Ardennes, N France
92 O3 **Revnosa** *headland* C Svalbard
Revolyutsii, Pik *see* Revolyutsiya, Qullai
147 T13 **Revolyutsiya, Qullai** *Rus.* Pik Revolyutsii. ▲ SE Tajikistan
111 L19 **Revúca** *Ger.* Grossrauschenbach, *Hung.* Nagyrőce. Banskobystrický Kraj, C Slovakia
154 K9 **Rewa** Madhya Pradesh, C India
152 I11 **Rewāri** Haryāna, N India
33 R14 **Rexburg** Idaho, NW USA
78 G13 **Rey Bouba** Nord, NE Cameroon
92 L3 **Reydharfjördhur** Austurland, E Iceland
57 K16 **Reyes** Beni, NW Bolivia
34 L8 **Reyes, Point** *headland* California, W USA
54 B12 **Reyes, Punta** *headland* SW Colombia
136 L17 **Reyhanlı** Hatay, S Turkey
43 U16 **Rey, Isla del** *island* Archipiélago de las Perlas, SE Panama
92 H2 **Reykhólar** Vestfirdhir, W Iceland
92 K2 **Reykjahlídh** Nordhurland Eystra, NE Iceland
92 I4 **Reykjanes** ⬖ *region* SW Iceland
197 O16 **Reykjanes Basin** *var.* Irminger Basin. *undersea feature* N Atlantic Ocean
197 N17 **Reykjanes Ridge** *undersea feature* N Atlantic Ocean
92 H4 **Reykjavík** *var.* Reikjavik. ● (Iceland) Höfudhborgarsvaedhi, W Iceland
18 D13 **Reynoldsville** Pennsylvania, NE USA
41 P8 **Reynosa** Tamaulipas, C Mexico
Reẕā'īyeh *see* Orūmīyeh
Reẕā'īyeh, Daryācheh-ye *see* Orūmīyeh, Daryācheh-ye
102 I8 **Rezé** Loire-Atlantique, NW France
118 K10 **Rēzekne** *Ger.* Rositten; *prev. Rus.* Rezhitsa. Rēzekne, SE Latvia
Rezhitsa *see* Rēzekne
117 N9 **Rezina** NE Moldova
114 N11 **Rezovo** *Turk.* Rezve. Burgas, E Bulgaria
114 N11 **Rezovska Reka** *Turk.* Rezve Deresi. ≈ Bulgaria/Turkey *see also* Rezve Deresi
Rezovska Reka *see* Rezve Deresi
Rezve *see* Rezovo
114 N11 **Rezve Deresi** *Bul.* Rezovska Reka. ≈ Bulgaria/Turkey *see also* Rezovska Reka
Rezve Deresi *see* Rezovska Reka
Rhadames *see* Ghadāmis
Rhaedestus *see* Tekirdağ
108 J10 **Rhaetian Alps** *Fr.* Alpes Rhétiques, *Ger.* Rätische Alpen, *It.* Alpi Retiche. ▲▲ C Europe
108 I8 **Rhätikon** ▲▲ C Europe
101 G14 **Rheda-Wiedenbrück** Nordrhein-Westfalen, W Germany
98 M12 **Rheden** Gelderland, E Netherlands
Rhegion/Rhegium *see* Reggio di Calabria
Rheims *see* Reims
Rhein *see* Rhine
101 E17 **Rheinbach** Nordrhein-Westfalen, W Germany
100 F13 **Rheine** *var.* Rheine in Westfalen. Nordrhein-Westfalen, NW Germany
Rheine in Westfalen *see* Rheine
Rheinfeld *see* Rheinfelden
101 F24 **Rheinfelden** Baden-Württemberg, S Germany
108 E6 **Rheinfelden** *var.* Rheinfeld. Aargau, N Switzerland
101 E17 **Rheinisches Schiefergebirge** *var.* Rhine State Uplands, *Eng.* Rhenish Slate Mountains. ▲▲ W Germany
101 D18 **Rheinland-Pfalz** *Eng.* Rhineland-Palatinate, *Fr.* Rhénanie-Palatinat. ⬖ *state* W Germany
101 G18 **Rhein/Main** ✕ (Frankfurt am Main) Hessen, W Germany
Rhénanie du Nord-Westphalie *see* Nordrhein-Westfalen
Rhénanie-Palatinat *see* Rheinland-Pfalz
98 K12 **Rhenen** Utrecht, C Netherlands
Rhenish Slate Mountains *see* Rheinisches Schiefergebirge
Rhétiques, Alpes *see* Rhaetian Alps
100 N10 **Rhin** ≈ NE Germany
Rhin *see* Rhine
84 F10 **Rhine** *Dut.* Rijn, *Fr.* Rhin, *Ger.* Rhein. ≈ W Europe
30 L5 **Rhinelander** Wisconsin, N USA
Rhineland-Palatinate *see* Rheinland-Pfalz
Rhine State Uplands *see* Rheinisches Schiefergebirge
100 N11 **Rhinkanal** *canal* NE Germany
81 F17 **Rhino Camp** NW Uganda
74 D7 **Rhir, Cap** *headland* W Morocco
106 D7 **Rho** Lombardia, N Italy
19 N12 **Rhode Island** *off.* State of Rhode Island and Providence Plantations, *also known as* Little Rhody, Ocean State. ⬖ *state* NE USA
19 O13 **Rhode Island** *island* Rhode Island, NE USA
19 O13 **Rhode Island Sound** *sound* Maine/Rhode Island, NE USA
Rhodes *see* Ródos
Rhode-Saint-Genèse *see* Sint-Genesius-Rode
84 L14 **Rhodes Basin** *undersea feature* E Mediterranean Sea
Rhodesia *see* Zimbabwe
114 I12 **Rhodope Mountains** *var.* Rodhópi Óri, *Bul.* Rhodope Planina, Rodopi, *Gk.* Orosirá Rodhópis, *Turk.* Dospad Dagh. ▲▲ Bulgaria/Greece
Rhodope Planina *see* Rhodope Mountains
101 I18 **Rhön** ▲▲ C Germany
103 Q10 **Rhône** ⬖ *department* E France
86 C12 **Rhône** ≈ France/Switzerland
103 R12 **Rhône-Alpes** ⬖ *region* E France
98 G13 **Rhoon** Zuid-Holland, SW Netherlands
96 G9 **Rhum** *var.* Rum. *island* W Scotland, UK
Rhuthun *see* Ruthin
97 J18 **Rhyl** NE Wales, UK
59 K18 **Rialma** Goiás, S Brazil
104 L3 **Riaño** Castilla-León, N Spain
105 O9 **Riansáres** ≈ C Spain
152 H6 **Riāsi** Jammu and Kashmir, NW India
168 K10 **Riau** *off.* Propinsi Riau. ⬖ *province* W Indonesia
Riau Archipelago *see* Riau, Kepulauan
168 M11 **Riau, Kepulauan** *var.* Riau Archipelago, *Dut.* Riouw-Archipel. *island group* W Indonesia
Riau, Propinsi *see* Riau
105 O6 **Riaza** Castilla-León, N Spain
105 N6 **Riaza** ≈ N Spain
81 K17 **Riba** *spring/well* NE Kenya
104 H4 **Ribadavia** Galicia, NW Spain
104 J2 **Ribadeo** Galicia, NW Spain
104 L2 **Ribadesella** Asturias, N Spain
104 G10 **Ribatejo** *former province* C Portugal
83 P15 **Ribáuè** Nampula, N Mozambique
97 K17 **Ribble** ≈ NW England, UK
95 F23 **Ribe** Ribe, W Denmark
95 F23 **Ribe** *off.* Ribe Amt, *var.* Ripen. ⬖ *county* W Denmark
Ribe Amt *see* Ribe
104 G3 **Ribeira** Galicia, NW Spain
64 O5 **Ribeira Brava** Madeira, Portugal, NE Atlantic Ocean
64 P3 **Ribeira Grande** São Miguel, Azores, Portugal, NE Atlantic Ocean
60 L8 **Ribeirão Preto** São Paulo, S Brazil
60 L11 **Ribeira, Rio** ≈ S Brazil
107 I24 **Ribera** Sicilia, Italy, C Mediterranean Sea
57 L14 **Riberalta** Beni, N Bolivia
105 W4 **Ribes de Freser** Cataluña, NE Spain
30 L6 **Rib Mountain** ▲ Wisconsin, N USA
109 U12 **Ribnica** *Ger.* Reifnitz. S Slovenia
117 N9 **Rîbniţa** *var.* Râbniţa, *Rus.* Rybnitsa. NE Moldova
100 M8 **Ribnitz-Damgarten** Mecklenburg-Vorpommern, NE Germany
111 D16 **Říčany** *Ger.* Ritschan. Středočesky Kraj, W Czech Republic
29 U7 **Rice** Minnesota, N USA
30 J5 **Rice Lake** Wisconsin, N USA
14 E8 **Rice Lake** ◎ Ontario, S Canada
14 I15 **Rice Lake** ◎ Ontario, SE Canada
23 V3 **Richard B. Russell Lake** ⊠ Georgia, SE USA
25 U6 **Richardson** Texas, SW USA
9 R11 **Richardson** ≈ Alberta, C Canada
10 I3 **Richardson Mountains** ▲▲ Yukon Territory, NW Canada
185 C21 **Richardson Mountains** ▲▲ South Island, New Zealand
42 F3 **Richardson Peak** ▲ SE Belize
76 G10 **Richard Toll** N Senegal
28 L5 **Richardton** North Dakota, N USA
14 F13 **Rich, Cape** *headland* Ontario, S Canada
102 L8 **Richelieu** Indre-et-Loire, C France
33 P15 **Richfield** Idaho, NW USA
36 K5 **Richfield** Utah, W USA
18 J10 **Richfield Springs** New York, NE USA
18 M6 **Richford** Vermont, NE USA
27 R6 **Rich Hill** Missouri, C USA
13 P14 **Richibucto** New Brunswick, SE Canada
108 G8 **Richisau** Glarus, NE Switzerland
23 S6 **Richland** Georgia, SE USA
27 U6 **Richland** Missouri, C USA
25 U8 **Richland** Texas, SW USA
32 K10 **Richland** Washington, NW USA
30 K8 **Richland Center** Wisconsin, N USA
21 W11 **Richlands** North Carolina, SE USA
21 Q7 **Richlands** Virginia, NE USA
25 R9 **Richland Springs** Texas, SW USA
183 S8 **Richmond** New South Wales, SE Australia
10 L17 **Richmond** British Columbia, SW Canada
14 L13 **Richmond** Ontario, SE Canada
15 Q12 **Richmond** Québec, SE Canada
185 I14 **Richmond** Tasman, South Island, New Zealand
35 N8 **Richmond** California, W USA
31 Q14 **Richmond** Indiana, N USA
20 M6 **Richmond** Kentucky, S USA
27 S4 **Richmond** Missouri, C USA
25 V11 **Richmond** Texas, SW USA
36 L1 **Richmond** Utah, W USA
21 W6 **Richmond** *state capital* Virginia, NE USA
14 H15 **Richmond Hill** Ontario, S Canada
185 J15 **Richmond Range** ▲▲ South Island, New Zealand
27 S12 **Rich Mountain** ▲ Arkansas, C USA
31 S13 **Richwood** Ohio, N USA
21 R5 **Richwood** West Virginia, NE USA
104 K5 **Ricobayo, Embalse de** ⊠ NW Spain
Ricomagus *see* Riom
Ridā' *see* Radā'
98 H13 **Ridderkerk** Zuid-Holland, SW Netherlands
33 N16 **Riddle** Idaho, NW USA
32 F14 **Riddle** Oregon, NW USA
14 L13 **Rideau** ≈ Ontario, SE Canada
35 T12 **Ridgecrest** California, W USA
18 L13 **Ridgefield** Connecticut, NE USA
22 K5 **Ridgeland** Mississippi, S USA
21 R15 **Ridgeland** South Carolina, SE USA
20 F8 **Ridgely** Tennessee, S USA
14 D17 **Ridgetown** Ontario, S Canada
21 R12 **Ridgeway** South Carolina, SE USA
Ridgeway *see* Ridgway
18 D13 **Ridgway** *var.* Ridgeway. Pennsylvania, NE USA
9 W16 **Riding Mountain** ▲▲ Manitoba, S Canada
Ried *see* Ried im Innkreis
109 R4 **Ried im Innkreis** *var.* Ried. Oberösterreich, NW Austria
109 X8 **Riegersburg** Steiermark, SE Austria
108 E6 **Riehen** Basel-Stadt, NW Switzerland
92 J9 **Riehppegáisá** *var.* Rieppe. ▲ N Norway
99 K18 **Riemst** Limburg, NE Belgium
Rieppe *see* Riehppegáisá
101 O15 **Riesa** Sachsen, E Germany
63 H24 **Riesco, Isla** *island* S Chile
107 K25 **Riesi** Sicilia, Italy, C Mediterranean Sea
83 F25 **Riet** ≈ SW South Africa
83 I23 **Riet** ≈ SW South Africa
118 D11 **Rietavas** Telšiai, W Lithuania
83 F19 **Rietfontein** Omaheke, E Namibia
107 I14 **Rieti** *anc.* Reate. Lazio, C Italy
84 D14 **Rif** *var.* Riff, Er Rif, Er Riff. ▲▲ N Morocco
Riff *see* Rif
37 Q4 **Rifle** Colorado, C USA
31 R7 **Rifle River** ≈ Michigan, N USA
81 H18 **Rift Valley** ⬖ *province* Kenya
Rift Valley *see* Great Rift Valley
118 F9 **Riga** *Eng.* Riga. ● (Latvia) Rīga, C Latvia
Rigaer Bucht *see* Riga, Gulf of
118 F6 **Riga, Gulf of** *Est.* Liivi Laht, *Ger.* Rigaer Bucht, *Latv.* Rīgas Jūras Līcis, *Rus.* Rizhskiy Zaliv; *prev. Est.* Riia Laht. *gulf* Estonia/Latvia
143 U12 **Rīgān** Kermān, SE Iran
Rīgas Jūras Līcis *see* Riga, Gulf of
15 N12 **Rigaud** ≈ Ontario/Québec, SE Canada
33 R14 **Rigby** Idaho, NW USA
148 M10 **Rīgestān** *var.* Registan. *desert region* S Afghanistan
32 M11 **Riggins** Idaho, NW USA
13 R8 **Rigolet** Newfoundland and Labrador, NE Canada
78 G9 **Rig-Rig** Kanem, W Chad
118 F4 **Riguldi** Läänemaa, W Estonia
Riia Laht *see* Riga, Gulf of
93 L19 **Riihimäki** Etelä-Suomi, S Finland
195 O2 **Riiser-Larsen Ice Shelf** *ice shelf* Antarctica
195 U2 **Riiser-Larsen Peninsula** *peninsula* Antarctica
65 P22 **Riiser-Larsen Sea** *sea* Antarctica
40 D2 **Riíto** Sonora, NW Mexico
112 B9 **Rijeka** *Ger.* Sankt Veit am Flaum, *It.* Fiume, *Slvn.* Reka; *anc.* Tarsatica. Primorje-Gorski Kotar, NW Croatia
99 I14 **Rijen** Noord-Brabant, S Netherlands
99 H15 **Rijkevorsel** Antwerpen, N Belgium
Rijn *see* Rhine
98 G11 **Rijnsburg** Zuid-Holland, W Netherlands
Rijssel *see* Lille
98 N10 **Rijssen** Overijssel, E Netherlands
98 G12 **Rijswijk** *Eng.* Ryswick. Zuid-Holland, W Netherlands
92 I10 **Riksgränsen** Norrbotten, N Sweden
165 U4 **Rikubetsu** Hokkaidō, NE Japan
165 R9 **Rikuzen-Takata** Iwate, Honshū, C Japan
27 O4 **Riley** Kansas, C USA
99 I17 **Rillaar** Vlaams Brabant, C Belgium
Rí, Loch *see* Ree, Lough
114 G11 **Rilska Reka** ≈ W Bulgaria
77 T12 **Rima** ≈ N Nigeria
141 N7 **Rimah, Wādī ar** *var.* Wādī ar Rummah. *dry watercourse* C Saudi Arabia
Rimaszombat *see* Rimavská Sobota
191 R12 **Rimatara** *island* Îles Australes, SW French Polynesia
111 L20 **Rimavská Sobota** *Ger.* Gross-Steffelsdorf, *Hung.* Rimaszombat. Bankobystrický Kraj, C Slovakia
9 Q15 **Rimbey** Alberta, SW Canada
95 P15 **Rimbo** Stockholm, C Sweden
95 M18 **Rimforsa** Östergötland, S Sweden
106 I11 **Rimini** *anc.* Ariminum. Emilia-Romagna, N Italy
Rîmnicu-Sărat *see* Râmnicu Sărat
Rîmnicu Vîlcea *see* Râmnicu Vâlcea
149 Y3 **Rimo Muztāgh** ▲▲ India/Pakistan
15 U7 **Rimouski** Québec, SE Canada
158 M16 **Rinbung** Xizang Zizhiqu, W China
Rinchinlhumbe *see* Dzöölön
62 I5 **Rincón, Cerro** ▲ N Chile
104 M15 **Rincón de la Victoria** Andalucía, S Spain
Rincón del Bonete, Lago Artificial de *see* Río Negro, Embalse del
105 Q4 **Rincón de Soto** La Rioja, N Spain
94 G8 **Rindal** Møre og Romsdal, S Norway
115 J20 **Rineia** *island* Kykládes, Greece, Aegean Sea
152 H11 **Rīngas** *prev.* Reengus, Rīngus. Rājasthān, N India
95 H24 **Ringe** Fyn, C Denmark
94 H11 **Ringebu** Oppland, S Norway
Ringen *see* Rõngu
186 K8 **Ringgi** Kolombangara, NW Solomon Islands
23 R1 **Ringgold** Georgia, SE USA
22 G5 **Ringgold** Louisiana, S USA
25 S5 **Ringgold** Texas, SW USA
95 E22 **Ringkøbing** Ringkøbing, W Denmark
95 E21 **Ringkøbing** *var.* Ringkøbing Amt. ⬖ *county* W Denmark
Ringkøbing Amt *see* Ringkøbing

◆ Country
● Country Capital
◇ Dependent Territory
○ Dependent Territory Capital
⬖ Administrative Regions
✕ International Airport
▲ Mountain
▲▲ Mountain Range
⛰ Volcano
≈ River
◎ Lake
⊠ Reservoir

RINGKØBING FJORD – ROOSEVELT, MOUNT

95 E22 **Ringkøbing Fjord** *fjord* W Denmark
33 S10 **Ringling** Montana, NW USA
27 N13 **Ringling** Oklahoma, C USA
94 H13 **Ringsaker** Hedmark, S Norway
95 I23 **Ringsted** Vestsjælland, E Denmark
Rīngus *see* Ringas
92 I9 **Ringvassøya** *Lapp.* Ráneš. *island* N Norway
18 K13 **Ringwood** New Jersey, NE USA
Rinn Duáin *see* Hook Head
100 H13 **Rinteln** Niedersachsen, NW Germany
115 E18 **Río Dytikí Ellás**, S Greece
Rio *see* Rio de Janeiro
56 C7 **Riobamba** Chimborazo, C Ecuador
60 P9 **Rio Bonito** Rio de Janeiro, SE Brazil
59 C16 **Rio Branco** *state capital* Acre, W Brazil
61 H18 **Río Branco** Cerro Largo, NE Uruguay
Rio Branco, Território de *see* Roraima
41 P8 **Río Bravo** Tamaulipas, C Mexico
63 G16 **Río Bueno** Los Lagos, C Chile
55 P5 **Río Caribe** Sucre, NE Venezuela
54 M5 **Río Chico** Miranda, N Venezuela
63 H18 **Río Cisnes** Aisén, S Chile
60 L9 **Rio Claro** São Paulo, S Brazil
45 V14 **Rio Claro** Trinidad, Trinidad and Tobago
54 J5 **Río Claro** Lara, N Venezuela
63 K15 **Río Colorado** Río Negro, E Argentina
62 K11 **Río Cuarto** Córdoba, C Argentina
60 P10 **Rio de Janeiro** *var.* Rio. *state capital* Rio de Janeiro, SE Brazil
60 P9 **Rio de Janeiro** *off.* Estado do Rio de Janeiro. ◆ *state* SE Brazil
Rio de Janeiro, Estado do *see* Rio de Janeiro
43 R17 **Río de Jesús** Veraguas, S Panama
34 K3 **Rio Dell** California, W USA
60 K13 **Rio do Sul** Santa Catarina, S Brazil
63 I23 **Río Gallegos** *var.* Gallegos, Puerto Gallegos. Santa Cruz, S Argentina
63 J24 **Río Grande** Tierra del Fuego, S Argentina
61 I18 **Rio Grande** *var.* São Pedro do Rio Grande do Sul. Rio Grande do Sul, S Brazil
40 L10 **Río Grande** Zacatecas, C Mexico
42 J9 **Río Grande** León, NW Nicaragua
45 V5 **Río Grande** E Puerto Rico
24 I9 **Rio Grande** ⚞ Texas, SW USA
25 R17 **Rio Grande City** Texas, SW USA
59 P14 **Rio Grande do Norte** *off.* Estado do Rio Grande do Norte. ◆ *state* E Brazil
Rio Grande do Norte, Estado do *see* Rio Grande do Norte
61 G15 **Rio Grande do Sul** *off.* Estado do Rio Grande do Sul. ◆ *state* S Brazil
Rio Grande do Sul, Estado do *see* Rio Grande do Sul
65 M17 **Rio Grande Fracture Zone** *tectonic feature* C Atlantic Ocean
65 J18 **Rio Grande Gap** *undersea feature* S Atlantic Ocean
Rio Grande Plateau *see* Rio Grande Rise
65 J18 **Rio Grande Rise** *var.* Rio Grande Plateau. *undersea feature* SW Atlantic Ocean
54 G4 **Ríohacha** La Guajira, N Colombia
43 S16 **Río Hato** Coclé, C Panama
25 T17 **Rio Hondo** Texas, SW USA
56 D10 **Rioja** San Martín, N Peru
41 Y11 **Río Lagartos** Yucatán, SE Mexico
103 P11 **Riom** *anc.* Ricomagus. Puy-de-Dôme, C France
104 F10 **Rio Maior** Santarém, C Portugal
103 O12 **Riom-ès-Montagnes** Cantal, C France
60 J12 **Rio Negro** Paraná, S Brazil
63 I15 **Río Negro** *off.* Provincia de Río Negro. ◆ *province* C Argentina
61 D18 **Río Negro** ◆ *department* W Uruguay
47 V12 **Río Negro, Embalse del** *var.* Lago Artificial de Rincón del Bonete. ⊠ C Uruguay
Río Negro, Provincia de *see* Río Negro
107 M17 **Rionero in Vulture** Basilicata, S Italy
137 S9 **Rioni** ⚞ W Georgia
105 P12 **Riópar** Castilla-La Mancha, C Spain
61 H16 **Rio Pardo** Rio Grande do Sul, S Brazil
37 R11 **Rio Rancho Estates** New Mexico, SW USA
42 L11 **Río San Juan** ◆ *department* S Nicaragua
54 E9 **Ríosucio** Caldas, W Colombia
54 C7 **Ríosucio** Chocó, NW Colombia
62 K10 **Río Tercero** Córdoba, C Argentina
54 J5 **Río Tocuyo** Lara, N Venezuela
Riouw-Archipel *see* Riau, Kepulauan
59 J19 **Rio Verde** Goiás, C Brazil
41 O12 **Río Verde** *var.* Rioverde. San Luis Potosí, C Mexico
Rioverde *see* Río Verde
35 O8 **Rio Vista** California, W USA
112 M11 **Ripanj** Serbia, N Serbia
106 J13 **Ripatransone** Marche, C Italy
Ripen *see* Ribe
22 M2 **Ripley** Mississippi, S USA
31 R15 **Ripley** Ohio, N USA
20 F9 **Ripley** Tennessee, S USA
21 Q4 **Ripley** West Virginia, NE USA
105 W4 **Ripoll** Cataluña, NE Spain
97 M16 **Ripon** N England, UK
30 M7 **Ripon** Wisconsin, N USA
107 L24 **Riposto** Sicilia, Italy, C Mediterranean Sea
99 L14 **Rips** Noord-Brabant, SE Netherlands
54 D9 **Risaralda** *off.* Departamento de Risaralda. ◆ *province* C Colombia
Risaralda, Departamento de *see* Risaralda
116 L8 **Rîşcani** *var.* Râşcani, *Rus.* Ryshkany. NW Moldova
152 J9 **Rishikesh** Uttaranchal, N India
165 S1 **Rishiri-tō** *var.* Risiri Tô. *island* NE Japan
165 S1 **Rishiri-yama** ⩘ Rishiri-tō, NE Japan
25 R7 **Rising Star** Texas, SW USA
31 Q15 **Rising Sun** Indiana, N USA
Risiri Tô *see* Rishiri-tō
102 L4 **Risle** ⚞ N France
Rîşno *see* Râşnov
27 V13 **Rison** Arkansas, C USA
95 G17 **Risør** Aust-Agder, S Norway
92 H10 **Risøyhamn** Nordland, C Norway
101 I23 **Riss** ⚞ S Germany
118 G4 **Risti** *Ger.* Kreuz. Läänemaa, W Estonia
15 V8 **Ristigouche** ⚞ Québec, SE Canada
93 N18 **Ristiina** Isä-Suomi, E Finland
93 N14 **Ristijärvi** Oulu, C Finland
188 C14 **Ritidian Point** *headland* N Guam
Ritschan *see* Říčany
35 R9 **Ritter, Mount** ▲ California, W USA
31 T12 **Rittman** Ohio, N USA
32 L9 **Ritzville** Washington, NW USA
Riva *see* Riva del Garda
61 A21 **Rivadavia** Buenos Aires, E Argentina
106 F7 **Riva del Garda** *var.* Riva. Trentino-Alto Adige, N Italy
106 B8 **Rivarolo Canavese** Piemonte, W Italy
42 K11 **Rivas** Rivas, SW Nicaragua
42 J11 **Rivas** ◆ *department* SW Nicaragua
103 R11 **Rive-de-Gier** Loire, E France
61 A22 **Rivera** Buenos Aires, E Argentina
61 F16 **Rivera** Rivera, NE Uruguay
61 F17 **Rivera** ◆ *department* NE Uruguay
35 P9 **Riverbank** California, W USA
76 K17 **River Cess** SW Liberia
28 M4 **Riverdale** North Dakota, N USA
30 I6 **River Falls** Wisconsin, N USA
9 T16 **Riverhurst** Saskatchewan, S Canada
183 O10 **Riverina** *physical region* New South Wales, SE Australia
80 G8 **River Nile** ◆ *state* NE Sudan
63 F19 **Rivero, Isla** *island* Archipiélago de los Chonos, S Chile
9 W16 **Rivers** Manitoba, S Canada
77 U17 **Rivers** ◆ *state* S Nigeria
185 D23 **Riversdale** Southland, South Island, New Zealand
83 F26 **Riversdale** Western Cape, SW South Africa
35 U15 **Riverside** California, W USA
25 W9 **Riverside** Texas, SW USA
37 U3 **Riverside Reservoir** ⊠ Colorado, C USA
10 K15 **Rivers Inlet** British Columbia, SW Canada
10 K15 **Rivers Inlet** *inlet* British Columbia, SW Canada
9 X15 **Riverton** Manitoba, S Canada
185 C24 **Riverton** Southland, South Island, New Zealand
30 L13 **Riverton** Illinois, N USA
36 L3 **Riverton** Utah, W USA
33 V15 **Riverton** Wyoming, C USA
14 G10 **River Valley** Ontario, S Canada
13 P14 **Riverview** New Brunswick, SE Canada
103 O17 **Rivesaltes** Pyrénées-Orientales, S France
36 H11 **Riviera** Arizona, SW USA
25 S15 **Riviera** Texas, SW USA
23 Z14 **Riviera Beach** Florida, SE USA
15 Q10 **Rivière-à-Pierre** Québec, SE Canada
15 T9 **Rivière-Bleue** Québec, SE Canada
15 T8 **Rivière-du-Loup** Québec, SE Canada
173 Y15 **Rivière du Rempart** NE Mauritius
45 R12 **Rivière-Pilote** S Martinique
173 O17 **Rivière St-Etienne, Point de la** *headland* SW Réunion
13 S10 **Rivière-St-Paul** Québec, E Canada
Rivière Sèche *see* Bel Air
116 K4 **Rivne** *Pol.* Równe, *Rus.* Rovno. Rivnens'ka Oblast', NW Ukraine
Rivne *see* Rivnens'ka Oblast'
116 K3 **Rivnens'ka Oblast'** *var.* Rivne, *Rus.* Rovenskaya Oblast'. ◆ *province* NW Ukraine
106 B8 **Rivoli** Piemonte, NW Italy
159 Q14 **Riwoqê** *var.* Racaka. Xizang Zizhiqu, W China
99 H19 **Rixensart** Walloon Brabant, C Belgium
Riyadh/Riyāḍ, Minṭaqat ar *see* Ar Riyāḍ
Riyāq *see* Rayak
Rizaiyeh *see* Orūmīyeh
137 P11 **Rize** Rize, NE Turkey
137 P11 **Rize** *prev.* Çoruh. ◆ *province* NE Turkey
161 R5 **Rizhao** Shandong, E China
Rizhskiy Zaliv *see* Riga, Gulf of
Rizokarpaso/Rizokárpason *see* Dipkarpaz
107 O21 **Rizzuto, Capo** *headland* S Italy
95 F15 **Rjukan** Telemark, S Norway
95 D16 **Rjuven** ▲▲ S Norway
76 H9 **Rkîz** Trarza, W Mauritania
115 Q23 **Ro** *prev.* Ágios Geórgios. *island* SE Greece
95 H14 **Roa** Oppland, S Norway
105 N5 **Roa** Castilla-León, N Spain
45 T9 **Road Town** ○ (British Virgin Islands) Tortola, C British Virgin Islands
96 F6 **Roag, Loch** *inlet* NW Scotland, UK
37 O5 **Roan Cliffs** *cliff* Colorado/Utah, W USA
21 P9 **Roan High Knob** *var.* Roan Mountain. ▲ North Carolina/Tennessee, SE USA
Roan Mountain *see* Roan High Knob
103 Q10 **Roanne** *anc.* Rodunma. Loire, E France
23 R4 **Roanoke** Alabama, S USA
21 S7 **Roanoke** Virginia, NE USA
21 Z9 **Roanoke Island** *island* North Carolina, SE USA
21 W8 **Roanoke Rapids** North Carolina, SE USA
21 X9 **Roanoke River** ⚞ North Carolina/Virginia, SE USA
37 O4 **Roan Plateau** *plain* Utah, W USA
37 R5 **Roaring Fork River** ⚞ Colorado, C USA
25 O5 **Roaring Springs** Texas, SW USA
42 J4 **Roatán** *var.* Coxen Hole, Coxin Hole. Islas de la Bahía, N Honduras
42 I4 **Roatán, Isla de** *island* Islas de la Bahía, N Honduras
Roat Kampuchea *see* Cambodia
Roazon *see* Rennes
143 T7 **Robāṭ-e Chāh Gonbad** Yazd, E Iran
143 R7 **Robāṭ-e Khān** Yazd, C Iran
143 T7 **Robāṭ-e Khvosh Āb** Yazd, E Iran
143 R8 **Robāṭ-e Posht-e Bādām** Yazd, NE Iran
143 Q8 **Ribāṭ-e Rīzāb** Yazd, C Iran
175 S8 **Robbie Ridge** *undersea feature* W Pacific Ocean
21 T10 **Robbins** North Carolina, SE USA
183 N15 **Robbins Island** *island* Tasmania, SE Australia
21 N10 **Robbinsville** North Carolina, SE USA
182 J12 **Robe** South Australia
21 W9 **Robersonville** North Carolina, SE USA
25 P8 **Robert Lee** Texas, SW USA
35 V5 **Roberts Creek Mountain** ▲ Nevada, W USA
93 J15 **Robertsfors** Västerbotten, N Sweden
27 R11 **Robert S. Kerr Reservoir** ⊠ Oklahoma, C USA
38 L12 **Roberts Mountain** ▲ Nunivak Island, Alaska, USA
83 F26 **Robertson** Western Cape, SW South Africa
194 H4 **Robertson Island** *island* Antarctica
76 J16 **Robertsport** W Liberia
182 J8 **Robertstown** South Australia
Robert Williams *see* Caála
15 P7 **Roberval** Québec, SE Canada
31 N15 **Robinson** Illinois, N USA
193 U11 **Róbinson Crusoe, Isla** *island* Islas Juan Fernández, Chile, E Pacific Ocean
180 J9 **Robinson Range** ▲▲ Western Australia
182 M9 **Robinvale** Victoria, SE Australia
105 P11 **Robledo** Castilla-La Mancha, C Spain
54 G5 **Robles** *var.* La Paz, Robles La Paz. Cesar, N Colombia
Robles La Paz *see* Robles
9 V15 **Roblin** Manitoba, S Canada
9 S17 **Robsart** Saskatchewan, S Canada
9 N15 **Robson, Mount** ▲ British Columbia, SW Canada
25 T14 **Robstown** Texas, SW USA
25 P6 **Roby** Texas, SW USA
104 E11 **Roca, Cabo da** *cape* C Portugal
Rocadas *see* Xangongo
41 S14 **Roca Partida, Punta** *headland* C Mexico
47 X6 **Rocas, Atol das** *island* E Brazil
107 L18 **Roccadaspide** *var.* Rocca d'Aspide. Campania, S Italy
Rocca d'Aspide *see* Roccadaspide
107 K15 **Roccaraso** Abruzzo, C Italy
106 H10 **Rocca San Casciano** Emilia-Romagna, C Italy
106 G13 **Roccastrada** Toscana, C Italy
61 G20 **Rocha** Rocha, E Uruguay
61 G19 **Rocha** ◆ *department* E Uruguay
97 L17 **Rochdale** NW England, UK
102 L11 **Rochechouart** Haute-Vienne, C France
99 J22 **Rochefort** Namur, SE Belgium
102 J11 **Rochefort** *var.* Rochefort sur Mer. Charente-Maritime, W France
Rochefort sur Mer *see* Rochefort
125 N10 **Rochegda** Arkhangel'skaya Oblast', NW Russian Federation
30 L10 **Rochelle** Illinois, N USA
25 Q9 **Rochelle** Texas, SW USA
15 V3 **Rochers Ouest, Rivière aux** ⚞ Québec, SE Canada
97 O22 **Rochester** *anc.* Durobrivae. SE England, UK
31 O12 **Rochester** Indiana, N USA
29 W10 **Rochester** Minnesota, N USA
19 O9 **Rochester** New Hampshire, NE USA
18 F9 **Rochester** New York, NE USA
25 P5 **Rochester** Texas, SW USA
31 S9 **Rochester Hills** Michigan, N USA
Rocheuses, Montagnes/Rockies *see* Rocky Mountains
64 M6 **Rockall** *island* N Atlantic Ocean, UK
64 L6 **Rockall Bank** *undersea feature* N Atlantic Ocean
84 B8 **Rockall Rise** *undersea feature* N Atlantic Ocean
84 C9 **Rockall Trough** *undersea feature* N Atlantic Ocean
35 U2 **Rock Creek** ⚞ Nevada, W USA
25 T10 **Rockdale** Texas, SW USA
195 N12 **Rockefeller Plateau** *plateau* Antarctica
30 K11 **Rock Falls** Illinois, N USA
23 Q5 **Rockford** Alabama, S USA
30 L10 **Rockford** Illinois, N USA
15 Q12 **Rock Forest** Québec, SE Canada
9 T17 **Rockglen** Saskatchewan, S Canada
181 Y8 **Rockhampton** Queensland, E Australia
21 R11 **Rock Hill** South Carolina, SE USA
180 I13 **Rockingham** Western Australia
21 T11 **Rockingham** North Carolina, SE USA
30 J11 **Rock Island** Illinois, N USA
25 U12 **Rock Island** Texas, SW USA
14 C10 **Rock Lake** Ontario, S Canada
29 O2 **Rock Lake** North Dakota, N USA
14 I12 **Rock Lake** ◎ Ontario, SE Canada
14 M12 **Rockland** Ontario, SE Canada
19 R7 **Rockland** Maine, NE USA
182 L11 **Rocklands Reservoir** ⊠ Victoria, SE Australia
35 O7 **Rocklin** California, W USA
23 R3 **Rockmart** Georgia, SE USA
31 N16 **Rockport** Indiana, N USA
27 Q1 **Rock Port** Missouri, C USA
25 T14 **Rockport** Texas, SW USA
32 I7 **Rockport** Washington, NW USA
29 S11 **Rock Rapids** Iowa, C USA
30 K11 **Rock River** ⚞ Illinois/Wisconsin, N USA
44 I3 **Rock Sound** Eleuthera Island, C Bahamas
25 P11 **Rocksprings** Texas, SW USA
33 U17 **Rock Springs** Wyoming, C USA
55 T9 **Rockstone** C Guyana
29 S12 **Rock Valley** Iowa, C USA
31 N14 **Rockville** Indiana, N USA
21 W3 **Rockville** Maryland, NE USA
25 U6 **Rockwall** Texas, SW USA
29 U13 **Rockwell City** Iowa, C USA
31 S10 **Rockwood** Michigan, N USA
20 M9 **Rockwood** Tennessee, S USA
25 Q8 **Rockwood** Texas, SW USA
37 U6 **Rocky Ford** Colorado, C USA
14 D9 **Rocky Island Lake** ◎ Ontario, S Canada
21 V9 **Rocky Mount** North Carolina, SE USA
21 S7 **Rocky Mount** Virginia, NE USA
33 Q8 **Rocky Mountain** ▲ Montana, NW USA
9 P15 **Rocky Mountain House** Alberta, SW Canada
37 T3 **Rocky Mountain National Park** *national park* Colorado, C USA
2 E12 **Rocky Mountains** *var.* Rockies, *Fr.* Montagnes Rocheuses. ▲▲ Canada/USA
42 H1 **Rocky Point** *headland* NE Belize
83 A17 **Rocky Point** *headland* NW Namibia
95 F14 **Rødberg** Buskerud, S Norway
95 I25 **Rødby** Storstrøm, SE Denmark
95 I25 **Rødbyhavn** Storstrøm, SE Denmark
13 T10 **Roddickton** Newfoundland, Newfoundland and Labrador, SE Canada
95 F23 **Rødding** Sønderjylland, SW Denmark
95 M22 **Rödeby** Blekinge, S Sweden
98 N6 **Roden** Drenthe, NE Netherlands
62 H9 **Rodeo** San Juan, W Argentina
103 O14 **Rodez** *anc.* Segodunum. Aveyron, S France
Rodholívos *see* Rodolívos
Rodhópi Óri *see* Rhodope Mountains
Ródhos *see* Ródos
Ródhos/Rodi *see* Ródos
Rodi *see* Ródos
107 N15 **Rodi Garganico** Puglia, SE Italy
101 N20 **Roding** Bayern, SE Germany
113 J19 **Rodinit, Kepi i** *headland* W Albania
116 I9 **Rodnei, Munţii** ▲▲ N Romania
184 L4 **Rodney, Cape** *headland* North Island, New Zealand
38 L9 **Rodney, Cape** *headland* Alaska, USA
124 M16 **Rodniki** Ivanovskaya Oblast', W Russian Federation
119 Q16 **Rodnya** *Rus.* Rodnya. Mahilyowskaya Voblasts', E Belarus
Rodó *see* José Enrique Rodó
114 H13 **Rodolívos** *var.* Rodholívos. Kentrikí Makedonía, NE Greece
Rodopi *see* Rhodope Mountains
115 O22 **Ródos** *var.* Ródhos, *Eng.* Rhodes, *It.* Rodi. Ródos, Dodekánisa, Greece, Aegean Sea
115 O22 **Ródos** *var.* Ródhos, *Eng.* Rhodes, *It.* Rodi; *anc.* Rhodos. *island* Dodekánisa, Greece, Aegean Sea
Rodosto *see* Tekirdağ
59 A14 **Rodrigues** Amazonas, W Brazil
173 P8 **Rodrigues** *var.* Rodriquez. *island* E Mauritius
Rodriquez *see* Rodrigues
Roebourne *see* Roanne
180 I7 **Roebourne** Western Australia
83 J20 **Roedtan** Limpopo, NE South Africa
98 H11 **Roelofarendsveen** Zuid-Holland, W Netherlands
Roepat *see* Rupat, Pulau
Roer *see* Rur
99 M16 **Roermond** Limburg, SE Netherlands
99 C18 **Roeselare** *Fr.* Roulers; *prev.* Rousselaere. West-Vlaanderen, W Belgium
9 P8 **Roes Welcome Sound** *strait* Nunavut, N Canada
Roeteng *see* Ruteng
Rofreit *see* Rovereto
Rogachëv *see* Rahachow
57 L15 **Rogagua, Laguna** ◎ NW Bolivia
95 C16 **Rogaland** ◆ *county* S Norway
25 Y9 **Roganville** Texas, SW USA
109 W11 **Rogaška Slatina** *Ger.* Rohitsch-Sauerbrunn; *prev.* Rogatec-Slatina. E Slovenia
Rogatec-Slatina *see* Rogaška Slatina
112 J13 **Rogatica** ◆ Republika Srpska, SE Bosnia and Herzegovina
Rogatin *see* Rohatyn
93 F17 **Rogen** ◎ C Sweden
27 S9 **Rogers** Arkansas, C USA
29 P5 **Rogers** North Dakota, N USA
25 T9 **Rogers** Texas, SW USA
31 R5 **Rogers City** Michigan, N USA
Roger Simpson Island *see* Abemama
35 T14 **Rogers Lake** *salt flat* California, W USA
21 Q8 **Rogers, Mount** ▲ Virginia, NE USA
33 O16 **Rogerson** Idaho, NW USA
9 O16 **Rogers Pass** *pass* British Columbia, SW Canada
21 O8 **Rogersville** Tennessee, S USA
99 L16 **Roggel** Limburg, SE Netherlands
Roggeveen *see* Roggewein, Cabo
193 R10 **Roggeveen Basin** *undersea feature* E Pacific Ocean
191 X16 **Roggewein, Cabo** *var.* Roggeveen. *cape* Easter Island, Chile, E Pacific Ocean
103 Y13 **Rogliano** Corse, France, C Mediterranean Sea
107 N21 **Rogliano** Calabria, SW Italy
92 G12 **Rognan** Nordland, C Norway
100 K10 **Rögnitz** ⚞ N Germany
Rogozhina/Rogozhinë *see* Rrogozhinë
110 G10 **Rogoźno** Wielkopolskie, C Poland
32 E15 **Rogue River** ⚞ Oregon, NW USA
116 I6 **Rohatyn** *Rus.* Rogatin. Ivano-Frankivs'ka Oblast', W Ukraine
189 O14 **Rohi** Pohnpei, E Micronesia
Rohitsch-Sauerbrunn *see* Rogaška Slatina
149 Q13 **Rohri** Sind, SE Pakistan
152 I10 **Rohtak** Haryāna, N India
Roi Ed *see* Roi Et
167 R9 **Roi Et** *var.* Muang Roi Et, Roi Ed. Roi Et, E Thailand
191 U9 **Roi Georges, Îles du** *island group* Îles Tuamotu, C French Polynesia
153 Y10 **Roing** Arunāchal Pradesh, NE India
118 E7 **Roja** Talsi, NW Latvia
61 B20 **Rojas** Buenos Aires, E Argentina
149 R12 **Rojhān** Punjab, E Pakistan
41 Q12 **Rojo, Cabo** *headland* C Mexico
45 Q10 **Rojo, Cabo** *cape* W Puerto Rico
168 K10 **Rokan Kiri, Sungai** ⚞ Sumatera, W Indonesia
118 I11 **Rokiškis** Panevėžys, NE Lithuania
165 R7 **Rokkasho** Aomori, Honshū, C Japan
111 B17 **Rokycany** *Ger.* Rokytzan. Plzeňský Kraj, W Czech Republic
117 P6 **Rokytne** Kyyivs'ka Oblast', N Ukraine
116 L3 **Rokytne** Rivnens'ka Oblast', NW Ukraine
Rokytzan *see* Rokycany
158 L11 **Rola Co** ◎ W China
29 V13 **Roland** Iowa, C USA
95 D15 **Røldal** Hordaland, S Norway
98 O7 **Rolde** Drenthe, NE Netherlands
29 O2 **Rolette** North Dakota, N USA
27 V6 **Rolla** Missouri, C USA
29 O2 **Rolla** North Dakota, N USA
108 A10 **Rolle** Vaud, W Switzerland
181 X8 **Rolleston** Queensland, E Australia
185 H19 **Rolleston** Canterbury, South Island, New Zealand
185 G18 **Rolleston Range** ▲▲ South Island, New Zealand
14 H8 **Rollet** Québec, SE Canada
22 J4 **Rolling Fork** Mississippi, S USA
20 L6 **Rolling Fork** ⚞ Kentucky, S USA
14 J11 **Rolphton** Ontario, SE Canada
Röm *see* Rømø
181 X10 **Roma** Queensland, E Australia
107 I15 **Roma** *Eng.* Rome. ● (Italy) Lazio, C Italy
95 P19 **Roma** Gotland, SE Sweden
21 T14 **Romain, Cape** *headland* South Carolina, SE USA
13 P11 **Romaine** ⚞ Newfoundland and Labrador/Québec, E Canada
25 R17 **Roma Los Saenz** Texas, SW USA
114 H8 **Roman** Vratsa, NW Bulgaria
116 L10 **Roman** *Hung.* Románvásár. Neamţ, NE Romania
64 M13 **Romanche Fracture Zone** *tectonic feature* E Atlantic Ocean
61 C15 **Romang** Santa Fe, C Argentina
171 R15 **Romang, Pulau** *var.* Pulau Roma. *island* Kepulauan Damar, E Indonesia
171 R15 **Romang, Selat** *strait* Nusa Tenggara, S Indonesia
116 J11 **Romania** *Bul.* Rumŭniya, *Ger.* Rumänien, *Hung.* Románia, *Rom.* România, *SCr.* Rumunjska, *Ukr.* Rumuniya, *prev.* Republica Socialistă România, Roumania, Rumania, Socialist Republic of Romania, *prev.Rom.* Romînia. ◆ *republic* SE Europe
România, Republica Socialistă *see* Romania
Romania, Socialist Republic of *see* Romania
117 T14 **Roman-Kash** ▲ S Ukraine
23 W16 **Romano, Cape** *headland* Florida, SE USA
44 G5 **Romano, Cayo** *island* C Cuba
123 O13 **Romanovka** Respublika Buryatiya, S Russian Federation
127 N8 **Romanovka** Saratovskaya Oblast', W Russian Federation
108 I6 **Romanshorn** Thurgau, NE Switzerland
103 R12 **Romans-sur-Isère** Drôme, E France
189 U12 **Romanum** *island* Chuuk, C Micronesia
Románvásár *see* Roman
39 S5 **Romanzof Mountains** ▲▲ Alaska, USA
Roma, Pulau *see* Romang, Pulau
103 S4 **Rombas** Moselle, NE France
23 R2 **Rome** Georgia, SE USA
18 I9 **Rome** New York, NE USA
Rome *see* Roma
31 S9 **Romeo** Michigan, N USA
Römerstadt *see* Rýmařov
Rometan *see* Romiton
103 P5 **Romilly-sur-Seine** Aube, N France
Rominia *see* Romania
146 L11 **Romiton** *Rus.* Rometan. Buxoro Viloyati, C Uzbekistan
21 U3 **Romney** West Virginia, NE USA
117 S4 **Romny** Sums'ka Oblast', NE Ukraine
95 E24 **Rømø** *Ger.* Röm. *island* SW Denmark
117 S5 **Romodan** Poltavs'ka Oblast', NE Ukraine
127 P5 **Romodanovo** Respublika Mordoviya, W Russian Federation
Romorantin *see* Romorantin-Lanthenay
103 N8 **Romorantin-Lanthenay** *var.* Romorantin. Loir-et-Cher, C France
94 F9 **Romsdal** *physical region* S Norway
94 F10 **Romsdalen** *valley* S Norway
94 E9 **Romsdalsfjorden** *fjord* S Norway
33 P8 **Ronan** Montana, NW USA
59 M14 **Roncador** Maranhão, E Brazil
186 M7 **Roncador Reef** *reef* N Solomon Islands
59 J17 **Roncador, Serra do** ▲▲ C Brazil
21 S6 **Ronceverte** West Virginia, NE USA
107 H14 **Ronciglione** Lazio, C Italy
104 L15 **Ronda** Andalucía, S Spain
94 G11 **Rondane** ▲▲ S Norway
104 L15 **Ronda, Serranía de** ▲▲ S Spain
95 H22 **Rønde** Århus, C Denmark
Ronde, Île *see* Round Island
Rōṇḍik *see* Rongrik Atoll
59 E16 **Rondônia** *off.* Estado de Rondônia; *prev.* Território de Rondônia. ◆ *state* W Brazil
Rondônia, Estado de *see* Rondônia
Rondônia, Território de *see* Rondônia
59 I18 **Rondonópolis** Mato Grosso, W Brazil
94 G11 **Rondslottet** ▲ S Norway
95 P20 **Ronehamn** Gotland, SE Sweden
160 L13 **Rong'an** *var.* Chang'an, Rongan. Guangxi Zhuangzu Zizhiqu, S China
Rongan *see* Rong'an
Rongcheng *see* Jianli, Hubei, China
189 R4 **Rongelap Atoll** *var.* Rōnlap. *atoll* Ralik Chain, NW Marshall Islands
Rongerik *see* Rongrik Atoll
160 K12 **Rongjiang** *var.* Guzhou. Guizhou, S China
160 L13 **Rong Jiang** ⚞ S China
Rongjiang *see* Nankang
Rong, Kas *see* Rŭng, Kaôh
167 P8 **Rong Kwang** Phrae, NW Thailand
189 T4 **Rongrik Atoll** *var.* Rōṇḍik, Rongerik. *atoll* Ralik Chain, N Marshall Islands
189 X2 **Rongrong** *island* SE Marshall Islands
160 L13 **Rongshui** *var.* Rongshui Miaozu Zizhixian. Guangxi Zhuangzu Zizhiqu, S China
Rongshui Miaozu Zizhixian *see* Rongshui
118 I6 **Rōngu** *Ger.* Ringen. Tartumaa, SE Estonia
160 L15 **Rongxian** *var.* Rongcheng. Guangxi Zhuangzu Zizhiqu, S China
Rong Xian *see* Rongxian, Guangxi, China
Rongzhag *see* Danba
Roniu *see* Ronui, Mont
189 N13 **Ronkiti** Pohnpei, E Micronesia
Rōnlap *see* Rongelap Atoll
95 L24 **Rønne** Bornholm, E Denmark
95 M22 **Ronneby** Blekinge, S Sweden
194 J7 **Ronne Entrance** *inlet* Antarctica
194 L6 **Ronne Ice Shelf** *ice shelf* Antarctica
99 E19 **Ronse** *Fr.* Renaix. Oost-Vlaanderen, SW Belgium
191 R8 **Ronui, Mont** *var.* Roniu. ▲ Tahiti, W French Polynesia
30 K14 **Roodhouse** Illinois, N USA
83 C19 **Rooibank** Erongo, W Namibia
Rooke Island *see* Umboi Island
65 N24 **Rookery Point** *headland* NE Tristan da Cunha
171 V13 **Roon, Pulau** *island* E Indonesia
173 V7 **Roo Rise** *undersea feature* E Indian Ocean
152 J9 **Roorkee** Uttaranchal, N India
99 H15 **Roosendaal** Noord-Brabant, S Netherlands
25 P10 **Roosevelt** Texas, SW USA
37 N3 **Roosevelt** Utah, W USA
47 T8 **Roosevelt** ⚞ W Brazil
195 O13 **Roosevelt Island** *island* Antarctica
10 L10 **Roosevelt, Mount** ▲ British Columbia, W Canada

◆ Country
● Country Capital
◇ Dependent Territory
○ Dependent Territory Capital
◆ Administrative Regions
✈ International Airport
▲ Mountain
▲▲ Mountain Range
⩘ Volcano
⚞ River
◎ Lake
⊠ Reservoir

- 9 P17 **Roosville** British Columbia, SW Canada
- 29 X10 **Root River** 🞰 Minnesota, N USA
- 111 N16 **Ropczyce** Podkarpackie, SE Poland
- 181 Q3 **Roper Bar** Northern Territory, N Australia
- 24 M5 **Ropesville** Texas, SW USA
- 102 K14 **Roquefort** Landes, SW France
- 61 C21 **Roque Pérez** Buenos Aires, E Argentina
- 58 E10 **Roraima** off. Estado de Roraima; prev. Território de Rio Branco, Território de Roraima. ◆ state N Brazil
  Roraima, Estado de see Roraima
- 58 F9 **Roraima, Mount** ▲ N South America
  Roraima, Território de see Roraima
- 94 I9 **Røros** Sør-Trøndelag, S Norway
- 108 I7 **Rorschach** Sankt Gallen, NE Switzerland
- 93 E14 **Rørvik** Nord-Trøndelag, C Norway
- 119 G17 **Ros'** Rus. Ross'. Hrodzyenskaya Voblasts', W Belarus
- 119 G17 **Ros'** Rus. Ross'. 🞰 W Belarus
- 117 O6 **Ros'** 🞰 N Ukraine
- 44 K7 **Rosa, Lake** ◎ Great Inagua, S Bahamas
- 32 M9 **Rosalia** Washington, NW USA
- 191 W15 **Rosalia, Punta** headland Easter Island, Chile, E Pacific Ocean
- 45 P12 **Rosalie** E Dominica
- 35 T14 **Rosamond** California, W USA
- 35 S14 **Rosamond Lake** salt flat California, W USA
- 61 B18 **Rosario** Santa Fe, C Argentina
- 40 J11 **Rosario** Sinaloa, C Mexico
- 40 G6 **Rosario** Sonora, NW Mexico
- 62 O6 **Rosario** San Pedro, C Paraguay
- 61 E20 **Rosario** Colonia, SW Uruguay
- 54 H5 **Rosario** Zulia, NW Venezuela
  Rosario see Nishino-shima
  Rosario see Rosarito
- 40 B4 **Rosario, Bahía del** bay NW Mexico
- 62 K6 **Rosario de la Frontera** Salta, N Argentina
- 61 C18 **Rosario del Tala** Entre Ríos, E Argentina
- 61 F16 **Rosário do Sul** Rio Grande do Sul, S Brazil
- 59 H18 **Rosário Oeste** Mato Grosso, W Brazil
- 40 B1 **Rosarito** var. Rosario. Baja California, NW Mexico
- 40 E7 **Rosarito** Baja California, NW Mexico
- 40 E7 **Rosarito** Baja California Sur, W Mexico
- 104 L9 **Rosarito, Embalse del** ◎ W Spain
- 107 N22 **Rosarno** Calabria, SW Italy
- 56 B5 **Rosa Zárate** var. Quinindé. Esmeraldas, SW Ecuador
  Roscianum see Rossano
- 29 O8 **Roscoe** South Dakota, N USA
- 25 P7 **Roscoe** Texas, SW USA
- 102 F5 **Roscoff** Finistère, NW France
  Ros Comáin see Roscommon
- 97 C17 **Roscommon** Ir. Ros Comáin. C Ireland
- 31 Q7 **Roscommon** Michigan, N USA
- 97 C17 **Roscommon** Ir. Ros Comáin. ◆ county C Ireland
  Ros. Cré see Roscrea
- 97 D19 **Roscrea** Ir. Ros. Cré. C Ireland
- 45 X12 **Roseau** prev. Charlotte Town. ● (Dominica) SW Dominica
- 29 S2 **Roseau** Minnesota, N USA
- 173 Y16 **Rose Belle** SE Mauritius
- 183 O16 **Rosebery** Tasmania, SE Australia
- 21 U11 **Roseboro** North Carolina, SE USA
- 25 T9 **Rosebud** Texas, SW USA
- 33 W10 **Rosebud Creek** 🞰 Montana, NW USA
- 32 F14 **Roseburg** Oregon, NW USA
- 22 J3 **Rosedale** Mississippi, S USA
- 99 H21 **Rosée** Namur, S Belgium
- 55 U8 **Rose Hall** E Guyana
- 173 X16 **Rose Hill** W Mauritius
- 80 H12 **Roseires, Reservoir** var. Lake Rusayris. ◎ E Sudan
  Rosenau see Rožnov pod Radhoštěm
  Rosenau see Rožňava
- 25 V11 **Rosenberg** Texas, SW USA
  Rosenberg see Olesno
  Rosenberg see Ružomberok
- 100 I10 **Rosengarten** Niedersachsen, N Germany
- 101 M24 **Rosenheim** Bayern, S Germany
  Rosenhof see Zilupe
- 105 X4 **Roses** Cataluña, NE Spain
- 105 X4 **Roses, Golf de** gulf NE Spain
- 107 K14 **Roseto degli Abruzzi** Abruzzo, C Italy
- 9 S16 **Rosetown** Saskatchewan, S Canada
  Rosetta see Rashid
- 35 O7 **Roseville** California, W USA
- 30 J12 **Roseville** Illinois, N USA
- 29 V8 **Roseville** Minnesota, N USA
- 29 R7 **Rosholt** South Dakota, N USA
- 106 F12 **Rosignano Marittimo** Toscana, C Italy
- 116 I14 **Roșiori de Vede** Teleorman, S Romania
- 114 K8 **Rositsa** 🞰 N Bulgaria
  Rositten see Rēzekne
- 95 J23 **Roskilde** Roskilde, E Denmark
- 95 I23 **Roskilde** off. Roskilde Amt. ◆ county E Denmark
  Roskilde Amt see Roskilde
  Ros Láir see Rosslare
- 126 H5 **Roslavl'** Smolenskaya Oblast', W Russian Federation
- 32 I8 **Roslyn** Washington, NW USA
- 99 K14 **Rosmalen** Noord-Brabant, S Netherlands
  Ros Mhic Thriúin see New Ross
- 113 P19 **Rosoman** C FYR Macedonia
- 102 F6 **Rosporden** Finistère, NW France

- 185 F17 **Ross** West Coast, South Island, New Zealand
- 10 J7 **Ross** 🞰 Yukon Territory, W Canada
  Ross' see Ros'
- 96 H8 **Ross and Cromarty** cultural region N Scotland, UK
- 107 O20 **Rossano** anc. Roscianum. Calabria, SW Italy
- 22 L5 **Ross Barnett Reservoir** ◎ Mississippi, S USA
- 9 W16 **Rossburn** Manitoba, S Canada
- 14 H13 **Rosseau** Ontario, S Canada
- 14 H13 **Rosseau, Lake** ◎ Ontario, S Canada
- 186 I10 **Rossel Island** prev. Yela Island. island SE Papua New Guinea
- 195 P12 **Ross Ice Shelf** ice shelf Antarctica
- 13 P16 **Rossignol, Lake** ◎ Nova Scotia, SE Canada
- 83 C19 **Rössing** Erongo, W Namibia
- 195 Q14 **Ross Island** island Antarctica
  Rossitten see Rybachiy
  Rossiyskaya Federatsiya see Russian Federation
- 9 N17 **Rossland** British Columbia, SW Canada
- 97 F20 **Rosslare** Ir. Ros Láir. Wexford, SE Ireland
- 97 F20 **Rosslare Harbour** Wexford, SE Ireland
- 101 M14 **Rosslau** Sachsen-Anhalt, E Germany
- 76 G10 **Rosso** Trarza, SW Mauritania
- 103 X14 **Rosso, Cap** headland Corse, France, C Mediterranean Sea
- 93 H16 **Rosvato** Jämtland, C Sweden
- 97 K21 **Ross-on-Wye** W England, UK
  Rossony see Rasony
- 126 L9 **Rossosh'** Voronezhskaya Oblast', W Russian Federation
- 181 Q7 **Ross River** Northern Territory, N Australia
- 10 J7 **Ross River** Yukon Territory, W Canada
- 195 O15 **Ross Sea** sea Antarctica
- 92 G13 **Røsvatnet** Lapp Reevhtse. ◎ C Norway
- 23 R1 **Rossville** Georgia, SE USA
  Rostak see Ar Rustāq
- 143 P14 **Rostāq** Hormozgān, S Iran
- 117 N5 **Rostavytsya** 🞰 N Ukraine
- 9 T15 **Rosthern** Saskatchewan, S Canada
- 100 M8 **Rostock** Mecklenburg-Vorpommern, NE Germany
- 124 L16 **Rostov** Yaroslavskaya Oblast', W Russian Federation
  Rostov see Rostov-na-Donu
- 126 L12 **Rostov-na-Donu** var. Rostov, Eng. Rostov-on-Don. Rostovskaya Oblast', SW Russian Federation
  Rostov-on-Don see Rostov-na-Donu
- 126 L10 **Rostovskaya Oblast'** ◇ province SW Russian Federation
- 93 J14 **Rosvik** Norrbotten, N Sweden
- 23 S3 **Roswell** Georgia, SE USA
- 37 U14 **Roswell** New Mexico, SW USA
- 94 K12 **Rot** Dalarna, C Sweden
- 101 I23 **Rot** 🞰 S Germany
- 104 J15 **Rota** Andalucía, S Spain
- 188 K9 **Rota** island S Northern Mariana Islands
- 25 P6 **Rotan** Texas, SW USA
  Rotcher Island see Tamana
- 100 I11 **Rotenburg** Niedersachsen, NW Germany
  Rotenburg see Rotenburg an der Fulda
- 101 I16 **Rotenburg an der Fulda** var. Rotenburg. Hessen, C Germany
- 101 L18 **Roter Main** 🞰 E Germany
- 101 K20 **Roth** Bayern, SE Germany
- 101 G16 **Rothaargebirge** ▲ W Germany
  Rothenburg see Rothenburg ob der Tauber
- 101 J20 **Rothenburg ob der Tauber** var. Rothenburg. Bayern, S Germany
- 194 H6 **Rothera** UK research station Antarctica
- 185 I17 **Rotherham** Canterbury, South Island, New Zealand
- 97 M17 **Rotherham** N England, UK
- 108 E7 **Rothrist** Aargau, N Switzerland
- 96 H12 **Rothesay** W Scotland, UK
- 194 H6 **Rothschild Island** island Antarctica
- 171 P17 **Roti, Pulau** island S Indonesia
- 183 O8 **Roto** New South Wales, SE Australia
- 184 N8 **Rotoiti, Lake** ◎ North Island, New Zealand
  Rotomagus see Rouen
- 107 N19 **Rotondella** Basilicata, S Italy
- 103 X15 **Rotondo, Monte** ▲ Corse, France, C Mediterranean Sea
- 185 I15 **Rotoroa, Lake** ◎ South Island, New Zealand
- 184 N8 **Rotorua** Bay of Plenty, North Island, New Zealand
- 184 N8 **Rotorua, Lake** ◎ North Island, New Zealand
- 101 N22 **Rott** 🞰 SE Germany
- 108 F10 **Rotten** 🞰 S Switzerland
- 109 T6 **Rottenmann** Steiermark, E Austria
- 98 H12 **Rotterdam** Zuid-Holland, SW Netherlands
- 18 K10 **Rotterdam** New York, NE USA
- 98 M21 **Rottnen** ◎ S Sweden
- 98 N4 **Rottumeroog** island Waddeneilanden, NE Netherlands
- 98 N4 **Rottumerplaat** island Waddeneilanden, NE Netherlands
- 101 G23 **Rottweil** Baden-Württemberg, S Germany
- 191 O7 **Rotui, Mont** ▲ Moorea, W French Polynesia
- 103 P1 **Roubaix** Nord, N France
- 111 C15 **Roudnice nad Labem** Ger. Raudnitz an der Elbe. Ústecký Kraj, NW Czech Republic
- 102 M4 **Rouen** anc. Rotomagus. Seine-Maritime, N France

- 171 X13 **Rouffaer Reserves** reserve Papua, E Indonesia
- 15 N10 **Rouge, Rivière** 🞰 Québec, SE Canada
- 20 J6 **Rough River** 🞰 Kentucky, S USA
- 20 J6 **Rough River Lake** ◎ Kentucky, S USA
  Rouhaïbé see Ar Ruḩaybah
- 102 K11 **Rouillac** Charente, W France
  Roulers see Roeselare
  Roumania see Romania
- 173 Y15 **Round Island** var. Ile Ronde. island NE Mauritius
- 14 J12 **Round Lake** ◎ Ontario, SE Canada
- 35 U7 **Round Mountain** Nevada, W USA
- 25 R10 **Round Mountain** Texas, SW USA
- 183 U5 **Round Mountain** ▲ New South Wales, SE Australia
- 25 S10 **Round Rock** Texas, SW USA
- 33 U10 **Roundup** Montana, NW USA
- 55 Y10 **Roura** NE French Guiana
  Rourkela see Räurkela
- 96 J4 **Rousay** island N Scotland, UK
  Rousselaere see Roeselare
- 103 O17 **Roussillon** cultural region S France
- 15 V7 **Routhierville** Québec, SE Canada
- 99 K25 **Rouvroy** Luxembourg, SE Belgium
- 14 I7 **Rouyn-Noranda** Québec, SE Canada
  Rouyuanchengzi see Huachi
- 92 L12 **Rovaniemi** Lappi, N Finland
- 106 E7 **Rovato** Lombardia, N Italy
- 125 N11 **Rovdino** Arkhangel'skaya Oblast', NW Russian Federation
- 117 Y8 **Roven'ky** var. Roven'ki. Luhans'ka Oblast', E Ukraine
  Rovenskaya Oblast' see Rivnens'ka Oblast'
  Rovenskaya Sloboda see Ruvyenskaya Slabada
- 106 G7 **Rovereto** Ger. Rofreit. Trentino-Alto Adige, N Italy
- 167 S12 **Rôviĕng Tbong** Préah Vihéar, N Cambodia
- 106 H8 **Rovigo** Veneto, NE Italy
- 112 A10 **Rovinj** It. Rovigno. Istra, NW Croatia
- 54 E10 **Rovira** Tolima, C Colombia
  Rovno see Rivne
- 127 P9 **Rovnoye** Saratovskaya Oblast', W Russian Federation
- 82 Q12 **Rovuma, Rio** var. Ruvuma. 🞰 Mozambique/Tanzania see also Ruvuma
  Rovuma, Rio see Ruvuma
- 119 O19 **Rovyenskaya Slabada** Rus. Rovenskaya Sloboda. Homyel'skaya Voblasts', SE Belarus
- 183 R5 **Rowena** New South Wales, SE Australia
- 21 T11 **Rowland** North Carolina, SE USA
- 9 P5 **Rowley** 🞰 Baffin Island, Nunavut, NE Canada
- 9 P6 **Rowley Island** island Nunavut, NE Canada
- 173 W8 **Rowley Shoals** reef NW Australia
  Równe see Rivne
- 171 O4 **Roxas** Mindoro, N Philippines
- 171 P5 **Roxas City** Panay Island, C Philippines
- 21 U8 **Roxboro** North Carolina, SE USA
- 185 D23 **Roxburgh** Otago, South Island, New Zealand
- 96 K13 **Roxburgh** cultural region SE Scotland, UK
- 182 H5 **Roxby Downs** South Australia
- 95 M17 **Roxen** ◎ S Sweden
- 25 V5 **Roxton** Texas, SW USA
- 15 P12 **Roxton-Sud** Québec, SE Canada
- 33 U8 **Roy** Montana, NW USA
- 37 U10 **Roy** New Mexico, SW USA
- 97 E17 **Royal Canal** Ir. An Chanáil Ríoga. canal C Ireland
- 30 L1 **Royale, Isle** island Michigan, N USA
- 37 S6 **Royal Gorge** valley Colorado, C USA
- 97 M20 **Royal Leamington Spa** var. Leamington, Leamington Spa. C England, UK
- 97 O23 **Royal Tunbridge Wells** var. Tunbridge Wells. SE England, UK
- 24 L9 **Royalty** Texas, SW USA
- 102 J11 **Royan** Charente-Maritime, W France
- 65 B24 **Roy Cove Settlement** West Falkland, Falkland Islands
- 103 O3 **Roye** Somme, N France
- 95 H15 **Røyken** Buskerud, S Norway
- 93 F14 **Røyrvik** Nord-Trøndelag, C Norway
- 25 U6 **Royse City** Texas, SW USA
- 97 O21 **Royston** E England, UK
- 23 U2 **Royston** Georgia, SE USA
- 114 L10 **Roza** prev. Gyulovo. Yambol, E Bulgaria
- 113 L16 **Rožaje** Montenegro
- 110 M10 **Różan** Mazowieckie, C Poland
- 117 O10 **Rozdil'na** Odes'ka Oblast', SW Ukraine
- 117 S12 **Rozdol'ne** Rus. Razdol'noye. Respublika Krym, S Ukraine
- 145 Q9 **Rozhdestvenka** Akmola, C Kazakhstan
- 116 J6 **Rozhnyativ** Ivano-Frankivs'ka Oblast', W Ukraine
- 116 J3 **Rozhyshche** Volyns'ka Oblast', NW Ukraine
  Roznau am Radhost see Rožnov pod Radhoštěm
- 111 I19 **Rožňava** Ger. Rosenau, Hung. Rozsnyó. Košický Kraj, E Slovakia
- 111 I18 **Rožnov pod Radhoštěm** Ger. Rosenau, Roznau an Radhost. Zlínský Kraj, E Czech Republic
  Rózsahegy see Ružomberok
  Rozsnyó see Râşnov
  Rozsnyó see Rožňava
- 113 K18 **Rranxë** Shkodër, NW Albania

- 113 L18 **Rrëshen** var. Rresheni, Rrshen. Lezhë, C Albania
  Rresheni see Rrëshen
- 113 K20 **Rrogozhina** var. Rogozhina, Rogozhinë, Rrogozhinë. Tiranë, W Albania
  Rrshen see Rrëshen
- 112 O13 **Rtanj** ▲ E Serbia
- 127 O7 **Rtishchevo** Saratovskaya Oblast', W Russian Federation
- 184 N12 **Ruahine Range** var. Ruarine. ▲ North Island, New Zealand
- 185 L14 **Ruamahanga** 🞰 North Island, New Zealand
  Ruanda see Rwanda
- 184 M10 **Ruapehu, Mount** ▲ North Island, New Zealand
- 185 C25 **Ruapuke Island** island SW New Zealand
  Ruarine see Ruahine Range
- 184 O9 **Ruatahuna** Bay of Plenty, North Island, New Zealand
- 184 Q8 **Ruatoria** Gisborne, North Island, New Zealand
- 184 K4 **Ruawai** Northland, North Island, New Zealand
- 15 N8 **Ruban** 🞰 Québec, SE Canada
- 81 I22 **Rubeho Mountains** ▲ C Tanzania
- 165 U3 **Rubeshibe** Hokkaidō, NE Japan
  Rubezhnoye see Rubizhne
- 113 L18 **Rubik** Lezhë, C Albania
- 54 H7 **Rubio** Táchira, W Venezuela
- 117 X6 **Rubizhne** Rus. Rubezhnoye. Luhans'ka Oblast', E Ukraine
- 81 F20 **Rubondo Island** island N Tanzania
- 122 I13 **Rubtsovsk** Altayskiy Kray, S Russian Federation
- 39 P9 **Ruby** Alaska, USA
- 35 W3 **Ruby Dome** ▲ Nevada, W USA
- 35 W4 **Ruby Lake** ◎ Nevada, W USA
- 35 W4 **Ruby Mountains** ▲ Nevada, W USA
- 33 Q12 **Ruby Range** ▲ Montana, NW USA
- 118 C10 **Rucava** Liepāja, SW Latvia
- 143 S13 **Rūdān** var. Dehbārez. Hormozgān, S Iran
- 119 G14 **Rūdiškės** Vilnius, S Lithuania
- 95 H24 **Rudkøbing** Fyn, C Denmark
- 125 S13 **Rudnichnyy** Kirovskaya Oblast', NW Russian Federation
  Rüdnichnyy see Koksu
- 114 N9 **Rudnik** Varna, E Bulgaria
  Rudny see Rudnyy
- 126 H4 **Rudnya** Smolenskaya Oblast', W Russian Federation
- 127 O8 **Rudnya** Volgogradskaya Oblast', SW Russian Federation
- 144 M7 **Rudnyy** var. Rudny. Kostanay, N Kazakhstan
- 122 K3 **Rudol'fa, Ostrov** island Zemlya Frantsa-Iosifa, NW Russian Federation
  Rudolf, Lake see Turkana, Lake
  Rudolfswert see Novo mesto
- 101 L17 **Rudolstadt** Thüringen, C Germany
- 31 Q4 **Rudyard** Michigan, N USA
- 33 S7 **Rudyard** Montana, NW USA
- 119 K16 **Rudzyensk** Rus. Rudensk. Minskaya Voblasts', C Belarus
- 104 L6 **Rueda** Castilla-León, N Spain
- 114 F10 **Ruen** ▲ Bulgaria/FYR Macedonia
- 80 G10 **Rufa'a** Gezira, C Sudan
- 102 L10 **Ruffec** Charente, W France
- 21 R14 **Ruffin** South Carolina, SE USA
- 81 J23 **Rufiji** 🞰 E Tanzania
- 61 A20 **Rufino** Santa Fe, C Argentina
- 76 F11 **Rufisque** W Senegal
- 83 K14 **Rufunsa** Lusaka, C Zambia
- 118 J9 **Rugāji** Balvi, E Latvia
- 161 R7 **Rugao** Jiangsu, E China
- 97 M20 **Rugby** C England, UK
- 29 N3 **Rugby** North Dakota, N USA
- 100 N7 **Rügen** cape NE Germany
  Ruhaybeh see Ar Ruḩaybah
- 81 E19 **Ruhengeri** NW Rwanda
  Ruhja see Rūjiena
- 100 M10 **Ruhner Berg** hill N Germany
- 118 F7 **Ruhnu** var. Ruhnu Saar, Swe. Runö. island SW Estonia
  Ruhnu Saar see Ruhnu
- 101 G15 **Ruhr** 🞰 W Germany
- 101 G15 **Ruhr Valley** industrial region W Germany
- 161 S11 **Rui'an** var. Rui an. Zhejiang, SE China
  Rui an see Rui'an
- 161 P10 **Ruichang** Jiangxi, S China
- 24 J11 **Ruidosa** Texas, SW USA
- 37 S14 **Ruidoso** New Mexico, SW USA
- 161 P12 **Ruijin** Jiangxi, S China
- 160 D13 **Ruili** Yunnan, SW China
- 98 N8 **Ruinen** Drenthe, NE Netherlands
- 99 D17 **Ruiselede** West-Vlaanderen, W Belgium
- 118 H7 **Rūjiena** Est. Ruhja, Ger. Rujen. Valmiera, N Latvia
- 79 I18 **Ruki** 🞰 W Dem. Rep. Congo
- 81 M21 **Rukwa** ◇ region SW Tanzania
- 81 F23 **Rukwa, Lake** ◎ SE Tanzania
- 25 P6 **Rule** Texas, SW USA
- 22 K3 **Ruleville** Mississippi, S USA
- 112 K10 **Ruma** Vojvodina, N Serbia
- 141 Q7 **Rumāḥ** Ar Riyāḍ, C Saudi Arabia
  Rumaitha see Ar Rumaythah
  Rumania/Rumänien see Romania
  Rumänisch-Sankt-Georgen see Sângeorz-Băi
- 139 Y13 **Rumaylah** SE Iraq
- 139 P2 **Rumaylah, Wādī** dry watercourse NE Syria
- 171 U11 **Rumbati** Papua, E Indonesia

- 81 E14 **Rumbek** El Buhayrat, S Sudan
  Rumburg see Rumburk
- 111 D14 **Rumburk** Ger. Rumburg. Ústecký Kraj, NW Czech Republic
- 44 J4 **Rum Cay** island C Bahamas
- 99 M26 **Rumelange** Luxembourg, S Luxembourg
- 99 D20 **Rumes** Hainaut, SW Belgium
- 19 P7 **Rumford** Maine, NE USA
- 110 I6 **Rumia** Pomorskie, N Poland
- 113 J17 **Rumija** ▲ S Montenegro
- 139 O6 **Rūmiyah** W Iraq
  Rummah, Wādī ar see Rimah, Wādī ar
  Rummelsburg in Pommern see Miastko
- 165 S3 **Rumoi** Hokkaidō, NE Japan
- 82 M12 **Rumphi** var. Rumpi. Northern, N Malawi
  Rumpi see Rumphi
- 29 V7 **Rum River** 🞰 Minnesota, N USA
- 188 F16 **Rumung** island Caroline Islands, W Micronesia
  Rumuniya/Rumūniya/ Rumunjska see Romania
- 185 G16 **Runanga** West Coast, South Island, New Zealand
- 184 P7 **Runaway, Cape** headland North Island, New Zealand
- 97 K18 **Runcorn** C England, UK
- 118 K10 **Rundāni** Ludza, E Latvia
- 83 E16 **Runde** var. Lundi. 🞰 SE Zimbabwe
- 83 C16 **Rundu** var. Runtu. Okavango, NE Namibia
- 93 I16 **Rundvik** Västerbotten, N Sweden
- 81 G20 **Runere** Mwanza, N Tanzania
- 25 S13 **Runge** Texas, SW USA
- 167 Q13 **Rŭng, Kaôh** prev. Kas Rong. island SW Cambodia
- 79 O16 **Rungu** Orientale, NE Dem. Rep. Congo
- 81 F23 **Rungwa** Rukwa, W Tanzania
- 81 G22 **Rungwa** Singida, C Tanzania
- 94 M13 **Runn** ◎ C Sweden
  Runö see Ruhnu
  Runtu see Rundu
- 158 L9 **Ruoqiang** var. Jo-ch'iang, Uigh. Charkhlik, Charkhliq, Qarkilik. Xinjiang Uygur Zizhiqu, NW China
- 159 S7 **Ruo Shui** 🞰 N China
- 92 L8 **Ruostekfielbmá** var. Rustefjelbma Finnmark. Finnmark, N Norway
- 93 L18 **Ruovesi** Länsi-Suomi, W Finland
- 112 B9 **Rupa** Primorje-Gorski Kotar, NW Croatia
- 182 M11 **Rupanyup** Victoria, SE Australia
- 168 K9 **Rupat, Pulau** prev. Roepat. island W Indonesia
- 168 K10 **Rupat, Selat** strait Sumatera, W Indonesia
- 116 J11 **Rupea** Ger. Reps, Hung. Kőhalom; prev. Cohalm. Braşov, C Romania
- 99 G17 **Rupel** 🞰 N Belgium
  Rupella see la Rochelle
- 33 P15 **Rupert** Idaho, NW USA
- 21 R5 **Rupert** West Virginia, NE USA
  Rupert House see Fort Rupert
- 12 J10 **Rupert, Rivière de** 🞰 Québec, C Canada
- 194 M13 **Ruppert Coast** physical region Antarctica
- 100 N11 **Ruppiner Kanal** canal NE Germany
- 55 S11 **Rupununi River** 🞰 S Guyana
- 101 D16 **Rur** Dut. Roer. 🞰 Germany/Netherlands
- 58 H13 **Rurópolis Presidente Medici** Pará, N Brazil
- 191 S12 **Rurutu** island Îles Australes, SW French Polynesia
- 83 L17 **Rusape** Manicaland, E Zimbabwe
  Rusayris, Lake see Roseires, Reservoir
  Ruschuk/Rusçuk see Ruse
- 114 K7 **Ruse** var. Ruschuk, Rustchuk, Turk. Rusçuk. Ruse, N Bulgaria
- 109 W10 **Ruše** NE Slovenia
- 114 L7 **Ruse** ◇ province N Bulgaria
- 114 K7 **Rusenski Lom** 🞰 N Bulgaria
- 97 G17 **Rush** Ir. An Ros. Dublin, E Ireland
- 161 S4 **Rushan** var. Xiacun. Shandong, E China
  Rushan see Rüshon
  Rushanskiy Khrebet see Rüshon, Qatorkühi
- 29 V7 **Rush City** Minnesota, N USA
- 37 V5 **Rush Creek** 🞰 Colorado, C USA
- 30 J13 **Rushford** Minnesota, N USA
- 14 D8 **Rush Lake** ◎ Ontario, S Canada
- 30 M7 **Rush Lake** ◎ Wisconsin, N USA
- 147 S13 **Rüshon** Rus. Rushan. SW Tajikistan
- 147 S14 **Rüshon, Qatorkühi** Rus. Rushanskiy Khrebet. ▲ SE Tajikistan
- 26 M12 **Rush Springs** Oklahoma, C USA
- 45 V15 **Rushville** Trinidad, Trinidad and Tobago
- 30 J13 **Rushville** Illinois, N USA
- 28 K12 **Rushville** Nebraska, C USA
- 183 O11 **Rushworth** Victoria, SE Australia
- 25 W8 **Rusk** Texas, SW USA
- 93 I14 **Rusksele** Västerbotten, N Sweden
- 118 C12 **Rusnė** Klaipėda, W Lithuania
- 114 M10 **Rusokastrenska Reka** 🞰 E Bulgaria
  Russadir see Melilla
- 109 X3 **Russbach** NE Austria
- 9 N11 **Russell** Manitoba, S Canada

- 184 K2 **Russell** Northland, North Island, New Zealand
- 26 L4 **Russell** Kansas, C USA
- 21 O4 **Russell** Arkansas, C USA
- 20 L7 **Russell Springs** Kentucky, S USA
- 23 O2 **Russellville** Alabama, S USA
- 27 T11 **Russellville** Arkansas, C USA
- 20 J7 **Russellville** Kentucky, S USA
- 101 G18 **Rüsselsheim** W Germany
  Russia see Russian Federation
  Russian America see Alaska
- 122 J11 **Russian Federation** off. Russian Federation var. Russia, Latv. Krievija, Rus. Rossiyskaya Federatsiya. ◆ republic Asia/Europe
  Russian Federation see Russian Federation
- 39 N11 **Russian Mission** Alaska, USA
- 34 M7 **Russian River** 🞰 California, W USA
- 194 L13 **Russkaya** Russian research station Antarctica
- 122 J5 **Russkaya Gavan'** Novaya Zemlya, Arkhangel'skaya Oblast', N Russian Federation
- 122 J5 **Russkiy, Ostrov** island N Russian Federation
- 109 Y5 **Rust** Burgenland, E Austria
  Rustaq see Ar Rustāq
- 137 U10 **Rust'avi** SE Georgia
- 21 T7 **Rustburg** Virginia, NE USA
  Rustchuk see Ruse
  Rustefjelbma Finnmark see Ruostekfielbmá
- 83 I21 **Rustenburg** North-West, N South Africa
- 22 H5 **Ruston** Louisiana, S USA
- 81 E21 **Rutana** S Burundi
- 62 I4 **Rutana, Volcán** ▲ N Chile
  Rutanzige, Lake see Edward, Lake
- 139 Y8 **Rutba** see Ar Ruţbah
- 104 M14 **Rute** Andalucía, S Spain
- 171 N16 **Ruteng** prev. Roeteng. Flores, C Indonesia
- 194 L8 **Rutford Ice Stream** ice feature Antarctica
- 35 X6 **Ruth** Nevada, W USA
- 101 G15 **Rüthen** Nordrhein-Westfalen, W Germany
- 14 D17 **Rutherford** Ontario, S Canada
- 21 Q10 **Rutherfordton** North Carolina, SE USA
- 108 G7 **Rüti** Zürich, N Switzerland
- 97 J18 **Ruthin** Wel. Rhuthun. NE Wales, UK
  Rutlam see Ratlam
- 18 M9 **Rutland** Vermont, NE USA
- 97 N19 **Rutland** cultural region C England, UK
- 21 N8 **Rutledge** Tennessee, S USA
- 158 G12 **Rutög** var. Rutok. Xizang Zizhiqu, W China
  Rutok see Rutög
- 79 P19 **Rutshuru** Nord Kivu, E Dem. Rep. Congo
- 98 L8 **Rutten** Flevoland, N Netherlands
- 127 Q17 **Rutul** Respublika Dagestan, SW Russian Federation
- 93 L14 **Ruukki** Oulu, C Finland
- 98 N11 **Ruurlo** Gelderland, E Netherlands
- 143 S15 **Ru'ūs al Jibāl** cape Oman/United Arab Emirates
- 138 I7 **Ru'ūs aţ Ţiwāl, Jabal** ▲ W Syria
- 81 H23 **Ruvuma** ◇ region SE Tanzania
- 81 I25 **Ruvuma, Rivière de** var. Rio Rovuma. 🞰 Mozambique/Tanzania see also Rovuma, Rio
  Ruvuma, Rio see Rovuma, Rio
- 138 L9 **Ruwayshid, Wadi ar** dry watercourse NE Jordan
- 141 Z10 **Ruways, Ra's ar** headland E Oman
- 79 P18 **Ruwenzori** ▲ Uganda/Dem. Rep. Congo
- 141 Y8 **Ruwī** NE Oman
- 114 F9 **Ruy** ▲ Bulgaria/Serbia and Montenegro
  Ruya see Luia, Rio
- 81 E20 **Ruyigi** E Burundi
- 127 P5 **Ruzayevka** Respublika Mordoviya, W Russian Federation
- 119 G18 **Ruzhany** Rus. Ruzhany. Brestskaya Voblasts', SW Belarus
- 114 I10 **Ruzhevo Konare** var. Ruzhevo Konare. Plovdiv, C Bulgaria
- 114 G7 **Ruzhintsi** Vidin, NW Bulgaria
- 161 N6 **Ruzhou** Henan, C China
- 117 N5 **Ruzhyn** Rus. Ruzhin. Zhytomyrs'ka Oblast', N Ukraine
- 111 K19 **Ružomberok** Ger. Rosenberg, Hung. Rózsahegy. Žilinský Kraj, N Slovakia
- 111 C16 **Ruzyně** ✈ (Praha) Praha, C Czech Republic
- 81 D19 **Rwanda** off. Rwandese Republic; prev. Ruanda. ◆ republic C Africa
  Rwandan Republic see Rwanda
  Ryasna see Rasna
- 126 L5 **Ryazan'** Ryazanskaya Oblast', W Russian Federation
- 126 L5 **Ryazanskaya Oblast'** ◇ province W Russian Federation
- 126 M6 **Ryazhsk** Ryazanskaya Oblast', W Russian Federation
- 118 B13 **Rybachiy** Ger. Rossitten. Kaliningradskaya Oblast', W Russian Federation
- 124 J2 **Rybachiy, Poluostrov** peninsula NW Russian Federation
  Rybach'ye see Balykchy
- 124 L15 **Rybinsk** prev. Andropov. Yaroslavskaya Oblast', W Russian Federation
- 124 K14 **Rybinskoye Vodokhranilishche** Eng. Rybinsk Reservoir, Rybinsk Sea. ◎ W Russian Federation

◆ Country | ◇ Dependent Territory | ◆ Administrative Regions | ▲ Mountain | 🗻 Volcano | ◎ Lake
● Country Capital | ◯ Dependent Territory Capital | ✈ International Airport | ▲▲ Mountain Range | 🞰 River | ☐ Reservoir

RYBINSK RESERVOIR/RYBINSK SEA – SAINT-JOHN

Rybinsk Reservoir/ Rybinsk Sea *see* Rybinskoye Vodokhranilishche
111 *I16* **Rybnik** Śląskie, S Poland
Rybnitsa *see* Rîbniţa
111 *F16* **Rychnov nad Kněžnou** *Ger.* Reichenau. Královéhradecký Kraj, N Czech Republic
110 *I12* **Rychwał** Wielkopolskie, C Poland
9 *O13* **Rycroft** Alberta, W Canada
95 *L21* **Ryd** Kronoberg, S Sweden
95 *L20* **Rydaholm** Jönköping, S Sweden
194 *I8* **Rydberg Peninsula** *peninsula* Antarctica
97 *P23* **Rye** SE England, UK
33 *T10* **Ryegate** Montana, NW USA
35 *S3* **Rye Patch Reservoir** ⊠ Nevada, W USA
95 *D15* **Ryfylke** *physical region* S Norway
95 *H16* **Rygge** Østfold, S Norway
110 *N13* **Ryki** Lubelskie, E Poland
Rykovo *see* Yenakiyeve
126 *I7* **Ryl'sk** Kurskaya Oblast', W Russian Federation
183 *S8* **Rylstone** New South Wales, SE Australia
111 *H17* **Rýmařov** *Ger.* Römerstadt. Moravskoslezský Kraj, E Czech Republic
144 *E11* **Ryn-Peski** *desert* W Kazakhstan
165 *N10* **Ryōtsu** *var.* Ryôtu. Niigata, Sado, C Japan
Ryôtu *see* Ryōtsu
110 *K10* **Rypin** Kujawsko-pomorskie, C Poland
Ryshkany *see* Rîşcani
Ryssel *see* Lille
Ryswick *see* Rijswijk
95 *M24* **Rytterknægten** *hill* E Denmark
Ryukyu Islands *see* Nansei-shotō
192 *G5* **Ryukyu Trench** *var.* Nansei Syotō Trench. *undersea feature* S East China Sea
110 *D11* **Rzepin** *Ger.* Reppen. Lubuskie, W Poland
111 *N16* **Rzeszów** Podkarpackie, SE Poland
124 *I16* **Rzhev** Tverskaya Oblast', W Russian Federation
Rzhishchev *see* Rzhyshchiv
117 *P5* **Rzhyshchiv** *Rus.* Rzhishchev. Kyyivs'ka Oblast', N Ukraine

S

138 *E11* **Sa'ad** Southern, W Israel
109 *P7* **Saalach** ≈ W Austria
101 *L14* **Saale** ≈ C Germany
101 *L17* **Saalfeld** *var.* Saalfeld an der Saale. Thüringen, C Germany
Saalfeld *see* Zalewo
Saalfeld an der Saale *see* Saalfeld
108 *C8* **Saane** ≈ W Switzerland
101 *D19* **Saar** *Fr.* Sarre. ≈ France/Germany
101 *E20* **Saarbrücken** *Fr.* Sarrebruck. Saarland, SW Germany
Saarburg *see* Sarrebourg
118 *D6* **Sääre** *var.* Sjar. Saaremaa, W Estonia
Saare *see* Saaremaa
118 *D5* **Saaremaa** *off.* Saare Maakond. ◐ *province* W Estonia
118 *E6* **Saaremaa** *Ger.* Oesel, Ösel; *prev.* Saare. *island* W Estonia
Saare Maakond *see* Saaremaa
92 *L12* **Saarenkylä** Lappi, N Finland
Saargemund *see* Sarreguemines
93 *L17* **Saarijärvi** Länsi-Soumi, C Finland
Saar in Mähren *see* Žd'ár nad Sázavou
92 *M10* **Saariselkä** *Lapp.* Suoločielgi. Lappi, N Finland
92 *L10* **Saariselkä** *hill range* NE Finland
101 *D20* **Saarland** *Fr.* Sarre. ◐ *state* SW Germany
Saarlautern *see* Saarlouis
101 *D20* **Saarlouis** *prev.* Saarlautern. Saarland, SW Germany
108 *E11* **Saaser Vispa** ≈ S Switzerland
137 *X12* **Saatlı** *Rus.* Saatly. C Azerbaijan
Saatly *see* Saatlı
Saaz *see* Žatec
45 *V9* **Saba** *island* N Netherlands Antilles
138 *J7* **Sab' Ābār** *var.* Sab'a Biyar, Sa'b Bi'ār. Ḥimş, C Syria
Sab'a Biyar *see* Sab' Ābār
112 *K11* **Šabac** Serbia, W Serbia
105 *W5* **Sabadell** Cataluña, E Spain
164 *K12* **Sabae** Fukui, Honshū, SW Japan
169 *V7* **Sabah** *prev.* British North Borneo, North Borneo. ◐ *state* East Malaysia
168 *J8* **Sabak** *var.* Sabak Bernam. Selangor, Peninsular Malaysia
Sabak Bernam *see* Sabak
38 *D16* **Sabak, Cape** *headland* Agattu Island, Alaska, USA
81 *J20* **Sabaki** ≈ S Kenya
142 *L2* **Sabalān, Kuhhā-ye** ▲ NW Iran
154 *H7* **Sabalgarh** Madhya Pradesh, C India
44 *E4* **Sabana, Archipiélago de** *island group* C Cuba
42 *H7* **Sabanagrande** *var.* Sabana Grande. Francisco Morazán, S Honduras
Sabana Grande *see* Sabanagrande
54 *E5* **Sabanalarga** Atlántico, N Colombia
41 *W14* **Sabancuy** Campeche, SE Mexico
45 *N8* **Sabaneta** NW Dominican Republic
54 *J4* **Sabaneta** Falcón, N Venezuela
188 *H4* **Sabaneta, Puntan** *prev.* Ushi Point. *headland* Saipan, S Northern Mariana Islands
171 *X14* **Sabang** Papua, E Indonesia
116 *L10* **Săbăoani** Neamţ, NE Romania
155 *J26* **Sabaragamuwa Province** ◐ *province* C Sri Lanka
Sabaria *see* Szombathely
154 *D10* **Sābarmati** ≈ NW India
171 *S10* **Sabatai** Pulau Morotai, E Indonesia
141 *Q15* **Sab'atayn, Ramlat as** *desert* C Yemen
107 *I16* **Sabaudia** Lazio, C Italy
57 *J19* **Sabaya** Oruro, S Bolivia
Sa'b Bi'ār *see* Sab' Ābār
Sabbioncello *see* Orebić
148 *I8* **Şāberī, Hāmūn-e** *var.* Daryācheh-ye Hāmun, Daryācheh-ye Sīstān. ◎ Afghanistan/Iran *see also* Sīstān, Daryācheh-ye
Şāberī, Hāmūn-e *see* Sīstān, Daryācheh-ye
27 *P2* **Sabetha** Kansas, C USA
75 *P10* **Sabhā** C Libya
67 *V13* **Sabi** *var.* Rio Save. ≈ Mozambique/Zimbabwe *see also* Save, Rio
Sabi *see* Save
118 *E8* **Sabile** *Ger.* Zabeln. Talsi, NW Latvia
31 *R14* **Sabina** Ohio, N USA
40 *I3* **Sabinal** Chihuahua, N Mexico
25 *Q12* **Sabinal** Texas, SW USA
25 *Q11* **Sabinal River** ≈ Texas, SW USA
105 *S4* **Sabiñánigo** Aragón, NE Spain
41 *N6* **Sabinas** Coahuila de Zaragoza, NE Mexico
41 *O8* **Sabinas Hidalgo** Nuevo León, NE Mexico
41 *N6* **Sabinas, Río** ≈ NE Mexico
22 *F9* **Sabine Lake** ◎ Louisiana/ Texas, S USA
92 *O3* **Sabine Land** *physical region* C Svalbard
25 *W7* **Sabine River** ≈ Louisiana/ Texas, SW USA
137 *X12* **Sabirabad** C Azerbaijan
Sabkha *see* As Sabkhah
171 *O4* **Sablayan** Mindoro, N Philippines
13 *P16* **Sable, Cape** *cape* Newfoundland and Labrador, SE Canada
23 *X17* **Sable, Cape** *headland* Florida, SE USA
13 *R16* **Sable Island** *island* Nova Scotia, SE Canada
14 *L11* **Sables, Lac des** ◎ Québec, SE Canada
14 *E10* **Sables, Rivière aux** ≈ Ontario, S Canada
102 *K7* **Sable-sur-Sarthe** Sarthe, NW France
125 *U7* **Sablya, Gora** ▲ NW Russian Federation
77 *U14* **Sabon Birnin Gwari** Kaduna, C Nigeria
77 *V11* **Sabon Kafi** Zinder, C Niger
104 *I6* **Sabor, Rio** ≈ N Portugal
14 *J8* **Sabourin, Lac** ◎ Québec, SE Canada
102 *J14* **Sabres** Landes, SW France
195 *X13* **Sabrina Coast** *physical region* Antarctica
140 *M11* **Sabt al Ulayā** 'Asīr, SW Saudi Arabia
104 *I8* **Sabugal** Guarda, N Portugal
29 *Z13* **Sabula** Iowa, C USA
141 *N13* **Şabyā** Jīzān, SW Saudi Arabia
Sabzawar *see* Sabzevār
Sabzawaran *see* Sabzvārān
143 *S4* **Sabzevār** *var.* Sabzawar. Khorāsān-Razavī, NE Iran
143 *T12* **Sabzvārān** *var.* Sabzawaran; *prev.* Jiroft. Kermān, SE Iran
Sacajawea Peak *see* Matterhorn
82 *C9* **Sacandica** Uíge, NW Angola
42 *A2* **Sacatepéquez** *off.* Departamento de Sacatepéquez. ◐ *department* S Guatemala
Sacatepéquez, Departamento de *see* Sacatepéquez
104 *F11* **Sacavém** Lisboa, W Portugal
29 *T13* **Sac City** Iowa, C USA
105 *P8* **Sacedón** Castilla-La Mancha, C Spain
116 *J12* **Săcele** *Ger.* Vierdörfer, *Hung.* Négyfalu; *prev. Ger.* Sieben Dörfer, *Hung.* Hétfalu. Braşov, C Romania
12 *C8* **Sachigo** Ontario, C Canada
12 *C7* **Sachigo** ≈ Ontario, C Canada
12 *C8* **Sachigo Lake** ◎ Ontario, C Canada
163 *Y16* **Sach'ŏn** *Jap.* Sansenhō; *prev.* Samch'ŏnpŏ. S South Korea
101 *O15* **Sachsen** *Eng.* Saxony, *Fr.* Saxe. ◐ *state* E Germany
101 *K14* **Sachsen-Anhalt** *Eng.* Saxony-Anhalt. ◐ *state* C Germany
109 *R9* **Sachsenburg** Salzburg, S Austria
Sachsenfeld *see* Žalec
8 *I5* **Sachs Harbour** Banks Island, Northwest Territories, N Canada
Sächsisch-Reen/Sächsisch-Regen *see* Reghin
18 *H8* **Sackets Harbor** New York, NE USA
13 *P14* **Sackville** New Brunswick, SE Canada
19 *P9* **Saco** Maine, NE USA
19 *P8* **Saco River** ≈ Maine/New Hampshire, NE USA
35 *O7* **Sacramento** *state capital* California, W USA
37 *T14* **Sacramento Mountains** ▲▲ New Mexico, SW USA
35 *N6* **Sacramento River** ≈ California, W USA
35 *N5* **Sacramento Valley** *valley* California, W USA
36 *I10* **Sacramento Wash** *valley* Arizona, SW USA
105 *N15* **Sacratif, Cabo** *cape* S Spain
116 *F9* **Săcueni** *prev.* Săcuieni, *Hung.* Székelyhid. Bihor, W Romania
Săcuieni *see* Săcueni
105 *R4* **Sádaba** Aragón, NE Spain
Sá da Bandeira *see* Lubango
138 *I6* **Şadad** Ḥimş, W Syria
141 *O13* **Şa'dah** NW Yemen
167 *O16* **Sadao** Songkhla, SW Thailand
142 *L8* **Sadd-e Dez, Daryācheh-ye** ◎ W Iran
19 *S3* **Saddleback Mountain** *hill* Maine, NE USA
19 *P6* **Saddleback Mountain** ▲ Maine, NE USA
141 *W13* **Sadḥ** S Oman
76 *J11* **Sadiola** Kayes, W Mali
149 *R12* **Sādiqābād** Punjab, E Pakistan
153 *Y10* **Sadiya** Assam, NE India
139 *W9* **Sa'dīyah, Hawr as** ◎ E Iraq
165 *N9* **Sado** *var.* Sadoga-shima. *island* C Japan
Sadoga-shima *see* Sado
104 *F12* **Sado, Rio** ≈ S Portugal
114 *I8* **Sadovets** Pleven, N Bulgaria
127 *O11* **Sadovoye** Respublika Kalmykiya, SW Russian Federation
105 *W9* **Sa Dragonera** *var.* Isla Dragonera. *island* Islas Baleares, Spain, W Mediterranean Sea
95 *H20* **Sæby** Nordjylland, N Denmark
105 *P9* **Saelices** Castilla-La Mancha, C Spain
Saena Julia *see* Siena
Saetabicula *see* Alzira
114 *O12* **Safaalan** Tekirdağ, NW Turkey
Safad *see* Ẕefat
Şafāqis *see* Sfax
192 *I16* **Safata Bay** *bay* Upolo, Samoa, C Pacific Ocean
Safed *see* Ẕefat
139 *X11* **Şaffāf, Ḥawr aş** *marshy lake* S Iraq
95 *J16* **Säffle** Värmland, C Sweden
37 *N15* **Safford** Arizona, SW USA
74 *E7* **Safi** W Morocco
143 *V9* **Safīdābeh** Khorāsān-e Janūbī, E Iran
148 *K5* **Safidkūh, Selseleh-ye** *Eng.* Paropamisus Range. ▲▲ W Afghanistan
142 *M4* **Safīd, Rūd-e** ≈ NW Iran
126 *I4* **Safonovo** Smolenskaya Oblast', W Russian Federation
136 *H11* **Safranbolu** Karabük, NW Turkey
139 *Y13* **Safwān** SE Iraq
158 *J16* **Saga** *var.* Gya'gya. Xizang Zizhiqu, W China
164 *C14* **Saga** Saga, Kyūshū, SW Japan
164 *C13* **Saga** *off.* Saga-ken. ◐ *prefecture* Kyūshū, SW Japan
165 *P10* **Sagae** Yamagata, Honshū, C Japan
166 *L3* **Sagaing** Sagaing, C Burma (Myanmar)
166 *L5* **Sagaing** ◐ *division* N Burma (Myanmar)
Saga-ken *see* Saga
165 *N13* **Sagamihara** Kanagawa, Honshū, S Japan
165 *N14* **Sagami-nada** *inlet* SW Japan
Sagan *see* Żagań
29 *Y3* **Saganaga Lake** ◎ Minnesota, N USA
155 *F18* **Sāgar** Karnātaka, W India
154 *I9* **Sāgar** *prev.* Saugor. Madhya Pradesh, C India
15 *S8* **Sagard** Québec, SE Canada
Sagarmāthā *see* Everest, Mount
Sagebrush State *see* Nevada
143 *V11* **Sāghand** Yazd, C Iran
19 *N14* **Sag Harbor** Long Island, New York, NE USA
Saghez *see* Saqqez
31 *R8* **Saginaw** Michigan, N USA
31 *R8* **Saginaw Bay** *lake bay* Michigan, N USA
144 *H11* **Sagiz** Atyrau, W Kazakhstan
64 *H6* **Saglek Bank** *undersea feature* W Labrador Sea
13 *P5* **Saglek Bay** *bay* SW Labrador Sea
Saglouc/Sagluk *see* Salluit
103 *X15* **Sagonne, Golfe de** *gulf* Corse, France, C Mediterranean Sea
105 *P13* **Sagra** ▲ S Spain
104 *F14* **Sagres** Faro, S Portugal
37 *S7* **Saguache** Colorado, C USA
44 *J7* **Sagua de Tánamo** Holguín, E Cuba
44 *E5* **Sagua la Grande** Villa Clara, C Cuba
15 *R7* **Saguenay** ≈ Québec, SE Canada
74 *C9* **Saguia al Hamra** *var.* As Saqia al Hamra. ≈ N Western Sahara
105 *S9* **Sagunto** *Cat.* Sagunt, *Ar.* Murviedro; *anc.* Saguntum. País Valenciano, E Spain
Sagunt/Saguntum *see* Sagunto
138 *H10* **Saḥāb** 'Ammān, NW Jordan
54 *E6* **Sahagún** Córdoba, NW Colombia
104 *L4* **Sahagún** Castilla-León, N Spain
141 *X8* **Saḥam** N Oman
68 *F9* **Sahara** *desert* Libya/Algeria
75 *U9* **Sahara el Gharbîya** *var.* Aş Şaḥrā' al Gharbīyah, *Eng.* Western Desert. *desert* C Egypt
75 *X9* **Sahara el Sharqîya** *var.* Aş Şaḥrā' ash Sharqīyah, *Eng.* Arabian Desert, Eastern Desert. *desert* E Egypt
Saharan Atlas *see* Atlas Saharien
152 *J9* **Sahāranpur** Uttar Pradesh, N India
64 *L10* **Saharan Seamounts** *var.* Saharian Seamounts. *undersea feature* E Atlantic Ocean
Saharian Seamounts *see* Saharan Seamounts
153 *Q13* **Saharsa** Bihār, NE India
67 *O7* **Sahel** *physical region* C Africa
153 *R14* **Sāhibganj** Jhārkhand, NE India
80 *N12* **Sahil** *off.* Gobolka Sahil. ◐ *region* N Somalia
139 *Q7* **Saḥīlīyah** C Iraq
138 *H4* **Sāḥilīyah, Jibāl as** ▲▲ NW Syria
114 *M13* **Şahin** Tekirdağ, NW Turkey
149 *U9* **Sāhīwāl** *prev.* Montgomery. Punjab, E Pakistan
149 *U8* **Sāhīwāl** Punjab, E Pakistan
141 *W11* **Saḥmah, Ramlat as** *desert* C Oman
139 *T13* **Şaḥrā' al Ḥijārah** *desert* S Iraq
40 *H5* **Sahuaripa** Sonora, NW Mexico
36 *M16* **Sahuarita** Arizona, SW USA
40 *L13* **Sahuayo** *var.* Sahuayo de José Mariá Morelos; *prev.* Sahuayo de Díaz, Sahuayo de Porfirio Díaz. Michoacán de Ocampo, SW Mexico
Sahuayo de Díaz/Sahuayo de José Mariá Morelos/ Sahuayo de Porfirio Díaz *see* Sahuayo
173 *W8* **Sahul Shelf** *undersea feature* N Timor Sea
167 *P17* **Sai Buri** Pattani, SW Thailand
74 *I6* **Saïda** NW Algeria
138 *G7* **Saïda** *var.* Şaydā, Sayida; *anc.* Sidon. W Lebanon
Sa'īdābād *see* Sīrjān
80 *B13* **Sa'id Bundas** Western Bahr el Ghazal, SW Sudan
186 *E7* **Saidor** Madang, N Papua New Guinea
153 *S13* **Saidpur** *var.* Syedpur. Rajshahi, NW Bangladesh
108 *C7* **Saignelégier** Jura, NW Switzerland
164 *H11* **Saigō** Shimane, Dōgo, SW Japan
Saigon *see* Hô Chi Minh
163 *P11* **SaihanTal** *var.* Sonid Youqi. Nei Mongol Zizhiqu, N China
162 *I12* **Saihan Toroi** Nei Mongol Zizhiqu, N China
Sai Hun *see* Syr Darya
92 *M11* **Saija** Lappi, NE Finland
164 *G14* **Saijō** Ehime, Shikoku, SW Japan
164 *E15* **Saiki** Ōita, Kyūshū, SW Japan
93 *N18* **Saimaa** ◎ SE Finland
93 *N18* **Saimaa Canal** *Fin.* Saimaan Kanava, *Rus.* Saymenskiy Kanal. *canal* Finland/Russian Federation
Saimaan Kanava *see* Saimaa Canal
40 *L10* **Saín Alto** Zacatecas, C Mexico
96 *L12* **St Abb's Head** *headland* SE Scotland, UK
9 *Y16* **St. Adolphe** Manitoba, S Canada
103 *O15* **St-Affrique** Aveyron, S France
15 *Q10* **St-Agapit** Québec, SE Canada
97 *O21* **St Albans** *anc.* Verulamium. E England, UK
18 *L6* **Saint Albans** Vermont, NE USA
21 *Q5* **Saint Albans** West Virginia, NE USA
St. Alban's Head *see* St Aldhelm's Head
9 *Q14* **St. Albert** Alberta, SW Canada
97 *M24* **St Aldhelm's Head** *var.* St. Alban's Head. *headland* S England, UK
15 *S8* **St-Alexandre** Québec, SE Canada
15 *O11* **St-Alexis-des-Monts** Québec, SE Canada
103 *P2* **St-Amand-les-Eaux** Nord, N France
103 *O9* **St-Amand-Montrond** *var.* St-Amand-Mont-Rond. Cher, C France
15 *Q7* **St-Ambroise** Québec, SE Canada
173 *P16* **St-André** NE Réunion
14 *M12* **St-André-Avellin** Québec, SE Canada
102 *K12* **St-André-de-Cubzac** Gironde, SW France
96 *K11* **St Andrews** E Scotland, UK
23 *Q9* **Saint Andrews Bay** *bay* Florida, SE USA
23 *W7* **Saint Andrew Sound** *sound* Georgia, SE USA
Saint Anna Trough *see* Svyataya Anna Trough
44 *J11* **St. Ann's Bay** C Jamaica
13 *T10* **St. Anthony** Newfoundland, Newfoundland and Labrador, SE Canada
33 *R13* **Saint Anthony** Idaho, NW USA
182 *M11* **Saint Arnaud** Victoria, SE Australia
185 *I15* **St. Arnaud Range** ▲▲ South Island, New Zealand
15 *T8* **St-Arsène** Québec, SE Canada
13 *R10* **St-Augustin** Québec, E Canada
23 *X9* **Saint Augustine** Florida, SE USA
97 *H24* **St Austell** SW England, UK
103 *T4* **St-Avold** Moselle, NE France
103 *N17* **St-Barthélemy** ▲▲ S France
102 *L17* **St-Béat** Haute-Garonne, S France
97 *I15* **St Bees Head** *headland* NW England, UK
173 *P16* **St-Benoit** E Réunion
103 *T13* **St-Bonnet** Hautes-Alpes, SE France
St.Botolph's Town *see* Boston
97 *G21* **St Brides Bay** *inlet* SW Wales, UK
102 *H5* **St-Brieuc** Côtes d'Armor, NW France
102 *H5* **St-Brieuc, Baie de** *bay* NW France
102 *L7* **St-Calais** Sarthe, NW France
15 *Q10* **St-Casimir** Québec, SE Canada
14 *H16* **St. Catharines** Ontario, S Canada
45 *S14* **St. Catherine, Mount** ▲ N Grenada
64 *C11* **St Catherine Point** *headland* E Bermuda
23 *X6* **Saint Catherines Island** *island* Georgia, SE USA
97 *M24* **St Catherine's Point** *headland* S England, UK
103 *N13* **St-Céré** Lot, S France
108 *A10* **St. Cergue** Vaud, W Switzerland
103 *R11* **St-Chamond** Loire, E France
33 *S16* **Saint Charles** Idaho, NW USA
27 *X4* **Saint Charles** Missouri, C USA
103 *P13* **St-Chély-d'Apcher** Lozère, S France
Saint Christopher and Nevis, Federation of *see* Saint Kitts and Nevis
Saint Christopher-Nevis *see* Saint Kitts and Nevis
31 *S9* **Saint Clair** Michigan, N USA
14 *D17* **St. Clair** ≈ Canada/USA
183 *O17* **St. Clair, Lake** ◎ Tasmania, SE Australia
14 *C17* **St. Clair, Lake** *var.* Lac à L'Eau Claire. ◎ Canada/USA
31 *S10* **Saint Clair Shores** Michigan, N USA
103 *S10* **St-Claude** *anc.* Condate. Jura, E France
45 *X6* **St-Claude** Basse Terre, SW Guadeloupe
23 *X12* **Saint Cloud** Florida, SE USA
29 *U8* **Saint Cloud** Minnesota, N USA
45 *T9* **Saint Croix** *island* S Virgin Islands (US)
30 *J4* **Saint Croix Flowage** ⊠ Wisconsin, N USA
19 *T5* **Saint Croix River** ≈ Canada/USA
29 *W7* **Saint Croix River** ≈ Minnesota/Wisconsin, N USA
45 *S14* **St. David's** SE Grenada
97 *H21* **St David's** SW Wales, UK
97 *G21* **St David's Head** *headland* SW Wales, UK
64 *C12* **St David's Island** *island* E Bermuda
173 *O16* **St-Denis** ○ (Réunion) NW Réunion
103 *U6* **St-Dié** Vosges, NE France
103 *R5* **St-Dizier** *anc.* Desiderii Fanum. Haute-Marne, N France
15 *N11* **St-Donat** Québec, SE Canada
15 *N11* **Ste-Adèle** Québec, SE Canada
15 *N11* **Ste-Agathe-des-Monts** Québec, SE Canada
9 *Y16* **Ste. Anne** Manitoba, S Canada
45 *R12* **Ste-Anne** Grande Terre, E Guadeloupe
45 *Y6* **Ste-Anne** SE Martinique
15 *Q10* **Ste-Anne** ≈ Québec, SE Canada
172 *I16* **Sainte Anne** *island* Inner Islands, NE Seychelles
15 *W6* **Ste-Anne-des-Monts** Québec, SE Canada
14 *M10* **Ste-Anne-du-Lac** Québec, SE Canada
15 *U4* **Ste-Anne, Lac** ◎ Québec, SE Canada
15 *S10* **Ste-Apolline** Québec, SE Canada
15 *U7* **Ste-Blandine** Québec, SE Canada
15 *R10* **Ste-Claire** Québec, SE Canada
15 *Q10* **Ste-Croix** Québec, SE Canada
108 *B8* **Ste. Croix** Vaud, SW Switzerland
103 *P14* **Ste-Énimie** Lozère, S France
27 *Y6* **Sainte Genevieve** Missouri, C USA
103 *S12* **St-Egrève** Isère, E France
39 *T12* **Saint Elias, Cape** *headland* Kayak Island, Alaska, USA
39 *U11* **Saint Elias, Mount** ▲ Alaska, USA
10 *G8* **Saint Elias Mountains** ▲▲ Canada/USA
55 *Y10* **St-Élie** N French Guiana
103 *O10* **St-Eloy-les-Mines** Puy-de-Dôme, C France
15 *S7* **Ste-Maguerite Nord-Est** ≈ Québec, SE Canada
15 *V4* **Ste-Marguerite, Pointe** *headland* Québec, SE Canada
15 *R10* **Ste-Marie** Québec, SE Canada
45 *Q11* **Ste-Marie** NE Martinique
173 *P16* **Ste-Marie** NE Réunion
103 *U6* **Ste-Marie-aux-Mines** Haut-Rhin, NE France
Sainte Marie, Cap *see* Vohimena, Tanjona
12 *J14* **Ste-Marie, Lac** ⊠ Québec, S Canada
172 *K4* **Sainte Marie, Nosy** *island* E Madagascar
102 *L8* **Ste-Maure-de-Touraine** Indre-et-Loire, C France
103 *R4* **Ste-Menehould** Marne, NE France
Ste-Perpétue *see* Ste-Perpétue-de-l'Islet
15 *S9* **Ste-Perpétue-de-l'Islet** *var.* Ste-Perpétue. Québec, SE Canada
45 *X11* **Ste-Rose** Basse Terre, N Guadeloupe
173 *P16* **Ste-Rose** E Réunion
9 *W15* **Ste. Rose du Lac** Manitoba, S Canada
102 *J11* **Saintes** *anc.* Mediolanum. Charente-Maritime, W France
45 *X7* **Saintes, Canal des** *channel* SW Guadeloupe
Saintes, Îles des *see* les Saintes
173 *P16* **Ste-Suzanne** N Réunion
15 *P10* **Ste-Thècle** Québec, SE Canada
103 *Q12* **St-Étienne** Loire, E France
102 *M4* **St-Étienne-du-Rouvray** Seine-Maritime, N France
Saint Eustatius *see* Sint Eustatius
14 *M11* **Ste-Véronique** Québec, SE Canada
15 *T7* **St-Fabien** Québec, SE Canada
15 *P7* **St-Félicien** Québec, SE Canada
15 *O11* **St-Félix-de-Valois** Québec, SE Canada
103 *Y14* **St-Florent** Corse, France, C Mediterranean Sea
103 *Y14* **St-Florent, Golfe de** *gulf* Corse, France, C Mediterranean Sea
103 *P6* **St-Florentin** Yonne, C France
103 *N9* **St-Florent-sur-Cher** Cher, C France
103 *P12* **St-Flour** Cantal, C France
26 *H2* **Saint Francis** Kansas, C USA
83 *H26* **St. Francis, Cape** *headland* S South Africa
27 *X10* **Saint Francis River** ≈ Arkansas/Missouri, C USA
22 *J8* **Saint Francisville** Louisiana, S USA
45 *Y6* **St-François** Grande Terre, E Guadeloupe
15 *Q12* **St-François** ≈ Québec, SE Canada
15 *R11* **St-François, Lac** ◎ Québec, SE Canada
27 *X7* **Saint Francois Mountains** ▲▲ Missouri, C USA
St-Gall *see* St-Gall/Saint Gall/St.Gallen
St-Gall/Saint Gall/St. Gallen *see* Sankt Gallen
102 *L16* **St-Gaudens** Haute-Garonne, S France
15 *R12* **St-Gédéon** Québec, SE Canada
181 *X10* **Saint George** Queensland, E Australia
64 *B12* **St George** N Bermuda
38 *K15* **Saint George** Saint George Island, Alaska, USA
21 *S14* **Saint George** South Carolina, SE USA
36 *J8* **Saint George** Utah, W USA
13 *R12* **St. George, Cape** *cape* Newfoundland, Newfoundland and Labrador, E Canada
186 *I6* **St. George, Cape** *headland* New Ireland, NE Papua New Guinea
38 *J15* **Saint George Island** *island* Pribilof Islands, Alaska, USA
23 *S10* **Saint George Island** *island* Florida, SE USA
99 *J19* **Saint-Georges** Liège, E Belgium
15 *R11* **St-Georges** Québec, SE Canada
55 *Z11* **St-Georges** E French Guiana
45 *R14* **St. George's** ● (Grenada) SW Grenada
13 *R12* **St. George's Bay** *inlet* Newfoundland, Newfoundland and Labrador, E Canada
97 *G21* **Saint George's Channel** *channel* Ireland/Wales, UK
186 *H6* **St. George's Channel** *channel* NE Papua New Guinea
64 *B11* **St George's Island** *island* E Bermuda
99 *I21* **Saint-Gérard** Namur, S Belgium
St-Germain *see* St-Germain-en-Laye
15 *P12* **St-Germain-de-Grantham** Québec, SE Canada
103 *N5* **St-Germain-en-Laye** *var.* St-Germain. Yvelines, N France
102 *H8* **St-Gildas, Pointe du** *headland* NW France
103 *R15* **St-Gilles** Gard, S France
102 *I9* **St-Gilles-Croix-de-Vie** Vendée, NW France
173 *O16* **St-Gilles-les-Bains** W Réunion
102 *M16* **St-Girons** Ariège, S France
Saint Gotthard *see* Szentgotthárd
108 *G9* **St. Gotthard Tunnel** *tunnel* Ticino, S Switzerland
97 *H22* **St Govan's Head** *headland* SW Wales, UK
34 *M7* **Saint Helena** California, W USA
65 *F24* **Saint Helena** ◇ *UK dependent territory* C Atlantic Ocean
67 *O12* **Saint Helena** *island* C Atlantic Ocean
83 *E25* **St. Helena Bay** *bay* SW South Africa
65 *M16* **Saint Helena Fracture Zone** *tectonic feature* C Atlantic Ocean
34 *M7* **Saint Helena, Mount** ▲ California, W USA
21 *S15* **Saint Helena Sound** *inlet* South Carolina, SE USA
31 *Q7* **Saint Helen, Lake** ◎ Michigan, N USA
183 *Q16* **Saint Helens** Tasmania, SE Australia
97 *K18* **St Helens** NW England, UK
32 *G10* **Saint Helens** Oregon, NW USA
32 *H10* **Saint Helens, Mount** Ѫ Washington, NW USA
97 *L26* **St Helier** ○ (Jersey) S Jersey, Channel Islands
15 *S9* **St-Hilarion** Québec, SE Canada
99 *K22* **Saint-Hubert** Luxembourg, SE Belgium
15 *T8* **St-Hubert** Québec, SE Canada
15 *P12* **St-Hyacinthe** Québec, SE Canada
St.Iago de la Vega *see* Spanish Town
31 *Q4* **Saint Ignace** Michigan, N USA
15 *O10* **St-Ignace-du-Lac** Québec, SE Canada
12 *D12* **St. Ignace Island** *island* Ontario, S Canada
108 *C7* **St. Imier** Bern, W Switzerland
97 *G25* **St Ives** SW England, UK
29 *U10* **Saint James** Minnesota, N USA
10 *I15* **St. James, Cape** *headland* Graham Island, British Columbia, SW Canada
15 *O13* **St-Jean** *var.* St-Jean-sur-Richelieu. Québec, SE Canada
55 *X9* **St-Jean** NW French Guiana
15 *R8* **St-Jean** ≈ Québec, SE Canada
Saint-Jean-d'Acre *see* 'Akko
102 *K11* **St-Jean-d'Angély** Charente-Maritime, W France
103 *N7* **St-Jean-de-Braye** Loiret, C France
102 *I16* **St-Jean-de-Luz** Pyrénées-Atlantiques, SW France
103 *T12* **St-Jean-de-Maurienne** Savoie, E France
102 *I9* **St-Jean-de-Monts** Vendée, NW France
103 *Q14* **St-Jean-du-Gard** Gard, S France
15 *Q7* **St-Jean, Lac** ◎ Québec, SE Canada
102 *I16* **St-Jean-Pied-de-Port** Pyrénées-Atlantiques, SW France
15 *S9* **St-Jean-Port-Joli** Québec, SE Canada
St-Jean-sur-Richelieu *see* St-Jean
15 *N12* **St-Jérôme** Québec, SE Canada
25 *T5* **Saint Jo** Texas, SW USA
13 *O15* **St. John** New Brunswick, SE Canada
26 *L6* **Saint John** Kansas, C USA
19 *Q2* **Saint John** *Fr.* Saint-John. ≈ Canada/USA
76 *K16* **Saint John** ≈ C Liberia
45 *T9* **Saint John** *island* C Virgin Islands (US)
Saint-John *see* Saint John

◆ Country
● Country Capital
◇ Dependent Territory
○ Dependent Territory Capital
◐ Administrative Regions
✈ International Airport
▲ Mountain
▲▲ Mountain Range
Ѫ Volcano
≈ River
◎ Lake
⊠ Reservoir

SAMANÁ, BAHÍA DE – SAN JOSÉ DE CÚCUTA

45 P8 **Samaná, Bahía de** *bay* E Dominican Republic
44 K4 **Samana Cay** *island* SE Bahamas
136 K17 **Samandağı** Hatay, S Turkey
149 P3 **Samangān** ◐ *province* N Afghanistan
Samangān *see* Āybak
165 T5 **Samani** Hokkaidō, NE Japan
54 C13 **Samaniego** Nariño, SW Colombia
171 Q5 **Samar** *island* C Philippines
127 S6 **Samara** *prev.* Kuybyshev. Samarskaya Oblast', W Russian Federation
127 T7 **Samara** ≈ W Russian Federation
127 S6 **Samara** ✈ Samarskaya Oblast', W Russian Federation
117 V7 **Samara** ≈ E Ukraine
186 G10 **Samarai** Milne Bay, SE Papua New Guinea
Samarang *see* Semarang
138 G9 **Samaria Hills** *hill range* N Israel
54 L9 **Samariapo** Amazonas, C Venezuela
169 V11 **Samarinda** Borneo, C Indonesia
Samarkand *see* Samarqand
Samarkandskaya Oblast' *see* Samarqand Viloyati
Samarkandski/ Samarkandskoye *see* Temirtau
Samarobriva *see* Amiens
147 N11 **Samarqand** *Rus.* Samarkand. Samarqand Viloyati, C Uzbekistan
146 M11 **Samarqand Viloyati** *Rus.* Samarkandskaya Oblast'. ◐ *province* C Uzbekistan
139 S6 **Sāmarrā'** C Iraq
127 R7 **Samarskaya Oblast'** *prev.* Kuybyshevskaya Oblast'. ◐ *province* W Russian Federation
153 Q13 **Samastīpur** Bihār, N India
76 L14 **Samatiguila** NW Ivory Coast
119 Q17 **Samatsevichy** *Rus.* Samotevichi. Mahilyowskaya Voblasts', E Belarus
Samawa *see* As Samāwah
137 Y11 **Şamaxı** *Rus.* Shemakha. E Azerbaijan
79 K18 **Samba** Equateur, NW Dem. Rep. Congo
79 N21 **Samba** Maniema, E Dem. Rep. Congo
152 H6 **Samba** Jammu and Kashmir, NW India
169 W10 **Sambaliung, Pegunungan** ▲▲ Borneo, N Indonesia
154 M11 **Sambalpur** Orissa, E India
67 X12 **Sambao** ≈ W Madagascar
169 Q10 **Sambas, Sungai** ≈ Borneo, N Indonesia
172 K2 **Sambava** Antsiranana, NE Madagascar
152 J10 **Sambhal** Uttar Pradesh, N India
152 H12 **Sāmbhar Salt Lake** ◎ N India
107 N21 **Sambiase** Calabria, SW Italy
116 H5 **Sambir** *Rus.* Sambor. L'vivs'ka Oblast', NW Ukraine
82 C13 **Sambo** Huambo, C Angola
Sambor *see* Sambir
61 E21 **Samborombón, Bahía** *bay* NE Argentina
99 H20 **Sambre** ≈ Belgium/France
43 V16 **Sambú, Río** ≈ SE Panama
163 Z14 **Samch'ŏk** *Jap.* Sanchoku. NE South Korea
Samch'ŏnpŏ *see* Sach'ŏn
81 I21 **Same** Kilimanjaro, NE Tanzania
108 J10 **Samedan** *Ger.* Samaden. Graubünden, S Switzerland
82 K12 **Samfya** Luapula, N Zambia
141 W13 **Samḥān, Jabal** ▲▲ SW Oman
115 C18 **Sámi** Kefallonía, Iónia Nisiá, Greece, C Mediterranean Sea
56 F10 **Samiria, Río** ≈ N Peru
Samirum *see* Semīrom
137 V11 **Şämkir** *Rus.* Shamkhor. NW Azerbaijan
167 S7 **Sam, Nam** *Vtn.* Sông Chu. ≈ Laos/Vietnam
Samnān *see* Semnān
Sam Neua *see* Xam Nua
75 P10 **Samnū** C Libya
192 H15 **Samoa** *off.* Independent State of Western Samoa, *var.* Sāmoa, *prev* Western Samoa. ◆ *monarchy* W Polynesia
192 L9 **Sāmoa** *island group* American Samoa
Sāmoa *see* Samoa
175 T9 **Samoa Basin** *undersea feature* W Pacific Ocean
112 D8 **Samobor** Zagreb, N Croatia
114 H10 **Samokov** *var.* Samakov. Sofiya, W Bulgaria
111 H21 **Šamorín** *Ger.* Sommerein, *Hung.* Somorja. Trnavský Kraj, W Slovakia
115 M19 **Sámos** *prev.* Limín Vathéos. Sámos, Dodekánisa, Greece, Aegean Sea
115 M20 **Sámos** *island* Dodekánisa, Greece, Aegean Sea
Samosch *see* Szamos
168 I9 **Samosir, Pulau** *island* W Indonesia
Samotevichi *see* Samatsevichy
Samothrace *see* Samothráki
115 K14 **Samothráki** Samothráki, NE Greece
115 J14 **Samothráki** *anc.* Samothrace. *island* NE Greece
115 A15 **Samothráki** *island* Iónia Nisiá, Greece, C Mediterranean Sea
Samotschin *see* Szamocin
Sampê *see* Xiangcheng
169 S13 **Sampit** Borneo, C Indonesia
169 S12 **Sampit, Sungai** ≈ Borneo, N Indonesia
Sampoku *see* Sanpoku
186 H7 **Sampun** New Britain, E Papua New Guinea
79 N24 **Sampwe** Katanga, SE Dem. Rep. Congo
25 X8 **Sam Rayburn Reservoir** ▨ Texas, SW USA
167 Q6 **Sam Sao, Phou** ▲▲ Laos/Thailand
95 H22 **Samsø** *island* E Denmark
95 H23 **Samsø Bælt** *channel* E Denmark
167 T7 **Sầm Sơn** Thanh Hoa, N Vietnam
136 L11 **Samsun** *anc.* Amisus. Samsun, N Turkey
136 K11 **Samsun** ◐ *province* N Turkey
137 R9 **Samtredia** W Georgia
59 E15 **Samuel, Represa de** ▨ W Brazil
167 O14 **Samui, Ko** *island* SW Thailand
Samundari *see* Samundri
149 U9 **Samundri** *var.* Samundari. Punjab, E Pakistan
137 X10 **Samur** ≈ Azerbaijan/Russian Federation
137 Y11 **Samur-Abşeron Kanalı** *Rus.* Sam ur-Apsheronskiy Kanal. *canal* E Azerbaijan
Sam ur-Apsheronskiy Kanal *see* Samur-Abşeron Kanalı
167 O11 **Samut Prakan** *var.* Muang Samut Prakan, Paknam. Samut Prakan, C Thailand
167 O11 **Samut Sakhon** *var.* Maha Chai, Samut Sakorn, Tha Chin. Samut Sakhon, C Thailand
Samut Sakorn *see* Samut Sakhon
167 O11 **Samut Songhram** *prev.* Meklong. Samut Songkhram, SW Thailand
77 N12 **San** Ségou, C Mali
111 O15 **San** ≈ SE Poland
141 O15 **Şan'ā'** *Eng.* Sana. ● (Yemen) W Yemen
112 F11 **Sana** ≈ NW Bosnia and Herzegovina
80 O12 **Sanaag** *off.* Gobolka Sanaag. ◐ *region* N Somalia
Sanaag, Gobolka *see* Sanaag
114 J8 **Sanadinovo** Pleven, N Bulgaria
195 P1 **Sanae** *South African research station* Antarctica
139 Y10 **Sanāf, Hawr as** ◎ S Iraq
79 E15 **Sanaga** ≈ C Cameroon
54 D12 **San Agustín** Huila, SW Colombia
171 R8 **San Agustin, Cape** *headland* Mindanao, S Philippines
37 Q13 **San Agustin, Plains of** *plain* New Mexico, SW USA
38 M16 **Sanak Island** *island* Aleutian Islands, Alaska, USA
193 U10 **San Ambrosio, Isla** *Eng.* San Ambrosio Island. *island* W Chile
San Ambrosio Island *see* San Ambrosio, Isla
171 Q12 **Sanana** Pulau Sanana, E Indonesia
171 Q12 **Sanana, Pulau** *island* Maluku, E Indonesia
142 K5 **Sanandaj** *prev.* Sinneh. Kordestān, W Iran
35 P8 **San Andreas** California, W USA
2 C13 **San Andreas Fault** *fault* W USA
54 G8 **San Andrés** Santander, C Colombia
61 C20 **San Andrés de Giles** Buenos Aires, E Argentina
37 R14 **San Andres Mountains** ▲▲ New Mexico, SW USA
41 S15 **San Andrés Tuxtla** *var.* Tuxtla. Veracruz-Llave, E Mexico
25 P8 **San Angelo** Texas, SW USA
107 A20 **San Antioco, Isola di** *island* W Italy
42 F4 **San Antonio** Toledo, S Belize
62 G11 **San Antonio** Valparaíso, C Chile
188 H6 **San Antonio** Saipan, S Northern Mariana Islands
37 R13 **San Antonio** New Mexico, SW USA
25 R12 **San Antonio** Texas, SW USA
54 M11 **San Antonio** Amazonas, S Venezuela
54 I7 **San Antonio** Barinas, C Venezuela
55 O5 **San Antonio** Monagas, NE Venezuela
25 S12 **San Antonio** ✈ Texas, SW USA
San Antonio *see* San Antonio del Táchira
San Antonio Abad *see* Sant Antonio de Portmany
San Antonio Abad *see* Sant Antoni de Portmany
25 U13 **San Antonio Bay** *inlet* Texas, SW USA
61 E22 **San Antonio, Cabo** *headland* E Argentina
44 A5 **San Antonio, Cabo de** *cape* W Cuba
105 T11 **San Antonio, Cabo de** *cape* E Spain
54 H7 **San Antonio de Caparo** Táchira, W Venezuela
62 J5 **San Antonio de los Cobres** Salta, NE Argentina
54 H7 **San Antonio del Táchira** *var.* San Antonio. Táchira, W Venezuela
35 T15 **San Antonio, Mount** ▲ California, W USA
63 K16 **San Antonio Oeste** Río Negro, E Argentina
25 T13 **San Antonio River** ≈ Texas, SW USA
54 J5 **Sanare** Lara, N Venezuela
103 T16 **Sanary-sur-Mer** Var, SE France
25 X8 **San Augustine** Texas, SW USA
San Augustine *see* Minami-Iō-jima
141 T13 **Sanāw** *var.* Sanaw. NE Yemen
41 O11 **San Bartolo** San Luis Potosí, C Mexico
107 L16 **San Bartolomeo in Galdo** Campania, S Italy
106 K13 **San Benedetto del Tronto** Marche, C Italy
42 E3 **San Benito** Petén, N Guatemala
25 T17 **San Benito** Texas, SW USA
54 E6 **San Benito Abad** Sucre, N Colombia
35 P11 **San Benito Mountain** ▲ California, W USA
35 O10 **San Benito River** ≈ California, W USA
108 H10 **San Bernardino** Graubünden, S Switzerland
35 U15 **San Bernardino** California, W USA
35 U15 **San Bernardino Mountains** ▲▲ California, W USA
62 H11 **San Bernardo** Santiago, C Chile
40 J8 **San Bernardo** Durango, C Mexico
164 G12 **Sanbe-san** ▲ Kyūshū, SW Japan
San Bizenti-Barakaldo *see* San Vicente de Barakaldo
40 J12 **San Blas** Nayarit, C Mexico
40 H8 **San Blas** Sinaloa, C Mexico
43 V14 **San Blas** *off.* Comarca de San Blas. ◐ *special territory* NE Panama
43 U14 **San Blas, Archipiélago de** *island group* NE Panama
23 Q10 **San Blas, Cape** *headland* Florida, SE USA
San Blas, Comarca de *see* San Blas
43 V14 **San Blas, Cordillera de** ▲▲ NE Panama
62 J8 **San Blas de los Sauces** Catamarca, NW Argentina
106 G8 **San Bonifacio** Veneto, NE Italy
29 S12 **Sanborn** Iowa, C USA
40 M7 **San Buenaventura** Coahuila de Zaragoza, NE Mexico
105 S5 **San Caprasio** ▲ N Spain
60 L19 **San Carlos** São Paulo, SE Brazil
62 G13 **San Carlos** Bío Bío, C Chile
40 E9 **San Carlos** Baja California Sur, W Mexico
41 N5 **San Carlos** Coahuila de Zaragoza, NE Mexico
41 P9 **San Carlos** Tamaulipas, C Mexico
42 L12 **San Carlos** Río San Juan, S Nicaragua
43 T16 **San Carlos** Panamá, C Panama
171 N3 **San Carlos** *off.* San Carlos City. Luzon, N Philippines
61 G20 **San Carlos** Maldonado, S Uruguay
36 M14 **San Carlos** Arizona, SW USA
54 K5 **San Carlos** Cojedes, N Venezuela
San Carlos *see* Quesada, Costa Rica
San Carlos *see* Luba, Equatorial Guinea
61 B17 **San Carlos Centro** Santa Fe, C Argentina
171 P6 **San Carlos City** Negros, C Philippines
San Carlos City *see* San Carlos
San Carlos de Ancud *see* Ancud
63 H16 **San Carlos de Bariloche** Río Negro, SW Argentina
61 B21 **San Carlos de Bolívar** Buenos Aires, E Argentina
54 H6 **San Carlos del Zulia** Zulia, W Venezuela
54 L12 **San Carlos de Río Negro** Amazonas, S Venezuela
San Carlos, Estrecho de *see* Falkland Sound
36 M14 **San Carlos Reservoir** ▨ Arizona, SW USA
42 M12 **San Carlos, Río** ≈ N Costa Rica
65 D24 **San Carlos Settlement** East Falkland, Falkland Islands
61 C23 **San Cayetano** Buenos Aires, E Argentina
103 O8 **Sancerre** Cher, C France
158 G7 **Sanchakou** Xinjiang Uygur Zizhiqu, NW China
Sanchoku *see* Samch'ŏk
41 O12 **San Ciro** San Luis Potosí, C Mexico
105 P10 **San Clemente** Castilla-La Mancha, C Spain
35 T16 **San Clemente** California, W USA
61 E21 **San Clemente del Tuyú** Buenos Aires, E Argentina
35 S17 **San Clemente Island** *island* Channel Islands, California, W USA
103 O9 **Sancoins** Cher, C France
61 B16 **San Cristóbal** Santa Fe, C Argentina
44 B4 **San Cristóbal** Pinar del Río, W Cuba
45 O9 **San Cristóbal** *var.* Benemérita de San Cristóbal. S Dominican Republic
54 H7 **San Cristóbal** Táchira, W Venezuela
187 N10 **San Cristobal** *var.* Makira. *island* SE Solomon Islands
San Cristóbal *see* San Cristóbal de Las Casas
41 U16 **San Cristóbal de Las Casas** *var.* San Cristóbal. Chiapas, SE Mexico
187 N10 **San Cristóbal, Isla** *var.* Chatham Island. *island* Galapagos Islands, Ecuador, E Pacific Ocean
42 D5 **San Cristóbal Verapaz** Alta Verapaz, C Guatemala
44 F6 **Sancti Spíritus** Sancti Spíritus, C Cuba
103 O11 **Sancy, Puy de** ▲ C France
95 D15 **Sand** Rogaland, S Norway
169 W7 **Sandakan** Sabah, East Malaysia
182 K9 **Sandalwood** South Australia
Sandalwood Island *see* Sumba, Pulau
94 D11 **Sandane** Sogn Og Fjordane, S Norway
114 G12 **Sandanski** *prev.* Sveti Vrach. Blagoevgradt, SW Bulgaria
76 J11 **Sandaré** Kayes, W Mali
95 J19 **Sandared** Västra Götaland, S Sweden
94 N12 **Sandarne** Gävleborg, C Sweden
186 B5 **Sandaun** *prev.* West Sepik. ◐ *province* NW Papua New Guinea
96 K4 **Sanday** *island* NE Scotland, UK
31 P15 **Sand Creek** ≈ Indiana, N USA
95 H15 **Sande** Vestfold, S Norway
95 H16 **Sandefjord** Vestfold, S Norway
77 O15 **Sandégué** E Ivory Coast
77 P14 **Sandema** N Ghana
37 O11 **Sanders** Arizona, SW USA
24 M11 **Sanderson** Texas, SW USA
23 U4 **Sandersville** Georgia, SE USA
92 H4 **Sandgerdhi** Sudhurland, SW Iceland
28 K14 **Sand Hills** ▲ Nebraska, C USA
25 S14 **Sandia** Texas, SW USA
35 T17 **San Diego** California, W USA
25 S14 **San Diego** Texas, SW USA
136 F14 **Sandıklı** Afyon, W Turkey
152 L12 **Sandīla** Uttar Pradesh, N India
San Dimitri Point *see* San Dimitri, Ras
121 N15 **San Dimitri, Ras** *var.* San Dimitri Point. *headland* Gozo, NW Malta
168 J13 **Sanding, Selat** *strait* W Indonesia
30 J3 **Sand Island** *island* Apostle Islands, Wisconsin, N USA
95 C16 **Sandnes** Rogaland, S Norway
92 F13 **Sandnessjøen** Nordland, C Norway
Sandø *see* Sandoy
79 L24 **Sandoa** Katanga, S Dem. Rep. Congo
111 N15 **Sandomierz** *Rus.* Sandomir. Świętokrzyskie, C Poland
Sandomir *see* Sandomierz
54 C13 **Sandoná** Nariño, SW Colombia
106 I7 **San Donà di Piave** Veneto, NE Italy
124 K14 **Sandovo** Tverskaya Oblast', W Russian Federation
166 K7 **Sandoway** Arakan State, W Burma (Myanmar)
97 M24 **Sandown** S England, UK
95 B19 **Sandoy** *Dan.* Sandø. *island* C Faeroe Islands
39 N16 **Sand Point** Popof Island, Alaska, USA
32 M7 **Sandpoint** Idaho, NW USA
65 N24 **Sand Point** *headland* E Tristan da Cunha
31 R7 **Sand Point** *headland* Michigan, N USA
93 H14 **Sandsele** Västerbotten, N Sweden
10 I14 **Sandspit** Moresby Island, British Columbia, SW Canada
27 P9 **Sand Springs** Oklahoma, C USA
29 W7 **Sandstone** Minnesota, N USA
36 K15 **Sand Tank Mountains** ▲▲ Arizona, SW USA
31 S8 **Sandusky** Michigan, N USA
31 S11 **Sandusky** Ohio, N USA
31 S12 **Sandusky River** ≈ Ohio, N USA
83 D22 **Sandverhaar** Karas, S Namibia
95 L24 **Sandvig** Bornholm, E Denmark
95 H15 **Sandvika** Akershus, S Norway
94 N13 **Sandviken** Gävleborg, C Sweden
30 M11 **Sandwich** Illinois, N USA
Sandwich Island *see* Éfaté
Sandwich Islands *see* Hawaiian Islands
153 V16 **Sandwip Island** *island* SE Bangladesh
9 U12 **Sandy Bay** Saskatchewan, C Canada
183 N16 **Sandy Cape** *headland* Tasmania, SE Australia
36 L3 **Sandy City** Utah, W USA
31 U12 **Sandy Creek** ≈ Ohio, N USA
146 J15 **Sandykachi** *var.* Sandykgachy, *Rus* Sandykachi. Maryyskiy Velayat, S Turkmenistan
21 O5 **Sandy Hook** Kentucky, S USA
18 K15 **Sandy Hook** *headland* New Jersey, NE USA
Sandykachi *see* Sandykachi
Sandykachi/Sandykgachy *see* Sandykgaçy
Sandykgachy *see* Sandykachi
146 J15 **Sandykgaçy** *var.* Sandykgachy, *Rus.* Sandykachi. Mary Welaýaty, S Turkmenistan
146 L13 **Sandykly Gumy** *Rus.* Peski Sandykly. *desert* E Turkmenistan
Sandykly, Peski *see* Sandykly Gumy
9 Q13 **Sandy Lake** Alberta, W Canada
12 B8 **Sandy Lake** Ontario, C Canada
12 B8 **Sandy Lake** ◎ Ontario, C Canada
23 S3 **Sandy Springs** Georgia, SE USA
24 H8 **San Elizario** Texas, SW USA
99 L25 **Sanem** Luxembourg, SW Luxembourg
42 K5 **San Esteban** Olancho, C Honduras
105 O6 **San Esteban de Gormaz** Castilla-León, N Spain
40 E5 **San Esteban, Isla** *island* NW Mexico
San Eugenio/San Eugenio del Cuareim *see* Artigas
62 H11 **San Felipe** *var.* San Felipe de Aconcagua. Valparaíso, C Chile
40 D3 **San Felipe** Baja California, NW Mexico
40 N12 **San Felipe** Guanajuato, C Mexico
54 K5 **San Felipe** Yaracuy, NW Venezuela
44 B5 **San Felipe, Cayos de** *island group* W Cuba
San Felipe de Aconcagua *see* San Felipe
San Felipe de Puerto Plata *see* Puerto Plata
37 R11 **San Felipe Pueblo** New Mexico, SW USA
San Feliú de Guixols *see* Sant Feliu de Guíxols
193 T10 **San Félix, Isla** *Eng.* San Felix Island. *island* W Chile
San Felix Island *see* San Félix, Isla
54 L11 **San Fernanado de Atabapo** Amazonas, S Venezuela
40 C4 **San Fernando** *var.* Misión San Fernando. Baja California, NW Mexico
41 P9 **San Fernando** Tamaulipas, C Mexico
171 N2 **San Fernando** Luzon, N Philippines
171 O3 **San Fernando** Luzon, N Philippines
104 J16 **San Fernando** *prev.* Isla de León. Andalucía, S Spain
45 U14 **San Fernando** Trinidad, Trinidad and Tobago
35 S15 **San Fernando** California, W USA
54 L7 **San Fernando** *var.* San Fernando de Apure. Apure, C Venezuela
San Fernando de Apure *see* San Fernando
62 L8 **San Fernando del Valle de Catamarca** *var.* Catamarca. Catamarca, NW Argentina
San Fernando de Monte Cristi *see* Monte Cristi
41 P9 **San Fernando, Río** ≈ C Mexico
23 X11 **Sanford** Florida, SE USA
19 P9 **Sanford** Maine, NE USA
21 T10 **Sanford** North Carolina, SE USA
25 N2 **Sanford** Texas, SW USA
39 T10 **Sanford, Mount** ▲ Alaska, USA
42 G8 **San Francisco** *var.* Gotera, San Francisco Gotera. Morazán, E El Salvador
43 R16 **San Francisco** Veraguas, C Panama
171 N2 **San Francisco** *var.* Aurora. Luzon, N Philippines
35 L8 **San Francisco** California, W USA
54 H5 **San Francisco** Zulia, NW Venezuela
34 M8 **San Francisco** ✈ California, W USA
35 N9 **San Francisco Bay** *bay* California, W USA
61 C24 **San Francisco de Bellocq** Buenos Aires, E Argentina
40 I6 **San Francisco de Borja** Chihuahua, N Mexico
42 J6 **San Francisco de la Paz** Olancho, C Honduras
40 J7 **San Francisco del Oro** Chihuahua, N Mexico
40 M12 **San Francisco del Rincón** Jalisco, SW Mexico
45 O8 **San Francisco de Macorís** C Dominican Republic
San Francisco de Satipo *see* Satipo
San Francisco Gotera *see* San Francisco
San Francisco Telixtlahuaca *see* Telixtlahuaca
107 K23 **San Fratello** Sicilia, Italy, C Mediterranean Sea
San Fructuoso *see* Tacuarembó
82 C12 **Sanga** Cuanza Sul, NW Angola
56 C5 **San Gabriel** Carchi, N Ecuador
159 S15 **Sa'ngain** Xizang Zizhiqu, W China
154 E13 **Sangamner** Mahārāshtra, W India
152 H12 **Sāngāner** Rājasthān, N India
Sangan, Koh-i- *see* Sangān, Kūh-e
149 N6 **Sangān, Kūh-e** *Pash.* Koh-i-Sangan. ▲ C Afghanistan
123 P10 **Sangar** Respublika Sakha (Yakutiya), NE Russian Federation
169 V11 **Sangasanga** Borneo, C Indonesia
103 N1 **Sangatte** Pas-de-Calais, N France
107 B19 **San Gavino Monreale** Sardegna, Italy, C Mediterranean Sea
57 D16 **Sangayan, Isla** *island* W Peru
30 L14 **Sangchris Lake** ▨ Illinois, N USA
171 N16 **Sangeang, Pulau** *island* S Indonesia
116 I10 **Sângeorgiu de Pădure** *prev.* Erdăt-Sângeorz, Singeorgiu de Pădure, *Hung.* Erdőszentgyörgy. Mureş, C Romania
116 I9 **Sângeorz-Băi** *var.* Singeroz Băi, *Ger.* Rumänisch-Sankt-Georgen, *Hung.* Oláhszentgyőrgy; *prev.* Singeorz-Băi. Bistriţa-Năsăud, N Romania
35 R10 **Sanger** California, W USA
25 T5 **Sanger** Texas, SW USA
Sângerei *see* Singerei
101 L15 **Sangerhausen** Sachsen-Anhalt, C Germany
45 S6 **San Germán** W Puerto Rico
San Germano *see* Cassino
161 N2 **Sanggan He** ≈ E China
169 Q11 **Sanggau** Borneo, C Indonesia
79 H16 **Sangha** ≈ Central African Republic/Congo
79 G16 **Sangha-Mbaéré** ◐ *prefecture* SW Central African Republic
149 Q15 **Sānghar** Sind, SE Pakistan
115 F22 **Sangiás** ▲ S Greece
Sangihe, Kepulauan *see* Sangir, Kepulauan
171 Q9 **Sangihe, Pulau** *var.* Sangir. *island* N Indonesia
54 G8 **San Gil** Santander, C Colombia
106 F12 **San Gimignano** Toscana, C Italy
148 M8 **Sangīn** *var.* Sangin. Helmand, S Afghanistan
Sangin *see* Sangīn
107 O21 **San Giovanni in Fiore** Calabria, SW Italy
107 M16 **San Giovanni Rotondo** Puglia, SE Italy
106 G12 **San Giovanni Valdarno** Toscana, C Italy
Sangir *see* Sangihe, Pulau
171 Q10 **Sangir, Kepulauan** *var* Kepulauan Sangihe. *island group* N Indonesia
Sangiyn Dalay *see* Erdenedalay, Dundgovĭ, Mongolia
Sangiyn Dalay *see* Erdene, Govĭ-Altay, Mongolia
Sangiyn Dalay *see* Nomgon, Ömnögovĭ, Mongolia
Sangiyn Dalay *see* Öldziyt, Övörhangay, Mongolia
163 Y15 **Sangju** *Jap.* Shōshū. C South Korea
167 R11 **Sângkha** Surin, E Thailand
169 W10 **Sangkulirang** Borneo, N Indonesia
169 W10 **Sangkulirang, Teluk** *bay* Borneo, N Indonesia
155 E16 **Sāngli** Mahārāshtra, W India
79 E16 **Sangmélima** Sud, S Cameroon
35 V15 **San Gorgonio Mountain** ▲ California, W USA
37 T8 **Sangre de Cristo Mountains** ▲▲ Colorado/New Mexico, C USA
61 A20 **San Gregorio** Santa Fe, C Argentina
61 F18 **San Gregorio de Polanco** Tacuarembó, C Uruguay
45 V14 **Sangre Grande** Trinidad, Trinidad and Tobago
159 N16 **Sangri** Xizang Zizhiqu, W China
152 H9 **Sangrūr** Punjab, NW India
44 I11 **Sangster** *off.* Sir Donald Sangster International Airport, *var.* Montego Bay. ✈ (Montego Bay) W Jamaica
59 G17 **Sangue, Rio do** ≈ W Brazil
105 R4 **Sangüesa** Navarra, N Spain
61 C16 **San Gustavo** Entre Ríos, E Argentina
Sangyuan *see* Wuqiao
40 C6 **San Hipólito, Punta** *headland* W Mexico
23 W15 **Sanibel** Sanibel Island, Florida, SE USA
23 V15 **Sanibel Island** *island* Florida, SE USA
60 F13 **San Ignacio** Misiones, NE Argentina
42 F2 **San Ignacio** *prev.* Cayo, El Cayo. Cayo, W Belize
57 L16 **San Ignacio** Beni, N Bolivia
57 O18 **San Ignacio** Santa Cruz, E Bolivia
42 M14 **San Ignacio** *var.* San Ignacio de Acosta. San José, W Costa Rica
40 E6 **San Ignacio** Baja California Sur, W Mexico
40 J10 **San Ignacio** Sinaloa, W Mexico
56 B9 **San Ignacio** Cajamarca, N Peru
San Ignacio de Acosta *see* San Ignacio
40 D7 **San Ignacio, Laguna** *lagoon* W Mexico
12 I6 **Sanikiluaq** Belcher Islands, Nunavut, C Canada
171 O3 **San Ildefonso Peninsula** *peninsula* Luzon, N Philippines
Saniquillie *see* Sanniquellie
61 D20 **San Isidro** Buenos Aires, E Argentina
43 N14 **San Isidro** *var.* San Isidro de El General. San José, SE Costa Rica
San Isidro de El General *see* San Isidro
54 E5 **San Jacinto** Bolívar, N Colombia
35 U16 **San Jacinto** California, W USA
35 V15 **San Jacinto Peak** ▲ California, W USA
61 F14 **San Javier** Misiones, NE Argentina
61 C16 **San Javier** Santa Fe, C Argentina
105 S13 **San Javier** Murcia, SE Spain
61 D18 **San Javier** Río Negro, W Uruguay
61 C16 **San Javier, Río** ≈ C Argentina
160 L12 **Sanjiang** *var.* Guyi, Sanjiang Dongzu Zizhixian. Guangxi Zhuangzu Zizhiqu, S China
Sanjiang *see* Jinping, Guizhou
Sanjiang Dongzu Zizhixian *see* Sanjiang
Sanjiaocheng *see* Haiyan
165 N11 **Sanjō** *var.* Sanzyô. Niigata, Honshū, C Japan
57 M15 **San Joaquín** Beni, N Bolivia
55 O6 **San Joaquín** Anzoátegui, NE Venezuela
35 O9 **San Joaquin River** ≈ California, W USA
35 P10 **San Joaquin Valley** *valley* California, W USA
61 A18 **San Jorge** Santa Fe, C Argentina
40 D3 **San Jorge, Bahía de** *bay* NW Mexico
63 J19 **San Jorge, Golfo** *var.* Gulf of San Jorge. *gulf* S Argentina
San Jorge, Gulf of *see* San Jorge, Golfo
61 F14 **San José** Misiones, NE Argentina
57 P19 **San José** *var.* San José de Chiquitos. Santa Cruz, E Bolivia
42 M14 **San José** ● (Costa Rica) San José, C Costa Rica
42 C7 **San José** *var.* Puerto San José. Escuintla, S Guatemala
40 G6 **San José** Sonora, NW Mexico
188 K8 **San Jose** Tinian, S Northern Mariana Islands
105 U11 **San José** Eivissa, Spain, W Mediterranean Sea
35 N9 **San Jose** California, W USA
54 H5 **San José** Zulia, NW Venezuela
42 M14 **San José** *off.* Provincia de San José. ◐ *province* W Costa Rica
61 E19 **San José** ◐ *department* S Uruguay
42 M13 **San José** ✈ Alajuela, C Costa Rica
San José *see* San José del Guaviare, Colombia
San Jose *see* Oleai
San Jose *see* Sant Josep de sa Talaia, Ibiza, Spain
San José *see* San José de Mayo, Uruguay
171 O3 **San Jose City** Luzon, N Philippines
San José de Chiquitos *see* San José
San José de Cúcuta *see* Cúcuta

◆ Country ● Country Capital ◇ Dependent Territory ○ Dependent Territory Capital ◐ Administrative Regions ✈ International Airport ▲ Mountain ▲▲ Mountain Range ⛰ Volcano ≈ River ◎ Lake ▨ Reservoir

317

San José de Feliciano – Santa María, Laguna de

61 D16 **San José de Feliciano** Entre Ríos, E Argentina
55 O6 **San José de Guanipa** var. El Tigrito. Anzoátegui, NE Venezuela
62 I9 **San José de Jáchal** San Juan, W Argentina
40 G10 **San José del Cabo** Baja California Sur, W Mexico
54 G12 **San José del Guaviare** var. San José. Guaviare, S Colombia
61 E20 **San José de Mayo** var. San José. San José, S Uruguay
54 I10 **San José de Ocuné** Vichada, E Colombia
41 O9 **San José de Raíces** Nuevo León, NE Mexico
63 K17 **San José, Golfo** gulf E Argentina
40 F9 **San José, Isla** island W Mexico
43 U16 **San José, Isla** island SE Panama
San Jose, Isla see Weddell Island
25 U14 **San Jose Island** island Texas, SW USA
San José, Provincia de see San José
62 I10 **San Juan** San Juan, W Argentina
45 N9 **San Juan** var. San Juan de la Maguana. C Dominican Republic
57 E17 **San Juan** Ica, S Peru
45 U5 **San Juan** ○ (Puerto Rico) NE Puerto Rico
62 H10 **San Juan** off. Provincia de San Juan. ◈ province W Argentina
45 U5 **San Juan** var. Luis Muñoz Marin. ✈ NE Puerto Rico
San Juan see San Juan de los Morros
62 O7 **San Juan Bautista** Misiones, S Paraguay
35 O10 **San Juan Bautista** California, W USA
San Juan Bautista see Villahermosa
San Juan Bautista Cuicatlán see Cuicatlán
San Juan Bautista Tuxtepec see Tuxtepec
79 C17 **San Juan, Cabo** cape S Equatorial Guinea
105 S12 **San Juan de Alicante** País Valenciano, E Spain
54 H7 **San Juan de Colón** Táchira, NW Venezuela
40 L9 **San Juan de Guadalupe** Durango, C Mexico
San Juan de la Maguana see San Juan
54 G4 **San Juan del Cesar** La Guajira, N Colombia
40 L15 **San Juan de Lima, Punta** headland SW Mexico
42 I8 **San Juan de Limay** Estelí, NW Nicaragua
43 N12 **San Juan del Norte** var. Greytown. Río San Juan, SE Nicaragua
54 K4 **San Juan de los Cayos** Falcón, N Venezuela
40 M12 **San Juan de los Lagos** Jalisco, C Mexico
54 L5 **San Juan de los Morros** var. San Juan. Guárico, N Venezuela
40 K9 **San Juan del Río** Durango, C Mexico
41 O13 **San Juan del Río** Querétaro de Arteaga, C Mexico
42 J11 **San Juan del Sur** Rivas, SW Nicaragua
54 M9 **San Juan de Manapiare** Amazonas, S Venezuela
40 E7 **San Juanico** Baja California Sur, W Mexico
40 D7 **San Juanico, Punta** headland W Mexico
32 G6 **San Juan Islands** island group Washington, NW USA
40 I6 **San Juanito** Chihuahua, N Mexico
40 I12 **San Juanito, Isla** island C Mexico
37 R8 **San Juan Mountains** ▲▲ Colorado, C USA
54 E5 **San Juan Nepomuceno** Bolívar, NW Colombia
44 E5 **San Juan, Pico** ▲ C Cuba
San Juan, Provincia de see San Juan
191 W15 **San Juan, Punta** headland Easter Island, Chile, E Pacific Ocean
42 M12 **San Juan, Río** ~ Costa Rica/Nicaragua
41 S15 **San Juan, Río** ~ SE Mexico
37 O8 **San Juan River** ~ Colorado/Utah, W USA
San Julián see Puerto San Julián
61 B17 **San Justo** Santa Fe, C Argentina
109 W5 **Sankt Aegyd am Neuwalde** Niederösterreich, E Austria
109 U9 **Sankt Andrä** Slvn. Šent Andraž. Kärnten, S Austria
Sankt Andrä see Szentendre
Sankt Anna see Sântana
108 K8 **Sankt Anton am Arlberg** Vorarlberg, W Austria
101 E16 **Sankt Augustin** Nordrhein-Westfalen, W Germany
Sankt-Bartholomäi see Palamuse
101 F24 **Sankt Blasien** Baden-Württemberg, SW Germany
109 R3 **Sankt Florian am Inn** Oberösterreich, N Austria
108 I7 **Sankt Gallen** var. St. Gallen, Eng. Saint Gall, Fr. St-Gall. Sankt Gallen, NE Switzerland
108 H8 **Sankt Gallen** var. St.Gallen, Eng. Saint Gall, Fr. St-Gall. ◈ canton NE Switzerland
108 J8 **Sankt Gallenkirch** Vorarlberg, W Austria
109 Q5 **Sankt Georgen** Salzburg, N Austria
Sankt Georgen see Đurđevac
Sankt-Georgen see Sfântu Gheorghe
109 R6 **Sankt Gilgen** Salzburg, NW Austria
Sankt Gotthard see Szentgotthárd
101 E20 **Sankt Ingbert** Saarland, SW Germany
Sankt-Jakobi see Viru-Jaagupi, Lääne-Virumaa, Estonia
Sankt-Jakobi see Pärnu-Jaagupi, Pärnumaa, Estonia
Sankt Johann see Sankt Johann in Tirol
109 T7 **Sankt Johann am Tauern** Steiermark, E Austria
109 Q7 **Sankt Johann im Pongau** Salzburg, NW Austria
109 P6 **Sankt Johann in Tirol** var. Sankt Johann. Tirol, W Austria
Sankt-Johannis see Järva-Jaani
108 L8 **Sankt Leonhard** Tirol, W Austria
Sankt Margarethen see Sankt Margarethen im Burgenland
109 Y5 **Sankt Margarethen im Burgenland** var. Sankt Margarethen. Burgenland, E Austria
Sankt Martin see Martin
109 X8 **Sankt Martin an der Raab** Burgenland, SE Austria
109 U7 **Sankt Michael in Obersteiermark** Steiermark, SE Austria
Sankt Michel see Mikkeli
Sankt Moritz see St. Moritz
108 E11 **Sankt Niklaus** Valais, S Switzerland
109 S7 **Sankt Nikolai** var. Sankt Nikolai im Sölktal. Steiermark, SE Austria
Sankt Nikolai im Sölktal see Sankt Nikolai
109 U9 **Sankt Paul** var. Sankt Paul im Lavanttal. Kärnten, S Austria
Sankt Paul im Lavanttal see Sankt Paul
Sankt Peter see Pivka
109 W9 **Sankt Peter am Ottersbach** Steiermark, SE Austria
124 J13 **Sankt-Peterburg** prev. Leningrad, Petrograd, Eng. Saint Petersburg, Fin. Pietari. Leningradskaya Oblast', NW Russian Federation
100 H8 **Sankt Peter-Ording** Schleswig-Holstein, N Germany
109 V4 **Sankt Pölten** Niederösterreich, N Austria
109 W7 **Sankt Ruprecht** var. Sankt Ruprecht an der Raab. Steiermark, SE Austria
Sankt Ruprecht an der Raab see Sankt Ruprecht
Sankt-Ulrich see Ortisei
109 T4 **Sankt Valentin** Niederösterreich, C Austria
Sankt Veit am Flaum see Rijeka
109 T9 **Sankt Veit an der Glan** Slvn. Št. Vid. Kärnten, S Austria
99 M21 **Sankt-Vith** var. Saint-Vith. Liège, E Belgium
101 E20 **Sankt Wendel** Saarland, SW Germany
109 R6 **Sankt Wolfgang** Salzburg, NW Austria
79 K21 **Sankuru** ~ C Dem. Rep. Congo
40 D8 **San Lázaro, Cabo** headland W Mexico
137 O16 **Şanlıurfa** prev. Sanli Urfa, Urfa; anc. Edessa. şanlıurfa, S Turkey
137 O16 **Şanlıurfa** prev. Urfa. ◈ province SE Turkey
Sanli Urfa see Şanlıurfa
137 O16 **Şanlıurfa Yaylası** plateau SE Turkey
61 B18 **San Lorenzo** Santa Fe, C Argentina
57 M21 **San Lorenzo** Tarija, S Bolivia
56 C5 **San Lorenzo** Esmeraldas, N Ecuador
42 H8 **San Lorenzo** Valle, S Honduras
56 A6 **San Lorenzo, Cabo** headland W Ecuador
105 N8 **San Lorenzo de El Escorial** var. El Escorial. Madrid, C Spain
40 E5 **San Lorenzo, Isla** island NW Mexico
57 C14 **San Lorenzo, Isla** island W Peru
63 G20 **San Lorenzo, Monte** ▲ S Argentina
40 I9 **San Lorenzo, Río** ~ C Mexico
104 J15 **Sanlúcar de Barrameda** Andalucía, S Spain
104 J14 **Sanlúcar la Mayor** Andalucía, S Spain
40 E6 **San Lucas** var. Cabo San Lucas. Baja California Sur, W Mexico
40 F11 **San Lucas** Baja California Sur, NW Mexico
40 G11 **San Lucas, Cabo** var. San Lucas Cape. headland W Mexico
San Lucas Cape see San Lucas, Cabo
62 J11 **San Luis** San Luis, C Argentina
42 E4 **San Luis** Petén, NE Guatemala
40 D2 **San Luis** var. San Luis Río Colorado. Sonora, NW Mexico
42 M7 **San Luis** Región Autónoma Atlántico Norte, NE Nicaragua
36 H15 **San Luis** Arizona, SW USA
37 T8 **San Luis** Colorado, C USA
54 J4 **San Luis** Falcón, N Venezuela
62 J11 **San Luis** off. Provincia de San Luis. ◈ province C Argentina
41 N12 **San Luis de la Paz** Guanajuato, C Mexico
40 K8 **San Luis del Cordero** Durango, C Mexico
40 D4 **San Luis, Isla** island NW Mexico
42 E6 **San Luis Jilotepeque** Jalapa, SE Guatemala
57 M16 **San Luis, Laguna de** ◎ NW Bolivia
35 P13 **San Luis Obispo** California, W USA
37 R7 **San Luis Peak** ▲ Colorado, C USA
41 N11 **San Luis Potosí** San Luis Potosí, C Mexico
41 N11 **San Luis Potosí** ◈ state C Mexico
San Luis, Provincia de see San Luis
35 O10 **San Luis Reservoir** ⊠ California, W USA
San Luis Río Colorado see San Luis
37 S8 **San Luis Valley** basin Colorado, C USA
107 C19 **Sanluri** Sardegna, Italy, C Mediterranean Sea
61 D23 **San Manuel** Buenos Aires, E Argentina
36 M15 **San Manuel** Arizona, SW USA
106 F11 **San Marcello Pistoiese** Toscana, C Italy
107 N20 **San Marco Argentano** Calabria, SW Italy
54 E6 **San Marcos** Sucre, N Colombia
42 M14 **San Marcos** San José, C Costa Rica
42 B5 **San Marcos** San Marcos, W Guatemala
42 F6 **San Marcos** Ocotepeque, SW Honduras
41 O16 **San Marcos** Guerrero, S Mexico
25 S11 **San Marcos** Texas, SW USA
42 A5 **San Marcos** off. Departamento de San Marcos. ◈ department W Guatemala
San Marcos de Arica see Arica
San Marcos, Departamento de see San Marcos
40 E6 **San Marcos, Isla** island W Mexico
106 H11 **San Marino** ● (San Marino) C San Marino
106 I11 **San Marino** off. Republic of San Marino. ◆ republic S Europe
San Marino, Republic of see San Marino
62 I11 **San Martín** Mendoza, C Argentina
54 F11 **San Martín** Meta, C Colombia
56 D11 **San Martín** off. Departamento de San Martín. ◈ department C Peru
194 I5 **San Martín** Argentinian research station Antarctica
63 H16 **San Martín de los Andes** Neuquén, W Argentina
San Martín, Departamento de see San Martín
104 M8 **San Martín de Valdeiglesias** Madrid, C Spain
63 G21 **San Martín, Lago** var. Lago O'Higgins. ◎ S Argentina
106 H6 **San Martino di Castrozza** Trentino-Alto Adige, N Italy
57 N16 **San Martín, Río** ~ N Bolivia
San Martín Texmelucan see Texmelucan
35 N9 **San Mateo** California, W USA
55 O6 **San Mateo** Anzoátegui, NE Venezuela
42 B4 **San Mateo Ixtatán** Huehuetenango, W Guatemala
57 Q18 **San Matías** Santa Cruz, E Bolivia
63 K16 **San Matías, Golfo** var. Gulf of San Matías. gulf E Argentina
San Matías, Gulf of see San Matías, Golfo
15 O8 **Sanmaur** Québec, SE Canada
161 T10 **Sanmen Wan** bay E China
160 M6 **Sanmenxia** var. Shan Xian. Henan, C China
Sânmiclăuş Mare see Sânnicolau Mare
61 D14 **San Miguel** Corrientes, NE Argentina
57 L16 **San Miguel** Beni, N Bolivia
42 G8 **San Miguel** San Miguel, SE El Salvador
40 L6 **San Miguel** Coahuila de Zaragoza, N Mexico
40 J9 **San Miguel** var. San Miguel de Cruces. Durango, C Mexico
43 U16 **San Miguel** Panamá, SE Panama
35 P12 **San Miguel** California, W USA
42 B9 **San Miguel** ◈ department E El Salvador
41 N13 **San Miguel de Allende** Guanajuato, C Mexico
San Miguel de Cruces see San Miguel
San Miguel de Ibarra see Ibarra
61 D21 **San Miguel del Monte** Buenos Aires, E Argentina
62 J7 **San Miguel de Tucumán** var. Tucumán. Tucumán, N Argentina
43 V16 **San Miguel, Golfo de** gulf S Panama
35 P15 **San Miguel Island** island California, W USA
42 L11 **San Miguelito** Río San Juan, S Nicaragua
43 T15 **San Miguelito** Panamá, C Panama
57 N18 **San Miguel, Río** ~ E Bolivia
56 D6 **San Miguel, Río** ~ Colombia/Ecuador
40 I7 **San Miguel, Río** ~ N Mexico
42 G8 **San Miguel, Volcán de** ⛰ SE El Salvador
161 Q12 **Sanming** Fujian, SE China
106 F11 **San Miniato** Toscana, C Italy
San Murezzan see St. Moritz
Sannār see Sennar
107 M15 **Sannicandro Garganico** Puglia, SE Italy
40 H6 **San Nicolás** Sonora, NW Mexico
61 C19 **San Nicolás de los Arroyos** Buenos Aires, E Argentina
35 R16 **San Nicolas Island** island Channel Islands, California, W USA
Sânnicolaul-Mare see Sânnicolau Mare
116 E11 **Sânnicolau Mare** var. Sânnicolaul-Mare, Hung. Nagyszentmiklós; prev. Sânmiclăuş Mare, Sînnicolau Mare. Timiş, W Romania
123 Q6 **Sannikova, Proliv** strait NE Russian Federation
76 K16 **Sanniquellie** var. Saniquillie. NE Liberia
165 R7 **Sannohe** Aomori, Honshū, C Japan
Sanntaler Alpen see Kamniško-Savinjske Alpe
111 O17 **Sanok** Podkarpackie, SE Poland
54 E5 **San Onofre** Sucre, NW Colombia
57 K21 **San Pablo** Potosí, S Bolivia
171 O4 **San Pablo** off. San Pablo City. Luzon, N Philippines
San Pablo Balleza see Balleza
35 N8 **San Pablo Bay** bay California, W USA
San Pablo City see San Pablo
40 C6 **San Pablo, Punta** headland W Mexico
43 R16 **San Pablo, Río** ~ C Panama
171 P4 **San Pascual** Burias Island, C Philippines
121 Q16 **San Pawl il-Bahar** Eng. Saint Paul's Bay. E Malta
61 C19 **San Pedro** Buenos Aires, E Argentina
62 K5 **San Pedro** Jujuy, N Argentina
60 G13 **San Pedro** Misiones, NE Argentina
42 H1 **San Pedro** Corozal, NE Belize
76 M17 **San-Pédro** S Ivory Coast
40 L8 **San Pedro** var. San Pedro de las Colonias. Coahuila de Zaragoza, NE Mexico
62 O5 **San Pedro** San Pedro, SE Paraguay
62 O6 **San Pedro** off. Departamento de San Pedro. ◈ department C Paraguay
44 G6 **San Pedro** ~ C Cuba
77 N16 **San Pedro** ✈ (Yamoussoukro) C Ivory Coast
San Pedro see San Pedro del Pinatar
42 D5 **San Pedro Carchá** Alta Verapaz, C Guatemala
35 S16 **San Pedro Channel** channel California, W USA
62 I5 **San Pedro de Atacama** Antofagasta, N Chile
San Pedro de Durazno see Durazno
40 G5 **San Pedro de la Cueva** Sonora, NW Mexico
San Pedro de las Colonias see San Pedro
56 B11 **San Pedro de Lloc** La Libertad, NW Peru
105 S13 **San Pedro del Pinatar** var. San Pedro. Murcia, SE Spain
45 P9 **San Pedro de Macorís** SE Dominican Republic
San Pedro, Departamento de see San Pedro
40 C3 **San Pedro Mártir, Sierra** ▲▲ NW Mexico
San Pedro Pochutla see Pochutla
42 D2 **San Pedro, Río** ~ Guatemala/Mexico
40 K10 **San Pedro, Río** ~ C Mexico
104 J10 **San Pedro, Sierra de** ▲▲ W Spain
42 G5 **San Pedro Sula** Cortés, NW Honduras
San Pedro Tapanatepec see Tapanatepec
62 I4 **San Pedro, Volcán** ⛰ N Chile
106 E7 **San Pellegrino Terme** Lombardia, N Italy
25 T16 **San Perlita** Texas, SW USA
San Pietro see Supetar
San Pietro del Carso see Pivka
107 A20 **San Pietro, Isola di** island W Italy
32 K7 **Sanpoil River** ~ Washington, NW USA
165 O9 **Sanpoku** var. Sampoku. Niigata, Honshū, C Japan
40 C3 **San Quintín** Baja California, NW Mexico
40 B3 **San Quintín, Bahía de** bay NW Mexico
40 B3 **San Quintín, Cabo** headland NW Mexico
62 I12 **San Rafael** Mendoza, W Argentina
41 N9 **San Rafael** Nuevo León, NE Mexico
34 M8 **San Rafael** California, W USA
37 Q11 **San Rafael** New Mexico, SW USA
54 H4 **San Rafael** var. El Moján. Zulia, NW Venezuela
42 J8 **San Rafael del Norte** Jinotega, NW Nicaragua
42 J10 **San Rafael del Sur** Managua, SW Nicaragua
36 M5 **San Rafael Knob** ▲ Utah, W USA
35 Q14 **San Rafael Mountains** ▲▲ California, W USA
42 M13 **San Ramón** Alajuela, C Costa Rica
57 E14 **San Ramón** Junín, C Peru
61 F19 **San Ramón** Canelones, S Uruguay
62 K5 **San Ramón de la Nueva Orán** Salta, N Argentina
57 O16 **San Ramón, Río** ~ E Bolivia
106 B11 **San Remo** Liguria, NW Italy
54 J3 **San Román, Cabo** headland NW Venezuela
61 C15 **San Roque** Corrientes, NE Argentina
188 I4 **San Roque** Saipan, S Northern Mariana Islands
104 K16 **San Roque** Andalucía, S Spain
25 R9 **San Saba** Texas, SW USA
25 Q9 **San Saba River** ~ Texas, SW USA
61 D17 **San Salvador** Entre Ríos, E Argentina
42 F7 **San Salvador** ● (El Salvador) San Salvador, SW El Salvador
42 A10 **San Salvador** ◈ department C El Salvador
44 K4 **San Salvador** prev. Watlings Island. island E Bahamas
42 F8 **San Salvador** ✈ La Paz, S El Salvador
62 J5 **San Salvador de Jujuy** var. Jujuy. Jujuy, N Argentina
42 F7 **San Salvador, Volcán de** ⛰ C El Salvador
77 Q14 **Sansanné-Mango** var. Mango. N Togo
45 S5 **San Sebastián** W Puerto Rico
63 J24 **San Sebastián, Bahía** bay S Argentina
Sansenhō see Sach'ŏn
106 H12 **Sansepolcro** Toscana, C Italy
107 M16 **San Severo** Puglia, SE Italy
112 F11 **Sanski Most** ◈ Federacija Bosna I Hercegovina, NW Bosnia and Herzegovina
171 W12 **Sansundi** Papua, E Indonesia
162 K9 **Sant** var. Mayhan. Övörhangay, C Mongolia
104 K11 **Santa Amalia** Extremadura, W Spain
60 F13 **Santa Ana** Misiones, NE Argentina
57 L16 **Santa Ana** Beni, N Bolivia
42 E7 **Santa Ana** Santa Ana, NW El Salvador
40 F4 **Santa Ana** Sonora, NW Mexico
35 T16 **Santa Ana** California, W USA
55 N6 **Santa Ana** Nueva Esparta, NE Venezuela
42 A9 **Santa Ana** ◈ department NW El Salvador
Santa Ana de Coro see Coro
35 U16 **Santa Ana Mountains** ▲▲ California, W USA
42 E7 **Santa Ana, Volcán de** var. La Matepec. ⛰ W El Salvador
42 G6 **Santa Bárbara** Santa Bárbara, W Honduras
40 J7 **Santa Barbara** Chihuahua, N Mexico
35 Q14 **Santa Barbara** California, W USA
54 L11 **Santa Bárbara** Amazonas, S Venezuela
54 I7 **Santa Bárbara** Barinas, W Venezuela
42 F5 **Santa Bárbara** ◈ department NW Honduras
Santa Bárbara see Iscuandé
35 Q15 **Santa Barbara Channel** channel California, W USA
Santa Bárbara de Samaná see Samaná
35 R16 **Santa Barbara Island** island Channel Islands, California, W USA
54 E5 **Santa Catalina** Bolívar, N Colombia
43 R15 **Santa Catalina** Bocas del Toro, W Panama
35 T17 **Santa Catalina, Gulf of** gulf California, W USA
40 F8 **Santa Catalina, Isla** island W Mexico
35 S16 **Santa Catalina Island** island Channel Islands, California, W USA
41 N8 **Santa Catarina** Nuevo León, NE Mexico
60 H13 **Santa Catarina** off. Estado de Santa Catarina. ◈ state S Brazil
Santa Catarina de Tepehuanes see Tepehuanes
Santa Catarina, Estado de see Santa Catarina
60 L13 **Santa Catarina, Ilha de** island S Brazil
45 Q16 **Santa Catherina** Curaçao, C Netherlands Antilles
44 E5 **Santa Clara** Villa Clara, C Cuba
35 N9 **Santa Clara** California, W USA
36 J8 **Santa Clara** Utah, W USA
Santa Clara see Santa Clara de Olimar
61 F18 **Santa Clara de Olimar** var. Santa Clara. Cerro Largo, NE Uruguay
61 A17 **Santa Clara de Saguier** Santa Fe, C Argentina
Santa Coloma see Santa Coloma de Gramanet
105 X5 **Santa Coloma de Farners** var. Santa Coloma de Farnés. Cataluña, NE Spain
Santa Coloma de Farnés see Santa Coloma de Farners
105 W6 **Santa Coloma de Gramanet** var. Santa Coloma. Cataluña, NE Spain
104 G2 **Santa Comba** Galicia, NW Spain
Santa Comba see Uaco Cungo
104 H8 **Santa Comba Dão** Viseu, N Portugal
82 C10 **Santa Cruz** Uíge, NW Angola
57 N19 **Santa Cruz** var. Santa Cruz de la Sierra. Santa Cruz, C Bolivia
62 G12 **Santa Cruz** Libertador, C Chile
42 K13 **Santa Cruz** Guanacaste, W Costa Rica
44 I12 **Santa Cruz** W Jamaica
64 P6 **Santa Cruz** Madeira, Portugal, NE Atlantic Ocean
35 N10 **Santa Cruz** California, W USA
63 H20 **Santa Cruz** off. Provincia de Santa Cruz. ◈ province S Argentina
57 O18 **Santa Cruz** ◈ department E Bolivia
Santa Cruz see Puerto Santa Cruz
Santa Cruz see Viru-Viru
Santa Cruz Barillas see Barillas
59 O18 **Santa Cruz Cabrália** Bahia, E Brazil
Santa Cruz de El Seibo see El Seibo
64 N11 **Santa Cruz de la Palma** La Palma, Islas Canarias, Spain, NE Atlantic Ocean
Santa Cruz de la Sierra see Santa Cruz
105 O9 **Santa Cruz de la Zarza** Castilla-La Mancha, C Spain
42 C5 **Santa Cruz del Quiché** Quiché, W Guatemala
105 N8 **Santa Cruz del Retamar** Castilla-La Mancha, C Spain
Santa Cruz del Seibo see El Seibo
44 G7 **Santa Cruz del Sur** Camagüey, C Cuba
105 O11 **Santa Cruz de Mudela** Castilla-La Mancha, C Spain
64 Q11 **Santa Cruz de Tenerife** Tenerife, Islas Canarias, Spain, NE Atlantic Ocean
64 P11 **Santa Cruz de Tenerife** ◈ province Islas Canarias, Spain, NE Atlantic Ocean
60 K9 **Santa Cruz do Rio Pardo** São Paulo, S Brazil
61 H15 **Santa Cruz do Sul** Rio Grande do Sul, S Brazil
57 C17 **Santa Cruz, Isla** var. Indefatigable Island, Isla Chávez. island Galapagos Islands, Ecuador, E Pacific Ocean
40 F8 **Santa Cruz, Isla** island W Mexico
35 Q15 **Santa Cruz Island** island California, W USA
187 Q10 **Santa Cruz Islands** island group E Solomon Islands
Santa Cruz, Provincia de see Santa Cruz
63 I22 **Santa Cruz, Río** ~ S Argentina
36 L15 **Santa Cruz River** ~ Arizona, SW USA
61 C17 **Santa Elena** Entre Ríos, E Argentina
42 F2 **Santa Elena** Cayo, W Belize
25 R16 **Santa Elena** Texas, SW USA
56 A7 **Santa Elena, Bahía de** bay W Ecuador
55 R10 **Santa Elena de Uairén** Bolívar, E Venezuela
42 K12 **Santa Elena, Península** peninsula NW Costa Rica
56 A7 **Santa Elena, Punta** headland W Ecuador
104 L11 **Santa Eufemia** Andalucía, S Spain
107 N21 **Santa Eufemia, Golfo di** gulf S Italy
105 S4 **Santa Eulalia de Gállego** Aragón, NE Spain
105 V11 **Santa Eulalia del Río** Ibiza, Spain, W Mediterranean Sea
61 B17 **Santa Fe** Santa Fe, C Argentina
44 C6 **Santa Fé** var. La Fe. Isla de la Juventud, W Cuba
43 R16 **Santa Fé** Veraguas, C Panama
105 N14 **Santa Fe** Andalucía, S Spain
37 S10 **Santa Fe** state capital New Mexico, SW USA
61 B15 **Santa Fe** off. Provincia de Santa Fe. ◈ province C Argentina
Santa Fe see Bogotá
Santa Fe de Bogotá see Bogotá
60 J7 **Santa Fé do Sul** São Paulo, S Brazil
57 B18 **Santa Fe, Isla** var. Barrington Island. island Galapagos Islands, Ecuador, E Pacific Ocean
Santa Fe, Provincia de see Santa Fe
23 V9 **Santa Fe River** ~ Florida, SE USA
59 M15 **Santa Filomena** Piauí, E Brazil
40 G10 **Santa Genoveva** ▲ W Mexico
153 S14 **Santahar** Rajshahi, NW Bangladesh
60 G11 **Santa Helena** Paraná, S Brazil
54 J5 **Santa Inés** Lara, N Venezuela
63 G24 **Santa Inés, Isla** island S Chile
62 J13 **Santa Isabel** La Pampa, C Argentina
43 U14 **Santa Isabel** Colón, N Panama
186 L8 **Santa Isabel** var. Bughotu. island N Solomon Islands
Santa Isabel see Malabo
58 D11 **Santa Isabel do Rio Negro** Amazonas, NW Brazil
61 C15 **Santa Lucia** Corrientes, NE Argentina
57 I17 **Santa Lucía** Puno, S Peru
61 F20 **Santa Lucía** var. Santa Lucia. Canelones, S Uruguay
42 B6 **Santa Lucía Cotzumalguapa** Escuintla, SW Guatemala
107 L23 **Santa Lucia del Mela** Sicilia, Italy, C Mediterranean Sea
35 O11 **Santa Lucia Range** ▲▲ California, W USA
40 D9 **Santa Margarita, Isla** island W Mexico
62 J7 **Santa María** Catamarca, N Argentina
61 G15 **Santa Maria** Rio Grande do Sul, S Brazil
35 P13 **Santa Maria** California, W USA
64 Q4 **Santa Maria** ✈ Santa Maria, Azores, Portugal, NE Atlantic Ocean
64 P3 **Santa Maria** island Azores, Portugal, NE Atlantic Ocean
Santa Maria see Gaua
Santa María Asunción Tlaxiaco see Tlaxiaco
40 G9 **Santa María, Bahía** bay W Mexico
83 L21 **Santa Maria, Cabo de** headland S Mozambique
104 G15 **Santa Maria, Cabo de** cape S Portugal
44 J4 **Santa Maria, Cape** headland Long Island, C Bahamas
107 J17 **Santa Maria Capua Vetere** Campania, S Italy
104 G7 **Santa Maria da Feira** Aveiro, N Portugal
59 M17 **Santa Maria da Vitória** Bahia, E Brazil
55 N9 **Santa María de Erebato** Bolívar, SE Venezuela
55 N6 **Santa María de Ipire** Guárico, C Venezuela
Santa Maria del Buen Aire see Buenos Aires
40 J8 **Santa María del Oro** Durango, C Mexico
41 N12 **Santa María del Río** San Luis Potosí, C Mexico
Santa Maria di Castellabate see Castellabate
107 Q20 **Santa Maria di Leuca, Capo** headland SE Italy
108 K10 **Santa Maria-im-Münstertal** Graubünden, SE Switzerland
57 B18 **Santa María, Isla** var. Isla Floreana, Charles Island. island Galapagos Islands, Ecuador, E Pacific Ocean
40 J3 **Santa María, Laguna de** ◎ N Mexico

◆ Country
● Country Capital
◇ Dependent Territory
○ Dependent Territory Capital
◈ Administrative Regions
✈ International Airport
▲ Mountain
▲▲ Mountain Range
⛰ Volcano
~ River
◎ Lake
⊠ Reservoir

Santa Maria, Rio – Saryyazynskoye Vodokhranilishche

61 G16 **Santa Maria, Rio** ≈ S Brazil
43 R16 **Santa María, Río** ≈ C Panama
36 J12 **Santa Maria River** ≈ Arizona, SW USA
107 G15 **Santa Marinella** Lazio, C Italy
54 F4 **Santa Marta** Magdalena, N Colombia
104 J11 **Santa Marta** Extremadura, W Spain
Santa Maura see Lefkáda
35 S15 **Santa Monica** California, W USA
116 F10 **Sântana** Ger. Sankt Anna, Hung. Újszentanna; prev. Sîntana. Arad, W Romania
61 F16 **Santana, Coxilha de** hill range S Brazil
61 H16 **Santana da Boa Vista** Rio Grande do Sul, S Brazil
61 F16 **Santana do Livramento** prev. Livramento. Rio Grande do Sul, S Brazil
105 N2 **Santander** Cantabria, N Spain
54 F8 **Santander** off. Departamento de Santander. ⬖ province C Colombia
Santander, Departamento de see Santander
Santander Jiménez see Jiménez
Sant'Andrea see Svetac
107 B20 **Sant'Antioco** Sardegna, Italy, C Mediterranean Sea
105 V11 **Sant Antonio de Portmany** Cas. San Antonio Abad. Ibiza, Spain, W Mediterranean Sea
105 Y10 **Sant Antoni de Portmany** Cas. San Antonio Abad. Ibiza, Spain, W Mediterranean
105 Y10 **Santanyí** Mallorca, Spain, W Mediterranean Sea
104 J13 **Santa Olalla del Cala** Andalucía, S Spain
35 R15 **Santa Paula** California, W USA
36 L4 **Santaquin** Utah, W USA
58 I12 **Santarém** Pará, N Brazil
104 G10 **Santarém** anc. Scalabis. Santarém, W Portugal
104 G10 **Santarém** ⬖ district C Portugal
44 F4 **Santaren Channel** channel W Bahamas
54 K10 **Santa Rita** Vichada, E Colombia
188 B16 **Santa Rita** SW Guam
42 H5 **Santa Rita** Cortés, NW Honduras
40 E9 **Santa Rita** Baja California Sur, W Mexico
54 H5 **Santa Rita** Zulia, NW Venezuela
59 I19 **Santa Rita de Araguaia** Goiás, S Brazil
Santa Rita de Cassia see Cássia
61 D14 **Santa Rosa** Corrientes, NE Argentina
62 K13 **Santa Rosa** La Pampa, C Argentina
61 G14 **Santa Rosa** Rio Grande do Sul, S Brazil
58 E10 **Santa Rosa** Roraima, N Brazil
56 B8 **Santa Rosa** El Oro, SW Ecuador
57 I16 **Santa Rosa** Puno, S Peru
34 M7 **Santa Rosa** California, W USA
37 U11 **Santa Rosa** New Mexico, SW USA
55 O6 **Santa Rosa** Anzoátegui, NE Venezuela
42 A3 **Santa Rosa** off. Departamento de Santa Rosa. ⬖ department SE Guatemala
Santa Rosa see Santa Rosa de Copán
63 J15 **Santa Rosa, Bajo de** basin E Argentina
42 F6 **Santa Rosa de Copán** var. Santa Rosa. Copán, W Honduras
54 E8 **Santa Rosa de Osos** Antioquia, C Colombia
Santa Rosa, Departamento de see Santa Rosa
35 Q15 **Santa Rosa Island** island California, W USA
23 O9 **Santa Rosa Island** island Florida, SE USA
40 E6 **Santa Rosalía** Baja California Sur, W Mexico
54 K6 **Santa Rosalía** Portuguesa, NW Venezuela
188 C15 **Santa Rosa, Mount** ▲ NE Guam
35 V16 **Santa Rosa Mountains** ⛰ California, W USA
35 T2 **Santa Rosa Range** ⛰ Nevada, W USA
62 M8 **Santa Sylvina** Chaco, N Argentina
Santa Tecla see Nueva San Salvador
61 B19 **Santa Teresa** Santa Fe, C Argentina
59 O20 **Santa Teresa** Espírito Santo, SE Brazil
107 M23 **San Teresa di Riva** Sicilia, Italy, C Mediterranean Sea
61 E21 **Santa Teresita** Buenos Aires, E Argentina
61 H19 **Santa Vitória do Palmar** Rio Grande do Sul, S Brazil
35 Q14 **Santa Ynez River** ≈ California, W USA
Sant Carles de la Rápida see Sant Carles de la Ràpita
105 U7 **Sant Carles de la Ràpita** var. Sant Carles de la Rápida. Cataluña, NE Spain
105 W5 **Sant Celoni** Cataluña, NE Spain
35 U17 **Santee** California, W USA
21 T13 **Santee River** ≈ South Carolina, SE USA
40 K15 **San Telmo, Punta** headland SW Mexico
107 O17 **Santeramo in Colle** Puglia, SE Italy
105 X5 **Sant Feliu de Guíxols** var. San Feliú de Guixols. Cataluña, NE Spain
105 W6 **Sant Feliu de Llobregat** Cataluña, NE Spain
106 C7 **Santhià** Piemonte, NE Italy
61 F15 **Santiago** Rio Grande do Sul, S Brazil
62 H11 **Santiago** var. Gran Santiago. ● (Chile) Santiago, C Chile
45 N8 **Santiago** var. Santiago de los Caballeros. N Dominican Republic
40 G10 **Santiago** Baja California Sur, W Mexico
41 O8 **Santiago** Nuevo León, NE Mexico
43 R16 **Santiago** Veraguas, S Panama
57 E16 **Santiago** Ica, SW Peru
104 G3 **Santiago** var. Santiago de Compostela, Eng. Compostella; anc. Campus Stellae. Galicia, NW Spain
62 H11 **Santiago** off. Región Metropolitana de Santiago, var. Metropolitan. ⬖ region C Chile
76 D10 **Santiago** var. São Tiago. island Ilhas de Sotavento, S Cape Verde
62 H11 **Santiago** ✈ Santiago, C Chile
104 G3 **Santiago** ✈ Galicia, NW Spain
Santiago see Santiago de Cuba, Cuba
Santiago see Grande de Santiago, Río, Mexico
42 B6 **Santiago Atitlán** Sololá, SW Guatemala
43 Q16 **Santiago, Cerro** ▲ W Panama
Santiago de Compostela see Santiago
44 I8 **Santiago de Cuba** var. Santiago. Santiago de Cuba, E Cuba
Santiago de Guayaquil see Guayaquil
62 K8 **Santiago del Estero** Santiago del Estero, C Argentina
61 A15 **Santiago del Estero** off. Provincia de Santiago del Estero. ⬖ province N Argentina
Santiago del Estero, Provincia de see Santiago del Estero
40 I8 **Santiago de los Caballeros** Sinaloa, W Mexico
Santiago de los Caballeros see Santiago, Dominican Republic
Santiago de los Caballeros see Ciudad de Guatemala, Guatemala
42 F8 **Santiago de María** Usulután, SE El Salvador
104 F12 **Santiago do Cacém** Setúbal, S Portugal
40 J12 **Santiago Ixcuintla** Nayarit, C Mexico
Santiago Jamiltepec see Jamiltepec
24 L11 **Santiago Mountains** ⛰ Texas, SW USA
40 J9 **Santiago Papasquiaro** Durango, C Mexico
Santiago Pinotepa Nacional see Pinotepa Nacional
Santiago, Región Metropolitana de see Santiago
56 C8 **Santiago, Río** ≈ N Peru
40 M10 **San Tiburcio** Zacatecas, C Mexico
105 N2 **Santillana** Cantabria, N Spain
54 I5 **San Timoteo** Zulia, NW Venezuela
Santi Quaranta see Sarandë
Santissima Trinidad see Chilung
105 O12 **Santisteban del Puerto** Andalucía, S Spain
105 U7 **Sant Jordi, Golf de** gulf NE Spain
105 U11 **Sant Josep de sa Talaia** var. San Jose. Ibiza, Spain, W Mediterranean Sea
162 G6 **Santmargats** var. Holboo. Dzavhan, W Mongolia
105 T8 **Sant Mateu** País Valenciano, E Spain
25 S7 **Santo** Texas, SW USA
Santo see Espiritu Santo
60 M10 **Santo Amaro, Ilha de** island SE Brazil
61 G14 **Santo Ângelo** Rio Grande do Sul, S Brazil
76 C9 **Santo Antão** island Ilhas de Barlavento, N Cape Verde
60 J10 **Santo Antônio da Platina** Paraná, S Brazil
58 C13 **Santo Antônio do Içá** Amazonas, N Brazil
57 Q18 **Santo Corazón, Río** ≈ E Bolivia
44 E5 **Santo Domingo** Villa Clara, C Cuba
45 O9 **Santo Domingo** prev. Ciudad Trujillo. ● (Dominican Republic) SE Dominican Republic
40 E8 **Santo Domingo** Baja California Sur, W Mexico
40 M10 **Santo Domingo** San Luis Potosí, C Mexico
42 L10 **Santo Domingo** Chontales, S Nicaragua
105 P4 **Santo Domingo de la Calzada** La Rioja, N Spain
56 B6 **Santo Domingo de los Colorados** Pichincha, NW Ecuador
Santo Domingo Tehuantepec see Tehuantepec
55 O6 **San Tomé** Anzoátegui, NE Venezuela
San Tomé de Guayana see Ciudad Guayana
105 R13 **Santomera** Murcia, SE Spain
105 O2 **Santoña** Cantabria, N Spain
Santorin see Santoríni
115 K22 **Santoríni** var. Santorin, prev. Thíra; anc. Thera. island Kykládes, Greece, Aegean Sea
60 M10 **Santos** São Paulo, S Brazil
65 J17 **Santos Plateau** undersea feature SW Atlantic Ocean
104 G6 **Santo Tirso** Porto, N Portugal
40 B2 **Santo Tomás** Baja California, NW Mexico
42 L10 **Santo Tomás** Chontales, S Nicaragua
42 G5 **Santo Tomás de Castilla** Izabal, E Guatemala
40 B2 **Santo Tomás, Punta** headland NW Mexico
57 H16 **Santo Tomás, Río** ≈ C Peru
57 B18 **Santo Tomás, Volcán** 🌋 Galapagos Islands, Ecuador, E Pacific Ocean
61 F14 **Santo Tomé** Corrientes, NE Argentina
Santo Tomé de Guayana see Ciudad Guayana
98 H10 **Santpoort** Noord-Holland, W Netherlands
Santurce see Santurtzi
105 O2 **Santurtzi** var. Santurce, Santurzi. País Vasco, N Spain
Santurzi see Santurtzi
63 G20 **San Valentín, Cerro** ▲ S Chile
42 F8 **San Vicente** San Vicente, C El Salvador
40 C2 **San Vicente** Baja California, NW Mexico
188 H6 **San Vicente** Saipan, S Northern Mariana Islands
42 B9 **San Vicente** ⬖ department E El Salvador
104 I10 **San Vicente de Alcántara** Extremadura, W Spain
105 N2 **San Vicente de Barakaldo** var. Baracaldo, Basq. San Bizenti-Barakaldo. País Vasco, N Spain
57 E15 **San Vicente de Cañete** var. Cañete. Lima, W Peru
104 M2 **San Vicente de la Barquera** Cantabria, N Spain
54 E12 **San Vicente del Caguán** Caquetá, S Colombia
42 F8 **San Vicente, Volcán de** 🌋 C El Salvador
43 O15 **San Vito** Puntarenas, SE Costa Rica
106 I7 **San Vito al Tagliamento** Friuli-Venezia Giulia, NE Italy
107 H23 **San Vito, Capo** headland Sicilia, Italy, C Mediterranean Sea
107 P18 **San Vito dei Normanni** Puglia, SE Italy
160 L17 **Sanya** var. Ya Xian. Hainan, S China
83 J16 **Sanyati** ≈ N Zimbabwe
25 Q16 **San Ygnacio** Texas, SW USA
160 L6 **Sanyuan** Shaanxi, C China
123 P11 **Sanyyakhtakh** Respublika Sakha (Yakutiya), NE Russian Federation
146 J15 **S. A.Nyýazow Adyndaky** Rus. Imeni S. A. Niyazova. Maryyskiy Velayat, S Turkmenistan
82 C10 **Sanza Pombo** Uíge, NW Angola
Sanzyô see Sanjō
104 G14 **São Bartolomeu de Messines** Faro, S Portugal
60 M10 **São Bernardo do Campo** São Paulo, S Brazil
61 F15 **São Borja** Rio Grande do Sul, S Brazil
104 H14 **São Brás de Alportel** Faro, S Portugal
60 M10 **São Caetano do Sul** São Paulo, S Brazil
60 L9 **São Carlos** São Paulo, S Brazil
59 P16 **São Cristóvão** Sergipe, E Brazil
61 F15 **São Francisco de Assis** Rio Grande do Sul, S Brazil
58 K13 **São Félix** Pará, NE Brazil
São Félix see São Félix do Araguaia
59 J16 **São Félix do Araguaia** var. São Félix. Mato Grosso, W Brazil
59 J14 **São Félix do Xingu** Pará, NE Brazil
60 Q9 **São Fidélis** Rio de Janeiro, SE Brazil
76 D10 **São Filipe** Fogo, S Cape Verde
60 K12 **São Francisco do Sul** Santa Catarina, S Brazil
60 K12 **São Francisco, Ilha de** island S Brazil
59 P16 **São Francisco, Rio** ≈ E Brazil
61 G16 **São Gabriel** Rio Grande do Sul, S Brazil
60 P10 **São Gonçalo** Rio de Janeiro, SE Brazil
81 H23 **Sao Hill** Iringa, S Tanzania
58 M12 **São João de Cortes** Maranhão E Brazil
60 R9 **São João da Barra** Rio de Janeiro, SE Brazil
104 G7 **São João da Madeira** Aveiro, N Portugal
58 M12 **São João de Cortês** Maranhão, E Brazil
59 M21 **São João del Rei** Minas Gerais, NE Brazil
59 N15 **São João do Piauí** Piauí, E Brazil
59 N14 **São João dos Patos** Maranhão, E Brazil
58 C11 **São Joaquim** Amazonas, NW Brazil
61 J14 **São Joaquim** Santa Catarina, S Brazil
60 L7 **São Joaquim da Barra** São Paulo, S Brazil
64 N2 **São Jorge** island Azores, Portugal, NE Atlantic Ocean
61 K14 **São José** Santa Catarina, S Brazil
60 M8 **São José do Rio Pardo** São Paulo, S Brazil
60 K8 **São José do Rio Preto** São Paulo, S Brazil
60 N10 **São Jose dos Campos** São Paulo, S Brazil
61 I17 **São Lourenço do Sul** Rio Grande do Sul, S Brazil
58 M12 **São Luís** state capital Maranhão, NE Brazil
58 F11 **São Luís** Roraima, N Brazil
58 M12 **São Luís, Ilha de** island NE Brazil
61 F14 **São Luiz Gonzaga** Rio Grande do Sul, S Brazil
104 I10 **São Mamede** ▲ C Portugal
São Mandol see São Manuel, Rio
47 U8 **São Manuel** ≈ C Brazil
59 H15 **São Manuel, Rio** var. São Mandol, Teles Pirés. ≈ C Brazil
58 C11 **São Marcelino** Amazonas, NW Brazil
58 N12 **São Marcos, Baía de** bay N Brazil
59 O20 **São Mateus** Espírito Santo, SE Brazil
60 J12 **São Mateus do Sul** Paraná, S Brazil
64 P3 **São Miguel** island Azores, Portugal, NE Atlantic Ocean
60 G13 **São Miguel d'Oeste** Santa Catarina, S Brazil
45 P9 **Saona, Isla** island SE Dominican Republic
172 H12 **Saondzou** ▲ Grande Comore, NW Comoros
103 R10 **Saône** ≈ E France
103 Q9 **Saône-et-Loire** ⬖ department C France
76 D9 **São Nicolau** Eng. Saint Nicholas. island Ilhas de Barlavento, N Cape Verde
60 M10 **São Paulo** state capital São Paulo, S Brazil
60 K9 **São Paulo** off. Estado de São Paulo. ⬖ state S Brazil
São Paulo de Loanda see Luanda
São Paulo, Estado de see São Paulo
São Pedro do Rio Grande do Sul see Rio Grande
104 H7 **São Pedro do Sul** Viseu, N Portugal
64 K13 **São Pedro e São Paulo** undersea feature C Atlantic Ocean
59 M14 **São Raimundo das Mangabeiras** Maranhão, E Brazil
59 Q14 **São Roque, Cabo de** headland E Brazil
São Salvador see Salvador, Brazil
São Salvador/São Salvador do Congo see M'Banza Congo, Angola
60 N10 **São Sebastião, Ilha de** island S Brazil
83 N19 **São Sebastião, Ponta** headland C Mozambique
104 F13 **São Teotónio** Beja, S Portugal
São Tiago see Santiago
79 B18 **São Tomé** ● (Sao Tome and Principe) São Tomé, S Sao Tome and Principe
79 B18 **São Tomé** ✈ São Tomé, S Sao Tome and Principe
79 B18 **São Tomé** Eng. Saint Thomas. island S Sao Tome and Principe
79 B17 **Sao Tome and Principe** off. Democratic Republic of Sao Tome and Principe. ◆ republic E Atlantic Ocean
Sao Tome and Principe, Democratic Republic of see Sao Tome and Principe
74 H9 **Saoura, Oued** ≈ NW Algeria
60 M10 **São Vicente** Eng. Saint Vincent. São Paulo, S Brazil
64 O5 **São Vicente** Madeira, Portugal, NE Atlantic Ocean
76 C9 **São Vicente** Eng. Saint Vincent. island Ilhas de Barlavento, N Cape Verde
104 F14 **São Vicente, Cabo de** Eng. Cape Saint Vincent, Port. Cabode São Vicente. cape S Portugal
São Vicente, Cabo de see São Vicente, Cabo de
Sápai see Sápes
Sapaleri, Cerro see Zapaleri, Cerro
Saparoea see Saparua
171 S13 **Saparua** prev. Saparoea. Pulau Saparau, C Indonesia
168 L11 **Sapat** Sumatera, W Indonesia
77 U17 **Sapele** Delta, S Nigeria
23 X7 **Sapelo Island** island Georgia, SE USA
23 X7 **Sapelo Sound** sound Georgia, SE USA
114 K13 **Sápes** var. Sápai. Anatolikí Makedonía kai Thráki, NE Greece
Sapiéntza see Sapiénza
115 D22 **Sapiénza** var Sapiéntza. island S Greece
Sapir see Sappir
61 I15 **Sapiranga** Rio Grande do Sul, S Brazil
114 K13 **Sápka** ⛰ NE Greece
105 X9 **Sa Pobla** Mallorca, Spain, W Mediterranean Sea
56 D11 **Saposoa** San Martín, N Peru
119 F16 **Sapotskin** Pol. Sopockinie, Rus. Sapotskino, Sopotskin. Hrodzyenskaya Voblasts', W Belarus
77 P13 **Sapoui** var. Sapouy. S Burkina
Sapouy see Sapoui
138 F12 **Sappir** var Sapir. Southern, S Israel
165 S4 **Sapporo** Hokkaidō, NE Japan
107 M19 **Sapri** Campania, S Italy
169 T16 **Sapudi, Pulau** island S Indonesia
27 P9 **Sapulpa** Oklahoma, C USA
142 J4 **Saqqez** var. Saghez, Sakiz, Saqqiz. Kordestān, NW Iran
Saqqiz see Saqqez
139 U8 **Sarābādī** E Iraq
167 P10 **Sara Buri** var. Saraburi. Saraburi, C Thailand
Saraburi see Sara Buri
Sarafjagān see Salafchegān
24 K9 **Saragosa** Texas, SW USA
Saragosa see Zaragoza
Saragt see Sarahs
56 B8 **Saraguro** Loja, S Ecuador
146 I15 **Sarahs** var. Saragt, Rus. Serakhs. Ahal Welaýaty, S Turkmenistan
126 M6 **Sarai** Ryazanskaya Oblast', W Russian Federation
Sarāi see Sarāy
154 M12 **Saraipāli** Chhattīsgarh, C India
149 T9 **Sarāi Sidhu** Punjab, E Pakistan
93 M15 **Säräisniemi** Oulu, C Finland
113 I14 **Sarajevo** ● (Bosnia and Herzegovina) Federacija Bosna I Hercegovina, SE Bosnia and Herzegovina
112 I13 **Sarajevo** ✈ Federacija Bosna I Hercegovina, C Bosnia and Herzegovina
143 V4 **Sarakhs** Khorāsān-Razavī, NE Iran
115 H17 **Sarakíniko, Ákrotírio** headland Évvoia, C Greece
115 I18 **Sarakinó** island Vóreioi Sporádes, Greece, Aegean Sea
127 V7 **Saraktash** Orenburgskaya Oblast', W Russian Federation
30 L15 **Sara, Lake** ⊠ Illinois, N USA
23 N8 **Saraland** Alabama, S USA
55 V9 **Saramacca** ⬖ district N Surinam
55 V10 **Saramacca Rivier** ≈ C Surinam
166 M2 **Saramati** ▲ N Burma (Myanmar)
145 R10 **Saran'** Kaz. Saran. Karaganda, C Kazakhstan
18 K7 **Saranac Lake** New York, NE USA
18 K7 **Saranac River** ≈ New York, NE USA
Saranda see Sarandë
113 L23 **Sarandë** var. Saranda, It. Porto Edda; prev. Santi Quaranta. Vlorë, S Albania
61 H14 **Sarandi** Rio Grande do Sul, S Brazil
61 F19 **Sarandí del Yí** Durazno, C Uruguay
61 F19 **Sarandí Grande** Florida, S Uruguay
171 Q8 **Sarangani Islands** island group S Philippines
127 P5 **Saransk** Respublika Mordoviya, W Russian Federation
115 C14 **Sarantáporos** ≈ N Greece
114 H9 **Sarantsi** Sofiya, W Bulgaria
127 T3 **Sarapul** Udmurtskaya Respublika, NW Russian Federation
Sarāqeb see Sarāqib
138 I3 **Sarāqib** Fr. Sarâqeb. Idlib, N Syria
54 J5 **Sarare** Lara, N Venezuela
55 O10 **Sarariña** Amazonas, S Venezuela
143 S10 **Sar Ashk** Kermān, C Iran
23 V13 **Sarasota** Florida, SE USA
117 O11 **Sarata** Odes'ka Oblast', SW Ukraine
116 I10 **Sărăţel** Hung. Szeretfalva. Bistriţa-Năsăud, N Romania
25 X10 **Saratoga** Texas, SW USA
18 K10 **Saratoga Springs** New York, NE USA
127 P8 **Saratov** Saratovskaya Oblast', W Russian Federation
127 P8 **Saratovskaya Oblast'** ⬖ province W Russian Federation
127 Q7 **Saratovskoye Vodokhranilishche** ⊠ W Russian Federation
Saravan/Saravane see Salavan
169 S9 **Sarawak** ⬖ state East Malaysia
Sarawak see Kuching
139 U6 **Sarāy** var. Sarāi. E Iraq
136 D10 **Saray** Tekirdağ, NW Turkey
76 J12 **Saraya** SE Senegal
143 W14 **Sarbāz** Sīstān va Balūchestān, SE Iran
143 U8 **Sarbīsheh** Khorāsān, E Iran
111 J24 **Sárbogárd** Fejér, C Hungary
Şarcad see Sarkad
27 S7 **Sarcoxie** Missouri, C USA
152 L11 **Sārda** Nep. Kali. ≈ India/Nepal
152 G10 **Sardārshahr** Rājasthān, NW India
107 C18 **Sardegna** Eng. Sardinia. ⬖ region Italy, C Mediterranean Sea
107 A18 **Sardegna** Eng. Sardinia. island Italy, C Mediterranean Sea
42 K13 **Sardinal** Guanacaste, NW Costa Rica
54 G7 **Sardinata** Norte de Santander, N Colombia
Sardinia see Sardegna
120 K8 **Sardinia-Corsica Trough** undersea feature Tyrrhenian Sea, C Mediterranean Sea
22 L2 **Sardis** Mississippi, S USA
22 L2 **Sardis Lake** ⊠ Mississippi, S USA
27 P12 **Sardis Lake** ⊠ Oklahoma, C USA
92 H12 **Sarek** ⛰ N Sweden
92 H11 **Sarektjåhkkå** ▲ N Sweden
149 N3 **Sar-e Pol** var. Sar-i-Pul. Sar-e Pol, N Afghanistan
149 O3 **Sar-e Pol** ⬖ province N Afghanistan
Sar-e Pol see Sar-e Pol-e Žahāb
142 J6 **Sar-e Pol-e Žahāb** var. Sar-e Pol, Sar-i Pul. Kermānshāhān, W Iran
Teluk Sarera see Cenderawasih, Teluk
92 H11 **Stortoppen** ▲ N Sweden
147 T13 **Sarez, Kŭli** Rus. Sarezskoye Ozero. ◎ SE Tajikistan
Sarezskoye Ozero see Sarez, Kŭli
64 G10 **Sargasso Sea** sea W Atlantic Ocean
149 U8 **Sargodha** Punjab, NE Pakistan
78 I13 **Sarh** prev. Fort-Archambault. Moyen-Chari, S Chad
143 P4 **Sārī** var. Sari, Sāri. Māzandarān, N Iran
115 N23 **Saría** island SE Greece
Sariasiya see Sariosiyo
40 F3 **Saric** Sonora, NW Mexico
188 K6 **Sarigan** island C Northern Mariana Islands
136 D14 **Sarıgöl** Manisa, SW Turkey
139 T6 **Sārihah** E Iraq
137 R12 **Sarıkamış** Kars, NE Turkey
169 R9 **Sarikei** Sarawak, East Malaysia
147 U12 **Sarikol Range** Rus. Sarykol'skiy Khrebet. ⛰ China/Tajikistan
181 Y7 **Sarina** Queensland, NE Australia
Sarine see La Sarine
105 S5 **Sariñena** Aragón, NE Spain
147 O13 **Sariosiyo** Rus. Sariasiya. Surkhondaryo Viloyati, S Uzbekistan
Sar-i-Pul see Sar-e Pol
Sar-i Pul see Sar-e Pol-e Žahāb
Sariqamish Kŭli see Sarygamyş Köli
149 V1 **Sarī Qūl** Rus. Ozero Zurkul', Taj. Zŭrkŭl. ◎ Afghanistan/ Tajikistan see also Zŭrkŭl
Sarī Qūl see Zŭrkŭl
75 Q12 **Sarīr Tībistī** var. Serir Tibesti. desert S Libya
25 S15 **Sarita** Texas, SW USA
163 W14 **Sariwŏn** SW North Korea
114 P12 **Sarıyer** İstanbul, NW Turkey
97 L26 **Sark** Fr. Sercq. island Channel Islands
111 N24 **Sarkad** Rom. Şărcad. Békés, SE Hungary
145 W14 **Sarkand** Almaty, SW Kazakhstan
Sarkaņi see Krasnogorskoye
152 D11 **Sarkāri Tala** Rājasthān, NW India
136 G15 **Şarkîkaraağaç** var. Şarki Karaağaç. Isparta, SW Turkey
Şarki Karaağaç see Şarkîkaraağaç
136 L13 **Şarkışla** Sivas, C Turkey
136 C11 **Şarköy** Tekirdağ, NW Turkey
Sárköz see Livada
Sarlat see Sarlat-la-Canéda
102 M13 **Sarlat-la-Canéda** var. Sarlat. Dordogne, SW France
109 S3 **Sarleinsbach** Oberösterreich, N Austria
Šarma see Ash Sharmah
171 Y12 **Sarmi** Papua, E Indonesia
63 I19 **Sarmiento** Chubut, S Argentina
63 H25 **Sarmiento, Monte** ▲ S Chile
94 J11 **Särna** Dalarna, C Sweden
108 F8 **Sarnen** Obwalden, C Switzerland
108 F9 **Sarner See** ◎ C Switzerland
14 D16 **Sarnia** Ontario, S Canada
116 L3 **Sarny** Rivnens'ka Oblast', NW Ukraine
171 O13 **Saroako** Sulawesi, C Indonesia
118 L13 **Sarochyna** Rus. Sorochino. Vitsyebskaya Voblasts', N Belarus
168 L12 **Sarolangun** Sumatera, W Indonesia
165 U3 **Saroma** Hokkaidō, NE Japan
165 V3 **Saroma-ko** ◎ Hokkaidō, NE Japan
Saronic Gulf see Saronikós Kólpos
115 H20 **Saronikós Kólpos** Eng. Saronic Gulf. gulf S Greece
106 D7 **Saronno** Lombardia, N Italy
136 B11 **Saros Körfezi** gulf NW Turkey
111 N20 **Sárospatak** Borsod-Abaúj-Zemplén, NE Hungary
127 O4 **Sarov** prev. Sarova. Respublika Mordoviya, SW Russian Federation
Sarova see Sarov
127 P12 **Sarpa** Respublika Kalmykiya, SW Russian Federation
127 P12 **Sarpa, Ozero** ◎ SW Russian Federation
113 M18 **Šar Planina** ⛰ FYR Macedonia/Serbia
95 I16 **Sarpsborg** Østfold, S Norway
139 U5 **Sarqalā** N Iraq
103 U4 **Sarralbe** Moselle, NE France
Sarre see Saar
Sarre see Saarland
103 U5 **Sarrebourg** Ger. Saarburg. Moselle, NE France
Sarrebruck see Saarbrücken
103 U4 **Sarreguemines** prev. Saargemund. Moselle, NE France
104 I3 **Sarria** Galicia, NW Spain
105 S8 **Sarrión** Aragón, NE Spain
42 F4 **Sarstoon** Sp. Río Sarstún. ≈ Belize/Guatemala
Sarstún, Río see Sarstoon
123 Q9 **Sartang** ≈ NE Russian Federation
103 X16 **Sartène** Corse, France, C Mediterranean Sea
102 K7 **Sarthe** ⬖ department NW France
102 K7 **Sarthe** ≈ N France
115 H15 **Sárti** Kentrikí Makedonía, N Greece
Sartu see Daqing
165 T1 **Sarufutsu** Hokkaidō, NE Japan
Saruhan see Manisa
152 G9 **Sarūpsar** Rājasthān, NW India
137 U13 **Şärur** prev. Il'ichevsk. SW Azerbaijan
Sarvani see Marneuli
111 G23 **Sárvár** Vas, W Hungary
143 P11 **Sarvestān** Fārs, S Iran
171 W12 **Sarwon** Papua, E Indonesia
Saryagach see Saryagash
145 P17 **Saryagash** var. Saryagach, Kaz. Saryaghash. Yuzhnyy Kazakhstan, S Kazakhstan
Saryaghash see Saryagash
Saryarqa see Kazakhskiy Melkosopochnik
147 W8 **Sary-Bulak** Narynskaya Oblast', C Kyrgyzstan
147 U10 **Sary-Bulak** Oshskaya Oblast', SW Kyrgyzstan
117 S14 **Sarych, Mys** headland S Ukraine
147 Z7 **Sary-Dzhaz** var. Aksu He. ≈ China/Kyrgyzstan see also Aksu He
Sary-Dzhaz see Aksu He
146 F8 **Sarygamyş Köli** Rus. Sarykamyshkoye Ozero, Uzb. Sariqamish Kŭli. salt lake Kazakhstan/Uzbekistan
144 G13 **Sarykamys** Kaz. Saryqamys. Mangistau, SW Kazakhstan
Sarykamyshkoye Ozero see Sarygamyş Köli
145 N7 **Sarykol'** prev. Uritskiy. Kustanay, N Kazakhstan
Sarykol'skiy Khrebet see Sarikol Range
144 M10 **Sarykopa, Ozero** ◎ C Kazakhstan
145 V15 **Saryozek** Kaz. Saryözek. Almaty, SE Kazakhstan
Saryqamys see Sarykamys
145 S13 **Saryshagan** Kaz. Saryshahan. Karaganda, SE Kazakhstan
Saryshahan see Saryshagan
145 O13 **Sarysu** ≈ S Kazakhstan
147 T11 **Sary-Tash** Oshskaya Oblast', SW Kyrgyzstan
145 T12 **Saryterek** Karaganda, C Kazakhstan
146 J15 **Saryýazy Suw Howdany** Rus. Saryyazynskoye Vodokhranilishche. ⊠ S Turkmenistan
Saryyazynskoye Vodokhranilishche see Saryýazy Suw Howdany

◆ Country · ● Country Capital · ◇ Dependent Territory · ○ Dependent Territory Capital · ⬖ Administrative Regions · ✈ International Airport · ▲ Mountain · ⛰ Mountain Range · 🌋 Volcano · ≈ River · ◎ Lake · ⊠ Reservoir

SARYESIK-ATYRAU, PESKI – SEELIG, MOUNT

145 *T14* **Saryesik-Atyrau, Peski** *desert* E Kazakhstan
106 *E10* **Sarzana** Liguria, NW Italy
188 *B17* **Sasalaguan, Mount** ▲ S Guam
153 *O14* **Sasarām** Bihār, N India
186 *M8* **Sasari, Mount** ▲ Santa Isabel, N Solomon Islands
164 *C13* **Sasebo** Nagasaki, Kyūshū, SW Japan
14 *I9* **Saseginaga, Lac** ◎ Québec, SE Canada
Saseno *see* Sazan
9 *R13* **Saskatchewan** ◈ *province* SW Canada
9 *U14* **Saskatchewan** ∿ Manitoba/Saskatchewan, C Canada
9 *T15* **Saskatoon** Saskatchewan, S Canada
9 *T15* **Saskatoon** ✈ Saskatchewan, S Canada
123 *N7* **Saskylakh** Respublika Sakha (Yakutiya), NE Russian Federation
42 *L7* **Saslaya, Cerro** ▲ N Nicaragua
38 *G17* **Sasmik, Cape** *headland* Tanaga Island, Alaska, USA
119 *N19* **Sasnovy Bor** *Rus.* Sosnovyy Bor. Homyel'skaya Voblasts', SE Belarus
127 *N5* **Sasovo** Ryazanskaya Oblast', W Russian Federation
25 *S12* **Saspamco** Texas, SW USA
109 *W9* **Sass** *var.* Sassbach. ∿ SE Austria
76 *M17* **Sassandra** S Ivory Coast
76 *M17* **Sassandra** *var.* Ibo, Sassandra Fleuve. ∿ S Ivory Coast
Sassandra Fleuve *see* Sassandra
107 *B17* **Sassari** Sardegna, Italy, C Mediterranean Sea
Sassbach *see* Sass
98 *H11* **Sassenheim** Zuid-Holland, W Netherlands
Sassmacken *see* Valdemārpils
100 *O7* **Sassnitz** Mecklenburg-Vorpommern, NE Germany
99 *E16* **Sas van Gent** Zeeland, SW Netherlands
145 *W12* **Sasykkol', Ozero** ◎ E Kazakhstan
117 *O12* **Sasyk Kunduk, Ozero** ◎ SW Ukraine
76 *J12* **Satadougou** Kayes, SW Mali
164 *C17* **Sata-misaki** Kyūshū, SW Japan
26 *I7* **Satanta** Kansas, C USA
155 *E15* **Sātāra** Mahārāshtra, W India
192 *G15* **Sātaua** Savai'i, NW Samoa
188 *M16* **Satawal** *island* Caroline Islands, C Micronesia
189 *R17* **Satawan Atoll** *atoll* Mortlock Islands, C Micronesia
23 *Y12* **Satellite Beach** Florida, SE USA
95 *M14* **Säter** Dalarna, C Sweden
Sathmar *see* Satu Mare
23 *V7* **Satilla River** ∿ Georgia, SE USA
57 *F14* **Satipo** *var.* San Francisco de Satipo. Junín, C Peru
122 *F11* **Satka** Chelyabinskaya Oblast', C Russian Federation
153 *T16* **Satkhira** Khulna, SW Bangladesh
146 *J13* **Şatlyk** *Rus.* Shatlyk. Mary Welaýaty, C Turkmenistan
154 *K9* **Satna** *prev.* Sutna. Madhya Pradesh, C India
103 *R11* **Satolas** ✈ (Lyon) Rhône, E France
111 *N20* **Sátoraljaújhely** Borsod-Abaúj-Zemplén, NE Hungary
145 *O12* **Satpayev** *prev.* Nikol'skiy. Karaganda, C Kazakhstan
154 *G11* **Sātpura Range** ▲▲ C India
167 *P12* **Sattahip** *var.* Ban Sattahip, Ban Sattahipp. Chon Buri, S Thailand
92 *L11* **Sattanen** Lappi, NE Finland
Satul *see* Satun
116 *H9* **Satulung** *Hung.* Kővárhosszúfalu. Maramureș, N Romania
Satul-Vechi *see* Staro Selo
116 *G8* **Satu Mare** *Ger.* Sathmar, *Hung.* Szatmárnémeti. Satu Mare, NW Romania
116 *G8* **Satu Mare** ◈ *county* NW Romania
167 *N16* **Satun** *var.* Satul, Setul. Satun, SW Thailand
192 *G16* **Satupaiteau** Savai'i, W Samoa
Sau *see* Sava
14 *F14* **Sauble** ∿ Ontario, S Canada
14 *F13* **Sauble Beach** Ontario, S Canada
61 *C16* **Sauce** Corrientes, NE Argentina
Sauce *see* Juan L. Lacaze
36 *K15* **Sauceda Mountains** ▲▲ Arizona, SW USA
61 *C17* **Sauce de Luna** Entre Ríos, E Argentina
63 *L15* **Sauce Grande, Río** ∿ E Argentina
40 *K6* **Saucillo** Chihuahua, N Mexico
95 *D15* **Sauda** Rogaland, S Norway
145 *Q16* **Saudakent** *Kaz.* Saūdakent; *prev.* Baykadam, *Kaz.* Bayqadam. Zhambyl, S Kazakhstan
92 *J2* **Saudhárkrókur** Nordhurland Vestra, N Iceland
141 *P9* **Saudi Arabia** *off.* Kingdom of Saudi Arabia, Al 'Arabīyah as Su'ūdīyah, *Ar.* Al Mamlakah al 'Arabīyah as Su'ūdīyah. ◆ *monarchy* SW Asia
Saudi Arabia, Kingdom of *see* Saudi Arabia
101 *D19* **Sauer** *var.* Sûre. ∿ NW Europe *see also* Sûre
Sauer *see* Sûre
101 *F15* **Sauerland** *forest* W Germany
14 *F14* **Saugeen** ∿ Ontario, S Canada
18 *K12* **Saugerties** New York, NE USA
Saugor *see* Sāgar
10 *K15* **Saugstad, Mount** ▲ British Columbia, SW Canada
Sāūjbulāgh *see* Mahābād
102 *J11* **Saujon** Charente-Maritime, W France
29 *T7* **Sauk Centre** Minnesota, N USA
30 *L8* **Sauk City** Wisconsin, N USA
29 *U7* **Sauk Rapids** Minnesota, N USA
55 *Y11* **Saül** C French Guiana
103 *O7* **Sauldre** ∿ C France
101 *I23* **Saulgau** Baden-Württemberg, SW Germany
103 *Q8* **Saulieu** Côte d'Or, C France
118 *G8* **Saulkrasti** Rīga, C Latvia
15 *S6* **Sault-aux-Cochons, Rivière du** ∿ Québec, SE Canada
31 *Q4* **Sault Sainte Marie** Michigan, N USA
12 *F14* **Sault Ste. Marie** Ontario, S Canada
145 *P7* **Saumalkol'** *prev.* Volodarskoye. Severnyy Kazakhstan, N Kazakhstan
190 *E13* **Sauma, Pointe** *headland* Île Alofi, W Wallis and Futuna
171 *T16* **Saumlaki** *var.* Saumlakki. Pulau Yamdena, E Indonesia
Saumlakki *see* Saumlaki
15 *R12* **Saumon, Rivière au** ∿ Québec, SE Canada
102 *K8* **Saumur** Maine-et-Loire, NW France
185 *F23* **Saunders, Cape** *headland* South Island, New Zealand
195 *N13* **Saunders Coast** *physical region* Antarctica
65 *B23* **Saunders Island** *island* NW Falkland Islands
65 *C24* **Saunders Island Settlement** Saunders Island, NW Falkland Islands
82 *F11* **Saurimo** *Port.* Henrique de Carvalho, Vila Henrique de Carvalho. Lunda Sul, NE Angola
55 *S11* **Sauriwaunawa** S Guyana
82 *D12* **Sautar** Malanje, NW Angola
45 *S13* **Sauteurs** N Grenada
102 *K13* **Sauveterre-de-Guyenne** Gironde, SW France
119 *O14* **Sava** *Rus.* Sava. Mahilyowskaya Voblasts', E Belarus
42 *J5* **Savá** Colón, N Honduras
84 *H11* **Sava** *Eng.* Save, *Ger.* Sau, *Hung.* Száva. ∿ SE Europe
33 *Y8* **Savage** Montana, NW USA
183 *N16* **Savage River** Tasmania, SE Australia
77 *R15* **Savalou** S Benin
30 *K10* **Savanna** Illinois, N USA
23 *X6* **Savannah** Georgia, SE USA
27 *R2* **Savannah** Missouri, C USA
20 *H10* **Savannah** Tennessee, S USA
21 *O12* **Savannah River** ∿ Georgia/South Carolina, SE USA
Savannakhét *see* Khanthabouli
44 *H12* **Savanna-La-Mar** W Jamaica
12 *B10* **Savant Lake** ◎ Ontario, S Canada
155 *F17* **Savanūr** Karnātaka, W India
93 *J16* **Sävar** Västerbotten, N Sweden
Savaria *see* Szombathely
154 *C11* **Sāvarkundla** *var.* Kundla. Gujarāt, W India
116 *F11* **Săvârșin** *Hung.* Soborsin; *prev.* Săvirșin. Arad, W Romania
136 *C13* **Savaştepe** Balıkesir, W Turkey
Savat *see* Savot
Savat *see* Savot
Sávdijári *see* Skaulo
77 *R15* **Savè** SE Benin
83 *N18* **Save** Inhambane, E Mozambique
102 *L16* **Save** ∿ S France
83 *L17* **Save** *var.* Sabi. ∿ Mozambique/Zimbabwe *see also* Sabi
Save *see* Sava
142 *M6* **Sāveh** Markazī, W Iran
116 *L8* **Săveni** Botoșani, NE Romania
103 *N16* **Saverdun** Ariège, S France
Save, Rio *see* Sabi
103 *U5* **Saverne** *var.* Zabern; *anc.* Tres Tabernae. Bas-Rhin, NE France
106 *B9* **Savigliano** Piemonte, NW Italy
Savigsivik *see* Savissivik
Savinichi *see* Savinichy
119 *Q16* **Savinichy** *Rus.* Savinichi. Mahilyowskaya Voblasts', E Belarus
109 *U10* **Savinja** ∿ N Slovenia
106 *H11* **Savio** ∿ C Italy
Săvirșin *see* Săvârșin
197 *O11* **Savissivik** *var.* Savigsivik. ◈ Avannaarsua, N Greenland
93 *N18* **Savitaipale** Etelä-Suomi, SE Finland
113 *J15* **Šavnik** C Montenegro
108 *I9* **Savognin** Graubünden, S Switzerland
103 *T12* **Savoie** ◈ *department* E France
106 *C10* **Savona** Liguria, NW Italy
93 *N17* **Savonlinna** *Swe.* Nyslott. Isä-Suomi, E Finland
93 *N17* **Savonranta** Isä-Suomi, E Finland
38 *K10* **Savoonga** Saint Lawrence Island, Alaska, USA
147 *P11* **Savot** *Rus.* Savat. Sirdaryo Viloyati, E Uzbekistan
147 *P11* **Savot** *Rus.* Savat. Sirdaryo Viloyati, E Uzbekistan
30 *M13* **Savoy** Illinois, N USA
117 *O8* **Savran'** Odes'ka Oblast', SW Ukraine
137 *R11* **Şavşat** Artvin, NE Turkey
95 *L19* **Sävsjö** Jönköping, S Sweden
Savu, Kepulauan *see* Sawu, Kepulauan
92 *M11* **Savukoski** Lappi, NE Finland
Savu, Pulau *see* Sawu, Pulau
187 *Y14* **Savusavu** Vanua Levu, N Fiji
171 *O17* **Savu Sea** *Ind.* Laut Sawu. *sea* S Indonesia
83 *H17* **Savute** North-West, N Botswana
139 *N7* **Şawāb Uqlat'** *well* W Iraq
138 *M7* **Sawāb, Wādī as** *dry watercourse* W Iraq
152 *H13* **Sawāi Mādhopur** Rājasthān, N India
Sawakin *see* Suakin
167 *R8* **Sawang Daen Din** Sakon Nakhon, E Thailand
167 *O8* **Sawankhalok** *var.* Swankalok. Sukhothai, NW Thailand
165 *P13* **Sawara** Chiba, Honshū, S Japan
37 *R5* **Sawatch Range** ▲▲ Colorado, C USA
141 *N12* **Sawdā', Jabal** ▲ SW Saudi Arabia
75 *P9* **Sawdā', Jabal as** ▲▲ C Libya
Sawdirī *see* Sodiri
97 *F14* **Sawel Mountain** ▲ C Northern Ireland, UK
Sawhāj *see* Sohâg
77 *O15* **Sawla** N Ghana
141 *X12* **Şawqirah** *var.* Suqrah. S Oman
141 *X12* **Şawqirah, Dawḩat** *var.* Ghubbat Sawqirah, Sukra Bay, Suqrah Bay. *bay* S Oman
Sawqirah, Ghubbat *see* Şawqirah, Dawḩat
183 *V5* **Sawtell** New South Wales, SE Australia
138 *K7* **Şawt, Wādī aş** *dry watercourse* S Syria
171 *O17* **Sawu, Kepulauan** *var.* Kepulauan Savu. *island group* S Indonesia
Sawu, Laut *see* Savu Sea
171 *O17* **Sawu, Pulau** *var.* Pulau Sawu. *island* Kepulauan Sawu, S Indonesia
105 *S12* **Sax** País Valenciano, E Spain
Saxe *see* Sachsen
108 *C11* **Saxon** Valais, SW Switzerland
Saxony *see* Sachsen
Saxony-Anhalt *see* Sachsen-Anhalt
77 *R12* **Say** Niamey, SW Niger
15 *V7* **Sayabec** Québec, SE Canada
Sayaboury *see* Xaignabouli
145 *U12* **Sayak** *Kaz.* Sayaq. Karaganda, E Kazakhstan
57 *D14* **Sayán** Lima, W Peru
129 *T6* **Sayanskiy Khrebet** ▲▲ S Russian Federation
Sayaq *see* Sayak
146 *K13* **Saýat** *Rus.* Sayat. Lebap Welaýaty, E Turkmenistan
42 *D3* **Sayaxché** Petén, N Guatemala
Şaydā/Sayida *see* Saïda
162 *J7* **Sayhan** *var.* Hüremt. Bulgan, C Mongolia
163 *N10* **Sayhandulaan** *var.* Öldziyt. Dornogovĭ, SE Mongolia
162 *K9* **Sayhan-Ovoo** *var.* Ongi. Dundgovĭ, C Mongolia
141 *T15* **Sayḩūt** E Yemen
29 *U14* **Saylorville Lake** ⊠ Iowa, C USA
Saymenskiy Kanal *see* Saimaa Canal
163 *N10* **Saynshand** Dornogovĭ, SE Mongolia
Saynshand *see* Sevrey
Sayn-Ust *see* Hohmorĭt
Say-Ötesh *see* Say-Utës
138 *J7* **Şayqal, Bahr** ◎ S Syria
Sayrab *see* Sayrob
158 *H4* **Sayram Hu** ◎ NW China
26 *K11* **Sayre** Oklahoma, C USA
18 *H12* **Sayre** Pennsylvania, NE USA
18 *K15* **Sayreville** New Jersey, NE USA
147 *N13* **Sayrob** *Rus.* Sayrab. Surkhondaryo Viloyati, S Uzbekistan
40 *L13* **Sayula** Jalisco, SW Mexico
141 *R14* **Say'ūn** *var.* Saywūn. C Yemen
144 *G14* **Say-Utës** *Kaz.* Say-Ötesh. Mangistau, SW Kazakhstan
10 *K16* **Sayward** Vancouver Island, British Columbia, SW Canada
Saywūn *see* Say'ūn
Sayyāl *see* As Sayyāl
139 *U8* **Sayyid 'Abīd** *var.* Saiyid Abid. E Iraq
113 *J22* **Sazan** *var.* Ishulli i Sazanit, *It.* Saseno. *island* SW Albania
Sazanit, Ishulli i *see* Sazan
Sazau/Sazawa *see* Sázava
111 *E17* **Sázava** *var.* Sazau, *Ger.* Sazawa. ∿ C Czech Republic
124 *J14* **Sazonovo** Vologodskaya Oblast', NW Russian Federation
102 *G6* **Scaër** Finistère, NW France
97 *J15* **Scafell Pike** ▲ NW England, UK
Scalabis *see* Santarém
96 *M2* **Scalloway** N Scotland, UK
38 *M11* **Scammon Bay** Alaska, USA
Scammon Lagoon/Scammon, Laguna *see* Ojo de Liebre, Laguna
84 *F7* **Scandinavia** *geophysical region* NW Europe
96 *K5* **Scapa Flow** *sea basin* N Scotland, UK
107 *K26* **Scaramia, Capo** *headland* Sicilia, Italy, C Mediterranean Sea
14 *H15* **Scarborough** Ontario, SE Canada
45 *Z16* **Scarborough** *prev.* Port Louis. Tobago, Trinidad and Tobago
97 *N16* **Scarborough** N England, UK
185 *I17* **Scargill** Canterbury, South Island, New Zealand
96 *E7* **Scarp** *island* NW Scotland, UK
Scarpanto *see* Kárpathos
Scarpanto Strait *see* Karpathou, Stenó
107 *G25* **Scauri** Sicilia, Italy, C Mediterranean Sea
Scealg, Bá na *see* Ballinskelligs Bay
Scebeli *see* Shebeli
100 *K10* **Schaale** ∿ N Germany
100 *K9* **Schaalsee** ◎ N Germany
99 *G18* **Schaerbeek** Brussels, C Belgium
108 *G6* **Schaffhausen** *Fr.* Schaffhouse. Schaffhausen, N Switzerland
108 *G6* **Schaffhausen** *Fr.* Schaffhouse. ◈ *canton* N Switzerland
Schaffhouse *see* Schaffhausen
98 *I8* **Schagen** Noord-Holland, NW Netherlands
Schaken *see* Šakiai
98 *M10* **Schalkhaar** Overijssel, E Netherlands
109 *R3* **Schärding** Oberösterreich, N Austria
100 *G9* **Scharhörn** *island* NW Germany
Schässburg *see* Sighișoara
Schaulen *see* Šiauliai
30 *M10* **Schaumburg** Illinois, N USA
Schebschi Mountains *see* Shebshi Mountains
98 *P6* **Scheemda** Groningen, NE Netherlands
100 *I10* **Scheessel** Niedersachsen, NW Germany
13 *N8* **Schefferville** Québec, E Canada
Schelde *see* Scheldt
99 *D18* **Scheldt** *Dut.* Schelde, *Fr.* Escaut. ∿ W Europe
35 *X5* **Schell Creek Range** ▲▲ Nevada, W USA
18 *K10* **Schenectady** New York, NE USA
99 *I17* **Scherpenheuvel** *Fr.* Montaigu. Vlaams Brabant, C Belgium
98 *K11* **Scherpenzeel** Gelderland, C Netherlands
25 *S12* **Schertz** Texas, SW USA
98 *G11* **Scheveningen** Zuid-Holland, W Netherlands
98 *G12* **Schiedam** Zuid-Holland, SW Netherlands
99 *M24* **Schieren** Diekirch, NE Luxembourg
98 *M4* **Schiermonnikoog** *Fris.* Skiermûntseach. Friesland, N Netherlands
98 *M4* **Schiermonnikoog** *Fris.* Skiermûntseach. *island* Waddeneilanden, N Netherlands
99 *K14* **Schijndel** Noord-Brabant, S Netherlands
Schil *see* Jiu
99 *H16* **Schilde** Antwerpen, N Belgium
Schillen *see* Zhilino
103 *V5* **Schiltigheim** Bas-Rhin, NE France
106 *G7* **Schio** Veneto, NE Italy
98 *H10* **Schiphol** ✈ (Amsterdam) Noord-Holland, C Netherlands
Schippenbeil *see* Sępopol
Schiria *see* Şiria
Schivelbein *see* Świdwin
115 *D22* **Schíza** *island* S Greece
175 *U3* **Schjetman Reef** *reef* Antarctica
Schlackenwerth *see* Ostrov
109 *R7* **Schladming** Steiermark, SE Austria
Schlan *see* Slaný
Schlanders *see* Silandro
100 *I7* **Schlei** *inlet* N Germany
101 *D17* **Schleiden** Nordrhein-Westfalen, W Germany
Schlelau *see* Szydłowiec
100 *I7* **Schleswig** Schleswig-Holstein, N Germany
29 *T13* **Schleswig** Iowa, C USA
100 *H8* **Schleswig-Holstein** ◈ *state* N Germany
Schlettstadt *see* Sélestat
108 *F7* **Schlieren** Zürich, N Switzerland
Schlochau *see* Człuchów
Schloppe *see* Człopa
101 *I18* **Schlüchtern** Hessen, C Germany
101 *J17* **Schmalkalden** Thüringen, C Germany
109 *W2* **Schmida** ∿ NE Austria
65 *P19* **Schmidt-Ott Seamount** *var.* Schmitt-Ott Seamount, Schmitt-Ott Tablemount. *undersea feature* SW Indian Ocean
Schmiegel *see* Śmigiel
Schmitt-Ott Seamount/Schmitt-Ott Tablemount *see* Schmidt-Ott Seamount
15 *V3* **Schmon** ∿ Québec, SE Canada
101 *M18* **Schneeberg** ▲ W Germany
Schneeberg *see* Veliki Snežnik
Schnee-Eifel *see* Schneifel
Schneekoppe *see* Sněžka
Schneidemühl *see* Piła
101 *D18* **Schneifel** *var.* Schnee-Eifel. *plateau* W Germany
Schnelle Körös/Schnelle Kreisch *see* Crişul Repede
100 *I11* **Schneverdingen** *var.* Schneverdingen (Wümme). Niedersachsen, NW Germany
Schneverdingen (Wümme) *see* Schneverdingen
Schoden *see* Skuodas
45 *Q12* **Schœlcher** W Martinique
18 *K10* **Schoharie** New York, NE USA
18 *K11* **Schoharie Creek** ∿ New York, NE USA
115 *J21* **Schoinoússa** *island* Kykládes, Greece, Aegean Sea
100 *L13* **Schönebeck** Sachsen-Anhalt, C Germany
Schöneck *see* Skarszewy
100 *O12* **Schönefeld** ✈ (Berlin) Berlin, NE Germany
101 *K24* **Schongau** Bayern, S Germany
100 *K13* **Schöningen** Niedersachsen, C Germany
Schönlanke *see* Trzcianka
Schönsee *see* Kowalewo Pomorskie
31 *P10* **Schoolcraft** Michigan, N USA
98 *O8* **Schoonebeek** Drenthe, NE Netherlands
98 *I12* **Schoonhoven** Zuid-Holland, C Netherlands
98 *H8* **Schoorl** Noord-Holland, NW Netherlands
Schooten *see* Schoten
101 *F24* **Schopfheim** Baden-Württemberg, SW Germany
101 *I21* **Schorndorf** Baden-Württemberg, S Germany
100 *F10* **Schortens** Niedersachsen, NW Germany
99 *H16* **Schoten** *var.* Schooten. Antwerpen, N Belgium
183 *Q17* **Schouten Island** *island* Tasmania, SE Australia
186 *C5* **Schouten Islands** *island group* NW Papua New Guinea
98 *E13* **Schouwen** *island* SW Netherlands
Schreiberhau *see* Szklarska Poręba
109 *U2* **Schrems** Niederösterreich, E Austria
101 *L22* **Schrobenhausen** Bayern, SE Germany
18 *L8* **Schroon Lake** ◎ New York, NE USA
108 *J8* **Schruns** Vorarlberg, W Austria
Schubin *see* Szubin
25 *U11* **Schulenburg** Texas, SW USA
Schuls *see* Scuol
108 *E8* **Schüpfheim** Luzern, C Switzerland
35 *S6* **Schurz** Nevada, W USA
101 *I24* **Schussen** ∿ S Germany
Schüttenhofen *see* Sušice
29 *R15* **Schuyler** Nebraska, C USA
18 *L10* **Schuylerville** New York, NE USA
101 *K20* **Schwabach** Bayern, SE Germany
Schwabenalb *see* Schwäbische Alb
101 *I23* **Schwäbische Alb** *var.* Schwabenalb, *Eng.* Swabian Jura. ▲▲ S Germany
101 *I22* **Schwäbisch Gmünd** *var.* Gmünd. Baden-Württemberg, SW Germany
101 *I21* **Schwäbisch Hall** *var.* Hall. Baden-Württemberg, SW Germany
101 *H16* **Schwalm** ∿ C Germany
109 *V9* **Schwanberg** Steiermark, SE Austria
108 *H8* **Schwanden** Glarus, E Switzerland
101 *M20* **Schwandorf** Bayern, SE Germany
109 *S5* **Schwanenstadt** Oberösterreich, NW Austria
169 *S11* **Schwaner, Pegunungan** ▲▲ Borneo, N Indonesia
109 *W5* **Schwarza** ∿ E Austria
109 *P9* **Schwarzach** ∿ S Austria
101 *M20* **Schwarzach** *Cz.* Černice. ∿ Czech Republic/Germany
Schwarzach *see* Schwarzach im Pongau
109 *Q7* **Schwarzach im Pongau** *var.* Schwarzach. Salzburg, NW Austria
Schwarzawa *see* Svratka
101 *N14* **Schwarze Elster** ∿ E Germany
Schwarze Körös *see* Crişul Negru
108 *D9* **Schwarzenburg** Bern, W Switzerland
83 *D21* **Schwarzrand** ▲▲ S Namibia
101 *G23* **Schwarzwald** *Eng.* Black Forest. ▲▲ SW Germany
Schwarzwasser *see* Wda
39 *P7* **Schwatka Mountains** ▲▲ Alaska, USA
109 *N7* **Schwaz** Tirol, W Austria
109 *Y4* **Schwechat** Niederösterreich, NE Austria
109 *Y4* **Schwechat** ✈ (Wien) Wien, E Austria
100 *P11* **Schwedt** Brandenburg, NE Germany
101 *D19* **Schweich** Rheinland-Pfalz, SW Germany
Schweidnitz *see* Świdnica
101 *J18* **Schweinfurt** Bayern, SE Germany
Schweiz *see* Switzerland
100 *L9* **Schwerin** Mecklenburg-Vorpommern, N Germany
Schwerin *see* Skwierzyna
100 *L9* **Schweriner See** ◎ N Germany
Schwertberg *see* Świecie
101 *F15* **Schwerte** Nordrhein-Westfalen, W Germany
Schwiebus *see* Świebodzin
100 *P13* **Schwielochsee** ◎ NE Germany
Schwihau *see* Švihov
Schwiz *see* Schwyz
108 *G8* **Schwyz** *var.* Schwiz. Schwyz, C Switzerland
108 *G8* **Schwyz** *var.* Schwiz. ◈ *canton* C Switzerland
14 *J11* **Schyan** ∿ Québec, SE Canada
Schyl *see* Jiu
107 *I24* **Sciacca** Sicilia, Italy, C Mediterranean Sea
Sciasciamana *see* Shashemenē
107 *L26* **Scicli** Sicilia, Italy, C Mediterranean Sea
97 *F25* **Scilly, Isles of** *island group* SW England, UK
111 *H17* **Ścinawa** *Ger.* Steinau an der Elbe. Dolnośląskie, SW Poland
Scio *see* Chíos
31 *S14* **Scioto River** ∿ Ohio, N USA
36 *L5* **Scipio** Utah, W USA
33 *X6* **Scobey** Montana, NW USA
183 *T7* **Scone** New South Wales, SE Australia
Scoresby Sound/Scoresbysund *see* Ittoqqortoormiit
Scoresby Sund *see* Kangertittivaq
Scorno, Punta dello *see* Caprara, Punta
34 *K3* **Scotia** California, W USA
47 *Y14* **Scotia Plate** *tectonic feature*
47 *V15* **Scotia Ridge** *undersea feature* S Atlantic Ocean
194 *H2* **Scotia Sea** *sea* SW Atlantic Ocean
29 *Q12* **Scotland** South Dakota, N USA
25 *R5* **Scotland** Texas, SW USA
96 *H11* **Scotland** *cultural region* Scotland, U K
21 *W8* **Scotland Neck** North Carolina, SE USA
195 *R13* **Scott Base** *NZ research station* Antarctica
10 *J16* **Scott, Cape** *headland* Vancouver Island, British Columbia, SW Canada
26 *I5* **Scott City** Kansas, C USA
27 *Y7* **Scott City** Missouri, C USA
195 *R14* **Scott Coast** *physical region* Antarctica
18 *C15* **Scottdale** Pennsylvania, NE USA
195 *Y11* **Scott Glacier** *glacier* Antarctica
195 *Q17* **Scott Island** *island* Antarctica
26 *L11* **Scott, Mount** ▲ Oklahoma, USA
32 *G15* **Scott, Mount** ▲ Oregon, NW USA
34 *M1* **Scott River** ∿ California, W USA
28 *I13* **Scottsbluff** Nebraska, C USA
23 *Q2* **Scottsboro** Alabama, S USA
31 *P15* **Scottsburg** Indiana, N USA
183 *P16* **Scottsdale** Tasmania, SE Australia
36 *L13* **Scottsdale** Arizona, SW USA
45 *O12* **Scotts Head Village** *var.* Cachacrou. S Dominica
192 *L14* **Scott Shoal** *undersea feature* S Pacific Ocean
20 *K7* **Scottsville** Kentucky, S USA
29 *U14* **Scranton** Iowa, C USA
18 *I13* **Scranton** Pennsylvania, NE USA
186 *B6* **Screw** ∿ NW Papua New Guinea
29 *R14* **Scribner** Nebraska, C USA
Scrobesbyrig' *see* Shrewsbury
14 *I14* **Scugog** ∿ Ontario, SE Canada
14 *I14* **Scugog, Lake** ◎ Ontario, SE Canada
97 *N17* **Scunthorpe** E England, UK
108 *K9* **Scuol** *Ger.* Schuls. Graubünden, E Switzerland
Scupi *see* Skopje
Scutari *see* Shkodër
113 *K17* **Scutari, Lake** *Alb.* Liqeni i Shkodrës, *SCr.* Skadarsko Jezero. ◎ Albania/Montenegro
Scyros *see* Skýros
Scythopolis *see* Bet She'an
25 *U13* **Seadrift** Texas, SW USA
21 *Y4* **Seaford** *var.* Seaford City. Delaware, NE USA
Seaford City *see* Seaford
14 *E15* **Seaforth** Ontario, S Canada
24 *M6* **Seagraves** Texas, SW USA
9 *X9* **Seal** ∿ Manitoba, C Canada
182 *M10* **Sea Lake** Victoria, SE Australia
83 *G26* **Seal, Cape** *headland* S South Africa
65 *D26* **Sea Lion Islands** *island group* SE Falkland Islands
19 *S8* **Seal Island** *island* Maine, NE USA
25 *V11* **Sealy** Texas, SW USA
35 *X12* **Searchlight** Nevada, W USA
27 *V11* **Searcy** Arkansas, C USA
19 *R7* **Searsport** Maine, NE USA
35 *N10* **Seaside** California, W USA
32 *F10* **Seaside** Oregon, NW USA
18 *K16* **Seaside Heights** New Jersey, NE USA
32 *H8* **Seattle** Washington, NW USA
32 *H9* **Seattle-Tacoma** ✈ Washington, NW USA
185 *J16* **Seaward Kaikoura Range** ▲▲ South Island, New Zealand
42 *J9* **Sébaco** Matagalpa, W Nicaragua
19 *P8* **Sebago Lake** ◎ Maine, NE USA
169 *S13* **Sebangan, Teluk** *bay* Borneo, C Indonesia
169 *S13* **Sebanganu, Teluk** *bay* Borneo, C Indonesia
Sebaste/Sebastia *see* Sivas
23 *Y12* **Sebastian** Florida, SE USA
40 *C5* **Sebastían Vizcaíno, Bahía** *bay* NW Mexico
19 *R6* **Sebasticook Lake** ◎ Maine, NE USA
34 *M7* **Sebastopol** California, W USA
Sebastopol *see* Sevastopol'
169 *W8* **Sebatik, Pulau** *island* N Indonesia
19 *R5* **Sebec Lake** ◎ Maine, NE USA
76 *K12* **Sébékoro** Kayes, W Mali
Sebenico *see* Šibenik
40 *G6* **Seberi, Cerro** ▲ NW Mexico
116 *H11* **Sebeş** *Ger.* Mühlbach, *Hung.* Szászsebes; *prev.* Sebeșu Săsesc. Alba, W Romania
Sebes-Körös *see* Crişul Repede
Sebeşu Săsesc *see* Sebeş
31 *R8* **Sebewaing** Michigan, N USA
124 *F16* **Sebezh** Pskovskaya Oblast', W Russian Federation
137 *N12* **Şebinkarahisar** Giresun, N Turkey
116 *F11* **Sebiş** *Hung.* Borossebes. Arad, W Romania
Sebkra Azz el Matti *see* Azzel Matti, Sebkha
19 *Q4* **Seboomook Lake** ◎ Maine, NE USA
74 *G6* **Sebou** *var.* Sebu. ∿ N Morocco
20 *I6* **Sebree** Kentucky, S USA
23 *X13* **Sebring** Florida, SE USA
Sebta *see* Ceuta
Sebu *see* Sebou
169 *U13* **Sebuku, Pulau** *island* N Indonesia
169 *W8* **Sebuku, Teluk** *bay* Borneo, N Indonesia
106 *F10* **Secchia** ∿ N Italy
10 *L17* **Sechelt** British Columbia, SW Canada
56 *C12* **Sechin, Río** ∿ W Peru
56 *A10* **Sechura, Bahía de** *bay* NW Peru
185 *A22* **Secretary Island** *island* SW New Zealand
155 *I15* **Secunderābād** *var.* Sikandarabad. Andhra Pradesh, C India
57 *L17* **Sécure, Río** ∿ C Bolivia
118 *D10* **Seda** Telšiai, NW Lithuania
27 *T5* **Sedalia** Missouri, C USA
103 *R3* **Sedan** Ardennes, N France
27 *P7* **Sedan** Kansas, C USA
105 *N3* **Sedano** Castilla-León, N Spain
104 *H10* **Seda, Ribeira de** *stream* C Portugal
185 *K15* **Seddon** Marlborough, South Island, New Zealand
185 *H15* **Seddonville** West Coast, South Island, New Zealand
143 *U7* **Sedeh** Khorāsān-e Janūbī, E Iran
138 *E11* **Sederot** Southern, S Israel
65 *B23* **Sedge Island** *island* NW Falkland Islands
76 *G12* **Sédhiou** SW Senegal
9 *U16* **Sedley** Saskatchewan, S Canada
Sedlez *see* Siedlce
117 *Q2* **Sedniv** Chernihivs'ka Oblast', N Ukraine
36 *L11* **Sedona** Arizona, SW USA
Sedunum *see* Sion
118 *F12* **Šeduva** Šiaulai, N Lithuania
141 *Y8* **Seeb** *var.* Muscat Sīb Airport. ✈ (Masqaţ) NE Oman
Seeb *see* As Sīb
108 *M7* **Seefeld in Tirol** Tirol, W Austria
83 *E22* **Seeheim Noord** Karas, S Namibia
Seeland *see* Sjælland
195 *N9* **Seelig, Mount** ▲ Antarctica

◆ Country
● Country Capital
◇ Dependent Territory
○ Dependent Territory Capital
◈ Administrative Regions
✈ International Airport
▲ Mountain
▲▲ Mountain Range
Volcano
∿ River
◎ Lake
⊠ Reservoir

SEEONEE – SHACKLETON ICE SHELF

Seeonee *see* Seoni
Seer *see* Dörgön
102 *L5* **Sées** Orne, N France
101 *J14* **Seesen** Niedersachsen, C Germany
Seesker Höhe *see* Szeska Góra
100 *J10* **Seevetal** Niedersachsen, N Germany
109 *V6* **Seewiesen** Steiermark, E Austria
136 *J13* **Şefaatli** *var.* Kızılkoca. Yozgat, C Turkey
149 *N3* **Sefīd, Darya-ye** *Pash.* Āb-i-safed. ≈ N Afghanistan
148 *K5* **Sefid Kūh, Selseleh-ye** *Eng.* Paropamisus Range. ▲ W Afghanistan
74 *G6* **Sefrou** N Morocco
185 *E19* **Sefton, Mount** ▲ South Island, New Zealand
171 *S13* **Segaf, Kepulauan** *island group* E Indonesia
169 *W7* **Segama, Sungai** ≈ East Malaysia
168 *L9* **Segamat** Johor, Peninsular Malaysia
77 *S13* **Ségbana** NE Benin
Segestica *see* Sisak
Segesvár *see* Sighişoara
171 *T12* **Seget** Papua, E Indonesia
Segewold *see* Sigulda
124 *J9* **Segezha** Respublika Kareliya, NW Russian Federation
Seghedin *see* Szeged
Segna *see* Senj
107 *I16* **Segni** Lazio, C Italy
Segodunum *see* Rodez
105 *S9* **Segorbe** País Valenciano, E Spain
76 *M12* **Ségou** *var.* Segu. Ségou, C Mali
76 *M12* **Ségou** ◐ *region* SW Mali
54 *E8* **Segovia** Antioquia, N Colombia
105 *N7* **Segovia** Castilla-León, C Spain
104 *M6* **Segovia** ◐ *province* Castilla-León, N Spain
Segoviao Wangkí *see* Coco, Río
124 *J9* **Segozero, Ozero** ◎ NW Russian Federation
102 *J7* **Segré** Maine-et-Loire, NW France
105 *U5* **Segre** ≈ NE Spain
Segu *see* Ségou
38 *I17* **Seguam Island** *island* Aleutian Islands, Alaska, USA
38 *I17* **Seguam Pass** *strait* Aleutian Islands, Alaska, USA
77 *Y7* **Séguédine** Agadez, NE Niger
76 *M15* **Séguéla** W Ivory Coast
25 *S11* **Seguin** Texas, SW USA
38 *E17* **Segula Island** *island* Aleutian Islands, Alaska, USA
62 *K10* **Segundo, Río** ≈ C Argentina
105 *Q12* **Segura** ≈ S Spain
105 *P13* **Segura, Sierra de** ▲▲ S Spain
83 *G18* **Sehithwa** North-West, N Botswana
154 *H10* **Sehore** Madhya Pradesh, C India
186 *G9* **Sehulea** Normanby Island, S Papua New Guinea
149 *P15* **Sehwān** Sind, SE Pakistan
109 *V8* **Seiersberg** Steiermark, SE Austria
26 *L9* **Seiling** Oklahoma, C USA
103 *S9* **Seille** ≈ E France
99 *J20* **Seilles** Namur, SE Belgium
93 *K17* **Seinäjoki** *Swe.* Östermyra. Länsi-Soumi, W Finland
12 *B12* **Seine** ≈ Ontario, S Canada
102 *M4* **Seine** ≈ N France
102 *K4* **Seine, Baie de la** *bay* N France
Seine, Banc de la *see* Seine Seamount
103 *O5* **Seine-et-Marne** ◐ *department* N France
102 *L3* **Seine-Maritime** ◐ *department* N France
84 *B14* **Seine Plain** *undersea feature* E Atlantic Ocean
84 *B15* **Seine Seamount** *var.* Banc de la Seine. *undersea feature* E Atlantic Ocean
102 *E6* **Sein, Île de** *island* NW France
171 *Y14* **Seinma** Papua, E Indonesia
Seisbierum *see* Sexbierum
109 *U5* **Seitenstetten Markt** Niederösterreich, C Austria
Seiyu *see* Chŏnju
95 *H22* **Sejerø** *island* E Denmark
110 *P7* **Sejny** Podlaskie, NE Poland
81 *G20* **Seke** Shinyanga, N Tanzania
164 *L13* **Seki** Gifu, Honshū, SW Japan
161 *U12* **Sekibi-sho** *island* China/Japan/Taiwan
165 *U3* **Sekihoku-tōge** *pass* Hokkaidō, NE Japan
Sekondi *see* Sekondi-Takoradi
77 *P17* **Sekondi-Takoradi** *var.* Sekondi. S Ghana
80 *J11* **Sek'ot'a** Amhara, N Ethiopia
Sekseūil *see* Saksaul'skiy
32 *I9* **Selah** Washington, NW USA
168 *J8* **Selangor** *var.* Negeri Selangor Darul Ehsan. ◐ *state* Peninsular Malaysia
Selânik *see* Thessaloníki
168 *K10* **Selapanjang** Pulau Rantau, W Indonesia
167 *R10* **Selaphum** Roi Et, E Thailand
171 *T16* **Selaru, Pulau** *island* Kepulauan Tanimbar, E Indonesia
171 *U13* **Selassi** Papua, E Indonesia
168 *J7* **Selatan, Selat** *strait* Peninsular Malaysia
39 *N8* **Selawik** Alaska, USA
39 *N8* **Selawik Lake** ◎ Alaska, USA
171 *N14* **Selayar, Selat** *strait* Sulawesi, C Indonesia
95 *C14* **Selbjørnsfjorden** *fjord* S Norway
94 *H8* **Selbusjøen** ◎ S Norway
97 *M17* **Selby** N England, UK
29 *N8* **Selby** South Dakota, N USA
21 *Z4* **Selbyville** Delaware, NE USA
136 *B15* **Selçuk** *var.* Akıncılar. İzmir, SW Turkey
39 *Q13* **Seldovia** Alaska, USA
107 *M18* **Sele** *anc.* Silarius. ≈ S Italy
83 *J19* **Selebi-Phikwe** Central, E Botswana
42 *B5* **Selegua, Río** ≈ W Guatemala
129 *X7* **Selemdzha** ≈ SE Russian Federation
129 *U7* **Selenga** *Mong.* Selenge Mörön. ≈ Mongolia/Russian Federation
79 *I19* **Selenge** Bandundu, W Dem. Rep. Congo
162 *K6* **Selenge** *var.* Ingettolgoy. Bulgan, N Mongolia
162 *L6* **Selenge** ◐ *province* N Mongolia
Selenge *see* Hyalganat, Bulgan, Mongolia
Selenge *see* Ih-Uul, Hövsgöl, Mongolia
Selenge Mörön *see* Selenga
123 *N14* **Selenginsk** Respublika Buryatiya, S Russian Federation
Selenica *see* Selenicë
113 *K22* **Selenicë** *var.* Selenica. Vlorë, SW Albania
123 *Q8* **Selennyakh** ≈ NE Russian Federation
100 *J8* **Selenter See** ◎ N Germany
Sele Sound *see* Soela Väin
103 *U6* **Sélestat** *Ger.* Schlettstadt. Bas-Rhin, NE France
Selety *see* Sileti
Seleucia *see* Silifke
92 *I4* **Selfoss** Sudhurland, SW Iceland
28 *M7* **Selfridge** North Dakota, N USA
76 *I15* **Seli** ≈ N Sierra Leone
76 *I11* **Sélibabi** *var.* Sélibaby. Guidimaka, S Mauritania
Sélibaby *see* Sélibabi
Selidovka/Selidovo *see* Selydove
124 *I15* **Seliger, Ozero** ◎ W Russian Federation
36 *J11* **Seligman** Arizona, SW USA
27 *S8* **Seligman** Missouri, C USA
80 *E6* **Selima Oasis** *oasis* N Sudan
76 *L13* **Sélingué, Lac de** ⊠ S Mali
Selinoús *see* Kréstena
18 *G14* **Selinsgrove** Pennsylvania, NE USA
Selishche *see* Syelishcha
124 *I16* **Selizharovo** Tverskaya Oblast', W Russian Federation
94 *C10* **Selje** Sogn Og Fjordane, S Norway
9 *X16* **Selkirk** Manitoba, S Canada
96 *K13* **Selkirk** SE Scotland, UK
96 *K13* **Selkirk** *cultural region* SE Scotland, UK
9 *O16* **Selkirk Mountains** ▲▲ British Columbia, SW Canada
193 *T11* **Selkirk Rise** *undersea feature* SE Pacific Ocean
115 *F21* **Sellasía** Pelopónnisos, S Greece
44 *M9* **Selle, Pic de la** *var.* La Selle. ▲ SE Haiti
102 *M8* **Selles-sur-Cher** Loir-et-Cher, C France
36 *K16* **Sells** Arizona, SW USA
Sellye *see* Sal'a
23 *P5* **Selma** Alabama, S USA
35 *Q11* **Selma** California, W USA
20 *G10* **Selmer** Tennessee, S USA
173 *N17* **Sel, Pointe au** *headland* W Réunion
Selselehye Kuhe Vākhān *see* Nicholas Range
127 *S2* **Selty** Udmurtskaya Respublika, NW Russian Federation
Selukwe *see* Shurugwi
62 *L9* **Selva** Santiago del Estero, N Argentina
9 *T9* **Selwyn Lake** ◎ Northwest Territories/Saskatchewan, C Canada
10 *K6* **Selwyn Mountains** ▲▲ Yukon Territory, NW Canada
181 *T6* **Selwyn Range** ▲▲ Queensland, C Australia
117 *W8* **Selydove** *var.* Selidovka, *Rus.* Selidovo. Donets'ka Oblast', SE Ukraine
Selzaete *see* Zelzate
Seman *see* Semanit, Lumi i
168 *M15* **Semangka, Teluk** *bay* Sumatera, SW Indonesia
113 *D22* **Semanit, Lumi i** *var.* Seman. ≈ W Albania
169 *Q16* **Semarang** *var.* Samarang. Jawa, C Indonesia
169 *Q10* **Sematan** Sarawak, East Malaysia
171 *P17* **Semau, Pulau** *island* S Indonesia
169 *V8* **Sembakung, Sungai** ≈ Borneo, N Indonesia
79 *G17* **Sembé** La Sangha, NW Congo
169 *S13* **Sembulu, Danau** ◎ Borneo, N Indonesia
Semendria *see* Smederevo
117 *R1* **Semenivka** Chernihivs'ka Oblast', N Ukraine
117 *S6* **Semenivka** *Rus.* Semenovka. Poltavs'ka Oblast', NE Ukraine
127 *O3* **Semenov** Nizhegorodskaya Oblast', W Russian Federation
Semenovka *see* Semenivka
169 *S17* **Semeru, Gunung** *var.* Mahameru. ▲ Jawa, S Indonesia
Semey *see* Semipalatinsk
Semezhevo *see* Syemyezhava
126 *L7* **Semiluki** Voronezhskaya Oblast', W Russian Federation
33 *W16* **Seminoe Reservoir** ⊠ Wyoming, C USA
27 *O11* **Seminole** Oklahoma, C USA
24 *M6* **Seminole** Texas, SW USA
23 *S8* **Seminole, Lake** ⊠ Florida/Georgia, SE USA
Semiozernoye *see* Auliyekol'
145 *V9* **Semipalatinsk** *Kaz.* Semey. Vostochnyy Kazakhstan, E Kazakhstan
143 *O9* **Semīrom** *var.* Samirum. Eşfahān, C Iran
38 *F17* **Semisopochnoi Island** *island* Aleutian Islands, Alaska, USA
169 *R11* **Semitau** Borneo, C Indonesia
81 *E18* **Semliki** ≈ Uganda/Dem. Rep. Congo
143 *P5* **Semnān** *var.* Samnān. Semnān, N Iran
143 *Q5* **Semnān** *off.* Ostān-e Semnān. ◐ *province* N Iran
Semnān, Ostān-e *see* Semnān
99 *K24* **Semois** ≈ SE Belgium
108 *E8* **Sempacher See** ◎ C Switzerland
Sena *see* Vila de Sena
30 *L12* **Senachwine Lake** ◎ Illinois, N USA
59 *O14* **Senador Pompeu** Ceará, E Brazil
Sena Gallica *see* Senigallia
59 *C15* **Sena Madureira** Acre, W Brazil
155 *L25* **Senanayake Samudra** ◎ E Sri Lanka
83 *G15* **Senanga** Western, SW Zambia
27 *Y9* **Senath** Missouri, C USA
22 *L2* **Senatobia** Mississippi, S USA
164 *C16* **Sendai** Kagoshima, Kyūshū, SW Japan
165 *Q10* **Sendai** Miyagi, Honshū, C Japan
165 *Q11* **Sendai-wan** *bay* E Japan
101 *J23* **Senden** Bayern, S Germany
154 *F11* **Sendhwa** Madhya Pradesh, C India
111 *H21* **Senec** *Ger.* Wartberg, *Hung.* Szenc; *prev.* Szempcz. Bratislavský Kraj, W Slovakia
27 *P3* **Seneca** Kansas, C USA
27 *R8* **Seneca** Missouri, C USA
32 *K13* **Seneca** Oregon, NW USA
21 *O11* **Seneca** South Carolina, SE USA
18 *G11* **Seneca Lake** ◎ New York, NE USA
31 *U13* **Senecaville Lake** ⊠ Ohio, N USA
76 *G11* **Senegal** *off.* Republic of Senegal, *Fr.* Sénégal. ◆ *republic* W Africa
76 *H9* **Senegal** *Fr.* Sénégal. ≈ W Africa
Senegal, Republic of *see* Senegal
31 *O4* **Seney Marsh** *wetland* Michigan, N USA
101 *P14* **Senftenberg** Brandenburg, E Germany
82 *L11* **Senga Hill** Northern, NE Zambia
158 *G13* **Sênggê Zangbo** ≈ W China
171 *Z13* **Senggi** Papua, E Indonesia
127 *R5* **Sengiley** Ul'yanovskaya Oblast', W Russian Federation
63 *I19* **Senguerr, Río** ≈ S Argentina
83 *J16* **Sengwa** ≈ C Zimbabwe
Senia *see* Senj
111 *H19* **Senica** *Ger.* Senitz, *Hung.* Szenice. Trnavský Kraj, W Slovakia
Seniça *see* Sjenica
106 *J11* **Senigallia** *anc.* Sena Gallica. Marche, C Italy
136 *F15* **Senirkent** Isparta, SW Turkey
Senitz *see* Senica
112 *C10* **Senj** *Ger.* Zengg, *It.* Segna; *anc.* Senia. Lika-Senj, NW Croatia
Senj *see* Örgön
92 *H9* **Senja** *prev.* Senjen. *island* N Norway
Senjen *see* Senja
161 *U12* **Senkaku-shotō** *island group* SW Japan
137 *R12* **Şenkaya** Erzurum, NE Turkey
83 *I16* **Senkobo** Southern, S Zambia
103 *O4* **Senlis** Oise, N France
167 *T12* **Senmonorom** Môndól Kiri, E Cambodia
80 *G10* **Sennar** *var.* Sannār. Sinnar, C Sudan
Senno *see* Syanno
Senones *see* Sens
109 *W11* **Senovo** E Slovenia
103 *P6* **Sens** *anc.* Agendicum, Senones. Yonne, C France
Sensburg *see* Mrągowo
167 *S11* **Sên, Stœng** ≈ C Cambodia
42 *F7* **Sensuntepeque** Cabañas, NE El Salvador
112 *L8* **Senta** *Hung.* Zenta. Vojvodina, N Serbia
Šent Andraž *see* Sankt Andrä
171 *Y13* **Sentani, Danau** ◎ Papua, E Indonesia
28 *J5* **Sentinel Butte** ▲ North Dakota, N USA
10 *M13* **Sentinel Peak** ▲ British Columbia, W Canada
59 *N16* **Sento Sé** Bahia, E Brazil
Šent Peter *see* Pivka
Št. Vid *see* Sankt Veit an der Glan
Seo de Urgel *see* La Seo d'Urgel
154 *I7* **Seondha** Madhya Pradesh, C India
154 *J11* **Seoni** *prev.* Seeonee. Madhya Pradesh, C India
Seoul *see* Sŏul
184 *I13* **Separation Point** *headland* South Island, New Zealand
169 *V10* **Sepasu** Borneo, N Indonesia
186 *B6* **Sepik** ≈ Indonesia/Papua New Guinea
Sepone *see* Muang Xépôn
110 *M7* **Sępopol** *Ger.* Schippenbeil. Warmińsko-Mazurskie, N Poland
116 *F10* **Şepreuş** *Hung.* Seprős. Arad, W Romania
Seprős *see* Şepreuş
Şepşi-Sângeorz/Sepsiszentgyörgy *see* Sfântu Gheorghe
15 *W4* **Sept-Îles** Québec, SE Canada
105 *N6* **Sepúlveda** Castilla-León, N Spain
104 *K8* **Sequeros** Castilla-León, N Spain
104 *L5* **Sequillo** ≈ NW Spain
32 *G7* **Sequim** Washington, NW USA
35 *S11* **Sequoia National Park** *national park* California, W USA
137 *Q14* **Şerafettin Dağları** ▲▲ E Turkey
127 *N10* **Serafimovich** Volgogradskaya Oblast', SW Russian Federation
171 *Q10* **Serai** Sulawesi, N Indonesia
99 *K19* **Seraing** Liège, E Belgium
Sêraitang *see* Baima
Serajgonj *see* Shirajganj Ghat
Serakhs *see* Sarahs
171 *W13* **Serami** Papua, E Indonesia
Seram, Laut *see* Ceram Sea
Serampore/Serampur *see* Shrīrāmpur
171 *S13* **Seram, Pulau** *var.* Serang, *Eng.* Ceram. *island* Maluku, E Indonesia
169 *N15* **Serang** Jawa, C Indonesia
Serang *see* Seram, Pulau
169 *P9* **Serasan, Pulau** *island* Kepulauan Natuna, W Indonesia
169 *P9* **Serasan, Selat** *strait* Indonesia/Malaysia
112 *M13* **Serbia** *off.* Federal Republic of Serbia; *prev.* Yugoslavia, *SCr.* Jugoslavija. ◆ *federal republic* SE Europe
112 *M12* **Serbia** *Ger.* Serbien, *Serb.* Srbija. ◐ *republic* Serbia
Serbia, Federal Republic of *see* Serbia
Serbien *see* Serbia
Sercq *see* Sark
146 *D12* **Serdar** *prev. Rus.* Gyzyrlabat, Kizyl-Arvat. Balkan Welaýaty, W Turkmenistan
Serdica *see* Sofiya
127 *O7* **Serdobsk** Penzenskaya Oblast', W Russian Federation
145 *X9* **Serebryansk** Vostochnyy Kazakhstan, E Kazakhstan
123 *Q12* **Serebryanyy Bor** Respublika Sakha (Yakutiya), NE Russian Federation
111 *H20* **Sered'** *Hung.* Szered. Trnavský Kraj, W Slovakia
117 *S1* **Seredyna-Buda** Sums'ka Oblast', NE Ukraine
118 *E13* **Seredžius** Tauragė, C Lithuania
136 *I14* **Şereflikoçhisar** Ankara, C Turkey
106 *D7* **Seregno** Lombardia, N Italy
103 *P7* **Serein** ≈ C France
168 *K9* **Seremban** Negeri Sembilan, Peninsular Malaysia
81 *H20* **Serengeti Plain** *plain* N Tanzania
82 *K13* **Serenje** Central, E Zambia
Seres *see* Sérres
116 *J5* **Seret** ≈ W Ukraine
Seret/Sereth *see* Siret
115 *I21* **Serfopoúla** *island* Kykládes, Greece, Aegean Sea
127 *P4* **Sergach** Nizhegorodskaya Oblast', W Russian Federation
29 *S13* **Sergeant Bluff** Iowa, C USA
163 *P7* **Sergelen** Dornod, NE Mongolia
Sergelen *see* Tuvshinshiree
168 *H8* **Sergeulangit, Pegunungan** ▲▲ Sumatera, NW Indonesia
122 *L5* **Sergeya Kirova, Ostrova** *island* N Russian Federation
Sergeyevichi *see* Syarhyeyevichy
145 *O7* **Sergeyevka** Severnyy Kazakhstan, N Kazakhstan
Sergiopol *see* Ayagoz
59 *P16* **Sergipe** *off.* Estado de Sergipe. ◐ *state* E Brazil
Sergipe, Estado de *see* Sergipe
126 *L3* **Sergiyev Posad** Moskovskaya Oblast', W Russian Federation
124 *K5* **Sergozero, Ozero** ◎ NW Russian Federation
146 *J17* **Serhetabat** *prev. Rus.* Gushgy, Kushka. Mary Welaýaty, S Turkmenistan
169 *Q10* **Serian** Sarawak, East Malaysia
115 *I21* **Sérifos** *anc.* Seriphos. *island* Kykládes, Greece, Aegean Sea
115 *I21* **Sérifou, Stenó** *strait* SE Greece
136 *F16* **Serik** Antalya, SW Turkey
106 *E7* **Serio** ≈ N Italy
Seriphos *see* Sérifos
Serir Tibesti *see* Sarīr Tibistī
Sêrkog *see* Sêrtar
127 *S5* **Sernovodsk** Samarskaya Oblast', W Russian Federation
127 *R2* **Sernur** Respublika Mariy El, W Russian Federation
110 *M11* **Serock** Mazowieckie, C Poland
61 *B18* **Serodino** Santa Fe, C Argentina
Seroei *see* Serui
105 *P14* **Serón** Andalucía, S Spain
99 *E14* **Serooskerke** Zeeland, SW Netherlands
105 *T6* **Seròs** Cataluña, NE Spain
122 *G10* **Serov** Sverdlovskaya Oblast', C Russian Federation
83 *I19* **Serowe** Central, SE Botswana
104 *H13* **Serpa** Beja, S Portugal
Serpa Pinto *see* Menongue
182 *A4* **Serpentine Lakes** *salt lake* South Australia
45 *T15* **Serpent's Mouth, The** *Sp.* Boca de la Serpiente. *strait* Trinidad and Tobago/Venezuela
Serpiente, Boca de la *see* Serpent's Mouth, The
126 *K4* **Serpukhov** Moskovskaya Oblast', W Russian Federation
60 *K13* **Serra do Mar** ▲▲
Sérrai *see* Sérres
107 *N22* **Serra San Bruno** Calabria, SW Italy
103 *S14* **Serres** Hautes-Alpes, SE France
114 *H13* **Sérres** *var.* Seres; *prev.* Sérrai. Kentrikí Makedonía, NE Greece
62 *J9* **Serrezuela** Córdoba, C Argentina
59 *O16* **Serrinha** Bahia, E Brazil
59 *M19* **Serro** *var.* Sêrro. Minas Gerais, NE Brazil
Sêrro *see* Serro
Sert *see* Siirt
104 *H9* **Sertã** *var.* Sertá. Castelo Branco, C Portugal
Sertá *see* Sertã
60 *L8* **Sertãozinho** São Paulo, S Brazil
160 *F7* **Sêrtar** *var.* Sêrkog. Sichuan, C China
171 *W13* **Serui** *prev.* Seroei. Papua, E Indonesia
83 *J19* **Serule** Central, E Botswana
169 *S12* **Seruyan, Sungai** *var.* Sungai Pembuang. ≈ Borneo, N Indonesia
115 *E14* **Sérvia** Dytikí Makedonía, N Greece
160 *E7* **Sêrxü** *var.* Jugar. Sichuan, C China
123 *R13* **Seryshevo** Amurskaya Oblast', SE Russian Federation
Sesana *see* Sežana
169 *V8* **Sesayap, Sungai** ≈ Borneo, N Indonesia
Sesdlets *see* Siedlce
79 *N17* **Sese** Orientale, N Dem. Rep. Congo
81 *F18* **Sese Islands** *island group* S Uganda
83 *H16* **Sesheke** *var.* Sesheko. Western, SE Zambia
Sesheko *see* Sesheke
106 *C8* **Sesia** *anc.* Sessites. ≈ NW Italy
104 *F11* **Sesimbra** Setúbal, S Portugal
115 *N22* **Seskliό** *island* Dodekánisa, Greece, Aegean Sea
30 *L16* **Sesser** Illinois, N USA
Sessites *see* Sesia
106 *G11* **Sesto Fiorentino** Toscana, C Italy
106 *E7* **Sesto San Giovanni** Lombardia, N Italy
106 *A8* **Sestriere** Piemonte, NE Italy
106 *D10* **Sestri Levante** Liguria, NW Italy
107 *C20* **Sestu** Sardegna, Italy, C Mediterranean Sea
112 *E8* **Sesvete** Zagreb, N Croatia
118 *G12* **Šeta** Kaunas, C Lithuania
Setabis *see* Xátiva
165 *Q4* **Setana** Hokkaidō, NE Japan
103 *Q16* **Sète** *prev.* Cette. Hérault, S France
58 *J11* **Sete Ilhas** Amapá, NE Brazil
59 *L20* **Sete Lagoas** Minas Gerais, NE Brazil
60 *G10* **Sete Quedas, Ilha das** *island* S Brazil
92 *I10* **Setermoen** Troms, N Norway
95 *E17* **Setesdal** *valley* S Norway
43 *W16* **Setetule, Cerro** ▲ SE Panama
21 *Q5* **Seth** West Virginia, NE USA
Setia *see* Sezze
74 *K5* **Sétif** *var.* Stif. N Algeria
164 *L5* **Seto** Aichi, Honshū, SW Japan
164 *G13* **Seto-naikai** *Eng.* Inland Sea. *sea* S Japan
165 *V16* **Setouchi** *var.* Setoushi. Kagoshima, Amami-Ō-shima, SW Japan
Setoushi *see* Setouchi
74 *F6* **Settat** W Morocco
79 *D20* **Setté Cama** Ogooué-Maritime, SW Gabon
9 *W13* **Setting Lake** ◎ Manitoba, C Canada
97 *L16* **Settle** N England, UK
189 *Y12* **Settlement** E Wake Island
104 *F11* **Setúbal** *Eng.* Saint Ubes, Saint Yves. Setúbal, W Portugal
104 *F11* **Setúbal** ◐ *district* S Portugal
104 *F12* **Setúbal, Baía de** *bay* W Portugal
Setul *see* Satun
12 *B10* **Seul, Lac** ◎ Ontario, S Canada
103 *R8* **Seurre** Côte d'Or, C France
137 *U11* **Sevan** C Armenia
137 *V12* **Sevana Lich** *Eng.* Lake Sevan, *Rus.* Ozero Sevan. ◎ E Armenia
Sevan, Lake/Sevan, Ozero *see* Sevana Lich
77 *N11* **Sévaré** Mopti, C Mali
117 *S14* **Sevastopol'** *Eng.* Sebastopol. Respublika Krym, S Ukraine
25 *R14* **Seven Sisters** Texas, SW USA
10 *K13* **Seven Sisters Peaks** ▲ British Columbia, SW Canada
99 *M15* **Sevenum** Limburg, SE Netherlands
103 *P14* **Séverac-le-Château** Aveyron, S France
14 *H13* **Severn** ≈ Ontario, S Canada
97 *L21* **Severn** *Wel.* Hafren. ≈ England/Wales, UK
125 *O11* **Severnaya Dvina** *var.* Northern Dvina. ≈ NW Russian Federation
127 *N16* **Severnaya Osetiya-Alaniya, Respublika** *Eng.* North Ossetia; *prev.* Respublika Severnaya Osetiya, Severo-Osetinskaya SSR. ◐ *autonomous republic* SW Russian Federation
Severnaya Osetiya, Respublika *see* Severnaya Osetiya-Alaniya, Respublika
122 *M5* **Severnaya Zemlya** *var.* Nicholas II Land. *island group* N Russian Federation
127 *T5* **Severnoye** Orenburgskaya Oblast', W Russian Federation
35 *S3* **Severn Troughs Range** ▲▲ Nevada, W USA
125 *W3* **Severnyy** Respublika Komi, NW Russian Federation
144 *I13* **Severnyy Chink Ustyurta** ▲▲ W Kazakhstan
125 *Q13* **Severnyye Uvaly** *var.* Northern Ural Hills. *hill range* NW Russian Federation
145 *O6* **Severnyy Kazakhstan** *off.* Severo-Kazakhstanskaya Oblast', *var.* North Kazakhstan, *Kaz.* Soltüstik Qazaqstan Oblysy. ◐ *province* N Kazakhstan
125 *V9* **Severnyy Ural** ▲▲ NW Russian Federation
Severo-Alichurskiy Khrebet *see* Alichuri Shimolí, Qatorkŭhi
123 *N12* **Severobaykal'sk** Respublika Buryatiya, S Russian Federation
Severodonetsk *see* Syeverodonets'k
124 *M8* **Severodvinsk** *prev.* Molotov, Sudostroy. Arkhangel'skaya Oblast', NW Russian Federation
Severo-Kazakhstanskaya Oblast' *see* Severnyy Kazakhstan
123 *U11* **Severo-Kuril'sk** Sakhalinskaya Oblast', SE Russian Federation
124 *J3* **Severomorsk** Murmanskaya Oblast', NW Russian Federation
Severo-Osetinskaya SSR *see* Severnaya Osetiya-Alaniya, Respublika
122 *M7* **Severo-Sibirskaya Nizmennost'** *var.* North Siberian Plain, *Eng.* North Siberian Lowland. *lowlands* N Russian Federation
122 *G10* **Severoural'sk** Sverdlovskaya Oblast', C Russian Federation
122 *L11* **Severo-Yeniseyskiy** Krasnoyarskiy Kray, C Russian Federation
122 *J12* **Seversk** Tomskaya Oblast', C Russian Federation
126 *M11* **Severskiy Donets** *Ukr.* Sivers'kyy Donets'. ≈ Russian Federation/Ukraine *see also* Sivers'kyy Donets'
Severskiy Donets *see* Sivers'kyy Donets'
92 *M9* **Sevettijärvi** Lappi, N Finland
36 *M5* **Sevier Bridge Reservoir** ⊠ Utah, W USA
36 *J4* **Sevier Desert** *plain* Utah, W USA
36 *J5* **Sevier Lake** ◎ Utah, W USA
21 *N9* **Sevierville** Tennessee, S USA
104 *J14* **Sevilla** *Eng.* Seville; *anc.* Hispalis. Andalucía, SW Spain
104 *J13* **Sevilla** ◐ *province* Andalucía, SW Spain
Sevilla de Niefang *see* Niefang
43 *O16* **Sevilla, Isla** *island* SW Panama
Seville *see* Sevilla
114 *J9* **Sevlievo** Gabrovo, N Bulgaria
Sevluš/Sevlyush *see* Vynohradiv
109 *V11* **Sevnica** *Ger.* Lichtenwald. E Slovenia
162 *J11* **Sevrey** *var.* Saynshand. Ömnögovĭ, S Mongolia
126 *I7* **Sevsk** Bryanskaya Oblast', W Russian Federation
76 *J15* **Sewa** ≈ E Sierra Leone
39 *R12* **Seward** Alaska, USA
29 *R15* **Seward** Nebraska, C USA
10 *G8* **Seward Glacier** *glacier* Yukon Territory, W Canada
197 *Q3* **Seward Peninsula** *peninsula* Alaska, USA
Seward's Folly *see* Alaska
62 *H12* **Sewell** Libertador, C Chile
98 *K5* **Sexbierum** *Fris.* Seisbierrum. Friesland, N Netherlands
9 *O13* **Sexsmith** Alberta, W Canada
41 *W13* **Seybaplaya** Campeche, SE Mexico
173 *N6* **Seychelles** *off.* Republic of Seychelles. ◆ *republic* W Indian Ocean
67 *Z9* **Seychelles** *island group* NE Seychelles
173 *N6* **Seychelles Bank** *var.* Le Banc des Seychelles. *undersea feature* W Indian Ocean
Seychelles, Le Banc des *see* Seychelles Bank
Seychelles, Republic of *see* Seychelles
172 *H17* **Seychellois, Morne** ▲ Mahé, NE Seychelles
92 *L2* **Seydhisfjördhur** Austurland, E Iceland
146 *J12* **Seýdi** *Rus.* Seydi; *prev.* Neftezavodsk. Lebap Welaýaty, E Turkmenistan
136 *G16* **Seydişehir** Konya, SW Turkey
136 *F15* **Seyfe Gölü** ◎ C Turkey
Seyhan *see* Adana
136 *K16* **Seyhan Barajı** ⊠ S Turkey
136 *K17* **Seyhan Nehri** ≈ S Turkey
136 *F12* **Seyitgazi** Eskişehir, W Turkey
126 *J7* **Seym** ≈ W Russian Federation
117 *S3* **Seym** ≈ N Ukraine
123 *T9* **Seymchan** Magadanskaya Oblast', E Russian Federation
114 *N12* **Seymen** Tekirdağ, NW Turkey
183 *O11* **Seymour** Victoria, SE Australia
83 *I25* **Seymour** Eastern Cape, S South Africa
29 *W16* **Seymour** Iowa, C USA
27 *U7* **Seymour** Missouri, C USA
25 *Q5* **Seymour** Texas, SW USA
114 *M12* **Şeytan Deresi** ≈ NW Turkey
109 *S12* **Sežana** *It.* Sesana. SW Slovenia
103 *P5* **Sézanne** Marne, N France
107 *I16* **Sezze** *anc.* Setia. Lazio, C Italy
Sfákia *see* Chóra Sfakíon
115 *D21* **Sfaktiria** *island* S Greece
116 *J11* **Sfântu Gheorghe** *Ger.* Sankt-Georgen, *Hung.* Sepsiszentgyörgy; *prev.* Şepşi-Sângeorz, Sfintu Gheorghe. Covasna, C Romania
117 *N13* **Sfântu Gheorghe, Braţul** *var.* Gheorghe Braţul. ≈ E Romania
75 *N6* **Sfax** *Ar.* Şafāqis. E Tunisia
75 *N6* **Sfax** ✈ E Tunisia
Sfintu Gheorghe *see* Sfântu Gheorghe
98 *H13* **'s-Gravendeel** Zuid-Holland, SW Netherlands
98 *F11* **'s-Gravenhage** *var.* Den Haag, *Eng.* The Hague, *Fr.* La Haye. ● (Netherlands-seat of government) Zuid-Holland, W Netherlands
98 *G12* **'s-Gravenzande** Zuid-Holland, W Netherlands
Shaan/Shaanxi Sheng *see* Shaanxi
159 *X11* **Shaanxi** *var.* Shaan, Shaanxi Sheng, Shan-hsi, Shenshi, Shensi. ◐ *province* C China
Shaartuz *see* Shahrtuz
Shaba *see* Katanga
Shabani *see* Zvishavane
81 *N17* **Shabeellaha Dhexe** *off.* Gobolka Shabeellaha Dhexe. ◐ *region* E Somalia
Shabeellaha Dhexe, Gobolka *see* Shabeellaha Dhexe
81 *L17* **Shabeellaha Hoose** *off.* Gobolka Shabeellaha Hoose. ◐ *region* S Somalia
Shabeellaha Hoose, Gobolka *see* Shabeellaha Hoose
Shabeelle, Webi *see* Shebeli
114 *O7* **Shabla** Dobrich, NE Bulgaria
114 *O7* **Shabla, Nos** *headland* NE Bulgaria
13 *N9* **Shabogama Lake** ◎ Newfoundland and Labrador, E Canada
79 *N20* **Shabunda** Sud Kivu, E Dem. Rep. Congo
141 *Q15* **Shabwah** C Yemen
158 *F8* **Shache** *var.* Yarkant. Xinjiang Uygur Zizhiqu, NW China
Shacheng *see* Huailai
195 *R12* **Shackleton Coast** *physical region* Antarctica
195 *Z10* **Shackleton Ice Shelf** *ice shelf* Antarctica

◆ Country ● Country Capital ◇ Dependent Territory ○ Dependent Territory Capital ◐ Administrative Regions ✈ International Airport ▲ Mountain ▲▲ Mountain Range Volcano ◎ Lake ≈ River ⊠ Reservoir

SHADDĀDĪ – SHISANJIANFANG

Shaddādī *see* Ash Shadādah
28 K7 **Shadehill Reservoir** ⊠ South Dakota, N USA
122 G11 **Shadrinsk** Kurganskaya Oblast', C Russian Federation
31 O12 **Shafer, Lake** ⊠ Indiana, N USA
35 R13 **Shafter** California, W USA
24 J11 **Shafter** Texas, SW USA
97 L23 **Shaftesbury** S England, UK
185 F22 **Shag** ≈ South Island, New Zealand
145 V9 **Shagan** ≈ E Kazakhstan
39 O11 **Shageluk** Alaska, USA
122 K14 **Shagonar** Respublika Tyva, S Russian Federation
185 F22 **Shag Point** *headland* South Island, New Zealand
144 J12 **Shagyray, Plato** *plain* SW Kazakhstan
Shāhābād *see* Eslāmābād
168 K9 **Shah Alam** Selangor, Peninsular Malaysia
117 O12 **Shahany, Ozero** ◎ SW Ukraine
138 H9 **Shahbā'** *anc.* Philippopolis. As Suwaydā', S Syria
Shahbān *see* Ad Dayr
149 P17 **Shāhbandar** Sind, SE Pakistan
149 P13 **Shāhdād Kot** Sind, SW Pakistan
143 T10 **Shahdād, Namakzār-e** *salt pan* E Iran
149 Q15 **Shāhdādpur** Sind, SE Pakistan
154 K10 **Shahdol** Madhya Pradesh, C India
161 N7 **Sha He** ≈ C China
Shahepu *see* Linze
153 N13 **Shāhganj** Uttar Pradesh, N India
152 C11 **Shāhgarh** Rājasthān, NW India
Sha Hi *see* Orūmīyeh, Daryācheh-ye
Shāhī *see* Qā'emshahr
139 Q6 **Shāhimah** *var.* Shahma. C Iraq
Shahjahanabad *see* Delhi
152 L11 **Shāhjahānpur** Uttar Pradesh, N India
Shahma *see* Shāhimah
149 U7 **Shāhpur** Punjab, E Pakistan
Shāhpur *see* Shāhpur Chākar
152 G13 **Shāhpura** Rājasthān, N India
149 Q15 **Shāhpur Chākar** *var.* Shāhpur. Sind, SE Pakistan
148 M5 **Shahrak** Ghowr, C Afghanistan
143 Q11 **Shahr-e Bābak** Kermān, C Iran
143 N8 **Shahr-e Kord** *var.* Shahr Kord. Chahār MaḨall va Bakhtīārī, C Iran
143 O9 **Shahreẓā** *var.* Qomisheh, Qumisheh, Shahriza; *prev.* Qomsheh. Eṣfahān, C Iran
147 S10 **Shahrikhon** *Rus.* Shakhrikhan. Andijon Viloyati, E Uzbekistan
147 P11 **Shahriston** *Rus.* Shakhristan. NW Tajikistan
Shahriza *see* Shahreẓā
Shahr-i-Zabul *see* Zābol
Shahr Kord *see* Shahr-e Kord
147 P14 **Shahrtuz** *Rus.* Shaartuz. SW Tajikistan
143 Q4 **Shāhrūd** *prev.* Emāmrūd, Emāmshahr. Semnān, N Iran
Shahsavār/Shahsawar *see* Tonekābon
Shaidara *see* Step' Nardara
Shaikh Ābid *see* Shaykh 'Ābid
Shaikh Fāris *see* Shaykh Fāris
Shaikh Najm *see* Shaykh Najm
138 K5 **Sha'īr, Jabal** ▲ C Syria
154 G10 **Shājāpur** Madhya Pradesh, C India
80 J8 **Shakal, Ras** *headland* NE Sudan
83 G17 **Shakawe** North West, NW Botswana
Shakhdarinskiy Khrebet *see* Shokhdara, Qatorkŭhi
Shakhrikhan *see* Shahrikhon
Shakhrisabz *see* Sharixon
Shakhristan *see* Shahriston
117 X8 **Shakhtars'k** *Rus.* Shakhtërsk. Donets'ka Oblast', SE Ukraine
Shakhtërsk *see* Shakhtars'k
145 R10 **Shakhtinsk** Karaganda, C Kazakhstan
126 L11 **Shakhty** Rostovskaya Oblast', SW Russian Federation
127 P2 **Shakhun'ya** Nizhegorodskaya Oblast', W Russian Federation
77 S15 **Shaki** Oyo, W Nigeria
81 J15 **Shakiso** Oromo, C Ethiopia
117 X8 **Shakmars'k** Donets'ka Oblast', E Ukraine
29 V9 **Shakopee** Minnesota, N USA
165 R3 **Shakotan-misaki** *headland* Hokkaidō, NE Japan
39 N9 **Shaktoolik** Alaska, USA
81 J14 **Shala Hāyk'** ◎ C Ethiopia
124 M10 **Shalakusha** Arkhangel'skaya Oblast', NW Russian Federation
145 U8 **Shalday** Pavlodar, NE Kazakhstan
127 P16 **Shali** Chechenskaya Respublika, SW Russian Federation
141 W12 **Shalim** *var.* Shelim. S Oman
Shaliuhe *see* Gangca
144 K12 **Shalkar** *var.* Chelkar. Aktyubinsk, W Kazakhstan
144 F9 **Shalkar, Ozero** *prev* Chelkar Ozero. ◎ W Kazakhstan
21 V12 **Shallotte** North Carolina, SE USA
25 N5 **Shallowater** Texas, SW USA
124 K11 **Shal'skiy** Respublika Kareliya, NW Russian Federation
160 F9 **Shaluli Shan** ▲▲ C China
81 F22 **Shama** ≈ C Tanzania
9 Z11 **Shamattawa** Manitoba, C Canada
12 F8 **Shamattawa** ≈ Ontario, C Canada
Shām, Bādiyat ash *see* Syrian Desert
Shamiya *see* Ash Shāmīyah
141 X8 **Shām, Jabal ash** *var.* Jebel Sham. ▲ NW Oman
Sham, Jebel *see* Shām, Jabal ash
Shamkhor *see* Şämkir
18 G14 **Shamokin** Pennsylvania, NE USA
25 P2 **Shamrock** Texas, SW USA
Sha'nabī, Jabal ash *see* Chambi, Jebel
139 Y12 **Shanāwah** E Iraq
Shancheng *see* Taining
159 T8 **Shandan** Gansu, N China
Shandī *see* Shendi
161 Q5 **Shandong** *var.* Lu, Shandong Sheng, Shantung. ◈ *province* E China
161 R4 **Shandong Bandao** *var.* Shantung Peninsula. *peninsula* E China
Shandong Sheng *see* Shandong
139 U8 **Shandrūkh** E Iraq
83 J17 **Shangani** ≈ W Zimbabwe
161 O15 **Shangchuan Dao** *island* S China
Shangchuankou *see* Minhe
163 P12 **Shangdu** Nei Mongol Zizhiqu, N China
161 O11 **Shanggao** *var.* Aoyang. Jiangxi, S China
161 S8 **Shanghai** *var.* Shang-hai. Shanghai Shi, E China
161 S8 **Shanghai Shi** *var.* Hu, Shanghai. ◈ *municipality* E China
161 P13 **Shanghang** Fujian, SE China
160 K14 **Shanglin** *var.* Dafeng. Guangxi Zhuangzu Zizhiqu, S China
160 L7 **Shangluo** *var.* Shangxian. Shaanxi, C China
160 L7 **Shangluo** *var.* Shangxian, Shangzhou. Shaanxi, C China
83 G15 **Shangombo** Western, W Zambia
Shangpai/Shangpaihe *see* Feixi
161 O6 **Shangqiu** *var.* Zhuji. Henan, C China
161 Q10 **Shangrao** Jiangxi, S China
Shangxian *see* Shangluo
Shangxian *see* Shangluo
161 S9 **Shangyu** *var.* Baiguan. Zhejiang, SE China
163 X9 **Shangzhi** Heilongjiang, NE China
Shangzhou *see* Shangluo
Shanhe *see* Zhengning
163 W9 **Shanhetun** Heilongjiang, NE China
Shan-hsi *see* Shaanxi, China
Shan-hsi *see* Shanxi, China
159 O6 **Shankou** Xinjiang Uygur Zizhiqu, W China
184 M13 **Shannon** Manawatu-Wanganui, North Island, New Zealand
97 C17 **Shannon** *Ir.* An tSionainn. ≈ W Ireland
97 B19 **Shannon** ✈ W Ireland
167 N6 **Shan Plateau** *plateau* E Burma (Myanmar)
158 M6 **Shanshan** *var.* Piqan. Xinjiang Uygur Zizhiqu, NW China
Shansi *see* Shanxi
167 N5 **Shan State** ◈ *state* E Burma (Myanmar)
Shantar Islands *see* Shantarskiye Ostrova
123 S12 **Shantarskiye Ostrova** *Eng.* Shantar Islands. *island group* E Russian Federation
161 Q14 **Shantou** *var.* Shan-t'ou, Swatow. Guangdong, S China
Shan-t'ou *see* Shantou
Shantung *see* Shandong
Shantung Peninsula *see* Shandong Bandao
163 O14 **Shanxi** *var.* Jin, Shan-hsi, Shansi, Shanxi Sheng. ◈ *province* C China
161 P6 **Shanxian** *var.* Shan Xian. Shandong, E China
Shan Xian *see* Sanmenxia
Shan Xian *see* Shanxian
Shanxi Sheng *see* Shanxi
160 L7 **Shanyang** Shaanxi, C China
161 N13 **Shanyin** *var.* Daiyue. Shanxi, C China E Asia
161 O13 **Shaoguan** *var.* Shao-kuan, *Cant.* Kukong; *prev.* Ch'u-chiang. Guangdong, S China
Shao-kuan *see* Shaoguan
161 Q11 **Shaowu** Fujian, SE China
161 S9 **Shaoxing** Zhejiang, SE China
160 M12 **Shaoyang** *var.* Tangdukou. Hunan, S China
160 M11 **Shaoyang** *var.* Baoqing, Shao-yang; *prev.* Pao-king. Hunan, S China
Shao-yang *see* Shaoyang
96 K5 **Shapinsay** *island* NE Scotland, UK
125 S4 **Shapkina** ≈ NW Russian Federation
Shāpūr *see* Salmās
158 M4 **Shaqiuhe** Xinjiang Uygur Zizhiqu, W China
139 T2 **Shaqlāwa** *var.* Shaqlāwah. E Iraq
Shaqlāwah *see* Shaqlāwa
138 I8 **Shaqqā** As Suwaydā', S Syria
141 P7 **Shaqrā'** Ar Riyāḍ, C Saudi Arabia
Shaqrā *see* Shuqrah
145 W10 **Shar** *var.* Charsk. Vostochnyy Kazakhstan, E Kazakhstan
149 O6 **Sharan** Dāikondī, SE Afghanistan
149 Q7 **Sharan** *var.* Zareh Sharan. Paktīkā, E Afghanistan
Sharaqpur *see* Sharqpur
Sharbaqty *see* Shcherbakty
141 X12 **Sharbatāt** S Oman
Sharbatāt, Ra's *see* Sharbithāt, Ras
141 X12 **Sharbithāt, Ras** *var.* Ra's Sharbatāt. *headland* S Oman
14 K14 **Sharbot Lake** Ontario, SE Canada
145 P17 **Shardara** *var.* Chardara. Yuzhnyy Kazakhstan, S Kazakhstan
Shardara Dalasy *see* Step' Nardara
162 F8 **Sharga** Govĭ-Altay, W Mongolia
Sharga *see* Tsagaan-Uul
116 M7 **Sharhorod** Vinnyts'ka Oblast', C Ukraine
Sharhulsan *see* Mandal-Ovoo
165 V3 **Shari** Hokkaidō, NE Japan
Shari *see* Chari
139 T6 **Shārī, Buḩayrat** ◎ C Iraq
147 N12 **Sharixon** *Rus.* Shakhrisabz. Qashqadaryo Viloyati, S Uzbekistan
Sharjah *see* Ash Shāriqah
118 K12 **Sharkawshchyna** *var.* Sharkowshchyna, *Pol.* Szarkowszczyzna, *Rus.* Sharkovshchina. Vitsyebskaya Voblasts', NW Belarus
180 G9 **Shark Bay** *bay* Western Australia
141 Y9 **Sharkh** E Oman
Sharkovshchina/Sharkowshchyna *see* Sharkawshchyna
127 U6 **Sharlyk** Orenburgskaya Oblast', W Russian Federation
Sharm ash Shaykh *see* Sharm el Sheikh
75 Y9 **Sharm el Sheikh** *var.* Ofiral, Sharm ash Shaykh. E Egypt
18 B13 **Sharon** Pennsylvania, NE USA
26 H4 **Sharon Springs** Kansas, C USA
31 Q14 **Sharonville** Ohio, N USA
Sharourah *see* Sharūrah
29 O10 **Sharpe, Lake** ⊠ South Dakota, N USA
Sharqī, Al Jabal ash/Sharqi, Jebel esh *see* Anti-Lebanon
Sharqīyah, Al Minṭaqah ash *see* Ash Sharqīyah
138 I6 **Sharqīyat an Nabk, Jabal** ▲ W Syria
149 W8 **Sharqpur** *var.* Sharaqpur. Punjab, E Pakistan
141 Q13 **Sharūrah** *var.* Sharourah. Najrān, S Saudi Arabia
125 O14 **Shar'ya** Kostromskaya Oblast', NW Russian Federation
145 V15 **Sharyn** *var.* Charyn. ≈ SE Kazakhstan
Sharyn *see* Charyn
83 J18 **Shashe** Central, NE Botswana
83 J18 **Shashe** *var.* Shashi. ≈ Botswana/Zimbabwe
81 J14 **Shashemenē** *var.* Shashemenne, Shashhamana, *It.* Sciasciamana. Oromo, C Ethiopia
Shashemenne/Shashhamana *see* Shashemenē
Shashi *see* Shashe
Shashi/Sha-shih/Shasi *see* Jingzhou, Hubei
35 N3 **Shasta Lake** ⊠ California, W USA
35 N2 **Shasta, Mount** ▲ California, W USA
127 O4 **Shatki** Nizhegorodskaya Oblast', W Russian Federation
Shatlyk *see* Şatlyk
Shatra *see* Ash Shaṭrah
119 K17 **Shatsk** *Rus.* Shatsk. Minskaya Voblasts', C Belarus
127 N5 **Shatsk** Ryazanskaya Oblast', W Russian Federation
26 J9 **Shattuck** Oklahoma, C USA
145 P16 **Shaul'der** Yuzhnyy Kazakhstan, S Kazakhstan
9 S17 **Shaunavon** Saskatchewan, S Canada
Shavat *see* Shovot
158 K4 **Shawan** Xinjiang Uygur Zizhiqu, NW China
14 G12 **Shawanaga** Ontario, S Canada
30 M6 **Shawano** Wisconsin, N USA
30 M6 **Shawano Lake** ◎ Wisconsin, N USA
15 P10 **Shawinigan** *prev.* Shawinigan Falls. Québec, SE Canada
Shawinigan Falls *see* Shawinigan
15 P10 **Shawinigan-Sud** Québec, SE Canada
138 J5 **Shawmarīyah, Jabal ash** ▲▲ C Syria
27 O11 **Shawnee** Oklahoma, C USA
14 K12 **Shawville** Québec, SE Canada
145 Q16 **Shayan** *var.* Chayan. Yuzhnyy Kazakhstan, S Kazakhstan
Shaykh *see* Ash Shakk
139 W9 **Shaykh 'Ābid** *var.* Shaikh Ābid. E Iraq
139 Y10 **Shaykh Fāris** *var.* Shaikh Fāris. E Iraq
139 T7 **Shaykh Ḥātim** E Iraq
Shaykh, Jabal ash *see* Hermon, Mount
139 X10 **Shaykh Najm** *var.* Shaikh Najm. E Iraq
139 W9 **Shaykh Sa'd** E Iraq
147 T14 **Shazud** SE Tajikistan
119 N18 **Shchadryn** *Rus.* Shchedrin. Homyel'skaya Voblasts', SE Belarus
119 H18 **Shchara** ≈ SW Belarus
Shchedrin *see* Shchadryn
Shcheglovsk *see* Kemerovo
126 K5 **Shchëkino** Tul'skaya Oblast', W Russian Federation
125 S7 **Shchel'yayur** Respublika Komi, NW Russian Federation
145 U8 **Shcherbakty** *Kaz.* Sharbaqty. Pavlodar, E Kazakhstan
126 K7 **Shchigry** Kurskaya Oblast', W Russian Federation
Shchitkovichi *see* Shchytkavichy
117 Q2 **Shchors** Chernihivs'ka Oblast', N Ukraine
117 T8 **Shchors'k** Dnipropetrovs'ka Oblast', E Ukraine
Shchuchin *see* Shchuchyn
145 Q7 **Shchuchinsk** *prev.* Shchuchye. Akmola, N Kazakhstan
Shchuchye *see* Shchuchinsk
119 G16 **Shchuchyn** *Pol.* Szczuczyn Nowogródzki, *Rus.* Shchuchin. Hrodzyenskaya Voblasts', W Belarus
119 K17 **Shchytkavichy** *Rus.* Shchitkovichi. Minskaya Voblasts', C Belarus
122 J13 **Shebalino** Respublika Altay, S Russian Federation
126 J9 **Shebekino** Belgorodskaya Oblast', W Russian Federation
Shebelē Wenz, Wabē *see* Shebeli
81 L14 **Shebeli** *Amh.* Wabē Shebelē Wenz, *It.* Scebeli, *Som.* Webi Shabeelle. ≈ Ethiopia/Somalia
113 M20 **Shebenikut, Maja e** ▲ E Albania
149 N2 **Sheberghān** *var.* Shibarghān, Shiberghan, Shiberghān. Jowzjān, N Afghanistan
144 F14 **Shebir** Mangistau, SW Kazakhstan
31 N8 **Sheboygan** Wisconsin, N USA
77 X15 **Shebshi Mountains** *var.* Schebschi Mountains. ▲▲ E Nigeria
Shechem *see* Nablus
Shedadi *see* Ash Shadādah
13 P14 **Shediac** New Brunswick, SE Canada
126 L15 **Shedok** Krasnodarskiy Kray, SW Russian Federation
80 N12 **Sheekh** Togdheer, N Somalia
38 M11 **Sheenjek River** ≈ Alaska, USA
96 D13 **Sheep Haven** *Ir.* Cuan na gCaorach. *inlet* N Ireland
35 X10 **Sheep Range** ▲▲ Nevada, W USA
98 M13 **'s-Heerenberg** Gelderland, E Netherlands
97 P22 **Sheerness** SE England, UK
13 Q15 **Sheet Harbour** Nova Scotia, SE Canada
185 H18 **Sheffield** Canterbury, South Island, New Zealand
97 M18 **Sheffield** N England, UK
23 O2 **Sheffield** Alabama, S USA
29 V12 **Sheffield** Iowa, C USA
25 N10 **Sheffield** Texas, SW USA
63 H22 **Shehuen, Río** ≈ S Argentina
Shekhem *see* Nablus
149 V8 **Shekhūpura** Punjab, NE Pakistan
Sheki *see* Şäki
124 L14 **Sheksna** Vologodskaya Oblast', NW Russian Federation
123 T5 **Shelagskiy, Mys** *cape* NE Russian Federation
27 V3 **Shelbina** Missouri, C USA
13 P16 **Shelburne** Nova Scotia, SE Canada
14 G14 **Shelburne** Ontario, S Canada
33 R7 **Shelby** Montana, NW USA
21 Q10 **Shelby** North Carolina, SE USA
31 S12 **Shelby** Ohio, N USA
30 L14 **Shelbyville** Illinois, N USA
31 P14 **Shelbyville** Indiana, N USA
20 L5 **Shelbyville** Kentucky, S USA
27 V2 **Shelbyville** Missouri, C USA
20 J10 **Shelbyville** Tennessee, S USA
25 X8 **Shelbyville** Texas, SW USA
30 L14 **Shelbyville, Lake** ⊠ Illinois, N USA
29 S12 **Sheldon** Iowa, C USA
38 M11 **Sheldons Point** Alaska, USA
Shelekhov Gulf *see* Shelikhova, Zaliv
123 U9 **Shelikhova, Zaliv** *Eng.* Shelekhov Gulf. *gulf* E Russian Federation
39 P14 **Shelikof Strait** *strait* Alaska, USA
Shelim *see* Shalīm
9 T14 **Shellbrook** Saskatchewan, S Canada
28 L3 **Shell Creek** ≈ North Dakota, N USA
Shellif *see* Chelif, Oued
22 I10 **Shell Keys** *island group* Louisiana, S USA
30 I4 **Shell Lake** Wisconsin, N USA
29 W12 **Shell Rock** Iowa, C USA
185 C26 **Shelter Point** *headland* Stewart Island, New Zealand
18 L13 **Shelton** Connecticut, NE USA
32 G8 **Shelton** Washington, NW USA
Shemakha *see* Şamaxı
145 W9 **Shemonaikha** Vostochnyy Kazakhstan, E Kazakhstan
127 Q4 **Shemursha** Chavash Respubliki, W Russian Federation
38 D16 **Shemya Island** *island* Aleutian Islands, Alaska, USA
29 T16 **Shenandoah** Iowa, C USA
21 U4 **Shenandoah** Virginia, NE USA
21 U4 **Shenandoah Mountains** *ridge* West Virginia, NE USA
21 V3 **Shenandoah River** ≈ West Virginia, NE USA
77 W15 **Shendam** Plateau, C Nigeria
80 G8 **Shendi** *var.* Shandī. River Nile, NE Sudan
76 I15 **Shenge** SW Sierra Leone
146 L10 **Shengeldi** *Rus.* Chingildi. Navoiy Viloyati, N Uzbekistan
146 L10 **Shengeldi** *Rus.* Chingildi. Navoiy Viloyati, N Uzbekistan
145 U15 **Shengel'dy** Almaty, SE Kazakhstan
113 K18 **Shëngjin** *var.* Shëngjini. Lezhë, NW Albania
Shëngjini *see* Shëngjin
Shengking *see* Liaoning
Sheng Xian/Shengxian *see* Shengzhou
161 S9 **Shengzhou** *var.* Shengxian, Sheng Xian. Zhejiang, SE China
Shenking *see* Liaoning
125 N11 **Shenkursk** Arkhangel'skaya Oblast', NW Russian Federation
160 L3 **Shenmu** Shaanxi, C China
113 L19 **Shën Noj i Madh** ▲ C Albania
160 L8 **Shennong Ding** *var.* Dashennongjia. ▲ C China
Shenshi/Shensi *see* Shaanxi
163 V12 **Shenyang** *Chin.* Shen-yang, *Eng.* Moukden, Mukden; *prev.* Fengtien. *province capital* Liaoning, NE China
Shen-yang *see* Shenyang
161 O15 **Shenzhen** Guangdong, S China
154 G8 **Sheopur** Madhya Pradesh, C India
116 L5 **Shepetivka** *Rus.* Shepetovka. Khmel'nyts'ka Oblast', NW Ukraine
Shepetovka *see* Shepetivka
25 W10 **Shepherd** Texas, SW USA
187 R14 **Shepherd Islands** *island group* C Vanuatu
20 K5 **Shepherdsville** Kentucky, S USA
183 O11 **Shepparton** Victoria, SE Australia
97 P22 **Sheppey, Isle of** *island* SE England, UK
Sherabad *see* Sherobod
97 L23 **Sherborne** S England, UK
76 H16 **Sherbro Island** *island* SW Sierra Leone
15 Q12 **Sherbrooke** Québec, SE Canada
29 T11 **Sherburn** Minnesota, N USA
78 H6 **Sherda** Borkou-Ennedi-Tibesti, N Chad
80 G7 **Shereik** River Nile, N Sudan
126 K3 **Sheremet'yevo** ✈ (Moskva) Moskovskaya Oblast', W Russian Federation
153 P14 **Shergāti** Bihār, N India
27 U12 **Sheridan** Arkansas, C USA
33 W12 **Sheridan** Wyoming, C USA
182 G8 **Sheringa** South Australia
25 U5 **Sherman** Texas, SW USA
194 J10 **Sherman Island** *island* Antarctica
19 S4 **Sherman Mills** Maine, NE USA
29 O15 **Sherman Reservoir** ⊠ Nebraska, C USA
147 N14 **Sherobod** *Rus.* Sherabad. Surkhondaryo Viloyati, S Uzbekistan
147 O13 **Sherobod** *Rus.* Sherabad. ≈ S Uzbekistan
153 T14 **Sherpur** Dhaka, N Bangladesh
37 T4 **Sherrelwood** Colorado, C USA
99 J14 **'s-Hertogenbosch** *Fr.* Bois-le-Duc, *Ger.* Herzogenbusch. Noord-Brabant, S Netherlands
28 M2 **Sherwood** North Dakota, N USA
9 Q14 **Sherwood Park** Alberta, SW Canada
56 F13 **Sheshea, Río** ≈ E Peru
143 T5 **Sheshtamad** Khorāsān-Razavī, NE Iran
29 S10 **Shetek, Lake** ◎ Minnesota, N USA
96 M2 **Shetland Islands** *island group* NE Scotland, UK
144 F14 **Shetpe** Mangistau, SW Kazakhstan
154 C11 **Shetrunji** ≈ W India
Shevchenko *see* Aktau
117 W5 **Shevchenkove** Kharkivs'ka Oblast', E Ukraine
81 H14 **Shewa Gīmīra** Southern, S Ethiopia
161 Q9 **Shexian** *var.* Huicheng, She Xian. Anhui, E China
She Xian *see* Shexian
161 R6 **Sheyang** *prev.* Hede. Jiangsu, E China
29 O4 **Sheyenne** North Dakota, N USA
29 P4 **Sheyenne River** ≈ North Dakota, N USA
96 G7 **Shiant Islands** *island group* NW Scotland, UK
123 U12 **Shiashkotan, Ostrov** *island* Kuril'skiye Ostrova, SE Russian Federation
31 R9 **Shiawassee River** ≈ Michigan, N USA
141 R14 **Shibām** C Yemen
Shibarghān *see* Sheberghān
165 O10 **Shibata** *var.* Sibata. Niigata, Honshū, C Japan
Shiberghan/Shiberghān *see* Sheberghān
Shibh Jazīrat Sīnā *see* Sinai
Shibīn al Kawm *see* Shibîn el Kôm
75 W8 **Shibîn el Kôm** *var.* Shibīn al Kawm. N Egypt
143 O13 **Shīb, Kūh-e** ▲▲ S Iran
12 D8 **Shibogama Lake** ◎ Ontario, C Canada
Shibotsu-jima *see* Zelënyy, Ostrov
164 B16 **Shibushi** Kagoshima, Kyūshū, SW Japan
189 U13 **Shichiyo Islands** *island group* Chuuk, C Micronesia
Shickshock Mountains *see* Chic-Chocs, Monts
145 S8 **Shiderti** *var.* Shiderty. Pavlodar, NE Kazakhstan
145 S9 **Shiderti** ≈ N Kazakhstan
Shiderty *see* Shiderti
96 G10 **Shiel, Loch** ◎ N Scotland, UK
164 J13 **Shiga** *off.* Shiga-ken, *var.* Siga. ◈ *prefecture* Honshū, SW Japan
Shiga-ken *see* Shiga
Shigatse *see* Xigazê
141 U13 **Shiḩan** *oasis* NE Yemen
Shih-chia-chuang/Shihmen *see* Shijiazhuang
158 K4 **Shihezi** Xinjiang Uygur Zizhiqu, NW China
Shiichi *see* Shyichy
113 K19 **Shijak** *var.* Shijaku. Durrës, W Albania
Shijaku *see* Shijak
161 O4 **Shijiazhuang** *var.* Shih-chia-chuang; *prev.* Shihmen. *province capital* Hebei, E China
165 R5 **Shikabe** Hokkaidō, NE Japan
149 Q13 **Shikārpur** Sind, S Pakistan
127 Q7 **Shikhany** Saratovskaya Oblast', W Russian Federation
189 V12 **Shiki Islands** *island group* Chuuk, C Micronesia
164 G14 **Shikoku** *var.* Sikoku. *island* SW Japan
192 H5 **Shikoku Basin** *var.* Sikoku Basin. *undersea feature* N Philippine Sea
164 G14 **Shikoku-sanchi** ▲▲ Shikoku, SW Japan
165 X4 **Shikotan, Ostrov** *Jap.* Shikotan-tō. *island* NE Russian Federation
Shikotan-tō *see* Shikotan, Ostrov
165 R4 **Shikotsu-ko** *var.* Sikotu Ko. ◎ Hokkaidō, NE Japan
81 N15 **Shilabo** Somali, E Ethiopia
127 X7 **Shil'da** Orenburgskaya Oblast', W Russian Federation
139 V3 **Shilēr, Āw-e** ≈ E Iraq
153 S12 **Shiliguri** *prev.* Siliguri. West Bengal, NE India
Shiliu *see* Changjiang
129 V7 **Shilka** ≈ S Russian Federation
18 H15 **Shillington** Pennsylvania, NE USA
153 V13 **Shillong** *state capital* Meghālaya, NE India
126 M5 **Shilovo** Ryazanskaya Oblast', W Russian Federation
164 C14 **Shimabara** *var.* Simabara. Nagasaki, Kyūshū, SW Japan
164 C14 **Shimabara-wan** *bay* SW Japan
164 F12 **Shimane** *off.* Shimane-ken, *var.* Simane. ◈ *prefecture* Honshū, SW Japan
164 G11 **Shimane-hantō** *peninsula* Honshū, SW Japan
Shimane-ken *see* Shimane
123 Q13 **Shimanovsk** Amurskaya Oblast', SE Russian Federation
Shimbir Berris *see* Shimbiris
80 O12 **Shimbiris** *var.* Shimbir Berris. ▲ N Somalia
165 T4 **Shimizu** Hokkaidō, NE Japan
164 M14 **Shimizu** *var.* Simizu. Shizuoka, Honshū, S Japan
152 I8 **Shimla** *prev.* Simla. *state capital* Himāchal Pradesh, N India
165 N14 **Shimoda** *var.* Simoda. Shizuoka, Honshū, S Japan
165 O13 **Shimodate** *var.* Simodate. Ibaraki, Honshū, S Japan
155 F18 **Shimoga** Karnātaka, W India
164 C15 **Shimo-jima** *island* SW Japan
164 B15 **Shimo-Koshiki-jima** *island* SW Japan
81 J21 **Shimoni** Coast, S Kenya
164 D13 **Shimonoseki** *var.* Simonoseki, *hist.* Akamagaseki, Bakan. Yamaguchi, Honshū, SW Japan
124 G14 **Shimsk** Novgorodskaya Oblast', NW Russian Federation
141 W7 **Shināṣ** N Oman
148 J6 **Shīndand** Herāt, W Afghanistan
Shinei *see* Hsinying
162 H10 **Shinejinst** *var.* Dzalaa. Bayanhongor, C Mongolia
25 T12 **Shiner** Texas, SW USA
167 N1 **Shingbwiyang** Kachin State, N Burma (Myanmar)
145 W11 **Shingozha** Vostochnyy Kazakhstan, E Kazakhstan
164 J15 **Shingū** *var.* Singû. Wakayama, Honshū, SW Japan
14 F8 **Shining Tree** Ontario, S Canada
165 P9 **Shinjō** *var.* Sinzyô. Yamagata, Honshū, C Japan
96 I7 **Shin, Loch** ◎ N Scotland, UK
21 S3 **Shinnston** West Virginia, NE USA
138 I6 **Shinshār** *Fr.* Chinnchâr. Ḩimş, W Syria
Shinshū *see* Chinju
165 T4 **Shintoku** Hokkaidō, NE Japan
81 G20 **Shinyanga** Shinyanga, NW Tanzania
81 G20 **Shinyanga** ◈ *region* N Tanzania
165 Q10 **Shiogama** *var.* Siogama. Miyagi, Honshū, C Japan
164 M12 **Shiojiri** *var.* Sioziri. Nagano, Honshū, S Japan
164 I15 **Shiono-misaki** *headland* Honshū, SW Japan
165 Q12 **Shioya-zaki** *headland* Honshū, C Japan
114 J9 **Shipchenski Prokhod** *pass* C Bulgaria
160 G14 **Shiping** Yunnan, SW China
13 P13 **Shippagan** *var.* Shippegan. New Brunswick, SE Canada
Shippegan *see* Shippagan
18 F15 **Shippensburg** Pennsylvania, NE USA
37 P9 **Shiprock** New Mexico, SW USA
37 O9 **Ship Rock** ▲ New Mexico, SW USA
15 R6 **Shipshaw** ≈ Québec, SE Canada
123 V10 **Shipunskiy, Mys** *cape* E Russian Federation
160 K7 **Shiquan** Shaanxi, C China
122 K13 **Shira** Respublika Khakasiya, S Russian Federation
153 T14 **Shirajganj Ghat** *var.* Serajgonj, Sirajganj. Rajshahi, C Bangladesh
165 P12 **Shirakawa** *var.* Sirakawa. Fukushima, Honshū, C Japan
164 M13 **Shirane-san** ▲ Honshū, S Japan
165 U14 **Shiranuka** Hokkaidō, NE Japan
195 N12 **Shirase Coast** *physical region* Antarctica
165 U3 **Shirataki** Hokkaidō, NE Japan
143 O11 **Shīrāz** *var.* Shirāz. Fārs, S Iran
83 N15 **Shire** *var.* Chire. ≈ Malawi/Mozambique
Shiree *see* Tsagaanhayrhan
Shireet *see* Bayandelger
165 W3 **Shiretoko-hantō** *headland* Hokkaidō, NE Japan
165 W3 **Shiretoko-misaki** *headland* Hokkaidō, NE Japan
127 N5 **Shiringushi** Respublika Mordoviya, W Russian Federation
148 M3 **Shīrīn Tagāb** Fāryāb, N Afghanistan
149 N2 **Shīrīn Tagāb** ≈ N Afghanistan
165 R6 **Shiriya-zaki** *headland* Honshū, C Japan
144 I12 **Shirkala, Gryada** *plain* W Kazakhstan
165 P10 **Shiroishi** *var.* Siroisi. Miyagi, Honshū, C Japan
Shirokoye *see* Shyroke
165 O10 **Shirone** *var.* Sirone. Niigata, Honshū, C Japan
164 L12 **Shirotori** Gifu, Honshū, SW Japan
197 T1 **Shirshov Ridge** *undersea feature* W Bering Sea
Shirshütür/Shirshyutyur, Peski *see* Şirşütür Gumy
143 T3 **Shīrvān** *var.* Shirwān. Khorāsān, NE Iran
Shirwa, Lake *see* Chilwa, Lake
Shirwān *see* Shīrvān
159 N5 **Shisanjianfang** Xinjiang Uygur Zizhiqu, W China

◆ Country
● Country Capital
◇ Dependent Territory
○ Dependent Territory Capital
◈ Administrative Regions
✈ International Airport
▲ Mountain
▲▲ Mountain Range
Volcano
≈ River
◎ Lake
⊠ Reservoir

SÎNGEORGIU DE PĂDURE – SMITHTON

Sîngeorgiu de Pădure see Sângeorgiu de Pădure
Singeorz-Băi/Singeroz Băi see Sângeorz-Băi
116 M9 Singerei var. Sângerei; prev. Lazovsk. N Moldova
Singhaburi see Sing Buri
81 H21 Singida Singida, C Tanzania
81 G22 Singida ◈ region C Tanzania
Singidunum see Beograd
166 M2 Singkaling Hkamti Sagaing, N Burma (Myanmar)
171 N14 Singkang Sulawesi, C Indonesia
168 J11 Singkarak, Danau ◎ Sumatera, W Indonesia
169 N10 Singkawang Borneo, C Indonesia
168 M11 Singkep, Pulau island Kepulauan Lingga, W Indonesia
168 H9 Singkilbaru Sumatera, W Indonesia
183 T7 Singleton New South Wales, SE Australia
Singora see Songkhla
Singû see Shingū
Sining see Xining
107 D17 Siniscola Sardegna, Italy, C Mediterranean Sea
113 F14 Sinj Split-Dalmacija, SE Croatia
Sinjajevina see Sinjavina
139 P3 Sinjār NW Iraq
139 P2 Sinjār, Jabal ▲▲ N Iraq
Sinja/Sinjah see Singa
113 K15 Sinjavina var. Sinjajevina. ▲▲ C Montenegro
80 I7 Sinkat Red Sea, NE Sudan
Sinkiang/Sinkiang Uighur Autonomous Region see Xinjiang Uygur Zizhiqu
Sînmartin see Târnăveni
163 V13 Sinmi-do island NW North Korea
101 I18 Sinn ≈ C Germany
Sinnamarie see Sinnamary
55 Y9 Sinnamary var. Sinnamarie. N French Guiana
80 G11 Sinnar ◈ state E Sudan
Sinneh see Sanandaj
18 E13 Sinnemahoning Creek ≈ Pennsylvania, NE USA
Sînnicolau Mare see Sânnicolau Mare
Sinoe, Lacul see Sinoie, Lacul
Sinoia see Chinhoyi
117 N14 Sinoie, Lacul prev. Lacul Sinoe. lagoon SE Romania
59 H16 Sinop Mato Grosso, W Brazil
136 K10 Sinop anc. Sinope. Sinop, N Turkey
136 J10 Sinop ◈ province N Turkey
136 K10 Sinop Burnu headland N Turkey
Sinope see Sinop
Sino/Sinoe see Greenville
163 Y12 Sinp'o E North Korea
101 H20 Sinsheim Baden-Württemberg, SW Germany
Sîntana see Sântana
169 R11 Sintang Borneo, C Indonesia
99 F14 Sint Annaland Zeeland, SW Netherlands
98 L5 Sint Annaparochie Friesland, N Netherlands
45 V9 Sint Eustatius Eng. Saint Eustatius. island N Netherlands Antilles
99 G19 Sint-Genesius-Rode Fr. Rhode-Saint-Genèse. Vlaams Brabant, C Belgium
99 F16 Sint-Gillis-Waas Oost-Vlaanderen, N Belgium
99 H17 Sint-Katelijne-Waver Antwerpen, C Belgium
99 E18 Sint-Lievens-Houtem Oost-Vlaanderen, NW Belgium
45 V9 Sint Maarten Eng. Saint Martin. island N Netherlands Antilles
99 F14 Sint Maartensdijk Zeeland, SW Netherlands
99 L19 Sint-Martens-Voeren Fr. Fouron-Saint-Martin. Limburg, NE Belgium
99 J14 Sint-Michielsgestel Noord-Brabant, S Netherlands
Sîn-Miclăuș see Gheorgheni
45 O16 Sint Nicholaas S Aruba
99 F16 Sint-Niklaas Fr. Saint-Nicolas. Oost-Vlaanderen, N Belgium
99 K14 Sint-Oedenrode Noord-Brabant, S Netherlands
25 T14 Sinton Texas, SW USA
99 G14 Sint Philipsland Zeeland, SW Netherlands
99 G19 Sint-Pieters-Leeuw Vlaams Brabant, C Belgium
104 E11 Sintra prev. Cintra. Lisboa, W Portugal
99 J18 Sint-Truiden Fr. Saint-Trond. Limburg, NE Belgium
99 H14 Sint Willebrord Noord-Brabant, S Netherlands
163 V13 Sinŭiju W North Korea
80 P13 Sinujiif Nugaal, NE Somalia
Sinus Aelaniticus see Aqaba, Gulf of
Sinus Gallicus see Lion, Golfe du
Sinyang see Xinyang
Sinyavka see Sinyawka
119 I18 Sinyawka Rus. Sinyavka. Minskaya Voblasts', SW Belarus
Sinying see Hsinying
Sinyukha see Synyukha
Sinzyô see Shinjō
111 I24 Sió ≈ W Hungary
171 O7 Siocon Mindanao, S Philippines
111 I24 Siófok Somogy, Hungary
Siogama see Shiogama
83 G15 Sioma Western, SW Zambia
108 D11 Sion Ger. Sitten; anc. Sedunum. Valais, SW Switzerland
103 O11 Sioule ≈ C France
29 S12 Sioux Center Iowa, C USA
29 R13 Sioux City Iowa, C USA
29 R11 Sioux Falls South Dakota, N USA
12 B11 Sioux Lookout Ontario, S Canada
29 T12 Sioux Rapids Iowa, C USA
Sioux State see North Dakota
Sioziri see Shiojiri
171 P6 Sipalay Negros, C Philippines
55 V11 Sipaliwini ◈ district S Surinam
45 U15 Siparia Trinidad, Trinidad and Tobago
Siphnos see Sífnos
163 V11 Siping var. Ssu-p'ing, Szeping; prev. Ssu-p'ing-chieh. Jilin, NE China
9 X12 Sipiwesk Manitoba, C Canada
9 W13 Sipiwesk Lake ◎ Manitoba, C Canada
195 O11 Siple Coast physical region Antarctica
194 K12 Siple Island island Antarctica
194 K13 Siple, Mount ▲ Siple Island, Antarctica
Sipoo see Sibbo
112 G12 Šipovo ◈ Republika Srpska, W Bosnia and Herzegovina
23 O4 Sipsey River ≈ Alabama, S USA
168 I13 Sipura, Pulau island W Indonesia
0 G16 Siqueiros Fracture Zone tectonic feature E Pacific Ocean
42 L10 Siquia, Río ≈ SE Nicaragua
43 N13 Siquirres Limón, E Costa Rica
54 J5 Siquisique Lara, N Venezuela
155 G19 Sīra Karnātaka, W India
95 D16 Sira ≈ S Norway
167 P12 Siracha var. Ban Si Racha, Si Racha. Chon Buri, S Thailand
Si Racha see Siracha
107 L25 Siracusa Eng. Syracuse. Sicilia, Italy, C Mediterranean Sea
Sirajganj see Shirajganj Ghat
Sirakawa see Shirakawa
9 N14 Sir Alexander, Mount ▲ British Columbia, W Canada
137 O12 Şiran Gümüşhane, NE Turkey
77 Q12 Sirba ≈ E Burkina
143 O17 Şīr Banī Yās island W United Arab Emirates
95 D17 Sirdalsvatnet ◎ S Norway
Sir Darya/Sirdaryo see Syr Darya
147 P10 Sirdaryo Sirdaryo Viloyati, E Uzbekistan
147 O11 Sirdaryo Viloyati Rus. Syrdar'inskaya Oblast'. ◈ province E Uzbekistan
Sir Donald Sangster International Airport see Sangster
181 S3 Sir Edward Pellew Group island group Northern Territory, NE Australia
116 K8 Siret Ger. Sereth, Hung. Szeret. Suceava, N Romania
116 K8 Siret var. Siretul, Ger. Sereth, Rus. Seret, Ukr. Siret. ≈ Romania/Ukraine
Siretul see Siret
140 K3 Sirhān, Wādī as dry watercourse Jordan/Saudi Arabia
152 I8 Sirhind Punjab, N India
116 F11 Şiria Ger. Schiria. Arad, W Romania
Siria see Syria
143 S14 Sīrīk Hormozgān, SE Iran
167 P8 Sirikit Reservoir ◎ N Thailand
58 K12 Sirituba, Ilha island NE Brazil
143 R11 Sīrjān prev. Sa'īdābād. Kermān, S Iran
182 H9 Sir Joseph Banks Group island group South Australia
92 K11 Sirkka Lappi, N Finland
Sirna see Sýrna
137 R16 Şırnak Şırnak, SE Turkey
137 S16 Şırnak ◈ province SE Turkey
Siroisi see Shiroishi
155 J14 Sironcha Mahārāshtra, C India
Sirone see Shirone
Síros see Sýros
Sirotino see Sirotsina
118 M12 Sirotsina Rus. Sirotino. Vitsyebskaya Voblasts', N Belarus
152 H9 Sirsa Haryāna, NW India
173 Y17 Sir Seewoosagur Ramgoolam ✈ (port Louis) SE Mauritius
155 E18 Sirsi Karnātaka, W India
146 K12 Şirşütür Gumy var. Shirshütür, Rus. Peski Shirshyutyur. desert E Turkmenistan
Sirte see Surt
182 A2 Sir Thomas, Mount ▲ South Australia
Sirti, Gulf of see Surt, Khalīj
142 J5 Sīrvān, Rūdkhāneh-ye var. Nahr Diyālá, Sirwan. ≈ Iran/Iraq see also Diyālá, Nahr
Sīrvān, Rudkhaneh-ye see Diyālá, Nahr
118 H13 Širvintos Vilnius, SE Lithuania
Sirwan see Diyālá, Nahr/Sīrvān, Rudkhaneh-ye
9 N15 Sir Wilfrid Laurier, Mount ▲ British Columbia, SW Canada
14 M10 Sir-Wilfrid, Mont ▲ Québec, SE Canada
Sisačko-Moslavačka Županija see Sisak-Moslavina
112 E9 Sisak var. Siscia, Ger. Sissek, Hung. Sziszek; anc. Segestica. Sisak-Moslavina, C Croatia
167 R10 Si Sa Ket var. Sisaket, Sri Saket. Si Sa Ket, E Thailand
Sisaket see Si Sa Ket
112 E9 Sisak-Moslavina off. Sisačko-Moslavačka Županija. ◈ province C Croatia
167 O8 Si Satchanala Sukhothai, NW Thailand
Siscia see Sisak
83 G22 Sishen Northern Cape, NW South Africa
137 V13 Sisian SE Armenia
197 N13 Sisimiut var. Holsteinborg, Holsteinsborg, Holstenborg, Holstensborg. ◈ Kitaa, S Greenland
30 M1 Siskiwit Bay lake bay Michigan, N USA
34 L1 Siskiyou Mountains ▲▲ California/Oregon, W USA
167 Q11 Sisŏphŏn Bătdâmbâng, NW Cambodia
108 E7 Sissach Basel-Land, NW Switzerland
186 B5 Sissano Sandaun, NW Papua New Guinea
Sissek see Sisak
29 R7 Sisseton South Dakota, N USA
143 W9 Sīstān, Daryācheh-ye var. Daryācheh-ye Hāmūn, Hāmūn-e Şāberī. ◎ Afghanistan/Iran see also Şāberī, Hāmūn-e
Sīstān, Daryācheh-ye see Şāberī, Hāmūn-e
143 V12 Sīstān va Balūchestān off. Ostān-e Sīstān va Balūchestān, var. Balūchestān va Sīstān. ◈ province SE Iran
Sīstān va Balūchestān, Ostān-e see Sīstān va Balūchestān
103 T14 Sisteron Alpes-de-Haute-Provence, SE France
32 H13 Sisters Oregon, NW USA
65 G15 Sisters Peak ▲ N Ascension Island
21 R3 Sistersville West Virginia, NE USA
Sistova see Svishtov
Sitakund see Sitakunda
153 V16 Sitakunda var. Sitakund. Chittagong, SE Bangladesh
153 P12 Sītāmarhi Bihār, N India
152 L11 Sītāpur Uttar Pradesh, N India
Sitaş Cristuru see Cristuru Secuiesc
115 L25 Siteía var. Sitía. Kríti, Greece, E Mediterranean Sea
105 V6 Sitges Cataluña, NE Spain
115 H15 Sithoniá peninsula NE Greece
Sitía see Siteía
54 F4 Sitionuevo Magdalena, N Colombia
39 X13 Sitka Baranof Island, Alaska, USA
39 Q15 Sitkinak Island island Trinity Islands, Alaska, USA
166 M7 Sittang var. Sittoung. ≈ S Burma (Myanmar)
99 L17 Sittard Limburg, SE Netherlands
Sitten see Sion
108 H7 Sitter ≈ NW Switzerland
109 U10 Sittersdorf Kärnten, S Austria
Sittoung see Sittang
166 K6 Sittwe var. Akyab. Arakan State, W Burma (Myanmar)
42 L8 Siuna Región Autónoma Atlántico Norte, NE Nicaragua
153 R15 Siuri West Bengal, NE India
Siut see Asyūt
123 Q13 Sivaki Amurskaya Oblast', SE Russian Federation
136 M13 Sivas anc. Sebastia, Sebaste. Sivas, C Turkey
136 M13 Sivas ◈ province C Turkey
137 O15 Siverek Şanlıurfa, S Turkey
117 X6 Sivers'k Donets'ka Oblast', E Ukraine
124 G13 Siverskiy Leningradskaya Oblast', NW Russian Federation
117 X6 Sivers'kyy Donets' Rus. Severskiy Donets. ≈ Russian Federation/Ukraine see also Severskiy Donets
Sivers'kyy Donets' see Severskiy Donets
125 W5 Sivomaskinskiy Respublika Komi, NW Russian Federation
136 G13 Sivrihisar Eskişehir, W Turkey
99 F22 Sivry Hainaut, S Belgium
123 V9 Sivuchiy, Mys cape E Russian Federation
75 U9 Siwa var. Sīwah. NW Egypt
Sīwah see Siwa
152 J9 Siwalik Range var. Shiwalik Range. ▲▲ India/Nepal
153 O13 Siwān Bihār, N India
43 O14 Sixaola, Río ≈ Costa Rica/Panama
Six Counties, The see Northern Ireland
103 T16 Six-Fours-les-Plages Var, SE France
161 Q7 Sixian var. Si Xian. Anhui, E China
Si Xian see Sixian
22 J9 Six Mile Lake ◎ Louisiana, S USA
139 V3 Siyāh Gūz E Iraq
155 L25 Siyambalanduwa Uva Province, SE Sri Lanka
137 Y10 Siyäzän Rus. Siazan'. NE Azerbaijan
Sizebolu see Sozopol
Sizuoka see Shizuoka
95 I24 Sjælland Eng. Zealand, Ger. Seeland. island E Denmark
Sjar see Sääre
113 L15 Sjenica Turk. Seniça. Serbia, SW Serbia
94 G11 Sjoa ≈ S Norway
95 K23 Sjöbo Skåne, S Sweden
94 E9 Sjøholt Møre og Romsdal, S Norway
92 O1 Sjuøyane island group N Svalbard
Skadar see Shkodër
Skadarsko Jezero see Scutari, Lake
117 R11 Skadovs'k Khersons'ka Oblast', S Ukraine
95 I24 Skælskør Vestsjælland, E Denmark
92 I2 Skagaströnd prev. Höfdhakaupstadhur. Nordhurland Vestra, N Iceland
95 H19 Skagen Nordjylland, N Denmark
Skagerak see Skagerrak
95 L16 Skagern ◎ C Sweden
197 T17 Skagerrak var. Skagerak. channel N Europe
94 G12 Skagget ▲ S Norway
32 H7 Skagit River ≈ Washington, NW USA
39 W12 Skagway Alaska, USA
92 K8 Skaidi Finnmark, N Norway
115 F21 Skála Pelopónnisos, S Greece
116 K6 Skalat Pol. Skałat. Ternopil's'ka Oblast', W Ukraine
95 J22 Skälderviken inlet Denmark/Sweden
124 J3 Skalistyy Murmanskaya Oblast', NW Russian Federation
92 I12 Skalka ◎ N Sweden
114 I12 Skalotí Anatolikí Makedonía kai Thráki, NE Greece
95 G22 Skanderborg Århus, C Denmark
95 K22 Skåne ◈ county S Sweden
75 N6 Skanès ✈ (Sousse) E Tunisia
95 C15 Skånevik Hordaland, S Norway
95 M18 Skänninge Östergötland, S Sweden
95 J23 Skanör med Falsterbo Skåne, S Sweden
115 H17 Skantzoúra island Vóreioi Sporádes, Greece, Aegean Sea
95 K18 Skara Västra Götaland, S Sweden
95 M17 Skärblacka Östergötland, S Sweden
95 I18 Skärhamn Västra Götaland, S Sweden
95 I14 Skarnes Hedmark, S Norway
119 M21 Skarodnaye Rus. Skorodnoye. Homyel'skaya Voblasts', SE Belarus
110 I8 Skarszewy Ger. Schöneck. Pomorskie, NW Poland
111 M14 Skarżysko-Kamienna Świętokrzyskie, C Poland
95 K16 Skattkärr Värmland, C Sweden
118 D12 Skaudvilė Tauragė, SW Lithuania
92 J12 Skaulo Lapp. Sávdijári. Norrbotten, N Sweden
111 K17 Skawina Małopolskie, S Poland
10 K12 Skeena ≈ British Columbia, SW Canada
10 J11 Skeena Mountains ▲▲ British Columbia, W Canada
97 O18 Skegness E England, UK
92 J4 Skeidharársandur coast S Iceland
93 J15 Skellefteå Västerbotten, N Sweden
93 I14 Skellefteälven ≈ N Sweden
93 J15 Skelleftehamn Västerbotten, N Sweden
25 O2 Skellytown Texas, SW USA
95 J19 Skene Västra Götaland, S Sweden
97 G17 Skerries Ir. Na Sceirí. Dublin, E Ireland
95 H15 Ski Akershus, S Norway
115 G17 Skíathos Skíathos, Vóreies Sporádes, Greece, Aegean Sea
115 G17 Skíathos island Vóreies Sporádes, Greece, Aegean Sea
27 P9 Skiatook Oklahoma, C USA
27 P9 Skiatook Lake ▣ Oklahoma, C USA
97 B22 Skibbereen Ir. An Sciobairín. Cork, SW Ireland
92 I9 Skibotn Troms, N Norway
119 F16 Skidal' Rus. Skidel'. Hrodzyenskaya Voblasts', W Belarus
97 K15 Skiddaw ▲ NW England, UK
Skidel' see Skidal'
25 T14 Skidmore Texas, SW USA
95 G16 Skien Telemark, S Norway
Skiermûntseach see Schiermonnikoog
110 L12 Skierniewice Łódzkie, C Poland
74 L5 Skikda prev. Philippeville. NE Algeria
30 M16 Skillet Fork ≈ Illinois, N USA
95 L19 Skillingaryd Jönköping, S Sweden
115 B19 Skinári, Akrotírio cape Zákynthos, Iónia Nisiá, Greece, C Mediterranean Sea
95 M15 Skinnskatteberg Västmanland, C Sweden
182 M12 Skipton Victoria, SE Australia
97 L16 Skipton N England, UK
Skiropoula see Skyropoúla
Skíros see Skýros
95 F21 Skive Viborg, NW Denmark
94 F11 Skjåk Oppland, S Norway
92 K2 Skjálfandafljót ≈ C Iceland
95 F22 Skjern Ringkøbing, W Denmark
95 F22 Skjern Å var. Skjern Aa. ≈ W Denmark
Skjern Aa see Skjern Å
92 G12 Skjerstad Nordland, C Norway
92 J8 Skjervøy Troms, N Norway
92 I10 Skjold Troms, N Norway
111 I17 Skoczów Śląskie, S Poland
109 T11 Škofja Loka Ger. Bischoflack. NW Slovenia
94 N12 Skog Gävleborg, C Sweden
95 K16 Skoghall Värmland, C Sweden
31 N10 Skokie Illinois, N USA
116 H6 Skole L'vivs'ka Oblast', W Ukraine
115 D19 Skóllis ▲ S Greece
167 S13 Skon Kâmpóng Cham, C Cambodia
115 H17 Skópelos Skópelos, Vóreies Sporádes, Greece, Aegean Sea
115 H17 Skópelos island Vóreies Sporádes, Greece, Aegean Sea
126 L5 Skopin Ryazanskaya Oblast', W Russian Federation
113 N18 Skopje var. Üsküb, Turk. Üsküp, prev. Skoplje; anc. Scupi. ● (FYR Macedonia) N FYR Macedonia
113 O18 Skopje ✈ N FYR Macedonia
Skoplje see Skopje
110 I8 Skórcz Ger. Skurz. Pomorskie, N Poland
Skorodnoye see Skarodnaye
93 H16 Skorped Västernorrland, C Sweden
95 G21 Skørping Nordjylland, N Denmark
95 K18 Skövde Västra Götaland, S Sweden
123 Q13 Skovorodino Amurskaya Oblast', SE Russian Federation
19 Q6 Skowhegan Maine, NE USA
9 W15 Skownan Manitoba, S Canada
94 H13 Skreia Oppland, S Norway
Skripón see Orchómenos
118 H9 Skrīveri Aizkraukle, S Latvia
118 J11 Skrudaliena Daugavpils, SE Latvia
118 D9 Skrunda Kuldīga, W Latvia
95 C16 Skudeneshavn Rogaland, S Norway
83 L20 Skukuza Mpumalanga, NE South Africa
97 B22 Skull Ir. An Scoil. SW Ireland
22 L3 Skuna River ≈ Mississippi, S USA
29 X15 Skunk River ≈ Iowa, C USA
Skuø see Skúvoy
118 C10 Skuodas Ger. Schoden, Pol. Szkudy. Klaipėda, NW Lithuania
95 K23 Skurup Skåne, S Sweden
Skurz see Skórcz
114 H8 Skŭt ≈ NW Bulgaria
94 O13 Skutskär Uppsala, C Sweden
95 B19 Skúvoy Dan. Skuø. island C Faeroe Islands
Skvira see Skvyra
117 O5 Skvyra Rus. Skvira. Kyyivs'ka Oblast', N Ukraine
39 Q11 Skwentna Alaska, USA
110 E11 Skwierzyna Ger. Schwerin. Lubuskie, W Poland
96 G9 Skye, Isle of island NW Scotland, UK
36 K13 Sky Harbour ✈ (Phoenix) Arizona, SW USA
32 I8 Skykomish Washington, NW USA
Skylge see Terschelling
63 F19 Skyring, Peninsula peninsula S Chile
63 H24 Skyring, Seno inlet S Chile
115 H17 Skyropoúla var. Skiropoula. island Vóreioi Sporádes, Greece, Aegean Sea
115 I17 Skýros var. Skíros. Skýros, Vóreioi Sporádes, Greece, Aegean Sea
115 I17 Skýros var. Skíros; anc. Scyros. island Vóreioi Sporádes, Greece, Aegean Sea
118 J12 Slabodka Rus. Slobodka. Vitsyebskaya Voblasts', NW Belarus
95 I23 Slagelse Vestsjælland, E Denmark
93 I14 Slagnäs Norrbotten, N Sweden
39 T10 Slana Alaska, USA
97 F20 Slaney Ir. An tSláine. ≈ SE Ireland
116 J13 Slănic Prahova, SE Romania
116 K11 Slănic Moldova Bacău, E Romania
113 H16 Slano Dubrovnik-Neretva, SE Croatia
124 F13 Slantsy Leningradskaya Oblast', NW Russian Federation
111 C16 Slaný Ger. Schlan. Střední Čechy, NW Czech Republic
111 K16 Śląskie ◈ province S Poland
12 C10 Slate Falls Ontario, S Canada
27 T4 Slater Missouri, C USA
112 H9 Slatina Hung. Szlatina; prev. Podravska Slatina. Virovitica-Podravina, NE Croatia
116 I14 Slatina Olt, S Romania
25 N5 Slaton Texas, SW USA
95 H14 Slattum Akershus, S Norway
9 R10 Slave ≈ Alberta/Northwest Territories, C Canada
68 E12 Slave Coast coastal region W Africa
9 P13 Slave Lake Alberta, SW Canada
122 I13 Slavgorod Altayskiy Kray, S Russian Federation
Slavgorod see Slawharad
Slavonia see Slavonija
112 G9 Slavonija Eng. Slavonia, Ger. Slawonien, Hung. Szlavonia, Szlavonország. cultural region NE Croatia
Slavonska Požega see Požega
112 H10 Slavonski Brod Ger. Brod, Hung. Bród; prev. Brod, Brod na Savi. Brod-Posavina, NE Croatia
116 L4 Slavuta Khmel'nyts'ka Oblast', NW Ukraine
117 P2 Slavutych Chernihivs'ka Oblast', N Ukraine
123 R15 Slavyanka Primorskiy Kray, SE Russian Federation
114 J8 Slavyanovo Pleven, N Bulgaria
Slavyansk see Slov"yans'k
126 K14 Slavyansk-na-Kubani Krasnodarskiy Kray, SW Russian Federation
119 N20 Slavyechna Rus. Slovechna. ≈ Belarus/Ukraine
119 O16 Slawharad Rus. Slavgorod. Mahilyowskaya Voblasts', E Belarus
110 G7 Sławno Zachodnio-pomorskie, NW Poland
Slawonien see Slavonija
29 S10 Slayton Minnesota, N USA
97 N18 Sleaford E England, UK
97 A20 Slea Head Ir. Ceann Sléibhe. headland SW Ireland
96 G9 Sleat, Sound of strait NW Scotland, UK
Sledyuki see Slyedzyuki
12 I5 Sleeper Islands island group Nunavut, C Canada
31 O6 Sleeping Bear Point headland Michigan, N USA
29 T10 Sleepy Eye Minnesota, N USA
39 O11 Sleetmute Alaska, USA
Sléibhe, Ceann see Slea Head
Slēmānī see As Sulaymānīyah
195 O5 Slessor Glacier glacier Antarctica
22 L9 Slidell Louisiana, S USA
18 K12 Slide Mountain ▲ New York, NE USA
98 I13 Sliedrecht Zuid-Holland, C Netherlands
121 P16 Sliema N Malta
97 G16 Slieve Donard ▲ SE Northern Ireland, UK
Sligeach see Sligo
97 D16 Sligo Ir. Sligeach. Sligo, NW Ireland
97 C16 Sligo Ir. Sligeach. ◈ county NW Ireland
97 C15 Sligo Bay Ir. Cuan Shligigh. inlet NW Ireland
18 B13 Slippery Rock Pennsylvania, NE USA
95 P19 Slite Gotland, SE Sweden
114 L9 Sliven var. Slivno. Sliven, C Bulgaria
114 L10 Sliven ◈ province C Bulgaria
114 G9 Slivnitsa Sofiya, W Bulgaria
Slivno see Sliven
114 L7 Slivo Pole Ruse, N Bulgaria
29 S13 Sloan Iowa, C USA
35 X12 Sloan Nevada, W USA
Slobodka see Slabodka
125 R14 Slobodskoy Kirovskaya Oblast', NW Russian Federation
Slobodzeya see Slobozia
117 O10 Slobozia Rus. Slobodzeya. E Moldova
116 L14 Slobozia Ialomiţa, SE Romania
98 O5 Slochteren Groningen, NE Netherlands
119 H17 Slonim Pol. Słonim, Rus. Slonim. Hrodzyenskaya Voblasts', W Belarus
Słonim see Slonim
98 K7 Sloter Meer ◎ N Netherlands
Slot, The see New Georgia Sound
97 N22 Slough S England, UK
111 J20 Slovakia off. Slovenská Republika, Ger. Slowakei, Hung. Szlovákia, Slvk. Slovensko. ◆ republic C Europe
Slovak Ore Mountains see Slovenské rudohorie
Slovechna see Slavyechna
109 S12 Slovenia off. Republic of Slovenia, Ger. Slowenien, Slvn. Slovenija. ◆ republic SE Europe
Slovenia, Republic of see Slovenia
Slovenija see Slovenia
109 V10 Slovenj Gradec Ger. Windischgraz. N Slovenia
109 W10 Slovenska Bistrica Ger. Windischfeistritz. NE Slovenia
Slovenská Republika see Slovakia
109 W10 Slovenska Konjice E Slovenia
111 K20 Slovenské rudohorie Eng. Slovak Ore Mountains, Ger. Slowakisches Erzgebirge, Ungarisches Erzgebirge. ▲▲ C Slovakia
Slovensko see Slovakia
117 Y7 Slov"yanoserbs'k Luhans'ka Oblast', E Ukraine
117 W6 Slov"yans'k Rus. Slavyansk. Donets'ka Oblast', E Ukraine
Slowakei see Slovakia
Slowakisches Erzgebirge see Slovenské rudohorie
Slowenien see Slovenia
110 D11 Słubice Ger. Frankfurt. Lubuskie, W Poland
119 K19 Sluch Rus. Sluch'. ≈ C Belarus
116 L4 Sluch ≈ NW Ukraine
99 D16 Sluis Zeeland, SW Netherlands
112 D10 Slunj Hung. Szluin. Karlovac, C Croatia
110 I11 Słupca Wielkopolskie, C Poland
110 G6 Słupia Ger. Stolpe. ≈ NW Poland
110 G6 Słupsk Ger. Stolp. Pomorskie, N Poland
119 K18 Slutsk Rus. Slutsk. Minskaya Voblasts', S Belarus
119 O16 Slyedzyuki Rus. Sledyuki. Mahilyowskaya Voblasts', E Belarus
97 A17 Slyne Head Ir. Ceann Léime. headland W Ireland
27 U14 Smackover Arkansas, C USA
95 L20 Småland cultural region S Sweden
95 K20 Smålandsstenar Jönköping, S Sweden
Small Malaita see Maramasike
13 O8 Smallwood Reservoir ◎ Newfoundland and Labrador, S Canada
119 N14 Smalyany Rus. Smolyany. Vitsyebskaya Voblasts', NE Belarus
119 L15 Smalyavichy Rus. Smolevichi. Minskaya Voblasts', C Belarus
74 C9 Smara var. Es Semara. N Western Sahara
119 I14 Smarhon' Pol. Smorgonie, Rus. Smorgon'. Hrodzyenskaya Voblasts', W Belarus
112 M11 Smederevo Ger. Semendria. Serbia, N Serbia
112 M12 Smederevska Palanka Serbia, C Serbia
95 M14 Smedjebacken Dalarna, C Sweden
116 L13 Smeeni Buzău, SE Romania
Smela see Smila
107 D16 Smeralda, Costa cultural region Sardegna, Italy, C Mediterranean Sea
111 J22 Śmigiel Ger. Schmiegel. Wielkopolskie, C Poland
117 Q6 Smila Rus. Smela. Cherkas'ka Oblast', C Ukraine
98 N7 Smilde Drenthe, NE Netherlands
9 S15 Smiley Saskatchewan, S Canada
25 T12 Smiley Texas, SW USA
Smilten see Smiltene
118 I8 Smiltene Ger. Smilten. Valka, N Latvia
123 T13 Smirnykh Ostrov Sakhalin, Sakhalinskaya Oblast', SE Russian Federation
9 Q13 Smith Alberta, W Canada
39 P4 Smith Bay bay Alaska, NW USA
12 I3 Smith, Cape cape Québec, NE Canada
26 L3 Smith Center Kansas, C USA
10 K13 Smithers British Columbia, SW Canada
21 V10 Smithfield North Carolina, SE USA
36 L1 Smithfield Utah, W USA
21 X7 Smithfield Virginia, NE USA
12 I3 Smith Island island Nunavut, C Canada
Smith Island see Sumisu-jima
20 H7 Smithland Kentucky, S USA
21 T7 Smith Mountain Lake var. Leesville Lake. ▣ Virginia, NE USA
34 L1 Smith River California, W USA
33 R9 Smith River ≈ Montana, NW USA
14 L13 Smiths Falls Ontario, SE Canada
33 N13 Smiths Ferry Idaho, NW USA
20 K7 Smiths Grove Kentucky, S USA
183 N15 Smithton Tasmania, SE Australia

324
◆ Country ● Country Capital ◇ Dependent Territory ○ Dependent Territory Capital ◈ Administrative Regions ✈ International Airport ▲ Mountain ▲▲ Mountain Range Volcano ≈ River ◎ Lake ▣ Reservoir

SMITHTOWN – SOUFLÍON

18 L14 **Smithtown** Long Island, New York, NE USA
20 K9 **Smithville** Tennessee, S USA
25 T11 **Smithville** Texas, SW USA
Šmohor *see* Hermagor
35 Q4 **Smoke Creek Desert** *desert* Nevada, W USA
9 O14 **Smoky** ~ Alberta, W Canada
182 E7 **Smoky Bay** South Australia
183 V6 **Smoky Cape** *headland* New South Wales, SE Australia
26 L4 **Smoky Hill River** ~ Kansas, C USA
26 L4 **Smoky Hills** *hill range* Kansas, C USA
9 Q14 **Smoky Lake** Alberta, SW Canada
94 E8 **Smøla** *island* W Norway
126 H4 **Smolensk** Smolenskaya Oblast', W Russian Federation
126 H4 **Smolenskaya Oblast'** ◈ *province* W Russian Federation
Smolensk-Moscow Upland *see* Smolensko-Moskovskaya Vozvyshennost'
126 J3 **Smolensko-Moskovskaya Vozvyshennost'** *var.* Smolensk-Moscow Upland. ▲▲ W Russian Federation
Smolevichi *see* Smalyavichy
115 C15 **Smólikas** *var.* Smolikás. ▲ W Greece
114 I12 **Smolyan** *prev.* Pashmakli. Smolyan, S Bulgaria
114 I12 **Smolyan** ◈ *province* S Bulgaria
Smolyany *see* Smalyany
33 S15 **Smoot** Wyoming, C USA
12 G12 **Smooth Rock Falls** Ontario, S Canada
Smorgon'/Smorgonie *see* Smarhon'
95 K23 **Smygehamn** Skåne, S Sweden
194 I7 **Smyley Island** *island* Antarctica
21 Y3 **Smyrna** Delaware, NE USA
23 S3 **Smyrna** Georgia, SE USA
20 J9 **Smyrna** Tennessee, S USA
Smyrna *see* İzmir
97 I16 **Snaefell** ▲ C Isle of Man
92 H3 **Snæfellsjökull** ▲ W Iceland
92 J3 **Snækollur** ▲ C Iceland
10 J4 **Snake** ~ Yukon Territory, NW Canada
29 O8 **Snake Creek** ~ South Dakota, N USA
183 P13 **Snake Island** *island* Victoria, SE Australia
35 Y6 **Snake Range** ▲▲ Nevada, W USA
32 K10 **Snake River** ~ NW USA
29 V6 **Snake River** ~ Minnesota, N USA
28 L12 **Snake River** ~ Nebraska, C USA
33 Q14 **Snake River Plain** *plain* Idaho, NW USA
93 F15 **Snåsa** Nord-Trøndelag, C Norway
21 O8 **Sneedville** Tennessee, S USA
98 K6 **Sneek** Friesland, N Netherlands
Sneeuw-gebergte *see* Maoke, Pegunungan
95 F22 **Snejbjerg** Ringkøbing, C Denmark
124 J3 **Snezhnogorsk** Murmanskaya Oblast', NW Russian Federation
122 K9 **Snezhnogorsk** Taymyrskiy (Dolgano-Nenetskiy) Avtonomnyy Okrug, N Russian Federation
Snezhnoye *see* Snizhne
111 G15 **Sněžka** *Ger.* Schneekoppe, *Pol.* Śnieżka. ▲ N Czech Republic/Poland
110 N8 **Śniardwy, Jezioro** *Ger.* Spirdingsee. ◎ NE Poland
Sniečkus *see* Visaginas
Śnieżka *see* Sněžka
117 R10 **Snihurivka** Mykolayivs'ka Oblast', S Ukraine
116 I5 **Snilov** ✈ (L'viv) L'vivs'ka Oblast', W Ukraine
111 O19 **Snina** *Hung.* Szinna. Prešovský Kraj, E Slovakia
117 Y8 **Snizhne** *Rus.* Snezhnoye. Donets'ka Oblast', SE Ukraine
94 G10 **Snøhetta** *var.* Snohetta. ▲ S Norway
92 G12 **Snøtinden** ▲ C Norway
97 I18 **Snowdon** ▲ NW Wales, UK
97 I18 **Snowdonia** ▲▲ NW Wales, UK
8 K10 **Snowdrift** ~ Northwest Territories, NW Canada
Snowdrift *see* Łutselk'e
37 N12 **Snowflake** Arizona, SW USA
21 Y5 **Snow Hill** Maryland, NE USA
21 W10 **Snow Hill** North Carolina, SE USA
194 H3 **Snowhill Island** *island* Antarctica
9 V13 **Snow Lake** Manitoba, C Canada
37 R5 **Snowmass Mountain** ▲ Colorado, C USA
18 M10 **Snow, Mount** ▲ Vermont, NE USA
34 M5 **Snow Mountain** ▲ California, W USA
Snow Mountains *see* Maoke, Pegunungan
33 N7 **Snowshoe Peak** ▲ Montana, NW USA
182 I8 **Snowtown** South Australia
36 K1 **Snowville** Utah, W USA
35 X3 **Snow Water Lake** ◎ Nevada, W USA
183 Q11 **Snowy Mountains** ▲▲ New South Wales/Victoria, SE Australia
183 Q12 **Snowy River** ~ New South Wales/Victoria, SE Australia
44 K5 **Snug Corner** Acklins Island, SE Bahamas
167 T13 **Snuŏl** Krâchéh, E Cambodia
116 J7 **Snyatyn** *Rus.* Snyatyn. Ivano-Frankivs'ka Oblast', W Ukraine
26 L12 **Snyder** Oklahoma, C USA
25 O6 **Snyder** Texas, SW USA
172 H3 **Soalala** Mahajanga, W Madagascar
172 J4 **Soanierana-Ivongo** Toamasina, E Madagascar
171 R11 **Soasiu** *var.* Tidore. Pulau Tidore, E Indonesia
54 G8 **Soatá** Boyacá, C Colombia
172 I5 **Soavinandriana** Antananarivo, C Madagascar
77 V13 **Soba** Kaduna, C Nigeria
163 Y16 **Sobaek-sanmaek** ▲▲ S South Korea
80 F13 **Sobat** ~ E Sudan
171 Z14 **Sobger, Sungai** ~ Papua, E Indonesia
171 V13 **Sobiei** Papua, E Indonesia
126 M3 **Sobinka** Vladimirskaya Oblast', W Russian Federation
127 S7 **Sobolevo** Orenburgskaya Oblast', W Russian Federation
Soborsin *see* Săvârşin
164 D15 **Sobo-san** ▲ Kyūshū, SW Japan
111 G14 **Sobótka** Dolnośląskie, SW Poland
59 O15 **Sobradinho** Bahia, E Brazil
Sobradinho, Barragem de *see* Sobradinho, Represa de
59 O16 **Sobradinho, Represa de** *var.* Barragem de Sobradinho. ⊡ E Brazil
58 O13 **Sobral** Ceará, E Brazil
105 T4 **Sobrarbe** *physical region* NE Spain
109 R10 **Soča** *It.* Isonzo. ~ Italy/Slovenia
110 L11 **Sochaczew** Mazowieckie, C Poland
126 L15 **Sochi** Krasnodarskiy Kray, SW Russian Federation
114 G13 **Sochós** *var.* Sohos, Sokhós. Kentrikí Makedonía, N Greece
Socialist People's Libyan Arab Jamahiriya *see* Libya
191 R11 **Société, Archipel de la** *var.* Archipel de Tahiti, Îles de la Société, *Eng.* Society Islands. *island group* W French Polynesia
Société, Îles de la/Society Islands *see* Société, Archipel de la
21 T11 **Society Hill** South Carolina, SE USA
Society Islands *see* Société, Archipel de la
175 W9 **Society Ridge** *undersea feature* C Pacific Ocean
62 I5 **Socompa, Volcán** ⛰ N Chile
Soconusco, Sierra de *see* Sierra Madre
54 G8 **Socorro** Santander, C Colombia
37 R13 **Socorro** New Mexico, SW USA
Socotra *see* Suquṭrā
167 S14 **Soc Trăng** *var.* Khanh Hung. Soc Trăng, S Vietnam
105 P10 **Socuéllamos** Castilla-La Mancha, C Spain
35 W13 **Soda Lake** *salt flat* California, W USA
92 L11 **Sodankylä** Lappi, N Finland
Sodari *see* Sodiri
33 R15 **Soda Springs** Idaho, NW USA
Soddo/Soddu *see* Sodo
20 L10 **Soddy Daisy** Tennessee, S USA
95 N14 **Söderfors** Uppsala, C Sweden
94 N12 **Söderhamn** Gävleborg, C Sweden
95 N17 **Söderköping** Östergötland, S Sweden
95 N17 **Södermanland** ◈ *county* C Sweden
95 O16 **Södertälje** Stockholm, C Sweden
80 D10 **Sodiri** *var.* Sawdirī, Sodari. Northern Kordofan, C Sudan
81 I14 **Sodo** *var.* Soddo, Soddu. Southern, S Ethiopia
94 N11 **Södra Dellen** ◎ C Sweden
95 M19 **Södra Vi** Kalmar, S Sweden
18 G9 **Sodus Point** *headland* New York, NE USA
171 Q17 **Soe** *prev.* Soë. Timor, C Indonesia
Soebang *see* Subang
Soekaboemi *see* Sukabumi
169 N15 **Soekarno-Hatta** ✈ (Jakarta) Jawa, S Indonesia
Soëla-Sund *see* Soela Väin
118 E5 **Soela Väin** *prev. Eng.* Sele Sound, *Ger.* Dagden-Sund, Soëla-Sund. *strait* W Estonia
Soemba *see* Sumba, Pulau
Soembawa *see* Sumbawa
Soemenep *see* Sumenep
Soengaipenoeh *see* Sungaipenuh
Soerabaja *see* Surabaya
Soerakarta *see* Surakarta
101 G14 **Soest** Nordrhein-Westfalen, W Germany
98 J11 **Soest** Utrecht, C Netherlands
100 F11 **Soeste** ~ NW Germany
98 J11 **Soesterberg** Utrecht, C Netherlands
115 E16 **Sofádes** *var.* Sofádhes. Thessalía, C Greece
Sofádhes *see* Sofádes
83 N18 **Sofala** Sofala, C Mozambique
83 N17 **Sofala** ◈ *province* C Mozambique
83 N18 **Sofala, Baia de** *bay* C Mozambique
172 J3 **Sofia** *seasonal river* NW Madagascar
Sofia *see* Sofiya
115 G19 **Sofikó** Pelopónnisos, S Greece
Sofi-Kurgan *see* Sopu-Korgon
114 G10 **Sofiya** *var.* Sophia, *Eng.* Sofia, *Lat.* Serdica. ● (Bulgaria) Sofiya-Grad, W Bulgaria
114 H9 **Sofiya** ◈ *province* W Bulgaria
114 G9 **Sofiya** ✈ Sofiya-Grad, W Bulgaria
114 G9 **Sofiya, Grad** ◈ *municipality* W Bulgaria
Sofiyevka *see* Sofiyivka
117 S8 **Sofiyivka** *Rus.* Sofiyevka. Dnipropetrovs'ka Oblast', E Ukraine
123 R13 **Sofiysk** Khabarovskiy Kray, SE Russian Federation
123 R12 **Sofiysk** Khabarovskiy Kray, SE Russian Federation
124 I6 **Sofporog** Respublika Kareliya, NW Russian Federation
115 L23 **Sofraná** *prev* Záfora. *island* Kykládes, Greece, Aegean Sea
165 Y14 **Sōfu-gan** *island* Izu-shotō, SE Japan
156 K10 **Sog** Xizang Zizhiqu, W China
54 G9 **Sogamoso** Boyacá, C Colombia
136 I11 **Soğanlı Çayı** ~ N Turkey
94 E12 **Sogn** *physical region* S Norway
Sogndal *see* Sogndalsfjøra
94 E12 **Sogndalsfjøra** *var.* Sogndal. Sogn Og Fjordane, S Norway
95 E18 **Søgne** Vest-Agder, S Norway
94 D12 **Sognefjorden** *fjord* NE North Sea
94 C12 **Sogn Og Fjordane** ◈ *county* S Norway
162 I11 **Sogo Nur** ◎ N China
159 T12 **Sogruma** Qinghai, W China
163 X17 **Sŏgwip'o** S South Korea
75 X10 **Soḥâg** *var.* Sawhāj, Suliag. C Egypt
Sohar *see* Ṣuḥār
64 H9 **Sohm Plain** *undersea feature* NW Atlantic Ocean
100 H7 **Soholmer Au** ~ N Germany
Sohos *see* Sochós
Sohrau *see* Żory
99 F20 **Soignies** Hainaut, SW Belgium
159 R15 **Soila** Xizang Zizhiqu, W China
103 P4 **Soissons** *anc.* Augusta Suessionum, Noviodunum. Aisne, N France
164 H13 **Sōja** Okayama, Honshū, SW Japan
152 F13 **Sojat** Rājasthān, N India
163 W13 **Sŏjosŏn-man** *inlet* W North Korea
116 I4 **Sokal'** *Rus.* Sokal. L'vivs'ka Oblast', NW Ukraine
163 Y14 **Sokch'o** N South Korea
136 B15 **Söke** Aydın, SW Turkey
189 N12 **Sokehs Island** *island* E Micronesia
79 M24 **Sokele** Katanga, SE Dem. Rep. Congo
147 R11 **Sokh** *Uzb.* Sūkh. ~ Kyrgyzstan/Uzbekistan
Sokh *see* So'x
Sokhós *see* Sochós
137 Q8 **Sokhumi** *Rus.* Sukhumi. NW Georgia
113 O14 **Sokobanja** Serbia, E Serbia
77 R15 **Sokodé** C Togo
123 T10 **Sokol** Magadanskaya Oblast', E Russian Federation
124 M13 **Sokol** Vologodskaya Oblast', NW Russian Federation
110 P9 **Sokółka** Podlaskie, NE Poland
76 M11 **Sokolo** Ségou, W Mali
111 A16 **Sokolov** *Ger.* Falkenau an der Eger; *prev.* Falknov nad Ohří. Karlovarský Kraj, W Czech Republic
111 O16 **Sokołów Małopolski** Podkarpackie, SE Poland
110 O11 **Sokołów Podlaski** Mazowieckie, C Poland
76 G11 **Sokone** W Senegal
77 T12 **Sokoto** Sokoto, NW Nigeria
77 T12 **Sokoto** ◈ *state* NW Nigeria
77 S12 **Sokoto** ~ NW Nigeria
Sokotra *see* Suquṭrā
147 U7 **Sokuluk** Chuyskaya Oblast', N Kyrgyzstan
116 L7 **Sokyryany** Chernivets'ka Oblast', W Ukraine
95 C16 **Sola** Rogaland, S Norway
187 R12 **Sola** Vanua Lava, N Vanuatu
95 C17 **Sola** ✈ (Stavanger) Rogaland, S Norway
81 H18 **Solai** Rift Valley, W Kenya
152 I8 **Solan** Himāchal Pradesh, N India
185 A25 **Solander Island** *island* SW New Zealand
Solano *see* Bahía Solano
155 F15 **Solāpur** *var.* Sholāpur. Mahārāshtra, W India
93 H16 **Solberg** Västernorrland, C Sweden
116 K9 **Solca** *Ger.* Solka. Suceava, N Romania
105 O16 **Sol, Costa del** *coastal region* S Spain
106 F5 **Solda** *Ger.* Sulden. Trentino-Alto Adige, N Italy
117 N9 **Şoldăneşti** *Rus.* Sholdaneshty. N Moldova
Soldau *see* Wkra
108 L8 **Sölden** Tirol, W Austria
27 P3 **Soldier Creek** ~ Kansas, C USA
39 R12 **Soldotna** Alaska, USA
110 I10 **Solec Kujawski** Kujawsko-pomorskie, C Poland
61 B16 **Soledad** Santa Fe, C Argentina
55 E4 **Soledad** Atlántico, N Colombia
35 O11 **Soledad** California, W USA
55 O7 **Soledad** Anzoátegui, NE Venezuela
61 H15 **Soledade** Rio Grande do Sul, S Brazil
Isla Soledad *see* East Falkland
103 Y15 **Solenzara** Corse, France, C Mediterranean Sea
Soleure *see* Solothurn
94 C12 **Solheim** Hordaland, S Norway
125 N14 **Soligalich** Kostromskaya Oblast', NW Russian Federation
Soligorsk *see* Salihorsk
97 L20 **Solihull** C England, UK
125 U13 **Solikamsk** Permskaya Oblast', NW Russian Federation
127 V8 **Sol'-Iletsk** Orenburgskaya Oblast', W Russian Federation
57 G17 **Solimana, Nevado** ▲ S Peru
58 E13 **Solimões, Rio** ~ C Brazil
113 E14 **Solin** *It.* Salona; *anc.* Salonae. Split-Dalmacija, S Croatia
101 E15 **Solingen** Nordrhein-Westfalen, W Germany
Solka *see* Solca
93 H16 **Sollefteå** Västernorrland, C Sweden
95 O15 **Sollentuna** Stockholm, C Sweden
105 x9 **Sóller** Mallorca, Spain, W Mediterranean Sea
94 L13 **Sollerön** Dalarna, C Sweden
101 I14 **Solling** *hill range* C Germany
95 O16 **Solna** Stockholm, C Sweden
126 K3 **Solnechnogorsk** Moskovskaya Oblast', W Russian Federation
123 R10 **Solnechnyy** Khabarovskiy Kray, SE Russian Federation
122 K13 **Solnechnyy** Krasnoyarskiy Kray, C Russian Federation
123 S13 **Solnechnyy** Respublika Sakha (Yakutiya), NE Russian Federation
Solo *see* Surakarta
107 L17 **Solofra** Campania, S Italy
168 J11 **Solok** Sumatera, W Indonesia
42 C6 **Sololá** Sololá, W Guatemala
42 A2 **Sololá** *off.* Departamento de Sololá. ◈ *department* SW Guatemala
Sololá, Departamento de *see* Sololá
81 J16 **Sololo** Eastern, N Kenya
42 C4 **Soloma** Huehuetenango, W Guatemala
38 M9 **Solomon** Alaska, USA
27 N4 **Solomon** Kansas, C USA
187 N9 **Solomon Islands** *prev.* British Solomon Islands Protectorate. ◆ *commonwealth republic* W Solomon Islands N Melanesia W Pacific Ocean
186 L7 **Solomon Islands** *island group* Papua New Guinea/Solomon Islands
26 M3 **Solomon River** ~ Kansas, C USA
186 H8 **Solomon Sea** *sea* W Pacific Ocean
31 U11 **Solon** Ohio, N USA
117 T8 **Solone** Dnipropetrovs'ka Oblast', E Ukraine
171 P16 **Solor, Kepulauan** *island group* S Indonesia
126 M4 **Solotcha** Ryazanskaya Oblast', W Russian Federation
108 D7 **Solothurn** *Fr.* Soleure. Solothurn, NW Switzerland
108 D7 **Solothurn** *Fr.* Soleure. ◈ *canton* NW Switzerland
124 J7 **Solovetskiye Ostrova** *island group* NW Russian Federation
105 V5 **Solsona** Cataluña, NE Spain
113 E14 **Šolta** *It.* Solta. *island* S Croatia
Soltānābād *see* Kāshmar
142 L4 **Solṭānīyeh** Zanjān, NW Iran
100 I11 **Soltau** Niedersachsen, NW Germany
124 G14 **Sol'tsy** Novgorodskaya Oblast', W Russian Federation
Soltüstik Qazaqstan Oblysy *see* Severnyy Kazakhstan
Solun *see* Thessaloníki
113 O19 **Solunska Glava** ▲ C FYR Macedonia
95 L22 **Sölvesborg** Blekinge, S Sweden
97 J15 **Solway Firth** *inlet* England/Scotland, UK
82 I13 **Solwezi** North Western, NW Zambia
165 Q11 **Sōma** Fukushima, Honshū, C Japan
136 C13 **Soma** Manisa, W Turkey
81 M14 **Somali** ◈ *province* E Ethiopia
81 O15 **Somalia** *off.* Somali Democratic Republic, *Som.* Jamuuriyada Demuqraadiga Soomaaliyeed, Soomaaliya; *prev.* Italian Somaliland, Somaliland Protectorate. ◆ *republic* E Africa
173 N6 **Somali Basin** *undersea feature* W Indian Ocean
Somali Democratic Republic *see* Somalia
80 N12 **Somaliland** ◈ *disputed territory* N Somalia
Somaliland Protectorate *see* Somalia
67 Y8 **Somali Plain** *undersea feature* W Indian Ocean
112 J8 **Sombor** *Hung.* Zombor. Vojvodina, NW Serbia
99 H20 **Sombreffe** Namur, S Belgium
40 L10 **Sombrerete** Zacatecas, C Mexico
45 V8 **Sombrero** *island* N Anguilla
151 Q21 **Sombrero Channel** *channel* Nicobar Islands, India
116 H9 **Şomcuta Mare** *Hung.* Nagysomkút; *prev.* Somcuţa Mare. Maramureş, N Romania
Somcuţa Mare *see* Şomcuta Mare
167 R9 **Somdet** Kalasin, E Thailand
99 L15 **Someren** Noord-Brabant, SE Netherlands
93 L19 **Somero** Länsi-Soumi, SW Finland
33 P7 **Somers** Montana, NW USA
64 A12 **Somerset** *var.* Somerset Village. W Bermuda
37 Q5 **Somerset** Colorado, C USA
20 M7 **Somerset** Kentucky, S USA
19 O12 **Somerset** Massachusetts, NE USA
97 K23 **Somerset** *cultural region* SW England, UK
Somerset East *see* Somerset-Oos
64 A12 **Somerset Island** *island* W Bermuda
197 N9 **Somerset Island** *island* Queen Elizabeth Islands, Nunavut, NW Canada
Somerset Nile *see* Victoria Nile
83 I25 **Somerset-Oos** *var.* Somerset East. Eastern Cape, S South Africa
Somerset Village *see* Somerset
83 E26 **Somerset-Wes** *var.* Somerset West. Western Cape, SW South Africa
Somerset West *see* Somerset-Wes
Somers Islands *see* Bermuda
18 J17 **Somers Point** New Jersey, NE USA
19 P9 **Somersworth** New Hampshire, NE USA
36 H15 **Somerton** Arizona, SW USA
18 J14 **Somerville** New Jersey, NE USA
20 F10 **Somerville** Tennessee, S USA
25 U10 **Somerville** Texas, SW USA
25 T10 **Somerville Lake** ⊡ Texas, SW USA
Someş/Somesch/Someşul *see* Szamos
103 N2 **Somme** ◈ *department* N France
103 N2 **Somme** ~ N France
95 L18 **Sommen** Jönköping, S Sweden
95 M18 **Sommen** ◎ S Sweden
101 K16 **Sömmerda** Thüringen, C Germany
Sommerein *see* Šamorín
Sommerfeld *see* Lubsko
55 Y11 **Sommet Tabulaire** *var.* Mont Itoupé. ▲ S French Guiana
111 H25 **Somogy** *off.* Somogy Megye. ◈ *county* SW Hungary
Somogy Megye *see* Somogy
Somorja *see* Šamorín
105 N7 **Somosierra, Puerto de** *pass* N Spain
187 Y14 **Somosomo** Taveuni, N Fiji
42 I9 **Somotillo** Chinandega, NW Nicaragua
42 I8 **Somoto** Madriz, NW Nicaragua
110 I11 **Sompolno** Wielkopolskie, C Poland
105 S3 **Somport** *var.* Puerto de Somport, *Fr.* Col du Somport; *anc.* Summus Portus. *pass* France/Spain
Somport *see* Somport, Col du
102 J17 **Somport, Col du** *var.* Puerto de Somport, *Sp.* Somport; *anc.* Summus Portus. *pass* France/Spain
Somport, Col du *see* Somport
Somport, Puerto de *see* Somport/Somport, Col du
99 K15 **Son** Noord-Brabant, S Netherlands
95 H15 **Son** ◈ Akershus, S Norway
154 L9 **Son** *var.* Sone. ~ C India
43 R16 **Soná** Veraguas, W Panama
Sonag *see* Zêkog
154 M12 **Sonapur** *prev.* Sonepur. Orissa, E India
95 G24 **Sønderborg** *Ger.* Sonderburg. Sønderjylland, SW Denmark
Sonderburg *see* Sønderborg
95 F24 **Sønderjylland** *var.* Sønderjyllands Amt. ◈ *county* SW Denmark
Sønderjyllands Amt *see* Sønderjylland
101 K15 **Sondershausen** Thüringen, C Germany
Søndre Strømfjord *see* Kangerlussuaq
106 E6 **Sondrio** Lombardia, N Italy
Sone *see* Son
Sonepur *see* Sonapur
57 K22 **Sonequera** ▲ S Bolivia
167 V12 **Sông Câu** Phu Yên, C Vietnam
167 R15 **Sông Đôc** Minh Hai, S Vietnam
81 H25 **Songea** Ruvuma, S Tanzania
163 X10 **Songhua Hu** ◎ NE China
163 Y7 **Songhua Jiang** *var.* Sungari. ~ NE China
161 S8 **Songjiang** Shanghai Shi, E China
Sŏngjin *see* Kimch'aek
167 O16 **Songkhla** *var.* Songkla, *Mal.* Singora. Songkhla, SW Thailand
Songkla *see* Songkhla
163 T13 **Song Ling** ▲▲ NE China
163 W14 **Songnim** SW North Korea
82 B10 **Songo** Uíge, NW Angola
83 M15 **Songo** Tete, NW Mozambique
79 F21 **Songololo** Bas-Congo, SW Dem. Rep. Congo
160 H7 **Songpan** *var.* Jin'an, *Tib.* Sungpu. Sichuan, C China
163 Y17 **Sŏngsan** S South Korea
161 R11 **Songxi** Fujian, SE China
160 M6 **Songxian** *var.* Song Xian. Henan, C China
Song Xian *see* Songxian
161 R10 **Songyang** *var.* Xiping; *prev.* Songyin. Zhejiang, SE China
Songyin *see* Songyang
163 V9 **Songyuan** *var.* Fu-yü, Petuna; *prev.* Fuyu. Jilin, NE China
Sonid Youqi *see* SaihanTal
Sonid Zuoqi *see* Mandalt
152 I10 **Sonipat** Haryāna, N India
93 M15 **Sonkajärvi** Itä-Suomi, C Finland
167 R6 **Sơn La** Sơn La, N Vietnam
149 O16 **Sonmiāni** Baluchistān, S Pakistan
149 O16 **Sonmiāni Bay** *bay* S Pakistan
101 K18 **Sonneberg** Thüringen, C Germany
101 N24 **Sonntagshorn** ▲ Austria/Germany
Sonoita *see* Sonoyta
40 E3 **Sonoita, Rio** *var.* Río Sonoyta. ~ Mexico/USA
35 N7 **Sonoma** California, W USA
35 T3 **Sonoma Peak** ▲ Nevada, W USA
35 P8 **Sonora** California, W USA
25 O10 **Sonora** Texas, SW USA
40 F5 **Sonora** ◈ *state* NW Mexico
35 X17 **Sonoran Desert** *var.* Desierto de Altar. *desert* Mexico/USA ***see also*** Altar, Desierto de
Sonoran Desert *see* Altar, Desierto de
40 G5 **Sonora, Río** ~ NW Mexico
40 E2 **Sonoyta** *var.* Sonoita. Sonora, NW Mexico
Sonoyta, Río *see* Sonoita, Rio
142 K6 **Sonqor** *var.* Sunqur. Kermānshāhān, W Iran
105 N9 **Sonseca** *var.* Sonseca con Casalgordo. Castilla-La Mancha, C Spain
Sonseca con Casalgordo *see* Sonseca
54 E9 **Sonsón** Antioquia, W Colombia
42 E7 **Sonsonate** Sonsonate, W El Salvador
42 A9 **Sonsonate** ◈ *department* SW El Salvador
188 A10 **Sonsorol Islands** *island group* S Palau
112 J9 **Sonta** *Hung.* Szond; *prev.* Szonta. Vojvodina, NW Serbia
167 S6 **Sơn Tây** *var.* Sontay. Ha Tây, N Vietnam
Sontay *see* Sơn Tây
101 J25 **Sonthofen** Bayern, S Germany
Soochow *see* Suzhou
80 O13 **Sool** *off.* Gobolka Sool. ◈ *region* N Somali
Soomaaliya/Soomaaliyeed, Jamuuriyada Demuqraadiga *see* Somalia
Soome Laht *see* Finland, Gulf of
23 V5 **Soperton** Georgia, SE USA
167 S6 **Sop Hao** Houaphan, N Laos
Sophia *see* Sofiya
171 S10 **Sopi** Pulau Morotai, E Indonesia
Sopianae *see* Pécs
171 U13 **Sopinusa** Papua, E Indonesia
81 B14 **Sopo** ~ W Sudan
Sopockinie/Sopotskin/Sopotskino *see* Sapotskin
114 I9 **Sopot** Plovdiv, C Bulgaria
110 I7 **Sopot** *Ger.* Zoppot. Pomorskie, N Poland
167 O8 **Sop Prap** *var.* Ban Sop Prap. Lampang, NW Thailand
111 G22 **Sopron** *Ger.* Ödenburg. Győr-Moson-Sopron, NW Hungary
147 U11 **Sopu-Korgon** *var.* Sofi-Kurgan. Oshskaya Oblast', SW Kyrgyzstan
152 H5 **Sopur** Jammu and Kashmir, NW India
107 J15 **Sora** Lazio, C Italy
154 N13 **Sorada** Orissa, E India
93 H17 **Söråker** Västernorrland, C Sweden
57 J17 **Sorata** La Paz, W Bolivia
Sorau/Sorau in der Niederlausitz *see* Żary
105 Q14 **Sorbas** Andalucía, S Spain
Sord/Sórd Choluim Chille *see* Swords
15 O11 **Sorel** Québec, SE Canada
183 P17 **Sorell** Tasmania, SE Australia
183 O17 **Sorell, Lake** ◎ Tasmania, SE Australia
106 E8 **Soresina** Lombardia, N Italy
95 D14 **Sørfjorden** *fjord* S Norway
94 N11 **Sörforsa** Gävleborg, C Sweden
103 R14 **Sorgues** Vaucluse, SE France
136 K13 **Sorgun** Yozgat, C Turkey
105 P5 **Soria** Castilla-León, N Spain
105 P6 **Soria** ◈ *province* Castilla-León, N Spain
61 D19 **Soriano** Soriano, SW Uruguay
61 D19 **Soriano** ◈ *department* SW Uruguay
92 O4 **Sørkapp** *headland* SW Svalbard
143 T5 **Sorkh, Kūh-e** ▲▲ NE Iran
95 I23 **Sorø** Vestsjælland, E Denmark
Soro *see* Ghazal, Bahr el
116 M8 **Soroca** *Rus.* Soroki. N Moldova
60 L10 **Sorocaba** São Paulo, S Brazil
Sorochino *see* Sarochyna
127 T7 **Sorochinsk** Orenburgskaya Oblast', W Russian Federation
Soroki *see* Soroca
188 H15 **Sorol** *atoll* Caroline Islands, W Micronesia
171 T12 **Sorong** Papua, E Indonesia
81 G17 **Soroti** C Uganda
Sørøy *see* Sørøya
92 J8 **Sørøya** *var.* Sørøy, *Lapp.* Sállan. *island* N Norway
104 G11 **Sorraia, Rio** ~ C Portugal
92 I10 **Sørreisa** Troms, N Norway
107 K18 **Sorrento** *anc.* Surrentum. Campania, S Italy
104 H10 **Sor, Ribeira de** *stream* C Portugal
195 T3 **Sør Rondane Mountains** ▲▲ Antarctica
93 H14 **Sorsele** Västerbotten, N Sweden
107 B17 **Sorso** Sardegna, Italy, C Mediterranean Sea
171 P4 **Sorsogon** Luzon, N Philippines
105 U4 **Sort** Cataluña, NE Spain
124 H11 **Sortavala** Respublika Kareliya, NW Russian Federation
107 L25 **Sortino** Sicilia, Italy, C Mediterranean Sea
92 G10 **Sortland** Nordland, C Norway
94 G9 **Sør-Trøndelag** ◈ *county* S Norway
95 I15 **Sørumsand** Akershus, S Norway
118 D6 **Sõrve Säär** *headland* SW Estonia
95 K22 **Sösdala** Skåne, S Sweden
105 R4 **Sos del Rey Católico** Aragón, NE Spain
93 F15 **Sösjöfjällen** ▲ C Sweden
126 K7 **Sosna** ~ W Russian Federation
62 H12 **Sosneado, Cerro** ▲ W Argentina
125 S9 **Sosnogorsk** Respublika Komi, NW Russian Federation
124 J8 **Sosnovets** Respublika Kareliya, NW Russian Federation
Sosnovets *see* Sosnowiec
127 Q3 **Sosnovka** Chavash Respubliki, W Russian Federation
125 S16 **Sosnovka** Kirovskaya Oblast', NW Russian Federation
124 M6 **Sosnovka** Murmanskaya Oblast', NW Russian Federation
126 M6 **Sosnovka** Tambovskaya Oblast', W Russian Federation
124 H12 **Sosnovo** *Fin.* Rautu. Leningradskaya Oblast', NW Russian Federation
Sosnovyy Bor *see* Sasnovy Bor
111 J16 **Sosnowiec** *Ger.* Sosnowitz, *Rus.* Sosnovets. Śląskie, S Poland
Sosnowitz *see* Sosnowiec
117 R2 **Sosnytsya** Chernihivs'ka Oblast', N Ukraine
109 V10 **Šoštanj** N Slovenia
122 G10 **Sos'va** Sverdlovskaya Oblast', C Russian Federation
54 D12 **Sotará, Volcán** ⛰ S Colombia
76 D10 **Sotavento, Ilhas de** *var.* Leeward Islands. *island group* S Cape Verde
93 N15 **Sotkamo** Oulu, C Finland
109 W11 **Sotla** ~ E Slovenia
41 P10 **Soto la Marina** Tamaulipas, C Mexico
41 P10 **Soto la Marina, Río** ~ C Mexico
95 B14 **Sotra** *island* S Norway
41 X12 **Sotuta** Yucatán, SE Mexico
79 F17 **Souanké** La Sangha, NW Congo
76 M17 **Soubré** S Ivory Coast
115 H24 **Soúda** *var.* Soúdha, *Eng.* Suda. Kríti, Greece, E Mediterranean Sea
Soúdha *see* Soúda
Soueida *see* As Suwaydā'
114 L12 **Souflí** *prev.* Souflíon. Anatolikí Makedonía kai Thráki, NE Greece
Souflíon *see* Souflí

◆ Country ● Country Capital ◇ Dependent Territory ○ Dependent Territory Capital ◈ Administrative Regions ✈ International Airport ▲ Mountain ▲▲ Mountain Range ⛰ Volcano ~ River ◎ Lake ⊡ Reservoir

Soufrière – Stade

45 S11 **Soufrière** W Saint Lucia
45 X6 **Soufrière** ▲ Basse Terre, S Guadeloupe
102 M13 **Souillac** Lot, S France
173 Y17 **Souillac** S Mauritius
74 M5 **Souk Ahras** NE Algeria
Souk el Arba du Rharb/ Souk-el-Arba-du-Rharb/ Souk-el-Arba-el-Rhab *see* Souk-el-Arba-Rharb
74 E6 **Souk-el-Arba-Rharb** *var.* Souk el Arba du Rharb, Souk-el-Arba-du-Rharb, Souk-el-Arba-el-Rhab. NW Morocco
Soukhné *see* As Sukhnah
163 X14 **Sŏul** *off.* Sŏul-t'ŭkpyŏlsi, *Eng.* Seoul, *Jap.* Keijō; *prev.* Kyŏngsŏng. ● (South Korea) NW South Korea
102 J11 **Soulac-sur-Mer** Gironde, SW France
Sŏul-t'ŭkpyŏlsi *see* Sŏul
99 L19 **Soumagne** Liège, E Belgium
18 M14 **Sound Beach** Long Island, New York, NE USA
95 J22 **Sound, The** *Dan.* Øresund, *Swe.* Öresund. *strait* Denmark/Sweden
115 H20 **Soúnio, Akrotírio** *cape* C Greece
138 F8 **Soûr** *var.* Şûr; *anc.* Tyre. SW Lebanon
Sources, Mont-aux- *see* Phofung
104 G8 **Soure** Coimbra, N Portugal
9 W17 **Souris** Manitoba, S Canada
13 Q14 **Souris** Prince Edward Island, SE Canada
28 L2 **Souris River** *var.* Mouse River. ∽ Canada/USA
25 X10 **Sour Lake** Texas, SW USA
115 F17 **Soúrpi** Thessalía, C Greece
104 H11 **Sousel** Portalegre, C Portugal
75 N6 **Sousse** *var.* Sūsah. NE Tunisia
14 H11 **South** ∽ Ontario, S Canada
South *see* Sud
83 G23 **South Africa** *off.* Republic of South Africa, *Afr.* Suid-Afrika. ◆ *republic* S Africa
South Africa, Republic of *see* South Africa
46-47 **South America** *continent*
2 J17 **South American Plate** *tectonic feature*
97 M23 **Southampton** *hist.* Hamwih, *Lat.* Clausentum. S England, UK
19 N14 **Southampton** Long Island, New York, NE USA
9 P8 **Southampton Island** *island* Nunavut, NE Canada
151 P20 **South Andaman** *island* Andaman Islands, India, NE Indian Ocean
13 Q6 **South Aulatsivik Island** *island* Newfoundland and Labrador, E Canada
182 E4 **South Australia** ◐ *state* S Australia
South Australian Abyssal Plain *see* South Australian Plain
192 G11 **South Australian Basin** *undersea feature* SW Indian Ocean
173 X12 **South Australian Plain** *var.* South Australian Abyssal Plain. *undersea feature* SE Indian Ocean
37 R13 **South Baldy** ▲ New Mexico, SW USA
23 Y14 **South Bay** Florida, SE USA
14 E12 **South Baymouth** Manitoulin Island, Ontario, S Canada
30 L10 **South Beloit** Illinois, N USA
31 O11 **South Bend** Indiana, N USA
25 R6 **South Bend** Texas, SW USA
32 F9 **South Bend** Washington, NW USA
South Beveland *see* Zuid-Beveland
South Borneo *see* Kalimantan Selatan
21 U7 **South Boston** Virginia, NE USA
182 F2 **South Branch Neales** *seasonal river* South Australia
21 U3 **South Branch Potomac River** ∽ West Virginia, NE USA
185 H19 **Southbridge** Canterbury, South Island, New Zealand
19 N12 **Southbridge** Massachusetts, NE USA
183 P17 **South Bruny Island** *island* Tasmania, SE Australia
18 L7 **South Burlington** Vermont, NE USA
44 M6 **South Caicos** *island* S Turks and Caicos Islands
South Cape *see* Ka Lae
23 V3 **South Carolina** *off.* State of South Carolina, *also known as* The Palmetto State. ◐ *state* SE USA
South Carpathians *see* Carpații Meridionali
South Celebes *see* Sulawesi Selatan
21 Q5 **South Charleston** West Virginia, NE USA
192 D7 **South China Basin** *undersea feature* SE South China Sea
169 R8 **South China Sea** *Chin.* Nan Hai, *Ind.* Laut Cina Selatan, *Vtn.* Biên Đông. *sea* SE Asia
33 Z10 **South Dakota** *off.* State of South Dakota, *also known as* The Coyote State, Sunshine State. ◐ *state* N USA
23 X10 **South Daytona** Florida, SE USA
37 R10 **South Domingo Pueblo** New Mexico, SW USA
97 N23 **South Downs** *hill range* SE England, UK
83 I21 **South East** ◐ *district* SE Botswana
65 H15 **South East Bay** *bay* Ascension Island, C Atlantic Ocean
183 O17 **South East Cape** *headland* Tasmania, SE Australia
38 K10 **Southeast Cape** *headland* Saint Lawrence Island, Alaska, USA
South-East Celebes *see* Sulawesi Tenggara
192 G12 **Southeast Indian Ridge** *undersea feature* Indian Ocean/ Pacific Ocean
Southeast Island *see* Tagula Island
193 P13 **Southeast Pacific Basin** *var.* Belling Hausen Mulde. *undersea feature* SE Pacific Ocean
65 H15 **South East Point** *headland* SE Ascension Island
183 O14 **South East Point** *headland* Victoria, S Australia
44 L5 **Southeast Point** *headland* Mayaguana, SE Bahamas
191 Z3 **South East Point** *headland* Kiritimati, NE Kiribati
South-East Sulawesi *see* Sulawesi Tenggara
9 U12 **Southend** Saskatchewan, C Canada
97 P22 **Southend-on-Sea** E England, UK
83 H20 **Southern** *var.* Bangwaketse, Ngwaketze. ◐ *district* SE Botswana
81 I15 **Southern** ◐ *region* S Ethiopia
138 E13 **Southern** ◐ *district* S Israel
83 N15 **Southern** ◐ *region* S Malawi
83 I15 **Southern** ◐ *province* S Zambia
185 E19 **Southern Alps** ⛰ South Island, New Zealand
190 K15 **Southern Cook Islands** *island group* S Cook Islands
180 K12 **Southern Cross** Western Australia
80 A12 **Southern Darfur** ◐ *state* W Sudan
186 B7 **Southern Highlands** ◐ *province* W Papua New Guinea
9 V11 **Southern Indian Lake** ◎ Manitoba, C Canada
80 E11 **Southern Kordofan** ◐ *state* C Sudan
187 Z15 **Southern Lau Group** *island group* Lau Group, SE Fiji
173 S13 **Southern Ocean** *ocean*
21 T10 **Southern Pines** North Carolina, SE USA
155 J26 **Southern Province** ◐ *province* S Sri Lanka
96 I13 **Southern Uplands** ⛰ S Scotland, UK
Southern Urals *see* Yuzhnyy Ural
183 P16 **South Esk River** ∽ Tasmania, SE Australia
9 U16 **Southey** Saskatchewan, S Canada
27 V2 **South Fabius River** ∽ Missouri, C USA
31 S10 **Southfield** Michigan, N USA
192 K10 **South Fiji Basin** *undersea feature* S Pacific Ocean
97 Q22 **South Foreland** *headland* SE England, UK
35 P7 **South Fork American River** ∽ California, W USA
28 K7 **South Fork Grand River** ∽ South Dakota, N USA
35 T12 **South Fork Kern River** ∽ California, W USA
39 Q7 **South Fork Koyukuk River** ∽ Alaska, USA
39 Q11 **South Fork Kuskokwim River** ∽ Alaska, USA
26 H2 **South Fork Republican River** ∽ C USA
26 L3 **South Fork Solomon River** ∽ Kansas, C USA
31 P5 **South Fox Island** *island* Michigan, N USA
20 G8 **South Fulton** Tennessee, S USA
195 U10 **South Geomagnetic Pole** *pole* Antarctica
65 J20 **South Georgia** *island* South Georgia and the South Sandwich Islands, SW Atlantic Ocean
65 K21 **South Georgia and the South Sandwich Islands** ◇ *UK Dependent Territory* SW Atlantic Ocean
47 Y14 **South Georgia Ridge** *var.* North Scotia Ridge. *undersea feature* SW Atlantic Ocean
181 Q1 **South Goulburn Island** *island* Northern Territory, N Australia
153 U16 **South Hatia Island** *island* SE Bangladesh
31 O10 **South Haven** Michigan, N USA
21 V7 **South Hill** Virginia, NE USA
South Holland *see* Zuid-Holland
21 P8 **South Holston Lake** ▣ Tennessee/Virginia, S USA
175 N1 **South Honshu Ridge** *undersea feature* W Pacific Ocean
26 M6 **South Hutchinson** Kansas, C USA
151 K21 **South Huvadhu Atoll** *atoll* S Maldives
173 U14 **South Indian Basin** *undersea feature* Indian Ocean/Pacific Ocean
9 W11 **South Indian Lake** Manitoba, C Canada
81 I17 **South Island** *island* NW Kenya
185 C20 **South Island** *island* S New Zealand
65 B23 **South Jason** *island* Jason Islands, NW Falkland Islands
South Kalimantan *see* Kalimantan Selatan
South Kazakhstan *see* Yuzhnyy Kazakhstan
163 X15 **South Korea** *off.* Republic of South Korea, *Kor.* Taehan Min'guk. ◆ *republic* E Asia
35 Q6 **South Lake Tahoe** California, W USA
25 N6 **Southland** Texas, SW USA
185 B23 **Southland** *off.* Southland Region. ◐ *region* South Island, New Zealand
Southland Region *see* Southland
29 N15 **South Loup River** ∽ Nebraska, C USA
151 K19 **South Maalhosmadulu Atoll** *atoll* N Maldives
14 E15 **South Maitland** ∽ Ontario, S Canada
192 E8 **South Makassar Basin** *undersea feature* E Java Sea
31 O6 **South Manitou Island** *island* Michigan, N USA
151 K18 **South Miladummadulu Atoll** *atoll* N Maldives
21 X8 **South Mills** North Carolina, SE USA
8 H9 **South Nahanni** ∽ Northwest Territories, NW Canada
39 P13 **South Naknek** Alaska, USA
14 M13 **South Nation** ∽ Ontario, SE Canada
44 F9 **South Negril Point** *headland* W Jamaica
151 K20 **South Nilandhe Atoll** *var.* Dhaalu Atoll. *atoll* C Maldives
36 L2 **South Ogden** Utah, W USA
18 M14 **Southold** Long Island, New York, NE USA
194 H1 **South Orkney Islands** *island group* Antarctica
137 S9 **South Ossetia** *former autonomous region* SW Georgia
South Pacific Basin *see* Southwest Pacific Basin
19 P7 **South Paris** Maine, NE USA
189 U13 **South Pass** *passage* Chuuk Islands, C Micronesia
33 U15 **South Pass** *pass* Wyoming, C USA
20 K10 **South Pittsburg** Tennessee, S USA
28 K15 **South Platte River** ∽ Colorado/Nebraska, C USA
31 T16 **South Point** Ohio, N USA
65 G15 **South Point** *headland* S Ascension Island
31 R6 **South Point** *headland* Michigan, N USA
South Point *see* Ka Lae
195 Q9 **South Pole** *pole* Antarctica
183 P17 **Southport** Tasmania, SE Australia
97 K17 **Southport** NW England, UK
21 V12 **Southport** North Carolina, SE USA
19 P8 **South Portland** Maine, NE USA
14 H12 **South River** Ontario, S Canada
21 U11 **South River** ∽ North Carolina, SE USA
96 K5 **South Ronaldsay** *island* NE Scotland, UK
36 L2 **South Salt Lake** Utah, W USA
65 L21 **South Sandwich Islands** *island group* SE South Georgia and South Sandwich Islands
65 K21 **South Sandwich Trench** *undersea feature* SW Atlantic Ocean
9 S16 **South Saskatchewan** ∽ Alberta/Saskatchewan, S Canada
65 I21 **South Scotia Ridge** *undersea feature* S Scotia Sea
9 V10 **South Seal** ∽ Manitoba, C Canada
194 G4 **South Shetland Islands** *island group* Antarctica
65 H22 **South Shetland Trough** *undersea feature* Atlantic Ocean/Pacific Ocean
97 M14 **South Shields** NE England, UK
29 R13 **South Sioux City** Nebraska, C USA
192 J9 **South Solomon Trench** *undersea feature* W Pacific Ocean
183 V3 **South Stradbroke Island** *island* Queensland, E Australia
South Sulawesi *see* Sulawesi Selatan
South Sumatra *see* Sumatera Selatan
184 K11 **South Taranaki Bight** *bight* SE Tasman Sea
South Tasmania Plateau *see* Tasman Plateau
36 M15 **South Tucson** Arizona, SW USA
12 H9 **South Twin Island** *island* Nunavut, C Canada
96 E9 **South Uist** *island* NW Scotland, UK
South-West *see* Sud-Ouest
South-West Africa/South West Africa *see* Namibia
65 F15 **South West Bay** *bay* Ascension Island, C Atlantic Ocean
183 N18 **South West Cape** *headland* Tasmania, SE Australia
185 B26 **South West Cape** *headland* Stewart Island, New Zealand
38 J10 **Southwest Cape** *headland* Saint Lawrence Island, Alaska, USA
Southwest Indian Ocean Ridge *see* Southwest Indian Ridge
173 N11 **Southwest Indian Ridge** *var.* Southwest Indian Ocean Ridge. *undersea feature* SW Indian Ocean
192 L10 **Southwest Pacific Basin** *var.* South Pacific Basin. *undersea feature* SE Pacific Ocean
44 H2 **Southwest Point** *headland* Great Abaco, N Bahamas
191 X3 **South West Point** *headland* Kiritimati, NE Kiribati
65 G25 **South West Point** *headland* SW Saint Helena
25 P5 **South Wichita River** ∽ Texas, SW USA
97 Q20 **Southwold** E England, UK
19 Q12 **South Yarmouth** Massachusetts, NE USA
116 J10 **Sovata** *Hung.* Szováta. Mureș, C Romania
107 N22 **Soverato** Calabria, SW Italy
121 O4 **Sovereign Base Area** *uk military installation* S Cyprus
Sovetabad *see* Ghafurov
126 C2 **Sovetsk** *Ger.* Tilsit. Kaliningradskaya Oblast', W Russian Federation
125 Q15 **Sovetsk** Kirovskaya Oblast', NW Russian Federation
127 N10 **Sovetskaya** Rostovskaya Oblast', SW Russian Federation
Sovetskoye *see* Ketchenery
146 I15 **Sovet"yab** *prev.* Sovet"yap. Ahal Welaýaty, S Turkmenistan
Sovet"yap *see* Sovet"yab
117 U12 **Sovyets'kyy** Respublika Krym, S Ukraine
83 I18 **Sowa** *var.* Sua. Central, NE Botswana
Sowa Pan *see* Sua Pan
83 J21 **Soweto** Gauteng, NE South Africa
147 R11 **So'x** *Rus.* Sokh. Farg'ona Viloyati, E Uzbekistan
Sōya-kaikyō *see* La Perouse Strait
165 T1 **Sōya-misaki** *headland* Hokkaidō, NE Japan
125 N7 **Soyana** ∽ NW Russian Federation
146 A8 **Soye, Mys** *var.* Mys Suz. *headland* NW Turkmenistan
82 A10 **Soyo** Dem. Rep. Congo, NW Angola
80 J10 **Soyra** ▲ C Eritrea
Sozaq *see* Suzak
119 P16 **Sozh** *Rus.* Sozh. ∽ NE Europe
114 N10 **Sozopol** *prev.* Sizebolu; *anc.* Apollonia. Burgas, E Bulgaria
99 L20 **Spa** Liège, E Belgium
194 I7 **Spaatz Island** *island* Antarctica
144 M14 **Space Launching Centre** *space station* Kzyl-Orda, S Kazakhstan
105 O7 **Spain** *off.* Kingdom of Spain, *Sp.* España; *anc.* Hispania, Iberia, *Lat.* Hispana. ◆ *monarchy* SW Europe
Spain, Kingdom of *see* Spain
Spalato *see* Split
97 O19 **Spalding** E England, UK
14 D11 **Spanish** Ontario, S Canada
36 L3 **Spanish Fork** Utah, W USA
64 B12 **Spanish Point** *headland* C Bermuda
14 E9 **Spanish River** ∽ Ontario, S Canada
44 K13 **Spanish Town** *hist.* St.Iago de la Vega. C Jamaica
35 Q5 **Sparks** Nevada, W USA
Sparnacum *see* Épernay
95 N16 **Sparreholm** Södermanland, C Sweden
23 U4 **Sparta** Georgia, SE USA
30 K16 **Sparta** Illinois, N USA
31 P9 **Sparta** Michigan, N USA
21 R8 **Sparta** North Carolina, SE USA
20 L9 **Sparta** Tennessee, S USA
30 I7 **Sparta** Wisconsin, N USA
Sparta *see* Spárti
21 Q11 **Spartanburg** South Carolina, SE USA
115 F21 **Spárti** *Eng.* Sparta. Pelopónnisos, S Greece
107 B21 **Spartivento, Capo** *headland* Sardegna, Italy, C Mediterranean Sea
9 P17 **Sparwood** British Columbia, SW Canada
126 I4 **Spas-Demensk** Kaluzhskaya Oblast', W Russian Federation
126 M4 **Spas-Klepiki** Ryazanskaya Oblast', W Russian Federation
Spasovo *see* Kulen Vakuf
123 R15 **Spassk-Dal'niy** Primorskiy Kray, SE Russian Federation
126 M5 **Spassk-Ryazanskiy** Ryazanskaya Oblast', W Russian Federation
115 H19 **Spáta** Attikí, C Greece
121 Q11 **Spátha, Akrotírio** *var.* Akrotírio Spánta. *headland* Kríti, Greece, E Mediterranean Sea
Špatrjan *see* Paternion
28 I9 **Spearfish** South Dakota, N USA
25 O1 **Spearman** Texas, SW USA
65 C25 **Speedwell Island** *island* S Falkland Islands
65 C25 **Speedwell Island Settlement** S Falkland Islands
65 G25 **Speery Island** *island* S Saint Helena
45 N14 **Speightstown** NW Barbados
106 I13 **Spello** Umbria, C Italy
39 R12 **Spenard** Alaska, USA
Spence Bay *see* Taloyoak
31 O14 **Spencer** Indiana, N USA
29 T12 **Spencer** Iowa, C USA
29 P12 **Spencer** Nebraska, C USA
21 S9 **Spencer** North Carolina, SE USA
20 L9 **Spencer** Tennessee, S USA
21 Q4 **Spencer** West Virginia, NE USA
30 K6 **Spencer** Wisconsin, N USA
182 G10 **Spencer, Cape** *headland* South Australia
39 V13 **Spencer, Cape** *headland* Alaska, USA
182 H9 **Spencer Gulf** *gulf* South Australia
18 F9 **Spencerport** New York, NE USA
31 Q12 **Spencerville** Ohio, N USA
115 E17 **Spercheiáda** *var.* Sperhiada, Sperkhiás. Stereá Ellás, C Greece
115 E17 **Spercheiós** ∽ C Greece
Sperhiada *see* Spercheiáda
95 G14 **Sperillen** ◎ S Norway
Sperkhiás *see* Spercheiáda
101 I18 **Spessart** *hill range* C Germany
Spétsai *see* Spétses
115 G21 **Spétses** *prev.* Spétsai. Spétses, S Greece
115 G21 **Spétses** *island* S Greece
96 J8 **Spey** ∽ NE Scotland, UK
101 G20 **Speyer** *Eng.* Spires; *anc.* Civitas Nemetum, Spira. Rheinland-Pfalz, SW Germany
101 G20 **Speyerbach** ∽ W Germany
107 N20 **Spezzano Albanese** Calabria, SW Italy
Spice Islands *see* Maluku
100 F9 **Spiekeroog** *island* NW Germany
109 W9 **Spielfeld** Steiermark, SE Austria
65 N21 **Spiess Seamount** *undersea feature* S Atlantic Ocean
108 E9 **Spiez** Bern, W Switzerland
98 G13 **Spijkenisse** Zuid-Holland, SW Netherlands
39 T6 **Spike Mountain** ▲ Alaska, USA
115 I25 **Spíli** Kríti, Greece, E Mediterranean Sea
108 D10 **Spillgerten** ▲ W Switzerland
118 F9 **Spilva** ✈ (Rīga) Rīga, C Latvia
107 N17 **Spinazzola** Puglia, SE Italy
149 O9 **Spīn Būldak** Kandahār, S Afghanistan
Spira *see* Speyer
Spirdingsee *see* Śniardwy, Jezioro
Spires *see* Speyer
29 T11 **Spirit Lake** Iowa, C USA
29 T11 **Spirit Lake** ◎ Iowa, C USA
9 N13 **Spirit River** Alberta, W Canada
9 S14 **Spiritwood** Saskatchewan, S Canada
27 R11 **Spiro** Oklahoma, C USA
111 L19 **Spišská Nová Ves** *Ger.* Neudorf, Zipser Neudorf, *Hung.* Igló. Košický Kraj, E Slovakia
137 T11 **Spitak** NW Armenia
92 O2 **Spitsbergen** *island* NW Svalbard
Spittal *see* Spittal an der Drau
109 R9 **Spittal an der Drau** *var.* Spittal. Kärnten, S Austria
109 V3 **Spitz** Niederösterreich, NE Austria
94 D9 **Spjelkavik** Møre og Romsdal, S Norway
25 W10 **Splendora** Texas, SW USA
113 E14 **Split** *It.* Spalato. Split-Dalmacija, S Croatia
113 E14 **Split** ✈ Split-Dalmacija, S Croatia
113 E14 **Split-Dalmacija** *off.* Splitsko-Dalmatinska Županija. ◐ *province* S Croatia
9 X12 **Split Lake** ◎ Manitoba, C Canada
Splitsko-Dalmatinska Županija *see* Split-Dalmacija
108 H10 **Splügen** Graubünden, S Switzerland
Spodnji Dravograd *see* Dravograd
25 P12 **Spofford** Texas, SW USA
118 J11 **Špoģi** Daugvapils, SE Latvia
32 L8 **Spokane** Washington, NW USA
32 L8 **Spokane River** ∽ Washington, NW USA
106 I13 **Spoleto** Umbria, C Italy
30 I4 **Spooner** Wisconsin, N USA
30 K12 **Spoon River** ∽ Illinois, N USA
21 W5 **Spotsylvania** Virginia, NE USA
32 L8 **Sprague** Washington, NW USA
170 J5 **Spratly Island** *island* SW Spratly Islands
192 E6 **Spratly Islands** *Chin.* Nansha Qundao. ◇ *disputed territory* SE Asia
32 J12 **Spray** Oregon, NW USA
112 I11 **Spreča** ∽ N Bosnia and Herzegovina
100 P13 **Spree** ∽ E Germany
100 P13 **Spreewald** *marshy woodland district* NE Germany
101 P14 **Spremberg** Brandenburg, E Germany
25 W11 **Spring** Texas, SW USA
31 Q10 **Spring Arbor** Michigan, N USA
83 E23 **Springbok** Northern Cape, W South Africa
18 I15 **Spring City** Pennsylvania, NE USA
20 L9 **Spring City** Tennessee, S USA
36 L4 **Spring City** Utah, W USA
35 W3 **Spring Creek** Nevada, W USA
27 S9 **Springdale** Arkansas, C USA
31 Q14 **Springdale** Ohio, N USA
100 I13 **Springe** Niedersachsen, N Germany
37 U9 **Springer** New Mexico, SW USA
37 W7 **Springfield** Colorado, C USA
23 W5 **Springfield** Georgia, SE USA
30 K14 **Springfield** *state capital* Illinois, N USA
20 L6 **Springfield** Kentucky, S USA
18 M12 **Springfield** Massachusetts, NE USA
29 T10 **Springfield** Minnesota, N USA
27 T7 **Springfield** Missouri, C USA
31 R13 **Springfield** Ohio, N USA
32 G13 **Springfield** Oregon, NW USA
29 Q12 **Springfield** South Dakota, N USA
20 J8 **Springfield** Tennessee, S USA
18 M9 **Springfield** Vermont, NE USA
30 K14 **Springfield, Lake** ▣ Illinois, N USA
55 T8 **Spring Garden** NE Guyana
30 K8 **Spring Green** Wisconsin, N USA
29 X11 **Spring Grove** Minnesota, N USA
13 P15 **Springhill** Nova Scotia, SE Canada
23 V12 **Spring Hill** Florida, SE USA
27 R4 **Spring Hill** Kansas, C USA
22 G4 **Springhill** Louisiana, S USA
20 I9 **Spring Hill** Tennessee, S USA
21 U10 **Spring Lake** North Carolina, SE USA
24 M4 **Springlake** Texas, SW USA
35 W11 **Spring Mountains** ⛰ Nevada, W USA
65 B24 **Spring Point** West Falkland, Falkland Islands
27 W9 **Spring River** ∽ Arkansas/ Missouri, C USA
27 S7 **Spring River** ∽ Missouri/ Oklahoma, C USA
83 J21 **Springs** Gauteng, NE South Africa
185 H16 **Springs Junction** West Coast, South Island, New Zealand
181 X8 **Springsure** Queensland, E Australia
29 W11 **Spring Valley** Minnesota, N USA
18 K13 **Spring Valley** New York, NE USA
29 N12 **Springview** Nebraska, C USA
18 D11 **Springville** New York, NE USA
36 L3 **Springville** Utah, W USA
Sprottau *see* Szprotawa
15 V4 **Sproule, Pointe** *headland* Québec, SE Canada
9 Q14 **Spruce Grove** Alberta, SW Canada
21 T4 **Spruce Knob** ▲ West Virginia, NE USA
35 X3 **Spruce Mountain** ▲ Nevada, W USA
21 P9 **Spruce Pine** North Carolina, SE USA
98 G13 **Spui** ∽ SW Netherlands
107 O19 **Spulico, Capo** *headland* S Italy
25 O5 **Spur** Texas, SW USA
97 O17 **Spurn Head** *headland* E England, UK
99 H20 **Spy** Namur, S Belgium
95 I15 **Spydeberg** Østfold, S Norway
185 J17 **Spy Glass Point** *headland* South Island, New Zealand
10 L17 **Squamish** British Columbia, SW Canada
19 O8 **Squam Lake** ◎ New Hampshire, NE USA
19 S2 **Squa Pan Mountain** ▲ Maine, NE USA
39 N16 **Squaw Harbor** Unga Island, Alaska, USA
14 E11 **Squaw Island** *island* Ontario, S Canada
107 O22 **Squillace, Golfo di** *gulf* S Italy
107 Q18 **Squinzano** Puglia, SE Italy
Sráid na Cathrach *see* Milltown Malbay
167 S11 **Srâlau** Stœ̆ng Trêng, N Cambodia
Srath an Urláir *see* Stranorlar
112 G10 **Srbac** ◐ Republika Srpska, N Bosnia and Herzegovina
Srbija *see* Serbia
Srbinje *see* Foča
112 K9 **Srbobran** *var.* Bácsszenttamás, *Hung.* Szenttamás. Vojvodina, N Serbia
Srbobran *see* Donji Vakuf
167 R13 **Srê Âmběl** Kaôh Kông, SW Cambodia
112 K13 **Srebrenica** ◐ Republika Srpska, E Bosnia and Herzegovina
112 I11 **Srebrenik** ◐ Federacija Bosna I Hercegovina, NE Bosnia and Herzegovina
114 K10 **Sredets** *prev.* Syulemeshlii. Stara Zagora, C Bulgaria
114 M10 **Sredets** *prev.* Grudovo. ◐ Burgas, E Bulgaria
114 M10 **Sredetska Reka** ∽ SE Bulgaria
123 U9 **Sredinnyy Khrebet** ⛰ E Russian Federation
114 N7 **Sredishte** *Rom.* Beibunar; *prev.* Knyazhevo. Dobrich, NE Bulgaria
114 I10 **Sredna Gora** ⛰ C Bulgaria
123 R7 **Srednekolymsk** Respublika Sakha (Yakutiya), NE Russian Federation
126 K7 **Srednerusskaya Vozvyshennost'** *Eng.* Central Russian Upland. ⛰ W Russian Federation
122 L9 **Srednesibirskoye Ploskogor'ye** *var.* Central Siberian Uplands, *Eng.* Central Siberian Plateau. ⛰ N Russian Federation
125 V13 **Sredniy Ural** ⛰ NW Russian Federation
167 T12 **Srê Khtŭm** Môndol Kiri, E Cambodia
110 G12 **Śrem** Wielkopolskie, C Poland
112 K10 **Sremska Mitrovica** *prev.* Mitrovica, *Ger.* Mitrowitz. Vojvodina, NW Serbia
167 R11 **Srêng, Stœ̆ng** ∽ NW Cambodia
167 R11 **Srê Noy** Siĕmréab, NW Cambodia
Srepok, Sông *see* Srêpôk, Tônle
167 T12 **Srêpôk, Tônle** *var.* Sông Srepok. ∽ Cambodia/Vietnam
123 P13 **Sretensk** Chitinskaya Oblast', S Russian Federation
169 R10 **Sri Aman** Sarawak, East Malaysia
117 R4 **Sribne** Chernihivs'ka Oblast', N Ukraine
155 J25 **Sri Jayawardanapura** *var.* Sri Jayawardenepura; *prev.* Kotte. Western Province, W Sri Lanka
Sri Jayawardenepura *see* Sri Jayawardanapura
155 M14 **Srīkākulam** Andhra Pradesh, E India
155 J25 **Sri Lanka** *off.* Democratic Socialist Republic of Sri Lanka; *prev.* Ceylon. ◆ *republic* S Asia
130 F14 **Sri Lanka** *island* S Asia
Sri Lanka, Democratic Socialist Republic of *see* Sri Lanka
153 V14 **Srimangal** Sylhet, E Bangladesh
Sri Mohangorh *see* Shri Mohangarh
152 H5 **Srīnagar** *state capital* Jammu and Kashmir, N India
167 N10 **Srinagarind Reservoir** ◎ W Thailand
155 F19 **Sringeri** Karnātaka, W India
155 K25 **Sri Pada** *Eng.* Adam's Peak. ▲ S Sri Lanka
Sri Saket *see* Si Sa Ket
111 G14 **Środa Śląska** *Ger.* Neumarkt. Dolnośląskie, SW Poland
110 H12 **Środa Wielkopolska** Wielkopolskie, C Poland
Srpska Kostajnica *see* Bosanska Kostajnica
113 G14 **Srpska, Republika** ◐ *republic* Bosnia and Herzegovina
Srpski Brod *see* Bosanski Brod
Ssu-ch'uan *see* Sichuan
Ssu-p'ing/Ssu-p'ing-chieh *see* Siping
Stablo *see* Stavelot
99 G15 **Stabroek** Antwerpen, N Belgium
Stackeln *see* Strenči
96 I5 **Stack Skerry** *island* N Scotland, UK
100 I9 **Stade** Niedersachsen, NW Germany

◆ Country
● Country Capital
◇ Dependent Territory
○ Dependent Territory Capital
◐ Administrative Regions
✈ International Airport
▲ Mountain
⛰ Mountain Range
Volcano
∽ River
◎ Lake
▣ Reservoir

STADLANDET – STROUDSBURG

94 C10 **Stadlandet** *peninsula* S Norway
109 R5 **Stadl-Paura** Oberösterreich, NW Austria
119 L20 **Stadolichy** *Rus.* Stodolichi. Homyel'skaya Voblasts', SE Belarus
98 P7 **Stadskanaal** Groningen, NE Netherlands
101 H16 **Stadtallendorf** Hessen, C Germany
101 K23 **Stadtbergen** Bayern, S Germany
108 G7 **Stäfa** Zürich, NE Switzerland
95 K23 **Staffanstorp** Skåne, S Sweden
101 K18 **Staffelstein** Bayern, C Germany
97 L19 **Stafford** C England, UK
26 L6 **Stafford** Kansas, C USA
21 W4 **Stafford** Virginia, NE USA
97 L19 **Staffordshire** *cultural region* C England, UK
19 N12 **Stafford Springs** Connecticut, NE USA
115 H14 **Stágira** Kentrikí Makedonía, N Greece
118 G7 **Staicele** Limbaži, N Latvia
Staierdorf-Anina *see* Anina
109 V8 **Stainz** Steiermark, SE Austria
Stájerlakanina *see* Anina
117 Y7 **Stakhanov** Luhans'ka Oblast', E Ukraine
108 E11 **Stalden** Valais, SW Switzerland
Stalin *see* Varna
Stalinabad *see* Dushanbe
Stalingrad *see* Volgograd
Staliniri *see* Ts'khinvali
Stalino *see* Donets'k
Stalinobod *see* Dushanbe
Stalinov Štít *see* Gerlachovský štít
Stalinsk *see* Novokuznetsk
Stalins'kaya Oblast' *see* Donets'ka Oblast'
Stalinski Zaliv *see* Varnenski Zaliv
Stalin, Yazovir *see* Iskŭr, Yazovir
111 N15 **Stalowa Wola** Podkarpackie, SE Poland
114 I11 **Stamboliyski** Plovdiv, C Bulgaria
114 J8 **Stamboliyski, Yazovir** ⊠ N Bulgaria
97 N19 **Stamford** E England, UK
18 L14 **Stamford** Connecticut, NE USA
25 P6 **Stamford** Texas, SW USA
25 Q6 **Stamford, Lake** ⊠ Texas, SW USA
108 I10 **Stampa** Graubünden, SE Switzerland
Stampalia *see* Astypálaia
27 T14 **Stamps** Arkansas, C USA
92 G11 **Stamsund** Nordland, C Norway
27 R2 **Stanberry** Missouri, C USA
195 O3 **Stancomb-Wills Glacier** *glacier* Antarctica
83 K21 **Standerton** Mpumalanga, E South Africa
31 R7 **Standish** Michigan, N USA
20 M6 **Stanford** Kentucky, S USA
33 S9 **Stanford** Montana, NW USA
95 P19 **Stånga** Gotland, SE Sweden
94 H13 **Stange** Hedmark, S Norway
83 L23 **Stanger** KwaZulu/Natal, E South Africa
Stanimaka *see* Asenovgrad
Stanislau *see* Ivano-Frankivs'k
35 P8 **Stanislaus River** ≈ California, W USA
Stanislav *see* Ivano-Frankivs'k
Stanislavskaya Oblast' *see* Ivano-Frankivs'ka Oblast'
Stanisławów *see* Ivano-Frankivs'k
Stanke Dimitrov *see* Dupnitsa
183 O15 **Stanley** Tasmania, SE Australia
65 E24 **Stanley** *var.* Port Stanley, Puerto Argentino. ○ (Falkland Islands) East Falkland, Falkland Islands
33 O13 **Stanley** Idaho, NW USA
28 L3 **Stanley** North Dakota, N USA
21 U4 **Stanley** Virginia, NE USA
30 J6 **Stanley** Wisconsin, N USA
79 G21 **Stanley Pool** *var.* Pool Malebo. *lake section of river* Congo/Dem. Rep. Congo
155 H20 **Stanley Reservoir** ⊠ S India
Stanleyville *see* Kisangani
42 G3 **Stann Creek** ◈ *district* SE Belize
Stann Creek *see* Dangriga
123 Q12 **Stanovoy Khrebet** ▲▲ SE Russian Federation
108 F8 **Stans** Unterwalden, C Switzerland
97 O21 **Stansted** ✕ (London) Essex, E England, UK
183 U4 **Stanthorpe** Queensland, E Australia
21 N6 **Stanton** Kentucky, S USA
31 Q8 **Stanton** Michigan, N USA
29 Q14 **Stanton** Nebraska, C USA
28 L5 **Stanton** North Dakota, N USA
25 N7 **Stanton** Texas, SW USA
32 H7 **Stanwood** Washington, NW USA
117 Y7 **Stanychno-Luhans'ke** Luhans'ka Oblast', E Ukraine
108 K7 **Stanzach** Tirol, W Austria
98 M9 **Staphorst** Overijssel, E Netherlands
14 D18 **Staples** Ontario, S Canada
29 T6 **Staples** Minnesota, N USA
28 M14 **Stapleton** Nebraska, C USA
25 S8 **Star** Texas, SW USA
111 M14 **Starachowice** Świętokrzyskie, C Poland
Stara Kanjiža *see* Kanjiža
111 M18 **Stará Ľubovňa** *Ger.* Altlublau, *Hung.* Ólubló. Prešovský Kraj, E Slovakia
112 L10 **Stara Pazova** *Ger.* Altpasua, *Hung.* Ópazova. Vojvodina, N Serbia
Stara Planina *see* Balkan Mountains
114 L9 **Stara Reka** ≈ C Bulgaria
116 M5 **Stara Synyava** Khmel'nyts'ka Oblast', W Ukraine
116 I2 **Stara Vyzhivka** Volyns'ka Oblast', NW Ukraine
Staraya Belitsa *see* Staraya Byelitsa
119 M14 **Staraya Byelitsa** *Rus.* Staraya Belitsa. Vitsyebskaya Voblasts', NE Belarus
127 R5 **Staraya Mayna** Ul'yanovskaya Oblast', W Russian Federation
119 O18 **Staraya Rudnya** *Rus.* Staraya Rudnya. Homyel'skaya Voblasts', SE Belarus
124 H14 **Staraya Russa** Novgorodskaya Oblast', W Russian Federation
114 K10 **Stara Zagora** *Lat.* Augusta Trajana. Stara Zagora, C Bulgaria
114 K10 **Stara Zagora** ◈ *province* C Bulgaria
29 S8 **Starbuck** Minnesota, N USA
191 W4 **Starbuck Island** *prev.* Volunteer Island. *island* E Kiribati
27 V13 **Star City** Arkansas, C USA
112 F13 **Staretina** ▲▲ W Bosnia and Herzegovina
Stargard in Pommern *see* Stargard Szczeciński
110 E9 **Stargard Szczeciński** *Ger.* Stargard in Pommern. Zachodnio-pomorskie, NW Poland
187 N10 **Star Harbour** *harbour* San Cristobal, SE Solomon Islands
Stari Bečej *see* Bečej
113 F15 **Stari Grad** *It.* Cittavecchia. Split-Dalmacija, S Croatia
124 J16 **Staritsa** Tverskaya Oblast', W Russian Federation
23 V9 **Starke** Florida, SE USA
22 M4 **Starkville** Mississippi, S USA
186 B7 **Star Mountains** *Ind.* Pegunungan Sterren. ▲▲ Indonesia/Papua New Guinea
101 L23 **Starnberg** Bayern, SE Germany
101 L24 **Starnberger See** ◎ SE Germany
Starobel'sk *see* Starobil's'k
117 X8 **Starobesheve** Donets'ka Oblast', E Ukraine
117 Y6 **Starobil's'k** *Rus.* Starobel'sk. Luhans'ka Oblast', E Ukraine
119 K18 **Starobin** *var.* Starobyn. Minskaya Voblasts', S Belarus
Starobyn *see* Starobin
126 H6 **Starodub** Bryanskaya Oblast', W Russian Federation
110 I8 **Starogard Gdański** *Ger.* Preussisch-Stargard. Pomorskie, N Poland
145 P16 **Staroikan** Yuzhnyy Kazakhstan, S Kazakhstan
Starokonstantinov *see* Starokostyantyniv
116 L5 **Starokostyantyniv** *Rus.* Starokonstantinov. Khmel'nyts'ka Oblast', NW Ukraine
126 K12 **Starominskaya** Krasnodarskiy Kray, SW Russian Federation
114 L7 **Staro Selo** *Rom.* Satul-Vechi; *prev.* Star-Smil. Silistra, NE Bulgaria
126 K12 **Staroshcherbinovskaya** Krasnodarskiy Kray, SW Russian Federation
127 V6 **Starosubkhangulovo** Respublika Bashkortostan, W Russian Federation
35 S4 **Star Peak** ▲ Nevada, W USA
Star-Smil *see* Staro Selo
97 J25 **Start Point** *headland* SW England, UK
Startsy *see* Kirawsk
Starum *see* Stavoren
119 L18 **Staryya Darohi** *Rus.* Staryye Dorogi. Minskaya Voblasts', S Belarus
Staryye Dorogi *see* Staryya Darohi
127 T2 **Staryye Zyatsy** Udmurtskaya Respublika, NW Russian Federation
117 U13 **Staryy Krym** Respublika Krym, S Ukraine
126 K8 **Staryy Oskol** Belgorodskaya Oblast', W Russian Federation
116 H6 **Staryy Sambir** L'vivs'ka Oblast', W Ukraine
101 L14 **Stassfurt** *var.* Staßfurt. Sachsen-Anhalt, C Germany
Staßfurt *see* Stassfurt
111 M15 **Staszów** Świętokrzyskie, C Poland
29 W13 **State Center** Iowa, C USA
18 E14 **State College** Pennsylvania, NE USA
18 K15 **Staten Island** *island* New York, NE USA
Staten Island *see* Estados, Isla de los
23 U8 **Statenville** Georgia, SE USA
23 W5 **Statesboro** Georgia, SE USA
States, The *see* United States of America
21 R9 **Statesville** North Carolina, SE USA
95 G16 **Stathelle** Telemark, S Norway
30 K15 **Staunton** Illinois, N USA
21 T5 **Staunton** Virginia, NE USA
95 C16 **Stavanger** Rogaland, S Norway
99 L21 **Stavelot** *Dut.* Stablo. Liège, E Belgium
95 G16 **Stavern** Vestfold, S Norway
Stavers Island *see* Vostok Island
98 J7 **Stavoren** *Fris.* Starum. Friesland, N Netherlands
115 K21 **Stavrí, Akrotírio** *var.* Akrotírio Stavrós. *headland* Naxos, Kykládes, Greece, Aegean Sea
126 M14 **Stavropol'** *prev.* Voroshilovsk. Stavropol'skiy Kray, SW Russian Federation
Stavropol' *see* Tol'yatti
126 M14 **Stavropol'skaya Vozvyshennost'** ▲▲ SW Russian Federation
126 M14 **Stavropol'skiy Kray** ◈ *territory* SW Russian Federation
115 H14 **Stavrós** Kentrikí Makedonía, N Greece
115 J24 **Stavrós, Akrotírio** *cape* Kríti, Greece, E Mediterranean Sea
Stavrós, Akrotírio *see* Stavrí, Akrotírio
114 I12 **Stavroúpoli** *prev.* Stavroúpolis. Anatolikí Makedonía kai Thráki, NE Greece
Stavroúpolis *see* Stavroúpoli
117 O6 **Stavyshche** Kyyivs'ka Oblast', N Ukraine
182 M11 **Stawell** Victoria, SE Australia
110 N9 **Stawiski** Podlaskie, NE Poland
14 G14 **Stayner** Ontario, S Canada
37 R3 **Steamboat Springs** Colorado, C USA
20 M8 **Stearns** Kentucky, S USA
39 N10 **Stebbins** Alaska, USA
108 K7 **Steeg** Tirol, W Austria
27 Y9 **Steele** Missouri, C USA
29 N5 **Steele** North Dakota, N USA
194 J5 **Steele Island** *island* Antarctica
30 K16 **Steeleville** Illinois, N USA
27 W6 **Steelville** Missouri, C USA
99 G14 **Steenbergen** Noord-Brabant, S Netherlands
Steenkool *see* Bintuni
9 O10 **Steen River** Alberta, W Canada
98 M8 **Steenwijk** Overijssel, N Netherlands
65 A23 **Steeple Jason** *island* Jason Islands, NW Falkland Islands
174 J8 **Steep Point** *headland* Western Australia
116 L9 **Ştefăneşti** Botoşani, NE Romania
Stefanie, Lake *see* Ch'ew Bahir
8 L5 **Stefansson Island** *island* Nunavut, N Canada
117 O10 **Ştefan Vodă** *Rus.* Suvorovo. SE Moldova
63 H18 **Steffen, Cerro** ▲ S Chile
108 D9 **Steffisburg** Bern, C Switzerland
95 J24 **Stege** Storstrøm, SE Denmark
116 G10 **Ştei** *Hung.* Vaskohsziklás. Bihor, W Romania
Steier *see* Steyr
Steierdorf/Steierdorf-Anina *see* Anina
109 T7 **Steiermark** *off.* Land Steiermark, *Eng.* Styria. ◈ *state* C Austria
Steiermark, Land *see* Steiermark
101 J19 **Steigerwald** *hill range* C Germany
99 L17 **Stein** Limburg, SE Netherlands
Stein *see* Stein an der Donau
Stein *see* Kamnik, Slovenia
108 M8 **Steinach** Tirol, W Austria
Steinamanger *see* Szombathely
109 W3 **Stein an der Donau** *var.* Stein. Niederösterreich, NE Austria
Steinau an der Elbe *see* Ścinawa
9 Y16 **Steinbach** Manitoba, S Canada
Steiner Alpen *see* Kamniško-Savinjske Alpe
99 L24 **Steinfort** Luxembourg, W Luxembourg
100 H12 **Steinhuder Meer** ◎ NW Germany
93 E15 **Steinkjer** Nord-Trøndelag, C Norway
Stejarul *see* Karapelit
99 F16 **Stekene** Oost-Vlaanderen, NW Belgium
83 E26 **Stellenbosch** Western Cape, SW South Africa
98 F13 **Stellendam** Zuid-Holland, SW Netherlands
39 T12 **Steller, Mount** ▲ Alaska, USA
103 Y14 **Stello, Monte** ▲ Corse, France, C Mediterranean Sea
106 F5 **Stelvio, Passo dello** *pass* Italy/Switzerland
103 R3 **Stenay** Meuse, NE France
100 L12 **Stendal** Sachsen-Anhalt, C Germany
118 E8 **Stende** Talsi, NW Latvia
182 H10 **Stenhouse Bay** South Australia
95 J23 **Stenløse** Frederiksborg, E Denmark
95 L19 **Stensjön** Jönköping, S Sweden
95 K18 **Stenstorp** Västra Götaland, S Sweden
95 I18 **Stenungsund** Västra Götaland, S Sweden
Stepanakert *see* Xankändi
137 T11 **Step'anavan** N Armenia
100 K9 **Stepenitz** ≈ N Germany
29 O10 **Stephan** South Dakota, N USA
29 S3 **Stephen** Minnesota, N USA
27 T14 **Stephens** Arkansas, C USA
184 J13 **Stephens, Cape** *headland* D'Urville Island, Marlborough, SW New Zealand
21 V3 **Stephens City** Virginia, NE USA
182 L6 **Stephens Creek** New South Wales, SE Australia
184 K13 **Stephens Island** *island* C New Zealand
31 N5 **Stephenson** Michigan, N USA
13 S12 **Stephenville** Newfoundland, Newfoundland and Labrador, SE Canada
25 S7 **Stephenville** Texas, SW USA
145 P17 **Step' Nardara** *Kaz.* Shardara Dalasy; *prev.* Shaidara. *grassland* S Kazakhstan
145 R8 **Stepnogorsk** Akmola, C Kazakhstan
127 O15 **Stepnoye** Stavropol'skiy Kray, SW Russian Federation
145 Q8 **Stepnyak** Akmola, N Kazakhstan
192 J17 **Steps Point** *headland* Tutuila, W American Samoa
115 F17 **Stereá Ellás** *Eng.* Greece Central. ◈ *region* C Greece
83 J24 **Sterkspruit** Eastern Cape, SE South Africa
127 U6 **Sterlibashevo** Respublika Bashkortostan, W Russian Federation
39 R12 **Sterling** Alaska, USA
37 V3 **Sterling** Colorado, C USA
30 K11 **Sterling** Illinois, N USA
26 M5 **Sterling** Kansas, C USA
25 O8 **Sterling City** Texas, SW USA
31 S9 **Sterling Heights** Michigan, N USA
21 W3 **Sterling Park** Virginia, NE USA
37 V2 **Sterling Reservoir** ⊠ Colorado, C USA
22 I5 **Sterlington** Louisiana, S USA
127 U6 **Sterlitamak** Respublika Bashkortostan, W Russian Federation
Sternberg *see* Šternberk
111 H17 **Šternberk** *Ger.* Sternberg. Olomoucký Kraj, E Czech Republic
141 V17 **Stēroh** Suquṭrā, S Yemen
Sterren, Pegunungan *see* Star Mountains
110 G11 **Stęszew** Wielkopolskie, C Poland
Stettin *see* Szczecin
Stettiner Haff *see* Szczeciński, Zalew
9 Q15 **Stettler** Alberta, SW Canada
31 V13 **Steubenville** Ohio, N USA
97 O21 **Stevenage** E England, UK
23 Q1 **Stevenson** Alabama, S USA
32 H11 **Stevenson** Washington, NW USA
182 E1 **Stevenson Creek** *seasonal river* South Australia
39 Q13 **Stevenson Entrance** *strait* Alaska, USA
30 L6 **Stevens Point** Wisconsin, N USA
39 R8 **Stevens Village** Alaska, USA
33 P10 **Stevensville** Montana, NW USA
93 E25 **Stevns Klint** *headland* E Denmark
10 J12 **Stewart** British Columbia, W Canada
10 J6 **Stewart** ≈ Yukon Territory, NW Canada
10 I6 **Stewart Crossing** Yukon Territory, NW Canada
63 H25 **Stewart, Isla** *island* S Chile
185 B25 **Stewart Island** *island* S New Zealand
Stewart Islands *see* Sikaiana
181 W6 **Stewart, Mount** ▲ Queensland, E Australia
10 H6 **Stewart River** Yukon Territory, NW Canada
27 R3 **Stewartsville** Missouri, C USA
9 S16 **Stewart Valley** Saskatchewan, S Canada
29 W10 **Stewartville** Minnesota, N USA
Steyerlak-Anina *see* Anina
109 T5 **Steyr** *var.* Steier. Oberösterreich, N Austria
109 T5 **Steyr** ≈ NW Austria
29 P11 **Stickney** South Dakota, N USA
98 L5 **Stiens** Friesland, N Netherlands
Stif *see* Sétif
27 Q11 **Stigler** Oklahoma, C USA
107 N18 **Stigliano** Basilicata, S Italy
95 N17 **Stigtomta** Södermanland, C Sweden
10 I11 **Stikine** ≈ British Columbia, W Canada
Stilida/Stilís *see* Stylída
95 G22 **Stilling** Århus, C Denmark
29 W8 **Stillwater** Minnesota, N USA
27 O9 **Stillwater** Oklahoma, C USA
35 S5 **Stillwater Range** ▲▲ Nevada, W USA
18 I8 **Stillwater Reservoir** ⊠ New York, NE USA
107 O22 **Stilo, Punta** *headland* S Italy
27 R10 **Stilwell** Oklahoma, C USA
113 N17 **Štimlje** Kosovo, S Serbia
25 N1 **Stinnett** Texas, SW USA
113 P18 **Štip** E FYR Macedonia
Stira *see* Stýra
96 J12 **Stirling** C Scotland, UK
96 I12 **Stirling** *cultural region* C Scotland, UK
180 J14 **Stirling Range** ▲▲ Western Australia
93 E16 **Stjørdalshalsen** Nord-Trøndelag, C Norway
Stochód *see* Stokhid
101 H24 **Stockach** Baden-Württemberg, S Germany
25 S12 **Stockdale** Texas, SW USA
109 X3 **Stockerau** Niederösterreich, NE Austria
93 H20 **Stockholm** ● (Sweden) Stockholm, C Sweden
95 O15 **Stockholm** ◈ *county* C Sweden
Stockmannshof *see* Pļaviņas
97 L18 **Stockport** NW England, UK
65 K15 **Stocks Seamount** *undersea feature* C Atlantic Ocean
35 O8 **Stockton** California, W USA
26 L3 **Stockton** Kansas, C USA
27 S6 **Stockton** Missouri, C USA
30 K3 **Stockton Island** *island* Apostle Islands, Wisconsin, N USA
27 S7 **Stockton Lake** ⊠ Missouri, C USA
97 M15 **Stockton-on-Tees** *var.* Stockton on Tees. N England, UK
Stockton on Tees *see* Stockton-on-Tees
24 M10 **Stockton Plateau** *plain* Texas, SW USA
28 M16 **Stockville** Nebraska, C USA
93 H17 **Stöde** Västernorrland, C Sweden
Stodolichi *see* Stadolichy
113 M19 **Stogovo Karaorman** ▲▲ W FYR Macedonia
Stoke *see* Stoke-on-Trent
97 L19 **Stoke-on-Trent** *var.* Stoke. C England, UK
182 M15 **Stokes Point** *headland* Tasmania, SE Australia
116 J2 **Stokhid** *Pol.* Stochód, *Rus.* Stokhod. ≈ NW Ukraine
Stokhod *see* Stokhid
92 I4 **Stokkseyri** Sudhurland, SW Iceland
92 G10 **Stokmarknes** Nordland, C Norway
Stol *see* Veliki Krš
113 H15 **Stolac** ◈ Federacija Bosna I Hercegovina, S Bosnia and Herzegovina
Stolbce *see* Stowbtsy
101 D16 **Stolberg** *var.* Stolberg im Rheinland. Nordrhein-Westfalen, W Germany
Stolberg im Rheinland *see* Stolberg
123 P6 **Stolbovoy, Ostrov** *island* NE Russian Federation
Stolbtsy *see* Stowbtsy
119 J20 **Stolin** *Rus.* Stolin. Brestskaya Voblasts', SW Belarus
95 K14 **Stöllet** *var.* Norra Ny. Värmland, C Sweden
Stolp *see* Słupsk
Stolpe *see* Słupia
Stolpmünde *see* Ustka
115 F15 **Stómio** Thessalía, C Greece
14 J11 **Stonecliffe** Ontario, SE Canada
96 L10 **Stonehaven** NE Scotland, UK
97 M23 **Stonehenge** *ancient monument* Wiltshire, S England, UK
23 T3 **Stone Mountain** ▲ Georgia, SE USA
9 X16 **Stonewall** Manitoba, S Canada
21 S3 **Stonewood** West Virginia, NE USA
14 D17 **Stoney Point** Ontario, S Canada
92 H10 **Stonglandseidet** Troms, N Norway
65 N25 **Stonybeach Bay** *bay* Tristan da Cunha, SE Atlantic Ocean
35 N5 **Stony Creek** ≈ California, W USA
65 N25 **Stonyhill Point** *headland* S Tristan da Cunha
14 I14 **Stony Lake** ◎ Ontario, SE Canada
9 Q14 **Stony Plain** Alberta, SW Canada
21 R9 **Stony Point** North Carolina, SE USA
18 G8 **Stony Point** *headland* New York, NE USA
9 T10 **Stony Rapids** Saskatchewan, C Canada
39 P11 **Stony River** Alaska, USA
Stony Tunguska *see* Podkamennaya Tunguska
12 G10 **Stooping** ≈ Ontario, C Canada
100 I9 **Stör** ≈ N Germany
95 M15 **Storå** Örebro, S Sweden
95 J16 **Stora Gla** ◎ C Sweden
95 I16 **Stora Le** *Nor.* Store Le. ◎ Norway/Sweden
92 I12 **Stora Lulevatten** ◎ N Sweden
92 H13 **Storavan** ◎ N Sweden
93 I20 **Storby** Åland, SW Finland
94 E10 **Stordalen** Møre og Romsdal, S Norway
95 H23 **Storebælt** *var.* Store Bælt, *Eng.* Great Belt, Storebelt. *channel* Baltic Sea/Kattegat
Store Bælt *see* Storebælt
Storebelt *see* Storebælt
95 M19 **Storebro** Kalmar, S Sweden
95 J24 **Store Heddinge** Storstrøm, SE Denmark
Store Le *see* Stora Le
93 E16 **Støren** Sør-Trøndelag, S Norway
92 O4 **Storfjorden** *fjord* S Norway
95 L15 **Storfors** Värmland, C Sweden
92 G13 **Storforshei** Nordland, C Norway
Storhammer *see* Hamar
100 L10 **Störkanal** *canal* N Germany
93 F16 **Storlien** Jämtland, C Sweden
183 P17 **Storm Bay** *inlet* Tasmania, SE Australia
29 T12 **Storm Lake** Iowa, C USA
29 S13 **Storm Lake** ◎ Iowa, C USA
96 G7 **Stornoway** NW Scotland, UK
Storojineţ *see* Storozhynets'
92 P1 **Storøya** *island* NE Svalbard
125 S10 **Storozhevsk** Respublika Komi, NW Russian Federation
Storozhinets *see* Storozhynets'
116 K8 **Storozhynets'** *Ger.* Storozynetz, *Rom.* Storojineţ, *Rus.* Storozhinets. Chernivets'ka Oblast', W Ukraine
Storozynetz *see* Storozhynets'
92 H11 **Storriten** ▲ C Norway
19 N12 **Storrs** Connecticut, NE USA
94 I11 **Storsjøen** ◎ S Norway
94 N13 **Storsjön** ◎ C Sweden
93 F16 **Storsjön** ◎ C Sweden
92 J9 **Storslett** Troms, N Norway
94 H11 **Storskrimten** ▲ S Norway
92 I9 **Storsteinnes** Troms, N Norway
95 I24 **Storstrøm** *var.* Storstrøms Amt. ◈ *county* SE Denmark
Storstrøms Amt *see* Storstrøm
93 J14 **Storsund** Norrbotten, N Sweden
94 J9 **Storsylen** *Swe.* Sylarna. ▲ Norway/Sweden
92 H11 **Stortoppen** ▲ N Sweden
93 H14 **Storuman** Västerbotten, N Sweden
93 H14 **Storuman** ◎ N Sweden
94 N13 **Storvik** Gävleborg, C Sweden
95 O14 **Storvreta** Uppsala, C Sweden
29 V13 **Story City** Iowa, C USA
9 V17 **Stoughton** Saskatchewan, S Canada
19 O11 **Stoughton** Massachusetts, NE USA
30 L9 **Stoughton** Wisconsin, N USA
97 L23 **Stour** ≈ E England, UK
97 P21 **Stour** ≈ S England, UK
27 T5 **Stover** Missouri, C USA
95 G21 **Støvring** Nordjylland, N Denmark
119 J17 **Stowbtsy** *Pol.* Stołbce, *Rus.* Stolbtsy. Minskaya Voblasts', C Belarus
25 X11 **Stowell** Texas, SW USA
97 P20 **Stowmarket** E England, UK
114 N8 **Stozher** Dobrich, NE Bulgaria
97 E14 **Strabane** *Ir.* An Srath Bán. W Northern Ireland, UK
121 S11 **Strabo Trench** *undersea feature* C Mediterranean Sea
27 T7 **Strafford** Missouri, C USA
183 N17 **Strahan** Tasmania, SE Australia
111 C18 **Strakonice** *Ger.* Strakonitz. Jihočeský Kraj, S Czech Republic
Strakonitz *see* Strakonice
100 N8 **Stralsund** Mecklenburg-Vorpommern, NE Germany
99 L16 **Stramproy** Limburg, SE Netherlands
83 E26 **Strand** Western Cape, SW South Africa
94 E10 **Stranda** Møre og Romsdal, S Norway
97 G15 **Strangford Lough** *Ir.* Loch Cuan. *inlet* E Northern Ireland, UK
95 N16 **Strängnäs** Södermanland, C Sweden
97 E14 **Stranorlar** *Ir.* Srath an Urláir. Donegal, NW Ireland
97 H14 **Stranraer** S Scotland, UK
9 U16 **Strasbourg** Saskatchewan, S Canada
103 V5 **Strasbourg** *Ger.* Strassburg; *anc.* Argentoratum. Bas-Rhin, NE France
37 U4 **Strasburg** Colorado, C USA
29 N7 **Strasburg** North Dakota, N USA
31 U12 **Strasburg** Ohio, N USA
21 U3 **Strasburg** Virginia, NE USA
117 N10 **Strășeni** *var.* Strasheny. C Moldova
Strasheny *see* Strășeni
109 T8 **Strassburg** Kärnten, S Austria
Strassburg *see* Strasbourg, France
Strassburg *see* Aiud, Romania
99 M25 **Strassen** Luxembourg, S Luxembourg
109 R5 **Strasswalchen** Salzburg, C Austria
14 F16 **Stratford** Ontario, S Canada
184 K10 **Stratford** Taranaki, North Island, New Zealand
35 Q11 **Stratford** California, W USA
29 V13 **Stratford** Iowa, C USA
27 O12 **Stratford** Oklahoma, C USA
25 N1 **Stratford** Texas, SW USA
30 K6 **Stratford** Wisconsin, N USA
Stratford *see* Stratford-upon-Avon
97 M20 **Stratford-upon-Avon** *var.* Stratford. C England, UK
183 O17 **Strathgordon** Tasmania, SE Australia
9 Q16 **Strathmore** Alberta, SW Canada
35 R11 **Strathmore** California, W USA
14 E16 **Strathroy** Ontario, S Canada
96 I6 **Strathy Point** *headland* N Scotland, UK
37 W4 **Stratton** Colorado, C USA
19 P6 **Stratton** Maine, NE USA
18 M10 **Stratton Mountain** ▲ Vermont, NE USA
101 N21 **Straubing** Bayern, SE Germany
100 O12 **Strausberg** Brandenburg, E Germany
32 K13 **Strawberry Mountain** ▲ Oregon, NW USA
29 X12 **Strawberry Point** Iowa, C USA
36 M3 **Strawberry Reservoir** ⊠ Utah, W USA
36 M4 **Strawberry River** ≈ Utah, W USA
25 R7 **Strawn** Texas, SW USA
113 P17 **Straža** ▲ Bulgaria/FYR Macedonia
111 I19 **Strážov** *Hung.* Sztrazsó. ▲ NW Slovakia
182 F7 **Streaky Bay** South Australia
182 E7 **Streaky Bay** *bay* South Australia
30 L12 **Streator** Illinois, N USA
Streckenbach *see* Świdnik
Strednogorie *see* Pirdop
111 C17 **Středočeský Kraj** ◈ *region* C Czech Republic
29 O6 **Streeter** North Dakota, N USA
25 U8 **Streetman** Texas, SW USA
116 G13 **Strehaia** Mehedinţi, SW Romania
Strehlen *see* Strzelin
114 I10 **Strelcha** Pazardzhik, C Bulgaria
122 L12 **Strelka** Krasnoyarskiy Kray, C Russian Federation
124 L6 **Strel'na** ≈ NW Russian Federation
118 H7 **Strenči** *Ger.* Stackeln. Valka, N Latvia
108 K8 **Strengen** Tirol, W Austria
106 C6 **Stresa** Piemonte, NE Italy
Streshin *see* Streshyn
119 N18 **Streshyn** *Rus.* Streshin. Homyel'skaya Voblasts', SE Belarus
95 B18 **Streymoy** *Dan.* Strømø. *island* N Faeroe Islands
95 G23 **Strib** Fyn, C Denmark
111 A17 **Stříbro** *Ger.* Mies. Plzeňský Kraj, W Czech Republic
186 B7 **Strickland** ≈ SW Papua New Guinea
Striegau *see* Strzegom
Strigonium *see* Esztergom
98 H13 **Strijen** Zuid-Holland, SW Netherlands
63 H21 **Strobel, Lago** ◎ S Argentina
61 B25 **Stroeder** Buenos Aires, E Argentina
115 C20 **Strofádes** *island* Iónioi Nísoi, Greece, C Mediterranean Sea
Strofilia *see* Strofyliá
115 G17 **Strofyliá** *var.* Strofilia. Évvoia, C Greece
100 O10 **Strom** ≈ NE Germany
107 L22 **Stromboli** ⚠ Isola Stromboli, SW Italy
107 L22 **Stromboli, Isola** *island* Isole Eolie, S Italy
96 H9 **Stromeferry** N Scotland, UK
96 J5 **Stromness** N Scotland, UK
Strømø *see* Streymoy
94 N11 **Strömsbruk** Gävleborg, C Sweden
29 Q15 **Stromsburg** Nebraska, C USA
95 K21 **Strömsnäsbruk** Kronoberg, S Sweden
95 I17 **Strömstad** Västra Götaland, S Sweden
93 G16 **Strömsund** Jämtland, C Sweden
93 G15 **Ströms Vattudal** *valley* N Sweden
27 V14 **Strong** Arkansas, C USA
Strongilí *see* Strongylí
107 O21 **Strongoli** Calabria, SW Italy
31 T11 **Strongsville** Ohio, N USA
115 Q23 **Strongylí** *var.* Strongilí. *island* SE Greece
96 K5 **Stronsay** *island* NE Scotland, UK
97 L21 **Stroud** C England, UK
27 O10 **Stroud** Oklahoma, C USA
18 I14 **Stroudsburg** Pennsylvania, NE USA

◆ Country
● Country Capital
◇ Dependent Territory
○ Dependent Territory Capital
◈ Administrative Regions
✕ International Airport
▲ Mountain
▲▲ Mountain Range
⚠ Volcano
≈ River
◎ Lake
⊠ Reservoir

◆ Country   ◇ Dependent Territory   ◆ Administrative Regions   ▲ Mountain   ☆ Volcano   ◎ Lake
● Country Capital   ○ Dependent Territory Capital   ✈ International Airport   ▲▲ Mountain Range   ~ River   ☒ Reservoir

Sur, Point – Tagant

35 *N11* **Sur, Point** *headland* California, W USA
187 *N15* **Surprise, Île** *island* N New Caledonia
61 *E22* **Sur, Punta** *headland* E Argentina
Surrentum *see* Sorrento
28 *M3* **Surrey** North Dakota, N USA
97 *O22* **Surrey** *cultural region* SE England, UK
21 *X7* **Surry** Virginia, NE USA
108 *F8* **Sursee** Luzern, W Switzerland
127 *P6* **Sursk** Penzenskaya Oblast', W Russian Federation
127 *P5* **Surskoye** Ul'yanovskaya Oblast', W Russian Federation
75 *P8* **Surt** *var.* Sidra, Sirte. N Libya
95 *I19* **Surte** Västra Götaland, S Sweden
75 *Q8* **Surt, Khalīj** *Eng.* Gulf of Sidra, Gulf of Sirti, Sidra. *gulf* N Libya
92 *I5* **Surtsey** *island* S Iceland
137 *N17* **Suruç** Şanlıurfa, S Turkey
168 *L13* **Surulangun** Sumatera, W Indonesia
147 *P13* **Surxondaryo** *Rus.* Surkhandar'ya. ≈ Tajikistan/Uzbekistan
Süs *see* Susch
106 *A8* **Susa** Piemonte, NE Italy
165 *E12* **Susa** Yamaguchi, Honshū, SW Japan
Susa *see* Shūsh
113 *E16* **Sušac** *It.* Cazza. *island* SW Croatia
Sūsah *see* Sousse
164 *G14* **Susaki** Kōchi, Shikoku, SW Japan
165 *I15* **Susami** Wakayama, Honshū, SW Japan
142 *K9* **Sūsangerd** *var.* Susangird. Khūzestān, SW Iran
Susangird *see* Sūsangerd
35 *P4* **Susanville** California, W USA
108 *J9* **Susch** *var.* Süs. Graubünden, SE Switzerland
137 *N12* **Suşehri** Sivas, N Turkey
Susiana *see* Khūzestān
111 *B18* **Sušice** *Ger.* Schüttenhofen. Plzeňský Kraj, W Czech Republic
39 *R11* **Susitna** Alaska, USA
39 *R11* **Susitna River** ≈ Alaska, USA
127 *Q3* **Suslonger** Respublika Mariy El, W Russian Federation
105 *N14* **Suspiro del Moro, Puerto del** *pass* S Spain
18 *H16* **Susquehanna River** ≈ New York/Pennsylvania, NE USA
13 *O15* **Sussex** New Brunswick, SE Canada
18 *J13* **Sussex** New Jersey, NE USA
21 *W7* **Sussex** Virginia, NE USA
97 *O23* **Sussex** *cultural region* S England, UK
183 *S10* **Sussex Inlet** New South Wales, SE Australia
99 *L17* **Susteren** Limburg, SE Netherlands
10 *K12* **Sustut Peak** ▲ British Columbia, W Canada
123 *S9* **Susuman** Magadanskaya Oblast', E Russian Federation
188 *H6* **Susupe** Saipan, S Northern Mariana Islands
136 *D12* **Susurluk** Balıkesir, NW Turkey
114 *M13* **Susuzmüsellim** Tekirdağ, NW Turkey
136 *F15* **Sütçüler** Isparta, SW Turkey
116 *L13* **Şuţeşti** Brăila, SE Romania
83 *F25* **Sutherland** Western Cape, SW South Africa
28 *L15* **Sutherland** Nebraska, C USA
96 *I7* **Sutherland** *cultural region* N Scotland, UK
185 *B21* **Sutherland Falls** *waterfall* South Island, New Zealand
32 *F14* **Sutherlin** Oregon, NW USA
149 *V10* **Sutlej** ≈ India/Pakistan
Sutna *see* Satna
35 *P7* **Sutter Creek** California, W USA
39 *R11* **Sutton** Alaska, USA
29 *Q16* **Sutton** Nebraska, C USA
21 *R4* **Sutton** West Virginia, NE USA
12 *F8* **Sutton** ≈ Ontario, C Canada
97 *M19* **Sutton Coldfield** C England, UK
21 *R4* **Sutton Lake** ⊠ West Virginia, NE USA
15 *P13* **Sutton, Monts** *hill range* Québec, SE Canada
12 *F8* **Sutton Ridges** ▲▲ Ontario, C Canada
165 *Q4* **Suttsu** Hokkaidō, NE Japan
39 *P15* **Sutwik Island** *island* Alaska, USA
Süüj *see* Dashinchilen
118 *H5* **Suure-Jaani** *Ger.* Gross-Sankt-Johannis. Viljandimaa, S Estonia
118 *J7* **Suur Munamägi** *var.* Munamägi, *Ger.* Eier-Berg. ▲ SE Estonia
118 *F5* **Suur Väin** *Ger.* Grosser Sund. *strait* W Estonia
147 *U8* **Suusamyr** Chuyskaya Oblast', C Kyrgyzstan
187 *X14* **Suva** ● (Fiji) Viti Levu, W Fiji
187 *X15* **Suva** ✈ Viti Levu, C Fiji
113 *N18* **Suva Gora** ▲▲ WFYR Macedonia
118 *H11* **Suvainiškis** Panevėžys, NE Lithuania
Suvalkai/Suvalki *see* Suwałki
113 *P15* **Suva Planina** ▲▲ SE Serbia
113 *M17* **Suva Reka** Kosovo, S Serbia
126 *K5* **Suvorov** Tul'skaya Oblast', W Russian Federation
117 *N12* **Suvorove** Odes'ka Oblast', SW Ukraine
Suvorovo *see* Ştefan Vodă
Suwaik *see* As Suwayq
Suwaira *see* Aş Şuwayrah
110 *O7* **Suwałki** *Lith.* Suvalkai, *Rus.* Suvalki. Podlaskie, NE Poland
167 *R10* **Suwannaphum** Roi Et, E Thailand
23 *V8* **Suwannee River** ≈ Florida/Georgia, SE USA
Şuwār *see* Aş Şuwār
190 *K14* **Suwarrow** *atoll* N Cook Islands
143 *R16* **Suwaydān** *var.* Sweiham. Abū Ẓaby, E United Arab Emirates
Suwaydá/Suwaydā', Muḩāfaẓat as *see* As Suwaydā'
Suwayqiyah, Hawr as *see* Shuwayjah, Hawr ash
Suways, Khalīj as *see* Suez, Gulf of
Suways, Qanāt as *see* Suez Canal
Suweida *see* As Suwaydā'
Suweon *see* Suwŏn
163 *X15* **Suwŏn** *var.* Suweon, *Jap.* Suigen. NW South Korea
Su Xian *see* Suzhou
143 *R14* **Sūzā** Hormozgān, S Iran
145 *P15* **Suzak** *Kaz.* Sozaq. Yuzhnyy Kazakhstan, S Kazakhstan
Suzaka *see* Suzuka
126 *M3* **Suzdal'** Vladimirskaya Oblast', W Russian Federation
161 *P7* **Suzhou** *var.* Su Xian. Anhui, E China
161 *R8* **Suzhou** *var.* Soochow, Su-chou, Suchow; *prev.* Wuhsien. Jiangsu, E China
Suzhou *see* Jiuquan
Suz, Mys *see* Soye, Mys
165 *M10* **Suzu** Ishikawa, Honshū, SW Japan
165 *K14* **Suzuka** Mie, Honshū, SW Japan
165 *N12* **Suzuka** *var.* Suzaka. Nagano, Honshū, S Japan
165 *M10* **Suzu-misaki** *headland* Honshū, SW Japan
Svågälv *see* Svågan
94 *M10* **Svågan** *var.* Svågälv. ≈ C Sweden
Svalava/Svaljava *see* Svalyava
92 *O2* **Svalbard** ◇ *Norwegian dependency* Arctic Ocean
92 *J2* **Svalbardhseyri** Nordhurland Eystra, N Iceland
95 *K22* **Svalöv** Skåne, S Sweden
116 *H7* **Svalyava** *Cz.* Svalava, Svaljava, *Hung.* Szolyva. Zakarpats'ka Oblast', W Ukraine
92 *O2* **Svanbergfjellet** ▲ C Svalbard
95 *M24* **Svaneke** Bornholm, E Denmark
95 *L22* **Svängsta** Blekinge, S Sweden
95 *J16* **Svanskog** Värmland, C Sweden
95 *L16* **Svartå** Örebro, C Sweden
95 *L15* **Svartälven** ≈ C Sweden
92 *G12* **Svartisen** *glacier* C Norway
117 *X6* **Svatove** *Rus.* Svatovo. Luhans'ka Oblast', E Ukraine
Svatovo *see* Svatove
Sväty Kríž nad Hronom *see* Žiar nad Hronom
167 *Q11* **Svay Chék, Stœng** ≈ Cambodia/Thailand
167 *S13* **Svay Riĕng** Svay Riĕng, S Cambodia
92 *O3* **Sveagruva** Spitsbergen, W Svalbard
95 *K23* **Svedala** Skåne, S Sweden
118 *H12* **Svėdesai** Utena, NE Lithuania
93 *G18* **Sveg** Jämtland, C Sweden
118 *C12* **Švėkšna** Klaipėda, W Lithuania
94 *C11* **Svelgen** Sogn Og Fjordane, S Norway
95 *H15* **Svelvik** Vestfold, S Norway
118 *I13* **Švenčionėliai** *Pol.* Nowo-Święciany. Vilnius, SE Lithuania
118 *I13* **Švenčionys** *Pol.* Swięciany. Vilnius, SE Lithuania
95 *H24* **Svendborg** Fyn, C Denmark
95 *K19* **Svenljunga** Västra Götaland, S Sweden
92 *P2* **Svenskøya** *island* E Svalbard
93 *G17* **Svenstavik** Jämtland, C Sweden
95 *G20* **Svenstrup** Nordjylland, N Denmark
118 *H12* **Šventoji** ≈ C Lithuania
117 *Z8* **Sverdlovs'k** *Rus.* Sverdlovsk; *prev.* Imeni Sverdlova Rudnik. Luhans'ka Oblast', E Ukraine
Sverdlovsk *see* Yekaterinburg
127 *W2* **Sverdlovskaya Oblast'** ◈ *province* C Russian Federation
122 *K6* **Sverdrup, Ostrov** *island* N Russian Federation
Sverige *see* Sweden
113 *D15* **Svetac** *prev.* Sveti Andrea, *It.* Sant'Andrea. *island* SW Croatia
Sveti Andrea *see* Svetac
Sveti Nikola *see* Sveti Nikole
113 *O18* **Sveti Nikole** *prev.* Sveti Nikola. C FYR Macedonia
Sveti Vrach *see* Sandanski
123 *T14* **Svetlaya** Primorskiy Kray, SE Russian Federation
126 *B2* **Svetlogorsk** Kaliningradskaya Oblast', W Russian Federation
122 *K9* **Svetlogorsk** Krasnoyarskiy Kray, N Russian Federation
Svetlogorsk *see* Svyetlahorsk
127 *N14* **Svetlograd** Stavropol'skiy Kray, SW Russian Federation
Svetlovodsk *see* Svitlovods'k
119 *A14* **Svetlyy** *Ger.* Zimmerbude. Kaliningradskaya Oblast', W Russian Federation
127 *Y8* **Svetlyy** Orenburgskaya Oblast', W Russian Federation
127 *P7* **Svetlyy** Saratovskaya Oblast', W Russian Federation
124 *G11* **Svetogorsk** *Fin.* Enso. Leningradskaya Oblast', NW Russian Federation
Svetozarevo *see* Jagodina
111 *B18* **Švihov** *Ger.* Schwihau. Plzeňský Kraj, W Czech Republic
112 *E13* **Svilaja** ▲▲ SE Croatia
112 *N12* **Svilajnac** Serbia, C Serbia
114 *L11* **Svilengrad** *prev.* Mustafa-Pasha. Khaskovo, S Bulgaria
Svinecea Mare, Munte *see* Svinecea Mare, Vârful
116 *F13* **Svinecea Mare, Vârful** *var.* Munte Svinecea Mare. ▲ SW Romania
Svinø *see* Svínoy
95 *B18* **Svínoy** *Dan.* Svinø. *island* NE Faeroe Islands
147 *N14* **Svintsovyy Rudnik** *Turkm.* Swintsowyy Rudnik. Lebap Welaýaty, E Turkmenistan
118 *I13* **Svir** *Rus.* Svir'. Minskaya Voblasts', NW Belarus
124 *I12* **Svir'** *canal* NW Russian Federation
Svir', Ozero *see* Svir, Vozyera
119 *I14* **Svir, Vozyera** *Rus.* Ozero Svir'. ◎ C Belarus
114 *J7* **Svishtov** *prev.* Sistova. Veliko Tŭrnovo, N Bulgaria
119 *F18* **Svislach** *Pol.* Świsłocz, *Rus.* Svisloch'. Hrodzyenskaya Voblasts', W Belarus
119 *M17* **Svislach** *Rus.* Svisloch'. Mahilyowskaya Voblasts', E Belarus
119 *L17* **Svislach** *Rus.* Svisloch'. ≈ E Belarus
Svisloch' *see* Svislach
111 *F17* **Svitavy** *Ger.* Zwittau. Pardubický Kraj, C Czech Republic
117 *S6* **Svitlovods'k** *Rus.* Svetlovodsk. Kirovohrads'ka Oblast', C Ukraine
Svizzera *see* Switzerland
123 *Q13* **Svobodnyy** Amurskaya Oblast', SE Russian Federation
114 *G9* **Svoge** Sofiya, W Bulgaria
92 *G11* **Svolvær** Nordland, C Norway
111 *F18* **Svratka** *Ger.* Schwarzawa. ≈ SE Czech Republic
113 *P14* **Svrljig** Serbia, E Serbia
197 *U10* **Svyataya Anna Trough** *var.* Saint Anna Trough. *undersea feature* N Kara Sea
124 *M4* **Svyatoy Nos, Mys** *headland* NW Russian Federation
119 *N18* **Svyetlahorsk** *Rus.* Svetlogorsk. Homyel'skaya Voblasts', SE Belarus
Swabian Jura *see* Schwäbische Alb
97 *P19* **Swaffham** E England, UK
23 *V5* **Swainsboro** Georgia, SE USA
83 *C19* **Swakop** ≈ W Namibia
83 *C19* **Swakopmund** Erongo, W Namibia
97 *M15* **Swale** ≈ N England, UK
Swallow Island *see* Nendö
99 *M16* **Swalmen** Limburg, SE Netherlands
12 *G8* **Swan** ≈ Ontario, C Canada
97 *L24* **Swanage** S England, UK
182 *M10* **Swan Hill** Victoria, SE Australia
9 *P13* **Swan Hills** Alberta, W Canada
65 *D24* **Swan Island** *island* C Falkland Islands
Swankalok *see* Sawankhalok
29 *U10* **Swan Lake** ◎ Minnesota, N USA
21 *Y10* **Swanquarter** North Carolina, SE USA
182 *J9* **Swan Reach** South Australia
9 *V15* **Swan River** Manitoba, S Canada
183 *P17* **Swansea** Tasmania, SE Australia
97 *J22* **Swansea** *Wel.* Abertawe. S Wales, UK
21 *R13* **Swansea** South Carolina, SE USA
19 *S7* **Swans Island** *island* Maine, NE USA
28 *L17* **Swanson Lake** ⊠ Nebraska, C USA
31 *R11* **Swanton** Ohio, N USA
110 *G11* **Swarzędz** Poznań, W Poland
Swatow *see* Shantou
83 *L22* **Swaziland** *off.* Kingdom of Swaziland. ◆ *monarchy* S Africa
Swaziland, Kingdom of *see* Swaziland
93 *G18* **Sweden** *off.* Kingdom of Sweden, *Swe.* Sverige. ◆ *monarchy* N Europe
Sweden, Kingdom of *see* Sweden
Swedru *see* Agona Swedru
25 *V12* **Sweeny** Texas, SW USA
33 *R6* **Sweetgrass** Montana, NW USA
32 *G12* **Sweet Home** Oregon, NW USA
25 *T12* **Sweet Home** Texas, SW USA
27 *T4* **Sweet Springs** Missouri, C USA
20 *M10* **Sweetwater** Tennessee, S USA
25 *P7* **Sweetwater** Texas, SW USA
33 *V15* **Sweetwater River** ≈ Wyoming, C USA
Sweiham *see* Suwaydān
83 *F26* **Swellendam** Western Cape, SW South Africa
111 *G15* **Świdnica** *Ger.* Schweidnitz. Wałbrzych, SW Poland
111 *O14* **Świdnik** *Ger.* Streckenbach. Lubelskie, E Poland
110 *F8* **Świdwin** *Ger.* Schivelbein. Zachodnio-pomorskie, NW Poland
111 *F15* **Świebodzice** *Ger.* Freiburg in Schlesien, Swiebodzice. Walbrzych, SW Poland
110 *E11* **Świebodzin** *Ger.* Schwiebus. Lubuskie, W Poland
Święciany *see* Švenčionys
110 *I9* **Świecie** *Ger.* Schwertberg. Kujawsko-pomorskie, C Poland
111 *L15* **Świętokrzyskie** ◈ *province* S Poland
9 *T16* **Swift Current** Saskatchewan, S Canada
98 *K9* **Swifterbant** Flevoland, C Netherlands
183 *Q12* **Swifts Creek** Victoria, SE Australia
96 *E13* **Swilly, Lough** *Ir.* Loch Súilí. *inlet* N Ireland
97 *M22* **Swindon** S England, UK
Swinemünde *see* Świnoujście
110 *D8* **Świnoujście** *Ger.* Swinemünde. Zachodnio-pomorskie, NW Poland
Swintsowyy Rudnik *see* Svintsovyy Rudnik
Świsłocz *see* Svislach
Swiss Confederation *see* Switzerland
108 *E9* **Switzerland** *off.* Swiss Confederation, *Fr.* La Suisse, *Ger.* Schweiz, *It.* Svizzera; *anc.* Helvetia. ◆ *federal republic* C Europe
97 *F17* **Swords** *Ir.* Sord, Sórd Choluim Chille. Dublin, E Ireland
18 *H13* **Swoyersville** Pennsylvania, NE USA
124 *I10* **Syamozera, Ozero** ◎ NW Russian Federation
124 *M13* **Syamzha** Vologodskaya Oblast', NW Russian Federation
118 *N13* **Syanno** *Rus.* Senno. Vitsyebskaya Voblasts', NE Belarus
119 *K16* **Syarhyeyevichy** *Rus.* Sergeyevichi. Minskaya Voblasts', C Belarus
124 *I12* **Syas'stroy** Leningradskaya Oblast', NW Russian Federation
Sycaminum *see* Hefa
30 *M10* **Sycamore** Illinois, N USA
126 *J3* **Sychëvka** Smolenskaya Oblast', W Russian Federation
111 *H14* **Syców** *Ger.* Gross Wartenberg. Dolnosląskie, SW Poland
14 *E17* **Sydenham** ≈ Ontario, S Canada
Sydenham Island *see* Nonouti
183 *T9* **Sydney** *state capital* New South Wales, SE Australia
13 *R14* **Sydney** Cape Breton Island, Nova Scotia, SE Canada
Sydney Island *see* Manra
13 *R14* **Sydney Mines** Cape Breton Island, Nova Scotia, SE Canada
Syedpur *see* Saidpur
119 *K18* **Syelishcha** *Rus.* Selishche. Minskaya Voblasts', C Belarus
119 *J18* **Syemyezhava** *Rus.* Semezhevo. Minskaya Voblasts', C Belarus
Syene *see* Aswân
117 *X6* **Syeverodonets'k** *Rus.* Severodonetsk. Luhans'ka Oblast', E Ukraine
100 *H11* **Syke** Niedersachsen, NW Germany
94 *D10* **Sykkylven** Møre og Romsdal, S Norway
Sykoúri *see* Sykoúrio
115 *F15* **Sykoúrio** *var.* Sikouri, Sykoúri; *prev.* Sikoúrion. Thessalía, C Greece
125 *R11* **Syktyvkar** *prev.* Ust'-Sysol'sk. Respublika Komi, NW Russian Federation
23 *Q4* **Sylacauga** Alabama, S USA
Sylarna *see* Storsylen
153 *V14* **Sylhet** Sylhet, NE Bangladesh
153 *V13* **Sylhet** ◈ *division* NE Bangladesh
100 *G6* **Sylt** *island* NW Germany
21 *O10* **Sylva** North Carolina, SE USA
125 *V15* **Sylva** ≈ NW Russian Federation
23 *W5* **Sylvania** Georgia, SE USA
31 *R11* **Sylvania** Ohio, N USA
9 *Q15* **Sylvan Lake** Alberta, SW Canada
33 *T13* **Sylvan Pass** *pass* Wyoming, C USA
23 *T7* **Sylvester** Georgia, SE USA
25 *P6* **Sylvester** Texas, SW USA
10 *L11* **Sylvia, Mount** ▲ British Columbia, W Canada
122 *K11* **Sym** ≈ C Russian Federation
115 *N22* **Sými** *var.* Simi. *island* Dodekánisa, Greece, Aegean Sea
117 *U8* **Synel'nykove** Dnipropetrovs'ka Oblast', E Ukraine
125 *U6* **Synya** Respublika Komi, NW Russian Federation
117 *P7* **Synyukha** *Rus.* Sinyukha. ≈ S Ukraine
195 *V2* **Syowa** *Japanese research station* Antarctica
26 *H6* **Syracuse** Kansas, C USA
29 *S16* **Syracuse** Nebraska, C USA
18 *H10* **Syracuse** New York, NE USA
Syracuse *see* Siracusa
Syrdar'inskaya Oblast' *see* Sirdaryo Viloyati
Syrdariya *see* Syr Darya
144 *L14* **Syr Darya** *var.* Sai Hun, Sir Darya, Syrdarya, *Kaz.* Syrdariya, *Rus.* Syrdar'ya, *Uzb.* Sirdaryo; *anc.* Jaxartes. ≈ C Asia
Syrdarya *see* Syr Darya
138 *J6* **Syria** *off.* Syrian Arab Republic, *var.* Siria, Syrie, *Ar.* Al-Jumhūrīyah al-'Arabīyah as-Sūrīyah, Sūrīya. ◆ *republic* SW Asia
Syrian Arab Republic *see* Syria
138 *L9* **Syrian Desert** *Ar.* Al Hamad, Bādiyat ash Shām. *desert* SW Asia
Syrie *see* Syria
115 *L22* **Sýrna** *var.* Sirna. *island* Kykládes, Greece, Aegean Sea
115 *I20* **Sýros** *var.* Síros. *island* Kykládes, Greece, Aegean Sea
93 *M18* **Sysmä** Etelä-Suomi, S Finland
125 *R12* **Sysola** ≈ NW Russian Federation
Syulemeshlii *see* Sredets
127 *S2* **Syumsi** Udmurtskaya Respublika, NW Russian Federation
114 *K10* **Syuyutliyka** ≈ C Bulgaria
Syvash, Zaliv *see* Syvash, Zatoka
117 *U12* **Syvash, Zatoka** *Rus.* Zaliv Syvash. *inlet* S Ukraine
127 *Q6* **Syzran'** Samarskaya Oblast', W Russian Federation
Szabadka *see* Subotica
111 *N21* **Szabolcs-Szatmár-Bereg** *off.* Szabolcs-Szatmár-Bereg Megye. ◈ *county* E Hungary
Szabolcs-Szatmár-Bereg Megye *see* Szabolcs-Szatmár-Bereg
110 *G10* **Szamocin** *Ger.* Samotschin. Wielkopolskie, C Poland
116 *H8* **Szamos** *var.* Someş, Someşul, *Ger.* Samosch, Somesch. ≈ Hungary/Romania
Szamosújvár *see* Gherla
110 *G11* **Szamotuły** Poznań, W Poland
Szarkowszczyzna *see* Sharkawshchyna
111 *M24* **Szarvas** Békés, SE Hungary
Szászmagyarós *see* Măieruş
Szászrégen *see* Reghin
Szászsebes *see* Sebeş
Szászváros *see* Orăştie
Szatmárrnémeti *see* Satu Mare
Száva *see* Sava
111 *P15* **Szczebrzeszyn** Lubelskie, E Poland
110 *D9* **Szczecin** *Eng./Ger.* Stettin. Zachodnio-pomorskie, NW Poland
110 *G8* **Szczecinek** *Ger.* Neustettin. Zachodnio-pomorskie, NW Poland
110 *D8* **Szczeciński, Zalew** *var.* Stettiner Haff, *Ger.* Oderhaff. *bay* Germany/Poland
111 *K15* **Szczekociny** Śląskie, S Poland
110 *N8* **Szczuczyn** Podlaskie, NE Poland
Szczuczyn Nowogródzki *see* Shchuchyn
110 *M8* **Szczytno** *Ger.* Ortelsburg. Warmińsko-Mazurskie, NE Poland
Szechuan/Szechwan *see* Sichuan
111 *K21* **Szécsény** Nógrád, N Hungary
111 *L25* **Szeged** *Ger.* Szegedin, *Rom.* Seghedin. Csongrád, SE Hungary
Szegedin *see* Szeged
111 *N23* **Szeghalom** Békés, SE Hungary
Székelyhid *see* Săcueni
Székelykeresztúr *see* Cristuru Secuiesc
111 *I23* **Székesfehérvár** *Ger.* Stuhlweissenberg; *anc.* Alba Regia. Fejér, W Hungary
Szeklerburg *see* Miercurea-Ciuc
Szekler Neumarkt *see* Târgu Secuiesc
111 *J25* **Szekszárd** Tolna, S Hungary
Szempcz/Szenc *see* Senec
Szenice *see* Senica
Szentágota *see* Agnita
111 *J22* **Szentendre** *Ger.* Sankt Andrä. Pest, N Hungary
111 *L24* **Szentes** Csongrád, SE Hungary
111 *F23* **Szentgotthárd** *Eng.* Saint Gotthard, *Ger.* Sankt Gotthard. Vas, W Hungary
Szentgyörgy *see* Đurđevac
Szenttamás *see* Srbobran
Széphely *see* Jebel
Szeping *see* Siping
Szered *see* Sered'
111 *N21* **Szerencs** Borsod-Abaúj-Zemplén, NE Hungary
Szeret *see* Siret
Szeretfalva *see* Sărăţel
110 *N7* **Szeska Góra** *var.* Szeskie Wygórza, *Ger.* Seesker Höhe. *hill* NE Poland
Szeskie Wygórza *see* Szeska Góra
111 *H25* **Szigetvár** Baranya, SW Hungary
Szilágysomlyó *see* Şimleu Silvaniei
Szinna *see* Snina
Sziszek *see* Sisak
Szitás-Keresztúr *see* Cristuru Secuiesc
111 *E15* **Szklarska Poręba** *Ger.* Schreiberhau. Dolnośląskie, SW Poland
Szkudy *see* Skuodas
Szlatina *see* Slatina
Szlavonia/Szlavonország *see* Slavonija
Szlovákia *see* Slovakia
Szluin *see* Slunj
111 *L23* **Szolnok** Jász-Nagykun-Szolnok, C Hungary
Szolyva *see* Svalyava
111 *G23* **Szombathely** *Ger.* Steinamanger; *anc.* Sabaria, Savaria. Vas, W Hungary
Szond/Szonta *see* Sonta
Szováta *see* Sovata
110 *F13* **Szprotawa** *Ger.* Sprottau. Lubuskie, W Poland
Sztálinváros *see* Dunaújváros
Sztrazsó *see* Strážov
110 *J8* **Sztum** *Ger.* Stuhm. Pomorskie, N Poland
110 *H10* **Szubin** *Ger.* Schubin. Kujawsko-pomorskie, C Poland
Szucsava *see* Suceava
Szurduk *see* Surduc
111 *M14* **Szydłowiec** *Ger.* Schlelau. Mazowieckie, C Poland

T

Taalintehdas *see* Dalsbruk
171 *O4* **Taal, Lake** ◎ Luzon, NW Philippines
95 *J23* **Taastrup** *var.* Tåstrup. København, E Denmark
111 *I24* **Tab** Somogy, W Hungary
171 *P4* **Tabaco** Luzon, N Philippines
186 *G4* **Tabalo** Mussau Island, NE PNG
104 *K5* **Tábara** Castilla-León, N Spain
186 *H5* **Tabar Islands** *island group* NE Papua New Guinea
Tabariya, Bahrat *see* Tiberias, Lake
143 *S7* **Ţabas** *var.* Golshan. Yazd, C Iran
43 *P15* **Tabasará, Serranía de** ▲▲ W Panama
41 *U15* **Tabasco** ◈ *state* SE Mexico
Tabasco *see* Grijalva, Río
127 *Q2* **Tabashino** Respublika Mariy El, W Russian Federation
58 *B13* **Tabatinga** Amazonas, N Brazil
74 *G9* **Tabelbala** W Algeria
9 *Q17* **Taber** Alberta, SW Canada
171 *V15* **Taberfane** Pulau Trangan, E Indonesia
95 *L19* **Taberg** Jönköping, S Sweden
191 *O3* **Tabiteuea** *prev.* Drummond Island. *atoll* Tungaru, W Kiribati
171 *O5* **Tablas Island** *island* C Philippines
184 *Q10* **Table Cape** *headland* North Island, New Zealand
13 *S13* **Table Mountain** ▲ Newfoundland, Newfoundland and Labrador, E Canada
173 *P17* **Table, Pointe de la** *headland* SE Réunion
27 *S8* **Table Rock Lake** ⊠ Arkansas/Missouri, C USA
36 *K14* **Table Top** ▲ Arizona, SW USA
186 *D8* **Tabletop, Mount** ▲ C Papua New Guinea
111 *D18* **Tábor** Jihočeský Kraj, S Czech Republic
123 *R7* **Tabor** Respublika Sakha (Yakutiya), NE Russian Federation
29 *S15* **Tabor** Iowa, C USA
81 *F21* **Tabora** Tabora, W Tanzania
81 *F21* **Tabora** ◈ *region* C Tanzania
21 *U12* **Tabor City** North Carolina, SE USA
147 *Q10* **Taboshar** NW Tajikistan
76 *L18* **Tabou** *var.* Tabu. S Ivory Coast
142 *J2* **Tabrīz** *var.* Tebriz; *anc.* Tauris. Āžarbāyjān-e Sharqi, NW Iran
Tabu *see* Tabou
191 *W1* **Tabuaeran** *prev.* Fanning Island. *atoll* Line Islands, E Kiribati
171 *O2* **Tabuk** Luzon, N Philippines
140 *J4* **Tabūk** Tabūk, NW Saudi Arabia
140 *J5* **Tabūk** *off.* Minţaqat Tabūk. ◈ *province* NW Saudi Arabia
Tabūk, Minţaqat *see* Tabūk
187 *Q13* **Tabwemasana, Mount** ▲ Espiritu Santo, W Vanuatu
95 *O15* **Täby** Stockholm, C Sweden
41 *N14* **Tacámbaro** Michoacán de Ocampo, SW Mexico
42 *A5* **Tacaná, Volcán** 🌋 Guatemala/Mexico
43 *X16* **Tacarcuna, Cerro** ▲ SE Panama
Tachau *see* Tachov
158 *J3* **Tacheng** *var.* Qoqek. Xinjiang Uygur Zizhiqu, NW China
54 *H7* **Táchira** *off.* Estado Táchira. ◈ *state* W Venezuela
Táchira, Estado *see* Táchira
161 *T13* **Tachoshui** N Taiwan
111 *A17* **Tachov** *Ger.* Tachau. Plveňský Kraj, W Czech Republic
171 *Q5* **Tacloban** *off.* Tacloban City. Leyte, C Philippines
Tacloban City *see* Tacloban
57 *I19* **Tacna** Tacna, SE Peru
57 *H18* **Tacna** *off.* Departamento de Tacna. ◈ *department* S Peru
Tacna, Departamento de *see* Tacna
32 *H8* **Tacoma** Washington, NW USA
18 *L11* **Taconic Range** ▲▲ NE USA
62 *L6* **Taco Pozo** Formosa, N Argentina
57 *M20* **Tacsara, Cordillera de** ▲▲ S Bolivia
61 *F17* **Tacuarembó** *prev.* San Fructuoso. Tacuarembó, C Uruguay
61 *E18* **Tacuarembó** ◈ *department* C Uruguay
61 *F17* **Tacuarembó, Río** ≈ C Uruguay
83 *I14* **Taculi** North Western, NW Zambia
171 *Q8* **Tacurong** Mindanao, S Philippines
77 *V8* **Tadek** ≈ NW Niger
74 *J9* **Tademaït, Plateau du** *plateau* C Algeria
187 *R17* **Tadine** Province des Îles Loyauté, E New Caledonia
80 *M11* **Tadjoura, Golfe de** *Eng.* Gulf of Tajura. *inlet* E Djibouti
80 *L11* **Tadjourah** E Djibouti
Tadmor/Tadmur *see* Tudmur
9 *W10* **Tadoule Lake** ◎ Manitoba, C Canada
15 *S8* **Tadoussac** Québec, SE Canada
155 *H18* **Tādpatri** Andhra Pradesh, E India
Tadzhikabad *see* Tojikobod
Tadzhikistan *see* Tajikistan
163 *Y14* **T'aebaek-sanmaek** ▲▲ E South Korea
163 *V15* **Taechŏng-do** *island* NW South Korea
163 *X13* **Taedong-gang** ≈ C North Korea
163 *Y16* **Taegu** *off.* Taegu-gwangyŏksi, *var.* Daegu, *Jap.* Taikyū. SE South Korea
Taegu-gwangyŏksi *see* Taegu
Taehan-haehyŏp *see* Korea Strait
Taehan Min'guk *see* South Korea
163 *Y15* **Taejŏn** *off.* Taejŏn-gwangyŏksi, *Jap.* Taiden. C South Korea
Taejŏn-gwangyŏksi *see* Taejŏn
193 *Z13* **Tafahi** *island* N Tonga
105 *Q4* **Tafalla** Navarra, N Spain
75 *M12* **Tafassâsset, Oued** ≈ SE Algeria
77 *W7* **Tafassâsset, Ténéré du** *desert* N Niger
55 *U11* **Tafelberg** ▲ S Surinam
97 *J21* **Taff** ≈ SE Wales, UK
Tafila/Ţafilah, Muḩāfaẓat aţ *see* Aţ Ţafilah
77 *N15* **Tafiré** N Ivory Coast
142 *M6* **Tafresh** Markazī, W Iran
143 *Q9* **Taft** Yazd, C Iran
35 *R13* **Taft** California, W USA
25 *T14* **Taft** Texas, SW USA
143 *W12* **Taftān, Kūh-e** ▲ SE Iran
35 *R13* **Taft Heights** California, W USA
189 *Y14* **Tafunsak** Kosrae, E Micronesia
192 *G16* **Tāga** Savai'i, SW Samoa
149 *O6* **Tagāb** Dāikondī, E Afghanistan
39 *O8* **Tagagawik River** ≈ Alaska, USA
165 *Q10* **Tagajō** *var.* Tagazyô. Miyagi, Honshū, C Japan
126 *K12* **Taganrog** Rostovskaya Oblast', SW Russian Federation
126 *K12* **Taganrog, Gulf of** *Rus.* Taganrogskiy Zaliv, *Ukr.* Tahanroz'ka Zatoka. *gulf* Russian Federation/Ukraine
Taganrogskiy Zaliv *see* Taganrog, Gulf of
76 *J8* **Tagant** ◈ *region* C Mauritania

◆ Country ● Country Capital ◇ Dependent Territory ○ Dependent Territory Capital ◈ Administrative Regions ✈ International Airport ▲ Mountain ▲▲ Mountain Range 🌋 Volcano ≈ River ◎ Lake ⊠ Reservoir

148 M14 **Tagas** Baluchistān, SW Pakistan

171 O4 **Tagaytay** Luzon, N Philippines

Tagazyō see Tagajō

171 P6 **Tagbilaran** var. Tagbilaran City. Bohol, C Philippines

Tagbilaran City see Tagbilaran

106 B10 **Taggia** Liguria, NW Italy

77 V9 **Taghouaji, Massif de** ▲ C Niger

107 J15 **Tagliacozzo** Lazio, C Italy

106 J7 **Tagliamento** ♒ NE Italy

149 N3 **Tagow Bāy** var. Bai. Sar-e Pol, N Afghanistan

146 H9 **Tagta** var. Tahta, Rus. Takhta. Daşoguz Welaýaty, N Turkmenistan

146 J16 **Tagtabazar** var. Takhtabazar. Mary Welaýaty, S Turkmenistan

59 L17 **Taguatinga** Tocantins, C Brazil

186 I10 **Tagula** Tagula Island, SE Papua New Guinea

186 I11 **Tagula Island** prev. Southeast Island, Sudest Island. island SE Papua New Guinea

171 Q7 **Tagum** Mindanao, S Philippines

54 C7 **Tagún, Cerro** elevation Colombia/Panama

105 P7 **Tagus** Port. Rio Tejo, Sp. Río Tajo. ♒ Portugal/Spain

64 M9 **Tagus Plain** undersea feature E Atlantic Ocean

191 S10 **Tahaa** island Îles Sous le Vent, W French Polynesia

191 U10 **Tahanea** atoll Îles Tuamotu, C French Polynesia

Tahanroz'ka Zatoka see Taganrog, Gulf of

74 K12 **Tahat** ▲ SE Algeria

163 U4 **Tahe** Heilongjiang, NE China

163 V12 **Ta He** ♒ NE China

Tahilt see Tsogt

191 T10 **Tahiti** island Îles du Vent, W French Polynesia

Tahiti, Archipel de see Société, Archipel de la

118 E4 **Tahkuna nina** headland W Estonia

148 K12 **Tāhlāb** ♒ W Pakistan

148 K12 **Tāhlāb, Dasht-i** desert SW Pakistan

27 R10 **Tahlequah** Oklahoma, C USA

35 Q6 **Tahoe City** California, W USA

35 Q6 **Tahoe, Lake** ◎ California/ Nevada, W USA

25 N6 **Tahoka** Texas, SW USA

32 F8 **Taholah** Washington, NW USA

77 T11 **Tahoua** Tahoua, W Niger

77 T11 **Tahoua** ◆ department W Niger

31 P3 **Tahquamenon Falls** waterfall Michigan, N USA

31 P4 **Tahquamenon River** ♒ Michigan, N USA

139 V10 **Taḩrīr** S Iraq

10 K17 **Tahsis** Vancouver Island, British Columbia, SW Canada

75 W9 **Taḩta** C Egypt

Tahta see Tagta

136 L15 **Tahtalı Dağları** ▲ C Turkey

57 I14 **Tahuamanu, Río** ♒ Bolivia/Peru

56 F13 **Tahuania, Río** ♒ E Peru

191 X7 **Tahuata** island Îles Marquises, NE French Polynesia

76 L17 **Taï** SW Ivory Coast

161 P5 **Tai'an** Shandong, E China

191 R8 **Taiarapu, Presqu'île de** peninsula Tahiti, W French Polynesia

Taibad see Tāybād

160 K7 **Taibai Shan** ▲ C China

105 Q12 **Taibilla, Sierra de** ▲ S Spain

Taibus Qi see Baochang

Taichū see T'aichung

161 S13 **T'aichung** Jap. Taichū; prev. Taiwan. C Taiwan

185 E23 **Taieri** ♒ South Island, New Zealand

115 E21 **Taÿgetos** ▲ S Greece

161 N4 **Taihang Shan** ▲ C China

184 M11 **Taihape** Manawatu-Wanganui, North Island, New Zealand

161 O7 **Taihe** Anhui, E China

161 O12 **Taihe** var. Chengjiang. Jiangxi, S China

Taihoku see T'aipei

161 P9 **Taihu** Anhui, E China

161 R8 **Tai Hu** ◎ E China

159 O9 **Taikang** var. Dorbod, Dorbod Mongolzu Zizhixian. Heilongjiang, NE China

161 O6 **Taikang** Henan, C China

165 T3 **Taiki** Hokkaidō, NE Japan

166 L8 **Taikkyi** Yangon, SW Burma (Myanmar)

Taikyū see Taegu

163 U8 **Tailai** Heilongjiang, NE China

168 I12 **Taileleo** Pulau Siberut, W Indonesia

182 I10 **Tailem Bend** South Australia

96 I8 **Tain** N Scotland, UK

161 S14 **T'ainan** Jap. Tainan; prev. Dainan. S Taiwan

115 E22 **Taínaro, Ákrotírio** cape S Greece

161 Q11 **Taining** var. Shancheng. Fujian, SE China

191 W7 **Taiohae** prev. Madisonville. Nuku Hiva, NE French Polynesia

161 T13 **T'aipei** Jap. Taihoku; prev. Daihoku. ● (Taiwan) N Taiwan

168 J7 **Taiping** Perak, Peninsular Malaysia

Taiping Ling ▲ see Taiping

163 S8 **Taisei** Hokkaidō, NE Japan

165 Q4 **Taisei** Hokkaidō, NE Japan

165 G12 **Taisha** Shimane, Honshū, SW Japan

109 R4 **Taiskirchen** Oberösterreich, NW Austria

63 F20 **Taitao, Península de** peninsula S Chile

Taitō see T'aitung

161 T14 **T'aitung** Jap. Taitō. S Taiwan

161 T14 **Taiwan** off. Republic of China, var. Formosa, Formo'sa. ◆ republic E Asia

192 F5 **Taiwan** var. Formosa. island E Asia

Taiwan see T'aichung

T'aiwan Haihsia/Taiwan Haixia see Taiwan Strait

Taiwan Shan see Chungyang Shanmo

161 R13 **Taiwan Strait** var. Formosa Strait, Chin. T'aiwan Haihsia, Taiwan Haixia. strait China/Taiwan

161 N4 **Taiyuan** var. T'ai-yuan, T'ai-yüan; prev. Yangku. province capital Shanxi, C China

T'ai-yuan/T'ai-yüan see Taiyuan

161 R7 **Taizhou** Jiangsu, E China

161 S10 **Taizhou** var. Jiaojiang; prev. Haimen. Zhejiang, SE China

Taizhou see Linhai

141 O16 **Ta'izz** SW Yemen

141 O16 **Ta'izz ✕** SW Yemen

75 P12 **Tājarhī** SW Libya

147 P13 **Tajikistan** off. Republic of Tajikistan, Taj. Jumhurii Tojikiston; prev. Tajik S.S.R. ◆ republic C Asia

Tajikistan, Republic of see Tajikistan

Tajik S.S.R see Tajikistan

165 O11 **Tajima** Fukushima, Honshū, C Japan

Tajoe see Tayu

Tajo, Río see Tagus

42 B5 **Tajumulco, Volcán** ▲ W Guatemala

105 P7 **Tajuña** ♒ C Spain

167 O9 **Tak** var. Rahaeng. Tak, W Thailand

189 U4 **Taka Atoll** var. Tōke. atoll Ratak Chain, N Marshall Islands

165 P12 **Takahagi** Ibaraki, Honshū, S Japan

165 H13 **Takahashi** var. Takahasi. Okayama, Honshū, SW Japan

Takahasi see Takahashi

189 P12 **Takaieu Island** island E Micronesia

184 I13 **Takaka** Tasman, South Island, New Zealand

170 M14 **Takalar** Sulawesi, C Indonesia

165 H13 **Takamatsu** var. Takamatu. Kagawa, Shikoku, SW Japan

Takamatu see Takamatsu

165 D14 **Takamori** Kumamoto, Kyūshū, SW Japan

165 D16 **Takanabe** Miyazaki, Kyūshū, SW Japan

170 M16 **Takan, Gunung** ▲ Pulau Sumba, S Indonesia

165 Q7 **Takanosu** Akita, Honshū, C Japan

Takao see Kaohsiung

165 L11 **Takaoka** Toyama, Honshū, SW Japan

184 N12 **Takapau** Hawke's Bay, North Island, New Zealand

191 U9 **Takapoto** atoll Îles Tuamotu, C French Polynesia

184 L5 **Takapuna** Auckland, North Island, New Zealand

165 J3 **Takarazuka** Hyōgo, Honshū, SW Japan

191 U9 **Takaroa** atoll Îles Tuamotu, C French Polynesia

165 N12 **Takasaki** Gunma, Honshū, S Japan

164 L12 **Takayama** Gifu, Honshū, SW Japan

164 K12 **Takefu** var. Takehu. Fukui, Honshū, SW Japan

Takehu see Takefu

164 C14 **Takeo** Saga, Kyūshū, SW Japan

164 C17 **Take-shima** island Nansei-shotō, SW Japan

142 M5 **Tākestān** var. Takistan; prev. Siadehan. Qazvin, N Iran

164 D14 **Taketa** Ōita, Kyūshū, SW Japan

167 R13 **Takêv** var. Takeo. Takêv, S Cambodia

167 O10 **Tak Fah** Nakhon Sawan, C Thailand

139 T13 **Takhādīd** well S Iraq

149 R3 **Takhār** ◆ province NE Afghanistan

Takhiatash see Takhiatosh

167 S13 **Ta Khmau** Kândal, S Cambodia

Takhta see Tagta

145 O8 **Takhtabrod** Severnyy Kazakhstan, N Kazakhstan

Takhtakupyr see Taxtako'pir

142 M8 **Takht-e Shāh, Kūh-e** ▲ C Iran

77 U12 **Takiéta** Zinder, S Niger

8 J8 **Takijuq Lake** ◎ Nunavut, NW Canada

165 S3 **Takikawa** Hokkaidō, NE Japan

165 U3 **Takinoue** Hokkaidō, NE Japan

185 B23 **Takitimu Mountains** ▲ South Island, New Zealand

165 R7 **Takko** Aomori, Honshū, N Japan

10 L13 **Takla Lake** ◎ British Columbia, SW Canada

Takla Makan Desert see Takla Makan Shamo

158 H9 **Taklimakan Shamo** Eng. Takla Makan Desert. desert NW China

167 T12 **Takôv Môndól** Kiri, E Cambodia

39 P10 **Takow** see Kaohsiung

123 O12 **Taksimo** Respublika Buryatiya, S Russian Federation

158 K10 **Taxkorgan** var. Taxkorgan Tajik Zizhixian. Xinjiang Uygur Zizhiqu, NW China

10 I10 **Taku** ♒ British Columbia, W Canada

166 M15 **Takua Pa** var. Ban Takua Pa. Phangnga, SW Thailand

77 W16 **Takum** Taraba, E Nigeria

191 V10 **Takume** atoll Îles Tuamotu, C French Polynesia

190 L16 **Takutea** island S Cook Islands

186 K6 **Takuu Islands** prev. Mortlock Group. island group NE Papua New Guinea

119 L18 **Tal'** Rus. Tal'. Minskaya Voblasts', S Belarus

40 L13 **Tala** Jalisco, C Mexico

61 F19 **Tala** Canelones, S Uruguay

Talabriga see Aveiro

119 N14 **Talachyn** Rus. Tolochin. Vitsyebskaya Voblasts', NE Belarus

149 U11 **Talagang** Punjab, E Pakistan

105 V11 **Talaia d'Alcúdia, Sa** ▲ W Mediterranean Sea

155 J23 **Talaimannar** Northern Province, NW Sri Lanka

117 X7 **Talalayivka** Chernihivs'ka Oblast', N Ukraine

43 O15 **Talamanca, Cordillera de** ▲ S Costa Rica

56 A9 **Talara** Piura, NW Peru

104 L11 **Talarrubias** Extremadura, W Spain

147 S8 **Talas** Talasskaya Oblast', NW Kyrgyzstan

147 S8 **Talas** ♒ W Kyrgyzstan

186 G7 **Talasea** New Britain, E Papua New Guinea

147 S8 **Talas Oblasty** var. Talasskaya Oblast'

147 S8 **Talasskaya Oblast'** Kir. Talas Oblasty. ◆ province

147 S8 **Talasskiy Alatau, Khrebet** ▲ Kazakhstan/Kyrgyzstan

77 U12 **Talata Mafara** Zamfara, NW Nigeria

171 R9 **Talaud, Kepulauan** island group E Indonesia

104 M9 **Talavera de la Reina** anc. Caesarobriga, Talabriga. Castilla-La Mancha, C Spain

104 J11 **Talavera la Real** Extremadura, W Spain

186 F7 **Talawe, Mount** ▲ New Britain, C Papua New Guinea

23 S5 **Talbotton** Georgia, SE USA

183 R7 **Talbragar River** ♒ New South Wales, SE Australia

62 G13 **Talca** Maule, C Chile

62 F13 **Talcahuano** Bío Bío, C Chile

154 N12 **Tālcher** Orissa, E India

25 W5 **Talco** Texas, SW USA

145 V14 **Taldykorgan** Kaz. Taldyqorghan; prev. Taldy-Kurgan. Taldykorgan, SE Kazakhstan

Taldy-Kurgan/ Taldyqorghan see Taldykorgan

147 Y7 **Taldy-Suu** Issyk-Kul'skaya Oblast', E Kyrgyzstan

147 U10 **Taldy-Suu** Oshskaya Oblast', SW Kyrgyzstan

Tal-e Khosravī see Yāsūj

193 Y15 **Taleki Tonga** island Otu Tolu Group, C Tonga

193 Y15 **Taleki Vavu'u** island Otu Tolu Group, C Tonga

102 J13 **Talence** Gironde, SW France

145 U16 **Talgar** Kaz. Talghar. Almaty, SE Kazakhstan

Talghar see Talgar

171 Q12 **Taliabu, Pulau** island C Indonesia

Taliar Kaz. see Dalian

115 L22 **Taliarós, Akrotírio** cape Astypálaia, Kykládes, Greece, Aegean Sea

27 Q12 **Talihina** Oklahoma, C USA

Talimardzhan see Tollimarjon

137 T12 **T'alin** Rus. Talin; prev. Verin T'alin. W Armenia

Talin see T'alin

81 E15 **Tali Post** Bahr el Gabel, S Sudan

Taliq-an see Tāloqān

Talış Dağları see Talish Mountains

142 L2 **Talish Mountains** Az. Talış Dağları, Per. Kūhhā-ye Ţāvālesh, Rus. Talyshskiye Gory. ▲ Azerbaijan/Iran

170 M16 **Taliwang** Sumbawa, C Indonesia

119 L17 **Tal'ka** Rus. Tal'ka. Minskaya Voblasts', C Belarus

39 R11 **Talkeetna** Alaska, USA

39 R11 **Talkeetna Mountains** ▲ Alaska, USA

Talkhof see Puurmani

92 H2 **Tálknafjördhur** Vestfirdhir, W Iceland

139 Q3 **Tall 'Abţaḩ** N Iraq

138 M2 **Tall Abyaḍ** var. Tell Abiad. Ar-Raqqah, N Syria

139 Q2 **Tall 'Afar** N Iraq

23 S8 **Talladega** Alabama, S USA

23 Q4 **Tallahassee** prev. Muskogean. state capital Florida, SE USA

22 L2 **Tallahatchie River** ♒ Mississippi, S USA

Tall al Abyaḍ see At Tall al Abyaḍ

139 W12 **Tall al Laḩm** S Iraq

183 P11 **Tallangatta** Victoria, SE Australia

23 R4 **Tallapoosa River** ♒ Alabama/Georgia, S USA

103 T13 **Tallard** Hautes-Alpes, SE France

23 Q5 **Tall ash Sha'īr** N Iraq

23 S8 **Tallassee** Alabama, S USA

138 I5 **Tall Bīsah** Ḩimṣ, W Syria

139 R3 **Tall Ḩassūnah** N Iraq

139 Q2 **Tall Ḩuqnah** var. Tell Ḩuqnah. N Iraq

Tallin see Tallinn

118 G3 **Tallinn** Ger. Reval, Rus. Tallin; prev. Revel. ● (Estonia) Harjumaa, NW Estonia

118 H3 **Tallinn ✕** Harjumaa, NW Estonia

138 H5 **Tall Kalakh** var. Tell Kalakh. Ḩimṣ, C Syria

Tall Kūchak see Tall Kūshik

139 R2 **Tall Küchek** S Iraq

139 P2 **Tall Kūshik** var. Tall Kūchak. Al Ḩasakah, E Syria

31 Q12 **Tallmadge** Ohio, N USA

22 J5 **Tallulah** Louisiana, S USA

139 V13 **Tall 'Uwaynāt** N Iraq

122 J13 **Tal'menka** Altayskiy Kray, S Russian Federation

122 K8 **Talnakh** Taymyrskiy (Dolgano-Nenetskiy) Avtonomnyy Okrug, N Russian Federation

117 P7 **Tal'ne** Rus. Tal'noye. Cherkas'ka Oblast', C Ukraine

Tal'noye see Tal'ne

80 E12 **Talodi** Southern Kordofan, C Sudan

188 B16 **Talofofo** SE Guam

188 B16 **Talofofo Bay** bay SE Guam

26 L9 **Taloga** Oklahoma, C USA

123 T10 **Talon** Magadanskaya Oblast', E Russian Federation

14 H11 **Talon, Lake** ◎ Ontario, S Canada

149 R2 **Tāloqān** var. Taliq-an. Takhār, NE Afghanistan

126 M8 **Talovaya** Voronezhskaya Oblast', W Russian Federation

9 N6 **Taloyoak** prev. Spence Bay. Nunavut, N Canada

25 Q8 **Talpa** Texas, SW USA

40 K13 **Talpa de Allende** Jalisco, C Mexico

23 S9 **Talquin, Lake** ◎ Florida, SE USA

Talsen see Talsi

118 E8 **Talsi** Ger. Talsen. Talsi, NW Latvia

143 V11 **Tal Siāh** Sīstān va Balūchestān, SE Iran

62 G6 **Taltal** Antofagasta, N Chile

8 K10 **Taltson** ♒ Northwest Territories, NW Canada

168 K11 **Taluk** Sumatera, W Indonesia

92 J8 **Talvik** Finnmark, N Norway

182 M7 **Talyawalka Creek** ♒ New South Wales, SE Australia

Talyshskiye Gory see Talish Mountains

29 W14 **Tama** Iowa, C USA

Tama Abu, Banjaran see Penambo, Banjaran

169 U9 **Tamabo, Banjaran** ▲ East Malaysia

190 B16 **Tamakautoga** SW Niue

127 N7 **Tamala** Penzenskaya Oblast', W Russian Federation

77 P15 **Tamale** C Ghana

191 P15 **Tamana** prev. Rotcher Island. atoll Tungaru, W Kiribati

74 K12 **Tamanrasset** var. Tamenghest. S Algeria

74 J13 **Tamanrasset** wadi Algeria/Mali

166 M2 **Tamanthi** Sagaing, N Burma (Myanmar)

97 I24 **Tamar** ♒ SW England, UK

54 H9 **Támara** Casanare, C Colombia

54 F7 **Tamar, Alto de** ▲ C Colombia

173 X16 **Tamarin** E Mauritius

105 T5 **Tamarite de Litera** var. Tararite de Litera. Aragón, NE Spain

116 L14 **Tăndărei** Ialomiţa, SE Romania

63 N14 **Tandil** Buenos Aires, E Argentina

78 H12 **Tandjilé** off. Préfecture du Tandjilé. ◆ prefecture SW Chad

Tandjilé, Préfecture du see Tandjilé

Tandjoeng see Tanjung

Tandjoengkarang see Bandar Lampung

Tandjoengpandan see Tanjungpandan

Tandjoengpinang see Tanjungpinang

Tandjoengredeb see Tanjungredeb

149 Q16 **Tando Allāhyār** Sind, SE Pakistan

149 Q17 **Tando Bāgo** Sind, SE Pakistan

149 Q16 **Tando Muhammad Khān** Sind, SE Pakistan

182 L7 **Tandou Lake** seasonal lake New South Wales, SE Australia

94 L11 **Tandsjöborg** Gävleborg, C Sweden

155 H15 **Tāndūr** Andhra Pradesh, C India

164 C17 **Tanega-shima** island Nansei-shotō, SW Japan

165 R7 **Taneichi** Iwate, Honshū, C Japan

Tanen Taunggyi see Tane Range

167 N8 **Tane Range** Bur. Tanen Taunggyi. ▲ W Thailand

111 P15 **Tanew** ♒ SE Poland

21 W2 **Taneytown** Maryland, NE USA

74 H12 **Tanezrouft** desert Algeria/Mali

81 L7 **Ţanf, Jabal aţ** ▲ SE Syria

81 J24 **Tanga** Tanga, E Tanzania

81 J22 **Tanga** ◆ region E Tanzania

153 T14 **Tangail** Dhaka, C Bangladesh

186 I5 **Tanga Islands** island group NE Papua New Guinea

Tanganyika see Tanzania

Tanganyika and Zanzibar see Tanzania

68 J13 **Tanganyika, Lake** ◎ E Africa

56 E7 **Tangarana, Río** ♒ N Peru

191 V16 **Tangaroa, Maunga** ▲ Easter Island, Chile, E Pacific Ocean

Tangdukou see Shaoyang

74 G5 **Tanger** var. Tangiers, Fr./Ger. Tangerk, Sp. Tánger; anc. Tingis. NW Morocco

169 N15 **Tangerang** Jawa, C Indonesia

100 M12 **Tangermünde** Sachsen-Anhalt, C Germany

159 O12 **Tanggulashan** var. Togton Heyan, var. Tuotuoheyan. Qinghai, C China

159 K10 **Tanggula Shan** var. Dangla, Tangla Range. ▲ W China

159 N13 **Tanggula Shan** ▲ W China

159 K10 **Tanggula Shankou** Tib. Dang La. pass W China

161 N7 **Tanghe** Henan, C China

149 T5 **Tāngi** North-West Frontier Province, NW Pakistan

Tangier see Tanger

159 H20 **Tangier Island** island Virginia, NE USA

Tangiers see Tanger

22 K8 **Tangipahoa River** ♒ Louisiana, S USA

Tangla Range see Tanggula

93 L18 **Tampere** Swe. Tammerfors. Länsi-Suomi, W Finland

41 Q11 **Tampico** Tamaulipas, C Mexico

171 P14 **Tampo** Pulau Muna, C Indonesia

167 V11 **Tam Quan** Bình Định, C Vietnam

162 J13 **Tamsag Muchang** Nei Mongol Zizhiqu, N China

Tamsal see Tamsalu

118 I4 **Tamsalu** Ger. Tamsal. Lääne-Virumaa, NE Estonia

109 S8 **Tamsweg** Salzburg, SW Austria

41 P12 **Tamuín** San Luis Potosí, C Mexico

188 C15 **Tamuning** NW Guam

183 T6 **Tamworth** New South Wales, SE Australia

97 M19 **Tamworth** C England, UK

81 K19 **Tana** SE Kenya

92 L8 **Tana** Deatnu/Tana

Tana see Deatnu

164 I15 **Tanabe** Wakayama, Honshū, SW Japan

92 L8 **Tana Bru** Finnmark, N Norway

39 T10 **Tanacross** Alaska, USA

92 L7 **Tanafjorden** Lapp. Deanuvuotna. fjord N Norway

38 G17 **Tanaga Island** island Aleutian Islands, Alaska, USA

38 G17 **Tanaga Volcano** ▲ Tanaga Island, Alaska, USA

107 M18 **Tanagro** ♒ S Italy

80 H11 **T'ana Häyk'** var. Lake Tana. ◎ NW Ethiopia

168 H11 **Tanahbela, Pulau** island Kepulauan Batu, W Indonesia

171 H13 **Tanahjampea, Pulau** island W Indonesia

168 H11 **Tanahmasa, Pulau** island Kepulauan Batu, W Indonesia

Tanais see Don

152 L10 **Tanakpur** Uttaranchal, N India

Tana, Lake see T'ana Häyk'

181 P5 **Tanami Desert** desert Northern Territory, N Australia

167 T14 **Tân An** Long An, S Vietnam

39 Q9 **Tanana** Alaska, USA

Tananarive see Antananarivo

39 Q9 **Tanana River** ♒ Alaska, USA

95 C16 **Tananger** Rogaland, S Norway

188 H5 **Tanapag** Saipan, S Northern Mariana Islands

188 H5 **Tanapag, Puetton** bay Saipan, S Northern Mariana Islands

106 C9 **Tanaro** ♒ N Italy

163 Y12 **Tanch'ŏn** E North Korea

40 M14 **Tancitaro, Cerro** ▲ C Mexico

153 N12 **Tända** Uttar Pradesh, N India

77 O15 **Tanda** E Ivory Coast

116 L14 **Tăndărei** Ialomiţa, SE Romania

63 N14 **Tandil** Buenos Aires, E Argentina

[continued]

164 J12 **Tango-hantō** peninsula Honshū, SW Japan

156 I10 **Tangra Yumco** var. Tangro Tso. ◎ W China

Tangro Tso see Tangra Yumco

157 T7 **Tangshan** var. T'ang-shan. Hebei, E China

T'ang-shan see Tangshan

77 R14 **Tanguiéta** NW Benin

163 X7 **Tangwang He** ♒ NE China

163 X7 **Tangyuan** Heilongjiang, NE China

92 M11 **Tanhua** Lappi, N Finland

171 U16 **Tanimbar, Kepulauan** island group Maluku, E Indonesia

Tanintharyi see Tenasserim

139 U4 **Tānjarō** ♒ E Iraq

129 T15 **Tanjong Piai** headland Peninsular Malaysia

Tanjore see Thanjāvūr

169 U12 **Tanjung** prev. Tandjoeng. Borneo, C Indonesia

169 W9 **Tanjung** N Indonesia

Tanjungkarang/ Tanjungkarang-Telukbetung see Bandar Lampung

169 N13 **Tanjungpandan** prev. Tandjoengpandan. Pulau Belitung, W Indonesia

168 M10 **Tanjungpinang** prev. Tandjoengpinang. Pulau Bintan, W Indonesia

169 V9 **Tanjungredeb** var. Tanjungredep; prev. Tandjoengredeb. Borneo, C Indonesia

171 R13 **Tanjungredep** see Tanjungredeb

149 S8 **Tänk** North-West Frontier Province, NW Pakistan

187 S15 **Tanna** island S Vanuatu

93 F17 **Tännäs** Jämtland, C Sweden

Tannenhof see Krynica

108 K7 **Tannheim** Tirol, W Austria

Tannu-Tuva see Tyva, Respublika

171 Q12 **Tano** Pulau Taliabu, E Indonesia

77 O17 **Tano** ♒ S Ghana

152 D10 **Tanot** Rājasthān, NW India

77 V11 **Tanout** Zinder, C Niger

Tân Phu see Đinh Quan

41 P12 **Tanquián** San Luis Potosí, C Mexico

77 R13 **Tansarga** E Burkina

167 T13 **Tan Son Nhat ✕** (Hồ Chí Minh) Tây Ninh, S Vietnam

75 V8 **Tanta** var. Tantā, Țanțā. N Egypt

74 D9 **Tan-Tan** SW Morocco

41 P12 **Tantoyuca** Veracruz-Llave, E Mexico

152 J12 **Tāntpur** Uttar Pradesh, N India

Tan-tung see Dandong

38 M12 **Tanunak** Alaska, USA

Ta-nyaung see Magwe

167 S5 **Tân Yên** Tuyên Quang, N Vietnam

81 F22 **Tanzania** off. United Republic of Tanzania, Swa. Jamhuri ya Muungano wa Tanzania; prev. German East Africa, Tanganyika and Zanzibar. ◆ republic E Africa

Tanzania, Jamhuri ya Muungano wa see Tanzania

Tanzania, United Republic of see Tanzania

163 T8 **Tao'er He** ♒ NE China

159 U11 **Tao He** ♒ C China

163 U9 **Taoan** var. Taoan, Tao'an. Jilin, NE China

Tao'an-an see Baicheng

Taongi see Bokaak Atoll

107 M23 **Taormina** anc. Tauromenium. Sicilia, Italy, C Mediterranean Sea

37 S9 **Taos** New Mexico, SW USA

77 O6 **Taoudenit** var. Taoudenni. Tombouctou, N Mali

74 G6 **Taounate** N Morocco

161 S13 **T'aoyüan** Jap. Tōen. N Taiwan

118 I3 **Tapa** Ger. Taps. Lääne-Virumaa, NE Estonia

41 V17 **Tapachula** Chiapas, SE Mexico

59 H14 **Tapajós, Río** var. Tapajóz. ♒ NW Brazil

Tapajóz see Tapajós, Río

61 C21 **Tapalqué** var. Tapalquén. Buenos Aires, E Argentina

Tapalquén see Tapalqué

55 W11 **Tapanahony Rivier** var. Tapanahoni. ♒ E Suriname

41 T16 **Tapanatepec** var. San Pedro Tapanatepec. Oaxaca, SE Mexico

185 D23 **Tapanui** Otago, South Island, New Zealand

59 H14 **Tapauá** Amazonas, N Brazil

47 R7 **Tapauá, Río** ♒ NW Brazil

185 I14 **Tapawera** Tasman, South Island, New Zealand

60 I16 **Tapes** Rio Grande do Sul, S Brazil

76 K16 **Tapeta** C Liberia

154 H11 **Tāpi** prev. Tāpti. ♒ W India

104 J2 **Tapia de Casariego** Asturias, N Spain

61 O10 **Tapiche, Río** ♒ N Peru

167 N15 **Tapi, Mae Nam** var. Luang. ♒ SW Thailand

186 E8 **Tapini** Central, S Papua New Guinea

59 H13 **Tapiraí** Amazonas, N Brazil

59 H13 **Tapiracó, Serra** ♒ N Brazil

59 H13 **Tapiracó, Serra** Port. Serra Tapiracó. ♒ Brazil/Venezuela

77 R13 **Tapoa** Benin/Niger

188 H5 **Tapochau, Mount** ▲ Saipan, S Northern Mariana Islands

111 H24 **Tapolca** Veszprém, W Hungary

21 X5 **Tappahannock** Virginia, NE USA

31 U13 **Tappan Lake** ◎ Ohio, N USA

◆ Country ◇ Dependent Territory ◆ Administrative Regions ▲ Mountain 🌋 Volcano ◎ Lake
● Country Capital ○ Dependent Territory Capital ✕ International Airport ▲ Mountain Range ♒ River ▨ Reservoir

165 Q6 **Tappi-zaki** *headland* Honshū, C Japan
Taps *see* Tapa
Tāpti *see* Tāpi
Tapuaemanu *see* Maiao
185 J16 **Tapuaenuku ▲** South Island, New Zealand
171 N8 **Tapul Group** *island group* Sulu Archipelago, SW Philippines
58 E11 **Tapurucuará** *var.* Tapuruquara. Amazonas, NW Brazil
Tapuruquara *see* Tapurmcuará
192 J17 **Taputapu, Cape** *headland* Tutuila, W American Samoa
141 W13 **Tāqah** S Oman
139 T3 **Taqtaq** N Iraq
61 J15 **Taquari, Rio ∠** C Brazil
Taquari, Rio Rio Grande do Sul, S Brazil
59 H19 **Taquari, Rio ∠** C Brazil
60 L8 **Taquaritinga** São Paulo, S Brazil
122 I11 **Tara** Omskaya Oblast', C Russian Federation
83 I16 **Tara** Southern, S Zambia
113 J15 **Tara ∠** Montenegro
112 K13 **Tara ∠** W Serbia
77 W15 **Taraba ✦** *state* E Nigeria
77 X15 **Taraba ∠** E Nigeria
75 O7 **Ṭarābulus** *var.* Ṭarābulus al Gharb, *Eng.* Tripoli. ● (Libya) NW Libya
75 O7 **Ṭarābulus ✈** NW Libya
Ṭarābulus al Gharb *see* Ṭarābulus
Ṭarābulus/Ṭarābulus ash Shām *see* Tripoli
105 O7 **Taracena** Castilla-La Mancha, C Spain
117 N12 **Taraclia** Rus. Tarakilya. S Moldova
139 V10 **Tarād al Kahf** SE Iraq
183 R10 **Tarago** New South Wales, SE Australia
162 J8 **Taragt** *var.* Hüremt. Övörhangay, C Mongolia
169 V8 **Tarakan** Borneo, C Indonesia
169 V9 **Tarakan, Pulau** *island* N Indonesia
Tarakilya *see* Taraclia
165 P16 **Tarama-jima** *island* Sakishima-shotō, SW Japan
184 K10 **Taranaki ✦** *region* North Island, New Zealand
184 K10 **Taranaki, Mount** *var.* Egmont. ▲ North Island, New Zealand
Taranaki Region *see* Taranaki
105 O9 **Tarancón** Castilla-La Mancha, C Spain
188 M15 **Tarang Reef** *reef* C Micronesia
96 E7 **Taransay** *island* NW Scotland, UK
107 P18 **Taranto** *var.* Tarentum. Puglia, SE Italy
107 O19 **Taranto, Golfo di** *Eng.* Gulf of Taranto. *gulf* S Italy
Taranto, Gulf of *see* Taranto, Golfo di
62 G3 **Tarapacá** *off.* Región de Tarapacá. ✦ *region* N Chile
Tarapacá, Región de *see* Tarapacá
187 N9 **Tarapaina** Maramasike Island, N Solomon Islands
56 D10 **Tarapoto** San Martín, N Peru
138 M6 **Ṭaraq an Na'jah** *hill range* E Syria
138 M6 **Ṭaraq Sidāwī** *hill range* E Syria
103 Q11 **Tarare** Rhône, E France
Tararite de Llitera *see* Tamarite de Litera
184 M13 **Tararua Range ▲▲** North Island, New Zealand
151 Q22 **Tārāsa Dwīp** *island* Nicobar Islands, India, NE Indian Ocean
103 Q15 **Tarascon** Bouches-du-Rhône, SE France
102 M17 **Tarascon-sur-Ariège** Ariège, S France
117 P6 **Tarashcha** Kyyivs'ka Oblast', N Ukraine
57 L18 **Tarata** Cochabamba, C Bolivia
57 I18 **Tarata** Tacna, SW Peru
190 H2 **Taratai** *atoll* Tungaru, W Kiribati
59 B15 **Tarauacá** Acre, W Brazil
59 B15 **Tarauacá, Rio ∠** NW Brazil
191 Q8 **Taravao** Tahiti, W French Polynesia
191 R8 **Taravao, Baie de** *bay* Tahiti, W French Polynesia
191 Q8 **Taravao, Isthme de** *isthmus* Tahiti, W French Polynesia
103 X16 **Taravo ∠** Corse, France, C Mediterranean Sea
190 J3 **Tarawa ▲** Tarawa, W Kiribati
190 H2 **Tarawa** *atoll* Tungaru, W Kiribati
184 N10 **Tarawera** Hawke's Bay, North Island, New Zealand
184 N8 **Tarawera, Lake ◎** North Island, New Zealand
184 N8 **Tarawera, Mount ▲** North Island, New Zealand
105 S8 **Tarayuela ▲** N Spain
145 R16 **Taraz** *prev.* Aulie Ata, Auliye-Ata, Dzhambul, Zhambyl. Zhambyl, S Kazakhstan
105 Q5 **Tarazona** Aragón, NE Spain
105 Q10 **Tarazona de la Mancha** Castilla-La Mancha, C Spain
145 X12 **Tarbagatay, Khrebet ▲▲** China/Kazakhstan
96 J8 **Tarbat Ness** *headland* N Scotland, UK
149 U5 **Tarbela Reservoir ⊞** N Pakistan
96 H12 **Tarbert** W Scotland, UK
96 F7 **Tarbert** NW Scotland, UK
102 K16 **Tarbes** *anc.* Bigorra. Hautes-Pyrénées, S France
21 W9 **Tarboro** North Carolina, SE USA
Tarca *see* Torysa
106 J6 **Tarcento** Friuli-Venezia Giulia, NE Italy
182 F5 **Tarcoola** South Australia
105 S5 **Tardienta** Aragón, NE Spain
102 L11 **Tardoire ∠** W France
183 U7 **Taree** New South Wales, SE Australia
92 K12 **Tärendö** *Lapp.* Deargget. Norrbotten, N Sweden

---

74 C9 **Tarfaya** SW Morocco
116 J13 **Târgovişte** *prev.* Tîrgovişte. Dâmboviţa, S Romania
Târgovište *see* Tŭrgovishte
116 M12 **Târgu Bujor** *prev.* Tîrgu Bujor. Galaţi, E Romania
116 H13 **Târgu Cărbuneşti** *prev.* Tîrgu. Gorj, SW Romania
116 L9 **Târgu Frumos** *prev.* Tîrgu Frumos. Iaşi, NE Romania
116 H13 **Târgu Jiu** *prev.* Tîrgu Jiu. Gorj, W Romania
116 H9 **Târgu Lăpuş** *prev.* Tîrgu Lăpuş. Maramureş, N Romania
Târgul-Neamţ *see* Târgu-Neamţ
Târgul-Săcuiesc *see* Târgu Secuiesc
116 I10 **Târgu Mureş** *prev.* Oşorhei, Tîrgu Mures, *Ger.* Neumarkt, *Hung.* Marosvásárhely. Mureş, C Romania
116 K9 **Târgu-Neamţ** *var.* Târgul-Neamţ; *prev.* Tîrgu-Neamţ. Neamţ, NE Romania
116 K11 **Târgu Ocna** *Hung.* Aknavásár; *prev.* Tîrgu Ocna. Bacău, E Romania
116 K11 **Târgu Secuiesc** *Ger.* Neumarkt, Szekler Neumarkt, *Hung.* Kezdivásárhely; *prev.* Chezdi-Oşorhei, Târgul-Săcuiesc, Tîrgu Secuiesc. Covasna, E Romania
145 X10 **Targyn** Vostochnyy Kazakhstan, E Kazakhstan
Tar Heel State *see* North Carolina
186 C7 **Tari** Southern Highlands, W Papua New Guinea
162 J6 **Tarialan** *var.* Badrah. Hövsgöl, N Mongolia
162 I7 **Tariat** *var.* Horgo. Arhangay, C Mongolia
143 P17 **Ṭarīf** Abū Ẓaby, C United Arab Emirates
104 K16 **Tarifa** Andalucía, S Spain
84 C14 **Tarifa, Punta de** *cape* SW Spain
57 M21 **Tarija** Tarija, S Bolivia
57 M21 **Tarija ✦** *department* S Bolivia
141 R14 **Tarim** C Yemen
Tarim Basin *see* Tarim Pendi
81 G19 **Tarime** Mara, N Tanzania
129 S8 **Tarim He ∠** NW China
159 H8 **Tarim Pendi** *Eng.* Tarim Basin. *basin* NW China
149 N7 **Tarīn Kowt** *var.* Terinkot. Orūzgān, C Afghanistan
171 O12 **Taripa** Sulawesi, C Indonesia
117 Q12 **Tarkhankut, Mys** *headland* S Ukraine
27 Q1 **Tarkio** Missouri, C USA
122 J9 **Tarko-Sale** Yamalo-Nenetskiy Avtonomnyy Okrug, N Russian Federation
77 P17 **Tarkwa** S Ghana
171 O3 **Tarlac** Luzon, N Philippines
95 F22 **Tarm** Ringkøbing, W Denmark
57 E14 **Tarma** Junín, C Peru
105 N15 **Tarn ✦** *department* S France
102 M15 **Tarn ∠** S France
111 L22 **Tarna ∠** C Hungary
92 G13 **Tärnaby** Västerbotten, N Sweden
149 P8 **Tarnak Rūd ∠** SE Afghanistan
116 J11 **Târnava Mare** *Ger.* Grosse Kokel, *Hung.* Nagy-Küküllő; *prev.* Tîrnava Mare. ∠ S Romania
116 I11 **Târnava Mică** *Ger.* Kleine Kokel, *Hung.* Kis-Küküllő; *prev.* Tîrnava Mică. ∠ C Romania
116 I11 **Târnăveni** *Ger.* Marteskirch, Martinskirch, *Hung.* Dicsőszentmárton; *prev.* Sînmartin, Tîrnăveni. Mureş, C Romania
102 L14 **Tarn-et-Garonne ✦** *department* S France
111 P18 **Tarnica ▲** SE Poland
111 N15 **Tarnobrzeg** Podkarpackie, SE Poland
125 N12 **Tarnogskiy Gorodok** Vologodskaya Oblast', NW Russian Federation
Tarnopol *see* Ternopil'
111 M16 **Tarnów** Małopolskie, S Poland
Tarnowice/Tarnowitz *see* Tarnowskie Góry
111 J16 **Tarnowskie Góry** *var.* Tarnowice, Tarnowskie Gory, *Ger.* Tarnowitz. Śląskie, S Poland
95 N14 **Tärnsjö** Västmanland, C Sweden
106 E9 **Taro ∠** NW Italy
186 I6 **Taron** New Ireland, NE Papua New Guinea
74 E8 **Taroudannt** *var.* Taroudant. SW Morocco
Taroudant *see* Taroudannt
23 V12 **Tarpon, Lake ◎** Florida, SE USA
23 V12 **Tarpon Springs** Florida, SE USA
107 G14 **Tarquinia** *anc.* Tarquinii, *hist.* Corneto. Lazio, C Italy
Tarquinii *see* Tarquinia
76 D10 **Tarrafal** Santiago, S Cape Verde
105 V6 **Tarragona** *anc.* Tarraco. Cataluña, E Spain
105 T7 **Tarragona ✦** *province* Cataluña, NE Spain
183 O17 **Tarraleah** Tasmania, SE Australia
23 P3 **Tarrant City** Alabama, S USA
185 D21 **Tarras** Otago, South Island, New Zealand
Tarrasa *see* Terrassa
105 U5 **Tàrrega** *var.* Tarrega. Cataluña, NE Spain
21 W9 **Tar River ∠** North Carolina, SE USA
Tarsatica *see* Rijeka
136 J17 **Tarsus** Mersin, S Turkey
Tartagal Salta, N Argentina
137 V12 **Tärtär** *Rus.* Terter. ∠ SW Azerbaijan
102 J15 **Tartas** Landes, SW France
139 Q6 **Tärtläsh ∠** *see* Prejmer
Tartlau *see* Prejmer
Tartous/Tartouss *see* Ṭarṭūs

---

118 J5 **Tartu** *Ger.* Dorpat; *prev. Rus.* Yurev, Yury'ev. SE Estonia
118 I5 **Tartumaa** *off.* Tartu Maakond. ✦ *province* E Estonia
Tartu Maakond *see* Tartumaa
138 H5 **Ṭarṭūs** *Fr.* Tartouss; *anc.* Tortosa. Ṭarṭūs, W Syria
138 H5 **Ṭarṭūs** *off.* Muḥāfaẓat Ṭarṭūs, *var.* Tartous, Tartus. ✦ *governorate* W Syria
Ṭarṭūs, Muḥāfaẓat *see* Ṭarṭūs
164 C16 **Tarumizu** Kagoshima, Kyūshū, SW Japan
126 K4 **Tarusa** Kaluzhskaya Oblast', W Russian Federation
117 N11 **Tarutyne** Odes'ka Oblast', SW Ukraine
162 I7 **Tarvagatyn Nuruu ▲▲** N Mongolia
106 J6 **Tarvisio** Friuli-Venezia Giulia, NE Italy
Tarvisium *see* Treviso
57 O19 **Tarvo, Río ∠** E Bolivia
14 G8 **Tarzwell** Ontario, S Canada
40 K5 **Tasajera, Sierra de la ▲▲** N Mexico
145 S13 **Tasaral** Karaganda, C Kazakhstan
Tasböget *see* Tasbuget
145 N15 **Tasbuget** *Kaz.* Tasböget. Kzylorda, S Kazakhstan
108 E11 **Täsch** Valais, SW Switzerland
Tasek Kenyir *see* Kenyir, Tasik
122 J14 **Tashanta** Respublika Altay, S Russian Federation
Tashauz *see* Daşoguz
Tashi Chho Dzong *see* Thimphu
153 U11 **Tashigang** E Bhutan
137 T11 **Tashir** *prev.* Kalinino. N Armenia
143 Q11 **Tashk, Daryācheh-ye** ◎ C Iran
Tashkent *see* Toshkent
Tashkentskaya Oblast' *see* Toshkent Viloyati
Tashkepri *see* Daşköpri
Tash-Kömür *see* Tash-Kumyr
147 S9 **Tash-Kumyr** *Kir.* Tash-Kömür. Dzhalal-Abadskaya Oblast', W Kyrgyzstan
127 T7 **Tashla** Orenburgskaya Oblast', W Russian Federation
122 J13 **Tashtagol** Kemerovskaya Oblast', S Russian Federation
95 H24 **Tåsinge** *island* C Denmark
12 M5 **Tasiujaq** Québec, E Canada
77 W11 **Tasker** Zinder, C Niger
145 W12 **Taskesken** Vostochnyy Kazakhstan, E Kazakhstan
136 J10 **Taşköprü** Kastamonu, N Turkey
Taskuduk, Peski *see* Tosquduq Qumlari
186 G5 **Taskul** New Ireland, NE Papua New Guinea
137 S13 **Taşlıçay** Ağrı, E Turkey
185 H14 **Tasman** *off.* Tasman District. ✦ *unitary authority* South Island, New Zealand
192 J12 **Tasman Basin** *var.* East Australian Basin. *undersea feature* S Tasman Sea
185 I14 **Tasman Bay** *inlet* South Island, New Zealand
Tasman District *see* Tasman
192 I13 **Tasman Fracture Zone** *tectonic feature* S Indian Ocean
185 E19 **Tasman Glacier** *glacier* South Island, New Zealand
Tasman Group *see* Nukumanu Islands
183 N15 **Tasmania** *prev.* Van Diemen's Land. ✦ *state* SE Australia
183 Q16 **Tasmania** *island* SE Australia
185 H14 **Tasman Mountains ▲▲** South Island, New Zealand
183 P17 **Tasman Peninsula** *peninsula* Tasmania, SE Australia
192 I11 **Tasman Plain** *undersea feature* W Tasman Sea
192 I12 **Tasman Plateau** *var.* South Tasmania Plateau. *undersea feature* SW Tasman Sea
192 I11 **Tasman Sea** *sea* SW Pacific Ocean
116 G9 **Tăşnad** *Ger.* Trestenberg, Trestendorf, *Hung.* Tasnád. Satu Mare, NW Romania
136 L11 **Taşova** Amasya, N Turkey
77 T10 **Tassara** Tahoua, W Niger
12 K4 **Tassialouc, Lac ◎** Québec, C Canada
74 L11 **Tassili du Hoggar** *see* Tassili ta-n-Ahaggar
74 L11 **Tassili-n-Ajjer** *plateau* E Algeria
74 K14 **Tassili ta-n-Ahaggar** *var.* Tassili du Hoggar. *plateau* S Algeria
59 M15 **Tasso Fragoso** Maranhão, E Brazil
Tåstrup *see* Taastrup
145 O9 **Tasty-Taldy** Akmola, C Kazakhstan
143 W10 **Tāsūkī** Sīstān va Balūchestān, SE Iran
111 I22 **Tata** *Ger.* Totis. Komárom-Esztergom, NW Hungary
74 E8 **Tata** SW Morocco
111 I22 **Tatabánya** Komárom-Esztergom, NW Hungary
191 X10 **Tatakoto** *atoll* Îles Tuamotu, C French Polynesia
75 N7 **Tataouine** *var.* Taţāwīn. E Tunisia
55 O5 **Tataracual, Cerro ▲** NE Venezuela
117 O12 **Tatarbunary** Odes'ka Oblast', SW Ukraine
119 M17 **Tatarka** *Rus.* Tatarka. Mahilyowskaya Voblasts', E Belarus
Tatar Pazardzhik *see* Pazardzhik
122 I12 **Tatarsk** Novosibirskaya Oblast', C Russian Federation
Tatarskaya ASSR *see* Tatarstan, Respublika
123 T13 **Tatarskiy Proliv** *Eng.* Tatar Strait. *strait* SE Russian Federation

---

127 R4 **Tatarstan, Respublika** *prev.* Tatarskaya ASSR. ✦ *autonomous republic* W Russian Federation
Tatar Strait *see* Tatarskiy Proliv
Taţāwīn *see* Tataouine
171 N12 **Tate** Sulawesi, N Indonesia
141 N11 **Tathlīth** 'Asīr, S Saudi Arabia
141 O11 **Tathlīth, Wādī** *dry watercourse* S Saudi Arabia
183 R11 **Tathra** New South Wales, SE Australia
127 P8 **Tatishchevo** Saratovskaya Oblast', W Russian Federation
39 S12 **Tatitlek** Alaska, USA
10 L15 **Tatla Lake** British Columbia, SW Canada
121 Q2 **Tatlısu** *Gk.* Akanthoú. N Cyprus
9 Z10 **Tatnam, Cape** *headland* Manitoba, C Canada
111 K18 **Tatra Mountains** *Ger.* Tatra, *Hung.* Tátra, *Pol./Slvk.* Tatry. ▲ Poland/Slovakia
Tatra/Tátra *see* Tatra Mountains
Tatry *see* Tatra Mountains
164 I13 **Tatsuno** *var.* Tatuno. Hyōgo, Honshū, SW Japan
145 S16 **Tatti** *var.* Tatty. Zhambyl, S Kazakhstan
Tatty *see* Tatti
60 L10 **Tatuí** São Paulo, S Brazil
37 V14 **Tatum** New Mexico, SW USA
25 X7 **Tatum** Texas, SW USA
Ta-t'ung/Tatung *see* Datong
137 R14 **Tatvan** Bitlis, SE Turkey
95 C16 **Tau** Rogaland, S Norway
192 L17 **Ta'ū** *island* Manua Islands, E American Samoa
193 W15 **Tau** *island* Tongatapu Group, N Tonga
59 O14 **Tauá** Ceará, E Brazil
60 N10 **Taubaté** São Paulo, S Brazil
101 I19 **Tauber ∠** SW Germany
101 I19 **Tauberbischofsheim** Baden-Württemberg, C Germany
144 E14 **Tauchik** *Kaz.* Taūshyq. Mangistau, SW Kazakhstan
191 W10 **Tauere** *atoll* Îles Tuamotu, C French Polynesia
101 H17 **Taufstein ▲** C Germany
190 I17 **Taukoka** *island* SE Cook Islands
184 L10 **Taumarunui** Manawatu-Wanganui, North Island, New Zealand
58 H22 **Taum Sauk Mountain ▲** Missouri, C USA
83 H22 **Taung** North-West, N South Africa
166 L6 **Taungdwingyi** Magwe, C Burma (Myanmar)
166 M6 **Taunggyi** Shan State, C Burma (Myanmar)
166 L5 **Taungtha** Mandalay, C Burma (Myanmar)
166 K7 **Taungup** Arakan State, W Burma (Myanmar)
149 S9 **Taunsa** Punjab, E Pakistan
97 K23 **Taunton** SW England, UK
19 O12 **Taunton** Massachusetts, NE USA
101 F18 **Taunus ▲▲** W Germany
101 G18 **Taunusstein** Hessen, W Germany
184 N9 **Taupo** Waikato, North Island, New Zealand
184 M9 **Taupo, Lake ◎** North Island, New Zealand
109 R8 **Taurach** *var.* Taurachbach. ∠ E Austria
Taurachbach *see* Taurach
118 D12 **Tauragė** *Ger.* Tauroggen. Tauragė, SW Lithuania
118 D13 **Tauragė ✦** *province* Lithuania
54 G10 **Tauramena** Casanare, C Colombia
184 N7 **Tauranga** Bay of Plenty, North Island, New Zealand
15 O9 **Taureau, Réservoir ⊞** Québec, SE Canada
107 N22 **Taurianova** Calabria, SW Italy
184 I2 **Tauroa Point** *headland* North Island, New Zealand
Tauroggen *see* Tauragė
Tauromenium *see* Taormina
Taurus Mountains *see* Toros Dağları
Taus *see* Domažlice
Taūshyq *see* Tauchik
105 R5 **Tauste** Aragón, NE Spain
191 V16 **Tautara, Motu** *island* Easter Island, Chile, E Pacific Ocean
191 R8 **Tautira** Tahiti, W French Polynesia
Tauz *see* Tovuz
137 U10 **T'bilisi** *Eng.* Tiflis. ● (Georgia) SE Georgia
137 T10 **T'bilisi ✈** S Georgia
79 E14 **Tchabal Mbabo ▲** W Cameroon
79 E14 **Tchad** *see* Chad
Tchad, Lac *see* Chad, Lake
82 G10 **Tchamba** Sverdlovskaya Oblast', C Russian Federation
82 G10 **Tavda ∠** C Russian Federation
105 T11 **Tavernes de la Valldigna** País Valenciano, E Spain
81 J20 **Taveta** Coast, S Kenya
187 Y14 **Taveuni** *island* N Fiji
147 R13 **Tavil'dara** var. Tavil'-Dara, Tovil'-Dora. C Tajikistan
104 H14 **Tavira** Faro, S Portugal
97 I24 **Tavistock** SW England, UK
167 N10 **Tavoy** *var.* Dawei. Tenasserim, S Burma (Myanmar)
Tavoy Island *see* Mali Kyun
115 E16 **Távropos, Techníti Límni ⊞** C Greece
136 M13 **Tavşanlı** Kütahya, NW Turkey
187 X14 **Tavua** Viti Levu, W Fiji
192 J23 **Tavua** SW England, UK, E Atlantic
185 L14 **Tawa** Wellington, North Island, New Zealand
25 V6 **Tawakoni, Lake ◎** Texas, SW USA
153 V15 **Tawang** Arunāchal Pradesh, NE India
169 R17 **Tawang, Teluk** *bay* Jawa, S Indonesia
31 R7 **Tawas Bay ◎** Michigan, N USA

---

31 R7 **Tawas City** Michigan, N USA
169 V8 **Tawau** Sabah, East Malaysia
141 U10 **Ṭawīl, Qalamat aṭ** *well* SE Saudi Arabia
171 N9 **Tawitawi** *island* Tawitawi Group, SW Philippines
Ṭawkar *see* Tokar
Tâwûq *see* Dāqūq
Tawzar *see* Tozeur
41 O15 **Taxco** *var.* Taxco de Alarcón. Guerrero, S Mexico
Taxco de Alarcón *see* Taxco
146 H8 **Takhiatosh** *Rus.* Takhiatash. Qoraqalpoghiston Respublikasi, W Uzbekistan
158 D9 **Taxkorgan** *var.* Taxkorgan Tajik Zizhixian. Xinjiang Uygur Zizhiqu, NW China
Taxkorgan Tajik Zizhixian *see* Taxkorgan
146 H7 **Taxtako'pir** *Rus.* Takhtakupyr. Qoraqalpog'iston Respublikasi, NW Uzbekistan
96 J10 **Tay ∠** C Scotland, UK
143 V6 **Ṭāybād** *var.* Taibad, Tāyyebād, Tayyebāt. Khorāsān-Razavī, NE Iran
Taybert at Turkz *see* Ṭayyibat at Turkī
124 J3 **Taybola** Murmanskaya Oblast', NW Russian Federation
81 M16 **Tayeeglow** Bakool, C Somalia
96 K11 **Tay, Firth of** *inlet* E Scotland, UK
122 J12 **Tayga** Kemerovskaya Oblast', S Russian Federation
Taygan *see* Delger
123 T9 **Taygonos, Mys** *cape* E Russian Federation
9 N12 **Taylor** British Columbia, W Canada
29 O14 **Taylor** Nebraska, C USA
18 I13 **Taylor** Pennsylvania, NE USA
25 T10 **Taylor** Texas, SW USA
37 Q11 **Taylor, Mount ▲** New Mexico, SW USA
37 R5 **Taylor Park Reservoir ⊞** Colorado, C USA
37 R6 **Taylor River ∠** Colorado, C USA
21 P11 **Taylors** South Carolina, SE USA
20 L5 **Taylorsville** Kentucky, S USA
21 R9 **Taylorsville** North Carolina, SE USA
30 L14 **Taylorville** Illinois, N USA
140 K5 **Taymā'** Tabūk, NW Saudi Arabia
122 M10 **Taymura ∠** C Russian Federation
123 O7 **Taymylyr** Respublika Sakha (Yakutiya), NE Russian Federation
122 L7 **Taymyr, Ozero ◎** N Russian Federation
122 M6 **Taymyr, Poluostrov** *peninsula* N Russian Federation
122 L8 **Taymyrskiy (Dolgano-Nenetskiy) Avtonomnyy Okrug** *var.* Taymyrskiy Avtonomnyy Okrug. ✦ *autonomous district* N Russian Federation
Taymyrskiy Avtonomnyy Okrug *see* Taymyrskiy (Dolgano-Nenetskiy)
167 S13 **Tây Ninh** Tây Ninh, S Vietnam
122 L12 **Tayshet** Irkutskaya Oblast', S Russian Federation
162 G8 **Tayshir** *var.* Tsagaan-Olom. Govĭ-Altay, C Mongolia
171 N5 **Taytay** Palawan, W Philippines
190 Q16 **Tayu** *prev.* Tajoe. Jawa, S Indonesia
Ṭāyybād/Tayyebāt *see* Ṭāybād
138 L5 **Ṭayyibah** *var.* At Taybé. Ḥimṣ, C Syria
138 I4 **Ṭayyibat at Turkī** *var.* Taybert at Turkz. Ḥamāh, W Syria
145 P7 **Tayynsha** *prev.* Krasnoarmeysk. Severnyy Kazakhstan, N Kazakhstan
122 K12 **Tegul'det** Tomskaya Oblast', C Russian Federation
35 S13 **Tehachapi** California, W USA
35 S13 **Tehachapi Mountains ▲▲** California, W USA
Tehama *see* Tihāmah
Teheran *see* Tehrān
77 O14 **Téhini** NE Ivory Coast
143 N5 **Tehrān** *var.* Teheran. ● (Iran) Tehrān, N Iran
143 N6 **Tehrān** *off.* Ostān-e Tehrān, *var.* Tehran. ✦ *province* N Iran
Tehrān, Ostān-e *see* Tehrān
152 K9 **Tehri** Uttaranchal, N India
Tehri *see* Tikamgarh
41 Q15 **Tehuacán** Puebla, S Mexico
41 S17 **Tehuantepec** *var.* Santo Domingo Tehuantepec. Oaxaca, SE Mexico
41 S17 **Tehuantepec, Golfo de** *var.* Gulf of Tehuantepec. *gulf* S Mexico
Tehuantepec, Gulf of *see* Tehuantepec, Golfo de
Tehuantepec, Isthmus of *see* Tehuantepec, Istmo de
41 T16 **Tehuantepec, Istmo de** *var.* Isthmus of Tehuantepec. *isthmus* SE Mexico
0 I16 **Tehuantepec Ridge** *undersea feature* E Pacific Ocean
41 S16 **Tehuantepec, Río ∠** SW Mexico
191 W10 **Tehuata** *atoll* Îles Tuamotu, C French Polynesia
64 O11 **Teide, Pico de ▲** Gran Canaria, Islas Canarias, Spain, NE Atlantic Ocean
181 V9 **Teifi ∠** SW Wales, UK
80 B9 **Teiga Plateau** *plateau* W Sudan
97 J24 **Teignmouth** SW England, UK
Teisen *see* Chech'ŏn
116 H1 **Teiuş** *Ger.* Dreikirchen, *Hung.* Tövis. Alba, C Romania
82 L13 **Tejakula** Bali, C Indonesia
146 I15 **Tejen** *Per.* Harīrūd, *Rus.* Tedzhen. Ahal Welaýaty, S Turkmenistan
146 I15 **Tejen** *Rus.* Tedzhen. ∠ Afghanistan/Iran *see also* Harīrūd

---

185 B22 **Te Anau, Lake ◎** South Island, New Zealand
41 Q15 **Teapa** Tabasco, SE Mexico
184 Q7 **Te Araroa** Gisborne, North Island, New Zealand
184 M7 **Te Aroha** Waikato, North Island, New Zealand
Teate *see* Chieti
190 A9 **Te Ava Fuagea** *channel* Funafuti Atoll, SE Tuvalu
190 B8 **Te Ava I Te Lape** *channel* Funafuti Atoll, SE Tuvalu
190 B9 **Te Ava Pua Pua** *channel* Funafuti Atoll, SE Tuvalu
184 M8 **Te Awamutu** Waikato, North Island, New Zealand
171 X12 **Teba** Papua, E Indonesia
104 L15 **Teba** Andalucía, S Spain
126 M15 **Teberda** Karachayevo-Cherkesskaya Respublika, SW Russian Federation
74 M6 **Tébessa** NE Algeria
62 O7 **Tebicuary, Río ∠** S Paraguay
168 L13 **Tebingtinggi** Sumatera, W Indonesia
168 I8 **Tebingtinggi** Sumatera, N Indonesia
Tebingtinggi, Pulau *see* Rantau, Pulau
Tebriz *see* Tabrīz
137 U9 **Tebulos Mt'a** *Rus.* Gora Tebulosmta. ▲ Georgia/Russian Federation
Tebulosmta, Gora *see* Tebulos Mt'a
41 Q14 **Tecamachalco** Puebla, S Mexico
40 B1 **Tecate** Baja California, NW Mexico
136 M13 **Tecer Dağları ▲▲** C Turkey
103 O17 **Tech ∠** S France
77 P16 **Techiman** W Ghana
117 N15 **Techirghiol** Constanţa, SE Romania
74 A12 **Techla** *var.* Techlé. SW Western Sahara
Techlé *see* Techla
63 H18 **Tecka, Sierra de ▲▲** SW Argentina
40 K13 **Tecolotlán** Jalisco, SW Mexico
41 N16 **Tecomán** Colima, SW Mexico
35 V12 **Tecopa** California, W USA
40 G5 **Tecoripa** Sonora, NW Mexico
41 N16 **Tecpan** *var.* Tecpan de Galeana. Guerrero, S Mexico
Tecpan de Galeana *see* Tecpan
40 J11 **Tecuala** Nayarit, C Mexico
116 L12 **Tecuci** Galaţi, E Romania
31 R10 **Tecumseh** Michigan, N USA
29 S16 **Tecumseh** Nebraska, C USA
27 O11 **Tecumseh** Oklahoma, C USA
Tedzhen *see* Harīrūd/Tejen
Tedzhen *see* Tejen
146 H15 **Tedzhenstroy** *Turkm.* Tejenstroy. Ahal Welaýaty, S Turkmenistan
97 L15 **Tees ∠** N England, UK
14 E15 **Teeswater** Ontario, S Canada
190 A10 **Tefala** *island* Funafuti Atoll, C Tuvalu
58 D13 **Tefé** Amazonas, N Brazil
74 K11 **Tefedest ▲▲** S Algeria
136 E16 **Tefenni** Burdur, SW Turkey
58 D13 **Tefé, Rio ∠** NW Brazil
169 P16 **Tegal** Jawa, C Indonesia
100 O12 **Tegel ✈** (Berlin) Berlin, NE Germany
99 M15 **Tegelen** Limburg, SE Netherlands
101 L24 **Tegernsee ◎** SE Germany
107 M18 **Teggiano** Campania, S Italy
77 U14 **Tegina** Niger, C Nigeria
42 I7 **Tegucigalpa ●** (Honduras) Francisco Morazán, SW Honduras
42 H7 **Tegucigalpa ✦** Central District, C Honduras
Tegucigalpa *see* Central District
Tegucigalpa *see* Francisco Morazán
77 U9 **Teguidda-n-Tessoumt** Agadez, C Niger
64 Q11 **Teguise** Lanzarote, Islas Canarias, Spain, NE Atlantic Ocean

TEJEN – THERMÍS

Tejen see Harīrūd
Tejenstroy see Tedzhenstroy
35 S14 Tejon Pass pass California, W USA
Tejo, Rio see Tagus
41 O14 Tejupilco var. Tejupilco de Hidalgo. México, S Mexico
Tejupilco de Hidalgo see Tejupilco
184 P7 Te Kaha Bay of Plenty, North Island, New Zealand
29 S14 Tekamah Nebraska, C USA
184 I1 Te Kao Northland, North Island, New Zealand
185 F20 Tekapo South Island, New Zealand
185 F19 Tekapo, Lake South Island, New Zealand
184 P9 Te Karaka Gisborne, North Island, New Zealand
184 L7 Te Kauwhata Waikato, North Island, New Zealand
41 X12 Tekax var. Tekax de Álvaro Obregón. Yucatán, SE Mexico
Tekax de Álvaro Obregón see Tekax
136 A14 Teke Burnu headland W Turkey
114 M12 Teke Deresi NW Turkey
146 D10 Tekedzhik, Gory hill range NW Turkmenistan
145 V14 Tekeli Almaty, SE Kazakhstan
145 R7 Teke, Ozero N Kazakhstan
158 I5 Tekes Xinjiang Uygur Zizhiqu, NW China
145 W16 Tekes Almaty, SE Kazakhstan
Tekes see Tekes He
158 H5 Tekes He Rus. Tekes. China/Kazakhstan
Teke/Tekendorf see Teaca
80 I10 Tekezē var. Takkaze. Eritrea/Ethiopia
Tekhtin see Tsyakhtsin
136 C10 Tekirdağ It. Rodosto; anc. Bisanthe, Raidestos, Rhaedestus. Tekirdağ, NW Turkey
136 C10 Tekirdağ province NW Turkey
155 N14 Tekkali Andhra Pradesh, E India
115 K15 Tekke Burnu Turk. İlyasbaba Burnu. headland NW Turkey
137 Q13 Tekman Erzurum, NE Turkey
32 M9 Tekoa Washington, NW USA
190 H16 Te Kou ▲ Rarotonga, S Cook Islands
Tekrit see Tikrīt
171 P12 Teku Sulawesi, N Indonesia
184 L9 Te Kuiti Waikato, North Island, New Zealand
42 H4 Tela Atlántida, NW Honduras
138 F12 Telalim Southern, S Israel
Telanaipura see Jambi
137 U10 T'elavi E Georgia
138 F10 Tel Aviv district W Israel
Tel Aviv-Jaffa see Tel Aviv-Yafo
138 F10 Tel Aviv-Yafo var. Tel Aviv-Jaffa. Tel Aviv, C Israel
138 F10 Tel Aviv-Yafo ✕ Tel Aviv, C Israel
111 E18 Telč Ger. Teltsch. Vysočina, C Czech Republic
186 B6 Telefomin Sandaun, NW Papua New Guinea
10 J10 Telegraph Creek British Columbia, W Canada
190 B10 Telele island Funafuti Atoll, C Tuvalu
60 J11 Telêmaco Borba Paraná, S Brazil
95 E15 Telemark county S Norway
62 J13 Telén La Pampa, C Argentina
Teleneshty see Telenești
116 M9 Telenești Rus. Teleneshty. C Moldova
104 J4 Teleno, El ▲ NW Spain
116 I15 Teleorman county S Romania
116 I14 Teleorman S Romania
25 V5 Telephone Texas, SW USA
35 U11 Telescope Peak ▲ California, W USA
Teles Pirés see São Manuel, Rio
97 L19 Telford W England, UK
108 L7 Telfs Tirol, W Austria
42 I9 Telica León, NW Nicaragua
42 J6 Telica, Río C Honduras
76 I13 Télimélé W Guinea
43 O14 Telire, Río Costa Rica/Panama
114 I8 Telish prev. Azizie. Pleven, N Bulgaria
41 R16 Telixtlahuaca var. San Francisco Telixtlahuaca. Oaxaca, SE Mexico
10 K13 Telkwa British Columbia, SW Canada
25 P4 Tell Texas, SW USA
Tell Abiad see Tall Abyaḍ
Tell Abiad/Tell Abyad see At Tall al Abyaḍ
31 O16 Tell City Indiana, N USA
38 M9 Teller Alaska, USA
Tell Huqnah see Tall Ḥuqnah
155 F20 Tellicherry var. Thalassery. Kerala, SW India
20 M10 Tellico Plains Tennessee, S USA
Tell Kalakh see Tall Kalakh
Tell Mardīkh see Ebla
54 E11 Tello Huila, C Colombia
Tell Shedadi see Ash Shadādah
37 Q7 Telluride Colorado, C USA
117 X9 Tel'manove Donets'ka Oblast', E Ukraine
Tel'man/Tel'mansk see Gubadag
162 H6 Telmen var. Övögdiy. Dzavhan, C Mongolia
162 H6 Telmen Nuur NW Mongolia
Teloekbetoeng see Bandar Lampung
41 O15 Teloloapán Guerrero, S Mexico
Telo Martius see Toulon
125 V8 Telposiz, Gora ▲ NW Russian Federation
Telschen see Telšiai
63 J17 Telsen Chubut, S Argentina
118 D11 Telšiai Ger. Telschen. Telšiai, NW Lithuania
118 D11 Telšiai province NW Lithuania
Teltsch see Telč
Telukbetung see Bandar Lampung
168 H10 Telukdalam Pulau Nias, W Indonesia
14 H9 Temagami Ontario, S Canada
14 G9 Temagami, Lake Ontario, S Canada
190 H16 Te Manga ▲ Rarotonga, S Cook Islands
191 W12 Tematangi atoll Îles Tuamotu, S French Polynesia
41 X11 Temax Yucatán, SE Mexico
171 E14 Tembagapura Papua, E Indonesia
129 U5 Tembenchi N Russian Federation
55 P6 Temblador Monagas, NE Venezuela
105 N9 Tembleque Castilla-La Mancha, C Spain
Temboni see Mitemele, Río
35 U16 Temecula California, W USA
168 K7 Temengor, Tasik Peninsular Malaysia
112 L9 Temerin Vojvodina, N Serbia
Temeschburg/Temeschwar see Timișoara
Temes-Kubin see Kovin
Temes/Temesch see Tamiš
Temesvár/Temeswar see Timișoara
Teminaboean see Teminabuan
171 U12 Teminabuan prev. Teminaboean. Papua, E Indonesia
145 P17 Temirlanovka Yuzhnyy Kazakhstan, S Kazakhstan
145 R10 Temirtau prev. Samarkandski, Samarkandskoye. Karaganda, C Kazakhstan
14 H10 Témiscaming Québec, SE Canada
Témiscamingue, Lac see Timiskaming, Lake
15 T8 Témiscouata, Lac Québec, SE Canada
127 N5 Temnikov Respublika Mordoviya, W Russian Federation
191 Y13 Temoe island Îles Gambier, E French Polynesia
183 Q9 Temora New South Wales, SE Australia
40 H7 Témoris Chihuahua, W Mexico
40 I5 Temósachic Chihuahua, N Mexico
187 Q10 Temotu var. Temotu Province. province E Solomon Islands
Temotu Province see Temotu
36 L14 Tempe Arizona, SW USA
Tempelburg see Czaplinek
107 C17 Tempio Pausania Sardegna, Italy, C Mediterranean Sea
42 K12 Tempisque, Río NW Costa Rica
25 T9 Temple Texas, SW USA
100 O12 Templehof ✕ (Berlin) Berlin, NE Germany
97 D19 Templemore Ir. An Teampall Mór. Tipperary, C Ireland
100 O11 Templin Brandenburg, NE Germany
41 P12 Tempoal var. Tempoal de Sánchez. Veracruz-Llave, E Mexico
Tempoal de Sánchez see Tempoal
41 P13 Tempoal, Río C Mexico
83 E14 Tempué Moxico, C Angola
126 J14 Temryuk Krasnodarskiy Kray, SW Russian Federation
99 G17 Temse Oost-Vlaanderen, N Belgium
63 F15 Temuco Araucanía, C Chile
185 G20 Temuka Canterbury, South Island, New Zealand
189 P13 Temwen Island island E Micronesia
56 C6 Tena Napo, C Ecuador
41 W13 Tenabo Campeche, E Mexico
Tenaghau see Aola
25 X7 Tenaha Texas, SW USA
39 X13 Tenake Chichagof Island, Alaska, USA
155 K16 Tenāli Andhra Pradesh, E India
Tenan see Ch'ŏnan
41 O14 Tenancingo var. Tenencingo de Degollado. México, S Mexico
191 X12 Tenararo island Groupe Actéon, SE French Polynesia
167 N12 Tenasserim Tenasserim, S Burma (Myanmar)
167 N11 Tenasserim var. Tanintharyi. division S Burma (Myanmar)
98 O5 Ten Boer Groningen, NE Netherlands
97 I21 Tenby SW Wales, UK
80 K11 Tendaho Āfar, NE Ethiopia
103 V14 Tende Alpes Maritimes, SE France
151 Q20 Ten Degree Channel strait Andaman and Nicobar Islands, India, E Indian Ocean
80 F11 Tendelti White Nile, E Sudan
76 G8 Te-n-Dghâmcha, Sebkhet var. Sebkha de Ndrhamcha, Sebkra de Ndaghamcha. salt lake W Mauritania
165 P10 Tendō Yamagata, Honshū, C Japan
74 H7 Tendrara NE Morocco
117 Q11 Tendrivs'ka Kosa spit S Ukraine
117 Q11 Tendrivs'ka Zatoka gulf S Ukraine
Tenencingo de Degollado see Tenancingo
77 N11 Ténenkou Mopti, C Mali
77 W9 Ténéré physical region C Niger
77 W9 Ténéré, Erg du desert C Niger
64 O11 Tenerife island Islas Canarias, Spain, NE Atlantic Ocean
74 J5 Ténès NW Algeria
170 M15 Tengah, Kepulauan island group C Indonesia
Tengcheng see Tengxian
169 V11 Tenggarong Borneo, C Indonesia
162 J15 Tengger Shamo desert N China
168 L8 Tenggul, Pulau island Peninsular Malaysia
Tengiz Köl see Tengiz, Ozero
145 P9 Tengiz, Ozero Kaz. Tengiz Köl. salt lake C Kazakhstan
76 M14 Tengréla var. Tingréla. N Ivory Coast
160 M14 Tengxian var. Tengcheng, Teng Xian. Guangxi Zhuangzu Zizhiqu, S China
Teng Xian see Tengxian
194 H2 Teniente Rodolfo Marsh Chilean research station South Shetland Islands, Antarctica
32 G9 Tenino Washington, NW USA
112 I9 Tenja Osijek-Baranja, E Croatia
188 B16 Tenjo, Mount ▲ W Guam
155 H23 Tenkāsi Tamil Nādu, SE India
79 N24 Tenke Katanga, SE Dem. Rep. Congo
Tenke see Tinca
123 Q7 Tenkeli Respublika Sakha (Yakutiya), NE Russian Federation
27 R10 Tenkiller Ferry Lake Oklahoma, C USA
77 Q13 Tenkodogo S Burkina
181 Q5 Tennant Creek Northern Territory, C Australia
20 G9 Tennessee off. State of Tennessee, also known as The Volunteer State. state SE USA
37 R5 Tennessee Pass pass Colorado, C USA
20 H10 Tennessee River S USA
23 N2 Tennessee Tombigbee Waterway canal Alabama/Mississippi, S USA
99 K22 Tenneville Luxembourg, SE Belgium
92 M11 Tenniöjoki NE Finland
92 L9 Tenojoki Lapp. Deatnu, Nor. Tana. Finland/Norway see also Deatnu
Tenojoki see Deatnu
169 U7 Tenom Sabah, East Malaysia
Tenos see Tínos
41 V15 Tenosique var. Tenosique de Pino Suárez. Tabasco, SE Mexico
Tenosique de Pino Suárez see Tenosique
22 I6 Tensas River Louisiana, S USA
23 O8 Tensaw River Alabama, S USA
74 E7 Tensift seasonal river W Morocco
171 O12 Tentena var. Tenteno. Sulawesi, C Indonesia
Tenteno see Tentena
183 U4 Tenterfield New South Wales, SE Australia
23 X16 Ten Thousand Islands island group Florida, SE USA
60 H9 Teodoro Sampaio São Paulo, S Brazil
59 N19 Teófilo Otoni var. Theophilo Ottoni. Minas Gerais, NE Brazil
116 K5 Teofipol' Khmel'nyts'ka Oblast', W Ukraine
191 Q8 Teohatu Tahiti, W French Polynesia
41 P14 Teotihuacán ruins México, S Mexico
Teotilán see Teotitlán del Camino
41 Q15 Teotitlán del Camino var. Teotilán. Oaxaca, S Mexico
190 G12 Tepa Île Uvea, E Wallis and Futuna
191 P8 Tepaee, Récif reef Tahiti, W French Polynesia
40 L14 Tepalcatepec Michoacán de Ocampo, SW Mexico
190 A16 Tepa Point headland SW Niue
40 L13 Tepatitlán var. Tepatitlán de Morelos. Jalisco, SW Mexico
Tepatitlán de Morelos see Tepatitlán
40 J9 Tepehuanes var. Santa Catarina de Tepehuanes. Durango, C Mexico
Tepelena see Tepelenë
113 L22 Tepelenë var. Tepelena, It. Tepeleni. Gjirokastër, S Albania
Tepeleni see Tepelenë
40 K12 Tepic Nayarit, C Mexico
111 C15 Teplice Ger. Teplitz; prev. Teplice-Šanov, Teplitz-Schönau. Ústecký Kraj, NW Czech Republic
Teplice-Šanov/Teplitz/Teplitz-Schönau see Teplice
117 O7 Teplyk Vinnyts'ka Oblast', C Ukraine
123 R10 Teplyy Klyuch Respublika Sakha (Yakutiya), NE Russian Federation
40 E5 Tepoca, Cabo headland NW Mexico
191 W9 Tepoto island Îles du Désappointement, C French Polynesia
92 L11 Tepsa Lappi, N Finland
190 B8 Tepuka atoll Funafuti Atoll, C Tuvalu
184 N7 Te Puke Bay of Plenty, North Island, New Zealand
40 L13 Tequila Jalisco, SW Mexico
41 O13 Tequisquiapan Querétaro de Arteaga, C Mexico
77 Q12 Téra Tillabéri, W Niger
104 J5 Tera NW Spain
191 V1 Teraina prev. Washington Island. atoll Line Islands, E Kiribati
81 F15 Terakeka Bahr el Gabel, S Sudan
107 J14 Teramo anc. Interamna. Abruzzi, C Italy
98 P7 Ter Apel Groningen, NE Netherlands
104 H11 Tera, Ribeira de S Portugal
185 K14 Terawhiti, Cape headland North Island, New Zealand
98 N12 Terborg Gelderland, E Netherlands
137 P13 Tercan Erzincan, NE Turkey
64 O2 Terceira ✕ Terceira, Azores, Portugal, NE Atlantic Ocean
64 O2 Terceira var. Ilha Terceira. island Azores, Portugal, NE Atlantic Ocean
Terceira, Ilha see Terceira
116 K6 Terebovlya Ternopil's'ka Oblast', W Ukraine
127 O15 Terek SW Russian Federation
Terekhovka see Tsyerakhowka
147 R9 Terek-Say Dzhalal-Abadskaya Oblast', W Kyrgyzstan
145 Z10 Terekty Kaz. Alekseevka. Vostochnyy Kazakhstan, E Kazakhstan
145 Z10 Terekty prev. Alekseevka, Alekseyevka. Vostochnyy Kazakhstan, E Kazakhstan
168 L7 Terengganu var. Trengganu. state Peninsular Malaysia
127 X7 Terensay Orenburgskaya Oblast', W Russian Federation
58 N13 Teresina var. Therezina. state capital Piauí, NE Brazil
60 P9 Teresópolis Rio de Janeiro, SE Brazil
110 P12 Terespol Lubelskie, E Poland
191 V16 Terevaka, Maunga Easter Island, Chile, E Pacific Ocean
103 P3 Tergnier Aisne, N France
43 O14 Teribe, Río NW Panama
124 K3 Teriberka Murmanskaya Oblast', NW Russian Federation
Terijoki see Zelenogorsk
Terinkot see Tarīn Kowt
145 O10 Tersakkan Kaz. Terisaqqan. C Kazakhstan
Terisaqqan see Tersakkan
24 K12 Terlingua Texas, SW USA
24 K11 Terlingua Creek Texas, SW USA
62 K7 Termas de Río Hondo Santiago del Estero, N Argentina
136 M11 Terme Samsun, N Turkey
Termez see Termiz
Termia see Kýthnos
107 J23 Termini Imerese anc. Thermae Himerenses. Sicilia, Italy, C Mediterranean Sea
41 V14 Términos, Laguna de lagoon SE Mexico
77 X10 Termit-Kaoboul Zinder, C Niger
147 O14 Termiz Rus. Termez. Surkhondaryo Viloyati, S Uzbekistan
107 L15 Termoli Molise, C Italy
Termonde see Dendermonde
98 P5 Termunten Groningen, NE Netherlands
171 R11 Ternate Pulau Ternate, E Indonesia
109 T5 Ternberg Oberösterreich, N Austria
99 E15 Terneuzen var. Neuzen. Zeeland, SW Netherlands
123 T14 Terney Primorskiy Kray, SE Russian Federation
107 I14 Terni anc. Interamna Nahars. Umbria, C Italy
109 X6 Ternitz Niederösterreich, E Austria
117 V7 Ternivka Dnipropetrovs'ka Oblast', E Ukraine
116 K6 Ternopil' Pol. Tarnopol, Rus. Ternopol'. Ternopil's'ka Oblast', W Ukraine
Ternopil' see Ternopil's'ka Oblast'
116 I6 Ternopil's'ka Oblast' var. Ternopil', Rus. Ternopol'skaya Oblast'. province NW Ukraine
Ternopol' see Ternopil'
Ternopol'skaya Oblast' see Ternopil's'ka Oblast'
123 U13 Terpeniya, Mys cape Ostrov Sakhalin, SE Russian Federation
Térraba, Río see Grande de Térraba, Río
10 J13 Terrace British Columbia, W Canada
12 D12 Terrace Bay Ontario, S Canada
107 I16 Terracina Lazio, C Italy
93 F14 Terråk Troms, N Norway
26 M13 Terral Oklahoma, C USA
107 B19 Terralba Sardegna, Italy, C Mediterranean Sea
Terranova di Sicilia see Gela
Terranova Pausania see Olbia
105 W5 Terrassa Cast. Tarrasa. Cataluña, E Spain
15 O12 Terrebonne Québec, SE Canada
22 J11 Terrebonne Bay bay Louisiana, SE USA
31 N14 Terre Haute Indiana, N USA
25 U6 Terrell Texas, SW USA
Terre Neuve see Newfoundland and Labrador
33 Q14 Terreton Idaho, NW USA
103 T7 Territoire-de-Belfort department E France
33 X9 Terry Montana, NW USA
28 I9 Terry Peak ▲ South Dakota, N USA
136 H14 Tersakan Gölü C Turkey
98 J4 Terschelling Fris. Skylge. island Waddeneilanden, N Netherlands
78 H10 Tersef Chari-Baguirmi, C Chad
147 X8 Terskey Ala-Too, Khrebet Kazakhstan/Kyrgyzstan
Terter see Tärtär
105 R8 Teruel anc. Turba. Aragón, E Spain
105 R7 Teruel province Aragón, E Spain
114 M7 Tervel prev. Kurtbunar, Rom. Curtbunar. Dobrich, NE Bulgaria
93 M16 Tervo Itä-Suomi, C Finland
92 L13 Tervola Lappi, NW Finland
Tervueren see Tervuren
99 H18 Tervuren var. Tervueren. Vlaams Brabant, C Belgium
162 G5 Tes var. Dzür. Dzavhan, W Mongolia
112 H11 Tešanj Federacija Bosna I Hercegovina, N Bosnia and Herzegovina
Teschen see Cieszyn
83 M19 Tesenane Inhambane, S Mozambique
80 I9 Teseney var. Tessenei. W Eritrea
39 P5 Teshekpuk Lake Alaska, USA
162 K6 Teshig Bulgan, N Mongolia
165 T2 Teshio Hokkaidō, NE Japan
165 T2 Teshio-sanchi Hokkaidō, NE Japan
Těšín see Cieszyn
Tesiyn Gol see Tes-Khem
129 T7 Tes-Khem var. Tesiyn Gol. Mongolia/Russian Federation
112 H11 Teslić Republika Srpska, N Bosnia and Herzegovina
10 I9 Teslin Yukon Territory, W Canada
10 I8 Teslin British Columbia/Yukon Territory, W Canada
77 Q8 Tessalit Kidal, NE Mali
77 V12 Tessaoua Maradi, S Niger
99 J17 Tessenderlo Limburg, NE Belgium
Tessenei see Teseney
14 L7 Tessier, Lac Québec, SE Canada
Tessin see Ticino
97 M23 Test S England, UK
Testama see Tõstamaa
55 P4 Testigos, Islas los island group N Venezuela
37 S10 Tesuque New Mexico, SW USA
103 O17 Têt var. Tet. S France
Tet see Têt
54 G5 Tetas, Cerro de las ▲ NW Venezuela
83 M15 Tete Tete, NW Mozambique
83 M15 Tete off. Província de Tete. province NW Mozambique
9 N15 Tête Jaune Cache British Columbia, SW Canada
184 O8 Te Teko Bay of Plenty, North Island, New Zealand
186 K9 Tetepare island New Georgia Islands, NW Solomon Islands
Tete, Província de see Tete
Teterev see Teteriv
116 M5 Teteriv Rus. Teterev. N Ukraine
100 M9 Teterow Mecklenburg-Vorpommern, NE Germany
114 I9 Teteven Lovech, N Bulgaria
191 T10 Tetiaroa atoll Îles du Vent, W French Polynesia
105 P14 Tetica de Bacares ▲ S Spain
Tetiyev see Tetiyiv
117 O6 Tetiyiv Rus. Tetiyev. Kyyivs'ka Oblast', N Ukraine
39 T10 Tetlin Alaska, USA
33 R8 Teton River Montana, NW USA
74 G5 Tétouan var. Tetouan, Tetuán. N Morocco
Tetova/Tetovë see Tetovo
114 L7 Tetovo Razgrad, N Bulgaria
113 N18 Tetovo Alb. Tetova, Tetovë, Turk. Kalkandelen. NW FYR Macedonia
115 E20 Tetrázio ▲ S Greece
Tetschen see Děčín
Tetuán see Tétouan
191 Q8 Tetufera, Mont ▲ Tahiti, W French Polynesia
127 R4 Tetyushi Respublika Tatarstan, W Russian Federation
108 I7 Teufen Sankt Gallen, NE Switzerland
40 L12 Teul var. Teul de Gonzáles Ortega. Zacatecas, C Mexico
107 B21 Teulada Sardegna, Italy, C Mediterranean Sea
Teul de Gonzáles Ortega see Teul
9 X16 Teulon Manitoba, S Canada
42 I7 Teupasenti El Paraíso, S Honduras
165 S2 Teuri-tō island NE Japan
100 G13 Teutoburger Wald Eng. Teutoburg Forest. hill range NW Germany
Teutoburg Forest see Teutoburger Wald
93 K17 Teuva Swe. Östermark. Länsi-Soumi, W Finland
107 H15 Tevere Eng. Tiber. C Italy
138 G9 Teverya var. Tiberias, Tverya. Northern, N Israel
96 K13 Teviot SE Scotland, UK
Tevli see Tewli
122 H11 Tevriz Omskaya Oblast', C Russian Federation
185 B24 Te Waewae Bay bay South Island, New Zealand
97 L21 Tewkesbury C England, UK
119 F19 Tewli Rus. Tevli. Brestskaya Voblasts', SW Belarus
159 U12 Têwo var. Dêngkagoin. Gansu, C China
25 U12 Texana, Lake Texas, SW USA
27 S14 Texarkana Arkansas, C USA
25 X5 Texarkana Texas, SW USA
25 N9 Texas off. State of Texas, also known as Lone Star State. state S USA
25 W12 Texas City Texas, SW USA
41 P14 Texcoco México, C Mexico
98 I6 Texel island Waddeneilanden, NW Netherlands
26 H8 Texhoma Oklahoma, C USA
25 N1 Texhoma Texas, SW USA
37 W12 Texico New Mexico, SW USA
24 L1 Texline Texas, SW USA
41 P14 Texmelucan var. San Martín Texmelucan. Puebla, S Mexico
27 O13 Texoma, Lake Oklahoma/Texas, C USA
25 N9 Texon Texas, SW USA
83 J23 Teyateyaneng NW Lesotho
124 M16 Teykovo Ivanovskaya Oblast', W Russian Federation
124 M16 Teza W Russian Federation
41 Q13 Teziutlán Puebla, S Mexico
153 W12 Tezpur Assam, NE India
9 N10 Tha-Anne Nunavut, NE Canada
83 K23 Thabana Ntlenyana var. Thabantshonyana, Mount Ntlenyana. ▲ E Lesotho
Thabantshonyana see Thabana Ntlenyana
83 J23 Thaba Putsoa ▲ C Lesotho
167 Q8 Tha Bo Nong Khai, E Thailand
103 T12 Thabor, Pic du ▲ E France
Tha Chin see Samut Sakhon
166 M7 Thagaya Pegu, C Burma (Myanmar)
Thai, Ao see Thailand, Gulf of
167 T6 Thai Binh Thai Binh, N Vietnam
167 S7 Thai Hoa var. Nghia Dan. Nghê An, N Vietnam
167 P9 Thailand off. Kingdom of Thailand, Th. Prathet Thai; prev. Siam. ◆ monarchy SE Asia
167 P13 Thailand, Gulf of var. Gulf of Siam, Th. Ao Thai, Vtn. Vinh Thai Lan. gulf SE Asia
Thailand, Kingdom of see Thailand
Thai Lan, Vinh see Thailand, Gulf of
167 T6 Thai Nguyên Bắc Thai, N Vietnam
167 S8 Thakhèk var. Muang Khammouan. Khammouan, C Laos
153 S13 Thakurgaon Rajshahi, NW Bangladesh
149 S6 Thal North-West Frontier Province, NW Pakistan
166 M15 Thalang Phuket, SW Thailand
Thalassery see Tellicherry
167 Q10 Thalat Khae Nakhon Ratchasima, C Thailand
109 Q5 Thalgau Salzburg, NW Austria
108 G7 Thalwil Zürich, NW Switzerland
83 I20 Thamaga Kweneng, SE Botswana
Thamarīd see Thamarīt
141 V13 Thamarīt var. Thamarīd, Thumrayt. SW Oman
141 P16 Thamar, Jabal ▲ SW Yemen
184 M6 Thames Waikato, North Island, New Zealand
14 D17 Thames Ontario, S Canada
97 O22 Thames S England, UK
184 M6 Thames, Firth of gulf North Island, New Zealand
14 D17 Thamesville Ontario, S Canada
141 S13 Thamūd N Yemen
167 N9 Thanbyuzayat Mon State, S Burma (Myanmar)
152 I9 Thānesar Haryāna, NW India
167 T7 Thanh Hoa Thanh Hoa, N Vietnam
Thanintari Taungdan see Bilauktaung Range
155 I21 Thanjāvūr prev. Tanjore. Tamil Nādu, SE India
Thanlwin see Salween
103 U7 Thann Haut-Rhin, NE France
167 O16 Tha Nong Phrom Phatthalung, SW Thailand
167 N13 Thap Sakae var. Thap Sakau. Prachuap Khiri Khan, SW Thailand
Thap Sakau see Thap Sakae
98 L10 't Harde Gelderland, E Netherlands
152 D11 Thar Desert var. Great Indian Desert, Indian Desert. desert India/Pakistan
181 V10 Thargomindah Queensland, C Australia
150 D11 Thar Pārkar desert SE Pakistan
139 S7 Tharthār al Furāt, Qanāt ath canal C Iraq
139 R7 Tharthār, Buḥayrat ath C Iraq
139 R5 Tharthār, Wādī ath dry watercourse N Iraq
167 N13 Tha Sae Chumphon, SW Thailand
167 N15 Tha Sala Nakhon Si Thammarat, SW Thailand
114 I13 Thásos Thásos, E Greece
115 I14 Thásos island E Greece
37 N14 Thatcher Arizona, SW USA
167 T5 Thât Khê var. Trâng Dinh. Lang Sơn, N Vietnam
166 M8 Thaton Mon State, S Burma (Myanmar)
167 S9 That Phanom Nakhon Phanom, E Thailand
167 R10 Tha Tum Surin, E Thailand
103 P16 Thau, Bassin de var. Étang de Thau. S France
Thau, Étang de see Thau, Bassin de
166 L3 Thaungdut Sagaing, N Burma (Myanmar)
167 O8 Thaungyin Th. Mae Nam Moei. Burma (Myanmar)/Thailand
167 R8 Tha Uthen Nakhon Phanom, E Thailand
109 W2 Thaya var. Dyje. Austria/Czech Republic see also Dyje
Thaya see Dyje
27 V8 Thayer Missouri, C USA
166 L6 Thayetmyo Magwe, C Burma (Myanmar)
33 S15 Thayne Wyoming, C USA
166 M5 Thazi Mandalay, C Burma (Myanmar)
Thebes see Thíva
44 L5 The Carlton var. Abraham Bay. Mayaguana, SE Bahamas
45 O14 The Crane var. Crane. S Barbados
32 I11 The Dalles Oregon, NW USA
28 M14 Thedford Nebraska, C USA
The Flatts Village see Flatts Village
The Hague see 's-Gravenhage
Theiss see Tisa/Tisza
8 M9 Thelon Northwest Territories, N Canada
9 V15 Theodore Saskatchewan, S Canada
23 N8 Theodore Alabama, S USA
36 L13 Theodore Roosevelt Lake Arizona, SW USA
Theodosia see Feodosiya
Theophilo Ottoni see Teófilo Otoni
11 V13 The Pas Manitoba, C Canada
31 T14 The Plains Ohio, N USA
Thera see Santoríni
172 H17 Thérèse, Île island Inner Islands, NE Seychelles
Therezina see Teresina
115 L20 Thérma Ikaría, Dodekánisa, Greece, Aegean Sea
Thermae Himerenses see Termini Imerese
Thermae Pannonicae see Baden
Thermaic Gulf/Thermaicus Sinus see Thermaïkós Kólpos
121 Q8 Thermaïkós Kólpos Eng. Thermaic Gulf; anc. Thermaicus Sinus. gulf N Greece
Thermiá see Kýthnos
115 L17 Thermís Lésvos, E Greece

332
◆ Country ● Country Capital ◇ Dependent Territory ○ Dependent Territory Capital Administrative Regions ✕ International Airport ▲ Mountain Mountain Range Volcano River Lake Reservoir

THÉRMO – TIVAOUANE

115 E18 **Thérmo** Dytikí Ellás, C Greece
33 V14 **Thermopolis** Wyoming, C USA
183 P10 **The Rock** New South Wales, SE Australia
195 O5 **Theron Mountains** ▲▲ Antarctica
The Sooner State *see* Oklahoma
115 G18 **Thespiés** Stereá Ellás, C Greece
115 E16 **Thessalía** *Eng.* Thessaly. ⬖ *region* C Greece
14 C10 **Thessalon** Ontario, S Canada
115 G14 **Thessaloníki** *Eng.* Salonica, *SCr.* Solun, *Turk.* Selânik. Kentrikí Makedonía, N Greece
115 G14 **Thessaloníki** ✈ Kentrikí Makedonía, N Greece
Thessaly *see* Thessalía
84 B12 **Theta Gap** *undersea feature* E Atlantic Ocean
97 P20 **Thetford** E England, UK
15 R11 **Thetford-Mines** Québec, SE Canada
113 K17 **Theth** *var.* Thethi. Shkodër, N Albania
Thethi *see* Theth
99 L20 **Theux** Liège, E Belgium
45 V9 **The Valley** ○ (Anguilla) E Anguilla
27 N10 **The Village** Oklahoma, C USA
The Volunteer State *see* Tennessee
25 W10 **The Woodlands** Texas, SW USA
Thiamis *see* Kalamás
Thian Shan *see* Tien Shan
Thibet *see* Xizang Zizhiqu
22 J9 **Thibodaux** Louisiana, S USA
29 S3 **Thief Lake** ◎ Minnesota, N USA
29 S3 **Thief River** ≈ Minnesota, N USA
29 S3 **Thief River Falls** Minnesota, N USA
Thièle *see* La Thielle
32 G14 **Thielsen, Mount** ▲ Oregon, NW USA
Thielt *see* Tielt
106 G7 **Thiene** Veneto, NE Italy
Thienen *see* Tienen
103 P11 **Thiers** Puy-de-Dôme, C France
76 F11 **Thiès** W Senegal
81 I19 **Thika** Central, S Kenya
Thikombia *see* Cikobia
151 K18 **Thiladhunmathi Atoll** *var.* Tiladummati Atoll. *atoll* N Maldives
Thimbu *see* Thimphu
153 T11 **Thimphu** *var.* Thimbu; *prev.* Tashi Chho Dzong. ● (Bhutan) W Bhutan
92 H2 **Thingeyri** Vestfirdhir, NW Iceland
92 I3 **Thingvellir** Sudhurland, SW Iceland
187 Q17 **Thio** Province Sud, C New Caledonia
103 T4 **Thionville** *Ger.* Diedenhofen. Moselle, NE France
115 K22 **Thíra** Santorini, Kykládes, Greece, Aegean Sea
Thíra *see* Santoríni
115 J22 **Thirasía** *island* Kykládes, Greece, Aegean Sea
97 M16 **Thirsk** N England, UK
14 F12 **Thirty Thousand Islands** *island group* Ontario, S Canada
Thiruvanathapuram *see* Trivandrum
95 F20 **Thisted** Viborg, NW Denmark
Thistil Fjord *see* Thistilfjördhur
92 L1 **Thistilfjördhur** *var.* Thistil Fjord. *fjord* NE Iceland
182 G9 **Thistle Island** *island* South Australia
Thithia *see* Cicia
Thiukhaoluang Phrahang *see* Luang Prabang Range
115 G18 **Thíva** *Eng.* Thebes; *prev.* Thívai. Stereá Ellás, C Greece
Thívai *see* Thíva
102 M12 **Thiviers** Dordogne, SW France
92 J4 **Thjórsá** ≈ C Iceland
9 N10 **Thlewiaza** ≈ Nunavut, NE Canada
8 L10 **Thoa** ≈ Northwest Territories, NW Canada
99 G14 **Tholen** Zeeland, SW Netherlands
99 F14 **Tholen** *island* SW Netherlands
26 L10 **Thomas** Oklahoma, C USA
21 T3 **Thomas** West Virginia, NE USA
27 U3 **Thomas Hill Reservoir** ⊠ Missouri, C USA
23 S5 **Thomaston** Georgia, SE USA
19 R7 **Thomaston** Maine, NE USA
25 T12 **Thomaston** Texas, SW USA
23 O6 **Thomasville** Alabama, S USA
23 T8 **Thomasville** Georgia, SE USA
21 S9 **Thomasville** North Carolina, SE USA
35 N5 **Thomes Creek** ≈ California, W USA
9 W12 **Thompson** Manitoba, C Canada
29 R4 **Thompson** North Dakota, N USA
0 F8 **Thompson** ≈ Alberta/British Columbia, SW Canada
33 O8 **Thompson Falls** Montana, NW USA
29 Q10 **Thompson, Lake** ◎ South Dakota, N USA
34 M3 **Thompson Peak** ▲ California, W USA
27 S2 **Thompson River** ≈ Missouri, C USA
185 A22 **Thompson Sound** *sound* South Island, New Zealand
8 J5 **Thomsen** ≈ Banks Island, Northwest Territories, NW Canada
23 V4 **Thomson** Georgia, SE USA
103 T10 **Thonon-les-Bains** Haute-Savoie, E France
103 O15 **Thoré** *var.* Thore. ≈ S France
Thore *see* Thoré
37 P11 **Thoreau** New Mexico, SW USA
Thorenburg *see* Turda
92 J3 **Thórisvatn** ◎ C Iceland
92 P4 **Thor, Kapp** *headland* S Svalbard
92 I4 **Thorlákshöfn** Sudhurland, SW Iceland
Thorn *see* Toruń
25 T10 **Thorndale** Texas, SW USA
14 H10 **Thorne** Ontario, S Canada
97 J14 **Thornhill** S Scotland, UK
25 U8 **Thornton** Texas, SW USA
Thornton Island *see* Millennium Island
14 H16 **Thorold** Ontario, S Canada
32 I9 **Thorp** Washington, NW USA
Thorshavn *see* Tórshavn
195 S3 **Thorshavnheiane** *physical region* Antarctica
92 L1 **Thórshöfn** Nordhurland Eystra, NE Iceland
Thospitis *see* Van Gölü
167 S14 **Thôt Nôt** Cân Thơ, S Vietnam
102 K8 **Thouars** Deux-Sèvres, W France
153 X14 **Thoubal** Manipur, NE India
102 K9 **Thouet** ≈ W France
Thoune *see* Thun
18 H7 **Thousand Islands** *island* Canada/USA
35 S15 **Thousand Oaks** California, W USA
114 L12 **Thrace** *cultural region* SE Europe
114 J13 **Thracian Sea** *Gk.* Thrakikó Pélagos; *anc.* Thracium Mare. *sea* Greece/Turkey
Thracium Mare/Thrakikó Pélagos *see* Thracian Sea
Thrá Lí, Bá *see* Tralee Bay
33 R11 **Three Forks** Montana, NW USA
162 M8 **Three Gorges Dam** *dam* Hubei, C China
160 L9 **Three Gorges Reservoir** ⊠ C China
9 Q16 **Three Hills** Alberta, SW Canada
183 N15 **Three Hummock Island** *island* Tasmania, SE Australia
184 H1 **Three Kings Islands** *island group* N New Zealand
175 P10 **Three Kings Rise** *undersea feature* W Pacific Ocean
77 O18 **Three Points, Cape** *headland* S Ghana
31 P10 **Three Rivers** Michigan, N USA
25 S13 **Three Rivers** Texas, SW USA
83 G24 **Three Sisters** Northern Cape, SW South Africa
32 H13 **Three Sisters** ▲ Oregon, NW USA
187 N10 **Three Sisters Islands** *island group* SE Solomon Islands
Thrissur *see* Trichūr
25 Q6 **Throckmorton** Texas, SW USA
180 M10 **Throssell, Lake** *salt lake* Western Australia
115 K25 **Thryptís** *var.* Thrýptis. ▲ Kríti, Greece, E Mediterranean Sea
167 T13 **Thu Dâu Môt** *var.* Phu Cüơng. Sông Be, S Vietnam
167 S6 **Thu Do** ✈ (Ha Nôi) Ha Nôi, N Vietnam
99 G21 **Thuin** Hainaut, S Belgium
149 Q12 **Thul** Sind, SE Pakistan
Thule *see* Qaanaaq
83 J18 **Thuli** *var.* Tuli. ≈ S Zimbabwe
Thumrayt *see* Thamarīt
108 D9 **Thun** *Fr.* Thoune. Bern, W Switzerland
12 C12 **Thunder Bay** Ontario, S Canada
30 M1 **Thunder Bay** *lake bay* S Canada
31 R6 **Thunder Bay** *lake bay* Michigan, N USA
31 R6 **Thunder Bay River** ≈ Michigan, N USA
27 N11 **Thunderbird, Lake** ⊠ Oklahoma, C USA
28 L8 **Thunder Butte Creek** ≈ South Dakota, N USA
108 E9 **Thuner See** ◎ C Switzerland
167 N15 **Thung Song** *var.* Cha Mai. Nakhon Si Thammarat, SW Thailand
108 H7 **Thur** ≈ N Switzerland
108 G6 **Thurgau** *Fr.* Thurgovie. ⬖ *canton* NE Switzerland
Thurgovie *see* Thurgau
Thuringe *see* Thüringen
108 J7 **Thüringen** Vorarlberg, W Austria
101 J17 **Thüringen** *Eng.* Thuringia, *Fr.* Thuringe. ⬖ *state* C Germany
101 J17 **Thüringer Wald** *Eng.* Thuringian Forest. ▲▲ C Germany
Thuringia *see* Thüringen
Thuringian Forest *see* Thüringer Wald
97 D19 **Thurles** *Ir.* Durlas. S Ireland
21 W2 **Thurmont** Maryland, NE USA
Thurø *see* Thurø By
95 H24 **Thurø By** *var.* Thurø. Fyn, C Denmark
14 M12 **Thurso** Québec, SE Canada
96 J6 **Thurso** N Scotland, UK
194 I10 **Thurston Island** *island* Antarctica
108 I9 **Thusis** Graubünden, S Switzerland
Thýamis *see* Kalamás
95 E21 **Thyborøn** *var.* Tyborøn. Ringkøbing, W Denmark
195 U3 **Thyer Glacier** *glacier* Antarctica
115 L20 **Thýmaina** *island* Dodekánisa, Greece, Aegean Sea
83 N15 **Thyolo** *var.* Cholo. Southern, S Malawi
183 U6 **Tia** New South Wales, SE Australia
54 H5 **Tía Juana** Zulia, NW Venezuela
Tiancheng *see* Chongyang
160 J14 **Tiandong** *var.* Pingma. Guangxi Zhuangzu Zizhiqu, S China
161 O3 **Tianjin** *var.* Tientsin. Tianjin Shi, E China
Tianjin *see* Tianjin Shi
161 P3 **Tianjin Shi** *var.* Jin, Tianjin, T'ien-ching, Tientsin. ⬖ *municipality* E China
159 S10 **Tianjun** *var.* Xinyuan. Qinghai, C China
160 J13 **Tianlin** *var.* Leli. Guangxi Zhuangzu Zizhiqu, S China
Tian Shan *see* Tien Shan
159 W11 **Tianshui** Gansu, C China
150 I7 **Tianshuihai** Xinjiang Uygur Zizhiqu, W China
161 S10 **Tiantai** Zhejiang, SE China
160 J14 **Tianyang** *var.* Tianzhou. Guangxi Zhuangzu Zizhiqu, S China
Tianzhou *see* Tianyang
159 U9 **Tianzhu** *var.* Huazangsi, Tianzhu Zangzu Zizhixian. Gansu, C China
Tianzhu Zangzu Zizhixian *see* Tianzhu
191 Q7 **Tiarei** Tahiti, W French Polynesia
74 J6 **Tiaret** *var.* Tihert. NW Algeria
77 N17 **Tiassalé** S Ivory Coast
192 I16 **Ti'avea** Upolu, SE Samoa
Tiba *see* Chiba
60 J11 **Tibagi** *var.* Tibají. Paraná, S Brazil
60 J10 **Tibagi, Rio** *var.* Rio Tibají. ≈ S Brazil
Tibají *see* Tibagi
Tibají, Rio *see* Tibagi, Rio
139 Q9 **Tibal, Wādī** *dry watercourse* S Iraq
54 G9 **Tibaná** Boyacá, C Colombia
79 F14 **Tibati** Adamaoua, N Cameroon
76 K15 **Tibé, Pic de** ▲ SE Guinea
Tiber *see* Tevere, Italy
Tiber *see* Tivoli, Italy
Tiberias *see* Teverya
138 G8 **Tiberias, Lake** *var.* Chinnereth, Sea of Bahr Tabariya, Sea of Galilee, *Ar.* Bahrat Tabariya, *Heb.* Yam Kinneret. ◎ N Israel
67 Q5 **Tibesti** *var.* Tibesti Massif, *Ar.* Tibistī. ▲▲ N Africa
Tibesti Massif *see* Tibesti
Tibet *see* Xizang Zizhiqu
Tibetan Autonomous Region *see* Xizang Zizhiqu
Tibet, Plateau of *see* Qingzang Gaoyuan
Tibistī *see* Tibesti
14 K7 **Tiblemont, Lac** ◎ Québec, SE Canada
139 X9 **Ţīb, Nahr aţ** ≈ S Iraq
Tibnī *see* At Tibnī
182 L4 **Tibooburra** New South Wales, SE Australia
95 L18 **Tibro** Västra Götaland, S Sweden
40 E5 **Tiburón, Isla** *var.* Isla del Tiburón. *island* NW Mexico
Tiburón, Isla del *see* Tiburón, Isla
23 W14 **Tice** Florida, SE USA
Tichau *see* Tychy
114 L8 **Ticha, Yazovir** ◎ NE Bulgaria
76 K9 **Tîchît** *var.* Tichitt. Tagant, C Mauritania
Tichitt *see* Tîchît
108 G11 **Ticino** *Fr./Ger.* Tessin. ⬖ *canton* S Switzerland
106 D8 **Ticino** ≈ Italy/Switzerland
108 H11 **Ticino** *Ger.* Tessin. ≈ SW Switzerland
Ticinum *see* Pavia
41 X12 **Ticul** Yucatán, SE Mexico
95 K18 **Tidaholm** Västra Götaland, S Sweden
Tidjikdja *see* Tidjikja
76 J8 **Tidjikja** *var.* Tidjikdja; *prev.* Fort-Cappolani. Tagant, C Mauritania
Tidore *see* Soasiu
171 R11 **Tidore, Pulau** *island* E Indonesia
Tîdra, Ile *see* Et Tîdra
77 N16 **Tiébissou** *var.* Tiebissou. C Ivory Coast
Tiebissou *see* Tiébissou
Tiefa *see* Diaobingshan
108 I9 **Tiefencastel** Graubünden, S Switzerland
Tiegenhof *see* Nowy Dwór Gdański
T'ieh-ling *see* Tieling
98 K13 **Tiel** Gelderland, C Netherlands
163 W7 **Tieli** Heilongjiang, NE China
163 V11 **Tieling** *var.* T'ieh-ling. Liaoning, NE China
152 L4 **Tielongtan** China/India
99 D17 **Tielt** *var.* Thielt. West-Vlaanderen, W Belgium
T'ien-ching *see* Tianjin Shi
99 I18 **Tienen** *var.* Thienen, *Fr.* Tirlemont. Vlaams Brabant, C Belgium
Tiên Giang, Sông *see* Mekong
147 X9 **Tien Shan** *Chin.* Thian Shan, Tian Shan, T'ien Shan, *Rus.* Tyan'-Shan'. ▲▲ C Asia
Tientsin *see* Tianjin
167 U6 **Tiên Yên** Quang Ninh, N Vietnam
95 O14 **Tierp** Uppsala, C Sweden
62 H7 **Tierra Amarilla** Atacama, N Chile
37 R9 **Tierra Amarilla** New Mexico, SW USA
41 R15 **Tierra Blanca** Veracruz-Llave, E Mexico
41 O16 **Tierra Colorada** Guerrero, S Mexico
63 J17 **Tierra Colorada, Bajo de la** *basin* SE Argentina
63 I25 **Tierra del Fuego** *off.* Provincia de la Tierra del Fuego. ⬖ *province* S Argentina
63 J24 **Tierra del Fuego** *island* Argentina/Chile
Tierra del Fuego, Provincia de la *see* Tierra del Fuego
54 D7 **Tierralta** Córdoba, NW Colombia
104 K9 **Tiétar** ≈ W Spain
60 L10 **Tietê** São Paulo, S Brazil
60 J8 **Tietê, Rio** ≈ S Brazil
32 I9 **Tieton** Washington, NW USA
32 J6 **Tiffany Mountain** ▲ Washington, NW USA
31 S12 **Tiffin** Ohio, N USA
31 Q11 **Tiffin River** ≈ Ohio, N USA
Tiflis *see* T'bilisi
23 U7 **Tifton** Georgia, SE USA
171 R13 **Tifu** Pulau Buru, E Indonesia
38 L17 **Tigalda Island** *island* Aleutian Islands, Alaska, USA
115 I15 **Tigáni, Ákrotírio** *headland* Límnos, E Greece
169 V6 **Tiga Tarok** Sabah, East Malaysia
117 O10 **Tighina** *Rus.* Bendery; *prev.* Bender. E Moldova
145 X9 **Tigiretskiy Khrebet** ▲▲ E Kazakhstan
79 F14 **Tignère** Adamaoua, N Cameroon
13 P14 **Tignish** Prince Edward Island, SE Canada
Tigranocerta *see* Siirt
80 I11 **Tigray** ⬖ *province* N Ethiopia
41 O11 **Tigre, Cerro del** ▲ C Mexico
56 F8 **Tigre, Río** ≈ N Peru
139 X10 **Tigris** *Ar.* Dijlah, *Turk.* Dicle. ≈ Iraq/Turkey
76 G9 **Tiguent** Trarza, SW Mauritania
74 M10 **Tiguentourine** E Algeria
77 V10 **Tiguidit, Falaise de** *ridge* C Niger
141 N13 **Tihāmah** *var.* Tehama. *plain* Saudi Arabia/Yemen
Tihert *see* Tiaret
Ti-hua/Tihwa *see* Ürümqi
41 Q13 **Tihuatlán** Veracruz-Llave, E Mexico
40 B1 **Tijuana** Baja California, NW Mexico
42 E2 **Tikal** Petén, N Guatemala
154 I9 **Tīkamgarh** *prev.* Tehri. Madhya Pradesh, C India
158 L7 **Tikanlik** Xinjiang Uygur Zizhiqu, NW China
77 P12 **Tikaré** N Burkina
39 O12 **Tikchik Lakes** *lakes* Alaska, USA
191 T9 **Tikehau** *atoll* Îles Tuamotu, C French Polynesia
191 V9 **Tikei** *island* Îles Tuamotu, C French Polynesia
126 L13 **Tikhoretsk** Krasnodarskiy Kray, SW Russian Federation
124 I13 **Tikhvin** Leningradskaya Oblast', NW Russian Federation
193 P9 **Tiki Basin** *undersea feature* S Pacific Ocean
76 K13 **Tikinsso** ≈ NE Guinea
184 Q8 **Tikitiki** Gisborne, North Island, New Zealand
79 D16 **Tiko** Sud-Ouest, SW Cameroon
139 S6 **Tikrīt** *var.* Tekrit. N Iraq
124 I8 **Tiksha** Respublika Kareliya, NW Russian Federation
124 I6 **Tikshozero, Ozero** ◎ NW Russian Federation
123 P7 **Tiksi** Respublika Sakha (Yakutiya), NE Russian Federation
Tiladummati Atoll *see* Thiladhunmathi Atoll
42 A6 **Tilapa** San Marcos, SW Guatemala
42 L13 **Tilarán** Guanacaste, NW Costa Rica
99 J14 **Tilburg** Noord-Brabant, S Netherlands
14 D17 **Tilbury** Ontario, S Canada
182 K4 **Tilcha** South Australia
Tilcha Creek *see* Callabonna Creek
29 Q14 **Tilden** Nebraska, C USA
25 R13 **Tilden** Texas, SW USA
14 H10 **Tilden Lake** Ontario, S Canada
116 G9 **Tileagd** *Hung.* Mezőtelegd. Bihor, W Romania
77 Q8 **Tilemsi, Vallée de** ≈ C Mali
123 V8 **Tilichiki** Koryakskiy Avtonomnyy Okrug, E Russian Federation
Tiligul *see* Tilihul
Tiligul'skiy Liman *see* Tilihul's'kyy Lyman
117 P9 **Tilihul** *Rus.* Tiligul. ≈ SW Ukraine
117 P10 **Tilihul's'kyy Lyman** *Rus.* Tiligul'skiy Liman. ◎ S Ukraine
Tilimsen *see* Tlemcen
Tilio Martius *see* Toulon
77 R11 **Tillabéri** *var.* Tillabéry. Tillabéri, W Niger
77 R11 **Tillabéri** ⬖ *department* SW Niger
Tillabéry *see* Tillabéri
32 F11 **Tillamook** Oregon, NW USA
32 E11 **Tillamook Bay** *inlet* Oregon, NW USA
151 Q22 **Tillanchāng Dwīp** *island* Nicobar Islands, India, NE Indian Ocean
95 N15 **Tillberga** Västmanland, C Sweden
Tillenberg *see* Dyleń
21 S10 **Tillery, Lake** ⊠ North Carolina, SE USA
77 T10 **Tillia** Tahoua, W Niger
23 N8 **Tillmans Corner** Alabama, S USA
14 F17 **Tillsonburg** Ontario, S Canada
115 N22 **Tílos** *island* Dodekánisa, Greece, Aegean Sea
183 N5 **Tilpa** New South Wales, SE Australia
Tilsit *see* Sovetsk
31 N13 **Tilton** Illinois, N USA
126 K7 **Tim** Kurskaya Oblast', W Russian Federation
54 D12 **Timaná** Huila, S Colombia
Timan Ridge *see* Timanskiy Kryazh
125 Q6 **Timanskiy Kryazh** *Eng.* Timan Ridge. *ridge* NW Russian Federation
185 G20 **Timaru** Canterbury, South Island, New Zealand
127 S6 **Timashevo** Samarskaya Oblast', W Russian Federation
126 K13 **Timashevsk** Krasnodarskiy Kray, SW Russian Federation
Timbaki/Timbákion *see* Tympáki
22 K10 **Timbalier Bay** *bay* Louisiana, S USA
22 K11 **Timbalier Island** *island* Louisiana, S USA
76 L10 **Timbedgha** *var.* Timbédra. Hodh ech Chargui, SE Mauritania
Timbédra *see* Timbedgha
32 G10 **Timber** Oregon, NW USA
181 O3 **Timber Creek** Northern Territory, N Australia
28 M8 **Timber Lake** South Dakota, N USA
54 D12 **Timbío** Cauca, SW Colombia
54 C12 **Timbiquí** Cauca, SW Colombia
83 O17 **Timbue, Ponta** *headland* C Mozambique
Timbuktu *see* Tombouctou
169 W8 **Timbun Mata, Pulau** *island* E Malaysia
77 P8 **Timétrine** *var.* Ti-n-Kâr. *oasis* C Mali
Timfi *see* Týmfi
Timfristos *see* Tymfristós
77 V9 **Timia** Agadez, C Niger
171 X14 **Timika** Papua, E Indonesia
74 I9 **Timimoun** C Algeria
Timiris, Cap *see* Timirist, Râs
76 F8 **Timirist, Râs** *var.* Cap Timiris. *headland* NW Mauritania
145 O7 **Timiryazevo** Severnyy Kazakhstan, N Kazakhstan
116 E11 **Timiş** ⬖ *county* SW Romania
14 H9 **Timiskaming, Lake** *Fr.* Lac Témiscamingue. ◎ Ontario/Québec, SE Canada
116 E11 **Timişoara** *Ger.* Temeschwar, Temeswar, *Hung.* Temesvár; *prev.* Temeschburg. Timiş, W Romania
116 E11 **Timisoara** ✈ Timiş, SW Romania
Timkovichi *see* Tsimkavichy
77 U8 **Ti-m-Meghsoï** ≈ NW Niger
100 K8 **Timmerdorfer Strand** Schleswig-Holstein, N Germany
14 F7 **Timmins** Ontario, S Canada
21 S12 **Timmonsville** South Carolina, SE USA
30 K5 **Timms Hill** ▲ Wisconsin, N USA
112 P12 **Timok** ≈ E Serbia
58 N13 **Timon** Maranhão, E Brazil
171 Q17 **Timor Sea** *sea* E Indian Ocean
Timor Timur *see* East Timor
Timor Trench *see* Timor Trough
192 G8 **Timor Trough** *var.* Timor Trench. *undersea feature* NE Timor Sea
61 A21 **Timote** Buenos Aires, E Argentina
54 I6 **Timotes** Mérida, NW Venezuela
25 X8 **Timpson** Texas, SW USA
123 Q11 **Timpton** ≈ NE Russian Federation
93 H17 **Timrå** Västernorrland, C Sweden
20 J10 **Tims Ford Lake** ⊠ Tennessee, S USA
168 L7 **Timur, Banjaran** ▲▲ Peninsular Malaysia
171 Q8 **Tinaca Point** *headland* Mindanao, S Philippines
54 K5 **Tinaco** Cojedes, N Venezuela
64 Q11 **Tinajo** Lanzarote, Islas Canarias, Spain, NE Atlantic Ocean
187 P10 **Tinakula** *island* Santa Cruz Islands, E Solomon Islands
54 K5 **Tinaquillo** Cojedes, N Venezuela
116 F10 **Tinca** *Hung.* Tenke. Bihor, W Romania
155 J20 **Tindivanam** Tamil Nādu, SE India
74 E9 **Tindouf** W Algeria
74 E9 **Tindouf, Sebkha de** *salt lake* W Algeria
104 J2 **Tineo** Asturias, N Spain
77 R9 **Ti-n-Essako** Kidal, E Mali
183 T5 **Tingha** New South Wales, SE Australia
Tingis *see* Tanger
Tinglett *see* Tinglev
95 F24 **Tinglev** *Ger.* Tinglett. Sønderjylland, SW Denmark
56 E12 **Tingo María** Huánuco, C Peru
Tingréla *see* Tengréla
158 K16 **Tingri** *var.* Xégar. Xizang Zizhiqu, W China
95 M21 **Tingsryd** Kronoberg, S Sweden
95 P19 **Tingstäde** Gotland, SE Sweden
62 H12 **Tinguiririca, Volcán** Ѫ C Chile
94 F9 **Tingvoll** Møre og Romsdal, S Norway
188 K8 **Tinian** *island* S Northern Mariana Islands
Ti-n-Kâr *see* Timétrine
Tinnevelly *see* Tirunelveli
95 G15 **Tinnoset** Telemark, S Norway
95 F15 **Tinnsjø** ◎ S Norway
Tino *see* Chino
115 J20 **Tínos** Tínos, Kykládes, Greece, Aegean Sea
115 J20 **Tínos** *anc.* Tenos. *island* Kykládes, Greece, Aegean Sea
153 R14 **Tinpahar** Jhārkhand, NE India
153 X11 **Tinsukia** Assam, NE India
76 K10 **Tîntâne** Hodh el Gharbi, S Mauritania
62 L7 **Tintina** Santiago del Estero, N Argentina
182 K10 **Tintinara** South Australia
104 I14 **Tinto** ≈ SW Spain
77 S8 **Ti-n-Zaouâtene** Kidal, NE Mali
Tiobraid Árann *see* Tipperary
28 K3 **Tioga** North Dakota, N USA
18 G12 **Tioga** Pennsylvania, NE USA
25 T5 **Tioga** Texas, SW USA
35 Q8 **Tioga Pass** *pass* California, W USA
18 G12 **Tioga River** ≈ New York/Pennsylvania, NE USA
Tioman Island *see* Tioman, Pulau
168 M9 **Tioman, Pulau** *var.* Tioman Island. *island* Peninsular Malaysia
18 C12 **Tionesta** Pennsylvania, NE USA
18 D12 **Tionesta Creek** ≈ Pennsylvania, NE USA
168 J13 **Tiop** Pulau Pagai Selatan, W Indonesia
77 O12 **Tiou** NW Burkina
18 H11 **Tioughnioga River** ≈ New York, NE USA
74 J5 **Tipasa** *var.* Tipaza. N Algeria
Tipaza *see* Tipasa
42 J10 **Tipitapa** Managua, W Nicaragua
31 R13 **Tipp City** Ohio, N USA
31 O12 **Tippecanoe River** ≈ Indiana, N USA
97 D20 **Tipperary** *Ir.* Tiobraid Árann. S Ireland
97 D19 **Tipperary** *Ir.* Tiobraid Árann. ⬖ *county* S Ireland
35 R12 **Tipton** California, W USA
31 P13 **Tipton** Indiana, N USA
29 Y14 **Tipton** Iowa, C USA
27 U5 **Tipton** Missouri, C USA
36 I10 **Tipton, Mount** ▲ Arizona, SW USA
20 F8 **Tiptonville** Tennessee, S USA
12 E12 **Tip Top Mountain** ▲ Ontario, S Canada
155 G19 **Tiptūr** Karnātaka, W India
Tiquisate *see* Pueblo Nuevo Tiquisate
58 L13 **Tiracambu, Serra do** ▲▲ E Brazil
Tirana *see* Tiranë
113 K19 **Tirana Rinas** ✈ Durrës, W Albania
113 L20 **Tiranë** *var.* Tirana. ● (Albania) Tiranë, C Albania
113 K20 **Tiranë** ⬖ *district* W Albania
140 I5 **Tirān, Jazīrat** *island* Egypt/Saudi Arabia
106 F6 **Tirano** Lombardia, N Italy
182 I2 **Tirari Desert** *desert* South Australia
117 O10 **Tiraspol** *Rus.* Tiraspol'. E Moldova
Tiraspol' *see* Tiraspol
184 M8 **Tirau** Waikato, North Island, New Zealand
136 C14 **Tire** İzmir, SW Turkey
137 O11 **Tirebolu** Giresun, N Turkey
96 F11 **Tiree** *island* W Scotland, UK
Tîrgovişte *see* Târgovişte
Tîrgu *see* Târgu Cărbuneşti
Tîrgu Bujor *see* Târgu Bujor
Tîrgu Frumos *see* Târgu Frumos
Tîrgu Jiu *see* Târgu Jiu
Tîrgu Lăpuş *see* Târgu Lăpuş
Tîrgu Mures *see* Târgu Mureş
Tîrgu-Neamţ *see* Târgu-Neamţ
Tîrgu Ocna *see* Târgu Ocna
Tîrgu Secuiesc *see* Târgu Secuiesc
149 T3 **Tirich Mīr** ▲ NW Pakistan
76 J5 **Tiris Zemmour** ⬖ *region* N Mauritania
Tirlemont *see* Tienen
127 W5 **Tirlyanskiy** Respublika Bashkortostan, W Russian Federation
Tîrnava Mare *see* Târnava Mare
Tîrnava Mică *see* Târnava Mică
Tîrnăveni *see* Târnăveni
Tírnavos *see* Týrnavos
Tirnovo *see* Veliko Tŭrnovo
154 J11 **Tirodi** Madhya Pradesh, C India
108 K8 **Tirol** *off.* Land Tirol, *var.* Tyrol, *It.* Tirolo. ⬖ *state* W Austria
Tirol, Land *see* Tirol
Tirolo *see* Tirol
Tirreno, Mare *see* Tyrrhenian Sea
107 B19 **Tirso** ≈ Sardegna, Italy, C Mediterranean Sea
95 H22 **Tirstrup** ✈ (Århus) Århus, C Denmark
155 I21 **Tiruchchirāppalli** *prev.* Trichinopoly. Tamil Nādu, SE India
155 H23 **Tirunelveli** *var.* Tinnevelly. Tamil Nādu, SE India
155 J19 **Tirupati** Andhra Pradesh, E India
155 I20 **Tiruppattūr** Tamil Nādu, SE India
155 H21 **Tiruppur** Tamil Nādu, SW India
155 I20 **Tiruvannāmalai** Tamil Nādu, SE India
112 L10 **Tisa** *Ger.* Theiss, *Hung.* Tisza, *Rus.* Tissa, *Ukr.* Tysa. ≈ SE Europe *see also* Tisza
Tisa *see* Tisza
Tischnowitz *see* Tišnov
9 U14 **Tisdale** Saskatchewan, S Canada
27 O13 **Tishomingo** Oklahoma, C USA
95 M17 **Tisnaren** ◎ S Sweden
111 F18 **Tišnov** *Ger.* Tischnowitz. Jihomoravský Kraj, SE Czech Republic
Tissa *see* Tisa/Tisza
74 J6 **Tissemsilt** N Algeria
153 S12 **Tista** ≈ NE India
112 L8 **Tisza** *Ger.* Theiss, *Rom./Slvn./SCr.* Tisa, *Rus.* Tissa, *Ukr.* Tysa. ≈ SE Europe *see also* Tisa
Tisza *see* Tisa
111 L23 **Tiszaföldvár** Jász-Nagykun-Szolnok, E Hungary
111 M22 **Tiszafüred** Jász-Nagykun-Szolnok, E Hungary
111 L23 **Tiszakécske** Bács-Kiskun, C Hungary
111 M21 **Tiszaújváros** *prev.* Leninváros. Borsod-Abaúj-Zemplén, NE Hungary
111 N21 **Tiszavasvári** Szabolcs-Szatmár-Bereg, NE Hungary
57 I17 **Titicaca, Lake** ◎ Bolivia/Peru
190 H17 **Titikaveka** Rarotonga, S Cook Islands
154 M13 **Titilāgarh** Orissa, E India
168 K8 **Titiwangsa, Banjaran** ▲▲ Peninsular Malaysia
Titograd *see* Podgorica
Titose *see* Chitose
Titova Mitrovica *see* Kosovska Mitrovica
Titovo Užice *see* Užice
113 M18 **Titov Vrv** ▲ NW FYR Macedonia
94 F7 **Titran** Sør-Trøndelag, S Norway
31 Q8 **Tittabawassee River** ≈ Michigan, N USA
116 J13 **Titu** Dâmboviţa, S Romania
79 M16 **Titule** Orientale, N Dem. Rep. Congo
23 X11 **Titusville** Florida, SE USA
18 C12 **Titusville** Pennsylvania, NE USA
76 G11 **Tivaouane** W Senegal

◆ Country
● Country Capital
◇ Dependent Territory
○ Dependent Territory Capital
⬖ Administrative Regions
✈ International Airport
▲ Mountain
▲▲ Mountain Range
Ѫ Volcano
≈ River
◎ Lake
⊠ Reservoir

113 *I17* **Tivat** SW Montenegro
14 *E14* **Tiverton** Ontario, S Canada
97 *J23* **Tiverton** SW England, UK
19 *O12* **Tiverton** Rhode Island, NE USA
107 *I15* **Tivoli** *anc.* Tiber. Lazio, C Italy
25 *U13* **Tivoli** Texas, SW USA
141 *Z8* **Ţīwī** NE Oman
41 *Y11* **Tizimín** Yucatán, SE Mexico
74 *K5* **Tizi Ouzou** *var.* Tizi-Ouzou. N Algeria
74 *D8* **Tiznit** SW Morocco
95 *F23* **Tjæreborg** Ribe, W Denmark
113 *I14* **Tjentište** ◆ Republika Srpska, SE Bosnia and Herzegovina
98 *L7* **Tjeukemeer** N Netherlands
Tjiamis *see* Ciamis
Tjiandjoer *see* Cianjur
Tjilatjap *see* Cilacap
95 *I18* **Tjörn** *island* S Sweden
92 *O3* **Tjuvfjorden** *fjord* S Svalbard
Tkvarcheli *see* Tqvarch'eli
40 *L8* **Tlahualillo** Durango, N Mexico
41 *P14* **Tlalnepantla** México, C Mexico
41 *Q13* **Tlapacoyán** Veracruz-Llave, E Mexico
41 *P16* **Tlapa de Comonfort** Guerrero, S Mexico
40 *L13* **Tlaquepaque** Jalisco, C Mexico
Tlascala *see* Tlaxcala
41 *P14* **Tlaxcala** *var.* Tlascala, Tlaxcala de Xicohténcatl.
41 *P14* **Tlaxcala** *state* S Mexico
Tlaxcala de Xicohténcatl *see* Tlaxcala
41 *P14* **Tlaxco** *var.* Tlaxco de Morelos. Tlaxcala, S Mexico
Tlaxco de Morelos *see* Tlaxco
41 *Q16* **Tlaxiaco** *var.* Santa María Asunción Tlaxiaco. Oaxaca, S Mexico
74 *I6* **Tlemcen** *var.* Tilimsen, Tlemsen. NW Algeria
Tlemsen *see* Tlemcen
138 *L4* **Tlété Ouâte Rharbi, Jebel** ▲ N Syria
116 *J7* **Tlumach** Ivano-Frankivs'ka Oblast', W Ukraine
127 *P17* **Tlyarata** Respublika Dagestan, SW Russian Federation
116 *K10* **Toaca, Vârful** *prev.* Vîrful Toaca. ▲ NE Romania
Toaca, Vîrful *see* Toaca, Vârful
187 *R13* **Toak** Ambrym, C Vanuatu
172 *J4* **Toamasina** *var.* Tamatave. Toamasina, E Madagascar
172 *J4* **Toamasina** ◆ *province* E Madagascar
172 *J4* **Toamasina** ✈ Toamasina, E Madagascar
21 *X6* **Toano** Virginia, NE USA
191 *U10* **Toau** *atoll* Îles Tuamotu, C French Polynesia
45 *T6* **Toa Vaca, Embalse** ◙ C Puerto Rico
62 *K13* **Toay** La Pampa, C Argentina
159 *R14* **Toba** Xizang Zizhiqu, W China
164 *K14* **Toba** Mie, Honshū, SW Japan
168 *I9* **Toba, Danau** ◎ Sumatera, W Indonesia
45 *Y16* **Tobago** *island* NE Trinidad and Tobago
149 *Q9* **Toba Kākar Range** ▲▲ NW Pakistan
105 *Q12* **Tobarra** Castilla-La Mancha, C Spain
149 *U9* **Toba Tek Singh** Punjab, E Pakistan
171 *R11* **Tobelo** Pulau Halmahera, E Indonesia
14 *E12* **Tobermory** Ontario, S Canada
96 *G10* **Tobermory** W Scotland, UK
165 *S4* **Tōbetsu** Hokkaidō, NE Japan
180 *M6* **Tobin Lake** ◎ Western Australia
9 *U14* **Tobin Lake** ◎ Saskatchewan, C Canada
35 *T4* **Tobin, Mount** ▲ Nevada, W USA
165 *O9* **Tobi-shima** *island* C Japan
169 *N13* **Tobooali** Pulau Bangka, W Indonesia
144 *M8* **Tobol** *Kaz.* Tobyl. Kustanay, N Kazakhstan
144 *L8* **Tobol** *Kaz.* Tobyl. ∿ Kazakhstan/Russian Federation
122 *H11* **Tobol'sk** Tyumenskaya Oblast', C Russian Federation
Tobruch/Tobruk *see* Ţubruq
125 *R3* **Tobseda** Nenetskiy Avtonomnyy Okrug, NW Russian Federation
Tobyl *see* Tobol
125 *Q6* **Tobysh** ∿ NW Russian Federation
54 *F10* **Tocaima** Cundinamarca, C Colombia
59 *K16* **Tocantins** *off.* Estado do Tocantins. ◆ *state* C Brazil
Tocantins, Estado do *see* Tocantins
59 *K15* **Tocantins, Rio** ∿ N Brazil
23 *T2* **Toccoa** Georgia, SE USA
165 *O12* **Tochigi** *off.* Tochigi-ken, *var.* Totigi. ◆ *prefecture* Honshū, S Japan
Tochigi-ken *see* Tochigi
165 *O11* **Tochio** *var.* Totio. Niigata, Honshū, C Japan
95 *I15* **Töcksfors** Värmland, C Sweden
42 *J5* **Tocoa** Colón, N Honduras
62 *H4* **Tocopilla** Antofagasta, N Chile
62 *I4* **Tocorpuri, Cerro de** ▲ Bolivia/Chile
183 *O10* **Tocumwal** New South Wales, SE Australia
54 *K4* **Tocuyo de La Costa** Falcón, NW Venezuela
152 *H13* **Toda Rāisingh** Rājasthān, N India
106 *H13* **Todi** Umbria, C Italy
108 *G9* **Tödi** ▲ NE Switzerland
171 *T12* **Todio** Papua, E Indonesia
165 *S9* **Todoga-saki** *headland* Honshū, C Japan
59 *P17* **Todos os Santos, Baía de** *bay* E Brazil
40 *F10* **Todos Santos** Baja California Sur, W Mexico

40 *B2* **Todos Santos, Bahía de** *bay* NW Mexico
Toeban *see* Tuban
Toekang Besi Eilanden *see* Tukangbesi, Kepulauan
Toeloenggagoeng *see* Tulungagung
Tōen *see* T'aoyüan
185 *D25* **Toetoes Bay** *bay* South Island, New Zealand
9 *U14* **Tofield** Alberta, SW Canada
10 *K17* **Tofino** Vancouver Island, SW Canada
189 *X17* **Tofol** Kosrae, E Micronesia
95 *J20* **Tofta** Halland, S Sweden
95 *H15* **Tofte** Buskerud, S Norway
95 *F24* **Toftlund** Sønderjylland, SW Denmark
193 *X15* **Tofua** *island* Ha'apai Group, C Tonga
187 *Q12* **Toga** *island* Torres Islands, N Vanuatu
80 *N13* **Togdheer** *off.* Gobolka Togdheer. ◆ *region* NW Somalia
Togdheer, Gobolka *see* Togdheer
164 *L11* **Togi** Ishikawa, Honshū, SW Japan
39 *N13* **Togiak** Alaska, USA
171 *O11* **Togian, Kepulauan** *island group* C Indonesia
77 *Q15* **Togo** *off.* Togolese Republic; *prev.* French Togoland. ◆ *republic* W Africa
Togolese Republic *see* Togo
162 *F8* **Tögrög** Govĭ-Altay, SW Mongolia
162 *F8* **Tögrög** *var.* Hoolt. Övörhangay, C Mongolia
Tögrög *see* Manhan
159 *N12* **Togton He** *var.* Tuotuo He. ∿ C China
Togton Heyan *see* Tanggulashan
144 *L7* **Toguzak** *Kaz.* Toghyzaq. ∿ Kazakhstan/Russian Federation
37 *P10* **Tohatchi** New Mexico, SW USA
191 *O7* **Tohiea, Mont** ▲ Moorea, W French Polynesia
137 *N14* **Tohma Çayı** ∿ C Turkey
93 *O17* **Tohmajärvi** Itä-Suomi, SE Finland
93 *L16* **Toholampi** Länsi-Soumi, W Finland
Tōhōm *see* Mandah
23 *X12* **Tohopekaliga, Lake** ◎ Florida, SE USA
164 *M14* **Toi** Shizuoka, Honshū, S Japan
190 *B15* **Toi** N Niue
93 *L19* **Toijala** Länsi-Suomi, SW Finland
171 *P12* **Toima** Sulawesi, N Indonesia
164 *D17* **Toi-misaki** *headland* Kyūshū, SW Japan
171 *Q17* **Toineke** Timor, S Indonesia
Toirc, Inis *see* Inishturk
35 *U6* **Toiyabe Range** ▲ Nevada, W USA
Tojikiston, Jumhurii *see* Tajikistan
147 *R12* **Tojikobod** *Rus.* Tadzhikabad. C Tajikistan
164 *G12* **Tōjō** Hiroshima, Honshū, SW Japan
39 *T10* **Tok** Alaska, USA
164 *K13* **Tōkai** Aichi, Honshū, SW Japan
111 *N21* **Tokaj** Borsod-Abaúj-Zemplén, NE Hungary
165 *N11* **Tōkamachi** Niigata, Honshū, S Japan
185 *D25* **Tokanui** Southland, South Island, New Zealand
80 *I7* **Tokar** *var.* Ṭawkar. Red Sea, NE Sudan
136 *L12* **Tokat** Tokat, N Turkey
136 *L12* **Tokat** ◆ *province* N Turkey
163 *X15* **Tŏkch'ŏk-gundo** *island group* NW South Korea
Tōke *see* Taka Atoll
190 *J9* **Tokelau** ◇ *NZ overseas territory* W Polynesia
Tŏketerebes *see* Trebišov
127 *R6* **Tol'yatti** *prev.* Stavropol'. Samarskaya Oblast', W Russian Federation
24 *M6* **Tokio** Texas, SW USA
Tokio *see* Tōkyō
189 *W11* **Toki Point** *point* NW Wake Island
Tokkuztara *see* Gongliu
147 *V7* **Tokmak** *Kir.* Tokmok. Chuyskaya Oblast', N Kyrgyzstan
117 *V9* **Tokmak** *var.* Velykyy Tokmak. Zaporiz'ka Oblast', SE Ukraine
Tokmok *see* Tokmak
184 *Q8* **Tokomaru Bay** Gisborne, North Island, New Zealand
165 *V3* **Tokoro** Hokkaidō, NE Japan
184 *M8* **Tokoroa** Waikato, North Island, New Zealand
76 *K14* **Tokounou** C Guinea
38 *M12* **Toksook Bay** Alaska, USA
Toksu *see* Xinhe
158 *L6* **Toksun** *var.* Toksum. Xinjiang Uygur Zizhiqu, NW China
147 *T8* **Toktogul** Talasskaya Oblast', NW Kyrgyzstan
147 *T9* **Toktogul'skoye Vodokhranilishche** ◙ W Kyrgyzstan
Toktomush *see* Tŭkhtamish
193 *Y14* **Toku** *island* Vava'u Group, N Tonga
165 *U16* **Tokunoshima** Kagoshima, Tokuno-shima, SW Japan
165 *U16* **Tokuno-shima** *island* Nansei-shotō, SW Japan
164 *I14* **Tokushima** *var.* Tokusima. Tokushima, Shikoku, SW Japan
164 *H14* **Tokushima** *off.* Tokushima-ken, *var.* Tokusima. ◆ *prefecture* Shikoku, SW Japan
Tokushima-ken *see* Tokushima
Tokusima *see* Tokushima
164 *E13* **Tokuyama** Yamaguchi, Honshū, SW Japan
165 *N13* **Tōkyō** *var.* Tokio. ● (Japan) Tōkyō, Honshū, S Japan

165 *O13* **Tōkyō** *off.* Tōkyō-to. ◊ *capital district* Honshū, S Japan
Tōkyō-to *see* Tōkyō
145 *T12* **Tokyrau** ∿ C Kazakhstan
149 *O3* **Tokzār** *Pash.* Tukzār. Sar-e Pol, N Afghanistan
145 *W13* **Tokzhaylau** *prev.* Dzerzhinskoye. Almaty, SE Kazakhstan
189 *U12* **Tol** *atoll* Chuuk Islands, C Micronesia
184 *Q9* **Tolaga Bay** Gisborne, North Island, New Zealand
172 *I7* **Tôlañaro** *prev.* Faradofay, Fort-Dauphin. Toliara, SE Madagascar
162 *D6* **Tolbo** Bayan-Ölgiy, W Mongolia
Tolbukhin *see* Dobrich
60 *G11* **Toledo** Paraná, S Brazil
54 *G8* **Toledo** Norte de Santander, N Colombia
105 *N9* **Toledo** *anc.* Toletum. Castilla-La Mancha, C Spain
30 *M14* **Toledo** Illinois, N USA
29 *W13* **Toledo** Iowa, C USA
31 *R11* **Toledo** Ohio, N USA
32 *F12* **Toledo** Oregon, NW USA
32 *G9* **Toledo** Washington, NW USA
42 *F3* **Toledo** ◆ *district* S Belize
104 *M9* **Toledo, Montes de** ▲ Castilla-La Mancha, C Spain
25 *Y7* **Toledo Bend Reservoir** ◙ Louisiana/Texas, SW USA
104 *M10* **Toledo, Montes de** ▲ C Spain
106 *J12* **Tolentino** Marche, C Italy
Toletum *see* Toledo
94 *H10* **Tolga** Hedmark, S Norway
158 *J3* **Toli** Xinjiang Uygur Zizhiqu, NW China
172 *H7* **Toliara** *var.* Toliary; *prev.* Tuléar. Toliara, SW Madagascar
172 *H7* **Toliara** ◆ *province* SW Madagascar
Toliary *see* Toliara
54 *D11* **Tolima** *off.* Departamento del Tolima. ◆ *province* C Colombia
Tolima, Departamento del *see* Tolima
171 *N11* **Tolitoli** Sulawesi, C Indonesia
95 *K22* **Tollarp** Skåne, S Sweden
100 *N9* **Tollense** ∿ NE Germany
100 *N10* **Tollensesee** ◎ NE Germany
36 *K13* **Tolleson** Arizona, SW USA
146 *M13* **Tollimarjon** *Rus.* Talimardzhan. Qashqadaryo Viloyati, S Uzbekistan
41 *U17* **Tolmezzo** Chiapas, SE Mexico
106 *J6* **Tolmezzo** Friuli-Venezia Giulia, NE Italy
109 *S11* **Tolmin** *Ger.* Tolmein, *It.* Tolmino. W Slovenia
Tolmino *see* Tolmin
111 *J25* **Tolna** *Ger.* Tolnau. Tolna, S Hungary
111 *I24* **Tolna** *off.* Tolna Megye. ◆ *county* SW Hungary
Tolna Megye *see* Tolna
Tolnau *see* Tolna
79 *I20* **Tolo** Bandundu, W Dem. Rep. Congo
190 *D12* **Toloke** Île Futuna, W Wallis and Futuna
30 *M13* **Tolono** Illinois, N USA
105 *Q3* **Tolosa** País Vasco, N Spain
Tolosa *see* Toulouse
171 *O13* **Tolo, Teluk** *bay* Sulawesi, C Indonesia
39 *R9* **Tolovana River** ∿ Alaska, USA
Tolsen *see* Tolmin
123 *U10* **Tolstoy, Mys** *cape* E Russian Federation
63 *G15* **Toltén** Araucanía, C Chile
63 *G15* **Toltén, Río** ∿ S Chile
54 *E6* **Tolú** Sucre, NW Colombia
41 *O14* **Toluca** *var.* Toluca de Lerdo. México, S Mexico
Toluca de Lerdo *see* Toluca
41 *O14* **Toluca, Nevado de** ▲ C Mexico
27 *Q4* **Tonganoxie** Kansas, C USA
39 *Y13* **Tongass National Forest** *reserve* Alaska, USA
193 *Y16* **Tongatapu** ✈ Tongatapu, S Tonga
193 *Y16* **Tongatapu** *island* Tongatapu Group, S Tonga
193 *Y16* **Tongatapu Group** *island group* S Tonga
175 *S9* **Tonga Trench** *undersea feature* S Pacific Ocean
161 *N8* **Tongbai Shan** ▲ C China
161 *P8* **Tongcheng** Anhui, E China
160 *L6* **Tongchuan** Shaanxi, C China
160 *L12* **Tongdao** *var.* Tongdao Dongzu Zizhixian; *prev.* Shuangjiang. Hunan, S China
Tongdao Dongzu Zizhixian *see* Tongdao
159 *T11* **Tongde** *var.* Gabasumdo. Qinghai, C China
99 *K19* **Tongeren** *Fr.* Tongres. Limburg, NE Belgium
163 *Y14* **Tonghae** NE South Korea
160 *G13* **Tonghai** *var.* Xiushan. Yunnan, SW China
163 *X8* **Tonghe** Heilongjiang, NE China
163 *W11* **Tonghua** Jilin, NE China
163 *Z6* **Tongjiang** Heilongjiang, NE China
163 *Y13* **Tongjosŏn-man** *prev.* Broughton Bay. *bay* E North Korea
163 *V7* **Tongken He** ∿ NE China
167 *T7* **Tongking, Gulf of** *Chin.* Beibu Wan, *Vtn.* Vịnh Bắc Bộ. *gulf* China/Vietnam
163 *U10* **Tongliao** Nei Mongol Zizhiqu, N China
161 *Q9* **Tongling** Anhui, E China
161 *R9* **Tonglu** Zhejiang, SE China
187 *R14* **Tongoa** *island* Shepherd Islands, S Vanuatu
63 *G14* **Tongoy** Coquimbo, C Chile
160 *L11* **Tongren** Guizhou, S China
159 *T11* **Tongren** *var.* Rongwo. Qinghai, C China
Tongres *see* Tongeren
37 *N9* **Tongsa** *var.* Tongsa Dzong. C Bhutan
Tongsa Dzong *see* Tongsa
Tongshan *see* Xuzhou, Jiangsu, China
Tongshan Fuding, Fujian, China

83 *J19* **Tom Burke** Limpopo, NE South Africa
146 *L9* **Tomdibuloq** *Rus.* Tamdybulak. Navoiy Viloyati, N Uzbekistan
146 *L9* **Tomditov-Tog'lari** ▲ N Uzbekistan
62 *G13* **Tomé** Bío Bío, C Chile
58 *L12* **Tomé-Açu** Pará, NE Brazil
95 *L23* **Tomelilla** Skåne, S Sweden
105 *O10* **Tomelloso** Castilla-La Mancha, C Spain
14 *H10* **Tomiko Lake** ◎ Ontario, S Canada
77 *N12* **Tominian** Ségou, C Mali
171 *N12* **Tomini, Gulf of** *var.* Teluk Tomini; *prev.* Teluk Gorontalo. *bay* Sulawesi, C Indonesia
Tomini, Teluk *see* Tomini, Gulf of
165 *Q11* **Tomioka** Fukushima, Honshū, S Japan
113 *G14* **Tomislavgrad** ◆ Federacija Bosna I Hercegovina, SW Bosnia and Herzegovina
181 *O9* **Tomkinson Ranges** ▲ South Australia/Western Australia
123 *Q11* **Tommot** Respublika Sakha (Yakutiya), NE Russian Federation
171 *Q11* **Tomohon** Sulawesi, N Indonesia
54 *K9* **Tomo, Río** ∿ E Colombia
113 *L21* **Tomorrit, Mali i** ▲ S Albania
9 *S17* **Tompkins** Saskatchewan, S Canada
20 *K8* **Tompkinsville** Kentucky, S USA
171 *N11* **Tompo** Sulawesi, N Indonesia
180 *I8* **Tom Price** Western Australia
122 *J12* **Tomsk** Tomskaya Oblast', C Russian Federation
122 *I11* **Tomskaya Oblast'** ◆ *province* C Russian Federation
18 *K16* **Toms River** New Jersey, NE USA
Tom Steed Lake *see* Tom Steed Reservoir
26 *L12* **Tom Steed Reservoir** *var.* Tom Steed Lake. ◙ Oklahoma, C USA
171 *U13* **Tomu** Papua, E Indonesia
158 *H6* **Tomur Feng** *var.* Pobeda Peak, *Rus.* Pik Pobedy. ▲ China/Kyrgyzstan *see also* Pobedy, Pik
Tomür Feng *see* Pobedy, Pik
189 *N13* **Tomworoahlang** Pohnpei, E Micronesia
41 *U17* **Tonalá** Chiapas, SE Mexico
106 *F6* **Tonale, Passo del** *pass* N Italy
164 *I11* **Tonami** Toyama, Honshū, SW Japan
58 *C12* **Tonantins** Amazonas, W Brazil
32 *K6* **Tonasket** Washington, NW USA
55 *Y9* **Tonate** *var.* Macouria. N French Guiana
18 *D10* **Tonawanda** New York, NE USA
171 *Q11* **Tondano** Sulawesi, C Indonesia
104 *H7* **Tondela** Viseu, N Portugal
95 *F24* **Tønder** *Ger.* Tondern. Sønderjylland, SW Denmark
Tondern *see* Tønder
143 *N4* **Tonekābon** *var.* Shahsawar, Tonkābon; *prev.* Shahsavār. Māzandarān, N Iran
Tonezh *see* Tonyezh
193 *Y14* **Tonga** *off.* Kingdom of Tonga, *var.* Friendly Islands. ◆ *monarchy* SW Pacific Ocean
193 *Y14* **Tonga** *island group* SW Pacific Ocean
83 *K23* **Tongaat** KwaZulu/Natal, E South Africa
Tonga, Kingdom of *see* Tonga
161 *Q13* **Tong'an** *var.* Datong, Tong an. Fujian, SE China
39 *Q11* **Tonga** *see* Tong'an
39 *Q11* **Torbert, Mount** ▲ Alaska, USA
31 *P6* **Torch Lake** ◎ Michigan, N USA
Törcsvár *see* Bran
Torda *see* Turda
104 *L6* **Tordesillas** Castilla-León, N Spain
92 *K13* **Töre** Norrbotten, N Sweden
95 *L17* **Töreboda** Västra Götaland, S Sweden
95 *J21* **Torekov** Skåne, S Sweden
92 *O3* **Torell Land** *physical region* SW Svalbard
101 *N14* **Torgau** Sachsen, E Germany
Torgay *see* Turgay
Torgay Üstirti *see* Turgayskaya Stolovaya Strana
99 *N22* **Torhamn** Blekinge, S Sweden
99 *C17* **Torhout** West-Vlaanderen, W Belgium
106 *B8* **Torino** *Eng.* Turin. Piemonte, NW Italy
165 *U15* **Tori-shima** *island* Izu-shotō, SE Japan
81 *F16* **Torit** Eastern Equatoria, S Sudan
186 *H6* **Toriu** New Britain, E Papua New Guinea
148 *M4* **Torkestān, Selseleh-ye Band-e** *var.* Bandi-i Turkistan. ▲ NW Afghanistan
104 *L7* **Tormes** ∿ W Spain
Tornacum *see* Tournai
Torneå *see* Tornio
92 *K12* **Torneälven** *var.* Tornionjoki, *Fin.* Tornionjoki. ∿ Finland/Sweden
92 *I11* **Torneträsk** ◎ N Sweden
13 *O4* **Torngat Mountains** ▲▲ Newfoundland and Labrador, NE Canada
92 *K13* **Tornio** *Swe.* Torneå. Lappi, NW Finland
92 *K13* **Tornio** ∿ Finland/Sweden
Torniojoki/Tornionjoki *see* Torneälven
61 *B23* **Tornquist** Buenos Aires, E Argentina
104 *L6* **Toro** Castilla-León, N Spain
63 *G16* **Toro, Cerro del** ▲ N Chile
77 *R12* **Torodi** Tillabéri, SW Niger

Tongshan *see* Xuzhou, Jiangsu, China
Tongshi *see* Wuzhishan
159 *P12* **Tongtian He** ∿ C China
96 *I6* **Tongue** N Scotland, UK
44 *M17* **Tongue of the Ocean** *strait* C Bahamas
33 *X10* **Tongue River** ∿ Montana, NW USA
33 *W11* **Tongue River Resevoir** ◙ Montana, NW USA
159 *V11* **Tongwei** Gansu, C China
159 *W9* **Tongxin** Ningxia, N China
163 *U9* **Tongyu** *var.* Kaitong. Jilin, NE China
160 *J11* **Tongzi** Guizhou, S China
162 *F8* **Tonhil** *var.* Dzüyl. Govĭ-Altay, SW Mongolia
40 *G5* **Tónichi** Sonora, NW Mexico
81 *D14* **Tonj** Warab, SW Sudan
152 *H13* **Tonk** Rājasthān, N India
27 *N8* **Tonkawa** Oklahoma, C USA
167 *Q12* **Tônlé Sap** *Eng.* Great Lake. ◎ W Cambodia
102 *L14* **Tonneins** Lot-et-Garonne, SW France
103 *Q7* **Tonnerre** Yonne, C France
Tonoas *see* Dublon
35 *U8* **Tonopah** Nevada, W USA
164 *H13* **Tonoshō** Okayama, Shōdo-shima, SW Japan
43 *S17* **Tonosí** Los Santos, S Panama
95 *H16* **Tønsberg** Vestfold, S Norway
39 *T11* **Tonsina** Alaska, USA
95 *D17* **Tonstad** Vest-Agder, S Norway
193 *X15* **Tonumea** *island* Nomuka Group, W Tonga
137 *N11* **Tonya** Trabzon, NE Turkey
119 *K20* **Tonyezh** *Rus.* Tonezh. Homyel'skaya Voblasts', SE Belarus
36 *L3* **Tooele** Utah, W USA
122 *L13* **Toora-Khem** Respublika Tyva, S Russian Federation
183 *O5* **Toorale East** New South Wales, SE Australia
83 *H25* **Toorberg** ▲ S South Africa
118 *G5* **Tootsi** Pärnumaa, SW Estonia
183 *U3* **Toowoomba** Queensland, E Australia
27 *Q4* **Topeka** *state capital* Kansas, C USA
111 *M18* **Topľa** *Hung.* Toplya. ∿ NE Slovakia
122 *J12* **Topki** Kemerovskaya Oblast', S Russian Federation
116 *J10* **Topliţa** *Ger.* Töplitz, *Hung.* Maroshévíz; *prev.* Topliţa Română, *Hung.* Oláh-Toplicza, *Hung.* Toplicza. Harghita, C Romania
Topliţa Română/Töplitz *see* Topliţa
Toplya *see* Topľa
111 *I20* **Topoľčany** *Hung.* Nagytapolcsány. Nitriansky Kraj, W Slovakia
40 *G8* **Topolobampo** Sinaloa, C Mexico
116 *I13* **Topoloveni** Argeş, S Romania
114 *L11* **Topolovgrad** *prev.* Kavakli. Khaskovo, S Bulgaria
Topolya *see* Bačka Topola
124 *I6* **Topozero, Ozero** ◎ NW Russian Federation
32 *J10* **Toppenish** Washington, NW USA
181 *P4* **Top Springs Roadhouse** Northern Territory, N Australia
189 *U11* **Tora** Chuuk, C Micronesia
Toraigh *see* Tory Island
189 *U11* **Tora Island Pass** *passage* Chuuk Islands, C Micronesia
143 *U5* **Torbat-e Ḥeydarīyeh** *var.* Turbat-i-Haidari. Khorāsān-Razavī, NE Iran
143 *V5* **Torbat-e Jām** *var.* Turbat-i-Jam. Khorāsān-Razavī, NE Iran
18 *L12* **Torrington** Connecticut, NE USA
33 *Z15* **Torrington** Wyoming, C USA
Torröjen *see* Torröjen
45 *V16* **Torröjen** *prev.* Torröjen. ◎ C Sweden
105 *O13* **Torrox** Andalucía, S Spain
94 *N13* **Torsåker** Gävleborg, C Sweden
95 *N21* **Torsås** Kalmar, S Sweden
95 *J14* **Torsby** Värmland, C Sweden
95 *N16* **Torshälla** Södermanland, C Sweden
95 *B19* **Tórshavn** *Dan.* Thorshavn. ● (Faeroe Islands) Streymoy, N Faeroe Islands
Torshiz *see* Kāshmar
146 *I9* **To'rtkok'l** *var.* Türtkül; *prev.* Petroaleksandrovsk, *Rus.* Turtkul'; *prev.* Petroaleksandrovsk. Qoraqalpog'iston Respublikasi, W Uzbekistan
Tortoise Islands *see* Colón, Archipiélago de
45 *T9* **Tortola** *island* C British Virgin Islands
106 *D9* **Tortona** *anc.* Dertona. Piemonte, NW Italy
107 *L23* **Tortorici** Sicilia, Italy, C Mediterranean Sea
105 *U7* **Tortosa** *anc.* Dertosa. Cataluña, E Spain
Tortosa *see* Ţarţūs
105 *U7* **Tortosa, Cap** *cape* E Spain
44 *L8* **Tortue, Île de la** *var.* La Tortuga Island. *island* N Haiti
55 *Y10* **Tortue, Montagne** ▲ C French Guiana
Tortuga, Isla *see* La Tortuga, Isla
Tortuga Island *see* Tortue, Île de la
54 *C11* **Tortugas, Golfo** *gulf* W Colombia
45 *T5* **Tortuguero, Laguna** *lagoon* N Puerto Rico
137 *Q12* **Tortum** Erzurum, NE Turkey
Torugart, Pereval *see* Turugart Shankou
136 *J13* **Torul** Gümüşhane, NE Turkey
110 *J10* **Toruń** *Ger.* Thorn. Toruń, Kujawsko-pomorskie, C Poland
95 *K20* **Torup** Halland, S Sweden
118 *A5* **Tõrva** *Ger.* Tõrwa. Valgamaa, S Estonia
Tõrwa *see* Tõrva
96 *D13* **Tory Island** *Ir.* Toraigh. *island* NW Ireland

Törökbecse *see* Novi Bečej
186 *J7* **Torokina** Bougainville Island, NE Papua New Guinea
111 *L23* **Törökszentmiklós** Jász-Nagykun-Szolnok, E Hungary
42 *G7* **Torola, Río** ∿ El Salvador/Honduras
Toronaíos, Kólpos *see* Kassándras, Kólpos
14 *H15* **Toronto** *province capital* Ontario, S Canada
31 *V12* **Toronto** Ohio, N USA
Toronto *see* Lester B. Pearson
27 *P6* **Toronto Lake** ◙ Kansas, C USA
35 *V16* **Toro Peak** ▲ California, W USA
124 *H16* **Toropets** Tverskaya Oblast', W Russian Federation
81 *G18* **Tororo** E Uganda
136 *H16* **Toros Dağları** *Eng.* Taurus Mountains. ▲ S Turkey
183 *N13* **Torquay** Victoria, SE Australia
97 *J24* **Torquay** SW England, UK
104 *M5* **Torquemada** Castilla-León, N Spain
35 *S5* **Torrance** California, W USA
104 *G12* **Torrão** Setúbal, S Portugal
104 *H8* **Torre, Alto da** ▲ C Portugal
107 *K18* **Torre Annunziata** Campania, S Italy
105 *T8* **Torreblanca** País Valenciano, E Spain
104 *L15* **Torrecilla** ▲ S Spain
105 *P4* **Torrecilla en Cameros** La Rioja, N Spain
105 *N13* **Torredelcampo** Andalucía, S Spain
107 *K17* **Torre del Greco** Campania, S Italy
104 *J6* **Torre de Moncorvo** *var.* Moncorvo, Tôrre de Moncorvo. Bragança, N Portugal
104 *J9* **Torrejoncillo** Extremadura, W Spain
105 *O8* **Torrejón de Ardoz** Madrid, C Spain
105 *N7* **Torrelaguna** Madrid, C Spain
105 *N2* **Torrelavega** Cantabria, N Spain
107 *M16* **Torremaggiore** Puglia, SE Italy
104 *M15* **Torremolinos** Andalucía, S Spain
182 *I6* **Torrens, Lake** *salt lake* South Australia
105 *S10* **Torrent** *Cas.* Torrente, *var.* Torrent de l'Horta. País Valenciano, E Spain
Torrent de l'Horta/Torrente *see* Torrent
40 *L8* **Torreón** Coahuila de Zaragoza, NE Mexico
105 *R13* **Torre Pacheco** Murcia, SE Spain
106 *A8* **Torre Pellice** Piemonte, NE Italy
105 *O13* **Torreperogil** Andalucía, S Spain
61 *J15* **Torres** Rio Grande do Sul, S Brazil
187 *Q11* **Torrès, Îles** *see* Torres Islands
104 *G9* **Torres Novas** Santarém, C Portugal
181 *V1* **Torres Strait** *strait* Australia/Papua New Guinea
104 *F10* **Torres Vedras** Lisboa, C Portugal
105 *S13* **Torrevieja** País Valenciano, E Spain
186 *B6* **Torricelli Mountains** ▲ NW Papua New Guinea
96 *G8* **Torridon, Loch** *inlet* NW Scotland, UK
106 *D9* **Torriglia** Liguria, NW Italy
104 *M9* **Torrijos** Castilla-La Mancha, C Spain
18 *L12* **Torrington** Connecticut, NE USA

TORYSA – TSAGAANNUUR

111 *N19* **Torysa** *Hung.* Tarca. ~ NE Slovakia
Torzburg *see* Bran
124 *J16* **Torzhok** Tverskaya Oblast', W Russian Federation
164 *F15* **Tosa-Shimizu** *var.* Tosasimizu. Kôchi, Shikoku, SW Japan
Tosasimizu *see* Tosa-Shimizu
164 *G15* **Tosa-wan** *bay* SW Japan
83 *H21* **Tosca** North-West, N South Africa
106 *F12* **Toscana** *Eng.* Tuscany. ◈ *region* C Italy
107 *E14* **Toscano, Arcipelago** *Eng.* Tuscan Archipelago. *island group* C Italy
106 *G10* **Tosco-Emiliano, Appennino** *Eng.* Tuscan-Emilian Mountains. ▲ C Italy
Tōsei *see* Tungshih
165 *N15* **To-shima** *island* Izu-shotō, SE Japan
147 *Q9* **Toshkent** *Eng./Rus.* Tashkent. ● Toshkent Viloyati, E Uzbekistan
147 *Q9* **Toshkent** ✈ Toshkent Viloyati, E Uzbekistan
147 *P9* **Toshkent Viloyati** *Rus.* Tashkentskaya Oblast'. ◈ *province* E Uzbekistan
124 *H13* **Tosno** Leningradskaya Oblast', NW Russian Federation
159 *Q10* **Toson Hu** ◎ C China
162 *H6* **Tosontsengel** Dzavhan, NW Mongolia
162 *J6* **Tosontsengel** *var.* Tsengel. Hövsgöl, N Mongolia
146 *I8* **Tosquduq Qumlari** *var.* Goshquduq Qum, Taskuduk, Peski. *desert* W Uzbekistan
105 *U4* **Tossal de l'Orri** *var.* Llorri. ▲ NE Spain
61 *A15* **Tostado** Santa Fe, C Argentina
118 *F6* **Tõstamaa** *Ger.* Testama. Pärnumaa, SW Estonia
100 *I10* **Tostedt** Niedersachsen, NW Germany
136 *J11* **Tosya** Kastamonu, N Turkey
95 *F15* **Totak** ◎ S Norway
105 *R13* **Totana** Murcia, SE Spain
94 *H13* **Toten** *physical region* S Norway
83 *G18* **Toteng** North-West, C Botswana
102 *M3* **Tôtes** Seine-Maritime, N France
Totigi *see* Tochigi
Totio *see* Tochio
Totis *see* Tata
189 *U13* **Totiw** *island* Chuuk, C Micronesia
125 *N13* **Tot'ma** *var.* Totma. Vologodskaya Oblast', NW Russian Federation
Tot'ma *see* Sukhona
55 *V9* **Totness** Coronie, N Surinam
42 *C5* **Totonicapán** Totonicapán, W Guatemala
42 *A2* **Totonicapán** *off.* Departamento de Totonicapán. ◈ *department* W Guatemala
Totonicapán, Departamento de *see* Totonicapán
61 *B18* **Totoras** Santa Fe, C Argentina
187 *Y15* **Totoya** *island* S Fiji
183 *Q7* **Tottenham** New South Wales, SE Australia
164 *I12* **Tottori** Tottori, Honshū, SW Japan
164 *H12* **Tottori** *off.* Tottori-ken. ◈ *prefecture* Honshū, SW Japan
Tottori-ken *see* Tottori
76 *I6* **Touâjil** Tiris Zemmour, N Mauritania
76 *L15* **Touba** W Ivory Coast
76 *G11* **Touba** W Senegal
74 *E7* **Toubkal, Jbel** ▲ W Morocco
32 *K10* **Touchet** Washington, NW USA
103 *P7* **Toucy** Yonne, C France
77 *O12* **Tougan** W Burkina
74 *L7* **Touggourt** NE Algeria
77 *Q12* **Tougouri** N Burkina
76 *J13* **Tougué** NW Guinea
76 *K12* **Toukoto** Kayes, W Mali
103 *S5* **Toul** Meurthe-et-Moselle, NE France
76 *L16* **Toulépleu** *var.* Toulobli. W Ivory Coast
161 *S14* **Touliu** C Taiwan
15 *U3* **Toulnustouc** ~ Québec, SE Canada
Toulobli *see* Toulépleu
103 *T16* **Toulon** *anc.* Telo Martius, Tilio Martius. Var, SE France
30 *K12* **Toulon** Illinois, N USA
102 *M15* **Toulouse** *anc.* Tolosa. Haute-Garonne, S France
102 *M15* **Toulouse** ✈ Haute-Garonne, S France
77 *N16* **Toumodi** C Ivory Coast
74 *G9* **Tounassine, Hamada** *hill range* W Algeria
166 *M7* **Toungoo** Pegu, C Burma (Myanmar)
102 *L8* **Touraine** *cultural region* C France
Tourane *see* Đà Nẵng
103 *P1* **Tourcoing** Nord, N France
104 *F2* **Touriñán, Cabo** *cape* NW Spain
76 *J6* **Tourine** Tiris Zemmour, N Mauritania
102 *J3* **Tourlaville** Manche, N France
99 *D19* **Tournai** *var.* Tournay, *Dut.* Doornik; *anc.* Tornacum. Hainaut, SW Belgium
102 *L16* **Tournay** Hautes-Pyrénées, S France
Tournay *see* Tournai
103 *R12* **Tournon** Ardèche, E France
103 *R9* **Tournus** Saône-et-Loire, C France
59 *Q14* **Touros** Rio Grande do Norte, E Brazil
102 *L8* **Tours** *anc.* Caesarodunum, Turoni. Indre-et-Loire, C France
183 *Q17* **Tourville, Cape** *headland* Tasmania, SE Australia
162 *L8* **Töv** ◈ *province* C Mongolia
54 *H7* **Tovar** Mérida, NW Venezuela
126 *L5* **Tovarkovskiy** Tul'skaya Oblast', W Russian Federation
Tovil'-Dora *see* Tavildara
Tövis *see* Teiuş
137 *V11* **Tovuz** *Rus.* Tauz. W Azerbaijan
165 *R7* **Towada** Aomori, Honshū, C Japan
184 *K3* **Towai** Northland, North Island, New Zealand
18 *H12* **Towanda** Pennsylvania, NE USA
29 *W4* **Tower** Minnesota, N USA
171 *N12* **Towera** Sulawesi, N Indonesia
Tower Island *see* Genovesa, Isla
180 *M13* **Tower Peak** ▲ Western Australia
35 *U11* **Towne Pass** *pass* California, W USA
29 *N3* **Towner** North Dakota, N USA
33 *R10* **Townsend** Montana, NW USA
181 *X6* **Townsville** Queensland, NE Australia
Towoeti Meer *see* Towuti, Danau
148 *K4* **Towraghoudī** Herāt, NW Afghanistan
21 *X3* **Towson** Maryland, NE USA
171 *O13* **Towuti, Danau** *Dut.* Towoeti Meer. ◎ Sulawesi, C Indonesia
Toxkan He *see* Ak-say
24 *K9* **Toyah** Texas, SW USA
165 *R4* **Tōya-ko** ◎ Hokkaidō, NE Japan
164 *L11* **Toyama** Toyama, Honshū, SW Japan
164 *L11* **Toyama** *off.* Toyama-ken. ◈ *prefecture* Honshū, SW Japan
Toyama-ken *see* Toyama
164 *L11* **Toyama-wan** *bay* W Japan
164 *H15* **Tōyo** Kōchi, Shikoku, SW Japan
Toyohara *see* Yuzhno-Sakhalinsk
164 *L14* **Toyohashi** *var.* Toyohasi. Aichi, Honshū, SW Japan
Toyohasi *see* Toyohashi
164 *L14* **Toyokawa** Aichi, Honshū, SW Japan
164 *I14* **Toyooka** Hyōgo, Honshū, SW Japan
164 *L13* **Toyota** Aichi, Honshū, SW Japan
165 *T1* **Toyotomi** Hokkaidō, NE Japan
147 *Q10* **To'ytepa** Toshkent Viloyati, E Uzbekistan
147 *Q10* **To'ytepa** *Rus.* Toytepa. Toshkent Viloyati, E Uzbekistan
Toytepa *see* To'ytepa
74 *M6* **Tozeur** *var.* Tawzar. W Tunisia
39 *Q8* **Tozi, Mount** ▲ Alaska, USA
137 *Q9* **Tqvarch'eli** *Rus.* Tkvarcheli. NW Georgia
Trâblous *see* Tripoli
137 *O11* **Trabzon** *Eng.* Trebizond; *anc.* Trapezus. Trabzon, NE Turkey
137 *O11* **Trabzon** *Eng.* Trebizond. ◈ *province* NE Turkey
13 *P13* **Tracadie** New Brunswick, SE Canada
Trachenberg *see* Żmigród
15 *O11* **Tracy** Québec, SE Canada
35 *O8* **Tracy** California, W USA
29 *S10* **Tracy** Minnesota, N USA
20 *K10* **Tracy City** Tennessee, S USA
106 *D7* **Tradate** Lombardia, N Italy
84 *F6* **Traena Bank** *undersea feature* E Norwegian Sea
29 *W13* **Traer** Iowa, C USA
104 *J16* **Trafalgar, Cabo de** *cape* SW Spain
Traiectum ad Mosam/Traiectum Tungorum *see* Maastricht
Tráigh Mhór *see* Tramore
9 *O17* **Trail** British Columbia, SW Canada
58 *B11* **Traíra, Serra do** ▲ NW Brazil
109 *V5* **Traisen** Niederösterreich, NE Austria
109 *W4* **Traisen** ~ NE Austria
109 *X4* **Traiskirchen** Niederösterreich, NE Austria
Trajani Portus *see* Civitavecchia
Trajectum ad Rhenum *see* Utrecht
119 *H14* **Trakai** *Ger.* Traken, *Pol.* Troki. Vilnius, SE Lithuania
Traken *see* Trakai
97 *B20* **Tralee** *Ir.* Trá Lí. SW Ireland
97 *A20* **Tralee Bay** *Ir.* Bá Thrá Lí. *bay* SW Ireland
Trá Lí *see* Tralee
Trälleborg *see* Trelleborg
Tralles Aydin *see* Aydın
61 *J16* **Tramandaí** Rio Grande do Sul, S Brazil
108 *C7* **Tramelan** Bern, W Switzerland
Trá Mhór *see* Tramore
97 *E20* **Tramore** *Ir.* Tráigh Mhór, Trá Mhór. Waterford, S Ireland
95 *L18* **Tranås** Jönköping, S Sweden
62 *J7* **Trancas** Tucumán, N Argentina
104 *I7* **Trancoso** Guarda, N Portugal
95 *H22* **Tranebjerg** Århus, C Denmark
95 *K19* **Tranemo** Västra Götaland, S Sweden
167 *N16* **Trang** Trang, S Thailand
171 *V15* **Trangan, Pulau** *island* Kepulauan Aru, E Indonesia
Trâng Dinh *see* Thât Khê
183 *Q7* **Trangie** New South Wales, SE Australia
94 *K12* **Trängslet** Dalarna, C Sweden
107 *N16* **Trani** Puglia, SE Italy
61 *F17* **Tranqueras** Rivera, NE Uruguay
63 *G17* **Tranqui, Isla** *island* S Chile
39 *V6* **Trans-Alaska pipeline** *oil pipeline* Alaska, USA
195 *Q10* **Transantarctic Mountains** ▲ Antarctica
Transcarpathian Oblast *see* Zakarpats'ka Oblast'
Transilvania *see* Transylvania
Transilvaniei, Alpi *see* Carpaţii Meridionali
Transjordan *see* Jordan
172 *L11* **Transkei Basin** *undersea feature* SW Indian Ocean
117 *O10* **Transnistria** *cultural region* E Moldavia
122 *E9* **Trans-Siberian Railway** *railway* Russian Federation
Transsylvanische Alpen/Transylvanian Alps *see* Carpaţii Meridionali
94 *K12* **Transtrand** Dalarna, C Sweden
116 *G10* **Transylvania** *Eng.* Ardeal, Transilvania, *Ger.* Siebenbürgen, *Hung.* Erdély. *cultural region* NW Romania
167 *S14* **Tra Ôn** Vinh Long, S Vietnam
107 *H23* **Trapani** *anc.* Drepanum. Sicilia, Italy, C Mediterranean Sea
167 *S12* **Trâpeăng Vêng** Kâmpóng Thum, C Cambodia
Trapezus *see* Trabzon
114 *L9* **Trapoklovo** Sliven, C Bulgaria
183 *P13* **Traralgon** Victoria, SE Australia
76 *H9* **Trarza** ◈ *region* SW Mauritania
Trasimenischersee *see* Trasimeno, Lago
106 *H12* **Trasimeno, Lago** *Eng.* Lake of Perugia, *Ger.* Trasimenischersee. ◎ C Italy
95 *J20* **Träslövsläge** Halland, S Sweden
Trás-os-Montes *see* Cucumbi
104 *I6* **Trás-os-Montes e Alto Douro** *former province* N Portugal
167 *Q12* **Trat** *var.* Bang Phra. Trat, S Thailand
Trá Tholl, Inis *see* Inishtrahull
Traù *see* Trogir
109 *T4* **Traun** Oberösterreich, N Austria
109 *S5* **Traun** ~ N Austria
Traun, Lake *see* Traunsee
101 *N23* **Traunreut** Bayern, SE Germany
109 *S5* **Traunsee** *var.* Gmundner See, *Eng.* Lake Traun. ◎ N Austria
Trautenau *see* Trutnov
21 *P11* **Travelers Rest** South Carolina, SE USA
182 *L8* **Travellers Lake** *seasonal lake* New South Wales, SE Australia
31 *P6* **Traverse City** Michigan, N USA
29 *R7* **Traverse, Lake** ◎ Minnesota/South Dakota, N USA
185 *I16* **Travers, Mount** ▲ South Island, New Zealand
9 *P17* **Travers Reservoir** ⊠ Alberta, SW Canada
167 *T14* **Tra Vinh** *var.* Phu Vinh. Tra Vinh, S Vietnam
25 *S10* **Travis, Lake** ⊠ Texas, SW USA
112 *H12* **Travnik** ◈ Federacija Bosna I Hercegovina, C Bosnia and Herzegovina
109 *V11* **Trbovlje** *Ger.* Trifail. C Slovenia
23 *V13* **Treasure Island** Florida, SE USA
Treasure State *see* Montana
186 *I8* **Treasury Islands** *island group* NW Solomon Islands
106 *D9* **Trebbia** *anc.* Trebia. ~ NW Italy
100 *N8* **Trebel** ~ NE Germany
103 *O16* **Trèbes** Aude, S France
Trebia *see* Trebbia
111 *F18* **Třebíč** *Ger.* Trebitsch. Vysočina, C Czech Republic
113 *I16* **Trebinje** ◈ Republika Srpska, S Bosnia and Herzegovina
Trebišnica *see* Trebišnjica
113 *H16* **Trebišnjica** *var.* Trebišnica. ~ S Bosnia and Herzegovina
111 *N20* **Trebišov** *Hung.* Tőketerebes. Košický Kraj, E Slovakia
Trebitsch *see* Třebíč
Trebizond *see* Trabzon
Trebnitz *see* Trzebnica
109 *V12* **Trebnje** SE Slovenia
111 *D19* **Třeboň** *Ger.* Wittingau. Jihočeský Kraj, S Czech Republic
104 *J15* **Trebujena** Andalucía, S Spain
100 *I7* **Treene** ~ N Germany
Tree Planters State *see* Nebraska
109 *S9* **Treffen** Kärnten, S Austria
Trefynwy *see* Monmouth
102 *G5* **Tréguier** Côtes d'Armor, NW France
61 *G18* **Treinta y Tres** Treinta y Tres, E Uruguay
61 *F18* **Treinta y Tres** ◈ *department* E Uruguay
122 *F11* **Trëkhgornyy** Chelyabinskaya Oblast', C Russian Federation
114 *F9* **Treklyanska Reka** ~ W Bulgaria
102 *K8* **Trélazé** Maine-et-Loire, NW France
63 *K17* **Trelew** Chubut, SE Argentina
95 *K23* **Trelleborg** *var.* Trälleborg. Skåne, S Sweden
113 *P15* **Trem** ▲ SE Serbia
15 *N11* **Tremblant, Mont** ▲ Québec, SE Canada
99 *H17* **Tremelo** Vlaams Brabant, C Belgium
107 *M15* **Tremiti, Isole** *island group* SE Italy
30 *K12* **Tremont** Illinois, N USA
36 *L1* **Tremonton** Utah, W USA
105 *U4* **Tremp** Cataluña, NE Spain
30 *J7* **Trempealeau** Wisconsin, N USA
15 *P8* **Trenche** ~ Québec, SE Canada
15 *O7* **Trenche, Lac** ◎ Québec, SE Canada
111 *I20* **Trenčiansky Kraj** ◈ *region* W Slovakia
111 *I19* **Trenčín** *Ger.* Trentschin, *Hung.* Trencsén. Trenčiansky Kraj, W Slovakia
Trencsén *see* Trenčín
Trengganu *see* Terengganu
Trengganu, Kuala *see* Kuala Terengganu
61 *A21* **Trenque Lauquen** Buenos Aires, E Argentina
14 *J14* **Trent** ~ Ontario, SE Canada
97 *N18* **Trent** ~ C England, UK
Trent *see* Trento
106 *F5* **Trentino-Alto Adige** *prev.* Venezia Tridentina. ◈ *region* N Italy
106 *G6* **Trento** *Eng.* Trent, *Ger.* Trient; *anc.* Tridentum. Trentino-Alto Adige, N Italy
14 *J15* **Trenton** Ontario, SE Canada
23 *V10* **Trenton** Florida, SE USA
23 *R1* **Trenton** Georgia, SE USA
31 *S10* **Trenton** Michigan, N USA
27 *S2* **Trenton** Missouri, C USA
28 *M17* **Trenton** Nebraska, C USA
18 *J15* **Trenton** *state capital* New Jersey, NE USA
21 *W10* **Trenton** North Carolina, SE USA
20 *G9* **Trenton** Tennessee, S USA
36 *L1* **Trenton** Utah, W USA
Trentschin *see* Trenčín
Treptow an der Rega *see* Trzebiatów
61 *C23* **Tres Arroyos** Buenos Aires, E Argentina
61 *J15* **Três Cachoeiras** Rio Grande do Sul, S Brazil
106 *E7* **Trescore Balneario** Lombardia, N Italy
41 *V17* **Tres Cruces, Cerro** ▲ SE Mexico
57 *K18* **Tres Cruces, Cordillera** ▲ W Bolivia
113 *N18* **Treska** ~ NW FYR Macedonia
113 *I14* **Treskavica** ▲ SE Bosnia and Herzegovina
59 *J20* **Três Lagoas** Mato Grosso do Sul, SW Brazil
40 *H12* **Tres Marías, Islas** *island group* C Mexico
59 *M19* **Três Marias, Represa** ⊠ SE Brazil
63 *F20* **Tres Montes, Península** *headland* S Chile
105 *O3* **Trespaderne** Castilla-León, N Spain
60 *G13* **Três Passos** Rio Grande do Sul, S Brazil
61 *A23* **Tres Picos, Cerro** ▲ E Argentina
63 *G17* **Tres Picos, Cerro** ▲ SW Argentina
60 *I12* **Três Pinheiros** Paraná, S Brazil
59 *M21* **Três Pontas** Minas Gerais, SE Brazil
Tres Puntas, Cabo *see* Manabique, Punta
60 *P9* **Três Rios** Rio de Janeiro, SE Brazil
Tres Tabernae *see* Saverne
Trestenberg/Trestendorf *see* Tăşnad
41 *R15* **Tres Valles** Veracruz-Llave, SE Mexico
94 *H12* **Tretten** Oppland, S Norway
Treuburg *see* Olecko
101 *K21* **Treuchtlingen** Bayern, S Germany
100 *N13* **Treuenbrietzen** Brandenburg, E Germany
95 *F16* **Treungen** Telemark, S Norway
63 *H17* **Trevelín** Chubut, SW Argentina
Treves/Trèves *see* Trier
106 *I13* **Trevi** Umbria, C Italy
106 *E7* **Treviglio** Lombardia, N Italy
104 *J4* **Trevinca, Peña** ▲ NW Spain
105 *P3* **Treviño** Castilla-León, N Spain
106 *I7* **Treviso** *anc.* Tarvisium. Veneto, NE Italy
97 *G24* **Trevose Head** *headland* SW England, UK
Trg *see* Feldkirchen in Kärnten
183 *P17* **Triabunna** Tasmania, SE Australia
21 *W4* **Triangle** Virginia, NE USA
83 *L18* **Triangle** Masvingo, SE Zimbabwe
115 *L23* **Tría Nisía** *island* Kykládes, Greece, Aegean Sea
Triberg *see* Triberg im Schwarzwald
101 *G23* **Triberg im Schwarzwald** *var.* Triberg. Baden-Württemberg, SW Germany
153 *P11* **Tribhuvan** ✈ (Kathmandu) Central, C Nepal
54 *C9* **Tribugá, Golfo de** *gulf* W Colombia
181 *W4* **Tribulation, Cape** *cape* Queensland, NE Australia
108 *M8* **Tribulaun** ▲ SW Austria
9 *U17* **Tribune** Saskatchewan, S Canada
26 *H5* **Tribune** Kansas, C USA
107 *N18* **Tricarico** Basilicata, S Italy
107 *Q19* **Tricase** Puglia, SE Italy
Trichinopoly *see* Tiruchchirāppalli
115 *D18* **Trichonída, Límni** ◎ C Greece
155 *G22* **Trichūr** *var.* Thrissur. Kerala, SW India
Tricorno *see* Triglav
183 *O8* **Trida** New South Wales, SE Australia
35 *S1* **Trident Peak** ▲ Nevada, W USA
Tridentum/Trient *see* Trento
109 *T6* **Trieben** Steiermark, SE Austria
101 *D19* **Trier** *Eng.* Treves, *Fr.* Trèves; *anc.* Augusta Treverorum. Rheinland-Pfalz, SW Germany
106 *K7* **Trieste** *Slvn.* Trst. Friuli-Venezia Giulia, NE Italy
Trieste, Golfo di/Triest, Golf von *see* Trieste, Gulf of
106 *J8* **Trieste, Gulf of** *Cro.* Tršćanski Zaljev, *Ger.* Golf von Triest, *It.* Golfo di Trieste, *Slvn.* Tržaški Zaliv. *gulf* S Europe
109 *W4* **Triesting** ~ W Austria
Triêu Hai *see* Quang Tri
Trifail *see* Trbovlje
116 *L9* **Trifeşti** Iaşi, NE Romania
109 *S10* **Triglav** *It.* Tricorno. ▲ NW Slovenia
104 *I14* **Trigueros** Andalucía, S Spain
115 *E16* **Tríkala** *prev.* Trikkala. Thessalía, C Greece
115 *E17* **Trikeriótis** ~ C Greece
Trikkala *see* Tríkala
Trikomo/Tríkomon *see* İskele
97 *F17* **Trim** *Ir.* Baile Átha Troim. Meath, E Ireland
108 *E7* **Trimbach** Solothurn, NW Switzerland
109 *Q5* **Trimmelkam** Oberösterreich, N Austria
29 *U11* **Trimont** Minnesota, N USA
Trimontium *see* Plovdiv
Trinacria *see* Sicilia
155 *K24* **Trincomalee** *var.* Trinkomali. Eastern Province, NE Sri Lanka
65 *K16* **Trindade, Ilha da** *island* Brazil, W Atlantic Ocean
47 *Y9* **Trindade Spur** *undersea feature* SW Atlantic Ocean
111 *J17* **Třinec** *Ger.* Trzynietz. Moravskoslezský Kraj, E Czech Republic
57 *M16* **Trinidad** Beni, N Bolivia
54 *H9* **Trinidad** Casanare, E Colombia
44 *E6* **Trinidad** Sancti Spíritus, C Cuba
61 *E19* **Trinidad** Flores, S Uruguay
37 *U8* **Trinidad** Colorado, C USA
45 *Y17* **Trinidad** *island* C Trinidad and Tobago
Trinidad *see* Jose Abad Santos
45 *Y16* **Trinidad and Tobago** *off.* Republic of Trinidad and Tobago. ◆ *republic* SE West Indies
Trinidad and Tobago, Republic of *see* Trinidad and Tobago
63 *F22* **Trinidad, Golfo** *gulf* S Chile
61 *B24* **Trinidad, Isla** *island* E Argentina
107 *N16* **Trinitapoli** Puglia, SE Italy
55 *X10* **Trinité, Montagnes de la** ▲ C French Guiana
25 *W9* **Trinity** Texas, SW USA
13 *U12* **Trinity Bay** *inlet* Newfoundland, Newfoundland and Labrador, E Canada
39 *P15* **Trinity Islands** *island group* Alaska, USA
35 *N2* **Trinity Mountains** ▲ California, W USA
35 *S4* **Trinity Peak** ▲ Nevada, W USA
35 *S5* **Trinity Range** ▲ Nevada, W USA
35 *N2* **Trinity River** ~ California, W USA
25 *V8* **Trinity River** ~ Texas, SW USA
Trinkomali *see* Trincomalee
173 *Y15* **Triolet** NW Mauritius
107 *O20* **Trionto, Capo** *headland* S Italy
Tripití, Ákra *see* Trypití, Akrotírio
115 *F20* **Trípoli** *prev.* Trípolis. Pelopónnisos, S Greece
138 *G6* **Tripoli** *var.* Tarābulus, Ṭarābulus ash Shām, Trâblous; *anc.* Tripolis. N Lebanon
29 *X12* **Tripoli** Iowa, C USA
Tripoli *see* Ṭarābulus
Trípolis *see* Trípoli, Greece
Tripolis *see* Tripoli, Lebanon
29 *Q12* **Tripp** South Dakota, N USA
153 *V15* **Tripura** *var.* Hill Tippera. ◈ *state* NE India
108 *K8* **Trisanna** ~ W Austria
100 *H8* **Trischen** *island* NW Germany
65 *M24* **Tristan da Cunha** ◇ *dependency of Saint Helena* SE Atlantic Ocean
67 *P15* **Tristan da Cunha** *island* SE Atlantic Ocean
65 *L18* **Tristan da Cunha Fracture Zone** *tectonic feature* S Atlantic Ocean
167 *S14* **Tri Tôn** An Giang, S Vietnam
167 *W10* **Triton Island** *island* S Paracel Islands
155 *G24* **Trivandrum** *var.* Thiruvanathapuram. *state capital* Kerala, SW India
111 *H20* **Trnava** *Ger.* Tyrnau, *Hung.* Nagyszombat. Trnavský Kraj, W Slovakia
111 *H20* **Trnavský Kraj** ◈ *region* W Slovakia
Trnovo *see* Veliko Tŭrnovo
Trobriand Island *see* Kiriwina Island
Trobriand Islands *see* Kiriwina Islands
9 *Q16* **Trochu** Alberta, SW Canada
109 *U7* **Trofaiach** Steiermark, SE Austria
93 *F14* **Trofors** Troms, N Norway
113 *E14* **Trogir** *It.* Traù. Split-Dalmacija, S Croatia
112 *F13* **Troglav** ▲ Bosnia and Herzegovina/Croatia
107 *M16* **Troia** Puglia, SE Italy
107 *K24* **Troina** Sicilia, Italy, C Mediterranean Sea
173 *O16* **Trois-Bassins** W Réunion
101 *E17* **Troisdorf** Nordrhein-Westfalen, W Germany
74 *H5* **Trois Fourches, Cap des** *cape* NE Morocco
15 *T8* **Trois-Pistoles** Québec, SE Canada
99 *L21* **Trois-Ponts** Liège, E Belgium
15 *P11* **Trois-Rivières** Québec, SE Canada
55 *Y12* **Trois Sauts** S French Guiana
99 *M22* **Troisvierges** Diekirch, N Luxembourg
122 *F11* **Troitsk** Chelyabinskaya Oblast', S Russian Federation
125 *T9* **Troitsko-Pechorsk** Respublika Komi, NW Russian Federation
127 *V7* **Troitskoye** Orenburgskaya Oblast', W Russian Federation
Troki *see* Trakai
94 *F9* **Trolla** ▲ S Norway
95 *J18* **Trollhättan** Västra Götaland, S Sweden
94 *G9* **Trollheimen** ▲ S Norway
94 *E9* **Trolltindane** ▲ S Norway
58 *H11* **Trombetas, Rio** ~ NE Brazil
128 *L16* **Tromelin, Île** *island* N Réunion
92 *I9* **Troms** ◈ *county* N Norway
92 *I9* **Tromsø** *Fin.* Tromssa. Troms, N Norway
84 *F5* **Tromsøflaket** *undersea feature* W Barents Sea
Tromssa *see* Tromsø
94 *H10* **Tron** ▲ S Norway
35 *U12* **Trona** California, W USA
63 *G16* **Tronador, Cerro** ▲ S Chile
94 *H8* **Trondheim** *Ger.* Drontheim; *prev.* Nidaros, Trondhjem. Sør-Trøndelag, S Norway
94 *H7* **Trondheimsfjorden** *fjord* S Norway
Trondhjem *see* Trondheim
107 *J14* **Tronto** ~ C Italy
121 *P3* **Troódos** *var.* Troodos Mountains. ▲ C Cyprus
Troodos *see* Ólympos
Troodos Mountains *see* Troódos
96 *I13* **Troon** W Scotland, UK
107 *M22* **Tropea** Calabria, SW Italy
36 *L7* **Tropic** Utah, W USA
64 *L10* **Tropic Seamount** *var.* Banc du Tropique. *undersea feature* E Atlantic Ocean
Tropique, Banc du *see* Tropic Seamount
Tropoja *see* Tropojë
113 *L17* **Tropojë** *var.* Tropoja. Kukës, N Albania
Troppau *see* Opava
95 *O16* **Trosa** Södermanland, C Sweden
118 *H12* **Troškūnai** Utena, E Lithuania
101 *G23* **Trossingen** Baden-Württemberg, SW Germany
117 *T4* **Trostyanets'** *Rus.* Trostyanets. Sums'ka Oblast', NE Ukraine
117 *N7* **Trostyanets'** *Rus.* Trostyanets. Vinnyts'ka Oblast', C Ukraine
Trostyanets *see* Trostyanets'
116 *L11* **Trotuş** ~ E Romania
44 *M8* **Trou-du-Nord** N Haiti
25 *W7* **Troup** Texas, SW USA
8 *I10* **Trout** ~ Northwest Territories, NW Canada
33 *N8* **Trout Creek** Montana, NW USA
32 *H10* **Trout Lake** Washington, NW USA
12 *B9* **Trout Lake** ◎ Ontario, S Canada
33 *T12* **Trout Peak** ▲ Wyoming, C USA
102 *L4* **Trouville** Calvados, N France
97 *L22* **Trowbridge** S England, UK
23 *Q6* **Troy** Alabama, S USA
27 *Q3* **Troy** Kansas, C USA
27 *W4* **Troy** Missouri, C USA
18 *L10* **Troy** New York, NE USA
21 *S10* **Troy** North Carolina, SE USA
31 *R13* **Troy** Ohio, N USA
25 *T9* **Troy** Texas, SW USA
114 *I9* **Troyan** Lovech, N Bulgaria
114 *I9* **Troyanski Prokhod** *pass* N Bulgaria
145 *N6* **Troyebratskiy** Severnyy Kazakhstan, N Kazakhstan
103 *Q6* **Troyes** *anc.* Augustobona Tricassium. Aube, N France
117 *X5* **Troyits'ke** Luhans'ka Oblast', E Ukraine
35 *W7* **Troy Peak** ▲ Nevada, W USA
113 *G15* **Trpanj** Dubrovnik-Neretva, S Croatia
Tršćanski Zaljev *see* Trieste, Gulf of
Trst *see* Trieste
113 *N14* **Trstenik** Serbia, C Serbia
126 *I6* **Trubchevsk** Bryanskaya Oblast', W Russian Federation
Trubchular *see* Orlyak
37 *S10* **Truchas Peak** ▲ New Mexico, SW USA
143 *P16* **Trucial Coast** *physical region* C United Arab Emirates
Trucial States *see* United Arab Emirates
35 *Q6* **Truckee** California, W USA
35 *R5* **Truckee River** ~ Nevada, W USA
127 *Q13* **Trudfront** Astrakhanskaya Oblast', SW Russian Federation
14 *I9* **Truite, Lac à la** ◎ Québec, SE Canada
42 *K4* **Trujillo** Colón, NE Honduras
56 *C12* **Trujillo** La Libertad, NW Peru
104 *K10* **Trujillo** Extremadura, W Spain
54 *I6* **Trujillo** Trujillo, NW Venezuela
54 *I6* **Trujillo** *off.* Estado Trujillo. ◈ *state* W Venezuela
Trujillo, Estado *see* Trujillo
Truk *see* Chuuk
Truk Islands *see* Chuuk Islands
29 *U10* **Truman** Minnesota, N USA
27 *X10* **Trumann** Arkansas, C USA
36 *J9* **Trumbull, Mount** ▲ Arizona, SW USA
114 *F9* **Trŭn** Pernik, W Bulgaria
183 *Q8* **Trundle** New South Wales, SE Australia
129 *U13* **Trung Phân** *physical region* S Vietnam
Trupcilar *see* Orlyak
13 *Q15* **Truro** Nova Scotia, SE Canada
97 *H25* **Truro** SW England, UK
25 *P5* **Truscott** Texas, SW USA
116 *K9* **Truşeşti** Botoşani, NE Romania
116 *H6* **Truskavets'** L'vivs'ka Oblast', W Ukraine
95 *H22* **Trustrup** Århus, C Denmark
10 *M11* **Trutch** British Columbia, W Canada
37 *Q14* **Truth Or Consequences** New Mexico, SW USA
111 *F15* **Trutnov** *Ger.* Trautenau. Královéhradecký Kraj, N Czech Republic
103 *P13* **Truyère** ~ C France
114 *K9* **Tryavna** Lovech, N Bulgaria
28 *M14* **Tryon** Nebraska, C USA
115 *J16* **Trypití, Akrotírio** *var.* Ákra Tripití. *headland* Ágios Efstrátios, E Greece
94 *J12* **Trysil** Hedmark, S Norway
94 *I11* **Trysilelva** ~ S Norway
112 *D10* **Tržac** ◈ Federacija Bosna I Hercegovina, NW Bosnia and Herzegovina
Tržaški Zaliv *see* Trieste, Gulf of
110 *G10* **Trzcianka** *Ger.* Schönlanke. Pila, Wielkopolskie, C Poland
110 *E7* **Trzebiatów** *Ger.* Treptow an der Rega. Zachodnio-pomorskie, NW Poland
111 *G14* **Trzebnica** *Ger.* Trebnitz. Dolnośląskie, SW Poland
109 *T10* **Tržič** *Ger.* Neumarktl. NW Slovenia
Trzynietz *see* Třinec
Tsabong *see* Tshabong
162 *G7* **Tsagaanchuluut** Dzavhan, C Mongolia
162 *M8* **Tsagaandelger** *var.* Haraat. Dundgovĭ, C Mongolia
Tsagaanders *see* Bayantümen
162 *G7* **Tsagaanhayrhan** *var.* Shiree. Dzavhan, W Mongolia
Tsagaannuur *see* Halhgol

◆ Country ● Country Capital ◇ Dependent Territory ○ Dependent Territory Capital ◈ Administrative Regions ✈ International Airport ▲ Mountain ▲ Mountain Range Volcano ~ River ◎ Lake ⊠ Reservoir

TSAGAAN-OLOM – TUSCUMBIA

Tsagaan-Olom *see* Tayshir
Tsagaan-Ovoo *see* Nariynteel
Tsagaantüngi *see* Altantsögts
162 H6 **Tsagaan-Uul** *var.* Sharga. Hövsgöl, N Mongolia
162 J5 **Tsagaan-Üür** *var.* Bulgan. Hövsgöl, N Mongolia
127 P12 **Tsagan Aman** Respublika Kalmykiya, SW Russian Federation
23 V11 **Tsala Apopka Lake** ◎ Florida, SE USA
Tsamkong *see* Zhanjiang
Tsangpo *see* Brahmaputra
Tsant *see* Deren
83 G17 **Tsao** North-West, NW Botswana
172 I4 **Tsaratanana** Mahajanga, C Madagascar
114 N10 **Tsarevo** *prev.* Michurin. Burgas, E Bulgaria
Tsarigrad *see* İstanbul
Tsaritsyn *see* Volgograd
124 G13 **Tsarskoye Selo** *prev.* Pushkin. Leningradskaya Oblast', NW Russian Federation
117 T7 **Tsarychanka** Dnipropetrovs'ka Oblast', E Ukraine
83 H21 **Tsatsu** Southern, S Botswana
81 J20 **Tsavo** Coast, S Kenya
83 E21 **Tsawisis** Karas, S Namibia
Tschakathurn *see* Čakovec
Tschaslau *see* Čáslav
Tschenstochau *see* Częstochowa
Tschernembl *see* Črnomelj
28 K6 **Tschida, Lake** ⊠ North Dakota, N USA
Tschorna *see* Mustvee
83 I17 **Tsebanana** Central, NE Botswana
162 G8 **Tseel** Govĭ-Altay, SW Mongolia
Tsefat *see* Ẕefat
126 M13 **Tselina** Rostovskaya Oblast', SW Russian Federation
Tselinograd *see* Astana
Tselinogradskaya Oblast *see* Akmola
Tsengel *see* Tosontsengel
162 J8 **Tsenher** *var.* Altan-Ovoo. Arhangay, C Mongolia
Tsenher *see* Mönhhayrhan
163 N8 **Tsenhermandal** *var.* Modot. Hentiy, C Mongolia
Tsentral'nyye Nizmennyye Garagumy *see* Merkezi Garagumy
Tsentral'nyye Nizmennyye Garagumy *see* Merkezi Garagumy
83 E21 **Tses** Karas, S Namibia
Tseshevlya *see* Tsyeshawlya
162 E7 **Tsetseg** *var.* Tsetsegnuur. Hovd, W Mongolia
Tsetsegnuur *see* Tsetseg
Tsetsen Khan *see* Öndörhaan
162 J6 **Tsetserleg** *var.* Hujirt. Arhangay, C Mongolia
162 J8 **Tsetserleg** Arhangay, C Mongolia
162 H6 **Tsetserleg** *var.* Halban. Hövsgöl, N Mongolia
77 R16 **Tsévié** S Togo
83 G21 **Tshabong** *var.* Tsabong. Kgalagadi, SW Botswana
83 G20 **Tshane** Kgalagadi, SW Botswana
Tshangalele, Lac *see* Lufira, Lac de Retenue de la
83 H17 **Tshauxaba** Central, C Botswana
79 F21 **Tshela** Bas-Congo, W Dem. Rep. Congo
79 K22 **Tshibala** Kasai Occidental, S Dem. Rep. Congo
79 J22 **Tshikapa** Kasai Occidental, SW Dem. Rep. Congo
79 L22 **Tshilenge** Kasai Oriental, S Dem. Rep. Congo
79 L24 **Tshimbalanga** Katanga, S Dem. Rep. Congo
79 L22 **Tshimbulu** Kasai Occidental, S Dem. Rep. Congo
Tshiumbe *see* Chiumbe
79 M21 **Tshofa** Kasai Oriental, C Dem. Rep. Congo
79 K18 **Tshuapa** ≋ C Dem. Rep. Congo
83 J21 **Tshwane** *var.* Epitoli; *prev.* Pretoria. ● Gauteng, NE South Africa
114 G7 **Tsibritsa** ≋ NW Bulgaria
Tsien Tang *see* Puyang Jiang
114 I12 **Tsigansko Gradishte** ▲ Bulgaria/Greece
Tsihombe *see* Tsiombe
8 H7 **Tsiigehtchic** *prev.* Arctic Red River. Northwest Territories, NW Canada
125 Q7 **Tsil'ma** ≋ NW Russian Federation
119 J17 **Tsimkavichy** *Rus.* Timkovichi. Minskaya Voblasts', C Belarus
126 M11 **Tsimlyansk** Rostovskaya Oblast', SW Russian Federation
127 N11 **Tsimlyanskoye Vodokhranilishche** *var.* Tsimlyansk Vodoskhovshche, *Eng.* Tsimlyansk Reservoir. ⊠ SW Russian Federation
Tsimlyansk Reservoir *see* Tsimlyanskoye Vodokhranilishche
Tsimlyansk Vodoskhovshche *see* Tsimlyanskoye Vodokhranilishche
Tsinan *see* Jinan
Tsing Hai *see* Qinghai Hu, China
Tsinghai *see* Qinghai, China
Tsingtao/Tsingtau *see* Qingdao
Tsingyuan *see* Baoding
Tsinkiang *see* Quanzhou
Tsintao *see* Qingdao
83 D17 **Tsintsabis** Otjikoto, N Namibia
172 H8 **Tsiombe** *var.* Tsihombe. Toliara, S Madagascar
123 O13 **Tsipa** ≋ S Russian Federation
172 H5 **Tsiribihina** ≋ W Madagascar
172 I5 **Tsiroanomandidy** Antananarivo, C Madagascar
189 U13 **Tsis** *island* Chuuk, C Micronesia
Tsitsihar *see* Qiqihar
127 Q3 **Tsivil'sk** Chuvashskaya Respublika, W Russian Federation
137 T9 **Ts'khinvali** *prev.* Staliniri. C Georgia
119 J19 **Tsna** ≋ SW Belarus
124 I15 **Tsna** *var.* Zna. ≋ W Russian Federation
162 G9 **Tsogt** *var.* Tahilt. Govĭ-Altay, W Mongolia
162 K10 **Tsogt-Ovoo** *var.* Doloon. Ömnögovĭ, S Mongolia
162 L10 **Tsogttsetsiy** Ömnögovĭ, S Mongolia
162 L10 **Tsogttsetsiy** *var.* Baruunsuu. Ömnögovĭ, S Mongolia
Tsoohor *see* Hürmen
164 K14 **Tsu** *var.* Tu. Mie, Honshū, SW Japan
165 O10 **Tsubame** *var.* Tubame. Niigata, Honshū, C Japan
165 V3 **Tsubetsu** Hokkaidō, NE Japan
165 O13 **Tsuchiura** *var.* Tutiura. Ibaraki, Honshū, S Japan
165 Q6 **Tsugaru-kaikyō** *strait* N Japan
164 E14 **Tsukumi** *var.* Tukumi. Ōita, Kyūshū, SW Japan
Tsul-Ulaan *see* Bayanuur
Tsul-Ulaan *see* Bayanuur
83 D17 **Tsumeb** Otjikoto, N Namibia
83 F17 **Tsumkwe** Otjozondjupa, NE Namibia
164 D15 **Tsuno** Miyazaki, Kyūshū, SW Japan
164 D12 **Tsuno-shima** *island* SW Japan
164 K12 **Tsuruga** *var.* Turuga. Fukui, Honshū, SW Japan
164 H12 **Tsurugi-san** ▲ Shikoku, SW Japan
165 P9 **Tsuruoka** *var.* Turuoka. Yamagata, Honshū, C Japan
164 C12 **Tsushima** *var.* Tsushima-tō, Tusima. *island group* SW Japan
Tsushima-tō *see* Tsushima
164 H12 **Tsuyama** *var.* Tuyama. Okayama, Honshū, SW Japan
83 G19 **Tswaane** Ghanzi, W Botswana
119 N16 **Tsyakhtsin** *Rus.* Tekhtin. Mahilyowskaya Voblasts', E Belarus
119 P19 **Tsyerakhowka** *Rus.* Terekhovka. Homyel'skaya Voblasts', SE Belarus
119 I17 **Tsyeshawlya** *Rus.* Cheshevlya, Tseshevlya. Brestskaya Voblasts', SW Belarus
Tsyurupinsk *see* Tsyurupyns'k
117 R10 **Tsyurupyns'k** *Rus.* Tsyurupinsk. Khersons'ka Oblast', S Ukraine
Tu *see* Tsu
186 C7 **Tua** ≋ C Papua New Guinea
Tuaim *see* Tuam
184 L6 **Tuakau** Waikato, North Island, New Zealand
97 C17 **Tuam** *Ir.* Tuaim. Galway, W Ireland
185 K14 **Tuamarina** Marlborough, South Island, New Zealand
Tuamotu, Archipel des *see* Tuamotu, Îles
193 Q9 **Tuamotu Fracture Zone** *tectonic feature* E Pacific Ocean
191 W9 **Tuamotu, Îles** *var.* Archipel des Tuamotu, Dangerous Archipelago, Tuamotu Islands. *island group* N French Polynesia
Tuamotu Islands *see* Tuamotu, Îles
175 X10 **Tuamotu Ridge** *undersea feature* C Pacific Ocean
167 R5 **Tuân Giao** Lai Châu, N Vietnam
171 O2 **Tuao** Luzon, N Philippines
190 B15 **Tuapa** NW Niue
43 N7 **Tuapí** Región Autónoma Atlántico Norte, NE Nicaragua
126 K15 **Tuapse** Krasnodarskiy Kray, SW Russian Federation
169 U6 **Tuaran** Sabah, East Malaysia
104 I6 **Tua, Rio** ≋ N Portugal
192 H15 **Tuasivi** Savai'i, C Samoa
185 B24 **Tuatapere** Southland, South Island, New Zealand
36 M9 **Tuba City** Arizona, SW USA
138 H11 **Ṭūbah, Qaṣr aṭ** *castle* 'Ammān, C Jordan
Tubame *see* Tsubame
169 R16 **Tuban** *prev.* Toeban. Jawa, C Indonesia
141 O16 **Tuban, Wādī** *dry watercourse* SW Yemen
61 K14 **Tubarão** Santa Catarina, S Brazil
98 O10 **Tubbergen** Overijssel, E Netherlands
Tubeke *see* Tubize
101 H22 **Tübingen** *var.* Tuebingen. Baden-Württemberg, SW Germany
127 W6 **Tubinskiy** Respublika Bashkortostan, W Russian Federation
99 G19 **Tubize** *Dut.* Tubeke. Walloon Brabant, C Belgium
76 J16 **Tubmanburg** NW Liberia
75 T7 **Tubruq** *Eng.* Tobruk, *It.* Tobruch. NE Libya
191 T13 **Tubuai** *island* Îles Australes, SW French Polynesia
Tubuai, Îles/Tubuai Islands *see* Australes, Îles
Tubuai-Manu *see* Maiao
40 F3 **Tubutama** Sonora, NW Mexico
54 K4 **Tucacas** Falcón, N Venezuela
59 P16 **Tucano** Bahia, E Brazil
57 P19 **Tucavaca, Río** ≋ E Bolivia
110 H8 **Tuchola** Kujawsko-pomorskie, C Poland
111 M17 **Tuchów** Małopolskie, S Poland
23 S3 **Tucker** Georgia, SE USA
27 W10 **Tuckerman** Arkansas, C USA
64 B12 **Tucker's Town** E Bermuda
Tuckum *see* Tukums
36 M15 **Tucson** Arizona, SW USA
62 J7 **Tucumán** *off.* Provincia de Tucumán. ◈ *province* N Argentina
Tucumán *see* San Miguel de Tucumán
Tucumán, Provincia de *see* Tucumán
37 V11 **Tucumcari** New Mexico, SW USA
58 H13 **Tucunaré** Pará, N Brazil
55 Q6 **Tucupita** Delta Amacuro, NE Venezuela
58 K13 **Tucuruí, Represa de** ⊠ NE Brazil
110 F9 **Tuczno** Zachodnio-pomorskie, NW Poland
Tuddo *see* Tudu
105 Q5 **Tudela** *Basq.* Tutera; *anc.* Tutela. Navarra, N Spain
104 M6 **Tudela de Duero** Castilla-León, N Spain
162 G6 **Tüdevtey** *var.* Oygon. Dzavhan, N Mongolia
138 K6 **Tudmur** *var.* Tadmur, Tamar, *Gk.* Palmyra, *Bibl.* Tadmor. Ḥimṣ, C Syria
118 J4 **Tudu** *Ger.* Tuddo. Lääne-Virumaa, NE Estonia
Tuebingen *see* Tübingen
122 J14 **Tuekta** Respublika Altay, S Russian Federation
104 I5 **Tuela, Rio** ≋ N Portugal
153 X12 **Tuensang** Nāgāland, NE India
136 L15 **Tufanbeyli** Adana, C Turkey
Tüffer *see* Laško
186 F9 **Tufi** Northern, S Papua New Guinea
193 O3 **Tufts Plain** *undersea feature* N Pacific Ocean
Tugalan *see* Kolkhozobod
67 V14 **Tugela** ≋ SE South Africa
21 P6 **Tug Fork** ≋ S USA
39 P15 **Tugidak Island** *island* Trinity Islands, Alaska, USA
171 O2 **Tuguegarao** Luzon, N Philippines
123 S12 **Tugur** Khabarovskiy Kray, SE Russian Federation
161 P4 **Tuhai He** ≋ E China
104 G4 **Tui** Galicia, NW Spain
77 O13 **Tui** *var.* Grand Balé. ≋ W Burkina
57 J16 **Tuichi, Río** ≋ W Bolivia
64 Q11 **Tuineje** Fuerteventura, Islas Canarias, Spain, NE Atlantic Ocean
43 X16 **Tuira, Río** ≋ SE Panama
Tuisarkan *see* Tüysarkān
Tujiabu *see* Yongxiu
127 W5 **Tukan** Respublika Bashkortostan, W Russian Federation
171 P14 **Tukangbesi, Kepulauan** *Dut.* Toekang Besi Eilanden. *island group* C Indonesia
147 V13 **Tükhtamish** *Rus.* Toktomush; *prev.* Tokhtamyshbek. SE Tajikistan
184 O12 **Tukituki** ≋ North Island, New Zealand
Tu-k'ou *see* Panzhihua
121 P12 **Tükrah** NE Libya
8 H6 **Tuktoyaktuk** Northwest Territories, NW Canada
168 I9 **Tuktuk** Pulau Samosir, W Indonesia
Tukumi *see* Tsukumi
118 E9 **Tukums** *Ger.* Tuckum. Tukums, W Latvia
81 G24 **Tukuyu** *prev.* Neu-Langenburg. Mbeya, S Tanzania
Tukzār *see* Tokzār
41 O13 **Tula** *var.* Tula de Allende. Hidalgo, C Mexico
41 O11 **Tula** Tamaulipas, C Mexico
126 K5 **Tula** Tul'skaya Oblast', W Russian Federation
Tulach Mhór *see* Tullamore
Tula de Allende *see* Tula
159 N10 **Tulage Ar Gol** ≋ W China
186 M9 **Tulaghi** *var.* Tulagi. Florida Islands, C Solomon Islands
Tulagi *see* Tulaghi
41 P13 **Tulancingo** Hidalgo, C Mexico
35 R11 **Tulare** California, W USA
29 P9 **Tulare** South Dakota, N USA
35 Q12 **Tulare Lake Bed** *salt flat* California, W USA
37 S14 **Tularosa** New Mexico, SW USA
37 P13 **Tularosa Mountains** ▲▲ New Mexico, SW USA
37 S15 **Tularosa Valley** *basin* New Mexico, SW USA
83 E25 **Tulbagh** Western Cape, SW South Africa
56 C5 **Tulcán** Carchi, N Ecuador
117 N13 **Tulcea** Tulcea, E Romania
117 N13 **Tulcea** ◈ *county* SE Romania
Tul'chin *see* Tul'chyn
117 N7 **Tul'chyn** *Rus.* Tul'chin. Vinnyts'ka Oblast', C Ukraine
Tuléar *see* Toliara
35 O1 **Tulelake** California, W USA
116 J10 **Tulgheş** *Hung.* Gyergyótölgyes. Harghita, C Romania
Tuli *see* Thuli
25 N4 **Tulia** Texas, SW USA
8 I9 **Tulita** *prev.* Fort Norman, Norman. Northwest Territories, NW Canada
20 J10 **Tullahoma** Tennessee, S USA
183 N12 **Tullamarine** ✕ (Melbourne) Victoria, SE Australia
183 Q7 **Tullamore** New South Wales, SE Australia
97 E18 **Tullamore** *Ir.* Tulach Mhór. Offaly, C Ireland
103 N12 **Tulle** *anc.* Tutela. Corrèze, C France
109 X3 **Tulln** *var.* Oberhollabrunn. Niederösterreich, NE Austria
109 W4 **Tulln** ≋ NE Austria
22 H6 **Tullos** Louisiana, S USA
97 F19 **Tullow** *Ir.* An Tullach. Carlow, SE Ireland
181 W5 **Tully** Queensland, NE Australia
124 J3 **Tuloma** ≋ NW Russian Federation
114 K10 **Tulovo** Stara Zagora, C Bulgaria
27 P9 **Tulsa** Oklahoma, C USA
153 N11 **Tulsipur** Mid Western, W Nepal
126 K6 **Tul'skaya Oblast'** ◈ *province* W Russian Federation
126 L14 **Tul'skiy** Respublika Adygeya, SW Russian Federation
186 E5 **Tulu** Manus Island, N Papua New Guinea
54 D10 **Tuluá** Valle del Cauca, W Colombia
116 M12 **Tulucești** Galați, E Romania
39 N12 **Tuluksak** Alaska, USA
41 Z12 **Tulum, Ruinas de** *ruins* Quintana Roo, SE Mexico
169 R17 **Tulungagung** *prev.* Toeloengagoeng. Jawa, C Indonesia
186 J6 **Tulun Islands** *var.* Kilinailau Islands; *prev.* Carteret Islands. *island group* NE Papua New Guinea
126 M4 **Tuma** Ryazanskaya Oblast', W Russian Federation
54 B12 **Tumaco** Nariño, SW Colombia
54 B12 **Tumaco, Bahía de** *bay* SW Colombia
Tuman-gang *see* Tumen
42 L8 **Tuma, Río** ≋ N Nicaragua
95 O16 **Tumba** Stockholm, C Sweden
Tumba, Lac *see* Ntomba, Lac
169 S12 **Tumbangsenamang** Borneo, C Indonesia
183 Q10 **Tumbarumba** New South Wales, SE Australia
56 A8 **Tumbes** Tumbes, NW Peru
56 A9 **Tumbes** *off.* Departamento de Tumbes. ◈ *department* NW Peru
Tumbes, Departamento de *see* Tumbes
19 P5 **Tumbledown Mountain** ▲ Maine, NE USA
9 N13 **Tumbler Ridge** British Columbia, W Canada
167 Q12 **Tumbŏt, Phnum** ▲ W Cambodia
182 G9 **Tumby Bay** South Australia
163 Y10 **Tumen** Jilin, NE China
163 Y11 **Tumen** *Chin.* Tumen Jiang, *Kor.* Tuman-gang, *Rus.* Tumyn'tszyan. ≋ E Asia
Tumen Jiang *see* Tumen
55 Q8 **Tumeremo** Bolívar, E Venezuela
155 G19 **Tumkūr** Karnātaka, W India
96 I10 **Tummel** ≋ C Scotland, UK
188 B15 **Tumon Bay** *bay* W Guam
77 P14 **Tumu** NW Ghana
58 I10 **Tumuc Humac Mountains** *var.* Serra Tumucumaque. ▲▲ N South America
Tumucumaque, Serra *see* Tumuc Humac Mountains
183 Q10 **Tumut** New South Wales, SE Australia
Tumyn'tszyan *see* Tumen
Tün *see* Ferdows
45 U14 **Tunapuna** Trinidad, Trinidad and Tobago
60 K11 **Tunas** Paraná, S Brazil
Tunbridge Wells *see* Royal Tunbridge Wells
114 L11 **Tunca Nehri** *Bul.* Tundzha. ≋ Bulgaria/Turkey *see also* Tundzha
Tunca Nehri *see* Tundzha
137 O14 **Tunceli** *var.* Kalan. Tunceli, E Turkey
137 O14 **Tunceli** ◈ *province* C Turkey
152 J12 **Tūndla** Uttar Pradesh, N India
81 I25 **Tunduru** Ruvuma, S Tanzania
114 L10 **Tundzha** *Turk.* Tunca Nehri. ≋ Bulgaria/Turkey *see also* Tunca Nehri
Tundzha *see* Tunca Nehri
162 I6 **Tünel** *var.* Bulag. Hövsgöl, N Mongolia
155 H17 **Tungabhadra** ≋ S India
155 F17 **Tungabhadra Reservoir** ◎ S India
191 P2 **Tungaru** *prev.* Gilbert Islands. *island group* W Kiribati
171 P7 **Tungawan** Mindanao, S Philippines
Tungdor *see* Mainling
T'ung-shan *see* Xuzhou
161 Q16 **Tungsha Tao** *Chin.* Dongsha Qundao, *Eng.* Pratas Island. *island* S Taiwan
161 S13 **Tungshih** *Jap.* Tōsei. N Taiwan
8 H9 **Tungsten** Northwest Territories, W Canada
Tung-t'ing Hu *see* Dongting Hu
56 A13 **Tungurahua** ◈ *province* C Ecuador
95 F14 **Tunhovdfjorden** ◎ S Norway
22 K2 **Tunica** Mississippi, S USA
75 N5 **Tunis** *var.* Tūnis. ● (Tunisia) NE Tunisia
75 N5 **Tunis, Golfe de** *Ar.* Khalīj Tūnis. *gulf* NE Tunisia
75 N6 **Tunisia** *off.* Republic of Tunisia, *Ar.* Al Jumhūrīyah at Tūnisīyah, *Fr.* République Tunisienne. ◆ *republic* N Africa
Tunisia, Republic of *see* Tunisia
Tunisienne, République *see* Tunisia
Tūnisīyah, Al Jumhūrīyah at *see* Tunisia
Tūnis, Khalīj *see* Tunis, Golfe de
54 G9 **Tunja** Boyacá, C Colombia
93 F14 **Tunnsjøen** *Lapp.* Dåtnejaevrie. ◎ C Norway
39 N12 **Tuntutuliak** Alaska, USA
197 P14 **Tunu** ◈ *province* E Greenland
147 U8 **Tunuk** Chuyskaya Oblast', C Kyrgyzstan
13 Q6 **Tunungayualok Island** *island* Newfoundland and Labrador, E Canada
62 H11 **Tunuyán** Mendoza, W Argentina
62 I11 **Tunuyán, Río** ≋ W Argentina
Tunxi *see* Huangshan
Tuodian *see* Shuangbai
Tuoji *see* Zhongba
35 P9 **Tuolumne River** ≋ California, W USA
Tuong Buong *see* Tương Đương
167 R7 **Tương Đương** *var.* Tuong Buong. Nghê An, N Vietnam
160 I13 **Tuoniang Jiang** ≋ S China
Tuotuo He *see* Togton He
Tuotuoheyan *see* Tanggulashan
Tüp *see* Tyup
60 J9 **Tupã** São Paulo, S Brazil
191 S10 **Tupai** *var.* Motu Iti. *atoll* Îles Sous le Vent, W French Polynesia
61 G15 **Tupanciretã** Rio Grande do Sul, S Brazil
22 M2 **Tupelo** Mississippi, S USA
59 K18 **Tupiraçaba** Goiás, S Brazil
57 L21 **Tupiza** Potosí, S Bolivia
9 N13 **Tupper** British Columbia, W Canada
18 J8 **Tupper Lake** ◎ New York, NE USA
146 J10 **Tuproqqal'a** Khorazm Viloyati, W Uzbekistan
146 J10 **Tuproqqal'a** *Rus.* Turpakkla. Xorazm Viloyati, W Uzbekistan
62 H11 **Tupungato, Volcán** 🌋 W Argentina
163 T9 **Tuquan** Nei Mongol Zizhiqu, N China
54 C13 **Túquerres** Nariño, SW Colombia
153 U13 **Tura** Meghālaya, NE India
122 M10 **Tura** Evenkiyskiy Avtonomnyy Okrug, N Russian Federation
122 G10 **Tura** ≋ C Russian Federation
140 M10 **Turabah** Makkah, W Saudi Arabia
55 O8 **Turagua, Cerro** ▲ C Venezuela
184 L12 **Turakina** Manawatu-Wanganui, North Island, New Zealand
185 K15 **Turakirae Head** *headland* North Island, New Zealand
186 B8 **Turama** ≋ S Papua New Guinea
122 K13 **Turan** Respublika Tyva, S Russian Federation
184 M10 **Turangi** Waikato, North Island, New Zealand
146 F11 **Turan Lowland** *var.* Turan Plain, *Kaz.* Turan Oypaty, *Rus.* Turanskaya Nizmennost', *Turk.* Turan Pesligi, *Uzb.* Turan Pasttekisligi. *plain* C Asia
Turan Oypaty/Turan Pesligi/Turan Plain/Turanskaya Nizmennost' *see* Turan Lowland
Turan Pasttekisligi *see* Turan Lowland
138 K7 **Ṭurāq al 'Ilab** *hill range* S Syria
119 K20 **Turaw** *Rus.* Turov. Homyel'skaya Voblasts', SE Belarus
140 L2 **Ṭurayf** Al Ḥudūd ash Shamālīyah, NW Saudi Arabia
Turba *see* Teruel
54 E5 **Turbaco** Bolívar, N Colombia
148 K15 **Turbat** Baluchistān, SW Pakistan
Turbat-i-Haidari *see* Torbat-e Ḥeydarīyeh
Turbat-i-Jam *see* Torbat-e Jām
54 D7 **Turbo** Antioquia, NW Colombia
Turčianský Svätý Martin *see* Martin
116 H10 **Turda** *Ger.* Thorenburg, *Hung.* Torda. Cluj, NW Romania
142 M7 **Ṭūreh** Markazī, W Iran
191 X12 **Tureia** *atoll* Îles Tuamotu, SE French Polynesia
110 I12 **Turek** Wielkopolskie, C Poland
93 L19 **Turenki** Etelä-Suomi, SW Finland
Turfan *see* Turpan
145 R8 **Turgay** *Kaz.* Torghay. Akmola, W Kazakhstan
145 N10 **Turgay** *Kaz.* Torgay. ≋ C Kazakhstan
144 M8 **Turgayskaya Stolovaya Strana** *Kaz.* Torgay Üstirti. *plateau* Kazakhstan/Russian Federation
Turgel *see* Türi
114 L8 **Türgovishte** *prev.* Eski Dzhumaya, Tărgovište. Türgovishte, N Bulgaria
114 L8 **Türgovishte** ◈ *province* N Bulgaria
136 C14 **Turgutlu** Manisa, W Turkey
136 L12 **Turhal** Tokat, N Turkey
118 H4 **Türi** *Ger.* Turgel. Järvamaa, N Estonia
105 S9 **Turia** ≋ E Spain
58 M12 **Turiaçu** Maranhão, E Brazil
Turin *see* Torino
116 I3 **Turiys'k** Volyns'ka Oblast', NW Ukraine
Turja *see* Tur"ya
116 H6 **Turka** L'vivs'ka Oblast', W Ukraine
81 H16 **Turkana, Lake** *var.* Lake Rudolf. ◎ N Kenya
145 P16 **Turkestan** *Kaz.* Türkistan. Yuzhnyy Kazakhstan, S Kazakhstan
147 Q12 **Turkestan Range** *Rus.* Turkestanskiy Khrebet. ▲▲ C Asia
Turkestanskiy Khrebet *see* Turkestan Range
111 M23 **Túrkeve** Jász-Nagykun-Szolnok, E Hungary
25 O4 **Turkey** Texas, SW USA
136 H14 **Turkey** *off.* Republic of Turkey, *Turk.* Türkiye Cumhuriyeti. ◆ *republic* SW Asia
181 N4 **Turkey Creek** Western Australia
26 M9 **Turkey Creek** ≋ Oklahoma, C USA
37 T9 **Turkey Mountains** ▲▲ New Mexico, SW USA
Turkey, Republic of *see* Turkey
29 X11 **Turkey River** ≋ Iowa, C USA
127 N7 **Turki** Saratovskaya Oblast', W Russian Federation
121 O1 **Turkish Republic of Northern Cyprus** ◇ *disputed territory* Cyprus
Türkistan *see* Turkestan
Turkistan, Bandi-i *see* Torkestān, Selseleh-ye Band-e
Türkiye Cumhuriyeti *see* Turkey
146 K12 **Türkmenabat** *prev.* *Rus.* Chardzhev, Chardzhou, Chardzhui, Lenin-Turkmenski, *Turkm.* Chärjew. Lebap Welaýaty, E Turkmenistan
146 A11 **Turkmen Aylagy** *Rus.* Turkmenskiy Zaliv. *lake gulf* W Turkmenistan
Turkmenbashi *see* Turkmenbaşy
146 A10 **Türkmenbaşy** *Rus.* Turkmenbashi; *prev.* Krasnovodsk. Balkan Welaýaty, W Turkmenistan
146 A10 **Türkmenbasy Aylagy** *prev.* *Rus.* Krasnovodskiy Zaliv, *Turkm.* Krasnowodsk Aylagy. *lake Gulf* W Turkmenistan
146 J14 **Turkmengala** *Rus.* Turkmen-kala; *prev.* Turkmen-Kala. Mary Welaýaty, S Turkmenistan
146 G13 **Turkmenistan** ; *prev.* Turkmenskaya Soviet Socialist Republic. ◆ *republic* C Asia
Turkmen-kala/Turkmen-Kala *see* Turkmengala
Turkmenskaya Soviet Socialist Republic *see* Turkmenistan
Turkmenskiy Zaliv *see* Turkmen Aylagy
136 L16 **Türkoğlu** Kahramanmaraş, S Turkey
44 L6 **Turks and Caicos Islands** ◇ *UK dependent territory* N West Indies
64 G10 **Turks and Caicos Islands** *UK dependant territory* N West Indies
45 N6 **Turks Islands** *island group* SE Turks and Caicos Islands
93 K19 **Turku** *Swe.* Åbo. Länsi-Soumi, SW Finland
81 H17 **Turkwel** *seasonal river* NW Kenya
27 P9 **Turley** Oklahoma, C USA
35 P9 **Turlock** California, W USA
118 I12 **Turmantas** Utena, NE Lithuania
Turmberg *see* Wieżyca
54 L5 **Turmero** Aragua, N Venezuela South America
184 N13 **Turnagain, Cape** *headland* North Island, New Zealand
Turnau *see* Turnov
42 H2 **Turneffe Islands** *island group* E Belize
18 M11 **Turners Falls** Massachusetts, NE USA
9 P16 **Turner Valley** Alberta, SW Canada
99 I16 **Turnhout** Antwerpen, N Belgium
109 V5 **Türnitz** Niederösterreich, E Austria
9 S12 **Turnor Lake** ◎ Saskatchewan, C Canada
111 E15 **Turnov** *Ger.* Turnau. Liberecký Kraj, N Czech Republic
Türnovo *see* Veliko Türnovo
116 I15 **Turnu Măgurele** *var.* Turnu-Măgurele. Teleorman, S Romania
Turnu Severin *see* Drobeta-Turnu Severin
Turócszentmárton *see* Martin
Turoni *see* Tours
Turov *see* Turaw
Turpakkla *see* Tuproqqal'a
158 M6 **Turpan** *var.* Turfan. Xinjiang Uygur Zizhiqu, NW China
Turpan Depression *see* Turpan Pendi
158 M6 **Turpan Pendi** *Eng.* Turpan Depression. *depression* NW China
158 M5 **Turpan Zhan** Xinjiang Uygur Zizhiqu, W China
Turpentine State *see* North Carolina
44 H8 **Turquino, Pico** ▲ E Cuba
27 Y10 **Turrell** Arkansas, C USA
43 N14 **Turrialba** Cartago, E Costa Rica
96 K8 **Turriff** NE Scotland, UK
139 V7 **Tursāq** E Iraq
Turshiz *see* Kāshmar
Tursunzade *see* Tursunzoda
147 P13 **Tursunzoda** *Rus.* Tursunzade; *prev.* Regar. W Tajikistan
Turt *see* Hanh
Türtkül/Turtkul' *see* To'rtko'l
29 O9 **Turtle Creek** ≋ South Dakota, N USA
30 K4 **Turtle Flambeau Flowage** ⊠ Wisconsin, N USA
9 S14 **Turtleford** Saskatchewan, S Canada
28 M4 **Turtle Lake** North Dakota, N USA
92 K12 **Turtola** Lappi, NW Finland
122 M10 **Turu** ≋ N Russian Federation
Turuga *see* Tsuruga
147 V10 **Turugart Pass** *pass* China/Kyrgyzstan
158 E7 **Turugart Shankou** *var.* Pereval Torugart. *pass* China/Kyrgyzstan
122 K9 **Turukhan** ≋ N Russian Federation
122 K9 **Turukhansk** Krasnoyarskiy Kray, N Russian Federation
139 N3 **Ṭurumbah** *well* NE Syria
Turuoka *see* Tsuruoka
144 H14 **Turush** Mangistau, SW Kazakhstan
60 K7 **Turvo, Rio** ≋ S Brazil
116 J2 **Tur"ya** *Pol.* Turja, *Rus.* Tur'ya. ≋ NW Ukraine
23 O4 **Tuscaloosa** Alabama, S USA
23 O4 **Tuscaloosa, Lake** ◎ Alabama, S USA
Tuscan Archipelago *see* Toscano, Arcipelago
Tuscan-Emilian Mountains *see* Tosco-Emiliano, Appennino
Tuscany *see* Toscana
35 V2 **Tuscarora** Nevada, W USA
18 F15 **Tuscarora Mountain** *ridge* Pennsylvania, NE USA
30 M14 **Tuscola** Illinois, N USA
25 P7 **Tuscola** Texas, SW USA
23 O2 **Tuscumbia** Alabama, S USA

◆ Country
● Country Capital
◇ Dependent Territory
○ Dependent Territory Capital
◈ Administrative Regions
✕ International Airport
▲ Mountain
▲▲ Mountain Range
🌋 Volcano
≋ River
◎ Lake
⊠ Reservoir

TUSENØYANE – UNDUR

92 O4 **Tusenøyane** *island group* S Svalbard
144 K13 **Tushybas, Zaliv** *prev.* Zaliv Paskevicha. *lake gulf* SW Kazakhstan
Tusima *see* Tsushima
171 Y15 **Tusirah** Papua, E Indonesia
23 Q5 **Tuskegee** Alabama, S USA
94 E8 **Tustna** *island* S Norway
39 R12 **Tustumena Lake** ◎ Alaska, USA
110 K13 **Tuszyn** Łódzkie, C Poland
137 S13 **Tutak** Ağrı, E Turkey
185 C20 **Tutamoe Range** ▲▲ North Island, New Zealand
Tutasev *see* Tutayev
124 L15 **Tutayev** *var.* Tutasev. Yaroslavskaya Oblast', W Russian Federation
Tutela *see* Tulle, France
Tutela *see* Tudela, Spain
Tutera *see* Tudela
155 H23 **Tuticorin** Tamil Nādu, SE India
113 L15 **Tutin** Serbia, S Serbia
184 O10 **Tutira** Hawke's Bay, North Island, New Zealand
Tutiura *see* Tsuchiura
122 K10 **Tutonchny** Evenkiyskiy Avtonomnyy Okrug, N Russian Federation
114 L6 **Tutrakan** Silistra, NE Bulgaria
29 N5 **Tuttle** North Dakota, N USA
26 M11 **Tuttle** Oklahoma, C USA
27 O3 **Tuttle Creek Lake** ⊠ Kansas, C USA
101 H23 **Tuttlingen** Baden-Württemberg, S Germany
171 R16 **Tutuala** East Timor
192 K17 **Tutuila** *island* W American Samoa
83 I18 **Tutume** Central, E Botswana
39 N7 **Tututalak Mountain** ▲ Alaska, USA
22 K3 **Tutwiler** Mississippi, S USA
162 L8 **Tuul Gol** ≈ N Mongolia
93 O16 **Tuupovaara** Itä-Suomi, E Finland
Tuva *see* Tyva, Respublika
190 E7 **Tuvalu** *prev.* Ellice Islands. ◆ *commonwealth republic* SW Pacific Ocean
Tuvinskaya ASSR *see* Tyva, Respublika
163 O9 **Tuvshinshiree** *var.* Sergelen. Sühbaatar, E Mongolia
141 P9 **Ṭuwayq, Jabal** ▲▲ C Saudi Arabia
138 H13 **Ṭuwayyil ash Shihāq** *desert* S Jordan
9 U16 **Tuxford** Saskatchewan, S Canada
167 U12 **Tu Xoay** Đắc Lắc, S Vietnam
40 L14 **Tuxpan** Jalisco, C Mexico
40 J12 **Tuxpan** Nayarit, C Mexico
41 Q12 **Tuxpán** *var.* Tuxpán de Rodríguez Cano. Veracruz-Llave, E Mexico
Tuxpán de Rodríguez Cano *see* Tuxpán
41 R15 **Tuxtepec** *var.* San Juan Bautista Tuxtepec. Oaxaca, S Mexico
41 U16 **Tuxtla** *var.* Tuxtla Gutiérrez. Chiapas, SE Mexico
Tuxtla *see* San Andrés Tuxtla
Tuxtla Gutiérrez *see* Tuxtla
Tuyama *see* Tsuyama
167 T5 **Tuyên Quang** Tuyên Quang, N Vietnam
167 U13 **Tuy Hoa** Binh Thuân, S Vietnam
167 V12 **Tuy Hoa** Phu Yên, S Vietnam
127 U5 **Tuymazy** Respublika Bashkortostan, W Russian Federation
Tuy Phong *see* Liên Hương
142 L6 **Tūysarkān** *var.* Tuisarkan, Tuyserkān. Hamadān, W Iran
Tuyserkān *see* Tūysarkān
145 W16 **Tuyuk** *Kaz.* Tuyyq. Taldykorgan, SE Kazakhstan
Tuyyq *see* Tuyuk
136 I14 **Tuz Gölü** ◎ C Turkey
125 Q15 **Tuzha** Kirovskaya Oblast', NW Russian Federation
113 K17 **Tuzi** S Montenegro
139 T5 **Tūz Khurmātū** N Iraq
117 N15 **Tuzla** Constanța, SE Romania
112 I11 **Tuzla** ◈ Federacija Bosna I Hercegovina, NE Bosnia and Herzegovina
137 T12 **Tuzluca** Iğdır, E Turkey
95 J20 **Tvååker** Halland, S Sweden
95 F17 **Tvedestrand** Aust-Agder, S Norway
124 J16 **Tver'** *prev.* Kalinin. Tverskaya Oblast', W Russian Federation
126 I15 **Tverskaya Oblast'** ◈ *province* W Russian Federation
124 I15 **Tvertsa** ≈ W Russian Federation
Tverya *see* Teverya
110 H13 **Twardogóra** *Ger.* Festenberg. Dolnośląskie, SW Poland
14 J14 **Tweed** Ontario, SE Canada
96 K13 **Tweed** ≈ England/Scotland, UK
98 O7 **Tweede-Exloërmond** Drenthe, NE Netherlands
183 V3 **Tweed Heads** New South Wales, SE Australia
98 M11 **Twello** Gelderland, E Netherlands
35 W15 **Twentynine Palms** California, W USA
25 P9 **Twin Buttes Reservoir** ⊠ Texas, SW USA
33 O15 **Twin Falls** Idaho, NW USA
39 N13 **Twin Hills** Alaska, USA
9 O11 **Twin Lakes** Alberta, W Canada
33 O12 **Twin Peaks** ▲ Idaho, NW USA
185 I14 **Twins, The** ▲ South Island, New Zealand
29 S5 **Twin Valley** Minnesota, N USA
100 G11 **Twistringen** Niedersachsen, NW Germany
185 E20 **Twizel** Canterbury, South Island, New Zealand
29 X5 **Two Harbors** Minnesota, N USA
9 R14 **Two Hills** Alberta, SW Canada
31 N7 **Two Rivers** Wisconsin, N USA
116 H8 **Tyachiv** Zakarpats'ka Oblast', W Ukraine
Tyan'-Shan' *see* Tien Shan
166 L3 **Tyao** ≈ Burma (Myanmar)/India
117 R6 **Tyas'myn** ≈ N Ukraine
23 X6 **Tybee Island** Georgia, SE USA
Tyborøn *see* Thyborøn
111 J16 **Tychy** *Ger.* Tichau. Śląskie, S Poland
111 O16 **Tyczyn** Podkarpackie, SE Poland
94 I8 **Tydal** Sør-Trøndelag, S Norway
115 H24 **Tyflós** ≈ Kríti, Greece, E Mediterranean Sea
21 S3 **Tygart Lake** ⊠ West Virginia, NE USA
123 Q13 **Tygda** Amurskaya Oblast', SE Russian Federation
21 Q11 **Tyger River** ≈ South Carolina, SE USA
32 I11 **Tygh Valley** Oregon, NW USA
94 F12 **Tyin** ◎ S Norway
29 S10 **Tyler** Minnesota, N USA
25 W7 **Tyler** Texas, SW USA
25 W7 **Tyler, Lake** ⊠ Texas, SW USA
22 K7 **Tylertown** Mississippi, S USA
117 P10 **Tylihuls'kyy Lyman** ◎ SW Ukraine
Tylos *see* Bahrain
115 C15 **Týmfi** *var.* Timfi. ▲ W Greece
115 E17 **Tymfristós** *var.* Timfristos. ▲ C Greece
115 J25 **Tympáki** *var.* Timbaki; *prev.* Timbákion. Kríti, Greece, E Mediterranean Sea
123 Q12 **Tynda** Amurskaya Oblast', SE Russian Federation
29 Q12 **Tyndall** South Dakota, N USA
97 L14 **Tyne** ≈ N England, UK
97 M14 **Tynemouth** NE England, UK
97 L14 **Tyneside** *cultural region* NE England, UK
94 H10 **Tynset** Hedmark, S Norway
39 Q12 **Tyonek** Alaska, USA
Tyôsi *see* Chōshi
Tyras *see* Dniester
Tyras *see* Bilhorod-Dnistrovs'kyy
Tyre *see* Soûr
95 G14 **Tyrifjorden** ◎ S Norway
95 K22 **Tyringe** Skåne, S Sweden
123 R13 **Tyrma** Khabarovskiy Kray, SE Russian Federation
Tyrnau *see* Trnava
115 F15 **Týrnavos** *var.* Tírnavos. Thessalía, C Greece
127 N16 **Tyrnyauz** Kabardino-Balkarskaya Respublika, SW Russian Federation
Tyrol *see* Tirol
18 E14 **Tyrone** Pennsylvania, NE USA
97 E15 **Tyrone** *cultural region* W Northern Ireland, UK
Tyros *see* Bahrain
182 M10 **Tyrrell, Lake** *salt lake* Victoria, SE Australia
84 H14 **Tyrrhenian Basin** *undersea feature* Tyrrhenian Sea, C Mediterranean Sea
120 L8 **Tyrrhenian Sea** *It.* Mare Tirreno. *sea* N Mediterranean Sea
94 J12 **Tyrsil** ≈ Hedmark, S Norway
Tysa *see* Tisa/Tisza
116 J7 **Tysmenytsya** Ivano-Frankivs'ka Oblast', W Ukraine
95 C14 **Tysnesøya** *island* S Norway
95 C14 **Tysse** Hordaland, S Norway
95 D14 **Tyssedal** Hordaland, S Norway
95 O17 **Tystberga** Södermanland, C Sweden
118 E12 **Tytuvėnai** Šiaulai, C Lithuania
144 D14 **Tyub-Karagan, Mys** *cape* SW Kazakhstan
147 V8 **Tyugel'-Say** Narynskaya Oblast', C Kyrgyzstan
122 H11 **Tyukalinsk** Omskaya Oblast', C Russian Federation
127 V7 **Tyul'gan** Orenburgskaya Oblast', W Russian Federation
122 G11 **Tyumen'** Tyumenskaya Oblast', C Russian Federation
122 H11 **Tyumenskaya Oblast'** ◈ *province* C Russian Federation
147 Y7 **Tyup** *Kir.* Tüp. Issyk-Kul'skaya Oblast', NE Kyrgyzstan
122 L14 **Tyva, Respublika** *prev.* Tannu-Tuva, Tuva, Tuvinskaya ASSR. ◈ *autonomous republic* C Russian Federation
117 N7 **Tyvriv** Vinnyts'ka Oblast', C Ukraine
97 J21 **Tywi** ≈ S Wales, UK
97 I19 **Tywyn** W Wales, UK
83 K20 **Tzaneen** Limpopo, NE South Africa
Tzekung *see* Zigong
115 I20 **Tziá** *prev.* Kéa, Kéos; *anc.* Ceos. *island* Kykládes, Greece, Aegean Sea
41 X12 **Tzucacab** Yucatán, SE Mexico

U

82 B12 **Uaco Cungo** *var.* Waku Kungo, *Port.* Santa Comba. Cuanza Sul, C Angola
UAE *see* United Arab Emirates
191 X7 **Ua Huka** *island* Îles Marquises, NE French Polynesia
58 E10 **Uaiacás** Roraima, N Brazil
Uamba *see* Wamba
Uanle Uen *see* Wanlaweyn
191 W7 **Ua Pu** *island* Îles Marquises, NE French Polynesia
81 L17 **Uar Garas** *spring/well* SW Somalia
58 G12 **Uatumã, Rio** ≈ C Brazil
Ua Uíbh Fhailí *see* Offaly
58 C11 **Uaupés, Rio** *var.* Río Vaupés. ≈ Brazil/Colombia *see also* Vaupés, Río
Uaupés, Rio *see* Vaupés, Río
145 X9 **Uba** ≈ E Kazakhstan
145 N6 **Ubagan** *Kaz.* Obagan. ≈ Kazakhstan/Russian Federation
186 G7 **Ubai** New Britain, E Papua New Guinea
79 J15 **Ubangi** *Fr.* Oubangui. ≈ C Africa
Ubangi-Shari *see* Central African Republic
116 M3 **Ubarts'** *Ukr.* Ubort'. ≈ Belarus/Ukraine *see also* Ubort'
Ubarts' *see* Ubort'
54 F9 **Ubaté** Cundinamarca, C Colombia
60 N10 **Ubatuba** São Paulo, S Brazil
149 R12 **Ubauro** Sind, SE Pakistan
171 Q6 **Ubay** Bohol, C Philippines
103 U14 **Ubaye** ≈ SE France
Ubayid, Wadi al *see* Ubayyiḍ, Wādī al
139 N8 **Ubaylah** W Iraq
139 O10 **Ubayyiḍ, Wādī al** *var.* Wadi al Ubayid. *dry watercourse* SW Iraq
98 L13 **Ubbergen** Gelderland, E Netherlands
164 E13 **Ube** Yamaguchi, Honshū, SW Japan
105 O13 **Úbeda** Andalucía, S Spain
109 V7 **Übelbach** *var.* Markt-Übelbach. Steiermark, SE Austria
59 L20 **Uberaba** Minas Gerais, SE Brazil
57 Q19 **Uberaba, Laguna** ◎ E Bolivia
59 K19 **Uberlândia** Minas Gerais, SE Brazil
101 H24 **Überlingen** Baden-Württemberg, S Germany
77 U16 **Ubiaja** Edo, S Nigeria
104 K3 **Ubiña, Peña** ▲ NW Spain
57 H17 **Ubinas, Volcán** ⛰ S Peru
Ubol Rajadhani/Ubol Ratchathani *see* Ubon Ratchathani
167 P9 **Ubolratna Reservoir** ⊠ C Thailand
167 S10 **Ubon Ratchathani** *var.* Muang Ubon, Ubol Rajadhani, Ubol Ratchathani, Udon Ratchathani. Ubon Ratchathani, E Thailand
119 L20 **Ubort'** *Bel.* Ubarts'. ≈ Belarus/Ukraine *see also* Ubarts'
Ubort' *see* Ubarts'
104 K15 **Ubrique** Andalucía, S Spain
Ubsu-Nur, Ozero *see* Uvs Nuur
79 M18 **Ubundu** Orientale, C Dem. Rep. Congo
146 J13 **Uçajy** *var.* Üchajy, *Rus.* Uch-Adzhi. Mary Welaýaty, C Turkmenistan
137 X11 **Ucar** *Rus.* Udzhary. C Azerbaijan
56 G13 **Ucayali** *off.* Departamento de Ucayali. ◈ *department* E Peru
Ucayali, Departamento de *see* Ucayali
56 F10 **Ucayali, Río** ≈ C Peru
Uccle *see* Ukkel
Uch-Adzhi/Üchajy *see* Uçajy
127 X4 **Uchaly** Respublika Bashkortostan, W Russian Federation
145 W13 **Ucharal** *Kaz.* Üsharal. Almaty, E Kazakhstan
164 C17 **Uchinoura** Kagoshima, Kyūshū, SW Japan
165 R5 **Uchiura-wan** *bay* NW Pacific Ocean
Uchkuduk *see* Uchquduq
Uchkurghan *see* Uchqŭrgon
147 S9 **Uchqo'rg'on** *Rus.* Uchkurghan. Namangan Viloyati, E Uzbekistan
146 K8 **Uchquduq** *Rus.* Uchkuduk. Navoiy Viloyati, N Uzbekistan
147 S9 **Uchqŭrgon** *Rus.* Uchkurghan. Namangan Viloyati, E Uzbekistan
Uchsay *see* Uchsoy
146 G6 **Uchsoy** *Rus.* Uchsay. Qoraqalpog'iston Respublikasi, NW Uzbekistan
Uchtagan Gumy/Uchtagan, Peski *see* Uçtagan Gumy
123 R11 **Uchur** ≈ E Russian Federation
100 O10 **Uckermark** *cultural region* E Germany
10 K17 **Ucluelet** Vancouver Island, British Columbia, SW Canada
146 D10 **Uçtagan Gumy** *var.* Uchtagan Gumy, *Rus.* Peski Uchtagan. *desert* NW Turkmenistan
122 M13 **Uda** ≈ S Russian Federation
123 R12 **Uda** ≈ E Russian Federation
123 N6 **Udachnyy** Respublika Sakha (Yakutiya), NE Russian Federation
155 G21 **Udagamandalam** *var.* Udhagamandalam; *prev.* Ootacamund. Tamil Nādu, SW India
152 F14 **Udaipur** *prev.* Oodeypore. Rājasthān, N India
Udayadhani *see* Uthai Thani
143 N16 **'Udayd, Khawr al** *var.* Khor al Udeid. *inlet* Qatar/Saudi Arabia
112 D11 **Udbina** Lika-Senj, W Croatia
95 I18 **Uddevalla** Västra Götaland, S Sweden
Uddjaur *see* Uddjaure
92 H13 **Uddjaure** *var.* Uddjaur. ◎ N Sweden
Udeid, Khor al *see* 'Udayd, Khawr al
99 K14 **Uden** Noord-Brabant, SE Netherlands
Uden *see* Udenhout
99 J14 **Udenhout** *var.* Uden. Noord-Brabant, S Netherlands
155 H14 **Udgīr** Mahārāshtra, C India
Udhagamandalam *see* Udagamandalam
152 H6 **Udhampur** Jammu and Kashmir, NW India
139 X14 **'Udhaybah, 'Uqlat al** *well* S Iraq
106 J7 **Udine** *anc.* Utina. Friuli-Venezia Giulia, NE Italy
175 T14 **Udintsev Fracture Zone** *tectonic feature* S Pacific Ocean
Udipi *see* Udupi
Udmurtia *see* Udmurtskaya Respublika
127 S2 **Udmurtskaya Respublika** *Eng.* Udmurtia. ◈ *autonomous republic* NW Russian Federation
124 J15 **Udomlya** Tverskaya Oblast', W Russian Federation
Udon Ratchathani *see* Ubon Ratchathani
167 Q8 **Udon Thani** *var.* Ban Mak Khaeng, Udorndhani. Udon Thani, N Thailand
Udorndhani *see* Udon Thani
189 U12 **Udot** *atoll* Chuuk Islands, C Micronesia
123 S12 **Udskaya Guba** *bay* E Russian Federation
155 E19 **Udupi** *var.* Udipi. Karnātaka, SW India
Udzhary *see* Ucar
100 O9 **Uecker** ≈ NE Germany
100 P9 **Ueckermünde** Mecklenburg-Vorpommern, NE Germany
164 M12 **Ueda** *var.* Uyeda. Nagano, Honshū, S Japan
79 L16 **Uele** *var.* Welle. ≈ NE Dem. Rep. Congo
123 W5 **Uelen** Chukotskiy Avtonomnyy Okrug, NE Russian Federation
Uele (upper course) *see* Kibali, Dem. Rep. Congo
Uele (upper course) *see* Uolo, Río, Equatorial Guinea/Gabon
100 J11 **Uelzen** Niedersachsen, N Germany
164 J14 **Ueno** Mie, Honshū, SW Japan
127 V4 **Ufa** Respublika Bashkortostan, W Russian Federation
127 V4 **Ufa** ≈ W Russian Federation
Ufra *see* Kenar
83 C18 **Ugab** ≈ C Namibia
118 D8 **Ugāle** Ventspils, NW Latvia
81 F17 **Uganda** *off.* Republic of Uganda. ◆ *republic* E Africa
Uganda, Republic of *see* Uganda
138 G4 **Ugarit** *Ar.* Ra's Shamrah. *site of ancient city* Al Lādhiqīyah, NW Syria
39 O14 **Ugashik** Alaska, USA
107 Q19 **Ugento** Puglia, SE Italy
105 O15 **Ugíjar** Andalucía, S Spain
103 T11 **Ugine** Savoie, E France
123 R13 **Uglegorsk** Amurskaya Oblast', S Russian Federation
125 V13 **Ugleural'sk** Permskaya Oblast', NW Russian Federation
124 L15 **Uglich** Yaroslavskaya Oblast', W Russian Federation
124 I14 **Uglovka** *var.* Okulovka. Novgorodskaya Oblast', W Russian Federation
126 I4 **Ugra** ≈ W Russian Federation
147 V9 **Ugyut** Narynskaya Oblast', C Kyrgyzstan
111 H19 **Uherské Hradiště** *Ger.* Ungarisch-Hradisch. Zlínský Kraj, E Czech Republic
111 H19 **Uherský Brod** *Ger.* Ungarisch-Brod. Zlínský Kraj, E Czech Republic
111 B17 **Úhlava** *Ger.* Angel. ≈ W Czech Republic
Uhorshchyna *see* Hungary
31 T13 **Uhrichsville** Ohio, N USA
Uhuru Peak *see* Kilimanjaro
96 G8 **Uig** N Scotland, UK
82 B10 **Uíge** *Port.* Carmona, Vila Marechal Carmona. Uíge, NW Angola
82 B10 **Uíge** ◈ *province* N Angola
193 Y15 **Uiha** *island* Ha'apai Group, C Tonga
189 U13 **Uijec** *island* Chuuk, C Micronesia
163 X14 **Ŭijŏngbu** *Jap.* Giseifu. NW South Korea
144 H10 **Uil** *Kaz.* Oyyl. Aktyubinsk, W Kazakhstan
144 H10 **Uil** *Kaz.* Oyyl. ≈ W Kazakhstan
36 M3 **Uinta Mountains** ▲▲ Utah, W USA
83 C18 **Uis** Erongo, NW Namibia
83 I25 **Uitenhage** Eastern Cape, S South Africa
98 H9 **Uitgeest** Noord-Holland, W Netherlands
98 I11 **Uithoorn** Noord-Holland, C Netherlands
98 O4 **Uithuizen** Groningen, NE Netherlands
98 O4 **Uithuizermeeden** Groningen, NE Netherlands
189 R6 **Ujae Atoll** *var.* Wūjae. *atoll* Ralik Chain, W Marshall Islands
111 I16 **Ujazd** Opolskie, S Poland
Új-Becse *see* Novi Bečej
Ujda *see* Oujda
189 N5 **Ujelang Atoll** *var.* Wujlān. *atoll* Ralik Chain, W Marshall Islands
111 N21 **Újfehértó** Szabolcs-Szatmár-Bereg, E Hungary
Újgradiska *see* Nova Gradiška
164 J13 **Uji** *var.* Uzi. Kyōto, Honshū, SW Japan
81 E21 **Ujiji** Kigoma, W Tanzania
154 G10 **Ujjain** *prev.* Ujain. Madhya Pradesh, C India
Újlak *see* Ilok
'Ujmān *see* 'Ajmān
Újmoldova *see* Moldova Nouă
Újszentanna *see* Sântana
Ujungpandang *see* Makassar
Ujung Salang *see* Phuket
Újvidék *see* Novi Sad
UK *see* United Kingdom
154 E11 **Ukāi Reservoir** ⊠ W India
81 G19 **Ukara Island** *island* N Tanzania
'Ukash, Wādī *see* 'Akāsh, Wādī
81 F19 **Ukerewe Island** *island* N Tanzania
139 S9 **Ukhaydhir** C Iraq
153 X13 **Ukhrul** Manipur, NE India
125 S9 **Ukhta** Respublika Komi, NW Russian Federation
34 L6 **Ukiah** California, W USA
32 K12 **Ukiah** Oregon, NW USA
99 G18 **Ukkel** *Fr.* Uccle. Brussels, C Belgium
118 G13 **Ukmergė** *Pol.* Wiłkomierz. Vilnius, C Lithuania
Ukraina *see* Ukraine
116 L6 **Ukraine** *off.* Ukraine, *Rus.* Ukraina, *Ukr.* Ukrayina; *prev.* Ukrainian Soviet Socialist Republic, Ukrainskay S.S.R. ◆ *republic* SE Europe
Ukraine *see* Ukraine
Ukrainian Soviet Socialist Republic *see* Ukraine
Ukrainskay S.S.R/Ukrayina *see* Ukraine
82 B13 **Uku** Cuanza Sul, NW Angola
164 B13 **Uku-jima** *island* Gotō-rettō, SW Japan
83 F20 **Ukwi** Kgalagadi, SW Botswana
118 M13 **Ula** *Rus.* Ulla. Vitsyebskaya Voblasts', N Belarus
136 C16 **Ula** Muğla, SW Turkey
118 M13 **Ula** *Rus.* Ulla. ≈ N Belarus
162 L7 **Ulaanbaatar** *Eng.* Ulan Bator; *prev.* Urga. ● (Mongolia) Töv, C Mongolia
Ulaan-Ereg *see* Bayanmönh
162 E5 **Ulaangom** Uvs, NW Mongolia
162 D5 **Ulaanhus** *var.* Bilüü. Bayan-Ölgiy, W Mongolia
Ulaantolgoy *see* Möst
Ulaan-Uul *see* Öldziyt, Bayanhongor, Mongolia
Ulaan-Uul *see* Erdene, Dornogovi, Mongolia
162 M14 **Ulan** *var.* Otog Qi. Nei Mongol Zizhiqu, N China
159 R10 **Ulan** *var.* Xireg; *prev.* Xiligou. Qinghai, C China
Ulan Bator *see* Ulaanbaatar
162 L13 **Ulan Buh Shamo** *desert* N China
Ulanhad *see* Chifeng
163 T8 **Ulanhot** Nei Mongol Zizhiqu, N China
127 Q14 **Ulan Khol** Respublika Kalmykiya, SW Russian Federation
162 M13 **Ulansuhai Nur** ◎ N China
123 N14 **Ulan-Ude** *prev.* Verkhneudinsk. Respublika Buryatiya, S Russian Federation
159 N12 **Ulan Ul Hu** ◎ C China
187 N9 **Ulawa Island** *island* SE Solomon Islands
138 J7 **'Ulayyānīyah, Bi'r al** *var.* Al Hilbeh. *well* S Syria
123 S12 **Ul'banskiy Zaliv** *strait* E Russian Federation
Ulbo *see* Olib
113 J18 **Ulcinj** S Montenegro
Uldz *see* Norovlin
Uleåborg *see* Oulu
Uleälv *see* Oulujoki
95 G16 **Ulefoss** Telemark, S Norway
Uleträsk *see* Oulujärvi
113 L19 **Ulëz** *var.* Ulëza. Dibër, C Albania
Ulëza *see* Ulëz
95 F22 **Ulfborg** Ringkøbing, W Denmark
98 N13 **Ulft** Gelderland, E Netherlands
162 G7 **Uliastay** *prev.* Jibhalanta. Dzavhan, W Mongolia
188 F8 **Ulimang** Babeldaob, N Palau
67 T10 **Ulindi** ≈ W Dem. Rep. Congo
188 H14 **Ulithi Atoll** *atoll* Caroline Islands, W Micronesia
112 N10 **Uljma** Vojvodina, NE Serbia
144 L11 **Ul'kayak** *Kaz.* Ölkeyek. ≈ C Kazakhstan
145 Q7 **Ul'ken-Karoy, Ozero** ◎ N Kazakhstan
Ülkenözen *see* Bol'shoy Uzen'
Ülkenqobda *see* Bol'shaya Khobda
104 G3 **Ulla** ≈ NW Spain
Ulla *see* Ula
183 S10 **Ulladulla** New South Wales, SE Australia
153 T14 **Ullapara** Rajshahi, W Bangladesh
96 H7 **Ullapool** N Scotland, UK
95 J20 **Ullared** Halland, S Sweden
105 T7 **Ulldecona** Cataluña, NE Spain
92 I9 **Ullsfjorden** *fjord* N Norway
97 K15 **Ullswater** ◎ NW England, UK
101 I22 **Ulm** Baden-Württemberg, S Germany
33 R8 **Ulm** Montana, NW USA
183 V5 **Ulmarra** New South Wales, SE Australia
116 K13 **Ulmeni** Buzău, C Romania
116 K14 **Ulmeni** Călărași, S Romania
42 L7 **Ulmukhuás** Región Autónoma Atlántico Norte, NE Nicaragua
188 C8 **Ulong** *var.* Aulong. *island* Palau Islands, N Palau
83 N14 **Ulonguè** *var.* Ulongwé. Tete, NW Mozambique
Ulongwé *see* Ulonguè
95 K19 **Ulricehamn** Västra Götaland, S Sweden
98 N5 **Ulrum** Groningen, NE Netherlands
163 Z16 **Ulsan** *Jap.* Urusan. SE South Korea
94 D10 **Ulsteinvik** Møre og Romsdal, S Norway
97 D15 **Ulster** ◈ *province* Northern Ireland, UK/Ireland
171 Q10 **Ulu** Pulau Siau, N Indonesia
123 Q11 **Ulu** Respublika Sakha (Yakutiya), NE Russian Federation
42 H5 **Ulúa, Río** ≈ NW Honduras
136 D12 **Ulubat Gölü** ◎ NW Turkey
136 E12 **Uludağ** ▲ NW Turkey
158 D7 **Ulugqat** Xinjiang Uygur Zizhiqu, W China
136 J16 **Ulukışla** Niğde, S Turkey
189 O15 **Ulul** *island* Caroline Islands, C Micronesia
83 L22 **Ulundi** KwaZulu/Natal, E South Africa
158 M3 **Ulungur He** ≈ NW China
158 K2 **Ulungur Hu** ◎ NW China
181 P8 **Uluru** *var.* Ayers Rock. *rocky outcrop* Northern Territory, C Australia
97 K16 **Ulverston** NW England, UK
183 O16 **Ulverstone** Tasmania, SE Australia
94 D13 **Ulvik** Hordaland, S Norway
93 J18 **Ulvila** Länsi-Suomi, W Finland
117 O8 **Ulyanivka** *Rus.* Ul'yanovka. Kirovohrads'ka Oblast', C Ukraine
Ul'yanovka *see* Ulyanivka
127 Q5 **Ul'yanovsk** *prev.* Simbirsk. Ul'yanovskaya Oblast', W Russian Federation
127 Q5 **Ul'yanovskaya Oblast'** ◈ *province* W Russian Federation
145 S10 **Ul'yanovskiy** Karaganda, C Kazakhstan
Ul'yanovskiy Kanal *see* Ul'yanow Kanali
146 M13 **Ul'yanow Kanali** *Rus.* Ul'yanovskiy Kanal. *canal* Turkmenistan/Uzbekistan
Ulyshylanshyq *see* Uly-Zhylanshyk
26 H6 **Ulysses** Kansas, C USA
145 O12 **Ulytau, Gory** ▲▲ C Kazakhstan
145 N11 **Uly-Zhylanshyk** *Kaz.* Ulyshylanshyq. ≈ C Kazakhstan
112 A9 **Umag** *It.* Umago. Istra, NW Croatia
Umago *see* Umag
41 W12 **Umán** Yucatán, SE Mexico
117 O7 **Uman'** *Rus.* Uman. Cherkas'ka Oblast', C Ukraine
189 V13 **Uman** *atoll* Chuuk Islands, C Micronesia
Uman *see* Uman'
Umanak/Umanaq *see* Uummannaq
'Umān, Khalīj *see* Oman, Gulf of
'Umān, Salṭanat *see* Oman
154 K10 **Umaria** Madhya Pradesh, C India
149 R16 **Umar kot** Sind, SE Pakistan
188 B17 **Umatac** SW Guam
188 A17 **Umatac Bay** *bay* SW Guam
139 S6 **Umayqah** C Iraq
124 J5 **Umba** Murmanskaya Oblast', NW Russian Federation
138 I8 **Umbāshī, Khirbat al** *ruins* As Suwaydā', S Syria
80 A12 **Umbelasha** ≈ W Sudan
106 H12 **Umbertide** Umbria, C Italy
61 B17 **Umberto** *var.* Humberto. Santa Fe, C Argentina
186 E7 **Umboi Island** *var.* Rooke Island. *island* C Papua New Guinea
124 J4 **Umbozero, Ozero** ◎ NW Russian Federation
106 H13 **Umbria** ◈ *region* C Italy
Umbrian-Machigian Mountains *see* Umbro-Marchigiano, Appennino
106 I12 **Umbro-Marchigiano, Appennino** *Eng.* Umbrian-Machigian Mountains. ▲▲ C Italy
93 J16 **Umeå** Västerbotten, N Sweden
93 H14 **Umeälven** ≈ N Sweden
39 Q5 **Umiat** Alaska, USA
83 K23 **Umlazi** KwaZulu/Natal, E South Africa
139 X10 **Umm al Baqar, Hawr** *var.* Birkat ad Dawaymah. *spring* S Iraq
141 U12 **Umm al Ḥayt, Wādī** *var.* Wādī Amilḥayt. *seasonal river* SW Oman
Umm al Qaiwain *see* Umm al Qaywayn
143 R15 **Umm al Qaywayn** *var.* Umm al Qaiwain. Umm al Qaywayn, NE United Arab Emirates
139 Q5 **Umm al Tūz** C Iraq
138 J3 **Umm 'Āmūd** Ḥalab, N Syria
141 Y10 **Umm ar Ruṣāṣ** *var.* Umm Ruṣayṣ. W Oman
141 X9 **Ummas Samīn** *sabkha* C Oman
141 V9 **Umm az Zumūl** *oasis* E Saudi Arabia
80 A9 **Umm Buru** Western Darfur, W Sudan
80 A12 **Umm Dafag** Southern Darfur, W Sudan
Umm Durmān *see* Omdurman
138 F9 **Umm el Fahm** Haifa, N Israel
80 F9 **Umm Inderab** Northern Kordofan, C Sudan
80 C10 **Umm Keddada** Northern Darfur, W Sudan
140 J7 **Umm Lajj** Tabūk, W Saudi Arabia
138 L10 **Umm Maḥfur** ≈ N Jordan
139 Y13 **Umm Qaṣr** SE Iraq
Umm Ruṣayṣ *see* Umm ar Ruṣāṣ
80 F11 **Umm Ruwaba** *var.* Umm Ruwābah, Um Ruwāba. Northern Kordofan, C Sudan
Umm Ruwābah *see* Umm Ruwaba
143 N16 **Umm Sa'īd** *var.* Musay'īd. S Qatar
138 K10 **Umm Ṭuways, Wādī** *dry watercourse* N Jordan
38 J17 **Umnak Island** *island* Aleutian Islands, Alaska, USA
32 F13 **Umpqua River** ≈ Oregon, NW USA
82 D13 **Umpulo** Bié, C Angola
154 I12 **Umred** Mahārāshtra, C India
139 Y10 **Umr Sawān, Hawr** ◎ S Iraq
Um Ruwāba *see* Umm Ruwaba
Umtali *see* Mutare
83 J24 **Umtata** Eastern Cape, SE South Africa
77 V17 **Umuahia** Abia, SW Nigeria
60 H10 **Umuarama** Paraná, S Brazil
Umvuma *see* Mvuma
83 K18 **Umzingwani** ≈ S Zimbabwe
112 D11 **Una** ≈ Bosnia and Herzegovina/Croatia
112 E12 **Unac** ≈ W Bosnia and Herzegovina
23 T6 **Unadilla** Georgia, SE USA
18 I10 **Unadilla River** ≈ New York, NE USA
59 L18 **Unaí** Minas Gerais, SE Brazil
39 N10 **Unalakleet** Alaska, USA
38 K17 **Unalaska Island** *island* Aleutian Islands, Alaska, USA
185 I16 **Una, Mount** ▲ South Island, New Zealand
82 N13 **Unango** Niassa, N Mozambique
Unao *see* Unnāo
92 L12 **Unari** Lappi, N Finland
141 O6 **'Unayzah** *var.* Anaiza. Al Qaṣīm, C Saudi Arabia
138 L10 **'Unayzah, Jabal** ▲ Jordan/Saudi Arabia
Unci *see* Almería
57 K19 **Uncía** Potosí, C Bolivia
37 Q7 **Uncompahgre Peak** ▲ Colorado, C USA
37 P6 **Uncompahgre Plateau** *plain* Colorado, C USA
95 L17 **Unden** ◎ S Sweden
28 M4 **Underwood** North Dakota, N USA
171 T13 **Undur** Pulau Seram, E Indonesia

◆ Country
● Country Capital
◇ Dependent Territory
○ Dependent Territory Capital
◈ Administrative Regions
✈ International Airport
▲ Mountain
▲▲ Mountain Range
⛰ Volcano
≈ River
◎ Lake
⊠ Reservoir

V

Country | ◇ Dependent Territory | ◆ Administrative Regions | ▲ Mountain | ≈ Volcano | ⊚ Lake
● Country Capital | ○ Dependent Territory Capital | ✈ International Airport | ▲▲ Mountain Range | ≈ River | ▨ Reservoir

VALDAY – VENDA NOVA

124 *I15* **Valday** Novgorodskaya Oblast', W Russian Federation
124 *I15* **Valdayskaya Vozvyshennost'** *var.* Valdai Hills. *hill range* W Russian Federation
104 *L9* **Valdecañas, Embalse de** ⊠ W Spain
118 *E8* **Valdemārpils** *Ger.* Sassmacken. Talsi, NW Latvia
95 *N18* **Valdemarsvik** Östergötland, S Sweden
105 *N8* **Valdemoro** Madrid, C Spain
105 *O11* **Valdepeñas** Castilla-La Mancha, C Spain
104 *L5* **Valderaduey** ≈ NE Spain
104 *L5* **Valderas** Castilla-León, N Spain
105 *T7* **Valderrobres** *var.* Vall-de-roures. Aragón, NE Spain
63 *K17* **Valdés, Península** *peninsula* SE Argentina
56 *C5* **Valdéz** *var.* Limones. Esmeraldas, NW Ecuador
39 *S11* **Valdez** Alaska, USA
Valdia *see* Weldiya
103 *U11* **Val d'Isère** Savoie, E France
63 *G15* **Valdivia** Los Lagos, C Chile
Valdivia Bank *see* Valdivia Seamount
65 *P17* **Valdivia Seamount** *var.* Valdivia Bank. *undersea feature* E Atlantic Ocean
103 *N4* **Val-d'Oise** ⬖ *department* N France
14 *J8* **Val-d'Or** Québec, SE Canada
23 *U8* **Valdosta** Georgia, SE USA
94 *G13* **Valdres** *physical region* S Norway
32 *L13* **Vale** Oregon, NW USA
116 *F9* **Valea lui Mihai** *Hung.* Érmihályfalva. Bihor, NW Romania
9 *N15* **Valemount** British Columbia, SW Canada
59 *O17* **Valença** Bahia, E Brazil
104 *F4* **Valença do Minho** Viana do Castelo, N Portugal
59 *N14* **Valença do Piauí** Piauí, E Brazil
103 *N8* **Valençay** Indre, C France
103 *R13* **Valence** *anc.* Valentia, Valentia Julia, Ventia. Drôme, E France
105 *S10* **Valencia** País Valenciano, E Spain
54 *K5* **Valencia** Carabobo, N Venezuela
105 *R10* **Valencia** *Cat.* València. ⬖ *province* País Valenciano, E Spain
105 *S10* **Valencia** ✈ Valencia, E Spain
104 *I10* **Valencia de Alcántara** Extremadura, W Spain
104 *L4* **Valencia de Don Juan** Castilla-León, N Spain
105 *U9* **Valencia, Golfo de** *var.* Gulf of Valencia. *gulf* E Spain
Valencia, Gulf of *see* Valencia, Golfo de
97 *A21* **Valencia Island** *Ir.* Dairbhre. *island* SW Ireland
Valencia/València *see* País Valenciano
103 *P2* **Valenciennes** Nord, N France
116 *K13* **Vălenii de Munte** Prahova, SE Romania
Valentia *see* Valence, France
Valentia *see* País Valenciano
Valentia Julia *see* Valence
103 *T8* **Valentigney** Doubs, E France
28 *M12* **Valentine** Nebraska, C USA
24 *J10* **Valentine** Texas, SW USA
Valentine State *see* Oregon
106 *C8* **Valenza** Piemonte, NW Italy
94 *I13* **Våler** Hedmark, S Norway
54 *I6* **Valera** Trujillo, NW Venezuela
192 *M11* **Valerie Guyot** *Undersea Feature* S Pacific Ocean
Valetta *see* Valletta
118 *I7* **Valga** *Ger.* Walk, *Latv.* Valka. Valgamaa, S Estonia
118 *I7* **Valgamaa** *var.* Valga Maakond. ⬖ *province* S Estonia
Valga Maakond *see* Valgamaa
43 *Q15* **Valiente, Península** *peninsula* NW Panama
103 *X16* **Valinco, Golfe de** *gulf* Corse, France, C Mediterranean Sea
112 *L12* **Valjevo** Serbia, W Serbia
Valjok *see* Válljohka
118 *I7* **Valka** *Ger.* Walk. Valka, N Latvia
Valka *see* Valga
93 *L18* **Valkeakoski** Länsi-Suomi, W Finland
93 *M19* **Valkeala** Etelä-Suomi, S Finland
99 *L18* **Valkenburg** Limburg, SE Netherlands
99 *K15* **Valkenswaard** Noord-Brabant, S Netherlands
119 *G15* **Valkininkai** Alytus, S Lithuania
117 *U5* **Valky** Kharkivs'ka Oblast', E Ukraine
41 *Y12* **Valladolid** Yucatán, SE Mexico
104 *M5* **Valladolid** Castilla-León, NW Spain
104 *L5* **Valladolid** ⬖ *province* Castilla-León, N Spain
103 *U15* **Vallauris** Alpes-Maritimes, SE France
Vall-de-roures *see* Valderrobres
Vall d'Uxo *see* La Vall d'Uixó
Vall D'Uxó *see* La Vall D'Uixó
95 *E16* **Valle** Aust-Agder, S Norway
105 *N2* **Valle** Cantabria, N Spain
42 *H8* **Valle** ⬖ *department* S Honduras
105 *N8* **Vallecas** Madrid, C Spain
37 *Q8* **Vallecito Reservoir** ⊠ Colorado, C USA
106 *A7* **Valle d'Aosta** ⬖ *region* NW Italy
41 *O14* **Valle de Bravo** México, S Mexico
55 *N5* **Valle de Guanape** Anzoátegui, N Venezuela
54 *M6* **Valle de La Pascua** Guárico, N Venezuela
54 *B11* **Valle del Cauca** *off.* Departamento del Valle del Cauca. ⬖ *province* W Colombia
Valle del Cauca, Departamento del *see* Valle del Cauca
41 *N13* **Valle de Santiago** Guanajuato, C Mexico
40 *J7* **Valle de Zaragoza** Chihuahua, N Mexico
54 *G5* **Valledupar** Cesar, N Colombia
76 *G10* **Vallée de Ferlo** ≈ NW Senegal
57 *M19* **Vallegrande** Santa Cruz, C Bolivia
41 *P8* **Valle Hermoso** Tamaulipas, C Mexico
35 *N8* **Vallejo** California, W USA
62 *G8* **Vallenar** Atacama, N Chile
95 *O15* **Vallentuna** Stockholm, C Sweden
121 *P16* **Valletta** *prev.* Valetta. ● (Malta) E Malta
27 *N6* **Valley Center** Kansas, C USA
29 *Q5* **Valley City** North Dakota, N USA
32 *I15* **Valley Falls** Oregon, NW USA
Valleyfield *see* Salaberry-de-Valleyfield
21 *S4* **Valley Head** West Virginia, NE USA
25 *T8* **Valley Mills** Texas, SW USA
75 *W10* **Valley of the Kings** *ancient monument* E Egypt
29 *R11* **Valley Springs** South Dakota, N USA
20 *K5* **Valley Station** Kentucky, S USA
9 *O13* **Valleyview** Alberta, W Canada
25 *T5* **Valley View** Texas, SW USA
61 *C21* **Vallimanca, Arroyo** ≈ E Argentina
92 *L9* **Válljohka** *var.* Valjok. Finnmark, N Norway
107 *M19* **Vallo della Lucania** Campania, S Italy
108 *B9* **Vallorbe** Vaud, W Switzerland
105 *V6* **Valls** Cataluña, NE Spain
94 *N11* **Vallsta** Gävleborg, C Sweden
94 *N12* **Vallvik** Gävleborg, C Sweden
9 *T17* **Val Marie** Saskatchewan, S Canada
118 *H7* **Valmiera** *Est.* Volmari, *Ger.* Wolmar. Valmiera, N Latvia
105 *N3* **Valnera** ▲ N Spain
102 *J3* **Valognes** Manche, N France
Valona *see* Vlorë
Valona Bay *see* Vlorës, Gjiri i
104 *G6* **Valongo** *var.* Valongo de Gaia. Porto, N Portugal
Valongo de Gaia *see* Valongo
104 *M5* **Valoria la Buena** Castilla-León, N Spain
119 *J15* **Valozhyn** *Pol.* Wołożyn, *Rus.* Volozhin. Minskaya Voblasts', C Belarus
104 *I5* **Valpaços** Vila Real, N Portugal
62 *G11* **Valparaíso** Valparaíso, C Chile
40 *L11* **Valparaíso** Zacatecas, C Mexico
23 *P8* **Valparaiso** Florida, SE USA
31 *N11* **Valparaiso** Indiana, N USA
62 *G11* **Valparaíso** *off.* Región de Valparaíso. ⬖ *region* C Chile
Valparaíso, Región de *see* Valparaíso
Valpo *see* Valpovo
112 *I9* **Valpovo** *Hung.* Valpo. Osijek-Baranja, E Croatia
103 *R14* **Valréas** Vaucluse, SE France
Vals *see* Vals-Platz
154 *D12* **Valsād** *prev.* Bulsar. Gujarāt, W India
Valsbaai *see* False Bay
171 *T12* **Valse Pisang, Kepulauan** *island group* E Indonesia
108 *H9* **Vals-Platz** *var.* Vals. Graubünden, S Switzerland
171 *X16* **Vals, Tanjung** *headland* Papua, SE Indonesia
93 *N15* **Valtimo** Itä-Suomi, E Finland
115 *D17* **Váltou** ▲▲ C Greece
127 *O12* **Valuyevka** Rostovskaya Oblast', SW Russian Federation
126 *K9* **Valuyki** Belgorodskaya Oblast', W Russian Federation
36 *L2* **Val Verda** Utah, W USA
64 *N12* **Valverde** Hierro, Islas Canarias, Spain, NE Atlantic Ocean
104 *I13* **Valverde del Camino** Andalucía, S Spain
95 *G23* **Vamdrup** Vejle, C Denmark
94 *L12* **Våmhus** Dalarna, C Sweden
93 *K18* **Vammala** Länsi-Soumi, SW Finland
Vámosudvarhely *see* Odorheiu Secuiesc
137 *S14* **Van** Van, E Turkey
25 *V7* **Van** Texas, SW USA
137 *T14* **Van** ⬖ *province* E Turkey
137 *T11* **Vanadzor** *prev.* Kirovakan. N Armenia
25 *U5* **Van Alstyne** Texas, SW USA
33 *W10* **Vananda** Montana, NW USA
116 *I11* **Vânători** *Hung.* Héjjasfalva; *prev.* Vînători. Mureş, C Romania
191 *W12* **Vanavana** *atoll* Îles Tuamotu, SE French Polynesia
Vana-Vändra *see* Vändra
122 *M11* **Vanavara** Evenkiyskiy Avtonomnyy Okrug, C Russian Federation
15 *Q8* **Van Bruyssel** Québec, SE Canada
27 *R10* **Van Buren** Arkansas, C USA
19 *S1* **Van Buren** Maine, NE USA
27 *W7* **Van Buren** Missouri, C USA
19 *T5* **Vanceboro** Maine, NE USA
21 *W10* **Vanceboro** North Carolina, SE USA
21 *O4* **Vanceburg** Kentucky, S USA
Vanch *see* Vanj
10 *L17* **Vancouver** British Columbia, SW Canada
32 *G11* **Vancouver** Washington, NW USA
10 *L17* **Vancouver** ✈ British Columbia, SW Canada
10 *K16* **Vancouver Island** *island* British Columbia, SW Canada
Vanda *see* Vantaa
171 *X13* **Van Daalen** ≈ Papua, E Indonesia
30 *L15* **Vandalia** Illinois, N USA
27 *V3* **Vandalia** Missouri, C USA
31 *R13* **Vandalia** Ohio, N USA
25 *U13* **Vanderbilt** Texas, SW USA
31 *Q10* **Vandercook Lake** Michigan, N USA
10 *L14* **Vanderhoof** British Columbia, SW Canada
18 *K8* **Vanderwhacker Mountain** ▲ New York, NE USA
181 *P1* **Van Diemen Gulf** *gulf* Northern Territory, N Australia
Van Diemen's Land *see* Tasmania
118 *H5* **Vändra** *Ger.* Fennern; *prev.* Vana-Vändra. Pärnumaa, SW Estonia
Vandsburg *see* Więcbork
34 *L4* **Van Duzen River** ≈ California, W USA
118 *F13* **Vandžiogala** Kaunas, C Lithuania
41 *N10* **Vanegas** San Luis Potosí, C Mexico
Vaner, Lake *see* Vänern
95 *K17* **Vänern** *Eng.* Lake Vaner; *prev.* Lake Vener. ◎ S Sweden
95 *J18* **Vänersborg** Västra Götaland, S Sweden
94 *F12* **Vang** Oppland, S Norway
172 *I7* **Vangaindrano** Fianarantsoa, SE Madagascar
137 *S14* **Van Gölü** *Eng.* Lake Van; *anc.* Thospitis. *salt lake* E Turkey
186 *L9* **Vangunu** *island* New Georgia Islands, NW Solomon Islands
24 *J9* **Van Horn** Texas, SW USA
187 *Q11* **Vanikolo** *var.* Vanikoro. *island* Santa Cruz Islands, E Solomon Islands
Vanikoro *see* Vanikolo
186 *A5* **Vanimo** Sandaun, NW Papua New Guinea
123 *T13* **Vanino** Khabarovskiy Kray, SE Russian Federation
155 *G19* **Vānīvilāsa Sāgara** ◎ SW India
147 *S13* **Vanj** *Rus.* Vanch. S Tajikistan
116 *G14* **Vânju Mare** *prev.* Vînju Mare. Mehedinţi, SW Romania
15 *N12* **Vankleek Hill** Ontario, SE Canada
Van, Lake *see* Van Gölü
93 *I16* **Vännäs** Västerbotten, N Sweden
93 *I15* **Vännäsby** Västerbotten, N Sweden
102 *H7* **Vannes** *anc.* Dariorigum. Morbihan, NW France
92 *I8* **Vanna** *island* N Norway
103 *T12* **Vanoise, Massif de la** ▲▲ E France
83 *E24* **Vanrhynsdorp** Western Cape, SW South Africa
21 *P7* **Vansant** Virginia, NE USA
94 *L13* **Vansbro** Dalarna, C Sweden
95 *D18* **Vanse** Vest-Agder, S Norway
9 *P7* **Vansittart Island** *island* Nunavut, NE Canada
93 *M20* **Vantaa** *Swe.* Vanda. Etelä-Suomi, S Finland
93 *L19* **Vantaa** ✈ (Helsinki) Etelä-Suomi, S Finland
32 *J9* **Vantage** Washington, NW USA
187 *Z14* **Vanua Balavu** *prev.* Vanua Mbalavu. *island* Lau Group, E Fiji
187 *R12* **Vanua Lava** *island* Banks Islands, N Vanuatu
187 *Y13* **Vanua Levu** *island* N Fiji
Vanua Mbalavu *see* Vanua Balavu
187 *R12* **Vanuatu** *off.* Republic of Vanuatu; *prev.* New Hebrides. ◆ *republic* SW Pacific Ocean
175 *P8* **Vanuatu** *island group* SW Pacific Ocean
Vanuatu, Republic of *see* Vanuatu
31 *Q12* **Van Wert** Ohio, N USA
187 *Q17* **Vao** Province Sud, S New Caledonia
Vapincum *see* Gap
117 *N7* **Vapnyarka** Vinnyts'ka Oblast', C Ukraine
103 *T15* **Var** ⬖ *department* SE France
103 *U14* **Var** ≈ SE France
95 *J18* **Vara** Västra Götaland, S Sweden
Varadinska Županija *see* Varaždin
118 *J10* **Varakļani** Madona, C Latvia
106 *C7* **Varallo** Piemonte, NE Italy
143 *O5* **Varāmīn** *var.* Veramin. Tehrān, N Iran
153 *N14* **Vārānasi** *prev.* Banaras, Benares, *hist.* Kasi. Uttar Pradesh, N India
125 *T3* **Varandey** Nenetskiy Avtonomnyy Okrug, NW Russian Federation
92 *M8* **Varangerbotn** Finnmark, N Norway
92 *M8* **Varangerfjorden** *Lapp.* Várjjatvuotna. *fjord* N Norway
92 *M8* **Varangerhalvøya** *Lapp.* Várnjárga. *peninsula* N Norway
Varannó *see* Vranov nad Topl'ou
107 *M15* **Varano, Lago di** ◎ SE Italy
118 *J13* **Varapayeva** *Rus.* Voropayevo. Vitsyebskaya Voblasts', NW Belarus
Varasd *see* Varaždin
112 *E7* **Varaždin** *Ger.* Warasdin, *Hung.* Varasd. Varaždin, N Croatia
112 *E7* **Varaždin** *off.* Varadinska Županija. ⬖ *province* N Croatia
106 *C10* **Varazze** Liguria, NW Italy
95 *J20* **Varberg** Halland, S Sweden
149 *P5* **Vardak** *var.* Wardak, *Pash.* Wardag. ⬖ *province* E Afghanistan
113 *Q19* **Vardar** *Gk.* Axiós. ≈ FYR Macedonia/Greece *see also* Axiós
Vardar *see* Axiós
95 *F23* **Varde** Ribe, W Denmark
137 *V12* **Vardenis** E Armenia
92 *N8* **Vardø** *Fin.* Vuoreija. Finnmark, N Norway
115 *E18* **Vardoúsia** ▲▲ C Greece
Vareia *see* Logroño
100 *G10* **Varel** Niedersachsen, NW Germany
119 *G15* **Varėna** *Pol.* Orany. Alytus, S Lithuania
15 *O12* **Varennes** Québec, SE Canada
103 *P10* **Varennes-sur-Allier** Allier, C France
112 *I12* **Vareš** ⬖ Federacija Bosna I Hercegovina, E Bosnia and Herzegovina
106 *D7* **Varese** Lombardia, N Italy
116 *J12* **Vârful Moldoveanu** *var.* Moldoveanul; *prev.* Vîrful Moldoveanu. ▲ C Romania
Varganzi *see* Warganza
95 *J18* **Vårgårda** Västra Götaland, S Sweden
54 *L4* **Vargas** *off.* Estado Vargas. ⬖ *state* N Venezuela
95 *J18* **Vargön** Västra Götaland, S Sweden
95 *C17* **Varhaug** Rogaland, S Norway
Várjjatvuotna *see* Varangerfjorden
93 *N17* **Varkaus** Itä-Suomi, C Finland
92 *J2* **Varmahlidh** Nordhurland Vestra, N Iceland
95 *J15* **Värmland** ⬖ *county* C Sweden
95 *K16* **Värmlandsnäs** *peninsula* S Sweden
114 *N8* **Varna** *prev.* Stalin; *anc.* Odessus. Varna, E Bulgaria
114 *N8* **Varna** ⬖ *province* E Bulgaria
114 *N8* **Varna** ✈ Varna, E Bulgaria
95 *L20* **Värnamo** Jönköping, S Sweden
114 *N8* **Varnenski Zaliv** *prev.* Stalinski Zaliv. *bay* E Bulgaria
114 *N8* **Varnensko Ezero** *estuary* E Bulgaria
118 *D11* **Varniai** Telšiai, W Lithuania
Várnjárga *see* Varangerhalvøya
Varnoús *see* Baba
111 *D14* **Varnsdorf** *Ger.* Warnsdorf. Ústecký Kraj, NW Czech Republic
111 *I23* **Várpalota** Veszprém, W Hungary
Varshava *see* Warszawa
118 *K6* **Värska** Põlvamaa, SE Estonia
98 *N12* **Varsseveld** Gelderland, E Netherlands
115 *D19* **Vartholomió** *prev.* Vartholomión. Dytikí Ellás, S Greece
Vartholomión *see* Vartholomió
137 *Q14* **Varto** Muş, E Turkey
95 *K18* **Vartofta** Västra Götaland, S Sweden
93 *O17* **Värtsilä** Itä-Suomi, E Finland
Värtsilä *see* Vyartsilya
117 *R4* **Varva** Chernihivs'ka Oblast', NE Ukraine
59 *H18* **Várzea Grande** Mato Grosso, SW Brazil
106 *D9* **Varzi** Lombardia, N Italy
Varzimanor Ayni *see* Ayní
124 *K5* **Varzuga** ≈ NW Russian Federation
103 *P8* **Varzy** Nièvre, C France
111 *G23* **Vas** *off.* Vas Megye. ⬖ *county* W Hungary
Vasa *see* Vaasa
190 *A9* **Vasafua** *island* Funafuti Atoll, C Tuvalu
111 *O21* **Vásárosnamény** Szabolcs-Szatmár-Bereg, E Hungary
104 *H13* **Vascão, Ribeira de** ≈ S Portugal
116 *G10* **Vaşcău** *Hung.* Vaskoh. Bihor, NE Romania
Vascongadas, Provincias *see* País Vasco
Vashess Bay *see* Vaskess Bay
Väsht *see* Khāsh
Vasilevichi *see* Vasilyevichy
115 *G14* **Vasiliká** Kentrikí Makedonía, NE Greece
115 *C18* **Vasilikí** Lefkáda, Iónioi Nísoi, Greece, C Mediterranean Sea
115 *K25* **Vasilikí** Kríti, Greece, E Mediterranean Sea
119 *G16* **Vasilishki** *Pol.* Wasiliszki, *Rus.* Vasilishki. Hrodzyenskaya Voblasts', W Belarus
Vasil Kolarov *see* Pamporovo
Vasil'kov *see* Vasyl'kiv
119 *N19* **Vasilyevichy** *Rus.* Vasilevichi. Homyel'skaya Voblasts', SE Belarus
191 *Y3* **Vaskess Bay** *var.* Vashess Bay. *bay* Kiritimati, E Kiribati
Vaskoh *see* Vaşcău
Vaskohsziklás *see* Ştei
116 *M10* **Vaslui** Vaslui, C Romania
116 *L11* **Vaslui** ⬖ *county* NE Romania
Vas Megye *see* Vas
31 *R8* **Vassar** Michigan, N USA
95 *E15* **Vassdalsegga** ▲ S Norway
60 *P9* **Vassouras** Rio de Janeiro, SE Brazil
95 *N15* **Västerås** Västmanland, C Sweden
93 *G15* **Västerbotten** ⬖ *county* N Sweden
94 *K12* **Västerdalälven** ≈ C Sweden
95 *O16* **Västerhaninge** Stockholm, C Sweden
94 *M10* **Västernorrland** ⬖ *county* C Sweden
95 *N19* **Västervik** Kalmar, S Sweden
95 *M15* **Västmanland** ⬖ *county* C Sweden
107 *L15* **Vasto** *anc.* Histonium. Abruzzo, C Italy
95 *J19* **Västra Götaland** ⬖ *county* S Sweden
95 *J16* **Västra Silen** ◎ S Sweden
111 *G23* **Vasvár** *Ger.* Eisenburg. Vas, W Hungary
117 *U9* **Vasylivka** Zaporiz'ka Oblast', SE Ukraine
117 *O5* **Vasyl'kiv** *var.* Vasil'kov. Kyyivs'ka Oblast', N Ukraine
122 *I11* **Vasyugan** ≈ C Russian Federation
103 *N8* **Vatan** Indre, C France
Vaté *see* Éfaté
115 *C18* **Vathy** *prev.* Itháki. Itháki, Iónia Nisiá, Greece, C Mediterranean Sea
107 *G15* **Vatican City** *off.* Vatican City State. ◆ *papal state* S Europe
Vatican City State *see* Vatican City
107 *M22* **Vaticano, Capo** *headland* S Italy
92 *K3* **Vatnajökull** *glacier* SE Iceland
95 *P15* **Vätö** Stockholm, C Sweden
187 *Z16* **Vatoa** *island* Lau Group, SE Fiji
172 *J5* **Vatomandry** Toamasina, E Madagascar
116 *J9* **Vatra Dornei** *Ger.* Dorna Watra. Suceava, NE Romania
116 *J9* **Vatra Moldoviţei** Suceava, NE Romania
Vatter, Lake *see* Vättern
95 *L18* **Vättern** *Eng.* Lake Vatter; *prev.* Lake Vetter. ◎ S Sweden
187 *X5* **Vatulele** *island* SW Fiji
117 *P7* **Vatutine** Cherkas'ka Oblast', C Ukraine
187 *W15* **Vatu Vara** *island* Lau Group, E Fiji
103 *R14* **Vaucluse** ⬖ *department* SE France
103 *S5* **Vaucouleurs** Meuse, NE France
108 *B9* **Vaud** *Ger.* Waadt. ⬖ *canton* SW Switzerland
15 *N12* **Vaudreuil** Québec, SE Canada
37 *T12* **Vaughn** New Mexico, SW USA
54 *I14* **Vaupés** *off.* Comisaría del Vaupés. ⬖ *province* SE Colombia
Vaupés, Comisaría del *see* Vaupés
54 *J13* **Vaupés, Río** *var.* Rio Uaupés. ≈ Brazil/Colombia *see also* Uaupés, Rio
Vaupés, Río *see* Uaupés, Rio
103 *Q15* **Vauvert** Gard, S France
9 *R17* **Vauxhall** Alberta, SW Canada
99 *K23* **Vaux-sur-Sûre** Luxembourg, SE Belgium
172 *J4* **Vavatenina** Toamasina, E Madagascar
193 *Y14* **Vava'u Group** *island group* N Tonga
76 *M16* **Vavoua** W Ivory Coast
127 *S2* **Vavozh** Udmurtskaya Respublika, NW Russian Federation
155 *K23* **Vavuniya** Northern Province, N Sri Lanka
119 *G17* **Vawkavysk** *Pol.* Wołkowysk, *Rus.* Volkovysk. Hrodzyenskaya Voblasts', W Belarus
119 *F17* **Vawkavyskaye Wzvyshsha** *Rus.* Volkovyskiye Vysoty. *hill range* W Belarus
95 *P15* **Vaxholm** Stockholm, C Sweden
95 *L21* **Växjö** *var.* Vexiö. Kronoberg, S Sweden
125 *T1* **Vaygach, Ostrov** *island* NW Russian Federation
137 *V13* **Vayk'** *prev.* Azizbekov. SE Armenia
Vazáš *see* Vittangi
125 *P8* **Vazhgort** *prev.* Chasovo. Respublika Komi, NW Russian Federation
45 *V10* **V. C. Bird** ✈ (St. John's) Antigua, Antigua and Barbuda
95 *C16* **Veavågen** Rogaland, S Norway
29 *Q7* **Veblen** South Dakota, N USA
98 *N9* **Vecht** *Ger.* Vechte. ≈ Germany/Netherlands *see also* Vechte
Vecht *see* Vechte
100 *G12* **Vechta** Niedersachsen, NW Germany
100 *E12* **Vechte** *Dut.* Vecht. ≈ Germany/Netherlands *see also* Vecht
Vechte *see* Vecht
118 *I8* **Vecpiebalga** Cēsis, C Latvia
118 *G9* **Vecumnieki** Bauska, C Latvia
Vedāvati *see* Hagari
95 *J20* **Veddige** Halland, S Sweden
116 *J15* **Vedea** ≈ S Romania
127 *P16* **Vedeno** Chechenskaya Respublika, SW Russian Federation
95 *C16* **Vedvågen** Rogaland, S Norway
98 *O6* **Veendam** Groningen, NE Netherlands
98 *K12* **Veenendaal** Utrecht, C Netherlands
99 *E14* **Veere** Zeeland, SW Netherlands
24 *M2* **Vega** Texas, SW USA
92 *E13* **Vega** *island* C Norway
45 *T5* **Vega Baja** C Puerto Rico
38 *D17* **Vega Point** *headland* Kiska Island, Alaska, USA
95 *F17* **Vegår** ◎ S Norway
99 *K14* **Veghel** Noord-Brabant, S Netherlands
Veglia *see* Krk
114 *E13* **Vegorítida, Límni** *var.* Límni Vegorítis. ◎ N Greece
Vegorítis, Límni *see* Vegorítida, Límni
9 *Q14* **Vegreville** Alberta, SW Canada
95 *K21* **Veinge** Halland, S Sweden
61 *B21* **Veinticinco de Mayo** *var.* 25 de Mayo. Buenos Aires, E Argentina
63 *I14* **Veinticinco de Mayo** La Pampa, C Argentina
119 *F15* **Veisiejai** Alytus, S Lithuania
95 *F23* **Vejen** Ribe, W Denmark
104 *K16* **Vejer de la Frontera** Andalucía, S Spain
95 *G23* **Vejle** Vejle, C Denmark
95 *F23* **Vejle** *off.* Vejle Amt. ⬖ *county* C Denmark
Vejle Amt *see* Vejle
114 *M7* **Vekilski** Shumen, NE Bulgaria
54 *G3* **Vela, Cabo de la** *headland* NE Colombia
Vela Goa *see* Goa
113 *F15* **Vela Luka** Dubrovnik-Neretva, S Croatia
61 *G19* **Velázquez** Rocha, E Uruguay
101 *E15* **Velbert** Nordrhein-Westfalen, W Germany
109 *S9* **Velden** Kärnten, S Austria
Veldes *see* Bled
99 *K15* **Veldhoven** Noord-Brabant, S Netherlands
112 *C11* **Velebit** ▲▲ C Croatia
114 *N11* **Veleka** ≈ SE Bulgaria
109 *V10* **Velenje** *Ger.* Wöllan. N Slovenia
190 *E12* **Vele, Pointe** *headland* Île Futuna, S Wallis and Futuna
113 *O18* **Veles** *Turk.* Köprülü. C FYR Macedonia
113 *M20* **Velešta** SW FYR Macedonia
115 *F16* **Velestíno** *prev.* Velestínon. Thessalía, C Greece
Velestínon *see* Velestíno
Velevshchina *see* Vyelyewshchyna
54 *F9* **Vélez** Santander, C Colombia
105 *Q13* **Vélez Blanco** Andalucía, S Spain
104 *M17* **Vélez de la Gomera, Peñon de** *island group* S Spain
105 *N15* **Vélez-Málaga** Andalucía, S Spain
105 *Q13* **Vélez Rubio** Andalucía, S Spain
Velha Goa *see* Goa
Velho *see* Porto Velho
112 *E8* **Velika Gorica** Zagreb, N Croatia
112 *C9* **Velika Kapela** ▲▲ NW Croatia
Velika Kikinda *see* Kikinda
112 *D10* **Velika Kladuša** ⬖ Federacija Bosna I Hercegovina, NW Bosnia and Herzegovina
112 *N11* **Velika Morava** *var.* Glavn'a Morava, Morava, *Ger.* Grosse Morava. ≈ C Serbia
112 *N12* **Velika Plana** Serbia, C Serbia
109 *U10* **Velika Raduha** ▲ N Slovenia
123 *V7* **Velikaya** ≈ NE Russian Federation
124 *F15* **Velikaya** ≈ W Russian Federation
Velikaya Berestovitsa *see* Vyalikaya Byerastavitsa
Velikaya Lepetikha *see* Velyka Lepetykha
Veliki Bečkerek *see* Zrenjanin
112 *P12* **Veliki Krš** *var.* Stol. ▲ E Serbia
114 *L8* **Veliki Preslav** *prev.* Preslav. Shumen, NE Bulgaria
112 *B9* **Veliki Risnjak** ▲ NW Croatia
109 *T13* **Veliki Snežnik** *Ger.* Schneeberg, *It.* Monte Nevoso. ▲ SW Slovenia
112 *J13* **Veliki Stolac** ▲ E Bosnia and Herzegovina
Velikiy Bor *see* Vyaliki Bor
124 *G16* **Velikiye Luki** Pskovskaya Oblast', W Russian Federation
124 *H14* **Velikiy Novgorod** *prev.* Novgorod. Novgorodskaya Oblast', W Russian Federation
125 *P12* **Velikiy Ustyug** Vologodskaya Oblast', NW Russian Federation
112 *N11* **Veliko Gradište** Serbia, NE Serbia
155 *I18* **Velikonda Range** ▲▲ SE India
Veliko Tărnovo *see* Veliko Tŭrnovo
114 *K9* **Veliko Tŭrnovo** *prev.* Tirnovo, Trnovo, Tŭrnovo, Veliko Tărnovo. Veliko Tŭrnovo, N Bulgaria
114 *K8* **Veliko Tŭrnovo** ⬖ *province* N Bulgaria
Velikovec *see* Völkermarkt
125 *R5* **Velikovisochnoye** Nenetskiy Avtonomnyy Okrug, NW Russian Federation
76 *H12* **Vélingara** C Senegal
76 *H11* **Vélingara** S Senegal
114 *H11* **Velingrad** Pazardzhik, C Bulgaria
126 *H3* **Velizh** Smolenskaya Oblast', W Russian Federation
111 *F16* **Velká Deštná** *var.* Deštná, Grosskoppe, *Ger.* Deschnaer Koppe. ▲ NE Czech Republic
111 *F18* **Velké Meziříčí** *Ger.* Grossmeseritsch. Vysočina, C Czech Republic
92 *N1* **Velkomstpynten** *headland* NW Svalbard
111 *K21* **Veľký Krtíš** Banskobystrický Kraj, C Slovakia
186 *J8* **Vella Lavella** *var.* Mbilua. *island* New Georgia Islands, NW Solomon Islands
107 *I15* **Velletri** Lazio, C Italy
95 *K23* **Vellinge** Skåne, S Sweden
155 *I19* **Vellore** Tamil Nādu, SE India
Velobriga *see* Viana do Castelo
115 *G21* **Velopoúla** *island* S Greece
98 *M12* **Velp** Gelderland, SE Netherlands
Velsen *see* Velsen-Noord
98 *H9* **Velsen-Noord** *var.* Velsen. Noord-Holland, W Netherlands
125 *N12* **Vel'sk** *var.* Velsk. Arkhangel'skaya Oblast', NW Russian Federation
Velsuna *see* Orvieto
98 *K10* **Veluwemeer** *lake channel* C Netherlands
28 *M3* **Velva** North Dakota, N USA
Velvendos/Velvendós *see* Velventós
115 *E14* **Velventós** *var.* Velvendos, Velvendós. Dytikí Makedonía, N Greece
117 *S5* **Velyka Bahachka** Poltavs'ka Oblast', C Ukraine
117 *S9* **Velyka Lepetykha** *Rus.* Velikaya Lepetikha. Khersons'ka Oblast', S Ukraine
117 *O10* **Velyka Mykhaylivka** Odes'ka Oblast', SW Ukraine
117 *W8* **Velyka Novosilka** Donets'ka Oblast', E Ukraine
117 *S9* **Velyka Oleksandrivka** Khersons'ka Oblast', S Ukraine
117 *T4* **Velyka Pysanivka** Sums'ka Oblast', NE Ukraine
116 *G6* **Velykyy Bereznyy** Zakarpats'ka Oblast', W Ukraine
117 *W4* **Velykyy Burluk** Kharkivs'ka Oblast', E Ukraine
Velykyy Tokmak *see* Tokmak
173 *P7* **Vema Fracture Zone** *tectonic feature* W Indian Ocean
65 *P18* **Vema Seamount** *undersea feature* SW Indian Ocean
93 *F17* **Vemdalen** Jämtland, C Sweden
95 *N19* **Vena** Kalmar, S Sweden
41 *N11* **Venado** San Luis Potosí, C Mexico
62 *L11* **Venado Tuerto** Entre Ríos, E Argentina
61 *A19* **Venado Tuerto** Santa Fe, C Argentina
107 *K16* **Venafro** Molise, C Italy
55 *Q9* **Venamo, Cerro** ▲ E Venezuela
106 *B8* **Venaria** Piemonte, NW Italy
103 *U15* **Vence** Alpes-Maritimes, SE France
104 *H5* **Venda Nova** Vila Real, N Portugal

◆ Country
● Country Capital
◇ Dependent Territory
○ Dependent Territory Capital
⬖ Administrative Regions
✈ International Airport
▲ Mountain
▲▲ Mountain Range
Volcano
≈ River
◎ Lake
⊠ Reservoir

Vendas Novas – Villa Cecilia

104 G11 Vendas Novas Évora, S Portugal
102 J9 Vendée ◐ department NW France
103 Q6 Vendeuvre-sur-Barse Aube, NE France
102 M7 Vendôme Loir-et-Cher, C France
Vendedig see Venezia
Vener, Lake see Vänern
106 I8 Veneta, Laguna lagoon NE Italy
Venetia see Venezia
39 S7 Venetie Alaska, USA
106 H8 Veneto var. Venezia Euganea. ◐ region NE Italy
114 M7 Venets Shumen, NE Bulgaria
126 L5 Venev Tul'skaya Oblast', W Russian Federation
106 I8 Venezia Eng. Venice, Fr. Venise, Ger. Venedig; anc. Venetia. Veneto, NE Italy
Venezia Euganea see Veneto
Venezia, Golfo di see Venice, Gulf of
Venezia Tridentina see Trentino-Alto Adige
54 K8 Venezuela off. Republic of Venezuela; prev. Estados Unidos de Venezuela, United States of Venezuela. ◆ republic N South America
Venezuela, Cordillera de see Costa, Cordillera de la
Venezuela, Estados Unidos de see Venezuela
54 I4 Venezuela, Golfo de Eng. Gulf of Maracaibo, Gulf of Venezuela. gulf NW Venezuela
Venezuela, Gulf of see Venezuela, Golfo de
64 F11 Venezuelan Basin undersea feature E Caribbean Sea
Venezuela, Republic of see Venezuela
Venezuela, United States of see Venezuela
155 D16 Vengurla Mahārāshtra, W India
39 O15 Veniaminof, Mount ▲ Alaska, USA
23 V14 Venice Florida, SE USA
22 L10 Venice Louisiana, S USA
Venice see Venezia
106 J8 Venice, Gulf of It. Golfo di Venezia, Slvn. Beneški Zaliv. gulf N Adriatic Sea
Venise see Venezia
94 K13 Venjan Dalarna, C Sweden
94 K13 Venjansjön ◎ C Sweden
155 J18 Venkatagiri Andhra Pradesh, E India
99 M15 Venlo prev. Venloo. Limburg, SE Netherlands
Venloo see Venlo
95 E18 Vennesla Vest-Agder, S Norway
107 M17 Venosa anc. Venusia. Basilicata, S Italy
Venoste, Alpi see Ötztaler Alpen
Venraij see Venray
99 M14 Venray var. Venraij. Limburg, SE Netherlands
118 C8 Venta Ger. Windau. ≈ Latvia/Lithuania
Venta Belgarum see Winchester
40 G9 Ventana, Punta Arena de la var. Punta de la Ventana. headland W Mexico
Ventana, Punta de la see Ventana, Punta Arena de la
61 B23 Ventana, Sierra de la hill range E Argentina
Ventia see Valence
191 S11 Vent, Îles du var. Windward Islands. island group Archipel de la Société, W French Polynesia
191 R10 Vent, Îles Sous le var. Leeward Islands. island group Archipel de la Société, W French Polynesia
106 B11 Ventimiglia Liguria, NW Italy
97 M24 Ventnor S England, UK
18 J17 Ventnor City New Jersey, NE USA
103 S14 Ventoux, Mont ▲ SE France
118 C8 Ventspils Ger. Windau. Ventspils, NW Latvia
54 M10 Ventuari, Río ≈ S Venezuela
35 R15 Ventura California, W USA
182 F8 Venus Bay South Australia
Venusia see Venosa
191 P7 Vénus, Pointe var. Pointe Tataaihoa. headland Tahiti, W French Polynesia
41 V16 Venustiano Carranza Chiapas, SE Mexico
41 N7 Venustiano Carranza, Presa ▣ NE Mexico
61 B15 Vera Santa Fe, C Argentina
105 Q14 Vera Andalucía, S Spain
63 K18 Vera, Bahía bay E Argentina
41 R14 Veracruz var. Veracruz Llave. Veracruz-Llave, E Mexico
Veracruz see Veracruz-Llave
41 Q13 Veracruz-Llave var. Veracruz. ◐ state E Mexico
Veracruz Llave see Veracruz
43 Q16 Veraguas off. Provincia de Veraguas. ◐ province W Panama
Veraguas, Provincia de see Veraguas
Veramin see Varāmīn
154 B12 Verāval Gujarāt, W India
106 C6 Verbania Piemonte, NW Italy
107 N20 Verbicaro Calabria, SW Italy
108 D11 Verbier Valais, SW Switzerland
Vercellae see Vercelli
106 C8 Vercelli anc. Vercellae. Piemonte, NW Italy
103 S13 Vercors physical region E France
Verdal see Verdalsøra
93 E16 Verdalsøra var. Verdal. Nord-Trøndelag, C Norway
Verde, Cabo see Cape Verde
44 J5 Verde, Cape headland Long Island, C Bahamas
104 M2 Verde, Costa coastal region N Spain
Verde Grande, Río/Verde Grande y de Belem, Río see Verde, Río
100 H11 Verden Niedersachsen, NW Germany
57 P16 Verde, Río ≈ Bolivia/Brazil
59 J19 Verde, Rio ≈ SE Brazil
40 M12 Verde, Río var. Río Verde Grande, Río Verde Grande y de Belem. ≈ C Mexico
41 Q16 Verde, Río ≈ SE Mexico
36 L13 Verde River ≈ Arizona, SW USA
Verdhikoúsa/Verdhikoússa see Verdikoússa
27 Q8 Verdigris River ≈ Kansas/Oklahoma, C USA
115 E15 Verdikoússa var. Verdhikoúsa, Verdhikoússa. Thessalía, C Greece
103 S15 Verdon ≈ SE France
15 O12 Verdun Québec, SE Canada
103 S4 Verdun var. Verdun-sur-Meuse; anc. Verodunum. Meuse, NE France
Verdun-sur-Meuse see Verdun
83 J21 Vereeniging Gauteng, NE South Africa
Veremeyki see Vyeramyeyki
125 T14 Vereshchagino Permskaya Oblast', NW Russian Federation
76 G14 Verga, Cap headland W Guinea
61 G18 Vergara Treinta y Tres, E Uruguay
108 G11 Vergeletto Ticino, S Switzerland
18 L8 Vergennes Vermont, NE USA
Veria see Véroia
104 I5 Verín Galicia, NW Spain
Verin T'alin see T'alin
118 K6 Veriora Põlvamaa, SE Estonia
117 T7 Verkhivtseve Dnipropetrovs'ka Oblast', E Ukraine
Verkhnedvinsk see Vyerkhnyadzvinsk
122 K10 Verkhneimbatsk Krasnoyarskiy Kray, N Russian Federation
124 I3 Verkhnetulomskiy Murmanskaya Oblast', NW Russian Federation
124 I3 Verkhnetulomskoye Vodokhranilishche ▣ NW Russian Federation
Verkhneudinsk see Ulan-Ude
123 P10 Verkhnevilyuysk Respublika Sakha (Yakutiya), NE Russian Federation
127 W5 Verkhniy Avzyan Respublika Bashkortostan, W Russian Federation
127 Q11 Verkhniy Baskunchak Astrakhanskaya Oblast', SW Russian Federation
127 W3 Verkhniye Kigi Respublika Bashkortostan, W Russian Federation
117 T9 Verkhniy Rohachyk Khersons'ka Oblast', S Ukraine
123 Q11 Verkhnyaya Amga Respublika Sakha (Yakutiya), NE Russian Federation
125 V6 Verkhnyaya Inta Respublika Komi, NW Russian Federation
125 O10 Verkhnyaya Toyma Arkhangel'skaya Oblast', NW Russian Federation
126 K6 Verkhov'ye Orlovskaya Oblast', W Russian Federation
116 I8 Verkhovyna Ivano-Frankivs'ka Oblast', W Ukraine
123 P8 Verkhoyanskiy Khrebet ▲▲ NE Russian Federation
117 T7 Verkn'odniprovs'k Dnipropetrovs'ka Oblast', E Ukraine
101 G14 Verl Nordrhein-Westfalen, NW Germany
92 N1 Verlegenhuken headland N Svalbard
82 A9 Vermelha, Ponta headland NW Angola
103 P7 Vermenton Yonne, C France
9 R14 Vermilion Alberta, SW Canada
31 T11 Vermilion Ohio, N USA
22 I10 Vermilion Bay bay Louisiana, S USA
29 V4 Vermilion Lake ◎ Minnesota, N USA
14 F9 Vermilion River ≈ Ontario, S Canada
30 L12 Vermilion River ≈ Illinois, N USA
29 R12 Vermillion South Dakota, N USA
29 R12 Vermillion River ≈ South Dakota, N USA
15 O9 Vermillon, Rivière ≈ Québec, SE Canada
115 E14 Vérmio ▲▲ N Greece
18 L8 Vermont off. State of Vermont, also known as Green Mountain State. ◐ state NE USA
113 K16 Vermosh var. Vermoshi. Shkodër, N Albania
Vermoshi see Vermosh
37 O3 Vernal Utah, W USA
14 G11 Verner Ontario, S Canada
102 M5 Verneuil-sur-Avre Eure, N France
114 D13 Vérno ▲▲ N Greece
9 N17 Vernon British Columbia, SW Canada
102 M4 Vernon Eure, N France
23 N3 Vernon Alabama, S USA
31 P15 Vernon Indiana, N USA
25 Q4 Vernon Texas, SW USA
32 G10 Vernonia Oregon, NW USA
14 G12 Vernon, Lake ◎ Ontario, S Canada
22 G7 Vernon Lake ▣ Louisiana, S USA
23 Y13 Vero Beach Florida, SE USA
Verőcze see Virovitica
Verodunum see Verdun
115 E14 Véroia var. Veria, Vérroia, Turk. Karaferiye. Kentrikí Makedonía, N Greece
106 E8 Verolanuova Lombardia, N Italy
14 K14 Verona Ontario, SE Canada
106 G8 Verona Veneto, NE Italy
29 P6 Verona North Dakota, N USA
30 L9 Verona Wisconsin, N USA
61 E20 Verónica Buenos Aires, E Argentina
22 J9 Verret, Lake ◎ Louisiana, S USA
Vérroia see Véroia
103 N5 Versailles Yvelines, N France
31 P15 Versailles Indiana, N USA
20 M5 Versailles Kentucky, S USA
27 U5 Versailles Missouri, C USA
31 Q13 Versailles Ohio, N USA
Versecz see Vršac
108 A10 Versoix Genève, SW Switzerland
15 Z6 Verte, Pointe headland Québec, SE Canada
111 I22 Vértes ▲▲ NW Hungary
44 G6 Vertientes Camagüey, C Cuba
114 G13 Vertískos ▲▲ N Greece
102 I8 Vertou Loire-Atlantique, NW France
Verulamium see St Albans
99 L19 Verviers Liège, E Belgium
103 Y14 Vescovato Corse, France, C Mediterranean Sea
99 L20 Vesdre ≈ E Belgium
117 U10 Vesele Rus. Veseloye. Zaporiz'ka Oblast', S Ukraine
111 D18 Veselí nad Lužnicí var. Weseli an der Lainsitz, Ger. Frohenbruck. Jihočeský Kraj, S Czech Republic
114 M9 Veselinovo Shumen, NE Bulgaria
126 L12 Veselovskoye Vodokhranilishche ▣ SW Russian Federation
Veseloye see Vesele
117 Q9 Veselynove Mykolayivs'ka Oblast', S Ukraine
Veseya see Vyasyeya
126 M10 Veshenskaya Rostovskaya Oblast', SW Russian Federation
127 Q5 Veshkayma Ul'yanovskaya Oblast', W Russian Federation
Vesisaari see Vadsø
Vesontio see Besançon
103 T7 Vesoul anc. Vesulium, Vesulum. Haute-Saône, E France
95 J20 Vessigebro Halland, S Sweden
95 D17 Vest-Agder ◐ county S Norway
23 P4 Vestavia Hills Alabama, S USA
84 F6 Vesterålen island NW Norway
92 G10 Vesterålen island group N Norway
87 V3 Vestervig Viborg, NW Denmark
92 H2 Vestfirdhir ◐ region NW Iceland
92 G11 Vestfjorden fjord C Norway
95 G16 Vestfold ◐ county S Norway
Vestmanhavn see Vestmanna
95 B18 Vestmanna Dan. Vestmanhavn. Streymoy, N Faeroe Islands
92 I4 Vestmannaeyjar Sudhurland, S Iceland
94 E9 Vestnes Møre og Romsdal, S Norway
95 I23 Vestsjælland off. Vestsjællands Amt. ◐ county E Denmark
Vestsjællands Amt see Vestsjælland
92 H3 Vesturland ◐ region W Iceland
92 G11 Vestvågøya island C Norway
Vesulium/Vesulum see Vesoul
Vesuna see Périgueux
107 K17 Vesuvio Eng. Vesuvius. Volcano S Italy
Vesuvius see Vesuvio
124 K14 Ves'yegonsk Tverskaya Oblast', W Russian Federation
111 I23 Veszprém Ger. Veszprim. Veszprém, W Hungary
111 H23 Veszprém off. Veszprém Megye. ◐ county W Hungary
Veszprém Megye see Veszprém
Veszprim see Veszprém
Vetka see Vyetka
95 M19 Vetlanda Jönköping, S Sweden
127 P1 Vetluga Nizhegorodskaya Oblast', W Russian Federation
125 P14 Vetluga ≈ NW Russian Federation
125 O14 Vetluzhskiy Kostromskaya Oblast', NW Russian Federation
127 P2 Vetluzhskiy Nizhegorodskaya Oblast', W Russian Federation
107 H14 Vetralla Lazio, C Italy
114 M9 Vetren prev. Zhitarovo. Burgas, E Bulgaria
114 M8 Vetrino Varna, E Bulgaria
Vetrino see Vyetryna
122 L7 Vetrovaya, Gora ▲ N Russian Federation
Vetter, Lake see Vättern
106 J13 Vettore, Monte ▲ C Italy
99 A17 Veurne var. Furnes. West-Vlaanderen, W Belgium
31 Q15 Vevay Indiana, N USA
108 C10 Vevey Ger. Vivis; anc. Vibiscum. Vaud, SW Switzerland
Vexiö see Växjö
103 S13 Veynes Hautes-Alpes, SE France
103 N11 Vézère ≈ W France
114 I9 Vezhen ▲ C Bulgaria
136 K11 Vezirköprü Samsun, N Turkey
57 J18 Viacha La Paz, W Bolivia
27 R10 Vian Oklahoma, C USA
Viana de Castelo see Viana do Castelo
104 H12 Viana do Alentejo Évora, S Portugal
104 I4 Viana do Bolo Galicia, NW Spain
104 G5 Viana do Castelo var. Viana de Castelo; anc. Velobriga. Viana do Castelo, NW Portugal
104 G5 Viana do Castelo var. Viana de Castelo. ◐ district N Portugal
98 J12 Vianen Utrecht, C Netherlands
167 Q8 Viangchan Eng./Fr. Vientiane. ● (Laos) C Laos
167 P6 Viangphoukha var. Vieng Pou Kha. Louang Namtha, N Laos
104 K13 Viar ≈ SW Spain
106 E11 Viareggio Toscana, C Italy
103 O14 Viaur ≈ S France
Vibiscum see Vevey
95 G21 Viborg Viborg, NW Denmark
29 R12 Viborg South Dakota, N USA
95 F21 Viborg off. Viborg Amt. ◐ county NW Denmark
Viborg Amt see Viborg
107 N22 Vibo Valentia prev. Monteleone di Calabria; anc. Hipponium. Calabria, SW Italy
105 W5 Vic var. Vich; anc. Ausa, Vicus Ausonensis. Cataluña, NE Spain
102 K16 Vic-en-Bigorre Hautes-Pyrénées, S France
40 K10 Vicente Guerrero Durango, C Mexico
41 P10 Vicente Guerrero, Presa var. Presa de las Adjuntas. ▣ NE Mexico
Vicentia see Vicenza
106 G8 Vicenza anc. Vicentia. Veneto, NE Italy
Vich see Vic
54 J10 Vichada off. Comisaría del Vichada. ◐ province E Colombia
Vichada, Comisaría del see Vichada
54 K10 Vichada, Río ≈ E Colombia
61 G17 Vichadero Rivera, NE Uruguay
Vichegda see Vychegda
124 M16 Vichuga Ivanovskaya Oblast', W Russian Federation
103 P10 Vichy Allier, C France
26 K9 Vici Oklahoma, C USA
31 P10 Vicksburg Michigan, N USA
22 J5 Vicksburg Mississippi, S USA
103 O12 Vic-sur-Cère Cantal, C France
59 I21 Víctor Mato Grosso do Sul, SW Brazil
29 X14 Victor Iowa, C USA
182 I10 Victor Harbor South Australia
61 C18 Victoria Entre Ríos, E Argentina
10 L17 Victoria province capital Vancouver Island, British Columbia, SW Canada
45 R14 Victoria NW Grenada
42 H6 Victoria Yoro, NW Honduras
121 O15 Victoria var. Rabat. Gozo, NW Malta
116 I12 Victoria Ger. Viktoriastadt. Braşov, C Romania
172 H17 Victoria ● (Seychelles) Mahé, SW Seychelles
25 U13 Victoria Texas, SW USA
183 N12 Victoria ◐ state SE Australia
174 K7 Victoria ≈ Western Australia
Victoria see Labuan, East Malaysia
Victoria see Masvingo, Zimbabwe
Victoria Bank see Vitória Seamount
9 Y15 Victoria Beach Manitoba, S Canada
Victoria de Durango see Durango
Victoria de las Tunas see Las Tunas
83 I16 Victoria Falls Matabeleland North, W Zimbabwe
83 I16 Victoria Falls waterfall Zambia/Zimbabwe
83 I16 Victoria Falls ✈ Matabeleland North, W Zimbabwe
Victoria Falls see Iguaçu, Salto do
63 F19 Victoria, Isla island Archipiélago de los Chonos, S Chile
8 K6 Victoria Island island Northwest Territories, NW Canada
182 L8 Victoria, Lake ◎ New South Wales, SE Australia
68 I12 Victoria, Lake var. Victoria Nyanza. ◎ E Africa
195 S13 Victoria Land physical region Antarctica
187 X14 Victoria, Mount ▲ Viti Levu, W Fiji
166 L5 Victoria, Mount ▲ W Burma (Myanmar)
186 E9 Victoria, Mount ▲ S Papua New Guinea
81 F17 Victoria Nile var. Somerset Nile. ≈ C Uganda
Victoria Nyanza see Victoria, Lake
42 G3 Victoria Peak ▲ SE Belize
185 H16 Victoria Range ▲▲ South Island, New Zealand
181 O3 Victoria River ≈ Northern Territory, N Australia
181 P3 Victoria River Roadhouse Northern Territory, N Australia
15 Q11 Victoriaville Québec, SE Canada
Victoria-Wes see Victoria West
83 G24 Victoria West Afr. Victoria-Wes. Northern Cape, W South Africa
62 J13 Victorica La Pampa, C Argentina
195 T3 Victor, Mount ▲ Antarctica
35 U14 Victorville California, W USA
62 G9 Vicuña Coquimbo, N Chile
62 K11 Vicuña Mackenna Córdoba, C Argentina
Vicus Ausonensis see Vic
Vicus Elbii see Viterbo
33 X7 Vida Montana, NW USA
23 V6 Vidalia Georgia, SE USA
22 J7 Vidalia Louisiana, S USA
95 F22 Videbæk Ringkøbing, C Denmark
60 I13 Videira Santa Catarina, S Brazil
116 J14 Videle Teleorman, S Romania
Videm-Krško see Krško
Vídeň see Wien
104 H12 Vidigueira Beja, S Portugal
114 J9 Vidima ≈ N Bulgaria
114 G7 Vidin anc. Bononia. Vidin, NW Bulgaria
114 F8 Vidin ◐ province NW Bulgaria
154 H10 Vidisha Madhya Pradesh, C India
25 Y10 Vidor Texas, SW USA
95 L20 Vidöstern ◎ S Sweden
92 J13 Vidsel Norrbotten, N Sweden
118 H9 Vidzemes Augstiene ▲▲ C Latvia
118 J12 Vidzy Rus. Vidzy. Vitsyebskaya Voblasts', NW Belarus
63 L16 Viedma Río Negro, E Argentina
63 H22 Viedma, Lago ◎ S Argentina
45 O11 Vieille Case var. Itassi. N Dominica
104 M2 Vieja, Peña ▲ N Spain
40 E4 Viejo, Cerro ▲ NW Mexico
56 B9 Viejo, Cerro ▲ N Peru
118 E10 Viekšniai Telšiai, NW Lithuania
105 U3 Vielha var. Viella. Cataluña, NE Spain
Viella see Vielha
99 L21 Vielsalm Luxembourg, E Belgium
Vieng Pou Kha see Viangphoukha
23 T6 Vienna Georgia, SE USA
30 L17 Vienna Illinois, N USA
27 V5 Vienna Missouri, C USA
21 Q3 Vienna West Virginia, NE USA
Vienna see Wien, Austria
Vienna see Vienne, France
103 R11 Vienne anc. Vienna. Isère, E France
102 L10 Vienne ◐ department W France
102 L9 Vienne ≈ W France
Vientiane see Viangchan
Vientos, Paso de los see Windward Passage
45 V6 Vieques var. Isabel Segunda. E Puerto Rico
45 V6 Vieques, Isla de island E Puerto Rico
45 V6 Vieques, Pasaje de passage E Puerto Rico
45 V5 Vieques, Sonda de sound E Puerto Rico
Vierdörfer see Săcele
93 M15 Vieremä Itä-Suomi, C Finland
99 M14 Vierlingsbeek Noord-Brabant, SE Netherlands
101 G20 Viernheim Hessen, W Germany
101 D15 Viersen Nordrhein-Westfalen, W Germany
108 G8 Vierwaldstätter See Eng. Lake of Lucerne. ◎ C Switzerland
103 N8 Vierzon Cher, C France
40 L8 Viesca Coahuila de Zaragoza, NE Mexico
118 H10 Viesīte Ger. Eckengraf. Jēkabpils, S Latvia
107 N15 Vieste Puglia, SE Italy
167 T8 Vietnam off. Socialist Republic of Vietnam, Vtn. Công Hoa Xã Hôi Chu Nghia Viêt Nam. ◆ republic SE Asia
Vietnam, Socialist Republic of see Vietnam
167 S5 Viêt Quang Ha Giang, N Vietnam
Vietri see Viêt Tri
167 S6 Viêt Tri var. Vietri. Vinh Phu, N Vietnam
30 L4 Vieux Desert, Lac ◎ Michigan/Wisconsin, N USA
45 Y13 Vieux Fort S Saint Lucia
45 X6 Vieux-Habitants Basse Terre, SW Guadeloupe
119 G14 Vievis Vilnius, S Lithuania
171 N2 Vigan Luzon, N Philippines
106 D8 Vigevano Lombardia, N Italy
107 N18 Viggiano Basilicata, S Italy
58 L12 Vigia Pará, NE Brazil
41 Y12 Vigía Chico Quintana Roo, SE Mexico
Vigie see George F L Charles
102 K17 Vignemale var. Pic de Vignemale. ▲ France/Spain
Vignemale, Pic de see Vignemale
106 G10 Vignola Emilia-Romagna, C Italy
104 G4 Vigo Galicia, NW Spain
104 G4 Vigo, Ría de estuary NW Spain
94 D9 Vigra island S Norway
95 C17 Vigrestad Rogaland, S Norway
93 L15 Vihanti Oulu, C Finland
149 U10 Vihāri Punjab, E Pakistan
102 K8 Vihiers Maine-et-Loire, NW France
111 O19 Vihorlat ▲ E Slovakia
93 L19 Vihti Etelä-Suomi, S Finland
Viipuri see Vyborg
93 M16 Viitasaari Länsi-Suomi, C Finland
118 K3 Viivikonna Ida-Virumaa, NE Estonia
155 K16 Vijayawāda prev. Bezwada. Andhra Pradesh, SE India
Vijosa/Vijosë see Aóos, Albania/Greece
Vijosa/Vijosë see Vjosës, Lumi i, Albania/Greece
92 J4 Vík Sudhurland, S Iceland
Vik see Vikøyri
94 L13 Vika Dalarna, C Sweden
92 L12 Vikajärvi Lappi, N Finland
94 L13 Vikarbyn Dalarna, C Sweden
95 J22 Viken Skåne, S Sweden
95 L17 Viken ◎ C Sweden
95 G15 Vikersund Buskerud, S Norway
114 G11 Vikhren ▲ SW Bulgaria
9 R15 Viking Alberta, SW Canada
84 E7 Viking Bank undersea feature N North Sea
95 M14 Vikmanshyttan Dalarna, C Sweden
94 D12 Vikøyri var. Vik. Sogn Og Fjordane, S Norway
93 H17 Viksjö Västernorrland, C Sweden
Viktoriastadt see Victoria
Vila see Port-Vila
Vila Arriaga see Bibala
Vila Artur de Paiva see Cubango
Vila Baleira see Porto Santo
Vila Bela da Santissima Trindade see Mato Grosso
58 B12 Vila Bittencourt Amazonas, NW Brazil
Vila da Ponte see Cubango
64 O2 Vila da Praia da Vitória Terceira, Azores, Portugal, NE Atlantic Ocean
Vila de Aljustrel see Cangamba
Vila de Almoster see Chiange
Vila de João Belo see Xai-Xai
Vila de Macia see Macia
Vila de Manhiça see Manhiça
Vila de Manica see Manica
Vila de Mocímboa da Praia see Mocímboa da Praia
83 N16 Vila de Sena var. Sena. Sofala, C Mozambique
104 F14 Vila do Bispo Faro, S Portugal
104 G6 Vila do Conde Porto, NW Portugal
Vila do Maio see Maio
64 P3 Vila do Porto Santa Maria, Azores, Portugal, NE Atlantic Ocean
83 K15 Vila do Zumbo prev. Vila do Zumbu, Zumbo. Tete, NW Mozambique
Vila do Zumbu see Vila do Zumbo
104 I6 Vila Flor var. Vila Flôr. Bragança, N Portugal
105 V6 Vilafranca del Penedès var. Villafranca del Panadés. Cataluña, NE Spain
104 F10 Vila Franca de Xira var. Vilafranca de Xira. Lisboa, C Portugal
Vila Gago Coutinho see Lumbala N'Guimbo
104 G3 Vilagarcía de Arousa var. Villagarcía de Arosa. Galicia, NW Spain
Vila General Machado see Camacupa
Vila Henrique de Carvalho see Saurimo
102 I7 Vilaine ≈ NW France
Vila João de Almeida see Chibia
118 K8 Viļaka Ger. Marienhausen. Balvi, NE Latvia
104 I2 Vilalba Galicia, NW Spain
Vila Marechal Carmona see Uíge
Vila Mariano Machado see Ganda
172 G3 Vilanandro, Tanjona headland W Madagascar
Vilanculos see Vilankulo
118 J10 Viļāni Rēzekne, E Latvia
83 N19 Vilankulo var. Vilanculos. Inhambane, E Mozambique
Vila Norton de Matos see Balombo
104 G6 Vila Nova de Famalicão var. Vila Nova de Famalicao. Braga, N Portugal
104 I6 Vila Nova de Foz Côa var. Vila Nova de Fozcôa. Guarda, N Portugal
Vila Nova de Fozcôa see Vila Nova de Foz Côa
104 F6 Vila Nova de Gaia Porto, NW Portugal
Vila Nova de Portimão see Portimão
105 V6 Vilanova i La Geltrú Cataluña, NE Spain
Vila Pereira de Eça see N'Giva
104 H6 Vila Pouca de Aguiar Vila Real, N Portugal
104 H6 Vila Real var. Vila Rial. Vila Real, N Portugal
104 H6 Vila Real ◐ district N Portugal
Vila-real de los Infantes see Villarreal
104 H14 Vila Real de Santo António Faro, S Portugal
104 J7 Vilar Formoso Guarda, N Portugal
Vila Rial see Vila Real
59 J15 Vila Rica Mato Grosso, W Brazil
Vila Robert Williams see Caála
Vila Salazar see N'Dalatando
Vila Serpa Pinto see Menongue
Vila Teixeira da Silva see Bailundo
Vila Teixeira de Sousa see Luau
104 H9 Vila Velha de Ródão Castelo Branco, C Portugal
104 G5 Vila Verde Braga, N Portugal
104 H11 Vila Viçosa Évora, S Portugal
57 G15 Vilcabamba, Cordillera de ▲▲ C Peru
Vilcea see Vâlcea
122 J4 Vil'cheka, Zemlya Eng. Wilczek Land. island Zemlya Frantsa-Iosifa, NW Russian Federation
95 F22 Vildbjerg Ringkøbing, C Denmark
Vileyka see Vilyeyka
93 H15 Vilhelmina Västerbotten, N Sweden
59 F17 Vilhena Rondônia, W Brazil
115 G19 Vília Attikí, C Greece
119 I14 Viliya Lith. Neris, Rus. Viliya. ≈ W Belarus
Viliya see Neris
118 H5 Viljandi Ger. Fellin. Viljandimaa, S Estonia
118 H5 Viljandimaa var. Viljandi Maakond. ◐ province SW Estonia
Viljandi Maakond see Viljandimaa
119 E14 Vilkaviškis Pol. Wyłkowyszki. Marijampolė, SW Lithuania
118 F13 Vilkija Kaunas, C Lithuania
197 V9 Vil'kitskogo, Proliv strait N Russian Federation
Vilkovo see Vylkove
57 L21 Villa Abecia Chuquisaca, S Bolivia
41 N5 Villa Acuña var. Ciudad Acuña. Coahuila de Zaragoza, NE Mexico
40 J4 Villa Ahumada Chihuahua, N Mexico
45 O9 Villa Altagracia C Dominican Republic
56 L13 Villa Bella Beni, N Bolivia
104 J3 Villablino Castilla-León, N Spain
54 K6 Villa Bruzual Portuguesa, N Venezuela
105 O9 Villacañas Castilla-La Mancha, C Spain
105 O12 Villacarrillo Andalucía, S Spain
104 M7 Villacastín Castilla-León, N Spain
Villa Cecilia see Ciudad Madero

◆ Country ● Country Capital ◇ Dependent Territory ○ Dependent Territory Capital ◐ Administrative Regions ✈ International Airport ▲ Mountain ▲▲ Mountain Range Volcano ≈ River ◎ Lake ▣ Reservoir

VILLACH – VOROSHILOVGRAD

109 S9 **Villach** *Slvn.* Beljak. Kärnten, S Austria
107 B20 **Villacidro** Sardegna, Italy, C Mediterranean Sea
Villa Concepción *see* Concepción
104 L4 **Villada** Castilla-León, N Spain
40 M10 **Villa de Cos** Zacatecas, C Mexico
54 L5 **Villa de Cura** *var.* Cura. Aragua, N Venezuela
Villa del Nevoso *see* Ilirska Bistrica
Villa del Pilar *see* Pilar
104 M13 **Villa del Río** Andalucía, S Spain
Villa de Méndez *see* Méndez
42 H6 **Villa de San Antonio** Comayagua, W Honduras
105 N4 **Villadiego** Castilla-León, N Spain
105 T8 **Villafames** País Valenciano, E Spain
41 U16 **Villa Flores** Chiapas, SE Mexico
104 J3 **Villafranca del Bierzo** Castilla-León, N Spain
105 S8 **Villafranca del Cid** País Valenciano, E Spain
104 J11 **Villafranca de los Barros** Extremadura, W Spain
105 N10 **Villafranca de los Caballeros** Castilla-La Mancha, C Spain
Villafranca del Panadés *see* Vilafranca del Penedès
106 F8 **Villafranca di Verona** Veneto, NE Italy
107 J23 **Villafrati** Sicilia, Italy, C Mediterranean Sea
Villagarcía de Arosa *see* Vilagarcía de Arousa
41 O9 **Villagrán** Tamaulipas, C Mexico
61 C17 **Villaguay** Entre Ríos, E Argentina
62 O6 **Villa Hayes** Presidente Hayes, S Paraguay
41 U15 **Villahermosa** *prev.* San Juan Bautista. Tabasco, SE Mexico
105 O11 **Villahermosa** Castilla-La Mancha, C Spain
64 O11 **Villahermoso** Gomera, Islas Canarias, Spain, NE Atlantic Ocean
Villa Hidalgo *see* Hidalgo
105 T12 **Villajoyosa** *Cat.* La Vila Joíosa. País Valenciano, E Spain
Villa Juárez *see* Juárez
Villalba *see* Collado Villalba
41 N8 **Villaldama** Nuevo León, NE Mexico
104 L5 **Villalón de Campos** Castilla-León, N Spain
61 A25 **Villalonga** Buenos Aires, E Argentina
104 L5 **Villalpando** Castilla-León, N Spain
40 K9 **Villa Madero** *var.* Francisco I. Madero. Durango, C Mexico
41 O9 **Villa Mainero** Tamaulipas, C Mexico
Villamaña *see* Villamañán
104 L4 **Villamañán** *var.* Villamaña. Castilla-León, N Spain
62 L10 **Villa María** Córdoba, C Argentina
61 C17 **Villa María Grande** Entre Ríos, E Argentina
57 K21 **Villa Martín** Potosí, SW Bolivia
104 K15 **Villamartín** Andalucía, S Spain
62 J8 **Villa Mazán** La Rioja, NW Argentina
Villa Mercedes *see* Mercedes
Villamil *see* Puerto Villamil
Villa Nador *see* Nador
54 G5 **Villanueva** La Guajira, N Colombia
42 H5 **Villanueva** Cortés, NW Honduras
40 L11 **Villanueva** Zacatecas, C Mexico
42 I9 **Villa Nueva** Chinandega, NW Nicaragua
37 T11 **Villanueva** New Mexico, SW USA
104 M12 **Villanueva de Córdoba** Andalucía, S Spain
105 O12 **Villanueva del Arzobispo** Andalucía, S Spain
104 K11 **Villanueva de la Serena** Extremadura, W Spain
104 L5 **Villanueva del Campo** Castilla-León, N Spain
105 O11 **Villanueva de los Infantes** Castilla-La Mancha, C Spain
61 C14 **Villa Ocampo** Santa Fe, C Argentina
40 J8 **Villa Ocampo** Durango, C Mexico
40 J7 **Villa Orestes Pereyra** Durango, C Mexico
105 N3 **Villarcayo** Castilla-León, N Spain
104 L5 **Villardefrades** Castilla-León, N Spain
105 S9 **Villar del Arzobispo** País Valenciano, E Spain
105 Q6 **Villaroya de la Sierra** Aragón, NE Spain
105 T9 **Villarreal** *var.* Vila-real de los Infantes. País Valenciano, E Spain
62 P6 **Villarrica** Guairá, SE Paraguay
63 G15 **Villarrica, Volcán** ▲ S Chile
105 P10 **Villarrobledo** Castilla-La Mancha, C Spain
105 O10 **Villarrubia de los Ojos** Castilla-La Mancha, C Spain
18 J17 **Villas** New Jersey, NE USA
105 O3 **Villasana de Mena** Castilla-León, N Spain
107 M23 **Villa San Giovanni** Calabria, S Italy
61 D18 **Villa San José** Entre Ríos, E Argentina
Villa Sanjurjo *see* Al-Hoceïma
105 P6 **Villasayas** Castilla-León, N Spain
107 C20 **Villasimius** Sardegna, Italy, C Mediterranean Sea
41 N6 **Villa Unión** Coahuila de Zaragoza, NE Mexico
40 K10 **Villa Unión** Durango, C Mexico
40 J10 **Villa Unión** Sinaloa, C Mexico
62 K12 **Villa Valeria** Córdoba, C Argentina
105 N8 **Villaverde** Madrid, C Spain
54 F10 **Villavicencio** Meta, C Colombia
104 L2 **Villaviciosa** Asturias, N Spain
104 L12 **Villaviciosa de Córdoba** Andalucía, S Spain
57 L22 **Villazón** Potosí, S Bolivia
14 J8 **Villebon, Lac** ◎ Québec, SE Canada
Ville de Kinshasa *see* Kinshasa
102 J5 **Villedieu-les-Poêles** Manche, N France
Villefranche *see* Villefranche-sur-Saône
103 N16 **Villefranche-de-Lauragais** Haute-Garonne, S France
103 N14 **Villefranche-de-Rouergue** Aveyron, S France
103 R10 **Villefranche-sur-Saône** *var.* Villefranche. Rhône, E France
14 H9 **Ville-Marie** Québec, SE Canada
102 M15 **Villemur-sur-Tarn** Haute-Garonne, S France
105 S11 **Villena** País Valenciano, E Spain
Villeneuve-d'Agen *see* Villeneuve-sur-Lot
102 L13 **Villeneuve-sur-Lot** *var.* Villeneuve-d'Agen, *hist.* Gajac. Lot-et-Garonne, SW France
103 P6 **Villeneuve-sur-Yonne** Yonne, C France
22 H8 **Ville Platte** Louisiana, S USA
103 R11 **Villeurbanne** Rhône, E France
101 G23 **Villingen-Schwenningen** Baden-Württemberg, S Germany
29 T15 **Villisca** Iowa, C USA
Villmanstrand *see* Lappeenranta
Vilna *see* Vilnius
119 H14 **Vilnius** *Pol.* Wilno, *Ger.* Wilna; *prev. Rus.* Vilna. ● (Lithuania) Vilnius, SE Lithuania
119 H14 **Vilnius** ✈ Vilnius, SE Lithuania
117 S7 **Vil'nohirs'k** Dnipropetrovs'ka Oblast', E Ukraine
117 U8 **Vil'nyans'k** Zaporiz'ka Oblast', SE Ukraine
93 L17 **Vilppula** Länsi-Suomi, W Finland
101 M20 **Vils** ~ SE Germany
118 C5 **Vilsandi Saar** *island* W Estonia
117 P8 **Vil'shanka** *Rus.* Olshanka. Kirovohrads'ka Oblast', C Ukraine
101 O22 **Vilshofen** Bayern, SE Germany
155 J20 **Viluppuram** Tamil Nādu, SE India
113 I16 **Vilusi** W Montenegro
99 G18 **Vilvoorde** *Fr.* Vilvorde. Vlaams Brabant, C Belgium
Vilvorde *see* Vilvoorde
119 J14 **Vilyeyka** *Pol.* Wilejka, *Rus.* Vileyka. Minskaya Voblasts', NW Belarus
122 V11 **Vilyuchinsk** Kamchatskaya Oblast', E Russian Federation
123 P10 **Vilyuy** ~ NE Russian Federation
123 P10 **Vilyuysk** Respublika Sakha (Yakutiya), NE Russian Federation
123 N10 **Vilyuyskoye Vodokhranilishche** ▣ NE Russian Federation
104 G2 **Vimianzo** Galicia, NW Spain
95 M19 **Vimmerby** Kalmar, S Sweden
102 L5 **Vimoutiers** Orne, N France
93 L16 **Vimpeli** Länsi-Soumi, W Finland
79 G14 **Vina** ~ Cameroon/Chad
62 G11 **Viña del Mar** Valparaíso, C Chile
19 R8 **Vinalhaven Island** *island* Maine, NE USA
105 T8 **Vinaròs** País Valenciano, E Spain
Vinátori *see* Vânători
31 N15 **Vincennes** Indiana, N USA
195 Y12 **Vincennes Bay** *bay* Antarctica
25 O7 **Vincent** Texas, SW USA
95 H24 **Vindeby** Fyn, C Denmark
93 I15 **Vindeln** Västerbotten, N Sweden
95 F21 **Vinderup** Ringkøbing, C Denmark
Vindhya Mountains *see* Vindhya Range
153 N14 **Vindhya Range** *var.* Vindhya Mountains. ▲▲ N India
Vindobona *see* Wien
20 K6 **Vine Grove** Kentucky, S USA
18 J17 **Vineland** New Jersey, NE USA
116 E11 **Vinga** Arad, W Romania
95 M16 **Vingåker** Södermanland, C Sweden
167 S8 **Vinh** Nghê An, N Vietnam
104 I5 **Vinhais** Bragança, N Portugal
167 T9 **Vinh Linh** Quang Tri, C Vietnam
Vinh Loi *see* Bac Liêu
167 S14 **Vinh Long** *var.* Vinhlong. Vinh Long, S Vietnam
Vinhlong *see* Vinh Long
113 Q18 **Vinica** NE FYR Macedonia
109 V13 **Vinica** SE Slovenia
114 G8 **Vinishte** Montana, NW Bulgaria
27 Q8 **Vinita** Oklahoma, C USA
Vinju Mare *see* Vânju Mare
98 I11 **Vinkeveen** Utrecht, C Netherlands
116 L6 **Vin'kivtsi** Khmel'nyts'ka Oblast', W Ukraine
112 I10 **Vinkovci** *Ger.* Winkowitz, *Hung.* Vinkovcze. Vukovar-Srijem, E Croatia
Vinkovcze *see* Vinkovci
Vinnitsa *see* Vinnytsya
Vinnitskaya Oblast'/ Vinnytsya *see* Vinnyts'ka Oblast'
116 M7 **Vinnyts'ka Oblast'** *var.* Vinnytsya, *Rus.* Vinnitskaya Oblast'. ◈ *province* C Ukraine
117 N6 **Vinnytsya** *Rus.* Vinnitsa. Vinnyts'ka Oblast', C Ukraine
117 N6 **Vinnytsya** ✈ Vinnyts'ka Oblast', N Ukraine
Vinogradov *see* Vynohradiv
194 L8 **Vinson Massif** ▲ Antarctica
94 G11 **Vinstra** Oppland, S Norway
116 K12 **Vintilă Vodă** Buzău, SE Romania
29 X13 **Vinton** Iowa, C USA
22 F9 **Vinton** Louisiana, S USA
155 J17 **Vinukonda** Andhra Pradesh, E India
Vioara *see* Ocnele Mari
83 E23 **Vioolsdrif** Northern Cape, SW South Africa
82 M13 **Viphya Mountains** ▲▲ C Malawi
171 Q4 **Virac** Catanduanes Island, N Philippines
124 K8 **Virandozero** Respublika Kareliya, NW Russian Federation
137 P16 **Viranşehir** Şanlıurfa, SE Turkey
154 D13 **Virār** Mahārāshtra, W India
9 W16 **Virden** Manitoba, S Canada
30 K14 **Virden** Illinois, N USA
Virdois *see* Virrat
102 J5 **Vire** Calvados, N France
102 J4 **Vire** ~ N France
83 A15 **Virei** Namibe, SW Angola
Vîrful Moldoveanu *see* Vârful Moldoveanu
35 R5 **Virgina Peak** ▲ Nevada, W USA
45 U9 **Virgin Gorda** *island* C British Virgin Islands
83 I22 **Virginia** Free State, C South Africa
30 K13 **Virginia** Illinois, N USA
29 W4 **Virginia** Minnesota, N USA
21 T6 **Virginia** *off.* Commonwealth of Virginia, *also known as* Mother of Presidents, Mother of States, Old Dominion. ◈ *state* NE USA
21 Y7 **Virginia Beach** Virginia, NE USA
33 R11 **Virginia City** Montana, NW USA
35 Q6 **Virginia City** Nevada, W USA
14 H8 **Virginiatown** Ontario, S Canada
Virgin Islands *see* British Virgin Islands
45 T9 **Virgin Islands (US)** *var.* Virgin Islands of the United States; *prev.* Danish West Indies. ◇ *US unincorporated territory* E West Indies
Virgin Islands of the United States *see* Virgin Islands (US)
45 T9 **Virgin Passage** *passage* Puerto Rico/Virgin Islands (US)
35 Y10 **Virgin River** ~ Nevada/ Utah, W USA
Virihaur *see* Virihaure
92 H12 **Virihaure** *var.* Virihaur. ◎ N Sweden
167 T11 **Virôchey** Rôtânôkiri, NE Cambodia
93 N19 **Virolahti** Etelä-Suomi, S Finland
30 J8 **Viroqua** Wisconsin, N USA
112 G8 **Virovitica** *Ger.* Virovititz, *Hung.* Verőcze; *prev. Ger.* Werowitz. Virovitica-Podravina, NE Croatia
112 G8 **Virovitica-Podravina** *off.* Virovitičko-Podravska Županija. ◈ *province* NE Croatia
Virovitičko-Podravska Županija *see* Virovitica-Podravina
Virovititz *see* Virovitica
113 J17 **Virpazar** S Montenegro
93 L17 **Virrat** *Swe.* Virdois. Länsi-Suomi, W Finland
95 M20 **Virserum** Kalmar, S Sweden
99 K25 **Virton** Luxembourg, SE Belgium
118 F5 **Virtsu** *Ger.* Werder. Läänemaa, W Estonia
56 C12 **Virú** La Libertad, C Peru
Virudhunagar *see* Virudunagar
155 H23 **Virudunagar** *var.* Virudhunagar. Tamil Nādu, SE India
118 I3 **Viru-Jaagupi** *Ger.* Sankt-Jakobi. Lääne-Virumaa, NE Estonia
57 N19 **Viru-Viru** *var.* Santa Cruz. ✈ (Santa Cruz) Santa Cruz, C Bolivia
113 E15 **Vis** *It.* Lissa; *anc.* Issa. *island* S Croatia
Vis *see* Fish
118 I12 **Visaginas** *prev.* Sniečkus. Utena, E Lithuania
155 M15 **Visākhapatnam** Andhra Pradesh, SE India
35 R11 **Visalia** California, W USA
Višău *see* Vişeu
95 P19 **Visby** *Ger.* Wisby. Gotland, SE Sweden
197 N9 **Viscount Melville Sound** *prev.* Melville Sound. *sound* Northwest Territories, N Canada
99 L19 **Visé** Liège, E Belgium
112 K13 **Višegrad** ◈ Republika Srpska, SE Bosnia and Herzegovina
58 L12 **Viseu** Pará, NE Brazil
104 H7 **Viseu** *prev.* Vizeu. Viseu, N Portugal
104 H7 **Viseu** *var.* Vizeu. ◈ *district* N Portugal
116 I8 **Vişeu** *Hung.* Visó; *prev.* Vişău. ~ NW Romania
116 I8 **Vişeu de Sus** *var.* Vişeul de Sus, *Ger.* Oberwischau, *Hung.* Felsővisó. Maramureş, N Romania
Vişeul de Sus *see* Vişeu de Sus
125 R10 **Vishera** ~ NW Russian Federation
95 J19 **Viskafors** Västra Götaland, S Sweden
95 J20 **Viskan** ~ S Sweden
95 L21 **Vislanda** Kronoberg, S Sweden
Vislinskiy Zaliv *see* Vistula Lagoon
Visó *see* Vişeu
112 H13 **Visoko** ◈ Federacija Bosna I Hercegovina, C Bosnia and Herzegovina
106 A9 **Viso, Monte** ▲ NW Italy
108 E10 **Visp** Valais, SW Switzerland
108 E10 **Vispa** ~ S Switzerland
95 M21 **Vissefjärda** Kalmar, S Sweden
100 I11 **Visselhövede** Niedersachsen, NW Germany
95 G23 **Vissenbjerg** Fyn, C Denmark
35 U17 **Vista** California, W USA
58 C11 **Vista Alegre** Amazonas, NW Brazil
114 J13 **Vistonída, Límni** ◎ NE Greece
Vistula *see* Wisła
119 A14 **Vistula Lagoon** *Ger.* Frisches Haff, *Pol.* Zalew Wiślany, *Rus.* Vislinskiy Zaliv. *lagoon* Poland/Russian Federation
114 I8 **Vit** ~ NW Bulgaria
Vitebsk *see* Vitsyebsk
Vitebskaya Oblast' *see* Vitsyebskaya Voblasts'
107 H14 **Viterbo** *anc.* Vicus Elbii. Lazio, C Italy
112 H12 **Vitez** ◈ Federacija Bosna I Hercegovina, C Bosnia and Herzegovina
167 S14 **Vi Thanh** Cân Thơ, S Vietnam
Viti *see* Fiji
186 E7 **Vitiaz Strait** *strait* NE Papua New Guinea
104 J7 **Vitigudino** Castilla-León, N Spain
187 W15 **Viti Levu** *island* W Fiji
123 O11 **Vitim** ~ C Russian Federation
123 O12 **Vitimskiy** Irkutskaya Oblast', C Russian Federation
109 V2 **Vitis** Niederösterreich, N Austria
59 O20 **Vitória** *state capital* Espírito Santo, SE Brazil
Vitoria *see* Vitoria-Gasteiz
Vitoria Bank *see* Vitória Seamount
59 N18 **Vitória da Conquista** Bahia, E Brazil
105 P3 **Vitoria-Gasteiz** *var.* Vitoria, *Eng.* Vittoria. País Vasco, N Spain
65 J16 **Vitória Seamount** *var.* Victoria Bank, Vitoria Bank. *undersea feature* C Atlantic Ocean
112 F13 **Vitorog** ▲ SW Bosnia and Herzegovina
102 J6 **Vitré** Ille-et-Vilaine, NW France
103 R5 **Vitry-le-François** Marne, N France
114 D13 **Vítsi** *var.* Vítsoi. ▲ N Greece
Vítsoi *see* Vítsi
118 N13 **Vitsyebsk** *Rus.* Vitebsk. Vitsyebskaya Voblasts', NE Belarus
118 K13 **Vitsyebskaya Voblasts'** *prev. Rus.* Vitebskaya Oblast'. ◈ *province* N Belarus
92 J11 **Vittangi** *Lapp.* Vazáš. Norrbotten, N Sweden
103 R8 **Vitteaux** Côte d'Or, C France
103 S6 **Vittel** Vosges, NE France
95 N15 **Vittinge** Västmanland, C Sweden
107 K25 **Vittoria** Sicilia, Italy, C Mediterranean Sea
Vittoria *see* Vitoria-Gasteiz
106 I7 **Vittorio Veneto** Veneto, NE Italy
175 Q9 **Vitu Levu** *island* W Fiji
175 Q7 **Vityaz Trench** *undersea feature* W Pacific Ocean
108 G8 **Vitznau** Luzern, W Switzerland
104 I1 **Viveiro** Galicia, NW Spain
105 S9 **Viver** País Valenciano, E Spain
103 Q13 **Viverais, Monts du** ▲▲ C France
122 L9 **Vivi** ~ N Russian Federation
22 F4 **Vivian** Louisiana, S USA
29 N10 **Vivian** South Dakota, N USA
103 R13 **Viviers** Ardèche, E France
Vivis *see* Vevey
83 K19 **Vivo** Limpopo, NE South Africa
102 L10 **Vivonne** Vienne, W France
Vizakna *see* Ocna Sibiului
105 O2 **Vizcaya** *Basq.* Bizkaia. ◈ *province* País Vasco, N Spain
Vizcaya, Golfo de *see* Biscay, Bay of
136 C10 **Vize** Kırklareli, NW Turkey
122 K4 **Vize, Ostrov** *island* Severnaya Zemlya, N Russian Federation
Vizeu *see* Viseu
155 M15 **Vizianagaram** *var.* Vizianagram. Andhra Pradesh, E India
Vizianagram *see* Vizianagaram
103 S12 **Vizille** Isère, E France
125 R11 **Vizinga** Respublika Komi, NW Russian Federation
116 M13 **Viziru** Brăila, SE Romania
113 K21 **Vjosës, Lumi i** *var.* Vijosa, Vijosë, *Gk.* Aóos. ~ Albania/ Greece *see also* Aóos
Vjosës, Lumi i *see* Aóos
99 H18 **Vlaams Brabant** ◈ *province* C Belgium
Vlaanderen *see* Flanders
98 G12 **Vlaardingen** Zuid-Holland, SW Netherlands
116 F10 **Vlădeasa, Vârful** *prev.* Vîrful Vlădeasa. ▲ NW Romania
Vlădeasa, Vîrful *see* Vlădeasa, Vârful
113 P16 **Vladičin Han** Serbia, SE Serbia
127 O16 **Vladikavkaz** *prev.* Dzaudzhikau, Ordzhonikidze. Respublika Severnaya Osetiya, SW Russian Federation
126 M3 **Vladimir** Vladimirskaya Oblast', W Russian Federation
144 M7 **Vladimirovka** Kostanay, N Kazakhstan
Vladimirovka *see* Yuzhno-Sakhalinsk
126 L3 **Vladimirskaya Oblast'** ◈ *province* W Russian Federation
126 I3 **Vladimirskiy Tupik** Smolenskaya Oblast', W Russian Federation
Vladimir-Volynskiy *see* Volodymyr-Volyns'kyy
123 Q7 **Vladivostok** Primorskiy Kray, SE Russian Federation
117 U13 **Vladyslavivka** Respublika Krym, S Ukraine
98 P6 **Vlagtwedde** Groningen, NE Netherlands
Vlajna *see* Kukavica
112 J12 **Vlasenica** ◈ Republika Srpska, E Bosnia and Herzegovina
112 G12 **Vlašić** ▲ C Bosnia and Herzegovina
111 D17 **Vlašim** *Ger.* Wlaschim. Středočeský Kraj, C Czech Republic
113 P15 **Vlasotince** Serbia, SE Serbia
123 Q7 **Vlasovo** Respublika Sakha (Yakutiya), NE Russian Federation
98 I11 **Vleuten** Utrecht, C Netherlands
98 I5 **Vlieland** *Fris.* Flylân. *island* Waddeneilanden, N Netherlands
98 I5 **Vliestroom** *strait* NW Netherlands
99 J14 **Vlijmen** Noord-Brabant, S Netherlands
99 E15 **Vlissingen** *Eng.* Flushing, *Fr.* Flessingue. Zeeland, SW Netherlands
Vlodava *see* Włodawa
Vlonë/Vlora *see* Vlorë
113 K22 **Vlorë** *prev.* Vlonë, *It.* Valona, Vlora. Vlorë, SW Albania
113 K22 **Vlorë** ◈ *district* SW Albania
113 K22 **Vlorës, Gjiri i** *var.* Valona Bay. *bay* SW Albania
Vlotslavsk *see* Włocławek
111 C16 **Vltava** *Ger.* Moldau. ~ W Czech Republic
126 K3 **Vnukovo** ✈ (Moskva) Gorod Moskva, W Russian Federation
146 L11 **Vobkent** Buxoro Viloyati, C Uzbekistan
146 L11 **Vobkent** *var.* Vabkent. Buxoro Viloyati, C Uzbekistan
25 Q9 **Voca** Texas, SW USA
109 R5 **Vöcklabruck** Oberösterreich, NW Austria
112 D13 **Vodice** Šibenik-Knin, S Croatia
124 K10 **Vodlozero, Ozero** ◎ NW Russian Federation
112 A10 **Vodnjan** *It.* Dignano d'Istria. Istra, NW Croatia
125 S9 **Vodnyy** Respublika Komi, NW Russian Federation
95 G20 **Vodskov** Nordjylland, N Denmark
92 H4 **Vogar** Sudhurland, SW Iceland
Vogelkop *see* Doberai, Jazirah
77 X15 **Vogel Peak** *prev.* Dimlang. ▲ E Nigeria
101 H17 **Vogelsberg** ▲ C Germany
106 D8 **Voghera** Lombardia, N Italy
112 I13 **Vogošća** ◈ Federacija Bosna I Hercegovina, SE Bosnia and Herzegovina
101 M17 **Vogtland** *historical region* E Germany
125 V12 **Vogul'skiy Kamen', Gora** ▲ NW Russian Federation
187 P16 **Voh** Province Nord, C New Caledonia
Vohémar *see* Iharaña
172 H8 **Vohimena, Tanjona** *Fr.* Cap Sainte Marie. *headland* S Madagascar
172 J6 **Vohipeno** Fianarantsoa, SE Madagascar
118 H5 **Võhma** *Ger.* Wõchma. Viljandimaa, S Estonia
81 J20 **Voi** Coast, S Kenya
76 K15 **Voinjama** N Liberia
103 S12 **Voiron** Isère, E France
109 V8 **Voitsberg** Steiermark, SE Austria
95 F24 **Vojens** *Ger.* Woyens. Sønderjylland, SW Denmark
112 K9 **Vojvodina** *Ger.* Wojwodina. Vojvodina, N Serbia
15 S6 **Volant** ~ Québec, SE Canada
Volaterrae *see* Volterra
43 P15 **Volcán** *var.* Hato del Volcán. Chiriquí, W Panama
Volcano Islands *see* Kazan-rettō
Volchansk *see* Vovchans'k
Volchya *see* Vovcha
94 D10 **Volda** Møre og Romsdal, S Norway
98 J9 **Volendam** Noord-Holland, C Netherlands
124 L15 **Volga** Yaroslavskaya Oblast', W Russian Federation
29 R10 **Volga** South Dakota, N USA
122 C11 **Volga** ~ NW Russian Federation
Volga-Baltic Waterway *see* Volgo-Baltiyskiy Kanal
Volga Uplands *see* Privolzhskaya Vozvyshennost'
124 L13 **Volgo-Baltiyskiy Kanal** *var.* Volga-Baltic Waterway. *canal* NW Russian Federation
126 M12 **Volgodonsk** Rostovskaya Oblast', SW Russian Federation
127 O10 **Volgograd** *prev.* Stalingrad, Tsaritsyn. Volgogradskaya Oblast', SW Russian Federation
127 N9 **Volgogradskaya Oblast'** ◈ *province* SW Russian Federation
127 P10 **Volgogradskoye Vodokhranilishche** ▣ SW Russian Federation
101 J19 **Volkach** Bayern, C Germany
109 U9 **Völkermarkt** *Slvn.* Velikovec. Kärnten, S Austria
124 I12 **Volkhov** Leningradskaya Oblast', NW Russian Federation
101 D20 **Völklingen** Saarland, SW Germany
Volkovysk *see* Vawkavysk
Volkovyskiye Vysoty *see* Vawkavyskaye Wzvyshsha
83 K22 **Volksrust** Mpumalanga, E South Africa
98 L8 **Vollenhove** Overijssel, N Netherlands
119 L16 **Volma** ~ C Belarus
Volmari *see* Valmiera
117 W9 **Volnovakha** Donets'ka Oblast', SE Ukraine
116 K6 **Volochys'k** Khmel'nyts'ka Oblast', W Ukraine
117 O6 **Volodarka** Kyyivs'ka Oblast', N Ukraine
117 W9 **Volodars'ke** Donets'ka Oblast', E Ukraine
127 R13 **Volodarskiy** Astrakhanskaya Oblast', SW Russian Federation
Volodarskoye *see* Saumalkol'
117 N8 **Volodars'k-Volyns'kyy** Zhytomyrs'ka Oblast', N Ukraine
116 K3 **Volodymerets'** Rivnens'ka Oblast', NW Ukraine
116 I3 **Volodymyr-Volyns'kyy** *Pol.* Włodzimierz, *Rus.* Vladimir-Volynskiy. Volyns'ka Oblast', NW Ukraine
124 L14 **Vologda** Vologodskaya Oblast', W Russian Federation
124 L12 **Vologodskaya Oblast'** ◈ *province* NW Russian Federation
126 K3 **Volokolamsk** Moskovskaya Oblast', W Russian Federation
126 K9 **Volokonovka** Belgorodskaya Oblast', W Russian Federation
115 G16 **Vólos** Thessalía, C Greece
124 M11 **Voloshka** Arkhangel'skaya Oblast', NW Russian Federation
Vološinovo *see* Novi Bečej
116 H7 **Volovets'** Zakarpats'ka Oblast', W Ukraine
114 K7 **Volovo** Ruse, N Bulgaria
Volozhin *see* Valozhyn
127 Q7 **Vol'sk** Saratovskaya Oblast', W Russian Federation
77 Q17 **Volta** ~ SE Ghana
Volta Blanche *see* White Volta
77 P16 **Volta, Lake** ▣ SE Ghana
Volta Noire *see* Black Volta
60 O9 **Volta Redonda** Rio de Janeiro, SE Brazil
Volta Rouge *see* Red Volta
106 F12 **Volterra** *anc.* Volaterrae. Toscana, C Italy
107 K17 **Volturno** ~ S Italy
113 I15 **Volujak** ▲▲ NW Montenegro
Volunteer Island *see* Starbuck Island
65 F24 **Volunteer Point** *headland* East Falkland, Falkland Islands
114 H13 **Vólvi, Límni** ◎ N Greece
Volyn *see* Volyns'ka Oblast'
116 I3 **Volyns'ka Oblast'** *var.* Volyn, *Rus.* Volynskaya Oblast'. ◈ *province* NW Ukraine
Volynskaya Oblast' *see* Volyns'ka Oblast'
127 Q3 **Volzhsk** Respublika Mariy El, W Russian Federation
127 O10 **Volzhskiy** Volgogradskaya Oblast', SW Russian Federation
172 I7 **Vondrozo** Fianarantsoa, SE Madagascar
114 K9 **Voneshta Voda** Veliko Tŭrnovo, N Bulgaria
39 P10 **Von Frank Mountain** ▲ Alaska, USA
115 C17 **Vónitsa** Dytikí Ellás, W Greece
118 J6 **Võnnu** *Ger.* Wendau. Tartumaa, SE Estonia
98 G12 **Voorburg** Zuid-Holland, W Netherlands
98 H11 **Voorschoten** Zuid-Holland, W Netherlands
98 M11 **Voorst** Gelderland, E Netherlands
98 K11 **Voorthuizen** Gelderland, C Netherlands
92 L2 **Vopnafjördhur** Austurland, E Iceland
92 L2 **Vopnafjördhur** *bay* E Iceland
Vora *see* Vorë
119 H15 **Voranava** *Pol.* Werenów, *Rus.* Voronovo. Hrodzyenskaya Voblasts', W Belarus
108 I8 **Vorarlberg** *off.* Land Vorarlberg. ◈ *state* W Austria
Vorarlberg, Land *see* Vorarlberg
109 X7 **Vorau** Steiermark, E Austria
98 N11 **Vorden** Gelderland, E Netherlands
108 H9 **Vorderrhein** ~ SE Switzerland
92 J2 **Vordhufell** ▲ N Iceland
95 I24 **Vordingborg** Storstrøm, SE Denmark
113 K19 **Vorë** *var.* Vora. Tiranë, W Albania
115 H17 **Vóreies Sporádes** *var.* Vóreioi Sporádes, Vórioi Sporádhes, *Eng.* Northern Sporades. *island group* E Greece
Vóreioi Sporádes *see* Vóreies Sporádes
115 J17 **Vóreion Aigaíon** *Eng.* Aegean North. ◈ *region* E Greece
115 G18 **Vóreios Evvoïkós Kólpos** *var.* Voreiós Evvoïkós Kólpos. *gulf* E Greece
197 S16 **Voring Plateau** *undersea feature* N Norwegian Sea
Vórioi Sporádhes *see* Vóreies Sporádes
125 W4 **Vorkuta** Respublika Komi, NW Russian Federation
95 I14 **Vorma** ~ S Norway
118 E4 **Vormsi** *var.* Vormsi Saar, *Ger.* Worms, *Swed.* Ormsö. *island* W Estonia
Vormsi Saar *see* Vormsi
127 N7 **Vorona** ~ W Russian Federation
126 L7 **Voronezh** Voronezhskaya Oblast', W Russian Federation
126 L7 **Voronezh** ~ W Russian Federation
126 K8 **Voronezhskaya Oblast'** ◈ *province* W Russian Federation
Voronovitsya *see* Voronovytsya
Voronovo *see* Voranava
117 N6 **Voronovytsya** *Rus.* Voronovitsa. Vinnyts'ka Oblast', C Ukraine
122 K7 **Vorontsovo** Taymyrskiy (Dolgano-Nenetskiy) Avtonomnyy Okrug, N Russian Federation
124 K3 **Voron'ya** ~ NW Russian Federation
Voropayevo *see* Varapayeva
Voroshilov *see* Ussuriysk
Voroshilovgrad *see* Luhans'k, Ukraine
Voroshilovgrad *see* Luhans'ka Oblast', Ukraine

◆ Country ● Country Capital ◇ Dependent Territory ○ Dependent Territory Capital ◈ Administrative Regions ✈ International Airport ▲ Mountain ▲▲ Mountain Range ▲ Volcano ~ River ◎ Lake ▣ Reservoir

WALVIS BAY – WEST ALLIS

83 *C19* **Walvis Bay** *Afr.* Walvisbaai. Erongo, NW Namibia
83 *B19* **Walvis Bay** *bay* NW Namibia
Walvish Ridge *see* Walvis Ridge
65 *O17* **Walvis Ridge** *var.* Walvish Ridge. *undersea feature* E Atlantic Ocean
171 *X16* **Wamal** Papua, E Indonesia
171 *U15* **Wamar, Pulau** *island* Kepulauan Aru, E Indonesia
79 *O17* **Wamba** Orientale, NE Dem. Rep. Congo
77 *V15* **Wamba** Nassarawa, C Nigeria
79 *H22* **Wamba** *var.* Uamba. ≈ Angola/Dem. Rep. Congo
27 *P4* **Wamego** Kansas, C USA
18 *I10* **Wampsville** New York, NE USA
42 *K6* **Wampú, Río** ≈ E Honduras
171 *X16* **Wan** Papua, E Indonesia
Wan *see* Anhui
183 *N4* **Wanaaring** New South Wales, SE Australia
185 *D21* **Wanaka** Otago, South Island, New Zealand
185 *D20* **Wanaka, Lake** ◎ South Island, New Zealand
171 *W14* **Wanapiri** Papua, E Indonesia
14 *F9* **Wanapitei** ≈ Ontario, S Canada
14 *F10* **Wanapitei Lake** ◎ Ontario, S Canada
18 *K14* **Wanaque** New Jersey, NE USA
171 *U12* **Wanau** Papua, E Indonesia
185 *F22* **Wanbrow, Cape** *headland* South Island, New Zealand
Wancheng *see* Wanning
Wanchuan *see* Zhangjiakou
171 *W13* **Wandai** *var.* Komeyo. Papua, E Indonesia
163 *Z8* **Wanda Shan** ▲▲ NE China
197 *R11* **Wandel Sea** *sea* Arctic Ocean
160 *D13* **Wanding** *var.* Wandingzhen. Yunnan, SW China
Wandingzhen *see* Wanding
99 *H20* **Wanfercée-Baulet** Hainaut, S Belgium
184 *L12* **Wanganui** Manawatu-Wanganui, North Island, New Zealand
184 *L11* **Wanganui** ≈ North Island, New Zealand
183 *P11* **Wangaratta** Victoria, SE Australia
160 *J8* **Wangcang** *var.* Donghe; *prev.* Fengjiaba, Hongjiang. Sichuan, C China
Wangda *see* Zogang
101 *I24* **Wangen im Allgäu** Baden-Württemberg, S Germany
Wangerin *see* Węgorzyno
100 *F9* **Wangerooge** *island* NW Germany
171 *W13* **Wanggar** Papua, E Indonesia
160 *J13* **Wangmo** *var.* Fuxing. Guizhou, S China
Wangolodougou *see* Ouangolodougou
161 *S9* **Wangpan Yang** *sea* E China
163 *Y10* **Wangqing** Jilin, NE China
167 *P8* **Wang Saphung** Loei, C Thailand
167 *O6* **Wan Hsa-la** Shan State, E Burma (Myanmar)
55 *W9* **Wanica** ◈ *district* N Surinam
79 *M18* **Wanie-Rukula** Orientale, C Dem. Rep. Congo
Wankie *see* Hwange
Wanki, Río *see* Coco, Río
81 *N17* **Wanlaweyn** *var.* Wanle Weyn, *It.* Uanle Uen. Shabeellaha Hoose, SW Somalia
Wanle Weyn *see* Wanlaweyn
180 *I12* **Wanneroo** Western Australia
160 *L17* **Wanning** *var.* Wancheng. Hainan, S China
167 *Q8* **Wanon Niwat** Sakon Nakhon, E Thailand
155 *H16* **Wanparti** Andhra Pradesh, C India
Wansen *see* Wiązów
160 *L11* **Wanshan** Guizhou, S China
99 *M14* **Wanssum** Limburg, SE Netherlands
184 *N12* **Wanstead** Hawke's Bay, North Island, New Zealand
Wanxian *see* Wanzhou
188 *F16* **Wanyaan** Yap, Micronesia
160 *K8* **Wanyuan** Sichuan, C China
161 *O11* **Wanzai** *var.* Kangle. Jiangxi, S China
99 *J20* **Wanze** Liège, E Belgium
160 *K9* **Wanzhou** *var.* Wanxian. Chongqing Shi, C China
31 *R12* **Wapakoneta** Ohio, N USA
12 *D7* **Wapaseese** ≈ Ontario, C Canada
32 *I10* **Wapato** Washington, NW USA
29 *Y15* **Wapello** Iowa, C USA
9 *N13* **Wapiti** ≈ Alberta/British Columbia, SW Canada
27 *X7* **Wappapello Lake** ⊠ Missouri, C USA
18 *K13* **Wappingers Falls** New York, NE USA
29 *X13* **Wapsipinicon River** ≈ Iowa, C USA
14 *L9* **Wapus** ≈ Québec, SE Canada
160 *H7* **Waqên** Sichuan, C China
21 *Q7* **War** West Virginia, NE USA
80 *D13* **Warab** Warab, SW Sudan
81 *D14* **Warab** ◈ *state* SW Sudan
155 *J15* **Warangal** Andhra Pradesh, C India
Waraždin *see* Varaždin
183 *O16* **Waratah** Tasmania, SE Australia
183 *O14* **Waratah Bay** *bay* Victoria, SE Australia
101 *H15* **Warburg** Nordrhein-Westfalen, W Germany
182 *I1* **Warburton Creek** *seasonal river* South Australia
180 *M9* **Warburton** Western Australia
99 *M20* **Warche** ≈ E Belgium
Wardag/Wardak *see* Vardak
32 *K9* **Warden** Washington, NW USA
154 *I12* **Wardha** Mahārāshtra, W India
Wardija Point *see* Wardija, Ras il-
121 *N15* **Wardija, Ras il-** *var.* Wardija Point. *headland* Gozo, NW Malta
139 *P3* **Wardiyah** N Iraq
185 *E19* **Ward, Mount** ▲ South Island, New Zealand
10 *L11* **Ware** British Columbia, W Canada
99 *D18* **Waregem** *var.* Waereghem. West-Vlaanderen, W Belgium
99 *J19* **Waremme** Liège, E Belgium
100 *N10* **Waren** Mecklenburg-Vorpommern, NE Germany
171 *W13* **Waren** Papua, E Indonesia
101 *F14* **Warendorf** Nordrhein-Westfalen, W Germany
21 *P12* **Ware Shoals** South Carolina, SE USA
98 *N4* **Warffum** Groningen, NE Netherlands
81 *O15* **Wargalo** Mudug, E Somalia
146 *M12* **Warganza** *Rus.* Varganzi. Qashqadaryo Viloyati, S Uzbekistan
Wargla *see* Ouargla
183 *T4* **Warialda** New South Wales, SE Australia
154 *F13* **Wāri Godri** Mahārāshtra, C India
167 *R10* **Warin Chamrap** Ubon Ratchathani, E Thailand
25 *R11* **Waring** Texas, SW USA
39 *O8* **Waring Mountains** ▲▲ Alaska, USA
110 *M12* **Warka** Mazowieckie, E Poland
184 *L5* **Warkworth** Auckland, North Island, New Zealand
171 *U12* **Warmandi** Papua, E Indonesia
83 *E22* **Warmbad** Karas, S Namibia
98 *H8* **Warmenhuizen** Noord-Holland, NW Netherlands
110 *M8* **Warmińsko-Mazurskie** ◈ *province* C Poland
97 *L22* **Warminster** S England, UK
18 *I15* **Warminster** Pennsylvania, NE USA
35 *V8* **Warm Springs** Nevada, W USA
32 *H12* **Warm Springs** Oregon, NW USA
21 *S5* **Warm Springs** Virginia, NE USA
100 *M8* **Warnemünde** Mecklenburg-Vorpommern, NE Germany
27 *Q10* **Warner** Oklahoma, C USA
35 *Q2* **Warner Mountains** ▲▲ California, W USA
23 *T5* **Warner Robins** Georgia, SE USA
57 *N18* **Warnes** Santa Cruz, C Bolivia
100 *M9* **Warnow** ≈ NE Germany
Warnsdorf *see* Varnsdorf
98 *M11* **Warnsveld** Gelderland, E Netherlands
154 *I13* **Warora** Mahārāshtra, C India
182 *L11* **Warracknabeal** Victoria, SE Australia
183 *O13* **Warragul** Victoria, SE Australia
183 *O4* **Warrego River** *seasonal river* New South Wales/Queensland, E Australia
183 *Q6* **Warren** New South Wales, SE Australia
9 *X16* **Warren** Manitoba, S Canada
27 *V14* **Warren** Arkansas, C USA
31 *S10* **Warren** Michigan, N USA
29 *R3* **Warren** Minnesota, N USA
31 *U11* **Warren** Ohio, N USA
18 *D12* **Warren** Pennsylvania, NE USA
25 *X10* **Warren** Texas, SW USA
97 *G16* **Warrenpoint** *Ir.* An Pointe. SE Northern Ireland, UK
27 *S4* **Warrensburg** Missouri, C USA
83 *H22* **Warrenton** Northern Cape, N South Africa
23 *U4* **Warrenton** Georgia, SE USA
27 *W4* **Warrenton** Missouri, C USA
21 *V8* **Warrenton** North Carolina, SE USA
21 *V4* **Warrenton** Virginia, NE USA
77 *U17* **Warri** Delta, S Nigeria
97 *L18* **Warrington** C England, UK
23 *O9* **Warrington** Florida, SE USA
23 *P3* **Warrior** Alabama, S USA
182 *L13* **Warrnambool** Victoria, SE Australia
29 *T2* **Warroad** Minnesota, N USA
183 *S6* **Warrumbungle Range** ▲▲ New South Wales, SE Australia
154 *J12* **Wārsa** Mahārāshtra, C India
31 *P11* **Warsaw** Indiana, N USA
20 *L4* **Warsaw** Kentucky, S USA
27 *T5* **Warsaw** Missouri, C USA
18 *E10* **Warsaw** New York, NE USA
21 *V10* **Warsaw** North Carolina, SE USA
21 *X5* **Warsaw** Virginia, NE USA
Warsaw/Warschau *see* Warszawa
81 *N17* **Warshiikh** Shabeellaha Dhexe, C Somalia
101 *G15* **Warstein** Nordrhein-Westfalen, W Germany
110 *M11* **Warszawa** *Eng.* Warsaw, *Ger.* Warschau, *Rus.* Varshava. ● (Poland) Mazowieckie, C Poland
110 *J13* **Warta** Sieradz, C Poland
110 *D11* **Warta** *Ger.* Warthe. ≈ W Poland
Wartberg *see* Senec
20 *M9* **Wartburg** Tennessee, S USA
108 *J7* **Warth** Vorarlberg, NW Austria
Warthe *see* Warta
169 *U12* **Waru** Borneo, C Indonesia
171 *T13* **Waru** Pulau Seram, E Indonesia
139 *N6* **Wa'r, Wādī al** *dry watercourse* E Syria
183 *U3* **Warwick** Queensland, E Australia
15 *Q11* **Warwick** Québec, SE Canada
97 *M20* **Warwick** C England, UK
18 *K13* **Warwick** New York, NE USA
29 *P4* **Warwick** North Dakota, N USA
19 *O12* **Warwick** Rhode Island, NE USA
97 *L20* **Warwickshire** *cultural region* C England, UK
14 *G14* **Wasaga Beach** Ontario, S Canada
77 *U13* **Wasagu** Kebbi, NW Nigeria
36 *M2* **Wasatch Range** ▲▲ W USA
35 *R12* **Wasco** California, W USA
29 *V10* **Waseca** Minnesota, N USA
14 *H13* **Washago** Ontario, S Canada
19 *S2* **Washburn** Maine, NE USA
28 *M5* **Washburn** North Dakota, N USA
30 *K3* **Washburn** Wisconsin, N USA
31 *S14* **Washburn Hill** *hill* Ohio, N USA
154 *H13* **Wāshīm** Mahārāshtra, C India
97 *M14* **Washington** NE England, UK
23 *U3* **Washington** Georgia, SE USA
30 *L12* **Washington** Illinois, N USA
31 *N15* **Washington** Indiana, N USA
29 *X15* **Washington** Iowa, C USA
27 *O3* **Washington** Kansas, C USA
27 *W5* **Washington** Missouri, C USA
21 *X9* **Washington** North Carolina, SE USA
18 *B15* **Washington** Pennsylvania, NE USA
25 *V10* **Washington** Texas, SW USA
36 *J8* **Washington** Utah, W USA
21 *V4* **Washington** Virginia, NE USA
32 *I9* **Washington** *off.* State of Washington, *also known as* Chinook State, Evergreen State. ◈ *state* NW USA
Washington *see* Washington Court House
31 *S14* **Washington Court House** *var.* Washington. Ohio, NE USA
21 *W4* **Washington DC** ● (USA) District of Columbia, NE USA
31 *O5* **Washington Island** *island* Wisconsin, N USA
Washington Island *see* Teraina
19 *O7* **Washington, Mount** ▲ New Hampshire, NE USA
26 *M11* **Washita River** ≈ Oklahoma/Texas, C USA
97 *O18* **Wash, The** *inlet* E England, UK
32 *L9* **Washtucna** Washington, NW USA
Wasiliszki *see* Vasilishki
110 *P9* **Wasilków** Podlaskie, NE Poland
39 *R11* **Wasilla** Alaska, USA
55 *U9* **Wasjabo** Sipaliwini, NW Surinam
9 *X11* **Waskaiowaka Lake** ◎ Manitoba, C Canada
9 *T14* **Waskesiu Lake** Saskatchewan, C Canada
25 *X7* **Waskom** Texas, SW USA
110 *G13* **Wąsosz** Dolnośląskie, SW Poland
42 *M6* **Waspam** *var.* Waspán. Región Autónoma Atlántico Norte, NE Nicaragua
Waspán *see* Waspam
165 *T3* **Wassamu** Hokkaidō, NE Japan
108 *G9* **Wassen** Uri, C Switzerland
98 *G11* **Wassenaar** Zuid-Holland, W Netherlands
99 *N24* **Wasserbillig** Grevenmacher, E Luxembourg
Wasserburg *see* Wasserburg am Inn
101 *M23* **Wasserburg am Inn** *var.* Wasserburg. Bayern, SE Germany
101 *I17* **Wasserkuppe** ▲ C Germany
103 *R5* **Wassy** Haute-Marne, N France
171 *N14* **Watampone** *var.* Bone. Sulawesi, C Indonesia
171 *R13* **Watawa** Pulau Buru, E Indonesia
Watenstedt-Salzgitter *see* Salzgitter
18 *M13* **Waterbury** Connecticut, NE USA
21 *R11* **Wateree Lake** ⊠ South Carolina, SE USA
21 *R12* **Wateree River** ≈ South Carolina, SE USA
97 *E20* **Waterford** *Ir.* Port Láirge. Waterford, S Ireland
31 *S9* **Waterford** Michigan, N USA
97 *E20* **Waterford** *Ir.* Port Láirge. ◈ *county* S Ireland
97 *E21* **Waterford Harbour** *Ir.* Cuan Phort Láirge. *inlet* S Ireland
98 *G12* **Wateringen** Zuid-Holland, W Netherlands
99 *G19* **Waterloo** Walloon Brabant, C Belgium
14 *F16* **Waterloo** Ontario, S Canada
15 *P12* **Waterloo** Québec, SE Canada
30 *K16* **Waterloo** Illinois, N USA
29 *X13* **Waterloo** Iowa, C USA
18 *G10* **Waterloo** New York, NE USA
30 *L4* **Watersmeet** Michigan, N USA
23 *V9* **Watertown** Florida, SE USA
18 *I8* **Watertown** New York, NE USA
29 *R9* **Watertown** South Dakota, N USA
30 *M8* **Watertown** Wisconsin, N USA
22 *L3* **Water Valley** Mississippi, S USA
27 *O3* **Waterville** Kansas, C USA
19 *Q7* **Waterville** Maine, NE USA
29 *V10* **Waterville** Minnesota, N USA
18 *I10* **Waterville** New York, NE USA
14 *E16* **Watford** Ontario, S Canada
97 *N21* **Watford** E England, UK
28 *K4* **Watford City** North Dakota, N USA
141 *X12* **Wāṭif** S Oman
18 *G11* **Watkins Glen** New York, NE USA
Watlings Island *see* San Salvador
171 *U15* **Watnil** Pulau Kai Kecil, E Indonesia
26 *M10* **Watonga** Oklahoma, C USA
9 *T16* **Watrous** Saskatchewan, S Canada
37 *T10* **Watrous** New Mexico, SW USA
79 *P16* **Watsa** Orientale, NE Dem. Rep. Congo
31 *N12* **Watseka** Illinois, N USA
79 *J19* **Watsikengo** Equateur, C Dem. Rep. Congo
182 *C5* **Watson** South Australia
9 *U15* **Watson** Saskatchewan, S Canada
195 *O10* **Watson Escarpment** ▲▲ Antarctica
10 *K9* **Watson Lake** Yukon Territory, W Canada
35 *N10* **Watsonville** California, W USA
167 *Q8* **Wattay** ✕ (Viangchan) Viangchan, C Laos
109 *N7* **Wattens** Tirol, W Austria
20 *M9* **Watts Bar Lake** ⊠ Tennessee, S USA
108 *H7* **Wattwil** Sankt Gallen, NE Switzerland
171 *T14* **Watubela, Kepulauan** *island group* E Indonesia
101 *N24* **Watzmann** ▲ SE Germany
186 *E8* **Wau** Morobe, C Papua New Guinea
81 *D14* **Wau** *var.* Wāw. Western Bahr el Ghazal, S Sudan
29 *Q8* **Waubay** South Dakota, N USA
29 *Q8* **Waubay Lake** ◎ South Dakota, N USA
183 *U7* **Wauchope** New South Wales, SE Australia
23 *W13* **Wauchula** Florida, SE USA
30 *M10* **Wauconda** Illinois, N USA
182 *J7* **Waukaringa** South Australia
31 *N10* **Waukegan** Illinois, N USA
30 *M9* **Waukesha** Wisconsin, N USA
29 *X11* **Waukon** Iowa, C USA
30 *L8* **Waunakee** Wisconsin, N USA
30 *L7* **Waupaca** Wisconsin, N USA
30 *M8* **Waupun** Wisconsin, N USA
26 *M13* **Waurika** Oklahoma, C USA
26 *M12* **Waurika Lake** ⊠ Oklahoma, C USA
30 *L6* **Wausau** Wisconsin, N USA
31 *R11* **Wauseon** Ohio, N USA
30 *L7* **Wautoma** Wisconsin, N USA
30 *M9* **Wauwatosa** Wisconsin, N USA
22 *L9* **Waveland** Mississippi, S USA
97 *Q20* **Waveney** ≈ E England, UK
184 *L11* **Waverley** Taranaki, North Island, New Zealand
29 *W12* **Waverly** Iowa, C USA
27 *T4* **Waverly** Missouri, C USA
29 *R15* **Waverly** Nebraska, C USA
18 *G12* **Waverly** New York, NE USA
20 *H8* **Waverly** Tennessee, S USA
21 *W7* **Waverly** Virginia, NE USA
99 *H19* **Wavre** Walloon Brabant, C Belgium
166 *M8* **Waw** Pegu, SW Burma (Myanmar)
Wāw *see* Wau
14 *B7* **Wawa** Ontario, S Canada
77 *T14* **Wawa** Niger, W Nigeria
75 *Q11* **Wāw al Kabīr** S Libya
43 *N7* **Wawa, Río** *var.* Rio Huahua. ≈ NE Nicaragua
186 *B8* **Wawoi** ≈ SW Papua New Guinea
25 *T7* **Waxahachie** Texas, SW USA
158 *L9* **Waxxari** Xinjiang Uygur Zizhiqu, NW China
Wayaobu *see* Zichang
23 *V7* **Waycross** Georgia, SE USA
180 *K10* **Way, Lake** ◎ Western Australia
31 *P9* **Wayland** Michigan, N USA
29 *R13* **Wayne** Nebraska, C USA
18 *K14* **Wayne** New Jersey, NE USA
21 *P5* **Wayne** West Virginia, NE USA
23 *V4* **Waynesboro** Georgia, SE USA
22 *M7* **Waynesboro** Mississippi, S USA
20 *H10* **Waynesboro** Tennessee, S USA
21 *U5* **Waynesboro** Virginia, NE USA
18 *B16* **Waynesburg** Pennsylvania, NE USA
27 *U6* **Waynesville** Missouri, C USA
21 *O10* **Waynesville** North Carolina, SE USA
26 *L8* **Waynoka** Oklahoma, C USA
Wazan *see* Ouazzane
Wazima *see* Wajima
149 *V7* **Wazīrābād** Punjab, NE Pakistan
Wazzan *see* Ouazzane
110 *I8* **Wda** *var.* Czarna Woda, *Ger.* Schwarzwasser. ≈ N Poland
187 *Q16* **Wé** Province des Îles Loyauté, E New Caledonia
97 *O23* **Weald, The** *lowlands* SE England, UK
186 *A9* **Weam** Western, SW Papua New Guinea
97 *L15* **Wear** ≈ N England, UK
Wearmouth *see* Sunderland
26 *L10* **Weatherford** Oklahoma, C USA
25 *S6* **Weatherford** Texas, SW USA
34 *M3* **Weaverville** California, W USA
27 *R7* **Webb City** Missouri, C USA
192 *G8* **Weber Basin** *undersea feature* S Ceram Sea
Webfoot State *see* Oregon
18 *F9* **Webster** New York, NE USA
29 *Q8* **Webster** South Dakota, N USA
29 *V13* **Webster City** Iowa, C USA
27 *X5* **Webster Groves** Missouri, C USA
21 *S4* **Webster Springs** *var.* Addison. West Virginia, NE USA
171 *S11* **Weda, Teluk** *bay* Pulau Halmahera, E Indonesia
65 *B25* **Weddell Island** *var.* Isla San José. *island* W Falkland Islands
65 *K22* **Weddell Plain** *undersea feature* SW Atlantic Ocean
65 *K23* **Weddell Sea** *sea* SW Atlantic Ocean
65 *B25* **Weddell Settlement** Weddell Island, W Falkland Islands
182 *M11* **Wedderburn** Victoria, SE Australia
100 *I9* **Wedel** Schleswig-Holstein, N Germany
92 *N3* **Wedel Jarlsberg Land** *physical region* SW Svalbard
100 *I12* **Wedemark** Niedersachsen, NW Germany
10 *M17* **Wedge Mountain** ▲ British Columbia, SW Canada
23 *R4* **Wedowee** Alabama, S USA
171 *U15* **Weduar** Pulau Kai Besar, E Indonesia
35 *N2* **Weed** California, W USA
15 *Q12* **Weedon Centre** Québec, SE Canada
18 *E13* **Weedville** Pennsylvania, NE USA
100 *F10* **Weener** Niedersachsen, NW Germany
29 *S16* **Weeping Water** Nebraska, C USA
99 *L16* **Weert** Limburg, SE Netherlands
98 *I10* **Weesp** Noord-Holland, C Netherlands
183 *S5* **Wee Waa** New South Wales, SE Australia
110 *N7* **Węgorzewo** *Ger.* Angerburg. Warmińsko-Mazurskie, NE Poland
110 *E9* **Węgorzyno** *Ger.* Wangerin. Zachodnio-pomorskie, NW Poland
110 *N11* **Węgrów** *Ger.* Bingerau. Mazowieckie, C Poland
98 *N5* **Wehe-Den Hoorn** Groningen, NE Netherlands
98 *M12* **Wehl** Gelderland, E Netherlands
Wehlau *see* Znamensk
168 *F7* **Weh, Pulau** *island* NW Indonesia
Wei *see* Weifang
161 *P1* **Weichang** *prev.* Zhuizishan. Hebei, E China
Weichang *see* Weishan
Weichsel *see* Wisła
101 *M16* **Weida** Thüringen, C Germany
Weiden *see* Weiden in der Oberpfalz
101 *M19* **Weiden in der Oberpfalz** *var.* Weiden. Bayern, SE Germany
161 *Q4* **Weifang** *var.* Wei, Wei-fang; *prev.* Weihsien. Shandong, E China
161 *S4* **Weihai** Shandong, E China
160 *K6* **Wei He** ≈ C China
Weihsien *see* Weifang
101 *G17* **Weilburg** Hessen, W Germany
101 *K24* **Weilheim in Oberbayern** Bayern, SE Germany
183 *P4* **Weilmoringle** New South Wales, SE Australia
101 *L16* **Weimar** Thüringen, C Germany
25 *U11* **Weimar** Texas, SW USA
160 *L6* **Weinan** Shaanxi, C China
108 *H6* **Weinfelden** Thurgau, NE Switzerland
101 *I24* **Weingarten** Baden-Württemberg, S Germany
101 *G20* **Weinheim** Baden-Württemberg, SW Germany
160 *H11* **Weining** *var.* Weining Yizu Huizu Miaozu Zizhixian. Guizhou, S China
Weining Yizu Huizu Miaozu Zizhixian *see* Weining
181 *V2* **Weipa** Queensland, NE Australia
9 *Y11* **Weir River** Manitoba, C Canada
21 *R1* **Weirton** West Virginia, NE USA
32 *M13* **Weiser** Idaho, NW USA
160 *F12* **Weishan** *var.* Weichang. Yunnan, SW China
161 *P6* **Weishan Hu** ◎ E China
101 *M15* **Weisse Elster** *Eng.* White Elster. ≈ Czech Republic/Germany
Weisse Körös/Weisse Kreisch *see* Crişul Alb
108 *L7* **Weissenbach am Lech** Tirol, W Austria
Weissenburg *see* Wissembourg
Weissenburg *see* Alba Iulia
101 *K21* **Weissenburg in Bayern** Bayern, SE Germany
101 *M15* **Weissenfels** *var.* Weißenfels. Sachsen-Anhalt, C Germany
109 *R9* **Weissensee** ◎ S Austria
Weissenstein *see* Paide
108 *E11* **Weisshorn** *var.* Flüela Wisshorn. ▲ SW Switzerland
Weisskirchen *see* Bela Crkva
23 *R3* **Weiss Lake** ⊠ Alabama, S USA
101 *Q14* **Weisswasser** *Lus.* Běla Woda. Sachsen, E Germany
99 *M22* **Weiswampach** Diekirch, N Luxembourg
109 *U2* **Weitra** Niederösterreich, N Austria
161 *O4* **Weixian** *var.* Wei Xian. Hebei, E China
Wei Xian *see* Weixian
159 *V11* **Weiyuan** Gansu, C China
Weiyuan *see* Shuangjiang
160 *F14* **Weiyuan Jiang** ≈ SW China
109 *W7* **Weiz** Steiermark, SE Austria
Weizhou *see* Wenchuan
160 *K16* **Weizhou Dao** *island* S China
110 *I6* **Wejherowo** Pomorskie, NW Poland
27 *Q8* **Welch** Oklahoma, C USA
24 *M6* **Welch** Texas, SW USA
21 *Q6* **Welch** West Virginia, NE USA
45 *O14* **Welchman Hall** C Barbados
80 *J11* **Weldiya** *var.* Waldia, *It.* Valdia. Amhara, N Ethiopia
21 *W8* **Weldon** North Carolina, SE USA
25 *V9* **Weldon** Texas, SW USA
99 *M19* **Welkenraedt** Liège, E Belgium
193 *O2* **Welker Seamount** *undersea feature* N Pacific Ocean
83 *I22* **Welkom** Free State, C South Africa
14 *H16* **Welland** Ontario, S Canada
14 *G16* **Welland** ≈ Ontario, S Canada
97 *O19* **Welland** ≈ C England, UK
14 *H17* **Welland Canal** *canal* Ontario, S Canada
155 *K25* **Wellawaya** Uva Province, SE Sri Lanka
Welle *see* Uele
181 *T4* **Wellesley Islands** *island group* Queensland, N Australia
99 *J22* **Wellin** Luxembourg, SE Belgium
97 *N20* **Wellingborough** C England, UK
183 *R7* **Wellington** New South Wales, SE Australia
14 *J15* **Wellington** Ontario, SE Canada
185 *L14* **Wellington** ● Wellington, North Island, New Zealand
83 *E26* **Wellington** Western Cape, SW South Africa
37 *T2* **Wellington** Colorado, C USA
27 *N7* **Wellington** Kansas, C USA
35 *R7* **Wellington** Nevada, W USA
31 *T11* **Wellington** Ohio, N USA
25 *P3* **Wellington** Texas, SW USA
36 *M4* **Wellington** Utah, W USA
185 *M14* **Wellington** *off.* Wellington Region. ◈ *region* (New Zealand) North Island, New Zealand
185 *L14* **Wellington** ✕ Wellington, North Island, New Zealand
Wellington *see* Wellington, Isla
63 *F22* **Wellington, Isla** *var.* Wellington. *island* S Chile
183 *P12* **Wellington, Lake** ◎ Victoria, SE Australia
Wellington Region *see* Wellington
29 *X14* **Wellman** Iowa, C USA
24 *M6* **Wellman** Texas, SW USA
97 *K22* **Wells** SW England, UK
29 *V11* **Wells** Minnesota, N USA
35 *X2* **Wells** Nevada, W USA
25 *W8* **Wells** Texas, SW USA
18 *F12* **Wellsboro** Pennsylvania, NE USA
21 *R1* **Wellsburg** West Virginia, NE USA
184 *K4* **Wellsford** Auckland, North Island, New Zealand
180 *L9* **Wells, Lake** ◎ Western Australia
181 *N4* **Wells, Mount** ▲ Western Australia
97 *P18* **Wells-next-the-Sea** E England, UK
31 *T15* **Wellston** Ohio, N USA
27 *O10* **Wellston** Oklahoma, C USA
18 *E11* **Wellsville** New York, NE USA
31 *V12* **Wellsville** Ohio, N USA
36 *L1* **Wellsville** Utah, W USA
36 *I14* **Wellton** Arizona, SW USA
109 *S4* **Wels** *anc.* Ovilava. Oberösterreich, N Austria
99 *K15* **Welschap** ✕ (Eindhoven) Noord-Brabant, S Netherlands
100 *P10* **Welse** ≈ NE Germany
22 *H9* **Welsh** Louisiana, S USA
97 *K19* **Welshpool** *Wel.* Y Trallwng. E Wales, UK
97 *O21* **Welwyn Garden City** E England, UK
79 *K18* **Wema** Equateur, NW Dem. Rep. Congo
81 *G21* **Wembere** ≈ C Tanzania
9 *N13* **Wembley** Alberta, W Canada
12 *I9* **Wemindji** *prev.* Nouveau-Comptoir, Paint Hills. Québec, C Canada
99 *G18* **Wemmel** Vlaams Brabant, C Belgium
32 *J8* **Wenatchee** Washington, NW USA
160 *M17* **Wenchang** Hainan, S China
161 *R11* **Wencheng** *var.* Daxue. Zhejiang, SE China
77 *P16* **Wenchi** W Ghana
Wen-chou/Wenchow *see* Wenzhou
160 *H8* **Wenchuan** *var.* Weizhou. Sichuan, C China
Wendau *see* Võnnu
Wenden *see* Cēsis
161 *S4* **Wendeng** Shandong, E China
81 *J14* **Wendo** Southern, S Ethiopia
36 *J2* **Wendover** Utah, W USA
14 *D9* **Wenebegon** ≈ Ontario, S Canada
14 *D8* **Wenebegon Lake** ◎ Ontario, S Canada
108 *E9* **Wengen** Bern, W Switzerland
161 *O13* **Wengyuan** *var.* Longxian. Guangdong, S China
189 *P15* **Weno** *prev.* Moen. Chuuk, C Micronesia
189 *V12* **Weno** *prev.* Moen. *atoll* Chuuk Islands, C Micronesia
158 *I13* **Wenquan** Qinghai, C China
159 *H4* **Wenquan** *var.* Arixang. Xinjiang Uygur Zizhiqu, NW China
Wenquan *see* Yingshan
160 *H14* **Wenshan** *var.* Kaihua. Yunnan, SW China
158 *H6* **Wensu** Xinjiang Uygur Zizhiqu, W China
182 *L8* **Wentworth** New South Wales, SE Australia
27 *W4* **Wentzville** Missouri, C USA
159 *V12* **Wenxian** *var.* Wen Xian. Gansu, C China
Wen Xian *see* Wenxian
161 *S10* **Wenzhou** *var.* Wen-chou, Wenchow. Zhejiang, SE China
34 *L4* **Weott** California, W USA
99 *I20* **Wépion** Namur, SE Belgium
100 *O11* **Werbellinsee** ◎ NE Germany
99 *L21* **Werbomont** Liège, E Belgium
83 *G20* **Werda** Kgalagadi, S Botswana
81 *N14* **Werdër** Somali, E Ethiopia
Werder *see* Virtsu
Werenów *see* Voranava
171 *U13* **Weri** Papua, E Indonesia
98 *I13* **Werkendam** Noord-Brabant, S Netherlands
101 *M20* **Wernberg-Köblitz** Bayern, SE Germany
101 *J18* **Werneck** Bayern, C Germany
101 *K14* **Wernigerode** Sachsen-Anhalt, C Germany
Werowitz *see* Virovitica
101 *J16* **Werra** ≈ C Germany
183 *N12* **Werribee** Victoria, SE Australia
183 *T6* **Werris Creek** New South Wales, SE Australia
Werro *see* Võru
Werschetz *see* Vršac
101 *K23* **Wertach** ≈ S Germany
101 *I19* **Wertheim** Baden-Württemberg, SW Germany
98 *J8* **Wervershoof** Noord-Holland, NW Netherlands
Wervicq *see* Wervik
99 *C18* **Wervik** *var.* Wervicq, Werwick. West-Vlaanderen, W Belgium
Werwick *see* Wervik
101 *D14* **Wesel** Nordrhein-Westfalen, W Germany
Weseli an der Lainsitz *see* Veselí nad Lužnicí
Wesenberg *see* Rakvere
100 *H12* **Weser** ≈ NW Germany
Wes-Kaap *see* Western Cape
25 *S17* **Weslaco** Texas, SW USA
14 *J13* **Weslemkoon Lake** ◎ Ontario, SE Canada
181 *R1* **Wessel Islands** *island group* Northern Territory, N Australia
29 *P9* **Wessington** South Dakota, N USA
29 *P10* **Wessington Springs** South Dakota, N USA
25 *T8* **West** Texas, SW USA
West *see* Ouest
30 *M9* **West Allis** Wisconsin, N USA

◆ Country ● Country Capital ◇ Dependent Territory ○ Dependent Territory Capital ◈ Administrative Regions ✕ International Airport ▲ Mountain ▲▲ Mountain Range ⛰ Volcano ≈ River ◎ Lake ⊠ Reservoir

Westall, Point – Wilsons Promontory

182 E8 **Westall, Point** *headland* South Australia
West Antarctica *see* Lesser Antarctica
14 G11 **West Arm** Ontario, S Canada
West Australian Basin *see* Wharton Basin
West Azerbaijan *see* Āzarbāyjān-e Gharbī
9 N17 **Westbank** British Columbia, SW Canada
138 F10 **West Bank** *disputed region* SW Asia
14 E11 **West Bay** Manitoulin Island, Ontario, S Canada
22 L11 **West Bay** *bay* Louisiana, S USA
30 M8 **West Bend** Wisconsin, N USA
153 R16 **West Bengal** ⬖ *state* NE India
West Borneo *see* Kalimantan Barat
29 Y14 **West Branch** Iowa, C USA
31 R7 **West Branch** Michigan, N USA
18 F13 **West Branch Susquehanna River** ≈ Pennsylvania, NE USA
97 L20 **West Bromwich** C England, UK
19 P8 **Westbrook** Maine, NE USA
29 T10 **Westbrook** Minnesota, N USA
29 Y15 **West Burlington** Iowa, C USA
96 L2 **West Burra** *island* NE Scotland, UK
30 J8 **Westby** Wisconsin, N USA
44 L6 **West Caicos** *island* W Turks and Caicos Islands
185 A24 **West Cape** *headland* South Island, New Zealand
174 L4 **West Caroline Basin** *undersea feature* SW Pacific Ocean
18 I16 **West Chester** Pennsylvania, NE USA
185 E18 **West Coast** *off.* West Coast Region. ⬖ *region* South Island, New Zealand
West Coast Region *see* West Coast
25 V12 **West Columbia** Texas, SW USA
29 W10 **West Concord** Minnesota, N USA
29 V14 **West Des Moines** Iowa, C USA
37 Q6 **West Elk Peak** ▲ Colorado, C USA
44 F1 **West End** Grand Bahama Island, N Bahamas
44 F1 **West End Point** *headland* Grand Bahama Island, N Bahamas
98 O7 **Westerbork** Drenthe, NE Netherlands
98 N3 **Westereems** *strait* Germany/Netherlands
98 O9 **Westerhaar-Vriezenveensewijk** Overijssel, E Netherlands
100 G6 **Westerland** Schleswig-Holstein, N Germany
99 I17 **Westerlo** Antwerpen, N Belgium
19 N13 **Westerly** Rhode Island, NE USA
81 G18 **Western** ⬖ *province* W Kenya
153 N11 **Western** ⬖ *zone* C Nepal
186 A8 **Western** ⬖ *province* SW Papua New Guinea
186 J8 **Western** *off.* Western Province. ⬖ *province* NW Solomon Islands
83 G15 **Western** ⬖ *province* SW Zambia
180 K8 **Western Australia** ⬖ *state* W Australia
80 A13 **Western Bahr el Ghazal** ⬖ *state* SW Sudan
Western Bug *see* Bug
83 F25 **Western Cape** *off.* Western Cape Province, *Afr.* Wes-Kaap. ⬖ *province* SW South Africa
Western Cape Province *see* Western Cape
80 A11 **Western Darfur** ⬖ *state* W Sudan
Western Desert *see* Sahara el Gharbîya
118 G9 **Western Dvina** *Bel.* Dzvina, *Ger.* Düna, *Latv.* Daugava, *Rus.* Zapadnaya Dvina. ≈ W Europe
81 D15 **Western Equatoria** ⬖ *state* SW Sudan
155 E16 **Western Ghats** ▲▲ SW India
186 C7 **Western Highlands** ⬖ *province* C Papua New Guinea
Western Isles *see* Outer Hebrides
80 C12 **Western Kordofan** ⬖ *state* C Sudan
21 T3 **Westernport** Maryland, NE USA
155 J26 **Western Province** ⬖ *province* SW Sri Lanka
Western Province *see* Western
Western Punjab *see* Punjab
74 B10 **Western Sahara** ◇ *disputed territory* N Africa
Western Samoa *see* Samoa
Western Samoa, Independent State of *see* Samoa
Western Sayans *see* Zapadnyy Sayan
Western Scheldt *see* Westerschelde
0 G13 **Western Sierra Madre** *var.* Western Sierra Madre. ▲▲ C Mexico
Western Sierra Madre *see* Western Sierra Madre
Western Sierra Madre *see* Sierra Madre Occidental
99 E15 **Westerschelde** *Eng.* Western Scheldt; *prev.* Honte. *inlet* S North Sea
31 S13 **Westerville** Ohio, N USA
101 F17 **Westerwald** ▲▲ W Germany
65 C25 **West Falkland** *var.* Gran Malvina. *island* W Falkland Islands
29 R5 **West Fargo** North Dakota, N USA
188 M15 **West Fayu Atoll** *atoll* Caroline Islands, C Micronesia
18 C11 **Westfield** New York, NE USA
30 L7 **Westfield** Wisconsin, N USA
West Flanders *see* West-Vlaanderen
27 S10 **West Fork** Arkansas, C USA
29 P16 **West Fork Big Blue River** ≈ Nebraska, C USA
29 U12 **West Fork Des Moines River** ≈ Iowa/Minnesota, C USA
25 S5 **West Fork Trinity River** ≈ Texas, SW USA
30 L16 **West Frankfort** Illinois, N USA
98 I8 **West-Friesland** *physical region* NW Netherlands
West Frisian Islands *see* Waddeneilanden
19 T5 **West Grand Lake** ◎ Maine, NE USA
18 M12 **West Hartford** Connecticut, NE USA
18 M13 **West Haven** Connecticut, NE USA
27 X12 **West Helena** Arkansas, C USA
28 M2 **Westhope** North Dakota, N USA
195 Y8 **West Ice Shelf** *ice shelf* Antarctica
47 R2 **West Indies** *island group* SE North America
West Irian *see* Papua
West Java *see* Jawa Barat
36 L3 **West Jordan** Utah, W USA
West Kalimantan *see* Kalimantan Barat
99 D14 **Westkapelle** Zeeland, SW Netherlands
West Kazakhstan *see* Zapadnyy Kazakhstan
31 O13 **West Lafayette** Indiana, N USA
31 T13 **West Lafayette** Ohio, N USA
West Lake *see* Kagera
29 Y14 **West Liberty** Iowa, C USA
21 O5 **West Liberty** Kentucky, S USA
Westliche Morava *see* Zapadna Morava
10 J13 **Westlock** Alberta, SW Canada
14 E17 **West Lorne** Ontario, S Canada
96 J12 **West Lothian** *cultural region* S Scotland, UK
99 H16 **Westmalle** Antwerpen, N Belgium
192 G6 **West Mariana Basin** *var.* Perece Vela Basin. *undersea feature* W Pacific Ocean
97 E17 **Westmeath** *Ir.* An Iarmhí, Na H-Iarmhidhe. ⬖ *county* C Ireland
27 Y11 **West Memphis** Arkansas, C USA
21 W2 **Westminster** Maryland, NE USA
21 O11 **Westminster** South Carolina, SE USA
22 I5 **West Monroe** Louisiana, S USA
18 D15 **Westmont** Pennsylvania, NE USA
27 O3 **Westmoreland** Kansas, C USA
35 W17 **Westmorland** California, W USA
186 E6 **West New Britain** ⬖ *province* E Papua New Guinea
West New Guinea *see* Papua
83 K18 **West Nicholson** Matabeleland South, S Zimbabwe
29 T14 **West Nishnabotna River** ≈ Iowa, C USA
175 P11 **West Norfolk Ridge** *undersea feature* W Pacific Ocean
25 P12 **West Nueces River** ≈ Texas, SW USA
West Nusa Tenggara *see* Nusa Tenggara Barat
29 T11 **West Okoboji Lake** ◎ Iowa, C USA
33 R16 **Weston** Idaho, NW USA
21 R4 **Weston** West Virginia, NE USA
97 J22 **Weston-super-Mare** SW England, UK
23 Z14 **West Palm Beach** Florida, SE USA
West Papua *see* Papua
188 E9 **West Passage** *passage* Babeldaob, N Palau
23 O9 **West Pensacola** Florida, SE USA
27 V8 **West Plains** Missouri, C USA
35 P7 **West Point** California, W USA
23 R5 **West Point** Georgia, SE USA
22 M3 **West Point** Mississippi, S USA
29 R14 **West Point** Nebraska, C USA
21 X6 **West Point** Virginia, NE USA
182 G10 **West Point** *headland* South Australia
65 B24 **Westpoint Island Settlement** Westpoint Island, NW Falkland Islands
23 R4 **West Point Lake** ⊠ Alabama/Georgia, SE USA
97 B16 **Westport** *Ir.* Cathair na Mart. Mayo, W Ireland
185 G15 **Westport** West Coast, South Island, New Zealand
32 F10 **Westport** Oregon, NW USA
32 F9 **Westport** Washington, NW USA
31 S15 **West Portsmouth** Ohio, N USA
West Punjab *see* Punjab
9 V14 **Westray** Manitoba, C Canada
96 J4 **Westray** *island* NE Scotland, UK
14 F9 **Westree** Ontario, S Canada
97 L16 **West Riding** *cultural region* N England, UK
West River *see* Xi Jiang
30 J7 **West Salem** Wisconsin, N USA
65 H21 **West Scotia Ridge** *undersea feature* W Scotia Sea
West Sepik *see* Sandaun
173 N4 **West Sheba Ridge** *undersea feature* W Indian Ocean
West Siberian Plain *see* Zapadno-Sibirskaya Ravnina
31 S11 **West Sister Island** *island* Ohio, N USA
West-Skylge *see* West-Terschelling
West Sumatra *see* Sumatera Barat
98 J5 **West-Terschelling** *Fris.* West-Skylge. Friesland, N Netherlands
64 J7 **West Thulean Rise** *undersea feature* N Atlantic Ocean
29 X12 **West Union** Iowa, C USA
31 R15 **West Union** Ohio, N USA
21 R3 **West Union** West Virginia, NE USA
31 N13 **Westville** Illinois, N USA
21 R3 **West Virginia** *off.* State of West Virginia, *also known as* Mountain State. ⬖ *state* NE USA
99 A17 **West-Vlaanderen** *Eng.* West Flanders. ⬖ *province* W Belgium
35 R7 **West Walker River** ≈ California/Nevada, W USA
35 P4 **Westwood** California, W USA
183 P9 **West Wyalong** New South Wales, SE Australia
171 Q16 **Wetar, Pulau** *island* Kepulauan Damar, E Indonesia
171 R16 **Wetar, Selat** *var.* Wetar Strait. *strait* Nusa Tenggara, S Indonesia
Wetar Strait *see* Wetar, Selat
9 Q15 **Wetaskiwin** Alberta, SW Canada
81 K21 **Wete** Pemba, E Tanzania
166 M4 **Wetlet** Sagaing, C Burma (Myanmar)
37 T6 **Wet Mountains** ▲▲ Colorado, C USA
101 E15 **Wetter** Nordrhein-Westfalen, W Germany
101 H17 **Wetter** ≈ W Germany
99 F17 **Wetteren** Oost-Vlaanderen, NW Belgium
108 F7 **Wettingen** Aargau, N Switzerland
27 P11 **Wetumka** Oklahoma, C USA
23 Q5 **Wetumpka** Alabama, S USA
108 G7 **Wetzikon** Zürich, N Switzerland
101 G17 **Wetzlar** Hessen, W Germany
99 C18 **Wevelgem** West-Vlaanderen, W Belgium
38 M6 **Wevok** *var.* Wewuk. Alaska, USA
23 R9 **Wewahitchka** Florida, SE USA
186 C6 **Wewak** East Sepik, NW Papua New Guinea
27 O11 **Wewoka** Oklahoma, C USA
Wewuk *see* Wevok
97 F20 **Wexford** *Ir.* Loch Garman. SE Ireland
97 F20 **Wexford** *Ir.* Loch Garman. ⬖ *cultural region* SE Ireland
30 L7 **Weyauwega** Wisconsin, N USA
9 U17 **Weyburn** Saskatchewan, S Canada
Weyer *see* Weyer Markt
109 U5 **Weyer Markt** *var.* Weyer. Oberösterreich, N Austria
100 H11 **Weyhe** Niedersachsen, NW Germany
97 L24 **Weymouth** S England, UK
19 P11 **Weymouth** Massachusetts, NE USA
99 H18 **Wezembeek-Oppem** Vlaams Brabant, C Belgium
98 M9 **Wezep** Gelderland, E Netherlands
184 M9 **Whakamaru** Waikato, North Island, New Zealand
184 O8 **Whakatane** Bay of Plenty, North Island, New Zealand
184 O8 **Whakatane** ≈ North Island, New Zealand
9 O9 **Whale Cove** Nunavut, C Canada
96 M2 **Whalsay** *island* NE Scotland, UK
184 L11 **Whangaehu** ≈ North Island, New Zealand
184 M6 **Whangamata** Waikato, North Island, New Zealand
184 Q9 **Whangara** Gisborne, North Island, New Zealand
184 K3 **Whangarei** Northland, North Island, New Zealand
184 K3 **Whangaruru Harbour** *inlet* North Island, New Zealand
25 V12 **Wharton** Texas, SW USA
173 U8 **Wharton Basin** *var.* West Australian Basin. *undersea feature* E Indian Ocean
185 E18 **Whataroa** West Coast, South Island, New Zealand
8 K10 **Wha Ti** *var.* Lac la Martre. Northwest Territories, W Canada
8 K10 **Wha Ti** *prev* Lac la Martre. Northwest Territories
184 K6 **Whatipu** Auckland, North Island, New Zealand
33 Y16 **Wheatland** Wyoming, C USA
14 D18 **Wheatley** Ontario, S Canada
30 M10 **Wheaton** Illinois, N USA
29 R7 **Wheaton** Minnesota, N USA
37 T4 **Wheat Ridge** Colorado, C USA
25 P2 **Wheeler** Texas, SW USA
23 O2 **Wheeler Lake** ⊠ Alabama, S USA
35 Y6 **Wheeler Peak** ▲ Nevada, W USA
37 T9 **Wheeler Peak** ▲ New Mexico, SW USA
31 S15 **Wheelersburg** Ohio, N USA
21 R2 **Wheeling** West Virginia, NE USA
97 L16 **Whernside** ▲ N England, UK
182 F9 **Whidbey, Point** *headland* South Australia
180 I7 **Whim Creek** Western Australia
10 L17 **Whistler** British Columbia, SW Canada
21 W8 **Whitakers** North Carolina, SE USA
14 H15 **Whitby** Ontario, S Canada
97 N15 **Whitby** N England, UK
10 G6 **White** ≈ Yukon Territory, W Canada
13 T11 **White Bay** *bay* Newfoundland, Newfoundland and Labrador, E Canada
20 I8 **White Bluff** Tennessee, S USA
28 J6 **White Butte** ▲ North Dakota, N USA
19 R5 **White Cap Mountain** ▲ Maine, NE USA
22 J9 **White Castle** Louisiana, S USA
182 M5 **White Cliffs** New South Wales, SE Australia
31 P8 **White Cloud** Michigan, N USA
9 P14 **Whitecourt** Alberta, SW Canada
25 O2 **White Deer** Texas, SW USA
White Elster *see* Weisse Elster
24 M5 **Whiteface** Texas, SW USA
18 K7 **Whiteface Mountain** ▲ New York, NE USA
29 W5 **Whiteface Reservoir** ⊠ Minnesota, N USA
33 O7 **Whitefish** Montana, NW USA
31 N9 **Whitefish Bay** Wisconsin, N USA
31 Q3 **Whitefish Bay** *lake bay* Canada/USA
14 E11 **Whitefish Falls** Ontario, S Canada
14 B7 **Whitefish Lake** ◎ Ontario, S Canada
29 U6 **Whitefish Lake** ◎ Minnesota, C USA
31 Q3 **Whitefish Point** *headland* Michigan, N USA
31 O4 **Whitefish River** ≈ Michigan, N USA
25 O4 **Whiteflat** Texas, SW USA
27 V12 **White Hall** Arkansas, C USA
30 K14 **White Hall** Illinois, N USA
31 O8 **Whitehall** Michigan, N USA
18 L9 **Whitehall** New York, NE USA
31 S13 **Whitehall** Ohio, N USA
30 J7 **Whitehall** Wisconsin, N USA
97 J15 **Whitehaven** NW England, UK
10 I8 **Whitehorse** *territory capital* Yukon Territory, W Canada
184 O7 **White Island** *island* NE New Zealand
14 K13 **White Lake** ◎ Ontario, SE Canada
22 H10 **White Lake** ◎ Louisiana, S USA
186 G7 **Whiteman Range** ▲▲ New Britain, E Papua New Guinea
183 Q15 **Whitemark** Tasmania, SE Australia
35 S9 **White Mountains** ▲▲ California/Nevada, W USA
19 N7 **White Mountains** ▲▲ Maine/New Hampshire, NE USA
80 F11 **White Nile** ⬖ *state* C Sudan
67 U7 **White Nile** *var.* Bahr el Jebel. ≈ S Sudan
81 E14 **White Nile** *Ar.* Al Baḩr al Abyaḑ, An Nīl al Abyaḑ, Bahr el Jebel. ≈ SE Sudan
25 W5 **White Oak Creek** ≈ Texas, SW USA
10 H9 **White Pass** *pass* Canada/USA
32 I9 **White Pass** *pass* Washington, NW USA
21 O9 **White Pine** Tennessee, S USA
18 K14 **White Plains** New York, NE USA
37 N13 **Whiteriver** Arizona, SW USA
28 M11 **White River** South Dakota, N USA
27 W12 **White River** ≈ Arkansas, SE USA
37 P3 **White River** ≈ Colorado/Utah, C USA
31 N15 **White River** ≈ Indiana, N USA
31 O8 **White River** ≈ Michigan, N USA
28 K11 **White River** ≈ South Dakota, N USA
25 O5 **White River** ≈ Texas, SW USA
18 M8 **White River** ≈ Vermont, NE USA
25 O5 **White River Lake** ⊠ Texas, SW USA
32 H11 **White Salmon** Washington, NW USA
18 I10 **Whitesboro** New York, NE USA
25 T5 **Whitesboro** Texas, SW USA
21 O7 **Whitesburg** Kentucky, S USA
White Sea *see* Beloye More
White Sea-Baltic Canal/White Sea Canal *see* Belomorsko-Baltiyskiy Kanal
63 I25 **Whiteside, Canal** *channel* S Chile
33 S10 **White Sulphur Springs** Montana, NW USA
21 R6 **White Sulphur Springs** West Virginia, NE USA
20 J6 **Whitesville** Kentucky, S USA
32 I10 **White Swan** Washington, NW USA
21 U12 **Whiteville** North Carolina, SE USA
20 F10 **Whiteville** Tennessee, S USA
77 Q13 **White Volta** *var.* Nakambé, *Fr.* Volta Blanche. ≈ Burkina/Ghana
30 M9 **Whitewater** Wisconsin, N USA
37 P14 **Whitewater Baldy** ▲ New Mexico, SW USA
23 X17 **Whitewater Bay** *bay* Florida, SE USA
31 Q14 **Whitewater River** ≈ Indiana/Ohio, N USA
9 V16 **Whitewood** Saskatchewan, S Canada
28 J9 **Whitewood** South Dakota, N USA
25 U5 **Whitewright** Texas, SW USA
97 I15 **Whithorn** S Scotland, UK
184 M6 **Whitianga** Waikato, North Island, New Zealand
19 N11 **Whitinsville** Massachusetts, NE USA
20 M8 **Whitley City** Kentucky, S USA
21 Q11 **Whitmire** South Carolina, SE USA
31 R10 **Whitmore Lake** Michigan, N USA
195 N9 **Whitmore Mountains** ▲▲ Antarctica
14 I12 **Whitney** Ontario, SE Canada
25 T8 **Whitney** Texas, SW USA
25 S8 **Whitney, Lake** ⊠ Texas, SW USA
35 S11 **Whitney, Mount** ▲ California, W USA
181 Y6 **Whitsunday Group** *island group* Queensland, E Australia
25 S6 **Whitt** Texas, SW USA
29 U12 **Whittemore** Iowa, C USA
39 R12 **Whittier** Alaska, USA
35 T15 **Whittier** California, W USA
83 I25 **Whittlesea** Eastern Cape, S South Africa
20 K10 **Whitwell** Tennessee, S USA
8 L10 **Wholdaia Lake** ◎ Northwest Territories, NW Canada
182 H7 **Whyalla** South Australia
Whydah *see* Ouidah
14 F13 **Wiarton** Ontario, S Canada
171 O13 **Wiau** Sulawesi, C Indonesia
111 H15 **Wiązów** *Ger.* Wansen. Dolnośląskie, SW Poland
33 Y8 **Wibaux** Montana, NW USA
27 N6 **Wichita** Kansas, C USA
25 R5 **Wichita Falls** Texas, SW USA
26 L11 **Wichita Mountains** ▲▲ Oklahoma, C USA
25 R5 **Wichita River** ≈ Texas, SW USA
96 K6 **Wick** N Scotland, UK
36 K13 **Wickenburg** Arizona, SW USA
24 L8 **Wickett** Texas, SW USA
180 I7 **Wickham** Western Australia
182 M14 **Wickham, Cape** *headland* Tasmania, SE Australia
20 G7 **Wickliffe** Kentucky, S USA
97 G19 **Wicklow** *Ir.* Cill Mhantáin. E Ireland
97 F19 **Wicklow** *Ir.* Cill Mhantáin. ⬖ *county* E Ireland
97 G19 **Wicklow Head** *Ir.* Ceann Chill Mhantáin. *headland* E Ireland
97 F18 **Wicklow Mountains** *Ir.* Sléibhte Chill Mhantáin. ▲▲ E Ireland
14 H10 **Wicksteed Lake** ◎ Ontario, S Canada
Wida *see* Ouidah
65 G15 **Wideawake Airfield** ✈ (Georgetown) SW Ascension Island
97 K18 **Widnes** NW England, UK
110 H9 **Więcbork** *Ger.* Vandsburg. Kujawsko-pomorskie, C Poland
101 E17 **Wied** ≈ W Germany
101 F16 **Wiehl** Nordrhein-Westfalen, W Germany
111 L17 **Wieliczka** Małopolskie, S Poland
110 H12 **Wielkopolskie** ⬖ *province* SW Poland
111 J14 **Wieluń** Sieradz, C Poland
109 X4 **Wien** *Eng.* Vienna, *Hung.* Bécs, *Slvk.* Vídeň, *Slvn.* Dunaj; *anc.* Vindobona. ● (Austria) Wien, NE Austria
109 X4 **Wien** *off.* Land Wien, *Eng.* Vienna. ⬖ *state* NE Austria
109 X5 **Wiener Neustadt** Niederösterreich, E Austria
Wien, Land *see* Wien
110 G7 **Wieprza** *Ger.* Wipper. ≈ NW Poland
98 O10 **Wierden** Overijssel, E Netherlands
98 I7 **Wieringerwerf** Noord-Holland, NW Netherlands
Wieruschow *see* Wieruszów
111 I14 **Wieruszów** *Ger.* Wieruschow. Łódzkie, C Poland
109 V9 **Wies** Steiermark, SE Austria
Wiesbachhorn *see* Grosses Wiesbachhorn
101 G18 **Wiesbaden** Hessen, W Germany
Wieselburg and Ungarisch-Altenburg/Wieselburg-Ungarisch-Altenburg *see* Mosonmagyaróvár
Wiesenhof *see* Ostrołęka
101 G20 **Wiesloch** Baden-Württemberg, SW Germany
100 F10 **Wiesmoor** Niedersachsen, NW Germany
110 I7 **Wieżyca** *Ger.* Turmberg. *hill* Pomorskie, N Poland
97 K17 **Wigan** NW England, UK
37 U3 **Wiggins** Colorado, C USA
22 M8 **Wiggins** Mississippi, S USA
Wigorna Ceaster *see* Worcester
97 I14 **Wigtown** S Scotland, UK
97 H14 **Wigtown** *cultural region* SW Scotland, UK
97 I15 **Wigtown Bay** *bay* SW Scotland, UK
98 L13 **Wijchen** Gelderland, SE Netherlands
92 N1 **Wijdefjorden** *fjord* NW Svalbard
98 M10 **Wijhe** Overijssel, E Netherlands
98 J12 **Wijk bij Duurstede** Utrecht, C Netherlands
98 J13 **Wijk en Aalburg** Noord-Brabant, S Netherlands
99 H16 **Wijnegem** Antwerpen, N Belgium
14 E11 **Wikwemikong** Manitoulin Island, Ontario, S Canada
108 H7 **Wil** Sankt Gallen, NE Switzerland
29 R16 **Wilber** Nebraska, C USA
32 K8 **Wilbur** Washington, NW USA
27 Q11 **Wilburton** Oklahoma, C USA
182 M6 **Wilcannia** New South Wales, SE Australia
18 D12 **Wilcox** Pennsylvania, NE USA
Wilczek Land *see* Vil'cheka, Zemlya
109 U6 **Wildalpen** Steiermark, E Austria
31 O13 **Wildcat Creek** ≈ Indiana, N USA
108 L9 **Wilde Kreuzspitze** *It.* Picco di Croce. ▲ Austria/Italy
Wildenschwert *see* Ústí nad Orlicí
98 O6 **Wildervank** Groningen, NE Netherlands
100 G11 **Wildeshausen** Niedersachsen, NW Germany
108 D10 **Wildhorn** ▲ SW Switzerland
9 R17 **Wild Horse** Alberta, SW Canada
27 N12 **Wildhorse Creek** ≈ Oklahoma, C USA
28 L14 **Wild Horse Hill** ▲ Nebraska, C USA
109 W8 **Wildon** Steiermark, SE Austria
24 M2 **Wildorado** Texas, SW USA
29 R6 **Wild Rice River** ≈ Minnesota/North Dakota, N USA
Wilejka *see* Vilyeyka
195 Y9 **Wilhelm II Coast** *physical region* Antarctica
195 X9 **Wilhelm II Land** *physical region* Antarctica
55 U11 **Wilhelmina Gebergte** ▲▲ C Surinam
18 B13 **Wilhelm, Lake** ⊠ Pennsylvania, NE USA
92 O2 **Wilhelmøya** *island* C Svalbard
Wilhelm-Pieck-Stadt *see* Guben
109 W4 **Wilhelmsburg** Niederösterreich, E Austria
100 G10 **Wilhelmshaven** Niedersachsen, NW Germany
Wilia/Wilja *see* Neris
18 H13 **Wilkes Barre** Pennsylvania, NE USA
21 R9 **Wilkesboro** North Carolina, SE USA
195 W15 **Wilkes Coast** *physical region* Antarctica
189 W12 **Wilkes Island** *island* N Wake Island
195 X12 **Wilkes Land** *physical region* Antarctica
9 S15 **Wilkie** Saskatchewan, S Canada
194 I6 **Wilkins Ice Shelf** *ice shelf* Antarctica
182 D4 **Wilkinsons Lakes** *salt lake* South Australia
Wilkomierz *see* Ukmergė
182 K11 **Willalooka** South Australia
32 G11 **Willamette River** ≈ Oregon, NW USA
183 O8 **Willandra Billabong Creek** *seasonal river* New South Wales, SE Australia
32 F9 **Willapa Bay** *inlet* Washington, NW USA
27 T7 **Willard** Missouri, C USA
37 S12 **Willard** New Mexico, SW USA
31 S12 **Willard** Ohio, N USA
36 L1 **Willard** Utah, W USA
186 G6 **Willaumez Peninsula** *headland* New Britain, E Papua New Guinea
37 N15 **Willcox** Arizona, SW USA
37 N16 **Willcox Playa** *salt flat* Arizona, SW USA
99 G17 **Willebroek** Antwerpen, C Belgium
99 G14 **Willemstad** Noord-Brabant, S Netherlands
45 P16 **Willemstad** ○ (Netherlands Antilles) Curaçao, Netherlands Antilles
9 S11 **William** ≈ Saskatchewan, C Canada
23 O6 **William "Bill" Dannelly Reservoir** ⊠ Alabama, S USA
182 G3 **William Creek** South Australia
181 T15 **William, Mount** ▲ South Australia
36 K11 **Williams** Arizona, SW USA
29 X14 **Williamsburg** Iowa, C USA
20 M8 **Williamsburg** Kentucky, S USA
31 R15 **Williamsburg** Ohio, N USA
21 X6 **Williamsburg** Virginia, NE USA
10 M15 **Williams Lake** British Columbia, SW Canada
21 P6 **Williamson** West Virginia, NE USA
31 N13 **Williamsport** Indiana, N USA
18 G13 **Williamsport** Pennsylvania, NE USA
21 W9 **Williamston** North Carolina, SE USA
21 P11 **Williamston** South Carolina, SE USA
20 M4 **Williamstown** Kentucky, S USA
18 L10 **Williamstown** Massachusetts, NE USA
18 J16 **Willingboro** New Jersey, NE USA
9 Q14 **Willingdon** Alberta, SW Canada
25 W10 **Willis** Texas, SW USA
108 F8 **Willisau** Luzern, W Switzerland
83 F24 **Williston** Northern Cape, W South Africa
23 V10 **Williston** Florida, SE USA
28 J3 **Williston** North Dakota, N USA
21 Q13 **Williston** South Carolina, SE USA
10 L12 **Williston Lake** ⊠ British Columbia, W Canada
34 L5 **Willits** California, W USA
29 T8 **Willmar** Minnesota, N USA
10 K11 **Will, Mount** ▲ British Columbia, W Canada
31 T11 **Willoughby** Ohio, N USA
9 U17 **Willow Bunch** Saskatchewan, S Canada
32 J11 **Willow Creek** ≈ Oregon, NW USA
39 R11 **Willow Lake** Alaska, USA
8 I9 **Willowlake** ≈ Northwest Territories, NW Canada
83 H25 **Willowmore** Eastern Cape, S South Africa
30 L5 **Willow Reservoir** ⊠ Wisconsin, N USA
35 N5 **Willows** California, W USA
27 V7 **Willow Springs** Missouri, C USA
182 I7 **Wilmington** South Australia
21 Y2 **Wilmington** Delaware, NE USA
21 V12 **Wilmington** North Carolina, SE USA
31 R14 **Wilmington** Ohio, N USA
20 M6 **Wilmore** Kentucky, S USA
29 R8 **Wilmot** South Dakota, N USA
Wilna/Wilno *see* Vilnius
101 G16 **Wilnsdorf** Nordrhein-Westfalen, W Germany
99 G16 **Wilrijk** Antwerpen, N Belgium
100 I10 **Wilseder Berg** *hill* NW Germany
67 Z12 **Wilshaw Ridge** *undersea feature* W Indian Ocean
21 V9 **Wilson** North Carolina, SE USA
25 N5 **Wilson** Texas, SW USA
182 A7 **Wilson Bluff** *headland* South Australia/Western Australia
35 Y7 **Wilson Creek Range** ▲▲ Nevada, W USA
23 O1 **Wilson Lake** ⊠ Alabama, S USA
26 M4 **Wilson Lake** ⊠ Kansas, SE USA
37 P7 **Wilson, Mount** ▲ Colorado, C USA
183 P13 **Wilsons Promontory** *peninsula* Victoria, SE Australia

◆ Country
● Country Capital
◇ Dependent Territory
○ Dependent Territory Capital
⬖ Administrative Regions
✈ International Airport
▲ Mountain
▲▲ Mountain Range
Volcano
≈ River
◎ Lake
⊠ Reservoir

Wilton – Xiamen

29 *Y14* **Wilton** Iowa, C USA
19 *P7* **Wilton** Maine, NE USA
28 *M5* **Wilton** North Dakota, N USA
97 *L22* **Wiltshire** *cultural region* S England, UK
99 *M23* **Wiltz** Diekirch, NW Luxembourg
180 *K9* **Wiluna** Western Australia
99 *M23* **Wilwerwiltz** Diekirch, NE Luxembourg
29 *P5* **Wimbledon** North Dakota, N USA
42 *K7* **Wina** *var.* Güina. Jinotega, N Nicaragua
31 *O12* **Winamac** Indiana, N USA
81 *G19* **Winam Gulf** *var.* Kavirondo Gulf. *gulf* SW Kenya
83 *I22* **Winburg** Free State, C South Africa
19 *N10* **Winchendon** Massachusetts, NE USA
14 *M13* **Winchester** Ontario, SE Canada
97 *M23* **Winchester** *hist.* Wintanceaster, *Lat.* Venta Belgarum. S England, UK
32 *M10* **Winchester** Idaho, NW USA
30 *J14* **Winchester** Illinois, N USA
31 *Q13* **Winchester** Indiana, N USA
20 *M5* **Winchester** Kentucky, S USA
18 *M10* **Winchester** New Hampshire, NE USA
20 *K10* **Winchester** Tennessee, S USA
21 *V3* **Winchester** Virginia, NE USA
99 *L22* **Wincrange** Diekirch, NW Luxembourg
10 *I5* **Wind** ≈ Yukon Territory, NW Canada
183 *S8* **Windamere, Lake** ◎ New South Wales, SE Australia
Windau *see* Ventspils
Windau *see* Venta
18 *D15* **Windber** Pennsylvania, NE USA
23 *T3* **Winder** Georgia, SE USA
97 *K15* **Windermere** NW England, UK
14 *C7* **Windermere Lake** ◎ Ontario, S Canada
31 *U11* **Windham** Ohio, N USA
83 *D19* **Windhoek** *Ger.* Windhuk. ● (Namibia) Khomas, C Namibia
83 *D20* **Windhoek** ✈ Khomas, C Namibia
Windhuk *see* Windhoek
15 *O8* **Windigo** Québec, SE Canada
15 *O8* **Windigo** ≈ Québec, SE Canada
Windischfeistritz *see* Slovenska Bistrica
109 *T6* **Windischgarsten** Oberösterreich, W Austria
Windischgraz *see* Slovenj Gradec
37 *T16* **Wind Mountain** ▲ New Mexico, SW USA
29 *T10* **Windom** Minnesota, N USA
37 *Q7* **Windom Peak** ▲ Colorado, C USA
181 *U9* **Windorah** Queensland, C Australia
37 *O10* **Window Rock** Arizona, SW USA
31 *N9* **Wind Point** *headland* Wisconsin, N USA
33 *U14* **Wind River** ≈ Wyoming, C USA
13 *P15* **Windsor** Nova Scotia, SE Canada
14 *C17* **Windsor** Ontario, S Canada
15 *Q12* **Windsor** Québec, SE Canada
97 *N22* **Windsor** S England, UK
37 *T3* **Windsor** Colorado, C USA
18 *M12* **Windsor** Connecticut, NE USA
27 *T5* **Windsor** Missouri, C USA
21 *X9* **Windsor** North Carolina, SE USA
18 *M12* **Windsor Locks** Connecticut, NE USA
25 *R5* **Windthorst** Texas, SW USA
45 *Z14* **Windward Islands** *island group* E West Indies
Windward Islands *see* Barlavento, Ilhas de, Cape Verde
Windward Islands *see* Vent, Îles du, Archipel de la Société, French Polynesia
44 *K8* **Windward Passage** *Sp.* Paso de los Vientos. *channel* Cuba/Haiti
55 *T9* **Wineperu** C Guyana
23 *O3* **Winfield** Alabama, S USA
29 *Y15* **Winfield** Iowa, C USA
27 *O7* **Winfield** Kansas, C USA
25 *W6* **Winfield** Texas, SW USA
21 *Q4* **Winfield** West Virginia, NE USA
29 *N5* **Wing** North Dakota, N USA
183 *U7* **Wingham** New South Wales, SE Australia
12 *G16* **Wingham** Ontario, S Canada
33 *T8* **Winifred** Montana, NW USA
12 *E8* **Winisk** ≈ Ontario, S Canada
12 *E9* **Winisk Lake** ◎ Ontario, C Canada
24 *L8* **Wink** Texas, SW USA
36 *M14* **Winkelman** Arizona, SW USA
9 *X17* **Winkler** Manitoba, S Canada
109 *Q9* **Winklern** Tirol, W Austria
Winkowitz *see* Vinkovci
32 *G9* **Winlock** Washington, NW USA
77 *P17* **Winneba** SE Ghana
29 *U11* **Winnebago** Minnesota, N USA
29 *R13* **Winnebago** Nebraska, C USA
30 *M7* **Winnebago, Lake** ◎ Wisconsin, N USA
30 *M7* **Winneconne** Wisconsin, N USA
35 *T3* **Winnemucca** Nevada, W USA
35 *R4* **Winnemucca Lake** ◎ Nevada, W USA
101 *H21* **Winnenden** Baden-Württemberg, SW Germany
29 *N11* **Winner** South Dakota, N USA
33 *U9* **Winnett** Montana, NW USA
14 *I9* **Winneway** Québec, SE Canada
22 *H6* **Winnfield** Louisiana, S USA
29 *U4* **Winnibigoshish, Lake** ◎ Minnesota, N USA
25 *X11* **Winnie** Texas, SW USA
9 *Y16* **Winnipeg** *province capital* Manitoba, S Canada
9 *X16* **Winnipeg** ✈ Manitoba, S Canada
0 *J8* **Winnipeg** ≈ Manitoba, S Canada
9 *X16* **Winnipeg Beach** Manitoba, S Canada
9 *W14* **Winnipeg, Lake** ◎ Manitoba, C Canada
9 *W15* **Winnipegosis** Manitoba, S Canada
9 *W15* **Winnipegosis, Lake** ◎ Manitoba, C Canada
19 *O8* **Winnipesaukee, Lake** ◎ New Hampshire, NE USA
22 *I6* **Winnsboro** Louisiana, S USA
21 *R12* **Winnsboro** South Carolina, SE USA
25 *W6* **Winnsboro** Texas, SW USA
29 *X10* **Winona** Minnesota, N USA
22 *L4* **Winona** Mississippi, S USA
27 *W7* **Winona** Missouri, C USA
25 *W7* **Winona** Texas, SW USA
18 *M7* **Winooski River** ≈ Vermont, NE USA
98 *P6* **Winschoten** Groningen, NE Netherlands
100 *J10* **Winsen** Niedersachsen, N Germany
36 *M11* **Winslow** Arizona, SW USA
19 *Q7* **Winslow** Maine, NE USA
18 *M12* **Winsted** Connecticut, NE USA
32 *F14* **Winston** Oregon, NW USA
21 *S9* **Winston Salem** North Carolina, SE USA
98 *N5* **Winsum** Groningen, NE Netherlands
Wintanceaster *see* Winchester
23 *W11* **Winter Garden** Florida, SE USA
10 *J16* **Winter Harbour** Vancouver Island, British Columbia, SW Canada
23 *W12* **Winter Haven** Florida, SE USA
23 *X11* **Winter Park** Florida, SE USA
25 *P8* **Winters** Texas, SW USA
29 *U15* **Winterset** Iowa, C USA
98 *O12* **Winterswijk** Gelderland, E Netherlands
108 *G6* **Winterthur** Zürich, NE Switzerland
29 *U9* **Winthrop** Minnesota, N USA
32 *J7* **Winthrop** Washington, NW USA
181 *V7* **Winton** Queensland, E Australia
185 *C24* **Winton** Southland, South Island, New Zealand
21 *X8* **Winton** North Carolina, SE USA
101 *K15* **Wipper** ≈ C Germany
101 *K14* **Wipper** ≈ C Germany
Wipper *see* Wieprza
182 *G6* **Wirraminna** South Australia
182 *F4* **Wirrida** South Australia
182 *F7* **Wirrulla** South Australia
Wirsitz *see* Wyrzysk
Wirz-See *see* Võrtsjärv
97 *O19* **Wisbech** E England, UK
Wisby *see* Visby
19 *Q8* **Wiscasset** Maine, NE USA
Wischau *see* Vyškov
30 *J5* **Wisconsin** *off.* State of Wisconsin, ***also known as*** Badger State. ◐ *state* N USA
30 *L8* **Wisconsin Dells** Wisconsin, N USA
30 *L8* **Wisconsin, Lake** ⊠ Wisconsin, N USA
30 *L7* **Wisconsin Rapids** Wisconsin, N USA
30 *L7* **Wisconsin River** ≈ Wisconsin, N USA
33 *P11* **Wisdom** Montana, NW USA
21 *P7* **Wise** Virginia, NE USA
39 *Q7* **Wiseman** Alaska, USA
96 *J12* **Wishaw** W Scotland, UK
29 *O6* **Wishek** North Dakota, N USA
32 *I11* **Wishram** Washington, NW USA
111 *J17* **Wisła** Śląskie, S Poland
110 *K11* **Wisła** *Eng.* Vistula, *Ger.* Weichsel. ≈ C Poland
Wiślany, Zalew *see* Vistula Lagoon
111 *M16* **Wisłoka** ≈ SE Poland
100 *L9* **Wismar** Mecklenburg-Vorpommern, N Germany
29 *R14* **Wisner** Nebraska, C USA
103 *V4* **Wissembourg** *var.* Weissenburg. Bas-Rhin, NE France
30 *J6* **Wissota, Lake** ⊠ Wisconsin, N USA
97 *O18* **Witham** ≈ E England, UK
97 *O17* **Withernsea** E England, UK
37 *Q13* **Withington, Mount** ▲ New Mexico, SW USA
23 *U8* **Withlacoochee River** ≈ Florida/Georgia, SE USA
110 *H11* **Witkowo** Wielkopolskie, C Poland
97 *M21* **Witney** S England, UK
101 *E15* **Witten** Nordrhein-Westfalen, W Germany
101 *N14* **Wittenberg** Sachsen-Anhalt, E Germany
30 *L6* **Wittenberg** Wisconsin, N USA
100 *L11* **Wittenberge** Brandenburg, N Germany
103 *U7* **Wittenheim** Haut-Rhin, NE France
180 *I7* **Wittenoom** Western Australia
Wittingau *see* Třeboň
100 *K12* **Wittingen** Niedersachsen, C Germany
101 *E18* **Wittlich** Rheinland-Pfalz, SW Germany
100 *F9* **Wittmund** Niedersachsen, NW Germany
100 *M10* **Wittstock** Brandenburg, NE Germany
186 *F6* **Witu Islands** *island group* E Papua New Guinea
110 *O7* **Wiżajny** Podlaskie, NE Poland
55 *W10* **W. J. van Blommesteinmeer** ⊠ E Surinam
110 *L11* **Wkra** *Ger.* Soldau. ≈ C Poland
110 *I6* **Władysławowo** Pomorskie, N Poland
Wlaschim *see* Vlašim
111 *E14* **Wleń** *Ger.* Lähn. Dolnośląskie, SW Poland
110 *J11* **Włocławek** *Ger./Rus.* Vlotslavsk. Kujawsko-pomorskie, C Poland
110 *P13* **Włodawa** *Rus.* Vlodava. Lubelskie, SE Poland
Włodzimierz *see* Volodymyr-Volyns'kyy
111 *K15* **Włoszczowa** Świętokrzyskie, C Poland
83 *C19* **Wlotzkasbaken** Erongo, W Namibia
15 *R12* **Woburn** Québec, SE Canada
19 *O11* **Woburn** Massachusetts, NE USA
Wocheiner Feistritz *see* Bohinjska Bistrica
Wöchma *see* Võhma
147 *S11* **Wodil** *var.* Vuadil'. Farg'ona Viloyati, E Uzbekistan
181 *V14* **Wodonga** Victoria, SE Australia
111 *I17* **Wodzisław Śląski** *Ger.* Loslau. Śląskie, S Poland
98 *I11* **Woerden** Zuid-Holland, C Netherlands
98 *I8* **Wognum** Noord-Holland, NW Netherlands
Wohlau *see* Wołów
108 *F7* **Wohlen** Aargau, NW Switzerland
195 *R2* **Wohlthat Mountains** ▲▲ Antarctica
Wojerecy *see* Hoyerswerda
Wōjjā *see* Wotje Atoll
Wojwodina *see* Vojvodina
171 *V15* **Wokam, Pulau** *island* Kepulauan Aru, E Indonesia
97 *N22* **Woking** SE England, UK
Woldenberg Neumark *see* Dobiegniew
188 *K15* **Woleai Atoll** *atoll* Caroline Islands, W Micronesia
Woleu *see* Uolo, Río
79 *E17* **Woleu-Ntem** *off.* Province du Woleu-Ntem, *var.* Le Woleu-Ntem. ◐ *province* W Gabon
Woleu-Ntem, Province du *see* Woleu-Ntem
32 *F15* **Wolf Creek** Oregon, NW USA
26 *K9* **Wolf Creek** ≈ Oklahoma/Texas, SW USA
37 *R7* **Wolf Creek Pass** *pass* Colorado, C USA
19 *O9* **Wolfeboro** New Hampshire, NE USA
25 *U5* **Wolfe City** Texas, SW USA
14 *L15* **Wolfe Island** *island* Ontario, SE Canada
101 *M14* **Wolfen** Sachsen-Anhalt, E Germany
100 *J13* **Wolfenbüttel** Niedersachsen, C Germany
109 *T4* **Wolfern** Oberösterreich, N Austria
109 *Q6* **Wolfgangsee** *var.* Abersee, St Wolfgangsee. ◎ N Austria
39 *P9* **Wolf Mountain** ▲ Alaska, USA
33 *X7* **Wolf Point** Montana, NW USA
22 *L8* **Wolf River** ≈ Mississippi, S USA
30 *M7* **Wolf River** ≈ Wisconsin, N USA
109 *U9* **Wolfsberg** Kärnten, SE Austria
100 *K12* **Wolfsburg** Niedersachsen, N Germany
57 *B17* **Wolf, Volcán** ◬ Galapagos Islands, Ecuador, E Pacific Ocean
100 *O8* **Wolgast** Mecklenburg-Vorpommern, NE Germany
108 *F8* **Wolhusen** Luzern, W Switzerland
110 *D8* **Wolin** *Ger.* Wollin. Zachodnio-pomorskie, NW Poland
109 *Y3* **Wolkersdorf** Niederösterreich, NE Austria
Wołkowysk *see* Vawkavysk
Wöllan *see* Velenje
8 *J6* **Wollaston, Cape** *headland* Victoria Island, Northwest Territories, NW Canada
63 *J25* **Wollaston, Isla** *island* S Chile
9 *U11* **Wollaston Lake** Saskatchewan, C Canada
9 *T10* **Wollaston Lake** ◎ Saskatchewan, C Canada
8 *J6* **Wollaston Peninsula** *peninsula* Victoria Island, Northwest Territories/Nunavut NW Canada
Wollin *see* Wolin
183 *S9* **Wollongong** New South Wales, SE Australia
Wolmar *see* Valmiera
100 *L13* **Wolmirstedt** Sachsen-Anhalt, C Germany
110 *M11* **Wołomin** Mazowieckie, C Poland
110 *G!3* **Wołów** *Ger.* Wohlau. Dolnośląskie, SW Poland
Wołożyn *see* Valozhyn
14 *G11* **Wolseley Bay** Ontario, S Canada
29 *P10* **Wolsey** South Dakota, N USA
110 *F12* **Wolsztyn** Wielkopolskie, C Poland
98 *M7* **Wolvega** *Fris.* Wolvegea. Friesland, N Netherlands
Wolvegea *see* Wolvega
97 *K19* **Wolverhampton** C England, UK
Wolverine State *see* Michigan
99 *G18* **Wolvertem** Vlaams Brabant, C Belgium
99 *H16* **Wommelgem** Antwerpen, N Belgium
186 *D7* **Wonenara** *var.* Wonerara. Eastern Highlands, C Papua New Guinea
Wonerara *see* Wonenara
Wongalara Lake *see* Wongalarroo Lake
183 *N6* **Wongalarroo Lake** *var.* Wongalara Lake. *seasonal lake* New South Wales, SE Australia
163 *Y15* **Wŏnju** *Jap.* Genshū. N South Korea
10 *M12* **Wonowon** British Columbia, W Canada
163 *X13* **Wŏnsan** SE North Korea
183 *O13* **Wonthaggi** Victoria, SE Australia
23 *N2* **Woodall Mountain** ▲ Mississippi, S USA
23 *W7* **Woodbine** Georgia, SE USA
29 *S14* **Woodbine** Iowa, C USA
18 *J17* **Woodbine** New Jersey, NE USA
21 *W4* **Woodbridge** Virginia, NE USA
183 *V4* **Woodburn** New South Wales, SE Australia
32 *G11* **Woodburn** Oregon, NW USA
20 *K9* **Woodbury** Tennessee, S USA
183 *V5* **Wooded Bluff** *headland* New South Wales, SE Australia
183 *V3* **Woodenbong** New South Wales, SE Australia
35 *R11* **Woodlake** California, W USA
35 *N7* **Woodland** California, W USA
19 *T5* **Woodland** Maine, NE USA
32 *G10* **Woodland** Washington, NW USA
37 *T5* **Woodland Park** Colorado, C USA
186 *I9* **Woodlark Island** *var.* Murua Island. *island* SE Papua New Guinea
Woodle Island *see* Kuria
9 *T17* **Wood Mountain** ▲▲ Saskatchewan, S Canada
30 *K15* **Wood River** Illinois, N USA
29 *P16* **Wood River** Nebraska, C USA
39 *R9* **Wood River** ≈ Alaska, USA
39 *O13* **Wood River Lakes** ◎ Alaska, USA
182 *C1* **Woodroffe, Mount** ▲ South Australia
21 *P11* **Woodruff** South Carolina, SE USA
30 *K4* **Woodruff** Wisconsin, N USA
25 *T14* **Woodsboro** Texas, SW USA
31 *U13* **Woodsfield** Ohio, N USA
181 *P4* **Woods, Lake** ◎ Northern Territory, N Australia
9 *Z16* **Woods, Lake of the** *Fr.* Lac des Bois. ◎ Canada/USA
25 *Q6* **Woodson** Texas, SW USA
13 *N14* **Woodstock** New Brunswick, SE Canada
14 *F16* **Woodstock** Ontario, S Canada
30 *M10* **Woodstock** Illinois, N USA
18 *M9* **Woodstock** Vermont, NE USA
21 *U4* **Woodstock** Virginia, NE USA
19 *N8* **Woodsville** New Hampshire, NE USA
184 *M12* **Woodville** Manawatu-Wanganui, North Island, New Zealand
22 *J7* **Woodville** Mississippi, S USA
25 *X9* **Woodville** Texas, SW USA
26 *K9* **Woodward** Oklahoma, C USA
29 *O5* **Woodworth** North Dakota, N USA
171 *W12* **Wool** Papua, E Indonesia
183 *V5* **Woolgoolga** New South Wales, E Australia
182 *H6* **Woomera** South Australia
19 *O12* **Woonsocket** Rhode Island, NE USA
29 *P10* **Woonsocket** South Dakota, N USA
31 *T12* **Wooster** Ohio, N USA
80 *L12* **Woqooyi Galbeed** *off.* Gobolka Woqooyi Galbeed. ◐ *region* NW Somalia
Woqooyi Galbeed, Gobolka *see* Woqooyi Galbeed
108 *E8* **Worb** Bern, C Switzerland
83 *F26* **Worcester** Western Cape, SW South Africa
97 *L20* **Worcester** *hist.* Wigorna Ceaster. W England, UK
19 *N11* **Worcester** Massachusetts, NE USA
97 *L20* **Worcestershire** *cultural region* C England, UK
32 *H16* **Worden** Oregon, NW USA
109 *O6* **Wörgl** Tirol, W Austria
171 *V15* **Workai, Pulau** *island* Kepulauan Aru, E Indonesia
97 *J15* **Workington** NW England, UK
98 *K7* **Workum** Friesland, N Netherlands
33 *V13* **Worland** Wyoming, C USA
Wormatia *see* Worms
99 *N25* **Wormeldange** Grevenmacher, E Luxembourg
98 *I9* **Wormer** Noord-Holland, C Netherlands
101 *G19* **Worms** *anc.* Augusta Vangionum, Borbetomagus, Wormatia. Rheinland-Pfalz, SW Germany
Worms *see* Vormsi
101 *K21* **Wörnitz** ≈ S Germany
25 *U8* **Wortham** Texas, SW USA
101 *G21* **Wörth am Rhein** Rheinland-Pfalz, SW Germany
109 *S9* **Wörther See** ◎ S Austria
97 *O23* **Worthing** SE England, UK
29 *S11* **Worthington** Minnesota, N USA
31 *S13* **Worthington** Ohio, N USA
35 *W8* **Worthington Peak** ▲ Nevada, W USA
171 *Y13* **Wosi** Papua, E Indonesia
171 *V13* **Wosimi** Papua, E Indonesia
189 *R5* **Wotho Atoll** *var.* Wōtto. *atoll* Ralik Chain, W Marshall Islands
189 *V5* **Wotje Atoll** *var.* Wōjjā. *atoll* Ratak Chain, E Marshall Islands
Wotoe *see* Wotu
Wottawa *see* Otava
Wōtto *see* Wotho Atoll
171 *O13* **Wotu** *prev.* Wotoe. Sulawesi, C Indonesia
98 *K11* **Woudenberg** Utrecht, C Netherlands
98 *I13* **Woudrichem** Noord-Brabant, S Netherlands
43 *N8* **Wounta** *var.* Huaunta. Región Autónoma Atlántico Norte, NE Nicaragua
171 *P14* **Wowoni, Pulau** *island* C Indonesia
81 *J17* **Woyamdero Plain** *plain* E Kenya
Woyens *see* Vojens
Wozrojdeniye Oroli *see* Vozrozhdeniya, Ostrov
Wrangel Island *see* Vrangelya, Ostrov
39 *Y13* **Wrangell** Wrangell Island, Alaska, USA
38 *C15* **Wrangell, Cape** *headland* Attu Island, Alaska, USA
39 *S11* **Wrangell, Mount** ▲ Alaska, USA
39 *T11* **Wrangell Mountains** ▲▲ Alaska, USA
197 *S7* **Wrangel Plain** *undersea feature* Arctic Ocean
96 *H6* **Wrath, Cape** *headland* N Scotland, UK
37 *W3* **Wray** Colorado, C USA
44 *K13* **Wreck Point** *headland* C Jamaica
83 *C23* **Wreck Point** *headland* W South Africa
23 *V4* **Wrens** Georgia, SE USA
97 *K18* **Wrexham** NE Wales, UK
27 *R13* **Wright City** Oklahoma, C USA
194 *J12* **Wright Island** *island* Antarctica
13 *N9* **Wright, Mont** ▲ Québec, E Canada
25 *X5* **Wright Patman Lake** ⊠ Texas, SW USA
36 *M16* **Wrightson, Mount** ▲ Arizona, SW USA
23 *U5* **Wrightsville** Georgia, SE USA
21 *W12* **Wrightsville Beach** North Carolina, SE USA
35 *T15* **Wrightwood** California, W USA
8 *H9* **Wrigley** Northwest Territories, W Canada
111 *G14* **Wrocław** *Eng./Ger.* Breslau. Dolnośląskie, SW Poland
110 *F10* **Wronki** *Ger.* Fronicken. Wielkopolskie, C Poland
110 *H11* **Września** Wielkopolskie, C Poland
110 *F12* **Wschowa** Lubuskie, W Poland
Wsetin *see* Vsetín
161 *O5* **Wu'an** Hebei, E China
180 *I12* **Wubin** Western Australia
163 *W9* **Wuchang** Heilongjiang, NE China
Wuchang *see* Wuhan
Wu-chou/Wuchow *see* Wuzhou
160 *M16* **Wuchuan** *var.* Meilu. Guangdong, S China
160 *K10* **Wuchuan** *var.* Duru, Gelaozu Miaozu Zhizhixian. Guizhou, S China
163 *O13* **Wuchuan** Nei Mongol Zizhiqu, N China
163 *V6* **Wudalianchi** *var.* Qingshan; *prev.* Dedu. Heilongjiang, NE China
159 *O11* **Wudaoliang** Qinghai, C China
141 *Q13* **Wuday'ah** *spring/well* S Saudi Arabia
77 *V13* **Wudil** Kano, N Nigeria
160 *G12* **Wuding** *var.* Jincheng. Yunnan, SW China
160 *L4* **Wuding He** ≈ C China
182 *G8* **Wudinna** South Australia
157 *P10* **Wudu** Gansu, C China
Wudu *see* Longnan
160 *L9* **Wufeng** Hubei, C China
161 *O11* **Wugong Shan** ▲▲ S China
157 *P7* **Wuhai** *var.* Haibowan. Nei Mongol Zizhiqu, N China
161 *O9* **Wuhan** *var.* Han-kou, Han-k'ou, Hanyang, Wuchang, Wu-han; *prev.* Hankow. *province capital* Hubei, C China
Wu-han *see* Wuhan
161 *Q7* **Wuhe** Anhui, E China
Wuhsien *see* Suzhou
Wuhsi/Wu-his *see* Wuxi
161 *Q8* **Wuhu** *var.* Wu-na-mu. Anhui, E China
Wūjae *see* Ujae Atoll
160 *K11* **Wu Jiang** ≈ C China
Wujlān *see* Ujelang Atoll
77 *W15* **Wukari** Taraba, E Nigeria
160 *H11* **Wulian Feng** ▲▲ SW China
160 *F13* **Wuliang Shan** ▲▲ SW China
160 *K11* **Wuling Shan** ▲▲ S China
109 *Y5* **Wulka** ≈ E Austria
Wulkan *see* Vulcan
109 *T3* **Wullowitz** Oberösterreich, N Austria
Wu-lu-k'o-mu-shi/Wu-lu-mu-ch'i *see* Ürümqi
79 *D14* **Wum** Nord-Ouest, NE Cameroon
160 *H12* **Wumeng Shan** ▲▲ SW China
160 *K14* **Wuming** Guangxi Zhuangzu Zizhiqu, S China
100 *I10* **Wümme** ≈ NW Germany
Wu-na-mu *see* Wuhu
171 *X13* **Wunen** Papua, E Indonesia
12 *D9* **Wunnummin Lake** ◎ Ontario, C Canada
80 *D13* **Wun Rog** Warab, S Sudan
101 *M18* **Wunsiedel** Bayern, E Germany
100 *I12* **Wunstorf** Niedersachsen, NW Germany
166 *M3* **Wuntho** Sagaing, N Burma (Myanmar)
101 *F15* **Wupper** ≈ W Germany
101 *E15* **Wuppertal** *prev.* Barmen-Elberfeld. Nordrhein-Westfalen, W Germany
160 *K5* **Wuqi** Shaanxi, C China
161 *P4* **Wuqiao** *var.* Sangyuan. Hebei, E China
101 *L23* **Würm** ≈ SE Germany
77 *T12* **Wurno** Sokoto, NW Nigeria
101 *I19* **Würzburg** Bayern, SW Germany
101 *N15* **Wurzen** Sachsen, E Germany
160 *L9* **Wu Shan** ▲▲ C China
158 *G7* **Wushi** *var.* Uqturpan. Xinjiang Uygur Zizhiqu, NW China
Wusih *see* Wuxi
65 *N18* **Wüst Seamount** *undersea feature* S Atlantic Ocean
Wusuli Jiang/Wusuri *see* Ussuri
161 *N3* **Wutai Shan** *var.* Beitai Ding. ▲ C China
160 *H10* **Wutongqiao** Sichuan, C China
159 *P6* **Wutongwozi Quan** *spring* NW China
99 *H15* **Wuustwezel** Antwerpen, N Belgium
186 *B4* **Wuvulu Island** *island* NW Papua New Guinea
159 *U9* **Wuwei** *var.* Liangzhou. Gansu, C China
161 *R8* **Wuxi** *var.* Wuhsi, Wu-hsi, Wusih. Jiangsu, E China
Wuxing *see* Huzhou
160 *L14* **Wuxuan** Guangxi Zhuangzu Zizhiqu, S China
Wuyang *see* Zhenyuan
160 *K11* **Wuyang He** ≈ S China
163 *X6* **Wuyiling** Heilongjiang, NE China
161 *Q11* **Wuyishan** *prev.* Chong'an. Fujian, SE China
157 *T12* **Wuyi Shan** ▲▲ SE China
162 *M13* **Wuyuan** Nei Mongol Zizhiqu, N China
160 *L17* **Wuzhishan** *prev.* Tongshi. Hainan, S China
160 *L17* **Wuzhi Shan** ▲ S China
159 *W8* **Wuzhong** Ningxia, N China
160 *M14* **Wuzhou** *var.* Wu-chou, Wuchow. Guangxi Zhuangzu Zizhiqu, S China
18 *H12* **Wyalusing** Pennsylvania, NE USA
182 *M10* **Wycheproof** Victoria, SE Australia
97 *K21* **Wye** *Wel.* Gwy. ≈ England/Wales, UK
Wyłkowyszki *see* Vilkaviškis
97 *P19* **Wymondham** E England, UK
29 *R17* **Wymore** Nebraska, C USA
182 *E5* **Wynbring** South Australia
181 *N3* **Wyndham** Western Australia
29 *R6* **Wyndmere** North Dakota, N USA
27 *X11* **Wynne** Arkansas, C USA
27 *N12* **Wynnewood** Oklahoma, C USA
183 *O15* **Wynyard** Tasmania, SE Australia
9 *U15* **Wynyard** Saskatchewan, S Canada
33 *V11* **Wyola** Montana, NW USA
182 *A4* **Wyola Lake** *salt lake* South Australia
31 *P9* **Wyoming** Michigan, N USA
33 *V14* **Wyoming** *off.* State of Wyoming, ***also known as*** Equality State. ◐ *state* C USA
33 *S15* **Wyoming Range** ▲▲ Wyoming, C USA
183 *T8* **Wyong** New South Wales, SE Australia
110 *G9* **Wyrzysk** *Ger.* Wirsitz. Wielkopolskie, C Poland
Wysg *see* Usk
110 *O10* **Wysokie Mazowieckie** Łomża, E Poland
110 *M11* **Wyszków** *Ger.* Probstberg. Mazowieckie, NE Poland
110 *L11* **Wyszogród** Mazowieckie, C Poland
21 *R7* **Wytheville** Virginia, NE USA
111 *L15* **Wyżyna Małopolska** *plateau*

X

80 *Q12* **Xaafuun** *It.* Hafun. Bari, NE Somalia
80 *Q12* **Xaafuun, Raas** *var.* Ras Hafun. *cape* NE Somalia
Xàbia *see* Jávea
42 *C4* **Xaclbal, Río** *var.* Xalbal. ≈ Guatemala/Mexico
137 *Y10* **Xaçmaz** *Rus.* Khachmas. N Azerbaijan
80 *O12* **Xadeed** *var.* Haded. *physical region* N Somalia
159 *O14* **Xagquka** Xizang Zizhiqu, W China
167 *Q6* **Xai** *var.* Muang Xay, Muong Sai. Oudômxai, N Laos
158 *F10* **Xaidulla** Xinjiang Uygur Zizhiqu, W China
167 *Q7* **Xaignabouli** *prev* Muang Xaignabouri, *Fr.* Sayaboury. Xaignabouli, N Laos
167 *R7* **Xai Lai Leng, Phou** ▲ Laos/Vietnam
158 *L15* **Xainza** Xizang Zizhiqu, W China
158 *L16* **Xaitongmoin** Xizang Zizhiqu, W China
83 *M20* **Xai-Xai** *prev.* João Belo, Vila de João Belo. Gaza, S Mozambique
Xalbal *see* Xaclbal, Río
80 *P13* **Xalin** Sool, N Somalia
146 *H7* **Xalqobod** *Rus.* Khalkabad. Qoraqalpog'iston Respublikasi, W Uzbekistan
167 *R6* **Xam Nua** *var.* Sam Neua. Houaphan, N Laos
82 *D11* **Xá-Muteba** *Port.* Cinco de Outubro. Lunda Norte, NE Angola
Xangda *see* Nangqên
83 *C16* **Xangongo** *Port.* Rocadas. Cunene, SW Angola
137 *W12* **Xankändi** *Rus.* Khankendi; *prev.* Stepanakert. SW Azerbaijan
137 *V11* **Xanlar** *Rus.* Khanlar. NW Azerbaijan
114 *J13* **Xánthi** Anatolikí Makedonía kai Thráki, NE Greece
60 *H13* **Xanxerê** Santa Catarina, S Brazil
81 *O15* **Xarardheere** Mudug, E Somalia
137 *Z11* **Xärä Zirä Adası** *Rus.* Ostrov Bulla. *Island* E Azerbaijan
162 *K13* **Xar Burd** *prev.* Bayan Nuru. Nei Mongol Zizhiqu, N China
163 *T11* **Xar Moron** ≈ NE China
Xarra *see* Xarrë
113 *L23* **Xarrë** *var.* Xarra. Vlorë, S Albania
82 *D12* **Xassengue** Lunda Sul, NW Angola
105 *S11* **Xátiva** *var.* Jativa; *anc.* Setabis. País Valenciano, E Spain
Xauen *see* Chefchaouen
60 *K10* **Xavantes, Represa de** *var.* Represa de Chavantes. ⊠ S Brazil
158 *I7* **Xayar** Xinjiang Uygur Zizhiqu, W China
Xäzär Dänizi *see* Caspian Sea
167 *S8* **Xé Bangfai** ≈ C Laos
167 *T9* **Xé Banghiang** *var.* Bang Hieng. ≈ S Laos
Xêgar *see* Tingri
31 *R14* **Xenia** Ohio, N USA
Xeres *see* Jeréz de la Frontera
115 *E15* **Xeriás** ≈ C Greece
115 *G17* **Xeró** ▲ Évvoia, C Greece
83 *H18* **Xhumo** Central, C Botswana
161 *N15* **Xiachuan Dao** *island* S China
Xiacun *see* Rushan
Xiaguan *see* Dali
159 *U11* **Xiahe** *var.* Labrang. Gansu, C China
161 *Q13* **Xiamen** *var.* Hsia-men; *prev.* Amoy. Fujian, SE China

◆ Country
● Country Capital
◇ Dependent Territory
○ Dependent Territory Capital
◐ Administrative Regions
✈ International Airport
▲ Mountain
▲▲ Mountain Range
◬ Volcano
≈ River
◎ Lake
⊠ Reservoir

Xi'an – Yellow Sea

160 *L6* **Xi'an** *var.* Changan, Sian, Signan, Siking, Singan, Xian. *province capital* Shaanxi, C China
160 *L10* **Xianfeng** *var.* Gaoleshan. Hubei, C China
Xiang *see* Hunan
161 *N7* **Xiangcheng** Henan, C China
160 *F10* **Xiangcheng** *var.* Sampê, *Tib.* Qagchêng. Sichuan, C China
160 *M8* **Xiangfan** *var.* Xiangyang. Hubei, C China
Xianggang *see* Hong Kong
161 *N10* **Xiang Jiang** ≈ S China
Xiangkhoang *see* Pèk
167 *Q7* **Xiangkhoang, Plateau de** *var.* Plain of Jars. *plateau* N Laos
161 *N11* **Xiangtan** *var.* Hsiang-t'an, Siangtan. Hunan, S China
161 *N11* **Xiangxiang** Hunan, S China
Xiangyang *see* Xiangfan
161 *S10* **Xianju** Zhejiang, SE China
Xianshui *see* Dawu
160 *F8* **Xianshui He** ≈ C China
161 *N9* **Xiantao** *var.* Mianyang. Hubei, C China
161 *R10* **Xianxia Ling** ▲▲ SE China
160 *K6* **Xianyang** Shaanxi, C China
158 *L5* **Xiaocaohu** Xinjiang Uygur Zizhiqu, W China
161 *O9* **Xiaogan** Hubei, C China
Xiaogang *see* Dongxiang
163 *W6* **Xiao Hinggan Ling** *Eng.* Lesser Khingan Range. ▲▲ NE China
160 *M6* **Xiao Shan** ▲▲ C China
160 *M12* **Xiao Shui** ≈ S China
Xiaoxi *see* Pinghe
161 *P6* **Xiaoxian** *var.* Longcheng, Xiao Xian. Anhui, E China
Xiao Xian *see* Xiaoxian
160 *G11* **Xichang** Sichuan, C China
41 *P11* **Xicoténcatl** Tamaulipas, C Mexico
Xieng Khouang *see* Pèk
Xieng Ngeun *see* Muong Xiang Ngeun
160 *J11* **Xifeng** *var.* Yongjing. Guizhou, S China
Xifeng *see* Qingyang
Xigang *see* Helan
158 *L16* **Xigazê** *var.* Jih-k'a-tse, Shigatse, Xigaze. Xizang Zizhiqu, W China
159 *W11* **Xihe** *var.* Hanyuan. Gansu, C China
160 *I8* **Xi He** ≈ C China
Xihuachi *see* Heshui
159 *W10* **Xiji** Ningxia, N China
160 *M14* **Xi Jiang** *var.* Hsi Chiang, *Eng.* West River. ≈ S China
159 *Q7* **Xijan Quan** *spring* NW China
160 *K15* **Xijin Shuiku** ⊠ S China
Xilagani *see* Xylaganí
Xiligou *see* Ulan
160 *I13* **Xilin** *var.* Bada. Guangxi Zhuangzu Zizhiqu, S China
163 *Q10* **Xilinhot** *var.* Silinhot. Nei Mongol Zizhiqu, N China
Xilinji *see* Mohe
Xilokastro *see* Xylókastro
Xin *see* Xinjiang Uygur Zizhiqu
161 *R10* **Xin'anjiang Shuiku** *var.* Qiandao Hu. ⊠ SE China
Xin'anzhen *see* Xinyi
Xin Barag Youqi *see* Altan Emel
Xin Barag Zuoqi *see* Amgalang
163 *W12* **Xinbin** *var.* Xinbin Manzu Zizhixian. Liaoning, NE China
Xinbin Manzu Zizhixian *see* Xinbin
161 *O7* **Xincai** Henan, C China
Xincheng *see* Zhaojue
Xindu *see* Luhuo
161 *O13* **Xinfeng** *var.* Jiading. Jiangxi, S China
161 *O14* **Xinfengjiang Shuiku** ⊠ S China
Xing'an *see* Ankang
Xingba *see* Lhünzê
163 *T13* **Xingcheng** Liaoning, NE China
Xingcheng *see* Xingning
82 *E11* **Xinge** Lunda Norte, NE Angola
161 *P12* **Xingguo** *var.* Lianjiang. Jiangxi, S China
159 *S11* **Xinghai** *var.* Ziketan. Qinghai, C China
161 *R7* **Xinghua** Jiangsu, E China
Xingkai Hu *see* Khanka, Lake
161 *P13* **Xingning** *var.* Xingcheng. Guangdong, S China
160 *I13* **Xingren** Guizhou, S China
161 *O4* **Xingtai** Hebei, E China
59 *J14* **Xingu, Rio** ≈ C Brazil
159 *P6* **Xingxingxia** Xinjiang Uygur Zizhiqu, NW China
160 *I13* **Xingyi** Guizhou, S China
158 *I6* **Xinhe** *var.* Toksu. Xinjiang Uygur Zizhiqu, NW China
163 *Q10* **Xin Hot** *var.* Abag Qi. Nei Mongol Zizhiqu, N China
Xinhua *see* Funing
163 *T12* **Xinhui** *var.* Aohan Qi. Nei Mongol Zizhiqu, N China
159 *T10* **Xining** *var.* Hsining, Hsi-ning, Sining. *province capital* Qinghai, C China
161 *O4* **Xinji** *prev.* Shulu. Hebei, E China
161 *P10* **Xinjian** Jiangxi, S China
Xinjiang *see* Xinjiang Uygur Zizhiqu
162 *D8* **Xinjiang Uygur Zizhiqu** *var.* Sinkiang, Sinkiang Uighur Autonomous Region, Xin, Xinjiang. ◈ *autonomous region* NW China
160 *H9* **Xinjin** *var.* Meixing, *Tib.* Zainlha. Sichuan, C China
Xinjin *see* Pulandian
Xinjing *see* Jingxi
163 *U12* **Xinmin** Liaoning, NE China
160 *M12* **Xinning** *var.* Jinshi. Hunan, S China
Xinpu *see* Lianyungang
Xinshan *see* Anyuan
161 *P5* **Xintai** Shandong, E China
Xinwen *see* Suncun
Xin Xian *see* Xinzhou
161 *N6* **Xinxiang** Henan, C China
161 *O8* **Xinyang** *var.* Hsin-yang, Sinyang. Henan, C China
161 *Q6* **Xinyi** *var.* Xin'anzhen. Jiangsu, E China
161 *Q6* **Xinyi He** ≈ E China
161 *O11* **Xinyu** Jiangxi, S China
158 *I5* **Xinyuan** *var.* Künes. Xinjiang Uygur Zizhiqu, NW China
Xinyuan *see* Tianjun
162 *M13* **Xinzhao Shan** ▲ N China
161 *N3* **Xinzhou** *var.* Xin Xian. Shanxi, C China
Xinzhou *see* Longlin
104 *H4* **Xinzo de Limia** Galicia, NW Spain
Xions *see* Książ Wielkopolski
161 *O7* **Xiping** Henan, C China
Xiping *see* Songyang
159 *T11* **Xiqing Shan** ▲▲ C China
59 *N16* **Xique-Xique** Bahia, E Brazil
Xireg *see* Ulan
115 *E14* **Xirovoúni** ▲ N Greece
162 *M13* **Xishanzui** *var.* Urad Qianqi. Nei Mongol Zizhiqu, N China
160 *J11* **Xishui** Guizhou, S China
Xi Ujimqin Qi *see* Bayan Ul
160 *K11* **Xiushan** *var.* Zhonghe. Chongqing Shi, C China
Xiushan *see* Tonghai
161 *O10* **Xiu Shui** ≈ S China
Xiuyan *see* Qingjian
146 *H9* **Xiva** *Rus.* Khiva, Khiwa. Xorazm Viloyati, W Uzbekistan
158 *J16* **Xixabangma Feng** ▲ W China
160 *M7* **Xixia** Henan, C China
Xixón *see* Gijón
Xixona *see* Jijona
Xizang *see* Xizang Zizhiqu
Xizang Gaoyuan *see* Qingzang Gaoyuan
160 *E9* **Xizang Zizhiqu** *var.* Thibet, Tibetan Autonomous Region, Xizang, *Eng.* Tibet. ◈ *autonomous region* W China
163 *U14* **Xizhong Dao** *island* N China
Xoi *see* Qüxü
146 *H8* **Xo'jayli** *Rus.* Khodzheyli. Qoraqalpog'iston Respublikasi, W Uzbekistan
Xolotlán *see* Managua, Lago de
147 *I9* **Xonqa** *var.* Khonqa, *Rus.* Khanka. Xorazm Viloyati, W Uzbekistan
146 *H9* **Xorazm Viloyati** *Rus.* Khorezmskaya Oblast'. ◈ *province* W Uzbekistan
159 *N9* **Xorkol** Xinjiang Uygur Zizhiqu, NW China
147 *P11* **Xovos** *var.* Ursat'yevskaya, *Rus.* Khavast. Sirdaryo Viloyati, E Uzbekistan
41 *X14* **Xpujil** Quintana Roo, E Mexico
161 *Q8* **Xuancheng** *var.* Xuanzhou. Anhui, E China
167 *T9* **Xuân Đuc** Quang Binh, C Vietnam
160 *L9* **Xuan'en** *var.* Zhushan. Hubei, C China
160 *K8* **Xuanhan** Sichuan, C China
161 *O2* **Xuanhua** Hebei, E China
161 *P4* **Xuanhui He** ≈ E China
Xuanzhou *see* Xuancheng
161 *N7* **Xuchang** Henan, C China
137 *X10* **Xudat** *Rus.* Khudat. NE Azerbaijan
81 *M16* **Xuddur** *var.* Hudur, *It.* Oddur. Bakool, SW Somalia
80 *O13* **Xudun** Sool, N Somalia
160 *L11* **Xuefeng Shan** ▲▲ S China
Xulun Hobot Qagan *see* Qagan Nur
42 *F2* **Xunantunich** *ruins* Cayo, W Belize
163 *W6* **Xun He** ≈ NE China
160 *L7* **Xun He** ≈ C China
160 *L14* **Xun Jiang** ≈ S China
163 *W5* **Xunke** *var.* Bianjing; *prev.* Qike. Heilongjiang, NE China
161 *P13* **Xunwu** *var.* Changning. Jiangxi, S China
161 *O3* **Xushui** Hebei, E China
160 *L16* **Xuwen** Guangdong, S China
160 *I11* **Xuyong** *var.* Yongning. Sichuan, C China
161 *P6* **Xuzhou** *var.* Hsu-chou, Suchow, Tongshan; *prev.* T'ung-shan. Jiangsu, E China
114 *K13* **Xylaganí** *var.* Xilaganí. Anatolikí Makedonía kai Thráki, NE Greece
115 *F19* **Xylókastro** *var.* Xilokastro. Pelopónnisos, S Greece

Y

160 *H9* **Ya'an** *var.* Yaan. Sichuan, C China
182 *L10* **Yaapeet** Victoria, SE Australia
79 *D15* **Yabassi** Littoral, W Cameroon
81 *J15* **Yabēlo** Oromo, C Ethiopia
114 *H9* **Yablanitsa** Lovech Oblast, N Bulgaria
43 *N7* **Yablis** Región Autónoma Atlántico Norte, NE Nicaragua
123 *O14* **Yablonovyy Khrebet** ▲▲ S Russian Federation
162 *J14* **Yabrai Shan** ▲▲ NE China
45 *U6* **Yabucoa** E Puerto Rico
160 *J11* **Yachi He** ≈ S China
32 *H10* **Yacolt** Washington, NW USA
54 *M10* **Yacuaray** Amazonas, S Venezuela
57 *M22* **Yacuiba** Tarija, S Bolivia
57 *K16* **Yacuma, Río** ≈ C Bolivia
155 *H16* **Yādgīr** Karnātaka, C India
21 *R8* **Yadkin River** ≈ North Carolina, SE USA
21 *R9* **Yadkinville** North Carolina, SE USA
127 *P3* **Yadrin** Chavash Respubliki, W Russian Federation
Yaegama-shotō *see* Yaeyama-shotō
Yaeme-saki *see* Paimi-saki
165 *O16* **Yaeyama-shotō** *var.* Yaegama-shotō. *island group* SW Japan
75 *O8* **Yafran** NW Libya
165 *S2* **Yagashiri-tō** *island* NE Japan
65 *H21* **Yaghan Basin** *undersea feature* SE Pacific Ocean
123 *S9* **Yagodnoye** Magadanskaya Oblast', E Russian Federation
Yagotin *see* Yahotyn
78 *G12* **Yagoua** Extrême-Nord, NE Cameroon
159 *Q11* **Yagradagzê Shan** ▲ C China
Yaguachi *see* Yaguachi Nuevo
56 *B7* **Yaguachi Nuevo** *var.* Yaguachi. Guayas, W Ecuador
Yaguarón, Río *see* Jaguarão, Rio
117 *Q11* **Yahorlyts'kyy Lyman** *bay* S Ukraine
117 *Q5* **Yahotyn** *Rus.* Yagotin. Kyyivs'ka Oblast', N Ukraine
40 *L12* **Yahualica** Jalisco, SW Mexico
79 *L17* **Yahuma** Orientale, N Dem. Rep. Congo
136 *K15* **Yahyalı** Kayseri, C Turkey
167 *N15* **Yai, Khao** ▲ SW Thailand
164 *M14* **Yaizu** Shizuoka, Honshū, S Japan
160 *G9* **Yajiang** *var.* Hekou, *Tib.* Nyagquka. Sichuan, C China
119 *O14* **Yakawlyevichi** *Rus.* Yakovlevichi. Vitsyebskaya Voblasts', NE Belarus
163 *S6* **Yakeshi** Nei Mongol Zizhiqu, N China
32 *I9* **Yakima** Washington, NW USA
32 *J10* **Yakima River** ≈ Washington, NW USA
114 *G7* **Yakimovo** Montana, NW Bulgaria
Yakkabag *see* Yakkabog'
147 *N12* **Yakkabog'** *Rus.* Yakkabag. Qashqadaryo Viloyati, S Uzbekistan
148 *L12* **Yakmach** Baluchistān, SW Pakistan
77 *O12* **Yako** W Burkina
39 *W13* **Yakobi Island** *island* Alexander Archipelago, Alaska, USA
79 *K15* **Yakoma** Equateur, N Dem. Rep. Congo
114 *H11* **Yakoruda** Blagoevgrad, SW Bulgaria
Yakovlevichi *see* Yakawlyevichi
127 *T2* **Yakshur-Bod'ya** Udmurtskaya Respublika, NW Russian Federation
165 *Q5* **Yakumo** Hokkaidō, NE Japan
164 *B17* **Yaku-shima** *island* Nansei-shotō, SW Japan
39 *V12* **Yakutat** Alaska, USA
39 *U12* **Yakutat Bay** *inlet* Alaska, USA
Yakutia/Yakutiya/Yakutiya, Respublika *see* Sakha (Yakutiya), Respublika
123 *Q10* **Yakutsk** Respublika Sakha (Yakutiya), NE Russian Federation
167 *O17* **Yala** Yala, SW Thailand
182 *D6* **Yalata** South Australia
31 *S9* **Yale** Michigan, N USA
180 *I11* **Yalgoo** Western Australia
114 *O12* **Yalıköy** İstanbul, NW Turkey
79 *L14* **Yalinga** Haute-Kotto, C Central African Republic
119 *M17* **Yalizava** *Rus.* Yelizovo. Mahilyowskaya Voblasts', E Belarus
44 *L13* **Yallahs Hill** ▲ E Jamaica
22 *L3* **Yalobusha River** ≈ Mississippi, S USA
79 *H15* **Yaloké** Ombella-Mpoko, W Central African Republic
160 *E7* **Yalong Jiang** ≈ C China
136 *E11* **Yalova** Yalova, NW Turkey
136 *E11* **Yalova** ◈ *province* NW Turkey
Yaloveny *see* Ialoveni
Yalpug *see* Ialpug
Yalpug, Ozero *see* Yalpuh, Ozero
117 *N12* **Yalpuh, Ozero** *Rus.* Ozero Yalpug. ◎ SW Ukraine
117 *T14* **Yalta** Respublika Krym, S Ukraine
163 *W12* **Yalu** *Chin.* Yalu Jiang, *Jap.* Oryokko, *Kor.* Amnok-kang. ≈ China/North Korea
Yalu Jiang *see* Yalu
136 *F14* **Yalvaç** Isparta, SW Turkey
165 *R9* **Yamada** Iwate, Honshū, C Japan
165 *D14* **Yamaga** Kumamoto, Kyūshū, SW Japan
165 *P10* **Yamagata** Yamagata, Honshū, C Japan
165 *P9* **Yamagata** *off.* Yamagata-ken. ◈ *prefecture* Honshū, C Japan
Yamagata-ken *see* Yamagata
164 *C16* **Yamagawa** Kagoshima, Kyūshū, SW Japan
164 *E13* **Yamaguchi** *var.* Yamaguti. Yamaguchi, Honshū, SW Japan
164 *E13* **Yamaguchi** *off.* Yamaguchi-ken, *var.* Yamaguti. ◈ *prefecture* Honshū, SW Japan
Yamaguchi-ken *see* Yamaguchi
Yamaguti *see* Yamaguchi
125 *X5* **Yamalo-Nenetskiy Avtonomnyy Okrug** ◈ *autonomous district* N Russian Federation
122 *J7* **Yamal, Poluostrov** *peninsula* N Russian Federation
165 *N13* **Yamanashi** *off.* Yamanashi-ken, *var.* Yamanasi. ◈ *prefecture* Honshū, S Japan
Yamanashi-ken *see* Yamanashi
Yamanasi *see* Yamanashi
Yamaniyah, Al Jumhūrīyah al *see* Yemen
127 *W5* **Yamantau** ▲ W Russian Federation
Yamasaki *see* Yamazaki
15 *P12* **Yamaska** ≈ Québec, SE Canada
192 *G4* **Yamato Ridge** *undersea feature* S Sea of Japan
164 *I13* **Yamazaki** *var.* Yamasaki. Hyōgo, Honshū, SW Japan
183 *V5* **Yamba** New South Wales, SE Australia
81 *D16* **Yambio** *var.* Yambiyo. Western Equatoria, S Sudan
Yambiyo *see* Yambio
114 *L10* **Yambol** *Turk.* Yanboli. Yambol, E Bulgaria
114 *M11* **Yambol** ◈ *province* E Bulgaria
79 *M17* **Yambuya** Orientale, N Dem. Rep. Congo
171 *T15* **Yamdena, Pulau** *prev.* Jamdena. *island* Kepulauan Tanimbar, E Indonesia
165 *O14* **Yame** Fukuoka, Kyūshū, SW Japan
166 *M6* **Yamethin** Mandalay, C Burma (Myanmar)
186 *C6* **Yaminbot** East Sepik, NW Papua New Guinea
181 *U9* **Yamma Yamma, Lake** ◎ Queensland, C Australia
76 *M16* **Yamoussoukro** ● (Ivory Coast) C Ivory Coast
37 *P3* **Yampa River** ≈ Colorado, C USA
117 *S2* **Yampil'** Sums'ka Oblast', NE Ukraine
116 *M8* **Yampil'** Vinnyts'ka Oblast', C Ukraine
123 *T9* **Yamsk** Magadanskaya Oblast', E Russian Federation
152 *J8* **Yamuna** *prev.* Jumna. ≈ N India
152 *I9* **Yamunānagar** Haryāna, N India
Yamundá *see* Nhamundá, Rio
145 *U8* **Yamyshevo** Pavlodar, NE Kazakhstan
159 *N16* **Yamzho Yumco** ◎ W China
123 *Q8* **Yana** ≈ NE Russian Federation
186 *H9* **Yanaba Island** *island* SE Papua New Guinea
155 *L16* **Yanam** *var.* Yanaon. Pondicherry, E India
160 *L5* **Yan'an** *var.* Yanan. Shaanxi, C China
Yanaon *see* Yanam
127 *U3* **Yanaul** Respublika Bashkortostan, W Russian Federation
118 *O12* **Yanavichy** *Rus.* Yanovichi. Vitsyebskaya Voblasts', NE Belarus
Yanboli *see* Yambol
140 *K8* **Yanbu 'al Baḩr** Al Madīnah, W Saudi Arabia
21 *T8* **Yanceyville** North Carolina, SE USA
161 *R7* **Yancheng** Jiangsu, E China
159 *W8* **Yanchi** Ningxia, N China
160 *L5* **Yanchuan** Shaanxi, C China
183 *O10* **Yanco Creek** *seasonal river* New South Wales, SE Australia
183 *O6* **Yanda Creek** *seasonal river* New South Wales, SE Australia
182 *K4* **Yandama Creek** *seasonal river* New South Wales/South Australia
161 *S11* **Yandang Shan** ▲▲ SE China
159 *O6* **Yandun** Xinjiang Uygur Zizhiqu, W China
76 *L13* **Yanfolila** Sikasso, SW Mali
79 *M18* **Yangambi** Orientale, N Dem. Rep. Congo
158 *M15* **Yangbajain** Xizang Zizhiqu, W China
Yangchow *see* Yangzhou
160 *M15* **Yangchun** *var.* Chuncheng. Guangdong, S China
161 *N2* **Yanggao** Shanxi, C China
Yanggeta *see* Yaqeta
Yangiabad *see* Yangiobod
Yangibazar *see* Dzhany-Bazar
Yangi-Bazar *see* Kofarnihon
Yangiklshak *see* Yangiqishloq
146 *M13* **Yangi-Nishon** *Rus.* Yang-Nishan. Qashqadaryo Viloyati, S Uzbekistan
147 *Q9* **Yangiobod** *Rus.* Yangiabad. Toshkent Viloyati, E Uzbekistan
147 *O10* **Yangiqishloq** *Rus.* Yangiklshak. Jizzax Viloyati, C Uzbekistan
147 *P11* **Yangiyer** Sirdaryo Viloyati, E Uzbekistan
147 *P9* **Yangiyo'l** *Rus.* Yangiyul'. Toshkent Viloyati, E Uzbekistan
Yangiyul' *see* Yangiyo'l
160 *M15* **Yangjiang** Guangdong, S China
Yangku *see* Taiyuan
Yang-Nishan *see* Yangi-Nishon
166 *L8* **Yangon** *Eng.* Rangoon. ● (Burma (Myanmar)) Yangon, S Burma (Myanmar)
166 *M8* **Yangon** *Eng.* Rangoon. ◈ *division* SW Burma (Myanmar)
161 *N4* **Yangquan** Shanxi, C China
161 *N13* **Yangshan** Guangdong, S China
167 *U12* **Yang Sin, Chu** ▲ S Vietnam
Yangtze *see* Chang Jiang
Yangtze *see* Chang Jiang/Jinsha Jiang
Yangtze *see* Jinsha Jiang
Yangtze Kiang *see* Chang Jiang
Yangtze Kiang *see* Chang Jiang
161 *R7* **Yangzhou** *var.* Yangchow. Jiangsu, E China
160 *L5* **Yan He** ≈ C China
163 *Y10* **Yanji** Jilin, NE China
Yanji *see* Longjing
Yanjing *see* Yangyuan
29 *Q12* **Yankton** South Dakota, N USA
161 *O12* **Yanling** *prev.* Lingxian, Ling Xian. Hunan, S China
Yannina *see* Ioánnina
123 *Q7* **Yano-Indigirskaya Nizmennost'** *plain* NE Russian Federation
Yanovichi *see* Yanavichy
155 *K24* **Yan Oya** ≈ N Sri Lanka
158 *K6* **Yanqi** *var.* Yanqi Huizu Zizhixian. Xinjiang Uygur Zizhiqu, NW China
Yanqi Huizu Zizhixian *see* Yanqi
161 *Q10* **Yanshan** *var.* Hekou. Jiangxi, S China
160 *H14* **Yanshan** *var.* Jiangna. Yunnan, SW China
161 *P2* **Yan Shan** ▲▲ E China
163 *X8* **Yanshou** Heilongjiang, NE China
123 *Q7* **Yanskiy Zaliv** *bay* N Russian Federation
183 *O4* **Yantabulla** New South Wales, SE Australia
161 *R4* **Yantai** *var.* Yan-t'ai; *prev.* Chefoo, Chih-fu. Shandong, E China
118 *A13* **Yantarnyy** *Ger.* Palmnicken. Kaliningradskaya Oblast', W Russian Federation
114 *J9* **Yantra** Gabrovo, N Bulgaria
114 *K9* **Yantra** ≈ N Bulgaria
160 *G11* **Yangyuan** *var.* Yanjing. Sichuan, C China
161 *P5* **Yanzhou** Shandong, E China
79 *E16* **Yaoundé** *var.* Yaunde. ● (Cameroon) Centre, S Cameroon
188 *I14* **Yap** ◈ *state* W Micronesia
188 *F16* **Yap** *island* Caroline Islands, W Micronesia
57 *M18* **Yapacani, Rio** ≈ C Bolivia
171 *W14* **Yapa Kopra** Papua, E Indonesia
Yapan *see* Yapen, Selat
Yapanskoye More East Sea/Japan, Sea of
77 *P15* **Yapei** N Ghana
12 *M10* **Yapeitso, Mont** ▲ Québec, E Canada
171 *W12* **Yapen, Pulau** *prev.* Japen. *island* E Indonesia
171 *W12* **Yapen, Selat** *var.* Yapan. *strait* Papua, E Indonesia
61 *E15* **Yapeyú** Corrientes, NE Argentina
136 *I11* **Yapraklı** Çankın, N Turkey
174 *M3* **Yap Trench** *var.* Yap Trough. *undersea feature* SE Philippine Sea
Yap Trough *see* Yap Trench
Yapurá *see* Caquetá, Río, Brazil/Colombia
Yapurá *see* Japurá, Rio, Brazil/Colombia
197 *I12* **Yaqaga** *island* N Fiji
197 *H12* **Yaqeta** *prev.* Yanggeta. *island* Yasawa Group, NW Fiji
40 *G6* **Yaqui** Sonora, NW Mexico
32 *E12* **Yaquina Bay** *bay* Oregon, NW USA
40 *G6* **Yaqui, Río** ≈ NW Mexico
54 *K5* **Yaracuy** *off.* Estado Yaracuy. ◈ *state* NW Venezuela
Yaracuy, Estado *see* Yaracuy
146 *E13* **Yarajy** *Rus.* Yaradzhi. Ahal Welaýaty, C Turkmenistan
Yaradzhi *see* Yarajy
125 *Q15* **Yaransk** Kirovskaya Oblast', NW Russian Federation
136 *F17* **Yardımcı Burnu** *headland* SW Turkey
97 *Q19* **Yare** ≈ E England, UK
125 *S9* **Yarega** Respublika Komi, NW Russian Federation
116 *I7* **Yaremcha** Ivano-Frankivs'ka Oblast', W Ukraine
189 *Q9* **Yaren** SW Nauru
125 *Q10* **Yarensk** Arkhangel'skaya Oblast', NW Russian Federation
155 *F16* **Yargatti** Karnātaka, W India
164 *M12* **Yariga-take** ▲ Honshū, S Japan
141 *O15* **Yarīm** W Yemen
54 *F14* **Yarí, Río** ≈ SW Colombia
54 *K5* **Yaritagua** Yaracuy, N Venezuela
Yarkand *see* Yarkant He
Yarkant *see* Shache
158 *E9* **Yarkant He** *var.* Yarkand. ≈ NW China
149 *U3* **Yarkhūn** ≈ NW Pakistan
Yarlung Zangbo Jiang *see* Brahmaputra
116 *L6* **Yarmolyntsi** Khmel'nyts'ka Oblast', W Ukraine
163 *T11* **Yar Moron** ≈ N China
13 *O16* **Yarmouth** Nova Scotia, SE Canada
Yarmouth *see* Great Yarmouth
Yaroslav *see* Jarosław
124 *L15* **Yaroslavl'** Yaroslavskaya Oblast', W Russian Federation
124 *K14* **Yaroslavskaya Oblast'** ◈ *province* W Russian Federation
123 *N11* **Yaroslavskiy** Respublika Sakha (Yakutiya), NE Russian Federation
183 *P13* **Yarram** Victoria, SE Australia
183 *O11* **Yarrawonga** Victoria, SE Australia
182 *L4* **Yarriarraburra Swamp** *wetland* New South Wales, SE Australia
122 *I8* **Yar-Sale** Yamalo-Nenetskiy Avtonomnyy Okrug, N Russian Federation
122 *K11* **Yartsevo** Krasnoyarskiy Kray, C Russian Federation
126 *I4* **Yartsevo** Smolenskaya Oblast', W Russian Federation
54 *E8* **Yarumal** Antioquia, NW Colombia
187 *W14* **Yasawa Group** *island group* NW Fiji
77 *V12* **Yashi** Katsina, N Nigeria
77 *S14* **Yashikera** Kwara, W Nigeria
147 *T14* **Yashilkŭl** *Rus.* Ozero Yashil'kul'. ◎ SE Tajikistan
Yashil'kul', Ozero *see* Yashilkŭl
165 *P9* **Yashima** Akita, Honshū, C Japan
127 *P13* **Yashkul'** Respublika Kalmykiya, SW Russian Federation
146 *F13* **Yashlyk** Ahal Welaýaty, C Turkmenistan
Yasinovataya *see* Yasynuvata
114 *N10* **Yasna Polyana** Burgas, E Bulgaria
167 *R10* **Yasothon** Yasothon, E Thailand
183 *R10* **Yass** New South Wales, SE Australia
Yassy *see* Iaşi
164 *H12* **Yasugi** Shimane, Honshū, SW Japan
143 *N10* **Yāsūj** *var.* Yesuj; *prev.* Tal-e Khosravī. Kohkīlūyeh va Būyer AḨmad, C Iran
136 *M11* **Yasun Burnu** *headland* N Turkey
117 *X8* **Yasynuvata** *Rus.* Yasinovataya. Donets'ka Oblast', SE Ukraine
136 *C15* **Yatağan** Muğla, SW Turkey
165 *Q7* **Yatate-tōge** *pass* Honshū, C Japan
187 *Q17* **Yaté** Province Sud, S New Caledonia
27 *P6* **Yates Center** Kansas, C USA
185 *B21* **Yates Point** *headland* South Island, New Zealand
9 *N9* **Yathkyed Lake** ◎ Nunavut, NE Canada
171 *T16* **Yatoke** Pulau Babar, E Indonesia
79 *M18* **Yatolema** Orientale, N Dem. Rep. Congo
164 *C15* **Yatsushiro** *var.* Yatusiro. Kumamoto, Kyūshū, SW Japan
164 *C15* **Yatsushiro-kai** *bay* SW Japan
138 *F11* **Yatta** *var.* Yuta. S West Bank
81 *J20* **Yatta Plateau** *plateau* SE Kenya
Yatusiro *see* Yatsushiro
57 *F17* **Yauca, Río** ≈ SW Peru
45 *S6* **Yauco** W Puerto Rico
Yaunde *see* Yaoundé
Yavan *see* Yovon
Yavarí *see* Javari, Rio
56 *G9* **Yavari Mirim, Río** ≈ NE Peru
40 *G7* **Yavaros** Sonora, NW Mexico
154 *I13* **Yavatmāl** Mahārāshtra, C India
54 *M9* **Yaví, Cerro** ▲ C Venezuela
43 *W16* **Yaviza** Darién, SE Panama
138 *F10* **Yavne** Central, W Israel
116 *H5* **Yavoriv** *Pol.* Jaworów, *Rus.* Yavorov. L'vivs'ka Oblast', NW Ukraine
Yavorov *see* Yavoriv
164 *F14* **Yawatahama** Ehime, Shikoku, SW Japan
Ya Xian *see* Sanya
136 *L17* **Yayladaği** Hatay, S Turkey
125 *V13* **Yayva** Permskaya Oblast', NW Russian Federation
125 *V12* **Yayva** ≈ NW Russian Federation
143 *Q9* **Yazd** *var.* Yezd. Yazd, C Iran
143 *Q8* **Yazd** *off.* Ostān-e Yazd, *var.* Yezd. ◈ *province* C Iran
Yazd, Ostān-e *see* Yazd
Yazgulemskiy Khrebet *see* Yazgulom, Qatorkŭhi
147 *S13* **Yazgulom, Qatorkŭhi** *Rus.* Yazgulemskiy Khrebet. ▲▲ S Tajikistan
22 *K5* **Yazoo City** Mississippi, S USA
22 *K5* **Yazoo River** ≈ Mississippi, S USA
127 *Q5* **Yazykovo** Ul'yanovskaya Oblast', W Russian Federation
109 *U4* **Ybbs** Niederösterreich, NE Austria
109 *U4* **Ybbs** ≈ C Austria
95 *G22* **Yding Skovhøj** *hill* C Denmark
115 *G20* **Ýdra** *var.* Ídhra, Idra. Ýdra, S Greece
115 *G21* **Ýdra** *var.* Ídhra. *island* Ýdra, S Greece
115 *G20* **Ýdras, Kólpos** *strait* S Greece
167 *N10* **Ye** Mon State, S Burma (Myanmar)
183 *O12* **Yea** Victoria, SE Australia
Yebaishou *see* Jianping
78 *I5* **Yebbi-Bou** Borkou-Ennedi-Tibesti, N Chad
158 *F9* **Yecheng** *var.* Kargilik. Xinjiang Uygur Zizhiqu, NW China
105 *R11* **Yecla** Murcia, SE Spain
40 *H6* **Yécora** Sonora, NW Mexico
Yedintsy *see* Edineţ
124 *J13* **Yefimovskiy** Leningradskaya Oblast', NW Russian Federation
126 *K6* **Yefremov** Tul'skaya Oblast', W Russian Federation
Yêgainnyin *see* Henan
137 *U12* **Yeghegis** *Rus.* Yekhegis. ≈ C Armenia
137 *U12* **Yeghegnadzor** C Armenia
145 *T10* **Yegindybulak** *Kaz.* Egindibulaq. Karaganda, C Kazakhstan
126 *L4* **Yegor'yevsk** Moskovskaya Oblast', W Russian Federation
Yehuda, Haré *see* Judaean Hills
81 *E15* **Yei** ≈ S Sudan
161 *P8* **Yeji** *var.* Yejiaji. Anhui, E China
Yejiaji *see* Yeji
122 *G10* **Yekaterinburg** *prev.* Sverdlovsk. Sverdlovskaya Oblast', C Russian Federation
Yekaterinodar *see* Krasnodar
Yekaterinoslav *see* Dnipropetrovs'k
123 *R13* **Yekaterinoslavka** Amurskaya Oblast', SE Russian Federation
127 *O7* **Yekaterinovka** Saratovskaya Oblast', W Russian Federation
76 *K16* **Yekepa** NE Liberia
Yekhegis *see* Yeghegis
127 *T3* **Yelabuga** Respublika Tatarstan, W Russian Federation
Yela Island *see* Rossel Island
127 *O8* **Yelan'** Volgogradskaya Oblast', SW Russian Federation
117 *Q9* **Yelanets'** *Rus.* Yelanets. Mykolayivs'ka Oblast', S Ukraine
126 *L7* **Yelets** Lipetskaya Oblast', W Russian Federation
125 *W4* **Yeletskiy** Respublika Komi, NW Russian Federation
76 *J11* **Yélimané** Kayes, W Mali
Yelisavetpol *see* Gäncä
Yelizavetgrad *see* Kirovohrad
123 *T12* **Yelizavety, Mys** *cape* SE Russian Federation
Yelizovo *see* Yalizava
127 *S5* **Yelkhovka** Samarskaya Oblast', W Russian Federation
96 *M1* **Yell** *island* NE Scotland, UK
155 *E17* **Yellāpur** Karnātaka, W India
9 *U17* **Yellow Grass** Saskatchewan, S Canada
Yellowhammer State *see* Alabama
9 *O15* **Yellowhead Pass** *pass* Alberta/British Columbia, SW Canada
8 *K10* **Yellowknife** *territory capital* Northwest Territories, W Canada
8 *K9* **Yellowknife** ≈ Northwest Territories, NW Canada
23 *P8* **Yellow River** ≈ Alabama/Florida, S USA
30 *K7* **Yellow River** ≈ Wisconsin, N USA
30 *I4* **Yellow River** ≈ Wisconsin, N USA
30 *J6* **Yellow River** ≈ Wisconsin, N USA
Yellow River *see* Huang He
157 *V8* **Yellow Sea** *Chin.* Huang Hai, *Kor.* Hwang-Hae. *sea* E Asia

◆ Country ◇ Dependent Territory ◈ Administrative Regions ▲ Mountain ⏶ Volcano ◎ Lake
● Country Capital ○ Dependent Territory Capital ✈ International Airport ▲▲ Mountain Range ≈ River ⊠ Reservoir

YELLOWSTONE LAKE – ZAGUNAO

33 S13 **Yellowstone Lake** ◎ Wyoming, C USA
33 T13 **Yellowstone National Park** *national park* Wyoming, NW USA
33 Y8 **Yellowstone River** ≈ Montana/Wyoming, NW USA
96 L1 **Yell Sound** *strait* N Scotland, UK
27 U9 **Yellville** Arkansas, C USA
122 K10 **Yeloguy** ≈ C Russian Federation
Yëloten *see* Ýolöten
119 M20 **Yel'sk** *Rus.* Yel'sk. Homyel'skaya Voblasts', SE Belarus
77 T13 **Yelwa** Kebbi, W Nigeria
21 R15 **Yemassee** South Carolina, SE USA
141 O15 **Yemen** *off.* Republic of Yemen, *Ar.* Al Jumhuriyah al Yamaniyah, Al Yaman. ◆ *republic* SW Asia
Yemen, Republic of *see* Yemen
116 M4 **Yemil'chyne** Zhytomyrs'ka Oblast', N Ukraine
124 M10 **Yemtsa** Arkhangel'skaya Oblast', NW Russian Federation
124 M10 **Yemtsa** ≈ NW Russian Federation
125 R10 **Yemva** *prev.* Zheleznodorozhnyy. Respublika Komi, NW Russian Federation
77 U17 **Yenagoa** Bayelsa, S Nigeria
117 X7 **Yenakiyeve** *Rus.* Yenakiyevo; *prev.* Ordzhonikidze, Rykovo. Donets'ka Oblast', E Ukraine
Yenakiyevo *see* Yenakiyeve
166 L6 **Yenangyaung** Magwe, W Burma (Myanmar)
167 S5 **Yên Bai** Yên Bai, N Vietnam
183 P9 **Yenda** New South Wales, SE Australia
77 Q14 **Yendi** NE Ghana
Yêndum *see* Zhag'yab
158 E8 **Yengisar** Xinjiang Uygur Zizhiqu, NW China
121 R1 **Yenierenköy** *var.* Yialousa, *Gk.* Agialoúsa. NE Cyprus
Yenipazar *see* Novi Pazar
136 E12 **Yenişehir** Bursa, NW Turkey
Yenisei Bay *see* Yeniseyskiy Zaliv
122 K12 **Yeniseysk** Krasnoyarskiy Kray, C Russian Federation
197 W10 **Yeniseyskiy Zaliv** *var.* Yenisei Bay. *bay* N Russian Federation
127 Q12 **Yenotayevka** Astrakhanskaya Oblast', SW Russian Federation
124 L4 **Yenozero, Ozero** ◎ NW Russian Federation
Yenping *see* Nanping
39 Q11 **Yentna River** ≈ Alaska, USA
180 M10 **Yeo, Lake** *salt lake* Western Australia
183 R7 **Yeoval** New South Wales, SE Australia
97 K23 **Yeovil** SW England, UK
40 H6 **Yepachic** Chihuahua, N Mexico
181 Y8 **Yeppoon** Queensland, E Australia
126 M5 **Yeraktur** Ryazanskaya Oblast', W Russian Federation
Yeraliyev *see* Kuryk
146 F12 **Yerbent** Ahal Welaýaty, C Turkmenistan
123 N11 **Yerbogachen** Irkutskaya Oblast', C Russian Federation
137 T12 **Yerevan** *Eng.* Erivan. ● (Armenia) C Armenia
137 U12 **Yerevan** ✈ C Armenia
127 O12 **Yergeni** *hill range* SW Russian Federation
Yeriho *see* Jericho
35 R6 **Yerington** Nevada, W USA
136 J13 **Yerköy** Yozgat, C Turkey
114 L13 **Yerlisu** Edirne, NW Turkey
Yermak *see* Aksu
145 R9 **Yermentau** *var.* Jermentau, *Kaz.* Ereymentaū. Akmola, C Kazakhstan
145 R9 **Yermentau, Gory** ▲▲ C Kazakhstan
125 R5 **Yermitsa** Respublika Komi, NW Russian Federation
35 V14 **Yermo** California, W USA
123 P13 **Yerofey Pavlovich** Amurskaya Oblast', SE Russian Federation
99 F15 **Yerseke** Zeeland, SW Netherlands
127 Q8 **Yershov** Saratovskaya Oblast', W Russian Federation
125 P9 **Yërtom** Respublika Komi, NW Russian Federation
56 D13 **Yerupaja, Nevado** ▲ C Peru
Yerushalayim *see* Jerusalem
105 R4 **Yesa, Embalse de** ⊠ NE Spain
144 F9 **Yesensay** Zapadnyy Kazakhstan, NW Kazakhstan
145 V15 **Yesik** *Kaz.* Esik; *prev.* Issyk. Almaty, SE Kazakhstan
145 O8 **Yesil'** *Kaz.* Esil. Akmola, C Kazakhstan
136 K15 **Yeşilhisar** Kayseri, C Turkey
136 L11 **Yeşilırmak** *var.* Iris. ≈ N Turkey
37 U12 **Yeso** New Mexico, SW USA
Yeso *see* Hokkaidō
127 N15 **Yessentuki** Stavropol'skiy Kray, SW Russian Federation
122 M9 **Yessey** Evenkiyskiy Avtonomnyy Okrug, N Russian Federation
105 P12 **Yeste** Castilla-La Mancha, C Spain
Yesuj *see* Yāsūj
183 T4 **Yetman** New South Wales, SE Australia
76 L4 **Yetti** *physical region* N Mauritania
166 M4 **Ye-u** Sagaing, C Burma (Myanmar)
102 H9 **Yeu, Île d'** *island* NW France
Yevlakh *see* Yevlax
137 W11 **Yevlax** *Rus.* Yevlakh. C Azerbaijan
117 S13 **Yevpatoriya** Respublika Krym, S Ukraine
Ye Xian *see* Laizhou
126 K12 **Yeya** ≈ SW Russian Federation
158 I10 **Yeyik** Xinjiang Uygur Zizhiqu, W China
126 K12 **Yeysk** Krasnodarskiy Kray, SW Russian Federation
Yezd *see* Yazd
Yezerishche *see* Yezyaryshcha
Yezhou *see* Jianshi
Yezo *see* Hokkaidō
118 N11 **Yezyaryshcha** *Rus.* Yezerishche. Vitsyebskaya Voblasts', NE Belarus
Yialí *see* Gyalí
Yialousa *see* Yenierenköy
163 V7 **Yi'an** Heilongjiang, NE China
Yiannitsá *see* Giannitsá
160 I10 **Yibin** Sichuan, C China
158 K13 **Yibug Caka** ◎ W China
160 M9 **Yichang** Hubei, C China
160 L5 **Yichuan** *var.* Danzhou. Shaanxi, C China
163 X6 **Yichun** *var.* I-ch'un. Heilongjiang, NE China
157 W3 **Yichun** Heilongjiang, NE China
161 O11 **Yichun** Jiangxi, S China
160 M9 **Yidu** *prev.* Zhicheng. Hubei, C China
Yidu *see* Qingzhou
188 C15 **Yigo** NE Guam
161 Q5 **Yi He** ≈ E China
163 X8 **Yilan** Heilongjiang, NE China
136 C9 **Yıldız Dağları** ▲▲ NW Turkey
136 L13 **Yıldızeli** Sivas, N Turkey
163 U4 **Yilehuli Shan** ▲▲ NE China
163 S7 **Yimin He** ≈ NE China
159 W8 **Yinchuan** *var.* Yinch'uan, Yin-ch'uan, Yinchwan. *province capital* Ningxia, N China
Yin-ch'uan/Yinch'uan *see* Yinchuan
Yinchwan *see* Yinchuan
Yindu He *see* Indus
Yingcheng *see* Yingde
161 N14 **Yingde** *var.* Yingcheng. Guangdong, S China
161 O7 **Ying He** ≈ C China
163 U13 **Yingkou** *var.* Ying-k'ou, Yingkow; *prev.* Newchwang, Niuchwang. Liaoning, NE China
Ying-k'ou *see* Yingkou
Yingkow *see* Yingkou
161 P9 **Yingshan** *var.* Wenquan. Hubei, C China
Yingshan *see* Guangshui
161 Q10 **Yingtan** Jiangxi, S China
Yin-hsien *see* Ningbo
158 H5 **Yining** *var.* I-ning, *Uigh.* Gulja, Kuldja. Xinjiang Uygur Zizhiqu, NW China
160 K11 **Yinjiang** *var.* Yinjiang Tujiazu Miaozu Zizhixian. Guizhou, S China
Yinjiang Tujiazu Miaozu Zizhixian *see* Yinjiang
166 L4 **Yinmabin** Sagaing, C Burma (Myanmar)
163 N13 **Yin Shan** ▲▲ N China
Yin-tu Ho *see* Indus
159 P15 **Yi'ong Zangbo** ≈ W China
Yioúra *see* Gyáros
81 J14 **Yirga 'Alem** *It.* Irgalem. Southern, S Ethiopia
61 E19 **Yí, Río** ≈ C Uruguay
81 E14 **Yirol** El Buhayrat, S Sudan
163 S8 **Yirshi** *var.* Yirxie. Nei Mongol Zizhiqu, N China
Yirxie *see* Yirshi
Yishan *see* Guanyun
161 Q5 **Yishui** Shandong, E China
Yisrael/Yisra'el *see* Israel
Yíthion *see* Gýtheio
Yitiaoshan *see* Jingtai
163 W10 **Yitong** *var.* Yitong Manzu Zizhixian. Jilin, NE China
Yitong Manzu Zizhixian *see* Yitong
159 P5 **Yiwu** *var.* Aratürük. Xinjiang Uygur Zizhiqu, NW China
163 U12 **Yiwulü Shan** ▲▲ N China
163 T12 **Yixian** *var.* Yizhou. Liaoning, NE China
161 N10 **Yiyang** Hunan, S China
161 Q10 **Yiyang** Jiangxi, S China
161 N13 **Yizhang** Hunan, S China
Yizhou *see* Yixian
93 K19 **Yläne** Länsi-Soumi, SW Finland
93 L14 **Yli-Ii** Oulu, C Finland
93 L14 **Ylikiiminki** Oulu, C Finland
92 N13 **Yli-Kitka** ◎ NE Finland
93 K17 **Ylistaro** Länsi-Soumi, W Finland
92 K13 **Ylitornio** Lappi, NW Finland
93 L15 **Ylivieska** Oulu, W Finland
93 L18 **Ylöjärvi** Länsi-Suomi, W Finland
95 N17 **Yngaren** ◎ C Sweden
25 T12 **Yoakum** Texas, SW USA
77 X13 **Yobe** ◐ *state* NE Nigeria
165 R3 **Yobetsu-dake** ⛰ Hokkaidō, NE Japan
80 L11 **Yoboki** C Djibouti
22 M4 **Yockanookany River** ≈ Mississippi, S USA
22 L2 **Yocona River** ≈ Mississippi, S USA
171 Y15 **Yodom** Papua, E Indonesia
169 Q16 **Yogyakarta** *prev.* Djokjakarta, Jogjakarta, Jokyakarta. Jawa, C Indonesia
169 P17 **Yogyakarta** *off.* Daerah Istimewa Yogyakarta, *var.* Djokjakarta, Jogjakarta, Jokyakarta. ◐ *autonomous district* S Indonesia
Yogyakarta, Daerah Istimewa *see* Yogyakarta
165 Q3 **Yoichi** Hokkaidō, NE Japan
42 G6 **Yojoa, Lago de** ◎ NW Honduras
79 G16 **Yokadouma** Est, SE Cameroon
164 K13 **Yokkaichi** *var.* Yokkaiti. Mie, Honshū, SW Japan
Yokkaiti *see* Yokkaichi
79 E15 **Yoko** Centre, C Cameroon
165 V15 **Yokoate-jima** *island* Nansei-shotō, SW Japan
165 R6 **Yokohama** Aomori, Honshū, C Japan
165 O14 **Yokosuka** Kanagawa, Honshū, S Japan
164 G12 **Yokota** Shimane, Honshū, SW Japan
165 Q9 **Yokote** Akita, Honshū, C Japan
77 Y14 **Yola** Adamawa, E Nigeria
79 L19 **Yolombo** Equateur, C Dem. Rep. Congo
146 J14 **Ýolöten** *Rus.* Yëloten; *prev.* Iolotan'. Mary Welaýaty, S Turkmenistan
165 Y15 **Yome-jima** *island* Ogasawara-shotō, SE Japan
76 K16 **Yomou** SE Guinea
171 Y15 **Yomuka** Papua, E Indonesia
188 C16 **Yona** E Guam
164 H12 **Yonago** Tottori, Honshū, SW Japan
165 N16 **Yonaguni** Okinawa, SW Japan
165 N16 **Yonaguni-jima** *island* Nansei-shotō, SW Japan
165 T16 **Yonaha-dake** ▲ Okinawa, SW Japan
163 X14 **Yonan** SW North Korea
165 P10 **Yonezawa** Yamagata, Honshū, C Japan
161 Q12 **Yong'an** *var.* Yongan. Fujian, SE China
Yong'an *see* Fengjie
159 T9 **Yongchang** Gansu, N China
161 P7 **Yongcheng** Henan, C China
163 Z15 **Yŏngch'ŏn** *Jap.* Eisen. SE South Korea
160 J10 **Yongchuan** Chongqing Shi, C China
159 U10 **Yongdeng** Gansu, C China
Yongding *see* Yongren
129 W9 **Yongding He** ≈ E China
161 P11 **Yongfeng** *var.* Enjiang. Jiangxi, S China
158 L5 **Yongfengqu** Xinjiang Uygur Zizhiqu, W China
160 L13 **Yongfu** Guangxi Zhuangzu Zizhiqu
163 X13 **Yŏnghŭng** E North Korea
159 U10 **Yongjing** Gansu, C China
Yongjing *see* Xifeng
163 Y15 **Yŏngju** *Jap.* Eishū. C South Korea
Yongning *see* Xuyong
160 E12 **Yongping** Yunnan, SW China
160 G12 **Yongren** *var.* Yongding. Yunnan, SW China
160 L10 **Yongshun** *var.* Lingxi. Hunan, S China
161 P10 **Yongxiu** *var.* Tujiabu. Jiangxi, S China
160 M12 **Yongzhou** *var.* Lengshuitan. Hunan, S China
Yongzhou *see* Zhishan
18 K14 **Yonkers** New York, NE USA
103 Q7 **Yonne** ◐ *department* C France
103 P6 **Yonne** ≈ C France
54 H9 **Yopal** *var.* El Yopal. Casanare, C Colombia
158 E8 **Yopurga** *var.* Yukuriawat. Xinjiang Uygur Zizhiqu, NW China
147 S11 **Yordan** *var.* Iordan, *Rus.* Jardan. Farg'ona Viloyati, E Uzbekistan
180 J12 **York** Western Australia
97 M16 **York** *anc.* Eboracum, Eburacum. N England, UK
23 N5 **York** Alabama, S USA
29 Q15 **York** Nebraska, C USA
18 G16 **York** Pennsylvania, NE USA
21 R11 **York** South Carolina, SE USA
14 J13 **York** ≈ Ontario, SE Canada
15 X6 **York** ≈ Québec, SE Canada
181 V1 **York, Cape** *headland* Queensland, NE Australia
182 I9 **Yorke Peninsula** *peninsula* South Australia
182 I9 **Yorketown** South Australia
19 P9 **York Harbor** Maine, NE USA
York, Kap *see* Innaanganeq
21 X6 **York River** ≈ Virginia, NE USA
97 M16 **Yorkshire** *cultural region* N England, UK
97 L16 **Yorkshire Dales** *physical region* N England, UK
9 V16 **Yorkton** Saskatchewan, S Canada
25 T12 **Yorktown** Texas, SW USA
21 X6 **Yorktown** Virginia, NE USA
30 M11 **Yorkville** Illinois, N USA
42 I5 **Yoro** Yoro, C Honduras
42 H5 **Yoro** ◐ *department* N Honduras
165 T16 **Yoron-jima** *island* Nansei-shotō, SW Japan
77 N13 **Yorosso** Sikasso, S Mali
35 R8 **Yosemite National Park** *national park* California, W USA
127 Q3 **Yoshkar-Ola** Respublika Mariy El, W Russian Federation
Yösönbulag *see* Altay
162 K8 **Yösöndzüyl** *var.* Mönhbulag. Övörhangay, C Mongolia
171 Y16 **Yos Sudarso, Pulau** *var.* Pulau Dolak, Pulau Kolepom; *prev.* Jos Sudarso. *island* E Indonesia
163 Y17 **Yŏsu** *Jap.* Reisui. S South Korea
165 R4 **Yotei-zan** ▲ Hokkaidō, NE Japan
97 D21 **Youghal** *Ir.* Eochaill. Cork, S Ireland
97 D21 **Youghal Bay** *Ir.* Cuan Eochaille. *inlet* S Ireland
18 C15 **Youghiogheny River** ≈ Pennsylvania, NE USA
160 K14 **You Jiang** ≈ S China
183 Q9 **Young** New South Wales, SE Australia
9 T15 **Young** Saskatchewan, S Canada
61 E18 **Young** Río Negro, W Uruguay
182 G5 **Younghusband, Lake** *salt lake* South Australia
182 J10 **Younghusband Peninsula** *peninsula* South Australia
184 Q10 **Young Nicks Head** *headland* North Island, New Zealand
185 D20 **Young Range** ▲▲ South Island, New Zealand
191 Q15 **Young's Rock** *island* Pitcairn Island, Pitcairn Islands
9 R16 **Youngstown** Alberta, SW Canada
31 V12 **Youngstown** Ohio, N USA
159 N9 **Youshashan** Qinghai, C China
Youth, Isle of *see* Juventud, Isla de la
77 N11 **Youvarou** Mopti, C Mali
160 K10 **Youyang** *var.* Zhongduo. Chongqing Shi, C China
163 Y7 **Youyi** Heilongjiang, NE China
147 P13 **Yovon** *Rus.* Yavan. SW Tajikistan
136 J13 **Yozgat** Yozgat, C Turkey
136 K13 **Yozgat** ◐ *province* C Turkey
62 O6 **Ypacaraí** *var.* Ypacaray. Central, S Paraguay
Ypacaray *see* Ypacaraí
62 P5 **Ypané, Río** ≈ C Paraguay
Ypres *see* Ieper
114 I13 **Ypsário** *var.* Ipsario. ▲ Thásos, E Greece
31 R10 **Ypsilanti** Michigan, N USA
34 M1 **Yreka** California, W USA
Yrendagüé *see* General Eugenio A. Garay
186 G5 **Ysabel Channel** *channel* N Papua New Guinea
14 K8 **Yser, Lac** ◎ Québec, SE Canada
147 Y8 **Yshtyk** Issyk-Kul'skaya Oblast', E Kyrgyzstan
Yssel *see* IJssel
103 Q12 **Yssingeaux** Haute-Loire, C France
95 K23 **Ystad** Skåne, S Sweden
Ysyk-Köl *see* Balykchy
Ysyk-Köl *see* Issyk-Kul', Ozero
Ysyk-Köl Oblasty *see* Issyk-Kul'skaya Oblast'
96 L8 **Ythan** ≈ NE Scotland, UK
Y Trallwng *see* Welshpool
94 C13 **Ytre Arna** Hordaland, S Norway
94 B12 **Ytre Sula** *island* S Norway
93 G17 **Ytterhogdal** Jämtland, C Sweden
Yu *see* Henan
Yuan *see* Red River
Yuan Jiang *see* Red River
161 S13 **Yüanlin** *Jap.* Inrin. C Taiwan
161 N3 **Yuanping** Shanxi, C China
Yuanquan *see* Anxi
Yuanshan *see* Lianping
161 O11 **Yuan Shui** ≈ S China
35 O6 **Yuba City** California, W USA
35 O6 **Yuba River** ≈ California, W USA
80 H13 **Yubdo** Oromo, C Ethiopia
126 L3 **Yubileynyy** Moskovskaya Oblast', W Russian Federation
41 X12 **Yucatán** ◐ *state* SE Mexico
47 O3 **Yucatan Basin** *var.* Yucatan Deep. *undersea feature* N Caribbean Sea
Yucatán, Canal de *see* Yucatan Channel
41 Y10 **Yucatan Channel** *Sp.* Canal de Yucatán. *channel* Cuba/Mexico
Yucatan Deep *see* Yucatan Basin
Yucatan Peninsula *see* Yucatán, Península de
41 X13 **Yucatán, Península de** *Eng.* Yucatan Peninsula. *peninsula* Guatemala/Mexico
36 I11 **Yucca** Arizona, SW USA
35 V15 **Yucca Valley** California, W USA
161 P4 **Yucheng** Shandong, E China
Yuci *see* Jinzhong
129 X5 **Yudoma** ≈ E Russian Federation
161 P12 **Yudu** *var.* Gaongjiang. Jiangxi, C China
Yue *see* Guangdong
Yuecheng *see* Yuexi
160 M12 **Yuecheng Ling** ▲▲ S China
Yuegaitan *see* Qumarlêb
181 P7 **Yuendumu** Northern Territory, N Australia
Yue Shan, Tai *see* Lantau Island
160 H10 **Yuexi** *var.* Yuecheng. Sichuan, C China
161 N10 **Yueyang** Hunan, S China
125 U14 **Yug** Permskaya Oblast', NW Russian Federation
125 P13 **Yug** ≈ NW Russian Federation
123 R10 **Yugorenok** Respublika Sakha (Yakutiya), NE Russian Federation
122 H9 **Yugorsk** Khanty-Mansiyskiy Avtonomnyy Okrug, C Russian Federation
122 H7 **Yugorskiy Poluostrov** *peninsula* NW Russian Federation
Yugoslavia *see* Serbia
146 K14 **Yugo-Vostochnyye Garagumy** *prev.* Yugo-Vostochnyye Karakumy. *desert* E Turkmenistan
Yugo-Vostochnyye Karakumy *see* Yugo-Vostochnyye Garagumy
Yuhu *see* Eryuan
161 S10 **Yuhuan Dao** *island* SE China
160 L14 **Yu Jiang** ≈ S China
Yujin *see* Qianwei
123 S7 **Yukagirskoye Ploskogor'ye** *plateau* NE Russian Federation
118 L11 **Yukhavichy** *Rus.* Yukhovichi. Vitsyebskaya Voblasts', N Belarus
126 J4 **Yukhnov** Kaluzhskaya Oblast', W Russian Federation
Yukhovichi *see* Yukhavichy
79 J20 **Yuki** *var.* Yuki Kengunda. Bandundu, W Dem. Rep. Congo
Yuki Kengunda *see* Yuki
26 M10 **Yukon** Oklahoma, C USA
0 F4 **Yukon** ≈ Canada/USA
Yukon *see* Yukon Territory
39 S7 **Yukon Flats** *salt flat* Alaska, USA
Yukon, Territoire du *see* Yukon Territory
10 I5 **Yukon Territory** *var.* Yukon, *Fr.* Territoire du Yukon. ◇ *territory* NW Canada
137 T16 **Yüksekova** Hakkâri, SE Turkey
123 N10 **Yukta** Evenkiyskiy Avtonomnyy Okrug, C Russian Federation
165 O13 **Yukuhashi** *var.* Yukuhasi. Fukuoka, Kyūshū, SW Japan
Yukuhasi *see* Yukuhashi
Yukuriawat *see* Yopurga
125 O9 **Yula** ≈ NW Russian Federation
181 P8 **Yulara** Northern Territory, N Australia
127 W6 **Yuldybayevo** Respublika Bashkortostan, W Russian Federation
23 W8 **Yulee** Florida, SE USA
158 K7 **Yuli** *var.* Lopnur. Xinjiang Uygur Zizhiqu, NW China
161 T14 **Yüli** C Taiwan
160 L15 **Yulin** Guangxi Zhuangzu Zizhiqu, S China
160 L4 **Yulin** Shaanxi, C China
161 T14 **Yüli Shan** ▲ E Taiwan
160 F11 **Yulong Xueshan** ▲ SW China
36 H14 **Yuma** Arizona, SW USA
37 W3 **Yuma** Colorado, C USA
54 K5 **Yumare** Yaracuy, N Venezuela
63 G14 **Yumbel** Bío Bío, C Chile
79 N19 **Yumbi** Maniema, E Dem. Rep. Congo
159 R8 **Yumen** *var.* Laojunmiao, Yümen. Gansu, N China
159 Q7 **Yumenzhen** Gansu, N China
158 J3 **Yumin** Xinjiang Uygur Zizhiqu, NW China
Yun *see* Yunnan
136 G14 **Yunak** Konya, W Turkey
45 O8 **Yuna, Río** ≈ E Dominican Republic
38 I17 **Yunaska Island** *island* Aleutian Islands, Alaska, USA
160 M6 **Yuncheng** Shanxi, C China
161 N14 **Yunfu** Guangdong, S China
57 L18 **Yungas** *physical region* E Bolivia
Yungki *see* Jilin
Yung-ning *see* Nanning
160 I12 **Yungui Gaoyuan** *plateau* SW China
Yunjinghong *see* Jinghong
160 M15 **Yunkai Dashan** ▲▲ S China
Yunki *see* Jilin
160 E11 **Yun Ling** ▲▲ SW China
161 N9 **Yunmeng** Hubei, C China
157 N14 **Yunnan** *var.* Yun, Yunnan Sheng, Yünnan, Yun-nan. ◐ *province* SW China
Yunnan *see* Kunming
Yunnan Sheng *see* Yunnan
Yünnan/Yun-nan *see* Yunnan
165 P15 **Yunomae** Kumamoto, Kyūshū, SW Japan
161 N8 **Yun Shui** ≈ C China
182 J7 **Yunta** South Australia
161 Q14 **Yunxiao** Fujian, SE China
160 K9 **Yunyang** Sichuan, C China
193 S9 **Yupanqui Basin** *undersea feature* E Pacific Ocean
Yuping *see* Libo
Yuping *see* Pingbian
Yuratishki *see* Yuratsishki
119 I15 **Yuratsishki** *Pol.* Juraciszki, *Rus.* Yuratishki. Hrodzyenskaya Voblasts', W Belarus
Yurev *see* Tartu
122 J12 **Yurga** Kemerovskaya Oblast', S Russian Federation
56 E10 **Yurimaguas** Loreto, N Peru
127 P3 **Yurino** Respublika Mariy El, W Russian Federation
41 N13 **Yuriria** Guanajuato, C Mexico
125 T13 **Yurla** Permskaya Oblast', NW Russian Federation
Yuruá, Río *see* Juruá, Rio
114 M13 **Yürük** Tekirdağ, NW Turkey
158 G10 **Yurungkax He** ≈ W China
125 Q14 **Yur'ya** *var.* Jarja. Kirovskaya Oblast', NW Russian Federation
Yury'ev *see* Tartu
125 N16 **Yur'yevets** Ivanovskaya Oblast', W Russian Federation
126 M3 **Yur'yev-Pol'skiy** Vladimirskaya Oblast', W Russian Federation
117 V7 **Yur"yivka** Dnipropetrovs'ka Oblast', E Ukraine
42 I7 **Yuscarán** El Paraíso, S Honduras
161 P12 **Yu Shan** ▲▲ S China
159 R13 **Yushu** *var.* Gyêgu. Qinghai, C China
127 P12 **Yusta** Respublika Kalmykiya, SW Russian Federation
124 I10 **Yustozero** Respublika Kareliya, NW Russian Federation
137 Q11 **Yusufeli** Artvin, NE Turkey
164 F14 **Yusuhara** Kōchi, Shikoku, SW Japan
125 T14 **Yus'va** Permskaya Oblast', NW Russian Federation
Yuta *see* Yatta
161 P2 **Yutian** Hebei, E China
158 H10 **Yutian** *var.* Keriya. Xinjiang Uygur Zizhiqu, NW China
62 K5 **Yuto** Jujuy, NW Argentina
62 P7 **Yuty** Caazapá, S Paraguay
160 G13 **Yuxi** Yunnan, SW China
161 O2 **Yuxian** *prev.* Yu Xian. Hebei, E China
Yu Xian *see* Yuxian
165 Q9 **Yuzawa** Akita, Honshū, C Japan
125 N16 **Yuzha** Ivanovskaya Oblast', W Russian Federation
Yuzhno-Alichurskiy Khrebet *see* Alichuri Janubí, Qatorkŭhi
Yuzhno-Kazakhstanskaya Oblast' *see* Yuzhnyy Kazakhstan
123 T13 **Yuzhno-Sakhalinsk** *Jap.* Toyohara; *prev.* Vladimirovka. Ostrov Sakhalin, Sakhalinskaya Oblast', SE Russian Federation
127 P14 **Yuzhno-Sukhokumsk** Respublika Dagestan, SW Russian Federation
145 Z10 **Yuzhnyy Altay, Khrebet** ▲▲ E Kazakhstan
Yuzhnyy Bug *see* Pivdennyy Buh
145 O15 **Yuzhnyy Kazakhstan** *off.* Yuzhno-Kazakhstanskaya Oblast', *Eng.* South Kazakhstan, *Kaz.* Ongtüstik Qazaqstan Oblysy; *prev.* Chimkentskaya Oblast'. ◐ *province* S Kazakhstan
123 U10 **Yuzhnyy, Mys** *cape* E Russian Federation
127 W6 **Yuzhnyy Ural** *var.* Southern Urals. ▲▲ W Russian Federation
159 V10 **Yuzhong** Gansu, C China
Yuzhou *see* Chongqing
103 N5 **Yvelines** ◐ *department* N France
108 B9 **Yverdon** *var.* Yverdon-les-Bains, *Ger.* Iferten; *anc.* Eborodunum. Vaud, W Switzerland
Yverdon-les-Bains *see* Yverdon
102 M3 **Yvetot** Seine-Maritime, N France
Ýylanly *see* Gurbansoltan Eje
Ýylanly *see* Gurbansoltan Eje

Z

147 T12 **Zaalayskiy Khrebet** *Taj.* Qatorkŭhi Pasi Oloy. ▲▲ Kyrgyzstan/Tajikistan
Zaamin *see* Zomin
Zaandam *see* Zaanstad
98 I10 **Zaanstad** *prev.* Zaandam. Noord-Holland, C Netherlands
Zabadani *see* Az Zabdānī
119 L18 **Zabalatstsye** *Rus.* Zabolot'ye. Homyel'skaya Voblasts', SE Belarus
112 L9 **Žabalj** *Ger.* Josefsdorf, *Hung.* Zsablya; *prev.* Józseffalva. Vojvodina, N Serbia
Zāb aş Şaghīr, Nahraz *see* Little Zab
123 P14 **Zabaykal'sk** Chitinskaya Oblast', S Russian Federation
Zāb-e Kūchek, Rūdkhāneh-ye *see* Little Zab
Zabeln *see* Sabile
Zabéré *see* Zabré
Zabern *see* Saverne
141 N16 **Zabīd** W Yemen
141 O16 **Zabīd, Wādī** *dry watercourse* SW Yemen
Żabinka *see* Zhabinka
Ząbkowice *see* Ząbkowice Śląskie
111 G15 **Ząbkowice Śląskie** *var.* Ząbkowice, *Ger.* Frankenstein, Frankenstein in Schlesien. Dolnośląskie, SW Poland
110 P10 **Zabłudów** Podlaskie, NE Poland
112 D8 **Zabok** Krapina-Zagorje, N Croatia
143 W9 **Zābol** *var.* Shahr-i-Zabul, Zabul; *prev.* Nasratabad. Sīstān va Balūchestān, E Iran
149 O7 **Zābol** *Pash.* Zābul. ◐ *province* SE Afghanistan
143 W13 **Zābolī** Sīstān va Balūchestān, SE Iran
Zabolot'ye *see* Zabalatstsye
77 Q13 **Zabré** *var.* Zabéré. S Burkina
111 G17 **Zábřeh** *Ger.* Hohenstadt. Olomoucký Kraj, E Czech Republic
111 J16 **Zabrze** *Ger.* Hindenburg, Hindenburg in Oberschlesien. Śląskie, S Poland
Zābul *see* Zābol
Zabul/Zābul *see* Zābol
42 E6 **Zacapa** Zacapa, E Guatemala
42 A3 **Zacapa** *off.* Departamento de Zacapa. ◐ *department* E Guatemala
Zacapa, Departamento de *see* Zacapa
40 M14 **Zacapú** Michoacán de Ocampo, SW Mexico
41 V14 **Zacatal** Campeche, SE Mexico
40 M11 **Zacatecas** Zacatecas, C Mexico
40 L10 **Zacatecas** ◐ *state* C Mexico
42 F8 **Zacatecoluca** La Paz, S El Salvador
41 P15 **Zacatepec** Morelos, S Mexico
41 Q13 **Zacatlán** Puebla, S Mexico
144 F8 **Zachagansk** Zapadnyy Kazakhstan, NW Kazakhstan
115 D20 **Zacháro** *var.* Zaharo, Zakháro. Dytikí Ellás, S Greece
22 J8 **Zachary** Louisiana, S USA
117 U6 **Zachepylivka** Kharkivs'ka Oblast', E Ukraine
Zachist'ye *see* Zachystsye
110 E9 **Zachodnio-pomorskie** ◐ *province* NW Poland
119 L14 **Zachystsye** *Rus.* Zachist'ye. Minskaya Voblasts', NW Belarus
40 L13 **Zacoalco** *var.* Zacoalco de Torres. Jalisco, SW Mexico
Zacoalco de Torres *see* Zacoalco
41 P13 **Zacualtipán** Hidalgo, C Mexico
112 C12 **Zadar** *It.* Zara; *anc.* Iader. Zadar, SW Croatia
112 C12 **Zadar** *off.* Zadarsko-Kninska Županija, Zadar-Knin. ◐ *province* SW Croatia
Zadar-Knin *see* Zadar
Zadarsko-Kninska Županija *see* Zadar
166 M14 **Zadetkyi Kyun** *var.* St.Matthew's Island. *island* Mergui Archipelago, S Burma (Myanmar)
67 Q9 **Zadié** *var.* Djadié. ≈ NE Gabon
159 Q13 **Zadoi** *var.* Qapugtang. Qinghai, C China
126 L7 **Zadonsk** Lipetskaya Oblast', W Russian Federation
75 X8 **Za'farâna** E Egypt
149 W7 **Zafarwāl** Punjab, E Pakistan
121 Q1 **Zafer Burnu** *var.* Cape Andreas, Cape Apostolas Andreas, *Gk.* Akrotíri Apostólou Andréa. *cape* NE Cyprus
107 J23 **Zafferano, Capo** *headland* Sicilia, Italy, C Mediterranean Sea
114 M7 **Zafirovo** Silistra, NE Bulgaria
Záfora *see* Sofraná
104 J12 **Zafra** Extremadura, W Spain
110 E13 **Żagań** *var.* Zagań, Żegań, *Ger.* Sagan. Lubuskie, W Poland
118 F10 **Žagarė** *Pol.* Żagory. Šiaulai, N Lithuania
75 W7 **Zagazig** *var.* Az Zaqāzīq. N Egypt
74 M5 **Zaghouan** *var.* Zaghwān. NE Tunisia
Zaghwān *see* Zaghouan
115 G16 **Zagorá** Thessalía, C Greece
Zagorod'ye *see* Zaharoddzye
Żagory *see* Žagarė
Zagrāb *see* Zagreb
112 E8 **Zagreb** *Ger.* Agram, *Hung.* Zágráb. ● (Croatia) Zagreb, N Croatia
112 E8 **Zagreb** *prev.* Grad Zagreb. ◐ *province* N Croatia
142 L7 **Zāgros, Kūhhā-ye** *Eng.* Zagros Mountains. ▲▲ W Iran
Zagros Mountains *see* Zāgros, Kūhhā-ye
112 O12 **Žagubica** Serbia, E Serbia
Zagunao *see* Lixian

◆ Country
● Country Capital
◇ Dependent Territory
○ Dependent Territory Capital
◐ Administrative Regions
✈ International Airport
▲ Mountain
▲▲ Mountain Range
⛰ Volcano
≈ River
◎ Lake
⊠ Reservoir

ZAGYVA – ZHUZHOU

111 L22 Zagyva ≈ N Hungary
Zaharo see Zacháro
119 G19 Zaharoddzye Rus. Zagorod'ye. physical region SW Belarus
143 W11 Zāhedān var. Zahidan; prev. Duzdab. Sīstān va Balūchestān, SE Iran
Zahidan see Zāhedān
Zaḩlah see Zahlé
138 H7 Zahlé var. Zaḩlah. C Lebanon
146 J14 Zähmet Rus. Zakhmet. Mary Welaýaty, C Turkmenistan
111 O20 Záhony Szabolcs-Szatmár-Bereg, NE Hungary
141 N13 Ẕahrān 'Asīr, S Saudi Arabia
139 R12 Ẕahrat al Baṭn hill range S Iraq
120 H11 Zahrez Chergui var. Zahrez Chergúi. marsh N Algeria
Zainlha see Xinjin
127 S4 Zainsk Respublika Tatarstan, W Russian Federation
82 A10 Zaire prev. Congo. ◐ province NW Angola
Zaire see Congo (river)
Zaire see Congo (Democratic Republic of)
112 P13 Zaječar Serbia, E Serbia
83 L18 Zaka Masvingo, E Zimbabwe
122 M14 Zakamensk Respublika Buryatiya, S Russian Federation
116 G7 Zakarpats'ka Oblast' Eng. Transcarpathian Oblast, Rus. Zakarpatskaya Oblast'. ◐ province W Ukraine
Zakarpatskaya Oblast' see Zakarpats'ka Oblast'
Zakataly see Zaqatala
Zakháro see Zacháro
Zakhidnyy Buh/Zakhodni Buh see Bug
Zakhmet see Zähmet
139 Q1 Zākhō var. Zākhū. N Iraq
Zākhū see Zākhō
Zákinthos see Zákynthos
111 L18 Zakopane Małopolskie, S Poland
78 J12 Zakouma Salamat, S Chad
115 L25 Zákros Kríti, Greece, E Mediterranean Sea
115 C19 Zákynthos var. Zákinthos. Zákynthos, W Greece
115 C20 Zákynthos var. Zákinthos, It. Zante. island Iónia Nísoi, Greece, C Mediterranean Sea
115 C19 Zakýnthou, Porthmós strait SW Greece
111 G24 Zala off. Zala Megye. ◐ county W Hungary
111 G24 Zala ≈ W Hungary
138 M4 Zalābiyah Dayr az Zawr, C Syria
111 G24 Zalaegerszeg Zala, W Hungary
104 K11 Zalamea de la Serena Extremadura, W Spain
104 J13 Zalamea la Real Andalucía, S Spain
Zala Megye see Zala
163 U7 Zalantun var. Butha Qi. Nei Mongol Zizhiqu, N China
111 G23 Zalaszentgrót Zala, SW Hungary
Zalatna see Zlatna
116 G9 Zalău Ger. Waltenberg, Hung. Zilah; prev. Ger. Zillenmarkt. Sălaj, NW Romania
109 V10 Žalec Ger. Sachsenfeld. C Slovenia
117 S9 Zalenodol's'k Dnipropetrovs'ka Oblast', E Ukraine
110 K8 Zalewo Ger. Saalfeld. Warmińsko-Mazurskie, NE Poland
141 N9 Ẓalim Makkah, W Saudi Arabia
80 A11 Zalingei var. Zalinje. Western Darfur, W Sudan
Zalinje see Zalingei
116 K7 Zalishchyky Ternopil's'ka Oblast', W Ukraine
Zallah see Zillah
98 J13 Zaltbommel Gelderland, C Netherlands
124 H15 Zaluch'ye Novgorodskaya Oblast', NW Russian Federation
Zamak see Zamakh
141 Q14 Zamakh var. Zamak. N Yemen
136 K15 Zamantı Irmağı ≈ C Turkey
Zambesi/Zambeze see Zambezi
83 G14 Zambezi North Western, W Zambia
83 K15 Zambezi var. Zambesi, Port. Zambeze. ≈ S Africa
83 O15 Zambézia off. Província da Zambézia. ◐ province C Mozambique
Zambézia, Província da see Zambézia
83 I14 Zambia off. Republic of Zambia; prev. Northern Rhodesia. ◆ republic S Africa
Zambia, Republic of see Zambia
171 O8 Zamboanga off. Zamboanga City. Mindanao, S Philippines
Zamboanga City see Zamboanga
54 E5 Zambrano Bolívar, N Colombia
110 N10 Zambrów Łomża, E Poland
83 L14 Zambué Tete, NW Mozambique
77 T13 Zamfara ≈ NW Nigeria
Zamkog see Zamtang
56 C9 Zamora Zamora Chinchipe, S Ecuador
104 K6 Zamora Castilla-León, NW Spain
104 K5 Zamora ◐ province Castilla-León, NW Spain
Zamora see Barinas
56 A13 Zamora Chinchipe ◐ province S Ecuador
40 M13 Zamora de Hidalgo Michoacán de Ocampo, SW Mexico
111 P15 Zamość Rus. Zamoste. Lubelskie, E Poland
Zamoste see Zamość
160 G7 Zamtang var. Zamkog; prev. Gamba. Sichuan, C China
75 O8 Zamzam, Wādī dry watercourse NW Libya
79 F20 Zanaga La Lékoumou, S Congo
41 T16 Zanatepec Oaxaca, SE Mexico
105 P9 Záncara ≈ C Spain
Zancle see Messina
158 G14 Zanda Xizang Zizhiqu, W China
98 H10 Zandvoort Noord-Holland, W Netherlands
39 P8 Zane Hills hill range Alaska, USA
31 T13 Zanesville Ohio, N USA
Zanga see Hrazdan
142 L4 Zanjān var. Zenjan, Zinjan. Zanjān, NW Iran
142 L4 Zanjān off. Ostān-e Zanjān, var. Zenjan, Zinjan. ◐ province NW Iran
Zanjān, Ostān-e see Zanjān
Zante see Zákynthos
81 J22 Zanzibar Zanzibar, E Tanzania
81 J22 Zanzibar ◐ region E Tanzania
81 J22 Zanzibar Swa. Unguja. island E Tanzania
81 J22 Zanzibar Channel channel E Tanzania
165 P10 Zaō-san ▲ Honshū, C Japan
161 N8 Zaoyang Hubei, C China
124 J2 Zaozërsk Murmanskaya Oblast', NW Russian Federation
161 Q6 Zaozhuang Shandong, E China
28 L4 Zap North Dakota, N USA
112 L13 Zapadna Morava Ger. Westliche Morava. ≈ C Serbia
124 H16 Zapadnaya Dvina Tverskaya Oblast', W Russian Federation
Zapadnaya Dvina see Western Dvina
Zapadno-Kazakhstanskaya Oblast' see Zapadnyy Kazakhstan
122 I9 Zapadno-Sibirskaya Ravnina Eng. West Siberian Plain. plain C Russian Federation
Zapadnyy Bug see Bug
144 E9 Zapadnyy Kazakhstan off. Zapadno-Kazakhstanskaya Oblast', Eng. West Kazakhstan, Kaz. Batys Qazaqstan Oblysy; prev. Ural'skaya Oblast'. ◐ province NW Kazakhstan
122 K13 Zapadnyy Sayan Eng. Western Sayans. ▲▲ S Russian Federation
63 H15 Zapala Neuquén, W Argentina
62 I4 Zapaleri, Cerro var. Cerro Sapaleri. ▲ N Chile
25 Q16 Zapata Texas, SW USA
44 D5 Zapata, Península de peninsula W Cuba
61 G19 Zapicán Lavalleja, S Uruguay
65 J19 Zapiola Ridge undersea feature SW Atlantic Ocean
65 L19 Zapiola Seamount undersea feature S Atlantic Ocean
124 I2 Zapolyarnyy Murmanskaya Oblast', NW Russian Federation
117 U8 Zaporizhzhya Rus. Zaporozh'ye; prev. Aleksandrovsk. Zaporiz'ka Oblast', SE Ukraine
Zaporizhzhya see Zaporiz'ka Oblast'
117 U9 Zaporiz'ka Oblast' var. Zaporizhzhya, Rus. Zaporozhskaya Oblast'. ◐ province SE Ukraine
Zaporozhskaya Oblast' see Zaporiz'ka Oblast'
Zaporozh'ye see Zaporizhzhya
40 L14 Zapotiltic Jalisco, SW Mexico
158 G13 Zapug Xizang Zizhiqu, W China
137 V10 Zaqatala Rus. Zakataly. NW Azerbaijan
159 P13 Zaqên Qinghai, W China
159 Q13 Za Qu ≈ C China
136 M13 Zara Sivas, C Turkey
Zara see Zadar
Zarafshan see Zarafshon
147 P12 Zarafshon Rus. Zeravshan. W Tajikistan
146 L9 Zarafshon Rus. Zarafshan. Navoiy Viloyati, N Uzbekistan
Zarafshon see Zeravshan
147 O12 Zarafshon, Qatorkŭhi Rus. Zeravshanskiy Khrebet, Uzb. Zarafshon Tizmasi. ▲▲ Tajikistan/Uzbekistan
Zarafshon Tizmasi see Zarafshon, Qatorkŭhi
54 E7 Zaragoza Antioquia, N Colombia
40 I5 Zaragoza Chihuahua, N Mexico
41 N6 Zaragoza Coahuila de Zaragoza, NE Mexico
41 O10 Zaragoza Nuevo León, NE Mexico
105 R5 Zaragoza Eng. Saragossa; anc. Caesaraugusta, Salduba. Aragón, NE Spain
105 R6 Zaragoza ◐ province Aragón, NE Spain
105 R5 Zaragoza ✈ Aragón, NE Spain
143 S10 Zarand Kermān, C Iran
148 J9 Zaranj Nīmrūz, SW Afghanistan
118 I11 Zarasai Utena, E Lithuania
62 N12 Zárate prev. General José F.Uriburu. Buenos Aires, E Argentina
105 Q2 Zarautz var. Zarauz. País Vasco, N Spain
Zarauz see Zarautz
Zaravecchia see Biograd na Moru
Zarāyīn see Zarēn
126 L4 Zaraysk Moskovskaya Oblast', W Russian Federation
55 N6 Zaraza Guárico, N Venezuela
Zarbdar see Zarbdor
147 P11 Zarbdor Rus. Zarbdar. Jizzax Viloyati, C Uzbekistan
142 M8 Zard Kūh ▲ SW Iran
124 I5 Zarechensk Murmanskaya Oblast', NW Russian Federation
127 P6 Zarechnyy Penzenskaya Oblast', W Russian Federation
Zareh Sharan see Sharan
39 Y14 Zarembo Island island Alexander Archipelago, Alaska, USA
139 V4 Zarēn var. Zarāyīn. E Iraq
149 Q7 Zarghūn Shahr var. Katawaz. Paktīkā, SE Afghanistan
77 V13 Zaria Kaduna, C Nigeria
116 K2 Zarichne Rivnens'ka Oblast', NW Ukraine
122 J13 Zarinsk Altayskiy Kray, S Russian Federation
116 J12 Zărneşti Hung. Zernest. Braşov, C Romania
115 J25 Zarós Kríti, Greece, E Mediterranean Sea
100 O9 Zarow ≈ NE Germany
Zarqa see Az Zarqā'
Zarqa/Muḩāfaẓat az Zarqā' see Az Zarqā'
111 G20 Záruby ▲ W Slovakia
56 B8 Zaruma El Oro, SW Ecuador
110 E13 Żary Ger. Sorau, Sorau in der Niederlausitz. Lubuskie, W Poland
54 D10 Zarzal Valle del Cauca, W Colombia
42 I7 Zarzalar, Cerro ▲ S Honduras
152 I5 Zāskār ≈ NE India
152 I5 Zāskār Range ▲▲ NE India
119 K15 Zaslawye Minskaya Voblasts', C Belarus
116 K7 Zastavna Chernivets'ka Oblast', W Ukraine
111 B16 Žatec Ger. Saaz. Ústecký Kraj, NW Czech Republic
Zaumgarten see Chrzanów
Zaunguzskiye Garagumy see Üngüz Angyrsyndaky Garagum
25 X9 Zavalla Texas, SW USA
99 H18 Zaventem Vlaams Brabant, C Belgium
99 H18 Zaventem ✈ (Brussel/Bruxelles) Vlaams Brabant, C Belgium
Zavertse see Zawiercie
114 L7 Zavet Razgrad, NE Bulgaria
127 O12 Zavetnoye Rostovskaya Oblast', SW Russian Federation
156 M3 Zavhan Gol ≈ W Mongolia
112 H12 Zavidovići ◐ Federacija Bosna I Hercegovina, N Bosnia and Herzegovina
123 R13 Zavitinsk Amurskaya Oblast', SE Russian Federation
Zawia see Az Zāwiyah
111 K15 Zawiercie Rus. Zavertse. Śląskie, S Poland
75 P11 Zawīlah var. Zuwaylah, It. Zueila. C Libya
138 I4 Zāwīyah, Jabal az ▲ NW Syria
109 Y3 Zaya ≈ NE Austria
166 M8 Zayatkyi Pegu, C Burma (Myanmar)
145 Y11 Zaysan Vostochnyy Kazakhstan, E Kazakhstan
Zaysan Köl see Zaysan, Ozero
145 Y11 Zaysan, Ozero Kaz. Zaysan Köl. ◎ E Kazakhstan
159 R16 Zayü var. Gyigang. Xizang Zizhiqu, W China
Zayyq see Ural
44 F6 Zaza ≈ C Cuba
116 K5 Zbarazh Ternopil's'ka Oblast', W Ukraine
116 J5 Zboriv Ternopil's'ka Oblast', W Ukraine
111 F18 Zbraslav Jihomoravský Kraj, SE Czech Republic
116 K6 Zbruch ≈ W Ukraine
Žďár see Žďár nad Sázavou
111 F17 Žďár nad Sázavou Ger. Saar in Mähren; prev. Žďár. Vysočina, C Czech Republic
116 K4 Zdolbuniv Pol. Zdolbunów, Rus. Zdolbunov. Rivnens'ka Oblast', NW Ukraine
Zdolbunov/Zdolbunów see Zdolbuniv
110 J13 Zduńska Wola Sieradz, C Poland
117 O4 Zdvizh ≈ N Ukraine
Zdzięciół see Dzyatlava
111 I16 Zdzieszowice Ger. Odertal. Opolskie, SW Poland
Zealand see Sjælland
188 K6 Zealandia Bank undersea feature C Pacific Ocean
63 H20 Zeballos, Monte ▲ S Argentina
83 K20 Zebediela Limpopo, NE South Africa
113 L18 Zebë, Mal var. Mali i Zebës. ▲ NE Albania
Zebës, Mali i see Zebë, Mal
21 V9 Zebulon North Carolina, SE USA
112 K8 Žednik Hung. Bácsjózseffalva. Vojvodina, N Serbia
99 C15 Zeebrugge West-Vlaanderen, NW Belgium
183 N16 Zeehan Tasmania, SE Australia
99 L14 Zeeland Noord-Brabant, SE Netherlands
29 N7 Zeeland North Dakota, N USA
99 E14 Zeeland ◐ province SW Netherlands
83 I21 Zeerust North-West, N South Africa
98 K10 Zeewolde Flevoland, C Netherlands
138 G8 Ẕefat var. Safed, Tsefat, Ar. Safad. Northern, N Israel
Zegań see Żagań
Zehden see Cedynia
100 O11 Zehdenick Brandenburg, NE Germany
Zē-i Bādīnān see Great Zab
Zeiden see Codlea
146 M14 Zeidskoye Vodokhranilishche ⊠ E Turkmenistan
Zē-i Kōya see Little Zab
181 P7 Zeil, Mount ▲ Northern Territory, C Australia
98 J12 Zeist Utrecht, C Netherlands
101 M16 Zeitz Sachsen-Anhalt, E Germany
159 T11 Zêkog var. Sonag. Qinghai, C China
Zelaya Norte see Atlántico Norte, Región Autónoma
Zelaya Sur see Atlántico Sur, Región Autónoma
99 F17 Zele Oost-Vlaanderen, NW Belgium
110 N12 Żelechów Lubelskie, E Poland
113 H14 Zelena Glava ▲ SE Bosnia and Herzegovina
113 I14 Zelengora ▲▲ S Bosnia and Herzegovina
124 I5 Zelenoborskiy Murmanskaya Oblast', NW Russian Federation
127 R3 Zelenodol'sk Respublika Tatarstan, W Russian Federation
122 J12 Zelenogorsk Krasnoyarskiy Kray, C Russian Federation
124 G12 Zelenogorsk Fin. Terijoki. Leningradskaya Oblast', NW Russian Federation
126 K3 Zelenograd Moskovskaya Oblast', W Russian Federation
118 B13 Zelenogradsk Ger. Cranz, Kranz. Kaliningradskaya Oblast', W Russian Federation
127 O15 Zelenokumsk Stavropol'skiy Kray, SW Russian Federation
165 X4 Zelënyy, Ostrov var. Shibotsu-jima. island NE Russian Federation
Železna Kapela see Eisenkappel
Železna Vrata see Demir Kapija
112 L11 Železniki Serbia, N Serbia
98 N12 Zelhem Gelderland, E Netherlands
113 N18 Želino NW FYR Macedonia
113 M14 Željin ▲▲ C Serbia
101 K17 Zella-Mehlis Thüringen, C Germany
109 P7 Zell am See var. Zell-am-See. Salzburg, S Austria
Zell-am-See see Zell am See
109 N7 Zell am Ziller Tirol, W Austria
Zelle see Celle
109 W2 Zellerndorf Niederösterreich, NE Austria
109 U7 Zeltweg Steiermark, S Austria
119 G17 Zel'va Pol. Zelwa. Hrodzyenskaya Voblasts', W Belarus
118 H13 Želva Vilnius, C Lithuania
Zelwa see Zel'va
99 E16 Zelzate var. Selzaete. Oost-Vlaanderen, NW Belgium
118 E11 Žemaičių Aukštumas physical region W Lithuania
118 C12 Žemaičių Naumiestis Klaipėda, SW Lithuania
119 L14 Zembin var. Zyembin. Minskaya Voblasts', C Belarus
127 N6 Zemetchino Penzenskaya Oblast', W Russian Federation
79 M15 Zémio Haut-Mbomou, E Central African Republic
41 R16 Zempoaltepec, Cerro ▲ SE Mexico
99 G17 Zemst Vlaams Brabant, C Belgium
112 L11 Zemun Serbia, N Serbia
Zendajan see Zendeh Jan
148 J5 Zendeh Jan var. Zendajan, Zindajān. Herāt, NW Afghanistan
Zengg see Senj
112 H12 Zenica ◐ Federacija Bosna I Hercegovina, C Bosnia and Herzegovina
Zenjan see Zanjān
Zen'kov see Zin'kiv
Zenshū see Chŏnju
Zenta see Senta
82 B11 Zenza do Itombe Cuanza Norte, NW Angola
112 H12 Žepče ◐ Federacija Bosna I Hercegovina, N Bosnia and Herzegovina
23 W12 Zephyrhills Florida, SE USA
158 F9 Zepu var. Poskam. Xinjiang Uygur Zizhiqu, NW China
147 Q12 Zeravshan Taj./Uzb. Zarafshon. ≈ Tajikistan/Uzbekistan
Zeravshan see Zarafshon
Zeravshanskiy Khrebet see Zarafshon, Qatorkŭhi
101 M14 Zerbst Sachsen-Anhalt, E Germany
145 P8 Zerenda Akmola, N Kazakhstan
110 H12 Żerków Wielkopolskie, C Poland
108 E11 Zermatt Valais, SW Switzerland
Zernest see Zărneşti
108 J9 Zernez Graubünden, SE Switzerland
126 L12 Zernograd Rostovskaya Oblast', SW Russian Federation
Zestafoni see Zestap'oni
137 S9 Zestap'oni Rus. Zestafoni. C Georgia
98 H12 Zestienhoven ✈ (Rotterdam) Zuid-Holland, SW Netherlands
113 J16 Zeta ≈ C Montenegro
8 L6 Zeta Lake ◎ Victoria Island, Northwest Territories, N Canada
98 L12 Zetten Gelderland, SE Netherlands
101 M17 Zeulenroda Thüringen, C Germany
100 H10 Zeven Niedersachsen, NW Germany
98 M12 Zevenaar Gelderland, SE Netherlands
99 H14 Zevenbergen Noord-Brabant, S Netherlands
129 X6 Zeya ≈ SE Russian Federation
Zeya Reservoir see Zeyskoye Vodokhranilishche
143 T11 Zeynalābād Kermān, C Iran
123 R12 Zeyskoye Vodokhranilishche Eng. Zeya Reservoir. ⊠ SE Russian Federation
104 H8 Zêzere, Rio ≈ C Portugal
Zgerzh see Zgierz
138 H6 Zgharta N Lebanon
110 K12 Zgierz Ger. Neuhof, Rus. Zgerzh. Łódź, C Poland
111 E14 Zgorzelec Ger. Görlitz. Dolnośląskie, SW Poland
158 I15 Zhabdün Xizang Zizhiqu, W China
119 F19 Zhabinka Pol. Żabinka, Rus. Zhabinka. Brestskaya Voblasts', SW Belarus
Zhaggo see Luhuo
159 R15 Zhag'yab var. Yêndum. Xizang Zizhiqu, W China
144 L9 Zhailma Kaz. Zhayylma. Kostanay, N Kazakhstan
145 V16 Zhalanash Almaty, SE Kazakhstan
Zhalashash see Dzhalagash
145 S7 Zhalauly, Ozero ◎ NE Kazakhstan
144 E9 Zhalpaktal prev. Furmanovo. Zapadnyy Kazakhstan, W Kazakhstan
119 G16 Zhaludok Rus. Zheludok. Hrodzyenskaya Voblasts', W Belarus
Zhaman-Akkol', Ozero see Akkol', Ozero
145 Q14 Zhambyl off. Zhambylskaya Oblast', Kaz. Zhambyl Oblysy; prev. Dzhambulskaya Oblast'. ◐ province S Kazakhstan
Zhambyl see Taraz
Zhambyl Oblysy/Zhambylskaya Oblast' see Zhambyl
Zhamo see Bomi
145 S12 Zhamshy ≈ C Kazakhstan
144 M15 Zhanadar'ya Kzylorda, S Kazakhstan
145 O15 Zhanakorgan Kaz. Zhangaqorghan. Kzylorda, S Kazakhstan
159 N16 Zhanang var. Chatang. Xizang Zizhiqu, W China
145 T12 Zhanaortalyk Karaganda, C Kazakhstan
144 F15 Zhanaozen Kaz. Zhangaözen; prev. Novyy Uzen'. Mangistau, W Kazakhstan
145 Q16 Zhanatas Zhambyl, S Kazakhstan
Zhangaözen see Zhanaozen
Zhangaqazaly see Ayteke Bi
Zhangaqorghan see Zhanakorgan
161 O2 Zhangbei Hebei, E China
Zhang-chia-k'ou see Zhangjiakou
Zhangdian see Zibo
Zhanggu see Danba
163 X9 Zhangguangcai Ling ▲▲ NE China
145 W10 Zhangiztobe Vostochnyy Kazakhstan, E Kazakhstan
159 W11 Zhangjiachuan Gansu, N China
160 L10 Zhangjiajie var. Dayong. Hunan, S China
161 O2 Zhangjiakou var. Changkiakow, Zhang-chia-k'ou, Eng. Kalgan; prev. Wanchuan. Hebei, E China
161 Q13 Zhangping Fujian, SE China
161 Q13 Zhangpu var. Sui'an. Fujian, SE China
163 U11 Zhangwu Liaoning, NE China
159 S8 Zhangye var. Ganzhou. Gansu, N China
161 Q13 Zhangzhou Fujian, SE China
163 W6 Zhan He ≈ NE China
144 D9 Zhanibek var. Zhänibek, Rus. Dzhanibek, Dzhanybek. Zapadnyy Kazakhstan, W Kazakhstan
160 L16 Zhanjiang var. Chanchiang, Chan-chiang, Cant. Tsamkong, Fr. Fort-Bayard. Guangdong, S China
Zhansügirov see Dzhansugurov
163 V8 Zhaodong Heilongjiang, NE China
Zhaoge see Qixian
160 H11 Zhaojue var. Xincheng. Sichuan, C China
161 N14 Zhaoqing Guangdong, S China
Zhaoren see Changwu
158 H5 Zhaosu var. Mongolküre. Xinjiang Uygur Zizhiqu, NW China
160 H11 Zhaotong Yunnan, SW China
163 V9 Zhaoyuan Heilongjiang, NE China
163 V9 Zhaozhou Heilongjiang, NE China
145 X13 Zharbulak Vostochnyy Kazakhstan, E Kazakhstan
158 J15 Zhari Namco ◎ W China
144 I12 Zharkamys Kaz. Zharqamys. Aktyubinsk, W Kazakhstan
145 W15 Zharkent prev. Panfilov. Taldykorgan, SE Kazakhstan
124 H17 Zharkovskiy Tverskaya Oblast', W Russian Federation
145 W11 Zharma Vostochnyy Kazakhstan, E Kazakhstan
144 F14 Zharmysh Mangistau, SW Kazakhstan
Zharqamys see Zharkamys
118 L13 Zhary Rus. Zhary. Vitsyebskaya Voblasts', N Belarus
Zhaslyk see Jasliq
158 J14 Zhaxi Co ◎ W China
Zhayylma see Zhailma
Zhdanov see Beyläqan
Zhdanov see Mariupol'
Zhe see Zhejiang
161 R10 Zhejiang var. Che-chiang, Chekiang, Zhe, Zhejiang Sheng. ◐ province SE China
Zhejiang Sheng see Zhejiang
145 S7 Zhelezinka Pavlodar, N Kazakhstan
119 C14 Zheleznodorozhnyy Ger. Gerdauen. Kaliningradskaya Oblast', W Russian Federation
Zheleznodorozhnyy see Yemva
122 K12 Zheleznogorsk Krasnoyarskiy Kray, C Russian Federation
126 J7 Zheleznogorsk Kurskaya Oblast', W Russian Federation
127 N15 Zheleznovodsk Stavropol'skiy Kray, SW Russian Federation
Zhëltyye Vody see Zhovti Vody
Zheludok see Zhaludok
Zhem see Emba
160 K7 Zhenba Shaanxi, C China
160 I13 Zhenfeng Guizhou, S China
Zhengjiatun see Shuangliao
159 X10 Zhengning var. Shanhe. Gansu, N China
Zhengxiangbai Qi see Qagan Nur
161 N6 Zhengzhou var. Ch'eng-chou, Chengchow; prev. Chenghsien. province capital Henan, C China
161 R8 Zhenjiang var. Chenkiang. Jiangsu, E China
163 U9 Zhenlai Jilin, NE China
160 I11 Zhenxiong Yunnan, SW China
160 K11 Zhenyuan var. Wuyang. Guizhou, S China
161 R11 Zherong var. Shuangcheng. Fujian, SE China
145 U15 Zhetigen prev. Nikolayevka. Almaty, SE Kazakhstan
Zhetiqara see Zhitikara
Zhetiqara see Zhitikara
144 F15 Zhetybay Mangistau, SW Kazakhstan
145 P17 Zhetysay var. Dzhetysay. Yuzhnyy Kazakhstan, S Kazakhstan
160 M11 Zhexi Shuiku ⊠ C China
145 O12 Zhezdy Karaganda, C Kazakhstan
145 O12 Zhezkazgan Kaz. Zhezqazghan; prev. Dzhezkazgan. Karaganda, C Kazakhstan
Zhezqazghan see Zhezkazgan
Zhicheng see Yidu
Zhidachov see Zhydachiv
159 Q12 Zhidoi var. Gyaijêpozhanggê. Qinghai, C China
122 M13 Zhigalovo Irkutskaya Oblast', S Russian Federation
127 R6 Zhigulevsk Samarskaya Oblast', W Russian Federation
118 D13 Zhilino Ger. Schillen. Kaliningradskaya Oblast', W Russian Federation
Zhiloy, Ostrov see Çiloy Adası
127 O8 Zhirnovsk Volgogradskaya Oblast', SW Russian Federation
160 M12 Zhishan prev. Yongzhou. Hunan, S China
Zhitarovo see Vetren
144 L8 Zhitikara Kaz. Zhetiqara; prev. Dzhetygara. Kostanay, NW Kazakhstan
144 L8 Zhitikara Kaz. Zhetiqara; prev. Džetygara. Kostanay, NW Kazakhstan
Zhitkovichi see Zhytkavichy
127 P10 Zhitkur Volgogradskaya Oblast', SW Russian Federation
Zhitomir see Zhytomyr
Zhitomirskaya Oblast' see Zhytomyrs'ka Oblast'
126 J5 Zhizdra Kaluzhskaya Oblast', W Russian Federation
119 N18 Zhlobin Homyel'skaya Voblasts', SE Belarus
Zhmerinka see Zhmerynka
116 M7 Zhmerynka Rus. Zhmerinka. Vinnyts'ka Oblast', C Ukraine
149 R9 Zhob var. Fort Sandeman. Baluchistān, SW Pakistan
149 R8 Zhob ≈ C Pakistan
Zhodino see Zhodzina
119 L15 Zhodzina Rus. Zhodino. Minskaya Voblasts', C Belarus
123 Q5 Zhokhova, Ostrov island Novosibirskiye Ostrova, NE Russian Federation
Zholkev/Zholkva see Zhovkva
Zholsaly see Dzhusaly
Zhondor see Jondor
158 I15 Zhongba var. Tuoji. Xizang Zizhiqu, W China
Zhongba see Jiangyou
160 F11 Zhongdian Yunnan, SW China
Zhongduo see Youyang
Zhonghe see Xiushan
Zhonghua Renmin Gongheguo see China
159 V9 Zhongning Ningxia, N China
Zhongping see Huize
161 N15 Zhongshan Guangdong, S China
195 X7 Zhongshan Chinese research station Antarctica
160 M6 Zhongtiao Shan ▲▲ C China
159 V9 Zhongwei Ningxia, N China
160 K9 Zhongxian var. Zhongzhou. Chongqing Shi, C China
161 N9 Zhongxiang Hubei, C China
Zhongzhou see Zhongxian
161 O7 Zhoukou var. Zhoukouzhen. Henan, C China
Zhoukouzhen see Zhoukou
161 S9 Zhoushan Zhejiang, S China
Zhoushan Islands see Zhoushan Qundao
161 S9 Zhoushan Qundao Eng. Zhoushan Islands. island group SE China
116 I5 Zhovkva Pol. Żółkiew, Rus. Zholkev, Zholkva; prev. Nesterov. L'vivs'ka Oblast', NW Ukraine
117 S7 Zhovti Vody Rus. Zhëltyye Vody. Dnipropetrovs'ka Oblast', E Ukraine
117 Q10 Zhovtneve Rus. Zhovtnevoye. Mykolayivs'ka Oblast', S Ukraine
Zhovtnevoye see Zhovtneve
114 K9 Zhrebchevo, Yazovir ⊠ C Bulgaria
163 V13 Zhuanghe Liaoning, NE China
159 W11 Zhuanglang var. Shuilocheng. Gansu, C China
145 P15 Zhuantobe Kaz. Zhūantöbe. Yuzhnyy Kazakhstan, S Kazakhstan
161 Q5 Zhucheng Shandong, E China
159 V12 Zhugqu Gansu, C China
161 N15 Zhuhai Guangdong, S China
Zhuizishan see Weichang
Zhuji see Shangqiu
126 I5 Zhukovka Bryanskaya Oblast', W Russian Federation
161 N7 Zhumadian Henan, C China
Zhuo Xian see Zhuozhou
161 O3 Zhuozhou prev. Zhuo Xian. Hebei, E China
162 L14 Zhuozi Shan ▲ N China
Zhuravichi see Zhuravichy
119 O17 Zhuravichy Rus. Zhuravichi. Homyel'skaya Voblasts', SE Belarus
145 Q8 Zhuravlevka Akmola, N Kazakhstan
117 Q4 Zhurivka Kyyivs'ka Oblast', N Ukraine
144 J11 Zhuryn Aktyubinsk, W Kazakhstan
145 T15 Zhusandala, Step' grassland SE Kazakhstan
160 L8 Zhushan Hubei, C China
Zhushan see Xuan'en
Zhuyang see Dazhu
161 N11 Zhuzhou Hunan, S China

◆ Country ● Country Capital ◇ Dependent Territory ○ Dependent Territory Capital ◐ Administrative Regions ✈ International Airport ▲ Mountain ▲▲ Mountain Range ⛰ Volcano ≈ River ◎ Lake ⊠ Reservoir

◆ Country   ◇ Dependent Territory   ◈ Administrative Regions   ▲ Mountain   ☈ Volcano   ☉ Lake
● Country Capital   ○ Dependent Territory Capital   ✈ International Airport   ▲▲ Mountain Range   ✍ River   ▨ Reservoir

Picture Credits

DORLING KINDERSLEY *would like to express their thanks to the following individuals, companies, and institutions for their help in preparing this atlas.*

Earth Resource Mapping Ltd., Egham, Surrey
Brian Groombridge, World Conservation Monitoring Centre, Cambridge
The British Library, London
British Library of Political and Economic Science, London
The British Museum, London
The City Business Library, London
King's College, London
National Meteorological Library and Archive, Bracknell
The Printed Word, London
The Royal Geographical Society, London
University of London Library
Paul Beardmore
Philip Boyes
Hayley Crockford
Alistair Dougal
Reg Grant
Louise Keane
Zoe Livesley
Laura Porter
Jeff Eidenshink
Chris Hornby
Rachelle Smith
Ray Pinchard
Robert Meisner
Fiona Strawbridge

Every effort has been made to trace the copyright holders and we apologize in advance for any unintentional omissions. We would be pleased to insert the appropriate acknowledgment in any subsequent edition of this publication.

Adams Picture Library: 86CLA; **G Andrews:** 186CR; **Ardea London Ltd:** K Ghana 150C; M Iljima 132TC; R Waller 148TR; Art Directors **Aspect Picture Library:** P Carmichael 160TR; 131CR(below); G Tompkinson 190TRB; **Axiom:** C Bradley 148CA, 158CA; J Holmes xivCRA, xxivBCR, xxviiCRB, 150TCR, 165C(below), 166TL, J Morris 75TL, 77CRB, J Spaull 134BL; **Bridgeman Art Library, London / New York:** Collection of the Earl of Pembroke, Wilton House xxBC; **The J. Allan Cash Photolibrary:** xlBR, xliiCLA, xlivCL, 10BC, 60CL, 69CLB, 70CL, 72CLB, 75BR, 76BC, 87BL, 109BR, 138BCL, 141TL, 154CR, 178BR, 181TR; **Bruce Coleman Ltd:** 86BC, 98CL, 100TC; S Alden 192BC(below); Atlantide xxviTCR, 138BR; E Bjurstrom 141BR; S Bond 96CRB; T Buchholz xvCL, 92TR, 123TCL; J Burton xxiiiC; J Cancalosi 181TRB; B J Coates xxvBL, 192CL; B Coleman 63TL; B & C Colhoun 2TR, 36CB; A Compost xxiiiCBR; Dr S Coyne 45TL; G Cubitt xviTCL, 169BR, 178TR, 184TR; P Davey xxviiCLB, 121TL(below); N Devore 189CBL; S J Doylee xxiiCRR; H Flygare xviiCRA; M P L Fogden 17C(above) ; Jeff Foott Productions xxiiiCRB, 11CRA; M Freeman 91BRA; P van Gaalen 86TR; G Gualco 140C; B Henderson 194CR; Dr C Henneghien 69C; HPH Photography, H Van den Berg 69CR; C Hughes 69BCL; C James xxxixTC; J Johnson 39CR, 197TR; J Jurka 91CA; S C Kaufman 28C; S J Krasemann 33TR; H Lange 10TRB, 68CA; C Lockwood 32BC; L C Marigo xxiiBC, xxviiCLA, 49CRA, 59BR; M McCoy 187TR; D Meredith 3CR; J Murray xvCR, 179BR; Orion Press 165CR(above); Orion Services & Trading Co. Inc. 164CR; C Ott 17BL; Dr E Pott 9TR, 40CL, 87C, 93TL, 194CLB; F Prenzel 186BC, 193BC; M Read 42BR, 43CRB; H Reinhard xxiiCR, xxviiTR, 194BR; L Lee Rue III 151BCL; J Shaw xixTL; K N Swenson 194BC; P Terry 115CR; N Tomalin 54BCL; P Ward 78TC; S Widstrand 57TR; K Wothe 91C, 173TCL; J T Wright 127BR; **Colorific:** Black Star / L Mulvehil 156CL; Black Star / R Rogers 57BR; Black Star / J Rupp 161BCR; Camera Tres / C. Meyer 59BRA; R Caputo / Matrix 78CL; J. Hill 117CLB; M Koene 55TR; G Satterley xliiCLAR; M Yamashita 156BL, 167CR(above); **Comstock:** 108CRB; Corbis UK Ltd: 170TR, 170BL; **D Cousens:** 147 CRA; **Sue Cunningham Photographic:** 51CR; S Alden 192BC(below) **James Davis Travel Photography:** xxxviTCB, xxxviTR, xxxviCL, 13CA, 19BC, 49TLB, 56BCR, 57CLA, 61BCL, 93BC, 94TC, 102TR, 120CB, 158BC, 179CRA, 191BR; **G Dunnet:** 124CA; **Environmental Picture Library:** Chris Westwood 126C; **Eye Ubiquitous:** xlCA; L. Fordyce 12CLA; L Johnstone 6CRA, 28BLA, 30CB; S. Miller xxiCA; M Southern 73BLA; **Chris Fairclough Colour Library:** xliBR; **Ffotograff:** N. Tapsell 158CL **FLPA -Images of nature:** 123TR; **Geoscience Features:** xviBCR, xviBR, 102CL, 108BC, 122BR; Solar Film 64TC; **gettyone stone**: 131BC, 133BR, 164CR(above); G Johnson 130BL; R Passmore 120TR; D Austen 187CL; G Allison 186CL; L Ulrich 17TL; M Vines 17BL; R Wells 193BL; **Robert Harding Picture Library:** xviiTC, xxivCR, xxxC, xxxvTC, 2TLB, 3CA, 15CRB, 15CR, 37BC, 38CRA, 50BL, 95BR, 99CR, 114CR, 122BL, 131CLA, 142CB, 143TL, 147TR, 168TR, 168CA, 166BR; P G. Adam 13TCB; D Atchison-Jones 70BLA; J Bayne 72BCL; B Schuster 80CR; C Bowman 50BR, 53CA, 62CL, 70CRL; C Campbell xxiBC; G Corrigan 159CRB, 161CRB; P Craven xxxvBL; R Cundy 69BR; Delu 79BC; A Durand 111BR; Financial Times 142BR; R Frerck 51BL; T Gervis 3BCL, 7CR; I Griffiths xxxCL, 77TL; T Hall 166CRA; D Harney 142CA; S Harris xliiiBCL; G Hellier xvCRB, 135BL; F Jackson 137BCR; Jacobs xxxviiTL; P Koch 139TR; F Joseph Land 122TR; Y Marcoux 9BR; S Massif xvBC; A Mills 88CLB; L Murray 114TR; R Rainford xlivBL; G Renner 74CB, 194C; C Rennie 48CL, 116BR; R Richardson 118CL; P Van Riel 48BR; E Rooney 124TR; Sassoon xxivCL, 148CLB; P Scholey 176TR; M Short 137TL; E Simanor xxviiCR; V Southwell 139CR; J Strachan 42TR, 111BL, 132BCR; C Tokeley 131CLA; A C Waltham 161C; T Waltham xviiBL, xxiiCLLL, 138CRB; Westlight 37CR; N Wheeler 139BL; A Williams xxxviiiBR, xlTR; A Woolfitt 95BRA; Paul Harris: 168TC; **Hutchison Library:** 131CR (above) 6BL; P. Collomb 137CR; C. Dodwell 130TR; S Errington 70BCL; P. Hellyer 142BC; J. Horner xxxiTC; R. Ian Lloyd 134CRA; N. Durrell McKenna xxviBCR; J.Nowell 135CLB, 143TC; A Zvoznikov xxiiCL; **Image Bank:** 87BR; J Banagan 190BCA; A Becker xxivBCL; M Khansa 121CR, M Isy-Schwart 193CR(above), 191CL; Khansa K Forest 163TR; Lomeo xxivTCR; T Madison 170TL(below); C Molyneux xxiiCRRR; C Navajas xviiiTR; Ocean Images Inc. 192CLB; J van Os xviiTCR; S Proehl 6CL; T Rakke xixTC, 64CL; M Reitz 196CA; M Romanelli 166CL(below); G A Rossi 151BCR, 176BLA; B Roussel 109TL; S Satushek xviiBCR; Stock Photos / J M Spielman xxivTRL; **Images Colour Library:** xxiiCLL, xxxixTR, xliCR, xliiiBL, 3BR, 19BR, 37TL, 44TL, 62TC, 91BR, 102CLB, 103CR, 150CL, 180CA; 164BC, 165TL; **Impact Photos:** J & G Andrews 186BL; C. Bluntzer 156BR; Cosmos / G. Buthaud 65BC; S Franklin 126BL; A. le Garsmeur 131C; A Indge xxviiTC; C Jones xxxiCB, 70BL; V. Nemirousky 137BR; J Nicholl 76TCR; C. Penn 187C(below); G Sweeney xviiBR, 196CB, 196TR, J & G Andrews 186TR; **JVZ Picture Library:** T Nilson 135TC; **Frank Lane Picture Agency:** xxiTCR, xxiiiBL, 93TR; A Christiansen 58CRA; J Holmes xivBL; S. McCutcheon 3C; Silvestris 173TCR; D Smith xxiiBCL; W Wisniewsli 195BR; **Leeds Castle Foundation:** xxxviiBC; **Magnum:** Abbas 83CR, 136CA; S Franklin 134CRB; D Hurn 4BCL; P. Jones-Griffiths 191BL; H Kubota xviBCL, 156CLB; F Maver xviBL; S McCurry 73CL, 133BCR; G. Rodger 74TR; C Steele Perkins 72BL; **Mountain Camera / John Cleare:** 153TR; C Monteath 153CR; **Nature Photographers:** E.A. Janes 112CL; **Natural Science Photos:** M Andera 110C; **Network Photographers Ltd.:** C Sappa / Rapho 119BL; **N.H.P.A.:** N. J. Dennis xxiiiCL; D Heuchlin xxiiiCLA; S Krasemann 15BL, 25BR, 38TC; K Schafer 49CB; R Tidman 160CLB; D Tomlinson 145CR; M Wendler 48TR; **Nottingham Trent University:** T Waltham xivCL, xvBR; **Novosti:** 144BLA; **Oxford Scientific Films:** D Allan xxiiTR; H R Bardarson xviiiBC; D Bown xxiiiCBLL; M Brown 140BL; M Colbeck 147CAR; W Faidley 3TL; L Gould xxiiiTRB; D Guravich xxiiiTR; P Hammerschmidy / Okapia 87CLA; M Hill 57TL, 195TR; C Menteath ; J Netherton 2CRB; S Osolinski 82CA; R Packwood 72CA; M Pitts 179TC; N Rosing xxiiiCBL, 9TR, 197BR; D Simonson 57C; Survival Anglia / C Catton 137TR; R Toms xxiiiBR; K Wothe xxiBL, xviiCLA; **Panos Pictures:** B Aris 133C; P Barker xxivBR; T Bolstao 153BR; N Cooper 82CB, 153TC; J-L Dugast 166C(below), 167BR; J Hartley 73CA, 90CL; J Holmes 149BC; J Morris 76CLB; M Rose 146TR; D Sansoni 155CL; C Stowers 163TL; **Edward Parker:** 49TL, 49CLB; **Pictor International:** xivBR, xvBRA, xixTCL, xxCL, 3CLA, 17BR, 20TR, 20CRB, 23BCA, 23CL, 26CB, 27BC, 30CA, 33TRB, 34BC, 34BR, 34CR, 38CB, 38CL, 43CL, 63BR, 65TC, 82CL, 83CLB, 99BR, 107CLA, 166TR, 171CL(above), 180CLB, 185TL; **Pictures Colour Library:** xxiBCL, xxiiBR, xxviBCL, 6BR, 15TR, 8TR, 16CL(above), 19TL, 20BL, 24C, 24CLA, 27TR, 32TRB, 36BC, 41CA, 43CRA, 68BL, 90TCB, 94BL, 99BL, 106CA, 107CLB, 107CR, 107BR, 117BL, 164BC, 192BL, K Forest 165TL(below); **Planet Earth Pictures:** 193CR(below); D Barrett 148CB, 184CA; R Coomber 16BL; G Douwma 172BR; E Edmonds 173BR; J Lythgoe 196BL; A Mounter 172CR; M Potts 6CA; P Scoones xxTR; J Walencik 110TR; J Waters 53BCL; **Popperfoto:** Reuters / J Drake xxxiiCLA; **Rex Features:** 165CR; Antelope xxxiiCLB; M Friedel xxiCR; I McIlgorm xxxCBR; J Shelley xxxCR; Sipa Press xxxCR; Sipa Press / Alix xxxCBL; Sipa Press / Chamussy 176BL; **Robert Harding Picture Library:** C. Tokeley 131TL; J Strachan 132BL; Franz Joseph Land 122TR; Franz Joseph Land 364/7088 123BL, 169C(above), 170C(above), 168CL, Tony Waltham 186CR(below), Y Marcoux 9BR; **Russia & Republics Photolibrary:** M Wadlow 118CR, 119CL, 124BC, 124CL, 125TL, 125BR, 126TCR; **Science Photo Library:** Earth Satellite Corporation xixTRB, xxxiCR, 49BCL; F Gohier xiCR; J Heseltine xviTCB; K Kent xvBLA; P Menzell xvBL; N.A.S.A. xBC; D Parker xivBC; University of Cambridge Collection Air Pictures 87CLB; RJ Wainscoat / P Arnold, Inc. xiBC; D Weintraub xiBL; **South American Pictures:** 57BL, 62TR; R Francis 52BL; Guyana Space Centre 50TR; T Morrison 49CRB, 49BL, 50CR, 52TR, 54TR, 60BL, 61C; **Southampton Oceanography:** xviiiBL; **Sovofoto / Eastfoto:** xxxiiCBR; **Spectrum Colour Library:** 50BC, 160BC; J King 145BR; **Frank Spooner Pictures:** Gamma-Liason/Vogel 131CL(above); 26CRB; E. Baitel xxxiiBC; Bernstein xxxiCL; Contrast 112CR; Diard / Photo News 113CL; Liaison / C. Hires xxxiiTCB; Liaison / Nickelsberg xxxiiTR; Marleen 113TL; Novosti 116CA; P. Piel xxxCA; N Quidu 135CL; H Stucke 188CLB, 190CA; Torrengo / Figaro 78BR; A Zamur 113BL; **Still Pictures:** C Caldicott 77TC; A Crump 189CL; M & C Denis-Huot xxiiBL, 78CR, 81BL; M Edwards xxiCRL, 53BL, 64CR, 69BLA, 155BR; J Frebet 53CLB; H Giradet 53TC; E Parker 52CL; M Gunther 121BC; **Tony Stone Images:** xxviTR, 4CA, 7BL, 7CL, 13CRB, 39BR, 58C, 97BC, 101BR, 106TR, 109CL, 109CRB, 164CLB, 165C,180CB, 181BR, 188BC, 192TR; G Allison 18TR, 31CRB, 187CRB; D Armand 14TCB; D Austen 180TR, 186CL, 187CL; J Beatty 74CL; O Benn xxviBR; K Biggs xxiTL; R Bradbury 44BR; R A Butcher xxviTL; J Callahan xxviiCRA; P Chesley 185BCL, 188C; W Clay 30BL, 31CRA; J Cornish 96BL, 107TL; C Condina 41CB; T Craddock xxivTR; P Degginger 36CLB; Demetrio 5BR; N DeVore xxivBC; A Diesendruck 60BR; S Egan 87CRA, 96BR; R Elliot xxiiBCR; S Elmore 19C; J Garrett 73CR; S Grandadam 14BR; R Grosskopf 28BL; D Hanson 104BC; C Harvey 69TL; G Hellier 110BL, 165CR; S Huber 103CRB; D Hughs xxxiBR; A Husmo 91TR; G Irvine 31BC; J Jangoux 58CL; D Johnston xviiTR; A Kehr 113C; R Koskas xviTR; J Lamb 96CRA; J Lawrence 75CRA; L Lefkowitz 7CA; M Lewis 45CLA; S Mayman 55BR; Murray & Associates 45CR; G Norways 104CA; N Parfitt xxviiCL, 68TCR, 81TL; R Passmore 121TR; N Press xviBCA; E Pritchard 88CA, 90CLR; T Raymond 21BL, 29TR; L Resnick 74BR; M Rogers 80BR; A Sacks 28TCB; C Saule 90CR; S Schulhof xxivTC; P Seaward 34CL; M Segal 32BL; V Shenai 152CL; R Sherman 26CL; H Sitton 136CR; R Smith xxvBLA, 56C; S Studd 108CLA; H Strand 49BR, 63TR; P Tweedie 177CR; L Ulrich 17BL; M Vines 17TC; A B Wadham 60CR; J Warden 63CLB; R Wells 23CRA, 193BL; G Yeowell 34BL; **Telegraph Colour Library:** 61CRB, 61TCR, 157TL; R Antrobus xxxixBR; J Sims 26BR; **Topham Picturepoint:** xxxiCBL, 162BR, 168TR, 168BC; **Travel Ink:** A Cowin 88TR; **Trip:** 140BR, 144CA, 155CRA; B Ashe 159TR; D Cole 190BCL, 190CR; D Davis 89BL; I Deineko xxxiTR; J Dennis 22BL; Dinodia 154CL; Eye Ubiquitous / L Fordyce 2CLB; A Gasson 149CR; W Jacobs 43TL, 54BL, 177BC, 178CLA, 185BCR, 186BL; P Kingsbury 112C; K Knight 177BR; V Kolpakov 147BL; T Noorits 87TL, 119BR, 146CL; R Power 41TR; N Ray 166BL, 168TC; C Rennie 116CLB; V Sidoropolev 145TR; E Smith 183BC, 183TL; **Woodfin Camp & Associates:** 92BLR; **World Pictures:** xvCRA, xviiCRA, 9CRB, 22CL, 23BC, 24BL, 35BL, 40TR, 51TR, 71BR, 80TCR, 82TR, 83BL, 86BCR, 96TC, 98BL, 100CR, 101CR, 103BC, 105TC, 157BL, 161BCL, 162CLB, 172CLB, 172BC, 179BL, 182CB, 183C, 184CL, 185CR; 121BR, 121TT; **Zefa Picture Library:** xviBLR, xviiBCL, xviiiCL, 3CL, 8BC, 8CT, 9CR, 13BC, 14TC, 16TR, 21TL, 22CRB, 25BL, 32TCR, 36BCR, 59BCL, 65TCL, 69CLA, 79TL, 81BR, 87CRB, 92C, 98C, 99TL, 100BL, 107TR, 118CRB, 120BL; 122C(below), 124CLA, 164BR, 183TR; Anatol 113BR; Barone 114BL; Brandenburg 5C; A J Brown 44TR; H J Clauss 55CLB; Damm 71BC; Evert 92BL; W Felger 3BL; J Fields 189CRA; R Frerck 4BL; G Heil 56BR; K Heibig 115BR; Heilman 28BC; Hunter 8C; Kitchen 10TR, 8CL, 8BL, 9TR; Dr H Kramarz 7BLA, 123CR(below); Mehlio 155BL; J F Raga 24TR; Rossenbach 105BR; Streichan 89TL; T Stewart 13TR, 19CR; Sunak 54BR, 162TR; D H Teuffen 95TL; B Zaunders 40BC. **Additional Photography:** Geoff Dann; Rob Reichenfeld; H Taylor; Jerry Young.

NORTH AMERICA

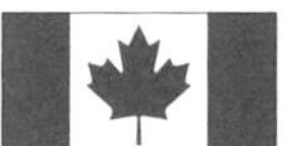

CANADA
PAGES 8–15

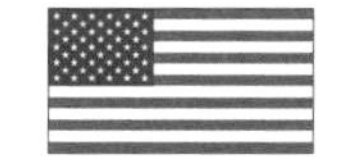

UNITED STATES OF AMERICA
PAGES 16–39

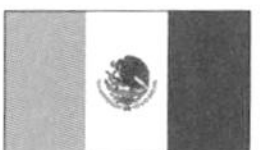

MEXICO
PAGES 40–41

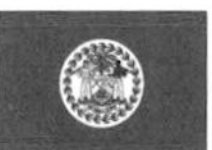

BELIZE
PAGES 42–43

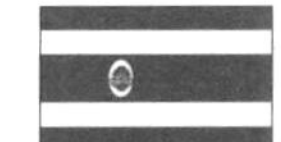

COSTA RICA
PAGES 42–43

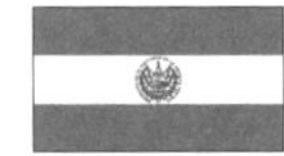

EL SALVADOR
PAGES 42–43

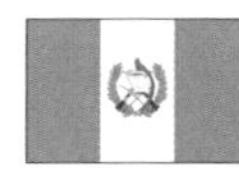

GUATEMALA
PAGES 42–43

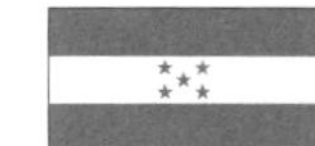

HONDURAS
PAGES 42–43

SOUTH AMERIC

GRENADA
PAGES 44–45

HAITI
PAGES 44–45

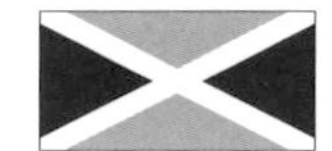

JAMAICA
PAGES 44–45

ST KITTS & NEVIS
PAGES 44–45

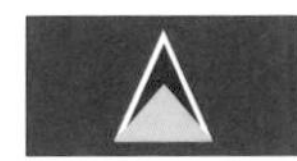

ST LUCIA
PAGES 44–45

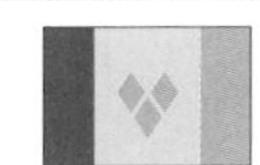

ST VINCENT & THE GRENADINES
PAGES 44–45

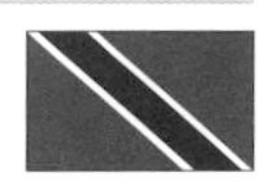

TRINIDAD & TOBAGO
PAGES 44–45

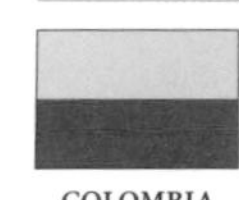

COLOMBIA
PAGES 54–55

AFRICA

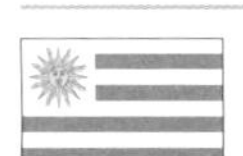

URUGUAY
PAGES 60–61

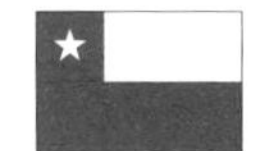

CHILE
PAGES 62–63

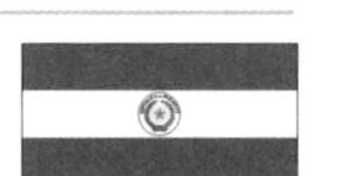

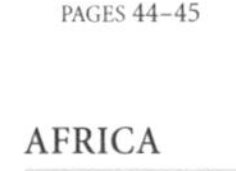

PARAGUAY
PAGES 62–63

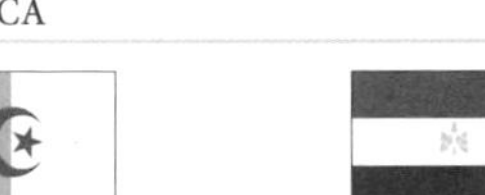

ALGERIA
PAGES 74–75

EGYPT
PAGES 74–75

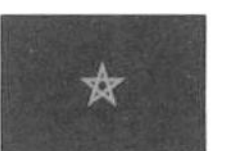

LIBYA
PAGES 74–75

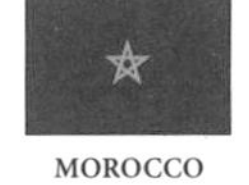

MOROCCO
PAGES 74–75

TUNISIA
PAGES 74–75

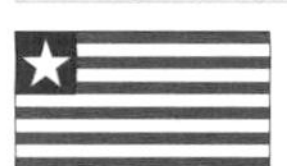

LIBERIA
PAGES 76–77

MALI
PAGES 76–77

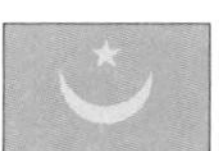

MAURITANIA
PAGES 76–77

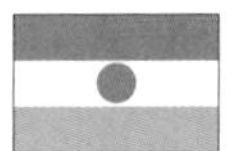

NIGER
PAGES 76–77

NIGERIA
PAGES 76–77

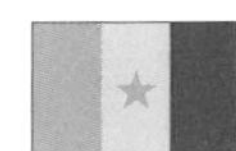

SENEGAL
PAGES 76–77

SIERRA LEONE
PAGES 76–77

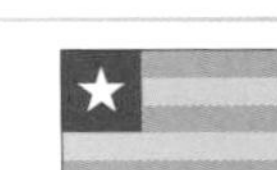

TOGO
PAGES 76–77

BURUNDI
PAGES 80–81

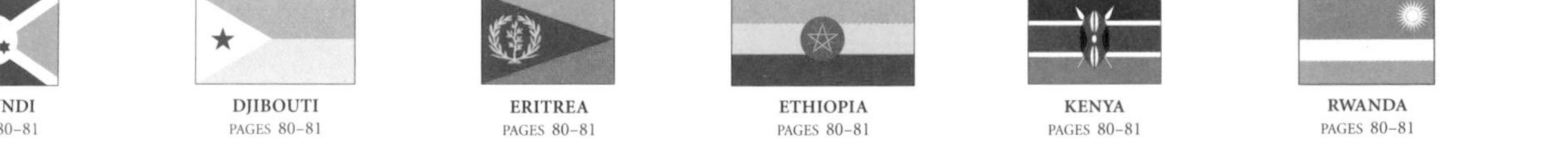

DJIBOUTI
PAGES 80–81

ERITREA
PAGES 80–81

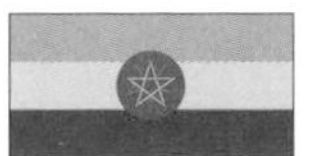

ETHIOPIA
PAGES 80–81

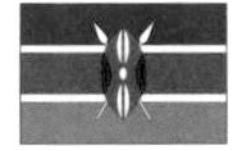

KENYA
PAGES 80–81

RWANDA
PAGES 80–81

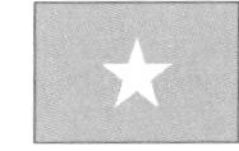

SOMALIA
PAGES 80–81

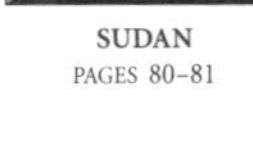

SUDAN
PAGES 80–81

EUROPE

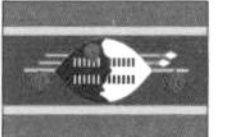

SOUTH AFRICA
PAGES 82–83

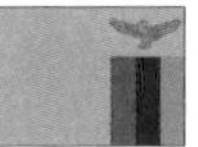

SWAZILAND
PAGES 82–83

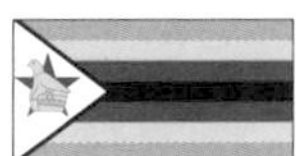

ZAMBIA
PAGES 82–83

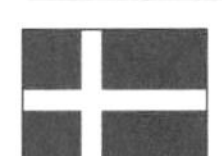

ZIMBABWE
PAGES 82–83

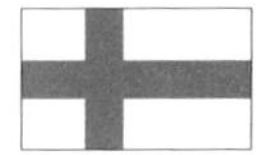

DENMARK
PAGES 92–93

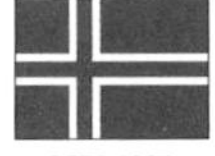

FINLAND
PAGES 92–93

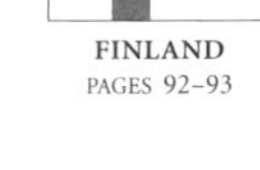

ICELAND
PAGES 92–93

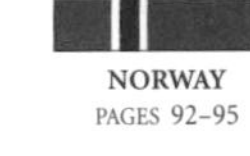

NORWAY
PAGES 92–95

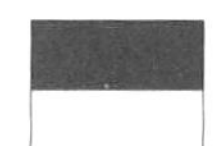

MONACO
PAGES 102–103

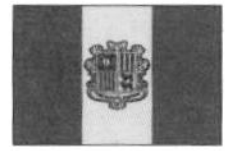

ANDORRA
PAGES 104–105

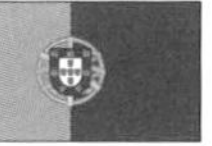

PORTUGAL
PAGES 104–105

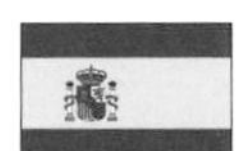

SPAIN
PAGES 104–105

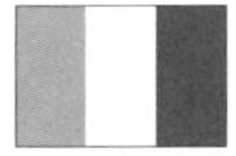

ITALY
PAGES 106–107

SAN MARINO
PAGES 106–107

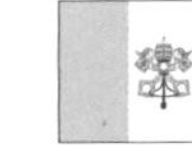

VATICAN CITY
PAGES 106–107

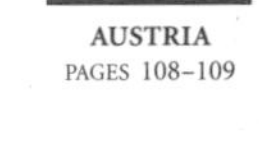

AUSTRIA
PAGES 108–109

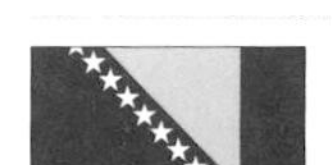

BOSNIA & HERZEGOVINA
PAGES 112–113

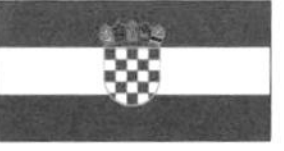

CROATIA
PAGES 112–113

MACEDONIA
PAGES 112–113

MONTENEGRO
PAGES 112–113

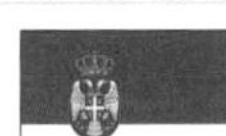

SERBIA
PAGES 112–113

BULGARIA
PAGES 114–115

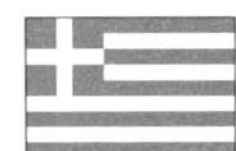

GREECE
PAGES 114–115

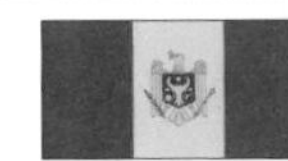

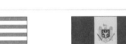

MOLDOVA
PAGES 116–117

ASIA

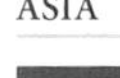

ARMENIA
PAGES 136–137

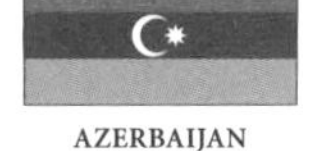

AZERBAIJAN
PAGES 136–137

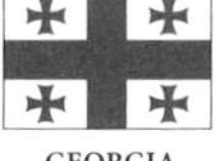

GEORGIA
PAGES 136–137

TURKEY
PAGES 136–137/114–115

IRAQ
PAGES 138–139

ISRAEL
PAGES 138–139

JORDAN
PAGES 138–139

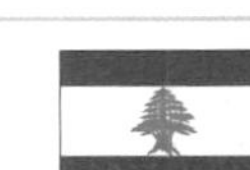

LEBANON
PAGES 138–139

IRAN
PAGES 142–143

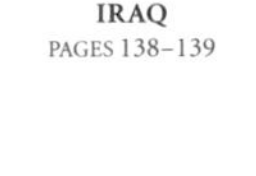

KAZAKHSTAN
PAGES 144–145

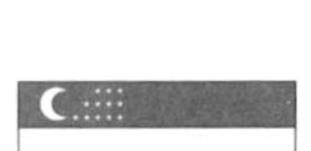

KYRGYZSTAN
PAGES 146–147

TAJIKISTAN
PAGES 146–147

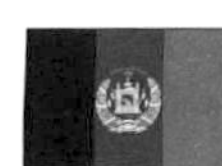

TURKMENISTAN
PAGES 146–147

UZBEKISTAN
PAGES 146–147

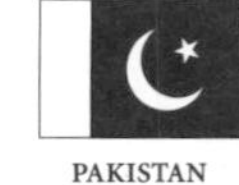

AFGHANISTAN
PAGES 148–149

PAKISTAN
PAGES 148–151

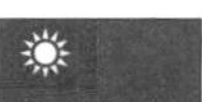

TAIWAN
PAGES 160–161

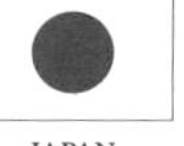

JAPAN
PAGES 164–165

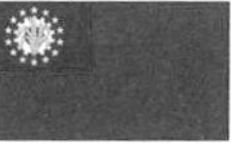

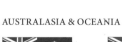

BURMA
PAGES 166–167

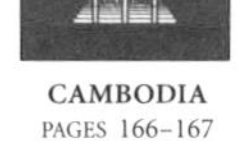

CAMBODIA
PAGES 166–167

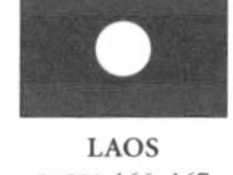

LAOS
PAGES 166–167

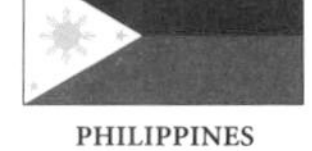

PHILIPPINES
PAGES 166–167

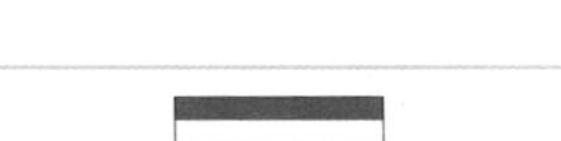

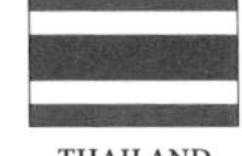

THAILAND
PAGES 166–167

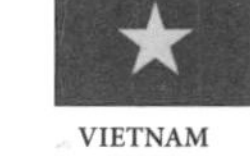

VIETNAM
PAGES 166–167

AUSTRALASIA & OCEANIA

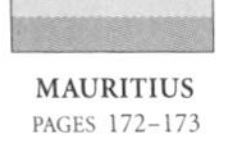

MAURITIUS
PAGES 172–173

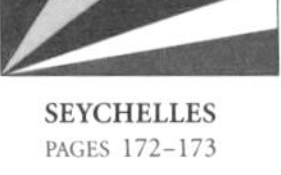

SEYCHELLES
PAGES 172–173

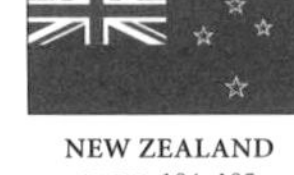

AUSTRALIA
PAGES 180–183

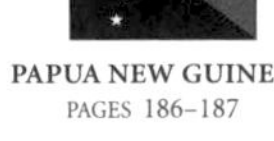

NEW ZEALAND
PAGES 184–185

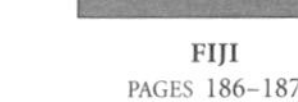

PAPUA NEW GUINEA
PAGES 186–187

FIJI
PAGES 186–187

SOLOMON ISLANDS
PAGES 186–187

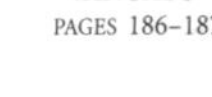

VANUATU
PAGES 186–187